ENGLISH AND SHORTHAND DICTIONARY

PITMAN'S
ENGLISH AND SHORTHAND DICTIONARY

BASED ON THE ORIGINAL WORK OF
SIR ISAAC PITMAN

WITH LISTS OF PROPER NAMES, GRAMMALOGUES AND CONTRACTIONS, AND AN ANALYTICAL INTRODUCTION ON THE FORMATION OF SHORTHAND OUTLINES TOGETHER WITH AN APPENDIX CONTAINING LISTS OF LATIN AND GREEK PREFIXES, COMMERCIAL TERMS IN FIVE LANGUAGE, AND FOREIGN WORDS PHRASES AND SAYINGS

THE DEFINITIONS BY
ARTHUR REYNOLDS, M.A., Oxon.

KALPAZ

ISBN: 978-93-5128-575-5(HB)

First Published in 1917
Indian Reprint in 2017

Published by

Kalpaz Publications
C-30, Satyawati Nagar,
Delhi – 110052
E-mail: kalpaz@hotmail.com
Website: kalpazpublications.com
Ph.: +91-9212142040

Cataloging in Publication Data--DK
Courtesy: D.K. Agencies (P) Ltd. <docinfo@dkagencies.com>

Pitman, Isaac, 1813-1897, author.
Pitman's English and shorthand dictionary : based on the original work of Sir Isaac Pitman : with lists of proper names, grammalogues and contractions, and an analytical introduction on the formation of shorthand outlines together with an appendix containing lists of Latin and Greek prefixes, commercial terms in five language, and foreign words, phrases and sayings / the definitions by Arthur Reynolds (M.A., Oxon.).
pages cm
"First published in 1917"--Title page verso.
ISBN 9789351285755 (HB)

1. Shorthand--Pitman--Dictionaries. I. Reynolds, Arthur, 1851- editor. II. Title. III. Title: English and shorthand dictionary.

Z55.5.P58 2017 DDC 653.42403 23

PREFACE

IN response to a demand often expressed by users of the Shorthand Dictionary, it was decided to add to the words it contained their ordinary meanings, with occasional notes concerning their origins. It was, in fact, impossible to resist the argument that it is vastly more convenient to use one book of reference than to have to use two, and accordingly the task of making the dictionary complete and self-contained was attempted, and has, it is hoped, been accomplished to the edification of those who may refer to it.

In order to keep the volume within reasonable limits, a great degree of economy had to be practised. Words have a tendency, the result of their handling sometimes by ordinary folk and sometimes by writers, to pass from their primary and obvious meanings to metaphorical senses. Only in a large and comprehensive dictionary would it be possible to follow every word into a variety of usages, and here this has been done sparingly; for, given one or two of its meanings, anyone meeting a word in a connection different from its natural setting would at once perceive that metaphor had been at work upon it, and be able to see how it had acquired this further meaning.

It is very tempting also to trace words to their earliest discoverable source, but again that process would result in extending the bulk as well as the scope of the present book. Its purpose is to furnish the writer of shorthand with a ready means of finding the common and regular signification of each word the shorthand outline of which he requires to learn. What such a student needs for his purpose is the immediate and obvious rather than the recondite.

Into the making of an English Dictionary Dr. Johnson introduced a delightful feature, the illustration of the meanings and usages of words by means of literary passages in which they occur. In a particular context, and especially when placed there by one of the makers of literature, a word is invested with a new life and power, and it needs the quotation for the lexicographer adequately to convey the acquired meaning. To attempt this here was also out of the question, and the modest *rôle* assumed confines the ambition of this Dictionary within the limit of a desire to explain simply and usefully the words of the vocabulary.

Subject, therefore, to these restrictions, the work is submitted to the public of shorthand writers and students in the hope and with the intention that it may be a real help to them.

The New Era edition, now presented to the public, must not be allowed to appear without a tribute of thanks to Mr. H. W. B. Wilson for his very valuable and skilful assistance in revising the Introduction and bringing it into conformity with the latest developments in Pitman's Shorthand.

A. R.

CONTENTS

INTRODUCTION

IN the present work standard forms are furnished for the words of the English language, written in accordance with the rules of Pitman's Shorthand (New Era Edition). Every writer of the system is aware that the use of the many regularized abbreviating devices which results in brief and facile outlines being obtained for the great majority of words without the help of any arbitrary abbreviation, also involves, in many instances, a choice between two or more possible forms, and the SHORTHAND DICTIONARY provides those outlines which experience has shown can be recommended for general adoption. Hence the importance and utility of the work as a book of reference for teachers, students, and practitioners.

In this edition of the Dictionary some further words have been incorporated in the Appendix.

Every effort has been made to render the Dictionary reliable and consistent in regard to pronunciation and the selection of the shorthand forms. There will, no doubt, be differences of opinion with regard to the outlines for certain words, since a form which is the most convenient to one writer is not invariably so to another writer. It is strongly recommended, however, that the closest possible adherence to Dictionary outlines be observed, since they have been decided upon as the result of experience and the most careful thought. No Dictionary outline, therefore, should be rejected in favour of another until an attempt has been made to ascertain whether there is not some special reason for its adoption. It is obvious that uniformity of outline is especially helpful in the case of writers who have to read or transcribe one another's notes.

PRONUNCIATION—REPRESENTATION OF VOWELS, ETC.

With respect to pronunciation, this has been carefully checked throughout, the *New English Dictionary* (edited by the late Sir James A. H. Murray, LL.D., and others) being taken as the authority in practically all cases, so far as that work is available.

The following observations with regard to the vowel sounds, etc., in certain classes of words may be found helpful—

(*a*) The sound of the vowel "*a*" in such words as b*a*r, h*a*rm, emb*a*rk, is *ah*.

There are, on the other hand, many words in which the vowel "*a*" before *r* has a short or indistinct sound; *e.g.*, 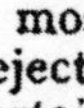 *tariff*, 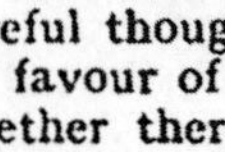 *globular*, 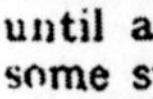 *pillar*. Compare  *tarry* (adjective) with 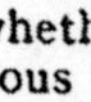 *tarry* (verb).

(*b*) *aw* and not *ah* is used in such words as *taunt, launch, saunter.*

(*c*) "*o*" when occurring medially and sounded indistinctly is represented by *ŭ*, as in *custom, mason, London, monopoly, gallop.*

A long vowel tends to become short when it is unaccented, and in some words, such as *proclaim, biograph,* the vowels *ō* and *ŭ* are practically indistinguishable as ordinarily pronounced. In others, however, *e.g., flotation, hotel, rotate, nobility,* the vowel is unmistakably *ō* although unaccented.

(*d*) The unaccented "*a*" in such words as *accurate, breakage, palace,* including most adjectives ending in *-ate*, is represented by *ĕ*.

Here, again, the long vowel tends to become short when it is unaccented. Compare *lace* with *palace.* In some cases, however, including all *verbs* ending in *-ate*, the vowel "*a*" is long, although it may be unaccented. Compare *moderate* (adjective) with *moderate* (verb).

(*e*) *ĭ* is used in *marriage, carriage,* etc.

(*f*) The diphthong *ī* is used in words ending in *-ization, e.g., realization, capitalization.*

(*g*) The vowel sound after *j* or *r* in such words as *Jew, juice, peruse,* is *ōō* and not *ū*. After *l*, also, *ū* is generally represented as *ōō* unless it begins a syllable; *e.g., include. flute. solution,* but *soluble, valuer.*

(*h*) In French words such as *patois, boudoir, soirée,* etc., *oi* is pronounced *wah.*

(*i*) *French eu.* When the usual sign representing the vowel sound of *eu* in French words cannot be conveniently employed, it may be treated as *ŭ*; thus, *raconteur, restaurateur.*

(*j*) In such words as *ranch, French, inch, punch,* with regard to which authorities differ, *ch,* which is believed to represent the more usual pronunciation, is employed.

NOTES AS TO THE PLACING OF VOWEL-SIGNS, ETC.

(1) DIPHTHONG *ū* BETWEEN TWO STROKES.—The diphthong *ū* when occurring between two strokes is treated in the same way as a third-place vowel; *i.e.,* it is always written before the second of the two strokes; thus, *Hercules, culinary, accurate, valueless.*

(2) DIPHTHONGS *ī* AND *oi*. The diphthong *ī* is written out of its

ordinary position for the purpose of joining finally to *n*, as in *deny*; and also in a few instances when following a third-place vowel; *e.g.*, *radii*, *nuclei*, *genii*. The diphthong *ow* is written out of its ordinary position for the purpose of joining initially to *l*, as in *owl*.

(3) DIPHTHONG *oi*.—It is permissible to write the first tick of the diphthong *oi* upward (i.e. as in the diphone *awi*), instead of horizontally, when it is more convenient to do so. This is the case especially when it is joined initially to *l*, thus, *oil*.

(4) The small circle used to represent a vowel occurring between the two consonants expressed by a stroke hooked for *r* or *l* is written *after* the stroke unless the presence of a hook or a stroke or of another vowel-sign renders the other side more convenient thus, *garnish*, but *regard*; *side car* but *motor-car*; *shilling*, but *virulent*; *parlour*, but *parallel*.

(5) THIRD-PLACE VOWEL OCCURRING ON SAME SIDE OF STROKE AS *shun* HOOK.—Any vowel- (or diphthongal-) sign other than a *dot* vowel is placed *outside final shun* hook thus *delusion*, *fusion*, *alleviation* (but *vision*). All third place signs are written inside medial *shun* hook; thus, *educational*.

(6) VOCALIZATION IN DERIVATIVE WORDS.—A vowel in a derivative word, whether occurring in a (grammatical) prefix or suffix, such as *re-*, *pre-*, *-able*, *-ance*, or in the portion representing the root word, follows the ordinary rules as regards the stroke to which it is to be placed, and if it is immediately followed by another vowel, a diphone is used; thus *prefigure*, *measurable*, *severance*, *singer*, *unopened*, *unaccented*, *re-examine*.

This does not apply to Compound Words, in which case the vowel signs are generally placed as in the original words unless there is some special reason to the contrary; thus, *headache*, *steam-engine*, *crab-apple*; but *seaman*, *black-eyed*, to avoid placing a vowel-sign in an angle.

SUPPLEMENTARY RULES FOR THE CHOICE OF OUTLINES

The following rules and explanations are given in order to show the practice which has been followed in the selection of the outlines for various classes of words—

DIPHTHONG Ū AND CONSONANT Y

Stroke is used whenever convenient in words beginning with the sound of *ū*; thus, *Europe*, *utilize*, *eulogy*, *unique*. Note, however, *usury* and *Euphrates*.

ABBREVIATED W USED MEDIALLY

The abbreviated form of the consonant *w* is not joined medially to a preceding stroke except in a few COMPOUNDS of "woman," in which it joins easily, such as *needlewoman*, *charwoman*, and in *sidewalk*; hence *woodwork*, *saleswoman*, *workwoman*, *silkworm*.

W (SEMICIRCLE AND STROKE)

Initial *w* followed by a DIPHONE or a TRIPHONE is represented by the stroke ; thus, *weigher*, *wooer*, *Wyoming*.

S (DIRECTION OF CIRCLE)

In writing *n s m* the circle *s* is placed *inside* the *m* in the following cases—

(*a*) In DERIVATIVES and COMPOUNDS from words in which the circle is written inside the *m*: *e.g.*, *unseemly*, *unsummoned*, *tinsmith* (compare *newsmonger*); also in the word *insomnia*.

(*b*) In words containing the syllable *-some*, *e.g.* *noisome*, *handsome*.

NOTE.—It will be found that, with only two or three exceptions, *e.g.*, *mincemeat*, *Norseman*, and *nursemaid*, the form is used for *n s m* and the form for *n z m*, most of the examples of the latter being words ending in *-ism*, *e.g.*, *communism*, *galvanism*.

S, Z (CIRCLE AND STROKE)

(I) Words ending in *-nese* and *-nize*, most of which are DERIVATIVES, are written with stroke *n* and circle *s* (*z*) whenever convenient;

thus, *Japanese*, *Americanize*, *humanize*, *modernize*. Note, however, *revolutionize*.

(2) Words ending in *-nism* are written with unless a better outline is obtained by writing hook *n* and The latter is found to be the more convenient form after (but not or or Examples: *Puritanism*, *religionism*, *anachronism*; but *mechanism*, *paganism*, *modernism*, *Wesleyanism*.

(3) Words ending in *-ess*. All words (feminines) ending in *-ess* cannot conveniently be treated uniformly, but the following shows the practice which has been followed—

(*a*) In words ending with the *syllable -ess*, stroke *s* is used if necessary for the purpose of distinguishing the feminine singular from the masculine plural when no other means of distinction is available; thus *poetess*, (*poets*), *heiress* (*heirs*), *Jewess*, (*Jews*).

(*b*) With regard to those words ending in *-eress*, *-oress*, *-dess*, *-n(t)ess* or *-fess* in which alternative methods of distinction are available, stroke *s* is used after or : thus, *archeress*, *manageress*, *tutoress*, *murderess*, *vicaress*, *deaconess*, *countess*, *championess*, *chiefess*: but in other cases the circle is written, *e.g.*, *viscountess*, *giantess*, *lioness*, *baroness*, *mayoress*, *authoress*.

(*c*) In words ending in *-ress* immediately preceded by a consonant, the final *s* sound is always represented by the circle; thus, *actress*, *waitress*, *tigress*.

(4) Words ending in *-zoon* are written with stroke *z*; thus, *epizoon*, *polyzoon* (plural *polyzoa*): but adjectives ending in *-zoic* have the circle; thus, *paleozoic*, *protozoic*,

(5) DERIVATIVES from words with outlines containing stroke *s* (see also paragraph 48 of the *Instructor* and No (3) below).

Derivatives formed by adding a suffix beginning with a vowel to a *primitive* word ending with *s* or *z* and a vowel retain stroke *s* or *z*: thus, *cosier*, *lazier*, *pursuance*, *Sadducean* *Puseyism*, *laziest*, *busiest*.

Compare—(*a*) *Secondary derivatives*, such as *spiciest*, *sauciest*, *glossier*, the primitives of which are written with circle *s*, and (*b*) Derivatives in which the suffix does not commence with a vowel; *e.g.*, *drowsiness*, *merciless*, *ensued*, *busily*.

S (STROKE AND CIRCLE): ST (AND LOOP)

(1) Initial *s* or *st* followed by a DIPHONE is written as follows—

(*a*) With stroke *s* or in DERIVATIVES such as *sower*, *seer*, *stayer*, *stowage*.

(*b*) With the circle or loop in other words, such as *sahib*, *stance*, *sienna*, *stoic*, *Styrian*.

Initial *s* or *st* followed by a TRIPHONE is written with stroke *s* or ; thus, *Siam*, *suet*, *Stuart*, *steward*, *Stowell*.

(2) Contrary to the general rule for words beginning with *s* vowel *s*, several words beginning with *sist* or (*con*)*sist* are more conveniently written with circle *s* first; *e.g.*, *system*, *cistern*, *consist*, *consistent*, *sisterly*.

(3) While words ending in *-ous* preceded by a diphthong are written with stroke *s* in accordance with paragraph 48 (*c*) of the *Instructor*, their DERIVATIVES ending in *-iously*, *-uously*, *-uousness* and *-uosity* are generally written with the circle: thus, *piously*, *strenuously*, *ambiguously*, *impetuosity*.

The following, however, are cases in which the stroke is retained for the purpose of distinction— *joyously*, *joyousness*, *ingenuously*, *ingenuousness*, *tenuously*, *tenuousness* *sinuosity*.

(3*a*) In other words containing *s*, *z* or *st* preceded by a TRIPHONE or by a DIPHONE, the circle or loop is used; *e.g.*, *bias*, *biased*, *quiesce*, *acquiesce*, *Genoese*, *essayist*, *truest*, *deist*, *Judaism*, *statuesque* The following are exceptions to this— *prowess*, (*principles*), *dais* *chaos* *newest*, (*next*), *highest*.

(4) Words ending in *-astic* or *-istic* are written as follows—

(*a*) With *st* loop after *t*, *d*, *j* or *l*, thus, *artistic* *deistic*, *logistic*, *elastic*

(*b*) With in other cases; thus *plastic*, *theistic*, *sophistic*

(5) is retained in DERIVATIVES from words with outlines containing , except the monosyllabic past tenses *stayed*, *stewed*, etc.; thus, *stowage*, *dustiness*, *majestic* *lustier*

ST (LOOP AND) ST)

Words ending in *-nest*, *-nist*, *-fest*, *-vest*, *-vist*, *-test*, *-tist*, *-dest*, etc., are written with the *st* loop unless a distinctly better outline is obtained by means of the stroke: thus, *keenest*, *greenest* *organist*, *briefest*, *bravest* *faintest*, *fondest*, *artist*, but *plainest*, *earnest*, *toughest*, *positivist*, *kindest*, *hardest*.

SST (, AND)

Words ending in *-cest*, *-cist* and *-sest* are generally written with : thus, *fiercest*, *publicist* *closest*; but is more convenient after *n* or *r*, as in *nicest*, *empiricist*; *densest*. is used in verbs ending in *-sist*, *e.g.*, *subsist*, *desist*.

SZD (AND)

COMPOUND WORDS ending in *-sized* are written with except when gives a better joining (as after *f*, *v*, or *n*); thus, *fair-sized*, *full-sized*, *large-sized*; but *oversized*, *undersized*.

SS, SZ (LARGE CIRCLE, AND)

(1) Words ending in *-sis* and *-sus* are written with the large circle; thus, *basis*, (plural *bases*), *narcissus*. Note also *Francis*.

(2) Words ending with the sound of *sĕs* or *zĕs*, or with *s* – $\frac{s}{z}$ separated by a diphthong or a diphone (including words ending in *-cess*, *-cize* and *-size*), are generally written with or ; thus, *access*, *possess*, *capsize*, *gaseous*; but after *th*, *n* or upward *r*, affords a better joining, *e.g.*, *Gothicize*, *princess*, *Frances*, *recess*, *exorcize*. The form is used also in *diocese* and *decease* for distinction; and the common words *success*, *exercise* and *emphasize*, are written with the large circle for convenience.

(3) Words ending in *-cism* are generally written with the large circle; thus, *fanaticism*, *Gallicism*; but after (*th*, *n* or *r*, the form gives more convenient and distinctive outlines; thus, *Gothicism*, *cynicism*, *laconicism*, *exorcism*, *Doricism*.

HOOKED STROKE AND STROKE R OR L

(1) Words ending in *-metry* and *-metric* are written with stroke *r* whenever practicable; thus, *geometry*, *barometric*, but *planimetry*.

(2) Words ending in *-able* or *-ible* are generally written with the hooked stroke ; thus, *obtainable*, *measurable*. The separate strokes , however, are used when a better outline is thus obtained; *e.g.*—

(*a*) After , , , or after a circle following a "right" curve (but not after or); thus, *excusable*, *accessible*, *invincible*, *reversible*, *forcible* (but *feasible*, *serviceable*).

(*b*) After or ; thus, *contestable*, *digestible*.

(*c*) After , or a downstroke hooked for *v*; thus, *explainable*, *discernible*, *provable*.

(*d*) After a half-length stroke hooked for *n*; thus, *accountable*, *lamentable*. (But note *insurmountable*.)

(*e*) After a *shun* hook; thus, *actionable*, but in *mentionable* disjoined is more convenient.

(3) Words ending in *-tal* or *-dal* preceded by *r* are written with stroke *l*; thus, *parietal*, *spheroidal* Compare the words *rattle*, *riddle*. A number of words ending in *-tal* preceded by *n* are also written with stroke *l*; *e.g.*, *mental*, *horizontal*. Compare the word *mantle*.

(4) Words ending in *-ful* and *-fully* are written with stroke *l* in cases where a distinction between the adjective and the adverb can easily be shown by means of the downward and the upward *l* respectively; *e.g.*, after —, —, ◡, ◡, or a straight upstroke; thus, *wakeful*, *wakefully*, *manful*, *wrongful*, *sorrowful*. In other words, including verbs, *fl* and *vl* occurring after the strokes mentioned above are represented by the hooked forms ; thus, *scuffle*, *interval*, *upheaval*.

(5) Words ending in *-shly* are generally written with , thus, *foolishly* *freshly* But note *harshly*, in which the stroke *l* is more convenient.

(6) On the other hand words beginning with *unr-*, *enr-*, *unl-*, *enl-*, formed by a prefix from words beginning with *r* or *l* generally retain the separate *r* or *l*; thus, *unrest*, *unreasoning*, *unleavened*, *enlist*. But note *enlighten* and *enliven*

(7) Words ending in *-ary*, *-ery*, *-ory*, etc., are treated as follows—

(*a*) The hooked strokes are used when they give a more easily written outline than the separate *r*; thus, *drapery*, *rookery*, *treasury*, *luminary*.

(*b*) The hooked strokes are retained in adjectives derived from words written with a final hooked stroke, such as *tottery*, *silvery*, *savoury*

(*c*) In other cases the separate *r* or *l* is written; thus, *statutory*, *notary*, *factory*, *fishery*.

(8) Derivatives ending in *-ally* and *-alize* from words written with a final hooked stroke retain the hooked form thus, *brutally*, *brutalize*, *locally*, *localize*. But note *totally* which is considered a more convenient form.

(9) Words ending in *-erate* or *-orate* are often written with separate *rt* if the latter gives an easily written outline and one which enables that of the past tense to be easily formed from it; thus, *exaggerate*, *exaggerated*; *adulterate*, *adulterated*; *enumerate*, *enumerated*. Compare *deliberate* *deliberated* *decorate*, *decorated*. The outline *elaborate* is necessary for distinction.

(10) Derivatives from words written with hooked forms of the *pr*, *pl* series are generally also written with the hooked forms if practicable, even if the *r* or *l* is no longer in the same syllable as the preceding consonant; thus, *tippler* *trampling*, *saddling*,

tackling, *doubly*. Compare such words as *seedling*, *duckling*, which are not so derived.

(11) In COMPOUND WORDS, when the second part of the compound begins with *r* or *l*, that *r* or *l* is, as a rule, not combined with the last letter of the first part: hence, *typewritten*, *bricklayer*, *necklace*. But note *typewriter* and *typewriting*.

(12) In the case of *verbs* the hooked forms are generally preferred so as to enable past tenses to be written on the same principle: thus, *bridle*, *bridled* (compare *bridal*), *model* *modelled*.

DUPLICATE FORMS FOR FR, VR, ETC.

(1) In DERIVATIVES and COMPOUNDS from words written with , etc., the form of *fr*, or *vr*, used in the primitive should, when convenient, also be used in the derivative or compound, without regard to the practice adopted in other words; thus, *freeness*, (compare *furnace*), *offerer* (compare *friar*).

Subject to the above—

(2) The "left" curves are used if more convenient for joining than the "right" curves. This is the case—

(*a*) When *fr* or *vr* occurs either before or after *t*, *d*, *ch*, *j*, *f*, *v*, *th*, *s* or *z*, as in *tougher*, *leverage*, *effervesce*, *survivor*, *froth*, *zephyr*.

(*b*) Generally before a character beginning with the same motion, viz. the "left" motion, as in *friable*, *freckle*, *frank*, *France*.

(3) In other cases the "right" curves are generally used, as *verbose*, *Africa*, *fresh*, *frame*.

(4) As regards *thr* and *THr*, are used initally when preceded by a vowel (*i.e.*, as when standing alone); thus, *Atherton*, *Atherley*, *otherwise*, and

(5) In other cases the "right" curves are used, as *thread*, *thrive*, *thrash*, *throttle*, *tether*, *zither*, *Arthur*.

DOUBLE CONSONANTS (VOCALIZED) AND SEPARATE R OR L

(1) Medial *r* or *l* preceded by a strongly-sounded vowel is generally represented by separate *r* or *l* unless a hooked form is necessary in order to avoid an awkward or a too lengthy outline: thus *ulterior*, *internal*, *fraternal*, *repel*, but *repulsive*.

(2) Words ending in *-torial* are generally written with separate *r*, but the hooked form is used in a few cases to avoid an awkward or a very lengthy outline; thus, *tutorial*, *equatorial*, *piscatorial*, but *reportorial*, *spectatorial*, *dictatorial*.

(3) Words ending in *-tarium*, *-torium*, etc., are generally written with the hooked *tr*; thus, *cometarium*, *moratorium*.

(4) Words ending in *-chord* are written with half-length *kr*: thus, *tetrachord*, *monochord*.

(5) Words ending in *-form* are written with the hooked form, or, after ... or ...: thus, *stalactiform* *spongiform*, *aciform*, *curviform*, *vermiform*. In other cases separate *r* is used; thus, *napiform*, *cuneiform*, *metalliform*, *variform*.

(6) Words ending in *-culate -gulate*, *-cular*, *-gular*, and *-culum* are generally written with the hooked strokes *kl* or *gl*; thus, *calculate*, *speculate*, *gesticulate*, *reticulate*, *articulate*, *circulate*, *matriculate*, *coagulate*, *regulate* *binocular*, *angular*, *singular*, *curriculum*.

(7) The prefix *for-* is represented by or, when this is inconvenient, by ; thus, *forsake*, *forbear*, but *forget*. This does not apply to the prefix *fore-*, which should be written with separate *r* (downward in preference) when convenient; thus, *forecast*, *forenoon*, *foresight* (compare *ferocity*); otherwise the hooked form is used: thus, *foretell*, *foreshorten*, *forewarn*.

(8) COMPOUND WORDS ending in *-bird* and *-board* are written with the half-length *br* whenever convenient; thus, *jailbird*, *mocking-bird*, *blackboard*, *switchboard*. But note *pasteboard*; also *keyboard*, for distinction.

FINAL N (STROKE AND HOOK)

(1) Words ending in *-nian* are generally written with the hook for the final *n*, even in the case of DERIVATIVES from words with outlines ending with hook *n*: thus, *Etonian*, *Hamiltonian*, but note *Gladstonian*, *Augustinian*, *Athenian*.

(2) Words ending in *-n nt* are generally written with hook *n* finally: thus, *anent*, *assonant*, *dissonant*. Final *-n nt* preceded by *p*, stroke *t* or *v*, or *m* is, however, written with stroke *nt* finally; thus, *pennant*, *tenant*, *convenient*, *dominant*, as are also the words *consonant* and *sonant*.

(3) Words ending in *-t n* or *-d n* are generally written with the hook for the final *n*: thus, *fatten*, *wheaten*, *abandon*.

(4) The final *n* is, however, represented by the stroke in the following cases—

(*a*) Words ending in *-rt n* or *-j st n*, such as *Spartan*, *martin*, *congestion*. Compare *puritan*, *baritone*, *Samaritan*, in which a vowel occurs between the *r* and the *t*.

(*b*) Most words ending in *-ntine*, *e.g.* *turpentine*.

(*c*) The words *fountain*, *mountain*, *plantain*, *pontoon*, *bounden*, and *garden*.

N PRECEDED BY TWO VOWEL-SOUNDS

Stroke *n* is used—(*a*) After a TRIPHONE consisting of *ū* and a vowel: thus, *genuine*, *constituent*, *pursuant*. Compare *lion*, *client*, *compliance*, *buoyancy*, in which the *n* is preceded by other triphones.

(*b*) After two separate vowel-signs; thus, *triune*.

(*c*) In the words *pioneer*, *giant*, *buoyant*, *heroine*, *ruin*, and several words ending in *-fluent*, *e.g.*, *fluent*, *mellifluent*. Compare other words in which *n* occurs after a diphone, *e.g.*, *crayon*, *cayenne*, *hygiene*.

Note also words like *recurrence*, *concurrent*, in which stroke *n* is used although the two vowel sounds do not occur together.

MEDIAL N

(1) In the absence of any special reason to the contrary, stroke *n* is used between *p*, *b*, *t*, *d*, *ch* or *j* and *full-length t* or *d*; thus, *pantaloon*, *bountiful*, *tantalize*, *dental*, *legendary*;

(2) But the hook is used between the same strokes and *half-length t* or *d*, unless the *n* is followed by a vowel; thus, *painted*, *potentate*, *daunted*, *enchanted*, *jointed*, but *penitent*, *originated*.

Note, however, *abandon* and *urbanity*, in which the other circular movement in the outlines renders the hook more convenient.

Stroke *n* is used after only one downstroke having an initial attachment on the opposite side; thus, *stranded*, *reprinted*, *branded*. Compare *disappointed*, *suspended*.

(3) Hook *n* is used between *r* and *n* in such words as *barrenness*, *modernness*, but stroke *n* is preferred between *sr* or *w* and *n*; thus, *sereneness*, *oneness*. Similarly *roundness*, but *windiness*.

(4) Stroke *n* is generally retained in DERIVATIVES from words written with the stroke, other than a few ending in *-ic* or *-cy;* thus, *funnier*, *puniness*; but *euphonic*, *subserviency*.

MEDIAL NS

(5) Stroke *n* is used medially before *s* or *z*, unless the hook is clearly more convenient; thus, *Wednesday*, *wainscot*, *caravansary*, but *ransom*, *lonesome*, *Ironside*.

(6) Two hooks together are generally avoided; hence *plunger*, *ranger*. They are, however, allowed in *kindred*, *hundred*, *manger*, *philanthropist*, and one or two uncommon words, as well as certain compound words (see next paragraph).

(7) In COMPOUND WORDS hook *n* is often retained medially, even where it would be avoided in other words; *e.g.*, *open-mouthed*, *penman*, *mainmast*, *rainproof*, *earthenware*.

F, V (HOOK AND STROKE)

(1) Words ending in *-tive* (other than those which are contracted) are generally written with ; thus, *receptive*, *inventive*. Exceptions to the above are *captive*, *plaintive*, *comparative*, and such words as *attentive*, *retentive*, *digestive*, *suggestive*.

(2) The stroke is used for *f* or *v* occurring between *p* or *b* (without an initial attachment) and *t* or *d;* thus, *pivot*, *buffet*. After or , however, the hook is more convenient; thus, *private*, *brevity*.

(3) Hook *f* or *v* is used between *t*, *d* or *ch* and *t* or *d* in DERIVATIVES as well as other words; thus *sanctified*, *Cheviot*. Note, however, *defied*, *edified* and *deified*, for distinction.

DIRECTION OF "SHUN" HOOK

Words like *probation*, *correction*, etc., are written in accordance with the principle of paragraph 95 of the *Instructor*: and *decoction*, *adoption*, *inaction*, etc., are also written in accordance with the spirit, though not the letter, of paragraph 96.

THE ASPIRATE

(1) Initial *h* followed by a TRIPHONE is represented by the upward or the downward stroke, and not by the tick; thus, *Higham*, *Howard*, *hierarchy*, *hyaline*, *Howell*.

(2) Downward *h* is used in a few cases to create a clear distinction of outline, as *heritor* (*inheritor*), *heritable* (*inheritable*), or to provide a more easily written form, as *heritage*.

(3) Words beginning with *hetero-* are written with except before — or , when is more convenient; thus, *heterogeneous*, *heterodox*; but *heterogamous*, *heteromorphous*, *heterology*.

(4) COMPOUND WORDS ending in *-house* are written as under—

(*a*) With if convenient for joining, *i.e.* after *p, b, t, d, l* or a straight upstroke; thus, *chop-house*, *club-house*, *gate-house*, *coffee-house*, *warehouse*, *hothouse*.

(*b*) With after *k, g, m* or *l*; thus, *workhouse*, *log-house*, *summer-house*, *ale-house*

(*c*) When stroke *s* gives a better joining than either or , *i.e.* after *ch, s, sh, n, ng*, a circle or a hook; thus, *coach-house*, *ice-house*, *wash-house*, *pigeon-house*, *alms-house*, *greenhouse*.

(5) Downward *h* is retained in DERIVATIVES and COMPOUNDS of words in which *h* is the only consonant, if a *syllable* is added to the primitive word; thus, *highness*, *highest*, *hoer*, *high-bred*,

hay-loft. Compare *hoed*, *hewn*, etc., in which there is no added syllable.

(6) Medial *h*. With regard to words ending in *-hold*, *-holed*, etc.—

(*a*) The form is used after *p*, *b*, *f*, *v*, TH, or *h*; thus, *uphold*, *copyhold*, *behold*, *foothold*, *overhauled*, *withhold*, *high-heeled*.

(*b*) In other cases dot *h* and either or, if more convenient, are written: thus, *pigeon-holed*, *stronghold*, *strangle-hold*, *leasehold*

UPWARD AND DOWNWARD R AND L

(1) Words beginning with *st* (*vowel*) *r* followed by stroke *n* have upward *r*: thus, *consternation*, *sternutation*, *Stornoway*.

(2) Final *r* is written upward (among other cases) after *kr*, *gr* or *lk*; thus, *crier*, *grower*, *luckier*; but downward after *sk*, or *fk*; thus, *obscure*, *fakir*.

(3) Final *r* in COMPOUNDS, as in other words is written upward after two downstrokes; thus, *tax-gatherer*, *shooting-star*

(4) In words ending in *-rest*, *-rist*, *-lest* or *-list* the *r* or *l* is written upward or downward as when followed by a final vowel; thus, *barest*, *fairest*, *imperialist*, *fullest*, *annalist*.

(5) Medial *r* is nearly always written downward before *m*; thus, *barium*, *emporium*, *forum*. After *th*, however, it is written upward; thus, *theorem*.

(6) Medial *r* is also written downward in most DERIVATIVES from words written with downward *r*; thus, *declarable*, *powerful*, *barely*, *furrier*, *maturely*; but in words ending in *-rial*, *-ral* or *-rhal* upward *r* is used; thus, *armorial*, *mayoral*, *catarrhal*.

(7) Final *l* after or is written as after ; thus, *egotistical*, *methodistical*, *logistical*, *fantastically*.

(8) *L* occurring finally, or with only a circle or loop following, is written downward after a half-length or double-length stroke if a more convenient outline is so obtained; thus, *completely*, *shiftless*, *vividly*, *pectoral*, *structural*. Note *actual* and *actually* for distinction.

(9) Final *l* is written upward after downward *l* in *genteelly*, *foully*, etc., but downward after *ld* or *lr* in *mildly*, *scholarly*, etc.

(10) Final *l* is written downward in COMPOUNDS of words written with upward *l* if the upward form would be quite inconvenient for joining, as in *sand-eel*, *train-oil*, but the upward form is retained if at all practicable, as in *port-hole*, *stock-list*.

(11) Medial *l* is written upward in *biliousness* and *superciliousness*, but downward in words ending in *-lescence* or *-lescent*; e.g., *opalescence*, *coalescent*. It is also written upward before whenever practicable; thus, *realism*, *imperialism*, but *sensationalism*, *naturalism*.

UPWARD AND DOWNWARD SH

(1) Final *sh* is written downward after *t* (or *st*); but upward after *d*; thus, *latish*, *coquettish*, *crustacea*, *moustache*, but *radish*, *Swedish*. Exception— *brutish*

(2) Final *-shŭs* is written upward after *t*, *d* or *sd*, but downward after *st*; thus, *fictitious* *seditious*, but *superstitious*.

(3) The words *mopish* and *mobbish* are written with upward *sh* on the same principle as *brush* (see *Instructor*, par. 120).

(4) Final *sh* or *sh s* after upward *l* is written downward: thus, *lash*, *slash*, *polish*, *malicious*; but in the past tenses *lashed*, *polished*, etc., upward *sh* is more convenient.

COMPOUND CONSONANTS

(1) *Wl* and *wh l*. The compound consonants and are used in all words beginning with *w l d* and *wh l d* respectively: thus, *wailed*, *weld*, *wild*, *wilder*, *wheeled*.

(2) *Rr*. The use of is strictly confined to derivatives from words written with final downward *r*; hence, *sorcerer*, *fruiterer*, *usurer*.

The compound consonant is not used after *l*; hence, *cellarer*.

(3) The word *queer* is so written in order to keep it quite distinct from *clear*.

(4) *Kw* and *mp*, *mb* in COMPOUND WORDS. A consonant at the end of the first part of a compound word is not combined with a consonant beginning the second part; hence *silk-worm*, *dumb-bell*, *tomboy*. An exception to this is the word *lukewarm*.

HALVING PRINCIPLE

(1) A stroke is not halved when a better outline is obtained by means of the full *t* or *d*; thus, *hotel*, *flotsam*, *graduation*, *indulge*, *integer*, *interior*, *tautology*, *litigious*, *lemonade*.

(2) Words ending in *-tatory*, *-datory*, *-ditary*, etc., are treated as follows—

(*a*) In the case of the termination *-tatory* the last *t* is generally written in full; thus, *rotatory*, *excitatory*, *saltatory*; but

(*b*) When the termination is *-datory*, *-ditary*, the halving principle is generally applied; thus, *consolidatory*, *hereditary*.

(3) Words ending in *-tively* following stroke *t* or *tr* are written with full *t*; thus, *authoritatively*, *illustratively*.

(4) Words ending in *-ctary*, *-ctory*, *-catory*, *-gatory*, *-clarian*, etc., are generally written with full *t*; thus, *directory*, *purgatory*, *Tractarian*. A better outline, however, is obtained by halving in such words as *secretary*, *migratory*.

(5) Words ending in *-taceous* and *-dacious* are written with full *t* or *d*; thus, *cretaceous*, *mendacious*.

(6) Although the halving principle is generally applied for the addition of either *t* or *d* in words of more than one syllable, in primitive words a thin stroke (other than or which can be thickened as well as halved) is not halved standing alone to add *d*, or a thick stroke standing alone to add *t*, unless there is a final hook or a joined diphthong: thus, *acrid*, *applaud*, *adroit*, *sedate*, *seclude*. Exceptions to this are— *convert*, *concord* and *conclude*.

In past tenses of more than one syllable, however, a thin stroke may generally be halved; thus, *seated*, *stated*, *uttered*, *offered*, *supplied*, *construed*, *committed*, *commuted*; but note *echoed* and *essayed*.

(7) The more common words ending in *-pid* are written with half-length *p*; thus, *tepid*, *insipid*; but

(8) Words ending in *-pade*, *-ped*, *-pede* or *-pod* are generally written with full *d*; thus, *escapade*, *uniped*, *centipede*, *tripod*. But note *quadruped*, to avoid a lengthy outline.

(9) Words ending in *k* (vowel) *d* are generally written with full *d*; thus, *arcade*, *naked*, *decoyed*; but half-length *k* is used in a few words of more than two syllables, *e.g.*, *barricade*, *cavalcade*, and in the word *rescued*.

(10) Words ending in *g* (vowel) *t*, however, are generally written with half-length *g*; thus, *frigate*, *target*, *nugget*.

(11) As a rule the halving principle is not applied if the resulting outline would not be capable of full vocalization. It is, however, applied in the case of a number of words ending in *-tism* or *-dism* in which a more facile outline is obtained by disregarding the " i," viz., *despotism*, *Jacobitism*, *patriotism*, *blackguardism*, *favouritism*, *scepticism*, and several words ending in *-matism* such as, *rheumatism*. Compare such words as *absolutism*, *conservatism*, etc., in which the full outline is quite convenient.

(12) The halving principle is, as a rule, applied when *t* or *d* is preceded by a DIPHONE ; thus, *create*, *druid*, *radiate* ; but the *t* is written in full in *poet*, *silhouette*, and a few uncommon words and proper names.

(13) Stroke *t* or *d* is retained when convenient in the following classes of DERIVATIVES, viz.—

(*a*) Words derived, either directly or indirectly, from *primitive* words with outlines containing stroke *t* or *d* and not more than one other stroke consonant : *e.g.*, *pitiful*, *cottony*, *gluttonous*, *bedeck*, *undivided*, *becloud*, *overrate*, *outspread*, *overcrowd*. The following are exceptional— *beautify*, *beautiful*, *written*, *writing*, *undefined*, *indebted*, *subdivide*

(*b*) Certain secondary derivatives from *primary derivatives* written with stroke *t* or *d*, in which the stroke is retained for the purpose of distinction ; *e.g.* *weightiness*, *greediness*, *heartily*, *flightiness*.

(*c*) In words ending in *-tieth*, in order to prevent the possibility of confusion between *seventieth* and *seventh* ; *fiftieth*, and *fifth*, etc.

(14) In COMPOUNDS of words with outlines ending in stroke *t* or *d* that *t* or *d* is generally expressed by halving; thus, *copyright*, *backbite*, *ice-boat*, *cow-hide*, *go-ahead*, *brush-wood*. Stroke *t* or *d* is, however, retained after one half-length stroke, as in *tit-bit*, *catboat*, and also in a few cases in which the full *t* or *d* gives a more distinct outline, *e.g.*, *rosewood*, *jolly-boat*, *row-boat*.

(15) In COMPOUNDS of words commencing with *t* or *d*, that *t* or *d* is not expressed by halving; thus, *time-table*, *grave-digger*, *quarter-deck*. Exceptions— *sometimes* and *beforetime*.

(16) *Lt* is generally written upward as in *fault*, *quilt*, *exult*; but it is written downward—

(*a*) When preceded by an initial vowel and followed by *m*, as in *ultimo*, and

(*b*) After *n*, *ng*, *vs* or *ns* as in *knelt*, *ringlet*, *vacillate*, *insult*; also in the word *dwelt*.

(17) *Rd*. With regard to final *rd*, the forms *veered*, *persevered*, etc., are adopted because, although not strictly in accordance with the rule, they are quite distinct and more convenient than the possible alternatives , , etc. On the other hand, in such words as *geared*, is a better form than , which latter would become indistinct in practice.

(18) In addition to cases in which would be actually inconvenient, is used for final *rd* in such past tenses as *rendered*, *surrendered*, *wintered*. (Compare *windward*.)

(19) *Ld*. When would be inconvenient *ld* is represented by the full form ; thus, *quarrelled*, *belittled*, *scheduled*, *leasehold*. Note: is sufficiently convenient in *retailed*, *mild*, *lulled*, etc.

DOUBLING PRINCIPLE

(1) The doubling principle is not applied in words ending in *-lateral* and *-literal*, double-length *l* being used only in words in which it occurs *finally* and in words derived from these: hence, *lateral* (compare *latterly*), *pluriliteral*, *poulterer* (compare *slaughterer*), *liturgy* (compare *lighterage*).

(2) The doubling principle, which is applied in the case of most common words ending in *-ture*, is not applied in the following instances— *literature*, *capture* (the outline being required for *captor*), *furniture*, and words like *departure* and *candidature*.

(3) When the vowel in the termination *tor* is sounded distinctly, as in the legal terms *grantor*, *vendor*, *guarantor*, the doubling principle is not applied.

(4) The doubling principle is applied in a few cases although there is an accented vowel between *t* and *r*; *e.g.* *interpret*, *enteric*, *dysenteric*, *tartaric*, *material*.

(5) The doubling principle is also applied in the following cases notwithstanding that there is no vowel between the *t* or *d* and the *r*—

(*a*) Several words containing *central*, *centri-* or *-centric*, *e.g.*, *central*, *concentric*, *eccentric*, *centrifugal*.

(*b*) *theatrical*, *cylindric*.

(6) Words ending in *-erate* or *-orate*, although derived from words written with a double-length stroke, are written by means of the halving principle (*i.e.*, in the same way as past tenses such as *centred*); thus, *directorate*, *stadtholderate*

(7) The doubling principle is not applied when *tr* is preceded by a triphone representing a diphthong and a long vowel; thus, *extenuator*, *punctuator*. Compare *proprietor*, *radiator*

(8) Joining of Strokes of Unequal Length. Paragraph 142 (*a*) of the *Instructor* applies to double-length as well as half-length strokes. Double-length *n*, however, is sufficiently distinct after *t* or downward *l*; thus, *detonator*, *alienator*.

(9) Double-length *l* is written upward, except after *n*, *ng*, *ns* or *sh*; thus, *filter*, *beholder*, *gilder*, but *penholder*, *ringleader*, *insulter*, *scolder*, *helter-skelter*.

(10) Double-length strokes may be used in such COMPOUND WORDS as the following— *backbiter*, *chaff-cutter*, *muzzle-loader*.

PREFIXES

Trans- is contracted by the omission of the *n* when it is followed by *p*, *m*, upward *l*, or the hooked letters *pl*, *kr*, *gr*, *fr*, and *fl*; thus, *transparent*, *transmit*, *translation*, *transplant*, *transcribe*, *transgress*, *transfer*, *transfluent*.

SUFFIXES

(1) With reference to *-ing* the stroke is used after, although it does not give a very convenient joining, as the dot might be mistaken for a vowel-sign; thus, *utilizing*, *releasing*.

(2) When adding *-ing*, the outline of the original word is almost invariably left unaltered; thus, *fancying*, *freezing*, *shelling*, *cleansing*, *hoeing*, *allowing*, *failing*, *piercing*, *pushing*, *rating*. Exceptions to this are *losing*, *lacing*, etc., *ailing*, *coalescing*, *convalescing*, and *writing*.

(3) When the outline of the present tense ends with a joined diphthong, the latter is not retained if stroke can be joined; thus, *renewing*, *pursuing*, *bowing*.

(4) Outlines containing stroke *ng*, when used in the representation of the suffix *-ing* are vocalized in the ordinary way, whether the vowel is a third-place vowel or otherwise; thus, *laying*, *gnawing*.

(5) *-ality*, *-ility*, *-arity*, etc., are expressed by means of a disjoined stroke in the great majority of cases, including practically all of the large number of words ending in *-bility*. The words which are written in full include—

(*a*) Words ending in *-alty*, *-iality*, *erty*, or *-iority*, if the full outline is quite convenient; thus, *penalty*, *cordiality*, *partiality*, *veniality*, *inferiority*.

(*b*) Words in which the full outline is particularly facile, especially after a half-length stroke; *e.g.*, *fertility*, *austerity*, *maturity*, *verticality*, *personality*.

(*c*) Words in which the *-ality*, etc., is preceded by only one stroke or by *s* or *shun*; thus, *hilarity*, *facility*, *nationality*.

(*d*) In a few cases for the purpose of distinction; *e.g.*, *juniority* (*geniality*), *locality* (*legality*), *disparity* (*disability*)

(*e*) *compatibility*, *accessibility*, *asperity*, and a few other miscellaneous words.

A vowel preceding the disjoined consonant indicating the suffix *-ality*, etc., may, if necessary, be disregarded; thus, *visibility*.

(6) *-ment* is represented by after or , or a hook to which the full form cannot conveniently be joined; thus, *consignment*, *preferment*, *effacement*, *commencement*, *enchantment*, *pavement*; also in *enlistment*. When can be made convenient, it is often written in preference to the contracted form; thus, *discernment*, *rescindment*, *amendment*, *assortment*.

(7) The suffix may be joined when occurring after full-length *r*, *n* or *ng*, also, when convenient, after a hook (the preceding part of the outline remaining unaltered); thus, *censorship*, *companionship*, *kingship*, *friendship*, *relationship*. *-Ship* is written in full after *l*, as in *fellowship*, also in *airship*.

(8) Disjoined may be used in COMPOUND and other words in which *-ship* is not grammatically a suffix: thus, *battleship*, *midshipman*, *lightship*.

(9) *-fulness* is represented by the disjoined suffix except in *delightfulness*, *doubtfulness* and *beautifulness*.

GRAMMALOGUES

DERIVATIVES and COMPOUNDS from grammalogues are written by retaining the logogram (unvocalized) in the outline whenever a convenient and legible form is so obtained; thus *golden*, *thankless*, *deliverer*, *advantageous*, *would-be*, *twofold*.

CONTRACTIONS

(1) With reference to the omission of medial *t* after *s*—see *Instructor*, par. 183 (*c*), when a vowel occurs immediately after the *t*, the latter is not omitted except in the following instances; viz. *postal*, *postage*, *post-office*, *testament*, *testimony*, *procrastinate*, *investigate*, *mistake*, *domestic*, *pessimistic*, *optimistic*, *euphemistic*, *mediumistic*, *bombastic*, *futuristic*, *substitute*, *substitution*, *destitute*, *destitution*, *institute*, *institution*, *celestial*, and derivatives from these words (*mistook* excepted). Compare *pistol*, *vestige*, *sophisticate*, *mystic*, *plastic*, *rustic*, etc., in which the *t* is expressed.

(2) In addition to the contractions appearing in the lists in the textbooks, contracted forms are also given in the Dictionary, as alternatives to the full outlines, for some other words, which are not considered to be of such frequent occurrence in general matter as to warrant their inclusion in the lists.

DERIVATIVE WORDS

The derivation of words must be regarded as one of a number of considerations affecting the choice of outlines, but while in the outlines of many derivatives the outline of the primitive word, or some particular feature of it, is retained, there are, on the other hand, many cases in which derivatives are written in accordance with the ordinary rules and principles of the system, without regard to derivation; *e.g.*, *remove*, *remover*; *bitter*, *embitter*. *hawk*, *hawker*. *ail*, *ailment*; *royal*, *royalist*.

Words described as "derivatives" are taken to include any words that are *apparently* derived from other English words.

In the above notes, attention is drawn by means of capitals to the treatment of certain classes of derivative and compound words.

DERIVATIVES ANTICIPATED

In certain cases, including some verbs previously mentioned, words are written in a particular way so that their outlines may agree with those of derivatives formed from them, *e.g.*, *meddle*, *meddled*; *wanton*, *wantonly*; *clandestine*, *clandestinely*; *captive*, *captivate*; *inadvertent*, *inadvertently*; *exist*, *existence*, *sister*, *sisterly*; *scientific*, *scientifically*; *shelter*, *sheltered*.

COMPOUND WORDS

A number of classes of compound words have already been dealt with in connection with the various principles involved. With regard to cases in which the outlines of the primary words will not join conveniently, they are written disjoined if a better outline is not obtainable by altering one or both of them so as to admit of joining. (See also next par.)

DISJOINING

(1) Disjoining is not resorted to if a better outline can otherwise be obtained; thus *tactics*, *locate*, *densely*, *rearrange*, but *misfeasance*, *steadfast*, *mentionable*, *deaf-mute*, *spendthrift*.

(2) Three straight strokes that would not make an angle are not joined together; hence *picture-gallery*, *turkey-cock*.

(3) Outlines in which one at least of three strokes is a curve are generally allowable although there is no angle; thus, *papacy*, *clockwork*; but the combination is avoided; hence, *tuckier*

(4) Sometimes an angle is shown in order to make a joining allowable; thus, *escheat*, *Hebraized*.

(5) More than two successive downstrokes including *p b*, *d t*, etc., are generally avoided by disjoining in such words as *top-boots*, *red-tapism*, *quarter-deck*. Compare *copy-book* *seed-time* *tea-dealer*, in which there are only two downstrokes.

OUTLINES AND VOWELS

Outlines, as a rule, are not varied in order to permit of a vowel-sign being placed exactly in its proper place; thus, *legislation*, *ceaseless*, *ingeniously*, *appropriately*, *meanwhile*. In a few cases, however, in which an outline that can be more accurately vocalized is a better one from a practical point of view, it is adopted, *e.g.*, *doubtless* *unsoiled*.

In certain cases in which it would be difficult to insert an intersected vowel-sign it is disregarded; *e.g.*, *figurative*, *calculated*, *partiality*

SPECIAL OUTLINES

It will be recognized that there are many pairs or groups of words which, from their meaning, are liable to clash, and every precaution is necessary in such cases to avoid the risk of confusion. In a great majority of cases the application of the ordinary rules of the system affords adequate means of distinction, but in a comparatively few of these pairs of words, such as *favoured*, *favourite*; *Australian*, *Australasian* *birth*, *burial*; which otherwise would be written with the same or a very similar form, a special outline is adopted for one of them in order to provide a clear distinction. Again, in a few instances, such as *solicitor*, *affidavit*, *oxyhydrogen*, *tartaric*, *sincerely*, *necessarily*, it has been found advisable, in order to secure the most convenient outline, to adopt a form which is not capable of being fully vocalized, or which is not written in accordance with the usual practice. A list of these special outlines, in addition to those already mentioned in this Introduction, is given below. It should be borne in mind that such outlines, except in the case of some derivatives from the words in question, must not necessarily be regarded as models for the formation of other outlines.

The following outlines are written out of their proper position for the purpose of distinction— *human*, *woman*, *permanent*.

The Index to the Introduction will be found most useful where it is desired to refer to any word or class of word

LIST OF SPECIAL OUTLINES

afresh
agent
alcohol
alkali
alliance
allowance
antithesis
assuredly
avert
avoidance
bachelor
bankrupt
beerhouse
bold
candlestick
capital
caused
*child*less
conciliatory
considerate
constitute
*dear*est
delightful
descriptions
desert
destiny
diffract
discern
downright
edification
editor
editorial
erudite
eventually
explode
eyesight
eyesore
fallen
farmer
fiscal
flannelette
foundation
further
futile
futurism
garnet
Gentile
girth
gradually
guidance
hardiest

heartily
hearty
hospital
hyoid
ignominy
illness
impercepti-ble
indigent
indolent
inert
inevitable
intromission
junior
marital
merchandise
moodily
moral
mortal
Mrs.
narrate
needful
needless
notable
officiated
omniscient
orator

ordinal
ornament
ornamental
outburst
oval
partake
*particular*ly
pattern
pennon
persecute
poorest
preciseness
pre-eminent
proprietary
Protestant
protestation
pure
qualify
quality
queerly
railroad
rebate
rebut
regret
revere
reverie

secretariat
separate
shortened
shrinker
sightseer
solitary
standardize
start
statute
subvert
swerved
synod
temperate
transept
trivial
undoubted
unlikely
unluckily
upright
ursiform
verbal
veritable
vesture
virile
vitiated
vitiation

PROPER NAMES

In connection with these the pronunciation has been checked from the *Century Cyclopedia of Proper Names*, the *Standard Dictionary*, and other sources. It should be remembered that proper names have frequently more than one accepted pronunciation. In some instances, such as *Grantham*, *Evesham*, etc., there is a local and also an "outside" pronunciation, and in the case of foreign names some have an anglicized pronunciation while others are given a native pronunciation only. From the shorthand point of view some proper names require special consideration, and the following observations will serve to indicate the practice which has been adopted in various groups of words—

(1) When the *nses* circle is used, the vowel is understood to be *ĕ*: it is therefore necessary to write stroke *n* and the *ses* circle when another vowel occurs, as in *Albigenses*, *Waldenses*.

(2) Proper names ending in *-ley* preceded by the sound of *k* are generally written with the hooked letter; thus, *Brockley*, *Hinckley*.

(3) Words ending in *-shire* are generally written with the hooked letter *shr*; thus, *Ayrshire*, *Aberdeenshire*.

(4) Words ending in *-ford* are generally written with the half-length hooked letter (or); thus, *Woodford*, *Catford*, *Oxford*. The separate however is used after etc., as in *Swinford*, *Cinderford*, *Chingford*.

(5) The hooked letter is used for the terminations *-borough*, *-burgh*, *-bury*, when it is more convenient than the separate *b-r*, including cases in which it occurs after *t*, *d*, *m*, *ms*, *l*, *ls*; thus, *Attleborough*, *Flamborough*, *Aldeburgh*, *Bloomsbury*, *Tilbury*, *Halsbury*.

(6) Proper names ending in *-ton* or *-don* are treated in the same way as other words having those terminations (see page xxi); thus, *Merton*, *Pemberton*, *Cheriton*, *Clifton*, *Bandon*.

(7) Words ending in *-field* are generally written with , but after / or / hook *f* is used; thus, *Duffield*, but *Lichfield*, *Sedgfield*.

(8) In the majority of words ending in *-ham* the *h* is silent, *e.g.*, *Clapham*, *Seaham*, *Ashburnham*, *Tottenham*, *Rotherham*, but in a few names of more than two syllables ending in *-ingham*, such as *Birmingham*, *Nottingham*, the aspirate is pronounced by some persons. There are also a number of names ending in *-sham* or *-tham* in which custom has sanctioned the sound of *sh* and *th* respectively, *e.g.*, *Horsham*, *Waltham*, *Bentham*, though in others the *s* or *t* sound is retained, *e.g.*, *Topsham*, *Cheetham*, *Greatham*.

(9) The *h* in the termination *-hurst* is generally represented by the dot; thus, *Lyndhurst*, *Billingshurst*. In a few instances, however, it is disregarded in order to obtain a more convenient outline, *e.g.*, *Pankhurst*, *Parkhurst*.

(10) After *k* (among other cases) the terminations *-wall*, *-well*, are most conveniently written with ; thus, *Kirkwall*, *Bakewell*. After upward *l*, however, is sufficiently convenient; as *Holywell*.

(11) When the vowel in the termination *-ville* is sounded distinctly, the separate *l* is written if convenient; thus, *Sackville*, *Granville*, but *Nashville*.

(12) The termination *-gate* is written with full *t*; thus, *Bishopsgate*, *Deansgate*, *Cripplegate*.

(13) *-wood*, however, is generally written with half-length *w*; thus, *Attwood*, *Kingswood*. Exception, *Heywood*, to distinguish from *Hayward*.

(14) Words having the termination *-worth* are written with ; thus, *Saddleworth*, *Nailsworth*; or when necessary to avoid an awkward or too lengthy outline, with vocalized with *wŭ*; thus, *Wandsworth*, *Wordsworth*.

(15) In words ending in *-ing*, the dot is used after or or after following another stroke; thus, *Epping*, *Wapping*, *Hastings*, *Twining*, *Spalding*. In other cases stroke is written; thus, *Tooting*, *Kettering*, *Hutchings* *Harding*, *Jennings*, *Behring*.

(16) In proper names *p* is not omitted when it occurs between *m* and *t* or *m* and *sh*; *e.g.*, *Hampstead* (*Hamstead*), *Ampthill*, *Compton*, *Assumption*, *Hampshire*. In *Campden* the *p* is silent.

(17) In proper names having their origin in uncontracted logograms the logograms are retained, but may be vocalized; thus, *Child*, *Gold*, *Short*. Proper names having their origin in contracted grammalogues are written in full; thus, *Lord*, *Liberty*, *Wordsworth*, *Yardley*, *Goodyear*, *Young*.

(18) In several place names such as *Kingston-on-Thames*, *Stratford-on-Avon*, *Burton-on-Trent*, *Clacton-on-Sea*, *Southend-on-Sea* the preposition may be omitted.

(19) The following are so written in order to obtain an easy or distinct outline— *Surat*, *Shetland*, *Thetford*, *Dudley* *Jedburgh*, *Ushant*, *London*, *Carruthers*, *Sutherland*, *Weymouth*.

DISTINGUISHING OUTLINES

The following distinguishing outlines should be noted— *Frances,* *Francis;* *Persia,* *Prussia;* *Tenby,* *Denbigh;* *Dunbar,* *Edinburgh;* *Didsbury,* *Dewsbury;* *Bute,* *Bude;* *Symonds,* *Simmons;* *Wyndham,* *Wenham;* *Cobbett,* *Cobb;* *Hindley,* *Huntley;* *Wales,* *Wells;* *Mather,* *Modder;* *Barmen,* *Bremen.*

NEW ERA CHANGES

The following is a summary of the changes introduced in the "New Era" edition of the system by practically all of which some simplification of a rule is effected—

"Right" semicircle used to express initial *w* before *k, g, m,* and *r* (upward or downward).

Triphones used to represent a diphthong and *any* vowel (either short or long).

St loop used in words like *steady, steadied,* etc.

Shr always written downward.

Shl always written upward.

Singer, wringer, etc., now vocalized regularly.

"Right" curves *fl* and *vl* discontinued except after *k, g, n, ng,* or a straight upstroke.

"Right" forms of *thl* and *THl* discontinued.

Words ending in *-cular* and *-gular* are now as a rule written with the hooked strokes.

(*Note.*—The contractions *regular* and *irregular* are retained.)

the case of *spr, str,* etc., following another stroke, the *r* hook is now shown whether the two strokes make an angle or not.

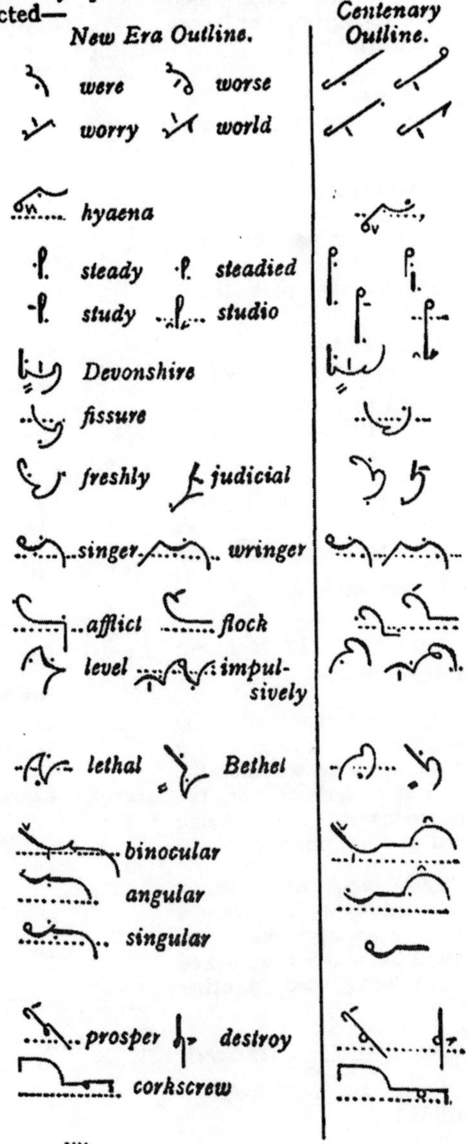

	New Era Outline.	*Centenary Outline.*
-uation. The outlines etc.. now vocalized with triphone.	*accentuation*	
Tick *h* no longer used before stroke *s* or *z* or before hooked strokes.	*Hesse* *hazy* *history* *Hastings* *hatred* *Huddersfield*	
Dot *h* no longer used initially.	*handed* *hundred*	
Final *sh* now written downward after upward *l* whether the word is a verb or not. (*Note.*—Upward *sh* retained in the past tenses *polished*, etc.)	*polish* *relish*	
Use of *rer* strictly confined to derivatives from words written with downward *r* finally.	*sorcerer* *fruiterer*	
Words in which the consonants are *h-ld* and *w-ld* now written with and respectively.	*held* *wild*	
Use of to represent *ld* discontinued.	*quarrelled* *mildly*	
Mpr, *mbr* represented by when following — *k* or an upstroke whether the word is a verb or not, the double-length being used in other cases.	*lumber* *Cumberland* *Humber*	
Ng-kr, *ng-gr* when occurring initially or following a circle or an upstroke represented by , the hooked stroke being used in other cases. (*Note.* *shrinker*, retained as a "special" outline.)	*anchor* *anchorage* *hanker* *linger* *conger*	

	New Era Outline.	Centenary Outline.
Doubling principle no longer applied to [outline] or [outline]	conqueror; slumberer	
Y diphthongs discontinued (with exception of diphthong *u*), and diphone [outline] used for *ia*, *ie*, etc., even when monosyllabic. (=*ya*, *ye*, etc.)	lawyer; vineyard; Spaniard; million	
W diphthongs restricted to medial use, and initial, joined semicircle used to represent consonant *w* only	water; washer; withstand; railway; walk	
Use of [outline] for *Wil-* discontinued.	Wilson; William	
Com in *-coming* is now indicated by disjoining.	becoming; becomingly; welcoming	
Inter- and *enter-* are now written in accordance with the rule for doubling and [outline] is given as a prefix representing *intro-*.	enterprise; intermingle; introduce	
The hook prefix *in-* is no longer used before *spr*.	inspiration	
Words which are uncontracted and are written in their regular position are excluded from the list of Grammalogues and a few other Grammalogues are discontinued.	happy; happen; children; suggest; suggested; suggestive; suggestion; journal; half; Heaven; initial; holy; whither; will; met; ye; youth; youths	
Logogram for *for* altered.	for	

A few other contracted logograms and a number of contractions are excluded from the lists and are now given in the Dictionary only as alternatives to the full outlines.

New Era Outline.	Centenary Outline.
or religious	
or religion	
or generation	
or Christian	
or Christianity	
or constitutional-ly	
or Phonography	
or saviour	
or scripture	

Logogram he now used only when joined to a preceding character.

In addition to the alterations referred to above. the outlines of a number of words have been regularized, *e.g.*, *travel*, *forefather* *vastly*, *income*. On the other hand, a few further words are given "special" outlines either for the purpose of distinction, *e.g.*, *burial*, *further*, *secretariat*, or for convenience, *e.g.*, *typewriter*.

Certain contractions which it has not been thought necessary to retain in the lists in the textbooks are now given in the Dictionary as alternatives to the full outlines; and alternative contracted forms are also given for some further words for which safe contractions may at times be desired.

INDEX TO INTRODUCTION

A. Subjects

B. Illustrative Words

Q

R

S

T

U

KEY TO ABBREVIATIONS USED IN THIS DICTIONARY

abbrev.	abbreviation
adj.	adjective
adv.	adverb
Amer.	American
anat.	anatomical
archit.	architectural
art.	article
astr.	astronomical
bel.	belonging
biol.	biological
chem.	chemical
colloq.	colloquial
comp.	comparative
conj.	conjunction
def.	definite
esp.	especially
fig.	figuratively
Fr.	French
Gr.	Greek
her.	heraldic
impers.	impersonal
indef.	indefinite
interj.	interjection
interrog	interrogative
i.q.	same as
Ital.	Italian
Lat.	Latin
leg.	legal
lit.	literally
med.	medical
mus.	musical
n.	noun
naut.	nautical
obs.	obsolete
orig.	originally
pers.	personal
pert.	pertaining
phr.	phrase
pl.	plural
p.p.	past participle
prep.	preposition
pres.	present
pret.	preterite
pron.	pronoun
pr.p.	present participle
p.t.	past tense
rel.	relating to; relative
Scot.	Scottish
sing.	singular
super.	superlative
usu.	usually
v.i.	verb intransitive
v. reflex.	verb reflexive
v.t.	verb transitive

NOTES

(*a*) All grammalogues and contractions, other than those which are fully vocalized (such as 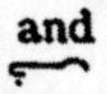 *cramped*), are printed in italic; also any portions of derivative or compound words for which logograms or contractions are retained.

(*b*) Only logograms and contractions (and their derivatives when the primitive forms are retained) occupying a first or a third position have their positions shown by a dotted line.

(*c*) Capitals are employed initially only where such is the ordinary usage, as in the case of proper names and terms. In botanical, zoological, and similar scientific terms, the names of genera are capitalized; with species bearing the same name a capital would not, of course, be used. For example, *Ranunculus*, the genus; but *ranunculus*, a plant of this genus.

Pitman's
English and Shorthand Dictionary

A

A, *indef. art.* or *adj.* (an before vowel or mute *h*), one, any.

Aaron'ic, } *adj.* pert.
Aaron'ical } to Aaron.

aback', *adv.*, behind, at the back. *Phr.* taken aback = surprised.

ab'acus, *n.*, now used only in architecture = the top portion of a pillar. Formerly used for arithmetical calculations, and consisted of beads or balls running on wires, and set in frame.

Abad'don, *n.*, the Destroying Angel; the bottomless pit.

abaft', *prep.* and *adv.*, astern, or towards the stern of a ship.

aban'don, *v.t.*, to give up, forsake, leave.

aban'doned, *p.p.*, abandon; *adj.*, shameless, profligate.

abandonee', *n.*, one to whom something is relinquished.

aban'doner, *n.*, one who abandons.

aban'doning, *pr.p.*, abandon.

aban'donment, *n.*, the act of abandoning; shamelessness.

abarticula'tion, *n.*, a dislocation.

abase', *v.t.*, to lower, degrade, humiliate.

abased', *p.p.*, abase.

abase'ment, *n.*, the act of lowering or humiliating; the state of humiliation.

abash', *v.t.*, to put to confusion or shame.

abashed', *p.p.*, abash.

abash'ing, *pr.p.*, abash.

abash'ment, *n.*, the state of being abashed.

aba'sing, *pr.p.*, abase.

abate', *v.t.* and *i.*, to diminish, decrease.

aba'ted, *p.p.*, abate.

abate'ment, *n.*, the act of abating, state of being abated, reduction of amount or quantity.

aba'ting, *pr.p.*, abate.

ab'atis, *n.*, a military obstruction of felled trees.

ab'atised, *adj.*, having an abatis.

abattoir', *n.*, a slaughter-house (*Fr.*).

abb, *n.*, a weaving term = yarn of warp.

Ab'ba, *n.*, Semitic word = father.

ab'bacy, *n.*, office of an abbot, an abbot's jurisdiction.

abba'tial, *adj.* } pert. to
abbat'ical, *adj.* } an abbot or abbey.

ab'bé, *n.*, French word for abbot; unbeneficed priests often have the title given them as a dignified appellation.

ab'bess, *n.*, the lady head of an abbey.

ab'bey, *n.*, a religious house under the rule of an abbot.

ab'bot, *n.*, the superior of an abbey. Also *abbat.*

abbre'viate, *v.t.*, to shorten.

abbre'viated, *p.p.*, abbreviate.

abbre'viating, *pr.p.*, abbreviate.

abbrevia'tion, *n.*, the act of shortening; the abbreviated state; a shortened formula, as B.A. for Bachelor of Arts.

abbre'viator, *n.*, one who abbreviates; the drafter of ecclesiastical briefs at the Vatican.

abbre'viatory, *adj.*, shortening.

abbre'viature, *n.*, the sign marking a contraction; also an abridgment.

Ab'derite, *n.*, an inhabitant of Abdera, a place noted for stupidity; a stupid person.

ab'dicant, *adj.*, abdicating, also *n.*, one who abdicates.

ab'dicate, *v.t.*, to resign, renounce.

ab'dicated, *p.p.*, abdicate.

ab'dicating, *pr.p.*, abdicate.

abdica'tion, *n.*, the act of abdicating.

ab'dicative, *adj.*, disposed to abdicate.

ab'dicator, *n.*, one who abdicates.

ab'ditory, *n.*, a place to hide things in.

abdo'men, *n.*, the belly, the receptacle of the viscera.

abdom'inal, *adj.*, bel. to the abdomen.

abdominos'copy, *n.*, surgical examination of the abdomen.

abdom'inous, *adj.*, rel. to the abdomen; gross.

abduce′, *v.t.*, to draw away or aside.

abduced′, *p.p.*, abduce.

abdu′cing, *pr.p.*, abduce.

abduct′, *v.t.*, to carry off forcibly or by stealth.

abduct′ed, *p.p.*, abduct.

abduct′ing, *pr.p.*, abduct.

abduc′tion, *n.*, the act of abducting.

abduct′or, *n.*, one who abducts.

abeam′, *adv.*, at right angles to the keel.

Abeceda′rian, *adj.*, rel. to the A.B.C., also *n.*, one who learns or teaches the A.B.C.

abed′, *adv.*, in bed.

abele′, *n.*, white poplar.

Abel′ian, *adj.*, of or pert. to Abel, the Norwegian mathematician; also *n.*, a member of the sect of Abelites or Abelians.

A′belite, *n.*, a member of the ancient African sect of followers of Abel.

aber′rancy, *n.*, a straying from truth.

aber′rant, *adj.*, straying from truth.

aberra′tion, *n.*, the act of straying from truth; mental confusion; deviation from type (*biol.*); an optical defect in a lens or mirror; the seeming displacement of a heavenly body (*astron.*).

abet′, *v.t.*, to aid, encourage, help in some action, frequently in misdeed. (The phrase in such a context is "to aid and abet.")

abet′ted, *p.p.*, abet.

abet′ting, *pr.p.*, abet.

abet′ter, **abet′tor**, *n.*, one who abets.

abey′ance, *n.*, suspension, the state of suspension or of being held over.

abey′ant, *adj.*, holding over.

abhor′, *v.t.*, to hate, abominate, shudder at.

abhorred′, *p.p.*, abhor.

abhor′rence, *n.*, hatred with loathing.

abhor′rent, *adj.*, repulsive, hateful.

abhor′rer, *n.*, one who abhors.

abhor′ring, *pr.p.*, abhor.

A′bib, *n.*, a Jewish month.

abi′dance, *n.*, an abiding.

abide′, *v.i.*, to stay, remain, dwell.

abi′der, *n.*, one who abides.

abi′ding, *pr.p.*, abide.

abi′dingly, *adv.*, permanently, continually.

ab′ies, *n.*, the fir-tree, a member of the pine-family.

Ab′igail, *n.*, the Bible name of a woman attendant; hence, by transference, denoting any lady's maid.

abil′ity, *n.*, the state of being able; capacity.

abintest′ate, *adj.* and *n.*, inheriting from (or the inheritor of) an intestate person.

abiogen′esis, *n.*, spontaneous generation.

ab′ject, *adj.*, sunk to a low state, grovelling, mean; also *n.* (but rare), a mean fellow.

abject′, *v.t.*, to degrade.

abjec′tion, *n.*, the state of one who is abject, or cast down.

ab′jectly, *adv.*, meanly, in a grovelling manner.

ab′jectness, *n.*, meanness, a grovelling attitude.

abjudica′tion, *n.*, judicial rejection.

abjura′tion, *n.*, a solemn denial or repudiation of some doctrine or opinion.

abju′ratory, *adj.*, of the nature of an abjuration.

abjure′, *v.t.*, to make a solemn denial or repudiation of some doctrine or opinion.

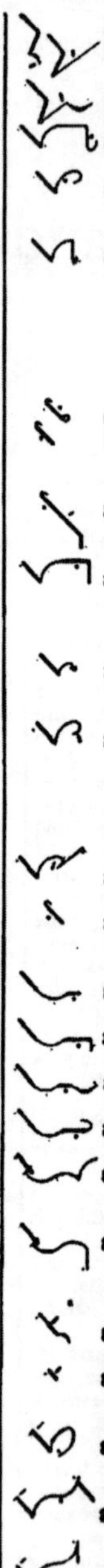

abjured′, *p.p.*, abjure.

abjur′er, *n.*, one who abjures.

abjur′ing, *pr.p.*, abjure.

ablacta′tion, *n.*, the act of weaning.

abla′tion, *n.*, the act of carrying off or removing.

ab′lative, *adj.*, tending to remove or separate. As a *n.* the ablative is the grammatical name for the case denoting separation.

ablaze′, *adv.*, on fire.

a′ble, *adj.*, having power, means, or capacity.

a′ble-bodied, *adj.*, in a physically fit condition.

ableg′ate, *n.*, a papal envoy, bearer to new cardinals of their insignia.

ab′luent, *adj.*, cleansing, purifying; *n.*, that which cleanses.

ablu′tion, *n.*, the act of cleansing. In ecclesiastical usage, the washing of the chalice and paten after Mass.

ablu′tionary, *adj.*, pert. to ablution.

a′bly, *adv.*, in an able manner, with ability.

ab′negate, *v.t.*, to give up, renounce.

ab′negated, *p.p.*, abnegate.

ab′negating, *pr.p.*, abnegate.

abnega′tion, *n.*, the act of abnegating.

abnor′mal, *adj.*, contrary to rule, unusual.

abnor′mity, *n.*, the state or quality of the abnormal; an irregularity.

aboard′, *adv.*, on board, on a vessel.

abode′, *n.*, a place of abiding or dwelling, the act of abiding.

abol′ish, *v.t.*, to destroy, put an end to.

abol′ishable, *adj.*, that which can be abolished.

abol′ished, *p.p.* abolish.

abol'isher, *n.*, one who abolishes.

abol'ishing, *pr.p.* abolish.

abol'ishment, *n.*, the act or state of abolishing.

aboli'tion, *n.*, *i.q.* abolishment.

aboli'tionism, *n.*, the anti-slavery doctrine or principle.

aboli'tionist, *n.*, one who opposes slavery.

abom'inable, *adj.*, detestable, hateful.

abom'inate, *v.t.*, to detest, abhor.

abom'inated, *p.p.*, abominate.

abomina'tion, *n.*, loathing; something detestable.

aborig'inal, *adj.*, indigenous; *n.*, a primitive native.

aborig'ines, *n.*, the original natives.

abor'tion, *n.*, a birth-miscarriage; the procuring of a miscarriage.

abor'tive, *adj.*, premature, ineffectual.

abor'tively, *adv.*, ineffectually.

abor'tiveness, *n.*, the state of being abortive.

abound', *v.i.*, to be in a state of plenty; to be in great quantity or numbers.

abound'ed, *p.p.*, abound.

abound'ing, *pr.p.*, abound.

about', *adv.*, around; nearly; *prep.*, around, concerning.

above' *adv.*, over, higher up; *prep.*, over, beyond, in excess of.

above'-board, *adv.* and *adj.*, without concealment, open.

abracadab'ra, *n.*, a cabalistic word used as a charm.

abrade', *v.t.*, to wear or scrape off.

abra'ded, *p.p.*, abrade.

abra'ding, *pr.p.*, abrade.

Abraham'ic, *adj.*, rel. to Abraham the patriarch.

A'brahamite, *n.*, a follower of the Gnostic preacher, Abraham.

abra'sion, *n.*, the act or operation of abrading, wearing, or rubbing off.

abra'sive, *adj.*, tending to abrasion; useful for abrading purposes.

abreast', *adv.*, on a level with, in line with.

abridge', *v.t.*, to shorten, epitomize.

abridged', *p.p.*, abridge.

abridg'ing, *pr.p.*, abridge.

abridg'ment, *n.*, the act or state of abridging; an epitome.

abroach', *adv.*, on tap, broached.

abroad', *adv.*, outside one's home or fatherland; in foreign parts.

ab'rogate, *v.t.*, to cancel, annul, repeal.

ab'rogated, *p.p.*, abrogate.

ab'rogating, *pr.p.*, abrogate.

abroga'tion, *n.*, the act of abrogating; repeal of a law.

abrupt', *adj.*, broken off short, precipitous, sudden, rude.

abrup'tion, *n.*, a sudden separation.

abrupt'ly, *adv.*, steeply, suddenly, rudely.

abrupt'ness, *n.*, steepness, rudeness.

ab'scess, *n.*, a sore, tumour.

abscind', *v.t.*, to sever, cut off.

abscis'sion, *n.*, the act of severance.

abscond', *v.i.*, to make off, flee into retirement.

abscond'ed, *p.p.*, abscond.

abscond'er, *n.*, one who absconds.

abscond'ing, *pr.p.*, abscond.

ab'sence, *n.*, the state of being away or absent; lack.

ab'sent, *adj.*, away; not present; inattentive.

absent', *v.t.*, to withdraw (oneself).

absent'ed, *p.p.*, absent.

absentee', *n.*, one who absents himself or is away; non-resident.

absentee'ism, *n.*, the practice of not residing on one's estate.

absent'ing, *pr.p.*, absent.

ab'sently, *adv.*, in an absent manner.

ab'sinth, *n.*, a liqueur made from wormwood and brandy.

absin'thian, *adj.*, rel. to absinth.

absin'thiate, *v.t.*, to make bitter with wormwood.

absin'thiated, *p.p.*, absinthiate.

absin'thin, *n.*, the bitter quality in absinth.

ab'sinthism, *n.*, the state induced by indulgence in absinth.

ab'solute, *adj.*, free, independent; unlimited; perfect; despotic.

ab'solutely, *adv.*, perfectly, quite; despotically.

ab'soluteness, *n.*, the quality of being absolute.

absolu'tion, *n.*, the act of loosing or absolving from sin.

ab'solutism, *n.*, the state or condition of the absolute; despotic rule.

ab'solutist, *n.*, one who advocates despotic rule.

absol'utory, *adj.*, able to absolve; loosing from sin.

absol'vatory, *adj.*, capable of absolving.

absolve', *v.t.*, to release from sin, to pardon.

absolved', *p.p.*, absolve.

absolv'er, *n.*, one who absolves.

absolv'ing, *pr.p.*, absolve.

ab'sonant, *adj.*, discordant; unreasonable.

absorb', *v.t.*, to draw in through the mouth, to swallow: to engross.
absorbabil'ity, *n.*, the condition of being absorbable.
absorb'able, *adj.*, capable of absorption.
absorbed' *p.p.*, absorb.
absorb'ent, *adj.*, absorbing; also *n.*, a substance capable of absorbing.
absorb'ing, *pr.p.*, absorb; *adj.*, engrossing.
absorp'tion, *n.*, the act of absorbing; mental preoccupation.
absorp'tive, *adj.*, capable of absorbing.
abstain', *v.i.*, to keep aloof from, to refrain.
abstained', *p.p.*, abstain.
abstain'er, *n.*, one who abstains, particularly from alcohol.
abstain'ing, *pr.p.*, abstain.
abste'mious, *adj.*, moderate in the use of drink.
abste'miously, *adv.*, with moderation in regard to drink.
abste'miousness, *n.*, the habit of moderation in regard to drink.
absten'tion, *n.*, the act of abstaining.
absterge', *v.t.*, to cleanse by wiping.
absterged', *p.p.*, absterge.
abster'gent, *adj.*, cleansing; also *n.*, that which cleanses.
abster'ging, *pr.p.*, absterge.
absterse', *adj.*, wiped clean.
abster'sion, *n.*, the act of wiping clean.
abster'sive, *adj.*, of cleansing property.
ab'stinence, *n.*, the act or state of abstaining.
ab'stinent, *adj.*, not self-indulgent.
ab'stinently, *adv.*, in a manner not self-indulgent.
abstract', *v.t.*, to draw away, to remove, to epitomize.
ab'stract, *adj.*, apart from matter (which is concrete); also *n.*, an epitome or summary.
abstract'ed, *p.p.*, abstract; also *adj.*, absent-minded.
abstract'edly, *adv.*, in an absent-minded way.
abstract'edness, *n.*, a mentally absent state.
abstract'er, *n.*, one who abstracts.
abstract'ing, *pr.p.*, abstract.
abstrac'tion, *n.* the act of abstracting; the state of being abstracted; mental concentration.
abstrac'tive, *adj.*, capable of abstracting.
ab'stractly, *adv.*, in an abstract manner.
ab'stractness, *n.*, the quality of being abstract.
abstruse', *adj.*, hidden, profound, hard to comprehend.
abstruse'ly, *adv.*, in an abstruse way.
abstruse'ness, *n.*, the quality of the abstruse.
absurd', *adj.*, irrational, ridiculous.
absurd'ity, *n.*, the absurd state, an absurd thing.
absurd'ly, *adv.*, in an absurd way.
absurd'ness, *n.*, the absurd state.
abun'dance, *n.*, plenty.
abun'dant, *adj.*, plentiful.
abun'dantly, *adv.*, plentifully, richly.
abuse', *v.t.*, to ill-treat, to violate, to insult, to misuse.
abuse', *n.*, ill-treatment, insult, misuse.
abused', *p.p.*, abuse.
abu'ser, *n.*, one who abuses.
abu'sing, *pr.p.*, abuse.
abu'sive, *adj.*, of the nature of abuse, insulting.
abu'sively, *adv.*, in an insulting way.
abu'siveness, *n.*, the abusive tendency.
abut', *v.t.*, to make to touch at the side or end; *v.i.*, to adjoin.
abut'ment, *n.*, the act of abutting; that which is abutted upon or abuts.
abut'tal, *n.*, the relation of abutting; abutment.
abut'ted, *p.p.*, abut.
abut'ting, *pr.p.*, abut.
abysm', *n.*, an abyss. gulf, vast depth.
abys'mal, *adj.*, profound, of vast depth.
abyss', *n.*, *i.q.* abysm.
Abyssin'ian, *adj.*, native to Abyssinia.
aca'cia, *n.*, a shrub so named (one kind yields gum arabic).
Aca'cian, *n.*, a follower of Acacius, Bishop of Caesarea in the 4th cent
acade'mian, *n.*, a member of an Academy: a disciple of Plato.
academ'ic, *adj.*, bel. or rel. to a University; bel. to the Platonic School.
academ'ical, *adj.*, *i.q.* academic.
Academic'ian, *n.*, a member of an Academy.
Acad'emist, *n.*, an academic philosopher.
acad'emy, *n.*, a place of higher learning; a University; the School of Plato.
Aca'dian, *adj.*, bel. to Acadia, or Nova Scotia.
Acale'phae, *n. pl.*, marine stinging zoophytes (sea-nettles and the like).
acan'tha, *n.*, a plant's prickle; a fish's fin; a spinous growth.
acantha'ceous, *adj.*, prickly.
acan'thine, *adj.*, rel. to the acanthus; *n.*, the acanthus-leaf ornament (*archit.*).
acar'diac, *adj.*, not having a heart.
ac'arus, *n.*, a mite.

acatalec'tic, *adj.*, not catalectic, *i.e.*, not lacking in metre.
acat'alepsy, *n.*, epilepsy.
acatalep'tic, *adj.*, in a state of acatalepsy.
acau'lous, *adj.*, without a stem.
Acca'dian, *n.*, the language of ancient Babylon.
accede', *v.i.*, to agree to.
acce'ded, *p.p.*, accede.
acce'ding, *pr.p.*, accede.
accel'erate, *v.t.* and *i.*, to quicken, hasten.
accel'erated, *p.p.*, accelerate.
accel'erating, *pr.p.*, accelerate.
accelera'tion, *n.*, quickening of speed.
accel'erative, *adj.*, causing acceleration.
accel'erator ped'al, *n.*, a pedal which quickens the speed of a motor.
accel'eratory, *adj.*, causing acceleration.
accend'ible, *adj.*, inflammable.
accen'sion, *n.*, the act of lighting altar candles.
ac'cent, *n.*, stress of voice; printed or written sign on a syllable or letter or musical note; peculiar distinction of speech or pronunciation.
accent', *v.t.*, to lay stress in speech or music.
accent'ed, *p.p.* accent.
accent'ing, *pr.p.*, accent.
accent'or, *n.*, a bird genus so named; a leading singer.
accent'ual, *adj.*, rel. to accent.
accent'uate, *v.t.*, to mark with an accent; to give prominence to.
accent'uated, *p.p.*, accentuate.
accent'uating, *pr.p.*, accentuate.
accentua'tion, *n.*, the act of accentuating.

accept', *v.t.*, to take or receive; to approve; to agree to pay.
acceptabil'ity, *n.*, the quality of being acceptable.
accept'able, *adj.*, able to be accepted; agreeable; welcome.
accept'ableness, *n.*, the state of being acceptable.
accept'ance, *n.*, the act of accepting; a state of acceptability; a bill of exchange; agreement to meet a bill.
accepta'tion, *n.*, the state of being accepted; meaning, sense.
accept'ed, *p.p.*, accept
accept'er, *n.*, one who accepts.
accept'ing, *pr.p.*, accept.
accep'tion, *n.*, favouritism.
accept'or, *n.*, one who accepts; one who has given his acceptance on a draft.
ac'cess, *n.*, approach or means of approach; increase; attack (of disease).
ac'cessary, *adj.*, aiding, contributing to; *n.*, an accomplice.
accessibil'ity, *n.*, the state or quality of being approached.
acces'sible, *adj.*, easy to be approached.
acces'sibly, *adv.*, in an accessible way.
acces'sion, *n.*, approach; the act of acceding; increase; a coming to the throne.
acces'sional, *adj.*, rel. to an accession.
acces'sive, *adj.*, tending to accession.
accesso'rial, *adj.*, rel. to an accessory.
ac'cessory, *adj.*, *i.q.* accessary; *n.*, something additional.
acciaccatu'ra, *n.*, a grace note struck with another note but instantly released, while the other continues to sound.
ac'cidence, *n.*, the rudimentary part of grammar.

ac'cident, *n.*, a chance occurrence; a mishap.
acciden'tal, *adj.*, happening by chance; fortuitous; *n.*, a musical sharp or flat not belonging to the key.
acciden'tally, *adv.*, by accident.
ac'cidie, *n.*, loss of interest; ennui.
accip'ient, *n.*, receiver.
accip'iter, *n.*, the hawk; also name for birds of prey.
accip'itrine, *adj.*, like the hawk.
acclaim', *v.t.*, to welcome or approve with shouting; *n.*, loud approval.
acclama'tion, *n.*, loud applause.
acclam'atory, *adj.*, expressing loud applause.
accli'mate, *v.t.*, to accustom to climate.
accli'mated, *p.p.*, acclimate.
accli'mating, *pr. p.*, acclimate.
acclima'tion, *n.*, the act of acclimating.
acclimatiza'tion, *n.*, the act of adapting to climate.
accli'matize, *v.t.*, to adapt to climate.
accli'matized, *p.p.*, acclimatize.
accli'matizing, *pr.p.*, acclimatize.
accli'mature, *n.*, the act of habituating to climate.
accliv'ity, *n.*, an upward slope; hill.
accli'vous, *adj.*, rising, sloping upwards.
accolade', *n.*, the stroke with the sword in conferring knighthood; the brace that couples musical staves together.
accom'modate, *v.t.*, to do a service or convenience; to fit, adapt.
accom'modated, *p.p.*, accommodate.
accom'modating, *pr.p.* accommodate.

accommoda'tion, *n.*, a favour, convenience; hospitality, room.

accom'modative, *adj.*, willing to accommodate.

accom'modator, *n.*, one who accommodates.

accom'panied, *p.p.*, accompany.

accom'panier, *n.*, one who accompanies.

accom'paniment, *n.*, something that accompanies. In music, an instrumental support to the voice or other instruments.

accom'panist, *n.*, one who plays the musical accompaniment.

accom'pany, *v.t.*, to go with. Musically, to play the accompaniment.

accom'panying, *p.p.*, accompany.

accom'plice, *n.*, a partner in crime.

accom'plish, *v.t.*, to perform, finish.

accom'plishable, *adj.*, able to be performed.

accom'plished, *p.p.*, accomplish; also *adj.*, = skilful, proficient.

accom'plisher, *n.*, one who accomplishes.

accom'plishing, *pr.p.*, accomplish.

accom'plishment, *n.*, the act or state of accomplishing; an elegant acquirement.

accord', *n.*, agreement, consent, harmony; *v.t.*, to grant; *v.i.*, agree.

accord'ance, *n.*, agreement, harmony.

accord'ancy, *n.*, *i.q.* accordance.

accord'ant, *adj.*, in a state of agreement.

accord'antly, *adv.*, agreeably.

accord'ed, *p.p.*, accord.

accord'er, *n.*, one who accords.

accord'ing, *pr.p.*, accord. (Helps to form prepositional phrase, "according to.")

accord'ingly, *adv.*, in agreement. In special sense = therefore.

accord'ion, *n.*, a reed instrument, so called.

accost', *n.*, to greet, address in words.

accost'able, *adj.*, able to be accosted.

accost'ed, *p.p.*, accost.

accost'ing, *pr.p.*, accost.

accou'chement, *n.*, bringing to bed (*Fr.*); confinement.

accoucheur', *n.*, a man midwife.

accoucheuse', *n.*, a midwife.

account', *n.*, sum, bill; description; *v.t.* and *i.*, to esteem, reckon.

accountabil'ity, *n.*, the state of being accountable; liability to be called to account.

account'able, *adj.*, able to account, responsible.

account'ableness, *n.*, the state of being accountable.

account'ant, *n.*, one who proves or keeps accounts.

account'antship, *n.*, the art or function of an accountant.

account'-book, *n.*, a book in which accounts are entered.

account'ed, *p.p.*, account.

account'ing, *pr.p.*, account.

accoup'le, *v.t.*, to join one thing to another.

accoup'led, *p.p.*, accouple.

accoup'ling, *pr.p.*, accouple.

accou'tre, *v.t.*, to clothe, equip.

accou'tred, *p.p.*, accoutre.

accou'trements, *n.*, military equipment.

accou'tring, *pr.p.*, accoutre.

accred'it, *v.t.*, to recommend, authorize.

accred'ited, *p.p.*, accredit.

accres'cence, *n.*, a growth, addition.

accres'cent, *adj.*, growing, being added.

accre'tion, *n.*, a growth, addition.

accre'tive, *adj.*, tending to growth.

accroach'ment, *n.*, usurpation.

accrue', *v.i.*, to increase, be added.

accrued', *p.p.*, accrue.

accru'ing, *pr.p.*, accrue.

accuba'tion, *n.*, the act of reclining.

accum'bent, *adj.*, reclining at table.

accu'mulate, *v.t.* and *i.*, to pile up, amass, grow.

accu'mulated, *p.p.*, accumulate.

accu'mulating, *pr.p.*, accumulate.

accumula'tion, *n.*, the act of accumulating; a piled up mass.

accu'mulative, *adj.*, tending to accumulate.

accu'mulatively, *adv.*, increasingly, in piles.

accu'mulator, *n.*, one who accumulates; a power-storing apparatus.

ac'curacy, *n.*, the state or faculty of being accurate.

ac'curate, *adj.*, careful, exact.

ac'curately, *adv.*, carefully, precisely.

ac'curateness, *n.*, the state of being accurate.

accurse', *v.t.*, to invoke curses against.

accursed', } **accurs'ed,** } *p.p.*, accurse.

accurs'ing, *pr.p.*, accurse.

accu'sable, *adj.*, able to be accused.

accu'sant, *adj.*, accusing; *n.*, an accuser.

accusa'tion, *n.*, a charge, indictment.

accu'sative, *adj.*, bringing a charge. In grammar, the name for the objective case.

accu'satively, *adv.*, in the manner of an accusation.
accu'satory, *adj.*, incriminating, accusing.
accuse', *v.t.*, to charge, indict.
accused', *p.p.*, accuse.
accus'er, *n.*, one who brings a charge.
accus'ing, *pr.p.*, accuse.
accus'tom, *v.t.*, to habituate.
accus'tomarily, *adv.*, habitually, in wonted manner
accus'tomary, *adj.*, habitual, wonted.
accus'tomed, *p.p.*, accustom.
accus'toming, *pr.p.*, accustom.
ace, *n.*, a single pip on playing-card; a unit.
ace'dia, *n.*, *see* accidie.
Acel'dama, *n.*, the field of blood.
acen'tric, *adj.*, without a centre.
Aceph'ala, *n.*, bivalves; headless molluscs.
aceph'alous, *adj.*, headless.
a'cer, *n.*, the maple-tree.
ac'erate, *adj.*, needle-pointed.
a'cerbate, *v.t.*, to embitter, exasperate.
acerb'ity, *n.*, bitter quality, bitterness.
ac'erose, *adj.*, needle-shaped.
a'cervate, *adj.*, massed or heaped together.
aces'cence, *n.*, a souring.
aces'cency, *n.*, the quality or state of turning sour.
aces'cent, *adj.*, turning sour.
aceta'rious, *adj.*, used in salad.
acet'ary, *n.*, the sour pulp in a pear, etc.
ac'etate, *v.a.*, salt of acetic acid.
ac'etated, *adj.*, combined with acetic acid.
ace'tic, *adj.*, of the nature of vinegar.
acet'ified, *p.p.*, acetify.
acet'ify, *v.t.*, to turn into vinegar; *v.i.*, to become sour.
acet'ifying, *pr.p.*, acetify.
acetom'eter, *n.*, an instrument for ascertaining the strength of acetic acid.
ac'etone, *n.*, an inflammable liquid, sharp-tasted.
ac'etose, *adj.*, producing or rel. to vinegar.
acetos'ity, *n.*, acidity.
ac'etous, *adj.*, *i.q.* acetose.
ace'tum, *n.*, vinegar (*Lat.*).
acet'ylene, *n.* and *adj.*, a colourless inflammable gas, so named.
Ache'an, *adj.*, bel. to Achea (a tribal district of ancient Greece).
Achai'an, *adj.*, bel. to the Achaioi, *i.q.* Achean.
ache, *n.* and *v.i.*, pain; to be painful.
ached, *p.p.*, ache.
A'cheron, *n.*, a fabled river in Hades.
achiev'able, *adj.*, able to be achieved.
achieve', *v.t.*, to accomplish by courage or skill or perseverance; to finish successfully.
achieved', *p.p.*, achieve.
achieve'ment, *n.*, something achieved.
achiev'er, *n.*, one who achieves.
achiev'ing, *pr.p.*, achieve.
ach'ing, *pr.p.*, ache.
a'chor, *n.*, a variety of eczema.
achromat'ic, *adj.*, colourless; forming images without their prismatic colouring.
achro'matism, *n.*, the achromatic state or quality.
achro'matize, *v.t.*, to make achromatic.
acic'ular, *adj.*, sharp-pointed.
acic'ulate, *adj.*, bearing prickles or bristles.
acic'uliform, *adj.*, needle-shaped.
ac'id, *n.* and *adj.*, sour, tart.
acidif'erous, *adj.*, acid-yielding.
acidifica'tion, *n.*, the act of converting to acid.
acid'ified, *p.p.*, acidify.
acid'ifier, *n.*, one who acidifies.
acid'ify, *v.t.* and *i.*, to make or become acid.
acid'ifying, *pr.p.*, acidify.
acidim'eter, *n.*, an apparatus for testing the strength of an acid.
acid'ity, *n.*, the acid quality, sourness.
acid'ulae, *n.*, cold acid mineral water-springs.
acid'ulate, *v.t.*, to make acid.
acid'ulated, *p.p.*, acidulate.
acid'ulating, *pr.p.*, acidulate.
acidula'tion, *n.*, the act of acidulating.
acid'ulous, *adj.*, slightly acid.
a'ciform, *adj.*, needle-shaped.
acknowl'edge, *v.t.*, to own, admit.
acknowl'edged, *p.p.*, acknowledge.
acknowl'edger, *n.*, one who acknowledges.
acknowl'edging, *pr.p.*, acknowledge.
acknowl'edgment, *n.*, the act of acknowledging; return of a favour.
ac'me, *n.*, highest point (a *Gr.* word).
ac'ne, *n.*, an eruption; maggot-pimple.
acock', *adv.*, cocked.
acol'ogy, *n.*, therapeutics, the science of remedies.
ac'olyte, *n.*, the attendant on a priest.
ac'onite, *n.*, the plant monk's-hood, or wolf's-bane.
acon'itine, *adj.*, of the quality of aconite.
a'corn, *n.*, the fruit of the oak.
a'corned, *adj.*, acorn-bearing.

acotyle′don, *n.*, a plant not having seed-lobes.

acotyle′donous, *adj.*, destitute of cotyledons (or seed-lobes).

acou′chy, *n.*, the Surinam rat.

acous′tic, *adj.*, rel. to hearing.

acoust′ical, *adj.*, rel. to hearing.

acquaint′, *v.t.*, to make known, to make oneself familiar with.

acquaint′ance, *n.*, the state of being acquainted; a person known, but not intimately.

acquaint′anceship, *n.*, *i.q.* acquaintance.

acquaint′ed, *p.p.*, acquaint; informed about.

acquaint′ing, *pr.p.*, acquaint.

acquest′, *n.*, property acquired otherwise than by inheritance.

acquiesce′, *v.i.*, to take passively, submit to.

acquiesced′, *p.p.*, acquiesce.

acquies′cence, *n.*, the state or act of acquiescing.

acquies′cent, *adj.*, ready to acquiesce or submit.

acquies′cing, *pr.p.*, acquiesce.

acquirabil′ity, *n.*, the state of being acquirable.

acquir′able, *adj.*, able to be acquired.

acquire′, *v.t.*, to obtain, attain, gain possession.

acquired′ *p.p.*, acquire.

acquire′ment, *n.*, the act or state of acquiring; a thing acquired.

acquir′er, *n.*, one who acquires.

acquir′ing, *pr.p.*, acquire.

acquisi′tion, *n.*, the act of acquiring; a valuable gain.

acquis′itive, *adj.*, of an acquiring tendency.

acquis′itively, *adv.*, in an acquisitive manner.

acquis′itiveness, *n.*, the acquiring tendency.

acquit′, *v.t.*, to free or clear, exculpate; reflexively, to bear oneself.

acquit′ment, *n.*, the act of acquitting.

acquit′tal, *n.*, the act or state of acquitting.

acquit′tance, *n.*, discharge, release.

acquit′ted, *p.p.*, acquit.

acquit′ting, *pr.p.*, acquit.

Ac′rasy, *n.*, intemperance personified.

a′cre, *n.*, a measure of surface, a field.

a′creage, *n.*, the extent in acres.

a′cred, *adj.*, possessing or containing acres.

ac′rid, *adj.*, sharp, pungent, corrosive.

acrid′ity, *n.*, the acrid state or quality.

ac′ridness, *n.*, the acrid quality.

acrimo′nious, *adj.*, full of bitterness, spiteful.

acrimo′niously, *adv.*, in an acrimonious way.

acrimo′niousness, *n.*, the acrimonious quality.

ac′rimony, *n.*, bitterness, spitefulness.

acrit′ical, *adj.*, without a crisis.

acroat′ic, *adj.* rel. to esoteric teaching.

ac′robat, *n.*, a gymnast—rope dancer, tumbler, and the like.

Acroceraun′nian, *adj.*, bel. to Acroceraunia, a Grecian promontory.

ac′rogen, *n.*, an organism that grows at the apex only.

acrog′enous, *adj.*, growing at the apex.

acrog′raphy, *n.*, the process of making a relief printing-block

ac′rolith, *n.*, a figure with a head made of stone.

Acrop′olis, *n.*, a city stronghold (*Gr.*).

ac′rospire, *v.i.*, to germinate; *n.*, the first sprout.

ac′rospired, *p.p.*, acrospire.

across′, *prep.* and *adv.*, athwart, to the opposite side, over.

acros′tic, *n.* and *adj.*, a composition, in which certain letters, usually the first in a line, make words.

acros′tically, *adv.*, acrostic-wise.

acrote′ria, *n. pl.*, ornaments above a building or pediment.

act, *n.*, a thing done or performed; the doing of a thing; a Parliamentary measure made law; a main division of a drama; *v.t.* and *i.*, to perform, do, play.

act′ed, *p.p.*, act.

Ac′tian, *adj.*, bel. to Actium (a promontory of ancient Greece).

act′ing, *pr.p.*, act; *n.*, an actor's business.

actin′ic, *adj.*, rel. to rays.

actin′iform, *adj.*, radiated.

ac′tinism, *n.*, radiation; the property of radiant energy.

actin′ograph, *n.*, a ray-recording instrument.

actinol′ogy, *n.*, the science or study of rays.

actinom′eter, *n.*, instrument for measuring rays.

ac′tion, *n.*, the state of doing or acting; the thing done; lawsuit.

ac′tionable, *adj.*, liable to an action or lawsuit.

ac′tionary, *n.*, a stockholder.

ac′tionist, *n.*, *i.q.* actionary.

ac′tionless, *adj.* without action.

ac′tive, *adj.*, full of action, lively.

ac′tively, *adv.*, in an active way.

activ'ity, *n.*, the active state.
act'or, *n.*, one who acts; a player (*dram.*).
act'ress, *n.*, a woman who acts.
act'ual, *adj.*, real, existing.
actual'ity, *n.*, the state of being actual.
act'ualize, *v.t.*, to make real.
act'ually, *adv.*, really, in fact.
actua'rial, *adj.*, rel. to an actuary.
actua'rially, *adv.*, by actuarial methods.
act'uary, *n.*, a registrar; one skilled in insurance business, rates of mortality, etc.
act'uate, *v.t.*, to move, influence.
act'uated, *p.p.*, actuate.
act'uating, *pr.p.*, actuate.
actua'tion, *n.*, the state of being actuated.
acu'leate, *adj.*, armed with a sting.
acu'leated, *adj.*, *i.q.* aculeate.
acu'men, *n.*, sharpness, wit, sagacity.
acu'minate, *adj.*, tapering.
acu'minated, *i.q.* acuminate.
acumina'tion, *n.*, the ending in a point.
acu'minous, *adj.*, pointed.
acupress'ure, *n.*, stopping bleeding by means of a suture.
acupunctura'tion, *n.*, the act of pricking with a needle.
acupunct'ure, *n.*, pricking with a needle.
acute', *adj.*, pointed, sharp; shrill.
acute'ly, *adv.*, sharply, cleverly.
acute'ness, *n.*, the state or quality of being acute.
adac'tyl, *adj.*, having neither fingers nor toes.
ad'age, *n.*, a common or old saying.
ada'gio, *adj.* and *adv.*, in slow (*mus.*) time; *n.*, a slow movement so named.
ad'amant, *n.*, a hard stone; the diamond.
adamante'an, *adj.*, like adaman ; hard-hearted.
adaman'tine, *adj.*, of adamant; hard-hearted.
Adam'ic, *adj.*, rel. to Adam.
Ad'amite, *n.*, human, sprung from Adam.
Adamit'ic, *adj.*, rel. to Adam.
Ad'am's-ap'ple, *n.*, the ball in the front of a man's throat.
adapt', *v.t.*, to fit, make suitable, alter.
adaptabil'ity, *n.*, the power to be adapted.
adapt'able, *adj.*, able to be adapted.
adapt'ableness, *n.*, the adaptable capacity.
adapta'tion, *n.*, the act of adapting; a thing adapted.
adapt'ed, *p.p.*, adapt.
adapt'er, *n.*, one who adapts.
adapt'ing, *pr.p.*, adapt
adapt'ive, *adj.*, capable of adapting.
add, *v.t.*, to put one thing to another; to say something more.
adden'da, *n.*, things to be added.
adden'dum, *n.*, a thing to be added.
ad'der, *n.*, a poisonous reptile; one who adds.
addibil'ity, *n.*, fitness to be added.
ad'dible, *adj.*, capable of addition.
addict', *v.t.*, to give over to.
addic'ted, *p.p.*, addict, generally in sense of prone to, given up to.
addict'edness, *n.*, the state of addicted.
addict'ing, *pr.p.*, addict.
addic'tion, *n.*, the act of addicting oneself.
addic'tive, *adj.*, inclined to addict.
ad'ding, *pr.p.*, add.
addit'ament, *n.*, an addition.
addi'tion, *n.*, the act of adding; a thing added.
addi'tional, *adj.*, added.
ad'dle, *v.t.*, to muddle, *v.i.*, become addled.
ad'dled, *p.p.*, addle; rotten, confused.
ad'dle-head'ed, *adj.*, with confused brain.
ad'dle-pa'ted, *adj.*, *i.q.* addle-headed.
ad'dling, *pr.p.*, addle; also *adj.*, confusing.
address', *v.t.*, to speak to; to direct something to; to prepare to strike (a golf ball); *n.*, a congratulatory speech or letter; a public lecture or discourse; skilfulness; manners; direction.
addressed', *p.p.*, address.
addressee', *n.*, one to whom a thing is addressed.
address'er, *n.*, one who addresses.
address'ing, *pr.p.*, address.
adduce', *v.t.*, to bring forward or cite.
adduced', *p.p.*, adduce.
addu'cent, *adj.*, drawing together.
addu'cer, *n.*, one who adduces.
addu'cible, *adj.*, able to be adduced.
addu'cing, *pr.p.*, adduce.
adduct', *v.t.*, to draw towards the axis of a limb or body.
adduc'tion, *n.*, the act of adducting, as of muscles.
adduc'tive, *adj.*, with power to adduct.
adduc'tor, *n.*, an adducting muscle.
ad'eling, *n.*, one of princely descent.
adel'opode, *adj.*, having concealed feet.
adel'phia, *n.*, brotherhood, or group of stamens.
ademp'tion, *n.*, the act of depriving.
adenog'raphy, *n.*, descriptive anatomy of the glands.
ad'enoid, *adj.*, glandiform glandular.

adenolog'ical, *adj.*, rel. to the study of the glands.
adenol'ogy, *n.*, the study of the glands.
adeno'ma, *n.*, a glandular kind of tumour.
ad'enose, *adj.*, glandular.
adenot'omy, *n.*, the cutting of a gland.
ad'enous, *adj.*, glandular.
ad'eps, *n.*, fat (*Lat.*).
adept', *adj.*, skilled, expert; *n.*, an expert person.
ad'equacy, *n.*, the state of being adequate.
ad'equate, *adj.*, equal to, competent, sufficient.
ad'equately, *adv.*, in an adequate manner or degree.
ad'equateness, *n.*, the state of being adequate.
adhere', *v.i.*, to stick to, cling to, support.
adhered', *p.p.*, adhere.
adhe'rence, *n.*, the act of adhering.
adhe'rency, *n.*, the tendency to adhere.
adhe'rent, *adj.*, sticking to; *n.*, a supporter.
adhe'rently, *adv.*, in a clinging or closely joined way.
adhe'rer, *n.*, one who supports or clings.
adhe'ring, *pr.p.*, adhere.
adhe'sion, *n.*, the act or quality of adhering; a thing that adheres.
adhe'sive, *adj.*, sticking, attached.
adhe'sively, *adv.*, with adhesion.
adhe'siveness, *n.*, the tendency to adhere.
adhib'it, *v.t.*, to let in; to attach; to use.
adhib'ited, *p.p.*, adhibit.
adhibi'tion, *n.*, the act of adhibiting.
adiaph'orous, *adj.*, opaque.
adieu', a *Fr.* phrase, à Dieu = farewell, used either as interjection or as noun.
adipoc'erate, *v.t.*, to convert into adipocere.
ad'ipocere, *n.*, a light fatty substance.
ad'ipose, *adj.* and *n.*, fat.
adipo'sity, *n.*, a tendency to fat.
ad'ipsy, *n.*, absence of thirst.
ad'it, *n.*, approach, entrance.
adja'cence, *n.*, the state of being near.
adja'cency, *n.*, neighbourhood.
adja'cent, *adj.*, situated near.
adja'cently, *adv.*, contiguously.
adject', *v.t.*, to join.
adject'ed, *p.p.*, adject.
adject'ing, *pr.p.*, adject.
adjec'tion, *n.*, the act of adjecting.
adjecti'val, *adj.*, of the nature of an adjective.
ad'jective, *n.*, the grammatical term for words denoting qualities or describing nouns.
ad'jectively, *adv.*, in the manner of adjectives.
adjoin', *v.t.*, to lie near, to be joined to.
adjoined', *p.p.*, adjoin.
adjoin'ing, *pr.p.*, adjoin; *adj.*, next to, contiguous.
adjourn', *v.t.* and *i.*, to put off to another time; to leave off.
adjourned', *p.p.*, adjourn.
adjourn'ing, *pr.p.*, adjourn.
adjourn'ment, *n.*, the act of adjourning.
adjudge', *v.t.*, to decide judicially.
adjudged', *p.p.*, adjudge.
adjudg'ing, *pr.p.*, adjudge.
adju'dicate, *v.t.*, to sit or decide as a judge.
adju'dicated, *p.p.*, adjudicate.
adju'dicating, *pr.p.*, adjudicate.
adjudica'tion, *n.*, the act of adjudicating.
adju'dicator, *n.*, one who adjudicates.
adjud'icature, *n.*, *i.q.* adjudication.
ad'junct, *n.*, something added.
adjunc'tion, *n.*, the act of joining; a thing joined.
adjunc'tive, *adj.*, tending to join.
adjunc'tively, *adv.*, in an adjunctive way.
adjunct'ly, *adv.*, as something added.
adjura'tion, *n.*, a solemn appeal; a solemn oath; the act of adjuring.
adju'ratory, *adj.*, of the nature of an adjuration.
adjure', *v.t.*, to make a solemn charge or appeal.
adjured', *p.p.*, adjure.
adjur'er, *n.*, one who adjures.
adjur'ing, *pr.p.*, adjure.
adjust', *v.t.*, to fit, make exact, settle.
adjust'able, *adj.*, able to be adjusted.
adjust'ed, *p.p.*, adjust.
adjust'er, *n.*, one who adjusts.
adjust'ing, *pr.p.*, adjust.
adjust'ive, *adj.*, capable of adjusting.
adjust'ment, *n.*, the act or state of adjusting; a regulating means, as in a watch; a settlement.
ad'jutancy, *n.*, the office or rank of adjutant.
ad'jutant, *n.*, an officer who helps the commanding officer.
ad'jutant-*gen'eral*, *n.*, the principal assistant to the commander of an army.
adju'tor, *n.*, a helper, assistant (*Lat.*).
adju'trix, *n.*, fem. of adjutor.
ad'juvant, *adj.*, assisting.
admeas'ure, *v.t.*, to apportion.
admeas'urement, *n.*, the act or state of admeasuring.
admin'ister, *v.t.*, to perform, execute; help.

admin'istered, *p.p.*, administer.

administe'rial, *adj.*, rel. to administration.

admin'istering, *pr.p.*, administer.

admin'istrable, *adj.*, able to be administered.

admin'istrate, *v.t.* to conduct, manage, govern.

administra'tion, *n.* the act of governing; the government.

admin'istrative, *adj.*, capable of administering.

admin'istrator, *n.*, one who administers.

admin'istrator-ship, *n.*, the function of administering.

admin'istratrix, *n.*, fem. of administrator.

admirabil'ity, *n.*, fitness to be admired.

ad'mirable, *adj.*, worthy to be admired.

ad'miral, *n.*, the commander of a fleet.

ad'miralship, *n.*, skill in commanding a fleet.

Ad'miralty, *n.*, the supreme authority in the navy; the governing board.

admira'tion, *n.*, wonder, regard.

admire', *v.t.*, to wonder at, esteem.

admired', *p.p.*, admire.

admir'er, *n.*, one who admires.

admir'ing, *pr.p.*, admire.

admir'ingly, *adv.*, like one who admires.

admissibil'ity, *n.*, the being admissible.

admis'sible, *adj.*, able to be admitted or permitted or conceived.

admis'sion, *n.*, the act of letting in or admitting; concession.

admis'sory, *adj.*, giving admission.

admit', *v.t.*, to let in; acknowledge, concede.

admit'table, *adj.*, able to be admitted.

admit'tance, *n.*, permission to enter.

admit'ted, *p.p.*, admit.

admit'ter, *n.*, one who admits.

admit'ting, *pr.p.*, admit.

admix', *v.t.*, to mix together.

admixed', *p.p.*, admix.

admix'tion, *n.*, the act or state of admixing.

admix'ture, *n.*, the act of admixing; an assembly of mixed things.

admon'ish, *v.t.*, to warn, reprove.

admon'ished, *p.p.*, admonish.

admon'isher, *n.*, one who admonishes.

admon'ishing, *pr.p.*, admonish.

admoni'tion, *n.*, the act of admonishing; warning.

admon'itor, *n.*, one who admonishes.

admon'itory, *adj.* rel. to admonition; warning.

admortiza'tion, *n.*, *i.q.* amortization.

adnas'cence, *n.*, adhesion, growing on to.

ad'nate, *adj.*, grown together.

adnom'inal, *adj.*, adjectival.

ado', *n.*, stir, trouble, fuss.

ado'be, *n.*, sun-dried brick; *adj.*, made of sun-dried brick.

adoles'cence, *n.*, state of growing up.

adoles'cency, *n.*, period of growing up.

adoles'cent, *adj.*, in the growing-up stage.

Adonai', *n.*, a Hebrew name for God.

Adone'an, *adj.*, *i.q.* Adonic.

Adon'ic, *adj.* rel. to Adonis.

adon'is, *n.*, a beauty, a dandy. (The original Adonis was beloved by Venus.)

adopt', *v.t.*, to take to oneself, to choose; to take as one's own child.

adopt'ed, *p.p.*, adopt.

adopt'er, *n.*, one who adopts.

adopt'ing, *pr.p.*, adopt

adop'tion, *n.*, the act of adopting.

adop'tionist, *n.*, one who believes that Our Lord is only God's adopted Son.

adop'tive, *adj.*, rel. to adoption.

ador'able, *adj.*, fit to be adored.

ador'ableness, *n.*, adorable state; fitness to be adored.

adora'tion, *n.*, the act of adoring.

adore', *v.t.*, to worship; love exceedingly.

adored', *p.p.*, adore.

ador'er, *n.*, one who adores.

ador'ing, *pr.p.*, adore.

ador'ingly, *adv.*, in an adoring way.

adorn', *v.t.*, to beautify, decorate.

adorned', *p.p.*, adorn.

adorn'er, *n.*, one who adorns.

adorn'ing, *pr.p.*, adorn.

adorn'ment, *n.*, act of adorning; an embellishment.

adoscula'tion, *n.*, impregnation of flowers or ova.

adown', *adv.* and *prep.*, down; down along.

adrift', *adv.*, driven by stream or wind.

adrip', *adv.*, in a dripping state.

adroga'tion, *n.*, adoption.

adroit', *adj.*, skilful, nimble.

adroit'ly, *adv.*, in adroit manner.

adroit'ness, *n.*, the adroit state or faculty.

adry', *adj.*, thirsty.

adsciti'tious, *adj.*, additional, unessential.

adsciti'tiously, *adv.*, in an adscititious way.

ad'script, *adj.*, written later; *n.*, a serf attached to the soil.

ad'ulate, *v.t.*, to bestow fulsome flattery on.

adula'tion, *n.*, fulsome flattery.

ad'ulator, *n.*, one who adulates.

ad'ulatory, *adj.*, fulsomely flattering.

adult', *n.*, one grown up; *adj.*, grown up, of full age.

adul'terant, *adj.*, adulterating; *n.*, a person or thing that adulterates.

adul'terate, *v.t.*, to corrupt, make impure.

adul'terated, *p.p.*, adulterate.

adul'terating, *pr.p.*, adulterate.

adultera'tion, *n.*, the act or effect of adulterating.

adul'terator, *n.*, one who adulterates.

adul'terer, *n.*, one who commits adultery.

adul'teress, *n.*, fem. of adulterer.

adul'terous, *adj.*, rel. to adultery.

adul'terously, *adv.*, in the manner of an adulterer.

adul'tery, *n.*, the act of breaking the marriage vows.

adult'ness, *n.*, maturity, the state of being grown up.

adum'bra, *n.*, the penumbra of an eclipse of the moon.

adum'brant, *adj.*, in outline, faintly shadowing.

ad'umbrate, *v.t.*, to sketch in outline, to typify.

ad'umbrated, *p.p.*, adumbrate.

ad'umbrating, *pr.p.*, adumbrate.

adumbra'tion, *n.*, the act of adumbrating; a faint sketch.

aduno'ate, *adj.*, hooked.

aduno'ous, *adj.*, hooked.

adust', *adj.*, burnt, dried up; *adv.*, in the dust.

advance', *v.t.* and *i.*, to put forward, move forward, give beforehand, increase (price).

advance', *n.*, the act of advancing, progress; payment in advance.

advanced', *p.p.*, advance.

advance'ment, *n.*, the act or state of advancing; promotion, furtherance.

advan'cer, *n.*, one who advances.

advan'cing, *pr.p.*, advance.

advan'cive, *adj.*, promoting advance.

advan'tage, *n.*, gain, profit, superiority; *v.t.*, to be of service to, to benefit.

advan'taged, *p.p.*, advantage.

advanta'geous, *adj.* profitable, useful.

advanta'geously, *adv.*, with profit or advantage.

advanta'geousness, *n.*, the state of being advantageous.

advant'aging, *pr.p.* advantage.

advene', *v.i.*, to come to, arrive; to be added.

adve'nient, *adj.*, additional.

ad'vent, *n.*, coming, arrival; the four weeks before Christmas.

adventi'tious, *adj.*, additional, casual.

adventi'tiously, *adv.*, additionally, casually.

adventi'tiousness, *n.*, the quality of being casual.

advent'ual, *adj.*, rel. to Advent.

adven'ture, *n.*, a hazardous enterprise, a risk; *v.t.* and *i.*, to embark on an enterprise.

adven'tured, *p.p.*, adventure.

adven'turer, *n.*, one who adventures; a trickster.

adven'turesome, *adj.*, prone to adventure.

adven'turess, *n.*, fem. of adventurer.

adven'turing, *pr.p.*, adventure.

adven'turous, *adj.*, bold, ready to take risks.

adven'turously, *adv.*, daringly.

adven'turousness, *n.*, boldness, daring.

ad'verb, *n.*, a word that qualifies verbs, adjectives, or adverbs.

adverb'ial, *adj.*, rel. to an adverb.

adverb'ially, *adv.*, in the manner of an adverb.

ad'versary, *n.*, opponent, enemy.

adver'sative, *adj.*, contrary, antithetical.

ad'verse, *adj.*, opposed, contrary to.

ad'versely, *adv.*, in a contrary or hostile way.

ad'verseness, *n.*, the adverse state.

adver'sity, *n.*, bad fortune, misfortune, misery.

advert', *v.t.* and *i.*, to turn, direct; to refer to.

advert'ed, *p.p.*, advert.

advert'ence, *n.*, attention.

advert'ency, *n.*, the attentive state.

advert'ent, *adj.*, attentive.

advert'ently, *adv.*, attentively.

advert'ing, *pr.p.*, advert.

ad'vertise, *v.t.*, to proclaim publicly, make known.

ad'vertised, *p.p.*, advertise.

adver'tisement, *n.*, publication, notice.

ad'vertiser, *n.*, one who advertises.

ad'vertising, *pr.p.*, advertise.

advice', *n.*, counsel, warning.

advisabil'ity, *n.*, the state of being advisable.

advis'able, *adj.*, able to be recommended; wise, prudent.

advis'ableness, *n.*, *i.q.* advisability.

advis'ably, *adv.*, wisely, in a way to be approved.

advise', *v.t.*, to give notice; to warn; to inform.

advised', *p.p.*, advise.

advis'edly, *adv.*, upon consideration, with all care.

advis'er, *n.*, one who advises.

advise'ment, *n.*, consultation, deliberation.

advis'ing, *pr.p.*, advise.

advis'ory, *adj.*, with power to advise.

ad'vocacy, *n.*, the act of advocating.

ad'vocate, *n.*, the pleader of a cause.

ad'vocate, *v.t.*, to plead, urge, support.

ad'vocated, *p.p.*, advocate.

ad'vocateship, *n.*, the office of advocate.

ad'vocating, *pr.p.*, advocate.

advoca'tion, *n.*, the act of transferring a law-case to another court (Scottish); appeal.

advow'ee, *n.*, a patron holding an advowson.

advow'son, *n.*, the right of presentation to a benefice.

adynam'ia, *n.*, loss of physical strength.

adynam'ic, *adj.*, rel. to adynamia; unaffected by force.

ad'ytum, *n.*, inner shrine; recess (*Lat.*).

adze, *n.*, an axe-like tool.

ae'dile, *n.*, a Roman magistrate entrusted with the care of public buildings, markets, games and so forth. Also *e'dile*.

Aege'an, *adj.*, rel. to the Archipelago.

ae'gis, *n.*, the protecting shield of Zeus.

aegro'tat, *n.*, a certificate of sickness.

Aene'id, *n.*, Virgil's poem on Aeneas.

Aeo'lian, *adj.*, bel. to Aeolia.

ae'on, *n.*, an age, great length of time.

a'erate, *v.t.*, to impregnate with air.

a'erated, *p.p.*, aerate.

a'erating, *pr.p.*, aerate.

aera'tion, *n.*, the process of aerating.

ae'rial, *adj.*, of the air; high up.

a'erie, *n.*, a bird of prey's nest.

aerifica'tion, *n.*, the process or state of aerifying.

a'erified, *p.p.*, aerify.

a'erify, *v.t.*, to fill with air.

a'erodrome, *n.*, a flying-machine course.

aerodynam'ics, *n.*, the science of the laws of motion of gases.

aerog'raphy, *n.*, description of the atmosphere.

a'erolite, *n.*, a meteoric stone.

a'erolith, *n.*, *i.q.* aerolite.

aerolit'ic, *adj.*, rel. to aerolites.

aerolog'ical, *adj.*, rel. to aerology.

aerol'ogist, *n.*, a student of aerology.

aerol'ogy, *n.*, the science of the atmosphere.

a'eromancy, *n.* divination of the sky.

aerom'eter, *n.*, an apparatus for discovering the tension of air.

aeromet'ric, *adj.*, rel. to aerometry.

aerom'etry, *n.*, the science of weighing and measuring air and gases.

a'eronaut, *n.*, a sky-sailor.

aeronau'tic, *adj.*, rel. to sky-sailing.

aeronau'tics, *n.*, the art and science of sky-sailing.

a'erophyte, *n.*, an air-plant, such as the orchid, that grows in the air.

a'eroplane, *n.*, a heavier than air flying-machine, with one or more planes or fixed surfaces.

a'eroplanist, *n.*, one who flies in an aeroplane.

aeros'copy, *n.*, observation of atmospheric phenomena.

a'erostat, *n.*, an air balloon.

aerostat'ics, *n.*, the statical science of air; ballooning.

aerosta'tion, *n.*, ballooning.

a'ery, *adj.*, high in air; spiritual.

Aescula'pian, *adj.*, rel. to Aesculapius.

Aescula'pius, *n.*, the Roman god of healing.

aesthet'ic, *adj.*, bel. to good taste or fine perception (*see* esthetic).

aesthet'ical, *adj.*, *i.q.* aesthetic.

afar', *adv.*, at a distance, far off.

afeard', *adj.*, afraid, frightened.

affabil'ity, *n.*, the quality of affable.

af'fable, *adj.*, ready to be spoken to, gracious.

af'fableness, *n.*, the quality of affable.

af'fably, *adv.*, graciously, agreeably.

affair', *n.*, a thing, matter, business, military engagement.

affect', *v.t.*, to influence, act upon; to assume, adopt, pretend.

affecta'tion, *n.*, an assumed pose, a pretence.

affect'ed, *p.p.*, affect; also *adj.*, showing affectation.

affect'edly, *adv.*, in an affected way.

affect'edness, *n.*, *i.q.*, affectation.

affectibil'ity, *n.*, an affectible condition.

affect'ible, *adj.*, capable of being affected.

affect'ing, *pr.p.*, affect.

affect'ingly, *adv.*, touchingly.

affec'tion, *n.*, love, tender feeling, fondness for; disease.

affec'tional, *adj.*, rel. to affections.

affec'tionate, *adj.*, loving, fond.

affec'tionately, *adv.*, lovingly, fondly.

affec'tionateness, *n.*, the quality of affectionate.

affec'tioned, *adj.*, disposed.

affec'tive, *adj.*, emotional; with power to affect.

affec'tively, *adv.*, in an affective way.

affi'ance, *n.*, promise, pledge, trust; *v.t.*, to plight faith, to betroth.

affi'anced, *p.p.*, affiance; *adj.*, betrothed.

affi'ancer, *n.*, one who affiances.

affi'ancing, *pr.p.*, affiance.

affiché, *n.*, a notice (*Fr.*).

affida'vit, *n.*, a sworn written statement.

affied', *adj.*, affianced.

affil'iate, *v.t.*, to adopt a child; to fix a child's parentage; to associate.

affil'iated, *p.p.*, affiliate.

affil'iating, *pr.p.*, affiliate.

affilia'tion, *n.*, the act of affiliating.

af'finage, *n.*, refining.

affin'ity, *n.*, near relationship; resemblance of nature; attraction (*chem.*).

affirm', *v.i.* and *t.*, to state confidently; to say yes.

affirm'able, *adj.*, able to be affirmed.

affirm'ably, *adv.*, in an affirmable manner.

affirm'ance, *n.*, ratification.

affirm'ant, *n.*, one who affirms.

affirma'tion, *n.*, the act of affirming; a positive statement.

affirm'ative, *adj.*, asserting; saying yes.

affirm'atively, *adv.*, in an affirmative way.

affirmed', *p.p.*, affirm.

affirm'er, *n.*, one who affirms.

affirm'ing, *pr.p.*, affirm.

affix', *v.t.*, to fix, to join.

af'fix, *n.*, an addition; a syllable or syllables added at the end of a word.

affixed', *p.p.*, affix.

affix'ing, *pr.p.*, affix.

affix'ture, *n.*, the act of affixing; that which is affixed.

affla'ted, *adj.*, inspired.

affla'tion, *n.*, inspiration.

affla'tus, *n.*, breath of wind; inspiration.

afflict', *v.t.*, to cause pain or grief to.

afflict'ed, *p.p.*, afflict.

afflict'er, *n.*, one who afflicts.

afflict'ing, *pr.p.*, afflict.

afflic'tion, *n.*, distress, grief, oppression.

afflict'ive, *adj.*, causing affliction.

af'fluence, *n.*, abundance, wealth.

af'fluency, *n.*, an affluent state.

af'fluent, *adj.*, abundantly wealthy.

af'flux, *n.*, a flowing towards; a concourse.

afford', *v.t.*, to bestow, to yield; to be able to spend.

afford'ed, *p.p.*, afford.

afford'ing, *pr.p.*, afford.

affor'est, *v.t.*, to turn into a forest by planting.

afforesta'tion, *n.*, the act of afforesting.

affran'chise, *v.t.*, to liberate.

affran'chisement, *n.*, the act of liberating.

affray', *n.*, an alarming or noisy fight; *v.t.*, to alarm.

affreight', *v.t.*, to charter a trading vessel.

affright', *n.*, terror, dread; *v.t.*, to cause terror.

affright'ed, *p.p.*, affright.

affright'er, *n.*, one who affrights.

affright'ing, *pr.p.*, affright.

affront', *n.*, an insult; *v.t.*, to insult.

affront'ed, *p.p.*, affront.

affront'ing, *pr.p.*, affront.

affront'ive, *adj.*, ready to insult.

affuse', *v.*, to pour (water) on.

affused', *p.p.*, affuse.

affus'ing, *pr.p.*, affuse.

affu'sion, *n.*, the pouring on (of water).

Af'ghan, *n.*, a native of Afghanistan.

afield', *adv.*, to a distance, far.

afire', *adv.*, on fire.

afloat', *adv.*, floating sailing.

afoot', *adv.*, on foot.

afore, *adv.*, formerly, before.

afore'going, *adj.*, previous, preceding.

afore'hand, *adv.*, previously, in anticipation.

afore'mentioned, *adj.*, previously spoken of.

afore'named, *adj.*, previously named.

afore'said, *adj.*, previously said or mentioned.

afore'thought, *adv.* and *adj.*, with premeditation.

afore'time, *adv.*, in former times.

a fortio'ri, *Lat. phr.* = from a stronger cause = much more therefore.

afoul', *adv.*, running foul.

afraid', *adj.*, frightened.

afresh', *adv.*, over again.

Af'ric, *adj.*, bel. to Africa.

Af'rican, *adj.*, *i.q.* Afric.

Af'ricander, *n.*, a white man born (of Dutch parentage) in Africa.

af'rit, *n.*, an evil spirit, demon.

afront', *adv.* and *prep.* in front (of).

aft', *adv.*, behind, in the stern of a ship; also *adj.*

aft'er, *adv.*, *conj.* and *prep.*, behind; later; later than; according to.

aft'er-ages, *n.*, futurity, the coming times.

aft'er-birth, *n.*, the placenta.

aft'er-clap, *n.*, an unexpected blow, when one has dropped one's guard.

aft'er-crop, *n.*, a later crop.

aft'er-damp, *n.*, choke damp (in a mine).

aft'erguard, *n.*, the sailors stationed abaft the mainmast.

aft'er-math, *n.*, a second crop.

aft'er-most, *adj.* and *adv.*, latest, last.

afternoon', *n.*, the period between midday and night.

aft'er-pains, *n.*, the pains after childbirth.

aft'er-piece, *n.*, a sequel; a farce succeeding a play.

aft'er-thought, *n.*, later reflection.

aft'erward, *adv.*, later in time.

aft'erwards, *adv.*, *i.q.* afterward.

aft'er-wit, *n.*, belated wisdom; wisdom after the event.

a'ga, *n.*, a Turkish gentleman or magistrate.

again', *adv.*, once more.

against', *prep.*, opposite, in opposition to

agal'ma, *n.*, an impression on a seal.

ag'amist, *n.*, one opposed to marriage.

ag'amous, *adj.*, unfit to marry; produced without sexual union.

ag'apae, *n.*, pl. of agape.

ag'ape, *n.*, a love feast.

agape', *adv.*, gaping, in astonishment.

Agapem'one, *n.*, the abode of Love.

ag'aric, *n.*, a fungus or mushroom.

agasp', *adv.*, gasping; *adj.*, eager for.

ag'ate, *n.*, a precious stone so named.

aga've, *n.*, an American plant so named.

agaze', *adv.*, in a gazing attitude.

agazed', *adj.*, astounded.

age, *n.*, a time-period; the length of a life; *v.i.*, to grow old.

a'ged, *adj.*, old.

a'gedly, *adv.*, like an old person.

a'geing, *pr.p.*, age.

a'gency, *n.*, the function of an agent.

agen'da, *n.*, things to be done or considered.

a'gent, *n.*, one who acts; an intermediary.

aggera'tion, *n.*, a heaping up.

agglom'erate, *v.t.* and *i.*, to gather into a mass, collect; *n.*, a heap.

agglom'erated, *p.p.*, agglomerate.

agglom'erating, *pr.p.*, agglomerate.

agglomera'tion, *n.*, the act of agglomerating.

agglu'tinant, *adj.*, tending to agglutinate.

agglu'tinate, *v.t.* and *i.*, to join (as if with glue).

agglu'tinated, *p.p.*, agglutinate.

agglu'tinating, *pr.p.*, agglutinate.

agglutina'tion, *n.*, the process of agglutinating.

agglu'tinative, *adj.*, tending to agglutination.

ag'grandize, *v.t.*, to increase; exalt.

ag'grandized, *p.p.*, aggrandize.

aggrand'izement, *n.*, increase, exaltation.

ag'grandizer, *n.*, one who aggrandizes.

ag'grandizing, *pr.p.*, aggrandize.

ag'gravate, *v.t.*, to make heavier or more serious; (less correctly) to annoy.

ag'gravated, *p.p.*, aggravate.

ag'gravating, *pr.p.*, aggravate.

aggrava'tion, *n.*, the making worse or more serious.

ag'gregate, *adj.*, taken together; *n.*, a total; *v.t.*, to collect.

ag'gregated, *p.p.*, aggregate.

ag'gregately, *adv.*, collectively.

ag'gregating, *pr.p.*, aggregate.

aggrega'tion, *n.*, the act of aggregating.

ag'gregative, *adj.*, tending to aggregate.

aggress', *v.i.*, to assault; open a quarrel; invade another man's rights.

aggressed', *p.p.*, aggress.

aggress'ing, *pr.p.*, aggress.

aggres'sion, *n.*, an unprovoked assault; an encroachment.

aggress'ive, *adj.*, assaulting, encroaching.

aggress'iveness, *n.*, a tendency to be aggressive.

aggress'or, *n.*, one who begins a quarrel, who invades another man's rights.

aggriev'ance, *n.*, offence.

aggrieve', *v.t.*, to offend, to give cause for complaint.

aggrieved', *p.p.*, aggrieve.

aggriev'ing, *pr.p.*, aggrieve.

aggroup', *v.t.*, to arrange in a group.

aggrouped', *p.p.*, aggroup.

aggroup'ing, *pr.p.*, aggroup.

aghast', *adj.* and *adv.*, wonder-struck and terrified.

ag'ile, *adj.*, nimble, active.

ag'ileness, *n.*, *i.q.*, agility.

agil'ity, *n.*, nimbleness, activity.

ag'io, *n.*, exchange premium; allowance on worn coin.

ag'iotage, *n.*, brokerage.

agist', *v.t.*, to look after cattle for hire; to assess for public purposes.

agist'ment, *n.*, the contract with an agistor; the agistor's profit; an assessment.

agist'or, *n.*, one who takes care of cattle for hire.

ag'itable, *adj.*, able to be agitated.

ag'itate, *v.t.*, to set in motion; perturb; excite.

ag'itated, *p.p.*, agitate.

ag'itating, *pr.p.*, agitate.

agita'tion, *n.*, an agitated state; disturbance; public movement.
ag'itative, *adj.*, causing agitation.
ag'itator, *n.*, one who excites the public.
a'glet, *n.*, the metal sheath at the end of a lace; a bullion ornament on a uniform; a particular kind of stay-lace (round and white).
aglow', *adv.*, glowing.
agmatol'ogy, *n.*, the study of fractures.
ag'nail, *n.*, a whitlow, a corn, misshapen finger-end.
ag'nate, *adj.*, related on the paternal side; akin; collaterally related.
agnat'ic, *adj.*, rel. to male descent.
agna'tion, *n.*, relationship through male descent.
agni'tion, *n.*, acknowledgment.
agno'men, *n.*, an additional name.
agnos'tic, *n.* and *adj.*, refusing to believe in the unknowable.
agnos'ticism, *n.*, the state of the agnostic.
ago', *adv.*, in time past.
agog', *adv.*, in an excited, eager state.
ago'ing, *adv.*, in movement.
agone', *adj.*, past.
agon'ic, *adj.*, without an angle.
ag'onist, *n.*, one who agonizes or contends.
agonis'tes, *n.*, one who strives.
agonis'tic, *adj.*, striving, agonizing.
agonis'tical, *adj.*, *i.q.* agonistic.
ag'onize, *v.i.* and *t.*, to endure anguish; to distress.
ag'onized, *p.p.*, agonize.
ag'onizing, *pr.p.*, agonize.
ag'onizingly, *adv.*, in a distressing manner.
ag'ony, *n.*, extreme pain anguish.
ag'ora, *n.*, a market-place, market (*Gr.*).
agou'ti, *n.*, a rodent, with three hind toes.
agraph'ia, *n.*, loss of power to write.
agra'rian, *adj.*, rel. to the land; *n.*, a supporter of agrarianism.
agra'rianism, *n.*, the doctrine of equal distribution of land.
agra'rianize, *n.*, to divide the land equally.
agree', *v.i.*, to consent, be of one mind with.
agreeabil'ity, *n.*, being agreeable.
agree'able, *adj.*, pleasant, consenting.
agree'ableness, *n.*, pleasantness.
agree'ably, *adv.*, pleasantly; in accordance with.
agreed', *p.p.*, agree.
agree'ing, *pr.p.*, agree.
agree'ment, *n.*, consent, a formal document of consent.
agres'tic, *adj.*, rel. to the country.
ag'riculter, *n.*, one who cultivates the land.
agricul'tural, *adj.*, rel. to agriculture.
ag'riculture, *n.*, land cultivation.
agricul'turist, *n.*, one engaged in agriculture.
ag'rimony, *n.*, the plant *agrimonia.*
agriol'ogy, *n.*, the study of uncivilized peoples.
agrostog'raphy, *n.*, the description of grasses.
agrostol'ogy, *n.*, the study of grasses.
aground', *adv.*, fixed to a sea or river bottom.
a'gue, *n.*, a feverish shivering complaint.
a'gued, *adj.*, suffering from ague.
a'guish, *adj.*, inclined to ague, shivering.
ah, *interj.*, expressing pain or surprise.
aha', *interj.*, expressing glee.
ahead', *adv.*, in advance, beyond.
aheap', *adv.*, piled up.
ahem', *interj.*, expressing hesitation or incredulity.
ahoy', *interj.*, a sailor's challenge of another ship.
ahull', *adv.*, lying almost broadside to wind and sea.
aid', *n.*, help, assistance; *v.t.*, to help, assist.
aid'ance, *n.*, *i.q.*, aid.
aid'ed, *p.p.*, aid.
aide'-de-camp, *n.*, a general officer's assistant.
aid'er, *n.*, one who aids.
aid'ful, *adj.*, helping.
aid'ing, *pr.p.*, aid.
aid'less, *adj.*, without help or aid.
ai'glet, *see* aglet.
ai'gret, *n.*, a heron or egret.
ai'grette, *n.*, an ornament of feathers or jewels worn on the head-dress.
ai'guille, *n.*, a sharp mountain peak; a drill.
ail, *v.i.*, to be ill.
ailed, *p.p.*, ail.
ail'ing, *pr.p.*, ail; *adj.*, in a sick state.
ail'ment, *n.*, an illness.
aim, *n.*, a striving to hit a mark; a thing aimed at; direction; intention; *v.i.*, to strive to hit a mark; *v.t.*, to point; direct.
aimed, *p.p.*, aim.
aim'ing, *pr.p.*, aim.
aim'less, *adj.*, without aim or intention.
aim'lessly, *adv.*, in an aimless way.
ain't, a vulgar phrase = am I not? is he, she, it not; are we, you, they not?
air, *n.*, the atmosphere; a person's bearing; a melody; *v.t.*, to expose to the air, to dry, to display boastfully.
air'-bed, *n.*, an inflated bed.
air'-brake, *n.*, a brake actuated by air.
air'-cells, *n.*, cells containing air.

air'-craft, *n.*, flying in the air; the flying service or industry; flying machines collectively.
aired, *p.p.*, air.
air'-gas, *n.*, the gas made by mixing air with petroleum vapour.
air'-gun, *n.*, a gun in which the force is air.
air'-hole, *n.*, an opening to admit air.
air'ily, *adv.*, lightly, gaily.
air'iness, *n.*, sprightliness, breeziness.
air'ing, *pr.p.*, air; *n.*, a walk or drive in the air.
air'less, *adj.*, without air.
air'-pump, *n.*, a pump for forcing out air.
air'-shaft, *n.*, a ventilating shaft.
air'ship, *n.*, a dirigible balloon.
air'-tight, *adj.*, excluding the air.
air'y, *adj.*, having plenty of air; light, sprightly.
aisle, *n.*, a division in a building flanking the central division.
ait, *n.*, a little island in a river.
ajar', *adv.*, slightly opened.
aj'utage, *n.*, a tub for discharging liquid.
akim'bo, *adv.*, with hands on hips and the elbows pointed outwards.
akin', *adj.*, rel. by blood; of like nature.
al'abaster, *n.*, a semi-transparent stone so named; *adj.*, made of alabaster.
alack', *interj.*, expressing grief.
alack'-a-day, interjectional phrase, expressing grief.
alac'rity, *n.*, speed, alertness, smartness
à la mode', *adv.*, in the fashion; *n.*, a thin silk material.
à la mort', *adv.*, to the death.
a'lar, *adj.*, winged.
alarm', *n.*, sudden fear; sense of coming danger; an alarum; *v.t.*, to cause sudden fright; to call to arms.
alarmed', *p.p.*, alarm.
alarm'ing, *pr.p.*, alarm; *adj.*, startling, disquieting.
alarm'ingly, *adv.*, startlingly.
alarm'ist, *n.*, one who without reason causes alarm.
alar'um, *n.*, a clock-work contrivance for waking people up.
a'lary, *adj.*, rel. to wings; wing-like.
alas', *interj.*, expressing sorrow.
a'late, *adj.*, winged.
alb, *n.*, a long, close-fitting white robe so named.
Alba'nian, *adj.*, bel. to Albania.
alba'ta, *n.*, a white alloy of nickel, zinc, and copper.
al'batross, *n.*, a great sea-bird so named; a German type of aeroplane.
albe'it, *conj.*, although, even granting that.
albes'cent, *adj.*, growing white.
Al'bin, *n.*, an old name for Scotland.
albi'ness, *n.*, fem. of albino.
al'binism, *n.*, the physical character of the Albino.
albi'no, *n.*, a man or beast having white hair and skin, and pink eyes; a plant deficient in colouring matter.
albi'noism, *n.*, *i.q.* albinism.
albugin'eous, *adj.*, rel. to the white of the eye.
albu'go, *n.*, an eye disease affecting the cornea.
al'bum, *n.*, a book of blank pages.
albu'men, *n.*, the white of an egg; nutritive matter found in a seed.
albu'min, *n.*, any substance composed like or resembling albumen; a proteid.
albu'minize, *v.t.*, to apply to paper an albuminous solution
albu'minized, *p.p.*, albuminize.
albu'minoid, *adj.*, resembling albumen.
albuminu'ria, *n.*, the presence of albumen in the urine.
albuminu'ric, *adj.*, rel. to albuminuria.
albu'minous, *adj.*, with the quality of albumin.
albur'num, *n.*, a tree's sap-wood.
alcade', *n.*, a Spanish, Portuguese, or Moorish Governor.
Alca'ic, *adj.*, in the metre of Alcaeus.
al'cazar, *n.*, a Spanish or Moorish palace.
alchem'ic, *adj.*, rel. to alchemy.
alchem'ical, *i.q.* alchemic.
al'chemist, *n.*, one who practises alchemy.
alchemis'tic, *adj.*, rel. to an alchemist.
al'chemy, *n.*, the spurious art of turning base metals into gold.
al'cohol, *n.*, a pure spirit so named.
al'coholate, *n.*, a compound having alcohol as its acid radical.
alcohol'ic, *adj.*, rel. to alcohol.
alcoholiza'tion, *n.*, the act of alcoholizing.
al'coholize, *v.t.*, to produce an alcoholic effect.
alcoholom'eter, *n.*, an instrument for testing the alcoholic strength of liquors.
Al'coran, *n.*, the sacred book of the Mohammedan religion.
Alcoran'ic, *adj.*, rel. to the Alcoran.
Alcoran'ist, *n.*, one who studies the Alcoran.
al'cove, *n.*, a recess.
Aldeb'aran, *n.*, one of the Hyades group of stars
al'dehyde, *n.*, a volatile liquid derived from alcohol.

al'der, *n.*, a tree so named.

al'derman, *n.*, a municipal dignitary so named.

alderman'ic, *adj.*, resembling, or bel. to, an alderman.

Al'dine, *adj.*, bel. to Aldus Manutius, the Venetian 16th cent. printer.

ale, *n.*, an intoxicating malt liquor, brewed with hops; beer.

aleak', *adv.*, having sprung a leak.

a'leatory, *adj.*, rel. to dicing and gambling.

alec'tryomancy, *n.*, divination by means of cocks.

alee', *adv.*, on or towards the lee side.

a'legar, *n.*, malt vinegar.

ale'hoof, *n.*, ground-ivy.

ale'house, *n.*, a place where ale is sold.

alem'bic, *n.*, a distilling vessel.

alem'broth, *n.*, a mixture used in alchemy.

alert', *adj.*, on the watch, spry.

alert'ness, *n.*, the quality of the alert.

alette', *n.*, a small wing in a building; a side of a pier.

aleu'romancy, *n.*, divination by means of flour.

aleurom'eter, *n.*, an instrument for testing the properties of flour.

Aleu'tian, *adj.*, rel. to the Aleuts, who live in the Aleutian islands of Alaska.

aleu'tic, *adj.*, *i.q.* Aleutian.

ale'wife, *n.*, a woman-seller of ale; an American herring-like fish.

Alexan'drian, *adj.*, bel. to Alexander or Alexandria.

Alexan'drine, *adj.*, bel. to Alexandria; *n.*, a twelve-syllabled iambic verse.

alexiphar'mic, *adj.*, antidotal.

alfres'co, an Italian phrase = in the fresh air.

Al'ga, *n.*, a species of sea-weed and water-weed.

al'gal, *adj.*, pert. to alga.

al'gebra, *n.*, the method of calculating by means of letters, signs, and figures.

algebra'ic, *adj.*, bel. to algebra.

algebra'ical, *adj.*, *i.q.* algebraic.

al'gebraist, *n.*, one skilled in algebra.

Algerine', *adj.*, bel. to Algiers.

Al'gol, *n.*, the variable star *Beta om Perseus*.

al'gor, *n.*, chilliness.

al'gorism, *n.*, Arabic numeration; arithmetic.

al'gum, *n.*, a Biblical tree, sandal-wood.

Alham'bra, *n.*, the famous Moorish palace at Granada.

a'lias, *adv.*, at another time; *n.*, a false name.

al'ibi, *adv.*, in another place; *n.*, the being in another place (*Leg.*).

a'lien, *adj.*, foreign, strange; *n.*, a foreigner, stranger.

alienabil'ity, *n.*, capacity to be alienated.

a'lienable, *adj.*, able to be alienated.

a'lienage, *n.*, the state of being an alien.

a'lienate, *v.t.*, to make over to another; to appropriate; to estrange.

a'lienated, *p.p.*, alienate.

a'lienating, *pr.p.*, alienate.

aliena'tion, *n.*, the act or state of alienating.

a'lienator, *n.*, one who alienates.

alienee', *n.*, one to whom a property is transferred.

a'lienism, *n.*, the state of being an alien; the treatment of mental derangement.

alif'erous, *adj.*, winged.

al'iform, *adj.*, wing-shaped.

alight', *v.i.*, to descend, light down, dismount; *adv.*, on fire.

alight'ed, *p.p.*, alight.

alight'ing, *pr.p.*, alight.

align', } *v.t.*, to ar-
aline', } range in line.

align'ment, *n.*, the act or state of aligning.

alike', *adj.*, resembling, like; *adv.*, in a similar way, equally.

al'iment, *n.*, nourishment, support.

aliment'al, *adj.*, rel. to aliment.

aliment'ary, *adj.*, rel. to aliment, giving nourishment.

alimenta'tion, *n.*, the giving of aliment.

aliment'iveness, *n.*, a liking for food and drink.

alimo'nious, *adj.*, nutritious.

al'imony, *n.*, support, a living allowance.

al'iped, *adj.*, wing-footed.

al'iquant, *adj.*, forming a fractional part of a number.

al'iquot, *adj.*, contained so many times in a whole; *n.*, an aliquot part.

a'lish, *adj.*, resembling ale.

alive', *adj.*, living, alert.

aliz'arine, *n.*, a coal product, used for red-dyeing.

al'kahest, *n.*, the universal solvent in alchemy.

alkales'cency, *n.*, tendency to become alkaline.

alkales'cent, *adj.*, becoming alkaline.

al'kali, *n.*, a chemical substance of a neutralizing nature.

al'kalifiable, *adj.*, able to be alkalified.

al'kalified, *p.p.*, alkalify.

al'kalify, *v.t.*, to change into an alkali.

al'kalifying, *pr.p.*, alkalify.

alkalig'enous, *adj.*, producing alkali.
alkalim'eter, *n.*, an apparatus for ascertaining the percentage of alkali in a solution.
alkalimet'ric, *adj.*, rel. to alkalimetry.
alkalimet'rical, *adj.*, *i.q.* alkalimetric.
alkalim'etry, *n.*, the process of discovering the percentage of alkali in a solution
al'kaline, *adj.*, rel. to alkali.
alkalin'ity, *n.*, the state of being alkaline.
alkaliza'tion, *n.*, the act or state of alkalizing.
al'kalize, *v.t.*, to turn into alkali.
al'kalized, *p.p.*, alkalize.
al'kalizing, *pr.p.*, alkalize.
al'kaloid, *n.*, a chemical substance with properties like those of alkali.
al'kanet, *n.*, the name of a plant producing red dye.
Al'koran, *see* Alcoran.
all, *adj.*, the entire number; the whole.
Al'lah, *n.*, the Mohammedan (Arabic) name for God.
al'lanite, *n.*, a mineral so named.
allanto'ic, *adj.*, rel. to the allantois.
allan'toid, *adj.*, like an allantois.
allan'tois, *n.*, a membranous appendage like a sac.
allay', *v.t.*, to lighten, make quiet, alleviate.
allayed', *p.p.*, allay.
allay'ing, *pr.p.*, allay.
allege', alledge', *v.t.*, to assert, make a statement.
allege'able, alledge'able, *adj.*, able to be alleged.
alleged', alledged' *p.p.*, allege.
alleg'er, alledg'er, *n.*, one who alleges.
alleg'ing, alledg'ing, *pr.p.*, allege.
allega'tion, *n.*, the act of alleging a charge.
alle'giance, *n.*, plighted loyalty.
allegor'ic, *adj.*, in the manner of allegory.
allegor'ical, *adj.*, *i.q.* allegoric.
allegor'ically, *adv.*, in an allegorical manner or sense.
al'legorist, *n.*, a writer of allegory.
al'legorize, *v.t.*, to make into allegory.
al'legorized, *p.p.*, allegorize.
al'legorizer, *n.*, one who allegorizes.
al'legorizing, *pr.p.*, allegorize.
al'legory, *n.*, a figurative story.
allegret'to, *adj.*, in fairly quick time (slower than allegro); *n.*, a movement in fairly quick time.
allegris'simo, *adj.*, in very fast time; *n.*, a movement in very fast time.
alle'gro, *adj.*, in fast time; *n.*, a fast movement.
allelu'ia, *interj.*, praise the Lord (*Heb.*)
aller'gic, *adj.*, highly susceptible to; having an aversion from.
alle'viate, *v.t.*, to lighten, assuage.
alle'viated, *p.p.*, alleviate.
alle'viating, *pr.p.*, alleviate.
allevia'tion, *n.*, the act of alleviating.
alle'viative, *adj.*, tending to alleviate.
alle'viator, *n.*, one who alleviates.
al'ley, *n.*, a narrow passage.
All Fools' Day, *n.*, April 1.
all-fours', *adv.*, on all four legs, or on hands and knees.
all-hail', *interj.*, expressing greeting.
All-Hal'lows, *n.*, the feast of All Hallows or Saints, Nov. 1.
allia'ceous, *adj.*, like or bel. to garlic.
alli'ance, *n.*, union by treaty.
allied', *p.p.*, ally.
allies', *n. pl.*, those who are closely or solemnly united.
alliga'tion, *n.*, the act of binding.
al'ligator, *n.*, the crocodile of America.
allit'erate, *v.t.*, to make alliterative;
allit'erate, *adj.*, alliterating in character
allit'erated, *p.p.*, alliterate.
allit'erating, *pr.p.*, alliterate.
allitera'tion, *n.*, repetition of a letter in a succession of words.
allit'erative, *adj.*, with a tendency to alliteration.
allit'eratively, *adv.*, in an alliterative way.
al'lium, *n.*, garlic; the name of a large class of *liliaceae.*
al'locate, *v.t.*, to assign a place or portion to.
al'located, *p.p.*, allocate.
al'locating, *pr.p.*, allocate.
alloca'tion, *n.*, the act of allocating.
alloca'tur, *n.*, a judge's allowance of an order of costs.
al'lochroite, *n.*, a species of garnet, so named from its changing colour under the blowpipe.
allocu'tion, *n.*, a spoken address.
allo'dial, *adj.*, rel. to absolute ownership.
allo'dium, *n.*, estate held in fee simple.
al'lograph, *n.*, a deed drawn by some one who is not a party to it.
allonge', *v.i.*, to lunge, *n.*, a lunge a paper slip attached to a bill of exchange, enabling the addition of further endorsements.
allopath'ic, *adj.*, rel to allopathy.
allopath'ically, *adv.*, on allopathic principles or methods.
allop'athist, *n.*, one who practises allopathy.

allop'athy, *n.*, the medical system which employs counter remedies, as distinguished from homoeopathy (*q.v.*).
allot', *v.t.*, to give as a portion or lot, to apportion.
allot'ment, *n.*, an allotted portion.
allot'ropy, *n.*, variation in physical properties.
allot'ted, *p.p.*, allot.
allot'ting, *pr.p.*, allot.
allow', *v.t.*, to permit; to concede or admit.
allow'able, *adj.*, able to be allowed.
allow'ableness, *n.*, state of the allowable.
allow'ably, *adv.*, in a way that can be allowed.
allow'ance, *n.*, permission, privilege; a grant; *v.t.*, to give a grant to.
allow'anced, *p.p.*, allowance.
allow'ancing, *pr.p.*, allowance.
allowed', *p.p.*, allow.
allow'ing, *pr.p.* allow.
alloy', *n.*, a mixture of metals; *v.t.*, to spoil by mixture of base with good.
alloy'age, *n.*, the act of alloying.
alloyed', *p.p.*, alloy.
alloy'ing, *pr.p.*, alloy.
All Saints' Day, *see* All Hallows.
all'-seeing, *adj.*, seeing all things.
All Souls' Day, *n.*, Nov. 2, when the faithful departed are commemorated.
all'spice, *n.*, the pepper-plant berry of Jamaica.
allude', *v.i.*, to refer to.
allud'ed, *p.p.*, allude.
allud'ing, *pr.p.*, allude.
allure', *v.t.*, to entice, draw on.
allured', *p.p.*, allure.
allure'ment, *n.*, the act of alluring.
allur'er, *n.*, one who allures.
allur'ing, *pr.p.*, allure.
allur'ingly, *adv.*, in an alluring way.
allu'sion, *n.*, reference to, hint at.
allu'sive, *adj.*, making reference.
allu'sively, *adv.*, in an allusive way.
allu'siveness, *n.*, the quality of being allusive.
allu'sory, *i.q.* allusive.
allu'vial, *adj.*, rel. to alluvium.
allu'vion, *n.*, the act of depositing soil.
allu'vium, *n.*, soil deposited by sea or river.
all-wise', *n.*, omniscient.
ally', *n.*, a person or state joined to another by compact; a close friend; *v.t.*, to attach, bind.
ally'ing, *pr.p.*, ally.
Al'magest, *n.*, the treatise of Pliny on astronomy; any learned treatise.
al'ma ma'ter, *n.*, one's university or college.
al'manac, *n.*, a year's kalendar.
al'mandine, *adj.*, rel. to the almandite.
al'mandite, *n.*, a species of garnet.
almight'iness, *n.*, the state of being almighty.
almight'y, *adj.*, omnipotent; *n.*, the Almighty, *i.e.*, God.
a'lmond, *n.*, the nut of the almond-tree.
al'moner, *n.*, a distributor of alms.
al'monry, *n.*, the place where alms are distributed.
al'most, *adv.*, nearly, all but.
alms, *n.*, a charitable gift.
alms'-house, *n.*, a house where poor persons are lodged.
al'muce, *n.*, *i.q.* amess.
al'mug, *n.*, *see* algum.
al'oe, *n.*, a bitter tropical plant.
aloet'ic, *adj.*, rel. to the aloe.
aloet'ical, *adj.*, *i.q.* aloetic.
aloft', *adv.*, up above, on high.
alogot'rophy, *n.*, irregular nutrition.
alone', *adj.* and *adv.*, solitary, solitarily, by oneself.
along', *adv.*, in line, in company with; *prep.*, from end to end or through a part of; forward.
along'side, *adv.* and *prep.*, side by side with.
aloof', *adv.*, at a distance, apart, aside.
aloof'ness, *n.*, a distant, stand-off manner.
alope'cia, *n.*, a form of baldness.
aloud', *adv.*, so as to be heard.
alp, *n.*, a mountain (*lit.*, snow-top).
alpac'a, *n.*, a Peruvian goat; the material made from its hair.
alp'enstock, *n.*, a mountaineer's staff.
al'pha, *n.*, the Greek A.
al'phabet, *n.*, all the letters of a language arranged in order.
alphabeta'rian, *n.*, the learner or maker of an alphabet.
alphabet'ic, *adj.*, in the order of the alphabet.
alphabet'ical, *adj.*, rel. to the alphabet.
al'phus, *n.*, a form of leprosy.
Alp'ine, *adj.*, bel. to the Alps.
alread'y, *adv.*, by this time.
Alsa'tia, *n.*, Alsace; also the name given to the Whitefriars in London, a famous sanctuary.
Alsa'tian, *adj.*, rel. to Alsatia.
al'sike, *n.*, a sort of clover.
al'so, *adv.*, in addition, as well.
Alta'ic, *adj.*, bel. to the Altaic mountains.
al'tar, *n.*, the stone or table of sacrifice.
al'tarage, *n.*, the endowments of an altar.
al'tar-cloth, *n.*, the cloth with which an altar is vested.

al'tar-piece, *n.*, a picture behind an altar.

al'ter, *v.t.*, to change, make different; *v.i.*, to become different.

alterabil'ity, *n.*, the alterable state.

al'terable, *adj.*, able to be altered.

al'terableness, *n.*, a tendency to change.

al'terably, *adv.*, with change.

al'terant, *adj.*, change-producing; *n.*, a substance that modifies a colour.

altera'tion, *n.*, change, variation.

al'terative, *n.*, a medicine which alters the bodily functions.

al'tercate, *v.i.*, to dispute.

al'tercating, *pr.p.*, altercate.

alterca'tion, *n.*, a dispute, wrangle.

al'tered, *p.p.*, alter.

al'tering, *pr.p.*, alter.

al'tern, *adj.*, with opposite parts alternating.

al'ternate, *v.t.* and *i.*, to make alternate; to be alternate; to change.

altern'ate, *adj.*, occurring one after the other in turn.

al'ternated, *p.p.*, alternate.

altern'ately, *adv.*, in succession.

al'ternating, *pr.p.*, alternate.

alterna'tion, *n.*, the act of alternating.

alter'native, *n.* and *adj.*, a choice between one and another.

altern'atively, *adv.*, one way or another.

Althae'a, *n.*, the marsh-mallow and other plants.

although', *conj.*, admitted, granted that; notwithstanding that.

altim'eter, *n.*, an instrument for measuring vertical angular elevation.

altim'etry, *n.*, the science of measuring vertical angular elevation.

altis'onant, *adj.*, high-sounding.

al'titude, *n.*, height.

al'to, *adj.*, high-pitched (of a male voice); *n.*, the alto part, an alto singer or instrument, as the viola.

altogeth'er, *adv.*, entirely, wholly.

alto-relie'vo, *adj.*, in high relief; *n.*, a carving in high relief.

alto-rilie'vo, *i.q.* alto-relievo.

al'truism, *n.*, doing something for another's sake.

al'truist, *n.*, one who professes altruism.

altruis'tic, *adj.*, rel. to altruism.

alu'del, *n.*, a pear-shaped glass vessel used in condensing.

al'um, *n.*, a chemical compound so named.

alu'mina, *n.*, aluminum oxide.

alu'minate, *v.t.*, to blend with a salt of aluminum.

aluminif'erous, *adj.*, producing alum, aluminum, or alumin.

alu'minite, *n.*, a white hydrous aluminum sulphate.

alumin'ium, *n.*, a whitish metallic element so named. Also *aluminum*.

alu'minous, *adj.*, rel. to aluminium, alumina, or alum.

al'umish, *adj.*, somewhat resembling alum.

alum'nus, *n.*, one who has been brought up in a college or a place of learning.

al'veary, *n.*, a bee-hive.

al'veolar, *adj.*, rel. to alveoli.

al'veolary, *adj.*, *i.q.* alveolar.

al'veolate, *adj.*, full of cavities.

al'veoli, *n.*, small cavities.

al'veolus, *n.*, a small cavity.

al'vine, *adj.*, rel. to the belly.

al'way } *adv.*, at all
al'ways } times.

am, *v.i.*, *pr.t.*, 1st pers. of to be.

am'adou, *n.*, a kind of tinder produced from fungi.

a'mah, *n.*, a child's nurse (*Indian*).

amain', *adv.*, with full strength.

amal'gam, *n.*, an alloy of a metal with mercury.

amal'gamate, *v.t.*, to mix up together.

amal'gamated, *p.p.*, amalgamate.

amal'gamating, *pr.p.*, amalgamate.

amalgama'tion, *n.*, the act of amalgamating; a compound.

amanuen'sis, *n.*, a writing secretary.

am'aranth, *n.*, the plant Love-lies-bleeding; a flower said in poetry never to fade.

amaranth'ine, *adj.*, rel. to amaranth.

amaranth'us, *n.*, also amarantus, which gives its name to the Amarantaceae (*Bot.*).

Amaryl'lis, *n.*, a Greek rustic nymph's name; a bulbous plant of South Africa.

amass', *v.t.*, to pile together.

amassed', *p.p.*, amass.

amass'ing, *pr.p.*, amass.

amass'ment, *n.*, the act or state of amassing.

am'ateur, *n.*, one who merely for love, not for a livelihood, pursues a study or art.

amateur'ish, *adj.*, unskilled, unprofessional.

amateu'rishly, *adv.*, in an unskilled way.

am'ative, *adj.*, sexually loving.

am'ativeness, *n.*, the amative state.

am'atory, *adj.*, of a loving tendency.

amauro'sis, *n.*, blindness.

amauro'tic, *adj.*, rel. to amaurosis.

amaze', *v.t.*, to astonish; stagger with surprise.
amazed, *p.p.*, amaze.
amaze'ment, *n.*, a state of astonishment.
amaz'ing, *pr.p.*, amaze; *adj.*, astonishing.
amaz'ingly, *adv.*, in an astonishing way.
Am'azon, *n.*, one of the race of women-warriors; the river of that name.
Amazo'nian, *adj.*, rel. to the Amazons; bold, mannish.
am'bage, *n.*, a circumlocution.
ambas'sador, *n.*, a representative, usually of a sovereign or state.
ambas'sadress, *n.*, fem. of ambassador.
am'ber, *n.*, a yellow, resinous substance, fossilized.
am'bergris, *n.*, a fragrant substance obtained from the sperm whale.
ambidex'ter, *adj.*, using both hands as right hands.
ambidexter'ity, *n.*, the power to use both hands equally well.
ambidex'trous, *adj.*, *i.q.* ambidexter.
ambidex'trously, *adv.*, in an ambidextrous way.
amb'ient, *adj.*, going about, surrounding.
ambigu'ity, *n.*, double meaning, uncertainty.
ambig'uous, *adj.*, of double meaning, uncertain.
ambig'uously, *adv.*, equivocally.
ambig'uousness, *n.*, a tendency to be ambiguous.
am'bit, *n.*, bounds, scope.
ambi'tion, *n.*, aiming at high things.
ambi'tious, *adj.*, inclined to ambition.
ambi'tiously, *adv.*, in an ambitious way.
am'ble, *v.i.*, to go at a slow pace; *n.*, the walk of certain quadrupeds.
am'bled, *p.p.*, amble.
am'bler, *n.*, one who ambles.
am'bling, *pr.p.*, amble.
amblyo'pia, *n.*, dimness of vision.
am'bo, *adj.*, both together; (*Lat.*), *n.*, a pulpit for the reading of the epistle or the gospel.
ambro'sia, *n.*, a divine drink or fragrance; a weed so named.
ambro'sial, *adj.*, rel. to ambrosia.
Ambro'sian, *adj.*, rel. to St. Ambrose.
am'brotype, *n.*, a photographic negative which, being thin, gave the effect of a positive.
am'bry, *n.*, a cupboard, locker. Also *aumbry*.
am'bulance, *n.*, a vehicle for conveying the sick or wounded.
am'bulant, *adj.*, walking.
ambula'tion, *n.*, the act of walking.
am'bulatory, *adj.*, rel. to walking; *n.*, a processional path round the altar of a church, or in a cloister.
am'bury, *n.*, a tumour affecting cattle and horses; a disease in turnips and some other plants.
ambuscade', *n.*, the act of hiding; or a place of hiding, for the purpose of a secret attack; the men in hiding; *v.t.*, to attack from an ambush.
ambusca'ded, *p.p.*, ambuscade.
ambusca'ding, *pr.p.*, ambuscade.
am'bush, *n.* and *v.t.*, *i.q.* ambuscade.
am'bushed, *p.p.*, ambush.
am'bushing, *pr.p.*, ambush.
am'bushment, *n.*, *i.q.* ambush.
ameer', **amir'**, *n.*, a Mohammedan ruler; the ruler of Afghanistan.
ame'liorate, *v.t.* and *i.*, to make better, improve.
ame'liorated, *p.p.*, ameliorate.
ame'liorating, *pr.p.*, ameliorate.
ameliora'tion, *n.*, the act or state of ameliorating.
ame'liorative, *adj.*, tending to ameliorate.
ame'liorator, *n.*, one who ameliorates.
amen', *interj.*, so be it; the ending of an oath or a prayer.
amenabil'ity, *n.*, the amenable quality.
ame'nable, *adj.*, submissive, adapting oneself to others' rule.
amend', *v.t.* and *i.*, to improve.
amend'able, *adj.*, capable of amending.
amend'ed, *p.p.*, amend.
amend'er, *n.*, one who amends.
amend'ing, *pr.p.*, amend.
amend'ment, *n.*, the act of amending; an alternative proposal
amends', *n. pl.*, satisfaction for a wrong done.
amen'ity, *n.*, pleasantness, agreeableness.
ament', *n.*, a catkin.
amenta'ceous, *adj.*, resembling the catkin.
amen'tia, *n.*, the state of being out of one's mind.
ament'um, *n.*, a catkin; *see* ament.
amerce', *v.t.*, to punish with a fine.
amerce'able, *adj.*, able or fit to be amerced.
amerced', *p.p.*, amerce.
amerce'ment, *n.*, the act of amercing.
amerc'er, *n.*, one who amerces.
amerc'ing, *pr.p.*, amerce.
Amer'ican, *adj.*, bel., or native, to America.
Amer'icanism, *n.*, something peculiar to Americans.

Amer'icanize, *v.t.* and *i.*, to change to American.

amess', *n.*, a hood with long ends in front, the mark of ecclesiastical rank; worn in choir.

am'ethyst, *n.*, a gem of a violet blue colour; a kind of quartz.

amethyst'ine, *adj.*, of, or like to, an amethyst.

Amhar'ic, *n.*, the court language of Abyssinia.

amiabil'ity, *n.*, lovableness, goodheartedness.

a'miable, *adj.*, lovable, good-hearted.

a'miableness, *n.*, the lovable quality.

a'miably, *adv.*, in a lovable way.

amian'thus, *n.*, a species of asbestos.

amicabil'ity, *n.*, an amicable tendency.

am'icable, *adj.*, of a friendly character.

am'icableness, *n.*, friendliness.

am'ice, *n.*, any kind of clothing or hooded mantle; the linen collar, with ornamental border, worn by the priest and ministers at the Mass.

amid', *prep.*, in the midst of, surrounded by.

am'idine, *n.*, a chemical compound so named; a solution of starch in hot water.

amid'ships, *adv.*, in the middle of a ship.

amidst', *prep.*, *i.q.* amid.

amiss', *adv.*, wrongly, in error, lacking.

am'ity, *n.*, friendship.

am'meter, *n.*, an instrument for measuring electric current.

ammo'nia, *n.*, a strong-smelling gas, much used in the arts and in medicine.

ammo'niac, *adj.*, rel. to ammonia.

ammoni'acal, *adj.*, *i.q.* ammonia.

am'monite, *n.*, a fossil shell-fish so named.

ammuni'tion, *n.*, means of defence, war material.

amne'sia, *n.*, loss of memory.

amne'sic, *adj.*, losing the memory.

am'nesty, *n.*, the act of overlooking an offence; pardon.

am'nion, *n.*, a membranous sac found in embryos.

amniot'ic, *adj.*, rel. to an amnion.

amoe'ba, *n.*, a class of Protozoans so named.

Amo'mum, *n.*, an aromatic herb of the ginger family.

among', *prep.*, in the midst of, together with.

amongst', *prep.*, *i.q.* among.

Amontilla'do, *n.*, a variety of sherry.

am'orist, *n.*, one with a propensity for amours.

amoro'so, *adj.* and *adv.*, in a tender way (*mus.*).

am'orous, *adj.*, excessively loving.

am'orously, *adv.*, in an amorous way.

am'orousness, *n.*, an amorous tendency.

amor'phism, *n.*, the state of being amorphous.

amor'phous, *adj.*, shapeless, without form.

amortiza'tion, *n.*, the act of conveying property to a corporation with perpetual succession; reduction of a debt by means of a sinking fund.

amor'tize, *v.t.*, to effect an amortization of.

amor'tizement, *n.*, *i.q.* amortization; the finishing off on the top of an architectural member.

amount', *n.*, sum, total; *v.i.*, to equal in total.

amount'ed, *p.p.*, amount.

amount'ing, *pr.p.*, amount.

amour', *n.*, a love adventure.

ampère', *n.*, the unit of electric current.

am'persand, *n.*, the sign &.

am'phi, a prefix = around, about.

Amphib'ia, *n.*, creatures that can live both on land and in water.

amphib'ian, *adj.*, of the nature of amphibia.

amphib'ious, *adj.*, *i.q.* amphibian.

amphib'iously, *adv.*, in the manner of amphibia.

amphib'iousness, *n.*, the quality of being amphibious.

amphibol'ogy, *n.*, ambiguity of expression.

amphib'olous, *adj.*, equivocal; spreading on both sides.

am'phibrach, *n.*, a metrical foot containing three syllables, of which the middle one is long and the others are short.

Amphictyon'ic, *adj.*, bel. to an amphictyony.

Amphic'tyons, *n.*, delegates to the Amphictyonic council.

Amphic'tyony, *n.*, an ancient Greek association for mutual defence.

amphisbae'na, *n.*, a fabled snake with a head at either end.

amphithe'atre, amphithe'ater, *n.*, a theatre with seats all round.

amphitheat'ric, *adj.*, in the form of an amphitheatre.

amphitheat'rical, *adj.*, *i.q.* amphitheatric.

am'phora, *n.*, a two-handled jar of earthenware.

am'phoral, *adj.*, rel. to an amphora.

am'ple, *adj.*, full, abundant, large, spacious.

am'pleness, *n.*, the condition of ample.

amplifica'tion, *n.*, an enlarging.

am'plified, *p.p.*, amplify.

am'plifier, *n.*, one who amplifies.

am'plify, *v.t.*, to enlarge; to add to a previous statement.

am'plifying, *pr.p.*, amplify.

am'plitude, *n.*, extent, largeness.

am'ply, *adv.*, abundantly, largely.

ampul'la, *n.*, a flask (*Lat.*).

am'putate, *v.t.*, to cut off (a limb).

am'putated, *p.p.*, amputate.

am'putating, *pr.p.*, amputate.

amputa'tion, *n.*, the operation of cutting off.

amuck', *adv.*, in a frenzied way, used in the phrase "to run amuck," or "amok."

am'ulet, *n.*, a charm consisting of a jewel or ornament.

amus'able, *adj.*, able to be amused.

amuse', *v.t.*, to entertain, delight.

amused', *p.p.*, amuse.

amuse'ment, *n.*, diversion, pleasure.

amus'er, *n.*, one who amuses.

amus'ing, *pr.p.*, amuse; *adj.* diverting.

amus'ingly, *adv.*, in an amusing way.

amus'ive, *adj.*, tending to amusement.

amyg'dalate, *n.* a salt of amygdalic acid; an emulsion of almonds; *adj.*, rel. to almonds.

amyg'daline, *adj.*, bel. to almonds, or the tonsils.

amyg'daloid, *adj.*, almond-shaped.

am'yl, *n.*, starch, fine flour.

amyla'ceous, *adj.*, starchy.

am'ylin, *n.*, starch-cellulose.

am'yss, *see* amess.

an, *art. indef.*; *a* before consonant.

an'a, *n.*, collected sayings; usually suffix, as Eliana.

Anabap'tism, *n.*, rebaptizing.

Anabap'tist, *n.*, one who re-baptizes a person already baptized. An A. is now called a Baptist.

Anabaptist'ic, *adj.*, rel. to Anabaptist teaching.

anab'olism, *n.*, a biological term describing "the upbuilding, constructive, synthetic processes" in the making of a cell.

anacamp'tic, *adj.*, reflecting.

anacathar'tic, *adj.*, purging upwards.

anach'ronism, *n.*, an error in point of time.

anachronis'tic, *adj.*, involving an error of time.

anaclas'tic, *adj.*, rel. to refraction.

anacolu'thon, *n.*, a mixture of syntactical constructions in a sentence.

anacon'da, *n.*, a large S. American water-snake.

Anacreon'tic, *adj.*, bel. to, or like, the poet Anacreon.

an'adem, *n.*, a band, fillet, garland.

anae'mia, *n.*, a bloodless condition.

anaem'ic, *adj.*, suffering from anaemia.

anaesthe'sia, *n.*, a state of insensibility to pain.

anaesthet'ic, *adj.* and *n.*, producing insensibility.

an'aglyph, *n.*, ornament in relief.

anaglyph'ic, *adj.*, rel. to anaglyph.

anaglyp'tic, *adj.*, *i.q.* anaglyphic.

anagno'sis, *n.*, recognition.

an'agogy, *n.*, mystical interpretation.

an'agram, *n.*, a rearrangement of the letters of a word to make a new word.

anagrammat'ic, *adj.*, of the nature of an anagram.

anagrammat'ical, *adj.*, *i.q.* anagrammatic.

anagram'matize, *v.t.*, to make an anagram out of a word.

an'agraph, *n.*, a recipe.

a'nal, *adj.*, rel. to the anus.

analec'ta, *n.*, *i.q.* analects.

analec'tic, *adj.*, composed of selections.

an'alects, *n. pl.*, selections, gleanings.

analem'ma, *n.*, a scale for finding the sun's declination on a given day; a surgical support.

an'alepsy, *n.*, a form of epilepsy.

analog'ical, *adj.*, of the nature of an analogy.

anal'ogist, *n.*, one who draws analogies.

anal'ogize, *v.i.*, to draw analogies.

anal'ogized, *p.p.*, analogize.

anal'ogizing, *pr.p.*, analogize.

anal'ogous, *adj.*, bearing a likeness or analogy to.

anal'ogously, *adv.*, in an analogous way.

an'alogue, *n.*, something that corresponds with another.

anal'ogy, *n.*, a correspondence or likeness of one thing to another.

anal'ysis, *n.*, the process of analysing.

an'alyst, *n.*, one who analyses.

analyt'ic, *adj.*, bel. to analysis.

analyt'ical, *adj.*, *i.q.* analytic.

an'alysable, *adj.*, capable of analysis.

analysa'tion, *n.*, the act of analysing.

an'alyse, *v.t.*, to separate into parts or elements; to trace a thing to the source.

an'alysed, *p.p.*, analyse.

an'alyser, *n.*, one who analyses.

an'alysing, *pr.p.*, analyse

anamor'phosis, *n.*, a distortion.

ana'nas, *n.*, the pineapple.

anan'drous, *adj.*, without stamens, a description of female plants.

an'apaest, an'apest, *n.*, a metrical foot, two short syllables before a long one.

anapaes'tic, anapes'tic, *adj.*, rel. to an anapest.

anaph'ora, *n.*, the portion of the liturgy of the Eastern Church which corresponds to the canon of the Western Church.

anarch'ic, *adj.*, tending to, or in a state of, anarchy.

anarch'ical, *adj.*, *i.q.* anarchic.

an'archism, *n.*, the state of, or tending to, anarchy.

an'archist, *n.*, one who teaches the overthrow of all government.

an'archy, *n.*, a state of lawlessness.

anar'throus, *adj.*, without the use of the article attached to a noun; without joints.

anasar'ca, *n.*, a dropsical condition of the cellular tissue; a somewhat similar affection of plants in wet weather.

anasar'cous, *adj.*, subject to anasarca.

anas'tasis, *n.*, resurrection, recovery.

anastat'ic, *adj.*, in relief.

anas'tomose, *v.t.*, to join by running together.

anas'tropha, *n.*, inversion.

anath'ema, *n.*, a solemn curse; the person or thing cursed.

anathemat'ical, *adj.*, rel. to anathema.

anath'ematism, *n.*, the pronouncing of anathemas.

anathematiza'tion, *n.*, the act of anathematizing.

anath'ematize, *v.t.*, to pronounce an anathema on.

anath'ematized, *p.p.*, anathematize.

anath'ematizer, *n.*, one who anathematizes.

anath'ematizing, *pr.p.* anathematize.

anatif'erous, *adj.*, geese-producing.

anatom'ic, *adj.*, rel. to anatomy.

anatom'ical, *adj.*, *i.q.* anatomic.

anat'omist, *n.*, one who studies or practises anatomy.

anatomiza'tion, *n.*, dissection.

anat'omize, *v.t.*, to practise anatomy; to cut into parts.

anat'omized, *p.p.*, anatomize.

anat'omizing, *pr.p.*, anatomize.

anat'omy, *n.*, the study or art of cutting a body to examine its structure; the structural arrangement of a body.

anatrep'tic, *adj.*, upsetting, refuting.

an'cestor, *n.*, one of an earlier generation, a forefather.

ancesto'rial, *adj.*, rel. to ancestors.

ances'tral, *adj.*, bel. to forefathers.

an'cestress, *n.*, fem. of ancestor.

an'cestry, *n.*, the line of one's ancestors.

anch'or, *n.*, the hook that holds a ship firm by gripping the water's bottom; also *v.i.* and *t.*, to come, or to bring a ship, to rest.

anch'orable, *adj.*, able to be anchored.

anch'orage, *n.*, a place where a vessel may be anchored or lie at anchor.

anch'ored, *p.p.*, anchor.

anch'oress, *n.*, fem. of anchoret or anchorite.

anch'oret, *n.*, one who retires from the world and often chooses to live in a perpetually enclosed chamber attached to a church.

anchoret'ic, *adj.*, rel. to an anchoret.

anchoret'ical, *adj.*, *i.q.* anchoretic.

anch'oring, *pr.p.*, anchor.

anch'orite, *n.*, *i.q.* anchoret.

ancho'vy, *n.*, a small fish, found in the Mediterranean.

an'chylose, *v.t.* and *i.*, to stiffen.

anchylo'sis, *n.*, the stiffening of a joint.

an'cient, *adj.*, bel. to long-past time; of great age; *n.*, a very old man; in old English, an ensign.

an'ciently, *adv.*, in ancient times.

an'cientry, *n.*, the people of old time.

an'cillary, *adj.*, serving (like a handmaid), and so helping.

ancip'ital, *adj.*, double headed, two edged.

ancip'itous, *adj.*, *i.q.* ancipital.

an'con, *n.*, a bracket, a quoin.

and, *conj.*, expressing addition.

andan'te, *adj.*, in moderately slow (musical) time; *n.*, a movement in moderately slow time.

andanti'no, *adj.*, not quite so slow as andante. (Properly, however, it means slower than andante.)

Ande'an, *adj.*, bel. to the Andes.

and'iron, *n.*, a fire-dog or iron bar supporting a log on a hearth.

andranat'omy, *n.* dissection of the (male) body.

androg'ynal, *adj.*, hermaphrodite.

androg'ynism, *n.*, the change in plants from dioecious to monoecious.

androg'ynous, *adj.*, hermaphrodite.

an'droid, *adj.*, like human; *n.*, an automaton.
android'al, *adj.* and *n.*, *i.q.* android.
an'dron, *n.*, the men's quarters in a Greek house.
an'ecdotal, *adj.*, rel. to anecdote.
an'ecdote, *n.*, a short tale or story.
anecdot'ic, *adj.*, with a tendency to anecdote.
aneodot'ical, *adj.*, *i.q.* anecdotic.
an'ecdotist, *n.*, one who tells anecdotes.
ane'mia, *n.*, a bloodless condition. Also *anaemia*.
anemog'raphy, *n.*, the recording of the wind's velocity.
anemol'ogy, *n.*, the study or science of winds.
anemom'eter, *n.*, a weather-gauge.
anemom'etry, *n.*, the art or science of gauging the winds.
anem'one, *n.*, the wind-flower.
anem'oscope, *n.*, an apparatus indicating the force and direction of the wind.
anent', *prep.*, towards, concerning.
an'eroid, *adj.*, without liquid (the barometric pressure being measured without the use of a fluid).
anesthe'sia, *n.*, a state of insensibility.
an'eurism, *n.*, a condition caused by the swelling of an artery.
anew', *adv.*, afresh, over again.
anfract'uous *adj.*, winding.
an'gel, *n.*, a heavenly messenger; an old coin so named.
angel'ic, *adj.*, like or rel. to the angels.
angel'ica, *n.*, an aromatic plant, used in medicine and sweets.
angel'ical, *adj.*, *i.q.* angelic.
angelol'ogy, *n.*, the study of angel ministry.
an'gelot, *n.*, the name of a coin and a musical instrument.
an'gelus, *n.*, the devotion so named, including the Ave Maria, recited morning, noon, and night. The bell rung for this devotion is often called the Angelus.
an'ger, *n.*, wrath, fury; *v.t.*, to provoke to wrath.
an'gered, *p.p.*, anger.
an'gering, *pr.p.*, anger.
an'gina, *n.*, quinsy; an intense pain.
angiocarp'ous, *adj.*, with fruit covered by an envelope.
angiog'raphy, *n.*, a description of the vascular system.
angiol'ogy, *n.*, the study of the vascular system and lymphatics.
angiot'omy, *n.*, the dissection of the vascular system.
an'gle, *n.*, a figure resulting from the inclination of one straight line to another; the inclination of two lines to one another; also a fishing hook, rod, and line; *v.i.*, to fish with rod and line.
an'gled, *p.p.*, angle.
an'gler, *n.*, one who angles.
An'glican, *adj.*, of the English type.
An'glicanism, *n.*, the method and spirit of the English Church.
An'glicè, *adv.* (*Lat.*), in the English way or language.
An'glicism, *n.*, a peculiarity of English speech and idioms.
an'glicize, *v.t.*, to convert into English.
an'glicized, *p.p.*, anglicize.
an'glicizing, *pr.p.*, anglicize.
an'gling, *pr.p.*, angle; *n.*, the fisherman's pursuit.
An'glomania, *n.*, a craze for imitating English ways.
An'glo-Sax'on, *adj.* and *n.*, bel. to the fused races of Angles and Saxons.
ango'la, *n.*, the wool of the Angora goat.
an'gor, *n.*, extreme distress.
ango'ra, *n.*, a fine kind of wool; a breed of cats.
an'grily, *adv.*, in an angry way.
an'gry, *adj.*, showing or feeling wrath or passion.
anguil'liform, *adj.*, like an eel in form.
anguin'eal, *adj.*, rel. to snakes.
an'guish, *n.*, acute pain or distress, physical or mental.
an'guished, *adj.*, feeling anguish.
an'guishing, *adj.*, causing anguish.
an'gular, *adj.*, pointed, corner-wise.
angular'ity, *n.*, an angular quality or character.
an'gularly, *adv.*, corner-wise, pointedly.
an'gulated, *adj.*, having angles.
anhela'tion, *n.*, a panting.
anhy'drous, *adj.*, waterless.
an'il, *n.*, an indigo plant found in the W. Indies.
an'ile, *adj.*, old-womanish.
an'iline, *n.*, a coal-tar product, from which certain dyes are made.
anil'ity, *n.*, old age in woman.
an'ima, *n.*, a breath, spirit.
animadver'sion, *n.*, consideration, reflexion, adverse comment.
animadvert', *v.i.*, to make comment on.
animadvert'ed, *p.p.*, animadvert.
animadvert'er, *n.*, one who animadverts.
animadvert'ing, *pr.p.*, animadvert.

an'imal, *adj.*, having life and will to move; brutal; rel. to animals; *n.*, a living creature; a brute; a carnal person.

animal'cula, *n.*, pl. of animalculum.

animal'cular, *adj.*, like or bel. to an animalcula.

animal'cule, *n.*, *i.q.* animalcula.

animal'culine, *adj.*, of the nature of animalcules.

animal'culist, *n.*, a student of animalcules.

animal'culum, *n.*, a diminutive animal.

an'imalism, *n.*, the condition of animal being; sensuality.

animal'ity, *n.*, the quality of animals.

animaliza'tion, *n.*, the act of animalizing.

an'imalize, *v.t.*, to turn into animals; to brutalize; to add an animal quality to anything.

an'imalized, *p.p.*, animalize.

animal'izing, *pr.p.*, animalize.

an'imate, *v.t.*, to quicken, give life or spirit to; *adj.*, having life.

an'imated, *p.p.*, animate; also *adj.*, lively, brisk.

an'imating, *pr.p.*, animate; also *adj.*, inspiriting.

an'imatingly, *adv.*, in an inspiriting way.

anima'tion, *n.*, life, vigour, briskness.

an'imative, *adj.*, causing animation.

an'imism, *n.*, the belief in the existence of a spiritual world apart from matter; the tendency to endow the material world and material objects with a soul.

an'imist, *n.*, a believer in animism.

animos'ity, *n.*, resentment, anger.

an'imus, *n.*, adverse feeling.

an'ion, *n.*, the name given by Faraday to the electrical component "which went up against the current."

an'ise, *n.*, an aromatic plant.

an'iseed, *n.*, the seed of anise.

an'isette, *n.*, a cordial made from aniseed.

an'ker, *n.*, a Dutch wine measure.

an'kle, *n.*, the part between the foot and the leg.

an'kle-bone, *n.*, the joint of the ankle.

an'kled, *adj.*, having ankles.

an'klet, *n.*, an ornamental ring for the ankle.

an'na, *n.*, a small Indian coin, 1-16th of a rupee.

an'nalist, *n.*, one who writes or compiles annals.

an'nalize, *v.t.*, to compile annals.

an'nals, *n.*, the record of yearly events.

an'nats (*Lat.* annates), *n.*, the first-fruits of a benefice, formerly payable to the Pope, later to Queen Anne's Bounty.

anneal', *v.t.*, to temper with furnace-heat.

annealed', *p.p.*, anneal.

anneal'ing, *pr.p.*, anneal.

annel'idan, *adj.*, rel. to Annelida (*i.e.*, earthworms and similar water-worms).

annex', *v.t.*, to join or add; *n.*, something (*usu.* a building) joined on.

annex'able, *adj.*, able to be annexed.

annexa'tion, *n.*, the act of annexing; appropriation.

annexa'tionist, *n.*, one who advocates annexation.

annexe' *n.*, *i.q.* annex.

annexed', *p.p.*, annex.

annex'ing, *pr.p.*, annex.

anni'hilable, *adj.*, able to be annihilated.

anni'hilate, *v.t.*, to reduce to nothing, destroy entirely.

anni'hilated, *p.p.*, annihilate.

anni'hilating, *pr.p.*, annihilate.

annihila'tion, *n.*, complete destruction.

anni'hilator, *n.*, one who annihilates.

anniver'sary, *n.*, a yearly commemoration.

an'no Dom'ini, *Lat.* phrase = in the year of Our Lord.

an'no mun'di, *Lat.* phrase = in the year of the world.

an'notate, *v.t.*, to make notes or comments on.

an'notated, *p.p.*, annotate.

an'notating, *pr.p.*, annotate.

annota'tion, *n.*, the act of making notes on; a note made.

an'notator, *n.*, one who annotates.

an'notatory, *adj.*, having annotation.

annot'to, *n.*, a yellowish-red dye.

announce', *v.t.*, to make publicly known.

announced', *p.p.*, announce.

announce'ment, *n.*, a thing announced; the act of announcing.

announc'er, *n.*, one who announces.

announc'ing, *pr.p.*, announce.

annoy', *v.t.*, to vex, irritate.

annoy'ance, *n.*, that which annoys; the act of annoying.

annoyed', *p.p.*, annoy.

annoy'er *n.*, one who annoys.

annoy'ing, *pr.p.*, annoy.

an'nual, *adj.*, yearly, happening year by year; *n.*, a plant that lives only for one year.

an'nually, *adv.*, year by year.

annu'itant, *n.*, one who receives an annuity.

annu'ity, *n.*, a yearly payment of money.

annul', *v.t.*, to cancel, make null and void.

an'nular, *adj.*, ring-like.

an'nulate, *adj.*, having rings, ringed.

an'nulated, *adj.*, *i.q.* annulate.

annula'tion, *n.*, the act or state of being ringed; ring formation.

an'nulet, *n.*, a little ring. In heraldry it denotes a fifth son.

annulled', *p.p.*, annul.

annul'ling, *pr.p.*, annul.

annul'ment, *n.*, the act of annulling.

Annulo'sa, *n.*, a class of animals under which arthropods and the higher worms are grouped.

an'nulose, *adj.*, ringed; rel. to the Annulosa.

an'nulus, *n.*, a ring.

annu'merate, *v.t.*, to add in.

annu'merated, *p.p.*, annumerate.

annu'merating, *pr.p.*, annumerate.

annumera'tion, *n.*, the process of annumerating.

annun'ciate, *v.t.*, to proclaim, publish tidings.

annun'ciated, *p.p.*, annunciate.

annun'ciating, *pr.p.*, annunciate.

annuncia'tion, *n.*, the act of announcing. The feast of the Annunciation of Our Lady commemorates the angel's announcement of Our Lord's coming birth.

annun'ciatory, *adj.*, bringing an announcement.

an'ode, *n.*, the point where the electric current enters.

an'odyne, *n.*, something that eases pain.

anoint', *v.t.*, to smear with oil or ointment; to administer the chrism.

anoint'ed, *p.p.*, anoint.

anoint'er, *n.*, one who anoints.

anoint'ing, *pr.p.*, anoint.

anoint'ment, *n.*, the act of anointing.

anom'alism, *n.*, an irregular tendency.

anom'alist, *n.*, one who commits irregularities.

anomalist'ic, *adj.*, tending to irregularity.

anomalist'ical, *adj.*, *i.q.* anomalistic.

anom'alous, *adj.*, irregular, exceptional.

anom'alously, *adv.*, irregularly.

anom'aly, *n.*, an irregularity; exceptional proceeding.

anon', *adv.*, immediately.

anonym'ity, *n.*, going without a name.

anon'ymous, *adj.*, dropping one's name, nameless.

anon'ymously, *adv.*, without a name.

anon'ymousness, *n.*, the act or state of anonymity.

anorex'ia, *n.*, want of appetite.

anos'mia, *n.*, inodorousness.

anoth'er, *adj.*, some person or thing else; one added.

anot'ta, *see* annotto.

an'serated, *adj.*, with terminations cleft and ornamented with birds' or reptiles' heads, etc.

an'serine, *adj.*, rel. to a goose; silly.

an'swer, *v.i.*, to make reply; to suit; to be a success.

an'swerable, *adj.*, held to account.

an'swered, *p.p.*, answer.

an'swerer, *n.*, one who answers.

an'swering, *pr.p.*, answer.

ant, *n.*, a tiny insect = an emmet.

an'ta, *n.*, a pilaster corresponding to one opposite.

antac'id, *adj.*, corrective of acidity.

antag'onism, *n.*, the act or state of opposing.

antag'onist, *n.*, one who strives against or opposes.

antagonist'ic, *adj.*, opposing.

antag'onize, *v.t.*, to resist, struggle against, neutralize.

antag'onized, *p.p.*, antagonize.

antag'onizing, *pr.p.*, antagonize.

antal'gic, *adj.*, pain-relieving.

antal'kali, *n.*, a substance that counteracts alkali.

Antarc'tic, *adj.*, the opposite to the Arctic; rel. to the South Pole.

antarthrit'ic, *adj.*, curing or relieving arthritis.

antasthmat'ic, *adj.*, relieving asthma.

ant'-eater, *n.*, a four-footed animal that devours ants.

antecede', *v.t.*, to go before.

antece'ded, *p.p.*, antecede.

antece'dence, *n.*, the act of going before.

antece'dent, *adj.*, going before; *n.*, something that has gone before; in *plur.* = past conduct.

antece'dently, *adv.*, previously.

antece'ding, *pr.p.*, antecede.

anteces'sor, *n.*, one who has anteceded.

an'techamber, *n.*, a room leading into another.

an'te-chapel, *n.*, the part of a chapel outside the screen.

an'tedate, *v.t.*, to anticipate the proper date.

an'tedated, *p.p.*, antedate.

an'tedating, *pr.p.*, antedate.

antedilu'vial, *adj.*, before the flood.

antedilu'vian, *adj.*, *i.q.* antediluvial; *n.*, one who lived before the flood.

an'telope, *n.*, a small kind of deer.

antemerid'ian, *adj.*, before mid-day.

antemun'dane, *adj.*, before the world's making.

antemu'ral, *adj.*, before the wall or walls.

anteni'cene, *adj.*, before the Council of Nicaea, A.D. 325.

anten'na, *n.*, a feeler or horn of a crustacean or an insect.

anten'nae, *n.*, pl. of antenna.

antenup'tial, *adj.*, before marriage.

antepas'chal, *adj.*, before Easter.

an'tepast, *n.*, food before a meal.

antepenult', *n.*, the last syllable but two.

antepenult'imate, *adj.* preceding the last but one.

antepilep'tic, *adj.*, rel. to the treatment of epilepsy.

ante'rior, *adj.*, preceding, earlier in date.

anterior'ity, *adj.*, precedence in date.

ante'riorly, *adv.*, earlier.

an'te-room, *n.*, an outer room leading into another.

an'them, *n.*, a solemn piece of vocal music for solo or chorus. It is the English Church form of the motet.

an'ther, *n.*, the part of a flower's stamen containing the pollen.

an'theroid, *adv.*, like an anther.

ant'-hill, *n.*, the mound raised by ants.

anthol'ogy, *n.*, a selection of choice literary passages.

an'thracite, *n.*, a smokeless kind of coal.

anthracit'ic, *adj.*, rel. to anthracite.

an'thrax, *n.*, a carbuncle; an infectious disease among sheep and cattle, and communicable to man.

anthropog'raphy, *n.*, the description of the human race.

an'thropoid, *adj.*, resembling the human.

anthropol'ogist, *n.*, a student of anthropology.

anthropol'ogy, *n.*, the study of humanity as a branch of natural science.

anthropomor'phism, *n.*, likening divine things to human.

anthropomor'phist, *n.* one who likens the divine to the human.

anthropomor'phize, *v.t.*, to liken the divine to the human.

anthropomor'phous, *adj.*, in human shape.

anthropop'athy, *n.*, the attribution of human passions to the Deity.

anthropoph'agi, *n.*, cannibals.

anthropoph'agous, *adj.*, cannibalistic.

anthropoph'agy, *n.*, cannibalism.

an'ti-, a Greek prefix = against, opposite to, instead of.

antibil'ious, *adj.*, corrective of bile.

an'tic, *adj.*, odd, quaint; *n.*, a buffoon; a merry caper.

An'tichrist, *n.*, the rival to Christ.

antichrist'ian, *adj.*, hostile to Christianity; rel. to Antichrist.

antic'ipant, *n.*, one who anticipates.

antic'ipate, *v.t.*, to act in advance; to forestall; to foresee.

antic'ipated, *p.p.*, anticipate.

antic'ipating, *pr.p.*, anticipate.

anticipa'tion, *n.*, the act of anticipating.

antic'ipative, *adj.*, anticipating.

antic'ipator, *n.*, one who anticipates.

antic'ipatory, *adj.*, forestalling, in advance.

anticli'max, *n.*, a drop from a previous ascent; bathos.

anticli'nal, *adj.*, bent with the convex side upward.

anticy'clone, *n.*, the opposite of a cyclone. (High pressure is at the centre, and the wind currents sweep outwards.)

an'tidotal, *adj.*, of the nature of an antidote.

an'tidote, *n.*, a remedy for poison or other trouble.

antidot'ical, *adj.*, rel. to antidotes.

antifeb'rile, *adj.*, fever-arresting.

antifed'eral, *adj.*, opposed to federalism.

antifed'eralism, *adj.*, a movement opposed to federalism.

antilog'arithm, *n.*, a number that corresponds to a given logarithm.

antil'ogy, *n.*, contradiction, inconsistency.

antimacas'sar, *n.*, a protection against soiling.

antimonarch'ical, *adj.* opposed to monarchy.

antimo'nial, *adj.*, rel. to antimony.

antimo'niate, *adj.*, having antimony in it.

antimo'nious, *adj.*, rel. to antimony.

an'timony, *n.*, a metallic element used in medicine, the arts, and alloys.

Antino'mian, *adj.*, opposed to law. The word is applied to those sectaries who hold that, in virtue of their belief, they are subject to no moral law.

Antino'mianism, *n.*, the theory or principles of Antinomians.

antin'omy, *n.*, a violation of law.

antipa'pal, *adj.*, opposed to the papacy.

antipathet'ic, *adj.*, repugnant, disliking.

antipath'ic, *adj.*, in a state of antipathy.

antip'athy, *n.*, a feeling of repugnance, dislike.

antiphlogis'tic, *adj.*, preventive of inflammation.

an'tiphon, *n.*, the passage sung or recited before and after psalms, canticles, and other portions of the Church's ritual.

antiph'onal, *adj.*, singing or reciting in alternate verses or passages; *n.*, a collection of antiphons.

antiph'ony, *n.*, alternate or responsory singing.

antiph'rasis, *n.*, the use of a word in a sense contrary to its proper meaning.

antip'odal, *adj.*, rel. to the antipodes.

an'tipode, *adj.*, the opposite.

antipode'an, *adj.*, in or of the Antipodes.

Antip'odes, *n.*, countries exactly on the opposite side of the globe; any extreme contrast.

antipyret'ic, *adj.*, relieving fever.

antipy'rin, *n.*, a preparation derived from coal tar, used in relief of fever.

antiqua'rian, *adj.*, rel. to antiquity; often incorrectly used as a noun for *antiquary*.

antiqua'rianism, *adj.*, a fondness for antiquarian research.

an'tiquary, *n.*, one who studies ancient things.

an'tiquate, *v.t.*, to make out-of-date; abolish.

an'tiquated, *p.p.*, antiquate; *adj.*, old-fashioned, out-of-date.

an'tiquating, *pr.p.*, antiquate.

antiqua'tion, *n.*, the act of antiquating.

antique', *adj.*, old, old-fashioned; *n.*, a specimen of old work, a curiosity.

antique'ly, *adv.*, in an old-fashioned way.

antique'ness, *n.*, age, old-world style.

antiq'uities, *n.*, relics of ancient times.

antiq'uity, *n.*, the olden days.

antirheumat'ic, *adj.*, relieving rheumatism.

antiscorbu'tic, *adj.*, remedial in cases of scurvy.

antiscript'ural, *adj.*, contrary to Holy Scripture.

antisep'tic, *adj.*, resisting or arresting putrefaction; *n.*, a substance with antiseptic properties.

antislav'ery, *n.*, a movement opposed to slavery.

antiso'cial, *adj.*, opposed to the interests of society.

antispasmod'ic, *adj.*, spasm-relieving.

antis'tasis, *n.*, a rhetorical argument that an act is justified on the ground that its omission would have led to something worse.

antis'trophe, *n.*, the lyrical passages that alternate with the strophe of a Greek chorus.

antistroph'ic, *adj.* rel. to antistrophe.

antith'eses, *n.*, pl. of antithesis.

antith'esis, *n.*, opposition, contrast.

antithet'ic, *adj.*, opposed to, in contrast with.

antithet'ical, *adj.*, *i.q.* antithetic.

antitox'in, *n.*, a substance that counteracts poison. The person affected is inoculated with it.

antitrinita'rian, *adj.*, opposed to belief in the Holy Trinity.

an'titype, *n.*, that which is represented by a type, *e.g.*, the Cross is the antitype to the Brazen Serpent in the Wilderness.

antityp'ical, *adj.*, corresponding to the type.

ant'ler, *n.*, a stag's horn.

ant'lered, *adj.*, having antlers.

ant'like, *adj.*, resembling an ant.

antonoma'sia, *n.*, the substitution of names.

ant'onym, *n.*, a word of opposite meaning.

Anu'bis, *n.*, the Egyptian dog-headed Deity.

a'nus, *n.*, the human posterior.

an'vil, *n.*, a blacksmith's hammering-block.

anxi'ety, *n.*, care, uneasiness, strong desire.

anx'ious, *adj.*, careworn, uneasy, desirous.

anx'iously, *adv.*, in an anxious way.

anx'iousness, *n.*, a state of anxiety.

an'y, *adj.*, some (one or more).

an'ybody, *pron.*, some individual.

an'yhow, *adv.*, in any way.

an'yone, *pron.*, anybody.

an'ything, *pron.*, some thing.

an'ywhere, *adv.*, in any place.

an'ywise, *adv.*, in any way.

Anz'ac, *adj.* and *n.*, a word coined during the Great War, and formed, like Cabal, out of initial letters, which represent Australian and New Zealand Army Corps.

Ao'nian *adj.*, bel. to Aonia. Mt. Helicon in Aonia was sacred to the Muses.

a'orist, *adj.* and *n.*, indefinite; *e.g.*, the aorist tense relates to no particular time.

aoris'tic, *adj.*, bel. to the aorist.

aor'ta, *n.*, the main artery, leading from the left side of the heart.

aorti'tis, *n.*, inflammation of the aorta.

apace', *adv.*, quickly, at a faster rate.

Apa'che, *n.*, a hooligan (*Fr.*).

apago'gè, *n.*, proof by showing the absurdity of the opposite.

ap'anage, *n.*, a perquisite; *orig.*, provision for maintenance of younger members of a family.

apart', *adv.*, separately, at a distance from each other.

apart'ment, *n.*, a room in a house.

apathet'ic, *adj.*, listless, indifferent.

apathet'ical, *adj.*, *i.q.* apathetic.

ap'athist, *n.*, one of an apathetic tendency.

ap'athy, *n.*, indifference, listlessness.

ap'atite, *n.*, a substance once used as a gem.

ape, *n.*, one of the monkey tribe; *v.t.*, to imitate, copy.

apeak', *adv.*, on the peak or summit of a flagstaff.

aped, *p.p.*, ape.

apel'lous, *adj.*, not skinned over, uncicatrized.

Ap'ennine, *adj.*, the name of a mountain range in Italy.

apep'sia, *n.*, inability to digest.

ape'rient, *adj.*, opening, laxative; *n.*, a laxative medicine.

aper'itive, *adj.*, having aperient properties.

ap'erture, *n.*, an opening.

a'pex, *n.*, top, summit.

apha'sia, *n.*, loss of speech.

aphe'lion, *n.*, the point most distant from the sun. Its opposite is the perihelion.

aphe'resis, *n.*, the elision of an unaccented syllable. Also *aphaeresis*.

aph'ides, *n.*, pl. of aphis.

a'phis, *n.*, the green-fly.

aphlogis'tic, *adj.*, non-inflammatory.

apho'nia, *n.*, soundlessness.

aph'orism, *n.*, a short saying; a maxim.

aph'orist, *n.*, an utterer of aphorisms.

aphorist'ic, *adj.*, in the manner of an aphorism.

aphorist'ical, *adj.*, *i.q.* aphoristic.

aph'orize, *v.i.*, to utter aphorisms.

aph'rite, *n.*, the foam-spar.

aph'thae, *n.*, small ulcerous vesicles, seen in the complaint called milk-thrush.

aph'thong, *n.*, a non-sounded letter or syllable of a word.

apia'rian, *adj.*, rel. to bees.

a'piarist, *n.*, a bee-keeper.

a'piary, *n.*, a bee-house.

ap'ices, *n.*, pl. of apex.

apic'ulated, *adj.*, pointed, peaked.

a'piculture, *n.*, bee-keeping.

apiece', *adv.*, in shares.

a'ping, *pr.p.*, ape.

a'pis, *n.*, a bee (*Lat.*).

a'pish, *adj.*, ape-like, imitative.

a'pishly, *adv.*, in an ape-like manner.

a'pishness, *n.*, an apish habit.

aplas'tic, *adj.*, not easily moulded.

aplomb', *adj.* and *adv.*, perpendicular; *n.*, cool self-possession.

apoc'alypse, *n.*, a revelation.

apocalyp'tic, *adj.*, rel. to or resembling apocalypse.

apocalyp'tical, *adj.*, *i.q.* apocalyptic.

apocar'pous, *adj.*, with separate carpels.

apoc'opate, *v.t.*, to perform apocope; to cut off or shorten.

apoc'opè, *n.*, a cutting off or elision of a final syllable or letter.

apocrus'tic, *adj.*, astringent.

Apoc'rypha, *n.*, the name given to the Deutero-canonical books of the Bible.

apoc'ryphal, *adj.*, rel. to the Apocrypha; of uncertain authority.

a'podal, *adj.*, not having ventral fins.

a'pode, *adj.*, without feet.

apod'osis, *n.*, the clause answering to an *if*-clause in syntax.

ap'ogee, *n.*, the point in the moon's orbit most distant from the earth.

ap'ograph, *n.*, an exact transcript.

Apol'lo, *n.*, a Greek and Roman deity, patron of music; worshipped as the sun-god, Phoebus Apollo.

Apoll'yon, *n.*, the great Power of Darkness.

apologet'ic, *adj.*, conveying an apology, making a defence.

apologet'ical, *adj.*, *i.q.* apologetic.

apologet'ics, *n.*, reasoning in defence (of Christianity).

apol'ogist, *n.*, one who makes an apology or defence.

apol'ogize, *v.i.*, to make an apology.

apol'ogized, *p.p.*, apologize.

apol'ogizer, *n.*, one who makes an apology.

apol'ogizing, *pr.p.*, apologize.

ap'ologue, *n.*, a fable with a moral.

apol'ogy, *n.*, a defence; an expression of regret; a makeshift.

ap'ophthegm, *n.*, a brief saying; a maxim.

apoph'yge, *n.*, a hollow curve at the base or top of a column.

apoplec'tic, *adj.*, rel. to apoplexy; *n.*, a sufferer from apoplexy.

apoplec'tical, *adj.*, *i.q.* apoplectic.

ap'oplexy, *n.*, a stroke caused by brain affection.
apos'tasy, *n.*, a falling away from, revolt against, one's religion.
apos'tate, *n.*, one who apostatizes.
apostat'ical, *adj.*, tending to apostasy.
apos'tatize, *v.i.*, to revolt against one's former faith.
apos'tatized, *p.p.*, apostatize.
apos'tatizing, *pr.p.*, apostatize.
a posterio'ri, *Lat.* phrase = arguing from effect to cause.
apos'til, *v.t.*, to annotate marginally; *n.*, a marginal note.
apos'tle, *n.*, one who is commissioned, esp. one of the Twelve Apostles; a leader in a movement or cause.
apos'tleship, *n.*, an apostle's office.
apos'tolate, *n.*, the order of apostles; an apostle's function.
apostol'ic, *adj.*, rel. to apostles.
apostol'ical, *adj.*, *i.q.* apostolic.
apostolic'ity, *n.*, the apostolic character.
apos'trophe, *n.*, an aside address to some person or thing; a typographical mark of possession.
apostroph'ic, *adj.*, rel. to apostrophe.
apos'trophize, *v.t.*, to address with an apostrophe.
apos'trophized, *p.p.*, apostrophize.
apos'trophizing, *pr.p.*, apostrophize.
apoth'ecary, *n.*, a storer of medicinal drugs; formerly an irregular practitioner in medicine.
ap'othegm, *n.*, *i.q.* apophthegm.
apothegmat'ic, *adj.*, of the nature of apothegm.
apotheo'sis, *n.*, deification, making into a god.
apothe'osize, *v.t.*, to deify.
apot'omy, apot'ome, *n.*, a major semitone.
appal', *v.t.*, to terrify, dismay.
Appalach'ian, *adj.*, bel. to the Appalachian mountains.
appalled', *p.p.*, appal.
appall'ing, *pr.p.*, appal; *adj.*, frightful.
appall'ingly, *adv.*, in an appalling way.
ap'panage, *n.*, a dependency.
appara'tus, *n.*, appliances for doing work.
appar'el, *n.*, clothing; embroidered work on alb and amice; *v.t.*, to clothe.
appar'elled, *or* **-eled,** *p.p.*, apparel; *adj.*, ornamented with apparels.
appar'elling, *pr.p.*, apparel.
appa'rent, *adj.*, visible, manifest, seeming.
appa'rently, *adv.*, clearly, seemingly.
appari'tion, *n.*, the act of appearing; something that appears, a ghost.
appar'itor, *n.*, an officer in a law court; a church beadle.
appeal', *v.i.*, to call upon; to carry a case to a superior court; *n.*, reference to a superior court, a call for aid.
appeal'able, *adj.*, able to be pleaded before a higher court.
appealed', *p.p.*, appeal.
appeal'er, *n.*, one who appeals.
appeal'ing, *pr.p.*, appeal; *adj.*, compelling interest.
appear', *v.i.*, to become visible; to seem.
appear'ance, *n.*, a showing, becoming visible; a seeming; outward aspect.
appeared', *p.p.*, appear.
appear'er, *n.*, one who appears.
appear'ing, *pr.p.*, appear.
appeas'able, *adj.*, able to be appeased.
appeas'ableness, *n.*, an appeasable state or temper.
appease', *v.t.*, to calm, allay.
appeased', *p.p.*, appease.
appease'ment, *n.*, the act of appeasing.
appeas'er, *n.*, one who appeases.
appeas'ing, *pr.p.*, appease.
appel'lant, *n.*, one who appeals.
appel'late, *adj.*, possessing appeal jurisdiction.
appella'tion, *n.*, a name.
appel'lative, *adj.*, rel. to appeal; *n.*, a nickname, title.
appel'latively, *adv.*, by way of an appeal.
appel'latory, *adj.*, conveying an appeal.
appellee', *n.*, the person against whom an appeal is lodged.
appel'lor, *n.*, *i.q.* appellant.
append', *v.t.*, to hang to, fix to, add.
append'age, *n.*, something appended.
append'ant, *n.*, *i.q.* appendage; *adj.*, joined to, added.
append'ed, *p.p.*, append.
append'ing, *pr.p.*, append.
appen'dices, pl. of appendix.
appendici'tis, *n.*, disease of the *vermiform appendix* to the great intestine.
appen'dix, *n.*, additional matter at the end of a book; a part of the great intestine so named.
appen'dixes, pl. of appendix.
appercep'tion, *n.*, self-consciousness; the faculty of the mind to be conscious of perceiving.
appertain', *v.i.*, to belong to, to be related to.
appertained', *p.p.*, appertain.
appertain'ing, *pr.p.*, appertain.

appertain'ment, *n.*, the state of appertaining.

ap'petence, *n.*, strong desire, appetite, tendency.

ap'petency, *n.*, *i.q.* appetence.

ap'petent, *adj.*, craving; impulsive.

ap'petite, *n.*, desire (chiefly for food).

ap'petitive, *adj.*, producing appetite.

ap'petise, *v.t.*, to excite appetite in a person.

ap'petizer, *n.*, something that promotes appetite.

ap'petizing, *adj.*, stimulating the appetite; tempting.

Ap'pian, *adj.*, named from Appius, as the Appian Way.

applaud', *v.t.*, to clap the hands at, to approve.

applaud'ed, *p.p.*, applaud.

applaud'er, *n.*, one who applauds.

applaud'ing, *pr.p.*, applaud.

applause', *n.*, the act of applauding, open praise.

applau'sive, *adj.*, expressing applause.

ap'ple, *n.*, the fruit so named; the pupil of an eye.

ap'ple-tree, *n.*, a tree bearing apples.

appli'ance, *n.*, something applied.

appli'ancy, *n.*, the habit of applying, adaptability.

applicabil'ity, *n.*, ability to be applied, fitness.

ap'plicable, *adj.*, able to be applied, fit.

ap'plicableness, *n.*, suitability, fitness to be applied.

ap'plicancy, *n.*, the state of applying.

ap'plicant, *n.*, one who applies for some gift or position.

applica'tion, *n.*, the act of applying; steady industry; the moral of a story or discourse.

ap'plicative, *adj.*, rel. to application; able to be applied.

ap'plicatory, *adj.*, fit for application.

applied', *p.p.*, apply.

appli'er, *n.*, one who applies.

appliqué', *n.*, something laid on.

apply', *v.t.* and *i.*, to put one thing to another, to exert; to request; to concern, be related to.

apply'ing, *pr.p.*, apply.

appoggiatu'ra, *n.*, an ornamental note in music, taking its time out of a principal note.

appoint', *v.t.*, to fix; confer office; settle.

appoint'ed, *p.p.*, appoint.

appointee', *n.*, a person appointed.

appoint'er, *n.*, one who appoints.

appoint'ing, *pr.p.* appoint.

appoint'ment, *n.*, the act of appointing; an office or post; an engagement.

appoint'ments, pl., of appointment = equipments.

Apollina'rian, *adj.*, rel. to Apollinarius; *e.g.*, the Apollinarian heresy.

appor'tion, *v.t.*, to assign portions or parts.

appor'tioned, *p.p.*, apportion.

appor'tioner, *n.*, one who apportions.

appor'tioning, *pr.p.*, apportion.

appor'tionment, *n.*, the act of apportioning.

appos'er, *n.*, one who apposes.

ap'posite, *adj.*, fitting, to the point.

ap'positely, *adv.*, fittingly, to the point.

ap'positeness, *n.*, applicability, the state of being to the point.

apposi'tion, *n.*, the act of placing side by side. In grammar, apposition is the juxtaposition of two nouns or equivalents in the same case, the latter explaining the former, as Victoria Regina.

appos'itive, *adj.*, rel. to apposition.

apprais'al, *n.*, the act of appraising.

appraise', *v.t.*, to take the value of, to price.

appraised', *p.p.*, appraise.

appraise'ment, *n.*, the act of appraising.

apprais'er, *n.*, a valuer, one who appraises.

apprais'ing, *pr.p.*, appraise.

appre'ciable, *adj.*, able to be appreciated.

appre'ciably, *adv.*, sensibly, in a way to be felt.

appre'ciate, *v.t.* and *i.*, to set a value on; to esteem highly; to increase in value.

appre'ciated, *p.p.*, appreciate.

appre'ciating, *pr.p.*, appreciate.

apprecia'tion, *n.*, the act of valuing, recognition of value; rise in price, a critique.

appre'ciative, *adj.*, showing appreciation.

appre'ciatory, *adj.*, *i.q.* appreciative.

apprehend', *v.t.*, to seize, to arrest; to understand; to anticipate with fear.

apprehend'ed, *p.p.*, apprehend.

apprehend'er, *n.*, one who apprehends.

apprehend'ing, *pr.p.*, apprehend.

apprehen'sible, *adj.*, able to be apprehended.

apprehen'sion, *n.*, nervous fear.

apprehen'sive, *adj.*, nervously fearful.

apprehen'sively, *adv.*, in an apprehensive way.

apprehen'siveness, *n.*, an apprehensive state.

appren'tice, *n.*, a young person

learning a trade or profession; *v.t.*, to bind a youth to an employer.

appren'ticed, *p.p.*, apprentice.

appren'ticeship, *n.*, the state of an apprentice; the period of being an apprentice.

appren'ticing, *pr.p.*, apprentice.

apprise', apprize', *v.t.*, to give notice of, inform.

apprised', *p.p.*, apprise.

appris'er, *n.*, one who apprises.

appris'ing, *pr.p.*, apprise.

approach', *v.t.* and *i.*, to come near to, make advances; *n.*, a coming near, path to.

approach'able, *adj.*, able to be approached, affable.

approached', *p.p.*, approach.

approach'er, *n.*, one who approaches.

approach'ing, *pr.p.*, approach.

approach'ment, *n.*, the act of approaching.

ap'probate, *v.t.*, to approve, sanction.

ap'probated, *p.p.*, approbate.

ap'probating, *pr.p.*, approbate.

approba'tion, *n.*, approval, sanction.

ap'probative, *adj.*, approving, sanctioning.

ap'probatively, *adv.*, in an approving way.

ap'probativeness, *n.*, a state of approving.

ap'probatory, *adj.*, *i.q.* approbative.

appro'priable, *adj.*, able to be appropriated.

appro'priate, *v.t.*, to make one's own; to set aside; *adj.*, fitting, suitable.

appro'priated, *p.p.*, appropriate.

appro'priately, *adv.*, in an appropriate way.

appro'priateness, *n.*, fitness, suitability.

appro'priating, *pr.p.*, appropriate.

appropria'tion, *n.*, the act of appropriating.

appro'priative, *adj.*, given to appropriating.

appro'priator, *n.*, one who appropriates.

approv'able, *adj.*, worthy to be approved.

approv'al, *n.*, approbation, sanction.

approve', *v.t.*, to think well of, sanction.

approved', *p.p.*, approve.

approve'ment, *n.*, the act of approving.

approv'er, *n.*, one who approves.

approv'ing, *pr.p.*, approve.

approv'ingly, *adv.*, in an approving way.

approx'imate, *v.i.*, to approach, come near to.

approx'imate, *adj.*, coming very near to, almost correct.

approx'imated, *p.p.*, approximate.

approx'imately, *adv.*, nearly, closely.

approx'imating, *pr.p.*, approximate.

approxima'tion, *n.*, the act of approximating; a calculation or statement almost exact.

approx'imative, *adj.*, coming close to, approaching.

appui', *n.*, support (*Fr.*).

appul'sion, *n.*, the act of striking against.

appur'tenance, *n.*, that which pertains or belongs.

appur'tenant, *adj.*, bel., pert. to.

a'pricot, *n.*, a fruit of the plum kind.

A'pril, *n.*, the fourth month of the year.

A'pril-fool, *n.*, one who is made a fool of on All Fools' Day, April 1.

a prio'ri, *Lat.* phrase = from something antecedent; *i.e.*, reasoning from cause to effect.

a'pron, *n.*, an outside garment protecting the front of the body.

a'proned, *adj.*, wearing an apron.

apropos', French phrase = to the purpose.

apse, *n.*, the round or multilateral end of a chancel, aisle, or chapel.

ap'sidal, *adj.*, rel. to an apse; in shape like an apse.

ap'sides, pl. of apsis.

ap'sis, *n.*, a point in an eccentric orbit furthest from or nearest to the centre of attraction; an apse.

apt, *adj.*, fit, apposite, liable to, well qualified.

ap'tera, *n.*, wingless creatures.

ap'teral, *adj.*, bel. to aptera.

ap'terous, *adj.*, wingless.

ap'teryx, *n.*, a bird with rudimentary wings.

apt'itude, *n.*, fitness, quickness, capacity for.

apt'ly, *adv.*, fitly, appropriately.

apt'ness, *n.*, a capacity for doing things, appropriateness.

ap'tote, *adj.*, not having case-endings.

a'qua, *n.*, water (*Lat.*).

aquafor'tis, *n.*, nitric acid.

aquarelle', *adj.*, water-colour.

aqua'rial, *adj.*, rel. to water.

aqua'rian, *adj.*, living in water.

aqua'rium, *n.*, a receptacle for water animals or plants.

Aqua'rius, *n.*, the water carrier—one of the signs of the Zodiac.

aquat'ic, *adj.*, rel. to, living in, water.

aq'uatint, *n.*, a special kind of engraving; an engraving printed from an aquatint plate.

a'qua vi'tae, *n.*, strong water, especially brandy, *eau de vie.*

a'queduct, *n.*, a channel for conveying water.

a'queous, *adj.*, watery, of water.

a'queousness, *n.*, a watery state.

a'quiline, *adj.*, eagle-like; hooked like an eagle's beak.

a'quilon, *n.*, the N.E. wind.

Ar'ab, *n.*, a native of Arabia.

arabesque', *n.*, ornamentation or carving in the Moorish style.

arabesqued', *adj.*, in the arabesque style.

Ara'bian, *adj.*, bel. to Arabia.

Ar'abic, *adj.*, *i.q.* Arabian; *n.*, the language of Persia.

ar'able, *adj.*, fit for the plough and tilling.

Arach'nida, *n.*, insects of the spider tribe.

arach'noid, *adj.*, spider-like.

arachnol'ogy, *n.*, the study of spider-nature.

ar'agonite, *n.*, a calcium carbonate.

Arama'ic, *adj.* and *n.*, the name of an ancient language of Syria.

Arame'an, *adj.*, bel. to Aram (Mesopotamia) or Aramaea.

ara'tion, *n.*, ploughing, tilling.

ar'balist, *n.*, a military engine so named; a crossbow.

ar'balister, *n.*, the man behind the arbalist.

ar'biter, *n.*, a judge or umpire.

ar'bitrable, *adj.*, able to go to arbitration.

arbit'rament, *n.*, decision, umpire's verdict.

ar'bitrarily, *adv.*, of one's own will, despotically.

ar'bitrariness, *n.*, an arbitrary temper.

ar'bitrary, *adj.*, acting on one's own will or decision.

ar'bitrate, *v.t.*, to decide between disputants.

ar'bitrated, *p.p.*, arbitrate.

ar'bitrating, *pr.p.*, arbitrate.

arbitra'tion, *n.*, the act of arbitrating.

ar'bitrator, *n.*, one who arbitrates.

ar'bitratrix, *n.*, fem. of arbitrator.

ar'bitress, *n.*, fem. of arbiter.

arbo'reous, *adj.*, bel. to trees.

arbores'cence, *n.*, the growth of trees.

arbore'tum, *n.*, a collection of trees for scientific study.

ar'boriculture, *n.*, scientific tree-culture.

arboricult'urist, *n.*, one engaged in arboriculture.

ar'boriform, *adj.*, tree-like.

ar'borist, *n.*, one who cultivates trees.

arboriza'tion, *n.*, an appearance like a tree.

ar'borous, *adj.*, rel. to trees.

ar'bour, ar'bor, *n.*, a tree-shaded bower.

ar'boured, *adj.*, recessed with arbours.

ar'buscle, *n.*, a tuft.

arbu'tean, *adj.*, bel. to the arbutus.

ar'butus, *n.*, the wild strawberry.

arc, *n.*, a curve, a part of the periphery of a circle or other curve.

arcade', *n.*, an arched structure; the range of arches in a church or other building; an arched passage with shops on either side.

arca'ded, *adj.*, in the form of an arcade.

Arca'dian, *adj.*, native to Arcadia; rustic, simple, pastoral.

arca'na, *n.*, secrets, mysteries.

arca'num, *n.*, a secret; something hidden.

arch, *n.*, a structural curve over an opening, or on the face of a wall; *adj.*, sly, roguish; *v.t.*, to form into an arch.

arch-, ar'chi-, a prefix denoting eminence, as archbishop.

archaeolog'ic, *adj.*, *i.q.* archaeological.

archaeolog'ical, *adj.*, rel. to archaeology.

archaeol'ogist, *n.*, one who studies archaeology.

archaeol'ogy, *n.*, the study of antiquities.

archa'ic, *adj.*, bel. to the remote past, obsolete.

ar'chaism, *n.*, an antiquated usage or expression.

archan'gel, *n.*, an angel of the highest rank.

archangel'ic, *adj.*, bel. or rel. to an archangel.

archbish'op, *n.*, a bishop who rules a province.

archbish'opric, *n.*, the office or rule of an archbishop.

archdea'con, *n.*, a chief deacon; the bishop's diocesan deputy.

archdea'conry, *n.*, an archdeacon's dignity or office.

archdea'conship, *n.*, an archdeacon's service.

archdi'ocese, *n.*, a term erroneously applied to an archbishop's diocese. It is unknown in the English Church.

archdru'id, *n.*, the chief of the Order of Druids.

archdu'cal, *adj.*, bel. to an archduke.

archduch'ess, *n.*, the fem. of archduke.

archduch'y, *n.*, an archduke's territory.

archduke', *n.*, a duke of the highest rank.

archduke'dom, *n.*, an archduke's office or territorial jurisdiction.

arched, *adj.*, covered with or forming an arch: *p.p.* arch.

arch'er, *n.*, one who shoots with a bow.

arch'eress, *n.*, fem. of archer.

arch'ery, *n.*, the sport of shooting with a bow.

ar'chetypal, *adj.*, rel. to an archetype.

ar'chetype, *n.*, the original on which a type is modelled.

archfiend', *n.*, the chief among the fiends, Satan.

arch'ical, *adj.*, governmental; original.

archidiac'onal, *adj.*, pert. to an archdeacon.

archiepis'copacy, *n.*, an archbishop's incumbency.

archiepis'copal, *adj.*, pert. to an archbishop.

ar'chil, *n.*, a lichen so named.

Archilo'chian, *adj.*, rel. to Archilochus, an ancient Greek satirical poet, inventor of the iambus.

archiman'drite, *n.*, the title of a Greek priest of the higher rank, ruler of a large monastery or of several smaller ones.

Archime'dean, *adj.*, rel. to Archimedes, the famous mathematician of antiquity.

arch'ing, *adj.*, curving; *pr.p.* arch.

archipel'ago, *n.*, a group of sea islands, esp. the islands in the Aegean Sea.

ar'chitect, *n.*, a master-builder, one who designs buildings.

ar'chitective, *adj.*, rel. to architecture; constructive.

architecton'ic, *adj.*, pert. to architecture; constructive.

architecton'ics, *n.*, the architectural science.

architect'ural, *adj.* rel. to architecture.

ar'chitecture, *n.*, the art or work of an architect.

ar'chitrave, *n.*, a principal beam, being the part of the entablature which rests on the capitals of the columns.

archi'val, *adj.*, rel. to archives.

ar'chives, *n. pl.*, ancient public records.

ar'chivist, *n.*, a student of archives.

ar'chivolt, *n.*, the under surface of an arch.

arch'ly, *adv.*, slyly, roguishly.

arch'ness, *n.*, slyness, roguishness.

ar'chon, *n.*, a magistrate, ruler (*Gr.*).

archpres'byter, *n.*, a presbyter of the higher rank.

archpres'bytery, *n.*, the office of an archpresbyter.

archpriest', *n.*, the title anciently given to the leading priest in a diocese. Sometimes, as at Haccombe in Devon, it was given to the head of a community. The rector of Haccombe retains the title.

arch'way, *n.*, a passage through an arch.

arch'wise, *adv.*, in the form of an arch.

ar'cograph, *n.*, a device for drawing circles without striking from a centre.

arcta'tion, *n.*, constriction, constipation.

Arc'tic, *adj.*, rel. to the Arctic or North Pole.

Arctu'rus, *n.*, the Great Bear constellation.

ar'cuate, *adj.*, arched in structure.

arcua'tion, *n.*, the arch formation

ar'dency, *n.*, fervent emotion, ardour.

ar'dent, *adj.*, heated, impetuous, zealous.

ar'dently, *adv.*, in an ardent way.

ar'dour, ar'dor, *n.*, heat, passion, zeal.

ar'duous, *adj.*, steep, difficult.

ar'duously, *adv.*, laboriously, with difficulty.

ar'duousness, *n.*, difficulty.

are, the pl. of the present tense of the copulative verb *to be.*

a'rea, *n.*, surface measurement; a space enclosed; the sunk space round a building; extent, range.

Ar'eca, *n.*, a kind of tropical palm.

arefac'tion, *n.*, withering.

ar'efy, *v.t.*, to wither up, dry up.

are'na, *n.*, the open space of a Roman amphitheatre; a place or scene of contest.

arena'ceous, *adj.*, sandy.

arena'tion, *n.*, the use of hot sand.

arenose', *adj.*, sandy.

are'ola, *n.*, a small space in the marking on insects' wings, veins of leaves, etc.

are'olate, *adj.*, marked with *areolae.*

areola'tion, *n.*, the act or state of being marked with *areolae.*

areom'eter, *n.*, a surface measuring instrument.

areomet'ric, *adj.*, rel. to surface measurement.

areomet'rical, *adj.*, *i.q.* areometric.

areom'etry, *n.*, the science of surface-measurement.

Areop'agist, *n.*, *i.q.* Areopagite.

Areop'agite, *n.*, a member of the Areopagus.

Areop'agus, *n.*, the Hill of Ares in Athens, on which the most ancient of the Courts was held. Called Mars' Hill in the Acts of the Apostles.

ar'gal, *conj.*, a corruption of *ergo* = therefore. Used in Shakespeare.

ar'gand, *adj.*, bel. to Argand's method of lighting.

ar'gent, *n.* and *adj.*, silver, silvery.

argent'al, *adj.* silvery.

argent'ic, *adj.*, rel. to silver.

argentif'erous, *adj.*, silver-producing.

ar'gentine, *adj.*, silvery; *n.*, a white metal so named.

Ar'gentine, *adj.*, rel. to Argentina; *n.*, a native of A.

ar'gil, *n.*, white clay.

argilla'ceous, *adj*, of white clay.

argillif'erous, *adj.*, producing white clay.

argil'lous, *adj.*, containing, or consisting of, white clay.

Ar'give, *adj.*, native of Argos.

ar'gol, *n.*, the grape-juice deposit in fermentation.

ar'gon, *n.*, an inert gas in the atmosphere.

Ar'gonaut, *n.*, a sailor on the mythical ship *Argo*.

Argonaut'ic, *adj.*, rel. to the Argonauts.

ar'gosy, *n.*, a richly-laden merchant vessel.

ar'got, *n.*, the French name for slang.

ar'guable, *adj.*, capable of being argued.

ar'gue, *v.t.* and *i.*, to discuss, to try to prove; to show.

ar'gued, *p.p.*, argue.

ar'guer, *n.*, one who argues.

ar'guing, *pr.p.*, argue.

ar'gument, *n.*, a debate, discussion, attempt to prove; summarized purport of a book or speech.

argumenta'tion, *n.*, a dispute.

argumen'tative, *adj.*, rel. to argument; fond of disputing.

argumen'tatively, *adv.* in an argumentative way.

argumen'tativeness, *n.*, a fondness for disputing.

ar'gus, *n.*, an E. Indian pheasant.

Ar'gus, *n.*, a Greek mythological being, having a hundred eyes.

a'ria, *n.*, a melody, song, air.

A'rian, *adj.*, rel. to Arius, the heretical leader opposed by St. Athanasius.

A'rianism, *n.*, the profession of Arian teaching.

ar'id, *adj.*, dry, parched, waste.

arid'ity, *n.*, a state of dryness.

ar'idness, *n.*, *i.q.* aridity.

A'ries, *n.*, the Ram, one of the signs of the Zodiac.

ariet'ta, *n.*, a short aria or melody.

aright', *adv.*, rightly, correctly.

ar'il, *n.*, a secondary covering of a seed.

arise', *v.i.*, to spring forth, to ascend, to leave one's bed.

aris'en, *p.p.*, arise.

aris'ing, *pr.p.*, arise.

ar'istarch, *n.*, a critic like Aristarchus.

aristarch'ian, *adj.*, rel. to Aristarchus.

aristoc'racy, *n.*, government by the best citizens; the aristocrats as a class or body.

ar'istocrat, *n.*, a member of the aristocracy; a person with pride of birth.

aristocrat'ic, *adj.* like an aristocrat.

aristocrat'ical, *adj.*, *i.q.* aristocratic.

Aristote'lian, *adj.*, belonging to Aristotle, the Greek philosopher.

Aristote'lic, *adj.*, *i.q.* Aristotelian.

ar'ithmancy, *n.*, divining by means of numbers.

arith'metic, *n.*, the science of numbers.

arithmet'ical, *adj.*, rel. to arithmetic.

arithmeti'cian, *n.*, one who practises arithmetic.

ark, *n.*, chest, box, (Noah's Ark was a large floating vessel); a place of refuge.

arm, *n.*, a limb of the body, an inlet of the sea; a weapon; *v.*, to furnish with weapons, equip for war.

arma'da, *n.*, a fleet of armed ships.

armadil'lo, *n.* a four-footed creature, small, having a horny shell.

ar'mament, *n.*, an armed force; the collected munitions of war; defence.

ar'mature, *n.*, defensive armour; part of an electrical machine.

arm'-chair, *n.*, a chair with supporting arms.

armed, *p.p.*, arm; *adj.*, having arms.

Arme'nian, *adj.*, native to, bel. to, Armenia.

arm'ful, *n.*, a gathering of things to fill the arms.

arm'hole, *n.*, a hole to let the arm through.

ar'miger, *n.*, the Lat. name for our Esquire; a person entitled to wear arms.

armig'erous, *adj.*, entitled to wear arms (heraldic).

armil'la, *n.*, a bracelet, ring.

armil'lary, *adj.*, rel. to an armilla.

arm'ing, *pr.p.*, arm.

Armin'ian, *adj.*, rel. to Arminius, a 16th cent. Dutch anti-Calvinist teacher.

Armin'ianism, *n.*, teaching of the school of Arminius.

armip'otence, *n.*, armed superiority.

armip'otent, *adj.*, superior in arms.

arm'istice, *n.*, a temporary suspension of hostilities.

arm'less, *adj.*, without arms.

arm'let, *n.*, a badge or ornament worn round the arm.

ar'mour, ar'mor, *n.*, defensive arms worn on the body, or used in the plating of a man-of-war.

ar'mourer, ar'morer, *n.*, one who makes armour

armo'rial, *adj.*, rel. to heraldic arms.

Armor'ic, *adj.*, rel. to Armorica.

Armor'ican, *n.*, *i.q.* Armoric.

ar'mourist, *n.*, an heraldic expert.

ar'mour-pla'ted, *adj.*, covered with defensive plates (a nautical term).

ar'moury, ar'mory, *n.* a place for the making or the keeping of arms.

arm'pit, *n.*, the hollow under the arms.

arms, pl. of arm.

arm's' - length, a phrase, "at arm's-length" = at a distance as long as one's arm.

ar'my, *n.*, an armed body of men; a large number.

ar'nica, *n.*, a medicinal herb so named, useful for bruises.

arnot'to, *n.*, an American tree resembling the Indian plum.

aroint', *v.i.* (generally found in the imperative), to remove, get out of the way.

aro'ma, *n.*, a fragrant smell or taste; metaphorically, an intangible quality.

aromat'ic, *adj.*, possessing aroma.

aromat'ical, *adj.*, *i.q.* aromatic.

aro'matize, *v.t.*, to season, perfume.

aro'matizer, *n.*, something that gives aroma.

aro'matous, *adj.*, *i.q.* aromatic.

arose', *p.t.*, arise.

around, *adv.* and *prep.*, all about, round.

arouse', *v.t.*, to stir up, awaken.

aroused', *p.p.*, arouse.

arous'ing, *pr.p.*, arouse.

arpeg'gio, *n.*, the harp-like striking of the notes of a chord separately.

ar'pent, *n.*, a former French land measure = an acre.

arquebusade', *n.*, a volley from arquebuses.

ar'quebuse, ar'quebus *n.*, an old fire-arm, supported on a rest.

arquebusier', *n.*, one who fires an arquebus.

ar'rack, *n.*, a heady liquor distilled from rice and other plants.

ar'ragonite, *n.* see aragonite.

arraign', *v.t.*, to indict before a judge.

arraigned', *p.p.*, arraign.

arraign'er, *n.*, one who arraigns.

arraign'ing, *pr.p.*, arraign.

arraign'ment, *n.*, a legal indictment.

arrange', *v.t.*, to place in order, settle.

arranged', *p.p.*, arrange.

arrange'ment, *n.*, the act of arranging; an agreed plan; a musical setting.

arrang'er, *n.*, one who arranges.

arrang'ing, *pr.p.*, arrange.

ar'rant, *adj.*, thorough, downright.

ar'rantly, *adv.*, in a downright way.

ar'ras, *n.*, tapestry (derived from Arras in France).

array', *n.*, order (as battle array), dress; *v.t.*, to vest, dress.

arrayed', *p.p.*, array.

array'er, *n.*, one who arrays.

array'ing, *pr.p.* array.

arrear', *n.*, position in the rear.

arrear'age, *n.*, the amount in arrear.

arrears', *n.*, an unpaid debt.

arrest', *v.t.*, to seize, to attract (the mind or attention); *n.*, a seizure by legal warrant, a stopping.

arrest'ed, *p.p.*, arrest.

arrest'er, arrest'or, *n.*, one who arrests.

arrest'ing, *pr.p.*, arrest.

arrest'ment, *n.*, the act of arresting.

ar'ris, *n.*, a ridge, as that between the channels of a Doric pillar.

arri'val, *n.*, a coming, act of arriving.

arrive', *v.i.*, to come, to reach a place.

arrived', *p.p.*, arrive.

arriv'ing, *pr.p.* arrive.

ar'rogance, *n.*, overbearing pride.

ar'rogancy, *n.*, *i.q.* arrogance.

ar'rogant, *adj.*, overbearingly proud, exacting.

ar'rogantly, *adv.*, in an arrogant way.

ar'rogate, *v.t.*, to claim unduly or in excess.

ar'rogated, *p.p.*, arrogate.

ar'rogating, *pr.p.*, arrogate.

arroga'tion, *n.*, the act of arrogating.

arrondisse'ment, *n.*, a French territorial division so named.

arro'sion, *n.*, destruction by biting.

ar'row, *n.*, a sharp-pointed missile, shot from a bow.

ar'row-head, *n.*, an arrow's pointed end.

ar'rowroot, *n.*, a starchy plant (*Maranta arundinacea*), very nutritious.

ar'row-shaped, *adj.*, shaped like an arrow.

ar'rowy, *adj.*, like an arrow.

ar'senal, *n.*, a manufactory or store of war munitions.

arse'niate, *n.*, an arsenic acid salt.

ar'senic, *n.*, a metal, a strong poison.

arsen'ical, *adj.*, containing or rel. to arsenic.

arsen'icate, *v.t.*, to charge with arsenic.

arsen'icated, *p.p.*, arsenicate.

arse'nious, *adj.*, pert. to arsenic.

ar'senite, *n.*, an arsenious acid salt.

ar'sis, *n.*, the stress of the voice where the accent comes; the conductor's beat at the beginning of a bar.

ar'son, *n.*, the act of wilfully setting on fire.

art, *n.*, skill, knowledge, cunning.

arte'rial, *adj.*, bel. to the arteries.

arterializa'tion, *n.*, the changing of venous into arterial blood.

arte'rialize, *v.t.*, to change venous into arterial blood.

arte'rialized, *p.p.*, arterialize.

arte'rializing, *pr.p.*, arterialize.

arteriol'ogy, *n.*, the study of the arteries.

arteriot'omy, *n.*, the act of cutting arteries

ar'tery, *n.*, a blood-vessel leading direct from the heart.

arte'sian, *adj.*, very deeply bored. (Artesian wells were first made in Artois.)

art'ful, *adj.*, cunning, designing.

art'fully, *adv.*, cunningly.

art'fulness, *n.*, cunning.

arthrit'ic, *adj.*, rel. to arthritis.

arthri'tis, *n.*, inflammation of a joint.

ar'tichoke, *n.*, an edible vegetable so named.

ar'ticle, *n.*, a separate part, a member, a thing or commodity, an agreed doctrine, a treaty-clause; a piece of literary work; *v.t.*, to bind by indenture.

ar'ticled, *p.p.*, article.

ar'ticling, *pr.p.*, article.

artic'ular, *adj.*, rel. to a joint or articulation.

artic'ularly, *adv.*, in an articulate way; in detail.

articula'ta, *n.*, creatures with segmented bodies.

artic'ulate, *adj.*, jointed; clear, distinct.

artic'ulate, *v.i.*, to speak distinctly.

artic'ulated, *p.p.*, articulate.

artic'ulately, *adv.*, with distinct utterance.

artic'ulating, *pr.p.*, articulate.

articula'tion, *n.*, a joint (*anat.*); clear utterance.

art'ifice, *n.*, contrivance, cunning device.

artif'icer, *n.*, one who practises an art, a workman.

artifi'cial, *adj.*, made by art, unreal.

artificial'ity, *n.*, artificial or unnatural character.

artifi'cialness, *n.*, i.q. artificiality.

artil'lerist, *n.*, an expert in artillery.

artil'lery, *n.*, originally the equipment of bow and arrows; now guns and cannons; also the men who use them.

artil'leryman, *n.*, a man in the artillery force.

ar'tisan, *n.*, one who practises a trade.

art'ist, *n.*, one who practises a fine art.

artiste', *n.*, the Fr. equivalent of artist, for which it is absurdly substituted in the case of public singers and actors.

artist'ic, *adj.*, rel. to art and artists.

artist'ical, *adj.*, i.q. artistic.

artist'ically, *adv.*, in an artistic way.

art'less, *adj.*, simple, natural.

art'lessly, *adv.*, simply, naturally.

art'lessness, *n.*, a simple state or character.

Arunde'lian, *adj.*, bel. to Arundel.

arundif'erous, *adj.*, reed-producing.

arus'pice, *n.*, a soothsayer, diviner.

arus'picy, *n.*, divining by means of the entrails of sacrificed beasts.

Ar'yan, *adj.* and *n.*, an Aryan is one who belongs to the great Indo-European family, for whom this name has been invented.

as, *n.*, a Roman coin and weight.

as, *adv.*, and *conj.*, denoting similarity or cause.

asafoet'ida, *n.*, an extract from the *Ferula* and other strong-smelling bitter plants.

asbes'tine, *adj.*, made of or rel. to asbestos.

asbes'tos, *n.*, a fire-proof substance.

as'caris, *n.*, a round worm.

ascend', *v.i.* and *t.*, to go up, mount.

ascend'able, *adj.*, able to be ascended.

ascend'ant, *n.*, a state of upward advance; predominance.

ascend'ent, *adj.*, mounting upward.

ascend'ed, *p.p.*, ascend.

ascend'ency, *n.*, a position of supremacy.

ascend'er, *n.*, one who ascends.

ascend'ing, *pr.p.*, ascend.

ascen'sion, *n.*, the act of ascending.

Ascen'sion Day, *n.*, the Day (otherwise Holy Thursday) of Our Lord's Ascension.

ascen'sional, *adj.*, rel. to ascension.

ascent', *n.*, a rising, climbing, degree of acclivity.

ascertain', *v.t.*, to find out for certain.

ascertain'able, *adj.*, capable of being ascertained.

ascertained', *p.p.*, ascertain.

ascertain'er, *n.*, one who ascertains.

ascertain'ing, *pr.p.*, ascertain.

ascertain'ment, *n.*, the act of ascertaining.

ascet'ic, *adj.*, practising severe self-denial; *n.*, one who lives the ascetic life.

ascet'icism, *n.*, the practice or life of an ascetic.

ascititious, *adj.*, additional, supplemental (also written *adscititious*).
ascrib'able, *adj.*, able to be ascribed.
ascribe, *v.t.*, to impute or attribute.
ascribed', *p.p.*, ascribe.
ascrib'ing, *pr.p.*, ascribe.
ascrip'tion, *n.*, the act of ascribing.
asep'sis, *n.*, absence of putrefaction.
asep'tic, *adj.*, not decaying or putrefying.
asex'ual, *adj.*, sexless.
ash, *n.*, the tree so named; burnt remains.
ashamed', *adj.*, filled with shame.
ash'en, *adj.*, bel. to or resembling the ash or ashes.
ash'ery, *n.*, an ash-bin.
ash'-hole, *n.*, a hole where ashes are thrown.
ash'lar, *n.*, hewn or squared stone.
ash'laring, *n.*, the wooden plaster-studs between the floor and the rafters of a garret; ashlar stone-work.
ashore', *adv.*, on shore.
ash'-pan, *n.*, a pan for ashes.
ash'pit, *n.*, a pit where ashes are flung.
Ash Wed'nesday, *n.*, the first day of Lent, when ashes are sprinkled on penitents' heads.
ash'y, *adj.*, pale, ash-like in colour.
A'sian, *adj.*, bel. to Asia.
Asiat'ic, *adj.*, *i.q.* Asian.
Asiat'icism, *n.*, an Asiatic peculiarity.
aside', *adv.*, on one side, apart; *n.*, a remark spoken aside.
as'inine, *adj.*, rel. to or resembling an ass.
asit'ia, *n.*, loss of appetite; lack of food.

ask, *v.t.*, to question, beg.
askance', *adv.*, sideways; with a suspicious look.
askant', *adv.*, *i.q.* askance.
asked, *p.p.*, ask.
askew', *adv.*, obliquely.
ask'ing, *pr.p.*, ask.
aslant', *adv.*, sloping, slanting.
asleep', *adv.*, in a state of sleep.
aslope', *adv.*, sloping.
Asmone'an, *adj.*, the name of a great Jewish family.
aso'matous, *adj.*, without body.
asp, *n.*, a venomous snake.
aspar'agine, *adj.*, rel. to asparagus.
aspar'agus, *n.*, a much relished vegetable.
as'pect, *n.*, sight, look, position, prospect.
as'pen, *n.*, a kind of poplar that shivers.
as'perate, *v.t.*, to make harsh, make uneven.
as'perated, *p.p.*, asperate.
as'perating, *pr.p.*, asperate.
aspera'tion, *n.*, the act or state of harshness, making uneven.
asper'ges, *n.*, the sprinkling with holy water. Its name is derived from the opening words of the ceremony—Asperges me, Thou shalt sprinkle me.
aspergil'lum, *n.*, the holy water sprinkler.
aspergil'lus, *n.*, a fungus.
asper'ity, *n.*, roughness, harshness.
asperm'ous, *n.*, not seeding.
asperse', *v.t.*, to accuse injuriously, to slander.
aspersed', *p.p.*, asperse.
aspers'er, *n.*, one who asperses.
aspers'ing, *pr.p.*, asperse.
asper'sion, *n.*, a slander.

aspers'ive, *adj.*, slanderous.
asperso'rium, *n.*, a holy water vessel.
aspers'ory, *n.*, *i.q.* aspersorium.
as'phalt, *n.*, a species of pitch.
asphal'tic, *adj.*, rel. to asphalt.
asphal'tum, *n.*, Lat. name of asphalt.
as'phodel, *n.*, a plant so named; the "fabulous asphodel" of Hades in Greek poetry.
asphyx'ia, *n.*, suffocation, temporary stoppage of breathing.
asphyx'iate, *v.t.*, to produce asphyxia.
asphyx'iated, *p.p.*, asphyxiate.
asphyx'iating, *pr.p.*, asphyxiate; *adj.*, causing asphyxia.
asphyx'y, *n.*, *i.q.* asphyxia.
as'pic, *n.*, a savoury jelly.
aspi'rant, *n.*, one who aspires.
as'pirate, *v.t.* to pronounce with a heavy breath.
as'pirate, *n.*, the sounded letter *h*.
as'pirated, *p.p.*, aspirate.
as'pirating, *pr.p.*, aspirate.
aspira'tion, *n.*, the act of aspiring; strong desire.
as'pirator, *n.*, an instrument for drawing in gas or air; also for drawing off fluid from abscesses, etc.
aspi'ratory, *adj.*, rel. to aspiration.
aspire', *v.i.*, to desire strongly, to strive after.
aspired', *p.p.*, aspire.
aspir'er, *n.*, one who aspires.
aspir'ing, *pr.p.*, aspire; also *adj.*, ambitious.
aspir'ingly, *adv.*, ambitiously.
asquint', *adv.*, with a squint.
ass, *n.*, the quadruped otherwise called the donkey.

as'sagai, *n.*, a Kaffir spear.
assa'i, *adv.*, a musical term = very.
assail', *v.t.*, to attack.
assail'able, *adj.*, open to attack.
assail'ant, *n.*, one who attacks.
assailed', *p.p.*, assail.
assail'er, *n.*, *i.q.* assailant.
assail'ing, *pr.p.*, assail.
assas'sin, *n.*, a secret murderer.
assas'sinate, *v.t.*, to murder secretly.
assas'sinated, *p.p.*, assassinate.
assas'sinating, *pr.p.*, assassinate.
assassina'tion, *n.*, the act of assassinating.
assas'sinator, *n.*, *i.q.* assassin.
assault', *v.t.*, to attack with violence; *n.*, an attack.
assay', *v.t.*, to try, test; *n.*, trial, test.
assayed', *p.p.*, assay.
assay'er, *n.*, one who assays.
assay'ing, *pr.p.*, assay.
assem'blage, *n.*, a gathering together.
assem'ble, *v.t.* and *i.*, to call or gather together; to meet together.
assem'bled, *p.p.*, assemble.
assem'bler, *n.*, one who assembles.
assem'bling, *pr.p.*, assemble.
assem'bly, *n.*, a meeting together.
assent', *v.i.*, to agree to, approve; *n.*, agreement, approval.
assent'ed, *p.p.*, assent.
assen'ter, *n.*, one who assents.
assen'tient, *adj.*, giving approval.
assent'ing, *pr.p.*, assent.
assert', *v.t.*, to affirm, state positively.
assert'ed, *p.p.*, assert.
assert'ing, *pr.p.*, assert.
asser'tion, *n.*, a positive affirmation.
assert'ive, *adj.*, making strong affirmation.
assert'ively, *adv.*, in an assertive way.
assert'or, *n.*, one who asserts.
assert'ory, *adj.*, rel. to assertion; affirmative.
assess', *v.t.*, to fix a value.
assess'able, *adj.*, liable to assessment.
assessed', *p.p.*, assess.
assess'ing, *pr.p.*, assess.
assess'ment, *n.*, valuation for rating or taxing purposes.
assess'or, *n.*, one who assesses.
as'sets, *n.*, property set against one's debts.
assev'erate, *v.t.*, to assert strongly.
assev'erated, *p.p.*, asseverate.
assev'erating, *pr.p.*, asseverate.
assevera'tion, *n.*, a strong assertion.
as'sident, *adj.*, usually present with; in constant attendance on.
assidu'ity, *n.*, steady diligence.
assid'uous, *adj.*, steadily diligent.
assid'uously, *adv.*, with untiring diligence.
assid'uousness, *n.*, *i.q.* assiduity.
assign', *v.t.*, to allot, make over to.
assign'able, *adj.*, able to be assigned.
as'signat, *n.* In the French Revolution *assignats*, or promissory notes, were issued on the security of the confiscated Church property.
assigna'tion, *n.*, an agreed meeting.
assigned', *p.p.*, assign.
assignee', *n.*, one to whom something is assigned.
assign'er, *n.*, one who assigns.
assign'ing, *pr.p.*, assign.
assign'ment, *n.*, a deed of transfer, the act of assigning.
assignor', *n.*, the party who assigns.
assigns', *n. pl.*, persons to whom property is transferred.
assim'ilable, *adj.*, able to be assimilated.
assim'ilate, *v.t.*, to make like; to absorb.
assim'ilated, *p.p.*, assimilate.
assim'ilating, *pr.p.*, assimilate.
assimila'tion, *n.*, the act of assimilating.
assim'ilative, *adj.*, capable of assimilating.
assim'ilatory, *adj.*, tending to assimilation.
assist', *v.t.* and *i.*, to help; to be present at a ceremony.
assist'ance, *n.*, help, aid; presence at a ceremony.
assist'ant, *n.*, one who assists, a helper.
assist'ed, *p.p.*, assist.
assist'ing, *pr.p.*, assist.
assize', *n.*, a court of justice, with judge and jury; *v.t.*, to fix price, weight and measure by authority.
assized', *p.p.*, assize.
assize'ment, *n.*, the act of assizing.
assiz'er, *n.*, one who assizes; one of a grand jury.
assiz'es, *n.*, pl. of assize.
assiz'or, *n.*, *i.q.* assizer.
associabil'ity, *n.*, the character of being associable.
asso'ciable, *adj.*, capable of being associated.
asso'ciate, *v.t* and *i.*, to join to oneself, or to be in company with; *n.*, one who is associated; *adj.*, connected.
asso'ciated, *p.p.*, associate.
asso'ciating, *pr.p.*, associate.
associa'tion, *n.*, the act of joining; a body of associated members.
associa'tional, *adj.*, rel. to an association.

asso'ciative, *adj.*, tending to association.

assoil'zie, *v.t.*, to give absolution (*obs.*).

as'sonance, *n.*, correspondence in sounds—consonants or vowels; any sort of correspondence.

as'sonant, *adj.*, making assonance.

assort', *v.t.*, to arrange in kinds, classify; *v.i.*, to agree, fall in with.

assort'ed, *p.p.*, assort.

assort'er, *n.*, one who assorts.

assort'ing, *pr.p.*, assort.

assort'ment, *n.*, an assorted portion.

assuage', *v.t.* and *i.*, to abate; subside.

assuaged', *p.p.*, assuage.

assuag'ement, *n.*, the act of allaying.

assuag'er, *n.*, one who assuages.

assuag'ing, *pr.p.*, assuage.

assua'sive, *adj.*, tending to assuage.

assume', *v.t.*, to take upon oneself; to accept without proof.

assumed', *p.p.*, assume.

assum'er, *n.*, one who assumes.

assum'ing, *pr.p.*, assume.

assum'ingly, *adv.*, in an assuming way.

assump'sit, *n.*, an unsealed agreement; an action at law rel. to such an agreement.

assump'tion, *n.*, the act of assuming; the taking for granted.

assump'tive, *adj.*, inclined to assume.

assump'tively, *adv.*, in an assumptive way.

assur'ance, *n.*, confidence; excessive confidence; a confident statement; life-security.

assure', *v.t.*, to make secure; to affirm with certainty; to take out a policy on.

assured', *p.p.*, assure.

assur'edly, *adv.*, certainly, without doubt.

assur'edness, *n.*, a confident state of mind.

assur'er, *n.*, one who assures.

assur'ing, *pr.p.*, assure, *adj.*, confidence-inspiring.

assur'ingly, *adv.*, in an assuring way.

Assyr'ian, *adj.*, bel. to Assyria.

Astar'te, *n.*, the Syro-Phoenician moon-goddess, also known as Ashtoreth.

astat'ic, *adj.*, in equilibrium; not tending to move in either direction.

as'ter, *n.*, a plant with star-shaped flora.

aste'ria, *n.*, a sapphire cut star-wise.

aste'riated, *adj.*, radiating like a star.

as'terisk, *n.*, a star-shaped mark of reference.

as'terism, *n.*, a cluster of three stars, marking a passage in a book.

astern', *adv.*, on the stern; *i.e.*, to the rear of a vessel.

as'teroid, *adj.*, star-like, like an aster.

asteroid'al, *adj.*, *i.q.* asteroid.

asthen'ia, *n.*, loss of power.

asthen'ic, *adj.*, suffering from loss of power.

asthenol'ogy, *n.*, the study of asthenia.

asth'ma, *n.*, a disease in which the patient breathes with difficulty.

asthmat'ic, *adj.*, suffering from asthma, rel. to asthma.

asthmat'ical, *adj.*, *i.q.* asthmatic.

astigmat'ic, *adj.*, rel. to astigmatism.

astig'matism, *n.*, a focal disorder of the sight.

astir' *adv.*, on the move.

aston'ied, *adj.*, dismayed, astounded (*obs.*).

aston'ish, *v.t.*, to fill with amazement, to cause excessive surprise.

aston'ished, *p.p.*, astonish.

aston'ishing, *pr.p.*, astonish.

aston'ishingly, *adv.*, surprisingly, amazingly.

aston'ishment, *n.*, surprise, amazement.

astound', *v.t.*, to amaze.

astound'ed, *p.p.*, astound.

astound'ing, *pr.p.*, astound.

astrad'dle, *adv.*, in straddling fashion.

as'tragal, *n.*, a convex (architectural) moulding.

as'tral, *adj.*, rel. to the stars; starry.

astray', *adv.*, out of the path.

astrict', *v.t.*, to bind; limit.

astrict'ed, *p.p.*, astrict.

astric'tion, *n.*, the act or state of astricting.

astrict'ing, *pr.p.*, astrict.

astric'tive, *adj.*, with power to astrict.

astride', *adv.* and *prep.*, with one foot only on either side of something.

astrin'gency, *n.*, the quality of binding.

astrin'gent, *adj.*, binding, contracting; *n.*, a binding medicine.

astrog'raphy, *n.*, star-mapping.

as'troid, *n.*, a star exceeding 5 points magnitude.

as'troite, *n.*, an ancient name for the sapphire.

as'trolabe, *n.*, an apparatus for finding the altitude of stars.

astrol'oger, *n.*, one who professes astrology.

astrolog'ic, *adj.*, rel. to astrology.

astrolog'ical, *adj.*, *i.q.* astrologic.

astrol'ogize, *v.t.*, to profess astrology.

astrol'ogy, *n.*, the pretended art of foretelling the future by the stars.
astron'omer, *n.*, one who practises astronomy.
astronom'ic, *adj.*, rel. to astronomy.
astronom'ical, *adj.*, *i.q.* astronomic.
astron'omy, *n.*, the science of the heavenly bodies.
as'troscope, *n.*, a celestial globe; a celestial telescope.
astrut', *adv.*, in strutting fashion.
astute', *adj.*, shrewd, cunning.
astute'ly, *adv.*, shrewdly, cunningly.
astute'ness, *n.* shrewdness, cunning.
asun'der, *adv.*, apart, in separate pieces.
asy'lum, *n.*, any place of refuge; a shelter for poor or afflicted persons.
asymmet'ric, *adj.*, lacking symmetry.
asymmet'rical, *adj.*, *i.q.* asymmetric.
asym'metry, *n.*, want of symmetry or proportion.
as'ymptote, *n.*, a straight line which an ever-approaching curve never reaches.
at, *prep.*, denoting station or position.
at'abal, *n.*, a Moorish name for a kettle-drum.
at'avism, *n.*, a reversion to ancestral type.
atax'ia, *n.*, disorder, loss of muscular control.
ate, *p.t.*, eat.
A'té, *n.*, retribution (*Gr.*).
atelier', *n.*, a workshop studio (*Fr.*).
athal'amous, *adj.*, without thalami.
Athana'sian, *adj.*, bel. to Athanasius.
a'theism, *n.*, the denial of God's existence.
a'theist, *n.*, a professor of atheism.
atheist'ic, *adj.*, rel. to atheists and atheism.
atheist'ical, *adj.*, *i.q.* atheistic.
ath'eling, *adj.*, of princely family (*obs.*).
athenae'um, *n.*, *orig.* the temple of Athene, now any institution for the promotion of culture.
Athe'nian, *adj.*, bel. to Athens.
athirst', *adj.*, in a thirsty state.
ath'lete, *n.*, one who is trained with muscular exercise.
athlet'ic, *adj.*, strong, exercised; rel. to athletes.
at-home, *adv.* phrase = in one's own house; familiar with.
athwart', *adv.* and *prep.*, across.
atilt', *adv.*, in tilting fashion.
Atlante'an, *adj.*, rel. to Atlas.
atlan'tes, *n.*, figures of men supporting, like caryatides, a superstructure.
Atlan'tic, *adj.* and *n.*, the name of one of the Oceans.
At'las, **at'las**, *n.*, a mountain in Asia; the mythological giant who bore the world on his shoulders; a book of maps.
atmol'ogy, *n.*, the study of vapour.
atmom'eter, *n.*, a vapour-measuring instrument.
at'mosphere, *n.*, the earth's air-envelope.
atmospher'ic, *adj.*, rel. to the atmosphere.
atmospher'ical, *adj.*, *i.q.* atmospheric.
atoll', *n.*, a ring-shaped coral island, with a lagoon inside it.
at'om, *n.*, an indivisible particle of matter; any very small thing.
atom'ic, *adj.*, rel. to atoms.
atom'ical, *adj.*, *i.q.* atomic.
at'omism, *n.*, the atomic theory; belief in that theory.
at'omist, *n.*, one who holds with atomism.
at'omize, *v.t.*, to reduce to atoms; to convert into spray.
atomol'ogy, *n.*, the study of atoms.
aton'able, *adj.*, able to be atoned for.
atone', *v.i.*, to make satisfaction for.
atoned', *p.p.*, atone.
atone'ment, *n.*, satisfaction, reconciliation.
aton'er, *n.*, one who atones.
aton'ic, *adj.*, wanting tone; unaccented.
aton'ing, *pr.p.*, atone.
at'ony, *n.*, want of tone.
atop', *adv.*, on the top.
atrabila'rian, *adj.*, *i.q.* atrabilious.
atrabil'ious, *adj.*, suffering from black bile, depressed, melancholy.
atramenta'ceous, *adj.*, inky.
atrament'al, *adj.*, rel. to ink.
atramenta'rious, *adj.*, inky.
atrament'ous, *adj.*, inky.
atrip', *adv.*, trippingly.
a'trium, *n.*, the central hall of a house (*Lat.*).
atro'cious, *adj.*, savage, brutal.
atro'ciously, *adv.*, savagely, brutally.
atro'ciousness, *n.*, savage character.
atroc'ity, *n.*, a brutal act; brutality.
at'rophied, *adj.*, wasting through lack of nourishment.
at'rophy, *n.*, a wasting away; *v.t.*, to cause wasting; *v.i.*, to waste away.
at'ropine, *n.*, an alkaloid contained in deadly nightshade.
attach', *v.t.*, to bind, fasten; to seize under warrant.
attach'able, *adj.*, able to be attached.
atta'ché, *n.*, one attached to a legation.
attached', *p.p.*, attach.
attach'ing, *pr.p.*, attach.

attach'ment, *n.*, a fastening; close tie of affection; legal seizure.
attack', *v.t.*, to assault; *n.*, an assault.
attack'able, *adj.*, liable to attack.
attacked', *p.p.*, attack.
attack'er, *n.*, one who attacks.
attack'ing, *pr.p.*, attack.
attain', *v.t.* and *i.*, to reach, arrive at.
attainabil'ity, *n.*, the being able to be attained.
attain'able, *adj.*, able to be attained.
attain'ableness, *n.*, *s.q.* attainability.
attaind'er, *n.*, forfeiture of civil rights.
attained', *p.p.*, attain.
attain'ing, *pr.p.*, attain.
attain'ment, *n.*, act of attaining, something attained; intellectual gift.
attaint', *v.t.*, to impose attainder upon; *n.*, act of attainting.
attaint'ed, *p.p.*, attaint.
attaint'ing, *pr.p.*, attaint.
attaint'ment, *n.*, act of attainting.
attaint'ure, *n.*, dishonouring imputation; attainder.
at'tar, *n.*, Oriental word for perfume made from flowers.
attem'per, *v.t.*, to modify, adapt.
attem'pered, *p.p.*, attemper.
attem'pering, *pr.p.*, attemper.
attempt', *v.t.* and *i.*, to try, endeavour; *n.*, an endeavour.
attempt'able, *adj.*, able to be attempted.
attempt'ed, *p.p.*, attempt.
attempt'er, *n.*, one who attempts.
attempt'ing, *pr.p.*, attempt.
attend', *v.t.* and *i.*, to wait on, wait for; to be present; to pay attention to.
attend'ance, *n.*, the act of attending; persons present.
attend'ant, *n.*, one who looks after persons or things.
attend'ed, *p.p.*, attend.
attend'ing, *pr.p.*, attend.
attent', *n.*, attention.
atten'tion, *n.*, the giving heed.
atten'tive, *adj.*, giving heed.
atten'tively, *adv.*, with attention.
atten'tiveness, *n.*, the character of being attentive.
atten'uant, *adj.*, making thin.
atten'uate, *v.t.*, to make thin.
atten'uated, *p.p.*, attenuate.
atten'uating, *pr.p.*, attenuate.
attenua'tion, *n.*, the act of making thin; thinness.
attest', *v.t.*, to bear witness to.
attesta'tion, *n.*, the act of attesting.
attest'ed, *p.p.*, attest.
attest'er, **attest'or**, *n.*, one who attests.
attest'ing, *pr.p.*, attest.
At'tic, *adj.*, bel. to Attica in Greece.
at'tic, *n.*, a room in the roof of a house; a low storey above the entablature.
At'ticism, *n.*, the usage of Attica or the Athenians.
At'ticize, *v.t.* and *i.*, to make Attic, to become Attic.
At'ticized, *p.p.*, atticize.
At'ticizing, *pr.p.*, atticize.
attire', *v.t.*, to dress, array; *n.*, dress, clothes.
attired', *p.p.*, attire.
attir'er, *n.*, one who attires.
attir'ing, *pr.p.*, attire.
at'titude, *n.*, posture; state of mind.
attitu'dinal, *adj.*, rel. to attitude.
attitu'dinize, *v.i.*, to posture, to assume false airs.
attitu'dinized, *p.p.*, attitudinize.
attitu'dinizing, *pr.p.*, attitudinize.
attol'lent, *adj.*, elevating.
attor'ney, *n.*, the legal agent for another.
Attor'ney-*Gen'eral*, *n.*, the highest legal adviser of the Crown.
attor'neyship, *n.*, the office or function of an attorney.
attract', *v.t.*, to draw, allure, charm.
attractabil'ity, *n.*, the state of being subject to attraction.
attract'able, *adj.*, subject to attraction.
attract'ed, *p.p.*, attract.
attract'ing, *pr.p.*, attract.
attract'ingly, *adv.*, in an attracting way.
attrac'tion, *n.*, the act of attracting; charm; the unseen force in Nature drawing particles to each other.
attract'ive, *adj.*, able to attract; charming.
attract'ively, *adv.*, charmingly.
attract'iveness, *n.*, a power to charm.
at'trahent, *adj.*, drawing to.
attrib'utable, *adj.*, able to be attributed.
at'tribute, *n.*, something attributed; a quality or property.
attrib'ute, *v.t.*, to impute, ascribe.
attrib'uted, *p.p.*, attribute.
attrib'uting, *pr.p.*, attribute.
attribu'tion, *n.*, the act of attributing.
attrib'utive, *adj.*, rel. to an attribute; expressing an attribute; assigned to; *n.*, an adjective.
attrib'utively, *adv.*, as an attribute.
attrite', *adj.*, worn down.
attri'tion, *n.*, wearing down by rubbing.
attune', *v.t.*, to make in tune.
attuned', *p.p.*, attune.

attun'ing, *pr.p.*, attune.

atyp'ical, *adj.*, acquired by specialization; not according to type.

aubin', *n.*, a kind of canter (*Fr.*).

au'burn, *adj.*, reddish brown in colour.

auc'tion, *n.*, a public sale, where the prices are raised by the bidders; a development of the game of bridge.

auctioneer', *n.*, one who sells by auction.

auctioneer'ing, *adj.*, rel. to auctioneers; *n.*, an auctioneer's profession.

auda'cious, *adj.*, bold, daring, impudent.

auda'ciously, *adv.*, daringly, impudently.

auda'ciousness, *n.*, impudence.

audac'ity, *n.*, daring, impudence.

audibil'ity, *n.*, ability to be heard.

au'dible, *adj.*, able to be heard.

au'dibleness, *n.*, *i.q.* audibility.

au'dibly, *adv.*, in a way that can be heard.

au'dience, *n.*, hearing; collected hearers.

audiom'eter, *n.*, an apparatus for testing the power of hearing.

au'diphone, *n.*, an instrument for conveying sound through the teeth.

au'dit, *n.*, an official inspection of accounts; *v.t.*, to hold an official examination of accounts.

au'dited, *p.p.*, audit.

au'diting, *pr.p.*, audit.

audi'tion, *n.*, the sense of hearing; listening.

au'ditor, *n.*, a hearer; one who conducts an audit.

audito'rium, *n.*, the part of a building occupied by the audience.

au'ditory, *n.*, a body of hearers; an auditorium.

au fait, adjectival phrase = versed in; instructed (*Fr.*).

Auge'an, *adj.*, rel. to Augeas, a mythical king whose stables Hercules cleansed.

au'ger, *n.*, a boring instrument.

au'get, *n.*, a priming-tube so named.

aught, *n.*, anything.

au'gite, *n.*, another name for pyroxene.

aug'ment, *n.*, the addition to, or lengthening of, an initial syllable.

augment', *v.t.*, to increase, make larger.

augment'able, *adj.*, able to be augmented.

augmenta'tion, *n.*, the act of augmenting; increase.

augment'ative, *adj.*, tending to increase.

augment'ed, *p.p.*, augment.

augment'er, *n.*, one who augments.

augment'ing, *pr.p.*, augment.

au'gur, *n.*, a Roman soothsayer who divined by the flight of birds; *v.t.* and *i.*, to practise augury; to foretell.

au'gural, *adj.*, bel. to an augur.

au'gured, *p.p.*, augur.

au'guring, *pr.p.*, augur.

au'gurship, *n.*, the office of an augur.

au'gury, *n.*, the art of an augur; an omen.

Au'gust, *n.*, the 8th month of the year, named from the Emperor Augustus.

august', *adj.*, grand, venerable.

august'ly, *adv.*, in an august manner.

Augus'tan, *adj.*, rel. to Augustus.

Augus'tine, *n.*, the saintly bishop of Hippo; also his later namesake, the Apostle of the English.

Augustin'ians, *n. pl.*, those who follow the rule of the Order named after St. Augustine.

august'ness, *n.*, stateliness, majesty.

auk, *n.*, an aquatic bird so named.

aula'rian, *adj.*, bel. to a hall.

au'lic, *adj.*, rel. to a court, as the Aulic Council.

aunt, *n.*, a female relative (a mother's or father's sister).

aunt'ie, *n.*, the childish name for aunt.

au'ra, *n.*, a breeze, air, subtle emanation.

au'ral, *adj.*, rel. to the ear.

au'rally, *adv.*, through the ear.

au'rated, *adj.*, eared.

au'reate, *adj.*, golden, gilded.

aure'lia, *n.*, a chrysalis.

aure'lian, *adj.*, in the chrysalis state.

aure'ola, *n.*, a halo; the sun's corona.

au'reole, *n.*, a halo or circlet of light.

au'ric, *adj.*, containing gold.

au'ricle, *n.*, the projecting body of an ear; one of the heart's cavities.

au'ricled, *adj.*, having auricles.

auric'ula, *n.*, the Alpine primrose; a little appendage, ear-shaped = auricle.

auric'ular, *adj.*, rel. to the ear or hearing; spoken into the ear, as in Confession.

auric'ularly, *adv.*, privately.

auric'ulate, *adj.*, having auricles.

auric'ulated, *adj.*, *i.q.* auriculate.

aurif'erous, *adj.*, gold-producing.

au'riform, *adj.*, ear-shaped.

aurig'raphy, *n.*, gold-engraving.

au'rist, *n.*, one who treats ear complaints.

au'rochs, *adj.*, the bison or wild ox of Europe.

auro'ra, *n.*, the dawn.

auro'ra borea'lis, *n.*, the northern lights.

auro'ral, *adj.*, rel. to the dawn.

au'rum, *n.*, gold (*Lat.*).

ausculta'tion, *n.*, hearing through a stethoscope.

aus'cultator, *n.*, one who examines a patient with a stethoscope.

auscult'ative, *adj.*, *i.q.*, auscultatory.

auscul'tatory, *adj.*, rel. to auscultation.

au'spicate, *v.t.*, to invoke good luck on.

au'spicated, *p.p.*, auspicate.

au'spicating, *pr.p.*, auspicate.

au'spice, *n.*, omen.

au'spices, *n. pl.*, influence, protection.

auspi'cious, *adj.*, lucky, of good omen.

auspi'ciously, *adv.*, luckily, with good omen.

auspi'ciousness, *n.*, a state of good omen.

austere', *adj.*, severe, stern, harsh.

austere'ly, *adv.*, severely, sternly, harshly.

auster'ity, *n.*, severity, sternness, harshness. [ern.

aus'tral, *adj.*, south-

Australa'sian, *adj.*, bel. to Australasia.

Austra'lian, *adj.*, bel. to Australia.

Aus'trian, *adj.*, pert. to Austria and the Austrians.

aus'tromancy, *n.*, divination by means of the wind.

authen'tic, *adj.*, true, real, actual.

authen'tical, *adj.*, *i.q.* authentic.

authen'ticate, *v.t.*, to verify, prove to be real.

authen'ticated, *p.p.*, authenticate.

authen'ticating, *pr.p.*, authenticate.

authentica'tion, *n.*, the act of authenticating.

authentic'ity, *n.* truth, reality.

au'thor, *n.*, a beginner, creator, writer.

au'thoress, *n.*, fem. of author.

author'itative, *adj.*, having authority.

author'itatively, *adv.*, as having authority.

author'itativeness, *n.*, the character of having authority or sanction.

author'ity, *n.*, power, right; a recognized expert; in pl. = the powers that be.

au'thorizable, *adj.*, able to be authorized.

authoriza'tion, *n.*, the granting of authority or sanction.

au'thorize, *v.t.*, to give authority to, to sanction.

au'thorized, *p.p.* authorize.

au'thorizing *pr.p.*, authorize.

au'thorship, *n.*, the writing of a book or article.

autobiog'rapher, *n.*, one who writes his own biography or life.

autobiograph'ic, *adj.*, rel. to autobiography.

autobiograph'ical, *adj* *i.q.* autobiographic.

autobiog'raphy, *n.*, a biography of oneself by oneself.

aut'ocar, *n.*, an automobile vehicle.

autoch'thon, *n.*, a native of the soil.

autoch'thonous, *adj.*, native, indigenous.

autoc'racy, *n.*, government by an absolute monarch.

au'tocrat, *n.*, one who rules absolutely.

autocrat'ic, *adj.*, ruling absolutely.

autocrat'ical, *adj.*, *i.q.* autocratic.

au'to-da-fé, *n.*, phrase = an act of faith.

autog'enous, *adj.*, self-producing.

au'tograph, *n.*, writing in one's own hand.

autograph'ic, *adj.*, written in one's own hand.

autograph'ical, *adj.*, *i.q.* autographic.

autog'raphy, *n.*, writing in one's own hand.

autom'ata, *n.*, pl. of automaton.

au'tomath, *n.*, a self-taught person.

automat'ic, *adj*, self-moving, self-acting.

automat'ical, *adj.*, *i.q.* automatic.

automat'ically, *adv.*, mechanically.

autom'atism, *n.*, the principle of self-action.

autom'aton, *n.*, a self-moving, self-acting instrument.

automobile', *adj.*, self-moving; *n.*, a carriage actuated by its own motive power.

au'tomotor, *n.*, a self-moving engine.

autonom'ic, *adj.*, *i.q.* autonomous.

auton'omize, *v.t.*, to make autonomous.

auton'omous, *adj.*, obeying one's own laws, self-governing.

auton'omy, *n.*, self-government, independence.

autop'sia, *n.*, personal examination (of a dead body).

autop'sy, *n.*, *i.q.* autopsia.

au'totype, *n.*, a facsimile; a photographic print in monochrome in a carbon pigment.

au'tumn, *n.*, the third of the seasons.

autum'nal, *adj.*, of the autumn.

auxil'iaries, *n.*, assistant troops, not forming part of the regular forces.

auxil'iary, *adj.*, helping; *n.*, a helper.

avail', *v.i.*, to profit, be of use, to serve a purpose.

availabil'ity, *n.*, ability to be used.

avail'able, *adj.*, able to be used.

avail'ableness, *n.* *i.q.* availability.

availed, *p.p.*, avail.

avail'ing, *pr.p.*, avail.
av'alanche, *n.*, a great fall of snow in mountains.
av'arice, *n.*, greed for gain.
avari'cious, *adj.*, greedy for gain.
avari'ciously, *adv.*, greedily.
avari'ciousness, *n.*, an avaricious temper.
avast', *interj.*, stop!
avatar', *n.*, a descent; incarnation.
avaunt', *interj.* = stand! keep off!
a've, an exclamation = Hail! *n.*, the act of devotion so named.
A've Mari'a, phrase = Hail Mary! the salutation to Our Lady.
avenge', *v.t.*, to exact satisfaction for a wrong.
avenged', *p.p.*, avenge.
aveng'er, *n.*, one who avenges.
aveng'ing, *pr.p.*, avenge.
av'ens, *n.*, a plant so named, bel. to the *Rosaceae*.
av'entail, *n.*, an air-hole, ventail.
av'enue, *n.*, an approach or passage, esp. through trees.
aver', *v.t.*, to state firmly.
av'erage, *n.*, a mean or middle; a general estimate; *adj.*, conforming to a general estimate, *v.t.* and *i.*, to get or conform to a general estimate.
av'eraged *p.p.*, average.
av'eraging *pr.p.*, average.
aver'ment, *n.*, a positive statement.
averred', *p.p.*, aver.
aver'ring, *pr.p.*, aver.
averse', *adj.*, turned away from; disinclined, unfavourable to.
averse'ly, *adv.*, disapprovingly.
aver'sion, *n.*, strong dislike.
avert', *v.t.*, to turn aside; to ward off.
avert'ed, *p.p.*, avert.
avert'er, *n.*, one who averts.
avert'ible, *adj.*, able to be averted.
avert'ing, *pr.p.*, avert.
a'viary, *n.*, a collection of birds; large cage.
avia'tion, *n.*, the art and science of aerial flight.
a'viator, *n.*, one who practises aviation.
av'id, *adj.*, greedy, very desirous.
avid'ious, *adj.*, *i.q.* avid.
avid'ity, *n.*, greediness, eagerness.
a'vion, *n.*, the earliest type of heavier-than-air machine.
avoca'tion, *n.*, strictly, the word means a recreation, a calling away from business. Nowadays it is used as the equivalent of vocation = employment.
avoc'ative, *adj.*, calling one aside.
av'ocet, *n.*, a wader-bird so named; also a humming-bird.
avoid', *v.t.*, to get away from, escape.
avoid'able, *adj.*, that can be avoided.
avoid'ably, *adv.*, in an avoidable way.
avoid'ance, *n.*, the act of avoiding.
avoid'ed, *p.p.*, avoid.
avoid'er, *n.*, one who avoids.
avoid'ing, *pr.p.*, avoid.
avoirdupois', *n.* and *adj.*, a standard of weight, reckoning 16 oz. to the lb.
av'oset, *n.*, *i.q.* avocet.
avoset'ta, *n.*, *i.q.* avocet.
avouch', *v.t.*, to affirm strongly.
avouched', *p.p.*, avouch.
avouch'er, *n.*, one who avouches.
avouch'ing, *pr.p.*, avouch.
avouch'ment, *n.*, a strong affirmation.
avow', *v.t.*, to state openly, confess.
avow'able, *adj.*, able to be avowed.
avow'al, *n.*, the act of avowing, an admission.
avowed', *p.p.*, avow.
avow'edly, *adv.*, admittedly, openly.
avowee', *n.*, a patron possessing an advowson.
avow'er, *n.*, one who avows.
avow'ing, *pr.p.*, avow.
avow'ry, *n.*, a law term for the acknowledgment of having taken the goods.
avulse', *v.t.*, to tear off.
avul'sion, *n.*, the act of rending.
avun'cular, *adj.*, rel. to an uncle.
await', *v.t.*, to wait for, expect.
await'ed, *p.p.*, await.
await'ing, *pr.p.*, await.
awake', *v.t.* and *i.*, to rouse from sleep, to rise from sleep; *adj.*, not asleep, alert.
awaked', *p.p.*, awake.
awa'ken, *v.t.*, to rouse from sleep.
awa'kened, *p.p.*, awaken.
awa'kening, *pr.p.*, awaken; *n.*, the act or effect of awakening.
awa'king, *pr.p.*, awake.
award', *v.t.*, to make over, adjudge; *n.*, a final judgment.
award'ed, *p.p.*, award.
award'er, *n.*, one who awards.
award'ing, *pr.p.* award.
aware', *adj.*, knowing, on the look out.
awash', *adv.* and *adj.*, just covered by the waves.
away', *adv.*, at a distance, to a distance, off.
awe, *n.*, reverential fear; *v.t.*, to strike awe into.
a-weath'er, *adv.*, towards the windy side.
awed, *p.p.*, awe.
a-weigh', *adv.*, said when the anchor just clears the bottom.
awe'less, *adj.*, without awe.

awe'some, *adj.*, *i.q.* awful.

awe'-struck, *adj.*, struck with awe.

aw'ful, *adj.*, producing awe, terrible.

aw'fully, *adv.*, terribly.

aw'fulness, *n.*, terrifying character.

awhile', *adv.*, for a time.

awhirl', *adv.*, in a whirling state.

aw'ing, *pr.p.*, awe.

awk'ward, *adj.*, clumsy, embarrassing.

awk'wardly, *adv.*, clumsily.

awk'wardness, *n.*, clumsiness, difficulty.

awl, *n.*, a cobbler's tool for piercing.

awn, *n.*, the beard of wheat.

awn'ing, *n.*, a cover for shelter.

awoke', *p.t.* awake.

awry', *adv.*, twisted aside.

axe, *n.*, a tool for cutting timber.

axe'-head, *n.*, the iron head of an axe.

ax'ial, *adj.*, rel. to an axis.

axif'erous, *adj.*, bearing an axis.

ax'iform, *adj.*, like an axis.

ax'il, *n.*, the angle at the junction of the upper side of a lateral member with the stem.

ax'ile, *adj.*, rel. to an axis.

axil'la, *n.*, the armpit.

ax'illar, *adj.*, *i.q.* axillary; *n.*, one of the under feathers of a bird where the wing joins the body.

ax'illary, *adj.*, rel. to an axil or axilla.

ax'inite, *n.*, a mineral so named.

ax'iom, *n.*, a universally agreed principle or proposition.

axiomat'ic, *adj.*, universally agreed upon, unarguable.

axiomat'ical, *adj.*, *i.q.* axiomatic.

ax'is, *n.*, a straight line on which a body revolves; the stem of a plant.

ax'le, *n.*, the pin round which a wheel turns.

ax'le-box, *n.*, the metal lining of a hub.

ax'led, *adj.*, having an axle.

ax'le-tree, *n.* *i.q.* axle.

ay, *interj.*, = yes.

a yah, *n.*, a Hindu female nurse.

aye, *adv.*, always, for ever.

aza'lea, *n.*, a flowering shrub so named.

az'imuth, *n.*, an arc of the horizon intercepted between the meridian and another vertical circle.

az'imuthal, *adj.*, rel. to an azimuth.

azo'ic, *adj.*, without organic life.

az'ote, *n.*, an older name for nitrogen.

az'oth, *n.*, the alchemist's name for mercury.

azot'ic, *adj.*, nitrogenous.

Az'tec, *n.*, one of the Aztec people.

az'ure, *adj.*, sky-blue; *n.*, the blue sky.

az'urine, *n.*, an aniline colour, deep blue.

az'ygous, *adj.*, unpaired.

az'ymite, *n.*, a user of unleavened bread.

az'ymous, *adj.*, rel. to unleavened bread.

B

baa, *interj.* and *n.*, the cry of a sheep.

Ba'al, *n.*, a Canaanitish deity, supposed to represent the sun.

bab'ble, *v.t.* and *i.*, to talk indistinctly or idly, to murmur; *n.*, idle talk.

bab'bled, *p.p.*, babble.

bab'blement, *n.*, babble.

bab'bler, *n.*, one who babbles, a teller of secrets.

bab'bling, *pr.p.*, babble.

babe, *n.*, an infant, young child of either sex.

Ba'bel, *n.*, the city where the confusion of tongues took place; a confused mixture of sounds; disorder.

ba'bery, *n.*, tawdry finery.

ba'boo, ba'bu, *n.*, Hindu word = master.

baboon', *n.*, a large species of ape or monkey.

ba'by, *n.*, a babe.

ba'byhood, *n.*, the state of being a baby; infancy.

ba'byish, *adj.*, childish.

Babylo'nian, *adj.*, bel. to Babylon or Babel.

Babylo'nish, *adj.*, Babylonian.

baccalau'reate, *n.*, the degree of Bachelor of Arts, etc.

baccara', baccarat', *n.*, a game of cards.

bac'cate, *adj.*, bearing berries; like a berry.

bac'chanal, *adj.*, *s.q.* bacchanalian; *n.*, a votary of Bacchus, a drunken reveller.

bacchana'lian, *adj.*, riotous, characterized by intemperate drinking.

bac'chant, *n.*, a priest of Bacchus.

bacchan'te, *n.*, a priestess of Bacchus, a female bacchanal.

bac'chic, *adj.*, rel. to Bacchus, drunken.

Bac'chus, *n.*, the classical god of wine.

baccif'erous, *adj.*, producing berries.

bacciv'orous, *adj.*, feeding on berries.

bach'elor, *n.*, an unmarried man; a university man who has taken his first degree.

bach'elorhood, *n.*, the state or period of being a bachelor.

bacil'li, *n.*, pl. of bacillus.

bacil'lus, *n.*, a microscopic organism, the source of disease, a bacterium.

back, *n.*, the hinder part; *adv.*, toward a former place, state, or condition; *adj.*, lying in the rear; *v.t.*, to support; to endorse; to move backward; *v.i.*, to move or go back.

back'bar, *n.*, a bar to support the back.

back'bite, *v.t.*, to slander an absent person.

back'biter, *n.*, one who backbites.

back'biting, *pr.p.*, backbite; *n.*, secret calumny.

back'board, *n.*, a board used to give erectness to the spine.

back'bone, *n.*, the spine; *fig.*, decision of character.

back'-door', *n.*, a door at the back of a building.

backed, *p.p.*, back; *adj.*, having a back.

back'er, *n.*, one who backs; one who bets in favour of a particular party in a contest.

back'fire, *v.i.*, to explode prematurely; *n.*, the act of backfiring.

back'fired, *p.p.*, backfire.

back'firing, *pr.p.*, backfire.

backgam'mon, *n.*, a game for two played on a prepared board with pieces or men and dice.

back'ground, *n.*, the part of a picture represented as farthest from the spectator; a state of being out of view.

back'handed, *adj.*, with the hand turned backward; oblique; sloping back; unfair.

back'hander, *n.*, an indirect blow.

back'house, *n.*, an outbuilding behind a house.

back'ing, *pr.p.*, back; *n.*, support.

back'lash, *n.*, the motion that has been missed between working parts of a machine.

back'side, *n.*, the back part of anything.

back'sight, *n.*, the rear sight of a gun, rifle, etc.

back'slide, *v.i.*, to fall away from religion or morality.

back'slider, *n.*, one who backslides.

back'sliding, *n.*, falling away from faith or practice.

back'stairs, *n.*, stairs in the back part of a house; *adj.*, secret and unfair, underhand.

back'stay, *n.*, a long rope from the top of a mast backwards to the side of a ship helping to support the mast.

back'sword, *n.*, a singlestick.

back'ward, *adv.* and *adj.*, toward the back; in a contrary manner or direction.

back'wardly, *adv.*, unwillingly.

back'wardness, *n.*, the state of being backward.

back'wards, *adv.*, backward.

back'wash, *n.*, the movement of a retiring wave.

back'water, *n.*, water turned back in its course by an obstruction; *v.i.*, to reverse the rowing.

back'woods, *n. pl.* (U.S.A. and Canada), forest districts remote from the more thickly settled parts.

back'woodsman, *n.*, inhabitant of the backwoods.

back'yard, *n.*, an enclosure in the rear of a house.

ba'con, *n.*, swine's flesh pickled and dried.

Baco'nian, *adj.*, pert. to Bacon, his philosophy and theories; *n.*, esp. one who believes that Bacon was the author of the works of Shakespeare.

bacte'ria, *n.*, pl. of bacterium.

bacte'rial, *adj.*, rel. to bacteria.

bacte'rian, *adj.*, *s.q.* bacterial.

bacteriol'ogy, *n.*, the science rel. to bacteria.

bacte'rium, *n.*, a minute organism found in organic matter, diseased animal tissues, etc.

bad, *adj.*, the opposite of good; wanting good qualities, physical or moral.

bade, *p.t.*, bid.

badge, *n.*, a mark or token worn to show connexion between the wearer and some other person, occupation, or condition.

badg'er, *n.*, a small mammal of nocturnal habits, carnivorous, and living in a burrow; *v.t.*, to worry or annoy.

badg'ered, *p.p.*, badger.

badg'ering, *pr.p.*, badger.

badi'geon, *n.*, a mixture of plaster and other substances used to fill up small holes in joiners' work.

bad'inage, *n.*, playful talk; chaff.

bad'ly, *adv.*, in a bad manner, unskilfully.

bad'minton, *n.*, a game like lawn-tennis, but played with shuttlecocks; a kind of claret-cup.

bad'ness, *n.*, the state of being bad.

baf'fle, *v.t.*, to elude or defeat.

baf'fled, *p.p.*, baffle.

baf'fler, *n.*, one who baffles.

baf'fling, *pr.p.*, baffle; *adj.*, baulking.

bag, *n.*, a sack; *v.t.*, to put into a bag; *v.i.*, to swell or hang like a bag.

bagatelle', *n.*, a trifle; a game played with a cue and balls on a board having nine holes at one end.

bag'gage, *n.*, luggage; the necessaries of an army.

bagged, *p.p.*, bag.

bag'ging, *pr.p.*, bag; *n.*, the cloth or other materials for bags.

bag'gy, *adj.*, puffy; looking like a bag.

bag'man, *n.*, a commercial traveller (slang).

bagn'io, *n.*, a bath; a brothel.

bag'pipe, *n.*, a musical wind instrument, consisting of a leather bag which receives air from the mouth or a bellows, and of pipes into which the air is driven by the performer's elbow.

bag'piper, *n.*, one who plays on a bagpipe.

bail, *n.*, a little stick placed on the stumps at cricket; legal security; *v.t.*, to free from water with a bucket or the like; to liberate from imprisonment on security.

bail'able, *adj.*, admitting of bail.

bailed, *p.p.*, bail.

bailee', *n.*, a person to whom goods are entrusted.

bail'er, *n.*, one who, or that which, bails.

bai'lie, *n.*, a Scottish alderman.

bai'liff, *n.*, a subordinate civil officer; an under-steward on an estate.

bail'ing, *pr.p.*, bail.

bai'liwick, *n.*, the precincts within which a bailiff has authority.

bail'ment, *n.*, the act of bailing an accused person.

bailor', *n.*, one who delivers goods or money to another in trust.

bairn, *n.*, a child.

bait, *v.t.*, to feed a beast when travelling; to lure fish or other animals; to harass by dogs; *n.*, a lure to catch fish.

bait'ed, *p.p.*, bait.

bait'ing, *pr.p.*, bait.

baize, *n.*, a coarse woollen stuff with a long nap.

bake, *v.t.*, to dry and harden by heat; to prepare in an oven.

baked, *p.p.*, bake.

bake'house, *n.*, a building for baking.

bake'meat, *n.*, meat cooked in an oven; a meat-pie.

bak'er, *n.*, one who bakes.

Bak'erloo, *n.*, a "portmanteau" word, the name of the railway line between Baker St. and Waterloo.

bak'ery *n.*, a bakehouse.

bak'ing, *pr.p.*, bake.

bak'sheesh, *n.*, a gratuity of money (an Eastern term).

bal'ance, *n.*, an instrument for ascertaining the weight of a body; surplus—the difference of two sums; the part of a clock that regulates the beats: *v.t.*, to weigh; to examine a merchant's books by summation; *v.i.*, to be equal on both sides of an account.

bal'anced. *p.p.*, balance.

bal'ancer, *n.*, one who, or that which, balances.

bal'ance-sheet, *n.*, a statement of assets and liabilities.

bal'ancing, *pr.p.*, balance.

bal'as-ru'by, *n.*, a species of ruby.

bal'ata, *n.*, a gum resembling rubber, and used for insulating purposes and as a substitute for shoe-leather.

bal'conied, *adj.*, having balconies.

bal'cony, *n.*, a projecting gallery in a theatre; a projecting platform, with a balustrade, on the outside of a building.

bald, *adj.*, without, or with little, hair; unadorned.

bal'dachin, *n.*, a canopy; also *baldachino* and *baudequin* (orig. the canopy was of cloth from Baldacca, *i.e.* Bagdad).

bal'derdash, *n.*, nonsense.

bald'head, *n.*, a man bald on the head.

bald'ly, *adv.*, meanly, inelegantly.

bald'ness, *n.*, the state of being bald.

bal'dric, *n.*, a broad belt worn diagonally across the body.

bale, *n.*, a bundle of goods; calamity; *v.t.*, to bail (water).

Balear'ic, *adj.*, pert. to a Spanish group of islands in the Mediterranean.

baled, *p.p.*, bale.

bale'-fire, *n.*, an alarm fire.

bale'ful, *adj.*, pernicious, calamitous.

bale'fully, *adv.*, in a baleful manner.

bale'fulness, *n.*, the state of being baleful.

bal'ing, *pr.p.*, bale.

balize', *n.*, a landmark or sea-beacon.

balk, *n.*, a thick beam; a disappointment; *v.t.*, to bar the way of. Also *baulk.*

balked, *p.p.*, balk.

balk'ing, *pr.p.*, balk.

ball, *n.*, a round body, a bullet; *v.t.* and *i.*, to form into a ball.

bal'lad, *n.*, a short narrative poem.

bal'lad-mon'ger, *n.*, a dealer in ballads, an inferior poet.

bal'last, *n.*, heavy matter carried in a ship which has no cargo; material between the rails of a railway: *v.t.*, to steady.

bal'lasted *p.p.*, ballast.

bal'lasting, *n.*, materials for ballast: *pr.p.*, ballast.

ball'-cock, *n.*, an automatic stop-cock consisting of a hollow sphere floating on the surface of a liquid and attached to a lever connected with the cock.

balled, *p.p.*, ball.

bal'let, *n.*, an elaborate dance in which several persons take part, the action conveying a story.

bal'let, *n.*, a little ball.

ball'ing, *pr.p.*, ball.

ballis'ta, *n.*, an ancient military engine for throwing heavy missiles; a sort of catapult; *pl.*, ballistae.

ballis'ter, *n.*, a crossbow.

ballis'tic, *adj.*, pert. to the ballista.

ballis'tics, *n.*, the science rel. to projectiles.

ballis'tite, *n.*, a very high explosive.

balloon', *n.*, a large hollow sphere, esp. a large bag filled with a light gas, capable of rising in the air.

balloon'ing, *n.*, the art of managing balloons.

balloon'ist, *n.*, one who ascends in a balloon.

bal'lot, *n.*, a ball or paper by which one votes secretly; the system of voting in this way; a lottery: *v.i.*, to vote secretly.

bal'lot-box, *n.* a box for receiving ballots.

bal'loted *p.p.*, ballot.

bal'loting, *pr.p.*, ballot.

ball'-room, *n.*, a large room for dancing.

balm, *n.*, a fragrant ointment; anything that soothes pain.

balm'ily, *adv.*, in a balmy manner.

balm'iness, *n.*, the quality of being balmy.

balm'y, *adj.*, fragrant; soothing; refreshing.

bal'neal, *adj.*, pert. to a bath.

bal'sam, *n.*, an aromatic, resinous substance flowing from certain plants, and used in medicine.

balsam'ic, *adj.*, having the qualities of balsam.

balsam'ical, *adj.*, balsamic.

balsamif'erous, *adj.*, producing balsam.

Bal'tic, *adj.*, pert. to the Baltic Sea.

bal'uster, *n.*, a small column used for balustrades.

bal'ustered, *adj.*, having balusters.

balustrade', *n.*, a row of balusters joined by a rail.

bambi'no, *n.* a baby; a figure of the Infant Jesus.

bamboo', *n.*, a tropical grass with large, jointed stems.

bamboo'zle, *v.t.*, to impose upon, deceive.

bamboo'zled, *p.p.*, bamboozle.

bamboo'zling, *pr.p.*, bamboozle.

ban, *n.*, a prohibition; a curse; *v.t.*, to put under a curse; proscribe.

ban'al, *adj.*, commonplace, vulgar.

banal'ity, *n.*, that which is banal.

bana'na, *n.*, a herbaceous plant akin to the plantain, bearing soft, luscious fruit.

ban'co, *n.*, a standard of money in which some banks keep their accounts; a seat or bench of justice.

band, *n.*, a connection; a narrow strip; a company of men, esp. soldiers, a body of instrumental musicians; *v.t.* and *i.*, to associate for some common purpose.

band'age, *n.*, a roller used in binding up wounds; *v.t.*, to put a bandage on.

band'aged, *p.p.*, bandage.

band'aging *pr.p.*, bandage.

bandan'na, *n.*, an Indian silk handkerchief.

band'box, *n.*, a light box of pasteboard for containing bonnets, etc.

band'eau, *n.*, a ribbon for the forehead.

band'ed, *p.p.*, band.

band'elet, *n.*, a small band or fillet.

ban'der, *n.*, one banded with others.

ban'derole, *n.*, a little flag; a military weapon; a trumpet.

ban'dicoot, *n.*, a large Indian rat eaten by coolies.

band'ied, *p.p.*, bandy.

band'ing, *pr.p.*, band.

ban'dit, *n.*, a robber, an outlaw.

bandit'ti, *n.*, pl. of bandit.

ban'dog, *n.*, a large, fierce dog, a mastiff, usually kept chained.

bandoleer', bandolier', *n.*, a shoulder-belt for cartridges.

bandore', *n.*, a stringed musical instrument, a sort of lyre.

band'roll, *n.*, a banderole.

bands'man, *n.*, a player in a band.

band-stand, *n.*, an open-air platform for a band of musicians.

ban'dy, *n.*, a sort of hockey-stick; the game played with these sticks and a ball; *v.t.*, to toss to and fro; *a.* bent.

ban'dying, *pr.p.*, bandy.

ban'dy-leg, *n.*, a bent or crooked leg.

ban'dy-legged, *adj.*, having bent legs.

bane, *n.*, any cause of destruction; deadly poison.

bane'ful, *adj.*, destructive, poisonous.

bane'fully, *adv.*, in a baneful way.

bane'fulness, *n.*, the quality of being baneful.

bang, *v.t.*, to beat; to make a loud noise; *n.*, a loud noise, a heavy blow.

banged, *p.p.*, bang.

bang'ing, *pr.p.*, bang.

ban'gle, *n.*, an ornamental ring for wrist or ankle.

bangue, *i.q.* bhang.

ban'ish, *v.t.*, to drive away, to exile.

ban'ished, *p.p.*, banish.

ban'isher, *n.*, one who banishes.

ban'ishing, *pr.p.*, banish.

ban'ishment, *n.*, exile; the act of banishing.

ban'ister, *n.*, a baluster, an upright in a stair-rail.

ban'jo, *n.*, a musical instrument with six strings, a body like a tambourine, and a neck like a guitar.

bank, *n.*, a mound; any acclivity; an establishment that trades in money; *v.i.*, to enclose with a bank, to put money in a bank; to turn quickly (an aircraft term).

bank'-bill, *n.*, a bill of exchange payable to order and negotiable.

bank'book, *n.*, a book in which debits and credits are entered by the officials of a bank.

banked, *p.p.*, bank.

bank'er, *n.*, one who keeps a bank.

bank'ing, *n.*, the business of a banker; making a turn with an aeroplane, inner side downwards; *pr.p.*, bank.

bank'-note, *n.*, a promissory note payable on demand, issued by a bank.

bank'rupt, *n.*, a person declared by legal authority to be unable to pay his debts.

bank'ruptcy, *n.*, the state of being a bankrupt.

bank'rupted, *adj.*, declared bankrupt.

bank'-stock, *n.*, a share or shares in the capital of a bank.

banned, *p.p.*, ban.

ban'ner, *n.*, a large square flag bearing heraldic devices.

ban'nered, *adj.*, having a banner.

ban'neret, *n.*, a knight intermediate in rank between a baron and a knight bachelor, raised to this rank for bravery in the field.

ban'nerol, *n.*, a little flag, a banderole.

ban'ning, *pr.p.*, ban.

ban'nock, *n.*, (*Scot.*), an unleavened cake made of meal and baked on an iron plate over a fire.

banns, *n. pl.*, a proclamation in church of an intended marriage.

ban'quet, *n.*, a feast; *v.t.* and *i.*, to feast.

ban'queted, *p.p.*, banquet.

ban'queter, *n.,* one who banquets.

ban'queting, *pr.p.,* banquet.

banquette', *n.,* a little raised bank inside the parapet of a fortification; the raised footway of a bridge.

bans, *n.,* pl. of ban.

ban'shee, *n.,* a female fairy whose appearance foretells a death (*Irish*).

ban'stickle, *n.,* a stickleback.

ban'tam, *n.,* a diminutive domestic fowl of great courage.

ban'ter, *v.t.,* to make fun of, to attack with jests; *n.,* humorous raillery, chaff.

ban'tered, *p.p.,* banter.

ban'terer, *n.,* one who banters.

ban'tering, *pr.p.,* banter.

bant'ling, *n.,* an infant (contemptuous).

ban'yan, *n.,* a kind of Indian fig tree whose branches send down shoots which take root and become trunks.

ba'obab, *n.,* a large African tree bearing a pulpy fruit called monkey-bread.

bap'tism, *n.,* immersion; the Sacrament of entrance into the Catholic Church.

baptis'mal, *adj.,* pert. to baptism.

Bap'tist, *n.,* one who baptizes, esp. St. John, the forerunner of Our Lord; a member of the Baptist sect.

bap'tistery, *n.,* a building or portion of a building where baptism is administered.

baptis'tic, *adj.,* rel. to baptism.

bapti'zable, *adj.,* capable of being baptized.

baptize', *v.t.,* to administer the sacrament of baptism to; to christen.

baptized', *p.p.,* baptize.

bapti'zer, *n.,* one who baptizes.

bapti'zing, *pr.p.,* baptize.

bar, *n.,* a pole; an obstruction; a bank of sand, etc., at the mouth of a river, the place in court where prisoners are placed; the profession of barrister; the enclosed place in a tavern where liquor is served; in music, a vertical line on the staff; *v.t.,* to fasten with a bar, to hinder, to exclude.

barb, *n.,* the sharp point projecting backwards of an arrow, fish hook, etc.; a Barbary horse; *v.t.,* to furnish with barbs, as an arrow.

bar'bacan, *n.,* a watch-tower; an advanced work before the gate of a walled town or castle.

Barba'dian, *adj.,* bel. to Barbados; *n.,* an inhabitant of Barbados.

barba'rian, *n.,* an uncivilized person; a brutal man.

barbar'ic, *adj.,* savage, wild; ornate, but not in good taste.

bar'barism, *n.,* an outrage; any offence against good taste; any form of speech contrary to correct idiom.

barbar'ity, *n.,* savageness, ferocity.

bar'barize, *v.i.,* to become barbarous; *v.t.* to make barbarous.

bar'barized, *p.p.,* barbarize.

bar'barizing, *pr.p.,* barbarize.

bar'barous, *adj.,* uncivilized, ignorant; cruel, brutal.

bar'barously, *adv.,* in a barbarous manner.

bar'barousness, *n.,* barbarity.

bar'bate, *adj.,* bearded.

bar'becue, *n.,* a large animal roasted whole; *v.t.,* to cook whole by roasting.

bar'becued, *p.p.,* barbecue.

bar'becuing, *pr.p.,* barbecue.

barbed, *adj.,* furnished with barbs; *p.p.,* barb.

bar'bel, *n.,* a fresh-water fish with four beard-like appendages on its upper jaw.

bar'bellate, *adj.,* having short, stiff hairs, often barbed.

bar'ber, *n.,* one whose occupation it is to shave the beard.

bar'berry, *n.,* a shrub bearing small acid berries, common in hedges.

bar'bet, *n.,* a dog with curly hair, a poodle.

barbette', *n.,* a platform in a fortification or on a ship of war, from which a cannon may be fired over the parapet instead of through an embrasure.

bar'bican, *n.,* a barbacan.

bar'bule, *n.,* a small barb; a little beard.

bar'carole, *n.,* a Venetian boat-song.

bard, *n.,* a poet, esp. a Celtic poet or singer.

bard'ic, *adj.,* pert. to bards.

bard'ism, *n.,* bardic lore.

bare, *adj.,* naked, empty, much worn; *v.t.,* to strip naked.

bare'bone, *adj.,* very lean.

bared, *p.p.,* bare.

bare'faced, *adj.,* impudent.

bare'facedness, *n.,* effrontery, impudence.

bare'foot, *adj.,* with bare feet.

bare'footed, *adj.,* barefoot.

barége', *n.,* a thin, gauze-like fabric.

bare'headed, *adj.,* having the head uncovered.

bare'ly, *adv.*, nakedly, without decoration; scarcely.

bare'ness, *n.*, the state of being bare.

bar'gain, *n.*, an agreement; the thing stipulated for; something bought or sold cheap; *v.i.*, to make an agreement.

bar'gained, *p.p.*, bargain.

bargainee, *n.*, the party who receives the property bargained for.

bar'gainer, *n.*, one who bargains.

bar'gaining, *pr.p.*, bargain.

barge, *n.*, a boat used ceremonially; a flat-bottomed boat for carrying goods.

barge'man, *n.*, a man who manages a barge.

baril'la, *n.*, an impure soda got by burning certain plants, esp. sea-weeds.

bar'ing, *pr.p.*, bare.

bar'-iron, *n.*, iron smelted from the ore in long rods.

bar'itone, *adj.*, between tenor and bass; *n.*, a baritone voice or singer.

ba'rium, *n.*, a metal.

bark, *n.*, the outer rind of a tree, shrub, etc.; a barque; the cry of a dog; *v.t.*, to peel; *v.i.*, to cry like a dog.

barked, *p.p.*, bark.

bar'keeper, *n.*, a server at a tavern bar.

bark'er, *n.*, one who barks; a pistol (slang).

bark'ery, *n.*, a tan-house.

bark'ing, *pr.p.*, bark.

bark'y, *adj.*, having the qualities of bark.

bar'ley, *n.*, a kind of grain.

bar'ley-broth, *n.*, broth containing barley.

bar'ley-corn, *n.*, a grain of barley; a measure equal to a third of an inch· a rifle foresight.

bar'ley-meal, *n.*, meal made by crushing barley.

barm, *n.*, yeast.

bar'maid, *n.*, a woman who serves in a tavern.

Bar'mecide, *adj.*, unreal, illusory.

barm'y, *adj.*, containing barm; frothy.

barn, *n.*, a covered building to contain farm produce.

bar'nacle, *n.*, a stalked sea shell-fish, often found attached to ships' bottoms; a species of goose.

bar'ograph, *n.*, a recording barometer.

bar'olite, *n.*, a kind of barytes.

barom'eter, *n.*, an instrument for measuring the weight or pressure of the atmosphere.

baromet'ric, *adj.*, pert. to the barometer.

baromet'rical, *adj.*, *i.q.* barometric.

barom'etry, *n.*, the science underlying the use of the barometer.

bar'on, *n.*, a peer holding the lowest rank in the hereditary peerage.

bar'onage, *n.*, the whole body of barons; the dignity of baron.

bar'oness, *n.*, a baron's lady.

bar'onet, *n.*, one holding hereditary rank below a baron, but not a peer, merely an hereditary knight.

bar'onetage, *n.*, the whole body of baronets.

bar'onetcy, *n.*, the title and dignity of a baronet.

baro'nial, *adj.*, pert. to a baron.

bar'ony, *n.*, the title or honour of a baron; in Ireland, a territorial division corresponding to the hundred.

bar'oscope, *n.*, an instrument for forecasting weather.

baroscop'ic, *adj.*, pert. to a baroscope.

baroscop'ical, *adj.*, *i.q.* baroscopic.

barouche', *n.*, a four-wheeled carriage with a falling top.

barque, *n.*, a three-masted sailing vessel, the two forward masts square-rigged, the mizzen mast rigged fore-and-aft.

bar'quentine, *n.*, a three-masted sailing vessel, the foremast square-rigged, the main and mizzen masts rigged fore-and-aft.

bar'racan, *n.*, a kind of camlet.

bar'rack, *n.*, a house for soldiers.

barracoon', *n.*, a negro barrack, a slave depôt.

bar'rage, *n.*, the formation of an artificial bar on a river or water course, to increase the depth of water; bar thus formed, esp. on the Nile.

bar'ras, *n.*, a kind of resin; galipot.

bar'rator, *n.*, an encourager of litigation; the master or any of the crew of a ship who commits barratry.

bar'ratrous, *adj.*, tainted with barratry.

bar'ratry, *n.*, fraud by the master of a ship who injures the owners, freighters, or insurers, as by sinking, deserting, or running away with the ship; encouragement of law-suits and quarrels.

barred, *p.p.*, bar; *adj.*, marked with thick lines.

bar'rel, *n.*, a cask; a hollow cylinder or tube.

bar'relage, *n.*, accommodation for barrels.

bar'relled, *adj.*, having a barrel or barrels.

bar'rel-organ, *n.*, a musical instrument

in which a barrel furnished with pegs opens valves as it turns and admits air to a set of pipes.

bar'ren, *adj.*, not fertile; unproductive.

bar'renness, *n.*, the state of being barren.

barricade', *n.*, a temporary fortification made of trees, earth, etc.; *v.t.*, to stop up by a barricade.

barrica'ded, *p.p.*, barricade.

barrica'ding, *pr.p.*, barricade.

bar'rier, *n.*, an obstruction, an obstacle.

bar'ring, *pr.p.*, bar; *prep.*, excepting.

bar'rister, *n.*, a lawyer who acts as an advocate.

bar'row, *n.*, a prehistoric sepulchral mound; a wheelbarrow.

bar'-shot, *n.* a double shot consisting of two round-shot united by a bar.

bar'ter, *v.t.*, to exchange one commodity for another and not for money; *n.*, the act of exchanging.

bar'tered, *p.p.*, barter.

bar'terer, *n.*, one who barters.

bar'tering, *pr.p.*, barter.

bartizan', *n.*, a turret for archers.

bar'ton, *n.*, a demesne; a farmyard.

bary'ta, *n.*, oxide of barium.

bary'tes, *n.*, baryta, or its sulphate (heavy-spar).

baryt'ic, *adj.*, containing baryta.

bar'ytone, *adj.*, baritone.

bary'tum, *n.*, barium.

ba'sal, *adj.*, pert. to a base.

basalt', *n.*, a black igneous rock.

basalt'ic, *adj.*, pert. to basalt.

basalt'iform, *adj.*, in the form of basalt; columnar.

basalt'ine, *adj.*, i.q. basaltic.

bas'anite, *n.*, touchstone.

base, *adj.*, worthless, low, mean; *n.*, the bottom of anything; a military depôt; *v.t.*, to lay the foundation of.

base'ball, *n.*, a ball-game like rounders.

base'born, *adj.*, of illegitimate birth.

based, *p.p.*, base.

base'less, *adj.*, without foundations.

base'ly, *adv.*, in a base manner.

base'ment, *n.*, the lowest story of a building.

base'ness, *n.*, meanness, vileness.

bashaw', *n.*, a pasha.

bash'ful, *adj.*, modest to excess; shy.

bash'fully, *adv.*, in a bashful manner.

bash'fulness, *n.*, excessive modesty; shyness.

bash'i-bazouk', *n.*, an irregular Turkish soldier.

ba'sic, *adj.*, rel. to a base.

bas'ified, *p.p.*, basify.

bas'ifier, *n.*, that which basifies.

bas'ify, *v.t.*, to convert into a chemical base.

bas'ifying, *pr.p.*, basify.

bas'il, *n.*, the slope at the edge of a cutting tool, a bezel; an aromatic pot-herb.

bas'ilar, *adj.*, basal.

bas'ilary, *adj.*, basal.

basil'ic, *adj.*, royal; kingly.

basil'ica, *n.*, a Roman public hall; a church with a similar plan.

basil'ical, *adj.*, pert. to a basilica.

basil'icon, *n.*, an ointment made of wax, pitch, and resin.

bas'ilisk, *n.*, a fabulous creature, a serpent or cockatrice.

ba'sin, *n.*, a round shallow vessel; a tract of country, drained by a river.

ba'sing, *pr.p.*, base.

ba'sis, *n.*, a base, a foundation.

bask, *v.i.*, to lie in warmth or at ease.

basked, *p.p.*, bask.

bas'ket, *n.*, a vessel made of plaited twigs, rushes, osiers, etc.

bask'ing, *pr.p.*, bask.

Basque, *n.*, the language of the Biscayans, French and Spanish; *adj.*, pert. to this language or people

bas-relief', *n.*, a sculpture in low relief.

bass, *n.*, a mat made of bast; a hassock; a sea-fish like a perch; a kind of bitter pale ale.

bass (in music), *n.*, the lowest part or male voice; *adj.*, pert. to this part.

bas'set, *n.*, a game at cards; a miner's term for an outcropping stratum; *v.i.*, to crop out.

bas'seted, *p.p.*, basset.

bas'seting, *pr.p.*, basset.

bassinet', **-ette'**, *n.*, a cradle or perambulator.

bassoon', *n.*, a bass wind instrument.

bassoon'ist, *n.*, a bassoon player.

bass'-viol, *n.*, a violoncello.

bass'wood, *n.*, the American lime-tree.

bast, *n.*, fibrous inner bark of the lime and other trees.

bas'tard, *n.*, an illegitimate child; *adj.*, spurious, not genuine.

bas'tardise, *v.t.*, to prove to be a bastard.

bas'tardised, *p.p.*, bastardize.

bas'tardising, *pr.p.*, bastardize.

bas'tardy, *n.*, the state of being a bastard.

baste, *v.t.*, to cudgel; to drip fat upon roasting meat; to sew slightly with long stitches.

bast'ed, *p.p.*, baste.

bastile', bastille', *n.*, a fortress, esp. the state prison in Paris destroyed in 1789.

bastina'do, *n.*, punishment in Mohammedan countries by beating the soles of the feet with a rod; *v.t.*, to inflict this punishment.

bastina'doed, *p.p.*, bastinado.

bast'ing, *pr.p.*, baste; *n.*, the long, loose stitches which fasten pieces of a garment together during the making.

bast'ion, *n.*, a mound standing out from the angle of a fortification.

bast'ioned, *adj.*, having bastions.

bas'yle, *n.*, a non-acid constituent of a compound.

bat, *n.*, a club used in the game of cricket and similar games; a winged mammal of nocturnal habits; *v.i.*, to play with a bat at cricket.

Bata'vian, *adj.*, pert. to Holland, or to Batavia in Java; *n.*, a Dutchman or inhabitant of Batavia.

batch, *n.*, a quantity of bread baked at one time; a number of individuals or articles similar to each other.

bate, *v.i.* and *t.*, to lessen.

bateau', *n.*, a light, broad flat-bottomed Canadian boat; the pontoon of a floating bridge.

ba'ted, *p.p.*, bate.

bath, *n.*, a vessel in which the body is washed; a Hebrew liquid measure; *Knights of the Bath*, a British order of knighthood.

bathe, *v.t.*, to immerse in a bath; *v.i.*, to take a bath.

bathed, *p.p.*, bathe.

bath'er, *n.*, one who bathes.

bath'ing, *pr.p.*, bathe.

bath'os, *n.*, a ludicrous descent from the elevated to the mean in literary composition; an anti-climax.

bath'-room, *n.*, a room for bathing in.

bat'ing, *pr.p.*, bate; *prep.*, excepting.

batiste', *n.*, a kind of cambric.

bat'let, *n.*, a small bat for beating linen in the wash.

bat'man, *n.*, a man in charge of the cooking utensils of a company of soldiers.

bat'on, *n.*, a truncheon; a conductor's rod; in heraldry, a diminutive of the band sinister, couped.

Batra'chia, *n. pl.*, a group of amphibious animals, including frogs and toads.

batra'chian, *adj.*, pert. to the Batrachia; *n.*, one of them.

bat'rachite, *n.*, a fossilized frog.

bat'rachoid, *adj.*, resembling a frog.

Batrachomyom'achy, *n.*, a Greek travesty of the Iliad; the battle between the frogs and the mice.

bats'man, *n.*, a cricketer using the bat.

bat'ta, *n.*, an extra allowance made to British officers in India.

battal'ia, *n. pl.*, an old plural of battalion.

battal'ion, *n.*, a body of infantry of about 1,000 men, forming one division of a regiment.

battal'ioned, *adj.*, formed into battalions.

bat'ted, *p.p.*, bat.

bat'teler, bat'tler, *n.*, an undergraduate who gets his battels free.

bat'tels, *n.*, food ordered from the buttery at an Oxford college.

bat'ten, *v.t.*, to fatten; to fasten with battens; *v.i.*, to grow fat, to gorge; *n.*, a long slip of wood.

bat'tened, *p.p.*, batten.

bat'tening, *pr.p.*, batten.

bat'ter, *n.*, a batsman; a mixture of flour, eggs, etc., beaten with some liquid into a paste; *v.t.*, to beat with successive blows.

bat'tered, *p.p.*, batter.

bat'terer, *n.*, one who batters.

bat'tering, *pr.p.*, batter.

bat'tering-ram, *n.*, an engine of war used to beat down walls.

bat'tery, *n.*, a number of guns placed near one another; a parapet, etc., to cover guns and gunners; an electric current-generator; personal assault.

bat'ting, *pr.p.*, bat.

bat'tish, *adj.*, like a bat.

bat'tle, *n.*, a great combat; *v.i.*, to fight.

bat'tle-array, *n.*, the arrangement of an army ready to give battle.

bat'tle-axe, *n.*, an axe used as a weapon.

bat'tled, *p.p.*, battle; *adj.*, furnished with battlements.

bat'tledore, *n.*, a racket used to strike a ball or shuttlecock.

bat'tle-field, *n.*, the scene of a battle.

bat'tlement, *n.*, an indented parapet.

bat'tlemented, *adj.*, having battlements.

bat'tler, *n.*, one who battles.

bat'tleship, *n.*, a large ship of war.

bat'tling, *pr.p.*, battle.

battol'ogy, *n.*, babbling; a needless repetition of words.

battue', *n.*, the shooting of driven game.

baubee', *n.*, a halfpenny (*Scot.*).

bau'ble, *n.*, a short stick bearing a fool's-head; a showy trifle.

baulk, *see* balk.

Bava'rian, *adj.*, pert. to Bavaria; *n.*, an inhabitant of Bavaria.

ba'vin, *n.*, a faggot of brushwood.

bawbee', *see* baubee.

bawd, *n.*, a brothel-keeper; a pander.

bawd'ily, *adv.*, in a bawdy manner.

bawd'y, *adj.*, lewd; obscene; unchaste.

bawl, *v.t.* and *i.*, to shout; *n.*, a vehement cry.

bawled, *p.p.*, bawl.

bawl'er, *n.*, one who bawls.

bawl'ing, *n.*, loud shouting; *pr.p.*, bawl.

bawn, *n.*, an enclosure with mud walls (for cattle).

bay, *n.*, an expanse of water between two headlands; the laurel-tree; the bark of a dog; a recess; a space between columns or buttresses, or projecting beyond the wall line, as a window; *v.t.* and *i.*, to bark; *adj.*, of a reddish chestnut colour.

bay'ard, *n.*, a bay horse.

bay'berry, *n.*, the wax-myrtle and its fruit.

bayed, *p.p.*, bay; *adj.*, having a bay or bays.

bay'ing, *pr.p.*, bay.

bay'onet, *n.*, a short sword to fix on the muzzle of a rifle; *v.t.*, to stab with a bayonet.

bay'oneted, *p.p.*, bayonet.

bay'oneting, *pr.p.*, bayonet.

bay'ou, *n.*, a channel proceeding from a lake (*American*).

bay'-salt, *n.*, salt obtained by evaporating sea-water.

bay'-tree, *n.*, a kind of laurel.

bay'-window, *n.*, a window forming a recess in a room, often polygonal in plan.

bazaar', bazar', *n.*, an Oriental street-market; a charity sale of miscellaneous articles.

bdell'ium, *n.*, an Arabian aromatic gum-resin.

be, *v.i.*, to exist; to become; to remain. (It forms a connection between the subject and predicate of a sentence; it also helps to form the compound tenses of other verbs.)

beach, *n.*, the strand; part of the shore washed by the tide; *v.t.*, to run (a vessel) on to the beach.

beached, *p.p.*, beach.

beach'ing, *pr.p.*, beach.

beach'y, *adj.*, having a beach.

bea'con, *n.*, an object, light, or signal used as a warning; *v.i.*, to serve as a beacon.

bea'conage, *n.*, money paid to maintain a beacon.

bea'coned, *adj.*, having a beacon; *p.p.*, beacon.

bea'coning, *pr.p.*, beacon.

bead, *n.*, a little perforated ball of gold, glass, etc., strung with others on a thread; any small globular body; *v.t.*, to adorn with beads; *v.i.*, to form into beads.

bead'ing, *n.*, a small round moulding in architecture or joinery; *pr.p.*, bead.

bead'le, *n.*, a subordinate officer of a court, church, or parish.

bead'-roll, *n.*, a list of persons for whose souls prayers are requested; a catalogue.

beads'-man, *n.*, one whose employment is to pray for another; a recipient of alms.

bea'gle, *n.*, a small hound kept to hunt hares.

beak, *n.*, the bill of a bird.

beaked, *adj.*, having a beak; beak-shaped.

beak'er, *n.*, a large drinking cup or glass.

beam, *n.*, a long straight piece of wood; a collection of parallel rays of light; *v.i.*, to emit rays of light; to show affection, satisfaction, etc.

beamed, *p.p.*, beam.

beam'ing, *pr.p.*, beam.

beam'less, *adj.*, emitting no rays of light.

beam'y, *adj.*, heavy, massive; radiant.

bean, *n.*, the seed of a leguminous plant; the plant itself.

bean-feast, *n.*, a holiday spent in merry-making.

bear, *v.t.*, to support; to convey; to bring forth; *n.*, a large carnivorous, flat-footed animal; a rude or uncouth man; a speculator on the Stock Exchange who tries to bring down the price of stock so as to be able to buy cheaply.

bear'able, *adj.*, able to be borne.

bear'-baiting, *n.*, the sport of baiting bears with dogs.

beard, *n.*, the hair on the face; *v.t.*, to defy.

beard'ed, *adj.*, having a beard; *p.p.*, beard.

beard'ing, *pr.p.*, beard.

beard'less, *adj.*, without a beard.

beard'lessness, *n.*, the state of being without a beard.

bear'er, *n.*, one who bears.

bear'-garden, *n.*, a place where bears are kept for sport; any place of disorder.

bear'ing, *pr.p.*, bear; *n.*, demeanour, mien; in an automobile it is the support in which a revolving part rotates.

bear'ish, *adj.*, resembling a bear; rude; surly.

bear'like, *adj.*, like a bear.

bear's'-foot, *n.*, a kind of hellebore.

bear's'-grease, *n.*, a pomade for the hair.

bear'skin, *n.*, the dressed fur of a bear.

beast, *n.*, any four-footed animal; a brutal or disgusting person.

beast'liness, *n.*, brutality; filthiness.

beast'ly, *adj.*, like a beast.

beat, *v.t.*, to strike; to overcome; *n.*, a stroke or blow; the round of a policeman.

beaten, *p.p.*, beat; *adj.*, made smooth by beating or treading.

beat'er, *n.*, one who beats.

beatif'ic, *adj.*, imparting bliss.

beatif'ical, *adj.*, beatific.

beatifica'tion, *n.*, blessedness; an act of the Pope by which he declares a person beatified but not canonized.

beat'ified, *p.p.*, beatify.

beat'ify, *v.t.*, to make blessed.

beat'ifying, *pr.p.*, beatify.

beat'ing, *pr.p.*, beat; *n.*, a defeat.

beat'itude, *n.*, consummate bliss; one of Our Lord's eight declarations of blessedness.

beau, *n.*, a fop; a sweetheart.

beau-ide'al, *n.*, highest type of excellence.

beau-monde', *n.*, the fashionable world.

beau'teous, *adj.*, beautiful.

beau'teously, *adv.*, in a beautiful manner.

beau'teousness, *n.*, [illegible]

beau'tified, *p.p.*, beautify.

beau'tifier, *n.*, one who beautifies.

beau'tiful, *adj.*, highly pleasing to the eye, the ear, or the mind.

beau'tifulness, *n.*, beauty.

beau'tify, *v.t.*, to render beautiful.

beau'tifying, *pr.p.*, beautify.

beau'ty, *n.*, an assemblage of perfections whereby an object is made pleasing to the eye; a beautiful woman or thing.

beau'ty-spot, *n.*, something that heightens beauty by contrast; a patch on the face to do this.

beaux, *n.*, pl. of beau.

bea'ver, *n.*, a quadruped about 2 ft. long, haunting rivers and lakes, valuable for its fur; the fur itself; the vizor of a helmet.

bea'vered, *adj.*, having a beaver or vizor.

bebee'rine, *n.*, the active principle of the bark of the *bebeeru*, a kind of laurel found in British Guiana.

becalm', *v.t.*, to render calm; to reduce (a ship) to motionlessness.

becalmed', *p.p.*, becalm.

becalm'ing, *pr.p.*, becalm.

became', *p.t.*, become.

because', *conj.*, by reason that.

beccafi'co, *n.*, a bird like the nightingale; the garden warbler.

bechance', *v.t.* and *i.*, to happen to; to happen.

bechanced', *p.p.*, bechance.

bechan'cing, *pr.p.*, bechance.

becharm', *v.t.*, to charm.

bêche'-de-mer, *n.*, the trepang, a sea-slug eaten by the Chinese.

beck, *n.*, a brook; a nod intended as a signal; *v.t.*, to call by a nod.

becked, *p.p.*, beck.

beck'et, *n.*, in ships a contrivance for fastening loose ropes.

beck'ing, *pr.p.*, to beck.

beck'on, *v.i.*, to make a sign with the hand or finger.

beck'oned, *p.p.*, beckon.

beck'oning, *pr.p.*, beckon.

becloud', *v.t.*, to cover with clouds; to render obscure.

beclou'ded, *p.p.*, becloud.

beclou'ding, *pr.p.*, becloud.

become', *v.i.*, to pass from one state to another; *v.t.*, to suit.

becom'ing, *pr.p.*, become; *adj.*, suitable.

becom'ingly, *adv.*, in a becoming manner.

becom'ingness, *n.*, suitability.

bed, *n.*, that on which one sleeps; a plot of ground in a garden; that on which anything rests; a layer; *v.t.*, to place in a bed; to plant.

bedab'ble, *v.t.*, to wet; to sprinkle.

bedab'bled, *p.p.*, bedabble.

bedab'bling, *pr.p.*, bedabble.

bedark'en, *v.t.*, to make dark.

bedash', *v.t.*, to bespatter.

bedaub', *v.t.*, to smear with anything thick or slimy.

bedaubed', *p.p.*, bedaub.

bedaub'ing, *pr.p.*, bedaub.

bedaz'zle, *v.t.*, to blind by excess of light.

bed'-*chair*, *n.*, a chair with a movable back which can be lowered so as to form a bed.

bed'chamber, *n.*, a bedroom.

bed'-clothes, *n. pl.*, blankets, coverlets, etc.

bed'ded, *p.p.*, bed.

bed'ding, *n.*, a bed and its furniture; *pr.p.*, bed.
bedeck', *v.t.*, to adorn.
bedecked', *p.p.*, bedeck.
bedeck'ing, *pr.p.*, bedeck.
bed'eguar, *n.*, a spongy excrescence found on roses, produced by insects.
be'del, be'dell, *n.*, a beadle in a university or law-court.
bedev'il, *v.t.*, to torment, as by evil spirits.
bedev'illed, bedev'iled, *p.p.*, bedevil.
bedev'illing, bedev'iling, *pr.p.*, bedevil.
bedew', *v.t.*, to moisten as with dew.
bedewed', *p.p.*, bedew.
bedew'ing, *pr.p.*, bedew.
bed'fellow, *n.*, one who occupies the same bed with another.
bed'-hangings, *n. pl.*, curtains hung about a bed.
bedight', *v.t.*, to dress gaily, *p.p.* bedight.
bedim', *v.t.*, to make dim; to obscure.
bedi'zen, *v.t.*, to deck in a tawdry manner.
bed'lam, *n.*, a madhouse (orig., Bethlehem Hospital).
bed'lamite, *n.*, a madman.
bed'maker, *n.*, a woman-servant who has the care of college rooms.
bed'mate, *n.*, a bedfellow.
Bed'ouin, *n.*, a nomadic Arab.
bed'-plate, *n.*, the foundation plate of an engine.
bed'-post, *n.*, one of the corner pillars of a bed.
bed'-quilt, *n.*, a coverlet or counterpane.
bedrag'gle, *v.t.*, to soil by dragging through mud.
bed'rid, *adj.*, long confined to bed.
bed'ridden, *adj.*, bedrid.
bed'room, *n.*, a sleeping room.
bed'side, *adj.*, beside a bed; *n.*, the space adjoining a bed.
bed'stead, *n.*, the framework of a bed.
bed'straw, *n.*, a plant growing wild in Britain, bearing yellow or white flowers.
bed'tick, *n.*, stout linen or cotton forming a bag to hold the packing of a bed.
bed'time, *n.*, the hour for bed.
bee, *n.*, an insect, one species of which is kept in hives for its wax and honey.
bee'bee, *n.*, a lady (*Hindustani*).
bee'bread, *n.*, the pollen of flowers collected by bees as food for their young.
beech, *n.*, a large, smooth-barked tree yielding a hard timber.
beech'en, *adj.*, bel. to the beech.
beech'-nut, *n.*, a nut or fruit of the beech.
beef, *n.*, the flesh of an ox.
beef'eater, *n.*, a yeoman of the guard.
beef'steak, *n.*, a slice of beef for broiling.
bee'hive, *n.*, a box used as a habitation for bees.
bee'house, *n.*, a house to contain bee-hives; an apiary.
beele, *n.*, an Indian tree akin to the quince.
bee'-line, *n.*, the direct path between two places.
Beel'zebub, *n.*, a Philistine god (O.T.); the prince of devils (N.T.).
bee'-master, *n.*, one who keeps bees.
been, *p.p.*, be.
beer, *n.*, a fermented alcoholic drink made from malted barley.
beer'-barrel, *n.*, a barrel to contain beer.
beer'-house, *n.*, a house where malt liquors are sold.
beer'-shop, *n.*, a shop where beer is sold.
beest'ings, *n.*, the first milk given by a cow after calving.
bees'-wax, *n.*, wax secreted by bees.
beet, *n.*, a plant with a thick, fleshy root, the red beet used as a kitchen vegetable, the white to produce sugar.
beet'le, *n.*, an insect with four wings, the front pair being horny; a wooden mallet; *v.i.*, to overhang.
beet'le-brow, *n.*, a prominent brow.
beet'led, *p.p.*, beetle.
beet'ling, *adj.*, overhanging (said of cliffs, etc.); *pr.p.*, beetle.
beet'-root, *n.*, the root of a beet; the plant itself.
beeves, *n. pl.*, oxen.
befall', *v.t.*, to happen to; *v.i.*, to come to pass.
befal'len, *p.p.*, befall.
befal'ling, *pr.p.*, befall.
befell', *p.t.*, befall.
befit, *v.t.*, to be suitable to.
befit'ted, *p.p.*, befit.
befit'ting, *pr.p.*, befit.
befog', *v.t.*, to involve in fog; to confuse.
befogged', *p.p.*, befog.
befogg'ing, *pr.p.*, befog.
befool', *v.t.*, to delude.
befooled', *p.p.*, befool.
befool'ing, *pr.p.*, befool.
before', *prep.*, in front of; *adv.*, previously; *conj.*, rather than; sooner than the time when.
before'hand, *adv.*, in advance.
before'time, *adv.*, formerly.
befoul', *v.t.*, to soil.
befriend', *v.t.*, to act as a friend to.
befriend'ed, *p.p.*, befriend.
befriend'ing, *pr.p.*, befriend.

befringe′, *v.t.*, to supply with a fringe.
beg, *v.t.* and *i.*, to ask for earnestly; to solicit alms; to assume.
began, *p.t.*, begin.
beget′, *v.t.*, to procreate; to produce.
beget′ter, *n.*, one who begets; a father.
beget′ting, *pr.p.*, beget.
beg′gar, *n.*, one who begs; *v.t.*, to reduce to beggary.
beg′gared, *p.p.*, beggar.
beg′garing, *pr.p.*, beggar.
beg′garliness, *n.*, meanness.
beg′garly, *adj.*, like a beggar.
beg′gary, *n.*, the state of a beggar.
begged, *p.p.*, beg.
beg′ging, *pr.p.*, beg.
begin′, *v.t.* and *i.*, to originate.
begin′ner, *n.*, one who begins; a tiro.
begin′ning, *n.*, origin; commencement; *pr.p.* begin.
begird′, *v.t.*, to surround with a girdle.
begird′ing, *pr.p.*, begird.
begirt′, *p.p.*, begird.
begone′, *interj.*, go away!
bego′nia, *n.*, a beautiful tropical plant.
begot′, *p.t.*, beget.
begot′ten, *p.p.*, beget.
begrime′, *v.t.*, to make grimy.
begrimed′, *p.p.*, begrime.
begrim′ing, *pr.p.*, begrime.
begrudge′, *v.t.*, to envy someone the possession of.
begrudged′, *p.p.*, begrudge.
begrudg′ing, *pr.p.*, begrudge.
beguile′, *v.t.*, to deceive; to while away (time).
beguiled′, *p.p.*, beguile.
beguile′ment, *n.*, the act or effect of beguiling.
beguil′er, *n.*, one who beguiles.
beguil′ing, *pr.p.*, beguile.
be′gum, *n.*, an Indian lady of high rank; a princess.
begun′, *p.p.*, begin.
behalf, *n.*, interest; support; defence.
behave′, *v.i.* and *refl.*, to conduct oneself.
behaved′ *p.p.*, behave.
beha′ving, *pr.p.*, behave.
behav′iour, behav′ior, *n.*, manner of behaving.
behead′, *v.t.*, to decapitate.
behead′ed, *p.p.*, behead.
behead′ing, *pr.p.*, behead.
beheld′, *p.p.*, behold.
be′hemoth, *n.*, a Biblical monster; perhaps the hippopotamus.
behest′, *n.*, a command.
behind′, *prep.* and *adv.*, at the back of; later.
behind′*hand*, *adv.*, insufficiently advanced; *adj.*, tardy.
behold′, *v.t.* and *i.*, to look at with attention; *interj.*, fix your attention on.
behold′en, *adj.*, bound in gratitude.
behold′er, *n.*, a spectator.
behold′ing, *pr.p.*, behold.
behoof′, *n.*, advantage; benefit.
behoove′, **behove′**, *v.t. impers.*, to be fit, meet, or necessary for.
behooved′, *i.q.* behoved.
behoved′, *p.t.*, behove.
be′ing, *pr.p.*, be; *n.*, existence; a living creature, usually human.
bela′bour, bela′bor, *v.t.*, to beat soundly.
bela′boured, *p.p.*, belabour.
bela′bouring, *pr.p.*, belabour.
belate′, *v.t.*, to make too late.
belat′ed, *p.p.*, belate; *adj.*, having lingered till late; benighted.
belay′, *v.t.*, to make fast by winding round something.
belayed′, *p.p.*, belay.
belay′ing, *pr.p.*, belay.
belch, *v.t.*, to eject wind from the stomach; *n.*, the act of belching.
belched, *p.p.*, belch.
belch′ing, *pr.p.*, belch; *n.*, the act of ejecting wind from the stomach.
bel′dam, bel′dame, *n.*, an ugly old woman.
belea′guer *v.t.*, to blockade with an army.
belea′guered, *p.p.*, beleaguer.
belea′guering, *pr.p.*, beleaguer.
belem′nite, *n.*, a dart-shaped fossil shell found in the chalk.
bel′fry, *n.*, a bell-tower; campanile.
Bel′gian, *n.*, an inhabitant of Belgium; *adj.*, pert. to Belgium.
Bel′gic, *adj.*, Belgian; pert. to the Belgae.
Be′lial, *n.*, wickedness; a wicked person; Satan.
belie′, *v.t.*, to show to be false; to calumniate.
belied′, *p.p.*, belie.
belief′, *n.*, an assent of the mind to the truth of a declared fact without personal knowledge of it; a creed.
***believ′*able** *adj.*, credible.
believe′, *v.t.* and *i.*, to be firmly persuaded of the truth of anything.
believed′, *p.p.*, believe.
believ′er, *n.*, one who believes.
***believ′*ing**, *pr.p.*, believe.
believ′ingly, *adv.*, in a believing manner.
belit′tle, *v.t.*, to disparage.
belit′tled, *p.p.*, belittle.
belit′tling, *pr.p.*, belittle.

bell, *n.*, a metallic vessel which gives a clear, musical sound on being struck; any bell-shaped thing; *v.t.*, to put a bell on.

belladon'na, *n.*, a poisonous medicinal British plant.

bell'-bird, *n.*, a South American bird; also an Australian bird of a different species.

belle, *n.*, a lady of distinguished beauty.

belles-let'tres, *n. pl.*, elegant literature.

bell'-founder, *n.*, a maker of bells.

bell'-foundry, *n.*, a bell-caster's works.

bell'-hanger, *n.*, one who fixes up bells in houses.

bel'licose, *adj.*, warlike; pugnacious.

bel'lied, *p.p.*, belly; *adj.*, protuberant.

bellig'erency, *n.*, warfare.

bellig'erent, *n.*, one engaged in fighting; *adj.*, carrying on war.

bell'man, *n.*, a public crier with a bell.

bell'-metal, *n.*, an alloy of copper and tin used in making bells.

bel'low, *v.i.*, to roar; to make a loud, hollow noise like a bull; *n.*, a loud outcry.

bel'lowed, *p.p.*, bellow.

bel'lower, *n.*, one who bellows.

bel'lowing, *pr.p.*, bellow; *n.*, the act or the sound itself.

bel'lows, *n.*, sing. or pl., an instrument for making a strong current of air.

bell'pull, *n.*, a bell-rope or wire and its attachment.

bell'ringer, *n.*, one who rings bells.

bell'-wether, *n.*, a sheep that leads the flock, having a bell on his neck.

bel'ly, *n.*, that part of the body below the thorax or chest; a protuberance, generally hollow; *v.i.*, to swell out.

bel'ly-band, *n.*, a band round the belly of a horse.

bel'lyful, *n.*, as much as satisfies the appetite.

bel'lying, *pr.p.*, belly.

belong', *v.i.*, to be the property of; to pertain to.

belonged', *p.p.*, belong.

belong'ing, *pr.p.*, belong.

belove', *v.t.*, to love.

beloved', *p.p.*, belove.

belov'ed, *adj.*, greatly loved.

below', *prep.* and *adv.*, under.

belt, *n.*, a girdle; a band, esp. one round two wheels transferring motion from one to the other; *v.t.*, to fasten or surround with a belt.

Bel'tane, *n.*, an ancient Celtic festival in which bonfires on hills were lighted.

bel'ted, *adj.*, wearing a belt; *p.p.*, belt.

belt'ing, *n.*, the materials of which belts for machinery are made; *pr.p.*, belt.

bel'vedere, *n.*, a summer-house on a knoll; a look-out turret.

bely'ing, *pr.p.*, belie.

bemire', *v.t.*, to soil with mud or mire.

bemired', *p.p.*, bemire.

bemir'ing, *pr.p.*, bemire.

bemoan', *v.t.*, to lament.

bemoaned', *p.p.*, bemoan.

bemoan'er, *n.*, one who bemoans.

bemoan'ing, *n.*, lamentation; *pr.p.*, bemoan.

bemuse', *v.t.*, to muddle or stupefy, as with liquor.

bemused', *p.p.*, bemuse.

bemus'ing, *pr.p.*, bemuse.

ben, *n.*, a mountain-peak (*Scot.*).

bench, *n.*, a long seat; a table on which carpenters, etc., do their work; a judge's seat, the judges, their court.

bench'er, *n.*, a senior barrister in an inn of court who is a governor of the society.

bend, *v.t.*, to curve or make crooked; *v.i.*, to deviate from the straight or the perpendicular; *n.*, a curve; one of the ordinaries in heraldry.

bend'able, *adj.*, capable of being bent.

bend'ed, *p.p.*, bend.

bend'er *n.*, one who bends.

bend'ing, *pr.p.*, bend; *n.*, the act.

bend'let, *n.*, a diminutive of a bend in heraldry.

bend'y, *adj.*, divided into an even number of bends of a shield in heraldry.

beneath', *prep.* and *adv.*, below; under.

Ben'edict, *n.*, a married man, esp. one who has been long a bachelor.

Benedic'tine, *adj.*, rel. to St. Benedict's rule; *n.*, a monk of the Order of St. Benedict; a kind of liqueur.

benedic'tion, *n.*, a blessing; a solemn invocation of happiness.

benedic'tive, *adj.*, *i.q.* benedictory.

benedic'tory, *adj.*, giving a blessing.

Benedic'tus, *n.*, the song of Zacharias in St. Luke i.; also the liturgical passage forming the ending of the *Sanctus*.

benefac'tion, *n.*, a charitable donation.

benefac'tor, *n.*, one who confers a benefit.

benefac'tress, *n.*, fem. of benefactor.

ben'efice, *n.*, an ecclesiastical endowment providing for the maintenance of divine service.

ben'eficed, *adj.*, possessed of a benefice.

benef'icence, *n.*, active charity.

benef'icent, *adj.*, performing acts of charity.

benef'icently, *adv.*, in a beneficent manner.

benefi'cial, *adj.*, advantageous.

benefi'cially, *adv.*, in a beneficial manner.

benefi'ciary, *n.*, one who is in the receipt of benefits or profits.

ben'efit, *n.*, an advantage or profit; *v.t.*, to do good to; *v.i.*, to gain advantage.

ben'efited, *p.p.*, benefit.

ben'efiting, *pr.p.*, benefit.

benev'olence, *n.*, charitableness; a euphemism for a tax illegally exacted.

benev'olent, *adj.*, charitable.

benev'olently, *adv.*, in a benevolent manner.

Bengalese', *adj.*, pert. to Bengal.

Bengal'i, *n.*, the language of Bengal; a native of Bengal.

benight', *v.t.*, to overtake with night.

benight'ed, *p.p.*, benight; *adj.*, morally dark, ignorant.

benight'ing, *pr.p.*, benight.

benign', *adj.*, kind; gracious; not severe.

benig'nant, *adj.*, gracious, kind.

benig'nantly, *adv.*, in a benignant manner.

benig'nity, *n.*, graciousness; kindness of superiors.

benign'ly, *adv.*, in a benign manner.

ben'ison, *n.*, a benediction.

ben'net, *n.*, the yellow avens.

bent, *n.*, a natural tendency; a wiry grass; *p.p.*, bend.

benth'al, *adj.*, pert to depth.

benumb', *v.t.*, to deprive of sensation.

benumbed', *p.p.*, benumb.

benumb'ing, *pr p.*, benumb.

ben'zene, *n.*, a solvent for grease prepared from coal tar.

ben'zine, *n.*, *i.q.* benzene.

benzo'ic, *adj.*, obtained from benzoin.

benzo'in, *n.*, gum-benjamin, obtained from the fragrant resin of a tree of Sumatra, used in incense, cosmetics, etc.

ben'zol, *n.*, *i.q.* benzene.

ben'zoline, *n.*, *i.q.* benzene.

bequeath', *v.t.*, to leave by will.

bequeathed', *p.p.*, bequeath.

bequeath'er, *n.*, one who bequeaths.

bequeath'ing, *pr.p.*, bequeath.

bequest', *n.*, a legacy; the act of bequeathing.

berate', *v.t.*, to scold.

berat'ed, *p.p.*, berate.

berat'ing, *pr.p.* berate.

ber'berine, *n.*, a yellow dye obtained from the root of the barberry tree.

Bere'an, *adj.*, bel. to Beroea.

bereave', *v.t.*, to deprive of something prized.

bereaved', *p.p.*, bereave.

bereave'ment, *n.*, deprivation, esp. loss by death.

bereav'ing, *pr.p.*, bereave.

bereft', *p.p.*, bereave.

ber'gamot, *n.*, a kind of pear; a fragrant oil or perfume prepared from lime fruit; a coarse tapestry.

ber'gander, *n.*, a wild duck.

berg'mote, *n.*, a Derbyshire miners' court for settling disputes.

ber'iberi, *n.*, an Indian disease.

Ber'nardine, *n.*, a Cistercian monk.

Bernese', *adj.*, pert. to Berne; *n.*, a citizen of Berne.

ber'ried, *adj.*, having berries.

ber'ry, *n.*, a small pulpy fruit.

ber'serker, *n.*, a Scandinavian warrior; a person of extreme violence.

berth, *n.*, a station in which a ship can lie; a small room in a ship; an appointment or situation, *v.t.*, to assign a ship's anchorage.

berthed', *p.p.*, berth.

berth'ing, *pr.p.*, berth.

Ber'thon-boat, *n.*, a collapsible boat.

ber'yl, *n.*, a kind of inferior emerald.

ber'ylline, *adj.*, like a beryl; bluish-green.

beseech', *v.t.*, to entreat.

beseech'er, *n.*, one who beseeches.

beseech'ing, *pr.p.*, beseech; *adj.*, entreating.

beseech'ingly, *adv.*, in a beseeching manner.

beseem', *v.t.*, to be worthy of.

beseemed', *p.p.*, beseem.

beseem'ing, *adj.*, becoming; fit; worthy of; *pr.p.*, beseem.

beseem'ingly, *adv.*, in a beseeming manner.

beset', *v.t.*, to hem in; to press hard upon.

beset'ting, *adj.*, habitually assailing.

beshrew', *v.t.*, to wish a curse to; to execrate mildly.

beside', *prep.*, at the side of; in comparison with.

besides', *prep.*, in addition to; *adv.*, moreover.

besiege', *v.t.*, to surround with armed forces so as to compel to surrender; to harass.

besieged', *p.p.*, besiege.

besieg'er, *n.*, one who besieges.

besieg'ing, *pr.p.*, besiege.

besmear', *v.t.*, to smear all over.

besmeared', *p.p.*, besmear.
besmear'ing, *pr.p.*, besmear.
be'som, *n.*, a broom; a brush of twigs.
besot', *v.t.*, to stupefy with drink.
besot'ted, *p.p.*, besot.
besot'ting, *pr.p.*, besot.
besought', *p.p.*, beseech.
bespang'le, *v.t.*, to adorn with spangles.
bespang'led, *p.p.*, bespangle.
bespang'ling, *pr.p.*, bespangle.
bespat'ter, *v.t.*, to soil by spattering.
bespat'tered, *p.p.*, bespatter.
bespat'tering, *pr.p.* bespatter.
bespeak', *v.t.*, to order beforehand; to betoken; *n.* (among actors), a benefit performance.
bespeak'er, *n.*, one who bespeaks.
bespeak'ing, *pr.p.*, bespeak.
bespoke', *p.t.*, bespeak.
bespok'en, *p.p.*, bespeak.
bespread', *v.t.*, to form a coating over.
besprin'kle, *v.t.*, to sprinkle over.
besprin'kled, *p.p.*, besprinkle.
besprin'kling, *pr.p.*, besprinkling.
Bes'semer, *adj.*, descriptive of steel made by Sir Henry Bessemer's process.
best, *adj.*, good in the highest degree; *v.t.*, to surpass, overcome.
bes'tial, *adj.*, brutal; brutish.
bestial'ity, *n.*, beastliness; the quality of a beast.
best'ialize, *v.t.*, to reduce to the condition of a beast.
bestir', *v.t.* and *refl.*, to put into brisk action.
bestirred', *p.p.*, bestir.
bestir'ring, *pr.p.*, bestir.
bestow', *v.t.*, to confer; to impart; to stow away.
bestow'al, *n.*, the act of bestowing.
bestowed', *p.p.*, bestow.
bestow'er, *n.*, one who bestows.
bestow'ing, *pr.p.*, bestow.
bestrad'dle, *v.t.*, to bestride.
bestrew', *v.t.*, to strew.
bestrewed', *p.p.*, bestrew.
bestrew'ing, *pr.p.*, bestrew.
bestrid', *p.p.*, bestride.
bestrid'den, *p.p.*, bestride.
bestride', *v.t.*, to stand or sit with the legs on each side of.
bestrid'ing, *pr.p.*, bestride.
bet, *v.t.*, to wager.
betake', *v.t. refl.*, to repair; to resort.
betak'en, *p.p.*, betake.
be'tel, *n.*, a kind of pepper, chewed in Malaysia.
beth'el, *n.*, a Dissenting place of worship.
bethink', *v.t. refl.*, to call or recall to mind.
bethink'ing, *pr.p.*, bethink.
bethought', *p.p.*, bethink.
betide', *v.t.*, to happen to; *v.i.*, to happen.
beti'ded, *p.p.*, betide.
beti'ding, *pr.p.*, betide.
betimes', *adv.*, seasonably; at an early hour.
beto'ken, *v.t.*, to serve as a token of; to foreshadow.
beto'kened, *p.p.*, betoken.
beto'kening, *pr.p.*, betoken.
bet'ony, *n.*, a British plant once used in medicine and dyeing.
betook', *p.t.* of betake.
betray', *v.t.*, to be unfaithful to.
betray'al, *n.*, the act of betraying.
betrayed', *p.p.*, betray.
betray'er, *n.*, one who betrays.
betray'ing, *pr.p.*, betray.
betray'ment, *n.*, *s.q.* betrayal.
betroth', *v.t.*, to contract with a view to marriage.
betroth'al, *n.*, the act of betrothing.
betrothed', *p.p.*, betroth.
betroth'ing, *pr.p.*, betroth.
bet'ted, *p.p.*, bet.
bet'ter, *adj.*, good in a higher degree; *adv.*, in a more excellent manner; *v.t.*, to improve; *n.*, a superior.
bet'tered, *p.p.*, better.
bet'tering, *pr.p.*, better.
bet'terment, *n.*, improvement.
bet'ters, *n. pl.*, superiors.
bet'ting, *pr.p.*, bet; *n.*, the act of wagering.
bet'ty, *n.*, a short jemmy; a Florence flask.
between', *prep.* and *adv.*, in the space or interval separating two things or groups.
betwixt', *prep.*, between.
bev'el, *n.*, the inclination of two surfaces of a solid body to one another; *v.t.*, to cut to a bevel.
bev'elled, **bev'eled**, *p.p.* bevel; *adj.*, having a bevel.
bev'elling, **bev'eling**, *pr.p.*, bevel.
bev'el-wheels, *n.*, machinery in which the shafts of two wheels that work on each other form an angle.
bev'erage, *n.*, a drink.
bev'y, *n.*, a flock of birds; a company of ladies.
bewail', *v.t.*, to lament.
bewail'able, *adj.*, worthy of being bewailed.
bewailed', *p.p.*, bewail.
bewail'er, *n.*, one who bewails.

bewail'ing, *n.*, lamentation; *pr.p.*, bewail.
beware', *v.i.*, to guard against; to be suspicious of.
bewil'der, *v.t.*, to puzzle, to confuse.
bewil'dered, *p.p.*, bewilder.
bewil'dering, *pr.p.*, bewilder.
bewil'derment, *n.*, state of being bewildered.
bewitch', *v.t.*, to subject to the influence of witchcraft; to charm.
bewitched', *p.p.*, bewitch.
bewitch'er, *n.*, one who bewitches.
bewitch'ery, *n.*, fascination; charm.
bewitch'ing, *adj.*, having power to bewitch; *pr.p.*, bewitch.
bewitch'ment, *n.*, *i.q.* bewitchery.
bewray', *v.t.*, to betray.
bey, *n.*, a Turkish governor.
beyond', *prep.* and *adv.*, on the farther side of.
bez'el, *n.*, that part of a finger ring which holds the stone; the groove in which the glass of a watch is set.
bezique', *n.*, a card game.
be'zoar, *n.*, intestinal concretions of certain animals, formerly believed to be antidotes to poison.
bezoar'dic, *adj.*, compounded with bezoar.
bhang, *n.*, a narcotic prepared from Indian hemp.
bian'gular, *adj.*, having two angles.
bi'as, *n.*, a weight let into a bowl which deflects it from running straight; prepossession; *v.t.*, to prejudice.
bi'as(s)ed, *p.p.*, bias.
bi'as(s)ing, *pr.p.*, bias.
biax'ial, *adj.*, having two axes.
bib, *v.t.*, to tipple; to drink frequently; *n.*, a chin-cloth worn by a child to protect its clothes.
biba'cious, *adj.*, addicted to drinking.
bibac'ity, *n.*, fondness for drinking.
bib'ber, *n.*, a tippler.
bib'itory, *adj.*, tippling.
Bi'ble, *n.*, the book of the Sacred Scriptures.
Bib'lical, *adj.*, pert. to the Bible.
Bib'licist, *n.*, one skilled in knowledge of the Bible.
bibliog'rapher, *n.*, one versed in bibliography.
bibliograph'ic, *adj.*, pert. to bibliography.
bibliograph'ical, *adj.*, *i.q.* bibliographic.
bibliog'raphy, *n.*, a history of the different editions of a book; a list of works on a given subject.
bibliol'atry, *n.*, excessive reverence for any book.
bibliolog'ical, *adj.*, rel. to bibliology.
bibliol'ogy, *n.*, Biblical literature.
bib'liomancy, *n.*, divination by means of a book, esp. the Bible.
biblioma'nia, *n.*, a passion for collecting old and rare books.
biblioma'niac, *n.*, one affected by bibliomania.
bibliomani'acal, *adj.*, pert. to bibliomania.
bibliom'anist, *n.*, *i.q.* bibliomaniac.
bib'liophile, *n.*, a lover of books.
bibliopho'bia, *n.*, a dislike of books
bib'liopole, *n.*, a bookseller.
bibliop'olism, *n.*, bookselling.
bibliop'olist, *n.*, *i.q.* bibliopole.
bibliothe'ca, *n.*, a library (*Lat.*).
bib'ulous, *adj.*, addicted to drinking.
bical'carate, *adj.*, having two spurs.
bicap'sular, *adj.*, having two capsules.
bicar'bonate, *n.*, a carbonate having two equivalents of carbon dioxide to one of a base.
bice, *n.*, a blue or green colour used by painters.
bicen'tenary, *n.*, two hundred years; the two-hundredth anniversary.
biceph'alous, *adj.*, having two heads.
bi'ceps, *n.*, a muscle of the arm or thigh, having two heads or origins.
bichro'mate, *n.*, a salt with two parts of chromic acid to one of the other ingredients.
bicip'ital, *adj.*, two-headed; pert. to the biceps.
bicip'itous, *adj.*, *i.q.* bicipital.
bick'er, *v.i.*, to quarrel; *n.*, a quarrel, brawl; flash; porringer.
bick'ered, *p.p.*, bicker.
bick'erer, *n.*, one who bickers.
bick'ering, *pr.p.*, bicker; *n.*, quarrelling.
bicon'jugate, *adj.*, in pairs; placed side by side.
bi'corn, *adj.*, having two horns.
bicorn'ous, *adj.*, *i.q.* bicorn.
bicor'poral, *adj.*, double-bodied.
bicru'ral, *adj.*, having two legs.
bicus'pid, *adj.*, two-fanged.
bi'cycle, *n.*, a light two-wheeled conveyance propelled by the rider.
bi'cyclist, *n.*, a bicycle rider.
bid, *v.t.*, to command; to pray; to offer as a price at an auction; *n.*, an offer of a price at an auction.
bid'den, *p.p.*, bid.
bid'der, *n.*, one who bids.
bid'ding, *pr.p.*, bid.

bide, *v.i.*, to remain in a place; *v.t.*, to wait for.
bid'ed, *p.p.*, bide.
bidet', *n.*, a soldier's baggage horse; a sort of small portable bath; a commode.
bid'ing, *pr.p.*, bide.
bien'nial, *adj.*, happening once in two years.
bien'nially, *adv.*, once in two years.
bier, *n.*, a frame for conveying a corpse to the grave.
bifa'rious, *adj.*, double; two-fold.
bif'erous, *adj.*, bearing twice a year.
bif'fin, *n.*, a cooking-apple.
bi'fid, *adj.*, cleft; forked.
bif'idate, *adj.*, *i.q.* bifid.
bif'idated, *i.q.* bifid.
biflo'rous, *adj.*, bearing two flowers.
bi'fold, *adj.*, two-fold; double.
bifo'liate, *adj.*, having two leaves.
bi'forate, *adj.*, having two perforations.
bif'orine, *n.*, a two-doored cell on the leaves of certain plants.
bi'form, *adj.*, double-bodied; having two shapes.
bi'formed, *adj.*, *i.q.* biform.
bi'furcate, *v.t.*, to fork; *adj.*, forked.
bi'furcated, *p.p.*, bifurcate.
bi'furcating, *pr.p.*, bifurcate.
bifurca'tion, *n.*, a forking.
bifur'cous, *adj.*, *i.q.* bifurcate.
big, *adj.*, great; pregnant; full.
big'amist, *n.*, one who has committed bigamy.
big'amy, *n.*, the crime or state of having more than one husband or wife at the same time.
big'arreau, big'aroon, *n.*, a white-heart cherry.
bigen'tial, *adj.*, rel. to two tribes.
big'gin, *n.*, a child's cap; a night-cap; a coif.
bight, *n.*, a bay, a loop.
big'ness, *n.*, the state of being big.
Bigno'nia, *n.*, a beautiful climbing shrub.
big'ot, *n.*, a person blindly attached to any opinion or creed.
big'oted, *adj.*, having the character of a bigot.
big'otry, *n.*, unreasoning zeal; intolerance.
big'wig, *n.*, a person of importance.
bijou', *adj.*, something small and pretty.
bijou'try, *n.*, jewellery; trinkets.
bi'jugate, *adj.*, having two pairs of leaflets.
bi'jugous, *adj.*, *i.q.* bijugate.
bila'biate, *adj.*, having two lips; applied to the corolla of a flower.
bilam'ellate, *adj.*, formed of two plates.
bilam'ellated, *adj.*, *i.q.* bilamellate.
bil'ander, *n.*, a two-masted Dutch canal boat.
bilat'eral, *adj.*, two-sided.
bil'berry, *n.*, the whortleberry.
bil'bo, *n.*, a sword.
bil'boes, *n. pl.*, a bar with shackles for the feet.
bile, *n.*, a yellow bitter liquid separated from the blood by the liver; ill-nature.
bile'-duct, *n.*, the tube conducting the bile.
bilge, *n.*, the floor of a ship's bottom; *v.i.*, to spring a leak in the bilge.
bilged, *p.p.*, bilge.
bilge'water, *n.*, water lying in a ship's bottom.
bilg'ing, *pr.p.*, bilge.
bil'iary, *adj.*, pert. to bile.
bilin'gual, *adj.*, expressed in two languages.
bilin'guist, *n.*, one who speaks two languages.
bil'ious, *adj.*, suffering from excess of bile.
bil'iousness, *n.*, the state of being bilious.
bilit'eral, *adj.*, consisting of two letters.
bilk, *v.t.*, to decamp without paying.
bilked, *p.p.*, bilk.
bilk'ing, *pr.p.*, bilk.
bill, *n.*, the beak of a fowl; a pruning instrument; a note of charges with amount due; an advertisement sheet; an order to pay; a parliamentary proposal; *v.i.*, to join bills, as doves do.
bill'book, *n.*, a book in which bills of exchange, etc., are noted.
billed, *p.p.*, bill.
bil'let, *n.*, a note in writing; a soldier's lodging; *v.t.*, to lodge a soldier in a private house.
billet-doux', *n.*, a love-letter.
bil'leted, *p.p.*, billet.
bil'leting, *pr.p.*, billet.
bill'hook, *n.*, a small hatchet with a hook.
bill'iard-room, *n.*, a room with a billiard table.
bill'iards, *n.*, a game played on a table with balls and cues.
bil'ling, *pr.p.*, bill.
bil'lingsgate, *n.*, foul language.
bil'lion, *n.*, a million millions.
bil'lot, *n.*, bullion in bar or mass.
bil'low, *n.*, a great wave; *v.i.*, to swell.
bil'lowy, *adj.* swelling into large waves.
bill'-poster, *n.*, *i.q.* bill-sticker.
bill'-sticker, *n.*, one who posts placards in public places.
bilo'bate, *adj.*, divided into two lobes.
bi'lobed, *i.q.* bilobate.

biloc'ular, *adj.*, divided into two cells.
bil'tong, *n.*, strips of dried lean meat.
bimac'ulate, *adj.*, marked with two spots.
bim'ana, *n. pl.*, animals having two hands.
bi'mane, *n.*, one of the bimana.
bim'anous, *adj.*, having two hands.
bime'dial, *adj.*, applied to lines which can only be summed in powers, being otherwise incommensurable.
bimes'trial, *adj.*, continuing two months
bimet'allism, bimet'alism, *n.*, a system of currency recognizing coins of two metals as legal tender to any amount.
bimonth'ly, *adj.* and *adv.*, occurring every two months.
bin, *n.*, a sub-division of a wine-cellar for bottles; a receptacle, as dust-bin, etc.
bi'nary, *adj.*, composed of two parts.
bi'nate, *adj.*, growing in pairs.
bind, *v.t.*, to fasten, esp. with anything flexible; to join together; to restrain.
bind'er, *n.*, one who binds, esp. books, sheaves, etc.
bind'ery, *n.*, a bookbinding workshop.
bind'ing, *n.*, the cover, etc., of a book; *pr.p.*, bind.
bind'weed, *n.*, the convolvulus.
biner'vate, *adj.*, two-nerved.
bin'nacle, *n.*, the ship's compass-box near the helm.
bin'ocle, *n.*, a field-glass; a telescope with two tubes, one for each eye.
binoc'ular, *adj.*, having two eyes; suited for the use of both eyes at once; *n.*, a binocle.
binoc'ulate, *adj.*, having two eyes.
bino'mial, *n.* and *adj.*, having two algebraic terms.
binom'inal, *adj.*, having two names.
binom'inous, *adj.*, *i.q.* binominal.
bi'nous, *adj.*, *i.q.*, binate.
bioc'ellate, *adj.*, marked with two eye-like spots.
biodynam'ics, *n.*, the doctrine of vital energy.
biogen'esis, *n.*, the doctrine that life can spring only from living organisms.
bi'ograph, *n.*, a kind of cinematograph.
biog'rapher, *n.*, one who writes a biography.
biograph'ic, *adj.*, pert. to biography.
biograph'ical, *adj.*, *i.q.* biographic.
biog'raphy, *n.*, a life history.
biolog'ical, *adj.*, pert. to biology.
biol'ogy, *n.*, the science that treats of the lives of animals and plants.
biolyt'ic, *adj.*, rel. to the destruction of life.
biom'etry, *n.*, calculation of expectation of life.
bi'oplasm, *n.*, germinal matter.
bi'otaxy, *n.*, the scientific classification of animals and plants.
bip'arous, *adj.*, bearing twins.
bipart'ible, *adj.*, capable of being divided into two.
bipart'ient, *adj.*, bearing twins.
bipart'ile, *adj.*, *i.q.* bipartible.
bipart'ite, *adj.*, having two corresponding parts.
biparti'tion, *n.*, the act of making bipartite.
bipec'tinate, *adj.*, having two toothed margins.
bi'ped, *n.*, an animal having two feet.
bi'pedal, *adj.*, having two feet.
bipel'tate, *adj.*, covered with a shell like a double shield.
bipen'nate, *adj.*, having two wings.
bipen'nated, *adj.*, *i.q.* bipennate.
bipet'alous, *adj.*, having two petals.
bipin'nate, *adj.*, doubly lobed.
bi'plane, *n.*, an aeroplane with an upper and a lower plane or carrying surface.
bipo'lar, *adj.*, doubly polar.
bipolar'ity, *n.*, bipolar quality.
bi'pont, *adj.*, rel. to books printed at Deuxponts (Bipontium or Zweibrücken).
bipont'ine, *i.q.* bipont.
bipunct'ual, *adj.*, having two points.
biquad'rate, *n.*, the square of the square; the fourth power.
biquint'ile, *n.*, an astronomical term applied to the relative positions of two planets separated by 144 degrees.
bira'diate, *adj.*, having two rays.
bira'mous, *adj.*, consisting of two branches.
birch, *n.*, a graceful tree with small leaves and whitish bark; an instrument of punishment; *v.t.*, to punish with the birch rod.
birched, *p.p.*, birch.
birch'en, *adj.*, consisting of birch.
birch'ing, *pr.p.* birch.
bird, *n.*, a feathered winged animal producing young from eggs.
bird'-cage, *n.*, a cage for a song-bird.
bird'catcher, *n.*, one who catches birds.
bird'-like, *adj.*, resembling a bird.
bird'-lime, *n.*, a sticky substance for entangling birds.
bird's'-eye, *n.*, a species of primrose; a kind of tobacco.
bi'reme, *n.*, a Greek or Roman vessel

with two tiers of oars.

biret'ta, *n.*, a square cap worn by ecclesiastics.

biros'trate, *adj.*, having a double beak.

biros'trated, *adj.*, *i.q.* birostrate.

birth, *n.*, the process of being born; lineage; origin.

birth'day, *n.*, the day on which anyone is born, or its anniversary.

birth'-mark, *n.*, a congenital mark.

birth'place, *n.*, the place of one's birth.

birth'right, *n.*, a right to which a person is entitled by birth.

Biscay'an, *adj.*, pert. to Biscay in Spain.

bis'cotin, *n.*, a confection made of flour, sugar, eggs, and marmalade.

bis'cuit, *n.*, a hard, dry, flat kind of bread that will keep; unglazed porcelain after the first baking.

bisect', *v.t.*, to cut into two parts; esp. into two equal parts.

bisect'ed, *p.p.*, bisect.

bisect'ing, *pr.p.*, bisect.

bisec'tion, *n.*, the act of bisecting.

biseg'ment, *n.*, one of the parts of a bisected line.

bise'rial, *adj.*, arranged in two series or rows.

biser'rate, *adj.*, having serrate serratures.

bise'tose, *adj.*, having two bristles.

bise'tous, *i.q.* bisetose.

bisex'ual, *adj.*, of both sexes.

bish'op, *n.*, a member of the highest order of the Christian ministry; a piece in the game of chess.

bish'opric, *n.*, the dignity of a bishop.

bisk, *n.*, soup made of several sorts of meat.

bis'muth, *n.*, a yellowish metal used in making printers' type.

bis'muthal, *adj.*, composed of bismuth.

bi'son, *n.*, a wild American ox.

bisque, *n.*, unglazed white porcelain; a point conceded to a tennis-player which he can claim when he chooses.

bissex'tile, *adj.*, pert. to leap-year.

bistip'uled, *adj.*, having two stipules.

bis'tort, *n.*, a plant with twisted roots; snakeweed or adder's-wort.

bis'toury, *n.*, a surgical instrument.

bis'tre, **bis'ter**, *n.*, a brown pigment.

bisul'cate, *adj.*, cloven footed.

bisul'phate, *n.*, a metallic salt of sulphuric acid in which one-half the hydrogen remains.

bisul'phuret, *n.*, a sulphide with two atoms of sulphur in the molecule.

bit, *p.t.* and *p.p.*, bite; *n.*, a small piece; a boring tool; the metal part of a horse's bridle.

bitch, *n.*, the female of canine animals, as the dog, fox, wolf.

bite, *v.t.*, to cut or crush with the teeth; *n.*, a wound made by biting; a mouthful.

bit'er, *n.*, one who bites.

bitern'ate, *adj.*, doubly ternate.

bit'ing, *pr.p.*, bite; *adj.*, sharp, sarcastic.

bitt, *n.*, a frame fastened to the deck of a vessel on which to secure cables; *v.t.*, to put round the bitts.

bit'ted, *adj.*, having bitts; *p.p.*, bitt.

bit'ten, *p.p.*, bite.

bit'ter, *adj.*, acrid; keen; reproachful; sarcastic.

bit'terish, *adj.*, rather bitter.

bit'terly, *adv.*, in a bitter manner.

bit'tern, *n.*, a wading-bird of the heron family.

bit'terness, *n.*, the quality of being bitter.

bit'ters, *n. pl.*, a liquor used as a stomachic, made of bitter herbs.

bit'tersweet, *n.*, the woody nightshade.

bit'terweed, *n.*, yellow gentian.

bit'ting, *pr.p.*, bitt.

bitts, *n. pl.*, short bifurcated posts used for securing a ship's cable.

bitu'men, *n.*, a mineral resin.

bitu'minate, *v.t.*, to impregnate with bitumen.

bitu'minated, *p.p.* bituminate.

bitu'minating, *pr.p.*, bituminate.

bitu'minize, *v.t.*, *i.q.* bituminate.

bitu'minous, *adj.*, containing bitumen.

bi'valve, *n.*, a shell-fish with two hinged valves.

bivalv'ous, *adj.*, *i.q.* bivalvular.

bivalv'ular, *adj.*, having two valves.

bivault'ed, *adj.*, having two arches.

biven'tral, *adj.*, having two bellies.

biv'ious, *adj.*, leading two ways.

biv'ouac, *n.*, an open-air encampment of soldiers without tents; *v.i.*, to encamp in bivouac.

biv'ouacked, *p.p.* bivouac.

biv'ouacking, *pr.p.*, bivouac.

biweek'ly, *adj.*, occurring every two weeks.

bizarre', *adj.*, odd, fantastic.

blab, *v.t.*, to let out secrets.

blabbed, *p.p.*, blab.

blab'ber, *n.*, one who blabs.

blab'bing, *pr.p.*, blab.

black, *adj.*, of the darkest colour; *v.t.*, to blacken.

black'amoor, *n.*, a negro.
black'art *n.*, magic.
black'ball, *v.t.*, to exclude or reject by vote.
black'balled, *p.p.*, blackball.
black'balling, *pr.p.*, blackball.
black'beetle, *n.*, a cockroach.
black'berry, *n.*, the berry of the bramble.
black'bird, *n.*, a song-bird of the thrush family with black plumage.
black'board, *n.*, a board used for instruction to receive drawing or writing in chalk.
black'-book, *n.*, a record of offences and punishments.
black'-cap, *n.*, a bird of the warbler family.
black'-cattle, *n.*, oxen reared for slaughter, no matter what their *colour* may be.
black'-death, *n.*, an Eastern plague which first visited England in the 14th century.
blacked, *p.p.*, black.
black'en, *v.t.*, to make black.
black'ened, *p.p.*, blacken.
black'ener, *n.*, a slanderer.
black'ening, *pr.p.*, blacken.
black'-eyed, *adj.*, having eyes with black or very dark irises.
black'fish, *n.*, a small whale.
black'*guard*, *n.*, a fellow of low character; *v.t.*, to use abusive language to.
black'*guardism*, *n.*, the conduct of a blackguard.
black'ing, *n.*, a black polish for leather.
black'ish, *adj.*, rather black.
black'-lead, *n.*, graphite; plumbago; *v.t.*, to polish with blacklead.
black'leg, *n.*, a cheat.
black'letter, *n.*, the Old English or Gothic type used in early printed books.

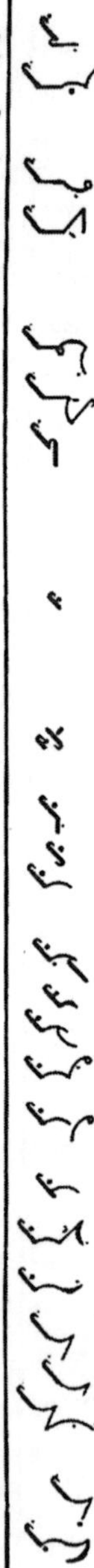

black'ly, *adv.*, in a black manner.
black'mail, *n.*, extortion by intimidation; *v.t.*, to levy blackmail on.
black'ness, *n.*, the state of being black.
Black' Rod, *n.*, the usher of the Order of the Garter; the usher of the Lords in Parliament.
black'smith, *n.*, an iron-smith.
black'thorn, *n.*, the sloe; a cudgel.
blad'der, *n.*, a thin membranous bag in the body of an animal containing the urine, the gall, etc.; any similar vesicle.
blade, *n.*, the cutting part of an instrument; a leaf of grass; the broad part of an oar; a rollicking fellow.
blade'-bone, *n.*, the shoulder-blade, the scapula.
blad'ed, *adj.*, having a blade.
blain, *n.*, a blister.
blame, *v.t.*, to censure or reproach; *n.*, imputation of a fault.
blame'able, *adj.*, deserving of blame.
blamed, *p.p.*, blame.
blame'ful, *adj.*, faulty; meriting blame.
blame'less, *adj.*, without fault.
blame'lessness, *n.*, the state of being blameless.
blam'er, *n.*, one who blames.
blame'worthy, *adj.*, culpable.
blam'ing, *pr.p.*, blame.
blanch, *v.t.* and *i.*, to whiten.
blanched, *p.p.*, blanch.
blanchim'eter, *n.*, an instrument for measuring bleaching power.
blanch'ing, *pr.p.*, blanch.
blancmange', *n.*, a kind of white jelly-like pudding.

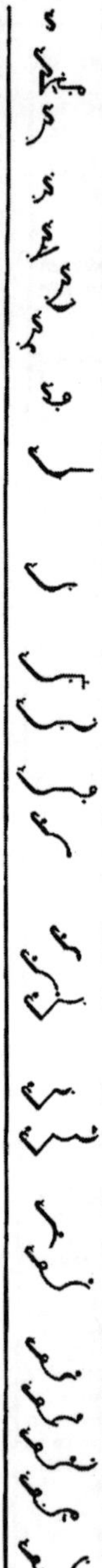

bland, *adj.*, mild; gentle; suave.
blandil'oquence, *n.*, flattering speech.
bland'ish, *v.t.* and *i.*, to caress or flatter; to render alluring.
bland'ished, *p.p.*, blandish.
bland'isher, *n.*, a flatterer.
bland'ishing, *pr.p.*, blandish.
bland'ishment, *n.*, artful caresses; cajolery; endearment.
bland'ness, *n.*, the state of being bland.
blank, *adj.*, white; empty; vacant; *n.*, an empty paper; an empty space on a paper; any void.
blank'et, *n.*, a soft, thick, woollen cloth used as a bed-covering.
blank'eted, *adj.*, covered with a blanket.
blank'eting, *n.*, material of which blankets are made.
blank'ness, *n.*, the state of being blank.
blare, *v.i.*, to make a loud trumpet-like noise; *v.t.*, to proclaim loudly; *n.*, a loud noise.
blared, *p.p.*, blare.
bla'ring, *pr.p.*, blare; *adj.*, harsh, loud.
blar'ney, *n.*, gross flattery; deceitful talk; *v.t.*, to humbug with talk.
blar'neyed, *p.p.*, blarney.
blar'neying, *pr.p.*, blarney; *n.*, the act of blarneying.
blasé, *adj.*, sated with pleasure.
blaspheme', *v.t.*, to speak impiously of; *v.i.*, to utter blasphemy.
blasphemed', *p.p.*, blaspheme.
blasphe'mer, *n.*, one who blasphemes.
blasphe'ming, *pr.p.*, blaspheme.
blas'phemous, *adj.*, impiously irreverent towards God.
blas'phemously, *adv.*, in a blasphemous manner.

blas'phemy, *n.*, grossly irreverent or outrageous language.

blast, *n.*, a gust of wind; the sound of blowing a wind-instrument; a blight; a violent explosion; *v.t.*, to injure by a blast or blight; to split by an explosion.

blast'ed, *p.p.*, blast.

blaste'ma, *n.*, the axis of growth of an embryo plant.

blast'er, *n.*, one who blasts.

blast'-furnace, *n.*, a smelting-furnace.

blast'ing, *pr.p.*, blast; *n.*, the operation of blasting.

blastocar'pous, *adj.*, having the germ beginning to grow inside the fruit.

blas'toderm, *n.*, the outside of the embryo in its earliest condition.

blast'pipe, *n.*, the pipe of a locomotive which carries the waste steam up the chimney.

bla'tant, *adj.*, noisy.

blat'ter, *v.i.*, to make a senseless noise.

blay, *n.*, a fish.

blaze, *n.*, a flame, a bursting out; a white spot on a horse's forehead; a white spot on a tree made by removing the bark; *v.i.*, to flame; *v.t.*, to proclaim; to make marks on trees to indicate a path.

blazed, *p.p.*, blaze.

blaz'ing, *pr.p.*, blaze.

bla'zon, *n.*, a heraldic figure; *v.t.*, to describe armorial bearings; to adorn; to proclaim.

bla'zoned, *p.p.*, blazon.

bla'zoner, *n.*, one who blazons; a herald; a scandal-monger.

bla'zoning, *pr.p.*, blazon.

bla'zonry, *n.*, the art of describing coats-of-arms.

bleach, *v.t.*, to whiten.

bleached, *p.p.*, bleach.

bleach'er, *n.*, one who bleaches.

bleach'ery, *n.*, an establishment where cloth is bleached.

bleach'ing, *n.*, the act or art of making textile fabrics white; *pr.p.*, bleach.

bleak, *adj.*, cold; chill; dreary.

bleak'ish, *adj.*, rather bleak.

bleak'ly, *adv.*, in a bleak manner.

bleak'ness, *n.*, the state of being bleak.

blear, *adj.*, sore (of the eyes); *v.t.*, to make sore so that the sight is dimmed.

blear'-eyed, *adj.*, sore-eyed; dim-sighted.

bleat, *v.i.*, to utter the cry of a sheep; *n.*, the cry of a sheep.

bleat'ed, *p.p.*, bleat.

bleat'er, *n.*, one who bleats.

bleat'ing, *n.*, the cry of a sheep; *pr.p.*, bleat.

bleb, *n.*, a blister.

bled, *p.p.*, bleed.

bleed, *v.i.*, to lose blood; *v.t.*, to take blood from.

bleed'ing, *n.*, the operation of letting blood.

blem'ish, *v.t.*, to impair or sully; *n.*, a defect.

blem'ished, *p.p.*, blemish.

blem'ishing, *pr.p.*, blemish.

blench, *v.i.*, to shrink; to flinch.

blenched, *p.p.*, blench.

blench'ing, *pr.p.*, blench.

blend, *v.t.*, to mingle; *v.i.*, to be mixed; *n.*, a mixture.

blende, *n.*, an ore of zinc.

blend'ed, *p.p.*, blend.

blend'er, *n.*, one who blends.

blend'ing, *pr.p.*, blend.

blen'ny, *n.*, a small fish found among rocks.

blent, *adj.*, another form of *blended*.

bles'-bok, *n.*, a white-faced South African antelope.

bless, *v.t.*, to invoke or bestow happiness on; to glorify for benefits received.

blessed, *p.p.*, bless.

bless'ed, *adj.*, favoured with blessings; sacred; holy.

bless'edly, *adv.*, in a blessed manner.

bless'edness, *n.*, happiness; God's favour.

bless'er, *n.*, one who blesses.

bless'ing, *n.*, the act of one who blesses; any good thing falling to one's lot; *pr.p.*, bless.

blest, *adj.*, another form of *blessed*.

blet, *n.*, over-ripeness in fruit.

blet'onism, *n.*, the faculty of water divination.

blet'onist, *n.*, a water diviner.

blew, *p.t.*, blow.

blight, *n.*, something that nips or destroys plants; *v.t.*, to blast; to frustrate.

blight'ed, *adj.*, smitten with blight; blasted; *p.p.*, blight.

blight'ing, *adj.*, destroying; *pr.p.*, blight.

blight'ingly, *adv.*, in a blighting manner.

blind, *adj.*, without sight; closed at one end; *v.t.*, to make blind; *n.*, something to hinder sight or to keep out light; the cover of a window; a pretext; a covert design.

blind'ed, *p.p.*, blind.

blind'er, *n.*, one who blinds; a horse's blinker.

blind'fold, *adj.*, having the eyes bandaged; *v.t.*, to cover the eyes with a bandage.

blind'folded, *adj.*, *i.q.* blindfold; *p.p.*, blindfold.

blind'folding, *pr.p.*, blindfold.

blind'ing, *adj.*, making blind; dazzling; *pr.p.*, blind.

blind'ly, *adv.*, without sight or understanding; in a reckless manner.

blind'man's-buff, *n.*, a child's game.

blind'ness, *n.*, the state of being blind.

blind'-side, *n.*, a weakness of character which allows one to be taken advantage of.

blink, *v.i.*, to wink; to glimmer; *v.t.*, to shut one's eyes to; to evade purposely; *n.*, a glance of the eye; a glimmer.

blink'ard, *n.*, one who blinks.

blinked, *p.p.*, blink.

blink'er, *n.*, one who blinks; a leather flap placed on either side of a horse's head to prevent him from seeing sideways or backwards.

blink'ing, *pr.p.*, blink.

bliss, *n.*, supreme happiness.

bliss'ful, *adj.*, full of bliss.

bliss'fulness, *n.*, extreme happiness.

blis'ter, *n.*, a thin vesicle on the skin containing watery matter; *v.t.*, to raise a blister on; *v.i.*, to become blistered.

blis'tered, *p.p.*, blister.

blis'tering, *adj.*, causing blisters; *pr.p.*, blister.

blis'tery, *adj.*, full of blisters.

blithe, *adj.*, gay; joyful; merry.

blithe'ful, *i.q.* blithe.

blithe'ly, *adv.*, in a blithe manner.

blithe'some, *adj.*, full of gaiety; cheerful.

blithe'someness, *n.*, gaiety.

bliz'zard, *n.*, a driving storm of sleet and snow.

bloat, *v.t.*, to make swollen; *v.i.*, to become swollen.

bloat'ed, *adj.*, swollen; unduly large; *p.p.*, bloat.

bloat'edness, *n.*, the state of being bloated.

bloat'er, *n.*, a smoke-dried herring.

bloat'ing, *pr.p.*, bloat.

blob'ber, *n.*, *i.q.* blubber.

blob'ber-lipped, *adj.*, having thick lips.

block, *n.*, a solid mass usually shaped with flat sides; an obstruction; a casing containing pulleys; a portion of a city enclosed by streets; a piece of wood or metal on which an engraving is cut; *v.t.*, to obstruct; to stop the ball with the bat at cricket.

blockade', *n.*, the prevention of ingress to a place by surrounding it with ships or troops; *v.t.*, to shut a place up in this way.

blockad'ed, *p.p.*, blockade.

blockad'ing, *pr.p.*, blockade.

block'-book, *n.*, a book printed from movable wooden blocks.

blocked, *p.p.*, block.

block'head, *n.*, a stupid fellow.

block'house, *n.*, a sort of fort.

block'ing, *pr.p.*, block.

block'ish, *adj.*, stupid.

block'-tin, *n.*, tin cast into ingots.

blond, blonde, *adj.*, of fair complexion.

blood, *n.*, the fluid in the arteries and veins of the body; consanguinity; *v.t.*, to bleed; to give a taste of blood.

blood'ed, *p.p.*, blood.

blood'-guiltiness, *n.*, murder.

blood'-heat, *n.*, the temperature of the human blood in health.

blood'hound, *n.*, a large dog of acute powers of scent.

blood'ily, *adv.*, in a bloody manner.

blood'iness, *n.*, murderousness.

blood'ing, *pr.p.*, blood.

blood'less, *adj.*, empty of blood; without shedding blood.

blood'-red, *adj.*, as red as blood.

blood'-relation, *n.*, one related by blood.

blood'root, *n.*, the tormentil.

blood'shed, *n.*, slaughter.

blood'shot, *adj.*, red and with congested veins (said of the eyes).

blood'stained, *adj.*, stained with blood.

blood'sucker, *n.*, any animal that sucks blood; an extortioner.

blood'thirsty, *adj.*, desirous to shed blood.

blood'-vessel, *n.*, a vein or artery.

blood'wort, *n.*, the bloody-veined dock.

blood'y, *adj.*, pert. to blood; bloodstained, cruel.

bloom, *n.*, a blossom; fullness of life and vigour; a glow or flush; the delicate powdery coating of certain fruits; *v.i.*, to put forth flowers; to show the beauty of youth.

bloom'ary, *n.*, the first forge in which iron is smelted.

bloomed, *p.p.*, bloom.

bloom'er, *n.*, a costume for women including loose trousers; *pl.*, the trousers alone.

bloom'ery, *n.*, *i.q.* bloomary.

bloom'ing, *adj.*, glowing as with youth and health; *pr.p.*, bloom.

bloom'ingly, *adv.*, in a blooming manner.

bloom'y, *adj.*, full of bloom.

blos'som, *n.*, the flower of a plant; *v.i.*, to put forth blossoms.

blos'somed, *adj.*, in bloom; *p.p.*, blossom.

blos'soming, *pr.p.*, blossom.

blot, *n.*, a spot or stain; *v.t.*, to stain; to dry by means of blotting-paper, etc.

blotch, *n.*, an irregular spot; *v.t.*, to mark with blotches.
blote, *v.t.*, to cure herrings.
blot'ted, *p.p.*, blot.
blot'ter, *n.*, one who or that which blots.
blot'ting, *pr.p.*, blot.
blouse, *n.*, a light, loose upper garment worn by workmen and children; a loose, outer bodice worn by women.
blow, *v.i.*, to make a current of air; to blossom; *v.t.*, to drive a current of air upon or into; *n.*, a stroke with the hand or a weapon; a calamity.
blow'er, *n.*, one who or that which blows.
blow'ing, *pr.p.*, blow.
blown, *p.p.*, blow.
blow'-pipe, *n.*, an instrument to produce intense heat; a tube through which savages blow poisoned darts.
blow'-valve, *n.*, a snifting valve.
blowzed, *adj.*, fat and ruddy.
blowz'y, *i.q.* blowzed.
blub'ber, *n.*, the fat of whales; *v.i.*, to weep so as to disfigure the face.
blub'bered, *p.p.*, blubber.
blub'bering, *pr.p.*, blubber.
bluch'er, *n.*, a strong leather half-boot or high shoe.
blud'geon, *n.*, a short stick with a heavy end used as a weapon; *v.t.*, to strike with a bludgeon.
blue, *adj.*, sky-coloured; *n.*, the colour of clear sky or deep sea; *v.t.*, to make blue.
blue'-bell, *n.*, the wild hyacinth or the hare-bell.
blue'berry, *n.*, a plant or shrub of the heath kind, bearing edible blue berries.
blue'-bird, *n.*, the blue robin (U.S.A.).
blue'book, *n.*, a British Government official report.
blue'bottle, *n.*, a fly with a large blue belly.
blue'-light, *n.*, a composition burning with a brilliant blue light, used as a flare.
blue'ness, *n.*, the quality of being blue.
blues, *n. pl.*, hypochondria; dejection.
blue'-stocking, *n.*, a literary lady; a female pedant.
blue'-stone, *n.*, sulphate of copper.
blu'ey, *adj.*, rather blue.
bluff, *adj.*, broad and full; frank and good-humoured; *n.*, a high bank with a steep front; bold words or acts meant to daunt an opponent; *v.t.*, to deceive with bluff.
bluffed, *p.p.*, bluff.
bluff'ing, *pr.p.*, bluff.
bluff'ness, *n.*, frankness; good-humour.
bluf'fy, *adj.*, having bold, projecting banks.
blu'ish, *adj.*, blue in a slight degree.
blu'ishly, *adv.*, in a bluish manner.
blun'der, *v.i.*, to make a gross mistake; to stumble; *n.*, a stupid mistake.
blun'derbuss, *n.*, a short gun or long pistol with a wide barrel.
blun'dered, *p.p.*, blunder.
blun'derer, *n.*, one who blunders.
blun'derhead, *n.*, a stupid fellow.
blun'dering, *pr.p.*, blunder.
blunt, *adj.*, dull, not sharp; having a thick edge or point; unceremonious; *v.t.*, to impair the keenness of.
blunt'ed, *p.p.*, blunt.
blunt'ing, *pr.p.*, blunt.
blunt'ish, *adj.*, rather blunt.
blunt'ly, *adv.*, in a blunt manner.
blunt'ness, *n.*, the state of being blunt.
blur, *n.*, a blot; a confused appearance; *v.t.*, to render indistinct.
blurred, *p.p.*, blur.
blur'ring, *pr.p.*, blur.
blurt, *v.t.*, to utter suddenly.
blurt'ed, *p.p.*, blurt.
blurt'ing, *pr.p.*, blurt.
blush, *v.i.*, to redden in the cheeks; *n.*, the act of blushing.
blushed, *p.p.*, blush.
blush'ing, *pr.p.*, blush; *adj.*, exhibiting blushes.
blush'ingly, *adv.*, with blushes.
blus'ter, *v.i.*, to roar; to bully.
blus'tered, *p.p.*, bluster.
blus'terer, *n.*, one who blusters.
blus'tering, *adj.*, noisy; swaggering; *pr.p.*, bluster.
blus'terous, **blus'trous**, *adj.*, noisy; tempestuous.
bo, *interj.*, a cry used to startle.
bo'a, *n.*, a very large species of serpents; a lady's neck-wrap.
bo'a-constric'tor, *n.*, one of the largest serpents, often 30 ft. long.
Boaner'ges, *n.*, a vociferous preacher.
boar, *n.*, a male pig.
board, *n.*, a piece of timber sawed thin and of considerable length and breadth compared with the thickness; daily food; *v.t.*, to go on to a vessel; to supply with board; *v.i.*, to live as a boarder.
board'able, *adj.*, capable of being boarded (as a ship).
board'ed, *p.p.*, board.
board'er, *n.*, one who boards a ship in action; one who has his daily food for payment at another's table.
board'ing, *pr.p.*, board.

board'ing-house, *n.*, a house where board and lodging is provided.

board'ing-*school*, *n.*, a school in which the pupils are boarded.

board'-wages, *n.*, wages allowed to servants in lieu of victuals.

boar'ish, *adj.*, pert. to a boar; swinish; brutal.

boast, *v.i.*, to speak in high praise of oneself or one's belongings; *n.*, a statement expressing vanity or pride.

boast'ed, *p.p.*, boast.

boast'er, *n.*, one who boasts.

boast'ful, *adj.*, addicted to boasting.

boast'fulness, *n.*, the state of being boastful.

boast'fully, *adv.*, in a boastful way.

boast'ing, *pr.p.*, boast; *n.*, the habit of being boastful.

boast'ingly, *adv.*, in a boasting manner.

boat, *n.*, a small vessel usually propelled by rowing; *v.i.*, to row or sail.

boat'able, *adj.*, fit to sail or row a boat on.

boat'bill, *n.*, a South American bird.

boat'builder, *n.*, a man who builds boats.

boat'ed, *p.p.*, boat.

boat'hook, *n.*, an iron hook for pulling or pushing a boat.

boat'ing, *n.*, rowing or sailing; *pr.p.*, boat.

boat'man, *n.*, a man who manages a boat.

boat'swain, *n.*, a ship's officer who summons the crew to their duty.

bob, *n.*, any small round object at the end of a string, chain, etc.; *v.t.*, to move jerkily; *v.i.*, to drop a curtsey.

bobbed, *p.p.*, bob.

bob'bin, *n.*, a small drum of wood on which thread is wound.

bob'binet, *n.*, a machine-made cotton net.

bob'bing, *pr.p.*, bob.

bob'olink, *n.*, the rice-bird of North America.

bob'stay, *n.*, a rope or chain attached to the bowsprit.

bob'tail, *n.*, a short tail; the rabble.

bob'tailed, *adj.*, having a tail cut short.

boc'asin, *n.*, a woollen stuff or calamanco.

Boche, *n.*, a name invented for the Germans by the French in the Great War.

bocking, *n.*, a coarse woollen fabric used as a floor-cloth.

bock'land, *n.*, a species of land-tenure.

bode, *v.i.*, to be ominous; *v.t.*, to portend; *p.p.*, bide.

bod'ed, *p.p.*, bode.

bode'ga, *n.*, a wine shop; a shop.

bod'ice, *n.*, the body part of a woman's dress.

bod'ied, *adj.*, having a body; *p.p.*, body.

bod'iless, *adj.*, having no material form; incorporeal.

bod'ily, *adj.*, concerning the body; *adv.*, completely.

bod'ing, *adj.*, ominous; *pr.p.*, bode.

bod'kin, *n.*, a blunt needle for drawing cord through a slot; a hair-pin.

Bodlei'an, *adj.*, rel. to Bodley, esp. describing the great university library at Oxford; *n.*, the library itself.

bod'y, *n.*, any entity; a human being; a corporation; substance; strength; *v.i.*, to invest with a body.

bod'y-clothes, *n. pl.*, attire, dress.

bod'y-*guard*, *n.*, a band of life-guards.

bod'ying, *pr.p.*, body.

bod'y-pol'itic, *n.*, the whole body of citizens.

Boeo'tian, *adj.*, pert. to Boeotia; stupid.

Boer, *n.*, a Dutch farmer or other colonist in South Africa.

bo'fors, *n.*, a type of naval gun.

bog, *n.*, a quagmire or morass; *v.t.*, to overwhelm in mire.

bo'gey, *n.*, *i.q.* bogy; also a fixed score-value for the holes on a golf course.

bogged, *p.p.*, bog.

bog'gle, *v.i.*, to hesitate; to shilly-shally.

bog'gled, *p.p.*, boggle.

bog'gler, *n.*, a waverer; an inconstant person.

bog'gling, *pr.p.*, boggle.

bog'gy, *adj.*, marshy; miry.

bo'gie, *n.*, a four-wheeled truck supporting the front or hind part of a wagon or locomotive.

bog'-land, *n.*, marshy land.

bo'gus, *adj.*, spurious; counterfeit.

bo'gy, *n.*, a hobgoblin; a wicked spirit.

boh, *interj.*, *i.q.* bo.

bohea', *n.*, an inferior black tea.

Bohe'mian, *n.*, a person, esp. an artist who despises conventionalities; *adj.*, pert. to Bohemia.

boil, *v.i.*, to bubble by the action of heat; to be violently agitated; *v.t.*, to subject to the action of heat in a liquid; *n.*, an inflamed, suppurating tumour.

boiled, *p.p.*, boil.

boil'er, *n.*, a vessel in which water is boiled or steam generated.

boil'er-plate, *n.*, iron plate for making boilers of engines.

boil'ery, *n.*, a place for boiling.

boil'ing, *pr.p.*, boil.

boil'ing-point, *n.*, the temperature at

which a liquid changes into a gas and *vice versâ*.

bois'terous, *adj.*, violent; stormy; turbulent.

bois'terously, *adv.*, in a boisterous manner.

bo'lar, *adj.*, clayey.

bold, *adj.*, daring; executed with courage; impudent; conspicuous.

bold'er, *adj.*, *comp.* of bold.

bold'est, *adj.*, *super.* of bold.

bold'ly, *adv.*, in a bold manner.

bold'ness, *n.*, the state or quality of being bold.

bole, *n.*, a tree-stem; a kind of yellow or brown earth containing iron oxide.

bole'ro, *n.*, a Spanish dance.

boll, *n.*, a Scottish dry measure containing about six bushels.

bol'lard, *n.*, a post or stanchion on a wharf or quay.

Bolognese', *adj.*, pert. to Bologna.

Bolo'gnian, *n.*, an inhabitant of Bologna; *adj.*, *i.q.* Bolognese.

bol'ster, *n.*, a kind of long under-pillow; *v.t.*, to support unworthily.

bol'stered, *p.p.*, bolster.

bol'stering, *pr.p.*, bolster.

bolt, *n.*, an arrow; a stream of lightning; a stout metallic pin for fastening objects together; a bar; *v.t.*, to fasten with a bolt; to swallow hurriedly; to sift; *v.i.*, to start and run off.

bolt'ed, *p.p.*, bolt.

bolt'er, *n.*, a horse given to bolting; a sieve.

bolt'ing, *pr.p.*, bolt.

bolt'ing-cloth, *n.*, sieve cloth.

bo'lus, *n.*, a round mass of medicinal matter to be swallowed at a gulp, larger and softer than a pill.

bomb, *n.*, a destructive projectile, hollow and filled with explosives; *v.t.*, to throw bombs at.

bom'bard, *n.*, a short, wide-mouthed cannon.

bombard', *v.t.*, to attack with bombs.

bombard'ed, *p.p.*, bombard.

bombardier', *n.*, a soldier who throws bombs; a non-commissioned artillery officer.

bombard'ing, *pr.p.*, bombard.

bombard'ment, *n.*, the act of bombarding.

bombasine', *n.*, a fabric partly worsted and partly silk or cotton.

bom'bast, *n.*, high-sounding words.

bombast'ic, *adj.*, high-sounding; turgid.

bombazette', *n.*, a thin woollen cloth.

bombazine', *n.*, *i.q.* bombasine.

bombed, *p.p.*, bomb.

bomb'ing, *pr.p.*, bomb.

bomb'-proof, *adj.*, secure against the action of bombs.

bomb'-shell, *n.*, a spherical bomb.

bom'byx, *n.*, a silkworm.

bon-accord', *n.*, goodwill (*Scot.*).

bo'na fi'de, *adj.* and *adv.*, in good faith.

bo'na fi'des, *n.*, good faith; honesty of purpose (*Lat.*).

bonan'za, *n.*, a rich mine; an unexpected prize.

Bonapart'ean, *adj.*, rel. to Bonaparte.

Bo'napartism, *n.*, support of the Bonaparte family in their claim to the French throne.

Bo'napartist, *n.*, one who supports the Bonapartes.

bona'sus, *n.*, the European bison; the aurochs.

bonas'sus, *n.*, *i.q.* bonasus.

bon'-bon, *n.*, a sugarplum.

bond, *n.*, anything that binds; the state of being bonded.

bond'age, *n.*, slavery.

bond'ed, *adj.*, applied to a licensed warehouse in which goods liable to government duties are stored.

bond'holder, *n.*, one who holds a bond or binding deed.

bond'ing, *adj.*, pert. to a bonder.

bond'maid, *n.*, a female slave.

bond'man, *n.*, a slave.

bond'servant, *n.*, a slave.

bonds'man, *n.*, *i.q.* bondman.

bond'woman, *n.*, a woman slave.

bone, *n.*, one of the pieces of which the skeleton of an animal is composed; *v.t.*, to take the bones out of; to put whalebone into.

boned, *p.p.*, bone.

bone'lace, *n.*, a linen lace.

bone'set, *v.t.*, to set broken bones.

bone'setter, *n.*, one who sets broken or dislocated bones.

bone'setting, *n.*, the art of setting bones.

bone'shaker, *n.*, an obsolete or defective bicycle.

bon'fire, *n.*, a fire made to express public joy.

bonhomie', *n.*, good humour.

Bon'iface, *n.*, a sleek, jolly innkeeper.

bon'ing, *pr.p.*, bone.

bon mot, *n.*, a witticism (*Fr.*).

bonne' bouche, *n.*, a titbit (*Fr.*).

bon'net, *n.*, a covering for the head; one for the top of anything; *v.t.*, to force the hat over the eyes of.

bon'neted, *adj.*, wearing a bonnet; *p.p.*, bonnet.

bon'netting, *pr.p.*, bonnet.

bon'nily, *adv.*, in a bonny manner.

bon'ny, *adj.*, handsome; pretty; fine.

bo'nus, *n.*, an extra payment made out of profits.

bon'y, *adj.*, having prominent bones.

bonze, *n.*, a Buddhist monk.

boo, *interj.*, a rude expression of contempt; *n.*, a hoot; *v.t.*, to insult with booing; *v.i.*, to hoot.

boo'by, *n.*, a stupid fellow; a bird of the pelican family.

boo'dle, *n.*, money; profit (*Amer. slang*).

book, *n.*, a number of sheets of paper stitched together and bound in a cover; *v.t.*, to register in a book; to buy a ticket for a journey.

book'-account, *n.*, a statement of debts.

book'binder, *n.*, one who binds books.

book'bindery, *n.*, a place where books are bound.

book'binding, *n.*, the art of binding books.

book'case, *n.*, a case of shelves for holding books.

book'-debt, *n.*, a debt against a person in an account-book.

booked, *p.p.*, book.

book'ing, *pr.p.*, book.

book'ish, *adj.*, studious; better acquainted with books than with the world.

book'ishness, *n.*, fondness for study.

book'-keeper, *n.*, one who keeps accounts.

book'-keeping, *n.*, the art of keeping accounts.

book'-knowledge, *n.*, knowledge derived from books.

book'land, *n.*, *i.q.* bockland.

book'let, *n.*, a little book.

book'-maker, *n.*, a maker of books; a betting-man who wagers on the defeat of a specified horse; a layer of odds as opposed to a backer.

book'mark, *n.*, a slip or strip to put between the leaves of a book to mark a place.

book'post, *n.*, the system of conveying books, etc., by post at a cheaper rate.

book'rack, *n.*, a rack for books.

book'seller, *n.*, one whose occupation is to sell books.

book'selling, *n.*, the business of selling books.

book'shelf, *n.*, a shelf to hold books.

book'stall, *n.*, a stall holding books offered for sale.

book'store, *n.*, a bookshop.

book'worm, *n.*, a worm or mite that eats holes in books; an over-studious person.

boom, *n.*, a long pole on which the bottom parts of sails are extended; a beam across a river which prevents ships from entering; a deep, hollow noise; *v.i.*, to advertise; to make a hollow noise.

boomed, *p.p.*, boom; having a boom.

boom'erang, *n.*, an Australian missile which returns to the thrower if it misses its mark.

boom'ing, *pr.p.*, boom.

boon, *n.*, a favour.

boor, *n.*, a rustic; an ill-mannered person.

boor'ish, *adj.*, awkward in manners.

boor'ishly, *adv.*, in a boorish manner.

boose, *v.i.*, *i.q.* booze.

boos'er, *n.*, *i.q.* boozer.

boos'y, *adj.*, *i.q.* boozy.

boot, *n.*, a covering for the foot and part of the leg; profit; *v.t.*, to avail (*impers.*).

boot'ed, *adj.*, wearing boots; *pr.p.*, boot.

bootee', *n.*, a child's knitted boot.

booth, *n.*, a temporary house or shed in a fair or market.

boot'ikin, *n.*, a child's legging.

boot'jack, *n.*, an instrument for drawing off boots.

boot'less, *adj.*, unprofitable; unavailing.

boot'lessly, *adv.*, in a bootless manner.

boot'-tree, *n.*, a contrivance to stretch and keep in shape a boot.

boot'y, *n.*, plunder.

booze, *v.i.*, to drink heavily.

boozed, *p.p.*, booze.

booz'er, *n.*, a heavy drinker.

booz'ing, *pr.p.*, booze.

booz'y, *adj.*, fuddled.

bopeep', *n.*, a game among children.

borac'ic, *adj.*, produced from borax.

bor'age, *n.*, a plant formerly infused in hot drinks, akin to the forget-me-not.

bo'rate, *n.*, a salt formed from boracic acid and a base.

bo'rax, *n.*, a crystalline compound of soda and boracic acid.

bor'der, *n.*, the outer edge of anything; *v.t.*, to have the edge adjoining.

bor'dered, *p.p.*, border.

bor'derer, *n.*, one who dwells on or near the border of a country.

bor'dering, *pr.p.*, border.

bor'der-land, *n.*, land forming a border or frontier.

bor'dure, *n.*, in heraldry, the border of a shield.

bore, *v.t.*, to penetrate by piercing; to weary by insufferable dulness; *n.*, the hole made by boring; the cavity of a tube; a dull person; a sudden tidal wave in a river; *p.t.*, bear.

bo'real, *adj.*, northern.
Bo'reas, *n.*, the North Wind.
bore'cole, *n.*, a hardy winter cabbage.
bored, *p.p.*, bore.
bore'dom, *n.*, the state of being bored.
bor'er, *n.*, one who, or that which, bores.
bo'ric, *adj.*, *i.q.* boracic.
bo'ring, *pr.p.*, bore; *adj.*, tedious, wearisome.
born, *p.p.*, bear (*to bring forth*).
borne, *p.p.*, bear (*to carry*).
bo'ron, *n.*, the characteristic element contained in borax.
bor'ough, *n.*, a corporate town.
bor'row, *v.t.*, to obtain on loan.
bor'rowed, *p.p.*, borrow.
bor'rower, *n.*, one who borrows.
bor'rowing, *pr.p.*, borrow.
Bor'stal system, *n.*, a method of reclaiming senior boy criminals.
bos, *n.*, an ox (*Lat.*).
bos'cage, *n.*, sylvan foliage.
bosh, *n.*, nonsense.
bosk'et, *n.*, a grove; a shrubbery.
bosk'y, *adj.*, covered with thickets; bushy.
bos'om, *n.*, the human breast; *adj.*, dear; *v.t.*, to embrace, embosom.
bos'omed, *p.p.*, bosom.
bos'oming, *pr.p.*, bosom.
boss, *n.*, a knob, protuberance; a master; *v.t.*, to order peremptorily.
bos'sage, *n.*, rustic work made of rough stones in building.
bossed, *p.p.*, boss; *adj.*, ornamented with bosses.
boss'ing, *pr.p.*, boss.
bos'sy, *adj.*, *i.q.* bossed.
Bos'well, *n.*, any biographer.
bot, *n.*, the maggot of a gadfly.
botan'ic, *adj.*, rel. to plants or botany.
botan'ical, *adj.*, *i.q.* botanic.
bot'anist, *n.*, one skilled in botany.
bot'anize, *v.i.*, to study plants.
bot'anized, *p.p.*, botanize.
bot'anizing, *pr.p.*, botanize.
bot'any, *n.*, the science which treats of the vegetable kingdom.
botar'go, *n.*, the salted roes of the mullet or tunny.
botch, *v.t.*, to mend or patch clumsily; *n.*, a swelling or blotch on the skin.
botched, *p.p.*, botch.
botch'er, *n.*, a clumsy workman at mending.
botch'ery, *n.*, clumsy workmanship.
botch'ing, *pr.p.*, botch.
botch'y, *adj.*, marked with botches.
bote, *n.*, compensation (*legal*).
bot'-fly, *n.*, a fly that produces bots.
both, *adj.*, *pron.*, *adv.* and *conj.*, the one and the other; the pair.
both'er, *v.t.*, to annoy; *n.*, a trouble.
both'ered, *p.p.*, bother.
both'ering, *pr.p.*, bother.
both'ie, both'y, *n.*, a building used as a lodging by workpeople (*Scot.*).
Both'nian, *adj.*, rel. to Bothnia.
Both'nic, *adj.*, *i.q.* Bothnian.
bot'ryoid, *adj.*, shaped like a bunch of grapes.
botryoid'al, *adj.*, *i.q.* botryoid.
bot'ryolite, *n.*, a variety of datolite.
bots, botts, *n. pl.*, the maggots of gadflies, causing a cattle disease.
bot'tine, *n.*, a half-boot; a surgical boot.
bot'tle, *n.*, a narrow-mouthed hollow vessel for containing liquids; *v.t.*, to put into bottles.
bot'tled, *p.p.*, bottle.
bot'tling, *pr.p.*, bottle.
bot'tom, *n.*, the lowest part of anything; the seat; the base; *adj.*, lowest; *v.t.*, to furnish with a bottom; reach the bottom of.
bot'tomed, *adj.*, having a bottom; *p.p.*, bottom.
bot'toming, *pr.p.*, bottom.
bot'tomless, *adj.*, fathomless.
bot'tomry, *n.*, the act of borrowing money by mortgaging or pledging a ship.
bouche, *v.t.*, to drill a new mouth in a spiked gun.
boudoir', *n.*, a small private room belonging to a lady.
bough, *n.*, a large branch of a tree.
bought, *p.p.*, buy.
bou'gie, *n.*, a wax taper; a surgical instrument for opening obstructed narrow passages.
bouil'li, *n.*, meat stewed with vegetables. [soup.
bouil'lon, *n.*, broth,
boul'der, *n.*, a water-worn, rounded stone, larger than a pebble; an ice-worn rock of large size found in clays and gravels of the Drift formation.
boul'evard, *n.*, a wide street shaded with trees; properly, a walk on the bulwarks or ramparts of a town.
bounce, *v.i.*, to make a sudden leap; to boast; *v.t.*, to drive suddenly and violently against anything; *n.*, a heavy blow; boasting.
bounced, *p.p.*, bounce.
bounc'er, *n.*, one that bounces; a braggart.
bounc'ing, *adj.*, vigorous; stout; *pr.p.*, bounce.
bounc'ingly, *adv.*, in a bouncing manner.
bound, *n.*, a limit; a leap; *v.t.*, to circumscribe; *v.i.*, to spring;

adj., prepared; destined; restrained; *p.p.*, bind.

bound'ary, *n.*, a limit.

bound'ed, *adj.*, limited; *p.p.*, bound.

bound'en, *adj.*, obligatory.

bound'er, *n.*, one who or that which bounds; a pretentious, vulgar fellow.

bound'ing, *pr. p.*, bound.

bound'less, *adj.*, illimitable; infinite.

bound'lessly, *adv.*, in unlimited degree.

bound'lessness, *n.*, the state of being boundless.

boun'teous, *adj.*, generous.

boun'teously, *adv.*, liberally.

boun'teousness, *n.*, the quality of being bounteous.

boun'tiful, *adj.*, munificent.

boun'tifulness, *n.*, the quality of being bountiful.

boun'ty, *n.*, generosity; a favour; a premium.

bouquet', *n.*, a bunch of flowers; an agreeable aroma.

Bour'bonism, *n.*, support of the claims of the Bourbon family to the French throne.

Bour'bonist, *n.*, a French royalist.

bour'geois, *n.*, a citizen, a man of middle rank; *adj.*, mediocre in taste or manners.

bourgeois', *n.*, small printing type, between brevier and long primer.

bourgeois'ie, *n.*, the middle class.

bour'geon, *v.i.* and *n.*, *i.q.* burgeon.

bourn, bourne, *n.*, a limit; a brook.

bourse, *n.*, an exchange where merchants meet to transact business.

boustrophe'don, *n.*, writing running in lines alternately from left to right and from right to left.

bout, *n.*, a set-to; a contest; a debauch.

bouts-rimés', *n. pl.*, words that rhyme given as the ends of lines of a stanza, the other parts to be filled in as an intellectual exercise.

bo'vine, *adj.*, pert. to oxen.

Bo'vril, *n.*, a patent preparation of beef essences.

bow, *n.*, part of a violin; a weapon; a looped knot; an arch or curve.

bow, *n.*, the front part of a ship; *v.t.*, to make to bend; *v.i.*, to bend the body.

bowd'lerize, *v.t.*, to alter a text by cutting out improprieties.

bowd'lerized, *p.p.*, bowdlerize.

bowd'lerizing, *pr.p.*, bowdlerize.

bowed, *p.p.*, bow.

bow'els, *n. pl.*, the intestines; compassion.

bow'er, *n.*, one who bows; one of two anchors at the bow of a ship; a boudoir; an arbour.

bow'ery, *adj.*, having bowers, arboured; a district of New York of evil reputation.

bow'ie-knife, *n.*, a strong knife used as a weapon in the United States.

bow'ing, *pr.p.*, bow.

bow'knot, *n.*, a slipknot.

bowl, *n.*, a hollow vessel, almost hemispherical; the hollow part of anything, as of a spoon or tobacco-pipe; a ball of wood used in a lawn game; *v.t.*, to deliver the ball at cricket; to roll a bowl.

bowled, *p.p.*, bowl.

bow'-leg, *n.*, a crooked leg.

bow'-legged, *adj.*, having crooked or bandy legs.

bowl'er, *n.*, one who plays at bowls; at cricket, the player who delivers or serves the ball to the batsman.

bow'line, *n.*, a rope attached to a square sail and fastened so as to stretch the sail tight forward towards the bow.

bowl'ing, *pr.p.*, bowl.

bowl'ing-green, *n.*, a level lawn for bowling.

bow'man, *n.*, an archer.

bowse, *v.t.*, to pull or haul hard.

bow'sprit, *n.*, the large spar projecting over the bow of a vessel.

bow'-string, *n.*, the string that bends a bow; a string used by Turkish executioners for strangling.

bow'-window, *n.*, a projecting window whose plan is a segment of a circle.

bow'-wow, *interj.*, the bark of a dog; *v.i.*, to bark.

box, *n.*, an evergreen shrub with hard wood; a case; a small room for spectators in a theatre; a shelter; the driver's seat on a carriage; a small house for sportsmen; *v.t.*, to enclose, as in a box; to fight with the fists.

boxed, *p.p.*, box.

box'er, *n.*, a pugilist.

box'ing, *pr.p.*, box.

box'-tree, *n.*, a hard-timbered, evergreen shrub.

box'-wood, *n.*, the fine, hard-grained timber of the box-tree.

boy, *n.*, a male child; a youth; a comrade.

boy'au, *n.*, a zig-zag trench in fortification.

boy'cott, *v.t.*, to ostracize; *n.*, ostracism.

boy'cotted, *p.p.*, boycott.

boy'cotting, *pr.p.*, boycott.

boy'hood, *n.*, the state of being a boy.

boy'ish, *adj.*, pert. to a boy; immature.

boy'ishly, *adv.*, in a boyish manner

boy'ishness, *n.*, the quality of being boyish.

boy's-play, *n.*, child's play; anything easy to accomplish.

brac'cate, *adj.*, feathered as to the feet.

brace, *n.*, that which holds two or more things tight together; a couple; *v.t.*, to tie closely; to strengthen.

braced, *p.p.*, brace.

brace'let, *n.*, an ornament for the wrist.

bra'cer, *n.*, a guard for the wrist.

brach'ial, *adj.* bel. to the arm.

brach'iate, *adj.*, having branches in pairs, each pair at right angles to the next.

brach'iopod, *n.*, a marine mollusc with breathing appendages on either side of its mouth.

brachyg'rapher, *n.*, a shorthand writer.

brachyg'raphy, *n.*, shorthand; stenography.

brachyl'ogy, *n.*, conciseness of expression.

bra'cing, *adj.*, invigorating; *pr.p.*, brace.

brack'en, *n.*, fern.

brack'et, *n.*, a short support projecting from a vertical surface; a gas-pipe projecting from a wall; one of two marks used by printers to enclose an interpolation, etc.; *v.t.*, to furnish with a bracket; to enclose within brackets.

brack'eted, *p.p.*, bracket.

brack'eting, *pr.p.*, bracket.

brack'ish, *adj.*, rather salt.

brack'ishness, *n.*, the quality of being brackish.

bract, *n.*, a modified leaf on the peduncle near the flower.

brac'tea, *n.* (*Lat.*), a thin plate of metal.

bract'eate, *adj.*, furnished with bracteae.

brad, *n.*, a small-headed nail used esp. by bootmakers.

brad'awl, *n.*, an awl to make holes for brads.

brad'ypod, *n.*, a sloth.

brag, *v.i.*, to boast; *n.*, a game at cards.

braggado'cio, *n.*, a braggart; empty boasting.

brag'gart, *n.*, a boaster.

bragged, *p.p.*, brag.

brag'ger, *n.*, one who brags.

brag'ging, *pr.p.*, brag.

Brah'ma, *n.*, a Hindu god; the Creator.

Brah'man, *n.*, a member of the Hindu sacred caste, noted for minute religious observances.

Brah'min, *n.*, *i.q.* Brahman.

Brahmin'ical, *adj.*, pert. to the Brahmins.

braid, *v.t.*, to plait; to intertwine; *n.*, a narrow plaited band.

braid'ed, *p.p.*, braid.

braid'ing, *n.*, trimming made of braid; *pr.p.*, braid.

brail, *n.*, a rope attached to a fore-and-aft sail; *v.t.*, to haul in by means of the brails.

Braille, *n.*, a system of reading for the blind by means of raised letters.

brain, *n.*, the soft, greyish matter contained in the skull; the understanding; *v.t.*, to beat out the brains of.

brained, *adj.*, furnished with brains; *p.p.*, brain.

brain'ing, *pr.p.*, brain.

brain'less, *adj.*, without understanding; silly.

brain'pan, *n.*, the skull.

braise, *v.t.* to stew with vegetables.

brake, *n.*, a thicket; an appliance to stop motion by friction; a heavy vehicle for breaking in young horses to harness; a wagonette.

brake'man, *n.*, a man whose business it is to attend to the brakes of a railway train.

brakes'man, *n.*, *i.q.* brakeman.

brak'y, *adj.*, full of brambles and shrubs.

bram'ble, *n.*, a prickly shrub; a blackberry.

bram'bling, *n.*, a British finch, larger than the chaffinch.

bram'bly, *adj.*, full of brambles.

bran, *n.*, the husk of grain.

branch, *n.*, a bough; an offshoot; a subdivision or department; *v.i.*, to send out branches; to diverge.

branched, *p.p.* branch.

bran'chial, *adj.*, rel. to the branchiae or gills of fishes.

branch'ing, *pr.p.*, branch.

branch'iopod, *n.*, a crustacean whose gills are on the feet, as in the water-fleas.

branch'less, *adj.*, without branches.

branch'y, *adj.*, having wide-spreading branches.

brand, *n.*, a sword; a piece of burning or partly burnt wood; a mark made by burning or otherwise to denote ownership, etc.; a trade-mark; a mark of infamy; *v.t.*, to mark; to stigmatize as infamous.

brand'ed, *p.p.*, brand.

brand'er, *n.*, one who brands.

bran'died, *adj.*, flavoured with brandy.

brand'ing, *pr.p.*, brand.

bran'dish, *v.t.*, to wave: to flourish.

bran'dished, *p.p.*, brandish.
bran'dishing, *pr.p.*, brandish.
brand'ling, *n.*, the parr; a young salmon.
brand'-new, *adj.*, absolutely new.
bran'dy, *n.*, a spirituous liquor distilled from wine.
bran'gle, *n.*, a squabble; *v.i.*, to wrangle.
bran'gled, *p.p.*, brangle.
bran'gler, *n.*, a squabbler.
bran'gling, *pr.p.*, brangle.
bran'lin, *n.*, a small red worm used as bait.
bran'ny, *adj.*, resembling or consisting of bran.
brant, *adj.*, *i.q.* brent.
brash, *n.*, a confused heap of fragments of broken rocks or of boughs of trees.
brass, *n.*, an alloy of copper and zinc; a monumental plate; impudence.
bras'sard, *n.*, an armlet.
bras'sart, *n.*, *i.q.* brassard.
brass'-band, *n.*, a company of musicians who perform on instruments of brass.
brasse, *n.*, a spotted fish resembling a perch.
brass'iness, *n.*, the state of being brassy.
brass'y, *adj.*, resembling or composed of brass; *n.*, a wooden golf club protected at the bottom by a brass plate.
brat, *n.*, a child; an apron (*Prov.*).
brava'do, *n.*, a boast.
brave, *adj.*, courageous; *n.*, a daring person; a North American Indian warrior; *v.t.*, to defy.
braved, *p.p.*, brave.
brave'ly, *adv.*, in a brave manner.
brave'ness, *n.*, the quality of being brave.
brav'er, *n.*, one who braves; *comp.* of brave.
brav'ery, *n.*, courage; splendour.
brav'est, *adj.*, *super.* of brave.
brav'ing, *pr.p.*, brave.
bra'vo, *interj.*, well done! *n.*, a hired assassin.
bravu'ra, *adj.* (in music), florid, elaborate.
brawl, *n.*, a noisy quarrel; *v.i.*, to quarrel noisily.
brawled, *p.p.*, brawl.
brawl'er, *n.*, one who brawls.
brawl'ing, *adj.*, quarrelsome; *pr.p.*, brawl.
brawn, *n.*, pig's cheek and ox feet, boiled and pickled, and pressed into a shape; muscular strength.
brawn'y, *adj.*, having large, strong muscles.
brax'y, *n.*, a disease of sheep.
bray, *v.t.*, to pound or grind small; *v.i.*, to utter the cry of an ass; *n.*, the roar of an ass.
brayed, *p.p.*, bray.
bray'er, *n.*, one that brays like an ass.
bray'ing, *pr.p.*, bray.
braze, *v.t.*, to solder with a hard alloy of brass and zinc; to cover or ornament with brass.
brazed, *p.p.*, braze.
bra'zen, *adj.*, made of brass; impudent.
bra'zen-faced, *adj.*, impudent.
bra'zenness, *n.*, brassiness; impudence.
bra'zier, *n.*, an open pan for burning wood or coal.
brazil', *n.*, a very heavy red tropical wood used in dyeing; a republic of South America.
Brazil'ian, *adj.*, pert. to Brazil.
bra'zing, *pr.p.*, braze.
breach, *n.*, the violation of a pledge; a gap, esp. in fortifications; a quarrel; *v.t.*, to make a breach in.
breaching, *pr.p.*, breach.
bread, *n.*, flour moistened, fermented, and baked into a food.
bread'-corn, *n.*, corn or grain of which bread is made.
bread'-fruit, *n.*, the fruit of a tree in Polynesia, used as a substitute for bread.
bread'stuff, *n.*, a collective name for all kinds of grain and flour out of which bread is made.
breadth, *n.*, extent from side to side; width.
bread'winner, *n.*, one whose labour supports a family.
break, *v.t.*, to divide by force; to train to obedience; to cashier or reduce in rank; to violate; *v.i.*, to become broken; to become bankrupt; *n.*, a breach; a brake.
break'able, *adj.*, capable of being broken.
break'age, *n.*, the act of breaking; allowance for accidental breaking.
break'-down, *n.*, an overthrow; a failure; a lively, noisy dance.
break'er, *n.*, one who breaks; a wave broken into foam near the shore; a small, flat water-cask.
break'fast, *n.*, the first meal of the day; *v.i.*, to eat breakfast.
break'fasted, *p.p.*, breakfast.
break'fasting, *pr.p.*, breakfast.
break'ing, *pr.p.* break.
break'man, *n.*, *i.q.* brakeman.
break'water, *n.*, a structure protecting a harbour by breaking the force of the waves.
bream, *n.*, a fresh-water fish of the

carp family; also a spiny sea-perch; *v.t.*, to clean a ship's bottom by fire.

breamed, *p.p.*, bream.

bream'ing, *pr.p.*, bream.

breast, *n.*, the fore-part of the body between the neck and the belly; the seat of the affections and emotions; *v.t.*, to meet in front boldly; to oppose with the breast.

breast'ed, *adj.*, having a breast; *p.p.*, breast.

breast'fast, *n.*, a cable used to fasten the midship part of a boat to a wharf.

breast'ing, *pr.p.*, breast.

breast'knot, *n.*, a knot of ribbon worn on the breast.

breast'pin, *n.*, a fastening or ornament worn on the breast.

breast'plate, *n.*, defensive armour covering the breast.

breast'wheel, *n.*, a water-wheel which delivers the water about half-way between the top and the bottom.

breast'work, *n.*, a breast-high parapet.

breath, *n.*, the air inhaled and exhaled during respiration; air in gentle motion.

breath'able, *adj.*, capable of being breathed.

breathe, *v.i.*, to take breath; to be alive; *v.t.*, to inhale; to utter.

breathed, *p.p.* breathe.

breath'er, *n.*, a sharp spell of exercise.

breath'ing, *n.*, respiration; in grammar, an aspirate; *pr.p.*, breathe.

breath'less, *adj.*, out of breath.

brec'cia, *n.*, a rock made of angular fragments united by a cement.

bred, *p.p.*, breed.

breech, *n.*, the hinder end of anything, esp. of a cannon; *v.t.*, to put into breeches; to flog; to fasten with a breeching.

breeched, *adj.*, having a breech or breeches; *p.p.*, breech.

breech'es, *n. pl.*, a garment worn by men to cover their hips and thighs.

breech'ing, *n.*, a strong rope to minimize the recoil of a gun; the part of harness round a horse's breech; *pr.p.*, breech.

breech'loader, *n.*, a firearm loaded at the breech instead of the muzzle.

breech'loading, *adj.*, loaded at the breech.

breed, *v.t.*, to produce; to bring up or rear; *v.i.*, to bear a child; *n.*, progeny from the same stock.

breed'er, *n.*, one who breeds young; one who takes care to raise a particular breed of animal.

breed'ing, *n.*, the act of producing young, of rearing live stock; upbringing; deportment; good manners; *pr.p.*, breed.

breeze, *n.*, a light wind; a horse-fly.

breez'y, *adj.*, fanned with light winds.

Bre'hon, *n.*, an ancient Irish judge.

brent, *adj.*, applied to a small wild goose which breeds in the north.

bret, *n.*, a kind of brill or turbot.

breth'ren, *n.*, pl. of brother.

bret'tice, *n.*, a partition in mining shafts to assist ventilation; a fence put round dangerous machinery.

breve, *n.*, in music, a note four minims in length.

brev'et, *adj.*, of temporary rank; *n.*, a patent or warrant; an honorary rank in the army; *v.t.*, to confer brevet rank upon.

brev'eted, *p.p.*, brevet.

brev'eting, *pr.p.*, brevet.

bre'viary, *n.*, a service book, containing the daily offices of the Church.

brevier', *n.*, a printing type between bourgeois and minion.

brev'iped, *adj.*, having short legs.

brevipen'nate, *adj.*, having short wings.

brev'ity, *n.*, shortness; conciseness; fewness of words.

brew, *v.t.*, to prepare by steeping, boiling, and fermentation; to mingle; to contrive; *n.*, the mixture formed by brewing.

brew'age, *n.*, a mixed drink.

brewed, *p.p.*, brew.

brew'er, *n.*, one who brews.

brew'ery, *n.*, a place where brewing is carried on.

brew'house, *n.*, a house in which beer is brewed.

brew'ing, *pr.p.*, brew; *n.*, the process of making beer, etc.; the quantity brewed at one time.

brew'is, *n.*, *i.q.* brew-house.

brew'ster, *n.*, one who brews; a brewer, esp. a female brewer.

bri'ar, *n.*, *i.q.* brier.

Bria'rean, *adj.*, pert. to Briareus, a giant with a hundred hands.

bribe, *n.*, a gift bestowed to corrupt the conduct; *v.t.*, to gain over by a bribe; *v.i.*, to practise bribery.

bribed, *p.p.*, bribe.

brib'er, *n.*, one who bribes.

brib'ery, *n.*, the act of giving or receiving a bribe.

brib'ing, *pr.p.*, bribe.

bric'-à-brac, *n.*, articles having interest or value because of their rarity, antiquity, etc.

brick, *n.*, a kind of artificial stone made by burning moistened and moulded clay; *adj.*, made of brick; *v.t.*, to cover with brick.
brick'bat, *n.*, a fragment of a brick.
brick'-kiln, *n.*, a furnace in which bricks are burned.
brick'layer, *n.*, one who builds with bricks.
brick'maker, *n.*, a maker of bricks.
brick'work, *n.*, masonry made of bricks.
brick'yard, *n.*, a yard in which bricks are stored for sale.
bri'dal, *n.*, a marriage.
bride, *n.*, a woman newly married or about to be married.
bride'cake, *n.*, the cake made for the guests at a wedding.
bride'chamber, *n.*, a nuptial apartment.
bride'groom, *n.*, a man newly married or about to be married.
bride'less, *adj.*, without a bride.
bride'maid, *n.*, a girl or woman who attends the bride at a wedding.
bride'man, *n.*, *i.q.* bridesman.
brides'maid, *n.*, *i.q.* bridesmaid.
brides'man, *n.*, a man who attends the bridegroom and bride at their marriage; a groomsman.
bride'well, *n.*, a prison for disorderly persons.
bridge, *n.*, a structure raised over a river or other depression to provide a suitable passage; a game at cards resembling whist; *v.t.*, to build a bridge over.
bridged, *p.p.*, bridge.
bridg'ing, *pr. p.*, bridge.
bri'dle, *n.*, head-harness for a horse; a restraint; *v.t.*, to restrain; *v.i.*, to toss the head, expressing indignation.
bri'dled, *p.p.*, bridle.
bri'dler, *n.*, one who bridles.
bri'dling, *pr.p.*, bridle.
bridoon', *n.*, a light snaffle with a distinct rein.
brief, *adj.*, short; *n.*, a summary of a case-at-law; a Papal letter; a circular appeal.
brief'er, *n.*, a solicitor who hands a brief to counsel; *adj.*, *comp.* of brief.
brief'est, *adj.*, *super.* of brief.
brief'less, *adj.*, having received no briefs.
brief'ly, *adv.*, concisely.
brief'ness, *n.*, conciseness.
bri'er, *n.*, a prickly shrub, esp. the wild rose.
bri'ered, *adj.*, set with briers.
bri'ery, *adj.*, full of briers; thorny.
brig, *n.*, a square-rigged, two-masted vessel.
brigade', *n.*, a number of battalions of troops.
brigadier', *n.*, the general commanding a brigade.
brig'and, *n.*, a robber, esp. one of those who live in bands in mountains.
brig'andage, *n.*, robbery by brigands.
brig'andine, *n.*, *i.q.* brigantine.
brig'antine, *n.*, a two-masted sailing vessel resembling a brig.
bright, *adj.*, shining; clever; cheerful.
bright'en, *v.t.*, to make bright or brighter; *v.i.*, to grow bright or brighter.
bright'ened, *p.p.*, brighten.
bright'ening, *pr. p.*, brighten.
bright'-eyed, *adj.*, having bright eyes.
bright'ly, *adv.*, in a bright manner.
bright'ness, *n.*, the state of being bright.
Bright's' disease', *n.*, a dangerous disease of the kidneys.
brigue, *n.* (*Fr.*), a cabal; a secret contrivance.
brill, *n.*, a flat-fish.
bril'liance, *n.*, great brightness; splendour.
bril'liancy, *n.*, *i.q.* brilliance.
bril'liant, *adj.*, sparkling; glittering; shining; *n.*, a fine-cut diamond.
bril'liantly, *adv.*, in a brilliant manner.
brim, *n.*, a margin; a rim; *v.t.*, to fill full; *v.i.*, to be full to overflowing.
brim'ful, *adj.*, full to the top.
brim'less, *adj.*, having no brim.
brimmed, *p.p.*, brim.
brim'mer, *n.*, a glass full to the brim.
brim'ming, *adj.*, full to the top; *pr.p.* brim.
brim'stone, *n.*, sulphur.
brind'ed, *i.q.* brindled.
brind'led, *adj.*, grey or tawny streaked with darker colour.
brine, *n.*, salt-water.
brine'pan, *n.*, a pit in which salt is formed by the evaporation of brine.
bring, *v.t.*, to fetch; to convey from a distant to a nearer place.
bring'er, *n.*, one who brings.
bring'ing, *pr.p.*, bring.
brin'ish, *adj.*, rather salt.
brink, *n.*, the edge of a steep place.
brin'y, *adj.*, consisting of brine.
brisk, *adj.*, lively; nimble; quick.
brisk'et, *n.*, the breast of an animal.
brisk'ly, *adv.*, in a brisk manner.
brisk'ness, *n.*, the state of being brisk.
bris'tle, *n.*, a stiff hair; *v.t.*, to stand on end like bristles.
bris'tled, *p.p.*, bristle.
bris'tling, *pr.p.*, bristle.
bris'tly, *adj.*, thick

set with hairs like bristles.

Britan'nic, *adj.*, pert. to Britain.

Brit'ish, *adj.*, pert. to Great Britain; sometimes applied specifically to the ancient Celtic inhabitants.

Brit'on, *n.*, a member of the British race.

brit'tle, *adj.*, easily broken; fragile.

brit'tleness, *n.*, fragility.

britz'ka, *n.*, an open carriage with a folding top.

broach, *n.*, a spit; a spire; *v.t.*, to open for the first time.

broached, *p.p.*, broach.

broach'er, *n.*, one who broaches, opens or utters.

broach'ing, *pr.p.*, broach.

broad, *adj.*, having extent from side to side; wide.

broad'-arrow, *n.*, a stamp resembling the head of an arrow marking government property.

broad'-axe, *n.*, a woodman's axe.

broad'cast, *adj.*, effected by casting the seed with the hand in sowing; *adv.*, far and wide; *v.t.*, to transmit from wireless stations to listeners-in (*q.v.*)

broad'cloth, *n.*, a fine woollen cloth.

broad'en, *v.t.*, to make broad or broader.

broad'ened, *p.p.*, broaden.

broad'ening, *pr.p.*, broaden.

broad'ish, *adj.*, rather broad.

broad'ly, *adv.*, widely; comprehensively.

broad'ness, *n.* breadth.

broad'side, *n.*, a simultaneous discharge of all the guns on one side of a ship; a sheet of paper printed on one side only, usually with popular matter.

broad'sword, *n.*, a sword with a broad blade and sharp edge, formerly the national weapon of the Highlanders.

Brobdingna'gian, *adj.*, rel. to the land of the Brobdingnags in *Gulliver's Travels*; gigantic.

brocade', *n.*, silk stuff richly embroidered.

brocad'ed, *adj.*, worked into a brocade; dressed in brocade.

broc'coli, *n.*, a cabbage resembling a cauliflower.

brochure', *n.*, a pamphlet.

brock, *n.*, a badger.

brock'et, *n.*, a red deer two years old.

brog, *n.*, a bradawl.

bro'gan, *n.*, a brogue.

brogue, *n.*, a shoe of rough hide; dialectical peculiarity.

broid'er, *v.t.*, to adorn with needlework.

broid'ered, *p.p.*, broider.

broid'ering, *pr.p.*, broider.

broil, *n.*, a noisy quarrel; *v.t.*, to cook over a fire on a gridiron; *v.i.*, to sweat with heat.

broiled, *p.p.*, broil.

broil'er, *n.*, one who broils.

broil'ing, *pr.p.*, broil.

broke, *p.t.*, break.

bro'ken, *p.p.*, break; *adj.*, interrupted.

bro'kenly, *adv.*, in a broken manner.

bro'kenness, *n.*, the state of being broken.

bro'ker, *n.*, an agent who buys or sells on commission.

bro'kerage, *n.*, a broker's commission.

bro'ma, *n.*, a form of prepared cocoa.

bro'mal, *n.*, a colourless, oily liquid obtained by the action of bromine on alcohol.

bro'mate, *n.*, a salt of bromic acid.

bromatol'ogy, *n.*, the science of alimentation.

bro'mide, *n.*, a compound of bromine and another element.

bro'mine, *n.*, a dark-reddish liquid element of strong odour.

bron'chia, *n. pl.*, the air-tubes leading to the lungs.

bron'chial, *adj.*, pert. to the bronchia.

bronchi'tis, *n.*, inflammation of the lining membrane of the bronchi or bronchia.

bron'chus, *n.*, one of the two bronchia.

bronze, *n.*, an alloy of copper, tin, and sometimes zinc; *v.t.*, to make to look like bronze; to brown; *v.i.*, to turn brown.

bronzed, *p.p.*, bronze.

bronz'ing, *pr.p.*, bronze.

brooch, *n.*, an ornamental clasp.

brood, *n.*, offspring; *v.i.*, to sit on eggs, as a hen; to dwell continuously on something with the mind.

brood'ed, *p.p.*, brood.

brood'ing, *adj.*, pondering; thinking deeply; *pr.p.*, brood.

brood'y, *adj.*, describing a sitting hen.

brook, *n.*, a small stream of water; *v.t.*, to endure.

brooked, *p.p.*, brook.

brook'ing, *pr.p.*, brook.

brook'let, *n.*, a little brook.

broom, *n.*, a shrub with yellow flowers growing on heaths; long-handled brush.

broom'stick, *n.*, the handle of a broom.

broom'y, *adj.*, full of broom.

brose, *n.*, a kind of Scotch broth or porridge.

broth, *n.*, liquor in which meat has been boiled, usually with certain vegetables.

broth'el, *n.*, a house of ill-fame.

broth'er, *n.*, the son of the same parents; a fellow-creature.

broth'erhood, *n.*, an association of men for any purpose.

broth'er-in-law, *n.*, the brother of one's husband or wife; a sister's husband.
broth'erliness, *n.*, the quality of being brotherly.
broth'erly, *adj.*, such as is natural for brothers.
brough'am, *n.*, a one-horse closed carriage.
brought, *p.p.*, bring.
brow, *n.*, the ridge over the eye; the forehead; the upper portion of a slope.
brow'beat, *v.t.*, to bully.
brow'beaten, *p.p.*, browbeat.
brow'beating, *pr.p.*, browbeat.
brown, *adj.*, a dark colour inclining to red; *v.t.*, to make brown; *v.i.*, to turn brown.
browned, *p.p.*, brown.
brown'ie, *n.*, a kind of fairy.
brown'ing, *n.*, a preparation of burnt sugar, etc., for colouring dishes; *pr.p.*, brown.
brown'ish, *adj.*, rather brown.
brown' stud'y, *n.*, a reverie.
browse, browze, *v.t.* and *i.*, to graze.
browsed, *p.p.*, browse.
brows'er, *n.*, one who browses.
brows'ing, *pr.p.*, browse.
bru'in, *n.*, a name given to the bear.
bruise, *v.t.*, to injure by a blow without laceration; *n.*, a contusion.
bruised, *p.p.*, bruise.
bruis'er, *n.*, one that bruises; a pugilist.
bruis'ing, *pr.p.*, bruise.
bruit, *n.*, a rumour; *v.t.*, to noise abroad.
bruit'ed, *p.p.*, bruit.
bruit'ing, *pr.p.*, bruit.
bru'mal, *adj.*, bel. to the winter.
brunette', *n.*, a woman of dark complexion.
brunt, *n.*, the heat or utmost violence of an onset.
brush, *n.*, an instrument made of bristles used for various purposes; a thicket of small trees and shrubs; the tail of a fox; a skirmish; *v.t.*, to rub as with a brush.
brushed, *p.p.*, brush.
brush'er, *n.*, one who brushes.
brush'ing, *pr.p.*, brush.
brush'wood, *n.*, small trees forming a coppice.
brush'y, *adj.*, rough; shaggy.
brusque, *adj.*, abrupt in manner.
brusque'ness, *n.*, an abrupt manner.
brus'querie, *n.*, brusqueness; a blunt expression.
Brus'sels sprouts', *n. pl.*, a variety of cabbage consisting of little clusters of leaves forming small heads.
bru'tal, *adj.*, savage; cruel.
brutal'ity, *n.*, gross cruelty.
bru'talize, *v.t.*, to degrade to the level of a brute.
bru'talized, *p.p.*, brutalize.
bru'talizing, *pr.p.*, brutalize.
bru'tally, *adv.*, in a brutal manner.
brute, *n.*, a beast; a savage in disposition or manners.
bru'tified, *p.p.*, brutify.
bru'tify, *v.t.*, to make a person a brute.
bru'tifying, *pr.p.*, brutify.
bru'tish, *adj.*, resembling a brute.
bru'tishly, *adv.*, in a brutish manner.
bru'tishness, *n.*, the state of being brutish.
bryol'ogy, *n.*, the science of mosses.
bry'ony, *n.*, one of two British climbing plants, one called *white*, the other *black*.
bub'ble, *n.*, a small vesicle of fluid containing air; *v.i.*, to rise in bubbles; *v.t.*, to cause to bubble.
bub'bled, *p.p.*, bubble.
bub'bling, *pr.p.*, bubble.
bub'bly, *adj.*, full of bubbles.
bu'bo, *n.*, an inflammatory tumour in the groin or armpit.
bubon'ic, *adj.*, characterized by buboes.
buc'cal, *adj.*, pert. to the cheek.
buccaneer', *n.*, a pirate, esp. an English or French pirate in the Spanish Main.
buccaneer'ing, *n.*, piracy.
buc'cinal, *adj.*, trumpet-like.
buccina'tor, *n.*, a muscle in the cheek used in blowing a wind instrument.
bucen'taur, *n.*, the Doge's state-barge at Venice; a mythical monster, half man and half ox.
bu'ceros, *n.*, a hornbill; a perching bird.
buck, *n.*, the male of various animals; a fop; bleaching-lye; *v.t.*, to wash in bleaching-lye; *v.i.*, to shy, to jib (of a horse).
bucked, *p.p.*, buck.
buck'et, *n.*, a vessel, now usu. of metal, for holding water; *v.i.*, to spurt (slang).
buck'etful, *n.*, as much as a bucket will hold.
buck'ing, *pr.p.*, buck.
buck'ish, *adj.*, foppish.
buc'kle, *n.*, an instrument, consisting of a rim, chape, and tongue, for fastening; *v.t.*, to fasten with a buckle; *v.t.* and *i.*, to crumple in.
buc'kled, *p.p.*, buckle.
buck'ler, *n.*, a kind of shield.
buck'ling, *pr.p.*, buckle.
buck'ram, *n.*, a coarse, stiff linen cloth.
buck'skin, *n.*, a soft yellowish or greyish leather, made of sheepskin.

buck'thorn, *n.*, a spiny British shrub of various species.
buck'wheat, *n.*, a herbaceous plant bearing small triangular seeds which are a valuable food.
bucol'ic, *adj.*, pastoral; *n.*, a pastoral poem.
bucol'ical, *i.q.* bucolic.
bud, *n.*, the early form of leaves or flowers before they expand; *v.i.*, to produce buds; *v.t.*, to graft with a leaf-bud instead of a shoot.
bud'ded, *p.p.*, bud.
Bud'dhism, *n.*, the chief religion of Asia.
Bud'dhist, *n.*, a worshipper of Buddha.
bud'ding, *pr.p.*, bud.
bud'dle, *n.*, a square frame used in washing metallic ore.
Bude'-light, *n.*, a brilliant light obtained by forcing oxygen into a coal or oil-gas flame.
budge, *v.i.*, to move away.
budged, *p.p.*, budge.
budg'er, *n.*, one who moves away.
budg'et, *n.*, a little sack; a stock (of news, etc.); the Chancellor of the Exchequer's annual statement.
budg'ing, *pr.p.*, budge.
bud'let, *n.*, a little bud springing from another bud.
buff, *n.*, a soft kind of leather; a light yellow colour.
buf'falo, *n.*, a large Oriental draught-ox; the bison of North America.
buf'fel, *n.*, a small duck.
buf'fer, *n.*, anything to deaden the impact between two bodies; a fellow (familiar and rather contemptuous).
buf'fet, *n.*, a refreshment room.
buf'fet, *n.*, a blow; *v.t.*, to beat.
buf'feted, *p.p.*, buffet.
buf'feter, *n.*, one who buffets.
buf'feting, *pr.p.*, buffet; *n.*, the act of buffeting.
buf'fo, *n.*, an operatic comic singer.
buffoon', *n.*, a jester.
buffoon'ery, *n.*, ridiculous pranks.
buffoon'ing, *n.*, *i.q.* buffoonery.
buf'fy, *adj.*, buff-coloured.
bug, *n.*, an insect of various kinds; esp. the domestic bug.
bug'bear, *n.*, something that causes terror.
bug'gy, *adj.*, abounding with bugs; *n.*, a light one-horse carriage.
bu'gle, *n.*, a hunting horn; a military musical brass wind instrument; a long black bead.
bu'gler, *n.*, one who plays a bugle.
bu'gloss, *n.*, a weed with purple flowers.
buhl, *n.*, inlaid ornamentation of gold, mother-of-pearl, etc.
buhl'-work, *n.*, cabinet work inlaid with buhl.
buhr'-stone, *n.*, stone used for millstones.
build, *v.t.*, to construct.
build'ed, *p.p.*, build; used poetically.
build'er, *n.*, one who builds.
build'ing, *n.*, the act of one who builds; the thing built; *pr.p.*, build.
built, *adj.*, shaped; *p.p.*, build.
bulb, *n.*, the rounded part of an onion or similar plant; any protuberance resembling a bulb.
bulbed, *adj.*, having a bulb.
bulbif'erous, *adj.*, producing bulbs.
bulb'let, *n.*, a bulb which separates from the stem of a plant.
bulb'ous, *adj.*, resembling a bulb in shape
bul'bul, *n.*, a nightingale (Persian).
bulb'ule, *n.*, a small or immature bulb.
bulge, *v.i.*, to swell out; a swelling out.
bulged, *p.p.*, bulge.
bulg'ing, *pr.p.*, bulge.
bulim'ia, *n.*, voracious appetite.
bulk, *n.*, size; the main mass; *v.i.*, to swell.
bulked, *p.p.*, bulk.
bulk'head, *n.*, a partition in a ship.
bulk'iness, *n.*, the quality of being bulky.
bulk'ing, *pr.p.*, bulk.
bulk'y, *n.*, large.
bull, *n.*, a male ox; on the stock exchange, one who works for a rise in the price of stock; a papal edict; a ludicrous inconsistency in language; *adj.*, male.
bul'la, *n.*, a leaden seal.
bul'lace, *n.*, a damson-like plum.
bull'dog, *n.*, a muscular, courageous, determined species of dog.
bul'let, *n.*, a projectile, usually leaden, to be discharged from small-arms.
bul'letin, *n.*, an official report.
bul'let-proof, *adj.*, able to resist bullets.
bull'-fight, *n.*, a combat between armed men and bulls.
bull'finch, *n.*, a British song-bird.
bull'frog, *n.*, a large American frog with a loud bass voice.
bul'lied, *p.p.*, bully.
bul'lion, *n.*, uncoined gold or silver; a kind of heavy silk and metallic fringe.
bul'lionist, *n.*, one who advocates an exclusive metallic currency.
bul'lock, *n.*, a young bull; an ox.
bull's-eye, *n.*, a circular opening in a building; a small lantern with a circular lens; the centre of a target, and

the shot that hits it; a kind of sweet.

bul'ly, *n.*, an arrogant domineering fellow; *v.t.* and *i.*, to act as a bully towards.

bul'lying, *pr.p.*, bully.

bul'rush, *n.*, a large rush that grows in marshes.

bulse, *n.*, in the East Indies, a bag for valuables.

bul'wark, *n.*, a rampart; a kind of wall round the deck of a ship

bum, *n.*, a humming sound; the podex; *v.i.*, to boom.

bumbail'iff, *n.*, an under-bailiff who serves writs for debt.

bum'ble-bee, *n.*, a large kind of bee.

bum'boat, *n.*, a boat for carrying provisions to a ship.

bum'kin, *n.*, a short boom or spar.

bump, *v.t.*, to strike; *v.i.*, to come into collision; *n.*, a protuberance; a shock from a collision.

bumped, *p.p.*, bump.

bump'er, *n.*, a glass filled to the brim.

bump'ing, *pr.p.* bump.

bump'kin, *n.*, an awkward, rustic lout; *i.q.* bumkin.

bump'tious, *adj.*, offensively self-assertive.

bump'tiously, *adv.*, in a bumptious way.

bump'tiousness, *n.*, the quality of being bumptious.

bun, *n.*, a little puffed cake; a chignon.

bunch, *n.*, a cluster; a protuberance; *v.t.*, to make into a bunch; *v.i.*, to cluster.

bunched, *p.p.*, bunch.

bunch'iness, *n.*, the state of being bunchy.

bunch'ing, *pr.p.*, bunch.

bunch'y, *adj.*, growing in a bunch.

bun'combe, *n.*, *i.q.* bunkum.

bun'dle, *n.*, a package; *v.t.*, to fasten into a rather shapeless package.

bun'dled, *p.p.*, bundle.

bun'dling, *pr.p.*, bundle.

bung, *n.*, a large cork; *v.t.*, to close up.

bun'galow, *n.*, a low verandahed house, common in India.

bung'-hole, *n.*, the hole in a cask through which it is filled.

bun'gle, *v.t.* and *i.*, to perform inefficiently.

bun'gled, *p.p.*, bungle.

bun'gler, *n.*, an unskilful performer.

bun'gling, *adj.*, clumsy; *pr.p.*, bungle.

bun'glingly, *adv.*, clumsily.

bun'ion, *n.*, an inflammatory swelling of the joint of the great toe.

bunk, *n.*, a sleeping-berth.

bunk'er, *n.*, a large bin.

bun'kum, *n.*, talking for talking's sake.

bun'ny, *n.*, a pet name for a rabbit.

bunt, *n.*, the belly of a sail; *v.i.*, to swell out.

bunt'ine, *n.*, a thin woollen stuff out of which flags are made.

bunt'ing, *n.*, a bird akin to the finch; *i.q.* buntine.

buoy, *n.*, a float used for various purposes; *v.t.*, to keep afloat.

buoy'ancy, *n.*, the quality of being buoyant.

buoy'ant, *adj.*, floating; light; cheerful.

buoy'antly, *adv.*, in a buoyant manner.

buoyed, *p.p.*, buoy.

bur, *n.*, *i.q.* burr.

bur'bot, *n.*, an English fresh-water cod, eel-shaped and bearded.

bur'den, *n.*, a load; the refrain of a song; *v.t.*, to load; to oppress.

bur'dened, *p.p.*, burden.

bur'dening, *pr.p.*, burden.

bur'densome, *adj.*, heavy; grievous to be borne.

bur'densomeness, *n.*, oppressiveness; heaviness.

bur'dock, *n.*, a large, rough-leaved, composite, perennial weed.

bureau', *n.*, a writing-table with drawers; a business office; a public department; a chest of drawers.

bureau'cracy, *n.*, the system of centralizing government, esp. when carried to excess.

bureaucrat'ic, *adj.*, rel. to bureaucracy.

bureaucrat'ical, *adj.*, *i.q.* bureaucratic.

bureau'cratist, *n.*, a supporter of bureaucracy.

burette', *n.*, a graduated pipette with a stop-cock.

burg, *n.*, a borough.

burg'age, *n.*, a system of land tenure.

burgee', *n.*, a small pennant.

bur'geon, *n.*, a bud; *v.i.*, to sprout.

bur'geoned, *p.p.*, burgeon.

bur'geoning, *pr.p.*, burgeon.

bur'gess, *n.*, a citizen or a parliamentary representative of a borough.

burgh, *n.*, a corporate town; a borough.

burgh'er, *n.*, an inhabitant of a burgh; a freeman.

burg'lar, *n.*, a nocturnal housebreaker.

burgla'rious, *adj.*, pert. to burglary.

burgla'riously, *adv.*, with intent to commit burglary.

burg'lary, *n.*, the crime of nocturnal housebreaking.

burg'mote, *n.*, a borough court held thrice yearly.

burg'omaster, *n.*, a Dutch, Flemish, or German mayor.

burgoo', *n.*, a kind of oatmeal porridge.

bur'grave, *n.*, an hereditary governor of a castle or town.
Bur'gundy, *n.*, a kind of wine.
bur'ial, *n.*, interment.
bur'ial-place, *n.*, a place of burial.
bur'ied, *p.p.*, bury.
bur'ier, *n.*, one who buries.
bu'rin, *n.*, an engraver's style or needle; a graver.
burke, *v.t.*, to smother; to shelve.
burked, *p.p.*, burke.
burk'er, *n.*, one who burks.
burk'ing, *pr.p.*, burke.
burl, *n.*, a small lump in thread or cloth; *v.t.*, to finish cloth by picking out burls.
burled, *p.p.*, burl.
burl'er, *n.*, one who picks burls out of cloth in finishing.
burlesque', *n.*, a dramatic or literary extravaganza; a travesty; a caricature; *adj.*, ludicrous because of contrast between subject and manner of treatment; *v.t.*, to turn into a burlesque.
burlesqued', *p.p.*, burlesque.
burlesqu'ing, *pr.p.*, burlesque.
burlet'ta, *n.*, a musical farce.
bur'liness, *n.*, the quality of being burly.
bur'ly, *n.*, great in bodily size.
Burmese', *adj.*, pert. to Burmah.
burn, *v.t.*, to consume or injure by fire; *v.i.*, to flame; *n.*, an injury caused by fire; a rivulet.
burn'able, *adj.*, capable of being burned.
burned, *p.p.*, burn.
burn'er, *n.*, one who burns; the jet-piece of a lamp.
burn'ing, *adj.*, flaming; causing ardour; *pr.p.*, burn.
bur'nish, *v.t.*, to polish and make shining.
bur'nished, *p.p.*, burnish.
bur'nisher, *n.*, one who or that which burnishes.
bur'nishing, *pr.p.*, burnish.
burnous', *n.*, a white woollen hood and mantle worn by Arabs.
burnt, *p.p.*, burn.
burnt'-offering, *n.*, a sacrifice or atonement for sin burnt on an altar.
burr, *n.*, the rough, prickly covering of certain seeds; the burdock; a guttural pronunciation of the sound *r*.
bur'ral, *n.*, *s.q.* burrel.
bur'rel, *n.*, the red-butter pear.
bur'rock, *n.*, a little weir or dam in a river.
bur'row, *n.*, a hole in the ground in which certain animals shelter; *v.t.*, to make a burrow or tunnel in the ground.
bur'rowed, *p.p.*, burrow.
bur'rowing, *pr.p.*, burrow.
bur'ry, *adj.*, covered with burrs.
bur'sar, *n.*, the treasurer of a college or monastery; a student to whom a bursary is paid.
bur'sary, *n.*, a scholarship or exhibition (usually Scottish); the treasury of a college or monastery.
burst, *v.i.*, to explode; *v.t.*, to break by violence; *n.*, a sudden explosion; *p.p.*, burst.
burst'er, *n.*, one who or that which bursts.
burst'ing, *n.*, the act of exploding; *pr.p.*, burst.
bur'then, *n.*, *s.q.* burden.
bur'ton, *n.*, a small tackle with two pulleys used in ships.
bur'y, *v.t.*, to cover with earth; to hide.
bur'ying, *pr.p.*, bury.
bur'ying-ground, *n.*, a cemetery.
bus, 'bus, *n.*, an abbreviation of *omnibus*, a street carriage.
bus'by, *n.*, a military fur head-dress.
bush, *n.*, a shrub with branches; a district overgrown with shrubs; a hard lining let into the axle-socket of a carriage; *v.i.*, to form a bush.
bushed, *p.p.*, bush.
bush'el, *n.*, a dry measure of eight gallons.
bush'iness, *n.*, the quality of being bushy.
bush'ing, *pr.p.*, bush.
bush'man, *n.*, a woodsman.
bush'ranger, *n.*, a robber in the bush country.
bush'y, *adj.*, like a bush.
bus'ied, *p.p.*, busy.
bus'ier, *adj.*, *comp.* of busy.
bus'iest, *adj.*, *super.* of busy.
bus'ily, *adv.*, in a busy manner.
bus'iness, *n.*, employment; concern; affair.
bus'iness-like, *adj.*, showing aptitude for affairs.
busk, *n.*, a support or stiffening in a woman's stays.
bus'ket, *n.*, a shrubbery.
bus'kin, *n.*, a high boot worn by ancient tragic actors.
bus'kined, *adj.*, wearing buskins; pert. to tragedy.
buss, *n.*, a kiss; a small vessel used in herring-fishing; *v.t.*, to kiss.
bust, *n.*, the figure down to just below the shoulders; the chest.
bus'tard, *n.*, a large bird.
bus'tle, *v.i.*, to be active and stirring; *n.*, activity with noise and agitation; a pad worn by

ladies below the waist behind.

bus'tled, *p.p.*, bustle.

bus'tler, *n.*, an active, stirring person.

bus'tling, *adj.*, busy; stirring; *pr.p.*, bustle.

bus'y, *adj.*, employed with constant attention; *v.t.*, to make or keep busy.

bus'ybody, *n.*, one who officiously concerns himself with the affairs of others.

bus'ying, *pr.p.*, busy.

but, *adv.*, *prep.*, and *conj.*, except, unless; only; on the contrary; however.

butch'er, *n.*, one who kills beasts for food; one who slays barbarously; *v.t.*, to kill for food or lust of slaughter.

butch'ered, *p.p.*, butcher.

butch'ering, *pr.p.*, butcher.

butch'erly, *adj.*, murderous.

butch'ery, *n.*, the business of slaughtering; barbarous and extensive bloodshed.

but'ler, *n.*, a domestic servant who takes charge of the wines, plate, etc.; a head man-servant.

but'lerage, *n.*, an ancient duty paid on imported wine.

but'lership, *n.*, the office of a butler.

but'lery, *n.*, a butler's pantry.

but'ment, *n.*, a buttress of an arch.

butt, *n.*, the larger end of a thing; a large cask; the object of aim or attack; a push with the head; *v.t.* and *i.*, to strike with the head.

butt'ed, *p.p.*, butt.

butt'-end, *n.*, the thicker end of anything.

but'ter, *n.*, an animal that butts; an oily substance obtained from cream or milk by churning; *v.t.*, to smear with butter; to flatter grossly.

but'tercup, *n.*, a yellow flower; the ranunculus.

but'tered, *p.p.*, butter.

but'terfly, *n.*, a diurnal lepidopterous insect with four coloured wings.

but'terine, *n.*, an artificial butter made from animal fat, yolks of eggs, etc., churned with milk.

but'tering, *pr.p.*, butter.

but'termilk, *n.*, the milk that remains after the butter is separated from it.

but'ter-tooth, *n.*, a broad fore-tooth.

but'tery, *n.*, a storeroom for wines, provisions, etc.; *adj.*, resembling butter.

butt'-hinge, *n.*, a door hinge.

but'ting, *pr.p.*, butt.

but'tock, *n.*, the rump.

but'ton, *n.*, a small round fastener for clothing; the disc at the end of a fencing foil; *v.t.*, to fasten with buttons.

but'toned, *p.p.*, button.

but'tonhole, *n.*, the hole or loop in which a button is fastened; a flower in a buttonhole; *v.t.*, to make buttonholes in; to detain.

but'toning, *pr.p.*, button.

but'tress, *n.*, a projecting support of masonry built on to a wall; any support or prop; *v.t.*, to prop.

but'tressed, *p.p.*, buttress.

but'tressing, *pr.p.*, buttress.

butts, *n. pl.*, the end of a rifle range where the targets are placed.

but'ty, *n.*, a man who raises coal by contract at a stated price per ton, employing others to do the work.

butyra'ceous, *adj.*, resembling butter.

butyr'ic, *adj.*, derived from butter.

bu'tyrin, *n.*, a fat contained in milk which gives butter its peculiar flavour.

bux'eous, *adj.*, pert. to the box-tree.

buxi'na, *n.*, an alkaloid obtained from the box-tree.

bux'ine, *n.*, *i.q.* buxina

bux'om, *adj.*, pliant; jolly; plump.

bux'omly, *adv.*, in a buxom manner.

bux'omness, *n.*, the quality of being buxom.

buy, *v.t.*, to acquire by paying a price to the seller.

buy'er, *n.*, one who buys.

buy'ing, *pr.p.*, buy.

buzz, *v.i.*, to make a low hissing sound; *v.t.*, to whisper; *n.*, a low whispering hum

buz'zard, *n.*, a large bird of the falcon family.

buzzed, *p.p.*, buzz.

buz'zer, *n.*, one who buzzes; one who tells tales secretly.

buz'zing, *pr.p.*, buzz.

buz'zingly, *adv.*, with a low, humming sound.

by, *prep.*, near; through; *adv.*, near; aside.

by *and* **by'**, *adv.*, in the near future.

bye, *n.*, a thing not directly aimed at; a run at cricket not due to a stroke of the bat.

by-elec'tion, *n.*, an election while Parliament is sitting, caused by death or resignation of the previous member.

by'-end, *n.*, secret purpose or advantage.

by'gone, *adj.*, past.

by'-lane, *n.*, a side-lane.

by'-law, *n.*, a local or private law; a law made by an incorporated body for the management of its own affairs.

by'-name, *n.*, a nickname.

by´-path, *n.*, a path secondary to a main road.

by´-prod´uct, *n.*, a secondary product.

bys´sine, *adj.*, of silky or flax-like appearance.

by´stander, *n.*, an onlooker.

by´-street, *n.*, a street secondary to a main street.

by the by´, *adv.*, by way of digression.

by´way, *n.*, a by-path.

by´word, *n.*, a common saying; a proverb; a name for reproach.

Byzan´tian, *adj.*, pert. to Byzantium.

Byzan´tine, *adj.*, *i.q.* Byzantian.

C

Ca'aba, *n.*, the great Mecca shrine; also *Kaaba*.

cab, *n.*, a vehicle so named; the shelter for an engine driver; a Jewish measure of capacity.

cabal', *n.*, a plotting combination, secret intrigue: *v.i.*, to plot.

cab'ala, *n.*, esoteric Rabbinism; inner teaching.

cab'alism, *n.*, occult doctrine.

cab'alist, *n.*, one who practises cabalism.

cabalis'tic, *adj.*, rel. to cabala.

cabal'ler, *n.*, one who joins a cabal.

cab'alline, *adj.*, rel. to horses.

cab'aret, *n.*, a tavern (*Fr.*).

cab'bage, *n.*, the vegetable so named; the head of a palm-tree; *v.t.*, to appropriate (a slang word).

cab'bala, *n.*, *i.q.* cabala.

ca'ber, *n.*, a spar of wood, flung in a Highland game.

cab'in, *n.*, a hut, small cottage or room; a room in a ship; *v.t.*, to confine in close quarters.

cab'in-boy, *n.*, a boy servant on board ship.

cab'ined, *p.p.*, cabin.

cab'inet, *n.*, a small room; a receptacle for articles of *vertu*; the select body of Ministers.

ca'ble, *n.*, a large and strong chain or rope: a submarine telegraph line; *v.t.*, to transmit a message by cable.

ca'bled, *p.p.*, cable.

ca'blegram, *n.*, a cable message.

ca'bling, *pr.p.*, cable.

cab'man, *n.*, the driver of a cab.

cabob', *v.t.*, to make into a cabob; *n.*, roast savoury meat.

cabochon', *n.*, a precious stone polished without facets.

caboose', *n.*, a ship's galley; a goods-train guard's van.

cabriolet', *n.*, a covered carriage (cab is the abbreviated form).

caca'o, *n.*, a tropical American and West Indian tree from the seed of which cocoa is prepared.

cach'alot, *n.*, the sperm whale.

cache, *n.*, a hiding-place.

ca'chet, *n.*, a seal, impress.

cachex'ia, *n.*, poor health, bad condition.

cachex'y, *n.*, *i.q.* cachexia.

cachinna'tion, *n.*, laughter.

cach'olong, *n.*, a pearl opal.

cachou', *n.*, an aromatic breath-sweetening pill.

cacique', *n.*, a tribal chief (W. Indian and S. American).

cack'le, *v.i.*, to make the sound of a hen or goose; to prattle.

cack'led, *p.p.*, cackle.

cack'ler, *n.*, one who cackles.

cack'ling, *pr.p.*, cackle.

cacochym'ic, *adj.*, suffering from cacochymy.

cac'ochymy, *n.*, a disordered condition of bodily fluids.

cacoe'thes, *n.*, a bad propensity (*Gr.*).

cacog'raphy, *n.*, bad writing.

cacol'ogy, *n.*, faulty pronunciation or use of words.

cacophon'ic, *adj.*, discordant, ill-sounding.

cacoph'onous, *adj.*, *i.q.* cacophonic.

cacoph'ony, *n.*, discordant noise.

cacta'ceous, *adj.*, rel. to or resembling the cactus.

cac'tus, *n.*, a flowering spiny and fleshy plant so named.

cad, *n.*, a low, mean fellow; an omnibus conductor.

cadaver'ic, *adj.*, pert. to a cadaver or carcass.

cadav'erous, *adj.*, corpse-like.

cadav'erously, *adv.*, in a cadaverous way.

cadav'erousness, *n.*, a cadaverous state.

cad'die, *n.*, one who carries for a golf player.

cad'dis, *n.*, the caddis-fly larva.

cad'dy, *n.*, a domestic box for holding tea.

cade, *n.*, a cask of capacity to hold 500 herrings or 1,000 sprats.

ca'dence, *n.*, the fall of the voice in speaking or reading; the close of a musical sentence.

ca'dency, *n.*, the precedence of younger members and branches of a great family.

caden'za, *n.*, an improvised or prepared addition before the close of a musical movement.

cadet', *n.*, a younger son; a young military student.

cadge, *v.i.*, to beg, sponge.

cadged, *p.p.*, cadge.

cadg'er, *n.*, one who cadges.

cadg'ing, *pr.p.*, cadge.

ca'di, *n.*, a Mohammedan judge.

cadil'lac, *n.*, a large kind of pear.

Cadme'an, *adj.*, pert. to Cadmus of Thebes: Theban.

cad'mia, *n.*, a zinc ointment.

cad'mium, *n.*, a metallic element so named.

cadre, *n.*, a regimental staff.

cadu'cean, *adj.*, rel. to the caduceus.

cadu'ceus, *n.*, Mercury's winged staff.

cadu'cous, *adj.*, dropping before ripened.

cae'cal, *adj.*, rel. to the caecum.

cae'cum, *n.*, a sort of pouch, closed at one end and attached to the great intestine.

Ca'en-stone, *n.*, a soft stone from Caen.

Cae'sarism, *n.*, absolute rule.

caesu'ra, *n.*, a break in a metrical foot, making a pause in the verse.

ca'fé, *n.*, a coffee-house, restaurant.

caffe'ic, *adj.*, rel. to coffee.

caf'feine, *n.*, a coffee-extract.

Caf'fre, *n.*, a native of a S. African tribe so named.

caf'tan, *n.*, a Turkish under-garment.

cage, *v.t.*, to confine in a cage, to keep within narrow limits; *n.*, an enclosure for birds or beasts; a contrivance for lowering and raising miners.

caged, *p.p.*, cage.

cag'ing, *pr.p.*, cage.

ca'hier, *n.*, loose sheets of paper collected; a committee's report.

caique', *n.*, a light Turkish skiff.

cairn, *n.*, a monument composed of piled stones.

cairngorm', *n.*, a species of rock-crystal.

cais'son, *n.*, an ammunition chest; a box for explosives in blasting; a casing for building under water.

cai'tiff, *adj.*, vile, despicable; *n.*, a vile fellow.

cajole', *v.t.*, to wheedle, flatter.

cajoled', *p.p.*, cajole.

cajole'ment, *n.*, the act of cajoling.

cajo'ler, *n.*, one who cajoles.

cajo'lery, *n.*, *i.q.* cajolement.

cajo'ling, *pr.p.*, cajole.

cake, *v.t.*, to make into a cake; *v.i.*, to harden; *n.*, a large or small mass of dough, sweetened, and either plain or containing various ingredients; a hardened mass.

caked, *p.p.*, cake.

cak'ing, *pr.p.*, cake.

cal'abash, *n.*, the fruit of a tropical tree, used for containing liquids.

Cala'brian, *adj.*, pert. to Calabria.

calaman'co, *n.*, a woollen material, brocaded or checkered.

cal'amar, *n.*, *i.q.* calamary.

cal'amary, *n.*, a cuttle-fish.

calamif'erous, *adj.*, reedy.

cal'amine, *n.*, a zinc silicate.

cal'amite, *n.*, a species of tremolite.

calam'itous, *adj.*, bringing calamity.

calam'itously, *adv.*, in a calamitous way.

calam'itousness, *n.*, the quality of calamity.

calam'ity, *n.*, disaster, misfortune.

cal'amus, *n.*, a cane-bearing palm; the sweet-flag.

calash', *n.*, a low-wheeled, hooded vehicle; a woman's hood.

cal'car, *n.*, a spur or a spur-like figure; a calcinating oven in glass-works.

calca'reous, *adj.*, rel. to limestone.

calca'reousness, *n.*, the calcareous quality.

cal'ceated, *adj.*, wearing shoes.

calceola'ria, *n. pl.*, a botanical genus; popularly known as slipperworts.

cal'cify, *v.i.*, to form lime.

calcin'able, *adj.*, able to be calcined.

calcina'tion, *n.*, the process of calcining.

calcin'atory, *adj.*, tending to calcination.

cal'cine, *v.t.*, to make friable by the application of heat; *v.i.*, to become friable.

cal'cined, *p.p.*, calcine.

cal'cining, *pr.p.*, calcine.

cal'cium, *n.*, a metallic element so named.

calcog'raphy, *n.*, drawing with pastels or chalks.

cal'culable, *adj.*, able to be calculated.

cal'culary, *n.*, concretions in fruit pulp.

cal'culate, *v.t.*, to reckon arithmetically; to estimate, plan, design.

cal'culated, *p.p.*, calculate.

cal'culating, *pr.p.*, calculate; *adj.*, designing.

calcula'tion, *n.*, the process of calculating; an arithmetical reckoning.

cal'culative, *adj.*, rel. to calculation.

cal'culator, *n.*, one who calculates; a calculating machine.

cal'culatory, *adj.*, rel. to calculation.

cal'culous, *adj.*, gritty.

cal'culus, *n.*, a stony growth in the body; a method of calculating by means of symbols.

cal'dron, *n.*, a large kettle.

Caledo'nian, *adj.*, bel. to Caledonia.

calefa'cient, *adj.*, producing warmth or heat.

calefac'tion, *n.*, the process of producing warmth.

calefac'tory, *adj.*, warmth-producing; *n.*, a chamber in a monastery where a fire is allowed; a chafing-dish or hot water sphere.

cal'endar, *v.t.*, to put into a calendar, to index; *n.*, a system of reckoning years, months, and days; an official list.

cal'ender, *v.t.*, to press in order to produce a glossy surface; *n.*, a paper-making machine giving a glossy surface; a Turkish dervish.

cal'endered, *p.p.*, calender.

cal'enderer, *n.*, one who calenders.

cal'endering, *pr.p.*, calender.

cal'ends, *n.*, the Latin name for the first day of the month. Also *kalends*.

cal'enture, *n.*, a delirious fever; hallucination.

cales'cence, *n.*, the process of growing warm.

calf, *n.*, a cow's offspring; the back of the leg below the knee.

calf's'-foot, *n.*, the wake-robin.

cal'ibrate, *v.t.*, to mark on a thermometer degrees of temperature.

calibra'tion, *n.*, the process of calibrating.

cal'ibre, cal'iber, *n.*, the bore of a tube; the size of bore; standard of ability.

cal'ico, *n.*, cotton cloth, whether plain or printed on one side; *adj.*, made of calico.

ca'lif, *n.*, *i.q.* caliph.

caligraph'ic, *adj.*, rel. to caligraphy.

calig'raphy, *n.*, good penmanship. Also *Calligraphy*.

cal'ipash, *n.*, the green gelatinous part of a turtle's flesh.

calipee', *n.*, the yellow gelatinous part of a turtle's flesh.

cal'iper, *n.*, an instrument for measuring diameters.

cal'iph, *n.*, a Mohammedan ruler.

cal'iphate, *n.*, the office, and tenure of office, of a caliph.

calisay'a, *n.*, a species of Peruvian bark.

calisthen'ics, callisthen'ics, *n. pl.*, easier gymnastic exercises, promoting gracefulness of body.

cal'ix, *n.*, a cavity in the shape of a cup.

calk, caulk, *v.t.*, to plug with oakum or other soft substance or to close up the seams of a ship by hammering; trace on transfer paper.

calked, *p.p.*, calk.

calk'er, *n.*, one who calks.

calk'ing, *pr.p.*, calk.

call, *v.t.*, to summon, arouse, proclaim, deem or style; *v.i.*, pay a short visit; *n.*, a cry, a demand, a vocation, a short visit.

called, *p.p.*, call.

call'er, *n.*, one who calls.

calligraph'ic, *adj.*, *i.q.* caligraphic.

callig'raphy, *n.*, *i.q.* caligraphy.

call'ing, *pr.p.*, call.

Calli'ope, *n.*, the chief of the Muses, patroness of epic poetry; a humming bird so named.

callos'ity, *n.*, a thickening of the skin; the state of being hardened.

cal'lous, *adj.*, hardened, insensible, indifferent.

cal'lously, *adv.*, in a callous way.

cal'lousness, *n.*, insensibility, indifference.

cal'low, *adj.*, unfledged.

cal'lus, *n.*, a hardened part, a callosity.

calm, *v.t.*, to tranquillize, soothe; *v.i.*, to become tranquil; *n.*, a state of smoothness or tranquillity; *adj.*, quiet, still, serene.

calmed, *p.p.*, calm.

calm'er, *n.*, one who calms.

calm'ing, *pr.p.*, calm.

calm'ly, *adv.*, with calmness.

calm'ness, *n.*, a state of calm.

cal'omel, *n.*, the purgative drug so named.

calores'cence, *n.*, generation of heat by reflection through a body partially transparent.

calor'ic, *n.*, heat.

calorif'ic, *adj.*, heat-producing, heat-carrying.

calorifica'tion, *n.*, the causing of heat.

calorim'eter, *n.*, a heat-measuring apparatus.

calotte', *n.*, a skull-cap, or other close-fitting cap.

cal'otype, *n.*, a photograph produced by a now antiquated process.

calum'ba, *n.*, a bitter vegetable tonic so named.

cal'umet, *n.*, the long reed-stemmed pipe of the N. American Indians.

calum'niate, *v.t.*, to defame, slander.

calum'niated, *p.p.*, calumniate.

calum'niating, *pr.p.*, calumniate.

calumnia'tion, *n.*, the act of calumniating.

calum'niator, *n.*, one who calumniates.

calum'niatory, *adj.*, defamatory, slanderous.

calum'nious, *adj.*, *i.q.* calumniatory.

calum'niously, *adv.*, slanderously.

calum'niousness, *n.*, a habit of slandering; the quality of being slanderous.

cal'umny, *n.*, a slanderous report or charge.

Cal'vary, *n.*, the place of Our Lord's Crucifixion; an open-air erection representing the Crucifixion.

calve, *v.t.*, to give birth to a calf; to throw off a part of an iceberg.

calved, *p.p.*, calve.

calves, *n.*, pl. of calf.

calves'-foot, *adj.*, made from the feet of a calf.

calv'ing, *pr.p.*, calve.

Cal'vinism, *n.*, the principles taught by John Calvin; the Calvinistic system.

Cal'vinist, *n.*, a follower of Calvin.

Calvinis'tic, *adj.*, rel. to Calvin or Calvinism.

Calvinis'tical, *adj.*, *i.q.* Calvinistic.

calx, *n.*, the residuum after calcination; chalk, lime; glass fragments for remelting.

cal'ycine, *adj.*, rel. to a calyx.

cal'ycle, *n.*, a supplementary calyx.

cal'yx, *n.*, the outer wrapping of a flower, composed of the sepals.

cam, *n.*, a revolving piece of machinery, giving a reciprocating motion.

cam'ber, *n.*, a slight convexity; a harbour (*obs.*); *v.t.*, to curve slightly upwards.

cam'bered, *p.p.*, camber.

cam'bering, *pr.p.*, camber.

cam'bial, *n.*, rel. to commercial exchange, or to cambium.

cam'bist, *n.*, an expert in exchange values; a book which shows the moneys, weights, and measures of foreign countries, with their equivalents.

cam'bistry, *n.*, the theory of commercial exchange.

cam'bium, *n.*, the organic source of new tissues in certain plants; property exchange.

camboose', *n.*, *i.q.* caboose.

Cam'brian, *adj.*, rel. to Cambria, or Wales.

cam'bric, *n.*, a fine white linen; also a cotton fabric made to look like linen.

came, *p.t.* come.

cam'el, *n.*, the well-known beast of burden, native to Arabia and Bactria.

camel'lia, *n.*, the flower named after G. J. Kamel.

camel'opard, *n.*, another name for the giraffe.

cam'eo, *n.*, a stone or shell so cut as to throw one layer into relief in one colour, the rest forming a background in a different colour.

cam'era, *n.*, the photographic box in which the image is received; a room, esp. a judge's private chamber.

cameralis'tic, *adj.*, pert. to high finance.

cam'erate, *adj.*, partitioned into rooms.

cam'erated, *adj.*, *i.q.* camerate.

camera'tion, *n.*, partition into rooms; a vaulting.

Camero'nian, *adj.*, pert. to the teaching of Richard Cameron; *n.*, a follower of Cameron.

Cam'isard, *n.*, a smock wearer, the nickname of the French Calvinists at the time of the revocation of the Edict of Nantes.

cam'isole, *n.*, a jacket, woman's wrapper.

cam'let, *n.*, a material made from camel's hair.

cam'omile, *n.*, a bitter aromatic plant, much used in medicine.

Camor'ra, *n.*, an Italian secret organization.

camp, *v.t.* and *i.*, to encamp; *n.*, an encampment, a place of encampment.

campaign', *n.*, a series or a period of military operations; any organized course of action.

campaign'er, *n.*, one engaged in a campaign.

campani'le, *n.*, a bell-tower, belfry.

campanol'ogy, *n.*, the science of bell-construction and bell-ringing.

campan'ula, *n.*, one of the bell-worts, as the Canterbury bell.

camped, *p.p.*, camp.

cam'phene, *n.*, oil of turpentine.

cam'phine, *n.*, *i.q.* camphene.

cam'phogen, *n.*, *i.q.* cymene.

cam'phor, *n.*, a medicinal resinous compound.

cam'phorate, *adj.*, impregnated with camphor.

cam'phorated, *adj.*, *i.q.*, camphorate.

camp'ing, *pr.p.*, camp.

cam'pion, *n.*, a member of the pink family (*Bot.*).

cam'shaft, *n.*, the shaft on which the cams are mounted.

can, a defective verb used as an auxiliary = to be able; *v.t.*, to preserve in cans.

can, *n.*, a vessel, usually of metal.

Ca'naanite, *n.*, an inhabitant of Canaan.

Ca'naanitish, *adj.*, bel. to Canaan.

Cana'dian, *adj.*, bel. to Canada.

canaille', *n.*, the vulgar, the rabble (*Fr.*).

canal', *n.*, an artificial watercourse; a channel, a groove.

canalic'ulate, *adj.*, having canaliculi, *i.e.*, small ducts.

canaliza'tion, *n.*, conversion into a canal.

ca'nalize, *v.t.*, to convert into a canal.

Ca'nanites, *n.*, a sect of Jewish zealots.

canard′, *n.*, a made-up sensational statement; a literary hoax (*Fr.*).

cana′ry, *n.*, a bird found in the Canary Islands.

can′cel, *v.t.*, to annul, cut out.

can′cellate, *adj.*, having a lattice-like appearance.

cancella′tion, *n.*, a lattice-like network; excision; annulment.

can′celled, *p.p.*, cancel.

can′celling, *pr.p.*, cancel.

can′cer, *n.*, a malignant growth so named.

can′cerate, *v.i.*, to become cancerous.

cancera′tion, *n.*, a cancerous state.

can′cerous, *adj.*, of the nature of cancer.

can′cerously, *adv.*, in a cancerous manner.

can′cerousness, *n.*, a tendency to cancer.

can′criform, *adj.*, crab-like.

can′crine, *adj.*, rel. to crabs.

can′crinite, *n.*, a silicate so named

candela′bra, *n.*, pl. of candelabrum.

candela′brum, *n.*, a branched candlestick.

can′dent, *adj.*, glowing, at white heat.

can′did, *adj.*, fair, frank.

can′didate, *n.*, an applicant for an office; one seeking Holy Orders, Confirmation, and the like.

can′didature, *n.*, a candidate's application.

can′didly, *adv.*, in a candid way.

can′didness, *n.*, a frank attitude.

can′died, *p.p.*, candy; *adj.*, made into candy, frosted.

can′dle, *n.*, a stick of wax or other preparation, with a central wick.

Can′dlemas, *n.*, the Feast of the Purification of Our Lady (Feb. 2), celebrated with the display of many candles.

can′dlestick, *n.*, a stand to hold a candle.

can′dour, can′dor, *n.*, fairness, frankness.

can′dy, *v.t.*, to turn into sugar crystals; to frost preserved fruits with sugar; *n.*, a confection of sugar.

can′dying, *pr.p.*, candy.

can′dytuft, *n.*, a plant of the mustard family.

cane, *v.t.*, to strike with a cane; *n.*, a species of reed or grass; a walking-stick.

cane′-brake, *n.*, land covered with growing canes.

caned, *p.p.*, cane.

cangue, cang, *n.*, a wooden yoke, used as a Chinese instrument of torture or punishment.

canic′ular, *adj.*, rel. to the dog-star.

can′ine, *adj.*, rel. to a dog; *n.*, a canine tooth.

ca′ning, *pr.p.*, cane; *n.*, the act of caning.

can′ister, *n.*, a box or case of metal.

can′ker, *v.t.*, to eat away, corrode; *v.i.*, to be infected with canker; *n.*, an eating and spreading ulcer.

can′kered, *p.p.*, canker.

can′kering, *pr.p.*, canker.

can′kerous, *adj.*, of the nature of canker.

can′ker-worm, *n.*, a destructive kind of caterpillar.

can′kery, *adj.*, affected with canker; cross, crabby.

can′nel-coal, *n.*, a coal that burns very brightly.

can′nibal, *n.*, one who eats human flesh.

can′nibalism, *n.*, a cannibal's state of life; the eating of human flesh.

can′nikin, *n.*, a little can.

can′non, *n.*, a large gun; a smooth horse bit; a stroke at billiards; *v.i.*, to glance off; to rebound from another object.

cannonade′, *n.*, a sustained attack with cannon; *v.t.*, to make an attack with cannon.

cannona′ded, *p.p.*, cannonade.

cannona′ding, *pr.p.*, cannonade.

cannoneer′, cannonier′, *n.*, a man who serves a cannon.

can′non-proof, *adj.*, impenetrable to cannon-shot.

can′non-shot, *n.*, a cannon-ball; the shooting of cannon; the range of a gun.

can′not, a phrase, the negative of *can*.

can′nula, *n.*, a surgical tube for conveying away pus.

can′nular, *adj.*, hollow, tubular.

can′ny, *adj.*, gentle, cautious, sagacious.

canoe′, *n.*, a boat propelled by the paddle.

can′on, *n.*, a rule or standard; a member of a Collegiate or Cathedral Chapter; the more solemn part of the Mass; the Church's standard of selection in regard to the Sacred Scriptures.

cañ′on, *n.*, a deep ravine.

can′oness, *n.*, a woman of rank in a conventual Chapter.

canon′ic, *adj.*, rel. to canons.

canon′ical, *adj.*, *s.q.* canonic; in accordance with rule. (The Canonical Scriptures are those which the Church has accepted.)

canon′icals, *n. pl.*, the vestments or habits prescribed by the canons for the clergy.

can'onist, *n.*, an expert in canon law.

canoniza'tion, *n.*, the act or state of canonizing.

can'onize, *v.t.*, to raise to the rank of a saint in the Kalendar.

can'onized, *p.p.* canonize.

can'onizing, *pr.p.*, canonize.

can'onry, *n.*, the office and dignity of a canon.

can'opied, *adj.*, having a canopy over.

can'opy, *v.t.*, to cover with a canopy; *n.*, an overhead covering.

cano'rous, *adj.*, tuneful, melodious.

canst, *v.*, a defective auxiliary verb, second person singular.

cant, *v.t.*, to tip up, to bevel; *v.i.*, to tilt; to whine like a beggar; *n.*, an inclination to one side; hypocritical talk.

can't, *v.*, an abbreviation for *cannot.*

Can'tab, *n.*, a Cantabrigian (or Cambridge man).

cantab'ile, *adj.*, smoothly flowing; *n.*, a smooth-flowing style in music.

Canta'brian *adj.*, pert. to Cantabria.

Cantabrig'ian, *adj.*, pert. to Cambridge.

can'taliver, *n.*, *i.q.* cantilever.

can'taloup, *n.*, a variety of melon.

cantan'kerous, *adj.*, quarrelsome, crusty, contrary.

canta'ta, *n.*, the musical setting of a poem or a drama.

canta'tion, *n.*, incantation.

cantatri'ce, *n.*, woman vocalist.

cant'ed, *p.p.*, cant.

canteen', *n.*, a soldier's drinking-flask; a military stores for food.

can'tel, *n.*, *i.q.* cantle.

can'ter, *v.t.*, to ride a horse at a canter; *v.i.*, to move at a canter; *n.*, a gentle gallop.

can'tered, *p.p.*, canter.

can'tering, *pr.p.*, canter.

canthar'ides, *n. pl.*, Spanish fly.

canthar'idin, *n.*, a compound extracted from Spanish fly and other insects.

can'ticle, *n.*, a prose song, such as *Magnificat.*

can'tilever, *n.*, a long bracket supporting a bridge roadway, a balcony, or other heavy structure.

can'tillate, *v.i.*, to chant.

cantilla'tion, *n.*, chanting.

cant'ing, *pr.p.*, cant; *adj.*, leaning; hypocritical.

can'tle, *n.*, a hunch of cheese or bread; the backbone of a saddle.

can'to, *n.*, a division in a long poem.

can'to fer'mo, *n.*, the plain song melody as distinguished from the faux bourdon.

can'ton, *v.t.*, to divide into districts; *n.*, a division of a country.

can'tonal, *adj.*, rel. to cantons.

can'toned *p.p.*, canton.

Can'tonese, *adj.*, rel. to Canton.

can'toning, *pr.p.*, canton.

canton'ment, *n.*, a military station, either temporary or permanent.

can'trip, *n.*, incantation, frolic.

can'vas, *adj.*, made of canvas; *n.*, a coarse cloth from which sails are made, or on which pictures are painted.

can'vass, *v.t.*, to examine closely; to solicit votes.

can'vassed, *p.p.*, canvass.

can'vasser, *n.*, one who canvasses.

can'vassing, *pr.p.*, canvass.

ca'ny, *adj.*, full of canes.

can'yon, *n.*, a deep ravine. Also *cañon.*

canzo'ne, *n.*, a Provençal type of madrigal.

canzonet', *n.*, a short song; a light operatic air.

caout'chouc, *n.*, india-rubber.

caout'choucin, *n.*, oil of caoutchouc.

cap, *v.t.*, to put a cap or cover on; to put a finishing touch to; to surpass; to salute; *n.*, a head covering; the top; anything like a cap.

capabil'ity, *n.*, skill, ability to do things.

cap'able, *adj.*, skilful, able.

ca'pableness *n.*, *i.q.* capability.

ca'pably, *adv.*. skilfully, ably.

capa'cious, *adj.*, roomy, wide, able to hold much.

capa'ciously, *adv.*, in a capacious way.

capa'ciousness, *n.*, the state of being capacious.

capac'itate, *v.t.*, to qualify, render capable.

capac'itated, *p.p.*, capacitate.

capac'itating, *pr.p.*, capacitate.

capac'ity, *n.*, cubic content; ability, skill; function or relation.

cap-à-pie', *adv.*, from head to foot.

capar'ison, *v.t.*, to cover with housings; *n.*, horse-trappings.

capar'isoned, *p.p.*, caparison.

capar'isoning, *pr.p.*, caparison.

cape, *n.*, a headland; a short circular cloak.

cap'elet, cap'ellet, *n.*, a swelling on a horse's hock.

ca'per, *v.i.*, to dance, leap about; *n.*, a frisky antic; a shrub with pungent flower-buds used for flavouring.

capercail'zie, *n.*, a large kind of grouse.
ca'pered, *p.p.*, caper.
ca'pering, *pr.p.*, caper.
cap'ias, *n.*, a writ authorizing the seizure of a person or goods.
capilla'ceous, *adj.*, hair-like.
capillaire', *n.*, a syrup, once made from the maidenhair fern.
capillar'ity, *n.*, capillary attraction.
cap'illary, *adj.*, rel. to the hair, hair-like; *n.*, a minute blood-vessel uniting the veins and arteries.
capil'liform, *adj.*, in the form of hair.
cap'ital, *adj.*, chief, at the head, rel. to the death penalty; *n.*, the head of a column; the chief city in a State; stock, money.
cap'italist, *n.*, one who possesses and employs capital.
capitaliza'tion, *n.*, the process of converting into capital.
cap'italize, *v.t.*, to convert into capital.
cap'italized, *p.p.*, capitalize.
cap'italizing, *pr.p.*, capitalize.
cap'itate, *adj.*, head-shaped; having a head.
capita'tion, *n.*, a grant made by heads.
Cap'itol, *n.*, the temple of Jupiter in Rome, called the Capitolium; the building at Washington in which the U.S.Congress meets.
Cap'itoline, *adj.*, rel. to the Capitolium.
capit'ular, *adj.*, pert. to a monastic or cathedral Chapter; *n.*, a collection of laws.
capit'ularly, *adv.*, in chapter form.
capit'ulary, *adj.* and *n.*, *i.q.* capitular.
capit'ulate, *v.i.*, to surrender on terms.
capit'ulated, *p.p.*, capitulate.
capit'ulating, *pr.p.*, capitulate.
capitula'tion, *n.*, the act of capitulating.
capit'ulator, *n.*, one who capitulates.
capit'ulum, *n.*, a little head; a chapter.
capi'vi, *n.*, a S. American balsam = copaiba.
cap'lin, *n.*, the part of a flail handle through which the thongs pass.
cap'nomor, *n.*, a compound distilled from wood-tars.
ca'pon, *n.*, a young cock fattened for table.
capote', *n.*, a cloak or coat with a hood; the hood of a vehicle.
capped, *p.p.*, cap.
cap'per, *n.*, one who caps.
cap'ping, *pr.p.*, cap.
caprice', *n.*, a whim, sudden change of mind.
capri'cious, *adj.*, subject to whims.
capri'ciously, *adv.*, in a capricious way.
capri'ciousness, *n.*, the state of being subject to sudden changes of mind.
Cap'ricorn, *n.*, the tenth of the signs of the Zodiac.
Cap'ricornus, *n.*, the Latin name for Capricorn = horned like a goat.
caprifica'tion, *n.*, artificial fertilization of the fig or date.
cap'riform, *adj.*, shaped like a goat.
cap'rine, *adj.*, goat-like.
cap'riole, *n.*, a leap, esp. of a trained horse.
cap'sicum, *n.*, the plant from which Cayenne pepper comes.
capsize', *v.t.* and *i.*, to overturn.
capsized', *p.p.*, capsize.
capsi'zing, *pr.p.*, capsize.
cap'stan, *n.*, an upright drum used in raising an anchor and other heavy weights.
cap'sular, *adj.*, rel. to or resembling a capsule.
cap'sulary, *adj.*, *i.q.* capsular.
cap'sule, *n.*, a plant's seed-vessel; a gelatinous bag containing medicine.
cap'tain, *n.*, a head officer; commander of a ship, a company of troops, a team or club; head boy of a school.
cap'taincy, *n.*, captain's rank or tenure of office.
cap'tainship, *n.*, a captaincy; skill as a captain.
cap'tion, *n.*, a title in a legal document, a chapter or section heading; an arrest.
cap'tious, *adj.*, making frivolous or vexatious objections.
cap'tiously, *adv.*, in a captious way.
cap'tiousness, *n.*, a tendency to be captious.
cap'tivate, *v.t.*, to make captive; to charm.
cap'tivated, *p.p.*, captivate.
cap'tivating, *pr.p.*, captivate.
captiva'tion, *n.*, the act of captivating; state of being captivated.
cap'tive, *adj.*, taken prisoner; held in captivity or bondage; *n.*, a prisoner.
captiv'ity, *n.*, the state of a captive.
cap'tor, *n.*, one who takes captive.
cap'ture, *n.*, the act of capturing; *v.t.*, to catch by force, arrest.
cap'tured, *p.p.*, capture.
cap'turing, *pr.p.*, capture.
Cap'uchin, *n.*, a monk of the Franciscan Order distinguished by his *capuche* or cowl.
cap'ulet, *n.*, a peasant woman's headgear worn in the S. of France.

car, *n.*, a generic name for many kinds of vehicles.

carabineer', *n.*, a soldier armed with a carbine. Also *carbineer*.

car'acal, *n.*, a species of Asiatic or African lynx.

car'ack, *n.*, a large armed Spanish or Portuguese trading vessel.

car'acole, *n.*, a quick half-turn made by a horseman; *v.i.*, to make sudden turns with horses.

car'acoly, *n.*, an alloy of gold, silver, and copper.

carafe', *n.*, a water-bottle.

car'amel, *n.*, burnt sugar for colouring; a form of sweet-meat.

car'at, *n.*, a unit of weight (= 4 grains) for precious stones; the one twenty-fourth part of gold purity.

car'avan, *n.*, an Oriental company of travellers for trade or other purposes; a house on wheels.

caravaneer', *n.*, one who uses a caravan.

car'avanner, *n.*, *i.q.* caravaneer.

caravan'sary, *n.*, *i.q.* caravanserai.

caravan'serai, *n.*, an enclosed shelter for caravans; an inn.

car'avel, *n.*, a small ship, formerly used in Spain and Portugal.

car'away, *n.*, a plant the seeds of which are used for flavouring.

car'bine, *n.*, a short rifle, used chiefly by cavalry.

carbineer', *n.*, a soldier using a carbine.

carbol'ic, *adj.*, produced from coal or coal-tar; *n.*, the product itself.

car'bolize, *v.t.*, to charge with carbolic.

car'bolized, *p.p.*, carbolize.

car'bolizing, *pr.p.*, carbolize.

car'bon, *n.*, pure charcoal.

carbona'ceous, *adj.*, producing carbon.

Carbona'ri, *n. pl.*, members of an Italian secret society.

car'bonate, *n.*, a carbonic acid salt; *adj.*, charged with carbonic.

carbon'ic, *adj.*, produced from carbon.

carbonif'erous, *adj.*, yielding coal or carbon.

carboniza'tion, *n.*, the process of converting into coal or carbon.

car'bonize, *v.t.*, to reduce to carbon.

car'bonized, *p.p.*, carbonize.

car'bonizing, *pr.p.*, carbonize.

car'boy, *n.*, a large bottle, enclosed in wicker-work, for carrying acids.

car'buncle, *n.*, a precious stone of a deep red colour; an ulcer so named.

car'buncled, *adj.*, set with carbuncles.

carbun'cular, *adj.*, of the nature of a carbuncle.

car'buret, *v.t.*, to impregnate with carbon; *n.*, a compound of carbon; carbide.

car'buretted, -ted, *p.p.*, carburet.

car'burettor, -ter, *n.*, an apparatus for carburetting.

car'burize, *v.t.*, *i.q.* carburet.

car'cajou, *n.*, the wolverine.

car'canet, *n.*, a jewelled chain or necklace.

car'cass, car'case, *n.*, a dead body; a framework.

carcinol'ogy, *n.*, the study of crustaceans.

carcino'ma, *n.*, a cancer.

carcino'matous, *adj.*, cancerous.

card, *v.t.*, to comb wool or flax; *n.*, a piece of pasteboard, intended for written or printed matter.

cardamine, *n.*, a perennial plant of the mustard family.

car'damom, *n.*, an aromatic East Indian and Chinese plant.

card'board, *n.*, thick card; *adj.*, made of cardboard.

card'-case, *n.*, a case containing calling-cards.

card'ed, *p.p.*, card.

card'er, *n.*, one who cards.

car'diac, *adj.*, rel. to the heart; *n.*, a cordial.

cardi'acal, *adj.*, *i.q.* cardiac.

cardiag'raphy, *n.*, the process of recording the strength of the heart's movements.

cardial'gia, *n.*, heart-burn.

cardial'gy, *n.*, *i.q.* cardialgia.

car'dinal, *adj.*, principal (*lit.*, that on which something hinges); of a red colour; *n.*, a member of the Sacred College at Rome. At St. Paul's Cathedral, London, two of the Minor Canons are called Cardinals.

car'dinalate, *n.*, the body of Cardinals, the rank of a cardinal, a cardinal's tenure of office.

card'ing, *pr.p.*, card.

cardiog'raphy, *n.*, *i.q.* cardiagraphy.

car'dioid, *n.*, a heart-shaped curve.

cardiol'ogy, *n.*, the science of the heart and of the heart's anatomy.

cardi'tis, *n.*, inflammation of the heart.

cardoon', *n.*, a perennial aster.

care, *v.i.*, to have regard; to be willing; *n.*, a state of anxiety, solicitude; charge; the object of one's care.

cared, *p.p.*, care.

careen', *v.t.*, to overturn a ship for the purpose of repairs, etc.; *v.i.*, to heel over.

careen'age, *n.*, the fee for careening; a place for careening purposes.

careened', *p.p.*, careen.

careen'ing, *pr.p.*, careen.

career', *n.*, a vocation, profession.

care'ful, *adj.*, full of care; conscientious in action; prudent.

care'fully, *adv.*, with care.

care'fulness, *n.*, the habit or state of taking care.

care'less, *adj.*, not taking care, indifferent; free from care.

care'lessly, *adv.*, in a careless way.

care'lessness, *n.*, the habit or state of not caring.

caress', *v.t.*, to fondle, stroke, pet; *n.*, an embrace, a fondling.

caressed', *p.p.*, caress.

caress'ing, *pr.p.*, caress.

caress'ingly, *adv.*, in a caressing way.

car'et, *n.*, a printer's or writer's mark of omission.

care'taker, *n.*, one who looks after a building or house.

care'worn, *adj.*, worn out with care.

car'go, *n.*, a ship's lading.

car'goose, *n.*, the crested grebe.

Car'ib, *n.*, one of an almost extinct American race, the Caribs, inhabiting the islands of the Caribbean Sea.

Caribbe'an, *adj.*, rel. to the Caribs and to the sea containing their islands.

Car'ibee, *n.*, *i.q.* Carib.

caribou', *n.*, the reindeer of N. America.

car'icature, *n.*, a likeness purposely distorted or exaggerated; *v.t.*, to represent in a ridiculous way.

car'icatured, *p.p.*, caricature.

car'icaturing, *pr.p.*, caricature.

car'icaturist, *n.*, one who caricatures.

car'icous *adj.*, fig-shaped.

ca'ries, *n.*, decay of teeth or bone.

car'illon, *n.*, a peal or chime of bells, acted upon by a performer or by mechanism.

cari'na, *n.*, a keel.

car'inate, *adj.*, keeled, keel-shaped.

car'inated, *adj.*, *i.q.* carinate.

car'ing, *pr.p.*, care.

car'iole, *n.*, a light one-horse vehicle.

carios'ity, *n.*, a carious state.

ca'rious, *adj.*, rotten, decaying.

cark, *v.t.*, to oppress with care; *n.*, anxiety, worry.

cark'ing, *pr.p.*, cark; *adj.*, worrying.

car'line, *adj.*, rel. to the Carlina; *n.*, a plant of the Carlina family; the short timber that joins the deck beams of a ship.

carl'ing, *n.*, the dish of fried peas, once peculiar to Carling Sunday.

Carlovin'gian, *adj.*, rel. to the dynasty of Charlemagne; *n.*, a member of the family of C.

car'man, *n.*, the driver of a car or cart.

Car'melite, *n.*, a member of the Order of Friars of Our Lady of Mount Carmel, known as the White Friars.

car'minate, *v.i.*, to emit internal wind.

car'minative, *adj.*, relieving flatulence.

car'mine, *n.*, a deep red colour made from cochineal.

car'nage, *n.*, great slaughter, butchery.

car'nal, *adj.*, rel. to the flesh, fleshly, sensual.

carnal'ity, *n.*, a sensual tendency or state.

car'nalize, *v.t.*, to make sensual.

car'nally, *adv.*, in a carnal way.

car'nal-mind'ed, *adj.*, disposed to sensuality.

carna'tion, *n.*, flesh-tint; the flowering plant so named.

carne'lian, *n.*, a red stone, much used for seals.

car'neous, *adj.*, fleshy.

car'ney, *n.*, a mouth disease in horses.

carnifica'tion, *n.*, a morbid conversion of tissue into flesh-like consistency.

car'nified, *p.p.*, carnify.

car'nify, *v.t.*, to convert into flesh; *v.i.*, to suffer carnification.

car'nifying, *pr.p.*, carnify.

car'nival, *n.*, the feast that precedes the Lenten fast; any sort of revel.

carniv'ora, *n.pl.*, flesh-eating creatures.

carniv'orous, *adj.*, flesh-eating.

carnos'ity, *n.*, fleshiness.

car'nous, *adj.*, fleshy.

car'ob, *n.*, the tree so named, bel. to the bean order.

car'ol, *v.i.*, to sing cheerfully, warble; *n.*, a joyous song, esp. the joyous songs of Christmas, Epiphany, and Easter.

car'olled, **-led**, *p.p.*, carol.

car'olling, **-ling**, *pr.p.*, carol.

carot'id, *adj.*, rel. to the carotids; *n.*, one of the great neck-arteries.

carou'sal, *n.*, a revel, drinking bout.

carouse', *v.i.*, to revel, hold a drinking-bout.

caroused', *p.p.*, carouse.

carous'er, *n.*, one who carouses.

carous'ing, *pr.p.*, carouse.

carp, *v.i.*, to cavil, criticize censoriously; *n.*, a fresh-water fish so named.

car'pal, *adj.*, rel. to the wrist

Carpa'thian, *adj.*, bel. to the Carpathian chain of mountains.

carped, *p.p.*, carp.

car'pel, *n.*, a simple pistil or seed-vessel.

car'pellary, *adj.*, resembling a carpel.

car'penter, *v.i.*, to do carpentry; *n.*, a worker in timber for all manner of uses.

car'pentry, *n.*, a carpenter's craft.

carp'er, *n.*, a caviller.

car'pet, *v.t.*, to cover with a carpet; *n.*, a woven floor-covering (formerly, a table cover).

car'peted, *p.p.*, carpet.

car'peting, *pr.p.*, carpet; also *n.*, carpet material, carpet goods; the act of carpeting.

carp'ing, *pr.p.*, carp.

car'polite, *n.*, fruit fossilized.

carpol'ogist, *n.*, a student of carpology.

carpol'ogy, *n.*, the study of fruits.

car'pus, *n.*, the wrist.

car'raway, *n.*, *see* caraway.

car'rel, *n.*, a recess in a cloister for a desk.

car'riage, *n.*, the act of carrying; cost of freight; a vehicle; bearing, demeanour; a thing carried (*obs.*).

car'ried, *p.p.*, carry.

car'rier, *n.*, one who carries; something that carries; one whose business it is to convey goods, parcels, etc.; part of a machine-gun.

car'rion *n.*, dead and putrefying flesh; any loathsome object.

carronade', *n.*, a short naval gun with large bore.

car'rot, *n.*, the edible vegetable so named.

car'roty, *adj.*, like a carrot, reddish-yellow.

car'ry, *v.t.*, to convey, bear; capture (a fort); involve, imply; hold up; to act as a bearer of anything; *n.*, portage; the range of a gun or missile.

car'rying, *pr.p.*, carry.

cart, *v.t.*, to carry in a cart, to convey; *n.*, a vehicle for carrying loads.

cart'age, *n.*, the carrying in a cart; cost of carrying.

carte, *n.*, a card, bill of fare; a term in fencing to denote a particular position.

carte blanche', *n.*, full permission to act as one pleases.

cart'ed, *p.p.*, cart.

carte-de-visite', *n.*, a visiting card; a small mounted photograph.

car'tel, *n.*, a written agreement for the interchange of prisoners; a written challenge.

cart'er, *n.*, one who drives a cart.

Carte'sian, *adj.*, rel. to Descartes and his philosophy.

Carte'sianism, *n.*, the philosophical system of Descartes.

Carthagin'ian, *adj.*, rel. to Carthage or the Carthaginians.

car'thamin, *n.*, a red dye.

cart'-horse, *n.*, a horse that draws a cart.

Carthu'sian, *adj.*, rel. to the Carthusians; *n.*, a monk of the Order of St. Bruno.

car'tilage, *n.*, gristle.

cartilag'inous, *adj.*, gristly.

cart'ing, *pr.p.*, cart.

cart'-load, *n.*, the contents of a cart.

cartog'rapher, *n.*, a map-maker.

cartograph'ic, *adj.*, rel. to cartography.

cartog'raphy, *n.*, the art of map-making.

car'ton, *n.*, a light cardboard box.

cartoon', *n.*, a large sketch for a picture; a picture representing, often comically, topical subjects.

cartoon'ist, *n.*, a drawer of cartoons.

cartouche, *n.*, a cartridge box; an inscribed tablet.

car'tridge, *n.*, a case in which is held the charge of a firearm.

car'tulary, *n.*, a register of charters and other records.

cart'way, *n.*, a road fit for carting purposes.

cart'wheel, *n.*, the wheel of a cart; a summersault.

cart'wright, *n.*, one who makes or repairs carts.

car'ucate, *n.*, a measure of plough land; it varied from 80 to 120 acres.

carun'cle, *n.*, a bird's wattles; the fleshy growth in the inner corner of the eye.

carun'cular, *adj.*, of the nature of a caruncle.

carun'culate, *adj.*, having caruncles.

carun'culated, *adj.*, *i.q.* caruncalate.

carve, *v.t.*, to cut, to fashion.

carved, *p.p.*, carve.

car'vel, *n.*, *see* caravel.

carv'er, *n.*, one who carves.

carv'ing, *pr.p.*, carve; also *n.*, the art or act of carving; a piece of carved work.

car'yate, *n.*, *i.q.* caryatid.

caryat'ic, *adj.*, rel. to caryatids.

caryat'id, *n.*, a female figure supporting (instead of a pillar) an entablature.

caryat'ides, *n.*, pl. of caryatid.

cas'cabel, *n.*, the loop at the breech of a cannon.

cascade', *n.*, a waterfall.

cascal'ho, *n.*, a Brazilian name for detritus.

cas'cara, *n.*, bark.

cascaril'la, *n.*, dimin. of cascara—an aromatic bark, useful as a tonic.

case, *n.*, a covering, sheath, book cover; something that happens; a condition; anyone under medical treatment; a law-suit; a grammatical name for the various relations of a noun; *v.t.*, to enclose, cover.

cased, *p.p.*, case.

case'harden, *v.t.*, to harden (iron) by making the surface into steel.

case'hardened, *p.p.*, caseharden.

case'hardening, *pr.p.*, caseharden; also *n.*, the act or state of casehardening.

ca'seic, *adj.*, rel. to cheese or casein.

ca'sein, *n.*, milk curd.

case'-knife, *n.*, a knife enclosed in a case or sheath.

case'mate, *n.*, a vaulted chamber in a fort; an armoured gun station in a ship.

case'mated, *adj.*, having casemates.

case'ment, *n.*, a hinged window, opening like a door.

case'mented, *adj.*, having casements.

ca'seous, *adj.*, like cheese.

casern', *n.*, a barrack.

case'-shot, *n.*, shrapnel or canister shot.

cash, *v.t.*, to change into money; *n.*, money of all kinds; a Chinese coin so named.

cash'-account, *n.*, a book-keeping record of money received and paid.

cash'-book, *n.*, the book recording receipts and payments of cash.

cash'-boy, *n.*, a boy who carries the cash from the counter to the cashier's desk and back again.

cashed, *p.p.*, cash.

cashew', *n.*, a nut-bearing tree (*see* cachou).

cash'-girl, *n.*, fem. of cash-boy.

cashier', *n.*, one who looks after the money in a shop or bank; *v.t.*, to dismiss with ignominy.

cashiered', *p.p.*, cashier.

cashier'ing, *pr.p.*, cashier.

cash'ing, *pr.p.*, cash.

cash'keeper, *n.*, a cashier.

cash'mere, *n.*, a fine fabric made from the wool of a Cashmere goat.

cashoo', *n.*, *see* catechu.

ca'sing, *n.*, a covering, framing; *pr.p.*, case.

casi'no, *n.*, a building for public entertainments.

cask, *v.t.*, to place in a cask; *n.*, a round, hooped vessel.

cas'ket, *n.*, a small box; a jewel-case; a coffin.

casque, *n.*, a helmet.

cassa'da, *n.*, *i.q.* cassava.

Cassan'dra, *n.*, the Trojan princess, whose prophecies went unheeded.

cas'sareep, *n.*, a condiment made from cassava.

cassa'tion, *n.*, reversal of a judicial sentence.

cassa'va, *n.*, the plant from which tapioca is derived.

cass'erole, *n.*, a stew-pan.

cas'sia, *n.*, the plant from which senna is obtained.

cas'simere, *n.*, *see* cashmere.

cassit'erite, *n.*, a tin dioxide.

cas'sock, *n.*, an ecclesiastical habit, close fitting and long.

cas'socked, *adj.*, wearing a cassock.

cas'sowary, *n.*, a large ostrich-like bird.

cast, *v.t.*, to throw, throw off, deposit; mould; reckon, calculate; *n.*, the act of throwing; the length of a throw; a squint; a type; a mould; the assignment of *dramatis personae*.

Casta'lian, *adj.*, rel. to Castalia, the spring sacred to the Muses.

cas'tanets, *n. pl.*, two wooden or ivory clappers, fastened to a dancer's thumb and rattled.

cast'away, *n.*, a person or ship that has been abandoned.

caste, *n.*, hereditary class; class distinction.

cas'tellan, *n.*, one in charge of a castle.

cas'tellany, *n.*, a castellan's jurisdiction.

cas'tellated, *adj.*, battlemented like a castle.

cas'ter, *n.*, one who casts; also *i.q.*, castor.

cas'tigate, *v.t.*, to chastize, criticize, emend.

cas'tigated, *p.p.*, castigate.

cas'tigating, *pr.p.*, castigate.

castiga'tion, *n.*, the act of castigating.

cas'tigator, *n.*, one who castigates.

cas'tigatory, *adj.*, rel. to castigation.

Castil'ian, *adj.*, bel. to Castile; *n.*, a native of Castile.

cast'ing, *pr.p.*, cast; *n.*, the act or result of casting.

cast'ing-net, *n.*, a net which is flung out and drawn back.

cast'ing-vote, *n.*, the chairman's extra vote when the sides are equal.

cast'-iron, *n.*, iron that has been melted; *adj.*, made of or like to cast-iron.

cas'tle, *v.t.*, to fortify; to exchange the places of the king and the castle at chess; *n.*, a fortress.

cas'tled, *p.p.*, castle; also *adj.*, having a castle on it.

cas'tling, *pr.p.*, castle.

cas'tor, *n.*, a beaver; a tall hat; a utensil for sprinkling (*e.g.*, a pepper castor); a small wheel for furniture legs; a substance secreted by the beaver.

cas'tor-oil, *n.*, a vegetable purgative.

castrameta'tion, *n.*, the act or method of measuring a camp.

cas'trate, *v.t.*, to emasculate.

cas'trated, *p.p.*, castrate.

cas'trating, *pr.p.*, castrate.

castra'tion, *n.*, the act or process of castrating.

cas'trel, *n.*, *see* kestrel.

cas'ual, *adj.*, accidental, happening by chance; unmethodical and careless; *n.*, a tramp.

cas'ualty, *n.*, a serious accident; loss through death or wounds.

cas'uist, *n.*, one who studies casuistry.

casuis'tic, *adj.*, rel. to casuistry.

casuis'tical, *adj.*, *i.q.* casuistic.

cas'uistry, *n.*, in moral science the study of cases of conscience; over-subtlety; sophistry.

cat, *v.t.*, to haul up; *n.*, the familiar animal so named.

catab'olism, *n.*, (*lit.*, a casting down); the change of protoplasm into other substances.

catachre'sis, *n.* a misuse of metaphors.

catachres'tic, *adj.*, of the nature of catachresis.

cat'aclysm, *n.*, a flood, deluge; any great upheaval.

cataclys'mic, *adj.*, rel. to cataclysms or to the cataclysmic theory.

cataclys'mist, *n.*, one who supports a particular view about cataclysms.

cat'acomb, *n.*, a subterranean cave-tomb.

catacous'tics, *n.*, the theory of reflected sound.

catadiop'tric, *adj.*, rel. to the reflection or refraction of light.

cat'afalque, *n.*, a temporary canopy over a corpse or coffin.

catagmat'ic, *adj.*, rel. to a fracture.

Cat'alan, *adj.*, bel. to Catalonia.

catalec'tic, *adj.*, lacking metrical completeness.

cat'alepsis, *n.*, *i.q.* catalepsy.

cat'alepsy, *n.*, a nervous affection; the patient loses consciousness, and his limbs become rigid, remaining where anyone fixes them.

catalep'tic, *adj.*, rel. or subject to catalepsy.

catallac'tics, *n.*, the theory of commercial exchange.

cat'alogue, *v.t.*, to make or to include in a list: *n.*, a list or detailed enumeration.

cat'alogued, *p.p.*, catalogue.

cat'aloguing, *pr.p.*, catalogue.

Catalo'nian, *adj.*, bel. to Catalonia.

Catal'pa, *n.*, a genus of trees so named.

catal'ysis, *n.*, a chemical process in which a stable agent changes a compound.

catalyt'ic, *adj.*, rel. to catalysis.

catamaran', *n.*, a surf-boat or raft.

catame'nia, *n. pl.*, the menses.

catame'nial, *adj.*, rel. to catamenia.

cat'amount, *n.*, the panther.

catapet'alous, *adj.*, with petals at the base of a group of stamens.

cat'aphract, *n.*, plate or scale armour.

cat'aplasm, *n.*, a poultice.

cat'apult, *n.*, originally a Roman engine for discharging heavy missiles; a modern toy.

catapult'ic, *adj.*, rel. to a catapult.

cat'aract, *n.*, a great waterfall, or rush of water; a disease of the eye.

catarac'tous, *adj.* cataract-like

catarrh', *n.*, an affection of the mucous membrane; a cold in the head.

catarrh'al, *adj.*, of the nature of catarrh.

catas'tasis, *n.*, the part in a Greek drama that next precedes the catastrophe.

catas'trophe, *n.*, in a drama = the *dénouement* or final conclusion; a disastrous ending, a calamity.

catastroph'ic, *adj.*, of the nature of catastrophe.

cat'bird, *n.*, the N. American mocking-thrush.

cat'boat, *n.*, a single-masted sailing boat.

cat'*call*, *n.*, a derisive outcry; *v.i.*, to raise this cry.

catch, *v.t.*, to lay hold of, seize; grasp meaning; hear sound; overtake; *n.*, anything that is caught; the act of catching, an impediment; a kind of musical form; a fastening.

catch'er, *n.*, one who catches.

catch'fly, *n.*, a plant so named from its glutinous stem.

catch'ing, *pr.p.*, catch

catch'ment, *n.*, drainage.

catch'penny, *adj.*, worthless; *n.*, a worthless article made only to sell.

catch'pole, *n.*, an instrument of medieval warfare for unhorsing an opponent.

catch'up, *n.*, *see* catsup.

catch'*word*, *n.*, a word or phrase designed to arrest the popular fancy; the first word of a page repeated at the foot of the preceding page.

catechet'ic, *adj.*, of the nature of a catechism.

catechet'ical, *adj.*, *i.q.* catechetic.

cat'echism, *n.*, instruction by question and answer.

cat'echist, *n.*, one who catechizes; a teacher of catechumens.

catechist'ic, *adj.*, rel. to catechizing.

catechiza'tion, *n.*, the act of catechizing.

cat'echize, *v.t.*, to teach by question and answer.

cat'echized, *p.p.*, catechize.

cat'echizer, *n.*, one who catechizes.

cat'echizing, *pr.p.*, catechize.

cat'echu, *n.*, an astringent extract.

catechu'men, *n.*, a person under instruction in the rudiments of the Catholic Faith.

catechumen'ic, *adj.*, in the relation of a catechumen.

catechumen'ical, *adj.*, *i.q.* catechumenic.

categoremat'ic, *adj.*, said of terms which are complete in themselves.

categor'ical, *adj.*, positive, unequivocal.

cat'egorize, *v.t.*, to classify.

cat'egory, *n.*, a class; general heading or grouping.

cate'na, *n.*, a chain, series.

catena'rian, *adj.*, rel. to a catenary.

cate'nary, *n.*, a mathematical curve so named; *adj.*, rel. to or like a catenary.

cat'enate, *v.t.*, to form into a chain or series.

cat'enated, *p.p.*, catenate.

catena'tion, *n.*, the act of catenating.

ca'ter, *v.i.*, to provide food; minister to any taste or desire.

cat'eran, *n.*, a Highland name for a freebooter.

ca'tered, *p.p.*, cater.

ca'terer, *n.*, one who caters.

ca'teress, *n.*, fem. of caterer.

ca'tering, *pr.p.*, cater.

cat'erpillar, *n.*, a grub; the larva of some insects.

cat'erwaul, *v.i.*, to make the cry of a cat; to raise any hideous cry.

cates, *n. pl.*, eatables; dainty meats.

cat'fish, *n.*, a fish so named from the purring sound it makes when caught.

cat'gut, *n.*, strong cord made from animals' intestines.

Cath'ari, *adj.*, a name corresponding to the Puritans.

cathar'sis, *n.*, purging.

cathar'tic, *adj.*, purging, purifying.

cathar'tical, *adj.*, *i.q.* cathartic.

cat'-head, *n.*, the projecting piece of timber or iron from which a ship's anchor hangs.

cathed'ra, *n.*, the Greek name for any seat; hence, the bishop's seat, stool, or throne.

cathe'dral, *adj.*, containing a *cathedra* or bishop's seat; *n.*, a church in which the bishop has his seat.

catheret'ic, *adj.*, destructive; erosive; *n.*, a caustic.

cath'eter, *n.*, a surgical instrument for insertion into passages.

cath'ode, *n.*, the negative pole or electrode of an electrical battery.

cathod'ic, *adj.*, rel. to a cathode.

cath'olic, *adj.*, universal. The Catholic Faith is so called not because it embraces all beliefs, but because the one belief is offered to the whole world without distinction of race. By a perversion of langua e a man who denies the Catholic Faith is often described as Catholic or Catholic-minded because he regards dogmatic belief as illiberal.

Cathol'icism, *n.*, the system and doctrines of the Catholic Church.

catholic'ity, *n.*, the Catholic character. It is sometimes perversely used in the sense of breadth, liberality.

Cathol'icize, *v.t.*, to make Catholic.

cathol'icon, *n.*, a universal remedy; a comprehensive book.

Catilina'rian, *adj.*, rel. to Catiline.

cat'ion, *n.*, Faraday's name for the element which in electrolysis makes its appearance at the cathode.

cat'kin, *n.*, the spikes of flowers on the willow and other trees.

cat'-like, *adj.*, like a cat.

cat'ling, *n.*, a kitten; a surgical knife so named.

cat'mint, *n.*, a kind of mint of which cats are fond.

cat'-nip, *n.*, *i.q.* catmint.

Cato'nian, *adj.*, rel. to Cato.

cat-o'-nine'-tails, *n.*, an obsolete instrument of punishment. It consisted of nine knotted cords attached to a handle.

catop'tric, *adj.*, reflecting.

cat's'-paw, *n.*, anyone made to do another's dirty work.

cat'sup, *n.*, a liquid aromatic condiment.

cat'tle, *n.*, domesticated live stock, particularly bovine.

cat'tle-show, *n.*, an exhibition of cattle.

Cauca'sian, *adj.*, rel. to the Caucasus region.

cau'cus, *n.*, a private association of political partisans.

cau'dal, *adj.*, rel. to the tail.

cau'date, *adj.*, tailed.

cau'dated, *adj.*, tailed.

cau'dle, *n.*, a warm concoction of wine, spices, etc., for a sick person.

cauf, *n.*, a basket in which fish are kept under water.

caught, *p.p.*, catch.

caul, *n.*, a fold of the peritoneum; a membranous covering of some infants' heads at child-birth; a hair-net.

caul'dron, *n.*, a large boiler or kettle.

caules'cent, *adj.*, having a stem.

cau'licle, *n.*, a little stem.

cau'licolous, *adj.*, living on stalks.

caul'icule, *n.*, *i.q.* caulicle.

caulif'erous, *adj.*, having a stem.

cau'liflower, *n.*, a cabbage with edible flowers. [like.

cau'liform, *adj.*, stem-

cau'line, *adj.*, growing on a stalk; the colouring matter in red cabbage.

caulk, *v.t.*, to make watertight (*see* calk).

caus'al, *adj.*, rel. to cause.

causal'ity, *n.*, the relation of cause and effect.

causa'tion, *n.*, *i.q.* causality; the act of causing.

caus'ative, *adj.*, producing effect from cause.

caus'atively, *adv.*, in a causative way.

cause, *n.*, an original source, reason, motive; a suit at law; a movement or principle; *v.t.*, to produce an effect; compel.

caused, *p.p.*, cause.

cause'less, *adj.*, without any just cause.

cause'lessly, *adv.*, in a causeless way.

cause'lessness, *n.*, an unreasonable condition or state.

caus'er, *n.*, one who causes.

cause'rie, *n.*, a chat, conversation (*Fr.*).

causeuse', *n.*, a seat for two people to chat on (*Fr.*).

cause'way, *n.*, a raised path.

cau'sey, *n.*, *i.q.* causeway.

cau'seyed, *adj.*, having a causeway.

causid'ical, *adj.*, rel. to advocacy.

caus'ing, *pr.p.*, cause.

caus'tic, *adj.*, burning; sarcastic; *n.*, a burning substance.

caustic'ity, *n.*, the quality of being caustic.

cau'tel, *n.*, caution; in ecclesiastical language, a precaution against defects or irregularities in saying Mass.

cau'ter, *n.*, a burning-iron.

cau'terant, *adj.*, of the character of a cautery.

cauteriza'tion, *n.*, the act of using a cautery.

cau'terize, *v.t.*, to burn with a cautery.

cau'terized, *p.p.*, cauterize.

cau'terizing, *pr.p.*, cauterize.

cau'tery, *n.*, burning with an acid or a hot iron; a searing iron or other agent.

cau'tion, *v.t.*, to admonish, warn; *n.*, prudence, consideration, advice, admonition.

cau'tionary, *adj.*, of the nature of warning.

cau'tioned, *p.p.*, caution.

cau'tioner, *n.*, one who cautions.

cau'tioning, *pr.p.*, caution.

cau'tious, *adj.*, wary, discreet.

cau'tiously, *adv.*, warily, discreetly.

cau'tiousness, *n.*, a wary, discreet characteristic.

cavalcade', *n.*, a train of horsemen.

cavalier', *n.*, an armed horseman; a lady's escort; a Royalist; *adj.*, like a cavalier, gay, off-hand; arrogant, abrupt.

cavalier'ly, *adv.*, in free and easy, haughty fashion.

cav'alry, *n.*, horse soldiers; *adj.*, rel. to cavalry.

cavass', *n.*, a Turkish military guard.

cavati'na, *n.*, a short aria without a repeat.

cave, *v.i.*, to fall in, collapse; *n.*, a hollow subterranean place.

ca'veat, *n.*, a legal process in delay of proceedings. (It means "let him beware.")

ca'veator, *n.*, one who files a caveat.

caved, *adj.*, hollowed; *p.p.*, cave.

cav'ern, *v.t.*, to excavate; enclose in a cavern; *n.*, an underground cave; any cavity.

cav'erned, *p.p.*, cavern.

cav'ernous, *adj.*, like a cavern; caverned.

cavet'to, *n.*, a grooved moulding.

caviar', **caviare'**, *n.*, sturgeon-roe prepared as a relish.

cav'icorn, *adj.*, with hollow horns.

cav'il, *v.i.*, to find needless fault, to be captious; *n.*, a captious objection, needless criticism.

cav'il(l)ed, *p.p.*, cavil.

cav'il(l)er, *n.*, one who cavils.

cav'il(l)ing, *pr.p.*, cavil.

cav'il(l)ingly, *adv.*, in a captious way.

cav'ing, *pr.p.*, cave.

cav'ity, *n.*, a hollow.

ca'vy, *n.*, a burrowing rodent, such as the guinea pig.

caw, *v.i.*, to make a sound like that of the crow, rook, jackdaw, or raven; *n.*, the cry of those birds.

cawed, *p.p.*, caw.

caw'ing, *pr.p.*, caw.

cawk, *v.i.* and *n.*, *i.q.* caw.

cax'on, *n.*, a chest.

Cayenne', *n.*, a town in French Guiana; (c-) a hot, red pepper, named from that place.

cay'man, *n.*, an American alligator.

cazique', *n.*, *see* cacique.

cease, *v.i.* and *t.*, to stop, desist, come to an end, bring to an end; *n.*, end, pause.

ceased, *p.p.*, cease.

cease'less, *adj.*, without cease.

cease'lessly, *adv.*, in a ceaseless way.

ceas'ing, *pr.p.*, cease.

ce'city, *n.*, blindness.

ce'dar, *n.*, a large tree of the pine and fir order; *adj.*, made of cedar wood.

ce'dared, *adj.*, cedar-covered.

ce'darn, *adj.*, made of cedar.

cede, *v.t.*, to give up, resign.

ce'ded, *p.p.*, cede.

ce'der, *n.*, one who cedes.

cedil'la, *n.*, the sign (,) beneath the letter *c*, softening it before *a*, *o*, *u*.

ce'ding, *pr.p.*, cede.

ce'drat, ce'drate, *n.*, the citron.

ce'drin, ce'drine, *n.*, the active principle of the cedron, a very bitter fruit.

ceil, *v.t.*, to cover with ceiling.

ceiled, *p.p.*, ceil.

ceil'ing, *pr.p.*, ceil; *n.*, the roof of a room.

cel'adon, *n.*, sea-green.

cel'andine, *n.*, the swallow-wort, a kind of poppy.

cel'ature, *n.*, the art of chasing and engraving.

cel'ebrant, *n.*, one who celebrates; the officiating priest or bishop at the Mass.

cel'ebrate, *v.t.*, to make famous; to observe with ceremonies; to commemorate; to officiate at the Mass.

cel'ebrated, *p.p.*, celebrate; *adj.*, famous.

cel'ebrating, *pr. p.*, celebrate.

celebra'tion, *n.*, the act of celebrating; the offering of the Holy Mysteries in the Mass.

cel'ebrator, *n.*, one who celebrates.

celeb'rity, *n.*, the state of being celebrated; a famous personage.

celer'iac, *n.*, turnip-rooted celery.

celer'ity, *n.*, speed, rapidity.

cel'ery, *n.*, the edible plant so named.

celes'tial, *adj.*, bel. or rel. to the sky or heavens.

ce'liac, *adj.*, rel. to the abdomen.

cel'ibacy, *n.*, the unmarried state; bachelorhood.

cel'ibate, *n.*, an unmarried person; *adj.*, not married; abstaining from marriage.

celidog'raphy, *n.*, the study or description of the sun's spots.

cell, *n.*, a small room (in a monastery or a prison); a cavity; a little mass of protoplasm enclosed in a sac; a division of an electric battery.

cel'lar, *n.*, an underground chamber for storage.

cel'larage, *n.*, a system or series of cellars; the capacity of a cellar; charge for storing.

cel'larer, *n.*, a monk in charge of the monastic cellar.

cel'laret, *n.*, a cabinet for holding wine or spirit decanters.

celled, *adj.*, containing cells.

'cell'ist, *n.*, abbreviation of violoncellist, one who plays the violoncello.

'cel'lo, *n.*, short for violoncello.

cel'lular, *adj.*, in cell formation.

cel'lulated, *adj.*, formed into cells.

cel'lule, *n.*, a little cell.

cellulif'erous, *adj.*, producing cellules.

cel'luloid, *n.*, a substance composed of camphor and guncotton.

cel'lulose, *adj.*, full of little cells; made of cellulose; *n.*, a white compound much used in the arts.

Cel'sius, *n.*, a thermometrical scale, named after the Swedish astronomer, Anders Celsius.

Celt, *n.*, a member of the Celtic race; a pre-historic stone, axe-like implement.

Celtibe'rian, *adj.*, pert. to the Celtiberi, a mixed people partly Celts, partly Iberians (Basques).

Celt'ic, *adj.*, bel. to the Celts.

Celt'icism, *n.*, something characteristic of a Celt.

Celt'ish, *adj.*, Celtic.

cement', *v.t.*, to join, unite closely; *n.*, a substance making things adhere; a kind of mortar; (metaphorically) a bond of union.

cementa'tion, *n.*, the process of cementing.

cement'atory, *adj.*, rel. to cement.

cement'ed, *p.p.*, cement.

cement'er, *n.*, one who cements.

cement'ing, *pr.p.*, cement.

cementi'tious, *adj.*, tending to cement.

cem'etery, *n.*, a graveyard, burial-ground.

cen'obite, *n.*, one who lives the common life, a monk, nun.

cenobit'ical, *adj.*, rel. to a cenobite.

cenog'amy, *n.*, community of wives or husbands.

cen'otaph, *n.*, a tomb not containing the

body of a person commemorated.

cense, *v.t.*, to offer incense to; to perfume.

censed, *p.p.*, cense.

cen'ser, *n.*, the vessel in which incense is burned.

cens'ing, *pr.p.*, cense.

cen'sor, *n.*, an ancient Roman official who looked after taxation and superintended the public morals; an official examiner of books, plays, etc.; one who criticizes with a moral purpose; *v.t.*, to reject after examination.

cen'sored, *p.p.*, censor.

censo'rial, *adj.*, rel. to a censor.

cen'soring, *pr.p.*, censor.

censo'rious, *adj.*, adversely critical.

censo'riously, *adv.*, in a censorious way.

censo'riousness, *n.*, the habit of criticizing.

cen'sorship, *n.*, the office of a censor; tenure of his office.

cen'sual, *adj.*, rel. to the census.

cen'surable, *adj.*, fit to be censured.

cen'sure, *v.t.*, to blame, reprove.

cen'sured, *p.p.*, censure.

cen'surer, *n.*, one who censures.

cen'suring, *pr.p.*, censure.

cen'sus, *n.*, a numbering of the people (in Roman times the census included a survey of property).

cent, *n.*, a hundred; the hundredth part of a dollar.

cent'age, *n.*, *i.q.* percentage.

cen'tal, *n.*, a weight of 100 lb.

cen'taur, *n.*, a fabled creature, half man, half horse.

cen'taury, *n.*, a plant of the gentian family.

centena'rian, *n.*, a person aged a hundred; *adj.*, rel. to a hundred years.

cen'tenary, *n.*, the hundredth anniversary.

centen'nial, *adj.*, rel. to a period of a hundred years.

cen'ter, *see* centre.

cen'tering, *pr.p.*, center.

centes'imal, *adj.*, hundredth; *n.*, a hundredth part.

centesima'tion, *n.*, the act of taking one in every hundred.

centifo'lious, *adj.*, hundred-leaved.

cen'tigrade, *adj.*, of a hundred degrees.

cen'tigramme, *n.*, a hundredth of a gram.

cen'tilitre, -ter, *n.*, a hundredth of a litre.

centime', *n.*, a hundredth of a franc.

cen'timetre, -ter, *n.*, a hundredth of a metre.

cen'tipede, *n.*, a creature with a hundred (*i.e.*, very many) feet.

cen'to, *n.*, a selection, patchwork.

cen'tral, *adj.*, rel. to, or placed at, the centre.

central'ity, *n.*, the state or relation of the central.

centraliza'tion, *n.*, the drawing to a centre; concentration of authority or administration in a single body or office.

cen'tralize, *v.t.*, to draw to a centre; to concentrate authority or administration.

cen'tralized, *p.p.*, centralize.

cen'tralizing, *pr.p.*, centralize.

cen'tre, *v.t.*, to fix on a centre, place at the centre; *v.i.*, to be at the centre; *n.*, the middle point of a circle; a point to which things converge.

cen'tre-bit, *n.*, a boring tool with a centre point.

cen'tred, *p.p.*, centre.

cen'tric, *adj.*, central.

cen'trical, *adj.*, *i.q.* centric.

centric'ity, *n.*, the centric relation.

centrif'ugal, *adj.*, flying off from the centre; radiating.

cen'tring, *pr.p.*, centre.

centrip'etal, *adj.*, tending towards the centre.

centum'vir, *n.*, a Roman judge so named. (The centumviri numbered 105, and were presided over by a praetor.)

centum'virate, *n.*, the body of centumvirs; the office, and tenure of office, of the centumvirs.

cen'tuple, *adj.*, a hundred-fold; *v.t.*, to increase a hundred-fold.

centu'rial, *adj.*, rel. to a century.

centu'rion, *n.*, a Roman military officer, commanding a hundred foot soldiers.

cen'tury, *n.*, a period of 100 years; a hundred in number; a Roman political division according to property.

ceorl, *n.*, a freeman (*see* churl).

cephalal'gic, *adj.*, rel. to headache; *n.*, a remedy for headache.

ceph'alalgy, *n.*, headache.

cephal'ic, *adj.*, rel. to the head.

ceph'alopod, *adj.*, rel. to the Cephalopods, molluscs with a subcentral head.

ceph'alous, *adj.*, having a head.

cera'ceous, *adj.*, waxen.

ceram'ic, *adj.*, rel. to pottery.

cer'asite, *n.*, a fossil resembling a cherry.

ce'rate, *adj.*, having a cere.

ce'rated, *adj.*, coated with wax.
cer'atin, *n.*, the essential element in the composition of horny tissue.
Cerbe'rean, *adj.*, rel. to Cerberus, the watch-dog of Hades.
cere, *v.t.*, to cover with wax or cerecloth; *n.*, wax; the waxy membrane on a bird's beak.
ce'real, *adj.*, rel. to Ceres; rel. to corn.
cerebel'lum, *n.*, the lower and back portion of the head.
cer'ebral, *adj.*, rel. to the brain.
cerebra'tion, *n.*, the action of brain.
cer'ebrum, *n.*, the brain.
cere'cloth, *n.*, a waxed cloth.
cere'ment, *n.*, a wrapping, esp. one covered with wax.
ceremo'nial, *adj.*, rel. to ceremony; *n.*, order of ceremonies; a book of ceremonies.
ceremo'nialism, *n.*, a fondness for ceremonial practices.
ceremo'nious, *adj.*, formal.
ceremo'niously, *adv.*, in a ceremonious way.
cer'emony, *n.*, the formal acts illustrating a rite or other observance; a way of showing respect or civility; regard for etiquette.
ce'reous, *adj.*, waxen.
ce'ric, *adj.*, rel. to wax.
ce'rin, *n.*, a compound obtained from cork.
cer'iph, *n.*, the little stroke projecting from the main strokes of a letter.
cerise', *adj.*, cherry-coloured; *n.*, the cherry colour.
ce'rite, *n.*, a cerium silicate.
ce'rium, *n.*, a rare metal of a steel-grey colour.
cerne, *v.t.*, to surround, *n.*, a circle.
cerog'raphy, *n.*, writing on wax.
ce'romancy, *n.*, divination by means of wax.
ceroplas'tic, *adj.*, modelled in wax; rel. to wax moulding.
cer'tain, *adj.*, sure, unquestionable; confident, convinced; appointed, one or some.
cer'tainly, *adv.*, truly, assuredly, inevitably.
cer'tainty, *n.*, the state or fact of being certain.
cer'tes, *adv.*, certainly (*obs.*).
certif'icate, *v.t.*, to give a certificate to; *n.*, a testimonial to character or proficiency.
certifica'tion, *n.*, the act of certifying; guarantee.
cer'tified, *p.p.*, certify.
cer'tifier, *n.*, one who certifies.
cer'tify, *v.t.*, to guarantee, make evident, testify.
cer'tifying, *pr.p.*, certify.
certiora'ri, *n.*, a writ from a higher court requiring the records from a lower court.
cer'titude, *n.*, assured belief; certainty.
ceru'lean, *adj.*, of a sky-blue colour.
ceru'men, *n.*, the wax in the ears.
ce'ruse, *n.*, white lead; *v.t.*, to paint with ceruse, a cosmetic made from white lead.
ce'rused, *p.p.*, ceruse.
cer'vical, *adj.*, rel. to the neck.
cer'vine, *adj.*, rel. to deer.
Cesa'rean, *adj.*, rel. to Caesar.
ces'pitous, *adj.*, turfy.
cess, *v.t.*, to assess, tax; *v.i.*, to surrender; *n.*, rate, tax.
cessa'tion, *n.*, a leaving off.
ces'ser, *n.*, ceasing to perform some duty.
ces'sion, *n.*, yielding up, surrender.
ces'sionary, *adj.*, giving up, surrendering.
ces'sor, *n.*, *i.q.* cesser.
cess'pool, *n.*, a covered well to receive the solid contents of a drain.
cest, *n.*, *i.q.* cestus.
ces'tui, *n.*, an old French expression = he: the man who.
ces'tus, *n.*, a girdle; a pugilist's fist-guard (*Lat.*).
cesu'ra, *n.*, a break or pause in a metrical foot. This break occurs at various points in a verse.
cesu'ral, *adj.*, rel. to, of the nature of, cesura.
Ceta'cea, *n. pl.*, marine animals, like the whale, the dolphin, etc.
ceta'cean, *adj.*, rel. to the cetacea; *n.*, one of these creatures.
ceta'ceous, *adj.*, *i.q.* cetacean.
ce'tic, *adj.*, rel. to the whale.
ce'tin, *n.*, a fatty compound containing spermacetti.
ce'tine, *n.* *i.q.* cetin.
cetol'ogy, *n.*, the study of cetaceans.
Chab'lis, *n.*, a French white wine from Chablis.
chad, *n.*, otherwise the shad, a young sea-bream.
chafe, *v.t.*, to rub sore, to gall; to annoy; to restore warmth; *v.i.*, to be hot with anger, to fume.
chafed, *p.p.*, chafe.
cha'fer, *n.*, one who chafes; also a common name for the cockchafer.
cha'fery, *n.*, a forge for the making of iron bars.
chaff, *v.t.*, to teaze, make fun of; *n.*, the husk of grain; cut straw or hay; banter.
chaff'-cutter, *n.*, a machine for cutting chaff.
chaffed, *p.p.*, chaff

chaf'fer, *v.t.*, to bargain, haggle; *n.*, bargaining.

chaf'fered, *p.p.*, chaffer.

chaf'ferer, *n.*, one who chaffers.

chaf'fering, *pr.p.*, chaffer.

chaf'finch, *n.*, a small British song-bird.

chaf'fy, *adj.*, like chaff, covered with chaff; disposed to banter.

cha'fing, *pr.p.*, chafe; *n.*, impatience, irritation.

cha'fing-dish, *n.*, a receptacle of live coals for heating purposes.

chagreen', *n.*, *see* shagreen.

chagrin', *v.t.* to vex, mortify; *n.*, disappointment; mortification.

chagrined', *p.p.*, chagrin.

chain, *v.t.*, to fasten with a chain, to fasten securely; to measure with a chain; *n.*, a series of links for the purpose of binding; bond, slavery; a connected series; a measuring line.

chained, *p.p.*, chain.

chain'ing, *pr.p.*, chain.

chain'-pump, *n.*, a pump with an endless chain to which buckets are attached.

chain'-shot, *n.*, cannon balls chained together.

chain'-stitch, *n.*, a loop-stitch.

chair, *v.t.*, to place in a chair; carry in a chair; *n.*, a single seat; an official seat; a sedan-chair.

chaired, *p.p.*, chair.

chair'ing, *pr.p.* chair.

chair'man, *n.*, the president of any assembly or company for whom a special chair is reserved; a sedan-chair bearer.

chair'manship, *n.*, the function, or term of office, of a chairman.

chaise, *n.*, a two-wheeled light carriage.

chalcedon'ic, *adj.*, rel. to, or resembling, the chalcedony.

chalced'ony, *n.*, a precious stone of the quartz kind.

chalcog'rapher, *n.*, one who engraves on copper.

chalcog'raphy, *n.*, copper engraving.

Chalda'ic, *adj.*, pert. to the Chaldees.

Chal'daism, *n.*, something characteristically Chaldean.

Chalde'an, *adj.*, bel. to Chaldea.

Chaldee', *adj.*, Chaldean; *n.*, a Chaldean.

chal'dron, *n.*, a coal and coke measure, of varying capacity according to country.

cha'let, *n.*, a Swiss mountain dwelling; any small country house built in imitation.

chal'ice, *n.*, a cup or bowl; pre-eminently the Eucharistic cup.

chal'iced, *adj.* cup-like.

chalk, *v.t.*, to mark with chalk; to treat with chalk; *n.*, a soft, white limestone.

chalked, *p.p.*, chalk.

chalk'iness, *n.*, chalky nature.

chalk'ing, *pr.p.* chalk.

chalk'-pit, *n.*, a pit from which chalk is extracted.

chalk'-stone, *n.*, a chalky formation in the body.

chalk'y, *adj.*, like chalk, rel. to, or made of, chalk.

chal'lenge, *v.t.*, to call out to combat, defy; demand proof; take exception to.

chal'lengeable, *adj.*, able to be challenged.

chal'lenged, *p.p.*, challenge.

chal'lenger, *n.*, one who challenges.

chal'lenging, *pr.p* challenge.

chalyb'eate, *adj.*, impregnated with iron.

cham, *n.*, a Tartar or Mogul chief.

chamade', *n.*, the trumpet or drum appeal for a parley.

cham'ber, *v.t.*, to furnish with chambers; *v.i.*, to act wantonly; *n.*, a room; an assembly.

cham'bered, *adj.*, provided with, or divided into, chambers; *p.p.*, chamber.

cham'ber-fellow, *n.*, one who shares chambers.

cham'bering, *pr.p.*, chamber; *n.*, wanton behaviour.

cham'berlain, *n.*, an officer in a royal or great household, who has charge of the chambers and the ceremonial.

cham'bermaid, *n.*, a domestic servant in charge of the chambers.

chame'leon, *n.*, a kind of lizard, possessed of the power to change colour.

cham'fer, *v.t.*, to groove, bevel; *n.*, a groove, bevel.

cham'fered, *p.p.*, chamfer.

cham'fering, *pr.p.*, chamfer.

cham'ois, *n.*, a species of mountain goat; a soft leather.

cham'omile, *n.*, *see* camomile.

champ, *v.t.* and *i.*, to gnash, crunch; *n.*, the act of champing.

champagne', *n.*, a sparkling wine from the Champagne district of France.

cham'paign, *adj.*, open country, unenclosed; *n.*, a plain, open country.

champed, *p.p.*, champ.

cham'perty, *n.*, a bargain between two litigants, to carry on a suit and share in the property.

champ'ing, *pr.p.*, champ.

cham'pion, *v.t.*, to act as a champion for, to defend a cause; *n.*, a defender.

cham'pioned, *p.p.*, champion.

cham'pioness, *n.*, fem. of champion.

cham'pioning, *pr.p.*, champion.

cham'pionship, *n.*, the act of a champion.

chance, *v.t.* and *i.*, to take the risk of; to happen by chance; *n.*, that which happens unexpectedly; an opportunity; a possibility.

chanced, *p.p.*, chance.

chan'cel, *n.*, the eastern section of a church.

chan'cellery, *n.*, the office of a chancellor; a court; a department of a legation.

chan'cellor, *n.*, an official who keeps the Great Seal; the head of a university; a cathedral dignitary so named; a diocesan judge.

chan'cellorship, *n.*, the office, and tenure of office, of a chancellor.

chan'cery, *n.*, a court of equity, now one of the divisions of the High Court.

chanc'ing, *pr.p.*, chance.

chan'cre, *n.*, an ulcer.

chan'crous, *adj.*, ulcerous.

chandelier', *n.*, a branched, suspended frame for holding candles.

chand'ler, *n.*, a maker of and dealer in candles; a general dealer.

chand'lery, *n.*, a chandler's shop; a chandler's goods.

chan'frin, *n.*, the forehead of a horse.

change, *v.t.* and *i.*, to alter, make or become different; to exchange; *n.*, alteration, exchange; smaller money for larger.

changeabil'ity, *n.*, a tendency to change.

change'able, *adj.*, prone to change.

change'ableness, *n.*, *i.q.* changeability.

change'ably, *adv.*, in a changeable way.

changed, *p.p.*, change.

change'ful, *adj.*, full of changes.

change'less, *adj.*, unchanging.

change'ling, *n.*, a substituted child.

chan'ger, *n.*, one who changes, esp. money.

chan'ging, *pr.p.*, change.

chan'nel, *v.t.*, to divide with channels; to groove; *n.*, the bed of a stream; a strait, estuary; a means or passage; line of action.

chan'nelled, *p.p.*, channel; *adj.*, having channels; channel-like.

chan'nelling, *pr.p.*, channel.

chan'son, *n.*, a song or ballad (*Fr.*).

chansonette', *n.*, a short ballad (*Fr.*).

chant, *v.t.* and *i.*, to sing; celebrate with praise; *n.*, a melody to which psalms and other nonmetrical words are sung.

chant'ed, *p.p.*, chant.

chant'er, *n.*, one who chants, a singer, a precentor; the finger-pipe on a bagpipe.

chant'ey, *n.*, a rhythmical song sung by sailors when at work.

chan'ticleer, *n.*, a cock.

chant'ing, *pr.p.*, chant.

chant'ress, *n.*, fem. of chanter.

chant'ry, *n.*, an endowment of a priest or priests to say mass for the soul of a founder or benefactor. Sometimes, but not quite correctly, the name is used for the chapel in which an endowed altar stood.

cha'os, *n.*, a formless and disordered state; utter confusion.

chaot'ic, *adj.*, like chaos, in utter confusion.

chap, *v.t.* and *i.*, to split, crack; *n.*, a split or crack in the skin; any fissure; a boy; a dealer; a jaw.

chape, *n.*, the tip of a scabbard; the part of a rein that goes into the buckle.

chapeau', *n.*, a hat (*Fr.*).

chap'el, *n.*, a small church or part of a church; a Dissenting place of worship; the collective journeymen in a printing office.

chap'elry, *n.*, a district in the jurisdiction of a chapel.

chap'eron, *v.t.*, to attend as a chaperon; *n.*, one who attends upon a lady.

chap'eronage, *n.*, the act or state of chaperoning.

chap'fallen, *adj.*, with drooping jaw, dejected.

chap'iter, *n.*, a pillar capital.

chap'lain, *n.*, a priest attached to a chapel, the forces, a ship, an institution, or company.

chap'laincy, *n.*, a chaplain's office or tenure of office.

chap'lainship, *n.*, *i.q.* chaplaincy.

chap'let, *n.*, a garland for the head; a part of a rosary.

chap'man, *n.*, a dealer in small wares.

chapped, *p.p.*, chap.

chap'py, *n.*, a little chap.

chaps, *n.*, pl. of chap.

chap'ter, *n.*, a chief division of a book; the collective name for the clergy of a cathedral or collegiate church; a local branch of a society.

chap'ter-house, *n.*, the building in

which a chapter assembles.

chap'trel, *n.*, an impost.

char, *v.t.*, to scorch; *v.i.*, to do household chores; *n.*, an odd job; a salmon-like fish.

char'-à-banc, *n.*, a large car with transverse seats.

char'acter, *v.t.*, to impress, engrave; to characterize; *n.*, a distinctive quality or set of qualities; a letter of the alphabet, reputation.

characterist'ic, *adj.*, distinctive, peculiarly marking; *n.*, a distinctive mark or quality.

characterist'ically, *adv.*, in a characteristic way.

characteriza'tion, *n.*, the act or effect of characterizing; description.

char'acterize, *v.t.*, to make distinguishable; to describe.

char'acterized, *p.p.*, characterize.

char'acterizing, *pr.p.*, characterize.

char'acterless, *adj.*, without character, not distinctive.

charade', *n.*, a riddle, word-puzzle; a play consisting of a word-puzzle.

char'coal, *n.*, charred wood; a drawing-pencil made of charcoal dust; a drawing in charcoal.

chard, *n.*, the white leaves or stalks of certain plants.

chare, *see* char.

charge, *v.t.*, to impose, lay upon; command; fill; accuse; debit, fix a price for; attack; *n.*, something imposed or put on; a command; accusation; demand of a price; attack.

chargeabil'ity, *n.*, a chargeable state.

charge'able, *adj.*, able to be charged.

charge'ably, *adv.*, expensively.

charged, *p.p.* charge.

chargé d'affaires', *n.*, a diplomatic official in charge of affairs, in place, or during the absence, of an ambassador.

char'ger, *n.*, one who charges; a war-horse; a large dish; a case for the charge of a machine gun.

charg'ing, *pr.p.*, charge.

cha'rily, *adv.*, in a chary way.

cha'riness, *n.*, a state of being chary.

char'iot, *n.*, a two-wheeled carriage, used in war and races; a state carriage.

charioteer', *n.*, the driver of a chariot.

char'ism, *n.*, a grace or power bestowed by the Holy Ghost.

charismat'ic, *adj.*, of the nature of a spiritual gift.

char'itable, *adj.*, apt at bestowing charity.

char'itableness, *n.*, a charitable temper.

char'ity, *n.*, love, esp. to one's neighbour; lenity of judgment.

chariva'ri, *n.*, a wild sort of serenade with a medley of noises.

char'latan, *n.*, an impostor, quack.

charlatan'ic, *adj.*, resembling a charlatan.

char'latanism, *n.*, the act or state of a charlatan.

char'latanry, *n.*, *s.q.* charlatanism.

Char'lie, *n.*, a night-watchman (*obs.*).

char'lock, *n.*, the wild mustard.

charm, *v.t.*, to enchant, cast a spell on, delight; *n.*, attractiveness, fascination, spell.

charmed, *p.p.*, charm.

charm'er, *n.*, one who charms.

charm'ing, *p.p.*, charm; *adj.*, delightful.

charm'ingly, *adv.*, delightfully.

char'nel, *adj.*, rel. to a corpse, ghastly; *n.*, a charnel-house.

char'nel-house, *n.*, a mortuary, a depository for bones.

char'pie, *n.*, lint.

char'poy, *n.*, a Hindu bed.

charred, *p.p.*, char.

char'ring, *pr.p.*, char.

char'ry, *adj.*, like charcoal.

chart, *v.t.*, to lay out on a chart; *n.*, a map of land, sea, or sky; a tabular sheet.

char'ta, *n.*, a parchment, writing.

charta'ceous, *adj.*, like paper.

char'ter, *v.t.*, to hire, engage; *n.*, a grant of titles, privileges, etc.

char'terage, *n.*, charges for chartering ships.

char'tered, *p.p.*, charter; *adj.*, authorized by charter.

char'terer, *n.*, one who charters.

Char'terhouse, *n.*, a Carthusian monastery; the name is the English equivalent of Chartreuse.

char'tering, *pr.p.*, charter.

char'ter-party, *n.*, agreement for hiring a ship or a part of a ship.

char'tism, *n.*, the principles of chartists.

char'tist, *n.*, an advocate of the so-called People's Charter.

chartog'rapher, *n.*, one who draws charts or maps.

chartog'raphy, *n.*, the art and practice of map-drawing.

chartom'eter, *n.*, an instrument for measuring distances on maps.

Chartreuse', *n.*, a Carthusian monastery; a liqueur distilled at La Grande Chartreuse in Grenoble.

Char'treux, *n.*, a Charterhouse.

char'tulary, *n.,* a record of property of a religious community.

char'woman, *n.,* a woman who chares, or does chores.

cha'ry, *adj.,* careful, cautious.

chas'able, chase'able, *adj.,* able to be chased.

chase, *v.t.,* to hunt, pursue, drive off; ornament metal by indenting; *n.,* hunting, pursuit; the part of a gun next to, and in front of, the trunnions.

chased, *p.p.,* chase.

chas'er, *n.,* one who chases.

chas'ing, *pr.p.,* chase.

chasm, *n.,* a gap in the earth's surface; any great breach or severance.

chasse'pot, *n.,* the French needle-gun, now out of date.

chasseur', *n.,* a French light-armed soldier.

chas'sis, *n.,* the lower frame of a motor-car; a type of gun-carriage.

chaste, *adj.,* pure, clean, refined.

chaste'ly, *adv.,* in a chaste way.

chast'en, *v.t.,* to purify, punish.

chast'ened, *p.p.,* chasten.

chast'ener, *n.,* one who chastens.

chast'ening, *pr.p.,* chasten; *n.,* punishment.

chastise', *v.t.,* to punish.

chastised', *p.p.,* chastise.

chas'tisement, *n.,* punishment.

chastis'er, *n.,* one who chastises.

chastis'ing, *p.p.,* chastise.

chas'tity, *n.,* the quality of being chaste.

chas'uble, *n.,* the vestment of the celebrant at Mass.

chat, *v.i.,* to talk informally, gossip; *n.,* informal talk, gossip.

château', *n.,* a French castle.

chat'elaine, *n.,* the lady of a castle; a lady's chain to which are attached a variety of trinkets, keys, etc.

chat'ellany, *n.,* the lordship of a castle-owner.

chat'ted, *p.p.,* chat.

chat'tel, *n.,* a movable article of property.

chat'ter, *v.i.,* to prattle, talk uselessly; shiver with cold (said of the teeth).

chat'terbox, *n.,* a garrulous person.

chat'tered, *p.p.,* chatter.

chat'terer, *n.,* one who chatters.

chat'tering, *pr.p.,* chatter.

chat'ting, *pr.p.* chat.

chat'ty, *adj.,* agreeably talkative, gossiping.

chat'wood, *n.,* twigs for burning.

Chauce'rian, *adj.,* rel. to, or resembling, Chaucer.

Chau'cerism, *n.,* a Chaucerian idiom or peculiarity.

chauf'feur, *n.,* a motor-car driver.

Chau'tauqua, *n.,* a mutual improvement union (*Amer.*).

chau'vinism, *n.,* the principles of a chauvinist.

chau'vinist, *n.,* one who says "My country, right or wrong" and despises every foreign country.

cheap, *adj.,* of low price, of little value, common, poor.

cheap'en, *v.t.,* to make cheap, lower the value; *v.i.,* to fall in price.

cheap'ened, *p.p.,* cheapen.

cheap'ener, *n.,* one who cheapens.

cheap'ening, *pr.p.,* cheapen.

cheap'ly, *adv.,* at a cheap rate.

cheap'ness, *n.,* the state or quality of being cheap.

cheat, *v.t.,* to deceive, defraud, mislead; *n.,* a fraudulent person, an act of cheating.

cheat'able, *adj.,* liable to be cheated.

cheat'ed, *p.p.,* cheat.

cheat'er, *n.,* one who cheats.

cheat'ing, *pr.p.,* cheat; *n.,* the act or practice of a cheat.

check, *v.t.,* to bring to a sudden stop; moderate; to verify by examination; to threaten a king in chess; *n.,* a sudden stoppage; something that stops; the American equivalent of English *cheque;* a crossed pattern in weaving; an identifying ticket or disc.

check'-book, *n.,* *i.q.* cheque-book.

checked, *p.p.,* check.

check'er, *n.,* one who checks; *v.t.,* to mark with a cross pattern; to fill with changes of fortune.

check'er-board, *n.,* *see* chequer-board.

check'ered, *p.p.,* checker; *adj.,* full of vicissitudes.

check'ering, *pr.p.,* checker.

check'ers, *n.,* *i.q.* chequers.

check'er-work, *n.,* work on a checkered pattern.

check'ing, *pr.p.,* check.

check'mate, *v.t.,* to beat at chess; to thwart, overcome; *n.,* defeat, thwarting.

check'mated, *p.p.,* checkmate.

check'mating, *pr.p.,* checkmate.

chee'-chee, *n.,* an Eurasian; an Eurasian's speech.

cheek, *v.t.,* to treat impudently; *n.,* the lower part of the side-face; impudence (*slang*).

cheek'-tooth, *n.,* a molar.

cheer, *v.t.*, to put heart into, inspirit, applaud; *n.*, a cry of applause, good entertainment, expression of countenance.

cheered, *p.p.*, cheer.

cheer'er, *n.*, one who cheers.

cheer'ful, *adj.*, hearty, gay.

cheer'fulness, *n.*, the state of being cheerful.

cheer'ily, *adv.*, brightly, gaily.

cheer'iness, *n.*, the state of being cheery.

cheer'ing, *pr.p.*, cheer; *adj.*, encouraging; *n.*, applause.

cheer'ingly, *adv.*, encouragingly.

cheer'less, *adj.*, gloomy, depressing.

cheer'y, *adj.*, bright, gay.

cheese, *n.*, the curd of milk compacted and dried.

cheese'-cake, *n.*, a sweet made of curd, sugar, and butter.

cheese'-cutter, *n.*, an instrument for cutting cheese.

cheese'-monger, *n.*, a dealer in cheeses.

cheese'-press, *n.*, a press used in making cheeses.

chee'sy, *adj.*, like cheese, or containing cheese.

chee'tah, *n.*, a kind of leopard used in hunting.

chef, *n.*, the head or chief; a head cook.

chef-d'œuvre', *n.*, a masterpiece.

Cheirop'tera, *n.*, bats.

cheirop'terous, *adj.*, having wings like hands.

chem'ic, *v.t.*, to apply chloride of lime; *n.*, chloride of lime; an alchemist.

chem'ical, *adj.*, rel. to chemistry; *n.*, a chemical substance.

chemise', *n.*, a woman's undergarment, a shift.

chemisette', *n.*, an under-bodice of feminine wear.

chem'ist, *n.*, one who is practised in chemistry.

chem'istry, *n.*, the science dealing with the composition of matter.

chenille', *n.*, a velvety cord of various materials.

cheque, *n.*, an order on a bank for payment of a named sum.

cheque'-book, *n.*, a book containing cheques and counterfoils.

cheq'uer-board, *n.*, the board with which chequers was played.

cheq'uer, *v.t.*, *i.q.* checker.

cheq'uers, *n. pl.*, a game once played with a board marked out with little squares.

cher'ish, *v.t.*, to treat with affection; retain in the memory.

cher'ished, *p.p.*, cherish.

cher'isher, *n.*, one who cherishes.

cher'ishing, *pr.p.*, cherish.

cheroot', *n.*, a form of cigar.

cher'ry, *n.*, the fruit of the cherry tree; *adj.*, cherry-coloured.

Cher'sonese, *n.*, the famous peninsula so named; any peninsula.

chert, *n.*, hornstone.

cher'ty, *adj.*, consisting of or like chert.

cher'ub, *n.*, an angel ranking next below a seraph; a beautiful child.

cheru'bic, *adj.*, cherub-like.

cher'ubim, *n.*, pl. of cherub.

cher'vil, *n.*, a potherb so named.

chess, *n.*, the game so named.

chess'-board, *n.*, the board on which chess is played; it has 64 squares.

chess'man, *n.*, one of the pieces used on a chess-board.

chest, *n.*, a box; the capacity of a chest; the thorax.

chest'ed, *adj.*, having a chest.

chest'nut, **ches'nut**, *n.*, the nut of the castanea; the tree so named; a reddish brown; a horse of chestnut colour; a venerable jest or story; *adj.*, of chestnut colour.

cheval'-glass, *n.*, a tall, swinging mirror.

chevalier', *n.*, a knight, horseman.

chevaux'-de-frise', *n.*, a spiked fence.

chev'ron, *n.*, an heraldic term; the V-shaped badge of a non-commissioned officer.

chev'ronal, *n.*, a narrow chevron.

chew, *v.t.*, to masticate, crush with the teeth.

chewed, *p.p.*, chew.

chew'ing, *pr.p.*, chew.

Chiant'i, *n.*, a red Italian wine.

chiaroscu'ro, *n.*, light and shade in painting; *adj.*, rel. to light and shade.

chib'bal, *n.*, the stone leek; *i.q.* cibol.

chibouk', **chibouque'**, *n.*, a Turkish pipe.

chic, *adj.*, in the mode, stylish; *n.*, stylishness, smartness.

chicane', *n.*, sophistry, a cunning way of hiding the truth; the holding of no trumps at cards.

chica'nery, *n.*, the employment of chicane.

chich, *adj.*, niggardly.

chich'ling, *n.*, *i.q.* chickling.

chick, *n.*, a young bird.

chick'abiddy, *n.*, a term of endearment for a child.

chick'en, *n.*, the chick of a domestic fowl.

chick'en-pox, *n.*, an eruptive childish disorder.

chick'ling, *n.*, a small chick.

chick'pea, *n.*, pulse.

chick'weed, *n.*, a wild flower so named.

chic'ory, *n.*, a perennial which, when roasted, is mixed with coffee.

chid, *p.t.*, chide.

chid'den, *p.p.*, chide.

chide, *v.t.*, to reprove.

chid'er, *n.*, one who chides.

chid'ing, *pr.p.*, chide.

chief, *adj.*, principal, foremost: *n.*, a leader.

chief'ess, *n.*, fem. of chief.

chief'ly, *adv.*, principally, first.

chief'tain, *n.*, a leader, head of a clan.

chief'tainship, *n.*, the office or rank of chieftain.

chiel, *n.*, a youth.

chield, *n.*, *i.q.* chiel.

chiffon, *n.*, a gauzy fabric.

chiffonier', *n.*, a rag-collector; a kind of sideboard.

chi'gnon, *n.*, a mode of dressing the back hair over a pad.

chil'blain, *v.t.*, to cause chilblains; *n.*, a sore produced by cold.

chil'blained, *adj.*, suffering from chilblains.

child, *n.*, a son or daughter, the human young; a person under age.

***child'*-bed**, *n.*, the time and place of delivery of a child.

***child'*-birth**, *n.*, *i.q.* child-bed.

childe, *n.*, a son, not yet knighted, of a great house.

Chil'dermas, *n.*, the Feast of Holy Innocents, Dec. 28.

***child'*hood**, *n.*, the childish period of life.

***child'*ish**, *adj.*, like a child, puerile, silly.

***child'*ishly**, *adv.*, like a child, sillily.

***child'*ishness**, *n.*, puerility.

***child'*less**, *adj.*, without a child.

***child'*like**, *adj.*, like a child, innocent.

***child'*ling**, *n.*, a little child.

chil'dren, *n.*, pl. of child.

chil'iad, *n.*, a group of 1,000; a thousand years.

chil'iagon, *n.*, a thousand-sided figure.

chil'iarch, *n.*, a commander of a thousand men.

chil'iasm, *n.*, the doctrine rel. to Our Lord's reign on earth for a thousand years.

chill, *v.t.*, to make cold; discourage; harden by cooling, *adj.*, feeling cold, discouraging; *n.*, a feeling of sudden cold; discouragement.

chilled, *p.p.*, chill.

chil'li, *n.*, dried capsicum-pod.

chil'liness, *n.*, the sensation or cause of chill.

chil'ling, *pr.p.*, chill; *adj.*, depressing.

chil'ly, *adj.*, *i.q.* chill.

chi'lopod, *adj.*, having 1,000 feet.

Chil'tern Hun'dreds, *n.*, Crown lands in Bucks, the stewardship of which, being a Crown appointment, vacates the holder's seat in Parliament.

chime, *v.t.* and *i.*, to make music with bells, to accord; *n.*, the sound of chiming bells; the chimed bells collectively; harmony.

chimed, *p.p.*, chime.

chi'mer, *n.*, a person or apparatus that chimes.

chime'ra, *n.*, a strange creation of the fancy.

chimere', *n.*, a sort of cope with armholes, and worn over academic and canonical habits.

chimer'ical, *adj.*, fantastic, impossible.

chi'ming, *pr.p.*, chime.

chim'ney, *n.*, a smoke vent, the tube of a lamp.

chim'ney-board, *n.*, a fire-board.

chim'ney-piece, *n.*, the outer frame of a chimney-opening.

chim'ney-pot, *n.*, a tubular added top to a chimney; a tall silk hat (*colloq.*).

chim'ney-sweep, *n.*, one who sweeps chimneys.

chimpan'zee, *n.*, an anthropoid ape from the W. Indies.

chin, *n.*, the face below the lips.

chi'na, *adj.*, made of china; *n.*, a fine porcelain.

chi'na-as'ter, *n.*, the aster of China.

chi'na-clay, *adj.*, a fine kind of clay.

chin'capin, *n.*, an American shrub, bearing edible nuts.

chinchil'la, *n.*, a small furry rodent; the fur of the chinchilla; *adj.*, made of chinchilla.

chin'-cough, *n.*, the whooping-cough.

chine, *v.t.*, to cut through the backbone; *v.i.*, to fissure; *n.*, an animal's backbone; a cliff fissure.

chined, *adj.*, having a chine; *p.p.*, chine.

Chinese', *adj.*, bel. to China; *n.*, a Chinaman.

chink, *v.t.* and *i.*, to rattle with a metallic sound; *n.*, the sound of rattled money; money (*slang*); a narrow opening.

chinked, *p.p.*, chink.

chink'ing, *pr.p.* chink.

chink'y, *adj.*, having chinks.

chinned, *adj.*, having a chin.

chinse, *v.t.*, to stop a ship's seams with oakum.

chintz, *adj.*, of chintz material; *n.*, a glazed cotton cloth.

chip, *v.t.*, to cut into little pieces; *v.i.*, to fly into little pieces; *n.*, a little piece of wood or stone, etc.; a kind of straw; *adj.*, made of chip.

chipped, *p.p.*, chip.
Chip'pendale, *adj.*, in the style invented by Chippendale; *n.*, a piece of Chippendale furniture.
chip'per, *adj.*, pert, smart (*Amer.*).
chip'ping, *pr.p.*, chip.
chip'py, *adj.*, having chips, dry.
chirag'ra, *n.*, gout in the hand.
chi'rograph, *adj.*, a piece of handwriting, a deed.
chirog'nomy, *n.*, judging character from the hand.
chirog'rapher, *n.*, an engrosser.
chirograph'ic, *adj.*, written by the hand.
chirog'raphist, *n.*, an expert in handwriting, a copyist.
chirog'raphy, *n.*, handwriting.
chirolog'ical, *adj.*, rel. to chirology.
chirol'ogy, *n.*, the art of sign-speech; the study of the hand.
chi'romancy, *n.*, palmistry.
chiroman'tic, *adj.*, rel. to palmistry.
chiron'omy, *n.*, gesticulation.
chi'roplast, *n.*, an apparatus for making the fingers supple.
chirop'odist, *n.*, one who doctors the feet and hands.
chiros'ophy, *n.*, palmistry.
chirp, *v.i.*, to make the short, shrill sound of a bird; *n.*, a bird's short, shrill note.
chirped, *p.p.*, chirp.
chirp'er, *n.*, one who chirps.
chirp'ing, *pr.p.*, chirp.
chir'rup, *v.i.*, *i.q.* chirp.
chir'ruped, *p.p.*, chirrup.
chir'ruping, *pr.p.*, chirrup.
chis'el, *v.t.*, to carve, cut with a chisel; *n.*, a bevel-edged tool used for cutting wood, stone, or iron.
chis'el(l)ed, *p.p.*, chisel; *adj.*, finely outlined; edged with a chisel.
chis'el(l)er, *n.*, one who chisels.
chis'el(l)ing, *pr.p.* chisel.
chiselly, *adj.*, gritty, gravelly.
Chis'leu, *n.*, a month in the Jewish Kalendar.
chit, *v.t.*, to remove sprouts· *n.*, a sprout, a child.
chit'-chat, *n.*, prattling talk, gossip.
chit'in, *n.*, the horny substance of certain beetles' shells.
chi'ton, *n.*, a Greek slave's tunic.
chit'terlings, *n.*, a pig's small intestines.
chit'ty, *adj.*, with sprouts, pimpled.
chiv'alric, *adj.*, rel. to chivalry.
chiv'alrous, *adj.*, rel. to chivalry; gallant, courteous.
chiv'alry, *n.*, the system of knighthood; gallant behaviour; courtesy.
chive, *n.*, a garden herb allied to the leek or onion; a piece cut off.
chlo'ral, *n.*, an oily liquid used to promote sleep.
chlo'rate, *n.*, a chloric acid salt.
chlo'ric, *adj.*, rel. to chlorine.
chlo'rid, chlo'ride, *n.*, chlorine compounded with some other element.
chlo'ridate, *v.t.*, to combine with a chlorid.
chlo'rine, *n.*, a chemical gaseous element.
chlo'rite, *n.*, a common appellation of several green stones.
chlorit'ic, *adj.*, containing chlorite.
chlo'rodyne, *n.*, an anodyne so named.
chlo'roform, *n.*, an anaesthetic so named; *v.t.*, to treat a patient with chloroform.
chlorom'eter, *n.*, an instrument for measuring the degree of chlorine.
chlorom'etry, *n.*, the process of using a chlorometer.
chlo'rophyl, chlo'rophyll, *n.*, the green colouring matter in plants.
chloro'sis, *n.*, a disease affecting girls at puberty, and marked by a greenish pallor.
chlo'rous, *adj.*, combined with chlorine.
chock, *v.t.*, to fasten with a chock; *n.*, a block or wedge of wood, to plug a hole or prevent something from slipping.
chock'-full, *adj.*, quite full.
choc'olate, *adj.*, of a dark reddish brown colour; *n.*, a preparation from the cacao plant.
choice, *adj.*, worthy to be chosen, select, precious; *n.*, the act or power of choosing, a thing chosen, determination.
choi'cer, *adj.*, *comp.* of choice.
choi'cest, *adj.*, *super.* of choice.
choir, *v.i.*, to sing in chorus; *n.*, a company of singers; the part of a church occupied by the singers.
choir'-organ, *n.*, the part of an organ containing soft stops for light accompaniment. (Formerly called *chair-organ.*)
choke, *v.t.*, to stop the breath, throttle, block up; *v.i.*, to be suffocated, become stopped up; *n.*, the inner part of the artichoke.
choke'-bore, *n.*, a gun-bore narrowed at the muzzle.
choked, *p.p.*, choke.
choke'-damp, *n.*, the poisonous carbonic acid gas often found in mines, wells, and quarries.
choke'-full, *adj.*, quite full, chock-full.

chok'er, *n.*, one who chokes; a crushing rejoinder; a large cravat.
chok'ing, *pr.p.*, choke.
chok'y, *adj.*, like choking, suffocating.
chol'er, *n.*, anger, passion.
chol'era, *n.*, a dangerous epidemic disease.
cholera'ic, *adj.*, rel. to cholera.
chol'era mor'bus *n.* *i.q.* cholera.
chol'eric, *adj.*, passionate, hasty-tempered.
chondri'tis, *n.*, inflammation of cartilage.
chondrom'eter, *n.*, a grain-weighing apparatus.
choose, *v.t.*, to make a choice; to select; to have a preference for.
choos'er, *n.* one who chooses.
choos'ing, *pr.p.*, choose.
chop, *v.t.*, to cut into pieces; to bargain over; *v.i.*, to shift or change suddenly; *n.*, a small piece cut off; a jaw, chap.
chop'-house, *n.*, a restaurant.
chop'in, *n.*, an earthenware drinking-vessel; a liquid measure.
chopine', *n.*, a high clog.
chopped, *p.p.*, chop.
chop'per, *n.*, one who chops, a chopping instrument.
chop'ping, *pr.p.*, chop.
chops, *n. pl.*, the cheeks or chaps.
chop'sticks, *n. pl.*, thin wooden or ivory sticks used by the Chinese at meals.
chorag'ic, *adj.*, belonging to a choragus.
chora'gus, *n.*, the leader or furnisher of a chorus.
cho'ral, *adj.*, rel. to a choir or chorus; *n.* a harmonized hymn tune of German type.
chorale', *n.*, *i.q.* choral.
cho'ralist, *n.*, one who makes or sings chorals.
chord, *n.*, the string of a musical instrument; a combination of musical notes; a straight line joining the ends of an arc or apse; *v.t.*, to string; *v.i.*, to accord.
chord'ed, *p.p.*, chord.
chord'ing *pr.p.* chord.
chore, *n.*, a small domestic job.
chore'a, *n.*, a nervous twitching, St. Vitus's dance.
choree', *n.*, a trochee.
choriam'bic, *adj.*, rel. to a choriambus.
choriam'bus, *n.* a metrical foot of four syllables, viz., a trochee followed by an iambus.
cho'rion, *n.*, an enveloping membrane of the fetus.
chor'ist, *n.*, a singer in a chorus.
chor'ister *n.*, a member of a choir.
chorog'rapher, *n.*, a surveyor.
chorograph'ic, *adj.*, rel. to surveys.
chorog'raphy, *n.*, the art or practice of regional surveying.
cho'roid, *adj.*, resembling the chorion.
cho'rus, *v.t.*, to sing the chorus of, to celebrate in concert; *n.*, a choir of singers; united song.
cho'rus(s)ed, *p.p.*, chorus.
cho'rus(s)ing, *pr.p.*, chorus.
chose, *p.t.*, choose.
chos'en, *p.p.*, choose.
chough, *n.*, a kind of jackdaw.
chouse *v.t.*, to swindle; *n.*, a swindle.
choused, *p.p.*, chouse.
chow-chow *adj.*, mixed up, miscellaneous; *n.*, a mixture of food; a breed of dogs.
chow'der, *n.*, a mixed dish; a picnic.
chrematis'tics, *n.*, political economy, the science of the distribution of wealth.
chrestom'athy, *n.*, a collection of useful extracts.
chrism, *n.*, the consecrated oil used in various Sacraments of the Church, and at the Sovereign's Consecration.
chris'mal, *n.*, a vessel containing chrism.
chris'matory, *adj.*, rel. to chrism or unction; *n.*, a case to carry the chrism vessels.
chris'om, *n.*, a baptismal robe.
chris'om-child, *n.*, a child dying in its first month was buried in its chrisom.
Christ, *n.*, the Anointed One, the Messiah.
Christ'-cross, *n.*, a mark or cross.
chris'ten, *v.t.*, to baptize, admit to the Christian family.
Chris'tendom, *n.*, all Christian countries collectively, all Christian people.
chris'tened, *p.p.*, christen.
chris'tening *pr.p.*, christen; *n.*, the baptismal ceremony.
Chris'tian, *adj.*, rel. to Christ's followers; *n.*, one of the baptized, a follower of Christ.
Christian'ity, *n.*, the practice or doctrines of the Christian faith ecclesiastical jurisdiction.
Christianiza'tion, *n.*, the act or state of Christianizing.
Christ'ianize, *v.t.*, to convert to Christianity.
Christ'ianized, *p.p.*, Christianize.
Christ'ianizing, *pr.p.*, Christianize.
Christ'ianly, *adv.*, in a Christian way.
Christ'mas, *n.*, the season of Our Lord's Birthday.
Christ'mas-box, *n.*, a Christmas gift.

Christ'mas-day', *n.*, the Feast of Our Lord's Birthday, Dec. 25.

Christol'ogy, *n.*, the study of the attributes and person of Christ.

chro'mate, *n.*, a chromic acid salt.

chromat'ic, *adj.*, rel. to colour; proceeding by semitones; *n.* a note modified by an accidental.

chromat'ics, *n.*, pl. of chromatic; the science of colour.

chromatog'raphy, *n.*, a work on colour.

chromatol'ogy, *n.*, the scientific study of colour.

chromatom'eter, *n.*, a colour-measuring scale.

chrome, *n.*, a yellow pigment.

chro'mic, *adj.*, rel. to chromium.

chro'mium, *n.*, a whitish metallic element so named.

chro'mograph, *n.*, a gelatine pad for multiplying writing.

chromolith'ograph, *n.*, a colour-printed lithograph.

chromolithog'raphy, *n.*, the art of making chromolithographs.

chro'mosphere, *n.*, a layer of glowing hydrogen through which the light of the sun has to pass.

chron'ic, *adj.*, lasting for a long time; firmly established.

chron'icle, *v.t.*, to record in order of time; *n.*, a record of events in order of time.

chron'icled, *p.p.*, chronicle.

chron'icler, *n.*, one who chronicles.

Chron'icles, *n.*, one of the books of the Old Testament.

chron'icling, *pr.p.*, chronicle.

chron'ogram, *n.*, an inscription in which a date can be read by the numeral letters (M. D. V. and the like) contained in the words.

chronogrammat'ic, *adj.*, in the style of a chronogram.

chron'ograph, *n.*, an accurate stop-watch; an instrument determining the muzzle velocity of a shot.

chronog'rapher, *n.*, a chronicler; a chronologist.

chronog'raphy, *n.*, the inquiry into dates and past history.

chronol'oger, *n.*, one versed in the study of dates and events.

chronolog'ic, *adj.*, in order of time.

chronolog'ical, **-ly**, *adj.* and *adv.*, in order of time.

chronol'ogist, *n.*, one who studies dates and events.

chronol'ogy, *n.*, the study of events and dates.

chronom'eter, *n.*, a specially accurate timekeeper.

chronomet'ric, *adj.*, rel. to the chronometer.

chronom'etry, *n.*, time-measurement.

chron'opher, *n.*, an electric apparatus for transmitting time-indications.

chron'oscope, *n.*, an instrument for ascertaining precise length of minute intervals of time.

chrys'alid, *adj.*, like a chrysalis.

chrys'alis, *n.*, a butterfly or moth in the grub state.

chrysan'themum, *n.*, the common name for a variety of flower of the aster type; the flower so named.

chrysog'raphy, *n.*, illuminating in gold.

chrys'olite, *n.*, a yellow topaz.

chrysol'ogy, *n.*, the science of wealth.

chry'soprase, *n.*, *i.q.* chrysoprasus.

chrysop'rasus, *n.*, a precious stone of apple-green colour.

chrys'otype, *n.*, a photographic proof in which gold chlorid is used.

chub, *n.*, a little river fish so named.

chubbed, *adj.*, *i.q.* chubby.

chub'by, *adj.*, plump, round.

chuck, *v.t.*, to throw, tip up, to call by clucking; *n.*, an upward pat, a throw, a part (of a lathe) for holding in position.

chucked, *p.p.*, chuck.

chuck'ing, *pr.p.*, chuck.

chuck'le, *v.i.*, to laugh to oneself.

chuck'led, *p.p.*, chuckle.

chuck'ling, *pr.p.*, chuckle.

chud'dar, *n.*, an Indian fine wool shawl.

chuff, *adj.*, churlish; chubby.

chuf'fily, *adv.*, churlishly.

chuf'finess, *n.*, surliness.

chuf'fy, *adj.*, chubby.

chum, *v.i.*, to share rooms with; *n.*, a chamber-fellow, close friend.

chump, *v.t.*, to munch; *n.*, a small block of wood; the thick end of a joint.

chu'nam, *v.t.*, to plaster with chunam; *n.*, a plaster of lime and sea sand.

chunk, *n.*, a short, thick piece.

chunk'y, *adj.*, like a chunk, in a small piece.

church, *v.t.*, to say the Office for the churching of women over a woman returning thanks for a safe delivery; *n.*, a building for church worship; the whole collection of Catholic Christians; a local assembly of Catholic Christians.

churched, *p.p.* church.

church'ing, *pr.p.*, church; *n.*, the

thanksgiving after childbirth.
church'man, *n.*, a member of the church; an ecclesiastic.
church'manship, *n.*, the status of a churchman.
church'-rate, *n.*, a rate levied for the maintenance of the church.
church'warden, *n.*, an officer who has the charge of a church and its property.
church'yard, *n.*, the area in which a church stands.
churl, *n.*, a rude rustic, a clown.
churl'ish, *adj.*, like a churl, ill-bred.
churl'ishly, *adv.*, rudely.
churl'ishness, *n.*, rudeness, ill-breeding.
churn, *v.t.*, to stir cream into butter; *n.*, a vessel in which butter is produced by agitating cream.
churned, *p.p.*, churn.
churn'ing, *pr.p.*, churn.
chute, *n.*, a rapid fall in a river; an inclined trough.
chut'ney, *n.*, a mixed Indian condiment.
chyla'ceous, *adj.*, of like nature with chyle.
chyle, *n.*, a milky fluid in the intestine.
chylifac'tive, *adj.*, rel. to chylification.
chylif'erous, *adj.*, chyle-carrying.
chylifica'tion, *n.*, the formation of chyle.
chy'lous, *adj.*, rel. to chyle.
chyme, *n.*, the pulp in the stomach resulting from the first act of digestion.
chymifica'tion, *n.*, the formation of chyme.
chym'ify, *v.t.* and *i.*, to turn into chyme.
ciba'rious, *adj.*, edible.
cib'ol, *n.*, the shallot.
cibo'rium, *n.*, a large covered cup used for the distribution of the Host; a tabernacle-like receptacle for a pyx; a canopy over an altar.
cica'da, *n.*, the harvest-fly, cricket, locust.
cic'atrice, *n.*, the scar of a healed wound.
cicatri'sive, *adj.*, tending to form a cicatrix.
cica'trix, *n.*, *i.q.* cicatrice (*Lat.*).
cicatriza'tion, *n.*, the forming of a cicatrix.
cic'atrize, *v.t.*, to form a cicatrix.
cic'atrized, *p.p.*, cicatrize.
cic'atrizing, *pr.p.*, cicatrize.
cic'ely, *n.*, a species of parsley.
cicero'ne, *n.*, a guide to the sights of a place.
Cicero'nian, *adj.*, in the style of Cicero.
cichoria'ceous, *adj.*, rel. to chicory.
Cid, *n.*, a leader, chief.
ci'der, *n.*, a drink from pressed apple juice.
ci'derist, *n.*, a judge or maker of cider.
ci-devant', *adj.*, previous, former.
cierge, *n.*, a wax taper.
cigar', *n.*, a roll of tobacco leaves for smoking.
cigarette', *n.*, tobacco rolled in paper, a diminutive cigar.
cil'ia, *n. pl.*, the hair-like growth on cells.
cil'iary, *adj.*, rel. to the eyelashes or to cilia.
cil'iate, *adj.*, having cilia.
cil'iated, *adj.*, *i.q.* ciliate.
cil'ice, *n.*, a hair-shirt.
Cili'cian, *adj.*, bel. to Cilicia.
cili'cious, *adj.*, made of hair.
cil'iform, *adj.*, like cilia.
cil'iograde, *adj.*, moving by means of cilia.
cil'ium, *n.*, the sing. of cilia.
ci'ma, *see* cyma.
Cim'bric, *adj.*, rel. to the Cimbri (or Cymri); Welsh.
Cimme'rian, *adj.*, rel. to the Cimmerii; profoundly dark.
cim'olite, *n.*, an aluminum silicate.
cinch, *v.t.*, to get a grip on, to compel; *n.*, a broad saddle-girth.
cincho'na, *n.*, the name of the tree from which quinine is produced.
cincho'nic, *adj.*, rel. to cinchona.
cin'chonine, *n.*, an alkaloid so named.
cinct'ure, *v.t.*, to girdle, surround; *n.*, a girdle, anything that encircles.
cinct'ured, *p.p.*, cincture.
cin'der, *n.*, the refuse of burnt coal.
cin'derous, *adj.*, like a cinder.
cin'dery, *adj.*, like, or abounding in, cinders.
cinefac'tion, *n.*, reduction to cinders.
cin'ema, *n.*, an apparatus for showing pictures in motion.
cinemat'ograph, *n.*, a moving picture.
cinera'ceous, *adj.*, ashy-coloured.
cinera'ria, *n.*, the family name for a variety of shrubs.
cin'erary, *adj.*, rel. to ashes, holding ashes.
cinera'tion, *n.*, reduction to ashes.
cine'rious, *adj.*, ashy-grey.
Cingalese', *adj.*, rel. to the Cingalese or Ceylon.
cin'nabar, *n.*, vermillion.
cin'nabarine, *adj.*, like cinnabar.
cin'namon, *n.*, the spicy inner bark of the cinnamon tree.
cinnamon'ic, *adj.*, consisting of cinnamon.
cinq, cinque, *adj.*, five.

cinque'-foil, *adj.*, having cinque-foils; *n.*, a five-cusped architectural ornament.
Cinque' Ports, *n.*, five English sea-ports charged with the defence of the realm.
ci'pher, *v.t.*, to calculate arithmetically; *v.i.*, to continue sounding (said of an organ-pipe); *n.*, the figure 0, the sign of zero· anything unimportant; a cryptic way of writing.
ci'phered, *p.p.*, cipher.
ci'phering, *pr.p.*, cipher.
cip'olin, *n.*, an Italian marble.
Circas'sian, *adj.*, bel. to Circassia; *n.*, a native of C.
Circe'an, *adj.*, rel. to Circe; bewitching.
Circen'sian, *adj.*, rel. to the (Roman) circus.
cir'cinal, *adj.*, circled back, coiled back on itself.
cir'cinate *adj.*, coiled inward.
cir'cle, *v.t.* and *i.*, to move circularly; to encircle; *n.*, a round figure, a ring, an assemblage of people sharing the same ideas or being of the same rank.
cir'cled, *p.p.*, circle.
cir'clet, *n.*, a little circle.
cir'cling, *pr.p.*, circle.
cir'cuit, *n.*, a going round; extent of circumference; a defined district; the passage of an electric current; *v.i.*, to circulate.
cir'cuited, *p.p.*, circuit.
cir'cuiting, *pr.p.*, circuit.
circu'itous, *adj.*, roundabout.
circu'itously, *adv.*, in a roundabout way.
circu'ity, *n.*, roundabout method.
cir'culable, *adj.*, able to be circulated.
cir'cular, *adj.*, round; of the nature of a circle; *n.*, a notice sent round.
cir'cularism, *n.*, the circular theory of the universe.
circular'ity, *n.*, the character of being circular.
cir'cularize, *v.t.*, to address a circular notice to; to make circular.
cir'cularly, *adv.*, in a circular way.
cir'culate, *v.t.*, to send round, to spread about; *v.i.*, to be spread about, to go round.
cir'culated, *p.p.*, circulate.
cir'culating, *p.p.*, circulate.
circula'tion, *n.*, the act of circulating; something circulated.
cir'culative, *adj.*, causing circulation.
cir'culatory, *adj.*, rel. to circulation.
circumam'bient, *adj.*, surrounding.
cir'cumcise, *v.t.*, to perform circumcision on.
cir'cumcised, *p.p.*, circumcise.
cir'cumciser, *n.*, one who circumcises.
cir'cumcising, *pr.p.*, circumcise.
circumci'sion, *n.*, the act of circumcising.
circumduct', *v.t.*, to lead round.
circum'ference, *n.*, the boundary line of a circle; the distance round.
circumferen'tial, *adj.*, in, or rel. to, the circumference.
circum'ferentor, *n.*, an instrument for measuring circumferences.
cir'cumflect, *v.t.*, to bend round.
cir'cumflex, *v.t.*, to accent with the circumflex; *n.*, an accent mark, combined of the acute and the grave.
circumflex'ion, *n.*, the act of circumflexing.
circum'fluence, *n.*, a flowing round.
circum'fluent, *adj.*, flowing round.
circum'fluous, *adj.*, *i.q.* circumfluent.
circumfuse', *v.t.*, to pour or spread round, to surround.
circumfused', *p.p.*, circumfuse.
circumfu'sile, *adj.*, able to be circumfused.
circumfu'sion, *n.*, the act of circumfusing.
circumgy'rate, *v.i.*, to revolve.
circumgyra'tion, *n.*, the act of revolving.
circumja'cence, *n.*, the relation of lying around.
circumja'cent, *adj.*, lying around, closely bordering.
circumlocu'tion, *n.*, a roundabout way of speaking; a redundant phrase.
circumloc'utory, *adj.*, redundant, roundabout.
circumnav'igable, *adj.* able to be sailed round.
circumnav'igate, *v.t.*, to sail round.
circumnav'igated, *p.p.* circumnavigate.
circumnav'igating, *pr.p.*, circumnavigate.
circumnaviga'tion, *n.*, the act of sailing round.
circumnav'igator, *n.*, one who circumnavigates.
circumpo'lar, *adj.*, round the pole.
circumrota'tion, *n.*, the act of revolving on an axis.
circumro'tary, *adj.*, revolving on an axis.
circumro'tatory, *adj.*, *i.q.* circumrotary.
circumscrib'able, *adj.*, able to be circumscribed.
circumscribe', *v.t.*, to confine within boundaries, to limit.
circumscribed', *p.p.*, circumscribe.
circumscrib'er, *n.*, one who circumscribes.
circumscrib'ing, *pr.p.*, circumscribe.

circumscrip'tion, *n.*, the act of circumscribing; state of being circumscribed.

circumscrip'tive, *adj.*, tending to circumscribe.

cir'cumspect, *adj.*, wary, discreet.

circumspec'tion, *n.*, wariness, discretion, vigilance.

circumspec'tive, *adj.*, watchful.

cir'cumspectly, *adv.*, warily, discreetly.

cir'cumspectness, *n.*, the habit of being circumspect.

cir'cumstance, *v.t.*, to place in particular circumstances; *n.*, an incident; an event; attendant condition.

cir'cumstanced, *p.p.*, circumstance.

circumstan'tial, *adj.*, containing full details; matter of fact.

circumstantial'ity, *n.*, the circumstantial character.

circumstan'tiate, *v.t.*, to confirm with facts or details.

circumstan'tiated, *p.p.*, circumstantiate.

circumstan'tiating, *pr.p.*, circumstantiate.

circumval'late, *v.t.*, to make a trench round, to fortify.

circumvalla'tion, *n.*, the act of circumvallating; a rampart and trench.

circumvent', *v.t.*, to outwit, get the better of.

circumvent'ed, *p.p.*, circumvent.

circumvent'ing, *pr.p.*, circumvent.

circumven'tion, *n.*, the act of circumventing.

circumven'tive, *adj.*, able to circumvent.

circumvola'tion, *n.*, the act of flying round.

circum'volute, *v.t.*, to wrap round.

circumvolu'tion, *n.*, the act of wrapping round.

circumvolve', *v.i.*, to roll round.

cir'cus, *n.*, a circular-ended race-course; hippodrome; a row of houses forming a circle or part of a circle.

cirrho'sis, *n.*, a morbid condition of tissue.

cirrif'erous, *adj.*, having cirri.

cir'riform, *adj.*, like a cirrus.

cirrig'erous, *adj.*, carrying cirri.

cir'riped, *adj.*, having cirrus-like feet.

cirro-cu'mulus, *n.*, a pile of small clouds, part cirrus, part cumulus.

cir'rose, *adj.*, having cirri.

cirro-stra'tus, *n.*, a mass of clouds terminating in cirri.

cir'rus, *n.*, a cloud-shape resembling a wisp of hair; a tendril.

cir'socele, *n.*, varicocele.

cisal'pine, *adj.*, on this (the Roman) side of the Alps.

cisatlan'tic, *adj.*, on this side of the Atlantic.

cismon'tane, *adj.*, on this side of the mountains.

cis'soid, *adj.*, within two intersecting curves; *n.*, a variety of curve so named.

cist, *n.*, a chest, box.

Cister'cian, *adj.*, bel. to the Cistercian Order; *n.*, a C. monk.

cis'tern, *n.*, a receptacle for holding liquid.

cis'tic, *see* cystic.

cit, *n.*, a Hindu name for the Universal Spirit; colloquial for a city man.

ci'table, *adj.*, able to be cited.

cit'adel, *n.*, a fortress within or defending a city.

cita'tion, *n.*, the act of citing, or quoting; a quotation; a summons.

ci'tatory, *adj.*, of the nature of a citation.

cite, *v.t.*, to call, quote, summon.

ci'ted, *p.p.*, cite.

ci'ter, *n.*, one who cites.

cith'ara, *n.*, the Greek lyre.

cith'er, *n.*, a zither.

cit'ified, *adj.*, having city airs.

cit'igrade, *adj.*, fast-running.

ci'ting, *pr.p.*, cite.

cit'izen, *n.*, the dweller in a city or country.

cit'izenship, *n.*, the status of a citizen.

cit'rate, *n.*, citric acid salt.

cit'rene, *n.*, a volatile oil so named.

cit'ric, *adj.*, consisting of fruit of the citron.

cit'ril, *n.*, a little bird so named.

cit'rine, *adj.*, lemon-coloured.

cit'ron, *n.*, the fruit of the citron tree.

cit'y, *n.*, a community of citizens; a place where citizens live.

civ'et, *n.*, a perfume so named; the civet-cat; a stew.

civ'et-cat, *n.*, *i.q.* civet.

civ'ic, *adj.*, rel. to a city or citizenship.

ci'vics, *n.*, the study of civil government.

civ'il, *adj.*, rel. to a city or state; polite, well-mannered.

civ'il engineer', *n.*, an engineer of roads, bridges, etc., for civil (not military) purposes.

civil'ian, *n.*, one engaged in civil (not military) occupations; an Indian Civil Servant.

civil'ity, *n.*, good manners, courteous treatment.

civ'ilizable, *adj.*, capable of civilization.

civiliza'tion, *n.*, the state of being civilized; the act of civilizing.

civ'ilize, *v.t.*, to bring under refining and progressive influences.

civ'ilized, *p.p.*, civilize.
civ'ilizer, *n.*, one who civilizes.
civ'ilizing, *pr.p.*, civilize; *adj.*, refining, progressive.
civ'illy, *n.*, courteously; in rel. to the State.
civ'ism, *n.*, the profession of devotion to the community.
clab'ber, *v.i.*, to curdle.
clack, *v.i.*, to rattle, babble; *n.*, a sudden noise, rattle, prattle.
clacked, *p.p.*, clack.
clack'er, *n.*, anything that clacks.
clack'ing, *pr.p.*, clack.
clad, *p.p.*, clothe.
claim, *v.t.*, to assert a right; to affirm; *n.*, an assertion of a right; anything claimed.
claim'able, *adj.*, able to be claimed.
claim'ant, *n.*, one who claims.
claimed, *p.p.*, claim.
claim'ing, *pr.p.*, claim.
clair-au'dience, *n.*, the alleged power of abnormal hearing.
clair-au'dient, *adj.*, able to hear abnormally.
clair-obscure', *see* chiaroscuro.
clairvoy'ance, *n.*, the alleged power of seeing absent persons and objects.
clairvoy'ant, *n.*, one who pretends to clairvoyance.
clam, *n.*, a bivalve shell-fish; *v.t.*, to starve.
cla'mant, *adj.*, loud, urgent.
clam'ber, *v.i.*, to climb with the hands and feet; *n.*, the act of clambering.
clam'bered, *p.p.*, clamber.
clam'bering, *pr.p.*, clamber.
clammed, *p.p.*, clam.
clam'ming, *pr.p.*, clam.
clam'miness, *n.*, a state or feeling of damp cold.
clam'my, *adj.*, damp, cold and sticky.
clam'or, clam'our, *v.i.*, to raise an outcry; *n.*, an outcry, vociferation.
clam'ored, clam'oured, *p.p.*, clamour.
clam'orer, clam'ourer, *n.*, one who clamours.
clam'oring, clam'ouring, *pr.p.*, clamour.
clam'orous, *adj.*, making an outcry, vociferous.
clamp, *v.t.*, to fasten tight, to secure; *n.*, a stiff fastening; the name of a variety of tools.
clamped, *p.p.*, clamp.
clamp'ing, *pr.p.*, clamp.
clan, *n.*, a tribe.
clandes'tine, *adj.*, secret, underhand.
clandes'tinely, *adv.*, secretly.
clang, *v.i.*, to make a ringing noise; *n.*, a ringing metallic sound.
clanged, *p.p.*, clang.
clang'ing, *pr.p.*, clang.
clan'gor, clan'gour, *n.*, a clanking sound.
clan'gorous, *adj.*, noisily sounding.
clank, *v.t.*, to make something clank; *v.i.*, to resound; *n.*, a metallic sort of sound.
clanked, *p.p.*, clank.
clank'ing, *pr.p.*, clank.
clan'nish, *adj.*, rel. to a clan; exclusive; united by prejudice.
clan'nishly, *adv.*, in clannish fashion.
clan'ship, *n.*, the rights of a member of a clan.
clans'man, *n.*, a member of a clan.
clap, *v.t.* and *i.*, to strike together; to strike suddenly; to applaud; *n.*, a sudden, sharp noise.
clap'board, *v.t.*, to protect with a clapboard; *n.*, a weather board.
clapped, *p.p.*, clap.
clap'per, *n.*, anything that claps; a bell's tongue.
clap'per-claw, *v.t.*, to scratch and slap; *n.*, a back-scratcher.
clap'ping, *pr.p.*, clap.
clap'trap, *n.*, balderdash, cheap talk.
claque, *n.*, a hired body of supporters in a theatre.
claqueur', *n.*, a hired applauder.
clarabel'la, *n.*, a sweet, soft-voiced organ-stop.
Clar'enceux, Clar'encieux, *n.*, the higher of the two provincial Kings-of-Arms. His province is South of the Trent.
clar'endon, *n.*, a heavy-faced printing type.
clar'et, *adj.*, claret-coloured; *n.*, a light red French wine.
clarifica'tion, *n.*, the process of clarifying.
clar'ified, *p.p.*, clarify.
clar'ifier, *n.*, anything that clarifies.
clar'ify, *v.t.*, to make clear, to purify.
clar'ifying, *pr.p.*, clarify.
clar'inet, *n.*, a keyed wind instrument so named.
clar'ion, *adj.*, like a clarion; *n.*, a form of trumpet.
clarionet', *n.*, *i.q.* clarinet.
clash, *v.t.*, to strike together; *v.i.*, to collide; *n.*, a noise of things striking together.
clashed, *p.p.*, clash.
clash'ing, *pr.p.*, clash.
clasp, *v.t.*, to embrace, fasten close; *n.*, an embrace, a fastening.
clasped, *p.p.*, clasp.
clasp'er, *n.*, anything that clasps.
clasp'ing, *pr.p.*, clasp.
clasp'-knife, *n.*, a knife, of which the blade shuts into the handle.
class, *v.t.*, to group together, to rank; *adj.*, rel. to class distinction; *n.*, a rank, group, division.

class'able, *adj.*, able to be classed.
classed, *p.p.*, class.
clas'sic, *adj.*, of the first rank, esp. in literature; rel. to the Greek or Latin classics; *n.*, a standard work or author.
clas'sical, *adj.*, *i.q.* classic.
classical'ity, *n.*, the classic nature or quality.
clas'sicism, *n.*, the style of the classics; an idiom of the classics.
clas'sicist, *n.*, one who favours or studies the ancient classical styles.
classifica'tion, *n.*, the act of classifying; a classified system.
clas'sified, *p.p.*, classify.
clas'sifier, *n.*, one who classifies.
clas'sify, *v.t.*, to group in classes.
clas'sifying, *pr.p.*, classify.
class'ing, *pr.p.*, class.
clas'sis, *n.*, a class.
class'man, *n.*, a member of a class; one who obtains university honours.
class'mate, *n.*, a fellow-member of a class.
clat'ter, *v.t.* and *i.*, to rattle; to prate; *n.*, a confused noise, prattle.
clat'tered, *p.p.*, clatter.
clat'terer, *n.*, one who clatters.
clat'tering, *pr.p.*, clatter.
clause, *n.*, a sentence or part of a sentence; an article in a contract or will.
claus'tral, *adj.*, rel. to a cloister, secluded.
clau'sular, *adj.*, containing clauses.
cla'vate, *adj.*, club-like.
cla'vated, *adj.*, *i.q.* clavate.
clave, *p.t.*, cleave.
clav'iary, *see* clavier.
clav'ichord, *n.*, an early stringed instrument with a keyboard.
clav'icle, *n.*, the collar-bone.
clavic'ular, *adj.*, rel. to the collar bone.
clavier', *n.*, a keyboard.
clav'iform, *adj.*, club-shaped.
clavig'erous, *adj.*, key-bearing.
cla'vis, *n.*, a key; a clue.
claw, *v.t.*, to seize, tear, scratch; *n.*, a hooked nail, the head of a hammer.
clawed, *p.p.*, claw.
claw'ing, *pr.p.*, claw.
clay, *v.t.*, to cover with clay; *n.*, stiff, damp soil.
clayed, *p.p.*, clay.
clay'ey, *adj.*, like clay, abounding in clay.
clay'ing, *pr.p.*, clay.
clay'ish, *adj.*, slightly clayey.
clay'more, *n.*, a Highlander's two-edged sword.
clead'ing, *n.*, a wooden lining.
clean, *v.t.*, to purify, cleanse; *adj.*, purified, free from dirt, smooth, morally pure; *adv.*, wholly, quite.
cleaned, *p.p.*, clean.
clean'er, *n.*, anything that cleans; *adj.*, *comp.* of clean.
clean'est, *adj.*, *super.* of clean.
clean'ing, *pr.p.*, clean.
clean'lily, *adv.*, in a cleanly way.
clean'liness, *n.*, the cleanly quality or habit.
clean'ly, *adj.*, habitually clean.
clean'ly, *adv.*, in a clean way.
clean'ness, *n.*, the state of being clean.
cleanse, *v.t.*, to make clean, to remove defilement.
cleansed, *p.p.*, cleanse.
cleans'er, *n.*, anything that cleanses.
cleans'ible, *adj.*, able to be cleansed.
cleans'ing, *pr.p.*, cleanse; *n.*, the act of cleansing.
clear, *v.t.*, to make bright; to free from blame, to remove; to gain over and above cost; *v.i.*, to become brighter; *adj.*, bright, pellucid, unobstructed, net, plainly manifest; *n.*, a clear space.
clear'age, *n.*, a clearing.
clear'ance, *n.*, the act of setting free; a cleared space.
cleared, *p.p.*, clear.
clear'er, *n.*, anything that clears; *adj.*, *comp.* of clear.
clear'est, *adj.*, *super.* of clear.
clear'ing, *pr.p.*, clear; *n.*, a cleared space; the settlement of bank balances.
clear'ing-house, *n.*, an office where bankers' balances are adjusted.
clear'ly, *adv.*, plainly, evidently.
clear'ness, *n.*, the state or quality of being clear.
clear'-sighted, *adj.*, having clear vision.
cleat, *v.t.*, to supply with a cleat; *n.*, a strip nailed across something to prevent slipping.
cleav'able, *adj.*, able to be cleft.
cleav'age, *n.*, the act of cleaving, a cleft.
cleave, *v.t.*, to split, divide; *v.i.*, to cling to.
cleaved, *p.p.*, cleave.
cleav'er, *n.*, one who cleaves, a chopper.
cleav'ing, *pr.p.*, cleave.
cledge, *n.*, clay.
cledg'y, *adj.*, clayey.
cleek, *n.*, a golf club with an iron head.
clef, *n.*, a musical sign to indicate pitch.
cleft, *p.p.*, cleave; *n.*, a fissure.
cleg, *n.*, a horse-fly.
clem'atis, *n.*, a climbing plant so named.
clem'ency, *n.*, the quality of gentleness, compassion.
clem'ent, *adj.*, gentle, compassionate.

Clem'entine, *adj.*, bel. to St. Clement.

clench, *v.t.*, to grasp, to double up, to brace.

clenched, *p.p.*, clench.

clen'cher, *n.*, anything that clenches.

clench'ing, *pr.p.*, clench.

clep'sydra, *n.*, a Greek water-clock.

clere'story, *n.*, the upper range of windows in a church.

cler'gy, *n.*, the collective name for clergymen as a body; the clerical status.

cler'gyman, *n.*, a member of the clergy.

cler'ic, *n.*, a clerk or clergyman.

cler'ical, *adj.*, rel. to the clergy; rel. to a clerk or writer.

clerk, *n.*, a cleric; a writer in an office; a scholar.

clerk'ly, *adj.*, scholarly; rel. to a clerk.

clerk'ship, *n.*, a clerk's office or function.

cle'romancy, *n.*, divination by lots.

clev'er, *adj.*, skilful, capable.

clev'erly, *adv.*, in a clever way.

clev'erness, *n.*, the quality of being clever.

clev'is, *n.*, an iron loop round a plough beam.

clew, *v.t.*, to roll up; *n.*, a ball of thread; a guide to a mystery; the lower corner of a sail.

cliché, *n.*, an electrotype or stereotype plate.

click, *v.t.*, to make to click; *v.i.*, to give forth a click; *n.*, short, sharp sound, non-metallic.

clicked, *p.p.*, click.

click'er, *n.*, anything that clicks; a foreman shoemaker.

click'et, *n.*, a latch.

click'ing, *pr.p.*, click.

cli'ent, *n.*, a dependent, a customer, one who consults a lawyer.

cli'entage, *n.*, a number of clients.

clientele', *n.*, a body of clients, followers, etc.

cliff, *n.*, a high steep rock.

clift, *n.*, *see* cleft.

climac'teric, *adj.*, rel. to a climax; *n.*, a critical period in life.

cli'mate, *n.*, local atmospheric conditions.

climat'ic, *adj.*, rel. to climate.

climat'ical, *adj.*, *i.q.* climatic.

cli'matize, *v.t.*, to accustom to a climate.

climatog'raphy, *n.*, a description of climate.

climatol'ogist, *n.*, an expert in climate.

climatol'ogy, *n.*, the study of climatic conditions.

cli'max, *n.*, an ascending scale. In modern usage it means incorrectly the highest point, acme.

climb, *v.t.*, to ascend, mount.

climb'able, *adj.*, able to be climbed.

climbed, *p.p.*, climb.

climb'er, *n.*, one who climbs.

climb'ing, *pr.p.*, climb.

clime, *n.*, a region, climate.

clinch, *v.t.*, to grasp, fasten tightly, set the teeth, settle; *n.*, a clinched bolt; a particular knot in a rope.

clinched, *p.p.*, clinch.

clinch'er, *n.*, a settler.

clinch'ing, *pr.p.*, clinch.

cling, *v.i.*, to hold on to, adhere to.

cling'er, *n.*, one who clings.

cling'ing, *pr.p.*, cling.

cling'stone, *adj.*, descriptive of a peach of which the pulp adheres to the stone.

cling'y, *adj.*, adhesive.

clin'ic, *adj.*, rel. to a bed; *n.*, a patient in bed; bedside teaching.

clin'ical, *adj.*, *i.q.* clinic.

clink, *v.t.*, to produce a tinkling sound; *v.i.*, to tinkle; *n.*, a sound as of metal on metal.

clinked, *p.p.*, clink.

clink'er, *n.*, one who clinks; a slag; *v.i.*, to form clinkers.

clink'ered, *p.p.*, clinker.

clink'ing, *pr.p.*, clink.

clinoceph'aly, *n.*, a flattening of the cranium.

cli'noid, *adj.*, like a bed.

clinom'eter, *n.*, an instrument for measuring angles of elevation and depression.

clinomet'ric, *adj.*, rel. to a clinometer.

clinomet'rical, *adj.*, *i.q.* clinometric.

clin'quant, *adj.*, tinselled.

clip, *v.t.*, to cut off, crop, shear; to embrace; *n.*, the act or result of clipping; a device for holding things fast; the holder for the charge of a magazine rifle.

clipped, *p.p.*, clip.

clip'per, *n.*, one who clips; an instrument for clipping; a fast sailing ship.

clip'ping, *pr.p.*, clip.

clique, *n.*, a small closely-united party.

cli'quish, *adj.*, exclusive, clannish.

cli'quism, *n.*, an exclusive tendency.

clish-ma-cla'ver, *n.*, gossip (*Scot.*).

cliv'ers, *n. pl.*, grass-tufts.

cloa'ca, *n.*, a sewer (*Lat.*).

cloa'cal, *adj.*, rel. to a sewer.

cloak, *v.t.*, to cover with a cloak, hide; *n.*, a loose outer garment; an excuse, disguise.

cloaked, *p.p.*, cloak.

cloak'ing, *pr.p.*, cloak.

clob'ber, *v.t.*, to patch up; *n.*, a black paste.

cloche, *n.*, a bell-glass.

clo'cher, *n.*, a belfry (*Fr.*).
clock, *n.*, a time-measuring instrument; an ornament on a stocking
clock'-maker, *n.*, a maker of clocks.
clock'-work, *adj.*, regular, accurate; *n.* a clock's mechanism.
clod, *v.t.*, to pelt with clods; to make clods of; *v.i.*, to form into clods; *n.*, a lump of earth or turf; a bumpkin.
clod'ded, *p.p.*, clod.
clod'ding, *pr.p.*, clod.
clod'dy, *adj.*, full of clods.
clod'-hopper, *n.*, a rustic, yokel.
clod'-hopping, *adj.*, loutish.
clod'pate, *n.*, a blockhead.
clod'pated, *adj.*, stupid.
clod'poll, *n.*, a stupid fellow.
cloff, *n.*, a small deduction of weight.
clog, *v.t.*, to choke up, impede; *v.i.*, to become clogged; *n.*, an impediment; a shoe with a wooden sole.
clogged, *p.p.*, clog.
clog'giness, *n.*, a tendency to clog.
clog'ging, *pr.p.*, clog.
clog'gy, *adj.*, apt to clog.
cloisonné, *n.*, a kind of enamel ware.
clois'ter, *v.t.*, to enclose in a monastery; *n.*, a covered walk, partly or wholly enclosed; a monastery.
clois'tered, *p.p.*, cloister.
clois'terer, *n.*, one who lives in a cloister.
clois'tering, *pr.p.*, cloister.
clois'tral, *adj.*, rel. to a cloister.
clon'ic, *adj.*, rel. to spasm.
close, *v.t.*, to shut up; to fill up; *v.i.*, to come near, come together.
close, *adj.*, near, attentive, confined, stifling, stingy. *n.*, an enclosure; an end; *adv.*, fast shut up, nearly, near.
close'-bodied, *adj.*, close-fitting.
closed, *p.p.*, close.
close'ly, *adv.*, in a close way, attentively, compactly.
close'ness, *n.*, the state of being close; proximity; stinginess.
clo'ser, *adj.*, *comp.* of close.
clos'est *adj.*, *super.* of close.
clos'et, *n.*, a closed chamber, a private room, *v.t.*, to shut in a closet.
clos'eted, *p.p.*, closet.
clos'eting, *pr.p.*, closet.
clos'ing, *pr.p.*, close.
clo'sure, *v.t.*, to put the closure on; *n.*, the sudden ending of a debate.
clot, *v.t.*, to make into clots; *v.i.*, to become clotted; *n.*, a thick coagulated mass of liquid matter.
clot'-bur, *n.*, the cockle-bur.
cloth, *n.*, woven material.
clothe, *v.t.*, to cover with a garment, invest.
clothed, *p.p.*, clothe.
clothes, *n. pl.*, dress, garments.
clothes'-basket, *n.*, a basket containing clothes.
clothes'-horse, *n.*, a rail to hang clothes on.
clothes'-line, *n.*, a line to hang clothes on.
cloth'ier, *n.*, a seller or maker of clothes.
cloth'ing, *pr.p.*, clothe; *n.*, garments.
clot'ted, *p.p.*, clot.
clot'ting, *pr.p.*, clot.
clot'ty, *adj.*, full of clots.
cloud, *v.t.*, to darken, overshadow; *n.*, vapour floating in the air; a dimmed effect; a soft wrap for the head.
cloud'-capt, **cloud'-capped**, *adj.*, having clouds on the summit.
cloud'ed, *p.p.*, cloud.
cloud'ily, *n.*, in a cloudy way.
cloud'iness, *n.*, the state of being cloudy.
cloud'ing, *pr.p.*, cloud.
cloud'less, *adj.*, without a cloud.
cloud'y, *adj.*, covered with clouds, lowering, not clear.
clough, *n.*, a sluice; a ravine.
clout, *v.t.*, to patch; to cuff; *n.*, a piece of cloth, a rag; a blow.
clout'ed, *p.p.*, clout.
clout'ing, *pr.p.*, clout.
clout'-nail, *n.*, a short nail used by cobblers.
clove, *p.t.* of cleave; *n.* a spice from the bud of the clove tree.
clo'ven, *p.p.*, cleave; *adj.*, divided.
clo'ven-footed, *adj.*, having the foot divided.
clo'ver, *n.*, a trefoil plant, used as fodder.
clo'vered, *adj.*, planted with clover.
clown, *n.*, a rustic, boor, buffoon.
clown'ish, *adj.*, like a clown.
clown'ishly, *adv.*, in a clown-like way.
clown'ishness, *n.*, the quality of a clown.
cloy, *v.t.*, to fill to excess.
cloyed, *p.p.*, cloy.
cloy'ing, *pr.p.*, cloy.
club, *v.t.*, to strike with a club; to use as a club; to contribute; *n.*, a heavy stick; an association.
club'bable, *adj.*, sociable.
clubbed, *p.p.*, club.
club'bist, *n.*, one who favours clubs.
club'-footed, *adj.*, having deformed feet.
club'-house, *n.*, a house in which a club meets.
club'-law, *n.*, rule by violence.
club'-room, *n.*, a room for a club's meetings

cluck, *v.i.*, to make the sound of a hen; *n.*, the sound made by a hen.
clucked, *p.p.*, cluck.
cluck'ing, *pr.p.*, cluck.
clue, *n.*, a guide, a means to solving a problem.
clum'ber, *n.*, a variety of spaniel.
clump, *v.t.*, to group; *v.i.*, to tramp; *n.*, a cluster, mass, a thick boot-sole.
clum'sily, *adv.*, in a clumsy way.
clum'siness, *n.*, the quality of being clumsy.
clum'sy, *adj.*, awkward, unwieldy.
clunch, *adj.*, stumpy; *n.*, indurated clay.
clung, *p.p.*, cling.
Clu'niac, *adj.*, rel. to the Cluniac Order; *n.*, a monk of Cluny.
clus'ter, *v.t.*, to gather into clusters; *v.i.*, to grow in clusters, form into clusters; *n.*, a bunch, group.
clus'tered, *p.p.*, cluster.
clus'tering, *pr.p.*, cluster.
clus'tery, *adj.*, having clusters.
clutch, *v.t.*, to grasp. *n.*, grasp, seizure; a mechanical device for putting parts into or out of action; a batch of eggs before laying.
clutched, *p.p.*, clutch.
clutch'ing, *pr.p.*, clutch.
clut'ter, *v.t.*, to disorder; *v.i.*, make a noise; *n.*, a heap of confusion.
clut'tered, *p.p.*, clutter.
clut'tering, *pr.p.*, clutter.
clys'mic, *adj.*, rel. to a deluge.
clys'ter, *n.*, an enema.
coach, *v.i.*, to travel by coach; to work under a tutor; *v.t.*, to tutor; *n.*, a large carriage, a railway carriage, a tutor.
coach'-horse, *n.*, a carriage horse.
coach'-house, *n.*, a building where a carriage is kept.
coach'man, *n.*, the driver of a carriage.
co-ac'tion, *n.*, joint action.
coac'tive, *adj.*, acting conjointly.
coadjust', *v.t.*, to accommodate mutually.
coad'jutant *adj.*, co-operating.
coadju'tor, *n.*, an assistant, colleague.
coadju'trix, *n.*, fem. of coadjutor.
coadven'ture, *v.i.*, to share in an adventure; *n.*, an adventure in company.
coag'ulable, *adj.*, able to coagulate.
coag'ulant, *adj.*, causing coagulation; *n.*, something that causes coagulation.
coag'ulate, *v.t.*, to curdle, thicken; *v.i.*, to become curdled.
coag'ulated, *p.p.*, coagulate.
coag'ulating, *pr.p.*, coagulate.
coagula'tion, *n.*, the act or state of coagulating.
coag'ulative, *adj.*, tending to coagulate.
coag'ulator, *n.*, something that causes coagulation.
coag'ulatory, *adj.*, *i.q.* coagulative.
coag'ulum, *n.*, a coagulant.
co'-aid, *n.*, mutual or joint help.
coal, *v.t.*, to furnish with coal; *v.i.*, to take in coal; *n.*, a black mineral used for fuel.
coal'-field, *n.*, a coal-bearing district.
coaled, *p.p.*, coal.
coalesce', *v.i.*, to grow together, combine.
coalesced', *p.p.*, coalesce.
coales'cence, *n.*, the act or state of coalescing.
coales'cent, *adj.*, growing together.
coalesc'ing, *pr.p.*, coalesce.
coal'ing, *pr.p.*, coal.
coali'tion, *n.*, the act of combining: a union of parties.
coali'tionist, *adj.*, rel. to coalition.
co-ally' *n.*, a joint ally.
coal'-mine, *n.*, a mine from which coal is hewn.
coal'-pit, *n.*, a pit from which coal is drawn.
coal'y, *adj.*, like, or containing, coal.
coam'ing, *see* comb-ing.
coapta'tion, *n.*, the fitting together of parts (of a broken bone).
coarc'tate, *adj.*, pressed together.
coarcta'tion, *n.*, stricture, contraction.
coarse, *adj.*, rough, of poor quality, unrefined.
coarse'ly, *adv.*, in a coarse way.
coarse'ness, *n.*, the quality of being coarse.
coars'er, *adj.*, *comp.* of coarse.
coars'est, *adj.*, *super.* of coarse.
coast, *v.i.*, to travel or sail along; to bicycle downhill without pedalling; *n.*, border, edge of land by the sea.
coast'ed, *p.p.*, coast.
coas'ter, *n.*, a vessel sailing from port to port on the same coast.
coast'-*guard*, *n.*, the guard stationed along the coast.
coast'ing, *pr.p.*, coast; *n.*, the sport of bicycling downhill without using the pedals.
coast'-line, *n.*, the line showing on a map the coast of a country.
coast'wise, *adv.* and *adj.*, along the coast.
coat, *v.t.*, to apply a coating to; to cover with a coat; *n.*, an outer covering; a layer.
coat'ed, *p.p.*, coat.
coatee', *n.*, a short coat.
coat'ing, *n.*, an outer layer; material for a coat; *pr.p.*, coat.

coax, *v.t.*, to wheedle, persuade by caresses.

coaxed, *p.p.*, coax.

coax'er, *n.*, one who coaxes.

coax'ing, *pr.p.*, coax; *adj.*, wheedling, fondling; *n.*, the act of one who coaxes.

coax'ingly, *adv.*, in a coaxing way.

cob, *v.t.*, to beat; *n.*, a roundish hump; a small sturdy horse, a head of wheat; a blow on the buttocks; a breakwater.

co'balt, *n.*, a mineral so named; a pigment made from the same.

cobalt'ic, *adj.*, rel. to cobalt.

cob'bing, *adj.*, vulgarly ostentatious; *n.*, copper-impregnated rubble.

cob'ble, *v.t.*, to patch up; to lay cobblestones on; *n.*, a variety of fishing-boat; a large round paving-stone.

cob'bled, *p.p.*, cobble.

cob'bler, *n.*, one who cobbles, a shoemender; a summer beverage so named.

cob'ble-stone, *n.*, a cobble for paving.

cob'bling, *pr.p.*, cobble.

cob'by, *adj.*, headstrong, ardent.

Cob'denism, *n.*, the doctrine of Cobden, *i.e.*, Free Trade.

Cob'denite, *n.*, a Free Trader.

cob'nut, *n.*, a variety of hazel-nut.

cob'ra, *n.*, an Indian snake, exceedingly venomous.

cob'web, *v.t.*, to cover with a cobweb; *n.*, a spider's web.

cob'webbed, *adj.*, covered with cobwebs.

co'ca, *n.*, the dried leaf of a Peruvian shrub.

co'caine, *n.*, an anaesthetic, produced from the coca plant.

coca'inism, *n.*, the effect of cocaine poisoning.

coc'culus, *n.*, a tropical plant bearing berries of a narcotic character.

coc'cyx, *n.*, the lower end of the spine.

coch'ineal, *n.*, a bright red dye, made from cochineal insects dried.

coch'lea, *n.*, one of the ear passages.

coch'lear, *adj.*, like a spoon; *n.*, the communion-spoon of the Greek Church.

cochlear'iform, *adj.*, spoon-shaped.

coch'leate, *adj.*, spiral like a snail-shell.

cock, *v.t.*, to set up on one side; to raise the hammer of a gun; *n.*, a male bird; a hay-pile; a jaunty tip.

cockade', *n.*, a knot of ribbons or other badge attached to a cap or hat.

cocka'ded, *adj.*, decorated with a cockade.

Cockaigne', *n.*, an imaginary country; London, the home of cockneys.

cockatoo', *n.*, a variety of parrot.

cock'atrice, *n.*, a fabulous snake-like creature, hatched from a cock's egg.

cock'bill, *v.t.*, to hang (an anchor) from the cathead; to raise the sign of mourning (*naut.*).

cock'boat, *n.*, a little rowing boat.

cock'chafer, *n.*, a winged beetle.

cock'-crow, *n.*, the early morning.

cock'-crowing, *n.*, *s.q.* cock-crow.

cocked, *p.p.*, cock.

cock'er, *n.*, a breed of spaniels; *v.t.*, to pamper, indulge.

cock'erel, *n.*, a young cock.

cock'et, *n.*, a seal of the custom house.

cock'-eyed, *adj.*, squinting.

cock'-fight, *n.*, a fight between cocks.

cock'-horse, *n.*, a hobby horse; anything across which a child can straddle.

cock'ing, *pr.p.*, cock.

cock'le, *n.*, a weed growing amid corn; a bivalve so named; *v.i.*, to wrinkle.

cock'led, *p.p.*, cockle.

cock'ling, *pr.p.*, cockle.

cock'ling, *see* cockerel.

cock'-loft, *n.*, a loft next to the roof.

cock'ney, *n.*, a Londoner.

cock'neyfied, *p.p.*, cockneyfy.

cock'neyfy, *v.t.*, to change to a Londoner.

cock'neyism, *n.*, the London manner and idiom.

cock'pit, *n.*, a ring for cock-fights.

cock'roach, *n.*, a black beetle.

cocks'comb, *see* coxcomb.

cock'sparrow, *n.*, a male sparrow.

cock'spur, *n.*, a spur on a cock's legs.

cock'swain, *see* coxswain.

cock'tail, *n.*, an American iced drink.

co'co, co'coa, *n.*, the palm tree; the seeds of the cacao tree.

co'coa-nib, *n.*, the roasted cacao seeds.

co'co-nut, *n.*, the fruit of the coco-palm.

cocoon', *n.*, an envelope spun by caterpillars.

cocoon'ery, *n.*, a place where silk is spun.

coc'tion, *n.*, the process of boiling.

cod, *n.*, a well-known edible fish.

co'da, *n.*, an additional ending to a piece of music; the finale of a fugue or sonata.

cod'dle, *v.t.*, to pamper; *n.*, one that is pampered.

cod'dled, *p.p.*, coddle.

cod'dling, *pr.p.*, coddle.

code, *n.*, a body of law; a system of signs for conveying messages briefly or in cipher.

co'deine, *n.*, an alkaloid so named.
co'dex, *n.*, an uncial MS.
cod'fish, *n.*, a cod.
codg'er, *n.*, an eccentric old person.
cod'icil, *n.*, a later note modifying or explaining a will.
codicil'lary, *adj.*, rel. to a codicil.
codifica'tion, *n.*, the systematizing of laws already in existence.
cod'ified, *p.p.*, codify.
cod'ifier, *n.*, one who codifies.
cod'ify, *v.t.*, to reduce existing enactments to a code.
cod'ifying, *pr.p.*, codify.
codil'la, *n.*, part of the flax or hemp.
codille', *n.*, a term used in the game of ombre.
cod'ling, *n.*, a young cod; a cooking apple.
co'don, *n.*, a bill; the mouth of a trumpet.
coeduca'tion, *n.*, the education of both sexes together.
co-effi'ciency, *n.*, combined efficiency.
coeffi'cient, *adj.*, cooperative, working with another; *n.*, a number placed commonly before another to multiply it.
coe'liac, *adj.*, rel. to the abdomen.
coemp'tion, *n.*, an old form of marriage by mutual purchase.
coenog'amy, *n.*, community of wives and husbands.
coe'qual, *adj.*, jointly equal.
coequal'ity, *n.*, the state of being coequal.
coerce', *v.t.*, to compel, force.
coerced', *p.p.*, coerce.
coer'cible, *adj.*, able to be coerced.
coer'cibleness, *n.*, the state of being coercible.
coerc'ing, *pr.p.*, coerce.
coer'cion, *n.*, the act of coercing.
coer'cive, *adj.*, producing coercion.
coessen'tial, *adj.*, having the same essence.
coessential'ity, *n.*, the quality or state of being coessential.
coeter'nal, *adj.*, equally eternal.
coeter'nity, *n.*, equal eternity.
coe'val, *adj.*, of the same generation, contemporary.
coexist', *v.i.*, to exist together.
coexist'ed, *p.p.*, coexist.
coexist'ence, *n.*, the state or fact of coexisting.
coexist'ent, *adj.*, coexisting.
coexist'ing, *pr.p.*, coexist.
coextend', *v.i.*, to be equally extensive.
coextend'ed, *p.p.*, coextend.
coextend'ing, *pr.p.*, coextend.
coexten'sion, *n.*, the act or state of coextending.
coexten'sive, *adj.*, coextending.
cof'fee, *n.*, the seeds of the coffee plant; the beverage made from them.
cof'fee-house, *n.*, a place of refreshment selling coffee.
cof'fee-pot, *n.*, a pot from which coffee is served.
cof'fer, *v.t.*, to shut in a chest; to sink panels in a ceiling; *n.*, a chest; a sunk panel.
cof'fer-dam, *n.*, a temporary dam.
cof'fered, *p.p.*, coffer; *adj.*, having coffers.
cof'ferer, *n.*, a treasurer.
cof'fin, *v.t.*, to place in a coffin; *n.*, a chest to hold a dead body.
cof'fined, *p.p.*, coffin.
cog, *v.t.*, to supply with cogs; to load (dice); to cheat; *n.*, a tooth on a wheel's surface; a projecting catch; a trick; a small fishing vessel.
co'gency, *n.*, the state or quality of the cogent.
co'gent, *adj.*, compelling, convincing.
co'gently, *adv.*, in a cogent way.
cogged, *adj.*, having cogs; *p.p.*, cog.
cog'ger, *n.*, one who builds mine-props.
cog'ging, *pr.p.*, cog.
cog'itable, *adj.*, able to be cogitated.
cog'itate, *v.t.*, to think over; *v.i.*, to reflect, meditate.
cog'itated, *p.p.*, cogitate.
cog'itating, *pr.p.*, cogitate.
cogita'tion, *n.*, the act or state of cogitating.
cog'itative, *adj.*, given to reflecting.
co'gnac, *n.*, fine French brandy.
cog'nate, *adj.*, of the same family or kind; allied.
cog'nateness, *n.*, the quality of being cognate.
cogna'tion, *n.*, family relationship.
cogni'tion, *n.*, clear apprehension, knowledge.
cog'nitive, *adj.*, rel. to cognition.
cog'nizable, *adj.*, able to be apprehended.
cog'nizance, *n.*, knowledge, recognition; a heraldic badge.
cog'nizant, *adj.*, perceiving, taking notice.
cog'nize, *v.t.*, to perceive, recognize.
cog'nized, *p.p.*, cognize.
cognizee', *n.*, one accepting the acknowledgment of a fine of lands.
cog'nizing, *pr.p.*, cognize.
cog'nizor, *n.*, one acknowledging a fine of lands.
cogno'men, *n.*, a surname, nickname.
cognom'inal, *adj.*, rel. to a cognomen; of the same name.
cog'-wheel, *n.*, a cogged or toothed wheel.

cohab'it, *v.i.*, to live together as married.
cohab'itant, *n.*, one who lives in the same place with another.
cohabita'tion, *n.*, the act or state of cohabiting.
cohab'ited, *p.p.*, cohabit.
cohab'iter, *n.*, *i.q.* cohabitant.
cohab'iting, *pr.p.*, cohabit.
coheir', *n.*, a joint heir.
coheir'ess, *n.*, fem. of coheir.
cohere', *v.i.*, to stick together.
cohered', *p.p.*, cohere.
coher'ence, *n.*, the act or state of cohering.
coher'ency, *n.*, a tendency to cohere; consistency.
coher'ent, *adj.*, sticking together; logically consistent.
coher'ently, *adv.*, in a coherent way.
coher'ing, *pr.p.*, cohere.
cohesibil'ity, *n.*, the state of being cohesible.
cohe'sible, *adj.*, able to cohere.
cohe'sion, *n.*, the act or state of cohering.
cohe'sive, *adj.*, with the power of cohering.
cohe'siveness, *n.*, the state of being cohesive.
cohib'it, *v.t.*, to restrain.
cohibi'tion, *n.*, the act or effect of cohibiting.
co'hobate, *v.t.*, to e-distil.
co'hort, *n.*, the tenth part of a Roman legion.
coif, *n.*, a form of head-gear, particularly as worn by serjeants-at-law.
coifed, *adj.*, wearing a coif.
coiffeur', *n.*, a hair-dresser.
coiffure, *n.*, head-dressing; a mode of dressing the hair.
coign, coigne, *n.*, a corner; corner-stone.
coil, *n.*, a rope gathered into a ring; a stir, noise; an electrical apparatus so named; *v.i.* and *t.*, to wind round.
coiled, *p.p.*, coil.
coil'ing, *pr.p.*, coil.
coin, *n.*, stamped money; *v.t.*, to stamp metal as money; to invent.
coin'age, *n.*, the process of stamping money; the money stamped; invention.
coincide', *v.i.*, to occur simultaneously; to agree exactly; to lie on the same line or point.
coincid'ed, *p.p.*, coincide.
coin'cidence, *n.*, the act of coinciding; a simultaneous occurrence.
coin'cident, *adj.*, simultaneously occurring.
coin'cidently, *adv.*, simultaneously.
coincid'ing, *pr.p.*, coincide.
coindica'tion, *n.*, a supplementary indication.
coined, *p.p.*, coin.
coin'er, *n.*, one who makes coins, esp. spurious ones.
co-inhab'itant, *n.*, a fellow-dweller.
coin'ing, *pr.p.*, coin.
coir, *n.*, cocoa-nut fibre.
coit, *n.*, *see* quoit.
coi'tion, *n.*, copulation, conjunction.
coju'ror, *n.*, a fellow-juryman.
coke, *n.*, coal residue after the withdrawal of the gas; *v.t.*, to turn into coke.
coked, *p.p.*, coke.
co'ker-nut, *n.*, the popular form of the name cocoa-nut.
cok'ing, *pr.p.*, coke.
col'ander, *n.*, a domestic strainer.
col'chicum, *n.*, meadow saffron.
col'cothar, *n.*, an iron peroxide.
cold, *adj.*, without heat; passionless; of a bluish tone; *n.*, absence of heat; the sensation of chill; a catarrh.
***cold'*-blooded**, *adj.*, having blood of a low temperature; cruel.
cold'er, *adj.*, *comp.* of cold.
cold'est, *adj.*, *super.* of cold.
***cold'*hearted**, *adj.*, without natural affection, cruel.
***cold'*ish**, *adj.*, somewhat cold.
***cold'*ly**, *adv.*, in a cold way.
***cold'*ness**, *n.*, the state of being cold; indifference.
cole, *n.*, a general name for cabbage-plants.
coleop'tera, *n. pl.*, insects with sheathed wings; beetles.
coleop'terist, *n.*, a collector of coleoptera.
coleop'terous, *adj.*, having sheathed wings.
cole'seed, *n.*, rape-seed.
col'et, *n.*, an acolyte.
cole'wort, *n.*, young cabbage.
col'ic, *n.*, violent pain of the bowels; *adj.*, rel. to the bowels.
col'icky, *adj.*, rel. to colic.
col'in, *n.*, a variety of quail.
Colise'um, *n.*, the great Flavian amphitheatre in Rome. Also *Colosseum*.
collab'orate, *v.i.*, to join with someone in a piece of work.
collab'orated, *p.p.*, collaborate.
collab'orating, *pr.p.*, collaborate.
collabora'tion, *n.*, the act of collaborating.
collab'orator, *n.*, one who collaborates.
collapse', *v.i.*, to fall down, break down, fail; *n.*, a breakdown, falling down; failure.
collapsed', *p.p.*, collapse.
collaps'ible, *adj.*, collapsing.

collaps'ing, *pr.p.*, collapse.

col'lar, *n.*, something worn round the neck; *v.t.*, to seize by the neck.

col'lared, *p.p.*, collar.

col'laret, collarette', *n.*, a fichu.

col'laring *pr.p.*, collar.

colla'table, *adj.*, able to be collated.

collate', *v.t.*, to compare a text or texts critically; to present to a benefice (said of a bishop exercising patronage).

colla'ted, *p.p.*, collate.

collat'eral, *adj.*, side by side; subsidiary; not in direct descent.

collat'eralness, *n.*, the state of being collateral.

collat'ing, *pr.p.*, collate.

colla'tion, *n.*, the act of collating; a light repast.

colla'tive, *adj.*, pert. to collation.

colla'tor, *n.*, one who collates.

col'league, *n.*, an associate in office, employment or undertaking.

col'lect, *n.*, a short liturgical prayer.

collect', *v.t.*, to gather together, assemble; *v.i.*, to assemble together.

collect'able, *adj.*, able to be collected.

collecta'nea, *n. pl.*, selected passages from books.

collecta'neous, *adj.*, selected.

collect'ed, *p.p.*, collect; also *adj.*, self-possessed.

collect'edly, *adv.*, with self-possession.

collect'edness, *n.*, a self-possessed attitude.

collect'ible, *adj.*, able to be collected.

collect'ing, *pr.p.*, collect.

collec'tion, *n.*, the act or state of collecting; a number of things collected together; a crowd; the gathering of alms; a college examination.

collect'ive, *adj.*, taken as a whole or in bulk.

collect'ively, *adv.*, altogether.

collect'iveness, *n.*, the state of being collective.

collect'ivism, *n.*, the political theory of collective ownership by the State.

collect'or, *n.*, one who collects.

collect'orate, *n.*, a collector's district.

collect'orship, *n.*, the office of a collector.

col'leen, *n.*, a girl (*Irish*).

col'lege, *n.*, a society, community; its hall or house of residence.

colle'gial, *adj.*, rel. to a college.

colle'gian, *n.*, the member of a college.

colle'giate, *adj.*, rel. to a college; corporately established.

col'let, *n.*, the part of a ring in which the stone is set.

collide', *v.i.*, to strike up against.

colli'ded, *p.p.*, collide.

colli'ding, *pr.p.*, collide.

col'lie, *n.*, a sheep-dog.

col'lier, *n.*, one who hews coal; a coaling vessel.

col'liery, *n.*, a coal mine.

col'ligate, *v.t.*, to fasten together.

colliga'tion, *n.*, the act of fastening together.

col'limate, *v.t.*, to make parallel.

collima'tion, *n.*, the act of collimating.

collinea'tion, *n.*, the act or state of bringing into line.

colliq'uative, *adj.*, marked by excessive purging.

colli'sion, *n.*, the act of colliding, concussion.

col'locate, *v.t.*, to place or arrange.

col'located, *p.p.*, collocate.

col'locating, *pr.p.*, collocate.

colloca'tion, *n.*, the act or state of collocating.

collocu'tion, *n.*, the act of making a colloquy.

collo'dion, *n.*, soluble gun-cotton treated with ether.

collo'dionize, *v.t.*, to prepare collodion.

col'loid, *adj.*, glue-like; *n.*, a glue-like substance.

col'lop, *n.*, a slice (of meat).

collo'quial, *adj.*, in the ordinary style of speech; rel. to conversation.

collo'quialism, *n.*, a colloquial expression.

col'loquist, *n.*, one who engages in a colloquy.

col'loquy, *n.*, a conversation.

col'lotype, *n.*, a photograph produced on gelatine; the collotype process; *v.t.*, to reproduce in collotype.

collude', *v.i.*, to be a partner to a collusion.

collu'ded, *p.p.*, collude.

collu'der, *n.*, one who colludes.

collu'ding, *pr.p.*, collude.

collu'sion, *n.*, a secret agreement to deceive.

collu'sive, *adj.*, fraudulently agreed, deceitful.

collu'sively, *adv.*, with collusion.

col'ly, *see* collie.

col'ocynth, *n.*, a purgative medicine.

colocyn'thin, *adj.*, rel. to colocynth.

co'lon, *n.*, the large intestine; a punctuation mark (:).

col'onel, *n.*, the head of a regiment.

col'onelcy, *n.*, a colonel's rank and office.

colo'nial, *adj.*, rel. to a colony.

col'onist, *n.*, a settler in a colony.
coloniza'tion, *n.*, the act or effect of colonizing.
coloniza'tionist, *n.*, an advocate of colonizing.
col'onize, *v.t.*, to form into a colony.
col'onized, *p.p.*, colonize.
col'onizing, *pr.p.*, colonize.
colonnade', *n.*, a row of columns.
col'ony, *n.*, a settlement.
col'ophon, *n.*, a device to mark the end of a book.
col'ophony, *n.*, a dark resin produced from turpentine.
col'or, col'our, *v.t.*, to tint, impart colour to; *v.i.*, to show colour; *n.*, tint, tinge, dye; a pretext; a flag.
col'orable, col'ourable, *adj.*, plausible, resembling.
col'orableness, col'ourableness, *n.*, the quality of being colourable.
col'orably, col'ourably, *adv.*, in a colourable way.
colora'tion, *n.*, the act or state of colouring.
col'orature, *n.*, colour in music.
col'ored, col'oured, *p.p.*, colour.
colorif'ic, *adj.*, producing colour.
col'oring, col'ouring, *pr.p.*, colour; *n.*, the act or art of applying colour; the colour applied.
col'orist, col'ourist, *n.*, an artist skilled in colouring.
col'orless, col'ourless, *adj.*, without colour, pale, white.
colos'sal, *adj.*, gigantic, huge.
Colosse'um, *n.*, the great amphitheatre of Rome (also spelt *Coliseum*).
Colos'sian, *adj.*, pert. to Colosse.
Colos'sus, *n.*, the gigantic statue at Rhodes

col'portage, *n.*, the distribution of books, tracts, etc.
col'porteur, *n.*, one who distributes books, tracts, etc.
colt, *n.*, a young male horse; an untrained youth; *v.t.*, to punish with a colt or rope's end.
colt'ish, *adj.*, like a colt, untamed.
colt'er, *see* coulter.
colts'foot, *n.*, a medicinal plant.
col'uber, *n.*, a serpent (*Lat.*).
col'ubrine, *adj.*, rel. to serpents.
colum'ba, *n.*, a pigeon; dove.
columba'rium, *n.*, a pigeon-house; dovecot; a set of niches for cinerary urns.
col'umbary, *n.*, *i.q.* columbarium.
Colum'bian, *adj.*, pert. to Columbus, Columbia, or the U.S.
colum'bic, *adj.*, pert. to columbium.
col'umbine, *n.*, a female pantomime dancer; a perennial plant.
colum'bium, *n.*, a dark grey metallic element.
columel'la, *n.*, a central column.
col'umn, *n.*, a cylindrical pillar; a large body of troops, a vertical row of figures; a division of a page.
colum'nar, *adj.*, rel. to columns.
col'umned, *adj.*, having columns.
columnia'tion, *n.*, the arrangement of columns.
colure', *n.*, the name of the two great circles in the celestial sphere.
col'za-oil, *n.*, oil from the seeds of a certain cabbage.
co'ma, *n.*, complete insensibility.
co'mate, *n.*, hairy; written *co-mate* it means companion.
co'matose, *adj.*, in a stupor, insensible.
comb, *v.t.*, to arrange the hair with a comb; *n.*, an instrument for adjusting the hair; a cock's crest.
com'bat, *v.t.*, to fight against; *n.*, a fight, contest.
com'batable, *adj.*, able to be combated.
com'batant, *n.*, one who combats.
com'bated, *p.p.*, combat.
com'bater, *n.*, *i.q.* combatant.
com'bating, *pr.p.*, combat.
com'bative, *adj.*, pugnacious, fond of fighting.
com'bativeness, *n.*, pugnacity.
combed, *p.p.*, comb.
comb'er, *n.*, anything that combs; a rolling breaker.
combin'able, *adj.*, able to be combined.
combina'tion, *n.*, the act or effect of combining; a union.
combine', *v.t.*, to join or associate together; *v.i.*, to unite, agree; *n.*, a secret association for the purpose of fraud.
combined', *p.p.*, combine.
combi'ner, *n.*, one who combines.
comb'ing, *pr.p.*, comb.
combin'ing, *pr.p.*, combine.
comb'less, *adj.*, lacking a comb.
combust', *adj.*, burnt.
combustibil'ity, *n.*, the state or quality of being combustible.
combus'tible, *adj.*, inflammable; *n.*, anything inflammable.
combus'tibleness, *n.*, *i.q.* combustibility.
combus'tion, *n.*, the act of burning; the condition of being burnt.
combus'tive, *adj.*, inflammatory.
come, *v.i.*, to draw near, arrive, happen; *v.t.*, to play the part of.
come'dian, *n.*, a writer or player of comedies.

comédienne′, *n.*, a comedy actress.
comediet′ta, *n.*, a short comedy.
come′-down, *n.*, a fall, drop.
com′edy, *n.*, a comic drama.
come′lier, *adj.*, *comp.* of comely.
come′liest, *adj.*, *super.* of comely.
come′lily, *adv.*, in a comely way.
come′liness, *n.*, beauty, grace.
come′ly, *adj.*, beautiful, graceful.
com′er, *n.*, one who comes.
comes′tible, *adj.*, eatable; *n.*, an article of food.
com′et, *n.*, a heavenly body with a luminous trail.
cometa′rium, *n.*, an instrument to measure a comet's motion.
com′etary, *adj.*, rel. to a comet.
comet′ic, *adj.*, *i.q.* cometary.
cometog′raphy, *n.*, the study of comets.
com′fit, *n.*, a dry sweetmeat.
com′fiture, *n.*, *i.q.* comfit.
com′fort, *v.t.*, to cheer, warm, solace; *n.*, solace, support, warmth.
com′fortable, *adj.*, imparting comfort, in a state of ease.
com′fortableness, *n.*, the quality of giving comfort.
com′forted, *p.p.*, comfort.
com′forter, *n.*, one who, anything that, comforts; a neck-wrap.
com′forting, *pr.p.*, comfort.
com′fortless, *adj.*, without comfort, dreary.
com′frey, *n.*, a hairy plant.
com′ic, *adj.*, ludicrous, exciting mirth.
com′ical, *adj.*, *i.q.* comic.
comical′ity, *n.*, ludicrousness, funniness
com′ically, *adv.*, in a comical way.
com′icalness, *n.*, *i.q.* comicality.
com′ing, *pr.p.*, come; *n.*, an arrival.
com′ity, *n.*, courtesy, civility.
com′ma, *n.*, a punctuation mark (,). In music a very small interval.
command′, *v.t.*, to order, lead; *n.*, an order; superior position, advantage; the charge of a naval or military force.
commandant′, *n.*, an officer in command of a garrison.
command′atory, *adj.*, mandatory.
command′ed, *p.p.*, command.
commandeer′, *v.t.*, to seize under military law.
commandeered′, *p.p.*, commandeer.
commandeer′ing, *pr.p.*, commandeer.
command′er, *n.*, one who commands; a naval officer so named.
command′ery, *n.*, a commander's office or sphere of jurisdiction; the rank of a Knight Commander; the name of a branch house of the Knights Templars.
command′ing, *pr.p.*, command; *adj.*, in a position of superiority, authoritative.
command′ingly, *adv.*, in a commanding way.
command′ment, *n.*, a command, precept, law.
comman′do, *n.*, a burgher military force.
commat′ic, *adj.*, terse, concise.
com′matism, *n.*, terseness, conciseness.
commeas′urable, *adj.*, commensurate.
commem′orable, *adj.*, worthy of commemoration.
commem′orate, *v.t.*, to celebrate the memory of.
commem′orated, *p.p.*, commemorate.
commem′orating, *pr.p.*, commemorate.
commemora′tion, *n.*, the act of commemorating.
commem′orative, *adj.* celebrating the memory of.
commem′orator, *n.*, one who commemorates.
commem′oratory, *adj.* *i.q.* commemorative.
commence′, *v.t.* and *i.*, to begin.
commenced′, *p.p.*, commence.
commence′ment, *n.*, a beginning; a university ceremony of granting degrees.
commenc′ing, *pr.p.*, commence.
commend′, *v.t.*, to name for approval, recommend, entrust
commend′able, *adj.*, worthy to be commended.
commend′ably, *adv.*, in a commendable way.
commen′dam, *n.*, a trust. Ecclesiastical livings have been sometimes held "in commendam," on trust until a permanent appointment is made.
commenda′tion, *n.*, the act of commending; approval.
commend′atory, *adj.*, laudatory, approving.
commend′ed, *p.p.*, commend.
commend′ing, *pr.p.*, commend.
commen′sal, *adj.*, sharing the same table.
commensurabil′ity, *n.*, the quality of being commensurable.
commen′surable, *adj.*, reducible to the same measure.
commen′surate, *adj.*, equal, proportionate.
commensura′tion, *n.*, the act of reducing to a common measure.

com'ment, *v.i.*, to remark on, make notes on; *n.*, an annotation, explanation.

com'mentary, *n.*, an exposition.

com'mentate, *v.t.*, to write expository notes.

commenta'tion, *n.*, the act of commenting.

com'mentator, *n.*, an expositor, annotator.

com'mented, *p.p.*, comment.

com'menter, *n.*, one who comments.

com'menting, *pr.p.*, comment.

commenti'tious, *adj.*, of the nature of a commentary.

com'merce, *n.*, trade, dealing, intercourse; *v.i.*, to have intercourse.

commer'cial, *adj.*, rel. to trade and commerce.

commer'cialism, *n.*, commercial ways, the commercial spirit.

commer'cialize, *v.t.*, to make commercial.

commer'cially, *adv.*, in the way of trade.

commina'tion, *n.*, a denouncement of sins and offences.

com'minatory, *adj.*, condemnatory.

commin'gle, *v.t.* and *i.*, to mingle together.

commin'gled, *p.p.*, commingle.

commin'gling, *pr.p.*, commingle.

com'minute, *v.t.*, to grind small, pulverize; *adj.*, ground small.

com'minuted, *p.p.*, comminute.

com'minuting, *pr.p.*, comminute.

comminu'tion, *n.*, the act or state of comminuting.

commis'erate, *v.t.*, to pity, compassionate

commis'erated, *p.p.*, commiserate.

commis'erating, *pr.p.*, commiserate.

commisera'tion, *n.*, the act of commiserating.

commis'erative, *adj.*, pitiful, compassionate.

commis'erator, *n.*, one who commiserates.

commissa'rial, *adj.*, rel. to commissary.

commissa'riat, *n.*, the provisioning department of an army.

com'missary, *n.*, a person charged with a commission, a delegate; an ordnance officer with honorary combatant rank.

com'missary - ***gen'eral***, *n.*, the head of the commissariat.

commis'sion, *v.t.*, to charge, entrust, authorize, *n.*, a charge, trust; the act of commissioning: a warrant; an appointment in the navy or the army; a body of commissioned persons.

commissionaire, *n.*, a military pensioner engaged as a messenger.

commis'sioned, *p.p.*, commission.

commis'sioner, *n.*, a member of a commission.

commis'sionership, *n.*, the office of a commissioner.

commis'sioning, *pr.p.*, commission.

com'missure, *n.*, a seam, point of union.

commit', *v.t.*, to entrust, consign, perpetrate, send to gaol or trial.

commit'ment, *n.*, *s.q.* committal; engagement, pledge.

commit'tal, *n.*, the act of committing.

commit'ted, *p.p.*, commit.

commit'tee, *n.*, a body of persons dealing with a particular business.

committee', *n.*, a person appointed to the guardianship of another's property.

commit'ter, *n.*, one who commits.

commit'ting, *pr.p.*, commit.

commit'tor, *n.*, one who commits.

commix', *v.t.* and *i.*, to intermingle.

commixed', *p.p.*, commix.

commix'ing, *pr.p.*, commix.

commix'tion, *n.*, the act or result of commixing.

commix'ture, *n.*, *s.q.* commixtion.

com'modate, *n.*, a form of loan, free of charge on return of loan undamaged.

commode', *n.*, a piece of furniture.

commo'dious, *adj.*, roomy, convenient, useful.

commo'diously, *adv.*, in a commodious way.

commo'diousness, *n.*, the quality of being commodious.

commod'ity, *n.*, something of use, an article of commerce; in *pl.*, goods, wares.

com'modore, *n.*, the commander of a naval squadron.

com'mon, *adj.*, belonging to two or more persons; vulgar; *n.*, an open space that is common property.

com'monable, *adj.*, having common pasturage rights.

com'monage, *n.*, pasturage rights.

com'monalty, *n.*, the collective people.

com'mon coun'cil, *n.*, the municipal body.

com'moner, *adj.*, *comp.* of common; *n.*, anyone not a peer; a M.P.; one who has joint rights in common lands; academically one who is admitted to commons but is not on the foundation.

com'monest, *adj.*, *super.* of common.

com'mon law, *n.*, English unwritten law.

com'monly, *adv.*, generally, usually, in common.

com'monness, *n.*, the quality of being common.

com'monplace, *adj.*, ordinary; *n.*, an obvious saying; anything ordinary.

com'monplace-book, *n.*, a book of notes for ready reference.

com'mons, *n.*, the name for food in the Oxford colleges; the common people of England; the House of Commons.

com'mon sense, *adj.*, marked by ordinary good sense; *n.*, sound sense, judgment.

com'monweal, *n.*, the well-being of the community; the commonwealth.

com'monwealth, *n.*, the body politic; in the Cromwellian usurpation it meant a republic.

com'morancy, *n.*, residence.

commo'tion, *n.*, tumult, disturbance.

com'munal, *adj.*, rel. to a commune.

com'munalize, *v.t.*, to make into a commune.

com'mune, *n.*, a self-governing community.

commune', *v.i.*, to hold intercourse.

communed', *p.p.*, commune.

communicabil'ity, *n.*, the state of being communicable.

commu'nicable, *adj.*, able to be communicated.

commu'nicant, *adj.*, communicating; *n.*, one who communicates in the Holy Eucharist.

commu'nicate, *v.t.*, to impart, reveal; *v.i.*, to share; to receive the Blessed Sacrament.

commu'nicated, *p.p.*, communicate.

commu'nicating, *pr.p.* communicate.

communica'tion, *n.*, the act of communicating; means of getting from place to place; news.

commu'nicative, *adj.*, fond of imparting information.

commu'nicator, *n.*, anything that communicates.

commu'nicatory, *adj.*, imparting information.

commu'ning, *pr.p.*, commune.

commun'ion, *n.*, intercourse, fellowship, a religious body, the reception of the Blessed Sacrament.

com'munism, *n.*, socialism.

com'munist, *n.*, an upholder of socialistic opinions.

communis'tic, *adj.*, rel. to communism.

commu'nity, *n.*, sharing a common society; a religious corporation.

com'munize, *v.t.*, to make public property.

commutabil'ity, *n.*, the quality of being commutable.

commu'table, *adj.*, able to be commuted.

commuta'tion, *n.*, the act of commuting; exchange.

commu'tative, *adj.*, rel. to commutation.

com'mutator, *n.*, contrivance for altering the course of an electrical current.

commute', *v.t.*, to exchange, buy off an obligation.

commu'ted, *p.p.*, commute.

commu'ter, *n.*, one who commutes.

commu'ting, *pr.p.*, commute.

compact', *v.t.*, to pack tight, press close; *adj.*, pressed close, solid.

com'pact, *n.*, an agreement.

compact'ed, *p.p.*, compact.

compact'edly, *adv.*, compactly.

compact'ing, *pr.p.*, compact.

compac'tion, *n.*, the state of being compacted.

compact'ly, *adv.*, closely, solidly.

compact'ness, *n.*, the quality of being compact.

compa'ges, *n.*, a structure of united parts; a joint (*Lat.*).

compag'inate, *v.t.*, to knit together.

compagina'tion, *n.*, the state of being compaginated.

compan'ion, *v.t.*, to accompany; *adj.*, attendant; *n.*, an associate, comrade; the shelter over the ship's ladder.

compan'ionable, *adj.*, sociable, agreeable.

compan'ionless, *n.*, without a companion.

compan'ionship, *n.*, the society of a comrade.

com'pany, *v.i.*, to associate with; *n.*, an assembly, society, fellowship, a trading firm, a crew, part of a regiment.

com'parable, *adj.*, able to be compared.

compar'ative, *adj.*, judged or measured by comparison; not positive; *n.*, the comparative degree.

compar'atively, *adv.*, by comparison; not positively.

compare', *v.t.*, to estimate one thing by reference to another; to examine; to form the degrees of comparison; *n.*, comparison.

compared', *p.p.*, compare.

compar'er, *n.*, one who compares.

compar'ing, *pr.p.*, compare.

compar'ison, *n.*, the act of comparing; a comparative estimate.

compart', *v.t.*, to subdivide.
compart'ed, *p.p.*, compart.
compart'ing, *pr.p.*, compart.
compart'ment, *n.*, a sub-division; a railway carriage; a panel.
com'pass, *v.t.*, to achieve, effect, encircle; *n.*, a circuit; enclosed space; a magnetic instrument determining the north; in *pl.*, instruments for drawing and dividing circles.
com'passable, *adj.*, able to be compassed.
com'passed, *p.p.*, compass.
com'passes, pl. compass.
com'passing, *pr.p.*, compass.
compas'sion, *n.*, pity, sympathy.
compas'sionate, *adj.*, pitiful, sympathetic.
compas'sionate, *v.t.*, to feel pity for.
compas'sionated, *p.p.*, compassionate.
compas'sionately, *adv.* with compassion.
compas'sionateness, *n.*, the quality of being compassionate.
compas'sionating, *pr.p.*, compassionate.
compatibil'ity, *n.*, the quality of being compatible.
compat'ible, *adj.*, consistent with, suitable.
compat'ibleness, *n.*, *i.q.*, compatibility.
compat'ibly, *adv.*, consistently, agreeably.
compat'riot, *n.*, a fellow-countryman.
compat'riotism, *n.*, the quality of fellow-countrymanship.
compel', *v.t.*, to force, drive.
compel'lable, *adj.*, able to be compelled.
compella'tion, *n.*, the act of addressing; a form of address.
compelled', *p.p.*, compel.
compel'ler, *n.*, anything that compels.
compel'ling, *pr.p.*, compel.
com'pend, *n.*, an abridgment.
compen'dious, *adj.*, summarized, abridged.
compen'diously, *adv.*, succinctly.
compen'diousness, *n.*, the quality of being compendious.
compen'dium, *n.*, an abridgment, summary.
com'pensate, *v.t.*, to remunerate, make amends for; *v.i.*, to make compensation.
com'pensated, *p.p.*, compensate.
com'pensating, *pr.p.*, compensate.
compensa'tion, *n.*, recompense, a set-off.
compen'sative, *adj.*, bringing recompense.
compen'satory, *adj.*, *i.q.*, compensative.
compete', *v.i.*, to contend in rivalry.
compet'ed, *p.p.*, compete.
com'petence, *n.*, ability, sufficiency.
com'petency, *n.*, *i.q.* competence.
com'petent, *n.*, sufficient, qualified.
com'petently, *adv.*, in a competent way.
compet'ing, *pr.p.*, compete.
competi'tion, *n.*, the act of competing, rivalry.
compet'itive, *adj.*, rel. to competition.
compet'itor, *n.*, one who competes.
compila'tion, *n.*, the act or result of compiling.
compile', *v.t.*, to bring together materials.
compiled', *p.p.*, compile.
compi'ler, *n.*, one who compiles.
compi'ling, *pr.p.*, compile.
compla'cence, *n.*, civility, affableness, self-satisfaction.
compla'cency, *n.*, *i.q.* complacence.
compla'cent, *adj.*, civil, affable.
compla'cently, *adv.*, in a complacent way.
complain', *v.i.*, to murmur, grumble, lament.
complain'ant, *n.*, a plaintiff.
complained', *p.p.*, complain.
complain'er, *n.*, one who complains.
complain'ing, *pr.p.*, complain.
complaint', *n.*, accusation, lament; ailment.
complais'ance, *n.*, courtesy.
complais'ant, *adj.*, courteous, agreeable.
complais'antly, *adv.*, in a complaisant way.
com'plement, *v.t.*, to complete a number or quantity; *n.*, the completion of a quantity or number.
complemen'tal, *adj.*, *i.q.* complementary.
complemen'tary, *adj.*, completing a quantity or number.
complete', *v.t.*, to perfect, finish; *adj.*, perfected, finished.
comple'ted, *p.p.*, complete.
complete'ly, *adv.*, entirely, wholly.
complete'ness, *n.*, the quality or state of being complete.
complet'ing, *pr.p.*, complete.
comple'tion, *n.*, the act or result of completing.
comple'tive, *adj.*, tending to completion.
comple'tory, *adj.*, *i.q.* completive.
com'plex, *adj.*, not simple, of many parts.
complex'ion, *n.*, colour of the skin, aspect.
complex'ional, *adj.*, rel. to the complexion.
complex'ioned, *adj.*, having a complexion.

complex'ity, *n.*, the state or quality of being complex.
com'plexness, *n.*, *i.q.* complexity.
complex'us, *n.*, the large muscle in the neck.
compli'able, *adj.*, *i.q.* compliant.
compli'ance, *n.*, an act of yielding; acquiescence.
compli'ant, *adj.*, ready to yield or acquiesce.
compli'antly, *adv.*, in a compliant way.
com'plicacy, *n.*, the state of being complicated.
com'plicate, *v.t.*, to involve, entangle; *adj.*, intricate.
com'plicated, *p.p.*, complicate.
com'plicating, *pr.p.*, complicate.
complica'tion, *n.*, the act or result of complicating.
complic'ity, *n.*, the being an accomplice.
complied', *p.p.*, comply.
compli'er, *n.*, one who complies.
com'pliment, *v.t.*, to praise, flatter; *n.*, praise, flattery.
compliment'al, *adj.*, *i.q.* complimentary.
compliment'ary, *adj.*, flattering.
com'plimenter, *n.*, one who pays compliments.
com'plin, com'pline, *n.*, the last day office of the Church.
complot, *v.i.*, to join in a plot; *n.*, a joint plot.
complot'ted, *p.p.*, complot.
complot'ter, *n.*, one who complots.
complot'ting, *pr.p.*, complot.
Compluten'sian, *adj.*, pert. to Complutum (in Spain) and the Polyglot Bible published there.
comply', *v.i.*, to yield, acquiesce.
comply'ing, *pr.p.*, comply.
com'po, *n.*, a sort of concrete; a material used in printing.
compo'nent, *adj.*, forming a part; *n.*, an ingredient.
comport', *v.t.*, to conduct, bear oneself; *v.i.*, to agree with.
comport'ed, *p.p.*, comport.
comport'ing, *pr.p.*, comport.
compose', *v.t.*, to put together, to write, to quiet, to arrange type.
composed', *p.p.*, compose; *adj.*, calm, self-possessed.
compo'sedly, *adv.*, calmly.
compo'sedness, *n.*, calmness, self-possession.
compo'ser, *n.*, one who composes a book or a piece of music.
compo'sing, *pr.p.*, compose.
com'posite, *adj.*, compound, made up of parts.
composi'tion, *n.*, the act or result of composing; an agreement, esp. for the acceptance by one's creditors of a smaller amount than the debt.
compos'itive, *adj.*, compound.
compos'itor, *n.*, a type-setter.
com'post, *n.*, a land-fertilizing mixture.
compo'sure, *n.*, calmness, sedateness.
compota'tion, *n.*, drinking in company.
com'pote, *n.*, stewed fruit.
compound', *v.t.*, to mix together; to settle; to condone; *v.i.*, to come to terms.
com'pound, *n.*, a mixture; the grounds of an Indian house; *adj.*, containing a mixture.
compound'able, *adj.*, able to be compounded.
compound'ed, *p.p.*, compound.
compound'er, *n.*, one who compounds.
compound'ing, *pr.p.*, compound.
compreca'tion, *n.*, a sharing in prayer; praying together.
comprehend', *v.t.*, to comprise; to understand.
comprehend'ed, *p.p.*, comprehend.
comprehend'er, *n.*, one who comprehends.
comprehend'ing, *pr.p.* comprehend.
comprehensibil'ity, *n.*, the state or quality of being comprehensible.
comprehen'sible, *adj.*, able to be comprehended.
comprehen'sibly, *adv.*, in a comprehensible way.
comprehen'sion, *n.*, the act or state of comprehending.
comprehen'sive, *adj.*, embracing, full.
comprehen'sively, *adv.* in a comprehensive way.
comprehen'siveness, *n.*, the quality of being comprehensive.
compress', *v.t.*, to press together.
com'press, *n.*, a surgical pad.
compressed', *p.p.*, compress.
compressibil'ity, *n.*, the quality of being compressible.
compress'ible, *adj.*, able to be compressed.
compress'ibleness, *n.*, *i.q.* compressibility.
compress'ing, *pr.p.*, compress.
compres'sion, *n.*, the act or result of compressing.
compress'ive, *adj.*, compressing.
compress'or, *n.*, anything that compresses.
compress'ure, *n.*, *i.q.* compression.
compris'al, *n.*, the act of comprising.
comprise', *v.t.*, to contain, include.
comprised', *p.p.*, comprise.

compris'ing, *pr.p.*, comprise.

com'promise, *v.t.*, to involve in risk; to settle by mutual concessions; *v.i.*, to make a compromise; *n.*, a settlement by mutual concessions.

com'promised, *p.p.*, compromise.

com'promiser, *n.*, one who compromises.

com'promising, *pr.p.*, compromise.

compromit', *v.t.*, to imperil, compromise.

compromit'ted, *p.p.*, compromit.

compromit'ting, *pr.p.* compromit.

compt'ograph, *n.*, a machine for adding up figures.

comptoir', *n.*, a counting-house, factory.

comptom'eter, *n.*, an adding machine.

comptrol'ler, *n.*, an examiner of public accounts. Also spelt *controller*.

compul'satory, *adj.*, forcible.

compul'sion, *n.*, the act of compelling, force.

compul'sive, *adj.*, compelling.

compul'sively, *adv.*, with compulsion.

compul'siveness, *n.*, the quality of being compulsive.

compul'sorily, *adv.*, by compulsion.

compul'sory, *adj.*, using compulsion, obligatory.

compunc'tion, *n.*, remorse, contrition.

compunc'tious, *adj.*, feeling compunction.

compurga'tion, *n.*, joint testimony to clear an accused person.

com'purgator, *n.*, one who testifies with others to clear an accused person.

compu'table, *adj.*, able to be computed.

computa'tion, *n.*, an estimate, reckoning.

compute', *v.t.*, to estimate, reckon.

compu'ted, *p.p.*, compute.

compu'ter, *n.*, one who computes.

compu'ting, *pr.p.*, compute.

com'rade, *n.*, a companion.

Com'tist, *n.*, a follower of Comte, a positivist; *adj.*, rel. to Comte and the positive philosophy.

con, *v.t.*, to peruse, study; *prep.*, short for Lat. *contra*, against; Italian word = with.

cona'tion, *n.*, endeavour.

cona'tive, *adj.*, endeavouring.

cona'tus, *n.*, an attempt (*Lat.*).

coax'ial, *adj.*, having the same axis.

concam'erate, *v.t.*, to divide into chambers.

concat'enate, *v.t.*, to link together.

concat'enated, *p.p.*, concatenate.

concat'enating, *pr.p.*, concatenate.

concatena'tion, *n.*, the act of concatenating; a series.

con'cave, *adj.*, with a curved hollow.

con'caved, *adj.*, *s.q.* concave.

con'cavely, *adv.*, in a concave way.

con'caveness, *n.*, the quality or state of being concave.

concav'ity, *n.*, *s.q.*, concaveness.

conceal', *v.t.*, to hide, cover.

conceal'able, *adj.*, able to be concealed.

concealed', *p.p.*, conceal.

conceal'er, *n.*, one who conceals.

conceal'ing, *pr.p.*, conceal.

conceal'ment, *n.*, the act of concealing; a hiding-place.

concede', *v.t.*, to grant, give up.

conce'ded, *p.p.*, concede.

conce'ding, *pr.p.*, concede.

conceit', *n.*, a notion; a quaint idea; vanity.

conceit'ed, *adj.*, vain.

conceit'edly, *adv.*, in a vain way.

conceit'edness, *n.*, the quality of being conceited.

conceiv'able, *adj.*, able to be conceived.

conceiv'ableness, *n.*, the quality of being conceivable

conceive', *v.t.*, to think, understand, form in the mind or in the womb; *v.i.*, to think; to become pregnant.

conceived', *p.p.*, conceive.

conceiv'er, *n.*, one who conceives.

conceiv'ing, *pr.p.*, conceive.

concent', *n.*, song in harmony.

con'centrate, *v.t.*, to bring to a common centre; to apply fixedly; to condense; *v.i.*, to fix all one's attention.

con'centrated, *p.p.*, concentrate.

con'centrating, *pr.p.*, concentrate.

concentra'tion, *n.*, the act or quality of being concentrated.

concen'trative, *adj.*, fixing (the mind) on one object.

concen'trativeness, *n.*, the quality of being concentrative.

con'centrator, *n.*, an apparatus for separating ore; an arrangement for narrowing the muzzle of a shot-gun.

concen'tre, **concen'ter**, *v.t.* and *i.*, to bring, or come, to the same centre.

concen'tric, *adj.*, having a common centre.

concen'trical, *adj.*, *s.q.* concentric.

concentric'ity, *n.*, the quality of being concentric.

con'cept, *n.*, an abstract conception.

concep'tacle, *n.*, that which contains: a follicle.

concep'tion, *n.*, the act of conceiving in the womb or in the mind; an idea.
concep'tive, *adj.*, capable of conception.
concern', *v.t.*, to relate to, to interest, to perturb; *n.*, business, solicitude.
concerned', *p.p.*, concern.
concern'edly, *adv.*, anxiously.
concern'ing, *pr.p.*, concern; *prep.*, with reference to.
concern'ment, *n.*, solicitude, business.
concert', *v.t.*, to arrange in association with someone.
con'cert, *n.*, a musical entertainment; concord; union.
concertan'te, *n.*, an orchestral piece with solo instruments.
concert'ed, *p.p.*, concert.
concerti'na, *n.*, a reed instrument.
concert'ing, *pr.p.*, concert.
concer'to, *n.*, a musical work for orchestra and solo instrument or instruments.
con'cert-pitch, *n.*, the standard musical pitch for concerts.
conces'sion, *n.*, the act of conceding; something conceded; territorial and other rights conceded by a government to a foreigner.
conces'sionary, *adj.*, rel. to concession.
conces'sionist, *n.*, one who favours concession.
conces'sive, *adj.*, conceding.
concess'sory, *adj.*, s.q. concessive.
conch, *n.*, a sea-shell.
con'cha, *n.*, the outer ear.
Conchif'era, *n.pl.*, the class name of bivalve molluscs.
conchif'erous, *adj.*, pert. to the Conchifera.
con'chite, *n.*, a fossil shell.
con'choid, *adj.*, curved like a shell; *n.*, a curve like a shell.
conchoi'dal, *adj.*, s.q. conchoid.
concholog'ical, *adj.*, rel. to conchology.
conchol'ogist, *n.*, a student of conchology.
conchol'ogy, *n.*, the science of molluscs and shells.
conchom'eter, *n.*, an instrument for measuring shells.
concierge', *n.*, a door-keeper (*Fr.*).
concil'iate, *v.t.*, to win over; reconcile.
concil'iated, *p.p.*, conciliate.
concil'iating, *pr.p.*, conciliate.
concilia'tion, *n.*, the act of conciliating.
concil'iator, *n.*, one who conciliates.
concil'iatory, *adj.*, tending to conciliation.
concin'nity, *n.*, agreeableness, elegance.
concise', *adj.*, terse, brief.
concise'ly, *adv.*, tersely, briefly.
concise'ness, *n.*, terseness, brevity.
conci'sion, *n.*, a cutting; abbreviation.
con'clave, *n.*, a private assembly.
conclude', *v.t.*, to close, end; to infer; settle.
conclu'ded, *p.p.*, conclude.
conclud'er, *n.*, one who concludes.
conclu'ding, *pr.p.*, conclude.
conclu'sion, *n.*, the act of ending; an end; an inference.
conclu'sive, *adj.*, final, decisive.
conclu'sively, *adv.*, decisively.
conclu'siveness, *n.*, the quality of being conclusive.
conclu'sory, *adj.*, s.q. conclusive.
concoct', *v.t.*, to mix with ingredients; to plot.
concoct'ed, *p.p.*, concoct.
concoct'er, *n.*, one who concocts.
concoct'ing, *pr.p.*, concoct.
concoc'tion, *n.*, the act or result of concocting.
concoc'tive, *adj.*, pert. to concocting.
concom'itance, *n.*, the state of being concomitant.
concom'itant, *adj.*, associated with, following, attendant; *n.*, an attendant circumstance.
con'cord, *n.*, harmony, agreement.
concord'ance, *n.*, an agreement; a dictionary of words and passages with reference marks.
concord'ant, *adj.*, agreeable to, in harmony.
concord'antly, *adv.*, agreeably, harmoniously.
concord'at, *n.*, a formal agreement between the Holy See and a secular power.
con'course, *n.*, an arrival together, a gathering, crowd.
concres'cence, *n.*, a growing together.
concres'cible, *n.*, able to grow together.
concrete, *v.t.*, to solidify; *adj.*, solid; not abstract; *n.*, a mass of lime, sand, etc.
concre'ted, *p.p.*, concrete; *adj.*, laid down with concrete.
con'cretely, *n.*, not abstractly.
con'creteness, *n.*, the quality of being concrete.
concre'ting, *pr.p.*, concrete.
concre'tion, *n.*, the act of concreting; a solidified mass.
concre'tional, *adj.*, rel. to concretion.
concre'tionary, *adj.*, marked by concretions.
concre'tive, *adj.*, tending to concretion.
concre'tor, *n.*, an apparatus for solidifying cane-juice.
concu'binage, *n.*, cohabitation without marriage.

concu'binary, *adj.*, rel. to concubinage.

con'cubine, *n.*, an unmarried woman cohabiting with a man.

concu'piscence, *n.*, carnal appetite.

concu'piscent, *adj.*, having carnal appetite.

concur', *v.i.*, to agree with, coincide.

concurred', *p.p.*, concur.

concur'rence, *n.*, the act or result of concurring.

concur'rent, *adj.*, coincident, simultaneous, acting in conjunction; *n.*, a contributory cause.

concur'rently, *adv.*, simultaneously, jointly.

concur'ring, *pr.p.*, concur.

concus'sion, *n.*, a shock, result of shock.

concus'sive, *adj.*, causing concussion.

condemn', *v.t.*, to find guilty, censure.

condem'nable, *adj.*, worthy of condemnation.

condemna'tion, *n.*, the act of condemning, censure.

condem'natory, *adj.*, expressing condemnation.

condemned', *p.p.*, condemn.

condemn'er, *n.*, one who condemns.

condemn'ing, *pr.p.*, condemn.

condensabil'ity, *n.*, the state or quality of being condensable.

condens'able, *adj.*, able to be condensed.

condens'ate, *v.t.*, to compress.

condens'ated, *p.p.*, condensate.

condens'ating, *pr.p.*, condensate.

condensa'tion, *n.*, the act or result of condensing.

condens'ative, *adj.*, producing condensation.

condense', *v.t.*, to compress; *v.i.*, to become dense.

condensed', *p.p.*, condense.

condens'er, *n.*, an apparatus for condensing gases; a storer of electricity; a concentrating lens.

condens'ing, *pr.p.*, condense.

condescend', *v.i.*, to come down, stoop, deign.

condescend'ed, *p.p.*, condescend.

condescend'ing, *pr.p.*, condescend.

condescend'ingly, *adv.* with condescension.

condescen'sion, *n.*, the act or state of condescending.

condign', *adj.*, thoroughly deserved.

condign'ly, *adv.*, deservedly.

condign'ness, *n.*, the quality of being condign.

con'diment, *n.*, a seasoning.

condi'tion, *v.t.*, to stipulate, to impose limitations; *n.*, a stipulation, limiting circumstance, state, etc.

condi'tional, *adj.*, depending on conditions.

condi'tionally, *adv.*, with limitations.

condi'tioned, *p.p.*, condition.

condi'tioning, *pr.p.*, condition.

condo'latory, *adj.*, conveying condolence.

condole', *v.i.*, to express sympathy with one in distress.

condoled', *p.p.*, condole.

condole'ment, *n.*, *i.q.* condolence.

condo'lence, *n.*, the act of condoling.

condo'ler, *n.*, one who condoles.

condo'ling, *pr.p.*, condole.

condona'tion, *n.*, the act of condoning.

condone', *v.t.*, to pardon, overlook.

condoned', *p.p.*, condone.

condon'ing, *pr.p.*, condone.

con'dor, *n.*, the great vulture of the Andes.

condottie're, *n.*, an Italian mercenary soldier.

conduce', *v.i.*, to promote an end, contribute to.

conduced', *p.p.*, conduce.

conducibil'ity, *n.*, the quality of being conducible.

condu'cible, *adj.*, tending to promote, contributory.

condu'cing, *pr.p.*, conduce.

condu'cive, *adj.*, *i.q.* conducible.

conduct', *v.t.*, to lead, direct; behave; transmit.

con'duct, *n.*, behaviour, management, right of passage.

conduct'ed, *p.p.*, conduct.

conductibil'ity, *n.*, the quality of being conductible.

conduct'ible, *adj.*, able to be conducted.

conduct'ing, *pr.p.*, conduct.

conduc'tion, *n.*, transmission by a conductor.

conduct'ive, *adj.*, conducting.

conductiv'ity, *n.*, the quality of being conductive.

conduct'or, *n.*, anything that conducts; a guide, guard on an omnibus; a transmitting medium.

conduct'ress, *n.*, fem. of conductor.

con'duit, *n.*, a water-pipe, canal for bringing water.

condu'plicate, *adj.*, doubled together.

con'dyle, *n.*, the round end of a bone.

con'dyloid, *adj.*, like, or rel. to, a condyle.

cone, *n.*, a solid body shaped like a sugar-loaf; the fruit of certain trees, as the pine.

cones, *n.*, a fine flour.

co'ney, *n.*, a rabbit.

confab'ulate, *v.i.*, to chat together.
confab'ulated, *p.p.*, confabulate.
confab'ulating, *pr.p.*, confabulate.
confabula'tion, *n.*, a chat.
confec'tion, *n.*, a sweet; something compounded with sugar; a dainty creation in millinery.
confec'tionary, *adj.*, rel. to confections.
confec'tioner, *n.*, one who makes and sells sweets.
confec'tionery, *n.*, sweetmeats, cakes, etc.
confed'eracy, *n.*, a league of any description.
confed'erate, *v.t.* and *i.*, to unite in a league.
confed'erate, *adj.*, united in a league; *n.*, a member of a confederation; an accomplice.
confed'erated, *p.p.*, confederate.
confed'erating, *pr.p.*, confederate.
confedera'tion, *n.*, the act of confederating; a league; an association of once independent states.
confed'erative, *adj.*, leading to confederation.
confer', *v.t.*, to bestow; *v.i.*, to consult with; hold conversation.
con'ference, *n.*, the act of conferring; a gathering for discussion; a lecture.
conferred', *p.p.*, confer.
confer'rer, *n.*, one who confers.
confer'ring, *pr.p.*, confer.
confess', *v.t.*, to own, admit; to hear confession; to make confession.
confess'ant, *n.*, one who confesses.
confessed', *p.p.*, confess.
confes'sedly, *adv.*, admittedly.
confess'ing, *pr.p.*, confess.
confes'sion, *n.*, the act of confessing; an avowal.
confes'sional, *adj.*, rel. to confession; *n.*, the place where confessions are heard; the system of confession.
confes'sionary, *adj.*, rel. to confession.
confess'or, *n.*, one who confesses; one who avows his faith at the risk of life; a priest who hears confessions.
confet'ti, *n. pl.*, comfits; pellets.
confidant', **confidante'**, *n.*, the sharer of one's secrets.
confide', *v.t.*, to entrust; *v.i.*, to repose trust in.
confi'ded, *p.p.*, confide.
con'fidence, *n.*, a feeling of trust; reliance.
con'fident, *adj.*, trustful, reliant.
confiden'tial, *adj.*, worthy of trust; said or done in confidence or secret.
con'fidently, *adv.*, with confidence.
confi'der, *n.*, one who confides.
confi'ding, *pr.p.*, confide.
config'urate, *v.t.*, to shape, fashion.
config'urated, *p.p.*, configurate.
config'urating, *pr.p.*, configurate.
configura'tion, *n.*, outward shape; relative position.
config'ure, *v.t.*, to shape according to a pattern.
config'ured, *p.p.*, configure.
confi'nable, *adj.*, able to be confined.
confine', *v.t.*, to place within limits; to imprison. In the passive, to be brought to child-bed.
con'fine, *n.*, a frontier.
confined', *p.p.*, confine.
confine'ment, *n.*, the act of confining; the state of being confined; child-bed.
confi'ner, *n.*, one who confines.
confi'ning, *pr.p.*, confine.
confirm', *v.t.*, to strengthen, support, ratify; to administer the Sacrament of Confirmation.
confirm'able, *adj.*, able to be confirmed.
confirma'tion, *n.*, the act of confirming; a further proof; the Sacrament of Confirmation.
confirm'ative, *adj.*, attesting.
confirm'atively, *adv.*, in a confirmative way.
confirm'atory, *adj.*, *i.q.* confirmative.
confirmed', *p.p.*, confirm.
confirm'edly, *adv.*, with confirmation.
confirmee', *n.*, a person confirmed or to whom something is confirmed.
confirm'er, *n.*, one who confirms.
confirm'ing, *pr.p.*, confirm.
confis'cable, *adj.*, able to be confiscated.
con'fiscate, *v.t.*, to appropriate to the public treasury.
con'fiscated, *p.p.*, confiscate.
con'fiscating, *pr.p.*, confiscate.
confisca'tion, *n.*, the act or result of confiscating.
con'fiscator, *n.*, one who confiscates.
confis'catory, *adj.*, in the nature of confiscation.
conflagra'tion, *n.*, a fire on a great scale.
conflict', *v.i.*, to fight, to be inconsistent with.
con'flict, *n.*, a fight.
conflict'ed, *p.p.*, conflict.
conflict'ing, *pr.p.*, conflict.
conflict'ive, *adj.*, conflicting.
con'fluence, *n.*, a meeting; the junction of two streams.
con'fluent, *adj.*, flowing to the same

point; *n.*, a tributary stream.

con'flux, *n.*, the junction of streams; a meeting.

conform', *v.t.*, to make alike, adapt; *v.i.*, to comply with.

conformabil'ity, *n.*, the state or quality of being conformable.

conform'able, *adj.*, compliant, corresponding.

conform'ably, *adv.*, correspondingly, compliantly.

conforma'tion, *n.*, structure.

conformed', *p.p.*, conform.

conform'ing, *pr.p.*, conform.

conform'ist, *n.*, one who conforms.

conform'ity, *n.*, compliance, resemblance.

confound', *v.t.*, to mix together, amaze, confuse.

confound'ed, *p.p.*, confound.

confound'er, *n.*, one who confounds.

confound'ing, *pr.p.*, confound.

confrater'nity, *n.*, a brotherhood.

confrère', *n.*, a colleague, associate.

confront', *v.t.*, to face, oppose.

confront'ed, *p.p.*, confront.

confront'er, *n.*, one who confronts.

confront'ing, *pr.p.*, confront.

Confu'cian, *adj.*, rel. to Confucius and his philosophy.

confuse', *v.t.*, to blend, jumble together, perplex, muddle.

confused', *p.p.*, confuse.

confu'sedly, *adv.*, in a confused way.

confu'sedness, *n.*, the state of being confused.

confu'sing, *pr.p.*, confuse.

confu'sion, *n.*, the act of confusing; tumult, disorder.

confu'sional, *adj.*, rel. to confusion.

confu'table, *adj.*, able to be confuted.

confuta'tion, *n.*, the act or result of confuting.

confute', *v.t.*, to convict of error.

confu'ted, *p.p.*, confute.

confu'ter, *n.*, one who confutes.

confu'ting, *pr.p.*, confute.

congé, *n.*, a bow; leave-taking permission.

congeal', *v.t.* and *i.*, to freeze, harden.

congeal'able, *adj.*, able to be congealed.

congealed', *p.p.*, congeal.

congeal'ing, *pr.p.*, congeal.

congeal'ment, *n.*, the act or effect of congealing.

con'gee, *n.*, boiled rice, rice-water.

congela'tion, *n.*, the act of congealing.

con'gener, *n.*, one of the same stock.

congener'ic, *adj.*, of the same stock.

conge'nial, *adj.*, of the same nature, agreeable.

congenial'ity, *n.*, the quality of being congenial.

conge'nialness, *n.*, *i.q.* congeniality.

congen'ital, *adj.*, existing at or from birth.

con'ger, *n.*, a sea-eel.

con'ger-eel', *n.*, *i.q.* conger.

conge'ries, *n.*, a mass of particles.

congest', *v.t.*, to accumulate.

congest'ed, *p.p.*, congest; *adj.*, crowded up; with an undue accumulation of blood.

congest'ible, *adj.*, able to be congested.

conges'tion, *n.*, overcrowding, stoppage; undue accumulation of blood.

congest'ive, *adj.*, causing congestion.

con'globate, *adj.*, spherical.

congloba'tion, *n.*, the act or effect of making spherical.

conglob'ulate, *adj.*, made spherical.

conglom'erate, *adj.*, gathered into a round mass; *n.*, a rock consisting of rounded and water-worn stones; *v.t.* and *i.*, to gather into a round mass.

conglom'erated, *p.p.*, conglomerate.

conglom'erating, *pr.p.*, conglomerate.

conglomera'tion, *n.*, the act or effect of conglomerating; a mixture.

conglu'tinant, *adj.*, cementing together.

conglu'tinate, *v.t.*, to cement together; to form into a single mass.

conglu'tinated, *p.p.*, conglutinate.

conglu'tinating, *pr.p.*, conglutinate.

conglutina'tion, *n.*, the act or effect of conglutinating.

conglu'tinative, *adj.*, causing conglutination.

Con'go, *n.*, the region so called.

con'gou, *n.*, a species of black China tea.

congrat'ulant, *adj.*, *i.q.* congratulatory.

congrat'ulate, *v.t.*, to felicitate, wish joy to.

congrat'ulated, *p.p.*, congratulate.

congrat'ulating, *pr.p.*, congratulate.

congratula'tion, *n.*, the act of congratulating.

congrat'ulator, *n.*, one who congratulates.

congrat'ulatory, *adj.*, expressing congratulation.

con'gregate, *v.t.*, to bring together; *v.i.*, to meet together.

con'gregated, *p.p.*, congregate.

con'gregating, *pr.p.*, congregate.

congrega'tion, *n.*, the act of congregating; an assembly.

congrega'tional, *adj.*, rel. to congregation.

Congrega'tionalism, *n.*, the Congregational system.

Congrega'tionalist, *n.*, one who adheres to Congregationalism.

con'gress, *n.*, a meeting, a legislative assembly.

congres'sional, *adj.*, rel. to congress.

congres'sionist, *n.*, one who supports a congress.

con'greve, *n.*, a rocket.

con'gruence, *n.*, the state or quality of being congruent.

con'gruent, *adj.*, accordant, suited.

congru'ity, *n.*, fitness, agreement.

con'gruous, *adj.*, *i.q.* congruent.

con'gruously, *adv.*, agreeably, in accordance.

con'gruousness, *n.*, *i.q.* congruity.

con'ic, *adj.*, cone-shaped, rel. to a cone.

con'ical, *adj.*, *i.q.* conic.

con'ically, *adv.*, in the form of a cone.

con'ic sec'tions, *n.*, the department of mathematics rel. to ellipses, parabolas and hyperbolas.

co'nifer, *n.*, a cone-bearing plant.

Conif'erae, *n.*, the family of conifers.

conif'erous, *adj.*, cone-bearing.

co'niform, *adj.*, cone-shaped.

conjec'turable, *adj.*, able to be conjectured.

conjec'tural, *adj.*, dubious; guessed.

conjec'ture, *v.t.*, to guess, surmise; *n.*, a guess, surmise.

conjec'tured, *p.p.*, conjecture.

conjec'turer, *n.*, one who conjectures.

conjec'turing, *pr.p.*, conjecture.

conjoin', *v.t.*, to join together.

conjoined', *p.p.*, conjoin.

conjoin'ing, *pr.p.*, conjoin.

conjoint', *adj.*, united in combination.

conjoint'ly, *adv.*, together.

conjoint'ness, *n.*, the state of being conjoint.

con'jugal, *adj.*, rel. to marriage.

conjugal'ity, *n.*, the state of marriage.

con'jugate, *v.t.*, to join; to inflect a verb; *adj.*, of kindred meaning.

con'jugated, *p.p.*, conjugate.

con'jugating, *pr.p.*, conjugate.

conjuga'tion, *n.*, union; the inflection of a verb.

conjuga'tional, *adj.*, rel. to conjugation.

conjunct', *adj.*, united, in association.

conjunc'tion, *n.*, the act or result of conjoining; a part of speech denoting a word that connects words and sentences.

conjunc'tional, *adj.*, rel. to a conjunction.

conjuncti'va, *n.*, the mucous membrane within the eyelid.

conjunc'tive, *adj.*, uniting; connected; *n.*, the grammatical mood so named.

conjunc'tively, *adv.*, in union.

conjunc'ture, *n.*, a point of time at which various circumstances or causes meet.

conjura'tion, *n.*, the act of conjuring; an incantation.

con'jure, *v.i.*, to practise a conjurer's arts.

conjure', *v.t.*, to bind by an oath; to exhort solemnly.

con'jured, *p.p.*, con'jure.

conjured', *p.p.*, conjure'.

con'jurer, *n.*, one who does tricks of sleight of hand.

conjur'er, *n.*, one who conjures'.

con'juring, *pr.p.*, con'jure.

conjur'ing, *pr.p.*, conjure'.

conjur'or, *n.*, one who takes oath in company.

connas'cent, *adj.*, having a common origin.

con'nate, *adj.*, united in the same body.

connat'ural, *adj.*, sharing the same nature.

connat'uralize, *v.t.*, to make of similar nature.

connect', *v.t.*, to join, bind.

connect'ed, *p.p.*, connect; *adj.*, coherent.

connect'edly, *adv.*, in a connected way.

connect'ing, *pr.p.*, connect.

connec'tion, *n.*, the act or result of connecting; a relation by marriage; intercourse; association; a religious body.

connect'ive, *adj.*, connecting; *n.*, that which connects.

connect'ively, *adv.*, in a connective way.

connect'or, *n.*, that which connects.

conned, *p.p.*, con.

con'ner, *n.*, one who cons.

connex'ion, *n.*, *i.q.* connection.

con'ning, *pr.p.*, con; *n.*, the act of directing a steersman.

con'ning-tower, *n.*, the pilot-house in an armoured ship.

conni'vance, *n.*, assumed ignorance of a plot; winking at a fault.

connive', *v.i.*, to wink at; to share secretly in a plot.

connived', *p.p.*, connive.

conni'ver, *n.*, one who connives.

conni'ving, *pr.p.*, connive.

connoisseur', *n.*, an expert judge in the fine arts.

connota'tion, *n.*, the implication of qualities.

connote', *v.t.*, to imply qualities or attributes.

conno'ted, *p.p.*, connote.

conno'ting, *pr.p.*, connote.

connu'bial, *adj.*, rel. to married life.

connubial'ity, *n.*, the connubial state.

connumera'tion, *n.*, the act of numbering together.

co'noid, *adj.*, cone-like; *n.*, anything cone-like.

conoi'dal, *adj.*, *i.q.* conoid.

conoi'dic, *adj.*, *i.q.* conoid.

co'noscope, *n.*, an instrument for examining crystals.

con'quer, *v.t.*, to overcome; *v.i.*, to win a victory.

con'querable, *adj.*, able to be conquered.

con'quered, *p.p.*, conquer.

con'quering, *pr.p.*, conquer.

con'queror, *n.*, one who conquers.

con'quest, *n.*, the act of conquering; victory.

consanguin'eal, *adj.*, *i.q.* consanguineous.

consanguin'eous, *adj.*, related in blood.

consanguin'ity, *n.*, relationship in blood.

con'science, *n.*, sense of right and wrong.

conscien'tious, *adj.*, having a conscience; scrupulous.

conscien'tiously, *n.*, scrupulously, exactly.

conscien'tiousness, *n.*, the quality of being conscientious.

con'scionable, *adj.*, in accordance with conscience; reasonable.

con'scious, *adj.*, aware; in possession of one's faculties.

con'sciously, *adv.*, with full knowledge.

con'sciousness, *n.*, the state or quality of being conscious.

conscript', *v.t.*, to enroll for military service.

con'script, *adj.*, enlisted; *n.*, one enlisted by conscription.

conscrip'tion, *n.*, the act of conscripting; compulsory service.

con'secrate, *v.t.*, to set apart for a sacred purpose; *adj.*, set apart.

con'secrated, *p.p.*, consecrate.

con'secrating, *pr.p.*, consecrate.

consecra'tion, *n.*, the act of consecrating.

con'secrator, *n.*, one who consecrates.

consec'tary, *adj.*, logically following; *n.*, a corollary.

consecu'tion, *n.*, consequence.

consec'utive, *adj.*, following in order.

consec'utively, *adv.*, in a consecutive way.

consec'utiveness, *n.*, the state or quality of being consecutive.

consen'sual, *adj.*, rel. to agreement of opinion.

consen'sus, *n.*, an agreement of opinion.

consent', *v.i.*, to be of one mind; to comply; *n.*, acquiescence, concurrence.

consenta'neous, *adj.*, accordant.

consent'ed, *p.p.*, consent.

consent'er, *n.*, one who consents.

consen'tient, *adj.*, agreeing in opinion.

consent'ing, *pr.p.*, consent.

con'sequence, *n.*, a result, effect; importance.

con'sequent, *adj.*, resulting, following.

consequen'tial, *adj.*, following as a consequence; self-important.

consequen'tially, *adv.*, in a consequential way.

con'sequently, *adv.*, naturally, as a consequence.

conserv'able, *adj.*, able to be conserved.

conserv'ancy, *n.*, preservation.

conserva'tion, *n.*, the act of preserving.

conserv'atism, *n.*, the political principle of preserving what is good in old institutions.

Conserv'ative, *n.*, one who professes Conservatism.

conserv'ative, *adj.*, preserving; politically opposed to violent change.

conserv'atively, *adv.*, in a conservative mood.

conserv'atoire, *n.*, a music-teaching institution.

conserv'atory, *n.*, a greenhouse.

conserve', *v.t.*, to save, preserve.

conserved', *p.p.*, conserve.

conserv'ing, *pr.p.*, conserve.

consid'er, *v.t.*, to think over, deliberate, deem.

consid'erable, *adj.*, worthy of consideration; valuable; more than a little.

consid'erably, *adv.*, more than a little.

consid'erate, *adj.*, thoughtful for others.

consid'erately, *adv.*, with thought for others.

consid'erateness, *n.*, the state or quality of being considerate.

considera'tion, *n.*, deliberation; respect for a person's claims; a *quid pro quo*.

consid'ered, *p.p.*, consider.

consid'erer, *n.*, one who considers.

consid'ering, *pr.p.*, consider.

consign', *v.t.*, to entrust; hand over.

consigned', *p.p.*, consign.

consignee', *n.*, one to whom anything is consigned.

consign'er, *n.*, one who consigns.

consign'ing, *pr.p.*, consign.

consign'ment, *n.*, the

act of consigning; goods consigned.

consignor', *n.*, *i.q.* consigner.

consist', *v.i.*, to be composed of; to coexist; to agree.

consist'ed, *p.p.*, consist.

consist'ence, *n.*, degree of density; agreement.

consist'ency, *n.*, *i.q.* consistence; conformity with.

consist'ent, *adj.*, solid; in conformity with; firm in principle.

consist'ently, *adv.*, conformably.

consist'ing, *pr.p.*, consist.

consisto'rial, *adj.*, rel. to a consistory.

consis'tory, *n.*, an assembly; the meeting of Cardinals; the court of a diocesan bishop.

conso'ciate, *v.t.*, to take into one's society; *v.i.*, to be in company.

conso'ciated, *p.p.*, consociate.

conso'ciating, *pr.p.*, consociate.

consocia'tion, *n.*, the act of consociating.

consol'able, *adj.*, willing to be consoled.

consola'tion, *n.*, comfort, alleviation of sorrow.

consol'atory, *adj.*, offering consolation, comforting.

console', *v.t.*, to comfort, cheer.

con'sole, *n.*, an ornamental bracket under a cornice.

consoled', *p.p.*, console.

conso'ler, *n.*, one who consoles.

consol'idate, *v.t.*, to make solid, combine; *v.i.*, to become solid.

consol'idated, *p.p.*, consolidate.

consol'idating, *pr.p.*, consolidate.

consolida'tion, *n.*, the act or result of consolidating.

consol'idator, *n.*, anything that consolidates.

consol'idatory, *adj.*, tending to consolidate.

consol'ing, *pr.p.*, console.

consols', *n. pl.*, consolidated stocks in the British National Debt.

consommé', *n.*, clear soup.

con'sonance, *n.*, concord, harmony.

con'sonancy, *n.*, *i.q.* consonance.

con'sonant, *adj.*, in harmony, accordant; *n.*, a letter which is sounded with a vowel.

consonan'tal, *adj.*, rel. to consonants.

con'sonantly, *adv.*, agreeably, harmoniously.

con'sonous, *adj.*, *i.q.* consonant.

consort', *v.i.*, to join company with.

con'sort, *n.*, a wife or husband; an attendant ship.

consort'ed, *p.p.*, consort.

consort'ing, *pr.p.*, consort.

conspec'tus, *n.*, a general view, an abstract.

conspic'uous, *adj.*, plainly seen, eminent.

conspic'uously, *adv.*, visibly, eminently.

conspic'uousness, *n.*, the state or quality of being conspicuous.

conspir'acy, *n.*, a combined plot.

conspira'tion, *n.*, the act of conspiring.

conspir'ator, *n.*, one who joins a conspiracy.

conspire', *v.i.*, to join in a conspiracy.

conspired', *p.p.*, conspire.

conspir'er, *n.*, one who conspires.

conspir'ing, *pr.p.*, conspire.

con'stable, *n.*, a high official (as Constable of the Tower); a peace-officer.

constab'ulary, *n.*, the police force.

con'stancy, *n.*, firmness, stability.

con'stant, *adj.*, firm, unvarying; *n.*, an invariable quantity of force.

con'stantly, *adv.*, regularly, without variation.

con'stellate, *v.t.*, to arrange in constellations; to cover with constellations.

constella'tion, *n.*, a group of fixed stars.

consterna'tion, *n.*, alarm, amazement.

con'stipate, *v.t.*, to bind, to make costive.

con'stipated, *p.p.*, constipate; *adj.*, costive.

con'stipating, *pr.p.*, constipate.

constipa'tion, *n.*, costiveness.

constit'uency, *n.*, a body of electors; an electoral division.

constit'uent, *adj.*, elemental, essential; *n.*, a member of a constituency.

con'stitute, *v.t.*, to form, compose; to appoint, establish.

con'stituted, *p.p.*, constitute.

con'stituting, *pr.p.*, constitute.

constitu'tion, *n.*, the act of constituting; that which is constituted; the fundamental laws of a nation; bodily condition.

constitu'tional, *adj.*, rel. to the constitution; fundamental; *n.*, a walk for exercise.

constitu'tionalism, *n.*, loyalty to the constitution.

constitu'tionalist, *n.*, an upholder of the constitution.

constitu'tionally, *adv.*, in accordance with the constitution.

constitu'tionist, *n.*, *i.q.* constitutionalist.

con'stitutive, *adj.*, essential, component.

con'stitutively, *adv.*, essentially.

con'stitutor, *n.*, that which constitutes.

constrain', *v.t.*, to compel, coerce.

constrain'able, *adj.*, able to be constrained.

constrained', *p.p.*, constrain.

constrain'er, *n.*, one who constrains.

constrain'ing, *pr.p.*, constrain.

constraint', *n.*, the act or effect of constraining; confinement.

constrict', *v.t.*, to narrow, cramp.

constrict'ed, *p.p.*, constrict.

constrict'ing, *pr.p.*, constrict.

constric'tion, *n.*, the act or effect of constricting.

constrict'ive, *adj.*, cramping, binding.

constrict'or, *n.*, that which constricts; the boa-constrictor.

constringe', *v.t.*, to contract, bind.

constringed', *p.p.*, constringe.

constrin'gent, *adj.*, binding, contracting.

constrin'ging, *pr.p.*, constringe.

construct', *v.t.*, to put together, build, compose.

construct'ed, *p.p.*, construct.

construct'er, *n.*, one who constructs.

construc'ting, *pr.p.*, construct.

construc'tion, *n.*, the act or result of constructing; an interpretation; the syntactical formation of a sentence.

construc'tional, *adj.*, rel. to construction.

construc'tionist, *n.*, one skilled in constructing.

construct'ive, *adj.*, with capacity for constructing; inferred.

construct'ively, *adv.*, in a constructive way.

construct'iveness, *n.*, capacity for constructing.

construct'or, *n.*, one who constructs.

con'strue, *v.t.*, to interpret, translate.

con'strued, *p.p.*, construe.

con'struing, *pr.p.*, construe.

consubstan'tial, *adj.*, of one substance or nature with.

consubstantial'ity, *n.*, the quality of being consubstantial.

consubstan'tiate, *v.t.*, to form into one substance with.

consubstan'tiated, *p.p.*, consubstantiate.

consubstan'tiating, *pr.p.*, consubstantiate.

consubstantia'tion, *n.*, the process by which, according to the Lutherans, the Body and Blood of Christ are consubstantiated with the elements of Bread and Wine.

con'suetude, *n.*, custom; intercourse.

consuetu'dinal, *adj.*, customary.

consuetu'dinary, *adj.*, *i.q.* consuetudinal.

con'sul, *n.*, a chief magistrate at Rome; the representative of a foreign State in another country, to look after the commercial interests and protect the subjects of his nation.

con'sulage, *n.*, the period of a consul's service.

con'sular, *adj.*, rel. to a consul.

con'sulate, *n.*, the office of a consul; a consul's official home.

con'sulship, *n.*, the office of a Roman consul.

consult', *v.t.*, to seek advice from, to deliberate with; regard.

consult'ant, *n.*, one who is consulted.

consulta'tion, *n.*, the act of consulting; the deliberation of two or more persons together.

consul'tative, *adj.*, deliberative.

consul'tatory, *adj.*, *i.q.* consultative.

consult'ed, *p.p.*, consult.

consult'er, *n.*, one who consults.

consult'ing, *pr.p.*, consult.

consu'mable, *adj.*, able to be consumed.

consume', *v.t.*, to destroy, devour; *v.i.*, to waste away.

consumed', *p.p.*, consume.

consu'mer, *n.*, one who consumes.

consu'ming, *pr.p.*, consume.

con'summate, *v.t.*, to accomplish, complete.

consum'mate, *adj.*, complete.

con'summated, *p.p.*, consummate.

consum'mately, *adv.*, completely, utterly.

con'summating, *pr.p.*, consummate.

consumma'tion, *n.*, the act or result of consummating; completion.

con'summator, *n.*, one who consummates.

consump'tion, *n.*, the act of consuming; decline.

consump'tive, *adj.*, causing consumption; suffering from phthisis.

consump'tively, *adv.*, in a consumptive way.

consump'tiveness, *n.*, the tendency to phthisis.

con'tact, *n.*, close touch, close union.

conta'gion, *n.*, disease conveyed by contact.

conta'gious, *adj.*, conveyed by contact.

conta'giously, *adv.*, in a contagious way.

conta'giousness, *n.*, the state of being contagious.

contain', *v.t.*, to hold within it, to hold up, keep within bounds; *v.i.*, to live continently.

contain'able, *adj.*, able to be contained.
contained', *p.p.*, contain.
contain'er, *n.*, that which contains.
contain'ing, *pr.p.*, contain.
contam'inable, *adj.*, able to be contaminated.
contam'inate, *v.t.*, to pollute, defile.
contam'inated, *p.p.*, contaminate.
contam'inating, *pr.p.*, contaminate.
contamina'tion, *n.*, pollution.
contam'inative, *adj.*, polluting.
contan'go, *n.*, a Stock Exchange term for the premium which a buyer pays to the broker for deferring settlement.
contemn', *v.t.*, to scorn, despise.
contemned', *p.p.*, contemn.
contem'ner, *n.*, one who contemns.
contemn'ing, *pr.p.*, contemn.
con'template, *v.t.*, to consider with attention, to think about, to intend.
con'templated, *p.p.*, contemplate.
con'templating, *pr.p.*, contemplate.
contempla'tion, *n.*, meditation, intention.
contem'plative, *adj.*, given to meditating.
contem'platively, *adv.*, thoughtfully.
contem'plativeness, *n.*, the state of being contemplative.
con'templator, *n.*, one who contemplates.
contempora'neous, *adj.*, existing at the same time with.
contempora'neousness, *n.*, coincidence in time.
contem'porary, *adj.* and *n.*, (one) of the same age or time.
contempt', *n.*, scorn, disregard.
contempt'ible, *adj.*, worthy of contempt.
contempt'ibly, *adv.*, in a contemptible way.
contemp'tuous, *adj.*, scornful, disdainful.
contemp'tuously, *adv.*, with contempt.
contemp'tuousness, *n.*, the state of being contemptuous.
contend', *v.i.*, to dispute, strive; affirm.
contend'ed, *p.p.*, contend.
contend'er, *n.*, one who contends.
contend'ing, *pr.p.*, contend.
content', *v.t.*, to gratify; *adj.*, satisfied; *n.*, what is contained; contented state.
content'ed, *p.p.*, content; *adj.*, satisfied.
content'edly, *adv.*, in a contented way.
content'edness, *n.*, the state of being contented.
content'ing, *pr.p.*, content.
conten'tion, *n.*, strife, argument.
conten'tious, *adj.*, leading to contention, quarrelsome.
conten'tiously, *adv.*, in a contentious way.
conten'tiousness, *n.*, the state or quality of being contentious.
content'ment, *n.*, contented state.
contents', *n.*, pl. of content.
conter'minable, *adj.*, able to be made conterminous.
conter'minous, *adj.*, bordering upon, contiguous.
contest', *v.t.* and *i.*, to dispute, litigate.
con'test, *n.*, a fight, struggle.
contest'able, *adj.*, debatable.
contest'ant, *n.*, one who contests.
contesta'tion, *n.*, disputation, emulation.
contest'ed, *p.p.*, contest.
contest'ing, *pr.p.*, contest.
con'text, *n.*, the whole from which a passage is quoted.
context'ual, *adj.*, rel. to context.
contex'tural, *adj.*, rel. to contexture.
contex'ture, *n.*, structure.
contigu'ity, *n.*, actual contact, close proximity.
contig'uous, *adj.*, closely adjacent.
contig'uously, *adv.*, adjacently.
con'tinence, *n.*, self-restraint, chastity.
con'tinency, *n.*, *i.q.* continence.
con'tinent, *adj.*, chaste; *n.*, the largest geographical division of land.
continen'tal, *adj.*, rel. to a continent.
con'tinently, *adv.*, chastely.
contin'gence, *n.*, *i.q.* contingency.
contin'gency, *n.*, chance, what may happen.
contin'gent, *adj.*, accidental, conditional; *n.*, something depending on chance; a body of troops.
contin'gently, *n.*, conditionally.
contin'uable, *adj.*, able to be continued.
contin'ual, *adj.*, continuing, lasting.
contin'ually, *adv.*, lastingly.
contin'uance, *n.*, permanence, duration.
contin'uant, *adj.*, continuing.
continua'tion, *n.*, the act or state of continuing; that which is continued.
contin'uative, *adj.*, continuing.
contin'uator, *n.*, one who continues.
contin'ue, *v.t.*, to carry on; *v.i.*, to persist, abide.
contin'ued, *p.p.*, continue.
contin'uer, *n.*, one who continues.
contin'uing, *pr.p.*, continue.
continu'ity, *n.*, the state of being continuous.
contin'uous, *adj.*,

uninterrupted, without a break.
contin'uously, *adv.*, uninterruptedly.
contort', *v.t.*, to twist.
contort'ed, *p.p.*, contort.
contort'ing, *pr.p.*, contort.
contor'tion, *n.*, a twisting, writhing.
contor'tionist, *n.*, a variety of acrobat.
con'tour, *v.t.*, to draw an outline; *n.*, outline.
con'tra, *prep.*, against (*Lat.*).
con'traband, *adj.*, illegal, prohibited.
contract', *v.t.*, to draw together, to narrow, to shorten; *v.i.*, to become shorter, to make an agreement.
con'tract, *n.*, an agreement.
contract'able, *adj.*, able to be contracted.
contract'ed, *p.p.*, contract.
contract'edly, *n.*, in a contracted way.
contract'edness, *n.*, the state of being contracted.
contractibil'ity, *n.*, the state or quality of being contractible.
contract'ible, *adj.*, able to be contracted.
contract'ile, *adj.*, having the power of contraction.
contractil'ity, *n.*, the state or quality of being contractile.
contract'ing, *pr.p.*, contract.
contrac'tion, *n.*, the act or result of contracting; abbreviation.
contract'or, *n.*, one who makes a contract.
contract'ual, *adj.*, of the nature of contract.
contrac'ture, *n.*, chronic shortening or stiffening.
con'tra-dance, *n.*, a country-dance in which the partners face one another.

contradict', *v.t.*, to gainsay, say the opposite to.
contradict'ed, *p.p.*, contradict.
contradict'ing, *pr.p.*, contradict.
contradic'tion, *n.*, the act of contradicting; denial.
contradic'tious, *adj.*, apt to contradict.
contradict'ive, *adj.*, *i.q.* contradictious.
contradict'orily, *adv.*, in a contradictory way.
contradict'ory, *adj.*, saying the opposite, giving the lie to, inconsistent with.
contradistinct', *adj.*, distinguished by opposite qualities.
contradistinc'tion, *n.*, distinguishing by opposite qualities.
contradistin'guish, *v.t.* to distinguish by opposite qualities.
contradistin'guished, *p.p.*, contradistinguish.
contradistin'guishing, *pr.p.*, contradistinguish.
contral'to, *n.*, the voice part between soprano and tenor; a contralto singer.
contrapun'tist, *n.*, a person skilled in counterpoint.
con'traries, *n. pl.*, opposites.
contrari'ety, *n.*, opposition, disagreement.
con'trarily, *n.*, in a contrary direction.
con'trariness, *n.*, *i.q.* contrariety.
con'trariwise, *adv.*, on the contrary, conversely.
con'trary, *adj.*, opposed, in an opposite direction; perverse; *n.*, something the opposite to others.
contrast', *v.t.*, to place in opposition or contrast.
con'trast, *n.*, opposition, dissimilitude.
contrast'ed, *p.p.*, contrast.
contrast'ing, *pr.p.*, contrast.

contravalla'tion, *n.*, a military defence-work made by the besiegers of a town.
contravene', *v.t.*, to transgress, to oppose.
contravened', *p.p.*, contravene.
contrave'ner, *n.*, one who contravenes.
contrave'ning, *pr.p.*, contravene.
contraven'tion, *n.*, the act of contravening.
con'tre-danse, *n.*, *see* contra-dance.
con'tretemps, *n.*, a mishap, a hitch.
contrib'ute, *v.t.*, to give to a common object or stock; *v.i.*, to lend support.
contrib'uted, *p.p.*, contribute.
contrib'uting, *pr.p.*, contribute.
contribu'tion, *n.*, the act of contributing; a share; a subscription; a writing in a review or paper.
contrib'utive, *adj.*, contributing.
contrib'utor, *n.*, one who contributes.
contrib'utory, *adj.*, *i.q.* contributive.
con'trite, *adj.*, repentant, sorry.
con'tritely, *adv.*, penitently.
contri'tion, *n.*, penitence, sorrow.
contri'vable, *adj.*, able to be contrived.
contri'vance, *n.*, the act of contriving; a device, apparatus.
contrive', *v.t.*, to devise, plan out, effect.
contrived', *p.p.*, contrive.
contri'ver, *n.*, one who contrives.
contri'ving, *pr.p.*, contrive.
control', *v.t.*, to check, guide, govern; *n.*, restraint, superintendence.
control'lable, *adj.*, subject to control.
controlled', *p.p.*, control.
control'ler, *n.*, one who controls; a device regulating an electric motor's

speed; a public official of accounts. Also *comptroller*.

control'lership, *n.*, the office of a controller.

control'ling, *pr.p.*, control.

control'ment, *n.*, the effect of controlling.

controver'sial, *adj.* rel. to controversy; disputatious.

controver'sialist, *n.*, one who engages in controversy.

con'troversy, *n.*, disputation.

controvert', *v.t.*, to oppose a statement; to refute.

controvert'ed, *p.p.*, controvert.

controvert'ible, *adj.*, refutable.

controvert'ing, *pr.p.*, controvert.

contuma'cious, *adj.*, perversely wilful, disobedient.

contuma'ciously, *adv.*, in a contumacious way.

contuma'ciousness, *n.*, the state of being contumacious.

con'tumacy, *n.*, wilfulness, disobedience to law.

contume'lious, *adj.*, contemptuously insolent.

con'tumely, *n.*, arrogant abuse.

contuse', *v.t.*, to crush, bruise.

contused', *p.p.*, contuse.

contu'sing, *pr.p.*, contuse.

contu'sion, *n.*, a bruise, the act of bruising.

conun'drum, *n.*, a riddle.

convalesce', *v.i.*, to recover from sickness.

convalesced', *p.p.*, convalesce.

convales'cence, *n.*, the state of recovering one's health.

convales'cency, *n.*, *i.q.* convalescence.

convales'cent, *adj.*, rel. to convalescence; recovering health.

convales'cing, *pr.p.*, convalesce.

convec'tion, *n.*, transmission; diffusion.

convec'tive, *adj.*, conveying.

conve'nable, *adj.*, capable of being convened.

convene', *v.t.*, to summon together; *v.i.*, to come together.

convened', *p.p.*, convene.

conve'ner, *n.*, one who convenes.

conve'nience, *n.*, fitness, accommodation.

conve'niency, *n.*, *i.q.* convenience.

conve'nient, *adj.*, fit, suitable, giving accommodation.

conve'niently, *adv.*, in a convenient way.

conve'ning, *pr.p.*, convene.

con'vent, *n.*, a community of religious, male or female; a nunnery or a monastery.

conven'ticle, *n.*, an irregular or schismatic assembly.

conven'ticler, *n.*, a frequenter of conventicles.

conven'tion, *n.*, an assembly, a contract; common usage.

conven'tional, *adj.*, rel. to convention; ordinary.

conven'tionalism, *n.*, the tendency to be conventional.

conven'tionalist, *n.*, one who is conventional.

conventional'ity, *n.*, the state or quality of being conventional; artificiality

conven'tionist, *n.*, one who makes a convention.

conven'tual, *adj.*, rel. or bel. to a convent.

converge', *v.i.*, to incline towards the same point.

converged', *p.p.*, converge.

conver'gence, *n.*, tendency to the same point.

conver'gency, *n.*, *i.q.* convergence.

conver'gent, *adj.*, inclining to the same point.

conver'ging, *pr.p.*, converge.

convers'able, *adj.*, fond of conversing.

convers'ableness, *n.*, the state or quality of being conversable.

con'versance, *n.*, familiarity with.

con'versant, *adj.*, familiar with, thoroughly informed about.

conversa'tion, *n.*, talk, discourse: habit of life.

conversa'tional, *adj.*, colloquial.

conversa'tionist, *n.*, a good talker.

convers'ative, *adj.*, social.

conversazio'ne, *n.*, a meeting for friendly talk.

converse', *v.i.*, to talk, join in conversation.

con'verse, *adj.*, opposite; *n.*, talk.

conversed', *p.p.*, converse.

con'versely, *adv.*, from the opposite point of view.

convers'ible, *adj.*, *i.q.* convertible.

convers'ing, *pr.p.*, converse.

conver'sion, *n.*, the act or result of converting.

convers'ive, *adj.*, leading to conversion.

convert', *v.t.*, to change, transmute; bring over to a change of belief or opinion; to apply to some use.

con'vert, *n.*, one who is converted.

convert'ed, *p.p.*, convert.

convert'er, *n.*, one who converts.

convertibil'ity, *n.*, the state or quality of being convertible.

convert'ible, *adj.*, able to be converted.

con'vex, *adj.*, rounded, swelling spherically.

con'vexed, *adj.*, *i.q.* convex.

convex'ity, *n.*, the quality or state of being convex.

con'vexly, *n.*, in a convex way.

convex'o - con'cave, *adj.*, convex on one side, concave on the other.

convey', *v.t.*, to carry; impart, transfer (property).

convey'able, *adj.*, able to be conveyed.

convey'ance, *n.*, the act of conveying; a deed of transfer; a vehicle.

convey'ancer, *n.*, one who negotiates the transfer of property.

convey'ancing, *n.*, the profession of a conveyancer.

conveyed', *p.p.*, convey.

convey'er, *n.*, anything that conveys.

convey'ing, *pr.p.*, convey.

convict', *v.t.*, to prove guilty.

con'vict, *n.*, one undergoing sentence.

convict'ed, *p.p.*, convict.

convict'ing, *pr.p.*, convict.

convic'tion, *n.*, the act of convicting; the state of being convicted; a firm belief.

convict'ive, *adj.*, tending to conviction.

convince', *v.t.*, to bring over to one's side by argument; persuade.

convinced', *p.p.*, convince.

convince'ment, *n.*, the state of being convinced.

convin'cer, *n.*, one who convinces.

convin'cible, *adj.*, open to conviction.

convin'cing, *pr.p.*, convince; *adj.*, persuasive.

convin'cingly, *adv.*, persuasively.

conviv'ial, *adj.*, sociable, fond of good fellowship.

conviv'ialist, *n.*, a convivial person.

convivial'ity, *n.*, good fellowship.

con'vocate, *v.t.*, to call together.

con'vocated, *p.p.*, convocate.

con'vocating, *pr.p.*, convocate.

convoca'tion, *n.*, the act of convocating; the assembly of the English clergy, and of certain universities.

convoca'tional, *adj.*, rel. to convocation.

convoke', *v.t.*, to summon together.

convoked', *p.p.*, convoke.

convo'king, *pr.p.*, convoke.

con'volute, *adj.*, twisted.

con'voluted, *adj.*, *i.q.* convolute.

convolu'tion, *n.*, a twisting.

convolve', *v.t.*, to roll together.

convolved', *p.p.*, convolve.

convolv'ing, *pr.p.*, convolve.

convol'vulus, *n.*, the twining plant so named.

convoy', *v.t.*, to protect while travelling by land or sea.

con'voy, *n.*, an escort.

convoyed', *p.p.*, convoy.

convoy'ing, *pr.p.*, convoy.

convulse', *v.t.*, to shake violently.

convulsed', *p.p.*, convulse.

convuls'ing, *pr.p.*, convulse.

convul'sion, *n.*, violent agitation; a sort of fit.

convul'sionary, *adj.*, causing convulsion.

convuls'ive, *adj.*, violently agitated.

convuls'ively, *adv.*, with violent agitation.

co'ny, co'ney, *n.*, a rabbit.

coo, *v.i.*, to produce the note of a pigeon; to speak wooingly; *n.*, the sound a pigeon makes.

cooed, *p.p.*, coo.

coo'ing, *pr.p.*, coo.

cook, *v.t.*, to heat prepared food.

cooked, *p.p.*, cook.

cook'ery, *n.*, the art and practice of cooking.

cook'ing, *pr.p.*, cook; *n.*, *i.q.* cookery.

cook'y, *n.*, a flat cake.

cool, *v.t.*, to reduce temperature; make cool; *v.i.*, to become cool; *adj.*, slightly cold, calm, calculating; *n.*, a state of moderate temperature.

cooled, *p.p.*, cool.

cool'er, *adj.*, *comp.* of cool; *n.*, a cooling receptacle.

cool'est, *adj.*, *super.* of cool.

cool'-headed, *adj.*, deliberate, calculating.

coo'lie, *n.*, a porter in India.

cool'ing, *pr.p.*, cool.

cool'ish, *adj.*, somewhat cool.

cool'ly, *adv.*, in a cool way.

cool'ness, *n.*, the state of being cool.

coom, *n.*, an old measure of capacity = 4 bushels.

coon, *n.*, a cunning person.

coop, *v.t.*, to cage, pen up; *n.*, a cage, pen.

cooped, *p.p.*, coop.

coop'er, *n.*, one who makes barrels; a malt liquor so named; a North Sea refreshment-selling vessel.

coop'erage, *n.*, a cooper's trade; payment for coopers' work.

co-op'erant, *adj.*, co-operating.

co-op'erate, *v.i.*, to work together.

co-op'erated, *p.p.*, co-operate.

co-op'erating, *pr.p.*, co-operate.

co-opera'tion, *n.*, the act of co-operating.

co-op'erative, *adj.*, associated, working in combination.

co-op'erator, *n.*, one who co-operates.

coop'ering, *n.*, a cooper's business.

coop'ery, *n.*, a cooper's trade.

co-opt', *v.t.*, to elect on to a committee (said of the existing members).

co-op'tate, *v.t.*, *i.q.* co-opt.

co-op'tion, *n.*, the act or result of co-opting.

co-or'dinance, *n.*, joint regulation.

co-or'dinate, *v.t.*, to range or class together; *adj.*, of the same order or class.

co-or'dinate, *n.*, an equal in rank; one of the geometrical elements defining the position of a point.

co-or'dinately, *adv.*, of the same order.

co-or'dinateness, *n.*, the state or quality of being co-ordinate

co-ordina'tion, *n.*, the act or result of co-ordinating.

coot, *n.*, a British aquatic bird.

copai'ba, *n.*, a S. American drug.

copai'vic, *adj.*, rel. to copaiba.

co'pal, *n.*, a resinous transparent substance used in varnishes.

copar'cenary, *n.*, an estate held by coheirs.

copar'cener, *n.*, a joint holder of an estate.

copart'ner, *n.*, a joint partner.

copart'nership, *n.*, the state of a copartner.

copart'nery, *n.*, *i.q.* copartnership.

copas'torate, *n.*, a joint pastorate.

cope, *v.i.*, to strive, contend successfully; *v.t.*, to add a coping to; *n.*, an ecclesiastical and academical hooded mantle.

co'peck, *n.*, a Russian copper coin, equal to an English halfpenny.

coped, *p.p.*, cope; *adj.*, wearing a cope.

Coper'nican, *adj.*, rel. to Copernicus and the Copernican system.

cope'-stone, *n.*, *i.q.* coping-stone.

cop'iable, *adj.*, able to be copied.

cop'ied, *p.p.*, copy.

cop'ier, *n.*, one who copies.

co'ping, *pr.p.*, cope; *n.*, the topmost course of a wall.

co'ping-stone, *n.*, the topmost course, or a stone in the topmost course, of a wall.

co'pious, *adj.*, abundant, plentiful.

co'piously, *adv.*, abundantly.

co'piousness, *n.*, the state of being copious.

copi'vi, *n.*, *i.q.* copaiba.

cop'per, *v.t.*, to overlay with copper; *n.*, a ductile metal of reddish colour; a copper coin; a boiler.

cop'peras, *n.*, green vitriol.

cop'pered, *p.p.*, copper.

cop'per-faced, *adj.*, faced with copper.

cop'perhead, *n.*, a poisonous N. American snake.

cop'pering, *pr.p.*, copper.

cop'perish, *adj.*, like copper.

cop'perize, *v.t.*, to treat like copper.

cop'perized, *p.p.*, copperize.

cop'perizing, *pr.p.*, copperize.

cop'perplate, *adj.*, printed on copperplate; *n.*, a plate of copper for engraving or etching.

cop'persmith, *n.*, a worker in copper.

cop'pery, *adj.*, *i.q.* copperish.

cop'pice, *n.*, a wood of low trees.

co-pres'ence, *n.*, presence together.

cop'rolite, *n.*, petrified dung.

cop'rolith, *n.*, *i.q.* coprolite.

coprolit'ic, *adj.*, rel. to coprolite.

coproph'agous, *adj.*, dung eating.

copse, *n.*, *i.q.* coppice.

cops'y, *adj.*, covered with copses; copselike.

Copt, *n.*, one of the original Egyptian stock.

Cop'tic, *adj.*, bel. to the Copts.

cop'ula, *n.*, the word expressing the relation of predicate to subject.

cop'ulate, *v.i.*, to unite; have intercourse with.

cop'ulated, *p.p.*, copulate.

cop'ulating, *pr.p.*, copulate.

copula'tion, *n.*, sexual intercourse.

cop'ulative, *adj.*, having the effect of joining; rel. to copulation.

cop'ulatively, *adv.*, with the effect of joining.

cop'y, *v.t.*, to imitate, reproduce exactly, transcribe; *n.*, an exact reproduction, transcription; one of a set of volumes; writing to be reproduced.

cop'y-book, *n.*, a book containing writing to be imitated.

cop'ygraph, *n.*, the duplication of MSS. or drawings.

cop'yhold, *n.*, holding of land on the strength of a copy of court roll.

cop'ying, *pr.p.*, copy.

cop'ying-press, *n.*, a press for multiplying copies.

cop'yist, *n.*, one who transcribes, or imitates.

cop'yright, *n.*, the exclusive publishing rights.

coquet', *v.i.*, to flirt, trifle.

co'quetry, *n.*, the arts of a coquette.

coquette', *n.*, a woman who coquets.

coquet'ted, *p.p.*, coquet.

coquet'ting, *pr.p.*, coquet.

coquet'tish, *adj.*, given to coquetry.
coquet'tishly, *adv.*, in a coquettish way.
cor'acle, *n.*, a wicker leather-covered boat.
cor'acoid, *adj.*, like a crow's beak; rel. to the C. bone; *n.*, a hook-like formation
cor'al, *adj.*, consisting of coral; *n.*, a hard structure in the sea composed of the skeletons of zoophytes; a child's coral toy.
coralla'ceous, *adj.*, made of coral.
corallif'erous, *adj.*, coral-producing.
coral'liform, *adj.*, branching like coral.
cor'alline, *adj.*, of, or like, coral; *n.*, a dye.
cor'allite, *n.*, fossilized coral.
coralloid'al, *adj.*, like coral.
cor'ban, *n.*, an offering.
cor'beil, cor'bel, *n.*, a little basket used in siege work.
cor'bel, *n.*, a projection or bracket.
cord, *v.t.*, to fasten; *n.*, a string, a wood measure.
cord'age, *n.*, a mass or collection of ropes.
cor'date, *adj.*, heart-shaped.
cord'ed, *adj.*, having cords; *p.p.*, cord.
cordelier', *n.*, a Franciscan (*Fr.*).
cordelle', *n.*, a tassel.
cor'dial, *adj.*, hearty, genial; *n.*, an invigorating medicine or liqueur.
cordial'ity, *n.*, cordial manner, geniality.
cor'dially, *adv.*, genially, heartily.
cor'diform, *adj.*, heart-shaped.
cordille'ra, *n.*, a mountain-chain.
cord'ing, *n.*, a ribbed surface; *pr.p.*, cord.
cor'dite, *n.*, smokeless powder.
cor'don, *n.*, a ribbon, a line.
cor'don bleu, *n.*, the top of a profession.
cor'dovan, *n.*, Spanish leather.
cor'duroy, *adj.*, made of corduroy; *n.*, a ribbed material of cotton or fustian; *v.t.*, to make a corduroy road.
cord'wainer, *n.*, a leather-worker, shoe-maker.
core, *v.t.*, to extract the core from; *n.*, the heart or inmost part.
cored, *adj.*, having a core; *p.p.* core.
co-re'gent, *n.*, a joint regent or ruler.
co-relig'ionist, *n.*, a professor of the same religion.
coreop'sis, *n.*, a genus of composite plants so named.
co-respond'ent, *n.*, a joint respondent.
corf, *n.*, a coal-heaving basket.
coria'ceous, *adj.*, leathery.
corian'der, *n.*, a seed-bearing plant so named.
co'ring, *pr.p.*, core.
Corin'thian, *adj.*, bel. to Corinth.
cork, *adj.*, made of cork; *n.*, the outer part of a cork-tree's bark; a stopper; *v.t.*, to stop with a cork.
cork'age, *n.*, an innkeeper's charge on wine belonging to guests.
corked, *adj.*, stopped with a cork; tasting of the cork; *p.p.*, cork.
cork'ing, *pr.p.*, cork.
cork'screw, *n.*, a cork-extractor.
cork'tree, *n.*, the tree from which cork is stripped.
cork'y, *adj.*, of, or like, cork.
cor'morant, *n.*, a fish-eating bird so named; a greedy person.
corn, *v.t.*, to cure or preserve; *n.*, grain of several varieties; a horny growth on the foot or toe.
corn'-chandler, *n.*, a retailer of corn.
corn'-cob, *n.*, the spike on the ear of maize.
corn'-cockle, *n.*, a weed that grows in corn.
corn'-crake, *n.*, the land-rail.
cor'nea, *n.*, the horny membrane of the eyeball.
corned, *adj.*, preserved, cured.
cor'nel, *n.*, a wild sort of cherry.
corne'lian, *adj.*, made of cornelian; *n.*, a sort of chalcedony.
cor'neous, *adj.*, horny.
cor'ner, *v.t.*, to drive into a corner or difficulty; to set up a monopoly; *n.*, an angle, a recess, a monopolizing ring.
cor'nered, *p.p.*, corner; *adj.*, having corners.
cor'nering, *pr.p.*, corner.
cor'ner-stone, *n.*, the principal stone.
cor'net, *n.*, a trumpet-like instrument; a junior cavalry officer.
cor'net-à-pis'ton, *n.*, a cornet on which the notes are produced by pistons.
cor'netcy, *n.*, the rank of a cornet.
corn'field, *n.*, a field for corn.
corn'flour, *n.*, fine meal from Indian corn.
corn'flower, *n.*, a wild plant so named.
cor'nice, *n*, a projection from the top of a wall or range of columns; overhanging snow.
cor'nicle, *n.*, the honey-duct of a plant louse.
cornic'ulate, *adj.*, having horns.
cor'niform, *adj.*, horn-shaped.
corn'ing, *n.*, meat-curing; *pr.p.*, corn.
Cor'nish, *adj.*, pert. to Cornwall.
cor'nist, *n.*, a player on the cornet.
corn'-land, *n*, corn-growing land.
corn'-laws, *n. pl.*, laws rel. to import and export of corn.

cor'no, *n.*, a horn.

corno'pean, *n.*, a musical instrument; an organ stop so named.

corn'-plaster, *n.*, a plaster for relieving corns.

cornuco'pia, *n.*, the horn of plenty.

cornute', *adj.*, horned.

cornu'ted, *adj.*, horned.

corn'y, *adj.*, horny; corn-producing.

cor'ody, *n.*, *i.q.* corrody.

corol'la, *n.*, a flower's inner envelope.

corolla'ceous, *adj.*, like a corolla.

corol'lary, *n.*, a further inference.

cor'ollate, *adj.*, having a corolla.

cor'ollated, *adj.*, *i.q.* corollate.

coro'na, *n.*, a crown; a halo.

cor'onach, *n.*, a dirge.

cor'onal, *adj.*, rel. to the corona; *n.*, a garland.

cor'onary, *adj.*, rel. to a crown; encircling.

cor'onated, *adj.*, having a corona.

corona'tion, *n.*, the ceremony of crowning.

cor'oner, *n.*, a Crown officer who holds inquests.

cor'onet, *n.*, a little or lesser crown.

cor'oneted, *adj.*, having a coronet.

coro'niform, *adj.*, crown-shaped.

cor'onoid, *adj.*, crown-like.

coro'nule, *n.*, the tuft of a seed.

cor'poral, *adj.*, pert. to the body; *n.*, a white linen cloth used at the altar; a non-commissioned officer so named.

corporal'ity, *n.*, the state of being corporal (*i.e.*, unspiritual).

cor'porally, *adv.*, bodily.

cor'poralship, *n.*, the office of corporal.

cor'porate, *adj.*, collective.

cor'porateness, *n.*, the state of being united in a body.

corpora'tion, *n.*, an authorized body, with powers to act as a single unit; (*slang*) a pot-belly.

cor'porative, *adj.*, corporate.

cor'porator, *n.*, a member, or cofounder, of a corporation.

corpo'real, *adj.*, having a body.

corporeal'ity, *n.*, the state of being corporeal.

corpo'really, *adv.*, in bodily form.

corpo'realness, *n.*, *i.q.* corporeality.

corpore'ity, *n.*, physical existence.

cor'posant, *n.*, the fireball seen on ships' masts in stormy weather.

corps, *n.*, a body, a company.

corpse, *n.*, a dead body.

cor'pulence, *n.*, excessive stoutness.

cor'pulency, *n.*, *i.q.* corpulence.

cor'pulent, *adj.*, excessively stout.

cor'pus, *n.*, a body; a whole.

cor'puscle, *n.*, a diminutive body, particle.

corpus'cular, *adj.*, consisting of corpuscles.

corpuscula'rian, *adj.*, rel. to corpuscles.

corral', *n.*, an enclosure for cattle, or for capturing wild elephants; *v.t.*, to enclose in a corral.

corralled', *p.p.*, corral.

corral'ling, *pr.p.*, corral.

correct', *v.t.*, to put right, punish; *adj.*, strictly accurate, right, proper.

correct'able, *adj.*, able to be corrected.

correct'ed, *p.p.*, correct.

correct'ing, *pr.p.*, correct.

correc'tion, *n.*, the process of correcting, the amending of an error, punishment.

correc'tional, *adj.*, with a correcting purpose.

correct'ive, *adj.*, tending to correction; *n.*, an antidote.

correct'ly, *adv.* rightly, properly, accurately.

correct'ness, *n.*, the state or habit of being correct.

correct'or, *n.*, one who corrects.

cor'relate, *v.t.*, to bring into reciprocal relation; *adj.*, correlated.

cor'related, *p.p.*, correlate.

cor'relating, *pr.p.*, correlate.

correla'tion, *n.*, the state of reciprocal relation.

correl'ative, *adj.*, reciprocally relative; *n.*, the antecedent to a relative pronoun.

correl'atively, *adv.*, in reciprocal relation.

correl'ativeness, *n.*, the state or quality of reciprocal relation.

correspond', *v.i.*, to answer, agree, be equal to; to write letters to.

correspond'ed, *p.p.*, correspond.

correspond'ence, *n.*, the act of corresponding; agreement; epistolary intercourse.

correspond'ent, *adj.*, equal, in agreement; *n.*, one who corresponds.

correspond'ing, *pr.p.*, correspond.

cor'ridor, *n.*, an open gallery or passage.

corrigen'da, *n.*, pl. of corrigendum.

corrigen'dum, *n.*, a point to be corrected.

corrigibil'ity, *n.*, the state of being corrigible.

cor'rigible, *adj.*, capable of reform or correction.

cor'rigibleness, *n.*, a willingness to be corrected.

corrob´orant, *adj.*, verifying, confirming.

corrob´orate, *v.t.*, to confirm, verify, establish.

corrob´orated, *p.p.*, corroborate.

corrob´orating, *pr.p.*, corroborate.

corrobora´tion, *n.*, the act of corroborating; a verification.

corrob´orative, *adj.*, confirming, supporting.

corrob´oratory, *adj.*, *i.q.* corroborative.

corroboree´, *n.*, an Australasian native war-dance.

corrode´, *v.t.*, to eat away, rust; *v.i.*, to rust.

corro´ded, *p.p.*, corrode.

corro´dible, *adj.*, liable to corrosion.

corro´ding, *pr.p.*, corrode.

cor´rody, *n.*, a founder's right of subsistence in his own monastery; provision.

corro´sible, *adj.*, *i.q.* corrodible.

corro´sibleness, *n.*, the state of being corrosible.

corro´sion, *n.*, the process of corroding.

corro´sive, *adj.*, tending to corrode.

corro´sively, *adv.*, in a corrosive way.

corro´siveness, *n.*, the corrosive power.

cor´rugant, *adj.*, wrinkling.

cor´rugate, *v.t.*, to wrinkle, or make folds in.

cor´rugated, *p.p.*, corrugate.

cor´rugating, *pr.p.*, corrugate.

corruga´tion, *n.*, the act of corrugating; a wrinkle.

cor´rugator, *n.*, something that corrugates.

corrupt´, *v.t.*, to make putrescent; to taint, spoil, make impure, deprave; *v.i.*, to become impure; *adj.*, tainted, depraved, full of errors.

corrupt´ed, *p.p.*, corrupt.

corrupt´er, *n.*, one who corrupts.

corruptibil´ity, *n.*, the state of being corruptible.

corrupt´ible, *adj.*, able to be corrupted; tending to decay.

corrupt´ibleness, *n.*, the state of being corruptible.

corrupt´ibly, *adv.*, in a corruptible way.

corrupt´ing, *pr.p.*, corrupt.

corrup´tion, *n.*, the process of corrupting; decay; dissolution.

corrupt´ive, *adj.*, with a corrupting tendency.

corrupt´ly, *adv.*, wrongly, in error, depravedly.

corrupt´ness, *n.*, the state or quality of being corrupt.

cor´sage, *n.*, a bodice.

cor´sair, *n.*, a pirate.

corse, *n.*, a dead body.

corse´let, *n.*, light armour for the body.

cor´set, *n.*, a body support, stays.

Cor´sican, *adj.*, pert. to Corsica.

cors´ned, *n.*, a piece of bread used as the test of guilt or innocence.

cortège´, *n.*, a train, procession.

Cor´tes, *n.*, the Parliament of Spain or Portugal.

cor´tex, *n.*, bark.

cor´tical, *adj.*, of, or like, bark; external.

cor´ticate, *adj.*, covered with bark.

cor´ticated, *adj.*, *i.q.* corticate.

cortici´ferous, *adj.*, bearing bark.

corun´dum, *n.*, a hard mineral so named.

corus´cant, *adj.*, glittering, sparkling.

cor´uscate, *v.i.*, to sparkle, glitter.

cor´uscated, *p.p.*, coruscate.

cor´uscating, *pr.p.*, coruscate.

corusca´tion, *n.*, a flash, sparkle.

corvée´, *n.*, the forced labour of feudalism.

corvette´, *n.*, a sloop.

cor´vine, *adj.*, like, or pert. to, a crow.

cor´vus, *n.*, a crow.

Cor´ybant, *n.*, a priest of Cybele.

Coryban´tic, *adj.*, rel. to the Corybants; wild, frenzied.

coryphae´us, *n.*, the leader of a Greek dramatic chorus.

coryphée´, *n.*, a ballet dancer.

cor´yphene, *n.*, a dolphin.

corypheu´s, *n.*, *i.q.*, coryphaeus.

cory´za, *n.*, a cold in the head.

cose´cant, *n.*, a trigonometrical function.

cosh´er, *v.t.* to pamper; *v.i.*, to cheat.

co´sily, *adv.*, in cosy fashion.

co´sine, *n.*, the sine of a complement of an angle or arc.

cosmet´ic, *adj.*, adorning; heightening beauty; *n.*, a dye or wash for adornment.

cos´mic, *adj.*, rel. to the cosmos or kosmos.

cos´mical, *adj.*, *i.q.* cosmic.

cos´mically, *adv.*, in the manner of the cosmos.

cosmog´onal, *adj.*, rel. to cosmogony.

cosmog´onist, *n.*, a student of cosmogonies.

cosmog´ony, *n.*, a work on the origin of the cosmos.

cosmog´rapher, *n.*, a student of cosmography.

cosmograph´ic, *adj.*, rel. to cosmography.

cosmog´raphy, *n.*, the science of the cosmos.

cos´molabe, *n.*, an astrolabe.

cosmol´atry, *n.*, worship of the cosmos.

cosmolog´ical, *adj.*, rel. to cosmology.

cosmol´ogist, *n.*, a student of cosmology.

cosmol'ogy, *n.*, the study of the origin of the cosmos.
cosmoplas'tic, *adj.*, rel. to the structure of the cosmos.
cosmopol'itan, *adj.*, claiming the citizenship of the world; *n.*, a citizen of the world.
cosmopol'itanism, *n.*, the claim to be a citizen of the world.
cosmop'olite, *n.*, *i.q.* cosmopolitan.
cosmora'ma, *n.*, a realistic representation of parts of the world.
cosmoram'ic, *adj.*, of the nature of cosmorama.
cos'mos, *n.*, order; the universe, world; the system of worlds.
Cos'sack, *n.*, a South Russian horseman; *adj.*, rel. to the Cossacks.
cos'set, *v.t.*, to pet up, cocker; *n.*, a pet lamb; a comforting drink.
cost, *v.t.*, to be valued at; to inflict; *n.*, an amount to be paid, charge.
cost'al, *adj.*, rel. to the ribs.
cos'tard, *n.*, a variety of apple.
cos'tate, *adj.*, ribbed.
cos'tated, *adj.*, ribbed.
cost'-book, *n.*, a list of partners in a mine.
cos'termonger, *n.*, a hawker of apples, also of other eatable things.
cost'ing, *pr.p.*, cost.
cos'tive, *adj.*, constipated.
cos'tively, *adv.*, in a costive way.
cos'tiveness, *n.*, constipation.
cost'liness, *n.*, high price.
cost'ly, *adj.*, costing much, high-priced.
cost'mary, *n.*, a fragrant plant so named.
cos'tume, *v.t.*, to put into costume; *n.*, dress, mode of dress.
costu'mer, *n.*, one who makes or provides costumes.
costu'mier, *n.*, *i.q.* costumer (*Fr.*).
co'sy, *adj.*, snug, comfortable; *n.*, a cover to a teapot.
cot, *n.*, a cottage; child's bed.
cotan'gent, *n.*, the tangent of the complement of an angle or arc.
cote, *n.*, a hut, sheepfold.
cotempora'neous, *see* contemporaneous.
cotem'porary, *see* contemporary.
co'terie, *n.*, a company, a party.
co-ter'minous, *see* conterminous.
cothurn'ate, *adj.*, wearing cothurni or buskins; pert. to tragedy.
cothur'nus, *n.*, a buskin, worn by Greek tragic actors; tragedy.
cotil'lion, *n.*, a variety of dance or dance-music; a black and white stuff.
co-trustee', *n.*, a joint trustee.
Cots'wold, *n.*, the name of a Gloucestershire range of hills.
cot'ta, *n.*, a truncated surplice.
cot'tage, *n.*, a little house.
cot'tager, *n.*, the occupant of a cottage, a rustic.
cot'tar, **cot'ter**, *n.*, *i.q.* cottager.
cot'tier, *n.*, *i.q.* cottar.
cot'ton, *adj.*, made of cotton; *n.*, a white material.
cot'ton-gin, *n.*, a machine for cleansing cotton.
cot'tony, *adj.*, cottonlike.
cotyle'don, *n.*, a seed lobe.
cotyle'donous, *adj.*, like a cotyledon.
cotyl'iform, *adj.*, cup-shaped.
cot'yloid, *adj.*, like a cup.
couch, *v.t.*, to hide; express in terms; to operate for cataract; *v.i.*, to lie down.
couch'ant, *adj.*, lying, crouching (*her.*).
couché', *adj.*, partly lying (*her.*).
couched, *p.p.*, couch.
couch'er, *n.*, one who couches.
couch'-grass, *n.*, a species of rapidly growing grass.
couch'ing, *pr.p.*, couch; *n.*, an operation for cataract.
cou'gar, *n.*, a panther.
cough, *v.i.*, to expel air from the lungs with violence; *n.*, a violent expulsion of air from the lungs.
coughed, *p.p.*, cough.
cough'er, *n.*, one who coughs.
cough'ing, *pr.p.*, cough.
could, *p.t.* of can.
coulisse', *n.*, a portcullis; a side-scene of a stage.
cou'loir, *n.*, a steep gorge.
coul'ter, *n.*, a ploughshare.
coun'cil, *n.*, a conference, assembly of councillors.
coun'cil-board, *n.*, the table at which councillors meet.
coun'cillor, **coun'cilor**, *n.*, a member of a council.
coun'sel, *v.t.*, to give advice to; *n.*, advice, deliberation; a barrister.
coun'selled, **coun'seled**, *p.p.*, counsel.
coun'selling, **coun'seling**, *pr.p.*, counsel.
coun'sellor, **coun'selor**, *n.*, one who gives counsel.
coun'sellorship, **coun'selorship**, *n.*, a counsellor's office or function.
count, *v.t.*, to reckon up, to esteem; *v.i.*, to rely upon; *n.*, reckoning; a particular charge; the title of a grade of nobility.
count'able, *adj.*, able to be counted.
count'ed, *p.p.*, count.

coun'tenance, *v.t.*, to approve, support; *n.*, the face, appearance, support.

coun'tenanced, *p.p.*, countenance.

coun'tenancer, *n.*, one who countenances.

coun'tenancing, *pr.p.*, countenance.

count'er, *adj.*, adverse, contrary; *v.t.*, to parry, oppose; *n.*, one who counts; part of a horse's breast; part of a ship's stern; a shop table.

counteract', *v.t.*, to defeat, neutralize.

counterac'ted, *p.p.*, counteract.

counteract'ing, *pr.p.*, counteract.

counterac'tion, *n.*, the act of counteracting.

counteract'ive, *adj.*, tending to counteract.

counteract'ively, *adv.*, with counteracting effect.

counter-attrac'tion, *n.*, attraction in an opposite direction.

counterbal'ance, *v.t.* to weigh against.

counterbal'anced, *p.p.*, counterbalance

counterbal'ancing, *pr.p.*, counterbalance.

count'erbrace, *v.t.*, to brace in opposite directions; *n.*, a device to relieve the stress on a mainbrace.

count'ercharge, *v.t.*, to charge in opposition; *n.*, an opposing charge.

count'ercharm, *n.*, a charm against a charm.

count'ercheck, *n.*, a check in opposition.

count'erclaim, *n.*, a claim against a claim.

count'erfeit, *v.t.*, to feign, to imitate, forge; *adj.*, spurious, feigned; *n.*, an imitation, forgery.

count'erfeited, *p.p.*, counterfeit.

count'erfeiter, *n.*, one who counterfeits.

count'erfeiting, *pr.p.*, counterfeit.

count'erfoil, *n.*, the part of a document or cheque retained by the drawer.

count'erguard, *n.*, a guard against a guard.

count'er-ir'ritant, *n.*, a plaster or other irritant to relieve pain in one part by causing it in another; *adj.*, producing counter-irritation.

count'er-jumper, *n.*, a shop assistant.

countermand', *v.t.*, to cancel an order; *n.*, the cancelling of an order.

countermand'ed, *p.p.*, countermand.

countermand'ing, *pr.p.*, countermand.

count'ermarch, *n.*, a march back.

count'ermark, *v.t.*, to put a countermark on; *n.*, an additional mark.

count'ermine, *v.t.*, to engineer a countermine; *n.*, a mine against a mine.

count'er-motion, *n.*, a motion in opposition.

count'ermure, *n.*, a strengthening wall.

count'erpane, *n.*, a bed-cover.

count'erpart, *n.*, a duplicate.

count'er-plea, *n.*, a plea in opposition.

count'erplot, *v.i.*, to meet a plot with a plot; *n.*, a plot against a plot.

count'erplotted, *p.p.*, counterplot.

count'erplotting, *pr.p.* counterplot.

count'erpoint, *n.*, a branch of musical science so named.

count'erpoise, *v.t.*, to balance; *n.*, balance.

count'erpoised, *p.p.*, counterpoise.

count'erpoising, *pr.p.*, counterpoise.

count'erscarp, *n.*, the slope of a ditch opposite to the scarp.

count'ersign, *v.t.*, to put an authenticating additional signature, *n.*, an additional signature; a sign corresponding to a sign.

count'ersigned, *p.p.*, countersign.

count'ersigning, *pr.p.*, countersign.

count'ersink, *v.t.*, to prepare a bed for the head of a screw or bolt.

count'er-stroke, *n.*, a stroke against a stroke.

count'er-tenor, *n.*, the voice part above the tenor.

countervail', *v.t.*, to counterbalance, compensate.

countervailed', *p.p.*, countervail.

countervail'ing, *pr.p.*, countervail.

countervalla'tion, *n.*, the act of opposing with a rampart; the rampart itself.

count'erview, *n.*, a contrary view.

count'erweigh, *v.t.*, to balance.

count'erweighed, *p.p.*, counterweigh.

count'erweighing, *pr.p.*, counterweigh.

count'erweight, *n.*, a balance.

count'erwork, *n.*, a work against a work.

count'ess, *n.*, fem. of earl or count.

count'ing, *pr.p.*, count.

count'ing-house, *n.*, a department of an office in which the accounts are kept.

count'less, *adj.*, innumerable.

count'rified, *adj.*, rustic; *p.p.*, countrify.

count'rify, *v.t.*, to make rustic.

count'rifying, *pr.p.*, countrify.

count'ry, *n.*, a region, the rustic districts, a native land.

count'ry-dance, *n.*, a contre-danse.

count'ryman, *n.*, a native of a country; a rustic.

coun'try-seat, *n.*, a house or estate in the country.
coun'ty, *n.*, a local division for political or administrative purposes.
coun'ty-court, *n.*, a court for small debt cases; *v.t.*, to sue.
coup, *n.*, a sudden stroke.
coup de grâce, *n.*, a final stroke (*Fr.*).
coup de main', *n.*, a sudden exercise of force (*Fr.*).
coup d'état', *n.*, a political sudden exercise of force (*Fr.*).
coupé', *n.*, the front part of a stage-coach; the end of a railway carriage; a four-wheeled carriage for two (*Fr.*).
coupee', *n.*, the salute in a dance (*Fr.*).
coup'er, *n.*, a lever on a loom.
coup'le, *v.t.*, to link, join; *v.i.*, to be joined; *n.*, a pair, two of the same kind, a man and his wife.
coup'led, *p.p.*, couple.
coup'ler, *n.*, one who couples, a thing that couples; an apparatus on an organ for linking keyboards together.
coup'let, *n.*, two successive lines of poetry.
coup'ling, *pr.p.*, couple; *n.*, links.
cou'pon, *n.*, a certificate; a ticket.
cour'age, *n.*, bravery, fortitude.
coura'geous, *adj.*, brave, spirited.
coura'geously, *adv.*, bravely.
coura'geousness, *n.*, courageous character.
cour'ant, *adj.*, running (*her.*).
cour'bash, *n.*, a whip made of hippopotamus hide.
cour'ier, *n.*, a messenger; an attendant.
course, *v.t.*, to chase with greyhounds; *n.*, a race, a racing-track; direction, line of movement, a stage in a meal; a range of masonry.
coursed, *p.p.*, course.
cours'er, *n.*, one who courses; a swift horse.
cours'ing, *pr.p.*, course; *n.*, chasing hares.
court, *v.t.*, to solicit, flatter, pay devotion to; *n.*, an inclosed space, a palace, a king's household; a place of justice, the judge.
court'-chaplain, *n.*, the chaplain of a sovereign.
court'ed, *p.p.*, court.
court'eous, *adj.*, polite, considerate.
court'eously, *adv.*, politely.
court'eousness, *n.*, the exercise of courtesy.
court'er, *n.*, one who courts.
court'esan, *n.*, a prostitute.
court'esy, *n.*, politeness, considerateness, civility.
court'-*hand*, *n.*, an old style of official handwriting.
court'-house, *n.*, a building in which a court is held.
court'ier, *n.*, one who is attached to a court; a person of courtly manners; one who seeks favours.
court'-lands, *n.*, the land of a lord of the manor.
court'-leet, *n.*, an old court of record.
court'liness, *n.*, the habit of courtesy.
court'ly, *adj.*, courteous, refined.
court-mar'tial, *n.*, a naval or military court of discipline.
court'-plaster, *n.*, a superior sticking-plaster.
court'ship, *n.*, the act or period of courting.
court'-yard, *n.*, an enclosure to a house.
cous'in, *n.*, an uncle's or aunt's son or daughter.
cous'in ger'man, *n.*, a first-cousin.
couteau, *n.*, a knife (*Fr.*).
couvade', *n.*, a primitive practice of putting to bed the father of a newly born infant and conveying to him sympathetic felicitations.
cove, *v.t.*, to arch; *n.*, a creek; a quiet corner; a hollowed moulding.
cov'enant, *v.i.*, to make a covenant; *n.*, a written agreement; a common pledge.
cov'enanted, *p.p.*, covenant; *adj.*, under agreement.
covenantee', *n.*, one with whom a contract is made.
cov'enanter, **cov'enantor**, *n.*, one who makes an agreement.
cov'enanting, *pr.p.*, covenant.
cov'er, *v.t.*, to lay something over, to hide; *n.*, something spread over; a shelter; a covert; furnished place for each guest at table.
cov'ered, *p.p.*, cover.
cov'erer, *n.*, one who covers.
cov'ering, *pr.p.*, cover; *n.*, something that covers.
cov'erlet, *n.*, a bed-quilt.
cov'ert, *adj.*, concealed, secret, underhand; protected; *n.*, a shelter, thicket, the hiding-place of wild animals.
cov'ertly, *adv.*, secretly.
cov'erture, *n.*, shelter; the protected state of a married woman.
cov'et, *v.t.*, to desire what is not one's own.
cov'etable, *adj.*, able to be coveted.
cov'eted, *p.p.*, covet.
cov'eter, *n.*, one who covets.
cov'eting, *pr.p.*, covet.
cov'etous, *adj.*, ardently desirous, avaricious.

cov'etously, *adv.*, in a covetous way.
cov'etousness, *n.*, the habit of coveting.
cov'ey, *n.*, a brood of birds, particularly partridges.
cov'in, *n.*, collusion in a fraud.
co'ving, *pr.p.*, cove; *n.*, the projection of a higher over a lower storey.
cov'inous, *adj.*, fraudulent.
cow, *v.t.*, to quell with fear; *n.*, the female ox.
cow'an, *n.*, an unapprenticed workman.
cow'ard, *n.*, one who lacks courage, a poltroon.
cow'ardice, *n.*, the act or state of a coward.
cow'ardliness, *n.*, *s.q.* cowardice.
cow'ardly, *adj.*, without courage, fearful.
cow'boy, *n.*, a boy in charge of cows; a ranchman.
cow-calf, *n.*, a female calf.
cow'catcher, *n.*, an apparatus in front of a locomotive for clearing away obstructions.
cowed, *p.p.*, cow.
cow'er, *v.i.*, to shudder, crouch down in fear.
cow'ered, *p.p.*, cower.
cow'ering, *pr.p.*, cower.
cow'gate, *n.*, the right to pasture cattle.
cow'hage, *n.*, a vermifuge.
cow'heel, *n.*, gelatine made from a cow's foot.
cow'herd, *n.*, one who has charge of cows.
cow'-hide, *n.*, leather made of cow's skin; a whip made of hide; *adj.*, made of cow-hide.
cow'ing, *pr.p.*, cow.
cowl, *n.*, a monk's hooded robe; a revolving top to a chimney pot.
cowled, *adj.*, wearing a cowl.

co-work'er, *n.*, a colleague, collaborator.
cow'-pox, *n.*, a disease affecting a cow's udders.
cow'rie, **cow'ry**, *n.*, shell money.
cow'slip, *n.*, a yellow flower so named.
cox'comb, *n.*, a conceited fellow.
coxcomb'ical, **coxcom'ical**, *adj.*, conceited, foppish.
cox'combry, *n.*, the act or nature of a coxcomb.
cox'swain, *n.*, one who steers a boat.
coy, *adj.*, bashful, demure.
coy'ish, *adj.*, playfully demure.
coy'ly, *adv.*, demurely, modestly.
coy'ness, *n.*, demureness.
coyo'te, *n.*, the prairie wolf.
coz'en, *v.t.*, to cheat.
coz'enage, *n.*, cheating, trickery.
coz'ened, *p.p.*, cozen.
coz'ener, *n.*, one who cozens.
coz'ening, *pr.p.*, cozen.
co'zily, *see* cosily.
co'zy, *see* cosy.
crab, *v.t.*, to catch crabs; to beat; to irritate; *n.*, a crustacean so named.
crab'-apple, *n.*, a small, very sour kind of apple.
crab'bed, *p.p.*, crab; *adj.*, sour, morose, difficult to read.
crab'bedly, *adv.*, morosely.
crab'bedness, *n.*, morosity.
crab'bing, *pr.p.*, crab.
crab'by, *adj.*, morose.
crab'stick, *n.*, a cudgel; a morose fellow.
crab'-tree, *n.*, a tree growing crab apples.
crab'-yaws, *n. pl.*, ulcers on the sole.
crack, *v.t.*, to make a fissure in, break open; *v.i.*, to split open; *n.*, a fissure, fracture, a sharp sound (as of a whip, etc.), a friendly chat.

crack'-brained, *adj.*, silly.
cracked, *p.p.*, crack; *adj.*, broken, imperfect; out of one's mind.
crack'er, *n.*, anything that cracks; a variety of biscuit; a firework.
crack'ing, *pr.p.*, crack.
crack'le, *v.i.*, to make a slight explosion; *v.t.*, to cover with cracks; *n.*, a cracking sound repeated.
crack'led, *p.p.*, crackle.
crack'ling, *pr.p.*, crackle; *n.*, a continued sound of slight explosion; the rind of roast pig.
crack'nel, *n.*, a variety of biscuit.
cracks'man, *n.*, a burglar.
cra'dle, *v.t.*, to put into a cradle; to bring up; *n.*, a babe's bed; native place; a timber-frame for launching vessels; a gold-washing apparatus.
cra'dled, *p.p.*, cradle.
cra'dling, *pr.p.*, cradle.
craft, *n.*, skill of hand, cunning.
craft'ily, *adv.*, cunningly.
craft'iness, *n.*, the act or quality of being crafty.
crafts'man, *n.*, a skilled worker, a member of a trade.
craft'y, *adj.*, cunning.
crag, *n.*, a steep, rough rock.
crag'ged, *adj.*, having crags.
crag'giness, *n.*, the quality of a crag.
crag'gy, *n.*, precipitous, rugged.
crags'man, *n.*, an expert crag-climber.
crake, *n.*, the corn-crake.
cram, *v.t.*, to stuff, fill to overflowing, get up for examination, tell falsehood to; *n.*, the act of cramming, a falsehood, getting up an examination.

cram'bo, *n.*, a family game of rhyming.
crammed, *p.p.*, cram.
cram'mer, *n.*, one who crams, esp. in preparing pupils for an examination.
cram'ming, *pr.p.*, cram.
cramp, *v.t.*, to confine, narrow; cause a muscular spasm; *n.*, a muscular spasm; a tool so named.
cramped, *p.p.*, cramp.
cramp'-fish, *n.*, the torpedo.
cramp'ing, *pr.p.*, cramp.
cramp'-iron, *n.*, a piece of iron, bent at the ends, to hold anything in place.
cram'pon, *n.*, a piece of iron fastened to a climber's shoes.
crampoon', *n.*, a weight-lifting apparatus.
cra'nage, *n.*, the right or cost of loading or unloading.
cran'berry, *n.*, a variety of whortleberry.
crane, *v.i.*, to stretch; *n.*, a tall bird so named; a weight-lifting machine.
cranes'bill, *n.*, a variety of geranium.
cra'nial, *adj.*, rel. to the skull.
craniog'nomy, *n.*, the science of skulls.
craniolog'ical, *adj.*, rel. to craniology.
craniol'ogist, *n.*, an expert in skulls.
craniol'ogy, *n.*, the study of skulls.
craniom'eter, *n.*, a skull-measuring instrument.
craniomet'rical, *adj.*, rel. to craniometry.
craniom'etry, *n.*, the scientific measurement of skulls.
cranios'copy, *n.*, the scientific study of skull formation.
cra'nium, *n.*, the skull.
crank, *adj.*, easily overturned; *n.*, a turn; an instrument for turning an axis; a monomaniac.
crank'le, *v.t.* and *i.*, to bend.
crank'led, *p.p.*, crankle.
crank'ling, *pr.p.*, crankle.
crank'y, *adj.*, shaky, loose, crotchety.
cran'nied, *adj.*, chinky.
cran'ny, *n.*, a chink.
crape, *v.t.*, to cover with crape; *n.*, a thin gauzy material.
crap'ulence, *n.*, sickness after a debauch.
crap'ulent, *adj.*, drunken.
crap'ulous, *adj.*, *i.q.* crapulent.
crash, *v.t.*, to dash; *v.i.*, to make a loud noise; *n.*, a loud alarming noise; coarse linen.
crashed, *p.p.*, crash.
crash'ing, *pr.p.*, crash.
cra'sis, *n.*, the formation of a long vowel or diphthong from two vowels.
crass, *adj.*, coarse, stupid.
crass'itude, *n.*, stupidity.
cratch, *n.*, a crib, a rack.
cratch'es, *n.*, a swelling on a horse's pastern or beneath the hoof.
crate, *n.*, a hamper, packing-frame.
cra'ter, *n.*, the hollow of a volcano.
crater'iform, *adj.*, cup-shaped.
craunch, *v.t.* and *i.*, *i.q.* crunch.
craunched, *p.p.*, craunch.
craunch'ing, *pr.p.*, craunch.
cravat', *n.*, a necktie.
crave, *v.t.*, to beg humbly, yearn for.
craved, *p.p.*, crave.
cra'ven, *adj.*, cowardly, dastardly.
cra'ver, *n.*, one who craves.
cra'ving, *pr.p.*, crave.
cra'vingly, *adv.*, with great yearning.
craw, *n.*, a bird's crop.
craw'-fish, *see* crayfish.
crawl, *v.i.*, to creep, move with difficulty; *n.*, a slow, difficult walk.
crawled, *p.p.*, crawl.
crawl'er, *n.*, anything that crawls.
crawl'ing, *pr.p.*, crawl.
cray'fish, *n.*, a fresh-water crustacean so named. (A corruption of the French *crevice*.)
cray'on, *adj.*, drawn in chalks; *n.*, a drawing chalk; a drawing in chalks; a carbon point.
cray'onist, *n.*, an artist in chalks.
craze, *v.i.*, to lose one's senses; *v.t.*, to drive out of one's wits; *n.*, a besetting whim, obsession; a crack.
crazed, *p.p.*, craze.
cra'zily, *adv.*, in crazy fashion.
cra'ziness, *n.*, a crazy condition.
cra'zing, *pr.p.*, craze.
cra'zy, *adj.*, demented; unsafe.
creak, *v.i.*, to make a sound of grating, *n.*, a grating noise.
creaked, *p.p.*, creak.
creak'ing, *pr.p.*, creak.
cream, *v.t.*, to skim; *v.i.*, to form cream; *n.*, the oily element of milk; the choicest part.
cream'-cheese', *n.*, cheese made from cream.
creamed, *p.p.*, cream.
cream'ery, *n.*, a shop where cream and butter are sold.
cream'ing, *pr.p.*, cream.
cream'y, *n.*, yielding cream; cream-like.
crease, *v.t.* and *i.*, to wrinkle; *n.*, a wrinkle; a line defining the batsman's and the bowler's position.
creased, *p.p.*, crease.
creas'er, *n.*, anything that creases.
creas'ing, *pr.p.*, crease.
crea'table, *adj.*, able to be created.
create', *v.t.*, to bring into being, make, originate, appoint.
crea'ted, *p.p.*, create.
crea'ting, *pr.p.*, create.

crea'tion, *n.*, the act of creating; all created things; a masterpiece; an elevation to rank.

crea'tive, *adj.*, with the faculty of creating.

crea'tiveness, *n.*, the faculty of creating.

crea'tor, *n.*, one who creates.

crea'tural, *adj.*, rel. to creatures.

crea'ture, *n.*, a created being; the tool of another.

crèche, *n.*, a public nursery.

cre'dence, *n.*, belief; a sidesanctuary table.

creden'da, *n.*, pl. of credendum.

creden'dum, *n.*, an article for belief.

cre'dent, *adj.*, believing.

creden'tial, *n.*, a testimonial, proof of identity and status.

credibil'ity, *n.*, the state of being credible.

cred'ible, *adj.*, worthy of belief.

cred'ibleness, *n.*, *i.q.* credibility.

cred'ibly, *adv.*, believably.

cred'it, *v.t.*, to believe, trust; acknowledge as owing; *n.*, belief; honour, permission to defer payment.

cred'itable, *adj.*, with honour.

cred'itably, *adv.*, to one's honour.

cred'ited, *p.p.*, credit.

cred'iting, *pr.p.*, credit.

cred'itor, *n.*, one to whom a debt is due.

credu'lity, *n.*, the state of being credulous.

cred'ulous, *adj.*, believing anything that is said.

cred'ulously, *adv.*, with credulity.

cred'ulousness, *n.*, *i.q.* credulity.

creed, *n.*, an accepted belief; articles of faith.

creek, *n.*, a small inlet of the sea.

creel, *n.*, a fishing-basket; *v.t.*, to place in a creel.

creep, *v.i.*, to crawl; move painfully; grow along the ground.

creep'er, *n.*, anything that creeps; a clinging plant.

creep'ing, *pr.p.*, creep.

creep'ingly, *adv.*, in a creeping way.

creese, *n.*, a Malayan knife.

cremate', *v.t.*, to burn a corpse.

crema'ted, *p.p.*, cremate.

crema'ting, *pr.p.*, cremate.

crema'tion, *n.*, the act of cremating.

cremato'rium, *n.*, a place for cremation.

Cremo'na, *n.*, a city in Italy; a violin by one of the great Cremona makers.

cre'nate, *adj.*, with notches.

cren'ature, *n.*, a notching.

cren'ellate, cren'elate, *v.t.*, to embattle; to decorate with indented mouldings.

cren'ellated, cren'elated, *p.p.*, crenellate.

cren'ellating, *pr.p.*, crenellate.

crenella'tion, crenela'tion, *n.*, decoration with indented mouldings.

crenelle', *n.*, an embrasure of a battlement.

cren'ulate, *adj.*, notched.

cre'ole, *adj.*, rel. to Creoles; *n.*, a European born in W. Indies or Span. America; in Louisiana a native of French or Spanish origin; a negro born there.

cre'osote, *n.*, an antiseptic product of wood-tar.

cre'pance, *n.*, a wound in a horse's hind leg produced by the other leg striking against it.

crep'itant, *adj.*, making a cracking or grinding sound.

crep'itate, *v.i.*, to make a cracking or grinding sound.

crep'itated, *p.p.*, crepitate.

crep'itating, *pr.p.*, crepitate.

crepita'tion, *n.*, the act or sound of crepitating.

crep'on, *n.*, a crape-like stuff.

crept, *p.p.*, creep.

crepus'cular, *adj.*, dim; twilight.

crepus'cule, *n.*, twilight.

crepus'culous, *adj.*, *i.q.* crepuscular.

crescen'do, *n.*, a growing volume of sound; *adv.*, with increasing volume.

cres'cent, *adj.*, growing; *n.*, a new moon; a moon-shaped emblem, the Moslem Empire.

cress, *n.*, the name for a variety of cruciferous plants.

cres'set, *n.*, a beacon-light; a stand for the light.

crest, *v.t.*, to top, surmount; *n.*, a top, ridge, plume; the emblem surmounting a helmet.

crest'ed, *p.p.*, crest; *adj.*, having a crest.

crest'fallen, *adj.*, depressed.

crest'ing, *n.*, a surmounting ornament; *pr.p.*, crest.

creta'ceous, *adj.*, chalky.

Cre'tan, *adj.*, bel. to Crete.

cre'tin, *n.*, one suffering from cretinism.

cre'tinism, *n.*, a disease producing deformity and idiocy.

cretonne', *n.*, a printed cotton fabric.

crevasse', *n.*, an opening in a glacier.

crev'et, *n.*, a pot for melting gold.

crev'ice, *n.*, a fissure.

crew, *p.t.*, crow; *n.*, the men of a ship or boat.

crew'el, *n.*, a material used for fancy work.

crib, *v.t.*, to confine; to appropriate; *n.*, a manger; a child's bed; a translation.

crib'bage, *n.*, a card game.

cribbed, *p.p.*, crib.
crib'bing, *pr.p.*, crib.
crib'ble, *v.t.*, to riddle; *n.*, a riddle; coarse meal.
crib'bled, *p.p.*, cribble; *adj.*, dotted or punctured.
crib'bling, *pr.p.* cribble.
crib'riform, *adj.*, like a sieve.
crick, *v.t.*, to twist; *n.*, a muscular twisting of the neck.
crick'et, *n.*, the game so named; the insect so named.
crick'eter, *n.*, one who plays cricket.
cri'coid, *adj.*, like a ring.
cried, *p.p.*, cry.
cri'er, *n.*, one who cries; an official who proclaims publicly.
crime, *n.*, an offence.
crim'inal, *n.*, one guilty of crime.
criminal'ity, *n.*, the state or quality of a criminal.
crim'inally, *adv.*, in a criminal way.
crim'inate, *v.t.*, to accuse, incriminate.
crim'inated, *p.p.*, criminate.
crim'inating, *pr.p.*, criminate.
crimina'tion, *n.*, the act of criminating.
crim'inative, *adj.*, tending to criminate.
crim'inatory, *adj.*, *i.q.* criminative.
criminol'ogy, *n.*, the study of crime and criminals.
crimp, *v.t.*, to make wavy; to contract; enlist by foul means; *n.*, one who crimps soldiers or sailors; the keeper of a low class of seamen's lodgings.
crimped, *p.p.*, crimp.
crimp'ing, *pr.p.*, crimp.
crimp'ing-iron, *n.*, an instrument for crimping.
crim'ple, *v.t.*, to crimp; *n.*, a wrinkle.
crim'pled, *p.p.*, crimple.
crim'pling, *pr.p.*, crimple.
crim'son, *v.t.*, to stain crimson; *v.i.*, to blush; *adj.*, the colour of crimson; *n.*, a deep red.
crim'soned, *p.p.*, crimson.
crim'soning, *pr.p.*, crimson.
cri'nal, *adj.*, rel. to hair.
cri'nate, *adj.*, having hairs.
cri'natory, *adj.*, rel. to hair.
cringe, *v.i.*, to bend down servilely; *n.*, servile self-abasement.
cringed, *p.p.*, cringe.
crin'ger, *n.*, one who cringes.
crin'ging, *pr.p.* cringe.
crin'gingly, *adv.*, in a cringing way.
crin'gle, *n.*, a loop.
crinicul'tural, *adj.*, concerning the cultivation of hair.
crinig'erous, *adj.*, hairy.
cri'nite, *adj.*, hairy.
crin'kle, *v.t.* and *i.*, to wrinkle; *n.*, a wrinkle.
crin'kled, *p.p.*, crinkle.
crin'kling, *pr.p.*, crinkle.
crin'kum - cran'kum, *n.*, a zig-zag.
crin'oid, *n.*, a stone-lily.
crinoi'dal, *adj.*, rel. to a crinoid.
crin'oline, *n.*, a hoop skirt.
crip'ple, *v.t.*, to maim, hamper; *n.*, one who is crippled.
crip'pled, *p.p.*, cripple.
crip'pling, *pr.p.*, cripple.
cri'sis, *n.*, a turning-point, extremity of danger.
crisp, *v.t.*, to make wavy; *adj.*, wavy, brittle, bright.
cris'pated, *adj.*, curled.
crisped, *p.p.*, crisp.
crisp'er, *n.*, anything that crisps.
Cris'pin, *n.*, the patron saint of shoemakers.
crisp'ing, *pr.p.*, crisp.
crisp'ly, *adv.*, in a crisp way.
crisp'ness, *n.*, the crisp state or quality.
crisp'y, *adj.*, somewhat crisp.
criss'-cross, *adj.*, backwards and forwards; *n.*, an intersection.
cris'tate, *adj.*, crested.
cris'tated, *adj.*, crested.
crite'ria, *n.*, pl. of criterion.
crite'rion, *n.*, a test, proof.
crit'ic, *n.*, a critical person.
crit'ical, *adj.*, exact; judging; censorious; at a crisis.
crit'ically, *adv.*, in a critical way.
crit'icalness, *n.*, the critical habit or quality.
crit'icism, *n.*, judgment, censure.
crit'icize, *v.t.*, to pass judgment on; to review; to censure.
crit'icized, *p.p.*, criticize.
crit'icizer, *n.*, one who criticizes.
crit'icizing, *pr.p.*, criticize.
critique', *n.*, a review of literary or artistic work.
criz'zle, *v.i.*, to become wrinkled.
croak, *v.i.*, to make a hoarse noise; to grumble; *n.*, a hoarse noise or cry.
croaked, *p.p.*, croak.
croak'er, *n.*, one who croaks; a grumbler.
croak'ing, *pr.p.*, croak.
Cro'at, *n.*, a native of Croatia.
Croa'tian, *adj.*, pert. to Croatia.
croche, *n.*, the top of an antler.
cro'chet, *v.t.*, to work at crochet; *n.*, work with a crochet hook.
cro'cheted, *p.p.*, crochet.
cro'cheting, *pr.p.*, crochet.
crock, *v.t.*, to overlay with soot; *n.*, an earthenware pot; soot on a pot.

crock'ery, *n.*, earthenware.

crock'et, *n.*, a projecting ornament on spires and canopy work.

croc'odile, *n.*, a large amphibian.

crocodil'ian, *adj.*, rel. to the crocodile.

cro'cus, *n.*, a spring flower so named.

croft, *n.*, a small field enclosure; a small farm holding; *v.t.*, to bleach.

croft'er, *n.*, a small farmer in the Highlands of Scotland.

croft'ing, *pr.p.*, croft.

crois'ant, *adj.*, crescent.

crom'lech, *n.*, a prehistoric stone circle.

cromor'na, *n.*, an organ reed-stop.

Cromwellian, *adj.*, rel. to Cromwell.

crone, *n.*, an old woman.

cro'ny, *n.*, a very intimate friend.

crook, *v.t.*, to bend; *v.i.*, to be bent; *n.*, a staff with a bent end; a sharper.

crooked, *p.p.*, crook.

crook'ed, *adj.*, not straight; unprincipled.

crook'edly, *adv.*, in a crooked way.

crook'edness, *n.*, the crooked state or quality.

crook'ing, *pr.p.*, crook.

crop, *v.t.*, to cut close, reap; lay under crops; *v.i.*, to sprout, appear suddenly; *n.*, the result of cropping; a bird's craw; close cut of hair; a hunting-whip.

cropped, *p.p.*, crop.

crop'per, *n.*, a cropping implement; one who crops; a bad fall (*slang*).

crop'ping, *pr.p.*, crop.

cro'quet, *v.t.*, to punish an opponent's ball; *n.*, the game so named.

crore, *n.*, a sum of Indian money = 100 lakhs.

cro'sier, **cro'zier**, *n.*, a bishop's staff or crook.

cro'siered, *adj.*, having a crosier.

cros'let, *n.*, a crucible.

cross, *v.t.*, to place across; pass over; mark crosswise; hinder; *n.*, an upright line crossed by another at right angles; the Christian emblem of Salvation; a great trial; a cross-breed.

cross'-action, *n.*, a counter-suit.

cross'-armed, *n.*, with crossed arms.

cross'-bar, *v.t.*, to draw a bar across; *n.*, a bar.

cross'-barred, *p.p.*, cross-bar.

cross'-bearer, *n.*, the bearer of a cross.

cross'bill, *n.*, a bird with a cruciform bill.

cross'bow, *n.*, an old cross-shaped bow.

cross'-breed, *n.*, an animal of mixed breed.

cross'-cut, *v.t.*, to intersect.

crossed, *p.p.*, cross.

cross-examina'tion, *n.*, the examination of a witness on behalf of the opposing party.

cross-exam'ine, *v.t.*, to examine a witness on behalf of the opposing party.

cross-exam'ined, *p.p.*, cross-examine.

cross-exam'ining, *pr.p.*, cross-examine

cross'-eyed, *adj.*, squinting.

cross'-grained, *adj.*, with irregular grain; of difficult temper.

cross'-head, *n.*, a beam crossing the top.

cross'ing, *pr.p.*, cross; *n.*, the act of crossing; a way over; a thwarting.

cross'-legged, *n.*, with the legs crossed.

cross'let, *see* croslet.

cross'ly, *adv.*, in a cross way.

cross'ness, *n.*, the cross quality; bad temper.

cross'-pur'pose, *n.*, a contrary purpose.

cross'-ques'tion, *v.t.*, *i.q.* cross-examine.

cross'-road, *n.*, a road meeting or crossing another.

cross'-tie, *n.*, a sleeper.

cross'-tree, *n.*, the short projections on a mast.

cross'ways, *n.*, a meeting-place of several roads.

cross'wise, *adv.*, across; like a cross.

crotch, *n.*, a hook.

crotched, *adj.*, hooked.

crotch'et, *n.*, a hook-shaped musical note; a foolish whim.

crotch'eted, *adj.*, consisting of crotchets.

crotch'ety, *adj.*, possessed by whims; odd.

cro'ton, *n.*, the E. Indian plant so named.

croton'ic, *adj.*, rel. to croton.

cro'ton-oil, *n.*, the oil from the seeds of croton.

crouch, *v.i.*, to bend down, stoop.

crouched, *p.p.*, crouch.

crouch'ing, *pr.p.*, crouch.

croup, *n.*, an affection of the trachea and larynx.

croupade', *n.*, a horse's leap in which the hind legs are drawn up.

crou'pier, *n.*, the man who handles the money at a gaming-table.

crow, *v.i.*, to make the sound of a cock; to exult over; *n.*, the sound of a cock; the bird so named.

crow'bar, *n.*, an iron lever.

crowd, *v.t.*, to press together; to oppress with numbers; *v.i.*, to assemble in great numbers; *n.*, a gathering of people or things; a Welsh stringed musical instrument.

crowd'ed, *p.p.*, crowd.

crowd'er, *n.*, one who crowds; a player on a crowd.

crowd'ing, *pr.p.*, crowd.

crowd'y, *n.*, thick gruel.

crowed, *p.p.*, crow.

crow'foot, *see* crow's-foot.

crow'ing, *pr.p.*, crow.

crown, *v.t.*, to place a crown on; to surmount; to complete; *n.*, a king's head-covering; royal power; a wreath; summit; a five-shilling piece; one of the sizes of paper and books.

crowned, *p.p.*, crown.

crown'er, *n.*, one who crowns; *see also* coroner.

crown'-glass, *n.*, best window glass.

crown'ing, *pr.p.*, crown; *adj.*, completing; supreme

crown' lawyer, *n.*, the Crown's legal adviser.

crown'less, *adj.*, without a crown.

crown'-post, *n.*, a king-post.

crown'prince, *n.*, the heir apparent.

crown'-wheel, *n.*, a variety of cog-wheel.

crow's'-foot, *n.*, the ranunculus; *n.*, a wrinkling of the skin beneath the eyes.

crow's'-nest, *n.*, a look-out on a mast.

cro'zier, *see* crosier.

cro'ziered, *see* crosiered.

cru'cial, *adj.*, rel. to a *crux* or cross; transverse; severe.

cru'ciate, *adj.*, cross-shaped.

cru'cible, *n.*, a melting-pot.

crucif'erous, *adj.*, with petals arranged in the form of a cross.

cru'cified, *p.p.*, crucify.

cru'cifier, *n.*, one who crucifies.

cru'cifix, *n.*, a cross with Our Lord's figure on it.

crucifix'ion, *n.*, the act of crucifying; terrible suffering.

cru'ciform, *adj.*, cross-shaped.

cru'cify, *v.t.*, to fasten to a cross; to torture; to subdue.

cru'cifying, *pr.p.* crucify.

crude, *adj.*, raw, coarse, uncultured.

crude'ly, *adv.*, in a crude way.

crude'ness, *n.*, the crude quality.

cru'dity, *n.*, *i.q.* crudeness.

cru'el, *adj.*, pitiless, fond of inflicting pain, severe.

cru'elly, *adv.*, in a cruel way.

cru'elty, *n.*, a cruel act.

cru'et, *n.*, a small vial.

cruise, *v.i.*, to sail about; *n.*, a voyage.

cruised, *p.p.*, cruise.

cruis'er, *n.*, a war vessel of high speed.

cruis'ing, *pr.p.*, cruise.

crumb, *v.t.*, to spread crumbs on; *n.*, a small fragment.

crumb'-cloth, *n.*, a cloth to protect against crumbs.

crumb'ing, *pr.p.*, crumb.

crum'ble, *v.t.*, to break up into crumbs; to shatter to pieces; *v.i.*, go to pieces.

crum'bled, *p.p.*, crumble.

crum'bling, *pr.p.*, crumble.

crum'my, *adj.*, full of crumbs; soft.

crump, *adj.*, crisp.

crum'pet, *n.*, a variety of tea-cake.

crum'ple, *v.t.*, to rumple, squeeze into folds; *v.i.*, to become crumpled.

crum'pled, *p.p.*, crumple.

crum'pling, *pr.p.*, crumple.

crunch, *v.t.*, to crush with the teeth; *v.i.*, to make a crunching noise; *n.*, the act of crunching.

crunched, *p.p.*, crunch.

crunch'ing, *pr.p.*, crunch.

crup'per, *n.*, a horse's buttocks; the leather loop passed under a horse's tail.

cru'ral, *adj.*, rel. to the thigh.

crusade', *n.*, an expedition of Crusaders; any vigorous concerted action; *v.i.*, to go on a crusade.

crusa'der, *n.*, a soldier under the emblem of the Cross fighting for the recovery of the Holy Land.

crusa'ding, *pr.p.*, crusade.

cruse, *n.*, a vessel, a dish.

crush, *v.t.*, to press, break, put down; *v.i.*, to go out of shape or into a smaller space; *n.*, a press, crowd.

crushed, *p.p.*, crush.

crush'er, *n.*, anything that crushes; a conclusive argument.

crush'ing, *pr.p.*, crush.

crust, *v.t.*, to overlay with crust; *v.i.*, to form a crust; *n.*, a hard outer layer or surface.

Crusta'cea, *n. pl.*, the generic name of shell-fish.

crusta'cean, *adj.*, rel. to the Crustacea; *n.*, one of the C.

crustaceol'ogy, *n.*, the study of Crustacea.

crusta'ceous, *adj.*, shell-covered.

crusta'ceousness, *n.*, the quality or state of being crustaceous.

crusta'ted, *adj.*, shell-covered.

crusta'tion, *adj.*, the act of forming a crust.

crust'ed, *adj.*, having a crust; *p.p.*, crust.

crust'ily, *adv.*, in a crusty way.

crust'iness, *n.*, surliness.

crust'ing, *pr.p.*, crust.

crust'y, *adj.*, crust-like, surly.

crutch, *n.*, a support for lameness; part of a lady's saddle.

crutched, *adj.*, having a crutch.

Crutched Fri'ars, *n.*, members of an

Order wearing a cross on their habits.

crux, *n.*, a cross; a trial; the crucial point.

cry, *v.t.*, to call out, proclaim; *v.i.*, to utter a cry, to exclaim, to weep; *n.*, a loud utterance, an attack of weeping, a party watchword, the noise of a pack of hounds on the chase.

cry'ing, *pr.p.*, cry.

crypt, *n.*, an underground vault.

crypt'ic, *adj.*, dark, mysterious.

crypt'ical, *adj.*, *i.q.* cryptic.

cryp'togam, *n.*, one of the cryptogamous plants.

Cryptoga'mia, *n.*, a name for flowerless plants.

cryptogam'ic, *adj.*, rel. to cryptogamia.

cryptog'amist, *n.*, a student of cryptogams.

cryptog'amous, *adj.*, pert. to the cryptogams.

cryptog'amy, *n.*, the cryptogamous state.

cryp'togram, *n.*, writing in cipher.

cryp'tograph, *n.*, a piece of writing in cipher.

cryptog'rapher, *n.*, one who writes in cipher.

cryptograph'ic, *adj.*, rel. to cryptography.

cryptograph'ical, *adj.*, *i.q.* cryptographic.

cryptog'raphy, *n.*, the art of writing in cipher.

crys'tal, *adj.*, made of crystal; transparent; *n.*, a definitely shaped piece of inorganic matter; very clear glass.

crys'talline, *adj.*, like crystal, transparent.

crys'tallite, *n.*, a spurious crystal formation.

crys'tallizable, *adj.*, able to be crystallized.

crystalliza'tion, *n.*, the act or state of crystallizing.

crys'tallize, *v.t.*, to turn into crystal; to give a permanent definite shape to; *v.i.*, to become crystal; to take definite shape.

crys'tallized, *p.p.*, crystallize.

crys'tallizing, *pr.p.*, crystallize.

crystallog'rapher, *n.*, an expert in the science of crystals.

crystallograph'ic, *adj.*, rel. to crystallography.

crystallog'raphy, *n.*, the science of crystal structure.

crys'talloid, *adj.*, like a crystal; *n.*, a protein crystal.

crystallol'ogy, *n.*, the science of crystals.

crys'tallotype, *n.*, a picture taken on glass or some transparent material.

cte'noid, *adj.*, having combs; *n.*, a fish with comb-like scales.

cub, *v.t.*, to produce cubs; *n.*, the young of a fox or other wild beast.

cu'bage, *n.*, the act of estimating cubic content; *n.*, the measure of cubic content.

Cu'ban, *adj.*, pert. to Cuba.

cuba'tion, *n.*, the act or period of lying.

cu'bature, *n.*, the cubic content; the process of ascertaining the cubic content.

cubbed, *p.p.*, cub.

cub'bing, *pr.p.*, cub; *adj.*, pert. to the chase of young foxes.

cub'by-hole, *n.*, a snug hiding place.

cube, *n.*, a solid body with six equal square faces; the multiple of the square of a quantity by the quantity itself; *v.t.*, to raise to the power of a cube.

cu'beb, *n.*, Java pepper.

cu'bic, *adj.*, rel. to a cube.

cu'bicle, *n.*, a bedroom.

cu'biform, *adj.*, cube-shaped.

cu'bit, *n.*, a measure roughly corresponding to the length of the forearm.

cu'bital, *adj.*, rel. to the cubit.

cu'boid, *adj.*, cube-like.

cuboi'dal, *adj.*, *i.q.* cuboid.

cuck'ing-stool, *n.*, a chair in which scolds were ducked under water.

cuck'old, *v.t.*, to seduce a man's wife; *n.*, a man whose wife is an adulteress.

cuck'oo, *n.*, the bird so named.

cu'cullate, *adj.*, hooded, hood-shaped.

cu'cullated, *adj.*, *i.q.* cucullate.

cu'cumber, *n.*, the creeping plant so named.

cucur'bit, *n.*, a generic name for pumpkins, melons, etc.; a gourd-shaped vessel

cud, *n.*, food returned from a ruminant's first stomach.

cud'bear, *n.*, a dye made from a cudbear lichen.

cud'dle, *v.t.*, to clasp closely; *v.i.*, to snuggle up; *n.*, an embrace.

cud'dled, *p.p.*, cuddle.

cud'dling, *pr.p.*, cuddle.

cud'dy, *n.*, a ship's galley.

cudg'el, *v.t.*, to strike with a cudgel; *n.*, a short, thick stick.

cudg'elled, **cudg'eled**, *p.p.*, cudgel.

cudg'el(l)er, *n.*, one who cudgels.

cudg'el(l)ing, *pr.p.*, cudgel.

cud'weed, *n.*, a plant so named.

cue, *n.*, a tail; the end words of an actor's part; a hint; a stick for driving a billiard ball.

cuff, *v.t.*, to slap; *n.*, a blow with the hand; a wrist-band.

cuffed, *p.p.*, cuff.

Cu'fic, *adj.*, pert. to the old Arabic written character.
cuff'ing, *pr.p.*, cuff.
cuirass', *n.*, a breastplate.
cuirassier', *n.*, a horse soldier wearing a cuirass.
cuish, *n.*, *i.q.* cuisse.
cuisine', *n.*, a kitchen; cookery.
cuisse, *n.*, armour for the thigh.
Cul'dee, *n.*, an early Order of religious.
cul-de-sac', *n.*, a passage with one outlet.
culic'iform, *adj.*, shaped like a gnat.
cu'linary, *adj.*, pert. to the kitchen.
cull, *v.t.*, to pick out, gather.
culled, *p.p.*, cull.
cul'lender, *n.*, *i.q.* colander.
cull'ing, *pr.p.*, cull.
cul'lion, *n.*, an orchid; a low person.
cul'lis, *n.*, a roof-gutter; a groove; *see* coulisse.
cul'ly, *v.t.*, to trick; *n.*, a dupe.
culm, *n.*, a grass-stem; poor kind of anthracite.
culmif'erous, *adj.*, having stems.
cul'minant, *adj.*, culminating.
cul'minate, *v.i.*, to reach the highest point.
cul'minated, *p.p.*, culminate.
cul'minating, *pr.p.*, culminate.
culmina'tion, *n.*, the act of culminating; the highest point attained.
culpabil'ity, *n.*, the state or quality of being culpable.
cul'pable, *adj.*, blameworthy, guilty.
cul'pableness, *n.*, *i.q.* culpability.
cul'pably, *adv.*, in a culpable way.
cul'prit, *n.*, a guilty person.
cult, *n.*, a system of worship; a particular devotion.
cul'tivable, *adj.*, able to be cultivated.
cul'tivatable, *adj.*, *i.q.* cultivable.
cul'tivate, *v.t.*, to bring under cultivation; to seek the society of.
cul'tivated, *p.p.*, cultivate.
cul'tivating, *pr.p.*, cultivate.
cultiva'tion, *n.*, the act of cultivating; a cultivated state; refinement.
cul'tivator, *n.*, anything that cultivates.
cul'trate, *adj.*, like a knife.
cul'trated, *adj.*, made like a knife.
cul'triform, *adj.*, knife-like.
cul'tural, *adj.*, tending or pert. to culture.
cul'ture, *n.*, tillage; intellectual improvement; the growing of bacteria.
cul'tured, *adj.*, cultivated, refined.
cul'tus, *n.*, a system of worship; cult.
cul'ver, *n.*, a wood-pigeon.
cul'verin, *n.*, an obsolete type of cannon.
cul'vert, *n.*, a subterranean drain.
cum'bent, *adj.*, reclining.
cum'ber, *v.t.*, to oppress, burden.
cum'bered, *p.p.*, cumber.
cum'berer, *n.*, one who cumbers.
cum'bering, *pr.p.*, cumber.
cum'bersome, *adj.*, troublesome, embarrassing.
cum'bersomely, *adv.*, in a cumbersome way.
cum'bersomeness, *n.*, the state or quality of being cumbersome.
Cum'brian, *n.*, pert. to Cumbria.
cum'brous, *adj.*, troublesome, heavy.
cum'brously, *adv.*, in a cumbrous way.
cum'brousness, *n.*, the state or quality of being cumbrous.
cum'in, cum'min, *n.*, an aromatic plant so named.
cum'merbund, *n.*, a sash, waistband.
cu'mulate *v.t.*, to pile up.
cu'mulated, *p.p.*, cumulate.
cu'mulating, *pr.p.*, cumulate.
cumula'tion, *n.*, the act of cumulating.
cu'mulative, *adj.*, increasing by addition.
cu'mulose, *adj.*, composed of cumuli.
cumulo-cirro-stra'tus, *n.*, a composite cloud - formation, consisting of cumulus and cirro-stratus.
cumulo-stra'tus, *n.*, a cloud half cumulus, half stratus.
cu'mulus, *n.*, a pile; a mass of round woolly clouds.
cu'neal, *adj.*, rel. to a wedge.
cu'neate, *adj.*, wedge-like.
cu'neated, *adj.*, *i.q.* cuneate.
cune'iform, *n.*, the ancient wedge-shaped Assyrian and Persian script.
cun'ning, *adj.*, sly, underhand, designing; *n.*, skill, craftiness.
cun'ningly, *adv.*, in a cunning way.
cun'ningness, *n.*, cunning conduct.
cup, *v.t.*, to bleed by cupping; *n.*, a vessel for drinking; anything shaped like a cup; a vessel used in surgical bleeding.
cup'bearer, *n.*, one who hands round a cup.
cup'board, *n.*, a shut-up closet.
cu'pel, *n.*, a refining vessel.
cupella'tion, *n.*, the act of refining.
cup'ful, *n.*, the quantity contained in a cup.
Cu'pid, *n.*, the Roman god of love.
cupid'ity, *adj.*, covetousness.

cu'pola, *n.*, a small domical lantern surmounting a building; a roof hemispherical or nearly so; a domical shot-proof ship's turret.
cupped, *p.p.*, cup.
cup'per, *n.*, one who cups.
cup'ping, *pr.p.*, cup.
cup'ping-glass, *n.*, a glass used in bleeding patients.
cu'preous, *adj.*, coppery.
cuprif'erous, *adj.*, yielding copper.
cu'prite, *n.*, red copper oxide.
cu'pule, *n.*, a small cup.
cupulif'erous, *adj.*, producing small cups.
cur, *n.*, a mongrel; a surly fellow.
curabil'ity, *n.*, a curable state.
cur'able, *adj.*, able to be cured.
cur'ableness, *n.*, *i.q.* curability.
curaçao', curaçoa', *n.*, a liqueur flavoured with orange-peel.
cu'racy, *n.*, a curate's office or sphere of work.
cura're, *n.*, a South American poison used for smearing arrows.
cu'rarize, *v.t.*, to smear with curare.
curas'sow, *n.*, a S. American bird so named.
cu'rate, *n.*, one with a cure of souls; the parish priest.
cur'ative, *adj.*, of curing effect.
cura'tor, *n.*, an officer in charge of a gallery or museum.
curb, *v.t.*, to restrain, hold; *n.*, anything that checks; a bit.
curbed, *p.p.*, curb.
curb'ing, *pr.p.*, curb.
curb'-roof, *n.*, a roof with two sets of rafters.
curb'stone, *see* kerbstone.
curcu'lio, *n.*, a weevil.
curd, *v.t.*, to make into curd; *v.i.*, to form curd; *n.*, the separated solid part of milk.
curd'ed, *p.p.*, curd.
curd'iness, *n.*, the state or quality of curd.
cur'dle, *v.t.*, to make into curd; *v.i.*, to become curd.
cur'dled, *p.p.*, curdle.
cur'dling, *pr.p.*, curdle.
curd'y, *adj.*, curdlike, curding.
cure, *v.t.*, to heal, remedy, preserve; to salt; *n.*, healing; spiritual charge; a benefice.
curé, *n.*, a French parish priest.
cured, *p.p.*, cure.
cure'less, *adj.*, past healing; without a cure.
cur'er, *n.*, one who cures.
curette', *n.*, a surgical instrument so named.
cur'few, *n.*, an old edict for the extinction of house fires at a fixed hour; the bell rung at curfew time.
cu'ria, *n.*, an assembly, a senate-house; the papal court.
cu'rial, *adj.*, rel. to a curia.
cur'ing, *pr.p.*, cure.
cu'rio, *n.*, a curiosity, bric-à-brac.
curios'ity, *n.*, the act or character of the curious.
curio'so, *n.*, a person skilled in an art or the arts.
cu'rious, *adj.*, inquisitive, exact, strange.
cu'riously, *adv.*, in a curious way.
cu'riousness, *n.*, the character of the curious.
curl, *v.t.*, to twist, bend; *v.i.*, to move spirally; become curled; play at curling.
curled, *p.p.*, curl.
curl'er, *n.*, one who curls; a player at curling.
cur'lew, *n.*, the bird so named.
curl'icue, *n.*, any queer, twisted thing.
cur'liness, *n.*, a tendency to curl.
curl'ing, *pr.p.*, curl; *n.*, the game so named played on ice.
curl'y, *adj.*, in curls; full of curls.
curmudg'eon, *n.*, a stingy fellow.
cur'rant, *n.*, a small dried grape; the shrub and fruit so named.
cur'rency, *n.*, circulation; the monetary system.
cur'rent, *adj.*, running; of the present time; common; *n.*, a flow, a stream, the set of a stream.
cur'rently, *adv.*, commonly, in the general opinion.
cur'ricle, *n.*, an old-fashioned two-wheeled, two-horsed vehicle.
curric'ula, *n.*, pl. of curriculum.
curric'ulum, *n.*, a prescribed course of studies.
cur'ried, *p.p.*, curry.
cur'rier, *n.*, a leather-dresser.
cur'rish, *adj.*, cur-like.
cur'ry, *v.t.*, to dress tanned leather, to clean a horse, to flavour with curry, to flatter.
cur'ry-comb, *v.t.*, to groom a horse; *n.*, a comb for grooming horses.
cur'rying, *pr.p.* curry.
curse, *v.t.*, to invoke evil against, to imprecate; *v.i.* to use bad language; *n.*, an imprecation against; a cause of trouble.
cursed, *p.p.*, curse.
curs'edness, *n.*, the state of being cursed.
curs'ing, *pr.p.*, curse.
cur'sitor, *n.*, once a clerk of the Chancery Court.
cur'sive, *adj.*, running.
cur'sorily, *adv.*, in a cursory way.
cur'soriness, *n.*, the quality of being cursory.

cur'sory, *adj.*, superficial.

curt, *adj.*, short, abrupt.

curtail', *v.t.*, to shorten at the end; reduce.

curtailed', *p.p.*, curtail.

curtail'er, *n.*, one who curtails.

curtail'ing *pr.p.*, curtail.

curtail'ment, *n.*, the act or effect of curtailing.

cur'tain, *v.t.*, to enclose with a curtain; *n.*, a screen; a castle wall between the towers.

cur'tained, *p.p.*, curtain.

cur'taining, *pr.p.*, curtain.

cur'tate, *adj.*, shortened.

curta'tion, *n.*, the difference between the curtate and the real distance of a planet from the sun or the earth.

cur'tilage, *n.*, the ground immediately connected with a house.

curt'ly, *adv.*, in a curt way.

curt'ness, *n.*, the act or state of being curt.

curt'sy, *v.i.*, to drop a curtsy; *n.*, a respectful dropping of the knees by women.

cu'rule, *adj.*, magisterial.

curv'ate, *adj.*, curved.

curv'ated, *adj.*, *i.q.* curvate.

curva'tion, *n.*, the act of curving.

curv'ature, *n.*, the act of bending; a bent state.

curve, *v.t.*, to bend; *v.i.*, to move in a curve; *n.*, a bent line, a bend.

curved, *p.p.*, curve.

cur'vet, *v.i.*, to prance; *n.*, a horse's prance.

cur'veted, *p.p.*, curvet.

cur'veting, *pr.p.*, curvet.

cur'viform, *adj.*, curved.

curvilin'eal, *adj.*, having curved lines.

curvilin'ear, *adj.*, *i.q.* curvilineal.

curv'ing, *pr.p.*, curve.

curv'ity, *n.*, the state of being curved.

cush'at, *n.*, a ring-dove.

cush'ion, *v.t.*, to put on a cushion, to furnish with cushions, *v.i.*, to go off the cushion at billiards; *n.*, a sort of pillow; the elastic padding round a billiard table.

cush'ioned, *p.p.*, cushion.

cush'ioning, *pr.p.*, cushion.

cush'iony, *adj.*, cushion-like, comfortable.

cusp, *n.*, a sharp point; an architectural spear-shaped ornament.

cusped, *adj.*, having cusps.

cus'pid, *n.*, a canine tooth.

cus'pidal, *adj.*, rel. to, of the nature of, a cusp.

cus'pidated, *adj.*, sharpened to a cusp.

cus'tard, *n.*, a confection of milk, eggs, sugar, and other things.

custo'dial, *adj.*, rel. to custody.

custo'dian, *n.*, one who has custody.

cus'tody, *n.*, guard, confinement, care, charge.

cus'tom, *n.*, what is usual; habit, wont; purchasing.

cus'tomable, *adj.*, liable to duty.

cus'tomarily, *adv.*, in a customary way.

cus'tomary, *adj.*, usual, wonted.

cus'tomed, *adj.*, accustomed.

cus'tomer, *n.*, a buyer; a person with some peculiarity.

cus'tom-house, *n.*, the place where customs duties are collected.

cus'toms, *n. pl.*, taxes on goods imported or exported

cus'tos, *n.*, a guardian, warden; a mark at the end of a musical line showing the first note on the following line.

cut, *v.t.*, to cleave, divide, make an incision; to refuse to recognize; put a spin on a ball; to hit a ball to the right; *n.*, an incision, gash; a stroke at cricket; a ditch; style; an engraving; a direct way; a spin on a ball; a snub.

cuta'neous, *adj.*, rel. to the skin.

cute, *adj.*, sharp, cunning.

cute'ness, *n.*, the quality of being cute.

cu'ticle, *n.*, the outer skin.

cutic'ular, *adj.*, rel. to the cuticle.

cu'tis, *n.*, the skin.

cut'lass, *n.*, a short, heavy sort of sword, slightly curved.

cut'ler, *n.*, one who makes or sells cutlery.

cut'lery, *n.*, a cutler's trade; cutting implements.

cut'let, *n.*, a slice of meat or fish for broiling.

cut'-out, *n.*, a switch to cut off an electric circuit.

cut'purse, *n.*, one who steals purses.

cut'ter, *n.*, anything that cuts; a small single-masted vessel; a small steamer used in the revenue service.

cut'throat, *n.*, an assassin.

cut'ting, *pr.p.*, cut; *adj.*, sharp-edged; *n.*, the act of cutting; an extract, a clipping.

cut'tle-fish, *n.*, the marine creature so named.

cut'ty, *adj.*, short; *n.*, a short thing, as a pipe, etc.

cut'-water, *n.*, the front part of a ship or boat.

cy'anate, *n.*, a cyanic acid salt.
cyan'ic, *adj.*, rel. to blue or to cyanogen.
cy'anid, *n.*, a compound formed with cyanogen.
cy'anide, *n.*, *i.q.* cyanid.
cyan'ogen, *n.*, a gas compounded of carbon and nitrogen.
cyanom'eter, *n.*, an apparatus for measuring the intensity of blue.
cyan'uret, *n.*, *i.q.* cyanid.
cyanu'ric, *adj.*, pert. to cyanogen and urea.
cyc'lamen, *n.*, a bulbous flowering plant so named.
cy'cle, *v.i.*, to move in a cycle; to bicycle; *n.*, a recurring period; a series; a bicycle or motor-cycle.
cy'cled, *p.p.*, cycle.
cyc'lic, *adj.*, moving in a fixed order, recurring in cycles; bel. to the epic cycle.
cyc'lical, *adj.*, *i.q.* cyclic.
cy'cling, *pr.p.*, cycle; *n.* the act of cycling.
cy'clist, *n.*, a bicyclist or motor-cyclist.
cy'clograph, *n.*, an apparatus for drawing arcs.
cy'cloid, *adj.*, like a circle; approaching the circular.
cycloi'dal, *adj.*, *i.q.* cycloid.
cyclom'eter, *n.*, an instrument that records a wheel's rotations.
cyclom'etry, *n.*, the art of measuring circles.
cy'clone, *n.*, a storm moving in a circle.
cyclope'an, *adj.*, rel. to the Cyclopes; gigantic.
cyclope'dia, *n.*, a dictionary of general knowledge, or of a special subject.
cyclope'dic, *adj.*, like a cyclopedia.
cyclope'dical, *adj.*, *i.q.* cyclopedic.
cyclop'ic, *adj.*, *i.q.* cyclopean.
Cy'clops, *n.*, one of the Cyclopes, fabulous one-eyed giants
cyg'net, *n.*, a young swan.
cyl'inder, *n.*, a solid, roll-like figure; a hollow cylinder-like vessel.
cylin'dric, *adj.*, pert. to a cylinder.
cylin'drical, *adj.*, *i.q.* cylindric.
cylin'driform, *adj.*, shaped like a cylinder.
cyl'indroid, *adj.*, like a cylinder.
cylindromet'ric, *adj.*, pert. to the measuring of cylinders.
cy'ma, *n.*, a curved moulding.
cym'bal, *n.*, one of a pair of brass plates clashed together for musical purposes.
cyme, *n.*, a form of inflorescence.
cy'mene, *n.*, an oily liquid compound obtained by distillation of camphor with phosphoric anhydrid.
cy'mose, *adj.*, of the nature of a cyme.
Cym'ric, *adj.*, rel. to the Cymri or Welsh.
cynan'che, *n.*, inflammation of the throat.
cynan'thropy, *n.*, the mental delusion of a man who believes himself to be a dog.
cyn'ic, *adj.*, rel. to Diogenes and the Cynics; *n.*, a sneering, captious person.
cyn'ical, *adj.*, sneering, captious.
cyn'icism, *n.*, the act or character of a cynic.
cyn'osure, *n.*, the Little Bear constellation; a centre of attraction.
cy'press, *n.*, a large, dark evergreen.
Cyp'rian, *adj.*, pert. to Cyprus and Venus.
cyp'rine, *adj.*, pert. to the cypress.
Cyp'riote, *n.*, a native of Cyprus.
Cyrena'ic, *adj.*, pert. to Cyrene.
Cyre'nian, *adj.*, *i.q.* Cyrenaic.
cyriolog'ic, *adj.*, rel. to hieroglyphics and capital letters.
cyst, *n.*, a sac of morbid matter in an animal body.
cyst'ic, *adj.*, rel. to cysts.
cysti'tis, *n.*, inflammation of the bladder.
cys'tocele, *n.*, a form of hernia.
cystot'omy, *n.*, an operation for cyst.
Cythere'an, *adj.*, connected with Cythera, and with Cytherea or Aphrodite (Venus).
Czar, *n.*, the title of the Emperor of Russia and the King of Bulgaria.
Czar'evitch, *n.*, a Czar's heir apparent.
Czarev'na, *n.*, the Czarevitch's consort.
Czari'na, *n.*, the Russian Empress.
Czech, *n.*, the name of the Bohemian Slavs.

D

dab, *v.t.*, to strike gently, or with something soft or moist; to deface; *n.*, a gentle blow; a piece of something soft.
dabbed, *p.p.*, dab.
dab'bing, *pr.p.*, dab.
dab'ble, *v.t.* and *i.*, to wet by dips or strokes; to work, but not in earnest.
dab'bled, *p.p.*, dabble.
dab'bler, *n.*, one who dabbles.
dab'bling, *pr.p.*, dabble.
dab'chick, *n.*, a small swimming bird.
dab'ster, *n.*, an adept; a proficient.
dace, *n.*, a small river fish.
dachs'hund, *n.*, a badger dog; small, short-legged, and long-bodied.
Da'cian, *adj.*, rel. to Dacia.
dacoit', *n.*, an East Indian brigand.
dac'tyl, *n.*, in poetry a foot containing one long and two short syllables:—(— ◡ ◡).
dac'tylar, *adj.*, pert. to a finger, toe, or claw; dactylic.
dactyl'ic, *adj.*, consisting of dactyls.
dactylog'raphy, *n.*, type-writing.
dactylol'ogy, *n.*, finger-language used by deaf mutes.
dad, *n.*, a childish name for father.
dad'dy, *n.*, a longer form of dad.
da'do, *n.*, the lower part of a wall when ornamented differently from the rest.
dae'dal, *adj.*, ingenious; intricate.
Daed'alus, *n.*, the builder of the Cretan Labyrinth.
daff, *v.t.*, to put off.
daf'fodil, *n.*, a kind of lily.
daft, *adj.*, crazy.

dag'ger, *n.*, a short sword for stabbing.
dag'gle, *v.t.* and *i.*, to draggle.
Da'gon, *n.*, the Philistine god.
daguer'rean, *adj.*, rel. to Daguerre or the daguerreotype.
daguerre'otype, *n.*, an early kind of photograph.
dahabee'yah, *n.*, a Nile passenger-boat.
dah'lia, *n.*, a flowering plant so named.
dai'ly, *adv.* and *adj.*, day by day.
dain'tily, *adv.*, in a dainty manner.
dain'tiness, *n.*, fineness of taste.
dain'ty, *adj.*, delicious; fastidious; elegant; trim; *n.*, something pleasant to the taste.
dai'ry, *n.*, a place for selling milk and making butter and cheese.
dai'rymaid, *n.*, a female servant doing dairy work.
da'is, *n.*, the raised end of a hall.
dais'ied, *adj.*, adorned with daisies.
dai'sy, *n.*, a small white flower with a yellow centre.
dak, *n.*, a relay of letter carriers, etc.; the post.
dale, *n.*, a hollow between hills.
dall, *n.*, a slab of marble.
dal'liance, *n.*, trifling; giving and receiving caresses.
dal'lied, *p.p.*, dally.
dal'lier, *n.*, one who dallies.
dal'ly, *v.i.*, to put off by doing little or nothing; to trifle.
dalmat'ic, *n.*, the deacon's Mass vestment, worn also by a bishop under the chasuble.

Dalto'nian, *n.*, one suffering from colour-blindness.
dal'tonism, *n.*, colour-blindness.
dam, *n.*, a bank to keep back water; a mother of four-footed animals; *v.t.*, to confine water by a bank.
dam'age, *n.*, harm; loss; *v.t.*, to injure.
dam'ageable, *adj.*, capable of being damaged.
dam'aged, *p.p.*, damage.
dam'aging, *pr.p.*, damage; *adj.*, injurious.
dam'ascene, *n.*, a damson; *v.t.*, *i.q.* damaskeen.
dam'ask, *n.*, cloth with woven figures on it; *adj.*, of a deep rose colour; *v.t.*, to variegate.
dam'asked, *p.p.*, damask.
damaskeen', *v.t.*, to ornament metals with inlaid gold or silver.
damaskeened', *p.p.*, damaskeen.
dam'assin, *n.*, damask with gold and silver flowers woven in.
dame, *n.*, a lady; a knight's or baronet's wife.
dammed, *p.p.*, dam.
dam'ming, *pr.p.*, dam.
damn, *v.t.*, to give over to everlasting punishment; to condemn.
damnabil'ity, *n.*, the quality of being damnable.
dam'nable, *adj.*, odious; detestable.
dam'nableness, *n.*, the state of being damnable.
dam'nably, *adv.*, in a damnable manner.
damna'tion, *n.*, punishment of the wicked.

dam'natory, *adj.*, condemnatory.
damned, *adj.*, detestable; *p.p.*, damn.
dam'nified, *p.p.*, damnify.
dam'nify, *v.t.*, to cause loss to.
dam'nifying, *pr.p.*, damnify.
dam'ning, *p.p.*, damn; *adj.*, convicting.
damp, *n.*, slight wetness; noxious gas in a coal-mine; *adj.*, feeling wet; *v.t.*, to make slightly wet; to depress.
damped, *p.p.*, damp.
damp'en, *v.t.*, to make damp.
damp'ened, *p.p.*, dampen.
damp'ening, *pr.p.*, dampen.
damp'er, *n.*, a plate in a chimney to regulate draught; a means of reducing sound in a musical instrument.
damp'ing, *pr.p.* damp; *adj.*, depressing.
damp'ish, *adj.*, rather damp.
damp'ness, *n.*, slight wetness.
dam'sel, *n.*, a girl.
dam'son, *n.*, a kind of plum.
dan, *n.*, an old title=master.
dance, *v.i.*, to move on foot to music; *n.*, a movement in time with music.
danced, *p.p.*, dance.
dan'cer, *n.*, one who dances.
dan'cing, *pr.p.*, dance; *n.*, the act of dancing.
dan'delion, *n.*, a herb with a yellow flower.
dan'der, *n.*, temper; a feeling of anger.
dan'dify, *v.t.*, to dress out like a dandy.
dan'dified, *p.p.*, dandify.
dan'dle, *v.t.*, to toss up and down gently.
dan'dled, *p.p.*, dandle.
dan'dler, *n.*, one who dandles.
dan'dling, *pr.p.*, dandle.
dan'druff, *n.*, scurf on the scalp.
dan'dy, *n.*, a fop.
dan'dyish, *adj.*, like a dandy.
dan'dyism, *n.*, foppishness.
Dane, *n.*, a native of Denmark.
Dane'geld, *n.*, the Danish exaction on our Saxon kings.
Dane'gelt, *n.*, *i.q.* Danegeld.
dane'wort, *n.*, dwarf elder.
dan'ger, *n.*, a state in which harm may happen.
dan'gerous, *adj.*, bringing or involving danger.
dan'gerously, *adv.*, in a dangerous manner.
dan'gerousness, *n.*, the state of being dangerous.
dan'gle, *v.t.* and *i.*, to hang loosely.
dan'gled, *p.p.*, dangle.
dan'gler, *n.*, one who hangs about women.
dan'gling, *pr.p.*, dangle.
Da'nish, *adj.*, pert. to Denmark.
dank, *adj.*, damp.
danseuse', *n.*, a female stage-dancer.
Danu'bian, *adj.*, rel. to the R. Danube.
dap, *v.i.*, to let bait fall gently into the water.
Daph'ne, *n.*, laurel.
dap'per, *adj.*, little and active; smart in dress.
dap'perling, *n.*, a little fellow; a dwarf.
dap'ple, *v.t.*, to mark with spots; *adj.*, spotted.
dap'pled, *p.p.*, dapple; *adj.*, variegated.
dap'pling, *pr.p.*, dapple.
dar, *n.*, the European black tern.
dare, *v.i.*, to be bold enough; *v.t.*, to defy; to challenge; *n.*, a dace.
dared, *p.p.*, dare.
dar'er, *n.*, one who dares.
dar'ic, *n.*, a Persian gold or silver coin.
dar'ing, *adj.*, bold; *n.*, courage: *pr.p.*, dare.
dar'ingly, *adv.*, in a daring manner.
dark, *adj.*, wanting light; *n.*, want of light.
dark'en, *v.t.*, to make dark; *v..*, to grow dark.
dark'ened, *p.p.*, darken.
dark'ener, *n.*, one who, or that which, darkens.
dark'ening, *pr.p.*, darken.
dark'er, *adj.*, *comp.* of dark.
dark'est, *adj.*, *super.* of dark.
dark'-eyed, *adj.*, having dark eyes.
dark'ish, *adj.*, dusky.
dark'ling, *adv.*, in the dark; *adj.*, black-looking; groping.
dark'ly, *adv.*, in a dark manner.
dark'ness, *n.*, the state of being dark.
dark'some, *adj.*, dark.
dar'ling, *n.*, one much beloved.
darn, *v.t.*, to mend a hole in cloth; *n.*, a place darned.
darned, *p.p.*, darn.
dar'nel, *n.*, a troublesome weed in corn.
darn'er, *n.*, one who darns.
darn'ing, *pr.p.*, darn; *n.*, the act of darning.
dart, *n.*, a pointed hand-missile; a sudden spring; *v.t.*, to throw suddenly; *v.i.*, to shoot out.
dart'ed, *p.p.*, dart.
dart'er, *n.*, one who darts; a tropical swimming bird.
dart'ing, *pr.p.*, dart.
Dar'winism, *n.*, the biological doctrines of Charles Darwin.
dash, *v.t.*, to strike strongly against; *v.i.* to rush; *n.*, a sudden rush; a mark (—) in printing or writing.
dash'-board, *n.*, a mud-catching board.
dashed, *p.p.*, dash.
dash'er, *n.*, one who, or that which, dashes.
dash'ing, *adj.*, showy; impetuous: *pr.p.*, dash.

das'tard, *n.*, a coward.
das'tardliness, *n.*, cowardliness.
das'tardly, *adj.*, cowardly.
das'tardy, *n.*, mean timorousness.
da'ta, *n. pl.*, facts given from which others may be inferred.
da'table, date'able, *adj.*, capable of being dated.
Data'ria, *n.*, an office in the papal court.
da'tary, *n.*, an officer having charge of the Dataria.
date, *n.*, the fruit of a kind of palm; a fixed point of time; *v.t.*, to note the time of.
da'ted, *p.p.*, date.
date'less, *adj.*, undated; of extreme antiquity; eternal.
da'ting, *pr.p.*, date.
da'tive, *adj.*, describing one of the cases of a noun; *n.*, the dative case.
da'tum, *n.*, sing. of data.
datu'ra, *n.*, a strong narcotic plant.
datu'rin, datu'rine, *n.*, atropin.
daub, *n.*, a coarse painting; *v.t.*, to smear with something soft.
daubed, *p.p.*, daub.
daub'er, *n.*, one who daubs; an indifferent painter.
daub'ing, *pr.p.*, daub.
daub'y, *adj.*, slimy; viscous.
daugh'ter, *n.*, a female child.
daugh'terly, *adj.*, dutiful; becoming a daughter.
daunt, *v.t.*, to intimidate.
daunt'ed, *p.p.*, daunt.
daunt'er, *n.*, one who daunts.
daunt'ing, *pr.p.*, daunt.
daunt'less, *adj.*, fearless.
daunt'lessly, *adv.*, in a bold, fearless manner.
daunt'lessness, *n.*, fearlessness.
dau'phin, *n.*, the French Heir Apparent.
dau'phiness, *n.*, the dauphin's wife.
dav'enport, *n.*, a small writing-table.
dav'it, *n.*, one of the two wooden or iron arms for hoisting or lowering a boat.
da'vy, *n.*, a safety lamp.
daw, *n.*, a bird of the crow kind.
daw'dle, *v.i.*, to waste time; to saunter.
daw'dled, *p.p.*, dawdle.
daw'dler, *n.*, a waster of time.
daw'dling, *pr.p.*, dawdle; *n.*, the act or habit of dawdling.
dawn, *n.*, the break of day; *v.i.*, to begin to show light.
dawned, *p.p.*, dawn.
dawn'ing, *n.*, the growing light in the morning; *pr.p.*, dawn.
day, *n.*, a period of 24 hours; the time of light between sunrise and sunset.
day'book, *n.*, a book recording daily sales and purchases.
day'break, *n.*, the beginning of the dawn.
day'-dream, *n.*, a reverie.
day'-labourer, *n.*, a worker for a daily wage.
day'light, *n.*, the light of the day; natural light.
day'spring, *n.*, the dawn.
day'-star, *n.*, the star that remains visible some time after dawn.
day'time, *n.*, the time of daylight.
day'-work, *n.*, work for a day's wage.
daze, *v.t.*, to make stupid.
dazed, *p.p.*, daze.
da'zing, *pr.p.*, daze.
daz'zle, *v.t.*, to dim the eyes by too strong light.
daz'zled, *p.p.*, dazzle.
daz'zling, *pr.p.*, dazzle; *adj.*, excessively brilliant.
dea'con, *n.*, a member of the third order of the clergy; a Presbyterian secular office-bearer.
dea'coness, *n.*, a female deacon, but not in Holy Orders.
dea'conry, *n.*, the office of a deacon.
dead, *adj.*, without life; *n.*, stillest time; *pl.*, those who are dead; *adv.*, completely.
dead'en, *v.t.*, to take away feeling; to soften.
dead'ened, *p.p.*, deaden.
dead'ening, *pr.p.*, deaden; *adj.*, depressing.
dead'eye, *n.*, a block pierced with three holes used on ships.
dead'head, *n.*, one who is admitted free to a theatre, etc.
dead'heat, *n.*, a race in which the competitors finish exactly side by side.
dead'-letter, *n.*, a law no longer enforced; a letter returned by the P.O.
dead'lier, *adj.*, *comp.* of deadly.
deadliest, *super.* of deadly.
dead'lift, *n.*, a direct lift of a dead-weight; an extreme emergency.
dead'light, *n.*, a shutter over a cabin window.
dead'liness, *n.*, the quality of being deadly.
dead'lock, *n.*, a complete standstill.
dead'ly, *adj.*, causing death.
dead'-march, *n.*, a funeral march.
dead'ness, *n.*, lifelessness.
dead'-weight, *n.*, an oppressive burden.
deaf, *adj.*, unable to hear.
deaf'en, *v.t.*, to make deaf.
deaf'ened, *p.p.*, deafen.
deaf'ening, *pr.p.*, deafen; *adj.*, extremely loud.

deaf'-mute, *n.*, a deaf and dumb person.
deaf'ness, *n.*, want of hearing.
deal, *n.*, a division; a thin cutting of wood; *v.t.*, to give out in parts; to carry on business; to distribute cards.
deal'er, *n.*, one who deals; a trader.
deal'ing, *pr.p.*, deal; *n.*, conduct; intercourse of business.
dealt, *p.p.*, deal.
dean, *n.*, the chief dignitary in a cathedral or collegiate church; the disciplinary official of a college; the president of an academic faculty.
dean'ery, *n.*, the charge of a dean; also his house; the area of a rural dean's authority.
dear, *adj.*, greatly beloved; costly.
dear'er, *adj. comp.* of dear.
dear'est, *adj., super.* of dear.
dear'ly, *adv.*, with great love; at a high price.
dear'ness, *n.*, high price; preciousness.
dearth, *n.*, scarcity.
dear'y, dear'ie, *n.*, a word of endearment.
dea'sil, *n.*, motion from east to west, as of the sun (*Scot.*).
death, *n.*, loss of life.
death'-bed, *n.*, the bed on which one dies.
death'less, *adj.*, that cannot die.
death'like, *adj.*, *s.q.* deathly.
death'ly, *adj.*, resembling death.
death'-rate, *n.*, the proportion of deaths in a specified area.
death's'-head, *n.*, a human skull.
death'-warrant, *n.*, an order for execution.
débâc'le, *n.*, a confused rout; a sudden breaking up of ice in a river (*Fr.*).
debar', *v.t.*, to shut out; to hinder.

debark', *v.t.* and *i.*, to land from a ship.
debarka'tion, *n.*, the act of landing.
debarked', *p.p.*, debark.
debark'ing, *pr.p.*, debark.
debarred', *p.p.*, debar.
debar'ring, *pr.p.*, debar.
debase', *v.t.*, to make of less value.
debased', *p.p.*, debase.
debase'ment, *n.*, the act of debasing.
deba'ser, *n.*, one who debases.
deba'sing, *pr.p.*, debase.
deba'table, *adj.*, that can be debated.
debate', *n.*, a contention in words; *v.t.*, to discuss.
deba'ted, *p.p.*, debate.
deba'ter, *n.*, one who debates.
deba'ting, *pr.p.*, debate.
debauch', *v.t.*, to lead away from virtue; *n.*, a course of intemperance or impurity.
debauched', *p.p.*, debauch; *adj.*, vitiated in morals.
debauchee', *n.*, a person given over to intemperance.
debauch'er, *n.*, one who debauches.
debauch'ery, *n.*, sinful indulgence.
debauch'ing, *pr.p.*, debauch.
deben'ture, *n.*, a document charging property with the repayment of a loan.
deben'tured, *adj.*, secured by debenture.
debil'itate, *v.t.*, to make weak.
debil'itated, *p.p.*, debilitate.
debil'itating, *adj.*, tending to weaken; *pr.p.*, debilitate.
debilita'tion, *n.*, the act of weakening.
debil'ity, *n.*, bodily weakness.
deb'it, *n.*, something recorded as owed; *v.t.*, to mark as due.

deb'ited, *p.p.*, debit.
deb'iting, *pr.p.*, debit.
debonair', *adj.*, accomplished; well-bred; courteous; affable.
debouch', *v.i.*, to emerge into open ground.
débris', *n.*, broken pieces of anything.
debt, *n.*, what one owes.
debt'less, *adj.*, free of debt.
debt'or, *n.*, one who owes.
début', *n.*, a first appearance.
débutant, *n.*, one who makes his début.
débutante, *n.*, fem. of débutant.
dec'achord, *n.*, a Greek ten-stringed musical instrument.
dec'adal, *adj.*, pert. to, or consisting of, tens.
dec'ade, *n.*, ten years; any group of ten.
dec'adence, *n.*, a growing worse.
dec'adency, *n.*, *i.q.* decadence.
dec'agon, *n.*, a plane figure with ten sides.
dec'agram, *n.*, a weight of ten grammes.
Decagyn'ia, *n. pl.*, plants having ten pistils.
decag'ynous, *adj.*, having ten pistils.
decahe'dral, *adj.*, having ten plane faces.
decahe'dron, *n.*, a solid figure with ten faces.
dec'alitre, dec'aliter, *n.*, a French measure of capacity.
Dec'alogue, *n.*, the Ten Commandments.
Decam'eron, *n.*, Boccaccio's famous collection of tales.
dec'ametre, dec'ameter, *n.*, a French measure of length.
decamp', *v.i.*, to go away secretly.
decamped', *p.p.*, decamp.
decamp'ing, *pr.p.*, decamp.

decamp'ment, *n.*, a marching off.
deca'nal, *adj.*, rel. to a dean.
Decan'dria, *n. pl.*, plants having ten stamens.
decan'drian, *adj.*, having ten stamens.
decan'drous, *adj.*, *i.q.* decanerian.
decan'gular, *adj.*, having ten angles.
deca'ni, *n.*, *lit.*, the Dean's side of the choir (a direction in ecclesiastical music)
decant', *v.t.*, to pour from one vessel to another.
decant'ed, *p.p.*, decant.
decant'er, *n.*, a glass bottle for wine or spirits.
decant'ing, *pr.p.*, decant.
decaphyl'lous, *adj.*, having ten leaves.
decap'itate, *v.t.*, to behead.
decap'itated, *p.p.*, decapitate.
decap'itating, *pr.p.*, decapitate.
decapita'tion, *n.*, the act of beheading.
dec'apod, *n.*, a crustacean with ten feet (crab, etc.).
decap'odous, *adj.*, having ten feet.
decar'bonate, *v.t.*, to deprive of carbon dioxide.
decar'bonated, *p.p.*, decarbonate.
decar'bonating, *pr.p.*, decarbonate.
decarboniza'tion, *n.*, the act of decarbonizing.
decar'bonize, *v.t.*, to deprive of carbon.
decar'bonized, *p.p.*, decarbonize.
decar'bonizing, *pr.p.*, decarbonize.
dec'astich, *n.*, a ten-line poem.
dec'astyle, *n.*, a portico of ten columns.
decasyllab'ic, *adj.*, having ten syllables.
decay', *v.i.*, to waste away; *n.*, a growing weak; withering.
decayed', *p.p.*, decay.
decay'ing, *pr.p.*, decay.

decease', *n.*, death; *v.i.*, to die.
deceased', *p.p.*, decease.
deceas'ing, *pr.p.*, decease.
deceit', *n.*, misrepresentation; trickery.
deceit'ful, *adj.*, addicted to deceit.
deceit'fulness, *n.*, tendency to deceive.
deceit'less, *adj.*, free of deceit.
deceiv'able, *adj.*, liable to be deceived.
deceive', *v.t.*, to mislead; to practise deceit on; to disappoint.
deceived', *p.p.*, deceive.
deceiv'er, *n.*, one who deceives.
deceiv'ing, *pr.p.*, deceive.
Decem'ber, *n.*, the last month of the year. (When the year's reckoning began in March, the name December, *i.e.* tenth month, was appropriate.)
decem'fid, *adj.*, divided into ten parts.
decem'vir, *n.*, one of ten magistrates in ancient Rome.
decem'viral, *adj.*, pert. to the decemvirs.
decem'virate, *n.*, the decemvirs collectively.
de'cency, *n.*, propriety, delicacy, becomingness.
decen'nary, *n.*, a period of ten years; *adj.*, pert. to a ten year period.
decen'nial, *adj.*, happening every ten years.
decen'nium, *n.*, *i.q.* decennary.
de'cent, *adj.*, acting in a proper way; becoming.
de'cently, *adv.*, in a decent manner.
decen'tralize, *v.t.*, to distribute what has been centralized.
decen'tralized, *p.p.*, decentralize.
decen'tralizing, *pr.p.*, decentralize.

decep'tion, *n.*, the act of deceiving.
decep'tive, *adj.*, tending to deceive.
decep'tively, *adv.*, in a manner to deceive.
decep'tiveness, *n.*, tendency to deceive.
decern', *v.i.* and *t.*, to pass judgment (*Scots law*).
deci'dable, *adj.*, able to be decided.
decide', *v.t.*, to determine; *v.i.*, to resolve.
deci'ded, *adj.*, with one's mind made up; unmistakable; *p.p.*, decide.
deci'dedly, *adv.*, in a decided way; certainly.
deci'der, *n.*, one who decides.
deci'ding, *pr.p.*, decide.
decid'uous, *adj.*, shedding leaves periodically.
decid'uousness, *n.*, the quality of being deciduous.
dec'igram, *n.*, a French weight.
dec'ilitre, dec'iliter, *n.*, a French measure of capacity.
decil'lion, *n.*, a number consisting of 1 followed by sixty ciphers.
decil'lionth, *n.*, one of a decillion equal parts.
dec'imal, *adj.*, counted by tens; *n.*, a fraction having some power of 10 as denominator.
dec'imalize, *v.t.*, to turn into a decimal.
dec'imate, *v.t.*, to kill every tenth man.
dec'imated, *p.p.*, decimate.
dec'imating, *pr.p.*, decimate.
decima'tion, *n.*, the act of decimating.
dec'imetre, dec'imeter, *n.*, a French measure of length.
deci'pher, *v.t.*, to read a cipher; to solve a difficulty in writing.
deci'pherable, *adj.*, able to be deciphered.
deci'phered, *p.p.*, decipher.

deci'pherer, *n.*, one who deciphers.

deci'phering, *pr.p.*, decipher.

deci'sion, *n.*, determination; a judgment.

deci'sive, *adj.*, ending dispute; quick in deciding.

deci'sively, *adv.*, in a decisive manner.

deci'siveness, *n.*, the quality of being decisive.

deck, *v.t.*, to cover; to adorn; *n.*, the upper platform of a ship; pack of cards.

decked, *adj.*, adorned; furnished with a deck: *p.p.*, deck.

deck'er, *n.*, a vessel with a deck or decks; one who decks.

deck'ing, *pr.p.*, deck.

declaim', *v.i.* and *t.*, to make a set speech.

declaimed', *p.p.*, declaim.

declaim'er, *n.*, one who speaks for effect.

declaim'ing, *pr.p.*, declaim.

declama'tion, *n.*, impassioned speech; the art of declaiming.

declam'atory, *adj.*, rel. to declamation.

declar'able, *adj.*, able to be declared.

declara'tion, *n.*, the act of declaring.

declar'ative, *adj.*, making declaration.

declar'atively, *adv.*, in a declarative manner.

declar'atory, *adj.*, distinctly expressive of opinions.

declare', *v.t.*, to affirm; to state fully.

declared', *p.p.*, declare.

declar'er, *n.*, one who declares.

declar'ing, *pr.p.*, declare.

declen'sion, *n.*, a falling off; deterioration; case-inflection; a noun-class.

decli'nable, *adj.*, having case inflections.

declina'tion, *n.*, deviation; one of the co-ordinates of a heavenly body; the deviation of the magnetic needle from the true north.

dec'linator, *n.*, an instrument for observing declination.

decli'natory, *adj.*, characterized by declining.

decline', *v.i.*, to sink or stoop to a lower level; to decay; *v.t.*, to refuse; to inflect so as to form the oblique cases; *n.*, a deterioration; consumption.

declined', *p.p.*, decline.

decli'ner, *n.*, one who declines.

decli'ning, *pr.p.*, decline.

declinom'eter, *n.*, an instrument for measuring the declination of the magnetic needle.

decli'nous, *adj.*, bending downwards (applied to stamens of a flower).

decliv'ity, *n.*, a slope downward.

decli'vous, *adj.*, sloping downward.

decoct', *v.t.*, to prepare by boiling.

decoct'ed, *p.p.*, decoct.

decoct'ible, *adj.*, able to be boiled.

decoct'ing, *pr.p.*, decoct.

decoc'tion, *n.*, the water in which a substance has been boiled; the act of boiling.

decoc'tive, *adj.*, having a tendency to decoct.

decol'late, *v.t.*, to behead.

decol'lated, *adj.*, beheaded; truncated; *p.p.*, decollate.

decol'lating, *pr.p.*, decollate.

decolla'tion, *n.*, the act of beheading.

décolleté', *adj.*, having the neck exposed (*Fr.*).

decol'orant, *n.*, a substance that bleaches.

decolora'tion, *n.*, removal of colour.

decol'orize, *v.t.*, *i.q.* decolour.

decol'orized, *p.p.*, decolorize.

decol'orizing, *pr.p.*, decolorize.

decol'our, **decol'or,** *v.t.*, to deprive of colour; to bleach.

decol'o(u)red, *p.p.*, decolour.

decol'o(u)ring, *pr.p.*, decolour.

decompo'sable, *adj.*, able to be decomposed.

decompose', *v.t.*, to resolve into original elements; *v.i.*, to decay.

decomposed', *p.p.*, decompose.

decompo'sing, *pr.p.*, decompose.

decom'posite, *adj.*, compounded a second time.

decomposi'tion, *n.*, analysis; disintegration; decay.

decompound', *adj.*, *i.q.* decomposite; *v.t.* to compound with things already compounded.

decompound'ed, *p.p.*, decompound.

decompound'ing, *pr.p.* decompound.

decon'secrate, *v.t.*, to unconsecrate; to secularise.

dec'orate, *v.t.*, to adorn.

dec'orated, *p.p.*, decorate.

dec'orating, *pr.p.*, decorate.

decora'tion, *n.*, ornamentation; a badge of honour.

dec'orative, *adj.*, adorning.

dec'orativeness, *n.*, quality of being decorative.

dec'orator, *n.*, one who decorates.

deco'rous, *adj.*, seemly; befitting.

deco'rously, *adv.*, in a becoming manner.

deco'rousness, *n.*, propriety of behaviour.

decor'ticate, *v.t.*, to strip the bark from.

decor'ticated, *p.p.*, decorticate.

decort'icating, *pr.p.*, decorticate.
decortica'tion, *n.*, the act of decorticating.
deco'rum, *n.*, decency of behaviour.
decoy', *n.*, a lure; a snare; *v.t.*, to entrap by deceit.
decoy'-duck, *n.*, a duck used to ensnare other ducks; *v.t.*, to entice, ensnare.
decoyed', *p.p.*, decoy.
decoy'ing, *pr.p.*, decoy.
decrease', *v.t.* and *i.*, to diminish; *n.*, gradual diminution.
decreased', *p.p.*, decrease.
decreas'ing, *pr.p.*, decrease.
decreas'ingly, *adv.*, by diminishing.
decree', *n.*, an edict; a judicial decision; *v.t.*, to determine judicially or legislatively.
decreed', *p.p.*, decree.
decre'er, *n.*, one who decrees.
decree'ing, *pr.p.*, decree.
dec'rement, *n.*, the small quantity by which a variable becomes less and less.
decrep'it, *adj.*, weakened with age.
decrep'itate, *v.i.*, to crackle when roasting.
decrep'itated, *p.p.*, decrepitate.
decrep'itating, *pr.p.*, decrepitate.
decrepita'tion, *n.*, the act of flying asunder with a crackling noise when strongly heated.
decrep'itude, *n.*, the state of being decrepit.
decres'cent, *adj.*, decreasing.
decre'tal, *n.*, a papal letter settling a point of ecclesiastical law.
decre'tist, *n.*, one who is skilled in knowledge of decretals or common law.
decre'tive, *adj.*, pert. to a decree.
decre'tory, *adj.*, established by a decree.
decri'al, *n.*, the act of decrying.
decried', *p.p.*, decry.
decrusta'tion, *n.*, the removal of a crust.
decry', *v.t.*, to discredit by fault-finding.
decry'ing, *pr.p.*, decry.
decum'bence, *n.*, the state of being decumbent.
decum'bency, *n.*, *i.q.* decumbence.
decum'bent, *adj.*, reclining; prostrate.
dec'uple, *adj.*, tenfold; *n.*, a number ten times repeated; *v.t.*, to multiply by 10.
dec'upled, *p.p.*, decuple.
dec'upling, *pr.p.*, decuple.
decu'rion, *n.*, a Roman officer over ten soldiers.
decur'rent, *adj.*, the base extended downwards along the stem (*Bot.*).
decur'sive, *adj.*, running down; decurrent.
decurve', *v.t.*, to make to curve downward.
decurved', *p.p.*, decurve.
decurv'ing, *pr.p.*, decurve.
decus'sate, *v.t.*, to intersect in a crosswise manner; *adj.*, *i.q.* decussated.
decus'sated, *adj.*, crossed; *p.p.*, decussate.
decus'sating, *pr.p.*, decussate.
decussa'tion, *n.*, the act of crossing at right angles.
decus'satively, *adv.* crosswise.
de'dal, *adj.*, *i.q.* daedal.
deda'lian, *adj.*, *i.q.* daedal.
ded'alous, *adj.*, having a margin with intricate windings (*Bot.*).
ded'icate, *v.t.*, to set apart, devote; inscribe to somebody.
ded'icated, *p.p.*, dedicate.
ded'icating, *pr.p.*, dedicate.
dedica'tion, *n.*, devotion; setting apart; use; an address prefixed to a book.
ded'icator, *n.*, one who dedicates.
ded'icatory, *adj.*, serving as a dedication.
deduce', *v.t.*, to infer; trace descent of.
deduced', *p.p.*, deduce.
deduce'ment, *n.*, deduction.
deducibil'ity, *n.*, the quality of being deducible.
dedu'cible, *adj.*, able to be deduced.
deduc'ing, *pr.p.*, deduce.
deduct', *v.t.*, to subtract.
deduct'ed, *p.p.*, deduct.
deduct'ing, *pr.p.*, deduct.
deduc'tion, *n.*, an inference from general to particular; a subtraction.
deduct'ive, *adj.*, deducible; rel. to deduction.
deed, *n.*, an act; a legal contract or agreement.
deed'less, *adj.*, inactive.
deem, *v.t.*, to believe; to judge; *v.i.*, to suppose.
deemed, *p.p.*, deem.
deem'ing, *pr.p.*, deem.
deem'ster, *n.*, one of two Manx justices.
deep, *adj.*, descending far downward; *n.*, the open sea.
deep'en, *v.t.*, to make deep or deeper; *v.i.*, to become deeper.
deep'ened, *p.p.*, deepen.
deep'ening, *pr.p.*, deepen.
deep'er, *adj.*, *comp.* of deep.
deep'est, *adj.*, *super.* of deep.
deep'ly, *adv.*, far below the surface; profoundly.
deep'ness, *n.*, depth.
deep'-seated, *adj.*, deep down.

deer, *n.*, a ruminant quadruped with branching horns.
deer'-stalker, *n.*, one who stalks deer.
deface', *v.t.*, to disfigure.
defaced', *adj.*, injured on the surface.
deface'ment, *n.*, injury to the surface.
defa'cer, *n.*, one who defaces.
defa'cing, *pr.p.*, deface.
de fac'to, phrase = actual (Lat.).
defal'cate, *v.t.*, to misappropriate money.
defal'cated, *p.p.*, defalcate.
defal'cating, *pr.p.*, defalcate.
defalca'tion, *n.*, a fraudulent deficiency in money matters.
de'falcator, *n.*, an embezzler.
defama'tion, *n.*, slander; calumny.
defam'atory, *adj.*, slanderous; calumnious.
defame', *v.t.*, to slander; to libel.
defamed', *p.p.*, defame.
defa'mer, *n.*, a slanderer.
defa'ming, *pr.p.*, defame.
default', *n.*, an omission of a duty; *v.t.*, to neglect an engagement.
default'ed, *p.p.*, default.
default'er, *n.*, one who makes default.
default'ing, *pr.p.*, default.
defea'sance, *n.*, a rendering null and void.
defea'sible, *adj.*, able to be annulled.
defea'sibleness, *n.*, the state of being defeasible.
defeat', *n.*, a frustration; an overthrow; *v.t.*, to overcome; to resist with success.
defeat'ed, *p.p.*, defeat.
defeat'ing, *pr.p.*, defeat.
def'ecate, *v.t.*, to purge of extraneous matter.
def'ecated, *p.p.*, defecate.
def'ecating, *pr.p.*, defecate.
defeca'tion, *n.*, the act of clarifying.
def'ecator, *n.*, one who or that which defecates.
defect', *n.*, a fault; something lacking; a shortcoming.
defect'ible, *adj.*, deficient.
defec'tion, *n.*, abandonment; apostasy.
defect'ive, *adj.*, imperfect.
defect'ively, *adv.*, imperfectly.
defect'iveness, *n.*, faultiness.
defence', *n.*, the act of defending; a protection; a vindication.
defenced', *adj.*, provided with a defence.
defence'less, *adj.*, without defence.
defence'lessness, *n.*, the state of being defenceless.
defend', *v.t.*, to protect against attack.
defend'able, *adj.*, able to be defended.
defendant, *n.*, one who opposes a charge or complaint.
defend'ed, *p.p.*, defend.
defend'er, *n.*, a champion; an advocate.
defend'ing, *pr.p.*, defend.
defensibil'ity, *n.*, the quality of being defensible.
defen'sible, *adj.*, able to be defended.
defen'sive, *adj.*, serving to defend.
defen'sively, *adv.*, in a defensive manner; *n.*, the state of being on defence.
defer', *v.t.*, to postpone; *v.i.*, to yield to another's opinion.
def'erence, *n.*, respect; courteous consideration.
def'erent, *n.*, an imaginary circle employed by Ptolemy in his system of astronomy.
deferen'tial, *adj.*, expressing deference.
deferred', *p.p.*, defer.
defer'rer, *n.*, one who defers.
defer'ring, *pr.p.*, defer.
defeu'dalize, *v.t.*, to deprive of feudal character.
defi'ance, *n.*, a challenging to fight; opposition to authority.
defi'ant, *adj.*, insolent, bold, disobedient.
defi'ciency, *n.*, want; something less than is necessary.
defi'cient, *adj.*, wanting, imperfect.
defi'ciently, *adv.*, in a defective manner.
def'icit, *n.*, a deficiency (in money).
defied', *p.p.*, defy.
defi'er, *n.*, one who defies.
defile', *v.t.*, to make unclean; *v.i.*, to march off in a line.
de'file, *n.*, a long, narrow pass.
defiled', *p.p.*, defile.
defile'ment, *n.*, the effect of defiling.
defi'ler, *n.*, one who defiles.
defi'ling, *pr.p.*, defile.
defi'nable, *adj.*, able to be defined.
define', *v.t.*, to determine the limits or meaning of.
defined', *p.p.*, define.
defi'ner, *n.*, one who defines.
defi'ning, *pr.p.*, define.
def'inite, *adj.*, certain; precise.
def'initely, *adv.*, in a definite manner.
def'initeness, *n.*, the state or character of being definite.
defini'tion, *n.*, a brief and exact description of a thing by its properties; clearness of outline.
defin'itive, *adj.*, determinate; conclusive.
defin'itively, *adv.*, conclusively; unconditionally.
deflagrabil'ity, *n.*, combustibility.

def'lagrable, *adj.*, combustible.
def'lagrate, *v.t.* and *i.*, to burn rapidly.
def'lagrated, *p.p.*, deflagrate.
def'lagrating, *pr.p.*, deflagrate.
deflagra'tion, *n.*, rapid combustion of a mixture.
def'lagrator, *n.*, an electrical instrument for producing the combustion of metallic substances.
deflate', *v.t.*, to withdraw the air from.
defla'ted, *p.p.*, deflate.
defla'ting, *pr.p.*, deflate.
defla'tion, *n.*, the act or effect of deflating; artificial depression of prices.
deflect', *v.t.* and *i.*, to turn from a straight line.
deflect'ed, *p.p.*, deflect.
deflect'ing, *pr.p.*, deflect.
deflec'tion, deflex'ion, *n.*, deviation.
deflect'or, *n.*, a diaphragm in a lamp or stove by means of which air and gas are mingled and made to burn completely.
deflo'rate, *adj.*, of plants, having shed their pollen on their flowers.
deflora'tion, *n.*, rape.
deflow'er, *v.t.*, to violate; to ravish.
deflow'ered, *p.p.*, deflower.
deflow'erer, *n.*, one who deflowers.
deflow'ering, *pr.p.*, deflower.
deflux'ion, *n.*, a catarrhal discharge.
defor'est, *v.t.*, to remove the trees from.
defor'ested, *p.p.*, deforest.
defor'esting, *pr.p.*, deforest.
deforesta'tion, *n.*, the act or practice of deforesting.
deform', *v.t.*, to disfigure.
deformed', *adj.*, misshapen; *p.p.*, deform.
deform'er, *n.*, one who deforms.
deform'ing, *pr.p.*, deform.
deform'ity, *n.*, the state of being deformed; any misshapen part of the body.
defraud', *v.t.*, to cheat.
defraud'ed, *p.p.*, defraud.
defraud'er, *n.*, one who defrauds.
defraud'ing, *pr.p.*, defraud.
defray', *v.t.*, to discharge; settle.
defrayed', *p.p.*, defray.
defray'er, *n.*, one who pays expenses.
defray'ing, *pr.p.*, defray.
deft, *adj.*, dexterous.
deft'ly, *adv.*, neatly; dexterously.
deft'ness, *n.*, dexterity.
defunct', *adj.*, dead.
defy', *v.t.*, to challenge; to set at nought.
defy'ing, *pr.p.*, defy.
degen'eracy, *n.*, a state of deterioration.
degen'erate, *adj.*, base; mean; having declined in natural or moral worth; *n.*, a creature that has so declined.
degen'erate, *v.i.*, to become of a lower type, physically or morally.
degen'erated, *p.p.*, degenerate.
degen'erately, *adv.*, in a degenerate manner.
degen'erateness, *n.* a degenerate state.
degen'erating, *pr.p.*, degenerate.
degenera'tion, *n.*, *i.q.* degeneracy.
degen'erative, *adj.*, causing degeneration.
deglu'tinate, *v.t.*, to unglue.
deglu'tinated, *p.p.*, deglutinate.
deglu'tinating, *pr.p.*, deglutinate.
degluti'tion, *n.*, the act or power of swallowing.
degrada'tion, *n.*, debasement; the act of degrading.
degrade', *v.t.*, to debase; to reduce from a higher to a lower rank; *v.i.*, to degenerate.
degra'ded, *adj.*, sunk to a vile state; *p.p.*, degrade.
degra'ding, *adj.*, dishonouring; *pr.p.*, degrade.
degra'dingly, *adv.*, in a degrading manner.
degree', *n.*, rank; station; extent; the 360th part of the circumference of a circle; a division marked on a scientific instrument; a university title of distinction.
dehisce', *v.i.*, to open (as the seed-vessels of plants).
dehis'cence, *n.*, the opening or splitting of certain organs in plants.
dehort'ative, *adj.*, dissuasive.
dehort'atory, *adj.*, *i.q.* dehortative.
de'icide, *n.*, the act of putting Jesus Christ to death; *n.*, one of Christ's murderers.
deifica'tion, *n.*, the act of deifying.
de'ified, *p.p.*, deify.
de'ifier, *n.*, one that deifies.
de'iform, *adj.*, of godlike form.
de'ify, *v.t.*, to make a god of.
de'ifying, *pr.p.*, deify.
deign, *v.i.*, to condescend.
deigned, *p.p.*, deign.
deign'ing, *pr.p.*, deign.
deil, *n.*, devil (*Scot.*).
deipnos'ophist, *n.*, a philosopher who cultivates learned conversation at meals.
de'ism, *n.*, the creed of a deist.
de'ist, *n.*, one who believes in a supreme being but denies revealed religion.
deis'tic, *adj.*, pert. to deism.

deis'tical, *adj.*, *i.q.* deistic.

de'ity, *n.*, divinity; Godhead; God; a fabulous god or goddess.

deject', *v.t.*, to cast down; to dispirit.

deject'ed, *adj.*, downcast; sorrowful.

deject'edly, *adv.*, sadly; heavily.

deject'edness, *n.*, dejection.

deject'er, *n.*, one who dejects.

deject'ing, *pr.p.*, deject.

dejec'tion, *n.*, lowness of spirits.

deject'ory, *adj.*, promoting the action of the bowels.

déjeuner, *n.*, breakfast; luncheon.

de ju're, *adv.* and *adj.*, by right; rightful (*Lat.*).

delaine', *n.*, a muslin made of cotton and wool, used chiefly as a printing cloth.

delay', *v.t.*, to retard; to hinder; *v.i.*, to linger; *n.*, a lingering or deferring.

delayed', *p.p.*, delay.

delay'er, *n.*, one who delays.

delay'ing, *pr.p.*, delay.

de'le, *v.t.*, blot out; erase; remove (*Lat.*).

delec'table, *adj.*, highly pleasing.

delecta'tion, *n.*, a giving delight; delight.

del'egate, *n.*, a representative; a deputy; *adj.*, representative.

del'egate, *v.t.*, to entrust to another's care and management.

del'egated, *p.p.*, delegate.

del'egating, *pr.p.*, delegate.

delega'tion, *n.*, appointment to act as deputy; a person or body of persons deputed to act for another or others.

delete', *v.t.*, to erase; to strike out with a pen or pencil.

delete'rious, *adj.*, noxious.

dele'tion, *n.*, the act of deleting; a passage deleted.

delf, *n.*, glazed earthenware dishes.

De'lian, *adj.*, rel. to Delos or to Apollo.

delib'erate, *adj.*, carefully considering probable consequences; not hasty; slow.

delib'erate, *v.i.*, to ponder; to reflect.

delib'erated, *p.p.*, deliberate.

delib'erately, *adv.*, in a deliberate manner.

delib'erateness, *n.*, the state or quality of being deliberate.

delib'erating, *pr.p.*, deliberate.

delibera'tion, *n.*, careful consideration; discussion and examination of pros and cons.

delib'erative, *adj.*, pert. to deliberation.

delib'erator, *n.*, one who deliberates.

del'ible, *adj.*, able to be deleted (more correctly spelt *deleble*).

del'icacy, *n.*, the quality of being delicate.

del'icate, *adj.*, dainty; easily injured; in weak health.

del'icately, *adv.*, daintily; tenderly.

del'icateness, *n.*, the state of being delicate.

delicatesse', *n.*, delicacy (*Fr.*).

deli'cious, *adj.*, affording exquisite pleasure.

deli'ciously, *adv.*, in a delicious manner.

deli'ciousness, *n.*, the quality of being delicious.

deliga'tion, *n.*, bandaging.

delight', *v.t.*, to please highly; *v.i.*, to be greatly pleased; *n.*, joy; the cause of joy.

delight'ed, *adj.*, overjoyed; *p.p.*, delight.

delight'ful, *adj.*, charming.

delight'fulness, *n.*, the quality of being delightful.

delight'ing, *pr.p.*, delight.

delight'some, *adj.*, *i.q.* delightful.

delim'it, *v.t.*, to fix boundaries of.

delimita'tion, *n.*, the fixing of boundaries.

delim'ited, *p.p.*, delimit.

delim'iting, *pr.p.*, delimit.

delin'eament, *n.*, portrayal either pictorially or in words.

delin'eate, *v.t.*, to depict or describe.

delin'eated, *p.p.*, delineate.

delin'eating, *pr.p.*, delineate.

delinea'tion, *n.*, the process of delineating.

delin'eator, *n.*, one who delineates.

delin'eatory, *adj.*, rel. to delineation.

delin'quency, *n.*, a misdeed, failure in duty.

delin'quent, *n.*, one who fails to perform his duty.

del'iquate, *v.i.*, to be dissolved; *v.t.*, to melt.

del'iquated, *p.p.*, deliquate.

del'iquating, *pr.p.*, deliquate.

deliqua'tion, *n.*, a melting.

deliquesce', *v.i.*, to become liquid by absorbing moisture from the air.

deliquesced', *p.p.*, deliquesce.

deliques'cence, *n.*, a gradual melting by absorption of moisture from the atmosphere.

deliques'cent, *adj.*, liquefying in the air.

deliques'cing, *pr.p.*, deliquesce.

delir'ious, *adj.*, affected with delirium.

delir'iously, *adv.*, in a delirious manner.

delir'ium, *n.*, a temporary disorder of the mind.

delir'ium tre'mens, *n.*, an affection of the brain caused by alcoholic excess.

deliv'er, *v.t.*, to rescue; to hand over; to resign; to utter; to disburden of a child.

deliv'erable, *adj.*, capable of being delivered.

deliv'erance, *n.*, release; verdict; delivered opinion.

deliv'ered, *p.p.*, deliver.

deliv'erer, *n.*, one who delivers.

deliv'ering, *pr.p.* deliver.

deliv'ery, *n.*, a giving up; utterance; manner of speaking; child-birth.

dell, *n.*, a small narrow valley.

Della-Crus'can, *adj.*, pert. to the Academia della Crusca in Florence; applied to a class of affected English writers.

Del'phian, *adj.*, rel. to Delphi; oracular.

Del'phic, *adj.*, *i.q.* Delphian.

del'ta, *n.*, the fourth letter of the Greek alphabet; an alluvial tract at the mouth of a river.

del'toid, *adj.*, triangular; in anatomy, applied to a muscle of the shoulder.

delude', *v.t.*, to mislead.

delu'ded, *p.p.*, delude.

delu'der, *n.*, a deceiver.

delu'ding, *pr.p.*, delude.

del'uge, *n.*, a flood; *v.t.*, to inundate.

del'uged, *p.p.*, deluge.

del'uging, *pr.p.*, deluge.

delu'sion, *n.*, a misleading of the mind; a false belief.

delu'sive, *adj.*, deceptive.

delu'sively, *adv.*, in a delusive manner.

delu'sory, *adj.*, apt to deceive.

delve, *v.i.* and *t.*, to dig.

delved, *p.p.*, delve.

delv'er, *n.*, one who delves.

delv'ing, *pr.p.*, delve.

demag'netize, *v.t.*, to deprive of magnetic influence.

demag'netized, *p.p.*, demagnetize.

demag'netizing, *pr.p.*, demagnetize.

demagog'ic, *adj.*, rel. to a demagogue.

dem'agogism, *n.*, demagogic principles.

dem'agogue, *n.*, one who acquires influence over the populace by playing on their ignorance.

demand', *v.t.*, to ask; to claim; to necessitate; *v.i.*, to inquire; *n.*, a request with authority.

demand'able, *adj.*, liable to demand.

demand'ant, *n.*, a plaintiff; one who demands.

demand'ed, *p.p.*, demand.

demand'er, *n.*, one who demands.

demand'ing, *pr.p.*, demand.

de'marcate, *v.t.*, to mark the boundaries of.

demarca'tion, *n.*, the process of marking off boundaries; separation.

demean', *v.t.*, to behave.

demeaned', *p.p.*, demean.

demean'ing, *pr.p.*, demean.

demean'our, demean'or, *n.*, behaviour.

dement'ed, *adj.*, insane.

demen'tia, *n.*, a form of insanity.

demer'it, *n.*, that which is blamable in moral conduct.

demersed', *adj.*, growing under water.

demer'sion, *n.*, the act of plunging into a liquid.

demesne', *n.*, land adjacent to a manor house.

dem'i, *prefix*, half.

dem'igod, *n.*, an inferior deity; one partly human, partly divine.

dem'ijohn, *n.*, a glass bottle with a large body and small neck, enclosed in wicker-work.

dem'ilune, *n.*, an outwork in fortification protecting a bastion.

dem'i-monde, *n.*, women of doubtful character living as ladies of position.

dem'iquaver, *n.*, *i.q.* semiquaver.

dem'irep, *n.*, a woman of doubtful chastity.

demisabil'ity, *n.*, capability of being demised.

demi'sable, *adj.*, able to be demised.

demise', *n.*, the death of a person of distinction; the conveyance of an estate in law; *v.t.*, to transfer, convey, or bequeath

demised', *p.p.* demise.

dem'isemiqua'ver, *n.*, the half of a semiquaver.

demi'sing, *pr.p.*, demise.

demis'sion, *n.*, a laying down of office; resignation.

demit', *v.t.*, to resign.

dem'itone, *n.*, *i.q.* semitone.

demo'bilize, *v.t.*, to disband troops.

democ'racy, *n.*, government by the people; the populace as rulers.

dem'ocrat, *n.*, one who adheres to democracy.

democrat'ic, *adj.*, pert. to democracy.

democrat'ical, *adj.*, *i.q.* democratic.

demo'graphy, *n.*, statistics, etc., rel. to population.

demoiselle', *n.*, a young lady.

demol'ish, *v.t.*, to destroy.

demol'ished, *p.t.*, demolish.

demol'isher, *n.*, one who demolishes.

demol'ishing, *pr.p.*, demolish.

demoli'tion, *n.*, destruction.

de'mon, *n.*, a malignant spirit.

demonetiza'tion, *n.*, the act of demonetizing.

demon'etize, *v.t.*, to deprive of standard value as money; to withdraw from circulation.

demon'etized, *p.p.*, demonetize.

demon'etizing, *pr.p.*, demonetize.

demo'niac, *adj.*, influenced by demons; *n.*, a human being possessed by a demon.

demoni'acal, *adj.*, *i.q.* demoniac.

demon'ic, *adj.*, rel. to a demon.

de'monism, *n.*, belief in demons.

de'monist, *n.*, a believer in demons.

de'monize, *v.t.*, to render diabolical.

de'monized, *p.p.*, demonize.

de'monizing, *pr.p.*, demonize.

demonol'atry, *n.*, devil-worship.

demonol'ogy, *n.*, knowledge regarding evil spirits.

demonstrabil'ity, *n.*, the state of being demonstrable.

demon'strable, *adj.*, capable of being demonstrated.

demon'strate, *v.t.*, to prove beyond doubt; to make evident.

demon'strated, *p.p.*, demonstrate.

demon'strating, *pr.p.*, demonstrate.

demon'stration, *n.*, a logical proof; a manifestation; a military operation intended to deceive the enemy.

demon'strative, *adj.*, proving by certain evidence; outwardly expressive of the emotions; pointing out.

demon'stratively, *adv.*, in a demonstrative manner.

dem'onstrator, *n.*, one who demonstrates.

demoraliza'tion, *n.*, the act of demoralizing; the state of being demoralized.

demor'alize, *v.t.*, to corrupt the morals of; to deprive (troops) of courage and self-reliance.

demor'alized, *p.p.*, demoralize.

demor'alizing, *pr.p.*, demoralize.

de'mos, *n.*, the common people.

Demosthen'ic, *adj.*, resembling Demosthenes; eloquent.

demot'ic, *adj.*, popular; said of the ordinary alphabet of ancient Egypt.

demount'able, *adj.*, able to be taken to pieces for convenience of transport.

demp'ster, *n.*, *i.q.* deemster.

demul'cent, *adj.*, mollifying; *n.*, a medicine which reduces the effects of irritation.

demul'sion, *n.*, the act of soothing.

demur', *v.i.*, to object hesitatingly; *n.*, hesitation.

demure', *adj.*, affectedly modest; consciously reserved.

demure'ly, *adv.*, in a demure manner.

demure'ness, *n.*, the state of being demure.

demur'rage, *n.*, time of detention of a vessel by the freighter beyond his agreement; corresponding compensation.

demurred', *p.p.*, demur.

demur'rer, *n.*, one who demurs; in law, a stop at some point in the pleadings and dependence on that point for the decision of the cause.

demur'ring, *pr.p.*, demur.

demy', *n.*, a particular size of paper, about 22 in. by 17½ in.; a scholar of Magdalen College, Oxford.

den, *n.*, a cave or pit used for shelter.

denar'cotize, *v.t.*, to deprive of narcotine.

denar'cotized, *p.p.*, denarcotize.

denar'cotizing, *pr.p.*, denarcotize.

dena'rius, *n.*, a Roman silver coin worth about 7½d.

den'ary, *adj.*, proceeding by tens.

dena'tionalize, *v.t.*, to divest of national rights or character.

dena'tionalized, *p.p.*, denationalize.

dena'tionalizing, *pr.p.* denationalize.

den'driform, *adj.*, shaped like a tree.

den'drite, *n.*, a mineral on, or in, which are figures resembling trees or mosses, the result of crystallization.

dendrit'ic, *adj.*, tree-like.

dendrit'ical, *adj.*, *i.q.* dendritic.

den'droid, *adj.*, resembling a small tree or shrub.

dendrol'ogist, *n.*, one acquainted with dendrology.

dendrol'ogy, *n.*, the natural history of trees.

den'gue, *n.*, a W. Indian epidemic fever resembling scarlet fever with rheumatism.

deni'able, *adj.*, capable of being denied.

deni'al, *n.*, contradiction; disownment.

denied', *p.p.*, deny.

deni'er, *n.*, one who denies.

den'igrate, *v.t.*, to blacken thoroughly.

deniza'tion, *n.*, the act of making one a denizen.

den'izen, *n.*, an inhabitant; a naturalized alien.

denom'inate, *v.t.*, to give a name to.

denom'inated, *p.p.*, denominate.

denom'inating, *pr.p.*, denominate.

denomina'tion, *n.*, a collection of individuals called by the same name; a religious sect.

denomina'tional, *adj.*, pert. to particular, esp. religious, denominations.
denom'inative, *adj.*, conferring a distinct appellation.
denom'inator, *n.*, the number below the line in a vulgar fraction.
deno'table, *adj.*, that may be denoted.
denota'tion, *n.*, the act of denoting; what a word or sign denotes.
denote', *v.t.*, to be the name of; to indicate.
deno'ted, *p.p.*, denote.
deno'ting, *pr.p.*, denote.
dénoue'ment, *n.*, the unravelling of a plot; the solution of a mystery; the issue of any course of conduct (*Fr.*).
denounce', *v.t.*, to accuse; terminate.
denounced', *p.p.*, denounce.
denounce'ment, *n.*, *i.q.* denunciation.
denounc'er, *n.*, one who denounces.
denounc'ing, *pr.p.*, denounce.
dense, *adj.*, compact; thick; stupid.
dense'ly, *adv.*, compactly.
dense'ness, *n.*, density; stupidity.
den'ser, *adj.*, *comp.* of dense.
den'sest, *adj.*, *super.* of dense.
den'sity, *n.*, closeness of constituent parts.
dent, *n.*, a depression made by a blow; *v.t.*, to make a dent in.
den'tal, *adj.*, rel. to the teeth; *n.*, a dental sound, as *d*, *t*, *th*.
den'talize, *v.t.*, to convert to a dental letter.
den'tate, *adj.*, toothed.
den'tated, *adj.*, *i.q.* dentate.
denta'tion, *n.*, a toothed form.
dent'ed, *p.p.*, dent.
dentelle', *n.*, lace.
den'ticle, *n.*, a small tooth or projecting point.
dentic'ulate, *adj.*, having small teeth.
dentic'ulated, *adj.*, *i.q.* denticulate.
denticula'tion, *n.*, the state of being denticulate.
den'tiform, *adj.*, tooth-like.
den'tifrice, *n.*, a powder for cleaning the teeth.
den'til, *n.*, a little square block cut on a Greek cornice.
dent'ing, *pr.p.*, dent.
den'tist, *n.*, one who extracts, cleans, repairs, and supplies teeth.
dentis'tic, *adj.*, rel. to dentistry.
den'tistry, *n.*, the profession or art of a dentist.
denti'tion, *n.*, the cutting of teeth in infancy; the system of teeth peculiar to an animal.
den'toid, *adj.*, shaped like a tooth.
den'ture, *n.*, a dentist's name for one or more artificial teeth.
den'udate, *adj.*, denuded; *v.t.*, *i.q.* denude.
den'udated, *adj.*, *i.q.* denudate; *p.p.*, denudate.
denuda'tion, *n.*, the act of denuding.
den'udating, *pr.p.*, denudate.
denude', *v.t.*, to make bare.
denu'ded, *p.p.*, denude.
denu'ding, *pr.p.*, denude.
denun'ciate, *v.t.*, to denounce.
denun'ciated, *p.p.*, denunciate.
denun'ciating, *pr.p.*, denunciate.
denuncia'tion, *n.*, a public menace or accusation.
denun'ciator, *n.*, one who denounces.
denun'ciatory, *adj.*, implying denunciation.
deny', *v.t.*, to declare not to be true; to refuse; *v.i.*, to answer in the negative.
deny'ing, *pr.p.*, deny.
deobstruct', *v.t.*, to remove obstructions from.
deob'struent, *adj.*, that opens the natural ducts and pores of the body.
deoc'ulate, *v.t.*, to make blind.
de'odand, *n.*, a chattel which, having caused the death of a person, was formerly confiscated by the king and devoted to religious uses.
de'odar, *n.*, the Indian cedar tree.
deodoriza'tion, *n.*, the act of deodorizing.
deo'dorize, *v.t.*, to deprive of smell, esp. of obnoxious smell.
deo'dorized, *p.p.*, deodorize.
deo'dorizer, *n.*, a substance which destroys fetid effluvia.
deo'dorizing, *pr.p.*, deodorize.
deontol'ogy, *n.*, the science of duty; ethics.
deox'idate, *v.t.*, to deprive of oxygen.
deox'idated, *p.p.*, deoxidate.
deox'idating, *pr.p.*, deoxidate.
deoxida'tion, *n.*, the process of reducing an oxide.
deox'idize, *v.t.*, *i.q.* deoxidate.
deox'idized, *p.p.*, deoxidize.
deox'idizing, *pr.p.*, deoxidize.
deox'ygenate, *v.t.*, *i.q.* deoxidate.
deox'ygenize, *v.t.*, *i.q.* deoxidate.
depart', *v.i.*, to go elsewhere.
depart'ed, *p.p.*, depart; *adj.*, gone; dead.
depart'er, *n.*, one who departs.
depart'ing, *pr.p.*, depart.
depart'ment, *n.*, a separate branch of business, science, etc.; a division of territory, as in France.

department'al, *adj.*, pert. to a department.

department'ally, *adv.*, in or by means of departments.

depar'ture, *n.*, the act of departing; deviation from a custom or plan.

depas'ture, *v.t.*, to put out to graze.

depau'perate *v.t.*, to impoverish.

depau'perize, *v.t.*, to free from pauperism.

depend', *v.i.*, to be sustained by being attached to something above; to hang down; to be contingent (on); to rely (upon).

depend'able, *adj.*, trustworthy.

depend'ant, *n.*, one who relies upon another for support.

depend'ed, *p.p.*, depend.

depend'ence, *n.*, the state of being dependent; confidence.

depend'ency, *n.*, a territory remote from the state to which it belongs, but subject to its government.

depend'ent, *adj.*, hanging down; at the disposal of; relying for support.

depend'ently, *adv.*, in a dependent manner.

depend'ing, *pr.p.*, depend.

dephos'phorize, *v.t.*, to remove phosphorus from.

dephos'phorized, *p.p.*, dephosphorize.

dephos'phorizing, *pr.p.*, dephosphorize.

depict', *v.t.*, to portray in colours or words; to describe.

depict'ed, *p.p.*, depict.

depict'er, *n.*, one who depicts.

depict'ing, *pr.p.*, depict.

depic'tion, *n.*, the act of depicting.

depic'ture, *v.t.*, to depict; to picture.

depic'tured, *p.p.*, depicture.

depic'turing *pr.p.*, depicture.

dep'ilate, *v.t.*, to strip of hair.

dep'ilated *p.p.*, depilate.

dep'ilating, *pr.p.*, depilate.

depila'tion, *n.*, the removal of hair.

depil'atory, *n.*, a cosmetic used to remove superfluous hairs.

deplete', *v.t.*, to exhaust by draining away.

deple'ted, *p.p.*, deplete.

deple'ting, *pr.p.*, deplete.

deple'tion, *n.*, the act of depleting.

deple'tory, *adj.*, causing depletion.

deplor'able, *adj.*, lamentable, contemptible.

deplor'ableness, *n.*, the state of being deplorable

deplor'ably, *adv.*, lamentably.

deplora'tion, *n.*, lamentation.

deplore', *v.t.*, to grieve for.

deplored', *p.p.*, deplore.

deplor'er, *n.*, one who deplores.

deplor'ing, *pr.p.*, deplore.

deplor'ingly, *adv.*, in a deploring manner.

deploy', *v.t.*, to extend in a line of small depth; *v.i.*, to form a more extended front.

deployed', *p.p.*, deploy.

deploy'ing, *pr.p.*, deploy.

deploy'ment, *n.*, the act of deploying

deplume', *v.t.*, to strip of feathers.

depo'larize, *v.t.*, to deprive of polarity.

depo'larized, *p.p.*, depolarize.

depo'larizing, *pr.p.*, depolarize.

depo'nent, *adj.*, laying down; *n.*, one who makes a deposition; a deponent verb, *i.e.*, a verb passive in form but active in meaning.

depop'ularize, *v.t.*, to make unpopular.

depop'ulate, *v.t.*, to deprive of inhabitants.

depop'ulated, *p.p.*, depopulate.

depop'ulating, *pr.p.*, depopulate.

depopula'tion, *n.*, the act of depopulating.

depop'ulator, *n.*, one who depopulates.

deport', *v.t.*, to banish; *refl.*, to behave.

deporta'tion, *n.*, banishment.

deport'ed, *p.p.*, deport.

deport'ing, *pr.p.*, deport.

deport'ment, *n.*, demeanour; conduct.

depo'sable, *adj.*, that may be deposed.

depose', *v.t.*, to remove from a throne or other high station; to bear witness in a court of law.

deposed', *p.p.*, depose.

depo'ser, *n.*, one who deposes.

depo'sing *pr.p.*, depose.

depos'it, *v.t.*, to lay down; to entrust; to put in a place for preservation; *n.*, that which is laid down; a pledge; a sum of money lodged in a bank.

depos'itary, *n.*, a person holding a deposit in trust.

depos'ited, *p.p.*, deposit

depos'iting, *pr.p.*, deposit.

deposi'tion, *n.*, the act of giving sworn evidence; the attested written testimony of a witness; the dethroning of a king; the act of depositing; something deposited.

depos'itor, *n.*, one who makes a deposit.

depos'itory, *n.*, a place where anything is lodged for preservation.

dep'ot, *n.*, a building where goods are stored; the headquarters of a regiment; a railway-station (*Amer.*).

deprava'tion, *n.*, the act of corrupting; deterioration.

deprave', *v.t.*, to corrupt.

depraved', *adj.*, vitiated; vicious; *p.p.*, deprave.

depra'ver, *n.*, one who depraves.

depra'ving, *pr.p.*, deprave.

deprav'ity, *n.*, a state of corrupted morals; wickedness.

dep'recate, *v.t.*, to argue earnestly against.

dep'recated, *p.p.*, deprecate.

dep'recating, *pr.p.*, deprecate.

dep'recatingly, *adv.*, in a deprecating manner.

depreca'tion, *n.*, disapproval.

dep'recative, *adj.*, *i.q.* deprecatory.

dep'recatory, *adj.*, serving to deprecate

depre'ciate, *v.t.*, to disparage; *v.i.*, to fall in value.

depre'ciated, *p.p.*, depreciate.

depre'ciating, *pr.p.*, depreciate.

deprecia'tion, *n.*, reduction in value.

depre'ciative, *adj.*, *i.q.* depreciatory.

depre'ciator, *n.*, one who depreciates.

depre'ciatory, *adj.*, tending to depreciate.

dep'redate, *v.t.*, to plunder.

dep'redated, *p.p.*, depredate.

dep'redating, *pr.p.*, depredate.

depreda'tion, *n.*, a robbing.

dep'redator, *n.*, a spoiler; a robber.

depred'atory, *adj.*, consisting in pillaging.

depress', *v.t.*, to press down; to lower; to make sad.

depressed', *p.p.*, depress; *adj.*, dispirited; sad, flattened in shape.

depress'ing, *pr.p.*, depress.

depress'ingly, *adv.*, in a depressing manner.

depres'sion, *n.*, the act of depressing; a hollow; dejection; a state of commercial dulness.

depress'ive, *adj.*, tending to depress.

depress'or, *n.*, that which depresses.

depri'vable, *adj.*, able to be deprived.

depriva'tion, *n.*, the act of depriving; a state of being deprived; want; the taking of a preferment from a clergyman.

deprive', *v.t.*, to dispossess.

deprived', *p.p.*, deprive.

depri'ver, *n.*, one who deprives.

depri'ving, *pr.p.*, deprive.

depth, *n.*, the distance from top to bottom, or from front to back, of a thing; profoundness; intensity.

depth'less, *adj.*, unfathomable.

depul'sion, *n.*, a thrusting away.

dep'urate, *v.t.*, to purify; *v.i.*, to turn pure.

dep'urated, *p.p.*, depurate.

dep'urating, *pr.p.*, depurate.

depura'tion, *n.*, the cleansing of a wound.

dep'urator, *n.*, one who, or that which, depurates.

depu'ratory, *adj.*, purifying the blood.

deputa'tion, *n.*, the person or persons deputed to transact business for another or others; the act of deputing.

depute', *v.t.*, to appoint as a substitute.

depu'ted, *p.p.*, depute.

depu'ting, *pr.p.*, depute.

dep'uty, *n.*, a representative or substitute.

derail', *v.t.*, to cause to leave the rails.

derailed', *p.p.*, derail.

derail'ing, *pr.p.*, derail.

derail'ment, *n.*, the state of being derailed.

derange', *v.t.*, to disorder.

derange'able, *adj.*, able to be deranged.

deranged', *p.p.*, derange.

derange'ment, *n.*, confusion; mental disorder.

deraug'ing, *pr.p.*, derange.

der'elict, *adj.*, abandoned, esp. at sea; *n.*, an article abandoned by the owner, esp. a vessel at sea.

derelic'tion, *n.*, abandonment.

deride', *v.t.*, to ridicule; to mock.

deri'ded, *p.p.*, deride.

deri'der, *n.*, a mocker.

deri'ding, *pr.p.*, deride.

deri'dingly, *adv.*, mockingly.

deris'ible, *adj.*, ridiculous.

deri'sion, *n.*, mockery; scorn.

deri'sive, *adj.*, mocking.

deri'sively, *adv.*, with mockery.

deri'siveness, *n.*, the state of being derisive.

deri'sory, *adj.*, *i.q.* derisive.

deri'vable, *adj.*, capable of being derived.

deriva'tion, *n.*, the act of deriving; etymology.

deriva'tional, *adj.*, rel. to derivation.

deriv'ative, *adj.*, taken from something preceding.

deriv'atively, *adv.*, by derivation.

derive', *v.t.*, to receive from a source; to trace the etymology of; *v.i.*, to trace origin from

derived', *p.p.*, derive.
deri'ver, *n.*, one who derives.
deri'ving, *pr.p.*, derive.
derm, *n.*, the true skin lying beneath the cuticle.
der'mal, *adj.*, pert. to, or consisting of, skin.
dermat'ic, *adj.*, pert. to the skin.
dermatog'raphy, *n.*, *i.q.* dermography.
der'matoid, *adj.* resembling skin.
dermatol'ogy, *n.*, the science of the skin and its diseases.
der'mic, *adj.*, rel. to the skin.
dermog'raphy, *n.*, a scientific description of the skin.
der'moid, *adj.*, resembling skin.
dermot'omy, *n.*, dissection of the skin.
der'nier, *adj.*, last (*Fr.*).
der'ogate, *v.t.*, to disparage; *v.i.*, to lessen by taking away a part.
der'ogated, *p.p.*, derogate.
der'ogating, *pr.p.* derogate.
deroga'tion, *n.*, disparagement.
derog'atory, *adj.*, lessening the effect or value.
der'rick, *n.*, a kind of crane for lifting weights.
der'ringer, *n.*, a short-barrelled pistol of large calibre.
der'vish, *n.*, a Mohammedan friar or monk.
des'cant, *n.*, melody, song; a contrapuntal ornamenting of a melody.
descant', *v.i.*, to discourse freely; to add a part to a melody.
descant'ed, *p.p.*, descant.
descant'er, *n.*, one who descants.
descant'ing, *pr.p.*, descant.
descend', *v.i.*, to move downward; *v.t.*, to pass from the top to the bottom of.
descend'ant, *n.*, an individual proceeding from an ancestor in any degree.
descend'ed, *p.p.*, descend.
descend'ent, *adj.*, descending.
descend'er, *n.*, one who descends.
descendibil'ity, *n.*, the quality of being descendible.
descend'ible, *adj.*, able to be passed down.
descend'ing, *adj.*, moving downwards; *pr.p.*, descend.
descen'sion, *n.*, descent; degradation.
descen'sional, *adj.*, pert. to descension.
descen'sive, *adj.*, tending downward.
descent', *n.*, the act of descending; declivity; an invasion; transmission by inheritance; lineage.
descri'bable, *adj.*, able to be described.
describe', *v.t.*, to trace out; to depict in words.
described', *p.p.*, describe.
descri'ber, *n.*, one who describes.
descri'bing, *pr.p.*, describe.
descried', *p.p.*, descry.
descri'er, *n.*, one who descries.
descrip'tion, *n.*, the act of describing; delineation in words; variety or kind.
descrip'tions, *n.*, pl. of description.
or **descrip'tive**, *adj.*, containing description.
descrip'tively, *adv.*, in a descriptive manner.
descry', *v.t.*, to espy.
descry'ing, *pr.p.*, descry.
des'ecrate, *v.t.*, to profane.
des'ecrated, *p.p.*, desecrate.
des'ecrating, *pr.p.*, desecrate.
desecra'tion, *n.*, profanation.
des'ert, *adj.*, lying waste; uncultivated and uninhabited; *n.*, a wilderness; a solitude; a vast sandy waste, almost destitute of vegetation.
desert', *v.t.*, to abandon; *v.i.*, to quit a post or service without permission; *n.*, reward or punishment merited.
desert'ed, *p.p.*, desert.
desert'er, *n.*, one who deserts, esp. a soldier or sailor.
desert'ing, *pr.p.*, desert.
deser'tion, *n.*, the act of deserting.
desert'less, *adj.*, undeserving.
deserve', *v.t.* and *i.*, to merit.
deserved', *p.p.*, deserve.
deserv'edly, *adv.*, justly.
deserv'er, *n.*, one who deserves.
deserv'ing, *adj.*, meritorious; *pr.p.*, deserve.
deserv'ingly, *adv.*, meritoriously.
deshabille', *n.*, the state of not being fully or properly dressed.
des'iccate, *v.t.*, to exhaust of moisture; *v.i.*, to become dry.
des'iccated, *p.p.*, desiccate.
des'iccating, *pr.p.*, desiccate.
desicca'tion, *n.*, the act of making dry.
des'iccative, *adj.*, drying; *n.*, an application that dries a sore.
des'iccator, *n.*, that which desiccates.
desid'erate, *v.t.*, to feel the want of; to desire.
desid'erated, *p.p.*, desiderate.
desid'erating, *pr.p.*, desiderate.
desid'erative, *adj.*, expressing desire; *n.*, a verb formed from another and expressing a desire of doing what the primitive verb implies.
desidera'tum, *n.*,

something much wanted.

design', *v.t.*, to sketch; to plan; to purpose; *n.*, a sketch; a scheme; intention.

design'able, *adj.*, able to be designed.

des'ignate, *v.t.*, to mark out by description; to select for a purpose.

des'ignated, *p.p.*, designate.

des'ignating, *pr.p.*, designate.

designa'tion, *n.*, the act of designating; a distinctive appellation.

des'ignator, *n.*, one who designates.

designed', *p.p.*, design.

design'edly, *adv.*, intentionally.

design'er, *n.*, one who designs.

design'ing, *adj.*, artful; *pr.p.*, design.

design'less, *adj.*, without intention.

desirabil'ity, *n.*, the quality of being desirable.

desir'able, *adj.*, worthy of desire.

desir'ableness, *n.*, *i.q.* desirability.

desire', *v.t.*, to covet; to request; *n.*, craving to obtain something; that which is desired.

desired', *p.p.*, desire.

desir'er, *n.*, one who desires.

desir'ing, *pr.p.*, desire.

desir'ous, *adj.*, wishful.

desist', *v.i.*, to discontinue.

desist'ance, *n.*, a ceasing to act.

desist'ed, *p.p.*, desist.

desist'ing, *pr.p.*, desist.

desi'tion, *n.*, an end or ending.

desk, *n.*, a kind of table for the use of writers and readers, often with a sloping upper surface.

desmol'ogy, *n.*, the anatomical study of sinews and ligaments.

des'olate, *adj.*, uninhabited; forlorn.

des'olate, *v.t.*, to lay waste; to ruin.

des'olated, *p.p.*, desolate.

des'olateness, *n.*, a state of being desolate.

des'olating, *pr.p.*, desolate.

desola'tion, *n.*, ruin; melancholy.

des'olator, *n.*, one who desolates.

despair', *v.i.*, to give up hope; *n.*, hopelessness.

despaired', *p.p.*, despair.

despair'ing, *adj.*, prone to despair; *pr.p.*, despair.

despair'ingly, *adv.*, in a despairing manner.

despatch', *v.t.*, to send; to hasten; to kill; *n.*, dismissal; speed; a letter on public business. Also *dispatch*.

despatched', *p.p.*, despatch.

despatch'ing, *pr.p.*, despatch.

despera'do, *n.*, a desperate fellow; a reckless ruffian.

des'perate, *adj.* beyond hope; reckless.

des'perately, *adv.*, in a desperate manner.

despera'tion, *n.*, the state of being desperate.

des'picable, *adj.*, contemptible.

des'picableness, *n.*, the quality of being despicable.

des'picably, *adv.*, vilely.

despi'sable, *adj.*, worthy of contempt.

despise', *v.t.*, to look down on; to scorn.

despised', *p.p.*, despise.

despi'ser, *n.*, one who despises.

despi'sing, *pr.p.*, despise.

despite', *n.*, extreme malice; contemptuous defiance; *prep.*, notwithstanding.

despite'ful, *adj.*, malignant.

despoil', *v.t.*, to rob; to strip.

despoiled', *p.p.*, despoil.

despoil'er, *n.*, a plunderer.

despoil'ing, *pr.p.*, despoil.

despoil'ment, *n.*, *i.q.* despoliation.

despolia'tion, *n.*, the act of despoiling.

despond', *v.i.*, to feel dejected; to lose heart.

despond'ed, *p.p.*, despond.

despond'ence, *n.*, *i.q.* despondency.

despond'ency, *n.*, the state of being despondent.

despond'ent, *adj.*, sinking into dejection.

despond'ing, *adj.*, *i.q.* despondent; *pr.p.*, despond.

des'pot, *n.*, an absolute monarch; a tyrant.

despot'ic, *adj.*, arbitrary; tyrannical.

despot'ical, *adj.*, *i.q.* despotic.

des'potism, *n.*, autocracy; tyranny.

des'potize, *v.i.*, to act as a despot.

des'pumate, *v.t.* and *i.*, to remove or throw off scum.

des'pumated, *p.p.*, despumate.

des'pumating, *pr.p.*, despumate.

despuma'tion, *n.*, the act of despumating.

des'quamate, *v.i.*, to peel off.

des'quamated, *p.p.*, desquamate.

des'quamating, *pr.p.*, desquamate.

desquama'tion, *n.*, a scaling off.

dessert', *n.*, a course of sweetmeats and fruit at the end of a dinner.

dessert'-spoonful, *n.*, as much as fills a dessert-spoon.

destina'tion, *n.*, the appointed end of a journey or voyage.

des'tine, *v.t.*, to fix unalterably; to doom.

des'tined, *p.p.*, destine.

des'tining, *pr.p.*, destine.

des'tiny, *n.*, fortune; doom; fate.

des'titute, *adj.*, devoid; in abject poverty.
destitu'tion, *n.*, a state of utter want.
destroy', *v.t.*, to demolish; to put an end to.
destroyed', *p.p.*, destroy.
destroy'er, *n.*, anything that destroys; a swift armed ship esp. designed against torpedo-boats.
destroy'ing, *pr.p.*, destroy.
destructibil'ity, *n.*, the state of being destructible.
destruc'tible, *adj.*, liable to destruction.
destruc'tion, *n.*, the act of destroying; the state of being destroyed.
destruc'tive, *adj.*, causing destruction.
destruc'tively, *adv.*, in a destructive manner.
destruc'tiveness, *n.*, a propensity to destroy.
destruc'tor, *n.*, a refuse-burner.
desuda'tion, *n.*, a profuse sweating.
des'uetude, *n.*, discontinuance of practice or custom.
des'ultorily, *adv.*, without method.
des'ultoriness, *n.*, the character of being desultory.
des'ultory, *adj.*, rambling; inconstant; unmethodical.
detach', *v.t.*, to separate.
detached', *adj.*, standing apart.
detach'ing, *pr.p.*, detach.
detach'ment, *n.*, a state of being detached; troops taken from the main army for some special service.
detail', *v.t.*, to recite the particulars of; to appoint to a special duty.
de'tail, *n.*, a fact; item; detachment.
detailed', *p.p.*, detail; *adj.*, exact; particular.
detail'ing, *pr.p.*, detail.
detain', *v.t.*, to keep back; to hold in custody.
detain'der, *n.*, a writ.
detained', *p.p.*, detain.
detain'er, *n.*, one who detains; in law, a keeping what belongs to another.
detain'ing, *pr.p.*, detain.
detect', *v.t.*, to discover.
detect'able, *adj.*, able to be detected.
detect'ed, *p.p.*, detect.
detect'er, -or, *n.*, one who, or that which, detects.
detect'ing, *pr.p.*, detect.
detec'tion, *n.*, discovery.
detec'tive, *n.*, a police officer whose special duty it is to detect crimes and apprehend criminals; *adj.*, pert. to detection.
detent', *n.*, a click or pawl in a clock, watch, or lock.
deten'tion, *n.*, the act of detaining; confinement; delay.
deter', *v.t.*, to prevent.
deterge', *v.t.*, to cleanse (a sore).
deterged', *p.p.*, deterge.
deter'gent, *adj.*, cleansing; *n.*, anything with cleansing power.
deter'ging, *pr.p.*, deterge.
dete'riorate, *v.i.*, to grow worse; *v.t.*, to make worse.
dete'riorated, *p.p.*, deteriorate.
dete'riorating, *pr.p.*, deteriorate.
deteriora'tion, *n.*, the process or state of growing worse.
deter'ment, *n.*, that which deters.
deter'minable, *adj.*, capable of being determined.
deter'minant, *adj.*, *i.q.* determinative; *n.*, in mathematics, an algebraical expression formed according to certain laws.
deter'minate, *adj.*, definite; conclusive.
deter'minately, *adv.*, precisely; in a determinate manner.
determina'tion, *n.*, decision; settled purpose; resoluteness.
deter'minative, *adj.*, having power to direct to a definite end.
deter'mine, *v.t.*, to fix or establish; to cause to come to a conclusion; *v.i.*, to resolve; to terminate.
deter'mined, *adj.*, resolute; *p.p.*, determine.
deter'minedly, *adv.*, in a determined manner.
deter'miner, *n.*, one who determines.
deter'mining, *pr.p.*, determine.
deter'minism, *n.*, the philosophical denial of free will.
deterred', *p.p.*, deter.
deter'rent, *adj.*, deterring; *n.*, that which deters.
deter'ring, *pr.p.*, deter.
deter'sion, *n.*, the act of cleansing.
deter'sive, *adj.*, *i.q.* detergent.
detest', *v.t.*, to hate extremely.
detest'able, *adj.*, very odious.
detesta'tion, *n.*, loathing.
detest'ed, *p.p.*, detest.
detest'er, *n.*, one who detests.
detest'ing, *pr.p.*, detest.
dethrone', *v.t.*, to depose.
dethroned', *p.p.*, dethrone.
dethrone'ment, *n.*, deposition.
dethro'ner, *n.*, one who dethrones.
dethro'ning, *pr.p.*, dethrone.
det'inue, *n.*, a thing or person detained;

an action for recovery.

det'onate, *v.t.* and *i.*, to explode, or cause to explode.

det'onated, *p.p.*, detonate.

det'onating, *adj.*, explosive; *pr.p.*, detonate.

detona'tion, *n.*, an explosion.

det'onator, *n.*, a capsule filled with some fulminating substance to fire a high explosive.

detoniza'tion, *n.*, the act of exploding.

det'onize, *v.t.*, *i.q.* detonate.

det'onized, *p.p.*, detonize.

det'onizing, *pr.p.* detonize.

detor'sion, *n.*, a wresting or perversion.

detort', *v.t.*, to distort to pervert.

detour', *n.*, a roundabout way (*Fr.*).

detract', *v.t.*, to take away from a whole; *v.i.*, to take away reputation.

detract'ed, *p.p.*, detract.

detract'ing, *pr.p.*, detract.

detrac'tion, *n.*, malicious depreciation.

detract'ive, *adj.*, having the power to take away.

detract'or, *n.*, one who detracts.

detract'ory, *adj.*, depreciatory.

detrain', *v.t.*, to remove troops from a train; *v.i.*, to alight.

detrained', *p.p.* detrain.

detrain'ing, *pr.p.*, detrain.

det'riment, *n.*, harm.

detrimen'tal, *adj.*, injurious.

detri'tal, *adj.*, pert. to detritus.

detri'tion, *n.*, the wearing down or weathering of rocks.

detri'tus, *n.*, disintegrated materials of rocks.

detrude', *v.t.*, to thrust down.

detrud'ed *p.p.*, detrude.

detrud'ing, *pr.p.* detrude.

detrun'cate, *v.t.*, to lop.

detrun'cated, *p.p.*, detruncate.

detrun'cating, *pr.p.*, detruncate.

detrunca'tion, *n.*, the act of detruncating.

detru'sion, *n.*, the act of detruding.

deuce, *n.*, a playing card or die with two spots; the devil.

deuterog'amist, *n.*, one who marries a second time.

deuterog'amy, *n.*, a second marriage; the marriage of a widow or widower.

Deuteron'omy, *n.*, the fifth book of the Pentateuch, containing a second version of the Law.

deuterop'athy, *n.*, the sympathetic affection of one part with another (*Med.*).

deutox'ide, *n.*, dioxide; binoxide.

devapora'tion, *n.*, the change of vapour into water.

dev'astate, *v.t.*, to ravage.

dev'astated, *p.p.*, devastate.

dev'astating, *pr.p.*, devastate.

devasta'tion, *n.*, havoc; desolation.

devel'op, *v.t.*, to unfold gradually; *v.i.*, to advance from stage to stage.

devel'oped, *p.p.*, develop.

devel'oper, *n.*, one who, or that which, develops.

devel'oping, *pr.p.*, develop.

devel'opment, *n.*, a gradual growth through progressive changes.

devest', *v.t.*, to divest; to alienate.

de'viate, *v.i.*, to diverge; to vary from uniform state.

de'viated, *p.p.*, deviate.

de'viating, *pr.p.*, deviate.

devia'tion, *n.*, a turning aside.

device', *n.*, a design, a scheme; an ornamental design; an emblem.

dev'il, *n.*, an evil spirit; the Evil One; a lawyer's, printer's, or author's assistant; *v.t.*, to pepper excessively and grill; *v.i.*, to work as devil for a printer, etc.

dev'ilish, *adj.*, pert. to the devil; very evil.

dev'ilishly, *adv.*, in a devilish manner.

dev'il(l)ed, *p.p.*, devil.

dev'il(l)ing, *pr.p.*, devil.

dev'ilry, *n.*, wicked mischief.

de'vious, *adj.*, rambling; going astray; circuitous.

de'viously, *adv.*, in a devious manner.

de'viousness, *n.*, the state of being devious.

devi'sable, *adj.*, able to be devised.

devise', *v.t.*, to invent or contrive; to bequeath; *v.i.*, to form a scheme; *n.*, a share of an estate bequeathed.

devised', *p.p.*, devise.

devisee', *n.*, the person to whom a devise is made.

devi'ser, *n.*, one who devises; a contriver.

devi'sing, *pr.p.*, devise.

devi'sor, *n.*, one who gives by will.

devi'talize, *v.t.*, to deprive of vitality.

devitrifica'tion, *n.*, the act of devitrifying.

devit'rify, *v.t.*, to deprive of the character of glass.

devo'calize, *v.t.*, to make toneless.

devoid', *adj.*, not possessing.

devoir', *n.*, service or duty; respect due to another (*Fr.*).

devolu'tion, *n.*, the act of devolving or transferring.

devolve', *v.t.* and *i.*, to pass, or make to pass, from one person to another.

devolved', *p.p.*, devolve.

devolv'ing, *pr.p.*, devolve.

Devo'nian, *adj.*, pert. to Devonshire; rel. to the Old Red Sandstone.

dev'onport, *n.*, a small writing table fitted with drawers, etc.

devote', *v.t.*, to set apart; to consecrate; to direct the attention entirely.

devo'ted, *adj.*, zealous; *p.p.*, devote.

devo'tedness, *n.*, the state of being devoted.

devotee', *n.*, an enthusiast, devout adherent; fanatic.

devo'ter, *n.*, one who devotes.

devo'ting, *pr.p.*, devote.

devo'tion, *n.*, ardent attachment; earnestness; a religious exercise.

devo'tional, *adj.*, pert. to devotion.

devour', *v.t.*, to eat up; to consume.

devoured', *p.p.*, devour.

devour'er, *n.*, one who devours.

devour'ing, *adj.*, consuming; destroying; *pr.p.*, devour.

devout', *adj.*, pious; religious; earnest.

devout'ly, *adv.*, in a devout manner.

devout'ness, *n.*, the state of being devout.

dew, *n.*, condensed atmospheric vapour on bodies colder than their surroundings.

dewan', *n.*, an Indian state treasurer.

dew'drop, *n.*, a drop of dew.

dew'iness, *n.*, a state of being dewy.

dew'lap, *n.*, a fold of skin hanging from the neck, esp. of cows.

dew'-point, *n.*, the temperature at which dew begins to form.

dew'y, *adj.*, partaking of the nature or appearance of dew.

dex'ter, *adj.*, situated on the right hand.

dexter'ity, *n.*, skill; expertness.

dex'terous, *adj.*, skilful; adroit; expert.

dex'terously, **dex'trously**, *adv.*, with dexterity.

dex'tral, *adj.*, right (as opposed to left).

dextral'ity, *n.*, right-handedness.

dex'trin(e), *n.*, the gummy matter into which the interior of starch globules is convertible.

dextrors'al, *adj.*, rising from left to right (as a climbing plant).

dex'trose, *n.*, grape-sugar.

dex'trous, *adj.*, *i.q.* dexterous.

Dey, *n.*, the title of the old governors of Algiers, Tunis, and Tripoli under the Sultan of Turkey.

dho'bi, *n.*, an Indian washerman.

dho'ti, *n.*, a Hindoo's loin-cloth.

dhow, *n.*, an Arab vessel, 150–250 tons burden, usually one-masted.

dhur'rie, *n.*, an Indian fringed cotton carpet.

diabe'tes, *n.*, a urinary disease.

diabe'tic, *adj.*, pert. to diabetes.

dia'blerie, *n.*, devilry; witchcraft.

diabol'ic, *adj.*, devilish; infernal; atrocious.

diabol'ical, *adj.*, *i.q.* diabolic.

diab'olism, *n.*, possession by the devil.

diab'olo, *n.*, a game of skill played with two sticks and a reel.

diacaus'tic, *adj.*, bel. to a class of caustic curves formed by refraction.

diach'ylon, *n.*, a medical plaster made of olive oil and powdered litharge.

diac'onal, *adj.*, rel. to a deacon.

diac'onate, *n.*, the office or dignity of a deacon.

diacous'tic, *adj.*, bel. to the refraction of sound.

diacrit'ic, *adj.*, distinguishing; distinctive.

diacrit'ical, *adj.*, *i.q.* diacritic.

di'adem, *n.*, a crown; a coronet.

diaer'esis, **dier'esis**, *n.*, mark (¨) over the latter of two vowels, making them two syllables.

diagno'sis, *n.*, the discrimination of diseases by their symptoms.

diagnos'tic, *adj.*, indicating the nature of a disease.

diag'onal, *adj.*, from angle to angle; *n.*, a straight line joining opposite corners of a figure.

diag'onally, *adv.*, in a diagonal direction.

di'agram, *n.*, an illustrative outline drawing.

diagrammat'ic, *adj.*, pert. to a diagram.

di'agraph, *n.*, an instrument which enables one to reproduce objects before one without requiring skill in drawing, a kind of *camera lucida*.

diagraph'ic, *adj.*, pert. to the diagraph.

di'al, *n.*, the face of a watch or other timekeeper; any similar face over which a pointer moves; *v.t.*, to measure with a dial.

di'alect, *n.*, a local idiom differing from the standard speech.

dialec'tic, *adj.*, pert. to a dialect or to dialectics; *n.*, reasoning.

dialec'tical, *adj.*, *i.q.* dialectic.

dialecti'cian, *n.*, a reasoner; a logician.

di'alist, *n.*, a maker or user of dials.

di'allage, *n.*, a foliated mineral akin to augite.

di'alling, **di'aling**, *n.*,

the art of constructing dials; the theory of the sundial.

dial'ogism, *n.*, oblique narration; dialogue in the third person.

dial'ogist, *n.*, a writer of dialogue; a speaker in a dialogue.

dialogis'tic, *adj.*, having the form of a dialogue.

dial'ogize, *v.i.*, to discourse in dialogue.

di'alogue, *n.*, a conversation between two or more persons, esp. in a stage-play.

di'al-plate, *n.*, the plate of a dial.

dial'ysis, *n.*, the separation of the crystalloid from the colloid elements of a body; debility; a solution of continuity.

diamagnet'ic, *adj.*, showing the peculiarity of pointing east and west under magnetic influence.

diam'eter, *n.*, a straight line through the centre of a body; thickness.

diam'etral, *adj.*, *i.q.* diametric.

diamet'ric, *adj.*, pert. to a diameter.

diamet'rical, *adj.*, *i.q.* diametric.

di'amond, *n.*, a very hard precious stone; a very small kind of printing type; a lozenge or rhombus.

Dian'dria, *n. pl.*, plants with two stamens.

dian'drian, *adj.*, having two stamens.

Dian'thus, *n.*, a genus of plants including the pink and carnation.

diapa'son, *n.*, an octave; the compass of a voice or instrument; an organ stop.

di'aper, *n.*, a linen or cotton fabric with a figured pattern; *v.t.*, to variegate with figures.

di'aphane, *n.*, a silk fabric with transparent figures.

diaphane'ity, *n.*, the quality of being diaphanous.

diaphanom'eter, *n.*, an instrument for measuring the transparency of the air.

diaph'anous, *adj.*, transparent pellucid.

diaphon'ic, *adj.*, diacoustic; rel. to sound-refraction.

diaphore'sis, *n.*, excessive perspiration.

diaphoret'ic, *adj.*, having the power to increase perspiration; *n.*, a sudorific.

di'aphragm, *n.*, the midriff; a partition.

diaph'ysis, *n.*, the shaft of a long bone.

dia'rian, *adj.*, rel. to a diary.

di'arist, *n.*, one who keeps a diary.

diarrhoe'a, diarrhe'a, *n.*, an ailment of the intestines; excessive looseness of the bowels.

diarrhoe'ic, *adj.*, rel. to diarrhoea.

diarrhoet'ic, *adj.*, producing diarrhoea.

diarthro'sis, *n.*, a joint capable of revolving in all directions, as the shoulder-joint.

di'ary, *n.*, a journal of daily transactions.

di'astase, *n.*, a substance in barley and oats after germination, which turns starch into sugar at 150° F.

dias'tole, *n.*, the dilatation of the heart; the lengthening of a short syllable.

di'astyle, *n.*, an arrangement of columns in classical architecture in which intercolumniation is equal to three diameters.

Diates'saron, *n.*, a harmony of the four gospels; an electuary or medicine containing four drugs; a musical interval.

diather'mal, *adj.*, penetrable by heat.

diather'manous, *adj.*, letting radiant heat pass through.

diath'esis, *n.*, habit of body; predisposition to certain diseases.

Diatoma'ceae, *n. pl.*, a family of minute unicellular algae, or primitive plant-forms.

diaton'ic, *adj.*, pert. to the major and minor scales in music.

di'atribe, *n.*, a long invective.

dib, *n.*, a small bone in a sheep's knee.

dib'ble, *n.*, a pointed tool used in gardening; *v.t.*, to dig with a dibble.

dib'bled, *p.p.*, dibble.

dib'bler, *n.*, one who dibbles.

dib'bling, *pr.p.*, dibble.

dib'stone, *n.*, a pebble used in a child's game (called *dibstones*).

dice, *n.*, pl. of die; *v.i.*, to play with dice.

dice'-box, *n.*, a box from which dice are thrown.

diced, *p.p.*, dice.

diceph'alous, *adj.*, having two heads.

di'cer, *n.*, a player at dice.

dichot'omize, *v.i.*, to become dichotomous.

dichot'omous, *adj.*, regularly dividing by pairs from top to bottom.

dichot'omy, *n.*, distribution of ideas by pairs; branching by continual forking.

dichromat'ic, *adj.*, having two colours.

di'cing, *pr.p.*, dice; *n.*, the practice or act of dicing.

dick'ens, *n.*, devil; deuce (*slang*).

dick'er, *n.*, ten hides or skins.

dick'ey, dick'y, *n.*, a false shirt-front; the driver's seat; a seat at the back of a carriage.

dicotyle'don, *n.*, a plant whose seeds contain a pair of seed-leaves.

dicotyle'donous, *adj.*, having two seed-leaves.

dictate', *v.t.*, to deliver a command; to instruct to be written.

dic'tate, *n.*, a rule suggested to the mind.

dicta'ted, *p.p.*, dictate.

dicta'ting, *pr.p.*, dictate.

dicta'tion, *n.*, the act of dictating.

dicta'tor, *n.*, one invested with absolute authority.

dictato'rial, *adj.*, over-bearing.

dicta'torship, *n.*, the office of a dictator.

dic'tion, *n.*, choice of words; mode of expression.

dic'tionary, *n.*, a book which contains the words of a language arranged alphabetically, with meanings, etc., attached.

dic'tum, *n.*, an authoritative saying.

did, *p.t.*, do.

didac'tic, *adj.*, intended to instruct.

didac'tical, *adj.*, *i.q.* didactic.

didac'tyl, *adj.*, two-toed; *n.*, a two-toed animal.

didac'tylous, *adj.*, two-toed or two-fingered.

did'dle, *v.t.*, to cheat; to dandle.

did'dled, *p.p.*, diddle.

did'dling, *pr.p.*, diddle; *n.*, cheating.

didecahe'dral, *adj.*, having ten planes at either extremity.

didst, *p.t.*, 2nd pers. sing., do.

did'ymous, *adj.*, twin; growing double.

didyna'mian, *adj.*, *i.q.* didynamous.

didyn'amous, *adj.*, having four stamens in pairs, one pair longer than the other.

die, *v.*, to cease to live; *n.*, a small cube used in gaming; a square body; a stamp used in coining, etc.

died, *p.p.*, die.

die'-hard, *n.*, a brave man who fights to the death.

die'-sinker, *n.*, an engraver of dies for embossing.

di'esis, *n.*, a very small interval in music.

di'et, *n.*, regular food and drink; a legislative session; a German or Austrian parliament; *v.t.*, to prescribe a diet.

di'etary, *n.*, a system of diet.

di'eted, *p.p.*, diet.

di'eter, *n.*, one who prescribes rules for eating.

dietet'ic, *adj.*, pert. to a regulated diet.

dietet'ical, *adj.*, *i.q.* dietetic.

di'etine, *n.*, a local assembly or diet.

di'eting, *pr.p.*, diet.

dif'fer, *v.i.*, to be unlike; to be of another opinion; to quarrel.

dif'fered, *p.p.*, differ.

dif'ference, *n.*, dissimilarity; a dispute; the remainder after arithmetical subtraction; *v.t.*, to cause a difference in; to discriminate.

dif'ferenced, *p.p.*, difference.

dif'ferencing, *pr.p.*, difference.

dif'ferent, *adj.*, distinct; separate; unlike.

differen'tia, *n.*, the characteristic attribute of a species.

differen'tial, *adj.*, making a difference, discriminating; a mathematical epithet applied to the infinitesimal difference between two values of a variable.

differen'tiate, *v.t.*, to distinguish by a difference; in mathematics, to obtain the differential coefficient of.

differen'tiated, *p.p.*, differentiate.

differen'tiating, *pr.p.*, differentiate.

differentia'tion, *n.*, the act of differentiating.

dif'ferently, *adv.*, in a different manner.

dif'ficult, *adj.*, not easy; hard to do or to understand.

dif'ficulty, *n.*, hardness to be done; embarrassment of affairs; a quarrel.

dif'fidence, *n.*, want of confidence; self-distrust.

dif'fident, *adj.*, not confident; bashful.

dif'form, *adj.*, irregular in form; anomalous.

diffract', *v.t.*, to bend from a straight line.

diffract'ed, *p.p.*, diffract.

diffract'ing, *pr.p.*, diffract.

diffrac'tion, *n.*, deflection of light.

diffuse', *adj.*, verbose; wanting in conciseness; *v.t.*, to send out in all directions.

diffused', *adj.*, spread; dispersed; *p.p.*, diffuse.

diffuse'ly, *adv.*, extensively; with too many words.

diffu'ser, *n.*, one who, or that which, diffuses.

diffusibil'ity, *n.*, the quality of being diffusible.

diffu'sible, *adj.*, capable of being spread in all directions.

diffu'sing, *pr.p.*, diffuse.

diffu'sion, *n.*, a spreading abroad; propagation.

diffu'sive, *adj.*, widely reaching.

diffu'sively, *adv.*, extensively; widely.

diffu'siveness, *n.*, the character of being diffusive.

dig, *v.t.*, to open and turn up with a spade; *v.i.*, to work with a spade or similar implement.

digam′ma, *n.*, a lost Greek letter, probably equivalent to *v* or *f*.

digas′tric, *adj.*, double bellied.

di′gest, *n.*, a collection of Roman laws, arranged by the Emperor Justinian; any similar collection.

digest′, *v.t.*, to arrange methodically for study; to dissolve in the stomach.

digest′ed, *p.p.*, digest.

digest′er, *n.*, one who arranges in order, that which assists the digestion of food; a vessel in which substances in water are exposed to great heat so as to extract their essences.

digestibil′ity, *n.*, the quality of being digestible.

digest′ible, *adj.*, capable of being digested.

digest′ing, *pr.p.*, digest.

diges′tion, *n.*, the act of methodizing; the process which food undergoes in the stomach.

digest′ive, *adj.*, having the power to promote digestion; *n.*, a stomachic.

digged, *p.p.*, dig; more commonly, *dug*.

dig′ger, *n.*, one who digs, esp. for gold.

dig′ging, *n.*, the act of digging; *pr.p.*, dig.

dig′gings, *n. pl.*, lodgings (*slang*).

dig′it, *n.*, a finger; any whole number less than ten.

dig′ital, *adj.*, pert. to the fingers; *n.*, a piano or organ key.

digita′lis, *n.*, a genus of plants including the foxglove.

dig′itate, *adj.*, branched out into divisions like fingers.

dig′itated, *adj.*, *i.q.* digitate.

digita′tion, *n.*, division into finger-like processes.

dig′itigrade, *n.*, an animal that walks on its toes.

di′glyph, *n.*, a projecting face with two channels sunk in it (*Arch.*).

dig′nified, *adj.*, stately in deportment; *p.p.*, dignify.

dig′nify, *v.t.*, to invest with dignity or high rank; to honour.

dig′nifying, *pr.p.*, dignify.

dig′nitary, *n.*, a person of exalted rank or office.

dig′nity, *n.*, nobleness of mind; an elevated office.

di′graph, *n.*, a union of two letters signifying one sound.

digress′, *v.i.*, to wander from a theme.

digressed′, *p.p.*, digress.

digress′ing, *pr.p.*, digress.

digres′sion, *n.*, a departure from a main subject.

digres′sional, *adj.*, consisting in digression.

digres′sive, *adj.*, *i.q.* digressional.

digyn′ian, *adj.*, having two pistils.

dig′ynous, *adj.*, *i.q.* digynian.

dihe′dral, *adj.*, having two plane faces, as a crystal.

dihe′dral an′gle, *n.*, the inclination to each other of an aeroplane's wings.

dihe′dron, *n.*, a figure with two planesides.

diju′dicate, *v.i.*, to judge; to adjudicate.

diju′dicated, *p.p.*, dijudicate.

diju′dicating, *pr.p.*, dijudicate.

dijudica′tion, *n.*, the act of adjudicating.

dike, *n.*, a ditch; a mound; *v.t.*, to surround with a dike; to secure by a bank.

diked, *p.p.*, dike.

di′king, *pr.p.*, dike.

dilac′erate, *v.t.*, to rend asunder.

dilac′erated, *p.p.*, dilacerate.

dilac′erating, *pr.p.*, dilacerate.

dilap′idate, *v.i.*, to fall to ruin; *v.t.*, to allow buildings to become ruinous by neglect.

dilap′idated, *adj.*, in a ruinous state; *p.p.*, dilapidate.

dilap′idating, *pr.p.* dilapidate.

dilapida′tion, *n.*, the state of being dilapidated; in ecclesiastical law, the decay of a building caused by the neglect of the incumbent.

dilap′idator, *n.*, one who dilapidates.

dilatabil′ity, *n.*, the quality of being dilatable.

dila′table, *adj.*, elastic; able to be dilated.

dilata′tion, *n.*, the act of expanding; the state of being distended.

dilate′, *v.t.* and *i.*, to expand; distend, enlarge on.

dila′ted, *p.p.*, dilate.

dila′ting, *pr.p.*, dilate.

dila′tion, *n.*, *i.q.* dilatation.

dil′atorily, *adv.*, in a dilatory manner.

dil′atoriness, *n.*, tardiness.

dil′atory, *adj.*, procrastinating, delaying.

dilem′ma, *n.*, a logical argument which catches an adversary between two fatal alternatives; an awkward situation.

dilettan′te, *n.*, an amateur; one who cultivates an art for amusement (pl. *dilettanti*).

dilettan′tism, *n.*, the character of a dilettante.

dil′igence, *n.*, industry; a four-wheeled stage-coach.

dil′igent, *adj.*, industrious; attentive.

dil′igently, *adv.*, in a diligent manner.

dill, *n.*, a European plant, the seeds of

which are used to cure flatulence.

dil'uent, *n.*, that which dilutes; a medicine to make the blood more fluid.

dilute', *v.t.*, to weaken by mixing with water: *adj.*, diluted.

dilu'ted, *p.p.*, dilute.

dilu'ter, *n.*, one who, that which, dilutes.

dilu'ting, *pr.p.*, dilute.

dilu'tion, *n.*, the act of diluting.

dilu'vial, *adj.*, pert. to a deluge, esp. to the Noachian Deluge.

dilu'vian, *adj.*, *i.q.* diluvial.

dilu'vium, *n.*, a deluge; a deposit caused by the extraordinary action of water.

dim, *adj.*, not seeing clearly; not clearly seen; obscure; *v.t.*, to obscure.

dime, *n.*, an American silver coin, the tenth of a dollar; ten cents; value about 5d.

dimen'sion, *n.*, extension in a single direction.

dim'eter, *n.*, a verse of two measures.

dimid'iate, *adj.* halved.

dimin'ish, *v.t.* and *i.*, to lessen.

dimin'ished, *adj.*, lessened in size or importance; *p.p.*, diminish.

dimin'ishing, *pr.p.*, diminish.

diminuen'do, *adv.*, diminishingly; *n.*, a lessening in volume of sound.

diminu'tion, *n.*, the act of diminishing.

dimin'utive, *adj.*, smaller than the normal size; *n.*, a word formed from another to express a little thing of the kind.

dim'issory, *adj.*, dismissing to another jurisdiction.

dim'ity, *n.*, a stout cotton fabric.

dim'ly, *adv.*, in a dim manner.

dimmed, *p.p.*, dim

dim'ming, *pr.p.*, dim.

dim'mish, *adj.*, somewhat dim.

dim'ness, *n.*, the state of being dim.

dimor'phism, *n.*, the property of having two distinct forms, exhibited by some crystalline minerals.

dimor'phous, *adj.*, exhibiting dimorphism.

dim'ple, *n.*, a small depression, esp. on the face; *v.i.*, to form dimples; *v.t.*, to mark with dimples.

dim'pled, *adj.*, having cheeks marked by dimples; *p.p.*, dimple.

dim'pling, *pr.p.*, dimple.

dim'ply, *adj.*, full of dimples.

din, *n.*, a loud, long-continued noise; *v.t.*, to stun with noise.

dine, *v.i.*, to take dinner; *v.t.*, to give a dinner to.

dined, *p.p.*, dine.

di'ner, *n.*, one who dines.

ding, *v.t.*, to dash.

ding'-dong, *n.*, the sound of bells; *adv.*, with alternating success.

dinged, *p.p.*, ding.

din'gey, din'ghy, *n.*, a ship's small boat; a pleasure boat.

din'giness, *n.*, the state of being dingy.

ding'ing, *pr.p.*, ding.

din'gle, *n.*, a little wooded valley.

din'go, *n.*, a wild Australian dog.

din'gy, *adj.*, soiled; dirty white.

di'ning, *pr.p.*, dine.

di'ning-room, *n.*, a room to dine in.

din'ner, *n.*, the principal meal of the day.

din'nerless, *adj.*, having no dinner.

din'ning, *pr.p.*, din.

dinothe'rium, *n.*, a gigantic extinct elephant.

dint, *n.*, the mark made by a blow; a dent; *v.t.*, to dent.

dint'ed, *p.p.*, dint.

dioc'esan, *adj.*, rel. to a diocese; *n.*, a bishop as related to his own diocese; one in a diocese in relation to the bishop.

di'ocese, *n.*, the extent of a bishop's jurisdiction.

Dioe'cia, *n. pl.*, a genus of plants, some being male and some female.

dioe'cian, *adj.*, having individuals of either sex.

diop'ter, *n.*, an optical instrument for taking altitudes.

diop'tric, *adj.*, pert. to dioptrics, that branch of optics which deals with refraction, esp. through lenses.

diop'trical, *adj.*, *i.q.* dioptric.

diora'ma, *n.*, a scenic spectacle produced by transmission and reflection of light.

diora'mic, *adj.*, pert. to diorama.

diortho'sis, *n.*, correction of a deformity; critical revision of a text.

diox'ide, *n.*, an oxide containing two atoms of oxygen and one of another element.

dip, *v.t.*, to put into a fluid and withdraw; *v.i.*, to sink; to slope; *n.*, an immersion; inclination; a rude kind of candle; a wash.

dipet'alous, *adj.*, two-petalled.

di'phone, *n.*, a phonographic sign representing two consecutive vowels, which are separately pronounced.

diphon'ic, *adj.*, rel. to a diphone.

diphthe'ria, *n.*, a disease of the throat.

diph'thong, *n.*, a union of two vowels to form a single sound.

diphthon'gal, *adj.*, bel. to a diphthong.

dip'loe, *n.*, the soft substance between

the plates of the skull.

diplo'ma, *n.*, a written document conferring a privilege or honour.

diplo'macy, *n.*, the art of conducting negotiations between nations.

dip'lomat, *n.*, a diplomatist.

diplomat'ic, *adj.*, rel. to diplomacy; tactful.

diplomat'ically, *adv.*, in a diplomatic manner; artfully.

diplo'matist, *n.*, a person skilled in diplomacy.

dipped, *p.p.*, dip.

dip'per, *n.*, one who, or that which, dips; an American Baptist; a water-ousel.

dip'ping, *pr.p.*, dip.

dips, pl. of dip (*n.*).

dipsoma'nia, *n.*, an uncontrollable mania for drinking stimulants.

Dip'tera, *n. pl.*, the class of animals having two wings only.

dip'teral, *adj.*, having two wings.

dip'tote, *n.*, a noun with only two cases.

dip'tych, *n.*, a carving or painting on two folding tablets.

diradia'tion, *n.*, the emission and diffusion of light.

dire, *adj.*, dreadful; dismal.

direct', *adj.*, straight; *v.t.*, to point in a straight line; to order; to address a letter.

direct'ed, *p.p.*, direct.

direct'ing, *pr.p.*, direct.

direc'tion, *n.*, the act of directing; course; management; the address on a letter.

direct'ive, *adj.*, having the power of directing.

direct'ly, *adv.*, in a direct manner; immediately.

direct'ness, *n.*, the quality of being direct.

direct'or, *n.*, one who directs, esp. a company; a spiritual adviser.

direct'orate, *n.*, a body of directors.

directo'rial, *adj.*, pert. to a director.

direct'ory, *n.*, a book containing an alphabetical list of persons, with certain particulars, such as their addresses.

direct'ress, *n.*, a woman who directs.

direct'rix, *n.*, a straight line of importance in the theory of conic sections.

dire'ful, *adj.*, *s.q.* dire.

dire'fulness, *n.*, the state of being dire.

dir'er, *adj.*, *comp.* of dire.

dir'est, *adj.*, *super.* of dire.

dirge, *n.*, a song expressing mourning.

dir'igible, *adj.*, able to be directed; *n.*, an airship capable of being steered.

dirk, *n.*, a dagger.

dirt, *n.*, any foul or filthy substance.

dirt'ied, *p.p.*, dirty.

dirt'ier, *adj.*, *comp.* of dirty.

dirt'iest, *adj.*, *super.* of dirty.

dirt'ily, *adv.*, in a dirty manner.

dirt'iness, *n.*, foulness; nastiness.

dirt'y, *adj.*, not clean; impure; *v.t.*, to defile, to soil.

dirt'ying, *pr.p.*, dirty.

Dis, *n.*, the god Pluto.

disabil'ity, *n.*, incapacity.

disa'ble, *v.t.*, to render incapable.

disa'bled, *p.p.*, disable.

disa'bling, *pr.p.*, disable.

disabuse', *v.t.*, to undeceive.

disabused', *p.p.*, disabuse.

disabus'ing, *pr.p.*, disabuse.

disadvan'tage, *n.*, injury, harm; damage; *v.t.* to affect injuriously.

disadvan'taged, *p.p.*, disadvantage.

disadvan'taging, *pr.p.*, disadvantage.

disadvanta'geous, *adj.*, unfavourable to success.

disadvanta'geously, *adv.*, in a disadvantageous manner.

disaffect', *v.t.*, to make unfriendly.

disaffect'ed, *adj.*, unfriendly, disloyal; *p.p.* disaffect.

disaffect'ing, *pr.p.*, disaffect.

disaffec'tion, *n.*, alienation of affection.

disaffirm', *v.t.*, to repudiate.

disaffirm'ance, *n.*, denial.

disaffirmed', *p.p.*, disaffirm.

disaffirm'ing, *pr.p.*, disaffirm.

disaffor'est, *v.t.*, to divest of forest laws.

disaffor'ested, *p.p.*, disafforest.

disaffor'esting, *pr.p.*, disafforest.

disagree', *v.i.*, to differ; to quarrel.

disagree'able, *adj.*, unpleasing.

disagree'ableness, *n.*, the quality of being disagreeable.

disagree'ably, *adv.*, unpleasantly.

disagreed', *p.p.*, disagree.

disagree'ing, *pr.p.*, disagree.

disagree'ment, *n.*, difference; a quarrel.

disallow', *v.t.*, to refuse permission for; to reject.

disallow'able, *adj.*, not to be permitted.

disallow'ance, *n.*, prohibition.

disallowed', *p.p.*, disallow.

disallow'ing, *pr.p.*, disallow.

disannul', *v.t.*, to cancel.

disannulled', *p.p.*, disannul.

disannul'ling, *pr.p.*, disannul.

disappear', *v.i.*, to vanish.

disappear'ance, *n.*, removal from sight.

disappeared', *p.p.*, disappear.
disappear'ing, *pr.p.*, disappear.
disappoint', *v.t.*, to belie expectation.
disappoint'ed, *p.p.*, disappoint.
disappoint'ing, *pr.p.*, disappoint; *adj.*, contrary to hope.
disappoint'ment, *n.*, failure of expectation.
disapproba'tion, *n.*, disapproval, censure.
disap'probatory, *adj.*, conveying disapprobation.
disappro'priate, *v.t.*, to release from individual ownership.
disapprov'al, *n.*, disapprobation; dislike.
disapprove', *v.t.*, to censure; *v.i.*, to express disapproval.
disapproved', *p.p.*, disapprove.
disapprov'ing, *pr.p.*, disapprove.
disapprov'ingly, *adv.*, in a disapproving manner.
disarm', *v.t.*, to take the arms from; to render harmless.
disarm'ament, *n.*, the act of disarming.
disarmed', *p.p.*, disarm.
disarm'ing, *pr.p.*, disarm.
disarrange', *v.t.*, to put out of order.
disarranged', *p.p.*, disarrange.
disarrange'ment, *n.*, disorder.
disarrang'ing, *pr.p.*, disarrange.
disarray', *v.t.*, to undress; to throw into disorder; *n.*, disorder; confusion.
disarrayed', *p.p.*, disarray.
disarray'ing, *pr.p.*, disarray.
disas'ter, *n.*, a great misfortune or calamity.
disas'trous, *adj.*, causing or accompanied by disaster.
disas'trously, *adv.*, in a disastrous manner.
disavow', *v.t.*, to repudiate; to disown.
disavow'al, *n.*, denial; repudiation.
disavowed', *p.p.*, disavow.
disavow'ing, *pr.p.*, disavow.
disband', *v.t.* and *i.*, to dismiss; to break up as a band of men.
disband'ed, *p.p.*, disband.
disband'ing, *pr.p.*, disband.
disband'ment, *n.*, the act of disbanding.
disbelief', *n.*, denial of belief.
disbelieve', *v.t.*, to hold not to be true; *v.i.*, to refuse to believe.
disbelieved', *p.p.*, disbelieve.
disbeliev'er, *n.*, an unbeliever.
disbeliev'ing, *pr.p.*, disbelieve.
disbur'den, *v.t.*, to remove a burden from.
disbur'dened, *p.p.*, disburden.
disbur'dening, *pr.p.*, disburden.
disburse', *v.t.*, to expend.
disbursed', *p.p.*, disburse.
disburse'ment, *n.*, a sum paid out.
disburs'er, *n.*, one who disburses.
disburs'ing, *pr.p.*, disburse.
disc, *n.*, a flat circular plate.
discard', *v.t.* and *i.*, to throw out of the hand cards not wanted in the game; to cast off.
discard'ed, *p.p.*, discard.
discard'ing, *pr.p.*, discard.
discern', *v.t.*, to discriminate by the eye or intellect.
discerned', *p.p.*, discern.
discern'er, *n.*, a clear-sighted observer.
discern'ible, *adj.*, able to be discerned.
discern'ing, *adj.*, sharp-sighted; acute of understanding; *pr.p.*, discern.
discern'ingly, *adv.*, in a discerning manner.
discern'ment, *n.*, acuteness of judgment, penetration.
discharge', *v.t.*, to free from a burden; to fire off; to pay (a debt); to dismiss; *n.*, release; dismissal, payment.
discharged', *p.p.*, discharge.
dischar'ger, *n.*, one who, or that which, discharges.
discharg'ing, *pr.p.*, discharge.
dis'ciform, *adj.*, disc-shaped.
disci'ple, *n.*, a pupil; a follower.
disci'pleship, *n.*, the state of being a disciple.
disciplina'rian, *n.*, one who enforces rigid discipline; a martinet.
dis'ciplinary, *adj.*, promoting discipline.
dis'cipline, *n.*, training; correction; chastisement; *v.t.*, to subject to discipline.
dis'ciplined, *p.p.*, discipline.
dis'ciplining, *pr.p.*, discipline.
disclaim', *v.t.*, to disavow.
disclaimed', *p.p.*, disclaim.
disclaim'er, *n.*, one who disclaims; an act of disclaiming.
disclaim'ing, *pr.p.*, disclaim.
disclose', *v.t.*, to reveal.
disclosed', *p.p.*, disclose.
disclo'ser, *n.*, one who discloses.
disclo'sing, *pr.p.*, disclose.
disclo'sure, *n.*, the act of revealing; the thing revealed.
dis'coid, *adj.*, resembling a disc.
discoi'dal, *adj.*, *i.q.* discoid.
discolora'tion, *n.*, the act of discolouring.

discol'our, discol'or, *v.t.*, to stain; *adj.*, differing in colour.

discol'oured, *p.p.*, discolour.

discol'ouring, *pr.p.*, discolour.

discom'fit, *v.t.*, to vanquish; to disconcert.

discom'fited, *p.p.*, discomfit.

discom'fiter, *n.*, one who discomfits.

discom'fiting, *pr.p.*, discomfit.

discom'fiture, *n.*, defeat; disappointment.

discom'fort, *n.*, absence of comfort; disturbance of peace; *v.t.*, to make uneasy.

discom'forted, *p.p.*, discomfort.

discom'forting *pr.p.*, discomfort.

discommode', *v.t.*, to put to inconvenience.

discommo'ded, *p.p.*, discommode.

discommo'ding, *pr.p.*, discommode; *adj.*, inconvenient.

discompose', *v.t.*, to disturb; to vex.

discomposed', *p.p.*, discompose.

discompo'sing, *pr.p.*, discompose.

discompo'sure, *n.*, agitation of mind.

disconcert', *v.t.*, to frustrate; to confuse.

disconcert'ed, *p.p.*, disconcert.

disconcert'ing, *pr.p.*, disconcert; *adj.*, upsetting.

disconnect', *v.t.*, to detach.

disconnect'ed, *p.p.*, disconnect.

disconnect'ing, *pr.p.*, disconnect.

disconnec'tion, *n.*, separation.

discon'solate, *adj.*, hopeless; sad.

discontent', *n.*, dissatisfaction.

discontent'ed, *adj.*, dissatisfied.

discontent'edly, *adv.*, in a discontented manner.

discontent'ing, *adj.*, causing discontent.

discontent'ment, *n.*, discontent.

discontin'uance, *n.*, cessation.

discontinua'tion, *n.*, *i.q.* discontinuance.

discontin'ue, *v.t.*, to put an end to; *v.i.*, to cease.

discontin'ued, *p.p.*, discontinue.

discontin'uing, *pr.p.*, discontinue.

discontinu'ity, *n.*, want of continuity.

discontin'uous, *adj.*, interrupted.

dis'cord, *n.*, disagreement; strife; a union of musical sounds disagreeable to the ear.

discord', *v.i.*, to be out of harmony or agreement.

discord'ance, *n.*, offence against harmony.

discord'ancy, *n.*, *i.q.* discordance.

discord'ant, *adj.*, disagreeing; not harmonious.

discos'tate, *adj.*, having ribs diverging radiately.

dis'count, *n.*, a deduction from a price or other sum of money to cover interest.

discount', *v.t.*, to deduct discount from; to discredit.

discount'able, *adj.*, capable of being discounted.

discount'ed, *p.p.*, discount.

discoun'tenance, *v.t.*, to discourage by disapproval.

discoun'tenanced, *p.p.* discountenance.

discoun'tenancing, *pr.p.*, discountenance.

dis'counter, *n.*, one who discounts bills, etc.

discount'ing, *pr.p.*, discount.

discour'age, *v.t.*, to dishearten; to dissuade.

discour'aged, *p.p.*, discourage.

discour'agement, *n.*, the act of discouraging; that which discourages.

discour'ager, *n.*, one who discourages.

discour'aging, *adj.*, disheartening; *pr.p.* discourage.

discourse', *n.*, conversation; a treatise; a sermon; *v.i.*, to communicate thoughts in a formal manner.

discoursed', *p.p.*, discourse.

discours'er, *n.*, one who discourses.

discours'ing, *pr.p.*, discourse.

discour'teous, *adj.*, uncivil.

discour'teously, *adv.*, uncivilly.

discour'tesy, *n.*, want of courtesy.

dis'cous, *adj.*, disc-shaped.

discov'er, *v.t.*, to have the first sight of; to detect.

discov'erable, *adj.*, able to be discovered.

discov'ered, *p.p.*, discover.

discov'erer, *n.*, one who discovers.

discov'ering, *pr.p.*, discover.

discov'erture, *n.*, in law, release of a woman from the coverture of her husband.

discov'ery, *n.*, a finding out; a revealing; that which is discovered.

discred'it, *n.*, disrepute; disbelief; *v.t.*, to disbelieve.

discred'itable, *adj.*, disgraceful.

discred'ited, *p.p.*, discredit.

discred'iting, *pr.p.*, discredit.

discreet', *adj.*, prudent; cautious.

discreet'ly, *adv.*, prudently.

discreet'ness, *n.*, the quality of being discreet.

discrep'ance, *n.*, *i.q.* discrepancy.

discrep'ancy, *n.*, inconsistency among facts.

discrep'ant, *adj.*, differing; inconsistent.

discrete', *adj.*, separate; distinct.
discre'tion, *n.*, discreetness; sound judgment; liberty of acting according to one's own judgment.
discre'tional, *adj.*, *i.q.* discretionary.
discre'tionary, *adj.*, left to one's own discretion.
discre'tive, *adj.*, denoting separation or opposition.
discrim'inate, *adj.*, having the power of noting minute distinctions.
discrim'inate, *v.t.*, to distinguish by observing differences; to select; *v.i.*, to note differences.
discrim'inated, *p.p.*, discriminate.
discrim'inately, *adv.*, with minute distinction.
discrim'inating, *adj.*, able to make nice distinctions; *pr.p.*, discriminate.
discrimina'tion, *n.*, the faculty of discriminating.
discrim'inative, *adj.*, characteristic; discriminating.
discrim'inator, *n.*, one who discriminates.
discrim'inatory, *adj.*, *i.q.* discriminative.
discrown', *v.t.*, to deprive of a crown.
discrowned', *p.p.*, discrown.
discrown'ing, *pr.p.*, discrown.
discur'sion, *n.*, the act of ranging from thought to thought in discourse.
discur'sive, *adj.*, passing rapidly from one subject to another.
discur'sively, *adv.*, in a discursive manner.
discur'sory, *adj.*, argumentative.
dis'cus, *n.*, a kind of ancient quoit; a disc.
discuss', *v.t.*, to debate; to argue.
discussed', *p.p.*, discuss.
discuss'er, *n.*, one who discusses.
discus'sing, *pr.p.*, discuss.
discus'sion, *n.*, debate; the act of discussing.
discuss'ive, *adj.*, having the power to discuss.
discu'tient, *n.*, a medicine or application which disperses a tumour.
disdain', *v.t.*, to scorn; *n.*, haughtiness; contempt.
disdained', *p.p.*, disdain.
disdain'ful, *adj.*, contemptuous; haughty.
disdain'fully, *adv.*, in disdainful manner.
disdain'ing, *pr.p.*, disdain.
disease', *n.*, any morbid state of the body.
diseased', *adj.*, affected with disease.
diseas'ing, *adj.*, causing discomfort.
disembark', *v.t.* and *i.*, to land.
disembarked', *p.p.*, disembark.
disembarka'tion, *n.*, the act of disembarking.
disembark'ing, *pr.p.*, disembark.
disembar'rass, *v.t.*, to free from embarrassment.
disembar'rassed, *p.p.*, disembarrass.
disembar'rassing, *pr.p.*, disembarrass.
disembar'rassment, *n.*, the act of disembarrassing.
disembod'ied, *p.p.*, disembody.
disembod'iment, *n.*, the act of disembodying.
disembod'y, *v.t.*, to disband (troops); to divest of the body.
disembod'ying, *pr.p.*, disembody.
disembogue', *v.i.*, to discharge water (as a stream) into the sea or a lake.
disembow'el, *v.t.*, to deprive of the viscera; to gut.
disembow'el(l)ed, *p.p.*, disembowel.
disembow'el(l)ing, *pr.p.* disembowel.
disembroil', *v.t.*, to extricate from confusion.
disembroiled', *p.p.*, disembroil.
disembroil'ing, *pr.p.*, disembroil.
disena'ble, *v.t.*, to disqualify.
disena'bled, *p.p.*, disenable.
disena'bling, *pr.p.*, disenable.
disenchant', *v.t.*, to free from fascination or pleasing delusion.
disenchant'ed, *p.p.*, disenchant.
disenchant'er, *n.*, one who disenchants.
disenchant'ing, *pr.p.*, disenchant.
disenchant'ment, *n.*, the act of disenchanting.
disencum'ber, *v.t.*, to free from encumbrance.
disencum'bered, *p.p.*, disencumber.
disencum'bering, *pr.p.* disencumber.
disencum'brance, *n.*, deliverance from encumbrance.
disendow', *v.t.*, to rob or deprive of endowments.
disendowed', *p.p.*, disendow.
disendow'ing, *pr.p.*, disendow.
disendow'ment, *n.*, the act of taking away an endowment.
disenfran'chise, *v.t.*, *i.q.* disfranchise.
disengage', *v.t.*, to disentangle; to free; to set free from an engagement.
disengaged', *adj.*, at leisure; not occupied; *p.p.*, disengage.
disengage'ment, *n.*, the state of being disengaged.
disengag'ing, *pr.p.*, disengage.
disentan'gle, *v.t.*, to unravel; to free from entanglements
disentan'gled, *p.p.*, disentangle.
disentan'gling, *pr.p.*, disentangle.
disenthrall', *v.t.*, to

rescue from slavery or oppression.

disenthralled', *p.p.*, disenthrall.

disenthrall'ing, *pr.p.*, disenthrall.

disestab'lish, *v.t.*, to cause to cease to be established.

disestab'lished, *p.p.*, disestablish.

disestab'lishing, *pr.p.*, disestablish.

disestab'lishment, *n.*, the act of disestablishing.

disesteem', *n.*, want of esteem; *v.t.*, to dislike slightly.

disesteemed', *p.p.*, disesteem.

disesteem'ing, *pr.p.*, disesteem.

disfa'vour, **disfa'vor**, *n.*, slight displeasure; a disobliging act; *v.t.*, to withdraw favour from.

disfa'voured, *p.p.*, disfavour.

disfa'vouring, *pr.p.*, disfavour.

disfigura'tion, *n.*, the act of disfiguring; disfigurement.

disfig'ure, *v.t.*, to injure the beauty of.

disfig'ured, *p.p.*, disfigure.

disfig'urement, *n.*, disfiguration; that which disfigures.

disfig'urer, *n.*, one who disfigures.

disfig'uring, *pr.p.*, disfigure.

disfran'chise, *v.t.*, to deprive of the rights of citizenship, esp. of the vote.

disfran'chised, *p.p.*, disfranchise.

disfran'chisement, *n.*, the state of being disfranchised.

disfran'chising, *pr.p.*, disfranchise.

disgorge', *v.t.*, to vomit; to surrender.

disgorged', *p.p.*, disgorge.

disgorge'ment, *n.*, the act of disgorging.

disgorg'ing, *pr.p.*, disgorge.

disgrace', *n.*, disfavour; shame; cause of shame; *v.t.*, to put out of favour; to dishonour.

disgraced', *p.p.*, disgrace.

disgrace'ful, *adj.*, shameful; infamous.

disgrace'fully, *adv.*, in a disgraceful manner.

disgrac'ing, *pr.p.*, disgrace.

disguise', *v.t.*, to conceal the ordinary appearance of; *n.*, a dress intended to conceal identity.

disguised', *p.p.*, disguise.

disgui'ser, *n.*, one who disguises.

disgui'sing, *pr.p.*, disguise.

disgust', *n.*, strong dislike; *v.t.*, to stir up loathing in.

disgust'ed, *p.p.*, disgust.

disgust'ful, *adj.*, exciting disgust.

disgust'ing, *pr.p.*, disgust; *adj.*, loathsome; nasty.

dish, *n.*, a broad, open vessel for serving food at table; *v.t.*, to put in a dish; to ruin (*slang*).

dishabille', *n.*, *i.q.* deshabille.

dish'-cloth, *n.*, a cloth for washing dishes.

disheart'en, *v.t.*, to discourage; to dispirit.

disheart'ened, *p.p.*, dishearten.

disheart'ening, *pr.p.*, dishearten.

disheart'enment, *n.*, discouragement.

dished, *p.p.*, dish.

dishev'el, *v.t.*, to allow (the hair) to hang negligently.

dishev'el(l)ed, *p.p.*, dishevel.

dishev'elling, *pr.p.*, dishevel.

dish'ing, *pr.p.*, dish.

dishon'est, *adj.*, not honest.

dishon'estly, *adv.*, fraudulently.

dishon'esty, *n.*, fraud; treachery.

dishon'our, **dishon'or**, *n.*, want of honour; disgrace; *v.t.*, to disgrace, treat with indignity; refuse to accept or pay (a cheque).

dishon'ourable, *adj.*, disgraceful.

dishon'oured, *p.p.*, dishonour.

dishon'ourer, *n.*, one who dishonours.

dishon'ouring, *pr.p.*, dishonour.

disillu'sion, *n.*, disenchantment; *v.t.*, to free from illusion.

disillu'sioned, *p.p.*, disillusion.

disillu'sioning, *pr.p.*, disillusion.

disinclina'tion, *n.*, unwillingness.

disincline', *v.t.*, to make unwilling.

disinclined', *p.p.*, disincline.

disincli'ning, *pr.p.*, disincline.

disincor'porate, *v.t.*, to deprive of corporate powers.

disincor'porated, *p.p.*, disincorporate.

disincor'porating, *pr.p.*, disincorporate.

disincorpora'tion, *n.*, the act of disincorporating.

disinfect', *v.t.*, to purify from contagious matter.

disinfect'ant, *n.*, a substance that disinfects.

disinfect'ed, *p.p.*, disinfect.

disinfect'ing, *pr.p.*, disinfect.

disinfec'tion, *n.*, purification from infecting matter.

disingen'uous, *adj.*, insincere.

disingen'uously, *adv.*, in a disingenuous manner.

disingen'uousness, *n.*, insincerity.

disinher'it, *v.t.*, to deprive of the right to an inheritance.

disinher'itance, *n.*, the act of disinheriting.

disinher'ited, *p.p.*, disinherit.

disinher'iting, *pr.p.*, disinherit.

disin'tegrable, *adj.*, that can be disintegrated.

disin'tegrate, *v.t.*, to reduce to fragments; *v.i.*, to lose coherence.

disin'tegrated, *p.p.*, disintegrate.
disin'tegrating, *pr.p.*, disintegrate.
disintegra'tion *n.*, the act of disintegrating.
disinter', *v.t.*, to take out of the earth.
disin'terested, *adj.*, unselfish; without personal motive.
disin'terestedly, *adv.*, in a disinterested manner.
disin'terestedness, *n.*, the state of being disinterested.
disinter'ment, *n.*, exhumation.
disinterred', *p.p.*, disinter.
disinter'ring. *pr.p.*, disinter.
disjoin', *v.t.*, to separate; *v.i.*, to part.
disjoined', *p.p.*, disjoin.
disjoin'ing, *pr.p.*, disjoin.
disjoint', *v.t.*, to separate at the joints; to render incoherent.
disjoint'ed, *adj.*, incoherent; out of order; *p.p.*, disjoint.
disjoint'ing, *pr.p.*, disjoint.
disjunct', *adj.*, separated.
disjunc'tion, *n.*, disunion; separation.
disjunct'ive, *adj.*, tending to separate; marking opposition.
disjunct'ively, *adv.*, in a disjunctive manner.
disk, *n.*, *i.q.* disc.
dislike', *n.*, antipathy; aversion; *v.t.*, to feel dislike towards.
disliked', *p.p.*, dislike.
disli'king, *pr.p.*, dislike.
dis'locate, *v.t.*, to displace; to put out of joint.
dis'located, *p.p.*, dislocate.
dis'locating, *pr.p.*, dislocate.
disloca'tion, *n.*, the act of dislocating or displacing.
dislodge', *v.t.*, to drive from the place occupied.
dislodged', *p.p.*, dislodge.
dislodg'ing, *pr.p.*, dislodge.
dislodg'ment, *n.*, the act of dislodging.
disloy'al, *adj.*, faithless; treacherous.
disloy'ally, *adv.*, in a disloyal manner.
disloy'alty, *n.*, infidelity.
dis'mal, *adj.*, gloomy.
dis'mally, *adv.*, in a dismal manner.
disman'tle, *v.t.*, to strip of equipments.
disman'tled *p.p.*, dismantle.
disman'tling, *pr.p.*, dismantle.
dismast', *v.t.*, to deprive of masts.
dismast'ed, *p.p.*, dismast.
dismast'ing, *pr.p.*, dismast.
dismay', *v.t.*, to discourage; *n.*, a complete loss of courage.
dismayed', *p.p.*, dismay.
dismay'ing, *pr.p.*, dismay.
disme, *n.*, a tenth part; the number ten.
dismem'ber, *v.t.*, to divide limb from limb.
dismem'bered, *p.p.*, dismember.
dismem'bering, *pr.p.*, dismember.
dismem'berment, *n.*, the act of dismembering.
dismiss', *v.t.*, to send away.
dismiss'al, *n.*, discharge.
dismissed', *p.p.*, dismiss.
dismiss'ing, *pr.p.*, dismiss.
dismis'sion, *n.*, the act of dismissing.
dismiss'ive, *adj.*, giving dismission.
dismiss'ory, *adj.*, granting permission to depart.
dismount', *v.i.*, to alight from a horse; *v.t.*, to unhorse.
dismount'ed, *p.p.*, dismount.
dismount'ing, *pr.p.*, dismount.
disobe'dience, *n.*, neglect or refusal to obey.
disobe'dient, *adj.*, guilty of disobedience.
disobe'diently, *adv.*, in a disobedient manner.
disobey', *v.t.*, to neglect or refuse to obey.
disobeyed', *p.p.*, disobey.
disobey'er, *n.*, one who disobeys.
disobey'ing, *pr.p.*, disobey.
disoblige', *v.t.*, to offend by failing to oblige.
disobliged', *p.p.*, disoblige.
disobli'ging, *adj.*, unaccommodating; *pr.p.*, disoblige.
disor'der, *n.*, want of order; confusion; sickness; *v.t.*, to throw into confusion.
disor'dered, *adj.*, irregular; deranged; *p.p.*, disorder.
disor'dering, *pr.p.*, disorder.
disor'derliness, *n.*, the state of being disorderly.
disor'derly, *adj.*, marked by disorder; unruly.
disorganiza'tion, *n.*, the state of being disorganized.
disor'ganize, *v.t.*, to throw into confusion.
disor'ganized, *p.p.*, disorganize.
disor'ganizer, *n.*, one who disorganizes.
disown', *v.t.*, to refuse to acknowledge.
disowned', *p.p.*, disown.
disown'ing, *pr.p.*, disown.
dispar'age, *v.t.*, to depreciate.
dispar'aged *p.p.*, disparage.
dispar'agement, *n.*, detraction; dishonour.
dispar'ager, *n.*, one who disparages.
dispar'aging, *pr.p.*, disparage.

dispar'agingly, *adv.*, in a manner to disparage.

dis'parate, *adj.*, dissimilar.

dispar'ity, *n.*, inequality.

dispark', *v.t.*, to turn (parkland) to some other use.

dispart', *v.t.*, to sever; *v.i.*, to open; *n.*, the difference between half the diameter of base ring and the muzzle of a gun; a muzzle sight.

dispart'ed, *p.p.*, dispart.

dispart'ing, *pr.p.*, dispart.

dispas'sion, *n.*, freedom from passion; apathy.

dispas'sionate, *adj.*, unmoved by feelings; impartial.

dispatch', *v.t.* and *n.*, *i.q.* despatch.

dispel', *v.t.*, to disperse.

dispelled', *p.p.*, dispel.

dispel'ling, *pr.p.*, dispel.

dispen'sable, *adj.*, able to be dispensed with.

dispen'sary, *n.*, a house in which medicines are compounded; a place where medicines and medical advice are given gratis.

dispensa'tion, *n.*, the act of dispensing; a system of religion and morals; the setting free from an obligation.

dispen'satory, *adj.*, having power to grant dispensations; *n.*, a pharmacopoeia.

dispense', *v.t.*, to distribute; to administer; to excuse from an obligation; to compound.

dispensed', *p.p.*, dispense.

dispen'ser, *n.*, one who dispenses.

dispen'sing, *adj.*, granting dispensation; *n.*, the act or practice of dispensing; *pr.p.*, dispense.

dispeo'ple, *v.t.*, to empty of inhabitants.

dispeo'pled, *p.p.*, dispeople.

disper'mous, *adj.*, two-seeded.

disperse', *v.t.* and *i.*, to scatter.

dispersed', *adj.*, scattered; *p.p.*, disperse.

disper'ser, *n.*, one who disperses.

disper'sing, *pr.p.*, disperse.

disper'sion, *n.*, the state of being scattered.

disper'sive, *adj.*, tending to scatter.

dispir'it, *v.t.*, to dishearten.

dispir'ited, *adj.*, depressed in spirits; *p.p.*, dispirit.

dispir'iting, *pr.p.*, dispirit; *adj.*, depressing.

displace', *v.t.*, to remove from its place.

displaced', *p.p.*, displace.

displace'ment, *n.*, removal; the quantity of water displaced by a floating body.

displac'ing, *pr.p.*, displace.

displant', *v.t.*, to pluck up what is planted.

displant'ed, *p.p.*, displant.

displant'ing, *pr.p.*, displant.

display', *v.t.*, to spread before the view; *n.*, exhibition; ostentatious show.

displayed', *p.p.*, display.

display'er, *n.*, one who displays.

display'ing, *pr.p.*, display.

displease', *v.t.*, to offend somewhat; to make slightly angry.

displeased', *p.p.*, displease.

displeas'er, *n.*, one who displeases.

displeas'ing, *adj.*, disagreeable; *pr.p.*, displease.

displeas'ure, *n.*, vexation; annoyance

displume', *v.t.*, to strip of feathers

displumed', *p.p.*, displume.

display'ing, *pr.p.*, displume.

dispone', *v.t.*, in Scots law, to convey (property) to another formally.

disponed', *p.p.*, dispone.

dispo'ner, *n.*, one who dispones.

dispon'ing, *pr.p.*, dispone.

disport', *n.*, sport; pastime; *v.t.*, to play; to sport.

disport'ed, *p.p.*, disport.

disport'ing, *pr.p.*, disport.

dispo'sable, *adj.*, free to be used when required.

dispo'sal, *n.*, arrangement; power of bestowing; the act of selling or parting with.

dispose', *v.t.*, to arrange; to incline; to apply to a particular purpose.

disposed', *adj.*, inclined; minded; *p.p.*, dispose.

dispo'ser, *n.*, one who disposes.

dispo'sing, *pr.p.*, dispose.

disposi'tion, *n.*, manner of arrangement; natural constitution of mind; propensity.

dispossess', *v.t.*, to deprive of ownership or occupancy.

dispossessed', *p.p.*, dispossess.

dispossess'ing, *pr.p.*, dispossess.

disposses'sion, *n.*, the act of dispossessing.

dispossess'or, *n.*, one who dispossesses.

dispraise', *n.*, blame; *v.t.*, to censure.

dispraised', *p.p.*, dispraise.

disprais'ing, *pr.p.*, dispraise.

disproof', *n.*, a proving to be false or erroneous.

dispropor'tion, *n.*, want of proportion or symmetry; inequality.

dispropor'tionable, *adj.*, not having due

proportion; unequal; inadequate.
dispropor'tional, *adj.*, *i.q.* disproportionable.
dispropor'tionate, *adj.*, *i.q.* disproportionable.
dispropor'tioned, *adj.*, wanting in symmetry.
disprov'able, *adj.*, capable of being disproved.
disprov'al, *n.*, the act of disproving.
disprove', *v.t.*, to prove to be false or erroneous.
disproved', *p.p.*, disprove.
disprov'er, *n.*, one who disproves.
disprov'ing, *pr.p.*, disprove.
dis'putable, *adj.*, controvertible.
dis'putant, *n.*, one who disputes or argues.
disputa'tion, *n.*, the act of disputing; controversy.
disputa'tious, *adj.*, inclined to dispute.
dispute', *v.i.*, to contend in argument; to wrangle; *v.t.*, to attempt to disprove; to call in question; to contest; *n.*, controversy; strife.
dispu'ted, *p.p.*, dispute.
dispu'ter, *n.*, one who disputes.
dispu'ting, *pr.p.*, dispute.
disqualifica'tion, *n.*, disability; that which disqualifies.
disqual'ified, *p.p.*, disqualify.
disqual'ify, *v.t.*, to incapacitate.
disqual'ifying, *pr.p.*, disqualify.
disqui'et, *n.*, uneasiness; anxiety; *v.t.*, to make uneasy; to harass.
disqui'eted, *p.p.*, disquiet.
disqui'eting, *adj.*, disturbing the mind; *pr.p.*, disquiet.
disqui'etude, *n.*, want of tranquillity; disquiet.

disquisi'tion, *n.*, a dissertation, essay, or treatise; an argumentative inquiry.
disquisi'tional, *adj.*, pert. to a disquisition.
disregard', *n.*, neglect; *v.t.*, to pay no heed to.
disregard'ed, *p.p.*, disregard.
disregard'ful, *adj.*, neglectful.
disregard'ing, *pr.p.*, disregard.
disrel'ish, *n.*, distaste; *v.t.*, to dislike the taste of.
disrel'ished, *p.p.*, disrelish.
disrel'ishing, *pr.p.*, disrelish.
disrepair', *n.*, a state of requiring to be repaired.
disrep'utable, *adj.*, dishonourable; low.
disrepute', *n.*, loss or want of reputation.
disrespect', *n.*, want of respect; rudeness.
disrespect'ful, *adj.*, wanting in respect.
disrespect'fully, *adv.*, in a disrespectful manner.
disrobe', *v.t.* and *i.*, to undress; to divest of a robe.
disrobed', *p.p.*, disrobe.
disro'ber, *n.*, one who disrobes.
disro'bing, *pr.p.*, disrobe.
disrup'tion, *n.*, the act of bursting and separating.
disrup'tive, *adj.*, causing or following disruption.
disrup'ture, *n.*, a rending asunder.
dissatisfac'tion, *n.*, discontent.
dissatisfac'tory, *adj.*, causing dissatisfaction.
dissat'isfied, *adj.*, discontented; *p.p.*, dissatisfy.
dissat'isfy, *v.t.*, to fail to satisfy; to render discontented.
dissat'isfying, *pr.p.*, dissatisfy.
dissect', *v.t.*, to divide with a cutting instrument; to analyse.
dissect'ed, *p.p.*, dissect.
dissect'ible, *adj.*, capable of being dissected.
dissect'ing, *adj.*, used in dissection; *pr.p.*, dissect.
dissec'tion, *n.*, the act or art of dissecting.
dissect'or, *n.*, one who dissects.
disseize', **disseise'**, *v.t.*, to dispossess wrongfully.
disseized', *p.p.*, disseize.
disseizee', *n.*, one who is disseized.
disseiz'in, *n.*, the act of disseizing.
disseiz'ing, *pr.p.*, disseize.
disseiz'or, *n.*, one who dispossesses another.
dissem'blance, *n.*, concealment by false pretences.
dissem'ble, *v.t.*, to hide by false pretences; *v.i.*, to put on an assumed manner.
dissem'bled, *p.p.*, dissemble.
dissem'bler, *n.*, one who dissembles.
dissem'bling, *pr.p.*, dissemble.
dissem'inate, *v.t.*, to diffuse; to spread by dispersion.
dissem'inated, *p.p.*, disseminate.
dissem'inating, *pr.p.*, disseminate.
dissemina'tion, *n.*, act of disseminating.
dissem'inator, *n.*, one who disseminates.
dissen'sion, *n.*, strife; quarrel; breach of friendship.
dissent', *v.i.*, to disagree in opinion; *n.*, difference of opinion; separation from the Church in England.
dissent'ed, *p.p.*, dissent.
dissent'er, *n.*, one who dissents; a separatist.

dissen'tient, *adj.*, declaring dissent; voting differently.

dissent'ing, *adj.*, disagreeing in opinion; bel. to a body of dissenters; *pr.p.*, dissent.

disserta'tion, *n.*, a treatise; a formal discourse.

disserve', *v.t.*, to do an ill-service to.

disserved', *pr.p.*, disserve.

disserv'ice, *n.*, an ill turn; an injury.

disserv'iceable, *adj.*, injurious.

disserv'ing, *pr.p.*, disserve.

dissev'er, *v.t.*, to part in two; to separate.

dissev'erance, *n.*, the act of dissevering.

dissevera'tion, *n.*, *s.q.* disseverance.

dissev'ered, *p.p.*, dissever.

dissev'ering, *pr.p.*, dissever.

dis'sidence, *n.*, dissent.

dis'sident, *adj.*, dissenting; *n.*, a dissenter.

dissil'ient, *adj.*, bursting (as the dry pod of a plant).

dissim'ilar, *adj.*, unlike.

dissimilar'ity, *n.*, unlikeness.

dissimila'tion, *n.*, the act of rendering dissimilar, esp. with reference to sounds in orthoepy.

dissimil'itude, *n.*, unlikeness; want of resemblance.

dissim'ulate, *v.i.*, to feign; to make pretence.

dissim'ulated, *p.p.*, dissimulate.

dissim'ulating, *pr.p.*, dissimulate.

dissimula'tion, *n.*, concealment of fact; hypocrisy.

dis'sipate, *v.t.*, to scatter; to drive away; to waste; *v.i.*, to vanish.

dis'sipated, *adj.*, extravagant; dissolute; *p.p.*, dissipate.

dis'sipating, *pr.p.*, dissipate.

dissipa'tion, *n.*, the act of dissipating, dissolute conduct.

disso'ciable, *adj.*, incongruous; not reconcilable.

disso'ciate, *v.t.*, to disunite; to part.

disso'ciated, *p.p.*, dissociate.

disso'ciating, *pr.p.*, dissociate.

dissocia'tion, *n.*, disunion; chemical decomposition.

dissolubil'ity, *n.*, the quality of being dissoluble.

dis'soluble, *adj.*, susceptible of decomposition.

dis'solute, *adj.*, debauched; given to vice or profligacy.

dis'solutely, *adv.*, in a dissolute manner.

dis'soluteness, *n.*, viciousness; dissipation.

dissolu'tion, *n.*, decomposition; death; the putting an end to the existence of an assembly.

dissolvabil'ity, *n.*, capability of being dissolved.

dissolv'able, *adj.*, able to be dissolved.

dissolve', *v.t.*, to melt; to liquefy; to destroy any connected system or body; *v.i.*, to melt; to break up.

dissolved', *p.p.*, dissolve.

dissolv'ent, *n.*, anything that dissolves.

dissolv'er, *n.*, one who, or that which, dissolves.

dissolv'ing, *pr.p.*, dissolve.

dis'sonance, *n.*, discord.

dis'sonancy, *n.*, *s.q.* dissonance.

dis'sonant, *adj.*, harsh sounding; incongruous.

dissuade', *v.t.*, to advise against; to turn from a purpose by argument.

dissua'ded, *p.p.*, dissuade.

dissua'der, *n.*, one who dissuades.

dissua'ding, *pr.p.*, dissuade.

dissua'sion, *n.*, advice in opposition to something.

dissua'sive, *adj.*, tending to dissuade; *n.*, an argument against.

dis'taff, *n.*, the staff to which a bunch of flax is tied, and from which the thread is drawn to be spun.

distain', *v.t.*, to stain.

distained', *p.p.*, distain.

distain'ing, *pr.p.*, distain.

dis'tance, *n.*, an interval of space or time; remoteness; *v.t.*, to outstrip.

dis'tanced, *p.p.*, distance.

dis'tancing, *pr.p.*, distance.

dis'tant, *adj.*, remote in place or time; not intimate.

dis'tantly, *adv.*, at a distance; with reserve.

distaste', *n.*, disrelish; disinclination.

distaste'ful, *adj.*, disagreeable.

distem'per, *n.*, a malady; a disease of young dogs; a kind of painting used for scene-painting and the decoration of walls, etc.; tempera; *v.t.*, to paint in tempera.

distem'perature, *n.*, confusion.

distem'pered, *adj.*, diseased in body or mind.

distem'pering, *pr.p.*, distemper.

distend', *v.t.*, to swell; *v.i.*, to become inflated.

distend'ed, *p.p.*, distend.

distend'ing, *pr.p.*, distend.

distensibil'ity, *n.*, the quality of being distensible.

disten'sible, *adj.*, capable of being distended.

disten'sion, *n.*, the act of distending; the state of being distended.

disten'sive, *adj., i.q.* distensible.
dis'tich, *n.,* a couplet.
distil', distill', *v.t.,* to yield in drops; to extract by distillation.
distil'lable, *adj.,* fit for distillation.
distil'late, *n.,* a fluid distilled.
distilla'tion, *n.,* the operation of extracting spirit from a substance by volatilization and condensation.
distil'latory, *adj.,* used in distillation, *n.,* a still.
distilled', *p.p.,* distil.
distil'ler, *n.,* one whose occupation is to extract spirit by distillation.
distil'lery, *n.,* the works where distilling is carried on.
distil'ling, *pr.p.,* distil; *n.,* the act or business of distilling.
distinct', *adj.,* well-defined; different; obvious.
distinc'tion, *n.,* a distinguishing quality; superiority; an honour of some kind.
distinct'ive, *adj.,* indicating difference.
distinct'ively, *adv.,* in a distinctive manner.
distinct'iveness, *n.,* the quality of being distinctive.
distinct'ly, *adv.,* clearly; obviously.
distinct'ness, *n.,* clearness; precision.
distin'guish, *v.t.,* to recognize the individuality of; to mark out from others by some point of difference, to confer an honour on.
***distin'guish*able,** *adj.,* capable of being distinguished.
distin'guished, *adj.,* eminent· *p.p.,* distinguish.
distin'guisher, *n.,* one who, or that which, distinguishes.
***distin'guish*ing,** *adj.,* characteristic; *pr.p.* distinguish.
distort', *v.t.,* to twist out of natural shape.
distort'ed, *adj.,* shaped abnormally; misshapen; *p.p.,* distort.
distort'ing, *pr.p.,* distort.
distor'tion, *n.,* a twisting out of natural shape or meaning.
distort'ive, *adj.,* causing distortion.
distract', *v.t.,* to turn from any object; to perplex; to render insane.
distract'ed, *adj.,* perplexed; crazy; *p.p.,* distract.
distract'ing, *pr.p.,* distract.
distrac'tion, *n.,* confusion of mind; diversion.
distract'ive, *adj.,* causing perplexity.
distrain', *v.t.,* to seize for debt.
distrain'able, *adj.,* liable to be distrained.
distrained', *p.p.,* distrain.
distrain'er, *n.,* one who distrains.
distrain'ing, *pr.p.,* distrain.
distrait', *adj.,* absent-minded (*Fr.*).
distraught', *adj.,* distracted.
distress', *n.,* anguish of mind or body; misery; seizure for debt; *v.t.,* to make miserable.
distressed', *adj.,* suffering distress; *p.p.,* distress.
distress'ful, *adj.,* inflicting or indicating distress.
distress'ing, *adj.,* very afflicting; *pr.p.,* distress.
distrib'utary, *adj., i.q.* distributive.
distrib'ute, *v.t.,* to divide among a number of recipients.
distrib'uted, *p.p.,* distribute.
distrib'uter, *n.,* one who distributes; a device for distributing electric current to the sparking plugs of a motor, or the compressed air of a self-starter to the cylinders.
distrib'uting, *pr.p.,* distribute.
distribu'tion, *n.,* the act of separating into distinct parts.
distrib'utive, *adj.,* serving to distribute.
distrib'utor, *n., i.q.* distributer.
dis'trict, *n.,* a region, locality, or quarter.
distrin'gas, *n.,* a writ authorizing distraint.
dis'trix, *n.,* a disease of the hair in which individual hairs split.
distrust', *v.t.,* to have no confidence in; to suspect; *n.,* doubt; suspicion.
distrust'ed, *p.p.,* distrust.
distrust'er, *n.,* one who distrusts.
distrust'ful, *adj.,* suspicious; wanting confidence.
distrust'ing, *pr.p.,* distrust.
disturb', *v.t.,* to agitate; to disquiet; to interfere with.
disturb'ance, *n.,* interruption of a settled state of things; confusion; a tumult.
disturbed', *p.p.,* disturb.
disturb'er, *n.,* one who disturbs.
disturb'ing, *pr.p.,* disturb.
disul'phate, *n.,* an acid salt of sulphuric acid.
disul'phuret, *n.,* a binary compound of sulphur, with two atoms of sulphur in the molecule.
disulphu'ric, *adj.,* applied to an acid containing two atoms of sulphur in each molecule.
disu'nion, *n.,* separation; dissension.
disu'nionist, *n.,* an advocate of disunion.
disunite', *v.t.,* to separate; to set at variance; *v.i.,* to fall asunder.

disunit'ed, *p.p.*, disunite.
disuni'ter, *n.*, anything that disjoins.
disuni'ting, *pr.p.*, disunite.
disu'nity, *n.*, want of unity.
disu'sage, *n.*, gradual cessation of use, custom, or practice.
disuse', *n.*, cessation of use.
disuse', *v.t.*, to cease to use.
disused', *p.p.*, disuse.
disus'ing, *pr.p.* disuse.
disyllab'ic, *adj.*, consisting of two syllables only.
disyl'lable, *n.*, a word of two syllables. Also *dissyllable.*
ditch, *n.*, a trench; *v.t.*, to dig a ditch; drain by a ditch.
ditched, *p.p.*, ditch.
ditch'er, *n.*, one who digs ditches.
ditch'ing, *pr.p.*, ditch.
ditch'-water, *n.*, water contained by a ditch; a simile for dulness.
di'theism, *n.*, the doctrine of the existence of good and evil principles in nature; Manicheism.
di'theist, *n.*, one who believes in ditheism.
ditheis'tic, *adj.*, rel. to ditheism.
dith'yramb, *n.*, a Bacchic hymn; an irregular poem of impetuous character.
dithyram'bic, *n.*, *i.q.* dithyramb; *adj.*, resembling a dithyramb; enthusiastic.
di'tone, *n.*, a musical interval measuring two tones.
dit'tany, *n.*, a plant of Southern Europe yielding a fragrant oil.
dit'to, *adj.*, same as aforesaid.
dit'ty, *n.*, a song; a little lyric poem.
diure'sis, *n.*, an excessive flow of urine.
diuret'ic, *adj.*, tending to excite the secretion of urine, *n.*, a medicine to stimulate the bladder or kidneys.
diur'nal, *adj.*, pert. to the daytime; daily.
divaga'tion, *n.*, a digression.
divan', *n.*, an Oriental court of justice, council, or council-chamber; a cushioned seat against the wall of a room; a café.
divar'icate, *v.t.* and *i.*, to branch, esp. at an obtuse angle.
divar'icated, *p.p.*, divaricate.
divar'icating, *pr.p.*, divaricate.
divarica'tion, *n.*, a forking.
dive, *v.i.*, to plunge into water head first; *n.*, a plunge; the act of diving.
dived, *p.p.*, dive.
di'ver, *n.*, one who dives; a marine swimming bird.
diverge', *v.i.*, to proceed in different directions from the same point; to deviate; to differ or vary.
diverged', *p.p.*, diverge.
diver'gence, *n.*, the act of diverging.
diver'gency, *n.*, *i.q.* divergence.
diver'gent, *adj.*, diverging, as lines separating from one another, proceeding from the same point.
diver'ging, *pr.p.*, diverge.
di'vers, *adj.*, different; several.
diverse', *adj.*, unlike.
diverse'ly, *adv.*, in different directions.
diversifica'tion, *n.*, the act of diversifying.
diver'sified, *adj.*, characterized by a variety of forms or objects; *p.p.*, diversified.
diver'siform, *adj.*, of various forms.
diver'sify, *v.t.*, to give variety to.
diver'sifying, *pr.p.*, diversify.
diver'sion, *n.*, the act of diverting; amusement; pastime; a feint to mislead an enemy.
diver'sity, *n.*, unlikeness; variety.
divert', *v.t.*, to turn aside; to amuse.
divert'ed, *p.p.*, divert.
divert'er, *n.*, one who diverts.
divert'ing, *pr.p.*, divert; *adj.*, entertaining.
divert'ive, *adj.*, amusing; interesting.
divest', *v.t.*, to deprive; to strip.
divest'ed, *p.p.*, divest.
divest'ing, *pr.p.*, divest.
divest'iture, *n.*, the deprivation or surrender of rights, property, etc.
divi'dable, *adj.*, capable of division.
divide', *v.t.*, to part; to set at variance; *v.i.*, to become separated; to open; to vote by the division of an assembly into two parts; *n.*, a watershed.
divi'ded, *adj.*, separated; at variance; *p.p.*, divide.
div'idend, *n.*, a number to be divided; profit made by a company to be divided among the shareholders; the share of each shareholder.
divi'der, *n.*, one who, or that which, divides.
divi'ding, *pr.p.*, divide.
divina'tion, *n.*, the act of divining.
div'inator, *n.*, a diviner.
divine', *adj.*, rel. to God, or to a heathen deity; godlike; holy; *n.*, a priest; a theologian; *v.t.*, to prognosticate; to guess; *v.i.*, to practise divination.
divined', *p.p.*, divine.
divine'ly, *adv.*, by the agency of God; in a supreme degree.
divi'ner, *n.*, a soothsayer; a guesser.

di'ving, *n.*, the art of descending into water to perform some work at the bottom; *pr.p.*, dive.

di'ving-bell, *n.*, an apparatus used in professional diving.

divi'ning, *pr.p.*, divine.

divin'ity, *n.*, godhead; divine nature; God; a celestial being; sacredness; the science of theology.

divisibil'ity, *n.*, the quality of being divisible.

divis'ible, *adj.*, capable of division.

divis'ibleness, *n.*, *i.q.* divisibility.

divi'sion, *n.*, a partition; a distinct segment or portion; a certain portion of an organized whole, as of an army; variance; one of the four fundamental rules of arithmetic.

divi'sional, *adj.*, bel. to division, or to a division or district.

divi'sive, *adj.*, tending to divide.

divi'sively, *adv.*, in a divisive manner.

divi'sor, *n.*, the number by which the dividend is divided.

divorce', *n.*, severance, sundering; *v.t.*, to separate.

divorced', *p.p.*, divorce.

divorce'ment, *n.*, *i.q.* divorce.

divor'cer, *n.*, one who divorces.

divor'cible, *adj.*, liable to be divorced.

divor'cing, *pr.p.*, divorce.

div'ot, *n.*, a sod or turf used in some places for roofing; the piece of turf a golf-player displaces.

divulge', *v.t.*, to reveal what was a secret.

divulged', *p.p.*, divulge.

divul'ger, *n.*, one who divulges.

divul'ging, *pr.p.*, divulge.

divul'sion, *n.*, a rending asunder; laceration.

di'zen, *v.t.*, to dress gaudily; to bedizen.

diz'ziness, *n.*, giddiness; vertigo.

diz'zy, *adj.*, giddy, heedless; causing giddiness.

do, *v.t.*, and *auxil.*, to effect; to cause to be, to cheat; to prepare.

dob'bin, *n.*, sea gravel mixed with sand; an old horse.

do'cent, *adj.*, teaching.

do'cile, *adj.*, teachable; tractable.

docil'ity, *n.*, the state of being docile.

doc'imasy, *n.*, metallurgy; the art of assaying metals.

docimas'tic, *adj.*, proving by experiments or tests; metallurgic.

docimol'ogy, *n.*, a treatise on the art of testing.

dock, *n.*, a weed with broad leaves; the place where a prisoner stands in court; an artificial basin for ships; *v.t.*, to bring into a dock; to shorten.

dock'age, *n.*, charges for the use of docks.

docked, *p.p.* dock.

dock'et, *n.*, a summary; any small written paper; *v.t.*, to mark the contents of a paper on the back.

dock'eted, *p.p.*, docket.

dock'eting, *pr.p.*, docket.

dock'ing, *pr.p.*, dock.

dock'yard, *n.*, an enclosure containing docks.

doc'tor, *n.*, a university graduate of the highest degree in any faculty; a physician; a teacher; *v.t.*, to treat medically; to falsify.

doc'toral, *adj.*, rel. to a doctor's degree.

doc'torate, *n.*, the degree of doctor.

doc'tored, *p.p.*, doctor.

doc'toring, *pr.p.*, doctor.

doc'tress, *n.*, a woman physician.

doctrinaire', *n.*, a theorist who ignores practical considerations.

doc'trinal, *adj.*, pert. to doctrine.

doc'trine, *n.*, a principle; a set of opinions or beliefs; esp. the truths of the gospel.

doc'ument, *n.*, an official or authoritative paper containing instructions or proof; any written or printed paper.

documen'tal, *adj.*, *i.q.* documentary.

documen'tary, *adj.*, consisting of documents.

doc'umented, *adj.*, illustrated with documentary proofs.

dod'der, *n.*, a leafless parasitic plant.

dod'dered, *adj.*, overgrown with dodder.

dod'dering, *adj.*, feeble, imbecile.

dodec'agon, *n.*, a regular polygon having twelve equal sides and angles.

dodecagyn'ian, *adj.*, having twelve styles.

dodecahe'dron, *n.*, a solid having twelve equal faces, each a regular pentagon.

dodecan'drian, *adj.*, having twelve stamens.

dodecan'drous, *adj.*, *i.q.* dodecandrian.

dodecasyl'lable, *n.*, a word of twelve syllables.

dodge, *v.i.*, to start suddenly aside; *v.t.*, to evade; to baffle; *n.*, a trick.

dodged, *p.p.*, dodge.

dodg'er, *n.*, one who dodges.

dodg'ing, *pr.p.*, dodge.

do'do, *n.*, an extinct bird of Mauritius.

doe, *n.*, the female of a buck.

do'er, *n.*, one who does or performs.

does, *v.t.* and *auxil.*, 3rd pers. sing. *pres.* of to do.

doe'skin, *n.*, the skin of a doe; a twilled

woollen cloth; *adj.*, made of doeskin.

doff, *v.t.*, to take off; *v.i.*, to take off the hat.

doffed, *p.p.*, doff.

doff'ing, *pr.p.*, doff.

dog, *n.*, an animal, akin to the wolf and fox, domesticated, and strongly attached to man; *v.t.*, to follow closely.

dog'berry, *n.*, the berry of the dogwood.

dog'-cart, *n.*, a two-seated gig, the rear occupants facing backwards.

dog'-days, *n. pl.*, the days from about July 3 to August 11; days of great heat.

doge, *n.*, the chief magistrate of the old republics of Venice and Genoa.

dog'-eared, *adj.*, having the corners turned down and crumpled.

dog'-fish, *n.*, a kind of small shark.

dogged, *p.p.*, dog.

dog'ged, *adj.*, obstinate; sullen.

dog'gedly, *adv.*, in a dogged manner.

dog'gedness, *n.*, the quality of being dogged.

dog'ger, *n.*, a Dutch two-masted fishing boat.

dog'gerel, *adj.*, defective in sense and rhythm; *n.*, extremely poor verses.

dog'gish, *adj.*, brutal; snappish.

dog'ma, *n.*, a doctrine received on authority.

dogmat'ic, *adj.*, pert. to dogmas; dictatorial.

dogmat'ical, *adj.*, *i.q.* dogmatic.

dogmat'icalness, *n.*, the quality of being dogmatic.

dogmat'ics, *n. pl.*, doctrinal theology.

dog'matism, *n.*, arrogant assertion.

dog'matist, *n.*, one who is dogmatic.

dog'matize, *v.i.*, to assert authoritatively.

dog'matized, *p.p.*, dogmatize.

dog'matizer, *n.*, one who dogmatizes.

dog'matizing, *pr.p.*, dogmatize.

dog'-rose, *n.*, the British wild rose.

dog's'-ear, *n.*, the corner of a leaf turned down by careless handling of a book; *v.t.*, to turn down and disfigure in this way.

dog's'-eared, *adj.*, with the corners crumpled.

dog's'-meat, *n.*, meat for, or only fit for, dogs.

dog'-star, *n.*, the star Sirius, of the first magnitude.

dog'tooth, *n.*, a canine tooth; an ornament characteristic of Early English architecture.

dog'-trot, *n.*, a gentle trot.

dog'-watch, *n.*, a watch of two turns on board ship.

dog'wood, *n.*, a British hedgerow shrub; the cornel.

dohl, *n.*, a kind of pulse like dried pease.

doi'ly, *n.*, a small ornamental table-mat.

do'ing, *pr.p.*, do.

do'ings, *n. pl.*, things done; performances; conduct.

doit, *n.*, a small Dutch copper coin; the old Scottish penny; any small coin.

dol'ce, *adj.* or *adv.*, soft and sweet, in music.

dol'drums, *n. pl.*, the equatorial belt of calms; low spirits.

dole, *n.*, a gratuity given in charity; grief; *v.t.*, to deal out in small quantities.

doled, *p.p.*, dole.

dole'ful, *adj.*, mournful.

dole'fulness, *n.*, the state of being doleful.

dole'some, *adj.*, doleful.

dole'somely, *adv.*, dolefully.

do'ling, *pr.p.*, dole.

do'-little, *n.*, an idler.

doll, *n.*, a little image used as a plaything.

dol'lar, *n.*, a silver coin of varying value; unit of currency used in the U.S.A. etc.

dolly, *n.*, a little doll.

dol'man, *n.*, a kind of Turkish robe; a lady's wide jacket.

dol'omite, *n.*, a rock, composed of the carbonates of lime and magnesia.

dolomit'ic, *adj.*, of the nature of dolomite.

dolorif'ic, *adj.*, causing grief.

dol'orous, *adj.*, sorrowful.

dol'orously, *adv.*, in a dolorous manner.

do'lour, do'lor, *n.*, sorrow.

dol'phin, *n.*, a name of several species of cetaceans; the grampus; a mooring buoy or post.

dolt, *n.*, a blockhead.

dolt'ish, *adj.*, stupid.

dolt'ishness, *n.*, stupidity.

domain', *n.*, a dominion; a landed estate; a demesne.

dome, *n.*, the hemispherical roof of a building; the rounded top of any building or chamber.

domed, *adj.*, provided with a dome.

Domes'day, *adj.*, rel. to the survey and census of William the Conqueror.

domes'tic, *adj.*, bel. to the home; tame; bel. to one's own country; *n.*, a household servant.

domes'ticate, *v.t.*, to make domestic; to tame; to reduce from a wild to a cultivated condition.

domes'ticated, *p.p.*, domesticate.

domes'ticating, *pr.p.*, domesticate.

domestica'tion, *n.*, the state of being domesticated.

domestic'ity, *n.*, the state of being domestic.

dom'icile, *n.*, a place of residence; a permanent abode; *v.t.*, to establish in a fixed residence.

dom'iciled, *p.p.*, domicile.

domicil'iary, *adj.*, rel. to a domicile.

domicil'iate, *v.t.*, *i.q.* domicile.

domicil'iated, *p.p.*, domiciliate.

domicil'iating, *pr.p.*, domiciliate.

domicilia'tion, *n.*, permanent residence.

dom'iciling, *pr.p.*, domicile.

dom'inant, *adj.*, prevailing; predominant; *n.*, the fifth tone of the diatonic scale.

dom'inate, *v.t.*, to have power over; to govern.

dom'inated, *p.p.*, dominate.

dom'inating, *pr.p.*, dominate.

domina'tion, *n.*, government; tyranny.

dom'inative, *adj.*, governing; imperious.

dom'inator, *n.*, one that dominates.

domineer', *v.i.* and *t.*, to rule or command insolently.

domineered', *p.p.*, domineer.

domineer'ing, *adj.*, overbearing; *pr.p.*, domineer.

Domin'ical, *adj.*, rel. to Sunday or the Lord's Day; *n.*, one of seven letters used in kalendars.

Domin'ican, *adj.*, rel. to St. Dominic or his religious Order of Preachers; *n.*, a member of this Order; a Black Friar.

dom'inie, *n.*, a Scottish schoolmaster.

domin'ion, *n.*, supreme authority; territory under a government; pl., an order of angels.

dom'ino, *n.*, a masquerade dress; a half-mask; a dotted tablet used in a game.

dom'inoes, *n. pl.*, a game played with dotted oblong tablets.

dom'inus, *n.*, a lord or master; an owner.

don, *n.*, a Spanish title of courtesy; a university dignitary; *v.t.*, to put on.

do'na, *n.*, the fem. of don; a sweetheart (*slang*).

donate', *v.i.* and *t.*, to give; to bestow.

dona'ted, *p.p.*, donate.

dona'ting, *pr.p.*, donate.

dona'tion, *n.*, a gratuity; a gift.

Don'atism, *n.*, the doctrines of Donatus.

Don'atist, *n.*, a follower of Donatus.

don'ative, *n.*, a gift; in law, a benefice bestowed by a patron without the intervention of a bishop.

done, *p.p.*, do.

donee', *n.*, the recipient of a grant or gift.

don'jon, *n.*, the principal tower of a castle; a keep.

don'key, *n.*, an ass

don'key-engine, *n.*, a small subsidiary steam engine.

don'na, *n.*, a lady.

donned, *p.p.*, don.

don'ning, *pr.p.*, don.

do'nor, *n.*, a giver.

doo'lie, doo'ly, *n.*, a palanquin.

doom, *n.*, final judgment; fate; ruin; *v.t.*, to condemn.

doomed, *p.p.*, doom.

doom'ing, *pr.p.*, doom.

dooms'day, *n.*, the day of doom.

door, *n.*, a frame of wood or other material which closes an opening.

door'-keeper, *n.*, a porter.

door'-nail, *n.*, the nail on which a door-knocker strikes.

door'-step, *n.*, the stone at a threshold.

door'way, *n.*, the entrance into a room or house.

dop'per, *n.*, an Anabaptist.

dor, dorr, *n.*, a British beetle.

Dor'cas, *adj.*, pert. to a society of ladies who make garments for the poor.

do'ree, *n.*, *i.q.* dory (the fish).

Do'rian, *adj.*, pert. to the Dorians, a people of Ancient Greece.

Dor'ic, *adj.*, *i.q.* Dorian; naming one of the ancient Greek orders of architecture; *n.*, a rustic dialect.

Dor'icism, *n.*, a peculiarity of the Doric dialect.

dor'mancy, *n.*, the state of being dormant.

dor'mant, *adj.*, sleeping; not in action; not claimed.

dor'mer, *n.*, a window in a roof.

dor'mitive, *n.*, a soporific; *adj.*, tending to cause sleep.

dor'mitory, *n.*, a building or room to sleep in.

dor'mouse, *n.*, a small rodent, torpid in the winter.

dor'my, *adj.*, a golf term implying that a person is up by as many holes as remain to play.

dor'sal, *adj.*, rel. to the back.

dor'sel, *n.*, a pannier; a hanging of rich stuff at the back of a throne or altar.

dor'sum, *n.*, a ridge; the back of an animal (*Lat.*).

do'ry, *n.*, a yellow European food-fish; a small boat.

do'sage, *n.*, the process of improving wine by additions of other substances.

dose, *n.*, the quantity of medicine to be taken at one time; *v.t.*, to physic.
dosed, *p.p.*, dose.
do'sing, *pr.p.*, dose.
dos'sal, *n.*, *s.q.* dorsel.
dossier', *n.*, a collection of all the papers rel. to some matter.
dos'sil, *n.*, a plug of lint for a wound.
dost, *v.t.* and *auxil.*, 2nd pers. sing. *pres.* of to do.
dot, *n.*, a speck; a small spot; *v.t.*, to mark with dots.
do'tage, *n.*, the childishness of old age.
do'tard, *n.*, a man whose mind is enfeebled by age.
dota'tion, *n.*, the bestowal of a dowry; endowment.
dote, *v.i.*, to be senile; to love to excess.
do'ted, *p.p.*, dote.
do'tel, *n.*, a dotard; silly fellow.
do'ter, *n.*, one who dotes.
doth, *v.t.* and *auxil.*, 3rd pers. sing. *pres.* of to do.
do'ting, *pr.p.*, dote.
do'tingly, *adv.*, with excessive fondness.
dot'tard, *n.*, an old, decayed tree.
dot'ted, *p.p.*, dot.
dot'ter, *n.*, a device for elevating a naval gun in accordance with the ship's roll.
dot'terel, *n.*, a kind of plover.
dot'ting, *pr.p.*, dot.
douane', *n.*, a customhouse (*Fr.*).
doub'le, *adj.*, twofold; twice as much; deceitful; *v.t.*, to make double; to pass round; *n.*, a duplicate; a quick step in marching.
doub'le-bar'rel(l)ed, *adj.*, having two barrels.
doub'led, *p.p.*, double.
doub'le-deal'ing, *n.*, duplicity; *adj.*, deceitful.
doub'le-face, *n.*, double dealing; hypocrisy.
doub'le-faced, *adj.*, hypocritical.
doub'leness, *n.*, the state of being double.
doub'let, *n.*, a kind of waistcoat; one of two words really the same but differing in form.
doub'ling, *pr.p.*, double.
doubloon', *n.*, a Spanish coin worth about a guinea; a double pistole.
doub'ly, *adv.*, to twice the extent.
doubt, *v.i.*, to be uncertain; *v.t.*, to distrust; *n.*, uncertainty of mind; want of belief; suspicion.
doubt'able, *adj.*, liable to be doubted.
doubt'ed, *p.p.*, doubt.
doubt'er, *n.*, one who doubts.
doubt'ful, *adj.*, undetermined; not certain.
doubt'fully, *adv.*, in a doubtful manner.
doubt'fulness, *n.*, the state of being doubtful.
doubt'ing, *pr. p.*, doubt.
doubt'ingly, *adv.*, in a doubting manner.
doubt'less, *adv.*, unquestionably.
douceur', *n.*, a gratuity; a bribe.
douche, *n.*, a kind of bath in which a jet of water or vapour is directed upon some part of the body.
dough, *n.*, paste of bread.
dough'nut, *n.*, a small round cake made of flour, eggs, sugar, and milk, and cooked in lard.
dough'tily, *adv.*, with doughtiness.
dough'tiness, *n.*, bravery; valour.
dough'ty, *adj.*, valiant; noble.
dough'y, *adj.*, like dough; flabby and pale.
douse, *v.t.*, to plunge into water; to extinguish.
doused, *p.p.*, douse.
dous'ing, *pr.p.*, douse.
dove, *n.*, a pigeon.
dove'-cot, *n.*, a house for doves.
dove'like, *adj.*, like a dove; gentle.
dove'tail, *n.*, a method of fastening boards at right angles; *v.t.* and *i.*, to unite in this way; to fit exactly.
dove'tailed, *p.p.*, dovetail.
dove'tailing, *pr.p.*, dovetail.
dow'able, *adj.*, entitled to dower.
dow'ager, *n.*, the widow of a person of rank whose heir has a wife.
dow'dy, *adj.*, ill-dressed.
dow'dyish, *adj.*, like a dowdy.
dow'el, *n.*, a wooden or iron pin used in fastening pieces of wood, etc., edgewise; *v.t.*, to fasten with dowels.
dow'elled, dow'eled, *p.p.*, dowel.
dow'elling, dow'eling, *pr.p.*, dowel.
dow'er, *n.*, a wife's portion; a widow's third; *v.t.*, to endow.
dow'ered, *p.p.*, dower.
dow'erless, *adj.*, without dower.
dow'las, *n.*, a coarse linen cloth.
down, *n.*, rising ground; a rounded, grassy hill; the soft covering of birds under the feathers; *prep.* and *adv.*, from a higher to a lower position.
down'cast, *adj.*, cast downward; dejected; *n.*, the ventilating shaft down which air passes into a mine.
down'fall, *n.*, a falling down; loss of fortune or fame; ruin.
down'haul, *n.*, a rope to haul down a sail.
down'hearted, *adj.*, dejected.
down'-hill, *adj.*, sloping downwards; *adv.*, down a slope.

down'iness, *n.*, the quality of being downy.

down'pour, *n.*, a continuous shower of rain.

down'right, *adj.*, plain; blunt; unceremonious; *adv.*, in plain terms; thoroughly.

down'sitting, *n.*, the act of sitting down.

down'stairs, *adj.*, rel. to the lower part of a house; *adv.*, below; down the stairs.

down'stroke, *n.*, a downward blow; the thick stroke of a letter.

down'ward, *adv.* and *adj.*, in a descending course.

down'y, *adj.*, covered with down; soothing.

dow'ry, *n.*, a wife's property at marriage.

dowse, *v.t.*, *i.q.* douse.

doxol'ogy, *n.*, a short hymn glorifying God.

dox'y, *n.*, a low word for sweetheart or mistress.

doyen', *n.*, a dean; the senior member of a body (*Fr.*).

doze, *v.i.*, to sleep lightly; *n.*, a light sleep.

dozed, *p.p.*, doze.

doz'en, *n.*, a collection of twelve, or about twelve, things or persons.

do'zer, *n.*, one who dozes.

do'ziness, *n.*, drowsiness.

do'zing, *pr.p.*, doze.

do'zy, *adj.*, sleepy.

drab, *n.*, a slut; a thick, dull-brown, woollen cloth; a dull-brown colour; *adj.*, dull-brown.

drab'ble, *v.t.*, to draggle; to wet and dirty.

drab'bled, *p.p.*, drabble.

drab'bling, *pr.p.*, drabble.

drachm, *n.*, a dram; three scruples.

drach'ma, *n.*, a Greek coin and weight.

Dracon'ic, *adj.*, rel. to Draco, the Athenian law-giver; extremely severe.

draff, *n.*, refuse; hogswash.

draff'y, *adj.*, consisting of draff; worthless.

draft, *n.*, a body of men drawn from a larger body; an order for payment; a document in outline; a sketch; *v.t.*, to make a draft of.

draft'ed, *p.p.*, draft.

draft'ing, *pr.p.*, draft.

drafts'man, *n.*, *i.q.* draughtsman.

drag, *v.t.*, to pull; to draw along the ground; *v.i.*, to be drawn along the ground; to proceed slowly; *n.*, a kind of grapnel for recovering articles lost in the water; an obstacle; a long, open carriage.

dragged, *p.p.*, drag.

drag'ging, *pr.p.*, drag.

drag'gle, *v.t.* and *i.*, to wet and dirty by drawing along the ground.

drag'gled, *p.p.*, draggle.

drag'gling, *pr.p.*, draggle.

drag'-net, *n.*, a fishing-net to be drawn along the bottom of a river or pond.

drag'oman, *n.*, an interpreter, esp. one attached to an embassy or consulate in the East.

drag'on, *n.*, a fabulous monster, a sort of winged crocodile.

drag'onet, *n.*, a small fish; a little goby.

drag'on-fly, *n.*, a kind of large insect.

drag'onish, *adj.*, like a dragon.

dragonnade', *n.*, a Protestant persecution under Louis XIV; *v.t.*, to use the military against citizens.

dragoon', *n.*, a cavalry soldier; *v.t.*, to compel by violence.

dragooned', *p.p.*, dragoon.

dragoon'ing, *pr.p.*, dragoon.

drain, *v.t.*, to exhaust; (of a liquid) to deprive by drawing off gradually; *v.t.*, to flow off gradually; *n.*, a trench to convey water from wet land; continuous outflow.

drain'able, *adj.*, capable of being drained.

drain'age, *n.*, a system of drains; the manner in which the waters of a country pass off by rivers.

drained, *p.p.*, drain.

drain'er, *n.*, one who, or that which, drains.

drain'ing, *pr.p.*, drain.

drain'-trap, *n.*, that which prevents foul air from escaping from drains.

drake, *n.*, a male duck.

dram, *n.*, the sixteenth part of an ounce avoirdupois; a drink of spirituous liquor.

dra'ma, *n.*, a stage-play; theatrical composition and representation.

dramat'ic, *adj.*, pert. to the drama; theatrical.

dramat'ical, *adj.*, *i.q.* dramatic.

dramat'ically, *adv.*, in a dramatic manner.

dram'atist, *n.*, a playwright.

dram'atize, *v.t.*, to make into a play.

dram'atized, *p.p.*, dramatize.

dram'atizing, *pr.p.*, dramatize.

dram'-drinker, *n.*, a person addicted to alcohol.

dram'-shop, *n.*, a shop where spirits are sold in small quantities.

drank, *p.t.*, drink.

drape, *v.t.*, to cover with drapery.

draped, *p.p.*, drape.

dra'per, *n.*, a dealer in cloths.

dra'pery, *n.*, the business of a draper; hangings.
dra'ping, *pr.p.*, drape.
dras'tic, *adj.*, powerful; efficacious.
draught, *n.*, the act of drawing; the act of drinking; a drink; a drawing or sketch; the depth a laden ship sinks in water; a current of air; *v.t.*, to sketch roughly. Also *draft*.
draught'-board, *n.*, a checkered board for the game of draughts.
draught'-engine, *n.*, a mining engine used for pumping, etc.
draught'-horse, *n.*, a horse used for drawing vehicles.
draught'iness, *n.*, the state of being draughty.
draughts, *n. pl.*, a game played with round pieces on a checkered board.
draughts'man, *n.*, one who draws designs and plans.
draught'y, *adj.*, exposed to draughts.
Dravid'ian, *adj.*, pert. to a family of languages spoken in Southern India and Ceylon.
draw, *v.t.*, to pull; to lead; to form a picture; to form a writing; *n.*, a contest in which both parties are equally successful.
draw'back, *n.*, a disadvantage; customs duties repaid.
draw'bridge, *n.*, a bridge that may be drawn up or aside.
drawee', *n.*, the person on whom a bill of exchange is drawn.
draw'er, *n.*, one who draws; a sliding box in a table or other piece of furniture.
draw'ers, *n. pl.*, a garment to cover the lower part of the body and the legs.
draw'ing, *n.*, the act of one who draws; pictorial representation; *pr.p.*, draw.
draw'ing-master, *n.*, one who teaches the art of drawing.
draw'ing-pen, *n.*, a pen for drawing lines.
draw'ing-room, *n.*, a reception room.
drawl, *v.i.*, to speak with slow utterance.
drawled, *p.p.*, drawl.
drawl'er, *n.*, one who drawls.
drawl'ing, *pr.p.*, drawl.
drawn, *p.p.*, draw.
draw'-net, *n.*, a net for catching birds.
dray, *n.*, a low cart on heavy wheels.
dray'-cart, *n.*, a dray.
dray'-horse, *n.*, a horse used in a dray.
dray'man, *n.*, a dray driver or attendant.
dread, *n.*, great fear; *adj.*, terrible; *v.t.* and *i.*, to fear greatly.
dread'ed, *p.p.*, dread.
dread'ful, *adj.*, terrible; *n.*, a book about crimes, frightful accidents, etc.
dread'fully, *adv.*, in a manner to be dreaded.
dread'fulness, *n.*, the quality of being dreadful.
dread'ing, *pr.p.*, dread.
dread'less, *adj.*, intrepid.
dread'lessness, *n.*, fearlessness.
dread'nought, *n.*, a thick rainproof cloth or garment; a very powerful armed ship.
dream, *n.*, the series of thoughts of a sleeping person; *v.i.*, to have images in the mind when asleep; *v.t.*, to see in a dream.
dreamed, *p.p.*, dream.
dream'er, *n.*, one who dreams; a visionary.
dream'iness, *n.*, the state of being dreamy.
dream'ing, *pr.p.*, dream.
dream'ingly, *adv.*, as though dreaming.
dream'less, *adj.*, free from dreams.
dreamt, *p.p.*, dream.
dream'y, *adj.*, full of dreams; dream-like.
drear, *adj.*, gloomy with solitude.
drear'ily, *adv.*, dismally.
drear'iness, *n.*, the state of being dreary.
drear'y, *adj.*, dismal; oppressively monotonous.
dredge, *n.*, an apparatus for clearing the bed of a channel; a drag-net; *v.t.*, to use a dredge; to sprinkle flour on roasting meat.
dredged, *p.p.*, dredge.
dredg'er, *n.*, one who, or that which, dredges.
dredg'ing, *pr.p.*, dredge.
dredg'ing-box, *n.*, a utensil for dredging flour.
dreg'gy, *adj.*, consisting of dregs; muddy.
dregs, *n. pl.*, the sediment of liquors; lees; the most worthless of human beings.
drench, *v.t.*, to wet thoroughly; to purge with a strong aperient medicine; *n.*, a purgative for an animal.
drenched, *p.p.*, drench.
drench'ing, *pr. p.*, drench.
Dres'den, *n.*, a town of Saxony; porcelain made there; *adj.*, pert. to china made near Dresden.
dress, *v.t.*, to put clothes on; to prepare, in a general sense; *v.i.*, to clothe oneself; to arrange oneself in a line with others; *n.*, garments; a lady's gown.
dress'coat, *n.*, a coat with narrow pointed tails worn at evening ceremonies.
dressed, *p.p.*, dress.

dress'er, *n.*, one who dresses; a hospital attendant; a kind of sideboard and low cupboard.
dress'ing, *n.*, an application to a wound; manure for land; preparation of food for cooking; a sauce or cream for a salad; *pr.p.*, dress.
dress'ing-case, *n.*, a case of toilet requisites.
dres'sing-gown, *n.*, a flowing coat worn to cover déshabille.
dres'sing-room, *n.*, an apartment in which one dresses oneself.
dres'sing-table, *n.*, a toilet table.
dress'maker, *n.*, a maker of ladies' dresses.
dress'y, *adj.*, wearing showy dress.
drib'ble, *v.t.*, to let fall in drops; to work a football forward with the feet; *v.i.*, to fall in a quick succession of drops; just to roll (into); *n.*, a trickle.
drib'bled, *p.p.*, dribble.
drib'bling, *pr.p.*, dribble.
drib'let, *n.*, a small part doled out as one of a series.
dried, *p.p.*, dry.
dri'er, *adj.*, *comp.* of dry; *n.*, one who dries.
dri'est, *adj.*, *super.* of dry.
drift, *n.*, a heap of matter driven together by wind or water; tendency; intention; *v.i.*, to be driven along by a current of water or air; *adj.*, drifted by wind or water.
drift'ed, *p.p.*, drift.
drift'ing, *pr.p.*, drift.
drift'wood, *n.*, wood drifted by water.
drill, *v.t.*, to bore; to train by frequent repetition of exercises; *n.*, a pointed instrument for boring holes; the exercises by which soldiers are trained.
drilled, *p.p.*, drill.
drill'ing, *n.*, a coarse linen or cotton cloth; *pr.p.*, drill.
drill'-plough, *n.*, a plough for sowing grain in drills or straight rows.
drill'-sergeant, *n.*, a sergeant who drills soldiers.
dri'ly, *adv.*, in a dry manner.
drink, *v.i.*, to swallow liquor; to be an habitual drunkard; *v.t.*, to imbibe; *n.*, liquor.
drink'able, *adj.*, fit for drink; *n.*, a liquor that may be drunk.
drink'er, *n.*, one who drinks.
drink'ing, *pr.p.*, drink.
drink'-offering, *n.*, a Jewish offering of wine.
drip, *v.i.*, to fall in drops; *n.*, the fall.
dripped, *p.p.*, drip.
drip'ping, *n.*, the fat which falls from roasting meat; *pr.p.* drip.
drip'ping-pan, *n.*, a pan to catch dripping.
drip'pings, *n. pl.*, that which drips from anything.
drive, *v.t.*, to urge forward· *v.i.*, to travel in a carriage; *n.*, a road prepared for driving; a sweeping blow.
driv'el, *v.i.*, to slaver; to be foolish; *n.*, silly, meaningless talk.
driv'el(l)ed, *p.p.*, drivel.
driv'el(l)er, *n.*, one who drivels; a fool.
driv'el(l)ing, *pr.p.*, drivel; *n.*, drivel.
driv'en, *p.p.*, drive.
dri'ver, *n.*, one who, or that which, drives; a wooden golf-club.
dri'ving, *pr.p.*, drive.
dri'ving-shaft, *n.*, a shaft from a driving-wheel setting a machine in motion.
driz'zle, *v.i.*, to rain in small drops; *n.*, a fine rain.
driz'zled, *p.p.*, drizzle.
driz'zling, *pr.p.*, drizzle.
driz'zly, *adj.*, shedding fine rain.
droll, *adj.*, laughable; *n.*, a jester.
droll'ery, *n.*, comicalness.
drom'edary, *n.*, the Arabian or single-humped camel.
drone, *n.*, male of the honey-bee; an idler; a humming sound; a bag-pipe's bass note; *v.i.*, to hum; *v.t.*, to speak in a dull, monotonous manner.
droned, *p.p.*, drone.
dro'ning, *pr.p.*, drone.
dro'nish, *adj.*, lazy; sluggish.
droop, *v.i.*, to bend downward as from weakness; *n.*, a drooping position.
drooped, *p.p.*, droop.
droop'ing, *pr.p.* droop.
droop'ingly, *adv.*, in a drooping manner.
drop, *n.*, a small portion of a liquid falling or about to fall; anything that hangs in the form of a drop; *v.t.*, to let fall; *v.i.*, to fall.
drop'let, *n.*, a little drop.
dropped, *p.p.*, drop.
drop'ping, *pr.p.*, drop.
drop'-scene, *n.*, a scenic picture suspended by pulleys which falls in front of the other scenery in theatres.
drop'sical, *adj.*, diseased with, inclined to, or resembling dropsy.
drop'sy, *n.*, an unnatural collection of water in any cavity or in the tissues of the body.
drosh'ky, *n.*, *i.q.* drosky.
dros'ky, *n.*, a light, four-wheeled carriage used in Russia.
dross, *n.*, waste or worthless matter; the refuse of metals.
dross'iness, *n.*, the quality of being drossy.

dross'y, *adj.*, worthless; impure; pert. to dross.

drought, *n.*, want of rain; aridness.

drought'y, *adj.*, full of drought.

drouth, *n.*, drought; thirst.

drove, *n.*, a number of animals driven in a body; *p.t.*, drive.

dro'ver, *n.*, one who drives cattle or sheep.

drown, *v.t.*, to kill by immersion in water; *v.i.*, to perish by suffocation in water.

drowned, *p.p.*, drown.

drown'ing, *pr.p.*, drown.

drowse, *v.i.*, to sleep imperfectly; *v.t.*, to make dull or stupid.

drowsed, *p.p.*, drowse.

drow'sily, *adv.*, in a drowsy manner.

drow'siness, *n.*, the state of being drowsy.

drows'ing, *pr.p.*, drowse.

drow'sy, *adj.*, sleepy; lulling.

drub, *v.t.*, to cudgel.

drubbed, *p.p.*, drub.

drub'bing, *pr.p.*, drub; *n.*, a sound beating.

drudge, *v.i.*, to work hard; *n.*, one who works hard and without pleasure.

drudged, *p.p.*, drudge.

drudg'er, *n.*, one who drudges; a taskmaster.

drudg'ery, *n.*, ignoble toil.

drudg'ing, *pr.p.*, drudge.

drudg'ingly, *adv.*, laboriously.

drug, *n.*, any substance used in the preparation of medicines; an article of slow sale; *v.t.*, to administer narcotics to and to stupefy.

drugged, *p.p.*, drug.

drug'get, *n.*, a woollen cloth for covering carpets or for use as a carpet.

drug'ging, *pr.p.*, drug.

drug'gist, *n.*, one who deals in drugs.

dru'id, *n.*, an ancient Celtic priest.

dru'idess, *n.*, a female druid.

druid'ic, *adj.*, pert. to the druids.

druid'ical, *adj.*, *s.q.* druidic.

dru'idism, *n.*, the doctrines and rites of the druids.

drum, *n.*, an instrument of music in the form of a hollow cylinder with ends covered with vellum; anything of the shape of a drum; *v.i.*, to beat a drum.

drum'head, *n.*, the head of a drum.

drum'-major, *n.*, the chief drummer of a regiment.

drummed, *p.p.*, drum.

drum'mer, *n.*, one who drums.

drum'ming, *pr.p.*, drum.

drum'stick, *n.*, the stick of a drum; the upper part of the leg of a cooked bird.

drunk, *adj.*, intoxicated by alcoholic liquor; *p.p.*, drink.

drunk'ard, *n.*, one given to over-indulgence in strong liquor.

drunk'en, *adj.*, drunk; proceeding from intoxication.

drunk'enness, *n.*, the state of being drunk; inebriety.

drupe, *n.*, stone fruit.

Druse, *n.*, one of a Syrian people and religious sect.

druse, *n.*, a cavity in a rock having its interior surface studded with crystals.

dry, *adj.*, destitute of moisture; uninteresting; quietly sarcastic; *v.t.*, to make dry; *v.i.*, to grow dry.

dry'ad, *n.*, a nymph of the woods.

dry'asdust, *adj.*, extremely uninteresting.

dry'-dock, *n.*, a graving dock from which the water is emptied in order that a vessel may be repaired.

dry'er, *n.*, one who, or that which, dries.

dry'-goods, *n. pl.*, cloths, etc.

dry'ing, *pr.p.*, dry.

dry'ly, *adv.*, without moisture, affection, or interest; sarcastically. Also *drily*.

dry'ness, *n.*, the state or quality of being dry.

dry'-nurse, *n.*, a nurse who tends but does not suckle; *v.t.*, to bring up in this way.

dry'-rot, *n.*, a disease of timber which reduces it to powder.

dry'salter, *n.*, a dealer in chemicals.

dry'-shod, *adv.*, without wetting the feet.

du'al, *adj.*, twofold; *n.*, the grammatical form used in some languages when two things are referred to.

du'alism, *n.*, the belief in two antagonistic principles governing human life.

du'alist, *n.*, a believer in dualism.

dual'ity, *n.*, the state of being dual.

dub, *v.t.*, to strike with a sword and make a knight; to give a new name to; to rub (leather) with grease.

du'bash, *n.*, a native Indian interpeter or commissionaire.

dubbed, *p.p.*, dub.

dub'ber, *n.*, one who dubs.

dub'bing, *n.*, grease used for smoothing and rendering leather watertight; *pr.p.*, dub.

dubi'ety, *n.*, doubtfulness.

du'bious, *adj.*, doubtful.

du'biously, *adv.*, in a dubious manner.

du'biousness, *n.*, the state of being dubious.

du'bitable, *adj.*, liable to be doubted.

dubita'tion, *n.*, the act of doubting or hesitating.
du'cal, *adj.*, pert. to a duke.
duc'at, *n.*, a gold or silver coin formerly used in many European countries.
ducatoon', *n.*, a silver coin once common on the Continent.
duch'ess, *n.*, the wife of a duke.
duch'y, *n.*, a dukedom.
duck, *n.*, a coarse cloth, usually white; a water-fowl; a bend of the head; *v.t.*, to dip in water and suddenly withdraw; *v.i.*, to stoop; to bow.
ducked, *p.p.*, duck.
duck'er, *n.*, one who ducks; a bathing-pond.
duck'ing, *pr.p.*, duck.
duck'ling, *n.*, a young duck.
duck'weed, *n.*, an aquatic plant that floats on the surface of still or gently running water.
duct, *n.*, a tube by which a fluid is conveyed.
duc'tile, *adj.*, capable of being drawn out into a thread.
ductil'ity, *n.*, the quality of being ductile.
dud'der, *v.i.*, to shiver; to tremble.
dude, *n.*, a fop (*Amer.*).
dudg'eon, *n.*, resentment.
due, *adj.*, demanding payment or performance; *n.*, a toll, tax, or tribute.
du'el, *n.*, a single combat.
du'el(l)er, *n.*, *i.q.* duellist.
du'el(l)ing, *n.*, the act or practice of engaging in duels.
du'el(l)ist, *n.*, one who engages in duels.
duel'lo, *n.*, a duel; the code of laws regulating duels.
duen'na, *n.*, an elderly woman who takes charge of a younger one.
duet', *n.*, a musical composition for two voices or instruments.
duet'to, *n.*, *i.q.* duet.
duff, *n.*, a stiff flour pudding boiled in a cloth.
duf'fel, *n.*, frieze; a coarse woollen cloth.
duf'fer, *n.*, a stupid person; a cheat.
dug, *n.*, the pap or nipple of an animal; *p.p.*, dig.
dug'out, *n.*, a shelter dug in the ground; a canoe hollowed out of a tree-trunk.
duke, *n.*, a nobleman of highest rank; a sovereign prince.
duke'dom, *n.*, the territory or rank of a duke.
dul'cet, *adj.*, melodious.
dul'cified, *p.p.*, dulcify.
dul'cify, *v.t.*, to render agreeable to the taste.
dul'cifying, *pr.p.*, dulcify.
dul'cimer, *n.*, a stringed musical instrument, played by being struck by two hammers.
duli'a, *n.*, veneration paid to saints or angels.
dull, *adj.*, without life or spirit; cheerless; dim; blunt; *v.t.*, to make dull.
dull'ard, *n.*, a blockhead.
dulled, *p.p.*, dull.
dull'er, *adj.*, *comp.* of dull.
dull'est, *adj.*, *super.* of dull.
dull'ing, *pr.p.*, dull.
dul'ly, *adv.*, in a dull manner.
dul'ness, *n.*, the character of being dull.
dulse, *n.*, an edible sea-weed.
du'ly, *adv.*, properly.
dumb, *adj.*, unable to utter articulate sounds; silent.
dumb'-bell, *n.*, a piece of gymnastic apparatus consisting of two balls with a short piece uniting them.
dumbfound', *v.t.*, to strike dumb; to confuse.
dumbfound'ed, *p.p.*, dumbfound.
dumbfound'ing, *pr.p.*, dumbfound.
dumb'ly, *adv.*, without speech.
dumb'ness, *n.*, the state of being dumb.
dumb'show, *n.*, gesture without words.
dum'dum, *n.*, a soft-cored bullet.
dum'my, *n.*, the exposed hand at bridge; any sham object; a lay-figure; *adj.*, fictitious.
dump, *v.t.*, to deposit carelessly; to sell cheaply in a foreign country owing to protection at home.
dumped, *p.p.*, dump.
dump'ing, *pr.p.*, dump.
dump'ish, *adj.*, melancholy.
dump'ling, *n.*, a mass of boiled paste.
dumps, *n. pl.*, low spirits.
dump'y, *adj.*, short and thick.
dun, *adj.*, dull brown; *v.t.*, to demand a debt in a pressing manner from; to importune; *n.*, one who duns.
dunce, *n.*, an ignoramus.
dun'der, *n.*, the dregs of sugar-cane juice used in distilling rum.
dune, *n.*, a low sand-hill on the coast.
dun'fish, *n.*, cured cod-fish.
dung, *n.*, the excrement of animals; *v.t.*, to manure with dung; *v.i.*, to void excrement.
dungaree', *n.*, a coarse blue calico used as a working dress by mechanics.
dunged, *p.p.*, dung.
dun'geon, *n.*, a deep, dark prison; a donjon or keep.
dung'hill, *n.*, a heap of dung; a mean abode.
dung'ing, *pr.p.*, dung.

dung'y, *adj.*, full of dung.

dung'-yard, *n.*, a yard in which dung is collected.

duniwas'sal, *n.*, a cadet of a Highland family of rank.

Dunlop', *n.*, a cheese made at Dunlop in Ayrshire; a kind of rubber tyre for a motor-car, etc.

dun'nage, *n.*, material laid in the hold of a ship to keep the cargo out of the bilge-water.

dunned, *p.p.*, dun.

dun'ner, *n.*, a debt-collector.

dun'ning, *pr.p.*, dun.

dun'nish, *adj.*, somewhat dun.

du'o, *n.*, a duet.

duodecen'nial, *adj.*, consisting of twelve years.

duodec'imal, *adj.*, reckoning by twelves.

duodec'imo, *adj.*, consisting of twelve leaves to a sheet; *n.*, a book made of sheets folded in this way.

duodec'uple, *adj.*, consisting of twelve.

duoden'ary, *adj.*, rel. to the number twelve; increasing by twelves.

duode'num, *n.*, the first portion of the small intestine.

duolit'eral, *adj.*, consisting of two letters only.

du'ologue, *n.*, a dialogue between two.

du'pable, *adj.*, gullible.

dupe, *n.*, a person easily led astray by his credulity; *v.t.*, to make a dupe of.

duped, *p.p.*, dupe.

du'pery, *n.*, the practice of duping.

du'ping, *pr.p.*, dupe.

du'ple, *adj.*, double.

du'plex, *adj.*, twofold.

du'plicate, *n.*, a second thing of the same kind; *adj.*, double; expressing proportion between squares.

du'plicate, *v.t.*, to double.

du'plicated, *p.p.*, duplicate.

du'plicating, *pr.p.*, duplicate.

duplica'tion, *n.*, the act of doubling.

du'plicative, *adj.*, having the quality of doubling.

du'plicator, *n.*, one who, or that which, duplicates; a copying machine.

du'plicature, *n.*, a doubling; a fold.

duplic'ity, *n.*, double-dealing; deceit.

durabil'ity, *n.*, the quality of being durable.

du'rable, *adj.*, not perishable.

du'rableness, *n.*, *s.q.* durability.

du'ra ma'ter, *n.*, the outer membrane of the brain.

du'rance, *n.*, imprisonment.

dura'tion, *n.*, continuance in time.

dur'bar, *n.*, an Indian state levée; an audience room in an Indian palace.

duress', *n.*, restraint of liberty; constraint by threats.

dur'ing, *prep.*, throughout the course of.

durst, *p.t.*, dare.

dusk, *adj.*, tending to darkness; *n.*, twilight.

dusk'ily, *adv.*, in a dusky manner.

dusk'iness, *n.*, the state of being dusky.

dusk'ish, *adj.*, rather dusky.

dusk'ishness, *n.*, the state of being duskish.

dusk'y, *adj.*, dark-coloured; not bright.

dust, *n.*, fine dry particles of matter; *v.t.*, to free from dust.

dust'-cart, *n.*, a cart for refuse.

dust'ed, *p.p.*, dust.

dust'er, *n.*, that which clears from dust.

dust'-hole, *n.*, a place for rubbish.

dust'iness, *n.*, the state of being dusty.

dust'ing, *pr.p.*, dust.

dust'man, *n.*, one whose business is to remove rubbish.

dust'-pan, *n.*, an utensil to hold dust swept up.

dust'y, *adj.*, covered with dust; dust-coloured.

Dutch, *adj.*, pert. to Holland.

Dutch'man, *n.*, a native of Holland.

du'teous, *adj.*, dutiful; obedient.

du'teously, *adv.*, in a duteous manner.

du'teousness, *n.*, the quality of being duteous.

du'tiable, *adj.*, subject to the imposition of duty or customs.

du'tiful, *adj.*, performing one's duty.

du'tifully, *adv.*, in a dutiful manner.

du'tifulness, *n.*, the character of being dutiful.

du'ty, *n.*, a moral obligation; a sum of money exacted by government in the course of trade.

duum'vir, *n.*, one of two Roman magistrates who performed the same duties.

duum'viral, *adj.*, pert. to the duumviri.

duum'virate, *n.*, the union of two men in the same office.

dux, *n.*, the head of a class or school (*Scot.*).

dwale, *n.*, the deadly nightshade.

dwarf, *n.*, a diminutive man or woman; anything much smaller than the ordinary size; *v.t.*, to stunt; to cause to look small or insignificant.

dwarfed, *p.p.*, dwarf.

dwarf'ing, *pr.p.*, dwarf.

dwarf'ish, *adj.*, below the common size or height.

dwell, *v.i.*, to live in a place.

dwelled, *p.p.*, dwell.

dwell'er, *n.*, an inhabitant.

dwell'ing, *n.*, a place of residence; *pr.p.*, dwell.

dwell'ing-house, *n.*, a house intended as a residence.

dwell'ing-place, *n.*, a place of residence.

dwelt, *p.p.*, dwell.

dwin'dle, *v.i.*, to diminish gradually.

dwin'dled, *adj.*, diminished in size; *p.p.* dwindle.

dwin'dling, *pr.p.*, dwindle.

Dy'ak, *n.*, an aboriginal inhabitant of Borneo.

dye, *v.t.*, to colour; *n.*, a stain.

dyed, *p.p.*, dye.

dye'-house, *n.*, a building in which dyeing is carried on.

dye'ing, *pr.p.*, dye.

dy'er, *n.*, one who dyes cloth.

dye'-stuff, *n.*, materials used in dyeing.

dye'-wood, *n.*, wood from which dye is extracted.

dy'ing, *adj.*, associated with death; *pr.p.*, die.

dyke, *n.*, *i.q.* dike.

dynam'eter, *n.*, an instrument for determining the magnifying power of telescopes.

dynamet'rical, *adj.*, pert. to a dynameter.

dynam'ic, *adj.*, pert. to force as a moving agency.

dynam'ical, *adj.*, *i.q.* dynamic.

dynam'ics, *n. pl.*, the science which deals with the nature and action of force.

dy'namite, *n.*, an explosive prepared from nitro-glycerine.

dy'namo, *n.*, an electric machine in which current is produced by power.

dynamom'eter, *n.*, an instrument for measuring force.

dyn'ast, *n.*, a ruler; a prince.

dynast'ic, *adj.*, rel. to a dynasty.

dyn'asty, *n.*, a line of kings.

dysenter'ic, *adj.*, pert. to dysentery.

dys'entery, *n.*, inflammation of the mucous membrane of the large intestine.

dyspep'sia, *n.*, indigestion.

dyspep'sy, *n.*, *i.q.* dyspepsia.

dyspep'tic, *adj.*, afflicted with dyspepsia; *n.*, a person so suffering.

dyspep'tical, *adj.*, *i.q.* dyspeptic.

dyspha'gia, *n.*, difficulty of swallowing.

dys'phony, *n.*, difficulty of speaking distinctly.

dyspnoe'a, *n.*, difficulty of breathing.

dysthe'sia, *n.*, a morbid feeling of discomfort.

dysthet'ic, *adj.*, pert. to dysthesia.

dys'ury, *n.*, difficulty in discharging urine.

E

each, *pron.*, every one (separately).

ea'ger, *adj.*, keen, earnest; ardently desirous: *n.*, *see* eagre.

ea'gerly, *adv.*, with eagerness.

ea'gerness, *n.*, a state of ardent desire.

ea'gle, *n.*, the large bird of prey so named.

ea'gle-eyed, *adj.*, with the eyes of an eagle; keen-sighted.

ea'glet, *n.*, a young eagle.

ea'gre, *n.*, a tidal wave.

eal'dorman, *n.*, the head of the assembly in Saxon times.

ear, *v.t.*, to plough; *n.*, the organ of hearing; an ear-like projection; fine perception; a corn-spike.

ear'-ache, *n.*, internal pain of the ear; otalgia.

ear'drum, *n.*, the tympanum.

eared, *p.p.*, ear; *adj.*, having ears.

ear'ing, *pr.p.*, ear; *n.*, the growth of an ear of corn; a small line for fastening (*naut.*).

earl, *n.*, the third highest rank of nobility.

earl'dom, *n.*, an earl's rank and territory.

ear'less, *adj.*, without ears.

ear'lier, *adj.*, *comp.* of early.

ear'liest, *adj.*, *super.* of early.

ear'liness, *n.*, the state of being early.

ear'ly, *adj.* and *adv.*, near the beginning; in good time; betimes; before the time.

ear'mark, *v.t.*, to mark specially; *n.*, an owner's mark on an animal; a mark of identification or appropriation.

earn, *v.t.*, to gain by service; to merit.

earned, *p.p.*, earn.

earn'er, *n.*, one who earns.

ear'nest, *adj.*, serious, determined; *n.*, seriousness, zeal: a pledge.

ear'nestly, *adv.*, in earnest.

ear'nest-money, *n.*, money paid to bind a bargain.

ear'nestness, *n.*, the state of being earnest.

earn'ing, *pr.p.*, earn.

earn'ings, *n. pl.*, wages, payment for service.

ear'-ring, *n.*, a ring hung from the ear.

ear'shot, *n.*, a distance to which the hearing reaches.

earth, *n.*, the ground, the globe on which we live: soil; a burrowing animal's hole; *v.t.*, to place in the earth, drive into the earth; mound up.

earth'-born, *adj.*, of earthly birth.

earthed, *p.p.*, earth.

earth'en, *adj.*, made of earth.

earth'enware, *n.*, domestic utensils made of burnt clay.

earth'liness, *n.*, the state or quality of being earthly.

earth'ling, *n.*, a worldling.

earth'ly, *adj.*, bel. to earth, gross, carnal.

earth'quake, *n.*, a disturbance of the earth's surface.

earth'worm, *n.*, the common worm.

earth'y, *adj.*, rel. to, or like, the earth; gross.

ear'-trumpet, *n.*, an instrument enabling the deaf to hear.

ear'-wax, *n.*, cerumen; wax in the ear.

ear'wig, *n.*, the insect so named.

ear'-witness, *n.*, one who testifies what he has heard.

ease, *v.t.*, to lighten, make looser; *n.* freedom from pain or trouble; comfort, rest.

eased, *p.p.*, ease.

ease'ful, *adj.*, full of ease.

ea'sel, *n.*, a stand for a picture, portfolio, etc.

ease'less, *adj.*, without ease.

ease'ment, *n.*, a right apart from ownership of the soil; relief.

eas'ier, *adj.*, *comp.* of easy.

eas'iest, *adj.*, *super.* of easy.

eas'ily, *adv.*, with ease.

eas'iness, *n.*, the state of being easy.

eas'ing, *pr.p.*, ease.

East, *adj.*, bel. to the East; *n.*, one of the cardinal points; an Eastern region.

East'er, *n.*, the greatest of the Christian Festivals, commemorating Our Lord's Resurrection.

Eas'terling, *n.*, a native of an Eastern country; formerly the English name for the Hanseatic traders.

east'erly, *adj.*, eastward; coming from the East.

east'ern, *adj.*, bel. to the East.

east'ward, *adv.*, toward the East.

eas'y, *adj.*, not difficult, comfortable, free from pain or trouble; unaffected.

eas'y-chair, *n.*, an arm-chair made to be especially comfortable.

eas'y-going, *adj.*, casual, good-natured.

eat, *v.t.*, to consume with the teeth; to wear away; *v.i.*, to take food; to taste.

eat'able, *adj.*, fit to eat; *n.*, anything edible.

eat'en, *p.p.*, eat.

eat'er, *n.*, anything that eats.

eat'ing, *pr.p.*, eat; *n.*, food.

eat'ing-house, *n.*, a restaurant.

eau-de-Cologne', *n.*, a perfume of that name.

eau-de-vie', *n.* brandy.

eaves, *n. pl.*, the overhanging part of a roof.

eaves'drop, *v.i.*, to listen secretly.

eaves'dropper, *n.*, one who listens secretly.

ebb, *v.i.*, to flow back, subside; decline; *n.*, the back flow of the tide; decline.

ebbed, *p.p.*, ebb.

ebb'ing, *pr.p.*, ebb.

ebb'tide, *n.*, low tide.

eb'on, *adj.*, made of ebony; *n.*, ebony.

eb'onize, *v.t.*, to make look like ebony.

eb'ony, *adj.*, made of ebony; *n.*, a hard black wood.

ebri'ety, *n.*, a state of drunkenness.

ebul'liency, *n.*, the state of being ebullient.

ebul'lient, *adj.*, bubbling over, excessively enthusiastic.

ebulli'tion, *n.*, the act of bubbling over; an outburst of enthusiasm.

écar'té, *n.*, a card game so named, for two.

ec'bole, *n.*, a digression.

eccen'tric, *adj.*, not in the centre; peculiar; *n.*, a device for alternating circular with rectilinear motion; a queer person.

eccen'trical, *adj.*, *i.q.* eccentric.

eccentric'ity, *n.*, the state or quality of being eccentric.

eccle'sia, *n.*, an assembly; the Church.

eccle'siarch, *n.*, a Church ruler.

Ecclesias'tes, *n.*, the name of one of the canonical Scriptures = the Preacher.

ecclesias'tic, *adj.*, rel. to the Church; *n.*, a Churchman (*i.e.*, in the sense of a person in Holy Orders).

ecclesias'tical, *adj.*, *i.q.* ecclesiastic.

ecclesias'ticism, *n.*, devotion to the Church; the ecclesiastical system.

Ecclesias'ticus, *n.*, one of the deutero-canonical Scriptures.

ecclesiolog'ical, *adj.*, rel. to ecclesiology.

ecclesiol'ogist, *n.*, a student of ecclesiology.

ecclesiol'ogy, *n.*, the study of church antiquities and church architecture.

ech'elon, *n.*, an arrangement of troops in a succession of receding lines, each to the right or left of the first; *v.t.*, to dispose in échelon; *v.i.*, to take up a position in échelon.

ech'inate, *adj.*, prickly, bristly.

echi'nus, *n.*, the sea-urchin; hedgehog.

ech'o, *v.t.*, to reflect back (a sound); *v.i.*, to resound; *n.*, a reflection of sound; an exact imitation.

ech'oed, *p.p.*, echo.

ech'oing, *pr.p.*, echo.

echom'eter, *n.*, an instrument for measuring sound-distance.

echom'etry, *n.*, the art of measuring sound-distance.

éclat', *n.*, brilliant effect, applause, distinction.

eclec'tic, *adj.*, selecting, picking and choosing; *n.*, one who is eclectic.

eclec'tical, *adj.*, *i.q.* eclectic.

eclec'ticism, *n.*, the eclectic spirit; selection from a variety of opinions.

eclipse', *v.t.*, to put under an eclipse; to obscure, throw into the shade; *n.*, an obscuration of a heavenly body.

eclipsed', *p.p.*, eclipse.

eclips'ing, *pr.p.*, eclipse.

eclip'tic, *adj.*, rel. to eclipses, or to the ecliptic; *n.*, the sun's apparent path.

ec'logue, *n.*, a simple, rustic poem.

econom'ic, *adj.*, pert. to economy.

econom'ical, *adj.*, careful of expenditure; also *i.q.* economic.

econom'ics, *n. pl.*, the science of wealth in relation to the state and the people; political economy.

econ'omist, *n.*, a student of economics.

econ'omize, *v.t.*, to husband, use thriftily; *v.i.*, to be thrifty.

econ'omized, *p.p.*, economize.

econ'omizing, *pr.p.*, economize.

econ'omy, *n.*, domestic management, saving; adjustment of means to ends; a system of government.

écraseur', *n.*, a surgical instrument so named.

écru', *adj.*, like unbleached linen; *n.*, coarse linen.

ec'stasis, *n.*, a trance.

ec'stasy, *n.*, a rapturous, exalted state.

ecstat'ic, *adj.*, exalted, rapturous, entrancing.

ecstat'ical, *adj.*, *i.q.* ecstatic.

ectro'sis, *n.*, arrestive treatment (*med.*).

écu, *n.*, an ancient coin of varying value.

ecumen'ical, *adj.*, bel. to the whole world, general. Also *oecumenical.*

ec'zema, *n.*, an inflamed state of the skin.

eczem'atous, *adj.*, of the nature of eczema.
eda'cious, *adj.*, voracious, destructive.
edac'ity, *n.*, voracity, greediness.
Ed'da, *n.*, the name of either of the two series of ancient Icelandic books.
ed'der, *v.t.*, to bind with edder; *n.*, a hedge; the binding for a hedge.
ed'died, *p.p.*, eddy.
ed'dy, *v.i.*, to whirl round and round; *n.*, a whirling current.
ed'dying, *pr.p.*, eddy.
ed'elweiss, *n.*, a small white Alpine flower.
edem'atous, *adj.*, puffy, swollen.
E'den, *n.*, Paradise.
eden'tate, *adj.*, without teeth.
eden'tated, *adj.*, deprived of teeth.
edge, *v.t.*, to put an edge to; to incite; *v.i.*, to sidle, come up slowly; *n.*, the sharp side of a blade; a sharp border; brink; fringe.
edged, *p.p.*, edge.
edge'less, *adj.*, without an edge.
edge'rail, *n.*, a rail on the edge of which wheels run.
edge'-tool, *n.*, a cutting-tool.
edge'ways, *adv.*, *i.q.* edgewise.
edge'wise, *adv.*, sideways.
edg'ing, *n.*, border.
ed'ible, *adj.*, eatable.
ed'ibleness, *n.*, the quality of being edible.
e'dict, *n.*, a proclamation by authority.
edifica'tion, *n.*, the act or effect of edifying.
ed'ifice, *n.*, a building, structure.
ed'ified, *p.p.*, edify.
ed'ify, *v.t.*, to build up, instruct, improve.
ed'ifying, *pr.p.*, edify.
e'dile, *n.*, *i.q.* aedile.
ed'it, *v.t.*, to look after the publication of a book; to prepare a book for publication.
ed'ited, *p.p.*, edit.
ed'iting, *pr.p.*, edit.
edi'tion, *n.*, the issue of a book to the public; the number of copies printed at one time.
ed'itor, *n.*, one who edits either a book or a newspaper, magazine, etc.
edito'rial, *adj.*, rel. to an editor.
ed'itorship, *n.*, the office of an editor.
ed'itress, *n.*, fem. of editor.
ed'ucable, *adj.*, capable of education.
ed'ucate, *v.t.*, to train, develop the mind and character.
ed'ucated, *p.p.*, educate.
ed'ucating, *pr.p.*, educate.
educa'tion, *n.*, the process or effect of educating.
educa'tional, *adj.*, rel. to education; instructive.
educa'tionist, *n.*, one who professes a knowledge of educational principles.
ed'ucator, *n.*, one who educates.
educe', *v.t.*, to draw out; make an inference.
educed', *p.p.*, educe.
edu'cible, *adj.*, able to be educed.
edu'cing, *pr.p.*, educe.
educ'tion, *n.*, the act or result of educing.
educ'tor, *n.*, anything that educes.
edul'corant, *adj.*, sweetening.
edul'corate, *v.t.*, to sweeten by reducing acidity.
edul'corator, *n.*, anything that edulcorates.
eel, *n.*, a snake-like fish so named.
e'en, *n.* and *adv.*, *see* even.
ee'rie, **ee'ry**, *adj.*, fear-inspiring; causing a feeling of loneliness.
efface', *v.t.*, to destroy the face of, blot out, remove from notice.
efface'able, *adj.*, able to be effaced.
effaced', *p.p.*, efface.
efface'ment, *n.*, the act of effacing.
effa'cing, *pr.p.*, efface.
effect', *v.t.*, bring to pass, accomplish; *n.*, a result, accomplishment.
effect'ed, *p.p.*, effect.
effect'ible, *adj.*, able to be effected.
effect'ing, *pr.p.*, effect.
effect'ive, *adj.*, effect-producing, successful.
effect'ively, *adv.*, in an effective way.
effect'iveness, *n.*, the quality of being effective.
effect'or, *n.*, that which effects.
effects', *n. pl.*, belongings, chattels.
effec'tual, *adj.*, producing intended effect.
effec'tually, *adv.*, in an effectual way.
effec'tuate, *v.t.*, to accomplish.
effec'tuated, *p.p.*, effectuate.
effec'tuating, *pr.p.*, effectuate.
effectua'tion, *n.*, the act or result of effectuating.
effem'inacy, *n.*, womanish character, unmanliness.
effem'inate, *adj.*, woman-like, unmanly.
effem'inate, *v.t.*, to weaken, render womanly.
effem'inated, *p.p.*, effeminate.
effem'inately, *adv.*, in an effeminate way.
effem'inateness, *n.*, the quality of being effeminate.
effem'inating, *pr.p.*, effeminate.
Effen'di, *n.*, a Turkish title, equivalent to *Mr.*
ef'ferent, *adj.*, discharging.
effervesce', *v.i.*, to bubble up, froth up.
effervesced', *p.p.*, effervesce.
efferves'cence, *n.*, the act or process of effervescing.

effervesʹcent, *adj.*, effervescing.

effete′, *adj.*, worn out by age.

efficaʹcious, *adj.*, able to produce intended result.

efficaʹciously, *adv.*, in an efficacious way.

efficaʹciousness, *n.*, the state or quality of being efficacious.

efʹficacy, *n.*, *i.q.* efficaciousness.

effiʹciency, *n.*, the state or quality of being efficient.

effiʹcient, *adj.*, able to produce intended effect; capable, vigorous.

effiʹciently, *adv.*, in an efficient way.

effigʹies, *n.*, a figure, effigy.

efʹfigy, *n.*, a figure, image.

effloresce′, *v.i.*, to blossom forth, flower.

effloresced′, *p.p.*, effloresce.

efflorésʹcence, *n.*, the state or period of efflorescing.

effloresʹcency, *n.*, the state or quality of being efflorescent.

effloresʹcent, *adj.*, blossoming forth, flowering.

effloresʹcing, *pr.p.*, effloresce.

efʹfluence, *n.*, a flowing out; that which flows out.

efʹfluent, *adj.*, flowing out; *n.*, an outlet, outflow.

effluʹvia, *n.*, pl. of effluvium.

effluʹvium, *n.*, an invisible vapour, generally from decaying matter.

efʹflux, *n.*, the act or process of outflowing.

effluxʹion, *n.*, a lapse; issue.

efʹfort, *n.*, an exertion of strength, attempt, achievement.

efʹfortless, *adj.*, without effort.

effrontʹery, *n.*, impudence, barefacedness.

efʹfulʹgence, *n.*, brightness, lustre.

efʹfulʹgent, *adj.*, shining forth, splendid.

effuse′, *v.t.*, to pour forth.

effused′, *p.p.*, effuse.

effuʹsing, *pr.p.*, effuse.

effuʹsion, *n.*, the act or result of effusing.

effuʹsive, *adj.*, exuberant in sentiment; gushing.

effuʹsively, *adv.*, in an effusive way.

effuʹsiveness, *n.*, gush.

eft, *n.*, a newt.

egesʹtion, *n.*, excretion.

egg, *v.t.*, to incite, goad on; *n.*, the rounded body containing the substance of the creature to be born from it.

egged, *p.p.*, egg.

eggʹing, *pr.p.*, egg.

eggʹ-shell, *n.*, the shell of the egg.

eʹgis, *see* aegis.

egʹlantine, *n.*, perhaps the sweetbriar or the honeysuckle.

egʹoism, *n.*, the self-regarding theory of morals.

egʹoist, *n.*, an upholder of egoism.

egʹotism, *n.*, a fondness for saying "I"; self-praise.

egʹotist, *n.*, one who speaks chiefly about himself; self-centred

egotisʹtic, *adj.*, self-centred, inordinately self-regarding.

egotisʹtical, *adj.*, *i.q.* egotistic.

egʹotize, *v.i.*, to indulge in egotism.

egreʹgious, *adj.*, remarkable, standing out of the crowd, (often used disparagingly).

egreʹgiously, *adv.*, in an egregious way.

eʹgress, *n.*, an exit, going out.

egresʹsion, *n.*, exit.

egʹret, *n.*, a variety of heron; a tuft of heron's feathers.

Egypʹtian, *adj.*, rel. to Egypt.

Egyptolʹogy, *n.*, the study of Egyptian history and antiquities.

eh, *interj.*, what!

eiʹcon, *n.*, a sacred picture. Also *icon.*

eiʹder, *n.*, a large sea-duck.

eiʹder-down, *n.*, the breast feathers of the eider; a bed-quilt.

eiʹder-duck, *n.*, *i.q.* eider.

eiʹdograph, *n.*, an apparatus for copying drawings.

eight, *adj.*, one of the cardinal numbers.

eighteen, *adj.*, one of the cardinal numbers.

eighteenth, *adj.*, the ordinal of eighteen.

eightʹfold, *adj.* and *adv.*, eight times repeated.

eighth, *adj.*, the ordinal of eight.

eighthʹly, *adv.*, in the eighth place.

eightʹieth, *adj.*, the ordinal of eighty.

eightʹscore, *adj.* and *n.*, eight times twenty.

eightʹy, *adj.*, a cardinal number.

eigne, *adj.*, eldest, elder (*Leg.*).

eireʹnicon, *n.*, an attempt (usually written) to bring about a reconciliation.

Eisteddʹfod, *n.*, a Welsh bardic assembly.

eiʹther, *pron.*, one or the other of two; *conj.*, in one of two cases.

ejacʹulate, *v.t.*, to jerk out words; speak in short sentences.

ejacʹulated, *p.p.*, ejaculate.

ejacʹulating, *pr.p.*, ejaculate.

ejaculaʹtion, *n.*, the act of ejaculating; a short, sharp exclamation.

ejacʹulatory, *adj.*, rel. to ejaculation.

eject′, *v.t.*, to throw out, dismiss, banish.

ejectʹed, *p.p.*, eject.

ejectʹing, *pr.p.*, eject.

ejecʹtion, *n.*, the act of ejecting.

ejectʹment, *n.*, removal (by law); dispossession.

eject'or, *n.*, one who ejects.

eke, *v.t.*, to make to suffice; *adv.*, equally, also.

eked, *p.p.*, eke.

e'king, *pr.p.*, eke.

elab'orate, *adj.*, made with much toil, highly finished.

elab'orate, *v.t.*, to work out with much pains; to add improvements to.

elab'orated, *p.p.*, elaborate.

elab'orately, *adv.*, in an elaborate way.

elab'orating, *pr.p.*, elaborate.

elabora'tion, *n.*, the act or process of elaborating.

elab'orative, *adj.*, tending to elaboration.

elab'orator, *n.*, one who elaborates.

ela'in, *n.*, an oily liquid compound. Also *olein*.

élan, *n.*, dash, ardour (*Fr.*).

e'land, *n.*, a S. African antelope.

elapse', *v.i.*, to pass away; end.

elapsed', *p.p.*, elapse.

elaps'ing, *pr.p.*, elapse.

elas'tic, *adj.*, having the power of returning to the state from which it has been disturbed by pressure, pulling, or distortion; *n.*, a strip or band of rubber.

elas'tically, *adv.*, in an elastic way.

elastic'ity, *n.*, the elastic property.

elate', *v.t.*, to exalt, elevate, make proud.

ela'ted, *p.p.*, elate.

ela'ting, *pr.p.*, elate.

ela'tion, *n.*, a state produced by elating.

el'bow, *v.t.*, to push aside, jostle; *n.*, the joint at the middle of the arm; any elbow-like bend.

el'bow-*chair*, *n.*, a chair with rests for the elbow.

el'bowed, *p.p.*, elbow; also *adj.*, elbow-shaped.

el'bowing, *pr.p.*, elbow.

el'bow-room, *n.*, space to turn round in.

el'der, *adj.*, older; *n.*, an old person; a functionary so named; the shrub so named.

el'derberry, *n.*, the fruit of the elder tree.

eld'erly, *adj.*, becoming old; rather aged.

eld'est, *adj.*, *super.* of elder.

El Dora'do, *n.*, a fabulous country rich in gold.

elecampane', *n.*, a variety of aster.

elect', *v.t.*, to choose, select (by vote); *adj.*, chosen; *n.*, one chosen.

elect'ed, *p.p.*, elect.

elect'ing, *pr.p.*, elect.

elec'tion, *n.*, the act or result or occasion of electing.

electioneer', *v.i.*, to organize an election; *n.*, one who organizes an election.

electioneered', *p.p.*, electioneer.

electioneer'ing, *pr.p.*, electioneer.

elec'tive, *adj.*, pert. to election.

elect'or, *n.*, one who has the right of electing.

elect'oral, *adj.*, bel. to an elector or election.

elect'orate, *n.*, the collective body of electors.

elec'tress, *n.*, fem. of elector.

***elec'tric*,** *adj.*, bel. to electricity; magnetic.

***elec'trical*,** *adj.*, *i.q.* electric.

***elec'trically*,** *adv.* by means of electricity.

electri'cian, *n.*, an expert in electrics.

elec'trics, *n. pl.*, the science of electricity

***electric'ity*,** *n.*, an energy - producing agency in nature.

elec'trifiable, *adj.*, able to be electrified.

electrifica'tion, *n.*, the process or result of electrifying.

elec'trified, *p.p.*, electrify.

elec'trify, *v.t.*, to charge with electricity; amaze.

elec'trifying, *pr.p.*, electrify.

elec'tro, *n.*, electroplate, an electrotype.

elec'trocute, *v.t.*, to execute by means of electricity.

elec'trode, *n.*, either of the poles or terminals of a galvanic battery or dynamo.

electrolier', *n.*, a holder of electric lamps.

electrol'ogy, *n.*, the science of electric phenomena.

electrol'ysis, *n.*, decomposition by means of electricity.

elec'trolyte, *n.*, a substance decomposable by electricity.

elec'trolyzable, *adj.*, able to electrolyze.

elec'trolyze, *v.t.*, to decompose by means of electricity.

elec'trolyzed, *p.p.*, electrolyze.

elec'trolyzing, *pr.p.*, electrolyze.

electro-mag'net, *n.*, a magnetized piece of soft metal.

electro - mag'netism, *n.*, the science dealing with the development of magnetism by electric currents.

electrom'eter, *n.*, an instrument for measuring the strength of an electric current.

electromo'tor, *n.*, a machine applying electricity as a motive power.

electrop'athy, *n.*, the treatment of disease with electricity.

electroph'orus, *n.*, an apparatus generating statical electricity by induction.

elec'troplate, *v.t.*, to cover with metal by means of electricity; *n.*, a piece of ware so coated.

elec'troplated, *p.p.*, electroplate.

elec'troplating, *pr.p.*, electroplate.

elec'troscope, *n.*, an instrument detecting the presence of electricity.

elec'trotype, *v.t.*, to make an electrotype of; *n.*, a reproduction in copper by means of electricity.

elec'trotyped, *p.p.*, electrotype.

elec'trotyper, *n.*, a maker of electrotypes.

elec'trotyping, *pr.p.*, electrotype.

elec'trum, *n.*, amber.

elec'tuary, *n.*, a medicine prepared as a confection.

eleemos'ynary, *adj.*, rel. to almsgiving; given from charity.

el'egance, *n.*, gracefulness, daintiness.

el'egancy, *n.*, *i.q.* elegance.

el'egant, *adj.*, graceful, refined.

el'egantly, *adv.*, with elegance.

elegi'ac, *adj.*, pert. to elegy and elegiacs; *n.*, elegiac verse.

elegi'acal, *adj.*, *i.q.* elegiac.

el'egist, *n.*, one who writes elegies.

el'egy, *n.*, a death-poem, funeral song.

el'eme, *adj.*, hand-picked, choice (*Turkish*).

el'ement, *n.*, one of the simplest parts; an unanalysable substance; a first principle; an ingredient; a natural environment.

elemen'tal, *adj.*, rel. to the elements.

elemen'tary, *adj.*, primary, simple.

el'ements, *n.*, pl. of element; rudiments of learning; the matter (bread and wine) of the Sacrament of the Altar.

el'emi, *n.*, a general name for gum resins.

elen'chus, *n.*, a refuting argument.

el'ephant, *n.*, the huge quadruped so named.

elephanti'asis, *n.*, a disease which makes the skin hard, rough and thick.

elephan'tine, *adj.*, rel. to or like an elephant.

elephan'toid, *adj.*, like an elephant.

Eleusin'ian, *adj.*, rel. to Eleusis and the Eleusinian mysteries.

el'evate, *v.t.*, to raise up, exalt, improve, cheer; *adj.*, elevated.

el'evated, *p.p.*, elevate; *adj.*, exalted; intoxicated.

el'evating, *pr.p.*, elevate.

eleva'tion, *n.*, the act or result of elevating.

el'evator, *n.*, anything that elevates; a lift; a limb-raising muscle; a horizontal plane, fore and aft, for steering an aeroplane upwards or downwards.

elev'en, *n.*, one more than ten. The complement of a cricket or Association football team.

elev'enth, *adj.*, the ordinal of eleven.

elf, *n.*, a small spirit, fairy.

elf'in, *adj.*, pert. to elves; *n.*, an elf, a playful child.

elf'ish, *adj.*, like an elf.

elf'ishness, *n.*, the state of being elfish.

elic'it, *v.t.*, to entice forth, to educe.

elic'ited, *p.p.*, elicit.

elic'iting, *pr.p.*, elicit.

elide', *v.t.*, to strike out, erase.

eli'ded, *p.p.*, elide.

eli'ding, *pr.p.*, elide.

eligibil'ity, *n.*, the state of being eligible.

el'igible, *adj.*, worthy of choice, desirable, qualified.

elim'inate, *v.t.*, to cast out or aside; to obtain by separation.

elim'inated, *p.p.*, eliminate.

elim'inating, *pr.p.*, eliminate.

elimina'tion, *n.*, the act or effect of eliminating.

el'iquate, *v.t.*, to melt out.

el'iquated, *p.p.*, eliquate.

el'iquating, *pr.p.*, eliquate.

eliqua'tion, *n.*, the process or effect of eliquating.

eli'sion, *n.*, the act or result of eliding.

élite', *adj.*, choice, select, the pick (*Fr.*).

elix'ir, *n.*, a liquor brewed by alchemists for preserving life indefinitely, or for converting baser metals into gold.

Elizabe'than, *adj.*, rel. to Queen Elizabeth and the Elizabethan period or architectural style.

elk, *n.*, the largest kind of deer.

ell, *n.*, an old cloth measure of varying lengths.

ellipse', *n.*, an oval-shaped figure.

ellip'sis, *n.*, the leaving out of words needed for the completion of the sense.

ellip'tic, *adj.*, rel. to or like an ellipse.

ellip'tical, *adj.*, *i.q.* elliptic.

elliptic'ity, *n.*, the state of being elliptic.

ellip'toid, *adj.*, like an ellipse.

elm, *n.*, the familiar tree so named.

elm'en, *adj.*, rel. to elms.

elm'y, *adj.*, covered with elms.

elocu'tion, *n.*, the art of speaking with correct and clear articulation.

elocu'tionary, *adj.*, rel. to elocution.

elocu'tionist, *n.*, one who professes elocution.

éloge', *n.*, a panegyric, encomium (*Fr.*).

el'ogy, *n.*, *i.q.* éloge.

El'ohim, *n.*, an Old Testament name for God, the true God, in all the fullness of deity.

e'longate, *v.t.*, to draw out, make longer.

e'longated, *p.p.*, elongate.

e'longating, *pr.p.*, elongate.

elonga'tion, *n.*, the process or result of elongating.

elope', *v.i.*, to run away clandestinely.

eloped', *p.p.*, elope.

elo'ping, *pr.p.*, elope.

elope'ment, *n.*, the act of eloping.

el'oquence, *n.*, the power of fine speech.

el'oquent, *adj.*, gifted with eloquence.

el'oquently, *adv.*, in an eloquent way.

else, *adv.*, in addition, also, instead.

else'where, *adv.*, in some other place.

elu'cidate, *v.t.*, to make clear, explain.

elu'cidated, *p.p.*, elucidate.

elu'cidating, *pr.p.*, elucidate.

elucida'tion, *n.*, the act or result of elucidating.

elu'cidative, *adj.*, explanatory, throwing light on.

elu'cidator, *n.*, one who elucidates.

elu'cidatory, *adj.*, *i.q.* elucidative.

elude', *v.t.*, to baffle, avoid by artifice.

elu'ded, *p.p.*, elude.

elu'dible, *adj.*, able to be eluded.

elu'ding, *pr.p.*, elude.

elu'sion, *n.*, the act of eluding.

elu'sive, *adj.*, baffling, hard to grasp.

elu'sively, *adv.*, in an elusive way.

elu'siveness, *n.*, the quality of being elusive.

elu'soriness, *n.*, the quality of being elusory.

elu'sory, *adj.*, *i.q.* elusive.

elves, *n.*, pl. of elf.

Elys'ian, *adj.*, bel. to Elysium; delightful, blessed.

Elys'ium, *n.*, the blissful place of the dead, the classic Paradise.

El'zevir, *adj.*, pert. to the Elzevirs, the famous 17th cent. Dutch publishers.

em, *n.*, a printer's unit of measurement.

ema'ciate, *v.t.*, to make thin, reduce to leanness; *v.i.*, to become lean.

ema'ciated, *p.p.*, emaciate.

ema'ciating, *pr.p.*, emaciate.

emacia'tion, *n.*, the state of being emaciated; extreme leanness.

em'anant, *adj.*, flowing from a source.

em'anate, *v.i.*, to flow from, proceed from.

em'anated, *p.p.*, emanate.

em'anating, *pr.p.*, emanate.

emana'tion, *n.*, the act of emanating; something that emanates.

em'anative, *adj.*, tending to emanate.

eman'cipate, *v.t.*, to set free from slavery or any oppression or bad influence.

eman'cipated, *p.p.*, emancipate.

eman'cipating, *pr.p.*, emancipate.

emancipa'tion, *n.*, the act or result of emancipating.

emancipa'tionist, *n.*, a supporter of the emancipation of slaves.

eman'cipator, *n.*, one who emancipates.

emas'culate, *v.t.*, to deprive of male strength; take out the vigour.

emas'culated, *p.p.*, emasculate.

emas'culating, *pr.p.*, emasculate.

emascula'tion, *n.*, the act of emasculating.

embale', *v.t.*, to make a bale of.

embaled', *p.p.*, embale.

emba'ling, *pr.p.*, embale.

embalm', *v.t.*, to preserve a corpse with spices and drugs.

embalmed', *p.p.*, embalm.

embalm'er, *n.*, one who embalms.

embalm'ing, *pr.p.*, embalm.

embank', *v.t.*, to build a bank around or against.

embanked', *p.p.*, embank.

embank'ing, *pr.p.*, embank.

embank'ment, *n.*, the act or result of embanking.

embarca'tion, *n.*, *see* embarkation.

embar'go, *v.t.*, to lay an embargo on; *n.*, an order forbidding a ship to leave a port.

embar'goed, *p.p.*, embargo.

embark', *v.t.*, to place on board; *v.i.*, to go on board; to begin an enterprise.

embarka'tion, *n.*, the act of embarking.

embarked', *p.p.*, embark.

embark'ing, *pr.p.*, embark.

embar'rass, *v.t.*, to hamper, trouble, perplex.

embar'rassed, *p.p.*, embarrass.

embar'rassing, *pr.p.*, embarrass; *adj.*, awkward, troublesome.

embar'rassment, *n.*, perturbation, perplexity, money trouble.

embas'sador, *n.*, *see* ambassador.

em'bassy, *n.*, an ambassador's mission; an ambassador's residence and the officials.

embat'tle, *v.t.*, to draw up in battle array.

embat'tled, *p.p.*, embattle; *adj.*, having battlements.

embat'tling, *pr.p.*, embattle.

embay', *v.t.*, to place in a bay.

embayed', *p.p.*, embay.

embay'ing, *pr.p.*, embay.

embed', *v.t.*, to lay in a bed.

embed'ded, *p.p.*, embed.

embed'ding, *pr.p.*, embed.

embel'lish, *v.t.*, to adorn, beautify.

embel'lished, *p.p.*, embellish.

embel'lisher, *n.*, one who embellishes.

embel'lishing, *pr.p.*, embellish.

embel'lishment, *n.*, the act or result of embellishing; an ornament.

em'ber, *n.*, a live coal; a remnant of a fire.

em'ber-week, *n.*, one of the four seasons of the ecclesiastical year, set apart for fasting and prayer. These are the times for admitting candidates to Holy Orders.

embez'zle, *v.t.*, to steal something entrusted to one's care.

embez'zled, *p.p.*, embezzle.

embez'zlement, *n.*, the act of embezzling.

embez'zler, *n.*, one who embezzles.

embez'zling, *pr.p.*, embezzle.

embit'ter, *v.t.*, to impart bitterness to; to intensify.

embit'tered, *p.p.*, embitter.

embit'tering, *pr.p.*, embitter.

emblaze', *v.t.*, to embellish, blazon.

emblazed', *p.p.*, emblaze.

embla'zing, *pr.p.*, emblaze.

embla'zon, *v.t.*, to adorn with heraldic figures, or with bright colours.

embla'zoned, *p.p.*, emblazon.

embla'zoner, *n.*, one who emblazons.

embla'zoning, *pr.p.*, emblazon.

embla'zonment, *n.*, *i.q.* emblazonry.

embla'zonry, *n.*, the act or art of emblazoning.

em'blem, *n.*, a type, figure, symbol.

emblemat'ic, *adj.*, typical, symbolical.

emblemat'ical, *adj.*, *i.q.* emblematic.

emblem'atize, *v.t.*, *i.q.* emblemize.

em'blements, *n. pl.*, profits on crops.

em'blemize, *v.t.*, to represent emblematically.

embod'ied, *p.p.*, embody.

embod'ier, *n.*, that which embodies.

embod'iment, *n.*, the act or result of embodying; a complete representation

embod'y, *v.t.*, to form into a body; to give concrete expression to.

embod'ying, *pr.p.*, embody.

embold'en, *v.t.*, to make bold, encourage, hearten.

embold'ened, *p.p.*, embolden.

embold'ening, *pr.p.*, embolden.

em'bolism, *n.*, the periodic intercalation of days or years; an obstruction caused by a clot of blood.

embolis'mal, *adj.*, rel. to an embolism.

embolis'mic, *adj.*, *i.q.* embolismal.

em'bolus, *n.*, an insertion; a blood-clot.

embonpoint', *adj.*, plump, well nourished; *n.*, plumpness.

embor'der, *v.t.*, to furnish with a border.

embos'om, *v.t.*, to receive into the bosom; to embrace, envelop.

embos'omed, *p.p.*, embosom.

embos'oming, *pr.p.*, embosom.

emboss', *v.t.*, to ornament with raised work.

embossed', *p.p.*, emboss.

emboss'ing, *pr.p.*, emboss.

emboss'ment, *n.*, the act or result of embossing.

embot'tle, *v.a.*, to put in a bottle.

embow'el, *v.t.*, to remove the entrails of; to bury.

embow'el(l)ed, *p.p.*, embowel.

embow'el(l)er, *n.*, one who embowels.

embow'el(l)ing, *pr.p.*, embowel.

embow'elment, *n.*, the act or result of embowelling.

embow'er, *v.t.*, to cover with a bower, shelter with trees.

embow'ered, *p.p.*, embower.

embow'ering, *pr.p.*, embower.

embrace', *v.t.*, to clasp with the arms; to adopt; to include; *n.*, the act of embracing; a clasping in the arms.

embraced', *p.p.*, embrace.

embra'cer, *n.*, anything that embraces.

embra'cery, *n.*, tampering with a jury.

embra'cing, *pr.p.*, embrace.

embra'sure, *n.*, an opening in a wall, with its sides bevelled, so that the opening widens inwards; a loop-hole.

em'brocate, *v.t.*, to apply a liquid medicine to the body.

em'brocated, *p.p.*, embrocate.

em'brocating, *pr.p.*, embrocate.

embroca'tion, *n.*, the act of embrocating; a liniment.

embro'glio, *n.*, *see* imbroglio.

embroid'er, *v.t.*, to ornament with needlework designs; to variegate.

embroid'ered, *p.p.*, embroider.

embroid'erer, *n.*, one who embroiders.

embroid'ering, *pr.p.*, embroider.

embroid'ery, *n.*, the art or act of embroidering; a piece of embroidered work.

embroil', *v.t.*, to involve in a quarrel.

embroiled', *p.p.*, embroil.

embroil'ing, *pr.p.*, embroil.

embroil'ment, *n.*, the act or result of embroiling.

em'bryo, *n.*, a rudimentary form; the vitalized germ in the first stage of development.

embryog'raphy, *n.*, a treatise on embryos.

embryol'ogy, *n.*, the study of embryos and the development of organisms.

em'bryonate, *adj.*, rel. to embryos.

em'bryonated, *adj.*, *i.q.* embryonate.

embryon'ic, *adj.*, in the state of an embryo; rel. to an embryo.

embryot'ic, *adj.*, *i.q.* embryonic.

embryot'omy, *n.*, the cutting or dissection of a foetus.

Emeer', *n.*, an Emir.

emend', *v.t.*, to correct.

emend'able, *adj.*, able to be emended.

emen'dals, *n. pl.*, money reserved for emergencies.

emenda'tion, *n.*, the act or result of emending; correction.

em'endator, *n.*, one who emends.

emend'atory, *adj.*, correcting.

emend'ed, *p.p.*, emend.

emend'ing, *pr.p.*, emend

em'erald, *adj.*, green like an emerald; *n.*, a green gem or colour; a printing type.

emerge', *v.i.*, to rise out of; come into view; result.

emerged', *p.p.*, emerge.

emer'gence, *n.*, the act of emerging.

emer'gency, *n.*, a sudden occurrence requiring instant action.

emer'gent, *adj.*, emerging.

emer'ging, *pr.p.*, emerge.

emer'iti, *adj.*, pl. of emeritus.

emer'itus, *adj.*, retired from office.

emer'itus-profes'sor, *n.*, an ex-professor.

em'erods, *n. pl.*, hemorrhoids.

em'eroid, *n.*, *i.q.* hemorrhoid.

emersed', *adj.*, standing out of the water; protruding.

emer'sion, *n.*, the act of emerging.

em'ery, *n.*, a hard mineral used in polishing.

em'esis, *n.*, vomiting.

emet'ic, *adj.*, producing vomiting; *n.*, a medicine that causes vomiting.

emet'ical, *adj.*, *i.q.* emetic.

e'meu, e'mu, *n.*, the Australian ostrich.

émeute', *n.*, a riot, outbreak.

em'igrant, *adj.*, migrating; *n.*, one who emigrates.

em'igrate, *v.i.*, to leave one's country in order to settle in another.

em'igrated, *p.p.*, emigrate.

em'igrating, *pr.p.*, emigrate.

emigra'tion, *n.*, the act of emigrating.

em'inence, *n.*, height, distinction; a title bestowed on cardinals.

em'inency, *n.*, *i.q.* eminence.

em'inent, *adj.*, towering above, exalted, distinguished.

em'inently, *adv.*, markedly, conspicuously.

Emir', *n.*, a Turkish or Arabic tribal ruler.

em'issary, *adj.*, rel. to a spy or an emissary; *n.*, one sent on a mission, a spy.

emis'sion, *n.*, the act or result of emitting.

emis'sive, *adj.*, leading to emission.

em'issory, *adj.*, *i.q.* emissive.

emit', *v.t.*, to send forth, put forth.

emit'ted, *p.p.*, emit.

emit'ting, *pr.p.*, emit.

em'met, *n.*, an ant.

emolles'cence, *n.*, the act or process of softening.

emol'liate, *v.t.*, to soften.

emol'liated, *p.p.*, emolliate.

emol'liating, *pr.p.*, emolliate.

emol'lient, *adj.*, softening in its effect; *n.*, an emollient substance.

emol'ument, *n.*, pay, reward.

emo'tion, *n.*, mental excitement, deep feeling.

emo'tional, *adj.*, rel. to the emotions; excitable.

emo'tionalism, *n.*, a tendency to be emotional.

emo'tive, *adj.*, causing emotion.

empale', *v.t.*, *see* impale.

empaled', *p.p.*, empale.

empale'ment, *n.*, the act of empaling.

empa'ling, *pr.p.*, empale.

empan'el, *v.t.*, *see* impanel.

empan'elled, empan'eled, *p.p.*, empanel.

empan'elling, empan'eling, *pr.p.*, empanel.

empark', *see* impark.

em'peror, *n.*, the ruler of an empire.

em'phasis, *n.*, stress, intensity.

em'phasize, *v.t.*, to lay stress on; call special attention to.

em'phasized, *p.p.*, emphasize.

em'phasizing, *pr.p.*, emphasize.

emphat'ic, *adj.*, laying stress, urgent.

emphat'ical, *adj.*, *i.q.* emphatic.

emphat'ically, *adv.*, with emphasis.

em'pire, *n.*, rule; the rule of an emperor; the territory of an empire; the nations composing an imperial whole.

empir'ic, *adj.*, rel. to experience; based on experience or mere observation.

empir'ical, *adj.*, *i.q.* empiric.

empir'icism, *n.*, the empirical method and characteristics.

empir'icist, *n.*, one who professes empiricism.

emplas'tic, *adj.*, adhesive; *n.*, a glutinous adhesive substance.

employ', *v.t.*, to engage in labour; *n.*, the state of being employed.

employed', *p.p.*, employ.

employé, *n.*, a male person employed.

employée, *n.*, a female employed.

employee', *n.*, one of either sex employed.

employ'er, *n.*, one who engages employees.

employ'ing, *pr.p.*, employ.

employ'ment, *n.*, the state of being employed; the act of employing; an occupation.

empoi'son, *v.t.*, to poison, envenom.

empo'rium, *n.*, a large store.

empow'er, *v.t.*, to authorize, entrust with power.

empow'ered, *p.p.*, empower.

empow'ering, *pr.p.*, empower.

em'press, *n.*, the fem. of emperor.

emp'tied, *p.p.*, empty.

emp'tier, *n.*, anything that empties; *adj.*, *comp.* of empty.

emp'tiest, *adj.*, *super.* of empty.

emp'tiness, *n.*, the state of being empty.

emp'ty, *adj.*, containing nothing; unsubstantial; unintelligent; vain.

emp'tying, *pr.p.*, empty.

emp'tyings, *n. pl.*, lees.

empur'ple, *v.t.*, to stain with purple.

empur'pled, *p.p.*, empurple.

empur'pling, *pr.p.*, empurple.

empye'ma, *n.*, suppuration.

empyr'eal, *adj.* and *n.*, *i.q.* empyrean.

empyre'an, *adj.*, pert. to the highest heaven; *n.*, the highest heaven.

empyreu'ma, *n.*, the smell of burning organic matter.

empyreumat'ic, *adj.*, rel. to empyreuma.

empyreumat'ical, *adj.*, *i.q.* empyreumatic.

e'mu, *n.*, the Australian ostrich.

em'ulate, *v.t.*, to vie with, to rival.

em'ulated, *p.p.*, emulate.

em'ulating, *pr.p.*, emulate.

emula'tion, *n.*, the act of emulating; rivalry.

em'ulative, *adj.*, inclined to emulating.

em'ulator, *n.*, one who emulates.

emul'gent, *adj.*, straining out.

em'ulous, *adj.*, trying to surpass or equal.

em'ulousness, *n.*, the state or quality of being emulous.

emul'sion, *n.*, a liquid composed of oil and water.

emul'sive, *adj.*, producing emulsion.

emunc'tory, *adj.*, excretory.

ena'ble, *v.t.*, to give power to; make able.

ena'bled, *p.p.*, enable.

ena'bling, *pr.p.*, enable.

enact', *v.t.*, to give Parliamentary sanction to; to perform.

enact'ed, *p.p.*, enact.

enact'ing, *pr.p.*, enact.

enact'ive, *adj.*, enacting.

enact'ment, *n.*, the act or result of enacting; a statute.

enact'or, *n.*, one who enacts.

enam'el, *v.t.*, to cover with enamel; *n.*, a smooth glossy material for laying over surfaces; the hard coating of teeth.

enam'elled, enam'eled, *p.p.*, enamel.

enam'elling, enam'eling, *pr.p.*, enamel; *n.*, a covering with enamel.

enam'eller, enam'eler, *n.*, one who enamels.

enam'our, enam'or, *v.t.*, to captivate, inspire with passion.

enam'oured, *p.p.*, enamour.

enam'ouring, *pr.p.*, enamour.

enarmed', *adj.*, armed.

enarthro'sis, *n.*, a ball-and-socket joint formation.

e'nate, *n.*, a relative on the maternal side.

encae'nia, ence'nia, *n. pl.*, a dedication festival. At Oxford, the encaenia are the yearly commemoration of founders and benefactors.

encage', *v.t.*, to confine in a cage.

encaged', *p.p.*, encage.

encag'ing, *pr.p.*, encage.

encamp', *v.t.*, to place in a camp; *v.i.*, to pitch a camp.

encamped', *p.p.*, encamp.

encamp'ing, *pr.p.*, encamp.

encamp'ment, *n.*, the act or place of encamping.

encan'this, *n.*, a tumour in the eye.

encar'pus, *n.*, a festoon of fruit and flowers.

encase', *v.t.*, to put into a case.

encased', *p.p.*, encase.

enca'sing, *pr.p.*, encase.

encaus'tic, *adj.*, burnt in; *n.*, encaustic work.

encave', *v.t.*, to shut into a cave.

enceinte', *adj.*, pregnant; *n.*, a surrounding wall, an enclosure.

encephal'ic, *adj.*, rel. to the encephalos.

enceph'alon, *n.*, the brain (*Gr.*).

enceph'alos, *n.*, *i.q.* encephalon.

enchain', *v.t.*, to bind with a chain.

enchained', *p.p.*, enchain.

enchain'ing, *pr.p.*, enchain.

enchant', *v.t.*, to cast a spell on; to charm, delight.

enchant'ed, *p.p.*, enchant.

enchant'er, *n.*, one who enchants.

enchant'ing, *pr.p.*, enchant; *adj.*, charming, delightful.

enchant'ingly, *adv.*, charmingly.

enchant'ment, *n.*, the act of enchanting; the state of being enchanted.

enchant'ress, *n.*, fem. of enchanter.

enchase', *v.t.*, to enclose in a border; to set in ornamental work; to ornament with embossed work; to chase.

enchased', *p.p.*, enchase.

encha'sing, *pr.p.*, enchase.

enchirid'ion, *n.*, a small handbook.

encho'rial, *adj.*, bel. to a country, indigenous.

encir'cle, *v.t.*, to surround.

encir'cled, *p.p.*, encircle.

encir'cling, *pr.p.*, encircle.

enclasp', *v.t.*, to embrace.

enclave', *n.*, a piece of territory in a foreign country.

enclit'ic, *adj.*, unaccented and attached to the final syllable of a preceding word; *n.*, a particle so attached.

enclit'ical, *adj.*, *i.q.* enclitic.

enclose', *v.t.*, to shut in, confine, frame. Also *inclose*.

enclosed', *p.p.*, enclose.

enclo'sing, *pr.p.*, enclose.

enclo'sure, *n.*, the act of enclosing; a space enclosed.

enco'miast, *n.*, one who pronounces an encomium.

encomias'tic, *adj.*, laudatory.

encomias'tical, *adj.*, *i.q.* encomiastic.

enco'mium, *n.*, an eulogy, praise.

encom'pass, *v.t.*, to encircle, surround.

encom'passed, *p.p.*, encompass.

encom'passing, *pr.p.*, encompass.

encore', *adv.*, again; *v.t.*, to demand a repetition of; *n.*, a call for a repetition.

encored', *p.p.*, encore.

encor'ing, *pr.p.*, encore.

encoun'ter, *v.t.*, to meet, engage with, experience.

encoun'tered, *p.p.*, encounter.

encoun'tering, *pr.p.*, encounter.

encour'age, *v.t.*, to cheer, hearten, incite.

encour'aged, *p.p.*, encourage.

encour'agement, *n.*, the act of encouraging, the state of being encouraged.

encour'ager, *n.*, one who encourages.

encour'aging, *pr.p.*, encourage; *adj.*, promising success, favourable.

encour'agingly, *adv.*, in an encouraging way.

encroach', *v.i.*, to trespass, invade.

encroached', *p.p.*, encroach.

encroach'er, *n.*, one who encroaches.

encroach'ing, *pr.p.*, encroach.

encroach'ment, *n.*, the act or result of encroaching.

encrust', *v.t.*, *see* incrust.

encum'ber, *v.t.*, to burden, hamper.

encum'bered, *p.p.*, encumber.

encum'bering, *pr.p.*, encumber.

encum'brance, *n.*, a hindrance.

encyc'lical, *adj.*, put into general circulation; *n.*, a letter from the Holy See to the Roman Catholic world.

encyclopae'dia, encyclope'dia, *n.*, a dictionary of general information.

encyclopae'dian, encyclope'dian, *adj.*, rel. to an encyclopaedia.

encyclopae'dic, encyclope'dic, *adj.*, *i.q.* encyclopaedian.

encyclopae'dist, encyclope'dist, *n.*, one who compiles an encyclopaedia; a man of universal knowledge.

encyst', *v.t.*, to surround with a cyst; *v.i.*, to be surrounded with a cyst.

encyst'ed, *p.p.*, encyst.

encyst'ing, *pr.p.*, encyst.

end, *v.t.*, to bring to an end, to terminate; *v.i.*, to come to an end; *n.*, the finish of anything, termination; object in view.

endan'ger, *v.t.*, to involve in danger.

endan'gered, *p.p.*, endanger.

endan'gering, *pr.p.*, endanger.

endear', *v.t.*, to make dear.

endeared', *p.p.*, endear.

endear'ing, *pr.p.*, endear; *adj.*, making dear.

endear'ment, *n.*, the act of endearing; affection.

endeav'our, endeav'or, *v.t.*, to try, attempt; *n.*, an attempt.

endeav'oured, endeav'ored, *p.p.*, endeavour.

endeav'ouring, endeav'oring, *pr.p.*, endeavour.

end'ed, *p.p.*, end.

endem'ic, *adj.*, peculiar to a people or

country; *n.*, a disease constantly prevailing in a locality.

endem'ical, *adj.*, *i.q.* endemic.

ender'mic, *adj.*, through the skin.

end'ing, *pr.p.*, end.

en'dive, *n.*, a garden herb, used in salads.

end'less, *adj.*, without end.

end'lessly, *adv.*, without end.

end'lessness, *n.*, the state of being endless.

end'long, *adv.*, lengthwise.

en'dogen, *n.*, a plant growing from within.

endog'enous, *adj.*, growing from within.

endorse', *v.t.*, to write one's name on the back of; to confirm, approve. Also *indorse.*

endorsed', *p.p.*, endorse.

endorse'ment, *n.*, the act of endorsing, a signature, a confirmation.

endors'er, *n.*, one who endorses.

endors'ing, *pr.p.*, endorse.

en'dosperm, *n.*, albumen in a seed.

endos'mose, *n.*, passage inward of liquid through the pores of a septum.

endow', *v.t.*, to furnish with a dowry, to give money for an endowment; to enrich.

endowed', *p.p.*, endow.

endow'er, *n.*, one who endows.

endow'ing, *pr.p.*, endow.

endow'ment, *n.*, the act of endowing; money given for the permanent income of a foundation; talent, grace.

Endozo'a, *n.pl.*, parasites.

endue', *v.t.*, to clothe, vest, endow.

endued', *p.p.*, endue.

endu'ing, *pr.p.*, endue.

endur'able, *adj.*, able to be endured.

endur'ance, *n.*, the faculty of enduring.

endure', *v.t.*, to bear, sustain; *v.i.*, to last, continue.

endured', *p.p.*, endure.

endur'ing, *pr.p.*, endure.

end'ways, *adv.*, *i.q.* endwise.

end'wise, *adv.*, with the end first or uppermost.

Ene'id, *see* Aeneid.

en'ema, *n.*, an injection, clyster.

en'emy, *n.*, a foe, an unfriendly person or people.

energet'ic, *adj.*, full of energy, active.

energet'ical, *adj.*, *i.q.* energetic.

en'ergize, *v.t.*, to make active or forceful; *v.i.*, to display energy.

en'ergized, *p.p.*, energize.

en'ergizer, *n.*, anything that energizes.

en'ergizing, *pr.p.*, energize.

en'ergy, *n.*, activity, force.

en'ervate, *v.t.*, to enfeeble; deprive of nerve or strength.

en'ervated, *p.p.*, enervate.

en'ervating, *pr.p.*, enervate.

enerva'tion, *n.*, the act or effect of enervating.

enfee'ble, *v.t.*, to reduce to weakness.

enfee'bled, *p.p.*, enfeeble.

enfee'blement, *n.*, the act or result of enfeebling.

enfee'bling, *pr.p.*, enfeeble.

enfeoff', *v.t.*, to convey (lands), transfer.

enfeoffed', *p.p.*, enfeoff.

enfeoff'ing, *pr.p.*, enfeoff.

enfeoff'ment, *n.*, the act of enfeoffing; the legal instrument of transference.

enfilade', *v.t.*, to rake with shot from the flank; *n.*, a line; gun fire from the flank.

enfila'ded, *p.p.*, enfilade.

enfila'ding, *pr.p.*, enfilade.

enfold', *v.t.*, to wrap up, to clasp.

enfold'ed, *p.p.*, enfold.

enfold'ing, *pr.p.*, enfold.

enforce', *v.t.*, to compel, give force to, put into practice.

enforce'able, *adj.*, able to be enforced.

enforced', *p.p.*, enforce.

enforc'edly, *adv.*, in an enforced way.

enforce'ment, *n.*, the act or result of enforcing.

enforc'er, *n.*, one who enforces.

enforc'ing, *pr.p.*, enforce.

enfran'chise, *v.t.*, to set free; to bestow the vote on.

enfran'chised, *p.p.*, enfranchise.

enfran'chisement, *n.*, the act or result of enfranchising.

enfran'chising, *pr.p.*, enfranchise.

engage', *v.t.*, to bind by promise; to employ; to entangle; *v.i.*, to promise, undertake; busy oneself; to join in a conflict.

engaged', *p.p.*, engage.

engage'ment, *n.*, an undertaking in words; a contract; a battle; a promise.

enga'ging, *p.p.*, engage; *adj.*, pleasing, attractive.

enga'gingly, *adv.*, pleasingly, attractively.

engen'der, *v.t.*, to beget, cause.

engen'dered, *p.p.*, engender.

engen'dering, *pr.p.*, engender.

en'gine, *n.*, a power-producing machine; an instrument or device.

engineer', *v.t.*, to organize, manage, carry through; *n.*, one who makes, repairs, uses, or drives engines; one who practises the art and science of engineering.

engineered', *p.p.*, engineer.

engineer'ing, *pr.p.*, engineer; *n.*, the science and art of construction.

en'ginery, *n.*, engines collectively; the art of working engines.

engird', *v.t.*, to encircle with a belt; surround.

engird'ed, *p.p.*, engird.

engird'ing, *pr.p.*, engird.

engir'dle, *v.t.*, to encircle, put a girdle on.

Eng'lish, *adj.*, rel. to England and the English; *n.*, the English language; English literature.

Eng'lishman, *n.*, a native of England; in a wider sense, a patriotic subject of the Crown of England.

engorge', *v.t.*, to fill up, congest; to consume voraciously.

engorged', *p.p.*, engorge.

engorge'ment, *n.*, the act or result of engorging.

engorg'ing, *pr.p.*, engorge.

engraft', *v.t.*, to graft; to impress upon the mind.

engraft'ed, *p.p.*, engraft.

engraft'ing, *pr.p.*, engraft.

engrail', *v.t.*, to indent.

engrailed', *p.p.*, engrail.

engrail'ing, *pr.p.*, engrail.

engrail'ment, *n.*, the arrangement of dots round a coin.

engrain', *see* ingrain.

engrave', *v.t.*, to cut a design or picture into metal or wood.

engraved', *p.p.*, engrave.

engra'ver, *n.*, one who engraves.

engra'ving, *pr.p.*, engrave; *n.*, a picture produced from an engraved plate.

engross', *v.t.*, to preoccupy, completely occupy; to write in a large, clear hand.

engrossed', *p.p.*, engross.

engross'er, *n.*, one who writes out documents in a large, clear hand.

engross'ing, *pr.p.*, engross; *n.*, the transcript of a document in a large hand; *adj.*, absorbing, enthralling.

engross'ment, *n.*, the act of engrossing; an engrossed document; mental absorption.

engulf', *v.t.*, to overwhelm, completely swallow up.

engulfed', *p.p.*, engulf.

engulf'ing, *pr.p.*, engulf.

enhance', *v.t.*, to increase in value, heighten.

enhanced', *p.p.*, enhance.

enhance'ment, *n.*, the act or result of enhancing.

enhan'cing, *pr.p.*, enhance.

enharmon'ic, *adj.*, with musical intervals smaller than a semitone.

enharmon'ical, *adj.*, *i.q.* enharmonic.

enheart'en, *v.t.*, to cheer up, inspirit.

enig'ma, *n.*, a riddle, word-puzzle.

enigmat'ic, *adj.*, puzzling, obscure.

enigmat'ical, *adj.*, *i.q.* enigmatic.

enig'matist, *n.*, one who makes or solves enigmas.

enig'matize, *v.i.*, to speak in enigmas.

enjoin', *v.t.*, to command, lay a charge upon.

enjoined', *p.p.*, enjoin.

enjoin'ing, *pr.p.*, enjoin.

enjoy', *v.t.*, to take pleasure in; to have possession of.

enjoy'able, *adj.*, delightful, causing enjoyment.

enjoyed', *p.p.*, enjoy.

enjoy'ing, *pr.p.*, enjoy.

enjoy'ment, *n.*, the act or state of enjoying; delight.

enkin'dle, *v.t.*, to set fire to; to rouse.

enkin'dled, *p.p.*, enkindle.

enkin'dling, *pr.p.*, enkindle.

enlarge', *v.t.*, to make larger, increase; to set at liberty; *v.i.*, to expatiate at length; to exaggerate.

enlarged', *p.p.*, enlarge.

enlarge'ment, *n.*, the act of enlarging; being set free.

enlar'ger, *n.*, one who enlarges.

enlar'ging, *pr.p.*, enlarge.

enlight'en, *v.t.*, to illuminate, give light to; throw light on.

enlight'ened, *p.p.*, enlighten.

enlight'ener, *n.*, one who enlightens.

enlight'ening, *pr.p.*, enlighten.

enlight'enment, *n.*, the act or result of enlightening.

enlist', *v.t.*, to put on a list or roll, to recruit; to win to one's side; *v.i.*, to join the colours.

enlist'ed, *p.p.*, enlist.

enlist'ing, *pr.p.*, enlist.

enlist'ment, *n.*, the act of enlisting.

enli'ven, *v.t.*, to put life into, add brightness to.

enli'vened, *p.p.*, enliven.

enli'vener, *n.*, one who enlivens.

enli'vening, *pr.p.*, enliven.

enmesh', *v.t.*, to entangle, snare.

en'mity, *n.*, hostility, unfriendliness.

en'neagon, *n.*, a nine-sided figure.

Ennean'dria, *n. pl.*, one of Linnaeus's grouping of plants. It contains flowers with nine stamens.

enno'ble, *v.t.*, to make noble, either morally or in rank.

enno'bled, *p.p.*, ennoble.

enno'blement, *n.*, the act of ennobling; state of being ennobled.

enno'bling, *pr.p.*, ennoble.

ennui', *n.*, boredom, lassitude.

enor'mity, *n.*, the state of being enormous; a monstrous offence.

enor'mous, *adj.*, excessively large, huge.

enor'mously, *adv.*, to an enormous degree.

enor'mousness, *n.*, the quality of being enormous.

enough', *adj.*, sufficient.

enounce', *v.t.*, to state, declare, enunciate.

enounced', *p.p.*, enounce.

enoun'cing, *pr.p.*, enounce.

enquire', *v.t.*, *see* inquire.

enrage', *v.t.*, to put into a rage, infuriate.

enraged', *p.p.*, enrage.

enra'ging, *pr.p.*, enrage.

enrap'ture, *v.t.*, to thrill with rapture.

enrap'tured, *p.p.*, enrapture.

enrap'turing, *pr.p.*, enrapture.

enrav'ish, *see* ravish.

enrav'ishment, *see* ravishment.

enrich', *v.t.*, to make wealthy; to add worth to; to ornament.

enriched', *p.p.*, enrich.

enrich'er, *n.*, one who enriches.

enrich'ing, *pr.p.*, enrich.

enrich'ment, *n.*, the act or result of enriching; ornamentation.

enrobe', *v.t.*, to deck with a robe.

enrobed', *p.p.*, enrobe.

enrob'ing, *pr.p.*, enrobe.

enrol', **enroll'**, *v.t.*, to place on a roll, enlist.

enrolled', *p.p.*, enrol.

enroll'er, *n.*, one who enrols.

enroll'ing, *pr.p.*, enrol.

enrol'ment, *n.*, the act or result of enroling.

enroot', *v.t.*, to cause to take root.

enroot'ed, *p.p.*, enroot.

enroot'ing, *pr.p.*, enroot.

ens, *n.*, an entity, an existing thing.

ensam'ple, *see* example.

ensan'guine, *v.t.*, to stain with blood.

ensconce', *v.t.*, to hide with safety.

ensconced', *p.p.*, ensconce.

enscone'ing, *pr.p.*, ensconce.

enseal', *v.t.*, to seal up.

ensealed', *p.p.*, enseal.

enseam', *v.t.*, to scar; sew up.

ensem'ble, *n.*, the whole (*Fr.*).

enshield', *v.t.*, to cover with a shield.

enshrine', *v.t.*, to set in a shrine; to cherish with affection.

enshrined', *p.p.*, enshrine.

enshrin'ing, *pr.p.*, enshrine.

enshroud', *v.t.*, to wrap in a shroud, envelop.

enshroud'ed, *p.p.*, enshroud.

enshroud'ing, *pr.p.*, enshroud.

en'siform, *adj.*, sword-shaped.

en'sign, *n.*, a standard, flag; a military officer who bore the flag of his regiment.

en'signcy, *n.*, the rank and office of an ensign.

en'silage, *n.*, storage in a silo.

enslave', *v.t.*, to make a slave of; captivate.

enslaved', *p.p.*, enslave.

ensla'ver, *n.*, one who enslaves.

enslave'ment, *n.*, the act or result of enslaving.

enslav'ing, *pr.p.*, enslave.

ensnare', *v.t.*, to entrap, entangle.

ensnared', *p.p.*, ensnare.

ensnar'er, *n.*, one who ensnares.

ensnar'ing, *pr.p.*, ensnare.

ensphere', *v.t.*, to place within a sphere.

ensphered', *p.p.*, ensphere.

enspher'ing, *pr.p.*, ensphere.

enstamp', *v.t.*, to stamp.

enstamped', *p.p.*, enstamp.

enstamp'ing, *pr.p.*, enstamp.

ensue', *v.t.* and *i.*, to follow.

ensued', *p.p.*, ensue.

ensu'ing, *pr.p.*, ensue.

ensure', *v.t.*, to make sure of, guarantee. Also *insure*.

entab'lature, *n.*, the topmost member (in a classical building) that rests upon the capitals of the pillars.

entail', *v.t.*, to settle in tail; to involve as a consequence; *n.*, settlement of an estate upon a named succession of inheritors.

entailed', *p.p.*, entail.

entail'ing, *pr.p.*, entail.

entail'ment, *n.*, the act or result of entailing.

entan'gle, *v.t.*, to twist together, to involve.

entan'gled, *pr.p.*, entangle.

entan'glement, *n.*, the act or result of entangling; a military obstruction of barbed wire, etc.

entan'gling, *pr.p.*, entangle.
en'tasis, *n.*, a slight convexity in the shaft of a column; a spasm.
entente', *n.*, understanding, agreement (*Fr.*).
en'ter, *v.t.* and *i.*, to come into; to make a record of; to name for a contest.
en'tered, *p.p.*, enter.
en'terer, *n.*, one who enters.
enter'ic, *adj.*, rel. to intestines; *n.*, an enteric inflammation.
enteri'tis, *n.*, inflammation of the small intestine.
en'tering, *pr.p.*, enter.
enterol'ogy, *n.*, the science of the intestines.
en'terprise, *v.t.*, to attempt; *n.*, bold attempt.
en'terprised, *p.p.*, enterprise.
en'terpriser, *n.*, one who is enterprising.
en'terprising, *pr.p.*, enterprise; *adj.*, bold, adventurous.
en'terprisingly, *n.*, in an enterprising way.
entertain', *v.t.*, to receive hospitably; to admit to one's thoughts; to amuse.
entertained', *p.p.*, entertain.
entertain'er, *n.*, one who entertains.
entertain'ing, *pr.p.*, entertain; *adj.*, amusing.
entertain'ment, *n.*, the act or result of entertaining.
enthral', *v.t.*, to captivate, charm.
enthralled', *p.p.*, enthral.
enthrall'ing, *pr.p.*, enthral.
enthrone', *v.t.*, to place on a throne.
enthroned', *p.p.*, enthrone.
enthrone'ment, *n.*, the act or result of enthroning.
enthro'ning, *pr.p.*, enthrone.
enthroniza'tion, *n.*, the ceremony of enthroning.
enthu'siasm, *n.*, a state or feeling of intense zeal or gratification.
enthu'siast, *n.*, one who shows himself enthusiastic.
enthusias'tic, *adj.*, full of enthusiasm; very zealous.
enthusias'tical, *adj.*, *i.q.* enthusiastic.
enthusias'tically, *adv.*, with enthusiasm.
entice', *v.t.*, to allure, draw on.
enticed', *p.p.*, entice.
entice'ment, *n.*, the act of enticing; a snare.
enti'cer, *n.*, one who entices.
enti'cing, *pr.p.*, entice; *adj.*, attractive.
enti'cingly, *adv.*, attractively, alluringly.
entire', *adj.*, whole, complete.
entire'ly, *adv.*, wholly, completely.
entire'ness, *n.*, the quality of being entire.
entire'ty, *n.*, completeness.
enti'tle, *v.t.*, to give a title or right to; to name.
enti'tled, *p.p.*, entitle.
enti'tling, *pr.p.*, entitle.
en'tity, *n.*, any individual existing thing; existence, essence.
entomb', *v.t.*, to place in a tomb.
entombed', *p.p.*, entomb.
entomb'ing, *pr.p.*, entomb.
entomb'ment, *n.*, the act or result of entombing.
entom'ic, *adj.*, rel. to insects.
entom'ical, *adj.*, *i.q.* entomic.
en'tomoid, *adj.*, insect-like.
entomolog'ical, *adj.*, rel. to entomology.
entomol'ogist, *n.*, one who studies entomology.
entomol'ogy, *n.*, the branch of natural history that relates to insects.
entomoph'agous, *adj.*, eating insects.
enton'ic, *adj.*, at high tension.
entourage', *n.*, surroundings, followers.
Entozo'a, *n. pl.*, internal parasites.
entozo'on, *n.*, sing. of entozoa.
en'tr'acte, *n.*, the interval between the acts; the music played in that interval.
en'trails, *n. pl.*, intestines, bowels.
entrain', *v.t.*, to put into a train; *v.i.*, to board a train.
entrained', *p.p.*, entrain.
entrain'ing, *pr.p.*, entrain.
entram'mel, *see* trammel.
entram'melled, **entram'meled**, *p.p.*, entrammel.
entram'melling, **entram'meling**, *pr.p.*, entrammel.
entrance', *v.t.*, to throw into a trance, charm.
en'trance, *n.*, the act of entering, admission, an opening into.
entranced', *p.p.*, entrance.
entranc'ing, *pr.p.*, entrance; *adj.*, charming.
en'trant, *adj.*, entering; *n.*, a novice.
entrap', *v.t.*, to catch in a trap.
entrapped', *p.p.*, entrap.
entrap'ping, *pr.p.*, entrap.
entreat', *v.t.*, to implore, beseech.
entreat'ed, *p.p.*, entreat.
entreat'er, *n.*, one who entreats.
entreat'ing, *pr.p.*, entreat.
entreat'ingly, *adv.*, pleadingly, beseechingly.
entreat'y, *n.*, an earnest request, prayer.
entrée', *n.*, entrance, privilege of entering; a made dish.

entremets', *n. pl.*, the viands that follow the *pièce de résistance* at a meal.
entrench', *v.t.*, to dig a trench; fortify with a trench; *v.i.*, to encroach.
entrenched', *p.p.*, entrench.
entrench'ing, *pr.p.*, entrench.
entrench'ment, *n.*, the act or result of entrenching.
en'trepôt, *n.*, a warehouse; a trade-distributing centre.
entrepreneur', *n.*, one who starts industrial schemes.
en'tresol, *n.*, a low storey between two higher ones; a mezzanine.
entrust', *v.t.*, to put into the care of; to charge with.
entrust'ed, *p.p.*, entrust.
entrust'ing, *pr.p.*, entrust.
en'try, *n.*, the act of entering; the place of entering; the act of entering in a ledger, register, etc.
entwine', *v.t.*, to interlace, twine round.
entwined', *p.p.*, entwine.
entwin'ing, *pr.p.*, entwine.
entwist', *v.t.*, to twist.
enu'cleate, *v.t.*, to extract; explain.
enu'cleated, *p.p.*, enucleate.
enu'cleating, *pr.p.*, enucleate.
enuclea'tion, *n.*, the act of enucleating; the extraction of a tumour.
enu'merate, *v.t.*, to reckon, count up, to mention severally.
enu'merated, *p.p.*, enumerate.
enu'merating, *pr.p.*, enumerate.
enumera'tion, *n.*, the act of enumerating; a list.
enu'merative, *adj.*, enumerating.
enu'merator, *n.*, one who enumerates.
enun'ciate, *v.t.*, to utter, declare, pronounce articulately.
enun'ciated, *p.p.*, enunciate.
enun'ciating, *pr.p.*, enunciate.
enuncia'tion, *n.*, the act of enunciating; clear articulation; the formal statement of a proposition.
enun'ciative, *adj.*, declaratory; rel. to enunciation.
enun'ciatory, *adj.*, *i.q.* enunciative.
envel'op, *v.t.*, to wrap round; surround.
en'velope, *n.*, a covering; the cover of a letter.
envel'oped, *p.p.*, envelop.
envel'oping, *pr.p.*, envelop.
envel'opment, *n.*, the act of enveloping; a covering.
enven'om, *v.t.*, to poison; put venom into.
enven'omed, *p.p.*, envenom.
enven'oming, *pr.p.*, envenom.
en'viable, *adj.*, the object of envy.
en'viably, *adv.*, in a way to be envied.
en'vied, *p.p.*, envy.
en'vier, *n.*, one who envies.
en'vious, *adj.*, feeling envy, jealous.
en'viously, *adv.*, with envy, jealously.
envi'ron, *v.t.*, to surround.
envi'roned, *p.p.*, environ.
envi'roning, *pr.p.*, environ.
envi'ronment, *n.*, surroundings; the external circumstances conditioning existence.
envi'rons, *n. pl.*, surrounding neighbourhood, suburbs.
en'voy, *n.*, a special messenger.
en'voyship, *n.*, the office of an envoy.
en'vy, *v.t.*, to be jealous of another's good fortune; *n.*, the feeling of jealousy of another's good position.
en'vying, *pr.p.*, envy.
enwrap', *v.t.*, to wrap closely.
enwreathe', *v.t.*, *i.q.* wreathe.
E'ocene, *adj.*, rel. to the Eocene period.
Eo'lian, *see* Aeolian.
e'on, *see* aeon.
Eozo'ic, *adj.*, pert. to the Eozoic or Upper Archaean rocks.
Eozo'on, *n.*, a foraminiferous fossil.
ep'act, *n.*, the name for the additional days to those of the polar lunar periods.
ep'arch, *n.*, a Greek or Russian ruler of an eparchy; a Russian metropolitan.
ep'archy, *n.*, a province.
epaule'ment, *n.*, a protective parapet.
ep'aulet, *or* -te, *n.*, a shoulder-ornament.
epen'thesis, *n.*, the addition of a syllable or a letter.
épergne', *n.*, a fruit or flower stand.
e'phah, *n.*, a Hebrew measure of capacity.
ephem'era, *n. pl.*, the May-fly; a genus of short-lived insects.
ephem'eral, *adj.*, lasting for a day; short-lived.
ephem'eris, *n.*, a day by day calculation of the motions of the heavenly bodies.
ephem'eron, *n.*, a May-fly.
Ephe'sian, *adj.*, rel. to Ephesus and the Ephesians.
eph'od, *n.*, a linen vestment of the Jewish ceremonial.
eph'or, *n.*, one of the five magistrates of Sparta.
ep'ic, *adj.*, rel. to heroic story; *n.*, a poem on heroic stories.
epican'thus, *n.*, a fold of skin in the corner of the eye.
ep'icarp, *n.*, the outer layer of a pericarp.

ep'icene, *adj.*, common to both sexes.

epicra'nium, *n.*, the covering of the skull.

Epicte'tian, *adj.*, rel. to Epictetus.

ep'icure, *n.*, a person fond of good eating.

Epicure'an, *adj.*, rel. to Epicurus; fond of good things.

Epicure'anism, *n.*, the practices of the Epicureans.

ep'icurism, *n.*, the practices of an epicure.

ep'icycle, *n.*, a circle centred on the circumference of another circle.

epicy'cloid, *n.*, a curve formed by a point in the circumference of a circle rolling on the exterior of another circle.

epidem'ic, *adj.*, spreading among the people, *n.*, an outbreak of disease among the people.

epidem'ical, *adj.*, rel. to epidemics.

epider'mal, *adj.*, rel. to epidermis.

epider'mis, *n.*, the outer skin, the scarf-skin.

epigas'tric, *adj.*, pert. to the abdomen.

epiglot'tic, *adj.*, pert. to the epiglottis.

epiglot'tis, *n.*, the cartilage at the tongue's root, partly closing the larynx.

ep'igram, *n.*, a terse, pithy saying; a short verse composition, satirical, antithetic or complimentary.

epigrammat'ic, *adj.*, rel. to or like an epigram.

epigrammat'ical, *adj.*, *i.q.* epigrammatic.

epigram'matist, *n.*, a writer of epigrams.

ep'igraph, *n.*, an inscription.

ep'ilepsy, *n.*, the "falling sickness," a nervous disorder accompanied by convulsive fits.

epilep'tic, *adj.*, rel. to or suffering from epilepsy; *n.*, one who suffers from epilepsy.

ep'ilogue, *n.*, a speech at the end of a play; the conclusion of a discourse.

Epiph'any, *n.*, the Feast of Our Lord's Manifestation, Jan. 6.

ep'iphyte, *n.*, a parasitical plant.

epis'copacy, *n.*, the principles or system of episcopal rule.

epis'copal, *adj.*, rel. to a bishop.

episcopa'lian, *adj.*, rel. to Episcopacy.

episcopa'lianism, *n.*, the doctrine of episcopal rule.

epis'copate, *n.*, a bishop's incumbency of his office; the collective bishops.

ep'isode, *n.*, a separate story or incident in a book or speech; any incident.

ep'isodial, *adj.*, of the nature of an episode.

ep'isperm, *n.*, a seed's outer covering.

epis'tle, *n.*, a letter.

epis'tolary, *adj.*, of the nature of a letter.

epis'tolize, *v.t.*, to write letters to.

ep'istyle, *n.*, an architrave.

ep'itaph, *n.*, an inscription on a tomb; a composition in honour of a dead person.

epithala'mium, *n.*, a wedding song.

epithe'lium, *n.*, the coating of the internal parts and organs of the body.

ep'ithet, *n.*, a word, usu. an adj., describing some quality of a person or thing.

epithet'ic, *adj.*, of the nature of epithet.

epit'ome, *n.*, an abbreviation, an abstract.

epit'omist, *n.*, one who makes an epitome.

epit'omize, *v.t.*, to reduce to an epitome.

epit'omized, *p.p.*, epitomize.

epit'omizer, *n.*, one who epitomizes.

epit'omizing, *pr.p.*, epitomize.

ep'itrite, *n.*, a metric foot containing one short and three long syllables variously arranged.

epizo'a, *n. pl.*, external parasites.

epizo'an, *adj.*, rel. to epizoa.

epizo'ic, *adj.*, *i.q.* epizoan.

epizoot'ic, *adj.*, spreading among animals.

ep'och, *n.*, a fixed point in time; an era.

ep'ochal, *adj.*, rel. to an epoch.

ep'ode, *n.*, the third number of a lyric ode; a kind of ode in which a long verse is followed by a shorter one.

epod'ic, *adj.*, rel. to an epode.

ep'onym, *n.*, the supposed or actual founder of a city named after him.

epon'ymous, *adj.*, giving a name to.

equabil'ity, *n.*, the quality of being equable.

e'quable, *adj.*, of even temper, calm.

e'quably, *adv.*, in an equable way.

e'qual, *adj.*, the same in size, amount, quality; *v.t.*, to make equal, be equal to.

equal'ity, *n.*, the state of being equal.

equaliza'tion, *n.*, the act or effect of equalizing.

e'qualize, *v.t.*, to make equal.

e'qualized, *p.p.*, equalize.

e'qualizer, *n.*, a device for giving lateral stability to an aeroplane.

e'qualizing, *pr.p.*, equalize.

e'qualled, e'qualed *p.p.*, equal.

e'qualling, e'qualing, *pr.p.*, equal.

e'qually, *adv.*, in the same degree.

equan'gular, *see* equiangular.

equanim'ity, *n.*, evenness of temper; calmness.

equate', *v.t.*, to form an equation with.

equa'ted, *p.p.*, equate.

equa'ting, *pr.p.*, equate.

equa'tion, *n.*, a proposition indicating equality between two quantities.

equa'tor, *n.*, an imaginary line round the earth dividing it into two equal parts.

equato'rial, *adj.*, rel. or bel. to the equator.

eq'uerry, *n.*, a court official under the Master of the Horse.

eques'trian, *adj.*, rel. to horsemanship.

eques'trianism, *n.*, horsemanship.

equian'gular, *adj.*, having equal angles.

equidis'tant, *adj.*, at an equal distance.

equilat'eral, *adj.*, having equal sides.

equili'brate, *v.t.* and *i.*, to balance equally.

equili'brated, *p.p.*, equilibrate.

equili'brating, *pr.p.*, equilibrate.

equilibra'tion, *n.*, the act of balancing: a state of equal balance.

equilib'rious, *adj.*, in equilibrium.

equil'ibrist, *n.*, a balancer, or tightrope walker.

equilib'rity, *n.*, the state of equilibrium.

equilib'rium, *n.*, equal balance, equipoise.

e'quine, *adj.*, pert. to a horse.

equinoc'tial, *adj.*, bel. to the time; the equinox.

e'quinox, *n.*, one of the two periods when day and night are equal.

equip', *v.t.*, to fit out, furnish, arm.

eq'uipage, *n.*, equipments, train of attendants.

equip'ment, *n.*, the state of being equipped; materials for equipping; outfit.

e'quipoise, *n.*, equality of weight; perfect balance.

equipol'lence, *n.*, equality of skill or influence.

equipol'lency, *n.*, *i.q.* equipollence.

equipol'lent, *adj.*, equally skilful or influential.

equipon'derance, *n.*, the state of being equal in weight.

equipon'derant, *adj.*, equal in weight.

equipped', *p.p.*, equip.

equip'ping, *pr.p.*, equip.

equiso'nance, *n.*, the concord of an octave.

equiso'nant, *adj.*, sounding in concord of an octave.

eq'uitable, *adj.*, just, fair.

eq'uitably, *adv.*, justly, fairly.

eq'uitant, *adj.*, on horseback, overlapping.

equita'tion, *n.*, the art of horsemanship.

eq'uites, *n. pl.*, the knights or members of the Roman equestrian order.

eq'uity, *n.*, fairness, impartiality. In the legal sense, it is the correction of what is defective in the broad statements of the law.

equiv'alence, *n.*, the state of being equivalent.

equiv'alency, *n.*, *i.q.* equivalence.

equiv'alent, *adj.*, of equal value to; *n.*, something of equal value.

equiv'ocal, *adj.*, having more than one meaning; questionable.

equiv'ocally, *adv.*, in an equivocal way.

equiv'ocate, *v.i.*, to use intentionally misleading words.

equiv'ocated, *p.p.*, equivocate.

equiv'ocating, *pr.p.*, equivocate.

equivoca'tion, *n.*, the act of equivocating; prevarication.

equiv'ocator, *n.*, one who equivocates.

e'quivoque, *n.*, an ambiguous expression; a pun.

equiv'orous, *adj.*, eating horse-flesh.

e'ra, *n.*, a period of time.

era'diate, *v.t.*, to shed as rays; *v.i.*, to radiate.

eradia'tion, *n.*, the act or effect of radiating.

erad'icable, *adj.*, able to be eradicated.

erad'icate, *v.t.*, to remove by the roots; destroy.

erad'icated, *p.p.*, eradicate.

erad'icating, *pr.p.*, eradicate.

eradica'tion, *n.*, the act or effect of eradicating.

erad'icative, *adj.*, utterly destructive.

era'sable, *adj.*, able to be erased.

erase', *v.t.*, to rub or cross out.

erased', *p.p.*, erase.

erase'ment, *n.*, erasure.

era'ser, *n.*, anything that erases.

era'sing, *pr.p.*, erase.

era'sion, *n.*, the act of erasing, erasure.

Eras'tian, *adj.*, rel. to Erastus and his teaching.

Eras'tianism, *n.*, the tenets of Erastus and his followers.

era'sure, *n.*, the act or effect of erasing; obliteration.

ere, *prep.* and *conj.*, sooner than, before.

Er'ebus, *n.*, an intermediate place of the dead.

erect', *v.t.*, to set upright, to build; *adj.*, upright.

erect'able, *adj.*, able to be erected.

erect'ed, *p.p.*, erect.

erect'ile, *adj.*, with power to erect.

erectil'ity, *n.*, the quality or state of being erectile.

erect'ing, *pr.p.*, erect.

erec'tion, *n.*, the act or result of erecting; a building.

erect'ly, *adv.*, straight upright.

erect'ness, *n.*, the quality of being erect.

erect'or, *n.*, anything that erects.

ere'long, *adv.*, shortly.

er'emite, *n.*, a hermit (*lit.*, dweller in the desert).

eremit'ic, *adj.*, rel. to hermits.

eremit'ical, *adj.*, *i.q.* eremitic.

er'ethism, *n.*, excessive excitability.

erg, *n.*, a unitary measure of energy.

er'go, *adv.*, therefore.

er'got, *n.*, a fungus on rye; a growth on a horse's fetlock.

er'gotism, *n.*, the growth of ergot; the effect of ergot as a medicine.

Eri'ca, *n.*, heath.

eriom'eter, *n.*, a measuring apparatus used in the textile industry.

er'mine, *n.*, a small furry animal; its fur worn by kings, peers and judges; *adj.*, made of ermine; *v.t.*, to invest with the ermine.

er'mined, *p.p.*, ermine.

erode', *v.t.*, to eat away.

ero'ded, *p.p.*, erode.

ero'dent, *adj.*, producing erosion.

ero'ding, *pr.p.*, erode.

ero'sion, *n.*, the act or result of eroding.

ero'sive, *adj.*, eating away, wearing away.

erot'ic, *adj.*, pert. to love; passionate.

erpetol'ogy, *see* herpetology.

err, *v.i.*, to go astray, to do wrong, to make a mistake.

er'rand, *n.*, a journey on someone's business, a commission.

er'rant, *adj.*, roving.

er'rantry, *n.*, a knight errant's service.

erra'ta, *n. pl.*, mistakes.

errat'ic, *adj.*, roving, uncertain, irregular.

errat'ical, *adj.*, *i.q.* erratic.

errat'ically, *adv.*, in an erratic way.

erra'tum, *n.*, sing. of errata.

er'rhine, *adj.*, causing sneezing.

erred, *p.p.*, err.

er'ring, *pr.p.*, err.

erro'neous, *adj.*, in error, mistaken.

erro'neously, *adv.*, incorrectly.

erro'neousness, *n.*, the state or quality of being erroneous.

er'ror, *n.*, a mistake, blunder, false belief.

Erse, *adj.*, rel. to Ireland and the Irish; *n.*, the native speech of Ireland.

erst, *adv.*, formerly, in the beginning.

erst'while, *adj.*, former; *adv.*, formerly.

erubes'cence, *n.*, a reddening, blushing.

erubes'cent, *adj.*, reddening, blushing.

eruct'ate, *v.t.*, to belch forth; *v.i.*, to belch.

eructa'tion, *n.*, the act of belching.

er'udite, *adj.*, learned, cultivated.

er'uditely, *adv.*, in an erudite way.

er'uditeness, *n.*, the state of being erudite.

erudi'tion, *n.*, learning; scholarship.

eru'ginous, *adj.*, rel. to verdigris.

erupt', *v.t.*, to cause to burst forth; *v.i.*, to burst forth.

erupt'ed, *p.p.*, erupt.

erupt'ing, *pr.p.*, erupt.

erup'tion, *n.*, the act or effect of erupting.

erup'tive, *adj.*, causing eruption.

erysip'elas, *n.*, a disease usually in the face or head, attended with inflammation and fever.

erysipel'atous, *adj.*, suffering from erysipelas.

erythe'ma, *n.*, excessive redness; a skin disease attended by redness.

escalade', *v.t.*, to attack by means of ladders; *n.*, an attack by means of ladders.

escala'ded, *p.p.*, escalade.

escala'ding, *pr.p.*, escalade.

es'calator, *n.*, a moving staircase.

escal'lop, *see* scallop.

escal'loped, *adj.*, charged with scallops (*Her.*).

escapade', *n.*, a frolic, flight.

escape', *v.t.*, to get clear from, avoid; *v.i.*, to get away safely; *n.*, flight, deliverance.

escaped', *p.p.*, escape.

escape'ment, *n.*, a part of the works of a time-piece controlling the revolutions of a cogged wheel that is actuated by the pendulum.

escap'ing, *p.p.*, escape.

escarp', *v.t.*, to form a steep slope; *n.*, the side of a ditch nearest to the rampart.

escarped', *p.p.*, escarp.

escarp'ing, *pr.p.*, escarp.

escarp'ment, *n.*, a steep side of a rock, hill, or rampart.

eschalot', *see* shallot.

es'char, *n.*, a slough.

eschatol'ogy, *n.*, the department of theology that deals with the last things, death, judgment, etc.

escheat', *v.t.*, to take over forfeited property; *v.i.*, to revert by forfeiture or failure of heirs; *n.*, the reversion by forfeiture or failure of heirs.

escheat'able, *adj.*, liable to escheat.

escheat'ed, *p.p*, escheat.

escheat'ing, *pr.p.*, escheat.

escheat'or, *n.*, an official who superintends escheating.

eschew', *v.t.*, to avoid.

eschewed', *p.p.*, eschew.

eschew'ing, *pr.p.*, eschew.

Esco'rial, *n.*, the royal palace near Madrid. Also written *Escurial*.

es'cort, *n.*, a guard of armed men, protection; a guide, attendant.

escort', *v.t.*, to accompany for protection.

escort'ed, *p.p.*, escort.

escort'ing, *pr.p.*, escort.

escritoire', *n.*, a writing-desk. Also written *écritoire*.

Escula'pian, *adj.*, rel. to Aesculapius; medical. Also written *Aesculapian*.

es'culent, *adj.*, eatable, fit for food; *n.*, anything eatable.

escutch'eon, *n.*, an heraldic shield; a plate round a keyhole.

escutch'eoned, *adj.*, furnished with an escutcheon.

Es'kimo, *see* Esquimau.

esoph'agus, *n.*, the gullet, conveying food and drink into the stomach (properly written *oesophagus*).

esoter'ic, *adj.*, inner, secret, mysterious; *n.*, a person initiated in esoteric principles.

espal'ier, *n.*, a trellis on which trees are trained; *n.*, a tree so trained.

espar'to, *n.*, a strong variety of grass.

espe'cial, *adj.*, special, particular, preeminent.

espe'cially, *adv.*, pre-eminently, particularly.

Esperan'to, *n.*, an invented universal language.

espi'al, *n.*, the act of spying, or keeping secret watch.

espied', *p.p.*, espy.

es'pionage, *n.*, the practice of a spy.

esplanade', *n.*, an open space for promenading; the level space between a citadel and a town.

espou'sal, *adj.*, rel. to a betrothal or marriage; *n.*, the act of espousing, betrothal.

espouse', *v.t.*, to take as a spouse, to betroth; to adopt a cause.

espoused', *p.p.*, espouse.

espous'er, *n.*, one who espouses.

espous'ing, *pr.p.*, espouse.

espy', *v.t.*, to catch sight of.

espy'ing, *pr.p.*, espy.

Es'quimau, *adj.*, the name of an indigenous people in Arctic regions; *n.*, one of the race.

esquire', *n.*, a shield-bearer, of the rank next below a knight; a gentleman entitled to arms.

essay', *v.t.*, to attempt.

es'say, *n.*, an endeavour; a short dissertation.

essayed', *p.p.*, essay.

essay'er, *n.*, one who essays.

essay'ing, *pr.p.*, essay.

es'sayist, *n.*, a writer of essays.

es'sence, *v.t.*, to perfume; *n.*, the true distinctive quality of anything; being in the abstract; a perfume.

es'senced, *p.p.*, essence.

es'sencing, *pr.p.*, essence.

Essene', *n.*, a member of a Jewish ascetic party.

essen'tial, *adj.*, rel. to the essence; necessary; *n.*, something necessary.

essential'ity, *n.*, the quality of being essential.

essen'tially, *n.*, necessarily.

estab'lish, *v.t.*, to settle, make firm or stable; to institute; to ratify; to prove.

estab'lished, *p.p.*, establish.

estab'lisher, *n.*, anything that establishes.

estab'lishing, *pr.p.*, establish.

estab'lishment, *n.*, the act of establishing; that which is established; an institution; a business or household.

estafette', *n.*, a courier.

estate', *n.*, condition, state, property.

esteem', *v.t.*, to value, prize; *n.*, favourable opinion, respect.

esteem'able, *adj.*, *i.q.* estimable.

esteemed', *p.p.*, esteem.

esteem'ing, *pr.p.*, esteem.

esthet'ic, *adj.*, *i.q.* aesthetic.

es'timable, *adj.*, worthy of esteem or respect.

es'timate, *v.t.*, to judge the value, height, weight, etc., of.

es'timate, *n.*, a valuation.

es'timated, *p.p.*, estimate.

es'timating, *pr.p.*, estimate.

estima'tion, *n.*, the act or result of estimating; esteem.

es'timator, *n.*, one who makes an estimate.

est'ival, *adj.*, rel. to summer. Also written *aestival*.

estiva'tion, *n.*, the act of spending the summer; dormancy in summer.

estop', *v.t.*, to bar, prevent, dam.

estopped', *p.p.*, estop.

estop'pel, *n.*, tow; prohibition.

estop'ping, *pr.p.*, estop.

esto'vers, *n. pl.*, necessaries allowed as such by law.

estrade′, *n.*, a low platform.
estrange′, *v.t.*, to make strange, alienate.
estranged′, *p.p.*, estrange.
estrange′ment, *n.*, the act of estranging; the state of being estranged.
estran′ging, *pr.p.*, estrange.
estrapade′, *n.*, a horse's kicking.
estray′, *n.*, an unclaimed horse or ox.
estreat′, *v.t.*, to levy a fine under an estreat; *n.*, a correct copy of the record under which a fine is levied.
estreat′ed, *p.p.*, estreat.
estreat′ing, *pr.p.*, estreat.
estrepe′ment, *n.*, waste committed on another man's lands, as by a tenant on his landlord's property.
es′tuary, *n.*, the wide, tidal mouth of a river.
es′tuate, *v.i.*, to boil up.
estua′tion, *n.*, the act of boiling up.
et cet′era, phrase = and the rest (*Lat.*).
etch, *v.t.*, to engrave with the use of a corrosive acid; to scratch lines with a sharp, needle-like instrument.
etched, *p.p.*, etch.
etch′er, *n.*, one who etches.
etch′ing, *pr.p.*, etch; *n.*, the process of etching; a printed impression.
eter′nal, *adj.*, without beginning or end; everlasting.
eter′nally, *adv.*, without end.
eter′nity, *n.*, infinite being or existence.
eter′nize, *v.t.*, to make perpetual.
eter′nized, *p.p.*, eternize.
eter′nizing, *pr.p.*, eternize.
ete′sian, *adj.*, annual.
eth′al, *n.*, cetyl alcohol.

e′ther, *n.*, the clear sky; the impalpable, invisible medium that fills all space; a mobile, colourless fluid.
ethe′real, *adj.*, rel. to the sky, light, airy.
ethe′realize, *v.t.*, to make ethereal.
ethe′realized, *p.p.*, etherealize.
ethe′realizing, *pr.p.*, etherealize.
e′theriform, *adj.*, of like nature with ether.
e′therism, *n.*, the effect of inhaling ether.
etheriza′tion, *n.*, the act or result of etherizing.
e′therize, *v.t.*, to bring under the influence of ether.
e′therized, *p.p.*, etherize.
e′therizing, *pr.p.*, etherize.
eth′ic, *adj.*, *i.q.* ethical.
eth′ical, *adj.*, moral.
eth′ically, *adv.*, morally.
eth′ics, *n.*, the science of morals and duties.
E′thiop, *n.*, an Ethiopian.
Ethio′pian, *adj.*, rel. to Ethiopia and the Ethiopians.
Ethiop′ic, *adj.*, *i.q.* Ethiopian.
eth′moid, *adj.*, sieve-like.
ethmoi′dal, *adj.*, *i.q.* ethmoid.
eth′narch, *n.*, a national ruler; a viceroy.
eth′nic, *adj.*, rel. to race.
eth′nical, *adj.*, *i.q.* ethnic.
ethnog′rapher, *n.*, one who describes races and peoples.
ethnograph′ic, *adj.*, rel. to ethnography.
ethnograph′ical, *adj.*, *i.q.* ethnographic.
ethnog′raphy, *n.*, description of races and peoples.
ethnolog′ic, *adj.*, rel. to ethnology.
ethnolog′ical, *adj.*, *i.q.* ethnologic.

ethnol′ogist, *n.*, one who studies ethnology.
ethnol′ogy, *n.*, the science rel. to races and peoples.
etholog′ic, *adj.*, rel. to ethology.
etholog′ical, *adj.*, *i.q.* ethologic.
ethol′ogist, *n.*, one who studies ethology.
ethol′ogy, *n.*, the science of human character.
e′tiolate, *v.t.*, to blanch; make sickly-looking; *v.i.*, to become pale.
etiol′ogy, *n.*, the science of causes.
et′iquette, *n.*, society formalities and rules.
Etne′an, *adj.*, pert. to Etna. Also written *Aetnean*.
Eto′nian, *adj.*, pert. to Eton; *n.*, a past or present Eton schoolboy.
Etrus′can, *adj.*, pert. to Etruria and the Etruscans.
etui′, *n.*, a lady's case for carrying small useful articles.
etymolog′ic, *adj.*, rel. to etymology.
etymolog′ical, *adj.*, *i.q.* etymologic.
etymolog′ically, *adv.*, according to etymology.
etymol′ogist, *n.*, a student of etymology.
etymol′ogy, *n.*, the science of word-growth and word-formation.
et′ymon, *n.*, the root form of a word.
eucalyp′tus, *n.*, the gum-tree of Australia.
eucalyp′tol, *n.*, a liquid found in eucalyptus oil.
Eu′charist, *n.*, the Mass or the Supper of the Lord; the Blessed Sacrament.
eucharis′tic, *adj.*, bel. to the Eucharist.
eucharis′tical, *adj.*, *i.q.* eucharistic.
eu′chre, *n.*, a card-game so named.

Euclid, *n.*, the Alexandrian geometer. the treatise which he wrote on geometry.

Euclid'ian, *adj.*, rel. to Euclid.

eu'crasy, *n.*, sound health.

eudiom'eter, *n.*, a vessel employed in the volumetric analysis of gases.

eudiomet'ric, *adj.*, rel. to eudiometry.

eudiom'etry, *n.*, the use of the eudiometer.

eugen'ic, *adj.*, rel. to eugenics.

Eugen'ics, *n.*, the theorizing about the physical improvement of the human race.

eu'logist, *n.*, one who pronounces a eulogy.

eulogis'tic, *adj.*, laudatory.

eulo'gium, *n.*, a laudation.

eu'logize, *v.t.*, to praise highly.

eu'logized, *p.p.*, eulogize.

eu'logizing, *pr.p.*, eulogize.

eu'logy, *n.*, a laudation.

eu'nomy, *n.*, law and order; a well-ordered constitution.

eu'nuch, *n.*, the guardian of a harem.

eupep'sia, *n.*, good digestion.

eupep'sy, *n.*, *i.q.* eupepsia.

eupep'tic, *adj.*, promoting a good digestion.

eu'phemism, *n.*, the use of an agreeable instead of an offensive expression.

eu'phemist, *n.*, one who uses euphemism.

euphemist'ic, *adj.*, of the nature of euphemism.

eu'phemize, *v.t.*, to describe euphemistically; *v.i.*, to speak euphemistically.

euphon'ic, *adj.*, sounding pleasantly.

eupho'nious, *adj.*, *i.q.* euphonic.

eu'phonism, *n.*, a concord of sweet sounds.

eu'phony, *n.*, pleasant sound; avoidance of harsh - sounding words in written or spoken words.

eu'phrasy, *n.*, eyebright.

eu'phuism, *n.*, affected speech (in the manner of Lyly's *Euphues*).

eu'phuist, *n.*, one who speaks affectedly.

euphuis'tic, *adj.*, rel. to, or marked by, Euphuism.

Eura'sian, *adj.*, rel. to Eurasia; (*i.e.*, Europe and Asia combined); half-caste.

eure'ka, *n.*, a Greek word = "I have found," the exclamation of Archimedes on making a scientific discovery.

eurhyth'my, *n.*, harmony, proportion.

euri'pus, *n.*, any arm of the sea like the original Euripus in Greece.

Euroc'lydon, *n.*, the N.E. wind.

Europe'an, *adj.*, rel. or bel. to Europe.

Eusta'chian, *adj.*, rel. to the Italian 16th cent. anatomist, Eustachio.

eu'style, *adj.*, *lit.* having good pillars—a term used with reference to intercolumniation.

eutec'tic, *adj.*, fusing at a low temperature.

Euter'pean, *adj.*, rel. to music.

euthana'sia, *n.*, an easy death.

euthan'asy, *n.*, *i.q.* euthanasia.

evac'uant, *adj.*, purgative; *n.*, a purging medicine; the safety-valve in organ bellows.

evac'uate, *v.t.*, to void, excrete; withdraw from.

evac'uated, *p.p.*, evacuate.

evac'uating, *pr.p.*, evacuate.

evacua'tion, *n.*, the act of evacuating.

evac'uative, *adj.*, causing evacuation.

evac'uator, *n.*, that which evacuates.

evade', *v.t.*, to get out of the way of; elude.

eva'ded, *p.p.*, evade.

eva'der, *n.*, one who evades.

eva'ding, *pr.p.*, evade.

evanes'cence, *n.*, a vanishing, passing away.

evanes'cent, *adj.*, vanishing, passing away.

evan'gel, *n.*, good tidings, the Gospel.

evangel'ic, *adj.*, rel. to the Gospel.

evangel'ical, *adj.*, *i.q.* evangelic. The word is appropriated by certain groups of Christians claiming to be the true professors of Gospel teaching.

evan'gelism, *n.*, the propagation of the Gospel.

evan'gelist, *n.*, a preacher of the Gospel, esp. applied to the writers of the four Gospels.

evangeliza'tion, *n.*, the act or process of evangelizing.

evan'gelize, *v.t.*, to instruct in the Gospel.

evan'gelized, *p.p.*, evangelize.

evan'gelizing, *pr.p.*, evangelize.

evan'ish, *v.i.*, to vanish.

evap'orable, *adj.*, able to be evaporated.

evap'orate, *v.t.*, to vaporize; *v.i.*, to become vapour and pass away.

evap'orated, *p.p.*, evaporate.

evap'orating, *pr.p.*, evaporate.

evapora'tion, *n.*, the process of evaporating.

evap'orative, *adj.*, causing evaporation.

eva'sible, *adj.*, able to be evaded.

eva'sion, *n.*, the act of evading, a sophistical excuse.

eva'sive, *adj.*, shifty, not straightforward.
eva'sively, *adv.*, shiftily.
eva'siveness, *n.*, the act or quality of evading.
eve, *n.*, evening; the day preceding a feast; the time immediately preceding an event.
evec'tion, *n.*, an inequality in the moon's motion.
e'ven, *v.t.*, to level, make equal; *v.i.*, to be even; *adj.*, equal, not odd, level, uniform; *adv.*, quite; to the same degree; *n.*, evening.
e'vened, *p.p.*, even.
e'vening, *pr.p.*, even.
eve'ning, *n.*, the end of day and beginning of night.
e'venly, *adv.*, equally, levelly, smoothly.
e'venness, *n.*, the state or quality of being even.
e'vensong, *n.*, the evening office of the English Church; vespers.
event', *n.*, something that happened; incident; issue or result; an item in a programme.
event'ful, *adj.*, full of incident, momentous.
event'fulness, *n.*, the state or quality of being eventful.
e'ventide, *n.*, the evening.
even'tual, *adj.*, following as a consequence.
even'tually, *adv.*, ultimately.
eventual'ity, *n.*, contingency, event, occurrence.
even'tuate, *v.i.*, to have an issue.
ev'er, *adv.*, at any time, at all times.
ev'ergreen, *adj.*, always green; *n.*, a tree always in leaf.
everlast'ing, *adj.*, always lasting.
everlast'ingly, *adv.*, without end.
ever-liv'ing, *adj.*, living for ever.
evermore', *adv.*, unendingly.
ever'sion, *n.*, a turning backward or inside out.
evert', *v.t.*, to turn inside out.
ev'ery, *adj.*, each one of all; very special.
ev'erybody, *n.*, each person, the whole world.
ev'eryday, *adj.*, suitable for each day.
ev'erything, *n.*, each one of all things.
everywhere, *adv.*, in every place.
evict', *v.t.*, to dispossess, expel.
evict'ed, *p.p.*, evict.
evict'ing, *pr.p.*, evict.
evic'tion, *n.*, the act or result of evicting; ejectment.
ev'idence, *v.t.*, to prove, show clearly; *n.*, testimony, a clear sign.
ev'idenced, *p.p.*, evidence.
ev'idencing, *pr.p.*, evidence.
ev'ident, *adj.*, clear, manifest.
eviden'tial, *adj.*, rel. to evidence; furnishing evidence.
ev'idently, *adv.*, manifestly, clearly.
e'vil, *adj.*, bad, wicked; *n.*, badness, wickedness; affliction, harm.
e'vil-doer, *n.*, one who commits evil deeds.
e'vil-eyed, *adj.*, possessing the evil eye.
evince', *v.t.*, to prove clearly; show plainly.
evinced', *p.p.*, evince.
evin'cible, *adj.*, capable of proof.
evinc'ing, *pr.p.*, evince.
evin'cive, *adj.*, capable of evincing or proving.
evis'cerate, *v.t.*, to take the entrails out of; disembowel.
evis'cerated, *p.p.*, eviscerate.
evis'cerating, *pr.p.*, eviscerate.
eviscera'tion, *n.*, the act or process of eviscerating.
ev'itable, *adj.*, avoidable.
evoke', *v.t.*, to call forth.
evoked', *p.p.*, evoke.
evo'king, *pr.p.*, evoke.
ev'olute, *n.*, a form of curve.
evolu'tion, *n.*, the act or result of evolving; development; ordered movement.
evolu'tionary, *adj.*, rel. to evolution.
evolu'tionist, *adj.*, rel. to evolution; *n.*, one who holds the doctrine of evolution, or who is skilled in the ordering of ships, soldiers, etc.
evolve', *v.t.*, to unroll, unfold, develop; throw off; *v.i.*, to open, develop.
evolved', *p.p.*, evolve.
evolve'ment, *n.*, *i.q.* evolution.
evolv'ing, *pr.p.*, evolve.
evul'sion, *n.*, plucking out; forcible extraction.
ewe, *n.*, a female sheep.
ew'er, *n.*, a large jug, pitcher.
ew'ery, *n.*, the room where ewers and napkins are kept.
ew'ry, *n.*, *i.q.* ewery.
exac'erbate, *v.t.*, to embitter, irritate.
exac'erbated, *p.p.*, exacerbate.
exac'erbating, *pr.p.*, exacerbate.
exacerba'tion, *n.*, the act of exacerbating; the exacerbated state.
exact', *v.t.*, to require, enforce, impose; *adj.*, precise, accurate.
exact'ed, *p.p.*, exact.
exact'er, *n.*, one who exacts.
exact'ing, *pr.p.*, exact; *adj.*, unreasonable in one's demands; laborious.
exac'tion, *n.*, the act of exacting; that which is unreasonably demanded.

exact'itude, *n.*, the state or quality of being exact.

exact'ly, *adv.*, precisely, accurately.

exact'ness, *n.*, *i.q.* exactitude.

exact'or, *n.*, one who exacts.

exag'gerate, *v.t.*, to make more of anything than it really is; to make a false representation.

exag'gerated, *p.p.*, exaggerate.

exag'gerating, *pr.p.*, exaggerate.

exaggera'tion, *n.*, the act of exaggerating; a false statement.

exalt', *v.t.*, to elevate, raise.

exalta'tion, *n.*, the act of exalting; the state of being exalted.

exalt'ed, *p.p.*, exalt.

exalt'edness, *n.*, the state of being exalted.

exalt'ing, *pr.p.*, exalt.

exam'inable, *adj.*, able to be examined.

examina'tion, *n.*, the act of examining.

exam'ine, *v.t.*, to look into carefully, to survey, test.

exam'ined, *pr.p.*, examine.

examinee', *n.*, one who is examined.

exam'iner, *n.*, one who examines.

exam'ining, *pr.p.*, examine.

exam'ple, *v.t.*, to illustrate with instances; *n.*, a sample, pattern, model of conduct, instance.

exanthe'ma, *n.*, a rash, eruption.

exanthem'atous, *adj.*, subject to exanthema.

exanthe'sis, *n.*, *i.q.* exanthema.

ex'arch, *n.*, a Byzantine provincial ruler; the ecclesiastical title in the East for a prelate next in rank below a patriarch.

ex'archate, *n.*, the office, or term or sphere of office, of an exarch.

exas'perate, *v.t.*, to ruffle the temper, provoke.

exas'perated, *p.p.*, exasperate.

exas'perating, *pr.p.*, exasperate; *adj.*, provoking.

exaspera'tion, *n.*, the act of exasperating; the state of being exasperated.

excandes'cent, *adj.*, at a white heat.

ex'cavate, *v.t.*, to hollow out, dig.

ex'cavated, *p.p.*, excavate.

ex'cavating, *pr.p.*, excavate.

excava'tion, *n.*, the act of excavating; a cavity made by digging.

ex'cavator, *n.*, one who excavates.

exceed', *v.t.*, to go beyond, surpass; *v.i.* to go beyond bounds.

exceed'ed, *p.p.*, exceed.

exceed'ing, *pr.p.*, exceed; *adj.*, very great.

exceed'ingly, *adv.*, very greatly.

excel', *v.t.*, to go beyond, outdo; *v.i.*, to be superior.

excelled', *p.p.*, excel.

ex'cellence, *n.*, the state or quality of excelling; superiority; an honorific title.

ex'cellency, *n.*, *i.q.* excellence.

ex'cellent, *adj.*, surpassing, very great or good.

ex'cellently, *adv.*, surpassingly, very greatly, very well.

excel'ling, *pr.p.*, excel.

excel'sior, *n.*, a variety of printing fount.

except', *v.t.*, to leave out, withdraw; *v.i.*, to raise objection; *prep.*, leaving out, but.

except'ed, *p.p.*, except.

except'ing, *pr.p.*, except.

excep'tion, *n.*, the act of excepting, the state of being excepted, an omission, a special case, objection.

excep'tionable, *adj.*, open to objection.

excep'tional, *adj.*, special, uncommon.

except'ive, *adj.*, rel. to an exception; captious.

except'or, *n.*, one who enters an exception.

excerpt', *v.t.*, to extract.

ex'cerpt, *n.*, an extract.

excerp'ta, *n. pl.*, extracts.

excerp'tion, *n.*, the act or process of excerpting; an excerpted passage.

excess', *n.*, the act of going beyond, overdoing, over-indulgence.

excess'ive, *adj.*, going to excess, passing the limit.

excess'ively, *adv.*, in an excessive degree.

excess'iveness, *n.*, the state or quality of being excessive.

***exchange'*,** *v.t.*, to give or take an equivalent; *v.i.*, to pass from one thing to another; *n.*, barter; the system of trading by means of credit, etc.; the passing from one state to another.

***exchange*abil'ity,** *n.*, the state or quality of being exchangeable.

***exchange'*able,** *adj.*, able to be exchanged.

***exchanged'*,** *p.p.*, exchange.

exchan'ger, *n.*, one who exchanges.

***exchan'ging*,** *pr.p.*, exchange.

excheq'uer, *n.*, the public treasury; any private resources.

exci'sable, *adj.*, able to be excised, dutiable.

excise', *v.t.*, to cut out; to levy duty on; *n.*, a duty on certain commodities.

excised', *p.p.*, excise.

excise'man, *n.*, an official who collects excise.

exci'sing, *p.p.*, excise.

exci'sion, *n.*, the act or result of excising.

excitabil'ity, *n.*, the state of being excitable.

exci'table, *adj.*, able to be excited, prone to excitement.

exci'tant, *adj.*, conducive to excitement.

excita'tion, *n.*, the act or state of excitement.

exci'tative, *adj.*, *i.q.* excitant.

exci'tatory, *adj.*, *i.q.* excitant.

excite', *v.t.*, to arouse, stimulate.

exci'ted, *p.p.*, excite.

excite'ment, *n.*, the act of exciting; the state of being excited; that which excites.

exci'ter, *n.*, one who excites.

exci'ting, *pr.p.*, excite; *adj.*, stirring, rousing.

exci'tingly, *adv.*, stirringly.

exclaim', *v.t.* and *i.*, to call out.

exclaimed', *p.p.*, exclaim.

exclaim'ing, *pr.p.*, exclaim.

exclama'tion, *n.*, the act of exclaiming; that which is exclaimed.

exclam'ative, *adj.*, expressing exclamation.

exclam'atory, *adj.*, *i.q.* exclamative.

exclude', *v.t.*, to shut out, bar, reject.

exclu'ded, *p.p.*, exclude.

exclu'ding, *pr.p.*, exclude.

exclu'sion, *n.*, the act of excluding; the state of being excluded.

exclu'sionist, *n.*, one who favours exclusion.

exclu'sive, *adj.*, with a tendency to exclude; exceptional; preferential; arrogant.

exclu'sively, *adv.*, specially, preferentially.

exclu'siveness, *n.*, the state of being exclusive.

excog'itate, *v.t.*, to think out, plan.

excog'itated, *p.p.*, excogitate.

excog'itating, *pr.p.*, excogitate.

excogita'tion, *n.*, the act or result of excogitating.

excommu'nicable, *adj.*, worthy to be excommunicated.

excommu'nicate, *v.t.*, to expel from communion; *n.*, a person so expelled.

excommu'nicated, *p.p.*, excommunicate.

excommu'nicating, *pr.p.*, excommunicate.

excommunica'tion, *n.*, the act of excommunicating; the state of being excommunicated.

excommu'nicator, *n.*, one who excommunicates.

exco'riate, *v.t.*, to flay, abrade.

exco'riated, *p.p.*, excoriate.

exco'riating, *pr.p.*, excoriate.

excoria'tion, *n.*, the act or result of excoriating.

excor'ticate, *v.t.*, to strip the bark from.

excortica'tion, *n.*, the act of excorticating.

ex'crement, *n.*, an animal discharge; the faeces.

excremen'tal, *adj.*, discharged as excrement.

excres'cence, *n.*, a superfluous growth.

excres'cent, *adj.*, growing superfluously.

excre'ta, *n. pl.*, matter eliminated.

excrete', *v.t.*, to eliminate waste matter.

excre'ted, *p.p.*, excrete.

excre'ting, *pr.p.*, excrete.

excre'tion, *n.*, the act or result of excreting.

excre'tive, *adj.*, conducive to excretion.

excre'tory, *adj.*, *i.q.* excretive.

excru'ciate, *v.t.*, to torture, agonize.

excru'ciated, *p.p.*, excruciate.

excru'ciating, *pr.p.*, excruciate; *adj.*, agonizing.

excrucia'tion, *n.*, agony.

excul'pable, *adj.*, able or worthy to be exculpated.

ex'culpate, *v.t.*, to acquit from blame.

ex'culpated, *p.p.*, exculpate.

ex'culpating, *pr.p.*, exculpate.

exculpa'tion, *n.*, the act of exculpating; the state of being exculpated.

excul'patory, *adj.*, leading to exculpation.

excur'sion, *n.*, a journey; a departure from the ordinary.

excur'sionist, *n.*, one who goes on an excursion.

excur'sive, *adj.*, wandering, disconnected.

excur'sus, *n.*, a supplementary treatise.

excu'sable, *adj.*, capable of excuse.

excu'sably, *adv.*, in an excusable way.

excu'satory, *adj.*, apologetic.

excuse', *v.t.*, to acquit of blame, pardon; *n.*, an exonerating plea; a justification; a reason for doing something.

excused', *p.p.*, excuse.

excuse'less, *adj.*, without excuse.

excu'ser, *n.*, one who excuses.

excu'sing, *pr.p.*, excuse.

ex'eat, *n.*, leave of absence (*Lat.*,= let him depart).

ex'ecrable, *adj.*, deserving execration; detestable; abominable.

ex'ecrably, *adv.*, outrageously, detestably.

ex'ecrate, *v.t.*, to invoke curses on.
ex'ecrated, *p.p.*, execrate.
ex'ecrating, *pr.p.*, execrate.
execra'tion, *n.*, the act of execrating; a curse, malediction.
ex'ecratory, *adj.*, of the nature of a curse.
exec'utant, *n.*, a performer on an instrument.
ex'ecute, *v.t.*, to perform, finish; put to death.
ex'ecuted, *p.p.*, execute.
ex'ecuting, *pr.p.*, execute.
execu'tion, *n.*, the act of executing; performance, dispatch.
execu'tioner, *n.*, one who executes, the headsman or the hangman.
exec'utive, *adj.*, rel. to execution, carrying into effect; *n.*, an official or officials charged with the duty of getting things done.
exec'utor, *n.*, one who carries out another's testamentary bequests.
executo'rial, *adj.*, rel. to an executor.
exec'utorship, *n.*, the office and duty of an executor.
exec'utory, *adj.*, administrative; rel. to the execution of the law.
exec'utrix, *n.*, fem. of executor.
exege'sis, *n.*, interpretation, exposition.
exeget'ic, *adj.*, interpretative, expository.
exeget'ical, *adj.*, *i.q.* exegetic.
exem'plar, *n.*, a pattern, model.
exem'plarily, *adv.*, in an exemplary way.
exem'plary, *adj.*, appearing as a model or typical.
exemplifica'tion, *n.*, the act or result of illustrating by example.
exem'plified, *p.p.*, exemplify.
exem'plifier, *n.*, one who exemplifies.
exem'plify, *n.*, to show by example, to illustrate.
exem'plifying, *pr.p.*, exemplify.
exempt', *v.t.*, to except, set free; *adj.*, released, not liable.
exempt'ed, *p.p.*, exempt.
exempt'ing, *pr.p.*, exempt.
exemp'tion, *n.*, the act and result of exempting.
exequa'tur, *n.*, an official warrant.
ex'equies, *n. pl.*, funeral ceremonies.
ex'ercisable, *adj.*, able to be exercised.
ex'ercise, *v.t.*, to practise, put forth; *v.i.*, to take exercise; *n.*, practising; training.
ex'ercised, *p.p.*, exercise.
ex'erciser, *n.*, one who exercises.
ex'ercising, *pr.p.*, exercise.
exercita'tion, *n.*, an exercise.
exergue', *n.*, the place on the reverse of a coin where the date, etc., is shown.
exert', *v.t.*, to put forth, employ.
exert'ed, *p.p.*, exert.
exert'ing, *pr.p.*, exert.
exer'tion, *n.*, effort, toil.
exfo'liate, *v.t.* and *i.*, to scale.
exfo'liated, *p.p.*, exfoliate.
exfo'liating, *pr.p.*, exfoliate.
exfolia'tion, *n.*, a scaling or peeling.
exfo'liative, *adj.*, causing exfoliation.
exha'lable, *adj.*, able to be exhaled.
exha'lant, *adj.*, exhaling.
exhala'tion, *n.*, the process of breathing out; that which is exhaled or given off.
exhale', *v.t.*, to breathe out, give off.
exhaled', *p.p.*, exhale.
exha'ling, *pr.p.*, exhale.
exhale'ment, *n.*, *i.q.* exhalation.
exhaust', *v.t.*, to draw completely off, to drain, to overcome with weariness; *n.*, the motive fluid escaping from a cylinder.
exhaust'ed, *p.p.*, exhaust.
exhaust'ible, *adj.*, able to be exhausted.
exhaust'ing, *pr.p.*, exhaust; *adj.*, causing exhaustion.
exhaustion, *n.*, the act or result of exhausting; extreme fatigue.
exhaust'ive, *adj.*, thorough; complete.
exhaust'less, *adj.*, inexhaustible.
exhib'it, *v.t.*, to show; *n.*, something exhibited.
exhib'ited, *p.p.*, exhibit.
exhib'iting, *pr.p.*, exhibit.
exhibi'tion, *n.*, the act of exhibiting; a public show; an academic endowment.
exhibi'tioner, *n.*, the holder of a college or university exhibition.
exhib'itive, *adj.*, exhibiting.
exhib'itor, *n.*, one who shows exhibits.
exhib'itory, *adj.*, *i.q.* exhibitive.
exhil'arant, *adj.*, exhilarating; *n.*, that which exhilarates.
exhil'arate, *v.t.*, to cheer, gladden.
exhil'arated, *p.p.*, exhilarate.
exhil'arating, *pr.p.*, exhilarate; *adj.*, cheerful, gladdening.
exhilara'tion, *n.*, the act of exhilarating; the state of one exhilarated.
exhort', *v.t.*, to admonish, entreat, incite.
exhorta'tion, *n.*, the act of exhorting; a hortatory address.

exhort'ative, *adj.*, exhorting.
exhort'atory, *adj.*, *i.q.* exhortative.
exhort'ed, *p.p.*, exhort.
exhort'er, *n.*, one who exhorts.
exhort'ing, *pr.p.*, exhort.
exhuma'tion, *n.*, the act of exhuming.
exhume', *v.t.*, to disinter.
exhumed', *p.p.*, exhume.
exhu'ming, *pr.p.*, exhume.
exigeant, *adj.*, exacting (*Fr.*).
ex'igency, *n.*, urgency, pressing necessity.
ex'igent, *adj.*, exacting, urgent.
exig'uous, *adj.*, small, insignificant.
ex'ile, *v.t.*, to banish from a country; *n.*, one banished; the state of being exiled.
ex'iled, *p.p.*, exile.
ex'iling, *pr.p.*, exile.
exinani'tion, *n.*, the act of emptying, the state of being emptied.
exist', *v.i.*, to be, or to go on being.
exist'ed, *p.p.*, exist.
exist'ence, *n.*, the state or continuance of being.
exist'ent, *adj.*, existing.
exist'ible, *adj.*, able to exist.
existibil'ity, *n.*, the state or quality of being existible.
exist'ing, *pr.p.*, exist.
ex'it, *n.*, a going out, a passage out.
ex-may'or, *n.*, a former mayor.
ex'ode, *n.*, the part of a Greek tragedy following the last choral ode; a farce in the Roman drama.
exo'dium, *n.*, *i.q.* exode.
Ex'odus, *n.*, the second book of the Old Testament, describing the escape of the Israelites. Hence, exodus generally means any going out or departing.
exog'amy, *n.*, marriage outside one's own tribe.
exog'amous, *adj.*, rel. to exogamy; marrying outside the tribe.
ex'ogen, *n.*, a plant that grows by the addition of concentric rings beneath the bark.
exog'enous, *adj.*, of the nature of an exogen.
exon'erate, *v.t.*, to acquit, free from blame.
exon'erated, *p.p.*, exonerate.
exon'erating, *pr.p.*, exonerate.
exonera'tion, *n.*, the act of exonerating; acquittal.
exon'erative, *adj.*, exonerating, freeing from blame.
exon'erator, *n.*, one who exonerates.
ex'orable, *adj.*, able to be entreated, relenting.
exor'bitance, *n.*, extravagance, excessive cost.
exor'bitancy, *n.*, *i.q.* exorbitance.
exor'bitant, *adj.*, extravagant, excessive.
exor'bitantly, *adv.*, extravagantly.
ex'orcise, *v.t.*, to allay (an evil spirit); *v.i.*, to practise exorcism.
ex'orcised, *p.p.*, exorcise.
ex'orciser, *n.*, one who exorcises.
ex'orcising, *pr.p.*, exorcise.
exor'cism, *n.*, the act of exorcising; a formula of exorcising.
exor'cist, *n.*, one who exorcises; one of the minor orders of the Church.
exor'dial, *adj.*, rel. to an exordium.
exor'dium, *n.*, an opening, beginning (of a speech).
exoter'ic, *adj.*, rel. to those outside the Mysteries (*i.e.*, the uninitiated); of a popular character.
exoter'ical, *adj.*, *i.q.* exoteric.
exot'ic, *adj.*, foreign; *n.*, a plant of foreign origin; not native.
exot'icism, *n.*, exotic nature.
expand', *v.t.*, to open out, spread out; *v.i.*, to become broader.
expand'ed, *p.p.*, expand.
expand'er, *n.*, that which expands.
expand'ing, *p.p.*, expand.
expanse', *n.*, something spread out; a stretch.
expansibil'ity, *n.*, the state or quality of being expansible.
expan'sible, *adj.*, able to be expanded.
expan'sion, *n.*, the act or result of expanding.
expan'sive, *adj.*, causing expansion; broad-minded.
expa'tiate, *v.i.*, to discourse at length, enlarge upon.
expa'tiated, *p.p.*, expatiate.
expa'tiating, *pr.p.*, expatiate.
expatia'tion, *n.*, the act of expatiating.
expa'tiator, *n.*, one who expatiates.
expa'tiatory, *adj.*, inclined to expatiation.
expa'triate, *v.t.*, to banish from one's country.
expa'triated, *p.p.*, expatriate.
expa'triating, *pr.p.*, expatriate.
expatria'tion, *n.*, the act or result of expatriating; exile.
expect', *v.t.*, to await, look for; suppose.
expect'ance, *n.*, *i.q.* expectancy.
expect'ancy, *n.*, a state of suspense and waiting.
expect'ant, *adj.*, in a state of expecting.
expect'antly, *adv.*, in an expectant way.
expecta'tion, *n.*, the state of expecting.

expect'ed, *p.p.*, expect.
expect'ing, *pr.p.*, expect.
expec'torant, *adj.*, promoting expectoration; *n.*, a medicine that promotes expectoration.
expec'torate, *v.t.*, to cough or spit out; *v.i.*, to discharge phlegm.
expec'torated, *p.p.*, expectorate.
expec'torating, *pr.p.*, expectorate.
expectora'tion, *n.*, the act or result of expectorating.
expe'dience, *n.*, *i.q.* expediency.
expe'diency, *n.*, advantageousness, policy.
expe'dient, *adj.*, advantageous, politic, suitable.
expe'diently, *adv.*, with advantage.
ex'pedite, *v.t.*, to hasten, facilitate, send forth; *adj.*, prompt.
ex'pedited, *p.p.*, expedite.
ex'peditely, *adv.*, promptly.
ex'pediting, *pr.p.*, expedite.
expedi'tion, *n.*, a journey (usually of a number of persons); speed, promptness.
expedi'tionary, *adj.*, rel. to an expedition.
expedi'tious, *adj.*, prompt, speedy.
expedi'tiously, *adv.*, promptly.
expel', *v.t.*, to drive forth, banish.
expel'lable, *adj.*, able to be expelled.
expelled', *p.p.*, expel.
expel'ler, *n.*, one who expels.
expel'ling, *pr.p.*, expel.
expend', *v.t.*, to spend, lay out, use up.
expend'ed, *p.p.*, expend.
expend'ing, *pr.p.*, expend.
expend'iture, *n.*, the act of expending; that which is expended.
expense', *n.*, cost, outlay.
expen'sive, *adj.*, costly, dear.
expen'sively, *adv.*, in an expensive way.
expen'siveness, *n.*, the state of being expensive.
expe'rience, *v.t.*, to make personal trial of, undergo; *n.*, knowledge gained from personal trial.
expe'rienced, *p.p.*, experience; *adj.*, practised, skilful.
expe'riencing, *pr.p.*, experience.
experien'tial, *adj.*, rel. to experience; empirical.
exper'iment, *v.i.*, to make experiments; *n.*, a trial for the purpose of discovery.
experimen'tal, *adj.*, of the nature of experiment.
experimen'talist, *n.*, one who makes experiments.
experimen'talize, *v.i.*, to make experiments.
experimen'tally, *adv.*, in an experimental way.
exper'imented, *p.p.*, experiment.
exper'imenter, *n.*, one who experiments.
exper'imenting, *pr.p.*, experiment.
exper'imentist, *n.*, *i.q.* experimentalist.
expert', *adj.*, adept, clever.
ex'pert, *n.*, one known for his special knowledge or skill.
expert'ly, *adv.*, in an expert way.
expert'ness, *n.*, skill.
ex'piable, *adj.*, able to be expiated.
ex'piate, *v.t.*, to atone for; make reparation for.
ex'piated, *p.p.*, expiate.
ex'piating, *pr.p.*, expiate.
expia'tion, *n.*, the act of expiating; reparation.
ex'piator, *n.*, one who expiates.
ex'piatory, *adj.*, making reparation.
expira'tion, *n.*, the act of breathing out; an end.
expir'atory, *adj.*, rel. to expiration.
expire', *v.t.*, to breathe out; *v.i.*, die; come to an end.
expired', *p.p.*, expire.
expir'ing, *pr.p.*, expire.
expi'ry, *n.*, an end, termination.
explain', *v.t.*, to make plain or clear.
explain'able, *adj.*, able to be explained.
explained', *p.p.*, explain.
explain'er, *n.*, one who explains.
explain'ing, *pr.p.*, explain.
explana'tion, *n.*, the act or result of explaining.
explan'atory, *adj.*, explaining.
ex'pletive, *adj.*, filling out, superfluous; *n.*, a superfluous word; an oath.
ex'pletory, *adj.*, superfluous.
ex'plicable, *adj.*, able to be explained.
ex'plicate, *v.t.*, to explain, unfold.
ex'plicated, *p.p.*, explicate.
ex'plicating, *pr.p.* explicate.
explica'tion, *n.*, the act or result of explicating.
ex'plicative, *adj.*, explanatory.
ex'plicatory, *adj.*, *i.q.* explicative.
explic'it, *adj.*, distinct, outspoken.
explic'itly, *adv.*, in an explicit way.
explic'itness, *n.*, distinctness, outspokenness.
explode', *v.t.*, to cause to burst with a loud noise; *v.i.*, to burst with a loud noise.
explo'ded, *p.p.*, explode; *adj.*, extinct.
explo'der, *n.*, anything that explodes.

explo'ding, *pr.p.*, explode.

exploit', *v.t.*, to put to one's own use, employ for one's own ends; *n.*, a brave deed, a great feat.

exploita'tion, *n.*, the act of exploiting; the development of a country's resources.

explora'tion, *n.*, the act of exploring.

explor'atory, *adj.*, exploring.

explore', *v.t.*, to search carefully, examine.

explored', *p.p.*, explore.

explor'er, *n.*, one who explores.

explor'ing, *pr.p.*, explore.

explo'sion, *n.*, the act of exploding; a bursting forth.

explo'sive, *adj.*, causing explosion; *n.*, that which explodes.

explo'sively, *adv.*, in an explosive way.

expo'nent, *adj.*, explaining, making clear; *n.*, one who explains; an algebraical symbol indicating the *power* of a quantity.

exponen'tial, *adj.*, pert. to exponents.

export', *v.t.*, to send out of the country.

ex'port, *n.*, that which is exported.

export'able, *adj.*, able or fit to be exported.

exporta'tion, *n.*, the act of exporting; an export.

export'ed, *p.p.*, export.

export'er, *n.*, one who exports.

export'ing, *pr.p.*, export.

expose', *v.t.*, to exhibit; lay open to view; place in danger.

exposé', *n.*, an exposure; an explanation (*Fr.*).

exposed', *p.p.*, expose.

expo'ser, *n.*, one who exposes.

expo'sing, *pr.p.*, expose.

exposi'tion, *n.*, the act of exposing or expounding; explanation, commentary; the working out of a climax.

expos'itive, *adj.*, rel. to exposition.

expos'itor, *n.*, one who expounds.

expos'itory, *adj.*, *i.q.* expositive.

expos'tulate, *v.i.*, to reason seriously with a person at fault.

expos'tulated, *p.p.*, expostulate.

expos'tulating, *pr.p.*, expostulate.

expostula'tion, *n.*, the act of expostulating.

expos'tulator, *n.*, one who expostulates.

expos'tulatory, *adj.*, in the nature of expostulation.

expo'sure, *n.*, the act or effect of exposing.

expound', *v.t.*, to explain, interpret.

expound'ed, *p.p.*, expound.

expound'er, *n.*, one who expounds.

expound'ing, *pr.p.*, expound.

ex-pres'ident, *n.*, a former president.

express', *v.t.*, to press out; make known; send by quick despatch; *adj.*, exact, emphatic, with despatch; *n.*, a fast train; an express message or messenger.

express'age, *n.*, the charge for expressing.

expressed', *p.p.*, express.

express'ible, *adj.*, able to be expressed.

express'ing, *pr.p.*, express.

expres'sion, *n.*, the act of expressing; what is said, a form of speech; outward aspect of features; the power of giving the spirit of a musical piece.

expres'sionless, *adj.*, lacking expression.

express'ive, *adj.*, showing a power of expression.

express'ively, *adv.*, with emphasis.

express'iveness, *n.*, the state or quality of being expressive.

express'ly, *adv.*, intentionally, emphatically, directly.

exprobra'tion, *n.*, reproach, censure.

expro'priate, *v.t.*, to dispossess, put out of one's possession.

expro'priated, *p.p.*, expropriate.

expro'priating, *pr.p.*, expropriate.

expropria'tion, *n.*, the act or result of expropriating.

expul'sion, *n.*, the act or result of expelling.

expul'sive, *adj.*, producing expulsion.

expunc'tion, *n.*, erasion.

expunge', *v.t.*, to erase.

expunged', *p.p.*, expunge.

expun'ging, *pr.p.*, expunge.

ex'purgate, *v.t.*, to cleanse from filth, purify.

ex'purgated, *p.p.*, expurgate.

ex'purgating, *pr.p.*, expurgate.

expurga'tion, *n.*, the act of expurgating; anything expurgated.

ex'purgator, *n.*, one who expurgates.

expur'gatory, *adj.*, making expurgation.

ex'quisite, *adj.*, choice, refined, fastidious, intense; *n.*, a fop.

ex'quisitely, *adv.*, in an exquisite way.

ex'quisiteness, *n.*, the state or quality of being exquisite.

exscind', *v.t.*, to cut out, sever.

exscind'ed, *p.p.*, exscind.

exscind'ing, *pr.p.*, exscind.

exsic'cant, *adj.*, drying up.

ex siccate, *v.t.*, to dry up.
exsicca'tion, *n.*, the act or result of exsiccating.
exsuc'tion, *n.*, a sucking out.
ex'tant, *adj.*, still existing.
extempora'neous, *adj.*, done at the moment, without preparation.
extem'porary, *adj.*, *i.q.* extemporaneous.
extem'pore, *adj.*, *i.q.* extemporaneous; *adv.*, at the moment.
extem'porize, *v.t.*, to make without preparation; *v.i.*, to speak or to perform without preparation.
extem'porized, *p.p.*, extemporize.
extem'porizer, *n.*, one who extemporizes.
extem'porizing, *pr.p.*, extemporize.
extend', *v.t.*, to stretch, enlarge, prolong; *v.i.*, to stretch out, be prolonged.
extend'ed, *p.p.*, extend.
extend'er, *n.*, one who extends.
extend'ible, *adj.*, *i.q.* extensible.
extend'ing, *pr.p.*, extend.
extensibil'ity, *n.*, the state or quality of being extensible.
exten'sible, *adj.*, capable of extension or expansion.
exten'sile, *adj.*, capable of extending.
exten'sion, *n.*, the act of extending; state of being extended; a logical term denoting, collectively, all the things of which a particular term can be predicated.
exten'sive, *adj.*, wide, comprehensive.
exten'sively, *adv.*, widely, comprehensively.
exten'siveness, *n.*, the quality or state of being extensive.
exten'sor, *n.*, a muscle that causes extension.

extent', *n.*, the measure of extension; size, compass.
exten'uate, *v.t.*, to lessen, weaken, tone down.
exten'uated, *p.p.*, extenuate.
exten'uating, *pr.p.*, extenuate.
extenua'tion, *n.*, the act of extenuating; palliation.
exten'uator, *n.*, a plea in extenuation.
exte'rior, *adj.*, outward, external; *n.*, the outside of anything.
exte'riorly, *adv.*, outwardly.
exter'minate, *v.t.*, to expel, utterly destroy.
exter'minated, *p.p.*, exterminate.
exter'minating, *pr.p.*, exterminate.
extermina'tion, *n.*, the act or result of exterminating.
exter'minator, *n.*, that which exterminates.
exter'minatory, *adj.*, causing extermination.
extern', *adj.*, external; *n.*, a day scholar.
exter'nal, *adj.*, on the outside of; foreign; on the surface.
exter'nalism, *n.*, a liking for externals in religion.
external'ity, *n.*, the quality of being external.
exter'nalize, *v.t.*, to make objective.
exter'nally, *adv.*, outwardly.
exter'sion, *n.*, erasion.
extinct', *adj.*, extinguished, dead.
extinc'teur, *n.*, a fire-extinguisher.
extinc'tion, *n.*, the act of extinguishing; death; annihilation.
extin'guish, *v.t.*, to put out, destroy, annihilate.
***extin'guish*able,** *adj.*, able to be extinguished.

extin'guished, *p.p.* extinguish.
extin'guisher, *n.*, anything that extinguishes.
***extin'guish*ing,** *pr.p.*, extinguish.
extin'guishment, *n.*, *i.q.* extinction.
ex'tirpate, *v.t.*, to root out, destroy.
ex'tirpated, *p.p.*, extirpate.
ex'tirpating, *pr.p.*, extirpate.
extirpa'tion, *n.*, the act or effect of extirpating.
ex'tirpator, *n.*, one who extirpates.
extol', *v.t.*, to praise very highly.
extolled', *p.p.*, extol.
extol'ler, *n.*, one who extols.
extol'ling, *pr.p.*, extol.
extor'sive, *adj.*, producing extortion.
extort', *v.t.*, to wring from a person by threat or force.
extort'ed, *p.p.*, extort.
extort'er, *n.*, one who extorts.
extort'ing, *pr.p.*, extort.
extor'tion, *n.*, an act of extorting; an overcharge.
extor'tionary, *adj.*, *i.q.* extortionate.
extor'tionate, *adj.*, oppressive; greatly overcharged.
extor'tioner, *n.*, one who practises extortion.
ex'tra, *adj.*, additional; *n.*, something additional.
extract', *v.t.*, to draw out; obtain by chemical means.
ex'tract, *n.*, something extracted; an essence.
extract'able, *adj.*, able to be extracted.
extract'ed, *p.p.*, extract.
extract'ing, *pr.p.*, extract.
extrac'tion, *n.*, the act of extracting.
extrac'tive, *adj.*, causing extraction.

extrac'tor, *n.*, that which extracts; a device for extracting unexploded cartridges from a gun, etc.

ex'tradite, *v.t.*, to deliver up to another State.

ex'tradited, *p.p.*, extradite.

ex'traditing, *pr.p.*, extradite.

extradi'tion, *n.*, the act of surrendering the custody of a person to another State.

extra'dos, *n.*, an arch's outer curve.

extrajudi'cial, *adj.*, outside the proper court.

extramun'dane, *adj.*, outside the world.

extramu'ral, *adj.*, outside the city walls.

extra'neous, *adj.*, external, not essential.

extra'neously, *adv.*, in an extraneous way.

extraor'dinarily, *adv.*, in an extraordinary degree.

extraor'dinary, *adj.*, out of the common order; strange, exceptional, amazing.

extrav'agance, *n.*, reckless spending; the exceeding of limits.

extrav'agant, *adj.*, exceeding limits, wastefully lavish.

extrav'agantly, *adv.*, in an extravagant way.

extravagan'za, *n.*, a fantastic composition.

extrav'asate, *v.t.*, to let out of the proper (blood) vessels; *v.i.*, to exude from the blood vessels.

extrav'asated, *p.p.*, extravasate.

extrav'asating, *pr.p.*, extravasate.

extravasa'tion, *n.*, the state of being extravasated.

extreme', *adj.*, at the utmost point, on the edge, furthest.

extreme'ly, *adv.*, in the highest degree.

extre'mist, *n.*, one who holds extreme views.

extrem'ity, *n.*, the very end; dire misfortune.

ex'tricable, *adj.*, able to be extricated.

ex'tricate, *v.t.*, to liberate; disentangle.

ex'tricated, *p.p.*, extricate.

ex'tricating, *pr.p.*, extricate.

extrica'tion, *n.*, the act of extricating.

extrin'sic, *adj.*, not essential or inherent.

extrin'sical, *adj.*, *i.q.* extrinsic.

extrin'sically, *adv.*, in an extrinsic way.

extrude', *v.t.*, to thrust out.

extru'ded, *p.p.*, extrude.

extru'ding, *pr.p.*, extrude.

extru'sion, *n.*, the act of extruding.

exu'berance, *n.*, the state of being exuberant.

exu'berant, *adj.*, abounding to excess; overflowing.

exu'berantly, *adv.*, in an exuberant way.

exuda'tion, *n.*, the act or state of exuding; that which has exuded.

exude', *v.t.*, to give out through pores; *v.i.*, to sweat or ooze slowly.

exu'ded, *p.p.*, exude.

exu'ding, *pr.p.*, exude.

exul'cerate, *v.t.*, to produce an ulcer; *v.i.*, to become ulcerated.

exul'cerated, *p.p.*, exulcerate.

exul'cerating, *pr.p.*, exulcerate.

exulcera'tion, *n.*, the act of forming an ulcer; the ulcerated state.

exult', *v.i.*, to feel great joy; to triumph.

exult'ant, *adj.*, triumphing.

exulta'tion, *n.*, a state of great joy.

exult'ed, *p.p.*, exult.

exult'ing, *pr.p.*, exult.

exult'ingly, *adv.*, in an exulting way.

exu'viae, *n. pl.*, cast-off skins of animals.

exu'vial, *adj.*, rel. to exuviae.

eye, *v.t.*, to look fixedly at; to make an eye-like hole in; *n.*, the organ of sight; a small hole; a catch for a hook; a bud.

eye'ball, *n.*, the ball or apple of the eye.

eye'brow, *n.*, the hairy growth over the eyes.

eyed, *p.p.*, eye; *adj.*, having eyes.

eye'-glass, *n.*, a single lens.

eye'ing, ey'ing, *pr.p.*, eye.

eye'lash, *n.*, the hair on the eyelids.

eye'less, *adj.*, without eyes, blind.

eye'let, *n.*, a small hole for laces, etc.

eye'let-hole, *n.*, *i.q.* eyelet.

eye'lid, *n.*, the outer covering of the eye.

eye'mark, *n.*, an object of vision.

eye'piece, *n.*, the part of a microscope or telescope nearest to the eye and containing the focussing lenses.

eye'pit, *n.*, the eye-socket.

eye'-salve, *n.*, an eye-ointment.

eye'-servant, *n.*, one who works only when under observation.

eye'-serve, *v.i.*, to work only under the master's eye.

eye'-server, *n.*, *i.q.* eye-servant.

eye'shot, *n.*, the range of vision.

eye'-service, *n.*, working only under the master's eye.

eye'sight, *n.*, vision.

eye'sore, *n.*, an affection of the eye; anything offensive to the sight.

eye'spot, *n.*, the rudimentary eye.

eye'string, *n.*, the muscle holding the eye.

eye'-tooth, *n.*, one of the two canines in the upper jaw.

eye'-water. *n.*, eye-wash.

eye'-witness, *n.*, one who testifies to what he nas actually seen; *v.i.*, to bear such witness.

eye'-witnessed, *p.p.*, eye-witness.

eye'-witnessing, *pr.p.*, eye-witness.

eyot, *n.*, a small river-island. Also written *ait.*

eyre, *n.*, a circuit.

ey'ry, *n.*, the nest of an eagle or other bird of prey.

F

Fa, *n.*, the fourth ascending note in the scale.

Fa'bian, *adj.*, rel. to Fabius; of the "wait and see" policy; *n.*, a member of the Fabian society.

fa'ble, *v.t.*, to speak untruthfully; *n.*, a moral story; an impossible tale.

fa'bled, *p.p.*, fable.

fa'bler, *n.*, an inventor of fables.

fa'bling, *pr.p.*, fable.

fab'ric, *n.*, a building; material.

fab'ricate, *v.t.*, to construct; invent falsely.

fab'ricated, *p.p.*, fabricate.

fab'ricating, *pr.p.*, fabricate.

fabrica'tion, *n.*, a made-up story.

fab'ricator, *n.*, one who fabricates.

fab'ulist, *n.*, a writer of fables.

fab'ulous, *adj.*, fictitious.

façade', *n.*, the front elevation of a building.

face, *v.t.*, to confront, oppose; to turn up with facings; *n.*, the visage; a surface.

faced, *p.p.*, face; *adj.*, with the surface covered or dressed.

fa'cer, *n.*, a blow in the face; a sudden difficulty.

fac'et, *v.t.*, to cut (a gem) with facets; *n.*, a small surface, one of the planes of a cut gem.

fac'eted, *adj.*, having facets.

face'tiae, *n. pl.*, amusing, witty sayings; books containing coarse but witty sayings.

face'tious, *adj.*, witty, jocular.

face'tiously, *adv.*, jocularly.

face'tiousness, *n.*, the quality of being facetious.

fa'cia, *n.*, the name plate on a shop front.

fa'cial, *adj.*, rel. to the face.

fac'ile, *adj.*, easy, pliant.

facil'itate, *v.t.*, to make easy.

facil'itated, *p.p.*, facilitate.

facil'itating, *pr.p.*, facilitate.

facilita'tion, *n.*, the act of making easy.

facil'ity, *n.*, easiness, dexterity, freedom.

fa'cing, *pr.p.*, face.

facsim'ile, *n.*, an exact copy.

fact, *n.*, something done or that has happened; reality.

fac'tion, *n.*, a political party, dissension.

fac'tious, *adj.*, promoting dissension, disorderly.

fac'tiously, *adv.*, in a factious way.

fac'tiousness, *n.*, a tendency to faction.

facti'tious, *adj.*, artificial.

facti'tiously, *adv.*, artificially.

fac'titive, *adj.*, causative.

fac'tor, *n.*, a business agent; an estate steward; one of the elements in an arithmetical product; *v.t.*, to resolve into factors.

fac'torage, *n.*, a factor's commission.

facto'rial, *adj.*, rel. to a factor.

fac'tory, *n.*, a manufactory.

facto'tum, *n.*, one who does all manner of work.

fac'ultative, *adj.*, permissive.

fac'ulty, *n.*, ability; a learned profession; an academic department, as theology, law, etc.

fad, *n.*, a crotchet.

fad'dist, *n.*, one who cherishes fads.

fad'dle, *v.i.*, to act in a trifling way.

fade, *v.i.*, to lose colour; to wither; to become indistinct.

fa'ded, *p.p.*, fade.

fade'less, *adj.*, unfading.

fa'ding, *pr.p.*, fade.

fae'cal, *adj.*, rel. to faeces.

fae'ces, *n. pl.*, excrement (*Lat.*).

faec'ula, *n.*, starch, chlorophyll. Also *fecula*.

fag, *v.t.*, to overwork; to compel to work; *v.i.*, to drudge, to grow weary; *n.*, a drudge; a boy who does menial work for a senior boy; drudgery; a cheap cigarette.

fag'-end, *n.*, the refuse or worthless part.

fagged, *p.p.*, fag.

fag'ging, *pr.p.*, fag.

fagg'ot, *n.*, a bundle of sticks bound up.

fagot'to, *n.*, a bassoon.

Fah'renheit, *n.*, a thermometrical scale, with 32 deg. as its freezing point and 212 deg. its boiling point.

faience', *n.*, glazed earthenware decorated.

fail, *v.i.*, to be deficient; to waste away; to become insolvent; *v.t.*, to desert, to be wanting to.

failed, *p.p.*, fail.

fail'ing, *pr.p.*, fail; *n.*, a fault, weakness.

faille, *n.*, a soft kind of silk.

fail'ure, *n.*, the act of failing, deficiency, omission, bankruptcy.

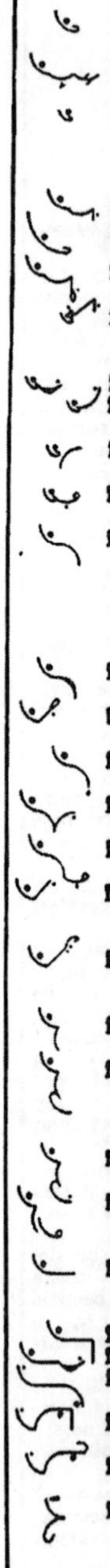

fain, *adv.*, gladly; *adj.*, willing.
fainéant', *adj.*, idle, feeble; *n.*, an idler.
faint, *v.i.*, to swoon; *adj.*, losing strength, weak, indistinct; *n.*, a swoon.
faint'ed, *p.p.*, faint.
faint'er, *adj.*, *comp.* of faint.
faint'est, *adj.*, *super.* of faint.
faint-heart'ed, *adj.*, wanting in courage or zeal.
faint'ing, *pr.p.*, faint.
faint'ish, *adj.*, somewhat faint.
faint'ly, *adv.*, weakly, dimly.
faint'ness, *n.*, a faint feeling.
fair, *adj.*, beautiful, comely; not dark; just, reasonable; moderately good; *n.*, a market at stated times.
fair'er, *adj.*, *comp.* of fair.
fair'est, *adj.*, *super.* of fair.
fair'ing, *n.*, a present from the fair.
fair'ly, *adv.*, justly, moderately.
fair'ness, *n.*, just conduct.
fair'y, *n.*, a sprite, elf; *adj.*, rel. to fairies.
fair'y-land, *n.*, the imaginary realm of the fairies.
faith, *n.*, belief, trust, fidelity.
faith'ful, *adj.*, loyal, honest; *n. pl.*, members of the Church.
faith'fully, *adv.*, with loyalty.
faith'fulness, *n.*, the quality of being faithful.
fake, *v.t.*, to fold; to fabricate; *n.*, a coil; a made-up thing.
faked, *p.p.*, fake.
fa'king, *pr.p.*, fake.
fakir', *n.*, an Indian mendicant.
fal'cate, *adj.*, sickle-shaped.
falca'tion, *n.*, sickle-shape formation.
fal'chion, *n.*, a short sword with a curved point.

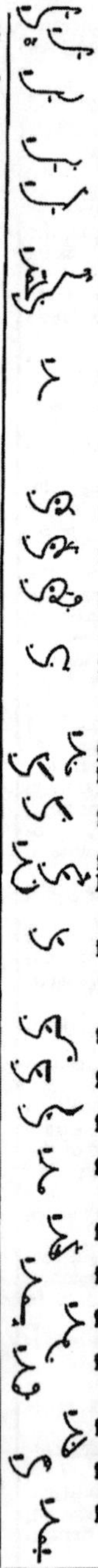

fal'con, *n.*, a bird of prey, trained for sport.
fal'coner, *n.*, one who manages or hunts with falcons.
fal'conet, *n.*, a small 15th cent. cannon.
fal'conry, *n.*, the sport of hunting with falcons.
fald'stool, *n.*, a bishop's folding chair.
Faler'nian, *adj.*, rel. to Mt. Falernus; *n.*, Falernian wine.
fall, *v.i.*, to drop, decline, ebb; *n.*, a downfall, a cascade, a drop in value; a veil; the autumn (*Amer.*).
falla'cious, *adj.*, deceptive, misleading.
falla'ciously, *adv.*, in a fallacious way.
falla'ciousness, *n.*, the quality of being fallacious.
fal'lacy, *n.*, a deceitful argument; logically defective reasoning; a sophism.
fall'en, *p.p.*, fall.
fallibil'ity, *n.*, liability to error.
fal'lible, *adj.*, liable to error.
fall'ing, *pr.p.*, fall.
Fallo'pian, *adj.*, rel. to the Fallopian ducts.
fal'low, *v.t.*, to make fallow; *adj.*, untilled, unsown; *n.*, unsown land.
fal'low-deer, *n.*, a variety of deer.
fal'lowed, *p.p.*, fallow.
fal'lowing, *pr.p.*, fallow.
false, *adj.*, untrue, dishonest, treacherous.
false'-hearted, *adj.*, treacherous.
false'hood, *n.*, a lie, an untruth.
false'ly, *adv.*, treacherously; in error.
false'ness, *n.*, the character of being false.
fal'ser, *adj.*, *comp.* of false.
fal'sest, *adj.*, *super.* of false.
falset'to, *n.*, an artificial voice above the natural compass.

falsifica'tion, *n.*, the act or result of falsifying.
fal'sified, *p.p.*, falsify.
fal'sifier, *n.*, one who falsifies.
fal'sify, *v.t.*, to make or prove to be false; to forge.
fal'sity, *n.*, the quality of being false; a lie.
fal'ter, *v.i.*, to waver, hesitate.
fal'tered, *p.p.*, falter.
fal'tering, *pr.p.*, falter.
fal'teringly, *adv.*, in a wavering manner.
fame, *n.*, celebrity, reputation, rumour.
famed, *adj.*, famous, renowned, rumoured.
famil'iar, *adj.*, intimate; domestic; unceremonious; accustomed; *n.*, an attendant spirit.
familiar'ity, *n.*, intimacy, acquaintance with; easy intercourse; an impertinence.
familiarisa'tion, *n.*, the act of familiarizing.
famil'iarize, *v.t.*, to make familiar.
famil'iarized, *p.p.*, familiarize.
famil'iarizing, *pr.p.*, familiarize.
famil'iarly, *adv.*, in a familiar way.
fam'ily, *n.*, a household; the children of a house; a race; high descent; a group of animals.
fam'ine, *n.*, dearth, hunger.
fam'ish, *v.t.*, to reduce to starvation; *v.i.*, to be starving.
fam'ished, *p.p.*, famish.
fam'ishing, *pr.p.*, famish.
fa'mous, *adj.*, celebrated; capital.
fa'mously, *adv.*, in a famous way; capitally.
fan, *v.t.*, to cool with a fan; to ventilate; to winnow; *n.*, a winnowing fan; an

instrument to agitate the air; a propeller.

fanat'ic, *adj.*, *i.q.* fanatical; *n.*, a wild enthusiast.

fanat'ical, *adj.*, wild, mad.

fanat'icism, *n.*, mad enthusiasm.

fan'cied, *p.p.*, fancy.

fan'cier, *n.*, a breeder of birds and animals.

fan'ciful, *adj.*, full of fancies, crotchety; fantastic.

fan'cifulness, *n.*, the quality of being fanciful.

fan'cy, *v.t.*, to conceive in the mind; to imagine; to conceive a liking for; *n.*, imagination; a liking.

fan'cying, *pr.p.*, fancy.

fandan'go, *n.*, a Spanish dance.

fane, *n.*, a temple, church.

fan'fare, *n.*, a flourish of trumpets.

fanfaronade', *n.* bluster; *v.i.*, to bluster.

fang, *n.*, a long tusk or tooth.

fanged, *adj.*, having fangs.

fan'gled, *adj.*, showy.

fang'less, *adj.*, without fangs.

fan'light, *n.*, a window over a door.

fanned, *p.p.*, fan.

fan'ner, *n.*, a ventilating apparatus; a winnowing machine.

fan'ning, *pr.p.*, fan.

fan'tail, *n.*, a variety of pigeons.

fanta'sia, *n.*, a musical reverie.

fan'tasm, *see* phantasm.

fantas'tic, *adj.*, fanciful, whimsical.

fantas'tical, *adj.*, *i.q.* fantastic.

fantas'tically, *adv.*, in a fantastic way.

fan'tasy, *n.*, fancy, imagination.

fan'tom, *see* phantom.

far, *adj.*, distant, remote; *adv.*, remotely; by many degrees.

far'ad, *n.*, a unit of electrical capacity.

faradiza'tion, *n.*, the excitation of a nerve with a magneto-electric current.

farce, *n.*, a short comical play; a ridiculous, futile proceeding.

farceur', *n.*, a wag.

far'cical, *adj.*, of the nature of a farce.

far'cin, *n.*, *i.q.* farcy.

far'cy, *n.*, a complaint of horses.

far'del, *n.*, a bundle.

fare, *v.i.*, to go, to succeed, to be fed; *n.*, food; the price for conveyance; a passenger.

fared, *p.p.*, fare.

farewell', *interj.*, good-bye; *n.*, leave-taking; an adieu.

far'-fetched, *adj.*, extravagant, forced.

fari'na, *n.*, meal, flour, starch.

farina'ceous, *adj.*, mealy, containing farina.

far'ing, *pr.p.*, fare.

far'inose, *adj.*, producing farina.

farm, *v.t.*, to cultivate land; to let out for a sum; *n.*, a tract of cultivated land.

farmed, *p.p.*, farm.

farm'er, *n.*, one who cultivates a farm; a collector of taxes who pays a certain sum.

farm'ery, *n.*, a farm and its buildings.

farm'house, *n.*, a farmer's dwelling.

farm'ing, *pr.p.*, farm; *n.*, the cultivation of land; the leasing of taxes.

farm'-labourer, *n.*, a worker on a farm.

farm'yard, *n.*, the yard of a farmhouse.

fa'ro, *n.*, a card game.

farra'ginous, *adj.*, jumbled.

farra'go, *n.*, a medley.

far'rier, *n.*, a shoer of horses; a horse doctor.

far'riery, *n.*, the trade of shoeing horses.

far'row, *v.t.*, to give birth to (pigs); *n.*, a litter of pigs; *adj.*, not calving.

farse, *v.t.*, to insert into a writing other words, such as—"Lord, have mercy, etc.," in the recital of the Decalogue.

far'-sighted, *adj.*, sagacious.

far'ther, *adj.* and *adv.*, *comp.* of far.

far'thermost, *adj.*, the most advanced.

far'thest, *adj.* and *adv.*, *super.* of far.

far'thing, *n.*, the fourth part of a penny.

far'thingale, *n.*, a hooped skirt.

fas'ces, *n.*, the emblem of the Roman magistrates; a bundle of rods with an axe in the middle.

fas'cia, *n.*, a fillet or band.

fas'cicle, *n.*, a small bundle; a division of a book.

fas'cicled, *adj.*, clustered.

fascic'ular, *adj.*, bel. to a cluster.

fascic'ulate, *adj.*, growing in clusters.

fascic'ulated, *adj.*, *i.q.* fasciculate.

fas'cinate, *v.t.*, to charm, bewitch.

fas'cinated, *p.p.*, fascinate.

fas'cinating, *pr.p.*, fascinate; *adj.*, charming.

fascina'tion, *n.*, charm, spell.

Fa'scist, a supporter of a form of dictatorship.

fash, *v.t.*, to annoy.

fash'ion, *v.t.*, to shape, mould; *n.*, style, shape; society.

fash'ionable, *adj.*, in the mode, stylish.

fash'ionably, *adv.*, stylishly.

fash'ioned, *p.p.*, fashion.

fash'ioner, *n.*, one who fashions.

fash'ioning, *pr.p.*, fashion.

fast, *v.i.*, to abstain from food; *adj.*, quick, firm, dissipated; *n.*, abstinence from food.

fast'-day, *n.*, a day of fasting.

fast'en, *v.t.*, to make secure, to cement.
fast'ened, *p.p.*, fasten.
fast'ening, *pr.p.*, fasten; *n.*, a bolt or clasp.
fast'er, *adj.*, *comp.* of fast.
fast'est, *adj.*, *super.* of fast.
fastid'ious, *adj.*, critical; hard to please.
fastid'iously, *adv.*, critically.
fastid'iousness, *n.*, squeamishness.
fast'ing, *pr.p.*, fast.
fast'ness, *n.*, firmness; a stronghold.
fat, *adj.*, fleshy, corpulent, greasy, affluent; *n.*, adipose matter; the unctuous part of animal flesh; *v.t.*, fatten.
fa'tal, *adj.*, fateful, destined, deadly.
fa'talism, *n.*, the doctrine of over-ruling fate.
fa'talist, *n.*, one who believes in fatalism.
fatalist'ic, *adj.*, leaning towards fatalism.
fatal'ity, *n.*, destiny; a fatal calamity.
fa'tally, *adv.*, in a fatal manner.
fate, *n.*, destiny, doom.
fa'ted, *adj.*, destined.
fate'ful, *adj.*, pregnant with destiny.
Fates, *n. pl.*, the three mythical dispensers of fate.
fa'ther, *v.t.*, to adopt, ascribe; *n.*, a male parent; an ancestor.
fa'thered, *p.p.*, father.
fa'therhood, *n.*, paternity.
fa'thering, *pr.p.*, father.
fa'ther-in-law, *n.*, the father of one's husband or wife.
fa'therland, *n.*, one's own country.
fa'therless, *adj.*, without a father.
fa'therliness, *n.*, the fatherly character.
fa'therly, *adj.*, like a father; rel. to a father.
fath'om, *n.*, a measure of depth equal to 6 ft.; *v.t.*, to sound, plumb.
fath'omable, *adj.*, capable of being sounded.
fath'omed, *p.p.*, fathom.
fath'oming, *pr.p.*, fathom.
fath'omless, *adj.*, bottomless.
fatigue', *v.t.*, to weary; *n.*, weariness; toil.
fatigued', *p.p.*, fatigue.
fatigu'ing, *adj.*, inducing fatigue.
fat'ling, *n.*, a young animal fattened for slaughter.
fat'ly, *adv.*, in a fat manner.
fat'ness, *n.*, plumpness; oiliness; fertility.
fat'ted, *adj.*, fattened for slaughter.
fat'ten, *v.t.*, to make fat; *v.i.*, to grow fat.
fat'tened, *p.p.*, fatten.
fat'tener, *n.*, one who, or that which, fattens.
fat'tening, *pr.p.*, fatten.
fat'ter, *adj.*, *comp.* of fat.
fat'test, *adj.*, *super.* of fat.
fat'tiness, *n.*, greasiness.
fat'ting, *pr.p.*, fat.
fat'tish, *adj.*, somewhat fat.
fat'ty, *adj.*, oily; composed of fat.
fatu'ity, *n.*, foolishness.
fat'uous, *adj.*, foolish.
fau'bourg, *n.*, a suburb; an urban district formerly a suburb (*Fr.*).
fau'ces, *n. pl.*, the windpipe (*Lat.*).
fau'cet, *n.*, a spigot; a pipe for drawing liquor from a cask.
faugh, *interj.*, an exclamation of disgust.
fault, *n.*, a slight offence; a defect; a lost scent (in hunting); a dislocation of geological strata.
fault'ily, *adv.*, in a faulty manner.
fault'iness, *n.*, the state of being faulty.
fault'less, *adj.*, without fault; perfect.
fault'lessly, *adv.*, in a faultless manner.
fault'lessness, *n.*, freedom from faults.
fault'y, *adj.*, defective; blamable.
faun, *n.*, a Roman rural deity.
fau'na, *n.*, a collective term for the animals peculiar to a region or period.
fau'nist, *n.*, one who describes the fauna of a district.
fauteuil', *n.*, an armchair.
faux pas, *n.*, a breach of manners or morals (*Fr.*).
fa'vour, **fa'vor**, *n.*, friendly disposition; an act of good-will; a token; a knot of ribbon; *v.t.*, to regard with kindness; to render easy.
fa'vourable, *adj.*, friendly, advantageous.
fa'vourably, *adv.*, in a favourable manner.
fa'voured, *adj.*, regarded with favour; featured; *p.p.*, favour.
fa'vourer, *n.*, one who favours.
fa'vouring, *pr.p.*, favour.
fa'vourite, *n.*, one greatly beloved; one unduly favoured; *adj.*, regarded with preference.
fa'vouritism, *n.*, the disposition to promote the interest of one person to the neglect of others with equal claims.
fawn, *v.i.*, to cringe and bow to gain favour.
fawned, *p.p.*, fawn.
fawn'er, *n.*, one who fawns.
fawn'ing, *adj.*, flattering, servile; *pr.p.*, fawn.
fawn'ingly, *adv.*, in a servile manner.
fay, *n.*, a fairy; *v.t.*, to fit two pieces of wood closely together.
fe'alty, *n.*, fidelity.

fear, *n.*, apprehension of danger; reverence; *v.t.*, to be afraid of; to venerate; *v.i.*, to be afraid.
feared, *p.p.*, fear.
fear'ful, *adj.*, afraid; timorous; terrible.
fear'fulness, *n.*, the quality of being fearful.
fear'ing, *pr.p.*, fear.
fear'less, *adj.*, courageous.
fear'lessly, *adv.*, in a fearless manner.
fear'lessness, *n.*, the state or quality of being fearless.
fear'some, *adj.*, exciting fear.
feasibil'ity, *n.*, practicability.
fea'sible, *adj.*, practicable.
fea'sibleness, *n.*, *i.q.* feasibility.
feast, *n.*, a banquet; a festival; *v.i.*, to take a sumptuous meal; *v.t.*, to entertain with sumptuous food.
feast'-day, *n.*, a day of celebration of a festival.
feast'ed, *p.p.*, feast.
feast'er, *n.*, one who feasts.
feast'ing, *pr.p.*, feast.
feat, *n.*, an exploit; *adj.*, neat; skilful.
feath'er, *n.*, a plume; *v.t.*, to fit or cover with feathers; to turn the blade of an oar horizontally.
feath'er-bed, *n.*, a bed stuffed with feathers.
feath'ered, *adj.*, covered or fitted with feathers; winged.
feath'er-edge, *n.*, the thinner edge of a plank.
feath'ering, *n.*, in Gothic architecture, an ornament consisting of small arcs separated by cusps; the act of turning an oar-blade; *pr.p.*, feather.
feath'ery, *adj.*, covered with or resembling feathers.
fea'ture, *n.*, a lineament of the face; a prominent part; *v.t.*, to resemble in face.
fea'tured, *adj.*, having a certain cast of features; *p.p.*, feature.
febrifa'cient, *adj.*, causing fever.
feb'rifuge, *n.*, medicine that removes fever.
feb'rile, *adj.*, indicating fever.
febril'ity, *n.*, feverishness.
Feb'ruary, *n.*, the second month of the year.
fe'cal, *adj.*, *i.q.* faecal.
fe'ces, *n. pl.*, *i.q.* faeces.
fec'ula, *n.*, powdery matter from plants; starch; farina.
fec'ulence, *n.*, sediment; dregs.
fec'ulent, *adj.*, muddy; turbid; foul.
fec'und, *adj.*, prolific.
fec'undate, *v.t.*, to make fruitful.
fecunda'tion, *n.*, the act of fecundating.
fecun'dity, *n.*, fertility; richness of invention.
fed, *p.p.*, feed.
fed'eral, *adj.*, pert. to a league; founded on alliance between States otherwise independent; *n.*, a member of the Northern party in the American Civil War, 1861-5.
fed'eralism, *n.*, the principles of federal government.
fed'eralist, *n.*, one who supports federalism; a federal.
fed'eralize, *v.t.* and *i.*, to unite in a federal compact.
fed'eralized, *p.p.*, federalize.
fed'eralizing, *pr.p.*, federalize.
fed'erate, *adj.*, leagued; *v.t.* and *i.*, to band together; to organize as a federal association.
federa'tion, *n.*, a league; a federal government.
fed'erative, *adj.*, forming a confederacy.
fee, *n.*, a reward for services; a fief; *v.t.*, to give a fee to.
fee'ble, *adj.*, weak.
fee'bleness, *n.*, weakness.
fee'bler, *adj.*, *comp.* of feeble.
fee'blest, *adj.*, *super.* of feeble.
fee'bly, *adv.*, in a feeble manner.
feed, *p.p.*, fee; *v.t.*, to give food to; *v.i.*, to eat; *n.*, food; fodder; an allowance of food.
feed'er, *n.*, one who feeds; that which supplies something.
feed'ing, *n.*, food; that which furnishes food for animals.
fee'-farm, *n.*, an estate in fee simple, subject to a perpetual rent.
fee'ing, *pr.p.*, fee.
feel, *v.t.*, to perceive by touch; to experience; *v.i.*, to have the sensibility excited; *n.*, sensation on being touched.
feel'er, *n.*, an organ of touch; a device to find out another's feelings or plans.
feel'ing, *adj.*, affecting; tender; *n.*, the sense of touch; tenderness of heart; sensitiveness.
feel'ingly, *adv.*, tenderly; keenly.
fee sim'ple, *n.*, an estate liable to alienation at the will of the owner.
feet, *n.*, pl. of foot.
fee' tail, *n.*, an estate limited to a man and the heirs of his body.
feign, *v.t.*, to counterfeit; to pretend.
feigned, *adj.*, simulated.
feign'edly, *adv.*, in a feigned manner.
feign'ing, *pr.p.*, feign.
feign'ingly, *adv.*, with pretence.
feint, *n.*, a pretence; a mock attack; *v.i.*, to make a mock attack.

feld'spar, *n.*, *i.q.* felspar.
felic'itate, *v.t.*, to congratulate.
felic'itated, *p.p.*, felicitate.
felic'itating, *pr.p.*, felicitate.
felicita'tion, *n.*, congratulation.
felic'itous, *adj.*, happy; extremely appropriate.
felic'itously, *adv.*, in a felicitous manner.
felic'ity, *n.*, blissfulness; appropriateness.
fe'line, *adj.*, rel. to cats.
fell, *p.t.* of fall; *adj.*, cruel; *n.*, a skin or hide; a seam or hem; a barren hill; *v.t.*, to sew a seam level with the cloth; to cause to fall; to hew or knock down.
fel'lah, *n.*, an Egyptian peasant.
fellaheen', *n.*, pl. of fellah.
felled, *p.p.*, fell.
fell'er, *n.*, one who fells.
fell'ing, *pr.p.*, fell.
fell'monger, *n.*, a dealer in hides.
fel'loe, *n.*, *i.q.* felly.
fel'low, *n.*, a companion; an equal; one of a pair; a member of a college or incorporated society; familiar for individual.
fel'low-creature, *n.*, one made by the same Creator.
fel'low-heir, *n.*, a joint inheritor.
fel'lowship, *n.*, companionship; a brotherhood; an establishment in a college entitling the holder to a share of its revenues.
fel'ly, *n.*, the circular rim of a wheel, or one of the parts thereof.
fe'lo-de-se, *n.*, a suicide.
fel'on, *n.*, a criminal; a whitlow; *adj.*, traitorous.
felo'nious, *adj.*, deliberately criminal.
felo'niously, *adv.*, in a felonious manner.
fel'ony, *n.*, a serious crime.
fel'spar, *n.*, a mineral—a constituent of granite, gneiss, etc.
felspath'ic, *adj.*, containing felspar.
felt, *p.p.*, feel; *n.*, wool compacted by rolling, beating, etc. *v.t.*, to make into felt.
felt'ed, *p.p.*, felt.
felt'er, *n.*, one who makes or covers with felt.
felt'ing, *n.*, the process by which, or the materials of which, felt is made; *pr.p.*, felt.
feluc'ca, *n.*, a long, narrow Mediterranean vessel with two large lateen sails.
fe'male, *n.*, an animal or plant that belongs to the sex which reproduces young or fruit; *adj.*, bel. to the sex which reproduces the race.
feminal'ity, *n.*, *i.q.* femininity.
fem'inine, *adj.*, pert. to the female sex.
feminin'ity, *n.*, the quality of being feminine.
fem'inize, *v.t.*, to make feminine; to give feminine qualities to.
fem'oral, *adj.*, bel. to the thigh.
fe'mur, *n.*, the thigh-bone.
fen, *n.*, low land covered partly with water; a marsh.
fence, *n.*, a boundary; the art of fencing; skill in repartee; a receiver of stolen goods; *v.t.*, to inclose with a fence; to hedge in; *v.i.*, to use a sword in order to learn attack and defence with it; to prevaricate.
fenced, *adj.*, inclosed with a fence; *p.p.*, fence.
fence'less, *adj.*, uninclosed; open.
fen'cer, *n.*, one who teaches or practises fencing with a sword or foil.
fen'cible, *n.*, a soldier for home defence only.
fen'cing, *n.*, the art of using a sword; material for making fences; *pr.p.*, fence.
fend, *v.t.*, to ward off.
fend'ed, *p.p.*, fend.
fend'er, *n.*, a utensil to keep live coals from rolling on to the floor; a contrivance hung over the side of a ship to protect it from injury by rubbing.
fend'ing, *pr.p.*, fend.
fenes'tral, *adj.*, pert. to a window.
fenes'trate, *adj.*, having windows or interstices.
fenes'trate, *v.t.*, to arrange windows in.
fenestra'tion, *n.*, the arrangement of windows in a building.
Fe'nian, *n.*, an Irish republican member of a secret society; *adj.*, of the Fenians.
Fe'nianism, *n.*, the principles of the Fenians.
fen'nel, *n.*, a fragrant plant.
fen'ny, *adj.*, marshy; boggy.
feoff, *n.*, a fief or fee.
feoffee', *n.*, the holder of land in fee.
feoff'er, *n.*, one who grants a fee.
feoff'ment, *n.*, the transference of a freehold estate; the deed by which a freehold is conveyed.
fera'cious, *adj.*, fruitful.
ferac'ity, *n.*, fruitfulness.
fe'rae, *n. pl.*, carnivorous mammals (*Lat.*).
fe'rial, *adj.*, pert. to holidays; ordinary.
fe'rine, *adj.*, rel. to a wild beast; savage.
Fering'hee, *n.*, Hindu name for European.

fer'ment, *n.*, any substance which produces the peculiar decomposition called fermentation; agitation.

ferment', *v.t.*, to cause fermentation; to excite; *v.i.*, to undergo fermentation; to work; to be agitated.

fermentabil'ity, *n.*, capability of being fermented.

ferment'able, *adj.*, capable of fermentation.

fermenta'tion, *n.*, the process by which grape juice is converted into wine, or a sweet infusion of malt into beer; any similar process; agitation; excitement.

ferment'ative, *adj.*, causing or produced by fermentation.

ferment'ed, *p.p.*, ferment.

ferment'ing, *pr.p.*, ferment.

fern, *n.*, a cryptogamous plant.

fern'ery, *n.*, a place where ferns are artificially grown.

fern'y, *adj.*, overgrown with fern.

fero'cious, *adj.*, fierce; savage.

fero'ciously, *adv.*, with savage cruelty.

fero'ciousness, *n.*, state of being ferocious.

feroc'ity, *n.*, *i.q.* ferociousness.

fer'reous, *adj.*, obtained from or containing iron.

fer'ret, *n.*, a domesticated sort of polecat, yellow, with red eyes; *v.t.*, to hunt rats or rabbits with ferrets; to search out cunningly.

fer'reted, *p.p.*, ferret.

fer'reting, *pr.p.*, ferret; *n.*, hunting with ferrets.

fer'riage, *n.*, the fare paid at a ferry.

fer'ric, *adj.*, pert. to, or extracted from, iron.

fer'ried, *p.p.*, ferry.

ferrif'erous, *adj.*, yielding iron.

ferru'ginated, *adj.*, having the colour or properties of iron-rust.

ferru'ginous, *adj.*, of the colour of iron-rust.

fer'rule, *n.*, a ring of metal put round anything to prevent splitting.

fer'ry, *v.t.*, to carry in a boat or raft over a river or other piece of water; *n.*, the place where passengers are ferried over a narrow piece of water; a ferry-boat.

fer'ry-boat, *n.*, a boat that plies at a ferry.

fer'ry-man, *n.*, one who keeps a ferry.

fer'rying, *pr.p.*, ferry.

fer'tile, *adj.*, fruitful.

fertil'ity, *n.*, fruitfulness.

fertiliza'tion, *n.*, the process of rendering fertile.

fert'ilize, *v.t.*, to make fertile.

fer'tilized, *p.p.*, fertilize.

fer'tilizer, *n.*, one who, or that which, fertilizes.

fer'tilizing, *pr.p.*, fertilize.

fer'ula, *n.*, a rod or cane with which light punishment is inflicted (*Lat.*).

ferula'ceous, *adj.*, having a stalk like a reed.

fer'ule, *n.*, a cane or rod for inflicting light punishment; *v.t.*, to punish with a ferule.

fer'vency, *n.*, ardour; warmth of devotion.

fer'vent, *adj.*, hot; ardent; earnest.

fer'vently, *adv.*, earnestly.

fer'vid, *adj.*, very hot; fervent.

fer'vidly, *adv.*, with glowing warmth.

fer'vour, fer'vor, *n.*, ardour; extreme earnestness.

fes'cue, *n.*, a kind of grass.

fesse, *n.*, a broad horizontal band across a shield (*her.*).

fes'tal, *adj.*, festive; pert. to a feast.

fes'ter, *v.i.*, to suppurate.

fes'tered, *p.p.*, fester.

fes'tering, *pr.p.*, fester.

fes'tival, *n.*, a time of feasting; an anniversary.

fes'tive, *adj.*, joyous; gay.

fes'tively, *adv.*, in a festive manner.

festiv'ity, *n.*, a festal celebration; social exhilaration.

festoon', *n.*, a garland; *v.t.*, to adorn with festoons.

festooned', *p.p.*, festoon.

festoon'ing, *pr.p.*, festoon.

fe'tal, *adj.*, pert. to a fetus.

fetch, *v.t.*, to bring; *n.*, a stratagem; the apparition of a living person.

fetched, *p.p.*, fetch.

fetch'ing, *pr.p.*, fetch.

fête, *n.*, a holiday; a festival day; *v.t.*, to honour with a festive entertainment.

fet'id, *adj.*, stinking.

fetif'erous, *adj.*, producing young.

fe'tish, fe'tich, *n.*, any object regarded with mysterious awe and worshipped by uncivilized races.

fet'lock, *n.*, a tuft of hair behind the pastern joint of a horse; the joint itself.

fe'tor, *n.*, stench (*Lat.*).

fet'ter, *n.*, a chain for the feet; a restraint; *v.t.*, to bind; to restrain.

fet'tered, *p.p.*, fetter.

fet'tering, *pr.p.*, fetter.

fe'tus, *n.*, the perfectly formed young of an animal before it is born or hatched.

feu, *n.*, a small piece of ground granted in perpetuity on payment of annual rent (*Scots law*).

feud, *n.*, a fief; hostility.

feu'dal, *adj.*, pert. to the system of holding lands by military services.

feu'dalism, *n.*, the feudal system.

feudaliza'tion, *n.*, the act of feudalizing.

feu'dalize, *v.t.*, to reduce to a feudal tenure.

feu'dalized, *p.p.*, feudalize.

feu'dalizing, *pr.p.*, feudalize.

feu'dary, *n.*, a feudatory; a vassal.

feu'datory, *adj.*, holding by feudal tenure; *n.*, a feudal tenant or vassal.

feuilleton', *n.*, that part of a French newspaper occupied by light literature; a serial story in a newspaper.

fe'ver, *n.*, a malady accompanied by increased temperature and a more rapid pulse; *v.i.*, to be seized with fever.

fe'vered, *p.p.*, fever.

fe'verfew, *n.*, a plant with much-divided leaves and a white flower.

fe'verish, *adj.*, slightly affected with fever; indicating fever.

fe'verishly, *adv.*, in a feverish manner.

fe'verishness, *n.*, the state of being feverish; anxious excitement.

few, *adj.*, not many.

few'er, *adj.*, *comp.* of few.

few'est, *adj.*, *super.* of few.

few'ness, *n.*, the state of being few.

fez, *n.*, a red Turkish cap.

fiacre, *n.*, a hackney cab with four wheels.

fiancé, fiancée, *n.*, a betrothed person.

fias'co, *n.*, an ignominious failure.

fi'at, *n.*, a command.

fib, *n.*, a falsehood; *v.i.*, to tell an untruth.

fibbed, *p.p.*, fib.

fib'ber, *n.*, one who tells fibs.

fib'bing, *pr.p.*, fib.

fi'bre, *n.*, a thread or filament.

fi'bril, *n.*, a small fibre.

fibril'la, *n.*, a hair on the root of a young plant.

fi'brillous, *adj.*, fibril-shaped.

fi'brin, *n.*, a substance contained in blood, causing it to clot.

fi'brinous, *adj.*, having the nature of fibrin.

fi'broid, *adj.*, made up of fibres.

fi'brous, *adj.*, consisting of fibres.

fib'ula, *n.*, a brooch or buckle; the smaller bone of the leg; a needle for sewing up wounds.

fi'chu, *n.*, a light kind of shawl.

fick'le, *adj.*, inconstant; changeable.

fick'leness, *n.*, inconstancy.

fi'co, *n.*, a fig; an insignificant trifle.

fic'tile, *adj.*, moulded by art; manufactured by a potter.

fictil'ia, *n. pl.*, ornamental articles moulded (*Lat.*).

fic'tion, *n.*, romances, novels, tales, etc.

fic'tionist, *n.*, a writer of fiction.

ficti'tious, *adj.*, imaginary; false.

ficti'tiously, *adv.*, in a fictitious manner.

ficti'tiousness, *n.*, the quality of being fictitious.

fi'cus, *n.*, a genus of trees and shrubs including the fig.

fid, *n.*, a block or pin of wood, used as a support.

fid'dle, *n.*, a violin; *v.i.*, to play on a fiddle; to trifle.

fid'dled, *p.p.*, fiddle.

fid'dler, *n.*, one who plays on a fiddle.

fid'dle-stick, *n.*, a fiddle-bow; *interj.*, nonsense!

fid'dling, *adj.*, trivial; fussy, *pr.p.*, fiddle; *n.*, playing the fiddle.

fidel'ity, *n.*, faithfulness.

fidg'et, *v.i.*, to be restless; *n.*, restlessness; a worrier.

fidg'eted, *p.p.*, fidget.

fidg'etily, *adv.*, restlessly.

fidg'etiness, *n.*, the state of being fidgety.

fidg'eting, *pr.p.*, fidget.

fidg'ety, *adj.*, restless; uneasy.

fidu'cial, *adj.*, undoubting; fiduciary.

fidu'ciary, *adj.*, trustful; held in trust; *n.*, a trustee.

fie, *interj.*, denoting impatience or contempt.

fief, *n.*, an estate held on feudal tenure.

field, *n.*, cleared or cultivated land; open country; a battle; the scene of military operations; scope; cricketers collectively; all the horses in a race; *v.i.*, to watch and recover the ball at cricket.

field'-book, *n.*, a surveyor's note-book.

field'er, *n.*, a player who fields at cricket.

field'fare, *n.*, a bird of the thrush family.

field'-glass, *n.*, a binocular glass for looking at distant objects.

field'-hos'pital, *n.*, a hospital in immediate touch with an army in the field.

field'-of'ficer, *n.*, a military officer above the rank of captain and below that of general.

field'-piece, *n.*, a gun used on the field of battle.

fiend, *n.*, a devil; a wicked person.

fiend'ish, *adj.*, devilish.

fiend'like, *adj.*, like a fiend; devilish.

fierce, *adj.*, violent; savage.

fierce'ly, *adv.*, furiously.
fierce'ness, *n.*, violence; fury, ferocity.
fierc'er, *adj.*, *comp.* of fierce.
fierc'est, *adj.* *super.* of fierce.
fi'eri-fa'cias, *n.*, a writ authorizing a sheriff to distrain.
fi'eriness, *n.*, the state of being fiery.
fi'ery, *adj.*, consisting of fire; blazing; impetuous; bright.
fife, *n.*, a small kind of flute; *v.i.*, to play on a fife.
fifed, *p.p.*, fife.
fi'fer, *n.*, one who plays on a fife.
fi'fing, *pr.p.*, fife.
fifteen, *adj.*, five and ten.
fifteenth, *adj.*, the fifth in order after the tenth; *n.*, one of fifteen equal parts into which a whole is divided.
fifth, *adj.*, next after the fourth; *n.*, one of five equal parts into which a whole is divided.
fifth'ly, *adv.*, in the fifth place.
fif'tieth, *adj.*, next in order after the forty-ninth; *n.*, one of fifty equal parts into which a whole is divided.
fif'ty, *adj.*, five times ten.
fig, *n.*, a fruit; something of very small value.
fight, *v.i.*, to contend; to strive; *v.t.*, to war against; *n.*, a contest; a battle.
fight'er, *n.*, a combatant.
fight'ing, *adj.*, trained for war; *pr.p.*, fight.
fig'-leaf, *n.*, a leaf of a fig-tree.
fig'ment, *n.*, something feigned or imagined.
fig'-tree, *n.*, a tree that bears figs.
figurabil'ity, *n.*, the quality of being figurable.
fig'urable, *adj.*, capable of being figured.
fig'ural, *adj.*, pert. to figures.
fig'urate, *adj.*, of a certain determinate shape; specifically applied to numbers representing some geometrical figure.
fig'urated, *adj.*, of definite form.
figura'tion, *n.*, the act of giving determinate form.
fig'urative, *adj.*, symbolical; not literal.
fig'uratively, *adv.*, metaphorically.
fig'ure, *n.*, form; shape; a character denoting a number; a rhetorical device; a trope; *v.t.*, to represent; to imagine; *v.i.*, to cipher.
fig'ured, *p.p.*, figure.
fig'ure-head, *n.*, the ornamental figure on a ship under the bowsprit.
fig'uring, *pr.p.*, figure.
fila'ceous, *adj.*, consisting of threads.
fil'acer, *n.*, an obsolete official of the Common Pleas, who made out and filed writs.
fil'ament, *n.*, a fine thread.
filamen'tous, *adj.*, like a thread; bearing filaments.
fil'ander, *n.*, a New Guinea kangaroo.
fil'atory, *n.*, a machine for spinning threads.
fil'ature, *n.*, a filatory; the reeling off of silk from cocoons.
fil'bert, *n.*, the fruit of a cultivated hazel tree.
filch, *v.t.*, to pilfer.
filched, *p.p.*, filch.
filch'er, *n.*, one who filches.
filch'ing, *adj.*, thievish; *n.*, thieving; *pr.p.*, filch.
file, *n.*, a collection of papers arranged for reference; a row of soldiers one behind another; a steel instrument for cutting or smoothing; *v.t.*, to place in a file; to cut with a file; *v.i.*, to march one by one.
filed, *p.p.*, file.
fil'emot, *adj.*, having the colour of a dead leaf.
fi'ler, *n.*, one who files.
fil'ial, *adj.*, becoming a child in relation to his parents; pert. to a son or daughter.
filia'tion, *n.*, adoption; the fixing of paternity.
fil'ibuster, *n.*, a buccaneer; an adventurer; *v.i.*, to act as a filibuster.
fil'ibustering, *pr.p.*, filibuster; *n.*, buccaneering.
fil'ibusterism, *n.*, the practice of filibustering.
fil'icoid, *adj.*, having the form of a fern.
fil'igree, *n.*, ornamental wire-work.
fil'igreed, *adj.*, ornamented with filigree.
fi'ling, *n.*, a particle rubbed off by a file; *pr.p.*, file.
Filio'que, *n.*, a clause (= "and the Son") added to the Nicene Creed which was one of the grounds for the schism between the Churches of the East and the West.
fill, *v.t.*, to occupy the whole space of; *v.i.*, to become full; *n.*, as much as fills.
filled, *p.p.*, fill.
fill'er, *n.*, that which, or one who, fills.
fil'let, *n.*, a narrow strip or band; meat rolled and tied round; *v.t.*, to bind with a fillet.
fil'leted, *p.p.*, fillet.
fil'leting, *n.*, material of which fillets are made; *pr.p.*, fillet.
fil'libeg, *n.*, a Scottish kilt.
fill'ing, *adj.*, able to fill or satisfy; *n.*, materials for stopping up a hole; *pr.p.*, fill.
fil'lip, *v.t.*, to strike smartly; *n.*, a smart blow; a stimulus.
fil'liped, *p.p.*, fillip.
fil'ly, *n.*, a young mare.

film, *n.*, a thin skin; a thin layer for receiving a photographic negative; a cinematographic ribbon; *v.t.*, to photograph for the cinematograph; *v.i.*, to cover with a film.

film'iness, *n.*, the state of being filmy.

film'y, *adj.*, like a film.

fi'lose, *adj.*, ending in a thread-like process.

fil'ter, *n.*, a strainer; *v.t.*, to purify by passing through a filter; *v.i.*, to percolate.

fil'tered, *p.p.*, filter.

fil'tering, *pr.p.*, filter.

filth, *n.*, dirt; foul matter.

filth'ily, *adv.*, in a filthy manner.

filth'iness, *n.*, the state of being filthy; impurity.

filth'y, *adj.*, foul; morally impure.

fil'trate, *v.t.*, to filter; *n.*, liquid passed through a filter.

fil'trated, *p.p.*, filtrate.

fil'trating, *pr.p.*, filtrate.

filtra'tion, *n.*, the process of filtering.

fim'briate, *adj.*, fringed; *v.t.*, to hem; to fringe.

fin, *n.*, a projecting wing-like organ or limb of a fish.

fi'nable, *adj.*, capable of being refined; admitting of a fine.

fi'nal, *adj.*, last, conclusive.

fina'le, *n.*, the last part of a musical concerto; the last scene.

final'ity, *n.*, the state of being final; a philosophical doctrine that everything exists for a determinate end.

fi'nally, *adv.*, lastly.

finance', *n.*, the science of revenue and expenditure, both public and private; *v.i.*, to conduct financial operations; *v.t.*, to support with pecuniary assistance.

financed', *p.p.*, finance.

finan'cing, *pr.p.*, finance.

finan'cial, *adj.*, pert. to money matters.

finan'cially, *adv.*, rel. to finance.

finan'cier, *n.*, one skilled in finance.

finch, *n.*, a small singing bird.

find, *v.t.*, to discover; *n.*, discovery of anything valuable; something found.

find'er, *n.*, one who, or that which, finds; a small telescope attached to a larger one.

find'ing, *n.*, discovery; a verdict; *pr.p.*, find.

fine, *adj.*, slender; very small; elegant; pure, free from clouds; *v.t.*, to refine; to punish by fine, *n.*, a payment in money imposed as a punishment.

fined, *p.p.*, fine.

fine'draw, *v.t.*, to sew up so as to conceal a rent.

fine'drawer, *n.*, one who finedraws.

fine'drawing, *pr.p.*, finedraw.

fine'drawn, *adj.*, drawn out too finely or subtly; *p.p.*, finedraw.

fine'ly, *adv.*, delicately; admirably.

fine'ness, *n.*, the state of being fine.

fi'ner, *n.*, one who refines or fines; *adj.*, *comp.* of fine.

fi'nery, *n.*, ornament, showy decoration; a forge in an ironworks.

fine'spun, *adj.*, drawn to a fine thread; over-elaborated.

finesse', *n.*, artifice; subtlety of contrivance; *v.t.* to use finesse.

finessed', *p.p.*, finesse.

finess'ing, *pr.p.*, finesse.

fi'nest, *adj.*, *super.* of fine.

fine'-still, *v.t.*, to distil spirit from molasses.

fin'ger, *n.*, one of the five extreme members of the hand; an index; *v.t.*, to touch with the fingers.

fin'gered, *adj.*, having fingers; *p.p.*, finger.

fin'gering, *n.*, the management of the fingers in playing on a musical instrument; the marking of the notes of a piece of music to guide the fingers in playing it; a kind of knitting worsted; *pr.p.*, finger.

fin'ger-ring, *n.*, a ring worn on a finger.

fin'ial, *n.*, the ornamental termination of a pinnacle or gable.

fin'ical, *adj.*, particular about trifles.

finical'ity, *n.*, the state of being finical.

fin'icalness, *n.*, *i.q.* finicality.

fin'icking, *adj.*, *i.q.* finical.

fin'ikin, *adj.*, *i.q.* finical.

fi'ning, *n.*, the process of refining or clarifying; the preparation used in clarifying; *pr.p.*, fine.

fi'nis, *n.*, conclusion.

fin'ish, *v.t.*, to bring to an end; *v.i.*, to come to an end; *n.*, careful elaboration.

fin'ished, *adj.*, perfectly polished; complete; *p.p.*, finish.

fin'isher, *n.*, one who finishes; that which gives the finishing touch.

fin'ishing, *pr.p.*, finish.

fi'nite, *adj.*, limited.

fi'nitely, *adv.*, in a finite manner.

fi'niteness, *n.*, the state of being finite.

fin'itude, *n.*, limitation; *i.q.* finiteness.

fin'less, *adj.*, destitute of fins.

Finn, *n.*, a native of Finland.

finned, *adj.*, possessing fins.
fin'ny, *adj.*, furnished with fins.
fin'-toed, *adj.*, having toes connected by a membrane.
fiord, fjord, *n.*, a long, narrow arm of the sea, common on the coast of Norway.
fir, *n.*, a coniferous tree; a pine.
fire, *n.*, heat and light produced by burning; a conflagration; vehemence; *v.t.*, to set on fire; to discharge a firearm.
fire'arm, *n.*, a weapon discharged by the combustion of powder.
fire'brand, *n.*, a piece of kindled wood; one who causes contention.
fire'-brick, *n.*, a clay brick capable of withstanding intense heat.
fire'-brigade, *n.*, an organized body of firemen.
fire'-clay, *n.*, a kind of clay capable of withstanding intense heat.
fire'-damp, *n.*, a highly explosive gas found in coal-mines.
fired, *p.p.*, fire.
fire'-engine, *n.*, an engine for extinguishing fires by pumping water on to the flames.
fire'fly, *n.*, a luminous winged insect.
fire'lock, *n.*, a musket with a flint-and-steel lock.
fire'man, *n.*, one whose work is to extinguish fires; a man who tends the fire of a steam-engine.
fire'-place, *n.*, a hearth.
fire'-plug, *n.*, a plug of a water-main.
fire'proof, *adj.*, rendered incombustible
fir'er, *n.*, one who, that which, fires.
fire'ship, *n.*, a vessel filled with combustibles to be set on fire so as to burn an enemy's ships.
fire'side, *n.*, the hearth; the home.
fire'stone, *n.*, any stone that resists the action of fire.
fire'-wood, *n.*, wood for fuel.
fire'work, *n.*, a preparation of gunpowder used for making a show.
fir'ing, *n.*, the act of discharging; fuel; *pr.p.*, fire.
fir'kin, *n.*, a small wooden cask; an old measure of capacity containing 7½ gals.
firm, *adj.*, compact; solid; steady; not easily moved; *n.*, a commercial house.
fir'mament, *n.*, the heavens.
firmamen'tal, *adj.*, pert. to the firmament.
fir'man, *n.*, a decree or licence of an Eastern monarch.
firm'er, *adj.*, *comp.* of firm.
firm'est, *adj.*, *super.* of firm.
firm'ly, *adv.*, in a firm manner.
firm'ness, *n.*, solidity; resolution.
first, *adj.* and *adv.*, preceding all others; foremost.
first'-born, *n.* and *adj.*, eldest; first brought forth.
first'-class, *adj.*, of the highest excellence.
first'-fruits, *n. pl.*, the first produce, profits or effect.
first'-hand, *adj.*, direct from the source.
first'ling, *n.*, the first-born of an animal.
first'ly, *adv.*, in the first place.
first'-rate, *adj.*, *s.q.* first-class.
firth, *n.*, a Scottish river-estuary, or arm or channel of the sea.
fir'-tree, *n.*, a coniferous tree; a pine-tree.
fisc, *n.*, a state treasury.
fis'cal, *adj.*, rel. to the public revenue.
fish, *n.*, an animal that lives in water, having gills and cold blood; *v.i.*, to catch fish.
fished, *p.p.*, fish.
fish'er, *n.*, one who fishes.
fish'erman, *n.*, one whose occupation is to catch fish.
fish'ery, *n.*, a place where fish are regularly caught.
fish'gig, *n.*, a kind of harpoon.
fish'-hook, *n.*, a hook for catching fish.
fish'ing, *n.*, the art of catching fish; *adj.*, used in fishing; *pr.p.*, fish.
fish'ing-line, *n.*, a line for catching fish.
fish'-market, *n.*, a market where fish is sold.
fish'monger, *n.*, a seller of fish.
fish'-pond, *n.*, a pond stocked with fresh-water fish.
fish'-tackle, *n.*, rods, lines, hooks, nets, etc., for fishing.
fish'-shop, *n.*, a shop where fish is sold.
fish'wife, *n.*, a woman who retails fish.
fish'y, *adj.*, having the qualities of fish; worn out, as by dissipation; suspiciously unsafe or treacherous.
fis'sile, *adj.*, readily splitting into flakes.
fissil'ity, *n.*, the quality of being fissile.
fis'sion, *n.*, the act of splitting.
fissip'arous, *adj.*, reproducing by fission or spontaneous division.
fis'siped, *adj.*, having toes separated to the base.
fis'sure, *n.*, a cleft, crack, or narrow chasm; *v.t.* and *i.*, to crack or fracture.
fis'sured, *p.p.*, fissure.
fist, *n.*, the clenched hand.
fist'ic, *adj.*, pugilistic.
fist'icuffs, *n. pl.*, a combat with fists.

fis'tula, *n.*, a morbid channel from an internal part to the surface of the skin; a musical pipe.
fis'tular, *adj.*, hollow; like a pipe or reed.
fis'tulary, *i.q.*, fistular.
fis'tulous, *adj.*, formed like a fistula.
fit, *n.*, a sudden, violent attack of disease; a paroxysm; a sudden activity followed by relaxation: *adj.*, suitable; *v.t.*, to adapt; to suit; *v.i.*, to be adjusted to shape.
fitch, *n.*, a vetch; a kind of bearded wheat; a pole-cat.
fitch'et, *n.*, a pole-cat.
fit'ful, *adj.*, spasmodic.
fit'ly, *adv.*, suitably.
fit'ness, *n.*, suitableness.
fit'ted, *p.p.*, fit.
fit'ter, *n.*, one who fits; one who puts the parts of machinery together; *adj.*, *comp.* of fit.
fit'test, *adj.*, *super.* of fit.
fit'ting, *adj.*, appropriate; *n.*, something fitted to another thing as an accessory; *pr.p.*, fit.
fit'tingly, *adv.*, suitably.
fit'tings, *n.*, pl. of fitting.
fitz, *adj.*, a prefix meaning "son of" used to form a patronymic surname.
five, *adj.*, four and one added.
five'fold, *adj.*, five times repeated.
fives'-court, *n.*, a court in which the game of fives (a kind of hand-tennis) is played.
fix, *v.t.*, to make firm; to fasten; *n.*, a dilemma.
fix'able, *adj.*, capable of being fixed.
fixa'tion, *n.*, the act of fixing.
fix'ative, *n.*, gum or glue.
fixed, *adj.*, established; fast; not volatile; *p.p.*, fix.
fix'edly, *adv.*, in a fixed manner.
fix'edness, *n.*, the state of being fixed.
fix'ing, *pr.p.*, fix.
fix'ings, *n. pl.*, accessories; equipment.
fix'ity, *n.*, fixed character; stability.
fix'ture, *n.*, anything fixed in position; part of the furniture of a house fixed to it with nails, screws, etc.
fiz'gig, *n.*, *i.q.* fishgig.
fizz, *v.i.*, to make a hissing sound; *n.*, a sparkling, effervescent wine (*slang*).
fizzed, *p.p.*, fizz.
fizz'ing, *pr.p.*, fizz.
fiz'zle, *v.i.*, *i.q.* fizz.
fiz'zled, *p.p.*, fizzle.
fiz'zling, *pr.p.*, fizzle.
fjeld, *n.*, a high, barren Norwegian plateau.
flab'bergast, *v.t.*, to astound.
flab'bergasted, *p.p.*, flabbergast.
flab'bergasting, *pr.p.*, flabbergast.
flab'biness, *n.*, the state of being flabby
flab'by, *adj.*, soft and yielding to the touch; hanging loose by its own weight.
flabel'late, *adj.*, fan-shaped.
flabella'tion, *n.*, fanning to keep fractured limbs and wounds cool.
flac'cid, *adj.*, lax; drooping.
flaccid'ity, *n.*, *i.q.* flaccidness.
flac'cidness, *n.*, the state of being flaccid.
flag, *n.*, a banner; a flat paving-stone; a kind of iris, having sword-shaped leaves; *v.i.*, to droop; to grow languid.
flagell'ant, *n.*, a fanatic who scourges himself.
flag'ellate, *v.t.*, to scourge.
flag'ellated, *p.p.*, flagellate.
flag'ellating, *pr.p.*, flagellate.
flagella'tion, *n.*, a flogging; the discipline of the scourge.
flageolet', *n.*, a small wind instrument resembling a flute.
flagged, *p.p.*, flag.
flag'giness, *n.*, the state of being flaggy
flag'ging, *pr.p.*, flag.
flag'gy, *adj.*, abounding in or resembling the plants called flags.
flagi'tious, *adj.*, grossly wicked.
flag'-officer, *n.*, an admiral.
flag'on, *n.*, a narrow-mouthed vessel for holding liquors.
fla'grance, *n.*, *i.q.* flagrancy.
fla'grancy, *n.*, heinousness; enormity.
fla'grant, *adj.*, glaring; notorious.
fla'grantly, *adv.*, in a flagrant manner.
flag'-ship, *n.*, the ship of a flag-officer.
flag'staff, *n.*, the pole on which a flag is displayed.
flag'-stone, *n.*, fissile sandstone; a large, flat paving-stone.
flail, *n.*, an instrument for threshing grain from the ear.
flair, *n.*, an intuitive perception; a power of scent.
flake, *n.*, a scale; a small fleecy particle; *v.i.*, to peel off.
flaked, *p.p.*, flake.
flake'-white, *n.*, a fine white pigment.
fla'kiness, *n.*, the state of being flaky.
fla'king, *pr.p.*, flake.
fla'ky, *adj.*, lying in flakes or thin layers.
flam, *n.*, a falsehood.
flam'beau, *n.*, a torch.
flamboy'ant, *adj.*, a term applied to Gothic architecture the chief feature of which is a wavy, flame-like tracery in the mouldings; extravagant.
flame, *n.*, a blaze; one beloved; *v.i.*, to blaze; to break out into violent passion.

flamed, *p.p.*, flame.
fla'men, *n.*, an ancient Roman priest (*Lat.*).
fla'ming, *pr.p.*, flame.
flamin'go, *n.*, a long-legged, web-footed, tropical bird with scarlet plumage.
Flamin'ian, *adj.*, pert. to C. Flaminius, a Roman censor.
flammabil'ity, *n.*, inflammability.
flam'mable, *adj.*, inflammable.
flam'meous, *adj.*, rel. to flame.
fla'my, *adj.*, consisting of flame.
flanch, *n.*, *i.q.* flange.
flange, *n.*, a projecting rim; *v.t.*, to make a flange on.
flank, *n.*, the side; *v.t.*, to be at the side of.
flanked, *p.p.*, flank.
flank'er, *n.*, one who, or that which, flanks.
flank'ing, *pr.p.*, flank.
flan'nel, *n.*, a soft, woollen cloth.
flannelette', *n.*, a cotton cloth resembling flannel.
flan'nelled, flan'neled, *adj.*, covered with flannel.
flap, *n.*, a loose, flat appendage hanging by the end or side and easily moved; the motion of anything broad and loose; a stroke; *v.t.*, to move or beat as with a flap; *v.i.*, to flutter.
flap'dragon, *n.*, *i.q.* snapdragon.
flapped, *p.p.*, flap.
flap'per, *n.*, a young wild duck; one who, or that which, flaps; a young girl whose hair hangs loose or in a plait (*colloq.*).
flare, *v.i.*, to burn brightly but waveringly; *n.*, a bright, unsteady light.
flared, *p.p.*, flare.
flar'ing, *pr.p.*, flare.
flash, *n.*, momentary brightness; an instant; *v.i.*, to give out a flash; to dart; *v.t.*, to convey instantaneously; *adj.*, gaudy; counterfeit.
flashed, *p.p.*, flash.
flash'er, *n.*, one who, or that which, flashes.
flash'-house, *n.*, a brothel.
flash'ily, *adv.*, in a flashy manner.
flash'ing, *pr.p.*, flash.
flash'y, *adj.*, tawdry.
flask, *n.*, a narrow-necked, globular glass bottle; a pocket spirit-bottle; a sportsman's gunpowder holder.
flas'ket, *n.*, a long, shallow basket.
flat, *adj.*, having a level surface; stale; dull; *n.*, a plain; a musical sign (♭); a floor; a simpleton; a barge; *v.t.*, to flatten.
flat'-boat, *n.*, a canal boat or barge.
flat'fish, *n.*, a fish with a flattened body.
flat'-iron, *n.*, a smoothing iron used in laundries.
flat'ly, *adv.*, positively.
flat'head, *n.*, a Chinook Indian; *adj.*, having a flat head produced artificially
flat'ness, *n.*, the quality of being flat.
flat'ted, *p.p.*, flat.
flat'ten, *v.t.*, to make flat.
flat'tened, *p.p.*, flatten.
flat'tening, *pr.p.*, flatten.
flat'ter, *v.t.*, to gratify; to inspire with false hopes; *adj.*, *comp.* of flat.
flat'tered, *p.p.*, flatter.
flat'terer, *n.*, one who flatters.
flat'tering, *pr.p.*, flatter; *n.*, *i.q.* flattery.
flat'tery, *n.*, insincere praise; adulation.
flat'test, *adj.*, *super.* of flat.
flat'ting, *n.*, a kind of house-painting.
flat'tish, *adj.*, somewhat flat.
flat'ulence, *n.*, the state of being flatulent.
flat'ulency, *n.*, *i.q.* flatulence.
flat'ulent, *adj.*, windy; affected with wind in the stomach.
fla'tus, *n.*, wind in the stomach.
flaunt, *v.i.*, to act ostentatiously; *v.t.*, to display.
flaunt'ed, *p.p.*, flaunt.
flaunt'er, *n.*, one who flaunts.
flaunt'ing, *adj.*, ostentatious; *pr.p.*, flaunt.
flaut'ist, *n.*, a player on the flute.
fla'vorous, *adj.*, having a rich flavour.
fla'vour, fla'vor, *n.*, taste; relish; *v.t.*, to season.
fla'voured, *adj.*, affecting the taste or smell; *p.p.*, flavour.
fla'vouring, *n.*, something that gives flavour to another thing; *pr.p.*, flavour.
fla'vourless, *adj.*, tasteless.
flaw, *n.*, a crack; a defect; a sudden, short gust of wind; *v.t.*, to produce a flaw in.
flaw'less, *adj.*, without defect.
flaw'y, *adj.*, faulty; full of flaws; subject to sudden gusts.
flax, *n.*, a plant of which the fibres are made into linen threads; the fibre prepared for spinning.
flax'en, *adj.*, made of flax; of the colour of flax; fair.
flax'seed, *n.*, the seed of flax; linseed.
flax'y, *adj.*, like flax.
flay, *v.t.*, to skin.
flayed, *p.p.*, flay.
flay'er, *n.*, one who flays.
flay'ing, *pr.p.*, flay.
flea, *n.*, an agile insect with a troublesome bite.
flea'bane, *n.*, a plant with a supposed power of driving away fleas.
flea'-bite, *n.*, the bite of a flea; a trifling inconvenience; a trifle.

fleam, *n.*, a farrier's lancet.
flea'wort, *n.*, a medicinal herb with seeds shaped like fleas.
fleck, *n.*, a spot; *v.t.*, to dapple.
flecked, *p.p.*, fleck.
fleck'er, *v.t.*, *i.q.* fleck.
fleck'less, *adj.*, spotless.
flec'tion, *n.*, the act of bending.
flec'tor, *n.*, a muscle that produces bending.
fled, *p.p.*, flee.
fledge, *v.t.*, to furnish with feathers.
fledged, *p.p.*, fledge.
fledge'ling, *n.*, a young bird just fledged.
fledg'ing, *pr.p.*, fledge.
flee, *v.i.*, to run away from; to seek shelter.
fleece, *n.*, the woollen coat of a sheep, *v.t.*, to rob pitilessly.
fleeced, *p.p.*, fleece.
flee'cer, *n.*, one who fleeces or robs of money.
flee'cing, *pr.p.*, fleece.
flee'cy, *adj.*, woolly.
fle'er, *n.*, one who flees.
fleer, *v.i.*, to sneer, *n.*, the act of mocking.
fleered, *p.p.*, fleer.
fleer'er, *n.*, a sneerer.
fleer'ing, *pr.p.*, fleer.
fleet, *n.*, a number of ships in company; *adj.*, swift; *v.i.*, to flit; to fly swiftly.
fleet'est, *adj.*, *super.* of fleet.
fleet'ing, *adj.*, transient; *pr.p.*, fleet.
fleet'ness, *n.*, rapidity.
Flem'ing, *n.*, a native of Flanders.
Flem'ish, *adj.*, pert. to Flanders; *n.*, the language of the Flemings; *pl.*, the people of Flanders.
flense, *v.t.*, to cut up and remove blubber from a whale.
flensed, *p.p.*, flense.
flens'ing, *pr.p.*, flense.
flesh, *n.*, the softer, solid part of the body of an animal; meat; mankind; carnal desire; the pulp of fruit; *v.t.*, to give the first taste of blood to; to use for the first time.
flesh'-colour, *n.*, the colour of flesh; carnation.
fleshed, *adj.*, having flesh of a particular kind; *p.p.*, flesh.
flesh'er, *n.*, a butcher (*Scot.*).
flesh'iness, *n.*, corpulence.
flesh'ings, *n. pl.*, tight drawers worn by dancers and actors, coloured to resemble the skin.
flesh'liness, *n.*, carnal appetites.
flesh'ly, *adj.*, carnal; not spiritual.
flesh'y, *adj.*, corpulent.
fletch, *v.t.*, to feather an arrow.
fleur-de-lis', *n.*, an heraldic lily; the iris.
flew, *p.p.*, fly.
flexibil'ity, *n.*, pliancy; readiness to comply.
flex'ible, *adj.*, pliant; yielding to pressure.
flex'ibly, *adv.*, in a flexible manner.
flex'ile, *adj.*, flexible; pliable.
flex'ion, *n.*, the act of bending; a part bent; an inflection.
flex'or, *n.*, a muscle that produces flexion.
flex'uous, *adj.*, having turns or windings.
flex'ure, *n.*, a bend; a part bent.
flib'bertigib'bet, *n.*, a restless, flighty person; a busy imp.
flick, *n.*, a sharp, sudden stroke, as with a whip; *v.t.*, to flip.
flick'er, *v.i.*, to waver; to flutter; *n.*, a wavering gleam.
flick'ered, *p.p.* flicker.
flick'ering, *pr.p.*, flicker.
fli'er, *n.*, one who flies.
flies, 3rd per. sing., *pres.*, fly; pl. of fly.
flight, *n.*, the act of fleeing or flying; a volley.
flight'iness, *n.*, extreme volatility.
flight'y, *adj.*, volatile; giddy; fickle.
flim'sily, *adv.*, in a flimsy manner.
flim'siness, *n.*, the quality of being flimsy.
flim'sy, *adj.*, unsubstantial; *n.*, a thin sort of paper.
flinch, *v.i.*, to shrink to wince.
flinched, *p.p.*, flinch.
flinch'ing, *pr.p.*, flinch.
fling, *v.t.*, to throw; *n.*, a Scottish dance; full enjoyment of pleasure.
fling'er, *n.*, one who flings.
fling'ing, *pr.p.*, fling.
flint, *n.*, a very hard stone, a kind of quartz.
flint'iness, *n.*, the quality of being flinty or very hard.
flint'y, *adj.*, containing flints; like flint; very hard; cruel.
flip, *n.*, a flick; a drink made of beer and spirits heated; *v.t.*, to flick.
flip'-flap, *n.*, a gigantic toy whereby people are raised to a great height.
flip'pancy, *n.*, the quality of being flippant.
flip'pant, *adj.*, pert; displaying levity.
flip'pantly, *adv.*, in a flippant manner.
flip'pantness, *n.*, *i.q.* flippancy.
flip'per, *n.*, the paddle of a turtle; the arm of a seal.
flirt, *v.t.*, to throw with a jerk; to play at courtship; *n.*, one who flirts or plays at love.
flirta'tion, *n.*, playing at courtship.
flirt'ed, *p.p.*, flirt.
flirt'ing, *pr.p.*, flirt.
flit, *v.i.*, to fly away quickly; to flutter; to migrate.
flitch, *n.*, a side of bacon.

flit'ted, *p.p.*, flit.
flit'ter, *v.t.* and *i.*, to flutter; *n.*, a rag; a tatter.
flit'ting, *prp.*, flit.
float, *v.i.*, to be supported by a fluid; *v.t.*, to cause to float; to launch a company or scheme; *n.*, that which floats on the surface of a fluid; a buoy; the cork on an angler's line; a raft.
float'age, *n.*, anything floating on water.
float'ed, *p.p.*, float.
float'er, *n.*, one that floats.
float'ing, *adj.*, resting on a fluid; not invested; unsettled; *pr.p.*, float.
floccilla'tion, *n.*, the picking of bed-clothes by a sick person in delirium.
floc'culence, *n.*, the state of being flocculent.
floc'culent, *adj.*, adhering in flakes or locks.
floc'cus, *n.*, a tuft of hair or feathers.
flock, *n.*, a lock of wool or hair; woollen refuse used for stuffing mattresses; a company of living creatures; *v.i.*, to crowd together.
flock'-bed, *n.*, a bed stuffed with flocks of wool or shredded cloth.
flocked, *p.p.*, flock.
flock'ing, *pr.p.*, flock.
flock'y, *adj.*, abounding with flocks.
floe, *n.*, a large mass of floating ice.
flog, *v.t.*, to beat or whip.
flogged, *p.p.*, flog.
flog'ger, *n.*, one who flogs.
flog'ging, *pr.p.*, flog; *n.*, a beating.
flood, *n.*, a great flow or overflow of water; the flowing in of the tide; abundance; *v.t.*, to overflow.
flood'ed, *p.p.*, flood.
flood'-gate, *n.*, a gate to be opened to let water flow, or shut to prevent it.
flood'ing, *n.*, the act of overflowing; *pr.p.*, flood.
floo'kan, / **flook'ing**, } *n.*, soft, clayey matter surrounding a vein of ore.
floor, *n.*, that part of a room on which we walk; a storey in a building; *v.t.*, to furnish with a floor; to knock down.
floored, *p.p.*, floor.
floor'ing, *n.*, materials for floors; *pr.p.*, floor.
flop, *v.i.*, to fall down suddenly; *n.*, a sudden sinking to the ground.
flopped, *p.p.*, flop.
flop'ping, *pr.p.*, flop.
flo'ra, *n.*, a collective term for the plants indigenous to a region.
flo'ral, *adj.*, pert. to flowers.
Flor'entine, *adj.*, rel. to Florence; *n.*, a native of Florence.
flores'cence, *n.*, a bursting into flower.
flores'cent, *adj.*, flowering.
flo'ret, *n.*, a single small flower in an inflorescence.
floricul'tural, *adj.*, pert. to floriculture.
flo'riculture, *n.*, cultivation of flowers.
flor'id, *adj.*, flushed with red; profusely ornamented.
flor'idness, *n.*, the state of being florid.
florif'erous, *adj.*, producing flowers.
flo'riform, *adj.*, in the form of a flower.
flor'in, *n.*, a two-shilling piece; a gold or silver coin of various countries, periods, and values.
flor'ist, *n.*, a dealer in, or cultivator of, flowers.
flos'cular, *adj.*, inflorescent.
flos'cule, *n.*, a floret.
flos'culus, *n.*, a floweret (*Lat.*).
floss, *n.*, a silky substance; small stream
flo'ta, *n.*, an old Spanish treasure-fleet.
flota'tion, *n.*, the science dealing with floating bodies; the act of launching a company.
flotil'la, *n.*, a little fleet; a fleet of small vessels.
flot'sam, *n.*, portions of a wreck that remain afloat.
flounce, *n.*, a jerking motion of the body indicating displeasure; a horizontal strip attached to a frock; *v.i.*, to move the body in jerks to show displeasure.
flounced, *p.p.*, flounce.
flounc'ing, *pr.p.*, flounce.
floun'der, *n.*, a flat-fish; *v.i.*, to roll or tumble about; to wallow.
floun'dered, *p.p.*, flounder.
floun'dering, *pr.p.*, flounder.
flour, *n.*, finely ground meal of grain; *v.t.*, to sprinkle with flour.
floured, *p.p.*, flour.
flour'ing, *pr.p.*, flour.
flour'ish, *v.i.*, to increase; to prosper; to make ornamental strokes; *v.t.*, to brandish; *n.*, an embellishment; a waving of something held in the hand; a fanfare.
flour'ished, *p.p.*, flourish.
flour'isher, *n.*, one who flourishes.
flour'ishing, *adj.*, thriving; *pr.p.*, flourish.
flour'y, *adj.*, covered with flour.
flout, *v.t.*, to treat with contempt.
flout'ed, *p.p.*, flout.
flout'er, *n.*, one who flouts.
flout'ing, *pr.p.*, flout.
flow, *v.i.*, to run smoothly, like water; to rise, as the tide; *n.*, a current; the rise of the tide; even movement.
flowed, *p.p.*, flow.
flow'er, *n.*, a blossom; youthful vigour;

v.i., to blossom; to flourish.

flower-de-luce′, *n.*, *i.q.* fleur-de-lis.

flow′ered, *adj.*, ornamented with flowers; *p.p.*, flower.

flow′eret, *n.*, a small flower.

flow′eriness, *n.*, the state of being flowery; figurative language.

flow′ering, *adj.*, producing flowers; *pr.p.*, flower.

flow′erless, *adj.*, having no flowers.

flow′ery, *adj.*, florid; full of flowers.

flow′ing, *pr.p.*, flow; *adj.*, fluent; smooth.

flow′ingly, *adv.*, in a flowing manner.

flown, *p.p.*, fly.

flu′can, **fluc′can**, *n.*, *i.q.*, flookan.

fluctif′erous, *adj.*, tending to produce waves.

fluc′tuate, *v.i.*, to move backward and forward; to rise and fall.

fluc′tuated, *p.p.*, fluctuate.

fluc′tuating, *adj.*, wavering; changeable; *pr.p.*, fluctuate.

fluctua′tion, *n.*, a rising and falling; unsteadiness.

flue, *n.*, a smoke-passage in a chimney; fluff.

flu′ency, *n.*, readiness of utterance.

flu′ent, *adj.*, flowing; voluble; smooth.

flu′ently, *adv.*, in a fluent manner.

fluff, *n.*, down or nap, generally loose.

fluff′y, *adj.*, downy; giving off fluff.

flu′id, *adj.*, liquid or gaseous; *n.*, a liquid or gas.

fluid′ity, *n.*, the state of being fluid.

flu′idize, *v.t.*, to convert into a fluid.

flu′idness, *n.*, *i.q.* fluidity.

fluke, *n.*, the part of an anchor which catches in the ground; a flounder; a parasite in sheep's liver; a variety of potato; an accidental success; *v.i.*, to make a fluke.

flu′ky, *adj.*, accidentally lucky.

flume, *n.*, an artificial channel for water to drive a mill or for gold-mining.

flu′minous, *adj.*, abounding in streams.

flum′mery, *n.*, a sort of jelly made from flour or meal; empty compliment.

flum′mox, *v.t.*, to embarrass.

flung, *p.p.*, fling.

flunk′ey, *n.*, a male servant in livery; a toady.

flunk′eyism, *n.*, servility.

flu′or, *n.*, a beautiful transparent mineral.

fluor′ic, *adj.*, pert. to fluor.

flu′oride, *n.*, a compound of fluorine and another element.

flu′orine, *n.*, an element existing in fluor.

flu′or-spar, *n.*, Derbyshire Spar; *i.q.* fluor.

flur′ried, *adj.*, agitated; *p.p.* flurry.

flur′ry, *n.*, agitation; a gust of wind; *v.t.*, to agitate.

flur′rying, *pr.p.*, flurry.

flush, *v.i.*, to blush; *v.t.*, to cause to redden suddenly; to elate; to wash out with water; *n.*, any warm colouring; a run of cards of the same suit; *adj.*, having the surface level with the adjacent surface; well supplied with money.

flushed, *p.p.*, flush.

flush′er, *n.*, one who, or that which, flushes.

flush′ing, *pr.p.*, flush.

flus′ter, *v.t.*, to confuse; *n.*, agitation of mind.

flus′tered, *p.p.*, fluster.

flus′tering, *pr.p.*, fluster.

flute, *n.*, a small musical wind instrument; a perpendicular furrow on the shaft of a column; *v.t.*, to make flutes or channels in.

flu′ted, *adj.*, channelled; *p.p.*, flute.

flu′ter, *n.*, one who makes grooves; a flutist.

flu′ting, *n.*, fluted work; *pr.p.*, flute.

flu′tist, *n.*, a flute-player.

flut′ter, *v.i.*, to move with quick vibrations or undulations; *v.t.*, to throw into confusion; *n.*, agitation of the mind.

flut′tered, *p.p.*, flutter.

flut′tering, *pr.p.*, flutter.

flu′ty, *adj.*, soft and clear in tone.

flu′vial, *adj.*, rel. to rivers.

flu′vialist, *n.*, one who explains geological phenomena by the action of streams.

flu′viatile, *adj.*, growing in a river.

flux, *n.*, the act of flowing; a discharge; a liquid state due to heat; *v.t.*, to fuse.

fluxa′tion, *n.*, a passing away.

fluxibil′ity, *n.*, the state of being fluxible.

flux′ible, *adj.*, capable of being fused.

flux′ion, *n.*, an excessive flowing or discharge; in mathematics, a differential.

flux′ional, *adj.*, variable.

flux′ionary, *adj.*, *i.q.*, fluxional.

flux′ionist, *n.*, one skilled in fluxions or the differential calculus.

fly, *v.i.*, to move through the air; to flee; *n.*, a winged insect; a hackney coach.

fly′blow, *n.*, the egg of a fly.

fly′-catcher, *n.*, that which catches flies; a kind of bird.

fly'er, *n.*, one that flies; part of a printing machine.
fly'ing, *pr.p.*, fly.
fly'ing-fish, *n.*, a fish that can fly through the air for a time by using its fins as planes.
fly'ing-machine', *n.*, a machine on which a man can fly; an aeroplane.
fly'-leaf, *n.*, a blank leaf at the beginning or end of a book.
fly'-shuttle, *n.*, the shuttle impelled by the weaver.
fly'-trap, *n.*, an American sensitive plant, the leaves of which close upon and capture insects.
fly'-wheel, *n.*, a heavy wheel which regulates the motion of an engine.
foal, *n.*, a young horse or mare; *v.i.*, to bring forth young, said of a mare or ass.
foaled, *p.p.*, foal.
foal'ing, *pr.p.*, foal.
foam, *n.*, froth; *v.i.*, to froth; to be angry.
foamed, *p.p.*, foam.
foam'ing, *pr.p.*, foam.
foam'y, *adj.*, frothy.
fob, *n.*, a watch-pocket; *v.t.*, to trick.
fobbed, *p.p.*, fob.
fob'bing, *pr.p.*, fob.
fo'cal, *adj.*, pert. to a focus.
focim'eter, *n.*, an instrument for finding the focus of a lens.
fo''c'sle, *n.*, *i.q.* forecastle.
fo'cus, *n.*, a point of concentration; *v.t.*, to bring to a focus.
fo'cus(s)ed, *p.p.*, focus.
fo'cus(s)ing, *pr.p.*, focus.
fod'der, *n.*, food for cattle; *v.t.*, to feed with fodder.
fod'dered, *p.p.*, fodder.
fod'dering, *pr.p.*, fodder.
foe, *n.*, an enemy.
foe'man, *n.*, an enemy in war; a personal antagonist.
foe'tal, *adj.*, *i.q.* fetal.
foe'tor, *n.*, *i.q.* fetor.
foe'tus, *n.*, *i.q.* fetus.
fog, *n.*, a dense, watery vapour darkening the atmosphere; *v.t.*, to envelop with fog.
fog'-bank, *n.*, a bank of fog at sea.
fogged, *p.p.*, fog.
fog'giness, *n.*, the state of being foggy.
fog'ging, *pr.p.*, fog.
fog'gy, *adj.*, abounding with fog; misty.
fog'-horn, *n.*, a warning in foggy weather.
fo'gy, *n.*, an old-fashioned fellow.
Foh, **foh**, *interj.*, an exclamation of impatience or dislike.
foi'ble, *n.*, the weak part of a sword; a slight moral weakness.
foil, *v.t.*, to frustrate; *n.*, a blunt sword for fencing; leaf metal; something enhancing beauty by contrast.
foiled, *p.p.*, foil; *adj.*, having arcs or hollow curves, said of a Gothic window.
foil'er, *n.*, one who foils.
foil'ing, *pr.p.*, foil.
foist, *v.t.*, to pass off as genuine.
foist'ed, *p.p.*, foist.
foist'er, *n.*, one who foists.
foist'ing, *pr.p.*, foist.
fold, *n.*, the doubling of cloth; an inclosure for sheep; *v.t.*, to lay one part over another of; to enfold; to confine in a sheepfold.
fold'age, *n.*, a manorial privilege rel. to sheepfolds.
fold'ed, *p.p.*, fold.
fold'er, *n.*, one who, or that which, folds.
fold'ing, *pr.p.*, fold.
folia'ceous, *adj.*, leafy.
fo'liage, *n.*, leaves collectively.
fo'liate, *v.t.*, to beat into a thin plate; to cover with tin-foil, etc.; *adj.*, furnished with leaves.
fo'liated, *adj.*, consisting of plates or laminae; in architecture, containing foils.
folia'tion, *n.*, the leafing of plants; the property in some rocks of splitting into laminae; the foils, cusps, etc., in a Gothic window.
fo'liature, *n.*, foliage.
fo'lier, *n.*, goldsmith's foil.
folif'erous, *adj.*, producing leaves.
fo'lio, *n.*, a book of the largest size; an opening of an account-book.
fo'liomort, *adj.*, having the colour of a dead leaf.
fo'lious, *adj.*, thin, like a leaf.
folk, *n.*, people in general.
'olk'land, *n.*, public land held in common by the people in ancient England.
folk'-lore, *n.*, rural superstitions, tales, traditions, etc.
folk'moot, *n.*, an assembly of the people in ancient England for legislative purposes.
folk'mote, *n.*, *i.q.* folkmoot.
fol'licle, *n.*, a dry seed-vessel opening on one side only; a vesicle; a gland.
follic'ular, *adj.*, rel. to follicles.
follic'ulated, *adj.*, having follicles.
follic'ulous, *adj.*, *i.q.* follicular.
fol'low, *v.t.*, to move behind in the same direction.
fol'lowed, *p.p.*, follow.
fol'lower, *n.*, one who follows; an adherent.
fol'lowing, *n.*, a body of followers; *adj.*, being next after; *pr.p.*, follow.
fol'ly, *n.*, foolish, weak conduct.
foment', *v.t.*, to apply warm lotions to; to abet.
fomenta'tion, *n.*, the act of fomenting; encouragement; a warm lotion.

foment'ed, *p.p.*, foment.

foment'er, *n.*, one who foments.

foment'ing, *pr.p.*, foment.

fond, *adj.*, foolish; loving ardently.

fon'dant, *n.*, a soft, moulded, sweet confection.

fond'le, *v.t.*, to caress.

fond'led, *p.p.*, fondle.

fond'ler, *n.*, one who fondles.

fond'ling, *n.*, a person or thing fondled.

fond'ly, *adv.*, affectionately; tenderly.

fond'ness, *n.*, great affection.

font, *n.*, an ecclesiastical vessel used in baptism; a complete assortment of printing types of one size.

font'al, *adj.*, pert. to a fount or source.

fontanelle', *n.*, a membranous interval between the bones of a child's skull.

food, *n.*, nutriment.

food'less, *adj.*, not having food.

fool, *n.*, an idiot; a professional jester; *v.t.*, to deceive.

fooled, *p.p.*, fool.

fool'ery, *n.*, folly.

fool'hardiness, *n.*, mad rashness.

fool'hardy, *adj.*, daring without judgment.

fool'ing, *pr.p.* fool.

fool'ish, *adj.*, unwise; silly.

fool'ishly, *adv.*, in a foolish manner.

fool'ishness, *n.*, folly.

fools'cap, *n.*, a dunce's cap; long folio printing paper.

foot, *n.*, the lower extremity of an animal's leg; the bottom; infantry; a length of 12 in.; a measure of a verse; *v.t.*, to add up; to pay; *v.i.*, to dance.

foot'ball, *n.*, a leather air-ball for kicking.

foot'-board, *n.*, a treadle; a foot-rest.

foot'boy, *n.*, a page.

foot'-bridge, *n.*, a narrow bridge for foot passengers.

foot'ed, *adj.*, provided with a foot or feet.

foot'fall, *n.*, a footstep.

foot'-*guards*, *n. pl.*, household infantry.

foot'hold, *n.*, firm standing; settlement.

foot'ing, *n.*, permanent settlement; foundation.

foot'lights, *n. pl.*, a row of lights on the front of the stage in a theatre.

foot'man, *n.*, an infantry soldier; a man-servant.

foot'mark, *n.*, the mark of a foot.

foot'-muff, *n.*, a muff for keeping the feet warm.

foot'-pace, *n.*, a slow step.

foot'-pad, *n.*, a highwayman on foot.

foot'-path, *n.*, a narrow path.

foot'print, *n.*, the mark of a foot.

foot'-soldier, *n.*, an infantryman.

foot'sore, *adj.*, having feet made tender by much walking.

foot'stalk, *n.*, a petiole; a peduncle.

foot'step, *n.*, a footprint; a footfall; the sound of a footfall.

foot'stool, *n.*, a stool for the feet.

foot'-warmer, *n.*, a contrivance for warming the feet.

foot'way, *n.*, a path for walkers.

foo'zle, *v.i.*, to play a shot badly at golf; *n.*, a bad shot.

fop, *n.*, a dandy.

fop'ling, *n.*, a petty fop.

fop'pery, *n.*, dandyism.

fop'pish, *adj.*, vain of dress; affected in manners.

fop'pishly, *adv.*, in a foppish manner.

fop'pishness, *n.*, the state of being foppish.

***for*,** *prep.*, instead of; for the sake of; with a view to, etc.; *conj.*, because.

for'age, *n.*, food for horses and cattle; *v.i.*, to search for forage.

for'aged, *p.p.*, forage.

for'ager, *n.*, one who forages.

for'aging, *pr.p.*, forage.

fora'men, *n.*, a small natural opening in animals and plants.

fora'minated, *adj.*, having foramina or little holes.

Foraminif'era, *n. pl.*, an order of minute animals having a perforated skull.

foraminif'erous, *adj.*, rel. to the Foraminifera.

***forasmuch'*,** *conj.*, seeing that; since.

for'ay, *v.i.*, to pillage; *n.*, a predatory excursion.

forbad', forbade', *p.t.*, forbid.

forbear', *v.i.*, to refrain.

for'bear, *n.*, an ancestor.

forbear'ance, *n.*, long-suffering; lenity.

forbear'ing, *adj.*, having forbearance; *pr.p.*, forbear.

forbid', *v.t.*, to prohibit.

forbid'den, *p.p.* forbid; *adj.*, prohibited.

forbid'der, *n.*, one who forbids.

forbid'ding, *adj.*, repulsive; *pr.p.*, forbid.

forbid'dingly, *adv.*, repulsively.

forbore', *p.t.* of forbear.

forborne', *p.p.*, forbear.

force, *n.*, power; strength; a body of troops or other organized body of men; a waterfall; *v.t.*, to compel; to stuff.

forced, *adj.*, constrained, unnatural; *p.p.*, force.

force'ful, *adj.*, powerful.

force'fulness, *n.*, determination.

force'less, *adj.*, feeble.
force'-meat, *n.*, stuffing used in cookery.
for'ceps, *n.*, a two-bladed instrument like tongs, used by surgeons, jewellers, etc.
force'-pump, *n.*, a pump which delivers the water by means of pressure.
for'cer, *n.*, one who, or that which, forces.
for'cible, *adj.*, powerful; violent.
for'cibly, *adv.*, in a forcible manner.
for'cing, *n.*, the art of raising plants earlier than their natural season; *pr.p.*, force.
for'cipated, *adj.*, formed like a forceps.
forcipa'tion, *n.*, torture by pinching with a forceps.
for'cite, *n.*, a kind of dynamite.
ford, *n.*, a shallow river-crossing; *v.t.*, to wade through.
ford'able, *adj.*, capable of being forded.
ford'ed, *p.p.*, ford.
ford'ing, *pr.p.*, ford.
fore, *adj.*, in front; *interj.*, a warning cry in the game of golf.
fore'arm, *n.*, that part of the arm between elbow and wrist.
forearm', *v.t.*, to arm before the time of need.
forebode', *v.t.*, to presage.
forebo'ded, *p.p.*, forebode.
forebo'der, *n.*, one who forebodes.
forebo'ding, *n.*, a feeling of apprehension; *pr.p.*, forebode.
fore'brace, *n.*, a rope fastened to the fore yard-arm.
forecast', *v.t.*, to calculate beforehand.
fore'cast, *n.*, a guess or estimate of the future.
forecast'ing, *pr.p.*, forecast.
fore'castle, *n.*, the forepart of a vessel.
fore'chains, *n. pl.*, a contrivance to carry the lower shrouds of a foremast outside the ship's side.
foreclose', *v.t.*, to prevent; to compel a mortgager to pay the money borrowed or forfeit his estate.
foreclosed', *p.p.*, foreclose.
foreclo'sing, *pr.p.*, foreclose.
foreclo'sure, *n.*, the act of foreclosing.
foredate', *v.t.*, to antedate.
foredat'ed, *p.p.*, foredate.
foredat'ing, *pr.p.*, foredate.
fore'-deck, *n.*, the forepart of the deck of a ship.
foredoom', *v.t.*, to predestinate.
fore'father, *n.*, an ancestor.
fore'finger, *n.*, the first or index finger.
fore'foot, *n.*, a front foot.
fore'front, *n.*, the foremost part.
forego', *v.t.*, to precede.
forego'ing, *adj.*, preceding.
foregone', *adj.*, predetermined.
fore'ground, *n.*, the front part of the scene in a picture.
fore'handed, *adj.*, beforehand; seasonable.
fore'head, *n.*, the brow.
for'eign, *adj.*, alien; irrelevant.
for'eigner, *n.*, an alien.
for'eignness, *n.*, the quality of being foreign.
forejudge', *v.t.*, to prejudge.
foreknew', *p.t.*, foreknow.
foreknow', *v.t.*, to have previous knowledge of.
foreknow'er, *n.*, one who foreknows.
foreknow'ing, *pr.p.*, foreknow.
foreknowl'edge, *n.*, prescience.
foreknown', *p.p.*, foreknow.
fore'land, *n.*, a promontory.
fore'lock, *n.*, the lock of hair that grows above the forehead.
fore'man, *n.*, a chief workman; the chief man of a jury.
fore'mast, *n.*, the front mast of a ship.
fore'most, *adj.*, first; most advanced.
fore'name, *n.*, a personal name preceding the surname.
fore'named, *adj.*, mentioned before.
fore'noon, *n.*, morning between sunrise and mid-day.
foren'sic, *adj.*, rel. to courts of justice.
foreordain', *v.t.*, to appoint beforehand.
foreordained', *p.p.*, foreordain.
foreordain'ing, *pr.p.*, foreordain.
foreordina'tion, *n.*, predetermination; predestination.
fore'part, *n.*, the first part in time or place.
fore'rank, *n.*, the front.
forerun', *v.t.*, to run before.
forerun'ner, *n.*, a harbinger.
forerun'ning, *pr.p.*, forerun.
fore'said, *adj.*, mentioned before.
fore'sail, *n.*, the chief sail on the foremast.
foresee', *v.t.*, to see beforehand.
foresee'ing, *pr.p.*, foresee.
foreseen', *p.p.*, foresee.
forese'er, *n.*, one who foresees.
foreshad'ow, *v.t.*, to typify beforehand.
foreshad'owed, *p.p.*, foreshadow.
foreshad'owing, *pr.p.*, foreshadow.
fore'-sheet, *n.*, the rope with which the foresail is set.
fore'shore, *n.*, the shore between high and low watermark.

foreshort'en, *v.t.*, to depict an object directed towards the spectator with the due expression of its length and relative position.

foreshort'ened, *p.p.*, foreshorten.

foreshort'ening, *pr.p.*, foreshorten.

foreshow', *v.t.*, to exhibit beforehand; to foretell.

foreshowed', *p.p.*, foreshow.

foreshow'ing, *pr.p.*, foreshow.

fore'side, *n.*, the front side.

fore'sight, *n.*, provident care for the future; the sight on the muzzle of a gun.

fore'skin, *n.*, the prepuce.

for'est, *n.*, a large tract of land covered with trees; a district devoted to the chase; *adj.*, pert. to a forest.

forestall', *v.t.*, to anticipate.

forestall'er, *n.*, one who forestalls.

for'ester, *n.*, one who has charge of a forest, or of the timber on an estate.

for'estry, *n.*, the art of managing growing trees.

foret', *n.*, a drill for making vents in ordnance.

fore'taste, *n.*, enjoyment in advance.

foretaste', *v.t.*, to taste before possession.

foretell', *v.t.*, to predict.

foretell'er, *n.*, one who foretells.

foretell'ing, *pr.p.*, foretell.

fore'thought, *n.*, provident care.

foreto'ken, *v.t.*, to foreshow.

foretold', *p.p.*, foretell.

fore'top, *n.*, the platform on the head of a foremast.

forev'er, *adv.*, permanently.

forewarn', *v.t.*, to give previous notice to.

forewarned', *p.p.*, forewarn.

forewarn'ing, *pr.p.*, forewarn.

fore'woman, *n.*, a woman who superintends others.

for'feit, *v.t.*, to lose the right to; *n.*, the act of forfeiting; that which is forfeited; a penalty; *adj.*, forfeited.

for'feitable, *adj.*, subject to forfeiture.

for'feited, *p.p.*, forfeit.

for'feiter, *n.*, one who forfeits.

for'feiting, *pr.p.*, forfeit.

for'feiture, *n.*, the losing of some right by an offence; the thing forfeited.

forfend', *v.t.*, to avert.

for'fex, *n.*, a pair of shears (*Lat.*).

forgath'er, *v.i.*, to meet; to convene.

forgave', *p.p.*, forgive.

forge, *n.*, a smithy; *v.t.*, to work metal into shape in a forge; to counterfeit a signature, etc.; *v.i.*, to commit forgery; to move on slowly.

forge'able, *adj.*, capable of being forged.

forged. *p.p.*, forge.

forge'man, *n.*, a man employed at a forge.

for'ger, *n.*, one who commits forgery.

for'gery, *n.*, the crime of counterfeiting handwriting, etc.; that which is forged.

forget', *v.t.*, to let go from the memory.

forget'ful, *adj.*, apt to forget.

forget'fulness, *n.*, the quality of being forgetful; oblivion.

forget'-me-not, *n.*, a small, bright-blue flower with a yellow eye.

forget'table, *adj.*, capable of being forgotten.

forget'ter, *n.*, one who forgets.

for'ging, *n.*, an article of metal forged; *pr.p.*, forge.

forgiv'able, *adj.*, pardonable.

forgive', *v.t.*, to pardon.

forgiv'en, *p.p.*, forgive.

forgive'ness, *n.*, pardon; willingness to forgive.

forgiv'er, *n.*, one who forgives.

forgiv'ing, *adj.*, inclined to overlook offences; *pr.p.*, forgive.

forgo', *v.t.*, to give up; to resign.

forgot', *p.p.* and *p.t.*, forget.

forgot'ten, *p.p.*, forget.

forjudge', *v.t.*, to prejudge; to expel from court.

fork, *n.*, an instrument with prongs for lifting something; one of the parts into which anything is bifurcated; *v.i.*, to divide into branches; *v.t.*, to dig or raise with a fork.

forked, *adj.*, having prongs or divisions like a fork.

fork'edness, *n.*, the quality of being forked.

fork'y, *adj.*, forked.

forlorn', *adj.*, abandoned; wretched.

forlorn'ness, *n.*, the state of being forlorn.

form, *n.*, shape; a long seat; the bed of a hare; *v.t.*, to shape.

form'al, *adj.*, ceremonious; conventional.

formal'dehyde, *n.*, a colourless, volatile liquid, chemically intermediate between formic acid and methyl alcohol.

form'alism, *n.*, strict adherence to form.

form'alist, *n.*, one given to formalism.

formal'ity, *n.*, a rule of proceeding; conventionality.

form'alize, *v.t.*, to render formal.

form'alized, *p.p.*, formalize.

form'alizing, *pr.p.*, formalize.

form'ally, *adv.*, in a formal manner; stiffly.
for'mat, *n.*, size of a book.
for'mate, *n.*, a salt of formic acid.
forma'tion, *n.*, production; arrangement.
form'ative, *adj.*, giving form.
forme, *n.*, type or plates fixed in a frame ready for printing.
formed, *p.p.*, form.
for'mer, *adj.*, preceding; earlier.
for'mer, *n.*, one who forms.
for'merly, *adv.*, before the present time.
for'mic, *adj.*, pert. to, or produced by, ants.
for'micate, *adj.*, pert. to an ant.
formica'tion, *n.*, a sensation like that of ants creeping on the skin.
for'midable, *adj.*, exciting fear or dread.
for'midably, *adv.*, in a formidable manner.
form'ing, *pr.p.*, form.
form'less, *adj.*, shapeless.
for'mula, *n.*, a prescribed form of words, doctrines, figures, or symbols expressing a rule or other statement.
for'mularize, *v.t.*, to formulate.
for'mulary, *n.*, a book containing prescribed forms.
for'mulate, *v.t.*, to express in a formula; to state precisely.
formula'tion, *n.*, the act of formulating.
for'nicate, *v.i.*, to have unlawful sexual intercourse.
for'nicated, *p.p.*, fornicate.
for'nicating, *pr.p.*, fornicate.
fornica'tion, *n.*, incontinence.
for'nicator, *n.*, one guilty of fornication.
for'nicatress, *n.*, an unmarried woman guilty of fornication.
for'nix, *n.*, the vault of the cranium (*Lat.*).
forsake', *v.t.*, to abandon.
forsa'ken, *p.p.*, forsake.
forsa'ker, *n.*, one who forsakes.
forsa'king, *pr.p.*, forsake.
forsook', *p.t.* of forsake.
forsooth', *adv.*, in truth (often ironical).
forswear', *v.t.*, to reject on oath; *v.i.*, to swear falsely.
forswear'er, *n.*, one who forswears; a perjurer.
forswore', *p.t.*, forswear.
forsworn', *p.p.*, forswear.
fort, *n.*, a small fortified place.
fort'alice, *n.*, a small outwork of a fortification.
for'te, *adv.*, loudly (in music).
forte, *n.*, the strong part of a sword-blade; chief excellence.
forth, *adv.*, onward in time, place, or order.
forth'coming, *adj.*, ready to appear.
forthwith', *adv.*, immediately.
for'tieth, *adj.*, next after the thirty-ninth; *n.*, one of forty equal parts into which a whole is divided.
for'tifiable, *adj.*, capable of being fortified.
fortifica'tion, *n.*, the art of strengthening military positions for defensive purposes; a fortified place.
for'tified, *p.p.*, fortify.
for'tifier, *n.*, one who fortifies.
for'tify, *v.t.*, to strengthen in any way.
for'tifying, *pr.p.*, fortify.
fortis'simo, *adv.*, in music, very loudly.
for'titude, *n.*, passive courage.
fort'night, *n.*, two weeks.
fort'nightly, *adj.* and *adv.*, once a fortnight.
for'tress, *n.*, a large fortified place.
fortu'itous, *adj.*, accidental.
fortu'itously, *adv.*, by chance.
fortu'itousness, *n.*, accident; chance.
fortu'ity, *n.*, *i.q.* fortuitousness.
for'tunate, *adj.*, lucky, successful.
for'tunately, *adv.*, luckily; happily.
for'tune, *n.*, chance; good luck; prosperity; great possessions.
for'tune-hunter, *n.*, a man who seeks to marry a rich woman.
for'tune-teller, *n.*, one who pretends to tell people their fortune in life.
for'ty, *adj.*, four times ten.
fo'rum, *n.*, a court, a tribunal.
for'ward, *adv.*, onward; *adj.*, being at the front, ready; pert; *v.t.*, to promote; to send to a destination.
for'warded, *p.p.*, forward.
for'warder, *n.*, one who forwards.
for'warding, *pr.p.*, forward.
for'wards, *adv.*, forward; to the front.
forzan'do, *adv.*, with emphasis (in music).
fosse, *n.*, a moat or ditch.
fosse'way, *n.*, one of the great Roman roads of England.
fos'sick, *v.i.*, to work waste heaps in hopes of finding gold; to rummage about for profit.
fos'sicker, *n.*, a miner who fossicks.
fos'sil, *n.*, petrified remains of animals and plants found in rocks.

fossilif'erous, *adj.*, containing fossils.

fossilifica'tion, *n.*, the act of fossilizing or becoming fossil.

fos'silist, *n.*, one versed in fossils.

fossiliza'tion, *n.*, the state of being fossilized.

fos'silize, *v.t.*, to convert into a fossil; *v.i.*, to become a fossil.

fos'silized, *p.p.*, fossilize.

fos'silizing, *pr.p.*, fossilize.

fossilol'ogy, *n.*, palaeontology.

fosso'rial, *adj.*, rel. to animals that dig in the ground for food and to make dwellings.

foss'way, *n.*, *i.q.* fosseway.

fos'ter, *v.t.*, to nourish; to encourage.

fos'terage, *n.*, the care of a foster-child.

fos'ter-brother, *n.*, one nursed at the same breast.

fos'ter-*child*, *n.*, a child nurtured by one who is not its father or mother.

fos'tered, *p.p.*, foster.

fos'terer, *n.*, one who fosters.

fos'ter-father, *n.*, one who adopts a child.

fos'tering, *pr.p.*, foster.

fos'terling, *n.*, a foster-child.

fos'ter-sister, *n.*, a girl or woman, not a sister, but nursed by the same person.

fos'ter-son, *n.*, an adopted son.

foth'er, *v.t.*, to stop a leak; *n.*, a weight for lead (19½ cwt.).

foth'ered, *p.p.*, fother.

fought, *p.p.*, fight.

foul, *adj.*, filthy; obscene; unfair; entangled; *v.t.*, to make foul; *v.i.*, to come into collision; *adv.*, in an irregular way; *n.*, a collision, an infringement of rules.

foulard', *n.*, a thin silk fabric.

fouled, *p.p.*, foul.

foul'ing, *pr.p.*, foul.

foul'ly, *adv.*, in a foul manner; shamefully

foul'ness, *n.*, filthiness.

fou'mart, *n.*, a polecat.

found, *p.p.*, find; *v.t.*, to lay the basis of; to form by melting a metal and pouring into a mould.

founda'tion, *n.*, the act of founding; a basis; an endowed institution.

founda'tioner, *n.*, one who derives support from the endowment of a school or college.

founda'tion-stone, *n.*, a stone of a public building laid in public with some ceremony.

found'ed, *p.p.*, found.

foun'der, *n.*, one who founds; *v.i.*, to fill and sink; to go lame; to miscarry.

foun'dered, *p.p.*, founder.

foun'derous, *adj.*, difficult to travel (of a road).

foun'dery, *n.*, *i.q.* foundry.

found'ing, *pr.p.*, found.

found'ling, *n.*, a child found without known parents.

found'ress, *n.*, a female founder.

foun'dry, *n.*, an establishment where metals are cast.

fount, *n.*, a spring of water; printing-type of the same kind.

foun'tain, *n.*, a spring of water; an artificial jet of water; a basin kept filled with water; origin or source.

foun'tain-head, *n.*, origin; primary source.

four, *adj.*, three and one.

fourchette', *n.*, the frog of a horse's hoof; part of the fingers of a glove.

four'fold, *adj.* and *adv.*, four times told.

four'-footed, *adj.*, having four feet.

Fou'rierism, *n.*, a socialistic system or form of communism.

four'-*in-hand*, *n.*, a vehicle with four horses and one driver.

four'-poster, *n.*, a large bed with four pillars for curtains.

four'score, *adj.*, eighty.

four'some, *n.*, a match at golf in which four people (two on either side) engage.

four'-square, *adj.*, square.

fourteen, *adj.*, four and ten.

fourteenth, *adj.*, the ordinal of fourteen; *n.*, one of fourteen equal parts into which a whole is divided.

fourth, *adj.*, the ordinal of four; *n.*, one of four equal parts into which a whole is divided.

fourth'ly, *adv.*, in the fourth place.

four'-wheeler, *n.*, a cab with four wheels.

fo'vea, *n.*, a little depression or pit.

fo'veate, *adj.*, pitted.

fo'veolate, *adj.*, *i.q.* foveate.

fovil'la, *n.*, the powder in a pollen grain that causes fertilization.

fowl, *n.*, a bird; a domestic cock or hen.

fowl'er, *n.*, a sportsman who pursues wild fowl.

fowl'ing, *n.*, the practice of pursuing wild fowl.

fowl'ing-piece, *n.*, a light gun for shooting birds.

fox, *n.*, a wild animal of the dog kind that preys on chickens and other small animals; a cunning fellow; *v.i.*, to turn sour; to become discoloured.

fox'-case, *n.*, the skin of a fox.

fox'-chase, *n.*, the hunting of a fox with hounds and horses.

foxed, *adj.*, marked with brownish spots, as paper.

fox'glove, *n.*, a plant with a spike of showy flowers.

fox'hound, *n.*, a hound for chasing foxes.

fox'iness, *n.*, cunning.

fox'like, *adj.*, resembling a fox.

fox'tail, *n.*, a grass with a close, cylindrical panicle of flowers resembling a fox's brush.

fox'y, *adj.*, cunning; sour (of beer, wine, etc.).

foyer', *n.*, a green-room or hall in a theatre (*Fr.*).

fracas, *n.*, a disturbance. (U.S.)

frac'tion, *n.*, a fragment; a part.

frac'tional, *adj.*, pert. to fractions.

frac'tious, *adj.*, peevish.

frac'tiously, *adv.*, snappishly.

frac'tiousness, *n.*, a fractious temper.

frac'ture, *n.*, a breakage; a crack; *v.t.*, to cause fracture in.

frac'tured, *p.p.*, fracture.

frac'turing, *pr.p.*, fracture.

frag'ile, *adj.*, easily broken; frail.

frag'ilely, *adv.*, in a fragile manner.

fragil'ity, *n.*, the quality of being fragile.

frag'ment, *n.*, a part broken off; anything left unfinished.

frag'mentary, *adj.*, composed of fragments; incomplete.

fra'grance, *n.*, pleasing scent.

fra'grancy, *n.*, *i.q.* fragrance.

fra'grant, *adj.*, sweet-smelling.

fra'grantly, *adv.*, with a sweet scent.

frail, *adj.*, fragile; perishable; not strong against temptation; *n.*, a basket made of rushes.

frail'ness, *n.*, the condition of being frail.

frail'ty, *n.*, frailness; infirmity; a fault proceeding from weakness.

fra'mable, *adj.*, capable of being framed.

frame, *v.t.*, to invent; to surround with a frame; *n.*, structure; a case for inclosing a picture, etc.; disposition of the mind.

framed, *p.p.*, frame.

fra'mer, *n.*, one who frames.

frame'work, *n.*, a structure acting as a support.

fra'ming, *n.*, a system of frames; *pr.p.*, frame.

franc, *n.*, the French unit of currency; formerly a silver coin.

fran'chise, *n.*, the right of voting at a parliamentary election.

fran'chisement, *n.*, *i.q.* enfranchisement.

Francis'can, *n.*, a Grey Friar or Minorite; *adj.*, of the Order of St. Francis of Assisi.

franc-tireur', *n.*, an irregular sharp-shooter or sniper; employed in guerrilla warfare.

frangibil'ity, *n.*, the quality of being frangible.

fran'gible, *adj.*, brittle.

fran'gipane, *n.*, pastry containing cream and almonds; a perfume.

frangipa'ni, *n.*, a perfume resembling the odour of a West Indian flower, or jasmine.

frank, *adj.*, candid; *v.t.*, to transmit free of cost; *n.*, one of the ancient German race of Franks.

franked, *p.p.*, frank.

frank'incense, *n.*, a gum obtained from an Indian tree resembling the sumach, which is aromatic when burned.

frank'ing, *pr.p.*, frank.

frank'lin, *n.*, a yeoman; a freeholder.

frank'ly, *adv.*, candidly.

frank'ness, *n.*, the quality of being frank.

fran'tic, *adj.*, mad; furious; distracted.

fran'ticly, *adv.*, in a frantic manner.

fran'ticness, *n.*, the state of being frantic.

frap, *v.t.*, to make fast by binding (a nautical term).

frater'nal, *adj.*, brotherly.

frater'nity, *n.*, a brotherhood; a society.

fraterniza'tion, *n.*, the act of fraternizing.

frat'ernize, *v.i.*, to hold sympathetic intercourse.

frat'ernized, *p.p.*, fraternize.

frat'ernizer, *n.*, one who fraternizes.

frat'ernizing, *pr.p.*, fraternize.

frat'ricidal, *adj.*, rel. to fratricide.

frat'ricide, *n.*, the crime of murdering a brother; one who commits such a murder.

fraud, *n.*, an act of deceit to gain unfair advantage.

fraud'ful, *adj.*, characterized by fraud.

fraud'ulence, *n.*, the quality of being fraudulent.

fraud'ulency, *n.*, *i.q.* fraudulence.

fraud'ulent, *adj.*, using fraud; founded on fraud.

fraud'ulently, *adv.*, in a fraudulent manner.

fraught, *adj.*, freighted; filled; abounding.

fray, *n.*, an affray; *v.t.*, to rub away the surface of.

frayed, *p.p.*, fray.

fray'ing, *pr.p.*, fray.

freak, *n.*, a whim or fancy; an odd, irregular thing.

freak'ish, *adj.*, whimsical; capricious.

freck'le, *n.*, a small yellowish spot in the skin; *v.t.* and *i.*, to mark or become marked with freckles.

freck'led, *adj.*, marked with freckles; *p.p.*, freckle.

freck'ling, *pr.p.*, freckle.

freck'ly, *adj.*, covered with freckles.

free, *adj.*, at liberty; liberal; gratuitous; exempt; *v.t.*, to set at liberty.

free'-bench, *n.*, a widow's right in copyhold; a kind of dower.

free'booter, *n.*, a plunderer.

free'-born, *adj.*, born free.

freed, *p.p.*, free.

freed'man, *n.*, a manumitted slave.

free'dom, *n.*, the state of being free; independence; particular privileges.

free'hold, *n.*, an estate the tenant of which owes no duty except to the crown; the tenure of such an estate.

free'holder, *n.*, the possessor of a freehold.

free'ing, *pr.p.*, free.

free'-liver, *n.*, one who indulges his appetite freely.

free'ly, *adv.*, in a free manner.

free'man, *n.*, a man who is free.

free'mason, *n.*, a member of a certain secret society.

free'masonry, *n.*, the mysteries into which freemasons are initiated.

free'-minded, *adj.*, unperplexed; free from care.

free'ness, *n.*, the state of being free.

free'port, *n.*, a port free of customs.

fre'er, *n.*, one who frees; *adj.*, *comp.* of free.

free'-spoken, *adj.*, accustomed to speak without reserve.

fre'est, *adj.*, *super.* of free.

free'stone, *n.*, sandstone.

free'thinker, *n.*, a sceptic; a deist.

freethink'ing, *adj.*, holding the principles of a freethinker.

free-*trade*, *n.*, trade free from imposts on imported articles.

free-tra'der, *n.*, an advocate of free-trade.

free-wheel, *n.*, a wheel which can be released from the driving gear so as to run freely.

free-will', *n.*, voluntariness; *adj.*, voluntary.

freeze, *v.t.*, to harden into ice; *v.i.*, to change from a liquid to a solid.

freez'ing, *pr.p.*, freeze.

freez'ing-point, *n.*, the temperature at which water becomes ice.

freight, *n.*, cargo; charge for transport of goods by water; *v.t.*, to load a ship.

freight'age, *n.*, money paid for freight.

freight'ed, *p.p.* freight.

freight'er, *n.*, one who freights.

freight'ing, *pr.p.*, freight.

French, *adj.*, pert. to France; *n.*, the language of France.

French' horn, *n.*, a musical instrument of brass with many curves.

French'ified, *p.p.*, Frenchify.

French'ify, *v.t.*, to make French; to infect with French manners.

French'man, *n.*, a man of the French nation.

frenet'ic, *adj.*, frenzied; frantic.

fren'ulum, *n.*, a little frenum or restraining band.

fren'zied, *adj.*, maddened; frantic.

fren'ziedly, *adv.*, distractedly.

fren'zy, *n.*, madness; delirium, distraction; *v.t.*, to drive to frenzy.

fre'quency, *n.*, the state of being frequent.

fre'quent, *adj.*, often seen, done, or happening.

frequent', *v.t.*, to visit often.

frequent'ed, *p.p.*, frequent.

frequent'er, *n.*, one who frequents.

frequent'ing, *pr.p.*, frequent.

fre'quently, *adv.*, often.

fres'co, *n.*, a method of painting on walls; *v.t.*, to paint in fresco, as walls.

fres'coed, *p.p.*, fresco.

fresh, *adj.*, lively; bright; in good condition; health-giving; pure and cool; new; not salt; re-invigorated.

fresh'en, *v.t.*, to make fresh; *v.i.*, to grow fresh.

fresh'ened, *p.p.*, freshen.

fresh'ening, *pr.p.*, freshen.

fresh'er, *comp.* of fresh.

fresh'est, *adj.*, *super.* of fresh.

fresh'et, *n.*, a small flood in a river.

fresh'ly, *adv.*, newly; recently.

fresh'man, *n.*, a first-year student.

fresh'ness, *n.*, the state of being fresh.

fret, *v.t.*, to eat into; to chafe; to irritate; *v.i.*, to be peevish; *n.*, vexation; a kind of ornament of interlacing bands.

fret'ful, *adj.*, ill-humoured.

fret'fully, *adv.*, peevishly.

fret'fulness, *n.*, peevishness.

fret'ted, *adj.*, adorned with fretwork; *p.p.*, fret.

fret'ter, *n.*, one who, or that which, frets.

fret'ting, *pr.p.*, fret.
fret'ty, *adj.*, adorned with fretwork.
fret'work, *n.*, ornamental work consisting of designs cut through thin wood.
friabil'ity, *n.*, the quality of being easily pulverized.
fri'able, *adj.*, easily crumbled.
fri'ar, *n.*, a member of a mendicant religious order.
fri'ary, *n.*, a convent of friars.
fria'tion, *n.*, the act of pulverizing.
frib'ble, *n.*, a frivolous, contemptible fellow; *v.i.*, to trifle.
frib'bler, *n.*, a trifler.
frib'bling, *adj.*, frivolous; trifling.
fricandeau', *n.*, a fricassee of veal.
fricassee', *n.*, a dish made by cutting meat into small fragments and cooking them with sauce or stock in a stewpan over a fire; *v.t.*, to cook in this way.
fricasseed', *p.p.*, fricassee.
fric'ative, *adj.*, a term applied to certain letters (*e.g.*, *s*, *z*, *f*, *v*).
fric'tion, *n.*, the rubbing of the surface of one body against that of another; the resistance a moving body experiences for this reason.
fric'tionless, *adj.*, having no friction.
Fri'day, *n.*, the sixth day of the week.
fried, *p.p.*, fry.
friend, *n.*, one attached to another by affection.
friend'less, *adj.*, destitute of friends.
friend'lier, *comp.* of friendly.
friend'liest, *adj.*, *super.* of friendly.
friend'liness, *n.*, goodwill; kindliness.
friend'ly, *adj.*, kind; not hostile.
friend'ship, *n.*, the feeling of mutual attachment that binds friends together.
frieze, *n.*, a coarse, woollen cloth with a shaggy nap; in architecture, an upper surface for ornament.
frig'ate, *n.*, an old man-of-war of considerable speed and great fighting power (less than a line-of-battle ship).
fright, *n.*, sudden fear; *v.t.*, to scare.
fright'en, *v.t.*, to terrify.
fright'ened, *p.p.*, frighten.
fright'ening, *pr.p.*, frighten.
fright'ful, *adj.*, causing fright; terrific.
fright'fully, *adv.*, terribly; shockingly.
fright'fulness, *n.*, dreadfulness.
frig'id, *adj.*, cold.
frigida'rium, *n.*, the cooling room of a Roman bath.
frigid'ity, *n.*, coldness.
frig'idly, *adv.*, in a frigid manner.
frig'idness, *n.*, the state of being frigid.
frigorif'ic, *adj.*, causing cold.
frill, *n.*, a ruffle or ornamental edging; *v.t.*, to decorate with a frill.
frilled, *p.p.*, frill.
frill'ing, *n.*, frill; ruffles; *pr.p.*, frill.
fringe, *n.*, a border consisting of loose threads attached at one end; a margin; *v.t.*, to border with a fringe.
fringed, *adj.*, bordered with a fringe; *p.p.*, fringe.
fring'ing, *pr.p.*, fringe.
fring'y, *adj.*, adorned with fringes.
frip'pery, *n.*, useless things; *adj.*, contemptible.
frisette', *n.*, a frizz of hair worn as a bang or front.
friseur', *n.*, a hairdresser.
frisk, *v.i.*, to gambol; *n.*, a frolic.
frisked, *p.p.*, frisk.
frisk'er, *n.*, one who frisks.
frisk'et, *n.*, a light frame hinged to the tympan in printing.
frisk'ily, *adv.*, in a frisky manner.
frisk'iness, *n.*, the state of being frisky.
frisk'ing, *pr.p.*, frisk.
frisk'y, *adj.*, frolicsome.
frit, *n.*, calcined material for glass-making.
frith, *n.*, *i.q.* firth.
frit'ter, *n.*, a small piece to be fried; *v.t.*, to break into small pieces; to waste on vain pursuits.
frit'tered, *p.p.*, fritter.
frit'tering, *pr.p.*, fritter.
frivol'ity, *n.*, levity of mind or disposition; an insignificant trifle.
friv'olous, *adj.*, trifling; trivial; of no importance.
friv'olously, *adv.*, in a frivolous manner.
friv'olousness, *n.*, the quality of being frivolous.
frizz, *v.t.*, to curl or crisp; *n.*, that which is frizzed.
frizzed, *p.p.*, frizz.
friz'zle, *v.t.* and *i.*, to curl or crisp; to fry with a spluttering noise; *n.*, a curl; a lock of hair crisped.
friz'zled, *p.p.*, frizzle.
friz'zler, *n.*, one who frizzles.
friz'zling, *pr.p.*, frizzle.
friz'zly, *adj.*, curly.
fro, *adv.*, from; away; back.
frock, *n.*, a gown of many sorts for masculine or feminine use.
frock'-coat, *n.*, a coat with full skirts reaching to the knees.
frocked, *adj.*, clothed in a frock.
Froebel'ian, *adj.*, rel. to the kindergarten system of education; *n.*, a kindergarten teacher.

frog, *n.*, an amphibious animal with great powers of leaping; a tender horn in a horse's hoof; a fastening for a coat in the form of a tassel or loop; *v.t.*, to ornament with frogs.
frog'hopper, *n.*, a small leaping insect.
frol'ic, *adj.*, full of mirth; *n.*, a merrymaking; *v.i.*, to gambol; to play merry tricks.
frol'icked, *p.p.*, frolic.
frol'icking, *pr.p.*, frolic.
frol'icsome, *adj.*, sportive.
frol'icsomeness, *n.*, sportiveness.
from, ***prep.***, out of; by reason of.
frond, *n.*, a fern-leaf.
frondesce', *v.i.*, to become leafy.
frondes'cence, *n.*, the act of bursting into leaf.
frondose', *adj.*, covered with leaves.
fron'dous, *adj.*, producing leaves and flowers on the same part.
front, *n.*, the part of anything directed forward; the foremost part; *adj.*, rel. to the front; *v.t.*, to face; to confront; to adorn in front.
front'age, *n.*, the whole extent of the front.
front'ager, *n.*, one who owns land abutting on a road.
fron'tal, *n.*, a fillet for the forehead; a frontlet; *adj.*, rel. to the forehead; directed towards the front.
front'ed, *p.p.*, front.
fron'tier, *n.*, the border of a country where it marches with another.
front'ing, *pr.p.*, front.
fron'tispiece, *n.*, an ornamental figure or picture at the beginning of a book.
front'less, *adj.*, wanting modesty; unblushing.
front'let, *n.*, a band worn on the forehead.
frost, *n.*, freezing weather; frozen dew; coldness; *v.t.*, to cover with anything resembling hoar-frost, such as white sugar.
frost'-bite, *n.*, a state of arrested circulation in any part of the body, due to exposure to frost.
frost'-bitten, *adj.*, affected with frostbite.
frost'ed, *p.p.*, frost.
frost'ily, *adv.*, in a frosty manner; coldly.
frost'iness, *n.*, the quality of being frosty.
frost'ing, *n.*, a covering resembling frost, esp. on a cake; *pr.p.* frost.
frost'work, *n.*, the beautiful covering of hoar-frost deposited on trees, etc.
frost'y, *adj.*, attended with frost; coldhearted.
froth, *n.*, foam; *v.i.*, to foam.
froth'ily, *adv.*, in a frothy manner.
froth'iness, *n.*, the state of being frothy.
froth'ing, *pr.p.*, froth.
froth'y, *adj.*, foamy; given to empty display.
frou'-frou, *n.*, a rustling, as of silk.
frounce, *v.t.*, to adorn with fringes, plaits, etc.; *n.*, a curl, plait, or flounce.
frounced, *p.p.*, frounce.
froun'cing, *pr.p.*, frounce.
fro'ward, *adj.*, perverse; disobedient; peevish.
fro'wardly, *adv.*, perversely; disobediently.
fro'wardness, *n.*, the quality of being froward.
frown, *v.i.*, to knit the brow; *n.*, a contraction or wrinkling of the brow, expressing displeasure.
frowned, *p.p.*, frown.
frown'ing, *pr.p.*, frown.
frown'ingly, *adv.*, in a frowning manner.
frow'zy, *adj.*, musty; dingy; slovenly.
froze, *p.t.*, freeze.
fro'zen, *p.p.*, freeze.
fructes'cence, *n.*, the fruiting season.
fructif'erous, *adj.*, producing fruit.
fructifica'tion, *n.*, the act of forming fruit; fecundation.
fruc'tified, *p.p.*, fructify.
fruc'tify, *v.t.*, to fertilize; *v.i.*, to produce fruit.
fruc'tifying, *pr.p.*, fructify.
fru'gal, *adj.*, thrifty; sparing.
frugal'ity, *n.*, a prudent and sparing use of anything.
fru'gally, *adv.*, in a frugal manner.
frugif'erous, *adj.*, producing fruit or crops.
frugiv'orous, *adj.*, feeding on fruit or seeds.
fruit, *n.*, the succulent edible product of certain plants, usually containing the seeds; seed; produce; result; *v.t.*, to cause to bear fruit; *v.i.*, to bear fruit.
fruit'age, *n.*, fruit collectively; produce.
fruit'erer, *n.*, a seller of fruits.
fruit'eress, *n.*, a woman who sells fruit.
fruit'ery, *n.*, a repository for fruit.
fruit'ful, *adj.*, prolific; fertile; productive.
fruit'fulness, *n.*, productiveness; fertility.
fruit'ing, *n.*, the process of forming fruit; *pr.p.*, fruit.
frui'tion, *n.*, use of anything, accompanied with pleasure.

fruit'less, *adj.*, destitute of fruit; vain.
fruit'lessly, *adv.*, in a fruitless manner.
fruit'lessness, *n.*, unprofitableness.
fruit'y, *adj.*, resembling fruit; having the taste of fruit.
frumenta'ceous, *adj.*, resembling wheat or some other cereal.
fru'menty, *n.*, *i.q.* furmenty.
frump, *n.*, a bad-tempered, old-fashioned, dowdy, old woman.
frus'trate, *v.t.*, to defeat; to balk.
frus'trated, *p.p.*, frustrate.
frus'trating, *pr.p.*, frustrate.
frustra'tion, *n.*, the act of frustrating.
frus'tum, *n.*, the part of a solid left after cutting off the top by a plane.
frutes'cence, *n.*, the quality of being shrub-like.
frutes'cent, *adj.*, shrubby.
fru'ticose, *adj.*, pert. to shrubs.
fru'ticous, *adj.*, *i.q.* fruticose.
frutic'ulose, *adj.*, branching like a shrub.
fry, *v.t.*, to cook in a pan over a fire; *n.*, anything fried; the young of fishes.
fry'er, *n.*, one who, or that which, fries.
fry'ing, *pr.p.*, fry.
fry'ing-pan, *n.*, a long-handled pan used for frying.
fu'ar, *n.*, one who holds a feu.
fu'cate, *adj.*, painted; disguised with paint.
fu'cated, *adj.*, *i.q.* fucate.
fuch'sia, *n.*, a flowering shrub with beautiful funnel-shaped, deciduous blossoms.
fuciv'orous, *adj.*, subsisting on sea-weed.
fu'coid, *adj.*, rel. to sea-weed
fucoi'dal, *adj.*, *i.q.* fucoid.
fu'cus, *n.*, a tough, leathery, brownish-green, sea-weed.
fud'dle, *v.t.*, to make tipsy; *v.i.*, to drink to excess.
fud'dled, *p.p.*, fuddle.
fud'dler, *n.*, a drunkard.
fud'dling, *pr.p.*, fuddle.
fudge, *v.t.*, to make up or fabricate; *n.*, a made-up story; nonsense.
Fue'gian, *n.*, a native of Terra del Fuego.
fu'el, *n.*, that which is used to feed fire.
fuga'cious, *adj.*, fleeting.
fugac'ity, *n.*, transitoriness.
fu'gal, *adj.*, rel. to fugue, containing repetitions or imitations of a given musical theme.
fu'gitive, *adj.*, fleeting; not fixed or durable; fleeing from danger, duty, etc.; *n.*, one who flees.
fu'gitively, *adv.*, in a fugitive manner.
fu'gleman, *n.*, a file-leader; any one who sets an example for others to follow.
fugue, *n.*, a musical composition in parts which follow each other regularly.
fu'guist, *n.*, a composer of fugues.
ful'crate, *adj.*, having a fulcrum.
ful'crum, *n.*, a support; the point about which a lever turns.
fulfil', *v.t.*, to accomplish; to perform; to complete.
fulfilled', *p.p.*, fulfil.
fulfil'ler, *n.*, one who fulfils.
fulfil'ling, *pr.p.*, fulfil.
fulfil'ment, *n.*, completion; performance.
ful'gency, *n.*, splendour.
ful'gent, *adj.*, dazzlingly bright.
fuli'ginous, *adj.*, sooty; dusky.
ful'gural, *adj.*, flashing like lightning.
full, *adj.*, having all it can contain; entire; *n.*, utmost extent; *adv.*, quite; *v.t.*, to thicken woollen fibres; to cleanse or bleach.
full'-aged, *adj.*, mature.
full'-blown, *adj.*, fully expanded.
fulled, *p.p.*, full.
full'er, *n.*, one who fulls cloth; one who bleaches; *adj.*, *comp.* of full.
fuller's earth', *n.*, a kind of clay useful in cleansing cloth.
full'ery, *n.*, a fulling-works.
full'est, *adj.*, *super.* of full.
full'ing, *pr.p.*, full; *n.*, the business of a fuller.
full'ing-mill, *n.*, a mill for fulling cloth.
full'-length, *adj.*, extending for the whole length.
full'ness, *n.*, *i.q.* fulness.
full'-swing, *adv.*, with haste and impetuosity.
full'y, *adv.*, completely.
ful'mar, *n.*, a marine swimming bird.
ful'minant, *adj.*, thundering; making a loud noise.
ful'minate, *v.i.*, to thunder; to explode with a loud noise; to threaten or denounce; *n.*, an explosive compound.
ful'minated, *p.p.*, fulminate.
ful'minating, *adj.*, thundering; exploding; detonating; *pr.p.*, fulminate.
fulmina'tion, *n.*, the act of fulminating; a menace; a censure.
ful'minatory, *adj.*, sending forth thunders.
ful'ness, *n.*, the state of being full or filled.
ful'some, *adj.*, offensive from excessive praise; nauseous.
ful'someness, *n.*, the state of being fulsome.

ful'vid, *adj.*, *i.q.* fulvous.
ful'vous, *adj.*, tawny yellow.
fum'atory, *adj.*, *i.q.* fumitory.
fum'ble, *v.i.*, to grope about; to use the hands awkwardly.
fum'bled, *p.p.*, fumble.
fum'bler, *n.*, one who fumbles.
fum'bling, *pr.p.*, fumble.
fume, *n.*, smoky, volatile matter, usually narcotic; mental agitation; *v.i.*, to pass off in a vapour; to be in a rage; *v.t.*, to fumigate.
fumed, *p.p.*, fume.
fumif'erous, *adj.*, producing smoke.
fu'migate, *v.t.*, to apply smoke to.
fu'migated, *p.p.*, fumigate.
fu'migating, *pr.p.*, fumigate.
fumiga'tion, *n.*, the act of fumigating.
fu'migator, *n.*, one who, or that which, fumigates.
fu'ming, *pr.p.*, fume.
fu'mitory, *n.*, a common plant with purple flowers.
fu'my, *adj.*, producing fumes; apt to fume or fret.
fun, *n.*, frolicsome amusement.
funam'bulate, *v.i.*, to walk on a rope.
funambula'tion, *n.*, rope-dancing.
funam'bulatory, *adj.*, pert. to rope-dancing.
funam'bulist, *n.*, a rope-walker.
func'tion, *n.*, office; duty; business; a formal ceremony; a mathematical quantity depending on another.
func'tional, *adj.*, rel. to a function or functions.
func'tionary, *n.*, one who has special duties to perform.
fund, *n.*, money used as capital; part of the national debt; a store; a supply; *v.t.*, to put into the form of bonds or stock bearing interest.
fun'dament, *n.*, a foundation; the buttocks.
fundamen'tal, *adj.*, essential; at the foundation of something; *n.*, a leading principle or rule.
fundamen'tally, *adv.*, essentially.
fund'ed, *p.p.*, fund.
fund'-holder, *n.*, one who has property in the public funds.
fund'ing, *pr.p.*, fund.
fun'dus, *n.*, the base of any hollow anatomical organ.
fu'neral, *n.*, burial; *adj.*, used at the interment of the dead.
fune'real, *adj.*, dismal; gloomy.
fun'gi, *n. pl.*, cryptogamous plants, including mushrooms, moulds, etc.
Fun'gia, *n.*, a genus of corals with radiating plates like the gills of a mushroom.
fun'gic, *adj.*, rel. to fungi.
fun'giform, *adj.*, having the form of a fungus.
fun'goid, *adj.*, like a fungus.
fun'gous, *adj.*, like a fungus; growing quickly but not durable.
fun'gus, *n.*, a vegetable parasite, usually spongy.
fu'nicle, *n.*, a little ligament attached to a seed.
funic'ular, *adj.*, depending on the tension of a cord; worked by a cable.
funk, *v.i.*, to flinch; to be frightened; *n.*, fear (*slang*).
fun'nel, *n.*, a hollow cone with a pipe leading from its apex; the chimney of a steamship.
fun'nier, *adj.*, *comp.* of funny.
fun'niest, *adj.*, *super.* of funny.
fun'ny, *adj.*, comical.
fun'ny-bone, *n.*, the bony projection of the elbow.
fur, *n.*, the short, soft hair growing on the skin of certain animals; *adj.*, made of fur; *v.t.* and *i.*, to cover with fur.
fur'below, *n.*, a kind of flounce or plaited border to a gown or petticoat.
fur'bish, *v.t.*, to brighten; to polish up.
fur'bished, *p.p.*, furbish.
fur'bisher, *n.*, one who, or that which, furbishes.
fur'bishing, *pr.p.*, furbish.
fur'cate, *adj.*, forked.
fur'cated, *adj.*, *i.q.* furcate.
furca'tion, *n.*, a forking or branching.
fur'fur, *n.*, scurf.
furio'so, *adv.*, with great vehemence.
fu'rious, *adj.*, raging; frenzied; violent.
fu'riously, *adv.*, in a furious manner.
fu'riousness, *n.*, the state of being furious.
furl, *v.t.*, to wrap (a sail) close and fasten.
furled, *p.p.*, furl.
furl'ing, *pr.p.*, furl.
fur'long, *n.*, the eighth part of a mile.
fur'lough, *n.*, leave of absence given to a soldier.
fur'menty, *n.*, a dish made of hulled wheat boiled in milk and seasoned.
fur'nace, *n.*, a structure containing a strong fire.
fur'nish, *v.t.*, to equip; to supply.
fur'nished, *p.p.*, furnish.
fur'nisher, *n.*, one who furnishes.
fur'nishing, *pr.p.*, furnish.
fur'niture, *n.*, equipment, esp. of chairs, tables, and utensils for domestic purposes.
fu'ror, *n.*, rage; mania.

furo're, *n.*, great excitement; enthusiasm.
furred, *p.p.*, fur.
fur'rier, *n.*, a dealer in furs.
fur'riery, *n.*, the trade of a furrier.
fur'ring, *pr.p.*, fur.
fur'row, *n.*, a groove; a wrinkle; *v.t.*, to plough; to mark with wrinkles.
fur'rowed, *adj.*, having grooves or furrows; *p.p.*, furrow.
fur'rowing, *pr.p.*, furrow.
fur'ry, *adj.*, covered with, or resembling, fur.
fur'ther, *adv.*, moreover; farther; *adj.*, remoter; added; *v.t.*, to promote.
fur'therance, *n.*, the act of furthering.
fur'thered, *p.p.*, further.
fur'therer, *n.*, a promoter.
fur'thering, *pr.p.*, further.
fur'ther*more*, *adv.*, moreover.
fur'ther*most*, *adj.*, furthest; most remote.
fur'thest, *adj.* and *adv.*, most distant.
fur'tive, *adj.*, stealthy.
fur'tively, *adv.*, stealthily.
fu'ry, *n.*, rage; madness.
furze, *n.*, gorse.
furz'y, *adj.*, overgrown with furze.
fusca'tion, *n.*, obscurity; darkening.
fus'cous, *adj.*, brown; dark-coloured.
fuse, *v.t.*, to liquefy by heat; to unite as if melted together by heat; *n.*, a tube filled with combustibles, used in discharging a shell and in blasting.
fused, *p.p.*, fuse.
fusee', *n.*, a small musket; a kind of match; a fuse; the conical piece in a watch or clock round which the chain or cord is wound.
fu'selage, *n.*, the framework of an aeroplane or dirigible; a part of a monoplane between the main body and the tail.
fusibil'ity, *n.*, the quality of being fusible.
fu'sible, *adj.*, capable of being fused or melted.
fu'siform, *adj.*, spindle-shaped.
fu'sil, *n.*, a light musket formerly used.
fusilier', *n.*, an infantry soldier; a rifleman.
fusillade', *n.*, a volley of musketry.
fu'sing, *pr.p.*, fuse.
fu'sion, *n.*, melting by heat; uniting as if melted together; complete union.
fuss, *n.*, unnecessary trouble; *v.i.*, to make much ado about nothing.
fussed, *p.p.*, fuss.
fuss'ily, *adv.*, in a fussy manner.
fuss'ing, *pr.p.*, fuss.
fuss'y, *adj.*, bustling; making ado.
fust, *n.*, a musty smell; *v.i.*, to become musty.
fus'tian, *n.*, a coarse cotton cloth with a pile like velvet, but shorter; inflated writing; bombast.
fus'tic, *n.*, the wood of a West Indian tree used in dyeing yellow.
fustiga'tion, *n.*, a cudgelling.
fust'iness, *n.*, the state of being fusty.
fust'y, *adj.*, musty; ill-smelling.
fu'tile, *adj.*, answering no useful purpose.
fu'tilely, *adv.*, in a futile manner.
futil'ity, *n.*, the quality of being futile.
fut'tock, *n.*, one of the timbers raised over the keel of a ship, forming its breadth.
fu'ture, *adj.*, that is to be hereafter; *n.*, time to come.
fu'turist, *n.*, one who believes that the Old Testament prophecies are yet to be fulfilled; an impressionist painter, sculptor, or poet who claims that his art is the art of the future.
futu'rity, *n.*, time yet to come.
fuze, *n.* and *v.t.*, *i.q.* fuse.
fuzz, *n.*, fine, light particles.
fuzz'ily, *adv.*, in a fuzzy manner.
fuzz'iness, *n.*, the state of being fuzzy.
fuzz'y, *adj.*, light and spongy; shaggy.
fy, *interj.*, *i.q.* fie.
fyrd, *n.*, the national army or militia, including all men able to bear arms (*Old Eng. Hist.*).

G

gab, *n.*, foolish chatter.

gab'ble, *v.i.*, to chatter without meaning; *v.t.*, to read hurriedly without attention to sense; *n.*, rapid talk.

gab'bled, *p.p.*, gabble.

gab'bler, *n.*, one who gabbles.

gab'bling, *pr.p.*, gabble.

ga'bel, *n.*, a tax on salt.

gab'erdine, *n.*, a coarse frock.

ga'bion, *n.*, a wickerwork cylinder containing earth.

gabionade', *n.*, a defensive work consisting of gabions.

ga'ble, *n.*, a triangular elevation in a building.

ga'bled, *adj.*, having gables.

ga'blet, *n.*, a little gable.

ga'by, *n.*, a fool.

gad, *v.i.*, to ramble purposelessly; *n.*, a pointed tool.

gad'ded, *p.p.*, gad.

gad'der, *n.*, one who gads.

gad'ding, *pr.p.*, gad.

gad'fly, *n.*, a fly that stings cattle.

Gael, *n.*, one of Gaelic stock.

Gael'ic, *adj.*, bel. to the Gaels; *n.*, the Gaelic language.

gaff, *v.t.*, to land a fish with the gaff; *n.*, an iron-hooked stick.

gaffed, *p.p.*, gaff.

gaf'fer, *n.*, a grandfather; a foreman.

gaf'fing, *pr.p.*, gaff.

gag, *v.t.*, to stop the mouth; *n.*, something stuffed into the mouth.

gage, *v.t.*, to wager, engage; measure; *n.*, a pledge, a challenge.

gaged, *p.p.*, gage.

ga'ger, *n.*, one who gages.

gagged, *p.p.*, gag.

gag'ger, *n.*, one who gags.

gag'ging, *pr.p.*, gag.

gag'gle, *v.i.*, to cackle.

gag'gled, *p.p.*, gaggle.

gag'gling, *pr.p.*, gaggle.

ga'ging, *pr.p.*, gage.

gai'ety, **gay'ety**, *n.*, mirth, cheerfulness, finery.

gai'ly, **gay'ly**, *adv.*, merrily, cheerfully, finely.

gain, *v.t.*, to acquire, obtain; *n.*, profit, advantage.

gained, *p.p.*, gain.

gain'er, *n.*, one who gains.

gain'ful, *adj.*, profitable.

gain'fulness, *n.*, the state of being gainful.

gain'less, *adj.*, without profit.

gain'ly, *adj.*, comely.

gain'said, *p.p.*, gainsay.

gain'say, *v.t.*, to contradict, oppose.

gain'sayer, *n.*, one who gainsays.

gain'saying, *pr.p.*, gainsay.

gair'ish, *see* garish.

gair'ishly, *see* garishly.

gair'ishness, *see* garishness.

gait, *n.*, manner of walking, bearing.

gait'er, *n.*, an ankle-covering.

ga'la, *n.*, show, festivity.

galac'tic, *adj.*, rel. to milk.

galactom'eter, *n.*, an instrument for measuring the density of milk. Also *lactometer*.

gal'antine, *n.*, a dish of white meat, boneless, tied up, and eaten cold.

Gala'tian, *adj.*, rel. to Galatia.

gal'axy, *n.*, the Milky Way; a notable assembly.

gal'banum, *n.*, a gum resin.

gale, *n.*, a violent wind-storm.

ga'lea, *n.*, a helmet (*Lat.*).

ga'leate, *adj.*, helmeted; helmet-like.

ga'leated, *adj.*, *i.q.* galeate.

gale'na, *n.*, the principal ore of lead.

Galen'ic, *adj.*, rel. to Galen (the Greek writer on medicine).

Ga'lenism, *n.*, the teaching of Galen.

Ga'lenist, *n.*, a disciple of Galen.

Gali'cian, *adj.*, rel. to Galicia.

Galile'an, *adj.*, rel. to Galilee or to Galileo.

gal'iot, *n.*, a variety of trading vessel.

gal'ipot, *n.*, a juice exuded from pine trees.

gall, *v.t.*, to fret, chafe; *n.*, the bile; rancour, malignity.

gal'lant, *adj.*, brave, spirited, chivalrous; *n.*, a fashionable person, a beau.

gallant', *adj.*, deferential to ladies; *v.t.*, to pay court to.

gallant'ing, *pr.p.*, gallant.

gal'lantly, *adv.*, bravely, chivalrously.

gallant'ly, *adv.*, politely.

gallant'ness, *n.*, the state or quality of being gallant.

gal'lantry, *n.*, bravery, chivalrousness.

galled, *p.p.*, gall.

gal'leon, *n.*, a Spanish three-decker.

gal'lery, *n.*, a corridor; a long room leading to others; a balcony in or round a room; a place for exhibiting works of art; spectators.

gal'ley, *n.*, a low, flat, oar-propelled vessel; a ship's kitchen; a frame for holding printing type.

gal'ley-slave, *n.*, a slave who rows a galley.

gal'liard, *n.*, a gay-spirited person.

Gal'lic, *adj.*, pert. to Gaul.

Gal'lican, *adj.*, *i.q.* Gallic.

Gal'licanism, *n.*, the system or principles of French Catholics who favoured the restriction of Papal interference.

Gal'licism, *n.*, a French idiom.

Gal'licize, *v.t.*, to make conformable to French.

galligas'kins, *n.*, leggings.

galliman'fry, *n.*, a medley.

gallina'ceous, *adj.*, rel. to domestic birds, pheasants, etc.

gall'ing, *pr.p.*, gall; *adj.*, irritating, vexing.

gal'linipper, *n.*, a species of mosquito.

gal'linule, *n.*, an American bird so named.

gal'lipot, *n.*, a glazed earthenware pot.

gallivant', *v.i.*, to go about flirting.

gallivan'ted, *p.p.*, gallivant.

gallivant'ing, *pr.p.*, gallivant.

gall'nut, *n.*, a round excrescence on the oak.

gal'lon, *n.*, a liquid measure of four quarts.

galloon', *n.*, a lace made of gold, silver, or silk.

gallooned', *adj.*, decorated with galloon.

gal'lop, *v.i.*, to run full speed; *n.*, a horse's full speed; a ride at full speed.

gallopade', *n.*, a rapid dance.

gal'loped, *p.p.*, gallop.

gal'loper, *n.*, one who gallops.

gal'loping, *pr.p.*, gallop.

gal'loway, *n.*, a horse of the Galloway breed.

gal'lows, *n.*, an erection for hanging criminals.

gall'stone, *n.*, a formation in the gall bladder.

gal'op, *n.*, a fast dance.

galore', *adj.*, abundant, in plenty.

galosh', *n.*, a rubber over-shoe. Also *golosh*.

galvan'ic, *adj.*, rel. to galvanism.

gal'vanism, *n.*, a species of electricity.

gal'vanist, *n.*, one who uses galvanism medically.

gal'vanize, *v.t.*, to produce galvanic effect on.

gal'vanized, *p.p.*, galvanize.

gal'vanizer, *n.*, anything that galvanizes.

gal'vanizing, *pr.p.*, galvanize.

galvanog'raphy, *n.*, an electrotype process of reproduction.

galvanol'ogist, *n.*, an expert in galvanology.

galvanol'ogy, *n.*, the study of galvanic phenomena.

galvanom'eter, *n.*, an instrument to measure the intensity of electric currents.

galvan'oscope, *n.*, a delicate instrument to measure electric currents.

Galwe'gian, *adj.*, rel. to Galway.

gam, *v.t.*, to pay a call to (nautical); *v.i.*, to gather together in schools (a whaling term); *n.*, a complimentary visit; a school of whales.

gam'ba, *n.*, an organ-stop; otherwise the *viol de Gamba.*

gambade', *n.*, a flourish.

gamba'do, *n.*, *i.q.* gambade.

gam'bit, *n.*, one of the openings in chess.

gam'ble, *v.t.*, to play away; to throw away; *v.i.*, to play for money; *n.*, a game of chance.

gam'bled, *p.p.*, gamble.

gam'bler, *n.*, one who gambles.

gam'bling, *pr.p.*, gamble.

gamboge', *n.*, a yellow gum-resin; *adj.*, of gamboge colour.

gambo'gian, *adj.*, rel. to gamboge.

gam'bol, *v.i.*, to frisk, frolic; *n.*, a frisking, a frolic.

gam'boled, -lled, *p.p.*, gambol.

gam'boling, -lling, *pr.p.*, gambol.

gam'brel, *n.*, a horse's hock; a bent stick.

game, *v.i.*, to play for a stake; *adj.*, sporting, plucky; *n.*, a sport or contest, play; wild animals pursued in sport.

game'-cock, *n.*, a fighting cock.

gamed, *p.p.*, game.

game'-fowl, *n.*, birds trained to fight.

game'ful, *adj.*, sportive.

game'keeper, *n.*, one who looks after game.

game'some, *adj.*, *i.q.* gameful.

game'ster, *n.*, a gambler.

gam'in, *n.*, a street urchin (*Fr.*).

ga'ming, *pr.p.*, game.

gam'ma, *n.*, the Greek letter G.

gam'mer, *n.*, grandmother (fem. of gaffer).

gam'mon, *v.t.*, to humbug, cheat; *n.*, smoked ham; a hoax; *interj.*, nonsense.

gam'moned, *p.p.*, gammon.

gam'moning, *pr.p.*, gammon.

gamopet'alous, *adj.*, with petals united at the base.

gamosep'alous, *adj.*, having the sepals cohering at the edges.

gamp, *n.*, a baggy umbrella (*slang*).

gam'ut, *n.*, the musical scale.

ga'my, *adj.*, high-flavoured; like game.

ganch, *v.t.*, to let fall on to sharp spikes.

ganched, *p.p.*, ganch.

ganch'ing, *pr.p.*, ganch.

gan'der, *n.*, the male of the goose.

gang, *n.*, a company, band; *v.i.*, to go (*Scot.*).

gang'er, *n.*, a foreman navvy or platelayer.

gan'gliac, *adj.*, pert. to ganglions.

gan'gliform, *adj.*, ganglion-shaped.

gan'glion, *n.*, a collection of nerves or nerve-cells.

gan'glioform, *adj.*, *i.q.* gangliform.

gan'glionary, *adj.*, rel. to ganglion.

ganglion'ic, *adj.*, *i.q.* ganglionary.

gan'grenate, *adj.*, gangrened.

gan'grene, *v.i.*, to mortify; *n.*, mortification of part of the body.

gan'grened, *p.p.*, gangrene.

gan'grening, *pr.p.*, gangrene.

gan'grenous, *adj.*, mortifying.

gangue, *see* gang.

gang'way, *n.*, a passage way.

gan'net, *n.*, a species of sea-bird.

gan'oid, *adj.*, rel. to the Ganoidei (the class of fish, like the sturgeon, having enamelled bony scales).

gant'let, *see* gauntlet.

gan'try, *n.*, a barrel-stand; a platform for a moving crane.

gaol, *n.*, a prison.

gaol'er, *n.*, a prison-keeper.

gap, *v.i.*, to yawn open; *n.*, an opening, breach.

gape, *v.i.*, to open the mouth wide, yawn, stare in amazement.

gaped, *p.p.*, gape.

ga'per, *n.*, one who gapes.

ga'ping, *pr.p.*, gape.

ga'pingly, *adv.*, in amazement.

gar, *v.t.*, to make, cause (*Scot.*).

garage, *n.*, a place for storing or repairing automobiles.

garb, *v.t.*, to clothe; *n.*, dress, fashion of dress.

gar'bage, *n.*, refuse, offal.

garbed, *p.p.*, garb.

garb'ing, *pr.p.*, garb.

gar'ble, *v.t.*, to sift for the purpose of selection. Incorrectly used in the sense of "to mutilate or pervert."

gar'bled, *p.p.*, garble.

gar'bler, *n.*, one who garbles.

gar'bling, *pr.p.*, garble.

garçon', a boy, a waiter (*Fr.*).

gar'dant, *adj.*, on guard, confronting (*Her.*).

gar'den, *v.i.*, to cultivate a garden; *n.*, cultivated ground for pleasure or for the growth of fruit and flowers.

gar'dened, *p.p.*, garden.

gar'dener, *n.*, one who gardens.

garde'nia, *n.*, a tropical plant with yellow or white flowers.

gar'dening, *pr.p.*, garden; *n.*, the care of a garden.

gare, *n.*, the coarse wool on a sheep's leg.

gar'fish, *n.*, a long sea-fish with a sharp snout.

Gargan'tuan, *adj.*, monstrous, enormous.

gar'garize, *v.i.*, to gargle.

gar'garism, *n.*, gargling.

gar'get, *n.*, a species of cattle-disease.

gar'gil, *n.*, a disease of geese.

gar'gle, *v.t.* and *i.*, to wash the inside of the throat; *n.*, a wash for the inside of the throat.

gar'gled, *p.p.*, gargle.

gar'gling, *pr.p.*, gargle.

gar'goyle, *n.*, a projecting water-spout.

gar'ish, *adj.*, gaudy, showy.

gar'ishly, *adv.*, gaudily.

gar'ishness, *n.*, the state or quality of being garish.

gar'land, *n.*, a wreath of flowers, *v.t.*, to wreathe.

gar'lic, *n.*, a species of onion.

gar'ment, *n.*, a piece of clothing.

gar'ner, *v.t.*, to store, to gather up; *n.*, a granary.

gar'nered, *p.p.*, garner.

gar'nering, *pr.p.*, garner.

gar'net, *n.*, a crystallized gem of reddish colour.

gar'nish, *v.t.*, to decorate, embellish.

gar'nished, *p.p.*, garnish.

garnishee', *n.*, the temporary holder of property pending the settlement of a third party's claim; *v.t.*, to secure by garnishment.

garnisheed', *p.p.*, garnishee.

garnishee'ing, *pr.p.*, garnishee.

gar'nisher, *n.*, one who garnishes.

gar'nishing, *pr.p.*, garnish; *n.*, decorations for a dish at table.

gar'nishment, *n.*, decoration, embellishment; a warning.

gar'niture, *n.*, decoration.

garotte', *see* garrotte.

ga'rous, *adj.*, rel. to garum.

gar'ret, *n.*, a small room at the top of a house.

garreteer', *n.*, a Grub-street writer, living in a garret.

gar'rison, *v.t.*, to furnish a fortified place with soldiers; *n.*, soldiers stationed in a fortified place.

gar'risoned, *p.p.*, garrison.

gar'risoning, *pr.p.*, garrison.

garrotte', *v.t.*, to strangle; to rob by strangling the person robbed; *n.*, a Spanish mode of execution by strangling.

garrot'ted, *p.p.*, garrotte.

garrot'ter, *n.*, one who garrottes.

garrot'ting, *pr.p.*, garrotte.

garru'lity, *n.*, talkativeness.

gar'rulous, *adj.*, talkative.

gar'rulously, *adv.*, talkatively.

gar'rulousness, *n.*, *i.q.* garrulity.

gar'ter, *v.t.*, to fasten with a garter; to invest with Order of the Garter; *n.*, a band round the stocking.

gar'tered, *p.p.*, garter.

gar'tering, *pr.p.*, garter.

garth, *n.*, an enclosure.

ga'rum, *n.*, pickled fish.

gas, *n.*, highly rarefied matter; *v.t.*, to supply, or apply, gas to; to poison with gas; *v.i.*, to talk boastfully.

Gas'con, *n.*, a native of Gascony.

gasconade', *v.i.*, to talk big; *n.*, boastfulness, bravado.

gasconaa'ded, *p.p.*, gasconade.

gasconaa'der, *n.*, a braggart.

gasconaa'ding, *pr.p.*, gasconade.

gaselier', *n.*, a frame for holding gas burners.

gas'eous, *adj.*, of the nature of gas.

gas'fitter, *n.*, one who attends to gas fittings.

gas'-fitting, *n.*, the trade of a gasfitter; in pl. gaslighting appliances.

gash, *v.t.*, to cut deep; *n.*, a deep cut.

gashed, *p.p.*, gash.

gash'ing, *pr.p.*, gash.

gas'-holder, *n.*, a gasometer.

gasifica'tion, *n.*, the act of bringing under the effect of gas.

gas'ified, *p.p.*, gasify.

gas'iform, *adj.*, like gas.

gas'ify, *v.t.*, to bring under gas.

gas'ifying, *pr.p.*, gasify.

gas'-jet, *n.*, a burner.

gas'ket, *n.*, a piece of rope for binding a furled sail to the yard or boom; packing for boiler-heads, etc.

gas'king, *n.*, hemp-packing.

gas'light, *n.*, the light of gas; a gas lamp.

gas'-meter, *n.*, an instrument for measuring the consumption of gas.

gas'ogen, *n.*, an apparatus for making aerated water.

gas'ogene, *n.*, *i.q.* gasogen.

gas'olene, *n.*, a product of petroleum.

gasom'eter, *n.*, a gas reservoir.

gasom'etry, *n.*, the system of measuring gas.

gasp, *v.i.*, to catch the breath, pant; *n.*, painful, convulsive breathing.

gasp'ing, *pr.p.*, gasp.

gasp'ingly, *adv.*, in a gasping way.

gassed, *p.p.*, gas.

gas'sing, *n.*, boastful talk; *pr.p.*, gas.

gas'sy, *adj.*, like gas, filled with gas.

gasterop'oda, *n. pl.*, molluscs having a foot beneath the belly.

gastral'gia, *n.*, stomach-ache.

gas'tric, *adj.*, rel. to the stomach.

gastril'oquist, *n.*, a ventriloquist.

gastril'oquy, *n.*, ventriloquism.

gastri'tis, *n.*, inflammation of the stomach.

gas'trocele, *n.*, stomach-hernia.

gastrol'ogy, *n.*, the art and science of cookery.

gas'tronome, *n.*, an epicure.

gastron'omer, *n.*, *i.q.* gastronome.

gastronom'ic, *adj.*, rel. to gastronomy.

gastron'omist, *n.*, *i.q.* gastronome.

gastron'omy, *n.*, the science of good eating.

gas'tropod, *see* gasteropoda.

gastrop'odous, *n.*, having a foot under the belly.

gas'-works, *n.*, a gas factory.

gate, *n.*, a fence closing an entrance or passage; a street (*Scot.*).

gate'house, *n.*, the outer entrance to a castle, monastery, etc.

gate'man, *n.*, the man in charge of a gate.

gate'way, *n.*, the entrance through a gate.

gath'er, *v.t.*, to collect, pluck; infer; *v.i.*, to assemble; to form pus; *n.*, a pleat, pucker.

gath'ered, *p.p.*, gather.

gath'erer, *n.*, one who gathers.

gath'ering, *pr.p.*, gather; *n.*, an assembly; an abscess.

gauche, *adj.*, awkward, the left (*Fr.*).

gaucherie', *n.*, awkwardness (*Fr.*).

Gau'cho, *n.*, a S. American cowboy.

gaud, *n.*, a piece of finery. Also *gawd.*

gaud'ily, *adv.*, in a gaudy way.

gaud'iness, *n.*, the state or quality of being gaudy.

gaud'y, *adj.*, showy.

gauf'fering, *n.*, fluted frilling; ornamented edging to a book. Also *goffering.*

gauge, *v.t.*, to measure capacity, estimate; *n.*, a measure of capacity; standard; a measuring instrument; a carpenter's tool to mark parallel lines.

gauge'able, *adj.*, capable of being gauged.
gauged, *p.p.*, gauge.
gau'ger, *n.*, an excise officer who measures the contents of casks.
gau'ging, *pr.p.*, gauge.
Gaul, *n.*, the country now called France; a native of Gaul.
Gaul'ish, *adj.*, rel. to Gaul.
gault, *n.*, a clay stratum so named.
gaunt, *adj.*, thin, lean.
gaunt'let, *n.*, a long glove.
gaunt'leted, *adj.*, wearing gauntlets.
gaunt'ly, *adv.*, with a pinched look.
gaunt'ry, *see* gantry.
gauze, *n.*, a thin, transparent fabric.
gauz'iness, *n.*, the state or quality of being gauzy.
gauz'y, *adj.*, like gauze, transparent.
gave, *p.t.* of give.
gav'el, *n.*, a mason's mallet; toll.
gav'elkind, *n.*, a form of land tenure under which, in a case of intestacy, all the sons share equally in the father's estate.
gavotte', *n.*, a lively dance.
gawk, *n.*, a lout; cuckoo.
gawk'y, *adj.* ungainly.
gay, *adj.*, sprightly, merry.
gay'est, *adj.*, *super.* of gay.
gay'ety, *see* gaiety.
gay'ly, *see* gaily.
gaze, *v.i.*, to look intently; *n.*, an intent look.
gazed, *p.p.*, gaze.
gazelle', *n.*, a small antelope.
ga'zer, *n.*, one who gazes.
gazette', *v.t.*, to announce officially; *n.*, an official or any other newspaper.
gazet'ted, *p.p.*, gazette.
gazetteer', *n.*, a geographical dictionary.
ga'zing, *pr.p.*, gaze.
ga'zing-stock, *n.*, an object of scorn and criticism.
gaz'ogene, *see* gasogen.
gear, *v.t.*, to put gear on; *n.*, tackle; toothed wheels; harness, dress.
geared, *p.p.*, gear.
gear'ing, *pr.p.*, gear; *n.*, toothed wheels working into each other.
gec'ko, *n.*, the wall-lizard.
gee, *v.i.*, to go on, move faster.
gee'-gee, *n.*, slang for a horse.
geese, *n.*, pl. of goose.
Gehen'na, *n.*, the valley of Hinnom; hell.
gei'sha, *n.*, a dancing-girl of Japan.
gelat'inate, *v.t.*, to turn into jelly; *v.i.*, to become jelly.
gelat'inated, *p.p.*, gelatinate.
gelat'inating, *pr.p.*, gelatinate.
gelatina'tion, *n.*, the act or effect of gelatinating.
gel'atine, *n.*, animal jelly.
gelat'inous, *adj.*, like gelatine.
gela'tion, *n.*, solidification with cold.
geld, *v.t.*, to castrate; deprive of essentials.
geld'ed, *p.p.*, geld.
geld'er, *n.*, one who gelds.
geld'ing, *pr.p.*, geld; *n.*, castration; a young horse that has been castrated.
gel'id, *adj.*, cold, freezing.
gem, *v.t.*, to adorn with jewels; *n.*, a precious stone; anything very choice.
Gema'ra, *n.*, the part of the Talmud following the Mishna, on which it is a commentary.
gemar'ic, *adj.*, rel. to the Gemara.
gem'el, *n.*, one of a pair of bars (*Her.*).
gemina'tion, *n.*, a doubling.
Gem'ini, *n. pl.*, the Zodiacal sign of the Twins (Castor and Pollux).
gem'ma, *n.*, a bud.
gem'mary, *adj.*, rel. to gems.
gem'mate, *adj.*, having buds.
gem'mated, *adj.*, *i.q.* gemmate.
gemma'tion, *n.*, the formation of buds.
gemmed, *adj.*, adorned with gems; *p.p.*, gem.
gem'meous, *adj.*, rel. to gems.
gemmif'erous, *adj.*, bearing buds.
gem'ming, *pr.p.*, gem.
gemmip'arous, *adj.*, producing buds.
gem'mule, *n.*, a small bud.
gem'my, *adj.*, set with gems; gemlike.
gems'bok, *n.*, the antelope of S. Africa.
gendarme', *n.*, a policeman (*Fr.*).
gendar'merie, *n.*, the police force (*Fr.*).
gendarm'ery, *n.*, *i.q.* gendarmerie.
gen'der, *n.*, a kind, sort, sex.
genealog'ical, *adj.*, pert. to genealogy.
genealog'ically, *adv.*, by descent.
geneal'ogist, *n.*, one who studies pedigrees.
geneal'ogy, *n.*, pedigree; the science of tracing pedigrees.
gen'era, *n.*, pl. of genus.
gen'eral, *adj.*, generic, rel. to the whole of a genus, class, or order; *n.*, the whole; a high commander.
generalis'simo, *n.*, a commander-in-chief.
general'ity, *n.*, the main body; the bulk.
generaliza'tion, *n.*, the act of generalizing; an induction.
gen'eralize, *v.t.* and *i.*, to extend from particulars to universals; to reduce to a genus.
gen'eralized, *p.p.*, generalize.

gen'eralizing, *pr.p.*, generalize.
gen'erally, *adj.*, universally, as a whole, commonly.
***gen'eral*ship**, *n.*, a general's rank or office; strategical skill.
gen'erant, *adj.*, generating.
gen'erate, *v.t.*, to produce, form.
gen'erated, *p.p.*, generate.
gen'erating, *pr.p.*, generate.
genera'tion, *n.*, the act of generating; offspring; period.
gen'erative, *adj.*, producing, forming.
gen'erator, *n.*, one who, or that which, generates; an apparatus for generating gas, electricity, steam.
genera'trix, *n.*, fem. of generator.
gener'ic, *adj.*, rel. to genus or kind.
gener'ical, *adj.*, *i.q.* generic.
generos'ity, *n.*, the quality of being generous; kindness.
gen'erous, *adj.*, kind, noble.
gen'erously, *adv.*, kindly.
Gen'esis, *n.*, the Book of Creation.
gen'esis, *n.*, creation, origin.
gen'et, *n.*, a small Spanish horse.
genet', *n.*, a civet cat; its fur.
geneth'liac, *adj.*, rel. to nativities; *n.*, a birthday ode.
genet'ic, *adj.*, rel. to genesis.
genet'ics, *n. pl.*, the science of heredity.
Gene'van, *adj.*, rel. to Geneva and to Calvinism.
Gene'vanism, *n.*, the Calvinistic system.
Genevese', *adj.*, rel. to Geneva; *n.*, a native of Geneva.
ge'nial, *adj.*, cheerful, kindly.
genial'ity, *n.*, cheeriness, kindliness.
ge'nially, *adv.*, in a genial way.
genic'ulate, *adj.*, having knee-like joints.
genic'ulated, *adj.*, *i.q.* geniculate.
ge'nie, *n.*, a jinn.
genis'ta, *n.*, the broom (*Lat.*).
gen'ital, *adj.*, pert. to reproduction.
gen'itive, *n.*, the grammatical case of relation, origin, and possession.
gen'itor, *n.*, a father.
gen'iture, *n.*, birth.
ge'nius, *n.*, a guardian spirit; mental talent; spirit; aptitude; a person of great natural gifts.
Genoese', *adj.*, rel. to Genoa; *n.*, a native of Genoa.
genre, *n.*, common life as represented in art; kind.
gens, *n.*, a clan, house (*Lat.*).
genteel', *adj.*, polite, well-bred.
genteel'ly, *adv.*, politely.
gen'tian, *n.*, a bitter medicinal herb.
Gen'tile, *adj.*, non-Jewish; *n.*, a heathen.
Gen'tilism, *n.*, heathenism.
gentil'ity, *n.*, the quality of good breeding.
gen'tle, *adj.*, well-born, mild-mannered, kindly, easy; *n.*, larva of the flesh-fly.
gen'tlefolk, *n.*, persons of good birth and breeding.
gen'tleman, *n.*, one of good birth and breeding.
***gen'tleman*like**, *adj.*, *i.q.* gentlemanly.
***gen'tleman*ly**, *adj.*, having the manners of a gentleman.
gen'tlemen, *n.*, pl. of gentleman.
gen'tleness, *n.*, the quality of being gentle.
gen'tlest, *adj.*, *super.* of gentle.
gen'tlewoman, *n.*, fem. of gentleman.
gen'tly, *adv.*, in a gentle way.
gen'try, *n.*, *i.q.* gentlefolk.
ge'nu, *n.*, the knee (*Lat.*).
gen'uflect, *v.i.*, to bend the knee (in worship).
gen'uflected, *p.p.*, genuflect.
gen'uflecting, *pr.p.*, genuflect.
genuflex'ion, *n.*, the act of genuflecting.
gen'uine, *adj.*, unadulterated, real, sincere.
gen'uinely, *adv.*, sincerely, really.
gen'uineness, *n.*, the quality of being genuine.
ge'nus, *n.*, a distinct class, group, or order.
geocen'tric, *adj.*, with the earth as centre.
geocen'trical, *adj.*, *i.q.* geocentric.
ge'ode, *n.*, a concretionary stone with crystal-lined cavity.
geodes'ic, *adj.*, rel. to geodesy.
geodes'ical, *adj.*, *i.q.* geodesic.
geod'esy, *n.*, the science of land-measurement.
geodet'ic, *adj.*, pert. to geodesy.
geodet'ical, *adj.*, *i.q.* geodetic.
geodif'erous, *adj.*, producing geodes.
geognos'tic, *adj.*, rel. to geognosy.
geognos'tical, *adj.*, *i.q.* geognostic.
geog'nosy, *n.*, knowledge of the earth.
geogon'ic, *adj.*, rel. to geogony.
geog'ony, *n.*, the study of the earth's formation.
geog'rapher, *n.*, a student of geography.
geograph'ic, *adj.*, rel. to geography.
geograph'ical, *adj.*, *i.q.* geographic.
geog'raphy, *n.*, the study of the earth's surface.
geolog'ical, *adj.*, rel. to geology.
geol'ogize, *v.i.*, to study geology.

geol'ogist, *n.*, an expert in geology.

geol'ogy, *n.*, the science of the earth's structure.

geom'eter, *n.*, a geometrician.

geomet'ric, *adj.*, rel. to geometry.

geomet'rical, *adj.*, *i.q.* geometric.

geomet'rically, *adv.*, in accordance with geometry.

geometri'cian, *n.*, *i.q.* geometer.

geom'etry, *n.*, the science which treats of the properties and relations of magnitudes.

geon'omy, *n.*, the study of the laws relating to the earth's structure.

George, *n.*, the jewel of a Knight of the Garter's collar.

Geor'gian, *adj.*, pert. to the reigns of the Georges; also to Georgia in Europe and the U.S.A.

geor'gic, *adj.*, rel. to rustic affairs; *n.*, a poem on agriculture.

Geor'gium Si'dus, *n.*, the planet Uranus, named after George III.

geora'ma, *n.*, a hollow globe showing a view of the earth's inner surface.

geos'copy, *n.*, observation of the earth's surface-matter.

geothermom'eter, *n.*, an instrument for taking the earth's temperature.

ge'rah, *n.*, a Jewish weight and coin.

gera'nium, *n.*, a genus of flowering plants.

ger'falcon, *n.*, a large kind of falcon.

germ, *n.*, a sprout; origin; first principle; microbe.

Ger'man, *adj.*, rel. to Germany; of the same family; *n.*, a native of Germany; the German language.

german'der, *n.*, a wild plant so named.

germane', *adj.*, near akin; closely allied.

German'ic, *adj.*, rel. to Germany and the Germans.

Ger'manism, *n.*, a German idiom.

Ger'manize, *v.t.*, to make German; *v.i.*, to adopt German ways.

ger'micide, *adj.*, destructive of germs.

ger'minal, *adj.*, pert. to germs.

ger'minant, *adj.*, sprouting.

ger'minate, *v.i.*, to sprout.

ger'minated, *p.p.*, germinate.

ger'minating, *pr.p.*, germinate.

germina'tion, *n.*, the act of germinating.

ger'mule, *n.*, a diminutive germ.

gerryman'der, *v.t.*, to tinker with the arrangement of constituencies.

ger'und, *n.*, a verbal noun which is one of the parts of a verb.

gerun'dial, *adj.*, rel. to a gerund.

ges'so, *n.*, a plaster (gypsum) used for painting, etc.

gesta'tion, *n.*, pregnancy.

ges'tatory, *adj.*, rel. to gestation.

gestic'ulate, *v.i.*, to accompany speech with gesture.

gestic'ulated, *p.p.*, gesticulate.

gestic'ulating, *pr.p.*, gesticulate.

gesticula'tion, *n.*, the act of gesticulating.

gestic'ulator, *n.*, one who gesticulates.

gestic'ulatory, *adj.*, rel. to gesticulation.

ges'ture, *n.*, gesticulation; movement expressing question or thought, etc.; *v.i.*, *i.q.* gesticulate.

get, *v.t.*, to obtain, acquire, meet with; *v.i.*, to arrive; go.

get'ter, *n.*, one who gets.

get'ting, *pr.p.*, get.

gew'-gaw, *n.*, a bauble, toy, showy trifle.

gey'ser, *n.*, an intermittent hot spring; an apparatus for heating water.

ghar'ry, *n.*, an Indian native cart.

ghast'lier, *adj.*, *comp.* of ghastly.

ghast'liness, *n.*, the state of being ghastly.

ghast'ly, *adj.*, deadly pale, cadaverous, horrible.

gha'zi, *n.*, a Turkish high commander.

ghee, *n.*, clarified butter.

gher'kin, *n.*, a small cucumber.

Ghet'to, *n.*, the Jews' quarter of a town.

Ghib'elline, *adj.*, rel. to the Ghibelline party.

ghost, *n.*, a spirit, a phantom.

ghost'like, *adj.*, like a ghost.

ghost'ly, *adj.*, *i.q.* ghostlike; spiritual.

ghoul, *n.*, an imaginary creature that feeds on human flesh.

ghoul'ish, *adj.*, rel. to a ghoul.

ghur'ry, *n.*, an Indian division of time.

gi'ant, *n.*, a being of monstrous size; an abnormally big and tall man; *adj.*, gigantic.

gi'antess, *n.*, fem. of giant.

giaour, *n.*, the Mohammedan name for an unbeliever.

gib, *v.t.*, to fasten or furnish with a gib; *n.*, a piece of metal for holding another in place.

gib'berish, *n.*, unintelligible talk.

gib'bet, *v.t.*, to hang on a gallows; to ridicule; *n.*, the gallows.

gib'beted, *p.p.*, gibbet.

gib'beting, *pr.p.*, gibbet.

gib'bon, *n.*, an ape.

gib'bose, *adj.*, *i.q.* gibbous.

gibbos'ity, *n.*, protuberance.

gib'bous, *adj.* humped, protuberant.

gibe, *v.t.* and *i.*, to scoff at, to mock; *v.t.*, to shift a sail; *v.i.*, to swing over; also *jibe* in these two senses; *n.*, a sarcastic jest.

gibed, *p.p.*, gibe.

gi'ber, *n.*, one who gibes.

gi'bing, *pr.p.*, gibe.

gib'let, *n.*, one of the edible viscera of poultry.

gib'staff, *n.*, a boat pole.

gid, *n.*, a disease in sheep.

gid'dier, *adj.*, *comp.* of giddy.

gid'diest, *adj.*, *super.* of giddy.

gid'dily, *adv.*, in a giddy way.

gid'diness, *n.*, the state of being giddy.

gid'dy, *adj.*, dizzy; thoughtless.

gift, *n.*, anything given; a present; mental endowment.

gift'ed, *adj.*, talented.

gig, *n.*, a two-wheeled one-horse trap; a contrivance for raising nap on woollen cloth; a ship's boat; a racing boat.

gigantesque', *adj.*, *i.q.* gigantic.

gigan'tic, *adj.*, huge, giant-like.

gig'gle, *v.i.*, to titter, laugh foolishly; *n.*, a foolish laugh.

gig'gled, *p.p.*, giggle.

gig'gler, *n.*, one who giggles.

gig'gling, *pr.p.*, giggle.

gig'ot, *n.*, a leg (*Fr.*).

Gilber'tian, *adj.*, rel. to Gilbert; serio-comic.

Gil'bertine, *adj.*, rel. to St. Gilbert of Sempringham and to his Order.

gild, *v.t.*, to overlay with gold; to make to appear bright; *n.*, *i.q.* guild.

gild'ed, *p.p.*, gild.

gild'er, *n.*, one who gilds.

gild'ing, *pr.p.*, gild. *n.*, the art of overlaying with gold; gold leaf.

gill, *n.*, the respiratory organ in a fish.

gill, *n.*, the fourth part of a pint; a young girl.

gil'lie, *n.*, a Highland attendant on a shooting party.

gil'lyflower, *n.*, a flower with a clove-like smell.

gil'py, *n.*, one who is frolicsome.

gilt, *adj.*, gilded; *n.*, gilding.

gim'bal, *n.*, a ring for suspending a ship's compass, etc.

gim'crack, *adj.*, worthless; *n.*, a trumpery thing.

gim'let, *n.*, a small boring tool.

gimp, *n.*, edging made of silk cord.

gin, *v.t.*, to snare, trap; *n.*, a trap; snare; an alcoholic liquor; a machine used in the preparation of cotton.

gin'gal, *n.*, a swivel gun; a Chinese or Indian light rest-musket.

gin'ger, *n.*, the spicy root of an Indian plant.

gingerade', *n.*, an effervescing beverage flavoured with ginger.

gin'gerbread, *n.*, a sort of cake variously flavoured.

gin'gerly, *adv.*, cautiously, delicately.

gin'gery, *adj.*, rel. to, or resembling, ginger.

ging'ham, *n.*, a kind of cotton or linen cloth; an umbrella.

gingi'val, *adj.*, rel. to the gums.

gin'gles, *n.*, shingles.

ginned, *p.p.*, gin.

gin'ning, *pr.p.*, gin.

gin'sang, *n.*, a Chinese aromatic root.

gip'sy, **gyp'sy**, *n.*, one of the wandering race so named; any swarthy person.

gip'syism, *n.*, a gipsy expression.

giraffe', *n.*, the camelopard.

gir'andole, *n.*, a branched candlestick.

gir'asol, *n.*, the fire-opal.

gird, *v.t.*, to bind round, encircle; *v.i.*, to gibe.

gird'ed, *p.p.*, gird.

gird'er, *n.*, the principal beam in a floor, bridge, etc.

gird'ing, *pr.p.*, gird.

gir'dle, *v.t.*, to bind with a girdle; to enclose; *n.*, a band for the waist; any girdle-like enclosure; a gridiron.

gir'dled, *p.p.*, girdle; *adj.*, wearing a girdle.

gir'dler, *n.*, a girdle-maker.

gir'dling, *pr.p.*, girdle.

girl, *n.*, a female child; a young woman.

girl'hood, *n.*, the state of being a girl.

girl'ish, *adj.*, like a girl, youthful.

girl'ishness, *n.*, the state or quality of being girlish.

Giron'dists, *n. pl.*, a moderate Republican group in the French Assembly, 1791-3.

girt, *p.p.*, gird.

girth, *n.*, a saddle-belt; circumference.

gist, *n.*, the main point of a question or action.

git'tern, *n.*, a cithern.

gius'to, *adj.*, steady (*Mus.*).

give, *v.t.*, to bestow, confer without reward, concede.

giv'en, *p.p.*, give.

giv'er, *n.*, one who gives.

giv'ing, *pr.p.*, give.

giz'zard, *n.*, a fowl's muscular stomach.

gla'brous, *adj.*, smooth, bald.

glacé, *adj.*, cooled, iced; *n.*, a thin, shiny, silk material.

gla'cial, *adj.*, consisting of, or rel. to, ice.

glac'ier, *n.*, accumulated mountain-ice and snow.

gla'cis, *n.*, the sloping outer branch of a fortified ditch.

glad, *v.t.*, *i.q.* gladden; *adj.*, delighted, cheery.

glad'den, *v.t.*, to make glad.

glad'dened, *p.p.*, gladden.

glad'dening, *pr.p.*, gladden.

glade, *n.*, an open, green space in a wood.

gla'diate, *adj.*, sword-like.

glad'iator, *n.*, a Roman fighter in the arena.

gladiato'rial, *adj.*, rel. to gladiators and the arena.

glad'iole, *n.*, *i.q.* gladiolus.

gladi'olus, *n.*, the sword-lily.

glad'ly, *adv.*, cheerily, willingly.

glad'ness, *n.*, the state of being glad.

glad'some, *adj.*, joyous, cheerful.

glad'someness, *n.*, joyousness.

Gladsto'nian, *adj.*, rel. to, or resembling, Gladstone.

glair, *n.*, white of egg; viscous matter; *v.t.*, to smear with glair.

glaired, *p.p.*, glair.

glair'ing, *pr.p.*, glair.

glair'y, *adj.*, gluey.

glaive, *n.*, a sort of halberd.

glam'orous, *adj.*, bewitching, fascinating.

glam'our, -or, *n.*, charm, witchery.

glance, *v.i.*, to shoot obliquely; to take a rapid view; *n.*, a rapid view: a look.

glanced, *p.p.*, glance.

glan'cing, *pr.p.*, glance.

gland, *n.*, a secreting organ.

glan'dered, *adj.*, affected with glanders.

glan'ders, *n. pl.*, a contagious disease in horses.

glandif'erous, *adj.*, acorn-bearing.

gland'iform, *adj.*, acorn-shaped.

glan'dular, *adj.*, pert. to, or resembling, glands.

glandula'tion, *n.*, glandular structure.

glan'dule, *n.*, a little gland.

glandulos'ity, *n.*, the quality of being glandulous.

glan'dulous, *adj.*, *i.q.* glandular.

glare, *v.i.*, to give a dazzling light, to look fiercely; *n.*, a dazzling light, lustre; fierce look.

glared, *p.p.*, glare.

glar'eous, *adj.*, gravelly.

glar'iness, *n.*, brilliance.

glar'ing, *pr.p.*, glare; *adj.*, dazzling, gaudy; conspicuous.

glar'y, *adj.*, bright, dazzling.

glass, *v.t.*, to reflect; *adj.*, vitreous, made of glass; *n.*, a transparent, brittle substance; a vessel made of glass; any sort of glass instrument.

glass'-blower, *n.*, one who blows glass.

glass'cutter, *n.*, one who cuts glass.

glass'ful, *n.*, as much as a glass holds.

glass'house, *n.*, a conservatory, greenhouse.

glas'siness, *n.*, the state or quality of being glassy.

glass'-works, *n.*, a glass-making factory.

glass'wort, *n.*, a plant used in glass-making.

glass'y, *adj.*, glass-like, slippery.

Glaswe'gian, *adj.*, rel. to Glasgow.

glau'cine, *n.*, an alkaloid in the horse-poppy.

glauco'ma, *n.*, dimness of sight.

glauco'matous, *adj.*, of the nature of glaucoma.

glauco'sis, *n.*, *i.q.* glaucoma.

glau'cous, *adj.*, sea-green; covered with a white bloom.

glaze, *v.t.*, to furnish with glass; *v.i.*, to become glassy; *n.*, vitreous coating.

glazed, *p.p.*, glaze.

gla'zer, *n.*, that which gives a glaze.

gla'zier, *n.*, one who sets glass.

gla'zing, *pr.p.*, glaze; *n.*, the act of setting glass; an enamel; window panes.

gleam, *v.i.*, to send out rays; *n.*, a sudden emission of light.

gleamed, *p.p.*, gleam.

gleam'ing, *pr.p.*, gleam.

glean, *v.t.*, to gather the leavings of reapers; to collect; *v.i.*, to pick up information.

gleaned, *p.p.*, glean.

glean'er, *n.*, one who gleans.

glean'ing, *pr.p.*, glean; *n.*, the act of gleaning; that which is gathered.

glebe, *n.*, a clod, soil, church landed property.

gle'by, *adj.*, pert. to glebe.

glee, *n.*, joyousness; a variety of part-song.

glee'ful, *adj.*, full of glee.

glee'some, *adj.*, *i.q.* gleeful.

gleet, *n.*, a mucous discharge.

glen, *n.*, a narrow valley.

gle'ne, *n.*, the eye-pupil.

glengar'ry, *n.*, a Scotch bonnet.

glenliv'et, *n.*, a brand of whisky.

gle'noid, *adj.*, having a cavity.

glib, *adj.*, smooth, flippant.

glib'ly, *adv.*, in a glib way.

glib'ness, *n.*, the quality of being glib.

glide, *v.i.*, to flow gently; to slide; *n.*, a sliding movement.

glid'dery, *adj.*, slippery.

gli'ded, *p.p.*, glide.

gli'der, *n.*, one who glides; an aerial apparatus for gliding.
gli'ding, *pr.p.*, glide.
gli'dingly, *adv.*, in a gliding manner.
glim'mer, *v.i.*, to give a faint light; *n.*, a faint light.
glim'mered, *p.p.*, glimmer.
glim'mering, *pr.p.*, glimmer; *n.*, a faint perception.
glimpse, *v.t.*, to catch a sudden sight of; *v.i.*, to appear momentarily; *n.*, a sudden flash; a faint idea.
glissade', *v.i.*, to slide downward; *n.*, the act of sliding down.
glis'ten, *v.i.*, to shine, sparkle; *n.*, a glitter.
glis'tened, *p.p.*, glisten.
glis'tening, *pr.p.*, glisten.
glis'ter, *v.i.*, *i.q.* glisten.
glis'tered, *p.p.*, glister.
glis'tering, *pr.p.*, glister; *adj.*, bright.
glit'ter, *v.i.*, to sparkle, to make a show.
glit'tered, *p.p.*, glitter.
glit'tering, *pr.p.*, glitter.
gloam'ing, *n.*, twilight, dusk.
gloat, *v.i.*, to stare admiringly or exultingly.
gloat'ed, *p.p.*, gloat.
gloat'ing, *pr.p.*, gloat.
glo'bate, *adj.*, globe-shaped.
glo'bated, *adj.*, *i.q.* globate.
globe, *n.*, a sphere, ball, the world; a model of the world or the heavens.
globe'-trotter, *n.*, a hurried traveller.
glo'bose, *adj.*, globe-shaped.
globos'ity, *n.*, the state or quality of being globose.
glo'bous, *adj.*, *i.q.* globular.
glob'ular, *adj.*, spherical.
glob'ule, *n.*, a small globe; a homoeopathic pill.
glob'ulin, *n.*, an albuminous particle found in blood and plants.
glob'ulous, *adj.*, *i.q.* globular.
glome, *n.*, part of the frog in a horse's foot.
glom'erate, *adj.*, gathered into a mass.
glomera'tion, *n.*, a cluster.
gloom, *v.i.*, to be or look gloomy; *v.t.*, to sadden; *n.*, partial darkness, sadness.
gloom'ier, *adj.*, *comp.* of gloomy.
gloom'iest, *adj.*, *super.* of gloomy.
gloom'ily, *adv.*, in a gloomy way.
gloom'iness, *n.*, the state or quality of being gloomy.
gloom'ing, *pr.p.*, gloom.
gloom'y, *adj.*, partially dark, dismal.
glo'ried, *p.p.*, glory.
glorifica'tion, *n.*, the act or effect of glorifying.
glo'rified, *p.p.*, glorify.
glo'rify, *v.t.*, to make glorious, magnify.
glo'rifying, *pr.p.*, glorify.
glo'rious, *adj.*, illustrious, celebrated.
glo'riously, *adv.*, in a glorious way.
glo'ry, *v.i.*, to exult, take pride in; *n.*, splendour, honour, fame.
glo'rying, *pr.p.*, glory.
gloss, *v.t.*, to excuse plausibly; to make notes on; make lustrous; *n.*, false lustre, comment.
glossal'gia, *n.*, pain in the tongue.
glossa'rial, *adj.*, rel. to a glossary.
glos'sarist, *n.*, the compiler of a glossary.
glos'sary, *n.*, a dictionary of special terms.
glossed, *p.p.*, gloss.
gloss'er, *n.*, one who glosses; a polisher.
gloss'ier, *adj.*, *comp.* of glossy.
gloss'iest, *adj.*, *super.* of glossy.
gloss'ily, *adv.*, in a glossy way.
gloss'iness, *n.*, the state or quality of being glossy.
gloss'ing, *pr.p.*, gloss.
glossi'tis, *n.*, inflammation of the tongue.
glossog'rapher, *n.*, one skilled in glossography.
glossograph'ical, *adj.*, rel. to glossography.
glossog'raphy, *n.*, the scientific description of the tongue.
glossolog'ical, *adj.*, rel. to glossology.
glossol'ogist, *n.*, one skilled in glossology.
glossol'ogy, *n.*, the science of languages.
gloss'y, *adj.*, having a gloss on it.
glot'tal, *adj.*, rel. to the glottis.
glot'tis, *n.*, the opening of the larynx.
glottol'ogy, *n.*, *i.q.* glossology.
glove, *v.t.*, to cover with a glove; *n.*, a covering of the hands.
gloved, *p.p.*, glove; *adj.*, covered with a glove.
glov'er, *n.*, a maker or seller of gloves.
glow, *v.i.*, to shine with intense heat; to become animated; *n.*, intense, shining heat; brightness; emotional warmth.
glowed, *p.p.*, glow.
glow'er, *v.i.*, to glare.
glow'ered, *p.p.*, glower.
glow'ering, *pr.p.*, glower.
glow'ing, *pr.p.*, glow.
glow'-worm, *n.*, a luminous grub.
gloxin'ia, *n.*, a tropical plant so named.
gloze, *v.t.*, to gloss over.
glozed, *p.p.*, gloze.
glo'zer, *n.*, one who glozes.
glo'zing, *pr.p.*, gloze.
glu'cic, *adj.*, sugary.
gluci'na, *n.*, glucinum oxide.
glu'cine, *adj.*, rel. to glucinum.
gluci'num, *n.*, a white

metal derived from beryl.

glu'cose, *n.*, sugar obtained from corn, grapes, etc.

glue, *v.t.*, to cement with glue; *n.*, a viscous cement.

glued, *p.p.*, glue.

glu'er, *n.*, anything that glues.

glu'ey, *adj.*, like glue.

glu'ing, *pr.p.*, glue.

glum, *adj.*, doleful, sullen.

gluma'ceous, *adj.*, pert. to glumes.

glume, *n.*, the husk of grasses and grain.

glu'mous, *adj.*, having glumes.

glut, *v.t.*, to fill to satiety; over-fill; *n.*, an over-supply.

glute'al, *adj.*, rel. to the buttocks.

glu'ten, *n.*, a viscid, elastic substance found in grain.

glu'tinate, *v.t.*, to cement.

glu'tinated, *p.p.*, glutinate.

glu'tinating, *pr.p.*, glutinate.

glu'tinous, *adj.*, viscous, gluey.

glut'ted, *p.p.*, glut.

glut'ting, *pr.p.*, glut.

glut'ton, *n.*, one who gluts himself with food.

glut'tonize, *v.i.*, to play the glutton.

glut'tonous, *adj.*, greedy over food.

glut'tony, *n.*, excess in eating.

glyc'erine, *n.*, a liquid extract from fatty matter.

glyco'nian, *adj.*, *i.q.* glyconic.

glycon'ic, *adj.*, pert. to the Glyconic metre; *n.*, a line in the Glyconic metre.

glyph, *n.*, upright fluting.

glyph'ic, *adj.*, rel. to sculpture.

glyph'ograph, *n.*, a reproduction in relief.

glyphog'rapher, *n.*, one skilled in glyphography.

glyphograph'ic, *adj.*, rel. to glyphography.

glyp'tic, *adj.*, rel. to glyptography.

glyptog'raphy, *n.*, the art of engraving gems.

glyptothe'ca, *n.*, a museum of sculptures.

gnarl, *v.t.*, to make knotty; *n.*, a knot on a tree.

gnarled, *p.p.*, gnarl; *adj.*, knotty.

gnarl'ing, *pr.p.*, gnarl.

gnarl'y, *adj.*, having gnarls.

gnash, *v.t.*, to strike together; *v.i.*, to grind the teeth.

gnashed, *p.p.*, gnash.

gnash'ing, *pr.p.*, gnash.

gnat, *n.*, a small, winged, stinging insect.

gnaw, *v.t.*, to eat away, bite, fret.

gnawed, *p.p.*, gnaw.

gnaw'er, *n.*, one who gnaws.

gnaw'ing, *pr.p.*, gnaw.

gneiss, *n.*, a crystalline rock.

gneiss'ose, *adj.*, of the nature of gneiss.

gnome, *n.*, an imaginary earth sprite; a sententious saying.

gno'mic, *adj.*, sententious, didactic.

gno'mon, *n.*, the rod, pillar, or pin of a sundial; what is left of a parallelogram when a smaller parallelogram has been taken out of it.

gnomon'ic, *adj.*, pert. to dials.

gnomon'ical, *adj.*, *i.q.* gnomonic.

gnomon'ics, *n.pl.*, the science and art of constructing dials.

gnomonol'ogy, *n.*, the science of dialling.

gno'sis, *n.*, higher knowledge.

gnos'tic, *adj.*, rel. to the Gnostics and Gnosticism.

Gnos'ticism, *n.*, a religious and philosophical system, partly Christian, partly pagan, prevalent in the first six centuries.

gnu, *n.*, a S. African ruminant of the antelope family, with a buffalo-like head.

go, *v.i.*, to walk, move, travel; *n.*, the mode; mettle.

goad, *v.t.*, to prick with a goad; to incite; *n.*, a pointed stick for driving oxen.

goad'ed, *p.p.*, goad.

goad'ing, *pr.p.*, goad.

go'-ahead, *adjectival phrase*, advanced, progressive.

goal, *n.*, the winning-post in a race; the end limit of a football field; any aim.

goat, *n.*, a horned, long-haired quadruped.

goatee', *n.*, a goat-beard.

goat'herd, *n.*, one who tends goats.

goat'ish, *adj.*, goat-like.

goat'sucker, *n.*, an insectivorous bird.

gob, *v.t.*, to spit; *n.*, spittle.

gobang', *n.*, a game played with counters.

gob'bet, *n.*, a lump.

gob'bing, *n.*, refuse.

gob'ble, *v.t.*, to swallow greedily; *v.i.*, to make the cry of a turkey; *n.*, a turkey's crop; a putt so played that, though it would have been expected to go beyond the hole, it drops in.

gob'bled, *p.p.*, gobble.

gob'bler, *n.*, one who gobbles.

gob'bling, *pr.p.*, gobble.

gob'elin, *n.*, tapestry of gobelin make or pattern.

gob'let, *n.*, a drinking vessel without a handle.

gob'lin, *n.*, an evil spirit; an elf; a fairy.

go'by, *n.*, a fish so named.

go'-by, *n.*, avoidance.

go'-cart, *n.*, a child's cart.

God, *n.*, the Supreme Deity.

god'child, *n.*, one for whom god-parents are sponsors in Holy Baptism.

god'daughter, *n.*, a female godchild.

god'dess, *n.*, a heathen female deity; a supremely beautiful woman.

Gode'tia, *n.*, a plant so named.

god'father, *n.*, a male god-parent.

God'head, *n.*, the Divine nature; divinity.

god'less, *adj.*, ungodly.

god'like, *adj.*, resembling God.

god'liness, *n.*, the state or quality of being godly.

god'ly, *adj.*, pious, holy.

god'mother, *n.*, a female god-parent.

godown', *n.*, an E. Indian warehouse.

god'-parent, *n.*, a child's sponsor at its baptism.

god'send, *n.*, a piece of providential good fortune.

god'son, *n.*, a male god-child.

God'-speed, *n.*, good success.

god'ward, *adv.*, towards God.

go'er, *n.*, one who goes.

gof'fer, *v.t.*, to crimp.

gof'fered, *p.p.*, goffer.

gof'fering, *pr.p.*, goffer; *n.*, fluting; ornamental edging to a book. Also *gauffering*.

gog'gle, *v.i.*, to roll the eyes; *n.*, a rolling of the eyes.

gog'gled, *p.p.*, goggle; *adj.*, wearing goggles.

gog'gling, *pr.p.*, goggle.

gog'gle-eyed, *adj.*, having big, rolling eyes.

gog'gles, *n.*, big spectacles.

gog'let, *n.*, an Indian water-cooler.

go'ing, *pr.p.*, go.

goi'tre, *n.*, a tumour or swelling in the throat.

goi'trous, *adj.*, affected with goitre.

golcon'da, *n.*, a rich gold-mine.

gold, *n.*, the chief precious metal.

gold'-beater, *n.*, one who beats out gold-leaf.

gold'en, *adj.*, made of gold, like gold.

gold'-field, *n.*, an auriferous district.

gold'finch, *n.*, a yellow singing-bird.

gold'fish, *n.*, a red-dish carp-like fish.

gold'-foil, *n.*, gold beaten thin.

gold'hammer, *n.*, the yellow-hammer bird.

gold'ilocks, *n.*, a name for the buttercup and other yellow flowers.

gold'-lace, *n.*, lace with a gold thread in it.

gold'plate, *n.*, gold vessels collectively.

gold'-size, *n.*, a size used in laying on gold-leaf.

gold'smith, *n.*, a worker in gold.

gold'-stick, *n.*, a Court official.

gold'thread, *n.*, an evergreen so named.

golf, *v.i.*, to play the game of golf; *n.*, a game played over links.

Goli'ath, *n.*, the Philistine giant.

golosh', *n.*, a rubber over-shoe.

gompho'sis, *n.*, socketing.

gomphi'asis, *n.*, looseness of the teeth.

gomu'ti, *n.*, a variety of fibre.

gon'dola, *n.*, a Venetian boat.

gondolier', *n.*, one who propels a gondola.

gone, *p.p.*, go.

gon'falon, *n.*, an ensign, standard.

gonfalonier', *n.*, a chief standard-bearer.

gong, *n.*, a tambourine-like bell struck with a padded stick.

goniom'eter, *n.*, an instrument for measuring angles.

goniomet'ric, *adj.*, rel. to goniometry.

goniomet'rical, *adj.*, *i.q.* goniometric.

goniom'etry, *n.*, the science of measuring angles.

good, *adj.*, excellent, beneficial, pious, kind; *n.*, benefit, advantage, prosperity.

good-bye', *interj.*, farewell; *n.*, a farewell.

good-day', *interj.*, a salutation at meeting or parting.

good-hu'moured, *adj.*, good-tempered.

good'ish, *adj.*, rather good.

good'iness, *n.*, the quality of being goody.

good'lier, *adj.*, *comp.* of goodly.

good'liest, *adj.*, *super.* of goodly.

good'liness, *n.*, the quality of being goodly.

good'ly, *adj.*, pleasing to behold; noble.

good'man, *n.*, the master of a household.

good-na'ture, *n.*, a kind disposition.

good-na'tured, *adj.*, kindly disposed.

good-na'turedly, *adv.*, in a good-natured way.

good'ness, *n.*, the quality of being good; kindness; piety.

good-night', an exclamation; *n.*, a late farewell.

goods, *n. pl.*, property; chattels, commodities.

goods'-train, *n.*, a freight train.

good'wife, *n.*, the mistress of a household.

goodwill', *n.*, kindliness; additional value; payment for goodwill.

good'y, *adj.*, feebly pious; namby-pamby.

Goor'kha, *n.*, one of the Goorkhas, the

chief Nepalese race. Also *Ghoorka*.

goosan'der, *n.*, a water-fowl.

goose, *n.*, a domestic web-footed water-fowl; a tailor's iron; a foolish person.

goose'berry, *n.*, a prickly shrub; its fruit.

goose'neck, *n.*, a piece of bent iron at the end of a boom or yard.

goos'ery, *n.*, a place for geese.

goose'-step, *n.*, the German military way of marching.

go'pher, *n.*, a variety of wood; a N. American rodent.

Gor'dian, *adj.*, rel. to Gordius, the Phrygian king.

Gor'dian knot, *n.*, Gordius's knot which Alexander cut with his sword.

gore, *v.t.*, to pierce with a horn; to make gores in a garment; *n.*, blood, clotted blood; a triangular piece of cloth; a strip of land.

gored, *p.p.*, gore.

gorge, *v.t.*, to swallow greedily; to satiate; *n.*, the throat; a narrow mountain pass.

gorged, *p.p.*, gorge.

gor'geous, *adj.*, splendid, glittering.

gor'geously, *adv.*, in a gorgeous way.

gor'geousness, *n.*, the quality of being gorgeous.

gor'get, *n.*, throat-armour.

gor'ging, *pr.p.*, gorge.

Gor'gon, *n.*, one of the three mythological sisters, the sight of whom turned the beholder to stone.

gorgo'nian, *adj.*, rel. to the Gorgons.

gorgonzo'la, *n.*, a variety of cheese.

goril'la, *n.*, the largest of the apes.

gor'ing, *pr.p.*, gore.

gor'mand, *n.*, a glutton.

gor'mandism, *n.*, gluttony.

gor'mandize, *v.t.*, to play the glutton.

gor'mandized, *p.p.*, gormandize.

gor'mandizer, *n.*, one who gormandizes.

gor'mandizing, *pr.p.*, gormandize.

gorse, *n.*, the furze.

gor'y, *adj.*, bloody.

gos'hawk, *n.*, a kind of hawk.

gos'ling, *n.*, a young goose.

gos'pel, *n.*, good tidings; the history of Our Lord's birth, ministry, and death; the Catholic faith; the portion from one of the four Gospels recited in the Eucharist.

gos'peller, *n.*, the English name for the deacon at Mass.

gos'samer, *n.*, a fine spider's web; any filmy substance.

gos'samery, *adj.*, filmy.

gos'sip, *v.i.*, to tattle, chat; *n.*, a godparent, a neighbour, a busy talker.

gos'siped, *p.p.*, gossip.

gossip'ing, *pr.p.*, gossip.

got, *p.p.*, get.

Goth, *n.*, one of an ancient Teutonic race.

Go'thamite, *n.*, one of the men of Gotham.

Goth'ic, *adj.*, like a Goth, barbarous; rel. to Gothic architecture; *n.*, the pointed style in European architecture; black-letter type.

Goth'icism, *n.*, the principles or idiom of the Gothic style.

Goth'icize, *v.t.*, to convert into Gothic.

got'ten, *p.p.*, get; *see* got.

gouge, *v.t.*, to scoop out with a gouge; *v.i.*, to force out the eye; *n.*, a chisel with a rounded edge.

gouged, *p.p.*, gouge.

gou'ging, *pr.p.* gouge.

gourd, *n.*, a large plant with bottle-shaped fruit; a drinking vessel.

gourd'y, *adj.*, having swollen legs.

gour'mand, *n.*, a glutton.

gourmet', *n.*, an epicure.

gout, *n.*, a disease of the joints.

goût, *n.*, taste, relish (*Fr.*).

gout'ily, *adv.*, in a gouty way.

gout'iness, *n.*, a tendency to gout.

gout'y, *n.*, affected with gout.

gov'ern, *v.t*, to control, rule over.

***gov'ern*able,** *adj.*, subject to control.

gov'ernance, *n.*, government.

gov'ernante, *n.*, a governess, duenna (*Fr.*).

gov'erned, *p.p.*, govern.

gov'erness, *n.* an instructress.

gov'erning, *pr.p.*, govern.

gov'ernment, *n.*, the act of governing; rule; the Ministry.

***govern*men'tal,** *adj.*, rel. to government.

gov'ernor, *n.*, one who governs; a tutor; a regulating appliance on an engine or other machine.

gov'ernor-*general*, *n.*, the ruler of a province.

gov'ernorship, *n.*, the office of a governor.

gow'an, *n.*, the daisy.

gown, *n.*, a long, loose garment; a woman's dress.

gowned, *adj.*, wearing a gown; dressed.

gown'man, *n.*, *i.q.* gownsman.

gowns'man, *n.*, one who wears a gown.

grab, *v.t.*, to seize with violence, snatch greedily; *n.*, the act of grabbing.

grabbed, *p.p.*, grab.

grab'bing, *pr.p.*, grab.

grab'ble, *v.i.*, to grope.

grace, *v.t.*, to adorn,

honour; *n.*, favour, charm, divine influence, a giving of thanks, an academic decree of permission.

graced, *p.p.*, grace.

grace'ful, *adj.*, elegant, charming.

grace'fully, *adv.*, charmingly.

grace'fulness, *n.*, the quality of being graceful.

grace'less, *adj.*, void of grace, abandoned.

grace'lessness, *n.*, the quality of being graceless.

Gra'ces, *n. pl.*, the three attendant nymphs of Venus.

gra'cing, *pr.p.*, grace.

gra'cious, *adj.*, elegant, kindly.

gra'ciously, *adv.*, in a gracious way.

gra'ciousness, *n.*, the quality of being gracious.

gradate', *v.t.*, to blend in grades.

grada'ted, *p.p.*, gradate.

grada'ting, *pr.p.*, gradate.

grada'tion, *n.*, a step in a series, gradual blending.

grada'tional, *adj.*, in gradation.

gra'datory, *adj.*, *i.q.* gradational.

grade, *v.t.*, to rank in order; *n.*, degree or rank.

gra'ded, *p.p.*, grade.

gra'dient, *n.*, the angle of incline in a road.

gradine', *n.*, one in a range of steps or of seats in tiers; a ledge over an altar.

gra'ding, *pr.p.*, grade.

grad'ual, *adj.*, advancing by steps, slow; *n.*, a prose anthem sung between the Epistle and Gospel; the book of Graduals.

grad'ually, *adv.*, slowly, regularly.

grad'uate, *v.i.*, to take an academic degree.

grad'uate, *n.*, the holder of a degree; *i.q.* gradate.

grad'uated, *p.p.*, graduate.

grad'uating, *pr.p.*, graduate.

gradua'tion, *n.*, admission to a degree; regular progression.

grad'uator, *n.*, an apparatus for the minute division of lines; an electromagnet.

gra'dus, *n.*, a dictionary of Prosody.

graf, graff, *v.t.*, *i.q.* graft.

graffi'ti, *n. pl.*, rough wall-sketches.

graffi'to, *n.*, sing. of graffiti.

graft, *v.t.*, to insert a shoot into another tree; to transfer tissue; *v.i.*, to take a bribe; *n.*, a grafted shoot; a bribe (*Amer.*).

graft'ed, *p.p.*, graft.

graft'er, *n.*, one who grafts.

graft'ing, *pr.p.*, graft.

grail, *n.*, a chalice; a dish; a Gradual book (*see* gradual).

grain, *v.t.*, to granulate; to paint in imitation of wood or marble; *n.*, a seed of corn; corn in general; a minute unit of weight.

grained, *p.p.*, grain.

grain'er, *n.*, one who grains.

grain'ing, *pr.p.*, grain; *n.*, the act of imitating in paint the grain of wood or marble.

grain'y, *adj.*, like grains.

gral'lic, *adj.*, rel. to the *Grallae* or Waders.

gral'loch, *v.t.*, to disembowel; *n.*, a deer's viscera.

gram, *n.*, *see* gramme.

gramin'eal, *adj.*, rel. to grass.

gramin'eous, *adj.*, consisting of grass.

graminif'erous, *adj.*, producing grass.

graminiv'orous, *adj.*, eating grass.

gram'malogue, *n.*, a word represented by a single shorthand sign.

gram'mar, *n.*, the art of correct speech or writing.

gramma'rian, *n.*, the writer of a grammar; an expert in grammar.

grammat'ic, *adj.*, rel. to grammar.

grammat'ical, *adj.*, *i.q.* grammatic.

grammat'ically, *adv.*, according to grammatical rule.

gram'matist, *n.*, a grammarian.

gramme, *n.*, a metric unit of weight (about 15½ grains, troy weight).

gram'ophone, *n.*, an apparatus for recording vocal sounds

gram'pus, *n.*, a porpoise-like cetacean.

gran'ary, *n.*, a store for grain.

grand, *adj.*, large, magnificent, exalted.

gran'dam, *n.*, a grandmother.

gran'dame, *n.*, *i.q.* grandam.

grand'-daughter, *n.*, the daughter of a son or daughter.

grandee', *n.*, one of the highest rank.

grand'er, *adj.*, *comp.* of grand.

grand'est, *adj.*, *super.* of grand.

gran'deur, *n.*, greatness, splendour.

grand'father, *n.*, a parent's father.

grandil'oquence, *n.*, bombastic talk.

grandil'oquent, *adj.*, bombastic.

gran'diose, *adj.*, affectedly grand.

grand-ju'ror, *n.*, member of a grand jury.

grand-ju'ry, *n.*, a jury to whom cases are referred from a court of first instance.

grand'ly, *adv.*, in a grand way.

grand'mother, *n.*, a parent's mother.

grand'parent, *n.*, a parent of a parent.

grand'sire, *n.*, a grandfather.

grand'son, *n.*, the son of a son or daughter.

grange, *n.*, a farmstead.
gran'ger, *n.*, a farmer.
gran'gerism, *n.*, the practice of illustrating a book with pictures lifted from other books.
gran'gerize, *v.t.*, to illustrate (books) with lifted pictures.
granif'erous, *adj.*, grain-producing.
gran'iform, *adj.*, like a grain.
gran'ite, *n.*, an igneous rock formation.
granit'ic, *adj.*, rel. to granite.
gran'itoid, *adj.*, like granite.
graniv'orous, *adj.*, grain-eating.
grant, *v.t.*, to concede, give, bestow; *n.*, a gift; a conveyance of property
grant'able, *adj.*, able to be granted.
grant'ed, *p.p.*, grant.
grantee', *n.*, the recipient of a grant.
grant'er, *n.*, one who grants.
grant'ing, *pr.p.*, grant.
grant'or, *n.*, one who conveys property.
gran'ular, *adj.*, consisting of, or resembling, grains.
gran'ulate, *v.t.*, to form into grains; *adj.*, *i.q.* granular.
gran'ulated, *p.p.*, granulate.
gran'ulating, *pr.p.*, granulate.
granula'tion, *n.*, the act or effect of granulating.
gran'ule, *n.*, a little grain.
gran'ulose, *n.*, an ingredient in starch convertible into sugar.
gran'ulous, *adj.*, *i.q.* granular.
grape, *n.*, the fruit of the vine; grape-shot.
gra'pery, *n.*, a vinery.
grape'-shot, *n.*, shot arranged in clusters.
grape'-sugar, *n.*, glucose.
grape'-vine, *n.*, the vine that yields the grape.
graph, *n.*, a diagram showing, by means of dots and lines, relationship; a gelatine copying appliance; *v.t.*, to copy by means of the graph.
graph'ic, *adj.*, rel. to writing or drawing; highly descriptive.
graph'ical, *adj.*, *i.q.* graphic.
graph'ically, *adv.*, in a graphic way.
graph'ite, *n.*, blacklead.
graph'olite, *adj.*, rel. to graphite.
grapholog'ic, *adj.*, rel. to graphology.
grapholog'ical, *adj.*, *i.q.* graphologic.
graphol'ogy, *n.*, the art of judging character from handwriting.
graphom'eter, *n.*, an instrument that measures angular degrees.
graphomet'ric, *adj.*, rel. to a graphometer.
graphomet'rical, *adj.*, *i.q.* graphometric.
graph'otype, *n.*, a printing process for producing relief blocks.
grap'nel, *n.*, a small anchor; large tongs.
grap'ple, *v.t.*, to seize; *v.i.*, to struggle; *n.*, a fight, seizure.
grap'pled, *p.p.*, grapple.
grap'pling, *pr.p.*, grapple.
grap'pling-iron, *n.*, a hook; grapnel.
grasp, *v.t.*, to seize with the hand; to perceive meaning; *n.*, a seizure, hold, intellectual apprehension.
grasp'able, *adj.*, able to be grasped.
grasped, *p.p.*, grasp.
grasp'er, *n.*, one who grasps.
grasp'ing, *pr.p.*, grasp; *adj.*, avaricious.
grass, *n.*, the common herbage of the field; *v.t.*, to cover with grass.
grassed, *p.p.*, grass.
grass'hopper, *n.*, a locust-like insect.
grass'iness, *n.*, the state of being grassy.
grass'ing, *pr.p.*, grass.
grass'-plot, *n.*, a grass-covered plot of ground.
grass'y, *adj.*, covered with grass; grass-like.
grate, *v.t.*, to rub; *v.i.*, to make a grinding noise; to jar; *n.*, a frame for holding fuel.
gra'ted, *p.p.*, grate.
grate'ful, *adj.*, full of gratitude, thankful; welcome.
grate'fully, *adv.*, in a grateful way.
grate'fulness, *n.*, gratitude.
gra'ter, *n.*, a utensil on which substances can be grated.
gratifica'tion, *n.*, the act of gratifying; pleasure, reward.
grat'ified, *p.p.*, gratify.
grat'ifier, *n.*, one who gratifies.
grat'ify, *v.t.*, to give satisfaction or pleasure.
grat'ifying, *pr.p.*, gratify; *adj.*, agreeable.
gra'ting, *pr.p.*, grate; *n.*, open bars; *adj.*, harsh.
gra'tingly, *adv.*, in a grating way.
gra'tis, *adv.*, without pay.
grat'itude, *n.*, the feeling of thankfulness.
gratu'itous, *adj.*, without pay; unprovoked.
gratu'itously, *adv.*, without pay or provocation.
gratu'ity, *n.*, a free gift.
grat'ulant, *adj.*, congratulating.
grat'ulate, *v.t.*, *i.q.* congratulate.
grat'ulated, *p.p.*, gratulate.
grat'ulating, *pr.p.*, gratulate.
gratula'tion, *n.*, *i.q.* congratulation.
grat'ulatory, *adj.*, *i.q.* congratulatory.
grava'men, *n.*, a complaint.
grave, *v.t.*, to carve,

engrave; *adj.*, heavy, serious, of low musical pitch; *n.*, a burial-place in the ground.

graved, *p.p.*, grave.

grav'el, *v.t.*, to lay gravel on; to embarrass; *n.*, small stones, usually mixed with sand; a disease of the kidneys and bladder.

grave'less, *adj.*, unburied.

grav'el(l)ed, *p.p.*, gravel.

grav'el(l)ing, *pr.p.*, gravel.

grav'elly, *adj.*, composed, or full, of gravel.

grave'ly, *adv.*, seriously.

gra'ven, *p.p.*, grave.

grave'ness, *n.*, the quality of being grave.

gra'ver, *n.*, an engraver; a burin; *adj.*, *comp.* of grave.

gra'vest, *adj.*, *super.* of grave.

grave'stone, *n.*, a stone over, or at the head of, a grave.

grave'yard, *n.*, a cemetery or churchyard.

gravim'eter, *n.*, an instrument for finding the specific gravity of bodies.

gra'ving, *pr.p.*, grave; *n.*, the act of engraving; the act of cleaning a ship's bottom.

gra'ving-dock, *n.*, a dock where a ship's bottom is cleaned.

grav'itate, *v.i.*, to tend towards.

grav'itated, *p.p.*, gravitate.

grav'itating, *pr.p.*, gravitate.

gravita'tion, *n.*, the process of gravitating; the force by which particles are made to tend toward each other.

grav'itative, *adj.*, causing or tending to gravitate.

grav'ity, *n.*, weightiness; seriousness; importance; the force drawing all bodies towards the earth's centre.

gra'vy, *n.*, the juice of roast meat.

gray, grey, *adj.*, a colour—white and black mixed.

gray'beard, *n.*, an old man.

gray'ish, *adj.*, somewhat gray.

gray'ling, *n.*, a freshwater fish.

grey'wacke, *n.*, a palaeozoic sandstone.

graze, *v.t.*, to use as pasture; to touch or rub very lightly; *v.i.*, to eat grass; *n.*, a slight rub.

grazed, *p.p.*, graze.

gra'zer, *n.*, anything that grazes.

gra'zier, *n.*, a cattle-breeder.

gra'zing, *pr.p.*, graze.

grease, *v.t.*, to smear with grease; to bribe; *n.*, animal fat; a disease of horses' heels.

greased, *p.p.*, grease.

greas'er, *n.*, a creole of Mexico.

greas'ier, *adj.*, *comp.* of greasy.

greas'iest, *adj.*, *super.* of greasy.

greas'ily, *adv.*, in a greasy way.

greas'iness, *n.*, the state of being greasy.

greas'ing, *pr.p.*, grease.

greas'y, *adj.*, like grease; smeared.

great, *adj.*, large, exalted, pregnant.

great'coat, *n.*, an overcoat.

great'er, *adj.*, *comp.* of great.

great'est, *adj.*, *super.* of great.

great'ly, *adv.*, much.

great'ness, *n.*, the quality of being great.

greaves, *n. pl.*, armour for the ankles.

grebe, *n.*, a diving-bird.

Gre'cian, *adj.*, Greek, rel. to Greece; *n.*, a Greek scholar; a sixth-form boy at Christ's Hospital.

Gre'cism, *n.*, a Greek idiom.

greed, *n.*, avarice.

greed'ily, *adv.*, in a greedy way.

greed'iness, *n.*, the state or quality of being greedy.

greed'y, *adj.*, avaricious, gluttonous.

Greek, *adj.*, *i.q.* Grecian; *n.*, a native of Hellas; the Greek language.

Greek'-fire, *n.*, an inflammable substance said to be inextinguishable.

green, *adj.*, of the colour of grass; new, fresh; *n.*, the colour of growing grass; a grassy space.

green'back, *n.*, American paper money.

green'er, *adj.*, *comp.* of green.

green'ery, *n.*, green things, vegetables.

green'est, *adj.*, *super.* of green.

green'-eyed, *adj.*, jealous.

green'ing, *n.*, a variety of apple.

green'gage, *n.*, a variety of plum.

green'grocer, *n.*, one who sells fruit, flowers, and vegetables.

green'horn, *n.*, a simpleton.

green'house, *n.*, a conservatory.

green'ish, *adj.*, almost green.

green'ness, *n.*, verdure, inexperience.

green'-room, *n.*, the actors' room behind the scenes.

greens, *n. pl.*, vegetables.

green'sand, *n.*, a green sandstone.

green'sward, *n.*, turf covered with green grass.

green'wood, *n.*, a wood in leaf.

greet, *v.t.*, to welcome, accost; *v.i.*, to greet; weep (*Scot.*).

greet'ed, *p.p.*, greet.

greet'er, *n.*, one who greets.

greet'ing, *pr.p.*, greet; *n.*, a salute, welcome.

greff'ier, *n.*, a registrar.
grega'rious, *adj.*, living in flocks; fond of company.
grega'riously, *adv.*, in a gregarious way.
Grego'rian, *adj.*, rel. to St. Gregory.
Grego'rian chant, *n.*, plainsong.
grenade', *n.*, a hollow shell filled with explosives; a fire-extinguisher.
grenadier', *n.*, a foot soldier armed with grenades.
gren'adine, *n.*, a thin, gauzy, dress fabric.
gresso'rial, *adj.*, capable of walking.
grew, *p.t.* of grow.
grey, *see* gray.
grey'beard, *see* graybeard.
grey'hound, *n.*, a slender, swift type of hound.
grey'ness, *n.*, the state of being grey.
grid'dle, *n.*, an iron plate; *see* girdle.
grid'dle-cake, *n.*, a cake baked on a griddle.
gride, *v.t.*, to jar.
gri'ded, *p.p.*, gride.
grid'elin, *n.*, a grey-violet colour.
gri'ding, *pr.p.*, gride.
grid'iron, *n.*, an iron grated cooking-utensil.
grief, *n.*, sorrow, compunction.
griev'ance, *n.*, a complaint.
grieve, *v.t.*, to cause grief; *v.i.*, to feel grief, to mourn.
grieved, *p.p.*, grieve.
griev'er, *n.*, one who grieves.
griev'ing, *pr.p.*, grieve.
griev'ous, *adj.*, causing grief; distressing; vexatious.
griev'ously, *adv.*, in a grievous way.
griev'ousness, *n.*, the quality of being grievous.
grif'fin, *n.*, a fabulous beast with eagle's wings and lion's body.
grig, *n.*, a small eel.
grill, *v.t.*, to broil; torture; *n.*, a gridiron; meat grilled.
grillade', *n.*, the act of grilling; grilled meat.
gril'lage, *n.*, timber foundations laid in marshy ground.
grille, grill, *n.*, an opening through bars.
grilled, *p.p.*, grill.
grill'ing, *pr.p.*, grill; *adj.*, scorching hot.
grilse, *n.*, a young Scotch salmon.
grim, *adj.*, forbidding, stern, hideous.
grimace', *v.i.*, to make faces; *n.*, a distortion of the countenance.
grimaced', *p.p.*, grimace.
grimac'ing, *pr.p.*, grimace.
grimal'kin, *n.*, an old cat.
grime, *v.t.*, to make grimy; *n.*, dirt, mud.
grimed, *p.p.*, grime.
gri'mier, *adj.*, *comp.* of grimy.
gri'miest, *adj.*, *super.* of grimy.
gri'mily, *adv.*, in a grimy way.
gri'miness, *n.*, the state or quality of being grimy.
gri'ming, *pr.p.*, grime.
grim'ly, *adv.*, in a grim way.
grim'mer, *adj.*, *comp.* of grim.
grim'mest, *adj.*, *super.* of grim.
grim'ness, *n.*, the quality of being grim.
gri'my, *adj.*, muddy, dirty.
grin, *v.i.*, to set the teeth together and withdraw the lips in anger or mirth; *n.*, a forced or sneering smile.
grind, *v.t.*, to sharpen; to reduce to powder; to oppress.
grind'er, *n.*, anything that grinds; a molar tooth.
grind'ery, *n.*, a place for grinding; material in leather trade.
grind'ing, *pr.p.*, grind; *n.*, the grinder's trade.
grind'stone, *n.*, a stone for sharpening tools.
grinned, *p.p.*, grin.
grin'ner, *n.*, one who grins.
grin'ning, *pr.p.*, grin.
grip, *v.t.*, to clutch, hold tight; *n.*, a grasp, pressure; part of a golf-club shaft held by the player; a handbag (*Amer.*).
gripe, *v.t.*, to hold in a clutch; to squeeze; *n.*, a grasp; colic pain.
griped, *p.p.*, gripe.
gri'per, *n.*, anything that gripes.
grippe, *n.*, influenza.
grip'per, *n.*, anything that grips.
grip'ping, *pr.p.*, grip.
grisaille', *n.*, a mode of painting in grey.
grisette', *n.*, a shop-girl; a smartly dressed working-girl (*Fr.*).
gris'kin, *n.*, the spine of pork.
gris'liness, *n.*, the quality of being grisly.
gris'ly, *adj.*, rather grey; hideous.
gris'on, *n.*, a weasel-like animal.
Grisons', *n. pl.*, Swiss cantons so named.
grist, *n.*, corn for grinding; supply.
gris'tle, *n.*, cartilage.
gris'tly, *adj.*, cartilaginous.
grit, *n.*, the coarse part of meal, sand, or gravel; endurance.
grit'-stone, *n.*, coarse sandstone.
grit'tiness, *n.*, the state or quality of being gritty.
grit'ty, *adj.*, full of grit.
griz'zle, *v.i.*, to complain (*slang*).
griz'zled, *p.p.*, grizzle; *adj.*, growing grey.
griz'zling, *pr.p.*, grizzle.
griz'zly, *adj.*, greyish; *n.*, a grizzly bear.
groan, *v.i.*, to utter a low sound of pain; *n.*, a low sound of pain.

groaned, *p.p.*, groan.

groan'ing, *pr.p.*, groan.

groat, *n.*, a coin worth fourpence.

groats, *n. pl.*, oats or wheat hulled.

gro'cer, *n.*, a dealer in tea, sugar, spice, etc.

gro'cery, *n.*, a grocer's shop; grocer's goods.

grog, *n.*, a mixture of spirits and water.

grog'gery, *n.*, a grog-shop (*Amer.*).

grog'giness, *n.*, the state of being groggy.

grog'gy, *adj.*, intoxicated; unsteady.

grog'ram, *n.*, a coarse fabric of silk, mohair, etc.

groin, *v.t.*, to construct groins; *n.*, the depressed part of the thigh; the line where two vaults intersect (*arch.*).

groined, *p.p.*, groin; *adj.*, having groins.

groin'ing, *pr.p.*, groin; *n.*, a system of intersecting vaults.

Gro'lieresque, *adj.*, in the Grolier style of binding.

grom'met, *n.*, a rope-bound ring; a cannon-wad.

groom, *v.t.*, to look after a horse; *n.*, one who has the care of a horse; a bridegroom.

groomed, *p.p.*, groom.

groom'ing, *pr. p.*, groom.

grooms'man, *n.*, a bridegroom's supporter.

groove, *v.t.*, to cut into channels; *n.*, a channel or furrow.

grooved, *p.p.*, groove.

groov'er, *n.*, anything that grooves.

groov'ing, *pr. p.*, groove.

grope, *v.i.*, to feel about in the dark.

groped, *p.p.*, grope.

gro'per, *n.*, one who gropes.

gro'ping, *pr.p.*, grope.

gross, *adj.*, coarse, big; *n.*, the bulk; twelve dozen.

gross'ly, *adv.*, in a gross way.

gross'ness, *n.*, coarseness.

grot, *n.*, a grotto.

grotesque', *adj.*, odd, fantastic.

grotesque'ly, *adv.*, oddly, ludicrously.

grotesque'ness, *n.*, the quality of being grotesque.

grot'to, *n.*, a cavern.

ground, *v.t.*, to fix, base, instruct in elements; *v.i.*, to run aground; *p.p.* and *p.t.*, grind; *adj.*, fundamental; *n.*, the earth's surface; a basis.

ground'age, *n.*, a port duty.

ground'-ash, *n.*, a young ash.

ground'ed, *p.p.*, ground.

ground'ing, *pr.p.*, ground; *n.*, elementary instruction.

ground'less, *adj.*, lacking proof or certainty; unreasonable.

ground'lessness, *n.*, the quality of being groundless.

ground'ling, *n.*, an uneducated person.

ground'-plan, *n.*, a drawing in flat of the divisions of a building on the ground level.

ground'-plot, *n.*, a plot of ground; *i.q.* ground-plan.

ground'-rent, *n.*, rent paid to a freeholder.

ground'sel, *n.*, a weed with yellow flowers.

ground'sill, *n.*, the lowest timber in a wooden framework.

ground'work, *n.*, the element of a subject.

group, *v.t.* and *i.*, to collect together, form into a group or cluster; *n.*, an assemblage, a cluster.

grouped, *p.p.*, group.

group'ing, *pr.p.*, group.

grouse, *v.i.*, to complain (*slang*); *n.*, a game-bird so named

grout, *v.t.*, to fill in the spaces between stone; *n.*, a coarse mortar.

grout'ed, *p.p.*, grout.

grout'ing, *pr.p.*, grout.

grove, *n.*, a wood; a shady avenue.

grov'el, *v.i.*, to lie prone, to be low or mean.

grov'elled, grov'eled, *p.p.*, grovel.

grov'eller, grov'eler, *n.*, one who grovels.

grov'elling, grov'eling, *pr.p.*, grovel.

grow, *v.t.*, to cultivate; *v.i.*, to increase, to vegetate.

grow'er, *n.*, a cultivator.

grow'ing, *pr.p.*, grow.

growl, *v.i.*, to snarl like a dog; *n.*, a dog's angry snarl.

growled, *p.p.*, growl.

growl'er, *n.*, one who growls; a four-wheeled cab (*slang*).

growl'ing, *pr.p.*, growl.

growl'ingly, *adv.*, in a growling way.

grown, *p.p.*, grow.

growth, *n.*, the act of growing; increase; result, effect.

grub, *v.t.*, to dig or root up; *v.i.*, to do dirty work; *n.*, the larva of an insect; a dirty-looking sloven; food (*slang*).

grubbed, *p.p.*, grub.

grub'ber, *n.*, one who grubs.

grub'bing, *pr.p.*, grub.

grudge, *v.t.*, to give or take reluctantly; *n.*, ill-will, envy; an old-standing offence

grudged, *p.p.*, grudge.

grudg'er, *n.*, one who grudges.

grudg'ing, *pr.p.*, grudge.

grudg'ingly, *adv.*, in a grudging way.

gru'el, *n.*, meal boiled in milk or water.

grue'some, *adj.*, horrible.

gruff, *adj.*, rough, harsh, hoarse.

gruff'ly, *adv.*, roughly, hoarsely.

gruff'ness, *n.*, the quality of being gruff.

grum'ble, *v.i.*, to growl, find fault.

grum'bled, *p.p.*, grumble.

grum'bler, *n.*, one who grumbles.

grum'bling, *pr.p.*, grumble.

grum'blingly, *adv.*, in a grumbling way.

grume, *n.*, a blood-clot.

grum'met, *n.*, a ring of twisted rope.

gru'mous, *adj.*, clotted, concreted.

grump, *n.*, a grumpy person.

grump'ily, *adv.*, in a grumpy way.

grump'y, *adj.*, surly, cross.

grunt, *v.i.*, to make the sound of a pig; *n.*, a pig's natural noise; an American edible fish.

grun'ted, *p.p.*, grunt.

grunt'er, *n.*, a pig.

grunt'ing, *pr.p.*, grunt.

Gruyère', *n.*, a variety of cheese.

gry'phon, *see* griffin.

guai'acum, *n.*, a resinous shrub.

guanif'erous, *adj.*, producing guano.

gua'no, *n.*, manure made from sea-fowls' dung.

guarantee', *v.t.*, to warrant, insure, be surety for; *n.*, a surety; one to whom a guaranty is given.

guaranteed', *p.p.*, guarantee.

guarantee'ing, *pr.p.*, guarantee.

guarantor', *n.*, one who guarantees.

guar'anty, *n.*, legal guarantee.

guard, *v.t.*, to protect, defend; *n.*, defence, attitude of defence; one in charge of a coach or train; soldiers on guard.

guard'ed, *p.p.*, guard; *adj.*, cautious.

guard'edly, *adv.*, cautiously, with reserve.

guard'edness, *n.*, cautiousness, circumspection.

guard'er, *n.*, one who guards.

guard'ian, *n.*, one who guards; a warden; *adj.*, guarding.

guard'ianship, *n.*, the office of a guardian.

guard'ing, *pr.p.*, guard.

gua'va, *n.*, a S. American tree with pear-shaped fruit.

gubernato'rial, *adj.*, rel. to a governor.

gudg'eon, *n.*, a fresh-water fish; a silly person.

guel'der-rose, *n.*, the snowball tree.

Guelph, *n.*, one of the great Italian party of Guelphs.

Guelph'ic, *adj.*, rel. to the Guelphs.

guer'don, *n.*, reward.

guerril'la, gueril'la, *n.*, irregular warfare; *adj.*, rel. to irregular warfare.

guess, *v.t.*, to conjecture, surmise; *n.*, a conjecture, surmise.

guessed, *p.p.*, guess.

guess'er, *n.*, one who guesses.

guess'ing, *pr.p.*, guess.

guess'-work, *n.*, guessing at random.

guest, *n.*, a visitor being entertained.

guffaw', *v.i.*, to laugh rudely; *n.*, a rude laugh.

guid'able, *adj.*, willing to be guided.

guid'ance, *n.*, leading, direction.

guide, *v.t.*, to lead, direct; *n.*, one who leads the way; a guide-book.

guide'-book, *n.*, a book directing the traveller.

guid'ed, *p.p.*, guide.

guide'-post, *n.*, a sign-post.

guid'er, *n.*, anything that guides.

guid'ing, *pr.p.*, guide.

guild, *n.*, a fraternity, association. Also *gild.*

guild'er, *n.*, the Dutch florin.

guild'hall, *n.*, the hall of a guild.

guile, *n.*, deceit, cunning.

guile'ful, *adj.*, deceitful, cunning.

guile'fulness, *n.*, the quality of being guileful.

guile'less, *adj.*, innocent of guile.

guile'lessly, *adv.*, in a guileless way.

guile'lessness, *n.*, freedom from guile.

guil'lemot, *n.*, a kind of auk.

guilloche', *n.*, a twisted ornament.

guillotine', *v.t.*, to behead with the guillotine; *n.*, an instrument for beheading.

guillotined', *p.p.*, guillotine.

guillotin'ing, *pr.p.*, guillotine.

guilt, *n.*, sin, crime.

guilt'ier, *adj.*, *comp.* of guilty.

guilt'iest, *adj.*, *super.* of guilty.

guilt'ily, *adv.*, in a guilty way.

guilt'iness, *n.*, the state or quality of being guilty.

guilt'less, *adj.*, innocent.

guilt'y, *adj.*, sinful, criminal.

guim'bard, *n.*, a jew's-harp.

guin'ea, *n.*, an old English coin worth 21s.

Guin'ea, *n.*, an African and S. American place-name.

guin'ea-fowl, *n.*, a bird found in the African Guinea.

guin'ea-pig, *n.*, a little rodent of S. America.

guise, *n.*, manner, appearance.

guitar', *n.*, a stringed instrument.

gulch, *n.*, a rocky valley.

gul'den, *n.*, the Austro-Hungarian florin.

gules, *n.* and *adj.*, heraldic for the colour red.

gulf, *n.*, a large bay; an abyss.

gull, *v.t.*, to trick, cheat; *n.*, a trick; a person easily tricked; a sea-bird.

gulled, *p.p.*, gull.

gul'let, *n.*, the throat.

gullibil'ity, *n.*, the quality of being gullible.
gul'lible, *adj.*, easily tricked.
gul'lied, *adj.*, channelled.
gul'ling, *pr.p.*, gull.
gul'ly, gul'ley, *n.*, a water-worn channel; a drain.
gulp, *v.t.*, to swallow eagerly; to suck down; *n.*, the act of gulping.
gulped, *p.p.*, gulp.
gulp'ing, *pr.p.*, gulp.
gum, *v.t.*, to stick with gum; *n.*, a resinous exudation; the fleshy socket of the teeth.
gum-ar'abic, *n.*, gum derived from the acacia.
gum'boil, *n.*, a boil on the gums.
gummed, *p.p.*, gum.
gummif'erous, *adj.*, yielding gum.
gum'miness, *n.*, the state or quality of being gummy.
gum'ming, *pr.p.*, gum.
gum'my, *adj.*, sticky, like gum.
gump'tion, *n.*, intelligent perception.
gum'-tree, *n.*, a gum-producing tree, esp. the eucalyptus.
gun, *n.*, a fire-arm.
gun'-barrel, *n.*, the barrel of a gun.
gun'boat, *n.*, a light war-ship with heavy guns.
gun'-carriage, *n.*, a carriage on which a gun is mounted.
gun'-cotton, *n.*, a high explosive.
gun'fire, *n.*, the fixed time for the morning and evening guns.
gun'-metal, *n.*, a copper and tin or zinc alloy.
gun'nel, *see* gunwale.
gun'ner, *n.*, an artilleryman; a naval warrant officer with charge of the ordnance.
gun'nery, *n.*, the science of artillery.
gun'ning, *n.*, game-shooting (*Amer.*).
gun'ny, *n.*, a coarse kind of sackcloth.
gun'powder, *n.*, an explosive powder.
gun'-room, *n.*, the junior officers' compartment in a ship.
gun'shot, *n.*, the range of a gun's fire.
gun'smith, *n.*, a manufacturer of guns.
gun'-stock, *n.*, the stock of a gun.
gun'wale, *n.*, the upper edge of a ship's side.
gur'gle, *v.i.*, to flow with a bubbling noise; *n.*, the sound of gurgling.
gur'gled, *p.p.*, gurgle.
gur'gling, *pr.p.*, gurgle.
Gur'kha, *see* Goorkha.
gur'nard, *n.*, *i.q.* gurnet.
gur'net, *n.*, a sea-fish.
gush, *v.i.*, to stream out violently; to overflow with sentiment; *n.*, a violent outflow; effusive sentiment.
gushed, *p.p.*, gush.
gush'ing, *pr.p.*, gush.
gush'ingly, *adv.*, in a gushing way.
gus'set, *n.*, a three-cornered inset of cloth.
gust, *n.*, a sudden blast of wind.
gus'tatory, *adj.*, rel. to taste.
gus'to, *n.*, relish.
gust'y, *adj.*, coming in blasts.
gut, *v.t.*, to eviscerate; to empty; *n.*, the intestinal canal; a strait.
gut'ta, *n.*, a drop.
gut'ta-per'cha, *n.*, a gum-resin.
gut'tate, *adj.*, spotted.
gut'ted, *p.p.*, gut.
gut'ter, *v.t.*, to form into channels; *v.i.*, to run in drops; *n.*, a water-channel.
gut'tered, *p.p.*, gutter.
gut'tering, *pr.p.*, gutter.
guttif'erous, *adj.*, yielding gum.
gut'ting, *pr.p.*, gut.
gut'tural, *adj.*, rel. to the throat; sounding deep in the throat; *n.*, a consonant pronounced in the throat.
gut'turally, *adv.*, in a guttural way.
gut'turalness, *n.*, the guttural quality.
gut'ty, *n.*, a golf-ball made of gutta-percha.
guy, *n.*, a steadying rope; a grotesque effigy; an odd-looking or queerly dressed person.
guz'zle, *v.i.*, to drink to excess; *n.*, a debauch.
guz'zled, *p.p.*, guzzle.
guz'zler, *n.*, one who guzzles.
guz'zling, *pr.p.*, guzzle.
gybe, *v.t.*, to shift a sail from one side of a ship to the other; *v.i.*, to swing to the other side.
gybed, *p.p.*, gybe.
gyb'ing, *pr.p.*, gybe.
gymkha'na, *n.*, sports.
gymna'siarch, *n.*, the superintendent of gymnasia.
gymna'sium, *n.*, a place of exercise; a school.
gym'nast, *n.*, one skilled in gymnastics.
gymnas'tic, *adj.*, rel. to gymnastics.
gymnas'tical, *adj.*, *i.q.* gymnastic.
gymnas'tics, *n. pl.*, gymnastic exercises.
gymnos'ophist, *n.*, a Hindu philosopher.
gym'nosperm, *n.*, a plant having seeds unprotected by vessels.
gymnosperm'ous, *adj.*, rel. to gymnosperms.
gym'note, *n.*, an electric eel.
gynaecol'ogy, *n.*, the science of women's diseases and functions.
gynan'drian, *adj.*, *i.q.* gynandrous.
gynan'drous, *adj.*, having stamens and pistils united, as in the orchids.
gyn'archy, *n.*, female government.
gyne'cian, *adj.*, rel. to women.

gynecoc'racy, *n.*, female rule.
gyp'seous, *adj.*, containing gypsum.
gypsif'erous, *adj.*, yielding gypsum.
gyp'sum, *n.*, hydrous sulphate of lime.
gyp'sy, *see* gipsy.
gy'ral, *adj.*, rotatory.
gy'rate, *adj.*, convoluted.
gyrate', *v.i.*, to revolve.
gyra'ted, *p.p.*, gyrate.
gyra'ting, *pr.p.*, gyrate.
gyra'tion, *n.*, the act of gyrating.
gy'ratory, *adj.*, revolving.
gyre, *v.i.*, to rotate; *n.*, a gyration.
gy'roscope, *n.*, an instrument demonstrating the laws of circular motion.
gy'rose, *adj.*, wavy.
gyve, *v.t.*, to fetter.
gyved, *p.p.*, gyve.
gyves, *n. pl.*, fetters.
gyv'ing, *pr.p.*, gyve.
gy'rostat, *n.*, a development of the gyroscope.

H

ha, *interj.*, expressing surprise, welcome, suspicion, etc.

ha'beas cor'pus, *Lat.* phrase (= you must have the body); a writ issued to a gaoler, requiring him to bring a prisoner into court.

hab'erdasher, *n.*, a dealer in small wares connected with dress.

hab'erdashery, *n.*, the wares sold by a haberdasher.

hab'ergeon, *n.*, a coat of mail, without sleeves.

habil'iment, *n.*, dress, attire.

habil'itate, *v.t.*, to supply capital to.

hab'it, *n.*, usage; fixed course of conduct; constitution of body or mind; dress (chiefly ecclesiastical or academic); *v.t.*, to dress.

habitabil'ity, *n.*, the state of being habitable.

hab'itable, *adj.*, fit to be lived in.

hab'itat, *n.*, the natural home of plants, etc.

habita'tion, *n.*, the act of inhabiting; abode

hab'ited, *p.p.*, habit.

hab'iting, *pr.p.* habit.

habit'ual, *adj.*, customary, usual.

habit'ually, *adv.*, customarily.

habit'uate, *v.t.*, to accustom.

habit'uated, *p.p.*, habituate.

habit'uating, *pr.p.*, habituate.

habitua'tion, *n.*, the act or effect of habituating.

hab'itude, *n.*, constitution of body or mind; custom.

habitué', *n.*, one who is a habitual visitor or frequenter.

hacien'da, *n.*, a Spanish - American homestead.

hack, *v.t.*, to hew; kick on the shins; *v.i.*, to ride in an ordinary way; to cough in a dry way; *n.*, a hired horse; a drudge; a mattock; a cut on the shins.

hacked, *p.p.*, hack.

hack'er, *n.*, one who hacks.

hack'ing, *pr.p.*, hack.

hack'le, *n.*, a comb for parting flax; a cock's neck feathers.

hack'ler, *n.*, a flax-dresser.

hack'ling, *pr. p.*, hackle.

hack'ly, *adj.*, rough.

hack'-matack, *n.*, a larch (*Amer.*).

hack'ney, *n.*, a horse for general use; a hireling; *v.t.*, to make common.

hack'ney-coach, *n.*, a hired coach.

hack'neyed, *p.p.*, hackney.

hack'neying, *pr.p.*, hackney.

had, *p.t.* and *p.p.*, have.

had'dock, *n.*, a sea-fish so named.

Ha'des, *n.*, the unseen world.

hadj, *n.*, the pilgrimage to Mecca.

hadj'i, *n.*, a pilgrim to Mecca.

hae'mal, *adj.*, rel. to blood.

hae'matic, *adj.*, rel. to blood; *n.*, a medicine acting on the blood.

hae'matin, *n.*, a blue-black substance contained in haemoglobin.

hae'matite, *n.*, an iron ore.

haemati'tic, *adj.*, rel. to haematite.

haemoglo'bin, *n.*, the colouring matter of the red corpuscles.

haem'orrhage, *n.*, bleeding from a blood-vessel.

haemorrhoi'dal, *adj.*, of the nature of haemorrhoids.

haem'orrhoids, *n. pl.*, bleeding veins, piles. Also *emerods*.

haft, *n.*, a handle.

haft'ed, *adj.*, having a handle.

hag, *n.*, a witch, an ugly old woman.

hag'gard, *adj.*, wild-looking, worried; *n.*, a young hawk.

hag'gis, *n.*, a Scottish pudding, made of sheep's entrails and oatmeal boiled in a maw.

hag'gish, *adj.*, hag-like.

hag'gle, *v.i.*, to wrangle, dispute; *n.*, wrangling.

hag'gled, *p.p.*, haggle.

hag'gler, *n.*, one who haggles.

hag'gling, *pr.p.*, haggle.

ha'giograph, *n.*, a sacred writing.

Hagiog'rapha, *n. pl.*, books of the Hebrew Scriptures other than the Law and the Prophets.

hagiog'rapher, *n.*, a writer on sacred things or of sacred books.

hagiog'raphy, *n.*, the writing of sacred books.

hagiol'ogist, *n.*, a writer about the saints.

hagiol'ogy, *n.*, knowledge about the saints.

hah, *interj.*, ha; *v.i.*, to hum.

ha'-ha, *n.*, a sunk fence.

hail, *v.t.*, to greet, call to; to rain down (blows); *v.i.*, to come down violently as hail; *n.*, frozen rain; *interj.*, of greeting.

hailed, *p.p.*, hail.

hail'ing, *pr.p.*, hail.

hail'stone, *n.*, a pellet of hail.

hail'storm, *n.*, a storm accompanied by hail.

hail'y, *adj.*, mixed with hail.

hair, *n.*, the filament growing out of the skin, esp. on the human head.

hair'-cloth, *n.*, cloth made of hairs.

hair'dresser, *n.*, one who cuts and dresses hair.

haired, *adj.*, covered with hair.

hair'iness, *n.*, the state of being hairy.

hair'less, *adj.*, bald.

hair'pin, *n.*, a pin to fasten up the hair.

hair's'-breadth, *n.*, a very small distance.

hair'y, *adj.*, covered with hairs, hirsute, rough.

hake, *n.*, a cod-like fish; a drying frame-work made of wood.

hal'berd, *n.*, an antique weapon, having a battle-axe on a long shaft.

halberdier', *n.*, a soldier using a halberd.

hal'cyon, *n.*, a fabulous bird; *adj.*, calm.

hale, *v.t.*, to drag, draw; *adj.*, robust, fresh-looking.

half, *adj.*, in value equal to a half; *adv.*, to the degree of a half; *n.*, one of the two equal divisions of anything.

half'blood, *adj.*, of mixed race; in the relation of persons having only one common parent; *n.*, a half-caste.

half'-caste, *n.*, of European father and Indian mother.

half'-pay, *n.*, reduced pay of an officer retired, or not on service for the time being.

half'pence, *n.*, one of the plurals of halfpenny.

half'penny, *n.*, the half of a penny.

half'way, *adj.*, midway.

half'witted, *adj.*, imbecile.

half'-year', *n.*, the period of half the year.

half'-year'ly, *adj.*, recurring each half-year.

hal'ibut, *n.*, a large flat fish.

hal'idom, *n.*, holiness; a sacred object.

halieu'tic, *adj.*, pert. to fishing.

hal'ing, *pr.p.*, hale.

hall, *n.*, a large room or building; a manor-house.

hallelu'jah, *see* Alleluia.

hal'liard, *see* halyard.

hall'mark, *n.*, the Goldsmiths' stamp on gold and silver; any standard of excellence.

halloo', *interj.*, calling someone's attention; urging hounds on; *v.i.*, to shout halloo. Also *hallo*. *See* holla.

hallooed', *p.p.*, halloo.

halloo'ing, *pr.p.*, halloo.

hal'low, *v.t.*, to make holy, venerate.

hal'lowed, *p.p.*, hallow.

Hallow-e'en', *n.*, the eve of All Saints' or All-Hallows' Day.

hal'lowing, *pr.p.*, hallow.

Hal'lowmas, *n.*, the feast of All-Hallows, Nov. 1.

hallucina'tion, *n.*, illusion.

hallu'cinatory, *adj.*, illusory.

ha'lo, *n.*, a luminous circle; the nimbus of a saint.

hal'ogen, *n.*, an ingredient in a saline compound.

halog'enous, *adj.*, rel. to halogen.

hal'oid, *adj.*, like common salt.

halt, *v.i.*, to walk lamely; to hesitate; *v.t.* and *i.*, to stop; *n.*, a stop; a limp; *adj.*, limping, lame.

halt'ed, *p.p.*, halt.

halt'er, *v.t.*, to secure with a halter; *n.*, a band round a horse's neck and head; a hangman's rope.

halt'ing, *pr.p.*, halt.

halt'ingly, *adv.*, in a halting way.

halve, *v.t.*, to share equally with another; to divide in two.

halved, *p.p.*, halve.

halves, *n.*, pl. of half.

halv'ing, *pr.p.*, halve.

hal'yard, *n.*, tackle for raising sails, etc.

ham, *n.*, the back of the thigh; the buttock.

hamadry'ad, *n.*, a wood nymph who dies with the tree she inhabits.

ha'mate, *adj.*, hooked.

ha'mated, *adj.*, furnished with hooks; hooked.

ham'ble, *v.t.*, to mutilate (dogs).

hames, *n. pl.*, the bars of metal attached to a horse's collar, and having the traces fastened to them.

Ham'ite, *n.*, a descendant of Ham.

Hamit'ic, *adj.*, descended from Ham; African.

ham'let, *n.*, a little village, usually without a church.

ham'mer, *v.t.*, to drive in with a hammer; to strike hard, to drive; *n.*, a tool for driving, striking or breaking.

ham'merable, *adj.*, able to be hammered.

ham'mercloth, *n.*, the cloth and hangings of a coach-box.

ham'mered, *p.p.*, hammer.

ham'merer, *n.*, one who hammers.

ham'mering, *pr.p.*, hammer.

ham'mer-man, *n.*, one who uses a hammer in metal-work.

ham'mock, *n.*, a canvas or network

couch or bed, slung at the ends.

ha'mous, *adj.*, *i.q.* hamate.

ham'per, *v.t.*, to obstruct, hinder; *n.*, rigging; a basket.

ham'pered, *p.p.*, hamper.

ham'pering, *pr.p.*, hamper.

ham'shackle, *v.t.*, to shackle a horse with a rope from the head to the foreleg.

ham'ster, *n.*, a rat-like rodent with pouched cheeks.

ham'string, *v.t.*, to disable by cutting the hamstring; *n.*, a tendon at the back of the knee.

ham'stringed, *p.p.*, hamstring. Also *hamstrung.*

ham'stringing, *pr.p.*, hamstring.

ham'strung, *p.p.*, hamstring. Also *hamstringed.*

han'aper, *n.*, a basket; a department of the Court of Chancery where certain documents were kept in a hanaper.

***hand*,** *n.*, the terminate part of the forearm; anything like a hand; a hand-worker; one of a ship's crew; a share in an enterprise; cards dealt to a player; the player himself; *v.t.*, to deliver; to help with the hand or arm.

***hand*'bill,** *n.*, a small printed notice or advertisement.

***hand*'book,** *n.*, a manual; guide-book.

***hand*'breadth,** *n.*, a space the breadth of the hand.

***hand*'cart,** *n.*, a cart drawn or driven by hand.

***hand*'cuff,** *v.t.*, to secure with hand-cuffs.

***hand*'cuffs,** *n. pl.*, steel manacles joined by a short chain.

***hand*'cuffed,** *p.p.*, handcuff.

hand'ed, *p.p.*, hand.

***hand*'ful,** *n.*, a quantity filling the hand.

***hand*'gallop,** *n.*, an easy gallop.

***hand*'icap,** *v.t.*, to impose a handicap; to impede; *n.*, a condition imposed on competitors with a view to equalizing their chances; a race where there is such handicap.

***hand*'icapper,** *n.*, one who decides the handicap.

***hand*'icraft,** *n.*, manual skill; a manual art.

***hand*'icraftsman,** *n.*, one who practises a handicraft.

***hand*'ier,** *adj.*, *comp.* of handy.

hand'iest, *adj.*, *super.* of handy.

***hand*'ily,** *adv.*, cleverly with the hands.

***hand*'iness,** *n.*, cleverness with the hands.

***hand*'ing,** *pr.p.*, hand.

hand'iwork, *n.*, something made with the hands.

hand'kerchief, *n.*, a square of some material, carried in the pocket or worn round the neck.

***hand*'le,** *v.t.*, to touch with the hands; to manage; to treat; to train; *n.*, the part by which anything is held; something that can be grasped.

***hand*'led,** *p.p.*, handle.

***hand*'ling,** *pr.p.*, handle.

***hand*'maid,** *n.*, a maid servant.

***hand*'maiden,** *n.*, *i.q.* handmaid.

***hand*'rail,** *n.*, a rail to support the hand.

***hand*'saw,** *n.*, a carpenter's saw.

***hand*'screw,** *n.*, a jackscrew.

***hand*'sel,** *v.t.*, to be the first to use; to use for the first time; *n.*, a gift at the New Year; earnest money.

***hand*'sel(l)ed,** *p.p.*, handsel.

***hand*'sel(l)ing,** *pr.p.*, handsel.

***hand*'some,** *adj.*, fine to the sight; generous.

***hand*'somely,** *adv.*, generously.

***hand*'someness,** *n.*, the state or quality of being handsome.

***hand*'spike,** *n.*, a kind of lever.

***hand*'work,** *n.*, work not done by machinery.

***hand*'writing,** *n.*, a person's autograph; style of penmanship

hand'y, *adj.*, deft; ready to hand.

hang, *v.t.*, to suspend, to execute on the gallows; to let droop; *v.i.*, to depend, to lag.

hang'ar, *n.*, a shed for airships, etc.

hang'dog, *n.*, a sneak; *adj.*, sneakish.

hanged, *p.p.*, hang (said of one who is executed).

hang'er, *n.*, anything by which something is hung; one who hangs (bells, etc.); a short sword; wood on a hill-slope.

hang'er-on, *n.*, a parasite, a follower.

hang'ing, *pr.p.*, hang.

hang'man, *n.*, an executioner.

hang'nail, *n.*, torn skin at the root of a finger nail.

hank, *v.t.*, to form into hanks; *n.*, a skein of yarn; a fastening.

hank'er, *v.i.*, to crave for a thing.

hank'ered, *p.p.*, hanker.

hank'ering, *pr.p.*, hanker; *n.*, a craving.

Hanove'rian, *adj.*, rel. to Hanover.

Han'sard, *n.*, the Parliamentary printed record.

hanse, *n.*, the Germanic league of trading cities.

Hanseat'ic, *adj.*, rel. to the hanse.

han'som, *n.*, a two-wheeled, one-horsed cab.

hap, *v.i.*, to happen; *n.*, an occurrence, chance.

haphaz'ard, *adj.*, accidental; *adv.*, at random; *n.*, mere chance.

hap'less, *adj.*, unlucky.

hap'ly, *adv.*, perchance, perhaps.

hap'pen, *v.i.*, to occur; to fall out by chance.

hap'pened, *p.p.*, happen.

hap'pening, *pr.p.*, happen.

hap'pier, *adj.*, *comp.* of happy.

hap'piest, *adj.*, *super.* of happy.

hap'pily, *adv.*, in a happy way, cheerfully, felicitously.

hap'piness, *n.*, the state of being happy.

hap'py, *adj.*, glad, cheerful, felicitous.

harangue', *v.t.*, to address in a speech; *v.i.*, to make a speech.

harangued', *p.p.*, harangue.

harang'uer, *n.*, one who harangues.

harang'uing, *pr.p.*, harangue.

har'ass, *v.t.*, to vex, annoy, worry.

har'assed, *p.p.*, harass.

har'assing, *pr.p.*, harass.

har'binger, *v.t.*, to proclaim, announce; *n.*, one who announces a coming person or thing.

har'bour, -or, *v.t.*, to shelter, cherish; *v.i.*, to seek shelter; *n.*, a haven, place of shelter.

har'boured, *p.p.*, harbour.

har'bourer, *n.*, one who harbours.

har'bouring, *pr.p.*, harbour.

har'bourless, *adj.*, without a harbour.

hard, *adj.*, solid, firm; difficult; severe, exacting; enduring; *adv.*, strenuously, tightly, nearly, etc.

hard'-earned, *adj.*, earned with difficulty.

hard'en, *v.t.*, to make hard; *v.i.*, to become hard.

hard'ened, *p.p.*, harden.

hard'ener, *n.*, anything that hardens.

hard'ening, *pr.p.*, harden.

hard'er, *adj.*, *comp.* of hard.

hard'est, *adj.*, *super.* of hard.

hard'-fought, *adj.*, fiercely fought.

hard'head, *n.*, a large round stone.

hard'-hearted, *adj.*, unkind, unfeeling.

hard'ier, *adj.*, *comp.* of hardy.

hard'iest, *adj.*, *super.* of hardy.

hard'ihood, *n.*, boldness, audacity.

hard'ily, *adv.*, in a hardy way.

hard'iness, *n.*, endurance, vigour.

hard'ly, *adv.*, harshly, severely, with difficulty.

hard'ness, *n.*, the quality of being hard.

hards, *n. pl.*, refuse of flax or wool.

hard'ship, *n.*, hardness of circumstances, injustice, suffering.

hard'ware, *n.*, metal manufactured articles.

hard'y, *adj.*, tough, capable of enduring, brave; *n.*, part of an anvil, a bar for cutting on.

hare, *n.*, a four-footed rodent with long ears and cleft upper lip.

hare'bell, *n.*, a bell-flower with round leaves.

hare'brained, *adj.*, giddy, rash.

hare'foot, *n.*, a foot like a hare's.

hare'lip, *n.*, a malformation of the upper lip.

ha'rem, *n.*, the women's quarter in a Turkish house; the women of the harem.

har'icot, *n.*, a ragout; French beans.

hark, *v.i.*, to listen, hearken; *n.*, the cry "Hark."

harl, *n.*, flaxen or hempen filament.

Harlei'an, *adj.*, rel. to Robert and Edward Harley, and the Harleian MSS.

har'lequin, *adj.*, fantastic; *n.*, a buffoon.

harlequinade', *n.*, the part, after a pantomime, in which harlequin appears.

har'lot, *n.*, a prostitute.

har'lotry, *n.*, a harlot's trade; lewdness.

harm, *v.t.*, to hurt, injure; *n.*, hurt, injury, mischief.

harmat'tan, *n.*, a dry W. African wind.

harmed, *p.p.*, harm.

harm'ful, *adj.*, hurtful, mischievous.

harm'fully, *adv.*, hurtfully, mischievously.

harm'fulness, *n.*, the quality of being harmful.

harm'ing, *p.p.*, harmful.

harm'less, *adj.*, free from offence; incapable of injury.

harm'lessly, *adv.*, in a harmless way.

harm'lessness, *n.*, the state or quality of being harmless.

harmon'ic, *adj.*, rel. to harmony; harmonious.

harmon'ica, *n. pl.*, a name given to several musical instruments.

harmon'ical, *adj.*, *i.q.* harmonic.

harmon'icon, *n.*, a mouth-organ.

harmo'nious, *adj.*, in harmony, concordant, symmetrical.

harmo'niously, *adv.*, in harmony, accordantly.

harmon'iphon, *n.*, a mouth-organ.

har'monist, *n.*, an expert in harmony; a writer on the agreements of writings, particularly the Sacred Scriptures.

harmo'nium, *n.*, a reed-organ.

har'monize, *v.t.*, to bring into agreement; to arrange in harmony; *v.i.*, to agree, accord with.
har'monized, *p.p.*, harmonize.
har'monizer, *n.*, one who harmonizes.
har'monizing, *pr.p.*, harmonize.
harmonom'eter, *n.*, an apparatus for measuring harmonic sound relations.
har'mony, *n.*, agreement; agreeable effect of arrangement; sound produced in chords.
har'most, *n.*, a Lacedaemonian provincial governor.
har'ness, *v.t.*, to put harness on; *n.*, the gear of a draught horse; armour; working equipments.
har'nessed, *p.p.*, harness.
har'nessing, *pr.p.*, harness.
harp, *n.*, a musical stringed instrument; *v.i.*, to play on the harp; to play tediously.
harped, *p.p.*, harp.
harp'er, *n.*, the player on a harp.
harp'ing, *pr.p.*, harp; *n.*, tedious dwelling on a theme; the act of playing the harp.
harp'ist, *n.*, *i.q.* harper.
harpoon', *v.t.*, to strike with a harpoon; *n.*, a missile attached to a line used by whalers.
harpooned', *p.p.*, harpoon.
harpoon'er, *n.*, one who harpoons.
harpoon'ing, *pr.p.*, harpoon.
harp'sichord, *n.*, an old musical instrument, the strings of which were plucked with quills set in motion from a finger-board.
har'py, *n.*, a rapacious monster; a grasping person.
har'quebus, *n.*, an antique gun. Also *arquebuse.*
har'ridan, *n.*, an old jade.
har'ried, *p.p.*, harry.
har'rier, *n.*, one who harries; a hound used for coursing hares.
har'row, *v.t.*, to draw the harrow over; to torment, lacerate the feelings of; to spoil; *n.*, an agricultural implement for turning or breaking clods.
har'rowed, *p.p.*, harrow.
har'rower, *n.*, one who harrows.
har'rowing, *pr.p.*, harrow; *adj.*, distressing.
har'ry, *v.t.*, to ravage, harass.
harsh, *adj.*, rough (in any sense), severe.
harsh'er, *adj.*, *comp.* of harsh.
harsh'est, *adj.*, *super.* of harsh.
harsh'ly, *adv.*, in a harsh way.
harsh'ness, *n.*, the quality of being harsh.
hars'let, *n.*, pig's fry. Also *haslet.*
hart, *n.*, a male deer.
harts'horn, *n.*, a preparation of ammonia (formerly distilled from a hart's horn).
har'um-scar'um, *adj.* and *n.*, wild, reckless conduct.
harus'pex, *n.*, a diviner (*Lat.*).
harus'pice, *n.*, *i.q.* haruspex.
harus'picy, *n.*, divination by inspection of animals' entrails.
har'vest, *v.t.*, to gather in and store; *n.*, the ingathering; the gathered crops; the time of ingathering; any reward of labour.
har'vested, *p.p.*, harvest.
har'vester, *n.*, a harvest labourer.
har'vesting, *pr.p.*, harvest.
has, *v.t.*, 3rd pers. sing., *pres.* of have.
hash, *v.t.*, to chop small; *n.*, a dish of meat chopped small; a medley.
hash'ish, *n.*, the tops and tender sprouts of hemp.
has'let, *n.*, pig's fry. Also *harslet.*
hasp, *v.t.*, to fasten with a hasp; *n.*, a door or lid fastening; a skein of yarn.
hasped, *p.p.*, hasp.
has'sock, *n.*, a kneeling cushion or footcushion; a tussock of grass.
hast, *v.t.*, 2nd pers. sing., *pres.* of have.
hast'ate, *adj.*, spear-shaped.
hast'ated, *adj.*, *i.q.* hastate.
haste, *v.i.*, to hurry, hasten; *n.*, hurry, celerity.
ha'sted, *p.p.*, haste.
ha'sten, *v.t.*, to urge forward, hurry; *v.i.*, to be quick.
ha'stened, *p.p.*, hasten.
ha'stener, *n.*, one who hastens; an old-fashioned screen round meat roasting before a fire.
ha'stening, *pr.p.*, hasten.
ha'stier, *adj.*, *comp.* of hasty.
ha'stiest, *adj.*, *super.* of hasty.
ha'stily, *adv.*, in haste.
ha'stiness, *n.*, the quality of being hasty.
ha'sting, *pr.p.*, haste.
ha'sty, *adj.*, quick-tempered, speedy.
ha'sty-pud'ding, *n.*, a pudding made with flour brought into a batter.
hat, *n.*, a head-covering.
hat'band, *n.*, a band for the hat.
hat'box, *n.*, a box for the hat.
hatch, *v.t.*, to produce young birds; to develop; to close with a hatch; to score with lines; *v.i.*, to come out of the egg; *n.*, engraved line; a half-door or wicket; a deck-opening.

hatched, *p.p.*, hatch.
hatch'el, *v.t.*, to hackle; *n.*, a sort of comb for cleaning flax, etc.
hatch'elled, -eled, *p.p.*, hatchel.
hatch'elling, -eling, *pr.p.*, hatchel.
hatch'er, *n.*, a bird that breeds; anything or person that hatches.
hatch'es, *n. pl.*, the openings to a ship's hold.
hatch'et, *n.*, a short axe.
hatch'ing, *pr.p.*, hatch; *n.*, the act of marking with incised lines.
hatch'ment, *n.*, an escutcheon.
hatch'way, *n.*, a hatch.
hate, *v.t.*, to dislike strongly; *n.*, strong dislike, malice.
hate'able, *adj.*, odious.
ha'ted, *p.p.*, hate.
hate'ful, *adj.*, detestable, odious.
hate'fully, *adv.*, detestably.
hate'fulness, *n.*, the quality of being hateful.
ha'ter, *n.*, one who hates.
hath, *v.t.*, 3rd pers. sing., *pres.* of have.
ha'ting, *pr.p.*, hate.
ha'tred, *n.*, the feeling of hate.
hat'ter, *n.*, one who sells or makes hats.
hatti-sherif', *n.*, a Turkish command countersigned by the Sultan.
hau'berk, *n.*, a coat of steel armour.
haugh, *n.*, a water-meadow.
haught'ily, *adv.*, in a haughty manner.
haugh'tiness, *n.*, arrogance, pride.
haugh'ty, *adj.*, proud, arrogant.
haul, *v.t.*, to pull, drag; to change a ship's course; *n.*, a pull; a "find," a catch of fish.
haul'age, *n.*, the act of hauling; charge for hauling.
hauled, *p.p.*, haul.
haul'er, *n.*, anything that hauls.
haul'ing, *pr.p.*, haul.
haulm, *n.*, a stalk, stem.
haunch, *n.*, the part between the ribs and the thigh; the side of an arch between the crown and the piers.
haunched, *adj.*, having haunches.
haunt, *v.t.*, to frequent, visit often; *n.*, a place of frequent resort; a favourite spot.
haunt'ed, *p.p.*, haunt, *adj.*, visited by ghosts.
haunt'er, *n.*, one who haunts.
haunt'ing, *pr.p.*, haunt.
haut'boy, *n.*, a wind wood instrument of reedy quality; an organ stop so named. Also *oboe*.
haut'eur, *n.*, *i.q.* haughtiness (*Fr.*).
haut-goût', *n.*, seasoning, taint (*Fr.*).
Havan'a, *n.*, a cigar imported from Havana or Cuba.
have, *v.t.*, to hold, possess.
ha'ven, *n.*, a harbour, shelter.
hav'ersack, *n.*, a soldier's sack for rations.
hav'ildar, *n.*, a Sepoy sergeant.
hav'ing, *pr.p.*, have.
hav'oc, *n.*, damage, devastation.
haw, *n.*, the fruit of a hawthorn; the sloe; an enclosure; the third eyelid or nictitating membrane.
Hawai'ian, *adj.*, rel. to the island of Hawaii; *n.*, a native of Hawaii.
haw-haw', *v.i.*, to guffaw.
hawk, *v.t.*, to cry for sale; *v.i.*, to clear the throat of phlegm; to practise falconry or hawking; *n.*, a clearing of the throat; a bird of prey so named; a mortar-board.
hawked, *p.p.*, hawk.
hawk'er, *n.*, a street trader; one who practises hawking.
hawk'ey, *n.*, a way of spelling *hockey*.
hawk'eyed, *adj.*, with exceptional powers of sight.
hawk'ing, *pr.p.*, hawk; *n.*, a hawker's trade.
hawk'weed, *n.*, a kind of aster; a species of groundsel.
hawse, *v.t.*, to hoist; *n.*, the part of a ship's bows where the hawse-holes are made.
hawse'-holes, *n. pl.*, holes for the cable to pass through.
haws'er, *n.*, a thick rope.
haw'thorn, *n.*, a thorny shrub so named.
hay, *n.*, cut and dried grass; *v.t.*, to make into hay; to feed with hay; *v.i.*, to make hay.
hay'cock, *n.*, a pile of hay in a field.
hay'field, *n.*, a field where hay is grown.
hay'ing, *pr.p.*, hay; *n.*, the work of making hay; the haymaking season.
hay'loft, *n.*, a loft for storing hay.
hay'maker, *n.*, one who makes hay.
hay'mow, *n.*, stored hay.
hay'rick, *n.*, *i.q.* haystack.
hay'stack, *n.*, a pile of stacked hay.
haz'ard, *v.t.*, to risk, imperil, venture; *n.*, exposure to risk; game of chance; the pocketing stroke at billiards; a difficulty on a golf-course.
haz'arded, *p.p.*, hazard.
haz'arding, *pr.p.*, hazard.
haz'ardous, *adj.*, risky.
haze, *v.i.*, to become hazy; *v.t.*, to bully, harass; *n.*, a dimming of the atmosphere; indistinctness.

hazed, *p.p.*, haze.

haz'el, *adj.*, made of hazel-wood; *n.*, a bush so named.

ha'ziness, *n.*, the state of being hazy.

ha'zing, *pr.p.*, haze.

ha'zy, *adj.*, misty; vague; partly intoxicated.

he, *pers. pron.*, the male referred to.

head, *v.t.*, to lead, stand at the head of; to intercept; to place at the top of; to move in a direction; to form a head; to lop off; *n.*, the upper part of an animal's body containing the brain; the top of anything; a single unit; a measure of stored force (as a head of water); a subject in a writing.

head'ache, *n.*, pain in the head.

head'band, *n.*, a band round the head; an ornamental band at the top or bottom of a bound book.

head'-dress, *n.*, an ornamental head-covering.

head'ed, *p.p.*, head.

head'er, *n.*, one who puts in heads (of barrels); a stone or brick laid endwise across the thickness of a wall; a plunge.

head'-gear, *n.*, anything worn on the head.

head'ily, *adv.*, in a heady way.

head'iness, *n.*, the state or quality of being heady.

head'ing, *pr.p.*, head; *n.*, a caption, title, or entry.

head'land, *n.*, a projecting cliff.

head'less, *adj.*, wanting a head.

head'line, *n.*, a line over a written or printed passage.

head'light, *n.*, a white light at the masthead; the front light of a locomotive or motor-car.

head'long, *adj.*, precipitate; *adv.*, precipitately, impetuously.

headmast'er, *n.*, the chief master in a school.

headquart'ers, *n. pl.*, a position where a command or group of officials is centred.

heads'man, *n.*, an executioner.

head'stall, *n.*, the bridle straps that pass round a horse's head.

head'stone, *n.*, a gravestone at the head of a grave.

head'strong, *adj.*, perverse, self-willed.

head'way, *n.*, forward movement; progress.

head'wind, *n.*, an opposing wind.

head'work, *n.*, brain-work.

head'y, *adj.*, impetuous, violent; intoxicating.

heal, *v.t.*, to restore to health; cure; *v.i.*, to become well.

heal'able, *adj.*, curable.

healed, *p.p.*, heal.

heal'er, *n.*, a physician; one who heals.

heal'ing, *pr.p.*, heal; *n.*, cure.

health, *n.*, the state of being whole or well.

health'ful, *adj.*, health-giving.

health'fully, *adv.*, in a healthful way.

health'fulness, *n.*, the quality of being healthful.

health'ier, *adj.*, *comp.* of healthy.

health'iest, *adj.*, *super.* of healthy.

health'ily, *adv.*, in a healthy way.

health'iness, *n.*, the state or quality of being healthy.

health'y, *adj.*, well, sound, in good condition; conducive to health.

heap, *v.t.*, to pile, load, accumulate; *n.*, a pile, mass of piled things; a large quantity or number.

heaped, *p.p.*, heap.

heap'ing, *pr.p.*, heap.

heap'y, *adj.*, in heaps.

hear, *v.t.*, to perceive with the ear; to listen to; to obey.

heard, *p.p.*, hear.

hear'er, *n.*, one who hears.

hear'ing, *pr.p.*, hear; *n.*, the sense of hearing; consideration.

heark'en, *v.i.*, to listen. Also *harken*.

heark'ened, *p.p.*, hearken.

heark'ening, *pr.p.*, hearken.

hear'say, *n.*, gossip, rumour.

hearse, *n.*, a carriage for coffins; a lattice-work canopy over a tomb, often stuck with tapers or herse lights. Also *herse*.

heart, *n.*, the organ that maintains the circulation of the blood; the seat of the affections; courage; pity; the centre or core.

heart'ache, *n.*, sorrow.

heart'broken, *adj.*, crushed with grief.

heart'burn, *n.*, a burning feeling in the lower part of the chest.

heart'-felt, *adj.*, sincere.

hearth, *n.*, the floor of a fireplace.

hearth'stone, *n.*, the slab forming the hearth; a soft stone for scouring purposes; *v.t.*, to scour with a hearthstone.

heart'ier, *adj.*, *comp.* of hearty.

heart'iest, *adj.*, *super.* of hearty.

heart'ily, *adv.*, in a hearty way.

heart'iness, *n.*, geniality, relish.

heart'less, *adj.*, unfeeling, cruel.

heart'lessness, *n.*, cruelty, want of heart.

heart'rending, *adj.*, distressing.

hearts'ease, *n.*, the pansy.

heart'-sick, *adj.*, sick at heart.

heart'y, *adj.*, genial, cordial, relishing.
heat, *v.t.*, to make hot, inflame, excite; *v.i.*, to become hot; *n.*, hotness, high temperature, flush, fury, excitement; a division of a race.
heat'ed, *p.p.*, heat; *adj.*, hot; excited.
heat'er, *n.*, anything that heats.
heath, *n.*, an open tract of uncultivated land overgrown with heath; a shrub of the *Erica* genus.
heath'en, *n.*, a pagan, a Gentile; an unenlightened person.
heath'endom, *n.*, heathens collectively; heathenism.
heath'enish, *adj.*, in the state of a heathen.
heath'enism, *n.*, the state of being a heathen.
heath'enize, *v.t.*, to make heathen.
heath'enized, *p.p.*, heathenize.
heath'enizing, *pr.p.*, heathenize.
heath'er, *n.*, the *Erica* plant.
heath'ery, *adj.*, like, or covered with, heather.
heath'y, *adj.*, like, or covered with, heath.
heat'ing, *pr.p.*, heat.
heave, *v.t.*, to lift, utter; *v.i.*, to rise and fall; to retch; *n.*, heaving, displacement.
heaved, *p.p.*, heave.
heav'en, *n.*, the sky, firmament, the abode of God.
heav'enly, *adj.*, rel. to heaven; blissful.
heav'enward, *adv.*, towards heaven.
heav'er, *n.*, one who heaves.
heaves, *n. pl.*, broken wind (in horses).
heav'ier, *adj.*, *comp.* of heavy.
heav'iest, *adj.*, *super.* of heavy.
heav'ily, *adv.*, with weight, oppressively
heav'iness, *n.*, weight; depression of spirit.
heav'ing, *pr.p.*, heave.
heav'y, *adj.*, weighty, ponderous, sad, overcast (of sky).
heav'y-la'den, *adj.*, overburdened.
hebdom'adal, *adj.*, weekly.
heb'etate, *v.t.*, to dull; *v.i.*, to become dull.
Hebra'ic, *adj.*, pert. to Hebrew or the Hebrews.
He'braism, *n.*, Hebrew idiom or attribute.
He'braist, *n.*, a Hebrew scholar; one who favours Hebrew religious thought.
Hebraist'ic, *adj.*, rel. to Hebrew religion or language.
He'braize, *v.t.*, to make Hebrew; *v.i.*, to conform to Hebraism.
He'braized, *p.p.*, Hebraize.
He'braizing, *pr.p.*, Hebraize.
He'brew, *adj.*, Israelitish, Jewish; *n.*, an Israelite, a Jew; the Jewish language.
He'brewess, *n.*, a Jewess.
Hebrid'ian, *adj.*, rel. to the Hebrides.
hec'atomb, *n.*, a large public sacrifice.
heck, *n.*, a device for stopping fish on a river.
heck'le, *v.t.*, to dress flax; to badger with questions.
hec'tare, *n.*, a metric unit of the French land measure.
hec'tic, *adj.*, constitutional; consumptive; *n.*, a fever accompanying consumption; a flush.
hec'tical, *adj.*, *i.q.* hectic.
hec'togramme, *n.*, weight of 100 grammes (*Fr.*).
hec'tograph, *n.*, a multiplying gelatine pad; *v.t.*, to copy with a hectograph.
hec'tolitre, -ter, *n.*, 100 litres (*Fr.*).
hec'tometre, -ter, *n.*, 100 metres (*Fr.*).
hec'tor, *v.t.*, to bully; *v.i.*, to bluster, play the bully; *n.*, a bully.
hec'tored, *p.p.*, hector.
hec'toring, *pr.p.*, hector.
hec'torism, *n.*, bullying conduct.
hed'dles, *n. pl.*, fine vertical wires or cords in a loom.
hedera'ceous, *adj.*, ivy-like.
hed'eral, *adj.*, rel. to ivy.
hederif'erous, *adj.*, ivy-growing.
hedge, *v.t.*, to fence round; to make or trim a hedge; *v.i.*, to bet on both sides; to avoid committing oneself; *n.*, a fence of bushes or low trees.
hedged, *p.p.*, hedge.
hedge'hog, *n.*, an insect-eating mammal armed with spines.
hedg'er, *n.*, one who makes or trims hedges; who hedges.
hedge'row, *n.*, a line of shrubs planted as a defence.
hedg'ing, *pr.p.*, hedge.
hedon'ic, *adj.*, rel. to pleasure.
hed'onism, *n.*, the pursuit of pleasure as the chief good.
heed, *v.t.*, to notice, pay attention to, care about; *n.*, attention, notice.
heed'ed, *p.p.*, heed.
heed'ful, *adj.*, attentive, considerate.
heed'ing, *pr.p.*, heed.
heed'less, *adj.*, not heeding.
heed'lessly, *adv.*, carelessly.
heed'lessness, *n.*, want of thought.
heel, *v.t.*, to put a heel to; to strike with the heel of a golf club; *v.i.*, to turn over on its side (of a ship); *n.*, the hinder part of the foot, or of a boot; anything like a heel.
heeled, *p.p.*, heel.
heel'ing, *pr.p.*, heel.

heel'tap, *v.t.*, to add thicknesses of leather to a heel; *n.*, a thickness of leather added to a heel; liquor left at the bottom of a glass.

heft, *v.t.*, to lift, to judge weight.

hegemon'ic, *adj.*, having dominion; supreme.

he'gemony, *n.*, supreme rule, leadership.

Heg'ira, -jira, *n.*, Mohammed's flight from Mecca; any flight.

heif'er, *n.*, a young cow.

heigh'-ho, *interj.*, expressing disappointment.

height, *n.*, elevation from a base; distance from top to bottom; eminence; rising ground.

height'en, *v.t.*, to make higher, to intensify, to advance; *v.i.*, to rise.

height'ened, *p.p.*, heighten.

height'ening, *pr.p.*, heighten.

hei'nous, *adj.*, atrocious, odious.

hei'nously, *adv.*, atrociously.

hei'nousness, *n.*, the quality of being heinous.

heir, *n.*, one entitled to succeed to another's estate; one who inherits anything.

heir-appa'rent, *n.*, one who will in due course be the heir.

heir'dom, *n.*, the state of being an heir.

heir'ess, *n.*, fem. of heir.

heir'less, *adj.*, without an heir.

heir'loom, *n.*, a chattel that comes to the heir.

heir'ship, *n.*, the right of inheritance.

held, *p.p.*, hold.

heli'acal, *adj.*, rel. to the sun.

hel'ical, *adj.*, spiral.

hel'icite, *n.*, a spiral fossil.

hel'icoid, *adj.*, spiral, like a snail shell; *n.*, a spiral surface.

Hel'icon, *n.*, the Boeotian mountain, abode of the Muses.

Helico'nian, *adj.*, rel. to Helicon and the Muses.

heliocen'tric, *adj.*, having the sun as centre.

he'liochrome, *n.*, a photograph in colours from nature.

he'liograph, *n.*, an apparatus for photographing the sun; a photograph obtained from exposure; a flash-light apparatus.

heliograph'ic, *adj.*, rel. to heliography.

heliog'raphy, *n.*, the use of a heliograph; a description of the sun's surface.

heliol'ater, *n.*, a sun-worshipper.

heliol'atry, *n.*, sun-worship.

heliom'eter, *n.*, an instrument for ascertaining the angular distance between stars.

he'lioscope, *n.*, a protected telescope for examining the sun.

he'liostat, *n.*, a mirror reflecting the sun.

he'liotrope, *n.*, a flowering shrub with clustered flowers; the heliotrope colour; the bloodstone.

heliotro'pic, *adj.*, turning toward the light.

he'liotype, *n.*, a picture from gelatine exposed to light.

helispher'ic, *adj.*, spherically spiral.

he'lium, *n.*, a supposed gas in the sun.

hel'ix, *n.*, a spiral; spiral ornament; the border of the external ear; a screw-thread.

hell, *n.*, the lower world; the place of evil spirits.

hel'lebore, *n.*, anciently a flower that cured madness; the Christmas rose and other species.

Helle'nian, *adj.*, Greek or Grecian.

Helle'nic, *adj.*, *s.q.* Hellenian.

Hel'lenism, *n.*, the Greek idiom; Greek culture.

Hel'lenist, *n.*, a Greek-speaking alien; a Greek scholar.

Hellenis'tic, *adj.*, rel. to Hellenists.

Hel'lenize, *v.t.*, to make Greek; *v.i.*, to adopt Greek ideas.

Hel'lenized, *p.p.*, Hellenize.

Hel'lenizing, *pr.p.*, Hellenize.

Hellespon'tine, *adj.*, rel. to the Hellespont or Dardanelles.

hell'hound, *n.*, a fiend.

hell'ish, *adj.*, hell-like, diabolical.

hell'ward, *adv.*, toward hell.

helm, *v.t.*, to steer; *n.*, a tiller; the wheel by which the rudder is moved; a helmet.

helm'et, *n.*, defensive head-gear.

helm'eted, *adj.*, wearing a helmet.

helmin'thic, *adj.*, pert. to worms.

helminthol'ogy, *n.*, the study of worms.

helms'man, *n.*, the man at the helm.

hel'ot, *n.*, a Spartan serf.

hel'otism, *n.*, the system of serfdom in ancient Sparta.

help, *v.t.*, to aid, assist; *n.*, aid, assistance.

helped, *p.p.*, help.

help'er, *n.*, one who helps.

help'ful, *adj.*, of assistance.

help'fully, *adv.*, usefully.

help'fulness, *n.*, usefulness.

help'less, *adj.*, incapable of self-help; without resource.

help'lessly, *adv.*, in a helpless way.

help'lessness, *n.*, the state of being helpless.

help'mate, *n.*, a helping partner.

help'meet, *n.*, *i.q.* help-mate.

hel'ter-skel'ter, *adv.*, in disordered hurry.

helve, *v.t.*, to fit with a handle; *n.*, a handle.

helved, *p.p.*, helve.

Helve'tian, *adj.*, Swiss.

Helvet'ic, *adj.*, *i.q.* Helvetian.

helv'ing, *pr.p.*, helve.

hem, *v.i.*, to clear the throat; express hesitation; *v.t.*, to sew a turned-down border; to enclose; *n.*, a border turned down and sewn over; an interjection: the sound of clearing the throat.

hem'achate, *n.*, a species of agate.

hem'atin, *n.*, dark colouring matter.

hem'atite, *n.*, iron-ore.

hematit'ic, *adj.*, rel. to hematite.

hemicra'nia, *n.*, pain on one side of the head; imperfect development of one side of the head.

hem'icycle, *n.*, a semi-circular arrangement of seating.

hemihe'dral, *adj.*, having half its complement of planes.

hemiop'sy, *n.*, half-blindness.

hemiple'gia, *n.*, paralysis of one side.

hem'iplegy, *n.*, *i.q.* hemiplegia.

hemip'teral, *adj.*, rel. to the hemiptera (an order of insects).

hemip'terous, *adj.*, *i.q.* hemipteral.

hem'isphere, *n.*, a half sphere; half the globe's surface.

hemispher'ic, *adj.*, like a half sphere.

hemispher'ical, *adj.*, *i.q.* hemispheric.

hemispher'oid, *n.*, a half-spheroid.

hemispheroid'al, *adj.*, like a hemispheroid.

hem'istich, *n.*, a half-verse.

hem'itrope, *adj.*, half inverted; *n.*, a twin crystal.

hem'lock, *n.*, an umbelliferous plant, poisonous and sedative.

hemmed, *p.p.*, hem.

hem'ming, *pr.p.*, hem; *n.*, hems; the stitching of hems.

hem'orrhage, *n.*, bleeding.

hemorrhoid'al, *n.*, pert. to hemorrhoids.

hem'orrhoids, *n. pl.*, piles. Also *haemorrhoids.*

hemostat'ic, *adj.*, pert. to blood-stagnation, or stoppage of bleeding.

hemp, *n.*, an Indian annual, fibre-producing.

hemp'en, *adj.*, made of hemp.

hemp'seed, *n.*, the seed of hemp.

hem'stitch, *v.t.*, to embroider with hemstitch; *n.*, ornamental stitching in a hem.

hen, *n.*, a female bird, esp. the domestic fowl.

hen'bane, *n.*, a poisonous, narcotic plant.

hence, *adv.*, from here; away.

henceforth', *adv.*, from this time onward.

hencefor'ward, *adv.*, *i.q.* henceforth.

hench'man, *n.*, a squire, attendant, supporter.

hen'coop, *n.*, a pen for fowls.

hendec'agon, *n.*, an eleven-sided plane rectilineal figure.

hendecasyll'able, *n.*, a verse of eleven syllables.

hen'house, *n.*, a place for fowls to live and roost in.

hen'na, *n.*, the Egyptian privet.

hen'otheism, *n.*, belief in one God; monotheism.

hen'peck, *v.t.*, to nag at; harass.

hepat'ic, *adj.*, rel. to the liver.

hepat'ical, *adj.*, *i.q.* hepatic.

hepatiza'tion, *n.*, change of tissue into liver substance.

hepatol'ogy, *n.*, the study of the liver.

hep'tachord, *n.*, a seven-stringed instrument; the major seventh.

hep'tagon, *n.*, a figure with seven angles and sides.

heptag'onal, *adj.*, seven-sided.

heptagyn'ia, *n.*, an order of plants with seven distinct styles.

heptahe'dron, *n.*, a seven-faced solid.

heptan'drian, *adj.*, having seven stamens.

heptan'gular, *adj.*, having seven angles.

hep'tarch, *n.*, the ruler of one of the kingdoms in a heptarchy.

hep'tarchy, *n.*, the rule of seven princes; a group of seven kingdoms.

her, *pers. pron.*, objective case of she; *possess. pron.*, bel. to her.

her'ald, *v.t.*, to announce, proclaim the advent; *n.*, an officer who carries messages from state to state; makes public proclamations; determines questions of precedence, etc.

her'alded, *p.p.*, herald.

heral'dic, *adj.*, rel. to heraldry.

her'alding, *pr.p.*, herald.

her'aldry, *n.*, the science of a herald; heraldic symbolism.

herb, *n.*, a plant with a non-persistent, non-woody stem.

herba'ceous, *adj.*, of the nature of herbs.

herb'age, *n.*, herbs collectively; pasturage.

herb'al, *adj.*, rel. to herbs; *n.*, a botany book.

herb'alism, *n.*, the knowledge of herbs.
herb'alist, *n.*, one skilled in herb-lore.
herba'rium, *n.*, any collection of dried plants.
her'bary, *n.*, a herb garden.
herbes'cent, *adj.*, becoming herb-like.
herbif'erous, *adj.*, herb-producing.
Herbiv'ora, *n. pl.*, creatures that feed on herbs.
herbiv'orous, *adj.*, feeding on herbs.
herboriza'tion, *n.*, botanical study.
her'borize, *v.i.*, to botanize.
her'borized, *p.p.*, herborize.
her'borizing, *pr.p.*, herborize.
herb'y, *adj.*, abounding in, or resembling, herbs.
Hercu'lean, *adj.*, rel. to Hercules; immensely strong; extremely arduous.
herd, *v.t.*, to tend, gather into a herd; *v.i.*, to go in a herd; *n.*, a group or flock of animals; a crowd of people; a herdsman.
herd'ed, *p.p.*, herd.
herd'er, *n.*, a herdsman.
herd'ing, *pr.p.*, herd.
herds'man, *n.*, the keeper of a herd.
here, *adv.*, in this place; present.
here'about, *adv.*, somewhere near here.
hereaf'ter, *adv.*, in the future.
hereat', *adv.*, at this spot.
hereby', *adv.*, near here; by this means.
hered'itable, *adj.*, that may be inherited.
heredit'ament, *n.*, heritable property.
hered'itary, *adj.*, inherited, transmitted by descent.
hered'ity, *n.*, transmission of qualities, etc., by descent.
herein', *adv.*, in this place, book, etc.
hereof', *adv.*, of this.
hereout', *adv.*, out of this.
her'esiarch, *n.*, the leader of a heresy.
heresiol'ogist, *n.*, one who writes about heresies.
her'esy, *n.*, doctrine opposed to orthodox standards.
her'etic, *n.*, one who holds heretical opinions.
heret'ical, *adj.*, of the nature of heresy.
heretofore', *adv.*, up to this time.
hereunto', *adv.*, up to here or now.
hereupon', *adv.*, following on this.
herewith', *adv.*, with this.
her'iot, *n.*, a payment to a lord on the death of a tenant.
her'iotable, *adj.*, liable to heriot.
her'isson, *n.*, a spiked revolving beam defending a gate.
her'itable, *adj.*, that can be inherited.
her'itage, *n.*, inherited property; share; transmitted quality.
her'itor, *n.*, one who inherits.
her'itrix, *n.*, fem. of heritor.
hermaph'rodite, *adj.*, bisexual; *n.*, a bisexual being.
hermaphrodit'ic, *adj.*, rel. to a hermaphrodite.
hermeneu'tical, *adj.*, interpretative.
hermeneu'tics, *n. pl.*, interpretation; the study of interpretation.
hermet'ic, *adj.*, rel. to alchemy; impervious to air.
hermet'ical, *adj.*, *i.q.* hermetic.
hermet'ically, *adv.*, by fusion.
her'mit, *n.*, a dweller apart, a recluse.
her'mitage, *n.*, a hermit's shelter; a French wine so named.
her'mitary, *n.*, a hermit's cell.
hermit'ical, *adj.*, rel. to a hermit.
her'nia, *n.*, rupture.
her'nial, *adj.*, pert. to hernia.
he'ro, *n.*, a demigod; a man of great valour; the principal character in a story, play, etc.
Hero'dian, *adj.*, rel. to Herod.
hero'ic, *adj.*, rel. to, or like, a hero.
hero'ical, *adj.*, *i.q.* heroic.
hero'ically, *adv.*, with heroism.
her'oine, *n.*, fem. of hero.
her'oism, *n.*, courage, fortitude.
her'on, *n.*, a wading bird.
her'onry, *n.*, a heron's breeding-place.
he'ro-worship, *n.*, worship of great men.
her'pes, *n.*, a skin-disease.
herpet'ic, *adj.*, of the nature of herpes.
herpetol'ogy, *n.*, the zoology of reptiles.
her'ring, *n.*, a sea-water fish.
hers, *possess. adj.*, the absolute form of *her*; used predicatively.
herse, *n.*, a portcullis; an heraldic charge like a harrow; a canopied framework over a bier.
herself', *pron.*, emphatic and reflexive substitute for *she* and *her*.
hes'itancy, *n.*, hesitation, vacillation.
hes'itant, *adj.*, hesitating, vacillating.
hes'itate, *v.i.*, to be undecided, doubtful, slow; to stammer.
hes'itated, *p.p.*, hesitate.
hes'itating, *pr.p.*, hesitate.
hes'itatingly, *adv.*, in a hesitating way.
hesita'tion, *n.*, uncertainty, indecision, shrinking.
hes'itative, *adj.*, hesitating.
Hes'per, *n.*, the evening star.

Hespe'rian, *adj.*, rel. to Hesperia; Western.

Hes'perus, *n.*, *i.q.* Hesper.

Hes'sian, *adj.*, rel. to Hesse; *n.*, a native of Hesse.

hetae'ra, *n.*, a Greek courtezan.

hetae'ria, *n.*, a Greek club or association.

heterocar'pous, *adj.*, bearing more than one kind of fruit.

heterochro'mous, *adj.* of more than one colour.

het'eroclite, *adj.*, irregularly declined; *n.*, an irregular noun.

heteroclit'ic, *adj.*, *i.q.* heteroclite.

heterodac'tyl, *adj.*, with the second toe irregular.

het'erodont, *adj.*, having teeth of different types.

het'erodox, *adj.*, not orthodox.

het'erodoxy, *n.*, unorthodox opinion.

heterog'amous, *adj.*, bearing bi-sexual flowers.

heterogene'ity, *n.*, the character of the heterogeneous.

heteroge'neous, *adj.*, not alike in character; not uniform in composition.

heterogen'esis, *n.*, spontaneous generation.

heterol'ogy, *n.*, abnormality.

heteromor'phic, *adj.*, of irregular form.

heteromor'phous, *adj.*, *i.q.* heteromorphic.

heteron'omy, *n.*, the opposite of autonomy; subjection to another's rule.

het'eronym, *n.*, a word spelt like another but pronounced differently.

heteropath'ic, *adj.*, rel. to heteropathy; of different effect.

heterop'athy, *n.*, allopathy.

heteropha'sia, *n.*, confusion of speech.

heuris'tic, *adj.*, helping discovery.

hew, *v.t.*, to cut (with an axe or sword); to fashion.

hewed, *p.p.*, hew.

hew'er, *n.*, one who hews.

hew'ing, *pr.p.*, hew.

hewn, *p.p.*, hew.

hex'achord, *n.*, a diatonic group of notes with a semitone between the third and the fourth.

hex'ad, *adj.*, of sixfold value.

hexadac'tylous, *adj.*, with six fingers or toes.

hexaë'meron, *n.*, the space of six days.

hex'agon, *n.*, a six-sided and six-angled figure.

hexag'onal, *adj.*, having six sides.

hexagyn'ial, *adj.*, having six styles.

hexag'ynous, *adj.*, *i.q.* hexagynial.

hexahe'dral, *adj.*, having six faces.

hexahe'dron, *n.*, a six-faced figure.

hexam'eter, *n.*, a line having six metrical feet.

hexamet'ric, *adj.*, rel. to hexameters.

hexamet'rical, *adj.*, *i.q.* hexametric.

hexan'dria, *n.*, flowers having six stamens.

hexan'drous, *adj.*, having six stamens.

hexan'gular, *adj.*, having six angles.

hexapet'alous, *adj.*, six-petalled.

hexaphyl'lous, *adj.*, six-leaved.

hex'apla, *n.*, a sixfold text in parallel columns.

hex'aplar, *adj.*, sixfold.

hex'apod, *adj.*, having six feet.

hex'astich, *n.*, a six-lined stanza.

hex'astyle, *adj.*, having six pillars.

Hex'ateuch, *n.*, the first six books of the Old Testament.

hey, *interj.*, expressing joy, surprise, and question; also calling attention.

hey'day, *interj.*, expressing joy, surprise, etc.; *n.*, the time of youth, prosperity, etc.

hia'tus, *n.*, a gap (*Lat.*)

hiber'nal, *adj.*, wintry.

hi'bernate, *v.i.*, to spend the winter (in torpor or inactivity).

hi'bernated, *p.p.*, hibernate.

hi'bernating, *pr.p.*, hiberaate.

hiberna'tion, *n.*, the state or period of hibernating.

Hiber'nian, *adj.*, Irish.

Hiber'nianism, *n.*, Irish idiom.

Hiber'nicism, *n.*, *i.q.* Hibernianism.

hic'cup, hic'cough, *v.i.*, to make a hiccup; *v.t.*, to utter with hiccups; *n.*, an involuntary spasm of the breathing organs.

hic'cuped, *p.p.*, hiccup.

hic'cuping, *pr.p.*, hiccup.

hick'ory, *n.*, a N. American tree allied to the walnut.

hick'wall, *n.*, a woodpecker.

hid, *p.p.*, hide.

hi'dage, *n.*, a tax on hides of land.

hidal'go, *n.*, a Spanish gentleman.

hid'den, *p.p.*, hide.

hid'denly, *adv.*, covertly.

hide, *v.t.*, to conceal, shelter; to flog; *v.i.*, to seek shelter, be concealed; *n.*, an animal's skin; a measure of land.

hide'bound, *adj.*, prejudiced, uncompromising.

hid'eous, *adj.*, frightful, ugly.

hid'eously, *adv.*, in a hideous way.

hi'der, *n.*, one who hides.

hi'ding, *pr.p.*, hide; *n.*, the act of hiding; concealment; a flogging.

hie, *v.t.*, to incite, urge on; *v.i.*, to hasten.

hied, *p.p.*, hie.

hi'erarch, *n.*, a chief priest.

hierarch'ical, *adj.*, rel. to hierarchy.
hi'erarchy, *n.*, a body of ecclesiastical rulers; government by an organized body of such rulers.
hierat'ic, *adj.*, sacerdotal.
hieroc'racy, *n.*, ecclesiastical rule.
hi'eroglyph, *n.*, picture writing.
hieroglyph'ic, *adj.*, represented by picture-signs; *n.*, *i.q.* hieroglyph.
hieroglyph'ical, *adj.*, *i.q.* hieroglyphic.
hi'erogram, *n.*, a sacred symbol.
hierogram'matist, *n.*, a writer of hierograms.
hierolog'ic, *adj.*, rel. to hierology.
hierol'ogist, *n.*, an expert in hierology.
hierol'ogy, *n.*, the study of ancient sacred writings.
hi'erophant, *n.*, a teacher of religious mysteries.
hig'gle, *v.i.*, to dispute, haggle.
hig'gled, *p.p.*, higgle.
hig'gledy - pig'gledy, *adv.*, in a muddled state.
hig'gler, *n.*, one who higgles.
hig'gling, *pr.p.*, higgle.
high, *adj.*, elevated, lofty; exalted; strong; tainted.
high'-born, *adj.*, of exalted birth.
high'-bred, *adj.*, of good pedigree.
high'-class, *adj.*, of superior order.
high'er, *adj.*, *comp.* of high.
high'est, *adj.*, *super.* of high.
high-falu'tin, *adj.*, bombastic; *n.*, bombast.
high'-flown, *adj.*, proud, extravagant.
high'-flyer, *n.*, an ambitious or extravagant person.
high-hand'ed, *adj.*, arbitrary.
high'-heeled, *adj.*, having high heels.
high'land, *n.*, a hilly or mountainous range. In pl., the Scottish range so named.
high'lander, *n.*, a native of the Highlands.
high'lows, *n. pl.*, ankle boots.
high'ly, *adv.*, greatly.
high'-minded, *adj.*, upright, well principled.
high'ness, *adj.*, the state of being high; a princely title.
high'-pressure, *adj.*, having high steam pressure.
high'-priest, *n.*, a chief priest.
high'-road, *n.*, a main road.
high'-spirited, *adj.*, impetuous, unrestrained.
high'-toned, *adj.*, honourable; high of pitch.
high'ty-tigh'ty, *see* hoity-toity.
high'-water, *n.*, the state of the tide when the water is highest.
high'-way, *n.*, the public main road.
high'wayman, *n.*, a highway robber.
high'wrought, *adj.*, elaborate; agitated.
hila'rious, *adj.*, loudly cheerful, festive.
hilar'ity, *n.*, cheerfulness, merriment.
Hil'ary, *n.*, St. Hilary of Poitiers. His day is Jan. 13 in the English and Jan. 14 in the Roman Kalendar.
hill, *n.*, elevated ground; a small mountain; a heap; *v.t.*, to bank up.
hill'iness, *n.*, the quality of being hilly.
hill'ock, *n.*, a little hill.
hill'side, *n.*, the slope of a hill.
hill'y, *adj.*, steep; abounding in hills.
hilt, *n.*, a sword-handle.
hilt'ed, *adj.*, having a hilt.
hi'lum, *n.*, the point where a seed is attached to a seed-vessel.
him, *pron.*, objective case of *he.*
Hima'layan, *adj.*, rel. to the Himalayas.
himself', *pron.* the reflexive of *he.*
hind, *adj.*, in the rear; posterior; *n.*, a female deer; a farm servant.
hind'er, *adj.*, posterior.
hin'der, *v.t.*, to prevent, retard.
hin'dered, *p.p.*, hinder.
hin'derer, *n.*, one who hinders.
hin'dering, *pr.p.*, hinder.
hind'er*most*, *adj.*, rearmost, furthest back.
hind'*most*, *adj.*, *i.q.* hindermost.
hin'drance, *n.*, a bar, impediment, check.
Hin'du, *adj.*, rel. to the Hindus; *n.*, a native of India.
Hin'duism, *n.*, the polytheistic religion of Hindus.
Hindusta'ni, *n.*, the official and general language of India.
hinge, *v.t.*, to fix with a hinge; to make to turn on a hinge; *v.i.*, to turn on a hinge.
hinged, *p.p.*, hinge.
hing'ing, *pr.p.*, hinge.
hin'ny, *v.i.*, to neigh; *n.*, a Scottish term of endearment.
hint, *v.t.*, to suggest slightly; *v.i.*, give a hint of; *n.*, a slight suggestion.
hint'ed, *p.p.*, hint.
hin'terland, *n.*, the region at the back of a coast or a river's bank.
hint'ing, *pr.p.*, hint.
hint'ingly, *adv.*, in an indirect way.
hip, *v.t.*, to depress; *n.*, the part of the body between the pelvis and the upper part of the thigh; the fruit of a rose; the blues; *interj.*, Hip, (hip, hurrah !).
hipped, *p.p.* hip.

hippocam'pus, *n.*, a sea-horse.

hip'pocras, *n.*, spiced wine.

Hippocrat'ic, *adj.*, pert. to Hippocrates.

hip'podrome, *n.*, a circus.

hip'pogriff, *n.*, a fabulous beast, part griffen, part horse.

hippoph'agy, *n.*, the eating of horse flesh.

hippopot'amus, *n.*, the river-horse, an African pachyderm.

hippu'ric, *adj.*, rel. to an acid in horse's urine.

hip'-roof, *n.*, a roof that rises direct from the wall-plate.

hip'shot, *adj.*, lame.

hir'cine, *adj.*, rel. to goats; goat-like; *n.*, a foetid, oily product of goat's fat.

hir'cus, *n.*, a goat (*Lat.*).

hire, *v.t.*, to engage for temporary service for pay; to bribe; *n.*, pay, bribe.

hired, *p.p.*, hire.

hire'ling, *n.*, a mercenary; a paid servant.

hir'er, *n.*, one who hires.

hir'ing, *pr.p.*, hire.

hir'sute, *adj.*, shaggy, hairy.

***his** possess. adj.* of *he*.

his'pid, *adj.*, bristly.

hiss, *v.t.*, to show disapproval of; *v.i.*, to make the sound of a goose or snake; *n.*, such a sound.

hissed, *p.p.*, hiss.

hiss'ing, *pr.p.*, hiss.

hist, *interj.*, hark! silence!

histog'raphy, *n.*, a description of tissues.

histolog'ical, *adj.*, rel. to histology.

histol'ogist, *n.*, an expert in histology.

histol'ogy, *n.*, the science of minute structure of organisms.

histor'ian, *adj.*, a writer or student of history.

histor'ic, *adj.*, rel. to, or famous in, history.

histor'ical, *adj.*, *i.q.* historic.

historic'ity, *n.*, truth to history; historical basis.

historiog'rapher, *n.*, an official writer of history.

historiog'raphy, *n.*, the writing of history.

hist'ory, *n.*, narration of past events.

histrion'ic, *adj.*, theatrical; rel. to actors.

hist'rionism, *n.*, acting; affected acting.

hit, *v.t.*, to strike, reach, suit; *n.*, a blow; lucky stroke.

hitch, *v.t.*, to hook, catch; *n.*, a catch, an impediment.

hitched, *p.p.*, hitch.

hitch'ing, *pr.p.*, hitch.

hith'er, *adv.*, to this place; *adj.*, on this nearest side.

hith'ermost, *adj.*, the nearest in this direction.

hitherto', *adv.*, up to this point (of time or place).

hith'erward, *adv.*, in this direction.

hit'ter, *n.*, one who hits.

hitt'ing, *pr.p.*, hit.

hive, *v.t.*, to place in a hive; *v.i.*, to assemble in a hive; *n.*, a bee-house; a swarm; a busy company.

hived, *p.p.*, hive.

hives, *n.pl.*, nettlerash

hiv'ing, *pr.p.*, hive.

ho, *interj.*, stop there!

hoar, *adj.*, gray-white; ancient.

hoard, *v.t.*, to store secretly, amass; *n.*, a secret store or pile.

hoard'ed, *p.p.*, hoard.

hoard'er, *n.*, one who hoards.

hoard'ing, *pr.p.*, hoard; *n.*, a fence of boards.

hoar'frost, *n.*, white frost.

hoar'-hound, *n.*, an aromatic herb.

hoar'iness, *n.*, the state or quality of being hoary.

hoarse, *adj.*, harsh-sounding.

hoarse'ly, *adv.*, in a hoarse way.

hoarse'ness, *n.*, harshness of voice.

hoar'y, *adj.*, white with age or frost.

hoax, *v.t.*, to play a trick upon; *n.*, a practical joke.

hoaxed, *p.p.*, hoax.

hoax'ing, *pr.p.*, hoax.

hob, *n.*, part of a grate for placing things upon; a sprite.

hob'ble, *v.t.*, to shackle; *v.i.*, to limp; *n.*, a limp.

hob'bled, *p.p.*, hobble.

hob'bledehoy, *n.*, a youth between a man and a boy; a raw youth.

hob'bler, *n.*, one who hobbles.

hob'bling, *pr.p.*, hobble.

hob'by, *n.*, a favourite pursuit; a breed of falcon.

hob'by-horse, *n.*, a child's toy (a stick with a horse's head).

hobgob'lin, *n.*, a fearful imp.

hob'nail, *n.*, a thick, roundheaded nail; a rustic.

hob'nailed, *adj.*, studded with hobnails.

hob'-nob, *v.i.*, to associate familiarly.

hock, *n.*, the joint at the lower extremity of the *tibia*; a Rhine wine.

hock'ey, *n.*, a ball game played with a curved stick.

ho'cus, *v.t.*, to take in; to trick.

ho'cus-po'cus, *n.*, a cheat, a juggling trick.

hod, *n.*, a bricklayer's trough for bricks or mortar.

hod'den-grey, *n.*, a coarse cloth made of natural wool.

hodge, *n.*, a rustic.

hodge'-podge', *n.*, a mixed mass; a medley.

hodiern'al, *adj.*, of to-day; modern.

hod'man, *n.*, the carrier of a hod.

hoe, *v.t.*, to clean with a hoe; *n.*, a garden tool for weeding.
hoed, *p.p.*, hoe.
hoe'ing, *pr.p.*, hoe.
hog, *v.t.*, to clip the hair short; *v.i.*, to dip at both ends; *n.*, a swine; a young sheep newly shorn; a swinish person.
hogged, *p.p.*, hog.
hog'gery, *n.*, a piggery.
hog'ging, *pr.p.*, hog.
hog'gish, *adj.*, swinish.
Hogmanay', *n.*, New Year's Eve.
hogs'head, *n.*, a measure of capacity; a large cask.
hoi'den, hoy'den, *n.*, a rude girl; *adj.*, ill-mannered; *v.i.*, to romp.
hoist, *v.t.*, to lift up, heave; *n.*, a hoisting apparatus; a lift.
hoist'ed, *p.p.*, hoist.
hoist'ing, *pr.p.*, hoist.
hoi'ty-toi'ty, *n. interj.*, expressing surprise, reproof, etc.
ho'key-po'key, *n.*, a cheap ice-cream.
hold, *v.t.*, to grasp, keep, consider, esteem, celebrate; *n.*, support, a clutch; the lowest part of a ship; a fortress.
hold'-all, *n.*, a traveller's bag.
hold'en, *p.p.*, hold.
hold'er, *n.*, anyone that holds; a handle.
hold'fast, *n.*, a catch, a hook; *adj.*, tenacious.
hold'ing, *pr.p.*, hold; *n.*, anything held; a tenure; influence.
hole, *n.*, a cavity, a perforation, a mean dwelling.
hol'iday, *n.*, a holy day; time of rest from labour; a festival.
ho'lier, *adj.*, *comp.* of holy.
ho'liest, *adj.*, *super.* of holy.
ho'lily, *adv.*, in a holy way.
ho'liness, *n.*, the quality or state of being holy; freedom from sin; sanctity.
hol'la, *v.i.*, to shout to someone far off; *n.*, a shout.
hol'laed, *p.p.*, holla.
hol'laing, *pr.p.*, holla.
Hol'lander, *n.*, a native of Holland.
hol'land, *n.*, a variety of linen unbleached.
hol'lands, *n.*, gin.
hol'loa, *see* holla.
hol'loaed, *p.p.*, holloa.
hol'loaing, *pr.p.*, holloa.
hol'low, *v.t.*, to scoop, excavate; *adj.*, empty inside; sunken; vain; *n.*, a cavity.
hol'lowed, *p.p.*, hollow.
hol'lowing, *pr.p.*, hollow.
hol'lowness, *n.*, the state or quality of being hollow.
hol'ly, *n.*, an evergreen tree or shrub.
hol'lyhock, *n.*, the rosemallow.
holm, *n.*, an evergreen oak; a river island.
hol'ocaust, *n.*, a burnt sacrifice.
hol'ograph, *n.*, a document entirely in the author's handwriting.
hol'ster, *n.*, a pistol case attached to a saddle.
hol'stered, *adj.*, furnished with holsters.
ho'ly, *adj.*, sacred, pure, devout.
ho'ly-day, *see* holiday.
ho'ly-rood, *n.*, the Sacred Cross.
ho'lystone, *v.t.*, to scrub with holystone; *n.*, a stone used for scrubbing a deck.
hom'age, *n.*, reverence, fealty.
home, *n.*, one's own dwelling-place; one's country; *adj.*, domestic.
home'-bred, *adj.*, bred at home.
home'-brewed, *adj.*, brewed at home.
home'less, *adj.*, without a home.
home'lessness, *n.*, the state of being homeless.
home'lier, *adj.*, *comp.* of homely.
home'liest, *adj.*, *super.* of homely.
home'liness, *n.*, the quality of being homely.
home'ly, *adj.*, domestic, plain of feature, uncultivated, simple.
home'-made, *adj.*, made at home.
Homer'ic, *adj.*, rel. to Homer.
home'sick, *adj.*, pining for home.
home'spun, *adj.*, plain, coarse; *n.*, homespun material.
home'stead, *n.*, a house and land.
home'ward, *adj.* and *adv.*, in the direction of home.
homici'dal, *adj.*, rel. to homicide.
hom'icide, *n.*, the killing of a man; a man-killer.
homilet'ic, *adj.*, of the nature of homily.
homilet'ics, *n. pl.*, literature relating to preaching.
hom'ilist, *n.*, a preacher.
hom'ily, *n.*, a sermon discourse.
ho'ming, *adj.*, returning home.
hom'iny, *n.*, maize hulled and broken.
hom'mock, *n.*, *see* hummock.
homocen'tric, *adj.*, concentric.
homochro'mous, *adj.*, of the same colour.
homoeopath'ic, *adj.*, pert. to homoeopathy.
homoeop'athist, *n.*, one who favours or practises homoeopathy.
homoeop'athy, *n.*, a medical system based on the doctrine that like cures like.
homog'amous, *adj.*, having only one kind of flower.
homogene'ity, *n.*, identity of nature.
homoge'neous, *adj.*, of the same kind or nature.

homol'ogate, *v.t.*, to confirm, allow.

homolog'ical, *adj.*, rel. to homology.

homol'ogous, *adj.*, identical in relative proportion, value, or structure.

hom'ologue, *n.*, an organ or part common to various animals but differing in function.

homol'ogy, *n.*, structural similarity.

hom'onym, *n.*, a word of similar sound to another but of different meaning.

homonym'ic, *adj.*, of the nature of a homonym.

homon'ymous, *adj.*, sounding alike.

homon'ymy, *n.*, the state of sounding alike.

hom'ophone, *n.*, a letter standing for the same sound as another.

homoph'onous, *adj.*, having the same sound.

homoph'ony, *n.*, the state of being homophonous.

homot'ropal, *adj.*, turned in the same direction.

hom'otype, *n.*, a corresponding part.

hone, *v.t.*, to sharpen; *n.*, a whetstone.

honed, *p.p.*, hone.

hon'est, *adj.*, upright, trustworthy, frank.

hon'estly, *adv.*, in an honest way.

hon'esty, *n.*, the quality of being honest.

hon'ey, *n.*, the flower-product collected by bees; an endearing term.

hon'ey-bee, *n.*, a honey-making bee.

hon'eycomb, *v.t.*, to riddle with holes; *n.*, the system of cells in a hive.

hon'eydew, *n.*, a saccharine secretion; a variety of tobacco.

hon'eyed, *adj.*, sweet, cajoling.

hon'eymoon, *n.*, the first month of married life.

hon'eysuckle, *n.*, a climbing fragrant plant.

hong, *n.*, a trading-place (*Chinese*); a foreign factory.

hon'ing, *pr.p.*, hone.

honora'rium, *n.*, a fee; a complimentary gift.

hon'orary, *adj.*, done or held as a mark of honour.

hon'our, hon'or, *v.t.*, to respect, revere, accept and pay; *n.*, respect, reverence, integrity, glory.

hon'ourable, *adj.*, worthy to be honoured; conferring honour; upright; with a sense of honour.

hon'ourably, *adv.*, in an honourable way.

hon'oured, *p.p.*, honour.

hon'ourer, *n.*, one who honours or confers honour.

hon'ouring, *pr.p.*, honour.

hon'oursman, *n.*, one who attains academic honours.

hood, *n.*, a covering for the head; a carriage cover; part of the academic costume; a suffix denoting state or quality.

hood'ed, *adj.*, having a hood.

hood'wink, *v.t.*, to impose on.

hoof, *n.*, the hard part of a quadruped's foot.

hoofed, *adj.*, having a hoof.

hook, *v.t.*, to catch with a hook; *v.i.*, to be bent; to catch on; *n.*, anything bent so as to hold on.

hook'ah, *n.*, a tobacco pipe, in which the smoke passes through water.

hooked, *p.p.*, hook; *adj.*, bent like a hook.

hook'ing, *pr.p.*, hook.

hook'er, *n.*, anything that hooks; a fishing craft.

hook'y, *adj.*, full of hooks; hooked.

hoo'ligan, *adj.*, rowdy; *n.*, a street rowdy.

hoop, *v.t.*, to bind round with hoops; *n.*, a band round a cask; a circular band; a child's toy.

hooped, *p.p.*, hoop.

hoop'er, *n.*, a cooper.

hoop'ing, *pr.p.*, hoop.

hoop'ing-cough, *see* whooping-cough.

hoo'poe, *n.*, a bird so named.

hoot, *v.t.*, to drive with shouts; *v.i.*, to make a hooting noise; *n.*, a derisive shout.

hoot'ed, *p.p.*, hoot.

hoot'ing, *pr.p.*, hoot.

hoove, *n.*, a cattle disease, attended with inflation of stomach.

hop, *v.i.*, to jump on one foot (or with both or all in the case of animals); *n.*, a spring; hopping; a dance; a climbing perennial.

hop'-bine, *n.*, the climbing stem of the hop.

hope, *v.t.*, to desire with expectation; *v.i.*, to be expectant; *n.*, expectant desire; confidence.

hoped, *p.p.*, hope.

hope'ful, *adj.*, confident, full of hope.

hope'fully, *adv.*, in a hopeful way.

hope'fulness, *n.*, the state of being hopeful.

hope'less, *adj.*, without hope, past hope.

hope'lessly, *adv.*, in a hopeless way.

hope'lessness, *n.*, the state of being hopeless.

hop'ing, *pr.p.*, hope.

hopped, *p.p.*, hop.

hop'per, *n.*, a hop-picker; one who hops; a funnel through which grain is passed.

hop'-picker, *n.*, a picker of hops; a hopper.

hop'ping, *pr.p.*, hop.

hop'ple, *v.t.*, to fetter the legs; *n.*, a leg-shackle; *see* hobble.

hop'-scotch, *n.*, a

child's game of hopping and at the same time kicking a stone over lines scotched on the ground.

ho'ral, *adj.*, hourly.

ho'rary, *adj.*, of the hours; hourly.

horde, *n.*, a troop, gang; *v.i.*, to be in a horde.

hori'zon, *n.*, the boundary line of earth and sky; the furthest limit.

horizon'tal *adj.*, of the horizon; parallel to the horizon.

horizon'tally, *adv.*, levelly.

horn, *v.t.*, to supply with horns; to gore; to adjust a ship's frame at right angles to line of keel; *n.*, the hard excrescence on an animal's head; a musical wind-instrument; a flask made of horn.

horn'beam, *n.*, a small tree so named.

horn'bill, *n.*, a large tropical bird, with a horn-like growth on the beak.

horn'blende, *n.*, a mineral, composed of silica, magnesia, etc.

horn'book, *n.*, a child's primer of the A, B, C, Paternoster, etc., mounted on a wooden tablet under a thin plate of transparent horn.

horned, *p.p.*, horn; *adj.*, having horns.

horn'er, *n.*, a horn-blower; a maker of horn utensils.

horn'et, *n.*, a large wasp-like insect.

horn'ing, *pr.p.*, horn.

horn'less, *adj.*, lacking horns.

horn'pipe, *n.*, an old wind-instrument; a lively dance.

horn'y, *adj.*, hard, like horn.

horog'raphy, *n.*, the art of making clock dials.

hor'ologe, *n.*, a time-piece.

horolog'ical, *adj.*, rel. to horology.

horologiog'raphy, *n.*, a description of time-pieces; the clock-maker's art.

horol'ogist, *n.*, a maker or seller of time-pieces.

horol'ogy, *n.*, the science of time-measuring and clock-making.

horom'eter, *n.*, a time-measuring instrument.

horom'etry, *n.*, the art of time-measuring.

hor'oscope, *n.*, the disposition of heavenly bodies at a given date.

horo'scopy, *n.*, the art of casting a horoscope.

hor'rent, *adj.*, bristling.

hor'rible, *adj.*, horrifying, shocking, hideous.

hor'ribleness, *n.*, the quality of being horrible.

hor'ribly, *adv.*, in a horrible way.

hor'rid, *adj.*, frightful; rough, bristling.

hor'ridly, *adv.*, in a horrid way.

horrif'ic, *adj.*, causing horror.

hor'rified, *p.p.*, horrify.

hor'rify, *v.t.*, to move with horror, scandalize.

hor'rifying, *pr.p.*, horrify.

hor'ror, *n.*, shuddering; extreme dislike.

horse, *v.t.*, to provide horses for; to mount on one's back; to punish; *n.*, a quadruped, solid-hoofed, and used for burden and draught or for riding.

horse'back, *n.*, the back of a horse; *adv.*, on a horse's back.

horse'-breaker, *n.*, one who breaks horses in.

horse'-chestnut, *n.*, a large tree with clustering white or pink flowers.

horse'-cloth, *n.*, a cloth covering for a horse.

horse'-coper, *n.*, a horse dealer.

horse'-flesh, *n.*, horses collectively; the flesh of horses.

horse'-guards, *n.*, the cavalry household troops; their head-quarters.

horse'hair, *n.*, the hair of horses; a fabric made of the same.

horse'-leech, *n.*, a large kind of leech; a greedy person.

horse'-litter, *n.*, a horse-drawn palanquin.

horse'man, *n.*, a rider; a clever rider.

horse'manship, *n.*, clever riding.

horse'-play, *n.*, rough and tumble play.

horse'-power, *n.*, a standard unit of measure of work.

horse'-radish, *n.*, a garden herb.

horse'shoe, *n.*, the iron shoe of a horse; anything shaped like it.

horse'tail, *n.*, a Turkish ensign.

horse'whip, *n.*, a whip for horses; *v.t.*, to flog with a horsewhip.

horse'woman, *n.*, fem. of horseman.

hors'ing, *n.*, a grinder's seat in a factory; punishment by mounting on someone's back.

hors'y, *adj.*, addicted to the turf; aping the dress and manners of a jockey.

horta'tion, *n.*, exhortation.

hort'ative, *adj.*, conveying exhortation.

hort'atory, *adj.*, *i.q.* hortative.

hort'icultor, *n.*, the cultivator of a garden.

horticul'tural, *adj.*, rel. to horticulture.

hort'iculture, *n.*, the cultivation of gardens.

horticul'turist, *n.*, one skilled in horticulture.

hor'tus sic'cus, *n.*, a herbarium.

hosan'na, *n.*, (save, pray) a cry of adoration.

hose, *v.t.*, to sprinkle with a hose; *n.*, a flexible pipe for watering purposes; stockings.

ho'sier, *n.*, one who sells hose and underwear.

ho'siery, *n.*, hosier's wares.

hos'pice, *n.*, a traveller's shelter; home for sick or destitute people.

hos'pitable, *adj.*, ready to entertain; hearty, sociable.

hos'pitably, *adv.*, in a hospitable way.

hos'pital, *n.*, a charitable institution of various types.

hospital'ity, *n.*, entertaining; readiness to welcome visitors.

hos'pitaller, *n.*, one of the Knights Hospitallers; the chaplain in some London hospitals.

hos'podar, *n.*, a lord.

host, *n.*, a victim· the consecrated wafer in the Blessed Sacrament; a large number; an army; one who entertains guests, innkeeper.

hos'tage, *n.*, a person taken as a security; a pledge.

hos'tel, *n.*, an inn; a students' hall of residence.

hos'teller, *n.*, the guest-master in a monastery.

hos'telry, *n.*, an inn.

host'ess, *n.*, a lady who entertains guests; the mistress of an inn.

hos'tile, *adj.*, of an enemy; showing ill-will; antagonistic.

hos'tilely, *adv.*, in a hostile way.

hostil'ity, *n.*, ill-will, antagonism; in pl., acts of war.

hos'tler, *n.*, *see* ostler.

hot, *adj.*, heated; at high temperature; fierce.

hot'bed, *n.*, a bed for forcing plants.

hot'-blooded, *adj.*, passionate.

hotch'pot, *n.*, the aggregation of property for division; a dish of several ingredients = hotchpotch.

hotch'-potch, *n.*, a cooked dish with many ingredients.

hot-cock'les, *n.*, an old game.

hotel', *n.*, a house for entertaining travellers.

hot'-head, *n.*, a fiery person.

hot'-headed, *adj.*, fiery, impetuous.

hot'house, *n.*, a forcing-house.

hot'ly, *adv.*, with heat.

hot'pot, *n.*, beef or mutton stewed in a covered pot with potatoes.

hot'press, *v.t.*, to press paper for smoothing purposes; *n.*, a press for bringing hot metal plates on to the surface of paper or other fabric.

hot'pressed, *p.p.*, hotpress.

hot'pressing, *pr.p.*, hotpress.

hot'spur, *n.*, an impetuous person.

Hot'tentot, *n.*, a native of what is now Cape Colony; a barbarian.

hot'ter, *adj.*, *comp.* of hot.

hot'test, *adj.*, *super.* of hot.

hough, *v.t.*, to hamstring; *n.*, *see* hock.

houghed, *p.p.*, hough.

hough'ing, *pr.p.*, hough.

hound, *v.t.*, to chase; to incite; *n.*, a dog for the chase; a worthless person.

hound'ish, *adj.*, like a hound.

hour, *n.*, the one-twenty-fourth part of a day; an appointed time.

***hour'*glass,** *n.*, a sand-glass marking the duration of an hour.

***hour'*-hand,** *n.*, the pointer that shows the hours on a dial.

hou'ri, *n.*, a nymph of the Mohammedan Paradise.

***hour'*ly,** *adj.*, occurring every hour; often.

house, *v.t.*, to give shelter to; place securely; *v.i.*, to seek shelter; *n.*, a building to dwell in; any place to house in; an assembly; a business firm.

house'boat, *n.*, a boat fitted up like a house.

house'breaker, *n.*, one who breaks into a house; one whose occupation is the breaking up of old houses.

house'breaking, *n.*, the occupation of a housebreaker.

housed, *p.p.*, house.

house'ful, *n.*, the full capacity of a house.

house'hold, *n.*, the inmates of a house; an establishment.

house'holder, *n.*, the occupier of a house; head of a family.

house'keeper, *n.*, one who manages the affairs of a household; one in charge of an office, etc.; a stay-at-home.

house'less, *adj.*, without a house.

house'maid, *n.*, a servant in charge of the rooms of a house.

house'-surgeon, *n.*, a resident hospital surgeon.

house'wife, *n.*, a mistress of a family; a case for needles, thread, etc.

house'wifery, *n.*, domestic economy.

hous'ing, *pr.p.*, house; *n.*, a covering for horses, usually ornamental.

hove, *p.t.*, heave.

hov'el, *n.*, a shed; a wretched dwelling.

hov'er, *v.i.*, to hang in the air; loiter about.

hov'ered, *p.p.*, hover.

hov'ering, *pr.p.*, hover.

how, *adv.*, in what manner or way; to what extent.

howbe'it, *conj.*, nevertheless.

how'dah, *n.*, a canopied seat on an elephant's back.

howev'er, *adv.*, in whatever way; to whatsoever extent; *conj.*, nevertheless.

how'itzer, *n.*, a short, light cannon for firing projectiles at a low elevation.

howl, *v.i.*, to make a sound of pain, rage, etc.; *n.*, the sound.

howled, *p.p.*, howl.

howl'er, *n.*, one who howls; an egregious blunder (*colloq.*).

howl'et, *n.*, an owlet.

howl'ing, *pr.p.*, howl.

howsoev'er, *adv.*, in whatsoever way or degree.

hoy, *n.*, a small coasting vessel; *interj.*, hallo!

hoy'den, *n.*, a rough girl.

hoy'denish, *adj.*, like a hoyden.

hub, *n.*, the central part of a wheel from which the spokes radiate; any central point.

hub'bub, *n.*, a stir, confusion, riot.

huck'aback, *n.*, a coarse, rough linen used for towelling.

huck'le, *n.*, the hip, haunch.

huck'lebacked, *adj.*, round-shouldered.

huck'leberry, *n.*, a N. American shrub bearing berries.

huck'ster, *v.t.* and *i.*, to sell, to higgle; *n.*, a pedlar; a venal person.

huck'stered, *p.p.*, huckster.

huck'stering, *pr.p.*, huckster.

hud'dle, *v.t.*, to crowd together disorderly; *v.i.*, to crowd promiscuously; *n.*, a confused heap or crowd.

hud'dled, *p.p.*, huddle.

hud'dler, *n.*, one who huddles.

hud'dling, *pr.p.*, huddle.

Hudibras'tic, *adj.*, in the style of Hudibras, the famous mock-heroic poem.

hue, *n.*, colour, shade of tint; a cry in pursuit.

huff, *v.t.*, to bully; to remove a piece from a chess-board or draughts-board; *v.i.*, to swell up; be puffed up; *n.*, a sudden taking of offence; the act of huffing.

huffed, *p.p.*, huff.

huff'ing, *pr.p.*, huff.

huff'iness, *n.*, the quality of being huffy.

huff'ish, *adj.*, petulant.

huf'fy, *adj.*, touchy.

hug, *v.t.*, to clasp tightly with the arms; to cherish; to keep near to; *n.*, a tight embrace.

huge, *adj.*, big, bulky.

huge'ly, *adv.*, very greatly.

hugged, *p.p.*, hug.

hug'ger-mug'ger, *v.t.* and *i.*, to hide; *adj.*, secret, confused; *n.*, secrecy, confusion.

hug'ging, *pr.p.*, hug.

Hu'guenot, *n.*, a French Protestant.

hulk, *v.t.*, to remove before blasting; *n.*, the body of a wrecked ship; anything big and clumsy.

hull, *v.t.*, to remove the hull from; to pierce a ship's hull; *n.*, the outer covering of fruit; a ship's frame.

hullabaloo', *n.*, uproar, hurly-burly.

hulled, *p.p.*, hull.

hul'ling, *pr.p.*, hull.

hum, *v.t.* and *i.*, to make the sound of bees; sing inarticulately; *n.*, a low, inarticulate sound or murmur.

hu'man, *adj.*, rel. to man.

humane', *adj.*, kind, compassionate.

humane'ly, *adv.*, in a humane way.

hu'manism, *n.*, literary culture; a system in which human affairs are the chief interest.

hu'manist, *n.*, a student of *literae humaniores*, or polite learning; a student of human affairs.

humanita'rian, *adj.*, rel. to humanitarianism; *n.*, a philanthropist.

humanita'rianism, *n.*, the principles of humanitarians or philanthropists.

human'ity, *n.*, human nature; the human race; philanthropy; mankind collectively.

humaniza'tion, *n.*, the act of humanizing; the humanized state.

hu'manize, *v.t.*, to make human, civilize.

hu'manized, *p.p.*, humanize.

hu'manizer, *n.*, one who humanizes.

hu'manizing, *pr.p.*, humanize.

hu'mankind, *n.*, mankind.

hu'manly, *adv.*, in a human way.

hum'ble, *v.t.*, to bring low, abase; *adj.*, lowly in mind or station.

hum'ble-bee, *n.*, the bumble-bee.

hum'bled, *p.p.*, humble.

hum'bleness, *n.*, the state of being humble; humility.

hum'bler, *adj.*, *comp.* of humble.

hum'blest, *adj.*, *super.* of humble.

hum'bling, *pr.p.*, humble.

hum'bly, *adv.*, in a humble way.

hum'bug, *v.t.*, to trick, impose upon; *n.*, sham, fraud.

hum'bugged, *p.p.*, humbug.

hum'bugging, *pr.p.*, humbug.

hum'drum, *adj.*,

monotonous, commonplace; *n.*, sameness, commonplaceness.

hu'meral, *adj.*, rel. to the humerus or shoulder; *n.*, a kind of veil worn over the shoulders by a minister in the Mass.

hu'merus, *n.*, the bone of the upper arm.

hum'hum, *n.*, a coarse Indian cotton cloth.

hu'mic, *adj.*, rel. to vegetable mould.

hu'mid, *adj.*, damp, moist.

humid'ify, *v.t.*, to moisten.

humid'ity, *n.*, dampness, moisture.

hu'mify, *v.t.*, to turn into mould.

humil'iate, *v.t.*, to abuse, put to shame.

humil'iated, *p.p.*, humiliate.

humil'iating, *pr.p.*, humiliate.

humilia'tion, *n.*, the act or effect of humiliating.

humil'ity, *n.*, *i.q.* humbleness.

hummed, *p.p.*, hum.

hum'mer, *n.*, one who hums.

hum'ming, *pr.p.* hum.

hum'ming-bird, *n.*, a bird whose vibrating wings make a humming sound.

hum'mock, *n.*, a hillock, knoll.

hu'moral, *adj.*, rel. to the fluids of the body.

hu'morist, *n.*, a humorous person.

hu'morous, *adj.*, displaying humour; with a sense of humour.

hu'morously, *adv.*, in a humorous way.

hu'mour, hu'mor, *v.t.*, to indulge the caprices of; to manage; *n.*, mental disposition; mood; drollery, comicality; a sense of the humorous; droll imaginativeness, distinguished from wit by being kindlier but less intellectual.

hu'moured, *p.p.*, humour.

hu'mouring, *pr.p.*, humour.

hu'mourless, *adj.*, lacking humour.

hu'moursome, *adj.*, crotchety, capricious.

hu'moursomely, *adv.*, capriciously.

hump, *v.t.*, to round or bend; *n.*, a protuberance; a rounded boss of earth.

hump'back, *n.*, a crooked back; one with a humpback.

hump'backed, *adj.*, having a humped back.

humped, *p.p.*, hump.

hump'ty-dump'ty, *adj.*, of stunted growth; *n.*, a dumpy person.

hu'mulin, *n.*, a hop-extract.

hu'mus, *n.*, mould.

Hun, *n.*, member of a wandering, ravaging race of Asiatic barbarians; anyone with like qualities.

hunch, *v.t.*, to crook; *n.*, a hump; a thick piece; a hunk.

hunch'back, *adj.* and *n.*, *see* humpback.

hunched, *p.p.*, bunch.

hun'dred, *adj.*, cardinal number = 10 × 10; *n.*, five score collectively; a county subdivision.

hun'dredfold, *n.*, a hundred times as many or much.

hun'dredth, *adj.*, the ordinal numeral of a hundred.

hun'dredweight, *n.*, 112 lb. avoirdupois.

hung, *p.p.*, hang.

Hunga'rian, *adj.*, rel. to Hungary; *n.*, a native of Hungary.

hun'ger, *v.i.*, to be hungry; to crave; to desire eagerly; *n.*, craving for food; eager desire.

hun'gered, *p.p.*, hunger.

hun'gering, *pr.p.*, hunger.

hun'grily, *adv.*, in a hungry way.

hun'gry, *adj.*, craving food; ardently desiring.

hunk, *n.*, a thick piece; a hunch.

hunks, *n.*, a miser.

hunt, *v.t.*, to chase, pursue; *n.*, a chase; a search; a company of huntsmen; a hunting district.

hunt'ed, *p.p.*, hunt.

hunt'er, *n.*, one who hunts; a huntsman; a horse for hunting.

hunt'ing, *pr.p.*, hunt; *n.*, the practice of the chase.

hunt'ress, *n.*, fem. of hunter.

hunts'man, *n.*, one who hunts; one in charge of a pack.

hur'dle, *v.t.*, to enclose or mark off with hurdles; *n.*, a movable framework of wood, strengthened with bars or withies.

hur'dled, *p.p.*, hurdle.

hur'dling, *pr.p.*, hurdle.

hur'dy-gur'dy, *n.*, a stringed musical instrument, actuated by means of a revolving wheel, or played with the fingers of one hand.

hurl, *v.t.*, to fling, throw with force.

hurl'bat, *n.*, a cudgel.

hurl'bone, *n.*, the whirlbone.

hurled, *p.p.*, hurl.

hurl'er, *n.*, one who hurls.

hurl'ing, *n.*, Irish hockey.

hurl'y-bur'ly, *n.*, tumult, uproar.

hurrah', *v.t.* and *i.*, to encourage by shouting hurrah! *interj.*, expressing joy, triumph, or approval.

hur'ricane, *n.*, a tempest; a violent cyclone.

hur'ried, *p.p.*, hurry.

hur'riedly, *adv.*, in a hurried way.

hur'rier, *n.*, one who hurries.

hur'ry, *v.t.*, to urge on; drive; *v.i.*, to move hastily; *n.*, excessive haste; eagerness.

hur'rying, *pr. p.*, hurry.

hur'ry-skur'ry, *adj.*, disorderly, confused; *n.*, disordered movement; bustle.

hurt, *v.t.*, to cause pain to; to injure; to grieve; *n.*, pain, harm, injury.

hurt'er, *n.*, one who hurts.

hurt'ful, *adj.*, injurious, harmful.

hurt'fulness, *n.*, the quality of being hurtful.

hur'tle, *v.t.*, to hurl; to push with violence; *v.i.*, to move with a clattering sound.

hur'tleberry, *n.*, the whortleberry.

hus'band, *v.t.*, to manage economically; to till; *n.*, a man in relation to his wife.

hus'banded, *p.p.*, husband.

hus'banding, *pr.p.*, husband.

hus'bandman, *n.*, a farmer.

hus'bandry, *n.*, farming; good management.

hush, *v.t.*, to silence; *v.i.*, to become silent; *n.*, stillness, silence.

hushed, *p.p.*, hush.

hush'ing, *pr.p.*, hush.

hush'-money, *n.*, a bribe for silence.

husk, *v.t.*, to take the husks from; *n.*, the outer covering of fruits or seeds.

husked, *p.p.*, husk.

husk'ier, *adj.*, *comp.* of husky.

husk'iest, *adj.*, *super.* of husky.

husk'ily, *adv.*, in a husky way.

husk'iness, *n.*, the quality of being husky.

husk'ing, *pr.p.*, husk.

husk'y, *adj.*, hoarse; harsh-voiced; like husk.

hussar', *n.*, a light cavalry soldier.

hus'sy, *n.*, an ill-behaved woman.

hust'ings, *n.*, a court of council; a stand on which Parliamentary candidates stood to speak.

hus'tle, *v.t.*, to push violently; jostle; *v.i.*, show alacrity.

hus'tled, *p.p.*, hustle.

hus'tler, *n.*, one who hustles.

hus'tling, *pr.p.*, hustle.

hut, *v.t.*, to lodge in huts; *n.*, a small house or cabin.

hutch, *v.t.*, to place in a hutch; to wash ore in a hutch; *n.*, a chest, cupboard, pen; a trough.

hutched, *p.p.*, hutch.

hutch'ing, *pr.p.*, hutch.

hut'ted, *p.p.*, hut.

hut'ting, *pr.p.*, hut.

huzza', *see* hurrah.

huzzaed', *p.p.*, huzza.

huzza'ing, *pr.p.*, huzza.

hy'acinth, *n.*, a bulbous fragrant plant.

hyacinth'ine, *adj.*, handsome, lovely.

Hy'ades, *n. pl.*, five stars in Taurus, said to bring rain at certain times.

Hy'ads, *n.*, *i.q.* Hyades

hyae'na, *n.*, a carnivorous, dog-like beast.

hy'aline, *adj.*, glassy, crystalline, clear.

hy'aloid, *adj.*, glassy; *n.*, a thin transparent membrane.

hy'brid, *adj.*, mongrel, of different species; *n.*, a mongrel; a word of mixed composition.

hy'bridize, *v.t.*, to produce a hybrid.

hy'bridized, *p.p.*, hybridize.

hy'bridizing, *pr.p.*, hybridize.

hybridiza'tion, *n.*, the act or effect of hybridizing.

hy'datid, *n.*, a bladder enclosing a tapeworm's larvae.

hy'datism, *n.*, the sound of moving pus.

hy'dra, *n.*, a water-serpent.

hydrac'id, *n.*, an acid containing hydrogen.

hy'dragogue, *n.*, a drug that promotes the secretion of water.

Hydran'gea, *n.*, a shrub producing a fine, clustering flower.

hy'drant, *n.*, a pipe for discharging water.

hydrar'gyrum, *n.*, quicksilver.

hy'drate, *v.t.*, to make into a hydrate; *n.*, a compound containing a definite proportion of water.

hy'drated, *p.p.*, hydrate.

hydraul'ic, *adj.*, rel. to moving fluids.

hydraul'ics, *n. pl.*, the science of fluids in motion.

hy'dride, *n.*, the combination of hydrogen with another element.

hydrobro'mic, *adj.*, containing bromin and hydrogen.

hydrocar'bon, *n.*, a compound of hydrogen and carbon.

hydrocar'bonate, *adj.*, containing carbon and hydrogen.

hy'drocele, *n.*, serous matter in the scrotum.

hydroceph'alous, *adj.*, suffering from water on the brain.

hydroceph'alus, *n.*, water in the head.

hydrochlo'rate, *n.*, a salt of hydrochloric acid.

hydrochlo'ric, *adj.*, containing hydrogen and chlorine.

hydrocy'anate, *n.*, a salt of hydrocyanic acid.

hydrodynam'ics, *n. pl.*, the science of motion in fluids.

hydro-elec'tric, *adj.*, producing electricity by friction of steam or water.

hydro-galvan'ic, *adj.*, rel. to galvanic currents produced by liquids.

hy'drogen, *n.*, a colourless, tasteless gas which, combined with oxygen, makes water.

hy'drogenize, *v.t.*, to make to combine with hydrogen.
hydrog'enous, *adj.*, rel. to hydrogen.
hydrog'rapher, *n.*, an expert in hydrography.
hydrograph'ic, *adj.*, rel. to hydrography.
hydrograph'ical, *adj.*, *i.q.* hydrographic.
hydrog'raphy, *n.*, the art of measuring and describing lakes, seas, etc.
hy'droid, *n.*, a hydra-like creature.
hydrolog'ical, *adj.*, rel. to hydrology.
hydrol'ogist, *n.*, an expert in hydrology.
hydrol'ysis, *n.*, decomposition of water where the two components are fixed in distinct compounds.
hy'dromel, *n.*, honey and water mixed.
hydrom'eter, *n.*, an instrument for measuring the specific gravity, etc., of fluids.
hydromet'ric, *adj.*, rel. to hydrometry.
hydrom'etry, *n.*, the measurement of the specific gravity, etc., of fluids.
hydropath'ic, *adj.*, rel. to hydropathy.
hydrop'athist, *n.*, one who practises hydropathy.
hydrop'athy, *n.*, the treatment of disease with water.
hy'drophane, *n.*, an opal which, when wet, loses its opacity.
hydroph'anous, *adj.*, translucent when wet.
hydropho'bia, *n.*, fear of water; madness caused by the bite of a dog, wolf, or fox.
hydropho'bic, *adj.*, pert. to hydrophobia.
hy'drophyte, *n.*, a water-plant.
hydrop'ic, *adj.*, dropsical.
hy'droplane, *n.*, a water-plane.
hy'drosalt, *n.*, a salt containing hydrogen.
hy'droscope, *n.*, an apparatus for detecting the presence of water in the air.
hy'drostat, *n.*, a contrivance for detecting the presence of water.
hydrostat'ic, *adj.*, pert. to hydrostatics.
hydrostat'ics, *n. pl.*, the science rel. to fluids at rest.
hydrot'ic, *adj.*, promoting a discharge of water.
hy'drous, *adj.*, containing water.
hydrox'ide, *n.*, a compound containing hydroxyl.
hydrox'yl, *n.*, a compound radical occurring in alcohol, etc.
hy'emal, *adj.*, wintry. Also *hiemal*.
hye'na, *see* hyaena.
hygei'an, *adj.*, rel. to health.
hy'giene, *n.*, the science treating of the preservation of health.
hygien'ic, *adj.*, health-preserving.
hygrol'ogy, *n.*, the science rel. to the presence of moisture in the air.
hygrom'eter, *n.*, an apparatus for measuring the extent of moisture in the air.
hygromet'ric, *adj.*, rel. to hygrometry.
hygrom'etry, *n.*, the measurement of the extent of water in the air.
hy'groscope, *n.*, an apparatus showing the moisture in the air.
hy'lobate, *n.*, a genus of apes.
hy'loist, *n.*, a materialist.
hy'lotheism, *n.*, pantheism.
hylozo'ic, *adj.*, rel. to hylozoism.
hylozo'ism, *n.*, materialism.
Hy'men, *n.*, the god of marriage.
hymene'al, *adj.*, rel. to marriage.
hymene'an, *adj.*, *i.q.* hymeneal.
Hymenop'tera, *n. pl.*, insects with fine membranous wings, as bees, etc.
hymenop'teral, *adj.*, rel. to the hymenoptera.
hymn, *v.t.*, to praise with song; *n.*, a song of praise or adoration.
hym'nal, *n.*, *i.q.* a hymn-book.
hymn'-book, *n.*, a collection of hymns.
hymned, *p.p.*, hymn.
hym'nic, *adj.*, lyrical.
hymn'ing, *pr.p.*, hymn.
hym'nody, *n.*, hymns and hymn-writing.
hymnog'rapher, *n.*, one who writes about hymns.
hymnol'ogist, *n.*, an expert in hymnology.
hymnol'ogy, *n.*, the study of hymn literature.
hy'oid, *n.*, the cartilaginous arch beneath the tongue.
Hyoscy'amus, *n.*, one of the night-shade group.
hyperbat'ic, *adj.*, transposed.
hyper'baton, *n.*, the transposition of words.
hyper'bola, *n.*, one of the conic sections.
hyper'bole, *n.*, an exaggeration.
hyperbol'ic, *adj.*, rel. to a hyperbola; exaggerated.
hyperbol'ical, *adj.*, *i.q.* hyperbolic.
hyperbol'ically, *adv.*, with exaggeration.
hyper'bolism, *n.*, a tendency to exaggeration.
hyper'bolist, *n.*, one given to exaggeration.
hyper'bolize, *v.i.*, to use hyperbole.
hyper'boloid, *n.*, a higher kind of hyperbola.
Hyperbo'rean, *adj.*, in the far north; arctically cold.

hypercar'bureted, *n.*, having an excessive quantity of gaseous hydrocarbons.

hypercatalec'tic, *adj.*, having an extra final syllable.

hypercrit'ic, *n.*, a severely critical person.

hypercrit'ical, *adj.*, unduly critical.

hypercrit'icism, *n.*, undue criticism.

hypercrit'icize, *v.t.*, to criticize unreasonably.

Hype'rion, *n.*, one of the Titan deities.

hyper'meter, *n.*, a metrically redundant verse.

hypermet'rical, *adj.*, rel. to a hypermeter.

hyper'trophy, *n.*, excessive physical development.

hy'phen, *v.t.*, to join with a hyphen; *n.*, a stroke (-) joining syllables or words.

hypnol'ogist, *n.*, an expert in hypnology.

hypnol'ogy, *n.*, the study of the phenomena of sleep.

hypnot'ic, *adj.*, rel. to hypnotism.

hyp'notism, *n.*, sleep produced by suggestion.

hyp'notize, *v.t.*, to send into a trance-like sleep.

hyp'notized, *p.p.*, hypnotize.

hyp'notizing, *pr.p.*, hypnotize.

hy'po-, a prefix = under.

hyp'ocaust, *n.*, an underground heating arrangement.

hypochon'dria, *n.*, a morbid state of low spirits.

hypochon'driac, *n.*, one suffering from hypochondria.

hypochondri'acal, *adj.*, morbidly low-spirited.

hypochondri'asis, *n.*, *i.q.* hypochondria.

hy'pocist, *n.*, a medicinal plant with astringent properties.

hypoc'risy, *n.*, false profession; dissimulation.

hyp'ocrite, *n.*, a false pretender.

hypocrit'ical, *adj.*, dissimulating, false.

hypoder'mic, *adj.*, injected beneath the skin.

hypogas'tric, *adj.*, pert. to the lowest part of the abdomen.

hyp'ogene, *adj.*, rel. to subterranean rock-formation.

hypoge'um, *n.*, an underground chamber.

hypophos'phate, *n.*, the lowest order of phosphates.

hypos'tasis, *n.*, underlying principle; substance.

hypostat'ic, *adj.*, essential, fundamental.

hypostat'ical, *adj.*, *i.q.* hypostatic.

hy'postyle, *n.*, a covered colonnade.

hypot'enuse, *n.*, the side of a right-angled triangle subtending the right angle.

hypoth'ec, *n.*, a pledge.

hypoth'ecate, *v.t.*, to pledge, mortgage.

hypoth'ecated, *p.p.*, hypothecate.

hypoth'ecating, *pr.p.*, hypothecate.

hypotheca'tion, *n.*, the act of hypothecating.

hypoth'esis, *n.*, an assumption, supposition.

hypothet'ic, *adj.*, conjectural, founded on assumption.

hypothet'ical, *adj.*, *i.q.* hypothetic.

hypothet'ically, *adv.*, by hypothesis.

hypsom'eter, *n.*, an apparatus for determining heights by the boiling point of water.

hy'son, *n.*, a green (China) tea.

hys'sop, *n.*, an aromatic plant.

hyste'ria, *n.*, a disorder of the nerves.

hyster'ic, *adj.*, rel. to hysteria.

hyster'ical, *adj.*, *i.q.* hysteric.

hyster'ics, *n. pl.*, *i.q.* hysteria.

hythe, *n.*, a small haven. Also *hithe*.

I

I, *pers. pron.*, myself.
i'amb, *n.*, *i.q.* iambus.
iam'bic, *adj.*, rel. to the iambus.
iam'bus, *n.*, a metrical foot, consisting of a short syllable followed by a long one.
Ibe'rian, *adj.*, bel. to Iberia; *n.*, a native of Spain.
i'bex, *n.*, a variety of wild goat.
ibi'dem, *adv.*, in the same place (*Lat.*).
i'bis, *n.*, a large wading-bird.
Ib'senism, *n.*, the teaching of Henrik Ibsen.
Ica'rian, *adj.*, rel. to Icarus; rash, presumptuous.
ice, *v.t.*, to cover with ice; to refrigerate; *n.*, frozen water.
ice'-age, *n.*, the glacial period.
ice'berg, *n.*, a great mass of floating ice.
ice'-boat, *n.*, a boat built specially strong to force its way through ice.
ice'-bound, *adj.*, frozen in.
ice-cream', *n.*, sweetened cream that has undergone a freezing process.
iced, *p.p.*, ice; *adj.*, coated with sugar.
ice'-floe, *n.*, a fragment of floating ice.
ice'-house, *n.*, a building for storing ice.
Ice'lander, *n.*, a native of Iceland.
Icelan'dic, *adj.*, rel. to Iceland.
ichneu'mon, *n.*, an Egyptian quadruped.
ich'nograph, *n.*, a ground-plan.
ichnograph'ic, *adj.*, rel. to ichnography.
ichnograph'ical, *adj.*, *i.q.* ichnographic.
ichnog'raphy, *n.*, the art of drawing plans, etc.
ichnolog'ical, *adj.*, rel. to ichnology.
ichno'logy, *n.*, the study of fossil foot-tracks.
i'chor, *n.*, the blood (or its equivalent) of the gods; the discharge from an ulcer.
i'chorous, *adj.*, pert. to ichor.
ichthyog'raphy, *n.*, a work on fishes.
ichthyol'ogist, *n.*, one interested in ichthyology.
ichthyol'ogy, *n.*, the study of fishes.
ichthyoph'agy, *n.*, the practice of fish-eating.
ichthyosau'rus, *n.*, a fossil marine creature.
i'cicle, *n.*, a hanging piece of ice.
i'ciness, *n.*, the state of being icy.
i'cing, *pr.p.*, ice; *n.*, a coating of sugar.
i'con, *n.*, a picture, image.
icon'oclasm, *n.*, the breaking of images.
icon'oclast, *n.*, a breaker of images.
iconoclast'ic, *adj.*, destruction of images; generally destructive.
iconograph'ic, *adj.*, rel. to iconography.
iconog'raphy, *n.*, the science of describing statues, pictures, likenesses, etc.
iconol'ater, *n.*, a worshipper of images.
iconol'atry, *n.*, the worship of images.
iconol'ogy, *n.*, the study of pictorial representation.
icosahe'dral, *adj.*, having twenty faces.
icosahe'dron, *n.*, a solid figure with twenty faces.
icosan'dria, *n. pl.*, plants with twenty or more unconnected stamens.
icosan'drous, *adj.*, rel. to icosandria.
icter'ic, *adj.*, suffering from jaundice.
icter'ical, *adj.*, *i.q.* icteric.
icteri'tious, *adj.*, jaundiced, yellow.
ic'tus, *n.*, a stroke, blow; musical beat.
i'cy, *adj.*, like ice; extremely cold.
ide'a, *n.*, a fancy, thought, intention.
ide'al, *adj.*, according to an idea; perfect; *n.*, a standard of perfection.
ide'alism, *n.*, the tendency to form ideals; the philosophical system which explains phenomena as modes of thought.
ide'alist, *n.*, one who forms ideals; an idealist philosopher.
idealis'tic, *adj.*, pert. to idealism.
ideal'ity, *n.*, the character of being ideal or unreal.
idealiza'tion, *n.*, the tendency to idealize.
ide'alize, *v.t.*, to refer things to an imaginary standard.
ide'alized, *p.p.*, idealize.
ide'alizing, *pr. p.*, idealize.
ide'ally, *adv.*, conceived as perfect.
idea'tion, *n.*, the shaping of ideas.
i'dem, *pron.*, the same man (*Lat.*).
id'em, *pron.*, the same thing (*Lat.*).
iden'tical, *adj.*, exactly the same.
iden'tically, *n.*, in an identical way or degree.

iden'tifiable, *adj.*, able to be identified.

identifica'tion, *n.*, the act or result of identifying.

iden'tified, *p.p.*, identify.

iden'tify, *v.t.*, to prove to be the same; recognize.

iden'tifying, *pr.p.*, identify.

iden'tity, *n.*, the state of being identical.

i'deograph, *n.*, a picture or symbol.

ideograph'ic, *adj.*, rel. to ideography.

ideograph'ical, *adj.*, *i.q.* ideographic.

ideog'raphy, *n.*, the pictorial representation of things or ideas.

ideolog'ical, *adj.*, rel. to ideology.

ideol'ogist, *n.*, one interested in ideology.

ideol'ogy, *n.*, the science and study of ideas.

ides, *n. pl.*, one of the fixed dates in the Roman month. In March, May, July, October, the Ides fall on the 15th; in the other months, on the 13th.

idioc'rasy, *n.*, *i.q.* idiosyncrasy.

idiocrat'ic, *adj.*, *i.q.* idiosyncratic.

id'iocy, *n.*, the state of being an idiot.

id'iograph, *n.*, a private signature; a trade mark.

idiograph'ic, *adj.*, rel. to an idiograph.

id'iom, *n.*, a usage peculiar to a particular language.

idiomat'ic, *adj.*, containing idiom; peculiar to a given language.

idiomat'ically, *n.*, in an idiomatic way.

idiopath'ic, *adj.*, rel. to idiopathy.

idiop'athy, *n.*, a primary disease.

idiosyn'crasy, *n.*, a personal peculiarity of mind.

idiosyncrat'ic, *adj.*, peculiar to an individual.

id'iot, *n.*, a person of undeveloped intellect.

idiot'ic, *adj.*, idiotlike, imbecile.

idiot'ical, *adj.*, *i.q.* idiotic.

idiot'icon, *n.*, a glossary of provincialisms.

id'iotism, *n.*, a barbarism; individual peculiarity of expression.

i'dle, *adj.*, doing nothing, lazy, vain, useless; *v.t.*, to spend in idleness; *v.i.*, to do nothing.

i'dled, *p.p.*, idle.

i'dleness, *n.*, the state of being idle.

i'dler, *n.*, one who idles; a sluggard.

i'dling, *pr.p.*, idle.

i'dly, *adv.*, lazily, vainly.

i'dol, *n.*, an image; a false appearance.

idol'ater, *n.*, an idol-worshipper.

idol'atress, *n.*, fem. of idolater.

idol'atrize, *v.t.*, to idolize; *v.i.*, to play the idolater.

idol'atrous, *adj.*, rel. to idolatry; loving to a morbid excess.

idol'atrously, *adv.*, in an idolatrous way or degree.

idol'atry, *n.*, image-worship; excessive fondness.

i'dolize, *v.t.*, to make an idol of; to love excessively.

i'dolized, *p.p.*, idolize.

i'dolizer, *n.*, one who idolizes.

i'dolizing, *pr.p.*, idolize.

i'dyll, *n.*, a short, simple, descriptive poem; a descriptive pastoral poem.

idyl'lic, *adj.*, rel. to idylls; resembling pastoral poetry.

if, *conj.*, implying condition or supposition.

ig'neous, *adj.*, fiery; caused by fire.

ignes'cent, *adj.*, scintillating.

ignif'erous, *adj.*, fire-producing.

ig'nis fat'uus, *n.*, a phosphorent gleam seen in marshy places; the will-o'-the-wisp.

ignite', *v.t.*, to kindle, cause to flame; *v.i.*, to take fire.

igni'table, *adj.*, able to be ignited.

igni'ted, *p.p.*, ignite.

igni'tible, *adj.*, *i.q.* ignitable.

igni'ting, *pr.p.*, ignite.

igni'tion, *n.*, the act of igniting.

igno'ble, *adj.*, not noble; base, mean.

igno'bly, *adv.*, basely, meanly.

ignomin'ious, *adj.*, bringing disgrace, shameful.

ignomin'iously, *adv.*, with ignominy.

ig'nominy, *n.*, shame, disgrace, infamy.

ignora'mus, *n.*, an ignorant person; a pretender to knowledge he does not possess.

ig'norance, *n.*, the state of being ignorant or uninformed.

ig'norant, *adj.*, without knowledge, uninformed, unaware.

ig'norantly, *adv.*, in an ignorant way.

ignore', *v.t.*, to regard as non-existent; leave out of consideration.

ignored', *p.p.*, ignore.

ignor'ing, *pr.p.*, ignore.

igua'na, *n.*, a large lizard of tropical America.

igua'nodon, *n.*, a fossil reptile, resembling the iguana.

il'eum, *n.*, the lower portion of the small intestine.

il'eus, *n.*, colic.

i'lex, *n.*, the holly; holm oak.

il'iac, *adj.*, rel. to the ilium.

Il'iad, *n.*, the Homeric Epic of the fall of Ilium or Troy.

il'ium, *n.*, the upper portion of the hip-bone.

ilk, *adj.* and *n.*, same.

ill, *adj.*, evil, disordered, sick; *adv.*, badly, poorly; *n.*, wrong, injury, misfortune, pain.

illa'tion, *n.*, the act of drawing an inference; the inference when made.

il'lative, *adj.*, inferential.

ill'-bred, *adj.*, badly brought up, rude.

ill-condi'tioned, *adj.*, badly disposed.

ille'gal, *adj.*, not legal, contrary to law.

illegal'ity, *n.*, the state or quality of being illegal.

ille'galize, *v.t.*, to make illegal.

ille'gally, *adv.*, in an illegal way.

illegibil'ity, *n.*, the quality of being illegible.

illeg'ible, *adj.*, not able to be deciphered.

illeg'ibly, *adv.*, in an undecipherable way.

illegit'imacy, *n.*, the state of being illegitimate.

illegi'timate, *adj.*, not in accordance with legal requirements; bastard; contrary to logic.

illegit'imate, *v.t.*, to pronounce illegitimate, bastardize.

illev'iable, *adj.*, unable to be levied.

ill-fa'voured, *adj.*, evil-looking, repulsive.

ill-hu'mour, *n.*, bad temper.

illib'eral, *adj.*, not liberal.

illiberal'ity, *n.*, the state of being illiberal.

illib'erally, *adv.*, in an illiberal way.

illic'it, *adj.*, unlawful.

illic'itly, *adv.*, unlawfully.

illic'itness, *n.*, the state of being illicit.

illimitabil'ity, *n.*, the quality of being illimitable.

illim'itable, *adj.*, not able to be limited; boundless.

illim'ited, *adj.*, not limited, boundless.

illini'tion, *n.*, the act of rubbing in.

illi'sion, *n.*, the act of striking against.

illit'eracy, *n.*, the state of being illiterate.

illit'erate, *adj.*, unlettered, uneducated.

illit'erateness, *n.*, *i.q.* illiteracy.

ill-man'nered, *adj.*, having bad manners.

ill-na'ture, *n.*, bad temper, peevishness.

ill-na'tured, *adj.*, bad-tempered, peevish.

ill'ness, *n.*, the state of being ill.

illog'ical, *adj.*, not logical.

ill-o'mened, *adj.*, of evil omen, inauspicious.

ill'-starred', *adj.*, born under an unlucky star; unfortunate.

ill-timed', *adj.*, untimely, unseasonable.

ill-treat', *v.t.*, to treat evilly; be cruel to.

illude', *v.t.*, to deceive, impose on.

illud'ed, *p.p.*, illude.

illud'ing, *pr.p.*, illude.

illume', *v.t.*, to lighten, illuminate.

illumed', *p.p.*, illume.

illu'minable, *adj.*, able to be illuminated.

illu'minant, *n.*, something that gives light.

illu'minate, *v.t.*, to throw light on, to enlighten; to embellish manuscripts.

illu'minated, *p.p.*, illuminate.

illumina'ti, *n. pl.*, "The Enlightened" (*i.e.*, members of certain secret societies); any who claim to possess superior knowledge.

illu'minating, *pr.p.*, illuminate.

illumina'tion, *n.*, the act or effect of illuminating.

illu'minative, *adj.*, illuminating.

illu'minator, *n.*, one who embellishes manuscripts.

illu'mine, *v.t.*, to throw light on, light up.

illu'mined, *p.p.*, illumine.

illu'ming, *pr. p.*, illume.

illu'mining, *pr.p.*, illumine.

illu'minism, *n.*, the doctrines of the illuminati; illumination.

illu'minize, *v.t.*, to make one of the illuminati.

ill'-used, *adj.*, badly treated.

illu'sion, *n.*, the act of illuding; a deception of the senses; a false show.

illu'sionism, *n.*, jugglery.

illu'sionist, *n.*, a dreamer; one who practises illusions (*e.g.*, as a juggler).

illu'sive, *adj.*, producing illusion.

illu'sively, *adv.*, in an illusive way.

illu'siveness, *n.*, the state or quality of being illusive.

illu'sory, *adj.*, producing illusion.

ill'ustrate, *v.t.*, to explain by examples; to embellish with pictures.

ill'ustrated, *p.p.*, illustrate.

ill'ustrating, *pr.p.*, illustrate.

illustra'tion, *n.*, the act of illustrating; a pictorial embellishment; an example.

illus'trative, *adj.*, tending to illustrate; explanatory.

illus'tratively, *adv.*, in an illustrative way.

ill'ustrator, ill'ustrater, *n.*, one who illustrates.

illus'trious, *adj.*, distinguished, glorious.

illus'triously, *adv.*, in an illustrious way.

illus'triousness, *n.*, the quality of being illustrious.

ill-will', *n.*, bad feeling, spite.

ill-wish'er, *n.*, one who wishes one ill.

im'age, *v.t.*, to form an image of, to represent, reflect; *n.*, a representation, statue, sculpture, mental picture.

im'ageable, *adj.*, imaginable.

im'aged, *p.p.*, image.

im'agery, *n.*, images in general; figurative writing or speech.

imag'inable, *adj.*, able to be imagined.

imag'inably, *adv.*, in an imaginable way.

imag'inary, *adj.*, not real, fancied.

imagina'tion, *n.*, the act or power of imagining.

imag'inative, *adj.*, given to imagining.

imag'ine, *v.t.*, to conceive mentally, form an idea; fancy.

imag'ined, *p.p.*, imagine.

imag'iner, *n.*, one who imagines.

im'aging, *pr.p.*, image.

imag'ining, *pr.p.*, imagine.

ima'go, *n.*, a winged insect fully developed.

imam', *n.*, a Mohammedan minister.

im'becile, *adj.*, mentally defective; physically and mentally weak.

imbecil'ity, *n.*, the state or quality of being imbecile.

imbed', *v.t.*, to lay in a mass of matter.

imbibe', *v.t.*, to drink in; take into the mind.

imbibed', *p.p.*, imbibe.

imbi'ber, *n.*, one who imbibes.

imbi'bing, *pr.p.*, imbibe.

imbibi'tion, *n.*, the act of imbibing.

imbo'som, *see* embosom.

im'bricate, *v.t.*, to lay so as to overlap; *adj.*, overlapping like tiles.

im'bricated, *p.p.*, imbricate; *adj.*, *i.q.* imbricate.

im'bricating, *pr.p.*, imbricate.

imbrica'tion, *n.*, a pattern that overlaps at the edges.

imbro'glio, *n.*, a complicated misunderstanding; an elaborate plot.

imbrue', *v.t.*, to wet, moisten, soak.

imbrued', *p.p.*, imbrue.

imbru'ing, *pr.p.*, imbrue.

imbrute', *v.t.*, to brutalize.

imbru'ted, *p.p.*, imbrute.

imbru'ting, *pr.p.*, imbrute.

imbue', *v.t.*, to impregnate, tinge; instruct.

imbued', *p.p.*, imbue.

imbu'ing, *pr.p.*, imbue.

imitabil'ity, *n.*, the quality of being imitable.

im'itable, *adj.*, capable of imitation.

im'itate, *v.t.*, to copy, emulate, mimic.

im'itated, *p.p.*, imitate.

im'itating, *pr.p.*, imitate.

imita'tion, *n.*, the act of imitating; a copy.

im'itative, *adj.*, copying, mimicking; following a pattern.

im'itatŏr, *n.*, one who imitates.

immac'ulate, *adj.*, spotless, absolutely pure.

immac'ulateness, *n.*, the state or quality of being immaculate.

im'manence, *n.*, the state of being immanent.

im'manency, *n.*, *i.q.* immanence.

im'manent, *adj.*, remaining in; inherent, present.

immate'rial, *adj.*, not material, incorporeal; of no importance.

immate'rialism, *n.*, the doctrine of the immaterial.

immate'rialist, *n.*, a believer in immaterialism.

immaterial'ity, *n.*, the quality of being immaterial.

immate'rially, *adv.*, in an immaterial way.

immature', *adj.*, not mature, unripe, undeveloped.

immatured', *adj.*, *i.q.* immature.

immature'ly, *adv.*, in an immature way.

immatur'ity, *n.*, the state of being immature.

immeas'urable, *adj.*, incapable of being measured.

immeas'urably, *adv.*, without measure.

imme'diate, *adj.*, instant, very close; direct, without external agency.

imme'diately, *adv.*, instantly, at once.

immed'icable, *adj.*, incurable.

immem'orable, *adj.*, unworthy of remembrance.

immemo'rial, *adj.*, old beyond record.

immense', *adj.*, boundless, illimitable, vast.

immense'ly, *adv.*, very greatly.

immense'ness, *n.*, the state or quality of the immense.

immen'sity, *n.*, *i.q.* immenseness; limitless space.

immensurabil'ity, *n.*, the state or quality of the immeasurable.

immen'surable, *adj.*, incapable of measurement.

immerge', *v.t.*, to immerse; *v.i.*, to vanish.

immerged', *p.p.*, immerge.

immer'ging, *pr.p.*, immerge.

immerse', *v.t.*, to dip or plunge into water; to engross.

immersed', *p.p.*, immerse.

immers'ing, *pr.p.*, immerse.

immer'sion, *n.*, the act of dipping; absorption.

immer'sionist, *n.*, a supporter of the practice of baptizing with immersion.

immethod'ical, *adj.*, unmethodical, untidy.
im'migrant, *n.*, one who immigrates.
im'migrate, *v.i.*, to come into a country to live in it.
im'migrated, *p.p.*, immigrate.
im'migrating, *pr.p.*, immigrate.
immigra'tion, *n.*, the act of immigrating.
im'minence, *n.*, the state or quality of being imminent.
im'minent, *adj.*, impending, close at hand, threatening.
im'minently, *adv.*, in an imminent way.
immin'gle, *v.t.*, to mix together.
immin'gled, *p.p.*, immingle.
immin'gling, *pr.p.*, immingle.
immiscibil'ity, *n.*, the state or quality of being immiscible.
immis'cible, *adj.*, incapable of mixture.
immis'sion, *n.*, the act of sending in; something injected.
immit'igable, *adj.*, unable to be mitigated.
immix', *v.t.*, to mix in.
immo'bile, *adj.*, not mobile, immovable.
immobil'ity, *n.*, the state or quality of being immobile.
immo'bilize, *v.t.*, to make immovable.
immo'bilized, *p.p.*, immobilize.
immo'bilizing, *pr.p.*, immobilize.
immod'erate, *adj.*, excessive, inordinate.
immod'erately, *adv.*, excessively.
immod'est, *adj.*, not modest, conceited, unreserved, impure.
immod'estly, *adv.*, in an immodest way.
immod'esty, *n.*, the lack of modesty; impurity.
im'molate, *v.t.*, to sacrifice.
im'molated, *p.p.*, immolate.
im'molating, *pr.p.*, immolate.
immola'tion, *n.*, the act of immolating.
im'molator, *n.*, a sacrificer.
immor'al, *adj.*, offending the divine or moral law; unscrupulous; unchaste.
immoral'ity, *n.*, the state or quality of being immoral.
immor'ally, *adv.*, in an immoral way.
immor'tal, *adj.*, not mortal, undying.
immortal'ity, *n.*, the state or quality of being immortal.
immortaliza'tion, *n.*, the state of being immortalized.
immor'talize, *v.t.*, to render immortal.
immor'talized, *p.p.*, immortalize.
immor'talizing, *pr.p.*, immortalize.
immortelle', *n.*, an everlasting flower (*Fr.*).
immovabil'ity, *n.*, the state or quality of being immovable.
immov'able, *adj.*, unable to be moved.
immov'ably, *adv.*, in an immovable way.
immune', *adj.*, free or exempt from, proof against.
immu'nity, *n.*, the state of being immune.
immuniza'tion, *n.*, the act or effect of rendering immune.
im'munize, *v.t.*, to render immune.
immure', *v.t.*, to wall up, imprison.
immured', *p.p.*, immure.
immur'ing, *pr.p.*, immure.
immutabil'ity, *n.*, the state or quality of being immutable.
immu'table, *adj.*, unchangeable.
immu'tably, *adv.*, unchangeably.
imp, *v.t.*, to help out; *n.*, a child; a mischievous sprite.
impact', *v.t.*, to press together.
im'pact, *n.*, the act of striking or colliding.
impact'ed, *p.p.*, impact.
impact'ing, *pr.p.*, impact.
impair', *v.t.*, to damage, lessen in value.
impaired', *p.p.*, impair.
impair'er, *n.*, one who impairs.
impair'ing, *pr.p.*, impair.
impale', *v.t.*, to run a stake through; fasten on a stake; fence round; place two coats of arms on one shield, side by side. Also *empale.*
impaled', *p.p.*, impale.
impale'ment, *n.*, the act of impaling; a space enclosed; the union of two coats of arms.
impa'ling, *pr.p.*, impale.
impalpabil'ity, *n.*, the state or quality of being impalpable.
impal'pable, *adj.*, not able to be felt or touched; unreal.
impana'tion, *n.*, embodiment in bread.
impan'el, *v.t.*, to enter names on a list; to form a jury.
impan'el(l)ed, *p.p.*, impanel.
impan'el(l)ing, *pr.p.*, impanel.
impar'adise, *v.t.*, to fill with transcendent joy.
imparisyllab'ic, *adj.*, not having the same number of syllables in all its cases.
impar'ity, *adj.*, inequality.
impark', *v.t.*, to enclose with a fence.
imparl'ance, *n.*, postponement of a suit.
impart', *v.t.*, to give a share of, communicate.
impart'ed, *p.p.*, impart.
impart'er, *n.*, one who imparts.
impart'ing, *pr.p.*, impart.
impar'tial, *adj.*, not partial; fair, equitable.
impartial'ity, *n.*, the state or quality of being fair.

impar'tially, *adv.*, equitably, fairly.

impar'tialness, *n.*, *i.q.* impartiality.

impartibil'ity, *n.*, the quality of being impartible.

impart'ible, *adj.*, incapable of partition.

impart'ment, *n.*, the act of imparting.

impas'sable, *adj.*, unable to be passed over or through.

impasse', *n.*, an insuperable obstacle (*Fr.*).

impassibil'ity, *n.*, the state or quality of being impassible.

impas'sible, *adj.*, incapable of feeling; apathetic.

impas'sion, *v.t.*, to fill with passion.

impas'sionate, *adj.*, impassioned.

impas'sioned, *p.p.*, impassion.

impas'sioning, *pr.p.*, impassion.

impas'sive, *adj.*, *i.q.* impassible.

impas'sively, *adv.*, in an impassive way.

impas'siveness, *n.*, *i.q.* impassivity.

impassiv'ity, *n.*, the state or quality of being impassive.

impasta'tion, *n.*, the act of turning into paste.

impaste', *v.t.*, to make into paste; to lay colours on thickly.

impa'sted, *p.p.*, impaste.

impa'sting, *pr.p.*, impaste.

impa'tience, *n.*, inability to endure pain or delay; restlessness.

impa'tient, *adj.*, unable to bear discomfort, pain, or delay; restless; opposed to restraint.

impa'tiently, *adv.*, with impatience.

impawn', *v.t.*, to place in pawn; to pledge.

impawned', *p.p.*, impawn.

impawn'ing, *pr.p.*, impawn.

impeach', *v.t.*, to charge, accuse; throw doubt on.

impeach'able, *adj.*, able to be impeached.

impeached', *p.p.*, impeach.

impeach'er, *n.*, one who impeaches.

impeach'ing, *pr.p.*, impeach.

impeach'ment, *n.*, the act of impeaching; a charge laid.

impearl', *v.t.*, to set with pearls; to make like pearls.

impearled', *p.p.*, impearl.

impearl'ing, *pr.p.*, impearl.

impeccabil'ity, *n.*, the state of being impeccable.

impec'cable, *adj.*, incapable of error or sinning.

impec'cancy, *n.*, sinlessness.

impec'cant, *adj.*, sinless.

impecunios'ity, *n.*, the state of being impecunious.

impecu'nious, *adj.*, without money.

impede', *v.t.*, to hamper, stop.

impe'ded, *p.p.*, impede.

impe'dient, *adj.*, hindering.

imped'iment, *n.*, a hindrance, obstacle.

impedimen'ta, *n. pl.*, baggage.

impedimen'tal, *adj.*, obstructing.

impe'ding, *pr.p.*, impede.

impel', *v.t.*, to drive forward, encourage.

impelled', *p.p.*, impel.

impel'lent, *adj.*, impelling.

impel'ler, *n.*, one who impels.

impel'ling, *pr.p.*, impel.

impen', *v.t.*, to enclose in a pen or fold.

impend', *v.i.*, to hang over, threaten, be imminent.

impend'ed, *p.p.*, impend.

impend'ence, *n.*, the state of being impendent.

impend'ency, *n.*, *i.q.* impendence.

impend'ent, *adj.*, imminent, hanging over.

impend'ing, *pr.p.*, impend.

impenetrabil'ity, *n.*, the state or quality of being impenetrable.

impen'etrable, *adj.*, unable to be penetrated or passed through.

impen'itence, *n.*, the state of being impenitent.

impen'itency, *n.*, *i.q.* impenitence.

impen'itent, *adj.*, unrepentant, stubborn.

impen'itently, *adv.*, in an impenitent way.

impen'nate, *adj.*, short-winged.

impen'nous, *adj.*, wingless.

imperati'val, *adj.*, rel. to the imperative mood.

imper'ative, *adj.*, commanding; having authority; necessary; obligatory; *n.*, the imperative mood.

imper'atively, *adv.*, urgently, with authority.

impera'tor, *n.*, a commander-in-chief. The later Latin title for Emperor.

imperato'rial, *adj.*, rel. to an imperator.

imper'atory, *adj.*, *i.q.* imperatorial.

imperceptibil'ity, *n.*, the quality or state of being imperceptible.

impercep'tible, *adj.*, unable to be perceived; invisible.

impercep'tibleness, *n.*, *i.q.* imperceptibility.

impercep'tibly, *adv.*, in an imperceptible way.

imper'fect, *adj.*, not perfect, incomplete.

imperfection, *n.*, incompleteness, blemish.

imper'fectly, *adv.*, in an imperfect way.

imper'fectness, *n.*, *i.q.* imperfection.

imper'forable, *adj.*, unable to be perforated.
imper'forate, *adj.*, without perforations.
imper'forated, *adj.*, *i.q.* imperforate.
imperfora'tion, *n.*, the state of being imperforate.
impe'rial, *adj.*, rel. to an emperor or empire; sovereign; *n.*, a tuft of hair beneath the lower lip; a large size of paper; the outside seat or a baggage-case on a diligence; a large size of photograph.
impe'rialism, *n.*, the principles or the system of Imperial Government; the spirit of empire.
impe'rialist, *n.*, one who professes imperialism.
impe'rialistic, *adj.*, pert. to imperialism.
impe'rialize, *v.t.*, to make imperial.
impe'rially, *adv.*, in an imperial way.
imper'il, *v.t.*, to bring into danger.
imper'illed, *p.p.*, imperil.
imper'illing, *pr.p.*, imperil.
impe'rious, *adj.*, dictatorial, commanding.
impe'riously, *adv.*, in an imperious way.
impe'riousness, *n.*, the state of being imperious.
imper'ishable, *adj.*, never perishing, everlasting.
imper'ishableness, *n.*, the state or quality of being imperishable.
imper'manence, *n.*, want of permanence.
imper'manent, *adj.*, without permanence.
impermeabil'ity, *adj.*, the quality of being impermeable.
imper'meable, *adj.*, impenetrable.
imper'sonal, *adj.*, not relating to any particular person.
impersonal'ity, *n.*, the quality of being impersonal.
imper'sonally, *adv.*, in an impersonal way.
imper'sonate, *v.t.*, to assume the part of someone; to represent.
imper'sonate, *adj.*, embodied in someone.
imper'sonated, *p.p.*, impersonate.
imper'sonating, *pr.p.*, impersonate.
imperson'a'tion, *n.*, the act of impersonating; that in which a thing is personified.
imper'tinence, *n.*, rudeness; uncivil behaviour; effrontery; something of no value.
imper'tinency, *n.*, *i.q.* impertinence.
imper'tinent, *adj.*, presuming, rude; irrelevant.
imper'tinently, *adv.*, rudely, with effrontery.
imperturbabil'ity, *n.*, the quality of being imperturbable.
impertur'bable, *adj.*, unable to be put out; unruffled.
imperturba'tion, *n.*, calmness.
imperviabil'ity, *n.*, the quality of being impervious.
imper'viable, *adj.*, *i.q.* imperviable.
imper'vious, *adj.*, unable to be passed through.
imper'viousness, *n.*, the quality of being impervious.
impeti'go, *n.*, a skin-disease.
im'petrate, *v.t.*, to gain by entreating.
impetra'tion, *n.*, the act of impetrating.
im'petratory, *adj.*, expressing entreaty.
impetuos'ity, *n.*, vehemence, rash energy.
impet'uous, *adj.*, vehement, rashly energetic.
impet'uously, *adv.*, in an impetuous way.
impet'uousness, *n.*, *i.q.* impetuosity.
im'petus, *n.*, momentum.
im'pi, *n.*, a small body of African warriors.
impi'ety, *n.*, the state or quality of being impious.
impinge', *v.i.*, to strike against, collide, touch upon.
impinged', *p.p.*, impinge.
impinge'ment *n.*, the act of impinging.
imping'ing, *pr.p.*, impinge.
im'pious, *adj.*, profane, irreverent.
im'piously, *adv.*, irreverently, profanely.
im'piousness, *n.*, *i.q.* impiety.
imp'ish, *adj.*, implike.
implacabil'ity, *n.*, the quality or state of being implacable.
impla'cable, *adj.*, unable to be appeased; unforgiving.
impla'cably, *adv.*, in an implacable way.
implant', *v.t.*, to plant into; to inculcate.
implanta'tion, *n.*, the act of implanting.
implant'ed, *p.p.*, implant.
implant'ing, *pr.p.*, implant.
implausibil'ity, *n.*, the quality of being implausible.
implau'sible, *adj.*, not readily believed or accepted.
implau'sibleness, *n.*, *i.q.* implausibility.
implead', *v.t.*, to bring an action against.
implead'ed, *p.p.*, implead.
implead'er, *n.*, one who impleads.
implead'ing, *pr.p.*, implead.
im'plement, *n.*, a tool or instrument.
implement'al, *adj.*, of the nature of an implement.
imple'tion, *n.*, the act of filling; state of being full.

im'plicate, *v.t.*, to entangle, involve.
im'plicate, *n.*, that which is involved.
im'plicated, *p.p.*, implicate.
im'plicating, *pr.p.*, implicate.
implica'tion, *n.*, deduction; that which is implied.
im'plicative, *adj.*, of the nature of implication.
implic'it, *adj.*, implied; unquestioning.
implic'itly, *adv.*, unquestioningly; inferentially.
implic'itness, *n.*, the state of being implicit.
implied', *p.p.*, imply.
implied'ly, *adv.*, by implication.
implora'tion, *n.*, the act of imploring.
implore', *v.t.*, to pray earnestly for.
implored', *p.p.*, implore.
implor'er, *n.*, one who implores.
implor'ing, *pr.p.*, implore.
implor'ingly, *adv.*, with earnest prayer.
imply', *v.t.*, signify, mean, convey.
imply'ing, *pr.p.*, imply.
impol'icy, *n.*, inexpediency.
impolite', *adj.*, rude, unpolished.
impolite'ly, *adv.*, rudely.
impolite'ness, *n.*, the state of being impolite.
impol'itic, *adj.*, inexpedient, not prudent.
imponderabil'ity, *n.*, the state or quality of being imponderable.
impon'derable, *adj.*, without perceptible weight; *n.*, something not appreciably heavy.
impon'derous, *adj.*, *i.q.* imponderable.
impo'nent, *adj.*, imposing.
imporos'ity, *n.*, solidity.
impo'rous, *adj.*, solid, without pores.
import', *v.t.*, to carry in; to signify.
im'port, *n.*, something imported; meaning; what is implied.
import'able, *adj.*, able to be imported.
impor'tance, *n.*, the quality of being important; significance, weight.
impor'tant, *adj.*, significant, weighty, of much consequence.
impor'tantly, *adv.*, in an important way.
importa'tion, *n.*, the act of importing; that which is imported.
import'ed, *p.p.*, import.
import'er, *n.*, one who imports.
import'ing, *pr.p.*, import.
impor'tunate, *adj.*, pressing, urgent, insistent.
impor'tunately, *adv.*, in an importunate way.
importune', *v.t.*, to solicit earnestly; to press.
importuned', *p.p.*, importune.
importu'ner, *n.*, one who importunes.
importu'ning, *pr.p.*, importune.
importu'nity, *n.*, the act of importuning; incessant entreaty.
impo'sable, *adj.*, able to be imposed.
impose', *v.t.*, to lay upon; *v.i.*, to practise deceit.
imposed', *p.p.*, impose.
impo'ser, *n.*, one who imposes.
impo'sing, *pr.p.*, impose; *adj.*, specious, showy, commanding.
impo'singly, *adv.*, in an imposing way.
impo'sing-stone, *n.*, a slab used by printers for imposing formes.
imposi'tion, *n.*, a laying on (as in Ordination and Confirmation); deceit; a punishment-task.
impossibil'ity, *n.*, the state or quality of being impossible; *n.*, something that is impossible.
impos'sible, *adj.*, not possible, unable to be done or thought.
im'post, *n.*, that which is imposed, as a tax; the resting of an arch on its support; the place where the arch rests.
imposthuma'tion, *n.*, the formation of an abscess.
impos'thume, *n.*, an abscess.
impos'tor, *n.*, a deceiver.
impos'ture, *n.*, a false pretence, fraud.
impos'tured, *adj.*, of the nature of fraud.
im'potence, *n.*, want of strength, feebleness.
im'potency, *n.*, *i.q.* impotence.
im'potent, *adj.*, without strength; without self-control.
im'potently, *adv.*, feebly.
impound', *v.t.*, to shut into a pound; to take legal possession of.
impound'ed, *p.p.*, impound.
impound'er, *n.*, one who impounds.
impound'ing, *pr.p.*, impound.
impov'erish, *v.t.*, to reduce to poverty; exhaust.
impov'erished, *p.p.*, impoverish.
impov'erisher, *n.*, one who impoverishes.
impov'erishing, *pr.p.*, impoverish.
impov'erishment, *n.*, the act of impoverishing; the impoverished state.
im*practicabil'ity*, *n.*, the state or quality of being impracticable.
im*prac'ticable*, *adj.*, not practicable; unable to be done; stubborn.
im'precate, *v.t.*, to curse.

im'precated, *p.p.*, imprecate.
im'precating, *pr.p.*, imprecate.
impreca'tion, *n.*, the act of imprecating; a curse.
im'precatory, *adj.*, expressing a curse.
impregnabil'ity, *n.*, the state of being impregnable.
impreg'nable, *adj.*, not to be taken by assault; capable of impregnation.
impreg'nably, *adv.*, in an impregnable way.
impreg'nate, *v.t.*, to make pregnant; to infuse qualities or particles; *adj.*, pregnant; filled with.
impreg'nated, *p.p.*, impregnate.
impreg'nating, *pr.p.*, impregnate.
impregna'tion, *n.*, the act of impregnating; state of being impregnated.
impresa'rio, *n.*, a manager or conductor of a troupe of singers or actors.
imprescrip'tible, *adj.*, independent of prescription.
impress', *v.t.*, to stamp, fix deeply in, influence.
im'press, *n.*, a mark, stamp.
impressed', *p.p.*, impress.
impressibil'ity, *n.*, the state or quality of being impressible.
impress'ible, *adj.*, able to be impressed.
impress'ing, *pr.p.*, impress.
impres'sion, *n.*, the act or effect of impressing; an indistinct recollection; a faint notion; a printing.
impres'sionable, *adj.*, susceptible of being impressed.
impres'sionism, *n.*, an artistic doctrine that a picture should convey a general impression, without particular regard to details.
impres'sionist, *n.*, one who practises impressionism.
impress'ive, *adj.*, impressing, striking, solemn.
impress'ively, *adv.*, in an impressive way.
impress'ment, *n.*, the act of pressing men for service; the state of being impressed.
impress'ure, *n.*, *i.q.* impression.
imprima'tur, *n.*, official permission to print a book.
impri'mis, *adv.*, in the first place.
imprint', *v.t.*, to print in; stamp in the mind.
im'print, *n.*, a stamp, impression; the name and address of a publisher at the foot of a title-page; a printer's name.
imprint'ed, *p.p.*, imprint.
imprint'ing, *pr.p.*, imprint.
impris'on, *v.t.*, to confine in prison; to shut in.
impris'oned, *p.p.*, imprison.
impris'oning, *pr.p.*, imprison.
impris'onment, *n.*, the act of imprisoning; state of being imprisoned.
improbabil'ity, *n.*, the state or quality of being improbable.
improb'able, *adj.*, not probable, unlikely.
improb'ably, *adv.*, not probably.
improb'ity, *n.*, dishonesty.
impromp'tu, *adj.*, unpremeditated; *adv.*, offhand; *n.*, something said or done on the spur of the moment.
improp'er, *adj.*, not proper, indecorous.
improp'erly, *adv.*, not properly.
impro'priate, *v.t.*, to take to private use —said of a layman or lay body holding Church property.
impro'priate, *adj.*, impropriated.
impro'priated, *p.p.*, impropriate.
impro'priating, *pr.p.*, impropriate.
impropria'tion, *n.*, the act of impropriating; that which is impropriated.
impro'priator, *n.*, one who holds impropriated property.
impropri'ety, *n.*, the state or quality of being improper; an improper act.
improvabil'ity, *n.*, the state or quality of being improvable.
improv'able, *adj.*, capable of improvement.
improv'ableness, *n.*, *i.q.* improvability.
improve', *v.t.*, to make better, reform; *v.i.*, to become better.
improved', *p.p.*, improve.
improve'ment, *n.*, the act or effect of improving.
improv'er, *n.*, anything that improves.
improv'idence, *n.*, the quality of being improvident; wastefulness.
improv'ident, *adj.*, wasteful, careless of the future.
improv'idently, *adv.*, in an improvident way.
improv'ing, *pr.p.*, improve.
improv'ingly, *adv.*, in an improving way.
improvisa'tion, *n.*, the act of improvising.
improvisato're, *n.*, one who improvises.
improvise', *v.t.*, to compose without preparation; to make something on the spur of the moment.
improvised', *p.p.*, improvise.
improvi'ser, *n.*, one who improvises.
improvi'sing, *pr.p.*, improvising.
impru'dence, *n.*, want of sagacity or thought; indiscretion.

impru'dent, *adj.*, lacking thought or sagacity; heedless.

impru'dently, *adv.*, in an imprudent way.

im'pudence, *n.*, shamelessness, audacity.

im'pudent, *adj.*, shameless, audacious.

im'pudently, *adv.*, in an impudent way.

impudic'ity, *n.*, immodesty.

impugn', *v.t.*, to attack, contradict.

impugned', *p.p.*, impugn.

impugn'er, *n.*, one who impugns.

impugn'ing, *pr.p.*, impugn.

im'pulse, *n.*, impelling force; a sudden motive.

impul'sion, *n.*, a sudden impetus; the act of impelling, the state of being impelled.

impul'sive, *adj.*, acting without waiting to reflect.

impul'sively, *adv.*, in an impulsive way.

impul'siveness, *n.*, the state or quality of being impulsive.

impu'nity, *n.*, freedom from punishment or injury.

impure', *adj.*, not pure, unclean, unchaste.

impure'ly, *adv.*, in an impure way.

impure'ness, *n.*, the state or quality of being impure.

impu'rity, *n.*, impureness; anything impure.

impur'ple, *v.t.*, to stain purple.

impu'table, *adj.*, able to be imputed.

imputa'tion, *n.*, the act of imputing; a charge or accusation.

impu'tative, *adj.*, imputed; able to be imputed.

impute', *v.t.*, to attribute, ascribe, place to one's account.

impu'ted, *p.p.*, impute.

impu'ter, *n.*, one who imputes.

impu'ting, *pr.p.*, impute.

imputres'cible, *adj.*, not liable to putrescence.

in, *prep.* and *adv.*, within; into.

inabil'ity, *n.*, the state of being unable.

inaccessibil'ity, *n.*, the state of being inaccessible.

inaccess'ible, *adj.*, unable to be approached.

inaccess'ibly, *adv.*, unapproachably.

inac'curacy, *n.*, the state or quality of being inaccurate; an error.

inac'curate, *adj.*, not exact, careless.

inac'curately, *adv.*, in an inaccurate way.

inac'tion, *n.*, a state of not acting.

inact'ive, *adj.*, not acting, idle.

inact'ively, *adv.*, idly.

inactiv'ity, *n.*, the quality of being inactive.

inad'equacy, *n.*, the state or quality of being inadequate.

inad'equate, *adj.*, insufficient, not competent.

inad'equately, *adv.*, insufficiently.

inad'equateness, *n.*, *i.q.*, inadequacy.

inadmissibil'ity, *n.*, the state or quality of being inadmissible.

inadmis'sible, *adj.*, unable to be admitted.

inadvert'ence, *n.*, heedlessness, carelessness, an act of carelessness.

inadvert'ent, *adj.*, not paying attention, careless.

inadvert'ently, *adv.*, carelessly.

ina'lienable, *adj.*, unable to be alienated.

inamora'ta, *n.*, a lady love.

inamora'to, *n.*, a lover.

inane', *adj.*, empty, foolish.

inan'imate, *adj.*, lifeless.

inan'imated, *adj.*, spiritless.

inani'tion, *n.*, a state of emptiness.

inan'ity, *n.*, the state of being inane or empty; silliness.

inap'petence, *n.*, lack of desire.

inap'petency, *n.*, *i.q.* inappetence.

inapplicabil'ity, *n.*, the state or quality of being inapplicable.

inap'plicable, *adj.*, unable to be applied; irrelevant.

inapplica'tion, *n.*, indolence.

inap'posite, *adj.*, irrelevant, unsuited.

inappre'ciable, *adj.*, not appreciable.

inapprecia'tion, *n.*, lack of appreciation.

inappro'priate, *adj.*, not appropriate, unsuited.

inapt', *adj.*, not fit or apt.

inapt'itude, *n.*, the state of being inapt.

inapt'ly, *adv.*, in an inapt way.

inapt'ness, *n.*, *i.q.* inaptitude.

inarch', *v.t.*, to graft by drawing the branch of one tree to the stock of another.

inartic'ulate, *adj.*, not jointed; indistinct.

inartic'ulately, *adv.*, indistinctly.

inarticula'tion, *n.*, the state of being inarticulate.

inartis'tic, *adj.*, not artistic.

inasmuch', *adv.*, seeing that, considering.

inatten'tion, *n.*, want of attention, carelessness.

inatten'tive, *adj.*, not attentive, careless.

inatten'tively, *adv.*, carelessly.

inatten'tiveness, *n.*, the state of being inattentive.

inaudibil'ity, *n.*, the state or quality of being inaudible.

inaud'ible, *adj.*, unable to be heard.
inau'gural, *adj.*, rel. to inauguration.
inau'gurate, *v.t.*, to open with formality.
inau'gurated, *p.p.*, inaugurate.
inau'gurating, *pr.p.*, inaugurate.
inaugura'tion, *n.*, the act of inaugurating; inaugural ceremonies.
inau'gurator, *n.*, one who inaugurates.
inauspi'cious, *adj.*, not auspicious, unlucky, ill-omened.
inauspi'ciously, *adv.*, unluckily, with ill-omen.
in'born, *adj.*, innate.
inbreathe', *v.t.*, to inspire; draw in breath.
in'bred, *adj.*, bred in; natural.
in'ca, *n.*, a Peruvian chief or emperor.
incage', *v.t.*, to shut in a cage.
incal'culable, *adj.*, unable to be calculated.
incales'cence, *n.*, the state or quality of being incalescent.
incales'cency, *n.*, *i.q.* incalescence.
incales'cent, *adj.*, growing warm.
incandes'cence, *n.*, the state or quality of being incandescent.
incandes'cent, *adj.*, growing white.
incanta'tion, *n.*, the use of a magical formula; enchantment.
incan'tatory, *adj.*, enchanting.
incapabil'ity, *n.*, the state of being incapable.
inca'pable, *adj.*, not capable, lacking power or fitness.
incapac'itate, *v.t.*, to render incapable; to disqualify.
incapac'itated, *p.p.*, incapacitate.
incapac'itating, *pr.p.*, incapacitate.
incapac'ity, *n.*, want of power or fitness.

incar'cerate, *v.t.*, to imprison.
incar'cerated, *p.p.*, incarcerate.
incar'cerating, *pr.p.*, incarcerate.
incarcera'tion, *n.*, imprisonment.
incar'nadine, *v.t.*, to dye crimson.
incar'nate, *v.t.*, to embody in flesh.
incar'nate, *adj.*, united with humanity; embodied.
incar'nated, *p.p.*, incarnate.
incar'nating, *pr.p.*, incarnate.
incarna'tion, *n.*, the act of incarnating; an embodiment.
incase', *v.t.*, to shut in a case, surround.
incased', *p.p.*, incase.
incas'ing, *pr.p.*, incase.
incau'tious, *adj.*, not cautious, unwary.
incau'tiously, *adv.*, without caution.
incau'tiousness, *n.*, want of caution.
in'cavated, *adj.*, hollowed.
incava'tion, *n.*, the act or effect of hollowing.
incen'diarism, *n.*, the act of setting fire.
incen'diary, *n.*, one who sets property on fire.
in'cense, *n.*, a preparation of aromatic gums, spices, etc., producing, when burnt, a fragrant fume.
incense', *v.t.*, to kindle rage; to bless with incense.
incen'sive, *adj.*, provoking.
incen'tive, *adj.*, stimulating; *n.*, stimulus.
incep'tion, *n.*, a beginning.
incep'tive, *adj.*, initial.
incep'tor, *n.*, a Cambridge B.A. when qualified for the M.A. degree.
incera'tion, *n.*, the process of covering with or making into wax.

incer'titude, *n.*, the state of uncertainty.
inces'sancy, *n.*, the state of not ceasing.
inces'sant, *adj.*, not ceasing, continual.
inces'santly, *adv.*, unceasingly.
in'cest, *n.*, intercourse within the prohibited degrees.
inces'tuous, *adj.*, of the nature of incest.
inch, *v.t.*, to mark with lines at intervals of an inch; *n.*, the one-twelfth part of a foot; an island.
inch'meal, *adv.*, by inches.
in'choate, *adj.*, begun, not nearly complete.
in'choately, *adv.*, incompletely, initially.
inchoa'tion, *n.*, the act of beginning.
incho'ative, *adj.*, initial.
in'cidence, *n.*, a falling; occurrence.
in'cident, *adj.*, falling upon, happening; *n.*, something that happens.
inciden'tal, *adj.*, casual, happening.
inciden'tally, *adv.*, in an incidental way.
incin'erate, *v.t.*, to burn to ashes.
incin'erated, *p.p.*, incinerate.
incin'erating, *pr.p.*, incinerate.
incinera'tion, *n.*, the act of cremating.
incip'ience, *n.*, *i.q.* incipiency.
incip'iency, *n.*, the initial stage, beginning.
incip'ient, *adj.*, beginning.
incip'iently, *adv.*, initially.
incise', *v.t.*, to cut in, engrave.
incised', *p.p.*, incise.
inci'sing, *pr.p.*, incise.
inci'sion, *n.*, the act or effect of incising.
inci'sive, *adj.*, cutting in; penetrating; trenchant.
inci'sor, *adj.*, rel. to the incisors; *n.*, one of the front or cutting teeth.
inci'sory, *adj.*, *i.q.* incisive.

incis'ure, *n.*, *i.q.* incision.

incita'tion, *n.*, the act of inciting; an incentive.

incite', *v.t.*, to arouse, urge on.

inci'ted, *p.p.*, incite.

incite'ment, *n.*, *i.q.* incitation.

inci'ter, *n.*, anything that incites.

inci'ting, *pr.p.*, incite.

incivil'ity, *n.*, lack of civility; rudeness.

inclasp', *v.t.*, to clasp.

inclasped', *p.p.*, inclasp.

inclasp'ing, *pr.p.*, inclasp.

inclem'ency, *n.*, harshness, severity.

inclem'ent, *adj.*, harsh, severe.

incli'nable, *adj.*, able to be inclined.

inclina'tion, *n.*, the act of inclining; preference, leaning, liking.

incli'natory, *adj.*, leaning.

incline', *v.t.*, to cause to lean; *v.i.*, to lean, give approval to; *n.*, a slope.

inclined', *p.p.*, incline; *adj.*, disposed to.

incli'ner, *n.*, anything that inclines.

incli'ning, *pr.p.*, incline.

inclinom'eter, *n.*, an apparatus for measuring slope.

inclose', *v.t.*, to shut in, fence round. Also *enclose*.

inclosed', *p.p.*, inclose.

inclo'sing, *pr.p.*, inclose.

inclo'sure, *n*, the act of inclosing; an inclosed space.

include', *v.t.*, to shut in, contain, embrace.

inclu'ded, *p.p.*, include.

inclu'ding, *pr.p.*, include.

inclu'sion, *n.*, the act or effect of including.

inclu'sive, *adj.*, including.

inclu'sively, *adv.*, so as to include.

incoer'cible, *adj.*, not able to be coerced.

incog', *abbrev.* for *incognito*.

incog'nita, *n.*, fem. of incognito.

incog'nito, *adj.*, unknown, in an assumed character; *adv.*, in disguise; *n.*, an assumed character.

incog'nizable, *adj.*, not cognizable.

incog'nizance, *n.*, inability to understand.

incog'nizant, *adj.*, failing to understand.

incoher'ence, *n.*, confusion, want of connexion.

incoher'ency, *n.*, *i.q.* incoherence.

incoher'ent, *adj.*, not cohering, loose, rambling.

incoher'ently, *adv.*, without connexion.

incombustibil'ity, *n.*, the state or quality of being incombustible.

incombus'tible, *adj.*, unable to be burned.

in'come, *n.*, means of living; money coming in.

in'coming, *n.*, entrance; *adj.*, coming in.

incommensurabil'ity, *n.*, the quality of being incommensurable.

incommen'surable, *adj.*, having no common measure.

incommen'surate, *adj.*, *i.q.* incommensurable.

incommode', *v.t.*, to inconvenience, worry.

incommo'ded, *p.p.*, incommode.

incommo'ding, *pr.p.*, incommode.

incommo'dious, *adj.*, not commodious, inconvenient, too small.

incommunicabil'ity, *n.*, the quality of being incommunicable.

incommu'nicable, *adj.*, unable to be imparted.

incommu'nicative, *adj.*, not communicative; reserved.

incommu'table, *adj.*, not commutable.

incom'parable, *adj.*, above comparison; unequalled.

incom'parably, *adv.*, beyond comparison.

incompatibil'ity, *n.*, the state or quality of being incompatible.

incompat'ible, *adj.*, not compatible; inconsistent with.

incom'petence, *n.*, a state of being not competent.

incom'petency, *n.*, *i.q.* incompetence.

incom'petent, *adj.*, not competent; unqualified, unable.

incom'petently, *adv.*, in an incompetent way.

incomplete', *adj.*, not complete, unfinished, imperfect.

incomplete'ly, *adv.*, in an incomplete way.

incomplete'ness, *n.*, the state of being incomplete.

incom'posite, *adj.*, not composite.

incomprehensibil'ity, *n.*, the quality of being incomprehensible.

incomprehen'sible, *adj.*, without limitations of time, space, etc.; (this is the meaning of the word in the Athanasian Creed: "The Father incomprehensible," etc.); unintelligible.

incomprehen'sive, *adj.*, limited.

incompressibil'ity, *n.*, the state or quality of being incompressible.

incompress'ible, *adj.*, not able to be compressed.

incompu'table, *adj.*, not to be computed.

inconceiv'able, *adj.*, beyond conception; not intelligible.

inconclu'sive, *adj.*, leading to no decision.

inconclu'sively, *adv.*, without finality.
incondens'able, *adj.*, not able to be condensed.
incon'gruent, *adj.*, incongruous.
incongru'ity, *n.*, want of harmony with; inconsistency; anything incongruous.
incon'gruous, *adj.*, incompatible with, inconsistent; odd.
incon'gruously, *adv.*, in an incongruous way.
incon'sequence, *n.*, illogicality, inconsistency.
incon'sequent, *adj.*, illogical, inconsistent.
inconsequen'tial, *adj.*, inconsequent.
inconsid'erable, *adj.*, not to be considered; quite unimportant.
inconsid'erate, *adj.* wanting in consideration; thoughtless.
inconsid'erately, *adv.*, without consideration.
inconsidera'tion, *n.*, want of forethought.
inconsist'ency, *n.*, the state or quality of being inconsistent; disagreement of two things.
inconsist'ent, *adj.*, not logically or morally consistent.
inconsist'ently, *adv.*, not consistently.
inconsol'able, *adj.*, unable to be consoled.
incon'sonance, *n.*, want of consonance.
inconspic'uous, *adj.*, not conspicuous.
inconspic'uously, *adv.*, not noticeably.
incon'stancy, *n.*, want of constancy or firmness.
incon'stant, *adj.*, not constant; unstable; wanting uniformity.
incon'stantly, *adv.*, in an inconstant way.
inconsum'able, *adj.*, unable to be consumed.
incontest'able, *adj.*, indisputable.
incon'tinence, *n.*, lack of self-restraint; loss of power to retain.
incon'tinent, *adj.*, without self-restraint; unceasing; unable to retain.
incon'tinently, *adv.*, without restraint; straightway.
incontrol'lable, *adj.*, uncontrollable.
incontrovertibil'ity, *n.*, the state or quality of being incontrovertible.
incontrovert'ible, *adj.*, unable to be controverted or disproved.
inconve'nience, *v.t.* to give trouble to; *n.*, the state or quality of being inconvenient.
inconve'nienced, *p.p.*, inconvenience.
inconve'niencing, *pr.p.*, inconvenience.
inconve'nient, *adj.*, not convenient, unsuitable, causing trouble.
inconvertibil'ity, *n.*, the state of being inconvertible.
inconvert'ible, *adj.*, not exchangeable; incapable of being (logically) converted.
inco-or'dinate, *adj.*, not co-ordinate.
inco-ordina'tion, *n.*, the state of being inco-ordinate.
incor'porate, *adj.*, formed into one body; embodied; not material.
incor'porate, *v.t.*, to form into one body; to admit to a society; *v.i.*, to join a body or society.
incor'porated, *p.p.*, incorporate.
incor'porating, *pr.p.*, incorporate.
incorpora'tion, *n.*, the act of incorporating; association.
incorpo'real, *adj.*, having no body; immaterial.
incorpore'ity, *n.*, the quality of being incorporeal.
incorrect', *adj.*, not correct, irregular.
incorrect'ly, *adv.*, erroneously.
incorrect'ness, *n.*, the state or quality of being incorrect.
incorrigibil'ity, *n.*, the state of being incorrigible.
incor'rigible, *adj.*, not submitting to correction; hopelessly bad.
incor'rigibleness, *n.*, *i.q.* incorrigibility.
incor'rigibly, *adv.*, in an incorrigible way.
incorro'dible, *adj.*, unable to be corroded.
incorrupt', *adj.*, pure, sound, undecayed.
incorruptibil'ity, *n.*, the state or quality of being incorruptible.
incorrupt'ible, *adj.*, not able to be corrupted.
incorrup'tion, *n.*, the state of being incorrupt.
incorrupt'ness, *n.*, *i.q.* incorruption.
incras'sate, *adj.*, thickened.
incras'sate, *v.t.*, to make thicker; *v.i.*, to become thick.
incrassa'tion, *n.*, the state of being incrassate.
incras'sative, *adj.*, causing a thickening.
in'crease, *n.*, growth of all kinds.
increase', *v.t.*, to make greater in any way; *v.i.*, to become greater.
increased', *p.p.*, increase.
increas'er, *n.*, that which increases.
increas'ing, *pr.p.*, increase.
increas'ingly, *adv.*, in an increasing degree.
incredibil'ity, *n.*, the quality of being incredible.
incred'ible, *adj.*, beyond belief.
incred'ibly, *adv.*, beyond belief.
incredu'lity, *n.*, the state of being incredulous.

incred'ulous, *adj.*, not credulous; unwilling to believe; sceptical.

incred'ulousness, *n.*, *i.q.* incredulity.

in'crement, *n.*, increase, augmentation; increased value

incremen'tal, *adj.*, rel. to augmentation.

incrim'inate, *v.t.*, to accuse, involve in a charge.

incrim'inated, *p.p.*, incriminate.

incrim'inating, *pr.p.*, incriminate.

incrim'inatory, *adj.*, incriminating.

incrust', *v.t.*, to cover with a crust or coating; to apply decorative materials.

incrust'ate, *adj.*, incrusted.

incrusta'tion, *n.*, an outer coating or crust.

incrust'ed, *p.p.*, incrust.

incrust'ing, *pr.p.*, incrust.

in'cubate, *v.t.*, to sit on eggs for hatching; to meditate on; *v.i.*, to brood.

in'cubated, *p.p.*, incubate.

in'cubating, *pr.p.*, incubate.

in'cubation, *n.*, the act of incubating.

in'cubator, *n.*, a contrivance for hatching chickens or for rearing abnormally delicate children.

in'cubus, *n.*, an oppressive weight.

in'culcate, *v.t.*, to impress upon the mind, to teach.

in'culcated, *p.p.*, inculcate.

in'culcating, *pr.p.*, inculcate.

inculca'tion, *n.*, the act of inculcating.

incul'pable, *adj.*, blameless.

incul'pate, *v.t.*, to accuse, blame.

incul'pated, *p.p.*, inculpate.

incul'pating, *pr.p.*, inculpate.

inculpa'tion, *n.*, the act or effect of inculpating.

incul'patory, *adj.*, criminatory.

incum'bency, *n.*, the office of an incumbent; the period of an incumbent's tenure.

incum'bent, *adj.*, leaning or resting on; obligatory; *n.*, the holder of an official position, ecclesiastical, legal, etc.

incur', *v.t.*, to become liable to; to run into.

incurabil'ity, *n.*, the state of being incurable.

incur'able, *adj.*, past cure or remedy.

incur'ably, *adv.*, in an incurable way.

incu'rious, *adj.*, not curious; indifferent.

incu'riously, *adv.*, indifferently.

incurred', *p.p.*, incur.

incur'ring, *pr.p.*, incur.

incur'sion, *n.*, invasion, raid.

incur'sive, *adj.*, invading, aggressive.

incurv'ate, *adj.*, curved inward.

incurv'ate, *v.t.*, to curve, bend.

incurv'ated, *p.p.*, incurvate.

incurv'ating, *pr.p.*, incurvating.

incurva'tion, *n.*, the state of being bent.

incurve', *v.t.* and *i.*, to bend inward; to bend.

incurved', *p.p.*, incurve.

incurv'ing, *pr.p.*, incurve.

indebt'ed, *adj.*, under debt or obligation.

indebt'edness, *n.*, the state of being indebted.

inde'cency, *n.*, unseemliness, indelicacy.

inde'cent, *adj.*, unbecoming, unseemly, immoral.

inde'cently, *adv.*, in an indecent way.

indecid'uous, *adj.*, not deciduous; perennial.

indeci'pherable, *adj.*, unable to be deciphered.

indeci'sion, *n.*, lack of decision; hesitation.

indeci'sive, *adj.*, uncertain, not final.

indeci'sively, *adv.*, in an indecisive way.

indecli'nable, *adj.*, not able to be declined.

indeco'rous, *adj.*, not decorous; unseemly.

indeco'rousness, *n.*, unseemliness.

indeco'rum, *n.*, impropriety.

indeed', *adv.*, truly, really; *interj.*, expressing surprise or doubt.

indefatigabil'ity, *n.*, the quality of being untiring.

indefat'igable, *adj.*, untiring.

indefat'igably, *adv.*, untiringly.

indefeasibil'ity, *n.*, the state or quality of being indefeasible.

indefea'sible, *adj.*, unable to be made void or defeated.

indefensibil'ity, *n.*, the quality of being indefensible.

indefen'sible, *adj.*, not to be defended.

indefen'sibly, *adv.*, in an indefensible way.

indefin'able, *adj.*, not able to be defined.

indefin'ably, *adv.*, in a way not to be defined.

indef'inite, *adj.*, not defined, indistinct, vague.

indef'initely, *adv.*, in an indefinite way.

indef'initeness, *n.*, the state or quality of being indefinite.

indelibil'ity, *n.*, the quality of being indelible.

indel'ible, *adj.*, unable to be erased or blotted out.

indel'ibly, *adv.*, in an indelible way.

indel'icacy, *n.*, want of delicacy or refinement.

indel'icate, *adj.*, unrefined, improper.

indel'icately, *adv.*, in an indelicate way.

indemnifica'tion, *n.*, the act of indemnifying.

indem'nified, *p.p.*, indemnify.

indem'nify, *v.t.*, to give compensation or security.

indem'nifying, *pr.p.*, indemnify.

indem'nity, *n.*, compensation; security; legal exemption from liability.

indent', *v.t.*, to notch; to begin a printed line short by the space of a word; to apprentice; *n.*, a notch, cut; an order for goods.

indenta'tion, *n.*, a small depression.

indent'ed, *adj.*, notched; apprenticed; *p.p.*, indent.

indent'ing, *pr.p.*, indent.

inden'ture, *n.*, a contract in writing; apprenticeship.

independ'ence, *n.*, the state of being independent.

independ'ent, *adj.*, not depending on; free; in easy circumstances.

independ'ently, *adv.*, separately.

indescri'bable, *adj.*, unable to be described.

indescri'bably, *adv.*, beyond description.

indestructibil'ity, *n.*, the quality of being indestructible.

indestruc'tible, *adj.*, not able to be destroyed.

indeter'minable, *adj.*, not able to be determined or classified.

indeter'minate, *adj.*, not determined, not precise.

indeter'minately, *adv.*, not precisely.

indetermina'tion, *n.*, hesitation, want of decision.

indevout', *adj.*, not devout.

in'dex, *v.t.*, to furnish with an index; *n.*, a pointer, sign, forefinger; an alphabetic table of entries.

in'dexed, *p.p.*, index.

in'dexer, *n.*, one who indexes.

in'dexes, *n.*, pl. of index.

index'ical, *adj.*, rel. to an index.

in'dexing, *pr.p.*, index.

indexter'ity, *n.*, lack of dexterity.

In'diaman, *n.*, a ship that trades with India.

In'dian, *adj.*, bel. to India; *n.*, a native of India.

in'dia-rub'ber, *n.*, caoutchouc.

in'dicate, *v.t.*, to point out, show.

in'dicated, *p.p.*, indicate.

in'dicating, *pr.p.*, indicate.

indica'tion, *n.*, the act or result of indicating; sign.

indic'ative, *adj.*, indicating, showing; *n.*, the indicative mood.

indic'atively, *adv.*, significantly.

in'dicator, *n.*, anything that indicates.

in'dicatory, *adj.*, showing.

ind'ices, *n. pl.*, figures or numbers indicating the power of a number.

indict', *v.t.*, to lay a charge against.

indict'able, *adj.*, liable to a charge.

indict'ed, *p.p.*, indict.

indict'er, *n.*, one who indicts.

indict'ing, *pr.p.*, indict.

indic'tion, *n.*, a period of fifteen years.

indict'ment, *n.*, a charge, accusation.

in*dif'ference*, *n.*, impartiality; unconcern.

in*dif'ferent*, *adj.*, impartial; unconcerned, not interested; passable.

in*dif'ferentism*, *n.*, the view that all religions are of equal merit.

in*dif'ferently*, *adv.*, impartially; passably.

in'digence, *n.*, the state of being indigent.

in'digene, *n.*, a native.

indig'enous, *adj.*, native to the soil.

in'digent, *adj.*, poor, needy.

indigest'ed, *adj.*, not digested.

indigestibil'ity, *n.*, the quality of being indigestible.

indigest'ible, *adj.*, not easy to be digested; unwholesome.

indiges'tion, *n.*, dyspepsia; inability to digest.

indig'nant, *adj.*, scornfully angry.

indig'nantly, *adv.*, angrily.

indigna'tion, *n.*, scornful anger.

indig'nity, *n.*, an undeserved slight; an insult.

in'digo, *adj.*, of the colour of indigo; *n.*, a vegetable dye; violet-blue.

indigom'eter, *n.*, an appliance for testing the strength of an indigo solution.

in'digotin, *n.*, the pure indigo.

indirect', *adj.*, not direct, misleading.

indirec'tion, *n.*, *i.q.* indirectness.

indirect'ly, *adv.*, not directly; through some other's intervention.

indirect'ness, *n.*, the state of being indirect.

indiscern'ible, *adj.*, not discernible, imperceptible.

indiscern'ibly, *adv.*, imperceptibly.

indis'cipline, *n.*, lack of discipline.

indiscreet', *adj.*, foolish, wanting in forethought.

indiscreet'ly, *adv.*, injudiciously.

indiscrete', *adj.*, not separate.

indiscre'tion, *n.*, want of forethought, imprudence; an act of imprudence.

indiscrim'inate, *adj.*, without distinction; promiscuous.

indiscrim'inately, *adv.*, promiscuously.

indiscrimina'tion, *n.*, want of discriminating power.

indispen'sable, *adj.* unable to be done without; completely necessary.

indispen'sably, *adv.*, necessarily.

indispose', *v.t.*, to turn one against; to disincline; to make unwell.

indisposed', *p.p.*, indispose; *adj.*, unwell.

indisposi'tion, *n.*, disinclination; a slight illness.

indis'putable, *adj.*, beyond dispute.

indis'putably, *adv.*, beyond dispute.

indissolubil'ity, *n.*, the quality of being indissoluble.

indis'soluble, *adj.*, not able to be dissolved or broken.

indis'solubly, *adv.*, in an indissoluble way.

indissol'vable, *adj.*, *i.q.* indissoluble.

indistinct', *adj.*, not distinct, obscure.

indistinct'ly, *adv.*, not distinctly.

indistinct'ness, *n.*, obscurity, faintness.

in*distin'guish*able, *adj.*, not to be distinguished.

indite', *v.t.*, to write, compose.

indi'ted, *p.p.*, indite.

indite'ment, *n.*, a composition.

indi'ter, *n.*, one who indites.

indi'ting, *pr.p.*, indite.

individ'ual, *adj.*, single, not divided, distinct; *n.*, a single object or person.

individ'ualism, *n.*, the political theory that the individual's rights are paramount; personal individual freedom.

individual'ity, *n.*, separate existence; distinctive character.

individualiza'tion, *n.*, the act of individualizing.

individ'ualize, *v.t.*, to distinguish from other persons or things.

individ'ualized, *p.p.*, individualize.

individ'ualizing, *pr.p.*, individualize.

individ'ually, *n.*, separately, one by one.

indivisibil'ity, *n.*, the quality of being indivisible.

indivis'ible, *adj.*, not able to be divided.

indo'cile, *adj.*, unteachable.

indocil'ity, *n.*, unteachableness.

indoc'trinate, *v.t.*, to instruct, acquaint.

indoc'trinated, *p.p.*, indoctrinate.

indoc'trinating, *pr.p.*, indoctrinate.

indoctrina'tion, *n.*, instruction.

in'dolence, *n.*, laziness, idleness.

in'dolent, *adj.*, lazy, idle.

in'dolently, *adv.*, lazily.

indom'itable, *adj.*, not to be subdued.

in'door, *adj.*, at home, within doors.

indoors', *adv.*, in or into a building.

indors'able, *adj.*, able to be indorsed.

indorse', *v.t.*, to sign on the back; approve, sanction. Also *endorse.*

indorsed', *p.p.*, indorse.

indorsee', *n.*, one in whose favour indorsement is made.

indorse'ment, *n.*, the signing on the back of a document; sanction, approval.

indors'er, *n.*, one who indorses.

indors'ing, *pr.p.*, indorse.

in'draught, *n.*, an inward flow of air, water, etc.

in'drawn, *adj.*, drawn in.

indu'bitable, *adj.*, beyond doubt, certain.

indu'bitably, *adv.*, certainly.

induce', *v.t.*, to lead on, persuade, cause.

induced', *p.p.*, induce.

induce'ment, *n.*, that which induces or persuades.

indu'cer, *n.*, one who induces.

indu'cible, *adj.*, able to be induced.

indu'cing, *pr.p.*, induce.

induct', *v.t.*, to put in possession, esp. to put a priest into the real, actual, and corporal possession of a church.

induct'ed, *p.p.*, induct.

induct'ile, *adj.*, not ductile.

inductil'ity, *n.*, the quality of being inductile.

induct'ing, *pr.p.*, induct.

induc'tion, *n.*, the ceremony of inducting; reasoning from particulars to general conclusions; a conclusion so arrived at; the causing of magnetization or electrification by means of a magnetized or electrified body not in contact with it.

induc'tive, *adj.*, rel. to induction.

induc'tively, *adv.*, by induction.

inductom'eter, *n.*, an apparatus measuring electric inductivity.

induct'or, *n.*, one who inducts.

indue', *v.t.*, to endow; to clothe. Also *endue.*

indued', *p.p.*, indue.

indu'ing, *pr.p.*, indue.

indulge', *v.t.*, to humour, gratify; *v.i.*, to yield to.

indulged', *p.p.*, indulge.

indul'gence, *n.*, the act of indulging; a favour granted; remission of temporal punishment.

indul'gent, *adj.*, exceedingly kind; readily yielding.

indul'gently, *adv.*, in an indulgent way.

indul'ging, *pr.p.*, indulge.

in'durate, *v.t.*, to harden; *v.i.*, to become hard.

in'durated, *p.p.*, indurate.

in'durating, *pr.p.*, indurate.

indura'tion, *n.*, hardening.

indus'trial, *adj.*, rel. to industry.

indus'trious, *adj.*, diligent, hard-working.

indus'triously, *adv.*, diligently.

in'dustry, *n.*, steady, hard work; a branch of trade.

in'dwelling, *adj.*, abiding or residing in.

ine'briant, *adj.*, intoxicating; *n.*, an intoxicant.

ine'briate, *v.t.*, to make drunk.

ine'briate, *adj.*, drunken; *n.*, a drunkard.

ine'briated, *p.p.*, inebriate.

ine'briating, *pr.p.*, inebriate.

inebria'tion, *n.*, the state of being drunk.

inebri'ety, *n.*, drunkenness.

ined'ited, *adj.*, not published; unrevised.

inef'fable, *adj.*, unspeakable, inexpressible.

inef'fableness, *n.*, the quality of being ineffable.

inef'fably, *adv.*, unspeakable.

ineffface'able, *adj.*, not to be effaced.

ineffec'tive, *adj.*, not effective.

ineffect'ual, *adj.*, not effective, unavailing.

ineffect'ually, *adv.*, without effect.

ineffica'cious, *adj.*, not efficacious.

inef'ficacy, *n.*, the state or quality of being inefficacious.

ineffi'ciency, *n.*, the state or quality of being inefficient.

ineffi'cient, *adj.*, lacking ability; not achieving an object.

ineffi'ciently, *adv.*, in an inefficient way.

inelas'tic, *adj.*, not elastic.

inelastic'ity, *n.*, want of elasticity.

inel'egance, *n.*, want of elegance or refinement.

inel'egant, *adj.*, wanting in elegance.

inel'egantly, *adv.*, in an inelegant way.

ineligibil'ity, *n.*, the quality of being ineligible.

inel'igible, *adj.*, not eligible; not qualified.

inept', *adj.*, unfit, foolish, inexpert.

inept'itude, *n.*, unfitness, foolishness.

inept'ly, *adv.*, in an inept way.

inept'ness, *n.*, *i.q.* ineptitude.

inequal'ity, *n.*, want of equality; unevenness; injustice.

ineq'uitable, *adj.*, not equitable; unjust.

inerad'icable, *adj.*, not to be eradicated.

inerrabil'ity, *n.*, the quality of being infallible.

inerr'able, *adj.*, incapable of error; infallible.

iner'rancy, *n.*, the quality of being inerrant.

iner'rant, *n.*, not erring; infallible.

inert', *adj.*, inactive, apathetic.

iner'tia, *n.*, sluggishness, inactivity.

inert'ly, *adv.*, sluggishly, inactively.

inert'ness, *n.*, the state of being inert.

inessen'tial, *adj.*, not essential. Also *unessential.*

ines'timable, *adj.*, beyond price; very valuable.

ines'timably, *adv.*, beyond reckoning.

inev'itable, *adv.*, not to be avoided.

inev'itably, *adv.*, unavoidably.

inexact', *adj.*, not exact, inaccurate.

inexact'ness, *n.*, inaccuracy.

inexcus'able, *adj.*, without excuse.

inexcu'sableness, *n.*, the state or quality of being inexcusable.

inexcu'sably, *adv.*, without excuse.

inexhaust'ible, *adj.*, not to be exhausted.

inexhaust'ibly, *adv.*, in an inexhaustible degree.

inex'orable, *adj.*, not to be won by entreaty; relentless.

inex'orably, *adv.*, relentlessly.

inexpe'diency, *n.*, unfitness, unadvisability.

inexpe'dient, *n.*, unadvisable, unfit.

inexpen'sive, *adj.*, not costly.

inexpe'rience, *n.*, lack of experience.

inexpe'rienced, *adj.*, without experience.

inexpert', *adj.*, not expert, unskilful.

inex'piable, *adj.*, past atoning for.

inex'plicable, *adj.*, not to be explained.

inex'plicably, *adv.*, past explanation.

inexplic'it, *adj.*, not distinctly expressed.

inexpress'ible, *adj.*, not to be told or uttered.

inexpress'ibly, *adv.*, beyond telling.

inexpress'ive, *adj.*, without significance.

inexpug'nable, *adj.*, not to be controverted.

inextin'guishable, *adj.*, unquenchable.

inex'tricable, *adj.*, unable to be disentangled.

inex'tricably, *adv.*, beyond disentangling.

infallibil'ity, *n.*, exemption from error.

infal'lible, *adj.*, incapable of error.

infal'libly, *adv.*, with absolute certainty.

in'famous, *adj.*, notoriously bad, disgraceful.

in'famously, *adv.*, disgracefully.

in'famy, *n.*, public disgrace, ignominy.

in'fancy, *n.*, the period of childhood; beginning.
in'fant, *n.*, a babe; one under the legal full age of 21 years.
infan'ta, *n.*, fem. of infante.
infan'te, *n.*, a Spanish or Portuguese prince.
infan'ticide, *n.*, child-murder.
in'fantile, *adj.*, child-like, rel. to children.
in'fantine, *adj.*, *i.q.* infantile.
in'fantry, *n.*, foot-soldiers.
infat'uate, *v.t.*, to affect with folly or passion.
infat'uated, *p.p.*, infatuate.
infat'uating, *pr.p.*, infatuate.
infatua'tion, *n.*, the state of being infatuated.
infect', *v.t.*, to taint, corrupt.
infect'ed, *p.p.*, infect.
infect'ing, *pr.p.*, infect.
infec'tion, *n.*, the act of infecting; pollution; the communication of disease.
infec'tious, *adj.*, spreading infection.
infec'tiously, *adv.*, in an infectious way.
infec'tiousness, *n.*, the character of being infectious.
infecun'dity, *n.*, barrenness.
infeft'ment, *n.*, the symbolical transfer of property.
infelic'itous, *adj.*, not felicitous, unfortunate.
infelicity, *n.*, misfortune, inappropriateness.
infer', *v.t.*, to draw a conclusion.
infer'able, *adj.*, capable of being inferred.
in'ference, *n.*, a deduction or conclusion.
inferen'tial, *adj.*, of the nature of an inference.
infe'rior, *adj.*, lower (in any relation).
inferior'ity, *n.*, the state or quality of being inferior; subordination.
infer'nal, *adj.*, bel. to the lower regions; outrageous.
infer'nally, *adv.*, outrageously.
infer'no, *n.*, the place or state of torment.
infer'rable, *adj.*, able to be inferred.
inferred', *p.p.*, infer.
infer'ring, *pr.p.*, infer.
infer'tile, *adj.*, not fertile.
infertil'ity, *n.*, barrenness.
infest', *v.t.*, to harass, overrun.
infesta'tion, *n.*, the act of infesting or overrunning.
infest'ed, *p.p.*, infest.
infest'er, *n.*, an invader.
infest'ing, *pr.p.*, infest.
in'fidel, *n.*, an unbeliever; an enemy to the Christian faith; *adj.*, unbelieving.
infidel'ity, *n.*, unfaithfulness; disbelief.
infil'trate, *v.t.*, to penetrate through pores.
infil'trated, *p.p.*, infiltrate.
infil'trating, *pr.p.*, infiltrate.
infiltra'tion, *n.*, the act of infiltrating; something that infiltrates.
in'finite, *adj.*, not bounded by space or time.
in'finitely, *adv.*, without limit.
in'finiteness *n.*, the state of the infinite; immensity.
infinites'imal, *adj.*, infinitely minute; *n.*, a quantity infinitesimally small.
infinites'imally, *adv.*, in infinitesimal degree.
infin'itive, *n.*, the infinitive mood.
infin'itude, *n.*, infinity.
infin'ity, *n.*, the state of being infinite; an infinite quantity.
infirm', *adj.*, weak, shaky.
infir'mary, *n.*, a house for the sick and infirm.
infir'mity, *n.*, the state of being infirm; a complaint; a fault.
infirm'ly, *adj.*, weakly.
infix', *v.t.*, to fix in; insert.
inflame', *v.t.*, to set on fire, kindle, excite.
inflamed', *p.p.*, inflame.
infla'ming, *pr.p.*, inflame.
inflammabil'ity, *n.*, the quality of being inflammable.
inflam'mable, *adj.*, capable of being inflamed.
inflamma'tion, *n.*, heated action of the blood, causing swelling, redness, and pain.
inflam'matory, *adj.*, producing inflammation; tending to passion, sedition, etc.
infla'table, *adj.*, able to be inflated.
inflate', *v.t.*, to fill with wind or breath; to elate; to raise prices artificially.
infla'ted, *p.p.*, inflate.
infla'ter, *n.*, anything that inflates.
infla'ting, *pr.p.*, inflate.
infla'tion, *n.*, the act or effect of inflating.
infla'tionary, *adj.*, producing inflation.
inflect', *v.t.*, to bend; to vary a noun or verb; to modulate the voice.
inflect'ed, *p.p.*, inflect.
inflec'tion, inflex'ion, *n.*, bending; modulation of the voice; the variations of the noun or verb.
inflec'tional, *adj.*, rel. to inflection.
inflec'tive, *adj.*, capable of bending.
inflexed', *adj.*, bent.
inflexibil'ity, *n.*, firmness, stiffness.
inflex'ible, *adj.*, unable to be bent, stiff; immovable.

inflex'ibly, *adv.*, firmly.

inflict', *v.t.*, to impose.

inflict'ed, *p.p.*, inflict.

inflict'ing, *pr.p.*, inflict.

inflic'tion, *n.*, the act of inflicting; calamity.

inflores'cence, *n.*, the general arrangement of blossoms.

in'fluence, *v.t.*, to affect, to modify, to bias; *n.*, favour, authority, sway.

in'fluenced, *p.p.*, influence.

in'fluencing, *pr.p.*, influence.

in'fluential, *adj.*, having influence or power.

influen'tially, *adv.*, in an influential way.

influen'za, *n.*, a catarrh (often epidemic).

in'flux, *n.*, a flowing into; infusion.

infold', *v.t.*, to envelop, clasp.

infold'ed, *p.p.*, infold.

infold'ing, *pr.p.*, infold.

inform', *v.t.*, to instruct, acquaint.

inform'al, *adj.*, unofficial, unceremonious.

informal'ity, *n.*, absence of formality.

inform'ally, *adv.*, in an informal way.

inform'ant, *n.*, one who gives information.

informa'tion, *n.*, intelligence given; instruction.

informed', *p.p.*, inform.

inform'er, *n.*, one who lays an information before a magistrate; a spy.

inform'ing, *pr.p.*, inform; *adj.*, instructive.

infract', *v.t.*, to make a breach in.

infrac'tion, *n.*, a breach, violation, infringement.

infran'gible, *adj.*, unbreakable; inviolable.

infre'quence, *n.*, rareness.

infre'quency, *n.*, *i.q.* infrequence.

infre'quent, *adj.*, rarely occurring, uncommon.

infringe', *v.t.*, to break in upon, violate.

infringed', *p.p.*, infringe.

infringe'ment, *n.*, the act of infringing; a breach.

infrin'ger, *n.*, one who infringes.

infrin'ging, *pr.p.*, infringe.

infruc'tuous, *adj.*, unfruitful.

infu'riate, *v.t.*, to rouse to fury; *adj.*, mad, raging.

infu'riated, *p.p.*, infuriate.

infu'riating, *pr.p.*, infuriate.

infuse', *v.t.*, to pour in, instil, make an infusion of.

infused', *p.p.*, infuse.

infu'ser, *n.*, one who infuses.

infusibil'ity, *n.*, state of being able to be infused.

infu'sible, *adj.*, capable of being infused.

infu'sing, *pr.p.*, infuse.

infu'sion, *n.*, the act of infusing; an extract made by steeping in liquid without boiling.

Infuso'ria, *n. pl.*, microscopic beings developed in infusions.

infuso'rial, *adj.*, rel. to Infusoria.

infu'sory, *adj.*, *i.q.* infusorial.

in'gather, *v.t.*, to harvest, gather in.

in'gathering, *pr.p.*, ingather; *n.*, the harvest.

inge'nious, *adj.*, clever, inventive.

inge'niously, *adv.*, cleverly.

inge'niousness, *n.*, cleverness, ingenuity.

ingénue', *n.*, an artless maiden.

ingenu'ity, *n.*, cleverness, inventiveness.

ingen'uous, *adj.*, natural, open, sincere.

ingen'uously, *adv.*, frankly, sincerely.

ingen'uousness, *n.*, frankness, naturalness.

ingest', *v.t.*, to take into the stomach.

inges'ta, *n. pl.*, food; things taken into the stomach.

inges'tion, *n.*, the act of taking in food.

in'gle, *n.*, the fireside.

inglo'rious, *adj.*, ignominious.

inglo'riously, *adv.*, ignominiously.

in'got, *n.*, a mass of cast metal.

ingraft', *v.t.*, to propagate by incision.

ingraft'ed, *p.p.*, ingraft.

ingraft'ing, *pr.p.*, ingraft.

ingraft'ment, *n.*, the act of ingrafting.

ingrain', *v.t.*, to dye deeply; to infix deeply.

ingrained', *p.p.*, ingrain.

ingrain'ing, *pr.p.*, ingrain.

in'grate, *n.*, a thankless person.

ingra'tiate, *v.t.*, to secure favour with some one.

ingra'tiated, *p.p.*, ingratiate.

ingra'tiating, *pr.p.*, ingratiate.

ingrat'itude, *n.*, unthankfulness.

ingre'dient, *n.*, part of a mixture.

in'gress, *n.*, entrance.

in'growing, *adj.*, growing inwards.

in'growth, *n.*, the act of growing inwards.

in'guinal, *adj.*, rel. to the groin.

ingulf', *v.t.*, to swallow up. Also *engulf.*

ingulfed', *p.p.*, ingulf.

ingulf'ing, *pr.p.*, ingulf.

ingur'gitate, *v.t.*, to swallow down; to guzzle.

ingurgita'tion, *n.*, a swallowing down, engulfing.

inhab'it, *v.t.*, to dwell in, occupy.
inhab'itable, *adj.*, fit to be dwelt in.
inhab'itancy, *n.*, residence, occupancy.
inhab'itant, *n.*, one who inhabits; a resident.
inhabita'tion, *n.*, permanent residence.
inhab'ited, *p.p.*, inhabit.
inhab'iter, *n.*, one who inhabits.
inhab'iting, *pr.p.*, inhabit.
inhab'itiveness, *n.*, love of home and country.
inhala'tion, *n.*, the act of inhaling; inspiration.
inhale', *v.t.*, to draw into the lungs.
inhaled', *p.p.*, inhale.
inha'ler, *n.*, an instrument for inhaling.
inha'ling, *pr.p.*, inhale.
inharmon'ic, *adj.*, discordant.
inharmo'nious, *adj.*, *i.q.* inharmonic.
inharmo'niously, *adv.*, discordantly.
inharmo'niousness, *n.*, unmusicalness, discordance.
inhere', *v.i.*, to be fixed or incorporated in.
inhered', *p.p.*, inhere.
inher'ence, *n.*, the state of inhering.
inher'ency, *n.*, *i.q.* inherence.
inher'ent, *adj.*, inhering.
inher'ently, *adv.*, innately.
inher'it, *v.t.*, to receive by descent or birth or legacy.
inher'itable, *adj.*, capable of being inherited.
inher'itance, *n.*, the act of inheriting; something inherited.
inher'ited, *p.p.*, inherit.
inher'iting, *pr.p.*, inherit.
inher'itor, *n.*, one who inherits.
inher'itrix, *n.*, fem. of inheritor.
inhib'it, *v.t.*, to restrain, hinder.
inhib'ited, *p.p.*, inhibit.
inhib'iting, *pr.p.*, inhibit.
inhibi'tion, *n.*, the act of inhibiting.
inhib'itory, *adj.*, forbidding, restraining.
inhos'pitable, *adj.*, not hospitable, unfriendly.
inhos'pitably, *adv.*, in an inhospitable manner.
inhospital'ity, *n.*, the lack of hospitality.
inhu'man, *adj.*, lacking humanity, cruel.
inhu'manly, *adv.*, cruelly.
inhuman'ity, *n.*, lack of humanity; cruelty.
inhuma'tion, *n.*, the act of burying.
inhume', *v.t.*, to bury, inter.
inhumed', *p.p.*, inhume.
inhu'ming, *pr.p.*, inhume.
inim'ical, *adj.*, unfriendly, hostile.
inim'ically, *adv.*, in an unfriendly way.
inim'itable, *adj.*, not to be imitated; unequalled.
inim'itably, *adv.*, in an inimitable way.
iniq'uitous, *adj.*, unjust, wicked.
iniq'uity, *n.*, injustice, wickedness.
ini'tial, *adj.*, beginning, inceptive; *n.*, a letter beginning a word; *v.t.*, to write one's initials on.
ini'tialled,-led, *p.p.*, initial.
ini'tialling, *pr.p.*, initial.
ini'tially, *adv.*, at the beginning.
ini'tiate, *v.t.*, to begin; to admit to an order, mystery, etc.
ini'tiate, *n.*, a novice.
ini'tiated, *p.p.*, initiate.
ini'tiating, *pr.p.*, initiate.
initia'tion, *n.*, the act of initiating; first admission.
ini'tiative, *adj.*, beginning; *n.*, a beginning; capacity for taking the first step.
ini'tiatory, *adj.*, introducing.
inject', *v.t.*, to throw into.
inject'ed, *p.p.*, inject.
inject'ing, *pr.p.*, inject.
injec'tion, *n.*, the act of injecting; something injected.
injudi'cious, *adj.*, indiscreet, unwise.
injudi'ciously, *adv.*, unwisely.
injunc'tion, *n.*, a command, behest; a restraining writ.
in'jure, *v.t.*, to hurt, do harm to.
in'jured, *p.p.*, injure.
in'jurer, *n.*, one who injures.
in'juring, *pr.p.*, injure.
inju'rious, *adj.*, causing injury.
inju'riously, *adv.*, harmfully.
in'jury, *n.*, mischief, hurt.
injus'tice, *n.*, violation of right.
ink, *v.t.*, to smear with ink.
ink'-horn, *n.*, an old receptacle for ink.
ink'iness, *n.*, the state of being inky.
ink'ling, *n.*, a hint.
ink'stand, *n.*, a stand for ink-bottles.
ink'y, *adj.*, smeared with ink; black.
inlace', *v.t.*, to lace; to ornament with lace.
inlaced', *p.p.*, inlace.
inla'cing, *pr.p.*, inlace.
inlaid, *p.p.*, inlay.
in'land, *adj.* and *adv.*, interior; away from the sea; *n.*, the interior of a country.
in'lander, *n.*, an inland inhabitant.
inlay', *v.t.*, to decorate with wood, ivory, etc.
in'lay, *n.*, inlaying material.
in'layer, *n.*, one who inlays.
inlay'ing, *pr.p.*, inlay; *n.*, the art of inlaying.
inlet', *v.t.*, to insert.
in'let, *n.*, a small bay; creek.

in'ly, *adv.*, inwardly.
in'mate, *n.*, a lodger; a dweller in.
in'most, *adj.* deepest within: innermost.
inn, *n.*, a place for entertaining travellers; a legal society.
innate', *adj.*, inborn, inbred.
innate'ly, *adv.*, naturally, inherently.
innate'ness, *n.*, the quality of being innate.
innav'igable, *adj.*, inaccessible to ships.
in'ner, *adj.*, interior.
in'ner*most*, *adj.*, inmost, deepest within.
inner'vate, *v.t.*, to give nervous stimulation to.
innerva'tion, *n.*, the disposition of the nervous system; nervous stimulus.
innerve', *v.t.*, to invigorate; give nervous stimulus to.
innerved', *p.p.*, innerve.
innerv'ing, *pr.p.*, innerve.
in'nings, *n.*, the period in which players are said to be in.
inn'keeper, *n.*, the keeper of an inn.
in'nocence, *n.*, harmlessness, guiltlessness, simplicity.
in'nocency, *n.*, *i.q.* innocence.
in'nocent, *adj.*, harmless, guiltless, simple.
in'nocently, *adv.*, in an innocent way.
innoc'uous, *adj.*, not hurtful.
innoc'uously, *adv.*, harmlessly.
innom'inate, *adj.*, nameless.
in'novate, *v.i.*, to introduce a change.
in'novated, *p.p.*, innovate.
in'novating, *pr.p.*, innovate.
innova'tion, *n.*, a novelty.
in'novator, *n.*, one who innovates.
innox'ious, *adj.*, harmless, safe.
innox'iously, *adv.*, harmlessly.

innuen'do, *n.*, an insinuation.
innu'merable, *adj.*, countless.
innu'merably, *adv.*, without number.
innu'merous, *adj.*, *i.q.* innumerable
innutri'tion, *n.*, the state of being innutritious.
innutri'tious, *adj.*, not nourishing.
innu'tritive, *adj.*, *i.q.* innutritious.
inobtru'sive, *adj.*, unobtrusive.
inobtru'sively, *adv.*, unobtrusively.
inobtru'siveness, *n.*, unobtrusiveness.
inoc'ulate, *v.t.*, to propagate by grafting; to vaccinate.
inoc'ulated, *p.p.*, inoculate.
inoc'ulating, *pr.p.*, inoculate.
inocula'tion, *n.*, the act of inoculating.
inoc'ulator, *n.*, one who inoculates.
ino'dorous, *adj.*, scentless, without smell.
inoffen'sive, *adj.*, harmless.
inoffen'sively, *adv.*, harmlessly.
inop'erative, *adj.*, not working; without effect.
inopportune', *adj.*, untimely; inconvenient.
inopportune'ly, *adv.*, in an inopportune way.
inor'dinate, *adj.*, irregular, immoderate.
inor'dinately, *adv.*, excessively.
inorgan'ic, *adj.*, not organic; without organs.
inos'culate, *v.t.*, to unite by contact.
inoscula'tion, *n.*, the act or effect of inosculating.
in'quest, *n.*, a judicial inquiry.
inqui'etude, *n.*, uneasiness, a disturbed state.
inquire', *v.i.* and *t.*, to ask, to make investigation. Also *enquire.*

inquired', *p.p.*, inquire.
inquiren'do, *n.*, power to hold inquiry (*leg.*)
inquir'er, *n.*, one who inquires.
inquir'ing, *pr.p.*, inquire.
inquir'y, *n.*, examination, investigation.
inquisi'tion, *n.*, a judicial examination; inspection.
inquisi'tional, *adj.*, rel. to an inquisition.
inquis'itive, *adj.*, curious, prying.
inquis'itively, *adv.*, curiously, in a prying way.
inquis'itiveness, *n.*, prying curiosity.
inquis'itor, *n.*, one who holds an inquisition.
inquisito'rial, *adj.*, in the manner of an inquisitor.
inquisito'rially, *adv.*, in an inquisitorial manner.
in'road, *n.*, an incursion, breach.
in'rush, *n.*, a rushing in.
insaliva'tion, *n.*, the action of saliva.
insalu'brious, *adj.*, unhealthy.
insalu'brity, *n.*, unhealthiness.
insal'utary, *adj.*, not salutary.
insane', *adj.*, out of the mind, mad.
insane'ly, *adv.*, like a madman.
insan'ity, *adj.*, madness.
insatiabil'ity, *n.*, the quality of being insatiable.
insa'tiable, *adj.*, never satisfied, greedy.
insa'tiableness, *n.*, *i.q.* insatiability.
insa'tiably, *adv.*, in an insatiable way.
insa'tiate, *adj.*, *i.q.* insatiable.
insa'tiately, *adv.*, *i.q.* insatiably.
insati'ety, *n.*, *i.q.* insatiableness.
inscribe', *v.t.*, to write on; to dedicate.
inscribed', *p.p.*, inscribe.

inscri'ber, *n.*, one who inscribes.
inscri'bing, *pr.p.*, inscribe.
inscrip'tion, *n.*, that which is inscribed.
inscrip'tive, *adj.*, inscribed.
inscroll', *v.t.*, to enter on a scroll.
inscrutabil'ity, *n.*, the quality of being inscrutable.
inscru'table, *adj.*, past finding out.
inseam', *v.t.*, to mark with a seam.
in'sect, *n.*, a small creeping or flying animal of the Insecta class.
insecta'rium, *n.*, a collection of insects for observation.
insec'ticide, *n.*, a poison for insects.
in'sectile, *adj.*, rel. to insects.
insec'tion, *n.*, incision.
insectiv'orous, *adj.*, devouring insects.
insecure', *adj.*, not secure, unsafe.
insecure'ly, *adv.*, unsafely.
insecu'rity, *n.*, danger.
insem'inate, *v.t.*, to impregnate.
insemina'tion, *n.*, impregnation.
insen'sate, *adj.*, lacking perception, mad.
in*sensibil'ity*, *n.* apathy; the state of being insensible.
in*sen'sible*, *adj.*, incapable of feeling; senseless.
in*sen'sibly*, *adv.*, in an insensible way.
insen'tient, *adj.*, not sentient.
inseparabil'ity, *n.*, the state of being inseparable.
insep'arable, *adj.*, that cannot be separated.
insep'arableness, *n.*, *i.q.* inseparability.
insep'arably, *adv.*, in an inseparable way.
insert', *v.t.*, to set or place in or among.
insert'ed, *p.p.*, insert.
insert'ing, *pr.p.*, insert.
inser'tion, *n.*, the act of inserting; something inserted.
Insesso'res, *n. pl.*, percher-birds
insesso'rial, *adj.*, perching.
in'set, *n.*, additional matter put into a book.
inset', *v.t.*, to set in.
in'shore, *adj.* and *adv.*, near or towards shore.
insicca'tion, *n.*, the act of drying in.
in'side, *adj.*, *prep.* and *adv.*, within; *n.*, the interior.
insi'der, *n.*, one who is inside.
insid'ious, *adj.*, lying in wait, treacherous, sly.
insid'iously, *adv.*, in an insidious way.
in'sight, *n.*, clear perception.
insig'nia, *n. pl.*, emblems of office.
in*signif'icance*, *n.*, want of meaning, unimportance.
in*signif'icancy*, *n.*, *i.q.* insignificance.
in*signif'icant*, *adj.*, without meaning, unimportant.
insincere', *adj.*, not sincere, false.
insincere'ly, *adv.*, without sincerity.
insincer'ity, *n.*, want of sincerity, falseness.
insin'uate, *v.t.*, to hint indirectly, to intimate; *v.i.*, to ingratiate oneself.
insin'uated, *p.p.*, insinuate.
insin'uating, *pr.p.*, insinuate.
insin'uatingly, *adv.*, in an insinuating way.
insinua'tion, *n.*, the act of insinuating; an artful, indirect hint.
insin'uative, *adj.*, conveying an insinuation.
insip'id, *adj.*, tasteless, flat, vapid.
insipid'ity, *n.*, absence of savour; vapidity.
insip'idly, *adv.*, in an insipid way.
insip'ience, *n.*, want of wisdom.
insip'ient, *adj.*, wanting wisdom, foolish.
insist', *v.i.*, to press a command, to persist.
insist'ed, *p.p.*, insist.
insist'ence, *n.*, the act of insisting.
insist'ency, *n.*, *i.q.* insistence.
insist'ent, *adj.*, urgent, imperative.
insist'ently, *adv.*, in an insistent way.
insist'ing, *pr.p.*, insist.
insi'tion, *n.*, ingrafting.
in si'tu, *adverbial phrase* = in position.
insnare', *v.t.*, to snare. Also *ensnare*.
insnared', *p.p.*, insnare.
insnar'er, *n.*, one who insnares.
insnar'ing, *pr.p.*, insnare.
insobri'ety, *n.*, intemperance.
in'solate, *v.t.*, to dry in the sun.
in'solated, *p.p.*, insolate.
insola'tion, *n.*, sun-drying.
in'solence, *n.*, arrogance; offensive rudeness.
in'solent, *adj.*, arrogant; rude.
in'solently, *adv.*, in an insolent way.
insolid'ity, *n.*, the quality of being not solid.
insolubil'ity, *n.*, the quality of being insoluble.
insol'uble, *adj.*, that cannot be dissolved.
insolv'able, *adj.*, unable to be solved or explained.
insolv'ency, *n.*, inability to meet one's creditors.
insolv'ent, *adj.*, unable to pay one's debts; *n.*, a bankrupt.
insom'nia, *n.*, inability to sleep.
insomuch', *adv.*, so, to such a degree.
insouciance', *n.*, indifference, carelessness (*Fr.*).

inspan′, *v.t.*, to yoke up, harness.

inspect′, *v.t.*, to view, superintend.

inspect′ed, *p.p.*, inspect.

inspect′ing, *pr.p.*, inspect.

inspec′tion, *n.*, close scrutiny, superintendence.

inspec′tor, *n.*, one who oversees.

inspec′tor-*gen′eral*, *n.*, an inspector of the highest rank.

inspi′rable, *adj.*, able to be inspired.

inspira′tion, *n.*, the act of inspiring.

inspir′atory, *adj.*, rel. to inspiration.

inspire′, *v.t.* and *i.*, to draw in breath; to breathe into; to influence the mind; to give official information to.

inspired′, *p.p.*, inspire.

inspi′rer, *n.*, one who inspires.

inspi′ring, *pr.p.*, inspire; *adj.*, stimulating to the mind.

inspir′it, *v.t.*, to hearten, encourage.

inspir′ited, *p.p.* inspirit.

inspir′iting, *pr.p.*, inspirit.

inspis′sate, *v.t.*, to thicken.

inspis′sated, *p.p.*, inspissate.

inspis′sating, *pr.p.*, inspissate.

inspissa′tion, *n.*, the act or effect of inspissating.

instabil′ity, *n.*, want of stability: inconstancy.

install′, *v.t.*, to put into an official place or office; to put gas or electricity into a building.

installa′tion, *n.*, the act of installing; an outfit of electric light, etc.; the introduction of machinery.

installed′, *p.p.*, instal.

install′ing, *pr.p.*, instal.

instal′ment, *n.*, the act of installing; part payment.

in′stance, *v.t.*, to quote an example; *n.*, an example; earnest entreaty.

in′stanced, *p.p.*, instance.

in′stancing, *pr.p.*, instance.

in′stant, *adj.*, insistent, earnest, immediate; *n.*, a particular point of time.

instanta′neous, *adj.*, occurring in an instant.

instanta′neously, *adv.*, at the moment.

instan′ter, *adv.*, immediately.

in′stantly, *adv.*, at once.

instate′, *v.t.*, to place in a particular rank.

instead′, *prep.* and *adv.*, in the place of.

in′step, *n.*, the upper side of the foot.

in′stigate, *v.t.*, to urge on, to prompt.

in′stigated, *p.p.*, instigate.

in′stigating, *pr.p.*, instigate.

instiga′tion, *n.*, the act of instigating; encouragement.

in′stigator, *n.*, one who instigates.

instil′, instill′, *v.t.*, to infuse by dropping in; to pour slowly in.

instilla′tion, *n.*, the act or effect of instilling.

instilled′, *p.p.*, instil.

instil′ler, *n.*, one who instils.

instil′ling, *pr.p.*, instil.

instinct′, *adj.*, animated by, stimulated.

in′stinct, *n.*, natural impulse.

instinc′tive, *adj.*, in accordance with natural impulse.

instinc′tively, *adv.*, in an instinctive way.

in′stitute, *v.t.*, to establish, found; to give spiritual authority to; *n.*, a maxim, principle; a society or building devoted to art, science, etc.

in′stituted, *p.p.*, institute.

in′stituting, *pr.p.*, institute.

institu′tion, *n.*, establishment; an established society; a building set apart for philanthropic, scientific, or other purposes.

institu′tional, *adj.*, rel. to institutions.

institu′tionary, *adj.*, *i.q.* institutional.

in′stitutive, *adj.*, tending to establish.

in′stitutor, *n.*, a founder.

instruct′, *v.t.*, to inform, teach, give orders.

instruct′ed, *p.p.*, instruct.

instruct′ing, *pr.p.*, instruct.

instruc′tion, *n.*, teaching, information, orders.

instruc′tive, *adj.*, teaching, informing.

instruct′or, *n.*, a teacher.

instruct′ress, *n.*, fem. of instructor.

in′strument, *n.*, that by which anything is effected; a tool; a contrivance for producing musical sounds; a deed (*leg.*).

instrumen′tal, *adj.*, conducing as means to an end; rel. to musical instruments.

instrument′alist, *n.*, a player on an instrument.

instrumental′ity, *n.*, agency.

instrument′ally, *adv.*, by means; played on an instrument.

instrumenta′tion, *n.*, the disposition and character of instrumental music.

in*subjec′tion*, *n.*, the state of not being subject.

insubor′dinate, *adj.*, unruly.

insubordina′tion, *n.*, unruliness.

in*substan′tial*, *adj.*, not substantial.

insubstantial′ity, *n.*, the quality of being insubstantial.

insubstan'tially, *adv.*, in an insubstantial way.

insuf'ferable, *adj.*, unendurable, intolerable.

insuf'ferably, *adv.*, intolerably.

insuffi'ciency, *n.*, a lack of sufficiency; inadequateness.

insuffi'cient, *adj.*, inadequate.

insuffi'ciently, *adv.* inadequately.

insuf'flate, *v.t.*, to breathe into or upon.

insuffla'tion, *n.*, the act of insufflating.

in'sufflator, *n.*, a blowing instrument.

in'sular, *adj.*, rel. to an island; narrow.

in'sularism, *n.*, the state or quality of being insular.

insular'ity, *n.*, *i.q.* insularism; narrowness of mind.

in'sulate, *v.t.*, to detach; to prevent the escape of electricity.

in'sulated, *p.p.*, insulate.

in'sulating, *pr.p.*, insulate.

insula'tion, *n.*, the act or effect of insulating.

in'sulator, *n.*, anything that insulates; a non-conductor.

insult', *v.t.*, to affront, outrage.

in'sult, *n.*, an affront, outrage.

insult'ed, *p.p.*, insult.

insult'er, *n.*, one who insults.

insult'ing, *pr.p.*, insult; *adj.*, abusive.

insult'ingly, *adv.*, in an insulting way.

insuperabil'ity, *n.*, the quality of being insuperable.

insu'perable, *adj.*, not to be overcome, insurmountable.

insu'perably, *adv.*, insurmountably.

insupport'able, *adj.*, not to be supported, unendurable.

insupport'ably, *adv.*, unendurably.

insuppres'sible, *adj.*, not to be suppressed.

insur'able, *adj.*, able to be insured.

insur'ance, *n.*, security against loss.

insure', *v.t.*, to make sure or secure.

insured', *p.p.*, insure.

insur'er, *n.*, one who insures.

insur'ing, *pr.p.*, insure.

insur'gent, *adj.*, rebellious; *n.*, a rebel.

insurmount'able, *adj.*, not to be surmounted or overcome.

insurmount'ably, *adv.*, in an insurmountable way.

insurrec'tion, *n.*, an act of rebellion.

insurrec'tionary, *adj.*, seditious.

insurrec'tionist, *n.*, one who takes part in insurrection.

insusceptibil'ity, *n.*, the state of being insusceptible.

insuscep'tible, *adj.*, not susceptible, not readily affected.

intact', *adj.*, untouched, uninjured.

inta'glio, *n.*, a figure cut in a gem.

in'take, *n.*, anything taken in; a narrowing-point; an inflow.

intangibil'ity, *n.*, the state of being intangible.

intan'gible, *adj.*, not perceptible to the touch; vague.

in'teger, *n.*, a whole number.

in'tegral, *adj.*, whole, entire; forming a whole.

in'tegrant, *adj.*, forming part of a whole.

in'tegrate, *v.t.* and *i.*, to combine the parts.

in'tegrated, *p.p.*, integrate.

in'tegrating, *pr.p.*, integrate.

integra'tion, *n.*, the act or effect of integrating.

integ'rity, *n.*, uprightness.

integ'ument, *n.*, a covering or membrane.

integumen'tary, *adj.*, pert. to an integument.

in'tellect, *n.*, the understanding.

intellec'tual, *adj.*, rel. to the intellect; endowed with intellect

intellec'tualism, *n.*, the doctrine of pure reason.

intellec'tualist, *n.*, one who professes intellectualism.

intellectual'ity, *n.*, the quality of being intellectual.

intellec'tually, *adv.*, on the score of intellect.

intel'ligence, *n.*, understanding; information.

intel'ligencer, *n.*, one who conveys news.

intel'ligent, *adj.*, understanding, mentally alert.

intelligen'tial, *adj.*, rel. to intelligence.

intel'ligently, *adv.*, with intelligence.

intelligibil'ity, *n.*, the quality of being intelligible.

intel'ligible, *adj.*, capable of being understood.

intel'ligibly, *adv.*, in a way to be understood.

intem'perance, *n.*, want of self-control, violence; drunkenness.

intem'perate, *adj.*, violent, excessive; given to drink.

intem'perately, *adv.*, in an intemperate way

intem'perateness, *n.*, *i.q.* intemperance.

intend', *v.t.*, to purpose, design.

intend'ancy, *n.*, superintendence.

intend'ant, *n.*, a superintendent.

intend'ed, *p.p.*, intend; *n.*, a betrothed lover.

intend'ing, *pr.p.*, intend.

intense', *adj.*, strained, vehement, earnest.

intense'ly, *adv.*, earnestly, strongly.

intense'ness, *n.*, the state of being intense.

intensifica'tion, *n.*, the act or effect of intensifying.

inten'sified, *p.p.*, intensify.

inten'sifier, *n.*, anything that intensifies.

inten'sify, *v.t.*, to render intense; to strengthen.

inten'sifying, *pr.p.*, intensify.

inten'sion, *n.*, connotation, logical content; exertion.

inten'sity, *n.*, density, force, vehemence.

inten'sive, *adj.*, tending to intensify; connoting.

intent', *adj.*, concentrated on; eager; *n.*, purpose, meaning.

inten'tion, *n.*, design, purpose.

inten'tional, *adj.*, intended, designed.

inten'tionally, *adv.*, on purpose.

inten'tioned, *adj.*, having intention, designed.

intent'ly, *adv.*, fixedly, earnestly.

intent'ness, *n.*, the state of being intent.

inter', *v.t.*, to bury.

interact', *v.i.*, to have mutual influence.

interbreed', *v.t.* and *i.*, to breed in, to crossbreed.

interbreed'ing, *pr.p.*, interbreed.

inter'calar, *adj.*, *i.q.* intercalary.

inter'calary, *adj.*, inserted, esp. in the Kalendar.

inter'calate, *v.t.*, to put between.

inter'calated, *p.p.*, intercalate.

inter'calating, *pr.p.*, intercalate.

intercala'tion, *n.*, the act of intercalating; an intercalated date.

intercede', *v.i.*, to intervene for; to plead in favour of.

interce'ded, *p.p.*, intercede.

interce'der, *n.*, one who intercedes.

interce'ding, *pr.p.*, intercede.

intercept', *v.t.*, to cut off, stop, obstruct.

intercept'ed, *p.p.*, intercept.

intercept'er, *n.*, one who intercepts.

intercept'ing, *pr.p.*, intercept.

intercep'tion, *n.*, the act of intercepting.

interces'sion, *n.*, the act of interceding; prayer on behalf of; mediation.

interces'sional, *adj.*, rel. to intercession.

interces'sor, *n.*, one who intercedes.

interces'sory, *adj.*, interceding.

interchange', *v.t.*, to exchange reciprocally.

in'terchange, *n.*, mutual exchange, commerce.

interchangeabil'ity, *n.*, the quality of being interchangeable.

interchange'able, *adj.*, able to be interchanged.

interchange'ableness, *n.*, *i.q.*, interchangeability.

interchange'ably, *adv.*, reciprocally.

interchanged', *p.p.*, interchange.

interchang'ing, *pr.p.*, interchange.

intercolo'nial, *adj.*, pert. to colonial intercourse.

intercolum'nar, *adj.*, between columns.

intercolumnia'tion, *n.*, architectural spacing between columns.

intercommu'nion, *n.*, sharing in communion.

intercommu'nicate, *v.i.*, to practise intercommunion.

intercommu'nity, *n.*, reciprocity.

intercos'tal, *adj.*, situated between the ribs.

in'tercourse, *n.*, fellowship, society, connexion, conversation.

intercur'rent, *adj.*, happening between.

interdepend'ence, *n.*, the state of being interdependent.

interdepend'ent, *adj.*, mutually dependent.

interdict', *v.t.*, to prohibit.

in'terdict, *n.*, a decree withholding the Sacraments.

interdict'ed, *p.p.*, interdict.

interdict'ing, *pr.p.*, interdict.

interdic'tion, *n.*, the act or result of interdicting.

interdict'ive, *adj.*, *i.q.* interdictory.

interdict'ory, *adj.*, interdicting, prohibitive.

in'terest, *v.t.*, to engage attention, to entertain; *n.*, concern, entertainment, advantage, premium for money loan.

in'terested, *p.p.*, interest.

in'teresting, *pr.p.*, interest; *adj.*, engaging, entertaining.

interfa'cial, *adj.*, between the faces of a many-sided figure.

interfere', *v.i.*, to meddle; intervene.

interfered', *p.p.*, interfere.

interfer'ence, *n.*, meddling.

interfer'er, *n.*, one who interferes.

interfer'ing, *pr.p.*, interfere; *adj.*, meddlesome.

interfer'ingly, *adv.*, meddlesomely.

interfuse', *v.t.* and *i.*, to spread between.

in'terim, *n.*, the meantime; *adv.*, meanwhile (*Lat.*).

inte'rior, *adj.*, inner; *n.*, the inside.

interja'cent, *adj.*, lying between.

interject', *v.t.*, to throw in, put between.

interject'ed, *p.p.*, interject.

interject'ing, *pr.p.*, interject.

interjec'tion, *n.*, a word thrown in; an exclamation.

interjec'tional, *adj.*, exclamatory.

interlace', *v.t.* and *i.*, to twine.

interlaced', *p.p.*, interlace.

interla'cing, *pr.p.*, interlace.

interlard', *v.t.*, to diversify with mixture.

interlard'ed, *p.p.*, interlard.

interlard'ing, *pr.p.*, interlard.

interleave', *v.t.*, to introduce blank leaves in.

interleaved', *p.p.*, interleave.

interleav'ing, *pr.p.*, interleave.

interline', *v.t.*, to write between the lines.

interlin'eal, *adj.*, written between the lines.

interlin'ear, *adj.*, *i.q.* interlineal.

interlinea'tion, *n.*, writing between the lines.

interlined', *p.p.*, interline.

interlin'ing, *pr.p.*, interline.

interlink', *v.t.*, to connect with links.

interlock', *v.t.*, to lock into one another.

interlocked', *p.p.*, interlock.

interlock'ing, *pr.p.*, interlock.

interloc'utor, *n.*, a questioner.

interloc'utory, *adj.*, questioning.

in'terloper, *n.*, an intruder.

interlu'cent, *adj.*, shining between.

in'terlude, *n.*, an interval in a play; music played in the interval.

interlu'nar, *adj.*, rel. to the period of the moon's invisibility.

interlu'nary, *adj.*, *i.q.* interlunar.

intermar'riage, *n.*, marriage with a member of the same tribe or family; also marriage between different tribes.

intermar'ried, *p.p.*, intermarry.

intermar'ry, *v.i.*, to marry with a member of the same tribe.

intermar'rying, *pr.p.*, intermarry.

intermed'dle, *v.i.*, to interfere.

intermed'dled, *p.p.*, intermeddle.

intermed'dler, *n.*, one who intermeddles.

intermed'dling, *pr.p.*, intermeddle.

interme'dial, *adj.*, intervening.

interme'diary, *adj.*, *i.q.* intermedial; *n.*, a go-between.

interme'diate, *v.i.*, to act as a go-between; *adj.*, lying between; intervening.

intermedia'tion, *n.*, the act of intermediating.

inter'ment, *n.*, burial.

intermez'zo, *n.*, an interlude.

inter'minable, *adj.*, endless, unlimited.

inter'minableness, *n.*, endlessness, boundlessness.

inter'minably, *adv.*, endlessly.

intermin'gle, *v.t.* and *i.*, to mix together.

intermin'gled, *p.p.*, intermingle.

intermin'gling, *pr.p.*, intermingle.

intermis'sion, *n.*, temporary cessation, pause.

intermis'sive, *adj.*, pausing for a space.

intermit', *v.t.*, to leave off for a space.

intermit'ted, *p.p.*, intermit.

intermit'tent, *adj.*, coming and going at intervals.

intermit'ting, *pr.p.*, intermit.

intermix', *v.t.* and *i.*, to intermingle.

intermixed', *p.p.*, intermix.

intermix'ing, *pr.p.*, intermix.

intermix'ture, *n.*, a mixed mass.

intermu'ral, *adj.*, between walls.

intern', *v.t.*, to place under arrest.

inter'nal, *adj.*, inner; domestic; not foreign.

inter'nally, *adv.*, inwardly.

interna'tional, *adj.*, rel. to intercourse between nations.

interna'tionalism, *n.*, the principle of a common interest among nations.

interna'tionalist, *n.*, one who advocates internationalism.

interna'tionally, *adv.*, by nations as a whole.

interne'cine, *adj.*, mutually destructive.

intern'ment, *n.*, the placing under arrest.

internun'cial, *adj.*, rel. to an internuncio.

internun'cio, *n.*, an ambassador.

interocean'ic, *adj.*, lying between oceans.

interpari'etal, *adj.*, lying between the parietal bones.

interpel'late, *v.i.*, to question.

interpel'lated, *p.p.*, interpellate.

interpella'tion, *n.*, a question.

interplan'etary, *adj.*, between planets.

interplead', *v.i.*, to discuss an incidental question at law.

interplead'er, *n.*, one who interpleads.

interplead'ing, *pr.p.*, interplead.

inter'polate, *v.t.*, to insert new or alien matter in a writing.

inter'polated, *p.p.*, interpolate.

inter'polater, *n.*, one who interpolates.

inter'polating, *pr.p.*, interpolate.

interpola'tion, *n.*, the act of interpolating; an interpolated passage.

interpose', *v.t.* and *i.*, to place between; to interfere, to mediate.

interposed', *p.p.*, interpose.

interpo'ser, *n.*, one who interposes.

interpo'sing, *pr.p.*, interpose.
interposi'tion, *n.*, intervention.
inter'pret, *v.t.*, to explain, translate.
inter'pretable, *adj.*, capable of explanation.
interpreta'tion, *n.*, explanation, exposition.
inter'preted, *p.p.*, interpret.
inter'preter, *n.*, one who interprets.
inter'pretive, *adj.*, explanatory.
interred', *p.p.*, inter.
interreg'num, *n.*, suspension of government; a period between two reigns.
inter'ring, *pr.p.*, inter.
inter'rogate, *v.t.*, to question.
inter'rogated, *p.p.*, interrogate.
interroga'tion, *n.*, a question.
interrog'ative, *adj.*, questioning.
inter'rogator, *n.*, a questioner.
interrog'atory, *adj.*, questioning.
interrupt', *v.t.*, to break off, hinder.
interrupt'ed, *p.p.*, interrupt.
interrupt'er, *n.*, one who interrupts.
interrupt'ing, *pr.p.*, interrupt.
interrup'tion, *n.*, an act of interrupting, a breaking off; obstruction.
interscap'ular, *adj.*, between the shoulder-blades.
interse'cant, *adj.*, cutting across; intersecting.
intersect', *v.t.*, to cut mutually; *v.i.*, to meet and cross each other.
intersect'ed, *p.p.*, intersect.
intersect'ing, *pr.p.*, intersect.
intersec'tion, *n.*, the point where lines cross each other.
intersec'tional, *adj.*, crossing and cutting.
in'terspace, *n.*, an intervening space.
intersperse', *v.t.*, to scatter among.
interspersed', *p.p.*, intersperse.
interspers'ing, *pr.p.*, intersperse.
intersper'sion, *n.*, the act of interpersing.
interstel'lar, *adj.*, between or amid stars.
interstel'lary, *adj.*, *s.q.* interstellar.
inter'stice, *n.*, a narrow chink, a crevice.
inter'stices, *n.*, pl. of interstice.
intersti'tial, *adj.*, having interstices.
intertex'ture, *n.*, interwoven texture.
intertri'bal, *adj.*, pert. to the relations between tribes.
intertrop'ical, *adj.*, between the tropics.
intertwine', *v.t.* and *i.*, to twist together.
intertwined', *p.p.*, intertwine.
intertwi'ning, *pr.p.*, intertwine.
intertwi'ningly, *adv.*, interlacing.
intertwist', *v.t.*, to twist together.
intertwist'ed, *p.p.*, intertwist.
intertwist'ing, *pr.p.*, intertwist.
in'terval, *n.*, an intervening space.
intervene', *v.i.*, to come between; to interfere.
intervened', *p.p.*, intervene.
interve'ner, *n.*, one who intervenes.
interve'nient, *adj.*, intervening.
interve'ning, *pr.p.*, intervene.
interven'tion, *n.*, the act of intervening; interference.
in'terview, *v.t.*, to hold an interview with; *n.*, a talk.
in'terviewed, *p.p.*, interview.
in'terviewer, *n.*, one who interviews.
in'terviewing, *pr.p.*, interview.
interweave', *v.t.*, to weave together.
interweaved', *p.p.*, interweave.
interweav'ing, *pr.p.*, interweave.
interwov'en, *p.p.*, interweave.
intes'table, *adj.*, not qualified to make a will.
intes'tacy, *n.*, the state of an intestate.
intes'tate, *adj.*, not having made a proper will; not legally bequeathed; *n.*, one who leaves no will.
intes'tinal, *adj.*, rel. to the intestines.
intes'tine, *adj.*, internal, domestic; *n.*, the alimentary canal. In pl., the internal organs.
in'timacy, *n.*, the state of being intimate; familiarity.
in'timate, *adj.*, closely associated; innermost; *n.*, a familiar friend and confidant.
in'timate, *v.t.*, to hint, make known indirectly.
in'timated, *p.p.*, intimate.
in'timately, *adv.*, closely, familiarly.
in'timating, *pr.p.*, intimate.
intima'tion, *n.*, an indirect hint, suggestion.
intim'idate, *v.t.*, to cause to be afraid; terrorize.
intim'idated, *p.p.*, intimidate.
intim'idating, *pr.p.*, intimidate.
intimida'tion, *n.*, terrorism.
intit'uled, *adj.*, entitled.
in'to, *prep.*, moving to and remaining in.
intol'erable, *adj.*, not to be tolerated; unendurable.
intol'erably, *adv.*, insufferably.
intol'erance, *n.*, want of forbearance.
intol'erant, *adj.*, not tolerant, bigoted.
intol'erantly, *adv.*, with intolerance.
in'tonate, *v.t.*, to intone, to sound the notes of a scale.

in'tonated, *p.p.*, intonate.

in'tonating, *pr.p.*, intonate.

intona'tion, *n.*, voice-modulation; the act of intoning; the introductory notes preceding the reciting note in plain-song.

in'tonator, *n.*, a monochord accurately divided into parts.

intone', *v.t.* and *i.*, to recite musically.

intoned', *p.p.*, intone.

intox'icant, *n.*, alcoholic drink; anything that causes high excitement.

intox'icate, *v.t.*, to make drunk; to elate greatly.

intox'icated, *p.p.*, intoxicate.

intox'icating, *pr.p.*, intoxicate.

intoxica'tion, *n.*, the state of drunkenness.

intractabil'ity, *n.*, the quality of being intractable.

intrac'table, *adj.*, unmanageable; obstinate.

intrac'tably, *adv.*, in an intractable way.

intra'dos, *n.*, a soffit.

intramu'ral, *adj.*, within a city's walls.

intranquil'lity, *n.*, restlessness.

intran'sigent, *adj.*, irreconcilable. Also *intransigeant.*

intran'sitive, *adj.*, not passing over to an object.

intransmis'sible, *adj.*, not able to be transmitted.

intrench', *v.t.*, to dig a trench; to fortify with a trench. Also *entrench.*

intrenched', *p.p.*, intrench.

intrench'ing, *pr.p.*, intrench.

intrench'ment, *n.*, the act of intrenching; an intrenched position.

intrep'id, *adj.*, fearless, dauntless.

intrepid'ity, *n.*, fearlessness.

intrep'idly, *adv.*, fearlessly.

in'tricacy, *n.*, entanglement, perplexity.

in'tricate, *adj.*, involved, entangled.

in'tricately, *adv.*, in an intricate way.

intrigue', *v.i.* to plot, scheme; *n.*, a plot, underhand scheme.

intrigued', *p.p.*, intrigue.

intrigu'er, *n.*, one who intrigues.

intrigu'ing, *pr.p.*, intrigue.

intrin'sic, *adj.*, inherent; in itself; essential.

intrin'sically, *adv.*, essentially; in itself.

introces'sion, *n.*, a depression.

introduce', *v.t.*, to bring in; to make known.

introduced', *p.p.*, introduce.

introdu'cer, *n.*, one who introduces.

introdu'cing, *pr.p.*, introduce.

introd'uction, *n.*, the act of introducing; something leading up, as the Introduction before a book.

introduc'tive, *adj.*, leading up to, beginning.

introduc'tory, *adj.*, *i.q.* introductive.

intro'it, *n.*, the anthem preceding the Mass.

intromis'sion, *n.*, insertion, introduction.

intromit', *v.t.*, to insert, place within.

intromit'ted, *p.p.*, intromit.

intromit'ting, *pr.p.*, intromit.

introrse', *adj.*, turned inwards.

introspect', *v.t.*, to look into; examine.

introspec'tion, *n.*, self-examination.

introspec'tive, *adj.*, self-examining.

introver'sion, *n.*, the act of turning inward.

introvert', *v.t.*, to turn inward.

introvert'ed, *p.p.*, introvert.

intrude', *v.t.*, to thrust in without permission; *v.i.*, to force oneself upon.

intru'ded, *p.p.*, intrude.

intru'der, *n.*, one who intrudes.

intru'ding, *pr.p.*, intrude.

intru'sion, *n.*, the act of intruding; encroachment.

intru'sive, *adj.*, coming in uninvited.

intrust', *see* entrust.

intuba'tion, *n.*, the process of inserting a tube.

intui'tion, *n.*, immediate perception; instinctive knowledge.

intu'itive, *adj.*, immediately perceptive; gained without conscious reasoning.

intu'itively, *adv.*, in an intuitive way.

intumesce', *v.i.*, to swell.

intumesced', *p.p.*, intumesce.

intumes'cence, *n.*, a swelling.

intumes'cing, *pr.p.*, intumesce.

intussuscep'tion, *n.*, the state of being received within; partial displacement of the intestine.

intwine', *see* entwine.

intwist', *see* entwist.

in'undate, *v.t.*, to flood, submerge, overwhelm.

in'undated, *p.p.*, inundate.

in'undating, *pr.p.*, inundate.

inunda'tion, *n.*, a deluge, overflow.

inure', *v.t.*, to accustom, harden.

inured', *p.p.*, inure.

inure'ment, *n.*, the act of inuring.

inur'ing, *pr.p.*, inure.

inurn', *v.t.*, to enclose in an urn.

inurned', *p.p.*, inurn.

inurn'ing, *pr.p.*, inurn.

inu'tile, *adj.*, useless.

inutil'ity, *n.*, uselessness.

invade', *v.t.*, to come into, attack, encroach upon.

inva'ded, *p.p.* invade.

inva'der, *n.*, one who invades.

inva'ding, *pr.p.*, invade.

in'valid, *n.*, a sick person; *adj.*, sick, weakly.

inval'id, *adj.*, not valid; without authority or legal force.

inval'idate, *v.t.*, to render invalid.

inval'idated, *p.p.*, invalidate.

inval'idating, *pr.p.*, invalidate.

invalid'ity, *n.*, the state of being null and void.

inval'uable, *adj.*, priceless; of the greatest value.

invariabil'ity, *n.*, the quality of being invariable.

inva'riable, *adj.*, not subject to variation; always the same.

inva'riableness, *n.*, *i.q.* invariability.

inva'riably, *adv.*, constantly.

inva'sion, *n.*, the act of invading; attack.

inva'sive, *adj.*, making invasion.

invec'tive, *adj.*, abusive; *n.*, vituperation, railing.

inveigh', *v.i.*, to rail against; to speak in denunciation.

inveighed', *p.p.*, inveigh.

inveigh'er, *n.*, one who inveighs.

inveigh'ing, *pr.p.*, inveigh.

invei'gle, *v.t.*, to entice, lead astray.

invei'gled, *p.p.*, inveigle.

invei'gler, *n.*, one who inveigles.

invei'gling, *pr.p.*, inveigle.

invent', *v.t.*, to find out, originate, contrive.

invent'ed, *p.p.*, invent.

invent'ing, *pr.p.*, invent.

inven'tion, *n.*, the act of inventing; something invented.

invent'ive, *adj.*, able to invent; rel. to invention.

invent'or, *n.*, one who invents.

in'ventory, *n.*, a list or schedule of household or other effects.

inverse', *adj.*, contrary, indirect.

inverse'ly, *adv.*, in an inverted order or degree.

inver'sion, *n.*, the act of inverting; the state of being inverted; a change of order or position.

invert', *v.t.*, to place upside down; to change the order of; to turn inside out.

invert'ant, *adj.*, reversed (*Her.*).

inver'tebral, *adj.*, *i.q.* invertebrate.

inver'tebrate, *adj.* and *n.*, backboneless, irresolute.

inver'tebrated, *adj.*, *i.q.* invertebrate.

invert'ed, *p.p.*, invert.

invert'edly, *adv.*, in an inverted way.

invert'ing, *pr.p.*, invert.

invest', *v.t.*, to lay out; to clothe with official garb and so to give authority; to besiege closely.

invest'ed, *p.p.*, invest.

inves'tigable, *adj.*, able to be investigated.

inves'tigate, *v.t.*, to track out, search into.

inves'tigated, *p.p.*, investigate.

inves'tigating, *pr.p.*, investigate.

investiga'tion, *n.*, careful search.

inves'tigative, *adj.*, making search.

inves'tigator, *n.*, one who investigates.

invest'ing, *pr.p.*, invest.

invest'iture, *n.*, the act or ceremony of conferring authority, esp. of delivering the ring and staff to a bishop.

invest'ment, *n.*, the laying out of money; money invested; the object on which money is laid out; a close siege.

invest'or, *n.*, one who invests.

invet'eracy, *adj.*, the state of being inveterate.

invet'erate, *adj.*, deep-rooted; of long standing.

invid'ious, *adj.*, exciting dislike or envy; offensive.

invid'iously, *adv.*, in an invidious way.

invig'orate, *v.t.*, to strengthen, brace.

invig'orated, *p.p.*, invigorate.

invig'orating, *pr.p.*, invigorate.

invigora'tion, *n.*, the effect of invigorating.

invincibil'ity, *n.*, the state of being invincible.

invin'cible, *adj.*, unconquerable.

invin'cibly, *adv.*, unconquerably.

inviolabil'ity, *n.*, the state of being inviolable.

invi'olable, *adj.*, not to be violated, or broken, or profaned.

invi'olably, *adv.*, in an inviolable way.

invi'olate, *adj.*, not violated, uninjured.

invisibil'ity, *n.*, the state of being invisible.

invis'ible, *adj.*, that cannot be seen.

invis'ibly, *adv.*, in an invisible way.

invita'tion, *n.*, the act of inviting.

invi'tatory, *adj.*, of the nature of an invitation; *n.*, a psalm inviting to worship (as Ps. xcv.), and farsed with additional words.

invite', *v.t.*, to bid, summon, ask to come.

invi'ted, *p.p.*, invite.

invi'ter, *n.*, one who invites.

invi'ting, *pr.p.*, invite; *adj.*, enticing, alluring.

invi'tingly, *adv.*, enticingly.

invit'rifiable, *adj.*, that cannot be vitrified.

in'vocate, *v.t.*, to call upon, to address in prayer.

invoca'tion, *n.*, the act of invoking; an incantation.

invoc'atory, *adj.*, invoking.

in'voice, *v.t.*, to make a bill of; *n.*, a list of the items of a bill.

in'voiced, *p.p.*, invoice.

in'voicing, *pr.p.*, invoice.

invoke', *v.t.*, to call upon, supplicate.

invoked', *p.p.*, invoke.

invo'king, *pr.p.*, invoke.

invol'ucel, *n.*, a diminutive involucre.

involucel'late, *adj.*, furnished with involucels.

involu'cral, *adj.*, having an involucre.

involu'crate, *adj.*, *i.q.* involucral.

in'volucre, *n.*, a whorl surrounding a flower.

in'volucred, *adj.*, having an involucre.

involu'cret, *n.*, a diminutive involucre; an involucel.

involu'crum, *n.*, an involucre.

invol'untarily, *adv.*, not of one's own will.

invol'untary, *adj.*, unintentioned; not of one's own will.

in'volute, *adj.*, twisted, turned inwards.

in'voluted, *adj.*, *i.q.* involute.

involu'tion, *n.*, a complication; the state of being involved.

involve', *v.t.*, to wrap round; include; entangle; imply.

involved', *p.p.*, involve.

involv'ing, *pr.p.*, involve.

invulnerabil'ity, *n.*, the state or quality of being invulnerable.

invul'nerable, *adj.*, that cannot be wounded.

in'ward, *adj.*, internal, inner; *adv.*, towards the interior.

in'wardly, *adv.*, internally.

in'wardness, *n.*, the true, inner meaning.

in'wards, *adv.*, *i.q.* inward.

inweave', *v.t.*, to entwine; weave into.

in'working, *n.*, operation from within.

inwo'ven, *p.p.*, inweave.

inwrap', *v.t.*, to envelop.

inwrapped', *p.p.*, inwrap.

inwrap'ping, *pr.p.*, inwrap.

inwrought', *adj.*, worked in (as in metal work).

i'odate, *n.*, an iodic acid salt.

iod'ic, *adj.*, containing iodine.

i'odide, *n.*, a compound of iodine.

i'odine, *n.*, a nonmetallic chemical element.

i'odize, *v.t.*, to treat with iodine.

i'odized, *p.p.*, iodize.

i'odizing, *pr.p.*, iodize.

io'doform, *n.*, a compound of iodine, with antiseptic properties.

i'olite, *n.*, a violet-coloured gem.

i'on, *n.*, a component part of a substance after electrolytic decomposition.

Io'nian, *adj.*, rel. to Ionia.

Ion'ic, *adj.*, *i.q.* Ionian; also the architectural term for one of the classical orders; *n.*, the Ionic dialect of Greek.

io'ta, *n.*, the ninth letter of the Greek alphabet; a very small part, a jot.

ipecacuan'ha, *n.*, a S. American shrub; the emetic made from its root.

ip'se dix'it, *n.*, a substantive phrase = he himself has said = a dictum.

ip'so fac'to, adverbial phrase = in very fact.

Ira'nian, *adj.*, Persian.

irascibil'ity, *n.*, irritability, hot temper.

iras'cible, *adj.*, hot-tempered.

iras'cibleness, *n.*, *i.q.* irascibility.

iras'cibly, *adv.*, irritably.

irate', *adj.*, angry.

ire, *n.*, anger, wrath.

ire'ful, *adj.*, very angry.

ire'fully, *adv.*, very angrily.

iren'ical, *adj.*, rel. to an irenicon.

ire'nicon, *n.*, a proposal of peace. Liturgically, it is a prayer for peace. Also *Eirenicon*.

i'rid, *n.*, one of the iris family.

i'rides, *n.*, pl. of iris.

irides'cence, *n.*, the state of being iridescent.

irides'cent, *adj.*, shining with the colours of the rainbow.

irid'ium, *n.*, a hard, white metallic element.

i'ris, *n.*, the rainbow; the coloured part of the eye showing through the pupil; a plant family so named.

i'risated, *adj.*, iridescent.

i'riscope, *n.*, a plate for showing the prismatic colours.

i'rises, *n.*, the English pl. of iris.

I'rish, *adj.*, pert. to Ireland and the Irish; *n.*, the Irish language.

I'rishism, *n.*, an Irish idiom.

I'rishman, *n.*, a native of Ireland.

I'rishry, *n.*, the Irish natives collectively.

iri'tis, *n.*, inflammation of the iris.

irk, *v.t.*, to weary.

irk'some, *adj.*, wearisome, disagreeable.

irk'someness, *n.*, troublesomeness.

i'ron, *v.t.*, to smooth with a hot iron; to fetter; *adj.*, made of iron, resembling iron; *n.*, the common metal so named; any iron weapon or tool.

i'ronclad, *n.*, an armour-plated war vessel.

i'roned, *p.p.*, iron.

i'roner, *n.*, anything that irons.

iron'ic, *adj.*, *i.q.* ironical.

iron'ical, *adj.*, of the nature of irony; meaning more than is said; sarcastic.

iron'ically, *adv.*, in an ironical way.

i'roning, *pr.p.*, iron.

i'ronmaster, *n.*, an iron manufacturer.

i'ronmonger, *n.*, a dealer in goods made of iron.

i'ronmongery, *n.*, goods made of iron.

i'ron-mould, *n.*, a stain of iron rust.

i'ronside, *n.*, a man of sturdy, resolute character.

i'ronwork, *n.*, anything made of iron.

i'rony, *adj.*, like iron.

i'rony, *n.*, saying something that means more than appears on the surface, and conceals sarcasm, contempt, ridicule, etc.

irra'diance, *n.*, the act or state of irradiating.

irra'diancy, *n.*, *i.q.* irradiance.

irra'diant, *adj.*, illuminating.

irra'diate, *v.t.*, to illuminate. [diate.

irra'diated, *p.p.*, irra-

irra'diating, *pr.p.*, irradiate.

irradia'tion, *n.*, illumination.

irra'tional, *adj.*, not rational, unreasoning, absurd.

irrational'ity, *n.*, the quality of being irrational.

irra'tionally, *adv.*, in an irrational way.

irreclaim'able, *adj.*, unable to be reclaimed.

irreclaim'ably, *adv.*, in an irreclaimable way.

irreconci'lable, *adj.*, not to be reconciled.

irreconci'lably, *adv.*, beyond reconciling.

irrec'onciled, *adj.*, unreconciled.

irrecov'erable, *adj.* unable to be recovered.

irrecov'erably, *adv.* beyond recovery.

irredeem'able, *adj.*, unable to be redeemed; not to be converted into cash.

irredeem'ably, *adv.*, past redemption.

irreden'ta, *adj.*, the full phrase is *Italia irredenta*, *i.e.*, unredeemed Italy, parts of Italy still subject to foreign rule.

Irreden'tist, *n.*, one of the Italian party called Irredentists, whose object is to establish a united Italy.

irredu'cible, *adj.*, unable to be reduced.

irrefragabil'ity, *n.*, the quality of being irrefragable.

irref'ragable, *adj.*, that cannot be broken; irrefutable.

irrefu'table, *adj.*, that cannot be refuted or disproved.

irreg'ular, *adj.*, not regular, not straight, not honourable.

irregular'ity, *n.*, departure from rule; improper conduct.

irreg'ularly, *adv.*, in an irregular way.

irrel'ative, *adj.*, unrelated, unconnected.

irrel'evance, *n.*, not being pertinent; something that is not pertinent.

irrel'evancy, *n.*, *i.q.* irrelevance.

irrel'evant, *adj.*, not pertinent; off the point.

irrelig'ion, *n.*, ungodliness, unbelief.

irrelig'ious, *adj.*, destitute of religion.

irreme'diable, *adj.*, past remedy.

irreme'diably, *adv.*, past remedy.

irremiss'ible, *adj.*, not remissible.

irremov'able, *adj.*, that cannot be removed.

irremov'ably, *adv.*, fixedly.

irreparabil'ity, *n.*, the quality of being irreparable.

irrep'arable, *adj.*, not to be repaired or made good.

irrep'arably, *adv.*, in an irreparable way.

irrepealabil'ity, *n.*, the state of being irrepealable.

irrepeal'able, *adj.*, irrevocable, not to be repealed.

irrepeal'ably, *adv.*, irrevocably.

irreplace'able, *adj.*, that cannot be replaced.

irreprehen'sible, *adj.*, blameless.

irrepres'sible, *adj.*, not to be repressed or kept down.

irreproach'able, *adj.*, beyond reproach

irreproach'ably, *adv.*, beyond reproach

irreprov'able, *adj.*, not to be reproved.

irresistibil'ity, *n.*, the quality of being irresistible.

irresist'ible, *adj.*, that cannot be resisted.

irresist'ibly, *adv.*, past resistance.

irres'oluble, *adj.*, that cannot be resolved.

irres'olute, *adj.*, hesitating, weak in purpose.

irresolu'tion, *n.*, weakness of purpose, hesitation.

irresolvabil'ity, *n.*, the quality of being irresolvable.

irresolv'able, *adj.*, *i.q.* irresoluble.

irrespec'tive, *adj.*, not having regard to; omitting.

irrespec'tively, *adv.*, excluding.

irresponsibil'ity, *n.*, the state or quality of being irresponsible.

irrespon'sible, *adj.*, not answerable; incapable of fulfilling obligations.

irretriev'able, *adj.*, that cannot be retrieved.
irretriev'ably, *adv.*, past retrieving.
irrev'erence, *n.*, want of reverence.
irrev'erent, *adj.*, wanting in reverence or respect.
irrev'erently, *adv.*, in an irreverent way.
irrevers'ible, *adj.*, that cannot be reversed.
irrevocabil'ity, *n.*, the state of being irrevocable.
irrev'ocable, *adj.*, beyond recall.
irrev'ocably, *adv.*, beyond recall.
ir'rigable, *adj.*, capable of being irrigated.
ir'rigate, *v.t.*, to supply land with water.
ir'rigated, *p.p.*, irrigate.
ir'rigating, *pr.p.*, irrigate.
irriga'tion, *n.*, the act or system of irrigating.
irrig'uous, *adj.*, water-supplying.
irritabil'ity, *n.*, the state of being irritable.
ir'ritable, *adj.*, easily provoked, excitable.
ir'ritant, *adj.*, causing irritation; *n.*, anything that causes irritation.
ir'ritate, *v.t.*, to vex, annoy, inflame.
ir'ritated, *p.p.*, irritate.
ir'ritating, *pr.p.*, irritate; *adj.*, annoying.
irrita'tion, *n.*, vexation, annoyance, inflammation.
ir'ritative, *adj.*, *i.q.* irritant.
ir'ritatory, *adj.*, *i.q.* irritant.
irrora'tion, *n.*, a small colour-marking.
irrup'tion, *n.*, a bursting in; invasion.
irrup'tive, *adj.*, bursting in.
Ir'vingite, *n.*, a follower of Edward Irving; *adj.*, pert. to the Irvingites.

is, *v.*, the third pers. sing., pres. tense, of the verb *to be.*
isagog'ics, *n.*, introductory writings.
ischiad'ic, *adj.*, sciatic.
is'chiagra, *n.*, sciatic gout.
ischuret'ic, *adj.*, relieving ischuria; *n.*, a remedy for ischuria.
ischu'ria, *n.*, retention of urine.
is'chury, *n.*, *i.q.* ischuria.
Ish'maelite, *n.*, a descendant of Ishmael; an outcast.
Ish'maelitish, *adj.*, like an Ishmaelite.
i'singlass, *n.*, a gelatinous product from the viscera of certain fish.
Is'lam, *n.*, the religion of Mohammed; the Mohammedan world
Is'lamism, *n.*, Mohammedanism.
Is'lamite, *n.*, a Musulman.
Islamit'ic, *adj.*, rel. to Mohammedanism.
is'land, *n.*, land surrounded by water.
is'lander, *n.*, a dweller on an island.
isle, *n.*, an island; *v.t.* and *i.*, to place or to live on an island.
is'let, *n.*, a little island.
ism, *n.*, a set of doctrines.
i'sobar, *n.*, a line drawn or supposed to be drawn through a number of places where the barometric pressure is the same.
isobar'ic, *adj.*, showing equal pressure.
isobaromet'ric, *adj.*, *i.q.* isobaric.
isochromat'ic, *adj.*, of the same colour.
isoch'ronal, *adj.*, of equal lengths of time.
isoch'ronism, *n.*, the quality of being isochronal.
isoch'ronous, *adj.*, *i.q.* isochronal.
i'sogon, *adj.*, having equal angles.
i'solate, *v.t.* to insulate; to place in a detached position; to separate.
i'solated, *p.p.*, isolate.
i'solating, *pr.p.*, isolate.
isola'tion, *n.*, the state of being isolated.
isomer'ic, *adj.*, having an homologous aggregate.
isom'erism, *n.*, the state of being isomeric.
isomet'ric, *adj.*, of equal measure.
isomet'rical, *adj.*, *i.q.* isometric.
isomor'phism, *n.*, the state of being isomorphous.
isomor'phous, *adj.*, identical in construction; like in form.
isonom'ic, *adj.*, having equal rights.
ison'omy, *n.*, equality of civil rights.
i'sopod, *n.*, one of the Isopoda.
isop'odous, *adj.*, rel. to the Isopoda.
isos'celes, *adj.*, having two equal sides.
isostem'onous, *adj.*, having as many stamens as petals and sepals.
isoth'eral, *adj.*, rel. to isothere.
i'sothere, *n.*, a line joining points where the same mean summer temperatures are shown.
i'sotherm, *n.*, a line joining places which have the same annual temperature.
isother'mal, *adj.*, rel. to an isotherm.
isoton'ic, *adj.*, with equal tones.
isotrop'ic, *adj.*, exhibiting the same properties in every direction.
Is'raelite, *n.*, a descendant of Jacob; a Hebrew.
Is'raelitic, *adj.*, *i.q.* Israelitish.
Is'raelitish, *adj.*, rel. to Israel.
is'suable, *adj.*, able to be issued, or to have a legal issue upon it.

is'sue, *v.i.*, to come out; to arise; to result; *v.t.*, to put forth, publish; *n.*, anything that issues; offspring; an end or result; a point of discussion or at law.

is'sued, *p.p.*, issue.

is'suer, *n.*, one who issues.

is'suing, *pr.p.*, issue.

Isth'mian, *adj.*, rel. to the Isthmus of Corinth.

isth'mus, *n.*, a narrow strip of land connecting two larger areas.

it, *pron.*, neuter of *he.*

Ital'ian, *adj.*, pert. to Italy and the Italians.

Ital'ianize, *v.t.*, to make Italian; *v.i.*, to become Italian.

Ital'ic, *adj.*, bel. to Italy; in the italic type; *n.*, a peculiar kind of printing type.

ital'icize, *v.t.*, to print in italic.

ital'icized, *p.p.*, italicize.

ital'icizing, *pr.p.*, italicize.

itch, *v.i.*, to suffer from skin irritation; to have a great desire for; *n.*, a distressing skin disease; feeling of skin irritation.

itched, *p.p.*, itch.

itch'ing, *pr.p.*, itch.

itch'y, *adj.*, having the itch.

i'tem, *adv.*, also; *n.*, a further entry in a list.

it'erant, *adj.*, repeating.

it'erate, *v.t.*, to repeat.

it'erated, *p.p.*, iterate.

it'erating, *pr.p.*, iterate.

itera'tion, *n.*, the act of iterating; a repetition.

it'erative, *adj.*, repeating.

itin'erancy, *n.*, the state of being itinerant.

itin'erant, *adj.*, journeying, wandering; *n.*, one who journeys.

itin'erary, *adj.*, rel. to travel; *n.*, the record of a journey; a road chart.

itin'erate, *v.i.*, to go travelling.

itin'erated, *p.p.*, itinerate.

itin'erating, *pr.p.*, itinerate.

its, *adj.*, possessive of *it.*

itself, *refl. pron.*, neuter of *himself.*

i'vied, *adj.*, overgrown with ivy.

i'vory, *adj.*, made of, or resembling, ivory; *n.*, the substance of which tusks of certain animals are composed.

i'vy, *n.*, a climbing evergreen.

Ix'ia, *n.*, a genus of S. African iris.

Ix'ora, *n.*, a genus of the madder family.

iz'ard, *n.*, the Pyrenean chamois.

iz'zard, *n.*, the letter Z.

J

jab'ber, *v.i.*, to talk rapidly and indistinctly; *v.t.*, to utter rapidly; *n.*, rapid, indistinct talk.

jab'bered, *p.p.*, jabber.

jab'berer, *n.*, one who jabbers.

jab'bering, *pr.p.*, jabber.

jac'amar, *n.*, a tropical American climbing bird.

jac'inth, *n.*, the gem also called hyacinth.

jack, *n.*, a contrivance, of various kinds, for raising weights, for turning a spit, for pulling off boots, etc.; the knave of a suit of cards; a flag; a pike (fish); a leather pitcher; a small bowl (the game of bowls).

jack-a-dan'dy, *n.*, a little, foppish fellow.

jack'al, *n.*, a carnivorous wild animal akin to the dog and the wolf.

Jack'-a-Lent, *n.*, a simple fellow.

jack'anapes, *n.*, an impertinent fellow.

jack'ass, *n.*, a male ass; a stupid fellow.

jack'-block, *n.*, a block fixed high in a ship, in the topgallant or royal rigging, and used for raising light spars, etc.

jack'-boots, *n. pl.*, large boots reaching up above the knee.

jack'daw, *n.*, a small species of crow.

jack'et, *n.*, a short coat; a cover of many kinds; *v.t.*, to provide with a jacket; to beat.

jack'eted, *adj.*, furnished with a jacket; *p.p.*, jacket.

jack'eting, *pr.p.*, jacket; *n.*, a beating.

jack'-knife, *n.*, a large pocket clasp-knife.

jack'-plane, *n.*, a large joiner's plane.

jack'-pudding, *n.*, a buffoon.

jack'-screw, *n.*, a jack for lifting heavy weights.

Jack-tar', *n.*, a sailor.

jack'-wood, *n.*, a heavy, fine-grained, yellow wood used in cabinet-making.

Jacobe'an, *adj.*, a term specially applied to early 17th cent. architecture.

Jac'obin, *n.*, a violent republican.

Jacobin'ic, *adj.*, resembling the French Jacobins of 1789.

Jacobin'ical, *adj.*, *s.q.* Jacobinic.

Jac'obinism, *n.*, the principles of Jacobins.

Jac'obite, *n.*, an adherent of James II of England and his descendants.

Jacobit'ical, *adj.*, rel. to the Jacobites.

Jac'obitism, *n.*, the principles of the Jacobites.

Ja'cob's-lad'der, *n.*, a cottage-garden flower; a ship's rope-ladder with wooden rungs.

jac'onet, *n.*, a light, soft muslin of open texture.

Jacquard', *adj.*, a term descriptive of a loom for weaving figured goods.

jacta'tion, *n.*, agitation of the body; morbid restlessness.

jactita'tion, *n.*, false assertion; a frequent tossing about of the body.

jac'ulator, *n.*, the archer fish.

jade, *n.*, a hard, greenish stone with an oily-looking surface, used for weapons and implements by rude nations; a mean woman, a hussy; *v.t.*, to fatigue.

ja'ded, *adj.*, wearied out; *p.p.*, jade.

ja'ding, *pr.p.*, jade.

jag, *v.t.*, to notch; *n.*, a notch; a sharp protuberance.

jagged, *p.p.*, jag.

jag'ged, *adj.*, having notches or teeth.

jag'gedness, *n.*, the state of being jagged.

jag'ger, *n.*, one who, or that which, jags.

jag'gy, *adj.*, set with jags or teeth; jagged.

jaghire', *n.*, in India, the assignment of the Government share of produce to an individual.

jag'uar, *n.*, the American tiger.

Jah, *n.*, Jehovah.

jail, *n.*, a prison. Also *gaol*.

jail'bird, *n.*, one who has been confined in jail.

jail'er, *n.*, a prison-keeper.

Jain, *n.*, one of a Hindu religious sect whose creed resembles Buddhism.

Jain'ism, *n.*, the doctrines of the Jains.

jal'ap, *n.*, a purgative medicine.

jalousie', *n.*, a kind of outside venetian blind (*Fr.*).

jam, *n.*, a preserve of fruit boiled with sugar and water; a press of people; *v.t.*, to wedge in; to squeeze tight.

jamb, *n.*, the vertical side-piece of an opening in a wall.

jammed, *p.p.*, jam.

jam'ming, *pr.p.*, jam.

jan'gle, *n.*, discordant sound; *v.t.*, to cause to sound harshly; *v.i.*, to sound inharmoniously; to quarrel in words.
jan'gled, *p.p.*, jangle.
jan'gler, *n.*, a babbler.
jan'gling, *pr.p.*, jangle.
jan'itor, *n.*, a doorkeeper.
janiza'rian, *adj.*, rel. to the janizaries.
jan'izary, *n.*, a soldier of the Turkish foot-guards.
Jan'senism, *n.*, the doctrine of the Jansenists.
Jan'senist, *n.*, a follower of Bishop Jansen of Ypres.
Jan'uary, *n.*, the first month of the year.
Japan', *n.*, a country of Asia; work varnished and figured as in Japan; lacquer; *v.t.*, to varnish with japan-lacquer.
Japanese', *adj.*, pert. to Japan; *n.*, a native of Japan; the language of Japan.
japanned', *p.p.*, japan.
japan'ner, *n.*, one who japans.
japan'ning, *pr.p.*, japan.
jape, *n.*, a coarse joke.
Japhet'ic, *adj.*, pert. to Japheth, one of the sons of Noah.
jar, *v.i.*, to sound discordantly; *v.t.*, to cause to shake; *n.*, a harsh sound; clash of opinion; a vessel of earthenware or glass.
jarara'ca, *n.*, a small poisonous Brazilian snake.
jarde, *n.*, a hard tumour on the leg of a horse.
jar'gon, *n.*, gibberish; professional slang.
jargonelle', *n.*, a variety of early pear.
jar'rah, *n.*, an Australian timber-tree.
jarred, *p.p.*, jar.
jar'ring, *pr.p.*, jar.
jar'ringly, *adv.*, in a jarring manner.
jar'vey, *n.*, a coach or cab driver.
jas'hawk, *n.*, a young hawk.
jas'mine, *n.*, a shrub with white or yellow sweet-smelling flowers.
jas'per, *n.*, a coloured opaque quartz.
jas'perated, *adj.*, containing particles of jasper.
jas'pery, *adj.*, resembling or mixed with jasper.
jaspid'ean, *adj.*, resembling, containing, or consisting of, jasper.
jaun'dice, *n.*, a disease of the liver causing yellowness of the skin; an emotion affecting the judgment; *v.t.*, to affect with prejudice or jealousy.
jaun'diced, *adj.*, affected with prejudice.
jaunt, *v.i.*, to ramble; *n.*, a short journey; an excursion.
jaun'ted, *p.p.*, jaunt.
jaun'tily, *adv.*, briskly; airily.
jaunt'ing, *pr.p.*, jaunt.
jaun'ty, *adj.*, sprightly
Javanese', *adj.*, rel. to Java; *n.*, a native, or the language, of Java.
jav'elin, *n.*, a light spear thrown from the hand.
jaw, *n.*, the bones of the mouth; *v.i.*, to gossip; to scold; *v.t.*, to lecture severely.
jaw'bone, *n.*, the bone of the jaw.
jawed, *adj.*, having jaws; *p.p.*, jaw.
jaw'ing, *pr.p.*, jaw; *n.*, a lecturing (*slang*).
jaw'y, *adj.*, rel. to the jaws.
jay, *n.*, a bird of the crow family.
jeal'ous, *adj.*, suspicious in love; anxiously careful.
jeal'ously, *adv.*, in a jealous manner.
jeal'ousy, *n.*, the quality of being jealous.
Jean, *n.*, a woman's name.
jean, *n.*, a twilled cotton cloth.
jeer, *v.t.* and *i.*, to mock; to deride; *n.*, a gibe.
jeered, *p.p.*, jeer.
jeer'er, *n.*, one who jeers.
jeer'ing, *pr.p.*, jeer.
Jeho'vah, *n.*, a name of God.
Jeho'vist, *adj.*, pert. to the Jehovistic portions of the Old Testament.
jejune', *adj.*, dry; uninteresting; barren.
jejune'ness, *n.*, the state of being jejune.
jel'lied, *adj.*, of the consistency of jelly.
jel'lify, *v.t.*, to make into or like jelly.
jel'ly, *n.*, a viscous, glutinous, transparent substance; *v.t.* and *i.*, to congeal.
jel'ly-fish, *n.*, a marine animal of jelly-like appearance.
jem'adar, *n.*, a native lieutenant in the Indian Army.
jem'my, *n.*, a short, stout crowbar used by housebreakers.
jen'net, *n.*, a small, Spanish horse. Also *gend.*
jen'neting, *n.*, an early apple.
jen'ny, *n.*, a machine for spinning moved by water or steam.
jeof'ail, *n.*, an oversight in pleading, and its acknowledgment.
jeop'ardize, *v.t.*, to expose to loss or injury.
jeop'ardized, *p.p.*, jeopardize.
jeop'ardizing, *pr.p.*, jeopardize.
jeop'ardous, *adj.*, hazardous.
jeop'ardy, *n.*, peril.
jerbo'a, *n.*, a small kind of rat with very long hind legs.
jeremi'ad, *n.*, a lamentation.
jer'falcon, *n.*, a bold and handsome kind of falcon.
jerk, *v.t.*, to give a sudden pull or push

to; to cut (beef) into long strips and dry in the sun; *n.*, a sudden pull or push.

jerked, *p.p.*, jerk.

jerked'-beef, *n.*, beef cut into strips and dried in the sun.

jerk'er, *n.*, one who jerks; an officer who searches ships for contraband.

jer'kin, *n.*, a jacket; a close waistcoat.

jerk'ing, *pr.p.*, jerk.

jer'ry, *adj.*, trashy; flimsy.

jer'ry-builder, *n.*, a builder of cheap and poorly constructed houses.

jer'sey, *n.*, a close-fitting, woollen upper shirt.

jess, *n.*, a short strap fastened round a hawk's leg.

jes'samine, *n.*, *i.q* jasmine.

Jes'se, *n.*, a genealogical representation in stained glass or stonework, showing Our Lord's human descent from David; a large brass candlestick with many branches, used in churches.

jest, *n.*, a joke; *v.i.*, to talk jokingly.

jest'ed, *p.p.*, jest.

jest'er, *n.*, a buffoon; a person formerly retained by men of rank to make sport for them.

jest'ing, *pr.p.*, jest; *n.*, making a joke.

jest'ingly, *adj.*, in a jesting manner; not in earnest.

Jes'uit, *n.*, a member of the Society of Jesus, a religious Order.

Jesuit'ic, *adj.*, pert. to, or resembling, the Jesuits.

Jesuit'ical, *adj.*, *i.q.* Jesuitic.

Jes'uitism, *n.*, the principles and practices of the Jesuits.

jet, *n.*, a hard, black mineral used for ornaments; a shooting forth; a pipe out of which a small stream of fluid issues; that which flows out of an orifice in a small stream; *v.i.*, to issue in a jet; to jut; *v.t.*, to spout forth.

jet d'eau', *n.*, an ornamental fountain (*Fr.*).

jet'sam, *n.*, goods thrown overboard to lighten a ship.

jet'tison, *n.*, *i.q.* jetsam; *v.t.*, to throw overboard.

jet'ty, *adj.*, made of, or black as, jet; *n.*, a kind of small pier.

jeu d'esprit', *n.*, an elegant literary trifle (*Fr.*).

Jew, *n.*, an Israelite.

jew'el, *n.*, a precious stone; an ornament of great value; *v.t.*, to adorn with jewels.

jew'el(l)ed, *p.p.*, jewel.

jew'el(l)er, *n.*, one who deals in jewels.

jew'ellery, *n.*, the art or trade of a jeweller; jewels in general.

jew'el(l)ing, *pr.p.*, jewel.

jew'el(l)y, *adj.*, jewel-like; brilliant.

jew'elry, *n.*, *i.q.*, jewellery.

Jew'ess, *n.*, a Hebrew woman.

Jew'ish, *adj.*, bel. to the Jews.

jew's'-ear, *n.*, a kind of fungus.

jew's'-harp, *n.*, a musical instrument held in the teeth and played by having a metal tongue struck or plucked.

Jez'ebel, *n.*, an unscrupulous, vicious woman.

jib, *n.*, a sail in front of the foremast; *v.t.*, to shift a sail from one side to the other; *v.i.*, to be restive; to pull against the bit.

jibbed, *p.p.*, jib.

jib'ber, *n.*, a horse that jibs.

jib'bing, *pr.p.*, jib.

jib'-boom, *n.*, a spar serving as a continuation of the bowsprit.

jibe, *v.t.* and *i.*, *i.q.* jib; to jeer.

jif'fy, *n.*, a moment.

jig, *n.*, a lively tune or dance; *v.i.*, to dance a jig.

jig'ger, *n.*, the chigoe; a kind of light tackle used in ships; a potter's wheel; a short rest for a billiard cue.

jig'ging, *pr.p.*, jig.

jill, *n.*, a sweetheart.

jilt, *n.*, a woman who leads a lover on and then leaves him; *v.t.*, to trick in love.

jilt'ed, *p.p.*, jilt.

jilt'ing, *pr.p.*, jilt.

jim'my, *n.*, *i.q.* jemmy.

jimp, *adj.*, neat; elegant.

jin'gal, *n.*, a small, portable cannon.

jin'gle, *v.i.* and *t.*, to sound like small bells; *n.*, a clinking sound; correspondence of sound in words.

jin'gled, *p.p.*, jingle.

jin'gling, *pr.p.*, jingle.

Jin'go, *n.*, a mild oath; a person clamorous for war.

Jin'goism, *n.*, the spirit of fighting.

jinn, *n.*, pl. of jinnee.

jin'nee, *n.*, a Mohammedan spirit, usually a demon.

jinrick'sha, *n.*, a light Eastern chaise drawn by a man.

jip'po, *n.*, a kind of corset.

job, *n.*, a bit of work for hire; public work bringing gain to a private person; *v.i.*, to buy and sell stocks; *v.t.*, to let out on hire; to stab or peck.

jobbed, *p.p.*, job.

job'ber, *n.*, one who jobs; one who lets out carriages and horses; a stock-jobber.

job'bery, *n.*, underhand dealing; the dishonest practice of turning a public office to private gain.

job'bing, *adj.*, a term applied to a person

who works by the job; *pr.p.*, job.

jock'ey, *n.*, one who rides horses in races; a horse-dealer; one who deals unfairly in business; *v.t.*, to jostle in riding; to treat unfairly.

jock'eyed, *p.p.*, jockey.

jock'eying, *pr.p.*, jockey.

jock'eyism, *n.*, the practice of jockeys.

jock'eyship, *n.*, the art of riding horses.

jocose', *adj.*, full of jokes or fun.

jocose'ly, *adv.*, in a jocose manner.

jocose'ness, *n.*, the quality of being jocose.

jocos'ity, *n.*, *i.q.* jocoseness.

joc'ular, *adj.*, fond of making jokes; facetious.

jocular'ity, *n.*, merriment; fondness for jokes.

joc'ularly, *adv.*, in a jocular manner.

joc'und, *adj*, cheerful; light-hearted.

jocund'ity, *n.*, the state of being jocund.

jog, *n.*, a push; a slight shake; *v.t.*, to push slightly; *v.i.*, to move along slowly with shakes and jolts.

jogged, *p.p.*, jog.

jog'ger, *n.*, one who jogs.

jog'ging, *pr.p.*, jog.

jog'gle, *v.t.*, to push slightly; *v.i.*, to totter; *n.*, a carpenter's joint made by means of notches.

jog'gled, *p.p.*, joggle.

jog'gling, *pr.p.*, joggle.

johan'nes, *n.*, a Portuguese gold coin.

join, *v.t.*, to bring or fix together; to engage in.

join'der, *n.*, a joining of parties as plaintiffs or defendants in a suit.

joined, *p.p.*, join.

join'er, *n.*, a worker in wood.

join'ery, *n.*, carpentry.

join'-*hand*, *n.*, writing in which the letters of a word are joined together.

join'ing, *n.*, a joint; *pr.p.*, join.

joint, *n.*, the place where two things are joined; a piece of meat cut; *v.t.*, to fix by joints; to divide by joints; *adj.*, shared in common.

joint'ed, *adj.*, provided with joints; formed with knots; *p.p.*, joint.

joint'er, *n.*, one who, or that which, joints.

joint'ing, *pr.p.*, joint.

joint'ly, *adv.*, together.

joint'ress, *n.*, a woman who has a jointure.

joint-ten'ant, *n.*, one who holds an estate with another and, if the other dies, takes the whole.

join'ture, *n.*, property settled on a woman at marriage; *v.t.*, to settle a jointure upon.

join'tured, *p.p.*, jointure.

join'turess, *n.*, *i.q.* jointress.

join'turing, *pr.p.*, jointure.

joist, *n.*, one of the beams upon which the boards of a floor or the laths of a ceiling are nailed; *v.t.*, to fit with joists.

joist'ed, *adj.*, having joists; *p.p.*, joist.

joist'ing, *pr.p.*, joist.

joke, *n.*, a jest; *v.i.*, to jest; *v.t.*, to rally.

joked, *p.p.*, joke.

jo'ker, *n.*, a merry fellow; one of the cards in certain card-games.

jo'king, *pr.p.*, joke.

jo'kingly, *adv.*, in a joking manner.

jole, *n.*, the jowl; the head.

jollifica'tion, *n.*, a merry-making.

jol'lily, *adv.*, in a jolly manner.

jol'lity, *n.*, mirth; joviality.

jol'ly, *adj.*, jovial; looking and feeling well; *n.*, a marine.

jol'ly-boat, *n.*, a ship's boat.

jolt, *v.i.*, and *t.*, to shake with sudden jerks; *n.*, a sudden shock or jerk.

jolt'ed, *p.p.*, jolt.

jolt'er, *n.*, one who, or that which, jolts.

jolt'ing, *pr.p.*, jolt.

jolt'ingly, *adv.*, in a jolting manner.

jon'quil, *n.*, a species of narcissus or daffodil.

jo'rum, *n.*, a bowl or drinking vessel with liquor in it.

joss, *n.*, a Chinese idol.

joss'-house, *n.*, a Chinese temple.

jos'tle, *v.t.*, to elbow; to hustle; *v.i.*, to shove about as in a crowd.

jos'tled, *p.p.*, jostle.

jos'tling, *pr.p.*, jostle.

jot, *n.*, an iota; the least possible quantity; *v.t.*, to make a memorandum of.

jot'ted, *p.p.*, jot.

jot'ting, *n.*, a short note; *pr.p.* jot.

joule, *n.*, a unit of work equal to ten million ergs.

jounce, *v.t.* and *i.*, to jolt; *n.*, a jolt.

jour'nal, *n.*, an account of a day's proceedings, or the paper in which they are recorded; a daily newspaper; that part of an axle which rests in the bearings.

jour'nalism, *n.*, the occupation of publishing, writing in, or conducting a journal.

jour'nalist, *n.*, a newspaper editor or contributor.

journalis'tic, *adj.*, rel. to journalism.

jour'nalize, *v.t.*, to enter in a journal.

jour'nalized, *p.p.*, journalize.

jour'nalizing, *pr.p.*, journalize.

jour'ney, *n.*, travel from one place to another; *v.i.*, to travel.

jour'neyed, *p.p.*, journey.

jour'neyer, *n.*, one who journeys.

jour'neying, *pr.p.*, journey.

jour'neyman, *n.*, a mechanic or workman who has learned his special trade.

jour'ney-work, *n.*, work done by a journeyman.

joust, *n.*, an encounter with spears on horseback as a trial of skill; *v.i.*, to tilt.

joust'ed, *p.p.*, joust.

joust'er, *n.*, one who jousts.

joust'ing, *pr.p.*, joust.

jo'vial, *adj.*, gay.

jovial'ity, *n.*, the quality of being jovial.

jo'vially, *adv.*, in a jovial manner.

jowl, *n.*, the cheek or jaw.

jowl'er, *n.*, a dog with large jowls; a beagle.

joy, *n.*, gladness; *v.i.*, to rejoice.

joyed, *p.p.*, joy.

joy'ful, *adj.*, full of joy.

joy'fully, *adv.*, in a joyful manner.

joy'fulness, *n.*, the state of being joyful.

joy'ing, *pr.p.*, joy.

joy'less, *adj.*, destitute of joy.

joy'lessly, *adv.*, in a joyless manner.

joy'lessness, *n.*, the state of being joyless.

joy'ous, *adj.*, joyful.

joy'ously, *adv.*, in a joyous manner.

joy'ousness, *n.*, the state of being joyous.

ju'bilant, *adj.*, shouting or singing with joy.

ju'bilate, *v.i.*, to rejoice; to triumph.

Jubila'te, *n.*, the 100th Psalm.

jubila'tion, *n.*, exultation.

ju'bilee, *n.*, rejoicing on the fiftieth anniversary of any event.

Juda'ic, *adj.*, pert. to the Jews.

Juda'ical, *adj.*, i.q. Judaic.

Ju'daism, *n.*, the Jewish system.

Judaiza'tion, *n.*, the act of Judaizing.

Ju'daize, *v.t.*, to convert to Judaism; *v.i.*, to practise Judaism.

Ju'daized, *p.p.*, judaize.

Ju'daizer, *n.*, one who judaizes.

Ju'daizing, *pr.p.*, judaize.

Ju'das, *n.*, a treacherous person; a hole for peeping into a room furtively.

judge, *n.*, one who hears and decides; *v.t.* and *i.*, to hear and determine; to estimate; criticize.

judged, *p.p.*, judge.

judg'er, *n.*, one who judges.

judge'ship, *n.*, the office of a judge.

judg'ing, *pr.p.*, judge.

judg'ment, *n.*, power of judging; the decision come to; a sentence passed on a prisoner.

ju'dicative, *adj.*, having power to judge.

ju'dicatory, *adj.*, bel. to a judge; *n.*, a court of justice.

ju'dicature, *n.*, the duties of a judge; the extent of a court's power; the body of judges.

judi'cial, *adj.*, bel. to a judge or a court; used in or enforced by a court; fitted for judging.

judi'cially, *adv.*, in a judicial manner.

judi'ciary, *adj.*, bel. to courts of justice; *n.*, the judges as a body.

judi'cious, *adj.*, wise; sound in judgment.

judi'ciously, *adv.*, in a judicious manner.

jug, *n.*, a vessel with a narrow mouth and swelling body, and, usually, a handle and a lip.

ju'gal, *adj.*, in the region of the cheekbone.

ju'gated, *adj.*, coupled together, as a pair of leaflets in a compound leaf.

Jug'gernaut, *n.*, an idol in India, underneath whose car people used to throw themselves as a sacrifice.

jug'gle, *v.i.*, to play tricks by sleight-of-hand.

jug'gled, *p.p.*, juggle.

jug'gler, *n.*, one who deceives by quickness of hand.

jug'glery, *n.*, the skill and tricks of a juggler.

jug'gling, *pr.p.*, juggle.

ju'gular, *adj.*, pert. to the neck or throat; *n.*, a large vein on each side of the neck.

jugula'tion, *n.*, the act of slitting a throat.

juice, *n.*, the watery part of vegetables, esp. fruits, and also of animal substances.

juice'less, *adj.*, destitute of juice.

jui'ciness, *n.*, the state of being juicy.

jui'cy, *adj.*, full of sap.

ju'jube, *n.*, a sweetmeat of gum and sugar; the fruit of a shrub of Southern Europe.

ju'lep, *n.*, a sweet liquid in which disagreeable medicines are taken; an American cocktail.

Ju'lian, *adj.*, derived from Julius Caesar, a term applied to the kalendar arranged by him.

julienne', *n.*, a soup containing vegetables cut into very small pieces.

July', *n.*, the seventh month of the year.

ju'mart, *n.*, the supposed offspring of a bull and a mare.

jum'ble, *v.t.*, to put together without order; *n.*, a mass without order.
jum'bled, *p.p.*, jumble.
jum'bler, *n.*, one who jumbles.
jum'bling, *pr.p.*, jumble.
jumelle', *adj.*, twin; paired; a term applied to binocular glasses, etc. (*Fr.*).
jump, *v.i.*, to leap; to accord; *v.t.*, to leap over; *n.*, a leap.
jumped, *p.p.*, jump.
jump'er, *n.*, one who jumps; a fanatical Calvinistic Methodist.
jump'ing, *pr.p.*, jump.
junc'tion, *n.*, the line or point where two things come together.
junc'ture, *n.*, an important point of time.
June, *n.*, the sixth month of the year.
jun'gle, *n.*, land covered with coarse, rank vegetation.
ju'nior, *adj.*, younger; lower in standing.
ju'niorate, *n.*, a state, or period, of probation in the Jesuit Order.
junior'ity, *n.*, the state of being junior.
ju'niper, *n.*, a shrub the berries of which are used in making gin.
junk, *n.*, pieces of old rope; salt beef; a Chinese ship.
junk'er, *n.*, a Prussian aristocrat; a young German nobleman.
jun'ket, *n.*, curds and cream; *v.i.*, to feast.
jun'keted, *p.p.*, junket.
jun'keting, *n.*, feasting; *pr.p.*, junket.
Ju'no, *n.*, a Roman goddess.
jun'ta, *n.*, a council; a grand council of state in Spain.
jun'to, *n.*, a secret council; a faction, a cabal.
jupe, *n.*, *i.q.* jupon.
Ju'piter, *n.*, a Roman god; one of the superior planets.
jupon, *n.*, a tight-fitting garment worn over armour; a petticoat.
Juras'sic, *adj.*, a geological term applied to certain limestone rocks.
ju'rat, *n.*, a kind of magistrate.
ju'ratory, *adj.*, rel. to an oath.
jurid'ical, *adj.*, bel. to a judge or a court of law.
jurid'ically, *adv.*, in a juridical manner.
jurisconsult', *n.*, anyone learned in jurisprudence.
jurisdic'tion, *n.*, legal authority and its extent.
jurisdic'tional, *adj.*, pert. to jurisdiction.
jurisdic'tive, *adj.*, having jurisdiction.
jurispru'dence, *n.*, a knowledge of law and its principles.
jurispru'dent, *adj.*, understanding law; *n.*, a jurist.
ju'rist, *n.*, a man learned in the civil law.
ju'ror, *n.*, a member of a jury.
ju'ry, *n.*, a body of men on oath, who judge of the facts stated at a trial.
ju'ryman, *n.*, a juror.
ju'ry-mast, *n.*, a mast to replace temporarily a broken one.
just, *v.i.*, *i.q.* joust; *adj.*, according to what is right; doing right; *adv.*, exactly; barely; a little while ago.
jus'tice, *n.*, justness; fairness; a judge or magistrate.
justi'ciary, *n.*, a chief-justice.
jus'tifiable, *adj.*, defensible; excusable.
jus'tifiably, *adv.*, excusably.
justifica'tion, *n.*, the act of justifying; acceptance of a sinner as righteous through the merits of Jesus Christ.
justif'icative, *adj.*, justifying.
justif'icatory, *adj.*, vindicatory.
jus'tified, *p.p.*, justify.
jus'tifier, *n.*, one who justifies.
jus'tify, *v.t.*, to make just, to prove to be right; to free from blame.
jus'tifying, *pr.p.*, justify.
jus'tle, *v.t.*, *i.q.* jostle.
jus'tled, *p.p.*, justle.
just'ling, *pr.p.*, justle.
just'ly, *adv.*, in a just manner.
just'ness, *n.*, the quality of being just.
jut, *v.i.*, to project.
jute, *n.*, a fibrous material resembling hemp.
jut'ted, *p.p.*, jut.
jut'ting, *pr.p.*, jut.
jut'ty, *n.*, a jetty.
Juvena'lian, *adj.*, pert. to Juvenal, the Roman satirist.
juvenes'cence, *n.*, the state of being juvenescent.
juvenes'cent, *adj.*, becoming young.
ju'venile, *adj.*, youthful; *n.*, a young person.
juvenil'ity, *n.*, youthfulness.
juxtaposi'tion, *n.*, proximity; the act of placing near or next to.

K

Ka'aba, *n.*, the shrine at Mecca.
kack'le, *v.t.*, to secure an end of a rope.
kad'dish, *n.*, a form of prayer used in the synagogue.
Kaf'ir, Kaf'fir, *n.*, one of the tribe of Kaffirs.
ka'go, *n.*, a Japanese palanquin.
kail, kale, *n.*, cabbage; broth made from cabbage.
Kai'ser, *n.*, the German title of an Emperor.
kale, *see* kail.
kalei'doscope, *n.*, a tube containing bits of coloured glass, which, being shaken and reflected in mirrors, produce symmetrical patterns.
kaleidoscop'ic, *adj.*, rel. to a kaleidoscope; constantly changing.
Kal'endar, *n.*, *see* Calendar.
Kal'ends, *n.*, *see* Calends.
ka'li, *n.*, the saltwort.
Kal'muck, *n.*, a Mongol race.
kamptu'licon, *n.*, cork carpet.
kam'sin, *n.*, a hot wind in Egypt. Also *khamsin.*
kangaroo', *n.*, a marsupial quadruped of Australia and Tasmania.
Kant'ian, *adj.*, rel. to Kant.
Kant'ism, *n.*, Kant's critical philosophy.
Kant'ist, *n.*, a disciple of Kant.
ka'olin, *n.*, fine white clay, from which porcelain is made.
kar'ma, *n.*, an act and its effects; destiny.
karoo', *n.*, a plateau covered with low scrub.
kaross', *n.*, an African garment; a skin-coat.
katab'olism, *n.*, destructive metabolism.
kath'ode, *n.*, the negative pole of a magnetic battery. Also *cathode.*
ka'tydid, *n.*, a long-horned insect.
kau'ri, *n.*, a New Zealand pine.
ka'va, *n.*, a strong intoxicant made from the kava root.
kavass', *n.*, a Turkish military guard or courier.
kay'ak, *n.*, an Esquimo canoe.
kea, *n.*, a New Zealand parrot.
keb, *v.i.*, to give birth to a lamb prematurely; *n.*, a ewe that has given birth prematurely.
keck, *v.i.*, to make the sound of vomiting; *n.*, the hollow stalk of a plant.
keck'le, *v.i.*, *i.q.* kackle.
keck'led, *p.p.*, keckle.
keck'ling, *pr. p.*, keckle.
keck'y, *adj.*, like a keck.
kedge, *v.t.*, to move (a ship) by pulling on an anchor grounded; *v.i.*, to move in this way (said of the ship); *n.*, a light anchor.
kedged, *p.p.*, kedge.
kedg'er, *n.*, a fisherman, cadger.
kedg'eree, *n.*, a stew of various ingredients; as fish, rice, eggs, etc.
kedg'ing, *pr.p.*, kedge.
keel, *v.t.*, to supply with a keel; *v.i.*, to turn keel upwards; *n.*, the lowest part of a ship's framework.
keel'age, *n.*, the payment for anchoring a vessel in port.
keeled, *p.p.*, keel.
keel'er, *n.*, a bargeman.
keel'haul, *v.t.*, to haul under the keel as a punishment.
keel'hauled, *p.p.*, keelhaul.
keel'hauling, *pr.p.*, keelhaul; *n.*, a former punishment in the navy.
keel'ing, *pr.p.*, keel.
keel'man, *n.*, a labourer on a barge.
keel'son, *n.*, a beam running longitudinally along the bottom of a ship.
keen, *v.t.*, to bewail; *v.i.*, to moan, wail; *n.*, an Irish dirge; *adj.*, sharp, pointed, intense, vigorous, intellectually alert.
keen'er, *n.*, one who keens; *adj.*, *comp.* of keen.
keen'est, *adj.*, *super.* of keen.
keen'ly, *adv.*, in a keen way.
keen'ness, *n.*, sharpness, vigour, acumen.
keep, *v.t.*, to retain, guard, employ, have habitually, have charge of; *n.*, a fortress; maintenance.
keep'er, *n.*, one who keeps; an attendant; a guard-ring.
keep'ing, *pr.p.*, keep.
keep'sake, *n.*, a souvenir.
keeve, *n.*, a large tub or vat.
keg, *n.*, a small barrel.
ke'lis, *n.*, a skin-disease.
kelp, *n.*, a large seaweed.
kel'pie, kel'py, *n.*, a water-sprite.
Kelt, *n.*, *see* Celt.
Kelt'ic, *n.*, *see* Celtic.
kemp, *n.*, knotty hair.

ken, *v.t.*, to recognize, to know; *n.*, range of sight or understanding; view; a low place of resort (*slang*).

ken'nel, *v.t.*, to house in a kennel; *v.i.*, to go to kennel; *n.*, a shelter for dogs; a mean dwelling; the gutter.

ken'nelled, *p.p.*, ken- [nel.

ken'nelling, *pr.p.*, kennel.

kenogen'esis, *n.*, development of fresh characteristics.

keno'sis, *n.*, an emptying, referring esp. to Our Lord's limiting of Himself in the Incarnation.

Kent'ish, *adj.*, pert. to Kent.

kent'ledge, *n.*, permanent ballast of pig-iron.

kep'i, *n.*, a French military cap with horizontal peak.

kept, *p.p.*, keep.

ker'atose, *adj.*, horny; *n.*, a horny substance.

kerb, *n.*, a pavement-edging; a raised pathway.

kerb'stone, *n.*, the stone of the kerb.

ker'chief, *n.*, a head-covering; a handkerchief.

ker'chiefed, *adj.*, wearing a kerchief.

kerf, *n.*, the groove made by a saw.

ker'mes, *n.*, an insect found on certain oaks; a red dye prepared from dead kermes.

kern, *n.*, an Irish foot-soldier; a boor.

ker'nel, *n.*, the inner edible part of a nut or fruit-stone; nucleus of a seed.

ker'nel(l)ed, *adj.*, having a kernel.

ker'nel(l)y, *adj.*, full of kernels.

ker'osene, *n.*, hydrocarbon lamp-oil.

ker'ril, *n.*, an E. Indian sea-snake.

ker'sey, *adj.*, homespun; *n.*, a cloth, smooth-faced and soft-napped.

ker'seymere, *n.*, a variety of Cashmere.

kes'trel, *n.*, a variety of hawk.

ketch, *n.*, a two-masted coaster.

ketch'up, *n.*, a sauce prepared from mushroom or tomato juice.

ket'tle, *n.*, a vessel for boiling or stewing.

ket'tle-drum, *n.*, a drum made hemispherical and having a parchment head; a ladies' tea-party.

kev'el, *n.*, a cleat.

kex, *n.*, a weed; a husk.

key, *v.t.*, to wedge, bolt; to regulate musical pitch of an instrument; *n.*, an instrument for working a lock; a solution of a problem; a series of related musical notes.

key'board, *n.*, a range of levers pressed by the fingers.

keyed, *p.p.*, key.

key'hole, *n.*, the hole into which the key is inserted.

key'less, *adj.*, having no key.

key'note, *n.*, the tonic note of a key.

key'stone, *n.*, the topmost stone of an arch, binding the whole structure.

kha'ki, *adj.*, dust-coloured; made of khaki-coloured material; *n.*, a dust-coloured cloth.

kham'sin, *n.*, *i.q.*, kamsin.

khan, *n.*, a Tartar, Turkish, and Mongolian sovereign; an official or gentleman in Afghanistan and India.

khan'ate, *n.*, a Tartar or Mongolian principality.

Khedive', *n.*, the title of the Egyptian viceroy.

kib'ble, *n.*, a bucket for hoisting; *v.t.*, to grind.

kib'bled, *p.p.*, kibble.

kib'bler, *n.*, one who kibbles stones.

kib'bling, *pr.p.*, kibble.

kibe, *n.*, an ulcerous chilblain.

kibed, *adj.*, chapped.

kibit'ka, *n.*, a Russian sledge; a Tartar's tent.

ki'by, *adj.*, chapped.

kib'lah, *n.*, the temple at Mecca towards which a Mussulman prays.

kick, *v.t.* and *i.*, to strike with the foot; *n.*, a blow with the foot; a gun's recoil; the depression in the bottom of a bottle.

kicked, *p.p.*, kick.

kick'er, *n.*, one who kicks.

kick'ing, *pr.p.*, kick; *n.*, act of a kicker.

kick'shaw, *n.*, a fancy dish; an unconsidered trifle.

kid, *v.t.* and *i.*, to bring forth a kid; to hoax (*slang*); *n.*, the young of a goat; leather made of kid's skin; a child (*slang*).

kid'der, *n.*, a forestaller.

Kid'derminster, *n.*, a manufacture of carpet named after the town.

kid'dle, *n.*, a fish-trap set in a weir.

kid'dow, *n.*, the guillemot.

kid'ling, *n.*, a young kid.

kid'nap, *v.t.*, to steal a child; to abduct.

kid'napped, *p.p.*, kidnap.

kid'napper, *n.*, one who kidnaps.

kid'napping, *pr.p.*, kidnap; *n.*, abduction.

kid'ney, *n.*, a urine-secreting organ.

kil'derkin, *n.*, a large cask, holding some 18 gallons.

kill, *v.t.*, to destroy the life of; slay; neutralize; consume; *n.*, the act of killing; that which is killed.

kill'dee, *n.*, the N. American plover.
killed, *p.p.*, kill.
kill'er, *n.*, that which kills.
kill'ing, *pr.p.*, kill; *adj.*, destructive, overpowering; extremely laughable (*slang*).
kiln, *v.t.*, to burn in a kiln; *n.*, an oven or furnace.
kiln'-dried, *adj.*, dried in a kiln; *p.p.*, kiln-dry.
kiln'-dry, *v.t.*, to dry in a kiln.
kiln'-drying, *pr.p.*, kiln-dry; *n.*, the act of kiln-drying.
kil'ogramme, kil'ogram, *n.*, a weight of 1,000 grammes.
kilogramme'tre, kilogramme'ter, *n.*, a unit of energy that raises one kilogramme to the height of one metre.
kil'olitre, kil'oliter, *n.*, a measure of 1,000 litres.
kil'ometre, kil'ometer, *n.*, a measure of 1,000 metres.
kilt, *v.t.*, to tuck up; to gather vertically in pleats; *n.*, a Scottish skirt.
kilt'ed, *p.p.*, kilt; *adj.*, wearing the kilt.
kilt'ing, *pr.p.*, kilt.
kim'bo, *v.t.*, to crook; *adv.*, akimbo.
kin, *n.*, consanguinity or affinity; kindred.
kind, *adj.*, considerate, benevolent, gentle; *n.*, sort, distinctive group.
kind'er, *adj.*, *comp.* of kind.
kin'dergarten, *n.*, a school for infants.
kind'est, *adj.*, *super.* of kind.
kind'hearted, *adj.*, benevolent.
kin'dle, *v.t.*, to ignite, inflame, inspire; *v.i.*, to burst into flames.
kin'dled, *p.p.*, kindle.
kin'dler, *n.*, that which kindles.
kind'lier, *adj.*, *comp.* of kindly.
kind'liest, *adj.*, *super.* of kindly.
kind'liness, *adj.*, benevolence.
kin'dling, *pr.p.*, kindle; *n.*, material for a fire.
kind'ly, *adj.*, good-natured, genial; natural; *adv.*, in a kind manner.
kind'ness, *n.*, benevolence.
kin'dred, *n.*, blood relationship; *adj.*, of like nature, congenial.
kine, *n.*, pl. of cow.
kinemat'ic, *adj.*, rel. to motion.
kinemat'ical, *adj.*, *s.q.* kinematic.
kinemat'ics, *n.*, *pl.*, the science of pure motion.
kinemat'ograph, *n.*, a contrivance showing on a screen a number of scenes in rapid succession, giving the semblance of motion. Also *cinematograph*.
kinet'ic, *adj.*, rel. to, or depending on, motion.
kinet'ics, *n. pl.*, the science of the relation of forces to the motions of bodies.
king, *v.t.*, to crown, enthrone; *v.i.*, to play the king; *n.*, a male sovereign.
king'-bird, *n.*, a bird of Paradise.
king'-crab, *n.*, a large crustacean.
king'craft, *n.*, the art of ruling as a king.
king'cup, *n.*, a buttercup.
king'dom, *n.*, a king's dominion; a monarchy; any separate sphere of authority.
king'fisher, *n.*, a small bird with beautiful plumage.
king'let, *n.*, a petty sovereign.
king'like, *adj.*, kingly.
king'liness, *n.*, the quality of being kingly.
king'ling, *n.*, a petty king; golden-crested wren.
king'ly, *adj.*, regal; like a king.
king'-post, *n.*, a vertical post between a tie-beam and the apex of a roof.
king's e'vil, *n.*, scrofula.
king'ship, *n.*, royal state.
kink, *v.t.*, to make to kink; *v.i.*, to form a kink; *n.*, a twist or curl; a queer mental twist.
kin'kajou, *n.*, a nocturnal carnivorous, arboreal animal.
ki'no, *n.*, an astringent gum.
kins'folk, *n.*, one's relatives.
kin'ship, *n.*, the status of a relative.
kins'man, *n.*, a relative.
kins'woman, *n.*, fem. of kinsman.
kiosk', *n.*, an open pavilion.
kip, *n.*, untanned calf-skin; a slight incline; a lodging (*slang*).
kip'per, *v.t.*, to cure; *n.*, a cured salmon; a herring smoked or dried in a special way.
kirk, *n.*, a church.
kirsch'wasser, *n.*, cherry-water.
kir'tle, *v.t.*, to dress in a kirtle; *n.*, a petticoat, a tunic.
kir'tled, *p.p.*, kirtle.
kis'met, *n.*, fate.
kiss, *v.t.*, to salute or caress with the lips; to touch; *n.*, a caress or salutation with the lips.
kissed, *p.p.*, kiss.
kiss'er, *n.*, one who kisses.
kiss'ing, *pr.p.*, kiss; *n.*, the act of kissing.
kit, *n.*, a wooden tub; a packing case; its contents; a small fiddle with three strings.
kit'cat, *n.*, a portrait, showing about half length, with the hands.
kitch'en, *n.*, an apartment for cooking.
kitch'ener, *n.*, a cooking-range.
kite, *n.*, a falcon-like bird; a flying toy.

kith, *n.*, acquaintance and kindred.
kit'ling, *n.*, a kitten.
kit'ten, *n.*, a young cat.
kit'tenish, *adj.*, kitten-like, playful.
ki'wi, *n.*, an apteryx.
kleptoma'nia, *n.*, a form of madness marked by the impulse to steal.
knack, *n.*, dexterity, a trick.
knack'er, *n.*, a horse-slaughterer.
knag, *n.*, a knob.
knag'gy, *adj.*, full of knots.
knap'sack, *n.*, a travelling-bag strapped to the back.
knap'weed, *n.*, a common European weed.
knar, *n.*, a knot in wood.
knarred, *adj.*, having knots.
knarled, *see* gnarled.
knave, *n.*, a rogue, a servant.
kna'very, *n.*, roguishness.
kna'vish, *adj.*, roguish.
kna'vishly, *adv.*, roguishly.
kna'vishness, *n.*, the conduct of a rogue.
knead, *v.t.*, to work up into a mass; to massage.
knead'ed, *p.p.*, knead.
knead'er, *n.*, one who kneads.
knead'ing, *pr.p.*, knead.
knee, *v.t.*, to touch with the knee; to fasten with knees; *n.*, the joint between the thigh and the lower leg; an angular beam or piece of iron.
knee'cap, *n.*, the patella; a covering for the knee.
kneed, *p.p.*, knee; *adj.*, gone at the knees.
knee'deep, *adj.* and *adv.*, up to the knees.
knee'joint, *n.*, the joint of the knee.
kneel, *v.i.*, to fall on the knees; to bend the knee.
kneeled, *p.t.*, kneel.
kneel'er, *n.*, one who kneels; a mat to kneel on.
kneel'ing, *pr.p.*, kneel.
knee'pan, *n.*, the patella.
knell, *v.t.* and *i.*, to toll; give a sad sound; *n.*, tolling; the last warning; a death omen.
knelt, *p.p.*, kneel.
knew, *p.t.*, know.
knick'erbockers, *n. pl.*, loose-fitting breeches.
knick'-nack, *n.*, a gimcrack; light article of furniture.
knife, *v.t.*, to stab, cut; *n.*, a cutting-blade set in a handle.
knife'-board, *n.*, a board for knife-cleaning; formerly, the longitudinal seat on an omnibus.
knife'-cleaner, *n.*, an apparatus for knife cleaning.
knife'-grinder, *n.*, a grinder of knives.
knight, *v.t.*, to confer knighthood on; *n.*, a person of rank devoted to military service.
knight'age, *n.*, a record of knights; knights as a whole.
knight'ed, *p.p.*, knight.
knight'-errant, *n.*, a knight wandering about for adventures; a quixotic person.
knight'-errantry, *n.*, the conduct of a knight errant.
knight'hood, *n.*, the dignity of a knight; chivalry; the whole body of knights.
knight'liness, *n.*, the quality of being knightly.
knight'ly, *adj.*, chivalrous.
knit, *v.t.*, to make a close texture with looped yarn; to contract; to make compact.
knit'ter, *n.*, one who knits; a knitting-machine.
knit'ting, *pr.p.*, knit; *n.*, the process of knitting.
knit'tle, *n.*, a small line made of twisted yarns.
knives, *n.*, pl. of knife.
knob, *v.t.*, to put knobs on; *v.i.*, to bulge out; *n.*, a round protuberance; a round handle; a lump.
knobbed, *p.p.*, knob; *adj.*, having knobs.
knob'biness, *n.*, the quality of being knobby.
knob'bing, *pr.p.*, knob.
knob'by, *adj.*, having knobs.
knock, *v.t.*, to strike, beat; *n.*, a stroke, a rap.
knocked, *p.p.*, knock.
knock'er, *n.*, one who knocks; a striker attached to a door.
knock'ing, *pr.p.*, knock.
knock'-kneed, *adj.*, weak in the knees.
knoll, *v.t.*, to toll, ring; *v.i.*, to sound out; *n.*, a low hill or mound.
knolled, *p.p.*, knoll.
knoll'ing, *pr.p.*, knoll.
knop, *n.*, a knob; bud.
knot, *v.t.*, to tie in a knot; *v.i.*, to form into knots; *n.*, an intertwining of parts of cord or rope; an ornamental knotted bow; a nautical measure of length; an excrescence; a hard formation in wood.
knot'berry, *n.*, the cloud-berry.
knot'-grass, *n.*, a trailing weed.
knot'ted, *p.p.*, knot.
knot'tiness, *n.*, the quality of being knotty.
knot'ting, *pr.p.*, knot.
knot'ty, *adj.*, knotted, full of knots.
knout, *v.t.*, to flog with the knout; *n.*, a scourge formerly used in Russia.
know, *v.t.*, to recognize with certainty; to be on intimate terms with; to understand.

know'able, *adj.*, able to be known.

know'ing, *pr.p.*, know; *adj.*, wide-awake, smart.

know'ingly, *adv.*, in a wide-awake way.

knowl'edge, *n.*, knowing; the result of knowing; mental apprehension.

known, *p.p.*, know.

knuck'le, *v.t.*, to press with the knuckles; *v.i.*, to give in; *n.*, the bone of the finger-joint; a calf's tarsal joint.

knuck'led, *p.p.*, knuckle.

knuck'le-duster, *n.*, a metal protection of the knuckles.

knuck'ling, *pr.p.*, knuckle.

knurl, *n.*, a knot, protuberance.

knurled, *adj.*, knobbed.

knur'ly, *adj.*, having knots or knobs.

ko'dak, *n.*, a portable photographic camera; *v.t.*, to photograph with a kodak.

kohl, *n.*, a powder for darkening the eyes.

kohl'rabi, *n.*, a variety of cabbage.

koo'doo, *n.*, a S. African antelope.

koo'lah, *n.*, an Australian sloth-like mammal.

ko'pek, *see* copeck.

kop'je, *n.*, a little hill.

Ko'ran, *n.*, the Mohammedan sacred book.

ko'sher, *adj.*, clean, pure, legally correct.

kotow', *v.i.*, to perform the kotow; *n.*, touching the ground with one's forehead in obeisance.

kou'miss, *n.*, fermented mare's milk.

kour'bash, *n.*, a hide whip.

kraal, *n.*, a group of native huts.

kra'ken, *n.*, a mythical sea monster.

krem'lin, *n.*, a Russian citadel, esp. that in Moscow.

kreut'zer, *n.*, a small German coin.

krieg'spiel, *n.*, the war game.

Krish'na, *n.*, a modern Hindu deity.

Krish'naism, *n.*, worship of Krishna.

krul'ler, *n.*, a cake fried in oil. Also *cruller*.

Krupp, *n.*, a production of the Krupp works at Essen.

ku'dos, *n.*, glory, credit (*Gr.*).

ku'fic, *n.*, an Arabic script.

ku'miss, *n.*, *see* koumiss.

kure, *n.*, a Japanese naval gun.

ku'ril, *n.*, a shearwater.

kur'saal, *n.*, a reception hall.

ky'anite, *n.*, *i.q.* cyanite.

ky'anize, *v.t.*, to impregnate (wood) with mercuric chloride.

ky'anized, *p.p.*, kyanize.

ky'anizing, *pr.p.*, kyanize.

Ky'rie, *n.*, the little litany at the beginning of Mass (*Kyrie eleison*, etc.).

kyriolog'ical, *adj.*, denoting things by arbitrary signs or the characters of the alphabet.

L

la, *n.*, the sixth note of the musical scale.

laa'ger, *v.t.* and *i.*, to form into a laager; to encamp; *n.*, an encampment within an enclosure of wagons.

laa'gered, *p.p.*, laager.

laa'gering, *pr.p.*, laager.

lab'arum, *n.*, Constantine's standard, bearing the sacred monogram.

la'bel, *v.t.*, to attach a label to; to classify; *n.*, a slip of some material, used for naming.

la'belled, la'beled, *p.p.*, label.

la'belling, la'beling, *pr.p.*, label.

label'lum, *n.*, a lower petal.

la'bent, *adj.*, gliding.

la'bial, *adj.*, rel. to, or produced by, the lips; *n.*, a sound produced by the lips.

la'biate, *adj.*, lipped.

labioden'tal, *adj.*, labial and dental.

lab'oratory, *n.*, a scientific workshop.

labo'rious, *adj.*, hard-working, difficult.

labo'riously, *adv.*, in a laborious way.

la'bour, la'bor, *v.i.*, to work hard, strive, to move with difficulty; *v.t.*, to elaborate, work out; *n.*, toil, hard work, difficulty; childbirth; the working classes collectively.

la'boured, *p.p.*, labour; *adj.*, done with labour; not spontaneous.

la'bourer, *n.*, one who labours.

la'bouring, *pr.p.*, labour.

Lab'radorite, *n.*, a variety of feldspar.

la'brose, *adj.*, thick-lipped.

labur'num, *n.*, a tree with clustering yellow flowers.

lab'yrinth, *n.*, a maze; an arrangement of tortuous passages.

labyrin'thian, *adj.*, like a labyrinth.

labyrin'thine, *adj.*, *i.q.* labyrinthian.

lac, *n.*, a dark-red resin; a hundred thousand (*Anglo-Ind.*); milk (*Lat.*).

lac'cic, *adj.*, rel. to lac.

lac'cin, *n.*, a compound contained in shellac.

lace, *v.t.*, to fasten, flavour; *v.i.*, compress waist; *n.*, string, cord, braid, fabric.

laced, *p.p.*, lace.

lac'erable, *adj.*, able to be lacerated.

lac'erate, *v.t.*, to tear, mangle, distress.

lac'erated, *p.p.*, lacerate.

lac'erating, *pr.p.*, lacerate.

lacera'tion, *n.*, the act of lacerating.

lac'erative, *adj.*, producing laceration.

Lacer'ta, *n.*, a lizard.

lacer'tian, *adj.*, lizard-like.

lacer'tine, *adj.*, *i.q.* lacertian.

lach'es, *n.*, neglect of duty; culpable negligence.

lach'rymal, *adj.*, rel. to tears.

lach'rymary, *adj.*, rel. to, or containing, tears.

lach'rymatory, *adj.*, causing tears; *n.*, a tear-vessel.

lach'rymose, *adj.*, tearful, given to weeping.

la'cing, *pr.p.*, lace; *n.*, cords used in aeroplanes to bind the covering of the planes.

lack, *v.t.*, to be without; *v.i.*, to be wanting; *n.*, want, deficiency.

lackadai'sical, *adj.*, languishing, sentimental.

lack'adaisy, *adj.*, *i.q.* lackadaisical.

lack'-a-day, *interj.*, of sorrow or pained surprise.

lacked, *p.p.*, lack.

lack'ey, lac'quey, *v.t.*, to attend upon; be servile to; *n.*, a footman; a servile follower.

lack'eyed, *p.p.*, lackey.

lack'eying, *pr.p.*, lackey.

lack'ing, *pr.p.*, lack.

lack'-lustre, *adj.*, dull.

lacon'ic, *adj.*, brief, concise.

lacon'ical, *adj.*, *i.q.* laconic.

lacon'ically, *adv.*, briefly, concisely.

lacon'icism, *n.*, brevity in expression.

la'conism, *n.*, *i.q.* laconicism; a brief saying.

lac'quer, lack'er, *v.t.*, to varnish with lacquer; *n.*, a gold-coloured varnish.

lac'quered, *p.p.*, lacquer.

lac'quering, *pr.p.*, lacquer; *n.*, the art of varnishing like lacquer; lacquer work.

lac'rimose, *see* lachrymose.

lacrosse', *n.*, an American ball game, played with a long, loosely-strung racquet.

lac'tarene, lac'tarine, *n.*, a preparation from milk curd, used in calico printing.

lac'tate, *v.t.*, to make into, or like, milk; *v.i.*, to secrete milk.

lacta'tion, *n.*, the act of secreting milk; suckling.

lac'teal, *adj.*, rel. to milk; conveying a milk-like fluid.

lac'tean, *adj.*, *i.q.* lacteal.

lactes'cence, *n.*, milkiness; milky juice.

lactes'cent, *n.*, milky; conveying milky juice.

lac'tic, *adj.*, re. to milk.

lactif'erous, *adj.*, milk producing.

lactom'eter, *n.*, an instrument for testing the purity of milk.

lacu'na, *n.*, a gap, blank, cavity (*Lat.*).

lacu'nar, *adj.*, pert. to a lacuna.

lac'unose, *adj.*, full of lacunae.

lacus'tral, *adj.*, *i.q.* lacustrine.

lacus'trine, *adj.*, rel. to lakes; growing in lakes.

lad, *n.*, a boy, youth.

lad'anum, *n.*, a species of resin.

lad'der, *n.*, a contrivance for climbing; a series of steps or rungs between two uprights.

lad'die, *n.*, Scottish for lad.

lade, *v.t.*, to fill with cargo; to load.

la'ded, *p.p.*, lade.

la'den, *p.p.*, lade.

la'ding, *pr.p.*, lade; *n.*, the act of lading; a cargo.

la'dle, *v.t.*, to remove in a ladle; *n.*, a long-handled spoon with a large bowl.

la'dleful, *n.*, the quantity a ladle contains.

la'dy, *n.*, a gentlewoman; a woman of rank; a wife.

la'dybird, *n.*, an insect so named.

La'dy Day, *n.*, the Feast of the Annunciation of Our Lady (March 25).

la'dylike, *adj.*, like a lady, refined.

la'dylove, *n.*, a sweetheart.

la'dy's-fin'ger, *n.*, the kidney vetch.

la'dyship, *n.*, being a lady; title of a lady of rank.

la'dy's-maid, *n.*, a personal attendant on a lady.

la'dy's-slipper, *n.*, a plant with yellow slipper-shaped flowers.

lag, *v.i.*, to go very slowly; to be left behind; *n.*, retardation.

la'ger beer, *n.*, a light German beer.

lag'gard, *n.*, one who lags.

lagged, *p.p.*, lag.

lag'ger, *n.*, *i.q.* laggard.

lag'ging, *pr.p.*, lag.

lagoon', *n.*, a salt-water lake separated by a sand-bank from the sea; the water within an atoll.

la'ic, *adj.*, the opposite to clerical; *n.*, a layman.

la'ical, *adj.*, non-clerical.

laiciza'tion, *n.*, the act of laicizing.

la'icize, *v.t.*, to make lay; to open to the laity.

laid, *p.p.*, lay.

lain, *p.p.*, lie.

lair, *n.*, a hiding-place, den; a shelter for cattle when being driven.

laird, *n.*, a Scottish landowner.

la'ity, *n.*, lay folk collectively.

lake, *n.*, a large expanse of landlocked water; a crimson pigment.

lake'let, *n.*, a diminutive lake.

lalla'tion, *n.*, a tendency to pronounce the letter *r* as *l*. Also *lambdacism*.

la'ma, *n.*, a Mongolian or Thibetan high priest. The Grand Lama is the head of the Thibetan religion.

La'maism, *n.*, the religion of Thibet.

La'maist, *n.*, a professor of Lamaism.

La'maite, *n.*, *i.q.* Lamaist.

lamb, *n.*, a young sheep.

lamb'dacism, *n.*, *see* lallation.

lam'bency, *n.*, brilliance.

lam'bent, *adj.*, playing over a surface, like a flame; soft, liquid.

lamb'ing, *n.*, the birth of lambs; the lambing season.

lamb'kin, *n.*, a little lamb.

lamb'-like, *adj.*, gentle.

lamb'skin, *adj.*, made of lambskin; *n.*, the skin of a lamb.

lamb's'-wool, *n.*, the wool of lambs.

lame, *v.t.*, to cripple; *adj.*, crippled, halting, inadequate.

lamed, *p.p.*, lame.

lamel'la, *n.*, a thin plate or film (*Lat.*).

lamel'lar, *adj.*, scale-like; forming a thin plate.

lam'ellate, *adj.*, composed of lamellae.

lam'ellated, *adj.*, *i.q.* lamellate.

lamel'liform, *adj.*, scale-like.

lame'ly, *adv.*, in a lame way.

lame'ness, *n.*, the state of being lame.

lament', *v.t.*, to grieve for; *v.i.*, to utter grief; *n.*, a passionate utterance of grief; a dirge.

lam'entable, *adj.*, mournful, deplorable.

lam'entably, *adv.*, in a lamentable way.

lamenta'tion, *n.*, the act of lamenting; a lament.

lament'ed, *p.p.*, lament.

lament'er, *n.*, one who laments.

lament'ing, *pr.p.*, lament.

lam'ina, *n.*, a thin plate or layer.

laminabil'ity, *n.*, the state of being laminable.

lam'inable, *adj.*, able to be hammered or rolled fine.

lam'inar, *adj.*, arranged in thin plates.

lam'inary, *adj.*, *i.q.* laminar.

lam'inate, *v.t.*, to roll or beat thin; *v.i.*, to become thin.

lam'inated, *p.p.*, laminate.

lam'inating, *pr.p.*, laminate.

lamina'tion, *n.*, the state of being laminated.

la'ming, *pr.p.*, lame.

laminif'erous, *adj.*, composed of laminae.

la'mish, *adj.*, somewhat lame.

Lam'mas, *n.*, Loaf-mass (the name for 1 Aug.).

lam'mergeyer, *n.*, the bearded vulture.

lamp, *n.*, an arrangement of great variety for giving light.

lam'pas, *n.*, a mouth disease in horses; a Chinese flowered silk.

lamp'black, *n.*, pigment from soot.

lam'per-eel, *n.*, a lamprey.

lamp'ic, *adj.*, rel. to a lamp or flame.

lamp'light, *n.*, the light from a lamp.

lamp'lighter, *n.*, one who lights lamps.

lampoon', *v.t.*, to satirize; *n.*, an abusive piece of satire.

lampooned', *p.p.*, lampoon.

lampoon'er, *n.*, a writer of a lampoon.

lampoon'ing, *pr.p.*, lampoon.

lampoon'ry, *n.*, the practice of lampooning.

lamp'-post, *n.*, the pillar which holds a street lamp.

lam'prey, *n.*, an eel-like fish.

la'nary, *n.*, a wool-store.

la'nate, *adj.*, woolly.

la'nated, *adj.*, *i.q.* lanate.

Lancaste'rian, *n.*, rel. to the Lancasterian school system.

Lancas'trian, *adj.*, rel. to Lancaster; *n.*, a native of the county of L., or an adherent of the Lancastrian party.

lance, *v.t.*, to cut or open with a lancet; *n.*, a long spear-headed shaft.

lance'-corporal, *n.*, a private with the temporary rank of corporal.

lanced, *p.p.*, lance.

lan'ceolar, *adj.*, shaped like a spear-head.

lan'ceolate, *adj.*, *i.q.* lanceolar.

lan'ceolated, *adj.*, *i.q.* lanceolar.

lan'cer, *n.*, a cavalry soldier armed with the lance.

lan'cet, *n.*, a surgical instrument for lancing.

lance'wood, *n.*, a W. Indian wood used for fishing-rods, carriage-shafts, etc.

lan'ciform, *adj.*, spear-like.

lan'cinate, *v.t.*, to pierce.

lancina'tion, *n.*, acute shooting pain.

lan'cing, *pr.p.*, lance.

land, *v.t.*, to bring to land, put on land; *v.i.*, to go ashore; *n.*, solid earth, landed estate.

lan'damman, *n.*, the President of the Diet in Switzerland.

lan'dau, *n.*, a four-wheeled carriage, the top of which can be opened and laid back.

landaulet', *n.*, a small single-seated landau.

land'ed, *p.p.*, land; *adj.*, possessing land.

land'er, *n.*, one who lands.

land'grave, *n.*, a German title, resembling that of a marquis.

landgra'viate, *n.*, the area of a landgrave's jurisdiction.

land'gravine, *n.*, fem. of landgrave.

land'holder, *n.*, one who holds land as owner or tenant.

land'ing, *pr.p.*, land; *n.*, the act of going ashore; a wharf; a stage on a stairway.

land'ing-chas'sis, *n.*, the under-body of an aeroplane.

land'lady, *n.*, the mistress of an inn; a keeper of lodgings, a woman who has tenants.

land'less, *adj.*, without lands.

land'locked, *adj.*, shut in by land.

land'loper, *n.*, a tramp.

land'*lord*, *n.*, the keeper of an inn or lodgings; one who has tenants.

land'*lord*ism, *n.*, the peculiar attitude of landlords.

land'lubber, *n.* one unused to the sea; a raw sailor.

land'mark, *n.*, a boundary mark.

land'owner, *n.*, an owner of landed property.

land'owning, *n.*, the ownership of land.

land'rail, *n.*, the corn crake.

land'reeve, *n.*, a farm bailiff.

land'scape, *n.*, a prospect of country.

land'slide, *n.*, *i.q.* landslip.

land'slip, *n.*, fall of a mass of a cliff or mountain.

lands'man, *n.*, the opposite to a seaman.

land'ward, *adv.*, toward land.

lane, *n.*, a narrow road.

lan'grage, *n.*, case-shot.

lan'grel, *n.*, *i.q.* langrage

langsyne', *adv.*, in the old days; *n.*, the old days.

***lan'guage*,** *n.*, speech, tongue.

Languedoc, *n.*, an old French province

lan'guid, *adj.*, inert, spiritless, faint.

lan'guidly, *adv.*, faintly, weakly.

lan'guish, *v.i.*, to become feeble, pine, be sentimentally tender.

lan'guished, *p.p.*, languish.

lan'guisher, *n.*, one who languishes.

lan'guishing, *pr.p.*, languish.

lan'guishment, *n.*, the state of being languid.

lan'guor, *n.*, faintness, weariness, dulness; heavy stillness.

lan'guorous, *adj.*, showing or causing languor.

lanif'erous, *adj.*, fleecy, wool-bearing.

lanig'erous, *adj.*, *i.q.* laniferous.

lank, *adj.*, spare, long and lean, limp.

lank'ness, *n.*, the state of being lank.

lank'y, *adj.*, excessively lank.

lan'ner, *n.*, a species of falcon.

lan'olin, *n.*, an ointment.

lans'quenet, *n.*, a game of cards.

lan'tern, *n.*, a case shielding a candle; the luminous chamber of a lighthouse; a cupola with glazed openings.

lan'ternist, *n.*, an operator with a magic-lantern.

lan'thanum, *n.*, a rare metal.

lan'thorn, *n.*, *i.q.* lantern.

lanu'ginous, *adj.*, downy.

lan'yard, *n.*, a small rope.

Laodice'an, *adj.*, rel. to Laodicea.

lap, *v.t.*, to fold, encircle, drink with the tongue; *v.i.*, to make a lapping sound, to break gently on the shore; *n.*, an overhanging flap; the waist to the knees of a seated person; the clothing of that part; overlapping; a single round in a running-track; an act of lapping.

lap'-dog, *n.*, a pet-dog.

lapel', *n.*, the reversed part of a coat-breast.

lap'ful, *n.*, the amount held in the lap.

lapida'rian, *adj.*, rel. to stones or stone-work; monumental.

lap'idary, *adj.*, *i.q.* lapidarian; *n.*, a cutter of gems.

lap'idate, *v.t.*, to stone; to cut and polish.

lapida'tion, *n.*, stoning.

lapidif'ic, *adj.*, petrifying.

lapid'ified, *adj.*, petrified.

lapid'ify, *v.t.*, to turn to stone, petrify.

la'pis, *n.*, a way of calico printing.

lap'is-laz'uli, *n.*, a blue mixture of minerals.

Lap'lander, *n.*, a native of Lapland.

Lapp, *n.*, *i.q.* Laplander.

lapped, *p.p.*, lap.

lap'per, *n.*, anything that laps.

lap'pet, *n.*, an overlapping piece.

lap'ping, *pr.p.*, lap.

lapse, *v.i.*, to fall back or away; to become void; to revert; to glide; *n.*, a fall, slip, slight error, flow, passage.

lapsed, *p.p.*, lapse.

laps'ing, *pr.p.*, lapse.

lap'sus, *n.*, a slip (*Lat.*).

Lapu'tan, *adj.*, rel. to Laputa; chimerical; *n.*, a native of Laputa.

lap'wing, *n.*, the peewit.

lar, *n.*, a Roman household god.

lar'board, *n.*, the port side of a vessel.

lar'ceny, *n.*, theft.

larch, *n.*, a coniferous tree.

lard, *v.t.*, to lace with strips of bacon; embellish with foreign words; *n.*, the half-solid oil of hog's fat.

larda'ceous, *adj.*, like lard.

lard'ed, *p.p.*, lard.

lard'er, *n.*, a storeroom for meat.

lard'ing, *pr.p.*, lard.

La'res, *n.*, pl. of lar.

large, *adj.*, great, broad, generous; *n.*, used in phrase "at large" (*i.e.*, at liberty).

large'ly, *adv.*, in a large way; to a great extent.

large'ness, *n.*, the quality of being large.

larg'er, *adj.*, *comp.* of large.

larg'ess(e), *n.*, a free gift.

larg'est, *adj.*, *super.* of large.

larghet'to, *adj.*, slow musical time; *n.*, a slow movement.

lar'go, *n.*, a slower time than larghetto; a largo movement; *adj.*, slow.

lar'iat, *n.*, a lasso.

lark, *n.*, a singing-bird; a frolic; *v.i.*, to frolic (*slang*).

lark'spur, *n.*, one of the Delphinia.

lar'mier, *n.*, a tear-bag.

lar'rikin, *n.*, a young hooligan.

lar'ry, *n.*, *i.q.* lorry.

lar'um, *n.*, *i.q.* alarum.

lar'va, *n.*, a grub.

lar'vae, *n.*, pl. of larva.

lar'val, *adj.*, rel. to larvae.

lar'vated, *adj.*, covered with a mask.

laryn'geal, *adj.*, rel. to the larynx.

laryn'gean, *adj.*, *i.q.* laryngeal.

laryngi'tis, *n.*, inflammation of the larynx.

laryn'goscope, *n.*, a mirror for examining the larynx.

laryngoscop'ic, *adj.*, rel. to laryngoscope.

laryngot'omy, *n.*, cutting into the larynx.

lar'ynx, *n.*, the seat of the vocal chords.

las'car, *n.*, an E. Indian seaman.

lasciv'ious, *adj.*, wanton, lustful.

lasciv'iously, *adv.*, lustfully.

lasciv'iousness, *n.*, wantonness, lustfulness.

lash, *v.t.*, to flog, whip; move suddenly; satirize; *n.*, a

stroke with a whip; the flexible end of a whip: an eyelash.
lashed, *p.p.*, lash.
lash'er, *n.*, one who lashes; a weir.
lash'ing, *pr.p.*, lash.
lash'ings, *n. pl.*, an abundance (*Scot.*).
lass, *n.*, a girl, sweetheart.
las'sie, *n.*, the Scottish form of "lass."
las'situde, *n.*, weariness, incapacity for exertion.
las'so, *v.t.*, to catch with a lasso; *n.*, a noosed rope.
last, *v.i.*, to endure, continue; *v.t.*, to suffice; *adj.* and *adv.*, at the end; after the rest; *n.*, a shoe-maker's model; a measure variously used in commerce.
last'ed, *p.p.*, last.
last'ing, *pr.p.*, last; *adj.*, permanent, durable.
last'ingly, *adv.*, permanently.
last'ly, *adv.*, finally.
latch, *v.t.*, to fasten with a latch; *n.*, the fastening of a door or gate, either dropping or shot.
latched, *p.p.*, latch.
latch'et, *n.*, a shoe fastening.
latch'ing, *pr.p.*, latch.
latch'-key, *n.*, a pocket door-key.
late, *adj.*, behind time, backward; far on in point of time; dead; recent; *adv.*, behind time; far on in time; hitherto.
lateen', *adj.*, of the lateen type (*i.e.*, triangular), on a long, tapering yard and a short mast; *n.*, a sail so rigged.
late'ly, *adv.*, recently.
la'tency, *n.*, the state of being latent.
late'ness, *n.*, the state of being late.
la'tent, *adj.*, secret, dormant.
la'tently, *adv.*, in a latent way.
la'ter, *adj.*, *comp.* of late.
lat'eral, *adj.*, rel. to the side; *n.*, a sprout.
lat'erally, *adv.*, in a lateral position; sideways.
Lat'eran, *adj.*, rel. to the Lateran; *n.*, the cathedral church (St. John Lateran) of Rome.
laterifo'lious, *adj.*, by the side of a leaf.
lateri'tious, *adj.*, of brick, or brick-like.
lath, *v.t.*, to overlay with laths; *n.*, a narrow strip of wood.
lathe, *n.*, a machine for turning wood, ivory, etc.
lathed, *p.p.*, lath.
lath'er, *n.*, froth of soap and water; froth-like sweat; *v.t.*, to spread lather on; to thrash; *v.i.*, to form into a lather; to sweat.
lath'ered, *p.p.*, lather.
lath'ering, *pr.p.*, lather; *n.*, a thrashing.
lath'ing, *pr.p.*, lath.
lath'y, *adj.*, slender, like a lath.
lat'iclave, *n.*, the purple stripe denoting a person of senatorial rank.
laticos'tate, *adj.*, broad-ribbed.
latiden'tate, *adj.*, broad-toothed.
latifo'lious, *adj.*, broad-leaved.
Lat'in, *adj.*, pert. to Latium and the Latins; *n.*, the L. language.
Lat'inism, *n.*, Latin idiom.
Lat'inist, *n.*, an accomplished Latin scholar.
Latin'ity, *n.*, the style in which one writes Latin; the Latin quality.
Lat'inize, *v.t.*, to turn into Latin; *v.i.*, to adopt Latin ways.
Lat'inized, *p.p.* Latinize.
Lat'inizing, *pr.p.*, Latinize.
la'tish, *adj.*, somewhat late.
lat'itude, *n.*, breadth, scope; distance from the equator.
latitu'dinal, *adj.*, rel. to latitude.
latitudina'rian, *adj.*, unorthodox.
latitudina'rianism, *n.*, unorthodoxy.
latitu'dinous, *adj.*, having width or scope.
la'trant, *adj.*, barking.
latri'a, *n.*, worship.
latrine', *n.*, a privy.
lat'ten, *adj.*, made of latten; *n.*, a mixed, brass-like metal.
lat'ter, *adj.*, of more recent date; the second of two things.
lat'terly, *adv.*, recently, of late.
lat'tice, *n.*, a screen or door made of laths crossed and showing interstices; *v.t.*, to supply with a lattice.
lat'ticed, *p.p.*, lattice.
lat'ticing, *pr.p.*, lattice.
laud, *v.t.*, to praise, extol.
laud'able, *adj.*, praiseworthy.
laud'ableness, *n.*, praiseworthiness.
laud'ably, *adv.*, praiseworthily.
laud'anum, *n.*, tincture of opium.
lauda'tion, *n.*, praise.
laud'atory, *adj.*, in praise, flattering.
laud'ed, *p.p.*, laud.
laud'ing, *pr.p.*, laud.
laugh, *v.i.*, to give expression to laughter; *n.*, an expression of joy, gaiety, pleasure, scorn.
laugh'able, *adj.*, ludicrous.
laugh'ably, *adv.*, ludicrously.
laughed, *p.p.*, laugh.
laugh'er, *n.*, one who laughs.
laugh'ing, *pr.p.*, laugh.
laugh'ingly, *adv.*, in a laughing way.
laugh'ter, *n.*, laughing, gaiety, merriment.
launch, *v.t.*, to hurl; set afloat; send off; *v.i.*, to begin an enterprise; *n.*, the act of launching; a war-ship's large open boat; an electric or steam boat.

launched, *p.p.*, launch.
launch'ing, *pr.p.*, launch.
laun'der, *v.t.*, to get up (linen); *n.*, a trough.
laun'derer, *n.*, one who gets up linen.
laun'dress, *n.*, fem. of launderer.
laun'dry, *n.*, a place where clothes are washed, etc.
lau'reate, *adj.*, wreathed with laurel; *n.*, a poet laureate.
lau'reated, *adj.*, *i.q.* laureate.
lau'reateship, *n.*, the office of laureate.
laurea'tion, *n.*, the act of conferring the laurel.
lau'rel, *n.*, an evergreen shrub.
lau'rel(l)ed, *adj.* laurel-crowned; laureate.
lau'rustine, *n.*, an evergreen shrub.
laurusti'nus, *n.*, *i.q.* laurustine.
la'va, *n.*, molten rock thrown up by a volcano.
lava'bo, *n.*, the ceremony of hand-washing in the Mass; the vessel for the water.
lav'atory, *n.*, a vessel for washing; a room for the purpose.
lave, *v.t.*, to bathe, wash.
lav'ender, *v.t.*, to lay up in lavender; *n.*, a lilac-leaved shrub.
la'ver, *n.*, an edible sea-weed.
la'ving, *pr.p.*, lave.
lav'ish, *v.t.*, to give in profusion, expend; *adj.*, profuse, prodigal.
lav'ished, *p.p.*, lavish.
lav'isher, *n.*, one who lavishes.
lav'ishing, *pr.p.*, lavish.
lav'ishly, *adv.*, profusely.
law, *n.*, a set of rules; enactment, precedent; rule of invariable sequence.
law'ful, *adj.*, in accordance with law; legal; allowable.
law'fully, *adv.*, in a lawful way.
law'fulness, *n.*, the quality of being lawful.
law'giver, *n.*, one who makes laws.
law'less, *adj.*, lacking laws; regardless of law, wild.
law'lessly, *adv.*, in a lawless way.
law'lessness, *n.*, the quality of being lawless.
lawn, *n.*, a glade; a surface of mown grass; a fine variety of linen.
lawn-ten'nis, *n.*, the variety of tennis played on a lawn instead of a court.
law'suit, *n.*, an action in a court of law.
law'yer, *n.*, a practitioner in the law; one versed in law.
lax, *adj.*, loose, flabby.
laxa'tion, *n.*, the act or effect of loosening.
lax'ative, *adj.*, purgative; *n.*, a purgative medicine.
lax'ity, *n.*, the quality of being lax.
lax'ly, *adv.*, loosely.
lay, *v.t.*, to place, cause to lie; to arrange in order; to deposit; *adj.*, non-clerical; non-professional, not expert· *n.*, a song.
lay'er, *n.*, one who lays; a stratum; thickness of something spread; a shoot not severed from its stem, and fastened into the ground; *v.t.*, to treat a plant thus.
lay'ering, *pr.p.*, layer.
layette', *n.*, a newly-born infant's outfit.
lay-fig'ure, *n.*, a model
lay'ing, *pr.p.*, lay.
lay'man, *n.*, not a clergyman nor one skilled in a particular profession referred to.
laz'ar, *n.*, a leper.
lazaret', *n.*, leper hospital; quarantine hospital.
lazaret'to, *n.*, *i.q.* lazaret.
Laz'arist, *n.*, one of the Order of St. Lazare for mission priests.
laze, *v.i.*, to be lazy (*colloq.*).
la'zier, *adj.*, *comp.* of lazy.
la'ziest, *adj.*, *super.* of lazy.
la'zily, *adv.*, in a lazy way.
la'ziness, *n.*, the state or quality of being lazy.
laz'uli, *n.*, *see* lapis-lazuli.
la'zy, *adj.*, slothful, idle.
lazzaro'ne, *n.*, a Neapolitan street-idler.
lea, *n.*, grass land; a yarn measure.
leach, *v.t.*, to wash by draining; *v.i.*, to percolate; *n.*, material leached.
leached, *p.p.*, leach.
leach'ing, *pr.p.*, leach.
lead, *n.*, a heavy, ductile metal; a thin strip of metal used to widen spaces in printed type.
lead, *v.t.*, to bring along, guide, go in front of; *n.*, direction given, example set; a water channel; the right to play first in a round of cards; the card or suit first played.
lead'ed, *adj.*, widened with leads.
lead'en, *adj.*, made of, or like lead.
lead'er, *n.*, one who leads; a leading article in a journal.
leaderette', *n.*, a short editorial.
lead'ership, *n.*, the function of a leader; guidance.
lead'ing, *pr.p.*, lead; *n.*, guidance; *adj.*, large type editorial; influential.
lead-pen'cil, *n.*, a pencil of wood encasing lead.
lead'ing-strings, *n. pl.*, supports for infants learning to walk.
leads'man, *n.*, a sailor who heaves the lead.
leaf, *n.*, an expansion from the side or

root of a plant stem; a petal; a single thickness of paper; a thin foil; flap of door or shutter.

leaf'age *n.*, foliage.

leafed, *adj.*, having leaves.

leaf'iness, *n.*, the quality of being leafy.

leaf'less, *adj.*, without leaves.

leaf'let, *n.*, a little leaf; a small printed leaf.

leaf'y, *adj.*, full of leaves.

league, *v.t.*, to combine in a league; *v.i.*, form a league; *n.*, an alliance, compact; a measure of three miles.

leagued, *p.p.*, league.

lea'guer, *n.*, a camp of besiegers.

lea'guing, *pr.p.*, league.

leak, *v.t.*, to allow to escape or pass through; *v.i.*, to pass out or through; *n.*, a hole letting water in or out.

leak'age, *n.*, the act of leaking; the quantity that has leaked out.

leaked, *p.p.*, leak

leak'iness, *n.*, the state or quality of being leaky.

leak'ing, *pr.p.*, leak.

leak'y, *adj.*, having a leak or leaks; unable to keep a secret.

leal, *adj.*, loyal.

lean, *v.t.*, to incline, support; *v.i.*, to incline oneself; to be inclined; to droop; *adj.*, thin, slender, meagre; *n.*, the non-fat part of meat.

leaned, *p.p.*, lean.

lean'er, *adj.*, *comp.* of lean.

lean'est, *adj.*, *super.* of lean.

lean'ing, *pr.p.*, lean.

lean'ness, *n.*, the quality of being lean.

leant, *p.p.*, lean.

lean'-to, *n.*, a penthouse.

leap, *v.i.*, to jump, spring; *n.*, a jump, spring.

leaped, *p.p.*, leap.

leap'er, *n.*, one who leaps.

leap'-frog, *n.*, a boy's game of leaping.

leap'ing, *pr.p.*, leap.

leap'-*year*, *n.*, every fourth year, to which is added the intercalary day, Feb. 29.

learn, *v.t.*, to come to know; get by heart; *v.i.*, to become instructed.

learned, *p.p.*, learn.

learn'ed, *adj.*, instructed, erudite, deeply versed.

learn'edly, *adv.*, in a learned way.

learn'ing, *pr.p.*, learn; *n.*, erudition, acquired knowledge, instruction.

learnt, *p.p.*, learn.

leas'able, *adj.*, able to be leased.

lease, *v.t.*, to convey to a tenant for a fixed time and rent; *n.*, the contract by which such conveyance is made; any terminable period; the crossing of warp-threads.

leased, *p.p.*, lease.

lease'hold, *n.*, tenure under lease.

lease'holder, *n.*, one who holds a lease.

leash, *v.t.*, to fasten in a leash; *n.*, a thong holding one or more hounds.

leashed, *p.p.*, leash.

leas'ing, *pr.p.*, lease; *n.*, lying.

least, *adj.* and *adv.*, smallest, slightest.

leath'er, *v.t.*, to cover with leather; to beat with a thong; *n.*, dressed hide.

leatherette', *n.*, imitation leather made of paper or cloth.

leath'ern, *adj.*, made of leather.

leath'ery, *adj.*, like leather.

leave, *v.t.*, to allow to remain; to depart from, to quit; to go away without; to deliver; *n.*, permission; a departure.

leaved, *adj.*, having leaves.

leav'en, *v.t.*, to cause to ferment; to influence imperceptibly; *n.*, something added to dough to cause fermentation; subtle influence.

leav'ened, *p.p.*, leaven.

leav'ening, *pr.p.*, leaven.

leaves, *n.*, pl. of leaf.

leav'ing, *pr.p.*, leave.

leav'ings, *n. pl.*, remnants, residue.

lech'er, *n.*, a debauchee.

lech'erous, *adj.*, debauched.

lech'ery, *n.*, debauchery.

lec'tern, *n.*, a desk for cantors or lectors.

lec'tion, *n.*, a portion read; a difference in text; *see* lesson.

lec'tionary, *n.*, a book of lections, or lists of lections.

lec'tor, *n.*, a reader (one of the minor orders of the Church).

lec'ture, *v.t.*, to admonish, reprove; *v.i.*, to deliver a discourse; *n.*, a discourse; admonition, reproof.

lec'tured, *p.p.*, lecture.

lec'turer, *n.*, one who lectures.

lec'tureship, *n.*, the office of a lecturer.

lec'turing, *pr.p.*, lecture.

led, *p.p.*, lead.

ledge, *n.*, a shelf or shelf-like projection; a ridge.

ledg'er, *n.*, the chief account book in a business establishment; a horizontal piece of wood used in scaffolding; *adj.*, in the phrase "ledger line," *i.e.*, an additional line above or below the musical stave.

led'-horse, *n.*, a horse without a rider and led.

lee, *n.*, shelter; side away from the wind.

leech, *v.t.*, to doctor; *n.*, a doctor; a blood-sucking worm; the sloping side of a sail.

leech'craft, *n.*, the art of healing.

leeched, *p.p.*, leech.

leech'ing, *pr.p.*, leech.

leek, *n.*, a culinary herb, like the onion.

leer, *v.i.*, to glance slyly or malignantly; *n.*, a lascivious or sly glance; an annealing chamber in glass-works.

leered, *p.p.*, leer.

leer'ing, *pr.p.*, leer.

leer'ingly, *adv.*, with a leer.

lees, *n. pl.*, deposit in a wine-glass; refuse.

lee shore, *n.*, the shore on the lee-ward side.

leet, *n.*, an old kind of English court.

lee'ward, *adj.* and *adv.*, on the lee side, *i.e.*, opposite to the windward side; *n.*, the leeward direction.

lee'wardly, *adj.*, unable to prevent falling to leeward.

lee'way, *n.*, drift to leeward; any falling off.

left, *p.p.*, leave; *adj.*, the side opposed to the right; *n.*, the left side; *adv.*, on or by the left.

left'-handed, *adj.*, using the left hand rather than the right; double-edged.

left'-off, *adj.*, disused.

leg, *v.i.*, to run (in the phrase, *leg it*); *n.*, a supporting and locomotive limb; any support or leg-like thing.

leg'acy, *n.*, a gift under a will; anything inherited.

le'gal, *adj.*, in accordance with, having the sanction of, law; rel. to law.

le'galism, *n.*, a theological preference of the Law to the Gospel.

le'galist, *n.*, a professor of legalism.

legal'ity, *n.*, lawfulness.

legaliza'tion, *n.*, the act or result of legalizing.

le'galize, *v.t.*, to make legal; to give the force of law to.

le'galized, *p.p.*, legalize.

le'galizing, *pr.p.*, legalize.

le'gally, *adv.*, in a legal way.

leg'ate, *n.*, an accredited envoy.

legate', *v.t.*, to bequeath.

legatee', *n.*, the recipient of a legacy.

lega'tion, *n.*, an embassy; an ambassador's residence.

lega'to, *adv.*, smoothly; without breaks.

lega'tor, *n.*, one who bequeaths; a testator.

leg'end, *n.*, a traditional story; an inscription.

leg'endary, *adj.*, of a mythical character.

leg'erdemain, *n.*, sleight of hand.

leg'er-line, *n.*, *see* ledger.

legged, *p.p.*, leg.

leg'ging, *pr.p.*, leg; *n.*, an outer covering for the lower leg.

leg'gy, *adj.*, lanky; all leg.

leghorn', *adj.*, made of leghorn straw; *n.*, a straw plait.

legibil'ity, *n.*, the quality of being legible.

leg'ible, *adj.*, readable, decipherable.

leg'ibly, *adv.*, clearly, decipherably.

le'gion, *n.*, a large division of the Roman army; a multitude.

le'gionary, *adj.*, rel. to legions; *n.*, a soldier of a legion.

leg'islate, *v.i.*, to pass laws.

leg'islated, *p.p.*, legislate.

leg'islating, *pr.p.*, legislate.

legisla'tion, *n.*, the enacting of laws.

leg'islative, *adj.*, that which enacts laws; law-making; *n.*, the authority that makes laws.

leg'islator, *n.*, a law-maker; a member of the legislature.

leg'islature, *n.*, the legislative body.

legit'imacy, *n.*, the state or quality of being legitimate.

legit'imate, *adj.*, lawful, regular; lawfully begotten.

legitimate', *v.t.*, to make legitimate by law or proof; to justify.

legit'imated, *p.p.*, legitimate.

legit'imately, *adv.*, lawfully.

legit'imating, *pr.p.*, legitimate.

legitima'tion, *n.*, the act of legitimating.

legit'imatize, *v.t.*, *i.q.* legitimate.

legit'imism, *n.*, the doctrine of succession by direct descent.

legit'imist, *n.*, an adherent of legitimism.

leg'ume, *n.*, the eatable part of a leguminous plant.

legu'men, *n.*, *i.q.* legume.

legu'min, *n.*, vegetable casein.

legu'minous, *adj.*, of the order of pulse.

lei'surable, *adj.*, vacant, idle.

lei'sure, *n.*, free time; spare time; freedom from fixed occupation.

lei'sured, *adj.*, disengaged; free to do as one likes.

lei'surely, *adj.*, deliberate, slow; *adv.*, deliberately.

lem'ma, *n.*, a theme for argument; a literary subject named in a heading.

lem'ming, *n.*, a sort of field mouse.

lem'on, *n.*, a pale yellow acid fruit of the orange family.

lemonade', *n.*, a beverage made from the lemon.

lem'on-sole, *n.*, a sort of plaice.

le'mur, *n.*, a monkey-like nocturnal mammal.

lend, *v.t.*, to give for temporary use; let out on interest; afford.

lend'able, *adj.*, able to be lent.

lend'er, *n.*, one who lends.

lend'ing, *pr.p.*, lend.

length, *n.*, longitudinal measurement; distance from end to end; degree or extent.

length'en, *v.t.*, to make longer; *v.i.*, to grow longer.

length'ened, *p.p.*, lengthen.

length'ening, *pr.p.*, lengthen.

length'ily, *adv.*, in a lengthy way.

length'iness, *n.*, prolixity.

length'wise, *adv.*, as measured in length.

length'y, *adj.*, prolix, wearisome.

le'niency, *n.*, gentleness, mildness.

le'nient, *adj.*, mild, gentle.

le'niently, *adv.*, gently.

le'nified, *p.p.*, lenify.

le'nify, *v.t.*, to appease, make gentle.

len'itive, *adj.*, soothing, palliating; *n.*, an assuaging remedy.

len'ity, *n.*, gentleness, mildness.

le'no, *n.*, a kind of gauze.

lens, *n.*, a piece of glass or transparent material, so shaped as to concentrate or disperse light-rays.

Lent, *n.*, the forty days of abstinence, from Ash Wednesday to Easter Eve.

lent, *p.p.*, lend.

lent'en, *adj.*, rel. to Lent.

lentic'ular, *adj.*, lentil-shaped; like a double-convex lens.

len'tiform, *adj.*, *i.q.* lenticular.

lentig'inous, *adj.*, dusty.

lenti'go, *n.*, freckles.

len'til, *n.*, a leguminous plant.

len'to, *adv.*, slowly (*mus.*).

Le'o, *n.*, the Lion, one of the signs of the Zodiac.

le'onid, *n.*, a meteor from Leo.

le'onine, *adj.*, like a lion, fierce; *n.*, a hexameter or pentameter line rhyming internally.

leop'ard, *n.*, a carnivorous mammal.

lep'er, *n.*, one afflicted with leprosy.

lep'idolite, *n.*, a scaly silicate.

Lepidop'tera, *n. pl.*, insects with scaly wings.

lepidop'terous, *adj.*, rel. to Lepidoptera.

lepido'sis, *n.*, a mild skin disease.

lep'idote, *adj.*, scurfy.

lep'orine, *adj.*, harelike.

lep'rosy, *n.*, a fearful wasting disease, accompanied by scales

lep'rous, *adj.*, rel. to leprosy.

leptodac'tyl, *adj.*, having long slender toes.

Les'bian, *adj.*, rel. to Lesbos.

lèse-majesté, *n.*, *i.q.* lese-majesty.

lese-maj'esty, *n.*, treason.

le'sion, *n.*, hurt, damage; morbid derangement of tissue or organ.

less, *adj.* and *adv.*, smaller; not so much.

lessee', *n.*, one to whom property is leased.

les'sen, *v.t.* and *i.*, to diminish.

les'sened, *p.p.*, lessen.

les'sening, *pr.p.*, lessen.

les'ser, *adj.*, *i.q.* less.

les'son, *v.t.*, to instruct, admonish; *n.*, a passage for reading; a lection; teaching; rebuke, punishment.

lessor', *n.*, one who leases out a property.

lest, *conj.*, for fear that; in order to prevent.

let, *v.t.*, to hinder; to grant use for rent; to permit, allow; *n.*, a hindrance; the letting of a house; the house let; a temporary arrest of a ball's progress (racquets or tennis).

le'thal, *adj.*, deadly.

lethar'gic, *adj.*, apathetic, drowsy.

leth'argy, *n.*, drowsiness, apathy.

Le'the, *n.*, a river in Hades; oblivion.

Lethe'an, *adj.*, rel. to Lethe.

lethif'erous, *adj.*, deadly.

let'-off, *n.*, a chance missed; a penalty remitted.

Lett, *n.*, a Lithuanian.

let'ter, *n.*, an alphabetical sign; an epistle; *v.t.*, to put lettering on.

let'tered, *adj.*, learned, literary: *p.p.*, letter.

let'tering, *pr.p.*, letter; *n.*, an inscription.

let'terpress, *n.*, printed matter.

let'ters, *n. pl.*, literature, learning.

let'ting, *pr.p.*, let.

let'tuce, *n.*, a garden herb used for salads.

Levant', *n.*, the Eastern Mediterranean; a variety of morocco.

levant', *v.i.*, to abscond.

levant'ed, *p.p.*, levant.

levant'er, *n.*, an absconder; a dweller in the Levant.

Levant'ine, *adj.*, rel. to the Levant.

levant'ing, *pr.p.*, levant.

leva'tor, *n.*, a lifting muscle.

lev'ee, *n.*, a reception; a court function for men only.

lev'el, *v.t.*, to make level, flat, or even; to make even with the ground; to point (a gun); *adj.*, horizontal; on an equality, even, uniform; *n.*, an instrument showing horizontality; a horizontal plane.

lev'elled, lev'eled, *p.p.*, level.

lev'eller, lev'eler, *n.*, one who would abolish inequalities.

lev'elling, lev'eling, *pr.p.*, level.

le'ver, *v.t.*, to lift or move with a lever; *n.*, a bar turning on a fulcrum and used for lifting up a weight.

le'verage, *n.*, power gained by levering; the action of a lever; added power.

lev'eret, *n.*, a young hare.

lev'iable, *adj.*, able to be levied upon.

levi'athan, *n.*, a huge sea-monster; anything immensely large.

lev'ied, *p.p.*, levy.

lev'igate, *v.t.*, to grind to powder; to make smooth, polish.

lev'igated, *p.p.*, levigate.

lev'igating, *pr.p.*, levigate.

leviga'tion, *n.*, the act of levigating.

lev'in, *n.*, lightning.

le'virate, *n.*, the Jewish practice requiring a dead man's brother or nearest kinsman to marry his wife.

lev'itate, *v.t.*, to make to float in the air; *v.i.*, to float in the air.

levita'tion, *n.*, the act of levitating.

Le'vite, *n.*, one of the priestly tribe of Levi.

Levit'ical, *adj.*, rel. to Levites and Leviticus.

Levit'icus, *n.*, one of the books of the Pentateuch.

lev'ity, *n.*, lightness; frivolity, trifling behaviour.

lev'y, *v.t.*, to collect tax; to enrol men for war; to proceed to take; *n.*, the collection or assessment of tax; enrolment.

lev'ying, *pr.p.*, levy.

lewd, *adj.*, obscene, lascivious.

lewd'ly, *adv.*, in a lewd way.

lewd'ness, *n.*, obscenity, indecency.

lew'is, *n.*, an iron device for hoisting heavy stones.

lex, *n.*, law (*Lat.*).

lex'ical, *adj.*, rel. to words and expressions; also to a lexicon.

lexicog'rapher, *n.*, the compiler of a lexicon.

lexicograph'ic, *adj.*, rel. to lexicography.

lexicograph'ical, *adj.*, *i.q.* lexicographic.

lexicog'raphy, *n.*, dictionary-making.

lexicol'ogy, *n.*, the study of words in a language.

lex'icon, *n.*, a dictionary.

lexigraph'ic, *adj.*, rel. to lexigraphy.

lexig'raphy, *n.*, the system of representing whole words by single signs.

ley, *n.*, produce.

Ley'den, *n.*, a city of Holland; a Leyden jar is a condenser.

li, *n.*, a Chinese weight and measure.

liabil'ity, *n.*, the state of being liable.

li'able, *adj.*, exposed or subject to some obligation or debt.

li'ableness, *n.*, *i.q.* liability.

liaison', *n.*, improper relations between the sexes. In French, it is the carrying on of the sound of an ordinarily silent consonant before a vowel or *h* mute.

li'ar, *n.*, one who lies.

li'as, *n.*, blue limestone rock.

liba'tion, *n.*, an offering of wine.

li'bel, *v.t.*, to defame with a libel; falsely accuse; *n.*, written and published slander; a declaration in writing.

li'bel(l)ant, *n.*, the institutor of an Admiralty suit.

li'bel(l)ed, *p.p.*, libel.

li'bel(l)er, *n.*, one guilty of libel.

li'bel(l)ing, *pr.p.*, libel.

li'bel(l)ous, *adj.*, of the nature of libel.

lib'er, *n.*, a book (*Lat.*); bark (*Lat.*).

lib'eral, *adj.*, generous; unstinted; wide in scope; unprejudiced; rel. to liberalism; *n.*, a professor of liberalism.

lib'eralism, *n.*, the profession of liberal opinions, or the Liberal policy.

liberal'ity, *n.*, generosity, bounty.

lib'eralize, *v.t.*, to make liberal.

lib'eralized, *p.p.*, liberalize.

lib'eralizing, *pr.p.*, liberalize.

lib'erally, *adv.*, generously.

lib'erate, *v.t.*, to set free.

lib'erated, *p.p.*, liberate.

lib'erating, *pr.p.*, liberate.

libera'tion, *n.*, deliverance.

lib'erator, *n.*, one who liberates.

liberta'rian, *adj.*, rel. to the freewill doctrine.

liber'ticide, *n.*, destruction of liberty; a destroyer of liberty.

lib'ertine, *adj.*, regardless of morals, dissolute; *n.*, a dissolute person.

lib'ertinism, *n.*, dissoluteness.

lib'erty, *n.*, freedom, exemption, immunity.

libid'inous, *adj.*, lustful.

Li'bra, *n.*, the Balance, one of the signs of the Zodiac.

libra'rian, *n.*, the custodian of a library.

libra'rianship, *n.*, a librarian's office.

li'brary, *n.*, a collection of books; a book-room.

li'brate, *v.i.*, to balance, be poised.

li'brated, *p.p.*, librate.
li'brating, *pr.p.*, librate.
libra'tion, *n.*, the act of balancing.
li'bratory, *adj.*, balancing.
libret'tist, *n.*, the writer of a libretto.
libret'to, *n.*, the words of an opera or oratorio.
Lib'yan, *adj.*, rel. to Libya; African.
lice, *n.*, pl. of louse.
li'cence, *n.*, official permission; excessive liberty; an irregularity; a certificate.
li'cense, *v.t.*, to grant permission.
li'censed, *p.p.*, license.
licensee', *n.*, the holder of a licence.
li'censer, *n.*, the granter of a licence.
li'censing, *pr.p.*, license.
licen'tiate, *n.*, the holder of an academic licence
licen'tious, *adj.*, irregular, lewd.
licen'tiously, *adv.*, in a licentious way.
licen'tiousness, *n.*, lewd behaviour.
lich, *n.*, a corpse.
lich'-gate, *n.*, the covered gateway at the entrance of a churchyard.
li'chen, *n.*, a parasitic fungus.
lichenog'raphy, *n.*, the description of lichens.
lic'it, *adj.*, lawful.
lic'itly, *adv.*, lawfully.
lick, *v.t.*, to smooth with the tongue; pass the tongue over; to overcome (*slang*); *n.*, the act of licking.
licked, *p.p.*, lick.
lick'er, *n.*, one who licks.
lick'erish, *adj.*, greedy; lecherous.
lick'ing, *pr.p.*, lick.
lick'spittle, *adj.*, toadying; *n.*, a toady.
lic'orice, *n.*, *see* liquorice.
lic'tor, *n.*, a Roman official attending the consuls and the dictator, and bearing the fasces (*Lat.*).
lid, *n.*, a cover, top.
lid'less, *adj.*, without a lid.
lie, *v.i.*, to be in a horizontal position, to be situated; to tell a falsehood; *n.*, a falsehood; position; in golf, the place or manner in which a ball happens to lie.
lied, *p.t.* and *p.*, lie, in the sense of telling a falsehood.
lief, *adv.*, willingly.
lief'er, *adv.*, sooner, rather.
liege, *adj.*, bound to service; claiming allegiance; *n.*, a vassal; a lord.
li'en, *n.*, a legal claim to hold property as security.
li'entery, *n.*, a form of diarrhoea.
lierne', *n.*, a cross-rib in vaulting (*Arch.*).
lieu, *n.*, place, stead.
lieuten'ancy, *n.*, the rank or office of lieutenant.
lieuten'ant, *n.*, a deputy, substitute; an officer in the navy and the army.
lieuten'ant, *n.*, *i.q.* the foregoing word, but pronounced by Americans "liutenant."
lieuten'ant-col'onel, *n.*, a military officer next below a colonel.
life, *n.*, the state of being alive; animation; existence; the living form; living things collectively.
life'-belt, *n.*, a life-preserving belt.
life'blood, *n.*, that which is essential to life.
life'boat, *n.*, a life-preserving boat.
life'-giving, *adj.*, inspiriting, animating.
life'guard, *n.*, a bodyguard of soldiers.
life'-insurance, *n.*, insurance on the chances of living.
life'less, *adj.*, dead, spiritless.
life'lessness, *n.*, the state of being lifeless.
life'like, *adj.*, true to reality.
life'-long, *adj.*, lasting through life
life'-preserver, *n.*, a loaded short stick.
life'time, *n.*, the period of a life.
lift, *v.t.*, to raise, hoist, steal; *v.i.*, to dispense, to rise; *n.*, the act of lifting; the extent of a rise; an elevator or hoist.
lift'ed, *p.p.*, lift.
lift'er, *n.*, anything that lifts.
lift'ing, *pr.p.*, lift.
lig'ament, *n.*, a tie; a binding membrane.
ligamen'tal, *adj.*, binding.
ligamen'tous, *adj.*, *i.q.* ligamental.
liga'tion, *n.*, the act of tying arteries, etc.
lig'ature, *n.*, *i.q.* ligation; that which unites or binds; a slur or tie in music.
light, *v.t.*, to set fire to, to illumine; *v.i.*, to take fire, to brighten; *adj.*, luminous, not dark; pale of hue; not heavy; elegant; easy to digest; trivial, thoughtless; *n.*, radiant energy acting on the sight: brightness; illuminant; illumination; a section of a window; a match or spill.
light'ed, *p.p.*, light.
light'en, *v.t.*, to make light; *v.i.*, to grow light; to emit lightning.
light'ened, *p.p.*, lighten.
light'ening, *pr.p.*, lighten.
light'er, *n.*, a boat for loading and unloading a ship; an appliance for lighting; *adj.*, *comp.* of light.
light'erage, *n.*, charge for unloading a ship.
light'erman, *n.*, one employed on a lighter.
light'est, *adj.*, *super.* of light.

light'-fingered, *adj.*, thievish, pilfering.
light'-footed, *adj.*, nimble.
light'-headed, *adj.*, delirious.
light'-hearted, *adj.*, cheerful.
light'-horse, *n.*, light-armed cavalry.
light'house, *n.*, a tower containing lamps; a pharos.
light'-in'fantry, *n.*, light-armed infantry.
light'ing, *pr.p.*, light; *n.*, artificial illumination.
light'ly, *adv.*, in a light way.
light'-minded, *adj.*, frivolous.
light'ness, *n.*, the state or quality of being light.
light'ning, *n.*, electric discharge between clouds, or between the clouds and the earth.
lights, *n. pl.*, lungs.
light'ship, *n.*, a ship carrying a warning light.
light'some, *adj.*, luminous, bright.
light'-spir'ited, *adj.*, cheerful.
lign-al'oes, *n.*, aloes wood.
lig'neous, *adj.*, woody.
lignifica'tion, *n.*, the state of being lignified.
lig'niform, *adj.*, like wood.
lig'nify, *v.t.*, to turn into wood; *v.i.*, to become wood.
lig'nified, *p.p.*, lignify.
lig'nifying, *pr.p.*, lignify.
lig'nin, *n.*, xylogen.
lig'nite, *n.*, brown coal.
lignit'ic, *adj.*, rel. to lignite.
lig'num vi'tae, *n.*, a tree producing very hard wood.
lig'ula, *n.*, a fillet; a tongue-like lobe (*Lat.*).
lig'ulate, *adj.*, having a ligula.
lig'ulated, *adj.*, *i.q.* ligulate.
lig'ure, *n.*, amber.
like, *v.t.*, to take a fancy to; to find agreeable; *v.i.*, to desire; *adj.*, resembling; equal; *prep.*, in the manner of; *n.*, anything equivalent
like'able, *adj.*, attractive.
liked, *p.p.*, like.
like'lihood, *n.*, probability.
like'liness, *n.*, probability.
like'ly, *adj.*, probable, reasonable, capable-looking; *adv.*, probably.
like'minded, *adj.*, in agreement.
li'ken, *v.t.*, to make like; to compare.
li'kened, *p.p.*, liken.
like'ness, *n.*, resemblance; a portrait.
li'kening, *pr.p.*, liken.
like'wise, *adv.*, in the same way; moreover.
li'king, *pr.p.*, like; *n.*, a fondness for; personal taste.
li'lac, *adj.*, lilac-coloured; *n.*, a flowering shrub; a pale purple colour.
lilia'ceous, *adj.*, pert. to lilies.
lil'ied, *adj.*, full of lilies.
lillibulle'ro, *n.*, an old English political song.
Lillipu'tian, *adj.*, rel. to the kingdom of Lilliput; tiny.
lilt, *v.t.*, to sing with a rhythm; *n.*, rhythmical, gay song.
lil'y, *n.*, a plant of the genus Lilium.
lima'ceous, *adj.*, slug-like.
li'mature, *n.*, polishing, filings.
limb, *n.*, a member (arm, leg, branch); an edge; *v.t.*, to disable.
lim'bate, *adj.*, having an edge of a different colour.
limbed, *p.p.*, limb; *adj.*, having limbs.
lim'ber, *v.t.*, to fasten limber to gun; *n.*, the front part of a gun-carriage; *adj.*, pliant, nimble.
lim'bered, *p.p.*, limber.
lim'bering, *pr.p.*, limber.
lim'berness, *n.*, pliancy, nimbleness.
limb'ing, *pr.p.*, limb.
lim'bo, *n.*, a shadowy region on the border of hell; prison, oblivion.
lim'bus, *n.*, an edge or border (*Lat.*).
lime, *v.t.*, to catch (birds) with a sticky substance; to manure with lime; to treat with lime and water; *n.*, calcium oxide from burnt limestone; a small fruit like the lemon.
lime'kiln, *n.*, a kiln for burning lime.
lime'light, *n.*, calcium light.
lim'erick, *n.*, a form of nonsense-verse.
lime'stone, *n.*, rock containing calcium carbonate.
lime'wash, *v.t.*, to whitewash.
lime'water, *n.*, an aqueous solution containing calcium hydrate.
lim'it, *v.t.*, to put bounds to; restrict; *n.*, a boundary, terminal point.
lim'itable, *adj.*, able to be limited.
lim'itary, *adj.*, limiting, subject to restriction.
limita'tion, *n.*, the act of limiting; a disabled or limited condition; defect.
lim'ited, *p.p.*, limit.
lim'iting, *pr.p.*, limit.
lim'itless, *adj.*, without limit.
limn, *v.t.*, to paint, draw.
lim'ner, *n.*, a painter.
lim'ning, *pr.p.*, limn.
limp, *v.i.*, to walk lamely; *n.*, a lame walk; *adj.*, not stiff; lacking energy.
limped, *p.p.*, limp.
lim'pet, *n.*, a mollusc that clings to rocks.
lim'pid, *adj.*, clear.
limpid'ity, *n.*, quality of clearness.
lim'pidness, *n.*, *i.q.* limpidity.
limp'ing, *pr.p.*, limp.

limp'ingly, *adv.*, in a limping way.

li'my, *adj.*, covered with, or resembling, lime.

lin, *n.*, a pool, esp. under a waterfall.

linch, *n.*, a ridge marking a boundary.

linch'pin, *n.*, the pin of an axle keeping the wheel on.

lin'den, *n.*, the lime tree.

line, *v.t.*, to mark with lines; to draw up a line; to put a lining to; *v.i.*, to form up in line; *n.*, fine long flax; cord; a long mark; a streak; a series or row; a metrical verse; troops deployed for action; railway track; department of business; lineage.

lin'eage, *n.*, lineal descent.

lin'eal, *adj.*, in direct succession.

lin'eally, *adv.*, by descent in line.

lin'eament, *n.*, feature.

lin'ear, *adj.*, rel. to line.

linear'ity, *n.*, the quality of being linear (*i.e.*, measured in one dimension).

linea'tion, *n.*, marking with lines.

lined, *p.p.*, line.

lin'en, *adj.*, made of flax; *n.*, cloth made from flax.

lin'en-draper, *n.*, one who deals in linen and calico goods.

li'ner, *n.*, a vessel bel. to a line of passenger ships.

li'nesman, *n.*, a member of a line regiment; in football and lawn tennis, a man who keeps eye for the umpire on the marked lines.

ling, *n.*, an edible sea-fish; heather.

lin'ger, *v.i.*, to delay starting; dally, drag on.

lin'gered, *p.p.*, linger.

lin'gering, *pr.p.*, linger.

lin'gerie, *n.*, underwear (*Fr.*).

lin'go, *n.*, a foreign tongue (a contemptuous expression).

lin'gual, *adj.*, rel. to the tongue; *n.*, a letter pronounced by the tongue.

lin'guiform, *adj.*, tongue-shaped.

lin'guist, *n.*, an expert in languages.

linguis'tic, *adj.*, rel. to languages.

linguis'tical, *adj.*, *i.q.* linguistic.

linguis'tics, *n. pl.*, the study of languages.

linguoden'tal, *adj.*, made with tongue and teeth.

lin'iment, *n.*, a liquid ointment.

li'ning, *pr.p.*, line; *n.*, an inner covering.

link, *v.t.*, to join; *v.i.*, to become joined; *n.*, a ring in a chain; a part of a connected series; a torch.

link'boy, *n.*, a torch-bearer.

linked, *p.p.*, link.

link'ing, *pr.p.*, link.

links, *n. pl.*, sandy ground near the sea, with turf and bents; a golf course.

Linne'an, *adj.*, pert. to Linnaeus, the 18th cent. botanist.

linn, *n.*, *i.q.* lin.

lin'net, *n.*, a singing-bird.

lino'leum, *n.*, a floor-cloth or oilcloth.

li'notype, *n.*, a machine producing a line of type cast in one piece.

lin'seed, *n.*, flax-seed.

lin'sey-wool'sey, *adj.*, made of linen and wool, or of cotton and linen with wool; *n.*, a dress made of the material.

lin'stock, *n.*, an iron-shod pike used in firing a gun.

lint, *n.*, ravelled linen used for dressing wounds.

lin'tel, *n.*, the horizontal top of a doorway or window.

li'on, *n.*, a large carnivorous beast.

li'oness, *n.*, fem. of lion.

li'on-hearted, *adj.*, courageous.

li'onize, *v.t.*, to show famous persons and places; *v.i.*, to visit show places.

li'onized, *p.p.*, lionize.

li'onizing, *pr.p.*, lionize.

lip, *v.t.*, to touch with the lip; touch the edge of; murmur; *n.*, the upper and lower edges of the mouth's opening.

lipped, *p.p.*, lip.

lip'pitude, *n.*, ophthalmia.

lip'salve, *n.*, ointment for sore lips.

liq'uable, *adj.*, able to be melted.

liqua'tion, *n.*, the act or effect of melting.

liquefac'tion, *n.*, *i.q.* liquation.

liquefi'able, *adj.*, able to be liquefied.

liq'uefied, *p.p.*, liquefy.

liq'uefier, *n.*, anything that liquefies.

liq'uefy, *n.*, to reduce to a liquid state; *v.i.*, to be melted.

liq'uefying, *pr.p.*, liquefy.

liques'cency, *n.*, the state of being liquescent.

liques'cent, *adj.*, in the act of becoming liquid.

liqueur', *n.*, a sweetened alcoholic cordial.

liq'uid, *adj.*, flowing; not solid nor gaseous; *n.*, a liquid substance.

liq'uidate, *v.t.*, to settle, pay off; to wind up a bankrupt's affairs.

liq'uidated, *p.p.*, liquidate.

liq'uidating, *pr.p.*, liquidate.

liquida'tion, *n.*, the act of liquidating; bankruptcy.

liq'uidator, *n.*, one who winds up a debtor's liabilities.

liquid'ity, *n.*, the state or quality of being liquid.

liq'uidize, *v.t.*, to render liquid.

liq'uidized, *p.p.*, liquidize.

liq'uidizing, *pr.p.*, liquidize.

liq'uor, *n.*, a fluid; a solution of dye; alcoholic drink.

liq'uorice, *n.*, the plant so named; a substance made from the *glycyrrhiza glabra*.

Lis'bon, *n.*, a wine named after the place.

lisp, *v.t.*, to pronounce with a lisp; to utter imperfectly; *v.i.*, to pronounce sibilants as *th*.

lisped, *p.p.*, lisp.

lisp'er, *n.*, one who lisps.

lisp'ing, *pr.p.*, lisp.

lis'som, *adj.*, lithe, agile.

list, *v.t.*, to register; to cover with list; to hear; to give heed to; to cause to careen; *v.i.*, to careen; to enlist; to listen; *n.*, a register or catalogue; selvage; the careening of a ship.

list'ed, *p.p.*, list.

lis'tel, *n.*, a fillet.

lis'ten, *v.i.*, to try to hear; to harken.

lis'tened, *p.p.*, listen.

lis'tener, *n.*, one who listens.

lis'tening, *pr.p.*, listen.

Lis'terism, *n.*, antiseptic surgery.

list'ing, *pr.p.*, list; *n.*, the act of listing.

list'less, *adj.*, apathetic, without interest.

list'lessly, *adv.*, in a listless way.

list'lessness, *n.*, apathy, lack of interest.

lists, *n. pl.*, palisades round a tournament ground.

lit, *p.p.*, light.

lit'any, *n.*, a supplication, esp. petitions sung by priests and people in procession.

lit'eracy, *n.*, ability to read and write.

lit'eral, *adj.*, in accordance with the letter; exact; expressed in letters.

lit'eralism, *n.*, the understanding of words in their simplest sense.

lit'eralist, *n.*, a matter-of-fact person.

lit'erally, *n.*, in a literal way.

lit'erary, *adj.*, rel. to, or engaged in, polite letters.

lit'erate, *adj.*, able to read and write; *n.*, a person acquainted with polite letters; one admitted to Holy Orders without possessing an academic degree.

litera'ti, *n. pl.*, learned people.

litera'tim, *n.*, letter for letter (a word taken to be a Latin one).

lit'erature, *n.*, the collective written works of all human minds; the profession of letters; the higher kind of writing; what has been written about a given subject.

lith'arge, *n.*, protoxide of lead.

lithe, *adj.*, supple, active.

lithe'ness, *adj.*, suppleness.

lithe'some, *adj.*, *see* lissom.

lith'ia, *n.*, lithium oxide.

lith'ic, *adj.*, rel. to the stone or to lithium.

lith'ium, *n.*, a metallic element, soft and white.

lith'oglyph, *n.*, carving on a gem; a carved gem.

lithoglyph'ic, *adj.*, rel. to a lithoglyph.

lith'ograph, *v.t.*, to reproduce on stone by lithography; *n.*, a picture so reproduced.

lith'ographed, *p.p.*, lithograph.

lithog'rapher, *n.*, one who lithographs.

lithograph'ic, *adj.*, rel. to lithography.

lithograph'ically, *adj.*, by lithography.

lith'ographing, *pr.p.*, lithograph.

lithog'raphy, *n.*, the art of printing on stone.

lith'oid, *adj.*, resembling stone.

lithoi'dal, *adj.*, *i.q.* lithoid.

litholog'ic, *adj.*, rel. to lithology.

litholog'ical, *adj.*, *i.q.* lithologic.

litholog'ically, *adv.*, in a lithological sense.

lithol'ogy, *n.*, the science of rock-structure and composition.

lithontrip'tic, *adj.*, remedial for calculi in the bladder; *n.*, a solvent of calculi.

lithoph'agous, *adj.*, eating or boring stone.

lith'ophane, *n.*, a transparency.

lith'otome, *n.*, a mineral resembling cut stone.

lithot'omist, *n.*, an operator who cuts for stone in bladder.

lithot'omy, *n.*, cutting for stone.

lithot'rity, *n.*, crushing stone in bladder.

lit'igant, *adj.*, engaged in litigation; *n.*, a party to a suit.

lit'igate, *v.t.*, to contest at law; *v.i.*, to go to law.

lit'igated, *p.p.*, litigate.

lit'igating, *pr.p.*, litigate.

litiga'tion, *n.*, the act of going to law.

lit'igator, *n.*, *i.q.* litigant.

liti'gious, *adj.*, addicted to litigation; legally disputable.

lit'mus, *n.*, a blue dye-stuff.

li'totes, *n.*, an ironical way of saying less than is intended, as *no little* for *much*.

litram'eter, *n.*, a device for ascertaining specific gravity of liquids.

li'tre, li'ter, *n.*, a metrical unit of capacity.

lit'ter, *v.t.*, to bring forth young; to make untidy with things scattered about; to provide a bed for cattle; *v.i.*, to bring forth a litter; *n.*, a palanquin; waste materials thrown about in disorder; the young of animals brought forth at one birth.

litte'rateur, *n.*, a literary person.

lit'tered, *p.p.*, litter.

lit'tering, *pr.p.*, litter.

lit'tle, *n.*, small, mean.

lit'tleness, *n.*, smallness; meanness.

lit'toral, *adj.*, rel. to the shore; *n.*, the country along the shore.

litur'gic, *adj.*, rel. to liturgy.

litur'gical, *adj.*, *i.q.* liturgic.

lit'urgy, *n.*, anciently a public service rendered voluntarily to the State. Now the rite of the Mass or Eucharist; also loosely used for the Book of Common Prayer.

live, *v.i.*, to be alive; have life; exist, subsist; *v.t.*, to spend, pass, act up to.

live, *adj.*, alive; burning.

live'-bait, *n.*, living fish for bait.

lived, *p.p.*, live.

lived, *adj.*, having a life.

live'lier, *adj.*, *comp.* of lively.

live'liest, *adj.*, *super.* of lively.

live'lihood, *n.*, means of living.

live'liness, *n.*, brightness, briskness.

live'long, *adj.*, whole, entire.

live'ly, *adj.*, live-like, brisk, vivid.

liv'er, *n.*, one who lives or dwells; a large glandular bile-secreting organ.

liv'eried, *adj.*, wearing livery.

liv'erwort, *n.*, a lichen.

liv'ery, *n.*, provision of food or clothing for dependents; the care and stabling of horses and carriages for payment; legal delivery of property to a ward; membership of a City Guild; the members collectively.

liv'eryman, *n.*, a member of a Livery Company.

lives, *n.*, pl. of life.

live'stock, *n.*, animals for use or sale.

liv'id, *adj.*, lead-coloured; discoloured as though bruised.

livid'ity, *n.*, the quality of being livid.

liv'idness, *n.*, *i.q.* lividity.

liv'ing, *pr.p.*, live; *adj.*, not dead; still alive; *n.*, livelihood, a parochial benefice.

Livo'nian, *adj.*, rel. to Livonia.

li'vre, *n.*, an old French coin = a franc.

lixiv'ial, *adj.*, of the nature of lixivium.

lixiv'iate, *v.t.*, to dissolve by lixiviating; to leach; *adj.*, leached.

lixiv'iated, *p.p.*, lixiviate.

lixivia'tion, *n.*, the act of extracting soluble from insoluble matter by means of washing; leaching.

lixiv'ium, *n.*, any mixture that has been leached.

liz'ard, *n.*, a reptile so named.

lla'ma, *n.*, a small kind of camel found in S. America; also its wool.

lo, *interj.*, see there! look!

loach, *n.*, an edible fresh-water fish.

load, *v.t.*, to heap upon; lay a burden on; fill with ammunition; *n.*, a burden; unit of weight or measure; the charge of a gun.

load'ed, *p.p.*, load.

load'ing, *pr.p.*, load; *n.*, something added to give weight.

load'star, *n.*, *see* lodestar.

load'stone, *n.*, *see* lodestone.

loaf, *v.i.*, to loiter idly; *n.*, a mass of bread or cake; a lump.

loaf'er, *n.*, an idle lounger.

loaf'ing, *pr.p.*, loaf.

loam, *v.t.*, to cover with loam; *n.*, a mixture of sand and clay.

loam'y, *adj.*, like loam.

loan, *n.*, something lent; the act of lending. In the U.S the verb "loan" is used for "lend."

loan'able, *adj.*, able to be lent.

loaned, *p.p.*, loan.

loan'ing, *pr.p.*, loan.

loan'-office, *n.*, a pawnbroker's shop (*Amer.*).

loath, loth, *adj.*, unwilling, reluctant.

loathe, *v.t.*, to detest, abominate.

loathed, *p.p.*, loathe.

loath'ing, *pr.p.*, loathe; *n.*, disgust, nausea.

loath'some, *adj.*, detestable, disgusting.

loath'someness, *n.*, the quality of being loathsome.

loaves, *n.*, pl. of loaf.

lob, *v.t.*, to bowl a slow or high-pitched ball; *v.i.*, to move clumsily; *n.*, a ball bowled underhand or struck high with a racket.

lo'bate, *adj.*, having lobes.

lo'bated, *adj.*, *i.q.* lobate.

lob'by, *v.t.*, to try to get a measure passed; *v.i.*, to use one's influence in the lobby; *n.*, a corridor or entrance hall, esp. where Members of Parliament meet their constituents, and where members divide.

lob'byist, *n.*, one who regularly practises lobbying.

lobe, *n.*, the projecting part of an ear; a sub-division of the liver or the lungs.

lobe'lia, *n.*, a herbaceous plant.

lob'lolly, *n.*, gruel.

lob'lolly boy, *n.*, a ship doctor's assistant.

lob'scouse, *n.*, a mess of salt meat, vegetables, and ship's biscuits.

lob'ster, *n.*, an edible crustacean.

lob'ular, *adj.*, having small lobes.

lob'ule, *n.*, a small lobe.

lo'cal, *adj.*, related to place.

local(e)', *n.*, scene or situation (*Fr.*).

lo'calism, *n.*, fondness for a place; narrowness of outlook; a local idiom.

local'ity, *n.*, position; aptitude for remembering places.

localiza'tion, *n.*, the act or result of localizing.

lo'calize, *v.t.*, to make local; to fix position of.

lo'calized, *p.p.*, localize.

lo'calizing, *pr.p.*, localize.

lo'cally, *n.*, with reference to place.

locate', *v.t.*, to establish in a place; (*Amer.*) to fix the place of.

loca'ted, *p.p.*, locate.

loca'ting, *pr.p.*, locate

loca'tion, *n.*, the act of locating; exact position; a plot of ground defined by boundaries (*Amer.*).

loc'ative, *adj.*, denoting the place where; indicating place in a series: *n.*, an old case-ending that related to place.

loch, *n.*, a Scottish lake or land-locked arm of the sea.

lock, *v.t.*, to fasten with a lock; encircle; *v.i.*, to become locked, to be held tight; *n.*, a fastening; contrivance for exploding a firearm; a portion of hair from the head; an arrangement for raising and lowering the levels of water in a canal.

lock'age, *n.*, toll for passage through a lock; difference of level of locks.

locked, *p.p.*, lock.

lock'er, *n.*, one who locks; a small cupboard; a sailor's clothes-chest.

lock'et, *n.*, a metal case for a miniature or lock of hair.

lock'ing, *pr.p.*, lock.

Lock'ist, *adj.*, rel. to John Locke and his metaphysical teaching.

lock'-jaw, *n.*, trismus; spasmodic permanent closure of the lower jaw.

lock'-out, *n.*, the shutting out of employees from a factory or mine.

lock'smith, *n.*, one who makes or repairs locks.

lock'-up, *n.*, a house of temporary detention; the act or time of locking up.

locomo'tion, *n.*, movement from place to place.

lo'comotive, *adj.*, rel. to locomotion; *n.*, an engine for drawing trains.

lo'comotor at'axy, *n.*, ataxia of the lower limbs; loss of power to walk.

loc'ulament, *n.*, *i.q.* loculus.

loc'ular, *adj.*, rel. to a loculus.

loc'ulus, *n.*, a small cavity or cell.

lo'cum-te'nens, *n.*, a substitute or deputy.

lo'cus, *n.*, locality, situation. In mathematics, a particular kind of curve.

lo'cust, *n.*, an edible insect; a N. American variety of bean.

locu'tion, *n.*, a mode of speech; a phrase.

loc'utory, *n.*, a monastic parlour; a grille.

lode, *n.*, a watercourse; a vein of metal.

lode'star, *n.*, a guiding star; the pole-star.

lode'stone, *n.*, magnetic iron ore.

lodge, *v.t.*, to give shelter to; to put in; *v.i.*, to reside in temporarily; to rest in or upon; *n.*, a small house; a gatekeeper's house or quarters; the residence of the Master of a College; an association of Freemasons.

lodged, *p.p.*, lodge.

lodg'er, *n.*, one who lives in lodgings.

lodg'ing, *pr.p.*, lodge; *n.*, hired room or rooms; abode.

lodg'ing-house, *n.*, a house where lodgings may be had.

lodg'ment, *n.*, a foothold; the act of lodging; that which has lodged.

loft, *v.t.*, to hit (a golf ball) up into the air; to provide with a loft; *n.*, a room next the roof; a raised floor or gallery; the tilt back of a golf-club's head.

loft'ier, *adj.*, *comp.* of lofty.

loft'iest, *adj.*, *super.* of lofty.

loft'ily, *adv.*, in a lofty way.

loft'iness, *n.*, height.

loft'y, *adj.*, high, towering, noble.

log, *v.t.*, to record in a log-book; to cut into logs; *n.*, a piece of felled timber; a float showing speed of a ship; a ship's record of daily progress.

log'arithm, *n.*, the index of the power of a fixed number (called the base) which must be raised to produce a given number.

logarith'mic, *adj.*, rel. to logarithms.

log'-book, *n.*, *see* log.

logged, *p.p.*, log; *adj.*, waterlogged.

log'gerhead, *n.*, a fool. (The phrase "at loggerheads" = quarrelling or disputing.)

log'gia, *n.*, a gallery or arcade having one side open.

log'ging, *pr.p.*, log.

log'house, *n.*, a building of logs used for military defence.

log'hut, *n.*, a wooden hut.

log'ic, *n.*, the science of correct thinking; correct use of argument; ability to argue correctly.

log'ical, *adj.*, in accordance with correct reasoning; rel. to logic.

log'ically, *adv.*, according to the rules of logic.

logi'cian, *n.*, an expert in logic.

logis'tic, *adj.*, rel. to calculation.

logis'tical, *adj.*, *i.q.* logistic.

log'line, *n.*, a line used for paying out the log.

log'ogram, *n.*, a shorthand sign representing a whole word.

logograph'ic, *adj.*, rel. to logography.

logog'raphy, *n.*, the use of logotypes in printing.

logom'achist, *adj.*, one who disputes about mere words.

logom'achy, *n.*, controversy over mere words.

logom'eter, *n.*, a logarithmic scale.

logomet'ric, *adj.*, rel. to a logometer.

Log'os, *n.*, the name in St. John i. for the Divine Word, the Second Person of the Blessed Trinity.

log'otype, *n.*, several letters or a word cast in one piece.

log'wood, *n.*, an American wood used in dyeing.

loin, *n.*, the part between the lower rib and the hip bone.

loi'ter, *v.i.*, to hang about, dawdle.

loi'tered, *p.p.*, loiter.

loi'terer, *n.*, one who loiters.

loi'tering, *pr.p.*, loiter.

loll, *v.t.*, to hang (the tongue) out; *v.i.*, to recline lazily, sit idly about.

Lol'lard, *n.*, one of Wyclif's followers.

Lol'lardism, *n.*, the doctrines of Wyclif.

lolled, *p.p.*, loll.

loll'ing, *pr.p.*, loll.

lol'lipop, *n.*, sugarplum.

Lom'bard, *n.* and *adj.*, native to Lombardy.

Lombar'dic, *adj.*, rel. to Lombardy, its people, and its school of artists; *n.*, a peculiar kind of script.

lo'ment, *n.*, a variety of pod.

Lon'doner, *n.*, an inhabitant or native of London.

lone, *adj.*, lonely, alone, unfrequented.

lone'lier, *adj.*, *comp.* of lonely.

lone'liest, *adj.*, *super.* of lonely.

lone'liness, *n.*, solitariness.

lone'ly, *adj.*, solitary, unfrequented.

lone'some, *adj.*, *i.q.* lonely.

lone'someness, *n.*, the state of being lonesome.

long, *v.i.*, to desire earnestly; *adj.*, great in measurement from end to end; tedious; delaying; *adv.*, for a long time.

long'-boat, *n.*, the large boat of a ship.

long'-bow, *n.*, a hand bow.

long'-cloth, *n.*, superior cotton cloth.

long'-clothes, *n. pl.*, an infant's first clothes.

longed, *p.p.*, long.

long'er, *n.*, one who longs.

lon'ger, *adj.* and *adv.*, *comp.* of long.

lon'gest, *adj.* and *adv.*, *super.* of long.

longe'val, *adj.*, long-lived.

longev'ity, *n.*, long life.

longe'vous, *adj.*, *i.q.* longeval.

long'hand, *n.*, ordinary writing, as distinct from shorthand.

long'-headed, *adj.*, shrewd.

longim'anous, *adj.*, long-handed.

long'ing, *pr.p.*, long; *n.*, a yearning.

long'ish, *adj.*, somewhat long.

lon'gitude, *n.*, distance E. or W. from an agreed meridian.

longitu'dinal, *adj.*, rel. to length; lengthwise.

long'lived, *adj.*, living for a long time.

long' run, *phrase* = the final issue.

long'-shore, *adj.*, working along the water-side.

long'-sight, *n.*, far sight.

long'-sighted, *adj.*, far-sighted.

long-sight'edness, *n.*, the state of being far-sighted.

long'-stop, *v.i.*, to be the long-stop; *n.*, the man behind the wicket-keeper.

long'-suffering, *adj.*, patient; *n.*, patience.

long'-winded, *adj.*, prolix.

long'wise, *adv.* and *adj.*, lengthwise.

loo, *v.t.*, to penalize at loo; *n.*, a round game at cards.

loo'by, *n.*, a stupid fellow; lubber.

loof, *n.*, *see* luff.

loo'fah, *n.*, a vegetable sponge.

look, *v.i.*, to use the eyes; to direct the gaze; to seem; to watch; *n.*, the act of looking or watching; appearance.

looked, *p.p.*, look.

look'er, *n.*, one who looks.

look'ing, *pr.p.*, look.

look'ing-glass, *n.*, a mirror.
look'out, *n.*, a place for observation; the observer.
loom, *v.i.*, to appear indistinctly; *n.*, an apparatus for weaving; the inboard portion of an oar; a guillemot.
loomed, *p.p.*, loom.
loom'ing, *pr.p.*, loom.
loon, *n.*, a dolt; grebe.
loop, *v.t.*, to bind into a loop; to fasten; *v.i.*, to move in loops; *n.*, a fold or doubling of cord, etc.; a curved piece of metal for a handle.
looped, *p.p.*, loop.
loop'er, *n.*, a caterpillar that loops itself.
loop'hole, *n.*, a narrow opening in a wall for archers or look-outs; a means of evasion; *v.t.*, to make loopholes in.
loop'holed, *p.p.*, loophole.
loop'ing, *pr.p.*, loop.
loose, *v.t.*, to set free, release; *adj.*, free, not attached; lax.
loose'ly, *adv.*, in a loose way.
loos'en, *v.t.*, to make loose, detach; *v.i.*, to come detached.
loos'ened, *p.p.*, loosen.
loose'ness, *n.*, the state or quality of being loose.
loos'er, *adj.*, *comp.* of loose.
loos'est, *adj.*, *super.* of loose.
loot, *v.t.*, to plunder; carry off as spoil; *n.*, plunder.
lop, *v.t.*, to cut at the top; to allow to hang down; *v.i.*, to hang down; to break in short waves; *n.*, something lopped; the lumpy break of a wave.
lopped, *p.p.*, lop.
lop'per, *n.*, one who, that which, lops.
lop'ping, *pr.p.*, lop.
lop'-sided, *adj.*, uneven, one-sided.
loqua'cious, *adj.*, talkative, garrulous.
loqua'ciously, *adv.*, talkatively.
loquac'ity, *n.*, talkativeness.
lor'cha, *n.*, a ship, European in build, but with Chinese rig.
lord, *v.t.*, to ennoble; *v.i.*, to be a ruler; *n.*, a ruler, master, husband, chief.
lord'ed, *p.p.*, lord.
lord'ing, *n.*, a little lord; *pr.p.*, lord.
***lord*'like,** *adj.*, haughty, imperious, grand.
***lord*'liness,** *n.*, the quality of being lordly.
***lord*'ling,** *n.*, a little lord.
***lord*'ly,** *adj.*, haughty, imperious, grand.
***lord*'ship,** *n.*, rule, ownership, a manor, the status or person of a lord.
***Lord's* Sup'per,** *n.*, the Mass or Eucharist.
lore, *n.*, teaching, erudition; the space between the eye and the beak of a bird.
lorgnette', *n.*, an opera-glass.
lor'icate, *adj.*, covered with armour.
lor'icated, *adj.*, *i.q.* loricate.
lorica'tion, *n.*, the state of being loricated; defensive armour.
lorn, *adj.*, desolate, forlorn.
lor'ry, *n.*, a long wagon; a truck.
lo'ry, *n.*, a variety of parrot.
lose, *v.t.*, to be parted from, to miss, fail to gain; *v.i.*, to be unsuccessful.
lo'sel, *n.*, a wastrel.
los'er, *n.*, one who loses.
los'ing, *pr.p.*, lose.
loss, *n.*, the act of losing or being lost; anything lost; misfortune.
lost, *p.p.*, lose.
lot, *v.t.*, to divide into lots; *n.*, a die; fortune; a divided portion of land; an item in a sale at auction; a number of collected things.
lo'ta, lo'tah, *n.*, an Indian round pot.
lote'-tree, *n.*, the lotus.
loth, *adj.*, *see* loath.
lotha'rio, *n.*, a rake.
lo'tion, *n.*, a liquid medicine externally applied.
lot'tery, *n.*, a scheme for distributing prizes by lot to ticket-holders.
lot'to, *n.*, an indoor game of chance.
lo'tus, *n.*, a plant of the water-lily family.
loud, *adj.*, having a great intensity of sound; noisy; flashy; *adv.*, = loudly.
loud'er, *adj.* and *adv.*, *comp.* of loud.
loud'est, *adj.* and *adv.*, *super.* of loud.
loud'ly, *adv.*, sonorously, very audibly.
loud'ness, *n.*, the quality of being loud.
lough, *n.*, a lake, or arm of the sea.
lou'is, *n.*, a French gold piece = 20 francs.
lou'is d'or', *n.*, *i.q.* louis.
lounge, *v.i.*, to saunter; loll; idle; *n.*, a stroll; a place or seat for lounging.
lounged, *p.p.*, lounge.
loung'er, *n.*, one who lounges.
loung'ing, *pr.p.*, lounge.
louse, *n.*, a small parasitic insect.
lou'sy, *adj.*, infected with lice.
lout, *n.*, a bumpkin; *v.i.*, to bow.
lout'ish, *adj.*, awkward, clownish.
lout'ishly, *adv.*, like a lout.
lou'ver, *n.*, a smoke vent; a lantern with cupola.
lou'ver-boards, *n. pl.*, openings in a window-space to admit air but not rain.
lov'able, *adj.*, worthy of love.

lov'age, *n.*, the herb *Levisticum.*
love, *v.t.*, to have affection or regard for; to cherish; to delight in; *n.*, affection, strong attachment, devotion; (in games) nothing, no score.
love'-apple, *n.*, the tomato.
love'-bird, *n.*, a small breed of parrot.
loved, *p.p.*, love.
love'-feast, *n.*, the ancient Christian Agapé, a common meal taken in brotherly love.
love'-knot, *n.*, a ribbon tied in a knot to signify love.
love'less, *adj.*, without love.
love'-letter, *n.*, a letter from or to a sweetheart.
love'lier, *adj.*, *comp.* of lovely.
love'liest, *adj.*, *super.* of lovely.
love'liness, *n.*, the quality of being lovely.
love'-lorn, *n.*, pining for a lover.
love'ly, *adj.*, attracting by its beauty, delightful.
lov'er, *n.*, one who loves; a sweetheart.
love'-sick, *adj.*, pining with love.
lov'ing, *pr.p.*, love; *adj.*, affectionate.
loving-kind'ness, *n.*, tenderness, compassion.
lov'ingly, *adv.*, tenderly.
low, *v.i.*, to make the cry of a cow; *n.*, a cow's cry; *adj.*, not high; deep, depressed; deep in pitch; moderate; mean, base.
low'-born, *adj.*, of humble birth.
low'-bred, *adj.*, ill-bred.
Low'-church, *adj.*, regarding as non-essential the three-fold order of ministry, Apostolic succession, and high views on the Sacraments.
lowed, *p.p.*, low.
low'er, *adj.* and *adv.*, *comp.* of low; *v.t.*, to let down, depress.
low'er, *v.i.*, to be gloomy and threatening.
low'ered, *p.p.*, lower.
low'ered, *p.p.*, lower.
low'ering, *pr.p.*, lower.
low'ering, *pr.p.*, lower; *adj.*, threatening.
lower'most, *adj.* and *adv.*, lowest.
low'ery, *adj.*, *i.q.* lowering.
low'est, *adj.* and *adv.*, *super.* of low.
low'ing, *pr.p.*, low.
low'land, *adj.*, of the low or level country. *n.* In pl. less elevated country.
Low'lander, *n.*, one who was born in the Lowlands.
low'lier, *adj.*, *comp.* of lowly.
low'liest, *adj.*, *super.* of lowly.
low'lily, *adv.*, in a lowly way.
low'liness, *n.*, humility.
low'ly, *adj.*, humble, unpretending.
low'-minded, *adj.*, base, vulgar.
low'-mindedness, *n.*, baseness, vulgarity.
low'ness, *n.*, the quality or state of being low.
low'-spirited, *n.*, depressed, melancholy.
low'-wines, *n.*, weak spirit after distillation of alcoholic substances.
loxodrom'ic, *adj.*, rel. to oblique sailing.
loy'al, *adj.*, faithful in allegiance.
loy'alist, *n.*, one who supports the lawful government.
loy'ally, *adv.*, in a loyal way.
loy'alty, *n.*, fidelity, constancy in allegiance.
loz'enge, *n.*, a rhombus, diamond figure; an unmarried woman's or a widow's escutcheon; a small tablet, either a sweetmeat or a medicine.
lub'ber, *n.*, a lout, a raw sailor.
lub'berly, *adj.*, loutish.
lu'bricant, *adj.*, lubricating; *n.*, anything that lubricates.
lu'bricate, *v.t.*, to make slippery by greasing.
lu'bricated, *p.p.*, lubricate.
lu'bricating, *pr.p.*, lubricate.
lubrica'tion, *n.*, the act of lubricating.
lu'bricator, *n.*, *i.q.* lubricant.
lubric'ity, *n.*, slipperiness, smoothness; lewdness.
lu'bricous, *adj.*, smooth, slippery.
luce, *n.*, a pike.
lu'cent, *adj.*, shining.
lucer'nal, *adj.*, rel. to a lamp.
lucerne', *n.*, a plant like clover, used for fodder.
lu'cid, *adj.*, clear.
lucid'ity, *n.*, clearness.
lu'cidly, *adv.*, clearly.
lu'cidness, *n.*, *i.q.* lucidity.
lu'cifer, *n.*, the morning star; a friction match.
lucif'erous, *adj.*, light-bringing.
lucif'ic, *adj.*, light-producing.
lu'ciform, *adj.*, like a light.
lucim'eter, *n.*, an apparatus for gauging the intensity of light.
luck, *n.*, chance, fortune.
luck'ier, *adj.*, *comp.* of lucky.
luck'iest, *adj.*, *super.* of lucky.
luck'ily, *adv.*, by good luck.
luck'less, *adj.*, unfortunate.
luck'y, *adj.*, fortunate.
lu'crative, *adj.*, bringing gain, profitable.
lu'cre, *n.*, pecuniary gain.
lu'cubrate, *v.t.*, to spend the midnight oil on; to write.

lucubra'tion, *n.*, the act of lucubrating; a literary product.
lu'culent, *adj.*, clear, lucid.
Lud'dite, *n.*, a rioter.
lu'dicrous, *adj.*, ridiculous.
lu'dicrously, *adv.*, ridiculously.
luff, *v.t.* and *i.*, to bring (a ship) into the wind; *n.*, a sail's foremost edge; the carved part of a ship's bow.
luffed, *p.p.*, luff.
luff'er, *n.*, *see* louver; a louver-board.
luff'ing, *pr.p.*, luff.
lug, *v.t.*, to pull, haul; *v.i.*, to pull hard at; *n.*, a pull; an ear; a square sail.
lug'gage, *n.*, baggage.
lugged, *p.p.*, lug.
lug'ger, *n.*, a small ship with lug sails.
lug'ging, *pr.p.*, lug.
lugu'brious, *adj.*, doleful.
luke'warm, *adj.*, neither hot nor cold; indifferent.
luke'warmness, *n.*, indifference.
lull, *v.t.*, to appease, make quiet; *v.i.*, to grow quiet; *n.*, a period of calm.
lull'aby, *n.*, a cradle song.
lulled, *p.p.*, lull.
lull'ing, *pr.p.*, lull.
lumachel'la, *n.*, limestone containing fossils (*Ital.*).
lu'machelle, *n.*, *i.q.* lumachella.
lumba'ginous, *adj.*, rel. to lumbago.
lumba'go, *n.*, rheumatic pain in the loins.
lum'bar, *adj.*, rel. to the loins.
lum'ber, *v.t.*, to fill with lumber; to encumber; *v.i.*, to trade in lumber; to go clumsily along; *n.*, litter, rubbish; cut and prepared timber; superfluous weight.
lum'bered, *p.p.*, lumber.
lum'bering, *pr.p.*, lumber; *adj.*, clumsy, moving heavily.
lum'berman, *n.*, a person engaged in the lumber trade.
lum'ber-room, *n.*, a room for useless articles.
lumbri'cal, *n.*, a muscle in the hand or foot.
lu'minary, *n.*, a light-giving body.
luminif'erous, *adj.*, light-producing.
luminos'ity, *n.*, the state or quality of being luminous.
lu'minous, *adj.*, yielding light.
lump, *v.t.*, to throw into a lump; *v.i.*, to grow lumpy; *n.*, a mass; the aggregate; a protuberance; a dull person.
lumped, *p.p.*, lump.
lump'er, *n.*, one who lumps.
lump'ing, *pr.p.*, lump.
lump'ish, *adj.*, dull, stupid.
lump'ishly, *adv.*, stupidly.
lump'y, *adj.*, having lumps.
Lu'na, *n.*, the Moon-goddess (*Lat.*).
lu'nacy, *n.*, madness.
lu'nar, *adj.*, pert. to the moon or month.
luna'rian, *n.*, a dweller in the moon; an expert in knowledge about the moon.
lu'nary, *adj.*, *i.q.* lunar.
lu'nate, *adj.*, crescent-shaped.
lu'nated, *adj.*, *i.q.* lunate.
lu'natic, *adj.*, insane; *n.*, a madman.
luna'tion, *n.*, the interval between one new moon and another.
lunch, *v.i.*, to take lunch; *n.*, a midday meal.
lunched, *p.p.*, lunch.
lunch'eon, *n.*, *i.q.* lunch.
lunch'ing, *pr.p.*, lunch.
lune, *n.*, a figure bounded by two arcs of circles.
lunette', *n.*, a moon-shaped opening, or a space in a dome or ceiling; a crescent-shaped holder in a monstrance.
lung, *n.*, a breathing organ.
lunge, *v.t.*, to break in with a lunge; *v.i.*, to make a thrust; *n.*, a long rope; a sudden thrust or hit out.
lunged, *p.p.*, lunge.
lun'ging, *pr.p.*, lunge.
lung'wort, *n.*, a borage-like herb.
lu'niform, *adj.*, crescent-shaped.
luniso'lar, *adj.*, caused by sun and moon combined.
lu'nular, *adj.*, like a small crescent.
lu'nulate, *adj.*, almost crescent-shaped.
lu'nulated, *adj.*, *i.q.* lunulate.
Lu'percal, *adj.*, rel. to Lupercus, the protector of shepherds.
lu'pine, *adj.*, wolfish, ravenous, rel. to wolves.
lu'pine, lu'pin, *n.*, a *lupinus* plant.
lu'pulin, *n.*, an alkaloid found in hops.
lu'pus, *n.*, an ulcerous skin disease.
lurch, *v.i.*, to swing, sway to one side; *n.*, a roll to one side; a stagger, an embarrassing position (as at cribbage).
lurched, *p.p.*, lurch.
lurch'er, *n.*, a poacher, swindler; a cross-breed of dogs.
lurch'ing, *pr.p.*, lurch.
lure, *v.t.*, to entice; to recall (a hawk); *n.*, a falconer's device for recalling a hawk with bait.
lured, *p.p.*, lure.
lu'rid, *adj.*, ghastly, stormy, dull red.
lu'ring, *pr.p.*, lure.
lurk, *v.i.*, to be in hiding; to be unnoticed.
lurked, *p.p.*, lurk.
lurk'er, *n.*, one who lurks.
lurk'ing, *pr.p.*, lurk.
lus'cious, *adj.*, rich and sweet.
lus'ciously, *adv.*, with a luscious flavour.

lus'ciousness, *n.*, luscious flavour.

lush, *adj.*, luxuriant; *n.*, drink (*slang*); *v.i.*, to indulge in wine (*slang*).

Lu'siad, *n.*, a Portuguese epic so named.

lust, *v.i.*, to desire inordinately; *n.*, inordinate desire.

lust'ed, *p.p.*, lust.

lust'ful, *adj.*, passionate, sensual.

lust'ier, *adj.*, *comp.* of lusty.

lust'iest, *adj.*, *super.* of lusty.

lust'ily, *adv.*, vigorously.

lust'iness, *n.*, sturdiness.

lust'ing, *pr.p.*, lust.

lus'tral, *adj.*, purifying.

lus'trate, *v.t.*, to purify ceremonially.

lustra'tion, *n.*, the act of lustrating.

lus'tre, *v.t.*, to put a gloss on; *n.*, gloss, sheen, glory; a dress material; a candelabrum with glass pendants; china or earthenware lustred; *i.q.* lustrum.

lus'tring, *n.*, a glossy silk fabric.

lus'trous, *adj.*, shining, splendid.

lus'trously, *adv.*, in a lustrous way.

lus'trum, *n.*, a quinquennium; period of five years.

lust'y, *adj.*, stout, vigorous.

lu'tanist, *n.*, a lute player.

luta'tion, *n.*, the process of luting.

lute, *v.t.*, to stop a hole with clay; to apply lute to; *n.*, stopping; also *v.i.*, to play on the lute; *n.*, a stringed instrument like the guitar.

lut'ed, *p.p.*, lute.

lu'teous, *adj.*, golden-yellow coloured.

lute'string, *n.*, a glossy silk fabric.

Lu'theran, *adj.*, bel. to Luther; *n.*, a follower of Luther.

Lu'theranism, *n.*, the doctrines of the Augsburg Confession.

lut'ing, *pr.p.*, lute.

lu'tose, *adj.*, muddy.

lu'tulent, *adj.*, muddy.

lux'ate, *v.t.*, to dislocate, displace.

lux'ating, *pr.p.*, luxate.

luxa'tion, *n.*, the act or result of luxating.

luxu'riance, *n.*, profuse growth, rankness.

luxu'riancy, *n.*, *i.q.* luxuriance.

luxu'riant, *adj.*, growing in profusion, rank.

luxu'riate, *v.i.*, to grow in profusion; to take extreme pleasure or delight.

luxu'riated, *p.p.*, luxuriate.

luxu'riating, *pr.p.*, luxuriate.

luxu'rious, *adj.*, given to luxury.

luxu'riously, *adv.*, in a luxurious way.

lux'ury, *n.*, excessive indulgence in costly things; enjoyment; a thing desired but not necessary; extravagance.

lycau'thropy, *n.*, the supposed power of changing from a man into a wolf.

lyce'um, *n.*, a grove near Athens where Aristotle taught the peripatetic philosophy; a literary institution or meeting-place.

lyd'dite, *n.*, a high explosive containing picric acid.

Lyd'ian, *adj.*, rel. to Lydia.

lye, *n.*, a leached solution from ashes; an alkaline solution used in various industries.

ly'ing, *pr.p.*, lie; *n.*, telling falsehoods; *adj.*, mendacious.

ly'ing-in', *n.*, childbirth.

lyke'-wake, *n.*, a night watch over the dead.

lymph, *n.*, water; the colourless alkaline fluid in the bodily tissues; virus of a disease.

lymphat'ic, *adj.*, rel. to or secreting lymph; of a phlegmatic temperament.

lynch, *v.t.*, to execute by mob law.

lynched, *p.p.*, lynch.

lynch'er, *n.*, one who lynches.

lynch'ing, *pr.p.*, lynch.

lynx, *n.*, a cat-like animal, possessed of very keen sight.

lynx'-eyed, *n.*, keen-sighted.

ly'ra, *n.*, one of the signs of the Zodiac.

ly'rate, *adj.*, lyre-shaped.

lyre, *n.*, an ancient kind of harp.

lyr'ic, *adj.*, to be sung to a lyre accompaniment; expressing emotion in verse; *n.*, a lyric poem, expressing the poet's own feelings and emotions and experiences.

lyr'ical, *adj.*, *i.q.* lyric.

lyr'icism, *n.*, lyric expression.

lyr'ist, *n.*, a player on the lyre; a lyric poet.

lyte'rian, *adj.*, showing the end.

M

Mab, *n.*, queen of the fairies.

macadamiza'tion, *n.*, the act or effect of macadamizing.

macad'amize, *v.t.*, to cover with broken stone.

macad'amized, *p.p.*, macadamize.

macad'amizing, *pr.p.* macadamize.

macaro'ni, macaro'ni, *n.*, long, slender tubes made of wheat flour; a fop.

macaron'ic, *adj.*, composed of Latin or Greek and a vernacular language given Latin or Greek forms; *n.*, a verse in macaronic.

macaroon', *n.*, a biscuit containing flour, eggs, almonds and sugar.

macaw', *n.*, a large kind of parrot.

Maccabe'an, *adj.*, rel. to the Maccabees.

ma'ccoboy, *n.*, a variety of snuff.

mace, *n.*, an emblem of power; a spice; a bagatelle cue; a spiked club.

mace'-bearer, *n.*, an officer who carries the mace.

Macedo'nian, *adj.*, rel. to Macedonia.

mac'erate, *v.t.*, to soften with fluid.

mac'erated, *p.p.*, macerate.

mac'erating, *pr.p.*, macerate.

macera'tion, *n.*, the act of macerating.

Machiavel'lian, *adj.*, rel. to Machiavelli; crafty.

Machiavel'lianism, *n.*, crafty policy.

Machiavel'lism, *n.*, *i.q.* Machiavellianism.

machic'olate, *v.t.*, to make machicolations on.

machic'olated, *p.p.*, machicolate.

machicola'tion, *n.*, an outer protection to the top of a fortress, with a space between it and the wall, enabling the defenders to drop boiling liquids, etc., down.

mach'inate, *v.t.*, to plan, contrive.

mach'inated, *p.p.*, machinate.

mach'inating, *pr.p.*, machinate.

machina'tion, *n.*, plot, contrivance.

machine', *v.t.*, to sew with a machine; *n.*, a mechanical contrivance.

machined', *p.p.*, machine.

machin'ery, *n.*, machines collectively; any contrivance by which action is maintained.

machin'ing, *pr.p.*, machine.

machin'ist, *n.*, a maker of machines; one skilled in machinery.

mack'erel, *n.*, a sea fish so named.

mack'intosh, *n.*, a waterproof overcoat.

mack'le, *v.t.*, to blur.

macrocephal'ic, *adj.*, long-headed.

mac'rocosm, *n.*, the universe.

macrom'eter, *n.*, an instrument for measuring distance.

mac'ula, *n.*, a spot (*Lat.*).

mac'ulate, *v.t.*, to spot.

mac'ulated, *p.p.*, maculate.

mac'ulating, *pr.p.*, maculate.

macula'tion, *n.*, the act or effect of maculating.

mad, *adj.*, angry, insane.

mad'am, mad'ame, *n.*, the title of a lady.

mad'cap, *n.*, a rash, thoughtless person.

mad'den, *v.t.*, to infuriate.

mad'dened, *p.p.*, madden.

mad'dening, *pr.p.*, madden; *adj.*, infuriating.

mad'der, *adj.*, *comp.* of mad; *n.*, a root yielding a red dye.

mad'dest, *adj.*, *super.* of mad.

mad'ding, *adj.*, *i.q.* maddening.

made, *p.p.*, make.

Madei'ra, *n.*, the island so named; the wine of M.

mademoiselle', *n.*, an unmarried lady (*Fr.*).

mad'house, *n.*, a lunatic asylum.

mad'ly, *adv.*, insanely.

mad'man, *n.*, a lunatic; an angry person.

mad'ness, *n.*, rage, fury, insanity.

madon'na, *n.*, an image of Our Lady.

mad'repore, *n.*, coral.

mad'rigal, *n.*, a choral song of special form.

mael'strom, *n.*, a whirlpool.

mae'nad, *n.*, a Bacchante.

maesto'so, *adv.*, majestically.

Mafi'a, *n.*, a Sicilian secret society.

magazine', *n.*, a storehouse; a periodical publication.

mag'dalen, *n.*, a penitent.

magen'ta, *n.*, a red dye.

mag'got, *n.*, a worm or grub; a whim.

mag'goty, *adj.*, full of maggots; whimsical.

Ma'gi, *n.*, the Wise Men of the East.

Ma'gian, *adj.*, rel. to the Magi.

mag'ic, *adj.*, rel. to magic; *n.*, sorcery, enchantment, witchcraft.

mag'ical, *adj.*, *i.q.* magic.

mag'ically, *adv.*, in a magical way.

magi'cian, *n.*, a sorcerer: one skilled in magic.

mag'ic lant'ern, *n.*, an optical apparatus, throwing objects magnified on to a screen.

magilp', *n.*, linseed oil and mastic varnish.

magiste'rial, *adj.*, rel. to a teacher or a magistrate; authoritative.

magiste'rially, *adv.*, authoritatively.

mag'istracy, *n.*, the office of a magistrate; magistrates collectively.

mag'istrate, *n.*, a public civil officer.

mag'ma, *n.*, a composite paste; dough-like mass.

Mag'na Car'ta, *n.*, the Great Charter of England.

magnanim'ity, *n.*, generosity; greatness of mind.

magnan'imous, *adj.*, great-minded, generous.

magnan'imously, *adj.*, with magnanimity.

mag'nate, *n.*, a grandee; one of the highest rank.

magne'sia, *n.*, a white powder, the oxide of magnesium.

magne'sian, *adj.*, rel. to magnesium.

magne'sium, *n.*, the metallic base of magnesia.

mag'net, *n.*, a steel bar having the properties of loadstone.

magnet'ic, *adj.*, rel. to magnetism.

mag'netism, *n.*, the properties of attracting and repelling; the science of magnetic phenomena.

mag'netize, *v.t.*, to imbue with magnetic properties.

mag'netized, *p.p.*, magnetize.

mag'netizer, *n.*, anything that magnetizes.

mag'netizing, *pr.p.*, magnetize.

magne'to - elec'tric, *adj.*, rel. to magneto-electricity.

magne'to-electric'ity, *n.*, electricity produced by magnetism.

magnetom'eter, *n.*, an apparatus measuring magnetic force.

magnetomet'ric, *adj.*, rel. to a magnetometer.

magnif'ic, *adj.*, *i.q.* magnificent.

magnif'ical, *adj.*, *i.q.* magnificent.

Magnif'icat, *n.*, the Song of the Blessed Virgin Mary.

magnifica'tion, *n.*, magnifying.

magnif'icence, *n.*, splendour, grandeur.

magnif'icent, *adj.*, splendid, grand.

magnif'icently, *adv.*, splendidly.

mag'nified, *p.p.*, magnify.

mag'nifier, *n.*, anything that magnifies.

mag'nify, *v.t.*, to enlarge, to exaggerate, to extol.

mag'nifying, *pr.p.*, magnify.

magnil'oquence, *n.*, pompous or lofty language.

magnil'oquent, *adj.*, talking big.

mag'nitude, *n.*, size, greatness.

magno'lia, *n.*, a flowering shrub.

mag'num, *n.*, a large size of bottle.

mag'pie, *n.*, a talking bird.

Mag'yar, *adj.*, rel. to the Magyars.

Mahara'ja, Mahara'jah, *n.*, the title of some Indian princes.

mahat'ma *n.*, a professor of esoteric Buddhism.

Mah'di, *n.*, a Mohammedan religious leader.

mahl'stick, *n.*, a painter's hand-rest.

Mah'mal, *n.*, the ceremonial car for conveying the Holy Carpet from Cairo to Mecca.

mahog'any, *adj.*, made of mahogany; *n.*, a reddish-brown wood.

Mahom'etan, *adj.*, rel. to Mahomet. Also *Mohammedan.*

Mahom'etanism, *n.*, the Mahometan religion. Also *Mohammedanism.*

mahout', *n.*, an elephant driver.

maid, *n.*, an unmarried woman; female servant.

maid'en, *n.*, a virgin, a girl; *adj.*, new, untried.

maid'enhair, *n.*, a variety of fern.

maid'enhood, *n.*, the state of being a maiden.

maid'enish, *adj.*, girlish.

maid'en-like, *adj.*, modest, gentle.

maid'enly, *adj.*, *i.q.* maiden-like.

Maid-Ma'rian, *n.*, a May Queen.

maid'servant, *n.*, a female domestic.

mail, *v.t.*, to arm with mail; to send by post; *n.*, armour; conveyance of letters; a batch of letters; tribute.

mail'cart, *n.*, a cart for carrying the mails; a child's light carriage.

mailed, *p.p.*, mail.

mail'ing, *pr.p.*, mail.

maim, *v.t.*, to injure, cripple.

maimed, *p.p.*, maim.

maim'ing, *pr.p.*, maim.

main, *adj.*, chief, leading; *n.*, the ocean; a chief conducting sewer-, gas-, or water-pipe; a match in cock-fighting; a throw of dice; *adv.*, greatly (*Prov.*).

main′land, *n.*, the land as distinguished from the sea or an island.
main′ly, *adv.*, chiefly.
main′mast, *n.*, the principal mast.
main′prize, *v.t.*, to release on recognizances; *n.*, the act of a surety in taking over the custody of a mainprized person.
main′sail, *n.*, the sail on the mainmast or bent to the mainyard.
main′spring, *n.*, the principal spring; source of power.
main′stay, *n.*, a chief support; the stay stretching from the foot of the foremast to the maintop.
maintain′, *v.t.*, to keep, defend, affirm.
maintain′able, *adj.*, able to be maintained.
maintained′, *p.p.*, maintain.
maintain′er, *n.*, one who maintains.
maintain′ing, *pr.p.*, maintain.
main′tenance, *n.*, support, livelihood.
main′top, *n.*, the top of a mainmast.
maisonette′, *n.*, a part of a house converted into a flat.
maize, *n.*, Indian corn.
majes′tic, *adj.*, stately, regal.
majes′tical, *adj.*, *i.q.* majestic.
majes′tically, *adv.*, in a majestic way.
maj′esty, *n.*, dignity, sovereignty, sublimity.
majol′ica, *n.*, fine earthenware painted.
ma′jor, *adj.*, greater; *n.*, a military officer, next above a captain.
ma′jor-do′mo, *n.*, a house-steward.
maj′or-gen′eral, *n.*, a military officer, next below a lieutenant-general.
major′ity, *n.*, the greater number; full legal age.
majus′cule, *n.*, an early Latin capital letter.
make, *v.t.*, to create, produce, cause; *n.*, form, structure.
make′bate, *n.*, Jacob's ladder (*Bot.*).
make′-believe, *n.*, pretence; *adj.*, unreal.
ma′ker, *n.*, one who makes.
make′shift, *n.*, an extemporized substitute; *adj.*, extemporized.
make′-up, *n.*, composition; an actor's disguise.
make′weight, *n.*, something thrown in.
ma′king, *pr.p.*, make.
mal′achite, *n.*, a carbonate of copper.
malacol′ogy, *n.*, the study of molluscs.
maladministra′tion, *n.*, mismanagement.
maladroit′, *adj.*, clumsy.
mal′ady, *n.*, a disease.
Mal′aga, *n.*, a kind of wine.
mal′anders, *n.*, a scurfy complaint in horses.
mal′apert, *adj.*, saucy.
malapropos′, *adj.*, inopportune.
ma′lar, *adj.*, rel. to the cheek.
mala′ria, *n.*, exhalations from swampy ground.
mala′rial, *adj.*, rel. to malaria.
mala′rious, *adj.*, producing malaria.
malassimila′tion, *n.*, imperfect assimilation.
Malay′, *adj.*, *i.q.* Malayan; *n.*, a Malayan native.
Malay′an, *adj.*, rel. to the Malays.
mal′content, *adj.*, discontented.
male, *adj.*, not female; of the begetting sex; *n.*, one of the male sex.
maledic′tion, *n.*, a curse.
mal′efactor, *n.*, a criminal.
mal′efactress, *n.*, fem. of malefactor.
malef′ic, *adj.*, baneful, evil.
malev′olence, *n.*, ill-will, spite.
malev′olent, *adj.*, spiteful, bearing ill-will.
malfea′sance, *n.*, an illegality.
malforma′tion, *n.*, mis-shapenness.
ma′lic, *adj.*, rel. to fruit — to apples particularly.
mal′ice, *n.*, spite, evil intent.
mali′cious, *adj.*, spiteful.
mali′ciously, *adv.*, spitefully.
mali′ciousness, *n.*, spitefulness, cruel intent.
malign′, *v.t.* to slander; *adj.*, hurtful.
malig′nancy, *n.*, the state of being malignant.
malig′nant, *adj.*, malicious, injurious.
maligned′, *p.p.*, malign.
malign′er, *n.*, one who maligns.
malign′ing, *pr.p.*, malign.
malig′nity, *n.*, malice, cruelty.
malign′ly, *adv.*, in a malign way.
malin′ger, *v.i.*, to shirk duty on pretence of illness.
malin′gered, *p.p.*, malinger.
malin′gerer, *n.*, one who malingers.
malin′gering, *pr.p.*, malinger.
mal′ison, *n.*, a curse.
mal′kin, *n.*, a cat, a mop, a scarecrow, a drab.
mall, *n.*, a mallet.
mall, *n.*, the place where pall-mall was played; a public walk.
mal′lard, *n.*, a wild duck.
malleabil′ity, *n.*, the quality of being malleable.
mal′leable, *adj.*, able to be hammered out.
mal′leate, *v.t.*, to hammer (metal).

mallea'tion, *n.*, the act of hammering.
malle'olar, *adj.*, rel. to the ankle.
mal'let, *n.*, a wooden hammer.
mal'low, *n.*, a plant of the Malva genus.
mal'lows, *n.*, *i.q.* mallow.
malm, *n.*, loam used in brickmaking.
malm'sey, *n.*, a species of grape; a wine made from the same.
malprac'tice, *n.*, evil.
malt, *v.t.*, to make into malt; *v.i.*, to become malt; *adj.*, made with malt; *n.*, grain fermented for brewing.
malt'ed, *p.p.*, malt.
Maltese', *adj.*, rel. to Malta; *n.*, a native of Malta.
mal'tha, *n.*, a sort of pitch.
Malthu'sian, *adj.*, rel. to Malthus and his theory.
malt'ing, *pr.p.*, malt.
maltreat', *v.t.*, to treat ill or cruelly.
maltreat'ed, *p.p.*, maltreat.
maltreat'ing, *pr.p.*, maltreat.
maltreat'ment, *n.*, cruel treatment.
malt'ster, *n.*, one who makes malt.
malt'y, *adj.*, like or containing malt.
Malva'ceae, *n. pl.*, an order of plants containing the mallows.
malva'ceous, *adj.*, rel. to Malvaceae.
malversa'tion, *n.*, fraudulent abuse of trust.
mama', *see* mamma.
mam'elon, *n.*, a mound.
mam'eluke, *n.*, one of the Egyptian cavalry.
mam'illary, *adj.*, *see* mammillary.
mam'illated, *adj.*, *see* mammillated.
mamma', *n.*, a familiar name for mother.
mam'mal, *n.*, an animal that suckles its young.
mamma'lia, *n.*, pl. of mammal.
mamma'lian, *adj.*, rel. to mammals.
mammal'ogist, *adj.*, rel. to mammalogy.
mammal'ogy, *n.*, the study of mammals.
mam'mary, *adj.*, rel. to the breasts.
mammif'erous, *adj.*, having breasts.
mam'miform, *adj.*, breast-shaped.
mam'millary, *adj.*, rel. to the breast.
mam'millated, *adj.*, having breasts, protuberant.
mam'mon, *n.*, worldly riches.
mam'monist, *n.*, a worshipper of mammon.
mam'moth, *adj.*, huge; *n.*, a huge extinct elephant.
man, *v.t.*, to furnish with men, to guard; *n.*, mankind collectively, a human being, a male.
man'acle, *v.t.*, to handcuff, fasten the hands; *n.*, a shackle for the hands.
man'acled, *p.p.*, manacle.
man'acling, *pr.p.*, manacle.
man'age, *v.t.*, to conduct, govern, contrive.
man'ageable, *adj.*, able to be managed.
man'aged, *p.p.*, manage.
man'agement, *n.*, superintendence, contrivance.
man'ager, *n.*, one who manages.
man'ageress, *n.*, fem. of manager.
manage'rial, *adj.*, rel. to management.
man'aging, *pr.p.*, manage.
man'akin, *n.*, a dwarf.
manatee', *n.*, the sea-cow.
Manchu', Manchoo', *n.*, one of the Manchus, the early conquerors of China.
man'ciple, *n.*, a steward.
manda'mus, *n.*, a writ from a higher to a lower court, or to a person.
man'darin, *n.*, a Chinese magistrate.
man'date, *n.*, a command, precept.
man'datary, *n.*, one to whom a mandate is issued.
man'datory, *adj.*, directing, ordering.
man'dible, *n.*, the upper jaw of an insect, lower of vertebrates.
mandib'ular, *adj.*, rel. to mandibles.
mandib'ulate, *adj.*, possessing mandibles.
Mandin'go, *n.*, the name of a S. African negro tribe.
man'dolin, *n.*, a kind of guitar.
man'drake, *n.*, a narcotic plant.
man'drel, *n.*, a revolving shank in a lathe.
man'dril, *n.*, *i.q.* mandrel.
man'ducate, *v.t.*, to eat, chew.
manduca'tion, *n.*, the act of eating.
mane, *n.*, the hair on the neck of a horse, lion, etc.
man'-eater, *n.*, a tiger that has tasted human flesh.
manège', *n.*, horsemanship.
ma'nes, *n. pl.*, the shades of the departed (*Lat.*).
man'ful, *adj.*, manly, courageous.
man'fully, *adv.*, courageously.
man'fulness, *n.*, courage, manliness.
man'gabey, *n.*, one of the monkey tribes.
man'ganese, *n.*, a hard and brittle grey metal.
mangane'sian, *adj.*, rel. to manganese.
mangan'ic, *adj.*, produced from manganese.
mange, *n.*, a skin disease in dogs and cattle.
man'gel-wur'zel, *n.*, a kind of beet.
man'ger, *n.*, a trough for cattle food.

man'giness, *n.*, the state of being mangy.
man'gle, *v.t.*, to lacerate, mutilate; to smooth linen; *n.*, a rolling press for smoothing linen.
man'gled, *p.p.*, mangle.
man'gler, *n.*, one who mangles; a mangling machine.
man'gling, *pr.p.*, mangle.
man'go, *n.*, a fruit-bearing tree.
man'grove, *n.*, an Indian fruit-bearing tree.
man'gy, *adj.*, suffering from mange.
man'hole, *n.*, an opening by which a sewer, etc., can be entered.
man'hood, *n.*, human nature; man's estate; courage.
ma'nia, *n.*, violent madness; insane desire.
ma'niac, *n.*, one suffering from mania.
mani'acal, *adj.*, suffering from mania.
Manichae'an, *adj.*, rel. to the Manichees.
Man'ichaeism, *n.*, the doctrine of the Manichees, or the dualistic theory of deity.
Manichee', *n.*, a believer in two Supreme Powers.
man'icure, *v.t.*, to care for the hands and nails; *n.*, the special treatment of the nails, etc.
man'icurist, *n.*, one who practises manicuring.
man'ifest, *v.t.*, to show, exhibit, reveal, give proof of; *adj.*, evident, plain, obvious; *n.*, an invoice of cargo.
man'ifestable, *adj.*, able to be manifested.
manifesta'tion, *n.*, discovery, display, proof.
man'ifested, *p.p.*, manifest.
man'ifesting, *pr.p.*, manifest.
man'ifestly, *adv.*, plainly, obviously.
manifes'to, *n.*, a public declaration.
man'ifold, *adj.*, multiplied many times; various; many; *adv.*, many times; *v.t.*, to duplicate.
man'ikin, *n.*, a little man; a model of the human form.
manil'la, *n.*, a variety of hemp; a cheroot.
man'ioc, *n.*, a plant from which tapioca is made.
man'iple, *n.*, a division of the Roman legion; a stole-like band worn round the left wrist in celebrating Mass.
manip'ular, *adj.*, rel. to handling.
manip'ulate, *v.t.*, to work with the hands, control, falsify.
manip'ulated, *p.p.*, manipulate.
manip'ulating, *pr.p.*, manipulate.
manipula'tion, *n.*, the act of manipulating; manual skill; falsification.
manip'ulative, *adj.*, done by manipulating.
manip'ulator, *n.*, one who manipulates.
ma'nis, *n.*, a variety of ant-eater.
man'itou, *n.*, the Great Spirit (N. Amer. Indian).
mankind', *n.*, human beings collectively; the human race.
man'lier, *adj.*, *comp.* of manly.
man'liest, *adj.*, *super.* of manly.
man'like, *adj.*, manly.
man'liness, *n.*, manly qualities.
man'ly, *adj.*, brave, noble.
man'na, *n.*, the Israelites' food in the wilderness; a saccharine substance obtained from a species of ash.
manned, *p.p.*, man.
man'ner, *n.*, form, custom, habit. In pl., morals; conduct.
man'nered, *adj.*, behaved.
man'nerism, *n.*, eccentricity of manner; affected style.
man'nerist, *n.*, one who shows mannerism.
man'nerliness, *n.*, politeness, courtesy.
man'nerly, *adj.*, polite, courteous.
man'ning, *pr.p.*, man.
man'nish, *adj.*, aping the masculine.
manoeu'vre, *v.t.*, to manage with address; *v.i.*, to conduct military operations; to scheme; *n.*, skilful movement, esp. in naval and military operations.
manoeu'vred, *p.p.*, manoeuvre.
manoeu'vrer, *n.*, one who manoeuvres.
manoeu'vring, *pr.p.*, manoeuvre.
man'-of-war', *n.*, a warship.
manom'eter, *n.* an instrument for measuring the rarefaction of elastic fluids.
manomet'rical, *adj.*, rel. to a manometer.
man'or, *n.*, a district under the jurisdiction of a lord; a lord's landed estate.
man'or-house, *n.*, the manorial lord's residence.
mano'rial, *adj.*, rel. to a manor.
man'sard, *n.*, a roof, an attic (*Fr.*).
manse, *n.*, a parsonage-house.
man'sion, *n.*, a large house.
man'slaughter, *n.*, the killing of a man without malice prepense.
man'suetude, *n.*, gentleness.
man'tel, *n.*, a shelf over a fireplace.
man'tel-board, *n.*, *i.q.* mantel.
man'telet, *n.*, a movable shelter for soldiers. Also *mantlet*.
man'telpiece, *n.*, *i.q.* mantel; a chimney-piece.

mantil la, *n.*, a Spanish veil or cloak.

man'tis, *n.*, the praying-inseet.

mantis'sa, *n.*, the decimal pa.t of a logarithm.

man'tle, *v.t.*. to cover with a mantle, to conceal; *v.i.*, to spread over; *n.*, a cloak.

man'tled, *p.p.*, mantle.

man'tling, *pr.p.*, mantle; *n.*, heraldic drapery round a shield.

man'trap, *n.*, a gin.

man'tua-maker, *n.*, a dressmaker.

man'ual, *adj.*, rel. to, or done with, the hands; *n.*, a handbook; an organ finger-board.

manufact'ory, *n.*, a workshop.

manufac'ture, *v.t.* and *i.*, to make by art and labour; *n.*, the making by art.

manufac'tured, *p.p.*, manufacture.

manufac'turer, *n.*, one engaged in manufacture.

manufac'turing, *pr.p.*, manufacture.

manumis'sion, *n.*, the act of setting free.

manumit', *v.t.*, to set free.

manumit'ted, *p.p.*, manumit.

manumit'ting, *pr.p.*, manumit.

manumo'tor, *n.*, a hand-driven carriage.

manure', *v.t.*, to fertilize with dung or other substances; *n.*, fertilizing substances.

manured', *p.p.*, manure.

manur'er, *n.*, a fertilizer.

manu'rial, *adj.*, rel. to manure.

manur'ing, *pr.p.*, manure.

man'uscript, *adj.*, hand-written; *n.*, a written paper or book.

Manx, *adj.*, rel. to the Isle of Man.

man'y, *adj.*, not few; composed of a great number.

Maori, *adj.*, rel. to the Maoris; *n.*, a M. native.

map, *v.t.*, to delineate geographically; to set out; *n.*, a delineation of a surface of the earth.

ma'ple, *n.*, a tree of the genus *Acer*.

mapped, *p.p.*, map.

map'ping, *pr.p.*, map.

mar, *v.t.*, to spoil, damage, deface.

mar'abou, *n.*, a species of stork.

Mar'about, *n.*, a Mohammedan saint.

marana'tha, Syriac phrase = the Lord is at hand; *see* 1 Cor. xvi.

maraschi'no, *n.*, a liqueur distilled from the cherry.

maras'mus, *n.*, atrophy.

maraud', *v.i.*, to raid.

maraud'ed, *p.p.*, maraud.

maraud'er, *n.*, a raider.

maraud'ing, *pr.p.*, maraud.

marave'di, *n.*, an old Spanish coin.

mar'ble, *v.t.*, to vein like marble; *adj.*, made of marble; cold, hard; *n.*, a calcareous stone, compact stone.

mar'bled, *p.p.*, marble.

mar'bler, *n.*, one who marbles.

mar'bling, *pr.p.*, marble.

marc, *n.*, fruit refuse after crushing (*Fr.*).

mar'casite, *n.*, white pyrites.

marces'cent, *adj.*, fading.

march, *v.i.*, to move by steps, or in military form; to border; *n.*, a military walk; advance; frontier; music for marching to.

marched, *p.p.*, march.

march'ing, *pr.p.*, march.

mar'chioness, *n.*, fem. of marquess or marquis.

march'pane, *n.*, *see* marzipan.

marco'nigram, *n.*, a wireless message.

mare, *n.*, fem. of horse.

mare's'-nest, *n.*, a fruitless discovery.

mare's'-tail, *n.*, a water-plant; a variety of cloud.

mar'garin, *n.*, imitation butter made from fats or nut oil.

mar'garine, *n.*, *i.q.* margarin.

mar'garite, *n.*, pearl mica.

mar'gin, *n.*, an edge, border, brink; something over.

mar'ginal, *adj.*, rel. to a margin.

margina'lia, *n.*, marginal notes.

mar'grave, *n.*, a German marquis.

mar'gravine, *n.*, fem. of margrave.

mar'guerite, *n.*, the daisy.

Ma'rian, *n.*, rel. to Mary.

mar'igold, *n.*, a yellow flower.

marinade', *n.*, a sort of pickle.

mar'inate, *v.t.*, to pickle in oil and vinegar.

marine', *adj.*, rel. to the sea.

mar'iner, *n.*, a seaman.

Mariol'ater, *n.*, one who worships Our Lady.

Mariol'atry, *n.*, worship of Our Lady.

marionette', *n.*, a puppet.

mar'ish, *n.*, a marsh.

Ma'rist, *n.*, one of the Marist Order.

mar'ital, *adj.*, rel. to a husband.

mar'itime, *adj.*, rel. to the sea; nautical.

mar'joram, *n.*, an aromatic herb.

mark, *v.t.*, to notify by a stamp; to notice; *n.*, a stamp, impression, sign.

marked, *p.p.*, mark.

mark'er, *n.*, one who marks; a scorer.

mar'ket, *v.t.*, to dispose of wares; *v.i.*, to go to market;

n., a space for buying and selling.

mar'ketable, *adj.*, saleable.

mar'ket-gar'den, *n.*, a garden producing for the market.

mar'ket-gar'dener, *n.*, the keeper of a market-garden.

mar'keting, *pr.p.*, market.

mar'ket-place, *n.*, the space for a market.

mark'ing, *pr.p.*, mark; *n.*, a mark; the arrangement of colouring.

marks'man, *n.*, a clever shot.

marks'manship, *n.*, skill at shooting.

marl, *v.t.*, to spread with marl; to wind with a marline; *n.*, earth containing carbonate of lime, etc.

marla'ceous, *adj.*, composed of marl.

marled, *p.p.*, marl.

mar'line, *n.*, a cord used in splicing.

mar'line-spike, *n.*, a piece of iron used in splicing.

mar'ling, *pr.p.*, marl.

mar'ly, *n.*, containing, or resembling, marl.

mar'malade, *n.*, a preserve.

marmora'ceous, *adj.*, containing marble.

marmo'real, *adj.*, rel. to marble.

marmo'rean, *adj.*, *i.q.* marmoreal.

mar'moset, *n.*, a small monkey.

mar'mot, *n.*, a variety of rat.

Mar'onite, *n.*, one of an Early Christian sect.

maroon', *v.t.*, to leave on a desert island; *n.*, a runaway slave; a reddish brown colour.

maroon'er, *n.*, one who maroons.

mar'plot, *n.*, one who spoils another's plan.

marque, *n.*, a licence to a private vessel to take reprisal.

marquee', *n.*, a large tent.

mar'quess, *n.*, a nobleman next in rank to a duke.

mar'queterie, *n.*, inlaid work.

mar'quetry, *n.*, *i.q.* marqueterie.

mar'quis, *n.*, *i.q.* marquess.

mar'quisate, *n.*, the lordship of a marquis.

marred, *p.p.*, mar.

mar'riage, *n.*, wedding, matrimony.

mar'riageable, *adj.*, fit to be married.

mar'ried, *p.p.*, marry.

mar'ring, *pr.p.*, mar.

mar'row, *n.*, oleaginous substance in bones.

mar'row-bone, *n.*, a bone containing marrow.

mar'rowfat, *n.*, a variety of pea.

mar'rowy, *adj.*, containing marrow.

mar'ry, *v.t.*, to take to wife; to perform the ceremony of a marriage; *v.i.*, to take a wife; to wed.

mar'rying, *pr.p.*, marry.

Mars, *n.*, the Roman war god; the planet Mars.

Marsa'la, *n.*, a kind of sherry.

Marseillaise', *n.*, rel. to Marseilles; *n.*, the French national song.

marsh, *n.*, a watery tract of land.

mar'shal, *v.t.*, to arrange, to rank in order; *n.*, a director of ceremonies; a military officer of the highest rank.

mar'shalcy, *n.*, the status of a marshal.

mar'shalled, mar'shaled, *p.p.*, marshal.

mar'shaller, mar'shaler, *n.*, one who marshals.

mar'shalling, mar'shaling, *pr.p.*, marshal.

Mar'shalsea, *n.*, an old debtors' prison in the Boro'.

marsh'iness, *n.*, the quality of being marshy.

marsh'-mallow, *n.*, a herb found in the salt marshes; a sweetmeat made of it.

marsh'-marigold, *n.*, a plant growing in damp meadows.

marsh'y, *adj.*, fenny, swampy.

marsu'pial, *adj.*, having an external pouch.

marsu'pium, *n.*, the external pouch of kangaroos and opossums.

mart, *n.*, a market; public sale.

martel'lo-tow'er, *n.*, an old type of coast defence.

mar'ten, *n.*, a furred animal, like the sable.

mar'tial, *adj.*, warlike, rel. to warfare.

Mar'tian, *adj.*, rel. to Mars.

mar'tin, *n.*, a kind of swallow.

martinet', *n.*, a severe disciplinarian.

mar'tingale, *n.*, a strap passing between a horse's forelegs, from the noseband to the girth.

Marti'ni, *n.*, a make of rifle.

Mar'tinmas, *n.*, the Feast of St. Martin (Nov. 11).

mart'let, *n.*, an heraldic bird, without beak or feet.

mar'tyr, *n.*, one who dies for his belief or cause; *v.t.*, to put to a martyr's death.

mar'tyrdom, *n.*, a martyr's death or suffering.

mar'tyred, *p.p.*, martyr.

mar'tyring, *pr.p.*, martyr.

martyrolog'ical, *adj.*, rel. to martyrology.

martyrol'ogist, *n.*, a writer on martyrology.

martyrol'ogy, *n.*, the history of martyrs.

mar'vel, *v.i.*, to wonder, be astonished; *n.*, something astonishing.

mar'velled, mar'veled, *p.p.*, marvel.

mar'vel(l)ing, *pr.p.*, marvel.
mar'vel(l)ous, *adj.*, wonderful, astonishing.
mar'vel(l)ously, *adv.*, wonderfully.
Marx'ism, *n.*, the teaching of Karl Marx, the State socialist.
mar'zipan, *n.*, a sweetmeat of nuts, sugar, and white of egg. Also *marchpane*.
mas'cle, *n.*, an heraldic perforated lozenge.
mas'cot, *n.*, something supposed to bring good luck; a charm.
mas'culine, *adj.*, male, manly.
mash, *v.t.*, to reduce to a pulpy state; to mix water and malt for brewing; *n.*, a blend of ingredients.
mashed, *p.p.*, mash.
mash'er, *n.*, a mashing machine.
mash'ie, *n.*, a light, iron golf-club so named.
mash'ing, *pr.p.*, mash.
mask, *v.t.*, to disguise with a mask; to conceal; *n.*, a face-cover, a blind.
masked, *p.p.*, mask; *adj.*, wearing a mask.
mask'er, *n.*, a masquerader.
mask'ing, *pr.p.*, mask.
ma'son, *n.*, one who builds with stone; a stone-worker; a freemason.
mason'ic, *adj.*, rel. to masons and masonry.
ma'sonry, *n.*, the work of a mason; freemasonry.
Maso'rah, *n.*, a body of Aramaic notes on the Old Testament.
Masoret'ic, *adj.*, rel. to the Masorah.
Mas'orite, *n.*, one of the contributors to the Masorah.
masquerade', *v.i.*, to assemble in masks; to pose; *n.*, a ball.
masquera'ded, *p.p.*, masquerade.
masquera'der, *n.*, one who masquerades.
masquera'ding, *p.p.*, masquerade.
Mass, mass, *n.*, the Holy Eucharist; a large quantity; a lump; *v.t.* and *i.*, to collect together.
mas'sacre, *v.t.*, to slay indiscriminately; *n.*, indiscriminate slaughter.
mas'sacred, *p.p.*, massacre.
mas'sacring, *pr.p.*, massacre.
massage, *n.*, medical rubbing or kneading: *v.t.*, to rub or knead.
mass'-book, *n.*, a missal.
masse'ter, *n.*, a muscle used in chewing.
masseur', *n.*, one who massages.
masseuse', *n.*, fem. of masseur.
mass'iness, *n.*, the quality of being massy.
mass'ive, *adj.*, bulky, weighty.
mass'ively, *adv.*, weightily, bulkily.
mass'iveness, *n.*, the quality of being massive.
mass'-meeting, *n.*, a large public gathering.
mass'y, *adj.*, *i.q.* massive.
mast, *n.*, an upright pole or tube supporting a sail; a vertical upright in the planes of an aeroplane; the fruit of the beech and the oak.
mast'ed, *adj.*, having a mast.
mas'ter, *v.t.*, to conquer, overcome, excel; *n.*, a governor, owner, teacher, captain of a merchantman, head of a house.
mas'tered, *p.p.*, master.
mas'terful, *adj.*, superior, domineering.
mas'tering, *pr.p.*, master.
mas'ter-key, *n.*, a key that fits many different locks.
mas'terless, *adj.*, without a master.
mas'terly, *adj.*, supremely skilful.
mas'terpiece, *n.*, a *chef-d'œuvre*; a consummate piece of work.
mas'tership, *n.*, the office of a master.
mas'ter-stroke, *n.*, a consummate achievement.
mas'tery, *n.*, victory, conquest, the upper hand.
mast'-head, *v.t.*, to send up to the mast-head (for punishment); *n.*, the top of a mast.
mas'tic, *n.*, a gum.
mas'ticable, *adj.*, able to be masticated.
mas'ticate, *v.t.*, to chew, crush with the teeth.
mas'ticated, *p.p.*, masticate.
mas'ticating, *pr.p.*, masticate.
mastica'tion, *n.*, the act of chewing.
mas'ticator, *n.*, anything that masticates; a mincing machine.
mas'ticatory, *adj.*, fit for chewing.
mas'tiff, *n.*, a large breed of dog.
mas'todon, *n.*, an extinct monster.
mas'toid, *adj.*, breast-like.
mat, *v.t.* and *i.*, to interweave, entangle; *n.*, a texture used for wiping the feet or putting things on.
mat'ador, *n.*, a bull-fighter; a card in the games of ombre and quadrille.
match, *v.t.*, to oppose as equal or alike; to equal; *v.i.*, to arrange a marriage with; *n.*, a contest, a completed game, an equal, a marriageable party, a matrimonial engagement, a lucifer.
match'able, *n.*, able to be matched.
matched, *p.p.*, match.
match'er, *n.*, one who matches.

match'ing, *pr.p.*, match.

match'less, *adj.*, inimitable.

match'lock, *n.*, an obsolete musket.

match'-maker, *n.*, one interested in getting people married.

match'-making, *adj.*, of the character of a match-maker; *n.*, the practice of a match-maker.

mate, *v.i.*, to match, to marry; *n.*, a companion; the final move in chess; a ship's officer.

ma'té, *n.*, a Brazilian tea.

ma'ted, *p.p.*, mate.

ma'telote, *n.*, a dish made of various fish.

ma'ter, *n.*, a membrane of the brain.

mate'rial, *adj.*, rel. to matter, corporeal, essential, that matters; *n.*, that of which a thing is made.

mate'rialism, *n.*, the denial of the spiritual in the world and man.

mate'rialist, *n.*, one who believes in materialism.

materialis'tic, *adj.*, rel. to materialism.

material'ity, *n.*, the material existence.

mate'rialize, *v.t.*, to make material; *v.i.*, to become material.

mate'rialized, *p.p.*, materialize.

mate'rializing, *pr.p.*, materialize.

mate'rially, *adv.*, substantially; seriously.

mate'ria med'ica, *n.*, the substances used in medicine.

matériel', *n.*, baggage, munitions.

mater'nal, *adj.*, motherly; rel. to a mother.

mater'nally, *n.*, in a motherly way.

mater'nity, *n.*, the relation of a mother.

mathemat'ic, *adj.*, *i.q.* mathematical.

mathemat'ical, *adj.*, rel. to mathematics.

mathemat'ically, *adv.*, according to mathematics.

mathemati'cian, *n.*, one skilled in mathematics.

mathemat'ics, *n. pl.*, the science of numbers and space.

mathe'sis, *n.*, learning.

mat'in, *adj.*, rel. to the morning.

mat'inée, *n.*, a morning performance or reception.

ma'ting, *pr.p.*, mate.

mat'ins, mat'tins, *n. pl.*, one of the day hours of the Church; morning prayer.

mat'rass, *n.*, a distilling vessel.

ma'trice, *n.*, *see* matrix.

mat'ricidal, *adj.*, rel. to matricide.

mat'ricide, *n.*, the murder of a mother.

matric'ulate, *v.t.*, to enter at a university; *v.i.*, to be entered at a university.

matric'ulated, *p.p.*, matriculate.

matric'ulating, *pr.p.*, matriculate.

matricula'tion, *n.*, the act of matriculating.

matrimo'nial, *adj.*, rel. to matrimony.

matrimo'nially, *adv.*, by matrimony.

mat'rimony, *n.*, the married state.

ma'trix, *n.*, a mould; the womb; the bed in which brasses are let into stone; the five basal colours in dyeing.

ma'tron, *n.*, a married woman; the woman head of an establishment.

ma'tronage, *n.*, matrons as a body.

ma'tronal, *adj.*, rel. to matrons.

ma'tronly, *adj.*, matron-like, elderly.

matronym'ic, *n.*, a name derived from a mother.

mat'ted, *p.p.*, mat.

mat'ter, *v.i.*, to signify, be important; *n.*, substance, a thing treated of.

mat'ting, *pr.p.*, mat; *n.*, mats as a whole; material used for mats.

mat'tock, *n.*, a pickaxe with one end flat.

mat'tress, *n.*, originally a case stuffed with straw or hair and used for bedding; now often a spring contrivance.

mat'urate, *v.t.*, to hasten on a boil.

matura'tion, *n.*, ripening.

matu'rative, *adj.*, with a ripening effect.

mature', *v.t.* and *i.*, to ripen; *adj.*, ripe, completed.

matured', *p.p.*, mature.

mature'ly, *adv.*, in a mature way.

mature'ness, *n.*, ripeness.

matures'cence, *n.*, the process of ripening.

matu'ring, *pr.p.*, mature.

matu'rity, *n.*, the mature state, ripeness, completion.

matuti'nal, *adj.*, early, of the morning.

maud, *n.*, a grey plaid.

maud'lin, *adj.*, fuddled, silly.

mau'gre, *prep.*, in spite of.

maul, *v.t.*, to bruise, beat; *n.*, a large wooden hammer.

mauled, *p.p.*, maul.

maul'ing, *pr.p.*, maul.

maul'stick, *n.*, *see* mahlstick.

maund, *n.*, a basket.

maund'er, *v.i.*, to ramble in speech.

maun'dered, *p.p.*, maunder.

maun'dering, *pr.p.*, maunder.

Maun'dy Thurs'day, *n.*, the Thursday in Holy Week.

Mau'ser, *n.*, a make of breech-loading magazine rifle.

mausole'um, *n.*, a magnificent tomb.

mauve, *n.*, a purple colour.

ma'vis, *n.*, the thrush.

maw, *n.*, an animal's stomach; a bird's craw.

mawk'ish, *adj.*, nauseous; sentimental.

maw'worm, *n.*, a worm in the intestines.

maxil'la, *n.*, the jawbone.

max'illar, *adj.*, rel. to the maxilla.

maxil'lary, *adj.*, *i.q.* maxillar.

maxil'liform, *adj.*, like a jawbone.

max'im, *n.*, an accepted principle; an adage; a variety of gun.

max'imum, *n.*, the greatest degree possible.

May, *n.*, the fifth month; hawthorn.

may, *v.i.*, to be permitted.

may'*be*, phrase = perhaps.

May'day, *n.*, the 1st of May.

May'flower, *n.*, the ship that bore the Pilgrim Fathers.

may'hap, phrase = perhaps.

may'hem, *n.*, injury by violence.

may'ing, *n.*, keeping May Day festival.

mayonnaise', *n.*, a sauce or dressing.

may'or, *n.*, the chief magistrate of a town.

may'oral, *adj.*, rel. to a mayor.

may'oralty, *n.*, a mayor's office, or period of office.

may'oress, *n.*, fem. of mayor.

May'pole, *n.*, a pole danced round on May Day.

maz'ard, *n.*, a variety of cherry.

mazarine', *adj.*, of mazarine colour; *n.*, a deep blue.

maze, *n.*, a labyrinth; confusion of thought; *v.t.*, to bewilder.

mazed, *p.p.*, maze.

ma'zily, *adv.*, winding about.

ma'ziness, *n.*, the state of being mazy.

ma'zing, *pr.p.*, maze.

mazur'ka, *n.*, a gay Polish dance.

ma'zy, *adj.*, intricate, winding.

me, *pron. pers.*, obj. case of "I."

mead, *n.*, a drink of fermented honey; a meadow.

mead'ow, *n.*, pasture land.

mead'ow-sweet, *n.*, one of the Spiraea.

mead'owy, *adj.*, like meadows; abounding in meadows.

mea'gre, *adj.*, lean, scanty.

mea'grely, *adv.*, scantily.

mea'greness, *n.*, leanness, scantiness.

meal, *n.*, a repast; the edible part of corn.

meal'ie, *n.*, an ear of Indian corn.

meal'iness, *n.*, the quality of being mealy.

meal'y, *adj.*, having the taste or quality of meal.

meal'y-mouthed, *n.*, soft-tongued, hypocritical.

mean, *v.t.*, to purpose, design, signify; *adj.*, worthless, contemptible, base; *n.*, a middle state.

mean'der, *v.i.*, to run in windings; to be intricate.

mean'dered, *p.p.*, meander.

mean'dering, *pr.p.*, meander.

mean'er, *adj.*, *comp.* of mean.

mean'est, *adj.*, *super.* of mean.

mean'ing, *pr.p.*, mean; *adj.*, significant; *n.*, sense, significance.

mean'ingless, *adj.*, senseless.

mean'ly, *adv.*, in a mean way.

mean'ness, *n.*, want of dignity, baseness, stinginess.

means, *n. pl.*, resources, property, instruments.

meant, *p.p.*, mean.

mean'time, *adv.*, in the intervening time; *n.*, the intervening time.

mean'while, *adv.*, and *n.*, *i.q.* meantime.

mea'sled, *adj.*, suffering from measles.

mea'sles, *n.*, a contagious febrile complaint.

mea'sly, *adj.*, affected with measles; shabby (*slang*).

meas'urable, *adj.*, able to be measured.

meas'urably, *adv.*, in a measurable degree.

meas'ure, *v.t.*, to ascertain by measuring; to mark out; compare with a standard; *n.*, a standard, rule, proportion, metre, Bill or Act of Parliament.

meas'ured, *p.p.*, measure.

meas'ureless, *adj.*, immeasurable.

meas'urement, *n.*, the act of measuring; dimension.

meas'urer, *n.*, one who measures.

meas'uring, *pr.p.*, measure.

meat, *n.*, animal food.

mechan'ic, *adj.*, *i.q.* mechanical; *n.*, one who practises a mechanical art.

mechan'ical, *adj.*, rel. to mechanics and machines; without thought.

mechan'ically, *n.*, automatically.

mechani'cian, *n.*, one skilled in mechanics and machinery.

mechan'ics, *n. pl.*, the science of the action of forces on bodies; the science of machinery.

mech'anism, *n.*, mechanical construction.

mech'anist, *n.*, a designer of machines.

Mech'lin, *n.*, a Belgian lace.

mecom'eter, *n.*, an instrument for measuring the length of a newly-born child.

meco'nium, *n.*, opium.

med'al, *n.*, a piece of metal, struck, and stamped with a device.

medal'lic, *adj.*, rel. to medals.

medal'lion, *n.*, a large medal; a round or oval tablet.

med'allist, *n.*, the winner of a medal; a medal engraver.

med'allurgy, *n.*, the art of making medals.

med'dle, *v.i.*, to interfere.

med'dled, *p.p.*, meddle.

med'dler, *n.*, a busybody.

med'dlesome, *adj.*, officiously interfering.

med'dling, *pr.p.*, meddle.

me'dia, *n.*, pl. of medium.

mediae'val, *adj.*, bel. to the Middle Ages.

mediae'valism, *n.*, the characteristics of the Middle Ages.

me'dial, *adj.*, denoting an average or mean.

me'dian, *adj.*, rel. to the middle.

me'diant, *n.*, the third note in the musical scale.

mediasti'num, *n.*, the intervening septum between two chief parts of an organ.

me'diate, *v.i.*, to interpose between two parties.

me'diate, *adj.*, opposite to immediate; effected by means.

me'diated, *p.p.*, mediate.

me'diately, *adv.*, by means.

me'diating, *pr.p.*, mediate.

media'tion, *n.*, the act of mediating; agency.

me'diatize, *v.t.*, to make a sovereign state a subject one, leaving to the prince or king his title and power of local government.

me'diatized, *p.p.*, mediatize.

me'diatizing, *pr.p.*, mediatize.

me'diator, *n.*, one who mediates; an intercessor.

mediato'rial, *adj.*, rel. to a mediator; intercessory.

media'trix, *n.*, fem. of mediator.

med'icable, *adj.*, curable.

med'ical, *adj.*, rel. to medicine.

med'ically, *adv.*, according to medicine.

med'icament, *n.*, a healing drug.

med'icate, *v.t.*, to tincture with anything medicinal.

med'icated, *p.p.*, medicate.

med'icating, *pr.p.*, medicate.

medica'tion, *n.*, the act or result of medicating.

medic'inal, *adj.*, rel. to physic or medicine.

medic'inally, *adv.*, medically.

med'icine, *n.*, a drug used as a remedy.

med'ico-le'gal, *adj.*, rel. to law in connexion with medicine.

medie'val, *adj.*, *see* mediaeval.

medie'valism, *n.*, *see* mediaevalism.

me'diocre, *adj.*, moderate, ordinary.

medioc'rity, *n.*, middle state or degree; a person of merely ordinary ability.

med'itate, *v.t.*, to plan, contrive, think about; *v.i.*, to ponder.

med'itated, *p.p.*, meditate.

med'itating, *pr.p.*, meditate.

medita'tion, *n.*, reflection, deep thought.

med'itative, *adj.*, reflecting; given to meditation.

Mediterra'nean, *adj.*, inland; lying between lands; *n.*, the Mediterranean Sea.

me'dium, *n.*, a mean; middle place; agency; space in which bodies move; a spiritualistic agent.

med'lar, *n.*, a fruit tree so named.

med'ley, *n.*, a mixture.

Médoc', *n.*, a French claret.

medul'la, *n.*, the marrow, pith.

med'ullary, *adj.*, rel. to the medulla.

medul'line, *n.*, pith, cellulose.

medu'sa, *n.*, a sea-nettle.

meed, *n.*, reward, desert.

meek, *adj.*, humble, mild.

meek'en, *v.t.*, to make meek.

meek'ly, *adv.*, with meekness.

meek'ness, *n.*, humility, mildness.

meer'schaum, *n.*, a silicated soft magnesian clay; a pipe made of it.

meet, *v.t.*, to encounter; to satisfy; *v.i.*, to come together; *adj.*, fitting; *n.*, a gathering of huntsmen.

meeting, *pr.p.*, meet; *n.*, an assembly, interview.

meet'ing-house, *n.*, a conventicle.

meet'ly, *adv.*, in a meet way.

meg'alith, *n.*, a large stone.

megalith'ic, *adj.*, composed of megaliths.

megalosau'rus, *n.*, a huge extinct lizard.

meg'aphone, *n.*, an extra-large speaking trumpet.

meg'ascope, *n.*, a sort of magic lantern.

megathe'rium, *n.*, a huge extinct monster.

me'grim, *n.*, sick headache.

meio'sis, *n.*, lessening; saying less than is meant (as "no small" for "great").

melancho'lia, *n.*, insanity accompanied by depression.

melanchol'ic, *adj.*, depressed.

mel'ancholy, *adj.*, depressed, sad; *n.*, depression of spirit, *i.q.* melancholia.

Melane'sian, *adj.*, rel. to the M. islands.

mel'anism, *n.*, excessive colouring in skin.

mel'anite, *n.*, a black garnet; a high explosive.

melas'ma, *n.*, a liver-patch on the skin.

meldom'eter, *n.*, a device for showing fusing points.

mêlée', *n.*, a scuffle, affray (*Fr.*).

mel'ilot, *n.*, a variety of clover.

me'liorate, *v.t.*, to improve, ameliorate.

meliora'tion, *n.*, improvement.

mellif'erous, *adj.*, honey-producing.

mellif'ic, *adj.*, *i.q.* melliferous.

mellif'luence, *n.*, smoothness.

mellif'luent, *adj.*, smooth, flowing like honey.

mellif'luous, *adj.*, *i.q.* mellifluous.

mel'lite, *n.*, honey stone.

mellit'ic, *adj.*, rel. to mellite.

mel'low, *v.t.*, to make mellow, to soften; *v.i.*, to ripen; *adj.*, soft with ripeness; semi-intoxicated.

mel'lowed, *p.p.*, mellow.

mel'lowing, *pr.p.*, mellow.

mel'lowness, *n.*, ripeness.

melo'deon, *n.*, a reed-organ.

melo'dious, *adj.*, tuneful, having a melody.

melo'diously, *adv.*, tunefully.

melo'diousness, *n.*, tunefulness.

mel'odist, *n.*, a maker of melody.

mel'odize, *v.t.*, to compose.

melodra'ma, *n.*, a sensational play.

melodramat'ic, *adj.*, rel. to melodrama.

melodramat'ical, *adj.*, *i.q.* melodramatic.

melodram'atist, *n.*, a writer of melodrama.

mel'ody, *n.*, tune, an air.

mel'on, *n.*, an edible fruit of the gourd kind.

melt, *v.t.*, to reduce to a liquid state, dissolve, soften; *v.i.*, to be liquefied or softened.

melt'ed, *p.p.*, melt.

melt'ing, *pr.p.*, melt.

melt'ingly, *adj.*, softly.

mem'ber, *n.*, a limb, a part; one of a society.

mem'bered, *adj.*, having members or limbs.

mem'bership, *n.*, the state of being a member.

membrana'ceous, *adj.*, rel. to membrane.

mem'brane, *n.*, a layer of tissue.

membranif'erous, *adj.*, producing membrane.

membra'niform, *adj.*, like membrane.

mem'branous, *adj.*, consisting of, or like to, membrane.

memen'to, *n.*, a souvenir.

mem'oir, *n.*, a record of personal history or scientific discovery.

memorabil'ia, *n. pl.*, things worth recording.

memorabil'ity, *n.*, the quality of being memorable.

mem'orable, *adj.*, worthy to be recorded or remembered.

mem'orably, *adv.*, in a memorable way.

memoran'da, *n. pl.*, notes of things to be remembered.

memoran'dum, *n.*, sing. of memoranda.

memo'rial, *adj.*, commemorative; rel. to memory; *n.*, a monument or tablet, or other commemorative emblem· a petition.

memo'rialist, *n.*, one who presents a petition.

memo'rialize, *v.t.*, to petition with a memorial.

memo'rialized, *p.p.*, memorialize.

memo'rializing, *pr.p.*, memorialize.

memor'iter, *adv.*, by memory (*Lat.*).

mem'orize, *v.t.*, to fix in the memory.

mem'orized, *p.p.*, memorize.

mem'orizing, *pr.p.*, memorize.

mem'ory, *n.*, the power of remembering; remembrance.

Mem'phian, *adj.*, rel. to Memphis.

men, *n.*, pl. of man.

men'ace, *v.t.*, to threaten; *n.*, a threat.

men'aced, *p.p.*, menace.

men'acing, *pr.p.*, menace; *adj.*, threatening.

men'acingly, *adv.*, threateningly.

ménage', *n.*, system, management (*Fr.*).

menag'erie, *n.*, a wild beast collection.

mend, *v.t.*, to put together again, repair, reform; *v.i.*, to grow better; *n.*, a repair.

mend'able, *adj.*, not past mending.

menda'cious, *adj.*, lying.

menda'ciously, *adv.*, with a lie.

menda'ciousness, *n.*, character for lying.

mendac'ity, *n.*, *i.q.* mendaciousness.

mend'ed, *p.p.*, mend.

mend'er, *n.*, one who mends.

men'dicancy, *n.*, begging.

men'dicant, *n.*, a beggar; *adj.*, begging.

mendic'ity, *n.*, *i.q.* mendicancy.

mend'ing, *pr.p.*, mend.

me'nial, *adj.*, servile, mean; *n.*, an inferior servant.

menin'geal, *adj.*, rel. to the meninges.

menin'ges, *n. pl.*, the membranes round the brain and spinal cord.

meningi'tis, *n.*, inflammation of the meninges.

menis'cal, *adj.*, rel. to a meniscus.

menis'coid, *adj.*, like a meniscus.

menis'cus, *n.*, a crescent; a lens with one surface convex, the other concave.

men'ses, *n. pl.*, the monthly flow.

men'strual, *adj.*, rel. to menses.

men'struate, *v.i.*, to discharge the menses.

menstrua'tion, *n.*, the act of menstruating.

men'struous, *adj.*, rel. to menses.

men'struum, *n.*, a solvent.

mensurabil'ity, *n.*, the quality of being mensurable.

men'surable, *adj.*, measurable.

men'sural, *adj.*, rel. to measurement.

mensura'tion, *n.*, the art of measuring.

men'tal, *adj.*, rel. to the mind.

mental'ity, *n.*, mental characteristics.

men'tally, *adv.*, in relation to mind.

men'thol, *n.*, a crystalline preparation.

men'tion, *v.t.*, to notice, name; *n.*, the act of mentioning, notice.

men'tionable, *adj.*, fit to be mentioned.

men'tioned, *p.p.*, mention.

men'tioning, *pr.p.*, mention.

men'tor, *n.*, a wise counsellor.

mento'rial, *adj.*, giving advice.

men'u, *n.*, a bill of fare.

Mephistophe'lian, *adj.*, like Mephistopheles; fiendishly cynical.

mephit'ic, *adj.*, noxious, poisonous.

mephit'ical, *adj.*, *i.q.* mephitic.

mephi'tis, *n.*, noxious fumes.

mer'cantile, *adj.*, commercial.

Mer'cédès, *n.*, a build of motor-cars.

mer'cenarily, *adv.*, in a mercenary spirit.

mer'cenary, *adj.*, with an eye to gain; sordid; *n.*, a hired soldier.

mer'cer, *n.*, a trader in textiles.

mer'cerize, *v.t.*, to make cotton fabric look like silk.

mer'cerized, *p.p.*, mercerize.

mer'cerizing, *pr.p.*, mercerize.

mer'cery, *n.*, a mercer's wares.

mer'chandise, *n.*, goods bought and sold.

mer'chant, *n.*, one who trades.

mer'chantable, *adj.*, fit for trading with.

mer'chantman, *n.*, a trading-ship.

mer'ciful, *adj.*, kind, pitiful.

mer'cifully, *adv.*, in a merciful way.

mer'ciless, *adj.*, pitiless, cruel.

mer'cilessly, *adv.*, pitilessly.

mercu'rial, *adj.*, volatile, flighty; rel. to mercury.

mercu'rialize, *v.t.*, to salivate.

mercu'rify, *v.t.*, to extract mercury; to mercurialize.

mer'cury, *n.*, quicksilver; the planet.

mer'cy, *n.*, pity, compassion.

mer'cy-seat, *n.*, the place where the Ark of the Covenant stood.

mere, *adj.*, simple, absolute; *n.*, a lake.

mere'ly, *adv.*, simply, absolutely.

meretri'cious, *adj.*, rel. to prostitutes; showily alluring; tawdry.

merge, *v.t.*, to swallow up; *v.i.*, to be swallowed up; to sink.

merged, *p.p.*, merge.

mer'ger, *n.*, the act of merging or combining.

merg'ing, *pr.p.*, merge.

merid'ian, *adj.*, rel. to midday; *n.*, midday; noon; the great circle on the earth's surface at right angles to the equator.

merid'ional, *adj.*, rel. to the meridian; southern.

meringue', *n.*, a sweet.

meri'no, *adj.*, made of merino wool; *n.*, a fine-wooled sheep; cloth made of the wool.

mer'it, *v.t.*, to deserve; *n.*, desert, excellence.

mer'ited, *p.p.*, merit.

mer'iting, *pr.p.*, merit.

merito'rious, *adj.*, praiseworthy, creditable.

merle, *n.*, the blackbird.

mer'lin, *n.*, a small falcon.

mer'ling, *n.*, the whiting.

mer'lon, *n.*, the space between embrasures.

mer'maid, *n.*, a fabulous creature, half woman, half fish.

mer'man, *n.*, masc. of mermaid.

merop'idan, *adj.*, rel. to the Meropidae or bee-eaters.

Merovin'gian, *adj.*, rel. to the Merovingian dynasty.

mer'rier, *adj.*, *comp.* of merry.

mer'riest, *adj.*, *super.* of merry.

mer'rily, *adv.*, gaily.

mer'riment, *n.*, gaiety, joyousness, mirth.

mer'ry, *adj.*, gay, joyous, mirthful.

merry-an'drew, *n.*, a buffoon.

mer'ry-making, *n.*, festivity.

mer'rythought, *n.*, the front bone in a fowl's breast.

mesdames', *n.*, pl. of madame.

mesdemoiselles', *n.*, pl. of mademoiselle.

meseems', phrase = methinks; it seems to me.

mesenter'ic, *adj.*, rel. to the mesentery.

mesenteri'tis, *n.*, inflammation of the mesentery.

mes'entery, *n.*, the membrane that keeps the intestines in their place.

mesh, *n.*, an interstice in a net; network; *v.t.*, to entangle.
meshed, *p.p.*, mesh.
mesh'ing, *pr.p.*, mesh.
mesh'y, *adj.*, entangling.
mesmer'ic, *adj.*, rel. to mesmerism.
mes'merism, *n.*, animal magnetism.
mes'merist, *n.*, one who mesmerizes.
mesmeriza'tion, *n.*, the act of mesmerizing.
mes'merize, *v.t.*, to throw into a mesmeric trance.
mes'merized, *p.p.*, mesmerize.
mes'merizer, *n.*, one who mesmerizes.
mes'merizing, *pr.p.*, mesmerize.
mesne, *adj.*, intervening.
mesoco'lon, *n.*, a continuation of the mesentery.
mes'osperm, *n.*, a seed's second membrane.
mesotho'rax, *n.*, the middle ring of an insect's thorax.
mesozo'ic, *adj.*, rel. to the Secondary era.
mess, *v.t.*, to dirty, to muddle; to feed; *v.i.*, to share food; *n.*, a state of dirt or muddle; a common meal.
mes'sage, *n.*, an errand, a communication.
messed, *p.p.*, mess.
mes'senger, *n.*, one who takes a message.
Messi'ah, *n.*, the Anointed, the Christ.
Messi'ahship, *n.*, the office of the Messiah.
Messian'ic, *adj.*, rel. to the Messiah.
mes'sieurs, *n.*, pl. of monsieur.
mess'ing, *pr.p.*, mess.
mess'mate, *n.*, the sharer of one's table.
mes'suage, *n.*, a dwelling-house and land.
mestee', *n.*, one born of a white and a quadroon.
mesti'zo, *n.*, one born of a Spaniard or Creole and an Indian.
met, *p.p.*, meet.
metab'asis, *n.*, transition.
metab'ola, *n. pl.*, insects that undergo transformation.
metabo'lian, *adj.*, rel. to metabola.
metabol'ic, *adj.*, subject to change or transformation.
metacar'pal, *adj.*, rel. to the metacarpus.
metacar'pus, *n.*, the part of the hand between the wrist and the fingers.
metach'ronism, *n.*, an error in date.
me'tage, *n.*, measurement; toll.
met'al, *v.t.*, to cover with broken stone; to macadamize; *n.*, an insoluble body, fusible by heat; small stone cubes.
met'alled, *p.p.*, metal.
metal'lic, *adj.*, rel. to metal; hard.
metallif'erous, *adj.*, metal-producing.
metal'liform, *adj.*, metal-like.
met'alline, met'aline, *adj.*, rel. to metal.
met'allist, met'alist, *n.*, a worker in metal.
met'allize, *v.t.*, to make into a metal.
metallog'raphy, *n.*, the science of metals; a description of metals.
met'alloid, *adj.*, like metal; *n.*, an elementary, non-metallic substance.
metalloid'al, *adj.*, *i.q.* metalloid.
metallur'gic, *adj.*, rel. to metallurgy.
metallur'gical, *adj.*, *i.q.* metallurgic.
met'allurgist, *n.*, one skilled in metallurgy.
met'allurgy, *n.*, working in metals.
met'al-man, *n.*, a worker in metals.
met'amere, *n.*, one of like segments of a body.
metamer'ic, *adj.*, rel. to a metamere.
metamor'phic, *adj.*, rel. to metamorphism.
metamor'phism, *n.*, the process of change in form or structure.
metamor'phose, *v.t.*, to transform.
metamor'phosed, *p.p.*, metamorphose.
metamor'phosing, *pr.p.*, metamorphose.
metamor'phosis, *n.*, transformation.
met'aphor, *n.*, a condensed simile.
metaphor'ic, *adj.*, figurative; of the nature of metaphor.
metaphor'ical, *adj.*, *i.q.* metaphoric.
metaphor'ically, *adv.*, not literally; figuratively.
met'aphrase, *n.*, close translation.
met'aphrast, *n.*, a literal translator.
metaphras'tic, *adj.*, literally translating.
metaphys'ic, *adj.*, rel. to metaphysics.
metaphys'ical, *adj.*, *i.q.* metaphysic.
metaphysi'cian, *n.*, a student of metaphysical philosophy
metaphys'ics, *n. pl.*, mental philosophy; ontology.
metapto'sis, *n.*, change in a disease.
metas'tasis, *n.*, change; removal of a disease from one part to another.
metastat'ic, *adj.*, rel. to metastasis.
metatar'sus, *n.*, the part of the foot between the tarsus and the toes.
metath'esis, *n.*, transposition.
metathet'ical, *adj.*, transposing.
metatho'rax, *n.*, the hindmost thoracic segment.
métayer, *n.*, a tenant who gives to his landlord part of the produce in return for stock, seed, etc.

mete, *v.t.*, to measure, allot.

me'ted, *p.p.*, mete.

metempsycho'sis, *n.*, transmigration of souls.

metempto'sis, *n.*, the solar equation.

me'teor, *n.*, a flying luminous body; a shooting star.

meteor'ic, *adj.*, rel. to meteors.

me'teorite, *n.*, a meteoric stone.

meteor'ograph, *n.*, an apparatus recording meteorological phenomena.

meteorograph'ic, *adj.*, rel. to meteorography.

meteorog'raphy, *n.*, the record of meteorological phenomena.

me'teoroid, *n.*, a body which becomes a meteor when it reaches the atmosphere.

me'teorolite, *n.*, a meteoric stone.

meteorolog'ical, *adj.*, rel. to meteorology.

meteorol'ogist, *n.*, an expert in meteorology.

meteorol'ogy, *n.*, the science of the atmosphere.

meteorom'eter, *n.*, an instrument that transmits meteorological records.

me'ter, *n.*, a measuring apparatus.

metheg'lin, *n.*, a beverage made of honey.

meth'ene, *n.*, marsh gas.

meth'ide, *n.*, a compound of methyl and an element.

methinks', *v., impers.*, I think; it seems to me.

meth'od, *n.*, rule, system, order.

method'ic, *adj.*, systematic, regular.

method'ical, *adj.*, *i.q.* methodic.

method'ically, *adv.*, systematically.

Meth'odism, *n.*, the principles of the Methodists.

Meth'odist, *n.*, a follower of Wesley and his Method, or rule of life.

methodis'tic, *adj.*, rel. to the Methodists.

methodis'tical, *adj.*, *i.q.* methodistic.

meth'odize, *v.t.*, to reduce to system.

meth'odized, *p.p.*, methodize.

meth'odizing, *pr.p.*, methodize.

methought', *v.impers.*, I thought; it seemed to me.

meth'yl, *n.*, wood spirit.

meth'ylated, *adj.*, containing methyl.

meth'ylene, *n.*, an inflammable liquid.

methyl'ic, *adj.*, containing methyl.

métier, *n.*, a business, trade (*Fr.*).

me'ting, *pr.p.*, mete.

meton'ic, *adj.*, rel. to Meton, the astronomer.

metonym'ic, *adj.*, rel. to metonymy.

meton'ymy, *n.*, the use of one word for another.

met'ope, *n.*, the space between triglyphs.

me'tre, me'ter, *n.*, rhythmic grouping of syllables; a unit of decimal measurement.

met'ric, *adj.*, rel. to decimal measurement.

met'rical, *adj.*, rel. to poetical or decimal metre.

met'rochrome, *n.*, a colour-measuring apparatus.

met'rograph, *n.*, an apparatus for gauging mileage.

metrol'ogy, *n.*, the science of measures and weights.

met'ronome, *n.*, an instrument measuring musical time.

metronom'ic, *adj.*, rel. to the metronome.

metronom'ical, *adj.*, *i.q.* metronomic.

metron'omy, *n.*, the art of measuring musical time.

metronym'ic, *n.*, called after one's mother.

metrop'olis, *n.*, a mother city or state; the seat of an archbishop.

metropol'itan, *adj.*, rel. to a metropolis: *n.*, the archbishop or chief bishop of a province.

met'tle, *n.*, ardour, spirit.

met'tled, *adj.*, *i.q.* mettlesome.

met'tlesome, *adj.*, high-spirited.

mew, *v.t.*, to shut up, confine; *v.i.*, to cry as a cat; *n.*, a seagull, a cage for hawks, the cry of a cat.

mewed, *p.p.*, mew.

mew'ing, *pr.p.*, mew.

mewl, *v.t.*, to cry as an infant; *n.*, an infant's cry.

mewled, *p.p.*, mewl.

mewl'er, *n.*, one who mewls.

mewl'ing, *pr.p.*, mewl.

mews, *n. pl.*, stables for carriage horses (*orig.* a place where hawks were kept).

Mex'ican, *adj.*, rel. to Mexico.

mez'zanine, *n.*, a low storey between higher ones.

mez'zo, *adj.*, half, middle.

mez'zotint, *n.*, a method of engraving on copper or steel; a print.

mezzotin'to, *n.*, *i.q.* mezzotint.

mias'ma, *n.*, a noxious exhalation; malaria.

mias'mal, *adj.*, malarious.

miasmat'ic, *adj.*, rel. to miasma.

miasmat'ical, *adj.*, *i.q.* miasmatic.

mias'matist, *n.*, one who studies malarious disorders.

mi'ca, *n.*, a mineral divisible into transparent flakes.

mica'ceous, *adj.*, containing, or like, mica.

mice, *n.*, pl. of mouse.

Mich'aelmas, *n.*, the Feast of St. Michael and All Angels (Sep. 29).

mick'le, *adj.*, much, great.
micracous'tic, *adj.*, making faint sounds audible.
mi'crobe, *n.*, a microscopic organism, such as bacteria, etc.
microceph'alous, *adj.*, small-skulled.
mi'crocosm, *n.*, a miniature world.
microcos'mic, *adj.*, like a microcosm.
microcos'mical, *adj.*, *i.q.* microcosmic.
micrograph'ophone, *n.*, an instrument recording the most delicate sounds.
microg'raphy, *n.*, description of microscopic objects.
microl'ogy, *n.*, the science of microscopic objects.
microm'eter, *n.*, an apparatus for measuring minute distances.
micromet'ric, *adj.*, rel. to the micrometer.
micronom'eter, *n.*, an instrument recording minute time-divisions. Also *microchronometer*.
mi'cro-or'ganism, *n.*, a microscopic organism.
mi'crophone, *n.*, an instrument that makes faint sounds audible.
microphon'ics, *n. pl.*, the study of minute sounds.
microph'onous, *adj.*, producing minute sounds.
mi'croscope, *n.*, an apparatus for magnifying minute objects.
microscop'ic, *adj.*, rel. to the microscope; infinitely small.
microscop'ical, *adj.*, *i.q.* microscopic.
micros'copist, *n.*, one who uses a microscope.
micros'copy, *n.*, the use of the microscope.
microzo'on, *n.*, a microscopic creature.
micturi'tion, *n.*, the voiding of urine.

mid, *adj.*, middle; *prep.*, amid.
mid'day, *n.*, noon.
mid'den, *n.*, a dunghill.
mid'dle, *adj.*, intermediate; equally distant; *n.*, a middle point or part.
mid'dle-aged, *adj.*, neither young nor old.
mid'dle-class, *adj.*, of the class between the highest and the lowest.
mid'dleman, *n.*, a trader between the producer and the consumer.
mid'dlemost, *adj.*, nearest the middle.
mid'dling, *adj.*, moderate; nothing very great.
mid'dy, *n.*, a midshipman.
midge, *n.*, a gnat.
midg'et, *n.*, a dwarf.
Mid'ianite, *adj.*, a native of Midian.
mid'land, *adj.*, in the interior of a country.
mid'most, *adj.*, nearest the middle.
mid'night, *n.*, the last moment of the day.
mid'rib, *n.*, a leaf's central rib.
mid'riff, *n.*, the diaphragm.
mid'ship, *adv.*, in the middle of a ship.
mid'shipman, *n.*, a junior naval officer.
midst, *n.*, the middle.
mid'stream, *adv.*, in the middle of a stream.
mid'summer, *n.*, the height of summer.
mid'way, *adj.* and *adv.*, in the middle of the way.
mid'-wicket, *adv.*, in the middle wicket.
mid'wife, *v.t.*, to assist in child-birth; *n.*, a woman who assists in child-birth.
mid'wifery, *n.*, obstetrics.
mien, *n.*, air, aspect, appearance.
miff, *v.t.*, to vex slightly; *adj.*, somewhat annoyed; *n.*, a display of vexation.

might, *n.*, power, strength; *p.p.*, may.
might'ier, *adj.*, *comp.* of mighty.
might'iest, *adj.*, *super.* of mighty.
might'ily, *adv.*, in a mighty degree; with much strength or vehemence.
might'iness, *n.*, the quality of being mighty.
might'y, *adj.*, powerful, exalted.
mignonette', *n.*, a fragrant plant.
migraine', *n.*, headache; *see* megrim.
mi'grate, *v.i.*, to leave one place for another.
mi'grated, *p.p.*, migrate.
mi'grating, *pr.p.*, migrate.
migra'tion, *n.*, removal.
mi'gratory, *adj.*, wandering.
Mika'do, *n.*, the Japanese Emperor.
Milanese', *adj.*, rel. to Milan.
milch, *adj.*, giving milk.
mild, *adj.*, gentle, indulgent.
mild'er, *adj.*, *comp.* of mild.
mild'est, *adj.*, *super.* of mild.
mil'dew, *v.t.*, to affect with mildew; *v.i.*, to be mildewed; *n.*, a plant disease; damp-produced spots.
mil'dewed, *p.p.*, mildew.
mil'dewing, *pr.p.*, mildew.
mild'ly, *adv.*, gently.
mild'ness, *n.*, gentleness, kindness.
mile, *n.*, a measure of distance = 1,760 yards.
mile'age, *n.*, a reckoning in miles.
Mile'sian, *adj.*, rel. to Miletus.
mile'stone, *n.*, a stone marking distance in miles.
mil'foil, *n.*, a plant so named.
mil'iary, *adj.*, like millet.

mil'itant, *adj.*, warring.
mil'itarism, *n.*, the military principle or system.
mil'itary, *adj.*, rel. to soldiers.
mil'itate, *v.i.*, to conflict.
mil'itated, *p.p.*, militate.
mil'itating, *pr.p.*, militate.
mili'tia, *n.*, an armed force for home service.
milk, *v.t.*, to draw milk; *n.*, a white secretion in female mammals.
milked, *p.p.*, milk.
milk'er, *n.*, a cow that gives milk.
milk'ier, *adj.*, *comp.* of milky.
milk'iest, *adj.*, *super.* of milky.
milk'iness, *adj.*, the quality of being milky.
milk'ing, *pr.p.*, milk.
milk'maid, *n.*, a woman who milks cows.
milk'man, *n.*, a man who supplies milk.
milk'sop, *n.*, an effeminate or weak-minded person.
milk'tooth, *n.*, one of the first growth of teeth.
milk'warm, *adj.*, warm as new milk.
milk'-white, *adj.*, white as milk.
milk'wort, *n.*, one of the Polygala.
milk'y, *adj.*, like milk.
mill, *v.t.*, to grind; to indent the edge of a coin; to roll (metal); *n.*, a machine for grinding; a place where grinding is done; a factory; a prize-fight (*slang*).
mill'-dam, *n.*, a dam in a mill-stream.
milled, *p.p.*, mill.
millena'rian, *adj.*, of a thousand years; rel. to the millennium.
mil'lenary, *n.*, the space of a thousand years; *adj.*, *i.q.* millenarian.
millen'nial, *adj.*, rel. to a millennium.
millen'nialist, *n.*, one who has peculiar views about the millennium.
millen'nium, *n.*, a period of a thousand years; esp. with reference to the reign of Christ with His Saints upon earth.
mil'lepede, *n.*, a many-footed insect.
mil'lepore, *n.*, a coral with many pores.
mill'er, *n.*, one who works a mill.
mill'erite, *n.*, an Adventist.
mill'er's-thumb, *n.*, a small fish.
milles'imal, *adj.*, having a thousand parts.
mil'let, *n.*, a hardy grass or grain.
mill'head, *n.*, a head of water for a mill.
mil'liard, *n.*, one thousand millions.
mil'liary, *adj.*, rel. to a Roman mile.
milli'gramme, **milli'gram**, *n.*, the thousandth part of a gramme.
milli'litre, **mill'ileter**, *n.*, the thousandth part of a litre.
mill'imetre, **mill'imeter**, *n.*, the thousandth part of a metre.
mil'liner, *n.*, one who sells, makes, or trims bonnets, etc.
mil'linery, *n.*, a milliner's wares.
mill'ing, *pr.p.*, mill; *n.*, the raised impression on the edge of a coin; the process of fulling cloth; the act of milling.
mil'lion, *n.*, a thousand thousands.
millionaire', *n.*, a person with a million of money.
mill'ionary, *adj.*, rel. to millions.
mil'lionth, *adj.*, the ordinal of a million.
mill'pond, *n.*, a pond supplying water-power to a mill.
mill'race, *n.*, the rush of water that drives a mill.
mill'stone, *n.*, a stone for grinding corn.
mill'wheel, *n.*, the wheel of a mill.
mill'wright, *n.*, a mill-builder.
mil'reis, *n.*, a Portuguese money value = 5s. (about).
milt, *n.*, the spleen; a fish's soft roe; *v.t.*, to impregnate.
Milton'ic, *adj.*, rel. to Milton.
mil'vine, *adj.*, rel. to kites.
mil'vus, *n.*, a kite (*Lat.*).
mime, *n.*, a type of drama ridiculing persons and things; an actor in a mime.
mim'eograph, *n.*, a copying machine.
mimet'ic, *adj.*, imitative.
mimet'ically, *adv.*, imitatively.
mim'ic, *v.t.*, to imitate; take off; *adj.*, imitative; *n.*, one who imitates or takes off.
mim'ical, *adj.*, *i.q.* mimic.
mim'icked, *p.p.*, mimic.
mim'icker, *n.*, *i.q.* mimic.
mim'icry, *n.*, the act of imitating.
mimog'rapher, *n.*, a writer of mimes.
mimo'sa, *n.*, a leguminous plant.
mina'cious, *adj.*, threatening.
minac'ity, *adj.*, threatening.
min'aret, *n.*, the turret of a mosque.
min'atory, *adj.*, threatening.
mince, *v.t.*, to chop small; *v.i.*, to speak affectedly; *n.*, a dish of finely-chopped meat.
minced, *p.p.*, mince.
mince'-meat, *n.*, meat chopped small and mixed with various ingredients.
mince-pie', *n.*, a Christmas pie containing mince-meat.
min'cing, *pr.p.*, mince; *adj.*, affectedly graceful.

min'cingly, *adv.*, in a mincing manner.

mind, *v.t.*, to mark, attend, heed; *v.i.*, to care; *n.*, the intellectual faculty; memory, intention.

mind'ed, *p.p.*, mind; *adj.*, disposed in mind.

mind'er, *n.*, one who keeps watch.

mind'ful, *adj.*, remembering, attentive.

mind'ing, *pr.p.*, mind.

mind'less, *adj.*, lacking intelligence.

mine, *v.t.*, to sap, undermine; *v.i.*, to do mining operations; *n.*, a deep excavation for minerals; *adj. possess.*, bel. to me.

mined, *p.p.*, mine.

mi'ner, *n.*, a worker in a mine.

min'eral, *adj.*, rel. to minerals; *n.*, any inorganic body.

min'eralist, *n.*, a collector of minerals.

mineraliza'tion, *n.*, the act or result of mineralizing.

min'eralize, *v.t.*, to turn into mineral; to impregnate minerally.

min'eralized, *p.p.*, mineralize.

min'eralizer, *n.*, that which mineralizes.

min'eralizing, *pr.p.*, mineralize.

mineralog'ic, *adj.*, rel. to mineralogy.

mineralog'ical, *adj.*, *i.q.* mineralogic.

mineral'ogist, *n.*, an expert in mineralogy.

mineral'ogy, *n.*, the science of minerals.

Miner'va, *n.*, the goddess of wisdom.

min'gle, *v.t.*, to mix, blend; *v.i.*, to join in.

min'gled, *p.p.*, mingle.

min'gling, *pr.p.*, mingle.

min'iate, *adj.*, vermilion-coloured.

min'iature, *adj.*, on a small scale; *n.*, a small portrait on ivory, etc.

min'iaturist, *n.*, an artist in miniatures.

Min'ié, *n.*, a Minié ball or rifle.

min'ify, *v.t.*, to reduce in size.

min'ikin, *n.*, any very small thing.

min'im, *n.*, half a semibreve; one-sixtieth of a dram.

min'imize, *v.t.*, to reduce to a minimum; make very little of.

min'imized, *p.p.*, minimize.

min'imizing, *pr.p.*, minimize.

min'imum, *n.*, the smallest possible amount.

mi'ning, *pr.p.*, mine; *adj.*, rel. to a mine; *n.*, the mining industry.

min'ion, *n.*, an obsequious dependent; a small printing type.

min'ister, *v.t.*, to supply, afford, administer; *v.i.*, to act as a minister or helper; *n.*, an assistant, agent; an officiant; the deacon or subdeacon at Mass; an administrator; an ambassador.

min'istered, *p.p.*, minister.

ministe'rial, *adj.*, rel. to a minister or ministry.

ministe'rialist, *n.*, a supporter of the Government party.

ministe'rially, *adv.*, in a ministerial capacity.

min'istering, *pr.p.*, minister.

min'istrant, *adj.*, acting as a minister.

ministra'tion, *n.*, the service or act of a minister.

min'istry, *n.*, the office of a minister; the Government.

min'ium, *n.*, red oxide of lead.

min'iver, *n.*, squirrel fur.

mink, *n.*, a weasel-like, fur-bearing mammal.

min'nesinger, *n.*, one of the lyric poets and singers of mediaeval Germany.

min'now, *n.*, a small fresh-water fish.

mi'nor, *adj.*, smaller, less, subordinate; *n.*, one under age.

Mi'norite, *n.*, a Franciscan brother.

minor'ity, *n.*, the status of a minor; the under-age period; the smaller number.

Min'otaur, *n.*, a fabulous monster, half bull, half man.

min'ster, *n.*, a monastery; sometimes applied to a Cathedral or other very large church.

min'strel, *n.*, a travelling poet or singer.

min'strelsy, *n.*, the minstrel's art; minstrels as a whole; ballad poetry.

mint, *v.t.*, to coin; stamp money, invent; *n.*, a place where money is coined; an aromatic plant.

mint'age, *n.*, the production of a mint; duty paid for coining.

mint'ed, *p.p.*, mint.

mint'er, *n.*, one who mints.

mint'ing, *pr.p.*, mint.

min'uend, *n.*, a number from which the subtrahend is taken.

minuet', *n.*, a stately dance; its music.

mi'nus, a Latin adverb = less, used prepositionally in the sense of "without"; *n.*, the sign (–) of subtraction.

min'ute, *v.t.*, to make a memorandum of; *n.*, a memorandum or entry of record; the sixtieth part of an hour.

minute', *adj.*, very small, exact, slender.

min'uted, *p.p.*, minute.

min'ute-book, *n.*, a memorandum book.

min'ute-gun, *n.*, a gun fired at intervals of a minute.

min'ute-hand, *n.*, a watch or clock hand pointing to the minutes.

minute'ly, *adv.*, exactly; on a small scale.

minute'ness, *n.*, exactness; the quality of being minute.

minu'tiae, *n. pl.*, small details.

min'uting, *pr.p.*, minute.

minx, *n.*, *i.q.* mink; also a pert girl.

Mi'ocene, *adj.*, less recent; rel. to the middle period of the Tertiary geological formation.

mir'acle, *n.*, a wonderful occurrence.

mirac'ulous, *adj.*, marvellous; of the nature of miracle.

mirac'ulously, *adv.*, as by a miracle.

mirac'ulousness, *n.*, the state of being miraculous.

mirage', *v.t.*, to reflect as in a mirror; *n.*, an atmospheric optical illusion.

mire, *v.t.*, to stain with mud; to plunge into mud; *v.i.*, to sink in mud; *n.*, mud; dirt mixed with water.

mired, *p.p.*, mire.

miri'fic, *adj.*, wondrous.

mi'riness, *n.*, the state or quality of being miry.

mir'ror, *v.t.*, to reflect in a mirror, or as in a mirror; *n.*, a looking-glass, a pattern.

mir'rored, *p.p.*, mirror.

mirth, *n.*, gaiety, merriment.

mirth'ful, *adj.*, gay, merry.

mirth'fully, *adv.*, gaily, merrily.

mirth'fulness, *n.*, the quality of being mirthful.

mirth'less, *adj.*, without mirth.

mir'y, *adj.*, full of, or smothered in, mire.

mir'za, *n.*, a Persian prince.

misadven'ture *n.*, mischance.

misadven'turous, *adj.*, unfortunate.

misadvised', *adj.*, ill-advised.

misalli'ance, *n.*, an ill-assorted marriage.

misallied', *adj.*, ill-assorted.

mis'anthrope, *n.*, a hater of mankind.

misanthrop'ic, *adj.*, anti-social.

misanthrop'ical, *adj.*, *i.q.* misanthropic.

misan'thropist, *n.*, *i.q.* misanthrope.

misan'thropy, *n.*, hatred of mankind.

misapplica'tion, *n.*, applying incorrectly.

misapplied', *p.p.*, misapply.

misapply', *v.t.*, to apply incorrectly.

misapply'ing, *pr.p.*, misapply.

misapprehend', *v.t.*, to misunderstand.

misapprehend'ed, *p.p.* misapprehend.

misapprehend'ing, *pr.p.*, misapprehend.

misapprehen'sion, *n.*, misunderstanding.

misappro'priate, *v.t.*, to apply wrongly.

misappro'priated, *p.p.* misappropriate.

misappro'priating, *pr.p.*, misappropriate.

misappropria'tion, *n.*, wrong application.

mis*become'*, *v.t.*, to suit ill.

mis*becom'ing*, *pr.p.*, misbecome; *adj.*, unfitting.

misbegot'ten, *adj.*, illegitimate; contemptible.

misbehave', *v.t.*, to behave badly.

misbehaved', *p.p.*, misbehave.

misbeha'ving, *pr.p.*, misbehave.

misbeha'viour, *n.*, ill-conduct.

misbelief', *n.*, false belief.

misbelieve', *v.t.*, to believe erroneously.

misbelieved', *p.p.*, misbelieve.

misbeliev'er, *n.*, one who misbelieves.

misbeliev'ing, *pr.p.*, misbelieve.

miscal'culate, *v.t.*, to calculate falsely.

miscal'culated, *p.p.*, miscalculate.

miscal'culating, *pr.p.*, miscalculate.

miscalcula'tion, *n.*, a false calculation.

miscall', *v.t.*, to call by a wrong name.

miscalled', *p.p.*, miscall.

miscall'ing, *pr.p.*, miscall.

miscar'riage, *n.*, failure; premature parturition.

miscar'ried, *p.p.*, miscarry.

miscar'ry, *v.i.*, to fail; to be delivered prematurely.

miscar'rying, *pr.p.*, miscarry.

miscellana'rian, *adj.*, rel. to miscellanies.

miscella'nea, *n. pl.*, a miscellaneous collection.

miscella'neous, *adj.*, composed of a variety of things; promiscuous.

miscella'neously, *adv.*, promiscuously.

miscel'lanist, *n.*, a writer of miscellany.

miscel'lany, *n.*, a mixture; a book on a variety of subjects.

mischance', *n.*, ill-luck.

mis'chief, *n.*, harm; intentional injury.

mis'chief-maker, *n.*, a busybody.

mis'chievous, *adj.*, harmful, pernicious.

mis'chievously, *adv.*, harmfully.

mischoose', *v.t.*, to make a wrong choice.

mis'cible, *adj.*, able to be mixed.

miscomputa'tion, *n.*, a wrong reckoning.

miscompute', *v.t.*, to reckon wrongly.

misconceive', *v.t.*, to have a false notion of.

misconceived', *p.p.*, misconceive.

misconceiv'ing, *pr.p.*, misconceive.

misconcep'tion, *n.*, a false notion; misunderstanding.

misconduct', *v. reflex.*, to behave oneself badly.

miscon'duct, *n.*, bad behaviour.

misconjec'ture, *n.*, a false conjecture.

misconstruc'tion, *n.*, a false construction.

miscon'strue, *v.t.*, to interpret wrongly.

miscon'strued, *p.p.*, misconstrue.

miscon'struing, *pr.p.*, misconstrue.

miscount', *v.t.*, to count wrongly; *n.*, an error in counting.

mis'creant, *n.*, a base wretch.

miscue', *v.i.*, to make a miscue; *n.*, a slip with a billiard cue.

misdate', *n.*, to date wrongly.

misdat'ed, *p.p.*, misdate.

misdat'ing, *pr.p.*, misdate.

misdeal', *v.t.*, to deal cards wrongly; *n.*, a false deal.

misdeed', *n.*, a wicked action.

misdemean', *v. reflex.*, to behave oneself ill.

misdemean'ant, *n.*, one guilty of a misdemeanour.

misdemean'our, *n.*, a petty crime; ill-behaviour.

misdirect', *v.t.*, to direct wrongly.

misdirect'ed, *p.p.*, misdirect.

misdirect'ing, *pr.p.*, misdirect.

misdirec'tion, *n.*, the act or result of misdirecting.

misdo', *v.t.*, to do amiss.

misdo'er, *n.*, one guilty of misdeeds.

misdo'ing, *pr.p.*, misdo; *n.*, evil conduct; *i.q.* misdeed.

mise, *n.*, expenses; settlement on terms.

misemploy', *v.t.*, to employ wrongly.

misemployed', *p.p.*, misemploy.

misemploy'ing, *pr.p.*, misemploy.

misemploy'ment, *n.*, the state of being misemployed; putting to a wrong use.

mi'ser, *n.*, one who hoards his money and lives miserably.

mis'erable, *adj.*, wretched, worthless.

mis'erably, *adv.*, in a miserable way.

misere're, *n.*, the 51st Psalm, and its musical setting.

miser'icord, *n.*, a projecting bracket beneath the folding seat of a choir stall (wrongly called a miserere); a room in a monastery where discipline was somewhat relaxed.

mi'serly, *adj.*, like a miser.

mis'ery, *n.*, wretchedness.

misfea'sance, *n.*, wrong performance; trespass.

misfire', *v.i.*, not to go off (said of a firearm).

misfit', *v.t.*, to fit badly; *n.*, a badly made garment.

misform', *v.t.*, to shape ill.

misformed', *p.p.*, misform.

misfor'tune, *n.*, bad luck, ill-fortune.

misgave', *p.t.* of misgive.

mis*give'*, *v.t.*, to arouse doubt; *v.i.*, to be apprehensive.

mis*giv'en*, *p.p.*, misgive.

mis*giv'ing*, *pr.p.*, misgive; *n.*, a feeling of doubt.

misgot'ten, *adj.*, ill-got.

mis*gov'ern*, *v.t.*, to govern badly.

mis*gov'erned*, *p.p.*, misgovern.

mis*governing*, *pr.p.*, misgovern.

mis*gov'ernment*, *n.*, bad government.

misguid'ance, *n.*, bad guidance, delusion.

misguide', *v.t.*, to delude, guide wrongly.

misguid'ed, *p.p.*, misguide; *adj.*, deluded, ill-advised.

misguid'ing, *pr.p.*, misguide.

mishap', *n.*, an unfortunate occurrence.

mishear', *v.t.*, to hear amiss.

misheard', *p.p.*, mishear.

mish'-mash, *n.*, a hotch-potch.

Mish'nah, *n.*, the Talmud text.

mish'nic, *adj.*, rel. to the Mishnah.

mis*inform'*, *v.t.*, to inform falsely.

mis*informed'*, *p.p.*, misinform.

mis*informa'tion*, *n.* false information.

misinter'pret, *v.t.*, to understand or interpret wrongly.

misinterpreta'tion, *n.*, a wrong construction.

misinter'preted, *p.p.*, misinterpret.

misinter'preter, *n.*, one who misinterprets.

misinter'preting, *pr.p.* misinterpret.

misjoin'der, *n.*, the joining of things or parties that should not be joined.

misjudge', *v.t.*, to judge wrongly; to mistake.

misjudged', *p.p.*, misjudge.

misjudg'ing, *pr.p.*, misjudge.

misjudg'ment, *n.*, a wrong determination.

mislaid', *p.p.*, mislay.

mislay', *v.t.*, to lay in a wrong place; to lose.

mislay'ing, *pr.p.*, mislay.

mislead', *v.t.*, to lead astray.

mislead'er, *n.*, one who misleads.

mislead'ing, *pr.p.*, mislead; *adj.*, deceptive.

misled', *p.p.*, mislead.

misman'age, *v.t.*, to manage or administer badly.

misman'aged, *p.p.*, mismanage.

misman'agement, *n.*, bad management.

misman'ager, *n.*, one who mismanages.

misman'aging, *pr.p.*, mismanage.

misname′, *v.t.*, to name wrongly.
misnamed′, *p.p.*, misname.
misnam′ing, *pr.p.*, misname.
misno′mer, *n.*, a wrong name.
misog′amist, *n.*, a hater of marriage.
misog′amy, *n.*, hatred of marriage.
misog′ynist, *n.*, a woman-hater.
misog′yny, *n.*, hatred of women.
mis′pickel, *n.*, arsenopyrite.
misplace′, *v.t.*, to put in the wrong place; bestow on the wrong object.
misplaced′, *p.p.*, misplace.
misplace′ment, *n.*, putting in the wrong place.
misplac′ing, *pr.p.*, misplace.
misplead′, *v.t.*, to plead wrongly.
misplead′ed, *p.p.*, misplead.
misplead′ing, *pr.p.*, misplead.
misprint′, *v.t.*, to make a printer's error; *n.*, a printer's error.
misprint′ed, *p.p.*, misprint.
misprint′ing, *pr.p.*, misprint.
mispri′sion, *n.*, concealment of a felony or treason.
mispronounce′, *v.t.*, to pronounce wrongly.
mispronounced′, *p.p.*, mispronounce.
mispronounc′ing, *pr.p.*, mispronounce.
mispronuncia′tion, *n.*, the art of mispronouncing; a word improperly pronounced.
mis*propor′tion*, *v.t.*, to proportion badly.
mis*propor′tioned*, *p.p.*, misproportion.
mis*propor′tioning*, *pr.p.*, misproportion.
misquota′tion, *n.*, the act of misquoting; a passage misquoted.
misquote′, *v.t.*, to quote incorrectly.
misquot′ed, *p.p.*, misquote.
misquot′ing, *pr.p.*, misquote.
misread′, *v.t.*, to read incorrectly.
misread′, *p.p.*, misread.
misread′ing, *pr.p.*, misread; *n.*, an error in a text.
misreck′on, *v.t.*, to reckon inaccurately.
mis*remem′ber*, *v.t.*, to remember uncertainly.
mis*remem′bered*, *p.p.*, misremember.
misreport′, *v.t.*, to report incorrectly.
misreport′ed, *p.p.*, misreport.
misreport′ing, *pr.p.*, misreport.
mis*represent′*, *v.t.*, to falsify; mis-state.
mis*representa′tion*, *n.*, the act or effect of misrepresenting.
mis*represent′ed*, *p.p.*, misrepresent.
mis*represent′ing*, *pr.p.*, misrepresent.
misrule′, *n.*, tumult, confusion, bad government.
miss, *v.t.*, to fail of hitting, finding, or obtaining; to feel the loss of; *v.i.*, to miss the mark; *n.*, a loss; an unmarried woman.
mis′sal, *n.*, the Mass-book.
missed, *p.p.*, miss.
mis′sel-thrush, *n.*, a thrush that eats mistletoe berries.
mis-shape′, *v.t.*, to shape ill.
mis-shaped′, *p.p.*, mis-shape.
mis-sha′pen, *adj.*, deformed, ugly.
mis′sile, *n.*, a weapon or thing thrown by the hand or from a gun.
miss′ing, *pr.p.*, miss.
mis′sion, *n.*, an errand, embassy; the act of sending or state of being sent on some high business; a missionary station; a series of religious services.
mis′sionary, *n.*, one sent abroad to preach religion; *adj.*, rel. to missionaries.
mis′sioner, *n.*, the conductor of a mission.
mis′sis, *n.*, the title (Mrs.).
mis′sive, *n.*, a letter despatched, a message; *adj.*, despatched.
mis-spell′, *v.t.*, to spell incorrectly.
mis-spelled′, *p.p.*, mis-spell.
mis-spell′ing, *pr.p.*, mis-spell; *n.*, an error in spelling.
mis-spelt′, *p.p.*, mis-spell.
mis-spend′, *v.t.*, to spend foolishly; waste.
mis-spend′ing, *pr.p.*, mis-spend; *adj.*, wasted.
mis-spent, *p.p.*, mis-spend.
mis-state′, *v.t.*, to state wrongly; falsify.
mis-sta′ted, *p.p.*, mis-state.
mis-state′ment, *n.*, an erroneous statement.
mis-sta′ting, *pr.p.*, mis-state.
mist, *n.*, a small, thin rain; fog.
mista′kable, *adj.*, capable of being mistaken.
mistake′, *v.t.*, to take one thing for another; *v.i.*, to err in judgment or opinion; *n.*, an error in judgment or opinion; a blunder; oversight.
mista′ken, *p.p.*, mistake; *adj.*, misunderstood; erroneous; ill-judged.
mista′king, *pr.p.*, mistake.
mistaught′, *p.p.*, misteach.
misteach′, *v.t.*, to teach wrongly.
misteach′ing, *pr.p.*, misteach; *n.*, false teaching.
mis′ter, *n.*, the title (Mr.).
mistimed′, *adj.*, inopportune, badly timed.
mist′iness, *n.*, the state of being misty.

mis'tletoe, *n.*, a parasitic evergreen plant.
mist'-like, *adj.*, like mist.
mis'took, *p.t.* of mistake.
mis'tral, *n.*, a N.W. wind that blows in the French Mediterranean provinces.
mistranslate', *v.t.*, to translate incorrectly.
mistransla'ted, *p.p.*, mistranslate.
mistransla'ting, *pr.p.*, mistranslate.
mistransla'tion, *n.*, an error in translating.
mis'tress, *n.*, a woman who governs; a female head of a house or school; a woman skilled in anything; a sweetheart; a concubine; the title of a married woman (pronounced *Missis* and written *Mrs.*).
mistrust', *v.t.*, to suspect, doubt; *n.*, doubt, suspicion.
mistrust'ed, *p.p.*, mistrust.
mistrust'ful, *adj.*, suspicious.
mistrust'ing, *pr.p.*, mistrust.
mist'y, *adj.*, covered with mist; cloudy; dim.
misunderstand', *v.t.*, to mistake, misconceive.
misunderstand'ing, *pr.p.*, misunderstand; *n.*, taking in a wrong sense.
misunder'stood, *p.p.*, misunderstand.
misu'sage, *n.*, a wrong usage.
misuse', *v.t.*, to make a wrong use of; treat improperly.
misuse', *n.*, a wrong use.
misused', *p.p.*, misuse.
misu'ser, *n.*, one who misuses.
misu'sing, *pr.p.*, misuse.
mite, *n.*, a very small insect; the smallest coin; anything tiny.
mi'ter, *see* mitre.
mit'igable, *adj.*, able to be assuaged.
mit'igant, *adj.*, assuaging.
mit'igate, *v.t.*, to assuage; render less severe.
mit'igated, *p.p.*, mitigate.
mit'igating, *pr.p.*, mitigate.
mitiga'tion, *n.*, abatement of anything painful or harsh.
mit'igative, *adj.*, causing mitigation.
mit'igator, *n.*, anything that mitigates.
mitrailleuse', *n.*, a machine gun.
mi'tral, *adj.*, rel. to, or like, a mitre.
mi'tre, *v.t.*, to cover with a mitre; to join two boards at an angle of 45°; *n.*, a head-dress of the Jewish high priest, a bishop, archbishop, or, in certain cases, an abbot.
mi'tred, *p.p.*, mitre; *adj.*, wearing the mitre; joined mitre-fashion.
mi'triform, *adj.* mitre-shaped, conical.
mi'tring, *pr.p.*, mitre.
mitt, *n.*, *i.q.* mitten.
mit'ten, *n.*, a fingerless glove; a wrist-covering.
mit'timus, *n.*, a warrant committing to prison, or transferring from one court to another.
mi'ty, *adj.*, full of mites.
mix, *v.t.*, to mingle, blend, confuse; *v.i.*, to combine.
mix'able, *adj.*, able to be mixed.
mixed, *p.p.*, mix.
mix'edly, *adv.*, confusedly.
mix'en, *n.*, a dunghill.
mix'er, *n.*, a bowl.
mix'ing, *pr.p.*, mix.
mixtilin'eal, *adj.*, combining straight and curved lines.
mixtilin'ear, *adj.*, *i.q.* mixtilineal.
mix'tion, *n.*, a mixture for fixing gold leaf.
mix'ture, *n.*, a mass formed by mixing.
miz'en, miz'zen, *n.*, the hindmost of the fore-and-aft sails.
miz'en-mast, *n.*, the mast abaft the mainmast.
miz'zle, *v.i.* to rain in small drops; *n.*, fine rain.
miz'zled, *p.p.*, mizzle.
miz'zling, *pr.p.*, mizzle.
miz'zly, *adj.*, drizzling.
mnemon'ic, *adj.*, memory-aiding.
mnemon'ical, *adj.*, *i.q.* mnemonic.
mnemon'ics, *n. pl.*, the cultivation of the memory.
mnem'otechny, *n.*, the art of memory.
moan, *v.i.*, to make a moaning sound; *n.*, a low sound of pain or grief.
moaned, *p.p.*, moan.
moan'ing, *pr.p.*, moan; *n.*, the act of moaning.
moat, *v.t.*, to surround with a moat; *n.*, a ditch round a castle or house.
moat'ed, *adj.*, having a moat.
mob, *v.t.*, to attack in a disorderly way; to crowd round; *n.*, a disorderly crowd; the populace.
mob'-cap, *n.*, a woman's head-dress.
mobbed, *p.p.*, mob.
mob'bing, *pr.p.*, mob.
mo'bile, *adj.*, moved or moving easily; changeable.
mobil'ity, *adj.*, the power of being moved; activity.
mobiliza'tion, *n.*, calling up for active service.
mo'biliza, *v.t.*, to call up for service; get troops ready.
mo'bilized, *p.p.*, mobilize.
mo'bilizing, *pr.p.*, mobilize.
mob'-law, *n.*, anarchy; the rule of the populace.
moboc'racy, *n.*, the rule of the mob; the populace.

moc'casin, *n.*, a N. American shoe of deer-skin.

mo'cha, *n.*, a particular kind of coffee.

mock, *v.t.*, to mimic, deride; *adj.*, false, counterfeit; *n.*, derision.

mocked, *p.p.*, mock.

mock'er, *n.*, one who mocks.

mock'ery, *n.*, derision, scorn.

mock'-hero'ic, *adj.*, pseudo-heroic.

mock'ing, *pr.p.*, mock.

mock'ing-bird, *n.*, a bird that mimics other birds.

mock'-orange, *n.*, syringa.

mock'-turtle, *n.*, veal made into soup resembling turtle-soup.

mo'co, *n.*, the rock cavy.

mo'dal, *adj.*, rel. to mode or form; (*musically*) bel. to one of the modes.

modal'ity, *n.*, difference in mode.

mode, *n.*, form, custom, manner; musical scale.

mod'el, *v.t.*, to shape, mould; *v.i.*, to do modelling; *n.*, a pattern, mould, a standard, an example; *adj.*, serving as a pattern.

mod'el(l)ed, *p.p.*, model.

mod'el(l)er, *n.*, one who models.

mod'el(l)ing, *pr.p.*, model; *n.*, the art of modelling.

mod'erate, *adj.*, temperate, reasonable, mild.

mod'erate, *v.t.*, to temper, abate, regulate; *v.i.*, to act as a moderator; to abate in violence.

mod'erated, *p.p.*, moderate.

mod'erately, *adv.*, in a moderate degree.

mod'erating, *pr.p.*, moderate.

modera'tion, *n.*, the act of moderating; the state or quality of being moderate; restraint.

Modera'tions, *n. pl.*, the first public examination at Oxford.

mod'eratism, *n.*, the principles of the Moderate party.

modera'to, *adj.* and *adv.*, at moderate speed (*mus.*).

mod'erator, *n.*, one who, or that which, moderates; the president of an assembly; an Oxford examiner; a Cambridge superintendent at examinations.

mod'ern, *adj.*, bel. to recent or present times.

mod'ernism, *n.*, a theological system which dispenses with the historical basis of Christian doctrines.

mod'ernist, *n.*, one who accepts modernism; a supporter of modern doctrines

moder'nity, *n.*, the quality of being modern.

moderniza'tion, *n.*, the act or result of modernizing.

mod'ernize, *v.t.*, to make modern.

mod'ernized, *p.p.*, modernize.

mod'ernizer, *n.*, one who modernizes.

mod'ernizing, *pr.p.*, modernize.

mod'ernness, *n.*, the quality or state of being modern.

mod'est, *adj.*, not self-assertive; chaste, simple.

mod'estly, *adv.*, in a modest way.

mod'esty, *n.*, modest behaviour, shyness, chastity.

mod'icum, *n.*, a small portion; a pittance.

modifiabil'ity, *n.*, the quality of being modifiable.

mod'ifiable, *adj.*, able to be modified.

modifica'tion, *n.*, the act of modifying; a modified state or form.

mod'ified, *p.p.*, modify.

mod'ifier, *n.*, that which modifies.

mod'ify, *v.t.*, to change the form of; to qualify.

mod'ifying, *pr.p.*, modify.

modil'lion, *n.*, a bracket under a cornice.

mo'dish, *adj.*, affecting the fashions.

mo'dishly, *adv.*, in a modish way.

mo'dist, *n.*, a follower of the fashions.

modiste', *n.*, a woman who makes fashionable dresses.

mod'ulate, *v.t.*, to inflict; *v.i.*, make a key-change (*mus.*).

mod'ulated, *p.p.*, modulate.

mod'ulating, *pr.p.*, modulate.

modula'tion, *n.*, the act of modulating; passage from one key to another (*mus.*).

mod'ulator, *n.*, a chart showing the musical scales.

mod'ule, *n.*, a unit for proportionate measurement.

mo'dus, *n.*, manner, means (*Lat.*).

Moesogoth'ic, *adj.*, rel. to the Moeso-Goths.

mofus'sil, *n.*, the country districts of India.

Mogul', *adj.*, rel. to the Moguls; *n.*, a Mongol.

mo'hair, *n.*, fabric made from the hair of the Angora goat.

Moham'medan, *adj.*, rel. to Mohammed and his followers.

Moham'medanism, *n.*, the religion of Mohammed.

Moham'medanize, *v.t.*, to convert to Mohammedanism; *v.i.*, to turn Mohammedan.

Mo'hawk, *n.*, one of the N. American tribe so-named.

Mo'hock, *n.*, an 18th century London street rowdy.

mo'hur, *n.*, an Indian gold piece = 15 rupees.

moi'dore, *n.*, a Portuguese gold piece = 27s.

moi'ety, *n.*, a half.

moil, *v.i.*, to toil.

moiled, *p.p.*, moil.

moil'ing, *pr.p.*, moil.

moi'neau, *n.*, a small bastion.

moire, *n.*, watered silk (*Fr.*).

moist, *adj.*, damp.

mois'ten, *v.t.*, to make moist.

mois'tened, *p.p.*, moisten.

mois'tening, *pr.p.*, moisten.

moist'ness, *n.*, dampness.

mois'ture, *n.*, dampness, moderate wetness.

mo'lar, *adj.*, grinding; *n.*, a grinding tooth.

molas'ses, *n.*, treacle.

mold, *n.*, crumbling, friable earth; a fungus growth; mustiness. Also *mould*.

mole, *n.*, a pier; a natural spot on the skin; a small burrowing quadruped.

molec'ular, *adj.*, rel. to molecules.

molecular'ity, *n.*, the quality of being molecular.

mol'ecule, *n.*, a minute particle of matter.

mole'-eyed, *adj.*, blind

mole'-hill, *n.*, the soil upturned by a mole.

mole'skin, *adj.*, made of moleskin; *n.*, a cloth resembling a mole's skin.

molest', *v.t.*, to annoy, disturb.

molesta'tion, *n.*, the act of molesting.

molest'ed, *p.p.*, molest.

molest'er, *n.*, one who molests.

molest'ing, *pr.p.*, molest.

Mol'inism, *n.*, the principles of the Jesuit Molina.

Mol'inist, *n.*, a follower of Molina.

mol'lah, *n.*, a teacher of Mohammedan law.

mol'lient, *adj.*, softening.

mol'lifiable, *adj.*, able to be mollified.

mollifica'tion, *n.*, the act or effect of mollifying.

mol'lified, *p.p.*, mollify.

mol'lifier, *n.*, one who, that which, mollifies.

mol'lify, *v.t.*, to soften, assuage.

mol'lifying, *pr.p.*, mollify.

mol'lusc, *n.*, one of the Mollusca.

Mollus'ca, *n. pl.*, invertebrates with soft bodies and a shelly covering.

mollus'can, *adj.*, rel. to the Mollusca.

mollus'cous, *adj.*, *i.q.* molluscan.

mol'lusk, *n.*, *i.q.* mollusc.

Mo'loch, *n.*, the god of fire.

molos'sus, *n.*, a foot of three long syllables.

mol'ten, *p.p.*, melt; *adj.*, made of molten metal.

mo'ly, *n.*, the Homeric herb that availed against Circe's spells

molyb'denous, *adj.*, rel. to molybdenum.

molybde'num, *n.*, a rare metal combined with lead and sulphur.

mo'ment, *n.*, an instant; importance.

mo'mentarily, *adv.*, in a moment of time.

mo'mentary, *adj.*, lasting for, or done in, a moment.

mo'mently, *adv.*, each moment.

momen'tous, *adj.*, of great importance.

momen'tum, *n.*, force of matter in motion.

Mo'mus, *n.*, the spirit of mockery.

mon'achal, *adj.*, rel. to monks.

mon'achism, *n.*, the monastic system.

mon'ad, *n.*, a primary constituent of matter; a simple, minute organism.

Monadel'phia, *n. pl.*, plants having their stamens united.

monadelph'ian, *adj.*, rel. to monadelphia.

monadelph'ous, *adj.*, *i.q.* monadelphian.

monad'ic, *adj.*, rel. to monads.

monad'ical, *adj.*, *i.q.* monadic.

monan'drian, *adj.*, having only one stamen.

monan'drous, *adj.*, *i.q.* monandrian.

mon'arch, *n.*, one who rules alone; a sovereign.

monar'chic, *adj.*, rel. to monarchy.

monar'chical, *adj.*, *i.q.* monarchic.

mon'archist, *n.*, a supporter of monarchy.

mon'archy, *n.*, the government of a single ruler.

monaste'rial, *adj.*, rel. to a monastery.

mon'astery, *n.*, a house of religious.

monas'tic, *adj.*, rel. to monks and monasteries.

monas'tical, *adj.*, *i.q.* monastic.

monas'ticism, *n.*, the monastic system.

monas'ticon, *n.*, a book about monasteries.

Mon'day, *n.*, the second day of the week.

mon'etary, *adj.*, rel. to money.

mon'etize, *v.t.*, to change into money; to standardize the value of.

mon'ey, *n.*, currency; metal coined; bank notes.

mon'eyed, *adj.*, wealthy.

mon'eyer, *n.*, a coiner.

mon'eyless, *adj.*, without money.

mon'ger, *n.*, a dealer.

Mon'gol, *adj.*, rel. to Mongolia.

Mongo'lian, *adj.*, *i.q.* Mongol.

mon'goose, *n.*, a snake-destroying ichneumon.

mon'grel, *adj.*, of mixed breed; hybrid; *n.*, a hybrid.

monil'iform, *adj.*, like a necklace.

mon'ism, *n.*, the theory that mind and matter are identical.
mon'ist, *n.*, a believer in monism.
monist'ic, *adj.*, rel. to monism.
moni'tion, *n.*, warning, instruction.
mon'itor, *n.*, one who warns; an elder boy who instructs the juniors; a build of man-of-war.
monito'rial, *adj.*, rel. to a monitor.
mon'itory, *adj.*, warning, giving notice.
mon'itress, *n.*, fem. of monitor.
monk, *n.*, a man who lives the monastic life.
monk'ery, *n.*, the monastic system.
mon'key, *n.*, a quadrumanous mammal.
monk'hood, *n.*, the monastic character.
monk'ish, *adj.*, rel. to monks.
monk's-hood, *n.*, aconite.
monocar'pous, *adj.*, bearing fruit only once.
monoceph'alous, *adj.*, having only one head.
monoc'eros, *adj.*, having one horn.
mon'ochord, *adj.*, having one string.
monochromat'ic, *adj.*, having only one colour.
mon'ochrome, *adj.*, *i.q.* monochromatic; *n.*, a painting in a single colour.
monochro'mic, *adj.*, in one colour.
mon'ocle, *n.*, a single eyeglass.
monocli'nous, *adj.*, dipping in one direction.
Monocotyle'don, *n.*, a plant having only one cotyledon.
monoc'racy, *n.*, autocracy.
mon'ocrat, *n.*, an autocrat.
monoc'ular, *adj.*, for use with one eye; having a single eye.
mon'ocule, *n.*, a creature with a single eye.
monoc'ulous, *adj.*, *i.q.* monocular.
Monodac'tylous, *adj.*, having one finger or toe.
mon'odist, *n.*, a writer or singer of monodies.
mon'odont, *adj.*, one-toothed.
mon'odrama, *n.*, a play for a single actor.
monodramat'ic, *adj.*, rel. to monodrama.
mon'ody, *n.*, a mournful song for a single voice.
monog'amist, *n.*, an advocate of monogamy.
monog'amous, *adj.*, having only one wife.
monog'amy, *n.*, marriage with one wife only.
monogen'esis, *n.*, reproduction from a single cell.
monogenet'ic, *adj.*, rel. to monogenesis.
monog'enism, *n.*, the theory that all men derive from one ancestor.
monog'enist, *n.*, a believer in monogenism.
monogenist'ic, *adj.*, rel. to monogenism.
mon'ogram, *n.*, two or more letters forming a cipher.
mon'ograph, *n.*, a treatise on a single subject.
monog'rapher, *n.*, the writer of a monograph.
monograph'ic, *adj.*, rel. to a monograph.
mon'olith, *n.*, an upright single stone.
monolith'ic, *adj.*, rel. to a monolith.
mon'ologue, *n.*, a soliloquy.
monoma'nia, *n.*, insanity on one particular subject.
monoma'niac, *n.*, one suffering from monomania.
monometal'lic, *adj.*, rel. to monometallism.
monomet'allism, *n.*, single currency.
monomet'allist, *n.*, an advocate of monometallism.
monom'eter, *adj.*, containing a single foot.
monomet'ric, *adj.*, *i.q.* monometer.
mono'mial, *adj.*, consisting of a single term.
monopet'alous, *adj.*, having a single petal.
monoph'onous, *adj.*, giving only one sound.
mon'ophthong, *n.*, a single vowel sound.
monophthon'gal, *adj.*, rel. to a monophthong.
monophyl'lous, *adj.*, single-leaved.
monoph'ysite, *adj.*, rel. to the theory that Our Lord had only a single nature.
mon'oplane, *n.*, an aeroplane of the single plane type.
monop'olism, *n.*, the practice of monopoly.
monop'olist, *n.*, one who monopolizes or favours monopoly.
monop'olize, *v.t.*, to obtain exclusive sale of; to engross entirely.
monop'olized, *p.p.*, monopolize.
monop'olizer, *n.*, one who monopolizes.
monop'olizing, *pr.p.*, monopolize.
monop'oly, *n.*, exclusive sale, or possession.
monop'teral, *adj.*, having only one wing.
mon'orail, *n.*, a railway running on a single rail.
mon'orime, mon'orhyme, *n.*, verse with a single rime.
monosep'alous, *n.*, having united sepals.
monosper'mous, *adj.*, one-seeded.
monospher'ical, *adj.*, rel. to a single sphere.

mon'ostich, *n.*, a one-versed composition.

monostroph'ic, *adj.*, having a single strophe.

monosyllab'ic, *adj.*, having a single syllable.

mon'osyllable, *n.*, a single syllable.

mon'otheism, *n.*, the worship of One God.

mon'otheist, *n.*, a worshipper of One God.

monotheis'tic, *adj.*, rel. to monotheism.

mon'otone, *n.*, singing at a uniform pitch; *v.t.* and *i.*, to recite on one note.

monot'onous, *adj.*, without variety; wearisome.

monot'ony, *n.*, wearisomeness, sameness.

mon'otype, *n.*, a composing machine that casts and sets up type.

monotyp'ic, *adj.*, rel. to monotype.

monox'ide, *n.*, an oxide with only one atom of oxygen in each molecule.

monseigneur', *n.*, a title of rank in France, as a bishop, the Dauphin, etc.

monsieur', *n.*, the French equivalent of Mr.

monsoon', *n.*, a periodical wind in the Indian Ocean.

mon'ster, *n.*, something out of the common order; *adj.*, huge.

mon'strance, *n.*, a transparent pyx in which the Sacred Host or a relic is shown.

monstros'ity, *n.*, the quality of being monstrous; something unnatural.

mon'strous, *adj.*, unnatural, shocking, huge.

mon'strously, *adv.*, hugely.

montan'ic, *adj.*, rel. to mountains.

Mon'tanism, *n.*, the heretical teaching of Montanus, a second century ascetic.

Mon'tanist, *n.*, a follower of Montanus.

mon'tant, *adj.*, mounting, increasing.

mon'te, *n.*, a Spanish gambling game.

mon'tem, *n.*, a famous ceremony at Eton, where every three years the scholars collected money on a hill for the support of one of their number at the University.

month, *n.*, the twelfth part of the year; four weeks.

month'ly, *adj.*, happening every month.

mon'ument, *n.*, a memorial.

monumen'tal, *adj.*, memorial; rel. to a monument; excessively great.

monumen'tally, *adv.*, as a memorial; hugely.

moo, *v.i.*, to make the noise of a cow; *n.*, a cow's lowing.

mood, *n.*, temper of mind; change in a verb; logical form of a syllogism.

mooed, *p.p.*, moo.

moo'ing, *pr.p.*, moo.

mood'ily, *adv.*, in a moody way.

mood'iness, *n.*, liability to strange moods.

mood'y, *adj.*, abstracted, gloomy; out of humour.

moon, *n.*, the earth's satellite; a month; *v.i.*, to roam or gaze around in an abstracted way.

moon'beam, *n.*, the moon's beam.

moon'-calf, *n.*, a dolt.

moon'less, *adj.*, without a moon.

moon'light, *n.*, the light of the moon.

moon'lighter, *n.*, one engaged in agrarian outrages in Ireland.

moon'lighting, *n.*, committing agrarian outrages.

moon'lit, *adj.*, lighted by the moon.

moon'-raker, *n.*, one who pursues foolish fancies.

moon'-raking, *n.*, the pursuit of foolish fancies.

moon'shee, *n.*, a Mohammedan scribe.

moon'shine, *n.*, moonlight; sheer nonsense; smuggled spirits.

moon'shiner, *n.*, a distiller of illicit whiskey.

moon'stone, *n.*, a yellowish white stone.

moon'struck, *adj.*, lunatic.

moon'wort, *n.*, a fern so named.

moon'y, *adj.*, crescent-shaped; sentimental.

moor, *v.t.*, to secure a ship with an anchor or cable; *v.i.*, to be so secured; *n.*, a native of Morocco; a large heathy tract.

moor'age, *n.*, a place for mooring.

moor'-cock, *n.*, red grouse.

moored, *p.p.*, moor.

moor'-fowl, *n.*, *i.q.* moor-cock.

moor'-grass, *n.*, a grass found on moors.

moor'-hen, *n.*, a water-fowl.

moor'ing, *pr.p.*, moor; *n.*, the act of mooring; in pl., the place of mooring.

Moor'ish, *adj.*, rel. to the Moors.

moor'land, *n.* and *adj.*, heathery land.

moor'-stone, *n.*, Cornish granite.

moor'y, *adj.*, like moorland.

moose, *n.*, a large animal allied to the elk.

moose'wood, *n.*, leatherwood.

moot, *v.t.*, to start a discussion; to debate, discuss; *n.*, a discussion; *adj.*, disputable.

moot'able, *adj.*, able to be mooted.

moot'-case, *n.*, a case for discussion.

moot'ed, *p.p.*, moot.
moot'ing, *pr.p.*, moot.
mop, *v.t.*, to rub with a mop; *n.*, a cloth broom for cleaning floors.
mope, *v.i.*, to be spiritless or silent.
moped, *p.p.*, mope.
mo'per, *n.*, one who mopes.
mo'ping, *pr.p.*, mope.
mo'pish, *adj.*, inclined to mope.
mo'pishness, *n.*, the state of being mopish.
mopped, *p.p.*, mop.
mop'pet, *n.*, a rag doll
mop'ping, *pr.p.*, mop.
moraine', *n.*, a line of stones and gravel at the edge of a glacier.
mor'al, *adj.*, rel. to morality; virtuous; probable; *n.*, the significance of a story; in pl. = ethics, morality, behaviour.
morale', *n.*, moral or mental condition.
mor'alist, *n.*, one who moralizes or makes moral reflections.
moral'ity, *n.*, the practice of moral duties; ethics; virtue; an allegorical play.
moraliza'tion, *n.*, the act or effect of moralizing.
mor'alize, *v.t.*, to give a moral meaning to; *v.i.*, to make moral reflections.
mor'alized, *p.p.*, moralize.
mor'alizer, *n.*, one who moralizes.
mor'alizing, *pr.p.*, moralize.
mor'ally, *adv.*, according to the moral law; practically.
mor'als, *n. pl.*, ethics, moral conduct.
morass', *n.*, a swamp, bog.
morass'y, *adj.*, swampy.
morato'rium, *n.*, an emergency device by which the State empowers the banks to withhold specie payments for a time named.

Mora'vian, *adj.*, rel. to Moravia.
Mora'vianism, *n.*, the religious system of the followers of John Hus.
mor'bid, *adj.*, diseased, sickly, unhealthy.
morbid'ity, *n.*, a diseased condition.
mor'bidly, *adv.*, in a morbid way.
mor'bidness, *n.*, a morbid tendency.
morbif'ic, *adj.*, causing disease.
morbil'lous, *adj.*, rel. to measles.
mor'bus, *n.*, disease (*Lat.*), as cholera morbus.
morceau', *n.*, a small piece (*Fr.*).
morda'cious, *adj.*, biting.
mordac'ity, *n.*, a tendency to biting.
mor'dant, *adj.*, biting, fixing colour, sarcastic.
more, *adj.*, greater in quantity or number; added; *adv.*, in greater degree; a second time.
moreen', *n.*, a strong woollen or cotton fabric.
morel', *n.*, an edible fungus; a variety of nightshade.
morel'lo, *n.*, a dark, bitter cherry.
moreo'ver, *adv.*, further, besides.
Moresque', *adj.*, Moorish (*Fr.*).
morganat'ic, *adj.*, rel. to a marriage in a royal house, when the wife renounces inheritance in their father's rank and property for her children, who, however, are legitimate.
morgue, *n.*, a French mortuary.
mor'ibund, *adj.*, in a dying condition.
moril'lon, *n.*, a choice dark grape.
mo'rion, *n.*, a visorless helmet.
Moris'co, *adj.*, Moresque; *n.*, a Moorish dance.
Mor'mon, *n.*, an adherent of the Mormon sect; *adj.*, rel. to Mormonism.

Mor'monism, *n.*, the principles of the Mormons; polygamy.
Mor'monite, *n.*, *i.q.* Mormon.
morn, *n.*, the earliest part of day.
morn'ing, *n.*, *i.q.* morn.
morn'ing-star, *n.*, Venus.
moroc'co, *n.*, a fine leather from Morocco.
morone', *n.*, a dark crimson.
morose', *adj.*, surly, sullen.
morose'ly, *adv.*, surlily.
morose'ness, *n.*, surliness.
Mor'pheus, *n.*, the god of sleep.
mor'phia, *n.*, the narcotic principle of opium.
mor'phine, *n.*, *i.q.* morphia.
mor'phinism, *n.*, the morphine habit.
morpholog'ic, *adj.*, pert. to morphology.
morpholog'ical, *adj.*, *i.q.* morphologic.
morpholog'ically, *adv.*, in a morphological sense.
morphol'ogy, *n.*, the science of forms.
mor'ris, *n.*, a rustic (originally, Moorish) dance.
mor'ris-dance, *n.*, *i.q.* morris.
mor'ris-pike, *n.*, a (supposed) Moorish pike.
mor'row, *n.*, morning; the day after today.
morse, *n.*, a clasp or brooch; the walrus.
mor'sel, *n.*, a small portion or bite.
mort, *n.*, the huntsman's note sounded when a deer is killed; a salmon in its third year.
mor'tal, *adj.*, subject to death, deadly; *n.*, a human being.
mortal'ity, *n.*, the state of being mortal; death.

mor'tar, *v.t.*, to cement with mortar; *n.*, a vessel for pounding; a piece of ordnance; cement.

mort'gage, *v.t.*, to make over to a creditor as security; *n.*, a grant or deed of property as security.

mort'gaged, *p.p.*, mortgage.

mortgagee', *n.*, one to whom a mortgage is given.

mort'gager, *n.*, one who gives a mortgage.

mort'gaging, *pr.p.*, mortgage.

mort'gagor, *n.*, *s.q.* mortgager.

mortif'erous, *adj.*, deadly.

mortifica'tion, *n.*, the effect of mortifying; gangrene; chagrin, humiliation.

mor'tified, *p.p.*, mortify.

mor'tify, *v.t.*, to humiliate, cause chagrin to; *v.i.*, to gangrene or decay.

mor'tifying, *pr.p.*, mortify; *adj.*, humiliating.

mor'tise, *v.t.*, to make a mortise in; *n.*, a hole in timber for the reception of a tenon or a lock.

mor'tised, *p.p.*, mortise.

mor'tising, *pr.p.*, mortise.

mort'main, *n.*, inalienable tenure; the state in which inalienable property is held.

mor'tuary, *n.*, a dead-house, charnel.

mo'rus, *n.*, the mulberry (*Lat.*).

Mosa'ic, *adj.*, rel. to Moses.

mosa'ic, *n.*, inlaid work of coloured glass or stones.

moschatel', *n.*, a plant with musk-like scent.

Moselle', *n.*, the river so named; a white wine.

Mos'lem, *n.*, a Mussulman; *adj.*, Mohammedan.

mosque, *n.*, a Mohammedan temple.

mosqui'to, *n.*, a variety of gnat.

moss, *n.*, a lichen; a morass.

moss'clad, *adj.*, overgrown with moss.

moss'iness, *n.*, the state of being mossy.

moss'-trooper, *n.*, a freebooter of the Scottish border.

moss'y, *adj.*, covered with moss; like moss.

most, *adj.*, greatest in quantity or number; *adv.*, the sign of the superlative degree; in the highest degree.

most'ly, *adv.*, for the most part.

mot, *n.*, a witticism (*Fr.*).

mote, *n.*, a small speck; a council.

moth, *n.*, a genus of nocturnal insects.

moth'-eaten, *adj.*, eaten by moths; decayed.

moth'er, *v.t.*, to be a mother to; *adj.*, in the relation of a mother; *n.*, a female parent.

moth'erhood, *n.*, a mother's office; maternity.

moth'ering, *pr.p.*, mother; *n.*, acting as a mother; celebrating Mothering Sunday.

moth'er-in-law, *n.*, a wife's or husband's mother.

moth'erless, *adj.*, without a mother.

mother'ly, *adj.*, like a mother.

moth'er-of-pearl, *n.*, a hard internal layer in shells.

moth'er tongue, *n.*, native speech; the vernacular.

moth'er-wit, *n.*, natural intelligence.

moth'y, *adj.*, infested with moths.

motif, *n.*, a musical subject (*Fr.*).

mo'tion, *v.i.*, to make a sign with head or hand; *n.*, movement, a proposal; action; course.

mo'tioned, *p.p.*, motion.

mo'tioning, *pr.p.*, motion.

mo'tionless, *adj.*, without movement.

mo'tive, *adj.*, causing movement; *n.*, that which is actuated; actuating purpose.

motiv'ity, *n.*, the quality of being motive.

mot'ley, *adj.*, of mixed colours; heterogeneous; *n.*, a coat of mixed colours, as worn by a jester.

mot'mot, *n.*, a S. American bird.

mo'tor, *n.*, a source of power; a machine actuated by steam, electricity, or oil.

mo'tor-bus, *n.*, an omnibus run with a motor.

mo'tor-car, *n.*, a car run with a motor.

mo'tor-cy'cle, *n.*, a cycle run with a motor.

moto'rial, *adj.*, rel. to motors.

mo'torist, *n.*, a motor-driver.

mo'tory, *adj.*, *s.q.* motorial.

mot'tle, *v.t.*, to mark with mottles; *n.*, an arrangement of various colours; a blotch.

mot'tled, *adj.*, speckled, blotched; *p.p.*, mottle.

mot'to, *n.*, a maxim; a sentence or quotation prefixed to a chapter, essay, book, etc., or appended to a coat of arms.

mouf'flon, *n.*, a mountain sheep.

mould, *v.t.*, to fashion, shape, model; *n.*, a matrix, shape; a spot; loose earth; fine surface soil; a fungus growth.

mould'able, *adj.*, able to be moulded.

mould'ed, *p.p.*, mould.

mould'er, *n.*, one who moulds; *v.i.*, to crumble away.

mould'ered, *p.p.*, moulder

mould'ering, *pr.p.*, moulder.
mould'iness, *n.*, the quality of being mouldy.
mould'ing, *pr.p.*, mould; *n.*, a term denoting the form of moulded objects, esp. in architecture.
mould'y, *adj.*, decaying with mould.
moult, *v.i.*, to shed feathers.
moult'ed, *p.p.*, moult.
moult'ing, *pr.p.*, moult; *n.*, the act or period of moulting.
mound, *v.t.*, to bank up; *n.*, an artificial bank.
mount, *v.t.*, to climb, ascend, get up on; to lend a horse to; to set up; *n.*, a mountain or hill; that on which something (*e.g.*, a picture) is mounted; a horse for riding.
mount'able, *adj.*, able to be mounted.
moun'tain, *n.*, a large hill.
moun'tain ash, *n.*, a tree with red berries
mountaineer', *v.i.*, to climb mountains; *n.*, a mountain climber; a dweller in mountains.
moun'tainous, *adj.*, pert. to a mountain; full of mountains.
mount'ebank, *n.*, a quack, impostor.
mount'ed, *p.p.*, mount
mount'er, *n.*, one who mounts.
mount'ing, *pr.p.*, mount; *n.*, the setting of a picture, etc.
mourn, *v.t.*, to grieve for; *v.i.*, to be sorrowful.
mourned, *p.p.*, mourn.
mourn'er, *n.*, one who mourns.
mourn'ful, *adj.*, sad, sorrowful.
mourn'fully, *adv.*, sadly.
mourn'fulness, *n.*, the state of being mournful.
mourn'ing, *pr.p.*, mourn; *n.*, a state of sorrow; funeral dress.
mourn'ing-ring, *n.*, a ring commemorating a dead person.
mouse, *v.i.*, to catch mice; *n.*, a small rodent.
moused, *p.p.*, mouse.
mouse'-ear, *n.*, hawkweed.
mous'er, *n.*, a cat good at catching mice.
mouse'-hole, *n.*, a hole by which a mouse passes to and fro.
mouse'-trap, *n.*, a trap for catching mice.
mous'ing, *pr.p.*, mouse.
moustache', *n.*, hair on the human upper lip.
mous'y, *adj.*, mouse-like; infested with mice.
mouth, *n.*, the orifice in a head through which food and speech pass; any orifice or opening, as the mouth of a river, etc.
mouth, *v.t.*, to speak words pompously; to take food with the mouth; *v.i.*, to grimace.
mouthed, *p.p.*, mouth.
mouth'er, *n.*, one who mouths.
mouth'ful, *n.*, the quantity that will fill a mouth.
mouth'ing, *pr. p.*, mouth.
mouth'piece, *n.*, that part of an instrument, pipe, etc., that is put into the mouth; one who speaks for another.
mouth'y, *adj.*, bombastic; ranting.
mov'able, move'able, *adj.*, able to be moved.
mov'ables, *n. pl.*, furniture, belongings.
move, *v.t.*, to put in motion; change the position of; to agitate; to put a resolution; *v.i.*, to change one's position; to propose; *n.*, an act of moving; the moving of a piece in chess, etc.; a scheme.
moved, *p.p.*, move.
move'less, *adj.*, motionless.
move'ment, *n.*, the act of moving; motional part in a machine; a tendency or fashion in thought; a division of a musical work; any kind of activity.
mov'er, *n.*, one who moves.
mov'ing, *pr.p.*, move; *adj.*, affecting.
mov'ingly, *adv.*, in an affecting way.
mow, *n.*, a stack of barley, hay, etc.; a store for these.
mow, *v.t.*, to cut down.
mow, *v.i.*, to grimace.
mow'er, *n.*, one who mows.
mow'ing, *pr.p.*, mow.
mown, *p.p.*, mow.
***Mr.*,** *n.*, the ordinary title prefixed to a man's name. A corruption of *Master*, and pronounced *Mister*.
Mrs., *n.*, the ordinary title of a married woman. Abbreviated from *Mistress*.
***much*,** *adj.* and *adv.*, in great quantity or degree.
much'ness, *n.*, greatness of degree or quantity.
mu'cid, *adj.*, slimy.
mu'ciform, *adj.*, like mucus.
mu'cilage, *n.*, gummy extract; gum.
mucilag'inous, *adj.*, of the nature of mucilage.
mucip'arous, *adj.*, producing mucus.
muck, *v.t.*, to dirty; *n.*, wet dung; dirt.
muck'er, *n.*, a bad cropper (*slang*).
muck'heap, *n.*, a dunghill.
muck'worm, *n.*, a larva found in dung-heaps.
muck'y, *adj.*, dirty.
mu'coid, *adj.*, like mucus.
mucos'ity, *n.*, the state of being mucous.
mu'cous, *adj.*, rel. to mucus.

mu'cronate, *adj.*, pointed.

mu'culent, *adj.*, slimy.

mu'cus, *n.*, a slimy secretion.

mud, *n.*, soft, wet earth; mire.

mud'dily, *adv.*, in a muddy way.

mud'diness, *n.*, the state of being muddy.

mud'dle, *v.t.*, to confuse; to mix up; *v.i.*, to do things in an ineffectual way.

mud'dled, *p.p.*, muddle.

mud'dler, *n.*, one who muddles.

mud'dling, *pr.p.*, muddle; *adj.*, confusing, perplexing.

mud'dy, *adj.*, stained with mud; in a state of mud; confused; dark; *v.t.*, to cover with mud.

muez'zin, *n.*, the Mohammedan who calls the hours of prayer from the minaret of a mosque.

muff, *n.*, a covering for the hands to keep them warm; a dull, clumsy person; a bungler; *v.t.*, to bungle at anything.

muf'fin, *n.*, a light kind of tea-cake.

muffineer', *n.*, a sugar or salt-castor.

muf'fle, *v.t.*, to wrap or cover up; to deaden (sound); *n.*, the upper lip of certain animals; a leather glove; a compartment in a pottery kiln.

muf'fled, *p.p.*, muffle.

muf'fler, *n.*, a wrap for the throat or mouth; anything that muffles.

muf'fling, *pr.p.*, muffle.

muf'ti, *n.*, a Mohammedan teacher of the law; civilian dress worn by a naval or military man.

mug, *n.*, a vessel for drinking; a silly person (*slang*); *v.i.*, to work hard at a subject; *v.t.*, to study hard (*slang*).

mug'ger, *n.*, an Indian crocodile so named.

mug'get, *n.*, the lily-of-the-valley.

Muggleto'nian, *n.*, an adherent of the Muggleton sect.

mug'gy, *adj.*, close, damp and warm.

mug'wump, *n.*, a man who holds himself superior to party.

mulat'to, *adj.*, tawny; *n.*, one of mixed parentage — European and negro.

mul'berry, *n.*, a fruit-bearing tree so named; the fruit of the same.

mulch, *n.*, litter.

mulched, *adj.*, having mulch spread.

mulct, *v.t.*, to fine; to take away from; *n.*, a fine.

mulct'ed, *p.p.*, mulct.

mulct'ing, *pr.p.*, mulct.

mulc'tuary, *adj.*, mulcting.

mule, *n.*, the offspring of a horse and an ass; any hybrid creature.

muleteer', *n.*, a mule driver.

mulieb'rity, *n.*, the womanish state or quality.

mu'lish, *adj.*, mule-like, stubborn.

mu'lishness, *n.*, stubbornness.

mull, *v.t.*, to concoct with sugar, spice, etc., into a drink; to make a muddle of (*slang*); *n.*, a failure (*slang*).

mull'ah, *n.*, a teacher of Mohammedan religion and law.

mulled, *p.p.*, mull.

mul'ler, *n.*, a sort of pestle.

mul'let, *n.*, a fish so named.

mulligataw'ny, *n.*, an E. Indian soup.

mul'ling, *pr.p.*, mull.

mul'lion, *n.*, a vertical division in a window.

multan'gular, *adj.*, having many angles.

multe'ity, *n.*, the quality of being numerous.

multiartic'ulate, *adj.*, many-jointed.

multicap'sular, *adj.*, many-capsuled.

multiden'tate, *adj.*, many-toothed.

multifa'rious, *adj.*, very various.

multifa'riously, *adv.*, in a variety of ways.

mul'tifid, *adj.*, with many clefts.

multiflo'rous, *adj.*, having more than three flowers.

mul'tifold, *adj.*, manifold.

mul'tiform, *adj.*, having many shapes.

multiform'ity, *n.*, the state of being multiform.

multilat'eral, *adj.*, many-sided.

multilin'eal, *adj.*, many-lined.

multil'oquence, *n.*, a flow of speech.

multil'oquent, *adj.*, speaking much.

multino'mial, *adj.*, having more than two terms.

multip'arous, *adj.*, having a numerous offspring.

multipar'tite, *adj.*, having many parts.

mul'tiped, *adj.*, many-footed.

mul'tiplane, *adj.*, having many planes.

mul'tiple, *adj.*, composed of many parts, etc.; *n.*, a quantity which exactly contains another so many times.

mul'tiplex, *adj.*, manifold.

mul'tipliable, *adj.*, able to be multiplied.

multiplicand', *n.*, a quantity to be multiplied.

mul'tiplicate, *adj.*, many-folded; composed of more than one.

multiplica'tion, *n.*, multiplying.

mul'tiplicative, *adj.*, multiplying.

mul'tiplicator, *n.*, the multiplying number.

multiplic'ity, *n.*, great variety.

mul'tiplied, *p.p.*, multiply.

mul'tiplier, *n.*, one who, or that which, multiplies.

mul'tiply, *v.t.*, to increase the number of; *v.i.*, to grow in number.

mul'tiplying, *pr.p.*, multiply.

multip'otent, *adj.*, very powerful.

multira'diate, *adj.*, having many rays.

multis'onous, *adj.*, loud-sounding; giving forth many sounds.

multispi'ral, *adj.*, with many rings.

mul'titude, *n.*, number; a crowd; the mob.

multitu'dinary, *adj.*, numerous.

multitu'dinous, *adj.*, numerous.

mul'tivalve, *adj.*, many-valved.

multival'vular, *adj.*, *i.q.* multivalve.

Multo'ca, *n.*, the Mohammedan legal code.

multoc'ular, *adj.*, many-eyed.

mum, *adj.*, silent; *v.i.*, to be silent; to play a mummer's part.

mum'ble, *v.t.* and *i.*, to utter indistinctly; to chew toothlessly.

mum'bled, *p.p.*, mumble.

mum'bler, *n.*, one who mumbles.

mum'bling, *pr.p.*, mumble.

mum'bo-jum'bo, *n.*, a hideous idol greatly venerated.

mummed, *p.p.*, mum.

mum'mer, *n*, a play-actor; buffoon.

mum'mery, *n.*, play-acting by mummers (esp. mystery and morality plays); buffoonery.

mummifica'tion, *n.*, the act or effect of mummifying.

mum'mified, *p.p.*, mummify.

mum'miform, *adj.*, like a mummy.

mum'mify, *v.t.*, to embalm as a mummy.

mum'ming, *pr.p.*, mum; *n.*, *i.q.* mummery.

mum'my, *n.*, an embalmed human body; a brown pigment; a child's pet name for mother.

mump, *v.i.*, to be sullenly silent; to be a beggar.

mumped, *p.p.*, mump.

mump'er, *n.*, one who mumps.

mump'ing, *pr.p.*, mump.

mump'ish, *adj.*, inclined to sulk.

mumps, *n. pl.*, a glandular disease of the neck; the sulks.

munch, *v.t.*, to chew.

munched, *p.p.*, munch

munch'er, *n.*, one who munches.

munch'ing, *pr.p.*, munch.

mun'dane, *adj.*, rel. to the world; worldly.

mun'datory, *adj.*, purifying; *n.*, a purificator for cleansing the chalice.

mundifica'tion, *n.*, cleansing.

mundif'icative, *adj.*, cleansing.

mun'go, *n.*, a superior sort of shoddy.

munic'ipal, *adj.*, bel. to a city or borough.

municipal'ity, *n.*, a self-governing town.

munif'icence, *n.*, splendid liberality.

munif'icent, *adj.*, giving generously.

munif'icently, *adv.*, with munificence.

mu'niment, *n.*, support; defence; a document.

mu'niment-room, *n.*, a place where documents are carefully kept.

muni'tion, *n.*, war materials; *v.t.*, to supply with munitions.

munjeet', *n.*, an E. Indian dye.

mun'nion, *n.*, *i.q* mullion.

mu'ral, *adj.*, rel. to a wall.

mur'der, *v.t.*, to kill with malice prepense; to slay; to spoil badly; *n.*, the act of murdering in all senses.

mur'dered, *p.p.*, murder.

mur'derer, *n.*, one who murders.

mur'deress, *n.*, fem. of murderer.

mur'dering, *pr.p.*, murder.

mur'derous, *adj.*, with intent to murder; of the nature of murder.

mur'derously, *adv.*, in a murderous way.

mu'riate, *n.*, chloride.

mu'riated, *adj.*, pickled; treated with chloride.

muriat'ic, *adj.*, of the nature of brine.

mu'ricate, *adj.*, rough-surfaced.

mu'ricated, *adj.*, *i.q.* muricate.

mu'riform, *adj.*, mouse-like.

mu'rine, *adj.*, rel. to mice.

murk, *adj.*, dark.

murk'ily, *adv.*, in a murky way.

murk'y, *adj.*, dark, gloomy.

mur'mur, *v.i.* and *t.*, to make a low sound; to mutter; *n.*, continued complaint; softly spoken word.

mur'mured, *p.p.*, murmur.

mur'murer, *n.*, one who murmurs.

mur'muring, *pr.p.*, murmur.

mur'murous, *adj.*, murmur-like.

mur'phy, *n.*, potato.

mur'rain, *n.*, a cattle-disease.

mur'rhine, mur'rine, *adj.*, made of fine glass.

mur'za, *n.*, a lower rank of Tartar nobility.

muscadel', *n.*, *i.q.* muscatel.

mus'cadine, *n.*, a grape with musk-like flavour.

muscar'dine, *n.*, a disease among silk-worms.

mus'cat, *n.*, a variety of grape; a wine made from muscadines.

muscatel', *n.*, the muscadine raisin.

mus'cle, *n.*, the fleshy contractile fibre in animals.

mus'cled, *adj.*, having muscles.

mus'coid, *adj.*, like moss.

muscol'ogy, *n.*, the science of mosses.

mus'cose, *adj.*, mossy.

muscos'ity, *n.*, mossiness.

muscova'do, *n.*, unrefined sugar.

Mus'covite, *adj.* and *n.*, Russian.

mus'cular, *adj.*, strong; rel. to muscles.

muscular'ity, *n.*, strength of muscle.

mus'culous, *adj.*, *i.q.* muscular.

muse, *v.i.*, to meditate; be pensive; *n.*, one of the nine nymphs who inspired the arts.

mused, *p.p.*, muse.

muse'ful, *n.*, silently thoughtful.

mu'ser, *n.*, one who muses.

muse'um, *n.*, a building or cabinet where curiosities are stored.

mush, *n.*, soft pulp; a food of maize meal.

mush'room, *n.*, an edible fungus; anything of rapid growth; *v.i.*, to go gathering mushrooms.

mu'sic, *n.*, the science of beautiful sound; melodious or harmonious sound.

mu'sical, *adj.*, rel. to music; melodious or harmonious.

mu'sically, *adv.*, in a melodious way.

mu'sic-hall, *n.*, a place where music is performed.

musi'cian, *n.*, one who composes or performs music.

mu'sic-master, *n.*, a teacher of music.

mu'sic-stool, *n.*, a seat for a player.

mu'sing, *pr.p.*, muse.

musk, *n.*, a strong-scented substance secreted by the musk-deer.

mus'ket, *n.*, an infantryman's gun.

musketeer', *n.*, one armed with a musket.

musketoon', *n.*, an old type of cavalry musket.

mus'ket-proof, *adj.*, resisting a musket-bullet.

mus'ketry, *n.*, muskets collectively; the art of shooting.

musk'iness, *n.*, the quality of being musky.

musk'-rat, *n.*, a N. American rodent.

musk'y, *adj.*, smelling of musk.

mus'lin *n.*, a fine cotton cloth; *adj.*, made of muslin.

muslinet(te)', *n.*, a thick muslin.

mus'quash, *n.*, *i.q.* musk-rat.

muss, *n.*, a mess; a squabble; *v.t.*, to disarrange (*Amer.*).

mus'sel, *n.*, a species of bivalve.

Mus'sulman, *adj.* and *n.*, Mohammedan.

must, *n.*, mouldiness; new unfermented wine; *v. aux.*, to be obliged to, or necessary.

mustache', *n.*, hair on the upper lip. Also *moustache.*

mustach'io, *n.*, a moustache.

mustach'ioed, *adj.*, wearing a moustache.

mus'tang, *n.*, a wild Californian or Mexican horse.

mus'tard, *n.*, a plant so named and its seed, used for various purposes.

mus'teline, *adj.*, rel. to weasels.

mus'ter, *v.t.* and *i.*, to assemble; to summon; *n.*, an assembling.

mus'tered, *p.p.*, muster.

mus'tering. *pr.p.*, muster.

mus'ter-roll, *n.*, a list of forces.

mus'tily, *adv.*, in a musty way.

mus'tiness, *n.*, the state or quality of being musty.

mus'ty, *adj.*, affected with mould; spoiled by damp or age.

mutabil'ity, *n.*, a liability to change.

mu'table, *adj.*, changeable.

mu'tably, *adv.*, in a mutable way.

mu'tage, *n.*, an arresting process in wine-fermentation.

mutate', *v.t.* and *i.*, to alter, change.

muta'ted, *p.p.*, mutate.

muta'tion, *n.*, change; the process of changing.

mute, *adj.*, dumb, silent; *n.*, one who is dumb; a hired mourner; *n.*, a contrivance for reducing the sound of musical instruments.

mute'ly, *adv.*, silently.

mute'ness, *n.*, speechlessness.

mu'tilate, *v.t.*, to deprive of a limb; to damage by cutting, etc.

mu'tilated, *p.p.*, mutilate.

mu'tilating. *pr.p.*, mutilate.

mutila'tion, *n.*, the act or effect of mutilating.

mu'tilator, *n.*, one who mutilates.

mutineer', *n.*, one who mutinies.

mu'tinied, *p.p.*, mutiny.

mu'tinous, *adj.*, guilty of, or inclined to, mutiny.

mu'tinously, *adv.*, in a mutinous way.

mu'tiny, *v.i.*, to rise against naval or military authority; *n.*, a revolt of sailors or soldiers.

mu'tinying, *pr.p.*, mutiny.

mu'tism, *n.*, dumbness.

mut'ter, *v.t.* and *i.*, to speak under one's

breath; to grumble: *n.*, muttered words.

mut'tered, *p.p.*, mutter.

mut'terer, *n.*, one who mutters.

mut'tering, *pr.p.*, mutter.

mut'ton, *n.*, the flesh of sheep.

mu'tual, *adj.*, reciprocal; in relation to one another.

mutual'ity, *n.*, the quality of being mutual.

mu'tually, *adv.*, reciprocally.

mu'tule, *n.*, a detail of a Doric cornice.

muz'zle, *v.t.*, to fasten the mouth; to silence (a person); *n.*, an animal's mouth; a fastening for the mouth.

muz'zled, *p.p.*, muzzle.

muz'zle-loader, *n.*, a gun loaded from the muzzle end.

muz'zling, *pr.p.*, muzzle.

my, *possess. adj.*, of, or belonging to, me.

my'all-wood, *n.*, a kind of acacia-wood.

mycolog'ic, *adj.*, rel. to mycology.

mycol'ogist, *n.*, a student of mycology.

mycol'ogy, *n.*, the study of fungi.

mynheer', *n.*, a Dutchman.

myog'raphy, *n.*, scientific description of muscles.

myolog'ic, *adj.*, rel. to myology.

myol'ogist, *n.*, a student of myology.

myolog'ical, *adj.*, *i.q.* myologic.

myol'ogy, *n.*, the science of the muscles.

my'ope, *n.*, a short-sighted person.

myo'pia, *n.*, short-sightedness.

myo'pic, *adj.*, short-sighted.

my'opy, *n.*, *i.q.* myopia.

my'osin, *n.*, a substance in muscular tissue.

myo'sis, *n.*, contraction of the pupil.

myosit'ic, *adj.*, pert. to myosis.

myot'omy, *n.*, dissection of the muscles.

myr'iad, *adj.* and *n.*, ten thousand; a number indefinitely large.

myr'iagram(me), *n.*, a weight of 10,000 grams.

myr'ialitre, myr'ialiter, *n.*, a measure of 10,000 litres.

myr'iametre, myr'iameter, *n.*, a measure of 10,000 metres.

myr'iapod, *n.* and *adj.*, many-legged.

myriora'ma, *n.*, a succession of views or pictures.

myr'ioscope, *n.*, a sort of kaleidoscope.

myr'midon, *n.*, a rough soldier; hired ruffian.

myrob'alan, *n.*, a sort of plum used by tanners and dyers.

myrrh, *n.*, an inspissated sap variously used.

myr'rhine, *adj.*, rel. to myrrh.

myr'tiform, *adj.*, like myrtle.

myr'tle, *n.*, a shrub so named.

myself', *pron.*, reflexive and emphatic.

mys'tagogue, *n.*, one who teaches mysteries.

myste'rious, *adj.*, full of mystery; obscure.

myste'riously, *adv.*, in a mysterious way.

mys'tery, *n.*, a sacrament; an esoteric truth; a deep religious rite; a secret; a handicraft.

mys'tic, *adj.*, rel. to mystery; *n.*, one who seeks communion with God in contemplation.

mys'tical, *adj.*, *i.q.* mystic; mysterious; secret.

mys'tically, *adv.*, in a mystical way.

mys'ticism, *n.*, the practice of the mystics.

mystifica'tion, *n.*, the act or result of mystifying.

mys'tified, *p.p.*, mystify.

mys'tify, *v.t.*, to render obscure or perplexing; to puzzle.

mys'tifying, *pr.p.*, mystify.

myth, *n.*, a fictitious story; a fable.

myth'ic, *adj.*, rel. to myth.

myth'ical, *adj.*, *i.q.* mythic.

myth'ically, *adv.*, in a mythical way.

mythog'rapher, *n.*, a myth-writer.

mythog'raphy, *n.*, the writing of myths.

mythol'oger, *n.*, an expert in mythology.

mytholog'ic, *adj.*, pert. to mythology.

mytholog'ical, *adj.*, *i.q.* mythologic.

mytholog'ically, *adv.*, in a mythological way.

mythol'ogist, *n.*, *i.q.* mythologer.

mythol'ogize, *v.t.*, to turn into myth; *v.i.*, to explain myth.

mythol'ogizing, *pr.p.*, mythologize.

mythol'ogy, *n.*, the study of myths; myths collectively.

myth'oplasm, *n.*, the earliest source of myth.

my'thus, *n.*, myth (*Lat.*).

N

nab, *v.t.*, to arrest (*slang*).

nabbed, *p.p.*, nab.

nab'bing, *pr.p.*, nab.

na'bob, *n.*, a Mogul governor; a wealthy retired Anglo-Indian.

nac'arat, *n.*, orange-red.

na'cre, *n.*, mother-o'-pearl.

nacré', *adj.*, like nacre; nacreous (*Fr.*).

na'creous, *adj.*, rel. to nacre.

na'dir, *n.*, the lowest point in the sky (the opposite to the zenith); any lowest point.

nae'vose, *adj.*, freckled.

nag, *v.i.*, to scold incessantly; *n.*, a small riding horse; a horse.

nagged, *p.p.*, nag.

nag'ging, *pr.p.*, nag; *n.*, incessant fault-finding.

Nai'ad, *n.*, a water-nymph.

naïf, *adj.*, *see* naïve.

nail, *v.t.*, to fasten with a nail, to secure; *n.*, the horny growth on the finger-ends; a piece of metal driven in with a hammer.

nail'-brush, *n.*, a brush for the finger-nails.

nailed, *p.p.*, nail.

nail'er, *n.*, a nail-maker; a consummately clever person (*slang*).

nail'ery, *n.*, a nail factory.

nail'ing, *pr.p.*, nail; *adj.*, excellent; supremely skilful (*slang*).

nail'-scissors, *n.*, scissors for trimming finger-nails.

nain'sook, *n.*, a fine cotton material.

naïve', **naive'**, *adj.*, simple, artless.

naïve'ly, *adv.*, artlessly.

naïveté', *n.*, artlessness, simplicity.

na'ked, *adj.*, bare, unclothed, plain.

na'kedly, *adv.*, in a naked way.

na'kedness, *n.*, the state of being naked.

nam'by-pam'by, *adj.*, affected, insipid, soft; *n.*, sentimental, affected talk.

name, *v.t.*, to give a name to; call by a name; to quote, specify, appoint; *n.*, an identifying word or title; reputation; a virtually non-existent thing.

na'm(e)able, *adj.*, fit to be named.

named, *p.p.*, name.

name'less, *adj.*, without a name; inglorious; unnamable.

name'ly, *adv.*, that is to say.

na'mer, *n.*, one who names.

name'sake, *n.*, one called by one's own name.

na'ming, *pr.p.*, name.

nankeen', *n.*, a yellow cotton fabric; pale buff colour.

Nantes, *n.*, brandy. Also *Nants*.

nap, *v.i.*, to take a short, slight sleep; to doze; *v.t.*, to put a nap on (cloth); *n.*, a short sleep; a raised surface; a card-game.

nape, *n.*, the back of the neck.

na'pery, *n.*, table linen.

naph'tha, *n.*, an inflammable oil.

naphthal'ic, *adj.*, rel. to naphtha.

naph'thaline, *n.*, a solid crystalline hydrocarbon.

na'piform, *adj.*, turnip-like.

nap'kin, *n.*, a square of linen; a small towel.

Napo'leon, *n.*, a French coin = 20 francs.

Napoleon'ic, *adj.*, rel. to, or resembling, Napoleon I.

nap'piness, *n.*, the quality of being nappy.

nap'ping, *pr.p.*, nap.

nap'py, *adj.*, foaming, heady.

Narcis'sus, *n.*, the son of Cephisus, the classical river god. At the sight of his own reflection in water, he faded away, and was changed into a flower (narcissus).

narco'sis, *n.*, the result of using a narcotic.

narcot'ic, *adj.*, inducing sleep or torpor; *n.*, a narcotic drug.

narcot'ical, *adj.*, *s.q.* narcotic.

nar'cotine, *n.*, a drug used in fevers.

nar'cotism, *n.*, the narcotized state.

nar'cotize, *v.t.*, to bring under narcotic influence.

nar'cotized, *p.p.*, narcotize.

nar'cotizing, *pr.p.*, narcotize.

nard, *n.*, ointment, spikenard.

nardine, *adj.*, rel. to nard.

na'res, *n.*, the nostrils (*Lat.*).

nar'ghile, *n.*, an Eastern tobacco pipe; a hookah.

narrate', *v.t.*, to relate, recite.

narra'ted, *p.p.*, narrate.

narra'ting, *pr.p.*, narrate.

narra'tion, *n.*, the act of narrating.

nar'rative, *n.*, a story, history; *adj.*, in the form of narration.

narra'tor, *n.*, a story-teller.

nar'row, *v.t.*, to reduce in width; *v.i.*, to be so reduced; *adj.*, small in width; cramped; illiberal; scrutinizing closely; *n.*, a strait.

nar'rowed, *p.p.*, narrow.

nar'rower, *adj., comp.* of narrow.

nar'rowest, *adj., super.* of narrow.

nar'rowing, *pr.p.*, narrow.

nar'rowly, *adv.*, with small breadth; parsimoniously; with close scrutiny.

nar'row-minded, *adj.*, illiberal, bigoted.

nar'row-mind'edness, *n.*, bigotry, illiberality.

nar'rowness, *n.*, lack of breadth.

nar'thex, *n.*, a vestibule; the part of a Christian basilica near the entrance, to which catechumens and penitents were restricted.

nar'whal, *n.*, an Arctic cetacean, with two teeth formed into one long tusk.

na'sal, *adj.*, rel. to the nose; *n.*, a nasal letter or sound (*i.e.*, pronounced through the nose).

nasal'ity, *n.*, the nasal quality.

nasaliza'tion, *n.*, giving a nasal sound.

na'salize, *v.t.*, to give a nasal sound to.

na'salized, *p.p.*, nasalize.

na'salizing, *pr.p.*, nasalize.

na'sally, *adv.*, through the nose.

nas'cent, *adj.*, beginning to be born.

na'sicornous, *adj.*, having a horn on the nose.

na'siform, *adj.*, in the form of a nose.

nasol'ogy, *n.*, the study of the nose.

nas'tier, *adj., comp.* of nasty.

nas'tiest, *adj., super.* of nasty.

nas'tily, *adv.*, in a nasty way.

nas'tiness, *n.*, the state or quality of being nasty.

nastur'tium, *n.*, a plant of the water-cress type; a garden plant with spurred flowers.

nas'ty, *adj.*, disgusting, dirty, ill-natured.

na'tal, *adj.*, rel. to birth.

natali'tial, *adj.*, rel. to a birthday.

na'tant, *adj.*, floating.

nata'tion, *n.*, swimming.

natato'rial, *adj.*, rel. to the Natatores or to swimming.

Natato'res, *n. pl.*, web-footed birds.

na'tatory, *adj.*, *i.q.* natatorial.

nath'less, *adv.*, nevertheless.

na'tion, *n.*, an individual people or race, of common origin, customs, and language; a state.

na'tional, *adj.*, rel. to a nation; *n.*, a member of a nation.

na'tionalism, *n.*, patriotism; the policy of national independence; the policy of nationalizing industry.

national'ity, *n.*, the quality of being national; membership of a nation; an independent people.

nationaliza'tion, *n.*, the act of nationalizing.

na'tionalize, *v.t.*, to make national; to make into a nation; to subject to the nation's control.

na'tionalized, *p.p.*, nationalize.

na'tionalizing, *pr.p.*, nationalize.

na'tionally, *n.*, by the nation collectively.

na'tionhood, *n.*, the condition of being a nation.

na'tive, *adj.*, born in a given place; indigenous; inherited; *n.*, one born in a place named; the cultivated oyster.

nativ'ity, *n.*, birth; a representation in art of Our Lord's Birth; a horoscope.

na'tron, *n.*, native sesquicarbonate of soda.

nat'ter-jack, *n.*, a variety of toad.

nat'tily, *adv.*, in a natty way.

nat'ty, *adj.*, trim, dainty.

nat'ural, *adj.*, according to nature; instinctive; unaffected, simple; not artificial; not sharped or flatted; *n.*, a note not marked as a sharp or flat; a white note on a keyboard; a born idiot.

nat'uralism, *n.*, conduct based on natural instincts; religious and philosophic theories opposed to supernaturalism.

nat'uralist, *n.*, a student of nature.

naturalis'tic, *adj.*, rel. to naturalism or to natural history.

naturaliza'tion, *n.*, the act or result of naturalizing.

nat'uralize, *v.t.*, to admit an alien to citizenship; to make natural; *v.i.*, to pursue natural history.

nat'uralized, *p.p.*, naturalize.

nat'uralizing, *pr.p.*, naturalize.

nat'urally, *adv.*, in a natural way; of course.

nat'uralness, *n.*, the quality of being natural; freedom from artificiality.

na'ture, *n.*, the collective phenomena of the material universe; the collective forces underlying these phenomena; the essential qualities of a thing; the unregenerate state of man.

naught, *adj.*, of no value; *n.*, nothing, a cipher.

naugh'tier, *adj., comp.* of naughty.

naugh'tiest, *adj., super.* of naughty.

naugh'tily, *adv.*, in a naughty way.

naugh'tiness, *n.*, disobedience, wilfulness, depravity.

naugh'ty, *adj.*, disobedient, wilful, wicked.

nau'sea, *n.*, a feeling of qualm, loathing.

nau'seant, *adj.*, nauseating.

nau'seate, *v.t.*, to produce nausea; *v.i.*, to turn sick.

nau'seated, *p.p.*, nauseate.

nau'seating, *pr.p.*, nauseate.

nausea'tion, *n.*, the state of being nauseated.

nau'seous, *adj.*, causing loathing, nasty.

nautch, *n.*, an Indian dancing entertainment.

nautch'-girl, *n.*, a dancing-girl.

nau'tical, *adj.*, rel. to sailors and navigation.

nau'tilite, *n.*, a fossil like the nautilus.

nau'tilus, *n.*, a cephalopod.

na'val, *adj.*, rel. to a navy or ships.

na'varch, *n.*, a (Greek) admiral.

na'varchy, *n.*, an admiral's office; skill in naval command.

nave, *n.*, the hub of a wheel; the body of a church.

na'vel, *n.*, the scar on the abdomen where the umbilical cord was cut.

navette', *n.*, an incense-boat (*Fr.*).

navic'ular, *adj.*, boat-shaped.

navigabil'ity, *n.*, the state of being navigable.

nav'igable, *adj.*, admitting navigation.

nav'igate, *v.t.*, to sail, manage, steer; *v.i.*, to sail a ship, make a voyage.

nav'igated, *p.p.*, navigate.

nav'igating, *pr.p.*, navigate.

naviga'tion, *n.*, the act or science of navigating.

nav'igator, *n.*, one who navigates, or is skilled in navigating; an explorer; a navvy.

nav'vy, *n.*, a labourer in the construction of canals, railways, etc. (abbreviated from preceding word).

navy, *n.*, the ships and the whole naval service bel. to a State.

nawab', *n.*, an Indian nobleman.

nay, *adv.*, no; *n.*, a denial or refusal; a negative vote or voter.

Nazarene', *adj.*, rel. to Nazareth; *n.*, a native of Nazareth.

Naz'arite, *n.*, a Hebrew ascetic, wearing long hair and abstaining from wine.

Naz'aritism, *n.*, the vows or practices of a Nazarite.

naze, *n.*, a headland.

neap, *v.i.*, to tend towards neap; *v.t.*, to leave a ship aground till the next high tide; *adj.*, low, lowest; *n.*, a neap tide, lowest ebb.

Neapol'itan, *adj.*, rel. to Naples.

neap'tide, *n.*, *s.q.* neap.

near, *v.t.*, to approach; *v.i.*, to draw near; *adj.*, not far off, not distant; closely related; intimate; closely following; stingy; *adv.*, close by, nigh, closely; *prep.*, close by, not far from.

neared, *p.p.*, near.

near'er, *adj., comp.* of near.

near'est, *adj., super.* of near.

near'ing, *pr.p.*, near.

near'ly, *adv.*, almost, not quite, closely.

near'ness, *n.*, proximity; the state of being near.

near'sighted, *adj.*, short-sighted; myopic.

neat, *adj.*, nice, elegantly simple, trim, tidy, clever, net, undiluted; *adj.*, bovine; *n.*, any kind of ox.

neat'-cattle, *n.*, bovine cattle.

neat'er, *adj., comp.* of neat.

neat'est, *adj., super.* of neat.

neat'herd, *n.*, a cowherd.

neat'ly, *adv.*, in a neat way.

neat'ness, *n.*, the quality of being neat.

neb, *n.*, a beak, nose, tip.

neb'ula, *n.*, a star-cluster; a speck on the cornea.

neb'ular, *adj.*, rel. to nebulae.

neb'ule, *n.*, an architectural moulding.

nebulos'ity, *n.*, the quality of being nebulous.

neb'ulous, *adj.*, confused, hazy, nebular.

necessa'rian, *adj.* and *n.*, *see* necessitarian.

nec'essarily, *adv.*, of necessity, inevitably.

nec'essariness, *n.*, the quality of being necessary.

nec'essary, *adj.*, indispensable, requisite, compulsory, inevitably resulting; *n.*, an indispensable thing.

necessita'rian, *adj.*, denying the doctrine of free will; *n.*, one who asserts that everything results from antecedent causes and denies free will.

neces'sitate, *v.t.*, to render necessary or inevitable.

neces'sitated, *p.p.*, necessitate.

neces'sitating, *pr.p.*, necessitate.

neces'sitous, *adj.*, needy, in straitened circumstances.

neces'sity, *n.*, the quality of being necessary; inevitability; compulsion, want, hardship, urgent need.

neck, *n.*, the part connecting a head with a trunk; anything resembling a neck, as a neck of land; the neck of a bottle, etc.

neck'cloth, *n.*, a cravat, necktie.

neck'erchief, *n.*, a kerchief for the neck.

neck'lace, *n.*, a neck ornament.

neck'let, *n.*, an ornament or covering for the neck.

neck'tie, *n.*, a cravat.

necrol'atry, *n.*, ancestor-worship.

necrolog'ic, *adj.*, rel. to necrology.

necrolog'ical, *adj.*, *s.q.* necrologic.

necrol'ogist, *n.*, one who records the names of the dead.

necrol'ogy, *n.*, a list of the names of the dead.

nec'romancer, *n.*, one who practises necromancy.

nec'romancy, *n.*, magic, divination through intercourse with the dead.

necromantic, *adj.*, rel. to necromancy.

necrop'olis, *n.*, a cemetery.

necro'scopy, *n.*, autopsy; post-mortem.

necro'sis, *n.*, mortification, gangrene.

necrot'omy, *n.*, dissection.

nec'tar, *n.*, the drink of the gods; any delicious drink; the honey of plants.

necta'real, *adj.*, rel. to nectar; deliciously sweet.

necta'rean, *adj.*, *s.q.* nectareal.

necta'reous, *adj.*, *s.q.* nectareal.

nectarif'erous, *adj.*, honey-producing.

nec'tarine, *n.*, a variety of peach with a smooth skin.

nec'tarize, *v.t.*, to sweeten.

nec'tary, *n.*, a plant's organ that secretes honey.

né (mas.) *or* **née** (fem.), *adj.*, born (*Fr.*).

need, *v.t.*, to require, be in need of; *v.i.*, to be under the necessity of; *n.*, lack, want, emergency, a thing needed.

need'ed, *p.p.*, need.

need'er, *n.*, one who needs.

need'ful, *adj.*, needed, requisite.

need'ier, *adj.*, *comp.* of needy.

need'iest, *adj.*, *super.* of needy.

need'ily, *adv.*, in a needy way.

need'iness, *n.*, the quality of being needy.

need'ing, *pr.p.*, need.

nee'dle, *v.t.*, to sew; to form needle-like crystals; *v.i.*, to sew, to crystallize; *n.*, a pointed instrument used for sewing, knitting, etc.; a piece of magnetized steel used as the indicator of a compass, or magnetic or electric apparatus; an instrument for etching — and many other senses.

nee'dle-book, *n.*, a needle-case like a book.

nee'dleful, *n.*, as much thread as can well be used at once.

nee'dle-gun, *n.*, a gun fired by a blow from a spring-needle.

nee'dle-shaped, *adj.*, long, narrow, and sharp-pointed.

need'less, *adj.* unnecessary.

need'lessly, *adv.*, unnecessarily.

need'lessness, *n.*, the quality of being needless.

nee'dle-woman, *n.*, a seamstress.

nee'dlework, *n.*, work done with a needle.

needs, *adv.*, of necessity.

need'y, *adj.*, in want; necessitous.

ne'er, *adv.*, never.

nefa'rious, *adj.*, wicked, heinous.

nega'tion, *n.*, the act of denying; a denial; absence of something positive.

neg'ative, *v.t.*, to veto, contradict, disprove; *adj.*, not positive; expressing negation or subtraction; reversing lights and shades; *n.*, a negative expression or statement; right of veto; a photographic picture where the lights and shades are reversed.

neg'atived, *p.p.*, negative.

neg'atively, *adv.*, in a negative way or sense.

neglect', *v.t.*, to slight; not do; *n.*, negligence.

neglect'ed, *p.p.*, neglect.

neglect'er, *n.*, one who neglects.

***neglect'*ful,** *adj.*, remiss, careless.

neglect'ing *pr.p.*, neglect.

negligé', *n.*, unceremonious dress.

neg'ligence, *n.*, carelessness, remissness, disregard.

neg'ligent, *adj.*, careless, remiss.

neg'ligently, *adv.*, carelessly.

neg'ligible, *adj.*, able to be disregarded.

negotiabil'ity, *n.*, the quality of being negotiable.

nego'tiable, *adj.*, able to be negotiated.

nego'tiate, *v.t.*, to arrange, bring about, convert into cash; *v.i.*, to transact business.

nego'tiated, *p.p.*, negotiate.

nego'tiating, *pr.p.*, negotiate.

negotia'tion, *n.*, a business transaction.

nego'tiator, *n.*, one who negotiates.

nego'tiatory, *adj.*, rel. to negotiation.

ne'gress, *n.*, an African black woman.
ne'gro, *adj.*, of the negro type; *n.*, an African black man.
ne'groid, *adj.*, negro-like.
Ne'gus, *n.*, the Emperor of Abyssinia.
ne'gus, *n.*, wine and water, hot and sweetened.
neigh, *v.i.*, to make a horse's sound.
neigh'bour -bor, *v.t.* and *i.*, to adjoin, border upon; *n.*, one who lives near; a friend; a person next to another.
neigh'bourhood, *n.*, the vicinity; the people of the vicinity; neighbourliness.
neigh'bouring, *pr.p.*, neighbour; *adj.*, adjacent.
neigh'bourliness, *n.*, kindliness.
neigh'bourly, *adj.*, kindly, sociable; *adv.*, in a neighbourly spirit.
neighed, *p.p.*, neigh.
neigh'ing, *pr.p.*, neigh.
nei'ther, *adj.* and *pron.*, not either; not the one or the other; *adv.*, not either, not on the one hand nor on the other; *conj.*, nor yet.
Neme'an, *adj.*, rel. to Nemea and the famous games.
Nem'esis, *n.*, retribution.
nen'uphar, *n.*, water-lily.
neog'raphy, *n.*, a new system of writing.
Ne'ocene, *adj.*, rel. to the later Tertiary.
neolith'ic, *adj.*, rel. to the later Stone Age.
neolo'gian, *adj.*, rel. to neology.
neolog'ical, *adj.*, *i.q.* neologian.
neol'ogism, *n.*, coining new words; adopting new and rationalistic opinions.
neol'ogist, *n.*, one who coins new words, or preaches new doctrines.
neol'ogize, *v.i.*, to coin new words or preach new doctrines.
neol'ogy, *n.*, the introducing of new words or doctrines.
ne'ophyte, *n.*, a novice; one lately converted.
Neoplaton'ic, *adj.*, pert. to Neoplatonism.
Neoplat'onism, *n.*, a philosophical system, taught in Alexandria in the 3rd cent. A.D., being a blend of Judaism and Christianity with Greek philosophy and the mysticism of the East.
Neoplat'onist, *n.*, one of the Neoplatonic school.
neoter'ic, *adj.*, recent; *n.*, a modern person.
Neozo'ic, *adj.*, pert. to the later rock series.
nepen'the, *n.*, the pitcher plant, narcotic in its effect. Also *nepenthes*.
neph'ew, *n.*, a sister's or brother's son.
neph'oscope, *n.*, an apparatus for observing cloud phenomena.
nephral'gia, *n.*, kidney neuralgia.
nephral'gy, *n.*, *i.q.* nephralgia.
neph'rite, *n.*, the kidney stone.
nephrit'ic, *adj.*, rel. to nephritis.
nephri'tis, *n.*, inflammation of the kidneys.
nephrol'ogy, *n.*, the study of kidney pathology.
nephrot'omy, *n.*, the cutting operation for stone in the kidneys.
nep'otal, *adj.*, rel. to nephews.
nep'otism, *n.*, favoritism towards relatives.
nep'otist, *n.*, one who practises nepotism.
Nep'tune, *n.*, the Roman god of the sea; the planet so named.
Neptu'nian, *adj.*, rel. to Neptune.
Nep'tunist, *n.*, a believer in the aqueous formation of certain rocks.
Ne'reid, *n.*, a sea-nymph.
ne'roli, *n.*, orange essence.
nerva'tion, *n.*, the distribution of the nerves.
nerve, *v.t.*, to inspirit; impart vigour to; *n.*, sinew or tendon.
nerved, *p.p.*, nerve.
nerve'less, *adj.*, without courage or vigour.
ner'vine, *n.*, a nerve-medicine.
nerv'ing, *pr.p.*, nerve.
ner'vous, *adj.*, rel. to the nerves; having nerve-force; easily perturbed.
nerv'ously, *adj.*, in a nervous way.
ner'vure, *n.*, a nerve or rib in architecture, or in botany.
nes'cience, *n.*, ignorance; agnosticism.
nes'cient, *adj.*, ignorant, agnostic.
ness, *n.*, a promontory.
nest, *v.t.* and *i.*, to place in a nest; to occupy a nest; *n.*, a place or structure where a bird lays its eggs or tends its young.
nest'ed, *p.p.*, nest.
nest'-egg, *n.*, an egg, natural or artificial, placed in a nest to induce a hen to lay.
nest'ing, *pr.p.*, nest.
nes'tle, *v.t.*, to cuddle; *v.i.*, to lie comfortably as in a nest.
nes'tled, *p.p.*, nestle.
nes'tling, *pr.p.*, nestle; *n.*, a very young bird.
Nes'tor, *n.*, a wise greybeard.
Nesto'rian, *adj.*, rel. to Nestorius.
Nesto'rianism, *n.*, the heretical system of Nestorius.
net, *v.t.*, to catch; to protect with a net; to make into network; to gain clear; *v.i.*, to make nets, do netting; *adj.*,

made of netting; clear after deduction of costs; not subject to discount; *n.*, a meshed fabric of cord, hair, etc.

neth'er, *adj.*, lower.

neth'ermost, *adj.*, *super.* of nether.

net'ted, *p.p.*, net.

net'ting, *pr.p.*, net; *n.*, network.

net'tle, *v.t.*, to sting, annoy; *n.*, the common stinging plant.

net'tled, *p.p.*, nettle.

net'tle-rash, *n.*, urticaria, a skin-eruption.

net'tle-wort, *n.*, one of the urticaceae.

net'tling, *adj.*, provoking; *pr.p.*, nettle.

net'work, *n.*, woven meshes.

neum, *n.*, a group of musical notes in plainsong notation.

neu'ral, *adj.*, rel. to the nerves.

neural'gia, *n.*, a painful affection of the nerves.

neural'gic, *adj.*, rel. to neuralgia.

neurasthe'nia, *n.*, nervous debility.

neuri'tis, *n.*, inflammation of a nerve.

neurol'ogist, *n.*, a student of neurology.

neurol'ogy, *n.*, the study of the nervous system.

Neurop'tera, *n.*, insects with membranous wings.

neurop'teran, *adj.*, rel. to neuroptera.

neuro'sis, *n.*, affection of the nerves, as epilepsy.

neurot'ic, *adj.*, nervous, abnormally sensitive; *n.*, a drug affecting the nerves.

neurot'omy, *n.*, the cutting of a nerve.

neu'ter, *adj.*, bel. to neither sex; *n.*, a sexless, sterile organism.

neu'tral, *adj.*, bel. to neither side; indifferent; not distinctly coloured; *n.*, a state that takes no side in a war.

neutral'ity, *n.*, the state of being neutral.

neutraliza'tion, *n.*, the act or effect of neutralizing.

neu'tralize, *v.t.*, to counteract; exclude from an area of hostilities.

neu'tralized, *p.p.*, neutralize.

neu'tralizer, *n.*, anything that neutralizes.

neu'tralizing, *pr.p.*, neutralize.

neu'trally, *adv.*, not taking sides.

nev'er, *adv.*, at no time; not ever.

nev'ermore, *adv.*, not again.

nevertheless', *adv.* and *conj.*, notwithstanding.

new, *adj.*, fresh, recent, strange.

new'-born, *adj.*, lately born.

new'-comer, *n.*, one who has lately come.

new'el, *n.*, the central pillar of a winding staircase; the top or bottom post of a stair hand-rail.

new'er, *adj.*, *comp.* of new.

new'est, *adj.*, *super.* of new.

newfan'gled, *adj.*, strange, of new fashion.

new-fash'ioned, *adj.*, of new fashion.

new'ish, *adj.*, somewhat new.

new'laid, *adj.*, freshly laid.

new'ly, *adv.*, recently, lately.

new'-made, *adj.*, recently made.

new'ness, *n.*, the state of being new; novelty.

news, *n.*, tidings, fresh information.

news'-agent, *n.*, a vendor of newspapers.

news'boy, *n.*, a boy who sells newspapers.

news'man, *n.*, one who reports news, or sells or delivers newspapers.

news'monger, *n.*, a gossip.

news'paper, *n.*, a public journal.

news'room, *n.*, a place where papers can be read.

news'vendor, *n.*, a seller of newspapers.

news'y, *adj.*, full of information (*slang*).

newt, *n.*, a small amphibian; an eft.

Newto'nian, *adj.*, rel. to Sir Isaac Newton and his philosophy.

next, *adj.*, nearest; immediately following; *adv.*, immediately following; *prep.*, adjoining, nearest to.

nex'us, *n.*, a bond, connexion. In plainsong, a melodic movement by intervals (*Lat.*).

nib, *v.t.*, to point (a pen); *n.*, a pen-point; pl., crushed cacao beans.

nibbed, *p.p.*, nib.

nib'ble, *v.t.* and *i.*, to take small bites of; to bite cautiously at; *n.*, the act of nibbling; a small bite.

nib'bled, *p.p.*, nibble.

nib'bler, *n.*, one who nibbles.

nib'bling, *pr.p.*, nibble.

nice, *adj.*, fastidious, particular, discerning, agreeable.

nice'ly, *adv.*, neatly, agreeably.

Ni'cene, *adj.*, rel. to Nicaea and the Nicene Councils (A.D. 325 and 787).

Ni'cene Creed, *n.*, the Catholic Creed formulated at the first Nicene Council, and recited in the Mass.

nice'ness, *n.*, the state of being nice.

ni'cer, *adj.*, *comp.* of nice.

ni'cest, *adj.*, *super.* of nice.

ni'cety, *n.*, *i.q.* niceness; something of subtle quality; minute distinction.

niche, *n.*, a recess in a wall, usually for a statue; any special place; *v.t.*, to put in a niche.

niched, *p.p.*, niche.
nick, *v.t.*, to indent, notch; to fit exactly: *n.*, a small cut at the edge; a notch.
nicked, *p.p.*, nick.
nick'el, *v.t.*, to nickel-plate; *adj.*, made of nickel; *n.*, a malleable and ductile white metal; a nickel coin.
nick'ing, *pr.p.*, nick.
nick'-nack, *n.*, *i.q.* knick-knack.
nick'name, *v.t.*, to call by a substituted name; *n.*, a familiar substitute for a person's real name.
nick'named, *p.p.*, nickname.
nick'naming, *pr.p.*, nickname.
Nicola'itan, *adj.*, rel. to the N. sect.
nico'tian, *adj.*, rel. to tobacco.
nico'tianin, *n.*, a compound distilled from tobacco.
nic'otine, *n.*, a poisonous alkaloid in tobacco and other plants.
nic'tate, *v.i.*, to wink the eyes.
nic'tated, *p.p.*, nictate.
nic'tating, *pr.p.*, nictate.
nicta'tion, *n.*, the act of nictating.
nic'titate, *v.i.*, *i.q.* nictate.
nictita'tion, *n.*, *i.q.* nictation.
nid'dering, *n.* and *adj.*, a coward, cowardly.
nide, *n.*, a brood of pheasants.
nid'get, *n.*, an idiot.
nid'ificate, *v.i.*, to build a nest.
nidifica'tion, *n.*, the act of nest-building.
nid'ify, *v.i.*, *i.q.*, nidificate.
nid'ulant, *adj.*, lying free, nestling.
nid'ulate, *v.i.*, *i.q.* nidificate.
nidula'tion, *n.*, the act of nidulating.
ni'dus, *n.*, a nest or breeding-place; a place where a disease is bred (*Lat.*).
niece, *n.*, the daughter of a brother or sister.
niel'lo, *n.*, a filling for engraved lines in metal; a piece of work so treated.
nig'gard, *n.*, a stingy fellow; *adj.*, stingy, in mean quantity.
nig'gardliness, *n.*, stinginess.
nig'gardly, *adj.*, *i.q.* niggard.
nig'ger, *n.*, a negro.
nig'gle, *v.i.*, to be over-exact; to worry over details.
nig'gler, *n.*, one who niggles.
nig'gling, *pr.p.*, niggle; *adj.*, petty, trifling.
nigh, *adj.*, *n.*, and *adv.*, near.
nigh'ness, *n.*, nearness.
night, *n.*, the period of darkness between sunset and sunrise.
night'cap, *n.*, a cap once used for sleeping or lounging in; the last draught before going to bed.
night'dress, *n.*, a garment worn in bed.
night'fall, *n.*, the approach of night.
night'gown, *n.*, *i.q.* nightdress.
night'ingale, *n.*, a migratory songster that sings by night as well as in the day.
night'jar, *n.*, the goat sucker.
night'-light, *n.*, a short, thick candle burnt through the night.
night'ly, *adj.* and *adv.*, at night.
night'man, *n.*, one who removes night-soil.
night'mare, *n.*, an oppressive or terrifying dream; an incubus.
night'marish, *adj.*, like a nightmare.
night'-piece, *n.*, a picture of a nightly scene.
night'-porter, *n.*, a porter on duty at night.
night'shade, *n.*, the name of several poisonous plants, as belladonna.
night'shirt, *n.*, a shirt worn in bed.
night'-stool, *n.*, a commode.
night'-time, *n.*, the period of night.
night'-walker, *n.*, one who walks by night.
night'-walking, *n.*, the act of walking by night.
night'-watch, *n.*, the act of watching by night; a body of night watchers.
night'-watcher, *n.*, one keeping watch by night.
nigres'cent, *adj.*, turning black.
ni'hilism, *n.*, an absolutely destructive scepticism; the doctrines of the nihilists.
ni'hilist, *n.*, one of an extremely revolutionary and anarchical party in Russia.
nihilis'tic, *adj.*, rel. to nihilism.
nihil'ity, *n.*, nothingness.
nil, **nill**, *n.*, nothing; no number.
Nilom'eter, *adj.*, a measured pillar marking the rise of the Nile.
Nilot'ic, *adj.*, pert. to the Nile.
nimbif'erous, *adj.*, cloud-bringing.
nim'ble, *adj.*, active, quick.
nim'bleness, *n.*, the quality of being nimble.
nim'bler, *adj.*, *comp.* of nimble.
nim'blest, *adj.*, *super.* of nimble.
nim'bly, *adv.*, actively, quickly.
nim'bus, *n.*, a cloud; a halo round the head of a deity or a saint.
nim'iny-piminy, *adj.*, prim, full of affectation.
nin'compoop, *n.*, a ninny.
nine, *adj.*, the cardinal number next above eight; *n.*, the number 9; a card with nine pips.

nine'fold, *adj.*, nine times repeated.
nine'pins, *n.*, a game resembling skittles.
nine'score, *adj.*, 20×9.
nineteen', *adj.*, one short of twenty.
nineteenth', *adj.*, ordinal of nineteen.
nine'tieth, *adj.*, ordinal of ninety.
nine'ty, *adj.*, nine times ten; *n.*, the number 90.
nin'ny, *n.*, a simpleton.
ninth, *adj.*, ordinal of nine.
ninth'ly, *adv.*, in the ninth place.
nip, *v.t.*, to pinch, pinch off, to take a small drink of; *n.*, a pinch, bite, a nipping air; a small draught of spirits.
nipped, *p.p.*, nip.
nip'per, *n.*, one who nips; a small boy.
nip'perkin, *n.*, a little cup.
nip'pers, *n. pl.*, small forceps.
nip'ping, *pr.p.*, nip; *adj.*, keen, biting.
nip'ple, *n.*, a teat; anything resembling a teat.
nip'py, *adj.*, keen, biting; nimble (*slang*).
Nirva'na, *n.*, the highest state of Buddhist perfection; absorption into the Deity.
Ni'san, *n.*, the Hebrew month so named.
ni'si pri'us, *n.*, a writ beginning with these two Latin words = "unless before"; a hearing of civil cases at the Assizes.
nit, *n.*, a small insect's egg.
ni'trate, *n.*, a salt having nitric acid as its base.
ni'trate, *v.t.*, to impregnate with nitric acid.
ni'tre, *n.*, potassium nitrate.
ni'tric, *adj.*, of nitre.
nitrifica'tion, *n.*, the act of nitrifying.
ni'trified, *p.p.*, nitrify.
ni'trify, *v.t.*, to turn into nitre; *v.i.*, to become nitrous.
ni'trifying, *pr.p.*, nitrify.
ni'trite, *n.*, a nitrous acid salt.
ni'trogen, *n.*, a gas without colour, scent, or taste constituting four-fifths of the atmosphere.
nitrog'enous, *adj.*, pert. to nitrogen.
nitrog'enize, *v.t.*, to impregnate with nitrogen.
nitro-glyc'erine, *n.*, a high explosive liquid, produced by the action of nitric acid.
nitromuriat'ic, *adj.*, rel. to nitric and hydrochloric acid.
ni'trous, *adj.*, pert. to nitre.
ni'trous ox'ide, *n.*, laughing gas.
nit'ty, *adj.*, full of nits.
niv'eous, *adj.*, like snow.
nix, *n.*, a water-elf; nothing (*Amer. slang*).
nix'ie, *n.*, *i.q.* nix.
Nizam', *n.*, the ruler of Hyderabad; a regular Turkish soldier.
no, *adj.*, not any; none; *adv. and neg. particle* of denial.
Noa'chian, *adj.*, rel. to Noah.
nob, *n.*, a knob, head; a swell (*slang*).
nob'ble, *v.t.*, to influence fraudulently; to come dishonestly by (*both slang*).
nobil'iary, *adj.*, pert. to the nobility; *n.*, the nobility.
nobil'ity, *n.*, the quality of being noble; the noble class.
no'ble, *adj.*, illustrious, of high birth, generous, magnificent; *n.*, one of the noble class.
no'bleman, *n.*, a peer.
no'bleness, *n.*, the quality of being noble.
noblesse', *n.*, the nobility; the class of nobles.
no'bly, *adv.*, in a noble way.
no'body, *n.*, no one; an insignificant person.
noctambula'tion, *n.*, the practice of night walking.
noctam'bulism, *n.*, the tendency to night walking.
noctam'bulist, *n.*, a night walker.
noctilu'cous, *adj.*, phosphorescent.
noctiv'agant, *adj.*, night wandering.
noctivaga'tion, *n.*, the act of night wandering.
noc'tograph, *n.*, an apparatus enabling the blind to write.
noc'tule, *n.*, a large bat.
noc'turn, *n.*, a section of the office of nocturns.
noctur'nal, *adj.*, nightly, by night.
noc'turne, *n.*, a musical reverie; a night-scene.
noc'uous, *adj.*, harmful.
nod, *v.t.*, to shake the head, assent, order; *v.i.*, to drop off to sleep, to decline from the perpendicular.
no'dal, *adj.*, rel. to nodes.
nod'ded, *p.p.*, nod.
nod'der, *n.*, one who nods.
nod'ding, *pr.p.*, nod.
nod'dle, *n.*, the head (*colloq.*).
nod'dy, *n.*, a fool; a sea-bird.
node, *n.*, a knot in timber; the point whence leaves spring, or where a planet's orbit intersects the ecliptic.
nodose', *adj.*, knotty.
nodos'ity, *adv.*, knottiness.
no'dous, *adj.*, *i.q.* nodose.
nod'ular, *adj.*, rel. to a nodule.
nodula'tion, *n.*, the formation of nodules.
nod'ule, *n.*, a little rounded lump; a small node.

nod'uled, *adj.*, having nodules.

No'el, *adj.*, Christmas. Also *Nowell.*

noet'ic, *adj.*, rel. to intellect; abstract; speculative.

nog, *n.*, a tree-snag; a wooden pin or peg.

nog'gin, *n.*, a small mug; a small liquid measure.

nog'ging, *n.*, a partition of scantling with a brick filling.

no'how, *adv.*, in no way.

noise, *n.*, excessive sound, clamour; *v.t.*, to publish abroad.

noised, *p.p.*, noise.

noise'less, *adv.*, silent.

noise'lessly, *adv.*, silently.

noise'lessness, *n.*, absence of sound.

noisette', *n.*, a small portion of meat cooked in a special way; a variety of rose.

nois'ily, *adv.*, loudly, with noise.

nois'iness, *n.*, the quality of being noisy.

nois'ing, *pr.p.*, noise.

noi'some, *adj.*, offensive, harmful.

noi'someness, *n.*, the quality of being noisome.

nois'y, *adj.*, making a noise, turbulent, loud.

no'lens vo'lens, *adv.*, willy-nilly.

nol'le pro'sequi, *n.*, stay of proceedings.

nom'ad, *adj.*, *i.q.* nomadic; *n.*, a wanderer.

nomad'ic, *adj.*, wandering hither and thither; migratory.

nom'adism, *n.*, the nomadic tendency.

nom'adize, *v.i.*, to become a nomad.

nom'adized, *p.p.*, nomadize.

nom'adizing, *pr.p.*, nomadize.

nom de guerre', *n.*, a pseudonym.

nom de plume', *n.*, an English invention for *nom de guerre.*

nome, *n.*, an ancient Greek and Egyptian territorial area.

no'menclator, *n.*, in ancient Rome a person who assigned the guests at a banquet their places; one who names things.

no'menclature, *n.*, the special names used in an art or science.

nom'ic, *adj.*, usual.

nom'inal, *adj.*, rel. to a noun or a name; existing in name only; of no significance.

nom'inalism, *n.*, the philosophic doctrine that abstract ideas are merely names.

nom'inalist, *n.*, a believer in nominalism.

nominalist'ic, *adj.*, pert. to nominalism.

nom'inally, *adv.*, in name only.

nom'inate, *v.t.*, to mention by name; appoint; propose for election.

nom'inated, *p.p.*, nominate.

nom'inating, *pr.p.*, nominate.

nomina'tion, *n.*, the act or right of nominating.

nominati'val, *adj.*, rel. to nominative; appointed by nomination.

nom'inative, *adj.*, rel. to nominative case; *n.*, the case of the grammatical subject.

nom'inator, *n.*, one who nominates.

nominee', *n.*, a person nominated.

nomolog'ical, *adj.*, pert. to nomology.

nomol'ogy, *n.*, the science of laws.

non-accept'ance, *n.*, refusal to accept.

non'age, *n.*, minority, immaturity.

nonagena'rian, *n.*, one between ninety and one hundred years of age.

nonages'imal, *adj.*, rel. to ninety or a nonagesimal; *n.*, the highest point of the ecliptic above the horizon.

non'agon, *n.*, a nine-sided and nine-angled plane figure.

non-appear'ance, *n.*, failure to appear.

non-arri'val, *n.*, failure to arrive.

non-attend'ance, *n.*, failure to attend.

nonce, *n.*, the time being.

non'chalance, *n.*, calm indifference.

non'chalant, *adj.*, calmly indifferent.

non'chalantly, *adv.*, in a nonchalant way.

non-com'batant, *adj.* and *n.*, civilian.

non-commis'sioned, *adj.*, not having naval or military commission.

non-commis'sioned of'ficer, *n.*, an officer of non-commissioned rank.

non-commit'tal, *adj.*, avoiding the taking of a side or committing oneself.

non-conduct'or, *n.*, a substance that resists the passage of heat or electricity.

Nonconform'ist, *adj.*, rel. to Nonconformity; *n.*, a Churchman who refused to conform to Church usages. (The term is now commonly applied to Separatists.)

Nonconform'ity, *n.* refusal to conform to the Church while claiming membership. (Now, the name for Dissent.)

non-content', *adj.*, opposed to a motion; *n.*, one who votes against.

non-deliv'ery, *n.*, failure to deliver.

non'descript, *adj.*, odd, neither one thing nor the other; *n.*, a person or thing hard to classify.

none, *adj.*, not any or one; *n.* and *pron.*, no one. Also *i.q. nones,* second meaning.

non-effect'ive, *adj.*, ineffective, disabled; *n.*, a disabled or unfit person.

non-effi'cient, *adj.*, incompetent; *n.*, one who is not qualified.

nonen'tity, *n.*, non-existence; a person of no account.

nones, *n. pl.*, the ninth day before the Roman Ides; the breviary office for the ninth hour (*i.e.*, 3 p.m.).

non-essen'tial, *adj.*, not essential.

none'such, *n.*, a paragon.

non-exist'ence, *n.*, the state of not being.

nonil'lion, *n.*, the ninth power of a million (in English reckoning); in Fr. reckoning, the tenth power of a thousand.

nonju'ring, *adj.*, refusing to take the oath of allegiance (to William III).

Nonju'ror, *n.*, one who refused allegiance to William III.

non-nat'ural, *adj.*, unnatural.

non-observ'ance, *n.*, failure to observe.

non-obe'dience, *n.*, failure to obey.

nonpareil', *adj.*, unique; *n.*, a paragon; a variety of printers' type; a variety of bird, apple, wheat, etc.

nonpay'ment, *n.*, omission to pay.

non-*perform'ance*, *n.*, failure to perform

non'plus, *v.t.*, to puzzle, perplex; *n.*, a perplexed condition

non'plussed, *p.p.*, nonplus.

non'plussing, *pr.p.*, nonplus.

non-*produc'tion*, *n.* failure to produce.

non-res'idence, *n.*, absenteeism.

non-res'ident, *adj.*, not residing on a benefice; not permanently settled.

non-resist'ance, *n.*, a passive attitude.

non'sense, *n.*, anything meaningless or ridiculous; *interj.*, ridiculous!

nonsen'sical, *adj.*, having no sense.

nonsen'sically, *adv.*, absurdly.

non-se'quitur, *n.*, the fallacy of a conclusion not warranted by the premises.

non'-stop, *adj.*, not stopping.

non'such, *n.*, a paragon; a variety of lucerne; *see* nonesuch.

non'suit, *v.t.*, to subject to a nonsuit; *n.*, the judicial stopping of a suit where there is no proper case.

non'suited, *p.p.*, nonsuit.

non'suiting, *pr.p.*, nonsuit.

noo'dle, *n.*, a simpleton.

nook, *n.*, a corner, recess.

noolog'ical, *adj.*, rel. to noology.

nool'ogist, *n.*, a student of noology.

nool'ogy, *n.*, the science of mental phenomena.

noon, *n.*, mid-day.

noon'day, *adj.*, rel. to mid-day; *n.*, *i.q.* noon.

noon'tide, *adj.* and *n.*, *i.q.* noonday.

noose, *v.t.*, to catch with a noose; *n.*, a loop with a running knot; a lasso.

noosed, *p.p.*, noose.

noos'ing, *pr.p.*, noose.

no'pal, *n.*, a variety of cactus used for breeding the cochineal insect.

***nor*,** *conj.*, and not; and not either.

norm, *n.*, a pattern, standard.

nor'ma, *n.*, the *Lat.* of norm.

nor'mal, *adj.*, according to type, regular; *n.*, the ordinary state, level, etc.

nor'malize, *v.t.*, to make conform to standard.

nor'mally, *adv.*, ordinarily, regularly.

Nor'man, *adj.*, rel. to the Normans; *n.*, a native of Normandy; the N. style of architecture.

norn, *n.*, one of the Scandinavian Fates.

Nor'roy, *n.*, the title of the Norroy King of Arms, whose jurisdiction lies North of the Trent.

Norse, *adj.*, Norwegian.

Norse'man, *n.*, a Norwegian.

north, *adj.*, in the north or northward; *n.*, the point opposite to the south.

north-east', *n.*, a point between N. and E.

north-east'er, *n.*, a N.E. wind.

north-east'erly, *adj.*, in, or from, a N.E. direction.

north-east'ern, *adj.*, rel. to the N.E.

north'erly, *adj.*, toward the N.; from the N.

***north'ern*,** *adj.*, in, or toward, the N.

north'erner, *adj.*, a native of the North country.

north'ern*most*, *adj.*, furthest N.

north'ing, *n.*, progress or drift northwards.

North'man, *n.*, a dweller in the North.

Northum'brian, pert. to Northumbria or Northumberland.

north'ward, *adj.* and *adv.*, toward the N.

north'wardly, *adv.*, toward the N.

north'wards, *adv.*, northward.

north-west', *adj.*, in or from the N.W.; *n.*, a point between N. and W.

north-west'er, *n.*, a N.-Westerly wind.

north-west'erly, *adj.*, from, or towards, the N.W.

north-west'ern, *adj.*, rel. to the N.W.

Norwe'gian, *adj.*, rel. to Norway and the Norwegians; *n.*, a native of N.

nose, *v.t.*, to smell or scent; *n.*, the organ of smell; a snout.

nose'bag, *n.*, a bag for fodder suspended to a horse's head.

nosed, *p.p.*, nose.

nose'gay, *n.*, a bouquet of flowers.

no'sing, *pr.p.*, nose.

nosog'raphy, *n.*, scientific description of diseases.

nosolog'ical, *adj.*, rel. to nosology.

nosol'ogist, *n.*, a student of nosology.

nosol'ogy, *n.*, classification of diseases.

nostal'gia, *n.*, home-sickness.

nostal'gic, *adj.*, pert. to nostalgia.

nos'tril, *n.*, a passage through the nose.

nos'trum, *n.*, a quack medicine; a pet project.

not, *adv.* of negation.

no'ta be'ne, *n.*, mark well or specially.

notabil'ia, *n. pl.*, things worthy of notice.

notabil'ity, *n.*, the quality of being notable; a notable person.

no'table, *adj.*, worthy of note, remarkable; *n.*, a person of distinction.

no'tably, *adv.*, in a way worthy of remark.

notal'gia, *n.*, backache.

nota'rial, *adj.*, rel. to a notary.

no'tary, *n.*, an official who attests writings.

nota'tion, *n.*, the act or system of noting by marks, figures, or characters.

notch, *v.t.*, to nick or cut into small hollows; *n.*, a cut so made.

notched, *p.p.*, notch.

notch'ing, *pr.p.*, notch.

note, *v.t.*, to set down, observe closely; *n.*, a mark; a short writing; a musical sound or character; a written acknowledgment of a debt with promise of payment.

note'-book, *n.*, a book for notes.

no'ted, *p.p.*, note; *adj.*, celebrated.

note'worthy, *adj.*, worthy to be noted.

noth'ing, *n.*, not anything; *n.*, a cipher.

noth'ingness, *n.*, non-existence, worthlessness.

no'tice, *v.t.*, to remark, observe, see; *n.*, remark, regard; information.

no'ticeable, *adj.*, worthy of observation.

no'ticeably, *adv.*, in a noticeable way.

no'tice-board, *n.*, a board on which notices are fixed.

no'ticed, *p.p.*, notice.

no'ticing, *pr.p.*, notice.

notifica'tion, *n.*, the act of giving notice; notice given.

no'tified, *p.p.*, notify.

no'tify, *v.t.*, to inform; make known to.

no'tifying, *pr.p.*, notify.

no'ting, *pr.p.*, note.

no'tion, *n.*, an idea, conception, opinion.

no'tional, *adj.*, rel. to notions; imaginary.

notori'ety, *n.*, the state of being notorious; publicity.

noto'rious, *adj.*, publicly known (commonly in a bad sense).

noto'riously, *adv.*, publicly, openly.

notwithstand'ing, *prep.*, in spite of; *adv.*, nevertheless; *conj.*, usu. with *that* = despite the fact that.

nougat', *n.*, a confection of sugar, nuts, etc.

nought, *i.q.* naught; *n.*, the figure 0.

nou'menal, *adj.*, pert. to noumena.

nou'menon, *n.*, something conceived in the mind, apart from external phenomena.

noun, *n.*, a name of anything.

nour'ish, *v.t.*, to feed, bring up.

nour'ishable, *adj.*, able to be nourished.

nour'ished, *p.p.*, nourish.

nour'isher, *n.*, one who nourishes.

nour'ishing, *pr.p.*, nourish; *adj.*, nutritious.

nour'ishment, *n.*, food

nous, *n.*, mind, intelligence; enlightened common sense (*Gr.*).

Nova'tian, *adj.*, rel. to the Novatian sect and its heresies.

Nova'tianism, *n.*, the doctrines of the Novatians.

nov'el, *adj.*, new, strange; *n.*, a tale of fiction.

novelette', *n.*, a short novel.

nov'elist, *n.*, a novel-writer.

nov'elty, *n.*, newness; a new thing.

Novem'ber, *n.*, the eleventh month of the year.

nove'na, *n.*, a religious devotion observed for a period of nine days.

nov'enary, *adj.*, pert. to a novena; also to the number nine; *n.*, a group of nine units.

noven'nial, *adj.*, happening every ninth year.

nov'ice, *n.*, a beginner, an initiate.

novi'ciate, *n.*, a novice's period of probation; the novices' quarters in a religious house.

novilu'nar, *adj.*, rel. to the new moon.

novi'tiate, *n.*, *i.q.* noviciate.

now, *adv.*, at the present time (used also without reference to time, in the sense of "It follows, then," "Beware," "Please do," etc.).

now'adays, *adv.*, in these times.

no'way, *adv.*, in no way; not at all.

now'el, *interj.*, expressing Christmas joy (*see* Noel); *n.*, the inner part of a large mould.

no'where, *adv.*, in no place.

no'wise, *adv.*, in no way.

nox'ious, *adj.*, harmful, deadly.

nox'iously, *adv.*, in a noxious way.

nox'iousness, *n.*, harmfulness.

noyau', *n.*, a liqueur flavoured with bitter almonds.

noz'zle, *n.*, a spout, end of a hose.

nuance', *n.*, a fine shade of meaning, colour, expression, etc.

Nu'bian, *adj.*, rel. to Nubia; *n.*, a Nubian negroid.

nubif'erous, *adj.*, cloud-bearing.

nu'bile, *adj.*, marriageable.

nucif'erous, *adj.*, nut-bearing.

nu'ciform, *adj.*, nut-shaped.

nu'cleal, *adj.*, rel. to a nucleus.

nu'clear, *adj.*, *i.q.* nucleal.

nu'cleate, *v.t.* and *i.*, to form into a nucleus.

nu'cleate, *adj.*, *i.q.* nucleated.

nu'cleated, *adj.*, having a nucleus; *p.p.*, nucleate.

nu'clei, *n.*, pl. of nucleus.

nu'cleiform, *adj.*, like a nucleus.

nu'cleus, *n.*, a central mass round which other matter accumulates; the body of a comet.

nuda'tion, *n.*, the act of making bare.

nude, *adj.*, naked, bare.

nude'ly, *adv.*, nakedly.

nude'ness, *n.*, the nude state.

nudge, *v.t.*, to jog with the elbow; to give a hint to; *n.*, a slight push.

nudged, *p.p.*, nudge.

nudg'ing, *pr.p.*, nudge.

nu'dity, *n.*, *i.q.* nudeness.

nu'gatory, *adj.*, of no force, trifling, futile.

nug'get, *n.*, a lump of metal or ore.

nui'sance, *n.*, that which annoys or offends.

null, *adj.*, void; of no force.

nul'lah, *n.*, a ravine with a water-course.

nullifica'tion, *n.*, the act of nullifying.

nullifid'ian, *adj.*, with no religious belief.

nul'lified, *p.p.*, nullify.

nul'lifier, *n.*, one who nullifies.

nul'lify, *v.t.*, to make void, cancel.

nul'lifying, *pr.p.*, nullify.

nul'lity, *n.*, invalidity, the state of being null; a nonentity.

numb, *v.t.*, to deprive of feeling; *adj.*, without feeling.

numbed, *p.p.*, numb.

numb'er, *adj.*, *comp.* of numb.

num'ber, *v.t.*, to count; reckon; mark numerically; *n.*, a single unit; a total of units; measure; one of a series; metre, verse.

num'bered, *p.p.*, number.

num'bering, *pr.p.*, number.

num'berless, *adj.*, innumerable.

Num'bers, *n. pl.*, one of the books of the Pentateuch; poetry, metre.

numb'ly, *adv.*, without feeling.

numb'ness, *n.*, loss of sensation.

nu'merable, *adj.*, able to be reckoned.

nu'meral, *adj.*, rel. to number; *n.*, a numerical symbol.

nu'merary, *adj.*, bel. to a number.

nu'merate, *v.t.*, to count; to read or point as a numerical expression.

nu'merated, *p.p.*, numerate.

nu'merating, *pr.p.*, numerate.

numera'tion, *n.*, the act or method of numbering.

nu'merator, *n.*, one who numbers; the figure or figures above the line of a fraction showing how many times the denominator is taken.

numer'ical, *adj.*, denoting numbers.

numer'ically, *adv.*, in number; by means of numbers.

nu'merous, *adj.*, composed of a number (as a numerous crowd, attendance, etc.); harmonious. It is wrongly used instead of "many."

nu'merously, *adv.*, in number.

numismat'ics, *n. pl.*, the science of coins and medals.

numis'matist, *n.*, one skilled in numismatics.

numismatol'ogy, *n.*, *i.q.* numismatics.

num'mular, *adj.*, rel. to coins.

num'mulary, *i.q.* nummular.

num'skull, *n.*, a blockhead.

nun, *n.*, a cloistered woman-religious; a variety of pigeon; a blue titmouse.

nun'cheon, *n.*, *i.q.* luncheon.

nun'ciature, *n.*, a nuncio's office.

nun'cio, *n.*, a papal envoy.

nun'cupative, *adj.*, oral, verbal.

nun'dinal, *adj.*, rel. to markets.

nun'nery, *n.*, a religious house of nuns.

nup'tial, *adj.*, rel. to marriage.

nup'tials, *n. pl.*, the marriage ceremony.

nurse, *v.t.*, to suckle or tend; bring up; tend a sick person; cherish; manage economically; *n.*, one who tends a child or sick patient.

nursed, *p.p.*, nurse.

nurse'-maid, *n.*, a servant with charge of a child.

nurs'ery, *n.*, a room for children; a plantation for young trees.

nurs'eryman, *n.*, the keeper of a nursery for young trees.

nurs'ing, *pr.p.*, nurse; *n.*, the business of a nurse.

nurs'ling, *n.*, an infant.

nur'ture, *v.t.*, to feed, educate; *n.*, that which nurtures; education.

nur'tured, *p.p.*, nurture.

nur'turing, *pr.p.*, nurture.

nut, *v.i.*, to go nutting; *n.*, a fruit consisting of a shell and a kernel; a metal block for securing a bolt; the tightener on a fiddle bow; a silly youth with affectations of dress, etc. (*slang*).

nu'tant, *adj.*, drooping.

nuta'tion, *n.*, nodding; the apparent vibratory motion of the earth's axis.

nut'-brown, *adj.*, brown as a nut.

nut'cracker, *n.*, an instrument for cracking nuts.

nut'-gall, *n.*, an excrescence on the oak.

nut'hatch, *n.*, a small bird that feeds on nuts.

nut'-hook, *n.*, a hook used in gathering nuts.

nut'meg, *n.*, the kernel of an aromatic nut.

nut'-oil, *n.*, oil got from nuts.

nu'trient, *adj.*, nutritious.

nu'triment, *n.*, nutritious food.

nutri'tion, *n.*, nourishment, food.

nutri'tious, *adj.*, nourishing.

nu'tritive, *adj.*, having the quality of nourishment.

nu'tritively, *adv.*, in a nourishing way.

nu'tritiveness, *n.*, the quality of being nourishing.

nut'shell, *n.*, the hard outside of a nut; something of small compass or capacity

nut'ted, *p.p.*, nut.

nut'ting, *pr.p.*, nut.

nux, *n.*, a nut (*Lat.*).

nux vom'ica, *n.*, an Indian fruit yielding strychnine.

nuz'zle, *v.i.*, to nose, burrow with the snout; *v.i.* to nestle, lie close.

nuz'zled, *p.p.*, nuzzle.

nuz'zling, *pr.p.*, nuzzle.

nyan'za, *n.*, a lake, marsh (*African*).

nyctalo'pia, *n.*, night-blindness.

nyc'talopy, *i.q.* nyctalopia.

nyl'ghau, *n.*, a variety of antelope.

nymph, *n.*, a semi-divine maiden dwelling in woods, streams, mountains, etc.; a young and lovely woman.

nym'pha, *n.*, a pupa, chrysalis.

nym'phal, *adj.*, rel. to nymphs.

nymphe'an, *adj.*, *i.q.* nymphal.

nymph'olepsy, *n.*, a state of ecstasy.

nympholep'tic, *adj.*, in a state of ecstasy.

O

O, *interj.*, with vocative case, or expressing wonder, pain, etc. The other form is "Oh," which is used when a punctuation mark is required, as, "Oh, must you go?"

oaf, *n.*, a changeling, a lout.

oaf'ish, *adj.*, loutish.

oak, *n.*, a tree of the genus *quercus*; oak timber.

oak'-apple, *n.*, an excrescence on the oak.

oak'en, *adj.*, made of oak.

oak'um, *n.*, old rope untwisted.

oar, *v.t.*, to propel by rowing; *n.*, a pole broadened at one end into a blade.

oar'age, *n.*, oars collectively.

oared, *p.p.*, oar; *adj.*, having oars.

oar'ing, *pr.p.*, oar.

oars'man, *n.*, a rower.

oa'sis, *n.*, a fertile spot in a desert.

oast, *n.*, a kiln for hop-drying.

oast'house, *n.*, the building containing an oast.

oat, *n.*, a cereal plant; the seed of the same; a shepherd's pipe.

oat'cake, *n.*, a cake made of oatmeal.

oat'en, *adj.*, made of, or pert. to, oats.

oath, *n.*, a solemn affirmation calling God to witness.

oat'meal, *n.*, meal made from oats.

obbliga'to, *adj.*, indispensable to the (musical) composition; *n.*, an additional accompaniment (*Ital.*).

obcor'date, *adj.*, inversely heart-shaped.

ob'duracy, *adj.*, stubbornness, hard-heartedness.

ob'durate, *adj.*, inflexibly hard.

ob'durately, *adv.*, in an obdurate way.

ob'durateness, *n.*, *i.q.* obduracy.

o'beah, *n.*, a form of sorcery among W. Indian negroes.

obe'dience, *n.*, submission to authority; compliance with command.

obe'dient, *adj.*, submissive, compliant.

obe'diently, *adv.*, submissively.

obei'sance, *n.*, an act of reverence; a bow.

obei'sant, *adj.*, reverential.

ob'elisk, *n.*, a rectangular tapering pillar; an old MS. mark (†) denoting corruptness of text.

ob'elus, *n.*, a critical sign, as the obelisk (†); or + as marking a passage for omission; or (—).

obese', *adj.*, fat.

obes'ity, *n.*, fatness, corpulence.

obey', *v.t.*, to comply with, perform a command.

obeyed', *p.p.*, obey.

obey'er, *n.*, one who obeys.

obey'ing, *pr.p.*, obey.

ob'fuscate, *v.t.*, to darken, obscure, bewilder.

ob'fuscated, *p.p.*, obfuscate.

ob'fuscating, *pr.p.*, obfuscate.

obfusca'tion, *n.*, darkening; confusion.

o'bi, *i.q.* obeah.

ob'it, *n.*, death; a year's mind or anniversary memorial of the dead.

ob'iter, *adv.*, by the way, incidentally.

obit'ual, *adj.*, rel. to obit.

obit'uary, *adj.*, rel. to a person's death; *n.*, a written notice of a person's death.

object', *v.t.*, to urge in opposition; *v.i.*, to express disapproval.

ob'ject, *n.*, anything visible or presented to the mind or senses; aim, purpose.

object'ed, *p.p.*, object.

object'ing, *pr.p.*, object.

objec'tion, *n.*, adverse reason.

objec'tionable, *adj.*, liable to objection; offensive.

objec'tive, *adj.*, pert. to an object; external to the mind; *n.*, the accusative case; the goal of an advancing army.

objec'tively, *adv.*, in an objective sense; externally to the mind.

objec'tivism, *n.*, the doctrine that the knowledge of the *non-ego* or external world comes before and is more important than the *ego*; an artist's or poet's power to give reality to what he is depicting.

objec'tivist, *adj.*, rel. to objectivism.

objectiv'ity, *n.*, the quality of being objective.

ob'jectless, *n.*, without a purpose.

object'or, *n.*, one who objects.

ob'jurgate, *v.t.*, to reprove, scold.

ob'jurgated, *p.p.*, objurgate.

ob'jurgating, *pr.p.*, objurgate.

objurga'tion, *n.*, reproof.

objur'gatory, *adj.*, reproving, scolding.

ob'late, *adj.*, broad, flattened out at the poles; *n.*, a secular person who has devoted himself to the service of a monastery; a member of the Order of Oblates.

obla'tion, *n.*, offering, sacrifice.

ob'ligate, *v.t.*, to hold (a person) to performance.

ob'ligated, *p.p.*, obligate.

ob'ligating, *pr.p.*, obligate.

obliga'tion, *n.*, the binding force of a vow, law, or pledge; a bond; indebtedness for a favour.

ob'ligatorily, *adv.*, in a binding way.

ob'ligatory, *adj.*, compulsory, binding.

oblige', *v.t.*, to constrain, bind; gratify.

obliged', *p.p.*, oblige.

obligee', *n.*, one to whom a bond is executed.

obli'ger, *n.*, one who obliges.

obli'ging, *pr.p.*, oblige; *adj.*, accommodating, polite.

obli'gingly, *adv.*, courteously.

ob'ligor, *n.*, one who gives a bond.

oblique', *adj.*, slanting; deviating from a right line.

oblique'ly, *adv.*, slantingly, not straightforward.

obliq'uity, *n.*, divergence from a straight line, or from the moral standard.

oblit'erate, *v.t.*, to blot out, efface.

oblit'erated, *p.p.*, obliterate.

oblit'erating, *pr.p.*, obliterate.

oblitera'tion, *n.*, effacement, extinction.

obliv'ion, *n.*, the state of forgetfulness or of being forgotten.

obliv'ious, *adj.*, forgetful, disregarding.

obliv'iously, *adv.*, with forgetfulness.

ob'long, *adj.*, longer than broad; *n.*, a rectangular figure longer than broad.

ob'loquy, *n.*, slander, calumnious language.

obmutes'cence, *n.*, taciturnity.

obnox'ious, *adj.*, liable; offensive.

o'boe, *n.*, a wood reed instrument; an organ stop so named = hautboy.

o'boist, *n.*, an oboe player.

ob'ol, *n.*, *i.q.* obolus.

ob'olus, *n.*, an old Greek coin, worth about 1½d.

obo'vate, *adj.*, inversely ovate.

obscene', *adj.*, filthy, grossly indecent.

obscene'ly, *adv.*, in an obscene way.

obscene'ness, *n.*, filthiness.

obscen'ity, *n.*, *i.q.* obsceneness.

obscur'ant, *n.*, one who opposes enlightenment.

obscur'antism, *n.*, resistance to enlightenment.

obscur'antist, *n.*, *i.q.* obscurant.

obscura'tion, *n.*, the act of darkening.

obscure', *v.t.*, to hide from view, darken, dim; *adj.*, dark; difficult to understand; humble.

obscured', *p.p.*, obscure.

obscure'ly, *adv.*, dimly, darkly.

obscure'ness, *n.*, the state of being obscure.

obscur'ing, *pr.p.*, obscure.

obscu'rity, *n.*, the state of being obscure; a humble position.

obsecra'tion, *n.*, a strong entreaty. The clauses in the Litany beginning with "By" are obsecrations.

ob'sequies, *n. pl.*, funeral rites.

obse'quious, *adj.*, servilely compliant.

obse'quiously, *adv.*, in an obsequious way.

obse'quiousness, *n.*, fawning, compliance; servility.

observ'able, *adj.*, worthy to be observed, remarkable.

observ'ably, *adv.*, in a remarkable way.

observ'ance, *n.*, the act of observing; performance of a rite, custom, or rule.

observ'ant, *adj.*, attentive, regardful; *n.*, a member of the Observants, a very strict section of the Franciscan Order.

observa'tion, *n.*, the act of observing; attention; a remark; notice.

observa'tional, *adj.*, pert. to observation.

observ'atory, *n.*, a place for astronomical observations.

observe', *v.t.*, to perform a rite, duty, etc.; to mark, watch, note; to say; *v.i.*, to make a remark.

observed', *p.p.*, observe.

observ'er, *n.*, one who observes; esp. an astronomer.

observ'ing, *pr.p.*, observe.

observ'ingly, *adv.*, attentively.

obsess', *v.t.*, to haunt, take complete possession of.

obsessed', *p.p.*, obsess.

obses'sion, *n.*, the state of being obsessed.

obsess'ing, *pr.p.*, obsess.

obsid'ian, *n.*, dark, glassy lava.

obsid'ional, pert. to a siege.

obsoles'cence, *n.*, the state of becoming obsolete.

obsoles'cent, *adj.*, growing obsolete.

ob'solete, *adj.*, gone out of use, antiquated; less developed than formerly.

ob'stacle, *n.*, a hindrance, bar.

obstet'ric, *adj.*, rel. to midwifery.
obstetri'cian, *adj.*, an accoucheur.
ob'stinacy, *n.*, stubbornness.
ob'stinate, *adj.*, stubborn, refractory.
ob'stinately, *adv.*, stubbornly.
obstrep'erous, *adj.*, noisy, unruly.
obstrep'erously, *adv.*, noisily.
obstruct', *v.t.*, to impede, block up.
obstruct'ed, *p.p.*, obstruct.
obstruct'er, *n.*, one who obstructs.
obstruct'ing, *pr.p.*, obstruct.
obstruc'tion, *n.*, the act of obstructing; a barrier, impediment.
obstruc'tionist, *n.*, one who hinders public business.
obstruc'tive, *adj.*, hindering.
ob'struent, *adj.*, obstructive; *n.*, an obstructive medicine.
obtain', *v.t.*, to get possession of; get; *v.i.*, to prevail, be in vogue.
obtain'able, *adj.*, able to be obtained.
obtained', *p.p.*, obtain.
obtain'er, *n.*, one who obtains.
obtain'ing, *pr.p.*, obtain.
obtain'ment, *n.*, acquisition.
obtest', *v.t.* and *i.*, to beseech, adjure.
obtesta'tion, *n.*, the act of obtesting.
obtest'ed, *p.p.*, obtest.
obtest'ing, *pr.p.*, obtest.
obtrude', *v.t.*, to force upon; *v.i.*, to enter unbidden.
obtru'ded, *p.p.*, obtrude.
obtru'der, *n.*, one who obtrudes.
obtru'ding, *pr.p.*, obtrude.
obtru'sion, *n.*, the act of obtruding.
obtru'sive, *adj.*, apt to obtrude.
obtru'sively, *adv.*, in an obtrusive way.
obtru'siveness, *n.*, a tendency to obtrude.
obtund', *v.t.*, to blunt.
obtund'ed, *p.p.*, obtund.
ob'turator, *n.*, that which closes up.
obtuse', *adj.*, blunt in form.
obtuse'-angled, *adj.*, containing an obtuse angle.
obtuse'-angular, *adj.*, forming an obtuse angle.
obtuse'ly, *adv.*, in an obtuse way.
obtuse'ness, *n.*, dulness, stupidity.
obtu'sion, *n.*, the act of blunting.
obverse', *adj.*, narrower at the bottom than at the top.
ob'verse, *n.*, the side of a coin stamped with the head: the opposite.
obverse'ly, *adv.*, in a contrary way.
obver'sion, *n.*, a turning toward; logical inference by change of quality of proposition.
obvert', *v.t.*, to turn toward; to infer (logically) by obversion.
obvert'ed, *p.p.*, obvert.
obvert'ing, *pr.p.*, obvert.
ob'viate, *v.t.*, to meet, prevent, remove.
ob'viated, *p.p.*, obviate.
ob'viating, *pr.p.*, obviate.
ob'vious, *adj.*, evident, palpable.
ob'viously, *adv.*, evidently, palpably.
ob'volute, *adj.*, covered over.
ocari'na, *n.*, a musical instrument made of terra-cotta.
occa'sion, *n.*, cause, need, opportunity, event; *v.t.*, to cause.
occa'sional, *adj.*, occurring at one time or another.
occa'sionalism, *n.*, a philosophical doctrine of the interaction of soul and body.
occa'sionally, *adv.*, now and again.
occa'sioned, *p.p.*, occasion.
occa'sioning, *pr.p.*, occasion.
occa'sive, *adj.*, western.
oc'cident, *n.*, the western world; the west.
occiden'tal, *adj.*, pert. to the west.
occip'ital, *adj.*, pert. to the occiput.
oc'ciput, *n.*, the hinder part of the head.
occlude', *v.t.*, to close; to absorb (gases).
occlud'ed, *p.p.*, occlude.
occlud'ing, *pr.p.*, occlude.
occlu'sion, *n.*, the act or effect of occluding.
occult', *adj.*, secret, mysterious; *v.t.*, to hide from view.
occulta'tion, *n.*, the act or effect of occulting.
occult'ed, *p.p.*, occult.
occult'ing, *pr.p.*, occult.
occult'ism, *n.*, esoteric teaching.
occult'ly, *adv.*, in an occult way.
occult'ness, *n.*, secrecy.
oc'cupancy, *n.*, the act of taking possession; the being in possession.
oc'cupant, *n.*, one in possession.
occupa'tion, *n.*, business, possession.
oc'cupied, *p.p.*, occupy; *adj.*, busy.
oc'cupier, *n.*, one who occupies.
oc'cupy, *v.t.*, to take possession of; to be in possession of; to fill; to employ; to use in business (*obs.*).
oc'cupying, *pr.p.*, occupy.
occur', *v.i.*, to happen; present itself to the mind or eye.
occurred', *p.p.*, occur.
occur'rence, *n.*, the act of occurring; something that has happened.

occur'rent, *adj.*, happening.

occur'ring. *pr.p.*, occur.

o'cean, *n.*, the great water area of the earth's surface.

Ocea'nia, *n.*, the islands between S. America and S.E. Asia.

Ocea'nian, *adj.*, pert. to Oceania and its islanders.

ocean'ic, *adj.*, rel. to the ocean.

o'ceanward, *adj.* and *adv.*, toward the ocean.

o'cellate, *adj.*, having eye-like spots.

o'cellated, *adj.*, *i.q.* ocellate.

o'celot, *n.*, an American wild cat.

ochra'ceous, *adj.*, ochre-coloured.

o'chre, o'cher, *n.*, a clay used as a pigment.

o'chreous, *adj.*, containing ochre.

o'chry, *adj.*, like ochre.

oc'tachord, *n.*, an eight-stringed instrument.

oc'tad, *n.*, a series of eight.

oc'tagon, *n.*, a figure of eight angles and sides.

octag'onal, *adj.*, having eight angles and sides.

octahe'dral, *adj.*, with eight equal plane faces.

octahe'dron, *n.*, a solid figure with eight plane faces.

octan'dria, *n. pl.*, flowers with eight stamens.

octan'drous, *adj.*, pert. to octandria.

oct'angle, *n.*, a plane figure with eight sides and angles.

octan'gular, *adj.*, having eight angles.

oc'tant, *n.*, the eighth part of a circle.

oc'tarch, *n.*, one of eight rulers in an octarchy.

oc'tarchy, *n.*, a government of eight; a country with eight governments.

oc'tateuch, *n.*, a group of eight books.

octa'val, *adj.*, pert. to an octave.

oc'tave, *n.*, an eighth in music; the interval between a note and the eighth above or below it; these two notes sounded together; the eighth day after a feast day; the period (inclusive) from the one day to the other; a liquid measure = one-eighth of a pipe of wine.

octa'vo, *adj.*, with eight leaves to a sheet when folded; *n.*, a book or pamphlet with eight leaves to a sheet.

octen'nial, *adj.*, occurring every eighth year; lasting eight years.

octet(te)', *n.*, a musical piece of eight parts or voices; a group of eight verses.

octil'lion, *n.*, the eighth power of a million. (In French reckoning, it is the ninth power of a thousand.)

Octo'ber, *n.*, the tenth month; ale brewed in October.

octodec'imo, *n.*, a book-size, eighteen leaves to the sheet.

octoden'tate, *adj.*, with eight teeth.

octogena'rian, *adj.*, aged eighty; *n.*, one aged eighty.

oc'tonary, *n.*, a group of eight; an eight-line stanza.

octopet'alous, *adj.*, having eight petals.

oct'opod, *n.*, one of the octopoda.

octop'oda, *n. pl.*, creatures with eight suckered arms.

oc'topus, *n.*, an octopod cuttle fish.

octoroon', *n.*, the progeny of a quadroon and a white; a person one-eighth negro and seven-eighths white.

octosper'mous, *adj.*, eight-seeded.

oc'tostyle, *n.*, an eight-columned building.

octosyllab'ic, *adj.*, composed of eight syllables.

octosyl'lable, *n.*, a word of eight syllables.

octroi', *n.*, duty levied at entrance to a city on trade wares; the station where the duty is levied.

oc'tuple, *adj.*, eightfold; *n.*, the product of multiplying eight times; *v.t.*, to multiply by eight.

oc'ular, *adj.*, pert. to the eyes; *n.*, the eye-piece of an optical instrument.

oc'ularly, *adv.*, by means of the eyes.

oc'ulate, *adj.*, having eyes.

oc'ulated, *adj.*, *i.q.* oculate.

oc'uliform, *adj.*, in the form of an eye.

oc'ulist, *n.*, an expert in eye-treatment.

od, *n.*, an assumed all-pervading force in nature.

o'dal, *n.*, a form of land tenure in Shetland and the Orkneys.

o'dalisque, *n.*, a female slave in a harem.

odd, *adj.*, not even in number; not matching; strange; remaining over.

Odd'fellows, *n.*, members of a friendly society so named.

odd'ity, *n.*, the quality of being odd; a queer, eccentric person.

odd'ly, *adv.*, strangely.

odd'ment, *n.*, something over and above, or casual.

odd'ness, *n.*, singularity.

odds, *n. pl.*, inequality; excess; advantage; variance.

ode, *n.*, a song; poem for singing.

ode'on, *n.*, a Greek or Roman hall for music performances; (in modern usage, a theatre is sometimes so named).

od´ic, *adj.*, rel. to od.

od´ically, *adv.*, as the effect of od.

O´din, *n.*, the Scandinavian chief of the gods.

o´dious, *adj.*, hateful, detestable.

o´diously, *adv.*, hatefully.

o´dium, *n.*, hatred, unpopularity.

o´dize, *v.t.*, to influence with od.

o´dized, *p.p.*, odize.

o´dizing, *pr.p.*, odize.

odom´eter, *n.*, a contrivance for measuring distance travelled.

odomet´rical, *adj.*, pert. to odometry.

odom´etry, *n.*, measurement of distance travelled.

odontal´gia, *n.*, toothache.

odontal´gic, *adj.*, rel. to toothache.

odontal´gy, *n.*, *i.q.* odontalgia.

odon´to, a form derived from the Greek word for *tooth*, and used in combination with many English scientific words.

odontolog´ical, *adj.*, pert. to odontology.

odontol´ogy, *n.*, the science of dentistry.

o´dorant, *adj.*, odorous.

odorif´erous, *adj.*, smelling, scented.

o´dorous, *adj.*, having an odour; fragrant.

o´dorously, *adv.*, fragrantly.

o´dour, o´dor, *n.*, smell, scent, fragrance.

o´dourless, *adj.*, without odour.

o´dyl, *n.*, *i.q.* od.

odyl´ic, *adj.*, rel. to odyl and od.

o´dylism, *n.*, the theory concerning odyl.

Od´yssey, *n.*, the great Greek epic (attributed to Homer) describing the wanderings of Odysseus.

oecumen´ic, *adj.*, pert. to the universal Church or Christian world.

oecumen´ical, *adj.*, *i.q.* oecumenic.

oenom´eter, *n.*, an apparatus for testing the alcoholic strength of wine.

o´er, *adv.* and *prep.*, *i.q.* over.

oesoph´agus, *n.*, the gullet.

of, *prep.*, denoting various relations of one word with another (*e.g.*, possession, origin, cause, partition, separation, privation, etc.)

off, *adv.*, away, at or to a distance; *prep.*, from, away from, distant from; *adj.*, far; *n.*, the off-side at cricket; *interj.*, away with you!

off´al, *n.*, food refuse, dregs.

off´chance, *n.*, a remote chance.

offence´, *n.*, the act of offending; a cause of stumbling; a sin, transgression; displeasure or a cause of displeasure; assault, attack.

offence´less, *adj.*, harmless.

offend´, *v.t.*, to cause to stumble; to transgress; to cause anger or displeasure; *v.i.*, to stumble; to be an offender.

offend´ed, *p.p.*, offend.

offend´er, *n.*, one who offends.

offend´ing, *pr.p.*, offend.

offen´sive, *adj.*, giving offence; repulsive; aggressive; *n.*, military operations of attack.

offen´sively, *adv.*, in an offensive way.

offen´siveness, *n.*, the quality of being offensive.

of´fer, *v.t.*, to present, to sacrifice; to attempt; to show for sale; *v.i.*, to attempt, to present itself; *n.*, an expressed willingness to do or give something; a price proposed by a seller or a buyer.

of´fered, *p.p.*, offer.

of´ferer, *n.*, one who offers.

of´fering, *pr.p.*, offer; *n.*, anything offered, a sacrifice or gift.

of´fertory, *n.*, the part of the Mass at which the oblations are offered; loosely used for the presentation of alms.

off´*hand*, *adj.*, unpremeditated, extempore, casual; *adv.*, without premeditation; casually.

of´fice, *n.*, service, duty, function, position of trust or authority; a ritual service; a place of business; a department of Government administration.

of´fice-bearer, *n.*, one who holds office.

of´fice-copy, *n.*, a duly certified copy.

of´ficer, *n.*, one who holds any office; esp. in the navy or army; *v.t.*, to furnish with officers; to take the command of.

of´ficered, *p.p.*, officer; *adj.*, staffed.

of´ficering, *pr.p.*, officer.

offi´cial, *adj.*, pert. to office; authoritative; *n.*, any officeholder; an officer of the ecclesiastical courts.

offi´cialism, *n.*, office-holding; red-tapeism; perfunctoriness.

offi´cially, *adv.*, in an official capacity; by authority.

offi´ciant, *n.*, a priest officiating.

offi´ciate, *v.i.*, to perform an office of the Church; to act in some official capacity.

offi´ciated, *p.p.*, officiate.

offi´ciating, *pr.p.*, officiate.

offi´ciator, *n.*, one who officiates.

offic'inal, *adj.*, used in the arts and medicine; on sale at a druggist's; *n.*, a drug prepared according to the pharmacopoeia.

offi'cious, *adj.*, fussy, intrusive; informal.

offi'ciously, *adv.*, intrusively.

offi'ciousness, *n.*, fussiness; informal intervention.

off'ing, *n.*, distance seaward; position away from the shore.

off'scouring, *n.*, anything scoured away, refuse, dregs.

off'scum, *n.*, refuse.

offset', *v.t.*, to balance; set over against.

off'set, *n.*, an equivalent; an off-shoot, spur of a mountain; a line drawn from a main to a subsidiary line for the purpose of surveying.

off'shoot, *n.*, a branch; a side issue.

off'-side, *adv.*, on the wrong side; *n.*, the side to a batsman's right as he faces the bowler; the right-hand side in riding and driving.

off'spring, *n.*, issue, a child.

off'ward, *adv.*, turned towards the sea.

oft, *adv.*, poetical for often.

oft'en, *adv.*, repeatedly, frequently, many times.

oft'ener, *adv.*, *comp.* of often.

oft'entimes, *adv.*, *i.q.* often.

oft'times, *adv.*, *i.q.* often.

ogee', *adj.*, characterized by the ogee curve; *n.*, a moulding which, seen in cross section, resembles the letter S.

og'ham, og'am, *n.*, an ancient British and Irish alphabet of twenty letters, found in inscriptions; any single letter of the ogham alphabet.

ogi'val, *adj.*, rel. to the ogive; descriptive of architecture in which the ogee occurs.

o'give, *n.*, a diagonal vaulting rib.

o'gle, *v.t.* and *i.*, to look amorously at; to cast a side glance; *n.*, a side glance.

o'gled, *p.p.*, ogle.

o'gler, *n.*, one who ogles.

o'gling, *pr.p.*, ogle.

o'gre, *n.*, a monster of fairy-tale that devours human beings.

o'gress, *n.*, fem. of ogre.

Ogyg'ian, *adj.*, prehistoric.

oh, *interj.*, expressing pain, pleasure, surprise, etc.

ohm, *n.*, the unit of electrical resistance.

oho', *interj.*, expressing astonishment.

oil, *v.t.*, to smear or anoint with oil; *n.*, a liquid unctuous substance obtained from various sources —animal, vegetable and mineral.

oil'cake, *n.*, a cattle-food made of substances from which oil has been expressed.

oil'cloth, *n.*, a cloth coated with a preparation of oil.

oiled, *p.p.*, oil.

oil'er, *n.*, one who oils; an oiling appliance.

oil'iness, *n.*, the state or quality of being oily.

oil'ing, *pr.p.*, oil.

oil'man, *n.*, a dealer in oils.

oil'-painting, *n.*, a painting in oil colours.

oil'-shop, *n.*, a shop where oil is sold.

oil'skin, *n.*, a waterproof cloth; a garment of that material.

oil'stone, *v.t.*, to polish or sharpen with oilstone; *n.*, a fine kind of stone.

oil'-tree, *n.*, any oil-yielding tree.

oil'y, *adj.*, full of oil, smeared with oil, like oil, unctuous (in any sense).

oint'ment, *n.*, any soft, unctuous matter.

Ojib'way, *n.*, a Chippeway Indian.

oka'pi, *n.*, a Central African ruminant.

o'konite, *n.*, an insulating material.

ok'ra, *n.*, an edible herb.

old, *adj.*, aged; having lived or been in use a long time; antiquated; of long standing.

old age, *n.*, the decline of life.

old'en, *adj.*, old, ancient.

old'er, *adj.*, *comp.* of old.

old'est, *adj.*, *super.* of old.

old-fash'ioned, *adj.*, antiquated; of the mode of an older day.

old'ish, *adj.*, rather old.

old'ness, *n.*, the state of being old.

old'-style, *adj.*, of an earlier mode or style.

old'wife, *n.*, an old woman who babbles; a variety of duck; a fish so named.

oleag'inous, *adj.*, oily.

olean'der, *n.*, an evergreen shrub so named.

oleas'ter, *n.*, the wild olive.

o'leate, *n.*, an oleic acid salt.

ole'fiant, *adj.*, oil-yielding.

ole'ic, *adj.*, pert. to oil.

oleif'erous, *adj.*, *i.q.* olefiant.

o'lein, *n.*, an oleaginous liquid, compound.

o'leo, a prefix meaning *oil* or *oily*.

o'leograph, *n.*, a coloured lithograph imitating an oil painting.

oleomar'garine, *n.*, an artificial butter made of various ingredients.

oleom'eter, *n.*, an apparatus for finding the purity and density of oil.

o'leoresin, *n.*, a preparation of oil with resin.

o'leous, *adj.*, oily.

olera'ceous, *adj.*, rel. to cooking herbs.

olfac'tion, *n.*, the sense of smell; the act of smelling.

olfac'tory, *adj.*, pert. to smelling.

olib'anum, *n.*, frankincense.

ol'igarch, *n.*, one of a government by the few.

oligarch'ic, *adj.*, rel. to oligarchy.

oligarch'ical, *adj.*, *s.q.* oligarchical.

ol'igarchy, *n.*, government by the few.

o'lio, *n.*, a medley.

ol'itory, *adj.*, pert. to pot-herbs; *n.*, a pot-herb.

oliva'ceous, *adj.*, pert. to the olive; olive-coloured.

ol'ive, *n.*, a tree producing oil; *adj.*, olive coloured.

ol'ive-branch, *n.*, the emblem of peace.

ol'iver, *n.*, an olive grove; a kind of hammer used in metal-work.

ol'ivine, *n.*, chrysolite.

ol'la, *n.*, a cooking-pot; an earthen jar.

olla podri'da, *n.*, a Spanish stew.

Olym'piad, *n.*, the period of four years between the holding of one Olympic festival and the next. The Greeks reckoned dates in Olympiads.

Olym'pian, *adj.*, rel. to Mt. Olympus; *n.*, any one of the twelve chief Greek deities.

Olym'pic, *adj.*, *s.q.* Olympian; also pert. to Olympia in Elis, where the Olympic games were held.

om'bre, *n.*, a Spanish gambling game with cards.

ombrom'eter, *n.*, a rain-gauge.

o'mega, *n.*, the long Greek O, the last letter in the alphabet.

om'elet, om'elette, *n.*, a fritter of eggs with or without other ingredients.

o'men, *n.*, a sign, favourable or the reverse; a prognostication; *v.t.*, to portend.

omen'tum, *n.*, a fold of the peritoneum.

o'mer, *n.*, a Biblical measure of capacity.

om'inous, *adj.*, foreboding ill.

om'inously, *adv.*, in an ominous way.

om'inousness, *n.*, the quality of being ominous.

omis'sible, *adj.*, that may be omitted.

omis'sion, *n.*, the act of omitting; something omitted.

omis'sive, *adj.*, omitting.

omit', *v.t.*, to leave out; pass over; overlook.

omit'ted, *p.p.*, omit.

omit'ting, *pr.p.*, omit.

om'nibus, *adj.*, all-embracing; covering many subjects; *n.*, a large public vehicle.

omnifa'rious, *adj.*, miscellaneous.

omnif'erous, *adj.*, producing every variety.

omnif'ic, *adj.*, all-creating.

om'niform, *adj.*, assuming every form.

omniform'ity, *n.*, the power of being omniform.

omnig'enous, *adj.*, containing all kinds.

omnipar'ity, *n.*, equality all round.

omnip'otence, *n.*, power without limit; the power of the Almighty.

omnip'otent, *adj.*, possessing all power.

omnipres'ence, *n.*, presence everywhere.

omnipres'ent, *adj.*, present everywhere.

omnis'cience, *n.*, unlimited knowledge.

omnis'cient, *adj.*, knowing everything.

om'nium, *n.*, the total value of the stocks of an English public loan; a what-not.

omniv'ora, *n. pl.*, omnivorous creatures.

omniv'orous, *adj.*, eating indiscriminately; all-devouring.

omophag'ic, *adj.*, living on raw flesh.

omphal'ic, *adj.*, rel. to the navel.

om'phalism, *n.*, centralization.

om'phalos, *n.*, the navel (*Gr.*).

omphalot'omy, *n.*, the cutting of the navel.

on, *prep.*, upon, at, near; *adv.*, forward, onward.

on'ager, *n.*, a wild ass.

once, *adv.*, at a single time; formerly; ever.

oncot'omy, *n.*, cutting a tumour or abscess.

one, *adj.*, single; any; a certain; *n.*, a single unit; the figure 1; an indefinite person.

one'-eyed, *adj.*, having only one eye.

one'-horse, *adj.*, drawn by a single horse; insignificant.

oneirocrit'ic, *adj.*, pert. to the power of interpreting dreams.

oneirol'ogy, *n.*, the study of dream phenomena.

onei'romancy, *n.*, divination by dreams.

oneiros'copy, *n.*, interpretation of dreams.

one'ness, *n.*, unity; the quality of being one.

on'erous, *adj.*, burdensome, heavy.

oneself', ***pron.***, the reflexive of *one*; one's self.

one'-sided, *adj.*, partial, imperfect.

on'ion, *n.* an edible bulb.

on'looker, *n.*, a spectator.

on'looking, *adj.*, in the position of a spectator.

on'ly, *adj.*, alone, single; *adv.*, singly, alone, merely.

on'omancy, *n.*, divination by means of names.

onomas'tic, *adj.*, pert. to a name.

onomas'ticon, *n.*, a dictionary (of names especially).

onomatol'ogy, *n.*, the study of names; nomenclature.

onomatoma'nia, *n.*, a peculiar form of madness connected with names.

onomatopoe'ia, *n.*, the representation of natural sounds by words which imitate them, as it were.

on'rush, *n.*, *i.q.* onset.

on'set, *n.*, a dash forward, attack.

on'slaught, *n.*, a murderous onset.

ontolog'ical, *adj.*, rel. to ontology; metaphysical.

ontol'ogism, *n.*, a theological doctrine attributing to the human mind an immediate consciousness of the Deity.

ontol'ogist, *n.*, one learned in ontology.

ontol'ogy, *n.*, the science of being.

o'nus, *n.*, a burden, responsibility (*Lat.*).

on'ward, *adj.*, progressive, advancing; *adv.*, forward, ahead.

on'yx, *n.*, a quartz stone, much used for cameos.

o'o-, o-, a prefix to many compound words; it means *egg*.

o'olite, *n.*, a variety of limestone.

oolit'ic, *adj.*, of oolite; pert. to oolite.

oolog'ical, *adj.*, pert. to oology.

ool'ogist, *n.*, one who makes a study of birds' eggs.

ool'ogy, *n.*, the study of birds' eggs and nidification.

Oo'pak, *n.*, a black tea so named.

ooze, *v.i.* and *t.*, to flow or distil gently; *n.*, soft mud.

oozed, *p.p.*, ooze.

oo'zing, *pr.p.*, ooze.

oo'zy, *adj.*, spongy and wet.

opac'ity, *n.*, the quality of being opaque.

o'pah, *n.*, a brightly coloured fish so named.

o'pal, *n.*, a precious stone so named.

opalesce', *v.i.*, to be iridescent like the opal.

opales'cence, *n.*, the iridescence of an opal.

opales'cent, *adj.*, iridescent like the opal.

o'paline, *adj.*, pert. to the opal; *n.*, a variety of glass or porcelain.

o'palize, *v.t.*, to change to opal.

o'palized, *p.p.*, opalize.

opaque', *adj.*, not transparent; resisting the passage of light.

ope, poetical for *open*.

o'pen, *v.t.* and *i.*, to unclose, expand, unfold; *adj.*, unshut, free, frank, accessible; *n.*, any unenclosed area.

open-air', *adj.*, out of doors.

o'pened, *p.p.*, open.

o'pener, *n.*, anything that opens.

o'pen-handed, *adj.*, generous, liberal.

o'pen-hearted, *adj.*, frank, sincere.

o'pening, *pr.p.*, open; *n.*, the act of opening; a hole, aperture, breach; a beginning; an opportunity.

o'penly, *adv.*, in an open way; publicly.

o'pen-mouthed, *adj.*, eagerly expecting; gaping with surprise

o'penness, *n.*, the quality of being open.

o'pen-work, *n.*, work with openings in it.

op'era, *n.*, musical drama.

op'era bouffe, *n.*, comic opera.

op'era-cloak, *n.*, a lady's wrap.

op'era-glass, *n.*, a binocular.

operam'eter, *n.*, a speed-indicator.

op'erant, *adj.*, acting, effective.

op'erate, *v.t.*, to make active, set working; *v.i.*, to work, act; perform a surgical operation.

op'erated, *p.p.*, operate.

operat'ic, *adj.*, pert. to opera.

operat'ically, *adv.*, in the manner of opera.

op'erating, *pr.p.*, operate.

opera'tion, *n.*, the process of operating; action; agency; a surgeon's act with the knife or other instrument.

op'erative, *adj.*, active, effective; *n.*, an artisan.

op'erator, *n.*, one who operates in any sense.

oper'cular, *adj.*, having, or forming, a lid.

oper'culate, *adj.*, having a lid.

oper'culated, *adj.*, *i.q.* operculate.

oper'culum, *n.*, a cover, lid (*Lat.*).

operet'ta, *n.*, a short, light opera.

op'erose, *adj.*, laborious.

oph'icleide, *n.*, a large brass instrument (*mus.*).

ophid'ian, *adj.*, rel. to snakes.

ophiol'ogist, *n.*, a student of ophiology.

ophiol'ogy, *n.*, the study of snakes and serpents.

Ophiu'chus, *n.*, the snake-bearer constellation.

ophthal'mia, *n.*, inflammation of the eye.

ophthal'mic, *adj.*, pert. to the eye.

ophthal'moscope, *n.*, an instrument used in examining the eye.

o'piate, *v.t.*, to drug, narcotize; *adj.*, containing opium; narcotic; *n.*, a narcotic.

opine', *v.t.* and *i.*, to think; hold an opinion.

opined', *p.p.*, opine.

opi'ning, *pr.p.*, opine.

opin'ion, *n.*, mental judgment; notion; conjecture; judicial decision.

opin'ionated, *adj.*, fond of expressing an opinion; conceited.

opin'ionative, *adj.*, *i.q.* opinionated.

opisom'eter, *n.*, an instrument for measuring the length of irregular lines.

opis'thograph, *n.*, a writing on both sides of a leaf or a slab.

o'pium, *n.*, the inspissated juice of the poppy.

o'pium-eater, *n.*, one who habitually consumes opium.

opodel'doc, *n.*, a saponaceous camphorated liniment.

opop'anax, *n.*, a gum resin; a herb so named.

opos'sum, *n.*, an American quadruped.

op'pidan, *adj.*, pert. to a town; *n.*, an Eton boy not on the foundation of the College.

oppo'nency, *n.*, the position of opponent in an academic dispute.

oppo'nent, *adj.*, opposing, opposite; *n.*, one who opposes; an antagonist.

opportune', *adj.*, timely, well-seasoned, fitting.

opportune'ly, *adv.*, at a fitting moment.

opportune'ness, *n.*, the quality of being opportune.

opportu'nism, *n.*, readiness to take advantage of the moment, often at the cost of consistency and principle.

opportu'nist, *n.*, one who practises opportunism.

opportu'nity, *n.*, a seasonable moment; a favourable chance.

oppo'sable, *adj.*, able to be opposed.

oppose', *v.t.*, to resist, withstand, dispute; to set up in opposition; *v.i.*, to offer resistance.

opposed', *p.p.*, oppose.

oppo'ser, *n.*, one who opposes.

oppo'sing, *pr.p.*, oppose.

op'posite, *adj.*, facing, confronting, contrary to, antagonistic.

opposi'tion, *n.*, the act of opposing; an obstacle; the party opposed to the Government.

opposi'tionist, *n.*, one belonging to the opposition.

oppos'itive, *adj.*, contrasting.

oppress', *v.t.*, to burden, press down, harass, tyrannize over.

oppressed', *p.p.*, oppress.

oppress'ing, *pr.p.*, oppress.

oppres'sion, *n.*, the act of oppressing; tyranny; a languid feeling.

oppress'ive, *adj.*, causing oppression; tyrannical; overpowering.

oppress'ively, *adv.*, in an oppressive way.

oppres'siveness, *n.*, the state of being oppressive.

oppress'or, *n.*, a tyrant.

oppro'brious, *adj.*, contumelious; contemptuously abusive.

oppro'briously, *adv.*, with opprobrium.

oppro'brium, *n.*, contemptuous abuse; infamy.

oppugn', *v.t.*, to contradict, attack, conflict with.

oppug'nancy, *n.*, opposition.

oppug'nant, *adj.*, opposing.

oppugned', *p.p.*, oppugn.

oppugn'er, *n.*, one who oppugns.

oppugn'ing, *pr.p.*, oppugn.

opsiom'eter, *n.*, *i.q.* optometer.

op'tative, *adj.*, pert. to wishing; *n.*, the optative or wishing mood.

op'tic, *adj.*, rel. to the eye and vision; *n.*, an eye.

op'tical, *adj.*, *i.q.* optic.

opti'cian, *n.*, a maker of optical instruments or glasses.

op'tics, *n. pl.*, the science of the nature and laws of vision.

op'tigraph, *n.*, an apparatus for copying a landscape.

op'timacy, *n.*, aristocracy.

optima'tes, *n. pl.*, the senatorial class in the Roman Republic (*Lat.*).

op'time, a Latin *adv.* meaning best; in very high degree. It is commonly found in the phrase *optime meritus*, "deserving in very high degree." At Cambridge, a winner of Second Class Mathematical Honours is called a Senior Optime; a third-class man Junior Optime.

op'timism, *n.*, a tendency to look always at the bright side of things; the belief that everything is ordered for the best.

op'timist, *n.*, one who practises optimism.

optimis'tic, *adj.*, practising optimism.

op'timise, *v.t.*, to reckon as best; *v.i.*, to be an optimist.

op'tion, *n.*, choice; liberty to choose.

op'tional, *adj.*, at one's discretion; left to choice.

optom'eter, *n.*, an apparatus for measuring the eye's focal range.

op'ulence, *n.*, wealth, abundance, luxuriance. [rich.

op'ulent, *adj.* wealthy,

op'us, *n.*, a work or composition (*Lat.*).

opus'cule, *n.*, a trifling work.

opus'culum, *n.*, *i.q.* opuscule (*Lat.*).

or, *prep.* and *conj.*, before, ere; *conj.*, uniting alternatives, as "this *or* that"; otherwise, else; *n.*, in heraldry, it represents the Fr. *or* = gold.

or'acle, *n.*, a sacred place from which a deity was said to deliver prophetic utterances; a prophecy so delivered; any solemn communication; an abnormally wise person.

orac'ular, *adj.*, pert. to, or, resembling, an oracle.

orac'ularly, *adv.*, in an oracular way.

ora'culum, *n.*, an oracle (*Lat.*).

o'ral, *adj.*, pert. to the mouth; verbal.

o'rally, *adv.*, verbally, by word of mouth.

or'ange, *n.*, the tree and its fruit so named; *adj.*, of the colour of an orange; bel. to the Orange political society.

orangeade', *n.*, a beverage made from oranges.

Or'angeism, *n.*, the principles of the Orange Society, named after William of Orange.

Or'angeman, *n.*, a member of the Orange political party.

or'angery, *n.*, a building containing orange trees.

orang'-outang', *n.*, a large ape.

ora'tion, *n.*, a speech, harangue; a way (direct or indirect) of speaking.

or'ator, *n.*, a speaker; an eloquent speaker.

orato'rial, *adj.*, rel. to oratory.

orator'ical, *adj.*, in the manner of oratory.

orator'ically, *adv.*, in the manner of an orator.

orato'rio, *n.*, a quasi-dramatic sacred cantata.

or'atory, *n.*, the art of speaking; rhetoric; a small church or chapel, esp. in a house. The Oratory is a R. C. Order of priests devoted to teaching and preaching; each establishment of theirs is known as an Oratory.

orb, *v.t.*, to gather into an orb; *n.*, once a circular disc, now a sphere; an eyeball; one of the regalia—a sphere surmounted by a cross.

orbed, *p.p.*, orb.

or'bic, *adj.*, circular.

or'bical, *adj.*, *i.q.* orbic.

orbic'ular, *adj.*, circular, spherical.

orbic'ulate, *adj.*, *i.q.* orbicular.

orb'ing, *pr.p.*, orb.

or'bit, *n.*, an eye socket; the course described by a planet, etc.

or'bital, *adj.*, pert. to an orb.

orc, **ork**, *n.*, a variety of sea monsters.

Orca'dian, *adj.*, rel. to the Orkneys; *n.*, a native of the O.

or'chard, *n.*, an enclosure for fruit-growing trees.

or'charding, *n.*, the care of an orchard.

or'chardist, *n.*, one who cultivates an orchard.

or'chestra, *n.*, a collection of instrumental players; the platform on which they play. Originally, the semi-circular area in front of a Greek stage.

orches'tral, *adj.*, pert. to an orchestra; set for a number of instruments.

orchestra'tion, *n.*, the art of composing for, or adapting to, an orchestra; instrumentation.

or'chid, *n.*, the name of an order of perennial herbaceous plants with tuberous roots.

orchida'ceous, *adj.*, pert. to the orchis.

or'chil, *n.*, a red or purple dyestuff derived from a lichen.

or'chis, *n.*, the name given to a genus of plants bel. to the Orchid family or order.

or'cin, *n.*, a substance obtained from lichen and used for dyeing.

ordain', *v.t.*, to appoint, destine; command; admit to Holy Orders.

ordained', *p.p.*, ordain.

ordain'er, *n.*, one who ordains.

ordain'ing, *pr.p.*, ordain.

or'deal, *n.*, a severe trial, as by fire, water, etc.; any trying experience.

or'der, *v.t.*, to put in order; draw up in array; regulate; command; *n.*, systematic arrangement; array; rank; class; sequence; a command; a fraternity or community under one rule; a type of architecture, as the Corinthian Order, etc.

or'dered, *p.p.*, order.

or'derer, *n.*, one who orders.

or'dering, *pr.p.*, order.

or'derliness, *n.*, the quality of being orderly; tidiness; method.

or'derly, *adj.*, methodical, tidy, well regulated; rel. to the carrying or execution of military orders; *n.*, a soldier whose duty it is to carry orders.

ordinaire', *n.*, ordinary wine; a common person (*Fr.*).

or'dinal, *n.*, a numeral marking order or succession, as fifth, seventh, etc.; a pontifical containing the Ordination rites; a book of directions for saying Mass.

or'dinance, *n.*, an authoritative order, a decree; a sacred rite.

or'dinand, *n.*, one selected for Holy Orders.

or'dinant, *n.*, an ordaining bishop.

or'dinarily, *adv.*, usually.

or'dinary, *adj.*, usual, customary, without rank; commonplace; *n.*, the part of the Mass preceding the Canon; a bishop or his deputy in a judicial capacity; in heraldry, any of the common charges; a table d'hôte.

or'dinate, *adj.*, regular; *n.*, one of two elements defining the position of a point in a plane.

ordina'tion, *n.*, the act of ordaining; that which is ordained; arrangement.

ord'nance, *n.*, cannon; the department concerned with military stores and equipments.

or'donnance, *n.*, correct arrangement; an ordinance (*Fr.*).

or'dure, *n.*, excrement, filth.

ore, *n.*, a metal-bearing mineral substance.

or'gan, *n.*, an instrument of action or motion; a means of expressing opinion, as in a newspaper, review, etc.; a musical wind instrument containing pipes of various kinds—flue and reed.

organ'ic, *adj.*, pert. to the bodily organs; having organs (as distinguished from inorganic); systematized; containing carbon.

organ'ical, *adj.*, *i.q.* organic.

organ'ically, *adv.*, in an organic way.

or'ganism, *n.*, organic structure.

or'ganist, *n.*, an organ-player.

or'ganizable, *adj.*, able to be organized.

organiza'tion, *n.*, the act or result of organizing; an organized system.

or'ganize, *v.t.* and *i.*, to form with organs, make organic; to put into order, make arrangements for; to unite in a body or force.

or'ganized, *p.p.* organize.

or'ganizer, *n.*, one who organizes.

or'ganizing, *pr.p.*, organize.

organog'raphist, *n.*, an expert in organography.

organog'raphy, *n.*, the description of organs.

organol'ogy, *n.*, the study of organs and structures.

or'ganon, *n.*, *i.q.* organum.

or'ganum, *n.*, an instrument of thought; system of logic.

or'ganzine, *n.*, a variety of silk thread; material made from it.

or'gasm, *n.*, violent excitement.

or'gies, *n.*, pl. of orgy.

orguinette', *n.*, a reed organ played through perforated paper.

or'gy, *n.*, a revel, debauch. (Usually found in plural.)

o'riel, *n.*, a projecting, overhanging window or recess.

o'rient, *adj.*, eastern, oriental; rising; *n.*, the East; the Eastern world.

orien'tal, *adj.*, eastern.

orien'talism, *n.*, the characteristics of the Eastern world; the study of Eastern matters.

orien'talist, *n.*, one learned in Eastern matters.

orien'talize, *v.t.*, to make Oriental.

orien'tate, *v.t.*, to set pointing eastward; *reflex.*, to determine one's position in regard to matters of opinion, etc.

orienta'tion, *n.*, the eastward lie of the axis of a building; situation in regard to the points of the compass; the act of discovering direction; determination of one's position in regard to opinions, beliefs, etc.

or'ifice, *n.*, an opening, vent.

or'iflamme, *n.*, the banner of St. Denis of France; the French royal ensign; any splendid symbol.

or'igan, *n.*, *i.q.* origanum.

orig'anum, *n.*, the wild marjoram.

Or'igenism, *n.*, the doctrines of Origen of Alexandria.

Or'igenist, *n.*, a disciple of Origen.

or'igin, *n.*, source, beginning, extraction.

orig'inal, *adj.*, first, primitive, novel; *n.*, a model or pattern; the first example of anything; an independent thinker.

original'ity, *n.*, the quality of being original; inventiveness.

orig'inally, *adv.*, at first, in the beginning.

orig'inate, *v.t.*, to initiate; *v.i.*, to have origin.

orig'inated, *p.p.*, originate.

orig'inating, *pr.p.*, originate.

origina'tion, *n.*, the act of originating; a beginning.

orig'inative, *adj.*, initiative; causing a beginning.

orig'inator, *n.*, one who originates.

o'riole, *n.*, a bird so named.

Ori'on, *n.*, a constellation so named.

or'ison, *n.*, a prayer.

orle, *n.*, a bearing; a bordure (*her.*).

or'lop, *n.*, a ship's lower deck.

or'molu, *n.*, brass or copper gilt; an alloy of copper, zinc, and tin; ormolu ware.

or'nament, *v.t.*, to adorn, decorate, beautify; *n.*, a decoration, adornment; (in ecclesiastical language) any accessory of worship or the church.

ornamen'tal, *adj.*, of the nature of ornament.

ornamenta'tion, *n.*, adornment.

or'namented, *p.p.*, ornament.

or'namenting, *pr.p.*, ornament.

ornate', *adj.*, splendid, highly ornamented, elegant.

ornith'olite, *n.*, a bird-fossil.

ornithol'ogist, *n.*, one who makes a study of birds.

ornithol'ogy, *n.*, the study of birds.

orni'thomancy, *n.*, augury.

ornithorhyn'cus, *n.*, the duck-billed platypus of Australia.

orog'eny, *n.*, the formation of mountains.

orog'raphy, *n.*, that department of geography which treats of mountains.

orol'ogy, *n.*, the study of mountains.

o'rotund, *adj.*, resonant, full.

or'phan, *v.t.*, to bereave of parents; *adj.*, bereft of parents; *n.*, a person bereft of parents.

or'phanage, *n.*, a home for orphans.

or'phaned, *p.p.*, orphan.

or'phaning, *pr.p.*, orphan.

Orphe'an, *adj.*, rel. to Orpheus; melodious.

Or'phic, *adj.*, pert. to Orpheus and the Orphic mystical sect; mysterious.

or'phrey, *n.*, embroidered border on an ecclesiastical vestment, etc.

or'piment, *n.*, a yellow mineral dye.

or'pine, or'pin, *n.*, a variety of stonecrop.

or'rery, *n.*, a mechanical apparatus showing the motions of planets.

or'ris, *n.*, a variety of the Iris.

or'thodox, *adj.*, holding right belief.

or'thodoxy, *n.*, soundness in belief and doctrine.

orthodrom'ic, *adj.*, pert. to orthodromy.

orthod'romy, *n.*, sailing in a great circle.

orthoep'ic, *adj.*, pronouncing correctly.

orthoep'ical, *adj.*, *i.q.* orthoepic.

or'thoepist, *n.*, one who is skilled in pronunciation.

or'thoepy, *n.*, the art of correct pronunciation.

orthog'rapher, *n.*, one who spells correctly.

orthograph'ic, *adj.*, pert. to right spelling; rightly spelt.

orthograph'ical, *adj.*, *i.q.* orthographic.

orthog'raphist, *n.*, *i.q.* orthographer.

orthog'raphy, *n.*, correct spelling; the science or art rel. to correct spelling, or to correct architectural drawing, or to perspective.

orthomet'ric, *adj.*, rel. to orthometry.

orthom'etry, *n.*, correct versification.

orthopae'dic, *adj.*, rel. to orthopaedy.

or'thopaedy, *n.*, the correction of children's deformities.

orthop'ter, *n.*, one of the orthoptera.

Orthop'tera, *n. pl.*, straight-winged creatures.

orthop'teran, *adj.*, pert. to orthoptera.

orthop'terous, *adj.*, *i.q.* orthopteran.

or'tive, *adj.*, rising.

or'tolan, *n.*, a garden bunting.

orts, *n. pl.*, refuse, scraps.

oryctog'raphy, *n.*, description of fossils.

oryctol'ogy, *n.*, the study of fossils.

os'cheocele, *n.*, scrotal dropsy.

os'cillate, *v.t.* and *i.*, to sway to and fro; vibrate.

os'cillated, *p.p.*, oscillate.

os'cillating, *pr.p.*, oscillate.

oscilla'tion, *n.*, a swaying to and fro.

os'cillatory, *adj.*, swinging like a pendulum.

os'citancy, *n.*, a tendency to yawning.

os'citant, *adj.*, yawning.

oscita'tion, *n.*, the act of yawning; negligence.

os'culant, *adj.*, kissing; clinging closely together; adherent.

os'culate, *v.t.* and *i.*, to kiss; to touch closely; to have closely resembling characters.

os'culated, *p.p.*, osculate.

os'culating, *pr.p.*, osculate.

oscula'tion, *n.*, kissing; contact.

os'culatory, *adj.*, kissing.

os'cule, *n.*, a vent.

o'sier, *n.*, a kind of willow used in basket-work; *adj.*, made from osier.

o'siered, *adj.*, abounding in osiers.

Osi'ris, *n.*, the Egyptian god so named.

Osman'li, *adj.* and *n.*, Ottoman; a Turkish official.

os'mic, *adj.*, rel. to osmium.

os'mium, *n.*, a metal so named from its pungent smell.

osmom'eter, *n.*, an apparatus for gauging the power of smell.

os'mose, *n.*, the mixture of percolating liquids.

osmot'ic, *adj.*, pert. to osmose.

Osmun'da, *n.*, flowering fern.

os'prey, *n.*, a bird of prey so named.

os'seous, *adj.*, bony, ossified.

Ossian'ic, *adj.*, rel. to Ossian, the Gaelic poet.

os'sicle, *n.*, a small bone, or small piece of bony substance.

ossif'erous, *adj.*, containing bone.

ossif'ic, *adj.*, bone-making.

ossifica'tion, *n.*, the process of turning into bone.

os'sified, *p.p.*, ossify.

os'sifrage, *n.*, the osprey.

os'sify, *v.t.* and *i.*, to change into bone.

os'sifying, *pr.p.*, ossify.

ossiv'orous, *adj.*, bone-eating.

os'suary, *n.*, a bone-urn; charnel house.

ostensibil'ity, *n.*, the quality of being ostensible.

osten'sible, *adj.*, not real but pretended; seeming.

osten'sibly, *adv.*, seemingly.

osten'sive, *adj.*, showing.

osten'sory, *n.*, a monstrance.

ostenta'tion, *n.*, display, vanity.

ostenta'tious, *adj.*, pretentious; vulgarly displaying.

ostenta'tiously, *adv.*, in an ostentatious way.

os'teocele, *n.*, a form of hernia.

osteog'raphy, *n.*, scientific description of the bones.

osteol'oger, *n.*, *i.q.* osteologist.

osteol'ogist, *n.*, one skilled in bone-anatomy.

osteol'ogy, *n.*, the science of bone-anatomy.

os'teophone, *n.*, an instrument helping the deaf to hear.

osteot'omy, *n.*, the dissection or dividing of a bone.

ostia'rius, *n.*, a door-keeper.

os'tiary, *n.*, *i.q.* ostiarius.

os'tler, *n.*, a man in charge of horses and stables. Also *hostler*.

os'tracism, *n.*, the act of ostracizing.

os'tracize, *v.t.*, to banish by vote; to exclude from society.

os'tracized, *p.p.*, ostracize.

os'tracizing, *pr.p.*, ostracize.

os'trich, *n.*, a large bird with valuable feathers.

Os'trogoth, *n.*, one of the Eastern Goths.

otacous'tic, *adj.*, aiding the hearing; *n.*, an ear-trumpet.

otal'gia, *n.*, earache.

otal'gic, *adj.*, pert. to otalgia.

otal'gy, *n.*, *i.q.* otalgia.

oth'er, *adj.*, *pron.*, *adv.*, not the same; different.

oth'erwise, *adv.*, else, differently.

otherworld'liness, *n.*, the character of living as for the future life.

o'tiose, *adj.*, idle, futile; with no practical purpose.

otograph'ic, *adj.*, pert. to otography.

otog'raphy, *n.*, the scientific description of the ear.

otol'ogy, *n.*, the science of the ear.

otop'athy, *n.*, a pathological condition of the ear.

otot'omy, *n.*, dissection of the ear.

ot'ter, *n.*, an aquatic mammal so named.

ot'to, *n.*, *i.q.* attar.

ot'toman, *n.*, a cushioned seat.

Ot'toman, *adj.*, rel. to Turkey; *n.*, a Turk.

oubliette', *n.*, a secret dungeon (*Fr.*).

ouch, *n.*, the setting of a gem; a jewelled clasp.

ought, *aux. v.*, to be bound to do or be.

ounce, *n.*, a unit of weight; a lynx.

our, *adj. possess.*, bel. to us.

ouranog'raphy, *adj.*, scientific description of the sky.

ourol'ogy, *n.*, *i.q.* urology.

ouros'copy, *n.*, *i.q.* uroscopy.

ours, *possess. pron.* and *adj.*, bel. to us.

ourselves, *reflex. pron.*, we or us in particular; not others.

oust, *v.t.*, to push aside, eject.

oust'ed, *p.p.*, oust.

oust'er, *n.*, one who ousts.

oust'ing, *pr.p.*, oust.

out, *v.t.*, to turn out; *v.i.*, to come out; *adv.*, the opposite to in; *adj.*, away from home; *n.*, in the pl., the Outs = the party not in office.

out*bal'ance*, *v.t.*, to outweigh.

outbid', *v.t.*, to make a larger bid than.

outblown', *adj.*, inflated.

outbound', *adj.*, outward bound.

out'break, *n.*, an outburst.

out'burst, *n.*, a violent outbreak.

out'cast, *n.*, one who is cast out; *adj.*, forlorn; ejected from society.

outclass', *v.t.*, to surpass in quality or skill.

out*'come*, *n.*, a result; issue.

out'crop, *n.*, appearance above ground; an exposed rock.

out'cry, *n.*, a loud cry; an auction.

outdo', *v.t.*, to surpass, excel.

outdone', *p.p.*, outdo.

out'door, *adj.*, in the open air.

outdoors′, *adv.*, in the open air; abroad.

out′er, *adj.*, external; away from the inside or middle.

out′er*most*, *adj.*, furthest outward; on the extreme part.

outface′, *v.t.*, to stare out of countenance; defy.

outfaced′, *p.p.*, outface.

outfa′cing, *pr.p.*, outface.

out′fall, *n.*, a river outlet.

out′fit, *n.*, equipment.

out′fitter, *n.*, one who supplies outfit.

outflank′, *v.t.*, to cut off on the flank.

out*gen′eral*, *v.t.*, to surpass in generalship.

outgo′, *v.t.*, to surpass.

out′going, *pr.p.*, outgo; *adj.*, going outward; *n.*, the act of going out.

out′goings, *n.*, pl. of outgoing; used in the sense of expenditure.

outgrow′, *v.t.*, to surpass in growth; to become too large or old for.

outgrow′ing, *pr.p.*, outgrow.

outgrown′, *p.p.*, outgrow.

out′growth, *n.*, that which grows out from something; an excrescence.

out-Her′od, *v.t.*, to outdo Herod in Herod-like acts.

out′house, *n.*, a detached building bel. to a larger building.

out′ing, *pr.p.*, out; *n.*, a holiday jaunt; an airing.

out′lander, *n.*, a foreigner.

outland′ish, *adj.*, foreign; barbarous.

outlast′, *v.t.*, to survive.

out′law, *v.t.*, to place outside the protection of the law; *n.*, a felon; a person proscribed.

out′lawed, *p.p.*, outlaw.

out′lawing, *pr.p.*, outlaw.

out′lawry, *n.*, the state of being an outlaw.

out′lay, *n.*, expenditure, disbursement.

out′let, *n.*, a passage outward, exit.

outlie′, *v.t.*, to surpass in lying; *v.i.*, to encamp under canvas.

out′lier, *n.*, something external to the main body.

out′line, *v.t.*, to sketch; draw in outline; *n.*, a sketch, rough plan; contour.

out′lined, *p.p.*, outline.

out′lining, *pr.p.*, outline.

outlive′, *v.t.*, to live longer than.

out′look, *n.*, prospect, view.

out′lying, *pr.p.*, outlie; *adj.*, situated apart; distant.

out′*most*, *adj.*, outermost.

out*num′ber*, *v.t.*, to be greater in number than.

out*num′bered*, *p.p.*, outnumber.

out*num′ber*ing, *pr.p.*, outnumber.

out-of-date′, adjectival and adverbial phrase = antiquated; behind the times.

out-of-doors′, adjectival and adverbial phrase = in the open air, abroad.

out′patient, *n.* a hospital patient not an inmate.

out′post, *n.*, a military advanced detachment; its station.

out′pour, *v.t.* and *i.*, to pour out; *n.*, an outpouring.

out′pouring, *pr.p.*, outpour; *n.*, a flowing out.

out′put, *n.*, the quantity put out or produced.

out′rage, *v.t.*, to insult; do violence to; *n.*, violence, insult.

out′raged, *p.p.*, outrage.

outra′geous, *adj.*, violent; grossly cruel; flagrant; immoderate.

outra′geously, *adv.*, in an outrageous way.

out′raging, *pr.p.*, outrage.

outrange′, *v.t.*, to surpass in range (said of a gun).

outré, *adj.*, odd, extravagant (*Fr.*).

outreach′, *v.t.*, to go beyond, overreach.

outride′, *v.t.*, to outstrip in riding.

out′rider, *n.*, an attendant on a carriage, mounted on horseback.

out′rigger, *n.*, a projection from a boat's side, such as the bracket supporting external rowlocks.

out′right, *adv.*, downright, absolutely.

outrun′, *v.t.*, to outstrip in a race.

outsail′, *v.t.*, to outstrip in sailing.

outsell′, *v.t.*, to sell at a better price than another.

out′set, *n.*, a start, beginning.

outshine′, *v.t.*, to eclipse; *v.i.*, to shine out.

out′side, *adj.*, external; *n.*, the exterior; *prep.*, external to; beyond the limits of.

outsi′der, *n.*, one who is excluded from any society, etc.; a layman; a person of no account; a horse not thought to have a chance of a place.

out′skirt, *n.*, the outer borders of a place.

out′span, *v.t.* and *i.*, to release the horses or oxen for the purpose of encamping; *n.*, the act of outspanning; the encampment.

out′spoken, *adj.*, bold, frank.

outspread′, *v.t.* and *i.*, to spread out; *adj.*, spread out, extended.

outstand'ing, *adj.*, still remaining; prominent, leading.

outstretch', *v.t.*, to extend.

outstretched', *p.p.*, outstretch.

outstretch'ing, *pr.p.*, outstretch.

outstrip', *v.t.*, to surpass in anything.

out-talk', *v.t.*, to talk a person down.

outvote', *v.t.*, to defeat by a majority of votes.

out'-voter, *n.*, one who lives in one constituency and votes in another.

outvo'ted, *p.p.*, outvote.

outvo'ting, *pr.p.*, outvote.

outwalk', *v.t.*, to walk faster than.

out'ward, *adj.*, outer, external; *adv.*, toward the exterior; *n.*, the exterior.

out'ward-bound, *adj.*, starting on a voyage.

out'wardly, *adv.*, externally; on the exterior or surface.

out'wards, *adv.*, *i.q.* outward.

outwear', *v.t.*, to last longer than.

outweigh', *v.t.*, to exceed the weight of.

outweighed' *p.p.*, outweigh.

outweigh'ing, *pr.p.*, outweigh.

outwit', *v.t.*, to get the better of with cunning.

outwit'ted, *p.p.*, outwit.

outwit'ting, *pr.p.*, outwit.

outwork', *v.t.*, to exceed in work.

out'work, *n.*, an advanced defence.

ou'zel, *n.*, the name of sundry small birds.

o'va, *n.*, pl. of ovum.

o'val, *adj.*, egg-shaped, ellipsoidal; *n.*, anything of oval shape.

ovalbu'men, *n.*, *i.q.* ovalbumin.

oval'bumin, *n.*, egg-albumin.

ova'rian, *adj.*, rel. to ovaries.

o'vary, *n.*, an organ in the female which produces ova.

o'vate, *adj.*, oval.

o'vate-oblong, *adj.*, combining the oval with the oblong.

ova'tion, *n.*, a secondary kind of triumph in ancient Rome; now used to mean a spontaneous acclamation, a joyous reception.

ov'en, *n.*, a cooking-chamber or box.

o'ver, *adj.*, upper; *adv.*, above, across, from one to another, from end to end, in excess, in addition, at an end; *prep.*, above, in command of, on the outside of, across, in excess of, extending over, beyond; *n.*, in cricket, a spell of bowling.

overact', *v.t.*, to overdo.

overact'ed, *p.p.*, overact.

overact'ing, *pr.p.*, overact.

o'verall, *n.*, an outer garment.

o'veralls, *n. pl.*, a workman's cover to protect his clothes.

overarch', *v.t.* and *i.*, to make an arch over.

overawe', *v.t.*, to fill with excessive awe.

overawed', *p.p.*, overawe.

overaw'ing, *pr.p.*, overawe.

overbal'ance, *v.t.*, to outbalance.

overbal'anced, *p.p.* overbalance.

overbal'ancing, *pr.p.*, overbalance.

overbear', *v.t.*, to domineer over; to overpower.

overbear'ing, *pr.p.*, overbear; *adj.*, domineering.

overblown', *adj.*, withered.

o'verboard, *adv.*, from off a ship into the water.

overborne', *p.p.*, overbear.

overbur'den, *v.t.*, to load too heavily; *n.*, an excessive load.

overcame', *p.t.*, overcome.

o'vercast, *v.t.*, to cover with clouds; *adj.*, darkened with clouds.

overcharge', *v.t.*, to charge too high a price.

o'vercharge, *n.*, an excessive charge.

overcloud', *v.t.*, to darken with clouds.

o'vercoat, *n.*, a great-coat, topcoat.

overcome', *v.t.*, to conquer, surmount.

overcom'ing, *pr.p.*, overcome.

overcrowd', *v.t.*, to crowd to overflowing.

overcrowd'ed, *p.p.*, overcrowd.

overcrowd'ing, *pr.p.*, overcrowd.

overdo', *v.t.*, to do to excess; carry too far.

overdo'ing, *pr.p.*, overdo.

overdone', *p.p.*, overdo.

overdose', *v.t.*, to administer an overdose to.

o'verdose, *n.*, an excessive dose.

o'verdraft, *n.*, an overdrawn account.

overdraw', *v.t.*, to draw upon one's banker in excess of one's account.

overdrawn', *p.p.*, overdraw.

overdue', *adj.*, past the date when due.

over-es'timate, *v.t.*, to value above worth.

over-es'timate, *n.*, an excessive estimate.

overflow', *v.t.* and *i.*, to flow over.

o'verflow, *n.*, an overflowing; flood; superabundance.

overflowed', *p.t.* and *p.p.*, overflow.

overflow'ing, *pr.p.*, overflow.

overgrow', *v.t.*, to grow all over; *v.i.*, to grow too fast or much.

overgrown', *p.p.*, overgrow.

o'vergrowth, *n.*, the state of being overgrown.

overhang', *v.t.*, to impend over; *v.i.*, to jut out.

o'verhang, *n.*, the extent to which a thing juts out.

overhaul', *v.t.*, to catch up with; to make a search in.

overhauled', *p.p.*, overhaul.

overhaul'ing, *pr.p.*, overhaul.

overhead', *adj.* and *adv.*, above one's head.

overhear', *v.t.*, to hear by listening unseen.

overheard', *p.p.*, overhear.

overheat', *v.t.*, to heat excessively.

overhung', *p.p.*, overhang.

overjoyed', *adj.*, rejoicing excessively.

overlaid', *p.p.*, overlay.

o'verland, *adj.* and *adv.*, by land.

overlap', *v.t.*, to extend over and beyond.

o'verlap, *n.*, an overlapping part; the extent of overlapping.

overlay', *v.t.*, to lay over a surface.

o'verlay, *n.*, something laid over; a coverlet.

overlay'ing, *pr.p.*, overlay.

overleap', *v.t.*, to leap over.

overlie', *v.t.*, to lie on; suffocate by lying on.

overload', *v.t.*, to load to excess.

o'verload, *n.*, an excessive load.

overlook', *v.t.*, to superintend; to ignore; to forgive.

overlooked', *p.p.*, overlook.

overlook'ing, *pr.p.*, overlook.

o'vermantel, *n.*, ornamental shelves above a chimney-piece.

overmas'ter, *v.t.*, to overpower.

overmatch', *v.t.*, to be more than a match for.

o'vermuch', *adj.* and *adv.*, to an excessive degree or amount.

overnight', *adj.* and *adv.*, during the previous evening.

overpaid', *p.p.*, overpay.

overpass', *v.t.*, to cross; to pass through.

overpay', *v.t.*, to pay more than is due.

o'verpay, *n.*, payment in excess.

o'verplus, *n.*, a surplus; an excess.

overpow'er, *v.t.*, to subdue, overcome.

overpow'ered, *p.p.*, overpower.

overpow'ering, *pr.p.*, overpower.

overpow'eringly, *adv.* very intensely.

over-ran', *p.t.*, overrun.

overrate', *v.t.*, to rate too highly.

overra'ted, *p.p.*, overrate.

overra'ting, *pr.p.*, overrate.

overreach', *v.t.*, to gain advantage over; to go beyond; extend over.

overreached', *p.p.*, overreach.

overreach'ing, *pr.p.*, overreach.

overrule', *v.t.*, to control, influence.

overruled', *p.p.*, overrule.

overru'ling, *pr.p.*, overrule.

overrun', *v.t.*, to run over; to pass; to alter the setting of printer's type by removing words from one line into another line, column, or page; *p.p.*, overrun.

overrun'ning, *pr.p.*, overrun.

oversee', *v.t.*, to superintend.

o'verseer, *n.*, a manager, superintendent.

overset', *v.t.*, to upset; to set too much printer's type.

o'verset, *n.*, too much printed type.

overshade', *v.t.*, to cast a shade over.

overshad'ow, *v.t.*, *i.q.* overshade; to throw into insignificance.

o'vershoe, *adj.* and *adv.*, above shoe-tops; *n.*, a golosh.

overshoot', *v.t.*, to shoot beyond the mark.

overshot', *p.p.*, overshoot.

o'versight, *n.*, neglect, omission.

oversleep', *v. reflex.*, to oversleep oneself (*i.e.*, to sleep beyond the proper time).

overslept', *p.p.*, oversleep.

overspent', *adj.*, wearied out.

overspread', *v.t.*, to spread over; *p.p.*, overspread.

overstep', *v.t.*, to transgress.

overstepped', *p.p.*, overstep.

overstock', *v.t.*, to put in too much stock.

o'verstock, *n.*, too much stock.

overstrain', *v.t.*, to strain unduly.

o'verstrain, *n.*, excessive strain.

overstrew', *v.t.*, to strew over.

overstrewn', *p.p.*, overstrew.

overstrung', *adj.*, too tensely strung; with the strings crossing obliquely.

o'vert, *adj.*, open.

overtake', *v.t.*, to catch up.

overta'ken, *p.p.*, overtake.

overtask', *v.t.*, to task unduly.

overtax', *v.t.*, to tax excessively.

o'vertax, *n.*, tax in excess.

overtaxed', *p.p.*, overtax.

overtax'ing, *pr.p.*, overtax.

overthrew', *p.t.*, overthrow.

overthrow', *v.t.*, to throw down; destroy.

o'verthrow, *n.*, demolition, defeat; a ball thrown in past the player to whom it is sent.

overthrow'ing, *pr.p.*, overthrow.

overthrown', *p.p.*, overthrow.

o'vertime, *adj.* and *adv.*, beyond the stipulated hours; *n.*, time in excess.

o'vertly, *adv.*, openly.

overtook', *p.t.*, overtake.

overtop', *v.t.*, to surmount; tower above.

overtrade', *v.i.*, to do business beyond one's means.

o'verture, *n.*, an offer, proposal; the introduction to an opera, oratorio, etc.

overturn', *v.t.*, to upset, destroy; *v.i.*, to capsize.

overturned', *p.p.*, overturn.

overween'ing, *adj.*, arrogant.

overweight', *v.t.*, to put too much weight on to.

o'verweight, *n.*, excess weight.

overwhelm', *v.t.*, to cover, spread over, subdue, overcome.

overwhelmed', *p.p.*, overwhelm.

overwhelm'ing, *pr.p.* overwhelm; *adj.*, crushing, overpowering.

o'verwise', *adj.*, excessively wise.

overwork', *v.t.*, to exact too much work from; to elaborate to excess.

o'verwork, *n.*, excessive labour.

o'verwrought', *adj.*, worked too hard; overstrained.

ovic'ular, *adj.*, pert. to an egg.

Ovid'ian, *adj.*, pert. to, in the style of, the Lat. poet, Ovid.

o'viduct, *n.*, the passage for the ova.

ovif'erous, *adj.*, egg-holding.

o'viform, *adj.*, egg-shaped; ovine.

ovig'erous, *adj.*, *i.q.* oviferous.

o'vine, *adj.*, pert. to sheep; like a sheep.

ovip'arous, *adj.*, egg-producing.

ovipos'itor, *n.*, the egg-depositing organ of insects.

o'void, *adj.*, egg-shaped.

ovoi'dal, *adj.*, *i.q.* ovoid.

o'volo, *n.*, a convex moulding found in Greek and Roman architecture.

ovo-vivip'arous, *adj.*, describes animals which hatch their eggs within their bodies.

o'vular, *adj.*, rel. to an ovule.

o'vule, *n.*, rudimentary seed; an unfertilized ovum.

o'vum, *n.*, an egg (*Lat.*); an animal female cell.

owe, *v.t.*, to be under a debt for; *v.i.*, to be in debt.

owed, *p.p.*, owe.

ow'elty, *n.*, equality (*Leg.*).

Ow'enite, *n.*, a follower of Robert Owen, the socialist.

owes, *pr.t.*, owe.

ow'ing, *pr.p.*, owe; *adj.*, due.

owl, *n.*, a raptorial bird so named.

owl'et, *n.*, a young owl.

owl'ing, *n.*, illegal export of wool (*obs.*).

owl'ish, *adj.*, owl-like, stupid.

owl'-like, *adj.*, *i.q.* owlish.

own, *v.t.*, to possess; to claim possession of; admit, confess; *adj.*, bel. to oneself; not another's.

owned, *p.p.*, own.

own'er, *n.*, one who owns.

own'erless, *adj.*, without owner; unclaimed.

own'ership, *n.*, possession.

own'ing, *pr.p.*, own.

ox, *n.*, any bovine animal; esp. the domesticated and castrated male ox.

ox'alate, *n.*, an oxalic acid salt.

oxal'ic, *adj.*, derived from wood-sorrel (oxalis).

ox'en, *n.*, pl. of ox.

ox'eye, *n.*, the name of several genera of the aster.

ox'-eyed, *adj.*, having large, gentle eyes.

oxidabil'ity, *n.*, the quality of being oxidable.

ox'idable, *adj.*, able to be converted into an oxide.

ox'idate, *v.t.*, to oxidize.

ox'idated, *p.p.*, oxidate.

ox'idating, *pr.p.*, oxidate.

oxida'tion, *n.*, the state or result of oxidating.

ox'idator, *n.*, an oxygen-generator.

ox'ide, *n.*, oxygen compounded with another element or with an organic radical.

ox'idizable, *adj.*, able to be oxidized.

ox'idize, *v.t.*, to make to combine with oxygen; to rust; *v.i.*, to rust.

ox'idized, *p.p.*, oxidize.

ox'idizement, *n.*, *i.q.* oxidation.

ox'idizing, *pr.p.*, oxidize.

ox'lip, *n.*, the sort of primrose so named.

Oxo'nian, *adj.*, rel. to Oxford; *n.*, a member of Oxford University.

ox'-tongue, *n.*, an ox's tongue; several kinds of plants so named.

oxyac'id, *n.*, an acid containing oxygen.

ox'ygen, *n.*, the colourless, tasteless, scentless gas so named.

ox'ygenate, *v.t.*, to treat with oxygen.

ox'ygenated, *p.p.*, oxygenate.

ox'ygenating, *pr.p.*, oxygenate.

oxygena'tion, *n.*, the

effect of oxygenating.

oxyg'enator, *n.*, an oxygen-generating apparatus.

oxygen'ic, *adj.*, pert. to oxygen.

ox'ygenizable, *adj.*, able to be oxygenized.

ox'ygenize, *v.t.*, *i.q.* oxygenate.

ox'ygenized, *p.p.*, oxygenize.

ox'ygenizement, *n.*, *i.q.* oxidation.

ox'ygenizing, *pr.p.*, oxygenize.

oxyg'enous, *adj.*, *i.q.* oxygenic.

ox'ygon, *n.*, a triangle with three acute angles.

oxyg'onal, *adj.*, acute-angled.

oxyhy'drogen, *adj.*, rel. to combination of oxygen with hydrogen.

ox'ymel, *n.*, a syrup made from vinegar and honey.

oxymu'riate, *n.*, a chloride.

oxymuriat'ic, *adj.*, rel. to oxygen and muriatic acid.

ox'yopy, *n.*, abnormally acute sight.

oxyph'ony, *n.*, shrillness.

oxyrhyn'cous, *adj.*, with pointed snout or beak.

ox'ytone, *adj.*, with the last syllable accented; *n.*, the accent so placed.

oy'er, *n.*, criminal trial by court of *oyer* and *terminer*.

oyes', oyez', *interj.*, the crier's demand for attention.

oys'ter, *n.*, an edible bivalve.

oys'ter-bed, *n.*, a bed where oysters are cultivated.

oys'ter-catcher, *n.*, a bird so named.

oys'ter-knife, *n.*, a knife for opening oysters.

oys'ter-shell, *n.*, the shell of an oyster.

oys'ter-woman, *n.*, a woman who sells oysters.

ozona'tion, *n.*, the effect of treating with ozone.

o'zone, *n.*, a colourless gas.

ozonif'erous, *adj.*, charged with ozone.

ozonifica'tion, *n.*, the act of treating with ozone.

o'zonize, *v.t.*, to treat with ozone.

o'zonized, *p.p.*, ozonize.

o'zonizing, *pr.p.*, ozonize.

ozonom'eter, *n.*, an apparatus measuring the quantity of ozone.

ozonomet'ric, *adj.*, pert. to ozonometry.

ozonom'etry, *n.*, the process of testing the presence of ozone.

P

pa, *n.*, a childish form of *Papa*.

pab'ular, *adj.*, pert. to food.

pabula'tion, *n.*, the act of providing food.

pab'ulous, *adj.*, *i.q.* pabular.

pab'ulum, *n.*, food (*Lat.*).

pac'a, *n.*, a large South American rodent animal used for food.

pace, *n.*, a step; speed of travelling; *v.i.*, to walk with measured steps; *v.t.*, to measure by steps.

paced, *p.p.*, pace.

pa'cer, *n.*, one that paces; a horse well-trained in pacing.

pacha', pasha', *n.*, a Turkish officer of high rank.

pacha'lic, pasha'lic, *n.*, a province governed by a pasha.

pachydac'tylous, *adj.*, thick-toed.

pach'yderm, *adj.*, pert. to thick-skinned animals; *n.*, an elephant, etc.

pachyder'mal, *adj.*, thick-skinned.

Pachyder'mata, *n.pl.*, an order of hoofed mammals.

pachyder'matous, *adj.* pert. to thick-skinned animals; not sensitive.

pacif'ic, *adj.*, making peace; at peace; *n.*, the name of an ocean.

pacifica'tion, *n.*, the act of pacifying.

pacif'icator, *n.*, a peacemaker.

pacif'icatory, *adj.*, conciliatory.

pacif'icist, *adj.*, advocating a peace policy; *n.*, one who advocates a peace policy.

pac'ified, *p.p.*, pacify.

pac'ifier, *n.*, one who pacifies.

pac'ify, *v.t.*, to calm.

pac'ifying, *pr.p.*, pacify.

pa'cing, *pr.p.*, pace.

pack, *n.*, that which is bound up to be carried; a set of cards; a number of hounds; a mass of floating ice; *v.t.*, to press into narrow space.

pack'age, *n.*, something packed.

packed, *p.p.*, pack.

pack'er, *n.*, one who packs.

pack'et, *n.*, a little package; a packet-boat.

pack'et-boat, *n.*, a vessel carrying mails, passengers, and goods on regular days of starting.

pack'et-ship, *n.*, *i.q.* packet-boat.

pack'horse, *n.*, a horse used for carrying packs of goods.

pack'ing, *n.*, the act of tying into a bundle; stuffing; material used to make the joints of machinery close.

pack'ing-case, *n.*, a deal box for moving and protecting goods.

pack'ing-needle, *n.*, a strong needle for sewing packages.

pack'man, *n.*, a man who carries a pack; a pedlar.

pack'thread, *n.*, a strong thread for sewing up packages.

pack'wax, *n.*, *i.q.* paxwax.

pa'co, *n.*, the alpaca.

pa'cos, *n.*, *i.q.* paco.

pact, *n.*, something agreed upon; a bargain.

pac'tion, *n.*, *i.q.* pact.

pac'tional, *adj.*, by way of agreement.

Pacto'lian, *adj.*, pert. to Pactolus, a river famous for its golden sands.

pad, *n.*, a soft bag or cushion; a number of leaves of paper laid together; an easy-going horse; *v.i.*, to walk slowly; *v.t.*, to stuff with something soft.

pad'ded, *p.p.*, pad.

pad'ding, *n.*, the soft stuffing of a cushion; matter of small value put into a book to extend it; *pr.p.*, pad.

pad'dle, *n.*, a broad-bladed oar; *v.i.* and *t.*, to row with a paddle; *v.i.*, to play in water with hands or feet.

pad'dle-box, *n.*, the covering of a paddle-wheel.

pad'dled, *p.p.*, paddle.

pad'dler, *n.*, one who paddles.

pad'dle-wheel, *n.*, a wheel with floats used in driving a steamship.

pad'dling, *pr.p.*, paddle.

pad'dock, *n.*, a toad or frog; a small grass park.

pad'dy, *n.*, rice in the husk.

pa'dishah, *n.*, a title of the Sultan of Turkey and of the Shah of Persia.

pad'lock, *n.*, a hanging lock with a clasp; *v.t.*, to fasten or provide with a padlock.

pad'locked, *p.p.*, padlock.

pa'dre, *n.*, father; a priest; a clergyman.

padro'ne, *n.*, master; an employer of labour.

pad'uasoy, *n.*, a kind of silk stuff.

pae'an, *n.*, a hymn of triumph.

paedobap′tism, *n.*, the baptism of infants.
paedobap′tist, *n.*, one who holds to infant baptism.
paedol′ogy, *n.*, *i.q.* paidology.
pae′on, *n.*, a metrical four-syllabled foot, with one syllable long.
pa′gan, *n.*, a heathen; *adj.*, rel. to false gods.
pa′ganish, *adj.*, heathenish.
pa′ganism, *n.*, the state of being a pagan.
pa′ganize, *v.t.*, to render heathenish.
pa′ganized, *p.p.*, paganize.
page, *n.*, a boy trained as a servant; a youth waiting on a person of rank; one side of a leaf; *v.t.*, to number pages.
pag′eant, *n.*, any great show; a stage on wheels; a picturesque play.
pag′eantry, *n.*, great display; a showy exhibition.
paged, *p.p.*, page.
pag′inal, *adj.*, consisting of pages.
pag′inate, *v.t.*, to indicate the pages of a book.
pag′inated, *p.p.*, paginate.
pag′inating, *pr.p.*, paginate.
pagina′tion, *n.*, the figures indicating the number of pages.
pa′ging, *pr.p.*, page.
pago′da, *n.*, a Buddhist temple; a coin formerly used in India.
pagu′rian, *n.*, a hermit-crab.
pah, *n.*, a fortified Maori camp; *interj.*, an exclamation of disgust.
paid, *p.p.*, pay.
paidol′ogy, *n.*, the scientific study of children.
pail, *n.*, a vessel of wood or metal in which water or milk is usually carried.
pail′ful, *n.*, as much as a pail will hold.
pain, *n.*, suffering; *v.t.*, to give pain to.
pained, *p.p.*, pain.
pain′ful, *adj.*, giving pain; requiring labour; careful.
pain′fully, *adv.*, in a painful manner.
pain′ing, *pr.p.*, pain.
pain′less, *adj.*, free from pain.
pain′lessly, *adv.*, in a painless manner.
pain′lessness, *n.*, the state of being painless.
pains, *n. pl.*, close application in working; penalties.
pains′taker, *n.*, one who takes pains.
pains′taking, *adj.*, laborious and careful; *n.*, careful labour.
paint, *v.t.*, to colour; to depict; *v.i.*, to practise painting; *n.*, a pigment.
paint′-box, *n.*, a colour-box.
paint′-brush, *n.*, a brush used in painting.
paint′ed, *p.p.*, paint.
paint′er, *n.*, one who paints; an artist in colour; a rope used to fasten a boat.
paint′ing, *n.*, the act or art of laying on colours; a painted picture; *pr.p.*, paint.
pair, *n.*, a couple; *v.i.*, to join in pairs; *v.t.*, to assort in twos.
paired, *p.p.*, pair.
pair′-horse, *adj.*, drawn by two horses.
pair′ing, *pr.p.*, pair.
pair′ing-off, *n.*, the act of departing from a company in couples.
pair′ing-time, *n.*, the time when birds couple.
paja′mas, *n. pl.*, a sleeping suit. Also *pyjamas*.
pal, *n.*, partner; chum (*slang*).
pal′ace, *n.*, the house in which a king or other distinguished person lives; a bishop's official residence; a stately mansion.
pal′adin, *n.*, a knight attached to a sovereign's court; a hero.
pal′aeograph, pal′eograph, *n.*, an ancient manuscript.
palaeog′rapher, paleog′rapher, *n.*, one skilled in palaeography.
palaeograph′ic, paleograph′ic, *adj.*, pert. to palaeography.
palaeog′raphist, paleog′raphist, *n.*, *i.q.* palaeographer.
palaeog′raphy, paleog′raphy, *n.*, the art of deciphering ancient writings.
palaeolith′ic, paleolith′ic, *adj.*, bel. to the earlier stone period of prehistoric time.
palaeolog′ical, paleo′-log′ical, *adj.*, pert. to palaeology.
palaeol′ogist, paleol′-ogist, *n.*, one conversant with paleology.
palaeol′ogy, paleol′-ogy, *n.*, archaeology.
palaeontol′ogy, paleontol′ogy, *n.*, that branch of biology which deals with organic fossil remains.
palaeothe′rium, *n.*, an extinct pachyderm found fossilized.
palaeozo′ic, paleozo′-ic, *adj.*, a term applied to the lowest division of stratified rocks.
palae′stra, *n.*, *i.q.* palestra.
palae′stric, *adj.*, *i.q.* palestric.
palankeen′, palanquin′, *n.*, a covered conveyance for one person, carried on poles on the shoulders of bearers.
pal′atable, *adj.*, agreeable to the taste.
pal′atal, *adj.*, pert. to the palate; *n.*, a sound pronounced with the aid of the palate.

pal'ate, *n.*, the roof of the mouth; taste.

pala'tial, *adj.*, magnificent.

palat'inate, *n.*, the seignory of a palatine.

pal'atine, *adj.*, possessing royal privileges; *n.*, a count palatine.

pala'ver, *n.*, a conference among some savage races; idle talk; *v.i.*, to talk idly; to hold a palaver.

pala'vered, *p.p.*, palaver.

pala'vering, *pr.p.*, palaver.

pale, *adj.*, whitish; dim; *v.i.*, to lose colour; *n.*, a pointed stake used in fencing; an enclosure; a district; in heraldry, a vertical stripe on a shield.

palea'ceous, *adj.*, consisting of chaff-like scales.

paled, *p.p.*, pale.

pale'-eyed, *adj.*, having pale eyes.

pale'-face, *n.*, a name among Red Indians for a white person.

pale'-faced, *adj.*, having a pale face; wan.

pale'ness, *n.*, the condition of being pale.

Palestin'ian, *adj.*, rel. to Palestine.

pales'tra, *n.*, a place for wrestling; the exercise of wrestling.

pales'tric, *adj.*, pert. to the palestra or to wrestling.

pal'etot, *n.*, an overcoat; a loose coat or long jacket.

pal'ette, *n.*, a thin board on which a painter lays his pigments.

pal'frey, *n.*, a riding horse; a small horse for a lady to ride.

Pa'li, *n.*, the sacred language of the Buddhists.

palil'logy, *n.*, the repetition of words to produce emphasis.

pal'impsest, *n.*, a parchment from which one writing, remaining faintly visible, has been removed in order to make room for another.

pal'indrome, *n.*, a word or sentence which reads the same backwards as forwards (*e.g.*, " madam ").

pa'ling, *n.*, a fence formed with pales; *pr.p.*, pale.

palingene'sia, *n.*, *i.q.* palingenesis.

palingen'esis, *n.*, a transformation; a metamorphosis; a great geological change.

pal'inode, *n.*, a recantation.

palisade', *n.*, a fence or fortification made of stakes; *v.t.*, to inclose or fortify with a palisade.

palisa'ded, *p.p.*, palisade.

palisa'ding, *pr.p.*, palisade; *n.*, *i.q.* palisade.

palisa'do, *n.*, *i.q.* palisade.

pa'lish, *adj.*, somewhat pale.

pall, *n.*, a mantle; an ecclesiastical vestment worn by archbishops; a large cloth to cover a coffin; *v.i.*, to become insipid; to lose charm.

Palla'dian, *adj.*, pert. to Palladio, a famous Italian architect, or to his style.

palla'dium, *n.*, a sacred image of Pallas; a guarantee of safety; a rare metal.

pal'let, *n.*, a small, rude bed; a palette; a wooden instrument used by potters and goldbeaters; part of the mechanism of a clock.

pal'lial, *adj.*, pert. to a mantle, esp. the mantle of a mollusc.

palliasse', *n.*, a straw mattress.

pal'liate, *v.t.*, to mitigate; extenuate.

pal'liated, *p.p.*, palliate.

pal'liating, *pr.p.*, palliate.

pallia'tion, *n.*, alleviation; extenuation.

pal'liative, *adj.*, serving to palliate; *n.*, that which palliates.

pal'liatory, *adj.*, *i.q.* palliative.

pal'lid, *adj.*, pale; deficient in colour.

pal'lidness, *n.*, paleness.

pall'ing, *pr.p.*, pall.

pal'lium, *n.*, the mantle of a mollusc; an archbishop's pall (*Lat.*).

pall-mall', *n.*, an ancient game played with balls and mallets.

pal'lor, *n.*, paleness.

palm, *n.*, the inside of the hand; a tropical tree of many species; a symbol of triumph; *v.t.*, to conceal in the palm of the hand; to impose by fraud.

pal'mar, *adj.*, of the breadth of the palm of the hand.

pal'mary, *adj.*, worthy of receiving the palm.

pal'mate, *n.*, a salt of palmic acid.

pal'mate, *adj.*, having the toes webbed; having the shape of the hand.

pal'mated, *adj.*, *i.q.* palmate.

palmed, *p.p.*, palm.

palm'er, *n.*, a pilgrim to the Holy Land.

palmet'to, *n.*, the West Indian cabbage-palm.

palm'ier, *adj.*, *comp.* of palmy.

palm'iest, *adj.*, *super.* of palmy.

pal'min, *n.*, ricinelaidin; a white fatty compound of castor-oil and nitric peroxide.

palm'ing, *pr.p.*, palm.

pal'miped, *adj.*, webfooted; *n.*, a bird with webbed feet.

palm'ist, *n.*, a fortune teller.

pal'mister, *n.*, one that practises palmistry.

pal'mistry, *n.*, the art of telling fortunes by the lines on the hand.
palm'-leaf, *n.*, the leaf of a palm.
palm'-oil, *n.*, a fatty substance resembling butter, obtained from the fruit of certain palms; a bribe (*slang*).
palm'-tree, *n.*, *s.q.* palm (a tree).
palm'y, *adj.*, flourishing.
palp, *n.*, a feeler on the head of an insect.
palpabil'ity, *n.*, obviousness.
pal'pable, *adj.*, perceptible; obvious.
pal'pably, *adv.*, obviously.
palpa'tion, *n.*, the act of feeling.
pal'pebral, *adj.*, pert. to the eyelid or eyebrow.
pal'pebrous, *adj.*, having heavy eyebrows.
pal'piform, *adj.*, having the form of palps or feelers.
palpig'erous, *adj.*, bearing palps.
pal'pitate, *v.i.*, to throb; to tremble.
pal'pitated, *p.p.*, palpitate.
pal'pitating, *pr.p.*, palpitate.
palpita'tion, *n.*, an abnormal pulsation of the heart.
pals'grave, *n.*, a count palatine.
pal'sied, *p.p.*, palsy; *adj.*, affected with palsy.
pal'sy, *n.*, paralysis; *v.t.*, to paralyse.
pal'sying, *pr.p.*, palsy.
pal'ter, *v.i.*, to equivocate.
pal'tered, *p.p.*, palter.
pal'terer, *n.*, an insincere dealer.
pal'tering, *pr.p.*, palter.
pal'trier, *adj.*, *comp.* of paltry.
pal'triest, *adj.*, *super.* of paltry.
pal'trily, *adv.*, in a paltry manner.
pal'triness, *n.*, the state of being paltry.
pal'try, *adj.*, worthless; contemptible.
palu'dal, *adj.*, pert. to a swamp; fenny.
palu'dinous, *adj.*, inhabiting marshes.
pa'ly, *adj.*, wanting colour; divided palewise (*her.*).
pam, *n.*, the knave of clubs in the game of loo.
pam'pas, *n. pl.*, the grassy, treeless plains of south-east South America.
pam'pas-grass, *n.*, a gigantic variety of ornamental grass.
pam'per, *v.t.*, to indulge to excess.
pam'pered, *adj.*, spoiled by indulgence or luxurious feeding; *p.p.*, pamper.
pam'perer, *n.*, one who pampers.
pam'pering, *pr.p.*, pamper.
pam'phlet, *n.*, a small book, stitched but not bound; a short treatise.
pamphleteer', *n.*, a writer of pamphlets; *v.i.*, to write pamphlets.
pamphleteer'ing, *pr.p.* pamphleteer; *n.*, the writing of pamphlets.
pam'pre, *n.*, an architectural ornament consisting of vine-leaves and grapes.
pan, *n.*, a broad, shallow dish; a Greek god of pastures, woods, etc.
panace'a, *n.*, a universal remedy.
panace'an, *adj.*, of the nature of a panacea.
pana'da, *n.*, bread-sop.
panama', *n.*, a thin, light, flexible hat made of fine straw or grass.
pan'cake, *n.*, a thin cake of batter cooked in a pan.
pancra'tium, *n.*, an ancient Greek gymnastic contest, consisting of boxing and wrestling.
pan'creas, *n.*, a large gland lying between the base of the stomach and the vertebrae; the sweetbread.
pancreat'ic, *adj.*, pert. to the pancreas.
Pande'an, *adj.*, pert. to Pan.
pan'dect, *n.*, a complete scientific treatise; in pl., the digest of Roman civil law made by order of Justinian.
pandem'ic, *adj.*, *s.q.* epidemic.
pandemo'nium, *n.*, a lawless, disorderly place or assemblage.
pan'der, *n.*, one who ministers to any of the baser passions; *v.i.*, to act as agent for the lusts of others.
pan'dered, *p.p.*, pander.
pan'dering, *pr.p.*, pander.
pandicula'tion, *n.*, the act of stretching oneself.
Pando'ra, *n.*, the name of the first woman, on whom all the gods and goddesses bestowed gifts.
pando'ra, *n.*, a marine bivalve.
pan'dour, *n.*, a savage Austrian foot soldier.
pan'dy, *n.*, a blow on the hand with a cane or strap.
pane, *n.*, a sunken panel surrounded by a border; a plate of glass inserted in a window.
paned, *adj.*, provided with, or composed of, panes.
panegyr'ic, *n.*, an elaborate encomium; *adj.*, eulogistic.
pan'egyrist, *n.*, a eulogist.
pan'egyrize, *v.t.*, to write or pronounce a eulogy on.
pan'el, *n.*, a compartment of a surface more or less distinct from the rest; a document containing the names of a jury; *v.t.*, to form with panels.

pan'el(l)ed, *p.p.*, panel.

pan'el(l)ing, *pr.p.*, panel; *n.*, panelled work.

pang, *n.*, a paroxysm of pain.

pangen'esis, *n.*, a hypothesis to explain the phenomena of organic development.

Pan-Ger'man, *adj.*, pert. to the union of all the German peoples in one State.

Pan-Ger'manism, *n.*, the Pan-German theory.

pango'lin, *n.*, an ant-eater.

Panhellen'ic, *adj.*, pert. to all Greeks.

Panhel'lenism, *n.*, the union of all the Greeks into one political body.

Panhel'lenist, *n.*, one who advocates Panhellenism.

pan'ic, *n.*, a sudden fright; a kind of grass.

pan'icle, *n.*, a branching inflorescence, as in lilac.

pan'ic-stricken, *adj.*, struck with sudden fear.

pan'ic-struck, *adj.*, *i.q.* panic-stricken.

Panislam'ic, *adj.*, pert. to a confederation of all the Mohammedan nations.

paniv'orous, *adj.*, bread-eating.

panjan'drum, *n.*, a high and mighty personage.

pan'nage, *n.*, the food of swine in the woods; beech-mast, acorns, etc.; the money paid for this.

pan'nel, *n.*, the accused in a criminal trial (*Scots law*).

pan'nier, *n.*, one of two baskets slung across a beast of burden; part of a lady's dress attached to the back of the skirt.

pan'nikin, *n.*, a small cup.

pan'oplied, *adj.*, having a full suit of armour.

pan'oply, *n.*, a full suit of armour.

panop'ticon, *n.*, Bentham's model prison; an exhibition of novelties.

panora'ma, *n.*, a picture in which all the objects visible from a point are represented on the inside of a cylinder.

panoram'ic, *adj.*, pert. to a panorama or complete view.

pan'-pipe, *n.*, a musical wind-instrument made of reeds of different lengths tied together.

Panslav'ic, *adj.*, pert. to all the Slavic races.

Panslav'ism, *n.*, a confederation of all the Slavic peoples.

Panslav'ist, *n.*, one who favours Panslavism.

pansoph'ical, *adj.*, pretending to universal knowledge.

pan'sophy, *n.*, Comenius's scheme of universal knowledge.

panstereora'ma, *n.*, a model in relief of a town or country.

pan'sy, *n.*, a garden violet; heartsease.

pant, *v.i.*, to breathe quickly; *n.*, a gasp.

pan'tagraph, *n.*, *i.q.* pantograph.

pantalettes', **pantalets'**, *n. pl.*, loose drawers.

pantaloon', *n.*, in modern pantomimes, a fatuous old man; *pl.*, a pair of trousers.

pantech'nicon, *n.*, a place where manufactured articles are exposed for sale; a van for removing furniture.

pant'ed, *p.p.*, pant.

pant'er, *n.*, one who pants.

pan'theism, *n.*, the doctrine that the universe is God.

pan'theist, *n.*, one who believes in pantheism.

pantheist'ic, *adj.*, rel. to pantheism.

pantheol'ogy, *n.*, a system of theology comprehending all religions.

Panthe'on, *n.*, a temple dedicated to all the gods.

pan'ther, *n.*, a kind of leopard.

pan'tile, *n.*, a tile with a cross section resembling the letter S.

pant'ing, *pr.p.*, pant.

pan'tler, *n.*, a servant in charge of the pantry.

pan'tofle, *n.*, a slipper.

pan'tograph, *n.*, an instrument for copying drawings to any scale.

pantograph'ic, *adj.*, pert. to a pantograph.

pantog'raphy, *n.*, copying by means of a pantograph.

pantolog'ic, *adj.*, rel. to pantology.

pantol'ogist, *n.*, one who aims at systematizing all branches of knowledge.

pantol'ogy, *n.*, universal knowledge.

pantom'eter, *n.*, an instrument for producing portraits in profile; an instrument for measuring angles.

pantom'etry, *n.*, the use of the pantometer.

pan'tomime, *n.*, dumb show; a Christmas theatrical entertainment of gorgeous scenery and costume and popular music.

pantomim'ic, *adj.*, rel. to pantomime.

pan'tomimist, *n.*, one who acts in pantomime.

pantomor'phic, *adj.*, assuming any shape.

pan'ton, *n.*, a kind of horse-shoe.

pantoph'agist, *n.*, one who eats anything edible.

pantoph'agy, *n.*, miscellaneous diet.

pan'try, *n.*, a room where provisions

are kept or where plate is cleaned.

pants, *n. pl.*, drawers or trousers.

pap, *n.*, soft food; a teat.

papa', *n.*, a child's word for father; the Latin name of the Pope.

pa'pacy, *n.*, the popedom.

pa'pal, *adj.*, rel. to the Pope.

papav'erous, *adj.*, pert. to the poppy family.

papaw', *n.*, a tropical tree.

pa'per, *n.*, a well-known substance for writing and printing on, wrapping, or covering; a newspaper; an essay; a document; *adj.*, made of paper; *v.t.*, to cover with paper.

pa'per-cutter, *n.*, a paper-knife; a machine for cutting paper; a "guillotine."

pa'pered, *p.p.*, paper.

pa'pering, *pr.p.*, paper.

pa'per-maker, *n.*, one who manufactures paper.

pa'per-weight, *n.*, a small weight to keep loose papers together.

pa'pery, *adj.*, like paper.

Pa'phian, *adj.*, rel. to Venus or her rites.

pa'pier-mâ'ché, *n.*, pulped paper moulded, dried, and japanned.

papiliona'ceous, *adj.*, resembling a butterfly.

papil'la, *n.*, a small pap or nipple; a little eminence on the skin; in pl., papillae

pap'illary, *adj.*, pert. to, or resembling, the nipple.

pap'illate, *v.t.*, to grow into a nipple.

pap'illate, *adj.*, covered with papillae.

pap'illose, *adj.*, *i.q.* papillary.

pa'pist, *n.*, a Roman Catholic; an adherent of the Papacy.

papis'tical, *adj.*, rel. to papists.

papoose', *n.*, a Red Indian baby or child.

pappes'cent, *adj.*, gradually becoming covered with down.

pap'pous, *adj.*, downy.

pap'py, *adj.*, soft, like pap.

Pap'uan, *adj.*, bel. to Papua or New Guinea.

pap'ula, *n.*, a pimple.

pap'ular, *adj.*, covered with pimples.

pap'ulous, *adj.*, *i.q.* papular.

papyra'ceous, *adj.*, made of papyrus.

papy'rograph, *n.*, a copying apparatus; a mimeograph.

papyrog'raphy, *n.*, the use of a papyrograph.

papy'rus, *n.*, a kind of sedge common in the Nile valley; a sort of paper made from its stems; a written scroll made of this material.

par, *n.*, state of equality; *i.q.* parr.

par'able, *n.*, a similitude; a fable or allegory with a moral.

parab'ola, *n.*, a plane figure formed when a cone intersects with a plane parallel to its side.

parabol'ic, *adj.*, pert. to a parabola or to a parable.

parabol'iform, *adj.*, having the shape of a parabola.

parab'olist, *n.*, a maker of parables.

parab'oloid, *n.*, the solid figure generated by the revolution of a parabola about its axis.

Paracel'sian, *adj.*, rel. to the doctrines of Paracelsus, the famous 16th cent. philosopher; *n.*, a follower of P.

parach'ronism, *n.*, a mistake in chronology which places an event later than its real date. (The opposite to an anachronism.)

par'achute, *n.*, an instrument enabling an aeronaut to leave his balloon and reach the ground in safety.

par'achutist, *n.*, one who uses a parachute.

par'aclete, *n.*, one called to aid; the Holy Spirit.

paracros'tic, *n.*, a poem in which the first verse contains in order the initial letters of all that follow.

parade', *n.*, display; the place where troops are drawn up for inspection; a public walk; *v.t.* and *i.*, to assemble in military order.

para'ded, *p.p.*, parade.

par'adigm, *n.*, a word displayed with all its inflections.

para'ding, *pr.p.*, parade.

paradisa'ical, *adj.*, pert. to Paradise.

par'adisal, *adj.*, *i.q.* paradisaical.

Par'adise, *n.*, the Garden of Eden; the abode of the blessed.

par'ados, *n.*, a parapet in the rear of a fortification.

par'adox, *n.*, a statement which seems contrary to common sense, but which is really true.

paradox'ical, *adj.*, rel. to a paradox.

par'affin, *n.*, a fatty substance used in making candles.

paragen'esis, *n.*, the origin of two things side by side.

parago'ge, *n.*, the addition of a letter or syllable to a word.

paragog'ic, *adj.*, lengthening a word by an affix.

par'agon, *n.*, a model of excellence.

par'agram, *n.*, a pun.

paragram'matist, *n.*, a punster.

par'agraph, *n.*, a portion of a writing dealing with one particular point.

paragraph'ic, *adj.*, rel. to a paragraph.

par'akeet, *n.*, *i.q.* parrakeet.

paral'dehyde, *n.*, a colourless liquid hypnotic.

paralip'sis, *n.*, a rhetorical figure involving a pretended omission.

paralipom'ena, *n. pl.*, a supplement containing omissions; the Books of Chronicles in the Bible.

parallac'tic, *adj.*, pert. to parallax.

par'allax, *n.*, apparent change of position due to change of point of view; angular difference between direction of a heavenly body as viewed from the surface and the centre of the earth (or sun).

par'allel, *adj.*, lying in the same direction and equidistant throughout; exactly similar; *n.*, one of such a pair of lines; a small circle on a globe parallel to its equator; likeness; comparison; *v.t.*, to compare; to equal.

parallelep'iped, *n.*, a solid shaped like a brick.

parallelepip'edon, *n.*, *i.q.* parallelepiped.

par'allelism, *n.*, the state of being parallel.

parallel'ogram, *n.*, a four-sided figure with its opposite sides parallel.

paral'ogism, *n.*, a piece of false reasoning.

paral'ogize, *v.i.*, to reason falsely.

paralysa'tion, *n.*, the action of paralysis.

par'alyse, *v.t.*, to affect with paralysis.

par'alysed, *p.p.*, paralyse.

par'alysing, *pr.p.*, paralyse.

paral'ysis, *n.*, a nervous disease producing loss of power or sensation.

paralyt'ic, *n.*, a person affected with paralysis; *adj.*, rel. to paralysis.

paramat'ta, *n.*, a light merino and cotton dress-fabric.

param'eter, *n.*, a constant in the equation of a curve.

par'amount, *adj.*, superior to all others; *n.*, chief.

par'amour, *n.*, a lover.

par'anymph, *n.*, a bridesman.

par'apegm, *n.*, a brass tablet for proclamations fixed to a pillar.

par'apet, *n.*, a breastwork; a wall placed at the edge of a bridge or platform to prevent people from falling over.

par'apeted, *adj.*, provided with a parapet.

par'aph, *n.*, a flourish under a signature.

parapherna'lia, *n. pl.*, appendages; trappings; a bride's private possessions.

par'aphrase, *n.*, a restatement in other and clearer terms; *v.i.* and *t.*, to explain fully; to make a paraphrase of.

par'aphrased, *p.p.*, paraphrase.

par'aphrasing, *pr.p.*, paraphrase.

par'aphrast, *n.*, one who paraphrases.

paraphras'tic, *adj.*, having the nature of a paraphrase.

paraple'gia, *n.*, paralysis of the lower limbs.

par'aplegy, *n.*, *i.q.* paraplegia.

par'asang, *n.*, an ancient Persian measure of length, equal to 30 stadia or about 3½ miles.

par'ascene, *n.*, *i.q.* parascenium.

parasce'nium, *n.*, one of the two projecting wings of a Greek theatre.

Parasce've, *n.*, Good Friday. (Literally, the Preparation for the Sabbath.)

parasele'ne, *n.*, a mock moon; a luminous ring round the moon.

par'asite, *n.*, a sycophant; a plant or animal that lives on or in other plants or animals and feeds upon their juices.

parasit'ic, *adj.*, having the nature of a parasite.

parasit'ical, *adj.*, *i.q.* parasitic.

par'asitism, *n.*, the state of being a parasite.

parasol', *n.*, a small umbrella or sunshade.

parath'esis, *n.*, grammatical apposition.

paravail', *adj.*, inferior; lowest (a feudal term).

par'boil, *v.t.*, to boil partly.

par'boiled, *p.p.*, parboil.

par'boiling, *pr.p.*, parboil.

par'buckle, *n.*, a single rope used in hoisting.

par'cel, *n.*, a package; a collection or group; a divided portion; *v.t.*, to divide into portions.

par'cel(l)ed, *p.p.*, parcel.

par'cel(l)ing, *pr.p.*, parcel.

par'cenary, *n.*, *i.q.* coparcenary.

par'cenar, *n.*, a coheir.

parch, *v.t.*, to dry extremely; *v.i.*, to grow very dry.

parched, *p.p.*, parch.

parch'ing, *pr.p.*, parch; *adj.*, causing extreme dryness or thirst.

parch'ment, *n.*, the skin of a young animal prepared for writing on.

pard, *n.*, a leopard or panther.

par'don, *v.t.*, to forgive; *n.*, forgiveness.
par'donable, *adj.*, excusable.
par'doned, *p.p.*, pardon.
par'doner, *n.*, one who pardons; one licensed to sell indulgences.
par'doning, *pr.p.*, pardon.
pare, *v.t.*, to trim or shave off the surface of.
pared, *p.p.*, pare.
paregor'ic, *n.*, a medicine assuaging pain; a tincture of opium.
parem'bole, *n.*, an explanatory phrase thrown into a sentence.
paren'chyma, *n.*, spongy and fibrous tissue of plants or animals.
parenchym'atous, *adj.*, of the nature of parenchyma.
parenet'ic, *adj.*, persuasive.
pa'rent, *n.*, a father or mother.
pa'rentage, *n.*, birth; origin.
paren'tal, *adj.*, characteristic of parents.
paren'thesis, *n.*, a detached explanatory sentence inserted into another and enclosed by brackets, dashes, or commas.
parenthet'ic, *adj.*, of the nature of a parenthesis.
parenthet'ical, *adj.*, *i.q.* parenthetic.
paren'ticide, *n.*, the killing of a parent.
pa'rentless, *adj.*, without parents; orphaned.
pa'rer, *n.*, one who, or that which, pares.
par'gasite, *n.*, a kind of hornblende.
par'get, *n.*, ornamental plaster; *v.t.* and *i.*, to ornament with plaster-work.
par'geter, *n.*, an ornamental plasterer.
par'geting, *n.*, ornamental plaster-work; *pr.p.*, parget.
parhe'lic, *adj.*, rel. to parhelia.
parhe'lion, *n.*, a mock sun.
pa'riah, *n.*, an outcast; one of the lowest class of Hindus.
pa'rial, *n.*, pair royal; three of a kind.
Pa'rian, *adj.*, rel. to the island of Paros and its marble.
pari'etal, *adj.*, pert. to a wall.
pari'etary, *n.*, the wall-pellitory.
pa'ring, *n.*, what is pared off; the rind; *pr.p.*, pare.
par'ish, *n.*, a district under a parson; *adj.*, pert. to a parish.
parish'ioner, *n.*, one bel. to a parish.
Paris'ian, *n.*, a native or inhabitant of Paris; *adj.*, rel. to Paris.
parisol'ogy, *n.*, the use of ambiguous language.
parisyllab'ic, *adj.*, having equal syllables.
par'ity, *n.*, equality; analogy.
park, *n.*, a large piece of pasture and woodland ground surrounding a mansion; a public pleasure garden; a train of artillery.
par'lance, *n.*, conversation; talk.
par'ley, *v.i.*, to confer with an enemy; *n.*, a conference with an enemy.
par'leyed, *p.p.*, parley.
par'leying, *pr.p.*, parley.
par'liament, *n.*, the supreme national council.
or
parliamenta'rian, *n.*, one of those who served the Parliament against Charles I.
parliamen'tary, *adj.*, pert. to parliament.
par'lour, *n.*, a sitting-room.
par'lous, *adj.*, risky; shocking.
par'lousness, *n.*, riskiness.
Parmesan', *adj.*, pert. to Parma and its cheese.
Parnas'sian, *adj.*, rel. to Mount Parnassus and the Muses.
paro'chial, *adj.*, bel. to a parish.
parod'ic, *adj.*, rel. to parody.
par'odied, *p.p.*, parody.
par'odist, *n.*, one who writes a parody.
par'ody, *n.*, a burlesque imitation of a serious composition; *v.t.*, to turn into a parody.
par'odying, *pr.p.*, parody.
parole', *n.*, word of honour.
par'onym, *n.*, a paronymous word.
paron'ymous, *adj.*, having the same sound but differing in spelling.
paron'ymy, *n.*, the quality of being paronymous.
par'oquet, *n.*, *i.q.* parrakeet.
parot'id, *n.*, a salivary gland on either side of the face.
paroti'tis, *n.*, mumps.
par'oxysm, *n.*, a convulsion; a fit.
paroxys'mal, *adj.*, marked by a paroxysm.
parquet', *n.*, that part of the floor of a theatre between the pit and the orchestra; *adj.*, of inlaid woodwork.
par'quet, *v.t.*, to ornament with parquetry.
par'quetry, *n.*, inlaid woodwork used for floors.
parr, *n.*, a young salmon.
par'rakeet, *n.*, a small eastern parrot with a long tail.
parrici'dal, *adj.*, committing parricide.
par'ricide, *n.*, the murder, or murderer, of a father.
par'ried, *p.p.*, parry.
par'rot, *n.*, a climbing bird with a hooked beak, sometimes able to imitate the human voice.

par'ry, *v.t.*, to ward off; *n.*, the act of parrying.

par'rying, *pr.p.*, parry.

parse, *v.t.*, to analyse a word grammatically.

parsed, *p.p.*, parse.

Parsee', *n.*, an Indian fire-worshipper.

Par'seeism, *n.*, the religion of the Parsees.

pars'er, *n.*, one who parses.

parsimo'nious, *adj.*, niggardly.

parsimo'niously, *adv.*, in a parsimonious manner.

parsimo'niousness, *n.*, the quality of being parsimonious.

par'simony, *n.*, niggardliness.

pars'ing, *n.*, the act of analysing a word grammatically; *pr.p.*, parse.

pars'ley, *n.*, a well-known garden vegetable.

pars'nip, *n.*, a plant with a white, edible root.

par'son, *n.*, the priest of a parish; the curate.

par'sonage, *n.*, the house of a parson; a benefice.

part, *n.*, a portion; *v.t.*, to divide; *adv.*, partly.

partake', *v.i.*, to participate.

parta'ken, *p.p.*, partake.

parta'ker, *n.*, a sharer.

parta'king, *pr.p.*, partake.

part'ed, *p.p.*, part.

part'er, *n.*, one who parts.

parterre', *n.*, a system of flower-beds; the pit of a theatre.

parthen'ic, *adj.*, born of an unmarried woman.

Par'thenon, *n.*, the temple of Athena on the Acropolis at Athens.

Parthen'ope, *n.*, one of the Sirens; the city of Naples.

par'tial, *adj.*, affecting a part only; inclined to favour; *n.*, a harmonic (*mus.*).

par'tialism, *n.*, the doctrine of the partialists.

par'tialist, *n.*, one who holds the doctrine that the Atonement was made for a part only of mankind.

partial'ity, *n.*, undue favour; fondness.

par'tially, *adv.*, in part; with undue bias.

part'ible, *adj.*, divisible.

partic'ipant, *n.*, *i.q.* partaker.

partic'ipate, *v.i.*, to have a share.

partic'ipated, *p.p.*, participate.

partic'ipating, *pr.p.*, participate.

participa'tion, *n.*, the state of sharing in common with others

partic'ipative, *adj.*, capable of participating.

partic'ipator, *n.*, one who participates.

particip'ial, *adj.*, having the nature of a participle.

par'ticiple, *n.*, a form of the verb which possesses some of the powers of an adjective.

par'ticle, *n.*, any very small portion; a word incapable of being inflected.

partic'ular, *adj.*, individual; special; circumstantial; precise; *n.*, a detail; a single instance.

partic'ularism, *n.*, the theological doctrine of particular election.

partic'ularist, *n.*, one who holds the doctrine of particularism.

particular'ity, *n.*, that which is particular; the state of being particular.

partic'ularize, *v.t.*, to specify.

partic'ularized, *p.p.*, particularize.

partic'ularizing, *pr.p.*, particularize.

partic'ularly, *adv.*, in a particular manner; specifically.

part'ing, *pr.p.*, part; *adj.*, given at parting; *n.*, a division.

par'tisan, *n.*, a kind of halbert or pike; an adherent of a party; *adj.*, biased.

par'tisanship, *n.*, the state of being a partisan.

par'tite, *adj.*, divided to the base.

parti'tion, *n.*, division; a wall of separation; a division; *v.t.*, to divide.

parti'tioned, *p.p.*, partition.

parti'tioning, *pr.p.*, partition.

par'titive, *adj.*, expressing the relation of a part to the whole.

part'let, *n.*, a 16th cent. garment for women; a hen.

part'ly, *adv.*, in part.

part'ner, *n.*, one who shares with another in a business, dance, etc.

part'nership, *n.*, the state of being a partner.

partook', *p.t.*, partake.

par'tridge, *n.*, a bird of the grouse family.

parts, *n.*, pl. of part; talent, ability.

partu'rient, *adj.*, bringing forth young.

parturi'tion, *n.*, the act of bringing forth young.

par'ty, *n.*, a number of persons united for some common purpose; *adj.*, divided into differently tinctured parts (*her.*).

par'ty-coloured, *adj.*, coloured differently in different parts.

par'ty-spirit, *n.*, the spirit that unites members of a party.

parure', *n.*, a set of ornaments.

par'venu, *n.*, an upstart; one newly risen.

pas, *n.*, a step; precedence (*Fr.*).

Pasch, *n.*, the Passover; Easter.

pas'chal, *adj.*, pert. to the Passover or to Easter.

pash, *v.t.*, to strike violently.

pasha', *n.*, a Turkish officer of high rank.

pasigraph'ic, *adj.*, rel. to pasigraphy.

pasig'raphy, *n.*, a system of universal writing; a universal language.

pasque'-flower, *n.*, a kind of anemone with large purple flowers.

pas'quin, *n.*, *i.q.* pasquinade.

pasquinade', *n.*, a lampoon; *v.t.* and *i.*, to satirize in writing.

pass, *n.*, a defile between two mountains; a ticket of free admission or passage; attainment of the qualifying standard in an examination; *v.t.* and *i.*, to proceed; vanish; go beyond or by; succeed in an examination.

pass'able, *adj.*, current; receivable; tolerable.

pass'ably, *adv.*, tolerably.

passade', *n.*, a thrust in fencing (*Fr.*).

pas'sage, *n.*, transit; a way or corridor through which one may pass; a portion of a book or poem quoted.

pas'sant, *adj.*, an heraldic term describing an animal which appears to be walking.

pass'-book, *n.*, a bank book.

passed, *p.p.*, pass.

passée', *adj.*, faded; a term applied to a woman who has lost the bloom of youth (*Fr.*).

pas'senger, *n.*, a traveller in a conveyance of any kind.

pass'er, *n.*, one that passes.

passer-*by',* *n.*, one who goes by.

pas'serine, *adj.*, rel. to the order of birds called passeres or perchers.

passibil'ity, *n.*, the quality of being passible.

pass'ible, *adj.*, impressionable.

pas'sim, *adv.*, here and there; in many places in a book (*Lat.*).

pass'ing, *adv.*, exceedingly; *pr.p.*, pass.

pass'ing-bell, *n.*, a bell rung when a parishioner is dying.

pas'sion, *n.*, the last suffering of the Saviour; a strong emotion; anger; ardour.

pas'sional, *n.*, a book describing the sufferings of saints and martyrs.

pas'sionate, *adj.*, irascible; vehement; emotional.

pas'sionately, *adv.*, ardently; angrily.

pas'sion-flower, *n.*, a plant with flowers supposed to symbolize the Passion.

pas'sionist, *n.*, a member of a Roman Catholic congregation devoted to keeping in memory the Passion of Christ.

pas'sionless, *adj.*, void of passion.

Pas'sion-play, *n.*, a miracle play representing scenes in the Passion.

Pas'sion Week, *n.*, the week before Holy Week and following Passion Sunday, the fifth Sunday in Lent.

pas'sive, *adj.*, unresisting; inert.

pas'sively, *adv.*, without action or resistance.

pas'siveness, *n.*, the quality of being passive.

passiv'ity, *n.*, *i.q.* passiveness.

Pass'over, *n.*, a Jewish Feast; the paschal lamb.

pass'port, *n.*, a safe-conduct granted to travellers.

pass'*word,* *n.*, a secret word by which a friend may be distinguished from a stranger.

past, *adj.*, existing no more; *n.*, a bygone time; *prep.*, after; beyond; by; *adv.*, by.

paste, *n.*, a soft mass; a kind of cement; a composition of which imitation precious stones are made; *v.t.*, to cement with paste.

paste'board, *n.*, cardboard.

pa'sted, *p.p.*, paste.

pas'tel, *n.*, a coloured crayon.

pas'tern, *n.*, that part of the leg of a horse between the hoof and the next joint; a shackle for horses while grazing.

Past'eurism, *n.*, a method of inoculation practised by Louis Pasteur.

Past'eurize, *v.t.*, to age wine or beer after Pasteur's method.

pastic'cio, *n.*, a picture painted by a master in imitation of the style of another artist; a medley or miscellany.

pas'til, *n.*, *i.q.* pastille.

pastille', *n.*, a little roll of paste which gives a fragrant smell when burned.

pas'time, *n.*, amusement; sport.

pa'sting, *pr.p.*, paste.

pas'tor, *n.*, a bishop. (Loosely used of other ministers of religion.)

pas'toral, *adj.*, rural; rel. to a pastor; *n.*, a bucolic poem.

pastora'le, *n.*, a melody or symphony in rustic style.

pas'torate, *n.*, the office of pastor.

pa'stry, *n.*, food made chiefly of paste.

pa'stry-cook, *n.*, one who makes and sells pastry.

pas'turable, *adj.*, fit for pasture.

pas'turage, *n.*, growing grass on which cattle are fed.

pas'ture, *n.*, a grazing ground; *v.t.*, to feed on growing grass.
pas'tured, *p.p.*, pasture.
pas'turing, *pr.p.*, pasture.
pas'ty, *n.*, a meat-pie covered with paste; *adj.*, like paste.
pat, *v.t.*, to tap with the fingers; *n.*, a light blow; a small shaped piece of butter; *adj.*, apt; *adv.*, fitly.
Patago'nian, *adj.*, pert. to Patagonia; *n.*, a native or inhabitant of Patagonia.
patch, *n.*, a piece of cloth sewn on a garment to repair it; a small plot of ground; *v.t.*, to mend by patching.
patched, *p.p.*, patch.
patch'er, *n.*, one who patches.
patch'ing *pr.p.*, patch.
patchou'li, *n.*, a perfume extracted from the leaves of an Indian and Chinese plant of the same name.
patch'work, *n.*, pieces of various shapes and colours sewn together.
patch'y, *adj.* full of patches.
pate, *n.*, the head; the top of the head.
pâté', *n.*, a little pie.
patel'la, *n.*, a small dish; the knee-pan.
patel'liform *adj.*, saucer-shaped.
pat'en, *n.*, a metal plate in which the Host is placed in the Sacrament of the Altar.
patent, *adj.*, evident; secured by law as an exclusive privilege; *n.*, a privilege conferring a limited monopoly; *v.t.*, to secure by a patent.
pat'entable, *adj.*, capable of being patented.
pat'ented, *p.p.*, patent.
patentee', *n.*, one who possesses patent-rights.
pat'enting, *pr.p.*, patent.
paterfamil'ias, *n.*, the father or head of a family.
pater'nal, *adj.*, fatherly; on the father's side.
pater'nity, *n.*, the relation of a father to his offspring.
pat'ernoster, *n.*, the Lord's Prayer; every tenth bead in a rosary; a rosary itself.
path, *n.*, a way.
Pathan', *n.*, an Afghan; an Indian of Afghan descent.
pathet'ic, *adj.*, exciting tender emotion.
pathet'ically, *adv.*, in a pathetic manner.
path'less, *adj.*, untrodden; having no beaten way.
pathog'eny, *n.*, the science of the origin and development of disease.
pathognomon'ic, *adj.*, characteristic of a particular disease.
pathog'nomy, *n.*, the science of the expression of the passions.
patholog'ic, *adj.*, *s.q.* pathological.
patholog'ical, *adj.*, pert. to pathology.
patholog'ically, *adv.*, in a pathological manner.
pathol'ogist, *n.*, one skilled in pathology.
pathol'ogy, *n.*, the science of the causes and symptoms of diseases.
pa'thos, *n.*, the quality that awakens the tender emotions.
path'way, *n.*, a path; a narrow way for foot-passengers.
pa'tience, *n.*, forbearance; constancy in labour.
pa'tient, *adj.*, bearing pain or affliction without murmuring; calmly diligent; *n.*, a person under medical treatment.
pa'tiently, *adv.*, uncomplainingly.
pat'ina, *n.*, the fine green rust of copper or bronze.
pat'ly, *adv.*, fitly.
patois', *n.*, a rustic or provincial mode of speech (*Fr.*).
pa'triarch, *n.*, the father and ruler of a family; an aged venerable man; a bishop of the highest rank, above an Archbishop or Metropolitan.
patriar'chal, *adj.*, bel. to a patriarch.
pat'riarchate, *n.*, the jurisdiction of a patriarch.
patriar'chic, *adj.*, *s.q.* patriarchal.
pa'triarchy, *n.*, *s.q.* patriarchate.
patri'cian, *adj.*, of noble birth; bel. to the senatorial order in ancient Rome; *n.*, a person of noble birth.
pat'ricidal, *adj.*, rel. to patricide.
pat'ricide, *n.*, the murder or murderer of a father.
patrimo'nial, *adj.*, inherited from ancestors.
pat'rimony, *n.*, a right or estate inherited from ancestors.
pat'riot, *n.*, a person who loves his country and zealously supports and defends it.
patriot'ic, *adj.*, having the feelings of a patriot.
patriot'ically, *adv.*, in a patriotic manner.
pat'riotism, *n.*, love of one's country.
Patripas'sian, *n.*, one of a sect of the Early Christian Church who taught that God the Father shared the sufferings of His Son.
patris'tic, *adj.*, pert. to the fathers of the Early Christian Church.
patrol', *n.*, the marching round of a military or police guard; a constable with a regular beat; *v.i.* and *t.*, to go the rounds.

patrolled', *p.p.*, patrol.
patrol'ling, *pr.p.*, patrol.
pa'tron, *n.*, a man of position who assists an inferior; one who has the gift of an ecclesiastical benefice.
pat'ronage, *n.*, the act of patronizing; the right of presentation to an ecclesiastical benefice.
pat'ronal, *adj.*, acting as a patron; bel. to a patron saint.
pa'troness, *n.*, a lady patron.
pat'ronize, *v.t.*, to act as, or to assume the air of, a patron.
pat'ronized, *p.p.*, patronize.
pat'ronizer, *n.*, one who patronizes.
pat'ronizing, *pr.p.*, patronize; *adj.*, condescending.
patronym'ic, *n.*, a personal name derived from that of a parent or ancestor; a surname.
patroon', *n.*, the proprietor of a manor in the State of New York.
pat'ten, *n.*, a wooden shoe standing on a ring, worn to keep the feet above the mud.
pat'ter, *v.i.*, to make a quick succession of small sounds; to mutter; *n.*, thieves' slang; rapid talk.
pat'tered, *p.p.*, patter.
pat'tering, *pr.p.*, patter.
pat'tern, *n.*, a model; an ornamental design on a woven fabric.
pat'ty, *n.*, a little pie.
pat'ty-pan, *n.*, a pan to bake patties in.
pat'ulous, *adj.*, opening widely.
pau'city, *n.*, fewness.
Paul'ine, *adj.*, pert. to St. Paul.
Paul'ist, *n.*, a member of the American Congregation of the Missionary Priests of St. Paul the Apostle.
paunch, *n.*, the belly.
pau'per, *n.*, a poor person, esp. one supported by law or charity.
pau'perism, *n.*, indigence.
pauperiza'tion, *n.*, the act of pauperizing.
pau'perize, *v.t.*, to reduce to the state of a pauper.
pau'perized, *p.p.*, pauperize.
pau'perizing, *pr.p.*, pauperize.
pause, *n.*, a temporary cessation; *v.i.*, to make a short stop.
paused, *p.p.*, pause.
paus'er, *n.*, one who pauses.
paus'ing, *pr.p.*, pause.
pave, *v.t.*, to floor with stone, wood, brick, etc.
pavé', *n.*, a street pavement (*Fr.*).
paved, *p.p.*, pave.
pave'ment, *n.*, a paved path or road.
pa'ver, *n.*, *i.q.* paviour.
pavil'ion, *n.*, a tent; a canopy.
pa'ving, *n.*, the laying of pavement; *pr.p.*, pave.
pa'viour, **pa'vior**, *n.*, one whose occupation is to pave.
pa'vo, *n.*, the Peacock—a constellation.
pav'onine, *adj.*, bel. to a peacock; iridescent.
paw, *n.*, the foot of a quadruped; *v.i.*, to draw the fore-foot along the ground.
pawed, *adj.*, having paws; *p.p.*, paw.
paw'ing, *pr.p.*, paw.
pawl, *n.*, a click which falls into the teeth of a ratchet-wheel.
pawn, *n.*, a piece of the lowest value at chess; a pledge; *v.t.*, to pledge with a pawnbroker.
pawn'broker, *n.*, a person licensed to lend money on goods deposited with him.
pawned, *p.p.*, pawn.
pawnee', *n.*, one with whom a pledge is deposited as security.
pawn'er, *n.*, one who pawns.
pawn'ing, *pr.p.*, pawn.
pawn'shop, *n.*, the place of business of a pawnbroker.
pawn'-ticket, *n.*, a ticket or receipt given by a pawnbroker to the pawner.
pax, *n.*, a small tablet engraved with sacred emblems which is first kissed by the priest and then passed to others to be kissed.
pax'wax, *n.*, a tendon in the neck of an animal. Also *packwax*.
pay, *v.t.*, to discharge a debt; *v.i.*, to be remunerative; *n.*, remuneration for goods purchased, services rendered, etc.
pay'able, *adj.*, suitable to be paid; due.
pay'-day, *n.*, the day for paying wages.
payee', *n.*, one to whom money is to be paid.
pay'er, *n.*, one who pays.
pay'ing, *pr.p.*, pay; *adj.*, advantageous.
pay'master, *n.*, an officer in the army or navy who regularly pays the officers and men.
pay'ment, *n.*, the discharge of a debt.
pay'nim, *n.*, a pagan.
pea, *n.*, a valuable vegetable; one of its seeds.
peace, *n.*, a state of tranquillity.
peace'able, *adj.*, disposed to peace.
peace'ably, *adv.*, in a peaceable manner.
peace'ful, *adj.*, possessing peace.
peace'fully, *adv.*, tranquilly.
peace'fulness, *n.*, the state or quality of being peaceful.
peace'maker, *n.*, one who reconciles parties in disagreement.

peace'-offering, *n.*, a propitiatory offering.
peace'-officer, *n.*, a civil officer to preserve the public peace.
peach, *n.*, a tree with a delicious fleshy fruit containing a stone; *v.i.*, to turn informer (*colloq.*).
pea-chick, *n.*, a young pea-fowl.
peach'-tree, *n.*, a tree bearing the fruit called peach.
peach'y, *adj.*, resembling a peach, esp. in colour and texture.
pea'cock, *n.*, a large gallinaceous bird of beautiful plumage.
pea'fowl, *n.*, the peacock or peahen.
pea'hen, *n.*, the female of the peacock.
pea'-jacket, *n.*, a thick, loose, woollen jacket worn by seamen.
peak, *n.*, the top of a hill that ends in a point; any projection, esp. of a cap; *v.i.*, to look thin and ill.
peaked, *adj.*, pointed; *p.p.*, peak.
peak'ish, *adj.*, thin-faced and sickly-looking.
peal, *n.*, a succession of loud sounds; *v.i.*, to utter a peal; *v.t.*, to cause to ring or sound.
pealed, *p.p.*, peal.
peal'ing, *pr.p.*, peal.
pean, *n.*, *i.q.* paean.
pea'nut, *n.*, the ground-nut or arachis.
pear, *n.*, a well-known tree and its fruit.
pearl, *n.*, a silvery, hard, smooth round or oval body produced by certain molluscs in their shells; an affection of the eye, also called cataract; a small printing type; *v.t.*, to set with pearls; to make like pearls; *v.i.*, to form into pearls; to dive for pearls.
pearl'-ash, *n.*, commercial potassium carbonate.
pearled, *adj.*, adorned with pearls; *p.p.*, pearl.
pearl'ing, *pr.p.*, pearl.
pearl'-stitch, *n.*, a seam-stitch in knitting.
pearl'y, *adj.*, containing or resembling pearls.
pear'main, *n.*, a kind of apple.
pear'-shaped, *adj.*, shaped like a pear.
pear'-tree, *n.*, a fruit-tree yielding pears.
peas'ant, *n.*, a countryman.
peas'antry, *n.*, country people collectively.
peas'cod, **pease'cod**, *n.*, the pod or shell of a pea.
pease, *n. pl.*, peas collectively.
pease'-pudding, *n.*, a pudding made chiefly of peas.
pea'-soup, *n.*, soup made from peas.
pea'shooter, *n.*, a tube through which peas are blown as missiles.
peat, *n.*, a kind of turf used as fuel.
peat'-moss, *n.*, a moss producing peat.
peat'y, *adj.*, resembling, composed of, or abounding in peat.
peb'ble, *n.*, a small rounded stone; agate; colourless, transparent rock-crystal.
peb'bled, *adj.*, abounding with pebbles.
peb'bly, *adj.*, full of pebbles.
peb'ble-stone, *n.*, a pebble.
pecan', *n.*, a kind of hickory.
peccabil'ity, *n.*, the state of being peccable.
pec'cable, *adj.*, liable to sin.
peccadil'lo, *n.*, a slight offence.
pec'cancy, *n.*, the state of being peccant.
pec'cant, *adj.*, sinning; corrupt.
pec'cary, *n.*, a pachydermatous American hog.
pecca'vi, *interj.*, an acknowledgment of fault. (This Lat. word=I have sinned.)
peck, *n.*, a quarter of a bushel; *v.t.*, to strike or pick up with the beak, or with a pointed instrument.
pecked, *p.p.*, peck.
peck'er, *n.*, one who, or that which, pecks.
peck'ing, *pr.p.*, peck.
pec'ten, *n.*, a marine bivalve the shells of which have diverging ribs and furrows.
pec'tinal, *adj.*, resembling a comb.
pec'tinate, *adj.*, toothed like a comb.
pec'tinated, *adj.*, *i.q.* pectinate.
pectina'tion, *n.*, the state of being pectinated.
pec'tine, *n.*, the basis of vegetable jelly.
pec'tolite, *n.*, a whitish sodium-calcium silicate.
pec'toral, *adj.*, pert. to the breast; *n.*, a breastplate.
pec'ulate, *v.i.*, to embezzle.
pec'ulated, *p.p.*, peculate.
pec'ulating, *pr.p.*, peculate.
pecula'tion, *n.*, embezzlement.
pec'ulator, *n.*, one who peculates.
pecu'liar, *adj.*, one's own; specially belonging; eccentric.
peculiar'ity, *n.*, a special characteristic; the state of being peculiar.
pecu'liarize, *v.t.*, to set apart; to appropriate.
pecu'liarly, *adv.*, in a manner not common to others.
pecu'niarily, *adv.*, in a pecuniary manner.
pecu'niary, *adj.*, rel. to money.

pedagog'ic, *adj.*, rel. to a pedagogue.

ped'agogism, *n.*, the business or manners of a pedagogue.

ped'agogue, *n.*, a schoolmaster.

ped'agogy, *n.*, the science of the principles of teaching.

ped'al, *adj.*, rel. to a foot or to a pedal; *n.*, a lever to be pressed down by the foot.

peda'lian, *adj.*, rel. to metrical feet.

pedal'ity, *n.*, measurement by paces.

ped'ant, *n.*, one who vainly displays his learning; a formalist.

pedan'tic, *adj.*, pert. to a pedant.

ped'antry, *n.*, boastful display of learning; obstinate adherence to rules.

ped'ate, *adj.*, having divisions like toes; divided into lobes.

ped'dle, *v.i.*, to retail small wares; to trifle; *v.t.*, to sell in small quantities while travelling about the country.

ped'dled, *p.p.*, peddle.

ped'dling, *pr.p.*, peddle.

ped'estal, *n.*, a basement or support for a statue, etc.

pedes'trial, *adj.*, bel. to the feet.

pedes'trian, *adj.*, going on foot; *n.*, a walker.

pedes'trianism, *n.*, the practice of walking.

pedes'trianize, *v.i.*, to tour on foot.

ped'icel, *n.*, the stalk of a single flower or leaf; the footstalk of a zoophyte.

ped'icel(l)ate, *adj.*, having a pedicel.

ped'icel(l)ed, *adj.*, having pedicels.

ped'icle, *n.*, *i.q.* pedicel.

pedic'ular, *adj.*, lousy.

pedicula'tion, *n.*, lousiness.

pedic'ulous, *adj.*, *i.q.* pedicular.

ped'icure, *n.*, the care and lesser surgery of the feet.

pedig'erous, *adj.*, having feet or legs.

ped'igree, *n.*, lineage; a genealogical tree.

ped'iment, *n.*, a gable in Greek architecture.

ped'imented, *adj.*, having a pediment.

ped'ipalp, *n.*, an arachnid; an appendage of a male spider.

ped'lar, *n.*, a travelling chapman.

ped'lary, *n.*, pedlar's wares; the employment of a pedlar.

pedobap'tism, *n.*, *i.q.* paedobaptism.

pedobap'tist, *n.* *i.q.* paedobaptist.

pedom'eter, *n.*, an instrument for numbering paces and so ascertaining distances travelled on foot.

pedomet'ric, *adj.*, pert. to a pedometer.

pedun'cle, *n.*, the stalk of a flower or fruit; the stem of a brachiopod.

pedun'cular, *adj.*, pert. to a peduncle.

pedun'culate, *adj.*, having a peduncle; growing on one.

peek, *v.i.*, to peep; *n.*, a woodpecker.

peel, *n.*, the rind of anything; a baker's shovel; a fortified tower; *v.t.*, to strip the rind or bark from; *v.i.*, to lose the skin or rind.

peeled, *p.p.*, peel.

peel'er, *n.*, one who peels; a policeman (*slang*).

peel'ing, *pr.p.*, peel; *n.*, the act of removing a rind; the rind removed.

peen, *n.*, the end of a hammer-head opposite the face.

peep, *v.i.*, to cry as a chicken; to look through a crevice or slyly; *n.*, a sly look.

peeped, *p.p.*, peep.

peep'er, *n.*, one that peeps.

peep'-hole, *n.*, a hole to peep through unseen.

peep'ing, *pr.p.*, peep.

peep'-show, *n.*, an exhibition of objects viewed through a lens.

peer, *n.*, an equal; a nobleman; *v.i.*, to peep.

peer'age, *n.*, the body of peers collectively; the rank of a peer.

peer'ess, *n.*, the consort of a peer; a noblewoman holding a title in her own right.

peer'ing, *pr.p.*, peer.

peer'less, *adj.*, unequalled.

peer'lessness, *n.*, the state of being without an equal.

pee'vish, *adj.*, fretful.

pee'vishly, *adv.*, in a peevish manner.

pee'vishness, *n.*, fretfulness.

pee'wit, pe'wit, *n.*, the lapwing.

peg, *n.*, a wooden pin; a pin on which to hang anything; a drink (*slang*); a degree in position or estimation (*colloq.*); *v.t.*, to fasten or mark with pegs.

Peg'asus, *n.*, a winged horse; the horse of the Muses, and, hence, connected with poetry.

pegged, *p.p.*, peg.

peg'ger, *n.*, one who pegs.

peg'ging, *pr.p.*, peg.

peg'-top, *n.*, a toy made to spin by a string.

peiram'eter, *n.*, an instrument to measure the resistance a road offers to a wheeled vehicle.

peiras'tic, *adj.*, tentative.

pek'an, *n.*, a North American marten.

pek'oe, *n.*, a fine, black tea.

pel'age, *n.*, the fur covering of a mammal.

Pela'gian, *n.*, a follower of Pelagius, a British monk who denied the doctrine of original sin; *adj.*, pert. to Pelagianism.

Pela'gianism, *n.*, the Pelagian heresy.
pelargo'nium, *n.*, a geranium or stork's-bill.
pel'erine, *n.*, a lady's long cape or tippet.
pelf, *n.*, money; filthy lucre.
pel'ican, *n.*, a large web-footed bird with a great pouched bill.
Pe'lion, *n.*, a mountain of Thessaly.
pelisse', *n.*, a robe of silk worn by ladies.
pell, *n.*, a skin; a roll of parchment.
pel'lage, *n.*, duty on hides or leather.
pella'gra, *n.*, a skin disease akin to leprosy.
pel'let, *n.*, a little ball.
pel'licle, *n.*, a thin skin; the outer covering of plants.
pellic'ular, *adj.*, pert. to a pellicle.
pel'litory, *n.*, a British plant.
pell-mell', *adv.*, in utter confusion.
pellu'cid, *adj.*, translucent.
pellucid'ity, *n.*, the quality of being pellucid.
Peloponne'sian, *adj.*, bel. to the southern peninsula of Greece.
pelt, *n.*, a raw hide; *v.t.*, to throw something at; *v.i.*, to drive; come down with violence (as rain, hail, etc.).
pel'tate, *adj.*, shield-shaped.
pel'tated, *adj.*, *i.q.* peltate.
pelt'ed, *p.p.*, pelt.
pelt'ing, *pr.p.*, pelt; *adj.*, driving; violent.
pelt'ry, *n.*, pelts collectively.
pel'vic, *adj.*, pert. to the pelvis.
pel'vis, *n.*, the bony framework of the lower part of the abdomen.
pem'mican, *n.*, lean venison or beef, dried, pounded into paste, and pressed into cakes.
pen, *n.*, an instrument used for writing; a small inclosure for animals or fowls; *v.t.*, to write; to encage.
pe'nal, *adj.*, entailing punishment.
pen'alty, *n.*, a punishment; a forfeiture.
pen'ance, *n.*, a punishment imposed for sin; one of the Seven Sacraments.
Pena'tes, *n. pl.*, household gods.
pence, *n.*, pl. of penny.
penchant', *n.*, a liking.
pen'cil, *n.*, an instrument formed of graphite, chalk, etc., for marking on paper; a collection of rays of light; *v.t.* and *i.*, to write with a pencil.
pen'cil(l)ed, *p.p.*, pencil; *adj.*, delicately marked, as with a pencil.
pen'cil(l)ing, *pr.p.*, pencil.
pen'-cutter, *n.*, a maker of pens.
pend'ant, *n.*, a suspended ornament; a flag borne at a mast-head; a hanging chandelier.
pend'ence, *n.*, *i.q.* pendency.
pend'ency, *n.*, the state of being pendent. [ing.
pend'ent, *adj.*, hang-
penden'tive, *n.*, the part of a groined ceiling springing from one impost; one of the spherical triangles resulting from the intersection of a dome by two pairs of opposite arches springing from the four imposts.
pen'dicle, *n.*, a croft or farm.
pend'ing, *adj.*, not terminated: *prep.*, during.
pendrag'on, *n.*, a chief leader among the ancient British.
pendulos'ity, *n.*, the state of being pendulous.
pen'dulous, *adj.*, hanging loosely.
pen'dulum, *n.*, the swinging piece in a clock.
penetrabil'ity, *n.*, the state of being penetrable.
pen'etrable, *adj.*, capable of being penetrated.
penetra'lia, *n. pl.*, a sanctuary; the inmost parts (*Lat.*).
pen'etrant, *adj.*, having the power to penetrate.
pen'etrate, *v.t.*, to enter into or pierce.
pen'etrated, *p.p.*, penetrate.
pen'etrating, *pr.p.*, penetrate; *adj.*, acute; discerning.
penetra'tion, *n.*, the act of penetrating; mental acuteness.
pen'etrative, *adj.*, sharp; subtle.
pen'guin, *n.*, a swimming bird with rudimentary wings.
pen'holder, *n.*, the stalk for holding a pen-nib.
pen'icil, *n.*, a pledget for wounds.
penicil'late, *adj.*, consisting of a bundle of short, compact fibres or hairs.
penin'sula, *n.*, a portion of land almost surrounded by water
penin'sular, *adj.*, rel. to a peninsula.
penin'sulate, *v.t.*, to form into a peninsula.
penin'sulated, *p.p.*, peninsulate.
pen'itence, *n.*, repentance.
pen'itencer, *n.*, a priest who hears confession; esp. in reserved cases.
pen'itency, *n.*, *i.q.* penitence.
pen'itent, *adj.*, contrite; *n.*, one who is contrite; one who confesses in the tribunal of penance.
peniten'tial, *adj.*, expressing penitence.
peniten'tiary, *adj.*, rel. to penance; *n.*, a place of discipline; a home for penitents; a R.C. office for the

consideration of questions of conscience, etc.
pen'itently, *adv.*, in a penitent manner.
pen'knife, *n.*, a pocket-knife.
pen'man, *n.*, a writer.
pen'manship, *n.*, the use of the pen.
pen'nant, *n.*, a pennon; a small flag.
pen'nate, *adj.*, formed like a feather.
penned, *p.p.*, pen.
pen'niform, *adj.*, resembling the barbs of a feather.
pennig'erous, *adj.*, bearing feathers or quills.
pen'niless, *adj.*, destitute of money.
pen'non, *n.*, a small pointed flag borne on a lance.
pen'ny, *n.*, a bronze coin, twelve of which make a shilling.
penny-a-li'ner, *n.*, a poor writer for hire.
pennyroy'al, *n.*, a British plant of the mint family.
pen'nyweight, *n.*, a weight equal to 24 grains.
pen'nywise, *adj.*, niggardly on unimportant occasions.
pen'nyworth, *n.*, as much as costs a penny.
penol'ogy, *n.*, the science and philosophy of public punishments.
pen'sile, *adj.*, hanging.
pen'sion, *n.*, an allowance made for past services; *v.t.*, to grant a pension to.
pension, *n.*, a Continental boarding-house or boarding-school (*Fr.*).
pen'sionary, *adj.*, receiving or consisting in a pension.
pen'sioned, *p.p.*, pension.
pen'sioner, *n.*, one who receives a pension; at Cambridge, one who pays for his commons.
pen'sioning, *pr.p.*, pension.
pen'sive, *adj.*, thoughtful and a little melancholy.
pen'sively, *adv.*, in a pensive manner.
pen'siveness, *n.*, the state of being pensive.
pent, *adj.*, penned; closely confined.
pen'tachord, *n.*, an ancient Greek five-stringed instrument of music; a scale of five diatonic intervals.
pen'tacle, *n.*, a five-pointed star.
pentacros'tic, *adj.*, containing five acrostics of the same word.
pentadac'tyl, *adj.*, five-fingered; five-toed.
pen'tagon, *n.*, a five-sided figure.
pentag'onal, *adj.*, having five angles.
pen'tagram, *n.*, *i.q.* pentacle.
pen'tagraph, *n.*, *i.q.* pantograph.
pentagyn'ia, *n. pl.*, plants with flowers having five styles.
pentahe'dral, *adj.*, having five equal faces.
pentahe'dron, *n.*, a solid with five equal faces.
pentam'eter, *n.*, a verse containing five feet.
pentan'dria, *n. pl.*, plants having flowers with five stamens.
pentan'gular, *adj.*, having five angles.
pentapet'alous, *adj.*, having five petals.
pentaphyl'lous, *adj.*, having five leaves.
pen'tarchy, *n.*, government by five persons.
pentasper'mous, *adj.*, containing five seeds
pen'tastich, *n.*, a poem of five verses.
pen'tastyle, *adj.*, having five columns in front.
Pen'tateuch, *n.*, the first five books of the Old Testament.
pentaton'ic, *adj.*, consisting of five tones.
Pen'tecost, *n.*, Whitsuntide; a solemn festival of the Jews coming fifty days after the Passover.
Pen'tecostal, *adj.*, pert. to Pentecost.
pent'house, *n.*, a shed sloping from another building.
penult', *n.*, the last syllable but one of a word.
penul'tima, *n.*, *i.q.* penult.
penul'timate, *adj.*, the last but one; *n.*, *i.q.* penult.
penum'bra, *n.*, a partial shadow outside of the total shadow.
penum'bral, *adj.*, pert. to a penumbra.
penu'rious, *adj.*, parsimonious.
penu'riously, *adv.*, in a penurious manner.
penu'riousness, *n.*, niggardliness.
pen'ury, *n.*, extreme poverty.
pe'on, *n.*, a Mexican day-labourer.
pe'onage, *n.*, the condition of a peon.
pe'ony, *n.*, a ranunculaceous garden-plant with gaudy flowers.
peo'ple, *n.*, the body of persons composing a nation or race; persons indefinitely; *v.t.*, to stock with inhabitants.
peo'pled, *p.p.*, people.
peo'pling, *pr.p.*, people.
pep, *n.*, the heart of an artificial flower.
pep'per, *n.*, a plant and its fruit, the latter having a hot, pungent taste; *v.t.*, to sprinkle with pepper; to pelt.
pep'percorn, *n.*, the berry of the pepper; an insignificant amount.
pep'pered, *p.p.*, pepper.
pep'pergrass, *n.*, a garden salad; the pillwort.
pep'pering, *pr.p.*, pepper; *n.*, a pelting.
pep'permint, *n.*, a plant of the mint family having a

pungent taste followed by a sense of coolness.

pep'pery, *adj.*, hot; irritable.

pep'sin, *n.*, the active principle of gastric juice.

pep'tic, *adj.*, digestive.

pep'toid, *adj.*, rel. to digestion.

pep'tone, *n.*, the substance into which the food is changed by the gastric juice.

per, *prep.*, through; by; by means of (*Lat.*).

peradven'ture, *adv.*, perhaps.

peram'bulate, *v.t.*, to walk through or over.

peram'bulated, *p.p.*, perambulate.

peram'bulating, *pr.p.*, perambulate.

perambula'tion, *n.*, a travelling survey.

peram'bulator, *n.*, a baby-carriage; one who perambulates.

per an'num, *adv.*, annually (*Lat. phrase*).

perceiv'able, *adv.*, *i.q.* perceptible.

perceive', *v.t.*, to see; to understand.

perceived', *p.p.*, perceive.

perceiv'er, *n.*, one who perceives.

perceiv'ing, *pr.p.*, perceive.

per cent.', *adv.*, abbreviation of *per centum* (*Lat.*).

percent'age, *n.*, the rate of interest on a hundred.

per cen'tum, *adv.*, by the hundred (*Lat.*).

per'cept, *n.*, that which is perceived.

perceptibil'ity, *n.*, the quality of being perceptible; the power of perceiving.

percep'tible, *adj.*, capable of being perceived.

percep'tibly, *adv.*, in a perceptible manner.

percep'tion, *n.*, the act or faculty of perceiving.

percep'tive, *adj.*, having the faculty of perception.

perceptiv'ity, *n.*, the power of perception.

perch, *n.*, a fresh-water fish; a measure of length containing 5½ yds.; a roost; *v.i.*, to roost; *v.t.*, to place on a perch.

perched, *p.p.*, perch.

perchance' *adv.*, perhaps.

perch'er, *n.*, one that perches; an insessorial bird.

perch'ing, *pr.p.*, perch.

perchlo'rate, *n.*, a salt of perchloric acid.

perchlo'ric, *adj.*, a term applied to an explosive acid.

perchlo'ride, *n.*, a chloride with the largest proportion of chlorine.

percip'ience, *n.*, perception.

percip'iency, *n.*, *i.q.* percipience.

percip'ient, *n.*, one who perceives; *adj.*, having the power of perception.

per'coid, *adj.*, bel. to the perch family.

per'colate, *v.t.*, to filter; *v.i.*, to pass through pores or small interstices.

per'colated, *p.p.*, percolate.

per'colating, *pr.p.*, percolate.

percola'tion, *n.*, the act of percolating.

per'colator, *n.*, a filter.

percuss', *v.t.*, to give a shock to; to strike against.

percussed', *p.p.*, percuss.

percuss'ing, *pr.p.*, percuss.

percus'sion, *n.*, forcible collision.

percus'sion-cap, *n.*, a small copper cup containing fulminating powder, used to explode gunpowder.

percuss'ive, *adj.*, acting by percussion.

percu'tient, *n.*, that which strikes.

perdi'tion, *n.*, utter destruction.

perdu', *adj.*, hid; in concealment (*Fr.*).

per'egrinate, *v.i.*, to travel.

peregrina'tion, *n.*, a journey.

per'egrinator, *n.*, a traveller.

per'egrine, *adj.*, foreign; *n.*, a kind of falcon.

per'emptorily, *adv.*, in a peremptory manner.

per'emptoriness, *n.*, the state of being peremptory.

per'emptory, *adj.*, authoritative; decisive; imperious.

peren'nial, *adj.*, lasting throughout the year; unceasing; *n.*, a plant whose roots remain alive longer than two years, but whose stems wither annually.

per'fect, *adj.*, finished; faultless; *v.t.*, to complete.

per'fected, *p.p.*, perfect.

per'fecter, *n.*, one who perfects.

perfectibil'ity, *n.*, the capacity of being made perfect.

perfect'ible, *adj.*, capable of being made perfect.

per'fecting, *pr.p.*, perfect.

perfec'tion, *n.*, the highest degree of excellence.

perfec'tionism, *n.*, the doctrine of the Perfectionists.

Perfec'tionist, *n.*, one who believes that moral perfection can be attained during life.

perfect'ive, *adj.*, tending to make perfect.

per'fectly, *adv.*, thoroughly.

per'fectness, *n.*, the quality of being perfect.

perfer'vid, *adj.*, very fervid.

perfi'cient, *adj.*, doing thoroughly.

perfid'ious, *adj.*, treacherous.

perfid'iously, *adv.*, in a perfidious manner.

perfid'iousness, *n.*, the quality of being perfidious.

per'fidy, *n.*, treachery.

perfo'liate, *adj.*, a term applied to a leaf whose base surrounds the stem.

perfo'liated, *adj.*, *i.q.* perfoliate.

per'forate, *v.t.*, to pierce.

per'forated *p.p.*, perforate.

per'forating, *pr.p.*, perforate.

perfora'tion, *n.*, the act of perforating; a hole pierced.

per'forative, *adj.*, having the power of piercing.

per'forator, *n.*, that which pierces.

perforce', *adv.*, of necessity.

perform', *v.t.*, to accomplish; *v.i.*, to act a part or play on a musical instrument.

perform'able, *adj.*, capable of being performed.

perform'ance, *n.*, a thing done; an entertainment; the act of performing.

performed', *p.p.*, perform.

perform'er, *n.*, one who performs; an actor, musician, etc.

perform'ing, *pr.p.*, perform.

perfume', *v.t.*, to scent.

per'fume, *n.*, a sweet odour.

perfumed', *p.p.*, perfume.

perfu'mer, *n.*, one who makes or sells perfumes.

perfu'mery, *n.*, perfumes collectively.

perfu'ming, *pr.p.*, perfume.

perfunc'torily, *adv.*, in a perfunctory manner.

perfunc'toriness, *n.*, the state of being perfunctory.

perfunc'tory, *adj.*, half-hearted; negligent.

perfuse', *v.t.*, to suffuse.

perfu'sive, *adj.*, adapted to perfuse.

pergame'neous, *adj.*, resembling parchment.

per'gola, *n.*, an arbour or bower on which plants may grow.

perhaps', *adv.*, possibly; maybe.

pe'ri, *n.*, a fallen angel; a kind of fairy (*Persian myth*).

per'ianth, *n.*, a combination of calyx and corolla in a flower.

pericar'diac, *adj.*, rel. to the pericardium.

pericar'dial, *adj.*, *i.q.* pericardiac.

pericar'dian, *adj.*, *i.q.* pericardiac.

pericar'dic, *adj.*, *i.q.* pericardiac.

pericardi'tis, *n.*, inflammation of the pericardium.

pericar'dium, *n.*, the membrane inclosing the heart.

per'icarp, *n.*, the seed-vessel of a plant.

pericar'pial, *adj.*, rel. to a pericarp.

per'iclase, *n.*, a transparent green magnesium oxide.

peric'ope, *n.*, an arrangement of the Epistles and Gospels to the needs of Sundays and Festivals.

pericra'nium, *n.*, the membrane surrounding the skull.

per'iderm, *n.*, a sort of outer layer or skin; the outer layer of bark.

per'idrome, *n.*, an ambulatory.

per'igee, *n.*, the point where the moon is nearest the earth.

perihe'lion, *n.*, a point nearest the sun in the orbit of a planet.

perihexahe'dral, *adj.*, having six equal faces.

per'il, *n.*, danger; *v.t.*, to risk.

per'il(l)ed, *p.p.*, peril.

per'il(l)ing, *pr.p.*, peril.

per'ilous, *adj.*, dangerous.

per'ilously, *adv.*, in a perilous manner.

per'ilousness, *n.*, the state of being perilous.

perim'eter, *n.*, the boundary of a figure, or the sum of its sides.

pe'riod, *n.*, an indefinite time; conclusion; a complete sentence; a full-stop or point.

period'ic, *adj.*, performed in a regular revolution; published at regular intervals.

period'ical, *adj.*, recurring or happening regularly; *n.*, a periodical publication.

period'ically, *adv.*, at stated periods.

periodic'ity, *n.*, the quality or state of being periodical.

perios'teum, *n.*, a vascular membrane surrounding a bone.

peripatet'ic, *adj.*, itinerant; Aristotelian.

periph'eral, *adj.*, pert. to a periphery.

peripher'ic, *adj.*, *i.q.* peripheral.

periph'ery, *n.*, circumference.

per'iphrase, *n.*, a periphrasis.

periph'rasis, *n.*, a circumlocution.

periphras'tic, *adj.*, characterized by periphrasis.

peripneumo'nia, *n.*, *i.q.* pneumonia.

peripneumon'ic, *adj.*, *i.q.* pneumonic.

peripneu'mony, *n.*, *i.q.* peripneumonia.

perip'teral, *adj.*, surrounded by a row of columns.

perip'terous, *adj.*, *i.q.* peripteral.

perip'tery, *n.*, a surrounding row of columns.

perique', *n.*, a dark tobacco from Louisiana.

per'iscope, *n.*, an optical instrument used by submarines and in trench warfare to survey objects on or above the water or from below parapets.

periscop'ic, *adj.*, viewing on all sides.

per'ish, *v.i.*, to die; to be destroyed.

per'ishable, *adj.*, subject to decay.

per'ished, *p.p.*, perish.

per'isperm, *n.*, the external skin of a seed.

perispher'ic, *adj.*, globular.

perissol'ogy, *n.* superfluity of words.

peristal'tic, *adj.*, contracting all round in successive circles (describing the movement of the intestines forcing their contents downwards).

peristreph'ic, *adj.*, rotatory.

per'istyle, *n.*, a row of surrounding columns.

perisys'tole, *n.*, the interval between the contraction and the dilatation of the heart.

perit'omous, *adj.*, cleaving in more directions than one.

peritone'um, *n.*, the membranous lining of the abdomen.

peritoni'tis, *n.*, inflammation of the peritoneum.

perit'ropal, *adj.*, rotatory.

perityphli'tis, *n.*, inflammation of the caecum or blind gut.

per'iwig, *n.*, a small wig.

per'iwinkle, *n.*, a British herbaceous plant with blue, white, or purple flowers and evergreen leaves; a small mollusc.

per'jure, *v.i.*, to forswear.

per'jured, *adj.*, guilty of perjury; *p.p.*, perjure.

per'jurer, *n.*, one that takes a false oath.

per'juring, *pr.p.*, perjure.

per'jury, *n.*, violation of an oath.

perk, *v.i.*, to hold up the head pertly.

perked, *p.p.*, perk.

per'kin, *n.*, weak perry.

perk'y, *adj.*, saucy.

per'manence, *n.*, the state or quality of being permanent.

per'manency, *n.*, *i.q.* permanence.

per'manent, *adj.*, remaining unaltered.

per'manently, *adv.*, in a permanent manner.

perman'ganate, *n.*, a salt of permanganic acid.

permeabil'ity, *n.*, the quality of being permeable.

per'meable, *adj.*, capable of being permeated.

per'meate, *v.t.*, to pass through the pores of.

per'meated, *p.p.*, permeate.

per'meating, *pr.p.*, permeate.

permea'tion, *n.*, the act of permeating.

permis'sible, *adj.*, allowable.

permissibility, *n.*, the quality of being permissible.

permis'sion, *n.*, authorization; leave.

permis'sive, *adj.*, permitting.

permis'sively, *adv.*, without prohibition.

permis'sory, *adj.*, *i.q.* permissive.

permit', *v.t.* and *i.*, to allow.

per'mit, *n.*, a written permission.

permit'ted, *p.p.*, permit.

permit'ter, *n.*, one who permits.

permit'ting, *pr.p.*, permit.

permu'table, *adj.*, exchangeable.

permuta'tion, *n.*, interchange; change of arrangement.

per'nancy, *n.*, in law, the taking or receiving of something.

perni'cious, *adj.*, destructive.

perni'ciously, *adv.*, in a pernicious manner.

perni'ciousness, *n.*, the state of being pernicious.

pernocta'tion, *n.*, the act of passing the night.

per'one, *n.*, the fibula.

perone'al, *adj.*, rel. to the fibula.

perora'tion, *n.*, the concluding part of a speech.

perox'ide, *n.*, an oxide containing the greatest possible quantity of oxygen.

perpend', *v.t.*, to consider attentively.

perpendic'ular, *adj.*, perfectly vertical; at right angles to.

perpendicular'ity, *n.*, the state of being perpendicular.

perpendic'ularly, *adv.*, in a perpendicular manner; vertically.

per'petrate, *v.t.*, to commit; to be guilty of.

per'petrated, *p.p.*, perpetrate.

per'petrating, *pr.p.*, perpetrate.

perpetra'tion, *n.*, the act of perpetrating.

per'petrator, *n.*, one who perpetrates.

perpet'ual, *adj.*, lasting for ever.

perpet'ually, *adv.*, for ever.

perpet'uate, *v.t.*, to make perpetual.

perpet'uated, *p.p.*, perpetuate.

perpet'uating, *pr.p.*, perpetuate.

perpetua'tion, *n.*, the act of making perpetual.

perpetu'ity, *n.*, the state or quality of being perpetual.

perphos'phate, *n.*, a phosphate formed by combining a peroxide with phosphoric acid.

perplex', *v.t.*, to puzzle.

perplexed', *p.p.*, perplex.

perplex'ing, *pr.p.*, perplex; *adj.*, embarrassing; difficult.

perplex'ity, *n.*, the state of being puzzled; or of being intricate.

per'quisite, *n.*, some sort of addition to wages or salary.

perquisi'tion, *n.*, a thorough inquiry.

per'ron, *n.*, an outside staircase leading to the main entrance of a building.

perroquet', *n.*, *i.q.* parrakeet.

per'ry, *n.*, a fermented drink made from the juice of pears.

perscruta'tion, *n.*, a minute inquiry or search.

per se', (*Lat.*) considered by itself.

per'secute, *v.t.*, to harass or afflict persistently.

per'secuted, *p.p.*, persecute.

per'secuting, *pr.p.*, persecute; *adj.*, addicted to persecution.

persecu'tion, *n.*, the act or practice of persecuting; the state of being persecuted.

per'secutor, *n.*, one who persecutes.

persecu'trix, *n.*, a female persecutor.

persever'ance, *n.*, persistence in any design.

persevere', *v.i.*, to continue resolutely any course begun.

persevered', *p.p.*, persevere.

perseve'ring, *pr.p.*, persevere; *adj.*, steadfast in purpose.

perseve'ringly, *adv.*, in a persevering manner.

Per'sian, *adj.*, pert. to Persia.

Per'sic, *adj.*, *i.q.* Persian.

persiflage', *n.*, idle banter (*Fr.*).

persist', *v.i.*, to continue steadily in the face of opposition.

persist'ed, *p.p.*, persist.

persist'ence, *n.*, steady continuance in a course.

persist'ency, *n.*, *i.q.* persistence.

persist'ent, *adj.*, tenacious of purpose.

persist'ing, *pr.p.* persist.

persist'ingly, *adv.*, in a persisting manner.

persist'ive, *adj.*, persistent.

per'son, *n.*, an individual human being; body; in grammar, the relation of a noun or pronoun to the act of speaking, doing, etc.

per'sonable, *adj.*, handsome.

per'sonage, *n.*, a person of distinction.

per'sonal, *adj.*, peculiar to an individual; disparaging a person; private.

personal'ity, *n.*, the state of being personal; the characteristics of an individual; a disparaging remark.

per'sonally, *adv.*, in person; as regards one's individuality.

per'sonalty, *n.*, personal property.

per'sonate, *v.t.*, to assume the character and appearance of.

per'sonated, *p.p.*, personate.

per'sonating, *pr.p.*, personate.

persona'tion, *n.*, the act of counterfeiting the person or character of another.

per'sonator, *n.*, one who personates.

personifica'tion, *n.*, the act of personifying.

person'ified, *p.p.*, personify.

person'ify, *v.t.*, to treat as a person; to impersonate.

person'ifying, *pr.p.*, personify.

personnel', *n.*, the body of persons employed in any occupation. (*Fr.*).

perspec'tive, *n.*, the art of drawing objects so that they appear to have their natural positions, sizes, and relations; a vista.

perspec'tograph, *n.*, an instrument to aid in perspective drawing.

perspectog'raphy, *n.*, the science or art of perspective.

perspica'cious, *adj.*, quick of understanding.

perspicac'ity, *n.*, penetration; acuteness of discernment.

perspicu'ity, *n.*, easiness of being understood.

perspic'uous, *adj.*, clear to the understanding.

perspirabil'ity, *n.*, the quality of being perspirable.

perspi'rable, *adj.*, capable of being perspired.

perspira'tion, *n.*, the act of perspiring; sweat.

perspir'atory, *adj.*, pert. to perspiration.

perspire', *v.i.*, to sweat.

perspired', *p.p.*, perspire.

perspi'ring, *pr.p.*, perspire.

persua'dable, *adj.*, capable of being persuaded.

persuade', *v.t.*, to advise; to convince by argument.

persua'ded, *p.p.*, persuade.

persua'ding, *pr.p.*, persuade.

persua'sible, *adj.*, *i.q.* persuadable.

persua'sion, *n.*, the act of persuading; a creed; a sect adhering to a creed.

persua'sive, *adj.*, having the power of persuading.

persua'sively, *adv.*, in a persuasive manner.

persua'siveness, *n.*, the quality of being persuasive.

persua'sory, *adj.*, persuasive.

persul'phate, *n.*, a sulphate of a metal containing as much of the acid as possible.

persulta'tion, *n.*, bloody sweat; exudation of blood through the skin.

pert, *adj.*, saucy; indecorously free.

pertain', *v.i.*, to belong.

pertained', *p.p.*, pertain.

pertain'ing, *pr.p.*, pertain.

pertina'cious, *adj.*, obstinate.

pertina'ciously, *adv.*, obstinately.

pertinac'ity, *n.*, obstinacy; resolution.

per'tinence, *n.*, fitness; appositeness.

per'tinency, *n.*, *i.q.* pertinence.

per'tinent, *adj.*, apposite.

per'tinently, *adv.*, to the purpose.

pert'ly, *adv.*, in a pert manner.

pert'ness, *n.*, sauciness; forwardness.

perturb', *v.t.*, to agitate.

perturb'ance, *n.*, *i.q.* perturbation.

perturba'tion, *n.*, disquiet of mind; disorder.

per'turbate, *v.t.*, *i.q.* perturb.

perturbed', *p.p.*, perturb.

perturb'ing, *pr.p.*, perturb.

peruke', *n.*, a periwig.

peru'sal, *n.*, the act of perusing.

peruse', *v.t.*, to read with attention.

perused', *p.p.*, peruse.

peru'ser, *n.*, one who peruses.

peru'sing, *pr.p.*, peruse.

Peru'vian, *adj.*, pert. to Peru.

pervade', *v.t.*, to be diffused throughout.

perva'ded, *p.p.*, pervade.

perva'ding, *pr.p.*, pervade.

perva'sion, *n.*, the act of pervading.

perva'sive, *adj.*, having power to pervade.

perverse', *adj.*, turned to evil; stubborn; untoward.

perverse'ly, *adv.*, obstinately in the wrong.

perverse'ness, *n.*, a disposition to thwart.

perver'sion, *n.*, the act of perverting; change to something worse.

perver'sity, *n.*, state or quality of being perverse.

perver'sive, *adj.*, tending to pervert.

pervert', *v.t.*, to turn from the right.

per'vert, *n.*, one who has been turned from one religion to another regarded as inferior.

pervert'ed, *p.p.*, pervert.

pervert'er, *n.*, one that perverts, distorts, or misapplies.

pervert'ible, *adj.*, capable of being perverted.

pervert'ing, *pr.p.*, pervert.

per'vious, *adj.*, penetrable.

per'viousness, *n.*, the quality of being pervious.

pesade', *n.*, the rearing of a horse (*Fr.*).

pes'sary, *n.*, an instrument for the treatment of *prolapsus uteri.*

pes'simism, *n.*, the opinion or doctrine that the present state of things tends to evil; looking to the dark side of things.

pes'simist, *n.*, one who holds pessimistic opinions.

pessimis'tic, *adj.*, pert. to pessimism.

pest, *n.*, a plague; anything or anybody noxious.

Pestaloz'zian, *adj.*, pert. to the system of elementary education devised by Pestalozzi.

pes'ter, *v.t.*, to annoy with vexatious trifles.

pes'tered, *p.p.*, pester.

pes'terer, *n.*, one who pesters.

pes'tering, *pr.p.*, pester.

pest'-house, *n.*, a hospital for plague patients.

pestif'erous, *adj.*, pestilential; malignant.

pes'tilence, *n.*, an epidemic malignant contagious disease.

pes'tilent, *adj.*, noxious to morals.

pestilen'tial, *adj.*, producing a pestilence; noxious.

pes'tle, *n.*, an instrument for pounding substances in a mortar.

pet, *n.*, a fit of peevishness; a fondling; *v.t.*, to fondle; to indulge; *adj.*, favourite.

pet'al, *n.*, a flower-leaf.

pet'al(l)ed, *adj.*, having petals.

petalif'erous, *adj.*, bearing petals.

petal'iform, *adj.*, shaped like a petal.

pet'aline, *adj.*, pert. to a petal.

pet'alite, *n.*, a mineral of foliated structure.

pet'alless, *adj.*, devoid of petals.

pet'aloid, *adj.*, resembling petals.

pet'alous, *adj.*, having petals.

petard', *n.*, an engine of war made of metal, to be loaded with powder and fixed to a barricade so as to break it down by explosion.

pet'asus, *n.*, Mercury's winged cap.

pete'chiae, *n. pl.*, purple spots due to malignant fever.

Peter's pence, *n. pl.*, a tribute to the Pope.

pe'tersham, *n.*, a thick, shaggy cloth fabric.

Pe'ter-wort, *n.*, St. Peter's-wort.

pet'iolar, *adj.*, proceeding from a leaf-stalk.

pet'iolate, *adj.*, having a petiole.

pet'iole, *n.*, a leaf-stalk.

petiol'ule, *n.*, a small or partial petiole.

petit', *adj.*, small in figure (*Fr.*).

petite', *adj.*, fem. of petit (*Fr.*).

peti'tion, *n.*, a supplication; *v.t.*, to address a petition to.

peti'tionary, *adj.*, offering or containing a petition.
peti'tioned, *p.p.*, petition.
peti'tioner, *n.*, one who presents a petition.
peti'tioning, *pr.p.*, petition.
petit mai'tre, *n.*, a fop.
petre'an, *adj.*, rel. to rock or stone.
pet'rel, *n.*, a web-footed sea-bird, found far from land.
petres'cence, *n.* the process of changing into stone.
petres'cent, *adj.*, changing into stony hardness.
petrifac'tion, *n.*, the process of converting into stone: a fossil.
petrifac'tive, *adj.*, having power to petrify.
petrif'ic, *adj.*, petrifactive.
pet'rified, *p.p.*, petrify.
pet'rify, *v.t.*, to convert into stone; to stupefy with fear or amazement.
pet'rifying, *pr.p.*, petrify.
Pe'trine, *adj.*, rel. to St. Peter.
pet'rol, *n.*, petroleum spirit.
petro'leum, *n.*, mineral oil.
pet'rolin, *n.*, a hydrocarbon akin to paraffin, found in Burmese petroleum.
petrolog'ical, *adj.*, pert. to petrology.
petrolog'ically, *adv.*, in a petrological manner.
petrol'ogist, *n.*, one versed in petrology.
petrol'ogy, *n.*, the chemical study of rocks.
pet'ronel, *n.*, a kind of carbine.
petrosi'lex, *n.*, rock flint.
petrosili'cious, *adj.*, consisting of petrosilex.
pet'rous, *adj.*, like stone; hard.
pet'ted, *p.p.*, pet.
pet'tichaps, *n. pl.*, a name applied to several British warblers.
pet'ticoat, *n.*, a loose undergarment worn by women.
pet'tier, *adj.*, *comp.* of petty.
pet'tiest, *adj.*, *super.* of petty.
pet'tifogger, *n.*, an inferior lawyer.
pet'tifoggery, *n.*, the practice of a pettifogger· mean tricks.
pet'tifogging, *adj.*, given to pettifoggery.
pet'tily, *adv.*, in a petty manner.
pet'tiness, *n.*, littleness.
pet'ting, *pr.p.*, pet.
pet'tish, *adj.*, proceeding from peevishness.
pet'tishly, *adv.*, in a pettish manner.
pet'tishness, *n.*, fretfulness.
pet'titoes, *n. pl.* the feet of a pig.
pet'to, *n.*, the breast (*Ital.*, *in petto* = with reserve).
pet'ty, *adj.*, small; inferior; insignificant.
pet'ulance, *n.*, pettishness.
pet'ulancy, *n.*, *i.q.* petulance.
pet'ulant, *adj.*, capricious; fretful.
pet'ulantly, *adv.*, in a petulant manner.
Petu'nia, *n.*, a genus of American herbaceous plants with beautiful flowers.
petunt'se, *n.*, Chinese fine clay.
pew, *n.*, a fixed seat in a church; *v.t.*, to provide with pews.
pewed, *adj.*, furnished with pews; *p.p.*, pew.
pe'wit, *n.*, see *peewit.*
pew'-opener, *n.*, a church attendant who opens the doors of pews.
pew'ter, *n.*, an alloy of tin and lead; vessels made of pewter.
pew'terer, *n.*, one who makes vessels of pewter.
pew'tery, *adj.*, resembling pewter.
pfen'nig, *n.*, a small German copper coin.
phac'oid, *adj.*, like a lentil; lenticular.
phaenog'amous, *adj.*, phanerogamous.
pha'eton, *n.*, an open four-wheeled carriage; an open touring motor-car.
phagede'na, *n.*, a spreading ulcer.
phageden'ic, *adj.*, pert. to phagedena.
phal'ange, *n.*, one of the small bones of the fingers and toes.
phalan'geal, *adj.*, bel. to the phalanges.
phalan'ger, *n.*, an Australian pouched animal living in trees.
phalan'ges, *n.*, pl. of phalanx.
phalan'gian, *adj.*, *i.q.* phalangeal.
phalanste'rian, *adj.*, pert. to a phalanstery; *n.*, a dweller in a phalanstery.
phal'anstery, *n.*, a socialistic community, as proposed by Fourier.
phal'anx, *n.*, a body of troops in close array; a phalange.
phal'lic, *adj.*, rel. to the phallus.
phal'lical, *adj.*, *i.q.* phallic.
phal'lus, *n.*, the emblem of the generative principle in nature carried in the Bacchic rites of ancient Greece.
phanerog'amous, *adj.*, bearing conspicuous flowers.
phan'tascope, *n.*, an optical contrivance for making fixed objects seem to be in motion.
phan'tasm, *n.*, a creation of the fancy: a phantom.
phantas'ma, *n.*, a phantasm; a day-dream.
phantasmago'ria, *n.*, illusive images; an exhibition of images as by the magic lantern.

phantasmagor'ic, *adj.*, rel. to a phantasmagoria.
phantas'mal, *adj.*, spectral; resembling a phantasm.
phantas'mascope, *n.*, *i.q.* phantascope.
phan'tasy, *n.*, *i.q.* fantasy.
phan'tom, *n.*, a ghost; something unreal.
Pharaon'ic, *adj.*, pert. to the Pharaohs.
Pharisa'ic, *adj.*, rel. to, or resembling, the Pharisees.
Pharisa'ical, *adj.*, *i.q.* pharisaic.
Phar'isaism, *n.*, the doctrines and conduct of the Pharisees; scrupulous observance of the forms of religion.
Pharise'an, *adj.*, *i.q.* pharisaic.
Phar'isee, *n.*, one of a sect among the Jews; a formalist.
Phar'iseeism, *n.*, *i.q.* pharisaism.
pharmaceu'tic, *adj.*, pert. to pharmacy.
pharmaceu'tical, *adj.*, *i.q.* pharmaceutic.
pharmaceu'tist, *n.*, an apothecary.
phar'macist, *n.*, one skilled in pharmacy.
phar'macolite, *n.*, a white mineral containing lime and arsenic.
pharmacol'ogist, *n.*, one skilled in pharmacology.
pharmacol'ogy, *n.*, the art of preparing medicines.
pharmacopoe'ia, *n.*, a book of directions for preparing medicines; an official list of drugs of the *Materia Medica*.
phar'macy, *n.*, the art of dispensing medicines; the occupation of an apothecary; a druggist's shop.
pha'ro, *n.*, *i.q.* faro.
Pha'ros, *n.*, a lighthouse.
pharyn'gal, *adj.*, *i.q.* pharyngeal.
pharyn'geal, *adj.*, pert. to the pharynx.
pharyngi'tis, *n.*, inflammation of the pharynx.
pharyngot'omy, *n.*, the operation of cutting into the pharynx to remove an obstruction.
phar'ynx, *n.*, part of the throat lying between the mouth and the oesophagus.
phase, *n.*, one of the appearances of the moon in respect of quantity of illumination of its disc; an aspect.
pha'sis, *n.*, a phase, in astromony.
pheas'ant, *n.*, a well-known gallinacecus game-bird.
pheas'antry, *n.*, a place for breeding pheasants.
phee'sy, *adj.*, fretful.
phen'gite, *n.*, colourless, translucent glucinum silicate.
phen'icin, *n.*, a brown dye.
phe'nix, *n.*, *i.q.* phoenix.
phenoga'mian, *adj.*, having flowers.
phenog'amous, *adj.*, *i.q.* phanerogamous.
phe'nol, *n.*, carbolic acid.
phenol'ogist, *n.*, one versed in phenology.
phenol'ogy, *n.*, the science of the distribution of plant and animal life according to climate.
phenom'ena, *n.*, pl. of phenomenon.
phenom'enal, *adj.*, rel. to phenomena.
phenom'enon, *n.*, a visible manifestation, fact, or occurrence; an unusual thing.
phe'on, *n.*, the barbed head of a dart (*her.*).
phi'al, *n.*, a small glass bottle; a vial.
Philadel'phian, *n.*, an inhabitant of Philadelphia; one of a 17th cent. sect of mystics; *adj.*, rel. to Philadelphia.
philan'der, *v.i.*, to flirt.
philan'derer, *n.*, a male flirt.
philan'dering, *pr.p.*, philander.
philanthrop'ic, *adj.*, benevolent.
philan'thropist, *n.*, one who does good to his fellow-men.
philan'thropy, *n.*, universal benevolence.
philatel'ic, *adj.*, rel. to philately.
philat'elist, *n.*, a stamp-collector.
philat'ely, *n.*, the science of collecting postage stamps.
philharmon'ic, *adj.*, fond of music.
Phil'hellene, *n.*, a friend of Greece.
Philhellen'ic, *adj.*, loving and supporting the Greeks against the Turks.
Philhel'lenism, *n.*, the principles of the Philhellenists.
Philhelle'nist, *n.*, one who supports the interests of the Greeks.
phil'ibeg, *n.*, the Highland kilt.
Philip'pian, *n.*, a native of Philippi.
philip'pic, *n.*, a speech attacking some one acrimoniously.
Phil'ippine, *adj.*, pert. to the Philippine Islands.
Phil'istine, *n.*, an inhabitant of Philistia in Syria; a person of narrow views, deficient in culture and taste.
Phil'istinism, *n.*, the characteristics of Philistines.
philol'oger, *n.*, *i.q.* philologist.
philolog'ic, *adj.*, *i.q.* philological.
philolog'ical, *adj.*, pert. to philology.
philol'ogist, *n.*, one versed in philology.
philol'ogy, *n.*, the study of language and literature; the science of language.
phil'omath, *n.*, a lover of learning.
philomath'ic, *adj.*, pert. to the love of learning.

philom'athy, *n.*, the love of learning.

phil'omel, *n.*, the nightingale.

Philome'la, *n.*, the daughter of Pandion, king of Athens, who was changed into a nightingale; the nightingale.

philope'na, *n.*, a game in which two persons eat the twin kernels of an almond and one pays a forfeit.

philopolem'ical, *adj.*, disputatious.

philoprogen'itiveness, *n.*, the love of offspring.

philos'opher, *n.*, one versed in philosophy; one who lives according to the rules of practical wisdom.

philosoph'ic, *adj.*, pert. to philosophy; calm; based on practical wisdom.

philosoph'ical, *adj.*, *i.q.* philosophic.

philosoph'ically, *adv.*, in a philosophical manner.

philos'ophism, *n.*, affectation of philosophy.

philos'ophist, *n.*, a would-be philosopher.

philos'ophize, *v.i.*, to reason like a philosopher.

philos'ophized, *p.p.*, philosophize.

philos'ophizing, *pr.p.*, philosophize.

philos'ophy, *n.*, the science which seeks to explain all things by ultimate causes; the calmness of the wise man.

philotech'nic, *adj.*, fond of the arts.

phil'tre, phil'ter, *n.*, a love potion.

phiz, *n.*, a humorous name for the face.

phlebi'tis, *n.*, inflammation of a vein.

phlebol'ogy, *n.*, that part of anatomy dealing with the veins.

phlebot'omist, *n.*, one who opens a vein to let blood.

phlebot'omy, *n.*, the practice of letting blood.

phlegm, *n.*, bronchial mucus; sluggishness.

phlegmat'ic, *adj.*, sluggish in temperament.

phleg'mon, *n.*, an inflammation.

phleme, *n.*, a flean; a farrier's lancet.

phlogis'tic, *adj.*, rel. to phlogiston.

phlogis'ton, *n.*, the hypothetical principle of inflammability, according to an obsolete theory.

phlox, *n.*, a genus of garden plants with red, white, or purple flowers.

pho'ca, *n.*, a seal (*Lat.*)

pho'cine, *adj.*, pert. to seals.

Phoe'bus, *n.*, Apollo; the sun.

Phoenic'ian, *adj.*, pert. to Phoenicia.

phoe'nix, *n.*, a mythical bird; a paragon.

'phone, *n.* and *v.t.*, an abbreviation of *telephone*.

phonet'ic, *adj.*, pert. to the voice; representing vocal sounds.

phonet'ically, *adv.*, in a phonetic manner.

phonet'ics, *n. pl.*, the science of vocal sounds and their representation.

phonetiza'tion, *n.*, the act of representing vocal sounds phonetically.

pho'nic, *adj.*, pert. to sound.

pho'nical, *adj.*, *i.q.* phonic.

pho'nics, *n. pl.*, the science of sounds; phonetics.

pho'nograph, *n.*, an instrument to register and reproduce sounds.

phonog'rapher, *n.*, or one skilled in Phonography.

phonograph'ic, *adj.*, or pert. to Phonography or to the phonograph.

Phonog'raphy, *n.*, or Pitman's phonetic shorthand.

pho'nolite, *n.*, clinkstone.

phonol'ogist, *n.*, one versed in phonology.

phonol'ogy, *n.*, phonetics.

phonom'eter, *n.*, an instrument for measuring the number in a given time of vibrations that produce a given sound.

pho'notype, *n.*, a character used in phonetic printing.

phonotyp'ic, *adj.*, pert. to phonotypy.

pho'notypist, *n.*, one who uses or advocates phonotypy.

pho'notypy, *n.*, phonetic printing.

phos'gene, *n.*, a suffocating gas produced by the action of light on chlorine and carbon dioxide.

phos'phate, *n.*, a salt of phosphoric acid.

phos'phene, *n.*, the spectrum or luminous image made by pressing the eyeball.

phos'phide, *n.*, a combination of phosphorus and some one other element.

phos'phite, *n.*, a salt of phosphorus acid.

phos'phor, *n.*, the morning star; phosphorus.

phos'phorate, *v.t.*, to impregnate with phosphorus.

phos'phorated, *p.p.*, phosphorate.

phos'phorating, *pr.p.*, phosphorate.

phosphoresce', *v.i.*, to give out phosphoric light.

phosphores'cence, *n.*, luminosity without combustion.

phosphores'cent, *adj.*, luminous without sensible heat.

phosphor'ic, *adj.*, rel. to phosphorus.

phos'phorous, *adj.*, obtained from phosphorus.

phos'phorus, *n.*, a solid non-metallic element found in bones.

phos'phuret(t)ed, *adj.*, combined with phosphorus.

pho'to, *n.*, an abbreviation of *photograph.*

photogen'ic, *adj.*, pert. to photogeny.

photog'eny, *n.*, photography.

pho'tograph, *n.*, a picture obtained by photography; *v.t.*, to produce a picture by photography.

photog'rapher, *n.*, one who photographs.

photograph'ic, *adj.*, rel. to photography.

photog'raphy, *n.*, the art of obtaining representations of objects by means of the action of light on certain chemicals.

photogravure', *n.*, a plate etched from a photograph; the process; the picture printed from the plate.

photo - lithog'raphy, *n.*, a mode of lithographing in which a photograph is transferred to a prepared stone.

photolog'ic, *adj.*, pert. to photology.

photol'ogy, *n.*, the science of light.

photom'eter, *n.*, an instrument to compare the intensity of different lights.

photomet'ric, *adj.*, pert. to a photometer.

photom'etry, *n.*, the measurement of the intensity of a light.

photopho'bia, *n.*, a dislike of light.

photop'sia, *n.*, a morbid affection of the sight in which sparks and flashes of light seem to play before the eyes.

pho'topsy, *n.*, *i.q.* photopsia.

pho'tosphere, *n.*, the luminous envelope of the sun.

pho'totype, *n.*, a plate on which a photograph has been etched with certain acids and used for printing copies from.

phototypog'raphy, *n.*, a photo-mechanical process of engraving which produces a plate that can be used on a printing machine.

photo - zincog'raphy, *n.*, the process of printing from a zinc plate on which a photograph has been etched.

phrase, *n.*, a short expression consisting of two or more words; *v.t.*, to express in words.

phrased, *p.p.*, phrase.

phra'seogram, *n.*, a combination of shorthand characters representing a phrase.

phra'seograph, *n.*, *i.q.* phraseogram.

phraseog'raphy, *n.*, the representation of phrases by means of shorthand signs.

phraseol'ogist, *n.*, a phrase-maker.

phraseol'ogy, *n.*, way of expression; diction.

phra'sing, *pr.p.*, phrase.

phrenet'ic, *adj.*, disordered in mind.

phren'ic, *adj.*, rel. to the diaphragm.

phreni'tis, *n.*, inflammation of the brain; frenzy.

phrenolog'ical, *adj.*, rel. to phrenology.

phrenol'ogist, *n.*, one versed in phrenology.

phrenol'ogy, *n.*, the science connecting different parts of the brain with different faculties of the mind.

phren'sy, *n.*, *i.q.* frenzy.

Phryg'ian, *adj.*, rel. to Phrygia.

phthis'ic, *n.*, consumption; a consumptive patient.

phthis'ical, *adj.*, suffering from phthisis or from asthma.

phthis'icky, *adj.*, asthmatic.

phthisiol'ogy, *n.*, the study of phthisis.

phthi'sis, *n.*, a wasting away of the lungs.

phylac'tery, *n.*, an amulet or charm worn by the ancient Jews.

phyllo'dium, *n.*, a leaf-stalk flattened and resembling a leaf.

phyl'lopod, *n.*, a crustacean with swimming limbs resembling leaves.

phyllox'era, *n.*, an insect which destroys vines.

phys'ic, *n.*, the art of healing; the science of medicine; a medicine; *v.t.*, to give medicine to.

phys'ical, *adj.*, rel. to nature or the material and sensible; rel. to the science of physics.

phys'ically, *adv.*, in a physical manner.

physi'cian, *n.*, one skilled in the art of healing.

phys'icist, *n.*, one skilled in physics.

phys'icked, *p.p.*, physic.

phys'icking, *pr.p.*, physic.

physico-log'ical, *adj.*, rel. to logic illustrated by physics.

physico-theol'ogy, *n.*, theology illustrated by physics.

phys'ics, *n. pl.*, the science of the laws and properties of matter.

physiognom'ic, *adj.*, pert. to physiognomy.

physiogn'omist, *n.*, one skilled in physiognomy.

physiogn'omy, *n.*, the art of reading character from the features; the face.

physiog'raphy, *n.*, a description of the natural features of the earth.

physiolog'ic, *adj.*, pert. to physiology.

physiolog'ical, *adj.*, *i.q.* physiologic.

physiolog'ically, *adv.*, according to the principles of physiology.

physiol'ogist, *n.*, one versed in physiology.

physiol'ogy, *n.*, the science of the phenomena of life.

physique', *n.*, a person's bodily structure or constitution.

phytiv'orous, *adj.*, eating plants.

phytog'eny, *n.*, the science of the generation of plants.

phytog'raphy, *n.*, a branch of botany dealing with the naming and description of plants.

phytolog'ical, *adj.*, rel. to phytology.

phytol'ogist, *n.*, a botanist.

phytol'ogy, *n.*, botany.

phyton'omy, *n.*, the science of the life of plants.

phytoph'agous, *adj.*, plant-eating.

phytot'omy, *n.*, the anatomy of plants.

Phytozo'a, *n. pl.*, zoophytes — plant-like animals, as sponges, etc.

phytozo'on, *n.*, a zoophyte.

pi, *n.*, the Greek letter *p*; a mathematical constant.

piac'ular, *adj.*, making atonement.

pi'a ma'ter, *n.*, the membrane surrounding the brain.

pi'anist, *n.*, a player on the piano.

pia'no, *adv.*, softly (a term used in music).

pian'o, *n.*, a pianoforte.

pianofor'te, *n.*, a musical instrument with metal strings struck by hammers set in motion from a keyboard.

pias'tre, pias'ter, *n.*, a coin of various values used in Italy, Turkey, Spain, etc.

piaz'za, *n.*, a rectangular open space; a colonnade.

pi'broch, *n.*, a Highland march played on the bagpipe.

pi'ca, *n.*, a large printing type.

picador', *n.*, a horseman, armed with a lance, who takes part in a bull-fight.

pic'amar, *n.*, an oily liquid contained in wood tar.

Pic'ard, *n.*, an inhabitant of Picardy, in North France.

picaroon', *n.*, a rogue; an adventurer.

picayune', *n.*, a coin in Florida and Louisiana, sixteen of which make a dollar.

Pic'cadilly, *n.*, a street in London; a collar or ruff.

pic'calilli, *n.*, a pungent pickle made of various vegetables.

pic'caninny, *n.*, a negro infant.

pic'colo, *n.*, a small or octave flute.

pick, *v.t.*, to strike with anything pointed; to choose; to steal; *v.i.*, to eat by morsels; *n.*, a sharp-pointed tool for loosening earth.

pick'aback, *adv.*, on the back like a pack.

pick'axe, *n.*, a long-handled instrument with a head consisting of a pick pointed at one end and bladed at the other.

picked, *p.p.*, pick.

pick'er, *n.*, one who picks or collects.

pick'erel, *n.*, a small fresh-water fish.

pick'et, *n.*, a peg for fastening a horse; a small body of soldiers for observation or to bring in stragglers; *v.t.*, to fasten to a peg; to post a guard.

pick'eted, *p.p.*, picket.

pick'eting, *pr.p.*, picket.

pick'ing, *n.*, perquisites; *pr.p.*, pick.

pick'le, *n.*, brine or vinegar for preserving food; food so preserved; a plight; a troublesome child; *v.t.*, to preserve in pickle.

pick'led, *p.p.*, pickle.

pick'ling, *pr.p.*, pickle.

pick'lock, *n.*, an instrument for picking a lock.

pick'-me-up, *n.*, a drug or dram to revive one's energies.

pick'pocket, *n.*, one who steals from the pocket.

pick'thank, *n.*, a parasite; a toady.

Pickwick'ian, *adj.*, rel. to Pickwick; used in a Pickwickian (*i.e.*, technical or constructive) sense.

pic'nic, *n.*, an open-air pleasure party; *v.i.*, to go on a picnic.

pic'nicking, *pr.p.*, picnic.

picotee', *n.*, a variety of carnation or pink.

pic'ric, *adj.*, having a bitter taste.

picric-ac'id, *n.*, a yellow and bitter compound, used in dyeing and the manufacture of explosives.

pic'rolite, *n.*, a fibrous or columnar kind of serpentine.

pic'romel, *n.*, a constituent of bile.

picrotox'in, *n.*, the bitter, poisonous principle of *Coccu-lus indicus*.

Pict, *n.*, a former inhabitant of north-east Scotland.

Pict'ish, *adj.*, pert. to the Picts.

pic'tograph, *n.*, a picture representing an idea.

picto'rial, *adj.*, rel. to pictures.

pic'ture, *n.*, a painted likeness; any likeness; *v.t.*, to paint; to describe clearly.

pic'ture-book, *n.*, a book for children containing many pictures.

pic'tured, *p.p.*, picture.

pic'ture-frame, *n.*, a border surrounding a picture.

pic'ture-gallery, *n.*, a large room in which pictures are exhibited.

picturesque′, *adj.*, suitable to form a pleasing picture; graphically written.

picturesque′ness, *n.*, the quality of being picturesque.

pic′turing, *pr.p.*, picture.

pic′ul, *n.*, a Chinese weight exceeding 1 cwt.

pid′dle, *v.i.*, to attend to trivialities.

pid′dled, *p.p.*, piddle.

pid′dler, *n.*, one who piddles or pettifogs.

pid′dling, *pr.p.*, piddle.

pid′gin, *n.*, a jargon of English expressed in a foreign idiom, esp. Chinese.

pie, *n.*, the magpie; paste cooked with something in it; disordered printing type.

pie′bald, *adj.*, having white spots all over the body.

piece, *n.*, a bit of anything; a composition; a gun; a coin; *v.t.*, to patch; to join together.

pieced, *p.p.*, piece.

piece′meal, *adv.*, bit by bit.

piece′ner, *n.*, one who feeds the slubbing-machine in a woollen mill.

piec′ing, *pr.p.*, piece.

pied, *adj.*, particoloured.

pier, *n.*, stonework supporting one side of an arch; a jetty or mole stretching into the sea.

pier′age, *n.*, toll paid for using a pier.

pierce, *v.t.*, to bore; to penetrate; to perforate.

pierce′able, *adj.*, capable of being pierced.

pierced, *p.p.*, pierce.

pier′cer, *n.*, an instrument, organ, or person that pierces.

pier′cing, *pr.p.*, pierce

pier′-glass, *n.*, a large mirror between windows.

Pie′rian, *adj.*, bel. to the Pierides or Muses.

pi′errot, *n.*, a buffoon or comic artist dressed in a loose white costume trimmed with black.

pier′-table, *n.*, a table between windows.

Pi′etism, *n.*, the practice or principles of the Pietists.

Pi′etist, pi′etist, *n.*, one of a religious party in Germany who sought to quicken piety in the Protestants; one who makes a display of religious feeling.

pietist′ic, *adj.*, rel. to pietists.

pi′ety, *n.*, sense of duty to God, parents, country, etc.

piezom′eter, *n.*, an instrument for measuring compressibility.

pig, *n.*, a swine; an oblong mass of unforged metal; *v.t.*, to farrow; *v.i.*, to live like pigs.

pig′eon, *n.*, a dove; a simpleton.

pig′eon-breasted, *adj.*, having a deformed chest with protuberant breast-bone.

pig′eongram, *n.*, a message carried by a pigeon.

pig′eon-hearted, *adj.*, timid; cowardly.

pig′eon-hole, *n.*, a compartment or nest in a case for papers.

pig′eon-house, *n.*, a dovecot.

pig′eonry, *n.*, a place for keeping pigeons.

pig′eon-toed, *adj.*, having the toes turning inwards.

pig′gery, *n.*, a collection of pigsties.

pig′gin, *n.*, a small wooden vessel with an erect handle.

pig′gish, *adj.*, like pigs.

pig′headed, *adj.*, stupidly obstinate.

pig′-iron, *n.*, iron in rough bars or pigs.

pig′-lead, *n.*, lead in pigs.

pigme′an, *adj.*, dwarfish.

pig′ment, *n.*, colouring matter; paint.

pigmen′tal, *adj.*, pert. to pigments.

pig′mentary, *adj.*, secreting pigment.

pigmenta′tion, *n.*, degeneration of tissues with discoloration.

pig′my, *n.*, a dwarf.

pignora′tion, *n.*, the practice or act of pawning.

pig′-nut, *n.*, the earth nut.

pig′skin, *n.*, the skin of a pig tanned into leather.

pig′sty, *n.*, a pen for pigs.

pig′tail, *n.*, the hair of the head tied into a tail; tobacco twisted into a rope.

pike, *n.*, a sharp-pointed weapon with a long shaft; a fresh-water fish with a long-pointed snout; a toll-bar.

piked, *adj.*, furnished with a pike.

pike′man, *n.*, a soldier armed with a pike.

pike′staff, *n.*, the shaft of a pike.

pilas′ter, *n.*, a square pillar, partly projecting from, partly engaged in, a wall.

pilas′tered, *adj.*, furnished with pilasters

pilau′, *n.*, an Oriental dish of rice cooked with butter or meat.

pilch, *n.*, a flannel cloth for an infant.

pil′chard, *n.*, a fish like a small herring.

pile, *n.*, a heap; a mass of buildings; a beam driven into soft earth to form a foundation; the nap of cloth; *v.i.*, to heap up.

pi′leate, *adj.*, having the form of a cap for the head.

pi′leated, *adj.*, *i.q.* pileate.

piled, *p.p.*, pile.

pile′-driver, *n.*, a machine for driving piles.

pi′ler, *n.*, one who piles.

piles, *n. pl.*, hemorrhoids; inflammation of the orifice of the rectum.

pil'fer, *v.t.* and *i.*, to steal by petty theft.
pil'fered, *p.p.*, pilfer.
pil'ferer, *n.*, one who pilfers.
pil'fering, *pr.p.*, pilfer; *n.*, petty theft.
pilgar'lick, *n.*, a person made bald by disease; a scurvy fellow.
pil'grim, *n.*, a traveller, esp. to holy places.
pil'grimage, *n.*, a journey undertaken by a pilgrim.
pilig'erous, *adj.*, bearing hairs, as a leaf.
pi'ling, *pr.p.*, pile.
pill, *n.*, a little ball of medicine to be swallowed whole.
pil'lage, *n.*, plunder; *v.t.*, to plunder.
pil'laged, *p.p.*, pillage.
pil'lager, *n.*, one who pillages.
pil'laging, *pr.p.*, pillage.
pil'lar, *n.*, a column; a support.
pil'lar-box, *n.*, a receptacle for letters to be sent by post.
pil'lared, *adj.*, having pillars.
pil'larist, *n.*, a stylite.
pill'-box, *n.*, a box for holding pills.
pil'lion, *n.*, a cushion for a woman to ride on behind a man on horseback.
pil'loried, *p.p.*, pillory.
pil'lory, *n.*, a wooden frame in which offenders were fastened and exhibited in public; *v.t.*, to punish in the pillory; to ridicule publicly.
pil'low, *n.*, a bed-cushion; *v.t.*, to rest on for support.
pil'low-case, *n.*, a case or sack covering a pillow.
pil'lowed, *p.p.*, pillow; *adj.*, provided with pillows.
pil'lowing, *pr.p.*, pillow.
pil'low-slip, *n.*, *i.q.* pillow-case.
pil'lowy, *adj.*, soft; yielding.
pi'lose, *adj.*, covered with hairs.
pilos'ity, *n.*, hairiness.
pi'lot, *n.*, a man who guides a vessel into a harbour or along a coast; *v.t.*, to act as pilot to.
pi'lotage, *n.*, the remuneration or the guidance of a pilot.
pi'loted, *p.p.*, pilot.
pi'lot-fish, *n.*, a fish which attends sharks at sea.
pi'loting, *pr.p.*, pilot.
pi'lous, *adj.*, *i.q.* pilose.
Pil'sener, *n.*, a kind of light German beer.
pil'ular, *adj.*, rel. to pills.
pi'lum, *n.*, a Roman javelin (*Lat.*).
pim'elite, *n.*, a variety of steatite, apple-green in colour.
pimen'ta, *n.*, allspice.
pimen'to, *n.*, *i.q.* pimenta.
pimp, *n.*, a pander; *v.i.*, to act as a pimp.
pimped, *p.p.*, pimp.
pim'pernel, *n.*, a little red-flowered plant common in cornfields.
pimp'ing, *pr.p.*, pimp.
pim'ple, *n.*, a little swelling on the skin.
pim'pled, *adj.*, having pimples on the skin.
pim'ply, *adj.*, full of pimples.
pin, *n.*, a short piece of pointed wire with a rounded head; *v.t.*, to fasten with a pin.
pin'afore, *n.*, a sort of apron to keep the front of a dress clean.
pinas'ter, *n.*, a kind of pine found in Southern Europe.
pin'-case, *n.*, a case for holding pins.
pince'-nez, *n. pl.*, a pair of eyeglasses supported by the bridge of the nose.
pin'cers, *n. pl.*, an instrument for gripping and drawing out nails.
pinch, *v.t.*, to grip with the fingers; *v.i.*, to be niggardly; *n.*, a compression, as with the finger and thumb; distress.
pinch'beck, *n.*, a yellow alloy of copper and zinc; *adj.*, sham.
pinched, *p.p.*, pinch.
pinch'er, *n.*, one who pinches.
pinch'ing, *pr.p.*, pinch.
pin'cushion, *n.*, a pad in which pins are stuck to preserve them.
Pindar'ic, *n.*, an irregular ode; *adj.*, rel. to Pindar, the great lyric poet of Greece.
Pin'darism, *n.*, a style of writing in imitation of Pindar.
Pin'darist, *n.*, one who models his style on Pindar.
pine, *n.*, a cone-bearing tree; *v.i.*, to waste away.
pin'eal, *adj.*, shaped like a pine-cone (applied to a gland in the brain which Descartes considered the seat of the soul).
pine'apple, *n.*, a tropical fruit.
pined, *p.p.*, pine.
pi'nery, *n.*, a hothouse for pineapples; a plantation of pine-trees.
pine'-tree, *n.*, an evergreen, cone-bearing, timber tree.
pi'ney, *adj.*, pert. to, or abounding in, pines.
pin'fold, *n.*, a pound for stray animals.
ping, *n.*, the sound made by a bullet passing through the air.
ping'-pong, *n.*, a kind of table-tennis.
pin'hole, *n.*, the puncture made by a pin; a very small hole.
pi'nic, *adj.*, derived from the pine-tree.
pi'ning, *pr.p.*, pine.
pin'ion, *n.*, a wing; the joint of a wing; a small toothed wheel; *v.t.*, to bind the arms of.
pin'ioned, *p.p.*, pinion.

pin'ioning, *pr.p.*, pinion.

pin'ite, *n.*, impure muscovite.

pink, *n.*, a garden flower—the carnation; a narrow-sterned vessel; *adj.*, coloured like the pink; *v.t.*, to ornament with holes and scollops; to stab with a rapier.

pinked, *p.p.*, pink.

pink'er, *n.*, one who pinks.

pink'ing, *pr.p.*, pink; *n.*, the process of decorating with holes and scollops.

pin'-money, *n.*, an allowance made to a wife for her own use.

pin'nace, *n.*, an eight-oared sea-boat; a small schooner-rigged vessel.

pin'nacle, *n.*, a pointed summit.

pin'nate, *adj.*, feather-shaped.

pin'nated, *adj.*, *i.q.* pinnate.

pinned, *p.p.*, pin.

pin'ner, *n.*, one who pins; pl., an 18th cent. female head-dress.

pin'ning, *pr.p.*, pin.

pin'niped, *n.*, a fin-footed animal.

pin'nock, *n.*, a hedge-sparrow; a titmouse.

pin'nule, *n.*, the barb of a feather; a leaflet.

pin'point, *n.*, a very small object.

pin'-prick, *n.*, a trifling injury or annoyance.

pint, *n.*, one-eighth of a gallon.

pin'tail, *n.*, a duck with a pointed tail.

pin'tle, *n.*, a pin or bolt, to prevent the recoil of a cannon; to hang a rudder to, to fasten a wheel to its axle, etc.

pi'ny, *adj.*, *i.q.* piney.

pioneer', *n.*, a soldier who goes before to clear the way; *v.i.*, to clear the way.

pioneered', *p.p.*, pioneer.

pioneer'ing, *pr.p.*, pioneer.

pi'ous, *adj.*, dutiful; doing the will of God.

pi'ously, *adv.*, in a pious manner.

pip, *n.*, a disease of fowls; the seed of a fruit; a spot on a playing card.

pipe, *n.*, a musical instrument formed of a long tube; any long tube; an instrument for smoking tobacco; a large cask; *v.i.*, to play on a pipe.

pipe'-case, *n.*, a case for a tobacco-pipe.

pipe'-clay, *n.*, white clay; *v.t.*, to whiten with pipe-clay.

piped, *p.p.*, pipe; *adj.*, tubular.

pipe'-fish, *n.*, a long, slender fish.

pipe'-laying, *n.*, the practice of putting down gas- or water-pipes.

pi'per, *n.*, one who plays on the pipes.

pip'erine, *n.*, a crystalline extract of pepper.

pipette', *n.*, a tube used by chemists for transferring liquids.

pi'ping, *pr.p.*, pipe; *n.*, pipes collectively; *adj.*, hissing with heat.

pipistrel', *n.*, the common bat.

pip'it, *n.*, a bird allied to the lark.

pip'kin, *n.*, a small earthen pot.

pip'pin, *n.*, an apple raised from the seed.

pi'quancy, *n.*, pungency.

pi'quant, *adj.*, stimulating to the taste; lively; sparkling.

piqué', *n.*, a figured cotton fabric.

pique, *n.*, wounded pride; *v.t.*, to wound the pride of.

piqued, *p.p.*, pique.

piqu'ing, *pr.p.*, pique.

pi'racy, *n.*, robbery at sea; literary theft.

pi'rate, *n.*, a sea-robber; a stealer of copyright; *v.i.* and *t.*, to act as a pirate.

pi'rated, *p.p.*, pirate.

pirat'ical, *adj.*, acting as a pirate.

pi'rating, *pr.p.*, pirate.

pirn, *n.*, a reel or bobbin.

pirogue', *n.*, a canoe made of a hollowed log.

pirouette', *n.*, a quick turn on the toes; *v.i.*, to whirl as a dancer.

pis'cary, *n.*, fishing rights.

piscato'rial, *adj.*, pert. to fish.

pis'catory, *adj.*, *i.q.* piscatorial.

Pis'ces, *n. pl.*, the constellation called The Fishes.

piscicul'ture, *n.*, the rearing of fish.

piscicul'turist, *n.*, one who practises pisciculture.

pis'ciform, *adj.*, fish-shaped.

pisci'na, *n.*, a small basin and drain near the altar in a church; a Roman fish-pond (*Lat.*).

pis'cinal, *adj.*, rel. to a fish-pond or to a piscina.

pis'cine, *adj.*, pert. to fishes.

pisciv'orous, *adj.*, feeding on fish.

pisé', *n.*, stiff clay rammed into moulds and used in building walls.

pish, *interj.*, a word expressing contempt.

pis'iform, *adj.*, pea-shaped; having a structure resembling peas.

pis'mire, *n.*, an ant.

pis'olite, *n.*, carbonate of lime of pisiform structure.

pista'chio, *n.*, a small southern tree and its nut.

pistareen', *n.*, an old Spanish silver coin worth about a franc.

pis'til, *n.*, the seed-bearing part of a flower.

pistilla'ceous, *adj.*, pert. to a pistil.

pis'tillate, *adj.*, having a pistil.

pistillif'erous, *adj.*, having a pistil and no stamens.

pis'tol, *n.*, a small gun held in one hand.
pistole', *n.*, a Spanish gold coin worth about 16s.
pis'tolet, *n.*, a small pistol.
pis'ton, *n.*, a rod or solid cylinder fitted to move up and down in the hollow cylinder of an engine.
pit, *n.*, a hole in the earth; a mine; the floor of a theatre; *v.t.*, to mark with small hollows.
pit'-a-pat, *adv.*, in a flutter.
pitch, *n.*, a black, sticky substance, prepared from tar; a throw; the height of a note; the slope of a roof; *v.t.*, to cover with pitch; to throw; to fix on to the ground; *v.i.*, to rise and fall, as a ship.
pitch'-black, *adj.*, as black or dark as pitch.
pitch'-blende, *n.*, a mineral containing radium, etc.
pitch'-dark, *adj.*, very dark.
pitched, *p.p.*, pitch.
pitch'er, *n.*, a vessel for holding water or other liquid.
pitch'er-plant, *n.*, a plant with pitcher-shaped leaves.
pitch'fork, *n.*, a fork with a long handle for pitching hay, etc.; a tuning-fork.
pitch'ing, *pr.p.*, pitch.
pitch'-pine, *n.*, a resinous pine from which pitch is produced.
pitch'-pipe, *n.*, a pipe for tuning.
pitch'y, *adj.*, black like pitch.
pit'eous, *adj.*, causing pity; showing pity.
pit'eously, *adv.*, in a piteous manner.
pit'fall, *n.*, a hidden pit; a snare.
pith, *n.*, the soft middle of a stem; life and strength.
pith'ily, *adv.*, in a pithy manner.
pith'iness, *n.*, the quality of being pithy.
pith'less, *adj.*, without force and energy.
pit'-hole, *n.*, a pock-mark.
pith'y, *adj.*, full of force and energy.
pit'iable, *adj.*, deserving pity.
pit'ied, *p.p.*, pity.
pit'ier, *n.*, one who pities.
pit'iful, *adj.*, tender-hearted; causing pity; contemptible.
pit'ifully, *adv.*, in a pitiful manner.
pit'iless, *adj.*, having no pity.
pit'ilessness, *n.*, the state of being pitiless.
pit'man, *n.*, one who works in a pit; a collier.
Pitman'ic, *adj.*, rel. to Phonography or Pitman's Shorthand
Pit'manite, *n.*, a writer of Phonography.
pit'-saw, *n.*, a large saw worked by two men, one standing below in a pit.
pit'tacal, *n.*, a dark-blue derivative of wood-tar.
pit'tance, *n.*, a small portion of money or food.
pit'ted, *p.p.*, pit; *adj.*, having little pits on the skin.
pit'ting, *pr.p.*, pit.
pitu'itary, *adj.*, secreting mucus.
pit'uite, *n.*, mucus; phlegm.
pitu'itous, *adj.*, resembling or consisting of mucus.
pit'y, *n.*, a tender feeling for suffering; a reason for feeling pity; *v.t.*, to feel tenderness for.
pit'ying, *pr.p.*, pity.
pit'yingly, *adv.*, compassionately.
pityri'asis, *n.*, a skin disease.
pit'yroid, *adj.*, resembling bran.
più, *adv.*, more (*Ital.*).
piv'ot, *n.*, a pin or shaft on which something turns; *v.i.*, to turn on a pivot.
piv'otal, *adj.*, bel. to a pivot.
pix, *n.*, *i.q.* pyx.
pix'ing, *v.t.*, *i.q.* pyxing.
pix'y, *n.*, a fairy.
placabil'ity, *n.*, the quality of being placable.
pla'cable, *adj.*, easily pacified.
pla'cableness, *n.*, *i.q.* placability.
plac'ard, *n.*, a written or printed paper stuck on a wall.
placard', *v.t.*, to stick up a placard.
placard'ed, *p.p.*, placard.
placard'ing, *pr.p.*, placard.
pla'cate, *v.t.*, to appease.
pla'cated, *p.p.*, placate.
pla'cating, *pr.p.*, placate.
place, *n.*, a broad, open space; rank; a passage in a book; *v.t.*, to fix or settle.
place'bo, *n.*, the first antiphon of the vespers for the dead; a medicine to humour or soothe.
placed, *p.p.*, place.
place'man, *n.*, an office-bearer.
placen'ta, *n.*, the spongy substance connecting a mother with her unborn young.
placen'tal, *adj.*, pert. to, or possessing, a placenta.
placenta'tion, *n.*, the disposition of the placenta.
pla'cer, *n.*, one who places; a place where gold-dust is found in the soil.
pla'cet, *n.*, a vote of assent.
plac'id, *adj.*, peaceful.
placid'ity, *n.*, calmness.
plac'idly, *adv.*, calmly.
pla'cing, *pr.p.*, place.
plac'itory, *adj.*, rel. to pleading in courts of law.
plack'et, *n.*, the opening or slit in a skirt.
plac'oid, *adj.*, having scales like detached plates (applied to fishes).

placoi'dian, *n.*, a placoid fish, as the shark.

plafond', *n.*, a ceiling; soffit (*Fr.*).

pla'gal, *adj.*, applied in music to a cadence in which the tonic chord follows that of the subdominant.

pla'giarism, *n.*, literary theft; that which is plagiarized.

pla'giarist, *n.*, one who plagiarizes.

pla'giarize, *v.t.* and *i.*, to steal the writings of another.

pla'giarized, *p.p.*, plagiarize.

pla'giarizing, *pr.p.*, plagiarize.

pla'giary, *n.*, *i.q.* plagiarist.

plagihe'dral, *adj.*, having oblique faces arranged spirally.

plague, *n.*, a deadly sickness; a troublesome person or thing; *v.t.*, to trouble

plagued, *p.p.*, plague.

pla'guer, *n.*, one who plagues.

pla'guily, *adv.*, vexatiously.

pla'guing, *pr.p.*, plague.

pla'guy, *adj.*, vexatious.

plaice, *n.*, a flat fish like a flounder.

plaid, *n.*, an outer woollen garment worn by Scottish Highlanders.

plaid'ing, *n.* a coarse twilled woollen cloth.

plain, *adj.*, flat; simple; unadorned; *n.*, a flat stretch of country.

plain'-chant, *n.*, *i.q.* plain-song.

plain'-dealing, *adj.*, honest; *n.*, honest speaking and acting.

plain'er, *adj.*, *comp.* of plain.

plain'est, *adj.*, *super.* of plain.

plain'ly, *adv.*, in a plain manner.

plain'ness, *n.*, the state or quality of being plain.

plain'-song, *n.*, vocal music in the old ecclesiastical modes, unmeasured in rhythm and sung in unison.

plain'-speaking, *n.*, straightforwardness of speech.

plain'-spoken, *adj.*, speaking what one thinks.

plaint, *n.*, an expression of sorrow; the written statement of a plaintiff in a court of law.

plain'tiff, *n.*, one who brings an action into court.

plain'tive, *adj.*, mournful; complaining.

plain'tively, *adv.*, in a plaintive manner.

plain'tiveness, *n.*, the quality or state of being plaintive.

plait, *n.*, a fold; twisted hair, wool, etc.; *v.t.*, to fold, to weave hairs, etc.

plait'ed, *adj.*, braided; interwoven.

plait'er, *n.*, one who plaits.

plait'ing, *pr.p.*, plait.

plan, *n.*, a sketch or design: the shape of anything on a flat surface; *v.t.*, to design.

pla'nary, *adj.*, pert. to a plane.

planch, *v.t.*, to cover with planks.

plan'chet, *n.*, a flat piece of metal to be stamped into a coin.

planchette', *n.*, a little tablet of wood running on wheels and provided with a lead-pencil, used as a kind of oracle.

plane, *n.*, a flat surface; a tool for making wood smooth; *adj.*, flat; *v.t.*, to make level or smooth.

planed, *p.p.*, plane.

pla'ner, *n.*, a wooden block to smooth a forme of type; a planing machine.

plan'et, *n.*, a heavenly body moving round the sun.

planeta'rium, *n.*, a machine representing the planets moving in their orbits.

plan'etary, *adj.*, pert. to the planets.

plan'etoid, *n.*, a very small planet.

plane'-tree, *n.*, a tree used for lining avenues, possessing a straight stem and palmate leaves.

plan'etule, *n.*, a little planet.

plan'gent, *adj.*, beating or dashing, as a wave.

planim'eter, *n.*, an instrument for measuring areas.

planimet'ric, *adj.*, pert. to planimetry.

planim'etry, *n.*, the mensuration of plane figures.

pla'ning, *pr.p.*, plane.

pla'ning-mill, *n.*, a machine with a revolving cutter for planing wood.

planipet'alous, *adj.*, having petals lying in the same plane.

plan'ish, *v.t.*, to make smooth.

plan'ished, *p.p.*, planish.

plan'ishing, *pr.p.*, planish.

plan'isphere, *n.*, a map showing the circles of the sphere.

plank, *n.*, a long, narrow, flat piece of wood; *v.t.*, to cover with planks.

planked, *p.p.*, plank.

plank'ing, *n.*, planks collectively.

planned, *p.p.*, plan.

plan'ner, *n.*, one who plans.

plan'ning, *pr.p.*, plan.

plano-con'cave, *adj.*, plane on one side and concave on the other.

plano-con'ical, *adj.*, plane on one side and conical on the other.

plant, *n.*, a vegetable with roots, stem, and leaves; the tools of a business; *v.t.*, to put in the ground for growth; to set.

plant'able, *adj.*, capable of being planted.

plan'tain, *n.*, a plant with broad leaves and a long flower-spike; a fruit akin to the banana.

plan'tar, *adj.*, rel. to the sole of the foot.

planta'tion, *n.*, a place planted with young trees; a colony.

plant'ed, *p.p.*, plant.

plant'er, *n.*, the owner of a plantation; one who, or that which, plants.

plant'icle, *n.*, an embryo plant.

plan'tigrade, *adj.*, walking on the sole, not on the toes.

plant'ing, *pr.p.*, plant.

plant'let, *n.*, a little rudimentary plant.

plant'ule, *n.*, a plant embryo.

plaque, *n.*, an ornamental plate.

plash, *n.*, a small, shallow pool; a dash of water; *v.i.*, to dabble in water.

plashed, *p.p.*, plash.

plash'ing, *pr.p.*, plash.

plash'y, *adj.*, watery; marshy.

plasm, *n.*, a mould or matrix; *i.q.* plasma.

plas'ma, *n.*, a green mineral; formless elementary matter; protoplasm.

plasmat'ic, *adj.*, pert. to plasma.

plas'ter, *n.*, a mixture of lime, sand, and water for covering walls; cloth spread with ointment; *v.t.*, to cover with plaster.

plas'tered, *p.p.*, plaster.

plas'terer, *n.*, one who plasters.

plas'tering, *pr.p.*, plaster; *n.*, plaster-work.

plas'tery, *adj.*, resembling or containing plaster.

plas'tic, *adj.*, easily moulded.

plas'ticine, *n.*, a substance used for teaching modelling.

plastic'ity, *n.*, the state of being plastic.

plastog'raphy, *n.*, the art of moulding or modelling; forgery of handwriting.

plas'tron, *n.*, a leather breast-plate used in fencing.

plat, *n.*, a piece of ground laid out with some sort of design; *v.t.*, to plait.

plat'band, *n.*, a flower border in a garden; a flat rectangular moulding.

plate, *n.*, a thin piece of metal; a nearly flat dish; household articles of gold or silver; *v.t.*, to cover with a thin coat of metal.

plateau', *n.*, a table-land.

pla'ted, *p.p.*, plate.

plate'ful, *n.*, as much as fills a plate.

plate'-glass, *n.*, thick glass used for windows, mirrors, etc.

plat'en, *n.*, the flat part of a printing-press.

pla'ter, *n.*, one who coats articles with gold or silver.

plate'-warmer, *n.*, a shelved case in which plates are warmed before the fire.

plat'form, *n.*, a floor or flat surface more or less elevated and used in various ways; a foundation; an agreed set of principles.

plat'ina, *n.*, *i.q.* platinum.

pla'ting, *n.*, a thin covering; *pr.p.*, plate.

platinif'erous, *adj.*, producing platinum.

plat'inize, *v.t.*, to combine or cover with platinum.

plat'inized, *p.p.*, platinize.

plat'inizing, *pr.p.*, platinize.

plat'inode, *n.*, a cathode.

plat'inoid, *n.*, a name given to any metal with which platinum is found associated.

plat'inotype, *n.*, a permanent photograph in platinum black.

plat'inous, *adj.*, containing or consisting of platinum.

plat'inum, *n.*, a valuable metal like dim silver but very heavy.

plat'itude, *n.*, a weak remark.

platom'eter, *n.*, a planimeter.

platon'ic, *adj.*, rel. to Plato or his philosophy; passionless.

Pla'tonism, *n.*, the philosophy of Plato.

Pla'tonist, *n.*, a follower of Plato.

Pla'tonize, *v.i.*, to adopt the philosophy of Plato.

Pla'tonized, *p.p.*, platonize.

Pla'tonizing, *pr.p.*, platonize.

platoon', *n.*, a firing party; a sub-division of a company of soldiers.

plat'ted, *p.p.*, plat.

plat'ter, *n.*, a large flat dish.

plat'ting, *n.*, woven or plaited strips of straw for hats.

plat'ypus, *n.*, the ornithorhynchus.

plau'dit, *n.*, an expression of praise.

plau'ditory, *adj.*, applauding.

plausibil'ity, *n.*, superficial reasonableness.

plau'sible, *adj.*, appearing reasonable.

plau'sibly, *adv.*, speciously.

plau'sive, *adj.*, manifesting praise.

play, *n.*, amusement; a scene or story for acting; scope; *v.t.*, to join in a game; to act; to make music; to keep in action.

play'bill, *n.*, a programme of a play in the form of a placard.

played, *p.p.*, play.

play'er, *n.*, one who plays; an actor; a gambler.

play'fellow, *n.*, a playmate.

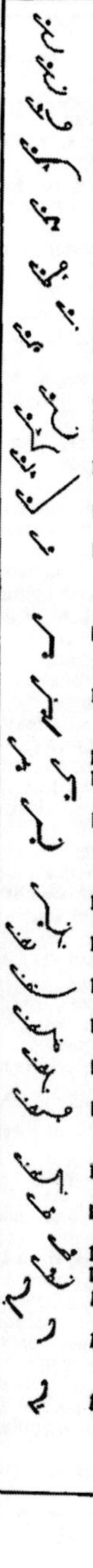

play'ful, *adj.*, fond of play or fun.
play'fully, *adv.*, in a playful manner.
play'fulness, *n.*, sportiveness.
play'goer, *n.*, one who frequents the theatre.
play'ground, *n.*, a piece of ground for recreation.
play'house, *n.*, a theatre.
play'ing, *pr.p.*, play.
play'mate, *n.*, one who plays along with another.
play'thing, *n.*, a toy.
play'time, *n.*, time set apart for play.
play'wright, *n.*, a maker of plays.
play'-*writer*, *n.*, a playwright.
plea, *n.*, a lawsuit; an answer to a charge; an urgent prayer.
plead, *v.t.* and *i.*, to use as a plea; to entreat.
plead'able, *adj.*, capable of being alleged in proof or defence.
plead'ed, *p.p.*, plead.
plead'er, *n.*, an advocate.
plead'ing, *p.p.*, plead; *n.*, advocacy; the statement of a litigant; *adj.*, imploring
plead'ingly, *adv.*, by pleading.
pleas'ant, *adj.*, giving pleasure; cheerful.
pleas'anter, *adj.*, *comp.* of pleasant.
pleas'antest, *adj.*, *super.* of pleasant.
pleas'antly, *adv.*, cheerfully.
pleas'antness, *n.*, the state of being pleasant.
pleas'antry, *n.*, lively talk; a jest.
please, *v.t.*, to cause joy to.
pleased, *p.p.*, please.
pleas'ing, *pr.p.*, please.
***pleas'urable*,** *adj.*, giving pleasure.
***pleas'ure*,** *n.*, delight; amusement; *v.t.*, to gratify.
***pleas'ure*-boat,** *n.*, a boat used for excursions and amusement.

***pleas'uring*,** *pr.p.*, pleasure.
pleat, *v.t.*, *i.q.* plait; *n.*, a fold.
plea'ted, *p.p.*, pleat.
plebe'ian, *adj.*, pert. to the common people; *n.*, one of the common people.
plebe'ianism, *n.*, vulgarity.
pleb'iscite, *n.*, a decision by the votes of the whole of the people.
plebs, *n.*, the common people (*Lat.*).
plec'trum, *n.*, a sort of comb for striking the strings of a lyre or other stringed instrument (*Lat.*).
pled, *p.p.*, plead.
pledge, *n.*, a promise; a security; *v.t.*, to promise; to pawn; to drink a health.
pledged, *p.p.*, pledge.
pledgee', *n.*, the person to whom anything is pledged.
pled'ger, *n.*, one who pledges.
pledg'et, *n.*, a compress laid on a wound.
pledg'ing, *pr.p.*, pledge.
Plei'ad, *n.*, one of the Pleiades.
Plei'ades, *n. pl.*, a group of seven stars.
Plei'ocene, *adj.*, more recent (*geol.*).
Pleiosau'rus, *n.*, an extinct saurian of great size.
Pleis'tocene, *adj.*, most recent (*geol.*).
ple'narily, *adv.*, in a plenary manner.
ple'narty, *n.*, the state of an ecclesiastical benefice when occupied.
ple'nary, *adj.*, complete.
plenilu'nar, *adj.*, rel. to the full moon.
plenip'otence, *n.*, completeness of power.
plenip'otent, *adj.*, possessing full power.
plenipoten'tiary, *n.*, a person who has full power to act for another; an ambassador with absolute power to make treaties, etc.

ple'nist, *n.*, one who believes that every portion of space is filled with matter.
plen'itude, *n.*, completeness.
plen'teous, *adj.*, abundant.
plen'teously, *adv.*, in a plenteous manner.
plen'tiful, *adj.*, abundant.
plen'tifully, *adv.*, abundantly.
plen'tifulness, *n.*, a state of plenty.
plen'ty, *n.*, a full supply; abundance.
ple'num, *n.*, that state of things in which every part of space is supposed to be full of matter.
ple'onasm, *n.*, redundancy of words.
pleonas'tic, *adj.*, redundant.
plesiomor'phism, *n.*, a state of crystallization which produces substances resembling one another closely, though they are not identical.
ple'siosaur, *n.*, an extinct gigantic long-necked saurian.
plesiosau'rus, *n.*, *i.q.* plesiosaur.
pleth'ora, *n.*, overfulness; too much blood.
plethor'ic, *adj.*, having too much blood.
pleu'ra, *n.*, the covering membrane of the lungs.
pleu'risy, *n.*, inflammation of the pleura.
pleurit'ic, *adj.*, pert. to pleurisy.
pleuro - pneumo'nia, *n.*, inflammation of the lungs and pleura.
plex'iform, *adj.*, formed like network.
plexim'eter, *n.*, a little instrument used in diagnosing disease by percussion of the body.
plex'ure, *n.*, an interweaving; a texture.
plex'us, *n.*, a network, as of nerves, fibres, etc. (*Lat.*).

pliabil'ity, *n.*, flexibility.
pli'able, *adj.*, easily bent or persuaded.
pli'ancy, *n.*, easiness to be bent or influenced.
pli'ant, *adj.*, pliable.
pli'ca, *n.*, a disease of the hair and of trees.
pli'cate, *adj.*, folded like a fan; plaited.
pli'cated, *adj.*, *i.q.* plicate.
plica'tion, *n.*, a fold; a folding.
plic'ature, *n.*, *i.q.* plication.
plied, *p.p.*, ply.
pli'er, *n.*, one who plies; *pl.*, an instrument for bending wire.
pli'form, *adj.*, having the form of a ply or fold.
plight, *n.*, condition; a state of risk: *v.t.*, to give as a pledge.
plight'ed, *p.p.*, plight.
plight'er, *n.*, one who plights.
plight'ing, *pr.p.*, plight.
plinth, *n.*, the lowest part of the base of a column; a thin course of masonry projecting near the base of a wall.
Pli'ocene, *adj.*, *i.q.* Pleiocene.
Pliosau'rus, *n.*, *i.q.* Pleiosaurus.
plod, *v.i.*, to go on slowly but without stopping.
plod'ded, *p.p.*, plod.
plod'der, *n.*, a slow, hard-working person.
plod'ding, *p.p.*, plod; *adj.*, patiently laborious.
plonge, *v.t.*, to cleanse a drain by stirring up the sediment.
plot, *n.*, a piece of ground; a secret plan or conspiracy; the story of a novel or play; *v.t.*, to represent in graphs; to map out or chart; *v.i.*, to plan mischief.
plot'ted, *p.p.*, plot.
plot'ter, *n.*, one who plots.
plot'ting, *pr.p.*, plot.
plough, *n.*, an instrument for turning up the soil; *v.t.* and *i.*, to turn up the soil with a plough.
plough'able, *adj.*, arable.
plough'boy, *n.* a boy who leads a team in ploughing.
ploughed, *p.p.*, plough.
plough'er, *n.*, one who ploughs.
plough'ing, *pr.p.*, plough.
plough'man, *n.*, a man who guides a plough.
plough'share, *n.*, the blade of a plough.
plough'-tail, *n.*, the handle of a plough.
plov'er, *n.*, a common wading-bird.
pluck, *n.*, courage; the heart, liver, etc., of an animal; *v.t.*, to strip off; to gather.
plucked, *p.p.*, pluck.
pluck'er, *n.*, one who plucks.
pluck'ier, *adj.*, *comp.* of plucky.
pluck'iest, *adj.*, *super.* of plucky.
pluck'ily, *adv.*, in a plucky manner.
pluck'iness, *n.*, the quality of being plucky.
pluck'ing, *pr.p.*, pluck.
pluck'y, *adj.*, courageous.
plug, *n.*, a stopper for a hole; *v.t.*, to stop with a plug.
plugged, *p.p.*, plug.
plug'ging, *pr.p.*, plug.
plum, *n.*, a fleshy fruit containing a stone; £100,000; a handsome fortune.
plu'mage, *n.*, the feathers of a bird.
plumassier', *n.*, a preparer of, or dealer in, feathers (*Fr.*).
plumb, *n.*, a leaden weight hung on a string; *adj.*, perpendicular; *v.t.*, to test with a plumb.
plumbag'inous, *adj.*, resembling or consisting of plumbago.
plumba'go, *n.*, black-lead; graphite.
plum'bean, *adj.*, leaden.
plum'beous, *adj.*, *i.q.* plumbean.
plumb'er, *n.*, a worker in lead.
plumb'ery, *n.*, works or manufactures of lead.
plum'bic, *adj.*, rel. to lead.
plumbif'erous, *adj.*, producing lead.
plumb'ing, *n.*, the art of working in lead.
plumb'-line, *n.*, a line with a plumb attached.
plum'-cake, *n.*, a raisin cake.
plume, *v.t.*, to adorn with feathers; to boast; *n.*, a crest, a feather.
plumed, *p.p.*, plume; *adj.*, having plumes.
plume'let, *n.*, a little plume.
plumig'erous, *adj.*, having plumes.
plu'miliform, *adj.*, in form like a feather.
plu'ming, *pr.p.*, plume.
plu'miped, *adj.*, with feathered feet.
plu'mist, *n.*, a feather-dresser.
plum'met, *v.t.*, to sound with a lead; *n.*, a leaden weight on a line for sounding.
plu'mous, *adj.*, having feathers. Also *plumose*.
plump, *v.i.*, to give all one's votes; *adj.*, round, sleek.
plump'er, *n.*, one who plumps.
plump'ness, *n.*, the quality of being plump.
plum'-pudding, *n.*, a pudding made with raisins and many ingredients.
plum'-tree, *n.*, a tree bearing plums.
plu'mule, *n.*, a down-feather; a rudimentary bud of an embryo plant.
plu'my, *adj.*, feathery.
plun'der, *v.t.*, to pillage, rob; *n.*, pillage, spoil.
plun'dered, *p.p.*, plunder.
plun'derer, *n.*, a pillager, robber.

plun'dering, *pr.p.*, plunder.

plunge, *v.t.*, to immerse; *v.i.*, to jump down; to gamble; *n.*, the act of plunging; a sudden drop.

plunged, *p.p.*, plunge.

plun'ger, *n.*, one who plunges, a piece of mechanism with plunging action.

plun'ging, *pr.p.*, plunge.

pluper'fect, *adj.*, denoting time previous to time already past; *n.*, the tense so named.

plu'ral, *adj.*, more than one; *n.*, the plural number.

plu'ralism, *n.*, the holding simultaneously of several offices.

plu'ralist, *n.*, one who holds several offices at once.

plural'ity, *n.*, more than one.

plu'ralize, *v.t.*, to make plural, or express in the plural.

plu'ralized, *p.p.*, pluralize.

plu'ralizing, *pr.p.*, pluralize.

plus, *adv.*, more; *prep.* with the addition of; *n.*, the sign(+); a positive quantity.

plush, *adj.*, made of plush; *n.*, a fabric with a long, soft nap.

plu'tarchy, *n.*, government by the rich.

plutoc'racy, *n.*, *i.q.* plutarchy; a wealthy ruling class.

plu'tocrat, *n.*, one who exerts the power of wealth.

Pluto'nian, *adj.*, rel. to Pluto and Hades; igneous.

Pluton'ic, *adj.*, *i.q.* Plutonian.

Plu'tonism, *n.*, the Plutonists' theory that rock-structure is chiefly the result of igneous action.

Plu'tonist, *n.*, an adherent of Plutonism.

plu'vial, *adj.*, rainy; rel. to rain.

pluviom'eter, *n.*, a rain-gauge.

plu'vious, *adj.*, *i.q.* pluvial.

ply, *v.t.*, to practise diligently; to wield; to assail (as with arguments); *v.i.*, to go backwards and forwards; *n.*, a layer or fold of cloth, strand of rope, etc.

ply'ing, *pr.p.*, ply.

pneumat'ic, *adj.*, rel. to air.

pneumat'ics, *n. pl.*, the science of airs and gases.

pneumatol'ogy, *n.*, the science of spiritual existence (embracing theology, demonology, and psychology).

pneumatom'eter, *n.*, a contrivance for measuring the amount of breath taken in at one inspiration.

pneumo'nia, *n.*, inflammation of the lungs.

pneumon'ic, *adj.*, rel. to the lungs.

pneumoni'tis, *n.*, inflammation of the lungs.

Pnyx, *n.*, the Athenian place of meeting.

po'a, *n.*, large grass.

poach, *v.t.*, to steal game; to boil (an egg) without the shell; to trample into holes; *v.i.*, to trespass.

poach'ard, *n.*, a diving-bird.

poached, *p.p.*, poach.

poach'er, *n.*, one who poaches.

poach'ing, *pr.p.*, poach; *n.*, stealing game and trespassing.

poach'y, *adj.*, sodden from trampling.

pock, *v.t.*, to score with pock-marks; *n.*, a mark left by certain diseases.

pock'et, *v.t.*, to put in one's pocket; to submit to; *n.*, a bag in a coat, etc., or on a billiard table; a cavity in a rock or the air.

pock'et-book, *n.*, a note-book for the pocket.

pock'et-compass, *n.*, a compass for the pocket.

pock'eted, *p.p.*, pocket.

pocket-hand'kerchief, *n.*, a handkerchief for the pocket.

pock'eting, *pr.p.*, pocket.

pock'et-knife, *n.*, a knife for the pocket.

pock'et-money, *n.*, money for small expenses.

pock'-mark, *n.*, the scar left by disease.

pock'y, *adj.*, pock-marked.

po'co, *adv.*, slightly (*mus.*).

poc'uliform, *adj.*, cup-shaped.

pod, *n.*, the seed-vessel of peas, beans, etc.; a small flock of seals; *v.t.*, to drive (seals) into a pod; *v.i.*, to fill out.

pod'agra, *n.*, gout in the foot.

pod'agral, *adj.*, pert. to gout.

podag'ric, *adj.*, *i.q.* podagral.

pod'ded, *adj.*, having pods.

podestà', *n.*, a magistrate (*Ital.*).

podg'y, *adj.*, soft and fat.

po'dium, *n.*, a base, plinth, continuous bench round a room.

podophyl'lin, *n.*, a purgative medicine made from the wild mandrake.

pod'osperm, *n.*, a seed's stalk.

poecilit'ic, *adj.*, variegated, mottled.

po'em, *n.*, a poetical composition.

po'esy, *n.*, the art of poetry; verse-making.

po'et, *n.*, a writer of poetry.

poetas'ter, *n.*, an indifferent poet.

po'etess, *n.*, fem. of poet.

poet'ic, *adj.*, rel. to poets and poetry.

poet'ical, *adj.*, *i.q.* poetic.

poet'ics, *n. pl.*, the study of the art of poetry.

po'et-lau'reate, *n.*, the Court poet.
po'etry, *n.*, verse; poems in general.
pog'gy, *n.*, a small whale.
pog'rom, *n.*, massacre of a section of the community in Russia.
poign'ancy, *n.*, sharpness, acuteness.
poign'ant, *adj.*, sharp, acute.
poign'antly, *adv.*, acutely.
poikilit'ic, *adj.*, *i.q.* poecilitic
poinset'tia, *n.*, a flower so named.
point, *v.t.*, to sharpen; to aim; to punctuate; to cement the joints of brickwork on the face; to arrange words for chanting; *n.*, a sharp end; a headland; a punctuation mark; a subject in an argument; the true bearing of an argument; one of the positions in the cricket-field.
point'blank, *adj.* and *adv.*, in direct line; flatly.
point'ed, *p.p.*, point; *adj.*, sharp-ended.
point'el, *n.*, a stilus.
point'ing, *pr.p.*, point; *n.*, the act of pointing in any sense.
point'er, *n.*, one who points; a variety of sporting dog; a stick for pointing with; one of the two stars so named in the Great Bear.
point'less, *adj.*, without point.
points'man, *n.*, a railwayman in charge of points on a line.
poise, *v.t.*, to weigh, balance; *n.*, weight, balance.
poised, *p.p.*, poise.
pois'ing, *pr.p.*, poise.
poi'son, *v.t.*, to kill by poison; to taint; *n.*, a deadly drug; venom.
poi'soned, *p.p.*, poison.
poi'soner, *n.*, one who administers poison.
poi'soning, *pr.p.*, poison.
poi'sonous, *adj.*, containing poison; venomous.
poi'trel, *n.*, a horse's breast-leather or breast-armour.
poke, *v.t.*, to thrust forward; to push; *n.*, a push; a bag or pouch.
poked, *p.p.*, poke.
po'ker, *n.*, a bar for poking the fire.
poke'weed, *n.*, a perennial herb.
po'king, *pr.p.*, poke.
po'ky, *adj.*, small, confined.
polac'ca, *n.*, *i.q.* polonaise.
po'lar, *adj.*, pert. to the pole or poles.
polarim'eter, *n.*, an apparatus for measuring the polarization of light.
polarim'etry, *n.*, the measuring of polarization.
polar'iscope, *n.*, *i.q.* polarimeter.
polar'ity, *n.*, the quality of having opposed poles; tendency towards the earth's magnetic poles; the quality of being attracted and repelled; modification of light and heat vibrations, so that the ray shows different qualities in different directions.
polariza'tion, *n.*, the effect of polarizing.
po'larize, *v.t.*, to give polarity to.
po'larized, *p.p.*, polarize.
po'larizer, *n.*, that which polarizes.
po'larizing, *pr.p.*, polarize.
pol'der, *n.*, reclaimed marsh land.
pole, *v.t.*, to propel with a pole; *n.*, a rod or shaft; a measure of length (5½ yds.); the North or the South Pole; a native of Poland.
pole'axe, *n.*, an axe on the end of a pole.
pole'cat, *n.*, a wild cat.
poled, *p.p.*, pole.
pol'emarch, *n.*, an ancient Greek military commander.
polem'ic, *adj.*, controversial; *n.*, a controversialist.
polem'ical, *adj.*, *i.q.* polemic.
polem'ics, *n. pl.*, controversial writings.
pole'-star, *n.*, the North Star.
police', *v.t.*, to guard with a police force; *n.*, a civil force.
policed', *p.p.*, police.
police'man, *n.*, a member of the police force.
pol'icy, *n.*, a scheme of governing; any course of action; an insurance contract; the pleasure-grounds of an estate.
po'ling, *pr.p.*, pole.
pol'ish, *v.t.*, to make bright by rubbing; *n.*, the result of polishing; a material for polishing papers; refinement of manners.
Po'lish, *adj.*, pert. to Poland and the Poles.
pol'ishable, *adj.*, that will take a polish.
pol'ished, *p.p.*, polish; *adj.*, refined.
pol'isher, *n.*, one who, or anything that, polishes.
pol'ishing, *pr.p.*, polish.
polite', *adj.*, gentle, courteous.
polite'ly, *adv.*, courteously.
polite'ness, *n.*, courteousness.
politesse', *n.*, good breeding (*Fr.*).
pol'itic, *adj.*, sagacious; well advised.
polit'ical, *adj.*, rel. to the state and to politics.
polit'ically, *adv.*, in regard to politics and the State.
politi'cian, *n.*, one who makes politics his business.
pol'itics, *n. pl.*, the art or science of governing.
pol'ity, *n.*, civil constitution.

pol'ka, *n.*, a Bohemian dance.

poll, *v.t.*, to crop the hair of; to take the votes of; to lop; *v.i.*, to give a vote; *n.*, the back of the head; votes taken and registered.

Poll (Polly), *n.*, pet name for Mary; a parrot.

poll'ack, *n.*, a kind of cod-fish.

pol'lard, *v.t.*, to lop trees; *n.*, a lopped tree; an animal that has lost its horns.

polled, *p.p.*, poll.

pol'len, *n.*, the dust of a flower.

poll'er, *n.*, one who polls.

pollicita'tion, *n.*, a revocable promise (*leg.*).

poll'ing, *pr.p.*, poll.

pollinif'erous, *adj.*, producing pollen.

pol'linose, *adj.*, covered with a pollen-like substance.

poll'-tax, *n.*, a tax on each member of a community.

pollute', *v.t.*, to defile, contaminate.

pollu'ted, *p.p.*, pollute.

pollu'ter, *n.*, one who pollutes.

pollu'ting, *pr.p.*, pollute.

pollu'tion, *n.*, contamination.

Pol'lux, *n.*, the twin-brother of Castor.

po'lo, *n.*, a ball game played by horsemen.

polonaise', *n.*, a Polish dance; a feminine dress.

polo'ny, *n.*, a variety of sausage.

poltroon', *n.*, an arrant coward; a dastard.

poltroon'ery, *n.*, dastardliness.

polyacous'tic, *adj.*, sound increasing.

Polyadel'phia, *n.pl.*, a class of plants with stamens joined in bundles.

polyan'dry, *n.*, the system under which a woman has several husbands.

polyan'thus, *n.*, a flowering plant so named.

pol'yarchy, *n.*, government by many.

polyba'sic, *adj.*, having more than two bases.

polycar'pous, *adj.*, having several carpels.

pol'ychord, *n.*, a ten-stringed musical instrument.

pol'ychroite, *n.*, saffranin; the colouring matter of saffron.

polychromat'ic, *adj.*, many-coloured.

pol'ychromy, *n.*, variegated colour.

polycotyle'don, *n.*, a plant with many cotyledons.

polydac'tyl, *adj.*, with an abnormal number of fingers.

polydip'sia, *n.*, excessive craving for drink.

polyg'amist, *n.*, the husband of several wives.

polyg'amous, *adj.*, having a plurality of wives.

polyg'amy, *n.*, plurality of wives.

polygas'tric, *adj.*, having many stomachs.

polyg'enous, *adj.*, heterogeneous.

pol'yglot, *adj.*, written in many languages; *n.*, a version in many languages.

pol'ygon, *n.*, a many-sided figure.

polyg'onal, *adj.*, with many sides or angles.

polyg'onous, *adj.*, *i.q.* polygonal.

Polyg'onum, *n.*, a plant genus—knot-grass, snakeweed, etc.

polyg'ony, *n.*, a plant of the polygonum genus.

pol'ygram, *n.*, a many-lined figure.

pol'ygraph, *n.*, a device for multiplying a writing.

polygraph'ic, *adj.*, rel. to polygraph.

polygraph'ical, *adj.*, *i.q.* polygraphic.

polyg'raphy *n.*, multiplying by means of a polygraph.

pol'ygyn, *n.*, a plant of the Polygynia order.

Polygyn'ia, *n. pl.*, an order of plants having many styles.

polyg'yny, *n.*, plurality of wives.

polyhe'dral, *adj.*, with many sides.

polyhe'dric, *adj.*, *i.q.* polyhedral.

polyhe'dron, *n.*, a many-sided solid.

polyhe'drous, *adj.*, *i.q.* polyhedral.

Polyhym'nia, *n.*, the Muse of sacred song.

pol'ymath, *n.*, a very learned person.

polymath'ic, *adj.*, pert. to polymathy.

polym'athy, *n.*, much learning.

polymor'phism, *n.*, the assumption of many forms.

polymor'phous, *adj.*, assuming many forms.

pol'yneme, *n.*, a thread fish.

Polyne'sian, *adj.*, rel. to Polynesia.

polyno'mial, *n.*, an algebraic expression of more than two terms.

polyon'ymous, *adj.*, having many names.

polyon'ymy, *n.*, multiplicity of names.

pol'yp, **pol'ype**, *n.*, an animal low in the scale of nature.

pol'ypary, *n.*, the structure supporting a cluster of polyps.

polyp'ean, *adj.*, pert. to a polyp.

polypet'alous, *adj.*, with many petals.

polyph'agous, *adj.*, eating many kinds of food.

polyphar'macy, *n.*, the blending of many medicinal drugs.

Polyphe'mus, *n.*, the one-eyed mythical Cyclops.

pol'yphone, *n.*, a written sign standing for more than one word.

polyphon'ic, *adj.*, with many sounds; with several melodies.

pol'yphonist, *n.*, a contrapuntist.

polyph'ony, *n.*, the blending of several strains.

polyphyl'lous, *adj.*, many-leaved.

Pol'ypi, *n.*, pl. of polypus.

pol'ypidom, *n.*, *i.q.* polypary.

pol'ypod, *adj.*, having many feet; *n.*, a many-footed creature.

pol'ypody, *n.*, genus of ferns.

pol'ypous, pert. to a polypus.

polyprismat'ic, *adj.*, showing many prisms.

pol'ypus, *n.*, a tumour.

polysep'alous, *adj.*, with many sepals.

pol'ysperm, *n.*, a tree of which the fruit has many seeds.

polysper'mous, *adj.*, having many seeds.

pol'ystyle, *adj.*, having many styles.

polysyllab'ic, *adj.*, many-syllabled.

polysyl'lable, *n.*, a word of many syllables.

polytech'nic, *n.*, comprising many arts; an institution where many arts are taught.

pol'ytheism, *n.*, worship of many gods.

pol'ytheist, *n.*, a worshipper of many gods.

polytheis'tic, *adj.*, pert. to polytheism.

polytheis'tical, *adj.*, *i.q.* polytheistic.

polyzo'nal, *adj.*, with many zones.

polyzo'on, *n.*, one of the polyzoa, or compound invertebrates

pom'ace, *n.*, the substance of apples and kindred fruit.

poma'ceous, *adj.*, pert. to pomace.

pomade', *n.*, a scented preparation for the hair.

poman'der, *n.*, a ball for carrying perfume.

poma'tum, *n.*, *i.q.* pomade.

pome, *n.*, a hollow metal sphere holding hot water to keep the hands warm; an apple-like fruit.

pomegran'ate, *n.*, the fruit so named.

pom'elo, *n.*, grape fruit.

pomif'erous, *n.*, pome-producing.

pom'mel, *v.t.*, to thump with the fists (also *pummel*); *n.*, the knob of a saddle-bow, or at the end of a sword-hilt.

pom'mel(l)ed, *p.p.*, pommel.

pom'mel(l)ing, *pr.p.*, pommel; *n.*, the act of pommelling.

pomolog'ical, *adj.*, rel. to pomology.

pomol'ogist, *n.*, an expert in pomology.

pomol'ogy, *n.*, the science of fruit culture.

Pomo'na, *n.*, the goddess of fruits (*Lat.*).

pomp, *n.*, show, display, pageantry.

pom'padour, *n.*, a style of coiffure; a mode of corsage; a shade of red.

Pompe'ian, *adj.*, rel. to Pompey and Pompeii.

pom'-pom, *n.*, a quick-firing, automatic gun.

pompos'ity, *n.*, an inflated manner.

pom'pous, *adj.*, inflated; affecting the grand.

pom'pously, *adv.*, in a pompous way.

pon'cho, *n.*, a Spanish cloak.

pond, *n.*, a body of stagnant water.

pon'der, *v.t.*, to meditate on; to think over.

ponderabil'ity, *n.*, the quality of being ponderable.

pon'derable, *adj.*, able to be weighed.

pon'dered, *p.p.*, ponder.

pon'derer, *n.*, one who ponders.

pon'dering, *pr.p.*, ponder.

ponderos'ity, *n.*, the quality of being ponderous.

pon'derous, *adj.*, heavy, weighty, important.

pond'weed, *n.*, a general name for weeds growing in still water.

po'nent, *adj.*, occidental.

pongee', *n.*, Chinese silk.

pon'go, *n.*, an African ape.

pon'iard, *n.*, a kind of dagger; *v.t.*, to stab with a poniard.

pon'tage, *n.*, a bridge-toll.

Pon'tic, *adj.*, rel. to the Pontus or Euxine.

pon'tiff, *n.*, a priest; a bishop; the Supreme Pontiff = the Pope.

pontif'ic, *adj.*, rel. to, or like, a pontiff.

pontif'ical, *adj.*, *i.q.* pontific; *n.*, a bishop's service book. In pl. = a bishop's vestments and insignia.

pontif'ically, *adv.*, in the character of a pontiff.

pontif'icate, *n.*, a pontiff's office, or term of office.

pontif'icate, *v.i.*, to celebrate, or assist at, Mass pontifically.

pontonier', *n.*, a soldier with charge of a pontoon or pontoon bridge.

pontoon', *n.*, a boat forming with others a floating bridge.

po'ny, *n.*, a little horse.

pood, *n.*, a Russian weight (36 lb. avoirdupois).

poo'dle, *n.*, a breed of performing dogs.

pooh, *n.*, an exclamation of contempt or derision.

pooh-pooh', *v.t.*, to treat with contempt as of no importance.

pooh-poohed', *p.p.*, pooh-pooh.

pooh-pooh'ing, *pr.p.*, pooh-pooh.

pool, *v.t.*, to share collectively; *n.*, a pond; a common fund; a billiard game.

pooled, *p.p.*, pool.

pool'er, *n.*, one who pools.

pool'ing, *pr.p.*, pool.

poop, *v.t.*, to break over a ship's stern; *n.*, the hinder part of a ship.

pooped, *p.p.*, poop.

poop'ing, *pr.p.*, poop.

poor, *adj.*, not rich, needy; barren, unproductive.

poor'-box, *n.*, an alms-box.

poor'er, *adj.*, *comp.* of poor.

poor'est, *adj.*, *super.* of poor.

poor'house, *n.*, the workhouse.

poor'-law, *n.*, the law rel. to the relief of the poor.

poor'ly, *adj.*, somewhat unwell; *adv.*, indifferently.

poor'ness, *n.*, poverty.

poor'-rate, *n.*, the rate appropriated to poor-relief.

poor'-relief, *n.*, the aid from public funds to the poor.

pop, *v.t.*, to put suddenly; *v.i.*, to make a small explosion; *n.*, a small, quick explosion; ginger beer (*colloq.*).

pope, *n.*, a Russian priest; the Holy Father.

pope'dom, *n.*, the rule of popes.

pope'-joan, *n.*, an antiquated card game.

pope'ling, *n.*, a little pope.

po'pery, *n.*, a name given to the beliefs and practices of the Roman Church and to anything assumed to resemble them.

pope's'-eye, *n.*, a gland in a sheep's or ox's thigh.

pop'-gun, *n.*, a child's toy that goes off with a pop.

pop'injay, *n.*, a parrot; a babbling fool; a bird used as an archery mark.

po'pish, *adj.*, rel. to popery.

pop'lar, *n.*, a tall, slender tree so named.

pop'lin, *n.*, a dress fabric.

poplit'ic, *n.*, rel. to the part behind the knee.

popped, *p.p.*, pop.

pop'pet, *n.*, a word of endearment; a short piece of timber.

pop'ping, *pr.p.*, pop; *n.*, the act of popping.

pop'py, *n.*, a plant from which opium is made.

pop'py-head, *n.*, a poppy's seed capsule; the carved end of a stall or seat. The latter use of the word is connected with *puppet*.

pop'ulace, *n.*, the multitude.

pop'ular, *adj.*, rel. to the people; generally esteemed.

popular'ity, *n.*, general esteem.

populariza'tion, *n.*, the act of popularizing.

pop'ularize, *v.t.*, to make known to and adopted by the multitude.

pop'ularized, *p.p.*, popularize.

pop'ularizing, *pr.p.*, popularize.

pop'ularly, *adv.*, in a popular way.

pop'ulate, *v.t.*, to fill with inhabitants.

pop'ulated, *p.p.*, populate.

pop'ulating, *pr.p.*, populate.

popula'tion, *n.*, inhabitants; the number of inhabitants.

pop'ulin, *n.*, a compound obtained from the aspen.

pop'ulist, *n.*, an advocate of collectivism.

pop'ulous, *adj.*, with a numerous population.

pop'ulousness, *n.*, the state of being populous.

por'cate, *adj.*, furrowed and ridged.

por'cated, *adj.*, *i.q.* porcate.

porce'lain, *n.*, the finest kind of earthenware.

porch, *n.*, the covered entrance to a building.

por'cine, *adj.*, rel. to pigs.

por'cupine, *n.*, a creature with a bristly hide and long quills.

pore, *v.i.*, to gaze with close and steady attention; *n.*, a passage through the skin.

pored, *p.p.*, pore.

po'riform, *adj.*, like pores.

po'ring, *pr.p.*, pore.

pork, *n.*, swine's flesh.

pork'-butcher, *n.*, a dealer in pork.

pork'er, *n.*, a wild pig.

pork'et, *n.*, a little hog.

pork'ling, *n.*, a little pig.

pornograph'ic, *adj.*, written obscenely.

pornog'raphy, *n.*, indecent literature.

poros'ity, *n.*, the state of being porous.

porot'ic, *adj.*, producing callus-formation.

po'rous, *adj.*, full of pores.

porphyrit'ic, *adj.*, pert. to porphyry.

por'phyry, *n.*, a hard rock, containing white and red crystals in a reddish ground.

por'poise, *n.*, a cetaceous creature with a short, rounded snout.

porra'ceous, *adj.*, leek-coloured.

porrect', *adj.*, stretched out.

por'ridge, *n.*, a mess of oatmeal.

porri'go, *n.*, scald-head.

por'ringer, *n.*, a porridge-bowl.

port, *v.t.*, to lay a ship over to the left side; to carry aslant; *n.*, a harbour; the left side of a ship; the wine of Oporto;

a gateway; deportment; an aperture for the escape of steam, etc.

portabil'ity, *n.*, the quality of being portable.

port'able, *adj.*, able to be carried.

port'age, *n.*, carriage; hire of transport; conveyance from one lake or river to another; *v.t.*, to convey in this way.

port'al, *n.*, a gate; a gateway.

portamen'to, *adv.*, sustaining the sound (*mus.*).

port-cray'on, *n.*, a pencil holder.

portcul'lis, *n.*, an open-work barrier drawn up and down in a castle gateway.

Porte, *n.*, the Ottoman court.

porte-monnaie, *n.*, a purse (*Fr.*).

portend', *v.t.*, to foretoken, presage.

portend'ed, *p.p.*, portend.

portend'ing, *pr.p.*, portend.

por'tent, *n.*, a presage, sign, omen.

porten'tous, *adj.*, ominous, alarming.

port'er, *n.*, one who carries for hire; a malt liquor; a gatekeeper.

port'erage, *n.*, a porter's hire.

port'fire, *n.*, a slow-match.

portfo'lio, *n.*, a case for loose papers, prints, etc.

port'-hole, *n.*, a ship's window.

port'ico, *n.*, a colonnade; a porch.

port'ière, *n.*, a doorway curtain.

por'tion, *v.t.*, to parcel; to endow; *n.*, a part; a dowry.

por'tioned, *p.p.*, portion.

por'tioning, *pr.p.*, portion.

por'tionist, *n.*, one who enjoys a portion; a joint incumbent.

por'tionless, *adj.*, without a portion.

port'liness, *n.*, the quality of being portly.

port'ly, *adj.*, large, dignified of mien.

portman'teau, *n.*, a travelling case.

por'trait, *n.*, a person's picture.

por'traiture, *n.*, the art of making portraits; vivid word-painting.

portray', *v.t.*, to represent; describe in a picture or as in a picture.

portray'al, *n.*, the act of portraying.

portrayed', *p.p.*, portray.

portray'er, *n.*, one who portrays.

portray'ing, *pr.p.*, portray.

port'reeve, *n.*, formerly the highest municipal officer.

port'ress, *n.*, a woman gatekeeper.

port'-toll, *n.*, a harbour toll.

port'-town, *n.*, a harbour town.

Portuguese', *adj.*, rel. to Portugal; a native of Portugal.

port-ward'en, *n.*, a harbour-master.

port wine', *n.*, the wine of Oporto.

pose, *v.t.*, to puzzle; to state; *v.i.*, to assume a character or attitude.

posa'da, *n.*, a Spanish inn.

posed, *p.p.*, pose.

po'ser, *n.*, a difficult problem.

po'sing, *pr.p.*, pose.

pos'it, *v.t.*, to place; to assume as fact.

pos'ited, *p.p.*, posit.

posi'tion, *n.*, situation; posture; place.

pos'iting, *pr.p.*, posit.

pos'itive, *adj.*, real, explicit; assertive.

pos'itively, *adv.*, in a positive way; really.

pos'itiveness, *n.*, a tendency to make statements dogmatically.

pos'itivism, *n.*, Comte's philosophical system of the co-ordination of the sciences.

pos'itivist, *n.*, an adherent of positivism.

pos'net, *n.*, a small basin.

posolog'ical, *adj.*, rel. to posology.

posol'ogy, *n.*, the science of quantity.

pos'se, *n.*, an armed force; potentiality.

possess', *v.t.*, to own; be master of; seize.

possessed', *p.p.*, possess; *adj.*, under the influence of an evil spirit.

possess'ing, *pr.p.*, possess.

posses'sion, *n.*, ownership; a thing owned; demoniacal control.

possess'ive, *adj.*, having or denoting possession; *n.*, the genitive case.

possess'or, *n.*, an owner, master.

possess'ory, *adj.*, rel. to possession.

pos'set, *n.*, a warm drink of milk curdled with wine, etc.

possibil'ity, *n.*, the quality of being possible.

pos'sible, *adj.*, that may exist or be done.

pos'sibly, *adv.*, within the limits of possibility.

post, *v.t.*, to despatch a letter; *v.i.*, to drive with post-horses; *n.*, a courier; postal service; a relay of post horses; an upright piece of timber; an office or situation; *prefix*, meaning after.

post'able, *adj.*, able to be posted.

post'age, *n.*, the fee for posting letters or parcels.

post'al, *adj.*, rel. to the post.

post'boy, *n.*, a post-chaise outrider.

post'-captain, *n.*, a naval captain of three years' standing.

post'card, *n.*, a card that can be stamped for postage.

post'-chaise, *n.*, a posting carriage.

post'date, *v.t.*, to name, on a document, etc., a later than the actual date.
post'dated, *p.p.*, postdate.
post'dating, *pr.p.*, post date.
post-dilu'vial, *adj.*, after the deluge.
post-dilu'vian, *adj.*, *i.q.* post-diluvial.
pos'tea, *n.*, the proceedings in a lawsuit between the joining of issue and the verdict.
post'ed, *p.p.*, post.
post'-entry, *n.*, a late or subsequent entry.
post'er, *n.*, an advertisement for posting up.
poste restante', *n.*, the branch of a post office where letters are kept to be called for.
poste'rior, *adj.*, subsequent in time or place; *n.*, the hinder parts.
posterior'ity, *n.*, the state of being posterior.
poste'riorly, *adv.*, subsequently.
poste'riors, *n. pl.*, the hinder parts.
poster'ity, *n.*, succeeding generations.
pos'tern, *adj.*, in the rear; private; *n.*, a small or secret gate or entrance.
post'-free, *adj.*, free of postage.
post-haste', *adv.*, at a rapid speed; in haste.
post'-horse, *n.*, a horse used in a post-chaise.
post'humous, *adj.*, born after a father's death; published after the author's death.
pos'til, *v.t.*, to make a marginal note or commentary on; *n.*, a marginal note.
postil'ion, postil'lion, *n.*, an outrider.
post'ing, *pr.p.*, post.
post'man, *n.*, a letter carrier.
post'mark, *n.*, the mark showing the offices through which a letter has passed.
post'master, *n.*, the head of a post office; one who jobs post-horses; a junior member of the foundation of Merton College, Oxford.
postmerid'ian, *adj.*, after mid-day.
post merid'iem, a Latin phrase = after mid-day.
post-mor'tem, *n.*, an autopsy after death.
postnup'tial, *adj.*, after marriage.
post-ob'it, *n.*, an agreement to repay a loan on the death of someone named in the bond.
post'-office, *n.*, a place for receiving and distributing letters, parcels, etc.
postpone', *v.t.*, to put off; delay for a while.
postponed', *p.p.*, postpone.
postpone'ment, *n.*, the act of putting off; a temporary delay.
postpo'ning, *pr.p.*, postpone.
postpran'dial, *adj.*, after dinner.
postsce'nium, *n.*, the part of a theatre behind the scenes.
post'script, *n.*, something added to a letter.
post'-town, *n.*, a town with a post office.
pos'tulant, *n.*, a candidate for admission to an order.
pos'tulate, *n.*, a self-evident proposition; something accepted as not needing proof.
pos'tulate, *v.t.*, to assume without proof.
pos'tulated, *p.p.*, postulate.
pos'tulating, *pr.p.*, postulate.
postula'tion, *n.*, the act of postulating.
pos'tulatory, *adj.*, assuming as self-evident.
pos'ture, *v.i.*, to pose; *n.*, attitude, state.
po'sy, *n.*, a nosegay; a motto.
pot, *v.t.*, to put into pots; to preserve; to shoot; *n.*, a vessel of metal or earthenware; a size of paper.
po'table, *adj.*, drinkable.
potage', *n.*, soup (*Fr.*)
potamog'raphy, *n.*, a description of river systems.
potamol'ogy, *n.*, the study of river systems.
pot'ash, *n.*, an alkali from wood ashes.
potas'sium, *n.*, a metallic element.
pota'tion, *n.*, a drinking bout; a large draught.
pota'to, *n.*, an esculent tuber.
po'tatory, *adj.*, rel. to potation.
pot'-boiler, *n.*, a piece of literary or artistic work done purely to make a little money.
pot'-boy, *n.*, a tavern servant.
potch, *v.t.*, to bleach.
poteen', *n.*, Irish whiskey.
po'tency, *n.*, the quality of being potent.
po'tent, *adj.*, powerful; intoxicating.
po'tentate, *n.*, a sovereign; exalted person.
poten'tial, *adj.*, possible (but not real); latent; powerful; indicating power.
potential'ity, *n.*, possibility.
poten'tially, *n.*, possibly (but not really).
po'tently, *adv.*, powerfully.
potheen', *n.*, *i.q.* poteen.
poth'er, *n.*, fuss, confusion; *v.i.*, to make a fuss; *v.t.*, to confuse.
pot'-herb, *n.*, a vegetable for cooking.
poth'ered, *p.p.*, pother
poth'ering, *pr.p.*, pother.
pot'hook, *n.*, a hook for hanging pots; one of the first signs learnt in writing.

pot'-house, *n.*, a low tavern.
pot'-hunter, *n.*, one who plays games for the sake of prizes.
po'tion, *n.*, a draught, dose.
pot'latch, *n.*, a N. American Indian feast.
pot-luck', *n.*, any food that is going.
pot'-man, *n.*, *i.q.* pot-boy.
potpourri', *n.*, a medley.
pot'sherd, *n.*, piece of a broken pot.
pot'tage, *n.*, a stew; porridge.
pot'ted, *p.p.*, pot.
pot'ter, *v.i.*, to spend time on trifles; *n.*, a maker of china and earthenware pottery.
pot'tered, *p.p.*, potter.
pot'tering, *pr.p.*, potter.
pot'tery, *n.*, all kinds of earthenware.
pot'ting, *pr.p.*, pot.
pot'tle, *n.*, a liquid measure = 2 qts.; a kind of fruit basket.
potwal'loper, *n.*, a roysterer.
potwal'loping, *n.*, hard and furious drinking.
pouch, *v.t.*, to pocket; *v.i.*, to swell; *n.*, a small bag; a sack.
pouched, *p.p.*, pouch.
pouch'ing, *pr.p.*, pouch.
pouchong', *n.*, a Chinese tea.
poulp, *n.*, an octopus.
poul'terer, *n.*, a vendor of poultry.
poul'tice, *v.t.*, to apply a poultice to; *n.*, a softening application.
poul'ticed, *p.p.*, poultice.
poul'ticing, *pr.p.*, poultice.
poul'try, *n.*, domestic fowls.
poul'try-*yard*, *n.*, a yard for poultry.
pounce, *v.i.*, to swoop down; *v.t.*, to sprinkle with powder; *n.*, powder once used for drying ink; a bird of prey's talon.
pounce'-box, *n.*, a box for holding pounce.
pounced, *p.p.*, pounce
poun'cet-box, *n.*, *i.q.* pounce-box.
pounc'ing, *pr.p.*, pounce.
pound, *v.t.*, to grind; shut in a pound; *n.*, a standard weight; a 20 shilling piece; an enclosure for stray cattle.
pound'age, *n.*, allowance of so much on the pound.
pound'ed, *p.p.*, pound
pound'er, *n.*, one who pounds.
pound'ing, *pr.p.*, pound.
pour, *v.t.*, to empty from a vessel; emit; utter; *v.i.*, to stream forth.
poured, *p.p.*, pour.
pour'er, *n.*, one who pours.
pour'ing, *pr.p.*, pour.
poussette', *n.*, one of the figures in a country dance.
pout, *v.i.*, to thrust out the lips; to look sullen; *n.*, an expression of sullenness by thrusting out the lips.
pout'ed, *p.p.*, pout.
pout'er, *n.*, one who pouts; a breed of pigeons.
pout'ing, *pr.p.*, pout.
pout'ingly, *adv.*, sullenly.
pov'erty, *n.*, the state of being poor; defect.
pow'der, *v.t.*, to pulverize; grind small; sprinkle, as with dust; *n.*, any substance pulverized; gunpowder.
pow'dered, *p.p.*, powder.
pow'der-horn, *n.*, a horn to carry gunpowder.
pow'dering, *pr.p.*, powder.
pow'der-magazine, *n.*, a store for gunpowder.
pow'der-mill, *n.*, a manufactory of gunpowder
pow'der-monkey, *n.*, a sailor-boy who carries powder for the guns.
pow'dery, *adj.*, like powder.
pow'er, *n.*, strength of body or mind; authority.
pow'erful, *adj.*, strong, influential.
pow'erfully, *adv.*, in a powerful way.
pow'erless, *adj.*, wanting power.
pow'wow, *v.i.*, to conjure; *n.*, a N. American Indian conjuror; incantation rites; a political meeting of a noisy kind.
pox, *n.*, an eruption of the skin.
poy, *n.*, a pole.
praam, pram, *n.*, a Dutch and Baltic lighter.
pram, *n.*, an abbreviation of perambulator.
***practica*bil'ity**, *n.*, the quality of being practicable.
prac'ticable, *adv.*, able to be put into practice; feasible.
prac'ticably, *adv.*, feasibly.
prac'tical, *adj.*, rel. to practice or use; able to do.
practical'ity, *n.*, the quality of being practical.
prac'tically, *adv.*, in effect; in practice.
prac'tice, *n.*, habitual action; acquired skill; action; one of the arithmetical rules.
prac'tise, *v.t.*, to do habitually; to do repeatedly; to exercise; *v.i.*, to acquire a habit; to be a practitioner
prac'tised, *p.p.*, practise; *adj.*, skilled
prac'tiser, *n.*, one who practises.
prac'tising, *pr.p.*, practise.
practi'tioner, *n.*, one who exercises a profession.
prae'cipe, *n.*, a legal writ demanding that a thing shall

be done, or why it has not been performed.

praecor'dia, *n. pl.*, the region of the heart.

praemuni're, *n.*, an offence against the royal prerogative; the writ against one so offending.

praeno'men, *n.*, a name preceding the family name (*Lat.*).

praetex'ta, *n.*, a white toga edged with purple stripes, the dress of priests, magistrates, and free-born youths in ancient Rome (*Lat.*).

prae'tor, *n.*, one of the high magistrates in ancient Rome (*Lat.*).

praeto'rian, *adj.*, rel. to praetors.

praeto'rium, *n.*, the general's headquarters; a Roman governor's residence (*Lat.*).

pragmat'ic, *adj.*, officious; busy.

pragmat'ical, *adj.*, *i.q.* pragmatic.

prag'matism, *n.*, a philosophic system which regards belief merely in its relation to human interests.

prag'matist, *n.*, one who adopts pragmatism.

prai'rie, *n.*, a vast tract of grass-covered land.

prai'rie-dog, *n.*, a small rodent found in prairies.

prai'rie-value, *n.*, the value of land in the wild state.

prai'rie-wolf, *n.*, the coyote.

praise, *v.t.*, to laud; express approval of; glorify; *n.*, high approval, laudation, worship.

praised, *p.p.*, praise.

prais'er, *n.*, one who praises.

praise'worthiness, *n.*, the state of being praiseworthy.

praise'worthy, *adj.*, deserving of praise.

prais'ing, *pr.p.*, praise.

prance, *v.i.*, to bound; to strut; *n.*, a bound.

pranced, *p.p.*, prance.

pranc'ing, *pr.p.*, prance.

pran'dial, *adj.*, rel. to dinner.

prank, *v.t.*, to dress out; *n.*, a frolic, trick.

pranked, *p.p.*, prank.

prank'ing, *pr.p.*, prank.

prank'ish, *adj.*, full of tricks.

prase, *n.*, a light green quartz.

pras'inous, *n.*, of the colour of grass.

prate, *v.i.*, to talk foolishly· to be garrulous.

pra'ted, *p.p.*, prate.

pra'ter, *n.*, one who prates.

pra'ting, *pr.p.*, prate; *n.*, loquacity.

prat'ique, *n.*, a licence to a ship to communicate or trade after quarantine.

prat'tle, *v.i.*, to chatter; talk childishly.

prat'tled, *p.p.*, prattle.

prat'tler, *n.*, one who prattles.

prat'tling, *pr.p.*, prattle.

prav'ity, *n.*, wickedness, depravity.

prawn, *n.*, a larger shrimp.

prax'is, *n.*, materials for exercise.

pray, *v.t.* and *i.*, to entreat: to offer prayer.

prayed, *p.p.*, pray.

prayer, *n.*, a petition, entreaty.

pray'er, *n.*, one who prays.

prayer'-book, *n.*, a book of prayers or devotions.

prayer'ful, *n.*, strong in prayer.

prayer'fully, *n.*, in a prayerful way.

prayer'fulness, *n.*, the quality of being prayerful.

prayer'less, *adj.*, not praying.

prayer'lessness, *n.*, the state of being prayerless.

prayer'-meeting, *n.*, a gathering for prayer.

pray'ing, *pr.p.*, pray.

preach, *v.t.*, to utter; *v.i.*, to deliver a sermon; to give advice.

preached, *p.p.*, preach.

preach'er, *n.*, one who preaches.

preach'ing, *pr.p.*, preach; *n.*, the delivery of sermons.

preach'ment, *n.*, a sermon delivered; a solemn harangue.

pre-acquaint', *v.t.*, to make acquainted in advance.

pre-acquaint'ance, *n.*, knowledge in advance.

pre-acquaint'ed, *p.p.*, pre-acquaint.

pre-acquaint'ing, *pr.p.* pre-acquaint.

pre-adam'ic, *adj.*, *i.q.* pre-adamite.

pre-ad'amite, *adj.*, previous to the birth of Adam.

preadmon'ish, *v.t.*, to admonish beforehand.

preadmon'ished, *p.p.*, preadmonish.

preadmoni'tion, *n.*, the act of preadmonishing.

pream'ble, *n.*, a preface; the introductory or explanatory part of a statute.

prearrange', *v.t.*, to arrange beforehand.

preassu'rance, *n.*, assurance beforehand.

preb'end, *n.*, a manor or estate attached to a stall in a cathedral or collegiate church.

preb'endal, *adj.*, rel. to a prebend or a prebendary.

preb'endary, *n.*, the holder of a prebend.

preca'rious, *adj.*, risky, uncertain, dubious.

preca'riously, *adv.*, riskily, uncertainly.

prec'ative, *adj.*, *i.q.* precatory.

prec'atory, *adj.*, suppliant.

precau'tion, *n.*, previous care; preventive measures.

precau'tionary, *adj.*, guarding in advance.

precede′, *v.t.* and *i.*, to go before in time or rank.
prece′ded, *p.p.*, precede.
prece′dence, *n.*, priority; superiority of rank.
prece′dency, *n.*, *i.q.* precedence.
prece′dent, *adj.*, going before.
prec′edent, *n.*, an example or rule; an earlier parallel.
prec′edented, *adj.*, having a precedent.
prece′ding, *pr.p.*, precede.
precen′tor, *n.*, a cathedral or collegiate dignitary who rules the choir; one who leads the singers.
precen′torship, *n.*, a precentor's office.
pre′cept, *n.*, an instruction, command, maxim.
precep′tive, *adj.*, rel. to precepts; didactic.
precep′tor, *n.*, a teacher.
precepto′rial, *adj.*, rel. to a preceptor.
precep′tory, *adj.*, didactic; *n.*, a subsidiary house of Knights Templars.
precep′tress, *n.*, a woman teacher.
preces′sion, *n.*, a going forward, esp. of the equinoxes.
pre′cinct, *n.*, an enclosure; a territorial division.
precios′ity, *n.*, affectation; over-fastidiousness.
pre′cious, *adj.*, of high price, valuable; affectedly superior in expression.
pre′ciously, *adv.*, in a precious way.
pre′ciousness, *n.*, value.
prec′ipice, *n.*, a steep place; an abrupt descent.
precip′itance, *n.*, *i.q.* precipitancy.
precip′itancy, *n.*, over-haste.
precip′itant, *adj.*, headlong, hasty; *n.*, in chemistry, an agent that solidifies a substance held in solution.
precip′itate, *v.t.*, to urge on with haste; to bring about before the time; to cause to sink to the bottom of a solution.
precip′itate, *adj.*, hasty, rash; *n.*, a precipitated substance.
precip′itated, *p.p.*, precipitate.
precip′itating, *pr.p.*, precipitate.
precipita′tion, *n.*, the act of precipitating.
precip′itous, *adj.*, abruptly steep.
precip′itously, *adv.*, steeply.
pré′cis, *n.*, a concise summary or abstract (*Fr.*).
precise′, *adj.*, exact, formal.
precise′ly, *adv.*, exactly, formally.
precise′ness, *n.*, formality, exactness, punctiliousness.
precis′ian, *n.*, a stickler for exactness; a purist.
precis′ion, *n.*, accuracy, exactness.
preci′sive, *adj.*, lopping, pruning.
preclude′, *v.t.*, to make impossible.
preclu′ded, *p.p.*, preclude.
preclu′ding, *pr.p.*, preclude.
preclu′sion, *n.*, prevention.
preclu′sive, *adj.*, preventive.
preco′cious, *adj.*, prematurely developed.
preco′ciousness, *n.*, *i.q.* precocity.
precoc′ity, *n.*, premature development, esp. of the mind.
precogni′tion, *n.*, previous knowledge; a preliminary examination of witnesses.
preconceive′, *v.t.*, to conceive in anticipation.
preconceived′, *p.p.*, preconceive.
preconceiv′ing, *pr.p.*, preconceive.
preconcep′tion, *n.*, the act of preconceiving; something preconceived.
preconcert′, *v.t.*, to concert or arrange beforehand.
preconcert′ed, *p.p.*, preconcert.
preconcert′ing, *pr.p.*, preconcert.
pre′conize, *v.t.*, to proclaim, summon by name; to give official approval to the appointment of a bishop.
precontract′, *v.t.* and *i.*, to contract beforehand.
precon′tract, *n.*, a contract beforehand.
precontract′ed, *p.p.*, precontract.
precontract′ing, *pr.p.*, precontract.
precord′ial, *adj.*, rel. to the parts in front of the heart.
precurs′ive, *adj.*, going before.
precurs′or, *n.*, a forerunner, as St. John Baptist.
precurs′ory, *adj.*, forerunning, anticipatory.
preda′cious, *adj.*, apt to plunder or to prey; predatory.
pred′atorily, *adv.*, in a predatory way.
pred′atory, *adj.*, preying, plundering.
predeces′sor, *n.*, one who had held a position before another.
predestina′rian, *adj.*, rel. to predestination and the predestinarian controversy; *n.*, a professor of the predestinarian controversy.
predes′tinate, *v.t.*, to foreordain.
predes′tinate, *adj.*, foreordained.
predes′tinated, *p.p.*, predestinate.
predes′tinating, *pr.p.*, predestinate.
predestina′tion, *n.*, foreordaining; divine appointment from eternity.
predes′tinator, *n.*, one who predestinates.

predes'tine, *v.t.*, *i.q.* predestinate.

predes'tined, *p.p.*, predestine.

predes'tining, *pr.p.*, predestine.

predeterm'inate, *adj.*, decreed beforehand.

predetermina'tion, *n.*, decree or decision beforehand.

predeterm'ine, *v.t.* and *i.*, to decree or decide beforehand.

predeterm'ined, *p.p.*, predetermine.

predeterm'ining, *pr.p.* predetermnie.

pre'dial, *adj.*, pert. to landed estates, agrarian; *n.*, a slave attached to the land.

predicabil'ity, *n.*, the quality of being predicable.

pred'icable, *adj.*, able to be predicted or affirmed.

predic'ament, *n.*, something predicated; a category; an awkward position, a fix.

pred'icant, *adj.*, preaching; *n.*, a preaching friar.

pred'icate, *n.*, that which is affirmed or denied; an attribute.

pred'icate, *v.t.*, to affirm or assert one thing of another.

pred'icated, *p.p.*, predicate.

pred'icating, *pr.p.*, predicate.

predica'tion, *n.*, an affirmation concerning anything.

predic'ative, *adj.*, affirming.

pred'icatory, *adj.*, *i.q.* predicative.

predict', *v.t.*, to foretell.

predict'ed, *p.p.*, predict.

predict'ing, *pr.p.*, predict.

predic'tion, *n.*, a foretelling.

predict'ive, *adj.*, predicting.

predilec'tion, *n.*, preference.

predispose', *v.t.*, to make liable or inclined.

predisposed', *p.p.*, predispose.

predispos'ing, *pr.p.*, predispose.

predisposi'tion, *n.*, a mental or physical condition of being liable or inclined.

predom'inance, *n.*, sway, preponderance.

predom'inancy, *n.*, *i.q.* predominance.

predom'inant, *adj.*, having superiority or preponderance.

predom'inate, *v.i.*, to have preponderance or superiority.

predom'inated, *p.p.*, predominate.

predom'inating, *pr.p.*, predominate.

predomina'tion, *n.*, preponderance, superiority, control.

predoom', *v.t.*, to destine, foredoom.

predoomed', *p.p.*, predoom.

predoom'ing, *pr.p.*, predoom.

pre-elect', *adj.*, forechosen; predestinate.

pre-elect'ed, *adj.*, *i.q.* pre-elect.

pre-elec'tion, *n.*, predestination.

pre-em'inence, *n.*, high superiority or excellence.

pre-em'inent, *adj.*, highly superior or excellent.

pre-empt', *v.t.*, to get by pre-emption.

pre-emp'tion, *n.*, purchase, or the right to purchase, before any other purchaser.

preen, *v.t.*, to trim with the beak; *reflex.* to trim oneself.

preened, *p.p.*, preen.

pre-engage', *v.t.* and *i.*, to engage beforehand.

pre-engage'ment, *n.*, a previous engagement.

preen'ing, *pr.p.*, preen.

pre-estab'lish, *v.t.*, to establish before.

pre-estab'lished, *p.p.* pre-establish.

pre-estab'lishing, *pr.p.*, pre-establish.

pre-exam'ine, *v.t.*, to examine beforehand

pre-exam'ined, *p.p.*, pre-examine.

pre-exam'ining, *pr.p.*, pre-examine.

pre-exist', *v.i.*, to exist previously.

pre-exist'ed, *p.p.*, pre-exist.

pre-exist'ence, *n.*, previous existence.

pre-exist'ent, *adj.*, existing before.

pre-exist'ing, *pr.p.*, pre-exist.

pref'ace, *v.t.*, to introduce (generally with a written or spoken word); *n.*, an introduction to a book; a prefatory note or remark; the beginning of the Canon of the Mass.

pref'aced, *p.p.*, preface.

pref'acer, *n.*, one who prefaces.

pref'acing, *pr.p.*, preface.

prefato'rial, *adj.*, pert. to a preface.

pref'atory, *adj.*, introductory.

pre'fect, *n.*, a Roman officer of high civil or military rank; the head of a French administrative department; a public school monitor.

pre'fecture, *n.*, a prefect's term of office, official residence, area of jurisdiction.

prefer', *v.t.*, to choose in preference; to promote; to bring forward; *v.i.*, to be more willing.

pref'erable, *adj.*, more desirable than another.

pref'erably, *adv.*, for choice.

pref'erence, *n.*, the liking of one thing more than another; a thing preferred; special favour; the right to be paid before other debts are paid.

preferen'tial, *adj.*, giving or receiving preference.

preferen'tially, *adv.*, in a preferential way.

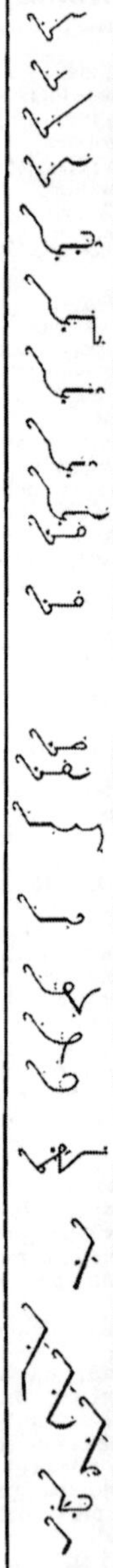

prefer'ment, *n.*, promotion to office.
preferred', *p.p.*, prefer.
prefer'rer, *n.*, one who prefers.
prefer'ring, *pr.p.*, prefer.
prefigura'tion, *n.*, representation through a type.
prefig'urative, *adj.*, representing by type.
prefig'ure, *v.t.*, to represent beforehand by type.
prefig'ured, *p.p.*, prefigure.
prefig'uring, *pr.p.*, prefigure.
prefix', *v.t.*, to place before; to add to in front.
pre'fix, *n.*, something prefixed, as a word or particle joined to the front of another word as *re*-place; a title.
prefixed', *p.p.*, prefix.
prefix'ing, *pr.p.*, prefixing.
preg'nancy, *n.*, the state of being pregnant; fullness of meaning.
preg'nant, *adj.*, being with young; gravid; full of meaning.
prehen'sible, *adj.*, able to be grasped.
prehen'sile, *adj.*, capable of grasping.
prehen'sion, *n.*, grasping, seizing, whether with the hand or with the mind.
prehistor'ic, *adj.*, antecedent to historic record.
prejudge', *v.t.*, to judge beforehand or prematurely.
prejudged', *p.p.*, prejudge.
prejudg'ing, *pr.p.*, prejudge.
prejudg'ment, *n.*, a judgment formed prematurely.
prejudica'tion, *n.*, *i.q.* prejudgment.
pre'judice, *v.t.*, to influence the mind of; to injure the validity of a case or claim; *n.*, bias; preconception; detriment.

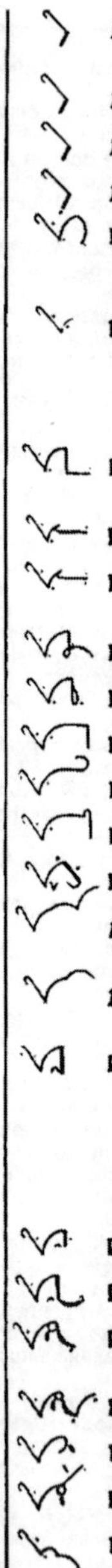

prej'udiced, *p.p.*, prejudice; *adj.*, biassed.
prejudi'cial, *adj.*, detrimental.
prejudi'cially, *adv.*, detrimentally.
prej'udicing, *pr.p.*, prejudice.
prel'acy, *n.*, the office or status of a prelate; prelatic government.
prel'ate, *n.*, one holding high rank in the Church—an archbishop, a cardinal, a bishop, an abbot, etc.
prelat'ic, *adj.*, pert. to prelates and prelacy.
prelat'ical, *adj.*, *i.q.* prelatic.
prelat'ically, *adv.*, in the manner of a prelate.
prel'atism, *n.*, *i.q.* prelacy.
prel'atist, *n.*, an advocate of prelacy.
prelect', *v.i.*, to lecture, discourse.
prelec'tion, *n.*, a discourse or lecture.
prelec'tor, *n.*, a lecturer.
preliba'tion, *n.*, a foretaste.
prelim'inarily, *adv.*, by way of a beginning.
prelim'inary, *adj.*, introductory; *n.* a first step.
prel'ude, *v.t.* and *i.*, to preface; introduce; to open with a (musical) prelude; *n.*, something introductory; an opening (musical) movement.
prel'uded, *p.p.*, prelude.
prel'uding, *pr.p.*, prelude.
prelu'sive, *adj.*, of the nature of a prelude; foreshadowing.
prelu'sively, *adv.*, in a prelusive way.
prelu'sion, *n.*, a premonition.
prelu'sory, *adj.*, *i.q.* prelusive.
premature', *adj.*, ripe before the time; occurring too soon; hasty.

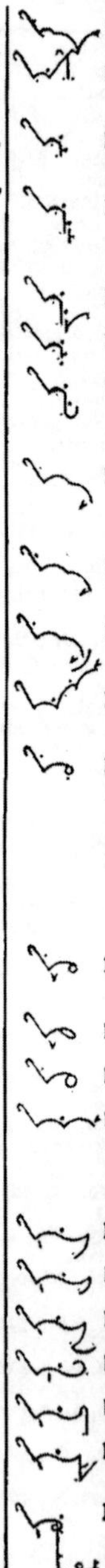

premature'ly, *adv.*, too soon.
prematur'ity, *n.*, the state of being premature.
premed'itate, *v.t.* and *i.*, to plan, think out, beforehand.
premed'itated, *p.p.*, premeditate; *adj.*, conceived beforehand.
premed'itatedly, *adv.*, with premeditation.
premed'itating, *pr.p.*, premeditate.
premedita'tion, *n.*, deliberate purpose; previous consideration.
prem'ier, *adj.*, first; of the first importance; *n.*, a Prime Minister.
première', *n.*, the first performance of a play (*Fr.*).
prem'iership, *n.*, the office of Prime Minister.
premillen'nial, *adj.*, before the millennium.
prem'ise, prem'iss, *n.*, a proposition from which another is inferred, as the major and minor premises in logic; the foregoing; in pl., a building and its adjuncts.
premise', *v.t.*, to state in introduction; to lay down premises.
premised', *p.p.*, premise.
prem'ises, *n. pl.*, *see* premise.
pre'mium, *n.*, a prize; a price paid; a value above par; excess value of one currency over another.
premon'ish, *v.t.*, to warn.
premon'ished, *p.p.*, premonish.
premon'ishing, *pr.p.*, premonish.
premoni'tion, *n.*, a warning; presage.
premon'itor, *n.*, one who premonishes.
premon'itory, *adj.*, conveying a warning.
Premonstraten'sian, *adj.*, pert. to the Order of Canons

Regular founded by St. Norbert, in 1119, at Prémontré in France; *n.*, a member of the Order.

premorse′, *adj.*, having the end truncated.

premuni′tion, *n.*, a defensive state.

preno′men, *n.*, *i.q.* praenomen.

prenom′inal, *adj.*, rel. to the prer omen.

pren′tice, *v.t.* and *n.*, *i.q.* apprentice.

preoc′cupancy, *n.*, the right or state of occupying beforehand.

preoccupa′tion, *n.*, preoccupancy; business more important than other matters; the state of being mentally engrossed.

preoc′cupied, *p.p.*, preoccupy.

preoc′cupy, *v.t.*, to engross (the mind).

preoc′cupying, *pr.p.*, preoccupy.

pre-ordain′, *v.t.*, to foreordain.

pre-ordained′, *p.p.*, pre-ordain.

pre-ordain′ing, *pr.p.*, pre-ordain.

pre-ordina′tion, *n.*, the act of pre-ordaining.

prepaid′, *p.p.*, prepay.

prep′arable, *adj.*, able to be prepared.

prepara′tion, *n.*, the state of preparing; something done to be in readiness; anything prepared, as food or medicine; getting up school lessons; preparing for a discord (*mus.*).

prepar′ative, *adj.*, *i.q.* preparatory.

prepar′atory, *adj.*, introductory; serving to prepare.

prepare′, *v.t.* and *i.*, to make ready; get ready.

prepared′, *p.p.*, prepare.

prepar′edly, *adv.*, in a state of readiness.

prepar′edness, *n.*, a state of readiness.

prepar′ing, *pr.p.*, prepare.

prepay′, *v.t.*, to pay in advance.

prepay′able, *adj.*, on which a charge is to be prepaid.

prepay′ing, *pr.p.*, prepay.

prepay′ment, *n.*, a payment in advance.

prepense′, *adj.*, premeditated, deliberate.

prepol′lence, *n.*, eminence, superiority.

prepol′lency, *n.*, *i.q.* prepollence.

prepol′lant, *adj.*, eminent, superior.

prepon′derance, *n.*, superiority in weight, force, number, etc.

prepon′derancy, *n.*, *i.q.* preponderance.

prepon′derant, *adj.*, preponderating.

prepon′derate, *v.i.*, to be superior in weight, force, number, etc.

prepon′derated, *p.p.*, preponderate.

prepon′derating, *pr.p.*, preponderate.

prepondera′tion, *n.*, *i.q.* preponderance.

preposi′tion, *n.*, a word which, placed before another, expresses its relation to some other word, as *in*, *by*, *from*.

preposi′tional, *adj.*, with the force of a preposition.

prepos′itive, *adj.*, that may be prefixed.

prepos′itor, *n.*, a school monitor, prefect. Also *praepostor*.

prepossess′, *v.t.*, to inspire; prejudice; to bias.

prepossessed′, *p.p.*, prepossess.

prepossess′ing, *pr.p.*, prepossess; *adj.*, engaging, charming.

prepossess′ion, *n.*, something preconceived; an antecedent bias in favour of some person or thing.

prepos′terous, *adj.*, contrary to nature, reason, or common sense; outrageously absurd.

prepos′terously, *adv.*, in a preposterous way.

prepo′tency, *n.*, predominating influence.

prepo′tent, *adj.*, with stronger influence.

pre′puce, *n.*, the foreskin.

Pre-Raph′aelite, *adj.*, rel. to the Pre-Raphaelite movement in favour of returning to the simplicity of the artists who preceded Raffaelle; *n.*, one of the Pre-Raphaelite brotherhood.

Pre-Raph′aelitism, *n.*, the Pre-Raphaelite principles.

prereq′uisite, *adj.*, antecedently required; *n.*, a preliminary condition or requirement.

prerog′ative, *adj.*, with the right of voting first; privileged; *n.*, peculiar right or privilege.

pres′age, *n.*, a portent, omen; presentiment.

presage′, *v.t.*, to portend, betoken, forebode.

presaged′, *p.p.*, presage.

presa′ging, *pr.p.*, presage.

pres′byope, *n.*, a sufferer from presbyopia.

presbyo′pia, *n.*, the long sight of old age.

pres′byter, *n.*, an elder; a Catholic priest.

presbyt′eral, *adj.*, pert. to presbyters.

presbyt′erate, *n.*, a presbyter's office, or term of service.

Presbyte′rian, *adj.*, rel. to the Presbyterian system; *n.*, a member of the Presbyterian body.

Presbyte′rianism, *n.*, the system of belief and polity adopted by Presbyterians.

pres'bytery, *n.*, the part of a church east of the choir; the place where the clergy sit or officiate; the whole body of presbyters; a priest's house.

pre'science, *n.*, foreknowledge.

pre'scient, *adj.*, foreknowing.

prescind', *v.t.*, to cut off, to abstract.

prescribe', *v.t.*, to lay down with authority; to impose; to recommend (a medicine); *v.i.*, to give directions of any kind.

prescribed', *p.p.*, prescribe.

prescri'ber, *n.*, one who prescribes.

prescri'bing, *pr.p.*, prescribe.

pre'script, *n.*, a direction, ordinance.

prescriptibil'ity, *n.*, fitness to be prescribed.

prescript'ible, *adj.*, fit to be prescribed.

prescrip'tion, *n.*, the act of prescribing; a doctor's recipe; direction; a right acquired by long, undisputed possession.

prescript'ive, *adj.*, prescribing; based on prescription.

pres'ence, *n.*, the being present; vicinity; aspect.

pres'ence - chamber, *n.*, a room where a sovereign receives visitors.

presence of mind', *n.*, calmness, self-possession.

present', *v.t.*, to introduce; to bestow; to offer; to level a weapon; to offer for judicial inquiry; to accuse; *n.*, the act of presenting arms.

pres'ent, *adj.*, in company; being now or here; *n.*, a gift, the present time.

present'able, *adj.*, fit to be presented; fit for society.

presenta'tion, *n.*, the act of presenting in any sense; dramatic exhibition; the statement of a case.

present'ative, *adj.*, serving to present; rel. to the right of an ecclesiastical patron to present to a benefice.

present'ed, *p.p.*, present.

presentee', *n.*, a Churchman presented to a benefice; a person recommended for office, presented at court, or receiving a present.

present'er, *n.*, one who presents.

present'ient, *adj.*, having a presentiment.

present'iment, *n.*, a foreboding.

present'ing, *pr.p.*, present.

present'ive, *adj.*, presenting to the mind.

pres'ently, *adv.*, soon, shortly. (In former times it often meant "at once; at the present time.")

present'ment, *n.*, the act of presenting in various senses; a grand jury's report; charges officially laid before the ecclesiastical authorities.

preserv'able, *adj.*, able to be preserved.

preserva'tion, *n.*, the act of preserving; the state of being preserved.

preserv'ative, *adj.*, aiding preservation; *n.*, anything that preserves.

preserv'atory, *adj.*, *i.q.* preservative.

preserve', *v.t.*, to keep safe; to secure the life of; to treat (fruit, meat, etc.) so as to keep them from decomposing; *n.*, jam; ground reserved for the protection of game, etc.

preserved', *p.p.*, preserve.

preserv'er, *n.*, one who preserves.

preserv'ing, *pr.p.*, preserve.

preside', *v.i.*, to occupy the chief seat.

presi'ded, *p.p.*, preside.

pres'idency, *n.*, the status, jurisdiction, term of office, and area of authority of a president.

pres'ident, *n.*, one who presides over a State, a College, a Society, etc.

presiden'tial, *adj.*, pert. to a president.

pres'identship, *n.*, a president's function or office.

presi'der, *n.*, one who presides.

presid'ial, *adj.*, pert. to a garrison.

presid'iary, *adj.*, *i.q.* presidial.

presi'ding, *pr.p.*, preside.

presignifica'tion, *n.*, presage.

presig'nified, *p.p.*, presignify.

presig'nify, *v.t.*, to foreshadow.

presig'nifying, *pr.p.*, presignify.

press, *v.t.*, to bring weight or force to bear upon or against; to impress; to squeeze or crush; to flatten; to follow closely; to push (an argument); *v.i.*, to bear weightily; to hurry on; to crowd; to importune; *n.*, a crowding; hurry; a cupboard with or without shelves; the art or practice of printing; a machine for printing; journalism and journalists collectively.

pressed, *p.p.*, press.

press'er, *n.*, that which presses.

press'-gang, *n.*, men who were formerly used to press or impress others into the navy or the army.

press'ing, *pr.p.*, press; *adj.*, urgent, weighty.

press'ingly, *adv.*, urgently.

press'man, *n.*, a journalist.

press'mark, *n.*, a mark in a book showing its exact place in the library shelves.

press'ure, *n.*, the exertion of force or influence; embarrassment; urgency.

press'-work, *n.*, the management of a printing-press; the output of the press.

prestidigita'tion, *n.*, sleight of hand.

prestidig'itator, *n.*, a conjuror.

prestige', *n.*, influence; importance, glamour.

prest'imony, *n.*, a fund, privately administered, for the maintenance of a priest.

prestis'simo, *adj.* and *adv.*, very fast; *n.*, a very rapid musical piece.

pres'to, *adj.* and *adv.*, fast; *n.*, a fast (musical) movement.

presu'mable, *adj.*, able to be presumed.

presu'mably, *adv.*, on reasonable assumption.

presume', *v.t.*, to take for granted; *v.i.*, to take a liberty.

presumed', *p.p.*, presume.

presu'ming, *pr.p.*, presume.

presump'tion, *n.*, the act of presuming; taking for granted; a reason for assuming; assurance; effrontery.

presump'tive, *adj.*, with reasonable grounds for presuming.

presump'tuous, *adj.*, arrogant, forward.

presump'tuously, *adv.*, in a presumptuous way.

presump'tuousness, *n.*, the state of being presumptuous.

presuppose', *v.t.*, to suppose before obtaining evidence; to take for granted.

presupposed', *p.p.*, presuppose.

presuppo'sing, *pr.p.*, presuppose.

presupposi'tion, *n.*, an act of presupposing.

pretence', *n.*, a claim; a pretext; a sham.

pretend', *v.t.*, to feign; make a false show of; to make a false statement; *v.i.*, to make believe.

pretend'ed, *p.p.*, pretend.

pretend'er, *n.*, one who makes a false claim.

pretend'ing, *pr.p.*, pretend.

preten'sion, *n.*, assertion of a claim; affectation.

preten'tious, *adj.*, making a false claim; showy, ostentatious.

preterhu'man, *adj.*, more than human.

preterimper'fect, *n.*, the imperfect tense in which an uncompleted action in the past is mentioned.

pret'erite, *adj.*, past; *n.*, a past tense.

pretermis'sion, *n.*, neglect, omission.

pretermit', *v.t.*, to neglect to do or mention.

pretermit'ted, *p.p.*, pretermit.

pretermit'ting, *pr.p.*, pretermit.

preternat'ural, *adj.*, beyond the natural order.

preterper'fect, *n.*, a past tense denoting an action completed.

preterpluper'fect, *n.*, a past tense denoting an action completed before a given point of time.

pre'text, *n.*, an excuse, pretence.

pretext', *v.t.*, to advance as a pretext.

pre'tor, *n.*, the consul as head of the Roman army; a civil magistrate so entitled. Also *praetor*.

preto'rial, *adj.*, rel. to a pretor.

preto'rian, *adj.*, bel. to a pretor or the pretorium: *n.*, a soldier of the Pretorian Guard.

preto'rium, *n.*, a general's headquarters; a provincial governor's residence (*Lat.*).

pret'tier, *adj.*, *comp.* of pretty.

pret'tiest, *adj.*, *super.* of pretty.

pret'tily, *adv.*, in a pretty way.

pret'tiness, *n.*, the quality of being pretty.

pret'ty, *adj.*, beautiful, dainty; moderate, sufficient; affected; *adv.*, fairly moderately.

prevail', *v.i.*, to be victorious; to predominate; to exist.

prevailed', *p.p.*, prevail.

prevail'ing, *pr.p.*, prevail; *adj.*, in general use or occurrence.

prev'alence, *n.*, the state of being prevalent; vogue.

prev'alency, *n.*, *i.q.* prevalence.

prev'alent, *adj.*, prevailing, commonly occurring.

prevar'icate, *v.i.*, to speak or act evasively.

prevar'icated, *p.p.*, prevaricate.

prevar'icating, *pr.p.*, prevaricate.

prevarica'tion, *n.*, evasion, quibble.

prevar'icator, *n.*, one who prevaricates.

preve'nient, *adj.*, going before, preceding, preventing.

prevent', *v.t.*, to stop, hinder; an early meaning was "to go before in aid," as in the Collect—"Prevent us, O Lord, in all our doings."

prevent'able, *adj.*, able to be prevented.

prevent'ative, *adj.* and *n.*, *i.q.* preventive.

prevent'ed, *p.p.*, prevent.

prevent'er, *n.*, one who prevents.

prevent'ing, *pr.p.*, prevent.

preven'tion, *n.*, the act or effect of preventing.

preven'tional, *adj.*, of a preventing nature.

prevent'ive, *adj.*, preventing; staving off; *n.*, a protective medicine or agent.

pre'vious, *adj.*, former, preceding.

pre'viously, *adv.*, before in time.

previse', *v.t.*, to foresee.

previ'sion, *n.*, foresight.

prey, *v.i.*, to seize food by violence; to exert a baneful influence on; *n.*, an animal seized by another for food; plunder; a victim.

preyed, *p.p.*, prey.

prey'ing, *pr.p.*, prey.

pri'apism, *n.*, sensuality.

price, *v.t.*, to estimate value of; to ask the price of; *n.*, equivalent value in exchange; the sum demanded or paid.

price'-current, *n.*, the ruling price of securities, investments, etc.

priced, *p.p.*, price.

price'less, *adj.*, beyond price, invaluable.

pri'cing, *pr.p.*, price.

prick, *v.t.*, to pierce slightly; puncture; sting; *n.*, the act or effect of pricking; a puncture; a point; a goad.

pricked, *p.p.*, prick.

prick'er, *n.*, one who pricks; a pricking implement.

prick'ing, *pr.p.*, prick.

prick'le, *v.t.*, to cause a pricking sensation; *v.i.*, to have the sensation; *n.*, a small, sharp point; a make of wicker basket.

prick'le-back, *n.*, the stickle-back.

prick'liness, *n.*, the quality of being prickly.

prick'ly, *adj.*, furnished with prickles; prickling.

prickly pear', *n.*, a pear-shaped fruit.

pride, *v. reflex.*, to be proud; *n.*, overweening estimate of self; arrogance; something to be proud of; the acme.

pri'ded, *p.p.*, pride.

pri'ding, *pr.p.*, pride.

pried, *p.p.*, pry.

prie-dieu, *n.*, a prayer-desk (*Fr.*).

pri'er, *n.*, one who pries.

priest, *n.*, one who offers sacrifice; a member of the clergy between a bishop and a deacon.

priest'craft, *n.*, priestly skill.

priest'ess, *n.*, a woman priest.

priest'hood, *n.*, the office or order of priests.

priest'like, *adj.*, like a priest; priestly.

priest'liness, *n.*, the quality of being priestly.

priest'ly, *adj.*, pert. to a priest.

priest'-ridden, *adj.*, under priestly influence.

prig, *n.*, a dull person, precise in manner and affectedly superior in virtue or wisdom.

prig'gery, *n.*, priggishness.

prig'gish, *adj.*, pert. to a prig.

prig'gishness, *n.*, assumption of superior knowledge or virtue.

prig'gism, *n.*, the quality of a prig.

prill, *n.*, a choice piece of ore.

prim, *v.t.*, to make to appear prim; *v.i.*, to appear prim; *adj.*, formal and precise in appearance and manner.

pri'macy, *n.*, chief place; the office of a primate.

pri'ma, *adj.*, first (*Lat.*).

pri'ma don'na, *n.*, the leading woman singer in opera.

pri'mage, *n.*, an additional percentage paid for freight on board ship.

pri'mal, *adj.*, early, primeval, fundamental.

pri'marily, *adv.*, originally, fundamentally.

pri'mary, *adj.*, original, fundamental, first in order.

pri'mate, *n.*, the head of an ecclesiastical province; an archbishop.

prima'tial, *adj.*, rel. to a primate.

primat'ical, *adj.*, *i.q.* primatial.

prime, *adj.*, chief, choice; *n.*, the early time (of day or life); the time of perfection; one of the day offices; the golden number; *v.t.*, to make ready, prepare; to charge a gun; to put on first coat of paint.

primed, *p.p.*, prime.

prime'ly, *adv.*, originally; highly.

prime'ness, *n.*, the quality of being prime.

pri'mer, *n.*, a reading book; a book of prayers and instruction; a size of type.

pri'mer, *n.*, that which, or one who, primes, esp. in regard to a gun.

prime'val, -ae'val, *adj.*, primitive; bel. to the earliest ages.

pri'ming, *pr.p.*, prime; *n.*, a gun-charge.

primi'tiae, *n.*, *pl.*, first fruits; the first fluid discharge at parturition (*Lat.*).

primi'tial, *adj.*, rel. to primitiae.

prim'itive, *adj.*, ancient, early, primary; *n.*, a radical, underived word.

prim'ness, *n.*, the quality of being prim.

primogen'itive, *adj.*, rel. to primogeniture.

primogen'itor, *n.*, remotest ancestor.

primogen'iture, *n.*, priority of birth; the status of the firstborn.

primord'ial, *adj.*, primeval.

prim'rose, *n.*, an early spring perennial, bearing yellow flowers.

prim'ula, *n.*, a herbaceous perennial.

pri'mum mo'bile, *n.*, the assumed outermost sphere in the universe; the original source of movement.

pri'mus, *n.*, the title of the presiding bishop of the Scottish Church.

prince, *n.*, a sovereign; the son of a king; a member of some of the highest ranks of nobility.

prince'dom, *n.*, a prince's sphere of authority.

prince'ly, *adj.*, princelike; magnificent, sumptuous.

prince's feath'er, *n.*, a tall, rich-looking annual so named.

prin'cess, *n.*, fem. of prince.

prin'cipal, *adj.*, chief in importance or station; leading; *n.*, one who takes the lead; a chief player; an employer; the head of a college, school, etc.; a soloist; an organ stop so named; capital; a main rafter.

principal'ity, *n.*, the jurisdiction of a prince; a State governed by a prince.

prin'cipally, *adv.*, chiefly.

prin'cipate, *n.*, *i.q.* principality.

princip'ia, *n. pl.*, first principles (*Lat.*).

prin'ciple, *n.*, an original source; a fundamental truth; a law of morals or of nature.

prin'cipled, *adj.*, having principles.

prink, *v.t.* and *i.*, to dress for display.

prinked, *p.p.*, prink.

prink'ing, *pr.p.*, prink.

print, *v.t.*, to impress; to put into type; to produce a photographic picture; *v.i.*, to be a printer; *n.*, an impress, printed type; a picture produced from the negative; a cotton fabric printed; a newspaper (*Amer.*).

print'ed, *p.p.*, print.

print'er, *n.*, one who prints.

print'ing, *pr.p.*, print; *n.*, a printer's art or trade.

print'ing-office, *n.*, an office where books, newspapers, etc., are printed.

print'ing-press, *n.*, a machine for printing.

pri'or, *adj.*, preceding, earlier (an objectionable modern use treats it also as an *adverb*, to express clumsily that for which the word " before " suffices); *n.*, a monastic officer ranking below an abbot. (In a religious house not an abbey the prior is the head.)

pri'orate, *n.*, the office, or tenure of office, of a prior.

pri'oress, *n.*, fem. of prior.

prior'ity, *n.*, precedence in time or position.

pri'ory, *n.*, a religious house governed by a prior or prioress.

prise, *v.t.*, *i.q.* prize.

prism, *n.*, a solid figure, having sides which are parallelograms and ends which are equal, similar, and parallel rectilineal figures.

prismat'ic, *adj.*, pert. to a prism.

prismat'ical, *adj.*, *i.q.* prismatic.

pris'moid, *n.*, a prism-like body, but differing from a prism in regard to its ends.

prismoid'al, *adj.*, pert. to a prismoid.

pris'on, *v.t.*, to place in captivity or confinement; *n.*, a place of confinement.

pris'oner, *n.*, one kept in prison; taken prisoner.

pris'oner's bars, *n.*, *i.q.* prisoner's base.

pris'oner's base, *n.*, a schoolboy game, in which each opposing party starts from a distinct base.

pris'on-van, *n.*, the van in which the gaol-birds are conveyed from prison to the court, and *vice-versa.*

pris'tine, *adj.*, former, ancient.

prith'ee, *interj.* = I pray thee; please.

pri'vacy, *n.*, the state of being in private.

pri'vate, *adj.*, unobserved; withdrawn from public; unofficial; reticent; special; *n.*, an ordinary soldier.

privateer', *n.*, an armed ship in private ownership and commissioned (by letters of marque) by a Government to act against an enemy nation.

privateer'ing, *n.*, the act of cruising in a privateer.

privateers'man, *n.*, a man on a privateer.

pri'vately, *n.*, in a private manner.

priva'tion, *n.*, the act of depriving; state of being deprived; loss, want.

priv'ative, *adj.*, denoting the loss or absence of; in grammar, it indicates a negative quality.

priv'et, *n.*, an evergreen shrub much used for hedges.

priv'ilege, *n.*, special right, advantage, or immunity; *v.t.*, to bestow a privilege on.

priv'ileged, *p.p.*, privilege.

priv'ileging, *pr.p.*, privilege.

priv'ily, *adv.*, secretly, privately.

priv'ity, *n.*, secrecy, privacy.

priv'y, *adj.*, secret, private, personal;

n., a person concerned in an action or matter.

prize, *v.t.*, to value greatly; to capture as a prize (of war); to force open; *n.*, a reward; a thing much valued; leverage.

prized, *p.p.*, prize.

prize'-fight, *n.*, a pugilistic contest for a prize.

prize'-fighter, *n.*, one who engages in a prize-fight.

prize'-fighting, *pr.p.*, prize-fight.

prize'man, *n.*, the winner of a prize.

prize'-money, *n.*, money paid for the proceeds of a maritime prize.

pri'zing, *pr.p.*, prize.

pro, *prep.*, for (*Lat.*).

pro'a, *n.*, a Malay sailing-boat.

prob'abilism, *n.*, the doctrine that a belief may be held on a probable basis.

prob'abilist, *n.*, a believer in probabilism.

probabil'ity, *n.*, the quality of being probable; likelihood.

prob'able, *adj.*, likely.

prob'ably, *adv.*, presumably; in all probability.

pro'bang, *n.*, a surgical implement for removing obstructions of the throat or oesophagus.

pro'bate, *n.*, official certifying of a will; a certified copy; a certified copy of a will; *adj.*, rel. to making proof.

proba'tion, *n.*, the act of testing; the state of being tested; novitiate.

proba'tional, *adj.*, under probation.

proba'tionary, *adj.*, done as a probation.

proba'tioner, *n.*, a person on approval, as a novice, etc.

pro'bative, *adj.*, evidential.

pro'batory, *adj.*, serving for a test.

probe, *v.t.*, to penetrate; examine with a probe; *n.*, a surgical instrument for exploring wounds.

probed, *p.p.*, probe.

pro'bing, *pr.p.*, probe.

prob'ity, *n.*, uprightness.

prob'lem, *n.*, a question for solution; a difficult matter.

problemat'ic, *adj.*, doubtful; calling for solution.

problemat'ical, *adj.*, *i.q.* problematic.

probos'cis, *n.*, an elephant's or tapir's trunk; the extended mouth of some insects.

proce'dure, *n.*, proceeding; method of doing.

proceed', *v.i.*, to advance, go on, come from.

proceed'ed, *p.p.*, proceed.

proceed'ing, *pr.p.*, proceed; *n.*, an action; conduct. In *pl.* = an action at law.

pro'ceeds, *n. pl.*, results; a resulting sum of money.

procella'rian, *adj.*, rel. to petrels; *n.*, a stormy petrel.

pro'cess, *n.*, progress, course of operation; series of movements; a legal writ, action at law.

proces'sion, *n.*, a movement in orderly array; the act of proceeding or emanating.

proces'sional, *adj.*, rel. to processions; a service-book for processional use.

proces'sionist, *n.*, one who joins in a procession.

pro'chronism, *n.*, giving an earlier than the true date; antedating.

proclaim', *v.t.*, to announce publicly or officially; to declare officially; to place under legal disqualifications.

proclaimed', *p.p.*, proclaim.

proclaim'er, *n.*, one who proclaims.

proclaim'ing, *pr.p.*, proclaim.

proclama'tion, *n.*, the act of proclaiming; an announcement.

procliv'ity, *n.*, a tendency.

procon'sul, *n.*, a provincial or colonial governor.

procon'sular, *adj.*, pert. to a proconsul.

procon'sulary, *adj.*, *i.q.* proconsular.

procon'sulate, *n.*, a proconsul's office or tenure of office.

procon'sulship, *n.*, *i.q.* proconsulate.

procras'tinate, *v.i.*, to put off, delay doing.

procras'tinated, *p.p.*, procrastinate.

procras'tinating, *pr.p.*, procrastinate.

procrastina'tion, *n.*, the act or habit of putting off.

procras'tinator, *n.*, one who procrastinates.

procras'tinatory, *adj.*, delaying, dilatory.

pro'creant, *adj.*, procreating.

pro'create, *v.t.*, to generate, beget.

pro'created, *p.p.*, procreate.

pro'creating, *pr.p.*, procreate.

procrea'tion, *n.*, the act or process of procreating.

pro'creative, *adj.*, generative, begetting.

pro'creator, *n.*, one who procreates.

Procrust'ean, *adj.*, rel. to Procrustes, the legendary robber who stretched or mutilated robbers to fit the bed he supplied for them; hence = enforcing rigid uniformity.

proc'tor, *n.*, the equivalent of the Lat. *procurator*; an agent, attorney; a university disciplinary official; a clerical representative in the Convocations of Canterbury and York; one practising in the ecclesiastical courts.

procto'rial, *adj.*, bel. to a proctor.

proc'torize, *v.t.*, said of a proctor who summons an undergraduate before him.

procum'bent, *adj.*, prostrate.

procur'able, *adj.*, able to be procured.

procura'tion, *n.*, obtaining, bringing about; power of attorney; provision of entertainment for a visiting bishop or official; a fee.

proc'urator, *n.*, a Roman imperial treasurer; an agent, proctor.

proc'uratory, *n.*, power of attorney.

procure', *v.t.*, to acquire; bring about; act as a procurer or procuress.

procured', *p.p.*, procure.

procure'ment, *n.*, attainment.

procur'er, *n.*, one who procures, esp. a man or woman who procures women for immoral purposes.

procur'ess, *n.*, fem. of procurer.

procur'ing, *pr.p.*, procure.

prod, *v.t.*, to poke; *n.*, a poke.

prod'ded, *p.p.*, prod.

prod'ding, *pr.p.*, prod.

prod'igal, *adj.*, lavish, wasteful; *n.*, a wastrel.

prodigal'ity, *n.*, lavishness, wastefulness.

prod'igally, *adv.*, lavishly.

prodig'ious, *adj.*, portentous, marvellous.

prodig'iously, *adv.*, marvellously.

prod'igy, *n.*, a marvel, portent; astonishingly clever person.

prodrom'ata, *n. pl.*, premonitory symptoms.

prod'romus, *n.*, a premonitory symptom.

prod'uce, *n.*, that which is produced; a yield.

produce', *v.t.*, to bring forth; call into existence; exhibit; yield; lengthen (a line).

produced', *p.p.*, produce.

produ'cer, *n.*, one who produces.

produ'cible, *adj.*, capable of being produced.

produ'cing, *pr.p.*, produce.

prod'uct, *n.*, something produced or yielded.

produc'tile, *adj.*, extensible.

produc'tion, *n.*, the act of producing; that which is produced; (in Scots law) evidential document.

produc'tive, *adj.*, yielding results; producing.

produc'tively, *adv.*, in a productive way.

produc'tiveness, *n.*, the quality of being productive.

pro'em, *n.*, an introduction, preface, preamble.

proe'mial, *adj.*, introductory.

profana'tion, *n.*, the act of profaning.

profane', *v.t.*, to desecrate, treat with irreverence; *adj.*, irreverent, secular.

profaned', *p.p.*, profane.

profane'ly, *adv.*, irreverently.

profane'ness, *n.*, the quality of being profane.

profa'ner, *n.*, one who profanes.

profa'ning, *pr.p.*, profane.

profan'ity, *n.*, a profane act; irreverence.

profess', *v.t.*, to avow openly; to pretend; to teach; *v.i.*, to be a teacher or professor of a subject.

professed', *p.p.*, profess; *adj.*, avowed; alleged.

profess'edly, *adv.*, avowedly; by pretence.

profess'ing, *pr.p.*, profess.

profes'sion, *n.*, the act of professing; declaration; a vocation, esp. a learned one.

profes'sional, *adj.*, the opposite to amateur; bel. to a profession.

profes'sionalism, *n.*, the character or habits of the professional person.

profes'sionally, *adv.*, in a professional capacity.

profes'sor, *n.*, one who professes in any sense; an authorized public teacher.

professo'rial, *adj.*, pert. to a professor.

professo'riate, *n.*, professors collectively; professorship.

profes'sorship, *n.*, the office of a professor.

prof'fer, *v.t.*, to propose, offer.

prof'fered, *p.p.*, proffer.

prof'fering, *pr.p.*, proffer.

profi'ciency, *n.*, skill, aptitude.

profi'cient, *adj.*, skilful, apt.

profi'ciently, *adv.*, skilfully.

pro'file, *n.*, the side face; a side view; *v.t.*, to make a drawing of in profile.

pro'filist, *n.*, one who draws profiles.

prof'it, *v.t.*, to be of advantage to; to help; *v.i.*, to reap advantage; *n.*, advantage, gain, help.

prof'itable, *adj.*, advantageous; lucrative.

prof'itably, *adv.*, with gain or profit.

prof'ited, *p.p.*, profit.

profiteer', *v.i.*, to make profits, usually by unscrupulous methods; *n.*, one who profiteers.

prof'iting, *pr.p.*, profit.
prof'itless, *adj.*, unprofitable.
prof'ligacy, *n.*, licentiousness; reckless wastefulness.
prof'ligate, *adj.*, licentious, recklessly wasteful; *n.*, a profligate person.
profound', *adj.*, deep; intense; showing great insight; *n.*, an abyss.
profound'er, *adj.*, *comp.* of profound.
profound'est, *adj.*, *super.* of profound.
profound'ly, *adv.*, deeply.
profun'dity, *n.*, depth in various senses.
profuse', *adj.*, lavish, abundant.
profuse'ly, *adv.*, lavishly, abundantly.
profuse'ness, *n.*, the quality of being profuse.
profu'sion, *n.*, abundance; exuberance.
prog, *v.i.*, to prod; *n.*, victuals (*slang*).
progen'itive, *adj.*, rel. to the generation of offspring.
progen'itor, *n.*, an ancestor; a predecessor.
progen'iture, *n.*, procreation.
prog'eny, *n.*, offspring.
prognath'ic, *adj.*, with projecting jaw.
prog'nathous, *adj.*, *i.q.* prognathic.
progno'sis, *n.*, *i.q.* prognostication.
prognos'tic, *adj.*, forecasting, predicting; *n.*, an omen.
prognos'ticable, *adj.*, able to be prognosticated.
prognos'ticate, *v.t.*, to foretell, forecast.
prognos'ticated, *p.p.*, prognosticate.
prognos'ticating, *pr.p.* prognosticate.
prognostica'tion, *n.*, the act of prognosticating; a prediction.
prognos'ticator, *n.*, one who prognosticates.
prognos'ticatory, *adj.*, of the nature of prognostication.
pro'gramme, **pro'gram**, *n.*, a list of items or events; a detailed plan of arrangements.
pro'gress, *n.*, advance; a royal or official tour.
progress', *v.i.*, to move onward; to make advance.
progressed', *p.p.*, progress.
progres'sing, *pr.p.*, progress.
progres'sion, *n.*, progress; an arithmetical or geometrical series; in music, the passing of a note or chord to another note or chord.
progres'sional, *adj.*, pert. to progress.
progres'sionist, *n.*, one who advocates progress.
progres'sive, *adj.*, tending to advance; moving forward; enlightened; *n.*, a supporter of progressive principles.
progres'sively, *adv.*, step by step; making advance.
progres'sivism, *n.*, progressive principles.
prohib'it, *v.t.*, to forbid, prevent.
prohib'ited, *p.p.*, prohibit.
prohib'iter, *n.*, one who prohibits.
prohib'iting, *pr.p.*, prohibit.
prohibi'tion, *n.*, the act of prohibition; a decree forbidding. (In the U.S. = a law forbidding the sale of intoxicating liquors.)
prohibi'tionary, *adj.*, forbidding.
prohibi'tionist, *n.*, one who favours the prohibition of alcoholic liquor.
prohib'itive, *adj.*, forbidding, preventing.
prohib'itively, *adv.*, in a prohibitive sense.
prohib'itory, *adj.*, *i.q.* prohibitive.
proj'ect, *n.*, a scheme, plan.
project', *v.t.*, to plan, contrive; to throw, cast; *v.i.*, to jut out; to form plans.
project'ed, *p.p.*, project.
project'ile, *adj.*, able to be shot forth or to impel; *n.*, a missile.
project'ing, *pr.p.*, project.
projec'tion, *n.*, casting; a jutting out; in geometry, the representation of a thing obtained by throwing its chief points forward upon a plane from a given point of sight.
project'or, *n.*, one who forms a project, esp. who starts a bubble company.
project'ure, *n.*, a projection.
projet, *n.*, a plan, scheme (*Fr.*).
prolapse', *v.i.*, to slip forward; *n.*, = prolapsus.
prolap'sus, *n.*, a falling forward or down of a bodily organ or part of an organ (*Lat.*).
pro'late, *adj.*, elongated.
prola'tion, *n.*, utterance; measure.
prola'tive, *adj.*, completing the predication of a sentence.
prolegom'ena, *n. pl.*, preliminary statements introducing the subject of a treatise.
prolegom'enary, *adj.*, introductory; pert. to prolegomena.
prolegom'enon, *n.*, sing. of prolegomena.
prolep'sis, *n.*, anticipation; esp. the use of an adjective or noun with a predicative force, as "they shot him *dead*," *i.e.*, so that he died.
prolep'tic, *adj.*, anticipatory.
proleta'rian, *adj.*, rel. to the proletariat; one of the people.
proleta'rianism, *n.*, the status or the principles of the people.

proleta'riat, *n.*, the people; the working class.
pro'letary, *adj.*, *i.q.* proletarian.
pro'licide, *n.*, the murder of offspring before or immediately after birth.
prolif'erous, *adj.*, productive of offspring; in botany, producing an excessive number of parts.
prolif'ic, *adj.*, fruitful; producing much offspring.
prolifica'tion, *n.*, generation; in botany, excessive production of parts.
pro'lix, *adj.*, long-winded, wordy.
prolix'ity, *n.*, wordiness, long-windedness.
pro'locutor, *n.*, a spokesman, esp. the President of the Lower House of Convocation of the Northern and Southern Provinces.
pro'logue, *n.*, an introduction, esp. to a play; an introductory event; *v.t.*, to furnish with a prologue.
prolong', *v.t.*, to lengthen, continue.
prolonge', *n.*, a rope for drawing a gun-carriage (*Fr.*).
prolonga'tion, *n.*, a lengthening.
prolonged', *p.p.*, prolong.
prolong'ing, *pr.p.*, prolong.
prolu'sion, *n.*, a preliminary essay; a prelude.
promenade', *v.i.*, to walk or ride, esp. as a social proceeding; *n.*, a walk or ride; a place for promenading.
promena'ded, *p.p.*, promenade.
promena'der, *n.*, one who promenades.
promena'ding, *pr.p.*, promenade.
Prome'thean, *adj.*, pert. to, or like, Prometheus.
prom'inence, *n.*, a jutting out; conspicuousness; distinction.
prom'inency, *n.*, *i.q.* prominence.
prom'inent, *adj.*, jutting out; conspicuous; distinguished.
prom'inently, *adv.*, in a prominent way.
promis'cuous, *adj.*, mixed in confusion; without distinction; casual.
promis'cuously, *adv.*, in a promiscuous way; casually.
prom'ise, *v.t.*, to covenant, pledge; to give ground for expectation; *n.*, a pledge, assurance; ground for expectation.
prom'ised, *p.p.*, promise.
promisee', *n.*, one to whom something is promised.
prom'iser, *n.*, one who promises.
prom'ising, *pr.p.*, promise; *adj.*, giving ground for expectation.
prom'issorily, *adv.*, by way of a promise.
prom'issory, *adj.*, of the nature of a promise or engagement.
prom'ontory, *n.*, a headland.
promote', *v.t.*, to advance; raise; forward.
promo'ted, *p.p.*, promote.
promo'ter, *n.*, one who promotes.
promo'ting, *pr.p.*, promote.
promo'tion, *n.*, the act of promoting; advancement.
promo'tive, *adj.*, causing advance; forwarding.
prompt, *adj.*, ready, quick, alert; *v.t.*, to instigate; suggest; help the memory of; remind; *n.*, a help given by a prompter.
prompt'-book, *n.*, the prompter's copy of a play.
prompt'ed, *p.p.*, prompt.
prompt'er, *n.*, one who prompts, esp. one who helps an actor's memory on the stage.
prompt'ing, *pr.p.*, prompt.
prompt'itude, *n.*, readiness, alertness.
prompt'ly, *adv.*, readily, punctually.
prom'ulgate, *v.t.*, to publish, proclaim.
prom'ulgated, *p.p.*, promulgate.
prom'ulgating, *pr.p.*, promulgate.
promulga'tion, *n.*, publication, proclamation.
prom'ulgator, *n.*, one who promulgates.
promulge', *v.t.*, *i.q.* promulgate.
promulged', *p.p.*, promulge.
promulg'er, *n.*, one who promulges.
promulg'ing, *pr.p.*, promulge.
pro'nate, *v.t.*, to lay prone.
pro'nated, *p.p.*, pronate.
prona'tion, *n.*, the act of pronating.
pro'nating, *pr.p.*, pronate.
prona'tor, *n.*, a muscle used in pronating.
prone, *adj.*, face downwards; disposed, inclined towards.
prone'ness, *n.*, disposition towards; leaning.
prong, *n.*, to use a prong upon; *n.*, a forked implement.
pronged, *p.p.*, prong; *adj.*, having prongs.
prong'ing, *pr.p.*, prong.
pronom'inal, *adj.*, rel. to a pronoun.
pro'noun, *n.*, a part of speech used instead of a proper noun.
pronounce', *v.t.*, to utter, declare formally, deliver, articulate.
pronounce'able, *adj.*, able to be pronounced.
pronounced', *p.p.*, pronounce; *adj.*, marked, decided.

pronounce'ment, *n.*, the act of pronouncing; a delivered judgment or statement.

pronounc'er, *n.*, one who pronounces.

pronounc'ing, *pr.p.*, pronounce.

pronunciamen'to, *n.*, a manifesto; public proclamation.

pronuncia'tion, *n.*, the act of pronouncing; the way in which words are pronounced.

pronunc'iatory, *adj.*, of the nature of a pronouncement.

proof, *adj.*, able to resist, impenetrable; rel. to printer's proof; *v.t.*, to make impenetrable; *n.*, clear evidence of fact; trial, test; impenetrability; standard of quality or strength; printer's or engraver's trial impression; a perfect impression of an engraved plate.

proof'-reader, *n.*, one who goes through a printer's proof to correct it.

proof'-sheet, *n.*, wide-margined paper on which a printer's proof is printed.

prop, *v.t.*, to support by leaning against something, or by putting something underneath; *n.*, a support.

propagan'da, *n.*, strictly, the name of the Congregation of Cardinals for propagating the faith (*de propaganda fide*); thence, any institution or association having for its object the propagation of certain doctrines or principles.

propagan'dism, *n.*, the spirit or methods of a propagandist.

propagan'dist, *n.*, one who is zealous in propagating a certain set of principles; *adj.*, pert. to propaganda.

prop'agate, *v.t.*, to breed, cause to multiply by generation; to diffuse, disseminate; to transmit.

prop'agated, *p.p.*, propagate.

prop'agating, *pr.p.*, propagate.

propaga'tion, *n.*, the act of propagating.

prop'agator, *n.*, one who propagates.

propel', *v.t.*, to push forward; cause to move forward.

propelled', *p.p.*, propel

propell'ent, *adj.*, propelling; *n.*, an explosive propelling bullet.

propel'ler, *n.*, one who, or that which, propels; esp. the driving screw of a ship (a bladed shaft revolving with a screw motion).

propel'ling, *pr.p.*, propel.

propend'ent, *adj.*, inclining forward.

propense', *adj.*, inclined, disposed.

propen'sion, *n.*, *i.q.* propensity.

propen'sity, *n.*, inclination, disposition, tendency.

prop'er, *adj.*, own; special; correct; natural; goodly.

prop'erly, *adv.*, in a proper way; correctly.

prop'erty, *n.*, something peculiarly one's own; possessions; a characteristic quality or function.

proph'ecy, *n.*, the power of prophesying; a prophetic utterance.

proph'esied, *p.p.*, prophesy.

proph'esier, *n.*, one who prophesies.

proph'esy, *v.t.*, to preach, proclaim; speak as a prophet; foretell; forecast.

proph'esying, *pr.p.*, prophesy.

proph'et, *n.*, one who speaks forth as a preacher or inspired teacher; one who predicts.

proph'etess, *n.*, fem. of prophet.

prophet'ic, *adj.*, rel. to prophecy and prophets.

prophet'ical, *adj.*, *i.q.* prophetic.

prophylac'tic, *adj.*, protective; *n.*, a medicine for warding off a disease.

propin'quity, *n.*, nearness, adjacence.

propi'tiable, *adj.*, able to be propitiated.

propi'tiate, *v.t.*, to appease; make favourable.

propi'tiated, *p.p.*, propitiate.

propi'tiating, *pr.p.*, propitiate.

propitia'tion, *n.*, atonement; conciliation.

propi'tiator, *n.*, one who propitiates.

propi'tiatory, *adj.*, pert. to propitiation.

propi'tious, *adj.*, favourable; auspicious.

propi'tiously, *adv.*, in a propitious way.

pro'plasm, *n.*, a matrix.

prop'olis, *n.*, bee-glue.

propone', *v.t.*, *i.q.* propose.

propo'nent, *adj.*, proposing.

propor'tion, *v.t.*, to make proportionate; *n.*, relation of a part to the whole; a comparative part; share.

propor'tionable, *adj.*, able to be proportioned.

propor'tional, *adj.*, in proportion; pert. to proportion.

propor'tionally, *adv.*, in due proportion.

propor'tionate, *adj.* in due proportion; according to a ratio.

propor'tionately, *adv.*, in proportion.

propor'tioned, *p.p.*, proportion.

propor'tioning, *pr.p.* proportion.

propor'tionment, *n.*, the act of proportioning.

propo'sal, *n.*, an offer of something to be done, accepted, or discussed; an offer of marriage.

propose', *v.t.*, to offer for acceptance, deliberation, etc.; *v.i.*, to intend; to offer marriage.

proposed', *p.p.*, propose.

propos'er, *n.*, one who proposes.

propos'ing, *pr.p.*, propose.

proposi'tion, *n.*, a proposed scheme; a subject offered for discussion; a judgment in words (logic); in mathematics, the statement of a problem or a theorem.

proposi'tional, *adj.*, pert. to a proposition.

propound', *v.t.*, to put forth for argument; to produce (a will).

propound'ed, *p.p.*, propound.

propound'er, *n.*, one who propounds.

propound'ing, *pr.p.*, propound.

propped, *p.p.*, prop.

prop'ping, *pr.p.*, prop.

proprae'tor, *n.*, an ex-praetor acting as provincial praetor in a district under civil rule.

propri'etary, *adj.*, rel. to a proprietor; *n.*, proprietorship.

propri'etor, *n.*, one with an exclusive right in anything; owner.

propri'etorship, *n.*, ownership.

propri'ety, *n.*, correctness, fitness.

pro-proc'tor, *n.*, a proctor's deputy.

propt, *p.p.*, prop. Also *propped*.

propul'sion, *n.*, the act or effect of propelling.

propul'sive, *adj.*, having propelling force.

propylae'um, *n.*, an entrance to a temple.

prop'ylon, *n.*, *i.q.* propylaeum.

pro ra'ta, Lat. phrase = proportionately.

pro-rec'tor, *n.*, a rector's deputy.

prorec'torate, *n.*, the office of a prorector.

proroga'tion, *n.*, the act of proroguing; adjournment.

prorogue', *v.t.*, to postpone, adjourn; to suspend (meetings of Parliament or Convocation).

prorogued', *p.p.*, prorogue.

progogu'ing, *pr.p.*, prorogue.

prosa'ic, *adj.*, prosy; like prose.

prosa'ical, *adj.*, *i.q.* prosaic.

pro'saism, *n.*, prose style.

pro'saist, *n.*, a prose writer; a prosy person.

prosce'nium, *n.*, a Greek stage; now the space in front of a drop scene.

proscribe', *v.t.*, to condemn as outside the protection of the law; to denounce.

proscribed', *p.p.*, proscribe.

proscrib'er, *n.*, one who proscribes.

proscrib'ing, *pr.p.*, proscribe.

proscrip'tion, *n.*, the act of proscribing; outlawry.

proscrip'tive, *adj.*, pert. to proscription.

prose, *n.*, non-metrical writing or speech; *adj.*, non-metrical; *v.i.* and *t.*, to write dully.

prosec'tor, *n.*, one who dissects for the purpose of an anatomical demonstration by a lecturer.

pros'ecute, *v.t.*, to accuse; take proceedings at law against; to follow up, pursue.

pros'ecuted, *p.p.*, prosecute.

pros'ecuting, *pr.p.*, prosecute.

prosecu'tion, *n.*, the act of prosecuting; the prosecuting party at law.

pros'ecutor, *n.*, one who prosecutes.

pros'ecutrix, *n.*, fem. of prosecutor.

prosed, *p.p.*, prose.

pros'elyte, *n.*, a new convert; *v.t.*, *i.q.* proselytize.

pros'elyted, *p.p.*, proselyte.

pros'elyting, *pr.p.*, proselyte.

pros'elytism, *n.*, the proselytizing spirit.

pros'elytize, *v.t.*, to endeavour to make converts.

pros'elytized, *p.p.*, proselytize.

pros'elytizing, *pr.p.*, proselytize.

pro'ser, *n.*, a dull talker; a bore.

pro'sily, *adv.*, in a dull, prosy fashion.

pro'siness, *n.*, dulness; tediousness.

pro'sing, *pr.p.*, prose.

pro-sla'very, *n.*, advocacy of slavery.

prosodi'acal, *adj.*, pert. to prosody.

proso'dial, *adj.*, *i.q.* prosodiacal.

proso'dian, *n.*, *i.q.* prosodist.

pros'odist, *n.*, an authority on prosody.

pros'ody, *n.*, the science of form in poetry.

prosopopoe'ia, *n.*, introducing a pretended speaker into a dialogue; personification.

prospect', *v.t.*, to survey a country for mining purposes; *v.i.*, to give promise.

pros'pect, *n.*, outlook; wide view; the future; promise.

prospec'tion, *n.*, prudence; foresight.

prospec'tive, *adj.*, rel. to the future; expected.

prospec'tively, *adv.*, with reference to the future.

prospec'tor, *n.*, one who prospects.

prospec'tus, *n.*, a published statement of objects or of any undertaking.

pros'per, *v.t.*, to forward; make successful; *v.i.*, to be successful; to do well.

pros'pered, *p.p.*, prosper.

pros'pering, *pr.p.*, prosper.

prosper'ity, *n.*, success; good fortune.

pros'perous, *adj.*, successful; thriving.

pros'perously, *adv.*, successfully.

pros'tate, *n.*, the prostate gland.

prostat'ic, *adj.*, rel. to the prostate.

pros'thesis, *n.*, the adding of a letter or letters to the beginning of a word.

prosthet'ic, *adj.*, rel. to prosthesis.

pros'titute, *v.t.*, to use for vile purposes; to debase; *n.*, a woman who uses her body for vile purposes.

pros'tituted, *p.p.*, prostitute.

pros'tituting, *pr.p.*, prostitute.

prostitu'tion, *n.*, the practice of prostituting in any sense.

pros'trate, *adj.*, prone; thrown down.

prostrate', *v.t.*, to throw down; to bring to ruin or exhaustion.

prostra'ted, *p.p.*, prostrate.

prostra'ting, *pr.p.*, prostrate.

prostra'tion, *n.*, the state of being prostrate.

pro'style, *n.*, a front portico.

pro'sy, *adj.*, dull, tedious.

prosyl'logism, *n.*, a syllogism proving a premise of another.

protag'onist, *n.*, the chief actor; a leader, champion.

prot'asis, *n.*, an antecedent clause, usu. conditional, leading up to the apodosis.

protat'ic, *adj.*, introductory.

pro'tean, *adj.*, rapidly changing; assuming many forms.

protect', *v.t.*, to guard, keep; support.

protect'ed, *p.p.*, protect.

protect'ing, *pr.p.*, protect.

protec'tion, *n.*, the act of protecting; safety; the policy of protecting home industries.

protec'tionist, *n.*, one who favours protection (in the political sense).

protect'ive, *adj.*, sheltering; defensive; *n.*, something that protects.

protect'or, *n.*, one who protects.

protect'oral, *adj.*, pert. to a protector.

protect'orate, *n.*, the office or jurisdiction of a protector.

protecto'rial, *adj.*, *i.q.* protectoral.

protect'ress, *n.*, fem. of protector.

protect'rix, *n.*, *i.q.* protectress.

pro'tégé, *n.*, a protected person (*Fr.*).

pro'tégée, *n.*, fem. of protégé (*Fr.*).

pro'teid, *n.*, *i.q.* protein.

pro'tein, *n.*, albuminoid.

pro tem'pore, *n.*, Lat. phrase = for the time being. Often written *pro tem.*

pro'test, *n.*, utterance of an objection or disagreement; a strong declaration; a notary's certificate of a bill's having been refused for acceptance.

protest', *v.t.* and *i.*, to affirm solemnly; to make a protest.

Prot'estant, *adj.*, professing, or rel. to, Protestantism; *n.*, one who professes Protestantism.

Prot'estantism, *n.*, the system and principles which grew out of the German protest against the decisions of the Diet of Spires (1529). Including, as it does, so wide a variety of beliefs and organizations, it defies definition.

protesta'tion, *n.*, a solemn declaration.

protest'ed, *p.p.*, protest.

protest'er, *n.*, one who protests.

protest'ing, *pr.p.*, protest.

protest'ingly, *adv.*, in the manner of one protesting.

Pro'teus, *n.*, a Greek sea-god who could transform himself into many shapes; any person or thing that changes capriciously; a certain variety of bacteria so named; an amphibian so named.

proth'esis, *n.*, in ecclesiastical language, the preparation for the offertory; the part of a church where the table of prothesis (our Credence) stands.

prothono'tary, *n.*, *i.q.* protonotary.

protho'rax, *n.*, the anterior section of the thorax.

pro'tocol, *n.*, the rough, original draft of a document, despatch, etc.; *v.t.* and *i.*, to draw up in protocol.

pro'togine, *n.*, an Alpine granite.

protomar'tyr, *n.*, the first of the martyrs, St. Stephen.

protono'tary, *n.*, a chief clerk or notary.

pro'toplasm, *n.*, the chief substance found in animal and vegetable cells.

protoplas'mic, *adj.*, pert. to protoplasm.

pro'toplast, *n.*, the earliest created man.

protoplas'tic, *adj.*, rel. to protoplasm.

pro'totype, *n.*, the original type or model.

protox'ide, *n.*, an oxide in which there is only one atom of oxygen.

protox'idize, *v.t.*, to form a protoxide by combining oxygen.

protox'idized, *p.p.*, protoxidize.
protox'idizing, *pr.p.*, protoxidize.
Protozo'a, *n. pl.*, animals of the simplest form.
protozo'ic, *adj.*, pert. to protozoa.
protozo'on, *n.*, sing. of protozoa.
protract', *v.t.*, to lengthen out; to continue to great length.
protract'ed, *p.p.*, protract.
protract'ile, *adj.*, able to be lengthened.
protract'ing, *pr.p.*, protract.
protrac'tion, *n.*, the act or effect of protracting.
protract'ive, *adj.*, causing protraction.
protract'or, *n.*, an angle-measuring instrument; a muscle so named.
protrude', *v.t.* and *i.*, to thrust forward; stick out.
protru'ded, *p.p.*, protrude.
protru'ding, *pr.p.*, protrude.
protru'sile, *adj.*, able to be thrust out.
protru'sion, *n.*, the act of protruding; a projection.
protru'sive, *adj.*, tending to protrude.
protu'berance, *n.*, a bulging out; that which bulges out.
protu'berant, *adj.*, bulging out.
protu'berate, *v.i.*, to bulge out.
protu'berated, *p.p.*, protuberate.
protu'berating, *pr.p.*, protuberate.
proud, *adj.*, haughty; vain; over-valuing self; highly gratified; splendid.
proud'er, *adj.*, *comp.* of proud.
proud'est, *adj.*, *super.* of proud.
proud'ly, *adv.*, with pride.
proud'ness, *n.*, the state of being proud.
prov'able, *adj.*, capable of proof.
prov'ably, *adv.*, in a way that can be proved.
prove, *v.t.*, to test; demonstrate; *v.i.*, to turn out to be.
proved, *p.p.*, prove.
provedore', *n.*, a caterer.
prov'en, *p.p.*, prove; also *adj.*, proved.
Proven'çal, *adj.*, pert. to Provence; *n.*, a native of P.
prov'ender, *n.*, fodder.
prov'er, *n.*, one who proves.
prov'erb, *n.*, an adage; saw; short wise saying in frequent use.
prover'bial, *adj.*, pert. to proverbs; commonly known.
prover'bialism, *n.*, a proverbial expression.
prover'bially, *adv.*, notoriously; in the manner of proverbs.
provide', *v.t.*, to prepare for or against; to supply; to stipulate; to appoint.
provi'ded, *p.p.*, provide; *conj.*, on condition that.
prov'idence, *n.*, foresight; care; thriftiness. The word is often used, rather absurdly, for the Deity.
prov'ident, *adj.*, foreseeing; thrifty.
providen'tial, *adj.*, pert. to divine care; lucky.
providen'tially, *adv.*, in a providential way.
prov'idently, *adv.*, in a provident way.
provi'der, *n.*, one who provides.
provi'ding, *pr.p.*, provide; *conj.*, on condition that.
prov'ince, *n.*, originally foreign territory under a Roman governor; a chief territorial division; an archbishop's or metropolitan's district; function; in pl. the country, not the capital.
provin'cial, *adj.*, pert. to a province; narrow, unpolished; *n.*, a dweller in the provinces; the ecclesiastical ruler of an order for a whole province.
provin'cialism, *n.*, the manners and speech of the provinces.
provincial'ity, *n.*, the manners, etc., of a provincial.
prov'ing, *pr.p.*, prove.
provi'sion, *v.t.*, to supply with food, etc.; *n.*, providing for; supply of anything; esp. in pl., supply of food, drink, etc.; a clause in a Bill or legal statement; appointment to a benefice before vacancy.
provi'sional, *adj.*, temporary.
provi'sionally, *adv.*, temporarily.
provi'sioned, *p.p.*, provision.
provi'sioning, *pr.p.*, provision; *n.*, the act of supplying provisions.
provi'so, *n.*, a stipulation or limiting clause.
provi'sory, *adj.*, conditional.
provoca'tion, *n.*, the act of provoking; irritation.
provoc'ative, *adj.*, challenging, irritating.
provo'kable, *adj.*, easy to provoke.
provoke', *v.t.*, to challenge; instigate; irritate; cause.
provoked', *p.p.*, provoke.
provo'ker, *n.*, one who provokes.
provo'king, *pr.p.*, provoke; *adj.*, irritating.
provo'kingly, *adv.*, in a provoking way.
prov'ost, *n.*, the title of the head of certain colleges, Scottish cathedrals and municipal corporations.
prow, *n.*, the front part of a ship's stem.
prow'ess, *n.*, bravery, gallantry.
prowl, *v.i.*, to go about for prey; to

wander about aimlessly.

prowled, *p.p.*, prowl.

prowl'er, *n.*, one who prowls.

prowl'ing, *pr.p.*, prowl.

prox'imal, *adj.*, in biology, it = situated near middle of body or point of attachment.

prox'imate, *adj.*, nearest in time, place, etc.

prox'imately, *adv.*, very nearly or closely.

proxim'ity, *n.*, nearness.

prox'imo, *adj.*, in the next (month).

prox'y, *n.*, agency.

prude, *n.*, an excessively proper woman in regard to speech and manners.

pru'dence, *n.*, foresight; sagacity.

pru'dent, *adj.*, sagacious; foreseeing.

pruden'tial, *adj.*, showing prudence or sagacity.

pru'dently, *adv.*, with prudence.

pru'dery, *n.*, the quality of a prude.

pru'dish, *adj.*, like a prude.

pru'dishly, *adv.*, in a prudish way.

pru'dishness, *n.*, *i.q.* prudery.

prune, *v.t.*, to trim (trees, etc.); remove anything superfluous; *n.*, a dried plum; the colour of a prune.

pruned, *p.p.*, prune.

prunel'la, *n.*, a stout, stiff fabric; a throat disease.

prunel'lo, *n.*, a choice sort of prune.

pru'ner, *n.*, one who prunes.

prunif'erous, *adj.*, plum-bearing.

pru'ning, *pr.p.*, prune.

pru'ning-hook, *n.*, an instrument for pruning purposes.

pru'rience, *n.*, a curiosity about lewd things.

pru'riency, *n.*, *i.q.* prurience.

pru'rient, *adj.*, curious about lewd things; with a lewd imagination.

prurig'inous, *adj.*, pert. to prurigo.

pruri'go, *n.*, itching.

Prus'sian, *adj.*, bel. to Prussia; *n.*, a native of P.

prus'siate, *n.*, a cyanide.

prus'sic, *adj.*, obtained from Prussian blue.

pry, *v.i.*, to look curiously into.

pry'ing, *pr.p.*, pry.

pry'ingly, *adv.*, in a prying way.

prytane'um, *n.*, a Greek town hall used for public entertainments.

pryt'anis, *n.*, the president of an ancient Greek State; one of the members of a presiding division of the Senate.

pryt'any, *n.*, presidency.

psalm, *n.*, a song to the music of the harp; a sacred song.

psalm'-book, *n.*, a book containing psalms and hymns.

psalm'ist, *n.*, a writer of psalms.

psalmod'ic, *adj.*, pert. to psalmody.

psalm'odist, *n.*, *i.q.* psalmist.

psalm'ody, *n.*, the art or practice of psalm-singing.

psalt'er, *n.*, a book of psalms; the Book of Psalms.

psalt'ery, *n.*, an ancient musical stringed instrument.

pseu'do, *prefix* = false; seeming.

pseu'dograph, *n.*, a forgery.

pseudog'raphy, *n.* false spelling.

pseudol'ogist, *n.*, a liar.

pseudol'ogy, *n.*, lying.

pseud'omorph, *n.*, a certain mineral externally like another mineral.

pseudomor'phous, *adj.*, pert. to a pseudomorph.

pseud'onym, *n.*, an assumed or false name; a *nom de guerre*.

pseudon'ymous, *adj.*, under an assumed name.

pseud'oscope, *n.*, an optical instrument which makes the convex appear concave or the concave appear convex.

pshaw, *interj.*, expressing impatience or contempt.

psilan'thropist, *n.*, one who affirms mere humanity of Our Lord.

psitt'acine, *adj.*, parrot-like; pert. to parrots.

pso'ra, *n.*, the itch.

psori'asis, *n.*, an irritating skin disease.

psor'ic, *adj.*, pert. to psora.

psych'ic, *adj.*, pert. to the mind or soul; occult.

psych'ical, *adj.*, *i.q.* psychic.

psycholog'ic, *adj.*, pert. to psychology.

psycholog'ical, *adj.*, *i.q.* psychologic.

psycholog'ically, *adv.*, in a psychological way or sense.

psychol'ogist, *n.*, a student of psychology.

psychol'ogy, *n.*, the study of the human mind or soul in its various operations.

psycho'sis, *n.*, mental or nervous derangement.

psychrom'eter, *n.*, a thermometer with a wet and a dry bulb.

psychrom'etry, *n.*, the measurement of the air's humidity.

ptar'migan, *n.*, a wild bird so named.

pter'o, a *prefix* denoting wing, plume.

pterodac'tyl, *n.*, an extinct winged creature so named.

pter'opod, *adj.*, having feet expanded into lobes like wings; *n.*, a creature so formed.

ptis'an, *n.*, a decoction such as barley-water; a weak drink for a sick person. Also *tisane*.

Ptolema'ic, *adj*., pert. to Ptolemy (the Alexandrian astronomer) and his system, which assumed that the earth is the stationary centre of the universe.

pto'maine, *n*., a poison resulting from putrefaction.

pty'alin, *n*., a constituent of saliva.

pty'alism, *n*., salivation.

pu'berty, *n*., the age at which procreation becomes possible.

pubesc'ence, *n*., the state of being pubescent.

pubesc'ent, *adj*., arrived at puberty; covered with down.

pu'bic, *adj*., rel. to the groin.

pub'lic, *adj*., rel. to the people; open to all; *n*., the collective people; a public-house.

pub'lican, *n*., a Roman farmer of taxes; a public-house keeper.

publica'tion, *n*., the act of publishing; something published.

public-house, *n*., a house of entertainment.

pub'licist, *n*., one acquainted with international law; a newspaper writer.

public'ity, *n*., the state of being made public; advertising.

pub'licly, *adv*., in a public way.

pub'lic-spirited, *adj*., animated by zeal for the common welfare.

pub'lish, *v.t*., to make openly known; to proclaim; to circulate; to issue (books, newspapers, etc.) for sale or free distribution.

pub'lished, *p.p*., publish.

pub'lisher, *n*., one who publishes, esp. books.

pub'lishing, *pr.p*., publish; *n*., a publisher's business.

puccoon', *n*., a N. American plant yielding red or orange dye.

puce, *adj*., of purplish brown colour.

puck, *n*., any hobgoblin, esp. Robin Goodfellow.

puck'er, *v.t*. and *i*., to contract into wrinkles; *n*., a wrinkling or contraction.

puck'ered, *p.p*., pucker.

puck'ering, *pr.p*., pucker.

puck'ery, *adj*., astringent.

pud'der, *v.t*. and *i*., to bother; *n*., bother.

pud'dering, *pr.p*., pudder.

pud'ding, *n*., a mixture of various ingredients, sometimes enclosed in a soft paste, or a skin.

pud'ding-stone, *n*., a composite rock containing rounded pebbles.

pud'dingy, *adj*., like pudding.

pud'dle, *v.t*., to make into wrought iron; *v.i*., to dabble; *n*., a little, dirty pool; a mess; puddled clay for lining embankments.

pud'dled, *p.p*., puddle.

pud'dler, *n*., one who puddles; a worker at puddling.

pud'dling, *pr.p*., puddle; *n*., the work of making molten iron malleable.

pud'dly, *adv*., full of puddles.

pu'dency, *n*., modesty.

pudic'ity, *n*., chasteness; delicacy.

pu'erile, *adj*., boyish, silly.

pueril'ity, *n*., boyishness; silliness.

puer'peral, *adj*., rel. to childbirth.

puer'perous, *adj*., parturient.

puff, *v.t*., to blow out; to inflate; to praise excessively; to smoke (a pipe, etc.); *v.i*., to emit short breaths; to swell; *n*., a short breath or pant; a piece of advertisement; something fluffy; a light pastry.

puff'-ball, *n*., a fungus so named.

puffed, *p.p*., puff.

puff'er, *n*., an advertiser; a fish so named.

puff'ery, *n*., advertising.

puff'in, *n*., a sea-bird so named.

puff'iness, *n*., the state of being puffy.

puff'ing, *pr.p*., puff.

puff'y, *adj*., gusty; inflated; panting.

pug, *v.t*., to puddle (clay); to deaden (sound) with clay, sawdust, etc.; *n*., a pug-dog; a goblin; clay worked with water.

pug'-dog, *n*., a breed of dog with short, snub nose.

pug'g(a)ree, *n*., a turban; a muslin scarf wound round a hat.

pugged, *p.p*., pug.

pug'ging, *pr.p*., pug.

pu'gil, *n*., a boxer (*Lat*.).

pu'gilism, *n*., the practice of boxing.

pu'gilist, *n*., a boxer; a prize-fighter.

pugilist'ic, *adj*., pert. to boxing.

pugna'cious, *adj*., fond of fighting.

pugnac'ity, *n*., a readiness to fight.

pug'-nose, *n*., a snub nose.

pug'nosed, *adj*., having a pug-nose.

puis'ne, *adj*., junior; subsequent; *n*., a junior or inferior judge.

pu'issance, *n*., power, influence.

pu'issant, *adj*., powerful; influential.

puke, *v.i*. and *t*., to vomit.

puked, *p.p*., puke.

pu'king, *pr.p*., puke.

pule, *v.i*., to whine feebly.

puled, *p.p*., pule.

pu'ler, *n*., a weakling.

pu'ling, *pr.p*., pule; *n*., a feeble cry.

pul'kha, *n.*, a Lapland sledge.
pull, *v.t.*, to draw; drag; extract; sunder; to row; take off a printer's proof; *v.i.*, to row; pull a rope; *n.*, the act of pulling; a tug; something pulled; the act of rowing; a printer's proof.
pull'-back, *n.*, a restraint; an arrangement for keeping in place the back folds of a dress.
pulled, *p.p.*, pull.
pull'er, *n.*, one who pulls; that which pulls.
pull'et, *n.*, a young hen.
pull'ey, *n.*, a wheel grooved for a cord or chain to pass over.
pull'ing, *pr.p.*, pull.
Pull'man-car, *n.*, a saloon car.
pull'ulate, *v.i.*, to sprout; develop.
pul'monary, *adj.*, pert. to the lungs.
pulmon'ic, *adj.*, *i.q.* pulmonary.
pulp, *v.t.*, to reduce to pulp; remove pulp; *v.i.*, to turn to pulp; *n.*, a soft, moist mass.
pulped, *p.p.*, pulp.
pulp'iness, *n.*, the state or quality of being pulpy.
pulp'ing, *pr.p.*, pulp.
pul'pit, *n.*, a raised platform for preaching.
pul'pitum, *n.*, a double choir-screen with a gallery over the intervening space.
pulp'y, *adj.*, consisting of pulp.
puls'ate, *v.i.*, to beat rhythmically.
puls'ated, *p.p.*, pulsate.
puls'atile, *adj.*, able to pulsate; actuated by percussion.
puls'ating, *pr.p.*, pulsate.
pulsa'tion, *n.*, the act of pulsating.
puls'ative, *adj.*, pulsating; causing pulsation.
puls'atory, *adj.*, pert. to pulsation; throbbing.
pulse, *v.i.*, to beat in rhythm; *n.*, rhythmic beating of arteries; any rhythmical repetition; edible seeds of legumens.
pulsed, *p.p.*, pulse.
pulse'less, *adj.*, without a pulse.
pulsif'ic, *adj.*, causing pulsation.
pulsim'eter, *n.*, an apparatus for measuring pulsations.
puls'ing, *pr.p.*, pulse.
pulsom'eter, *n.*, a vacuum pump.
pulta'ceous, *adj.*, pappy, pulpy.
pulv'erable, *adj.*, able to be pulverized.
pulvera'ceous, *adj.*, with a powdery surface.
pulv'erine, *n.*, barilla ashes.
pulveriza'tion, *n.*, the act or effect of pulverizing.
pulv'erize, *v.t.*, to reduce to powder or spray; demolish.
pulv'erized, *p.p.*, pulverize.
pulv'erizer, *n.*, anything that pulverizes.
pulv'erizing, *pr.p.*, pulverize.
pulv'erous, *adj.*, dusty; dust-like.
pulver'ulent, *adj.*, powdery; powdered.
pulv'inated, *adj.*, swelling out like a cushion.
pulv'is, *n.*, dust (*Lat.*).
pu'ma, *n.*, a large American carnivore.
pum'ice, *v.t.*, to clean with pumice; *n.*, a light lava, used for cleaning or polishing.
pum'mel, *v.t.*, to beat with the fists. Also *pommel.*
pump, *v.t.*, to draw up with a pump; to pour forth; to question for information, *n.*, a machine for raising water and for many other uses; a light shoe.
pumped, *p.p.*, pump.
pump'er, *n.*, one who pumps.
pump'ernickel, *n.*, rye bread.
pump'-handle, *n.*, the handle of a pump.
pump'ing, *pr.p.*, pump
pum'pion, *n.*, *i.q.* pumpkin.
pump'kin, *n.*, a trailing plant so named, and its large, round, yellow fruit.
pun, *v.t.*, to ram; *v.i.*, to play on words; *n.*, a play on words; paronomasia.
punch, *v.t.*, to hit with the fist; to pierce a hole; *n.*, a blow with the fist; a tool for perforating, etc.; a hot beverage with mixed ingredients; a variety of draught horse.
punched, *p.p.*, punch.
punch'eon, *n.*, a large cask; a prop in a coal mine.
punch'er, *n.*, one who, that which, punches.
punchinel'lo, *n.*, the principal character in a puppet-show (*Ital.*).
punch'ing, *pr.p.*, punch.
punct'ate, *adj.*, having points or dots.
punct'ated, *adj.*, *i.q.* punctate.
punct'iform, *adj.*, like a point or dot.
punctil'io, *n.*, a fine point of ceremony or behaviour.
punctil'ious, *adj.*, scrupulously exact in ceremony.
punct'ual, *adj.*, exact in point of time; pert. to a *punctum* or point.
punctual'ity, *n.*, the quality of always being in time.
punct'ually, *adv.*, to the precise moment.
punct'uate, *v.t.*, to mark with the necessary stops or points; to emphasize.
punct'uated, *p.p.*, punctuate.
punct'uating, *pr.p.*, punctuate.
punctua'tion, *n.*, the act of punctuating; the insertion of stops or points.

punct'uator, *n.*, one skilled in punctuating.

punct'ure, *v.t.* and *i.*, to pierce; make a hole; *n.*, a prick; a hole made by a prick.

punct'ured, *p.p.*, puncture.

punct'uring, *pr.p.*, puncture.

pun'dit, *n.*, a Brahmin scholar; a pretender to learning.

pung, *n.*, a low one-horse sled.

pun'gence, *n.*, the quality of being pungent.

pun'gency, *n.*, *i.q.* pungence.

pun'gent, *adj.*, pointed; biting; caustic; exciting to the taste, smell, etc.

Pu'nic, *adj.*, Carthaginian.

pu'nier, *adj.*, *comp.* of puny.

pu'niest, *adj.*, *super.* of puny.

pu'niness, *n.*, smallness; weakness.

pun'ish, *v.t.*, to chastise; impose penalty on; strike with severe blows.

pun'ishable, *adj.* that can, or ought to, be punished.

pun'ished, *p.p.*, punish.

pun'isher, *n.*, one who punishes.

pun'ishing, *pr.p.*, punish.

pun'ishment, *n.*, the act or effect of punishing.

pu'nitive, *adj.*, of the nature, or with the purpose of, punishment.

pu'nitory, *adj.*, *i.q.* punitive.

punk, *n.*, rotting wood used for tinder.

pun'ka, *n.*, an E. Indian fan; an arrangement for keeping a place cool.

punned, *p.p.*, pun.

pun'ner, *n.*, a ramming implement.

pun'net, *n.*, a small, round fruit-basket.

pun'ning, *pr.p.*, pun; *n.*, the practice of making puns.

pun'ster, *n.*, a maker of puns.

punt, *v.t.* and *i.*, to propel a punt; to kick a dropping football; *v.i.*, to gamble; *n.*, a flat-bottomed, square-ended boat, propelled by poling or paddling.

punt'er, *n.*, one who punts; a gambler.

punt'ing, *n.*, the art or practice of propelling a punt.

pu'ny, *adj.*, undersized, feeble.

pup, *v.i.*, to bring forth; *n.*, a whelp.

pu'pa, *n.*, a chrysalis.

pu'pil, *n.*, a young scholar; a minor under a guardian; the apple of an eye.

pu'pilage, *n.*, the condition of being a pupil.

pu'pil(l)ary, *adj.*, rel. to a pupil.

pupip'arous, *adj.*, bringing forth in the pupa state.

pupiv'orous, *adj.*, feeding on pupae.

pupped, *p.p.*, pup.

pup'pet, *n.*, a small figure moved by wires; one whose actions, etc., are controlled by another.

pup'pet-show, *n.*, a dramatic exhibition of puppets.

pup'ping, *pr.p.*, pup.

pup'py, *n.*, *dim.* of pup; a coxcomb.

pup'pyism, *n.*, the state of being a puppy.

pura'na, *n.*, one of the sacred Sanskrit poems.

puran'ic, *adj.*, rel. to puranas.

pur'blind, *adj.*, partially blind.

pur'chasable, *adj.*, for sale.

pur'chase, *v.t.*, to buy; gain, acquire; to haul up; *n.*, buying; something bought; leverage.

pur'chased, *p.p.*, purchase.

pur'chase-money, *n.*, payment for property acquired.

pur'chaser, *n.*, a buyer.

pur'chasing, *pr.p.*, purchase.

pure, *adj.*, unadulterated, clean, simple, sheer.

pure'ly, *adv.*, in a pure way; absolutely, simply.

pure'ness, *n.*, the state of being pure.

pur'er, *adj.*, *comp.* of pure.

pur'est, *adj.*, *super.* of pure.

pur'fle, *v.t.*, to embroider or adorn the edge of; to beautify; *n.*, an ornament on the edge.

purga'tion, *n.*, the act of purging, or cleansing; the old method of clearing oneself by ordeal or sworn word.

pur'gative, *adj.*, having a purging quality; *n.*, a purging draught.

purgato'rial, *adj.*, pert. to purgatory.

pur'gatory, *adj.*, cleansing; *n.*, the place where departed souls are cleansed.

purge, *v.t.*, to make clean; to clear out cathartically; *n.*, a cathartic medicine.

purged, *p.p.*, purge.

pur'ger, *n.*, one who, or that which, purges.

pur'ging, *pr.p.*, purge; *n.*, diarrhoea.

purifica'tion, *n.*, the act of purifying; ritual cleansing.

pur'ificative, *adj.*, producing purification.

pur'ificator, *n.*, a napkin used by the celebrant at Mass.

pur'ificatory, *adj.*, *i.q.* purification.

pur'ified, *p.p.*, purify.

pur'ifier, *n.*, one who, or that which, purifies.

pur'iform, *adj.*, like pus.

pur'ify, *v.t.*, to make pure; to cleanse.

pur'ifying, *pr.p.*, purify.

Pur'im, *n.*, the Jewish Feast of Lots, in

memory of the failure of Haman's attempt.

pur'ism, *n.*, pedantic insistence on purity of language.

pur'ist, *n.*, one noticeable for purism.

Pur'itan, *adj.*, rel. to Puritans and puritanism; *n.*, one of the 16th and 17th cent. professors of pure religion as they conceived it.

puritan'ic, *adj.*, rel. to the Puritans; strait-laced.

puritan'ical, *adj.*, *i.q.* puritanic.

Pur'itanism, *n.*, the principles of the Puritans.

pur'ity, *n.*, cleanness, pureness.

purl, *v.t.*, to purfle; *v.i.*, to make a rippling sound; *n.*, an embroidered edge; a backward stitch; a rippling sound; hot beer with sundry ingredients.

purled, *p.p.*, purl.

pur'lieu, *n.*, outskirts (usually in pl.).

pur'lin, *n.*, a horizontal roof timber supporting rafters or boards.

purl'ing, *pr.p.*, purl.

purloin', *v.t.*, to pilfer.

purloined', *p.p.*, purloin.

purloin'er, *n.*, one who pilfers.

purloin'ing, *pr.p.*, purloin.

purpar'ty, *n.*, a share (*leg.*).

pur'ple, *v.t.*, to make purple; *adj.*, of purple colour; *n.*, a colour mixed of red and blue in various proportions; (formerly)crimson. Emperors, kings, cardinals affecting purple robes, the word *purple* stands for their rank.

pur'ples, *n. pl.*, a disease of wheat.

pur'pled, *p.p.*, purple.

pur'pling, *pr.p.*, purple.

pur'plish, *adj.*, inclining to purple.

purport', *v.t.*, to mean, signify.

pur'port, *n.*, meaning, signification.

purport'ed, *p.p.*, purport.

purport'ing, *pr.p.*, purport.

pur'pose, *v.t.* and *i.*, to intend, design; *n.*, intention; object.

pur'posed, *p.p.*, purpose.

pur'poseful, *adj.*, full of determination.

pur'poseless, *adj.*, without any object.

pur'posely, *adv.*, with intention.

pur'poser, *n.*, one who purposes.

pur'posing, *pr.p.*, purpose.

purpres'ture, *n.*, encroachment on the king's highway.

pur'pura, *n.*, a disease indicated by purple spots on the skin.

pur'pure, *n.*, purple (*her.*).

purpu'real, *adj.*, purple.

pur'purin, *n.*, red colouring matter.

purr, *v.i.*, to make the sound of purring; *v.t.*, to speak words as if purring; *n.*, the sound a cat makes when pleased.

purred, *p.p.*, purr.

pur'ree, *n.*, yellow colouring matter.

pur'ring, *pr.p.*, purr; *n.*, the act of purring.

purse, *v.t.* and *i.*, to contract, wrinkle; *n.*, a pouch or bag for money.

pursed, *p.p.*, purse.

purse'ful, *n.*, the contents of a full purse.

purse'-net, *n.*, a net with a mouth closing like a purse.

purse'-pride, *n.*, pride of wealth.

purse'-proud, *adj.*, proud of one's wealth.

purs'er, *n.*, a ship's officer with charge of accounts and provisions.

purs'ing, *pr.p.*, purse.

purs'lane, *n.*, a succulent pot-herb.

pursu'able, *adj.*, able to be pursued.

pursu'al, *n.*, pursuit.

pursu'ance, *n.*, the act of pursuing, or following out.

pursu'ant, *adj.*, following out; *adv.*, in consequence.

pursue', *v.t.*, to follow up; to chase, hunt; seek; to prosecute (*Scots law*); *v.i.*, to continue.

pursued', *p.p.*, pursue.

pursu'er, *n.*, one who pursues; a prosecutor.

pursu'ing, *pr.p.*, pursue.

pursuit', *n.*, the act of pursuing; an occupation or recreation.

pur'suivant, *n.*, an attendant; an official at the Heralds' College, next in rank to the heralds.

purs'y, *adj.*, fat and short of breath.

pur'tenance, *n.*, an animal's inwards (*obs.*).

pur'ulence, *n.*, suppuration.

pur'ulency, *n.*, *i.q.* purulence.

pur'ulent, *adj.*, suppurating.

purvey', *v.t.*, to provide; supply.

purvey'ance, *n.*, supply; the act of purveying; the State's right to demand supplies.

purveyed', *p.p.*, purvey.

purvey'ing, *pr.p.*, purvey.

purvey'or, *n.*, one who purveys. (The word is applicable only to a person supplying provisions on a large scale.)

pur'view, *n.*, purport, scope; visual range; the active parts of a statute as distinct from defining clauses.

pus, *n.*, morbid suppurating matter (*Lat.*).

Pu'seyism, *n.*, a polemical term denoting the principles of the Tractarians.

Pu'seyite, *n.*, a Tractarian; a disciple of Dr. Pusey, the most capable of the Tract writers.
push, *v.t.*, to thrust; cause to move away; to advance; *v.i.*, to be pushing for one's own ends; *n.*, a thrust; an advance; additional effort; self-interested activity.
pushed, *p.p.*, push.
push'er, *n.*, one who pushes (in any sense).
push'ful, *adj.*, bent on getting on (*slang*).
push'ing, *pr.p.*, push; *adj.*, pushful.
push'-pin, *n.*, a child's game.
pusillanim'ity, *n.*, faint-heartedness; poor-spiritedness.
pusillan'imous, *adj.*, poor-spirited; faint-hearted.
puss, *n.*, a cat; a hare; (*colloq.*) a girl.
pus'sy, *n.*, a cat.
pus'tular, *adj.*, rel. to pustules.
pus'tulate, *adj.*, having pustules.
pus'tulate, *v.t.* and *i.*, to form pustules.
pus'tulated, *p.p.*, pustulate.
pustula'tion, *n.*, formation of pustules.
pus'tule, *n.*, a pimple; excrescence.
pus'tulous, *adj.*, *i.q.* pustulate.
put, *v.t.* and *i.*, to lay; set; place; propose (an argument); to start; *n.*, a cast or throw.
put, *v.t.* and *i.*, to send a golf ball towards the putting-hole; *p.p.*, put; *n.*, the shot for the hole.
puta'men, *n.*, shell of a stone-fruit's stone.
pu'tative, *adj.*, reputed; imagined.
pu'teal, *n.*, the fencing of a wall.
pu'tid, *adj.*, stinking.
put'log, *n.*, one of the short timbers supporting a scaffold.
put'-off, *n.*, an evasive excuse.

putrefac'tion, *n.*, the process of putrefying.
putrefac'tive, *adj.*, putrefying.
pu'trefied, *p.p.*, putrefy.
pu'trefy, *v.t.*, to make putrid; cause to decay; *v.i.*, to become putrid.
pu'trefying, *pr.p.*, putrefy.
putres'cence, *n.*, the process of rotting.
putres'cent, *adj.*, in a rotting state.
putres'cible, *adj.*, liable to becoming rotten.
pu'trid, *adj.*, rotten; stinking.
putrid'ity, *n.*, the state or quality of being putrid.
put'ted, *p.p.*, put.
put'tee, *n.* (usu. in pl.), a strip of cloth wound round and round the leg.
put'ter, *n.*, a golf-club used for putting.
put'tied, *p.p.*, putty.
put'ting, *pr.p.*, put.
put'ting, *pr.p.*, put.
put'ty, *v.t.*, to fasten with putty; *n.*, a plaster for fixing glass, or polishing jewels, or stopping cracks.
put'tying, *pr.p.*, putty.
puz'zle, *v.t.*, to perplex, mystify; *v.i.*, to try to solve; *n.*, a thing difficult to understand; an enigma; a toy, the pieces of which have to be arranged.
puz'zled, *p.p.*, puzzle.
puz'zle-headed, *adj.*, bewildered; stupid.
puz'zler, *n.*, that which puzzles.
puz'zling, *pr.p.*, puzzle; *adj.*, bewildering
puzzola'no, *n.*, volcanic ash from Pozzuoli. Also *poz-z(u)olana.*
pyae'mia, *n.*, blood-poisoning.
pyo'nite, *n.*, a variety of topaz.
pyc'nostyle, *adj.*, having pillars set closely; *n.*, a close arrangement of pillars.

pye, *n.*, a magpie.
py'garg, *n.*, the osprey.
pygmae'an, pygme'an, *adj.*, pert. to pygmies; dwarfish.
pyg'my, *adj.*, diminutive, dwarfish; *n.*, one of the race of dwarfs called Pygmies; any dwarf.
pyja'mas, *n.*, loose trousers; a sleeping-suit. Also *pajamas*.
pylo'ric, *adj.*, pert. to the pylorus.
pylo'rus, *n.*, the opening from the stomach to the smaller intestine.
py'racanth, *n.*, an evergreen thorn.
pyr'amid, *n.*, a solid structure, square at base, with triangular sides mounting to an apex.
pyram'idal, *adj.*, rel. to, or resembling, a pyramid.
pyramid'ical, *adj.*, *i.q.* pyramidal.
pyre, *n.*, a funeral pile.
Pyrene'an, *adj.*, rel. to the Pyrenees.
Pyre'thrum, *n.*, feverfew.
pyret'ic, *adj.*, febrile; *n.*, a febrifuge.
pyretol'ogy, *n.*, the science of the study of fevers.
pyrex'ia, *n.*, fever.
pyrex'ial, *adj.*, rel. to fever.
pyr'gom, *n.*, a mineral so named.
pyr'idine, *n.*, a liquid alkaloid, used in asthma cases.
py'riform, *adj.*, pear-shaped.
pyrita'ceous, *adj.*, pyritic.
pyri'tes, *n.*, one of the metallic sulphides of iron or copper.
pyrit'ic, *adj.*, pert. to pyrites.
pyro-ac'id, *n.*, acetin.
py'ro-elec'tric, *adj.*, rel. to pyro-electricity.
py'ro-electric'ity, *n.*, electrification produced by heating or cooling.
pyrog'enous, *adj.*, igneous.

pyrol'atry, *n.*, fire-worship.

pyrolig'neous, *adj.*, in a state produced by fire on wood.

pyrolith'ic, *adj.*, cyanuric.

pyrol'ogist, *n.*, a student of pyrology.

pyrol'ogy, *n.*, the science of examination by means of heat.

py'romancy, *n.*, divination by fire.

pyroman'tic, *adj.*, rel. to pyromancy.

pyrom'eter, *n.*, an apparatus for measuring high degrees of heat.

pyromet'ric, *adj.*, pert. to pyrometry.

pyrom'etry, *n.*, the science of measuring high temperatures.

pyromorph'ous, *adj.*, crystallizing by means of fire.

py'rope, *n.*, a kind of garnet.

pyroph'orous, *adj.*, yielding fire.

pyroph'orus, *n.*, a spontaneously combustible compound.

py'roscope, *n.*, an instrument for measuring the intensity of heat radiation.

pyro'sis, *n.*, a catarrhal state of the stomach.

pyrotech'nic, *adj.*, rel. to fireworks.

pyrotech'nics, *n. pl.*, fireworks; the manufacture of them.

pyrotech'nist, *n.*, one who makes fireworks.

py'rotechny, *n.*, the art of making fireworks.

pyroxyl'ic, *adj.*, produced, by distillation, from wood.

pyrox'ylin, *n.*, any explosive made from vegetable fibre to which nitric acid is applied.

Pyr'rhic, *adj.*, rel. to Pyrrhus; costly.

pyr'rhonism, *n.*, scepticism. The word is derived from Pyrrho, an ancient Greek sceptical teacher.

pyr'rhonist, *n.*, a follower of Pyrrho; a sceptic.

Pythagore'an, *adj.*, pert. to Pythagoras, who taught the doctrine of the transmigration of souls.

Pythag'orism, *n.*, the doctrines of Pythagoras.

Pyth'ian, *adj.*, rel. to the Delphic oracle of Apollo.

py'thon, *n.*, a fabulous serpent slain by Apollo; a large snake that kills by crushing; a soothsayer, oracle.

py'thoness, *n.*, fem. of python.

python'ic, *adj.*, rel. to python.

py'thonism, *n.*, soothsaying: ventriloquism.

pyx, *n.*, a box, esp. that in which the Host is kept.

pyxid'ium, *n.*, a lidded capsule.

pyx'is, *n.*, a casket; also *i.q.* pyxidium.

Q

qua, *conj.*, as; in the character or position of.

quab, *n.*, the miller's thumb.

quack, *v.i.*, to make a duck's sound; to prate; *n.*, an ignorant professor of surgery or physic; a charlatan; a duck's sound.

quacked, *p.p.*, quack.

quack'ery, *n.*, the tricks of a quack.

quack'ish, *adj.*, like a quack.

quack'salver, *n.*, *i.q.* quack (in sense of charlatan).

quad, *n.*, *i.q.* quadrat; also *i.q.* quadrangle (of which words it is an abbreviation).

quad'ra, *n.*, the border of a square panel; a fillet on an Ionic base; a plinth.

Quadrages'ima, *n.*, the first Sunday in Lent; the forty days of Lent. (The name = fortieth.)

quad'rangle, *n.*, a figure with four sides; a court enclosed by four sides.

quadran'gular, *adj.*, having four sides.

quad'rans, *n.*, the fourth part of a Roman *as* (*Lat.*).

quad'rant, *n.*, a quarter circumference of a circle; the figure contained between an arc and two radii at a right angle.

quad'rat, *n.*, a little block used in the spacing of type.

quad'rate, *adj.*, rectangular, square; *n.*, a bone or muscle so named.

quadrate', *v.t.*, to square, or make square.

quadrat'ic, *adj.*, involving a second and no higher power; *n.*, a quadratic equation.

quad'rature, *n.*, the process of expressing in terms of square measure the dimensions of any area.

quadren'nial, *adj.*, in every four years; lasting four years.

quad'rible, *adj.*, able to be squared.

quadricap'sular, *adj.*, with four capsules.

quad'ricorn, *adj.*, with four horns.

quadriden'tate, *adj.*, with four rows of teeth.

quad'rifid, *adj.*, with four lobes or divisions.

quad'rifoil, *adj.*, with four foliations.

quad'riform, *adj.*, four-fold.

quadri'ga, *n.*, a four-horse chariot (*Lat.*).

quadrilat'eral, *adj.*, having four sides; *n.*, a figure with four sides.

quadrilit'eral, *adj.*, having four letters.

quadrille', *n.*, a square dance; an old card game for four hands.

quadrill'ion, *n.*, a million to the fourth power.

quadrilo'bate, *adj.*, having four lobes.

quad'rilobed, *adj.*, *i.q.* quadrilobate.

quadriloc'ular, *adj.*, four-celled, four-chambered.

quadrino'mial, *adj.*, having four algebraical terms.

quadripart'ite, *adj.*, having four parts.

quadriphyl'lous, *adj.*, with four leaves.

quad'rireme, *n.*, a vessel with four banks of rowers.

quadrisyllab'ic, *adj.*, composed of four syllables.

quadrisyl'lable, *n.*, a word with four syllables.

quad'rivalve, *adj.*, having four valves.

quadrivalv'ular, *adj.*, having four valves.

quadriv'ial, *adj.*, rel. to the quadrivium.

quadriv'ium, *n.*, the mediaeval course of four studies.

quadroon', *n.*, a person whose blood is one-quarter black; any hybrid with one quarter not pure.

Quadru'mana, *n. pl.*, mammals having feet like hands.

quad'rumane, *n.*, one of the Quadrumana.

quadru'manous, *adj.*, four-handed; rel. to Quadrumana.

quad'rune, *n.*, a gritstone.

quad'ruped, *adj.*, having four feet; *n.*, a four-footed animal.

quad'ruple, *v.t.*, to multiply by four; *adj.*, multiplied by four; *n.*, a quantity four times that of one given.

quad'rupled, *p.p.*, quadruple.

quadru'plicate, *adj.*, fourfold; four times over.

quadru'plicate, *v.t.*, to multiply by four; to quadruple.

quadru'plicated, *p.p.*, quadruplicate.

quadru'plicating, *pr.p.*, quadruplicate.

quadruplica'tion, *n.*, a making fourfold.

quad'rupling, *pr.p.*, quadruple.

quaest'or, *n.*, an ancient Roman financial magistrate (*Lat.*).

quaff, *v.t.*, to take a draught of.

quaffed, *p.p.*, quaff.

quaff'er, *n.*, one who quaffs.

quaff'ing, *pr.p.*, quaff.

quag, *n.*, *i.q.* quagmire.

quag'ga, *n.*, a sort of zebra.

quag'gy, *adj.*, boggy.

quag'mire, *n.*, a bog, morass.

quail, *v.i.*, to shrink, cower; *n.*, a small bird so named.

quailed, *p.p.*, quail.

quail'ing, *pr.p.*, quail.

quaint, *adj.*, odd, whimsical, antique.

quaint'ly, *adv.*, in a quaint way.

quaint'ness, *n.*, the state or quality of being quaint.

quake, *v.i.*, to tremble, shake, vibrate; *n.*, the act of quaking.

quaked, *p.p.*, quake.

qua'ker, *n.*, one who quakes. The name was once given contemptuously to a member of the Society of Friends, but it has lost its offensive meaning.

qua'keress, *n.*, fem. of quaker.

Qua'kerish, *adj.*, like the Quakers.

Qua'kerism, *n.*, the principles and system of the Society of Friends.

qua'king, *pr.p.*, quake.

qual'ifiable, *adj.*, able to be qualified.

qualifica'tion, *n.*, a limiting or conditioning circumstance; a proof of fitness.

qual'ificative, *adj.*, qualifying.

qual'ificator, *n.*, an ecclesiastical official, charged with the duty of preparing disputed cases with theological precision.

qual'ified, *p.p.*, qualify.

qual'ifier, *n.*, one who, or that which, qualifies.

qual'ify, *v.t.*, to fit; to modify, moderate; *v.i.*, to come up to standard.

qual'ifying, *pr.p.*, qualify.

qual'itative, *adj.*, pert to quality.

quality, *n.*, kind, nature, standard of excellence.

qualm, *n.*, momentary sickness; twinge of conscience; hesitancy.

qualm'ish, *adj.*, inclined to sickness.

qualm'ishly, *adv.*, in a qualmish way.

quan'dary, *n.*, a state of perplexity; a fix.

quantifica'tion, *n.*, the act of quantifying.

quan'titative, *adj.*, rel. to quantity.

quan'tity, *n.*, the measure of how much, whether size, weight, amount, extension, or number.

quan'tum, *n.*, a share; sufficient amount.

qua'rantine, *v.t.*, to isolate travellers who are sick or supposed to be capable of spreading infection; *n.*, the state, or period, of being quarantined.

quar'rel, *v.i.*, to complain against; to fall out, contend; *n.*, a complaint; a falling out, a dispute; a cross-bow bolt.

quar'rel(l)ed, *p.p.*, quarrel.

quar'rel(l)er, *n.*, one who quarrels.

quar'rel(l)ing, *pr.p.*, quarrel.

quar'relsome, *adj.*, ready to quarrel; touchy.

quar'ried, *p.p.*, quarry.

quar'rier, *n.*, one who quarries.

quar'ry, *v.t.* and *i.*, to take stone or marble from its bed; to do research work; *n.*, a place whence stone is extracted; prey.

quar'rying, *pr.p.*, quarry; *n.*, the act of quarrying.

quart, *n.*, a quarter of a gallon; two pints; *n.*, *i.q.* carte (a fencing term); a sequence in piquet.

quar'tan, *adj.*, recurring after every three days; *n.*, a quartan fever.

quarta'tion, *n.*, the addition of one part gold to three parts silver in assaying.

quar'ter, *v.t.*, to divide into four parts; to billet; to add a coat of arms to one's own (*her.*); to range over; *v.i.*, to be in billets; to avoid ruts in a road; *n.*, a fourth part; a district; the haunches; the side of a ship between the main chains and the stern; mercy to a fallen enemy; in *pl.*, billets; *adj.*, one-fourth in measure.

quar'terage, *n.*, payment at quarter day; a quarter's allowance.

quar'ter-day, *n.*, one of the four statutory days on which payments are due.

quar'ter-deck, *n.*, the part of a deck reserved for officers.

quar'tered, *p.p.*, quarter.

quar'terfoil, *n.*, *i.q.* quatrefoil.

quar'tering, *pr.p.*, quarter; *n.*, the division of a shield to enable the addition of other arms (*her.*).

quar'terly, *adj.* and *adv.*, every quarter; in the four quarters or the diagonally opposite quarters of a shield (*her.*); *n.*, a periodical issued every three months.

quar'termaster, *n.*, a staff officer whose duty is to assign quarters, see to rations, etc.

quar'tern, *n.*, a measure of capacity of differing values; *n.*, a four-pound loaf.

quarteroon', *n.*, *i.q.* quadroon.

quar'ters, *n.pl.*, billets.

quar'ter-ses'sions, *n.*, a quarterly court.

quar'terstaff, *n.*, a heavy pole used for defence or sport.

quartet', **-ette'**, *n.*, a combination of four performers or instruments; a composition for four performers; any group of four.

quar'to, *n.*, a size of paper resulting from two foldings; a page or book of this size.

quartodec'iman, *adj.*, rel. to the observance of Easter on the 14th day of the month Nisan, whatever day of the week it might be.

quar'tole, *n.*, a series of four notes to be played in the time of three or six (*mus.*).

quartz, *n.*, a name for minerals consisting of silicon dioxide.

quartzif'erous, *adj.*, producing quartz.

quartz'ose, *adj.*, containing quartz.

quartz'y, *adj.*, *i.q.* quartzose.

quash, *v.t.*, to annul, cancel.

quashed, *p.p.*, quash.

quash'ee, *n.*, a W. Indian negro.

quash'ing, *pr.p.*, quash.

qua'si, *conj.* and *prefix*, as if; seemingly.

quas'sia, *n.*, a bitter wood.

quas'sin, *n.*, the bitter principle of quassia.

quater'nary, *adj.*, consisting of four parts; rel. to the number four.

quater'nion, *n.*, a body of four soldiers; a set of four; *adj.*, four-fold.

quater'nity, *n.*, a group of four.

quat'orzain, *n.*, a fourteen-line sonnet.

quat'rain, *n.*, a four-line stanza.

quat'refoil, *n.*, an architectural form with four cusps.

qua'ver, *v.i.*, to shake, tremble, vibrate, trill; *n.*, a trilly, shaky speech; a note of the value of half a crotchet (*mus.*).

qua'vered, *p.p.*, quaver.

qua'verer, *n.*, one who quavers.

qua'vering, *pr.p.*, quaver.

quay, *n.*, a wharf; a landing-stage.

quay'age, *n.*, wharfage.

queach'y, *adj.*, quaking (as a bog).

quean, *n.*, an impudent woman; a girl.

quea'siness, *n.*, the state of being queasy.

quea'sy, *adj.*, nauseating; qualmish.

queen, *v.t.*, to make queen; to convert a pawn into a queen; *v.i.*, to play a queen's part; *n.*, a king's consort; a female sovereign; a piece in chess so named; a fully developed female bee, etc.

queen'ing, *pr.p.*, queen; *n.*, a variety of apple.

queen'like, *adj.*, *i.q.* queenly.

queen'ly, *adj.*, resembling a queen.

queen'post, *n.*, one of two upright posts in a roof-truss.

queer, *adj.*, odd, strange; of doubtful character; feeling faint; *v.t.* (*slang*), to interfere with, spoil.

queer'ish, *adj.*, rather queer.

queer'ly, *adv.*, in a queer way.

quell, *v.t.*, to put down; silence; suppress.

quelled, *p.p.*, quell.

quell'er, *n.*, one who quells.

quell'ing, *pr.p.*, quell.

quench, *v.t.*, to extinguish; cool; suppress.

quench'able, *adj.*, able to be quenched.

quenched, *p.p.*, quench.

quench'er, *n.*, one who, or that which, quenches.

quench'ing, *pr.p.*, quench.

quench'less, *adj.*, unquenchable.

quer'cine, *adj.*, pert. to oaks.

quer'citron, *n.*, the black oak; a dye made from the same.

que'ried, *p.p.*, query.

querimo'nious, *adj.*, full of grievances.

que'rist, *n.*, a questioner.

quern, *v.t.* and *i.*, to grind (corn); *n.*, a hand-mill.

quer'ulous, *adj.*, full of complaints; peevish.

quer'ulously, *adv.*, peevishly.

quer'ulousness, *n.*, the state of being querulous.

que'ry, *v.t.* and *i.*, to question; to call in question; *n.*, a question; an objection.

que'rying, *pr.p.*, query.

quest, *v.t.* and *i.*, to go on quest (for); *n.*, search, inquiry; official investigation (as Crowner's Quest).

ques'tion, *v.t.*, to interrogate; express disbelief in or doubt about; *n.*, an interrogation; a subject for discussion; torture.

ques'tionable, *adj.*, open to doubt or objection; of doubtful propriety.

ques'tionableness, *n.*, the quality of being questionable.

ques'tionably, *adv.*, in a questionable way.

ques'tioned, *p.p.*, question.

ques'tioner, *n.*, one who questions.

ques'tioning, *pr.p.*, question.

ques'tionist, *n.*, a candidate for a degree at Cambridge.

ques'tionless, *adj.*, unquestioning; *adv.*, without doubt.

questionnaire', *n.*, a list of questions.

quest'man, *n.*, an inspector; a sidesman.

ques'tor, *n.*, *i.q.* quaestor.

queue, *n.*, a pig-tail; a file of people.

quib'ble, *v.i.*, to evade an argument; to

shuffle; *n.*, an evasion of the point by playing with words.

quib'bled, *p.p.* quibble.

quib'bler, *n.*, one who quibbles.

quib'bling, *pr.p.*, quibble; *n.*, evasion of the point of an argument.

quick, *adj.*, alive; living; alert; fast; pregnant; *n.*, the living part; a vital, sensitive part; *adv.*, quickly.

quick'en, *v.t.*, to give life to; to animate; to stimulate; *v.i.*, to come to life.

quick'ened, *p.p.*, quicken.

quick'ener, *n.*, one who, or that which, quickens.

quick'ening, *pr.p.*, quicken.

quick'er, *adj.*, and *adv.*, *comp.* of quick.

quick'-grass, *n.*, couch grass.

quick'lime, *n.*, a result of expelling, by means of heat, the carbon dioxide from limestone, etc.

quick'ly, *adv.*, with speed, rapidly.

quick'ness, *n.*, celerity.

quick'sand, *n.*, loose, moving sand.

quick'set, *adj.*, made of living shrubs; *n.*, a hedge so formed.

quick'-sighted, *adj.*, having quick sight.

quick'silver, *n.*, mercury; *v.t.*, to coat with quicksilver.

quick'step, *n.*, a quick marching step.

quick'-witted, *adj.*, with nimble wits.

Quicun'que vult', *n.*, the Athanasian Creed. (The name= Whosoever will.)

quid, *n.*, a lump of tobacco for chewing; a something; (*slang*) a sovereign.

quid'dity, *n.*, the essential nature of a thing; cavilling.

quid'dle, *v.i.*, to quiver (*Amer.*).

quid'nunc, *n.*, a gossip; newsmonger.

quid pro quo', substantival phrase = a set off, compensation.

quiesce', *v.i.*, to become silent.

quies'cence, *n.*, the state of becoming or being silent.

quies'cency, *n.*, *i.q.* quiescence.

quies'cent, *adj.*, silent, inert.

qui'et, *v.t.*, to calm, appease; *v.i.*, to become quiet; *adj.*, calm, peaceful, silent, unobtrusive; *n.*, calmness, stillness, soundlessness.

qui'eted, *p.p.*, quiet.

qui'eter, *adj.*, *comp.* of quiet.

qui'etest, *adj.*, *super.* of quiet.

qui'eting, *pr.p.*, quiet.

qui'etism, *n.*, the principle of passivity; mysticism; quiet devotional contemplation.

qui'etist, *n.*, one who practises quietism.

quietist'ic, *adj.*, rel. to quietism.

qui'etly, *adv.*, in a quiet way.

qui'etness, *n.*, the state of being quiet.

qui'etude, *n.*, rest; tranquillity.

quie'tus, *n.*, a final blow; acquittance.

quill, *v.t.* and *i.*, to goffer; *n.*, a large wing or tail feather; a pen made of such; a plectrum; one of a porcupine's spines; a musical pipe.

quill'-driver, *n.*, a writer.

quilled, *p.p.*, quill; *adj.*, having quills.

quil'let, *n.*, a quibble.

quill'ing, *pr.p.*, quill; *n.*, goffering; fluted muslin or lace.

quill'wort, *n.*, a variety of aquatic plant so named.

quilt, *v.t.*, to line or cover with padded material; *n.*, a bed-cover; a quilted garment.

quilt'ed, *p.p.*, quilt.

quilt'er, *n.*, one who quilts.

quilt'ing, *pr.p.*, quilt; *n.*, quilted work; material to be quilted.

qui'nary, *adj.*, pert. to five; containing five.

qui'nate, *adj.*, having five leaflets.

quince, *n.*, a hard, acid, yellowish fruit so named.

quince'-tree, *n.*, the shrub that bears quinces.

quincun'cial, *adj.*, arranged in quincunx form.

quin'cunx, *n.*, an arrangement of five things in a square in the manner of the five on dice or playing cards.

quindec'agon, *n.*, a figure with fifteen angles and sides.

quinine', *n.*, the invaluable drug made from Peruvian bark.

Quinquages'ima, *n.*, the Sunday next before Lent. (See note on Septuagesima.)

quinquan'gular, *adj.*, five-angled.

quinquefo'liate, *adj.*, five-leaved.

quinquelit'eral, *adj.*, five-lettered.

quinquen'nial, *adj.*, recurring every five years; lasting five years.

quinquepar'tite, *adj.*, divided into five parts.

quin'quereme, *n.*, a galley with five banks of oars.

quinquesyll'able, *n.*, a five-syllable word.

quin'quevalve, *adj.*, having five valves.

quin'quifid, *adj.*, cleft in five.

quinqui'na, *n.*, Peruvian bark.

quin'sy, *n.*, amygdalitis; inflammation of the tonsils.

quint, *n.*, a fifth (*in mus.*); an organ stop sounding the fifth; in piquet, a sequence of five cards of one suit.

quin'tain, *n.*, an old tilting sport.

quin'tal, *n.*, a hundredweight.
quin'tan, *adj.*, returning every fifth day.
quintess'ence, *n.*, concentrated essence; orig. the fifth substance in addition to the four elements.
quintessen'tial, *adj.*, pert. to quintessence.
quintet', -ette', *n.*, a combination of five voices or instruments (*mus.*); a musical composition for five performers.
quintil'lion, *n.*, a million to the fifth power. In France, it is only a million million million.
quin'tuple, *v.t.*, to multiply by five; *adj.*, five-fold; *n.*, a five-fold amount.
quintu'plicate, *v.t.*, to make five times the original amount.
quintu'plicate, *adj.*, pert. to five separate parts; five-fold.
quin'zaine, *n.*, a composition containing fifteen lines.
quip, *v.t.* and *i.*, to gibe; *n.*, a gibe, quibble.
qui'pu, quip'pu, *n.*, the old Peruvian substitute for writing. It consisted of knotted threads of various colours.
quire, *v.t.*, to fold in quires; to mark the quires; *v.i.*, to sing in chorus; *n.*, the one-twentieth of a ream; a book; a choir, whether the singers or the place where they sing.
Quiri'nal, *n.*, one of the hills of ancient Rome.
Quir'inal, *n.*, the modern palace of the Kings of Italy on the Quirinal Hill (now pronounced *Quir'inal*).
quirk, *v.t.*, to hollow out; *n.*, a quibble; conceit; in architecture, a groove.
quirked, *p.p.*, quirk.
quirt, *n.*, a riding whip peculiar to S. America.
quit, *v.t.*, to acquit; conduct (*reflex.*); to desist from; to let go; to leave; to repay; *adj.*, clear, released from obligation. In pl. it = even.
quitch'-grass, *n.*, couch-grass.
quit'claim, *n.*, renouncement of claim; release in full.
quite, *adv.*, totally; without reservation, completely.
quit'-rent, *n.*, rent paid by a copyholder, who was thus released from service.
quits, *n. pl.*, *see* quit.
quit'table, *adj.*, able to be quitted.
quit'tance, *n.*, release; requital.
quit'ted, *p.p.*, quit.
quit'ter, *n.*, one who quits.
quit'ting, *pr.p.*, quit.
quiv'er, *v.i.*, to be agitated; to shake; vibrate; *n.*, an arrow-holder; vibration, shaking.
quiv'ered, *adj.*, having a quiver; *p.p.*, quiver.
quiv'erful, *n.*, the contents of a quiver.
quiv'ering, *pr.p.*, quiver.
quiv'eringly, *adv.*, in a quivering way.
qui vive', Fr. phrase, "That who may live?" = "Who goes there?"; *n.*, the alert.
Quixot'ic, *adj.*, rel. to Don Quixote; like Q. in being visionary, chivalrous and unpractical.
quixot'ically, *adv.*, in a quixotic fashion.
quix'otism, *n.*, quixotic ideals.
quix'otry, *n.*, *i.q.* quixotism.
quiz, *v.t.*, to make fun of; to gibe; to stare at; *n.*, a ridiculous person; one given to quizzing; a hoax, chaff.
quizzed, *p.p.*, quiz.
quiz'zer, *n.*, one who quizzes.
quiz'zical, *adj.*, mocking, chaffing.
quiz'zing, *pr.p.*, quiz.
quiz'zing-glass, *n.*, a monocle affected by a quiz.
quo'ad, *prep.* (*Lat.*), as regards.
quod'libet, *n.*, a subject for argument; a subtle point.
quoin, *v.t.*, to bind with a quoin; *n.*, the outer angle of a building; cornerstone; a wedge for the type in a forme, or for raising a gun's level.
quoit, *n.*, an iron disc open in the middle and thrown by the player at a peg.
quon'dam, *adv.* (*Lat.*), used as an *adj.* = sometime, former.
quo'rum, *n.*, a specified required number.
quo'ta, *n.*, an individual share or contribution to a whole.
quo'table, *adj.*, able, or fit, to be quoted.
quota'tion, *n.*, the act of quoting; a passage quoted; a statement of price.
quote, *v.t.*, to repeat someone's written or spoken words; to adduce authority from a writer; to state a price.
quo'ted, *p.p.*, quote.
quo'ter, *n.*, one who quotes.
quoth, *v.t.*, an old past tense of an obsolete verb = I, he, she said.
quo'tha, *interj.*, an old word = forsooth.
quotid'ian, *adj.*, daily; ordinary.
quo'tient, *n.*, the figure that shows how many times one number is contained in another.
quo'ting, *pr.p.*, quote.
Qurân', *n.*, *i.q.* Koran.

R

rab, *n.*, a mason's rod for mixing hair with mortar.

rab'bet, *n.*, a groove cut on the end of a board so that another may fit into it; *v.t.*, to cut a board in this way.

rab'beted, *p.p.*, rabbet.

rab'beting, *pr.p.*, rabbet.

rab'bi, *n.*, a Jewish doctor or teacher.

rab'bin, *n.*, *i.q.* rabbi.

Rabbin'ic, *n.*, a dialect of Hebrew; later Hebrew.

rabbin'ic, *adj.*, pert. to the rabbis, or to the non-canonical Hebrew writings.

rabbin'ical, *adj.*, *i.q.* rabbinic.

rab'binism, *n.*, a rabbinic expression or phrase.

rab'binist, *n.*, a Jew who adheres to the Talmud and rabbinic traditions.

rab'bit, *n.*, a rodent mammal that burrows in the earth.

rab'ble, *n.*, a disorderly crowd; the lowest class of the people.

rab'blement, *n.*, a tumultuous crowd of low people.

rabdol'ogy, *n.*, the art of computing by means of "Napier's Rods."

Rabelai'sian, *adj.*, like, pert. to, the great satirist, Rabelais, and his style; grotesque in humour.

rab'id, *adj.*, mad with rage; intolerant.

rab'idly, *adv.*, in a rabid manner.

rab'idness, *n.*, the state of being rabid.

ra'bies, *n.*, madness of dogs and related animals, causing hydrophobia.

ra'ca, *adj.*, a Syriac epithet of contempt meaning worthless.

raccoon', *n.*, a North American animal with valuable fur.

race, *n.*, a speed contest; a mill-stream; a rapid current in the sea; people related by descent; a breed or stock; a root; *v.i.*, to run swiftly; to contend in a race.

race'-course, *n.*, the ground on which races, esp. horse-races, are run.

raced, *p.p.*, race.

race'-horse, *n.*, a horse kept for racing.

raceme', *n.*, a cluster of flowers growing out of a common slender axis.

ra'cer, *n.*, one who races; a race-horse.

rachil'la, *n.*, the zigzag axis on a grass-spikelet along which the florets are arranged.

ra'chis, *n.*, the vertebral column; the shaft of a feather; the stalk of a fern-frond.

ra'cial, *adj.*, pert. to a race.

ra'cier, *adj.*, *comp.* of racy.

ra'ciest, *adj.*, *super.* of racy.

ra'cily, *adv.*, in a racy manner.

ra'ciness, *n.*, the quality of being racy.

ra'cing, *pr.p.*, race; *n.*, the pastime of attending horse-races; *adj.*, pert. to races.

rack, *v.t.*, to strain vehemently; to torture; to draw pure liquor off from its sediment; *n.*, a framework; an instrument of torture; a bar with a toothed edge working in the teeth of a wheel; thin flying clouds; destruction; *i.q.* arrack.

racked, *p.p.*, rack.

rack'et, *n.*, clamour; a battledore used in such games as tennis, racquets, etc.; *v.i.*, to make a confused noise; to frolic.

rack'eted, *p.p.*, racket

rack'eting, *pr.p.*, racket.

rack'ety, *adj.*, making a tumultuous noise.

rack'ing, *pr.p.*, rack.

rack'-rent, *n.*, full annual rent of a property; the market value of the property at the time in question; *v.t.*, to impose rack-rent upon.

rack'-renter, *n.*, a landlord who rack-rents his tenants.

raconteur', *n.*, a story teller (*Fr.*).

racoon', *n.*, *i.q.* raccoon.

racqu'et, *n.*, *i.q.* racket.

ra'cy, *adj.*, having a strong, piquant flavour; spirited.

rad'dle, *v.t.*, to interweave; to paint with raddle; *n.*, an interwoven or pleached hedge; a red pigment.

ra'dial, *adj.*, pert. to a radius.

ra'diance, *n.*, vivid brightness.

ra'diancy, *n.*, *i.q.* radiance.

ra'diant, *adj.*, brilliant; giving out rays.

ra'diantly, *adv.*, in a radiant manner.

ra'diary, *n.*, a radiate.

Radia'ta, *n. pl.*, a division of the animal kingdom according to Cuvier.

ra'diate, *v.i.*, to proceed in rays from a point or surface;

v.t., to emit in direct lines from a point or surface.

ra'diate, *adj.*, having rays; *n.*, a member of the Radiata.

ra'diated, *p.p.*, radiate.

ra'diating, *pr.p.*, radiate.

radia'tion, *n.*, the act of radiating.

ra'diator, *n.*, that which radiates; part of a heating apparatus.

rad'ical, *adj.*, pert. to the root; fundamental; thoroughgoing; *n.*, one who advocates thorough social or political reform; a root word.

rad'icalism, *n.*, the doctrines of the radicals or advanced liberals.

radical'ity, *n.*, the quality of being radical.

rad'ically, *adv.*, fundamentally.

rad'icant, *adj.*, taking root on or above the ground.

rad'icate, *adj.*, deeply rooted.

rad'icate, *v.t.*, to plant deeply; to cause to take root.

rad'icated, *p.p.*, radicate; *adj.*, *i.q.* radicate.

rad'icating, *pr.p.*, radicate.

radica'tion, *n.*, the process of taking root deeply.

rad'icle, *n.*, that part of a seed which becomes the root; the fibrous parts of a root.

radic'ular, *adj.*, pert. to a radicle.

ra'dii, *n.*, pl. of radius.

radiom'eter, *n.*, an instrument for measuring radiant energy.

rad'ish, *n.*, a cruciferous plant with an edible root.

ra'dius, *n.*, a straight line drawn from the centre of a circle to the circumference; the smaller bone of the forearm.

ra'dix, *n.*, a root; a mathematical base.

raf'fia, *n.*, a fibre used in basketry, etc.

raf'fish, *adj.*, dissipated; worthless.

raf'fle, *n.*, a kind of lottery; *v.t.*, to dispose of by means of a raffle.

raf'fled, *p.p.*, raffle.

raf'fler, *n.*, one who raffles.

raf'fling, *pr.p.*, raffle.

raft, *n.*, a float made of planks, barrels, etc.; *v.t.*, to carry on a raft.

raft'er, *n.*, one of the sloping timbers of a roof; *v.t.*, to provide with rafters.

raft'ered, *adj.*, furnished with rafters; *p.p.*, rafter.

raft'ing, *pr.p.*, raft.

rafts'man, *n.*, a man who manages a raft.

rag, *n.*, a shred of cloth; a tatter; a kind of hard, rough stone; *v.t.* and *i.*, to tease; to indulge in horse-play (*slang*).

rag'amuffin, *n.*, a ragged or worthless fellow.

rage, *n.*, furious anger; something eagerly sought after; *v.i.*, to act violently.

raged, *p.p.*, rage.

ra'ger, *n.*, one who rages.

rag'-fair, *n.*, a place of cheap shops.

rag'ged, *adj.*, tattered.

rag'gedness, *n.*, the state of being ragged.

rag'ging, *pr.p.*, rag.

ra'ging, *pr.p.*, rage; *adj.*, furious.

rag'lan, *n.*, a loose overcoat with wide sleeves.

rag'man, *n.*, a collector of and dealer in rags.

ragout', *n.*, a highly seasoned stew (*Fr.*).

rag'-shop, *n.*, a shop where rags, bones, and other rubbish are bought in small quantities.

rag'stone, *n.*, a siliceous rock with a rough fracture.

rag'wort, *n.*, a coarse weed with ragged leaves and a yellow flower.

raid, *n.*, a hostile attack; *v.t.*, to invade, esp. for plunder.

rail, *n.*, a bar of wood or iron; one of the metals of a railway; *v.t.*, to fence off with rails; *v.i.*, use reproachful words.

railed, *p.p.*, rail.

rail'er, *n.*, one who rails.

rail'ing, *n.*, a fence made of posts and rails; *adj.*, reproachful and insulting; *n.*, abuse; *pr.p.*, rail.

rail'lery, *n.*, banter.

rail'road, *n.*, a railway (chiefly Amer. and Colonial).

rail'way, *n.*, a road with rails on which the wheels of vehicles run.

rai'ment, *n.*, clothing.

rain, *n.*, water dropping from the clouds; *v.i.*, to fall in drops from the clouds; to fall like rain.

rain'bow, *n.*, an arc of a circle, coloured prismatically, seen in a rain-cloud opposite to the sun.

rain'drop, *n.*, a drop of rain.

rained, *p.p.*, rain.

rain'fall, *n.*, the amount of rain that falls in a certain time.

rain'-gauge, *n.*, an instrument for measuring rainfall.

rain'ier, *adj.*, *comp.* of rainy.

rain'iest, *adj.*, *super.* of rainy.

rain'iness, *n.*, the state of being rainy.

rain'ing, *pr.p.*, rain.

rain'less, *adj.*, without rain.

rain'-proof, *adj.*, impermeable by rain.

rain'-water, *n.*, water fallen from the clouds as rain.

rain'y, *adj.*, showery; abounding with rain.

rais'able, *adj.*, capable of being raised.

raise, *v.t.*, to elevate.
raised, *p.p.*, raise.
rais'er, *n.*, one who, or that which, raises.
rai'sin, *n.*, a dried grape.
rais'ing, *pr.p.*, raise.
ra'ja, *n.*, a Hindu chief or prince.
ra'jah, *n.*, *i.q.* raja.
Rajpoot', *n.*, an inhabitant of Rajputana, in India.
rake, *n.*, a toothed gardening and farming tool; a dissolute fellow; a slope or inclination (a naut. term); *v.t.*, to apply a rake to; *v.i.*, to lead a dissolute life; to slope.
raked, *p.p.*, rake.
rakee', *n.*, an Oriental spirituous liquor.
rake'-hell, *n.*, a dissolute fellow; a profligate.
ra'ker, *n.*, one who, or that which, rakes.
ra'king, *pr.p.*, rake; *adj.*, inclined; enfilading; scouring or cannonading along a line from end to end.
ra'kish, *adj.*, dissolute; having a rake or inclination of the masts forward or aft (*naut.*).
ra'kishness, *n.*, the quality of being rakish.
râle, *n.*, a noise made by air passing through mucus in the lungs.
ral'lied, *p.p.*, rally.
ral'lier, *n.*, one who rallies.
ral'ly, *v.t.*, to re-unite; to tease; *v.i.*, to re-form in order; *n.*, a stand made by retreating troops.
ral'lying, *pr.p.*, rally.
ram, *n.*, the male of the sheep; a battering-ram; the piston of a hydraulic press; *v.t.*, to strike with a ram; to force in.
Ramadan', *n.*, the ninth month of the Mohammedan year; the great annual Mohammedan fast.
ram'ble, *n.*, a roving or aimless excursion; *v.i.*, to wander; to think or talk incoherently.
ram'bled, *p.p.*, ramble.
ram'bler, *n.*, one who rambles; a plant which grows without restraint; a climbing rose or other plant.
ram'bling, *p.p.*, ramble; *adj.*, straggling; confused in language or ideas; *n.*, a ramble.
ram'ekin, *n.*, a mixture of eggs and cheese, etc., cooked and served on bread.
ra'meous, *adj.*, bel. to, or growing on, a branch.
ramifica'tion, *n.*, the act of ramifying; a subordinate branch.
ram'ified, *p.p.*, ramify.
ram'iform, *adj.*, shaped like a branch.
ram'ify, *v.i.*, to branch out; to be subdivided.
ram'ifying, *pr.p.*, ramify.
rammed, *p.p.*, ram.
ram'mer, *n.*, one who, or that which, rams; a ramrod.
ram'ming, *pr.p.*, ram.
ram'mish, *adj.*, ramlike; stinking; lascivious.
ram'my, *adj.*, *i.q.* rammish.
ra'mous, *adj.*, branched; full of branches.
ramp, *v.i.*, to climb, as a plant; to rear on the hind-legs; to rage.
rampa'cious, *adj.*, boisterous.
rampage', *v.i.*, to prance about furiously; *n.*, a state of passion or excitement.
rampaged', *p.p.*, rampage.
rampa'ging, *pr.p.*, rampage.
ram'pancy, *n.*, the state of being rampant.
ram'pant, *adj.*, rank in growth; standing on one hind-leg, as if attacking (*her.*).
ram'part, *n.*, a bulwark or defence; a raised fortification round a place.
ramped, *p.p.*, ramp.
ramp'ing, *pr.p.*, ramp
ram'pion, *n.*, a perennial bell-flower.
ram'rod, *n.*, a rod for ramming down the charge of a firearm.
ram'shackle, *adj.*, rickety; ill-made.
ram'sons, *n. pl.*, wild garlic.
ram'ulous, *adj.*, having many small branches.
ra'mus, *n.*, branch (*Lat.*).
ran, *p.t.* of to run.
rances'cent, *adj.*, becoming rancid or sour.
ranch, *n.*, an Amer. horse or cattle farm.
ranch'man, *n.*, a man employed on a ranch.
ran'cho, *n.*, *i.q.* ranch.
ran'cid, *adj.*, having a rank smell (said of oils and fats).
rancid'ity, *n.*, the quality of being rancid.
ran'cidness, *n.*, *i.q.* rancidity.
ran'corous, *adj.*, full of rancour.
ran'corously, *adv.*, in a rancorous manner.
ran'co(u)r, *n.*, spite; malice; malignant hatred.
rand, *n.*, a sort of beefsteak; a thin inner sole for a shoe; highlands.
randan', *n.*, a four-oared boat with three rowers, the middle rower pulling two oars.
ran'dom, *adj.*, fortuitous; *n.*, a course without direction.
ra'nee, *n.*, an Indian princess, wife of a rajah.
rang, *p.t.* of to ring.
range, *v.t.*, to set in a row or rows; to pass over; *v.i.*, to rank; *n.*, a row; extent; a kitchen grate; a place for rifle practice.

ranged, *p.p.*, range.
ran'ger, *n.*, one who ranges; the keeper of a royal park or forest.
ran'ging, *pr.p.*, range.
ra'nine, *adj.*, rel. to frogs.
rank, *n.*, a row; a line of soldiers; a social class or order; high social position; *v.t.*, to classify; *adj.*, luxuriant; strong-scented; gross.
ranked, *p.p.*, rank.
rank'er, *n.*, a private soldier; one raised from the ranks.
rank'ing, *pr.p.*, rank.
ran'kle, *v.i.*, to fester; to cause bitterness or irritation.
ran'kled, *p.p.*, rankle.
ran'kling, *pr.p.*, rankle.
rank'ly, *adv.*, with vigorous growth; coarsely; grossly.
rank'ness, *n.*, the state of being rank.
ran'sack, *v.t.*, to rummage; to search thoroughly; to strip by plundering.
ran'sacked, *p.p.*, ransack.
ran'sacker, *n.*, one who ransacks.
ran'sacking, *pr.p.*, ransack.
ran'som, *n.*, price of freedom from captivity; redemption; *v.t.*, to pay a ransom for.
ran'somed, *p.p.*, ransom.
ran'somer, *n.*, one who ransoms.
ran'soming, *pr.p.*, ransom.
ran'somless, *adj.*, free from ransom.
rant, *n.*, bombast; *v.i.*, to use extravagant language; to declaim.
rant'ed, *p.p.*, rant.
rant'er, *n.*, one who rants; a noisy preacher.
Rant'erism, *n.*, the doctrines and practices of the Ranters, a fanatical sect which sprang up in 1645.
rant'ing, *pr.p.*, rant.
rant'y, *adj.*, boisterous.
Ranun'culus, *n.*, one of the crows-foot genus of plants.
rap, *n.*, a quick, smart knock; a small thing of little value; *v.i.*, to knock; *v.t.*, to give a knock to; to affect with ecstasy.
rapa'cious, *adj.*, wont to seize property violently; grasping.
rapa'ciously, *adv.*, in a rapacious manner.
rapa'ciousness, *n.*, disposition to plunder or oppress.
rapac'ity, *n.*, the quality of being rapacious.
rape, *n.*, snatching by force; carnal intercourse procured by violence; refuse skins of raisins; a plant of the cabbage family; a division of the county of Sussex
Raph'aelism, *n.*, the methods and principles of Raffaelle.
Raph'aelite, *n.*, an artist who adopts the methods and principles of Raffaelle.
Raph'aelitism, *n.*, *i.q.* Raphaelism.
ra'phe, *n.*, a suture or line of junction, in botany and zoology.
raph'ides, *n. pl.*, needle-shaped crystals occurring in plant-cells.
raph'igraph, *n.*, an obsolete typewriter for the blind.
rap'id, *adj.*, very swift; *n.*, a swift current in a river where the bed slopes down steeply.
rapid'ity, *n.*, swiftness.
rap'idly, *adv.*, with great swiftness.
ra'pier, *n.*, a sword used only in thrusting.
rap'ine, *n.*, the act of plundering.
rapparee', *n.*, a wild Irish robber.
rapped, *p.p.*, rap.
rappee', *n.*, a strong kind of snuff.
rap'per, *n.*, one who raps; a door-knocker.
rap'ping, *pr.p.*, rap.
rapport', *n.*, correspondence; harmony (*Fr.*).
rapprochement, *n.*, a reconciliation (*Fr.*).
rapscal'lion, *n.*, a low, mean fellow.
rapt, *adj.*, in an ecstasy.
rap'tor, *n.*, one of the Raptores, or birds of prey.
rapto'rial, *adj.*, living by rapine; pert. to the Raptores or birds of prey.
rapto'rious, *adj.*, *i.q.* raptorial.
rap'ture, *n.*, extreme joy.
rap'turous, *adj.*, ecstatic; extremely delightful.
ra'ra a'vis, *n.*, a rare bird = a very uncommon thing (*Lat.*).
rare, *adj.*, uncommon; sparse; excellent.
rarefac'tion, *n.*, expansion by separation of constituent particles.
rar'efiable, *adj.*, capable of being rarefied.
rar'efied, *p.p.*, rarefy.
rar'efy, *v.i.*, to become less dense; *v.t.*, to make less dense.
rar'efying, *pr.p.*, rarefy.
rare'ly, *adv.*, seldom; in a rare manner or degree.
rare'ness, *n.*, uncommonness; tenuity; value due to scarcity.
rar'er, *adj.*, *comp.* of rare.
rar'ity, *n.*, the quality of being rare; a thing valued for its excellence or scarcity.
ras'cal, *n.*, a scoundrel; a rogue; a lean deer.
rascal'ity, *n.*, mean trickiness; dishonesty.
rascal'lion, *n.*, *i.q.* rapscallion.
ras'cally, *adj.*, like a rascal; vile.

rase, *v.t.*, to graze; to erase; to raze or level with the ground.

rash, *n.*, an eruption of red spots or patches on the skin; *adj.*, precipitate; acting without caution.

rash'er, *n.*, a slice of bacon; *adj.*, *comp.* of rash.

rash'ly, *adv.*, in a rash manner.

rash'ness, *n.*, precipitation; a rash act.

raso'rial, *adj.*, pert. to the Rasores or gallinaceous birds (scratchers).

rasp, *n.*, a coarse kind of file; *v.t.*, to rub with something rough; to vex.

rasp'atory, *n.*, a surgeon's rasp.

rasp'berry, *n.*, a well-known British fruit.

rasped, *p.p.*, rasp.

rasp'er, *n.*, a scraper; one who, or that which, rasps.

rasp'ing, *pr.p.*, rasp.

ra'sure, *n.*, the act of scraping or erasing.

rat, *n.*, a small rodent mammal; a political deserter; *v.i.*, to catch rats; to desert a party from selfish motives.

ratafi'a, *n.*, a spirit flavoured with the kernels of cherries, peaches, etc.

ratan', *n.*, *i.q.* rattan.

rat'any, *n.*, a Peruvian shrub used in medicine.

ratch, *n.*, a rack-bar with teeth in which a pawl falls, used to prevent the motion of a machine from being reversed.

ratch'et, *n.*, a little bar which catches in the teeth of a toothed wheel and holds it; a pawl.

ratch'il, *n.*, gravelly stone.

rate, *n.*, a proportion or standard; degree as regards speed or other variable; a local tax; *v.t.*, to fix the value of; to scold.

rateabil'ity, *n.*, the quality of being rateable.

rate'able, *adj.*, liable to taxation; reckoned according to a certain rate.

rate'ably, *adv.*, by rate or proportion.

rate'-book, *n.*, a book containing the rate-accounts.

ra'ted, *p.p.*, rate.

rate'payer, *n.*, one who pays rates.

rate'payers, *n.*, pl. of ratepayer.

ra'ter, *n.*, one who rates.

rath'er, *adv.*, sooner; more readily or properly; somewhat.

ratifica'tion, *n.*, the act of ratifying; authorization.

rat'ified, *p.p.*, ratify.

rat'ifier, *n.*, one who ratifies.

rat'ify, *v.t.*, to confirm; to make valid.

rat'ifying, *pr.p.*, ratify.

ra'ting, *pr.p.*, rate; *n.*, the act of estimating; rank, esp. of men and ships in the Navy.

ra'tio, *n.*, the measure of a quantity in terms of another, often expressed as a fraction.

ratioc'inate, *v.i.*, to reason; to argue.

ratiocina'tion, *n.*, the process of deductive reasoning.

ratioc'inative, *adj.*, characterized by ratiocination.

ra'tion, *n.*, a soldier or sailor's daily allowance of food; *v.t.*, to supply with rations.

ra'tional, *adj.*, endowed with reason; agreeable to reason; *n.*, an algebraical or arithmetical quantity expressible in finite terms.

rationa'le, *n.*, a statement of reasons or principles.

ra'tionalism, *n.*, a system of religious opinions which denies inspiration or revelation.

ra'tionalist, *n.*, one who adheres to rationalism.

rationalist'ic, *adj.*, rel. to rationalism.

rational'ity, *n.*, reasonableness.

ra'tionalize, *v.t.*, to interpret as a rationalist; *v.i.*, to act as a rationalist.

ra'tionally, *adv.*, reasonably; sensibly.

rat'lin, *n.*, a small rope used in rope-ladders in the rigging of a ship.

ratoon', *n.*, a sprout from the root of a cut sugar-cane.

rats'bane, *n.*, poison for rats.

rat'-tail, *n.*, a disease of horses affecting the hair of the tail.

rattan', *n.*, a cane or walking-stick made of the flexible stem of an Eastern palm; the continuous roll of a drum.

rat'ted, *p.p.*, rat.

ratteen', *n.*, a thick twilled woollen stuff

rat'ten, *v.t.*, to destroy or take away maliciously tools or machinery.

rat'ter, *n.*, one who catches rats: a terrier.

rat'ting, *pr.p.* rat.

rat'tle, *v.i.*, to make a rapid series of sharp sounds; *n.*, a rapid succession of sharp sounds; an instrument for producing a rattling sound; a chatterer.

rat'tled, *p.p.*, rattle.

rat'tler, *n.*, a babbler; a rattlesnake.

rat'tlesnake, *n.*, a venomous American snake with a rattling tail.

rat'tling, *pr.p.*, rattle.

rau'city, *n.*, hoarseness; harshness of sound.

rau'cous, *adj.*, hoarse; harsh.

rav'age, *n.*, devastation; *v.t.*, to lay waste by force.

rav'aged, *p.p.*, ravage.

rav'ager, *n.*, one who ravages.

rav'aging, *pr.p.*, ravage.

rave, *v.i.*, to be delirious; to speak enthusiastically.

raved, *p.p.*, rave.

rav'el, *v.t.*, to unweave; to disentangle; to make intricate.

rave'lin, *n.*, a separate work in fortification, triangular in plan.

rav'el(l)ed, *p.p.*, ravel.

rav'el(l)ing, *pr.p.*, ravel; *n.*, a thread detached in the process of untwisting.

ra'ven, *n.*, a large black bird of the crow family; *adj.*, black.

rav'en, *n.*, prey; *v.i.*, to prey with rapacity; *v.t.*, to devour.

rav'ened, *p.p.*, raven.

rav'ener, *n.*, one who ravens.

rav'ening, *pr.p.*, raven.

rav'enous, *adj.*, furiously hungry.

rav'enously, *adv.*, in a ravenous manner.

ra'ver, *n.*, one who raves.

rav'in, *n.* and *v.*, *i.q.* rav'en.

ravine', *n.*, a deep, narrow gorge; a gully.

ra'ving, *pr.p.*, rave; *adj.*, mad; *n.*, incoherent talk.

rav'ish, *v.t.*, to seize and carry away by force; to commit a rape upon; to enrapture.

rav'ished, *p.p.*, ravish

rav'isher, *n.*, one who ravishes.

rav'ishing, *pr.p.*, ravish; *adj.*, very delightful.

rav'ishment, *n.*, ecstasy.

raw, *adj.*, uncooked; not manufactured; not diluted; inexperienced; cold and damp; *n.*, a sore place.

raw'-boned, *adj.*, lean; gaunt.

raw'-head, *n.*, a spectre to frighten children with: a death's head.

raw'ish, *adj.*, somewhat raw.

raw'ness, *n.*, the state of being raw.

ray, *n.*, a line of light; a diverging radius; a radiating spine in the fin of a fish; one of a genus of fishes to which the skate belongs.

ra'yah, *n.*, in Turkey, a non-Mohammedan who pays the poll-tax.

rayed, *adj.*, adorned with rays.

ray'less, *adj.*, dark.

raze, *v.t.*, to graze; to level with the ground. Also *rase*.

razed, *p.p.*, raze.

razee', *n.*, a ship of war cut down to a smaller size.

ra'zing, *pr.p.*, raze.

ra'zor, *n.*, a keen knife used in shaving.

ra'zor-bill, *n.*, the common auk.

reabsorb', *v.t.*, to absorb again.

reabsorp'tion, *n.*, the act of reabsorbing.

reach, *v.t.*, to touch by stretching towards; to arrive at; to give with the hand; *v.i.*, to extend; *n.*, the distance one can reach; scope; a straight portion of a river between bends.

reach'able, *adj.*, within reach.

reached, *p.p.*, reach.

reach'er, *n.*, one who reaches.

reach'ing, *pr.p.*, reach.

react', *v.i.*, to resist action by an opposing force; to act mutually upon each other.

reac'tion, *n.*, the resistence made by a body to anything tending to change its state; the mutual action of chemical agents on each other; a retrograde tendency; depression after excitement; response to a stimulus.

reac'tionary, *adj.*, rel. to reaction.

react'ive, *adj.*, able to react.

read, *v.t.*, to peruse; to understand; to study; to explain; *v.i.*, to stand written or printed; to study.

read, *p.p.*, read.

read'able, *adj.*, worth reading; legible.

readdress', *v.t.*, to address again; to correct a wrong address.

readdressed' *p.p.*, readdress.

readdress'ing, *pr.p.*, readdress.

read'er, *n.*, one who reads; a reading-book; a corrector of the press; one who reads lessons, lectures, etc.

read'ier, *adj.*, *comp.* of ready.

read'iest, *adj.*, *super.* of ready.

read'ily, *adv.*, quickly; willingly.

read'iness, *n.*, the state of being ready; due preparation; alacrity.

read'ing, *p.p.*, read; *adj.*, given to the study of books; *n.*, the act of one who reads; a particular version of a passage; the recital of a Bill in Parliament.

read'ing-book, *n.*, a school-book containing exercises in reading.

read'ing-room, *n.*, a room appropriated to books, newspapers, etc., for readers.

readjust', *v.t.*, to adjust again.

readjust'ed, *p.p.*, readjust.

readjust'ing, *pr.p.*, readjust.

readjust'ment, *n.*, the act of readjusting.

readmis'sion, *n.*, the act of admitting again.

readmit', *v.t.*, to admit again.

read'y, *adj.*, prepared; prompt: willing.

read'y-made, *adj.*, kept in stock ready for use.
reaffirm', *v.t.*, to affirm again.
reaffor'est, *v.t.*, to convert again into a forest.
rea'gent, *n.*, anything that produces a reaction.
re'al, *adj.*, actual; not imaginary; pert. to things that are permanent and immovable, as lands and tenements.
real'gar, *n.*, red orpiment; a brilliant red pigment.
re'alism, *n.*, the principles of a realist.
re'alist, *n.*, in metaphysics, one who holds that external objects exist apart from our conceptions of them; in art and letters, one who reproduces nature or describes real life exactly as it appears to him.
realist'ic, *adj.*, rel. to realism.
real'ity, *n.*, the quality of being real; truth; fact.
re'alizable, *adj.*, capable of being realized.
realiza'tion, *n.*, the act of realizing.
re'alize, *v.t.*, to make real; to accomplish; to gain; to convert into money.
re'alized, *p.p.*, realize.
re'alizing, *pr.p.*, realize.
re'ally, *adv.*, actually; in truth.
realm, *n.*, a kingdom, region, or sphere.
re'alty, *n.*, real property; lands, tenements, etc.
ream, *n.*, a package of paper, containing 20 quires; *v.t.*, to enlarge the bore, as of a cannon.
rean'imate, *v.t.*, to resuscitate.
rean'imated, *p.p.*, reanimate.
rean'imating, *pr.p.*, reanimate.
reanima'tion, *n.*, the act of reanimating.
reannex', *v.t.*, to annex again.
reannexa'tion, *n.*, the act of annexing again.
reap, *v.t.*, to cut down and gather, as wheat, etc.; to receive as a reward.
reaped, *p.p.*, reap.
reap'er, *n.*, one who reaps; a reaping-machine.
reap'ing, *pr.p.*, reap.
reap'ing-hook, *n.*, a sickle.
reappear', *v.i.*, to appear again.
reappear'ance, *n.*, a new appearance.
reappoint', *v.t.*, to appoint again.
reappoint'ing, *pr.p.*, reappoint.
reappoint'ment, *n.*, a renewed appointment.
reappor'tion, *v.t.*, to apportion again.
rear, *n.*, the part behind; the background; *adj.*, in the rear; hindermost; *v.t.*, to erect; to educate; to breed; *v.i.*, to rise on the hind legs.
rear-ad'miral, *n.*, an admiral of the third degree or rank.
reared, *p.p.*, rear.
rear'er, *n.*, one who rears.
rear'-guard, *n.*, part of an army which follows the main body to protect it.
rear'ing, *pr.p.*, rear; *n.*, the act of one who rears.
rear'mouse, *n.*, the leather-winged bat.
re-arrange', *v.t.*, to arrange again.
re-arranged', *p.p.*, re-arrange.
re-arrang'ing, *pr.p.*, re-arrange.
re-arrange'ment, *n.*, a second arrangement.
rear'ward, *n.*, the rear-guard; *adj.* and *adv.*, towards the rear.
reascend', *v.i.*, to ascend again.
rea'son, *n.*, a cause acting on the mind; an explanation; a faculty of the mind; fairness; *v.i.*, to argue; *v.t.*, to examine argumentatively.
rea'sonable, *adj.*, rational; agreeable to reason; equitable.
rea'sonableness, *n.*, the quality of being reasonable.
rea'sonably, *adv.*, in a reasonable manner; moderately.
rea'soned, *p.p.*, reason.
rea'soner, *n.*, one who reasons or argues.
rea'soning, *pr.p.*, reason; *n.*, the act of exercising the reason; arguments, proofs, or reasons.
reassem'ble, *v.t.*, to collect again; *v.i.*, to meet together again.
reassert', *v.t.*, to assert again.
re-assess', *v.t.*, to assess again.
reassign', *v.t.*, to assign again.
reassign'ing, *pr.p.*, reassign.
reassign'ment, *n.*, a renewed assignment
reassume', *v.t.*, to resume; to take again.
reassu'rance, *n.*, confirmation repeated; reinsurance.
reassure', *v.t.*, to restore courage to; to reinsure.
reast'y, *adj.*, rusty and rancid (salt meat).
rebaptize', *v.t.*, to baptize a second time.
rebate', *v.t.*, to make a discount or deduction from; to blunt.
re'bate, *n.*, *i.q.* rebatement.
reba'ted, *p.p.*, rebate.
rebate'ment, *n.*, diminution in price.
reba'ting, *pr.p.*, rebate.
re'beck, *n.*, a sort of Moorish violin.
reb'el, *n.*, one who revolts; *adj.*, rebellious.
rebel', *v.i.*, to revolt; to refuse to obey.
rebelled', *p.p.*, rebel.

rebel'ling, *pr.p.*, rebel

rebell'ion, *n.*, act of rebelling; refusal to obey lawful authority; an armed rising against a government.

rebell'ious, *adj.*, characterized by rebellion.

rebound', *v.i.*, to spring back; *n.*, resilience; a spring back.

re-bound', *adj.*, bound again.

rebound'ed, *p.p.*, rebound.

rebound'ing, *pr.p.*, rebound.

rebuff', *n.*, a repulse; *v.t.*, to repel the advances of.

rebuffed', *p.p.*, rebuff.

rebuff'ing, *pr.p.*, rebuff.

rebuild', *v.t.*, to build again.

rebuild'ing, *pr.p.*, rebuild.

rebuilt', *p.p.*, rebuild.

rebuke', *v.t.*, to reprimand; *n.*, reproof.

rebuked', *p.p.*, rebuke.

rebu'ker, *n.*, one who rebukes.

rebu'king, *pr.p.*, rebuke.

re'bus, *n.*, a set of words expressed by figures or pictures the names of which resemble in sound the words or syllables of which it is composed.

rebut', *v.t.*, to refute.

rebut'tal, *n.*, the act of rebutting; confutation.

rebut'ted, *p.p.*, rebut.

rebut'ter, *n.*, the answer of a defendant to the surrejoinder of a plaintiff.

rebut'ting, *pr.p.*, rebut.

recal'citrant, *adj.*, refractory.

recal'citrate, *v.i.*, to be refractory.

recal'citrated, *p.p.*, recalcitrate.

recal'citrating, *pr.p.*, recalcitrate.

recalcitra'tion, *n.*, act of recalcitrating; refractoriness.

recalesce', *v.i.*, to grow warm again.

recales'cence, *n.*, renewed warmth.

recall', *v.t.*, to call back; to revoke; to bring back to memory; *n.*, a calling back.

recalled', *p.p.*, recall.

recall'ing, *pr.p.*, recall.

recant', *v.t.* and *i.*, to unsay; to retract.

recanta'tion, *n.*, a declaration contradicting a previous one.

recant'ed, *p.p.*, recant.

recant'er, *n.*, one who recants.

recant'ing, *pr.p.*, recant.

recapit'ulate, *v.t.*, to repeat or summarize.

recapit'ulated, *p.p.*, recapitulate.

recapit'ulating, *pr.p.*, recapitulate.

recapitula'tion, *n.*, the act of recapitulating; a summary.

recapit'ulatory, *adj.*, containing recapitulation.

recap'tion, *n.*, the re-taking, without force or violence, of one's property from a person illegally detaining it.

recap'ture, *n.*, the act of re-taking; *v.t.*, to re-take.

recast', *v.t.*, to mould anew.

recede', *v.i.*, to move back; *v.t.*, to yield to a former possessor.

rece'ded, *p.p.*, recede.

rece'ding, *pr.p.*, recede.

receipt', *n.*, the act of receiving; a recipe; a plan or scheme; a written acknowledgment of something received; *v.t.*, to give a receipt for.

receipt'-book, *n.*, a book containing receipt-forms.

receipt'ed, *p.p.*, receipt.

receipt'ing, *pr.p.*, receipt.

receiv'able, *adj.*, such as may be received.

receive', *v.t.*, to accept; to contain; to take from a thief, knowing the thing received to have been stolen.

received', *p.p.*, receive.

receiv'er, *n.*, one who receives; a person appointed to receive rents, profits, etc.; a person who takes stolen goods from a thief; a vessel for receiving liquids or gases.

receiv'ership, *n.*, the office of a receiver.

receiv'ing, *pr.p.*, receive.

re'cency, *n.*, *i.q.* recentness.

recen'sion, *n.*, a critical revision of a text.

re'cent, *adj.*, of late origin; modern; fresh.

re'cently, *adv.*, lately; not long since.

re'centness, *n.*, the state of being recent.

recep'tacle, *n.*, a repository.

receptac'ular, *adj.*, pert. to a receptacle.

receptibil'ity, *n.*, receivableness.

recep'tible, *adj.*, capable of being received.

recep'tion, *n.*, a receiving; welcome; an entertainment.

recep'tive, *adj.*, able to take in or contain.

receptiv'ity, *n.*, the quality of being receptive.

recess', *n.*, a moving back; a public holiday or suspension of business; a niche; an alcove; *v.t.*, to make a recess in.

recessed', *p.p.*, recess; *adj.*, having a recess or recesses.

reces'sion, *n.*, the act of receding.

reces'sional, *adj.*, pert. to recession.

Rech'abite, *n.*, a member of a friendly society of total abstainers.

recharge', *v.t.*, to charge again.

réchauffé, *n.*, a warmed-up dish; a concoction of old materials.

recheat', *n.*, a call to hounds on a huntsman's horn.

recherché, *adj.*, exquisite; choice (*Fr.*).

rechoose', *v.t.*, to choose again; to make a second choice.

recid'ivist, *n.*, a relapsed criminal.

rec'ipe, *n.*, a prescription or receipt for making any mixture.

recip'iency, *n.*, act or capacity of receiving.

recip'ient, *n.*, one who receives; *adj.*, receiving.

recip'rocal, *adj.*, mutual; inverse; *n.*, a quantity which results from dividing unity by another, to which it is said to be reciprocal.

reciprocal'ity, *n.*, the quality of being reciprocal.

recip'rocally, *adv.*, mutually; inversely.

recip'rocate, *v.i.*, to alternate; *v.t.*, to give and return mutually.

recip'rocated, *p.p.*, reciprocate.

recip'rocating, *pr.p.*, reciprocate; *adj.*, moving backwards and forwards alternately.

reciproca'tion, *n.*, interchange of acts; alternation.

reciproc'ity, *n.*, the character of being reciprocal; equal rights mutually yielded and enjoyed, esp. commercial privileges between two nations.

reci'sion, *n.*, the act of cutting off.

reci'tal, *n.*, the act of reciting; that which is recited; a narrative; a musical entertainment given by a single performer.

recita'tion, *n.*, the act of reciting; a composition learned by heart and delivered before an audience.

recitative', *n.*, a musical recitation or declamatory piece.

recitati'vo, *n.*, *i.q.* recitative (*It.*).

recite', *v.t.*, to repeat from memory; to narrate; *v.i.*, to rehearse a composition committed to memory.

reci'ted, *p.p.*, recite.

reci'ter, *n.*, one who recites; a narrator.

reci'ting, *pr.p.*, recite.

reck, *v.i.*, to heed.

recked, *p.p.*, reck.

reck'ing, *pr.p.*, reck.

reck'less, *adj.*, heedless of consequences.

reck'lessly, *adv.*, in a reckless manner.

reck'lessness, *n.*, the quality of being reckless.

reck'on, *v.t.*, to count; to calculate; *v.i.*, to compute; to suppose.

reck'oned, *p.p.*, reckon.

reck'oner, *n.*, one who reckons; a help in reckoning.

reck'oning, *pr.p.*, reckon; *n.*, calculation; charges.

reclaim', *v.t.*, to claim back; to bring under cultivation; to reform.

reclaim'able, *adj.*, capable of being reclaimed.

reclaimed', *p.p.*, reclaim.

reclaim'ing, *pr.p.*, reclaim.

reclama'tion, *n.*, the act of reclaiming.

réclame, *n.*, an advertisement; a puff (*Fr.*).

rec'linate, *adj.*, (of a leaf) bent downward.

reclina'tion, *n.*, a surgical operation in the treatment of cataract.

recline', *v.t.*, to lay down to rest; *v.i.*, to repose in a recumbent position.

reclined', *p.p.*, recline.

recli'ner, *n.*, one who reclines.

recli'ning, *pr.p.*, recline; *adj.*, leaning back or sideways.

reclose', *v.t.*, to close again.

recluse', *n.*, a person who lives in seclusion; a hermit.

reclu'sion, *n.*, retirement from the world.

reclu'sive, *adj.*, affording retirement.

recoal', *v.i.*, to fill up bunkers with coal.

recogni'tion, *n.*, the act of recognizing; acknowledgment.

rec'ognizable, *adj.*, capable of being recognized.

recog'nizance, *n.*, a personal legal obligation entered into under a penalty; a token.

rec'ognize, *v.t.*, to perceive the identity of; to acknowledge.

rec'ognized, *p.p.*, recognize.

rec'ognizer, *n.*, one who recognizes.

rec'ognizing, *pr.p.*, recognize.

rec'ognizor, *n.*, one who gives recognizances.

recoil', *v.i.*, to fall back after an advance or forward impetus; *n.*, a rebound.

recoiled', *p.p.*, recoil.

recoil'er, *n.*, one who recoils.

recoil'ing, *pr.p.*, recoil; *n.*, *i.q.* recoilment.

recoil'ment, *n.*, the act of recoiling.

recoin', *v.t.*, to melt and mint anew.

recoin'age, *n.*, the act of recoining.

recollect', *v.t.*, to bring back to the mind; to remember.

re-collect', *v.t.*, to collect what has been scattered.

recollect'ed, *p.p.*, recollect.

re-collect'ed, *p.p.*, re-collect.

recollect'ing, *pr.p.*, recollect.

re-collect'ing, *pr.p.*, re-collect.

recollec'tion, *n.*, remembrance.

re-collec'tion, *n.*, the act of collecting what has been scattered.

recollect'ive, *adj.*, having the power of recollection.

recombina'tion, *n.*, combination for the second time.

recombine', *v.t.*, to combine again.

recommence', *v.t.*, to begin again.

recommenced', *p.p.*, recommence.

recommenc'ing, *pr.p.*, recommence.

recommend', *v.t.*, to put favourably before another.

recommend'able, *adj.*, worthy of recommendation.

recommenda'tion, *n.*, a favourable representation; that which recommends.

recommend'atory, *adj.*, serving to recommend.

recommend'ed, *p.p.*, recommend.

recommend'er, one who recommends.

recommend'ing, *pr.p.*, recommend.

recommit', *v.t.*, to commit again (to prison); to refer again (to a committee).

recommit'ted, *p.p.*, recommit.

recommit'ting, *pr.p.*, recommit.

recommit'ment, *n.*, a second commitment; a reference.

recommit'tal, *n.*, *i.q.* recommitment.

rec'ompense, *v.t.*, to reward; to compensate; *n.*, a reward; a compensation.

rec'ompensed, *p.p.*, recompense.

rec'ompensing, *pr.p.*, recompense.

recompose', *v.t.*, to compose again.

recomposed', *p.p.*, recompose.

recompos'ing, *pr.p.*, recompose.

recomposi'tion, *n.*, the act of bringing separated elements together again.

rec'oncilable, *adj.*, capable of being brought again to friendly feelings, or made to agree.

rec'oncilably, *adv.*, harmoniously; consistently.

rec'oncile, *v.t.*, to restore to friendship after estrangement; to harmonize.

rec'onciled, *p.p.*, reconcile.

rec'oncilement, *n.*, renewal of friendship.

rec'onciler, *n.*, one who reconciles.

reconcilia'tion, *n.*, the act of reconciling enemies; the act of making consistent.

reconcil'iatory, *adj.*, tending to reconcile.

rec'onciling, *pr.p.*, reconcile.

rec'ondite, *adj.*, abstruse.

reconduct', *v.t.*, to conduct back.

recon'naissance, *n.*, a preliminary survey of an enemy's position.

reconnoi'tre, *v.t.*, to make a preliminary military survey of.

reconnoi'tred, *p.p.*, reconnoitre.

reconnoi'tring, *pr.p.*, reconnoitre.

recon'quer, *v.t.*, to conquer again; to recover.

reconsid'er, *v.t.*, to consider again.

reconsidera'tion, *n.*, the act of reconsidering.

reconsid'ered, *p.p.*, reconsider.

reconsid'ering, *pr.p.*, reconsider.

reconstruct', *v.t.*, to construct again.

reconstruct'ed, *p.p.*, reconstruct.

reconstruct'ing, *pr.p.*, reconstruct.

reconstruc'tion, *n.*, the act of constructing again.

reconvert', *v.t.*, to convert again.

reconvey', *v.t.*, to transfer to a former owner or place.

reconvey'ance, *n.*, the act of reconveying.

recop'y, *v.t.*, to copy again.

record', *v.t.*, to write down for preservation; to note.

rec'ord, *n.*, something written down to preserve the memory of anything; a public document; the highest achievement up till now.

record'ed, *p.p.*, record

record'er, *n.*, one who records; a borough or city chief judge; an old musical instrument like a flageolet; a registering apparatus.

record'ing, *pr.p.*, record; *adj.*, registering.

recount', *v.t.*, to narrate; to count again; *n.*, a counting over again.

recount'ed, *p.p.*, recount.

recount'ing, *pr.p.*, recount.

recoup', *v.t.*, to keep back as a set-off; to indemnify (oneself).

recouped', *p.p.*, recoup.

recoup'ing, *pr.p.*, recoup.

recoup'ment, *n.*, the act of recouping.

recourse', *n.*, a going to, as for protection or help.

recov'er, *v.t.*, to regain; *v.i.*, to grow well again; to regain a former condition.

re-cov'er, *v.t.*, to cover again.

recov'erable, *adj.*, capable of being recovered.

recov'ered, *p.p.*, re-cover.

re-cov'ered, *p.p.*, re-cover.

recov'erer, *n.*, one who recovers.

recov'ering, *pr.p.*, recover.

re-cov'ering, *pr.p.*, re-cover.

recov'ery, *n.*, the act or power of getting again; restoration from sickness or any low condition.

rec'reancy, *n.*, cowardice.

rec'reant, *adj.*, cowardly; false; *n.*, one who yields basely.

rec'reate, *v.t.*, to reanimate; to amuse; *v.i.*, to take recreation.

re-create', *v.t.*, to form anew.

rec'reated, *p.p.*, recreate.

re-crea'ted, *p.p.*, re-create.

rec'reating, *pr.p.*, recreate.

re-crea'ting, *pr.p.*, re-create.

recrea'tion, *n.*, refreshment of strength and spirits after labour; amusement.

re-crea'tion, *n.*, the act of forming anew.

rec'reative, *adj.*, tending to recreate; diverting.

rec'rement, *n.*, superfluous matter separated from that which is useful; dross.

recremen'tal, *adj.*, drossy.

recrementi'tial, *adj.*, *i.q.* recremental.

recrementi'tious, *adj.*, *i.q.* recremental.

recrim'inate, *v.i.*, to make a counter-accusation.

recrimina'tion, *n.*, a counter-accusation.

recrim'inative, *adj.*, retorting accusation

recrudes'cence, *n.*, growing raw, sore, or painful again; increased severity of a disease after temporary remission; a breaking out afresh.

recruit', *v.t.*, to repair by fresh supplies; to refresh; to supply with new men; *n.*, a newly enlisted soldier.

recruit'ed, *p.p.*, recruit.

recruit'er, *n.*, one who recruits.

recruit'ing, *pr.p.*, recruit; *n.*, the act of enlisting new soldiers.

rec'tal, *adj.*, rel. to the rectum.

rect'angle, *n.*, a right-angled parallelogram.

rect'angled, *adj.*, having right angles.

rectan'gular, *adj.*, right-angled.

rectangular'ity, *n.*, the state of being rectangular.

rec'tifiable, *adj.*, capable of being rectified.

rectifica'tion, *n.*, the operation of rectifying; the process of purifying by distillation.

rec'tified, *p.p.*, rectify

rec'tifier, *n.*, one who rectifies.

rec'tify, *v.t.*, to put right; to refine by distillation.

rec'tifying, *pr.p.*, rectify.

rectilin'eal, *adj.*, bounded by or consisting of straight lines.

rectilin'ear, *adj.*, *i.q.* rectilineal.

rec'titude, *n.*, honesty; uprightness; rightness of principle.

rec'tor, *n.*, a clergyman who possesses parsonage and predial tithes; the head of a college or university, or (in Scotland) a great public school.

rec'torate, *n.*, the office or rank of a rector.

recto'rial, *adj.*, pert. to a rector or rectory.

rec'tory, *n.*, a rector's benefice or dwelling.

rec'tum, *n.*, the part of the large intestine leading to the anus.

recum'bence, *n.*, the state or posture of being recumbent; repose.

recum'bency, *n.*, *i.q.* recumbence.

recum'bent, *adj.*, reclining; lying down.

recu'perate, *v.i.*, to regain health; to recover.

recu'perated, *p.p.*, recuperate.

recu'perating, *pr.p.*, recuperate.

recupera'tion, *n.*, recovery.

recu'perative, *adj.*, tending to recovery.

recu'perator, *n.*, that which revives or restores vigour.

recur', *v.i.*, to return; to occur again.

recurred', *p.p.*, recur.

recur'rence, *n.*, the act of recurring; return; recourse.

recur'rent, *adj.*, returning from time to time.

recur'ring, *pr.p.*, recur; *adj.*, returning again; circulating.

recurv'ate, *adj.*, curved backward or outward.

recurv'ous, *adj.*, bent backward.

rec'usancy, *n.*, the state of being a recusant; nonconformity.

rec'usant, *adj.*, refusing to acknowledge authority; *n.*, one who will not conform to general opinion; a dissenter.

recusa'tion, *n.*, refusal; challenging the impartiality of a judge.

red, *adj.*, of a bright, warm colour; *n.*, one of the primary colours.

rédacteur', *n.*, an editor (*Fr.*).

redac'tion, *n.*, preparation for publication; an editorial staff.

redan', *n.*, a simple field fortification with a salient angle.

red'breast, *n.*, a bird commonly called robin.

red'cap, *n.*, the goldfinch; a kind of spectre haunting Scottish castles.

red'coat, *n.*, a soldier.

red'-cross, *adj.*, wearing the Cross of St. George.

red'den, *v.t.*, to make red; *v.i.*, to become red.

redden'dum, *n.*, a particular clause in a lease.

red'dened, *p.p.*, redden.

red'dening, *pr.p.*, redden.

red'dish, *adj.*, somewhat red.

red'dle, *n.*, red chalk; a pigment used to mark sheep with.

redeem', *v.t.*, to buy back; to ransom; to rescue; to atone for.

redeem'able, *adj.*, capable of being redeemed.

redeemed', *p.p.*, redeem.

redeem'er, *n.*, one who redeems; Our Saviour.

redeem'ing, *pr.p.*, redeem.

redemp'tible, *adj.*, redeemable.

redemp'tion, *n.*, the act of redeeming; the state of being redeemed.

redemp'tionary, *n.*, one who may be redeemed.

redemp'tioner, *n.*, one who, in former times, in order to emigrate to America, sold himself into bondage for a limited time.

redemp'tive, *adj.*, serving to redeem.

Redemp'torist, *n.*, one of a religious congregation which devotes itself to education.

redemp'tory, *adj.*, paid for ransom.

red'-eye, *n.*, the red-eyed vireo or greenlet, an American singing-bird.

red'-gum, *n.*, an infantile eruptive skin disease.

red'-handed, *adj.*, caught in the very act.

red'head, *n.*, a person with red hair; an American duck; the red-headed woodpecker; a kind of milkweed.

redhibi'tion, *n.*, the annulling of a sale and return of the purchase on account of some defect.

redhib'itory, *adj.*, pert. to redhibition.

red'-hot, *adj.*, heated to redness.

red'ingote, *n.*, a long, plain, double-breasted overcoat for women.

redin'tegrate, *v.t.*, to make whole again.

redin'tegrated, *p.p.*, redintegrate.

redin'tegrating, *pr.p.*, redintegrate.

redintegra'tion, *n.*, restoration to a sound state.

redispose', *v.t.*, to dispose again.

redistrib'ute, *v.t.*, to distribute again.

redistribu'tion, *n.*, a new distribution.

red'-letter, *adj.*, marked by red letters; fortunate.

red'ness, *n.*, the quality of being red; red colour.

red'olence, *n.*, fragrance.

red'olency, *n.*, *i.q.* redolence.

red'olent, *adj.*, fragrant.

redoub'le, *v.t.*, to increase by repeated additions; *v.i.*, to become twice as much.

redoubt', *n.*, a small, inclosed field-work.

redoubt'able, *adj.*, formidable valiant.

redoubt'ed, *adj.*, valiant; formidable.

redound', *v.i.*, to flow back as a wave; to contribute.

redound'ed, *p.p.*, redound.

redound'ing, *pr.p.*, redound.

redraw', *v.t.*, to draw again; *v.i.*, to draw a new bill of exchange.

redress', *v.t.*, to remedy; to compensate; *n.*, reparation.

redress'able, *adj.*, capable of being redressed.

redressed', *p.p.*, redress.

redress'ing, *pr.p.*, redress.

redress'ive, *adj.*, affording redress.

red'root, *n.*, the name of many species of American plants with red roots.

red'shank, *n.*, a long-legged bird like a snipe.

red'-short, *adj.*, brittle when red-hot (said of certain kinds of iron).

red'skin, *n.*, a North American Indian.

red'start, *n.*, a singing bird akin to the robin.

red'-streak, *n.*, a sort of apple.

red'-tape, *n.*, excessive regard to routine.

red-ta'pish, *adj.*, pedantically formal.

red-ta'pism, *n.*, excessive officialism.

red'top, *n.*, a valuable pasture grass grown in the U.S.A., called also English grass and herd's grass.

reduce', *v.t.*, to bring to any state or condition; to make less or lower; to subdue; to separate metal from dross; to replace a broken bone or dislocation.

reduced', *p.p.* reduce.

redu'cent, *adj.*, tending to reduce.

redu'cible, *adj.*, capable of being reduced; convertible.

redu'cing, *pr.p.*, reduce.

reduc'tion, *n.*, conversion into another state or denomination; diminution; subjugation; the process of obtaining metal from ore.

reduc'tive, *adj.*, tending to reduce.

redun'dance, *n.*, superfluity; that which is redundant.

redun'dancy, *n.*, *i.q.* redundance.

redun'dant, *adj.*, superfluous.

redu'plicate, *v.t.*, to double; to multiply; to repeat.

redu'plicated, *p.p.*, reduplicate.

redu'plicating, *pr.p.*, reduplicate.

reduplica'tion, *n.*, the act of reduplicating; the repetition of a root, prefix, or initial syllable.

redu'plicative, *adj.*, tending to reduplicate.

red'wing, *n.*, a kind of thrush passing through Britain in winter.

re-ech'o, *v.t.* and *i.*, to reverberate again; *n.*, the echo of an echo.

re-ech'oed, *p.p.*, re-echo.

re-ech'oing, *pr.p.*, re-echo.

reed, *n.*, a tall, broad-leaved plant with a hollow stem; a musical instrument made from a reed; a little tube in a wind instrument; a thin plate of metal which vibrates in a harmonium, etc.; part of a loom.

reed'en, *adj.*, made of reeds.

reed'ing, *n.*, a small, convex, architectural moulding; the milling on the edge of a coin.

reed'less, *adj.*, destitute of reeds.

reed'y, *adj.*, abounding with reeds; resembling a reed; having a thin, harsh tone.

reef, *n.*, a mass of rocks in the sea near the surface; a gold-bearing vein of quartz; part of a sail capable of being drawn together by small ropes; *v.t.*, to reduce the size of a sail by folding part of it.

reefed, *p.p.*, reef.

reef'er, *n.*, one who reefs; a midshipman; a thick, short jacket.

reef'ing, *pr.p.*, reef.

reef'y, *adj.*, abounding in reefs.

reek, *n.*, smoke; vapour; *v.i.*, to smoke; to emit vapour.

reeked, *p.p.*, reek.

reek'ing, *pr.p.*, reek; *adj.*, emitting vapour.

reek'y, *adj.*, smoky.

reel, *n.*, a bobbin; a revolving frame on which a line may be wound; a lively Scottish dance; a staggering motion; *v.i.*, to dance a reel; to stagger in walking.

re-elect', *v.t.*, to elect again.

re-elect'ed, *p.p.*, re-elect.

re-elect'ing, *pr.p.*, re-elect.

re-elec'tion, *n.*, election a second time.

reeled, *p.p.*, reel.

re-el'igible, *adj.*, capable of re-election.

reel'ing, *pr.p.*, reel; *adj.*, staggering.

re-embark', *v.i.* and *t.*, to embark again.

re-embarked', *p.p.*, re-embark.

re-embark'ing, *pr.p.*, re-embark.

re-enact', *v.t.*, to enact again.

re-enact'ment, *n.*, the passing of a law a second time.

re-enforce', *v.t.*, to enforce anew.

re-enforced', *p.p.*, re-enforce.

re-enforce'ment, *n.*, the act of re-enforcing.

re-engage', *v.t.* and *i.*, to engage a second time.

re-en'ter, *v.t.*, to enter again; to cut incisions deeper.

re-en'tered, *p.p.*, re-enter.

re-en'tering, *pr.p.*, re-enter; *adj.*, (of an angle) pointing inwards.

re-en'trance, *n.*, the act of entering again.

re-en'try, *n.*, retaking possession of lands, etc., lately lost.

reer'-mouse, *n.*, a bat.

re-estab'lish, *v.t.*, to establish anew.

re-estab'lished, *p.p.*, re-establish.

re-estab'lishing, *pr.p.*, re-establish.

re-estab'lishment, *n.*, the act of re-establishing.

reeve, *n.*, a bailiff; a steward; a bird, the female of the ruff; *v.t.* and *i.*, to pass a rope through a hole.

reeved, *p.p.*, reeve.

reev'ing, *pr.p.*, reeve.

re-examina'tion, *n.*, a renewed examination.

re-exam'ine, *v.t.*, to examine anew.

re-exam'ined, *p.p.*, re-examine.

re-exam'ining, *pr.p.*, re-examine.

re-export', *v.t.*, to export after having imported.

re-ex'port, *n.*, any commodity re-exported.

refash'ion, *v.t.*, to form into shape a second time.

refash'ioned, *p.p.*, refashion.

refash'ioning, *pr.p.*, refashion.

refec'tion, *n.*, refreshment; a repast.

refec'tive, *adj.*, refreshing.

refec'tory, *n.*, a dining-room, esp. in convents.

refer', *v.t.*, to assign; to trace back; to impute; *v.i.*, to allude; to direct the attention.

ref'erable, *adj.*, considered as belonging.

referee', *n.*, an arbitrator.

ref'erence, *n.*, the act of referring; a note in a book which refers a reader to another passage.

referen'dary, *adj.*, rel. to a referendum.

referen'dum, *n.*, a reference to the people of a measure passed by their representatives, for final approval.

referen'tial, *adj.*, having reference.

referred', *p.p.*, refer.

refer'rer, *n.*, one who refers.

refer'rible, *adj.*, considered as belonging.

refer'ring, *pr.p.*, refer.

refill', *v.t.* and *i.*, to fill again; *n.*, a filling again.

refine', *v.t.*, to purify; to separate from other metals or dross; to give culture to; to polish (the manners).

refined', *p.p.*, refine; *adj.*, elegant in character.

refi'nedly, *adv.*, in a refined manner.

refine'ment, *n.*, the act of refining; elegance of manners, language, etc.; over-nicety.

refi'ner, *n.*, one who refines liquors, metals, sugar, etc.

refi'nery, *n.*, a place for refining metals, sugar, etc.

refi'ning, *pr.p.*, refine.

refit', *v.t.*, to restore after damage.

refit'ted, *p.p.*, refit.

refit'ting, *pr.p.*, refit.

reflect', *v.t.*, to direct back after striking a surface; to give back an image; *v.i.*, to return rays (of light, heat, sound, etc.); to consider seriously; to bring reproach.

reflect'ed, *p.p.*, reflect.

reflect'ible, *adj.*, capable of being reflected.

reflect'ing, *pr.p.*, reflect; *adj.*, throwing back light, as a mirror; meditative.

reflec'tion, *n.*, the act of reflecting or the state of being reflected; an image formed by a reflecting surface; continued meditation; a reproach.

reflect'ive, *adj.*, throwing back rays; exercising reflection; reflexive.

reflect'or, *n.*, one who or that which, reflects; a reflecting telescope.

re'flex, *n.*, an image produced by reflection; *adj.*, having a backward direction; performed involuntarily.

reflex', *v.t.*, to bend back.

reflexed', *adj.*, bent back; *p.p.*, reflex.

reflexibil'ity, *n.*, the quality of being reflexible.

reflex'ible, *adj.*, capable of being reflected or reflexed.

reflex'ive, *adj.*, (of a verb) having as its direct object a pronoun standing for the subject (also applied to pronouns of this type).

reflores'cence, *n.*, a second blossoming.

ref'luence, *n.*, a flowing back.

ref'luent, *adj.*, flowing back; ebbing.

re'flux, *n.*, a flowing back; the ebb; *adj.*, flowing back.

reform', *v.t.*, to amend; *v.i.*, to amend one's behaviour; *n.*, amendment of what is defective or bad; a change in the regulations affecting parliamentary representation.

re-form', *v.t.*, to give another arrangement to.

reform'able, *adj.*, capable of being reformed.

reforma'tion, *n.*, amendment of life, manners, etc.; the religious revolution of the sixteenth century.

re-forma'tion, *n.*, the act of forming again; a second, and different, formation.

reform'ative, *adj.*, tending to reform.

reform'atory, *adj.*, tending to reform; *n.*, an institution for the reformation of young criminals.

reformed', *p.p.*, reform; *adj.*, amended; changed.

reform'er, *n.*, one who reforms; one who promotes political reform; one of those who brought about the Reformation.

reform'ing, *pr.p.*, reform.

reform'ist, *n.*, a political reformer.

refract', *v.t.*, to deflect a ray on passing from one medium to another.

refract'ed, *p.p.*, refract; *adj.*, turned from a direct course.

refract'ing, *pr.p.*, refract; *adj.*, serving to refract.

refrac'tion, *n.*, the act of refracting or state of being refracted.

refract'ive, *adj.*, pert. to refraction.

refrac'torily, *adv.*, in a refractory manner.

refrac'toriness, *n.*, the quality of being refractory.

refrac'tory, *adj.*, stubborn and unmanageable.

re-frac'ture, *n.*, a second fracture of the same thing.

ref'ragable, *adj.*, capable of being resisted or refuted.

refrain', *n.*, the burden of a song; a kind of musical repetition; *v.t.*, to restrain; *v.i.*, to forbear; to abstain.

refrained', *p.p.*, refrain.

refrain'ing, *pr.p.*, refrain.

refrangibil'ity, *n.*, the quality of being refrangible.

refran'gible, *adj.*, subject to, or capable of, refraction.

refresh', *v.t.*, to give new strength to; to freshen.

refreshed', *p.p.*, refresh.

refresh'er, *n.*, one who, or that which, refreshes; an additional fee paid to counsel when a case is adjourned.

refresh'ing, *pr.p.*, refresh; *adj.*, invigorating.

refresh'ment, *n.*, the act of refreshing; that which refreshes; that which reinvigorates, as food or drink.

refrig'erant, *adj.* and *n.*, *i.q.* refrigerative.
refrig'erate, *v.t.*, to cool.
refrig'erated, *p.p.*, refrigerate.
refrig'erating, *pr.p.*, refrigerate.
refrigera'tion, *n.*, the act of refrigerating.
refrig'erative, *adj.*, cooling; *n.*, a cooling medicine.
refrig'erator, *n.*, that which keeps cool or refrigerates; a machine for making ice; a cold chest.
refrig'eratory, *adj.*, cooling.
reft, *adj.*, bereft.
ref'uge, *n.*, shelter from distress; a house of refuge; an expedient to secure protection.
refugee', *n.*, one who flees for refuge.
reful'gence, *n.*, splendour; brilliancy.
reful'gency, *n.*, *i.q.* refulgence.
reful'gent, *adj.*, shining; splendid.
refund', *v.t.*, to pay back; *n.* repayment.
refund'ed, *p.p.*, refund.
refund'ing, *pr.p.*, refund.
refund'ment, *n.*, the act of paying back.
refu'sable, *adj.*, capable of being refused.
refu'sal, *n.*, denial of a request; option or pre-emption.
refuse', *v.t.*, to deny the request of; *v.i.*, not to comply; to decline.
ref'use, *adj.*, left as worthless; *n.*, waste matter.
refused', *p.p.*, refuse.
refu'ser, *n.*, one who refuses.
refu'sing, *pr.p.*, refuse
refu'table, *adj.*, capable of being refuted.
refuta'tion, *n.*, overthrow by argument.
refu'tatory, *adj.*, tending to refute.
refute', *v.t.*, to disprove; to prove to be false.
refu'ted, *p.p.*, refute.
refu'ting, *pr.p.*, refute.

regain', *v.t.*, to recover something lost; to reach again.
regained', *p.p.*, regain.
regain'ing, *pr.p.*, regain.
re'gal, *adj.*, royal.
regale', *v.t.*, to entertain sumptuously; to gratify; *v.i.*, to fare sumptuously.
regaled', *p.p.*, regale.
regale'ment, *n.*, entertainment; gratification.
rega'lia, *n. pl.*, the symbols of royalty; improperly, the insignia of a society, such as the Oddfellows, etc.; a brand of cigars.
rega'ling, *pr.p.*, regale.
regal'ity, *n.*, kingship; a Scottish territorial jurisdiction.
re'gally, *adv.*, in a regal manner.
regard', *v.t.*, to look upon; to observe; to pay attention to; to respect or esteem; to view in the light of; *n.*, attention; esteem; reference.
regard'ant, *adj.*, watching; epithet applied to an animal in heraldry looking backward.
regard'ed, *p.p.*, regard.
regard'ful, *adj.*, paying regard.
regard'ing, *pr.p.*, regard; *prep.*, in reference to.
regard'less, *adj.*, heedless.
regat'ta, *n.*, a meeting at which sailing or rowing races take place.
Re'gel, *n.*, a fixed star of the first magnitude in the left foot of Orion.
regela'tion, *n.*, the freezing together of two pieces of ice.
re'gency, *n.*, the office or jurisdiction of a regent.
regen'eracy, *n.*, the state of being regenerated.

regen'erate, *n.*, a convert; one changed spiritually; *adj.*, reproduced; changed spiritually.
regen'erate, *v.t.*, to reproduce; to change the affections from indifference to love of God.
regen'erated, *p.p.*, regenerate.
regen'erating, *pr.p.*, regenerate.
regenera'tion, *n.*, the act of regenerating.
regen'erative, *adj.*, producing regeneration.
regen'erator, *n.*, one who regenerates.
regen'eratory, *adj.*, regenerative.
re'gent, *adj.*, exercising vicarious authority; *n.*, one who rules during the minority or disability of a king; an old university term for a teaching M.A.
regermina'tion, *n.*, a second germination or vegetation.
reg'icidal, *adj.*, pert. to regicide.
reg'icide, *n.*, one who kills a king; the murder of a king.
régime', *n.*, system of government or administration.
reg'imen, *n.*, orderly government; regulation of diet, habits, etc.
reg'iment, *n.*, a body of soldiers commanded by a colonel. (Formerly it meant government.)
regimen'tal, *adj.*, bel. to a regiment.
regimen'tals, *n. pl.*, the uniform of a regiment.
re'gion, *n.*, a tract of land of indefinite but considerable extent; a division of the body.
reg'ister, *n.*, a record; a list; a contrivance for regulating combustion in a stove or range; the compass of a voice or musical instrument;

a set of pipes in an organ; *v.t.*, to enter in a register; *v.i.*, to correspond exactly, in colour-printing.

reg'istered, *p.p.*, register; *adj.*, enrolled; entered in a list.

reg'istering, *pr.p.*, register.

reg'istrar, *n.*, a keeper of records.

reg'istrarship, *n.*, the office of a registrar.

reg'istrary, *n.*, *i.q.* registrar (a term used by Cambridge University).

registra'tion, *n.*, the act of inserting in a register.

reg'istry, *n.*, the place where a register is kept.

re'gius, *adj.*, royal (*Lat.*).

Re'gium Do'num, *n.*, a Parliamentary grant formerly paid for the sustentation of Presbyterian ministers in Ireland.

re'gius profes'sor, *n.*, one of certain professors at Oxford and Cambridge appointed by the Crown.

reg'let, *n.*, a strip used in printing to separate pages in the chase; a flat, narrow moulding between panels.

reg'nal, *adj.*, pert. to the reign of a monarch.

reg'nancy, *n.*, sovereignty; rule.

reg'nant, *adj.*, reigning as sovereign; prevalent.

regorge', *v.t.*, to swallow again; to vomit up.

regorged', *p.p.*, regorge.

regrant', *v.t.*, to grant back; *n.*, a new grant.

regrate', *v.t.*, to buy and sell again in (or near) the same market, so raising the price; to corner locally.

regra'ted, *p.p.*, regrate.

regra'ter, *n.*, one who buys provisions and sells them in the same market.

regra'ting, *pr.p.*, regrate.

re'gress, *n.*, power of returning.

regres'sion, *n.*, the act of passing back.

regress'ive, *adj.*, passing back.

regret', *n.*, sorrowful longing; remorse; *v.t.*, to look back at with sorrowful longing.

regret'ful, *adj.*, full of regret.

regret'table, *adj.*, to be regretted.

regret'ted, *p.p.*, regret.

regret'ting, *pr.p.*, regret.

reg'ular, *adj.*, in accordance with rule; methodical; uniform; symmetrical; bel. to and bound by the rules of a monastic order; *n.*, a soldier of a permanent army; one who has taken monastic vows.

regular'ity, *n.*, the quality of being regular.

reg'ularize, *v.t.*, to make regular or conformable to rule.

reg'ularly, *adv.*, in a regular manner.

reg'ulate, *v.t.*, to adjust by rule; to direct; to cause to act properly.

reg'ulated, *p.p.*, regulate.

reg'ulating, *pr.p.*, regulate.

regula'tion, *n.*, the act of regulating; a rule.

reg'ulative, *adj.*, tending to regulate.

reg'ulator, *n.*, one who, or that which, regulates; the governor of a steam-engine.

reg'ulus, *n.*, an old name for antimony; a bright star in Leo; a petty king.

regur'gitate, *v.t.*, to cause to surge back; *v.i.*, to surge back.

regurgita'tion, *n.*, the act of regurgitating; the rising into the mouth of part of the contents of the stomach.

rehabil'itate, *v.t.*, to reinstate; to re-establish in the esteem of others.

rehabil'itated, *p.p.*, rehabilitate.

rehabilita'tion, *n.*, the act of rehabilitating.

rehang', *v.t.*, to hang again.

rehash', *v.t.*, to work up old material in a new form; *n.*, old material newly made up.

rehear', *v.t.*, to hear again; to try (a case) a second time.

reheard', *p.p.*, rehear.

rehear'ing, *pr.p.* rehear; *n.*, a further trial.

rehears'al, *n.*, a trial performance; the act of rehearsing.

rehearse', *v.t.*, to recite; to repeat experimentally before engaging in a public performance.

rehearsed', *p.p.*, rehearse.

rehears'er, *n.*, one who rehearses.

rehears'ing, *pr.p.*, rehearse.

reheat', *v.t.*, to heat again.

Reichs'rath, *n.*, former Imperial Austrian Parliament.

Reichs'tag, *n.*, former Imperial Parliament of Germany.

reign, *v.i.*, to exercise sovereign power; *n.*, sovereignty; the time during which a sovereign reigns.

reigned, *p.p.*, reign.

reign'ing, *pr.p.*, reign.

reimburse', *v.t.*, to refund; to pay back to.

reimbursed', *p.p.*, reimburse.

reimburse'ment, *n.*, repayment.

reimburs'ing, *pr.p.*, reimburse.

reimprint', *v.t.*, to imprint or print again.

rein, *n.*, the strap of a bridle by which a horse is controlled;

restraint; *v.t.*, to guide; to control.

reincarna'tion, *n.*, the act of taking a human body as residence by a spirit for a second time.

rein'deer, *n.*, a deer of Northern Europe used as a domestic animal.

reined, *p.p.*, rein.

reinforce', *v.t.*, to strengthen, esp. with more troops, ships, etc.

reinforced', *p.p.*, reinforce.

reinforce'ment, *n.*, additional forces to strengthen an army or fleet.

reinforc'ing, *pr.p.*, reinforce.

rein'ing, *pr.p.*, rein.

rein'less, *adj.*, without reins; uncontrolled.

reins, *n. pl.*, the kidneys; the loins; formerly the supposed seat of the affections and passions; pl. of rein.

reinsert', *v.t.*, to insert a second time.

reinspec'tion, *n.*, the act of inspecting a second time.

reinstall', *v.t.*, to install again.

reinstate', *v.t.*, to place again in a former state.

reinstat'ed, *p.p.*, reinstate.

reinstate'ment, *n.*, reestablishment.

reinstat'ing, *pr.p.*, reinstate.

reinsur'ance, *n.*, a renewed or second insurance; an insurance to cover risks undertaken by a first insurance.

reinsure', *v.t.*, to insure again.

reintroduce', *v.t.*, to introduce again.

reintroduc'tion, *n.*, a second introduction.

reinvest', *v.t.*, to invest anew.

reinvest'ment, *n.*, the act of reinvesting the proceeds of a realised investment.

reis'sue, *v.i.*, to go forth again; *v.t.*, to issue a second time; *n.*, a second or renewed issue.

reis'sued, *p.p.*, reissue.

reis'suing, *pr.p.*, reissue.

reit'erate, *v.t.*, to repeat again and again.

reit'erated, *p.p.*, reiterate.

reit'erating, *pr.p.*, reiterate.

reitera'tion, *n.*, repetition.

reit'erative, *n.*, a word signifying repeated or intense action; a part of a word repeated so as to form a reduplicated word.

reject', *v.t.*, to discard; to refuse to receive or grant.

reject'able, *adj.*, capable of being rejected.

reject'ed, *p.p.*, reject.

reject'er, *n.*, one who rejects.

reject'ing, *pr.p.*, reject.

rejec'tion, *n.*, the act of rejecting; refusal to grant or accept.

reject'ive, *adj.*, tending to reject.

reject'ment, *n.*, the act of rejecting.

rejoice', *v.i.*, to be joyful; *v.t.*, to gladden.

rejoiced', *p.p.*, rejoice.

rejoi'cing, *pr.p.*, rejoice; *n.*, joy, gladness.

rejoin', *v.t.*, to join again; to reply; *v.i.*, to answer to a reply.

rejoin'der, *n.*, an answer to a reply.

rejoined', *p.p.*, rejoin.

rejoin'ing, *pr.p.*, rejoin.

reju'venate, *v.t.*, to make young again.

reju'venated, *p.p.*, rejuvenate.

reju'venating, *pr.p.*, rejuvenate.

rejuvenes'cence, *n.*, a renewal of youth.

rejuvenes'cent, *adj.*, becoming young again.

rekin'dle, *v.t.*, to kindle again.

rekin'dled, *p.p.*, rekindle.

rekin'dling, *pr.p.*, rekindle.

relaid', *p.p.*, relay.

relais', *n.*, a narrow ledge between the foot of a rampart and the scarp of the ditch.

relapse', *v.i.*, to backslide; *n.*, a falling back into a former bad state.

relapsed', *p.p.*, relapse; *adj.*, an epithet describing a heretic who, after abjuring his heresy, has fallen back into it again.

relaps'er, *n.*, one who relapses.

relaps'ing, *pr.p.*, relapse.

relate', *v.t.*, to tell; to narrate; to ally by kindred or connections; *v.i.*, to have reference (to).

rela'ted, *p.p.*, relate; *adj.*, connected by blood or alliance; standing in some relation.

rela'ting, *pr.p.*, relate.

rela'tion, *n.*, the act of relating; narrative; a certain position of one thing with regard to another; a kinsman or kinswoman.

rela'tional, *adj.*, indicating some relation.

rela'tionship, *n.*, kinship.

rel'ative, *adj.*, pertinent; not absolute; *n.*, a kinsman or kinswoman; a word which relates to another, or refers to a preceding statement.

rel'atively, *adv.*, in relation to; comparatively.

rela'tor, *n.*, one who relates.

relax', *v.t.* and *i.*, to slacken; to become less severe; to relieve from constipation; to unbend.

relaxa'tion, *n.*, the act of relaxing; recreation; an occupation to give relief after toil.

relax'ative, *adj.*, laxative; *n.*, a laxative medicine.

relaxed', *p.p.*, relax.

relax'ing, *pr.p.*, relax; *adj.*, enervating; causing languor.

relay', *n.*, a supply of horses on the road to relieve others; a number of men who work at stated intervals.

re-lay', *v.t.*, to lay again.

releas'able, *adj.*, capable of being released.

release', *v.t.*, to liberate; *n.*, liberation from bondage or obligation.

released', *p.p.*, release.

release'ment, *n.*, the act of releasing.

releas'er, *n.*, one who releases.

releas'ing, *pr.p.*, release.

rel'egate, *v.t.*, to send out of the way; to banish.

rel'egated, *p.p.*, relegate.

rel'egating, *pr.p.*, relegate.

relega'tion, *n.*, the act of relegating; banishment.

relent', *v.i.*, to become more mild; to yield.

relent'ed, *p.p.*, relent.

relent'ing, *pr.p.*, relent.

relent'less, *adj.*, implacable; pitiless.

relent'lessly, *adv.*, without pity.

relet', *v.t.*, to let again (as a house).

rel'evance, *n.*, pertinence.

rel'evancy, *n.*, *i.q.* relevance.

rel'evant, *adj.*, pertinent; applicable.

reliabil'ity, *n.*, the quality of being reliable.

reli'able, *adj.*, to be depended on.

reli'ance, *n.*, trust; confidence.

reli'ant, *adj.*, having reliance; self-relying.

rel'ic, *n.*, a remaining fragment; a memento.

rel'ict, *n.*, a widow.

relied', *p.p.*, rely.

relief', *n.*, succour; that which mitigates some evil; help given to a pauper; in painting, an appearance of solidity; in sculpture and architecture, prominence above the ground or plane on which a figure is formed; the surface elevations of a country.

reli'er, *n.*, one who relies.

reliev'able, *adj.*, capable of being relieved.

relieve', *v.t.*, to alleviate pain, etc.; to help the poor, etc.; to set off by contrast; to give an appearance of solidity to; to release from duty by substituting another person.

relieved', *p.p.*, relieve.

reliev'ing, *pr.p.*, relieve; *adj.*, serving to relieve.

relie'vo, *n.*, the prominence of a figure above the ground on which it is formed—in sculpture and architecture.

relight', *v.t.*, to rekindle.

relig'ion, *n.*, piety; any system of belief and worship.

relig'ionism, *n.*, affected religion.

relig'ionist, *n.*, a religious bigot; one who deals much in religious discourse.

religios'ity, *n.*, a morbidly religious state.

relig'ious, *adj.*, rel. to religion; pious; devoted by vows to the service of God; scrupulously faithful; *n.*, a member of a religious order; a monk or nun.

relig'iously, *adv.*, piously; reverently; conscientiously.

relin'quish, *v.t.*, to abandon; to desist from; to renounce a claim to.

relin'quished, *p.p.*, relinquish.

relin'quishing, *pr.p.*, relinquish.

relin'quishment, *n.*, the act of relinquishing.

rel'iquary, *n.*, a casket in which relics are kept.

relique', *n.*, *i.q.* relic.

rel'ish, *v.t.*, to like the flavour of; *v.i.*, to have a pleasing flavour; *n.*, savour; taste; liking; something taken with food to give it a flavour.

rel'ishable, *adj.*, capable of being relished.

rel'ished, *p.p.*, relish.

rel'ishing, *pr.p.*, relish.

relive', *v.i.*, to live again.

reloan', *n.*, a repeated loan.

relu'cent, *adj.*, luminous.

reluc'tance, *n.*, unwillingness.

reluc'tant, *adj.*, unwilling.

reluc'tantly, *adv.*, unwillingly.

relume', *v.t.*, to light again.

relumed', *p.p.*, relume.

relu'mine, *v.t.*, *i.q.* relume.

relu'mined, *p.p.*, relumine.

relu'ming, *pr.p.*, relume.

relu'mining, *pr.p.*, relumine.

rely', *v.i.*, to trust; to have confidence.

rely'ing, *pr.p.*, rely.

remade', *p.p.*, remake.

remain', *v.i.*, to stay.

remain'der, *n.*, that which remains.

remained', *p.p.*, remain.

remain'ing, *pr.p.*, remain.

remains', *n. pl.*, a dead body; the literary works of a dead author; anything that is left.

remake', *v.t.*, to make over again.

re'make, *n.*, anything re-made.
remand', *v.t.*, to send (an accused person) back to gaol till further evidence is forthcoming; *n.*, the state of being remanded. [mand.
remand'ed, *p.p.*, re-
remand'ing, *pr.p.*, remand.
remand'ment, *n.*, a remand.
rem'anent, *adj.*, remaining.
rem'anet, *n.*, a postponed case for trial.
remark', *n.*, observation; a comment; *v.t.*, to observe; to utter as a comment.
re-mark', *v.t.*, to mark a second time.
remark'able, *adj.*, worthy of notice; extraordinary; conspicuous.
remark'ably, *adv.*, surprisingly; in a remarkable manner.
remarked', *p.p.*, remark.
remark'ing, *pr.p.*, remark.
remar'riage, *n.*, a second marriage.
remar'ried, *p.p.*, remarry.
remar'ry, *v.t.*, to marry again; *v.i.*, to be married again.
remar'rying, *pr.p.*, remarry.
reme'diable, *adj.*, capable of being remedied.
reme'dial, *adj.*, affording a remedy.
rem'edied, *p.p.*, remedy.
rem'ediless, *adj.*, incurable; irreparable.
rem'edy, *n.*, a cure; redress; *v.t.*, to cure; to redress.
rem'edying, *pr.p.*, remedy.
remem'ber, *v.t.*, to keep in the mind; to recollect; *v.i.*, to bear in mind.
remem'bered, *p.p.*, remember.
remem'bering, *pr.p.*, remember.
remem'brance, *n.*, power of remembering; what is remembered; a keepsake.
remem'brancer, *n.*, an officer in the Exchequer who makes records and processes; a recorder; an officer of the Corporation of London.
rem'iform, *adj.*, oar-shaped.
remi'grate, *v.i.*, to migrate again.
remind', *v.t.*, to cause to remember.
remind'ed, *p.p.*, remind.
remind'er, *n.*, one who, or that which, reminds.
remind'ful, *adj.*, tending to remind.
remind'ing, *pr.p.*, remind.
reminis'cence, *n.*, recollection; a narration of what is recollected.
reminis'cent, *adj.*, calling to mind; having remembrance.
rem'iped, *n.*, an aquatic animal that uses its feet as oars.
remise', *n.*, a surrender or release (of a claim); a covered fly or carriage; a coach-house.
remise', *v.t.*, to resign or surrender by deed.
remised', *p.p.*, remise.
remis'ing, *pr.p.*, remise.
remiss', *adj.*, negligent.
remissibil'ity, *n.*, capability of being remitted.
remiss'ible, *adj.*, capable of being remitted.
remis'sion, *n.*, the act of remitting; abatement; forgiveness.
remiss'ive, *adj.*, relaxing; pardoning.
remiss'ly, *adv.*, carelessly.
remiss'ness, *n.*, the quality of being remiss.
remiss'ory, *adj.*, pert. to remission; tending to remit.
remit', *v.t.*, to abate; to forgive; to send back or send; to transmit money, etc.; *v.i.*, to become less intense.
remit'tal, *n.*, a sending of money to a distance.
remit'tance, *n.*, the act of sending money to a distance as a payment; the sum so sent.
remit'ted, *p.p.*, remit.
remit'tent, *adj.*, ceasing temporarily.
remit'ter, *n.*, one who remits. [mit.
remit'ting, *pr.p.*, re-
rem'nant, *n.*, that which remains after the removal of the rest; esp. a piece of cloth remaining after the rest has been sold; a fragment.
remod'el, *v.t.*, to model anew.
remod'el(l)ed, *p.p.*, remodel.
remod'el(l)ing, *pr.p.*, remodel.
remon'etize, *v.t.*, to make again the standard money of account.
remon'strance, *n.*, the act of remonstrating; a strong statement of reasons against.
remon'strant, *adj.*, expostulatory.
remon'strate, *v.t.*, to expostulate.
remon'strated, *p.p.*, remonstrate.
remon'strating, *pr.p.*, remonstrate.
remon'strator, *n.*, one who remonstrates.
rem'ora, *n.*, the sucking-fish.
remorse', *n.*, anguish caused by a sense of guilt.
remorse'ful, *adj.*, full of remorse.
remorse'less, *adj.*, pitiless.
remote', *adj.*, distant; inconsiderable.
remote'ly, *adv.*, at a distance; slightly.
remote'ness, *n.*, distance; state of being remote.
remo'ter, *adj.*, *comp.* of remote.

remo'test, *adj.*, *super.* of remote.

remould', *v.t.*, to mould or shape anew.

remount', *v.t.* and *i.*, to mount again; *n.*, a fresh horse to mount.

removabil'ity, *n.*, the quality of being removable.

remov'able, *adj.*, capable of being removed.

remov'al, *n.*, a moving from one place to another; displacing from an office; putting an end to.

remove', *v.t.*, to move from its place in any manner; *v.i.*, to change place; *n.*, a removal; a step in any scale of gradation; a dish moved from table to table to make room for something else.

removed', *p.p.*, remove.

remov'ing, *pr.p.*, remove.

remunerabil'ity, *n.*, capability of being remunerated.

remu'nerable, *adj.*, capable of being remunerated.

remu'nerate, *v.t.*, to reward; to recompense.

remu'nerated, *p.p.*, remunerate.

remu'nerating, *pr.p.*, remunerate.

remunera'tion, *n.*, something given to remunerate; the act of remunerating.

remu'nerative, *adj.*, affording remuneration.

remu'neratory, *adj.*, rewarding.

Renaissance', *n.*, any revival; esp. the revival of learning in the fifteenth century.

re'nal, *adj.*, pert. to the kidneys.

rename', *v.t.*, to give a new name to.

ren'ard, *n.*, *i.q.* reynard.

renas'cence, *n.*, *i.q.* Renaissance; the state of being renascent.

renas'cent, *adj.*, springing again into existence.

rencon'tre, *n.*, a chance meeting; a slight hostile engagement.

rencoun'ter, *n.*, a rencontre; *v.i.*, to meet (an enemy) unexpectedly; to fight hand to hand.

rend, *v.t.*, to tear; to tear asunder.

ren'der, *n.*, one who rends; *v.t.*, to give back; to invest with qualities; to translate; represent.

ren'dered, *p.p.*, render.

ren'dering, *pr.p.*, render; *n.*, a translation; a representation.

ren'dezvous, *n.*, a meeting-place; *v.i.*, to assemble at a particular place (*Fr.*).

rend'ible, *adj.*, capable of being torn asunder.

rend'ing, *pr.p.*, rend.

rendi'tion, *n.*, translation; reproducing artistically; surrender.

ren'egade, *n.*, an apostate; a deserter. Also *runagate.*

renew', *v.t.*, to restore; to make again; to begin again; *v.i.*, to become new; to grow afresh.

renew'able, *adj.*, capable of being renewed.

renew'al, *n.*, the act of renewing.

renewed', *p.p.*, renew.

renew'er, *n.*, one who renews.

renew'ing, *pr.p.*, renew.

ren'iform, *adj.*, kidney-shaped.

reni'tency, *n.*, the state of being renitent.

reni'tent, *adj.*, resisting pressure; persistently opposed.

ren'net, *n.*, a kind of apple; a preparation for curdling milk.

renounce', *v.t.*, to disown; to abjure; to cast off; *v.i.*, to revoke.

renounced', *p.p.*, renounce.

renounce'ment, *n.*, renunciation.

renoun'cer, *n.*, one who renounces.

renoun'cing, *pr.p.*, renounce.

ren'ovate, *v.t.*, to repair; to renew.

ren'ovated, *p.p.*, renovate.

ren'ovating, *pr.p.*, renovate.

renova'tion, *n.*, the act of renovating; repair; restoration.

ren'ovator, *n.*, one who, or that which, renovates.

renown', *n.*, fame; *v.t.*, to make famous.

renowned', *adj.*, famous.

rent, *p.p.*, rend; *n.*, a hole torn; money paid to an owner by a tenant for occupation; *v.t.*, to let for rent; *v.i.*, to be let for rent.

rent'able, *adj.*, capable of being rented.

rent'al, *n.*, a schedule of rents; amount of rent.

rente, *n.*, French Government Stock (*Fr.*).

rent'ed, *p.p.*, rent.

rent'er, *n.*, one who pays rent; a lessee.

rent'ing, *pr.p.*, rent.

rent'-roll, *n.*, a list of rents.

renum'ber, *v.t.*, to number again or anew.

renum'bered, *p.p.*, renumber.

renuncia'tion, *n.*, the act of renouncing; disclaiming; disowning.

reoc'cupy, *v.t.*, to occupy anew.

reo'pen, *v.t.* and *i.*, to open again.

reo'pened, *p.p.*, reopen.

reo'pening, *pr.p.*, reopen.

reordain', *v.t.*, to ordain again, the first ordination being defective.

reorganiza'tion, *n.*, the act of organizing again.

reor'ganize, *v.t.*, to organize anew.

reor'ganized, *p.p.*, reorganize.

reor'ganizing, *pr.p.*, reorganize.

rep, *n.*, a dress fabric of ribbed appearance.

repack', *v.t.*, to pack again.

repaid', *p.p.*, repay.

repair', *v.t.*, to restore; mend; make amends for; *v.i.*, to go to.

repair'able, *adj.*, able to be repaired.

repaired', *p.p.*, repair.

repair'er, *n.*, one who repairs.

repair'ing, *pr.p.*, repair.

repand', *adj.*, describing a leaf with an unequal edge.

rep'arable, *adj.*, *i.q.* repairable.

repara'tion, *n.*, amends, compensation, atonement.

repar'ative, *adj.*, repairing.

repartee', *n.*, a smart retort.

repass', *v.t.*, to pass again.

repassed', *p.p.*, repass.

repass'ing, *pr.p.*, repass.

repast', *n.*, a meal; food.

repay', *v.t.*, to pay back; make a return for.

repay'able, *adj.*, able to be repaid; that must be repaid.

repay'ing, *pr.p.*, repay.

repay'ment, *n.*, payment of a debt.

repeal', *v.t.*, to cancel; revoke; abrogate.

repealabil'ity, *n.*, the quality of being repealable.

repeal'able, *adj.*, able to be repealed.

repealed', *p.p.*, repeal.

repeal'er, *n.*, one who repeals; esp. one who favoured the repeal of the Union of Great Britain and Ireland.

repeal'ing, *pr.p.*, repeal.

repeat', *v.t.*, to do or to say over again; to recite; *n.*, repetition; a musical sign directing the repetition of a passage.

repeat'ed, *p.p.*, repeat; *adj.*, frequent.

repeat'edly, *adv.*, frequently.

repeat'er, *n.*, one who repeats; a revolver; a watch that repeats by striking the hours, minutes, and seconds; a recurring decimal.

repeat'ing, *pr.p.*, repeat.

repel', *v.t.*, to drive away; to check; to disgust.

repel'lant, *adj.*, disgusting; repulsive; driving back.

repelled', *p.p.*, repel.

repel'lence, *n.*, the repellent character.

repel'lency, *n.*, *i.q.* repellence.

repel'lent, *adj.*, *i.q.* repellant.

repel'ler, *n.*, one who repels.

repel'ling, *pr.p.*, repel.

repent', *v.i.*, to be sorry for an offence.

repent'ance, *n.*, sorrow for an offence; change of heart.

repent'ant, *adj.*, in a state of repentance.

repent'ed, *p.p.*, repent.

repent'ing, *pr.p.*, repent.

repeo'ple, *v.t.*, to populate afresh.

repercuss', *v.t.*, to re-echo; *v.i.*, to reverberate.

repercussed', *p.p.*, repercuss.

repercuss'ing, *pr.p.*, repercuss.

repercus'sion, *n.*, reverberation.

repercus'sive, *adj.*, reverberating.

répertoire', *n.*, a store of music, stories, etc.

rep'ertory, *n.*, a storehouse.

rep'etend, *n.*, the part repeated in a recurring decimal.

repeti'tion, *n.*, the act of repeating; reiteration; passages committed to memory.

repeti'tious, *adj.*, repeating.

repine', *v.i.*, to grieve; be discontented; murmur.

repined', *p.p.*, repine.

repi'ner, *n.*, one who repines.

repi'ning, *pr.p.*, repine; *n.*, expressing discontent; murmuring.

replace', *v.t.*, to put back into its place. (In recent usage, to substitute one thing for another.)

replaced', *p.p.*, replace.

replace'ment, *n.*, the act of replacing.

repla'cing, *pr.p.*, replace.

replant', *v.t.*, to plant afresh.

replen'ish, *v.t.*, to fill afresh; to stock.

replen'ished, *p.p.*, replenish.

replen'ishing, *pr.p.*, replenish.

replen'ishment, *n.*, the act of replenishing; the replenished state.

replete', *adj.*, full.

replete'ness, *n.*, the state of being replete.

reple'tion, *n.*, the state of being overfull.

replev'iable, *adj.*, able to be replevied.

replev'ied, *p.p.*, replevy.

replev'in, *n.*, an action at law for the recovery by writ of wrongfully seized goods.

replev'y, *v.t.*, to recover goods by replevin.

replev'ying, *pr.p.*, replevy.

rep'lica, *n.*, a duplicate of a work of art by the artist himself.

rep'licant, *adj.*, folding back.

rep'licate, *adj.*, folded back; *n.*, anything folded back.

rep'licate, *v.t.*, to fold back; to echo.
rep'licated, *p.p.*, replicate.
rep'licating, *pr.p.*, replicate.
replica'tion, *n.*, the act or effect of replicating; echo; a plaintiff's reply to the defendant.
replied', *p.p.*, reply.
repli'er, *n.*, one who replies.
reply', *v.i.*, to answer; *n.*, an answer.
reply'ing, *pr.p.*, reply.
report', *v.t.*, to bring back a message; to relate; to take down in writing; to announce; *n.*, rumour; a formal statement; a description; a loud noise (as of a gun).
report'ed, *p.p.*, report.
report'er, *n.*, one who reports, esp. one who takes down a speech, or gives an account of any proceedings.
report'ing, *p.p.*, report; *n.*, the business of a reporter; the art of reporting.
reporto'rial, *adj.*, rel. to reporters.
repos'al, *n.*, the state of being in repose.
repose', *v.t.*, to lay to rest; to place (trust or confidence); *v.i.*, to lie down to rest; to sleep; *n.*, sleep; a restful attitude.
reposed', *p.p.*, repose.
repose'ful, *adj.*, restful.
repo'sing, *pr.p.*, repose.
repos'it, *v.t.*, to place in security.
repos'ited, *p.p.*, reposit.
repos'iting, *pr.p.*, reposit.
repos'itory, *n.*, a place of storage; a warehouse.
repossess', *v.t.*, to regain possession.
reposses'sion, *n.*, possession regained.
repoussé, *adj.*, said of metal worked in relief; *n.*, metal so worked and chased.
reprehend', *v.t.*, to censure.
reprehend'ed, *p.p.*, reprehend.
reprehend'ing, *pr.p.*, reprehend.
reprehen'sible, *adj.*, worthy of censure; blameworthy.
reprehen'sion, *n.*, the act of reprehending.
reprehen'sive, *adj.*, reproving.
reprehen'sory, *adj.*, *i.q.* reprehensive.
represent', *v.t.*, to show in a picture; to personate; to act on behalf of; to make a report of.
re-present, *v.t.*, to present anew.
represent'able, *adj.*, able to be represented.
representa'tion, *n.*, the act of representing; a likeness; an account; a theatrical performance.
represent'ative, *adj.*, personating; acting or standing for; typical; *n.*, one who acts on behalf of others, esp. a Member of Parliament; an heir.
represent'ed, *p.p.*, represent.
represent'ing, *pr.p.*, represent.
repress', *v.t.*, to check; restrain; put down.
repressed', *p.p.*, repress.
repress'er, *n.*, one who represses.
repress'ing, *pr.p.*, repress.
repres'sion, *n.*, the act of repressing; state of being repressed.
repress'ive, *adj.*, tending to repress.
reprieve', *v.t.*, to order suspension of punishment; *n.*, respite.
reprieved', *p.p.*, reprieve.
repriev'ing, *pr.p.*, reprieve.
reprimand', *v.t.*, to reprove severely.
rep'rimand, *n.*, a severe reproof.
reprimand'ed, *p.p.*, reprimand.
reprimand'ing, *pr.p.*, reprimand.
reprint', *v.t.*, to print again.
re'print, *n.*, a printing repeated.
reprint'ed, *p.p.*, reprint.
reprint'ing, *pr.p.*, reprint.
repri'sal, *n.*, retaliation.
reprise', *n.*, payment out of an estate.
reproach', *v.t.*, to blame, rebuke; *n.*, blame, rebuke.
reproach'able, *adj.*, blameworthy.
reproached', *p.p.*, reproach.
reproach'ful, *adj.*, expressing rebuke.
reproach'fully, *adv.*, in a reproachful way.
reproach'ing, *pr.p.*, reproach.
rep'robate, *adj.*, depraved; abandoned; *n.*, a depraved sinner.
rep'robate, *v.t.*, to condemn; to denounce.
rep'robated, *p.p.*, reprobate.
rep'robating, *pr.p.*, reprobate.
reproba'tion, *n.*, condemnation.
rep'robative, *adj.*, condemnatory.
reproduce', *v.t.*, to produce in facsimile; to make a likeness of; to bring forth.
reproduced', *p.p.*, reproduce.
reproduc'tion, *n.*, the act or result of reproducing.
reproduc'tive, *adj.*, reproducing.
reproof', *n.*, blame, rebuke.
reprov'able, *adj.*, worthy of reproof.
reprov'al, *n.*, the act of reproving.
reprove', *v.t.*, to rebuke; take to task.
reproved', *p.p.*, reprove.
reprov'er, *n.*, one who reproves.
reprov'ing, *pr.p.*, reprove.
reprov'ingly, *adv.*, by way of reproof.
repta'tion, *n.*, creeping.

rep'tatory, *adj.*, creeping.

rep'tile, *adj.*, crawling; creeping; grovelling; *n.*, one of the Reptilia; a grovelling person.

Repti'lia, *n. pl.*, creatures that creep or crawl.

reptil'ian, *adj.*, rel. to reptiles.

repub'lic, *n.*, the commonwealth; a government by the people.

repub'lican, *adj.*, pert. to a republic; *n.*, one who is opposed to the rule of a sovereign.

repub'licanism, *n.*, the principles of republicans.

repub'licanize, *v.t.*, to change to a republic; to indoctrinate with republican principles.

repub'licanized, *p.p.*, republicanize.

repub'licanizing, *pr.p.*, republicanize.

republica'tion, *n.*, the act of republishing; a fresh issue of a book.

repub'lish, *v.t.*, to publish afresh; to issue again.

repub'lished, *p.p.*, republish.

repub'lishing, *pr.p.*, republish.

repu'diable, *adj.*, able to be repudiated.

repu'diate, *v.t.*, to reject; disavow; refuse to acknowledge (a debt).

repu'diated, *p.p.*, repudiate.

repu'diating, *pr.p.*, repudiate.

repudia'tion, *n.*, the act of repudiating; disavowal.

repu'diator, *n.*, one who repudiates.

repug'nance, *n.*, distaste; aversion.

repug'nancy, *n.*, *i.q.* repugnance.

repug'nant, *adj.*, distasteful; offensive.

repulse', *v.t.*, to beat back; repel; *n.*, a driving back; refusal; denial.

repulsed', *p.p.*, repulse.

repuls'ing, *pr.p.*, repulse.

repul'sion, *n.*, the act or effect of repulsing; a feeling of loathing.

repul'sive, *adj.*, tending to repulse; loathsome.

repul'sively, *adv.*, in a repulsive manner.

repul'siveness, *n.*, the quality of being repulsive.

repur'chase, *v.t.*, to buy back.

rep'utable, *adj.*, of good repute.

rep'utably, *adv.*, in a reputable way.

reputa'tion, *n.*, good name; credit.

repute', *v.t.*, to estimate; think; *n.*, character; estimation.

repu'ted, *p.p.*, repute.

repu'ting, *pr.p.*, repute.

request', *v.t.*, to ask for; *n.*, a prayer, petition, demand.

request'ed, *p.p.*, request.

request'ing, *pr.p.*, request.

req'uiem, *n.*, a funeral mass; the music for the same. (The name comes from the first word of the Introit: *requiem aeternam dona eis, Domine.*)

requir'able, *adj.*, able to be required.

require', *v.t.*, to need; to demand.

required', *p.p.*, require

require'ment, *n.*, something required.

requir'ing, *pr.p.*, require.

req'uisite, *adj.*, indispensable; *n.*, anything indispensable.

requisi'tion, *v.t.*, to demand; *n.*, the act of requiring; a demand.

requisi'tioned, *p.p.*, requisition.

requisi'tioning, *pr.p.*, rescue.

requi'tal, *n.*, the act of requiting.

requite', *v.t.*, to recompense; make a return to.

requi'ted *p.p.*, requite

requi'ting, *pr.p.*, requite.

rere'dos, *n.*, a hanging or structure behind an altar.

re-resolve', *v.i.*, to resolve afresh.

rere'ward, *n.*, a rearguard. Also *rearward.*

resale', *n.*, sale over again.

rescind', *v.t.*, to cancel; revoke.

rescind'able, *adj.*, able to be rescinded.

rescind'ed, *p.p.*, rescind.

rescind'ing, *pr.p.*, rescind.

rescind'ment, *n.*, *i.q.* rescission.

rescis'sion, *n.*, the act of rescinding.

recis'sory, *adj.*, annulling.

rescribe', *v.t.*, to write an answer.

re'script, *n.*, a reply in writing; a papal decree on a question submitted; an official announcement; a palimpsest.

rescrip'tive, *adj.*, in the nature of a rescript.

rescrip'tively, *adv.*, in a rescriptive way.

res'cuable, *adj.*, able to be rescued.

res'cue, *v.t.*, to save from danger; to recover by force (*leg.*); *n.*, deliverance; recovery by force (*leg.*).

res'cued, *p.p.*, rescue.

res'cuer, *n.*, a deliverer.

res'cuing, *pr.p.*, rescue

research', *v.t.* and *i.*, to search again; *n.*, investigation; deep and learned inquiry.

reseat', *v.t.*, to replace in a seat; to put a new seat in.

resect', *v.t.*, to pare.

Rese'da, *n.*, a genus of herbs.

reseize', *v.t.*, to take possession of again.

resell', *v.t.*, to sell again.

resem'blance, *n.*, likeness, similarity.

resem'ble, *v.t.*, to be like to.

resem'bled, *p.p.*, resemble.
resem'bling, *pr.p.*, resemble.
resent', *v.t.*, to feel indignation at.
resent'ed, *p.p.*, resent.
resent'ful, *adj.*, retaining a sense of injury.
resent'ing, *pr.p.*, resent.
resent'ment, *n.*, a sense of injury.
reserva'tion, *n.*, the act of reserving; a right reserved; something held back; a setting apart; the withholding of absolution; the reserving of the Blessed Sacrament.
reserve', *v.t.*, to hold back; to keep possession of; to book (seats); *n.*, something kept back for later use, esp. troops; reticence; speaking less than the truth.
reserved', *p.p.*, reserve; *adj.*, reticent; understating.
reserv'edly, *adv.*, in a reserved manner; with reserve.
reserv'ing, *pr.p.*, reserve.
reserv'ist, *n.*, one held in reserve, as troops, players in games, etc.
res'ervoir, *n.*, an artificial lake for water-supply; any receptacle in which a liquid supply is kept.
reset', *v.t.*, to set again; *v.t.* and *i.*, to shelter a criminal; to receive stolen goods.
reset'ter, *n.*, one who resets.
reset'ting, *pr.p.*, reset.
reset'tle, *v.t.* and *i.*, to settle again.
reset'tlement, *n.*, the act of resettling; the state of being resettled.
reship', *v.t.* and *i.*, to ship again.
reship'ment, *n.*, the act of reshipping.
reside', *v.i.*, to dwell; to inhere.
resi'ded, *p.p.*, reside.
res'idence, *n.*, the act of residing; place of dwelling.
res'idency, *n.*, the official dwelling of the Indian Governor-General's agent at a native court.
res'ident, *adj.*, residing; *n.*, one who resides; an agent of the Indian Governor-General residing at a native court.
residen'tial, *adj.*, used for residences.
residen'tiary, *adj.*, residing; required to reside, esp. said of canons held to specified terms of residence at their cathedral or collegiate churches; *n.*, one required to reside officially.
resi'der, *n.*, one who resides.
resi'ding, *pr.p.*, reside
resid'ual, *adj.*, leaving a remainder; pert. to a residuum.
resid'uary, *adj.*, *i.q.* residual.
res'idue, *n.*, a remainder after subtraction.
resid'uum, *n.*, that which remains; dregs.
resign', *v.t.* and *i.*, to give up; renounce claim on; retire.
resigna'tion, *n.*, the act of resigning; acceptance of the inevitable.
resigned', *p.p.*, resign.
resign'edly, *adv.*, with resignation.
resignee', *n.*, one to whom something is resigned.
resign'er, *n.*, one who resigns.
resign'ing, *pr.p.*, resign.
resile', *v.i.*, to recoil.
resil'ience, *n.*, elasticity; recuperative power; the power of springing back to previous state.
resil'iency, *n.*, *i.q.* resilience.
resil'ient, *adj.*, elastic.
res'in, *n.*, a gummy substance that exudes from plants or is made chemically.
resinif'erous, *adj.*, producing resin.
res'inous, *adj.*, containing resin; like resin.
resist', *v.t.* and *i.*, to oppose, withstand; *n.*, a protective coating.
resist'ance, *n.*, the act of resisting; opposition; power to resist; non-conductivity.
resist'ant, *adj.*, having power to resist.
resist'ed, *p.p.*, resist.
resist'er, *n.*, one who resists.
resistibil'ity, *n.*, the quality of being resistible.
resist'ible, *adj.*, able to be resisted.
resist'ing, *pr.p.*, resist.
resist'ive, *adj.*, having power to resist.
resist'less, *adj.*, irresistible.
res'oluble, *adj.*, able to be resolved.
res'olute, *adj.*, firm, determined, bold.
res'olutely, *adv.*, boldly, determinedly.
resolu'tion, *n.*, analysis; gradual improvement of morbid conditions; the change of a chord from discord to concord (*mus.*); a firm resolve; a motion adopted by a meeting; fixed purpose.
resolvabil'ity, *n.*, the quality or state of being resolvable.
resolv'able, *adj.*, capable of analysis or solution.
resolve', *v.t.*, to change the form of; to break up into parts; to make intelligible; to cause dispersion of pus; *v.i.*, to decide; to come to a determination; *n.*, a fixed purpose; resolution.
resolved', *p.p.*, resolve; *adj.*, determined.
resolv'ent, *adj.*, reducing tumours, etc.; solvent; *n.*, an agent that is resolvent.

resolv'er, *n.*, one who, or that which, resolves.

resolv'ing, *pr.p.*, resolve.

res'onance, *n.*, the quality of being resonant; echoing sound.

res'onant, *adj.*, returning or prolonging sound; full of sound.

res'onator, *n.*, a contrivance which, responding to a particular note, detects its presence in a mixed sound; an apparatus giving greater resonance.

resorb', *v.t.*, to absorb again.

resorbed', *p.p.*, resorb

resorb'ent, *adj.*, having the power to resorb.

resorb'ing, *pr.p.*, resorb.

resorp'tion, *n.*, the act or effect of resorbing.

resort', *v.i.*, to have recourse; to go often; *n.*, recourse; an expedient.

resort'ed, *p.p.*, resort.

resort'ing, *pr.p.*, resort.

resound', *v.t.*, to repeat sound of; to celebrate; *v.i.*, to make a loud sound; to be resonant; to be celebrated.

resound'ed, *p.p.*, resound.

resound'ing, *pr.p.*, resound.

resource', *n.*, something to fall back upon for aid; resort; ingenuity. In pl. it = means, pecuniary or other.

resource'less, *adj.*, without resources.

respect', *v.t.*, to treat with deference; to heed; to refer to; *n.*, deference; relation.

***respect'*ability,** *n.*, the quality of being respectable.

***respect'*able,** *adj.*, worthy of respect; of good name; moderately good, passable.

***respect'*ably,** *adv.*, in a respectable way.

respect'ant, *adj.*, confronting (*her.*).

respect'ed, *p.p.*, respect.

respect'er, *n.*, one who respects.

***respect'*ful,** *adj.*, deferential, humble.

***respect'*fully,** *adv.*, with deference.

***respect'*fulness,** *n.*, the quality of being respectful.

***respect'*ing,** *pr.p.*, respect; *prep.*, in regard to.

respect'ive, *adj.*, individual, separate.

***respect'*ively,** *adv.*, individually.

respell', *v.t.*, to spell again.

respirabil'ity, *n.*, the quality of being respirable.

respir'able, *adj.*, fit to breathe.

respira'tion, *n.*, the act of breathing.

respira'tional, *adj.*, rel. to respiration.

res'pirator, *n.*, a covering for the mouth to keep out cold air, fog, etc.

respir'atory, *adj.*, rel. to respiration.

respire', *v.t.* and *i.*, to breathe; inhale and exhale.

respired', *p.p.*, respire

respir'ing, *pr.p.*, respire.

res'pite, *n.*, a postponement; reprieve; temporary relief; *v.t.*, to grant respite.

res'pited, *p.p.*, respite

res'piting, *pr.p.*, respite.

resplen'dence, *n.*, splendour, magnificence.

resplen'dency, *n.*, *i.q.* resplendence.

resplen'dent, *adj.*, splendid, magnificent.

respond', *v.i.*, to answer; reply; *n.*, liturgically, the responds were antiphons recited after each lesson in the Divine Service; in architecture, a pilaster or column attached to a wall and supporting an arch.

respond'ed, *p.p.*, respond.

respond'ence, *n.*, analogy.

respond'ent, *adj.*, responding; *n.*, one who supports an opposing argument; a defendant.

respond'ing, *pr.p.*, respond.

response', *n.*, an answer; liturgically, the answer to the priest's versicle.

responsibil'ities, *n.pl.*, obligations.

responsibil'ity, *n.*, obligation; charge.

respon'sible, *adj.*, involving responsibilities; answerable; morally and mentally capable; trustworthy.

Respon'sions, *n. pl.*, the name of the first academic examination at Oxford, colloquially called Smalls.

respon'sive, *adj.*, giving answer; sympathetic.

respon'sively, *adv.*, in a responsive way.

respon'siveness, *n.*, the quality of being responsive.

rest, *v.t.*, to lay to rest; to place; *v.i.*, to cease from work or movement or care; *n.*, repose; cessation from work or worry or movement; remainder; that on which a thing can be rested; an interval of silence shown by an appropriate sign (*mus.*).

res'taurant, *n.*, a place of refreshment.

restau'rateur, *n.*, a restaurant-keeper (*Fr.*).

rest'ed, *p.p.*, rest.

rest'ful, *adj.*, producing a sense of ease and rest.

rest'fully, *adv.*, in a restful way.

rest'fulness, *n.*, the quality of being restful.

rest'ing, *pr.p.*, rest.

restitu'tion, *n.*, an act of reparation; restoring to lawful owner; compensation.

rest'ive, *adj.*, stubborn; unmanageable; refractory.

rest'ively, *adv.*, in a restive way.

rest'iveness, *n.*, stubbornness; refractoriness.

rest'less, *adj.*, without rest; fidgety; uneasy.

rest'lessly, *adv.*, in a restless way.

rest'lessness, *n.*, fidgetiness; uneasiness.

resto'rable, *adj.*, able to be restored.

restora'tion, *n.*, the act, or effect, of restoring; a renewal; re-establishment.

restora'tionism, *n.*, the belief in the final happiness of mankind.

restora'tionist, *n.*, a believer in restorationism.

restor'ative, *adj.*, restoring in its effect; *n.*, something that revives or restores.

restore', *v.t.*, to make restitution; to re-establish; to present anew in what is believed to have been the original state.

restored', *p.p.*, restore.

restor'er, *n.*, one who restores.

restor'ing, *pr.p.*, restore.

restrain', *v.t.*, to hold back, check, confine.

restrain'able, *adj.*, able to be restrained

restrained', *p.p.*, restrain; *adj.*, reserved.

restrain'edly, *adv.*, in a restrained manner.

restrain'er, *n.*, one who restrains.

restrain'ing, *pr.p.*, restrain.

restraint', *n.*, the act of restraining; the state of being restrained; self-control; confinement.

restrict', *v.t.*, to limit; confine.

restrict'ed, *p.p.*, restrict.

restrict'ing, *pr.p.*, restrict.

restric'tion, *n.*, limitation, confinement.

restrict'ive, *adj.*, tending to restrict.

restrict'ively, *adv.*, with restriction.

restring', *v.t.*, to fit a racket with fresh gut.

restring'ing, *pr.p.*, restring; *n.*, refitting with gut.

restrung', *p.p.*, restring.

rest'y, *adj.*, *i.q.* restive.

result', *v.i.*, to arise; to issue; to follow as a consequence; *n.*, a consequence, effect.

result'ant, *adj.*, resulting; *n.*, a force which is the result of two or more forces combined.

result'ed, *p.p.*, result.

resu'mable, *adj.*, able to be resumed.

resume', *v.t.*, to take up again; to recover; *v.i.*, to begin speaking again.

résumé', *n.*, a summary, abstract, précis (*Fr.*).

resumed', *p.p.*, resume.

resu'ming, *pr.p.*, resume.

resump'tion, *n.*, the act of resuming.

resump'tive, *adj.*, taking back or up again.

resu'pinate, *adj.*, inverted.

resur'gence, *n.*, the act of surging back.

resur'gent, *adj.*, surging back.

resurrec'tion, *n.*, the act of rising again; a revival; body-snatching.

resurrec'tionist, *n.*, a body-snatcher.

resurvey', *v.t.*, to survey afresh.

resus'citant, *adj.*, tending to revive.

resus'citate, *v.t.*, to revive; bring back to consciousness; reanimate.

resus'citated, *p.p.*, resuscitate.

resus'citating, *pr.p.*, resuscitate.

resuscita'tion, *n.*, the act or effect of resuscitating.

resus'citative, *adj.*, aiding recovery.

resus'citator, *n.*, one who, or that which, resuscitates.

ret, *v.t.*, to macerate fibrous plants.

reta'ble, *n.*, an altarpiece; reredos.

re'tail, *adj.* (the opposite to wholesale), sold in small quantities; *n.*, sale in small quantities.

retail', *v.t.*, to sell at retail; to repeat; recount.

retailed', *p.p.*, retail.

retail'er, *n.*, one who retails; one who sells at retail.

retail'ing, *pr.p.*, retail.

retain', *v.t.*, to hold in possession; to keep; to engage for fee.

retain'able, *adj.*, able to be retained.

retained', *p.p.*, retain.

retain'er, *n.*, one who retains; a servant in a great household; a camp-follower; a fee for services engaged; legal retention or authority to retain.

retain'ing, *pr.p.*, retain.

retake', *v.t.*, to take back or again.

reta'ken, *p.p.*, retake.

reta'king, *pr.p.*, retake.

retal'iate, *v.t.*, to repay in kind; *v.i.*, to return evil for evil; to impose fiscal duties; to make rejoinder.

retal'iated, *p.p.*, retaliate.

retal'iating, *pr.p.*, retaliate.

retalia'tion, *n.*, the act of retaliating; revenge.

retal'iative, *adj.*, of the nature of retaliation.

retal'iatory, *adj.*, *i.q.* retaliative.

retard', *v.t.*, to arrest the progress of; to

diminish velocity of; *v.i.*, to delay; *n.*, delay, esp. in regard to the motion of tides, waves, celestial bodies, etc.

retarda'tion, *n.*, the act or effect of retarding.

retard'ative, *adj.*, tending to retard.

retard'ed, *p.p.*, retard.

retard'ing, *pr.p.*, retard.

retch, *v.i.*, to strain as with vomiting.

retched, *p.p.*, retch.

retch'ing, *pr.p.*, retch; *n.*, straining as with vomiting.

reten'tion, *n.*, the act of retaining; holding back; power of retaining.

reten'tive, *adj.*, with power to retain, esp. in the memory.

reten'tively, *adv.*, in a retentive way.

reten'tiveness, *n.*, the power of retaining; good memory.

re'tiary, *adj.*, web-spinning; *n.*, a spinning spider.

ret'icence, *n.*, silence, reserve, taciturnity.

ret'icent, *adj.*, silent, reserved, taciturn.

ret'icle, *n.*, fine lines, like network, drawn across an object glass.

retic'ular, *adj.*, having interstices.

retic'ulate, *adj.*, consisting of, or like, network.

retic'ulate, *v.t.*, to divide in network-fashion.

retic'ulated, *p.p.*, reticulate; *adj.*, *i.q.* reticulate.

retic'ulating, *pr.p.*, reticulate.

reticula'tion, *n.*, network.

ret'icule, *n.*, *i.q.* reticle; also a lady's hand-bag.

retic'ulum, *n.*, a ruminant animal's second stomach.

re'tiform, *adj.*, like network.

ret'ina, *n.*, a coat at the back of the eye-ball sensitive to light.

ret'inal, *adj.*, pert. to the retina.

retini'tis, *n.*, inflammation of the retina.

ret'inoid, *adj.*, resembling resin.

ret'inue, *n.*, a body of attendants or retainers.

retire', *v.t.*, to withdraw; remove from active service; *v.i.*, to withdraw oneself in several senses.

retired', *p.p.*, retire; *adj.*, returned to private life.

retire'ment, *n.*, the act of retiring; the retired state; a secluded place.

retir'ing, *pr.p.*, retire; *adj.*, shy, unobtrusive.

retort', *v.t.*, to turn back upon another; *v.i.*, to make a sharp reply: *n.*, a sharp reply; a vessel used for distillation and other purposes.

retort'ed, *p.p.*, retort.

retort'ing, *pr.p.*, retort.

retor'tion, *n.*, a bending back.

retouch', *v.t.*, to touch over again; to improve.

retouched', *p.p.*, retouch.

retouch'ing, *pr.p.*, retouch.

retour', *n.*, a copy of a return to the Chancery Court (*Scot.*).

retrace', *v.t.*, to trace back; to repeat.

retrace'able, *adj.*, able to be retraced.

retraced', *p.p.*, retrace.

retra'cing, *pr.p.*, retrace.

retract', *v.t.* and *i.*, to draw back; take back; recant; *n.*, the pricking of a horse's hoof by driving a nail into it.

retractabil'ity, *n.*, the state or quality of being retractable.

retract'able, *adj.*, able to be retracted.

retract'ed, *p.p.*, retract.

retract'ible, *adj.*, *i.q.* retractable.

retract'ile, *adj.*, able to be drawn back.

retract'ing, *pr.p.*, retract.

retrac'tion, *n.*, the act of withdrawing.

retract'ive, *adj.*, retracting; able to draw back.

retract'or, *n.*, that which retracts; a retracting muscle or instrument.

retread', *v.t.*, to tread again.

retreat', *v.i.*, to withdraw, retire, go back; *n.*, withdrawal, retirement; a place of retirement.

retreat'ed, *p.p.*, retreat.

retreat'er, *n.*, one who retreats.

retreat'ing, *pr.p.*, retreat.

retrench', *v.t.*, to cut down, curtail; *v.i.*, to economize.

retrenched', *p.p.*, retrench.

retrench'ing, *pr.p.*, retrench.

retrench'ment, *n.*, economizing; cutting down expenses.

retribu'tion, *n.*, requital; punishment.

retrib'utive, *adj.*, punitive; in the way of requital.

retrib'utory, *adj.*, making retribution.

retriev'able, *adj.*, able to be retrieved.

retriev'al, *n.*, restoration.

retrieve', *v.t.*, to bring back; to restore; remedy; *v.i.*, to be a retriever (said of a dog).

retrieved', *p.p.*, retrieve.

retriev'er, *n.*, one who retrieves; a breed of dogs used in shooting game.

retriev'ing, *pr.p.*, retrieve.

ret'ro-, a prefix = backward.

retroac'tion, *n.*, reverse action.

retroact'ive, *adj.*, retrospective; rel. to past transactions.
retrocede', *v.t.*, to give back, restore.
retroce'ded, *p.p.*, retrocede.
retroce'dent, *adj.*, giving back.
retroce'ding, *pr.p.*, retrocede.
retroces'sion, *n.*, the act of giving back, or restoring.
re'trochoir, *n.*, the part of a church behind the high altar in the choir, but exclusive of a chapel further east.
retroduc'tion, *n.*, a drawing back.
ret'roflex, *adj.*, bent back.
ret'roflexed, *adj.*, *i.q.* retroplex.
retrograda'tion, *n.*, the act of retrograding.
ret'rograde, *v.i.*, to go back; to deteriorate; *adj.*, going back; deteriorating; *n.*, a degenerate.
ret'rograded, *p.p.*, retrograde.
ret'rograding, *pr.p.*, retrograde.
retrogres'sion, *n.*, a retrograde process.
retrogres'sive, *adj.*, retrograding.
retropul'sive, *adj.*, pushing backward.
retrorse', *adj.*, turned backward.
retrorse'ly, *adv.*, in a retrorse way.
ret'rospect, *v.t.*, and *i.*, to survey the past; *n.*, a survey of the past.
retrospec'tion, *n.*, the act of retrospecting.
retrospec'tive, *adj.*, looking back on the past; embracing the past.
retrospec'tively, *adv.*, in a retrospective way.
retrous'sé, *adj.*, turned up at the end; tip-tilted (*Fr.*).
retrover'sion, *n.*, the state of being tipped back; a tipping backward.
ret'rovert, *v.t.*, to turn back.
ret'roverted, *p.p.*, retrovert.
ret'roverting, *pr.p.*, retrovert.
return', *v.t.*, to turn again; repay; requite; pay; elect; transmit (a statement, etc.); to send back (a tennis-ball) into the opponent's court; *v.i.*, to come or go back; reply; turn again; *n.*, a coming or going back; restoration; requital; formal statement or list; election; a side of a building receding from the front. In pl., profits; a variety of tobacco.
return'able, *adj.*, able to be returned; due.
returned', *p.p.*, return; *adj.*, used in an architectural sense, as "returned stalls," *i.e.*, arranged L shape.
return'ing, *pr.p.*, return.
retuse', *adj.*, broadened at the end and depressed in the middle (*bot.*).
reun'nion, *n.*, a reuniting; state of being reunited; a social meeting.
reunite', *v.t.* and *i.*, to unite again.
reuni'ted, *p.p.*, reunite.
revac'cinate, *v.t.*, to vaccinate again.
revaccina'tion, *n.*, vaccination repeated.
reveal', *v.t.*, to bring into the light; to display; divulge.
reveal'able, *adj.*, able to be revealed.
revealed', *p.p.*, reveal.
reveal'er, *n.*, one who reveals.
reveal'ing, *pr.p.*, reveal.
reveil'lé, *n.*, the morning bugle call.
rev'el, *v.i.*, to indulge in wild festivities; to delight greatly; *n.*, wild festivities; carousal.
revela'tion, *n.*, the act of revealing; something revealed; Apocalypse.
rev'el(l)ed, *p.p.*, revel.
rev'el(l)er, *n.*, one who holds revel.
revel'lent, *adj.*, causing revulsion.
rev'e(l)ling, *pr.p.*, revel.
rev'elry, *n.*, revelling; riotous festivity.
revendica'tion, *n.*, a suit demanding back lost property, etc.
revenge', *v.t.*, to exact vengeance for; to inflict punishment for; *n.*, the act of revenging; retaliation; vindictiveness.
revenged', *p.p.*, revenge.
revenge'ful, *adj.*, vindictive.
reven'ger, *n.*, one who takes revenge.
reven'ging, *pr.p.*, revenge.
rev'enue, *n.*, income, public or private.
rever'berant, *adj.*, resounding.
rever'berate, *v.t.* and *i.*, to echo; to reflect or be reflected.
rever'berated, *p.p.*, reverberate.
rever'berating, *pr.p.*, reverberate.
reverbera'tion, *n.*, the act or effect of reverberating.
rever'beratory, *adj.*, *i.q.* reverberant.
revere', *v.t.*, to reverence; to respect greatly.
revered', *p.p.*, revere.
rev'erence, *v.t.*, to treat or regard with veneration; *n.*, veneration, honour; an act of respect; a reverend person, as in the expression *Your Reverence, his Reverence,* etc. (*colloq.*).
rev'erenced, *p.p.*, reverence.
rev'erencing, *pr.p.*, reverence.
rev'erend, *adj.*, worthy of reverence; an ecclesiastical title of a person in Holy Orders, a

Mother Superior, etc.

rev'erent, *adj.*, showing reverence.

reveren'tial, *adj.* expressive of reverence.

reveren'tially, *adv.*, in a reverential way.

rev'erently, *adv.*, in a reverent way.

reve'rer, *n.*, one who reveres.

rev'erie, *n.*, day-dreaming; musing without method.

revers', *n.*, a lapel.

revers', *n.*, pl. of revers.

revers'al, *n.*, the act or effect of reversing; defeat.

reverse', *v.t.*, to turn back; to change the order or position of; to annul; *adj.*, opposite, reversed, annulled; *n.*, the opposite; the back of a medal (as distinguished from the obverse); a change to the contrary; defeat.

reversed', *p.p.*, reverse.

reverse'ly, *adv.*, in a reverse way.

revers'ible, *adj.*, able to be reversed.

revers'ing, *pr.p.*, reverse.

rever'sion, *n.*, a return to a former state; right of inheritance; a deferred annuity.

rever'sionary, *adj.*, rel. to reversion.

rever'sioner, *n.*, one who is entitled to a reversion.

revert', *v.i.*, to return; to come back to the original owner.

revert'ed, *p.p.*, revert.

revert'ible, *adj.*, able to revert.

revert'ing, *pr.p.*, revert.

revert'ive, *adj.*, retiring.

revest', *v.t.*, to clothe again; to reinvest in a title or office; *v.i.*, to take effect again.

revest'ry, *n.*, *i.q.* vestry.

review', *v.t.*, to view again; to go over in memory; to scrutinize, criticize; to inspect; *n.*, a looking back, retrospect; critical examination; an inspection; a written criticism; a literary periodical.

review'able, *adj.*, able to be reviewed.

review'al, *n.*, a review.

reviewed', *p.p.*, review.

review'er, *n.*, a writer of reviews.

review'ing, *pr.p.*, review; *n.*, the business of a reviewer.

revile', *v.t.*, to slander, abuse.

reviled', *p.p.*, revile.

revi'ler, *n.*, one who reviles.

revi'ling, *pr.p.*, revile; *n.*, abuse.

revi'sal, *n.*, revision.

revise', *v.t.*, to reconsider for the purpose of correction; to alter; *n.*, a revision.

revised', *p.p.*, revise.

revi'ser, *n.*, one who revises.

revi'sing, *pr.p.*, revise.

revis'ion, *n.*, the act of revising; that which has been revised.

revis'ional, *adj.*, of the nature of revision.

revis'ionary, *adj.*, *i.q.* revisional.

revis'it, *v.t.*, to visit again.

revi'val, *n.*, the act of reviving; restoration; recovery.

revi'valism, *n.*, a movement advocating spiritual revival by peculiar methods.

revi'valist, *n.*, an advocate of revivalism.

revive', *v.t.*, to restore to animation; to bring back to life; to bring back from oblivion; *v.i.*, to recover; to regain animation.

revived', *p.p.*, revive.

revi'ver, *n.*, that which revives.

revivifica'tion, *n.*, the act of revivifying.

reviv'ified, *p.p.*, revivify.

reviv'ify, *v.t.*, to vivify again; to quicken again.

reviv'ifying, *pr.p.*, revivify.

revi'ving, *pr.p.*, revive; *adj.*, restorative.

revivis'cence, *n.*, renewal of life.

revivis'cent, *adj.*, returning to life.

revi'vor, *n.*, the process of reviving a dormant judgment or suspended action (*leg.*).

revocabil'ity, *n.*, the state of being revocable.

rev'ocable, *adj.*, able to be revoked or recalled.

revoca'tion, *n.*, the act or effect of revoking; annulment.

rev'ocatory, *adj.*, revoking.

revoke', *v.t.*, to recall; to cancel; to withdraw; *v.i.*, to make a revoke (at cards); *n.*, neglect to follow suit.

revoked', *p.p.*, revoke

revo'king, *pr.p.*, revoke.

revolt', *v...*, to shock; *v.i.*, to rebel; to mutiny; to be nauseated; *n.*, a rebellion, mutiny.

revolt'ed, *p.p.*, revolt.

revolt'er, *n.*, one who revolts.

revolt'ing, *pr.p.*, revolt; *adj.*, shocking.

rev'olute, *adj.*, rolled backwards.

revolu'tion, *n.*, a rolling backward; a completeturnround; a complete reversal; a wholesale change of principles of government.

revolu'tionary, *adj.*, rel. to a revolution.

revolu'tionist, *n.*, one who advocates, or takes part in, a revolution.

revolu'tionize, *v.t.*, to change completely; *v.i.*, to pass through a revolution.

revolu'tionized, *p.p.*, revolutionize.

revolu'tionizing, *pr.p.* revolutionize.

revolve', *v.t.*, to make go round; to ponder; *v.i.*, to rotate; to recur in a cycle.

revolved', *p.p.*, revolve.

revolv'er, *n.*, a pistol having a revolving cylinder in the breech; anything that revolves.

revolv'ing, *pr.p.*, revolve.

revul'sion, *n.*, a violent change of feeling; removal of a disease from one part to another.

revul'sive, *adj.*, producing a revulsion.

reward', *v.t.*, to recompense; requite; *n.*, a recognition of merit; a requital.

reward'able, *adj.*, worthy of reward.

reward'ed, *p.p.*, reward.

reward'er, *n.*, one who rewards.

reward'ing, *p.p.*, reward.

rewrite', *v.t.*, to write over again.

rewrit'ten, *p.p.*, rewrite.

rex, *n.*, a king (*Lat.*).

rey'nard, *n.*, a name for the fox as the most cunning of beasts. Also *renard*.

rhabar'barate, *adj.*, tinctured with rhubarb (*rhabarbarum*).

rhabdol'ogy, *n.*, calculating by means of Napier's rods.

rhab'domancy, *n.*, divination by means of rods.

Rhadaman'thine, *adj.*, rel. to Rhadamanthus, the judge in Hades; rigorous, exact.

Rhae'tian, Rhe'tian, *adj.*, naming the Alps near the Engadine.

rhapsod'ic, *adj.*, pert. to rhapsody.

rhapsod'ical, *adj.*, *i.q.* rhapsodic.

rhap'sodist, *n.*, one who recites or makes rhapsodies.

rhap'sodize, *v.t.* and *i.*, to recite; to make rhapsodies.

rhap'sodized, *p.p.*, rhapsodize.

rhap'sodizing, *pr.p.*, rhapsodize.

rhap'sody, *n.*, a long epic poem for recitation in whole or part.

Rhen'ish, *adj.*, pert. to the Rhine; *n.*, Rhine wine.

rheom'eter, *n.*, an instrument for measuring blood-circulation.

rheom'etry, *n.*, the science of measuring blood-circulation.

rhe'ostat, *n.*, an instrument to regulate force of currents.

Rhe'tian, *adj.*, *i.q.* Rhaetian.

rhet'oric, *n.*, the art of discourse; oratory; the science of persuasive speech; insincere or exaggerated speech or writing.

rhetor'ical, *adj.*, rel. to rhetoric; artificial or extravagant in speech or writing.

rhetor'ically, *adv.*, in a rhetorical way.

rhetori'cian, *n.*, one who speaks or writes rhetoric.

rheum, *n.*, catarrhal discharge.

rheumat'ic, *adj.*, pert. to, suffering from, rheumatism; *n.*, one so suffering.

rheum'atism, *n.*, a painful disease affecting the joints or muscles.

rheum'y, *adj.*, pert. to rheum; damp.

rhi'no, *n.*, money (*slang*); also a *prefix* meaning nose.

rhinoce'rial, *adj.*, rhinoceros-like; pug.

rhinoc'eros, *n.*, a huge mammal, with a thick, plated skin and a horned nose.

rhi'noscope, *n.*, an instrument for the examination of the nose.

rhinos'copy, *n.*, the art of examining the nose.

rhizo'ma, *n.*, *i.q.* rhizome.

rhi'zome, *n.*, a prostrate stem producing roots, etc.

rhizoph'agous, *adj.*, root-eating.

Rho'dian, *adj.*, rel. to Rhodes; a native of Rhodes.

rho'dium, *n.*, a greyish element used in alloys.

Rhododen'dron, *n.*, an evergreen shrub with large, fine flowers.

rhodomontade', *n.*, *see* rodomontade.

rhomb, *n.*, a parallelogram, equilateral and oblique-angled.

rhom'bic, *adj.*, like a rhomb.

rhom'boid, *adj.*, like a rhomb; *n.*, a parallelogram that is neither rectangular nor rhombic.

rhom'boidal, *adj.*, *i.q.* rhomboid.

rhom'bus, *n.*, *i.q.* rhomb; the turbot or brill.

rhu'barb, *n.*, a purgative root imported from Turkey, China and Tibet; a garden-stalk used in cookery.

rhumb, *n.*, one of the thirty-two points in a mariner's compass.

rhyme, *n.*, *see* rime.

rhymed, *p.p.*, rhyme; *see* rimed.

rhym'er, *n.*, one who rhymes; a versifier.

rhyme'less, *adj.*, not rhyming.

rhyme'ster, *n.*, a composer of rhymes.

rhym'ic, *adj.*, pert. to rhyme.

rhym'ing, *pr.p.*, rhyme; versification in rhyme.

rhythm, *n.*, metrical movement; measured flow of words or musical notes; proper correlation of structural parts (*arch.*); regular succession of strong and weak elements in movement; periodicity.

rhyth'mic, *adj.*, marked by rhythm.

rhyth'mical, *adj.*, *i.q.* rhythmic.

rhyth'mus, *n.*, *i.q.* rhythm (*Gr.*).

Rial'to, *n.*, the old business quarter of Venice; the bridge over the Grand Canal.

ri'ant, *adj.*, bright, smiling.

rib, *v.t.*, to furnish with ribs; *n.*, one of the curved bones extending from the spine and encircling the body; anything like a rib, as the vein of a leaf, a wave-mark on sand, etc.

rib'ald, *adj.*, profane, irreverent; obscene in speech.

rib'aldry, *n.*, profanity, obscenity in speech.

rib'and, rib'band, *n.*, *i.q.* ribbon.

ribbed, *p.p.*, rib; *adj.*, having ribs.

rib'bing, *pr.p.*, rib; *n.*, an arrangement of ribs; a method of ploughing.

rib'bon, *v.t.*, to deck with ribbons; *v.i.*, to run to ribbons (as melting wax); *n.*, a strip of silk or other material for a variety of uses.

rib'boned, *p.p.*, ribbon; *adj.*, decorated with a ribbon.

rib'boning, *pr.p.*, ribbon.

Rib'bonism, *n.*, the principles of the secret society of Ribbonmen, Irishmen organized to oppose the Orange societies.

Ri'bes, *n.*, a plant genus which includes the gooseberry and the currant.

Rib'ston pip'pin, *n.*, a variety of eating apple.

rice, *n.*, a cereal producing a seed much used for food.

rice'-bird, *n.*, the bobolink.

rice'-paper, *n.*, paper made from a Formosan plant and much used by Chinese artists.

rice'-water, *n.*, water in which rice has been boiled.

rich, *adj.*, wealthy, affluent; costly; luxuriant; abounding in; deep and full; very amusing.

rich'er, *adj.*, *comp.* of rich.

rich'es, *n.*, wealth, possessions.

rich'est, *adj.*, *super.* of rich.

rich'ly, *adv.*, in a rich way; sumptuously; fully.

rich'ness, *n.*, the quality of being rich.

ricinela'idin, *n.*, a compound of castor-oil and nitric peroxide.

rick, *v.t.*, to make into ricks; *n.*, a stack of hay, etc.

rick'ets, *n.*, an infantine disease, accompanied by softening of the bones, esp. of the spine; rachitis.

rick'ety, *adj.*, afflicted with rickets; tottering, unsafe.

rick'ing, *pr.p.*, rick.

rick'shaw, *n.*, a hand-carriage; the jinricksha.

ric'ochet, *v.i.*, to glance off, rebound; *n.*, the glancing off of a bullet, etc., after striking some object.

ricochet'ted, *p.p.*, richochet.

ricochet'ting, *pr.p.*, ricochet.

rid, *v.t.*, to free, relieve, abolish; *adj.*, free; disencumbered.

rid'dance, *n.*, the act of ridding; relief, freedom.

rid'dels, *n. pl.*, side-curtains of an altar.

rid'den, *p.p.*, ride.

rid'der, *n.*, one who, or that which, rids.

rid'ding, *pr.p.*, rid.

rid'dle, *v.t.*, to pierce with holes; to sift; to solve; *n.*, a large sort of sieve; an enigma; puzzle.

rid'dled, *p.p.*, riddle.

rid'dler, *n.*, one who riddles.

rid'dling, *pr.p.*, riddle.

ride, *v.t.*, to be carried on the back of; to sit on or in (as a carriage); *v.i.*, to travel on horseback, etc., or in a conveyance; to float; to work its way up.

ride'able, *adj.*, able to be ridden.

rideau', *n.*, a curtain (*Fr.*).

ri'der, *n.*, one who rides a horse, bicycle, etc.; a supplementary writing, statement, clause of a Parliamentary Bill; a corollary; a mathematical problem for solution according to principles previously taught.

ri'derless, *adj.*, without a rider.

ridge, *v.t.* and *i.*, to form into ridges; *n.*, the top of two slopes which meet, as on a mountain, a furrow, and so forth.

ridged, *p.p.*, ridge; *adj.*, having ridges.

ridge'way, *n.*, a road along a ridge.

ridg'ing, *pr.p.*, ridge.

rid'icule, *v.t.*, to make fun of; laugh at; satirize; *n.*, derisive laughter; an object of derision.

rid'iculed, *p.p.*, ridicule.

rid'iculer, *n.*, one who ridicules.

rid'iculing, *pr.p.*, ridicule.

ridic'ulous, *adj.*, absurd, laughable, contemptible.

ridic'ulously, *adv.*, in an absurd fashion.

ridic'ulousness, *n.*, absurdity.

ri'ding, *pr.p.*, ride; *n.*, the act or state of riding; a procession; an administrative division of Yorkshire and Lincolnshire.

ri'ding-hood, *n.*, a rider's head-covering.

ri'ding-master, *n.*, a teacher of riding.

ridot'to, *n.*, a masked ball; a public ball-room; a shortened score (*mus.*); *adj.*, abbreviated from full score (*mus.*).

rife, *adj.*, commonly occurring; current; abundant.

riff'raff, *n.*, the mob, rabble; rubbish.

ri'fle, *v.t.*, to rob, plunder; to groove (a firearm); *n.*, a firearm having its bore grooved (or rifled).

ri'fle-corps, *n.*, a body of troops armed with rifles.

ri'fled, *p.p.*, rifle.

ri'fleman, *n.*, a soldier armed with a rifle.

ri'fler, *n.*, one who rifles; a robber.

ri'fle-shot, *n.*, the length to which a rifle carries.

ri'fling, *pr.p.*, rifle.

rift, *v.t.*, to cleave, split; *n.*, a fissure, split.

rift'ed, *p.p.*, rift.

rift'ing, *pr.p.*, rift.

rift'less, *adj.*, without a rift.

rif'ty, *adj.*, full of fissures.

rig, *v.t.*, to furnish with sails, ropes, etc.; to equip; to manipulate the market fraudulently; *n.*, a ship's equipment; costume; tackle; a dodge.

rigadoon', *n.*, an old Provençal dance and its music.

Ri'gel, *n.*, the star *Beta*, in *Orion*.

riges'cent, *adj.*, stiffening.

rigged, *p.p.*, rig.

rig'ger, *n.*, one who rigs; a handwheel.

rig'ging, *pr.p.*, rig; *n.*, a ship's equipment of spars, sails, etc.

right, *v.t.*, to put right; to remedy a wrong; *adj.*, straight; just; morally good; fitting, correct; *n.*, just or proper conduct; that which is essentially right; just claim; the side opposite to the left; *adv.*, correctly; justly; greatly.

right'-about, *n.*, the opposite direction.

right'-angle, *n.*, an angle of 90°.

right'-angled, *adj.*, containing right angles.

right'ed, *p.p.*, right.

right'eous, *adj.*, just, virtuous, upright.

right'eously, *adv.*, justly, uprightly.

right'eousness, *n.*, the quality of being righteous.

right'er, *adj.*, *comp.* of right; *n.*, one who rights.

right'ful, *adj.*, with a just claim; just.

right'fully, *adv.*, by right.

right'fulness, *n.*, the quality of being rightful.

right'-*hand*, *adj.*, lying to the right side.

right'-handed, *adj.*, using chiefly the right hand.

right'ing, *pr.p.*, right.

right'ly, *adv.*, properly, strictly.

right'-minded, *adj.*, upright in disposition.

right'-mindedness, *n.*, the quality of being right-minded.

right'ness, *n.*, the quality of being right.

rig'id, *adj.*, stiff; not flexible.

rigid'ity, *n.*, stiffness; inflexibility.

rig'idly, *adv.*, stiffly.

rig'idness, *n.*, *i.q.* rigidity.

rig'marole, *n.*, incoherent, rambling talk or writing.

ri'gor, *n.*, stiffness, rigidity; a violent chill with shivering (*Lat.*).

rig'orist, *n.*, an austere person of strict principles.

rig'orous, *adj.*, austere, strict; inclement.

rig'orously, *adv.*, in a rigorous way.

rig'our, *n.*, severity, austerity; strictness; the quality or state of being inclement.

Rig-ve'da, *n.*, the chief of the Vedas, or hymns in praise of the powers of nature.

rile, *v.t.*, to annoy, exasperate (*slang*).

riled, *p.p.*, rile.

rilie'vo, *n.*, a relief (in sculpture) (*Ital.*).

ri'ling, *pr.p.*, rile; *adj.*, exasperating.

rill, *v.i.*, to run in a small stream; *n.*, a brooklet.

rilled, *p.p.*, rill.

rill'et, *n.*, diminutive of rill.

rill'ing, *pr.p.*, rill.

rim, *v.t.*, to put a rim to; *n.*, an edging; the circumference of a wheel; a frame.

rime, *v.t.*, to produce identity of sounds in words; to versify; *n.*, versification; identity of sounds in words. Also spelt *rhyme*.

rime, *v.t.*, to cover with rime; *n.*, a hoar-frost.

rimed, *p.p.*, rime.

ri'mer, *n.*, a versifier.

rime'ster, *n.*, a would-be poet.

ri'ming, *pr.p.*, rime.

rimmed, *p.p.*, rim; *adj.*, having a rim.

rim'ming, *pr.p.*, rim.

rimose', *adj.*, chinky.

rimos'ity, *n.*, the quality or state of being rimose.

ri'mous, *adj.*, *i.q.* rimose.

rim'ple, *v.t.* and *i.*, to wrinkle.

rim'pled, *p.p.*, rimple.

rim'pling, *pr.p.*, rimple.

ri'my, *adj.*, frosty, cold.

rind, *n.*, the peel or outer coating of fruit, flesh, etc.

rin'derpest, *n.*, a cattle-disease.

rin'dle, *n.*, a runnel.

ring, *v.t.*, to cause to sound clearly; to sound; to encircle; to put a ring in or upon; *v.i.*, to give forth a clear song; to move in spirals;

to resound; *n.*, a circle; a circular band for the finger; a peal of bells; a combination for controlling the market.

ring′-bolt, *n.*, an eye-bolt with a ring.

ring′-bone, *n.*, a disease in horses marked by a bony growth on the pastern-bones.

ring′-dove, *n.*, a wood-pigeon.

ringed, *p.p.*, ring; *adj.*, marked with a ring.

rin′gent, *adj.*, grinning, gaping.

ring′er, *n.*, one who rings bells; an apparatus for ringing; a quoit that encircles the pin; a hunted fox that runs in rings.

ring′-fence, *n.*, a fence entirely surrounding a park, etc.

ring′ing, *pr.p.*, ring; *adj.*, giving forth a clear metallic sound; *n.*, the act of ringing; the sound of bells.

ring′leader, *n.*, one who heads a rebellion, riot, etc.

ring′let, *n.*, a little ring; a spiral lock of hair.

ring′-shaped, *adj.*, shaped like a ring.

ring′tail, *n.*, the female of the hen-harrier; the golden eagle.

ring′-tailed, *adj.*, having a tail marked with rings.

ring′worm, *n.*, a skin disease in circular patches.

rink, *v.i.*, to skate on a rink; *n.*, a curling-ground; an artificial skating surface.

rinked, *p.p.*, rink.

rink′er, *n.*, one who rinks.

rink′ing, *pr.p.*, rink; *n.*, the act or art of rinking.

rinse, *v.t.*, to swill; cleanse with liquid.

rinsed, *p.p.*, rinse.

rins′ing, *pr.p.*, rinse; *n.*, the act of rinsing; a liquid for rinsing.

ri′ot, *v.i.*, to make a tumult; to behave violently; to luxuriate; *n.*, tumult, disorder, luxuriant growth.

ri′oted, *p.p.*, riot.

ri′oter, *n.*, one who riots; a tumultuous person.

ri′oting, *pr.p.*, riot; *n.*, tumult.

ri′otous, *adj.*, tumultuous; dissipated; profligate.

ri′otously, *adv.*, in a riotous way.

ri′otousness, *n.*, the quality of being riotous.

rip, *v.t.*, to tear, divide; pull off; lay bare; *v.i.*, to be torn; to rush along; *n.*, a dissipated person (*colloq.*).

ripa′rian, *adj.*, rel. to a river-bank.

ripe, *v.t.* and *i.*, to ripen; *adj.*, mature; ready to be reaped or gathered.

ripe′ly, *adv.*, maturely

ri′pen, *v.t.* and *i.*, to bring or come to maturity.

ri′pened, *p.p.*, ripen.

ripe′ness, *n.*, maturity; the state of being ripe.

ri′pening, *pr.p.*, ripen.

ri′per, *adj.*, *comp.* of ripe.

ripie′no, *adj.*, reinforced, *i.e.*, having the (musical) parts doubled or still further supplemented.

riposte′, *v.i.*, to make a quick return; *n.*, a quick return with a rapier or the tongue; repartee.

ripped, *p.p.*, rip.

rip′per, *n.*, one who, or that which, rips; someone or something very delightful (*slang*).

rip′ping, *pr.p.*, rip; *adj.*, delightful (*slang*).

rip′ple, *v.t.*, to ruffle (the surface); *v.i.*, to make a ripple; *n.*, a ruffling of the surface of water; anything resembling a ripple.

rip′pled, *p.p.*, ripple.

rip′pling, *pr.p.*, ripple.

rip′-rap, *v.t.*, to reinforce with rip-rap; *n.*, broken stones for strengthening or making foundations

rise, *v.t.*, to bring above the horizon; to lift a fish to the top of the water; *v.i.*, to ascend; to get up from a lying posture; to advance in height in any sense, as to be promoted; to slope upward; to come to the surface (as a fish); *n.*, an ascent; promotion; a fish's ascent for bait; the height of a step; any kind of upward advance; humiliation by ridicule (*slang*).

ris′en, *p.p.*, rise.

ri′ser, *n.*, one who, or that which, rises; the upright piece between two stair-treads.

risibil′ity, *n.*, the quality of being risible.

ris′ible, *adj.*, disposed to laugh.

ris′ibly, *adv.*, in a risible way.

ri′sing, *pr.p.*, rise; *n.*, a getting up; an insurrection.

risk, *v.t.* and *i.*, to hazard; *n.*, hazard; taking one's chance.

risked, *p.p.*, risk.

risk′ing, *pr.p.*, risk.

risk′y, *adj.*, hazardous, dangerous; somewhat improper.

ris′sole, *n.*, meat or fish cooked in a sausage-like roll or cake.

ritardan′do, *adv.*, slower (*mus.*).

rite, *n.*, a prescribed form of words used in liturgical worship and ceremonial observances. (Rite must be distinguished from ceremony as it is distinguished on the title-page of the Book of Common Prayer.)

ritornel'lo, *n.*, an instrumental interlude, prelude, or refrain.

rit'ual, *adj.*, pert. to rites; *n.*, prescribed order of religious service; a book of rites.

rit'ualism, *n.*, a system based on rites as opposed to informal or non-liturgical worship.

Rit'ualist, *n.*, one learned in liturgiology or the study of rites. (In the sixties and seventies of last century it was contemptuously, but incorrectly, applied to the advocates of ceremonial in the English Church.)

ritualis'tic, *adj.*, rel. to ritual and ritualism.

rit'ually, *adv.*, according to ritual; with rites.

ri'val, *v.t.*, to emulate, oppose; equal; *n.*, one who competes for a prize coveted by another; *adj.*, in competition.

ri'val(l)ed, *p.p.*, rival.

ri'val(l)ing, *pr.p.*, rival.

ri'valry, *n.*, an act or state of competing.

ri'valship, *n.*, *i.q.* rivalry.

rive, *v.t.* and *i.*, to split.

rived, *p.t.* and *p.*, rive.

riv'en, *p.p.*, rive.

riv'er, *n.*, a large stream of flowing water.

riv'er-horse, *n.*, the hippopotamus.

riv'et, *v.t.*, to fix, fasten, clinch; *n.*, a bolt or nail fixing metal plates together.

riv'eted, *p.p.*, rivet.

riv'eting, *pr.p.*, rivet; *n.*, the act of joining with rivets; a whole system of rivets.

rivière', *n.*, a necklace of diamonds or other gems.

ri'ving, *pr.p.*, rive.

riv'ulet, *n.*, a very small stream.

rix'-dollar, *n.*, a silver coin of Denmark and other countries.

roach, *n.*, a freshwater fish.

road, *n.*, a track, path, highway.

road'hog, *n.*, one who drives a motor or rides a motor-cycle to the danger of the public.

roads, *n.*, pl. of road; *i.q.* roadstead.

road'side, *n.*, the side of a road.

road'stead, *n.*, an open place of anchorage.

road'ster, *n.*, a horse or bicycle, etc., for travelling on roads.

road'way, *n.*, the middle of a road.

roam, *v.i.*, to go from place to place, to wander; *v.t.*, to wander over.

roamed, *p.p.*, roam.

roam'er, *n.*, one who roams.

roam'ing, *pr.p.*, roam

roan, *adj.*, of a colour combining chestnut, bay, or sorrel with grey or white; *n.*, the roan colour; a roan-coloured horse; a soft sheepskin leather used in bookbinding.

roar, *v.i.*, to utter a loud, prolonged sound; *v.t.*, to shout out something; *n.*, a loud, prolonged sound.

roared, *p.p.*, roar.

roar'er, *n.*, one who roars, esp. a horse afflicted with roaring.

roar'ing, *pr.p.*, roar; *adj.*, boisterous; riotously merry; highly successful (*slang*); *n.*, a disease of the larynx affecting horses.

roast, *v.t.*, to cook by subjecting to fire; to parch; to banter (*slang*); *adj.*, roasted; *n.*, roasted meat, or meat for roasting. (Hence the phrase, "To rule the roast.")

roast'ed, *p.p.*, roast.

roast'er, *n.*, one who roasts; an oven or other apparatus for roasting.

roast'ing, *pr.p.*, roast.

rob, *v.t.*, to plunder; to steal from; to deprive; *v.i.*, to be a thief.

robbed, *p.p.*, rob.

rob'ber, *n.*, a thief, plunderer.

rob'bery, *n.*, the act of robbing.

rob'bin, *n.*, a package of rice, spice, etc.

rob'bing, *pr.p.*, rob.

robe, *v.t.*, to dress; invest ceremoniously with dress; *v.i.*, to put on dress; *n.*, a dress, esp. an official garment; a costume; a woman's dress-fabric in a single piece.

robed, *p.p.*, robe.

rob'in, *n.*, a small bird with a red breast.

rob'inet, *n.*, the chaffinch; an old engine of war.

ro'bing, *pr.p.*, robe.

rob'in-red'breast, *n.*, the robin.

ro'borant, *adj.*, strengthening.

ro'burite, *n.*, an explosive so named.

robust', *adj.*, vigorous, stout, strenuous.

robust'ious, *adj.*, sturdy, boisterous.

robust'ly, *adv.*, vigorously.

robust'ness, *n.*, the quality of being robust.

roc, *n.*, a fabulous Eastern bird of vast size and strength.

roc'ambole, *n.*, Spanish garlic.

Roccel'la, *n. pl.*, the name of certain lichens.

roccel'lic, *adj.*, rel. to Roccella.

roch'et, *n.*, an ecclesiastical linen vestment, close-fitting, worn by ecclesiastics of various ranks.

rock, *v.t.*, to move from side to side; to move (a cradle); *v.i.*, to sway one way and another; *n.*, the hard crust of the earth; a foundation.

rock'-bound, *adj.*, fenced round with rocks.

rock'-crystal, *n.*, transparent quartz.

rocked, *p.p.*, rock.

rock'er, *n.*, anything that rocks; one of the curved pieces beneath a rocking-chair; a rocking-chair; an automobile lever.

rock'ery, *n.*, rock-work.

rock'et, *v.i.*, to shoot up like a rocket; *n.*, a firework that shoots straight up into the air; a plant so named.

rock'iness, *n.*, the quality of being rocky.

rock'ing, *pr.p.*, rock.

rock'ing-*chair*, *n.*, a chair that swings on rockers.

rock'ing-horse, *n.*, a child's toy-horse on rockers.

rock'ing-stone, *n.*, a stone that rocks without falling over.

rock'-oil, *n.*, petroleum.

rock'-salt, *n.*, halite.

rock'work, *n.*, a structure imitating rock; a rockery.

rock'y, *adj.*, hard, like rock; abounding in rocks.

roco'co, *adj.*, in the rococo style; *n.*, a debased, over-decorated, architectural style.

rod, *n.*, *v.t.*, to supply with rods; *n.*, a straight slip of wood; a switch; a birch-rod; a lightning-rod; a measure of length; anything rod-like.

rode, *p.t.*, ride.

ro'dent, *adj.*, gnawing; *n.*, a mammal with incisor and no canine teeth.

Roden'tia, *n. pl.*, rodent mammals, as the beaver, rat, etc.

rodomontade', *v.i.*, to rant; *n.*, rant, bluster.

roe, *n.*, spawn; the eggs of fishes; the roebuck; female of the hart.

roe'buck, *n.*, a small kind of deer.

roga'tion, *n.*, the act of supplicating.

Roga'tion-days, *n.pl.*, the Monday, Tuesday, and Wednesday preceding Ascension Day.

Roga'tion-tide, *n.*, the period of the rogation-days.

Roga'tion-week, *n.*, the week in which the rogation-days occur.

rogue, *v.t.*, to trick; *n.*, a knave, swindler, vagabond.

rogu'ery, *n.*, the conduct of a rogue; mischievous playfulness.

rogu'ish, *adj.*, inclined to roguery.

rogu'ishly, *adv.*, in a roguish way.

rogu'ishness, *n.*, the quality of being roguish.

roil, *v.t.*, to muddy; to annoy.

roiled, *p.p.*, roil.

roil'ing, *pr.p.*, roil.

roil'y, *adj.*, muddy.

roist'er, *v.i.*, to rollick.

roist'erer, *n.*, a rollicking fellow.

rôle, *n.*, a character or part in a play; a function (*Fr.*).

roll, *v.t.*, to move by turning round and round; to wrap; to fold cylindrically; to flatten by rolling; *v.i.*, to move onward by revolving; to rotate; to thunder; *n.*, anything rolled into cylindrical form; an official list; a strip of material that can be rolled; a cake formed by rolling; a printer's tool; a rolling sound, as of thunder or drums.

roll'-*call*, *n.*, a calling over of names on a roll.

rolled, *p.p.*, roll.

roll'er, *n.*, anything with which rolling is done.

roll'er-skate, *n.*, a skate on wheels.

rol'lick, *v.i.*, to indulge in boisterous amusement.

rol'licked, *p.p.*, rollick.

rol'licking, *pr.p.*, rollick; *adj.*, boisterous, frolicsome.

roll'ing, *pr.p.*, roll; *adj.*, moving circularly; undulating.

roll'ing-pin, *n.*, a kitchen utensil for rolling out paste, etc.

roll'ing-stock, *n.*, a railway company's carriages, trucks, etc.

ro'ly-po'ly, *n.*, pastry rolled round jam or fruit.

Roma'ic, *adj.*, rel. to modern Greek; *n.*, the modern Greek language.

romal', *n.*, a Spanish-American thong used instead of a whip.

Ro'man, *adj.*, pert. to Rome and the Romans; like an ancient Roman, stern; *n.*, a citizen of Rome; a kind of type.

Ro'man Cath'olic, *adj.*, bel. to the Roman Church; *n.*, one who belongs to the Roman obedience.

romance', *v.i.*, to fabricate stories; *n.*, an imaginative story about chivalry, whether in verse or prose; the sentiment of chivalry or love or mystery.

Romance', *adj.*, rel. to languages deriving from Latin.

romanced', *p.p.*, romance.

roman'cer, *n.*, one who romances.

roman'cing, *pr.p.*, romance.

roman'cist, *n.*, *i.q.* romancer.

Romanesque', *adj.*, rel. to Romanesque architecture; *n.*, Romanesque architecture, which was developed out of the earlier Roman style, and became what is known in England as Norman.

Roman'ic, *adj.*, *i.q.* Romance.

Ro'manism, *n.*, the Roman Catholic system.

Ro'manist, *adj.*, pert. to Romanism; *n.*, an adherent of the Roman Catholic Church.

Ro'manize, *v.t.*, to make Roman in any sense; *v.i.*, to become Roman Catholic.

Ro'manized, *p.p.*, Romanize.

Ro'manizing, *pr.p.*, Romanize.

roman'tic, *adj.*, pert. to romance; full of mysterious suggestion; appealing to the historic sentiment; sentimental.

roman'tically, *adv.*, in a romantic way.

roman'ticism, *n.*, a romantic style of writing; the appeal to mediaevalism.

roman'ticist, *n.*, one who leans to romanticism.

Rom'any, *adj.*, pert. to the gipsies; *n.*, a gipsy; gipsy speech.

Ro'mic, *n.*, a phonetic system based on the Roman alphabet.

Ro'mish, *adj.*, Roman Catholic (in popular language). In the Thirty-nine Articles the word seems to describe some popular mediaeval errors.

romp, *v.i.*, to play roughly; to gain an easy win; *n.*, one who romps; esp. a tom-boy.

romped, *p.p.*, romp.

romp'ing, *pr.p.*, romp.

romp'ish, *adj.*, given to romping.

ron'deau, *n.*, a poetical form, consisting of ten or thirteen lines with two rimes only and two refrains.

ron'del, *n.*, a poetical form, more or less resembling the rondeau, but differing esp. in treatment of the refrain.

Rönt'gen rays, *n. pl.*, rays which penetrate many substances otherwise impervious to light.

rood, *n.*, the Cross, with or without the Figure of Christ upon it, esp. the Crucifix with its attendant figures of Our Lady and St. John, placed on a rood-screen; a square land-measure; an old measure of length = rod.

roof, *v.t.*, to cover with a roof in any sense; *n.*, the upper covering of a house or any building; the top of an omnibus or coach.

roofed, *p.p.*, roof; *adj.*, covered with a roof.

roof'ing, *pr.p.*, roof; *n.*, structural materials of a roof.

roof'less, *adj.*, uncovered; without a roof.

roof'-tree, *n.*, a ridge-pole; a roof.

roof'y, *adj.*, roofed.

rook, *v.t.*, to swindle; overcharge (*slang*); *n.*, a kind of crow; a swindler (*slang*); the castle in chess.

rooked, *p.p.*, rook.

rook'ery, *n.*, a colony of rooks, penguins, seals, etc.

room, *n.*, space enough for a given purpose; opportunity; a chamber, apartment; stead.

room'ful, *n.*, as many, or much, as a room holds.

room'iness, *n.*, the quality of being roomy or spacious.

room'y, *adj.*, spacious

roost, *v.i.*, to sit on a perch; *n.*, a perch; a garret (*Scot.*).

roost'ed, *p.p.*, roost.

roost'er, *n.*, a domestic cock.

roost'ing, *pr.p.*, roost.

root, *v.t.*, to plant; to dig up; *v.i.*, to get fixed in the soil; to turn up with the snout; *n.*, a plant's growth beneath the soil, giving it fixity and nourishing it from the soil; foundation; source; the primitive of a word; a number that, being multiplied by itself a given number of times, gives its power; a chord's fundamental note (*mus.*).

root'ed, *p.p.*, root; *adj.*, established, fixed.

root'-house, *n.*, a place for storage of roots.

root'ing, *pr.p.*, root.

root'let, *n.*, a little root.

root'-stock, *n.*, rhizome; an original root.

root'y, *adj.*, full of roots.

ropal'ic, *adj.*, containing words each a syllable longer than the preceding word. Also *rhopalic*.

rope, *v.t.*, to fasten with a rope, enclose with a rope; *v.i.*, to become ropy; *n.*, fibres twisted into a thick cord; anything rope-like, as a rope of hair.

roped, *p.p.*, rope.

rope'-maker, *n.*, one who makes ropes.

rope'-making, *n.*, the trade of making ropes.

ro'per, *n.*, a rope-maker; one who binds with rope.

ro'pery, *n.*, a rope-walk.

rope's end, *v.t.*, to beat with an end of rope.

rope'walk, *n.*, a place where rope is made.

rope'-yarn, *n.*, fibres forming a smaller strand.

ro'piness, *n.*, the state or quality of being ropy.

ro'ping, *pr.p.*, rope; *n.*, cordage.

ro'py, *adj.*, stringy, viscous.

roqu'elaure, *n.*, an eighteenth century French cloak for men.

ro'ral, *adj.*, pert. to dew.

rorif'erous, *adj.*, dew-producing.

ror'qual, *n.*, a variety of whale, having a dorsal fin.

Rosa'ceae, *n. pl.*, the generic name for flowers of the rose type.

rosa'ceous, *adj.*, pert. to the *Rosaceae*.

ro'sary, *n.*, a rose-garden; a chaplet of roses; a devotion in which are commemorated the chief events in the life of Our Lord and His Virgin Mother; the string or chain of beads used in the devotion.

rose, *p.t.*, rise; *n.*, a plant bel. to the *Rosaceae*; the flower of this shrub; rose-colour; the nozzle of a watering-pot.

ro'seal, *adj.*, *i.q.* roseate.

ro'seate, *adj.*, rose-coloured.

rose'bud, *n.*, the bud of a rose.

rose'-colour, *n.*, the colour of the rose.

rose'-coloured, *adj.*, of the colour of the rose.

rose'mary, *n.*, a sweet-scented evergreen shrub.

rose'ola, *n.*, a red rash.

rosette', roset', *n.*, a rose-shaped badge or architectural ornament.

rose'-water, *n.*, a perfume prepared from roses.

rose'wood, *n.*, the name of a Brazilian timber much used in cabinet work.

Rosicru'cian, *adj.*, rel. to the Rosicrucians and their magic; *n.*, one of the Rosicrucians, an esoteric society of occult philosophers.

ros'ied, *adj.*, made rosy.

ro'sier, *adj.*, *comp.* of rosy.

ro'siest, *adj. super.* of rosy.

ros'in, *v.t.*, to rub with rosin; *n.*, *i.q.* resin, particularly that which results from the distillation of oil of turpentine from crude turpentine.

ros'iny, *adj.*, like, or covered with, rosin.

ross, *v.t.*, to remove bark; *n.*, a rough surface of bark.

ros'tel, *n.*, a small beak or beak-like protuberance.

ros'tellate, *adj.*, having a rostel.

ros'ter, *n.*, a list of military or regimental duties.

ros'tral, *adj.*, ornamented with beaks; rel. to rostrum.

ros'trate, *adj.*, having a rostrum.

ros'trated, *adj.*, *i.q.* rostrate.

ros'trum, *n.*, a beak; a platform (*Lat.*).

ros'ulate, *adj.*, arranged like the petals of roses.

ro'sy, *adj.*, of the colour of red roses; cheerful, bright.

rot, *v.i.*, to become rotten, to decay, to pine; to pretend to be serious (*slang*); *v.t.*, to make to rot; to spoil (*slang*); to banter; *n.*, decay, rottenness; absurdity (*slang*).

ro'ta, *n.*, a list or order of names or duties; *i.q.* roster.

ro'tary, *adj.*, revolving on its axis; rotating; *n.*, a rotary machine.

rotate', *v.t.*, to cause to revolve on its axis; to vary the order of (crops); *v.i.*, to revolve; to recur.

ro'tate, *adj.*, wheel-shaped.

rota'ted, *adj.*, *i.q.* rotate; *p.p.*, rotate.

rota'ting, *pr.p.*, rotate.

rota'tion, *n.*, the act of rotating; recurrence or succession in a regular order.

rota'tor, *n.*, a revolving apparatus or a piece of one; a muscle that enables a limb to rotate.

ro'tatory, *adj.*, revolving.

rote, *n.*, repetition for the purpose of fixing in the memory; mere memory.

ro'tifer, *n.*, one of the rotifera.

Rotif'era, *n. pl.*, animalcules having rotatory organs.

rot'ted, *p.p.*, rot.

rot'ten, *adj.*, decaying, putrid, corrupt (in any sense).

rot'tenness, *n.*, the state or quality of being rotten.

rot'ting, *pr.p.*, rot.

rotund', *adj.*, round; sonorous.

rotun'da, *n.*, a round building, usually domed.

rotund'ity, *n.*, roundness.

rotund'ness, *n.*, *i.q.* rotundity.

rou'ble, *n.*, a Russian silver coin; the R. monetary unit.

rou'cou, *n.*, a dye from the roucou tree.

rou'é, *n.*, a dissipated person; a rake.

rouge, *v.t.* and *i.*, to stain with rouge; *n.*, a red powder; *adj.*, red (*her.*).

rouged, *p.p.*, rouge.

Rouge Croix', *n.*, one of the two pursuivants in the College of Arms.

Rouge Drag'on, *n.*, one of the two pursuivants in the College of Arms.

rouge-et-noir', *n.*, a gambling card-game, so named from the stakes being placed on red and black marks.

rough, *v.t.*, to turn up; to rub the wrong way; to treat a horse's hoofs so as to prevent him from slipping; make a rough sketch of; *adj.*, uneven, not level; coarse; shaggy; rude; violent; harsh; imperfect; preliminary; *n.*, a hooligan.

rough'-cast, *adj.*, covered with lime and gravel mixed; not completely worked out.

rough'-draft, *n.*, a draft not completely worked out.

rough'-draw, *v.t.*, to draw in outline.

rough'en, *v.t.*, to make rough.

rough'ened, *p.p.*, roughen.

rough'ening, *pr.p.*, roughen.

rough'er, *adj.*, *comp.* of rough.

rough'-hew, *v.t.*, to shape incompletely.

rough'-hewed, *p.p.*, rough-hew.

rough'-hewing, *pr.p.*, rough-hew.

rough'-hewn, *p.p.*, rough-hew.

rough'ing, *pr.p.*, rough.

rough'ish, *adj.*, somewhat rough.

rough'ly, *adv.*, in a rough way.

rough'ness, *n.*, the quality of being rough.

rough'-rider, *n.*, one who can ride any sort of horse; an irregular horse-soldier.

rough'shod, *adj.*, having the nails of the hoof projecting; *adv.*, in a domineering way.

roug'ing, *pr.p.*, rouge.

roulade', *n.*, a series of rapid runs; a vocal flourish.

rouleau', *n.*, coins packed cylindrically; a roll.

roulette', *n.*, a gambling game; a wheel used in engraving and perforating.

rounce, *n.*, a card-game; a cylindrical contrivance for moving the bed of a hand-press.

roun'cival, *n.*, the name for a variety of pea.

round, *v.t.*, to make round; to make complete and symmetrical; *adj.*, spherical; circular; cylindrical; complete; considerable; *n.*, anything round; circumference; a circuit or series; a musical piece for three or more equal voices; a kind of canon (*mus.*); *adv.*, rotatorily; about; *prep.*, about, surrounding.

round'about, *adj.*, circuitous; circumlocutory; *n.*, a kind of jacket; a merry-go-round; circumlocution.

round'ed, *p.p.*, round.

round'el, *n.*, *i.q.* rondeau; a medallion.

round'elay, *n.*, a song with refrain.

round'er, *n.*, one who rounds; in pl., a game with bat and ball.

round'-hand, *adj.*, bowling with the arm horizontally swung.

Round'head, *n.*, one of the seventeenth century Puritans.

round'house, *n.*, a lock-up; a range of cabins in an old sailing-ship.

round'ing, *pr.p.*, round.

round'ish, *adj.*, somewhat round.

round'ly, *n.*, in a round way; very thoroughly.

round'ness, *n.*, the quality of being round.

round-rob'in, *n.*, a petition the signatures to which are arranged in a circle.

round' - shouldered, *adj.*, with curved back.

roup, *v.t.*, to sell by auction; *n.*, an auction sale (*Scot.*); a disease in poultry.

rouse, *v.t.*, to awaken, excite, stir up; *v.i.*, to awake; to haul (*naut.*); *n.*, a reveillé, a bumper.

roused, *p.p.*, rouse.

rous'er, *n.*, one who, or that which, rouses.

rous'ing, *pr.p.*, rouse; *adj.*, startling, outrageous.

rout, *v.t.*, to put to disorderly flight; to fetch out; *n.*, disorderly flight; an unlawful assembly; an evening party (*obs.*).

route, *n.*, road, direction; marching orders.

rout'ed, *p.p.*, rout.

routine', *n.*, regular, ordered succession of tasks or procedure.

rout'ing, *pr.p.*, rout.

rout' seat, *n.*, a seat or chair for a ball or evening party.

rove, *v.i.*, to wander, stray; to rave (*Scot.*); *v.t.*, to stray through; to ravel out; to reduce in diameter; *p.t.*, reeve; *n.*, a strand of fibre.

roved, *p.p.*, rove.

ro'ver, *n.*, one who roves; a pirate or brigand; the name of a croquet player or ball when all the hoops have been made.

ro'ving, *pr.p.*, rove.

row, *v.t.*, to propel with oars; to place in line; *n.*, a line; rank, or file; a series.

row, *v.t.*, to abuse; rebuke severely (*colloq.*); *v.i.*, to make a disturbance; *n.*, a brawl; a loud noise.

row'an, *n.*, the mountain ash.

row'-boat, *n.*, a boat propelled with oars.

row'dy, *adj.*, boisterous, rough; *n.*, a rough, disorderly person.

row'dyish, *adj.*, inclined to rowdyism.

row'dyism, *n.*, turbulence.

rowed, *p.p.*, row.

row'el, *n.*, the little toothed wheel in a spur; *v.t.*, to prick with a spur.

row'el(l)ed, *p.p.*, rowel

row'el(l)ing, *pr.p.*, rowel.

row'en, *n.*, an aftermath of hay.

row'er, *n.*, one who rows with an oar.

row'ing, *pr.p.*, row (oars).

row'ing, *pr.p.*, row (noise).

row'lock, *n.*, a contrivance on a gunwale for giving the oars their motive power.

roy'al, *adj.*, kingly; pert. to kings; regal; *n.*, a size of paper; the sail immediately above the top-gallant mast.

roy'alism, *n.*, adherence to the principles of monarchy.

roy'alist, *n.*, a supporter of monarchy, esp. a supporter of the Crown against the Cromwellian usurpation.

roy'ally, *adv.*, in a royal way.

roy'alty, *n.*, the rank or office of a sovereign; the sovereign's privileges; kingly character; princes collectively (strictly, the word belongs to a sovereign, but in common modern usage any prince of the blood is called a royalty); payment to an author or patentee on the proceeds of his book, etc.

roys'terer, *n.*, *i.q.* roisterer.

rub, *v.t.*, to apply friction by moving something over the surface of; to chafe; polish; graze; erase by rubbing; to take a copy by rubbing; *v.i.*, to graze, scrape; make difficult progress; *n.*, the act of rubbing; a cause of difficulty; the rubber at whist or bridge.

rubbed, *p.p.*, rub.

rub'ber, *adj.*, made of rubber; *n.*, one who rubs; any appliance for rubbing; a masseur; caoutchouc; the winning game at cards; a series of games; a collision (in the game of bowls); *v.t.*, to apply a rubber coating to.

rub'bing, *pr.p.*, rub; *n.*, the act of rubbing; a reproduction of a brass, drawing, etc., obtained by rubbing heel-ball or graphite over paper placed above the design, etc.

rub'bish, *n.*, waste matter, refuse, trash; *interj.*, nonsense.

rub'bishy, *adj.*, worthless.

rub'ble, *n.*, broken stone; water-worn stones.

rub'bly, *adj.*, full of rubble.

rubefa'cient, *adj.*, producing redness or blushing; *n.*, a counter-irritant.

ru'bellite, *n.*, a red silicate.

rube'ola, *n.*, measles.

rubes'cence, *n.*, the state of being rubescent.

rubes'cent, *adj.*, growing red.

ru'bican, *adj.*, with grey or white flecks.

ru'bicel, *n.*, a precious stone resembling a ruby.

Ru'bicon, *n.*, the river in Italy separating it from Caesar's Gaulish province. In his quarrel with Pompey, he crossed the river and so committed himself to a war. Hence, the word means any irrevocable decision or proceeding.

ru'bicund, *adj.*, ruddy; flushed.

rubicun'dity, *n.*, the state of being rubicund.

ru'bied, *adj.*, ornamented with rubies.

rubif'ic, *adj.*, *i.q.* rubefacient.

ru'biform, *adj.*, reddish.

ru'bify, *v.t.*, to redden.

rubig'inous, *adj.*, rusty; rust-coloured.

ru'bric, *n.*, a heading or caption; a liturgical direction written in red.

ru'brical, *adj.*, rel. to, of the nature of, a rubric.

ru'bricate, *v.t.*, to illuminate with red.

ru'bricist, *n.*, a stickler for rubrics.

rub'stone, *n.*, stone of which whetstones are made; a whetstone.

ru'by, *n.*, a gem of varying degrees of red; a size of printer's type.

ruche, *n.*, a frill; *v.t.*, to ornament with a frill.

ruch'ing, *n.*, *i.q.* ruche

ruck, *v.t.* and *i.*, to crease; *n.*, a crease; a heap; a crowd in the end of a race.

ruc'tion, *n.*, trouble; a row.

rudd, *n.*, a fresh-water fish.

rud'der, *n.*, a steering apparatus.

rud'dier, *adj.*, *comp.* of ruddy.

rud'diest, *adj.*, *super.* of ruddy.

rud'diness, *n.*, the quality of being ruddy.

rud'dle, *n.*, red ochre.

rud'dock, *n.*, a robin; a red apple.

rud'dy, *adj.*, inclined to red; florid; *v.t.*, to make ruddy.

rude, *adj.*, rough, barbarous, impolite, uncultivated, robust.

rude'ly, *adv.*, in a rude way.

rude'ness, *n.*, impoliteness.

ruden'ture, *n.*, cabling.

ru'der, *adj.*, *comp.* of rude.

ru'dest, *adj.*, *super.* of rude.

ru'diment, *n.*, an element; first principle; something undeveloped.

rudimen'tal, *adj.*, *i.q.* rudimentary.

rudimen'tary, *adj.*, elementary; undeveloped.

rue, *v.t.*, to lament for; repent of; *n.*, a bitter herb.

rued, *p.p.*, rue.

rue'ful, *adj.*, dolorous, mournful.

rue'fully, *adv.*, mournfully.
rue'fulness, *n.*, sadness.
rue'ing, *pr.p.*, rue.
rufes'cent, *adj.*, tending to yellow redness.
ruff, *v.t.*, to ruffle; to play a trump card instead of following suit; *n.*, a frilled neck ornament; a fresh-water fish; a snipe; a pigeon.
ruffed, *p.p.*, ruff.
ruf'fian, *n.*, a coarse villian.
ruf'fianism, *n.*, the character of a ruffian.
ruf'fianly, *adj.*, brutal
ruff'ing, *pr.p.*, ruff.
ruf'fle, *v.t.*, to disorder, flutter; put out of temper; put a ruffle on; to make a drum roll; *v.i.*, to become rough; to flutter; to fall out of temper; *n.*, a laced or plaited article of dress.
ruf'fled, *p.p.*, ruffle.
ruf'fling, *pr.p.*, ruffle.
ru'fous, *adj.*, yellowish red.
rug, *n.*, a wrap, coverlet.
ru'gate, *adj.*, *i.q.* rugous.
rug'ged, *adj.*, rough; uneven; uncouth; shaggy.
rug'gedly, *adv.*, in a rugged way.
rug'gedness, *n.*, the quality or state of being rugged.
ru'gous, *adj.*, wrinkled
ru'in, *v.t.*, to destroy, overthrow; bring to poverty; *n.*, destruction, overthrow; moral or financial destruction; a ruinous building.
ru'inate, *adj.*, ruined.
ruina'tion, *n.*, destruction.
ru'ined, *p.p.*, ruin.
ru'ining, *pr.p.*, ruin.
ru'inous, *adj.*, in a ruined state; leading to ruin.
rule, *v.t.*, to govern; to give a decision on; to mark with lines; *v.i.*, to be a ruler; to prevail; *n.*, a standard, law, regulation; regular mode; an order of court; an instrument for ruling lines.
ruled, *p.p.*, rule.
ru'ler, *n.*, one who rules; an instrument for ruling lines.
ru'ling, *pr.p.*, rule.
rum, *n.*, an alcoholic liquor distilled from sugar-cane juice; *adj.*, queer, strange (*slang*).
rum'ble, *v.i.*, to make a prolonged heavy sound; *n.*, a long, heavy sound; a servant's seat behind a carriage.
rum'bled, *p.p.*, rumble.
rum'bling, *pr.p.*, rumble; *n.*, *i.q.* rumble.
ru'men, *n.*, a ruminant's first stomach.
ru'minal, *adj.*, chewing the cud.
ru'minant, *adj.*, *i.q.* ruminal; *n.*, a cud-chewing animal.
ru'minate, *v.i.*, to chew the cud; to ponder.
ru'minated, *p.p.*, ruminate.
ru'minating, *pr.p.*, ruminate.
rumina'tion, *n.*, the act of ruminating.
ru'minator, *n.*, one who ponders.
rum'mage, *v.t.*, to ransack; *v.i.*, to search with care; *n.*, a close search.
rum'maged, *p.p.*, rummage.
rum'mage-sale, *n.*, a sale of old odds and ends for charity.
rum'maging, *pr.p.*, rummage.
rum'mer, *n.*, a drinking glass for toddy.
ru'mour, ru'mor, *v.t.*, to report; *n.*, report; current story.
ru'moured, ru'mored, *p.p.*, rumour.
ru'mouring, rum'oring, *pr.p.*, rumour.
rump, *n.*, the buttocks; fag-end.
rum'ple, *v.t.*, to make uneven; to plait; *n.*, a plait.
rum'pled, *p.p.*, rumple.
rum'pling, *pr.p.*, rumple.
rum'pus, *n.*, a great fuss; a disturbance.
run, *v.i.*, to move swiftly above a walk; to flow, melt; to go on continuously; *v.t.*, to make to run; to push; to carry on; *n.*, the act of running; a distance covered by running or sailing; a sudden demand; a space for running in; continuance; a score for running the distance between wickets.
run'agate, *n.*, a renegade (of which *runagate* is an altered form); a fugitive.
run'away, *adj.*, running away; *n.*, a fugitive.
run'cinate, *adj.*, having leaves convex on one side and straight on the other.
run'dle, *n.*, a rung in a ladder.
rund'let, *n.*, a wine-cask; a measure of wine. Also *runlet*.
rune, *n.*, a Runic letter or poem.
rung, *p.p.*, ring; *n.*, a step in a ladder.
ru'nic, *adj.*, pert. to runes; *n.*, a primitive Teutonic alphabet.
run'let, *n.*, a little stream; a small barrel.
run'nel, *n.*, a small brook.
run'ner, *n.*, one who runs; a scout; the keel on which a sleigh runs; a shooting sprig; a millstone that revolves; a supplementary rope in mechanical tackle.
run'net, *n.*, *i.q.* rennet.
run'ning, *pr.p.*, run; *n.*, the act of running; that which flows; a flow of pus; competitors who win places in a race.
runt, *n.*, a stunted animal; a stump.

rupee′, *n.*, an Indian silver monetary unit.

rup′tion, *n.*, *i.q.* rupture.

rup′ture, *v.t.*, to break, burst; sever; to produce hernia; *n.*, a breach, severance; hernia.

rup′tured, *p.p.*, rupture.

rup′turing, *pr.p.*, rupture.

ru′ral, *adj.*, pert. to the country; rustic.

ru′ralist, *n.*, a dweller in the country.

ru′ralize, *v.i.*, to adopt the country life; *v.t.*, to make rural.

ru′rally, *adv.*, in rustic fashion.

ruse, *n.*, a trick, dodge.

rush, *v.t.*, to make to move rapidly; *v.i.*, to move in great haste or violence; *n.*, a hasty movement; a marsh plant; something worthless.

rushed, *p.p.*, rush.

rush′er, *n.*, one who rushes.

rush′ing, *pr.p.*, rush.

rush′light, *n.*, a candle made from rushes.

rush′y, *adj.*, rush-like; abounding in rushes.

rusk, *n.*, a sort of biscuit.

Russ, *n.* and *adj.*, *i.q.* Russian.

rus′set, *adj.*, reddish-brown; homespun; *n.*, a reddish-brown colour; homespun fabric; a variety of apple.

rus′seting, *n.*, russet clothes; a rustic.

rus′sety, *adj.*, russet-coloured.

Rus′sia-leather, *n.*, a choice leather treated with birch-oil.

Rus′sian, *adj.*, rel. to Russia; *n.*, a native of Russia.

Rus′sianism, *n.*, Russian idiom.

rust, *v.t.*, to affect with rust; to impair; *v.i.*, to be affected by rust; to lose power through inactivity; *n.*, red oxide of iron forming on steel and iron; mildew, degeneration.

rust′ed, *p.p.*, rust.

rus′tic, *adj.*, rural; simple; rude; *n.*, a peasant.

rus′ticate, *v.t.*, to send away temporarily from college; *v.i.*, to dwell in the country.

rus′ticated, *p.p.*, rusticate.

rus′ticating, *pr.p.*, rusticate.

rustica′tion, *n.*, expulsion for a time from college; life in the country.

rustic′ity, *n.*, the rustic state or character; the ways of a peasant.

rust′iness, *n.*, the state or quality of being rusty.

rust′ing, *pr.p.*, rust.

rus′tle, *v.i.*, to produce the sound of soft things, as leaves, rubbing together; *n.*, the sound itself.

rus′tled, *p.p.*, rustle.

rus′tling, *pr.p.*, rustle.

rust′y, *adj.*, affected by rust; weakened by disuse or idleness; of the colour of rust.

rut, *v.t.*, to make ruts in; *v.i.*, to have sexual desire (said of deer); *n.*, a groove; a wheel-track; the sexual desire of a deer.

ruth, *n.*, pity, sorrow.

ruthe′nium, *n.*, an element derived from platinum ore.

ruth′less, *adj.*, pitiless, cruel.

ruth′lessly, *adv.*, without pity.

ruth′lessness, *n.*, cruelty; pitilessness.

ru′tile, *adj.*, digging, burrowing.

rut′tish, *adj.*, wanton.

rye, *n.*, a cereal plant.

ry′ot, *n.*, a Hindu agriculturist.

S

sabadil'la, *n.*, a drug prepared from the seeds of the sabadilla or cevadilla plant, found in S. America.

Sabae'an, Sabe'an, *adj.*, rel. to Saba or Yemen; Arabian.

Sab'aoth, *n. pl.*, hosts; armies.

Sabbata'rian, *adj.*, rel. to the Sabbath and Sabbatarianism; *n.*, a precisian in regard to Sabbath observance.

Sabbata'rianism, *n.*, the principles of Sabbatarians.

Sab'bath, *n.*, the Jewish rest on the seventh day of the week; Saturday.

Sabbat'ic, *adj.*, rel. to the Sabbath.

Sabbat'ical, *adj.*, *i.q.* Sabbatic.

Sab'batism, *n.*, observance of the Sabbath rest.

Sabe'an, *adj.*, *i.q.* Sabaean.

Sa'beism, *n.*, *i.q.* Sabianism.

Sabel'lian, *adj.*, pert. to Sabellius, an African heretic who affirmed that there was only one Person in the Godhead.

Sabel'lianism, *n.*, the heresy of Sabellius.

Sa'bian, *adj.*, rel. to Sabianism.

Sa'bianism, *n.*, a system of nature-worship, in which the heavenly hosts were taken to symbolize God.

Sab'ine, *adj.*, rel. to the Sabines, an old Italian tribe.

sa'ble, *adj.*, black; of dark hue; *n.*, a species of weasel esteemed for its fine fur; in pl., mourning attire.

sabot', *n.*, a rustic wooden shoe (*Fr.*).

sabotage', *n.*, a violent and destructive strike (*Fr.*).

sa'bre, *v.t.*, to put to the sword; *n.*, a cavalryman's sword

sab'retache, *n.*, a cavalryman's leather bag attached to the left side of his sword-belt.

sac, *n.*, a bag; cyst; a manorial lord's privilege of holding a court.

saccade', *n.*, a jerk on a bridle; pressure with a violin bow.

sac'cate, *adj.*, bag-shaped.

acchar'ic, *adj.*, rel. to sugar.

sacchar'ify, *v.t.*, to change into sugar.

saccharim'eter, *n.* an apparatus showing the quantity of saccharine matter in liquids. Also *saccharometer*.

sac'charin, *n.*, a compound prepared from coal-tar.

sac'charine, *adj.*, sugary; rel. to sugar.

sac'charoid, *adj.*, resembling loaf sugar.

sac'cule, *n.*, a small cyst or sac.

sacerdo'tal, *adj.*, rel. to a priest; priestly.

sacerdo'talism, *n.*, the priestly system.

sacerdo'tally, *adv.*, in a priestly way or sense.

sa'chem, *n.*, a chief (Amer. Indian).

sachet', *n.*, a scent-bag (*Fr.*).

sack, *n.*, a bag, pouch; a sackful; a loose garment; an old wine so named; plunder of a besieged place; dismissal from service (*colloq.*); *v.t.*, to pillage; to fill sacks with; to dismiss (*colloq.*).

sack'age, *n.*, plundering.

sack'but, *n.*, an ancient musical instrument resembling a lyre; a sort of trombone.

sack'cloth, *adj.*, cloth of which sacks are made; a sign of sorrow.

sacked, *p.p.*, sack.

sack'er, *n.*, a pillager.

sack'ful, *n.*, what a sack will hold.

sack'ing, *pr.p.*, sack; *n.*, the material of which sacks are made.

sacque, *n.*, a woman's robe.

sac'rament, *n.*, originally a military oath; a mystery; "an outward and visible sign of an inward and spiritual grace given unto us."

sacramen'tal, *adj.*, rel. to sacraments; of the nature of a sacrament; *n.*, something akin to a sacrament.

sacramen'talist, *n.*, one with exalted views on the Sacraments.

sacramenta'rian, *adj.*, rel. to Sacraments; *n.*, a professor of Zwinglian doctrines.

Sacramen'tary, *n.*, an ancient ritual book rel. to the celebration of Mass; *adj.*, *i.q.* sacramentarian.

sacra'rium, *n.*, a piscina; anciently, a shrine (*Lat.*).

sa'cred, *adj.*, consecrated; holy; inviolate.

sa'credly, *adv.*, in a sacred way.

sa'credness, *n.*, the state or quality of being sacred.

sac'rifice, *v.t.*, to offer as an act of worship; to suffer a loss for the sake of gaining something; to make a sale below value; *v.i.*, to make an offering; *n.*, an offering in worship; that which is sacrificed; loss with a purpose; a sale below value.

sac'rificed, *p.p.*, sacrifice.

sac'rificer, *n.*, one who sacrifices; a priest.

sacrifi'cial, *adj.*, of the nature of sacrifice.

sac'rificing, *pr.p.*, sacrifice.

sac'rilege, *n.*, an act of impiety in a sacred place; diversion of sacred property to secular uses.

sacrile'gious, *adj.*, of the nature of sacrilege.

sacrile'gist, *n.*, a sacrilegious person.

Sa'crist, *n.*, a minor canon who is the sacristan.

sac'ristan, *n.*, a church official whose duties are connected with the altar and its ornaments; sexton.

sac'risty, *n.*, the part of a church where the vestments are kept and the altar vessels are prepared.

sac'rosanct, *adj.*, peculiarly sacred; inviolable.

sa'crum, *n.*, the bone at the lower end of the vertebral column (*Lat.*).

sad, *adj.*, sorrowful, depressed, grave; of dark hue.

sad'den, *v.t.*, to make sad; *v.i.*, to become sad.

sad'der, *adj.*, *comp.* of sad.

sad'dest, *adj.*, *super.* of sad.

sad'dle, *n.*, a rider's seat on a horse or bicycle; a wooden block attached to a yard-arm; *v.t.*, to lay a saddle on; to encumber.

sad'dle-bag, *n.*, a bag carried on a saddle.

sad'dle-bow, *n.*, the curved part of a saddle or pommel.

sad'dled, *p.p.*, saddle.

sad'dler, *n.*, one who makes or repairs harness.

sad'dlery, *n.*, articles made by a saddler; a saddler's shop.

sad'dle-shaped, *adj.*, shaped like a saddle.

sad'dle-tree, *n.*, the frame of a saddle.

sad'dling, *pr.p.*, saddle.

Sadducе'an, *adj.*, rel. to the Sadducees.

Sad'ducee, *n.*, a member of a Jewish sect which, in particular, denied the resurrection.

Sad'duceeism, *n.*, the principles and system of the Sadducees.

sad'-iron, *n.*, a flat-iron, usually containing a heater.

sad'ly, *adv.*, in a mournful way; unhappily; excessively

sad'ness, *n.*, the state of being sad.

safe, *adj.*, secure; in shelter; harmless; *n.*, a strong chest.

safe-con'duct, *n.*, a permit or guard guaranteeing a safe journey.

safe'-guard, *v.t.*, to protect, secure; *n.*, a protector; protection; guarantee of safety.

safe'-keeping, *n.*, care, protection.

safe'ly, *adv.*, out of danger; securely.

sa'fer, *adj.*, *comp.* of safe.

sa'fest, *adj.*, *super.* of safe.

safe'ty, *n.*, security, shelter, freedom from danger.

safe'ty-lamp, *n.*, a miner's lamp protected by gauze.

safe'ty-valve, *n.*, a valve that allows steam to escape when the pressure becomes dangerous.

saf'flower, *n.*, a kind of thistle used for the dye which it yields.

saf'fron, *n.*, a plant which yields a yellow dye; yellow; *adj.*, of the colour of saffron.

saf'frony, *adj.*, yellowish; orange-coloured.

sag, *v.i.*, to sink in; to incline to one side or to leeward; *v.t.*, to make to sag; *n.*, a tendency to sink or incline.

sa'ga, *n.*, a Scandinavian prose epic.

saga'cious, *adj.*, prudent, clear-sighted.

saga'ciously, *adv.*, in a sagacious way.

sagac'ity, *n.*, prudence, clear-sightedness.

sag'amore, *n.*, a chief (N. Amer. Indian).

sage, *adj.*, wise, discreet; *n.*, an elder noted for wisdom; an aromatic garden herb.

sage'ly, *adv.*, in a sage way.

sag'ger, sag'gar, *n.*, a fireclay casing used in a kiln. Also *seggar*.

sagit'ta, *n.*, an arrow (*Lat.*).

sag'ittal, *adj.*, arrow-like.

Sagitta'rius, *n.*, the Archer, one of the signs of the Zodiac.

sag'ittary, *adj.*, arrow-like.

sag'ittate, *adj.*, arrow-shaped.

sa'go, *n.*, a starch-like article of food prepared from the pith of a species of palm.

sagoin', *n.*, a variety of monkey.

sa'gy, *adj.*, flavoured with sage.

sah'ib, *n.*, the title of a European gentleman in India or Persia.

sa'ic, *n.*, a Levantine sailing-vessel.

saice, *n.*, a Bengalese word for groom.

said, *p.p.* and *t.*, say.

sail, *v.t.*, to cause to sail; to navigate; traverse with a ship; *v.i.*, to be carried in a boat or ship; to start on a voyage;

n., a canvas sheet stretched out to catch the breeze; a ship; a pleasure trip on the water.

sail'able, *adj.*, fit for sailing.

sail'cloth, *n.*, canvas or other fabric of which sails are made.

sailed, *p.p.*, sail.

sail'er, *n.*, a sailing ship.

sail'ing, *pr.p.*, sail; *n.*, navigation; starting on a voyage.

sail'-loft, *n.*, a place for the storage of sails.

sail'maker, *n.*, a maker of sails.

sail'or, *n.*, a mariner; seaman.

sain'foin, *n.*, a plant so named and grown for fodder.

saint, *v.t.*, to canonize; *n.*, a person of especial sanctity; one of the blest in Paradise; one who has been canonized.

saint'ed, *p.p.*, saint; *adj.*, holy; dead.

saint'like, *adj.*, resembling a saint.

saint'liness, *n.*, the quality of being a saint.

saint'ly, *adj.*, saintlike.

Saint-Simo'nian, *adj.*, rel. to St.-Simonism.

Saint-Si'monism, *n.*, the socialistic doctrines of Saint-Simon, a French writer and thinker (1760-1825).

Saint-Si'monist, *n.*, a disciple of Saint-Simon.

Saint-Si'monite, *n.*, *i.q.* Saint-Simonist.

Saint Vi'tus's dance, *n.*, *i.q.* chorea.

saith, *v.t.*, the old 3rd pers. sing., *pr.t.* say.

sake, *n.*, purpose; cause; account.

sak'é, *n.*, fermented liquor obtained from rice, a Japanese beverage.

sa'ker, *n.*, a large breed of falcon.

sal, *n.*, the Lat. name for salt, used frequently as a prefix.

salaam', *v.i.*, to make obeisance or greeting; *n.*, an exclamation of greeting or obeisance.

sala'cious, *adj.*, lustful.

sala'ciousness, *n.*, *i.q.* salacity.

salac'ity, *n.*, lustfulness.

sal'ad, *n.*, uncooked herbs, shredded and mixed with oil, etc.

sal'ad-days, *n. pl.*, the time of inexperienced youth.

salaman'der, *n.*, a kind of newt, reputed in ancient times to live in fire.

salaman'drine, *adj.*, pert. to, or resembling, a salamander.

sal'aried, *adj.*, in receipt of a salary.

sal'ary, *n.*, stipend, pay.

sale, *n.*, selling; exchange of a commodity for money; demand.

sale'able, *adj.*, that can be sold.

sale'ableness, *n.*, the quality of being saleable.

sal'ep, *n.*, a farinaceous meal obtained from the tubers of certain orchids.

salera'tus, *n.*, cooking-soda.

sale'-room, *n.*, a place where goods are sold at auction.

sales'man, *n.*, one who makes purchases for a firm, or sells in a shop.

sales'woman, *n.*, fem. of salesman.

Sal'ic, *adj.*, rel. to the Salii, an ancient Frankish tribe. The Salic law prohibited a woman's accession to the throne.

sal'icin, sal'icine, *n.*, an extract from the willow or poplar.

sali'cylate, *n.*, a salt of salicylic acid.

salicyl'ic, *adj.*, rel. to willows or derived from some of them.

sa'lient, *adj.*, leaping; prominent; at an angle less than two right angles; *n.*, a projection in a military line or fortification.

salif'erous, *adj.*, producing salt.

sal'ifiable, *adj.*, able to be salified.

salifica'tion, *n.*, the act or effect of salifying.

sal'ified, *p.p.*, salify.

sal'ify, *v.t.*, to impregnate with a salt.

sal'ifying, *pr.p.*, salify.

salina'tion, *n.*, the act of steeping in a saline liquor.

sa'line, *adj.*, possessing the properties of salt; *n.*, a salt spring.

sali'va, *n.*, the secretion of the mouth.

sali'val, *adj.*, rel. to saliva.

sal'ivant, *adj.* promoting the secretion of saliva; *n.*, that which promotes saliva.

sal'ivary, *adj.*, pert. to saliva.

sal'ivate, *v.t.*, to cause a large secretion of saliva.

sal'ivated, *p.p.*, salivate.

sal'ivating, *pr.p.*, salivate.

saliva'tion, *n.*, the act of secreting saliva in abnormal quantity.

sal'landers, *n. pl.*, an eruption on a horse's hind leg.

sal'let, *n.*, a light helmet.

sal'lied, *p.p.*, sally.

sal'low, *adj.*, pallid, yellowish; *n.*, a small willow-like tree.

sal'lowness, *n.*, the state of being sallow.

sal'ly, *v.i.*, to rush forth suddenly; *n.*, a sudden dash out from a besieged place; an excursion; a lively encounter of wits; raillery.

sal'lying, *pr.p.*, sally.

sally-lunn', *n.*, a variety of tea-cake.

sal'ly-port, *n.*, a postern for the passage of troops.

salmagun'di, *n.*, a dish of mixed ingredients; a medley.
salm'on, *n.*, a choice fish so named.
salm'onet, *n.*, a young salmon; parr.
salm'onoid, *adj.*, like a salmon.
salm'on-trout, *n.*, a marine trout, resembling the salmon.
salon', *n.*, a saloon; an art gallery; a social or literary circle.
saloon', *n.*, a state apartment; a large room; a divan.
saloop', *n.*, a medicinal infusion of sassafras.
sal'picon, *n.*, a rechauffé of meat, bread, and vegetables.
sal'pinx, *n.*, the Eustachian tube (*Gr.*).
sal'sify, *n.*, the oyster-plant, chiefly valued for its edible root.
salsil'la, *n.*, an edible plant resembling the Jerusalem artichoke.
salt, *n.*, a mineral found in the earth or obtained from the sea by evaporation; chloride of sodium; an acid combined with a base; wit; flavour; a seaman; *adj.*, saline; impregnated or flavoured with salt; *v.t.*, to sprinkle salt upon; to season.
sal'tant, *adj.*, leaping, dancing (*her.*).
sal'tate, *v.i.*, to dance, leap.
salta'tion, *n.*, the act of leaping or dancing.
saltato'rial, *adj.*, rel. to dancing.
saltato'rious, *adj.*, *i.q.* saltatorial.
sal'tatory, *adj.*, *i.q.* saltatorial.
salt'-cellar, *n.*, a receptacle for table-salt.
salt'ed, *p.p.*, salt.
salt'er, *n.*, a dealer in salt, a fish-curer.
salt'ern, *n.*, a salt factory.
sal'tier, *n.*, *i.q.* saltire.
Saltigra'da, *n. pl.*, a genus of leaping spiders.
salt'ing, *pr.p.*, salt.
sal'tire, *n.*, a St. Andrew's Cross (×) used in heraldry.
salt'ish, *adj.*, somewhat salt.
salt'less, *adj.*, insipid.
salt'ness, *n.*, the saline quality.
saltpe'tre, *n.*, nitre.
salt'y, *adj.*, tasting of salt.
salu'brious, *adj.*, healthy.
salu'briousness, *n.*, *i.q.* salubrity.
salu'brity, *n.*, the quality of being salubrious.
sal'utarily, *adv.*, in a salutary way.
sal'utariness, *n.*, the quality of being salutary.
sal'utary, *adj.*, healthful; wholesome.
saluta'tion, *n.*, the act of saluting; a word of greeting.
salu'tatory, *adj.*, greeting, saluting.
salute', *v.t.*, to greet; welcome; pay military or naval honour to; *v.i.*, to make a salute; *n.*, an act of greeting; a sign of respect to a superior or to a flag, etc.
salu'ted, *p.p.*, salute.
salu'ter, *n.*, one who salutes.
salutif'erous, *adj.*, health-giving.
salu'ting, *pr.p.*, salute
salvabil'ity, *adj.*, the state of being salvable.
sal'vable, *adj.*, able to be saved.
sal'vage, *n.*, reward for saving a cargo, vessel, or other property; the property saved.
salva'tion, *n.*, the act of saving; rescue; spiritual saving.
Salva'tionist, *adj.*, rel. to the Salvation Army; *n.*, a member of the Salvation Army.
salve, *v.t.*, to save from loss or destruction.
salve, *v.t.*, to remedy, soothe; *n.*, a soothing remedy, usually an ointment.
Sal've Regi'na, *n.*, the title, taken from the opening words, of the great breviary hymn addressed to Our Lady.
salved, *p.p.*, salve.
sal'ver, *n.*, a tray.
salv'ing, *pr.p.*, salve.
sal'vo, *n.*, an artillery salute; a reservation.
sal volat'ile, *n.*, spirit of ammonia.
sam'ara, *n.*, winged fruit, as of the elm, etc.
Samar'itan, *adj.*, rel. to Samaria; *n.*, a native of S.
Sam'bo, *n.*, the child of a negro and a mulatto.
same, *adj.*, identical; already mentioned.
same'ness, *n.*, identity; similarity.
Sa'mian, *adj.*, rel. to the island of Samos; *n.*, a native of S.
sa'miel, *n.*, the simoom.
sam'ite, *n.*, a silk or satin fabric.
sam'let, *n.*, a small salmon.
Samothra'cian, *adj.*, rel. to Samothrace; *n.*, a native of S.
samp, *n.*, maize boiled in milk (*Amer.*).
sam'pan, *n.*, a Chinese or Javanese fisherman's boat and house combined.
sam'phire, *n.*, a marine plant.
sam'ple, *n.*, a specimen, example; *v.t.*, to take as a specimen; to exhibit a thing of the same kind.
sam'pler, *n.*, a piece of needlework made as a pattern, or as an example of a beginner's work; one who samples.
sanabil'ity, *n.*, the state of being sanable.

san'able, *adj.*, curable

san'ative, *adj.*, curative.

sanato'rium, *n.*, a home where patients are placed for cure.

san'atory, *adj.*, conducive to cure or health.

sanctifica'tion, *n.*, the act of sanctifying; the sanctified state.

sanc'tified, *p.p.*, sanctify.

sanc'tifier, *n.*, one who sanctifies; the Holy Ghost.

sanc'tify, *v.t.*, to make holy; to consecrate; to make into a means of sanctity.

sanc'tifying, *pr.p.*, sanctify.

sanctil'oquent, *adj.*, speaking of holy things.

sanctimo'nious, *adj.*, affectedly pious.

sanctimo'niousness, *n.*, affected piety.

sanc'timony, *n.*, *i.q.* sanctimoniousness.

sanc'tion, *n.*, the act of authorizing or sanctioning; authority; a compelling principle; *v.t.*, to authorize, permit.

sanc'tioned, *p.p.*, sanction.

sanc'tioning, *pr.p.*, sanction.

sanc'titude, *n.*, holiness.

sanc'tity, *n.*, holiness; inviolability.

sanc'tuary, *n.*, a sacred place; a place of privileged asylum; the part of a church where the altar stands.

sanc'tum, *n.*, a specially private room; a study.

sanc'tus, *n.*, the prose anthem, "Sanctus, Sanctus, Sanctus," in the Eucharist; the "Ter Sanctus" (*Lat.*).

sand, *n.*, rock worn into minute particles; *v.t.*, to sprinkle sand over.

san'dal, *n.*, a shoe strapped to the foot; a kind of slipper.

san'dal(l)ed, *adj.*, wearing sandals.

san'dal-wood, *n.*, a white wood used by cabinet-makers.

san'darac, *n.*, a resinous gum.

sand'-bag, *n.*, a bag filled with sand and used for defensive purposes.

sand'blind, *adj.*, semi-blind.

sand'ed, *p.p.*, sand.

Sandema'nian, *adj.*, rel. to the teaching of Robert Sandeman, an 18th cent. preacher in Scotland and America of what are known as the Glassite doctrines.

sand'-eel, *n.*, an eel that disappears into the sand at ebb-tide.

san'derling, *n.*, a little wading-bird.

san'ders, *n.*, a red sandal-wood.

san'dever, *n.*, *i.q.* sandiver.

sand'hill, *n.*, sand mounded.

sand'iness, *n.*, the quality of being sandy.

sand'ing, *pr.p.*, sand.

san'diver, *n.*, glass-gall.

sand'-paper, *n.*, paper on which sand is fixed; *v.t.*, to rub or polish with sand-paper.

sand'-piper, *n.*, a snipe or woodcock.

sand'stone, *n.*, rock composed of quartz and silica.

sand'wich, *n.*, meat, etc., between two slices of bread; *v.t.*, to put one thing between two others.

sand'y, *adj.*, full of, or resembling, sand; shifting; sand-coloured.

sane, *adj.*, of sound mind; reasonable.

sane'ness, *n.*, soundness of mind; reasonableness.

sang, *p.t.*, sing.

sangaree', *n.*, spiced brandy and water.

sang-froid', *n.*, coolness, composure (*Fr.*).

san'giac, *n.*, a Turkish administrative area. Also *Sanjac.*

Sangrail', -greal', *n.*, the Holy Grail, a sacred chalice containing the True Blood, and said to have been borne to Glastonbury by St. Joseph of Arimathea. Also *Sangraal.*

sanguif'erous, *adj.*, conveying blood.

sanguifica'tion, *n.*, the production of blood.

san'guify, *v.t.*, to form blood.

san'guinarily, *adv.*, in a sanguinary way; with much bloodshed.

san'guinary, *adj.*, bloody; with much bloodshed.

san'guine, *adj.*, of blood colour; ardent; hopeful; *v.t.*, to stain with blood.

san'guinely, *adv.*, in a sanguine temper.

sanguin'eous, *adj.*, bloody.

sanguiniv'orous, *adj.*, living on blood. Also *sanguivorous.*

sanguisu'gous, *adj.*, blood-sucking.

San'hedrim, *n.*, the Jewish Council of judges, presided over by the High Priest.

San'hedrin, *n.*, *i.q.* Sanhedrim.

san'icle, *n.*, a perennial herb so named.

sa'nies, *n.*, blood from a wound.

sa'nious, *adj.*, resembling or producing sanies.

sanita'rian, *adj.*, *i.q.* sanitary.

san'itary, *adj.*, rel. to health; hygienic.

sanita'tion, *n.*, hygiene.

san'ity, *n.*, mental soundness; reasonableness.

san'jak, *n.*, *i.q.* sangiac.

sank, *p.t.*, sink.

san'pan, *n.*, *i.q.* sampan.

sans, *prep.*, without (*Fr.*).

sansculotte', *n.*, a person without breeches, a term contemptuously applied to a French Revolutionist (*Fr.*).

San'skrit, *n.*, the ancient Aryan language of India. Also *Sanscrit.*

sans souci', a French phrase = without care.

san'talin, *n.*, red colouring matter derived from sandalwood.

san'tonin, *n.*, a vermifuge obtained from the plant santonica.

sap, *n.*, the vital juice in the stem of a plant or tree; any vital fluid; a trench dug for besiegers to approach a fort under shelter; one who studies hard (*colloq.*); *v.t.*, to undermine; to impair the vitality of.

sap'ajou, *n.*, a S. Amer. monkey.

sap'an-wood, *n.*, the wood of an E. Indian tree, the sappan.

sap'id, *adj.*, savoury.

sapid'ity, *n.*, flavour, savour.

sa'pience, *n.*, wisdom; knowledge.

sa'pient, *adj.*, wise, learned.

sapien'tial, *adj.*, rel. to wisdom, esp. the Jewish Sapiential writings, as Proverbs, Book of Wisdom, etc.

sapinda'ceous, *adj.*, bel. to the *Sapindaceae*, the soapberry family.

sap'less, *adj.*, without sap.

sap'ling, *n.*, a young tree.

sapodil'la, *n.*, a tropical tree so named.

sapona'ceous, *adj.*, soapy.

saponac'ity, *n.*, soapiness.

sapon'ifiable, *adj.*, able to be saponified.

saponifica'tion *n.*, the state of being saponified; change into soap.

sapon'ified, *p.p.*, saponify.

sapon'ify, *v.t.*, to change into soap.

sapon'ifying, *pr.p.*, saponify.

sap'onin, -ine, *n.*, an extract from soapwort, horse-chestnut and other plants.

sap'onule, *n.*, a magnesium-aluminium silicate.

sa'por, sa'pour, *n.*, taste.

saporif'ic, *adj.*, producing taste.

saporos'ity, *n.*, the power of producing taste.

sapped, *p.p.*, sap.

sap'per, *n.*, one who saps; a private of the Royal Engineers.

Sap'phic, *adj.*, rel. to Sappho, the Greek poetess, and to the metre associated with her name.

sap'phire, *n.*, a blue gem so named.

sap'phirine, *adj.*, resembling sapphire.

sap'piness, *n.*, the quality of being sappy.

sap'ping, *pr.p.*, sap.

sap'py, *adj.*, full of sap.

saproph'agan, *adj.*, eating rotten food.

sap'-wood, *n.*, new wood, next the bark.

sar'aband, *n.*, a Spanish dance and its music.

Sar'acen, *n.*, the old name for a Turk.

Saracen'ic, *adj.*, rel. to the Saracens.

sar'casm, *n.*, a caustic expression.

sarcas'tic, *adj.*, caustic, biting, satirical.

sarcas'tically, *adv.*, in a sarcastic way.

sarce'net, *n.*, a fine silken fabric.

sar'cocarp, *n.*, the flesh of a fruit.

sar'cocele, *n.*, a tumour of the testicles.

sar'cocol, *n.*, an African gum-resin.

sar'code, *n.*, animal protoplasm.

sar'colite, *n.*, mineral of the colour of flesh.

sarcol'ogy, *n.*, the study of flesh or the soft bodily tissue.

sarco'ma, *n.*, a fleshy tumour.

sarco'matous, *adj.*, rel. to sarcoma.

sarcoph'agi, *n. pl.*, flesh-eaters.

sarcoph'agus, *n.*, a stone coffin.

sarcoph'agy, *n.*, the habit of eating flesh.

sar'cous, *adj.*, pert. to flesh.

sard, *n.*, a deep red stone.

sar'dine, *n.*, *i.q.* sard.

sardine', *n.*, a Mediterranean fish like the pilchard; the young of the herring, etc., prepared.

Sardin'ian, *adj.*, pert. to Sardinia; *n.*, a native of S.

sar'dius, *n.*, a precious stone so named; *see* sardine.

sardon'ic, *adj.*, forced and harsh (said of a grin or cruel laugh).

sar'donyx, *n.*, a kind of agate.

sargas'sum, *n.*, a weed growing in the N. Atlantic. Also *sargasso.*

sark, *n.*, a shirt (*Scot.*).

sark'ing, *n.*, material for sarks; thin boarding.

sar'lak, *n.*, a Tartary yak.

Sarma'tian, *adj.*, pert. to Sarmatia; *n.*, a Sarmatian or Pole.

Sarmat'ic, *adj.*, *i.q.* Sarmatian.

sar'ment, *n.*, a runner.

sar'plar, *n.*, a large woolsack, containing 2,240 lbs.

sar'rasin, *n.*, a portcullis.

sarsaparil'la, *n.*, a Mexican medicinal shrub.

sar'sen, *adj.*, a term applied to druidical stones on the Chalk Downs.

sarse'net, *n.*, *i.q.* sarcenet.

sar'tor, *n.*, a tailor (*Lat.*).

sarto'rial, *adj.*, rel. to tailors and tailoring.

sarto'rius, *n.*, a muscle in the thigh used in crossing the legs as a tailor crosses them.

sash, *n.*, a scarf or band worn over the shoulder or round the waist; the framework of window-glass; *v.t.*, to fit with sashes.

sashed, *adj.*, wearing a sash; *p.p.*, sash.

sash'-frame, *n.*, the framework enclosing a sash window.

sash'-line, *n.*, a cord for raising or depressing a sash.

sas'safras, *n.*, a fragrant tree so named.

Sas'senach, *adj.*, Saxon; *n.*, a Saxon (a Gaelic word).

sas'soline, *n.*, a natural boracic acid.

sas'tra, *n. pl.*, laws, institutes, esp. those of the Brahmins.

sat, *p.t.*, sit.

Sa'tan, *n.*, the Devil.

satan'ic, *adj.*, pert. to, or resembling, Satan; devilish.

satan'ical, *adj.*, *i.q.* Satanic.

satch'el, *n.*, a light bag suspended from the arm or slung over the shoulder.

sate, *v.t.*, to satisfy (a desire or appetite).

sa'ted, *p.p.*, sate.

sateen', *n.*, an imitation satin.

sat'ellite, *n.*, an attendant; a small planet revolving round a larger one.

sa'tiable, *adj.*, able to be sated.

sa'tiate, *v.t.*, to fill to the full; to glut.

sa'tiate, *adj.*, glutted.

sa'tiated, *p.p.*, satiate.

sa'tiating, *pr.p.*, satiate; *adj.*, glutting.

satia'tion, *n.*, quenching; surfeit.

sati'ety, *n.*, overfulness.

sat'in, *n.*, a smooth, glossy fabric of silk.

satinet(te)', *n.*, an imitation thin satin.

sa'ting, *pr.p.*, sate.

sat'in-wood, *n.*, a wood with a satin-like surface.

sat'iny, *adj.*, like satin.

sat'ire, *n.*, ridicule, sarcasm; poetry holding folly or vice up to ridicule.

satir'ic, *adj.*, of the nature of satire.

satir'ical, *adj.*, *i.q.* satiric.

satir'ically, *adv.*, in a satirical way.

sat'irist, *n.*, a writer of satire.

sat'irize, *v.t.*, to ridicule with satire.

sat'irized, *p.p.*, satirize.

sat'irizing, *pr.p.*, satirize.

satisfac'tion, *n.*, the giving of content; complete content; appeasing.

satisfac'torily, *adv.* in a satisfactory way.

satisfac'tory, *adj.*, giving satisfaction; removing doubt.

sat'isfiable, *adj.*, able to be satisfied.

sat'isfied, *p.p.*, satisfy

sat'isfier, *n.*, one who makes satisfaction.

sat'isfy, *v.t.*, to give satisfaction to; to content; to make full discharge; to remove doubt; *v.i.*, to make atonement.

sat'isfying, *pr.p.*, satisfy; *adj.*, contenting.

sa'trap, *n.*, a Persian provincial governor.

sa'trapy, *n.*, the office or province of a satrap.

Sat'suma, *n.*, a yellow Japanese ware.

sat'urable, *adj.*, able to be saturated.

sat'urant, *adj.*, saturating; *n.*, an antacid substance.

sat'urate, *adj.*, saturated; impregnated.

sat'urate, *v.t.*, to impregnate, soak.

sat'urated, *p.p.*, saturate.

sat'urating, *pr.p.*, saturate.

satura'tion, *n.*, the act or effect of saturating.

Sat'urday, *n.*, the seventh day of the week; the Sabbath; (named after Saturn).

Sat'urn, *n.*, the most ancient of the Roman deities; god of creation; a planet so named.

Saturna'lia, *n. pl.*, the festival in honour of Saturn, attended by great revelry and licence, hence=noisy revel.

Saturna'lian, *adj.*, rel. to Saturnalia; riotous.

Satur'nian, *adj.*, rel. to Saturn and the Golden Age of primitive goodness and happiness.

sat'urnine, *adj.*, grim, morose; rel. to the influence of the planet Saturn.

sat'yr, *n.*, a fabulous creature, half man, half goat, attending on Bacchus.

sauce, *n.*, a liquid preparation for flavouring purposes; a relish; impertinence (*colloq.*); *v.t.*, to add as a relish to; to be impertinent to (*colloq.*).

sauce'-boat, *n.*, a boat-shaped piece of table-ware to hold a sauce or gravy.

sauce'-box, *n.*, an impertinent person (*colloq.*).

sauced, *p.p.*, sauce.

sauce'pan, *n.*, a pan for cooking purposes.

sau'cer, *n.*, a shallow piece of ware to hold a cup.

sau'cier, *adj.*, *comp.* of saucy.

sau'ciest, *adj.*, *super.* of saucy.

sau'cily, *adv.*, impertinently.

sau'ciness, *n.*, pertness; impertinence.

sauc'ing, *pr.p.*, sauce.

saucisse', *n.*, a fuse; faggots in a bundle to keep earth in a trench from falling in.

saucisson', *n.*, *i.q.* saucisse; fascine.
sau'cy, *adj.*, pert; impertinent.
sauer'kraut, *n.*, decayed cabbage in pickle.
Saumur, *n.*, a white wine so named.
saun'ter, *v.i.*, to stroll; walk idly; *n.*, a stroll; a place for rambling in.
saun'tered, *p.p.*, saunter.
saun'terer, *n.*, one who saunters.
saun'tering, *pr.p.*, saunter.
Sau'ria, *n. pl.*, an order of scaly, four-footed reptiles, as the crocodile, etc.
sau'rian, *n.*, one of the Sauria.
sau'roid, *adj.*, like a saurian.
sau'sage, *n.*, chopped meat or other ingredients packed in an animal's gut.
sausage-roll', *n.*, a roll filled with sausage meat.
sauté, *adj.*, cooked in a frying pan and tossed.
Sauterne', *n.*, a French white wine.
sa'vable, **save'able**, *adj.*, able to be saved.
sav'age, *adj.*, fierce, wild, barbarous; angry; *n.*, an uncivilized man or woman; a cruel person; *v.t.*, to bite.
sav'agely, *adv.*, fiercely, angrily.
sav'ageness, *n.*, fierceness.
sav'agery, *n.*, the acts of a savage; the state of a savage.
savan'nah, *n.*, an open plain.
savant', *n.*, a learned or scientific person (*Fr.*).
save, *v.t.*, to rescue, redeem; prevent; put by; *v.i.*, to practise economy; *prep.*, excepting.
saved, *p.p.*, save.
sav'eloy, *n.*, a kind of sausage cooked.
sa'ver, *n.*, one who saves or economizes.
sav'in, **sav'ine**, *n.*, an evergreen shrub, the leaves of which have medicinal properties.
sa'ving, *pr.p.*, save; *n.*, economy; *prep.*, except; *adj.*, excepting, reserving.
sa'vingly, *adv.*, in a saving way.
sa'vings, *n.pl.*, money economized.
sa'vings-bank, *n.*, a bank where savings are deposited.
sa'viour, *n.*, one who saves; (S-) Our Lord Jesus Christ.
sa'vour, **sa'vor**, *n.*, flavour; relish; scent; *v.t.*, to taste or smell agreeably; *v.i.*, to possess an agreeable taste or smell.
sa'voured, *p.p.*, savour.
sa'vourily, *adv.*, in a savoury way.
sa'vouriness, *n.*, the quality of being savoury.
sa'vouring, *pr.p.*, savour.
sa'vourless, *n.*, insipid.
sa'voury, *adj.*, good to taste or smell.
savoy', *n.*, a winter cabbage.
Savoy'ard, *n.*, a native of Savoy.
saw, *p.t.*, see; *n.*, a serrated instrument for cutting; a wise saying; *v.t.*, to cut with a saw; *v.i.*, to yield to the saw.
saw'dust, *n.*, the dust produced by sawing.
sawed, *p.t.*, saw.
saw'fish, *n.*, a fish with a spined snout.
saw'ing, *pr.p.*, saw.
saw'mill, *n.*, a factory where timber is sawn.
sawn, *p.p.*, saw.
saw'ney, *n.*, an idiot, lout; a rude nickname for a Scot.
saw'-pit, *n.*, a pit in which sawyers work.
saw'yer, *n.*, a workman who saws wood.
sax'atile, *adj.*, pert. to rocks.
sax'horn, *n.*, a brass wind-instrument.
saxic'avous, *adj.*, rock-boring.
sax'ifrage, *n.*, a genus of rock-grown plants.
Sax'on, *adj.*, pert. to Saxony and the Saxons; *n.*, a native of Saxony; an Anglo-Saxon.
Sax'onism, *n.*, Saxon idiom.
say, *v.t.*, to speak, recite, declare, pronounce; *v.i.*, to speak, answer; *n.*, remark, speech.
say'est, 2nd pers. sing., *pr.t.* say.
say'ing, *pr.p.*, say; *n.*, something said; a proverb.
says, 3rd pers. sing., *pr.t.*, say.
scab, *n.*, a cover formed over a wound; a disease in sheep; one who stands out of a workmen's strike.
scab'bard, *n.*, the sheath of a sword; *v.t.*, to sheathe.
scabbed, *adj.*, troubled with scab.
scab'bier, *adj.*, *comp.* of scabby.
scab'biest, *adj.*, *super.* of scabby.
scab'biness, *n.*, the condition of being scabby.
scab'by, *adj.*, covered with scabs; suffering from scab.
sca'bies, *n.*, the itch.
sca'bious, *adj.*, troubled with scabies; *n.*, a plant.
sca'brous, *adj.*, rough, scaly, dotted.
scad, *n.*, the shad.
scaf'fold, *n.*, a raised platform or stage; the place for the gallows; a political programme.
scaf'folder, *n.*, one who builds scaffolding.
scaf'folding, *n.*, the timber, poles, etc., for a scaffold; the framework of a scaffold.
scagl'ia, *n.*, a special kind of limestone.

scaglio'la, *n.*, plaster imitating scaglia.

sca'la, *n.*, a ladder or staircase (*Lat.*).

scal'able, *adj.*, able to be scaled.

scald, *v.t.*, to burn with hot liquid or steam; to heat (cream); to let the fire taint what is being boiled; *n.*, a burn from hot liquid or steam; scurf; a Scandinavian minstrel.

scald'ed, *p.p.*, scald.

scald'er, *n.*, one who, or that which, scalds.

scald'-head, *n.*, scab on the head.

scal'dic, *adj.*, rel. to the Scalds.

scald'ing, *pr.p.*, scald.

scale, *v.t.*, to mount, ascend; to remove scales from; *v.i.*, to come off in layers; to weigh (so much); *n.*, the pan of a balance; a weighing instrument; one of the small plates on a fish's body; any scale-like layer; a graduated measure; a complete series of musical intervals; a standard of measurement.

scaled, *p.p.*, scale.

scalene', *adj.*, having unequal angles and sides.

sca'ler, *n.*, one who scales.

sca'liness, *n.*, the quality of being scaly.

sca'ling, *pr.p.*, scale.

scal'lawag, *n.*, *i.q.* scallywag.

scall'ion, *n.*, the eschalot.

scal'lop, *n.*, a sea bivalve; a recessed border; *v.t.*, to cut a border with curves or recesses.

scal'loped, *p.p.*, scallop; *adj.*, said of oysters baked with bread crumbs.

scal'loping, *pr.p.*, scallop.

scal'lop-shell, *n.*, the shell of a scallop, the emblem of a pilgrim to the Shrine of St. Iago of Compostella; the emblem of St. James.

scal'lywag, *n.*, a poor, lean animal; a scamp. Also *scallawag*.

scalp, *n.*, the skin on the top of a head; that part torn or cut off by Red Indians; *v.t.*, to cut off the scalp from; *v.i.*, to profit quickly on market fluctuations (*colloq.*).

scalped, *p.p.*, scalp.

scal'pel, *n.*, a small, sharp knife.

scalp'er, *n.*, one who scalps.

scalp'ing, *pr.p.*, scalp.

scalp'ing-knife, *n.*, a knife used for the purpose of scalping.

scal'y, *adj.*, covered with scales; scale-like.

scam'ble, *v.i.*, to trespass on hospitality (*Scot.*).

scam'bled, *p.p.*, scamble.

scam'bler, *n.*, an intruder who scambles (*Scot.*).

scam'bling, *pr.p.*, scamble.

scam'mony, *n.*, a cathartic obtained from the sap of a convolvulus-like plant.

scamp, *n.*, a worthless fellow; rascal; *v.t.*, to stint labour on a task.

scam'per, *v.i.*, to run very fast; to hurry off; *n.*, a hurried flight; a quick run or ride.

scam'pered, *p.p.*, scamper.

scam'pering, *pr.p.*, scamper.

scan, *v.t.*, to run the eyes over; to survey; to examine the metre of; *v.i.*, to obey the rules of scansion.

scan'dal, *n.*, offence; cause of offence; defamatory talk; disgrace.

scan'dalize, *v.t.*, to shock.

scan'dalized, *p.p.*, scandalize.

scan'dalizing, *pr.p.*, scandalize.

scan'dal-monger, *n.*, one who talks scandal.

scan'dalous, *adj.*, causing scandal; infamous.

scan'dalously, *adv.*, in a scandalous way.

scan'dent, *adj.*, climbing.

Scandina'vian, *adj.*, rel. to Scandinavia; *n.*, a native of S.

scanned, *p.p.* scan.

scan'ning, *pr.p.*, scan; *n.*, *i.q.* scansion.

scan'sion, *n.*, the act of scanning; *i.e.*, of marking the metrical construction of verse.

Scanso'res, *n. pl.*, climbing birds, as the woodpecker, etc.

scanso'rial, *adj.*, rel. to Scansores, climbing.

scant, *adj.*, *i.q.* scanty; *n.* lack; stint; *v.t.*, to stint, limit; *v.i.*, to fall off in quantity or amount.

scant'ier, *adj.*, *comp.* of scanty.

scant'iest, *adj.*, *super.* of scanty.

scant'ily, *adv.*, in a scanty way.

scant'iness, *n.*, stint; insufficiency.

scant'ing, *pr.p.*, scant.

scan'tle, *v.t.*, to partition; *n.*, a gauge used in slate-making.

scant'ling, *n.*, a small piece of sawn timber; the size to which it should be sawn.

scant'ly, *n.*, barely; insufficiently.

scant'ness, *n.*, bareness, insufficiency.

scant'y, *adj.*, not abundant; not sufficing; scant.

scape, *n.*, the part of a pillar immediately above the base; a peduncle.

scape'goat, *n.*, orig., a goat which was sent out into the wilderness, the Jewish

High Priest having confessed the sins of the people over it; any one on whom blame for others is cast.

scape'grace, *n.*, a ne'er-do-well.

scape'ment, *n.*, *i.q.* escapement.

scaph'oid, *adj.*, boat-shaped.

scap'ple, *v.t.*, to rough-dress stone.

scap'ula, *n.*, the shoulder-blade.

scap'ular, *adj.*, rel. to the shoulder-blade; *n.*, a part of the religious habit worn over the shoulders.

scap'ulary, *n.*, *i.q.* scapular.

scar, *v.t.*, to make a mark upon; *v.i.*, to form a scar; *n.*, a mark, scratch; a steep rock.

scar'ab, *n.*, a beetle, scarabaeus; an Egyptian beetle-shaped charm.

scar'abee, *n.*, *i.q.* scarab.

scar'amouch, *n.*, a buffoon dressed in black; a bragging, cowardly character in Old Italian comedy.

scarce, *adj.*, rare, stinted.

scarce'ly, *adv.*, hardly, stintedly.

scarce'ness, *n.*, want, rarity; the state of being scarce.

scar'city, *n.*, *i.q.* scarceness.

scare, *v.t.*, to frighten, terrify; *n.*, a fright, panic.

scare'crow, *n.*, anything set up to frighten birds away; a ridiculous figure.

scared, *p.p.*, scare.

scarf, *n.*, a neck-wrap or tie; a sash; *v.t.*, to cover with a scarf; to dovetail.

scarfed, *p.p.*, scarf.

scarf'ing, *pr.p.*, scarf; *n.*, the straight joining of two pieces of timber.

scarf'skin, *n.*, the cuticle.

scarifica'tion, *n.*, the act of scarifying.

scar'ificator, *n.*, a scarifying surgical instrument.

scar'ified, *p.p.*, scarify.

scar'ifier, *n.*, anything that scarifies; *i.q.*, scarificator; an implement used in agriculture.

scar'ify, *v.t.*, to cut or scratch a surface, whether the skin or the soil.

scar'ifying, *pr.p.*, scarify.

sca'ring, *pr.p.*, scare.

sca'rious, *adj.*, dry, scaly.

scarlati'na, *n.*, a mild type of scarlet fever.

scarlati'nous, *adj.*, of the nature of scarlatina.

scar'let, *adj.*, bright red; *n.*, a bright red colour; a scarlet-coloured robe or material.

scarp, *n.*, a steep slope; the sloping ground beneath a parapet; *v.t.*, to cut like a scarp.

scarped, *p.p.*, scarp.

scarred, *p.p.*, scar.

scar'ring, *pr.p.*, scar.

scathe, *v.t.*, to injure; *n.*, a hurt, injury.

scathed, *p.p.*, scathe.

scathe'less, *adj.*, unhurt.

sca'thing, *pr. p.*, scathe; *adj.*, cutting, severe, injurious.

scat'ter, *v.t.*, to disperse; throw broadcast; *v.i.*, to be broken up or dispersed.

scat'ter-brained, *adj.*, frivolous, giddy.

scat'tered, *p.p.*, scatter.

scat'terer, *n.*, one who, or that which, scatters.

scat'tering, *pr.p.*, scatter.

scaup, *n.*, a certain kind of duck.

scav'enge, *v.t.* and *i.*, to cleanse (streets) from filth.

scav'enger, *n.*, one who scavenges; a refuse-eating animal.

scav'enging, *pr.p.*, scavenge.

sce'na, *n.*, an Italian operatic scene.

scenar'io, *n.*, a sketch of the plot or libretto of a play.

scene, *n.*, a spectacle; show; disagreeable exhibition of quarrelling; the general setting of an action or occurrence.

scene'-painter, *n.*, one who paints stage-scenery.

sce'nery, *n.*, the general aspect of ground or country; stage-paintings.

scene'-shifter, *n.*, one who moves the scenery in a theatre.

sce'nic, *adj.*, rel. to scenery and the stage.

sce'nical, *adj.*, *i.q.* scenic.

scenograph'ic, *adj.*, drawn perspectively.

scenog'raphy, *n.*, drawing in perspective.

scent, *v.t.*, to detect by the smell; to perfume; *n.*, smell, odour, perfume; the sense of smell.

scent'ed, *p.p.*, scent; *adj.*, odorous, fragrant.

scent'ing, *pr.p.*, scent.

scent'less, *adj.*, inodorous; without smell.

scep'tic, skep'tic, *n.*, one who accepts nothing on trust, but enquires into truth or falsehood; a doubter.

scep'tical, *adj.*, doubting, enquiring; disbelieving.

scep'tically, *adv.*, in a sceptical way.

scep'ticism, *n.*, the philosophical position that experience is the only test of truth; doubt, negation.

scep'tre, *n.*, a staff, the emblem of royal power; *v.t.*, to give a sceptre to.

scep'tred, *p.p.*, sceptre; *adj.*, wielding a sceptre.

scep'treless, *adj.*, without a sceptre.

(U.S.) **sched'ule**, *n.*, a document containing an inventory or list; a document appended to another; *v.t.*, to enter in a schedule.

sched'uled, *p.p.*, schedule.

sche'ma, *n.*, an outline, plan; type; syllogistic figure.

schemat'ic, *adj.*, rel. to a schema.

sche'matism, *n.*, outline; design.

scheme, *n.*, a plan, purpose, plot; *v.t.*, to design; *v.i.*, to form a plot or design.

schemed, *p.p.*, scheme.

sche'mer, *n.*, a designing person.

sche'ming, *pr.p.*, scheme.

scherzan'do, *adv.*, in a sportive way (*mus.*).

scher'zo, *n.*, a quick, bright, musical movement.

Schiedam', *n.*, Holland gin.

schism, *n.*, a rent, division; specifically a splitting off from the Catholic Church.

schismat'ic, *adj.*, rel. to schism; *n.*, one guilty of schism.

schismat'ical, *adj.*, *i.q.* schismatic.

schist, *n.*, fissile rock.

schist'ose, *adj.*, fissile; schist-like.

schist'ous, *adj.*, *i.q.* schistose.

schnapps, schnaps, *n.*, Dutch gin.

schol'ar, *n.*, one who goes to school; a learner; a man of learning; a title of an undergraduate foundationer in a college.

schol'arlike, *adj.*, *i.q.* scholarly.

schol'arly, *adj.*, learned.

schol'arship, *n.*, learning, erudition; an exhibition held by a scholar of a college.

scholas'tic, *adj.*, rel. to schools and scholars; bel. to the mediaeval philosophy of the Schoolmen; *n.*, their philosophical system.

scholas'tically, *adv.*, in a scholastic way.

scholas'ticism, *n.*, *i.q.* scholastic.

scho'liast, *n.*, a commentator.

scho'lium, *n.*, the comment or annotation of a scholiast.

school, *n.*, a place of instruction; a group of adherents to a particular set of opinions; a great collection, a shoal, of fish; *v.t.*, to train; to discipline.

***school'*-board**, *n.*, a board of persons charged with the care of schools.

***school'*-book**, *n.*, a book of instruction.

***school'*boy**, *n.*, a boy under instruction at school.

***school'*-days**, *n.*, the time of life when one is at school.

schooled, *p.p.*, school.

***school'*fellow**, *n.*, a contemporary at school.

***school'*girl**, *n.*, fem. of schoolboy.

***school'*house**, *n.*, a schoolmaster's residence.

***school'*ing**, *pr.p.*, school; *n.*, education.

***school'*man**, *n.*, a mediaeval teacher of scholastic.

***school'*master**, *n.*, a teacher.

***school'*mate**, *n.*, *i.q.* schoolfellow.

***school'*mistress**, *n.*, fem. of schoolmaster.

***school'*room**, *n.*, a room where school is kept.

***school'*-teacher**, *n.*, a teacher in a school.

***school'*-teaching**, *n.*, a school teacher's profession.

schoon'er, *n.*, a vessel with two or three masts and fore and aft rigging.

schottische', *n.*, a variety of polka.

sci'agraph, *n.*, the interior of a building shown in section.

sciagraph'ic, *adj.*, rel. to a sciagraph.

sciag'raphy, *n.*, the art of representing shadows.

sciat'ic, *adj.*, rel. to the hip.

sciat'ica, *n.*, neuralgia affecting the sciatic nerve.

sciat'ical, *adj.*, rel. to the hip and sciatica.

sci'ence, *n.*, knowledge; systematised discoveries in nature or other departments of enquiry.

scien'tial, *adj.*, pert. to science.

scientif'ic, *adj.*, pert. to science; versed in science.

scientif'ical, *adj.*, *i.q.* scientific.

scientif'ically, *adv.*, in a scientific way.

sci'entist, *n.*, a man of science.

sci'licet, *conj.*, namely, to wit (*Lat.*).

scim'itar, *n.*, a curved Oriental sword.

scintil'la, *n.*, a spark (*Lat.*).

scin'tillant, *adj.*, sparkling.

scin'tillate, *v.i.*, to sparkle; emit sparks.

scin'tillated, *p.p.*, scintillate.

scin'tillating, *pr.p.*, scintillate.

scintilla'tion, *n.*, the act of scintillating; a flash; twinkle.

sci'olism, *n.*, shallow learning.

sci'olist, *n.*, a false pretender to learning.

sci'on, *n.*, a branch, shoot; a descendant.

sciop'tic, *adj.*, rel. to a *camera obscura*.

scirrhos'ity, *n.*, hardness.

scir'rhous, *adj.*, hardened.

scir'rhus, *n.*, a hard cancer.

scis'sel, *n.*, clippings of metal.

scis'sile, *adj.*, with cutting power.

scis'sion, *n.*, a cutting; the act of cutting.

scis'sors, *n. pl.*, a smaller kind of shears.

scis'sure, *n.*, a cut.

sci'urine, *adj.*, pert. to squirrels.

Sclavo'nian, *adj.*, rel. to Sclavs. Also *Slavonian.*

Sclavon'ic, *adj.*, *i.q.* Sclavonian. Also *Slavonic.*

scler'ogen, *n.*, the thickening substance in wood cells.

sclero'sis, *n.*, a hardening; thickening.

sclerot'ic, *adj.*, hard.

scobs, *n.*, the raspings of hard substances.

scoff, *v.t.*, to deride; *v.i.*, to be derisive; *n.*, derision; ridicule

scoffed, *p.p.*, scoff.

scoff'er, *n.*, one who scoffs.

scoff'ing, *pr.p.*, scoff.

scold, *v.t.* and *i.*, to reprove angrily; to find fault; *n.*, a woman who habitually finds fault.

scold'ed, *p.p.*, scold.

scold'er, *n.*, one who scolds.

scold'ing, *pr.p.*, scold; *n.*, a chiding.

sco'lecite, *n.*, a fossilized worm.

sco'lex, *n.*, tapeworm larva (*Gr.*).

scol'lop, *n.*, *see* scallop.

Scolopen'dra, *n. pl.*, a centipede venomous insect.

sconce, *v.t.*, to inflict a penalty on; *n.*, a bulwark; protection; a candle or lampholder; a head; a penalty.

scone, *n.*, a kind of tea-cake.

scoop, *v.t.*, to shovel up; to hollow; *n.*, a shovel, ladle, scuttle; a substantial gain (*colloq.*).

scooped, *p.p.*, scoop.

scoop'er, *n.*, anything that scoops.

scoop'ing, *pr.p.*, scoop.

scope, *n.*, range; outlook; room for action; aim.

scorbu'tic, *adj.*, rel. to scurvy.

scorch, *v.t.* and *i.*, to singe; shrivel up with heat; *v.i.*, to cycle or motor at high speed (*slang*).

scorched, *p.p.*, scorch.

scorch'er, *n.*, one who cycles or motors at high speed; anything extreme (*slang*); that which scorches.

scorch'ing, *pr.p.*, scorch.

scorch'ingly, *adv.*, with scorching effect.

score, *v.t.*, to mark; notch; to reckon up; to win (a number of runs, etc.); *n.*, a mark; notch; a reckoning; behalf; the number 20; musical parts written down.

scored, *p.p.*, score.

scor'er, *n.*, one who scores; a record of scores.

sco'ria, *n.*, volcanic débris; slag.

scoria'ceous, *adj.*, rel. to scoria.

scorifica'tion, *n.*, formation of scoria.

sco'rified, *p.p.*, scorify.

sco'riform, *adj.*, like scoria.

sco'rify, *v.t.* and *i.*, to form scoria.

sco'rifying, *pr.p.*, scorify.

scor'ing, *pr.p.*, score.

sco'rious, *adj.*, *i.q.* scoriaceous.

scorn, *v.t.*, to contemn; *n.*, contempt, disdain.

scorned, *p.p.*, scorn.

scorn'er, *n.*, one who scorns.

scorn'ful, *adj.*, disdainful, contemptuous.

scorn'fully, *adv.*, in a scornful way.

scorn'ing, *pr.p*, scorn.

Scor'pio, *n.*, the Scorpion, one of the signs of the Zodiac.

scor'pion, *n.*, a creature with claws like a lobster and a sting in its tail.

scor'tatory, *adj.*, rel. to prostitution.

Scot, *n.*, a Scotsman.

scot, *n.*, a fine; tax.

Scotch, *adj.*, *i.q.* Scottish. In pl. as a noun, it means the Scots, the people of Scotland.

scotch, *v.t.*, to score, hack; to cripple; to block; to frustrate; *n.*, a cut; a chock or block.

scotched, *p.p.*, scotch.

scotch'ing, *pr.p.*, scotch.

Scotch'man, *n.*, a Scot.

sco'ter, *n.*, a variety of sea-duck.

scot'-free', *adj.*, free from duty of paying scot; unpunished; safe and sound.

sco'tia, *n.*, a hollow moulding in a pillar-base in classical architecture.

Sco'tia, *n.*, the Latin name for Scotland.

Scot'icè, *adv.*, after the Scottish manner; in Scots speech.

Sco'tist, *n.*, a disciple of Duns Scotus, the famous 13th cent. philosopher.

sco'tograph, *n.*, a contrivance enabling the blind to read or anyone to write in the dark.

scoto'ma, *n.*, vertigo; difficulty in discerning objects.

Scots, *adj.*, Scottish; *n.*, the speech of Scotland; pl. of Scot.

Scots'man, *n.*, a Scot.

Scot'ticism, *n.*, Scottish idiom.

Scot'tish, *adj.*, Scots, Scotch.

scoun'drel, *n.*, a villain, rascal.

scoun'drelism, *n.*, the conduct of a scoundrel; rascality.

scoun'drelly, *adj.*, like a scoundrel.

scour, *v.t.*, to cleanse by rubbing or polishing; to range over; sweep along; *n.*, the effect of rushing water on a channel; something used for scouring.

scoured, *p.p.*, scour.

scour'er, *n.*, one who, or that which, scours.

scourge, *v.t.*, to lash, punish with scourging, harass; *n.*, a whip for flogging; any plague or vengeance.

scourged, *p.p.*, scourge

scour'ger, *n.*, one who scourges.

scour'ging, *pr.p.*, scourge.

scour'ing, *pr.p.*, scour; *n.*, the act of scouring in all senses.

scout, *v.t.*, to reject or dismiss with contempt; *v.i.*, to mock; to act as a scout; *n.*, someone sent out to reconnoitre and bring information; a look-out; a member of the great organization of Boy Scouts; a college servant at Oxford.

scout'ed, *p.p.*, scout.

scout'ing, *pr.p.*, scout

scov'el, *n.*, a mop to clean ovens.

scow, *n.*, a flat-bottomed boat, square-ended.

scowl, *v.i.*, to put on a sullen look; to frown angrily; *n.*, an angry frown.

scowled, *p.p.*, scowl.

scowl'ing, *pr.p.*, scowl.

scrab'ble, *v.t.*, to scratch writings on; *v.i.*, to scrawl, scribble; to scramble; *n.*, scrambling.

scrab'bled, *p.p.*, scrabble.

scrab'bling, *pr.p.*, scrabble.

scrag, *v.t.*, to kill by hanging (*colloq.*); to collar (at football); *n.*, a lean person or thing; the thin end of a neck of mutton.

scragged, *p.p.*, scrag.

scrag'gily, *adv.*, in a scraggy way.

scrag'giness, *n.*, the condition of being scraggy.

scrag'gy, *adj.*, lean.

scram'ble, *v.t.*, to cook eggs broken into a pan and mixed with butter, etc.; to gather up in confusion; *v.i.*, to clamber on hands and feet; to struggle; to run in all directions, as a creeper; *n.*, a struggle; a clambering.

scram'bled, *p.p.*, scramble.

scram'bler, *n.*, one who scrambles.

scramb'ling, *pr.p.*, scramble.

scranch, *v.t.*, to crunch (*colloq.*).

scrap, *v.t.*, to throw away as refuse; to engage in a fight (*slang*); *n.*, something scraped off; a fragment; a small portion; a fight (*slang*).

scrap'-book, *n.*, a book of extracts, cuttings, pictures, etc.

scrape, *v.t.*, to scratch; take the surface off; rub hard on; to gather up by scraping; *v.i.*, to rub a surface; to save money; to make a bow by scraping the feet; to play a fiddle indifferently; *n.*, the act of scraping; a troublesome situation created by one's own fault; a movement with the foot in making a bow.

scraped, *p.p.*, scrape.

scra'per, *n.*, that which scrapes; an appliance for scraping mud off one's shoes.

scra'ping, *pr.p.*, scrape.

scratch, *v.t.*, to tear or abrade a surface; to write clumsily; to erase from a list; *n.*, a mark of scratching; the sound of scratching; a slight wound; the starting line in a race; *adj.*, chosen indiscriminately; having no handicap allowance.

scratched, *p.p.*, scratch.

scratch'ing, *pr.p.*, scratch.

scratch'y, *adj.*, making the sound of scratching; poorly drawn.

scrawl, *v.t.*, to scribble, write more or less illegibly; *n.*, a piece of bad writing.

scrawled, *p.p.*, scrawl.

scrawl'er, *n.*, one who scrawls.

scrawl'ing, *pr.p.*, scrawl.

scrawl'y, *adj.*, badly written.

scrawn'y, *adj.*, skinny.

scray, *n.*, a tern.

scream, *v.t.*, to utter in a piercing voice; *v.i.*, to make a piercing cry; *n.*, a piercing cry or sound.

screamed, *p.p.*, scream

scream'er, *n.*, one who screams; anything that excites great laughter or astonishment (*slang*)

scream'ing, *pr.p.*, scream; *adj.*, provoking great laughter (*slang*).

scree, *n.*, a mountain slope of loose stones.

screech, *v.t.*, to utter in a screaming voice; *v.i.*, to make a sharp, screaming sound or cry.

screeched, *p.p.*, screech.

screech'ing, *pr.p.*, screech.

screech'-owl, *n.*, an owl that screeches.

screed, *n.*, a long, boring tale; a strip of mortar or wood fixed at intervals on a surface to be plastered, and showing the compartments of the plastering.

screen, *v.t.*, to cover, conceal, protect; to riddle; *n.*, a barrier of any kind protecting against heat, cold, etc.; the barrier between nave and choir, or between one division of a church and another; a sheet on to which a magic lantern or shadow picture is thrown.

screened, *p.p.*, screen.

screen'ing, *pr.p.*, screen.

screes, *n. pl.*, loose stones; *see* scree.

screw, *v.t.*, to apply a screw or a screwing motion to; to use pressure with; to distort; to put a twist on a ball; *v.i.*, to turn screw-fashion; to be a miser; *n.*, a cylindrical piece of wood or metal, spirally grooved on the outside or inside; a miser; a broken-down horse.

screw′-driver, *n.*, a tool for forcing a screw in.

screwed, *p.p.*, screw.

screw′ing, *pr.p.*, screw.

screw′-jack, *n.*, a lifting jack with a screw; a dentist's apparatus for changing the position of overcrowded teeth.

screw′-pine, *n.*, a plant with spiral leaves.

scrib′ble, *v.t.* and *i.*, to write hastily or carelessly; *v.i.*, to be a writer or scribbler; to card wool; *n.*, hasty writing; poor literature.

scrib′bled, *p.p.*, scribble.

scrib′bler, *n.*, one who scribbles; an indifferent author; a machine for scribbling wool.

scrib′bling, *pr.p.*, scribble; *n.*, wool-carding.

scribe, *n.*, a writer, penman; specifically an expounder and recorder of the Jewish law and tradition; *v.t.*, to scratch with a marking tool, for the purpose of guiding a saw, etc.

scribed, *p.p.*, scribe.

scri′bing, *pr.p.*, scribe

scrim′mage, *v.i.*, to join in a scrimmage (*colloq.*); *n.*, a tussle, row, skirmish.

scrimp, *v.t.* and *i.*, to stint, skimp; *adj.*, skimped; *n.*, a niggard.

scrimped, *p.p.*, scrimp

scrim′shaw, *v.t.* and *i.*, to decorate ivory, shells, etc., with coloured drawings; *n.*, a shell, etc., so decorated.

scrip, *n.*, a bag, wallet; a document showing the holder's title to payment of interest, dividend, etc.

scrip′-holder, *n.*, the owner of a piece of scrip.

script, *n.*, writing; style of writing; imitation writing; a draft.

scripto′rial, *adj.*, rel. to writing or authorship.

scripto′rium, *n.*, a part of a monastery where manuscripts are written.

Scrip′tural, *adj.*, rel. to the Sacred Scriptures.

Scrip′turalist, *n.*, one who interprets the Sacred Scriptures in the most literal sense.

Scrip′turally, *adv.*, according to Scripture.

Scrip′ture, *n.*, writing, esp. the Bible; a passage from the Bible.

Scrip′ture-reader, *n.*, a layman who instructs the poor and unlearned.

Scrip′turist, *n.*, one learned in the Scriptures.

scriv′ener, *n.*, a person who draws up deeds, drafts documents, lends money, or acts as a notary.

scriv′enery, *n.*, a scrivener's calling.

scrobic′ulate, *adj.*, furrowed, marked.

scrof′ula, *n.*, morbid predisposition to glandular tumours. (Formerly known as King's Evil, because patients were brought to the Sovereign, who was held to possess a healing touch for this complaint.)

scrof′ulous, *adj.*, suffering from scrofula; of the nature of scrofula.

scroll, *v.t.*, to write in a scroll; to draft; to curl up; to adorn with scrolls; *v.i.*, to curl up in a roll; *n.*, a roll; an artistic scroll-like ornament; anything resembling a scroll, as a fiddle-head.

scrolled, *p.p.*, scroll; *adj.*, decorated with scrolls; like a scroll; encased in a scroll.

scroll′work, *n.*, ornamental scroll-like design.

scro′tum, *n.*, the pouch containing the testicles.

scrub, *v.t.* and *i.*, to cleanse by rubbing; *v.i.*, to be a drudge; *n.*, the act of scrubbing; a stunted shrub; ground covered with stunted trees or shrubs; any person or thing particularly mean.

scrubbed, *p.p.*, scrub.

scrub′ber, *n.*, one who, or that which, scrubs.

scrub′bier, *adj.*, *comp.* of scrubby.

scrub′biest, *adj.*, *super.* of scrubby.

scrub′bing, *pr.p.*, scrub; *n.*, a cleaning.

scrub′by, *adj.*, mean, undersized, shabby.

scruff, *n.*, the back of the neck.

scrum, *n.*, *colloq.* for scrummage.

scrum′mage, *n.*, *i.q.* scrimmage.

scrump′tious, *adj.*, especially delightful or beautiful (*colloq.*).

scru′ple, *v.i.*, to hesitate on conscientious grounds; *n.*, hesitation on moral or conscientious grounds; an apothecaries' weight-unit (= 20 grains).

scru′pled, *p.p.*, scruple.

scru′pling, *pr.p.*, scruple.

scrupulos′ity, *n.*, *i.q.* scrupulousness.

scru′pulous, *adj.*, conscientious, punctilious.

scru′pulously, *adv.*, conscientiously.

scru′pulousness, *n.*, the state or quality of being scrupulous.

scruta'tor, *n.*, a careful enquirer or examiner (*Lat.*).

scru'tatory, *adj.*, scrutinizing.

scrutineer', *n.*, a scrutinizer; one who conducts a scrutiny, particularly at Parliamentary or municipal elections.

scru'tinize, *v.t.*, to investigate or examine closely.

scru'tinized, *p.p.*, scrutinize.

scru'tinizer, *n.*, one who scrutinizes.

scru'tinizing, *pr.p.*, scrutinize.

scru'tiny, *n.*, close investigation; strict enquiry; examination of voting-papers at an election; a mode of electing the Pope.

scrutoire', *n.*, a writing-table; escritoire.

scud, *v.i.*, to drive along swiftly; *n.*, a rapid rushing; light cloud or spray driven before the wind.

scud'ded, *p.p.*, scud.

scud'ding, *pr.p.*, scud.

scu'di, *n.*, pl. of scudo.

scu'do, *n.*, an old Italian silver-piece, value about a dollar.

scuf'fle, *v.i.*, to struggle in a disorderly contest; *v.t.*, to hustle; *n.*, a disordered struggle.

scuf'fled, *p.p.*, scuffle.

scuf'fler, *n.*, one who scuffles.

scuf'fling, *pr.p.*, scuffle.

sculk, *v.i.*, *i.q.* skulk.

sculked, *p.p.*, *i.q.* skulked.

sculk'er, *n.*, *i.q.* skulker.

sculk'ing, *pr.p.*, *i.q.* skulking.

scull, *v.t.* and *i.*, to urge on a boat with oars or sculls; *n.*, a small oar used by one hand only.

sculled, *p.p.*, scull.

scull'er, *n.*, one who sculls.

scull'ery, *n.*, the part of a house where dishes, etc., are washed up.

scull'ing, *pr.p.*, scull; *n.*, the practice or art of rowing with sculls.

scull'ion, *n.*, a cook's help, the boy who washes dishes, etc.

sculp, *v.t.* and *i.*, to carve, practise a sculptor's art.

scul'pin, *n.*, an American sea-fish.

sculp'tor, *n.*, an artist who carves in stone, models in clay; an artist in sculpture.

sculp'tural, *adj.*, pert. to sculpture.

sculp'ture, *n.*, the art of carving in stone, marble, etc.; modelling in clay, casting in metals; a piece of sculptured work; *v.t.*, to carve; to represent; to adorn with sculpture.

sculp'tured, *p.p.*, sculpture; *adj.*, with superficial marking.

sculpturesque', *adj.*, with the manner or appearance of a sculptured work.

sculp'turing, *pr.p.*, sculpture *n.*, *i.q.* sculpture.

scum, *v.t.*, to skim; *v.i.*, to form a scum; *n.*, impurities that have risen to the surface of boiling liquid; refuse; offscouring.

scum'ble, *v.t.*, to soften the colours or hard outlines of a picture; *n.*, the softening of colours or outlines.

scum'bled, *p.p.*, scumble.

scumb'ling, *pr.p.*, scumble.

scummed, *p.p.*, scum.

scum'mings, *n. pl.*, skimmings.

scun'ner, *n.*, loathing (*Scot.*).

scup'per, *n.*, an opening in the side of a ship to let water off the deck.

scurf, *n.*, skin flaked off; scaly matter on a surface.

scurf'ier, *adj.*, *comp.* of scurfy.

scurf'iest, *adj.*, *super.* of scurfy.

scurf'iness, *n.*, the state of being scurfy.

scurf'y, *adj.*, covered with scurf; forming scurf.

scur'rile, *adj.*, *i.q.* scurrilous.

scurril'ity, *n.*, gross or obscene abuse.

scur'rilous, *adj.*, grossly or obscenely abusive.

scur'rilously, *adv.*, in a scurrilous way.

scur'ried, *p.p.*, scurry.

scur'ry, *v.i.*, to run hastily; scamper; *n.*, a hurried run; a whirl.

scur'rying, *pr.p.*, scurry.

scur'vily, *adv.*, shabbily; basely.

scur'viness, *n.*, meanness; shabbiness.

scur'vy, *adj.*, mean, base; covered with scurf; *n.*, a distressing complaint affecting the blood and producing painful effects internally and externally.

scut, *n.*, a short tail, as of a rabbit, etc.

scu'tage, *n.*, an old English assessment of feudal landlords in lieu of personal service.

scu'tate, *adj.*, buckler-shaped; covered with shield-shaped scales.

scutch, *v.t.*, to dress fibrous material by beating; to beat (*Scot.*); *n.*, a scutching machine; tow separated by scutching.

scutched, *p.p.*, scutch.

scutch'eon, *n.*, *i.q.* escutcheon; a metal plate on a door, etc.; the cover of a keyhole.

scutch'er, *n.*, a scutching implement.

scutch'ing, *pr.p.*, scutch.

scute, *n.*, *i.q.* scutum.

scu'tel, *n.*, *i.q.* scutellum.

scu'tellate, *adj.*, like a scutellum; platter-like.

scu'tellated, *adj.*, *i.q.* scutellate.

scutel'lum, *n.*, a little plate, shield, or scale formed on insects, birds, plants, etc.
scutif'erous, *adj.*, shield-bearing.
scu'tiform, *adj.*, shield-shaped; peltate.
scut'ter, *v.i.*, *i.q.* scurry.
scut'tle, *v.t.*, to make holes in a ship in order to sink it; *v.i.*, to run in a hurry; *n.*, a hatchway; any hole; a vessel to hold coal; a running in haste.
scut'tled, *p.p.*, scuttle.
scut'tling, *pr.p.*, scuttle.
scu'tum, *n.*, a shield (*Lat.*); a knee-pan; a shield-like plate or scale on turtles, alligators, etc.
scym'itar, *n.*, *i.q.* scimitar.
scy'phus, *n.*, a Greek drinking-cup; in botany, a cup-shaped organ.
scythe, *v.t.*, to mow; to arm with a scythe; *n.*, an implement for mowing and reaping.
scythed, *p.p.*, scythe; *adj.*, having scythes fixed to the axles.
Scyth'ian, *adj.*, pert. to Scythia; *n.*, a native of S.
sea, *n.*, a large body of salt water covering the greater part of the earth's surface; the ocean; a large inland lake.
sea'board, *n.*, coast, sea-shore.
sea'-born, *adj.*, born of the sea.
sea'-borne, *adj.*, carried by sea.
sea'-breach, *n.*, the bursting of a dyke.
sea'-breeze, *n.*, a breeze coming from the sea.
sea'-captain, *n.*, the captain of a ship.
sea'-chart, *n.*, a marine map.
sea'-coast, *n.*, the land where it fringes the sea; the shore.
sea'-cow, *n.*, the walrus.
sea'-dog, *n.*, the harbour-seal; a tough old sailor.
sea'-elephant, *n.*, an elephant-seal.
sea'farer, *n.*, a mariner.
sea'faring, *adj.*, living a sailor's life; *n.*, the life of a sailor.
sea'-fight, *n.*, a battle at sea.
sea'-gauge, *n.*, a sounding apparatus; a ship's draught.
sea'-girt, *adj.*, surrounded by the sea.
sea'-green, *adj.*, green like the sea; *n.*, the colour of the sea.
sea'-gull, *n.*, a gull; large tern.
sea'-horse, *n.*, walrus; hippocampus.
sea'-kale, *n.*, a perennial edible herb.
sea'-king, *n.*, an ancient Scandinavian sea-rover. (The word perhaps owes its origin to a misunderstanding of the name Vikings, which means "dwellers in creeks.")
seal, *v.t.*, to impress with a stamp bearing a device; to close; to confirm; to sign with the cross; *v.i.*, to affix a seal; to go sealing; *n.*, a stamp for making impressions in wax, lead, etc.; the impression thus made; a pledge; a ratification; an amphibious marine mammal, much prized for its fur.
sealed, *p.p.*, seal.
sea'-leopard, *n.*, a variety of seal marked with spots.
seal'er, *n.*, one who seals in any sense; a ship used in sealing.
sea'-level, *n.*, the level of a line halfway between high and low tide.
seal'ing, *pr.p.*, seal; *n.*, the occupation of hunting seals.
seal'ing-wax, *n.*, wax to receive the impression of a seal.
sea'-lion, *n.*, a variety of seal.
seal'skin, *n.*, the skin and fur of a seal; *adj.*, made of sealskin.
seam, *v.t.*, to join with a seam; to mark, scar; to produce a seam-like appearance in knitting; *n.*, a line showing the junction of two parts; a line of fissure; a thin stratum of rock or coal.
sea'man, *n.*, a mariner, sailor.
sea'manship, *n.*, the mariner's art; skill in navigating.
sea'-mark, *n.*, a lighthouse, beacon, etc.
seamed, *p.p.*, seam.
seam'er, *n.*, one who seams; a machine for seaming.
sea'-mew, *n.*, a gull.
seam'ing, *pr.p.*, seam.
seam'less, *adj.*, without seam.
sea'-mouse, *n.*, an iridescent sea-worm.
seam'ster, *n.*, one whose business it is to sew.
seam'stress, *n.*, *i.q.* seamster.
seam'y, *adj.*, having or showing seams; also used figuratively as in the phrase "the seamy side," *i.e.*, the worst aspect.
séance', *n.*, a sitting, session; esp. the sitting of spiritualists.
sea'-pie, *n.*, a sailor's dish of meat and crust in layers.
sea'plane, *n.*, a variety of aeroplane used in the naval service.
sea'port, *n.*, a harbour; a town or city with a harbour.
sear, *v.t.*, to wither, scorch; *adj.*, dry, withered (also *sere*); *n.*, the catch that keeps a gun-hammer at half cock.
search, *v.t.*, to explore, overhaul; ransack, investigate; *n.*, the act of searching;

investigation; enquiry.

search'able, *adj.*, able to be searched.

searched, *p.p.*, search.

search'er, *n.*, one who searches.

search'ing, *pr. p.*, search; *adj.*, penetrating, critical.

search'light, *n.*, a strong electric light in a reflector, projecting a beam of great length.

seared, *p.p.*, sear.

sear'ing, *pr.p.*, sear.

sea'-room, *n.*, space enough for a ship to move freely.

sea'-rover, *n.*, a pirate or pirate-ship.

sea'scape, *n.*, a picture of a marine subject.

sea'-serpent, *n.*, a wonderful monster of the deep, usually heard of in the "silly season" of the year, together with the "big gooseberry."

sea'-shell, *n.*, the shell of a marine creature.

sea'shore, *n.*, the land by the sea; the coast.

sea'sick, *adj.*, suffering from sea-sickness.

sea'-sickness, *n.*, a miserable complaint among travellers by sea, the result of the ship's motion.

sea'side, *n.*, the land near the sea; *adj.*, adjacent to the sea.

sea'-snail, *n.*, a marine snail-like gasteropod.

sea'son, *n.*, a period of time; a division of the year; the fitting time; *v.t.*, to spice, flavour, temper, inure.

sea'sonable, *adj.*, fitting to the season.

sea'soned, *p.p.*, season.

sea'soner, *n.*, that which seasons.

sea'soning, *pr.p.*, season.

sea'son-ticket, *n.*, a railway or other ticket allowing the holder to use it for a stated season.

seat, *n.*, that on which one sits, as a chair, sofa, etc., the buttocks; the part of pants, trousers, etc., that covers the buttocks; a place where a landowner resides or anything is situated; a constituency; the right to sit; *v.t.*, to place in a seat; to establish.

seat'ed, *p.p.*, seat.

sea-term, *n.*, a nautical expression.

seat'ing, *pr.p.*, seat; *n.*, the collective seats, or method of arranging them, in a building; material for seat-covering.

sea'-urchin, *n.*, the echinus.

sea'-wall, *n.*, a wall built to keep out the sea.

sea'ward, *adj.* and *adv.*, toward the sea.

sea'-water, *n.*, the water of the sea.

sea'-weed, *n.*, a plant that grows in sea-water.

sea'worthiness, *n.*, the state or quality of being seaworthy.

sea'worthy, *adj.*, fit to go to sea; in sound condition.

seba'ceous, *adj.*, pert. to fat.

sebac'ic, *adj.*, fatty; made from fat.

se'bate, *n.*, a sebacic acid salt.

sebun'dy, *n.*, an Anglo-Indian word for the native militia and police.

se'cant, *adj.*, cutting, intersecting.

secede', *v.i.*, to withdraw, separate.

sece'ded, *p.p.*, secede.

sece'der, *n.*, one who secedes; a separatist.

sece'ding, *pr.p.*, secede.

secern', *v.t.*, to distinguish.

secerned', *p.p.*, secern.

secern'ing, *pr.p.*, secern.

seces'sion, *n.*, the act of seceding.

seces'sionist, *n.*, a supporter of secession; esp. a supporter of the doctrine that a State had the right to secede from the United States of America.

seclude', *v.t.*, to shut up; put into retirement; remove from intercourse.

seclu'ded, *p.p.*, seclude; *adj.*, retired.

seclu'ding, *pr.p.*, seclude.

seclu'sion, *n.*, the act of secluding; retirement; solitariness.

seclu'sive, *adj.*, having a tendency to seclude.

sec'ond, *adj.*, the ordinal of two; next after the first; *n.*, a short interval (one-sixtieth of a minute); a duellist's supporter; an inferior to the first; a subordinate part; *v.t.*, to support, promote.

second', *v.t.*, to retire (an officer) temporarily before appointing him to some duty outside his regiment.

sec'ondarily, *adv.*, in a secondary degree.

sec'ondary, *adj.*, of lower rank, influence or grade; less important; delegated; subsequent; *n.*, a delegate; a minor official in a cathedral; one of an insect's hind wings; a feather on the second joint of a bird's wings.

sec'ond-best, *adj.*, not quite the first; inferior.

sec'onded, *p.p.*, sec'ond.

second'ed, *p.p.*, second'.

sec'onder, *n.*, one who seconds or formally supports a resolution.

sec'ond-*hand*, *adj.*, not new; previously

owned; indirect; not original; *n.*, the pointer that indicates the seconds on a clock or watch dial.

sec'onding, *pr.p.*, second.

second'ing, *pr.p.*, second'.

sec'ondly, *adv.*, in the second place.

sec'ond-rate, *adj.*, not first rate; of indifferent quality.

sec'onds, *n. pl.*, an article or articles not of the first quality, as seconds in flour or tobacco.

sec'ond-sight, *n.*, a supposed faculty of seeing future or distant events.

se'crecy, *n.*, concealment, seclusion, secretiveness.

se'cret, *adj.*, concealed, hidden, private, reticent; *n.*, something not revealed; mystery; something not to be told; liturgically, a prayer privately said by the celebrant at Mass.

secrétaire', *n.*, a writing desk; *i.q.* escritoire.

secreta'rial, *adj.*, pert. to a secretary and his duties.

secreta'riat, *n.*, a secretary's functions or the place where his work is done.

sec'retary, *n.*, one who acts as the confidential assistant of another; or attends to the correspondence and records of a society; or superintends a Department of State.

sec'retary-bird, *n.*, a S. African bird with a crest that suggests a quill pen.

sec'retaryship, *n.*, a secretary's post.

secrete', *v.t.*, to place in concealment; to separate from blood and sap by secretion.

secre'ted, *p.p.*, secrete

secre'ting, *pr.p.*, secrete.

secre'tion, *n.*, the act or result of secreting; the process by which materials are separated from blood and sap and made into new substances, as milk, urine, etc.

secre'tive, *adj.*, reserved, reticent.

secre'tiveness, *n.*, the quality of being secretive.

se'cretly, *adv.*, in a secret way.

se'cretness, *n.*, the quality or state of being secret.

secre'tory, *adj.*, secreting.

sect, *n.*, a body that dissents from the Church or sets up its own particular standard of religion or philosophy.

secta'rian, *adj.*, pert. to sects and sectarianism.

secta'rianism, *n.*, the spirit of sects.

secta'rianize, *v.t.*, to make sectarian.

sect'arist, *n.*, *i.q.*, sectary.

sect'ary, *n.*, the adherent of a sect, religious, philosophical, etc.

sec'tile, *adj.*, able to be cut.

sec'tion, *n.*, the act of cutting; a portion cut or marked off.

sec'tional, *adj.*, pert. to a section; divided into sections; rel. to a portion of a community or territory.

sec'tor, *n.*, a plane figure contained within two radii of a circle and the subtending arc; a mathematical rule consisting of two flat pieces strongly jointed at one end and marked with lines to represent sines, tangents, etc.

sec'ular, *adj.*, pert. to this age or world, and so the opposite to religious; recurring through the ages; happening once in a century; non-monastic; *n.*, a non-monastic priest.

sec'ularism, *n.*, the quality of being secular; the principles of the secularists.

sec'ularist, *n.*, one who repudiates religion and worship; specifically, one who opposes religious teaching in schools.

secular'ity, *n.*, the quality or state of being secular.

seculariza'tion, *n.*, the act or effect of secularizing.

sec'ularize, *v.t.*, to make secular; exclude religion from.

sec'ularized, *p.p.*, secularize.

sec'ularizing, *pr.p.*, secularize.

sec'ularly, *adv.*, in a secular way.

sec'und, *adj.*, having organs on one side only.

sec'undine, *n.*, the inside coat of an ovule.

secur'able, *adj.*, able to be secured.

secure', *adj.*, free from care or anxiety; safe; sure of; firm; *v.t.*, to make secure; guarantee; obtain; get hold of.

secured', *p.p.*, secure.

secure'ly, *n.*, in safety.

secu'rer, *n.*, one who secures; *adj.*, *comp.* of secure.

secu'riform, *adj.*, hatchet-shaped.

secu'ring, *pr.p.*, secure.

secu'rity, *n.*, freedom from anxiety; safety; guarantee; something hypothecated; documentary proof of loan.

sedan', *n.*, a portable chair borne on poles.

sedate', *adj.*, dignified, grave, composed.

sedate'ly, *adv.*, in a sedate manner.

sedate'ness, *n.*, the quality of being sedate.

sed'ative, *adj.*, soothing; *n.*, a soothing drug.

sed'entarily, *adv.*, in a sedentary way.

sed'entariness, *n.*, the sedentary habit.

sed'entary, *adj.*, not active; requiring or involving much sitting.

sede'runt, *v.i.* (*Lat.*), *p.t.*, 3rd per. pl. ="there sat" or "were present" (said of persons attending at a council, meeting, etc.); thence used as a *n.*, a session, sitting.

sedge, *n.*, a general name for many water-side plants.

sedg'y, *adj.*, abounding in, or like, sedge.

sedi'le, *n.*, a seat (*Lat.*); specifically a seat let into a church wall near an altar for the priest's use.

sedil'ia, *n.*, pl. of sedile, the group of seats (three, four, or even five in number) for the celebrant and his ministers at Mass.

sed'iment, *n.*, a deposit at the bottom of a liquid; lees.

sedimen'tary, *adj.*, of the nature of sediment.

sedi'tion, *n.*, revolt, strife.

sedi'tionary, *adj.*, pert. to sedition.

sedi'tious, *adj.*, of the character of sedition; engaged in sedition.

seduce', *v.t.*, to draw away; to tempt, esp. to corrupt a woman.

seduced', *p.p.*, seduce.

seduce'ment, *n.*, *i.q.* seduction.

sedu'cer, *n.*, one who seduces.

sedu'cible, *adj.*, able to be seduced.

sedu'cing, *p.p.*, seduce.

seduc'tion, *n.*, the act of seducing; enticement.

seduc'tive, *adj.*, attractive, enticing.

seduc'tively, *adv.*, in a seductive way.

sedu'lity, *n.*, industry, diligence.

sed'ulous, *adj.*, diligent, industrious, busy.

sed'ulously, *adv.*, in a sedulous way.

see, *v.t.*, to perceive with the eyes; to perceive with the mind; to understand; to visit; to attend upon; *v.i.*, to perceive; to reflect, consider; *n.*, the seat of a bishop's jurisdiction.

seed, *n.*, the germ of a plant; semen; milt; progeny; *v.t.*, to plant with seed; to extract the seeds from; *v.i.*, to yield seed.

seed'-bud, *n.*, the ovule of a seed.

seed'ed, *p.p.*, seed; *adj.*, bearing seed.

seed'ier, *adj.*, *comp.* of seedy.

seed'iest, *adj.*, *super.* of seedy.

seed'iness, *n.*, the state of being seedy.

seed'less, *adj.*, without seeds.

seed'ling, *n.*, grown or raised from the seed.

seeds'man, *n.*, one who sells seeds.

seed'-time, *n.*, the time for sowing.

seed'-vessel, *n.*, the pericarp.

seed'y, *adj.*, full of seed; running to seed; having the flavour of weeds growing among (grape) vines; shabby, mean; unwell (*colloq.*).

see'ing, *pr.p.*, see; *adj.*, intelligent; understanding.

seek, *v.t.*, to go in quest of; look for; aim at acquiring; ask for; *v.i.*, to make search or enquiry.

seek'er, *n.*, one who seeks.

seek'ing, *pr.p.*, seek.

seem, *v.i.*, to appear; to present the appearance of being.

seemed, *p.p.*, seem.

seem'ing, *pr.p.*, seem; *adj.*, apparent; not real or genuine.

seem'ingly, *adv.*, apparently.

seem'lier, *adj.*, *comp.* of seemly.

seem'liest, *adj.*, *super.* of seemly.

seem'liness, *n.*, the quality of being seemly.

seem'ly, *adj.*, fitting, becoming, decorous.

seen, *p.p.*, see.

se'er, *n.*, one who sees.

seer, *n.*, a prophet; one who has preternatural vision.

sees, *v.t.* and *i.*, 3rd per. sing., *pr.t.* see.

see'-saw, *adj.* and *adv.*, with a backward and forward or upward and downward movement; *v.i.*, to move up and down or backward and forward; *n.*, a children's game with a plank balanced, so that the players move up and down alternately.

see'-sawed, *p.p.*, see-saw.

see'-sawing, *pr.p.*, see-saw.

seethe, *v.t.* and *i.*, to boil.

seethed, *p.p.*, seethe.

seeth'er, *n.*, one who, or that which, seethes.

seeth'ing, *pr. p.*, seethe; *adj.*, agitated.

seg'gar, *n.*, a baking-case in a kiln.

seg'ment, *n.*, a portion cut off or marked off.

segment'al, *adj.*, of the nature of a segment.

segmenta'tion, *n.*, the act of dividing into segments.

seg'regate, *v.t.*, to place apart; to isolate; *v.i.*, to separate

seg'regated, *p.p.*, segregate.

seg'regating, *pr.p.*, segregate.

segrega'tion, *n.*, the act or result of segregating.

Seid'litz, *adj.*, pert. to Seidlitz, in Bohemia, noted for its alkaline waters.

seign'eur, *n.*, a feudal manorial lord.

seigneu'rial, *adj.*, rel. to a seigneur and a seigneurie.

seign'ior, *n.*, *i.q.* seigneur.

sei'gniorage, *n.*, the prerogatives of a seigneur.

sei'gniory, *n.*, lordship; sovereign authority.

seine, *n.*, a large fishing-net; *v.t.*, to fish with a seine.

sein'er, *n.*, a fisher with a seine.

sein'ing, *pr.p.*, seine.

seis'in, *n.*, possession; freehold.

seis'mic, *adj.*, pert. to earthquakes.

seis'mograph, *n.*, an instrument for recording the phenomena of earthquakes.

seismom'eter, *n.*, an apparatus for measuring the length, etc., of a seismic wave.

seiz'able, *adj.*, able to be seized.

seize, *v.t.*, to take hold or possession of; to grasp, snatch; to perceive the meaning of.

seized, *p.p.*, seize.

seiz'er, *n.*, one who seizes.

sei'zin, *n.*, *i.q.* seisin.

seiz'ing, *pr.p.*, seize.

sei'zure, *n.*, the act or result of seizing; an attack of apoplexy, etc.

se'lah, *n.*, a supposed Hebrew musical direction.

sel'dom, *adv.*, infrequently; rarely; not often.

select', *adj.*, picked, chosen; exclusive; *v.t.*, to pick out.

select'ed, *p.p.*, select.

select'ing, *pr.p.*, select

selec'tion, *n.*, the act of selecting; anything selected.

select'ive, *adv.*, tending to select.

select'man, *n.*, one of three New England urban officials.

select'ness, *n.*, the quality of being select; exclusiveness.

select'or, *n.*, one who, or that which, selects.

sel'enate, *n.*, a selenic acid salt.

selen'ic, *adj.*, pert. to selenium.

sel'enide, *n.*, a compound of selenium and a radical or element.

selenif'erous, *adj.*, producing selenium.

sel'enite, *n.*, a variety of gypsum; a selenious acid gas.

selenit'ic, *adj.*, rel. to selenite.

sele'nium, *n.*, a nonmetallic element.

selenog'rapher, *n.*, one who studies the moon's surface.

selenograph'ic, *adj.*, pert. to selenography.

selenog'raphy, *n.*, the study or mapping of the moon.

self, *adj.*, identical, same; unmixed; *n.*, personal individuality; a person or thing regarded from its individual point of view.

self-con'fident, *adj.*, relying upon oneself; bumptious.

self-con'scious, *adj.*, thinking too much about other people's opinion of oneself.

self-con'sciousness, *n.*, the quality of being self-conscious.

self-control', *adj.*, command over oneself.

self-defence', *n.*, protection of oneself.

self-deni'al, *n.*, unselfishness; denying oneself.

self-esteem', *n.*, too good an opinion of oneself.

self-ev'ident, *adj.*, obvious; needing no outside proof.

self-help', *n.*, independence.

self-*in'terest*, *n.*, one's own interest.

self-*in'terested*, *adj.*, with an eye to one's own interest.

***self'ish*,** *adj.*, loving self and disregarding others.

***self'ishly*,** *adv.*, in a selfish way.

***self'ishness*,** *n.*, the quality of being selfish.

self-love', *n.*, love of self.

self-made', *adj.*, made by one's own efforts.

self-possessed', *adj.*, with perfect command of oneself.

self-posses'sion, *n.*, command of oneself.

self-reli'ance, *n.*, reliance on one's own strength.

self-reli'ant, *adj.*, relying on one's own strength.

self-rely'ing, *adj.*, *i.q.* self-reliant.

self-right'eous, *adj.*, righteous in one's own eyes; pharisaical.

self-right'eousness, *n.*, the quality of being self-righteous.

self'same, *adj.*, the very same.

self-will', *n.*, obstinacy; wilfulness.

self-willed', *adj.*, obstinate; following one's own will exclusively.

sell, *v.t.*, to barter for a consideration; to betray; to disappoint by not doing what was expected or promised (*slang*); *n.*, the disappointment caused (*slang*).

sell'er, *n.*, one who sells.

sell'ing, *pr.p.*, sell.

sel'vage, sel'vedge, *n.*, the edge of woven fabric; *v.t.*, to finish with a selvage.

sel'vaged, sel'vedged, *p.p.*, selvage; *adj.*, having a selvage.

sel'vagee, *n.*, a strap or ring of rope yarns.

selves, *n.*, pl. of self.

sem'aphore, *n.*, an apparatus for signalling, having movable arms, disks, etc.

semaphor'ic, *adj.*, pert. to a semaphore.

sematol'ogy, *n.*, the study of signs or characters.

sem'blance, *n.*, outward appearance; something imaginary.

semée, *adj.*, covered with small (heraldic) bearings.

semeiog'raphy, *n.*, the science of morbid symptoms.

semeiolog'ical, *adj.*, pert. to semeiology.

semeiol'ogy, *n.*, that department of pathology that relates to symptoms.

semeiot'ic, *adj.*, symptomatic.

semes'ter, *n.*, a six months' academic course.

semes'tral, *adj.*, pert. to a semester.

semi-an'nual, *adj.*, half-yearly.

sem'ibreve, *n.*, a note half the length of a breve.

sem'icircle, *n.*, a half-circle.

semicir'cular, *adj.*, in the form of a half-circle.

semico'lon, *n.*, a punctuation mark (;), ranking in importance between a comma and a full-stop.

semi-detached', *adj.*, joined at one side, free on the other.

semi-diam'eter, *n.*, a half-diameter.

semilu'nar, *adj.*, crescent-shaped.

sem'inal, *adj.*, rel. to seed and reproduction.

sem'inarist, *n.*, a member of a seminary, esp. one bel. to the Jesuits.

sem'inary, *n.*, a place of education.

semina'tion, *n.*, seeding.

seminif'erous, *adj.*, producing seed.

seminif'ic, *adj.*, *i.q.* seminiferous.

sem'iped, *n.*, a half-foot.

sem'iquaver, *n.*, a note of half the value of a quaver.

Se'mite, *n.*, one bel. to a race alleged to be descended from Shem, as the Hebrews.

Semit'ic, *adj.*, pert. to the Semites.

sem'itone, *n.*, a half tone interval (*mus.*).

semivow'el, *n.*, a sound half vowel and half consonant (as *w* and *y*).

semoli'na, *n.*, what remains of wheat when the flour has been bolted.

sempervi'rent, *adj.*, evergreen.

sempiter'nal, *adj.*, everlasting.

sem'pre, *adv.*, always, throughout (*Ital.*).

semp'ster, *n.*, a seamster. (This is the original feminine form. Later, the new feminine, *sempstress*, was made.)

semp'stress, *n.*, fem. of sempster.

se'nary, *adj.*, pert. to six.

sen'ate, *n.*, the supreme council at Rome; the upper legislative chamber in modern States; the governing body of some universities.

sen'ate-house, *n.*, the meeting-place of a senate.

sen'ator, *n.*, a member of a senate.

senato'rial, *adj.*, pert. to a senate and senators.

sen'atorship, *n.*, the office or rank of a senator.

send, *v.t.*, to dispatch, dismiss; order to go; to throw; to grant; cause to be so-and-so; *v.i.*, to dispatch a messenger; *n.*, a forward impulse.

send'er, *n.*, one who sends.

send'ing, *pr.p.*, send.

sen'ega, *n.*, an expectorant drug made from senega or snake-root.

senes'cence, *n.*, the state of growing old.

sen'eschal, *n.*, a steward in a great establishment.

sen'green, *n.*, the houseleek.

se'nile, *adj.*, decaying with age.

senil'ity, *n.*, the state of being senile; old age.

se'nior, *adj.*, older; superior in age or standing; *n.*, one who is older, or superior on account of age or standing.

senior'ity, *n.*, the state of being senior; priority in age or dignity.

sen'na, *n.*, an aperient drug, being the dried leaves of the Cassia.

sen'night, *n.*, a week.

sen'nit, *n.*, braided cord.

senoc'ular, *adj.*, with six eyes.

señor', *n.*, the Spanish equivalent of Sir or Mr.

seño'ra, *n.*, fem. of señor.

señori'ta, *n.*, the Spanish equivalent of Miss.

sen'sate, *adj.*, apprehended by the senses; perceptible to the senses.

sensa'tion, *n.*, perception by the senses; feeling; a condition of excitement or interest.

sensa'tional, *adj.*, rel. to sensation; exciting, thrilling.

sensa'tionalism, *n.*, a pandering to excitement; the theory that ideas are but sensations transformed.

sensa'tionalist, *adj.*, of a sensational character; *n.*, a believer in the theory of sensationalism; a sensational writer.

sensa'tionary, *adj.*, *i.q.* sensational.

sense, *n.*, perception of objects; understanding; meaning.

sense'less, *adj.*, unable to feel; unconscious; silly; contrary to reason.

sense'lessly, *adv.*, in a senseless fashion.

sense'lessness, *n.*, the quality of being senseless.

sensibil'ity, *n.*, the state or quality of being sensible; ability to be sensitive; fine feeling.

sen'sible, *adj.*, apprehended by the senses; of good judgment; reasonable.

sen'sibly, *adv.*, judiciously, reasonably; perceptibly.

sensif'erous, *adj.*, conveying sense impressions.

sensif'ic, *adj.*, causing sensation.

sen'sitive, *adj.*, readily perceptive of objects; easily affected by the acts, words, and attitude of others; responsive to external impressions.

sen'sitively, *adv.*, in a sensitive way.

sen'sitiveness, *n.*, the state or quality of being sensitive.

sen'sitize, *v.t.*, to make sensitive; esp. to cause to be acted upon by the sun's actinic rays.

sen'sitized, *p.p.*, sensitize.

sen'sitizing, *pr.p.*, sensitize.

senso'rial, *adj.*, rel. to the sensorium.

senso'rium, *n.*, the brain.

sen'sory, *adj.*, *i.q.* sensorial.

sen'sual, *adj.*, controlled by the senses and fleshy appetites; licentious; carnal.

sen'sualism, *n.*, sensual conduct.

sen'sualist, *n.*, a sensual person.

sensual'ity, *n.*, *i.q.* sensualism.

sen'sualize, *v.t.*, to make sensual.

sen'sualized, *p.p.*, sensualize.

sen'sualizing, *pr.p.*, sensualize.

sen'sually, *adv.*, in a sensual way.

sen'suous, *adj.*, pert. to the senses; rel. to the objects of sense.

sent, *p.t.* and *p.*, send.

sen'tence, *n.*, judgment; meaning; the judgment of a court; a complete verbal expression of a thought or judgment; *v.t.*, to condemn from the judicial bench.

sen'tenced, *p.p.*, sentence.

sen'tencing. *pr.p.*, sentence.

senten'tial, *adj.*, pert. to a sentence.

senten'tious, *adj.*, composed of sentences; full of maxims; axiomatic.

senten'tiously, *adv.*, in a sententious style.

senten'tiousness, *n.*, the quality of being sententious.

sen'tience, *n.*, *i.q.* sentiency.

sen'tiency, *n.*, the state or quality of being sentient.

sen'tient, *adj.*, capable of feeling and perceiving.

sen'timent, *n.*, a thought influenced by emotion; an opinion; common opinion; a toast.

sentimen'tal, *adj.*, emotional; led by emotion rather than by reason; inclined to the romantic.

sentimen'talism, *n.*, a tendency to the romantic and emotional.

sentimen'talist, *n.*, one who thinks or pretends to think sentimentally.

sentimental'ity, *n.*, *i.q.* sentimentalism.

sentimen'talize, *v.i.*, to act or think in a sentimental way.

sentimen'talized, *p.p.*, sentimentalize.

sentimen'talizing, *pr.p.*, sentimentalize.

sentimen'tally, *n.*, in a sentimental way.

sen'tinel, *n.*, one on guard, esp. on military guard; *v.t.*, to guard; to appoint a sentinel for.

sen'try, *n.*, a sentinel's post and duty; a sentinel.

sen'try-box, *n.*, a sentry's shelter.

sep'al, *n.*, a division of a calyx (*bot.*).

sep'aloid, *adj.*, like a sepal.

separabil'ity, *n.*, the quality or state of being separable.

sep'arable, *adj.*, able to be parted or separated.

sep'arate, *adj.*, parted, divided, distinct.

sep'arate, *v.t.*, to divide; to part; to set apart; *v.i.*, to disperse; to come apart.

sep'arated, *p.p.*, separate.

sep'arately, *adv.*, apart; individually; in a separate way.

sep'arateness, *n.*, the state or quality of being separate.

sep'arating, *pr.p.*, separate.

separa'tion, *n.*, the act of separating; state of being separate.

sep'aratism, *n.*, the principles of the separatists.

sep'aratist, *n.*, one who advocates separation; specifically, one who has parted from the Church.

sep'arative, *adj.*, disjunctive.

sep'arator, *n.*, one who, that which, separates.

sep'aratory, *adj.*, tending to separate; *n.*, an instrument used in surgery; an apparatus for the chemical separation of liquors.

se'pia, *n.*, a brown pigment; a cuttle-fish; *adj.*, of the colour of sepia; drawn in sepia.

se'poy, *n.*, an Indian native soldier.

sept, *n.*, a tribe, clan; *adj.*, *i.q.* septangular.

septan'gular, *adj.*, having seven angles.

septa'ria, *n. pl.*, geological nodules.
sep'tate, *adj.*, divided by septa.
Septem'ber, *n.*, the ninth month.
Septem'brist, *n.*, a French Revolutionist who took part in the massacre of Sept. 3, 1792.
septem'vir, *n.*, one of a commission of seven in ancient Rome. (In pl., *septemviri*.)
sep'tenary, *adj.*, rel. to, or lasting for, seven years.
septen'nial, *adj.*, recurring every seven years; lasting seven years.
septen'trional, *adj.*, rel. to the north.
septet', septette', *n.*, a musical piece for seven instruments.
sept'foil, *n.*, the tormentil (*bot.*); an architectural ornament resembling seven leaves.
sep'tic, *adj.*, causing putrefaction; *n.*, that which causes putrefaction.
septicae'mia, *n.*, putrefaction in the blood; blood-poisoning.
sep'tical, *adj.*, putrefying.
sep'ticidal, *adj.*, splitting through septa.
septic'ity, *n.*, septic condition.
septifa'rious, *adj.*, in seven different ways.
septif'erous, *adj.*, conveying septic poison.
septilat'eral, *adj.*, seven-sided.
septin'sular, *adj.*, having seven islands.
septuagena'rian, *adj.*, seventy years old; *n.*, a person seventy years of age.
septuage'nary, *adj.*, composed of seventy; *n.*, the number 70.
Septuages'ima, *n.*, the name of the third Sunday (and its week) before Lent. (Strictly, the name means seventieth, but it is due to a feeling in favour of round numbers. Quadragesima (40th) is the first Sunday in Lent. Then, working backward, we have Quinquagesima, Sexagesima, Septuagesima.)
Sep'tuagint, *n.*, the great Greek version of the Old Testament Scriptures. The name means 70, the traditional number of the translators employed.
sep'tum, *n.*, a barrier; partition; the membranous partition between organs or cavities. (In pl., *septa*.)
sep'tuple, *adj.*, sevenfold.
sepul'chral, *adj.*, rel. to sepulchres or tombs; hollow-sounding.
sep'ulchre, *n.*, a tomb, grave; *v.t.*, to bury.
sep'ulture, *n.*, burial.
sequa'cious, *adj.*, following.
sequac'ity, *n.*, the quality of being sequacious.
se'quel, *n.*, something that follows as a consequence; a continuation to a story or incident.
seque'la, *n.*, a morbid state consequent on another.
se'quence, *n.*, successive order; a series; cards of successive values in the same suit; a musical phrase repeated at another pitch; a hymn following the gradual and immediately preceding the Gospel (*e.g.*, the *Dies Irae*) on certain occasions.
se'quent, *adj.*, following in sequence; *n.*, a sequence.
sequen'tial, *adj.*, in succession.
sequen'tially, *adv.*, in succession.
seques'ter, *v.t.*, to take away temporarily; to seclude; *v.i.*, to forgo a wife's claim on her husband's estate.
seques'tered, *p.p.*, sequester; *adj.*, remote, secluded.
seques'tering, *pr.p.*, sequester.
seques'trate, *v.t.*, to withhold for a time the income of a benefice from the incumbent; to take under State control a debtor's property for the benefit of the creditors.
seques'trated, *p.p.*, sequestrate.
seques'trating, *pr.p.*, sequestrate.
sequestra'tion, *n.*, the act or effect of sequestrating.
se'questrator, *n.*, one who sequesters property.
se'quin, *n.*, an old Venetian gold coin.
sera'glio, *n.*, a harem.
sera'i, *n.*, an Eastern inn.
seralbu'men, *n.*, albumen in the blood.
ser'aph, *n.*, an angelic being of highest rank.
seraph'ic, *adj.*, pert. to, or resembling, a seraph.
seraph'ically, *adv.*, like a seraph.
ser'aphim, *n. pl.*, seraphs.
ser'aphine, *n.*, a small instrument of the harmonium type.
seras'kier, *n.*, a high military authority in the Turkish army.
Ser'bian, *adj.*, *i.q.* Servian.
Serbo'nian, *adj.*, pert. to Serbonis, an Egyptian bog that swallowed everything up.
sere, *adj.* and *v.t.*, *i.q.* sear.
serenade', *n.*, outdoor evening music; a song sung by a lover at the window of his inamorata; *v.t.*, to honour with a serenade.
serena'ded, *p.p.*, serenade.
serena'der, *n.*, one who serenades.

serena'ding, *pr.p.*, serenade.

serena'ta, *n.*, a cantata to be performed in the open air; a form of symphony.

serendip'ity, *n.*, the character of a bibliophile and collector of curios.

serene', *adj.*, calm, unruffled.

serene'ly, *adv.*, calmly

serene'ness, *n.*, the quality or state of being serene.

seren'ity, *n.*, *i.q.* sereneness.

serf, *n.*, a slave attached to the land; a villein.

serf'dom, *n.*, the state of being a serf.

serge, *n.*, a woollen fabric.

ser'geancy, *n.*, a sergeant's office. Also *sergeantcy*.

ser'geant, *n.*, a non-commissioned military officer.

ser'geant-ma'jor, *n.*, a warrant officer attending on the adjutant.

ser'geantship, *n.*, *i.q.* sergeancy.

se'rial, *adj.*, bel. to a series; *n.*, a story appearing in parts.

se'rially, *adv.*, in part publication.

se'riate, *v.t.*, to arrange in order.

se'riate, *adj.*, arranged in order.

seria'tim, *adv.*, in order (a spurious Latin word).

seri'ceous, *adj.*, silky.

se'ries, *n.*, connected or related order; succession.

ser'in, *n.*, a finch.

serio-com'ic, *adj.*, combining grave and comic.

se'rious, *adj.*, grave, earnest.

se'riously, *adv.*, in a serious way.

se'riousness, *n.*, the quality of being serious.

ser'jeant, *n.*, a member of a now extinct order of serjeants-at-law, from whom the judges were selected. They were chiefly distinguished by the coif, a relic of which is the black patch in a judge's wig.

ser'jeanty, *n.*, a mode of legal tenure so named.

ser'mon, *n.*, a homily or discourse, usually on a text.

ser'monize, *v.i.*, to preach; *v.t.*, to address.

ser'monized, *p.p.*, sermonize.

ser'monizer, *n.*, one who sermonizes.

ser'monizing, *pr.p.*, sermonize.

seron', *n.*, a crate for dried fruits. Also *seroon*.

seros'ity, *n.*, the state or quality of being serous; *n.*, the thin exudation from serum.

ser'otine, *n.*, a reddish-coloured bat.

se'rous, *adj.*, pert. to serum.

ser'pent, *n.*, a reptile of the snake order; a musical instrument of brass; a firework; anyone of snake-like qualities.

serpen'tiform, *adj.*, shaped like a snake.

ser'pentine, *adj.*, rel. to, resembling, a snake in form or movement; *n.*, a variety of rock formation.

ser'pentry, *n.*, a place of serpents.

serpi'ginous, *adj.*, suffering from herpes; creeping.

serpi'go, *n.*, herpes.

ser'rate, *adj.*, like a saw; with toothed edge.

ser'rated, *adj.*, *i.q.* serrate.

ser'rature, *n.*, saw-like edging; a serrated structure.

ser'ried, *adj.*, in close order; packed.

ser'rulate, *adj.*, finely notched.

serrula'tion, *n.*, an arrangement of fine notches.

se'rum, *n.*, the fluid secretion of serous membranes.

serv'ant, *n.*, one who serves in any capacity.

serve, *v.t.*, to be the servant of; to worship; to wait upon; to deliver (food) to; to conduce to; *v.i.*, to be a servant; to fit; to hold an office.

served, *p.p.*, serve.

serv'er, *n.*, one who serves, esp. who assists the priest at the altar.

Ser'vian, *adj.*, rel. to Servia (or Serbia); *n.*, a native of S.

serv'ice, *n.*, the status or occupation of a servant; a kind office; naval and military employ; an outfit of plate, china or crockery; regular traffic between place and place; waiting at table; waiters collectively; a religious office; a musical setting (not in chant form) of the Canticles.

serv'iceable, *adj.*, handy, convenient.

serv'iceableness, *n.*, the quality of being serviceable.

serv'iceably, *adv.*, in a serviceable manner.

serviette', *n.*, a table-napkin.

serv'ile, *adj.*, slavish; mean; obsequious.

serv'ilely, *adv.*, in a servile way.

servil'ity, *n.*, the quality of being servile.

serv'ing, *pr.p.*, serve.

serv'ing-man, *n.*, a man-servant.

serv'itor, *n.*, a servant, retainer; formerly the name for certain undergraduates at Oxford who performed some menial offices in return for their keep. In old letters, often the writer courteously so subscribes himself.

serv'itorship, *n.*, the office of a servitor.
serv'itude, *n.*, the state of slavery.
ses'ame, *n.*, an oil-yielding plant.
ses'amoid, *adj.*, like sesame.
ses'amum, *n.*, *i.q.* sesame.
sesquial'tera, *n.*, an organ-stop of several ranks.
sesquial'teral, *adj.*, being one-half more.
sesquidu'plicate, *adj.*, in the ratio of 2½ to 1.
sesquip'edal, *adj.*, *i.q.* sesquipedalian.
sesquipeda'lian, *adj.*, a foot and a half long; expressed in long words.
ses'quitone, *n.*, the interval of a minor third.
sess, *n.*, *i.q.* cess.
ses'sile, *adj.*, not having a foot-stalk.
ses'sion, *n.*, the act of sitting; a meeting; a period of being assembled (as a Session of Parliament). In pl., the sittings of magistrates.
ses'sional, *adj.*, rel. to a session.
ses'terce, *n.*, an old Roman coin (the *sestertius*) = 2d.
sestet', sestette', *n.*, a composition for six voices or instruments; the last six lines of the second section of a sonnet.
set, *v.t.*, to fix, place, plant; to spread (sails); to give a start to; to adjust; to appoint; to arrange printer's type; *v.i.*, to decline (said of the heavenly bodies); to become fixed or congealed; to take a certain direction; *adj.*, fixed regular; resolute; prescribed; *n.*, the act of setting; tendency or direction; the sinking of a heavenly body; a clique; a group; the number of games in lawn tennis that must be scored by the winner or winners.
se'ta, *n.*, a bristle (*Lat.*).
seta'ceous, *adj.*, bristly.
setif'erous, *adj.*, having bristles.
se'tiform, *adj.*, like a bristle.
set'-off, *n.*, a counterbalance; a *quid pro quo*.
se'ton, *n.*, a surgical contrivance for keeping a sore open.
se'tous, *adj.*, bristly. Also *setose*.
sett, *n.*, mines leased in a number; wood or metal laid on the top of a pile too short for the hammer to reach it otherwise.
settee', *n.*, a lounge-seat; a Mediterranean boat.
set'ter, *n.*, one who, or that which, sets; a breed of sporting dog.
set'ting, *pr.p.*, set; *n.*, the act of setting; environment; the mount of a jewel.
set'tle, *v.t.*, to make to remain at rest; to establish; to make to sink; to adjudicate; to compose; to discharge (a debt); to colonize; *v.i.*, to steady down and remain at rest; to alight; to sink to the bottom; to pay an account; to colonize; to set up a home with a wife; *n.*, a high-backed bench with arms.
set'tled, *p.p.*, settle.
set'tlement, *n.*, the act or effect of settling; a composition or agreement; a colony; money legally assigned to a wife.
set'tler, *n.*, a colonist; a decisive act or occurrence.
set'tling, *pr.p.*, settle.
set'tlor, *n.*, one who settles an estate.
set'-to, *n.*, a contest; a bout of fencing, boxing, etc.
set'wall, *n.*, the valerian.
sev'en, *n.*, a cardinal number = 6 + 1; the symbol 7; *adj.*, containing seven persons or things.
sev'enfold, *adj.*, seven times over.
sev'ennight, *n.*, *i.q.* sennight.
seventeen, *n.*, a cardinal number = 7 + 10; the symbol 17; *adj.*, containing seven + ten.
seventeenth, *n.*, the ordinal of seventeen; *adj.*, the next after the sixteenth.
sev'enth, *adj.*, the ordinal of seven; the next after the sixth.
sev'enthly, *adv.*, in the seventh place.
sev'entieth, *adj.*, the ordinal of seventy; *n.*, next after the sixty-ninth.
sev'enty, *n.*, the cardinal number next after 69 = 7 × 10; in pl., one of the years in the seventh decade; *adj.*, containing seven × ten persons or things.
Seventy, The, *n. pl.*, the traditional 70 translators of the Septuagint, which is often referred to under the symbol LXX.
sev'er, *v.t.*, to cut; part; divide; *v.i.*, to come apart.
sev'eral, *adj.*, separate, distinct; composed of more than two but only a few.
sev'erally, *adv.*, separately.
sev'eralty, *n.*, the state of being several.
sev'erance, *n.*, the act of severing; state of being severed.
severe', *adj.*, harsh; stern; inclement; hard to bear; extremely critical.
sev'ered, *p.p.*, sever.
severe'ly, *adv.*, in a severe way.
seve'rer, *adj.*, *comp.* of severe.

seve'rest, *adj., super.* of severe.
sev'ering, *pr.p.,* sever.
sever'ity, *n.,* harshness, strictness; inclemency; rigour.
sew, *v.t.,* to stitch together with a needle and thread; *v.i.,* to use a needle and thread.
sew'age, *n.,* matter discharged into a sewer.
sewed, *p.t.,* sew.
sew'er, *n.,* one who sews.
sew'er, *n.,* a drain; an attendant at a banquet who tasted dishes, placed guests, etc.
sew'erage, *n.,* the system of sewers; drainage.
sew'ing, *pr.p.,* sew; *n.,* the act of sewing; work done with a thread and needle.
sew'ing-machine, *n.,* a machine that sews.
sewn, *p.p.,* sew.
sex, *n.,* the difference between male and female.
sexagena'rian, *adj.,* sixty years old; *n.,* a person of that age.
sexag'enary, *adj.,* rel. to the number sixty.
Sexages'ima, *n.,* the second Sunday before Lent. (See note on Septuagesima.)
sexan'gular, *adj.,* having six angles.
sexen'nial, *adj.,* occurring every six years; lasting six years.
sex'less, *adj.,* of no sex.
Sext, *n.,* the Breviary office for mid-day (the sixth hour).
sex'tain, *n.,* a stanza containing six lines.
sex'tant, *n.,* the one-sixth of a circle; a mathematical instrument for finding angular distances between objects. It is mostly used by mariners.
sextet', *n., i.q.* sestet.
sex'tile, *adj.,* rel. to the position of planets at a distance of 60 degrees from each other.
sextil'lion, *n.,* a million raised to the sixth power.
sex'ton, *n.,* originally a sacristan; later a grave-digger and lower official of a church.
sex'toness, *n.,* fem. of sexton, whose duties are to look after the church.
sex'tuple, *adj.,* six times multiplied.
sex'ual, *adj.,* pert. to sex and the relations between the sexes.
sex'ualist, *n.,* one who is interested in sex problems.
sexual'ity, *n.,* the quality or state of being sexual.
sex'ually, *adv.,* in relation to the sexes.
sforza'to, *adv.,* forcibly, emphatically (*mus.*).
sfuma'to, *adj.,* misty in appearance; blurred in outline (*Ital.*).
sgraffi'to, *adj.,* painted in lines cut through a white overlaid surface down to a dark stucco beneath (*Ital.*).
shab, *n., i.q.* scab.
shab'bier, *adj., comp.* of shabby.
shab'biest, *adj., super.* of shabby.
shab'bily, *adv.,* in a mean, shabby way.
shab'biness, *n.,* the quality or state of being shabby.
shab'by, *adj.,* with a worn-out appearance; mean.
shab'rack, *n.,* a cavalry officer's horse-covering.
shack, *n.,* right of pasturage in the winter; a tramp; a log cabin.
shack'le, *n.,* a fetter; the bar of a padlock; *v.t.,* to fetter; to impede.
shack'led, *p.p.,* shackle.
shack'les, *n.,* pl. of shackle.
shack'ling, *pr.p.,* shackle.
shad, *n.,* a small fish so named.
shad'dock, *n.,* an orange-like fruit.
shade, *n.,* the darkened state resulting from the sun's rays being screened off; a gradation of colour; a ghost; *v.t.,* to screen from heat or light; to darken parts of a map, drawing, etc.
sha'ded, *p.p.,* shade.
shades, *n. pl.,* wine vaults.
sha'dier, *adj., comp.* of shady.
sha'diest, *adj., super.* of shady.
sha'dily, *adv.,* in a shady way.
sha'diness, *n.,* the quality of being shady.
sha'ding, *pr.p.,* shade; *n.,* the act of shading; the act of depicting the effect of light and shade.
shad'ow, *n.,* shade that more or less resembles the form of the object that casts it; a dark part of a painting, drawing, etc.; safety; a close attendant; a wasted body; *v.t.,* to darken; to pursue closely.
shad'owed, *p.p.,* shadow.
shad'owing, *pr.p.,* shadow.
shad'owy, *adj.,* giving shade; dim; unreal.
sha'dy, *adj.,* spreading a shade; covering; of questionable character (*colloq.*).
shaft, *n.,* an arrow; the straight length of a spear; a mine entrance; a straight chimney; a handle; the middle members of a column.
shaft'ed, *adj.,* having a shaft.
shaft'ing, *n.,* power-transmitting shafts.
shag, *n.,* a tobacco.
shag'giness, *n.,* the quality of being shaggy.
shag'gy, *adj.,* with rough or long hair.

shagreen', *n.*, leather made of, or resembling, shark's skin; *adj.*, made of shagreen.

shah, *n.*, the sovereign of Persia.

shake, *v.t.*, to make to shiver; to move with short, quick jerks; to weaken; to cause to vibrate; *v.i.*, to shiver; to tremble; to put a quiver into a musical note with voice or instrument.

sha'ken, *adj.*, weakened; broken.

sha'ker, *n.*, one who shakes; a member of the fanatical sect of Shakers.

Sha'kerism, *n.*, the system of the Shaker sect.

sha'kier, *adj.*, *comp.* of shaky.

sha'kiest, *adj.*, *super.* of shaky.

sha'kiness, *n.*, the quality or state of being shaky.

sha'king, *pr.p.*, shake; *n.*, the act of shaking.

shak'o, *n.*, a soldier's cap.

Shakspe'rian, *adj.*, rel. to Shakspere. Also *Shakspearian, Shakespearean.*

sha'ky, *adj.*, in a shaking condition; unsafe; unsound.

shale, *n.*, loose flaked stone; a husk.

shall, *v. aux.*, *future tense*, to be about to do or be = to intend.

shalloon', *n.*, a worsted fabric.

shal'lop, *n.*, a small boat.

shallot', **shalot'**, *n.*, *i.q.* eschalot.

shal'low, *adj.*, not deep; not intellectually profound; without deep feeling; insincere; *n.*, a part of a river, etc., where the water is not deep; a shoal; *v.i.*, to lessen in depth.

shal'lower, *adj.*, *comp.* of shallow.

shal'lowest, *adj.*, *super.* of shallow.

shal'lowness, *n.*, want of depth in all senses.

shalt, *v. aux.*, *pr.t.*, 2nd per. sing.; *see* shall.

sha'ly, *adj.*, abounding in, or resembling, shale.

sham, *adj.*, false; imitation; *n.*, a person or thing that is false or counterfeit; *v.i.*, to pretend.

sha'man, *n.*, a priestly practitioner of Shamanism.

Sha'manism, *n.*, a system of doctrines and functions based on a belief in good and evil spiritual agencies and in magic.

sham'ble, *v.i.*, to shuffle along with a clumsy gait.

sham'bled, *p.p.*, shamble.

sham'bles, *n. pl.*, a place where meat is sold or cattle are slaughtered.

sham'bling, *pr.p.*, shamble; *adj.*, with a clumsy gait.

shame, *v.t.*, to disgrace; to confound; to put to the blush; *n.*, the sense of having done something wrong or improper; disgrace; infamy.

shamed, *p.p.*, shame.

shame'faced, *adj.*, modest, bashful.

shame'ful, *adj.*, disgraceful, shocking.

shame'fully, *adv.*, in a shameful way.

shame'less, *adj.*, without shame; immodest.

shame'lessness, *n.*, the quality of being shameless.

sha'ming, *pr. p.*, shame.

shammed, *p.p.*, sham.

sham'mer, *n.*, one who shams.

sham'ming, *pr.p.*, sham; *n.*, pretending.

sham'my, *n.*, chamois leather.

shampoo', *n.*, a wash for the hair; friction and pressure of the limbs and joints; *v.t.*, to subject to the process of shampooing.

shampooed', *p.p.*, shampoo.

shampoo'er, *n.*, one who shampoos.

shampoo'ing, *pr.p.*, shampoo.

sham'rock, *n.*, a trefoil plant, beloved by the Irish, who make it their national emblem.

shan'dygaff, *n.*, a beverage of ale and ginger beer combined.

shank, *n.*, the part of the leg between the knee and the ankle; the shaft of a column; the part of a tool between the head and the handle; the straight part of a fish hook; *v.i.*, to drop off in decay.

shanked, *adj.*, having a shank; *p.p.*, shank.

shank'er, *n.*, one who makes shanks.

shank'ing, *pr.p.*, shank

shan't, *v. aux.*, an abbreviation for *shall not.*

shan'ty, *n.*, a rough sort of dwelling.

shape, *n.*, form, outline, figure; *v.t.*, to form, to fashion; *v.i.*, to conform to a type or pattern.

shaped, *p.p.*, shape.

shape'less, *adj.*, without any particular shape.

shape'liness, *n.*, the quality of being shapely.

shape'ly, *adj.*, well formed.

sha'ping, *pr.p.*, shape.

shard, *n.*, a piece of broken earthenware; a potsherd.

share, *n.*, a portion, part; an investment with a company; a ploughshare; *v.t.*, to divide into portions; to enjoy in partnership; *v.i.*, to have a share.

shared, *p.p.*, share.

share'holder, *n.*, one who holds a share in a company's business.

sha'rer, *n.*, one who shares.

sha'ring, *pr.p.*, share.

shark, *n.*, a fierce fish; a cunning cheat; *v.t.* and *i.*, to swallow greedily.

sharked, *p.p.*, shark.

shark'er, *n.*, one who sharks.

shark'ing, *pr.p.*, shark

sharp, *adj.*, pointed, penetrating, piercingly shrill; subtle; higher in musical pitch; *n.*, a musical mark (♯) indicating that the note against which it stands must be raised by a semitone; *v.t.*, *i.q.* sharpen; *v.i.*, to be a sharper.

sharped, *p.p.*, sharp.

sharp'-edged, *adj.*, having a sharp, cutting edge.

sharp'en, *v.t.*, to make sharp; to raise by a semitone; *v.i.*, to become sharp.

sharp'ened, *p.p.*, sharpen.

sharp'ening, *pr.p.*, sharpen.

sharp'er, *n.*, a swindler; *adj.*, *comp.* of sharp.

sharp'est, *adj.*, *super.* of sharp.

sharp'ing, *pr.p.*, sharp.

sharp'ly, *adv.*, in a sharp way.

sharp'ness, *n.*, the quality of being sharp.

sharp'-set, *adj.*, keen; eager; ravenous.

sharp'shooter, *n.*, a sniper.

sharp-sight'ed, *adj.*, with quick, keen sight.

sharp-wit'ted, *adj.*, of keen wit.

shas'ter, *n.*, a commentary on the Vedas. Also *Shastra*.

shat'ter, *v.t.*, to shake or break to pieces.

shat'tered, *p.p.*, shatter.

shat'tering, *pr.p.*, shatter.

shat'ters, *n. pl.* fragments.

shat'tery, *adj.*, brittle.

shave, *v.t.*, to remove hairs with a razor; to pare; to go very close to; *v.i.*, to use a razor; *n.*, removal of a beard, etc.; a tool for shaving wood; a narrow escape.

shaved, *p.p.*, shave.

shave'ling, *n.*, a tonsured cleric; a monk.

sha'ven, *adj.*, shaved.

sha'ver, *n.*, one who, or that which, shaves; a small boy (*colloq.*).

sha'ving, *pr.p.*, shave; *n.*, the act of shaving; thin slice of iron or metal shaved off.

sha'ving-brush, *n.*, a lather-brush used in shaving.

shawl, *n.*, a loose wrap for the shoulders, etc.; *v.t.*, to wrap in a shawl.

shawm, *n.*, a Biblical wind-instrument.

she, *n.*, the fem. of the personal pronoun, he.

sheaf, *n.*, a bundle of gathered wheat, etc.; a quiverful of arrows; *v.i.*, to make up into sheaves.

shear, *v.t.*, to clip the wool from; to reap.

sheared, *p.t.* and *p.*, shear.

shear'er, *n.*, one who, or that which, shears.

shear'ing, *pr.p.*, shear; *n.*, the act or the time of shearing.

shear'man, *n.*, a man who shears.

shears, *n. pl.*, a double instrument used for cutting or shearing; a mechanical weight-raising apparatus.

shear'-steel, *n.*, drawn steel.

shear'water, *n.*, a kind of puffin.

sheat'-fish, *n.*, a catfish.

sheath, *n.*, a scabbard; an outside casing; enveloping membrane, skin, etc.

sheathe, *v.t.*, to enclose in a scabbard or a casing.

sheathed, *p.p.*, sheathe

sheath'er, *n.*, one who sheathes.

sheath'ing, *pr.p.*, sheathe.

sheath'y, *adj.*, like a sheathe.

sheave, *n.*, a pulley wheel, grooved; *v.t.*, to make up into sheaves.

shebeen', *n.*, a drinking den.

Shechi'nah, *n.*, *i.q.* Shekinah.

shed, *v.t.*, to drop off; to let fall; to spread abroad; *n.*, a sloping surface (as a watershed); a one-storeyed building to shelter cattle, goods, etc.

shed'der, *n.*, one who sheds.

shed'ding, *pr.p.*, shed.

sheen, *n.*, brightness, radiance.

sheen'y, *adj.*, radiant, bright.

sheep, *n.*, an ovine ruminant.

sheep'-cot, *n.*, a pen for sheep.

sheep'-dog, *n.*, a shepherd's dog.

sheep'fold, *n.*, an enclosure for sheep.

sheep'-hook, *n.*, a shepherd's crook.

sheep'ish, *adj.*, like a sheep; bashful and silly-looking.

sheep'ishly, *adv.*, in a sheepish way.

sheep'ishness, *n.*, the quality of being sheepish.

sheep'-pen, *n.*, a pen to hold sheep.

sheep'-run, *n.*, a pasturage ground.

sheep's'-eye, *n.*, an amorous look.

sheep'skin, *n.*, the skin of a sheep; parchment.

sheep'-stealer, *n.*, one who steals sheep.

sheep'-stealing, *n.*, the practice of stealing sheep.

sheer, *adj.*, downright; mere; precipitous; *adv.*, precipitously; *n.*, the slope upwards of a ship's lines towards bow or stern; a swerving course; *v.i.*, to turn from a course. In pl., a hoisting apparatus.

sheered, *p.p.*, sheer.

sheer'-hulk, *n.*, a dismasted ship used for hoisting purposes.

sheer'ing, *pr.p.*, sheer.

sheers, *n. pl.*, *see* sheer

sheer'water, *n.*, *i.q.* shearwater.

sheet, *n.*, a thin expanse of anything, as linen, paper, etc., esp. a rectangular piece of linen cloth used as one of the bed-clothes; a stretch of water; a rope attached to the lower corner of a sail; *v.t.*, to cover with a sheet.

sheet'-anchor, *n.*, an emergency anchor.

sheet'ing, *pr.p.*, sheet; *n.*, material of which bed-sheets are made.

sheets, *n.*, pl. of sheet.

sheik, sheikh, *n.*, an Arab or Mohammedan chief.

shek'el, *n.*, an ancient Hebrew coin or weight.

Shek'i'nah, *n.*, the Divine glory over the Mercy-seat.

shel'drake, *n.*, a variety of wild duck.

shel'duck, *n.*, the female sheldrake.

shelf, *n.*, a slab or board let into a wall; a book-case or a cupboard to stand things upon.

shelf'y, *adj.*, abounding in, resembling, shelves.

shell, *n.*, the outer case or covering of nuts, fruits, seeds, eggs, molluscs, etc.; the walls of a ruined or partly finished building; an inner coffin; the case of an explosive; a projectile; *v.t.*, to take out of its shell; to fire at with shells; *v.i.*, to throw off scales.

shellac', shell'-lac, *n.*, thin flakes of lac used for varnish.

shelled, *p.p.*, shell.

shell'-fish, *n.*, a crustacean or mollusc.

shell'ing, *pr.p.*, shell.

shell'work, *n.*, ornamentation with shells.

shell'y, *adj.*, resembling, abounding in, shells.

shel'ter, *n.*, protection against danger, wind, rain, etc., a place of refuge; *v.t.*, to protect; *v.i.*, to seek refuge.

shel'tered, *p.p.*, shelter.

shel'tering, *pr.p.*, shelter.

shel'terless, *adj.*, without shelter.

shel'tie, shel'ty, *n.*, a Shetland pony.

shel'ty, *n.*, a rough cabin.

shelve, *v.t.*, to put aside or on a shelf; *v.i.*, to slope gradually.

shelved, *p.p.*, shelve.

shelves, *n.*, pl. of shelf.

shelv'ing, *pr.p.*, shelve; *adj.*, gently sloping.

shelv'y, *adj.*, sloping.

Shem'ite, *adj.*, *i.q.* Semite.

Shemit'ic, *adj.*, *i.q.* Semitic.

She'ol, *n.*, the place of the dead; the Hebrew Hades.

shep'herd, *v.t.*, to care for as a shepherd; to watch over; *n.*, one who tends sheep.

shep'herdess, *n.*, fem. of shepherd.

shep'py, *n.*, a pen for sheep.

sher'bet, *n.*, an Oriental drink, composed of fruit juice with flavouring, and cooled with snow. The English imitation is effervescing.

sherd, *n.*, a broken piece of pottery, *i.q.* shard.

shereef',-rif', *n.*, one descended from Mohammed through Fatima, and distinguished by a green turban or veil; the chief magistrate of Mecca.

sher'iff, *n.*, a shire-reeve; the chief administrative officer of a shire or county. His duties are partly judicial, partly concerned with the issue of writs, presiding at elections, etc.

sher'ry, *n.*, a white wine from Xeres, in Southern Spain.

shew, *v.t.*, *i.q.* show.

Shi'ah, *n.*, one of the two great Mohammedan sects, Sunni and Shiah. A Shiite professes to be a follower of Ali as the first legitimate Imam.

shib'boleth, *n.*, a test-word; a party phrase. (The word is first found in the Book of Judges, xii. 6.)

shield, *n.*, a body protection, worn on the left arm; any protective person or thing, such as a screen in machinery or gunnery; an escutcheon; *v.t.*, to protect, defend, screen.

shield'ed, *p.p.*, shield.

shield'ing, *pr.p.*, shield.

shield'less, *adj.*, without a shield.

shiel'ing, *n.*, a shelter, a hut (*Scots.*).

shift, *v.t.*, to move from one place to another; to substitute one for another; *v.i.*, to change one's position; to equivocate; to do as well as one can for oneself; *n.*, a change; a substitution; a relay; a dodge, device; a chemise.

shift'ed, *p.p.*, shift.

shift'er, *n.*, one who shifts, esp. who shifts scenes in a theatre.

shift'ier, *adj.*, *comp.* of shifty.

shift'iest, *adj.*, *super.* of shifty.

shift'ing, *pr.p.*, shift.

shift'less, *adj.*, helpless; without resource; incapable.

shift'y, *adj.*, prevaricating; crafty; evasive.

Shi'ite, *n.*, a member of the Shiah sect.

shille'la(g)h, shilla'lah *n.*, an Irish blackthorn cudgel.

shil'ling, *n.*, an English silver coin worth twelve pence; the one-twentieth of a sovereign.

shil'ly-shally, *v.i.*, to waste time in making up one's mind; to vacillate; *n.*, indecision, vacillation.

Shi'loh, *n.*, a Hebrew word meaning Rest.

shi'ly, *adv.*, *i.q.*, shyly.

shim'mer, *v.i.*, to give a faint quivering light; to gleam tremulously; *n.*, a tremulous gleam; a faint quiveringlight.

shim'mered, *p.p.*, shimmer.

shim'mering, *pr.p.*, shimmer.

shin, *n.*, the front part of the leg from the knee downward; the shank; *v.t.*, to kick or hit on the shin; *v.i.*, to climb.

shin'dy, *n.*, a row, brawl (*slang*).

shine, *v.t.*, to make to shine; to polish (*colloq.*); *v.i.*, to give light; to be bright; to be brilliant (in any sense); *n.*, light, brightness, polish; *i.q.* shindy.

shined, *p.p.*, shine, in sense of polishing.

shi'ner, *n.*, one who or that which, shines; esp. a gold coin (*colloq.*).

shin'gle, *n.*, rounded beach pebbles; a wooden roof-tile; *v.t.*, to roof with shingles.

shin'gled, *p.p.*, shingle; *adj.*, covered with shingles.

shin'gles, *n.*, herpes; a nervous cutaneous affection, marked by an eruption partly encircling the body.

shin'gling, *n.*, a process in puddling, which consists in pressing or hammering out iron impurities.

shin'gly, *adj.*, composed of shingles; covered with shingles; like shingles.

shi'nier, *adj.*, *comp.* of shiny.

shi'niest, *adj.*, *super.* of shiny.

shi'ning, *pr.p.*, shine; *adj.*, radiant, eminent.

Shinto, *n.*, the earliest religion of Japan

shi'ny, *adj.*, bright, polished.

ship, *n.*, a sea-vessel; anything resembling a ship, esp. the incense-boat; *v.t.*, to place on board for transport; to take (a crew) on board; to draw (oars) in from the water; *v.i.*, to go aboard; to join a ship as a common sailor.

ship'board, *n.*, a ship's deck or side; the ship itself.

ship'-builder, *n.*, a builder of ships.

ship'-building, *n.*, the shipbuilder's craft; naval construction.

ship'-carpenter, *n.*, a carpenter on board ship or employed in building ships.

ship'-chandler, *n.*, a dealer in ship-requirements, as canvas, cordage, etc.

ship'master, *n.*, the commander of a merchant-vessel.

ship'mate, *n.*, a member of one's own crew.

ship'ment, *n.*, the act of shipping; anything shipped.

ship'-money, *n.*, a tax imposed on coast towns and villages, compelling them to provide the King with ships.

ship'-owner, *n.*, one who owns ships.

shipped, *p.p.*, ship.

ship'per, *n.*, one who ships; a commodity that can safely be sent by sea.

ship'ping, *pr.p.*, ship; *n.*, ships collectively

ship'-shape, *adj.*, neat and tidy as is customary in ships; *adv.*, in perfect order.

ship'wreck, *n.*, the wrecking of a ship; complete ruin; *v.t.*, to destroy by wrecking; to ruin.

ship'wrecked, *p.p.*, shipwreck.

ship'wright, *n.*, a builder of ships.

ship'yard, *n.*, a place where ships are built or repaired.

shire, *adj.*, a political division of Great Britain, corresponding to a county.

shire'-town, *n.*, the chief town of a shire or county.

shirk, *v.t.*, to evade; try to wriggle out of; *v.i.*, to be a shirker; *n.*, *i.q.* shirker.

shirked, *p.p.*, shirk.

shirk'er, *n.*, one who evades his duty.

shirk'ing, *pr.p.*, shirk.

shirt, *n.*, a body garment, usually of underwear for men and of outer wear for women.

shirt'ed, *adj.*, wearing, or covered with, a shirt.

shirt'ing, *n.*, material for shirts.

shirt'less, *adj.* without a shirt.

shit'tah, *n.*, a kind of acacia.

shit'tim-wood, *n.*, the timber of the shittah.

shive, *n.*, a shiver or thin fragment.

shiv'er, *v.t.*, to break or smash to shivers; *v.i.*, to shudder or tremble with cold; *n.*, a trembling with cold.

shiv'ered, *p.p.*, shiver.

shiv'ering, *pr.p.*, shiver; *n.*, an attack of shivers.

shiv'ery, *adj.*, like a shiver; feeling cold and inclined to shiver.

shoad, *n.*, a fragment of ore.

shoal, *v.t.*, to make shallow; *v.i.*, to run shallow; to swarm; *n.*, a school or multitude of fishes; any throng; shallow water; a sand-bar; *adj.*, shallow.

shoal'iness, *n.*, the state of being shoaly

shoal'y, *adj.*, abounding in shoals.

shoat, *n.*, a young pig.

shock, *n.*, a concussion; a sudden shaking or collision; the effect of a sudden blow or concussion, or of the passage of an electric current: sheaves set up to ripen; a disordered mass(as of hair); *v.t.*, to jar; shake; horrify; *v.i.*, to collide.

shocked, *p.p.*, shock.

shock'-headed, *n.*, with rough, tumbled hair.

shock'ing, *adj.*, *pr.p.*, shock; *adj.*, disgusting, horrifying.

shod, *p.p.*, shoe.

shod'dy, *n.*, old fabrics and rags shredded and made up into a cloth; sham; *adj.*, made of shoddy; sham; *v.t.*, to convert into shoddy cloth.

shode, *n.*, *i.q.* shoad.

shoe, *n.*, a low outer covering for the foot; anything resembling a shoe in shape or use; *v.t.*, to supply with shoes; to put a ferrule on.

shoe'black, *n.*, one who polishes shoes with blacking.

shoe'horn, *n.*, an instrument made of horn or other substance, to enable a shoe to be put on.

shoe'ing, *pr.p.*, shoe; *n.*, the act of shoeing a horse, etc.

shoe'-leather, *n.*, material for making shoes.

shoe'less, *adj.*, without shoes.

shoe'maker, *n.*, one who makes shoes.

shoe'making, *n.*, a shoemaker's or cobbler's craft.

sho'er, *n.*, one who shoes, esp. horses.

shoe'-string, *n.*, the lace of a shoe.

shone, *p.t.* and *p.*, shine.

shoo, *v.t.*, to scare birds with the voice; *v.i.*, to make the sound *shoo*; *interj.*, the sound *shoo.*

shook, *p.t.*, shake.

shoon, *n.*, pl. of shoe (*obs.*).

shoot, *v.t.*, to discharge a missile; to hit or kill by shooting; to put forth; to protrude; to discharge; to shoot [game] over (*colloq.*); *v.i.*, to fire a gun or pistol; to let fly an arrow; to dart; to grow up quickly; to project; *n.*, a young growth, a sprout; a swift flow of water; a sloping passage down which things can be shot; a district owned or hired for shooting game; a shooting party.

shoot'er, *n.*, one who, or that which, shoots.

shoot'ing, *pr.p.*, shoot; *n.*, the act of shooting; the ownership of land where game can be shot; the land so owned or hired.

shoot'ing-box, *n.*, a lodge where a shooting-party lives temporarily.

shoot'ing-star, *n.*, a star-like meteoric discharge.

shop, *n.*, a place where goods of any sort are sold; a building or room where artisan's or craftsman's work is done; unseasonable talk about one's profession or business (*colloq.*); *v.i.*, to visit shops.

shop'keeper, *n.*, a tradesman.

shop'lifter, *n.*, one who steals from a shop.

shop'man, *n.*, one who serves in a shop.

shopped, *p.p.*, shop.

shop'ping, *pr.p.*, shop; *n.*, the act or practice of visiting shops.

shop'walker, *n.*, a superior person who walks about a shop instructing customers how and where to obtain what they want.

shop'-woman, *n.*, fem. of shopman.

shore, *v.t.*, to prop up; to surround with a shore; *n.*, land skirting the sea; a prop to hold up a structure.

shored, *p.p.*, shore.

shore'less, *adj.*, without a shore; boundless.

shore'ward, *adv.*, toward the shore.

shor'ing, *pr.p.*, shore; *n.*, the act of shoring; an arrangement of props.

shorn, *p.p.*, shear.

short, *v.t.* and *i.*, to shorten; *adj.*, the opposite to long; insufficient; in want of, or inadequately supplied with; quick-tempered; crisp or brittle; unmixed; *n.*, something short, essence or pith; a syllable pronounced short; *adv.*, not enough; abruptly.

short'age, *n.*, deficiency.

short'coming, *n.*, failure; defect; delinquency.

short'en, *v.t.*, to make shorter; curtail; to check; *v.i.*, to become shorter.

short'ened, *p.p.*, shorten.

short'ener, *n.*, one who shortens.

short'ening, *pr.p.*, shorten.

short'er, *adj.*, *comp.* of short.

short'est, *adj.*, *super.* of short.

short'hand, *n.*, a method or system of writing compendiously and in a labour-saving way; stenography.

***short*-han'ded,** *adj.*, without enough helpers.

***short'*horn,** *n.*, a special breed of cattle.

***short'*horned,** *adj.*, having short horns.

***short'*-lived,** *adj.*, living only for a short time.

***short'*ly,** *adv.*, immediately; curtly.

***short'*ness,** *n.*, the quality or state of being short.

shorts, *n. pl.*, a poorer quality of hemp; small-clothes; truncated trousers.

***short'*-sighted,** *adj.*, myopic; near-sighted; not discerning.

***short*-sight'edness,** *n.*, the state or quality of being short-sighted.

shot, *p.p.*, shoot; *n.*, a missile (non-explosive) discharged from a cannon, gun, or pistol; an act of shooting; one who shoots; a reckoning.

shote, *n.*, a young hog. Also *shoat.*

shot'-free, *adj.*, free of cost. Also *scot-free.*

shot'ted, *adj.*, loaded with shot.

should, *past* and *conditional* of shall; sometimes implying further action as contemplated in the past; sometimes forming the apodosis of a conditional sentence; sometimes implying obligation.

shoul'der, *v.t.*, to raise on to one's shoulder; to hustle, push aside; *n.*, that part of a body to which an arm, wing, or fore-leg is joined; anything like a shoulder, as, *e.g.*, an abutment.

shoul'der-belt, *n.*, a belt worn over one shoulder and across back and chest.

shoul'der-blade, *n.*, the scapula; one of the large, flat bones in the upper back.

shoul'dered, *p.p.*, shoulder; *adj.*, having a shoulder or shoulders.

shoul'dering, *pr.p.*, shoulder.

shoul'der-knot, *n.*, a distinctive badge or ornament worn on the shoulders.

shout, *v.t.*, to pronounce loudly; *v.i.*, to speak with a loud voice; to cry out lustily; *n.*, a loud cry or call.

shout'ed, *p.p.*, shout.

shout'er, *n.*, one who shouts.

shout'ing, *pr.p.*, shout.

shove, *v.t.* and *i.*, to thrust, push; *n.*, the act of shoving; a push.

shoved, *p.p.*, shove.

shov'el, *n.*, a spade-like implement for scooping up earth, coal, etc.; *v.t.*, to scoop up.

shov'elful, *n.*, as much as a shovel holds.

shov'el(l)ed, *p.p.*, shovel.

shov'el(l)er, *n.*, one who, or that which, shovels.

shov'el(l)ing, *pr.p.*, shovel.

shov'ing, *pr.p.*, shove.

show, *v.t.*, to make to be seen; to reveal; to prove; to exhibit; *v.i.*, to be seen; *n.*, an exhibition; spectacle; display; appearance.

show'bill, *n.*, a placard advertising an exhibition.

show'bread, *n.*, the twelve loaves laid every Sabbath on a table near the altar of incense in the tabernacle and the Temple. Also *shewbread.*

show'-case, *n.*, a case containing samples.

showed, *p.t.*, show.

show'er, *n.*, one who shows.

show'er, *n.*, a short fall (of rain, hail, etc.); *v.t.*, to discharge as in a shower; to sprinkle; *v.i.*, to fall in a shower.

show'er-bath, *n.*, a bath with an apparatus for letting water fall from above.

show'ered, *p.p.*, shower.

show'ering, *pr.p.*, shower.

show'erless, *adj.*, without a shower.

show'ery, *adj.*, coming in showers, not in steady rain.

show'ily, *adv.*, in a showy way.

show'iness, *n.*, the quality of being showy.

show'ing, *pr.p.* show.

show'man, *n.*, one who gives an exhibition.

shown, *p.p.*, show.

show'room, *n.*, a room where articles for sale, etc., are exhibited.

show'y, *adj.*, gaudy; ostentatious.

shrank, *p.t.*, shrink.

shrap'nel, *n.*, bullets contained in an explosive shell.

shred, *n.*, a torn piece; any small bit; *v.t.*, to tear into fragments.

shred'ded, *p.p.*, shred.

shred'ding, *pr.p.*, shred.

shrew, *n.*, a scold, usually a woman.

shrewd, *adj.*, sagacious, far-seeing, judicious.

shrewd'ly, *adv.*, in a shrewd way.

shrewd'ness, *n.*, the quality of being shrewd.

shrew'ish, *adj.*, inclined to be a scold.

shrew'-mole, *n.*, an American mole.

shrew'-mouse, *n.*, a very small mouse-like insect-eating creature.

shriek, *v.i.* and *t.*, to call out in piercing or agonized tones; to laugh uncontrollably; *n.*, a wild, shrill cry.

shrieked, *p.p.*, shriek.

shriek'ing, *pr.p.*, shriek.

shrie'valty, *n.*, the office, and term of office, of a sheriff.

shrift, *n.*, absolution after confession.
shrike, *n.*, the butcher-bird, which impales its victims on thorns.
shrill, *v.t.*, to utter shrilly; *v.i.*, to make a shrill sound; *adj.*, high-sounding; *n.*, a high, penetrating sound.
shrill'ness, *n.*, the quality of being shrill.
shril'ly, *adv.*, in a shrill way.
shrimp, *n.*, a small sea-water crustacean; anyone very small; *v.i.*, to catch shrimps.
shrimp'ing, *pr.p.*, shrimp; *n.*, catching shrimps.
shrine, *v.t.*, *i.q.* enshrine; *n.*, a chest, casket, or tomb containing relics; a place hallowed by a saint's relics; a place of pilgrimage.
shrink, *v.t.*, to cause to shrink; *v.i.*, to become smaller, to recoil.
shrink'age, *n.*, contraction, diminution.
shrink'er, *n.*, one who shrinks.
shrink'ing, *pr.p.*, shrink.
shrive, *v.t.*, to minister to in the tribunal of penance; to absolve.
shrived, *p.t.* and *p.*, shrive.
shriv'el, *v.t.*, to cause to contract or wither; *v.i.*, to contract; wither.
shriv'el(l)ed, *p.p.*, shrivel.
shriv'el(l)ing, *pr.p.*, shrivel.
shriv'en, *p.p.*, shrive.
shri'ving, *pr.p.*, shrive.
shri'ving-pew, *n.*, the mediaeval predecessor of the confessional-box.
shroff, *v.t.*, to inspect coins and coining.
shroff'age, *n.*, the inspection of coins and coining, and the cost of making it.
shroud, *n.*, a wrapper for a corpse; *v.t.*, to cover, conceal; in pl., ship's ropes steadying the mast.
shroud'ed, *p.p.*, shroud.
shroud'ing, *pr.p.*, shroud.
Shrove'tide, *n.*, the period for being shriven.
Shrove Tues'day, *n.*, the day before Ash Wednesday. Its name comes from the fact that at this season penitents especially made their confession.
shrub, *n.*, a plant growth of smaller size than a tree, and commonly springing from several stems; a kind of liqueur made generally of rum with fruit juices.
shrub'bery, *n.*, a place abounding in shrubs.
shrub'biness, *n.*, the quality of being shrubby.
shrub'by, *adj.*, abounding in shrubs; like shrubs.
shrug, *v.t.*, to lift the shoulders slightly by way of expressing contempt, annoyance, etc.; *n.*, this gesture.
shrugged, *p.p.*, shrug.
shrug'ging, *pr.p.*, shrug.
shrunk, *p.p.*, shrink.
shrunk'en, *adj.*, contracted, diminished.
shud'der, *v.i.*, to shiver with fear, horror, etc.; *n.*, a quivering with fear or horror.
shud'dered, *p.p.*, shudder.
shud'dering, *pr.p.*, shudder.
shuf'fle, *v.t.*, to move in a disordered way; to change the positions of ; *v.i.*, to scramble along; to prevaricate; to be evasive.
shuf'fled, *p.p.*, shuffle.
shuf'fler, *n.*, one who shuffles; a prevaricator.
shuf'fling, *pr.p.* shuffle.
shu'mac, *n.*, dried leaves, ground, and used in dyeing processes. Also *sumac*.
shun, *v.t.*, to avoid.
shunned, *p.p.*, shun.
shun'ning, *pr.p.*, shun.
shunt, *v.t.*, to remove from a main to a side line; to divert; *v.i.*, to diverge; *n.*, the act of shunting or state of being shunted; an electric conductor, by means of which the current may in different degrees be diverted.
shunt'ed, *p.p.*, shunt.
shunt'er, *n.*, one who, or that which, shunts.
shunt'ing, *pr.p.*, shunt
shut, *v.t.*, to close, lock, bar; *v.i.*, to be closed; *p.p.*, shut.
shut'ter, *n.*, one who, that which, shuts; a cover to a window.
shut'ting, *pr.p.*, shut.
shut'tle, *n.*, a weaving implement.
shut'tlecock, *n.*, a feathered cork, used in the game of battledore and shuttlecock.
shwan'pan, *n.*, a Chinese calculating apparatus.
shy, *adj.*, nervously retiring; bashful; reserved; *v.i.*, to start aside in fear; *v.t.*, to throw (*colloq.*); *n.*, a throw (*colloq.*); a starting aside.
shy'er, *n.*, one who shies; *adj.*, *comp.* of shy.
shy'est, *adj.*, *super.* of shy.
shy'ing, *pr.p.*, shy; *n.*, the act of shying; *adj.*, apt to shy.
shy'ly, *adv.*, in a shy way.
shy'ness, *n.*, the character of being shy.
si, *n.*, the seventh note in the musical scale.
sial'agogue, *n.*, a saliva-inducing agent.
Siamese', *adj.*, pert. to Siam and the Siamese; *n.*, a native of Siam; the language of Siam.

Sibe'rian, *adj.*, pert. to Siberia; *n.*, a native of Siberia.
sib'ilance, *n.*, the state or quality of being sibilant.
sib'ilancy, *n.*, *i.q.* sibilance.
sib'ilant, *adj.*, hissing; *n.*, a sibilant consonant.
sibila'tion, *n.*, pronouncing with a sibilant sound.
sib'yl, *n.*, a woman who prophesies.
sib'ylline, *adj.*, pert. to a Sibyl.
sic, *adv.*, thus; so (*Lat.*); *adj.*, such (*Scot.*).
sic'ca, *n.*, an Indian jeweller's weight.
sic'cative, *adj.*, drying.
sic'city, *n.*, aridity.
sice, *n.*, the number six in dicing.
Sicil'ian, *adj.*, pert. to Sicily; *n.*, a native of Sicily.
sick, *adj.*, ill, unwell, vomiting, disgusted.
sick'-bed, *n.*, a bed of illness.
sick'en, *v.t.*, to disgust; make sick; *v.i.*, to be on the point of becoming ill; to feel disgust.
sick'ened, *p.p.*, sicken
sick'ening, *pr.p.*, sicken; *adj.*, disgusting.
sick'ish, *adj.*, inclined to sickness.
sick'le, *n.*, a reaper's hook.
sick'led, *adj.*, supplied with a sickle.
sickle'wort, *n.*, heal-all (*bot.*).
sick'lied, *adj.*, made to look sickly.
sick'liness, *n.*, a tendency to ill-health; the state or quality of being sickly.
sick'-list, *n.*, a list of persons regarded as ill.
sick'ly, *adj.*, ailing; causing nausea; *adv.*, in a sick way.
sick'ness, *n.*, illness; nausea.
sick'-room, *n.*, a room containing a sick person.
side, *n.*, a surface of a solid body; the part from the shoulder to the hip; a hill-slope; a party; the bias given to a billiard ball struck not quite in the centre; arrogance (*slang*); *v.i.*, to take a side (*i.e.*, to support a party).
side'board, *n.*, a buffet.
si'ded, *p.p.*, side.
side'ling, *adj.*, sloping
side'long, *adj.*, on the side; *adv.*, laterally.
si'deral, *adj.*, *i.q.* sidereal.
side'real, *adj.*, rel. to stars.
sid'erite, *n.*, a meteoric stone.
siderog'raphy, *n.*, an engraving on steel.
sid'eroscope, *n.*, a scientific apparatus for discovering iron particles.
side'-saddle, *n.*, a lady's saddle.
sides'man, *n.*, a church official assistant to the churchwardens; one who takes sides.
side'-table, *n.*, a supplementary table.
side'walk, *n.*, a footpath (*Amer.*).
side'wise, *adv.*, laterally.
si'di, *n.*, an E. Indian word used in addressing a Mohammedan gentleman.
si'ding, *pr.p.*, side; *n.*, a railway line off the main track.
si'dle, *v.i.*, to walk sideways.
si'dled, *p.p.*, sidle.
si'dling, *pr.p.*, sidle.
siege, *v.t.*, *i.q.* besiege; *n.*, an attempt to reduce a fortified place to surrender; the floor in a glass furnace.
sieg'ing, *pr.p.*, siege.
si'enite, *n.*, *i.q.* syenite
sien'na, *n.*, a reddish-brown pigment brought from Sienna.
sier'ra, *n.*, a serrated range of mountains.
sies'ta, *n.*, a mid-day rest or sleep.
sieve, *n.*, an implement used for straining out finer particles.
sift, *v.t.*, to separate by means of a sieve; to investigate closely.
sift'ed, *p.p.*, sift.
sift'er, *n.*, one who, or that which, sifts.
sift'ing, *pr.p.*, sift.
sigh, *v.i.*, to breathe deep and long; to mourn; *n.*, a long, deep breath; a sound of grief or sorrow.
sighed, *p.p.*, sigh.
sigh'er, *n.*, one who sighs.
sigh'ing, *pr.p.*, sigh; *n.*, the act of sighing.
sight, *n.*, the power of seeing; vision; appearance; a contrivance for improving one's aim with a gun; a spectacle; *v.t.*, to catch sight of; to adjust the sight of (a gun).
sight'ed, *p.p.*, sight.
sight'ing, *pr.p.*, sight.
sight'less, *adj.*, blind.
sight'lessness, *n.*, blindness.
sight'liness, *n.*, the quality of being sightly.
sight'ly, *adj.*, good to look on.
sight'-seeing, *n.*, going to see places and things worth seeing.
sight'-seer, *n.*, one who indulges in sight-seeing.
sig'il, *n.*, a seal or signature.
sigilla'ria, *n. pl.*, coal-fossils.
sigil'lum, *n.*, a seal (*Lat.*).
sig'ma, *n.*, the Greek equivalent of the letter S.
sig'moid, *adj.*, like a S.
sigmoid'al, *adj.*, *i.q.* sigmoid.
sign, *n.*, a mark; token; indication; wonder; a board bearing a device and hung outside a shop or inn; *v.t.*, to mark with a signature; *v.i.*, to signal.
sig'nal, *n.*, a means of giving notice or

warning; *adj.*, worthy of note; remarkable; *v.t.* and *i.*, to convey (a message) by signals.

sig'nalize, *v.t.*, to make noteworthy.

sig'nalized, *p.p.*, signalize.

sig'nalizing, *pr.p.*, signalize.

sig'nal(l)ed, *p.p.*, signal.

sig'nal(l)er, *n.*, one who gives signals.

sig'nal(l)ing, *pr.p.*, signal; *n.*, the act of signalling.

sig'nally, *adv.*, in a conspicuous manner.

sig'nalman, *n.*, a man who attends to railway signals.

sig'natory, *adj.*, signing; *n.*, one who appends his name to a document.

sig'nature, *n.*, a name subscribed to a letter or document; a stamp; the indication of a musical key by means of signs—flats and sharps.

sign'-board, *n.*, a board bearing a device and hung outside a shop or inn.

signed, *p.p.*, sign.

sign'er, *n.*, one who signs.

sig'net, *n.*, a ring bearing a device and used for sealing.

signif'icance, *n.*, the state or quality of being significant; meaning; importance.

signif'icancy, *n.*, *i.q.* significance.

signif'icant, *adj.*, full of meaning; important; *n.*, a symbol.

signif'icantly, *adv.*, meaningly; with importance.

significa'tion, *n.*, the act or effect of signifying; import.

signif'icative, *adj.*, *i.q.* significant.

sig'nificator, *n.*, one who, or that which, signifies.

signif'icatory, *adj.*, signifying.

sig'nified, *p.p.*, signify.

sig'nify, *v.t.*, to indicate; exhibit; imply; *v.i.*, to have importance.

sig'nifying, *pr.p.*, signify.

sign'ing, *pr.p.*, sign.

si'gnior, *n.*, a lord; the Italian for Mr. or Sir.

sign'-manual, *n.*, an autograph signature.

si'gnor, *n.*, *i.q.* signior.

signo'ra, *n.*, fem. of signor (*Ital.*).

signori'na, *n.*, a young lady; Miss (*Ital.*).

si'gnory, *n.*, a lordship.

sign'-painter, *n.*, an artist in sign-boards

sign'-post, *n.*, a post with pointers showing direction to places.

Sikh, *n.*, one of the Sikhs, a great fighting race in the Punjaub.

si'lence, *n.*, absence of sound; stillness; hush; *v.t.*, to reduce to silence.

si'lenced, *p.p.*, silence

si'lencer, *n.*, one who silences.

si'lencing, *pr.p.*, silence.

si'lent, *adj.*, without sound; still; mute; reserved.

si'lently, *adv.*, noiselessly.

sile'sia, *n.*, a cloth, so named from Silesia, whence it originally came.

Sile'sian, *adj.*, bel. to Silesia; *n.*, a native of Silesia.

si'lex, *n.*, *i.q.* silica.

silhouette', *n.*, a profile portrait; a likeness cast on a wall or other surface; *v.t.*, to show in profile or silhouette.

sil'ica, *n.*, silicon dioxide.

sil'icate, *n.*, a silicic acid salt.

sil'icated, *adj.*, impregnated with silica.

sili'ceous, *adj.*, containing, or pert. to, silica.

silicif'erous, *adj.*, producing silica.

silic'ified, *p.p.* silicify.

silic'ify, *v.t.*, to change into silica.

silic'ifying, *pr.p.*, silicify.

silic'ium, *n.*, *i.q.* silicon.

sil'icle, *n.*, a small pod.

sil'icon, *n.*, a non-metallic element.

silic'ulose, *adj.*, pod-like.

sil'iqua, *n.*, a pod (*Lat.*).

sil'iquiform, *adj.*, like a siliqua.

sil'iquose, *adj.*, pod-like.

silk, *n.*, a fibrous substance produced by silkworms in forming their cocoons; cloth or thread made of silk; the silk gown of a K.C.; the lustre of certain precious stones; *adj.*, made of silk.

silk'en, *adj.*, made of silk; like silk; soft and smooth.

silk'iness, *n.*, the state or quality of being silky.

silk'worm, *n.*, the worm (*bombyx mori*) that produces silk.

silk'y, *adj.*, like silk; smooth, soft, and lustrous.

sill, *n.*, a horizontal base of a window or door.

sil'labub, syl'labub, *n.*, milk or cream curded by the addition of wine, and often whipped.

Sil'lery, *n.*, a champagne.

sil'lier, *adj.*, *comp.* of silly.

sil'liest, *adj.*, *super.* of silly.

sil'lily, *adv.*, in a silly way.

sil'liness, *n.*, the quality of being silly.

sillom'eter, *n.*, a nautical instrument for ascertaining a ship's rate of sailing.

sil'ly, *adj.*, simple, foolish, senseless, imbecile.

si'lo, *n.*, an airtight enclosure, whether a pit or a building, in which green fodder can be stored and kept fit for eating after going through a process of fermentation; *v.t.*, to treat in this way; to turn to ensilage.

silt, *n.*, sediment carried down by flowing water; *v.t.*, to choke up with an earthy deposit; *v.i.*, to become so choked up.

silt'ed, *p.p.*, silt.

silt'ing, *pr.p.*, silt.

Silu'rian, *adj.*, pert. to the Silures, early Celtic inhabitants of Wales; bel. to the Silurian geological division of the Palaeozoic period.

sil'va, *n.*, a wood, forest, glade (*Lat.*).

sil'van, *adj.*, wooded; pert. to forests and woods; rural.

sil'ver, *n.*, one of the precious metals, white and lustrous; silver coin; a sheen as of silver; *v.t.*, to coat or cover with silver; *v.i.*, to become silvery.

sil'vered, *p.p.*, silver

sil'verer, *n.*, one who silvers.

sil'ver-grey, *adj.*, grey with a look of silver.

sil'vering, *pr.p.*, silver; silver-plating; the art of silvering.

sil'verling, *n.*, an ancient silver coin.

sil'versmith, *n.*, a worker in silver.

sil'ver-stick, *n.*, a field officer of the Life Guards in attendance at Court, whose emblem of office is a silver wand.

sil'very, *adj.*, like silver; containing silver.

simar', *n.*, a kind of scarf.

Sim'ia, *n.*, an anthropoid genus of apes.

sim'ian, *adj.*, apelike; pert. to apes.

sim'ilar, *adj.*, like, resembling.

similar'ity, *n.*, likeness; the state of being similar.

sim'ilarly, *adv.*, in like manner.

sim'ile, *n.*, a comparison; the likening of one thing to another in express words; (a metaphor is a simile condensed into a single word or phrase); *adv.*, in similar style (*mus.*).

simil'itude, *n.*, likeness; appearance.

sim'ilize, *v.t.*, to compare by means of a simile; *v.i.*, to use similes.

sim'ilor, *n.*, an alloy of copper and zinc.

sim'ious, *adj.*, *i.q.* simian.

sim'itar, *n.* *i.q.* scimitar.

sim'mer, *v.t.*, to keep near the boiling point; *v.i.*, to keep gently boiling; *n.*, the simmering state.

sim'mered, *p.p.*, simmer.

sim'mering, *pr.p.*, simmer.

sim'nel-cake, *n.*, a rich cake, often decorated, and eaten principally on Mothering Sunday, but also at Christmas and Easter.

simo'niac, *n.*, one who has committed an act of simony.

simoni'acal, *adj.*, of the nature of simony.

Simo'nian, *adj.*, rel. to Simon Magus; *n.*, a member of an Early Christian heretical sect.

sim'ony, *n.*, the sin of Simon Magus; purchasing preferment in the Church.

simoom', *n.*, a hot, dry wind met with mostly in the Arabian desert.

simoon', *n.*, *i.q.* simoom.

si'mous, *adj.*, snubnosed.

sim'per, *v.i.*, to laugh or smile in a silly fashion; to smirk; *n.*, a silly, affected smile.

sim'pered, *p.p.*, simper.

sim'perer, *n.*, one who simpers.

sim'pering, *pr.p.*, simper.

sim'ple, *adj.*, not combined with another thing; single; unaffected; plain; easy; unlettered; uncultivated; ordinary; *n.*, an element; a medicinal herb; ecclesiastically, a feast of the lowest rank.

sim'ple-minded, *adj.*, ingenuous.

simple-mind'edness, *n.*, ingenuousness.

sim'pleness, *n.*, the quality of being simple.

sim'pler, *adj.*, *comp.* of simple.

sim'plest, *adj.*, *super.* of simple.

sim'pleton, *n.*, a silly person; a dolt.

simplic'ity, *n.*, *i.q.* simpleness.

simplifica'tion, *n.*, the act or effect of simplifying.

sim'plified, *adj.*, *p.p.*, simplify.

sim'plify, *v.t.*, to make simple; to explain.

sim'plifying, *pr.p.*, simplify.

sim'plism, *n.*, affected simplicity.

sim'ply, *adv.*, in a simple way; merely.

simula'crum, *n.*, an image, likeness, ghost, pretender (*Lat.*).

sim'ulant, *adj.*, simulating.

sim'ulate, *v.t.*, to pretend; to present oneself in the character of; to assume the form of.

sim'ulated, *p.p.*, simulate.

sim'ulating, *pr.p.*, simulate.

simula'tion, *n.*, the act of simulating.

simulta'neous, *adj.*, occurring at the same moment.

simulta'neously, *adv.*, at the same moment.

sin, *n.*, offence against God and right;

transgression; *v.i.*, to offend against divine or moral law.

Sinait'ic, *adj.*, pert. to Sinai or the Peninsula of Sinai.

sin'apism, *n.*, a mustard plaster.

since, *adv.*, ago; from a past time till now; *prep.*, throughout the interval between then and now; *conj.*, from a past time till now and during the interval; because.

sincere', *adj.*, ingenuous; honest; without deceit.

sincere'ly, *adv.*, with sincerity.

sincer'ity, *n.*, the state or quality of being sincere.

sincip'ital, *adj.*, rel. to the sinciput.

sin'ciput, *n.*, the front part of the top of the head.

sin'don, *n.*, a fine Oriental fabric; a robe made of sindon.

sine, *n.*, a line drawn from one end of an arc perpendicular to radius at the other end; *adv.*, ago (*Scot.*).

si'ne, *prep.*, without (*Lat.*).

si'necure, *n.*, a post or office with no duties, esp. an ecclesiastical benefice without cure of souls.

si'necurism, *n.*, the state of being the holder of a sinecure.

si'necurist, *n.*, one who holds a sinecure.

si'ne di'e, *adv. phrase*, without a day, *i.e.*, with no date assigned (*Lat.*).

sine quâ non', *n. phrase*, something absolutely indispensable (*Lat.*).

sin'ew, *n.*, a tendon or cord-like tissue.

sin'ewed, *adj.*, having sinews.

sin'ewy, *adj.*, strong, well-knit.

sinfo'nia, *n.*, a symphony (*mus.*).

sin'ful, *adj.*, wicked.

sin'fully, *adv.*, wickedly.

sin'fulness, *n.*, wickedness; a state of sin.

sing, *v.t.*, to celebrate in song or verse; *v.i.*, to utter a song; to make a sound as of singing.

sing'able, *adj.*, that can be sung.

singe, *v.t.* and *i.*, to scorch; to burn superficially; *n.*, the act or effect of singeing.

singed, *p.p.*, singe.

singe'ing, *pr.p.*, singe.

sin'ger, *n.*, one who singes.

sing'er, *n.*, one who sings; a cantor or chorister.

Singhalese', *adj.*, pert to the people of Ceylon; *n.*, a native of Ceylon. Also *Sinhalese* and *Cingalese*.

sing'ing, *pr.p.*, sing.

sing'ing-book, *n.*, a song-book.

sing'ing-master, *n.*, an instructor in singing.

sing'ing-school, *n.*, a song-school.

sin'gle, *adj.*, individual; one only; unmarried; unaided; ingenuous; *n.*, a game in which each opponent is single; a hit for one in cricket; *v.t.*, to pick out as typical or exemplary.

sin'gled, *p.p.*, single.

sin'gle-handed, *adj.*, having only one hand; unaided.

sin'gle-hearted, *adj.*, sincere.

sin'gle-minded, *adj.*, *i.q.* single-hearted.

single-mind'edness, *n.*, the quality of being single-minded; sincerity.

sin'gleness, *n.*, the state of being single or distinct; simplicity, ingenuousness.

sin'gle-stick, *n.*, a thick cudgel; esp. a stick used in a kind of fencing game.

sing'let, *n.*, a kind of unlined waistcoat.

sin'gling, *pr.p.*, single.

sin'gly, *adv.*, one at a time; by oneself.

sing'song, *adj.*, monotonous, droning; *n.*, a monotonous, droning kind of speech; an amateur, free-and-easy concert.

sin'gular, *adj.*, not plural; single; remarkable; strange.

singular'ity, *n.*, the quality of being singular.

sin'gularly, *adv.*, in a surprising way.

sin'ical, *adj.*, pert. to a sine.

sin'ister, *adj.*, of ill-omen; malignant; villainous; on the left side (*her.*).

sin'istral, *adj.*, pert. to the left hand.

sin'istrous, *adj.*, towards the left.

sink, *v.t.*, to submerge; to excavate downward; to lower or degrade; to suppress; to engrave; *v.i.*, to descend, decline; to fall towards the bottom; *n.*, a drain for dirty water, etc.

sink'er, *n.*, one who, that which, sinks; a weight attached to a fishing or sounding line.

sink'hole, *n.*, the hole in a sink for the outflow.

sink'ing, *pr.p.*, sink; *n.*, an internal feeling of hunger or exhaustion.

sink'ing-fund, *n.*, a reserve of money, the accumulation of which will, at maturity, pay off a debt.

sin'less, *adj.*, without sin; pure.

sin'lessness, *n.*, the state or quality of being sinless.

sinned, *p.p.*, sin.

sin'ner, *n.*, one who sins.

sin'net, *n.*, cordage plaited. Also *sennit*.

sin'ning, *pr.p.*, sin.

sin'-offering, *n.*, a sacrifice in atonement for sin.

sin'ter, *n.*, a siliceous deposit in springs.

Sin'too, *n.*, *i.q.* Shinto.

sin'uate, *adj.*, with a margin curving inward and outward.

sin'uated, *adj.*, *i.q.* sinuate.

sinua'tion, *n.*, curving inward and outward.

sin'uose, *adj.*, wavy.

sinuos'ity, *n.*, waviness.

sin'uous, *adj.*, curving, winding.

si'nus, *n.*, a bay; a depression; fistula (*Lat.*).

sip, *v.t.*, to drink lightly and in small draughts; to taste; *n.*, a small draught; taste.

si'phon, *n.*, a bent tube with one part shorter than the other, used for drawing water, etc., down to a lower level; an aerated water bottle containing a siphon; a tube-like organ. Also *syphon*.

siphon'ic, *adj.*, pert. to a siphon.

si'phuncle, *n.*, a canal-like tube in certain molluscs and shells; a tube with which some insects suck.

siphun'cular, *adj.*, pert. to a siphuncule.

sipped, *p.p.*, sip.

sip'ping, *pr.p.*, sip.

si'quis, a *Lat.* phrase = If any (of you know cause or impediment, etc.). It denotes specifically the asking in church whether there is any reason why so-and-so may not be admitted to the diaconate or the priesthood.

sir, *n.*, the title of address in speaking to every gentleman; courtesy title of a knight or baronet.

sir'car, *or* **sir'kar,** *n.*, an E. Indian name for the Government or the head of a business house.

sir'dar, *n.*, a military commander; a chief.

sire, *n.*, the title of address in speaking to the sovereign; a father; a male animal; *v.t.*, to be the father of.

si'ren, *n.*, a nymph who lured mariners to destruction; a ship's fog-horn; *adj.*, enchanting, bewitching.

sirene', *n.*, an apparatus that marks the vibrations of a musical note.

siri'asis, *n.*, sunstroke; a sun-bath.

Sir'ius, *n.*, the dog-star.

sir'loin, *n.*, the upper part of a loin of beef.

siroc'co, *n.*, a hot, dry wind rising in the Libyan desert.

sir'rah, *n.*, an angry or scornful expression.

sir'up, *n.*, *i.q.* syrup.

sir'upy, *adj.*, *i.q.* syrupy.

sis'kin, *n.*, a variety of finch.

sis'ter, *n.*, a daughter of the same parents as those of another person; the title of a woman belonging to a religious or a nursing order; one of the same kind, as "the sister university."

sis'terhood, *n.*, the relation of a sister; a religious community of sisters; sisters collectively.

sis'ter-in-law, *n.*, a wife's or a husband's sister; a brother's wife.

sis'terly, *adj.*, like a sister.

Sis'tine, *adj.*, rel. specifically to Pope Sixtus IV and the Sistine Chapel named after him and built by him in Rome.

sis'trum, *n.*, a sort of musical rattle (*Lat.*).

Sisyphe'an, *adj.*, pert. to Sisyphus and his perpetual punishment of having to push uphill a stone that continually rolled back; hopelessly laborious.

sit, *v.t.*, to have a firm seat on; *v.i.*, to support the body on the buttocks; to rest; to weigh upon; to enter for an examination; to represent a constituency; to hold a court; to incubate.

site, *n.*, a place where a building stands or is about to be erected.

sith, *conj.*, since.

sithe, *n.*, old form of the word *scythe*.

sitol'ogy, *n.*, the science of food and diet.

sit'ter, *n.*, one who sits, esp. to an artist, etc.; a brooding hen.

sit'ting, *pr.p.*, sit; *n.*, the act of sitting; a seat in a church; a session; the collective eggs under a sitting hen.

sit'ting-room, *n.*, a room to sit in.

sit'uate, *v.t.*, to place; *adj.*, placed.

sit'uated, *p.p.*, situate; *adj.*, *i.q.* situate.

situa'tion, *n.*, position, place; a post of service.

sitz'-bath, *n.*, a bath in which one sits.

Si'vaism, *n.*, the worship of Siva.

Si'vaite, *n.*, a worshipper of the Hindu deity, Siva.

Sivan', *n.*, a month in the Hebrew Kalendar.

six, *n.*, the number next above five; the sign 6; *adj.*, exceeding five by one.

six'fold, *adj.*, six times as many; multiplied by six.

six'pence, *n.*, the value of six pennies; a coin of that value.

six'penny, *adj.*, worth sixpence.

six'score, *adj.*, multiplied by 120; six times twenty.

sixteen', *adj.*, six added to ten.

sixteenth, *adj.*, the ordinal of sixteen.
sixth, *adj.*, the ordinal of six.
sixth'ly, *adv.*, in the sixth place.
six'tieth, *adj.*, the ordinal of sixty.
six'ty, *adj.*, six times ten.
si'zable, *adj.*, proper as regards size.
si'zar, *n.*, an undergraduate at Cambridge or Dublin holding a small benefaction from his college.
size, *n.*, bulk, dimensions; a sort of g[illegible]; *v.t.*, to group according to size; to cover with size; *v.i.*, to draw food supplies from a college buttery at Cambridge.
size'able, *adj.*, *i.q.* sizable.
sized, *p.p.*, size.
siz'el, *n.*, metal-clippings.
si'zer, *n.*, one who sizes.
si'zing, *pr.p.*, size; *n.*, the act of sizing in all senses; the materials used in the process of sizing.
si'zy, *adj.*, like, or containing, size.
sjam'bok, *n.*, a S. African Boer's whip; *v.t.*, to flog with a sjambok.
skald, *n.*, an old Scandinavian bard. Also *scald*.
skate, *n.*, a flat fish; an attachment to the foot enabling the wearer to travel over ice; *v.i.*, to travel on skates.
ska'ted, *p.p.*, skate.
ska'ter, *n.*, one who skates.
ska'ting, *pr.p.*, skate.
skedad'dle, *v.i.*, to make one's escape; clear off (*Amer.*).
skeel, *n.*, a Scottish wooden milk vessel.
skeet, *n.*, a scoop.
skein, *n.*, silk, thread, etc., in a coil.
skel'eton, *n.*, the bony structure of animals when stripped of the flesh; an outline; a fleshless person.

skelp, *n.*, a smart smack; *v.t.*, to hit or smack (*Scot.*).
skep'tic, *adj.* and *n.*, *i.q.* sceptic.
sker'ry, *n.*, a reef (*Scot.*).
sketch, *n.*, an incomplete or rapid drawing; a rough draft; *v.t.*, to draw in rough outline; to make a sketch of; *v.i.*, to act as a sketcher.
sketch'-book, *n.*, a book in which sketches can be drawn.
sketched, *p.p.*, sketch.
sketch'er, *n.*, one who sketches.
sketch'ily, *adv.*, in a sketchy way.
sketch'ing, *pr. p.*, sketch; *n.*, the occupation of a sketcher.
sketch'y, *adj.*, in outline; imperfect.
skew, *adj.*, slanting; *adv.*, slantwise.
skew'-back, *n.*, the bevelled support at the spring of a segmented arch.
skew'-bridge, *n.*, a bridge crossing a road or river slantwise.
skewed, *p.p.*, skew.
skew'er, *n.*, a metal or wooden pin for holding meat together.
ski, *n.*, a long snowshoe; *v.i.*, to slide on skis.
skid, *v.i.*, to side-slip; *v.t.*, to check with a skid; *n.*, a drag on a wheel; a ship's fender; part of an aeroplane's running gear.
skid'ded, *p.p.*, skid.
skid'ding, *pr.p.*, skid.
skiff, *n.*, a small boat.
ski'-ing, *pr.p.*, ski.
skil'ful, *adj.*, clever; handy; expert.
skil'fully, *adv.*, with skill.
skil'fulness, *n.*, cleverness, dexterity.
skill, *n.*, cleverness; expertness.
skilled, *adj.*, expert; skilful.
skil'let, *n.*, a small cooking utensil.

skil'ly, *n.*, a thin gruel in which meat has been boiled; prison fare.
skim, *v.t.*, to take the scum off; to remove cream from; *v.i.*, to pass quickly and lightly over anything.
skimmed, *p.p.*, skim.
skim'mer, *n.*, one who, or that which, skims.
skim'-milk, *n.*, milk from which the cream has been skimmed.
skim'ming, *pr.p.*, skim.
skim'mington, *n.*, orig. a rowdy demonstration against a henpecked man; a row; now, any disturbance.
skin, *n.*, an animal's outer covering; anything like a skin; *v.t.*, to remove the skin; to flay; *v.i.*, to form a coating.
skin'-deep, *adj.* and *adv.*, only just below the surface.
skin'flint, *n.*, a screw; a niggardly person.
skin'ful, *n.*, as much as one can hold of food or drink.
skink, *n.*, a variety of lizard.
skin'less, *adj.*, having little or no skin; having a thin skin.
skinned, *p.p.*, skin.
skin'ner, *n.*, a dealer in skins.
skin'nier, *adj.*, *comp.* of skinny.
skin'niest, *adj.*, *super.* of skinny.
skin'niness, *n.*, the quality or state of being skinny.
skin'ning, *pr.p.*, skin.
skin'ny, *adj.*, lean; mean (*slang*); niggardly.
skip, *v.i.*, to take light leaps; *v.t.*, to omit (passages from a book or letter); *n.*, a light leap; an omission; a basket.
skipped, *p.p.*, skip.
skip'per, *n.*, one who skips; a sea-captain.
skip'ping, *pr.p.*, skip.

skir'mish, *n.*, a small fight; a brush; *v.i.*, to engage in a small fight, not a regular battle.
skir'mished, *p.p.*, skirmish.
skir'misher, *n.*, one who skirmishes.
skir'mishing, *pr.p.*, skirmish.
skir'ret, *n.*, a water-parsnip.
skirt, *n.*, the lower part of any garment; the part of a frock from the waist downward; a border; *v.t.*, to go close by anything; *v.i.*, to extend along.
skirt'ed, *p.p.*, skirt; *adj.* having a skirt attached.
skirt'ing, *pr.p.*, skirt; *n.*, dress material; *i.q.* skirting-board.
skirt'ing-board, *n.*, upright boarding laid along the bottom of an inner wall.
skit, *n.*, a take-off; a satire.
skit'tish, *adj.*, playful; wanton; easily startled.
skit'tishly, *adv.*, in a skittish way.
skit'tle-alley, *n.*, an alley in which skittles or nine-pins are played.
skit'tles, *n. pl.*, the game of ninepins.
ski'ver, *n.*, an instrument used in leather dressing; split sheep skin.
skow, *n.*, a flat-bottomed boat. Also *scow*.
skulk, *v.i.*, to keep out of sight; to hang back; to idle; *n.*, an idler.
skulked, *p.p.*, skulk.
skulk'er, *n.*, one who skulks.
skulk'ing, *pr.p.*, skulk.
skull, *n.*, the bony structure containing the brain.
skull'cap, *n.*, a cap fitting close to the skull.
skunk, *n.*, a carnivorous American beast, highly malodorous when chased; a mean, worthless person.
skur'ry, *v.i.*, *i.q.* scurry
sky, *n.*, the upper air; the ethereal vault; *v.t.*, to hang (pictures) too high to be properly seen.
sky'-blue, *adj.*, blue like the colour of the sky.
sky'ey, *adj.*, like the sky; up in the sky.
sky'-high, *adj.* and *adv.*, high up towards the sky.
sky'ish, *adj.*, sky-like.
sky'lark, *n.*, a soaring lark; *v.i.*, to indulge in a frolic (*colloq.*).
sky'larking, *pr.p.*, skylark.
sky'light, *n.*, a window in a roof.
sky'rocket, *n.*, a rocket with a high flight.
sky'-sail, *n.*, a light sail above the royal.
sky'-scraper, *n.*, an immensely high building; a sail above the royal.
slab, *n.*, a flat piece of stone; mire; *adj.*, thick, sticky.
slab'ber, *v.i.*, to dribble saliva; *n.*, saliva. Also *slobber*.
slab'bered, *p.p.*, slabber.
slab'berer, *n.*, one who slabbers.
slab'bering, *pr.p.*, slabber.
slab'biness, *n.*, the quality of being slabby.
slab'by, *adj.*, viscous; sloppy.
slack, *adj.*, loose; unenergetic; idle; at ease; *v.i.*, to be lazy (*colloq.*); *n.*, the loose part of a rope.
slacked, *p.p.* slack.
slack'en, *v.t.*, to make looser; *v.i.*, to become looser; to relax in effort.
slack'ened, *p.p.*, slacken.
slack'ening, *pr.p.*, slacken.
slack'ing, *pr.p.*, slack.
slack'ly, *adv.*, loosely, lazily.
slack'ness, *n.*, the state or quality of being slack.
slag, *n.*, metal refuse; cinders vitrified.
slag'gy, *adj.*, containing or resembling slag.
slain, *p.p.*, slay.
slake, *v.t.*, to quench (thirst); to weaken by watering; *v.i.*, to be watered.
slaked, *p.p.*, slake.
slake'less, *adj.*, unquenchable.
sla'king, *pr.p.*, slake.
slam, *v.t.*, to bang to with a noise; *v.i.*, to close with a noise; *n.*, a loud bang.
slammed, *p.p.*, slam.
slam'ming, *pr.p.*, slam
slan'der, *n.*, calumny; spiteful rumour; *v.t.*, to defame; to speak untruth about spitefully.
slan'dered, *p.p.*, slander.
slan'derer, *n.*, one who slanders.
slan'dering, *pr.p.*, slander; *n.*, calumniation.
slan'derous, *adj.*, calumnious; speaking slander.
slan'derously, *adv.*, in a slanderous manner.
slang, *n.*, the use of words not bearing the literary hall-mark; colloquial jargon; argot; *v.t.*, to address abusively (*colloq.*).
slanged, *p.p.*, slang.
slang'ing, *pr.p.*, slang.
slang'y, *adj.*, given to the use of slang.
slant, *adj.*, oblique, sloping; *v.t.*, to make to slope; *v.i.*, to slope; *n.*, a sloping direction; an inclined plane.
slant'ed, *p.p.*, slant.
slant'ing, *pr.p.*, slant.
slant'ingly, *adv.*, in a slanting way; slantwise; aslant.
slant'wise, *adv.*, *i.q.* slantingly.
slap, *n.*, a blow with the open hand; *v.t.*, to deliver such a blow; *adv.*, directly.
slap'-dash, *adj.*, done at random.
slapped, *p.p.*, slap.
slap'ping, *pr.p.*, slap.

slash, *v.t.*, to cut with repeated strokes; to slit; to whip savagely; *v.i.*, to use a whip at random; *n.*, a slit.
slashed, *p.p.*, slash.
slash'er, *n.*, one who slashes.
slash'ing, *pr.p.*, slash; *adj.*, caustic, severely critical.
slat, *n.*, a narrow metal or wooden fastening between larger pieces.
slatch, *n.*, the slack of a rope; the duration of a transitory breeze.
slate, *n.*, laminated rock that can be used in place of roof-tiles or for writing upon; *v.t.*, to roof with slates; to scold (*slang*).
sla'ted, *p.p.*, slate.
slate'-pencil, *n.*, a pencil for writing on a slate.
sla'ter, *n.*, a man who slates roofs; a leather-dresser's implement for removing the hair from hides.
sla'ting, *pr.p.*, slate; *n.*, a scolding (*slang*).
slat'tern, *n.*, a slovenly woman.
slat'ternliness, *n.*, slovenliness.
slat'ternly, *adj.*, slovenly; *adv.*, untidily.
sla'ty, *adj.*, like, or abounding in, slate.
slaugh'ter, *n.*, killing on a large scale; massacre; the killing of cattle; *v.t.*, to slay; to kill (cattle) for eating.
slaugh'tered, *p.p.*, slaughter.
slaugh'terer, *n.*, one who kills cattle for the butcher.
slaugh'ter-house, *n.*, an abattoir.
slaugh'tering, *pr.p.*, slaughter.
slaugh'terous, *adj.*, murderous.
Slav, *n.*, a member of the Slavonic race in Central Europe.
slave, *n.*, a person held in bondage; a serf; a downtrodden person; *v.i.*, to drudge; to work laboriously.
slaved, *p.p.*, slave.
slave'-driver, *n.*, one who compels slaves to work; anyone like him.
slave'holder, *n.*, an owner of slaves.
slave'holding, *n.*, the practice of keeping slaves.
slave'-owner, *n.*, *i.q.* slave-holder.
sla'ver, *n.*, a dealer in slaves; a ship for exporting slaves.
slav'er, *n.*, dribbled saliva; *v.t.*, to foul with dribble; *v.i.*, to dribble.
slav'ered, *p.p.*, slaver.
slav'erer, *n.*, one who slavers.
slav'ering, *pr.p.*, slaver.
sla'very, *n.*, the condition of being a slave.
slave'-ship, *n.*, a ship used in the slave-trade; *i.q.* slaver.
slave'-trade, *n.*, traffic in slaves.
sla'ving, *pr.p.*, slave.
sla'vish, *adj.*, like a slave; abject.
sla'vishly, *adv.*, abjectly.
sla'vishness, *n.*, abjectness.
Slavon'ic, *adj.*, rel. to the Slavs.
slay, *v.t.*, to kill, destroy.
slay'er, *n.*, one who kills.
slay'ing, *pr.p.*, slay.
sleave, *n.*, floss; entangled thread.
slea'zy, slee'zy, *adj.*, flimsy.
sled, *n.*, a sledge; *v.t.*, to carry in a sled.
sled'ded, *p.p.*, sled.
sled'ding, *pr.p.*, sled.
sledge, *n.*, *i.q.* sled; *i.q.* sledge-hammer.
sledge'-hammer, *n.*, a great heavy hammer.
sleek, *adj.*, smooth, shiny; *v.t.*, to smooth; to put a gloss on.
sleeked, *p.p.*, sleek.
sleek'ing, *pr.p.*, sleek.
sleek'ly, *adv.*, in a sleek way.
sleek'ness, *n.*, smoothness, glossiness.
sleep, *n.*, slumber; *v.i.*, to slumber; to rest in sleep or in death; to become motionless.
sleep'er, *n.*, one who sleeps; one of the timbers on which railway metals are laid.
sleep'ier, *adj.*, *comp.* of sleepy.
sleep'iest, *adj.*, *super.* of sleepy.
sleep'ily, *adv.*, in a sleepy way.
sleep'iness, *n.*, the state of being sleepy.
sleep'ing, *pr.p.*, sleep.
sleep'less, *adj.*, unable to sleep.
sleep'lessness, *n.*, the state of being sleepless; insomnia.
sleep'-walker, *n.*, one who walks in his sleep; a somnambulist.
sleep'-walking, *n.*, the habit of walking in sleep; somnambulism.
sleep'y, *adj.*, wanting to go to sleep; tired; slow; over-ripe.
sleet, *n.*, driving snow or hail mixed with rain; *v.i.*, to come in a shower of sleet.
sleet'iness, *n.*, the state of being sleety.
sleet'y, *adj.*, falling in sleet.
sleeve, *n.*, an arm-covering; *v.t.*, to put sleeves into a garment.
sleeve'-links, *n. pl.*, a contrivance for fastening cuffs.
sleigh, *v.i.*, to ride in a sleigh or sledge; *n.*, a sledge.
sleigh'-bell, *n.*, a bell on a horse drawing a sleigh.
sleigh'ing, *pr. p.*, sleigh; *n.*, driving in a sleigh.
sleight, *n.*, dexterity; prestidigitation.
slen'der, *adj.*, thin, tapering, slight.
slen'derly, *adv.*, slightly.
slen'derness, *n.*, the quality of being slender.

slept, *p.p.*, sleep.
sleuth, *n.*, trail.
sleuth'-hound, *n.*, a bloodhound.
slew, *p.t.*, slay.
sley, *n.*, a weaver's reed.
slice, *n.*, a piece cut out of or off something; a table-implement for serving fish; the flight of a sliced golf-ball; *v.t.*, to cut into slices; to hit a golf-ball so that it flies off to the right.
sliced, *p.p.*, slice.
sli'cer, *n.*, one who, or that which, slices.
sli'cing, *pr.p.*, slice.
slick, *n.*, metal ore in a state to be worked; *adv.*, right away; entirely.
slid, *p.t.*, slide.
slid'der, *n.*, slipperiness (*Scot.*).
slide, *v.i.*, to skim over ice or any other smooth surface; *v.t.*, to slip a thing along; *n.*, smooth ice on which one can slide; a slip; a slope; a magic lantern picture on glass.
sli'der, *n.*, one who slides.
sli'ding, *pr.p.*, slide; *n.*, a slider's pastime.
sli'ding-scale, *n.*, a graduated scale.
slight, *adj.*, slim, frail, small; insignificant; *n.*, contemptuous treatment; an affront; *v.t.*, to treat contemptuously; to affront.
slight'ed, *p.p.*, slight.
slight'er, *adj.*, *comp.* of slight.
slight'est, *adj.*, *super.* of slight.
slight'ing, *pr.p.*, slight.
slight'ingly, *adv.*, in a slighting way.
slight'ly, *adv.*, in small degree; insignificantly.
slight'ness, *n.*, the quality or condition of being slight.
sli'ly, *adv.*, in a sly way.
slim, *adj.*, slender, thin; crafty (*colloq.*).
slime, *n.*, sticky mud; any sticky substance; *v.t.*, to daub; *v.i.*, to become slimy.
slimed, *p.p.*, slime.
sli'miness, *n.*, the state or quality of being slimy.
sli'ming, *pr.p.*, slime.
slim'ness, *n.*, the state or quality of being slim.
sli'my, *adj.*, viscous, sticky; covered with slime.
sling, *n.*, an implement for hurling stones; a contrivance for supporting an injured arm or hand.
sling'er, *n.*, one who slings.
sling'ing, *pr.p.*, sling.
slink, *v.i.*, to steal away; to sneak off; *v.t.*, to give birth prematurely to (said of the lower animals).
slink'ing, *pr.p.*, slink.
slip, *v.t.*, to let loose; to omit; *v.i.*, to miss one's footing; to fall; to move unperceived; to commit a fault; *n.*, a fall; a fault; an omission; a twig; a young growth or shoot; a petticoat; the cover of a pillow, etc.; a little sole; one of the fielders in cricket; a position in the cricket field.
slip'-knot, *n.*, a running-knot.
slipped, *p.p.*, slip.
slip'per, *n.*, a loose, easy shoe; one who slips.
slip'periness, *n.*, the quality of being slippery.
slip'pery, *adj.*, excessively smooth, causing one to slip; infirm; crafty.
slip'ping, *pr.p.*, slip.
slip'shod, *adj.*, careless, slovenly.
slip'-slop, *adj.*, *i.q.* slipshod; *n.*, a poor, weak drink; careless work.
slit, *n.*, a narrow cut or opening; *v.t.*, to make a slit in.
slith'er, *v.i.*, to slip, slide.
slit'ter, *n.*, one who, that which, slits.
slit'ting, *pr.p.*, slit.
slit'ting-mill, *n.*, a mill where metal plates are slit.
sliv'er, *v.t.*, to cut up small; *n.*, a small piece cut from something.
sloam, *n.*, earth between coal layers.
sloat, *n.*, *i.q.* slot.
slob'ber, *v.i.*, *i.q.* slabber.
slob'bered, *i.q.* slabbered.
slob'berer, *i.q.* slabberer.
slob'bering, *i.q.* slabbering.
sloe, *n.*, a bitter sort of plum.
slog, *v.t.* and *i.*, to strike hard and wildly (*colloq.*); *n.*, a wild hit.
slo'gan, *n.*, a war-cry of a clan (*Scot.*).
slogged, *p.p.*, slog.
slog'ger, *n.*, one who slogs.
slog'ging, *pr.p.*, slog.
sloid, **sloyd**, *n.*, Swedish drill.
sloop, *n.*, a single-masted vessel rigged fore and aft.
slop, *n.*, spilt liquid; drink or liquid food of poor quality; *v.t.*, to spill carelessly or by accident; to wet.
slop'-basin, *n.*, a basin into which slops can be poured.
slope, *n.*, a declivity; *v.t.*, to make to incline; to cause to slant; *v.i.*, to slant.
sloped, *p.p.*, slope.
slo'ping, *pr.p.*, slope; *adj.*, slanting.
slop'-pail, *n.*, a pail to hold dirty water.
slopped, *p.p.*, slop.
slop'piness, *n.*, the state or quality of being sloppy.
slop'ping, *pr.p.*, slop.
slop'py, *adj.*, wet, slopped, splashed.
slops, *n. pl.*, ready-made, reach-me-down clothes.
slop'-shop, *n.*, a shop where ready-made clothes are sold.

slosh, *n.*, mud, slush (*colloq.*).
slosh'y, *adj.*, muddy (*colloq.*).
slot, *n.*, a slit or aperture; a mortise; a deer's trail; a stage trap-door; *v.t.*, to furnish with a slot; to track.
sloth, *n.*, inertness, laziness; a S. American quadruped that lives in trees.
sloth'ful, *adj.*, inert, lazy.
sloth'fully, *adv.*, lazily
sloth'fulness, *n.*, idleness, inertness.
slot'ted, *p.p.*, slot.
slot'ting, *pr.p.*, slot.
slouch, *v.t.*, to tilt to one side; *v.i.*, to walk in an ungainly way; *n.*, a stoop with the head or shoulders; an awkward gait; a clumsy fellow.
slouched, *p.p.*, slouch.
slouch'-hat, *n.*, a hat that tilts down.
slouch'ing, *pr.p.*, slouch.
slough, *n.*, a bog.
slough, *n.*, a skin that is cast by a snake; that which comes away from a malignant sore; *v.i.*, to come away from the skin; to cast off a skin.
sloughed, *p.p.*, slough.
slough'ing, *pr.p.*, slough.
slough'y, *adj.*, miry.
slough'y, *adj.*, sloughing; tending to slough.
slov'en, *n.*, a careless, untidy person.
slov'enliness, *n.*, the quality of being slovenly.
slov'enly, *adj.*, carelessly untidy.
slow, *adj.*, not quick; behind in point of time; dull.
slow'ly, *adv.*, not quickly.
slow'ness, *n.*, the quality of being slow.
slow'-worm, *n.*, the blind-worm.
slub, *v.t.*, to give (wool) a slight twist; *n.*, wool so twisted.
slub'ber, *v.t.* and *n.*, *i.q.* slub.
slub'bered, *p.p.*, slubber.
slub'bering, *pr.p.*, slubber.
sludge, *n.*, slush.
slue, *v.t.* and *i.*, to turn or twist round.
slued, *p.p.*, slue.
slug, *n.*, a kind of snail without a shell; a form of bullet; *i.q.* sluggard.
slug'gard, *n.*, one who loves lying abed; a lazy fellow.
slug'gish, *adj.*, torpid; inert, slow.
slug'gishly, *adv.*, in a sluggish way.
slug'gishness, *n.*, laziness, idleness, inactivity.
sluice, *n.*, a barrier in a river, etc., controlling the water's flow; the rush of water through a flood-gate; *v.t.*, to throw water over oneself.
slui'cy, *adj.*, rushing out like water from a sluice.
slu'ing, *pr.p.*, slue.
slum, *n.*, a wretchedly poor quarter in a town; *v.i.*, to visit the slums.
slum'ber, *n.*, sleep; *v.i.*, to sleep; to doze.
slum'bered, *p.p.*, slumber.
slum'berer, *n.*, one who slumbers.
slum'bering, *pr.p.*, slumber.
slum'berous, *adj.*, inducing sleep; sleeping; quiet.
slum'ming, *pr.p.*, slum.
slump, *n.*, a rapid fall in prices, etc.; a fall through a coating of ice; *v.i.*, to sink through ice or into mud; to fall in value; to fail.
slung, *p.t.* and *p.*, sling.
slunk, *p.p.*, slink.
slur, *n.*, a disparaging remark; stigma; a curve over two or more musical notes which are to be sung to the same syllable or played without a break; *v.t.*, to disparage; to speak or write indistinctly; to do anything carelessly; to sing with a slur.
slurred, *p.p.*, slur.
slur'ring, *pr.p.*, slur.
slush, *n.*, wet snow; soft mud.
slush'y, *adj.*, full of slush.
slut, *n.*, an untidy, dirty girl or woman; a slattern.
slut'tish, *adj.*, inclined to be a slattern.
slut'tishly, *adv.*, in a slatternly way.
sly, *adj.*, cunning, hypocritical, playful.
sly'-boots, *n.*, a sly person or animal.
sly'ly, *adv.*, in a sly way.
sly'ness, *n.*, the quality of being sly.
smack, *v.t.*, to hit with the hand; to make a cracking noise with; to part the lips with an explosive noise; *v.i.*, to have a flavour; *n.*, a blow with the hands; a noise made with the lips; a flavour or taste; a small fishing-boat; *adv.*, clean, outright; with a smacking noise.
smacked, *p.p.*, smack.
smack'ing, *pr.p.*, smack; *n.*, a smack or succession of smacks.
small, *adj.*, not large; of little size; amount, quantity, etc.; weak; mild, humble; *n.*, a small part, esp. of the back; *adv.*, in a low tone.
small'age, *n.*, wild celery.
small'-arms, *n. pl.*, military weapons of the smaller kind, as rifles, etc.
small'er, *adj.*, *comp.* of small.
small'est, *adj.*, *super.* of small.
small'ness, *n.*, the quality of being small.

small'pox, *n.*, a virulent and highly infectious disease.

smalt, *n.*, glass of a deep cobalt-blue colour; when pulverized, it is used for a pigment.

smarag'dine, *adj.*, of emerald green.

smart, *adj.*, alert; trim; fashionably attired; sharp; *v.t.*, to feel an acute pain, generally superficial; to induce a feeling of pain; *n.*, an acute feeling of pain, physical or mental.

smart'ed, *p.p.*, smart.

smart'en, *v.t.*, to brisk up; improve the appearance of.

smart'ened, *p.p.*, smarten.

smart'ening, *pr.p.*, smarten.

smart'er, *adj.*, *comp.* of smart.

smart'est, *adj.*, *super.* of smart.

smart'ing, *pr.p.*, smart.

smart'ly, *adv.*, in a smart way.

smart'-money, *n.*, exemplary legal damages.

smart'ness, *n.*, the quality or state of being smart.

smash, *v.t.*, to break in pieces; to hit downward with violence; *v.i.*, to become bankrupt; to fall in pieces; *n.*, a breaking to pieces; a great fall; bankruptcy.

smashed, *p.p.*, smash.

smash'er, *n.*, one who smashes; a smashing or complete blow.

smash'ing, *pr.p.*, smash.

smat'ter, *v.t.*, to show only a superficial knowledge of; *v.i.*, to have a smattering; *n.*, scanty and superficial knowledge.

smat'tered, *p.p.*, smatter.

smat'terer, *n.*, one who has a superficial knowledge.

smat'tering, *pr.p.*, smatter; *n.*, a slight superficial knowledge.

smear, *v.t.*, to daub with some sticky or greasy substance; to mark with a stain, smudge, or blot; *n.*, a daub, stain, spot.

smeared, *p.p.*, smear.

smear'ing, *pr.p.*, smear.

smear'y, *adj.*, smeared

smec'tite, *n.*, a clay used for cleaning purposes.

smell, *n.*, the nasal sense; an odour; *v.t.*, to perceive an odour; *v.i.*, to emit an odour.

smelled, *p.p.*, smell.

smell'er, *n.*, one who, or that which, smells; the nose (*slang*).

smell'ing, *pr.p.*, smell; *adj.*, odoriferous.

smell'ing-bottle, *n.*, a bottle containing smelling-salts.

smell'ing-salts, *n.*, an olfactory stimulant made of ammonium carbonate and scented.

smell'-less, *adj.*, inodorous.

smelt, *n.*, extract from ore; a small edible fish; *p.p.*, smell; *v.t.*, to extract metal from ore.

smelt'ed, *p.p.*, smelt.

smelt'er, *n.*, one who works at smelting.

smelt'ery, *n.*, a factory where metal is extracted from ore by roasting.

smelt'ing, *pr.p.*, smelt; *n.*, the process of smelting.

smew, *n.*, a variety of merganser.

smi'lax, *n.*, a climbing shrub of the Liliaceae.

smile, *n.*, a kind, pleased, or contemptuous expression on the face; *v.i.*, to show pleasure, kindness, or contempt with a facial expression; to be favourable; to be auspicious.

smiled, *p.p.*, smile.

smi'ler, *n.*, one who smiles.

smi'ling, *pr.p.*, smile; *adj.*, favourable, auspicious.

smi'lingly, *adv.*, with a pleased expression.

smirch, *v.t.*, to stain, pollute, defame.

smirched, *p.p.*, smirch.

smirch'ing, *pr.p.*, smirch.

smirk, *v.i.*, to smile in a silly way; to simper.

smirked, *p.p.*, smirk.

smirk'ing, *pr.p.*, smirk.

smit, an obsolete *p.p.* of smite.

smite, *v.t.*, to strike, hit; *n.*, a blow; a bit.

smi'ter, *n.*, one who smites.

smith, *n.*, one who works in metals, esp. iron.

smithereens', *n. pl.*, fragments.

smith'ery, *n.*, the smith's art.

smith'ing, *n.*, *i.q.* smithery.

smith'y, *n.*, a blacksmith's shop; a forge.

smi'ting, *pr.p.*, smite.

smit'ten, *p.p.*, smite.

smock, *n.*, a shift; a smock-frock; an insertion like the collar of a smock-frock; *v.t.*, to dress in a smock; to gather with pleats.

smock'-frock, *n.*, an old-fashioned rustic outer garment.

smoke, *n.*, volatilized product of combustion; vapour; fume; the act of smoking; a cigarette or cigar; *v.t.*, to cure by smoking; to blacken with smoke; to inhale smoke from a pipe, a cigar, or a cigarette; *v.i.*, to emit smoke; to perform the act of smoking; to rage.

smoked, *p.p.*, smoke; *adj.*, smoke-cured.

smoke'less, *adj.*, free from smoke.

smo'ker, *n.*, one who, or that which, smokes.

smo'kier, *adj., comp.* of smoky.

smo'kiest, *adj., super.* of smoky.

smo'kily, *adv.,* in a smoky way.

smo'kiness, *n.,* the state or quality of being smoky.

smo'king, *pr.p.,* smoke; *n.,* the act of a smoker.

smo'ky, *adj.,* full of, resembling, smoke; smoke-stained.

smooth, *adj.,* with even, not rough, surface; easy, without obstructions; easily flowing; hairless; not aspirated; *v.t.,* to remove roughness, obstructions, difficulties, etc.

smoothed, *p.p.,* smooth.

smooth'er, *adj., comp.* of smooth.

smooth'est, *adj., super.* of smooth.

smooth'-faced, *adj.,* beardless; hypocritical.

smooth'ing, *pr.p.,* smooth.

smooth'ly, *adv.,* in a smooth way.

smooth'ness, *n.,* the state or quality of being smooth.

smooth'-spoken, *adj.,* plausible.

smorzan'do, *adv.,* decreasing in tone.

smorza'to, *adv., i.q.* smorzando.

smote, *p.t.,* smite.

smoth'er, *v.t.,* to suffocate; to overwhelm; cover up; conceal; *n.,* stifling dust; the state of being smothered.

smoth'ered, *p.p.,* smother.

smoth'ering, *pr.p.,* smother; *adj.,* suffocating.

smoul'der, *v.i.,* to burn slowly without flame; to burn inwardly; to exist but not to be outwardly perceived.

smoul'dered, *p.p.,* smoulder.

smoul'dering, *pr.p.,* smoulder.

smoul'dry, *adj.,* smouldering.

smudge, *n.,* an ugly stain; a smear; *v.t.,* to draw a smudge over; *v.i.,* to show smears.

smudged, *p.p.,* smudge

smudg'ing, *pr.p.,* smudge.

smug, *adj.,* affectedly correct; self-satisfied; *n.,* an outsider (*colloq.*); a person not interested in games and society doings.

smug'gle, *v.t.,* to convey secretly; to import or export goods without paying duty.

smug'gled, *p.p.,* smuggle.

smug'gler, *n.,* one who smuggles.

smug'gling, *pr.p.,* smuggle; *n.,* the practices of a smuggler.

smut, *n.,* a sooty stain; a floating particle of soot; a disease in corn and other plants; filthy talk; *v.t.,* to stain with soot; to induce the disease of smut; *v.i.,* to be infected with smut.

smutch, *v.t.,* to soil; *n.,* a stain; defilement.

smutched, *p.p.,* smutch.

smutch'ing, *pr.p.,* smutch.

smut'ted, *p.p.,* smut.

smut'tily, *adv.,* in a smutty way.

smut'tiness, *n.,* the state or quality of being smutty.

smut'ting, *pr.p.,* smut.

smut'ty, *adj.,* stained or infected with smut; lewd.

snack, *n.,* a small portion of food; a hasty luncheon; a small fives-ball.

snaf'fle, *n.,* a light bridle without a curb.

snaf'fled, *adj.,* having a snaffle bit.

snag, *n.,* a jagged projection from a tree-stump or a broken tooth; a sunken piece of timber just below the surface of water and dangerous to boats.

snag'gy, *adj.,* full of, resembling, snags.

snail, *n.,* a slimy gasteropod mollusc.

snail'-like, *adj.,* like a snail.

snail'-shell, *n.,* the shell of a snail.

snake, *n.,* a serpent; any person or thing resembling a snake; *v.i.,* to steal along in snake-like fashion.

snake'-root, *n.,* the name for some medicinal plants useful in cases of snake-bite.

snake'-stone, *n.,* ammonite.

snake'-wood, *n.,* a climbing plant, from the root of which is derived a medicine for snake-bite.

sna'kish, *adj.,* like a snake.

sna'ky, *adj., i.q.* snakish; infested with snakes.

snap, *v.t.,* to bite suddenly and with a sound; to break with a jerk; to cut off short; *v.i.,* to make a short crackling sound; to come apart with a short, sharp sound; to rap out a cross word; *n.,* an act of biting or attempting to bite; a touch of frost; a breaking; vigorous style of writing; *adj.,* done off-hand.

snap'dragon, *n.,* an antirrhinum; a Christmas game.

snapped, *p.p.,* snap.

snap'per, *n.,* one who, or that which, snaps; a fish of that name.

snap'ping, *pr.p.,* snap.

snap'pish, *adj.,* inclined to be cross or peevish.

snap'pishly, *adv.,* in a snappish way.

snap'-shot, *n.,* a random shot; an instantaneous photograph; *v.t.,* to photograph instantaneously.

snap'py, *adj.*, *i.q.* snappish.

snapt, *p.p.*, snap.

snare, *v.t.*, to trap; to entangle; *n.*, a trap, a gin.

snared, *p.p.*, snare.

sna'rer, *n.*, one who snares.

sna'ring, *pr.p.*, snare.

snarl, *v.i.*, to growl as a dog does; to speak harshly or angrily; *v.t.*, to say in harsh tones; *n.*, the angry growl of a dog; also *v.t.* to entangle; to emboss; *v.i.*, to become entangled; *n.*, tangled thread, hair, etc.; a knot in timber.

snarled, *p.p.*, snarl.

snarl'er, *n.*, one who snarls.

snarl'ing, *pr.p.*, snarl.

sna'ry, *adj.*, entangling.

snatch, *v.t.*, to seize quickly or rudely; *n.*, the act of snatching; a fragment; a short spell; a short fragment of song or speech.

snatched, *p.p.*, snatch.

snatch'er, *n.*, one who snatches.

snatch'ing, *pr.p.*, snatch.

snatch'ingly, *adv.*, in a snatching way.

snath, *n.*, a scythe-handle.

sneak, *v.t.*, to steal (*colloq.*); *v.i.*, to go about stealthily; to act in an underhand way; to tell tales (*colloq.*); *n.*, a furtive person; a tell-tale; a daisy-cutter.

sneaked, *p.p.*, sneak.

sneak'er, *n.*, one who sneaks.

sneak'ier, *adj.*, *comp.* of sneaky.

sneak'iest, *adj.*, *super.* of sneaky.

sneak'ing, *pr.p.*, sneak.

sneak'ingly, *adv.*, in a sneaking way.

sneak'y, *adj.*, like a sneak.

sneer, *v.i.*, to express contempt in the face or in speech; to deride; *n.*, a contemptuous look or word.

sneered, *p.p.*, sneer.

sneer'er, *n.*, one who sneers.

sneer'ing, *pr.p.*, sneer.

sneer'ingly, *adv.*, in a sneering way.

sneeze, *v.i.*, to emit a spasmodic noise from mouth or nostrils; *n.*, the sound of sneezing.

sneezed, *p.p.*, sneeze.

sneez'ing, *pr.p.*, sneeze.

snell, *adj.*, cold; harsh (*Scot.*).

snick, *v.t.*, to notch; cut a small notch in; to hit (a cricket ball) with a slight deflection; *n.*, a notch; a slightly deflected hit.

snick'er, *v.i.*, *i.q.* snigger.

snick'ered, *p.p.*, snicker.

snick'ering, *pr.p.*, snicker.

snick'ersnee, *n.*, a comic word for a knife.

sniff, *v.t.* and *i.*, to draw into the nostrils; to make a contemptuous sound through the nostrils; *n.*, an expression of contempt; a slight smell; the act of sniffing.

sniffed, *p.p.*, sniff.

sniff'ing, *pr.p.*, sniff.

snif'fle, *v.i.*, *i.q.* snuffle.

snig'ger, *v.i.*, to laugh in a silly way or sly way; *n.*, a silly or sly laugh.

snig'gered, *p.p.*, snigger.

snig'gering, *pr.p.*, snigger.

snig'gle, *v.i.*, to fish for eels by baiting their hiding-holes.

snig'gled, *p.p.*, sniggle

snig'gling, *pr.p.*, sniggle.

snip, *v.t.*, to cut off quickly; *n.*, a cut with scissors; a small portion.

snipe, *n.*, a bird of the fens; *v.t.*, to kill one by one (said of a sharpshooter).

snipped, *p.p.*, snip.

snip'pet, *n.*, a small piece or share.

snip'ping, *pr.p.*, snip.

sniv'el, *v.i.*, to run at the nose; to cry from fear or misery; *n.*, discharge from the nose; cant, humbug.

sniv'el(l)ed, *p.p.* snivel

sniv'el(l)er, *n.*, one who snivels.

sniv'el(l)ing, *pr.p.*, snivel.

snob, *n.*, one who gives himself airs for his supposed social distinction; one who affects to be of higher standing than he is; a journeyman shoemaker.

snob'bery, *n.*, the conduct of a snob.

snob'bish, *adj.*, like a snob.

snob'bishly, *adv.*, in a snobbish way.

snood, *n.*, a hair-ribbon.

snooze, *v.i.*, to sleep lightly and for a short spell; to nap; *n.*, a nap.

snore, *v.i.*, to breathe heavily and stertorously in sleep; *n.*, a stertorous noise.

snored, *p.p.*, snore.

snor'er, *n.*, one who snores.

snor'ing, *pr.p.*, snore; *n.*, the act of snoring.

snort, *v.i.*, to make a sound through the nostrils, expressing anger, contempt, surprise, etc.; *n.*, the sound itself.

snort'ed, *p.p.*, snort.

snort'er, *n.*, one who snorts.

snort'ing, *pr.p.*, snort.

snot'ters, *n.*, a turkey-cock's wattles.

snout, *n.*, a beast's nose.

snow, *n.*, frozen vapour in the air; *v.i.*, to come down as snow.

snow'ball, *n.*, snow packed into a ball; *v.t.*, to pelt with snowballs.

snow'bird, *n.*, the snow-bunting.

snow'blind, *adj.*, made blind by the snow.

snow'blindness, *n.*, the state of being snowblind.

snow'-drift, *n.*, a drift of snow.

snow'-drop, *n.*, an early white flower.

snowed, *p.p.*, snow.

snow'flake, *n.*, a flake of snow.

snow'ing, *pr.p.*, snow.

snow'line, *n.*, the height at which snow becomes perpetual.

snow'-shoe, *n.*, a long shoe for travelling over snow.

snow'-slip, *n.*, an avalanche.

snow'-storm, *n.*, a storm accompanied by snow.

snow'-white, *adj.*, white as snow.

snow'y, *adj.*, like snow; full of, covered with, snow.

snub, *v.t.*, to put a person down with a slight; *n.*, an intentional slight; a reproof.

snubbed, *p.p.*, snub.

snub'bing, *pr.p.*, snub *n.*, a reprimand.

snuff, *v.t.*, to draw up into the nose; to smell; to cut the wick of a candle; *n.*, tobacco in the form of powder; burnt wick.

snuff'-box, *n.*, a box to hold snuff.

snuffed, *p.p.*, snuff.

snuff'er, *n.*, a person addicted to snuff-taking.

snuff'ers, *n. pl.*, a scissors-like instrument for snuffing a candle.

snuff'er-tray, *n.*, a small tray to hold the snuffers.

snuff'ing, *pr.p.*, snuff; *n.*, snuff-taking.

snuf'fle, *v.i.*, to breathe or speak through the nose; *n.*, the noise of breathing through the nose; a nasal way of speaking; cant.

snuf'fled, *p.p.*, snuffle.

snuf'fles, *n. pl.*, an attack of snuffling.

snuf'fling, *pr.p.*, snuffle.

snuff'-taker, *n.*, *i.q.* snuffer.

snuff'y, *adj.*, covered or stained with snuff.

snug, *adj.*, concealed; cosy; comfortable; *v.i.*, to snuggle.

snugged, *p.p.*, snug.

snug'gery, *n.*, a cosy room.

snug'ging, *pr.p.*, snug.

snug'gle, *v.i.*, to lie close; *v.t.*, to clasp close for warmth.

snug'gled, *p.p.*, snuggle.

snug'gling, *pr.p.*, snuggle.

snug'ly, *adv.*, cosily.

so, *adv.*, thus; in such way or degree; thereabouts; on that condition; *conj.*, provided that; *interj.*, stay there; stop.

soak, *v.t.*, to make to absorb moisture; to steep; *v.i.*, to become wet through; to drink to excess.

soak'age, *n.*, the extent of soaking.

soaked, *p.p.*, soak.

soak'er, *n.*, a hard drinker (*colloq.*).

soak'ing, *pr.p.*, soak.

soap, *n.*, a manufactured article from fats and alkali; *v.t.*, to cleanse with soap; to cajole.

soap'-bubble, *n.*, a bubble produced by blowing through soapy water.

soaped, *p.p.*, soap.

soap'ier, *adj.*, *comp.* of soapy.

soap'iest, *adj.*, *super.* of soapy.

soap'ing, *pr.p.*, soap.

soap'-stone, *n.*, steatite.

soap'-suds, *n. pl.*, the scum of soapy water.

soap'wort, *n.*, a perennial, juice from the roots of which produces a lather.

soap'y, *adj.*, like soap; covered with soap; softly flattering.

soar, *v.i.*, to rise or fly upwards; *n.*, a flight.

soared, *p.p.*, soar.

soar'ing, *pr.p.*, soar.

sob, *v.i.*, to utter a sound of grief convulsively with weeping; *n.*, the sound.

sobbed, *p.p.*, sob.

sob'bing, *pr.p.*, sob.

so'ber, *adj.*, not given to drunkenness; grave; earnest; quiet; *v.t.*, to make sober; *v.i.* to become sober.

so'bered, *p.p.*, sober.

so'bering, *pr.p.*, sober.

so'berly, *adv.*, sedately; in a sober way.

so'berness, *n.*, the state of being sober.

sobri'ety, *n.*, abstinence from intemperance; seriousness.

so'briquet, *n.*, a nickname (*Fr.*).

soc, *n.*, feudal tenant-right; the lord of the manor's power of holding a court. Also *soke*.

soc'age, *n.*, a feudal form of tenure.

so'-called, *adj.*, pretended; not as in fact.

sociabil'ity, *n.*, the quality of being sociable.

so'ciable, *adj.*, fond of company; agreeable; friendly; *n.*, a friendly party; a vehicle for two.

so'ciably, *adv.*, in a sociable way.

so'cial, *adj.*, pert. to society; sociable; convivial.

so'cialism, *n.*, the principles of socialists, who advocate community of property and co-operation of labour.

so'cialist, *n.*, an advocate of community of property and co-operation of labour.

socialist'ic, *adj.*, pert. to socialists and socialism.

social'ity, *n.*, conviviality; the state or quality of being social.

so'cialize, *v.t.*, to bring under socialistic conditions.

so'cialized, *p.p.*, socialize.

so'cializing, *pr.p.*, socialize.

so'cially, *adv.*, in a social way; in rel. to society.

soci'ety, *n.*, company; fraternity; people collectively; an association for a common purpose and with common interests; people collectively of the higher, wealthier, and more educated class.

Socin'ian, *adj.*, pert. to Socinus, a 16th cent. writer, who advocated Unitarianism.

Socin'ianism, *n.*, the doctrines of Socinus; Unitarianism.

sociolog'ical, *adj.*, pert. to sociology.

sociol'ogist, *n.*, a student of sociology.

sociol'ogy, *n.*, the study of social phenomena; social science.

sock, *n.*, originally a low shoe, worn by the players in a classical comedy; a shortened stocking; a removable lining to a boot.

sock'et, *n.*, a tube-like arrangement into which a bolt, bar, etc., fits.

so'cle, *n.*, a low plinth

soc'man, *n.*, one whose tenure is by socage.

Soc'otrine, *adj.*, pert. to Socotra, an island E. of Africa.

Socrat'ic, *adj.*, pert. to Socrates and his philosophy.

Socrat'ical, *adj.*, *i.q.* Socratic.

Socrat'ically, *adv.*, after the manner of Socrates.

Soc'ratism, *n.*, the method of Socrates.

sod, *n.*, turf; *v.t.*, to put turf on.

so'da, *n.*, sodium oxide.

sodal'ity, *n.*, a brotherhood, company.

so'da-water, *n.*, water impregnated with bicarbonate of soda and aerated.

sod'ded, *p.p.*, sod.

sod'den, *adj.*, boiled; soaked with wet; flabby.

sod'ding, *pr.p.*, sod.

sod'dy, *adj.*, turfy.

so'dium, *n.*, a metallic element.

soev'er, a separable suffix giving an indefinite and general meaning to adjectives, adverbs, and relative pronouns.

so'fa, *n.*, a kind of couch.

sof'fit, *n.*, the under-surface of an arch, cornice, etc.

sof'ism, *n.*, the doctrines of the Sofis or dervishes. Also *Sufism.*

soft, *adj.*, not hard; yielding to pressure; smooth; subdued; weak-headed; *adv.*, gently.

sof'ten, *v.t.*, to make soft; *v.i.*, to become soft.

sof'tened, *p.p.*, soft.

sof'tener, *n.*, one who, that which, softens.

sof'tening, *pr.p.*, soften.

soft'ly, *adv.*, in a soft way.

soft'ness, *n.*, the state or quality of being soft.

sog'gy, *adj.*, wet.

soho', *interj.*, used by huntsmen.

soi-disant', *adj.*, pretended; self-styled.

soil, *n.*, surface earth; land; stain; impurity; *v.t.*, to stain, defile, damage; *v.i.*, to become soiled.

soiled, *p.p.*, soil.

soil'ing, *pr.p.*, soil.

soirée', *n.*, an evening entertainment (*Fr.*).

soj'ourn, *n.*, a visit, stay; *v.i.* to stay in a place for a while.

soj'ourned, *p.p.*, sojourn.

soj'ourner, *pr.p.*, a visitor to a place.

soj'ourning, *pr.p.*, sojourn.

soke, *i.q.* soc.

so'ken, *n.*, territory held in socage.

Sol, *n.*, the Sun (*Lat.*); the fifth note in the diatonic scale (*mus.*)

so'la, *adj.*, fem. of solus, "alone" (*Lat.*); *n.*, the hat-plant of India and its pith; a sun-helmet made of the pith.

sol'ace, *n.*, comfort, consolation; *v.t.*, to comfort, console.

sol'aced, *p.p.*, solace.

sol'acement, *n.*, *i.q.* solace.

sol'acing, *pr.p.*, solace.

Solana'ceae, *n. pl.*, plants of the nightshade family.

solana'ceous, *adj.*, pert. to the Solanaceae.

solan'der, *n.*, a case for papers, documents, drawings, etc.

so'lan-goose, *n.*, the gannet.

sol'anine, *n.*, a poisonous compound derived from the solanum.

sola'no, *n.*, a hot wind felt in the Mediterranean.

Sola'num, *n.*, a plant genus including the nightshade and the potato.

so'lar, *adj.*, pert. to the sun; *n.*, the dwelling-room in a mediaeval house.

sola'rium, *n.*, *i.q.* solar; a sun-bath.

solariza'tion, *n.*, the act or effect of solarizing.

so'larize, *v.t.*, to expose too long to the sun's light.

so'larized, *p.p.*, solarize.

so'larizing, *pr.p.*, solarize.

sola'tium, *n.*, compensation (*Lat.*).

sold, *p.p.*, sell.

sol'dan, *n.*, Sultan.

sol'der, *n.*, a fusible cement for joining metal; *v.t.*, to join metal.

sol'dered, *p.p.*, solder.

sol'derer, *n.*, one who solders.

sol'dering, *pr.p.*, solder

sol'dier, *n.*, a fighting man; a private; *v.i.*, to act as a soldier.

sol'diering, *pr.p.*, soldier; *n.*, the profession of arms.

sol'dierly, *adj.*, like a true soldier.

sol'diery, *n.*, soldiers collectively.

sole, *n.*, a flat fish; the bottom of the foot or shoe; *v.t.*, to put a sole on (a shoe); *adj.*, alone; single.

sol'ecism, *n.*, an offence against the rules of a language; an impropriety.

sol'ecist, *n.*, one who commits a solecism.

solecis'tic, *adj.*, of the nature of a solecism.

sol'ecize, *v.i.*, to commit a solecism.

soled, *p.p.*, sole.

sole'ly, *adv.*, singly; by oneself, alone.

sol'emn, *adj.*, ceremonial; grave; awful; reverential.

sol'emness, *n.*, the quality of being solemn.

solem'nity, *n.*, *i.q.* solemness; a solemn rite.

solemniza'tion, *n.*, the act of solemnizing.

sol'emnize, *v.t.*, to give solemnity to; to perform (a rite, as marriage).

sol'emnized, *p.p.*, solemnize.

sol'emnizer, *n*, one who solemnizes.

sol'emnizing, *pr.p.*, solemnize.

sol'emnly, *adv.*, with solemnity.

so'len, *n.*, the razor-shell mollusc.

so'lenite, *n.*, a fossil solen.

so'lenoid, *adj.*, like a solen.

sole'noid, *n.*, a cylindrical wire magnet.

sol'-fa, *n.*, the name for the gamut or diatonic scale; *v.i.*, to sing the scale.

sol'-faing, *pr.p.*, sol-fa.

solfata'ria, *n.*, a sulphur mine (*Ital.*).

solfata'ra, *n.*, a vent in a volcano (*Ital.*).

solic'it, *v.t.*, to importune, beg.

solic'itant, *adj.*, importuning.

solicita'tion, *n.*, the act of soliciting.

solic'ited, *p.p.*, solicit.

solic'iting, *pr.p.*, solicit.

solic'itor, *n.*, a member of the legal profession who acts on one's behalf in the courts.

solic'itor-gen'eral, *n.*, the second in rank of the law officers of the Crown.

solic'itous, *adj.*, concerned for; anxious.

solic'itously, *adv.*, concernedly; anxiously.

solic'itude, *n.*, concern; anxiety.

sol'id, *adj.*, substantial; firm; compact; the opposite to hollow; unanimous; *n.*, a body having its particles closely compacted.

solidar'ity, *n.*, community of interests; *esprit de corps.*

solidifica'tion, *n.*, the act or effect of solidifying.

solid'ified, *p.p.*, solidify.

solid'ify, *v.t.*, to make solid; *v.i.*, to become solid.

solid'ifying, *pr.p.*, solidify.

sol'idism, *n.*, the theory of the solidists.

sol'idist, *n.*, one who believes in the theory that diseases are due to morbid alterations in the solid parts of the system.

solid'ity, *n.*, the state or quality of being solid.

sol'idly, *adv.*, in a solid way.

solidun'gulous, *adj.*, having the hoof solid.

solifid'ian, *adj.*, rel. to the belief that faith only (*i.e.*, without works) suffices for salvation.

solifid'ianism, *n.*, the belief in faith alone, without works.

solil'oquize, *v.i.*, to speak in soliloquy.

solil'oquized, *p.p.*, soliloquize.

solil'oquizing, *pr.p.*, soliloquize.

solil'oquy, *n.*, speaking to oneself.

sol'iped, *adj.*, *i.q.* solidungulate.

solip'edous, *adj.*, *i.q.* soliped.

sol'ipsism, *n.*, the theory that the universe exists only in a person's mind.

solitaire', *n.*, a button; a single stone in its setting; a solo game.

solita'rian, *n.*, a recluse.

sol'itarily, *adv.*, in a solitary way.

sol'itariness, *n.*, the state of being solitary.

sol'itary, *adj.*, lonely, single; *n.*, a recluse.

sol'itude, *n.*, loneliness; remoteness from habitations.

soliv'agant, *adj.*, wandering solitary.

sol'mizate, *v.i.*, to sing the scale with the use of syllables as the names of the notes; to sol-fa.

solmiza'tion, *n.*, the use of syllables as the names of the notes in the musical scale.

so'lo, *n.*, music performed by a single player or singer, or for a single instrument.

so'loist, *n.*, one who performs a solo.

Solomon's-seal', *n.*, a plant so named.

sol'stice, *n.*, one of the two half-yearly periods when the sun seems to pause after reaching its farthest distance N. and S. of the equator (these occur about June 21 and Dec. 22); one of the two points in the ecliptic which the sun reaches at the time of solstice.

solsti'tial, *adj.*, pert. to the solstices.

solubil'ity, *n.*, the state or quality of being soluble.

sol'uble, *adj.*, able to be solved or dissolved.

so'lus, *adj.*, alone (*Lat.*).

solute', *adj.*, separated.

solu'tion, *n.*, the act or effect of solving or dissolving.

solvabil'ity, *n.*, the quality of being solvable.

solv'able, *adj.*, capable of solution.

solve, *v.t.*, to work out (a problem or puzzle); to explain.

solved, *p.p.*, solve.

solv'ency, *n.*, the state of being solvent.

solv'end, *n.*, something to be solved.

solv'ent, *adj.*, able to pay all debts; able to dissolve; *n.*, an agent that dissolves another substance.

solv'er, *n.*, one who solves.

solv'ing, *pr.p.*, solve.

somatol'ogy, *n.*, the study of the properties of material bodies.

somatot'omy, *n.*, dissection of bodies.

som'bre, *adj.*, dark, lowering, gloomy.

som'breness, *n.*, the state or quality of being sombre.

som'brous, *adj.*, gloomy.

some, a suffix indicating degree; *adj.*, to a certain extent; describing without defining a number, amount, extent, etc.; approximately.

some'body, *n.*, someone; an important person.

some'how, *adv.*, in some way or other.

some'one, *n.*, *i.q.* somebody.

som'ersault, *n.*, a turning head over heels; *v.i.*, to do a somersault.

som'erset, *n.* and *v.i.*, *i.q.* somersault; also *n.*, a padded saddle.

some'thing, *n.*, a thing alluded to but not specified; a part; *adv.*, somewhat; to a certain extent.

some'time, *adv.*, at one time or another; once upon a time.

some'times, *adv.*, at times; occasionally.

some'what, *adv.*, to some extent.

some'where, *adv.*, in some place or other.

some'while, *adv.*, at some time or other; formerly.

so'mite, *n.*, a segment of a vertebrate.

somnambulate, *v.i.*, to walk in sleep.

somnambula'tion, *n.*, sleep-walking.

somnam'bulator, *n.*, *i.q.* somnambulist.

somnam'bulism, *n.*, *i.q.* somnambulation.

somnam'bulist, *n.*, a sleep-walker.

somnif'erous, *adj.*, producing sleep.

somnif'ic, *adj.*, *i.q.* somniferous.

somnil'oquence, *n.*, talking in sleep.

somnil'oquism, *n.*, *i.q.* somniloquence.

somnil'oquist, *n.*, a talker in sleep.

somnip'athy, *n.*, sleep produced by hypnotism.

som'nolence, *n.*, sleepiness.

som'nolency, *n.*, *i.q.* somnolence.

som'nolent, *adj.*, sleepy, drowsy.

son, *n.*, male offspring or descendant.

so'nance, *n.*, sounding, resonance.

so'nant, *adj.*, sounding.

sona'ta, *n.*, a musical composition, of a particular structure, performed on a solo instrument.

sonati'na, *n.*, a simpler form of the sonata.

son'cy, *adj.*, buxom, plump (*Scot.*); lucky. Also *sonsy*.

song, *n.*, that which is sung or intended for singing; verse; a lyric; a bird's vocal utterance; a bagatelle.

song'ster, *n.*, a singer, esp. a bird.

song'stress, *n.*, fem. of songster.

sonif'erous, *adj.*, producing a sound; conducting sound.

son'-in-law, *n.*, the husband of one's daughter.

son'net, *n.*, a lyrical composition of fourteen lines, conforming to several different types; *v.i.*, to write sonnets.

sonneteer', *n.*, a writer of sonnets.

son'neting, *n.*, the writing of sonnets; *pr.p.*, sonnet.

Son'nite, *adj.*, rel. to the Sunnites; *n.*, an orthodox Mohammedan who accepts tradition (Sunna) as well as the Koran.

sonom'eter, *n.*, an instrument for ascertaining sound-values, or for testing the hearing capacity.

sonorif'ic, *adj.*, producing sound.

sono'rous, *adj.*, resounding; clearly audible; deep.

sono'rously, *adv.*, clearly, loudly.

son'ship, *n.*, the relation of a son to a father.

Soo'der, *n.*, *i.q.* Sudra.

Soo'dra, *n.*, *i.q.* Sudra.

soo'fee, *n.*, *i.q.* sufi.

soo'feeism, *n.*, *i.q.* sufism.

soon, *adv.*, in a short time hence; shortly; immediately.

soon'er, *adv.*, more quickly; in preference.

soot, *n.*, a product of coal combustion; *v.t.*, to cover with soot.

soot'ed, *p.p.*, soot.

sooth, *n.*, truth.

soothe, *v.t.*, to stroke, calm, allay; blandish.

soothed, *p.p.*, soothe.

sooth'er, *n.*, one who, or that which, soothes.

sooth'ing, *pr.p.*, soothe; *adj.*, comforting.

sooth'ingly, *adv.*, in a soothing way; with soothing effect.

sooth'say, *v.i.*, to prognosticate.

sooth'sayer, *n.*, a prophet, foreteller.

sooth'saying, *pr.p.*, soothsay; *n.*, the profession of a soothsayer.

soot'ier, *adj.*, *comp.* of sooty.

soot'iest, *adj.*, *super.* of sooty.

soot'iness, *n.*, the state or quality of being sooty.

soot'y, *adj.*, full of, covered with, soot.

sop, *n.*, something dipped and soaked in broth, etc.; something intended to appease; *v.t.*, to dip into broth; to absorb.

soph, *n.*, an abbreviation of sophister and sophomore.

so'phi, *n.*, *i.q.* sufi.

soph'ism, *n.*, a false argument; a fallacy.

soph'ist, *n.*, an ancient Greek teacher of philosophy and rhetoric. The sophists were noted for their specious and fallacious arguments; hence a sophist now means a false reasoner.

soph'ister, *n.*, a second or third year man at Cambridge.

sophis'tic, *adj.*, pert. to sophists; fallacious.

sophis'tical, *adj.*, *i.q.* sophistic.

sophis'ticate, *v.t.*, to obscure with sophistry; to mislead; to adulterate.

sophis'ticated, *p.p.*, sophisticate.

sophis'ticating, *pr.p.*, sophisticate.

sophistica'tion, *n.*, the state or quality of being sophisticated.

sophis'ticator, *n.*, one who indulges in sophistry.

soph'istry, *n.*, the practices of sophists; deception, quibbling; perverted casuistry.

soph'omore, *n.*, a second-year man in an American University.

sophomor'ic, *adj.*, pert. to a sophomore; callow.

soporif'erous, *adj.*, producing sleep.

soporif'ic, *adj.*, *i.q.* soporiferous; *n.*, an anodyne producing sleep.

so'porous, *adj.*, *i.q.* soporiferous.

sopped, *p.p.*, sop.

sop'ping, *pr.p.*, sop; *adj.*, wet through.

sopra'nist, *n.*, a soprano vocalist.

sopra'no, *n.*, the highest treble voice; one who sings soprano.

sorb, *n.*, the service-tree or its fruit.

Sor'bet, *n.*, water-ice flavoured (*Fr.*).

Sorbonne', *n.*, originally, the theological faculty in the University of Paris, and named after its founder, Robert de Sorbon, a 13th cent. theologian; now Richelieu's building, in which lectures are given by learned societies.

sor'cerer, *n.*, one who uses magic, enchantments, etc.

sor'ceress, *n.*, fem. of sorcerer.

sor'cerous, *adj.*, pert. to sorcery.

sor'cery, *n.*, magic arts, wizardry, witchcraft.

sor'des, *n.*, foul discharge from ulcers, etc.

sor'det, *n.*, *i.q.* sordine.

sor'did, *adj.*, filthy, squalid, mercenary.

sor'didly, *adv.*, in a sordid way.

sor'didness, *n.*, the quality or state of being sordid.

sor'dine, *n.*, a mute, a damper.

sordi'ni, *n.*, pl. of sordino.

sordi'no, *n.*, *i.q.* sordine; a kit (*Ital.*).

sore, *adj.*, morbidly sensitive to pain; causing pain; offended; *n.*, a sore place on the body; something rankling in the mind; *adv.*, *i.q.* sorely.

sore'ly, *adv.*, in a sore manner; in a way to cause distress; very greatly.

sore'ness, *n.*, the state or quality of being sore.

sor'er, *adj.*, *comp.* of sore.

sor'est, *adj.*, *super.* of sore.

sor'go, *n.*, a kind of sugar-cane; the sorghum.

sori'tes, *n.*, an extended syllogism or chain of syllogisms; a sophistical method of leading a person to the acceptance of an absurd conclusion.

sorn, *v.i.*, to sponge on friends for hospitality (*Scot.*).

sorned, *p.p.*, sorn.

sorn'er, *n.*, one who sorns.

sorn'ing, *pr.p.*, sorn.

soro'sis, *n.*, a fleshy kind of fruit, such as the pine-apple, mulberry, etc.

sor'rel, *n.*, a perennial herb with a slightly sour taste.

sor'rier, *adj.*, *comp.* of sorry.

sor'riest, *adj.*, *super.* of sorry.

sor'rily, *adv.*, in a sorry way.

sor'row, *n.*, grief; repentance; misfortune; *v.i.*, to feel sorrow.

sor'rowed, *p.p.*, sorrow.

sor'rowful, *adj.*, full of sorrow; sad.

sor'rowfully, *adv.*, sadly, mournfully.

sor'rowing, *pr.p.*, sorrow.

sor'ry, *adj.*, filled with regret; poor, mean, shabby.

sort, *n.*, kind, class, way; in printer's type, a letter or portion of fount; a group; *v.t.*, to separate into groups; to pick out from a mixed number; *v.i.*, to correspond.

sort'able, *adj.*, able to be sorted.

sort'ed, *p.p.*, sort.

sort'er, *n.*, one who sorts.

sor'tie, *n.*, a sally; a dash out from a besieged place (*Fr.*).

sor'tilege, *n.*, divination by casting lots.

sortile'gious, *adj.*, pert. to sortilege.

sort'ing, *pr.p.*, sort.

so'-so, *adj.*, not up to much; indifferent.

sostenu'to, *adv.*, in a sustained way (*mus.*)

sot, *n.*, a drunkard, toper; *v.i.*, to be a toper.

soteriol'ogy, *n.*, the branch of theological science rel. to the scheme of salvation.

so'thic, *adj.*, pert. to the dog-star (of which Sothis was the Egyptian name).

sot'tish, *adj.*, like a sot; characteristic of a sot.

sot'tishness, *n.*, habitual drunkenness.

sot'to vo'ce, adverbial phrase = under the breath; aside (*Ital.*).

sou, *n.*, a French coin, now valued at five centimes.

soubrette', *n.*, a French actress in the character of a pert maid-servant or lady's maid.

souchong', *n.*, a black tea.

soufflé', *adj.*, mottled; prepared with white of egg beaten; *n.*, a dish so prepared (*Fr.*).

souf'fle, *n.*, a low murmur heard in auscultation of an organ or part.

sough, *n.*, a gentle, whistling or sighing sound as of wind; *v.i.*, to make such sound.

sought, *p.p.* and *t.*, seek.

soul, *n.*, the spiritual part, as distinct from the material part, of a man; a human being; the vital principle and mental powers common to all the animal world; the essence; the animating influence; emotional feeling.

soul'ful, *adj.*, full of soul; emotional.

soul'fully, *adv.*, in a soulful way.

soul'fulness, *n.*, the quality of being soulful.

soul'less, *adj.*, without emotional feeling; heartless.

soul'lessly, *adv.*, in a soulless way.

soul'lessness, *n.*, the quality of being soulless.

soul'-stirring, *adj.*, rousing, exciting.

sound, *n.*, the sensation produced through the hearing; tone; noise; ear-shot; one of a series of articulate utterances, as vowel sounds; a strait; *adj.*, healthy; to be relied upon; judicious; solvent; *v.i.*, to give forth a sound; to appear like; *v.t.*, to make a sound with; to express by means of sound; to celebrate; to auscultate; to try the depth of; to inquire into.

sound'board, *n.*, a canopy over a pulpit or platform to enable the voice to carry; a thin piece of wood in some musical instruments to improve the resonance; in a pianoforte, the wood on which the strings are stretched; in an organ, the top of the wind-chest having the pipes inserted into it. Also *sounding-board.*

sound'ed, *p.p.*, sound.

sound'er, *adj.*, *comp.* of sound.

sound'est, *adj.*, *super.* of sound.

sound'ing, *pr.p.*, sound; *adj.*, resonant; *n.*, the act of sounding in any sense; the dive of a fish when hooked; the taking of the depth of water.

sound'ing-board, *n.*, *i.q.* sound-board.

sound'ings, *n. pl.*, the result of making a sounding; specimens brought up as the result of sounding.

sound'less, *adj.*, without a sound; still; silent.

sound'ly, *adv.*, in a sound way.

sound'ness, *n.*, the quality of being sound.

soup, *n.*, a liquid food produced by boiling meat, vegetables, etc., in water.

soupçon', *n.*, a very small quantity; just a taste. (The French word properly means "a suspicion.")

sour, *adj.*, acid, tart; without sweetness of temper; peevish, morose; bad for crops; *v.t.* and *i.*, to turn sour.

source, *n.*, a spring, fount, origin.

soured, *p.p.*, sour.

sour'ing, *pr.p.*, sour.

sour'ish, *adj.*, inclined to be sour.

sour'krout (or -**crout**), *n.*, *i.q.*, sauerkraut.

sour'ly, *adv.*, in a sour way.

sour'ness, *n.*, the quality of being sour.

sous, *prep.*, under (*Fr.*).

souse, *v.t.*, to plunge or dip in water; to give a wetting to; to steep in vinegar; to put into pickle made with salt.

soused, *p.p.*, souse.

sous'ing, *pr.p.*, souse.

soutane', *n.*, a cassock (*Fr.*).

sou'terrain, *n.*, a cellar, grotto (*Fr.*).

south, *n.*, the point of the compass opposite to the north; *adj.*, bel. to the south; situated in, or looking towards, the south; *adv.*, southward; from the south; *v.i.*, to cross the meridian of a place.

Southcott'ian, *n.*, a follower of Joanna Southcott, an 18th and early 19th cent. religious impostor.

Soutn'down, *adj.*, pert. to a district of Sussex and Hants. known as the Southdowns; *n.*, the mutton of Southdown sheep.

south-east', *adj.*, *adv.*, and *n.*, midway between S. and E.

south-east'er, *n.*, a wind blowing from the S.E.

south-east'erly, *adj.*, blowing from the S.E.

south-east'ern, *adj.*, pert. to the S.E.

south'erly, *adj.*, in or towards the south; blowing from the south.

south'ern, *adj.*, rel. to, situated in, looking or tending towards, the south.

south'erner, *n.*, one who lives in the south country, esp. in the southern part of the U.S. of America.

south'ing, *pr.p.*, south; *n.*, the difference of latitude in sailing south.

south'*most*, *adj.* and *adv.*, furthest south.

south'ron, *n.*, a dweller in the south; esp. south of the Scottish border. (It was supposed, in Scotland, to be felt in England as a term of contempt.)

south'ward, *adj.* and *adv.*, toward the S.

south-west', *adj.*, *n.*, and *adv.*, midway between S. and W.

south-west'er, *n.*, a S.W. wind.

south-west'erly, *adj.*, toward, or blowing from, the S.W.

south-west'ern, *adj.*, situated in, pert. to, the S.W.

souvenir', *n.*, a memento; recollection (*Fr.*).

sov'ereign, *adj.*, supreme; pre-eminent; very potent; *n.*, a supreme ruler; an English gold coin (20s.).

sov'ereignty, *n.*, the state or quality of being sovereign.

sow, *n.*, fem. of pig.

sow, *v.t.*, to scatter seeds on; to plant.

sowar', *n.*, a native trooper of the irregular cavalry in British India.

sow'bread, *n.*, a variety of cyclamen.

sowed, *p.p.*, sow.

sow'ens, *n.*, a Scottish flummery; a paste used by weavers.

sow'er, *n.*, one who, or that which, sows; one who causes.

sow'ing, *pr.p.*, sow; *n.*, the act of sowing; the thing sown.

sown, *p.p.*, sow.

soy, *n.*, a sauce or flavouring used by the Chinese and the Japanese. It is made from the soy bean or pea.

spa, *n.*, any place where there is a mineral spring.

space, *n.*, continuous extension; the interval between one point and another, whether of time or material objects; a printer's device to separate words; room; *v.t.*, to arrange in such a way that a space separates each object or group of objects.

spaced, *p.p.*, space.

spa'cing, *pr.p.*, space; *n.*, the act of spacing; the distance spaced.

spa'cious, *adj.*, vast in extent; roomy; with scope for activity.

spa'ciously, *adv.*, in a spacious way.

spa'ciousness, *n.*, roominess, extent.

spad'dle, *n.*, a little spade.

spade, *n.*, an implement for digging; the name of one of the suits in a pack of cards; *v.t.*, to dig over.

spade'ful, *n.*, as much as a spade will hold.

spadi'ceous, *adj.*, pert. to a spadix.

spadille', *n.*, the ace of spades in the games of quadrille and ombre.

spa'dix, *n.*, a spike of flowers having a fleshy axis, which is usually enclosed in a spathe.

spado'ne, *n.*, a light broadsword.

spaghet'ti, *n. pl.*, a smaller kind of macaroni (*Ital.*).

spa'hi, *n.*, an old name for a corps of irregular Turkish cavalry; an irregular Turkish cavalryman.

spake, *p.t.*, speak.

spall, *v.t.*, to break up; to chip; *v.i.*, to chip; *n.*, a flake, chip.

spalt, *n.*, a white, scaly mineral of use in fusing metals.

span, *n.*, any interval of space or time; extreme distance from one fixed point to another, as, for instance, the width of an arch or of the space between the abutments of a bridge; *v.t.*, to measure; to cover the width of; to hobble; *v.i.*, to extend.

span'drel, *n.*, the space between the shoulder of an arch and the rectangular moulding surrounding it, or the space between adjoining arches.

span'gle, *n.*, a little glittering piece of metal, often used as a dress ornament; *v.t.*, to ornament with spangles.

span'gled, *p.p.*, spangle.

span'gling, *pr.p.*, spangle.

Span'iard, *n.*, a native of Spain.

span'iel, *n.*, a sporting dog.

Span'ish, *adj.*, rel. to Spain and the Spaniards.

spank, *v.t.*, to smack; *v.i.*, to career along; *n.*, a smack.

spanked, *p.p.*, spank.

spank'er, *n.*, one who spanks; an after-sail.

spank'ing, *pr.p.*, spank; *n.*, a smacking.

spanned, *p.p.*, span.

span'ner, *n.*, one who, or that which, spans; a tool for tightening screws.

span'ning, *pr.p.*, span.

spar, *n.*, a shining mineral; a ship's mast, boom, etc.; a boxing contest; a verbal dispute; *v.i.*, to engage in a contest of blows or words.

spare, *adj.*, meagre, thin, economical; *v.t.*, to show mercy to; to do without; to part with; *v.i.*, to live in a poor way; to forbear.

spared, *p.p.*, spare.

spare'ness, *n.*, the quality or state of being spare.

spa'rer, *n.*, one who spares.

spare'rib, *n.*, a joint of pork consisting of ribs specially treated.

sparge, *v.t.*, to sprinkle.

spar'ger, *n.*, a sprinkler, used esp. by brewers.

spa'ring, *pr.p.*, spare; *adj.*, parsimonious.

spa'ringly, *adv.*, in a sparing way.

spark, *n.*, a flash of light as from a fire; a smart youth; a beau; *v.i.*, to give off sparks when electric continuity is broken.

spark'ing-plug, *n.*, an automobile device causing an electric spark to leap between two electrodes, thus exploding the charge in the cylinder.

spark'le, *n.*, a coruscation; a flash; *v.i.*, to flash, coruscate.

spark'led, *p.p.*, sparkles.

spark'ler, *n.*, one who, or that which, sparkles.

spark'ling, *pr. p.*, sparkle.

spark'lingly, *adv.*, in a sparkling way.

spar'ling, *n.*, a smelt.

sparred, *p.p.*, spar.

spar'ring, *pr.p.*, spar.

spar'row, *n.*, a small bird of that name.

spar'row-hawk, *n.*, a small bird that preys on sparrows and other small birds.

spar'ry, *adj.*, like, full of, spar.

sparse, *adj.*, thin, scanty.

sparse'ly, *adv.*, scantily.

sparse'ness, *n.*, the state or quality of being sparse.

Spar'tan, *adj.*, pert. to Sparta and the Spartans; austere; hardy.

spasm, *n.*, a sudden, violent muscular contraction.

spasmod'ic, *adj.*, sudden and violent; convulsive.

spasmod'ical, *adj.*, *i.q.* spasmodic.

spasmod'ically, *adv.*, in a spasmodic way.

spasmol'ogy, *n.*, the study of spasms.

spas'tic, *adj.*, *i.q.* spasmodic.

spastic'ity, *n.*, the state or quality of being spastic.

spat, *p.t.*, spit; *n.*, spawn of shell-fish.

spatha'ceous, *adj.*, producing or resembling spathes.

spathe, *n.*, the calix of a spadix.

spath'ic, *adj.*, like spar.

spath'iform, *adj.*, like a spathe.

spats, *n. pl.*, truncated gaiters.

spat'ter, *v.t.*, to drench by sprinkling; to destroy the character of.

spat'terdashes, *n. pl.*, leather gaiters.

spat'tered, *p.p.* spatter.

spat'tering, *pr.p.*, spatter.

spat'ula, *n.*, a knife used in spreading plasters, mixing paints, etc.

spat'ulate, *adj.*, like a spatula.

spav'in, *n.*, a disease in a horse's hock; *v.t.*, to affect with spavin.

spav'ined, *p.p.*, spavin.

spawn, *n.*, offspring; ova; the mycelium of mushrooms and other fungi.

spawned, *p.p.*, spawn.

spawn'er, *n.*, one who, or that which, spawns.

spawn'ing, *pr.p.*, spawn.

spay, *n.*, a red deer stag of the third year; *v.t.*, to remove ovaries from a female animal; to castrate.

spayed, *p.p.*, spay.

spay'ing, *pr.p.*, spay.

speak, *v.t.*, to utter, say, reveal; *v.i.*, to indulge in speech; to talk; to deliver an oration.

speak'able, *adj.*, able to be spoken.

speak'er, *n.*, one who speaks, notably the Speaker of the House of Commons.

speak'ing, *pr.p.*, speak; *adj.*, life-like.

speak'ing-trumpet, *n.*, a device enabling deaf persons to hear.

speak'ing-tube, *n.*, a tube conveying the voice.

spear, *n.*, a pointed weapon; anything resembling it; *v.t.*, to pierce with a spear.

speared, *p.p.*, spear.

spear'ing, *pr.p.*, spear

spear'mint, *n.*, the ordinary mint in use.

spear'wort, *n.*, a variety of ranunculus.

spec'ial, *adj.*, pert. to a species; appropriate to a particular end; distinctive.

spec'ialist, *n.*, a professional man who devotes himself to a particular department of his work; an expert in a particular subject.
special'ity, *n.*, a distinct department; a special aptitude.
spec'ialize, *v.i.*, to act as a specialist.
spec'ialized, *p.p.*, specialize.
spec'ializing, *pr.p.*, specialize.
spec'ially, *n.*, in a special manner or degree.
spec'ialty, *n.*, a special characteristic or obligation.
spe'cie, *n.*, coin.
spe'cies, *n.*, a group within a genus; kind.
specif'ic, *adj.*, rel. to a species; detailed; *n.*, a cure for a disease.
specif'ically, *adv.*, in detail; precisely.
specifica'tion, *n.*, the act or result of specifying; the setting out of the details of a plan for a building, an organ, etc.
spec'ified, *p.p.*, specify.
spec'ify, *v.t.*, to particularize; to give details of.
spec'ifying, *pr.p.*, specify.
spec'imen, *n.*, a proof, example, exhibit.
spe'cious, *adj.*, outwardly attractive; plausible.
spe'ciously, *adv.*, in a specious way.
speck, *n.*, a small spot; a flaw; *v.t.*, to spot.
specked, *p.p.*, speck.
speck'ing, *pr.p.*, speck.
speck'le, *n.*, a small spot; *v.t.*, to cover with speckles; to variegate.
speck'led, *p.p.*, speckle.
speck'ling, *pr.p.*, speckle.
spec'tacle, *n.*, a sight; a show.
spec'tacled, *adj.*, wearing spectacles.
spec'tacles, *n. pl.*, a pair of eyeglasses framed.
spectac'ular, *adj.*, pert. to a spectacle; shown in picture; scenic.
specta'tor, *n.*, one who looks on.
spectato'rial, *adj.*, pert. to spectators.
specta'tress, *n.*, fem. of spectator.
specta'trix, *n.*, *i.q.* spectatress.
spec'tral, *adj.*, rel. to a spectre; ghostly.
spec'tre, *n.*, a ghost.
spectrol'ogy, *n.*, the study of spectrum analysis.
spec'troscope, *n.*, a scientific instrument for the examination of spectrum.
spec'trum, *n.*, light rays passed through a prism and shown on a screen.
spec'ular, *adj.*, like a mirror or speculum.
spec'ulate, *v.i.*, to meditate; to invest money for profit.
spec'ulated, *p.p.*, speculate.
spec'ulating, *pr.p.*, speculate.
specula'tion, *n.*, meditation; theorizing; investment of money for profit.
spec'ulative, *adj.*, meditative; theorizing; involving risk.
spec'ulator, *n.*, one who speculates.
spec'ulatory, *adj.*, theoretical.
spec'ulum, *n.*, a mirror; a surgical instrument used in internal examinations
sped, *p.t.* and *p.*, speed.
speech, *n.*, articulate utterance; an oration; language.
speech'ified, *p.p.*, speechify.
speech'ify, *v.i.*, to make speeches.
speech'ifying, *pr.p.*, speechify.
speech'less, *adj.*, unable to speak; silent; dumb.
speed, *n.*, haste; swiftness; success; *v.t.*, to give a good send-off to; to accelerate; *v.i.*, to move swiftly; to prosper.
speed'ily, *adv.*, quickly.
speed'ing, *pr.p.*, speed.
speed'well, *n.*, veronica.
speed'y, *adj.*, quick, hasty.
speiss, *n.*, a compound obtained in smelting certain ores.
spell, *v.t.*, to write or recite the separate letters of a word; mean; *v.i.*, to make words from letters; to signify; *n.*, a charm, incantation; a turn of labour; a period of working.
spell'-bound, *adj.*, charmed, fascinated.
spelled, *p.p.*, spell.
spell'er, *n.*, one who spells; a spelling-book.
spell'ing, *pr.p.*, spell; *n.*, the act of spelling.
spell'ing-book, *n.*, a book from which spelling is learnt.
spelt, *p.p.*, spell; *n.*, a variety of wheat.
spel'ter, *n.*, zinc.
spen'cer, *n.*, a short overcoat; a bodice.
Spence'rian, *adj.*, pert. to Herbert Spencer and his philosophy.
spend, *v.t.*, to lay out; pay out; to pass; use; *v.i.*, to spend money.
spend'er, *n.*, one who spends; an extravagant person.
spend'ing, *pr.p.*, spend; *n.*, the habit of spending.
spend'thrift, *n.*, *i.q.* spender.
Spense'rian, *adj.*, pert. to Edmund Spenser and his poetry.
spent, *p.p.*, spend; *adj.*, exhausted.
sperm, *n.*, a sperm whale; semen.
spermace'ti, *n.*, a secretion in the head of a sperm whale.
spermat'ic, *adj.*, pert. to sperm or semen.
spermatozo'a, *n. pl.*, one of the living fertilizing elements in semen.

spew, *v.t.* and *i.*, to vomit; spit forth; to droop at the muzzle (said of a gun).
spewed, *p.p.*, spew.
spew'ing, *pr.p.*, spew.
sphac'elate, *v.i.*, to make gangrenous; *v.i.*, to become gangrenous.
sphacela'tion, *n.*, a gangrenous condition.
sphac'elus, *n.*, gangrene (*Gr.*).
sphag'nous, *adj.*, covered with bog-moss.
sphe'nogram, *n.*, a cuneiform sign.
sphe'noid, *adj.*, wedge-shaped.
sphenoid'al, *adj.*, *i.q.* sphenoid.
sphere, *n.*, a solid body, every point on the surface of which is equally distant from the centre; a globe; ball; the sky; a celestial body; range of duty; social position; *v.t.*, to include in a sphere or among the heavenly bodies; to make spherical.
sphered, *p.p.*, sphere.
spher'ic, *adj.*, pert. to, resembling, a sphere.
spher'ical, *adj.*, *i.q.* spheric.
spher'ically, *adv.*, in a spherical way.
spheric'ity, *n.*, the state or quality of being spherical.
spher'icle, *n.*, a small sphere.
spher'ics, *n. pl.*, spherical geometry and trigonometry.
sphe'ring, *pr.p.*, sphere.
sphe'roid, *adj.*, sphere-like.
spheroi'dal, *adj.*, *i.q.* spheroid.
spherom'eter, *n.*, an apparatus for measuring the length of the radii of spherical surfaces.
spher'ule, *n.*, a small sphere.
spher'ulite, *n.*, glassy globules in some rock-formations.
sphe'ry, *adj.*, starry.
sphinc'ter, *n.*, a muscle that closes an opening or a tube.
sphinx, *n.*, the winged monster of Thebes; the name also of Egyptian figures with lion's body and human face; any mysterious person.
sphragis'tics, *n. pl.*, the study of engraved seals.
sphyg'mic, *adj.*, rel. to the pulse.
sphyg'mograph, *n.*, an instrument that records pulse-beats.
sphygmom'eter, *n.*, a contrivance for ascertaining the blood pressure in the arteries.
spi'cate, *adj.*, like a spike; consisting of spikes.
spi'cated, *adj.*, *i.q.* spicate.
spicca'to, *adv.*, the opposite to legato (*mus.*).
spice, *n.*, aromatic vegetable substance; anything that adds a flavour or zest; *v.t.*, to season with spice.
spiced, *p.p.*, spice.
spi'cer, *n.*, one who deals in spices.
spi'cery, *n.*, spices collectively; a store of spices; the quality of spice.
spi'cier, *adj.*, *comp.* of spicy.
spi'ciest, *adj.*, *super.* of spicy.
spi'ciness, *n.*, the quality of being spicy.
spi'cing, *pr.p.*, spice.
spick, *adj.*, fresh, smart.
spic'ular, *adj.*, pert. to a spicule; pointed; pungent.
spic'ulate, *adj.*, having spicules.
spic'ulate, *v.t.*, to point.
spic'ule, *n.*, a thin, pointed body.
spic'uliform, *adj.*, shaped like a spicule.
spiculig'enous, *adj.*, bearing spicules.
spic'y, *adj.*, aromatic, pungent, piquant; showy; indelicate (*colloq.*).
spi'der, *n.*, an arachnid, one of the Araneids; the name for various objects with spider-like legs.
spig'ot, *n.*, the plug of a vent in a cask.
spike, *n.*, a sharp point or end; a flower-cluster; *v.t.*, to fasten, supply, pierce, with spikes.
spiked, *p.p.*, spike.
spike'let, *n.*, a subordinate spike.
spike'nard, *n.*, costly aromatic ointment.
spi'king, *pr.p.*, spike.
spi'ky, *adj.*, like a spike; set with spikes.
spile, *n.*, a spigot; a wooden pile; *v.t.*, to make a hole for a spigot.
spil'likin, *n.*, a little pin.
spill, *v.t.*, to let liquid drop; upset; *n.*, a fall; a thin roll or strip of paper or wood for lighting a candle, etc.
spilled, *p.p.*, spill.
spill'er, *n.*, one who spills; a small mackerel-net inside a large one.
spill'ing, *pr.p.*, spill.
spilt, *p.p.*, spill.
spin, *v.t.*, to twist into threads; to form a web; to make to revolve; to compose; to reject a candidate in an examination (*colloq.*); *v.i.*, to practise the art of spinning; to make webs; to troll; *n.*, a whirl; short, brisk run or walk.
spina'ceous, *adj.*, like spinach.
spin'ach, *n.*, a garden vegetable.
spi'nal, *adj.*, rel. to the spine.
spin'dle, *n.*, a pin that twists and winds thread on a spinning wheel; a bar used in the same manner in hand spinning; *v.i.*, to grow like a spindle.
spin'dle-tree, *n.*, a tree or shrub so named.

spin'dling, *pr.p.*, spindle; *n.*, a shoot on a plant.

spine, *n.*, the column of the vertebrae; backbone; a ridge.

spined, *adj.*, having a spine or spines.

spin'el, *n.*, the name of certain minerals found in regular crystals.

spine'less, *adj.*, without a spine; invertebrate.

spines'cent, *adj.*, ending in a spine.

spin'et, *n.*, an old musical instrument resembling a harpsichord.

spinif'erous, *adj.*, producing spines.

spin'naker, *n.*, a large supplementary sail carried on the mainmast and used by racing yachts.

spin'ner, *n.*, one who, or that which, spins, or turns in a lathe.

spin'neret, *n.*, a spinning organ in silkworms, etc.

spin'nery, *n.*, a spinning-mill.

spin'ney, *n.*, a thicket.

spin'ning, *pr.p.*, spin.

spin'ning-jenny, *n.*, a machine for spinning two or more strands at once.

spin'ning-wheel, *n.*, an old family implement with which yarn or thread was spun.

spi'nose, *adj.*, *i.q.* spinous.

spinos'ity, *n.*, the state or quality of being spinous.

spi'nous, *adj.*, having spines.

Spino'zism, *n.*, the philosophical doctrines of Spinoza (died 1677).

Spino'zist, *n.*, a follower of Spinoza.

spin'ster, *n.*, orig. a woman who spins; now an unmarried one.

spin'ule, *n.*, a small spine.

spin'ulose, *adj.*, *i.q.* spinulous.

spin'ulous, *adj.*, having spinules.

spi'ny, *adj.*, full of spines; thorny.

spi'racle, *n.*, a breathing-hole; a blow-hole.

spi'ral, *adj.*, twisted, coiled, winding round and round; *n.*, a curve; a spring, a spiral formation in shells, etc.; *v.t.*, to make spiral.

spi'rally, *adv.*, in a spiral way.

spi'rant, *adj.*, produced by the breath; *n.*, a consonant pronounced through a not quite closed aperture of the mouth and continued.

spira'tion, *n.*, breathing.

spire, *n.*, a tapering pyramidal body; a pyramidal termination to a church-tower; a shoot; *v.t.*, to furnish with spires; *v.i.*, to shoot upward.

spir'it, *n.*, breath, soul; a ghost; an incorporeal, rational being; energy, courage; inner meaning; state of mind; unseen influence; strong distilled liquor; *v.t.*, to convey away secretly; to inspirit.

spir'ited, *p.p.*, spirit; *adj.*, dashing, courageous.

spir'iting, *pr.p.*, spirit.

spir'itist, *n.*, a spiritualist; a medium.

spir'itless, *adj.*, tame; without fire or energy.

spirito'so, *adv.*, with spirit (*mus.*).

spir'itous, *adj.*, of the nature of spirits.

spir'itual, *adj.*, pert. to the spirit; the opposite to the material; inspired or divinely bestowed; marked by the highest qualities of soul; ecclesiastical; *n.*, something pert. to the spirit.

spir'itualism, *n.*, the belief in the power to hold intercourse with the dead; the philosophic doctrine that spirit alone exists.

spir'itualist, *n.*, a believer in spiritualism.

spiritualis'tic, *adj.*, pert. to spiritualism and spiritualists.

spiritual'ity, *n.*, the quality of being spiritual.

spiritual'ities, *n. pl.*, sources of revenue arising out of the performance of ecclesiastical functions (as the spiritualities of a see).

spiritualiza'tion, *n.*, the act or result of spiritualizing.

spiritualize, *v.t.*, to make spiritual; to raise morally, intellectually, or religiously; to interpret in a spiritual rather than a literal sense.

spir'itualized, *p.p.*, spiritualize.

spir'itualizer, *n.*, one who spiritualizes.

spir'itualizing, *pr.p.*, spiritualize.

spir'itually, *adv.*, in a spiritual way.

spir'itualty, *n.*, the clergy.

spirituelle', *adj.*, pure; spiritual.

spir'ituous, *adj.*, of the nature of spirit; alcoholic.

spi'rograph, *n.*, an instrument to record the movements in breathing.

spirom'eter, *n.*, an instrument to measure lung capacity.

spirt, *v.t.* and *i.*, to pour in a sudden stream. Also *spurt*.

spirt'ed, *p.p.*, spirt.

spirt'ing, *pr.p.*, spirt.

spi'ry, *adj.*, like a spire; tapering.

spis'sated, *adj.*, thickened.

spis'situde, *n.*, thickness.

spit, *n.*, a pointed piece of metal on which meat can be roasted; a pointed shoal of sand; *v.t.*, to put on a spit for roasting; to impale; to send out from the mouth; *v.i.*, to discharge saliva; to drizzle.

spite, *n.*, a feeling of envy or hatred; a grudge; *v.t.*, to injure maliciously and in revenge.

spi'ted, *p.p.*, spite.

spite'ful, *adj.*, malicious; full of spite.

spite'fully, *adv.*, in a spiteful way.

spite'fulness, *n.*, the state or quality of being spiteful.

spit'fire, *n.*, one who habitually expresses his anger.

spi'ting, *pr.p.*, spite.

spit'ted, *p.p.*, spit (in sense of impaling or putting on a spit).

spit'ter, *n.*, one who spits.

spit'ting, *pr.p.*, spit.

spit'tle, *n.*, saliva.

spittoon', *n.*, an antiquated smoking-room accessory with an obvious purpose.

splanchnol'ogy, *n.*, the study of the internal organisms.

splash, *n.*, water or other liquid dashed up or down; *v.t.*, to wet with water thrown upon a person or thing; *v.i.*, to dash water about; to brag (*colloq.*).

splash'-board, *n.*, a protection at the front of a driver's seat to catch splashed mud.

splashed, *p.p.*, splash.

splash'er, *n.*, one who, or that which, splashes.

splash'ing, *pr.p.*, splash.

splash'y, *adj.*, splashing.

splay, *n.*, a sloping surface; *adj.*, sloping or spreading inwards or outwards; *v.t.*, to slant; to put out of joint.

splayed, *p.p.*, splay; *adj.*, widening outwards or inwards.

splay'-foot, *n.*, a foot which turns outwards.

splay'-footed, *adj.*, having splay feet.

spleen, *n.*, an internal organ, believed by the ancients to be the seat of some of the feelings; melancholy; suppressed spite; bad temper.

spleen'ish, *adj.*, ill-humoured; melancholy.

spleen'y, *adj.*, *i.q.* spleenish.

splen'dent, *adj.*, shining; gleaming.

splen'did, *adj.*, shining; bright; glorious.

splen'didly, *adv.*, in a splendid way.

splen'dour, *n.*, brightness, glory, magnificence.

splenet'ic, *adj.*, given to spleen; melancholy; peevish.

splenet'ical, *adj.*, *i.q.* splenetic.

splen'ic, *adj.*, pert. to the spleen.

sple'nocele, *n.*, rupture of the spleen.

splenol'ogy, *n.*, the study of the spleen.

spleu'chan, *n.*, a bag; pouch (*Scot.*).

splice, *n.*, the joining of a fracture; the binding together of two rope-ends; *v.t.*, to join together by uniting the strands (of two ropes); to bind round a juncture; to unite in marriage (*slang.*).

spliced, *p.p.*, splice.

spli'cing, *pr.p.*, splice.

splint, *n.*, *i.q.* splinter; a piece of wood used for keeping fractured limbs, etc., in position; a growth on a horse's shank-bone.

splin'ter, *n.*, a small piece broken off longitudinally; any fragment; *v.t.* and *i.*, to break into splinters.

splin'tered, *p.p.*, splinter.

splin'tering, *pr.p.*, splinter.

splin'tery, *adj.*, like splinters.

split, *n.*, a fissure; cleavage; *v.t.* and *i.*, to make a fissure; to rupture or be ruptured; to give away a secret.

split'ter, *n.*, one who, or that which, splits.

splotch, *n.*, a daub; a splash.

splotch'y, *adj.*, dauby.

splutter', *n.*, an inarticulate, confused noise; muddle; *v.i.*, to speak in an indistinct and rapid way; to shed ink (said of a pen).

splut'tered, *p.p.*, splutter.

splut'tering, *pr.p.*, splutter.

spod'omancy, *n.*, divination with dust.

spoil, *n.*, plunder; pillage; *v.t.*, to plunder; to pillage; to mar; to vitiate; *v.i.*, to deteriorate.

spoiled, *p.p.*, spoil.

spoil'er, *n.*, one who spoils.

spoil'ing, *pr.p.*, spoil.

spoilt, *p.t.*, spoil.

spoke, *p.t.*, speak; *n.*, one of the parts of a wheel connecting the nave with the rim; a rung in a ladder; *v.t.*, to fit with spokes.

spo'ken, *p.p.*, speak.

spoke'-shave, *n.*, a two-handled plane.

spokes'man, *n.*, one who acts as a mouthpiece.

spo'liate, *v.t.*, to despoil.

spo'liated, *p.p.*, spoliate.

spo'liating, *pr.p.*, spoliate.

spolia'tion, *n.*, plundering; pillaging.

spo'liative, *adj.*, having the effect of pillage.

spo'liator, *n.*, a plunderer.

sponda'ic, *adj.*, pert. to a spondee.

sponda'ical, *adj.*, *i.q.* spondaic.

spon'dee, *n.*, a metrical foot consisting of two long syllables

spon'dyl, -dyle, *n.*, a vertebra.

sponge, *n.*, a porous, elastic, and fibrous growth; a gun-mop; a horseshoe point; a cadger; *v.t.*, to cleanse with a sponge; *v.i.*, to cadge.

sponged, *p.p.*, sponge.

spon'ger, *n.*, one who, or that which, sponges.

spon'giform, *adj.*, like a sponge.

spon'giness, *n.*, the state or quality of being spongy.

spong'ing, *pr.p.*, sponge.

spon'ging-house, *n.*, a house where debtors were kept by the bailiff before being committed to prison.

spon'giole, *n.*, sponge-like material in plant roots.

spon'giolite, *n.*, a fossilized sponge.

spon'gious, *adj.*, sponge-like.

spon'gy, *adj.*, like sponge; oozing.

spon'sal, *adj.*, pert. to god-parents or sureties.

spon'sion, *n.*, the act of a sponsor; a solemn undertaking.

spon'sor, *n.*, a surety; a god-parent.

sponso'rial, *adj.*, pert. to a sponsor.

spon'sorship, *n.*, the office of a sponsor.

spontane'ity, *n.*, the quality or state of being spontaneous.

sponta'neous, *adj.*, of one's own accord; done as the result of natural impulse.

sponta'neously, *adv.*, in a spontaneous way.

spook, *n.*, a ghost (*colloq.*).

spool, *n.*, a cylinder round which thread is wound.

spoon, *n.*, a smaller ladle for domestic or table use; a variety of golf club; *v.t.*, to lift with a spoon; *v.i.*, to play the lover (*colloq.*).

spoon'bill, *n.*, a wading-bird.

spoon'ful, *n.*, the quantity contained in a spoon.

spoon'meat, *n.*, food conveyed in a spoon.

spoon'y, *adj.*, foolishly amatory; idiot-like; *n.*, an idiot.

spoor, *n.*, scent; trail.

sporad'ic, *adj.*, scattered; occurring here and there.

spore, *n.*, a minute seed in plants and other organisms.

spor'ran, *n.*, a Highlander's pouch.

sport, *n.*, a game; jest; mockery; exercises like hunting, shooting, etc.; athletics; a freak; *v.i.*, to indulge in games or frolics; to hunt, shoot, etc.; *v.t.*, to wear or exhibit (*colloq.*).

sport'ed, *p.p.*, sport.

sport'ful, *adj.*, fond of jest; merry.

sport'fully, *adv.*, in a sportful way.

sport'fulness, *n.*, the quality or state of being sportful.

sport'ing, *pr.p.*, sport; *adj.*, fond of sport.

sport'ing chance, *n.*, the off-chance.

sport'ive, *adj.*, merry, lively.

sport'iveness, *n.*, frolicsomeness.

sports'man, *n.*, one addicted to sport; a man who "plays the game."

sports'manship, *n.*, the skill of a sportsman.

spor'ule, *n.*, a granule with spore.

sporulif'erous, *adj.*, producing sporules.

spot, *n.*, a speck; a blemish; a mark, place, or locality; the spot-stroke at billiards; *v.t.*, to blemish; to mark with spots; to detect (*colloq.*); *v.i.*, to become spotty.

spot'less, *adj.*, without spot or blemish; pure; innocent.

spot'lessness, *n.*, the state or quality of being spotless.

spot'ted, *p.p.*, spot.

spot'ter, *n.*, one who, or that which, spots.

spot'tiness, *n.*, the state or quality of being spotty.

spot'ting, *pr.p.*, spot.

spot'ty, *adj.*, marked with spots.

spou'sal, *adj.*, nuptial.

spousals, *n. pl.*, nuptials; the marriage ceremony.

spouse, *n.*, a married person; husband or wife.

spout, *n.*, the lip of a can, jug, etc.; a projecting pipe for discharging a liquid; *v.t.*, to discharge liquid as from a pipe; to deposit with a pawnbroker; *v.i.*, to gush forth; to make a speech (*colloq.*).

spout'ed, *p.p.*, spout.

spout'er, *n.*, one who makes speeches (*colloq.*).

spout'ing, *pr.p.*, spout.

sprack, *adj.*, vivacious (*Scot.*).

sprag, *n.*, a salmon-peel or codling.

sprain, *n.*, a violent straining of muscles or ligaments; *v.t.*, to strain the muscles or ligaments violently.

sprained, *p.p.*, sprain.

sprain'ing, *pr.p.*, sprain.

sprang, *p.t.*, spring.

sprat, *n.*, a diminutive fish.

sprawl, *v.i.*, to stretch oneself loosely or awkwardly; to spread out.

sprawled, *p.p.*, sprawl.

sprawl'er, *n.*, one who, or that which, sprawls.

sprawl'ing, *pr.p.*, sprawl.

spray, *n.*, water or liquid perfume blown into small particles; a small branch; a number of small shoots; *v.t.*, to sprinkle.

spray'er, *n.*, one who, or that which, sprays.

spread, *v.t.*, to extend; scatter; unfurl; circulate; furnish a table; *p.t.* and *p.*, spread; *v.i.*, to be stretched or extended; *n.*, measure of extension; a feast (*colloq.*).

spread'-eagle, *adj.*, tall-talking; *n.*, the emblem of the U.S.

spread'er, *n.*, one who, that which, spreads.

spread'ing, *pr.p.*, spread.

spree, *n.*, a frolic (*slang*).

sprent, *adj.*, sprinkled; scattered.

sprig, *n.*, a young shoot; a small nail or brad; *v.t.*, to drive sprigs into.

sprigged, *p.p.*, sprig.

sprig'ging, *pr.p.*, sprig.

sprig'gy, *adj.*, full of, resembling, sprigs.

spright, *n.*, *i.q.* sprite.

spright'liness, *n.*, the state or quality of being sprightly.

spright'ly, *adj.*, lively, vivacious, alert, gay; *adv.*, in a sprightly way.

spring, *n.*, the earliest season of the year; a leap; bound; an elastic piece of mechanism; a dart forward or a recoil; a fountain or source; a crack in the handle of a cricket bat, etc.; *v.i.*, to arise; take origin; leap; bound; fly back or forward; *v.t.*, to arouse; start; strain.

spring'bok, *n.*, a S. African variety of deer.

springe, *n.*, a gin.

spring'er, *n.*, one who, or that which, springs; architecturally, the part where an arch begins to curve; the impost; the bottom stone laid on the impost; the lowest of the stones in a gable; a rib in a vault.

spring'-halt, *n.*, a sort of chorea in horses.

spring'iness, *n.*, the state of being springy.

spring'ing, *pr.p.*, spring.

spring'-tide, *n.*, the tide about the new and the full moon.

spring'-time, *n.*, *i.q.* the season of spring.

spring'y, *adj.*, soft, elastic.

sprin'kle, *v.t.*, to scatter into drops; to pour over; *v.i.*, to fall in thin drops; as a light rain; *n.*, a light fall in drops.

sprin'kled, *p.p.*, sprinkle.

sprin'kler, *n.*, one who, that which, sprinkles.

sprin'kling, *pr.p.*, sprinkle; *adj.*, in small drops; *n.*, a small quantity dropping; any small quantity or number.

sprint, *v.i.*, to run at top speed for a short spurt; *n.*, a short run at top speed.

sprit, *n.*, a shoot; a small spar.

sprite, *n.*, a spirit, fairy, elf. Also *spright.*

sprit'sail, *n.*, a sail stretched on a sprit.

sprock'et, *n.*, a little toothed wheel in an automobile.

sprod, *n.*, a second year salmon.

sprout, *n.*, a young growth; a shoot; *v.i.*, to shoot.

sprout'ed, *p.p.*, sprout.

sprout'ing, *pr.p.*, sprout.

sprouts, *n. pl.*, Brussels sprouts.

spruce, *adj.*, trim, tidy, smart; *n.*, the spruce fir; a fermented drink produced from spruce-leaves; *v.t.*, to make spruce.

spruced, *p.p.*, spruce.

spruce'ly, *adv.*, in a spruce manner.

spruce'ness, *n.*, the state or quality of being spruce.

spru'cing, *pr.p.*, spruce.

sprue', *n.*, a passage for metal being moulded to flow through.

sprung, *p.p.*, spring.

spry, *adj.*, alert.

spud, *n.*, a small weeding spade.

spue, *v.t.* and *i.*, *i.q.* spew.

spume, *n.*, foam, froth; *v.i.*, to throw off froth.

spumed, *p.p.*, spume.

spumes'cence, *n.*, the state of being spumescent.

spumes'cent, *adj.*, foaming.

spumif'erous, *adj.*, producing froth.

spu'miness, *n.*, the state or quality of being spumous.

spu'ming, *pr.p.*, spume.

spu'mous, *adj.*, frothy, foamy.

spun, *p.p.*, spin.

spunge, *n.* and *v.t.*, *i.q.* sponge.

spunk, *n.*, courage; spirit.

spur, *n.*, a rowelled instrument attached to the heel for pricking a horse; anything spur-like, as a projection from a mountain or a flower, etc.; *v.t.*, to prick (a horse); to stimulate; to put spurs on to.

spur'gall, *n.*, a gall produced by spurring.

spurge, *n.*, a type of plant, acrid, milky, and juicy.

spu'rious, *adj.*, false; sham.

spu'riously, *adv.*, in a spurious way.

spu'riousness, *n.*, the state or quality of being spurious.

spurl'ing-line, *n.*, a cord connecting the steering-wheel with the index.

spurn, *v.t.* and *i.*, to scorn; contemn; reject; *n.*, contempt.

spurned, *p.p.*, spurn.

spurn'er, *n.*, one who spurns.

spurn'ing, *pr.p.*, spurn.

spurred, *p.p.*, spur.

spur'rer, *n.*, one who spurs.

spur'rier, *n.*, a spur-maker.

spur'ring, *pr.p.*, spur.

spur'royal, *n.*, an old coin of James the First's reign, stamped with a device resembling the rowel of a spur.

spur'ry, *n.*, the name for certain kinds of plants, esp. the common weed, the corn-spurry.

spurt, *v.t.*, to make to flow; *v.i.*, to flow suddenly in a jet; to make a sudden and fresh start or effort; *n.*, such a fresh effort.

spurt'ed, *p.p.*, spurt.

spurt'ing, *pr.p.*, spurt.

spu'ta, *n.*, pl. of sputum.

sput'ter, *v.t.*, to utter incoherently or excitedly; *v.i.*, to speak with a spitting noise; *n.*, rapid, incoherent talk.

sput'tered, *p.p.*, sputter.

sput'terer, *n.*, one who sputters.

sput'tering, *pr.p.*, sputter.

spu'tum, *n.*, saliva; matter expectorated.

spy, *n.*, an alien who secretly keeps watch on an enemy's movements, and communicates the results of his observations to his own country; one who informs against anyone; *v.t.*, to catch sight of; perceive; *v.i.*, to play the spy.

spy'-glass, *n.*, a hand telescope.

spy'ing, *pr.p.*, spy.

squab, *adj.*, squat; *n.*, a squat person; a young pigeon.

squab'bish, *adj.*, somewhat squat.

squab'ble, *v.i.*, to bicker; wrangle; *n.*, a quarrel.

squab'bled, *p.p.*, squabble.

squab'bler, *n.*, one who squabbles.

squab'bling, *pr.p.*, squabble; *n.*, the act of squabbling.

squab'by, *adj.*, dumpy

squad, *n.*, a small force of soldiers, etc.

squad'ron, *n.*, a division of a cavalry regiment, containing two troops; a group of war-vessels detached for particular service; *v.t.*, to set in array.

squal'id, *adj.*, dirty, mean, wretched-looking.

squalid'ity, *n.*, *i.q.* squalidness.

squal'idness, *n.*, the state or quality of being squalid.

squall, *v.t.* and *i.*, to cry out; to scream; *v.i.*, to blow a squall; *n.*, a scream; a sudden storm of wind, often accompanied by rain or snow.

squalled, *p.p.*, squall.

squall'er, *n.*, one who squalls.

squall'ing, *pr. p.*, squall.

squall'y, *adj.*, stormy; blustering.

squa'loid, *adj.*, shark-like.

squal'or, *n.*, wretched appearance; poverty; destitution.

squa'ma, *n.*, a scale, or a scale-like structure (*Lat.*).

squama'ceous, *adj.*, scaly.

squa'miform, *adj.*, like scales.

squamig'erous, *adj.*, having scales.

squa'mipen, *n.*, a penguin.

squa'moid, *adj.*, scaly.

squa'mous, *adj.*, covered with, resembling, scales.

squan'der, *v.t.*, to waste; spend extravagantly.

squan'dered, *p.p.*, squander.

squan'derer, *n.*, one who squanders.

squan'dering, *pr.p.*, squander.

square, *adj.*, having four equal sides and four right-angles; rectangular; honest, outright; ample (*colloq.*); multiplied by itself; *n.*, a rectangular equilateral figure; an open area surrounded by buildings, even if the true square-shape is not preserved; any square-shaped figure; the product of a number or quantity multiplied by itself; a T-shaped rule for finding right angles; *v.t.*, to multiply a number by itself; to make square or rectangular with four equal sides; to make to balance; to adjust; to bribe, win over; to lay (yards) at right angles to the keel; *v.i.*, to be at right angles; to agree; to take a boxer's attitude; *adv.*, squarely.

squared, *p.p.*, square.

square'ly, *adv.*, in a square way; fairly.

square'ness, *n.*, the state or quality of being square.

squar'er, *n.*, one who squares; *adj.*, *comp.* of square.

square'-rigged, *adj.*, having the principal sails rigged on horizontal yards suspended by the middle from the mast.

squar'est, *adj.*, *super.* of square.

squar'ing, *pr. p.*, square.

squar'ish, *adj.*, inclined to the square.

squarrose', *adj.*, *i.q.* squarrous.

squar'rous, *adj.*, rough and having scale-like processes.

squash, *v.t.*, to squeeze and make pulpy (*colloq.*); *v.i.*, to become pulpy; to crowd; *n.*, a close crowd; the name of certain gourds.

squashed, *p.p.*, squash.

squash'er, *n.*, one who, or that which, squashes.

squash'ing, *pr.p.*, squash.

squash'y, *adj.*, soft, pulpy.

squat, *adj.*, dwarfish, dumpy; squatting; *n.*, the posture of squatting; *v.i.*, to crouch in a sitting posture; to settle in a new country.

squat'ted, *p.p.*, squat.

squat'ter, *n.*, a settler; one who squats.

squat'ting, *pr.p.*, squat.

squaw, *n.*, an American Indian woman or girl.

squawk, *v.t.*, to make a shrill, harsh cry of fear or pain; *n.*, the cry.

squawked, *p.p.*, squawk.

squawk'er, *n.*, one who squawks.

squawk'ing, *pr.p.*, squawk.

squeak, *v.i.*, to make a thin, small noise; *n.*, the noise.

squeaked, *p.p.*, squeak

squeak'er, *n.*, one who, that which, squeaks.

squeak'ing, *pr.p.*, squeak.

squeak'y, *adj.*, making the sound of squeaking.

squeal, *v.t.* and *i.*, to utter with a sharp, loud noise, as in pain, fear, etc.; *n.*, the noise of squealing.

squealed, *p.p.*, squeal.

squeal'ing, *pr.p.*, squeal.

squeam'ish, *adj.*, readily nauseated; over - scrupulous; disgusted.

squeam'ishly, *adv.*, in a squeamish way.

squeam'ishness, *n.*, the state or quality of being squeamish.

squee'gee, *n.*, an implement for absorbing and removing wet. Also *squilgee*.

squeez'able, *adj.*, able to be squeezed.

squeeze, *v.t.*, to crush, press; to extract by pressing; to extort; to take an impression of; *v.i.*, to press one's way; to penetrate by pressing; *n.*, the act of squeezing; a tight fit.

squeezed, *p.p.*, squeeze

squeez'er, *n.*, one who, that which, squeezes.

squeez'ing, *pr.p.*, squeeze.

squelch, *v.t.*, to suppress.

squib, *v.t.*, to throw squibs at; to lampoon; *n.*, a small explosive firework; a lampoon.

squib'bing, *pr.p.*, squib.

squid, *n.*, a cuttle-fish.

squil'gee, *n.*, *i.q.* squeegee.

squill, *n.*, a medicinal bulbous plant; its sliced bulb.

squint, *v.i.*, to look obliquely; to suffer from strabismus; *adj.*, having a squint; *n.*, strabismus; a difference between the axes of the two eyes; a hurried look; a hagioscope.

squint'ed, *p.p.*, squint

squint'er, *n.*, one who squints.

squint'-eyed, *adj.*, having cross-eyes.

squint'ing, *pr.p.*, squint.

squire, *n.*, the attendant on a knight; an esquire; a country gentleman with a landed estate; *v.t.*, to attend upon.

squire'archy, *n.*, squires collectively as county magnates.

squireen', *n.*, a smaller landowner, particularly in Ireland.

squire'ship, *n.*, the position of a squire.

squirm, *v.i.*, to wriggle; to cower and shudder; *n.*, a wriggle.

squirmed, *p.p.*, squirm

squirm'ing, *pr.p.*, squirm; *n.*, the act of squirming.

squir'rel, *n.*, a rodent with bushy tail.

squirt, *v.t.*, to throw water or other liquid with a syringe; *v.i.*, to be thrown as from a syringe; *n.*, a syringe; a jet.

squirt'ed, *p.p.*, squirt.

squirt'ing, *pr.p.*, squirt

stab, *v.t.* and *i.*, to pierce with a knife, dagger, etc.; to cause a stabbing pain; *n.*, a blow with a knife; a stabbing pain.

Sta'bat Ma'ter, *n.*, a Latin sequence for Passion-tide; the music of the same.

stabbed, *p.p.*, stab.

stab'ber, *n.*, one who, that which, stabs.

stab'bing, *pr.p.*, stab.

stabil'ity, *n.*, firmness; strength; steadfastness; equilibrium.

sta'bilize, *v.t.*, to make stable.

sta'ble, *adj.*, firm, steady, lasting; *n.*, a shed or other building to shelter horses or cattle; *v.t.* and *i.*, to shelter in a stable.

sta'bled, *p.p.*, stable.

sta'ble-keeper, *n.*, one who keeps stables and hires out horses.

sta'bleness, *n.*, *i.q.* stability.

sta'bling, *pr.p.*, stable; *n.*, accommodation for horses.

stab'lish, *v.t.*, *i.q.* establish.

sta'bly, *adv.*, in a stable way.

stacca'to, *adv.*, played abruptly and in a detached manner.

stack, *v.t.*, to arrange in stacks; to file; *n.*, a pile of wheat sheaves or of hay or straw; anything piled; a smoke-funnel or chimney.

stacked, *p.p.*, stack.

stack'er, *n.*, one who stacks.

stack'ing, *pr.p.*, stack.

stac'te, *n.*, a spice used as an ingredient of incense.

sta'dia, *n.*, an instrument for measuring distances. Also the pl. of stadium.

sta'dium, *n.*, an ancient Greek measure of length; a racecourse; in medicine, the period of a disease.

stadt'holder, *n.*, a Netherlander provincial governor.

staff, *n.*, a stick, a support; a pole; a body of officers closely attached to headquarters, or of persons employed in a firm, school, etc.; the musical stave, consisting of lines with spaces between, indicating relative pitch of notes.

stag, *n.*, a male deer; a bull castrated when fully grown.

stage, *n.*, a platform for actors; the theatrical profession; any sort of platform; a storey; a halting-place; distance between two places in a journey; a defined period; *i.q.* stage-coach; *v.t.*, to mount a play.

stage'-coach, *n.*, a public conveyance travelling from one place to another by stages.

staged, *p.p.*, stage.

stage'-player, *n.*, an actor.

sta'ger, *n.*, a stage-horse.

stage'-struck, *adj.*, morbidly desirous of becoming an actor.

sta'gey, *adj.*, theatrical; unnatural.

stag'ger, *v.t.*, to shake; to dismay; to cause to doubt; to arrange spokes of wheels; *v.i.*, to reel; to waver; *n.*, a reeling movement; in *pl.*, a brain disease in cattle and horses; a state of giddiness.

stag'gered, *p.p.*, stagger.

stag'gering, *pr.p.*, stagger.

stag'hound, *n.*, a hound used in stag-hunting.

sta'ging, *pr.p.*, stage; *n.*, scaffolding.

Stag'irite, *n.*, a native of Stageira, esp. Aristotle, who is often alluded to as the Stagirite.

stag'nancy, *n.*, the state or quality of being stagnant.

stag'nant, *adj.*, motionless; not flowing; lifeless; dull.

stag'nate, *v.i.*, to have no movement; to become inert.

stag'nated, *p.p.*, stagnate.

stag'nating, *pr.p.*, stagnate.

stagna'tion, *n.*, the state of being stagnant.

sta'gy, *adj.*, *i.q.* stagey.

staid, *adj.*, steady, sober.

stain, *n.*, spot, blemish, discoloration; colouring for wood, walls, etc.; *v.t.*, to discolour; blemish; colour.

stained, *p.p.*, stain.

stain'er, *n.*, one who stains or paints.

stain'ing, *pr.p.*, stain; *n.*, the act of staining; stained work.

stain'less, *adj.*, unblemished.

stain'lessness, *n.*, the state or quality of being stainless.

stair, *n.*, a step, or series of ascending or descending steps.

stair'case, *n.*, a set of stairs.

stair'-rod, *n.*, a rod to keep a stair-carpet in its place.

stair'way, *n.*, *i.q.* staircase.

staith(e), *n.*, a wharf.

stake, *n.*, a pole, stick, pale with sharpened end; an upright post; a hazard; wager; *v.t.*, to impale; to defend with stakes; to wager; to curry (a skin).

staked, *p.p.*, stake.

stake'holder, *n.*, one who holds the wagers of two or more parties.

sta'king, *pr.p.*, stake.

stalac'tic, *adj.*, formed by dripping deposit.

stalac'tiform, *adj.*, like a stalactite.

stal'actite, *n.*, a mineral pendulous formation, the result of a dripping deposit.

stalactit'ic, *adj.*, *i.q.* stalactic.

stal'agmite, *n.*, a deposit on the ground, formed by a drip from above, and sometimes growing till it meets the gradually descending stalactite and joins with it.

stalagmit'ic, *adj.*, rel. to stalagmites.

stal'der, *n.*, a cask-stand.

stale, *adj.*, vapid through age; worn out; trite; *n.*, urine of cattle; a broom-handle; *v.t.*, to make stale; take the life out of; *v.i.*, to become stale; to urinate.

stale'mate, *v.t.*, to reduce to a stalemate; *n.*, a position (in chess) where neither side can claim a win.

stale'ness, *n.*, the state or quality of being stale.

stalk, *v.t.*, to pursue stealthily; to pass with a stately step; *v.i.*, to walk in a stately way; to pursue game stealthily; *n.*, a stem; a gait.

stalked, *p.p.*, stalk.

stalk'er, *n.*, one who stalks.

stalk'ing, *pr.p.*, stalk; *n.*, the act of stalking.

stalk'less, *adj.*, without a stalk.

stalk'y, *adj.*, like a stalk; with a large stalk.

stall, *v.t.*, to put into a stall; to put stalls into; to fix in a drift or mud; *v.i.*, to be stuck in mud, etc.; *n.*, a compartment in a row of seats in a choir or a theatre; a compartment in a stable; a thief's confederates.

stall'age, *n.*, stall-accommodation; payment for right to erect stalls at a fair.

stalled, *p.p.*, stall.

stall'-fed, *adj.*, fed in a stable; *p.p.*, stall-feed.

stall'-feed, *v.t.*, to feed cattle in a stable or stall.

stall'-feeding, *pr.p.*, stall-feed.

stall'ing, *pr.p.*, stall.

stal'lion, *n.*, a horse not castrated and kept for breeding purposes.

stal'wart, *adj.*, sturdy, strong, bold: *n.*, a strong partisan.

sta'men, *n.*, the organ that contains the pollen of a flowering plant (*Lat.*).

stam'ina, *n.*, strength of constitution; lasting power.

stam'inal, *adj.*, pert. to stamina and stamens.

stam'inate, *adj.*, having stamens.

stam'inate, *v.t.*, to invigorate.

stamin'eous, *adj.*, rel. to stamens.

staminif'erous, *adj.*, having stamens.

stam'mer, *v.t.* and *i.*, to speak with a stammer; *n.*, defective, stuttering speech; utterance with an impediment.

stam'mered, *p.p.*, stammer.

stam'merer, *n.*, one who stammers.

stam'mering, *pr.p.*, stammer; *n.*, stuttering.

stamp, *n.*, a pattern, impress; a stamping machine; an official mark on deeds, bills, etc.; an official paper marked as receipt for payment of fee for postage, etc.; character; heavy pressure with the foot; *v.t.*, to make an impress; to affix a stamp; *v.i.*, to press heavily with the foot.

stamped, *p.p.*, stamp.

stampede', *n.*, a wild flight in alarm; *v.t.*, to cause to stampede; *v.i.*, to run wildly away in a frightened crowd.

stamp'er, *n.*, one who, or that which, stamps.

stamp'ing, *pr.p.*, stamp.

stance, *n.*, the position of a golf-player in making a stroke.

stanch, *v.t.*, to stop the flow; to check the flow of blood from; *adj.*, firm, loyal, vigorous. Also *staunch*.

stanched, *p.p.*, stanch.

stanch'ing, *pr.p.*, stanch.

stan'chion, *n.*, a vertical support; an upright bar; *v.t.*, to enclose (cattle) with a stanchion; to secure with stanchions.

stand, *v.t.*, to set upright; to bear; to give as a treat; *v.i.*, to assume an upright position; to keep one's footing; to endure; to be still; to be based; *n.*, a firm position; a halt; resistance; a support; a platform; a rack; a set of shelves.

stand'ard, *n.*, a measure, rule, type; a flag; an educational grade; an upright shrub or tree not supported; *adj.*, according to pattern or recognized degree of quality or excellence.

stand'ard-bearer, *n.*, one who carries a standard.

standardiza'tion, *n.*, the act or effect of standardizing.

stand'ardize, *v.t.*, to make according to one pattern; to obtain analytically the specific value of, for the purpose of comparing with other solutions, etc.

stand'ardized, *p.p.*, standardize.

stand'ardizing, *pr.p.*, standardize.

stand'er, *n.*, one who, or that which, stands.

stand'ing, *pr.p.*, stand; *n.*, rank, position, repute; *adj.*, permanent; stock.

stand'ish, *n.*, an inkstand.

stand'point, *n.*, a point from which one views a question.

stand'still, *n.*, a halt.

stan'hope, *n.*, a light, open carriage.

stank, *p.t.*, stink.

stan'nary, *n.*, a tin mine; a tin mining district; *adj.*, pert. to tin mining.

stan'nate, *n.*, a stannic acid salt.

stan'nic, *adj.*, pert. to tin.

stannif'erous, *adj.*, producing tin.

stann'yel, *n.*, the kestrel. Also *staniel*.

stan'za, *n.*, a group of rimed lines, forming a single division of equal length with other divisions in a poem.

stanza'ic, *adj.*, arranged in, pert. to, stanzas.

staph'yline, *adj.*, rel. to the uvula.

staphylo'ma, *n.*, a protrusion of the cornea or other surface of the eye.

sta'ple, *adj.*, regularly on the market; principal; *n.*, a leading article of commerce; chief element; cotton-fibre; a great mart; a monopoly; a piece of metal, pointed at both ends and driven into a door, etc., to receive a hook or hasp; *v.t.*, to fasten with a staple.

sta'pled, *p.p.*, staple.

sta'pler, *n.*, one who sorts wool; a wool merchant with a monopoly.

star, *n.*, a luminous heavenly body—(strictly, a star is a fixed star, but a wider meaning is given to the name by the inclusion of planets)—anything like a star; an asterisk; the principal actor in a company; any outstanding member of a profession; *v.t.*, to adorn with stars; to mark with an asterisk; to break so as to produce a starlike appearance; *v.i.*, to play a leading part as an actor; to get a new innings in the game of pool.

star'board, *n.*, the right-hand side of a ship; *v.t.*, to turn a ship to the right.

starch, *n.*, white powder found in all plants except fungi; in its prepared form, when mixed with boiling water, it is used for stiffening linen, etc.; *adj.*, prim, stiff; *v.t.*, to stiffen.

Star' Chamber, *n.*, a former ancient legal tribunal, so named from a chamber with a star-spangled roof in which it met. (Abolished 1640.)

starched, *p.p.*, starch

starch'er, *n.*, one who, or that which, starches.

starch'ing, *pr.p.*, starch.

starch'y, *adj.*, stiff in any sense.

stare, *n.*, a fixed look expressing horror, fright, astonishment, etc.; *v.i.*, to look with a stare; *v.t.*, to put out of countenance.

stared, *p.p.*, stare.

sta'rer, *n.*, one who stares.

star'fish, *n.*, an echinoderm with radiating arms.

star'-flower, *n.*, any star-shaped flower.

star'-gazer, *n.*, an astronomer; an astrologer.

star'-gazing, *adj.*, studying the stars; *n.*, astronomy; the study of the stars; absent-mindedness.

sta'ring, *pr.p.*, stare; *adj.*, with a stare; prominent; gaudy.

stark, *adj.*, stiff; downright; *adv.*, quite.

star'less, *adj.*, without **stars**; dark.

star'light, *n.*, the light of the stars.

star'like, *adj.*, like a star.

star'ling, *n.*, a bird so named and noted for its powers of imitation; an arrangement of piles round a bridge-pier.

star'lit, *adj.*, illuminated by the stars.

star'ost, *n.*, a Polish noble.

star'osty, *n.*, a Polish noble's seigniory.

starred, *p.p.*, star.

star'riness, *n.*, the state or quality of being starry.

star'ring, *pr.p.*, star.

star'ry, *adj.*, bright with stars.

star'-spangled, *adj.*, spangled or dotted over with stars.

start, *v.t.*, to cause to begin; to make a beginning of; *v.i.*, to make a beginning; set out on a journey; spring up in alarm, surprise, etc.; *n.*, a beginning; a setting out; distance allowed on a handicap.

start'ed, *p.p.*, start.

start'er, *n.*, one who starts; one who gives the signal to competitors in a race; anything that sets machinery in motion.

start'ful, *adj.*, skittish.

start'ing, *pr.p.*, start.

start'ing-point, *n.*, a point or place from which one starts.

start'ing-post, *n.*, a post from which racers start.

start'le, *v.t.*, to fill with sudden alarm; to surprise.

start'led, *p.p.*, startle.

start'ling, *pr.p.*, startle; *adj.*, alarming; surprising.

starva'tion, *n.*, the act or effect of starving; the starved state.

starve, *v.t.*, to destroy with hunger or cold; to deprive of necessaries; *v.i.*, to perish of hunger or cold.

starved, *p.p.*, starve.

starve'ling, *adj.*, starving; improperly fed; *n.*, a starving or ill-fed person.

starv'ing, *pr.p.*, starve

star'wort, *n.*, an aster.

state, *n.*, condition; mode of existence; a community with an organized government; *adj.*, pert. to the State; ceremoniously formal; *v.t.* and *i.*, to say expressly in word or writing; to fix definitely.

state'craft, *n.*, skill in government.

sta'ted, *p.p.*, state; *adj.*, fixed; regular.

sta'tedly, *adv.*, expressly.

state'lier, *adj.*, *comp.* of stately.

state'liest, *adj.*, *super.* of stately.

state'liness, *n.*, the state or quality of being stately.

state'ly, *adj.*, majestic, dignified.

state'ment, *n.*, the act of stating; that which is stated.

sta'ter, *n.*, one who states; an old Greek coin varying in value.

state'room, *n.*, an officer's sleeping-room in a ship; a private sleeping-room in a passenger ship.

States *Gen'eral*, *n. pl.*, a general legislative body representing various estates of the citizens.

states'man, *n.*, one engaged or skilled in government.

states'manlike, *adj.*, showing skill in government.

states'manship, *n.*, the quality of being statesmanlike.

stat'ic, *adj.*, pert. to bodies in equilibrium and at rest, or to electricity at rest; acting as weight without motion.

stat'ical, *adj.*, *i.q.* static.

stat'ics, *n. pl.*, the study or science of bodies at rest.

sta'ting, *pr.p.*, state.

sta'tion, *n.*, a position or place where people stay or it is appointed for them to stay or halt; rank; the collected officers and society residing at a military post in India; a point from which surveying measurements are taken; a stated fast on Wednesday or Friday; a halting-point in a procession; a church to which processions go in Rome; one of the set of fourteen pictures or sculptures illustrating the events of Our Lord's Passion; *v.t.*, to place; assign a position to.

sta'tional, *adj.*, rel. to a station.

sta'tionary, *adj.*, standing still; not moving or advancing.

sta'tioned, *p.p.*, station.

sta'tioner, *n.*, one who sells paper, pens, pencils, etc.

sta'tionery, *n.*, writing materials.

sta'tioning, *pr.p.*, station.

sta'tist, *n.*, one who handles statistics; *i.q.* statistician.

statis'tic, *n.*, sing. of statistics.

statis'tical, *adj.*, pert. to statistics.

statis'tically, *adv.*, in a statistical way.

statisti'cian, *n.*, one who compiles and tabulates statistics.

statis'tics, *n. pl.*, numerical facts compiled and systematically tabulated.

sta'tive, *adj.*, pert. to a permanent camp.

stat'uary, *n.*, statues collectively; the sculptor's art; a sculptor; *adj.*, rel. to statues.

stat'ue, *n.*, a sculptured, cast, or moulded representation of a human or animal figure; *v.t.*, to represent as a statue.

stat'ued, *p.p.*, statue.

statuesque', *n.*, like a statue for grace, or dignity, or repose.

statuette', *n.*, a little statue.

stat'ure, *n.*, height, chiefly of a human being.

sta'tus, *n.*, position, standing.

stat'utable, *adj.*, *i.q.* statutory.

stat'ute, *n.*, a legislative enactment; a law; *adj.*, pert. to statutes; authorized by statute.

stat'ute-book, *n.*, a book recording legal enactments.

stat'utory, *adj.*, regulated by statute; having the authority of law.

staunch, *adj.*, and *v.t.*, *i.q.* stanch.

staur'o-, a Greek prefix denoting a cross.

staur'oscope, *n.*, an optical instrument for determining the effect of polarized light on crystals.

stau'rotypous, *adj.*, with markings like crosses.

stave, *n.*, one of the bent timbers in the side of a cask; a staff (*mus.*); a verse or stanza; *v.t.*, to break the staves or sides of; to fix with staves; (with the word *off*) to avert; *v.i.*, to be broken in.

staved, *p.p.*, stave.

sta'ving, *pr.p.*, stave.

stay, *v.t.*, to stop; arrest; support; *v.i.*, to remain (in a place); to stand still; *n.*, a support; continuance (in a place); suspension of proceedings (*leg.*); a rope, supporting a mast or sail.

stayed, *p.p.*, stay.

stay'er, *n.*, one who stays; one who can last.

stay'ing, *pr.p.*, stay.

stay'lace, *n.*, the lace of a corset.

stay'-maker, *n.*, a corset-maker.

stays, *n. pl.*, a corset; the act of going about (*naut.*).

stay'sail, *n.*, a sail on a stay.

stead, *n.*, place or room; avail.

stead'fast, sted'fast, *adj.*, firm, loyal.

stead'fastly, *adv.*, loyally, firmly.

stead'fastness, *n.*, firmness, loyalty.

stead'ied, *p.p.*, steady

stead'ier, *adj.*, *comp.* of steady.

stead'iest, *adj.*, *super.* of steady.

stead'ily, *adv.*, in a steady way.

stead'iness, *n.*, the state or quality of being steady.

stead'y, *adj.*, not easily shaken; firm; temperate; regular; *v.t.*, to make steady; to keep (a ship) firm in its course; *n.*, a support.

stead'ying, *pr.p.*, steady.

steak, *n.*, a cut from flesh-meat or fish.

steal, *v.t.*, to take by theft or by surprise; to take secret or complete possession of; *v.i.*, to be a thief; to move secretly or silently.

steal'er, *n.*, one who steals.

steal'ing, *pr.p.*, steal; *n.*, theft.

stealth, *n.*, secrecy or silence.

stealth'ily, *adv.*, in a stealthy way.

stealth'iness, *n.*, the quality of being stealthy.

stealth'y, *adj.*, surreptitious; furtive.

steam, *n.*, vapour of water; the gas emanating from boiling water; any exhalation like steam; energy; *v.t.*, to treat or cook with steam; *v.i.*, to give forth steam; to travel by means of steam.

steam'boat, *n.*, a boat driven by steam-power.

steamed, *p.p.*, steam.

steam'-engine, *n.*, an engine worked by steam.

steam'er, *n.*, one who, that which, steams; a steamship.

steam'-gauge, *n.*, a gauge showing the steam pressure in a boiler.

steam'-gun, *n.*, a gun in which steam is used to propel the projectile.

steam'-hammer, *n.*, a hammer worked by steam.
steam'ing, *pr.p.*, steam
steam'-pipe, *n.*, a pipe providing for the escape of steam.
steam'-ship, *n.*, a ship propelled by steam.
steam'-tug, *n.*, a tug propelled by steam.
steam'y, *adj.*, like steam; full of steam.
ste'arate, *n.*, a stearic acid salt.
stear'ic, *adj.*, pert. to stearin.
ste'arin, *n.*, the principal ingredient in animal and vegetable fats; stearic acid for candles.
ste'atite, *n.*, soapstone.
steatit'ic, *adj.*, pert. to steatite.
steato'ma, *n.*, a fatty tumour.
steatom'atous, *adj.*, pert. to a steatoma.
steato'sis, *n.*, fatty degeneration.
steed, *n.*, a horse.
steel, *n.*, a malleable alloy of iron; *adj.*, made of, or resembling steel; *v.t.*, to harden.
steeled, *p.p.*, steel.
steel'iness, *adj.*, the quality of being steely.
steel'ing, *pr.p.*, steel.
steel'-plated, *adj.*, protected with steel plates.
steel'y, *adj.*, like steel; inflexible.
steel'yard, *n.*, a weighing apparatus with a short arm from which the thing to be weighed is suspended, and a long arm that is graduated and along which a weight slides until it registers the exact weight of the suspended object.
steen'ing, *n.*, the stone casing of a well.
steep, *adj.*, greatly inclining; sheer; precipitous; outrageous, exorbitant (*colloq.*); *n.*, a precipice, mountain, ascent; *v.t.*, to soak in a liquid; to impregnate; *n.*, liquid for steeping; the process of steeping.
steeped, *p.p.*, steep.
steep'ing, *pr.p.*, steep.
stee'ple, *n.*, a tower and spire.
stee'plechase, *n.*, a horse race over obstacles.
steep'ness, *n.*, the state or quality of being steep.
steep'y, *adj.*, steep.
steer, *v.t.*, to direct the course of (a ship or boat); *v.i.*, to guide the rudder; to direct one's course; *n.*, a young male ox.
steer'age, *n.*, the act of steering; the action of a ship's helm; the part of a passenger ship where the cheaper berths are placed, or where the quarters of junior officers on a warship are situated.
steered, *p.p.*, steer.
steer'er, *n.*, one who steers.
steer'ing, *pr.p.*, steer.
steers'man, *n.*, *i.q.* steerer.
steeve, *n.*, the angle a bowsprit makes with the horizon; a spar used in shifting cargo; *v.t.* and *i.*, to make an angle with the horizon; *v.i.*, to work with a steeve.
steeved, *p.p.*, steeve.
steev'ing, *pr.p.*, steeve.
steganog'raphy, *n.*, cryptic writing; cipher.
stegnot'ic, *adj.*, constipating.
ste'la, *n.*, *i.q.* stele.
ste'le, *n.*, a plain pillar with neither base nor capital (*Gr.*).
stel'lar, *adj.*, pert. to the stars.
stel'lary, *adj.*, *i.q.* stellar.
stel'late, *adj.*, starlike, radiating.
stel'lated, *adj.*, *i.q.* stellate.
stellif'erous, *adj.*, starry.
stel'liform, *adj.*, shaped like a star.
stel'lular, *adj.*, radiated.
stelog'raphy, *n.*, writing on stelae.
stem, *n.*, the trunk of a tree; the main axis of any plant; any stem-like thing (as the stem of a pipe); the forepart of a ship; the uninflected base of a word; *v.t.*, to arrest; oppose; dam; *v.i.*, to go forward.
stem'less, *adj.*, without stem.
stemmed, *p.p.*, stem.
stem'ming, *pr.p.*, stem
stem'ple, *n.*, a crossbar enabling miners to ascend and descend in a pit.
stench, *n.*, smell, stink.
sten'cil, *n.*, a piece of metal or cardboard perforated with a pattern or lettering; *v.t.*, to mark by means of stencilling.
sten'cil(l)ed, *p.p.*, stencil.
sten'cil(l)ing, *pr.p.*, stencil.
stenog'rapher, *n.*, a writer of stenography or shorthand.
stenograph'ic, *adj.*, pert. to stenography.
stenograph'ical, *adj.*, *i.q.* stenographic.
stenog'raphist, *n.*, *i.q.* stenographer.
stenog'raphy, *n.*, the art and practice of shorthand writing.
sten'otype, *n.*, shorthand print.
sten'otypy, *n.*, shorthand printing.
sten'tor, *n.*, a loud-lunged person.
stento'rian, *adj.*, loud-lunged; like the ancient Greek herald, Stentor.
step, *n.*, a movement of the foot in walking; a footstep; the distance measured by the foot in stepping; a rung in a ladder; a stair; *v.i.*, to move on foot; to

walk; *v.t.*, to measure a distance by pacing it; to make a step of; to fix up (a mast).

step'brother, *n.*, a brother by marriage only; the son of one's father or mother by a later or previous marriage.

step'*child*, *n.*, the child of one's wife or husband by a previous marriage.

step'dame, *n.*, a grandmother by marriage only.

step'daughter, *n.*, the daughter of one's wife or husband by a previous marriage.

step'father, *n.*, the husband of one's mother by a later marriage.

stephano'tis, *n.*, a climbing, white-flowered plant.

step'mother, *n.*, the wife of one's father by a later marriage.

steppe, *n.*, a Russian plain.

stepped, *p.p.*, step.

step'per, *n.*, one who steps.

step'ping, *pr.p.*, step.

step'ping-stone, *n.*, a stone used for mounting.

step'sister, *n.*, the daughter of one's father or mother by a previous or later marriage.

step'son, *n.*, the son of a wife or husband by a previous marriage.

stercora'ceous, *adj.*, pert. to dung.

ster'corary, *adj.*, *i.q.* stercoraceous.

stere, *n.*, a cubic measure unit.

ster'eo, a prefix = hard, solid, firm; *n.*, short for stereotype.

stereograph'ic, *adj.*, rel. to stereography.

stereog'raphy, *n.*, showing solid figures on a plane.

stereom'eter, *n.*, a scientific apparatus for finding specific gravity.

stereomet'ric, *adj.*, pert. to stereometry.

stereom'etry, *n.*, the art of finding the specific gravity of bodies, or their cubical contents.

stereop'ticon, *n.*, a magic lantern that appears to represent objects in relief.

ster'eoscope, *n.*, an optical binocular apparatus showing a picture as though in relief.

stereoscop'ic, *adj.*, pert. to stereoscopes.

stereos'copist, *n.*, one who makes stereoscopes.

ster'eotype, *n.*, a metal casting of matter printed in movable types; *v.t.*, to make such a casting; to make permanent; *adj.*, rel. to stereotype.

ster'eotyped, *p.p.*, stereotype.

ster'eotyper, *n.*, one who stereotypes.

stereotyp'ic, *adj.*, in stereotype.

ster'eotyping, *pr.p.*, stereotype.

stereotypog'raphy, *n.*, stereotyping.

ster'ile, *adj.*, barren, unfruitful.

steril'ity, *n.*, the state of being sterile.

ster'ilize, *v.t.*, to make sterile; make incapable of reproduction.

ster'ilized, *p.p.*, sterilize.

ster'ilizing, *pr.p.*, sterilize.

ster'ling, *adj.*, pure; of the best quality; according to the English money standard.

stern, *adj.*, severe; harsh; in the stern; *n.*, the after part of a ship or boat; hindquarters.

ster'nal, *adj.*, rel. to the sternum.

stern'-board, *n.*, a board on a vessel's stern.

stern'-chase, *n.*, pursuit from the rear.

stern'er, *adj.*, *comp.* of stern.

stern'est, *adj.*, *super.* of stern.

stern'ly, *adv.*, in a stern way.

stern'*most*, *adj.*, furthest in the rear.

stern'ness, *n.*, the quality of being stern; severity.

sternocos'tal, *adj.*, pert. to the chest and ribs.

stern'-post, *n.*, the timber support of the stern.

stern'-sheets, *n. pl.*, the part of a ship devoted to the passengers' seats.

ster'num, *n.*, the breast-bone (*Lat.*).

sternuta'tion, *n.*, sneezing.

sternu'tative, *adj.*, exciting a sneeze.

sternu'tatory, *adj.* pert. to sneezing.

ster'torous, *adj.*, snoring.

stet, *v.i.*, *pr. subjunct.* 3rd pers. sing. of the Latin word for *stand* = "let it stand." It has become an English transitive verb, meaning to leave uncorrected anything that has been corrected.

stethom'eter, *n.*, an instrument measuring the chest in the act of respiration.

steth'oscope, *n.*, an instrument enabling the user to hear sounds in a patient's thorax.

stethoscop'ic, *adj.*, pert. to a stethoscope.

stethoscop'ical, *adj.* stethoscopic.

ste'vedore, *n.*, a man engaged in loading or unloading cargo.

stew, *v.t.*, to cook meat slowly in a pan; to let it simmer; *v.i.*, to be cooked in this way; *n.*, meat so cooked.

stew'ard, *n.*, one who looks after the domestic accounts of a family or master; one who manages a landed estate; one who superintends the culinary affairs of a ship, a club, etc.; one who performs duties akin to those of a steward.

stew'ardess, *n.*, a woman attendant on a ship.

stew'ardship, *n.*, the office of a steward.

stewed, *p.p.*, stew.

stew'ing, *pr.p.*, stew; *adj.*, excessively hot (*colloq.*).

sthen'ic, *adj.*, showing a morbid condition of the heart and blood vessels.

stib'ial, *adj.*, like antimony.

stib'iated, *adj.*, *i.q.* stibious.

stib'ious, *adj.*, containing antimony.

stib'ium, *n.*, antimony (*Lat.*).

stich, *n.*, a metrical line or verse.

stich'ic, *adj.*, pert. to a stich.

stichom'etry, *n.*, verse-measurement.

stick, *v.t.*, to cause to adhere; to fasten; to stab; to set with points; to compose (type); *v.i.*, to adhere; to remain; to be unable to move; *n.*, a cutting from a tree; a walking-staff; a printer's composing stick; a dull fellow (*colloq.*).

stick'er, *n.*, one who, or that which, sticks.

stick'iness, *n.*, the state or quality of being sticky.

stick'ing, *pr.p.*, stick.

stick'le, *v.i.*, to insist on an unimportant point; to cling tenaciously to some observance or rule.

stick'leback, *n.*, a small fish with a spiny back.

stick'led, *p.p.*, stickle.

stick'ler, *n.*, one who stickles.

stick'ling, *pr.p.*, stickle

stick'y, *adj.*, adhesive; viscous.

stiff, *adj.*, unyielding to the touch; firm; violent; precise; severe.

stiff'en, *v.t.*, to make stiff; *v.i.*, to become stiff.

stiff'ened, *p.p.*, stiffen

stiff'ening, *pr.p.*, stiffen; *n.*, material that makes something stiff.

stiff'er, *adj.*, *comp.* of stiff.

stiff'ly, *adv.*, in a stiff way.

stiff'-neck, *n.*, an obstinate person.

stiff'necked, *adj.*, stubborn; obstinate.

stiff'ness, *n.*, the state or quality of being stiff.

sti'fle, *v.t.*, to smother; suffocate; deaden; *v.i.*, to be suffocated; *n.*, the joint next below a horse's buttock.

sti'fled, *p.p.*, stifle.

sti'fling, *pr.p.*, stifle; *adj.*, suffocating.

stig'ma, *n.*, a mark; a stamp; brand of censure or of shame; the top of a pistil.

stig'mata, *n.*, pl. of stigma, the marks of Our Lord's wounds which some of His Saints have borne in their bodies.

stigmat'ic, *adj.*, pert. to a stigma.

stigmat'ical, *adj.*, *i.q.* stigmatic.

stig'matize, *v.t.*, to brand with a stigma; to hold up to infamy.

stig'matized, *p.p.*, stigmatize.

stig'matizing, *pr.p.*, stigmatize.

stile, *n.*, a fence with steps; an upright in panelled work; a gnomon.

stilet'to, *n.*, a small dagger; a pointed instrument for making eyelet holes.

still, *adj.*, quiet; calm; not effervescent; *adv.*, continuing now; nevertheless; *v.t.*, to make still; to calm; *n.*, a distilling appliance.

still'-born, *adj.*, born dead.

stilled, *p.p.*, still.

still'er, *adj.*, *comp.* of still; *n.*, one who, or that which, stills.

still'ing, *pr.p.*, still.

still life, *n.*, inanimate objects in art.

still'ness, *n.*, the state or quality of being still.

still'-room, *n.*, a room in a house for making or storing drinks

stil'ly, *adj.*, *i.q.* still.

stilt, *n.*, one of two poles with a notch some way up each of them, on which the foot can be rested; *v.t.*, to place on stilts.

stilt'ed, *p.p.*, stilt; *adj.*, artificial; pompous; in architecture, elongated.

stilt'ing, *pr.p.*, stilt.

Stil'ton, *n.*, a choice make of cheese.

stim'ulant, *adj.*, stimulating; *n.*, that which stimulates, esp. an alcoholic liquor.

stim'ulate, *v.t.*, to give a stimulus to; to spur on; to inspirit.

stim'ulated, *p.p.*, stimulate.

stim'ulating, *pr.p.*, stimulate.

stimula'tion, *n.*, the act or effect of stimulating.

stim'ulative, *adj.*, giving a stimulus.

stim'ulator, *n.*, one who, or that which, stimulates.

stim'ulus, *n.*, an impetus; a spur; an incentive (*Lat.*).

sting, *n.*, the poisonous pointed weapon of certain creatures; *v.t.*, to cause pain with a sting; to provoke.

sting'er, *n.*, one who, or that which, stings.

stin'gier, *adj.*, *comp.* of stingy.

stin'giest, *adj.*, *super.* of stingy.

stin'gily, *adv.*, in a stingy way.

stin'giness, *n.*, the quality of being stingy.

sting'ing, *pr.p.*, sting.

sting'less, *adj.*, harmless; without a sting.

stin'go, *n.*, strong ale.

stin'gy, *adj.*, niggardly, mean, parsimonious.
sting'y, *adj.*, apt to sting.
stink, *n.*, a foul smell; stench; *v.t.*, to make to stink; *v.i.*, to give forth a foul smell.
stink'ard, *n.*, an offensive person.
stink'er, *n.*, one who, or that which, stinks.
stink'ing, *pr.p.*, stink; *adj.*, foully smelling; offensive.
stint, *n.*, niggardly or scanty supply; *v.t.*, to supply in scanty or niggardly amount or quantity.
stint'ed, *p.p.*, stint.
stint'er, *n.*, one who stints.
stint'ing, *pr.p.*, stint.
stipe, *n.*, a stalk.
sti'pend, *n.*, pay; fixed salary, esp. that of a priest.
stipend'iary, *adj.*, in receipt of a fixed stipend; *n.*, one so paid, esp. a police magistrate.
stip'ple, *n.*, dotted work; *v.t.* and *i.*, to employ dots for lines in engraving, drawing, or painting.
stip'pled, *p.p.*, stipple.
stip'pling, *pr.p.*, stipple; *n.*, the act of engraving, etching, etc., in dots.
stipula'ceous, *adj.*, *i.q.* stipular.
stip'ular, *adj.*, growing on stipules; near or resembling stipules.
stip'ulary, *adj.*, *i.q.* stipular.
stip'ulate, *adj.*, having stipules.
stip'ulate, *v.t.* and *i.*, to require as the terms of agreement; to demand.
stip'ulated, *p.p.*, stipulate.
stip'ulating, *pr.p.*, stipulate.
stipula'tion, *n.*, the act of stipulating; terms demanded.
stip'ulator, *n.*, one who stipulates.
stip'ule, *n.*, an appendage at the base of some leaves.
stip'uled, *adj.*, having stipules.
stir, *v.t.*, to move particles round and round; to arouse, stimulate; *v.i.*, to arouse oneself; to move; *n.*, a bustle, disturbance, public interest.
stirk, *n.*, a bovine yearling.
stirred, *p.p.*, stir.
stir'rer, *n.*, one who stirs.
stir'ring, *pr.p.*, stir; *adj.*, exciting, busy; *n.*, the act of stirring
stir'rup, *n.*, a rider's foot-rest suspended from the saddle.
stitch, *n.*, one passing of the needle and thread in sewing; a peculiar sharp pain in the side; *v.t.* and *i.*, to sew; to pass thread through and back.
stitched, *p.p.*, stitch.
stitch'er, *n.*, one who, or that which, stitches.
stitch'ing, *pr.p.*, stitch.
stith'y, *n.*, a forge.
stive, *v.t.*, to stew; *n.*, a stew; flour-dust.
stived, *p.p.*, stive.
sti'ver, *n.*, a Dutch coin of the very smallest value.
sti'ving, *pr.p.*, stive.
sto'a, *n.*, a Greek portico, esp. one in the market-place of Athens, where Zeno and his school expounded their philosophy. Hence the name *Stoics*.
stoat, *n.*, the ermine.
stock, *n.*, a tree-trunk or stem; lineage; animals on a farm; company capital; accumulated goods; a handle; the part of a gun supporting the barrel, etc.; a stiff neck-band; a variety of gillyflower; *adj.*, always in store; commonplace; *v.t.*, to furnish with cattle or goods or seed; to fit with a handle or support.
stockade', *n.*, a fortification of stakes; a palisade; *v.t.*, to fence with stakes.
stock'-broker, *n.*, one who negotiates the purchase and sale of stocks.
stock'-dove, *n.*, a wood pigeon.
stocked, *p.p.*, stock.
stock'-fish, *n.*, dried, salted fish.
stock'holder, *n.*, one who holds stocks.
stockinet', *n.*, an elastic material.
stock'ing, *pr.p.*, stock; *n.*, a leg-covering.
stock'-in-*trade*, *n.*, a dealer's collective goods.
stock'ish, *adj.*, stunted.
stock'-jobber, *n.*, a dealer or speculator in stocks.
stock'-jobbing, *n.*, a stock-jobber's business.
stock'list, *n.*, a list of stocks and shares.
stocks, *n. pl.*, public funds; an old instrument of punishment, the offender's legs being confined in a wooden frame.
stock'still, *adj.*, absolutely at rest; motionless.
stock'-taking, *n.*, a periodical overhauling of one's possessions or merchandise.
stock'y, *adj.*, stumpy.
stock'-yard, *n.*, an enclosure for cattle on a ranch, etc.
Sto'ic, *n.*, a disciple of Zeno and the Stoic philosophers; *adj.*, pert. to the Stoa and the Stoics; (-s) contemptuous of pain.
sto'ical, *adj.*, *i.q.* stoic.
stoicheiol'ogy, *n.*, the study of first principles.
stoicheiom'etry, *n.*, the art of calculating the weight of atoms in chemical elements.
sto'icism, *n.*, the doctrines of the Stoics; indifference to pain and misfortune.

stoke, *v.t.* and *i.*, to make up a fire.

stoked, *p.p.*, stoke.

stoke'-hole, *n.*, the part of a ship's interior where the engine-furnaces are worked.

sto'ker, *n.*, a furnace-man on an engine.

sto'king, *pr.p.*, stoke; *n.*, the act or business of a stoker.

stole, *n.*, a long, narrow strip of silk or other material worn scarf-fashion by the Sacred Ministers at Mass and in other Sacramental rites; *p.t.*, steal.

stoled, *adj.*, vested in a stole.

sto'len, *p.p.*, steal.

stol'id, *adj.*, unmoving, slow, stupid.

stolid'ity, *n.*, the state or quality of being stolid.

sto'lon, *n.*, a branch which trails or a sucker which takes root.

stom'ach, *n.*, the chief digestive organ; appetite; liking; pride; *v.t.*, to tolerate.

stom'achal, *adj.*, pert. to the stomach.

stom'ached, *p.p.*, stomach.

stom'acher, *n.*, a lady's breast-covering.

stomach'ic, *adj.*, pert. to the stomach; appetising; good for the stomach; *n.*, a stomach medicine.

stomach'ical, *adj.*, *i.q.* stomachic.

stom'achless, *adj.*, without a stomach.

stom'ach-pump, *n.*, an instrument for evacuating the stomach.

sto'mapod, *n.*, one of the stomapoda, an order of crustaceans.

stone, *n.*, hard earth formation; a gem; stony matter in the bladder; the hard seed-shell of stone-fruit; a weight (14 lb.); *v.t.*, to throw stones at; to extract the stones from; to pave, etc., with stones.

stone'-blind, *adj.*, absolutely sightless.

stone'chat, *n.*, a little bird so named.

stone'-*cold*, *adj.*, as cold as stone.

stone'crop, *n.*, a plant so named.

stone'-cutter, *n.*, a cutter of stone.

stoned, *p.p.*, stone.

stone'-fruit, *n.*, fruit containing a hard seed-shell.

stone'-mason, *n.*, a worker in stone.

sto'ner, *n.*, one who stones.

stone's'-throw, *n.*, the average distance to which a stone is thrown.

stone'-still, *adj.*, absolutely still.

stone'-waller, *n.*, a cricketer who keeps his wickets up for a long time, but makes few runs.

stone'ware, *n.*, a common kind of pottery.

sto'niness, *n.*, the state or quality of being stony.

sto'ning, *pr.p.*, stone.

sto'ny, *adj.*, hard like stone; abounding in stone.

sto'ny-heart'ed, *adj.*, hard-hearted.

stood, *p.t.* and *p.*, stand.

stook, *n.*, corn-sheaves gathered into a shock; *v.t.*, to gather into shocks.

stool, *n.*, a movable seat unbacked; the seat of a commode, etc.; *v.i.*, to evacuate the bowels.

stoop, *n.*, a bending down and forward; a bird's swoop; a verandah or porch (*Amer.*); *v.i.*, to incline the body; to abase oneself; to condescend; to make submission; to swoop.

stooped, *p.p.*, stoop.

stoop'er, *n.*, one who stoops.

stoop'ing, *pr.p.*, stoop

stoop'ingly, *adv.*, in a stooping way.

stop, *n.*, cessation of movement; arrest, a standstill; a punctuation mark; a slide opening or closing a range of pipes in an organ; *v.t.*, to bring to rest; to hinder; to punctuate; to withhold payment; *v.i.*, to come to a standstill.

stop'-cock, *n.*, a tap by means of which the flow of water can be controlled.

stop'gap, *n.*, that which fills any gap or vacancy.

stop'page, *n.*, the effect or act of stopping; a hindrance; a suspension of pay.

stopped, *p.p.*, stop.

stop'per, *n.*, one who, or that which, stops; esp. which closes the mouth of a bottle.

stop'ping, *pr.p.*, stop; *n.*, stoppage; that which stops.

stop'ple, *n.*, a plug; *v.t.*, to plug.

stop'-watch, *n.*, a watch that can be stopped at will.

sto'rage, *n.*, accommodation for goods of all kinds; the storing of electricity; charge for storing.

sto'rax, *n.*, a resin.

store, *n.*, a collection of things that are to be kept; abundance; a miscellaneous shop; *v.t.*, to place in a warehouse; to accumulate; to furnish with stores.

stored, *p.p.*, store.

store'house, *n.*, a place for storing.

store'keeper, *n.*, one who keeps a store.

store'room, *n.*, an apartment where stores are kept.

store'ship, *n.*, a ship carrying stored goods.

sto'rey, sto'ry, *n.*, a stage in a building.

sto'ried, *adj.*, supplied with stories; told in story.

sto'ring, *pr.p.*, store.
stork, *n.*, a wading bird so named.
stork's-bill, *n.*, the long, pointed bill of a stork.
storm, *n.*, a violent outburst of wind, rain, thunder, passion, etc.; attack on a fortified position; *v.i.*, to make much noise in angry abuse; *v.t.*, to besiege.
stormed, *p.p.*, storm.
storm'ier, *adj., comp.* of stormy.
storm'iest, *adj., super.* of stormy.
storm'iness, *n.*, the state or quality of being stormy.
storm'ing, *pr.p.*, storm.
storm'y, *adj.*, tempestuous; threatening storm.
Stor'thing, *n.*, the Parliament of Norway.
sto'ry, *n.*, history; narrative; a tale; a novel; a report; the plot of a book, play, etc.; a lie; *v.t.*, to chronicle; celebrate in history.
sto'ry-book, *n.*, a book of stories for children.
sto'ry-teller, *n.*, one who tells stories either in a good or in a bad sense.
sto'ry-telling, *n.*, the art or practice of telling stories.
stoup, *n.*, a drinking-vessel; a holy-water receptacle.
stout, *adj.*, corpulent; strongly built; firm, resolute; *n.*, a dark ale or porter.
stout'er, *adj., comp.* of stout.
stout'est, *adj., super.* of stout.
stout'ly, *adv.*, firmly, solidly.
stout'ness, *n.*, the state or quality of being stout.
stove, *p.t.*, stave; *v.t.*, to force (plants) in a hothouse; *n.*, a closed or partially closed fire-box, used for heating, cooking, etc.
stove'-pipe, *n.*, a pipe from a stove into a chimney; a tall, silk hat (*colloq.*).
stow, *v.t.*, to pack; to fill compactly and neatly; to leave off doing (*slang*).
stow'age, *n.*, the act of stowing; capacity; charge for stowing.
stow'away, *n.*, one who secretes himself on a ship.
stowed, *p.p.*, stow.
stow'ing, *pr.p.*, stow.
stra'bism, *n.*, *i.q.* strabismus.
strabis'mus, *n.*, a squint.
strad'dle, *v.t.*, to sit across; *v.i.*, to stand, ride, sit with the legs far apart; *n.*, a straddling posture; the extent to which the legs are stretched apart; an arrangement in the Stock Exchange by which a purchaser secures the right to call or deliver stock.
strad'dled, *p.p.*, straddle.
strad'dling, *pr.p.*, straddle.
Stradiva'rius, *n.*, a violin or some other stringed instrument by the famous 18th cent. maker, Stradivarius of Cremona. Also colloquially abbreviated to *Strad.*
strag'gle, *v.i.*, to go astray from a company or main body; to ramble; to grow irregularly and be spread; to occur irregularly.
strag'gled, *p.p.*, straggle.
strag'gler, *n.*, one who, or that which, straggle.
strag'gling, *pr.p.*, straggle.
straight, *adj.*, lying evenly between any two points; keeping to one direction; not bent nor curving; erect; upright, frank; *n.*, a straight part; a reach in a river; the condition of being straight; a sequence at poker.
straight'en, *v.t.*, to make straight; *v.i.*, to become straight.
straight'ened, *p.p.*, straighten.
straight'ener, *n.*, one who, or that which, straightens.
straight'ening, *pr.p.*, straighten.
straightfor'ward, *adj.*, honest, frank, ingenuous.
straightfor'wardness, *n.*, the quality of being straightforward.
straight'ly, *adv.*, without deviating.
straight'ness, *n.*, the state or quality of being straight.
straight'way, *adv.*, immediately, forthwith.
strain, *v.t.*, to apply tension to; to exert to the utmost; to over-exert; to pass through a sieve or colander; *v.i.*, to exert oneself greatly; to percolate; *n.*, the act or effect of straining; stress; tension; a snatch of poetry or musical sound; a style of speaking, thinking, or writing; family descent; a natural disposition.
strained, *adj.*, strain.
strain'er, *n.*, one who, or that which, strains; a sieve-like utensil; a strengthening support behind the panel of a carriage.
strain'ing, *pr.p.*, strain; *n.*, the act of straining.
strait, *adj.*, narrow; strict; *n.*, a narrow waterway connecting two seas; in pl., difficulties; narrow means.
strait'en, *v.t.*, to narrow, confine; tighten.
strait'ened, *p.p.*, straiten.
strait'-jacket, *n.*, a strong jacket confining the wearer's arms.

strait'-laced, *adj.*, tightly laced; prim; prudish.

strait'ly, *adv.*, narrowly, strictly.

strait'ness, *n.*, narrowness; poverty.

strait'-waistcoat, *n.*, *i.q.* strait-jacket.

strake, *n.*, a single breadth of the planking in a ship continuously from end to end.

stramin'eous, *adj.*, like straw.

stramo'nium, *n.*, a narcotic weed akin to the nightshade, used medicinally in asthma cases.

stram'ony, *n.*, *i.q.* stramonium.

strand, *n.*, a shore; a fibre; a loose hair; one of the strings or wires in a rope; *v.t.*, to run (a vessel) ashore; to leave in difficulties.

strand'ed, *p.p.*, strand; *adj.*, hopelessly in difficulties.

strand'ing, *pr.p.*, strand.

strange, *adj.*, alien; unfamiliar; extraordinary; eccentric.

strange'ly, *adv.*, in a strange manner.

strange'ness, *n.*, the state or quality of being strange.

stran'ger, *adj.*, *comp.* of strange; *n.*, an alien; a foreigner.

stran'gle, *v.t.*, to choke; to throttle; to suppress; *v.i.*, to be throttled.

stran'gled, *p.p.*, strangle.

stran'gles, *n. pl.*, a catarrhal affection in horses.

stran'gling, *pr.p.*, strangle.

stran'gulate, *v.t.*, to strangle; to constrict.

stran'gulated, *p.p.*, strangulate.

strangula'tion, *n.*, the act or effect of strangulating.

stran'gury, *n.*, difficulty in passing urine; a swelling in plants as the result of bandaging.

strap, *n.*, a leather thong, usually with a buckle or some means of fastening; a strip or band, etc., for joining or holding things together; *v.t.*, to bind with a strap; to flog; to whet; to close a wound by strapping.

straphang'er, *n.*, a passenger in a tram-car or railway carriage who, unable to get a seat, hangs on to straps suspended for the purpose.

strappa'do, *n.*, torture by hanging the victim up to a pulley, letting him down with violence, and pulling him up again; *v.t.*, to torture in this way.

strapped, *p.p.*, strap.

strap'per, *n.*, one who straps; a big, lusty person.

strap'ping, *pr.p.*, strap; *adj.*, big, bulky, lusty.

strass, *n.*, silk refuse.

stra'ta, *n.*, pl. of stratum.

strat'agem, *n.*, a cunning plan to trick an enemy.

stratarith'metry, *n.*, the art of estimating the number of men enclosed in a geometrical space.

strateget'ical, *adj.*, *i.q.* strategic.

strateg'ic, *adj.*, pert. to strategy.

strateg'ical, *adj.*, *i.q.* strategic.

strat'egist, *n.*, one skilled in strategy.

strat'egy, *n.*, generalship; military science; the art of planning movements of armies so as to prevent the enemy from choosing his own time and place for fighting.

strath, *n.*, a mountain valley or river-course.

strathspey', *n.*, a Scottish dance of a lively character and resembling a reel.

stratifica'tion, *n.*, the arrangement of strata; the act or effect of laying sedimentary deposits.

strat'ified, *p.p.*, stratify.

strat'iform, *adj.*, formed like a stratum.

strat'ify, *v.t.*, to deposit sedimentary layers; *v.i.*, to form in layers.

strat'ifying, *pr.p.*, stratify.

stratoc'racy, *n.*, government by the military.

stratog'raphy, *n.*, a description of an army.

stra'tum, *n.*, a layer naturally deposited.

stra'tus, *n.*, a layer of cloud near to the horizon.

straw, *n.*, the dry stalk of cut wheat, barley, oats, etc.; something valueless; *adj.*, made of straw; *v.t.*, to strew.

straw'berry, *n.*, a perennial plant so named and its fruit.

straw'-colour, *n.*, a straw-like colour.

straw'y, *adj.*, made of, resembling, straw.

stray, *v.i.*, to wander, straggle; *adj.*, wandering; sporadic; *n.*, a domestic animal gone astray; escheated property of a deceased person.

strayed, *p.p.*, stray.

stray'er, *n.*, one who strays.

stray'ing, *pr.p.*, stray.

streak, *n.*, a line or stripe; a trace; *v.t.*, to mark with streaks; to make stripes on; *v.i.*, to stretch.

streaked, *p.p.*, streak.

streak'ing, *pr.p.*, streak.

streak'y, *adj.*, in layers or stripes.

stream, *n.*, running water; the flow of any liquid or gas; current; continuous flow (of speech, people moving, etc.); *v.i.*, to flow in a stream or like a stream.

streamed, *p.p.*, stream

stream'er, *n.*, anything that streams; a flag, pennon, ribbon, etc.

stream'ing, *pr.p.*, stream.

stream'let, *n.*, a small stream.

stream'y, *adj.*, abounding in streams; stream-like

street, *n.*, orig. a paved road; now, a road through a town or village.

strength, *n.*, physical power; the state of being strong.

strength'en, *v.t.*, to make strong; *v.i.*, to become stronger.

strength'ened, *p.p.*, strengthen.

strength'ener, *n.*, one who, or that which, strengthens.

strength'ening, *pr.p.*, strengthen; *adj.*, nourishing; invigorating.

strength'less, *adj.*, weak; without strength.

stren'uous, *adj.*, vigorous; exacting; calling for exertion.

stren'uously, *adv.*, in a strenuous way.

stren'uousness, *n.*, the quality of being strenuous.

stress, *n.*, force; pressure; need of effort; emphasis; in mechanics, force acting between adjoining bodies or parts of bodies; *v.t.*, to emphasize; accentuate.

stretch, *v.t.*, to strain, tighten; make longer or wider; extend; use extra effort; *v.i.*, to extend oneself; exaggerate; *n.*, the act of stretching; state of being stretched; extent of country or expanse of water; a measured period.

stretched, *p.p.*, stretch

stretch'er, *n.*, one who, or that which, stretches; a contrivance for carrying disabled persons; a foot-rest in a boat; a brick or stone set in a wall so as to show its side; a lie (*colloq.*).

stretch'ing, *pr.p.*, stretch.

strew, *v.t.*, to scatter; shower; partly cover.

strewed, *p.p.*, strew.

strew'ing, *pr.p.*, strew

stri'a, *n.*, superficial marking; line; low ridge.

stri'ae, *n.*, pl. of stria.

stri'ate, *v.t.*, to mark with striae.

stri'ate, *adj.*, *i.q.* striated.

stri'ated, *adj.*, marked with striae.

stria'tion, *n.*, marking with striae.

strick'en, *adj.*, afflicted; *p.p.*, strike.

strick'le, *n.*, a straight-edged piece of metal or wood for levelling the top of a measure of grain.

strict, *adj.*, severe, formal, precise, ascetic.

strict'er, *adj.*, *comp.* of strict.

strict'est, *adj.*, *super.* of strict.

strict'ly, *adv.*, in a strict way; accurately, precisely.

strict'ness, *n.*, the state or quality of being strict.

stric'ture, *n.*, contraction of some bodily organ; animadversion; censure.

stric'tured, *adj.*, suffering from stricture

strid'den, *p.p.*, stride.

stride, *n.*, a long step; the space covered in a stride; *v.t.*, to span in striding; *v.i.*, to walk in strides or long steps.

stri'dent, *adj.*, harsh; raucous.

stri'ding, *pr.p.*, stride.

stri'dulate, *v.i.*, to make a creaking noise, like that of a grasshopper, cricket., etc.

stri'dulous, *adj.*, creaking.

strife, *n.*, dissension, feud, quarrel.

stri'ga, *n.*, in botany, a hair-like scale; in architecture, fluting

strig'il, *n.*, a flesh-scraper; a brush (*Lat.*).

stri'gose, *adj.*, having strigae.

stri'gous, *adj.*, *i.q.* strigose.

strike, *v.t.*, to hit, beat; create an impression on; occur to; haul down, and many metaphorical senses; *v.i.*, to come in sudden contact; to give out a sound that results from striking; to refuse to work; to impinge, etc.; *n.*, a blow; a refusal to work; *i.q.* strickle; flax ready for heckling; full measure of ale.

stri'ker, *n.*, one who, or that which, strikes.

stri'king, *pr.p.*, strike; *adj.*, remarkable; noteworthy.

stri'kingly, *adv.*, in a striking manner.

string, *n.*, fine cord; anything like string, as a fiddle-string or piano-string; a series of things strung together, as beads or a string of people; a billiard scoring-board, on which the scored numbers slide; *v.t.*, to thread; to supply with strings; to tighten up; *v.i.*, to form a string or continuous line.

string'-board, *n.*, *i.q.* string-course.

string'-course, *n.*, a projecting moulding on a building.

stringed, *adj.*, furnished with strings (*mus.*).

strin'gency, *n.*, the state or quality of being stringent.

stringen'do, *adv.*, quickening up (*mus.*)

strin'gent, *adj.*, exacting; severe; difficult.

string'er, *n.*, one who, or that which, strings; supporting timber running along the length of a structure.

string'-halt, *n.*, a form of chorea in horses; *i.q.* spring-halt.

string'iness, *n.*, the quality of being stringy.

string'ing, *pr.p.*, string.

string'y, *adj.*, like string; fibrous.

strip, *v.t.*, to remove the outer covering from; to despoil; to denude; to cut into strips; *v.i.*, to take off one's clothes; to peel off; *n.*, a narrow piece.

stripe, *n.*, a distinguishing line or band; a blow; *v.t.*, to mark with stripes; *adj.*, marked with stripes.

striped, *p.p.*, stripe.

stri'ping, *pr.p.*, stripe.

strip'ling, *n.*, a youth; one not fully matured.

stripped, *p.p.*, strip.

strip'per, *n.*, one who, or that which, strips

strip'ping, *pr.p.*, strip.

stript, *p.p.*, strip.

strive, *v.i.*, to endeavour; struggle; dispute; quarrel.

striv'en, *p.p.*, strive.

stri'ver, *n.*, one who strives.

stri'ving, *pr.p.*, strive.

strob'ile, *n.*, pine-cone

strode, *p.t.*, stride.

stroke, *v.t.*, to move the hand gently along; to smooth; to flatter; to be the stroke oarsman of; *n.*, the act of striking; repeated action; a line, etc., made by a single movement of the hand; accident; a paralytic seizure; the stroke oarsman or his place in a boat.

stroked, *p.p.*, stroke.

stro'ker, *n.*, one who, or that which, strokes.

strokes'man, *n.*, a man who rows stroke, *i.e.*, who sits nearest the stern and sets the pace and strength.

stro'king, *pr.p.*, stroke.

stroll, *v.i.*, to take a ramble.

strolled, *p.p.*, stroll.

stroll'er, *n.*, one who strolls.

stroll'ing, *pr.p.*, stroll.

stro'ma, *n.*, connecting tissue in the framework of a cell, etc.

stromat'ic, *adj.*, pert. to a stroma.

stromb, *n.*, a gastropod so named.

strom'bite, *n.*, a fossil stromb.

strom'bus, *n.*, *i.q.* stromb.

strong, *adj.*, vigorous; full of strength; healthy; loud; clear; staunch; inflecting or modifying the stem rather than the endings of words; *adv.*, *i.q.* strongly.

stron'ger, *adj.*, *comp.* of strong.

stron'gest, *adj.*, *super.* of strong.

strong'hold, *n.*, a fortified place.

strong'ish, *adj.*, rather strong.

strong'ly, *adv.*, with strength; firmly.

strong'minded, *adj.*, not squeamish; courageous.

strong - mind'edness, *n.*, the quality of being strongminded.

strong'room, *n.*, a room to keep things safely.

stron'tia, *n.*, a strontium oxide.

stron'tian, *adj.*, pert. to strontium.

stron'tium, *n.*, a metallic element so named.

strop, *n.*, a leather strap to sharpen razors on; *v.t.*, to sharpen (a razor) by stropping.

stro'phe, *n.*, in the Greek drama, one section of a song chanted by the chorus; the first of two stanzas.

stroph'ic, *adj.*, pert. to a strophe.

stroph'iolate, *adj.*, having a strophiole.

stroph'iolated, *adj.*, *i.q.* strophiolate.

stroph'iole, *n.*, an appendage to the base of some seeds.

strove, *p.t.*, strive.

strow, *v.t.*, to spread or scatter on the ground. Also *strew*.

strowed, *p.p.*, strow.

strow'ing, *pr.p.*, strow.

strown, *p.p.*, strow.

struck, *p.t.* and *p.*, strike.

struc'tural, *adj.*, pert. to structure.

struc'ture, *n.*, construction; building; make; disposition of parts in animal or vegetable substance.

strug'gle, *n.*, a striving; great effort; pain; labour; *v.i.*, to make a great effort; strive with difficulty.

strug'gled, *p.p.*, struggle.

strug'gling, *pr.p.*, struggle.

strum, *v.t.* and *i.*, to play casually and with noise.

stru'ma, *n.*, scrofula.

strummed, *p.p.*, strum.

strum'ming, *pr.p.*, strum.

stru'mous, *adj.*, affected with struma.

strum'pet, *n.*, a courtesan.

strung, *p.p.* and *t.*, string.

strut, *v.i.*, to march about in a proud way; *n.*, such a walk; a wooden support.

stru'thious, *adj.*, pert. to the struthio genus of birds.

strut'ted, *p.p.*, strut.

strut'ter, *n.*, one who struts.

strut'ting, *pr.p.*, strut.

strych'nia, *n.*, *i.q.* strychnin.

strych'nin, -nine, *n.*, a poisonous extract of *nux vomica*.

stub, *v.t.*, to root up; *n.*, a tree-stump; a stub-nail.

stubbed, *p.p.*, stub; *adj.*, full of stubs; broken off short.

stub'bing, *pr.p.*, stub.

stub'ble, *n.*, what is left in a corn-field after reaping.
stub'bly, *adj.*, like stubble; covered with stubble.
stub'born, *adj.*, obstinate; mulish; difficult to work.
stub'bornly, *adv.*, in a stubborn way.
stub'bornness, *n.*, the state or quality of being stubborn.
stub'by, *adj.*, short and thick.
stuc'co, *n.*, plaster for overlaying wall surfaces; stucco-work; *v.t.*, to overlay with plaster.
stuc'coed, *p.p.*, stucco.
stuc'coer, *n.*, a worker or dealer in stucco.
stuc'coing, *pr.p.*, stucco.
stuck, *p.t.* and *p.*, stick.
stuck'-up, *adj.*, conceited.
stud, *n.*, a knob; a button; a fastener; a collection of horses for racing or breeding purposes; *v.t.*, to furnish with studs; to ornament.
stud'ded, *p.p.*, stud.
stud'ding, *pr.p.*, stud.
stu'dent, *n.*, one who studies; a scholar.
stud'ied, *p.p.*, study; *adj.*, premeditated; precise.
stu'dio, *n.*, an artist's work-room.
stu'dious, *adj.*, given to study; zealous.
stu'diously, *adv.*, in a studious way.
stud'y, *n.*, mental application to learning; a learned pursuit; a preliminary sketch; a room to study in; *v.t.*, to apply the mind to; to look minutely into; to think about; to be mindful of.
stud'ying, *pr.p.*, study
stu'fa, *n.*, steam exhaling from the ground.
stuff, *n.*, fabric or material; furniture; worthless material; nonsense; *v.t.*, to pack; to cram into; to put stuffing into; to fill a dead animal's skin so as to retain its natural appearance; *v.i.*, to overeat oneself.
stuffed, *p.p.*, stuff.
stuff'er, *n.*, one who stuffs; a taxidermist
stuff'ier, *adj.*, *comp.* of stuffy.
stuff'iest, *adj.*, *super.* of stuffy.
stuff'iness, *n.*, the state or quality of being stuffy.
stuff'ing, *pr.p.*, stuff; *n.*, force-meat; anything used for the purpose of stuffing.
stuff'y, *adj.*, stifling; without proper ventilation.
stultifica'tion, *n.*, the act or effect of stultifying.
stul'tified, *p.p.*, stultify.
stul'tifier, *n.*, one who stultifies.
stul'tify, *v.t.*, to make foolish; to make of no effect.
stul'tifying, *pr.p.*, stultify.
stum, *n.*, must; grape juice before fermentation.
stum'ble, *v.i.*, to trip up; to walk haltingly; to fall; *n.*, a false step; a trip.
stum'bled, *p.p.*, stumble.
stum'bler, *n.*, one who stumbles.
stum'bling, *pr.p.*, stumble.
stum'bling-block, *n.*, a cause of offence.
stummed, *p.p.*, stum.
stum'ming, *pr.p.*, stum.
stump, *n.*, what is left above ground of a tree cut down; a mutilated limb; an artist's pencil; one part of the wicket on a cricket ground; *v.t.*, to reduce to a stump; to hit a wicket down while the batsman is out of his ground; to baffle (*colloq.*); *v.i.*, to make a round of speeches or lectures; to walk stiffly and heavily.
stumped, *p.p.*, stump.
stump'iness, *n.*, the state or quality of being stumpy.
stump'ing, *pr.p.*, stump.
stump-or'ator, *n.*, one who stumps the country making speeches.
stump-or'atory, *n.*, a stump-orator's performances.
stump'y, *adj.*, stunted; abounding in stumps
stun, *v.t.*, to make senseless with a violent blow; to deafen; to overwhelm with surprise, grief, etc.
Stund'ist, *n.*, one of a Russian religious sect resembling Puritans.
stung, *p.t.* and *p.*, sting.
stunk, *p.t.* and *p.*, stink.
stunned, *p.p.*, stun.
stun'ner, *n.*, one who, that which, stuns.
stun'ning, *pr.p.*, stun; *adj.*, overwhelming; delightful (*colloq.*).
stunt, *v.t.*, to shorten the growth of; *v.i.*, to have the growth arrested; *n.*, the arrest of growth.
stunt'ed, *p.p.*, stunt.
stunt'ing, *pr.p.*, stunt.
stupe, *n.*, a compress.
stupefa'cient, *adj.*, stupefying.
stupefac'tion, *n.*, the act or effect of stupefying.
stupefac'tive, *adj.*, causing stupefaction.
stu'pefied, *p.p.*, stupefy.
stu'pefier, *n.*, one who, that which, stupefies.
stu'pefy, *v.t.*, to reduce to a state of stupor; to make insensible to pain, etc.; to make stupid.
stu'pefying, *pr.p.*, stupefy.
stupen'dous, *adj.*, amazing in greatness.
stupen'dously, *adv.*, in a stupendous way.
stu'pid, *adj.*, dull; insensible; unreasonable; obstinate.

stupid'ity, *n.*, the state or quality of being stupid.
stu'pidly, *adv.*, in a stupid way.
stu'por, *n.*, insensibility; lethargy.
stu'pose, *adj.*, with tow-like hairs.
stu'prate, *v.t.*, to ravish.
stupra'tion, *adj.*, ravishing.
stur'dier, *adj.*, *comp.* of sturdy.
stur'diest, *adj.*, *super.* of sturdy.
stur'dily, *adv.*, in a sturdy way.
stur'diness, *n.*, the state or quality of being sturdy.
stur'dy, *adj.*, strong; well-set; vigorous.
stur'geon, *n.*, a large fish so named, much valued for its roe, from which caviare is made.
stut'ter, *v.t.*, to say with a stammer; *v.i.*, to stammer.
stut'tered, *p.p.*, stutter.
stut'terer, *n.*, one who stutters.
stut'tering, *pr.p.*, stutter; *n.*, hesitation in speaking.
sty, *n.*, a pig's shelter; a swelling on the eye; *v.t.*, to enclose in a sty.
Styg'ian, *adj.*, rel. to the Styx, the river of Hades; hellish.
stylagalma'ic, *adj.*, like a caryatid.
sty'lar, *adj.*, pert. to a style.
style, *n.*, a pointed instrument for writing on waxen tablets; fashion; mode; a distinctive title; stalk between a flower's ovary and stigma; *v.t.*, to address; call by a distinctive name.
styled, *p.p.*, style.
sty'let, *n.*, a small style.
sty'liform, *adj.*, like a style.
sty'ling, *pr.p.*, style.
sty'lish, *adj.*, smart; in the fashion.
sty'lishly, *adv.*, in a stylish way.
sty'list, *n.*, one who is particular in regard to style in writing.
sty'lite, *n.*, an eremite who lived on the top of a pillar, as St. Simeon Stylites.
sty'lobate, *n.*, the base of a row of pillars.
sty'lograph, *n.*, a stylographic pen.
stylograph'ic, *adj.*, pert. to a stylograph and stylography.
stylog'raphy, *n.*, writing with a style.
sty'loid, *adj.*, like a style or a pillar.
sty'lus, *n.*, a style for writing.
styp'tic, *adj.*, having the effect of staunching blood; *n.*, a substance that stops bleeding.
styptic'ity, *n.*, the quality of being styptic.
Styx, *n.*, the river of Hades (*Lat.*).
suabil'ity, *n.*, the state of being suable
su'able, *adj.*, in a position to be sued.
sua'sion, *n.*, advice, entreaty.
sua'sive, *adj.*, conveying advice or entreaty.
suave, *adj.*, gentle, bland.
suave'ly, *adv.*, in a suave way.
suav'ity, *n.*, gentleness; blandness.
sub, a Lat. preposition = "under," used in many words as a prefix, meaning *under, beneath, somewhat.*
subac'etate, *adj.*, somewhat acetate.
sub-a'gency, *n.*, an agency under another agent.
sub-a'gent, *n.*, an agent's deputy.
subal'pine, *adj.*, situated below the Alps.
sub'altern, *adj.*, inferior; *n.*, a commissioned officer below a captain's rank.
subalter'nate, *adj.*, alternate, but with tend·ncy to become opposite; a broad proposition (*Logic*).
suba'queous, *adj.*, beneath the water.
subas'tral, *adj.*, beneath the stars.
subaudi'tion, *n.*, the understanding of something not expressed, as St. Paul's, the word Cathedral being understood.
sub'base, *n.*, a lower base.
subbra'chial, *adj.*, having ventrals under pectorals.
subbra'chian, *adj.*, *i.q.* subbrachial.
subcla'vian, *adj.*, below the shoulder.
sub-commit'tee, *n.*, an inner committee.
sub-con'scious, *adj.*, partially conscious; pert. to acts done without full consciousness.
sub-con'tract, *n.*, a contract within another.
subcon'trary, *adj.*, contrary in lesser degree.
subcor'date, *adj.*, below the heart.
subcos'tal, *adj.*, below the ribs.
subcuta'neous, *adj.*, beneath the skin.
sub'deacon, *n.*, a minister next below the deacon. At Mass he reads the Epistle.
sub'dean, *n.*, the dean's deputy. In some of the cathedrals, he is a Minor Canon; in others, he is one of the higher dignitaries.
subdivide', *v.t.*, to divide what has been already divided.
subdivi'ded, *p.p.*, subdivide.
subdivi'ding, *pr.p.*, subdivide.
subdivis'ible, *adj.*, capable of subdivision.
subdivi'sion, *n.*, division into still smaller parts after a first division.
subdom'inant, *adj.*, below the dominant; *n.*, the fourth note in the scale.

subdu'able, *adj.*, able to be subdued.
subdu'al, *n.*, the act or result of subduing.
subduce', *v.t.*, to withdraw.
subduced', *p.p.*, subduce.
subdu'cing, *pr.p.*, subduce.
subduct', *v.t.*, to withdraw. [duct.
subduct'ed, *p.p.*, sub-
subduct'ing, *pr.p.*, subduct.
subduc'tion, *n.*, the act of subducting; that which is subducted.
subdue', *v.t.*, to overcome; conquer; lower.
subdued', *p.p.*, subdue; *adj.*, depressed; lowered.
subdu'er, *n.*, one who subdues. [due.
subdu'ing, *pr.p.*, sub-
sub-ed'itor, *n.*, one who attends to the make-up of a newspaper.
su'berate, *adj.*, *i.q.* suberic.
suber'ic, *adj.*, rel. to cork.
su'berin, -ine, *n.*, cellular tissue of cork.
su'berose, *adj.*, *i.q.* suberous.
su'berous, *adj.*, pert. to cork; elastic.
sub'genus, *n.*, a genus within a genus.
su'bito, *adv.*, suddenly; quickly (*mus.*).
subja'cent, *adj.*, lying close to, or below.
sub'ject, *adj.*, under another's authority; liable to; *n.*, one who is under another's authority; a matter for discussion, writing, etc.; a musical theme; a design; the *Ego* as distinguished from the object.
***subject'*,** *v.t.*, to reduce to submission; to expose.
subject'ed, *p.t.*, subject.
subject'ed, *p.p.*, subject.
subject'ing, *pr.p.*, subject.
subjec'tion, *n.*, subjugation; the state of being subjected.
subjec'tive, *adj.*, rel. to the subject, or to one's own consciousness.
subjec'tively, *adv.*, in a subjective sense.
subjec'tivism, *n.*, the teaching of thinkers who believe that knowledge is relative.
subjectiv'ity, *n.*, the state or quality of being subjective. Also *subjectiveness.*
sub'ject-matter, *n.*, a theme or question under discussion or written about.
subjoin', *v.t.*, to add; affix. [join.
subjoined', *p.p.*, sub-
subjoin'ing, *pr.p.*, subjoin.
sub ju'dice, *Lat. phrase* = still before a judge; not yet determined.
sub'jugate, *v.t.*, to conquer, subdue.
sub'jugated, *p.p.*, subjugate.
sub'jugating, *pr.p.*, subjugate.
subjuga'tion, *n.*, the act or effect of subjugating.
sub'jugator, *n.*, one who subjugates.
subjunc'tion, *n.*, the act or effect of subjoining.
subjunc'tive, *adj.*, denoting contingency; *n.*, the verbal mood which expresses contingency
sublapsa'rian, *adj.*, rel. to sublapsarianism.
sublapsa'rianism, *n.*, the opinions of sublapsarians, or moderate Calvinists, who hold that election was subsequent to the Fall.
sublate', *v.t.*, to deny in argument.
subla'tion, *n.*, the act of sublating.
sublease', *v.t.*, said of a leasehold tenant who leases his house to another holder; *n.*, a lease within a lease.
sublet', *v.t.*, said of the occupant of a rented house who lets the house to another tenant; *n.*, a let within a let.
subleva'tion, *n.*, removal.
sub-libra'rian, *n.*, a librarian's assistant.
sub'limate, *adj.*, said of a substance that has been sublimated *n.*, a sublimated substance.
sub'limate, *v.t.*, to reduce a solid to vapour and then condense it.
sub'limated, *p.p.*, sublimate.
sub'limating, *pr.p.*, sublimate.
sublima'tion, *n.*, the process of sublimating.
sublime', *adj.*, high, exalted, awe-inspiring; *n.*, the awe-inspiring as distinct from the beautiful; *v.t.*, to elevate; ennoble; *v.i.*, to be able to be sublimated. [lime.
sublimed', *p.p.*, sub-
sublime'ly, *pr.p.*, in a sublime way.
sublim'inal, *adj.*, behind or beneath the conscious state.
subli'ming, *pr.p.*, sublime.
sublim'ity, *n.*, the state or quality of being sublime.
sublu'nar, *adj.*, *i.q.* sublunary.
sub'lunary, *adj.*, beneath the moon.
sub'marine, *adj.*, beneath the sea; *n.*, a submarine boat.
submax'illary, *adj.*, lying under the maxilla.
subme'diant, *n.*, the sixth note in the scale.
submerge', *v.t.*, to sink or depress below water; overwhelm; *v.i.*, to sink below the water.
submerged', *p.p.*, submerge.
submer'gence, *n.*, the act of submerging; state of being submerged.

submer'ging, *pr.p.*, submerge.

submerse', *v.t.*, *i.q.* submerge.

submersed', *p.p.*, submerse.

submers'ing, *pr.p.*, submerse.

submer'sion, *n.*, *i.q.* submergence.

submis'sion, *n.*, subjection; yielding; deference.

submiss'ive, *adj.*, yielding; obedient.

submiss'ively, *adv.*, in a submissive way.

submiss'iveness, *n.*, the state of being submissive.

submit', *v.t.*, to place under another's authority; to yield; to offer for judgment; *v.i.*, to yield; to place oneself under another.

submit'ted, *p.p.*, submit.

submit'ting, *pr.p.*, submit.

submul'tiple, *n.*, a quantity or number contained within another an exact number of times.

subnas'cent, *adj.*, growing underneath

subor'dinacy, *n.*, the state of being subordinate.

subor'dinate, *adj.*, of lower rank; under authority; *n.*, a person under authority.

subor'dinate, *v.t.*, to place in subjection; to rank as of lower importance.

subor'dinated, *p.p.*, subordinate.

subor'dinating, *pr.p.*, subordinate.

subordina'tion, *n.*, the act of subordinating; submissiveness.

suborn', *v.t.*, to make to give false witness; to obtain by collusion.

suborna'tion, *n.*, the act of suborning.

suborned', *p.p.*, suborn.

suborn'er, *n.*, one who suborns.

suborn'ing, *pr.p.*, suborn.

subo'vate, *adj.*, slightly ovate.

subpoe'na, *n.*, a command from a law-court for the appearance of a witness; *v.t.*, to summon a witness under a penalty.

subpoe'naed, *p.p.*, subpoena.

subpoe'naing, *pr.p.*, subpoena.

subprin'cipal, *adj.*, principal in a secondary degree.

subrep'tion, *n.*, the act of snatching away.

subroga'tion, *n.*, succession; substitution.

sub ro'sa, adverbial *Lat.* phrase = under the rose (*i.e.*, in secret).

sub'salt, *adj.*, slightly salt.

subscribe', *v.t.*, to sign; to contribute; to get a book published by subscription; *v.i.*, to consent.

subscribed', *p.p.*, subscribe.

subscri'ber, *n.*, one who subscribes.

subscri'bing, *pr.p.*, subscribe.

sub'script, *adj.*, written underneath.

subscrip'tion, *n.*, the act of subscribing; something subscribed; formal assent.

sub'section, *n.*, a section within a section.

sub'sequence, *n.*, the act or state of being subsequent.

sub'sequent, *adj.*, following on; later.

sub'sequently, *adv.*, later.

subserve', *v.t.*, to be to the interest of; to promote.

subserved', *p.p.*, subserve.

subserv'ience, *n.*, the state of being subservient.

subserv'iency, *n.*, *i.q.*, subservience.

subserv'ient, *adj.*, helping; subordinate to.

subside', *v.i.*, to sink down; to collapse; grow calm.

subsi'ded, *p.p.*, subside.

subsi'dence, *n.*, the act or result of subsiding.

subsid'iarily, *adv.*, in a subsidiary way.

subsid'iary, *adj.*, aiding; additional; auxiliary.

subsi'ding, *pr.p.*, subside.

sub'sidize, *v.t.*, to help with a money grant.

sub'sidized, *p.p.*, subsidize.

sub'sidizing, *pr.p.*, subsidize.

sub'sidy, *n.*, money granted in aid.

subsist', *v.i.*, to live; to inhere.

subsist'ed, *p.p.*, subsist.

subsist'ence, *n.*, the act or state of subsisting; livelihood.

subsist'ent, *adj.*, subsisting.

subsist'ing, *pr.p.*, subsist.

sub'soil, *n.*, soil beneath the surface.

subspe'cies, *n.*, a species within a species.

sub'stance, *n.*, matter; meaning; wealth.

substan'tial, *adj.*, pert. to substance; solid; bodily; having plenty of means.

substantial'ity, *n.*, the state or quality of being substantial.

substan'tially, *adv.* in a substantial way or sense.

substan'tials, *n. pl.*, parts that are of the essence of a thing.

substan'tiate, *v.t.*, to prove the truth of.

substan'tiated, *p.p.*, substantiate.

substan'tiating, *pr.p.*, substantiate.

substantia'tion, *n.*, the act or effect of substantiating.

sub'stantive, *adj.*, denoting existence or reality; material; *n.*, a noun, denoting individual things, actions, qualities.

sub'stantively, *adv.*, in a substantive way or sense.

sub'stitute, *v.t.*, to put (one thing) in the place of another; *n.*, a person or thing taking the place of another.
sub'stituted, *p.p.*, substitute.
sub'stituting, *pr.p.*, substitute.
substitu'tion, *n.*, the act or result of substituting.
substitu'tional, *adj.*, pert. to substitution.
substitu'tionary, *adj.*, *i.q.* substitutional.
sub'stitutive, *adj.*, effecting substitution.
sub'strate, *adj.*, lying beneath.
substra'tum, *n.*, a lower stratum.
substruc'ture, *n.*, a structure supporting another.
subsul'phate, *n.*, a salt allied to a sulphate.
subtan'gent, *n.*, that part of a curve's axis which is intercepted between the tangent and the ordinate.
subtend', *v.t.*, to lie opposite to.
subtend'ed, *p.p.*, subtend.
subtend'ing, *pr.p.*, subtend.
subtense', *adj.*, subtending.
subter'fluent, *adj.*, flowing beneath.
sub'terfuge, *n.*, an evasion; a dodge.
subterra'nean, *adj.*, underground.
subterra'neous, *adj.*, *i.q.* subterranean.
sub'tile, *adj.*, cunning; penetrating; acute; refined; tenuous.
subtil'ity, *n.*, the state or quality of being subtile.
subtiliza'tion, *n.*, the act or effect of subtilizing.
sub'tilize, *v.t.*, to make subtile.
sub'tilized, *p.p.*, subtilize.
sub'tilizing, *pr.p.*, subtilize.
sub'tle, *adj.*, clever; cunning; refined.
sub'tlety, *n.*, cunning; acuteness.
sub'tly, *adv.*, in a subtle way.
subton'ic, *n.*, the leading note of the diatonic scale.
subtract', *v.t.*, to take from; to take a smaller from a larger number or quantity.
subtract'ed, *p.p.*, subtract.
subtract'er, *n.*, one who subtracts.
subtract'ing, *pr.p.*, subtract.
subtrac'tion, *n.*, the act of subtracting; one of the rules of arithmetic.
subtract'ive, *adj.*, having the effect of subtracting.
sub'trahend, *n.*, the smaller number or amount to be subtracted from a larger.
su'bulate, *adj.*, like an awl.
sub'urb, *n.*, a part adjacent to a city.
subur'ban, *adj.*, pert. to a suburb.
sub'urbs, *n. pl.*, the environs of a town.
subven'tion, *n.*, a grant; subsidy.
subver'sion, *n.*, the act or result of subverting.
subver'sive, *adj.*, tending to subvert.
subvert', *v.t.*, to overthrow; turn upside down; demoralize.
subvert'ed, *p.p.*, subvert.
subvert'er, *n.*, one who subverts.
subvert'ible, *adj.*, able to be subverted.
subvert'ing, *pr.p.*, subvert.
sub'way, *n.*, an underground passage.
succeda'neous, *adj.*, substitutional.
succeda'neum, *n.*, a deputy; a substitute.
succeed', *v.t.*, to follow next after; *v.i.*, to come after; to prosper; to do what one attempts to do.
succeed'ed, *p.p.*, succeed.
succeed'ing, *pr.p.*, succeed.
succen'tor, *n.*, one who acts for a precentor. (In some churches he is called sub-chanter.)
success', *n.*, the accomplishment of an endeavour; prosperity.
success'ful, *adj.*, having success.
success'fully, *adv.*, with success.
succes'sion, *n.*, the act of following; the right to take another's place or possessions; rotation.
succes'sional, *adj.*, pert. to succession.
succes'sionist, *n.*, one who believes in some principle of succession.
succes'sive, *adj.*, consecutive; repeated.
succes'sively, *adv.*, consecutively.
success'or, *n.*, one who takes another's place or property.
succif'erous, *adj.*, producing sap or juice.
suc'cinate, *n.*, a salt of succinic acid.
suc'cinated, *adj.*, *i.q.* succinate.
succinct', *adj.*, brief; terse.
succinct'ly, *adv.*, tersely.
succinct'ness, *n.*, the state or quality of being succinct.
succin'ic, *adj.*, derived from amber; contained in amber.
suc'cinite, *n.*, amber.
suc'cinous, *adj.*, sappy; juicy.
suc'cour, -cor, *n.*, help, aid; *v.t.*, to help.
suc'coured, -cored, *p.p.*, succour.
suc'courer, -corer, *n.*, a helper.
suc'couring, -coring, *pr.p.*, succour.
suc'culence, *n.*, juiciness.
suc'culency, *n.*, *i.q.* succulence.
suc'culent, *adj.*, juicy.

succumb', *v.i.*, to give in; yield.
succumbed', *p.p.*, succumb.
succumb'ing, *pr.p.*, succumb.
succus'sion, *n.*, a shaking.
succus'sive, *adj.*, shaking.
such, *adj.*, of that kind or degree; certain; so great.
suck, *v.t.*, to extract with the lips; *v.i.*, to draw a mother's milk; *n.*, the act of sucking; breast-milk.
sucked, *p.p.*, suck.
suck'er, *n.*, one who sucks; that which sucks or by which anything is sucked; a shoot thrown out by a plant at its stem.
suck'ing, *pr.p.*, suck.
suck'le, *v.t.*, to feed from the breast.
suck'led, *p.p.*, suckle.
suck'ling, *pr.p.*, suckle; *n.*, a child at the breast.
suc'tion, *n.*, the act of sucking or of drawing liquids or air.
suc'tion-stroke, *n.*, in a motor engine, the outward movement of the piston.
sucto'rial, *adj.*, living by sucking.
sucto'rian, *adj.*, *i.q.* suctorial.
Sudanese', *adj.*, pert. to the Sudan; *n.*, a native of the Sudan.
suda'tion, *n.*, sweating.
su'datory, *adj.*, promoting sweat.
sud'den, *adj.*, happening unexpectedly or in an instant.
sud'denly, *adv.*, instantaneously; unexpectedly.
sud'denness, *n.*, the quality of being sudden.
sudorif'erous, *adj.*, causing sweat.
sudorif'ic, *adj.*, *i.q.* sudoriferous.
sudorip'arous, *adj.*, *i.q.* sudoriferous.
Su'dra, *n.*, the lowest Hindu caste.
suds, *n. pl.*, dirty soapy water.
sue, *v.t.*, to take out a summons against; *v.i.*, to petition; court; take out a summons.
sued, *p.p.*, sue.
suède, *n.*, leather, undressed, and used for glove-making, boots and shoes.
su'er, *n.*, one who sues.
su'et, *n.*, fatty substance in oxen and sheep, used for a variety of purposes.
su'ety, *adj.*, like, abounding in, suet.
suf'fer, *v.t.*, to endure (pain,hardship,etc.); to permit; *v.i.*, to have pain; to be injured.
suf'ferable, *adj.*, able to be suffered.
suf'ferance, *n.*, tolerance; contemptuous permission.
suf'fered, *p.p.*, suffer.
suf'ferer, *n.*, one who suffers.
suf'fering, *pr.p.*, suffer; *n.*, pain, misery.
suffice', *v.t.*, to content; satisfy; *v.i.*, to be enough.
sufficed', *p.p.*, suffice.
suffi'ciency, *n.*, the state or quality of being sufficient; adequate means; self-satisfaction.
suffi'cient, *adj.*, enough, satisfying.
suffi'ciently, *adv.*, enough.
suffi'cing, *pr.p.*, suffice.
suf'fix, *n.*, a syllable or word added to the end of a word.
suffix', *v.t.*, to add to the end of a word.
suffixed', *p.p.*, suffix.
suffix'ing, *pr.p.*, suffix.
suffla'tion, *n.*, filling with air.
suf'focate, *v.t.*, to stifle; stop the breathing of.
suf'focated, *p.p.*, suffocate.
suf'focating, *pr.p.*, suffocate.
suffoca'tion, *n.*, the act or effect of suffocating.
suf'focative, *adj.*, causing suffocation.
suf'fragan, *adj.*, assistant (*lit.*, voting with), said of the bishops of a Province, who are the supporters of their Metropolitan; *n.*, a bishop.
suf'fragette, *n.*, a woman who demands the Parliamentary vote.
suf'frage, *n.*, the vote; franchise; a vote given at any discussion.
suf'fragism, *n.*, the theory that women ought to share the franchise.
suf'fragist, *n.*, an advocate of wider franchise.
suffuse', *v.t.*, to tinge.
suffused', *p.p.*, suffuse.
suffu'sing, *pr.p.*, suffuse.
suffu'sion, *n.*, the act or effect of suffusing.
su'fi, *n.*, a dervish; one of the Persian Shah's titles. Also *sofi*.
Su'fism, *n.*, the doctrines of the dervishes.
sug, *n.*, a parasite of the trout.
sug'ar, *n.*, a sweet extract from cane, beet, etc.; adulation; *adj.*, made of sugar; *v.t.*, to sweeten.
sug'ar-cane, *n.*, the cane from which sugar is extracted.
sug'ared, *p.p.*, sugar; *adj.*, flattering.
sug'ariness, *n.*, the state or quality of being sugary; sweetness.
sug'aring, *pr.p.*, sugar.
sug'ar-loaf, *n.*, sugar made into a conical pyramid.
sug'ar-plum, *n.*, a plum preserved and covered with sugar.
sug'ary, *adj.*, full of, resembling, sugar.
suggest', *v.t.*, to convey a thought or hint; to intimate.
suggest'ed, *p.p.*, suggest.
suggest'er, *n.*, one who suggests.
suggest'ing, *pr.p.*, suggest.

sugges'tion, *n.*, the act of suggesting; a hint.
sugges'tive, *adj.*, conveying a suggestion; implying.
suggest'ively, *adv.*, in a suggestive way.
suici'dal, *adj.*, self-destructive.
su'icide, *n.*, one who takes his own life; the act of taking one's own life.
su'ing, *pr.p.*, sue.
suit, *n.*, a set of garments; an action-at-law to recover something; a series of cards of the same name; *v.t.*, to fit; to accord with; to please; *v.i.*, to agree.
suitabil'ity, *n.*, the state or quality of being suitable.
suit'able, *adj.*, fitting; convenient.
suit'ableness, *n.*, *i.q.* suitability.
suit'ably, *adv.*, fittingly.
suite, *n.*, a company of followers or attendants; a series; a set (of rooms, furniture, etc.).
suit'ed, *p.p.*, suit.
suit'ing, *pr.p.*, suit; *n.*, materials for suits of clothes.
suit'or, *n.*, one who makes an application; a wooer; a plaintiff.
sul'cate, *adj.*, furrowed; grooved.
sul'cated, *adj.*, *i.q.* sulcate.
sulk, *v.i.*, to be angrily silent.
sulk'ily, *adv.*, in a sulky way.
sulk'iness, *n.*, the state or quality of being sulky.
sulks, *n. pl.*, a sulky fit.
sulk'y, *adj.*, sullen and silent; *n.*, a light carriage for one person (*Amer.*).
sul'len, *adj.*, morose; refusing to speak.
sul'lenly, *adv.*, in a sullen way.
sul'lenness, *n.*, the state of being sullen.
sul'lied, *p.p.*, sully.
sul'ly, *v.t.*, to stain; defile; tarnish.
sul'lying, *pr.p.*, sully.
sul'phate, *n.*, a sulphurous acid salt.
sulphat'ic, *adj.*, pert. to sulphate.
sul'phide, *n.*, sulphur and some element or metal combined.
sul'phite, *n.*, a sulphurous acid salt.
sul'phoral, *n.*, a narcotic compound.
sul'phur, *n.*, an element, non-metallic, yellow, not soluble in water.
sul'phurate, *adj.*, rel. to, resembling, sulphur; *n.*, a sulphurate substance.
sul'phurate, *v.t.*, to impregnate or to act upon with sulphur.
sul'phurated, *p.p.*, sulphurate.
sul'phurating, *pr.p.*, sulphurate.
sulphura'tion, *n.*, the act or effect of sulphurating.
sulphu'reous, *adj.*, full of, resembling, sulphur.
sul'phuret, *n.*, *i.q.* sulphide.
sul'phuretted, *adj.*, treated with sulphur.
sulphu'ric, *adj.*, pert. to, containing, sulphur.
sul'phuring, *pr.p.*, sulphur.
sul'phurous, *adj.*, produced by sulphur; like sulphur.
sul'tan, *n.*, the head of the Ottoman Empire; any Mohammedan ruler.
sulta'na, *n.*, fem. of sultan; a variety of raisin.
sul'taness, *n.*, *i.q.* sultana.
sul'tanship, *n.*, the office or rank of a sultan.
sul'trily, *adv.*, in a sultry way.
sul'triness, *n.*, the state or quality of being sultry.
sul'try, *adj.*, hot and oppressive.
sum, *n.*, a total amount; the whole; an arithmetical problem; an aggregate of money; *v.t.*, to reckon up the total; to summarize.
su'mac, su'mach, *n.*, a plant used in dyeing, tanning, etc.
Suma'tran, *adj.*, pert. to Sumatra; *n.*, a native of S.
sum'marily, *adv.*, in a summary fashion.
sum'marize, *v.t.*, to reduce to a concise statement.
sum'marized, *p.p.*, summarize.
sum'marizing, *pr.p.*, summarize.
sum'mary, *adj.*, done on the spot or at once; abrupt; concise; *n.*, a concise abstract.
summa'tion, *n.*, the act of summing; aggregate.
summed, *p.p.*, sum.
sum'mer, *n.*, the second season of the year; a timber on which the end of a joint rests; *v.i.*, to pass the summer.
sum'mered, *p.p.*, summer.
sum'mer-house, *n.*, a shelter in a garden.
sum'mering, *pr.p.*, summer.
sum'mersault, *n.*, *i.q.* somersault.
sum'merset, *n.*, *i.q.* somersault.
sum'ming, *pr.p.*, sum.
sum'mit, *n.*, the top; highest point.
sum'mon, *v.t.*, to call upon; to command the appearance of; to rally.
sum'moned, *p.p.*, summon.
sum'moner, *n.*, one who summons.
sum'moning, *pr.p.*, summon.
sum'mons, *n. pl.*, a writ commanding appearance in court; a call.
sum'mum bo'num, *Lat.* phrase = the highest good.
sumph, *n.*, a stupid fellow (*Scot.*).
sump'ter, *n.*, a baggage-horse; *adj.*,

used for carrying baggage.

sump'tuary, *adj.*, rel. to expenditure and in restraint of extravagance.

sump'tuous, *adj.*, costly, luxurious.

sump'tuously, *adv.*, in a sumptuous way.

sump'tuousness, *n.*, costliness; magnificence.

sun, *n.*, the great orb which is the centre of our solar system; any central orb; the sunshine; *v.t.*, to expose to the sun's influence.

sun'beam, *n.*, a ray from the sun.

sun'burnt, *adj.*, tanned by the sun.

Sun'day, *n.*, the first day of the week; the Lord's Day; the *dies dominica* (*Fr.*, dimanche); *adj.*, pert. to Sunday.

sun'der, *v.t.*, to sever; divide.

sun'dial, *n.*, a dial showing the time by means of a shadow cast by the sun.

sun'down, *n.*, sunset.

sun'dried, *adj.*, dried in the sun.

sun'dries, *n. pl.*, odds and ends; a variety of things.

sun'dry, *adj.*, several; various.

sun'fish, *n.*, a fish so named.

sun'flower, *n.*, a yellow flower with ray-like petals.

sung, *p.p.*, sing.

sunk, *p.p.*, sink.

sunk'en, *adj.*, sunk; pressed down.

sun'light, *n.*, the light of the sun.

sun'like, *adj.*, like a [sun.

sun'lit, *adj.*, lighted by the sun.

Sun'na, *n.*, traditional Mohammedan laws orally handed down.

sun'nier, *adj.*, *comp.* of sunny.

sun'niest, *adj.*, *super.* of sunny.

sun'niness, *n.*, the state or quality of being sunny.

sun'ning, *pr.p.*, sun.

Sun'nite, *n.*, a Mohammedan adherent of the precepts of the Sunna.

sun'ny, *adj.*, bright; warmed and brightened by the sun; cheerful.

sun'rise, *n.*, the dawn.

sun'rising, *n.*, the coming of the dawn.

sun'set, *n.*, the decline of the sun.

sun'shade, *n.*, a parasol.

sun'shine, *n.*, the shining of the sun; warmth and brightness.

sun'shiny, *adj.*, full of sunshine.

sun'stroke, *n.*, a brain affection caused by excessive exposure to sun-heat.

sup, *v.i.*, to take supper; *v.t.*, to sip; *n.*, a small quantity of liquid food.

su'per, *Lat. prep.* used as a prefix in the sense of *over*, *to excess*, *beyond*; *n.*, a supernumerary actor (*slang*).

su'perable, *adj.*, able to be overcome.

superabound', *v.i.*, to abound to excess.

superabun'dance, *n.*, abundance beyond what is needed.

superabun'dant, *adj.*, abounding to excess.

superadd', *v.t.*, to add over and above.

superaddi'tion, *n.*, addition over and above.

superangel'ic, *adj.*, above ordinary angelic rank.

superan'nuate, *v.t.*, to discharge on account of age.

superan'nuated, *p.p.*, superannuate.

superan'nuating, *pr.p.* superannuate.

superannua'tion, *n.*, dismissal on account of age.

superb', *adj.*, proud, magnificent.

superb'ly, *adv.*, in a superb way.

supercar'go, *n.*, one who has the charge of the cargo on a merchant vessel.

supercil'ious, *adj.*, disdainful; haughty.

supercil'iously, *adv.*, in a supercilious way.

supercil'iousness, *n.*, the state or quality of being supercilious

superem'inence, *n.*, very high eminence.

superem'inent, *adj.*, very eminent.

superoga'tion, *n.*, doing more than one is called upon to do.

supererog'atory, *adj.*, of the nature of supererogation.

superex'cellence, *adj.*, excellence in a high degree.

superex'cellent, *adj.*, excellent in a high degree.

superfi'cial, *adj.*, rel. to the surface; shallow; unsound; not thorough.

superficial'ity, *n.*, the state or quality of being superficial.

superfi'cially, *n.*, in a superficial way; on the surface.

superfi'cies, *n.*, surface; superficial area.

su'perfine, *adj.*, exceedingly fine; very choice.

superflu'ity, *n.*, an over-abundance.

super'fluous, *adj.*, over-abundant.

superhu'man, *adj.*, more than human.

superimpose', *v.t.*, to lay on the top.

superimposed', *p.p.*, superimpose.

superimpo'sing, *pr.p.*, superimpose.

superincum'bent, *adj.*, lying on the top.

superinduce', *v.t.*, to bring on in addition.

superinduced', *p.p.*, superinduce.

superindu'cing, *pr.p.*, superinduce.

superintend', *v.t.*, to look after; have the oversight of.

superintend'ed, *p.p.*, superintend.

superintend'ence, *n.*, the act of superintending; the duty of a superintendent.

superintend'ency, *n.*, *i.q.* superintendence

superintend'ent, *n.*, one who superintends.

superintend'ing, *pr.p.*, superintend.

supe'rior, *adj.*, higher; of better quality; surpassing; affectedly better than others; *n.*, the head of a community.

superior'ity, *n.*, the state or quality of being superior; advantage.

super'lative, *adj.*, excellent in the highest degree; *n.*, a degree of comparison denoting the highest.

super'latively, *adv.*, in a superlative degree.

superlu'nar, *adj.*, above the moon.

superlu'nary, *adj.*, *i.q.* superlunar.

su'perman, *n.*, an ideal superior man.

supermun'dane, *adj.*, above the world.

super'nal, *adj.*, pert. to the upper regions; heavenly.

superna'tant, *adj.*, floating above the surface.

supernat'ural, *adj.*, outside and above the ordinary laws of nature.

supernat'uralism, *n.*, the state or quality of being supernatural; the teaching that God is known only through revelation.

supernat'uralist, *n.*, a believer in supernaturalism.

supernat'urally, *adv.*, in a supernatural way or sense.

supernu'merary, *adj.*, additional beyond a required number; *n.*, a person taken on above the full complement.

superphos'phate, *n.*, a phosphate of extra strength as regards the proportion of phosphoric acid.

superpose', *v.t.*, to put on the top.

superposed', *p.p.*, superpose.

superposi'tion, *n.*, the act of superposition; state of being superposed.

superroy'al, *adj.*, more than royal.

superscribe', *v.t.*, to write over, or at the head.

superscribed', *p.p.*, superscribe.

superscri'bing, *pr.p.*, superscribe.

superscrip'tion, *n.*, the act of superscribing; that which is superscribed.

supersede', *v.t.*, to take the place of; depose.

superse'deas, *n.*, legal permission to supersede (*Lat.*).

superse'ded, *p.p.*, supersede.

superse'ding, *pr.p.*, supersede.

supersen'sual, *adj.*, above the senses.

superses'sion, *n.*, the act or result of superseding.

supersti'tion, *n.*, excessive devotion to false beliefs or unworthy religious observances.

supersti'tious, *adj.*, believing in false gods or supposed spiritual agencies.

supersti'tiously, *adv.*, in a superstitious way.

superstra'tum, *n.*, a layer over another.

superstruc'ture, *n.*, a structure over a substructure.

superton'ic, *n.*, the second note in the diatonic scale.

supervene', *v.i.*, to come on, not as a consequence but merely as an after event.

supervened', *p.p.*, supervene.

superve'nient, *adj.*, supervening.

superve'ning, *pr.p.*, supervene.

superven'tion, *n.*, the act or state of supervening.

supervi'sal, *n.*, *i.q.* supervision.

supervise', *v.t.*, to superintend; look after as an overseer.

supervised', *p.p.*, supervise.

supervi'sing, *pr.p.*, supervise.

supervi'sion, *n.*, the act of supervising; an overseer's duty.

supervi'sor, *n.*, one who supervises.

supervi'sory, *adj.*, of the nature of supervision.

su'pinate, *v.t.*, to turn on its back.

supina'tion, *n.*, the act of laying on its back; state of being so placed.

supine', *adj.*, lying on the back; indolent.

su'pine, *n.*, one of the two Lat. verbal nouns in *-um* and *-u*.

supine'ly, *adv.*, in a supine way.

supine'ness, *n.*, the state or quality of being supine.

supped, *p.p.*, sup.

sup'per, *n.*, an evening meal.

sup'perless, *adj.*, without a supper.

sup'ping, *pr.p.*, sup.

supplant', *v.t.*, to supersede; take another's place.

supplanta'tion, *n.*, the act of supplanting.

supplant'ed, *p.p.*, supplant.

supplant'er, *n.*, one who supplants.

supplant'ing, *pr.p.*, supplant.

sup'ple, *adj.*, lissom; obsequious; *v.t.*, to make flexible; *v.i.*, to become flexible.

sup'pled, *p.p.*, supple.

sup'plement, *n.*, something added to fill up; an addition at the end of a book or treatise; an extra sheet or sheets in a newspaper; *v.t.*, to make additions to.

supplemen'tal, *adj.*, rel. to a supplement; additional.

supplemen'tary, *adj.*, *i.q.* supplemental.

sup'pleness, *n.*, the state or quality of being supple; flexibility.

sup'pliant, *n.*, a petitioner; one who supplicates.

sup'plicant, *adj.*, supplicating; *n.*, *i.q.* suppliant.

sup'plicate, *v.t.*, to implore; entreat humbly.

sup'plicated, *p.p.*, supplicate.

sup'plicating, *pr.p.*, supplicate.

supplica'tion, *n.*, the act of supplication.

sup'plicator, *n.*, one who supplicates.

sup'plicatory, *adj.*, making supplication; in the character of a suppliant.

supplied', *p.p.*, supply

suppli'er, *n.*, one who supplies.

supplies', *n.pl.*, stores; provisions; money for necessary purposes.

supply', *v.t.*, to furnish; give what is necessary; to stand for; to fill a vacant post; *n.*, an adequate amount or quantity.

supply'ing, *pr.p.*, supply.

support', *v.t.*, to hold up; to defend; take the side of; supply with maintenance; *n.*, help; countenance; maintenance; confirmation.

support'able, *adj.*, able to be supported

support'ed, *p.p.*, support.

support'er, *n.*, one who, that which, supports. In pl., the savage men, or strange beasts, or other heraldic emblems (as the lion and the unicorn) supporting certain privileged coats of arms.

support'ing, *pr.p.*, support.

suppo'sable, *adj.*, able to be supposed.

suppose', *v.t.* and *i.*, to imagine; assume; think.

supposed', *p.p.*, suppose.

suppo'sing, *pr.p.*, suppose.

supposi'tion, *n.*, the act of supposing; that which is supposed.

supposi'tional, *adj.*, of the nature of supposition.

suppositi'tious, *adj.*, imaginary; false.

suppos'itive, *adj.*, making supposition.

suppos'itory, *adj.*, a solid medicine introduced into the body through a canal, cavity, etc.

suppress', *v.t.*, to crush down; to quell; to conceal.

suppressed', *p.p.*, suppress.

suppress'ing, *pr.p.*, suppress.

suppres'sion, *n.*, the act or effect of suppressing.

suppress'ive, *adj.*, with the effect of suppressing.

suppress'or, *n.*, one who suppresses.

sup'purate, *v.i.*, to discharge pus.

sup'purated, *p.p.*, suppurate.

sup'purating, *pr.p.*, suppurate.

suppura'tion, *n.*, discharge of pus.

sup'purative, *adj.*, suppurating.

supra-ax'illary, *adj.*, above the armpit.

supracil'iary, *adj.*, above the eyelids.

supralapsa'rian, *adj.*, rel. to the high Calvinistic doctrine that election was decreed before the Fall.

supramun'dane, *adj.*, above the world or the worldly.

supra-or'bital, *adj.*, above the orbit.

suprem'acy, *n.*, the state or quality of being supreme; position of command.

supreme', *adj.*, highest above all; utmost.

supreme'ly, *adv.*, in the highest degree.

su'ra, *n.*, a division of the Koran.

su'rah, *n.*, a silky material.

su'ral, *adj.*, rel. to the calf of the leg.

surat', *n.*, a coarse make of cotton.

surbase', *v.t.*, to flatten.

sur'base, *n.*, mouldings, etc., on the base of a column, etc.

surbase'ment, *n.*, a flattened state.

surbed', *v.t.*, to lay stone in a different position from that in its bed.

surcharge', *v.t.*, to charge in excess.

sur'charge, *n.*, an overcharge.

surcharged', *p.p.*, surcharge.

surcharg'ing, *pr.p.*, surcharge.

sur'cingle, *n.*, a girdle, etc.

sur'coat, *n.*, a top-coat.

surd, *n.*, in mathematics, a quantity not to be expressed in rational numbers; *adj.*, not to be expressed in rational numbers.

sure, *adj.*, certain; reliable; safe; *adv.*, *i.q.* surely.

***sure'*-footed**, *adj.*, steady on the foot; not tripping.

***sure'*ly**, *adv.*, certainly; truly; without danger.

***sure'*ness**, *n.*, the state or quality of being sure.

***sur'*er**, *adj.*, *comp.* of sure.

***sur'*est**, *adj.*, *super.* of sure.

***sure'*ty**, *n.*, a sponsor; one who gives guarantees; bail; surety.

***sure'*tyship**, *n.*, the office or obligation of a surety.

surf, *n.*, broken water on a shore.

sur'face, *n.*, the upper or outside face of a thing; superficies.

sur'feit, *n.*, fulness to satiety; eating and drinking to excess; *v.t.*, to fill to satiety; *v.i.*, to eat and drink to excess.

sur'feited, *p.p.*, surfeit.

sur'feiting, *pr.p.*, surfeit.

surge, *v.i.*, to flow in a great wave; *n.*, a great wave; a swell.

surged, *p.p.*, surge.

sur'geon, *n.*, a manual operator in bodily diseases or injuries. (The old name, *chirurgeon*, of Greek derivation, means a manual operator.)

sur'geoncy, *n.*, an army or naval surgeon's position.

sur'gery, *n.*, a place where a surgeon can be consulted and keeps his drugs.

sur'gical, *adj.*, pert. to surgeons and surgery.

sur'ging, *pr.p.*, surge.

sur'gy, *adj.*, surging.

sur'liness, *n.*, the state or quality of being surly.

sur'ly, *adj.*, morose; gruff; ill-conditioned

surmise', *v.t.*, to conjecture; suppose; suspect; *n.*, conjecture; suspicion.

surmised', *p.p.*, surmise.

surmi'sing, *pr.p.*, surmise.

surmount', *v.t.*, to overcome; ascend above.

surmount'able, *adj.*, able to be surmounted.

surmount'ed, *p.p.*, surmount.

surmount'er, *n.*, one who surmounts.

surmount'ing, *pr.p.*, surmount.

sur'name, *n.*, the family name. (A person's name is that given in baptism; the family name is additional); *v.t.*, to give this additional name.

sur'named, *p.p.*, surname.

sur'naming, *pr.p.*, surname.

surpass', *v.t.*, to go beyond; to exceed; to excel.

surpass'able, *adj.*, able to be surpassed.

surpassed', *p.p.*, surpass.

surpass'ing, *pr.p.*, surpass; *adj.*, exceeding.

sur'plice, *n.*, a white linen ecclesiastical vesture.

sur'plus, *n.*, an overplus; something over and above what is necessary.

sur'plusage, *n.*, the amount of a surplus.

surpri'sal, *n.*, the act of surprising; the state of being surprised.

surprise', *v.t.*, to take unexpectedly; to attack suddenly; to amaze; *n.*, the state of being caught unawares; astonishment.

surprised', *p.p.*, surprise.

surpri'sing, *pr.p.*, surprise; *adj.*, astonishing.

surrebut', *v.i.*, to answer a rebut.

surrebut'ted, *p.p.*, surrebut.

surrebut'ter, *n.*, one who surrebuts.

surrebut'ting, *pr.p.*, surrebut.

surrejoin', *v.i.*, to reply to a rejoinder.

surrejoin'der, *n.*, a reply to a rejoinder.

surren'der, *v.t.*, to resign possession of or claim to; to yield; *v.i.*, to yield; give up; *n.*, the act of surrendering.

surren'dered, *p.p.*, surrender.

surrenderee', *n.*, one to whom anything is surrendered.

surren'derer, *n.*, one who surrenders.

surren'dering, *pr.p.*, surrender.

surrepti'tious, *adj.*, stealthy; underhand; secret.

surrepti'tiously, *adv.*, in a surreptitious way.

sur'rogate, *n.*, a bishop's official, having licensing powers.

surround', *v.t.*, to encircle; encompass; invest.

surround'ed, *p.p.*, surround.

surround'ing, *pr.p.*, surround.

surtax', *v.t.*, to overtax. [tax.

sur'tax, *n.*, an over-

surtout', *n.*, a long coat (*Fr.*).

surveil'lance, *n.*, supervision; oversight (*Fr.*).

survey', *v.t.*, to overlook; to scan; to estimate by measurement a land surface.

sur'vey, *n.*, the act of surveying; an examination.

survey'al, *n.*, the act of surveying.

surveyed', *p.p.*, survey.

survey'ing, *pr.p.*, survey; *n.*, the profession of a surveyor.

survey'or, *n.*, one who surveys; one engaged in land surveying.

survey'orship, *n.*, the office of a surveyor.

survi'val, *n.*, the act of surviving; that which has survived.

survive', *v.t.* and *i.*, to outlive; to live on

survived', *p.p.*, survive.

survi'ving, *pr.p.*, survive.

survi'vor, *n.*, one who has survived.

survi'vorship, *n.*, the state of being a survivor; a reversion that depends upon some life.

susceptibil'ity, *n.*, the state of being susceptible.

suscep'tible, *adj.*, able to be influenced by changes, appeals to the affection, sensations, etc.; capable of being impressed; having sensibility.

suscep'tibly, *adv.*, in a susceptible way.

suscep'tive, *adj.*, *s.q.* susceptible.

sus'pect, *n.*, a suspected person.

suspect', *v.t.*, to have under suspicion; to believe, but without proof; to mistrust.

suspect'able, *adj.*, able to be suspected.

suspect'ed, *p.p.*, suspect.

suspect'er, *n.*, one who suspects.

suspect'ing, *pr.p.*, suspect.

suspend', *v.t.*, to hang up; defer; debar from office.

suspend'ed, *p.p.*, suspend.

suspend'er, *n.*, one who, that which, suspends.

suspen'ders, *n. pl.*, braces to hold up trousers, stockings, etc.

suspend'ing, *pr.p.*, suspend.

suspense', *n.*, an anxious state of mind while something is awaited; reservation of judgment; temporary abeyance of one's rights.

suspensibil'ity, *n.*, the state of being suspensible.

suspen'sible, *adj.*, able to be suspended or held up.

suspen'sion, *n.*, the act of suspending; state of being suspended or in suspense; abeyance; in music, the holding of a note while passing from one chord to another.

suspen'sor, *n.*, that which suspends, esp. a supporting bandage.

suspen'sory, *adj.*, having the effect of holding up or delaying.

suspi'cion, *n.*, a feeling of mistrust; a conjecture; a hint; just a little; a soupçon.

suspi'cious, *adj.*, feeling suspicion; arousing suspicion.

suspi'ciously, *adv.*, in a suspicious way.

suspira'tion, *n.*, sighing.

suspire', *v.i.*, to sigh.

suspired', *p.p.*, suspire.

suspi'ring, *pr.p.*, suspire.

sustain', *v.t.*, to support; to bear; to nourish; continue.

sustain'able, *adj.*, able to be sustained.

sustained', *p.p.*, sustain.

sustain'er, *n.*, one who, that which, sustains.

sustain'ing, *pr.p.*, sustain; *adj.*, nourishing.

sustain'ment, *n.*, the act or result of sustaining.

sus'tenance, *n.*, support; means of living; nourishment.

sustenta'tion, *n.*, support; relief.

sut'ler, *n.*, a camp follower who sells provisions, etc.

suttee', *n.*, the old Hindu custom for a widow to offer her life on her husband's funeral pyre.

suttee'ism, *n.*, the system of suttee.

sut'tle, *n.*, weight after the deduction of tare before tret has been reckoned.

su'tural, *adj.*, pert. to a suture.

su'ture, *n.*, a joint by sewing; the markings of the skull's joints; a seam.

su'zerain, *n.*, a supreme ruler; an overlord.

su'zerainty, *n.*, the rank or office of a suzerain.

swab, *n.*, a ship's mop; a lout; *v.t.*, to mop up.

swabbed, *p.p.*, swab.

swab'ber, *n.*, one who swabs.

swab'bing, *pr.p.*, swab

swad'dle, *v.t.*, to wrap in long loose robes; to swathe.

swad'dled, *p.p.*, swaddle.

swad'dling, *pr.p.*, swaddle.

swad'dling-clothes, *n.*, a newborn infant's wrapping.

swag, *v.i.*, to sink down heavily; *n.*, a sagging movement; a thief's booty (*slang*).

swagged, *p.p.*, swag.

swag'ger, *n.*, bragging; walking in a conceited way; *v.i.*, to give oneself airs; walk with a strut.

swag'gered, *p.p.*, swagger.

swag'gerer, *n.*, one who swaggers.

swag'gering, *pr.p.*, swagger.

swag'ging, *pr.p.*, swag.

swain, *n.*, a rustic; a lover.

swale, *v.t.*, *i.q.* sweal.

swaled, *p.p.*, swale.

swa'ling, *pr.p.*, swale.

swal'low, *n.*, a migratory bird so named; the act of swallowing; the amount swallowed; *v.i.*, to take down through the mouth; to engulf; to submit to; to accept with credulity.

swal'lowed, *p.p.*, swallow.

swal'lower, *n.*, one who swallows.

swal'lowing, *pr.p.*, swallow.

swal'lowtail, *n.*, something resembling a swallow's tail; a dress-coat.

swal'low-tailed, *adj.*, shaped like a swallow's tail.

swal'lowwort, *n.*, tame poison; celandine.

swam, *p.t.*, swim.

swamp, *n.*, a marsh; morass; *v.t.*, to plunge into a swamp; to overturn a boat; to overwhelm.

swamped, *p.p.*, swamp

swamp'ing, *pr.p.*, swamp.

swamp'y, *adj.*, marshy

swan, *n.*, a web-footed aquatic bird so named.

swan'pan, *n.*, a Chinese abacus.

swans'down, *n.*, the soft down of a swan.

swap, *v.t.*, to barter; exchange; *n.*, barter; a blow; *adv.*, of a sudden.

swapped, *p.p.*, swap.

swap'ping, *pr.p.*, swap.

sward, *n.*, a stretch of grass.

sware, *p.t.*, swear (*obs.*).

swarm, *n.*, a moving crowd; a cluster, esp. of bees; *v.i.*, to move in crowds; to grow multitudinously; to migrate from a hive; *v.t.*, (with the added word *up*) to climb.

swarmed, *p.p.*, swarm

swarm'ing, *pr.p.*, swarm.

swart, *adj.*, *i.q.* swarthy.

swarth, *n.*, a phantom; *adj.*, *i.q.* swarthy.

swarth'ily, *adv.*, in a swarthy way.

swarth'iness, *n.*, the state or quality of being swarthy.

swarth'y, *adj.*, dark-complexioned.

swash, *n.*, water dashed about; *v.t.*, to make a splash with water.

swash'-buckler, *n.*, a swaggering soldier of fortune.

swash'ing, *pr.p.*, swash.

swas'tika, *n.*, the fylfot; the ancient emblem, a cross with equal arms, the ends of which are returned at right angles.

swath, *n.*, the sweep of a scythe; the line where a scythe has mown.

swathe, *n.*, a rolled bandage; *v.t.*, to wrap a bandage round.

swathed, *p.p.*, swathe.

swa'thing, *pr.p.*, swathe.

sway, *n.*, rule, dominion; inclination of a balance; *v.t.*, to rule; to influence; *v.i.*, to waver; fall on one side, or backward and forward.

swayed, *p.p.*, sway.

sway'ing, *pr.p.*, sway.

sweal, *v.t.*, to scorch; singe; *v.i.*, to melt away.

swealed, *p.p.*, sweal.

sweal'ing, *pr.p.*, sweal.

swear, *v.t.*, to cause to take oath; *v.i.*, to take oath; to use bad language.

swear'er, *n.*, one who swears.

swear'ing, *pr.p.*, swear.

sweat, *n.*, perspiration; toil; *v.i.*, to perspire; to labour; *v.t.*, to overwork and underpay.

sweat'ed, *p.p.*, sweat.

sweat'er, *n.*, one who sweats; a thick jersey.

sweat'iness, *n.*, the state of being sweaty.

sweat'ing, *pr. p.*, sweat; *n.*, employing people for an inadequate wage.

sweat'y, *adj.*, perspiring; covered with sweat.

Swede, *n.*, a Swedish native; S. turnip.

Swedenbor'gian, *adj.*, rel. to Emanuel Swedenborg and his doctrines.

Swedenbor'gianism, *n.*, the religious system of Swedenborg's followers; the New Jerusalem.

Swe'dish, *adj.*, pert. to Sweden and the Swedes; *n.*, the language of Sweden.

sweep, *v.t.*, to clear up with a broom; to drive or carry off with a violent rush; to graze; *v.i.*, to rush along with violence or majestically; to make a long or wide movement; *n.*, the act of sweeping; range; force of a blow; a large-sized oar; a chimney sweep; a low fellow (*colloq.*).

sweep'er, *n.*, one who, that which, sweeps.

sweep'ing, *pr.p.*, sweep; *adj.*, wide in its application.

sweep'ings, *n. pl.*, what is swept up.

sweep'stakes, *n. pl.*, money betted at a horse-race.

sweet, *adj.*, sugary; agreeable to taste; luscious; kind; gentle; fresh (*i.e.*, not stale); dear; in pl., as a *n.*, confectionery.

sweet'bread, *n.*, the pancreas in a calf.

sweet'-brier,-briar, *n.*, eglantine.

sweet'en, *v.t.*, to make sweet in any sense.

sweet'ened, *p.p.*, sweeten.

sweet'ener, *n.*, one who, that which, sweetens.

sweet'ening, *pr.p.*, sweeten; *n.*, something used in order to sweeten.

sweet'er, *adj.*, *comp.* of sweet.

sweet'est, *adj.*, *super.* of sweet.

sweet'heart, *n.*, a lover; *v.t.*, to court.

sweet'ing, *n.*, *i.q.* sweetheart (*obs.*).

sweet'ish, *adj.*, somewhat sweet.

sweet'ly, *adv.*, in a sweet way.

sweet'meat, *n.*, a sugary confection.

sweet'ness, *n.*, the state or quality of being sweet.

sweet'pea, *n.*, a flowering pea.

sweet'-scented, *adj.*, fragrant.

sweet'-smelling, *adj.*, fragrant.

sweet-will'iam, *n.*, a flowering plant so named.

swell, *v.t.*, to make to expand; to fill out; to increase; *v.i.*, to be inflated; to expand; to grow stronger or more violent; *n.*, the state of swelling; increase; rising of waves; a part of an organ in which the pipes are screened off by shutters, the gradual opening of which produces a swelling sound; a personage; a dandy (*colloq.*); *adj.*, distinguished; dandified (*colloq.*).

swelled, *p.p.*, swell.

swell'ing, *pr.p.*, swell; *n.*, a tumorous growth.

swel'ter, *v.i.*, to sweat excessively; to be overcome with heat.

swel'tered, *p.p.*, swelter.

swel'tering, *pr.p.*, swelter; *adj.*, overpoweringly hot.

swel'try, *adj.*, sultry.

swept, *p.p.*, sweep.

swerve, *v.i.*, to turn aside; *n.*, a turning aside; a deviation.

swerved, *p.p.*, swerve.

swerv'ing, *pr.p.*, swerve.

swift, *adj.*, fast; rapid; sudden; *n.*, a kind of swallow; a rapid current.

swift'er, *adj.*, *comp.* of swift.

swift'est, *adj.*, *super.* of swift.

swift'ly, *adv.*, rapidly, suddenly, fast.

swift'ness, *n.*, the state or quality of being swift.

swig, *v.t.*, to drink off; *v.i.*, to be a drinker.

swill, *v.t.*, to wash by pouring water over; *v.t.* and *i.*, to drink to excess.

swilled, *p.p.*, swill.

swill'er, *n.*, one who, that which, swills.

swill'ing, *pr.p.*, swill.

swim, *v.t.*, to make to swim or float; *v.i.*, to float and move through water; to be full to overflowing; to become dizzy; *n.*, the act of swimming; a fish's air-bladder.

swim'mer, *n.*, one who, that which, swims.

swim'ming, *pr.p.*, swim; *n.*, supporting and moving oneself in the water by moving the hands and feet.

swim'mingly, *adv.*, easily; with success.

swin'dle, *v.t.*, to cheat, esp. in money matters; *v.i.*, to be a swindler; *n.*, the act of a swindler.

swin'dled, *p.p.*, swindle.

swin'dler, *n.*, one who swindles; a fraudulent person who cheats over money dealings.

swin'dling, *pr.p.*, swindle; *n.*, the practices of a swindler.

swine, *n.*, a pig or pigs (the pl. form being the same).

swine'herd, *n.*, one who tends swine.

swing, *v.t.*, to move to and fro an object suspended or uplifted; *v.i.*, to move to and fro; to oscillate; to be hanged; *n.*, the act of swinging; the state of being swung; a hanging seat that can be swung to and fro.

swinge, *v.t.*, to thrash; *n.*, movement to and fro; sway.

swinged, *p.p.*, swinge.

swinge'ing, *pr.p.*, swinge.

swin'gel, *n.*, the striking part of a flail.

swing'er, *n.*, one who swings.

swing'ing, *pr.p.*, swing.

swin'gle, *v.t.*, to beat flax; *v.i.*, to be pendent.

swin'gled, *p.p.*, swingle.

swin'gling, *pr.p.*, swingle.

swi'nish, *adj.*, like a swine; beastly.

swipe, *v.t.* and *i.*, to hit with a wild stroke; *n.*, a sweeping blow with a cricket bat.

swipes, *n. pl.*, thin beer.

swirl, *v.i.*, to eddy; *n.*, the motion of eddying water.

swirl'ed, *p.p.*, swirl.

swirl'ing, *pr.p.*, swirl.

swish, *v.t.*, to flog; *n.*, the sound of a stroke with a birch, etc.

Swiss, *adj.*, pert. to Switzerland and the Swiss; *n.*, a native of Switzerland.

switch, *v.t.*, to shunt; turn on or off; thrash; *n.*, a thin rod; a device for shunting on a railway; a device for controlling electric currents.

switch'back, *n.*, an up-and-down track; *adj.*, with a succession of ascents and descents.

switch'band, *n.*, a contrivance for cutting or making an electric current.

switch'board, *n.*, a board on which electric switches are placed, showing their controls.

switched, *p.p.*, switch.

switch'ing, *pr.p.*, switch.

switch'man, *n.*, a man in charge of switches.

Swit'zer, *n.*, a Swiss.

swiv'el, *n.*, something that revolves within another; a revolving cannon; *v.t.*, to make to move on a pivot; *v.i.*, to turn.

swoll'en, *p.p.*, swell.

swoon, *v.i.*, to faint; *n.*, a fainting-fit.

swooned, *p.p.*, swoon.

swoon'ing, *pr.p.*, swoon; *n.*, syncope.

swoop, *v.t.* and *i.*, to fly or spring down upon a thing; *n.*, the act of swooping and seizing.

swooped, *p.p.*, swoop.

swoop'ing, *pr.p.*, swoop.

swop, *v.t.*, to barter, exchange; *n.*, exchange, barter. Also *swap*.

swopped, *p.p.*, swop.

swop'ping, *pr.p.*, swop

sword, *n.*, a cutting and stabbing weapon; the emblem of war, power of life and death, justice, etc.

sword'-bayonet, *n.*, a bayonet shaped like a short sword.

sword'-belt, *n.*, a belt from which a sword is suspended.

sword'-blade, *n.*, the blade of a sword.

sword'-cane, *n.*, a cane containing a sword.

sword'fish, *n.*, a fish with a sword-like projection.

sword'-shaped, *adj.*, shaped like a sword.

swords'man, *n.*, one skilled in the use of the sword.

swore, *p.t.*, swear.
swora, *p.p.*, swear.
swum, *p.p.*, swim.
swung, *p.t.* and *p.*, swing.
Syb'arite, *n.*, a luxurious person; a voluptuary; a native of the ancient Italian city, Sybaris, notorious for the extravagance of its inhabitants.
Sybarit'ic, *adj.*, like a Sybarite.
syc'amine, *n.*, a black mulberry tree.
syc'amore, *n.*, a bushy tree so named.
sycee', *n.*, Chinese silver currency.
syc'ophancy, *n.*, the act or character of a sycophant.
syc'ophant, *n.*, a flatterer; parasite.
sycophan'tic, *adj.*, like a sycophant.
syc'ophantize, *v.i.*, to play the sycophant.
sy'enite, *n.*, an Egyptian granite rock.
syenit'ic, *adj.*, pert. to syenite.
syllaba'rium, *n.*, a list of the root syllables of a language.
syl'labary, *n.*, *i.q.* syllabarium.
syllab'ic, *adj.*, pert. to syllables.
syllab'ically, *adv.*, syllable by syllable.
syllabica'tion, *n.*, formation into syllables.
syl'lable, *n.*, a letter or group of letters that can be pronounced by a single vocal effort.
syl'labub, *n.*, cream and wine, etc., mixed and curded. Also *sillabub*.
syl'labus, *n.*, a conspectus; abstract.
syl'logism, *n.*, a logical term describing the drawing of a conclusion from two premises.
syllogis'tic, *adj.*, pert. to syllogism; in the form of a syllogism.
syllogiza'tion, *n.*, the act of making syllogisms.
syl'logize, *v.i.*, to make syllogisms; *v.t.*, to throw into the form of a syllogism.
syl'logized, *p.p.*, syllogize.
syl'logizer, *n.*, one who syllogizes.
syl'logizing, *pr.p.*, syllogize.
sylph, *n.*, a fairy; sprite.
sylph'id, *adj.*, sylph-like.
syl'va, *n.*, a wood; forest (*Lat.*). Also *silva*.
syl'van, *adj.*, rel. to woods; rustic; shady.
syl'vanite, *n.*, a tellurid.
sym'bol, *n.*, a token; pledge; sign; creed.
symbol'ic, *adj.*, pert. to symbol; expressed in symbols.
symbol'ical, *adj.*, *i.q.* symbolic.
symbol'ically, *adv.*, in a symbolic way.
symbol'ics, *n. pl.*, the study of creeds.
sym'bolism, *n.*, expression by means of symbols; meaning of a thing symbolized.
sym'bolist, *n.*, one who studies creeds.
symboliza'tion, *n.*, the use of symbols.
sym'bolize, *v.t.*, to mean symbolically.
sym'bolized, *p.p.*, symbolize.
sym'bolizing, *pr.p.*, symbolize.
symmet'ric, *adj.*, commensurate; in exact proportion; harmonious.
symmet'rical, *adj.*, *i.q.* symmetric.
symmet'rically, *adv.*, in a symmetrical way.
sym'metrize, *v.t.*, to make symmetrical.
sym'metrized, *p.p.*, symmetrize.
sym'metrizing, *pr.p.*, symmetrize.
sym'metry, *n.*, perfect proportion of parts; regularity of form; harmony.
sympathet'ic, *adj.*, being in sympathy; compassionate; congenial.
sympathet'ical, *adj.*, sympathetic.
sympathet'ically, *adv.*, in a sympathetic way.
sym'pathize, *v.i.*, to show or feel sympathy or compassion.
sym'pathized, *p.p.*, sympathize.
sym'pathizer, *n.*, one who sympathizes.
sym'pathizing, *pr.p.*, sympathize.
sym'pathy, *n.*, compassion; a feeling for another's sorrow or sharing in his pleasure; reciprocal action of bodily organs.
symphon'ic, *adj.*, pert. to symphony; concordant.
sympho'nious, *adj.*, *i.q.* symphonic.
sym'phonist, *n.*, composer of symphonies (*mus.*).
sym'phony, *n.*, harmony; concord of sounds; a musical orchestral work of a particular form; an instrumental beginning or ending to a vocal work.
sym'physis, *n.*, union of parts; coalescence.
sympiesom'eter, *n.*, a barometer working by compression.
sympo'siac, *adj.*, pert. to a symposium.
sympo'siarch, *n.*, the master of a banquet.
sympo'siast, *n.*, one who shares in a literary symposium.
sympo'sium, *n.*, a drinking in company; banquet; a joint literary article.
symp'tom, *n.*, a perceptible sign of a hidden cause; a token.
symptomat'ic, *adj.*, betokening.
symptomatol'ogy, *n.*, the study of symptoms.
syn, a Greek prefix = with, together.
synae'resis, *n.*, the combination of two vowels into a single sound.

synagog'ic, *adj.*, pert. to a synagogue.

synagog'ical, *adj.*, *i.q.* synagogic.

syn'agogue, *n.*, a congregation; assembly; a Jewish place of non-sacrificial worship, as distinct from the Temple.

syn'archy, *n.*, joint rule.

synarthro'sis, *n.*, congestion.

syncar'pous, *adj.*, having coherent carpels.

syn'chronal, *adj.*, *i.q.* synchronous.

syn'chronism, *n.*, coincidence of dates.

syn'chronise, *v.t.*, to date simultaneously; *v.i.*, to occur simultaneously.

syn'chronized, *p.p.*, synchronize.

syn'chronizing, *pr.p.*, synchronize.

syn'chronous, *adj.*, simultaneous.

syncli'nal, *adj.*, pert. to a line that inclines till it meets a common line or point.

syn'copal, *adj.*, pert. to syncope.

syn'copate, *v.t.*, to shorten by cutting something out; in music, to borrow from a following note part of its accent and throw it on to part of the preceding note; to carry the sound of the last note of a bar into the first beat of the next bar.

syn'copated, *p.p.*, syncopate.

syn'copating, *pr.p.*, syncopate.

syncopa'tion, *n.*, the act of syncopating; the result of syncopating.

syn'cope, *n.*, a cutting out from the middle of a word; a fainting fit.

syn'copist, *n.*, one who practises syncopation.

syncret'ic, *adj.*, pert. to syncretism.

syn'cretism, *n.*, the act of harmonizing contradictory beliefs; the result so obtained.

syn'cretist, *n.*, one who makes a syncretism.

syndac'tylous, *adj.*, having the same kind of toes or fingers.

syndesmo'sis, *n.*, a binding together.

syn'dic, *n.*, a Government official; chief magistrate; one charged with special business duties.

syn'dicalism, *n.*, a socialistic labour doctrine, insisting on the control of all industries by the workers.

syn'dicate, *n.*, syndics in council; business men combined in a speculation.

synec'doche, *n.*, taking a part for the whole, or a whole for the part.

syner'esis, *n.*, *i.q.* synaeresis.

synerget'ic, *adj.*, working or energizing in union.

syn'ergy, *n.*, correlation of different organs; co-operation.

syngen'esis, *n.*, the view that the male and the female jointly produce the embryo.

synize'sis, *n.*, pronouncing as one syllable two vowels, which do not form a diphthong.

syn'od, *n.*, a formal gathering of the clergy under their bishop; a Presbyterian council.

syn'odal, *adj.*, *i.q.* synodic.

syn'odals, *n. pl.*, a money payment of the clergy to the bishop at Easter.

synod'ic, *adj.*, pert. to a synod; done in synod.

synod'ical, *adj.*, *i.q.* synodic.

syn'odist, *n.*, a member of a synod.

syn'onym, *n.*, a word that has the same meaning as another.

synonym'ic, *adj.*, being synonymous.

synon'ymize, *v.i.*, to use a synonym; *v.t.*, to make synonymous.

synon'ymous, *adj.*, having identical meaning.

synon'ymously, *adv.*, in a synonymous way.

synon'ymy, *n.*, the state of being synonymous.

synop'sis, *n.*, a general view; summary.

synop'tic, *adj.*, in the nature of a synopsis; agreeing in point of view and in statement, with special reference to the first three Gospels; *n.*, each of the writers of the first three Gospels.

synop'tical, *adj.*, *i.q.* synoptic.

synop'tically, *adv.*, in a synoptic way.

synop'tist, *n.*, a name given to St. Matt. St. Mark, and St. Luke; *see* synoptic.

syno'via, *n.*, fluid secretion in joints.

syno'vial, *adj.*, pert. to synovia.

synovi'tis, *n.*, inflammation of a synovial membrane.

syntac'tic, *adj.*, pert. to syntax.

syntac'tical, *adj.*, *i.q.* syntactic.

syn'tax, *n.*, the rules of grammatical construction.

syntax'is, *n.*, *i.q.* syntax.

synther'mal, *adj.*, of the same temperature.

syn'thesis, *n.*, a combination; composition; the opposite to analysis; the result of combining into a whole.

synthet'ic, *adj.*, not analytic; pert. to synthesis.

synthet'ical, *adj.*, *i.q.* synthetic.

synthet'ically, *adv.*, by way of synthesis.

syn'tomy, *n.*, brevity.

synton'ic, *adj.*, alike in tone.

syph'ilis, *n.*, a venereal disease.

syphilit'ic, *adj.*, pert. to syphilis.

sy'phon, *n.*, *i.q.* siphon.

sy'ren, *n.*, *i.q.* siren.

Syr'iac, *adj.*, pert. to Syria; *n.*, the old language of Syria.

Syr'iacism, *n.*, the Syriac idiom.

Syr'ian, *adj.*, bel. to Syria; *n.*, a native of Syria.

Syr'ianism, *n.*, *i.q.* Syriacism.

syrin'ga, *n.*, a plant genus so named.

syr'inge, *n.*, a small pump or squirt; *v.t.*, to inject.

syr'inged, *p.p.*, syringe

syr'inging, *pr. p.*, syringe.

syringot'omy, *n.*, cutting for fistula.

syr'inx, *n.*, fistula; the lower larynx; Pan pipes.

syr'tic, *adj.*, pert. to a syrtis.

syrt'is, *n.*, a quicksand (*Lat.*).

syr'up, *n.*, sugar saturated in water; a liquid product of sugar.

syr'upy, *adj.*, like, full of, syrup.

systal'tic, *adj.*, pulsing.

sys'tem, *n.*, a whole in relation to parts; regular arrangement; method; a code of doctrines, etc.

systemat'ic, *adj.*, methodical; regular.

systemat'ical, *adj.*, *i.q.* systematic.

systemat'ically, *adv.*, in a systematic way.

sys'tematism, *n.*, the attempt to systematize.

sys'tematist, *n.*, one who systematizes.

sys'tematize, *v.t.*, to reduce to system.

sys'tematized, *p.p.*, systematize.

sys'tematizer, *n.*, one who systematizes.

sys'tematizing, *pr.p.*, systematize.

systemiza'tion, *n.*, the act or result of systematizing.

sys'temize, *v.t.*, *i.q.* systematize.

sys'temized, *p.p.*, systemize.

sys'temizer, *n.*, *i.q.* systematizer.

sys'tem-maker, *n.*, one who makes systems.

sys'tole, *n.*, the shortening of a long syllable; one of the heart movements, consisting of the contraction of the auricles and ventricles.

systol'ic, *adj.*, pert. to systole.

sys'tyle, *adj.*, with pillars closely set in a row; with pillars placed at a distance from each other of two diameters.

syz'ygy, *n.*, a conjunction. In pl., the point of conjunction of the moon or a planet with the sun.

T

Taal, *n.*, a S. African Dutch dialect.
tab, *n.*, a border, shoe latchet, tag.
tab'ard, *n.*, a short coat worn over a suit of armour, and still worn by heralds.
tab'aret, *n.*, a striped upholstering fabric.
tabasheer', *n.*, an Oriental drug extracted from bamboo.
tab'bied, *p.p.*, tabby.
tab'binet, *n.*, a mixed fabric used in upholstery.
tab'by, *v.t.*, to give a waved appearance to; *adj.*, brindled, wavy; *n.*, a wavy silken fabric; stone, etc., mixed with mortar; a brindled cat.
tab'bying, *pr.p.*, tabby; *n.*, a calendering process producing a wavy appearance.
tabefac'tion, *n.*, consumption, wasting.
Tab'erdar, *n.*, the title of certain scholars of Queen's College, Oxford.
tab'ernacle, *v.i.*, to dwell for a while; sojourn; *n.*, a tent; specifically the Tabernacle in the Wilderness; a shrine for the Reserved Sacrament.
tab'ernacled, *p.p.*, tabernacle.
tab'ernacle-work, *n.*, carved or sculptured canopy-work.
tab'ernacling, *pr.p.*, tabernacle.
ta'bes, *n.*, a wasting away (*Lat.*).
tabet'ic, *adj.*, atrophied.
tab'idly, *adv.*, wasting away.
tab'idness, *n.*, a state of wasting.
tabif'ic, *adj.*, causing wasting away.
tab'lature, *n.*, decorative painting; the division of the skull.
ta'ble, *v.t.*, to place (a document, etc.) on a table; to register or index; *v.i.*, to share a table; *n.*, a flat board on legs; any flat surface; food; an index or catalogue.
tableau', *n.*, a picture; lively scene.
tableau'-vivant', *n.*, a living picture.
tab'le-cloth, *n.*, a cloth to cover a table.
ta'bled, *p.p.*, table.
ta'ble d'hôte, *n.*, a set meal for a fixed price.
ta'ble-land, *n.*, high, flat land; a plateau.
ta'ble-spoon, *n.*, a large spoon used at table.
tab'let, *n.*, a little table; a flat surface for inscriptions or for memoranda; a cake of soap, etc.
ta'ble-talk, *n.*, conversation of a desultory kind.
ta'ble-turning, *n.*, an amusement in vogue among spiritualists.
ta'bling, *pr.p.*, table.
taboo', *n.*, a barbarous rite of consecration; *v.t.*, to pronounce inviolable; prohibit the use of. Also *tabu*.
tabooed', *p.p.*, taboo.
taboo'ing, *pr.p.*, taboo.
ta'bor, *n.*, a little drum.
tab'oret, *n.*, a diminutive tabor.
tab'ouret, *n.*, a footstool of ornamental work.
tab'ret, *n.*, *i.q.* taboret.
tab'ular, *adj.*, pert. to a table; like a table; laminated; in catalogue or index form.
tab'ula ra'sa, *n.*, a blank page (*Lat.*).
tab'ularize, *v.t.*, to arrange in tabular form.
tab'ulate, *v.t.*, to put a flat surface on; to reduce to tabular form.
tab'ulated, *p.p.*, tabulate.
tab'ulating, *pr.p.*, tabulate.
tabula'tion, *n.*, the act of tabulating; a tabular arrangement.
tab'ulator, *n.*, one who tabulates.
tac'amahac, *n.*, a resin.
tac'ca, *n.*, a species of arrowroot.
ta'cet, *n.*, a musical term indicating a silence.
tache, *v.t.*, to mark; blemish; *n.*, a blemish.
tache, *n.*, a pan used in sugar making.
tachom'eter, *n.*, a speed-measuring instrument.
tachygraph'ic, *adj.*, pert. to tachygraphy.
tachyg'raphy, *n.*, stenography.
tachym'eter, *n.*, a rapidly measuring instrument.
tac'it, *adj.*, silent, secret, unspoken.
tac'itly, *adv.*, in a tacit way.
tac'iturn, *adj.*, gloomily silent.
taciturn'ity, *n.*, the quality or state of being taciturn.
tack, *n.*, a small kind of nail; something appended; a boat's or ship's sailing direction; *v.t.*, to drive a tack into; to append; *v.i.*, to change a ship's sailing direction.
tacked, *p.p.*, tack.
tack'er, *n.*, one who tacks.

tack'ing, *pr.p.*, tack; *n.*, a ship's change of direction.

tack'le, *n.*, a ship's outfit of rigging, etc.; an arrangement of pulleys; fishing implements; *v.t.*, to grapple with; to harness.

tack'led, *p.p.*, tackle.

tack'ling, *pr.p.*, tackle; *n.*, gear; sails, ropes, etc., on a ship.

tacks'man, *n.*, a Scottish leaseholder.

tact, *n.*, skilfulness in handling a difficult position without giving offence.

tact'ful, *adj.*, possessing tact.

tact'fully, *adv.*, in a tactful way.

tac'tic, *adj.*, *i.q.* tactical.

tac'tical, *adj.*, rel. to tactics.

tactic'ian, *n.*, one skilled in tactics.

tac'tics, *n. pl.*, that part of military science which relates to movements of ships or troops in battle.

tac'tile, *adj.*, sensible to the touch; that can be touched.

tactil'ity, *n.*, the quality of being tactile.

tac'tion, *n.*, the act of touching.

tac'tual, *adj.*, rel. to touch.

tad'pole, *n.*, a young frog.

tael, *n.*, a Chinese coin (= about 6s.).

tae'nia, *n.*, the tapeworm; a fillet or band ornament on a Doric architrave (*Lat.*).

taff'erel, *n.*, *i.q.* taffrail.

taff'eta, *n.*, a thin silken fabric with a glossy surface.

taff'rail, *n.*, the rail of a boat's stern.

taf'fy, *n.*, a Welshman (*colloq.*).

tafi'a, *n.*, a species of rum.

tag, *n.*, the metal tubing at the end of a lace; an appendage; a trite quotation of a familiar passage; *v.t.*, to append.

tagged, *p.p.*, tag; *adj.*, having tags.

tag'ging, *pr.p.*, tag.

tag'lia, *n.*, a pulley arrangement.

Tagliaco'tian, *adj.*, pert. to the 16th cent. Bolognese surgeon, Taliacotius, and the operation for making a new nose.

tag'rag, *n.*, the multitude; rabble.

tail, *n.*, an appendage to an animal's backbone; anything hanging down or appended; limitation; *v.i.*, to dwindle

tail'age, *n.*, *i.q.* tallage.

tailed, *p.p.*, tail; *adj.*, having a tail.

tail'ing, *pr.p.*, tail; *n.*, that part of a projecting brick or stone which does not project from the wall; stamped ore refuse.

tail'less, *adj.*, lacking a tail.

tail'or, *n.*, a man who makes clothes; *v.t.*, to make clothes for; *v.i.*, to practise tailoring.

tail'ored, *p.p.*, tailor; *adj.*, turned out by one's tailor.

tail'oress, *n.*, fem. of tailor.

tail'oring, *pr.p.*, tailor; *n.*, a tailor's trade; tailor's materials.

tail'-piece, *n.*, an appendage to a page or chapter.

tail'zie, *n.*, the legal cutting of entail (*Scots Law*).

taint, *v.t.*, to infect with an odour or bad taste; to tinge; *n.*, an infecting smell or taste.

taint'ed, *p.p.*, taint.

taint'ing, *pr.p.*, taint.

taint'less, *adj.*, without a taint.

taint'ure, *n.*, stain.

take, *v.t.*, assume possession of; lay hands on; seize; adopt; regard; obtain; contract; apprehend; conduct; go across or through; *v.i.*, to derogate from; to have effect; to form a liking for; to make a good picture; *n.*, a catch (as of fish); amount of copy furnished to a compositor; takings.

take'-in, *n.*, a trick, deception.

ta'ken, *p.p.*, take.

take'-off, *n.*, a satirical representation; a piece of mimicry; a drawback; a starting-point.

ta'ker, *n.*, one who takes.

ta'king, *pr.p.*, take; *adj.*, attractive, pleasing.

ta'kingly, *adv.*, attractively.

ta'kingness, *n.*, agreeableness, charm.

ta'kings, *n. pl.*, money received for seats in a theatre or by sales in a business.

tal'apoin, *n.*, a species of monkey; a Siamese bonza.

tal'bot, *n.*, a variety of hunting-dog, noted for its quick scent.

talc, *n.*, a flaky substance, hydrous silicate of magnesia.

talck'y, *adj.*, *i.q.*, talcose.

talc'ose, *adj.*, *i.q.* talcous.

talc'ous, *adj.*, of the nature of talc.

tale, *n.*, a story, anecdote; a reckoning; number.

tale'bearer, *n.*, one who carries gossip from one person to another.

tale'bearing, *adj.*, idly gossiping; *n.*, idle gossip.

tal'ent, *n.*, in the classical age, a weight, coin, sum of money; mental endowment; intellectual gifts.

tal'ented, *adj.*, intellectually endowed; clever.

ta'les, *n. pl.*, a writ for summoning extra jurors; a list of them.

ta'lesman, *n.*, an extra juryman.

tal'iped, *adj.*, club-footed.

tal'iput, *n.*, an Indian giant palm. Also *talipot.*

tal'isman, *n.*, a stone or metal charm, defensive against evil or productive of great good.

talisman'ic, *adj.*, of the nature of a talisman.

talk, *v.t.*, to utter; converse about; *v.i.*, to speak, converse; babble.

talk'ative, *adj.*, too much given to talking.

talk'atively, *adv.*, in a talkative way.

talked, *p.p.*, talk.

talk'ee-talk'ee, *n.*, rubbish, nonsense.

talk'er, *n.*, one who talks, esp. one who talks overmuch.

talk'ing, *pr.p.*, talk; *n.*, the act of talking; conversation.

tall, *adj.*, lofty; high of stature; exaggerated (*slang*).

tall'age, *n.*, toll, tax. Also *tailage.*

tall'er, *adj.*, *comp.* of tall.

tall'est, *adj.*, *super.* of tall.

tal'lied, *p.p.*, tally.

tall'ness, *n.*, loftiness; height of stature.

tal'low, *v.t.*, to smear with tallow; *n.*, melted fat; material for candles.

tal'low-chandler, *n.*, one who sells tallow candles.

tal'lowy, *adj.*, pert. to tallow.

tal'ly, *n.*, a notched stick once used for keeping accounts, something that matches; *v.t.* and *i.*, to match.

tally-ho', *n.*, a huntsman's cry.

tal'lying, *pr.p.*, tally; *n.*, the act of tallying.

tal'lyman, *n.*, a seller of goods for payment in instalments

Tal'mud, *n.*, a Rabbinical book, consisting of the Mishna and the Gemara, and treating of Jewish traditions, law, etc.

Talmud'ic, *adj.*, pert. to the Talmud.

Tal'mudist, *n.*, one learned in the Talmud.

tal'on, *n.*, a bird's claw.

tal'oned, *adj.*, furnished with talons.

talook', taluk', *n.*, an Indian territorial area.

talook'dar, taluk'dar, *n.*, one who holds a talook.

ta'lus, *n.*, the ankle-bone; a slope; sloping débris below a rock.

tamabil'ity, *n.*, the quality of being tamable.

ta'mable, tame'able, *adj.*, able to be tamed; gentle.

ta'mableness, tame'ableness, *n.*, the quality of being tamable.

tam'arach, *n.*, the black larch of America.

tam'arin, *n.*, a species of monkey.

tam'arind, *n.*, a leguminous tree.

tam'arisk, *n.*, a shrub so named.

tam'bour, *n.*, a drum; a drum-shaped structure; an embroidery frame; *v.t.*, to embroider on a tambour.

tambourine', *n.*, a musical instrument, tapped with the hand, and having jingling cymbals in the encircling frame.

tame, *v.t.*, to bring under control; to change from wild to gentle; to subdue; *adj.*, subdued; rendered gentle; dull; without spirit.

tameabil'ity, tamabil'ity, *n.*, *i.q.* tamableness.

tamed, *p.p.*, tame.

tame'less, *adj.*, untamable.

tame'ly, *adv.*, in a tame manner.

tame'ness, *n.*, gentleness; insipidity.

ta'mer, *n.*, one who tames, esp. wild animals.

Tam'il, *n.*, a language spoken in Ceylon and S.E. India.

ta'ming, *pr.p.*, tame.

Tam'many, *n.*, an American political organization.

Tam-o'-Shan'ter, *n.*, a soft flat cap.

tamp, *v.t.*, to stop a blasting-hole; to hammer gently.

tamped, *p.p.*, tamp.

tam'per, *v.t.*, to meddle; interfere; bribe.

tam'pered, *p.p.*, tamper.

tam'perer, *n.*, one who tampers.

tam'pering, *pr.p.*, tamper.

tamp'ing, *pr.p.*, tamp.

tam'pion, *n.*, a stopper, esp. of a cannon's mouth.

tam'poe, *n.*, an edible Malayan fruit.

tam'tam, *n.*, a native drum; *i.q.* tom-tom.

tan, *n.*, bark of a tree, esp. the oak, used for the preparation of hides; *adj.*, brown like tan; *v.t.*, to make leather from hides treated with an infusion of bark; to sunburn; to beat (*colloq.*); *v.i.*, to be browned by the sun.

tan'ager, *n.*, an American finch-like bird.

tan'dem, *adv.*, with one horse in front of another; *n.*, a carriage drawn by two horses, one in front of the other; a bicycle for two or more riders seated tandem-fashion.

tang, *n.*, a strong flavour; the part of a knife, tool, etc., that goes into the handle; the sound of a bell; *v.i.*, to give forth a bell-like sound.

tan'gency, *n.*, contact.

tan'gent, *adj.*, touching; *n.*, a straight line which touches a curve but, being produced beyond the point of contact, does not cut the curve or circle.

tangen'tial, *adj.*, pert. to a tangent.

tangerine', *n.*, a small orange with a peculiar taste.

tangibil'ity, *n.*, the quality of being tangible.

tan'gible, *adj.*, able to be touched, attained, or perceived; real.

tan'gle, *v.t.*, to twist into a confused knot; to complicate; *v.i.*, to become entangled; *n.*, a confused knot; a complication; a seaweed.

tan'gled, *p.p.*, tangle.

tan'gling, *pr.p.*, tangle

tan'gly, *adj.*, in a tangle.

tan'ist, *n.*, an Irish popularly elected head of a clan or landowner.

tan'istry, *n.*, the custom of electing tanists.

tank, *n.*, a reservoir or large cistern; a strange armoured car used by the British Army in the war with the Central Empires.

tank'ard, *n.*, a drinking vessel.

tan'nage, *n.*, the process of tanning.

tan'nate, *n.*, a tannic acid salt.

tanned, *p.p.*, tan.

tan'ner, *n.*, one who makes hides into leather; sixpence (*slang*).

tan'nery, *n.*, a yard where hides are tanned.

tan'nic, *adj.*, rel. to, or got from, bark.

tan'nier, *n.*, the spoon-flower.

tan'nin, *n.*, tannic acid.

tan'ning, *pr.p.*, tan; *n.*, the tanning industry.

tan'sy, *n.*, an aromatic herb so named.

tantaliza'tion, *n.*, tantalizing; being tantalized.

tan'talize, *v.t.*, to tempt with vain hopes.

tan'talized, *p.p.*, tantalize.

tan'talizer, *n.*, one who tantalizes.

tan'talizing, *pr.p.*, tantalize; *adj.*, provoking.

tan'talum, *n.*, a scarce element so named.

tan'talus, *n.*, an open stand for spirit decanters secured with a lock.

tan'tamount, *adj.*, equal; equivalent.

tan'tivy, *n.*, a gallop; *adv.*, at a gallop.

tan'trum, *n.*, a pet, passion.

tan'yard, *n.*, *i.q.* tannery.

tap, *v.t.*, to beat or hammer lightly; to make an opening in a vessel for the liquid to flow out; to sole or heel a shoe; to bore; *n.*, a light blow with a hammer or the hand; an outlet for fluid; the part of a tavern where liquor is drawn.

tape, *n.*, a strip of linen or cotton cloth.

ta'per, *v.t.*, to narrow; *v.i.*, to become slender towards one end; *n.*, a candle that tapers.

ta'pered, *p.p.*, taper.

ta'pering, *pr.p.*, taper; *adj.*, narrowing towards one end.

tap'estry, *n.*, a woven fabric with figures, pictures, etc., worked in.

tap'et, *n.*, a S. Amer. hare.

tape'worm, *n.*, an intestinal worm like a tape.

tap'house, *n.*, a beer-house.

tapio'ca, *n.*, a product from cassava root.

ta'pir, *n.*, a quadruped of the hog genus.

tap'is, *n.*, a carpet (*Fr.*). (Originally, carpets were used to cover a table or an altar, not a floor. Hence the phrase *sur le tapis*, "on the carpet," means laid on the table for debate.)

tapped, *p.p.*, tap.

tap'per, *n.*, one who, that which, taps. (Formerly it meant a drawer of wine or ale.)

tap'pet, *n.*, a little lever arrangement, altering or regulating motion.

tap'ping, *pr.p.*, tap.

tap'-room, *n.*, a public-house bar.

tap'-root, *n.*, a plant's chief root.

tap'ster, *n.*, one who draws liquor. (This word originally was the feminine form of tapper, women being often employed as drawers.)

tar, *n.*, a thick, black, oily substance distilled from coal, pine, etc.; a sailor; *v.t.*, to cover with tar.

tarantel'la, *n.*, a fast Neapolitan dance and its music.

tar'antism, *n.*, an affection produced by the bite of a tarantula.

taran'tula, *n.*, a great poisonous spider, alleged to affect with a dancing madness those whom it bites.

tarax'acum, *n.*, a plant genus, containing the dandelion.

tarboosh', *n.*, a blue-tasselled fez.

tar'digrade, *n.*, one of the Tardigrada, such as the sloth.

tar'dily, *adv.*, slowly; hesitatingly.

tar'diness, *n.*, slowness, dilatoriness.

tar'dy, *adj.*, slow; belated; dilatory.

tare, *n.*, a darnel; allowance for the weight of a cask, wrapper, case, etc., after it has been weighed with its contents.

tar'entism, *n.*, *i.q.* tarantism.

tar'get, *n.*, a marked disk or butt used in archery and rifle or artillery practice; a light shield; neck and breast of lamb (as a joint for the table).
targeteer', *n.*, one armed with a target.
Tar'gum, *n.*, the Chaldaic version of the Old Testament Scriptures.
Tar'gumist, *n.*, one learned in the Targum.
tar'iff, *n.*, list of dutiable commodities, whether imports or exports.
tar'iff-reform', Tar'iff Reform', *n.*, a change in existing tariffs; a movement to tax imports.
tar'in, *n.*, a French bird so named.
tar'latan, *n.*, a fine dress fabric.
tarn, *n.*, a small mountain lake.
tar'nish, *v.t.*, to sully; stain; *v.i.*, to be sullied.
tar'nished, *p.p.*, tarnish.
tar'nishing, *pr.p.*, tarnish.
tarpau'lin, *n.*, heavy canvas waterproof.
Tarpe'ian, *adj.*, rel. to Tarpeia and the rock named after her at Rome.
tar'ragon, *n.*, a vinegar.
tarred, *p.p.*, tar.
tar'ried, *p.p.*, tarry.
tar'rier, *n.*, one who tarries.
tar'rier, *adj.*, *comp.* of tarry.
tar'ring, *pr.p.*, tar.
tar'rock, *n.*, a young kittiwake.
tar'ry, *adj.*, like tar; covered with tar.
tar'ry, *v.i.*, to wait; linger; in older English, *v.t.*, to wait for; await.
tar'rying, *pr.p.*, tarry.
tar'sal, *adj.*, rel. to the tarsus.
tarse, *n.*, *i.q.* tarsus.
tar'sus, *n.*, the instep.
tart, *adj.*, sharp; acid; cutting; *n.*, an uncovered pie.
tar'tan, *n.*, a many-coloured plaid.
Tar'tar, tar'tar, *n.*, a native of Tartary; a dangerous-tempered person; a dental deposit; *adj.*, bel. to Tartary.
Tarta'rean, *adj.*, pert. to Tartarus.
tar'tar-emet'ic, *n.*, a compound of antimony, potassium, and tartaric acid.
Tar'tarus, *n.*, Hades; the darkest of the infernal regions.
tart'ish, *adj.*, somewhat tart.
tart'ly, *adv.*, in a tart manner.
tart'ness, *n.*, the state or quality of being tart.
tar'trate, *n.*, a tartaric acid salt.
Tartuffe', *n.*, one of Molière's comic characters; a precise hypocrite.
Tartuf'fish, *adj.*, like Tartuffe.
tar'-water, *n.*, a decoction from tar.
task, *n.*, an imposed piece of work; something to be learnt; *v.t.*, to impose a task upon; to try severely.
tasked, *p.p.*, task.
task'er, *n.*, one who imposes a task.
task'ing, *pr.p.*, task.
task'master, *n.*, *i.q.* tasker.
task'-work, *n.*, a definite amount of work required to be done.
Tasma'nian, *adj.*, pert. to Tasmania; *n.*, a native of Tasmania.
tas'sel, *n.*, a hanging ornament made of cord, gold lace, etc.; a male goshawk; anything like a tassel.
tas'selled, tas'seled, *adj.*, ornamented with tassels.
tas'selling, tas'seling, *n.*, ornamentation with tassels.
ta'stable, taste'able, *adj.*, able to be tasted.
taste, sensation by means of the tongue and palate; relish; flavour; savour; experimental trial; fine discrimination and a sense of the good and beautiful; *v.t.*, to experience the sensation of tasting; to make trial of; just to eat or sip a little of.
ta'sted, *p.p.*, taste.
taste'ful, *adj.*, marked by good taste.
taste'fully, *adv.*, in a tasteful way.
taste'less, *adj.*, without taste (in any sense).
taste'lessness, *n.*, the state or quality of being tasteless.
ta'ster, *n.*, one who tastes, esp. an expert in wines, teas, etc.
ta'stily, *adv.*, in a tasty way.
ta'sting, *pr.p.*, taste.
ta'sty, *adj.*, pleasant to the taste; exhibiting good taste.
tat, *n.*, a cloth of jute; *v.t.* and *i.*, to do tatting.
ta'-ta', *n.*, a nursery word for an airing; *interj.* = good-bye (*colloq.*).
tat'ter, *n.*, one who tats; a torn fragment.
tatterdema'lion, *n.*, a fellow in rags.
tat'tered, *adj.*, torn and ragged.
tat'ting, *pr.p.*, tat; *n.*, a sort of hand lace-work; the act of tatting.
tat'tle, *v.i.*, to prattle; talk small scandal; *n.*, prating talk.
tat'tled, *p.p.*, tattle.
tat'tler, *n.*, one who tattles.
tat'tling, *pr.p.*, tattle.
tattoo', *n.*, pictorial and emblematic drawings in colour worked into the skin after puncturing; drum-beat; *v.t.*, to mark the skin with tattoo.
tattooed', *p.p.*, tattoo.

tattoo'ing, *pr.p.*, tattoo; *n.*, the act of tattooing; tattoo marks.
taught, *p.t.* and *p.*, teach.
taunt, *n.*, a bitter, spiteful reproach; *v.t.*, to level reproach at.
taunt'ed, *p.p.*, taunt.
taunt'er, *n.*, one who taunts.
taunt'ing, *pr.p.*, taunt.
taunt'ingly, *adv.*, in a taunting way.
tau'riform, *adj.*, like a ball.
tau'rine, *adj.*, pert. to balls.
tau'rocol, *n.*, glue made from a bull's hide.
Tau'rus, *n.*, the Bull, one of the signs of the Zodiac (*Lat.*).
taut, *adj.*, stretched; tight; secure.
tautolog'ical, *n.*, saying the same thing repeatedly; meaning the same thing.
tautolog'ically, *adv.*, in a tautological way.
tautol'ogist, *n.*, one who tautologizes.
tautol'ogize, *v.i.*, to say the same thing in different words.
tautol'ogized, *p.p.*, tautologize.
tautol'ogizing, *pr.p.*, tautologize.
tautol'ogy, *n.*, saying the same thing though in different words.
tautophon'ical, *adj.*, identical in sound or speech.
tautoph'ony, *n.*, identity of sound or speech.
tav'ern, *n.*, an inn.
tav'ern-keeper, *n.*, an innkeeper.
taw, *v.t.*, to make white leather from skins; *n.*, a marble for playing.
taw'drily, *adv.*, in a tawdry way.
taw'driness, *n.*, the state or quality of being tawdry.
taw'dry, *adj.*, cheap, showy, gaudy. The word is derived from St. Audrey (Etheldreda), on whose festival St. Audrey (called tawdry) beads were sold
tawed, *p.p.*, taw.
taw'er, *n.*, a leather-dresser.
taw'ery, *n.*, a place where tawing is done.
taw'ing, *pr.p.*, taw.
taw'niness, *n.*, the state or quality of being tawny.
taw'ny, *adj.*, brown, with a tinge of yellow.
taws, *n.pl.*, a Scottish instrument for punishing youth. It consists of a leather strap with a fringed end.
tax, *n.*, an impost; *v.t.*, to impose a tax on income, etc.; to oppress; to put a strain on; to accuse.
taxabil'ity, *n.*, the state of being taxable.
tax'able, *adj.*, subject to tax.
taxa'tion, *n.*, the act of taxing; imposed rate; the process of reviewing costs.
taxed, *p.p.*, tax.
tax'er, *n.*, one who taxes.
tax'-gatherer, *n.*, a collector of taxes.
tax'i, *n.*, an abbreviation for taxicab.
tax'icab, *n.*, a motor-cab.
taxider'mic, *adj.*, rel. to taxidermy.
tax'idermist, *n.*, one who stuffs dead beasts, birds, etc.
tax'idermy, *n.*, the art of preserving the natural appearance of dead beasts, etc., by stuffing them.
taxim'eter, *n.*, a register of the fare on a taxicab or other public vehicle.
tax'in, *n.*, a resin obtained from yew trees.
tax'ing, *pr.p.*, tax.
taxon'omy, *n.*, classification—a department of natural history.
tax'payer, *n.*, one who pays tax.
tax'za, *n.*, a wide, open bowl, with or without handles.
tea, *n.*, a plant so named; the dried leaves of the same; a drink made by an infusion of the leaves; any infusion of the kind; *v.i.*, to take or drink tea.
tea'-caddy, *n.*, a small chest to contain the dried leaves of the tea plant.
teach, *v.t.*, to instruct; inform; *v.i.*, to practise as a teacher.
teach'able, *adj.*, able to be taught; apt to learn.
teach'ableness, *n.*, the state of being teachable.
teach'er, *n.*, one who teaches.
tea'-chest, *n.*, a box in which tea is packed.
teach'ing, *pr.p.*, teach; *n.*, the act or profession of teaching.
tea'cup, *n.*, a cup to hold tea.
tea'cupful, *n.*, the quantity of tea that will fill a cup.
tea'-dealer, *n.*, one who deals in tea.
tea'-garden, *n.*, a pleasure garden where tea can be drunk.
teak, *n.*, an Indian tree and its timber.
tea'kettle, *n.*, a kettle to hold boiling water for the making of tea.
teal, *n.*, a fresh-water wild duck.
team, *n.*, horses harnessed for driving a plough, etc.; players in a game.
team'ster, *n.*, the driver of a team.
tea'pot, *n.*, a pot from which tea is poured.
tear, *n.*, a drop of fluid secreted from the lachrymal gland
tear, *n.*, a rent; *v.t.*, to rend; make a tear in; snatch away *v.i.*, to be rent; come apart.
tear'er, *n.*, one who tears.
tear'ful, *adj.*, weeping.

tear'fully, *adv.*, in a tearful way.
tear'fulness, *n.*, the state of being tearful.
tear'ing, *pr.p.*, tear.
tease, *v.t.*, to annoy by frequent provocation or raillery; irritate; to unravel (flax, etc.); *n.*, one given to teasing.
teased, *p.p.*, tease.
teas'el, tea'zle, *n.*, a plant so named, and used in wool manufacture.
teas'er, *n.*, one who teases; a difficult problem.
tea'-service, *n.*, the appliances of a tea-table.
teas'ing, *pr.p.*, tease.
tea'spoonful, *n.*, the quantity that a teaspoon will contain. (In pl., *teaspoonfuls.*)
teat, *n.*, the nipple of a female mammal's breast.
tea'-table, *n.*, a table on which tea is served.
tea'-urn, *n.*, an urn containing tea, or used in making tea.
tea'zle, *n.*, *i.q.* teasle; *v.t.*, to raise the nap of woollen cloth.
tea'zled, *p.p.*, teazle.
tea'zler, *n.*, one who, that which, teazles.
tea'zling, *pr.p.*, teazle.
Tebet', *n.*, a Jewish month.
Tebeth', *n.*, *i.q.* Tebet.
tech'ily, *adv.*, in a techy way.
tech'iness, *n.*, the state of being techy.
tech'nical, *adj.*, pert. to handicrafts, art, science, or any profession.
technical'ity, *n.*, the quality of being technical; something exclusively relating to a particular industry, art, etc.
tech'nically, *adv.*, in a technical sense or manner.
tech'nics, *n. pl.*, studies rel. to the arts.

technique', *n.*, skill in an art (*Fr.*).
technolog'ic, *adj.*, pert. to technology.
technolog'ical, *adj.*, *i.q.* technologic.
technol'ogist, *n.*, a student of technology.
technol'ogy, *n.*, the science or study of the arts in industry.
tech'y, *adj.*, easily vexed; irritable.
tecton'ic, *n.*, pert. to construction.
tecton'ics, *n. pl.*, the science of construction.
ted, *v.t.*, to spread out: to dry.
ted'ded, *p.p.*, ted.
ted'der, *n.*, one who, that which, teds.
ted'ding, *pr.p.*, ted.
Ted'dy-bear, *n.*, a modern toy. (Its name comes from Theodore Roosevelt, a former President of the U.S.)
Te De'um, *n.*, the great prose-hymn of the Church, recited in the daily offices, and sung solemnly on occasions of victory and national rejoicing.
te'dious, *adj.*, wearisome; boring; lengthy.
te'diously, *adv.*, in a tedious way.
te'dium, *n.*, wearisomeness.
tee, *n.*, the starting-place for each hole in a golf-course; the mark aimed at in curling and quoits; a short length of piping; *v.t.*, to set up a golf ball on a raised bit of sand.
teem, *v.i.*, to be very full; to be fertile.
teemed, *pr.p.*, teem.
teem'ing, *pr.p.*, teem.
teens, *n. pl.*, the years numbered from thirteen to nineteen.
teeth, *n.*, pl. of tooth.
teethe, *v.i.*, to cut the teeth; to go through the process of dentition.
teethed, *p.p.*, teeth.
teeth'ing, *pr.p.*, teethe; *n.*, dentition.

teeto'tal, *adj.*, completely abstaining from alcohol.
teeto'tal(l)er, *n.*, a total abstainer from alcohol.
teeto'talism, *n.*, total abstinence from alcohol.
teeto'tum, *n.*, a child's spinning toy.
teg, *n.*, a young sheep; a second-year doe.
teg'men, *n.*, a covering; in botany, the under layer of a seed's coating (*Lat.*).
tegmen'tum, *n.*, a covering; protection (*Lat.*).
teg'ular, *adj.*, like a tile; covering.
teg'ument, *n.*, a covering; envelope; skin.
tegumen'tal, *adj.*, in the nature of a tegument.
tegumen'tary, *adj.*, *i.q.* tegumental.
tehee', *n.*, a comic titter; *v.i.*, to titter in an absurd way.
teil, *n.*, the linden.
tei'noscope, *n.*, a telescope furnished with prisms to connect the chromatic aberration of light.
telamo'nes, *n. pl.*, in architecture, figures of men used as pillars or pilasters.
tela'rian, *adj.*, spinning a web.
telaut'ograph, *n.*, handwriting transmitted by telegraph.
tel'egram, *n.*, a message transmitted by telegraph.
tel'egraph, *n.*, an instrument for transmitting messages; *v.t.*, to transmit a message; *v.i.*, to make use of the telegraph.
tel'egraphed, *p.p.*, telegraph.
telegraph'ic, *adj.*, rel. to telegraphy.
tel'egraphing, *pr.p.*, telegraph.
teleg'raphist, *n.*, a telegraphic operator.
teleg'raphy, *n.*, the system or science of the telegraph.

teleolog'ical, *adj.*, pert. to teleology.

teleol'ogy, *n.*, the philosophy of final causes.

Teleosau'rus, *n.*, a genus of Oolitic fossil reptiles.

telepath'ic, *adj.*, rel. to telepathy.

telep'athist, *n.*, one who has the gift of telepathy.

telep'athy, *n.*, thought transference by an effort of the mind.

tel'ephone, *n.*, an instrument conveying sound by means of electricity.

telephon'ic, *adj.*, rel. to, transmitted by, the telephone.

tel'escope, *n.*, instrument making distant objects visible; *v.t.*, to crush in; *v.i.*, to slide together.

telescop'ic, *adj.*, pert. to the telescope.

teles'copist, *n.*, one who makes skilled use of the telescope.

teles'copy, *n.*, the use of the telescope.

telesmat'ic, *adj.*, magical.

tel'estich, *n.*, an acrostic at the end of the lines.

tel'ewriter, *n.*, an instrument transmitting *facsimile* telegrams.

tel'ic, *adj.*, rel. to the final cause.

tell, *v.t.*, to convey in words; relate; count; *v.i.*, to lay information; to be effective; produce an effect.

tell'er, *n.*, one who tells; a bank official at the counter; one who counts votes in the Parliamentary lobbies.

tell'ing, *pr.p.*, tell; *adj.*, effective.

tell'-tale, *n.*, one who reveals secrets; an automatic means of checking; *adj.*, telling tales.

tellu'ral, *adj.*, *i.q.* telluric.

tel'lurate, *n.*, a telluric acid salt.

tellu'rian, *adj.*, rel. to tellurium.

tellu'ric, *adj.*, pert. to the earth.

tellu'rid, *n.*, tellurium compounded with an organic radical.

tellu'rium, *n.*, a rare metal so named.

tel'lurous, *adj.*, pert. to tellurium.

temera'rious, *adj.*, rash; foolhardy.

temer'ity, *n.*, rashness

tem'per, *n.*, quality of metal; state of mind; natural tendency; passion; *v.t.*, to reduce to sufficient strength, coolness, etc.; to calm.

tem'pera, *n.*, a method of painting on a prepared medium. Also *distemper*.

tem'perament, *n.*, mental qualities.

temperamen'tal, *adj.*, pert. to temperament.

temperamen'tally, *adv.*, according to temperament.

tem'perance, *n.*, self-restraint in all matters.

tem'perate, *adj.*, self-restrained; moderate; not excessive.

tem'perately, *adv.*, in a temperate way.

tem'perative, *adj.*, restraining; gratifying.

tem'perature, *n.*, degree of warmth or cold.

tem'pered, *p.p.*, temper.

tem'pering, *pr.p.*, temper.

tem'pest, *n.*, a violent storm.

tempes'tuous, *adj.*, stormy; violent.

tempes'tuously, *adv.*, in a tempestuous way.

tempes'tuousness, *n.*, the state or quality of being tempestuous.

tem'plar, *n.*, a knight of the Order of Templars; a student in law attached to the Inner or the Middle Temple, London.

tem'ple, *n.*, a place of divine worship, esp. the Temple in Jerusalem; one of the flat sides of the head by the forehead.

tem'plet, *n.*, a shaping pattern; a gauge.

tem'po, *n.*, rate of musical speed (*Ital.*).

tem'poral, *adj.*, bel. to time; secular.

temporal'ity, *n.*, the state or quality of being temporal.

temporal'ities, *n.*, the revenues from ecclesiastical property.

tem'porally, *adv.*, in a temporal way or sense.

tem'porarily, *adv.*, for a time only.

tem'porary, *adj.*, lasting only for a time.

temporiza'tion, *n.*, the act of temporizing.

tem'porize, *v.i.*, to go with the times; to be a trimmer.

tem'porized, *p.p.*, temporize.

tem'porizer, *n.*, one who temporizes.

tem'porizing, *pr.p.*, temporize.

tempt, *v.t.*, to try; persuade to wrong; allure.

temptabil'ity, *n.*, the state of being temptable.

tempt'able, *adj.*, able to be tempted.

tempta'tion, *n.*, the act of tempting; state of being tempted; something alluring or enticing to wrong.

tempt'ed, *p.p.*, tempt.

tempt'er, *n.*, one who tempts, esp. Satan.

tempt'ing, *pr.p.*, tempt; *adj.*, alluring; attractive.

tempt'ress, *n.*, fem. of tempter.

ten, *n.*, the cardinal number next above nine; *adj.*, one more than nine.

tenabil'ity, *n.*, the state or quality of being tenable.

ten'able, *adj.*, able to be held.

ten'ace, *n.*, a peculiar combination in a whist hand.

tena'cious, *adj.*, grasping; clinging; obstinate.

tena'ciously, *adv.*, in a tenacious way.

tenac'ity, *n.*, the quality of being tenacious.

tenac'ulum, *n.*, a surgical hooked instrument.

ten'ancy, *n.*, the status of a tenant; temporary occupancy.

ten'ant, *n.*, a temporary occupant of land or premises; *v.t.*, to hold in tenancy.

ten'antable, *adj.*, fit for occupation.

ten'anted, *p.p.*, tenant

ten'anting, *pr.p.*, tenant.

ten'antless, *adj.*, unoccupied.

ten'antry, *n.*, collective tenants.

tench, *n.*, a fresh-water fish so named.

tend, *v.t.*, to look after; care for.

tend'ed, *p.p.*, tend.

ten'dency, *n.*, disposition; proneness; direction.

ten'der, *adj.*, soft; kind-hearted; sore; *n.*, a detachable part of a locomotive engine, containing the fuel, etc.; an attendant ship; a proposal or offer; *v.t.*, to offer; propose; *v.t.*, to send in an estimate for the performance of work or supply of goods.

ten'dered, *p.p.*, tender.

ten'derer, *adj.*, *comp.* of tender.

ten'der-hearted, *adj.*, compassionate; easily moved to pity.

ten'dering, *pr.p.*, tender.

ten'derly, *adv.*, in a tender way.

ten'derness, *n.*, the state or quality of being tender.

tend'ing, *pr.p.*, tend.

ten'dinous, *adj.*, rel. to a tendon.

ten'don, *n.*, sinew; the connecting link between bone and muscle.

ten'dril, *n.*, a feeler thrown out by a plant.

Ten'ebrae, *n.*, the offices of matins and lauds for Thursday, Friday, and Saturday in Holy Week.

ten'ebrous, *adj.*, dark, gloomy.

ten'ement, *n.*, a building held by a tenant; esp. a room or set of rooms in a house; permanent property.

tenemen'tal, *adj.*, pert. to a tenement.

tenemen'tary, *adj.*, *i.q.* tenemental.

ten'et, *n.*, a belief; an accepted principle.

ten'fold, *adj.*, ten times as much or great.

te'nioid, *adj.*, like a band.

ten'nis, *n.*, an old game known as court tennis; also a modern game known as lawn tennis.

ten'nis-court, *n.*, a court where tennis is played.

ten'nis-lawn, *n.*, a lawn where lawn tennis is played.

ten'on, *n.*, the wedge-shaped end of a timber so shaped for mortising.

ten'or, *n.*, course; drift; purport; male voice between bass and alto; *adj.*, rel. to the tenor voice or pitch.

tenot'omy, *n.*, cutting a tendon.

ten'pence, *n.*, the amount or value of ten pennies.

ten'penny, *adj.*, worth or costing tenpence.

tense, *adj.*, on the stretch; *n.*, one of the verb inflections varying in relation to the time expressed, whether past, present, or future.

tense'ly, *adv.*, in a tense way.

tense'ness, *n.*, the state or quality of being tense.

tensibil'ity, *n.*, the state or quality of being tensible.

ten'sible, *adj.*, able to be stretched.

ten'sile, *adj.*, ductile.

ten'sion, *n.*, the act of stretching; the state of being stretched or tense; suspense; mental excitement.

ten'sity, *n.*, *i.q.* tenseness.

ten'sive, *adj.*, producing tension.

ten'sor, *n.*, a muscle that stretches.

tent, *n.*, a movable habitation or shelter; a surgical roll; a variety of wine.

ten'tacle, *n.*, an organ by means of which certain invertebrates feel, move, etc.

tentac'ular, *adj.*, of the nature of tentacles.

tentac'ulum, *n.*, a tentacle (*Lat.*).

ten'tative, *adj.*, attempting; making experiment.

ten'tatively, *adv.*, in a tentative way.

tent'ed, *adj.*, having tents.

ten'ter, *n.*, a frame holding tenter-hooks; *v.t.*, to hang on tenter-hooks.

ten'ter-hook, *n.*, a hook to hang clothes, etc., on. In pl., a state of strain.

tenth, *adj.*, the ordinal of ten; next after ninth.

tenth'ly, *adv.*, in the tenth place.

tent'ing, *n.*, material for making tents.

tento'rium, *n.*, a tent (*Lat.*): a tent-like formation between the cerebrum and the cerebellum.

tenuifo'lious, *adj.*, having thin leaves.

tenu'ity, *n.*, thinness; rarity.

ten'uous, *adj.*, thin; slender.

ten'uously, *adv.*, in a tenuous way.

ten'uousness, *n.*, the state or quality of being tenuous.
ten'ure, *n.*, holding; occupancy; rights or conditions of occupancy.
tepefac'tion, *n.*, the act of tepefying; state of being tepefied.
tep'efied, *p.p.*, tepefy.
tep'efy, *v.t.*, to warm; make tepid.
tep'efying, *pr.p.*, tepefy.
tep'id, *adj.*, neither hot nor cold; fairly warm.
tepid'ity, *n.*, the state of being tepid.
ter'aph, *n.*, a household god, or image of one.
ter'aphim, *n.*, pl. of teraph.
teratol'ogy, *n.*, the study of abnormal animal or plant structures.
terce, *n.*, a large cask (42 gallons); a card sequence of the same colour; a musical interval of a third; one of the day offices said at the third hour (*i.e.*, 9 a.m.).
ter'cel, *n.*, the male falcon. Also *tiercel.*
tercen'tenary, *adj.*, rel. to a period of 300 years; *n.*, the three hundredth anniversary.
ter'ebinth, *n.*, the turpentine tree.
terebin'thine, *adj.*, bel. to a terebenth; like turpentine.
Tere'do, *n.*, a boring worm; the shipworm.
terete', *adj.*, cylindrical.
tergem'inal, *adj.*, three times double.
tergem'inate, *adj.*, three times double.
tergif'erous, *adj.*, bearing on the back.
ter'giversate, *v.i.*, to shuffle; evade.
tergiversa'tion, *n.*, evasion; shuffling.
ter'gum, *n.*, the upper surface of an insect's abdomen (*Lat.*).
term, *n.*, an end; limit; subject or predicate of a logical proposition; the number of a compound mathematical quantity; an expression; a period; the time when the law courts are open, or residence or attendance at lectures counts at a university; *v.t.*, to name; to phrase.
ter'magancy, *n.*, the conduct of a termagant.
ter'magant, *n.*, a violent, loud-tongued woman; *adj.*, noisily violent.
termed, *p.p.*, term.
Ter'mes, *n.*, a variety of insects, as white ants, etc.
ter'minable, *adj.*, able to be terminated.
ter'minal, *adj.*, rel. to a term or to an end; disposed according to termination; *n.*, a boundary; an end of a circuit on a dynamo.
ter'minate, *adj.*, limited; bounded.
ter'minate, *v.t.*, to put a finish to; to end; *v.i.*, to be limited; to end.
ter'minated, *p.p.*, terminate.
ter'minating, *pr.p.*, terminate.
termina'tion, *n.*, the act of terminating; an end.
termina'tional, *adj.*, pert. to a termination.
ter'minative, *adj.*, placing a limit; fixing an end.
ter'minator, *n.*, one who, that which, terminates; the line marking the division between the bright and the dark parts of the moon.
ter'minatory, *adj.*, *i.q.* terminative.
ter'miner, *n.*, the act of determining.
term'ing, *pr.p.*, term.
ter'minism, *n.*, the teaching that the period of Divine grace is limited.
ter'minist, *n.*, a believer in terminism.
terminolog'ical, *adj.*, rel. to terms.
terminolog'ically, *adv.* according to terminology.
terminol'ogy, *n.*, the definition or use of special terms.
ter'minus, *n.*, an end; a boundary; a railway station where a line begins or ends.
ter'mite, *n.*, white ant.
ter'mites, *n.*, pl. of termes.
term'less, *adj.*, without a term.
tern, *n.*, a kind of gull; *adj.*, containing three; threefold.
ter'nary, *adj.*, going in threes; *n.*, the number three.
ter'nate, *adj.*, grouped in threes.
Terpsichore'an, *n.*, pert. to Terpsichore the Muse of dancing.
ter'ra, *n.*, the earth (*Lat.*).
ter'race, *n.*, ground levelled on a hill or sloping ground; a row of houses; the flat top of an Eastern house; *v.t.*, to make a terrace of.
ter'raced, *p.p.*, terrace.
ter'racing, *pr.p.*, terrace.
ter'ra-cot'ta, *n.*, burnt clay and sand, used for making statues, medallions, architectural ornaments, etc.
ter'ra fir'ma, *n.*, the land as distinct from water.
ter'ra incog'nita, *n.*, an unknown, strange land.
ter'rapin, *n.*, an edible fresh-water tortoise.
terra'queous, *adj.*, consisting of land and water.
ter'ras, *n.*, a flaw in marble, which being removed, the cavity is filled in with a substitute. Also *trass.*

terrene, *adj.*, pert. to the earth.

ter'reous, *adj.*, earthy.

terre'plein, *n.*, the terrace behind a rampart.

terres'trial, *adj.*, bel. to the earth or the world, as distinct from celestial.

ter'rible, *adj.*, fearful; frightful; dreadful.

ter'ribly, *adv.*, in a terrible degree.

ter'rier, *n.*, a canine breed; a scheduled statement of landed property.

terrif'ic, *adj.*, terrifying.

ter'rified, *p.p.*, terrify

ter'rify, *v.t.*, to fill with terror; to frighten.

ter'rifying, *pr.p.*, terrify.

terrig'enous, *adj.*, earth-born.

territo'rial, *adj.*, rel. to territory or a specified district.

territo'rialism, *n.*, the principle of territorial division.

territo'rially, *adv.*, in a territorial way.

Territo'rials, *n. pl.*, a military force created in 1908.

ter'ritory, *n.*, the area contained within the jurisdiction of a king, bishop, etc.; a large extent of land; a region. In the U.S., land not yet raised to the rank of a state.

ter'ror, *n.*, fear, alarm; a frightful person.

ter'rorism, *n.*, ruling by fear; intimidation.

ter'rorist, *n.*, one who advocates terrorism.

ter'rorize, *v.t.* and *i.*, to rule by fear; to intimidate.

Ter Sanc'tus, *n.*, the liturgical hymn, "Holy, Holy, Holy," etc., more commonly called the Sanctus.

terse, *adj.*, neat; concise.

terse'ly, *adv.*, neatly, concisely.

terse'ness, *n.*, neatness; elegance; conciseness.

ter'tial, *adj.*, bel. to the third row.

ter'tian, *adj.*, recurring on each third day; *n.*, a fever or ague recurring each third day.

ter'tiary, *adj.*, of the third order etc.; rel. to geological strata that overlie the chalk; *n.*, a member of the third order of St. Francis or St. Dominic.

ter'za-ri'ma, *n.*, an Italian poetic form in which the middle line of the first triplet rimes with a first and third of the next triplet.

terzet'to, *n.*, a short three-voice composition (*mus.*).

tes'sellate, *v.t.*, to cover with tile-work.

tes'sellated, *p.p.*, tessellate.

tes'sellating, *pr.p.*, tessellate.

tessella'tion, *n.*, the act of tessellating; the state of being tessellated.

tes'sera, *n.*, one of the cubes in a piece of mosaic.

tes'seral, *adj.*, rel. to tesserae.

tes'sular, *adj.*, of equal measure.

test, *n.*, a trial; proof; experiment; *v.t.*, to put to the proof; make trial of; experiment with; refine.

tes'ta, *n.*, a tile; the integument of a seed; the shell of testaceae (*Lat.*).

test'able, *adj.*, able to be tested.

testa'cea, *n.*, a mollusc. (In pl., testaceae.)

testa'cean, *adj.*, pert. to testaceae.

testacel'la, *n.*, a slug-like gastropod.

testaceol'ogy, *n.*, the study of testacean creatures.

testa'ceous, *adj.*, covered with a shell.

tes'tacy, *n.*, the position of leaving a proper will.

tes'tament, *n.*, a will; one of the two sections of the Bible, the Old and the New Testament.

testamen'tary, *adj.*, pert. to a will; bequeathed.

tes'tate, *adj.*, leaving a valid will; *n.*, one whose will is valid.

testa'tor, *n.*, one who bequeathes property by will.

testa'trix, *n.*, fem. of testator.

test'ed, *p.p.*, test.

test'er, *n.*, one who tests; the old name for sixpence; a canopy.

tes'ticle, *n.*, a gland that secretes spermatozoa.

testifica'tion, *n.*, the act of testifying; witness.

tes'tified, *p.p.*, testify.

tes'tifier, *n.*, one who testifies.

tes'tify, *v.i.*, to bear witness; give evidence; *v.t.*, to state in evidence.

tes'tifying, *pr.p.*, testify.

tes'tily, *adv.*, in a testy way.

testimo'nial, *n.*, an expression of approval; witness to character; a gift to mark high esteem; *adj.*, rel. to testimony.

tes'timony, *n.*, witness's evidence.

tes'tiness, *n.*, the state or quality of being testy.

test'ing, *pr.p.*, test; *n.*, assay; trial.

test'-paper, *n.*, a sensitive paper used in chemical experiments.

testu'dinal, *adj.*, like a tortoise.

testu'dinate, *adj.*, arched tortoise-like.

testu'do, *n.*, an ancient Roman device of locking shields together, under cover of which soldiers advanced to a siege; a tortoise (*Lat.*).

tes'ty, *adj.*, quick-tempered and peevish; irritable.

tetan'ic, *adj.*, rel. to tetanus.

tet'anus, *n.*, lockjaw.

tetch'ily, *adv.*, in a tetchy way.

tech'iness, *n.*, the state of being tetchy

tetch'y, *adj.*, *i.q.* techy.

tête, *n.*, a head (*Fr.*).

tête'-à-tête', *n.*, a private conversation; *adv.*, in private conversation.

teth'er, *n.*, a rope for fastening animals up; liberty of action up to a point; *v.t.*, to confine.

teth'ered, *p.p.*, tether.

teth'ering, *pr.p.*, tether.

tet'ra, a *Gr.* prefix = four.

tetrabran'chiate, *adj.*, with four gills or branchiae.

tet'rachord, *n.*, the four notes of the half-scale.

tet'rad, *n.*, the number four; a group of four.

tet'radrachm, *n.*, a coin of four drachmae value.

tet'ragon, *n.*, a four-sided figure having four angles.

tetrag'onal, *adj.*, rel. to a tetragon.

tetrahe'dral, *adj.*, with four sides.

tetrahe'dron, *n.*, a solid figure with four triangular surfaces.

tetram'eter, *n.*, a metrical verse of four feet.

tet'rapla, *n.*, the Holy Scriptures set out in four parallel columns each containing a different version.

tet'rapod, *n.*, a quadrupedal insect.

tet'rarch, *n.*, a Roman governor of the fourth part of a province.

tet'rarchate, *n.*, the rule or term of office, of a tetrarch.

tet'rarchy, *n.*, province of a tetrarch.

tet'rastich, *n.*, a stanza of four lines.

tet'rastyle, *n.*, a structure fronted by four pillars.

tetrasyl'lable, *n.*, a four-syllabled word.

tet'ter, *n.*, a skin disease; herpes.

Teu'ton, *adj.*, *i.q.* Teutonic; *n.*, a German.

Teuton'ic, *adj.*, German.

Teu'tonism, *n.*, German idiom.

tew'el, tu'el, *n.*, a tuyère.

te'whit, *n.*, the lapwing.

Tex'an, *adj.*, bel. to Texas; *n.*, a native of Texas.

text, *n.*, a subject of discourse; a writing.

text'book, *n.*, an authoritative book of instruction.

text'-*hand*, *n.*, a large style of handwriting.

tex'tile, *adj.*, woven; *n.*, a woven fabric.

texto'rial, *adj.*, rel. to weaving.

tex'tual, *adj.*, rel. to text.

tex'tualist, *n.*, a student of text.

textual'ity, *n.*, the quality of being textual.

tex'tually, *n.*, according to text.

tex'tuary, *adj.*, *i.q.* textual.

tex'ture, *n.*, weaving; a thing woven; a manner of weaving.

thal'amus, *n.*, the reputed starting-point of a nerve; the receptacle of a flower (*Lat.*).

tha'ler, *n.*, a German dollar.

Thali'a, *n.*, the Muse of Comedy.

Thali'an, *adj.*, rel. to Thalia; comic.

thal'lium, *n.*, a metallic element so named.

Tham'muz, Tam'muz, *n.*, an ancient deity.

than, *conj.*, used in comparisons, as *more than, greater than.*

thane, *n.*, an Anglo-Saxon landowner.

thank, *v.t.*, to profess gratitude to.

thanked, *p.p.*, thank.

thank'ful, *adj.*, grateful.

thank'fully, *adv.*, gratefully.

***thank'*fulness,** *n.*, gratitude.

***thank'*ing,** *pr.p.*, thank.

***thank'*less,** *adj.*, ungrateful; earning no return of thanks.

***thank'*lessness,** *n.*, the state or quality of being thankless.

***thank'*offering,** *n.*, a sacrifice in gratitude

thanks, *n. pl.*, the expression of gratitude.

***thanks'*giving,** *n.*, the act of giving thanks; a public festival of thanks.

***thank'*worthy,** *adj.*, deserving of gratitude.

that, *demonstrative pron.* and *adj.*, yonder one; not this; *conj.*, because; since. The word is also used as a *relative pron.* = who or which.

thatch, *n.*, a straw covering for houses, sheds, etc.; *v.t.*, to protect with thatch.

thatched, *p.p.*, thatch

thatch'er, *n.*, a man who thatches houses, stacks, etc.

thatch'ing, *pr.p.*, thatch.

thau'matrope, *n.*, an optical device causing an impression of a visible object to remain after its actual withdrawal.

thaumatur'gic, *adj.*, wonder-working; rel. to miracles.

thaumatur'gist, *n.*, a wonder-worker.

thau'maturgy, *n.*, wonder-working; performing of miracles; sleight of hand.

thaw, *v.i.*, to melt; to become milder; *v.t.*, to melt; *n.*, a state in which ice melts when the temperature rises above freezing-point.

thawed, *p.p.*, thaw.

thaw′ing, *pr.p.*, thaw.

thaw′y, *adj.*, inclined to thaw.

the, *adj.*, the definite article.

The′a, *n.*, the tea plant.

thean′thropism, *n.*, a belief that deity and humanity can be combined in one person.

the′archy, *n.*, government by God.

The′atine, *n.*, a member of the Theatine Order, which was founded in order to promote the Counter-reformation.

the′atre, the′ater, *n.*, a place for spectacular or dramatic exhibitions; a scene of action; a room arranged theatre-wise for lectures, demonstrations, operations, etc.

theat′ric, *adj.*, pert. to a theatre.

theat′rical, *adj.*, *i.q.* theatric; histrionic; affected like an actor.

theat′rically, *adv.*, in a theatrical way.

theat′ricals, *n. pl.*, dramatic performances (usually amateur).

The′ban, *adj.*, rel. to Thebes; *n.*, a native of Thebes.

the′ca, *n.*, a sheath; a fern's seed-case (*Gr.*)

the′codont, *adj.*, with sheathed teeth.

thee, *pers. pron.*, accusative or objective case of thou.

theft, *n.*, the act of stealing.

the′ine, *n.*, the essential principle of tea.

their, *poss. adj.*, bel. to them.

theirs, *pers. pron.*, genitive or possessive case of they.

the′ism, *n.*, belief in a personal God.

the′ist, *n.*, a believer in a personal God.

theist′ic, *adj.*, rel. to theism.

theist′ical, *adj.*, *i.q.* theistic.

them, *pers. pron.*, objective or accusative case of they.

theme, *n.*, a subject for discourse or argument; a short essay; a musical subject.

Them′is, *n.*, the Greek goddess of justice.

themselves′, *reflexive pron.*, pl. of himself, etc.

then, *adv.*, at that time; immediately; in addition or next after; *conj.*, therefore; so; in consequence.

thence, *adv.*, from that place or time.

thenceforth′, *adv.*, from that time forward.

thencefor′ward, *adv.*, from that time or place forward.

theobro′ma, *n.*, a genus of trees from which cacao is derived.

theobro′mine, *n.*, an alkaloid obtained from the chocolate nut.

theoc′racy, *n.*, government by God; a kingdom ruled directly by God.

theocrat′ic, *adj.*, rel. to theocracy.

theocrat′ical, *adj.*, *i.q.* theocratic.

theod′icy, *n.*, the justification of God's Providence.

theod′olite, *n.*, a surveying instrument.

theodolit′ic, *adj.*, rel. to the use of the theodolite.

theog′ony, *n.*, the study of the origin of heathen deities; a poem on the subject.

theolo′gian, *n.*, a student or professor of theology.

theolog′ical, *adj.*, pert. to theology.

theolog′ically, *adv.*, according to theology.

theol′ogist, *n.*, *i.q.* theologian.

the′ologue, *n.*, *i.q.* theologian.

theol′ogy, *n.*, the study of divinity.

theom′achy, *n.*, a strife among deities.

theop′athy, *n.*, the sufferings of a deity.

theoph′any, *n.*, a visible appearance of a deity.

theophilosoph′ic, *adj.*, philosophizing about religion.

theopneus′tic, *adj.*, divinely inspired.

theopneu′sty, *n.*, divine inspiration.

theor′bo, *n.*, a double lute.

the′orem, *n.*, a proposition for proof.

theoret′ic, *adj.*, pert. to theory; speculative.

theoret′ical, *adj.*, *i.q.* theoretic.

theoret′ically, *adv.*, in a theoretical way.

the′orist, *n.*, one who theorizes.

the′orize, *v.i.*, to indulge in theories; to speculate.

the′orized, *p.p.*, theorize.

the′orizer, *n.*, *i.q.* theorist.

the′orizing, *pr.p.*, theorize.

the′ory, *n.*, speculation, hypothesis; abstract principles.

theosoph′ic, *adj.*, pert. to theosophy.

theosoph′ical, *adj.*, *i.q.* theosophic.

theos′ophist, *n.*, one who practises theosophy.

theos′ophy, *n.*, an esoteric system of philosophy which affects a privileged knowledge of the occult powers of nature.

therapeu′tic, *adj.*, curative.

therapeu′tical, *adj.*, *i.q.* therapeutic.

therapeu′tics, *n. pl.*, that part of medical science which relates to the curative treatment of disease.

there, *adv.*, yonder; not here; at that point.

there'about, *adv.*, somewhere in that direction.
thereaf'ter, *adv.*, after that time; subsequently.
thereat', *adv.*, at that
thereby', *adv.*, by that; consequently.
there'fore, *adv.* and *conj.*, because of that; for that reason
therefrom', *adv.*, from that time, place, or cause.
therein', *adv.*, in that.
thereof', *adv.*, of that.
thereon', *adv.*, upon that; subsequently.
thereout', *adv.*, from out of that.
thereto', *adv*, to that; in addition.
thereupon', *adv.*, consequently.
therewith', *adv.*, with that.
therewithal', *adv.*, *i.q.* therewith; *n.*, means.
the'riac, *adj.*, pert. to the lower animals.
theri'acal, *adj.*, *i.q.* theriac.
theriot'omy, *n.*, the anatomy of lower animals.
ther'mae, *n. pl.*, hot springs; baths (*Gr.*).
ther'mal, *adj.*, rel. to temperatures; warm
ther'mic, *adj.*, rel. to thermae.
Thermidor', *n.*, the eleventh month in the Kalendar of the French Revolutionists.
thermo-dynam'ics, *n. pl.*, the science of the dynamics of heat.
thermo-electric'ity, *n.*, electricity in relation to heat.
thermol'ogy, *n.*, the study of heat phenomena.
thermom'eter, *n.*, an apparatus showing degrees of temperature.
thermomet'ric, *adj.*, pert. to a thermometer.
thermomet'rical, *adj.*, *i.q.* thermometric.
ther'moscope, *n.*, an apparatus recording relative differences of temperature.
ther'mostat, *n.*, an instrument which automatically regulates temperature.
thermot'ic, *adj.*, pert. to heat.
thermot'ics, *n. pl.*, the study of heat phenomena.
ther'motypy, *n.*, the developing of pictures by the application of heat.
thesau'rus, *n.*, a treasury; dictionary; lexicon (*Gr.* and *Lat.*).
these, *demonstrative pron.*, pl. of this.
the'sis, *n.*, a subject for an essay, or for treatment as an academic exercise; the exercise or essay itself.
Thes'pian, *adj.*, pert. to Thespis, the reputed originator of the drama; dramatic.
Thessalo'nian, *adj.*, pert. to Thessalonica; *n.*, a native of T.
thet'ic, *adj.*, rel. to a thesis.
thet'ical, *adj.*, *i.q.* thetic.
theur'gic, *adj.*, rel. to theurgy.
theur'gist, *n.*, one who professes theurgy.
the'urgy, *n.*, magic.
thews, *n. pl.*, muscles; physical strength.
they, *pers. pron.*, pl. of he, she, it.
Thibe'tan, *adj.*, pert. to Thibet; *n.*, a native of T. Also *Tibetan.*
thick, *adj.*, not thin; dense; closely compacted; cloudy; not transparent; quickly following; *adv.*, indistinctly; in rapid succession; *n.*, the thick part.
thick'en, *v.t.*, to make thick; *v.i.*, to become thicker.
thick'ened, *p.p.*, thicken.
thick'ening, *pr.p.*, thicken.
thick'er, *adj.*, *comp.* of thick.
thick'est, *adj.*, *super.* of thick.
thick'et, *n.*, a copse; close group of trees.
thick'head, *n.*, a dolt; stupid fellow.
thick'headed, *adj.*, stupid; mentally dense.
thick'ish, *adj.*, somewhat thick.
thick'ly, *adv.*, in a thick way.
thick'ness, *n.*, the state or quality of being thick.
thick'-set, *adj.*, stoutly built; closely planted; *n.*, a closely planted hedge.
thief, *n.*, one who steals.
thieve, *v.t.* and *i.*, to steal.
thieved, *p.p.*, thieve.
thiev'ery, *n.*, stealing.
thieves, *n.*, pl. of thief.
thiev'ing, *pr.p.*, thieve; *n.*, the art or practice of a thief.
thiev'ish, *adj.*, inclined to stealing; stolen.
thigh, *n.*, the upper leg between the knee and the body.
thigh'bone, *n.*, the bone of the thigh.
thill, *n.*, a cart or carriage shaft; a mine floor.
thill'er, *n.*, a shaft horse.
thills, *n. pl.*, shafts.
thim'ble, *n.*, a finger-guard used in sewing; a ring on a sail.
thim'bleful, *n.*, a mere drop; very minute draught.
thim'blerig, *n.*, a juggling trick with a pea and three thimbles; *v.t.*, to play the trick on.
thim'blerigged, *p.p.*, thimblerig.
thim'blerigger, *n.*, one who thimblerigs.
thim'blerigging, *pr.p.*, thimblerig.
thin, *adj.*, not thick; spare; narrow; fine; clear but not strong; meagre; *v.t.*, to make thin; *v.i.*, to become thin.

thine, *possess. adj.*, bel. to thee.

thing, *n.*, that which exists as imaginable or manifest to the senses; an inanimate object; a contemptible object; a Scandinavian legislative assembly.

think, *v.t.*, to conceive in the mind; hold in opinion; decide; purpose; *v.i.*, to imagine; ponder; be of opinion.

***think*'able,** *adj.*, able to be thought.

think'er, *n.*, one who thinks; a philosopher.

***think*'ing,** *pr.p.*, think; *adj.*, contemplative; philosophic; *n.*, contemplation; foresight.

thin'ly, *adv.*, in a thin way.

thinned, *p.p.*, thin.

thin'ner, *adj., comp.* of thin.

thin'ness, *n.*, the state or quality of being thin.

thin'nest, *adj., super.* of thin.

thin'ning, *pr.p.*, thin.

thin'nish, *adj.*, somewhat thin.

thin'-skinned, *adj.*, having a thin skin; morbidly sensitive and touchy.

third, *adj.*, the ordinal of three; the next after the second; rel. to one of three equal parts; *n.*, a third part; a musical interval of three diatonic sounds.

***third*'ing,** *n.*, a third part or division. (Politically, it = a Riding.)

***third*'ly,** *adv.*, in the third place.

thirds, *n.*, pl. of third.

thirl'age, *n.*, a mill-owner's power to make his tenants bring their corn to his mill.

thirst, *n.*, a desire for drink; any strong desire; *v.i.*, to have a desire for drink; to be thirsty.

thirst'ed, *p.p.*, thirst.

thirst'er, *n.*, one who thirsts.

thirst'ier, *adj., comp.* of thirsty.

thirst'iest, *adj., super.* of thirsty.

thirst'ily, *adv.*, in a thirsty way.

thirst'iness, *n.*, the state of being thirsty.

thirst'ing, *pr.p.*, thirst.

thirst'y, *adj.*, feeling thirst; eagerly desiring.

thirteen', *adj.*, ten plus three; *n.*, the cardinal number next after twelve.

thirteenth', *adj.*, the ordinal of thirteen; next after twelfth.

thir'tieth, *adj.*, the ordinal of thirty; next after twenty-ninth.

thir'ty, *adj.*, three times ten; *n.*, the cardinal number = 10 × 3.

this, *pron.* and *adj.*, that which is here or now, or last referred to.

this'tle, *n.*, a plant of the Carduus genus.

this'tly, *adj.*, full of, resembling, thistles.

thith'er, *adv.*, in that direction.

thith'erward, *adv.*, towards that end or direction.

thole, *n.*, a pin on which a boat's oar turns; *v.t.*, to put up with (*Scot.*).

thole'-pin, *n.*, *i.q.* thole.

Thomae'an, *adj.*, pert. to Thomism.

Tho'mism, *n.*, the teachings of the scholastic doctor, St. Thomas Aquinas (13th cent.).

Tho'mist, *n.*, a disciple of St. Thomas Aquinas.

Tho'mite, *n.*, *i.q.* Thomist.

thong, *n.*, a thin leather strip for various purposes; a lash.

Thor, *n.*, the Scandinavian god of thunder, etc., whose name is perpetuated in Thursday.

thorac'ic, *adj.*, pert. to the thorax.

tho'rax, *n.*, the chest; a breastplate (*Gr.*).

tho'rium, *n.*, a metallic element so named.

thorn, *n.*, a prickly growth on certain trees and shrubs; a prickly shrub or tree; anything that annoys.

thorn'-apple, *n.*, stramonium.

thorn'-bush, *n.*, a thorn-bearing bush.

thorn'-hedge, *n.*, a hedge composed of thorns.

thorn'y, *adj.*, covered with, resembling, thorns; full of difficulty and trouble.

thor'ough, *adj.*, complete; entire; insisting on perfection.

thor'oughbass, *n.*, the science of harmony; a kind of musical shorthand, in which chords are represented by figures.

thor'oughbred, *adj.*, bred from the best stock; high-spirited; *n.*, an animal of the best breeding.

thor'oughfare, *n.*, a road open to traffic.

thor'oughgoing, *adj.*, uncompromising; complete.

thor'oughly, *adv.*, completely; entirely.

thor'oughness, *n.*, the state or quality of being thorough.

thor'ough-paced, *adj.*, complete.

thor'oughwort, *n.*, a plant so named.

thorp, *n.*, a hamlet. Also *thorpe.*

those, *pron.* and *adj.*, pl. of this.

Thoth, *n.*, the Egyptian god of wisdom.

thou, *pers. pron.*, 2nd person, you.

though, *conj.* (implying concession), granted that; notwithstanding the fact that; *i.q.* although; *adv.*, however.

thought, *p.t.* and *p.*, think; *n.*, the act of thinking; that which one thinks; reflection; circumspection; regard for others.
thought'ful, *adj.*, reflecting; considerate; anxious.
thought'fully, *adv.*, in a thoughtful way.
thought'fulness, *n.*, the state of being thoughtful.
thought'less, *adj.*, inconsiderate; reckless; unthinking.
thought'lessly, *adv.*, in a thoughtless way.
thought'lessness, *n.*, the state of being thoughtless.
thou'sand, *adj.*, ten hundred; *n.*, the cardinal number = 100 × 10.
thou'sandfold, *adj.*, a thousand times as many.
thous'andth, *adj.*, the ordinal of 1,000; next after 999th.
Thra'cian, *adj.*, rel. to Thrace; *n.*, a native of Thrace.
thral'dom, *n.*, servitude.
thrall, *n.*, a serf.
thrap'ple, *n.*, the windpipe (*Scot.*).
thrash, *v.t.*, to beat corn in order to extract the grain; to flog; *v.i.*, to do thrashing.
thrashed, *p.p.*, thrash.
thrash'er, *n.*, one who, that which, thrashes.
thrash'ing, *pr.p.*, thrash; *n.*, a flogging; the process of beating corn.
thrason'ical, *adj.*, resembling Thraso, a braggart soldier in Terence's *Eunuchus;* bragging.
thrave, *n.*, a drove.
thread, *n.*, very fine line of silk, cotton, etc., filament; unbroken continuity in a story, an argument, etc.; the spiral of a screw; *v.t.*, to pass thread through; to penetrate; to string together.
thread'bare, *adj.*, worn out; shabby; hackneyed.
thread'ed, *p.p.*, thread
thread'en, *adj.*, made of thread.
thread'ing, *pr.p.*, thread.
thread'shaped, *adj.*, like a thread.
thread'y, *adj.*, like thread.
threap, *v.i.*, to cry out; complain.
threat, *n.*, a menace; *v.t.*, to menace.
threat'en, *v.t.*, to try to frighten by menacing; to give sinister indications (as of storm, rain, etc.).
threat'ened, *p.p.*, threaten.
threat'ener, *n.*, one who threatens.
threat'ening, *pr.p.*, threaten; *adj.*, indicating the approach of danger, storm, etc.
three, *adj.*, containing one more than two; *n.*, the cardinal number 3.
three'-cornered, *adj.*, having three corners; in which three parties are engaged.
three'-decker, *n.*, an old man-of-war; an absurd old structure in a church, having desks in three tiers, for the clerk, the reader, and the preacher respectively.
three'fold, *adj.*, three times multiplied.
three'-legged, *adj.*, having three legs.
three'pence, *n.*, the amount of three pennies; the smallest English silver coin now in use.
three'penny, *adj.*, costing threepence; *n.*, the coin of that value (*colloq.*).
three'score, *adj.*, sixty; 20 × 3.
three'some, *n.*, a game of golf in which one player takes on two opponents.
threne, *n.*, a lament.
thren'ody, *n.*, a song of lamentation; a dirge.
thresh, *v.t.*, *i.q.* thrash, in sense of beating out grain.
thresh'er, *n.*, one who threshes; a machine for threshing.
thresh'old, *n.*, a door sill; entrance to a house.
threw, *p.t.*, throw.
thrice, *adv.*, three times.
thrid, *v.t.*, to thread one's way through.
thrift, *n.*, economy; frugality; improvement of property.
thrift'ily, *adv.*, in a thrifty way.
thrift'iness, *n.*, the quality of being thrifty.
thrift'less, *adj.*, not thrifty; wasteful.
thrift'lessness, *n.*, the quality of being thriftless.
thrift'y, *adj.*, economical; saving; industrious.
thrill, *n.*, the feeling of being pierced; something exciting; *v.t.*, to pierce; to fill with excitement; *v.i.*, to feel excited; to quiver.
thrilled, *p.p.*, thrill.
thrill'ing, *pr.p.*, thrill, *adj.*, exciting.
thrive, *v.i.*, to prosper; grow; grow strong; grow rich.
thrived, *p.t.* and *p.*, thrive.
thriv'en, *p.p.*, thrive.
thri'ving, *pr.p.*, thrive; *adj.*, prosperous.
throat, *n.*, the front part of an animal's neck through which food is taken and breath drawn.
throat'iness, *n.*, the quality of being throaty.
throat'wort, *n.*, a plant so named.
throat'y, *adj.*, produced by the throat; guttural.
throb, *v.i.*, to beat; pulsate; *n.*, a pulsation.
throbbed, *p.p.*, throb.
throb'bing, *pr.p.*, throb.

throe, *n.*, great pain; agony; *v.i.*, to be in extreme pain.

thrombo'sis, *n.*, a clotted condition of blood-vessels (*Gr.*).

throm'bus, *n.*, a clot of blood.

throne, *n.*, a seat of authority, as a king's, a bishop's, etc.; *v.t.*, to enthrone.

throned, *p.p.*, throne.

throng, *n.*, a crowd; a press; *v.t.*, to fill with a multitude; to press; *v.i.*, to come in crowds.

thronged, *p.p.*, throng.

throng'ing, *pr.p.*, throng.

thro'ning, *pr.p.*, throne.

thros'tle, *n.*, a song-thrush; a machine used in a cotton mill.

thros'tling, *n.*, a throat disease in cattle.

throt'tle, *v.t.*, to seize by the throat and strangle; *n.*, the windpipe; a valve regulating the flow of gas to the engine of a motor.

throt'tled, *p.p.*, throttle.

throt'tle-valve, *n.*, *i.q.* throttle (last meaning).

throt'tling, *pr.p.*, throttle.

through, *prep.*, from one end of a thing to the other; by means of; *adv.*, from end to end.

throughout', *adv.*, all the time; from beginning to end; *prep.*, during the whole of.

throve, *p.t.*, thrive.

throw, *v.t.*, to fling; cast; hurl; bring down; cast off; overturn; spin; *n.*, the act of throwing; a cast of the dice; length that a thing is thrown.

throw'er, *n.*, one who throws; that which throws.

throw'ing, *p.p.*, throw

thrown, *p.p.*, throw.

throw'ster, *n.*, a gamester; a silk-thrower.

thrum, *n.*, coarse yarn; fringe; the sound of strumming; *v.t.*, to tuft; to beat out a tune.

thrummed, *p.p.*, thrum.

thrum'ming, *pr.p.*, thrum.

thrush, *n.*, a song-bird so named; an infantine complaint affecting the mouth and throat.

thrust, *v.t.*, to push; project; drive; *v.i.*, to make a push; to aim a blow with a rapier, bayonet, etc., *n.*, a push; a stab.

thrust'er, *n.*, one who thrusts.

thrust'ing, *pr.p.*, thrust.

thrust'ings, *n. pl.*, white whey pressed out of curd.

thud, *n.*, the heavy sound of a falling body.

thud'ded, *p.p.*, thud.

thud'ding, *pr.p.*, thud.

Thug, *n.*, one of a secret band of Indian assassins.

Thug'gee, *n.*, the Thug's method of murder.

Thug'gery, *n.*, *i.q.* Thuggee.

Thug'gism, *n.*, *i.q.* Thuggee.

Thu'le, *n.*, the ancient classical name for the remotest north (*Ultima Thule*).

thumb, *n.*, the short, thick digit of the human hand; *v.t.*, to soil by rubbing with the thumb; *v.i.*, to handle things awkwardly.

thumbed, *p.p.*, thumb.

thumb'ing, *pr.p.*, thumb.

thumb'screw, *n.*, an instrument of torture by violent pressure of the thumb.

thumb'-stall, *n.*, a cover for a bandaged thumb.

thum'mim, *n. pl.*, the mysterious ornament of the Jewish high-priest's breastplate.

thump, *v.t.*, to deal hard blows upon; *v.i.*, to beat heavily; *n.*, a heavy blow.

thumped, *p.p.*, thump.

thump'er, *n.*, one who, that which, thumps; a lie; a very big thing (*colloq.*).

thump'ing, *pr.p.*, thump; *adj.*, very big (*colloq.*).

thun'der, *n.*, the noisy discharge of electricity from clouds; any very loud noise; *v.i.*, to make a thundering noise; *v.t.*, to utter in loud denunciation.

thun'derbolt, *n.*, a lightning discharge; something startling for its suddenness or violence; a belemnite.

thun'derclap, *n.*, a clap of thunder.

thun'dered, *p.p.*, thunder.

thun'derer, *n.*, one who thunders.

thun'dering, *pr.p.*, thunder; *adj.*, emitting the sound of thunder; very big (*colloq.*).

thun'der-shower, *n.*, a shower accompanied by thunder.

thun'der-storm, *n.*, a storm accompanied by thunder.

thun'derstruck, *adj.*, overcome with sudden astonishment.

thun'dery, *adj.*, inclined to thunder; accompanied by thunder.

thu'rible, *n.*, a censer.

thu'rifer, *n.*, one who carries and swings the censer in church ceremonies.

thurif'erous, *adj.*, producing incense.

thurifica'tion, *n.*, the production of incense.

thurl, *v.t.*, to bore; *n.*, a perforation.

Thurs'day, *n.*, the fifth day of the week.

thus, *adv.*, in this way; so.

thwack, *v.t.*, to beat with a flat, heavy thing; *n.*, a blow so delivered.

thwacked, *p. p.*, thwack.

thwack'ing, *pr.p.*, thwack.

thwaite, *n.*, land reclaimed for tilling.

thwart, *v.t.*, to cross; to frustrate; *adj.* and *adv.*, crosswise; *n.*, a rower's seat across a boat.

thwart'ed, *p.p.*, thwart

thwart'ing, *pr.p.*, thwart.

thy, *poss. adj.*, bel. to thee.

thy'ine, *adj.*, producing Sandarac.

thyme, *n.*, an aromatic herb so named.

thy'mus, *n.*, a generic name of certain shrubs; a gland of the neck and thorax.

thym'y, *adj.*, abounding in, smelling of, thyme.

thy'roid, *adj.*, like a shield; *n.*, a laryngeal cartilage.

thyrse, *n.*, *i.q.* thyrsus.

thyr'soid, *adj.*, thyrsus-shaped.

thyr'sus, *n.*, the emblem of Bacchus—a wand adorned with ivy, vine leaves, and grape-clusters.

thyself', *pron.*, an emphatic form of thou or thee.

tia'ra, *n.*, a head-ornament; diadem; esp. the Pope's triple tiara.

Tibe'tan, *adj.* and *n.*, *i.q.* Thibetan.

tib'ia, *n.*, the shin bone (*Lat.*).

tib'ial, *adj.*, pert. to the tibia.

tic, *n.*, neuralgia.

tic'-douloureux', *n.*, *i.q.* tic.

tick, *n.*, a parasitic insect; a cover for bedding; a little mark; the beat of a clock or watch; credit (*colloq.*); *v.i.*, to make a short, quick beat (as a clock, etc.); *v.t.*, to put a tick against.

ticked, *p.p.*, tick.

tick'en, *n.*, *i.q.* ticking.

tick'et, *n.*, a card, etc., marked in a way to show the owner's right to something; a label; a political party programme; *v.t.*, to label; to mark.

tick'eted, *p.p.*, ticket.

tick'eting, *pr.p.*, ticket.

tick'ing, *pr.p.*, tick; *n.*, the cover of bedding.

tick'le, *v.t.*, to cause to laugh by touching lightly in a sensitive part; to amuse; *v.i.*, to have the feeling of tickling.

tick'led, *p.p.*, tickle.

tick'ler, *n.*, one who, that which, tickles; a difficult problem.

tick'ling, *pr.p.*, tickle.

tick'lish, *adj.*, having the feeling of being tickled; easily tickled; awkward; critical.

tick'seed, *n.*, a plant with prickly joints to its pods.

tick'-tack, *n.*, a mode of signalling on a racecourse; a tapping sound; *adv.*, with a sound of tapping.

tid, *adj.*, nice; soft.

ti'dal, *adj.*, rel. to tide.

tid'bit, *n.*, a dainty morsel. Also *tit-bit*.

tide, *n.*, the rise and fall of the sea or a river; season (as Eastertide, etc.); drift; *v.t.*, to drive with the tide; *v.i.*, to drift.

ti'ded, *p.p.*, tide.

tide'-gauge, *n.*, an apparatus showing the degrees in the rise and fall of tides.

tide'less, *adj.*, having no tides.

tide'mill, *n.*, a mill worked by the tide.

tides'man, *n.*, an official of the custom house whose duty is to see to the discharge of ships.

tide'waiter, *n.*, *i.q.* tidesman.

tide'way, *n.*, the passage in a river where vessels can use the tides.

ti'dier, *adj.*, *comp.* of tidy.

ti'diest, *adj.*, *super.* of tidy.

ti'dily, *adv.*, in a tidy way.

ti'diness, *n.*, the state or quality of being tidy.

ti'ding, *pr.p.*, tide.

ti'dings, *n. pl.*, news.

ti'dy, *adj.*, neat; trim; orderly; *n.*, a toilet receptacle for odds and ends; a movable chair cover.

tie, *n.*, a fastening; band; knot; close connexion; obligation; a mark showing that a musical note is held for the duration of the following note; *v.t.*, to fasten, join; *v.i.*, to be equal in a contest.

tied, *p.p.*, tie.

ti'er, *n.*, one who, that which, ties.

tier, *n.*, a row, esp. one of a series of ascending stages.

tierce, *n.*, a 42 gal. cask; a fencing thrust; a musical third; an organ stop sounding the seventeenth above the diapason; in card games, a sequence of three cards of the same colour.

tier'cel, *n.*, the male hawk. Also *tercel*.

tierce'let, *n.*, a male bird of prey. Also *tercelet*.

tiff, *n.*, a quarrel; wordy dispute; a sip; *v.t.*, to sip; *v.i.*, to be peevish.

tif'fany, *n.*, a thin gauze fabric.

tif'fin, *n.*, the Anglo-Indian name for luncheon.

tig, *n.*, a childish game.

tige, *n.*, the shaft of a pillar.

ti'ger, *n.*, a fierce carnivore; a boy groom.

ti'ger-cat, *n.*, a wild-cat.

ti'gerish, *adj.*, like a tiger.

ti'ger-lily, *n.*, a variety of lily so named.

tight, *adj.*, drawn close together; constricted; close fitting; not leaking; difficult; drunk (*colloq.*).

tight'en, *v.t.*, to make tight; *v.i.*, to become tight.

tight'ened, *p.p.*, tighten.

tight'ening, *pr.p.*, tighten.

tight'er, *adj.*, *comp.* of tight.

tight'est, *adj.*, *super.* of tight.

tight'ly, *adv.*, in a tight way.

tight'ness, *n.*, the state or quality of being tight.

tights, *n. pl.*, an actor's very close-fitting underclothes.

ti'gress, *n.*, fem. of tiger.

ti'grine, *adj.*, rel. to tigers.

tike, *n.*, a dog; a Yorkshireman (*colloq.*). Also *tyke*.

til'bury, *n.*, a variety of carriage.

tile, *n.*, a thin flat slab, used for roofing, flooring, etc.; a hat (*colloq.*); *v.t.*, to guard (the door of a Masonic lodge); to roof or cover with tiles.

tile'-earth, *n.*, a clay.

tiled, *p.p.*, tile.

til'er, *n.*, one who lays tiles; a Masonic door-keeper.

til'ing, *pr.p.*, tile; *n.*, the act of tiling; roofing.

till, *v.t.*, to plough; to cultivate; *n.*, a money-receptacle in a shop-counter; a stiff clay.

till, *prep.*, until; as far as.

till'able, *adj.*, fit for tilling.

till'age, *n.*, agriculture; tilled land.

tilled, *p.p.*, till.

till'er, *n.*, one who tills; a rudder-handle; *v.i.*, to send out a number of stems from the root.

till'ering, *pr.p.*, tiller.

till'ing, *pr.p.*, till.

tilt, *n.*, a tent cover; cover of a wagon or a boat's stern; a jousting; an incline upwards; *v.t.*, to cover with a tilt; to level a tilting-lance; to make to incline; *v.i.*, to incline; to joust.

tilt'ed, *p.p.*, tilt.

tilt'er, *n.*, one who tilts.

tilth, *n.*, tilled land.

tilt'-hammer, *n.*, a large steam or hydraulic hammer.

tilt'ing, *pr.p.*, tilt; *n.*, the act of tilting; forging with a tilt-hammer.

tim'bal, **tym'bal**, *n.*, a kettle-drum.

tim'ber, *n.*, wood; trees collectively; *v.t.*, to lay timber on

tim'bered, *p.p.*, timber; *adj.*, covered with trees.

tim'bering, *pr.p.*, timber.

tim'bre, *n.*, the quality of sound in a voice or musical instrument (*Fr.*)

tim'brel, *n.*, a Hebrew drum.

time, *n.*, measured continuance; a date; period; the opposite to eternity; season; duration of opportunity; measured musical beats; *v.t.*, to measure time; to do at the fitting moment.

timed, *p.p.*, time.

time'-honoured, *adj.*, honoured for a long past time; venerable.

time'ist, *n.*, one who observes strict time (*mus.*).

time'-keeper, *n.*, a person who records the time when employees begin and leave off work; a watch or clock.

time'less, *adj.*, eternal

time'liness, *n.*, the state or quality of being timely.

time'ly, *adj.*, in good or convenient time; seasonable.

time'piece, *n.*, a clock.

time'-server, *n.*, one who takes selfish advantage of every opportunity with no regard to principles.

time'-serving, *adj.*, looking after one's own interests without reference to principles; *n.*, self-interest.

time'-table, *n.*, a register of the times at which trains start and arrive, work is to be done, etc.

time'-worn, *adj.*, ancient and decaying.

tim'id, *adj.*, fearful; nervous; cowardly.

timid'ity, *n.*, faint-heartedness; lack of courage.

tim'idly, *adv.*, in a timid way.

ti'ming, *pr.p.*, time.

ti'mist, *n.*, *i.q.* timeist.

timoc'racy, *n.*, form of polity under which property is a qualification for office.

timoneer', *n.*, a look-out man; a helmsman.

tim'orous, *adj.*, dreading danger.

tim'orously, *adv.*, in a timorous way.

Timoth'ean, *adj.*, bel. to Timotheus.

tim'othy, *n.*, a species of fodder-grass.

tin, *n.*, a white, malleable metal; a vessel made of tin; money (*slang*); *v.t.*, to overlay with tin; to preserve in tins.

tin'cal, *n.*, native borax.

tincto'rial, *adj.*, pert. to colouring and dyeing.

tinc'ture, *n.*, colouring; a medical solution; the colouring in a shield (*her.*); *v.t.*, to tinge; colour.

tinc'tured, *p.p.*, tincture.

tinc'turing, *pr.p.*, tincture.

tin'der, *n.*, rotten wood, etc., for kindling into a flame.

tin′der-box, *n.*, a box to contain tinder.
tine, *n.*, a spike; prong.
tin′ea, *n.*, a moth (*Lat.*); ringworm.
tin′foil, *n.*, tin beaten exceedingly thin.
ting, *n.*, a sound as of a bell; *v.i.*, to give forth such a sound.
tinge, *v.t.*, to stain; infect with a faint colour, etc.; *n.*, a colouring; a slight addition of taste, colour, etc.
tinged, *p.p.*, tinge.
tinge′ing, *pr.p.*, tinge.
ting′ing, *pr.p.*, ting.
tin′gle, *v.i.*, to have a pricking sensation; *n.*, such a sensation.
tin′gled, *p.p.*, tingle.
tin′gling, *pr.p.*, tingle.
tink, *v.i.*, to chink; *n.*, a chinking or tinkling sound.
tinked, *p.p.*, tink.
tink′er, *n.*, one who repairs pots and pans; *v.t.*, to mend pots, etc.; to botch; *v.i.*, to be meddlesome.
tink′ered, *p.p.*, tinker.
tink′ering, *pr.p.*, tinker.
tink′ing, *pr.p.*, tink.
tin′kle, *n.*, a sound as of ringing; *v.t.*, to set tinkling.
tin′kled, *p.p.*, tinkle.
tin′kling, *pr.p.*, tinkle.
tin′man, *n.*, a worker in tin.
tinned, *p.p.*, tin; *adj.*, packed or preserved in tins or cans.
tin′ner, *n.*, a worker in a tin mine.
tin′ning, *pr.p.*, tin.
tin′ny, *adj.*, like tin; making the sound of tin when beaten.
tin′plate, *n.*, iron-plate overlaid with tin; *adj.*, made of tin-plate.
tin′sel, *n.*, cloth with gold or silver woven in; thin metal work; gaudy, cheap ornament; *adj.*, cheap and gaudy; very showy; *v.t.*, to adorn with tinsel.
tin′selled, tin′seled, *p.p.*, tinsel.
tin′selling, tin′seling, *pr.p.*, tinsel.
tin′smith, *n.*, a worker in tin.
tint, *n.*, a colour; hue; shade of colour; *v.t.*, to impart a colour to.
tint′ed, *p.p.*, tint.
tint′ing, *pr.p.*, tint.
tintinnab′ulary, *adj.*, rel. to bells.
tintinnabula′tion, *n.*, the sound of bells.
ti′ny, *adj.*, minute; very small.
tip, *n.*, the point of a thing; a tilt; a gift (*colloq.*); a private hint; *v.t.*, to point; put a tip to; to give a present to (*colloq.*); to help with a private hint.
tip′-cat, *n.*, a boy's game with a stick and a small piece of wood pointed at the ends.
tipped, *p.p.*, tip.
tip′per, *n.*, one who, that which, tips (in all senses); a Sussex brew of ale.
tip′pet, *n.*, a shoulder-wrap of fur or other material, esp. the scarf-like tippet of silk or stuff worn by the English clergy with surplice for choir offices and with the gown for outdoor use.
tip′ping, *pr.p.*, tip; *n.*, the practice of giving tips or gratuities (*colloq.*).
tip′ple, *v.t.* and *i.*, to drink as a habit; *n.*, alcoholic drink; any sort of drink.
tip′pled, *p.p.*, tipple.
tip′pler, *n.*, a habitual drinker; a soaker.
tip′pling, *pr.p.*, tipple; *n.*, the alcoholic habit.
tip′sily, *adv.*, in a tipsy way.
tip′staff, *n.*, a sheriff's officer; a constable.
tip′sy, *adj.*, partially intoxicated; fuddled; inclined to turn topsy-turvy.
tip′toe, *n.*, the toe-tips; *adj.*, standing on tip-toe; stealthy.
tip′-top, *adj.*, supremely good; *n.*, the very summit; *adv.*, in first-rate style (*colloq.*).
tirade′, *n.*, a long-drawn-out declamation; a prolonged scolding; a diatonic run completing the interval between two notes.
tirailleur′, *n.*, a skirmisher; sharpshooter; marksman (*Fr.*).
tire, *v.t.*, to weary; to attire; *v.i.*, to grow weary; *n.*, a band round the fellies of wheels.
tired, *p.p.*, tire; *adj.*, weary.
tire′less, *adj.*, without a tire. The word is sometimes used in the sense of untiring.
tire′lessness, *n.*, the state of being tireless.
tire′some, *adj.*, worrying, annoying, tedious.
tire′someness, *n.*, the state or quality of being tiresome.
ti′ring, *pr.p.*, tire; *adj.*, wearisome.
Tiro′nian, *adj.*, pert. to Tiro, Cicero's freedman, the inventor of the shorthand system long known by his name and long in use. It is said to have contained 5,000 shorthand signs.
'tis, an abbreviation for "it is."
Tish′ri, *n.*, a Jewish month — ecclesiastically the seventh, civilly the first. Also *Tisri.*
Tis′ri, *n.*, *i.q.* Tishri.
tis′sue, *n.*, fabric woven, and sometimes crossed with gold or silver threads; a fine texture; closely connected cellular substance; a connected series, as "a tissue of lies"; *v.t.*, to form into a tissue.
tis′sued, *p.p.*, tissue.
tis′suing, *pr.p.*, tissue.

tit, *n.*, a morsel; a little horse; a titmouse; the name of several small songsters.

Ti'tan, *n.*, one of the fabled classical giants; a giant.

Tita'nian, *adj.*, *i.q.* Titanic; rel. to titanium.

Titan'ic, *adj.*, rel. to the Titans; gigantic; immensely strong.

titanif'erous, *adj.*, producing titanium.

tita'nium, *n.*, a hard metal so named.

tit'-bit, *n.*, *i.q.* tid-bit.

ti'thable, *adj.*, subject to payment of tithe.

tithe, *n.*, a tenth part; tax to the amount of one-tenth of profits; *v.t.*, to levy such a tax.

tithe'-barn, *n.*, a barn where were deposited tithe-payments in kind instead of money.

tithed, *p.p.*, tithe.

ti'ther, *n.*, one who tithes.

ti'thing, *pr.p.*, tithe; *n.*, the levying of tithe; a group of ten householders, whose duty it was to keep order in their district; a civil territorial division corresponding to the Hundred.

ti'thing-man, *n.*, the head of a tithing.

tit'illate, *v.t.*, to tickle.

tit'illated, *p.p.*, titillate.

tit'illating, *pr.p.*, titillate.

titilla'tion, *n.*, the act or effect of titillating.

tit'ivate, *v.t.* and *i.*, to make (oneself) smart

tit'lark, *n.*, a small songster.

ti'tle, *n.*, an inscription or heading; name; distinctive or honorific appellation; a right to anything; a spiritual charge as a condition of admission to Holy Orders; *v.t.*, *i.q.* entitle.

ti'tled, *p.p.*, title; *adj.*, possessing an honorific title, as *Sir*, *Lord*, etc.

ti'tle-deed, *n.*, a document establishing a person's claim to possession.

ti'tle-page, *n.*, the front page of a book setting out its name, description, authorship, imprint, etc.

ti'tling, *pr.p.*, title.

tit'mouse, *n.*, a little bird so named.

tit'rate, *v.t.*, to measure by volume.

tit'rated, *p.p.*, titrate.

tit'rating, *pr.p.*, titrate.

tit'ter, *v.i.*, to laugh in a silly way; *n.*, a giggle.

tit'tered, *p.p.*, titter.

tit'tering, *pr.p.*, titter.

tit'tle, *n.*, a tiny particle.

tit'tle-tattle, *n.*, small-talk; silly gossip; *v.i.*, to gossip.

tit'ular, *adj.*, rel. to title; nominal; *n.*, a person who has an empty title and no authority.

tit'ulary, *adj.*, *i.q.* titular.

tiv'y, *adv.*, a hunting term = at full gallop.

tme'sis, *n.*, a cutting into two of a compound word (*Gr.*).

to, *prep.*, towards; in the direction of; as far as.

toad, *n.*, a frog-like reptile; the bufo.

toad'-eater, *n.*, a sycophant.

toad'ied, *p.p.*, toady.

toad'stone, *n.*, a variety of rock.

toad'stool, *n.*, a fungus; one of the agarics.

toad'y, *n.*, a sycophant; parasite; *v.t.* to flatter; curry favour of; fawn upon.

toad'ying, *pr.p.*, toady.

toad'yism, *n.*, sycophancy; fawning.

toast, *n.*, bread roasted; a health; *v.t.*, to make into toast; to warm before the fire; to drink a health to a person, country, cause, etc., honoured at a banquet by toasting.

toast'ed, *p.p.*, toast.

toast'er, *n.*, one who, that which, toasts.

toast'ing, *pr.p.*, toast.

toast'ing-fork, *n.*, a fork on which bread is held before a fire.

toast'-master, *n.*, a person who proclaims the toasts at a banquet.

toast'-rack, *n.*, a rack in which pieces of toast are served.

tobac'co, *n.*, a plant of the genus *Nicotiana*, the leaves of which are smoked in various forms, or ground into snuff.

tobac'conist, *n.*, one who sells tobacco, cigars, pipes, etc.

tobog'gan, *n.*, a sort of sledge for coasting down inclines; *v.i.*, to slide in a toboggan.

tobog'ganing, *pr.p.*, toboggan.

too'sin, *n.*, a bell to sound an alarm.

tod, *n.*, a measure of wool (28 lbs.).

to-day', *adv.*, on this present day; in our time.

tod'dle, *v.i.*, to walk with short, weak steps; *n.*, such a manner of walking.

tod'dled, *p.p.*, toddle.

tod'dler, *n.*, one who toddles; an infant.

tod'dling, *pr.p.*, toddle.

tod'dy, *n.*, a palm-juice; hot spirits and water with sugar, etc.

to-do', *n.*, a fuss.

to'dy, *n.*, a little bird so named.

toe, *n.*, one of the separate ends of the forepart of a foot; anything like a toe; *v.t.*, to touch with the toe (as "to toe the line").

tof'fee, **tof'fy**, *n.*, a sweetmeat made with butter, sugar, etc.

toft, *n.*, a grove.

to'ga, *n.*, the robe of a Roman citizen (*Lat.*).

togeth'er, *adv.*, in company; all united or combined.

tog'gery, *n.*, clothes (*colloq.*).

tog'gle, *n.*, a tapering pin of wood grooved in the middle.

toil, *n.*, labour; a snare; *v.i.*, to labour.

toiled, *p.p.*, toil.

toil'er, *n.*, one who labours.

toi'let, *n.*, the business of dressing; attire.

toilinet(te'), *n.*, a cloth of woollen yarn with cotton and silk interwoven.

toil'ing, *pr.p.*, toil.

toil'less, *adj.*, without toil.

toil'some, *adj.*, laborious.

toil'-worn, *adj.*, worn out with labour.

Toison-d'Or', *n.*, the Order of the Golden Fleece.

Tokay', *n.*, a choice wine of Hungary.

to'la, *n.*, an Indian gold and silver weight (180 grs. troy).

told, *p.t.* and *p.*, tell.

tole, *v.t.*, to attract.

Tole'do, *n.*, a sword of Toledo, a Spanish city noted for its manufacture of finely - tempered sword blades.

tol'erable, *adj.*, endurable; moderately good.

tol'erably, *adv.*, to a tolerable degree.

tol'erance, *n.*, *i.q.* toleration, patience.

tol'erant, *adj.*, patient; indulgent.

tol'erate, *v.t.*, to endure; allow; not to interfere with.

tol'erated, *p.p.*, tolerate.

tol'erating, *pr.p.*, tolerate.

tolera'tion, *n.*, the act of tolerating; putting up with things not approved; patience with opinions one dislikes.

toll, *n.*, the slow sound of a bell at intervals; a charge at turnpikes, bridges, etc.; duty demanded; *v.i.*, to sound a bell solemnly and at intervals.

toll'-booth, *n.*, a prison (*Scot.*).

toll'-bridge, *n.*, a bridge on which passengers are charged a fee.

tolled, *p.p.*, toll.

toll'er, *n.*, one who, that which, tolls.

toll'-gate, *n.*, a gate across a road where a fee is demanded of passengers.

toll'-gatherer, *n.*, a collector of tolls.

toll'-house, *n.*, a toll-gatherer's house.

toll'ing, *pr.p.*, toll.

toll'man, *n.*, *i.q.* toll-gatherer.

tolt, *v.t.*, to remove; *n.*, in old English law, a writ withdrawing a case from the Court baron to the County Court.

tolu', *n.*, a balsam.

tol'zey, *n.*, *i.q.* toll-booth.

tom'ahawk, *n.*, a N. Amer. Indian hatchet; *v.t.*, to hit with a tomahawk.

toma'to, *n.*, a plant so named; its fruit.

tomb, *n.*, a grave; a sepulchral monument; *v.t.*, to place in a tomb.

tom'bac, *n.*, copper and zinc alloy.

tombed, *p.p.*, tomb.

tom'boy, *n.*, a rough girl.

tomb'stone, *n.*, a stone over a grave.

tom'-cat, *n.*, a male cat.

tom'-cod, *n.*, a small variety of cod.

tome, *n.*, a large volume.

tomen'tous, *adj.*, covered with nap. Also *tomentose*.

tom'-fool, *n.*, an idiot; a silly fellow.

tomfool'ery, *n.*, nonsense; silly conduct.

tomin', *n.*, a weight of 12 grs., used in the jewellery trade.

tom-nod'dy, *n.*, a fool.

to-mor'row, *adv.*, on the day after to-day

tom'pion, *n.*, a cannon's stopper.

tom'-tit', *n.*, the titmouse.

tom'-tom, *n.*, a kind of drum used by African and Indian natives.

ton, *n.*, twenty cwts., 40 cubic ft. (*naut.*).

ton, *n.*, fashion: the mode (*Fr.*).

to'nal, *adj.*, rel. to tone.

tonal'ity, *n.*, key relationship.

tone, *n.*, sound and its quality; note; style; a healthy condition; blend of colours; a musical interval of two semitones; one of the plainsong chant-melodies; *v.t.*, to invigorate; to temper; to blend the colours of; *v.i.*, to agree in colour or shade.

toned, *p.p.*, tone.

tone'less, *adj.*, lacking tone.

ton'ga, *n.*, a British-Indian two-wheeled carriage.

tongs, *n. pl.*, an appliance for grasping objects.

tongue, *n.*, the organ of taste; that with which one speaks; a language; anything tongue-like, as a tongue of land, or a low promontory; *v.i.*, to use the tongue in any sense; to produce a staccato effect on a flute, etc., by using the tongue.

tongued, *p.p.*, tongue; *adj.*, having a tongue.

tongue'-shaped, *adj.*, like a tongue in shape.

tongue'-tied, *adj.*, mum; silent.

tongu'ing, *pr.p.*, tongue.

ton'ic, *adj.*, invigorating; rel. to the keynote; *n.*, a medicine that gives tone; the keynote.

ton'ically, *adv.*, in a tonic sense or relation.
tonic'ity, *n.*, the quality of being tonic.
to-night', *adv.*, on this present night.
to'ning, *pr.p.*, tone.
ton'ka, *n.*, a scent derived from the Tonka bean.
ton'nage, *n.*, capacity or weight reckoned in tons; ship-duty; shipping collectively.
ton'sil, *n.*, one of the glands attached to the sides of the throat.
ton'sillar, **ton'silar**, *adj.*, pert. to the tonsils.
tonsillit'ic, *adj.*, pert. to tonsillitis.
tonsilli'tis, *n.*, inflammation of the tonsils.
tonso'rial, *adj.*, rel. to shaving and barbers.
ton'sure, *n.*, the act of shaving the head; the crown left round the head after the top has been shaven; a mark of admission to the clerical status; *v.t.*, to confer the tonsure upon.
ton'sured, *p.p.*, tonsure.
tontine', *n.*, an arrangement by which the last survivor of a number of annuitants succeeds to the whole amount secured.
to'ny, *adj.*, fashionable (*slang*).
too, *adv.*, also; in addition; excessively.
took, *p.t.*, take.
tool, *n.*, an implement; anyone of whom another makes use for his own purposes; *v.t.*, to use a tool upon (esp. in book-binding); to drive.
tooled, *p.p.*, tool.
tool'ing, *pr.p.*, tool; *n.*, work done with a tool (esp. by a bookbinder).
toon, **tun**, *n.*, town (*Scot.*).
toon'wood, *n.*, a dark kind of cedar.
toot, *v.t.*, to blow a horn, flute, etc.; *n.*, a single sound on a horn, flute, etc.
toot'ed, *p.p.*, toot.
toot'er, *n.*, one who, that which, toots.
tooth, *n.*, a bony outgrowth from the jaws with which an animal chews and bites; anything tooth-like; *v.t.*, to supply with tooth-like indentations.
tooth'ache, *n.*, pain in the teeth.
tooth'-brush, *n.*, a brush for cleansing the teeth.
toothed, *p.p.*, tooth; *adj.*, indented.
tooth'ing, *pr.p.*, tooth.
tooth'less, *adj.*, having no teeth.
tooth'let, *n.*, a small tooth.
tooth'leted, *adj.*, having small teeth.
tooth'pick, *n.*, a quill or metal pointed instrument for picking the teeth.
tooth'some, *adj.*, good to taste.
tooth'wort, *n.*, a plant with toothed or indented leaves.
toot'ing, *pr.p.*, toot.
top, *n.*, the summit; the highest part; a revolving toy; *v.t.*, to put a top on; to surpass; to remove the top from.
to'paz, *n.*, a gem so named.
top'-boots, *n. pl.*, boots with tops coming well up the leg.
top'-coat, *n.*, an overcoat.
tope, *n.*, a grove; a Buddhist sepulchral monument; *v.i.*, to be a drunkard.
toped, *p.p.*, tope.
to'per, *n.*, a hard drinker.
to'ping, *pr.p.*, tope.
topgal'lant, *adj.*, above the gallant mast; *n.*, a topgallant mast or sail.
toph, *n.*, chalky formation round the teeth and on the surface of joints. Also *tophus*.
topha'ceous, *adj.*, pert. to toph.
top'-heavy, *adj.*, with too much weight on the top.
To'phet, *n.*, the place in the valley of Hinnom where Moloch was worshipped with a perpetual fire; hell.
to'phus, *n.*, *i.q.* toph.
top'ic, *n.*, a subject of talk or discourse.
top'ical, *adj.*, rel. to a place; rel. to current events.
top'knot, *n.*, a knot of hair on the top of the head.
top'man, *n.*, one who is posted in the tops (*naut.*).
top'mast, *n.*, the upper mast.
top'most, *adj.*, the highest.
topog'rapher, *n.*, an expert in topography.
topograph'ic, *adj.*, rel. to topography.
topog'raphy, *n.*, the study of places.
topped, *p.p.*, top.
top'per, *n.*, one who, that which, tops; a tall hat; a superfine person or thing (*slang*).
top'ping, *pr.p.*, top; supremely good (*slang*).
top'ple, *v.t.*, to overthrow; knock down; *v.i.*, to fall over.
top'pled, *p.p.*, topple.
top'pling, *pr.p.*, topple.
top'sail, *n.*, an upper sail.
topsy-tur'vy, *adj.*, upside down; in a muddle.
toque, *n.*, a lady's close-fitting hat.
tor, *n.*, a high rock or hill.
torch, *n.*, a portable light.
torch'-bearer, *n.*, one who carries a torch.
torch'-light, *n.*, the light of a torch.
tore, *p.t.*, tear.
toreu'tic, *adj.*, sculptured; worked in bas-relief on metal.

tor'ment, *n.*, torture; pain.

torment', *v.t.*, to torture, cause anguish to.

torment'ed, *p.p.*, torment.

torment'er, *n.*, one who torments.

tor'mentil, *n.*, an astringent drug.

torment'ing, *pr.p.*, torment.

torment'or, *n.*, *i.q.* tormenter.

torment'ress, *n.*, fem. of tormenter.

torn, *p.p.*, tear.

torna'do, *n.*, a tempest.

to'rous, *adj.*, knobby.

torpe'do, *n.*, a crampfish; a projectile discharged from a submarine; *v.t.*, to discharge a torpedo at.

tor'pid, *adj.*, sleepy; sluggish; inactive.

torpid'ity, *n.*, the state or quality of being torpid.

tor'pified, *p.p.*, torpify.

tor'pify, *v.t.*, to make torpid or numb.

tor'pifying, *pr.p.*, torpify.

tor'pitude, *n.*, a state of torpor.

tor'por, *n.*, the state of being torpid; numbness.

tor'quated, *adj.*, furnished with a collar.

torque, *n.*, a barbaric neck-ornament.

torqued, *adj.*, having a torque.

torrefac'tion, *n.*, the act of torrefying; state of being torrefied.

tor'refied, *p.p.*, torrefy.

tor'refy, *v.t.*, to heat.

tor'refying, *pr.p.*, torrefy.

tor'rent, *n.*, a strongly rushing stream; a copious flood.

torren'tial, *adj.*, pert. to, resembling, a torrent.

Torricel'lian, *adj.*, rel. to Torricelli, the 17th cent. inventor of the barometer.

tor'rid, *adj.*, scorching; scorched.

torse, *n.*, a wreath (*her.*).

tor'sel, *n.*, scroll-work; a wooden insertion in a wall to support a joist, etc.

tor'sion, *n.*, the act of twisting or wrenching.

tor'so, *n.*, in sculpture, a mutilated statue; the trunk lacking a head or limbs.

tort, *n.*, injury, damage (*leg.*).

torteau', *n.*, a circular heraldic emblem.

tor'tile, *adj.*, twisted; twined.

tor'tious, *adj.*, rel. to a tort.

tor'tive, *adj.*, twisted.

tor'toise, *n.*, a shell-covered reptile so named; a testudo.

tor'toise-shell, *n.*, the shell of a tortoise; *adj.*, made of polished tortoise-shell.

tortuos'ity, *n.*, the state or quality of being tortuous.

tor'tuous, *adj.*, twisting, winding; crooked; deceitful.

tor'ture, *n.*, extreme pain; pain cruelly inflicted; *v.t.*, to inflict cruel pain for the purpose of extorting a confession or evidence; to pervert.

tor'tured, *p.p.*, torture.

tor'turer, *n.*, one who inflicts torture.

tor'turing, *pr.p.*, torture.

tor'ulous, *adj.*, ridged; swelling.

to'rus, *n.*, a semicircular moulding at the bottom of a pillar; the support of carpels in a flower.

To'ry, *n.*, once, a Church and King man; now, more vaguely, a Conservative.

To'ryism, *n.*, the principles professed by Tories.

toss, *v.t.*, to heave up into the air; to jerk upward; *v.i.*, to pitch; roll; *n.*, an upward throw.

tossed, *p.p.*, toss.

toss'ing, *pr.p.*, toss.

tos'to, *adj.*, fast (*mus.*).

tot, *n.*, a tiny thing; *v.t.*, to add up; *see* tots.

to'tal, *adj.*, aggregate; complete; *n.*, the sum; amount.

total'ity, *n.*, the state or quality of being total; completeness.

to'talize, *v.t.*, to work out the total.

to'tally, *adv.*, completely; entirely.

to'tem, *n.*, a beast regarded as the emblem or distinguishing mark of a barbaric tribe.

to'temism, *n.*, the practice of distinguishing families or tribes by their totem.

toth'er, *pron.* = the other (*colloq.*).

tot'ter, *v.i.*, to shake as though on the point of falling.

tot'tered, *p.p.*, totter.

tot'tering, *pr.p.*, totter.

tot'tery, *adj.*, shaky; staggery.

toucan', *n.*, a bird so named.

touch, *n.*, the sense of feeling; the act of touching; close relation; power of impression through the hand or fingers; a stroke with a painter's brush, sculptor's chisel, etc.; *v.t.*, to apply the hand to; to feel; to reach; to affect emotionally or injuriously; *v.i.*, to be in close relation; to put in with a ship.

touched, *p.p.*, touch.

touch'er, *n.*, one who, that which, touches.

touch'-hole, *n.*, the hole in a firearm where the charge was ignited.

touch'iness, *n.*, the state or quality of being touchy.

touch'ing, *pr.p.*, touch; *adj.*, affecting; moving; *pr.p.*, in regard to.

touch'-me-not, *n.*, a plant so named.

touch'stone, *n.*, a testing stone; a test.

touch'wood, *n.*, any dried wood for kindling.

touch'y, *adj.*, quick to take offence; irritable.

tough, *adj.*, hard to break; not easily chewed; sturdy; capable of endurance; *n.*, a hooligan (*Amer.*).

tough'en, *v.t.*, to harden; make tough; *v.i.*, to become tough.

tough'ened, *p.p.*, toughen.

tough'ening, *pr.p.*, toughen.

tough'er, *adj.*, *comp.* of tough.

tough'est, *adj.*, *super.* of tough.

tough'ish, *adj.*, somewhat tough.

tough'ly, *adv.*, in a tough way.

tough'ness, *n.*, the state or quality of being tough.

toupee', *n.*, a diminutive wig.

toupet', *n.*, *i.q.* toupee (*Fr.*).

tour, *n.*, a continued journey; travel; *v.i.*, to go on a tour.

tourbil'lion, *n.*, a revolving firework.

tour'ing, *pr.p.*, tour; *n.*, travel.

tour'ist, *n.*, one who goes on a tour.

tour'maline, *n.*, a mineral so named.

tour'nament, *n.*, a contest of mounted knights; any exhibition of competitors.

tour'ney, *n.*, *i.q.* tournament.

tour'niquet, *n.*, a surgical appliance for stopping the flow of blood from a severed artery.

tournure', *n.*, shape; figure.

tou'sle, tou'zle, *v.t.*, to disarray; disorder.

tou'sled, tou'zled, *p.p.*, tousle.

tou'sling, tou'zling, *pr.p.*, tousle.

tout, *n.*, a person who hangs about to give information, get tips, etc.; *v.t.*, to act as a tout.

tout'ed, *p.p.*, tout.

tout'er, *n.*, one who touts; a tout.

tout'ing, *pr.p.*, tout.

tow, *n.*, coarse hemp or flax; *v.t.*, to haul a boat; *n.*, the action of towing.

tow'age, *n.*, a charge for towing.

to'ward, *adv.*, close at hand; *prep.*, in the direction of; in regard to.

to'wardly, *adj.*, agreeable.

to'wardness, *n.*, the quality of being towardly.

to'wards, *prep.*, *i.q.* toward.

towed, *p.p.*, tow.

tow'el, *n.*, a cloth for washing purposes.

tow'elling, tow'eling, *n.*, material for towels.

tow'er, *n.*, a fortress-like tall building, or part of a building; *v.i.*, to stand up very high.

tow'ered, *p.p.*, tower.

tow'ering, *pr.p.*, tower; *adj.*, tall.

tow'ery, *adj.*, like a tower.

tow'ing, *pr.p.*, tow.

to-wit', phrase = that is to say.

tow'-line, *n.*, a rope for towing.

town, *n.*, an inhabited place larger than a village; the capital.

town-clerk', *n.*, an official in charge of municipal business.

town'-crier, *n.*, an official who makes public announcements.

town-hall', *n.*, a municipal assembly hall.

town'-house, *n.*, a residence in town.

towns'-folk, *n.*, inhabitants of a town.

town'ship, *n.*, a town; in the U.S., a territorial division of the county.

towns'man, *n.*, a dweller in a town.

towns'people, *n.*, inhabitants of a town.

town'-talk', *n.*, the talk of a town.

tow'ser, *n.*, one who worries or creates a disturbance. (Once a common name for a dog.)

tow'y, *adj.*, like tow; full of tow.

tox'ic, *adj.*, poisonous.

tox'ical, *adj.*, *i.q.* toxic.

toxicol'ogist, *n.*, an expert in toxicology

toxicol'ogy, *n.*, the study of poisons.

toxoph'ilite, *n.*, an amateur archer; *adj.*, rel. to archery.

toy, *n.*, a plaything; something worthless; *v.i.*, to play; trifle.

toyed, *p.p.*, toy.

toy'ing, *pr.p.*, toy.

toy'-shop, *n.*, a shop where toys are sold.

trabea'tion, *n.*, structural arrangement on horizontal lines.

trace, *n.*, a mark; trail; footprint; vestige; *v.t.*, to track; copy by following marks.

trace'able, *adj.*, able to be traced.

traced, *p.p.*, trace.

tra'cer, *n.*, one who traces.

tra'cery, *n.*, the ornamental work in Gothic windows and arches.

tra'ces, *n. pl.*, the bands or ropes by which horses, oxen, etc., draw a vehicle, plough, etc.

trache'a, *n.*, the windpipe.

trache'ae, *n. pl.*, the tubes through which insects breathe.

tra'cheal, *adj.*, pert. to the trachea.

trache'ocele, *n.*, tracheal hernia.

tracheot'omy, *n.*, the operation of opening the windpipe.

tra'chyte, *n.*, a certain kind of igneous rock.

tra'cing, *pr.p.*, trac ; *n.*, a copy through thin paper of a picture, etc., beneath.

tra'cing-paper, *n.*, thin paper used for tracing purposes.

track, *n.*, a trail; footmark; an unmade road; a running path; a railroad; *v.t.*, to follow in the trail of.

tracked, *p.p.*, track.

track'ing, *pr.p.*, track.

track'less, *adj.*, showing no track.

tract, *n.*, a pamphlet; short treatise; a large extent of country; deliberateness.

tractabil'ity, *n.*, the state or quality of being tractable.

tract'able, *adj.*, docile, manageable.

tract'ably, *adv.*, in a tractable way.

Tracta'rian, *adj.*, rel. to the "Tracts for the Times," which were published during the period 1833-41, the most famous of the writers being Pusey and Newman; *n.*, a High Churchman.

Tracta'rianism, *n.*, the principles laid down and defended in the "Tracts," which developed into what is known as the Oxford or the Catholic Movement.

trac'tate, *n.*, a treatise

trac'tile, *adj.*, *i.q.* ductile.

tractil'ity, *n.*, the state or quality of being tractile.

trac'tion, *n.*, the act of drawing; the state of being drawn

trac'tive, *adj.*, drawing.

trac'tor, *n.*, that which draws.

trac'tory, *adj.*, *i.q.* tractive.

tract'rix, *n.*, a special kind of curve.

***trade*,** *n.*, traffic; commerce; a business or craft; *v.t.*, to traffic in; *v.i.*, to engage in commerce.

tra'ded, *p.p.*, trade.

***trade'*-mark,** *n.*, a mark protecting a trader's manufacture against the makers of similar, but not genuine, articles.

***trade'*-price,** *n.*, the price charged to a retailer.

tra'der, *n.*, one who trades; a trading-vessel.

trade'-sale, *n.*, an auction confined to the members of a particular trade.

***trades'*folk,** *n. pl.*, tradespeople.

***trades'*man,** *n.*, one following a trade.

***trades*-u'nion,** *n.*, an organized mutual association of the workmen of a particular industry.

***trades*-u'nionism,** *n.*, the principle of association among workers.

***trade'*wind,** *n.*, a wind that blows steadily for periods in the same direction along ocean trade routes.

***tra'ding*,** *pr.p.*, trade; *adj.*, rel. to trade.

tradi'tion, *n.*, unwritten delivery of a doctrine or story from generation to generation; an orally transmitted legend or doctrine.

tradi'tional, *adj.*, according to or by tradition.

tradi'tionally, *adv.*, by tradition.

tradi'tionary, *adj.*, *i.q.* traditional.

tradi'tionist, *n.*, one who favours tradition.

trad'itor, *n.*, one who, to save his life, makes surrender of sacred property.

traduce', *v.t.*, to slander; grossly to misrepresent.

traduced', *p.p.*, traduce.

tradu'cer, *n.*, a slanderer.

tradu'cing, *pr.p.*, traduce.

traduc'tion, *n.*, the act of traducing.

traduc'tive, *adj.*, slanderous.

traf'fic, *n.*, trade; goods being conveyed; concourse; thronging; *v.t.*, to exchange; *v.i.*, to do business.

traf'ficked, *p.p.*, traffic.

traf'ficker, *n.*, one who traffics.

traf'ficking, *pr.p.*, traffic.

trag'acanth, *n.*, a species of gum.

trage'dian, *n.*, a writer or actor of tragedies.

trag'edy, *n.*, a drama of an exalted character, illustrating the working out of fate; an overwhelmingly sad event.

trag'ic, *adj.*, pert. to tragedy; terrible.

trag'ical, *adj.*, *i.q.* tragic.

trag'ically, *adv.*, in a tragical way.

tragi-com'edy, *n.*, a play containing both tragedy and comedy.

tragi-com'ic, *adj.*, partly tragic and partly comic.

tragi-com'ical, *adj.*, *i.q.* tragi-comic.

trag'ule, *n.*, a small hornless deer.

trail, *n.*, a track; scent; a string of things; *v.t.*, to drag on the ground; *v.i.*, to be dragged along; to climb or depend (as a creeping plant)

trailed, *p.p.*, trail.

trail'er, *n.*, a trail-car.

trail'ing, *pr.p.*, trail.

train, *n.*, a body of followers; retinue; railway carriages linked up together; a trailing robe; state of preparedness; gunpowder laid up to a firing-point; *v.t.*, to discipline; educate; aim a cannon; *v.i.*, to prepare oneself for any athletic performance.

train'able, *adj.*, able to be trained.

train'-band, *n.*, an old English volunteer force.

train'-bearer, *n.*, one who supports a train (in the sense of a robe).
trained, *p.p.*, train.
train'er, *n.*, one who trains people,horses, etc.
train'ing, *pr.p.*, train; *n.*, preparation.
train'-oil, *n.*, whale-oil.
traipse, *v.i.*, to walk idly or slovenly; *n.*, a saunter; a sloven. Also *trapes*.
trait, *n.*, a characteristic.
trai'tor, *n.*, one who betrays a cause; who is guilty of treason or treachery
trai'torous, *adj.*, pert. to a traitor.
trai'torously, *adv.*, in a traitorous way.
trai'tress, *n.*, fem. of traitor.
traject', *v.t.*, to throw across.
traj'ect, *n.*, *i.q.* trajectory; a ford.
trajec'tion, *n.*, the act of trajecting or transporting; a passage.
traject'ory, *n.*, the curve of a flying missile, comet, etc.
tram, *n.*, *i.q.* tram-car; a tram-line; *v.i.*, to go in a tram-car.
tram'-car, *n.*, a car running on tram lines.
tram'mel, *v.t.*, to encumber; impede; *n.*, a fishing or fowling net; an impediment.
tram'mel(l)ed, *p.p.*, trammel.
tram'mel(l)ing, *pr.p.*, trammel.
tramon'tane, *adj.*, beyond the mountains; *n.*, a bitter north wind from the Alps.
tramp, *v.t.*, to travel over; *v.i.*, to walk with a regular and heavy tread; to go for a long walk; *n.*, a vagrant; the beat of feet on the ground; a long walk.
tramped, *p.p.*, tramp.
tramp'ing, *pr.p.*, tramp.
tram'ple, *v.t.*, to tread under foot; to treat with rude contempt.
tram'pled, *p.p.*, trample.
tram'pler, *n.*, one who tramples.
tram'pling, *pr.p.*, trample.
tram'-road, *n.*, *i.q.* tramway.
tram'way, *n.*, a track for trams to run on.
trance, *n.*, a condition in which, though unconscious, one sees visions; a cataleptic state; *v.t.*, to throw into a trance.
tran'quil, *adj.*, calm; peaceful.
tranquil'lity, *n.*, the state of being tranquil.
tranquilliza'tion, *n.*, the act of tranquillizing; state of being tranquillized.
tran'quillize, *v.t.*, to make tranquil; appease; calm.
tran'quillized, *p.p.*, tranquillize.
tran'quillizer, *n.*, one who, that which, tranquillizes.
tran'quillizing, *pr.p.*, tranquillize.
tran'quilly, *adv.*, in a tranquil way.
trans, a *Lat. prep.*, across; used as a prefix to many words.
transact', *adj.*, to perform; carry through; negotiate.
transact'ed, *p.p.*, transact.
transact'ing, *pr.p.*, transact.
transac'tion, *n.*, the process of transacting; negotiation; an affair carried through.
transac'tor, *n.*, one who transacts.
transal'pine, *adj.*, on the other side of the Alps.
transatlan'tic, *adj.*, across the Atlantic.
transcend', *v.t.*, to surpass; exceed.
transcend'ed, *p.p.*, transcend.
transcend'ence, *n.*, the state or quality of being transcendent.
transcend'ency, *n.*, *i.q.* transcendence.
transcend'ent, *adj.*, surpassing; supereminent.
transcenden'tal, *adj.*, outside or beyond experience; metaphysical.
transcenden'talism, *n.*, the Kantian *a priori* philosophy.
transcenden'talist, *n.*, an adherent of transcendentalism.
transcenden'tally, *adv.*, in a transcendental way.
transcen'dently, *adv.*, in a transcendent way.
transcend'ing, *pr.p.*, transcend.
transcribe', *v.t.*, to make an exact copy of.
transcribed', *p.p.*, transcribe.
transcri'ber, *n.*, a copyist; one who transcribes.
transcri'bing, *pr.p.*, transcribe.
tran'script, *n.*, an exact copy in writing.
transcrip'tion, *n.*, the act of transcribing; *i.q.* transcript.
transcrip'tive, *adj.*, transcribing.
tran'sept, *n.*, a part of a building that crosses another part at right angles.
transfer', *v.t.*, to remove from one place to another; to hand over; to reproduce, as in lithography.
trans'fer, *n.*, a handing over from one person to another; a reproduction of a picture by printing; a soldier drafted into another regiment, etc.
trans'ferable, *adj.*, able to be transferred.
transferee', *n.*, one to whom property is transferred by a deed of conveyance.

trans'ference, *n.*, the act of transferring; state of being transferred.

trans'feror, *n.*, one who transfers property.

transferred', *p.p.*, transfer.

transfer'rer, *n.*, one who transfers (in a general sense).

transfer'ring, *pr.p.*, transfer.

transfigura'tion, *n.*, the act of transfiguring; the change wrought by transfiguring; esp. Our Lord's Transfiguration on the Mount.

transfig'ure, *v.t.*, to change in form and appearance.

transfig'ured, *p.p.*, transfigure.

transfig'uring, *pr.p.*, transfigure.

transfix', *v.t.*, to pierce through.

transfixed', *p.p.*, transfix.

transfix'ing, *pr.p.*, transfix.

transfix'ion, *n.*, the act of transfixing; the state of being transfixed.

trans'fluent, *adj.*, flowing through or across.

transform', *v.t.*, to change completely.

transform'able, *adj.*, capable of transformation.

transforma'tion, *n.*, the act of transforming; state of being transformed.

transform'ative, *adj.*, producing transformation.

transformed', *p.p.*, transform.

transform'er, *n.*, one who transforms.

transform'ing, *pr.p.*, transform.

transfuse', *v.t.*, to remove (liquid) from one vessel to another; to convert into a new form; medically, to take blood from a person's veins and inject it into a patient

transfused', *p.p.*, transfuse.

transfu'sible, *adj.*, able to be transfused.

transfu'sing, *pr.p.*, transfuse.

transfu'sion, *n.*, the act of transfusing.

transfu'sive, *adj.*, effecting transfusion.

transgress', *v.t.*, to overstep; offend against; *v.i.*, to sin; offend.

transgressed', *p.p.*, transgress.

transgress'ing, *pr.p.*, transgress.

transgres'sion, *n.*, the act of transgressing; an offence; sin.

transgres'sional, *adj.*, rel. to transgression.

transgress'ive, *adj.*, transgressing; guilty.

transgress'or, *n.*, one who transgresses; a sinner.

tranship', *v.t.* and *i.*, to remove from one ship to another. Also *transship.*

tranship'ment, *n.*, the act or process of transhipping.

tran'sience, *n.*, *i.q.* transientness.

tran'sient, *adj.*, passing; ephemeral.

tran'siently, *adv.*, in a transient way.

tran'sientness, *n.*, the state or quality of being transient.

transil'ience, *n.*, the state of being transilient.

transil'iency, *n.*, transilience.

transil'ient, *adj.*, leaping or stretching from one supporting point to another

trans'it, *n.*, passage; conveyance; the apparent passage of a celestial body over the meridian of a place.

transi'tion, *n.*, the act of passing; the state of passing; change; period of change or of changing style; in music, change from key to key; or from major to relative minor and *vice versâ.*

transi'tional, *adj.*, pert. to, or in a stage of, transition. Often esp. applied to the architectural period when Norman was giving way to First Pointed.

trans'itive, *adj.*, acting directly upon an object (said of a verb which expresses an effect upon some person or thing and requires to be followed by the objective or accusative case).

trans'itorily, *adv.*, in a transitory way.

trans'itoriness, *n.*, the state or quality of being transitory.

trans'itory, *adj.*, *i.q.* transient; cursory.

transla'table, *adj.*, able to be translated.

translate', *v.t.*, to convey from one language to another; to remove or promote from one position (as a bishopric) to another; to change the form of; to carry away; to transform; to retransmit (a telegraphic message).

transla'ted, *p.p.*, translate.

transla'ting, *pr.p.*, translate.

transla'tion, *n.*, the act of translating; something translated; removal; nonrotating motion.

transla'tive, *adj.*, metaphorical.

transla'tor, *n.*, one who translates; an instrument converting one form of energy to another; a telegraph repeater; a cobbler who converts old shoes into new ones (*colloq.*). In pl., old shoes so converted (*colloq.*).

transla'tory, *adj.*, pert. to, of the nature of, translation.

translit'erate, *v.t.*, to reproduce a foreign word in the alphabetic characters of one's own language according to the sound.

transloca'tion, *n.*, the act of changing position.

translu'cence, *n.*, the state or quality of being translucent.

translu'cency, *n.*, *i.q.* translucence.

translu'cent, *adj.*, letting light through but not being quite transparent. (The word, however, is often used in the sense of transparent.)

translu'cid, *adj.*, *i.q.* translucent.

transmarine', *adj.*, situated across the sea.

trans'migrate, *v.i.*, to pass from one place or state to another.

trans'migrated, *p.p.*, transmigrate.

trans'migrating, *pr.p.*, transmigrate.

transmigra'tion, *n.*, the act of transmigrating, esp. the passing of a soul from one state or body into another; metempsychosis.

trans'migrator, *n.*, one who transmigrates.

transmi'gratory, *adj.*, passing from one state into another.

transmissibil'ity, *n.*, the state or quality of being transmissible.

transmis'sible, *adj.*, able to be transmitted.

transmis'sion, *n.*, the act of transmitting, esp. of allowing the passage of ether-waves through a medium.

transmis'sive, *adj.*, permitting transmission; derivable.

transmit', *v.t.*, to convey through or across; to hand down or on; to convey ether-waves through a medium.

transmit'tal, *n.*, the act of transmitting.

transmit'ted, *p.p.*, transmit.

transmit'ter, *n.*, one who, that which, transmits; a telegraphic instrument for transmitting messages; also a telephonic instrument.

transmit'tible, *adj.*, able to be transmitted.

transmit'ting, *pr.p.*, transmit.

transmutabil'ity, *n.*, the state or quality of being transmutable.

transmu'table, *adj.*, able to be transmuted.

transmuta'tion, *n.*, the act or result of transmuting, esp. the alchemistic pretended conversion of base metals into gold; change of one species into another.

transmuta'tionist, *n.*, one who holds the biological theory that one species can be changed into another; an alchemist.

transmute', *v.t.*, to change in form, nature, or substance.

transmu'ted, *p.p.*, transmute.

transmu'ter, *n.*, one who, that which, transmutes.

transmu'ting, *pr.p.*, transmute.

tran'som, *n.*, a horizontal wood or stone bar across a window or a doorhead; a beam across a ship; stern-post; a beam across a sawpit.

tran'somed, *adj.*, having a transome.

transpa'dane, *adj.*, situated on the other side of the Po (Padus).

transpa'rence, *n.*, the state or quality of being transparent.

transpa'rency, *n.*, *i.q.* transparence; lucidity; a picture, etc., on a thin canvas or muslin allowing the light to come through it; a photograph, etc., on glass to be seen with the light behind it.

transpa'rent, *adj.*, admitting the light through without diffusion; clear; easy to see through; frank.

transpierce', *v.t.*, to pierce through.

transpierced', *p.p.*, transpierce.

transpierc'ing, *pr.p.*, transpierce.

transpi'rable, *adj.*, able to be transpired.

transpira'tion, *n.*, the process of transpiring; exhalation.

transpi'ratory, *adj.*, exhaling.

transpire', *v.t.*, to emit through the excretory organs of the lungs or the skin; to exhale; *v.i.*, to be exhaled; (incorrectly and vulgarly) to happen; occur.

transpired', *p.p.*, transpire.

transpi'ring, *pr.p.*, transpire.

transplant', *v.t.*, to remove from one place and to plant in another; in surgery, to take tissue from one part of a person's body, or that of another body, and plant it where it is needed.

transplanta'tion, *n.*, the process of transplanting.

transplant'ed, *p.p.*, transplant.

transplant'er, *n.*, one who, that which, transplants.

transplant'ing, *pr.p.*, transplant.

transplend'ent, *adj.*, very resplendent.

transport', *v.t.*, to convey from one place to another; to take or send across, esp. across the sea; to carry away emotionally.

trans'port, *n.*, transportation; conveyance; a convict condemned to transportation; a ship to carry troops, stores, etc.; rapture.

transportabil'ity, *n.*, the state of being transportable.

transport'able, *adj.*, able to be transported.

transporta'tion, *n.*, the act of transporting; the state of being transported.

transport'ed, *p.p.*, transport.

transport'er, *n.*, one who transports.

transport'ing, *pr.p.*, transport.

transpo'sal, *n.*, the act of transposing; a piece of music written or played in a different key from the original.

transpose', *v.t.*, to change the position or order of; to write or play a piece of music in another key than the original.

transposed', *p.p.*, transpose.

transpo'sing, *pr.p.*, transpose.

transposi'tion, *n.*, the act of transposing; state of being transposed.

transposi'tional, *adj.*, rel. to transposition.

transpos'itive, *adj.*, causing or caused by transposition.

tranship', *v.t.*, to remove from one ship to another.

transship'ment, *n.*, the act of transshipping.

transshipped', *p.p.*, transship.

transship'ping, *pr.p.*, transship.

transubstan'tiate, *v.t.*, to change the substance of; esp. to change the substance (*i.e.*, the essential, non-material nature) of Bread and Wine in the Eucharist into the Body and Blood of Christ.

transubstan'tiated, *p.p.*, transubstantiate.

transubstan'tiating, *pr.p.*, transubstantiate.

transubstantia'tion, *n.*, the act of transubstantiating, esp. the change in the Eucharistic elements.

transuda'tion, *n.*, passage of fluid through pores or membranes.

transu'datory, *adj.*, rel. to transudation.

transude', *v.i.*, to pass through pores or membranes.

transu'ded, *p.p.*, transude.

transu'ding, *pr.p.*, transude.

transvec'tion, *n.*, the act of transporting.

transver'sal, *adj.*, transverse; *n.*, a straight line that cuts a system of lines.

transverse', *v.t.*, to transpose; *adj.*, lying across or in a crosswise relation; *n.*, anything transverse; a muscle so named.

transverse'ly, *adv.*, in a transverse direction; crosswise.

transvola'tion, *n.*, the act of flying across.

trap, *v.t.*, to snare; take in a trap; to prevent the escape of (liquid, gas, etc.); *v.i.*, to snare game; *n.*, a snare; gin; pitfall; an arrangement within a pipe to prevent the escape of foul smell, noxious gas, etc.; a carriage (*colloq.*).

trapan', *v.t.*, *i.q.* trepan.

trapanned', *p.p.*, trapan.

trapan'ning, *pr.p.*, trapan.

trap'-door', *n.*, a hinged door in a roof, floor, deck, etc.

trapeze', *n.*, a bar hung from two ropes and used by athletes, acrobats, etc.

trape'zian, *adj.*, with opposed trapeziform faces.

trape'ziform, *adj.*, like a trapezium.

trape'zium, *n.*, a quadrilateral figure having no two sides parallel.

trapezohe'dron, *n.*, a solid with all its faces bounded by trapezoids.

trap'ezoid, *n.*, a quadrilateral plane figure with two sides parallel but not the others.

trapezoid'al, *adj.*, like a trapezoid.

trap'pean, *adj.*, pert. to trap rock.

trapped, *p.p.*, trap.

trap'per, *n.*, one who traps; a hunter of fur-bearing game; a miner whose duty it is to look after the air-doors.

trap'ping, *pr.p.*, trap; *n.*, the trade of supplying traps; the pursuit of furred game; harness; outward adornment.

trap'pings, *n.*, pl. of trapping; in the sense of harness, adornment.

Trap'pist, *n.*, a member of the extremely severe Order of Trappists, a reformed Cistercian Order. Among its most ascetic requirements is the obligation of perpetual silence.

trap'pous, *adj.*, *i.q.* trappean.

trap'-rock, *n.*, an igneous rock useful for road-making and railway ballast.

traps, *n. pl.*, belongings; luggage.

trash, *n.*, nonsense; worthless stuff.

trash'y, *adj.*, worthless; rubbishy.

trass, *n.*, an earth used in the making of hydraulic cement.

traumat'ic, *adj.*, pert. to wounds.

trav'ail, *n.*, labour; toil; labour in childbirth; anguish; *v.i.*, to labour.

trav'ailing, *pr.p.*, travail.

trav'el, *v.t.*, to pass over in travelling;

to convey (books, articles, etc.,) for orders; *v.i.*, to journey; to move; to go about for a business house; *n.*, journeying. In pl., a story of wanderings.

trav'el(l)ed, *p.p.*, travel; *adj.*, having visited many countries.

trav'el(l)er, *n.*, one who, that which, travels; one who has visited many countries; one who travels for a business house.

trav'el(l)ing, *pr.p.*, travel.

trav'ersable, *adj.*, able to be traversed.

trav'erse, *v.t.*, to go across or over; to wander over; to question; to oppose; *v.i.*, to swivel; *n.*, a crosspiece; transom, etc.; a gallery across a building; a screened bench; a ship's zig-zag course.

trav'ersed, *p.p.*, traverse.

trav'erser, *n.*, one who traverses.

trav'erse-table, *n.*, a nautical table for dealing with traverses; a railway turn-table.

trav'ersing, *pr.p.*, traverse.

trav'ertine, trav'ertin, *n.*, a porous yellow Italian rock, quarried for building purposes.

trav'estied, *p.p.*, travesty.

trav'esty, *n.*, a caricature; ridiculous imitation; *v.t.*, to imitate in an absurd way and make ridiculous.

trav'estying, *pr.p.*, travesty.

trav'is, *n.*, a bar; beam; transom. Also *trevis*.

trawl, *n.*, a drag net; *v.t.*, to fish with a trawl.

trawled, *p.p.*, trawl.

trawl'er, *n.*, one who trawls; a boat for trawling.

trawl'ing, *pr.p.*, trawl; *n.*, the business of fishing with a trawl.

trawl'-net, *n.*, a large bag net for trawling or dragging.

tray, *n.*, a flat portable, shallow vessel for carrying things on; a movable shelf in a trunk.

treach'erous, *adj.*, traitorous; betraying; false.

treach'ery, *n.*, betrayal; perfidy.

trea'cle, *n.*, syrup derived from sugar.

tread, *n.*, the planting of one's foot on the ground; manner of walking; sound of feet; upper surface of a stair; the part of a wheel that touches the ground or a rail; a male bird's act of copulation; *v.t.*, to walk on; press with the feet; crush; copulate with (said of the male bird); *v.i.*, to step.

tread'er, *n.*, one who treads.

tread'ing, *pr.p.*, tread.

tread'le, *n.*, a lever worked by the foot; *v.i.*, to operate a treadle.

tread'mill, *n.*, a mechanical device for obtaining rotation by means of walking up steps.

trea'son, *n.*, active disloyalty to the State; treachery.

trea'sonable, *adj.*, guilty of treason; involving treason.

treas'ure, *n.*, accumulated and hoarded wealth; a highly valued possession; *v.t.*, to hoard; to value very highly; to preserve.

treas'ured, *p.p.*, treasure.

treas'urer, *n.*, an official who receives and pays out the money of a household, society, etc.

treas'ure-trove, *n.*, treasure of unknown ownership found anywhere.

treas'uring, *pr.p.*, treasure.

treas'ury, *n.*, a repository of treasure; the department of public finance and revenue.

treat, *n.*, something to give enjoyment; *v.t.*, to act or behave towards; deal with; entertain; *v.i.*, to arrange terms.

treat'able, *adj.*, able to be treated.

treat'ed, *p.p.*, treat.

treat'er, *n.*, one who treats.

treat'ing, *pr.p.*, treat.

trea'tise, *n.*, a tract; essay on a special subject.

treat'ment, *n.*, the act or manner of dealing with a person or thing.

treat'y, *n.*, an arrangement of terms between nations or persons.

treb'le, *adj.*, threefold; soprano; *n.*, the treble voice or part (*mus.*); *v.t.*, to multiply by three; *v.i.*, to increase threefold.

treb'le clef, *n.*, the uppermost clef (*mus.*).

treb'led, *p.p.*, treble.

treb'ling, *pr.p.*, treble.

treb'ly, *adv.*, threefold.

treb'uchet, *n.*, an old military engine for hurling heavy missiles; a scale-balance that tilts; a small tilting-trap for birds.

tree, *n.*, a branching plant growing from one stem; the Cross; *v.t.*, to compel to take refuge in a tree; to place in an embarrassing position.

tree'-frog, *n.*, an arboreal amphibian.

tree'-nail, *n.*, a wooden timber-fastener.

tref'le, *n.*, *i.q.* trefoil.

tre'foil, *n.*, a three-leaved plant, such as the clover; an architectural ornament so named.

treil'lage, *n.*, an espalier.

trek, *v.i.*, to migrate in wagons; *n.*, a migration. (A Dutch S. African word.)

trel'lis, *n.*, latticework for fencing, etc.; *v.t.*, to cover with trellis work.

trel'lised, *p.p.*, trellis.

trel'lising, *pr.p.*, trellis.

trel'lis-work, *n.*, wooden laths arranged crosswise.

treman'do, *adv.*, trembling (*mus.*).

trem'ble, *v.i.*, to quake with fear, cold, etc.; to quaver; *n.*, a fit of shaking.

trem'bled, *p.p.*, tremble.

trem'bler, *n.*, one who trembles.

trem'bling, *pr.p.*, tremble.

Tremel'la, *n.*, a genus of fungi of jelly-like substance.

tremen'dous, *adj.*, alarming; terrible; amazing.

tremen'dously, *adv.*, in tremendous degree.

trem'olite, *n.*, a species of hornblende.

trem'olo, *n.*, a quavering effect produced by the voice, or mechanically (*mus.*).

trem'or, *n.*, a shaking fit; a thrill; a seismic wave.

trem'ulous, *adj.*, trembling; quavering; timid.

trem'ulousness, *n.*, the state of being tremulous.

trench, *n.*, an extended excavation; a drain; a dug-out; *v.t.*, to cultivate with trenches; to excavate; *v.i.*, to encroach.

trench'ant, *adj.*, cutting; severe.

trenched, *p.p.*, trench.

trench'er, *n.*, one who trenches; a wooden plate; a college cap.

trench'erman, *n.*, one blest with a good appetite.

trench'ing, *pr.p.*, trench.

trend, *n.*, tendency in a certain direction; bearing; *v.i.*, to tend in a certain direction.

trend'ed, *p.p.*, trend.

trend'ing, *pr.p.*, trend.

tren'tal, *n.*, thirty things in a series; a daily succession of thirty masses.

trepan', *v.t.*, to perforate (the skull); *n.*, the surgical instrument used in trepanning. Also *trephine* and *trapan*.

trepang', *n.*, bêche-de-mer; a sea-slug.

trepanned', *p.p.*, trepan.

trepan'ner, *n.*, one who trepans.

trepan'ning, *pr.p.*, trepan; *n.*, the surgical operation of trepanning.

trephine', *n.* and *v.t.*, *i.q.* trepan.

trepida'tion, *n.*, sudden alarm; state of panic.

tres'pass, *n.*, a transgression; sin; intrusion in another's domain; offence; *v.i.*, to transgress; intrude into another's domain; offend against custom, etc.

tres'passed, *p.p.*, trespass.

tres'passer, *n.*, one who trespasses.

tres'passing, *pr.p.*, trespass.

tress, *n.*, a lock of hair.

tressed, *adj.*, having tresses.

tress'ure, *n.*, a heraldic border.

tress'ured, *adj.*, bordered with a tressure.

tress'y, *adj.*, covered with tresses.

tres'tle, *n.*, a support; the movable underpart of a temporary table.

tres'tle-board, *n.*, a designing-board for a draughtsman.

tres'tle-tree, *n.*, a wooden support of the cross-trees (*naut.*).

tret, *n.*, a rebate on the price of certain commodities as compensation for damage in transport.

trev'et, *n.*, *i.q.* trivet.

trey, *n.*, a three in dice or cards.

tri'able, *adj.*, able to be tried.

tri'ad, *n.*, a group of three; the common chord of a tone, its third and fifth (*mus.*); in chemistry, an atom, etc., with a combining power of three.

tri'al, *n.*, putting to the proof; test; a trying affliction; examination in a court of law.

tri'alogue, *n.*, a conversation among three speakers.

trian'drian, *adj.*, with three equal stamens.

trian'drous, *adj.*, *i.q.* triandrian.

tri'angle, *n.*, a plain three-sided figure with three angles; a triangular musical instrument of percussion; a military instrument of punishment.

tri'angled, *adj.*, *i.q.* triangular.

trian'gular, *adj.*, in the form of a triangle.

triangular'ity, *n.*, the state or quality of being triangular.

trian'gularly, *adv.*, in a triangular way.

trian'gulate, *v.t.*, to survey by dividing into triangles.

trian'gulated, *p.p.*, triangulate.

trian'gulating, *pr.p.*, triangulate.

triangula'tion, *n.*, the process of triangulating; a survey.

tri'archy, *n.*, a province governed by three persons; the rule of three persons.

Tri'as, tri'as, *n.*, the lowest division of the Mesozoic period.

Trias'sic, *adj.*, pert. to the Trias; *n.*, *i.q.* trias.

tri'bal, *adj.*, pert. to a tribe or tribes.
tribe, *n.*, a group of related families under one chief; a political group; an ethnical division.
trib'let, *n.*, a mandrel for forging rings, nuts, etc.
tribom'eter, *n.*, an apparatus for measuring sliding motion.
trib'rach, *n.*, a metrical foot consisting of three short syllables.
tribula'tion, *n.*, great trouble; affliction.
tribu'nal, *n.*, a seat of authority; a court of justice.
trib'unary, *adj.*, pert. to a tribune.
trib'unate, *n.*, the office of a tribune; term of a tribune's office.
trib'une, *n.*, an old Roman officer chosen by the people as the guardian of their rights and liberties; a platform.
tribuni'cial, *adj.*, *i.q.* tribunary.
trib'utarily, *adv.*, in a tributary way.
trib'utary, *adj.*, paying tribute; contributing; *n.*, a nation or prince in subjection to another; a smaller river running into a larger one.
trib'ute, *n.*, tax; impost; acknowledgment.
tricap'sular, *adj.*, having three capsules.
trice, *n.*, an instant of time; *v.t.*, to fasten up.
tricen'tenary, *adj.*, pert. to a period of three hundred years; *n.*, the commemoration of an event of three hundred years ago.
trichi'na, *n.*, a parasite in swine and human beings.
trichino'sis, *n.*, a disease produced by the trichina.
tri'chord, *adj.*, having three strings; *n.*, an instrument of three strings; a pianoforte having three strings to each note.
trichot'omous, *adj.*, pert. to trichotomy.
trichot'omy, *n.*, division into three.
trick, *n.*, a deception; dodge; imposition; piece of legerdemain; a completed single round in a game of cards; *v.t.*, to deceive; impose upon; adorn.
tricked, *p.p.*, trick.
trick'ery, *n.*, deceit; imposition; stratagem.
trick'ing, *pr.p.*, trick.
trick'ish, *adj.*, *i.q.* tricky.
trick'ishness, *n.*, the quality of being trickish.
trick'le, *v.t.*, to cause to flow in a thin stream or in drops; *v.i.*, to flow in a thin stream or in drops; *n.*, a thin flow.
trick'led, *p.p.*, trickle.
trick'ling, *pr.p.*, trickle.
trick'ster, *n.*, one who plays tricks.
trick'sy, *adj.*, up to tricks; pretty.
trick-track, *n.*, an old game so named.
trick'y, *adj.*, full of tricks; puzzling; difficult.
triclinate, *adj.*, asymmetric; *i.q.* triclinic.
triclin'ic, *adj.*, with three unequal axes intersecting obliquely.
triclin'ium, *n.*, the Roman arrangement of a dining-room, having three couches arranged as three sides of a square or oblong.
tricoc'cous, *adj.*, with three carpels.
tri'colour, *n.*, a flag in three colours arranged in equal stripes.
tri'coloured, *adj.*, having three colours.
tricor'poral, *adj.*, having three bodies.
tricus'pid, *adj.*, having three cusps.
tricus'pidate, *adj.*, three-pointed.
tri'cycle, *n.*, a three-wheeled cycle; *v.i.*, to ride a tricycle.
tridac'tylous, *adj.*, having three toes or fingers.
tri'dent, *n.*, a three-pronged sceptre; the emblem of Neptune and of sovereignty over the sea.
triden'tate, *adj.*, three-pronged.
Triden'tine, *adj.*, rel. to the Council of Trent.
tridiapa'son, *n.*, a triple octave.
tried, *p.p.*, try; *adj.*, tested; proved; afflicted.
trien'nial, *adj.*, occurring every three years; lasting for three years.
trien'nially, *adv.*, once every three years.
tri'er, *n.*, one who tries; a trial.
tri'erarch, *n.*, the commander of an ancient Greek trireme; one who performed the *leitourgia* or liturgy of supplying a trireme to the State.
trifa'rious, *adj.*, arranged in three upright rows.
tri'fid, *adj.*, split into three.
trifist'ulary, *adj.*, with three pipes.
tri'fle, *n.*, something of little or no value; a sweet dish; *v.i.*, to dally; to be frivolous; *v.t.*, to waste in idleness.
tri'fled, *p.p.*, trifle.
tri'fler, *n.*, one who trifles.
tri'fling, *pr.p.*, trifle; *adj.*, of no importance.
tri'flingly, *adv.*, in a trifling way.
triflo'ral, *adj.*, bearing three flowers.
triflo'rous, *adj.*, *i.q.* trifloral.
trifo'liate, *adj.*, having three leaves.
trifo'liated, *adj.*, *i.q.* trifoliate.

trifo'liolate, *adj.*, with three leaves.

Trifo'lium, *n.*, a botanical genus containing the clovers.

tri'foly, *n.*, *i.q.* trefoil (*obs.*).

trifo'rium, *n.*, a gallery in the space between the inner vault of an aisle and the outer roof.

tri'form, *adj.*, in three divisions.

triform'ity, *n.*, the state of being triform.

tri'furcated, *adj.*, with three forks.

trig, *adj.*, neat; trim; *v.t.*, to stop; skid.

trig'amous, *adj.*, pert. to trigamy; bearing three kinds of flowers.

trig'amy, *n.*, the state of being married three times, or of having three wives or husbands at once.

trigged, *p.p.*, trig.

trig'ger, *n.*, the contrivance in a pistol lock or gun lock by which the hammer is caused to act.

trig'ging, *pr.p.*, trig.

tri'glyph, *n.*, a Doric frieze ornament vertically grooved, alternating with the metopes.

tri'gon, *n.*, a triangle.

trig'onal, *adj.*, triangular.

trigonomet'ric, *adj.*, pert. to trigonometry.

trigonom'etry, *n.*, a department of mathematics rel. to the angles and sides of triangles. [graph.

tri'gram, *n.*, *i.q.* tri-

trigrammat'ic, *adj.*, containing three letters or groups of letters.

tri'graph, *n.*, a group of three letters for one sound.

Trigyn'ia, *n. pl.*, Linnaeus's third order in his plant system.

trihe'dral, *adj.*, with three intersecting surfaces as sides.

trihe'dron, *n.*, a three-sided figure.

trilat'eral, *adj.*, three-sided.

trilin'gual, *adj.*, speaking three languages.

trilit'eral, *adj.*, containing three letters.

tri'lith, *n.*, *i.q.* trilithon.

tri'lithon, *n.*, a monumental structure of two upright stones supporting a horizontal stone.

trill, *n.*, a tremulous, quavering sound; a musical shake; *v.t.*, to sound with a quaver; to pipe; to roll (certain sounds, as the *r*); *v.i.*, to sound tremulously.

trilled, *p.p.*, trill.

trill'ing, *pr.p.*, trill.

tril'lion, *n.*, a cardinal number, a million million millions. In France and elsewhere, a million millions.

trilo'bate, *adj.*, having three lobes.

tri'lobed, *adj.*, *i.q.* trilobate.

tri'lobite, *n.*, one of the trilobites, a very early and common order of fossils.

triloc'ular, *adj.*, with three cells.

tril'ogy, *n.*, a series of three tragedies illustrating in order three stages in the same story.

trim, *adj.*, tidy; spruce; *n.*, state or condition as regards being in good order; *v.t.*, to put in good order; to adjust; to make shapely by cutting off ragged edges; to clip; to prune; to adorn.

trimes'ter, *n.*, a quarterly period.

trimes'tral, *adj.*, quarterly; every three months.

trimes'trial, *adj.*, *i.q.* trimestral.

trim'eter, *n.*, a verse of three metrical feet; or of trimetrical lines.

trimet'ric, *adj.*, pert. to trimeter.

trim'ly, *adv.*, in a trim way.

trimmed, *p.p.*, trim.

trim'mer, *n.*, one who trims; a time-serving person who changes sides when it suits his purpose.

trim'ming, *pr.p.*, trim; *n.*, decoration.

trim'ness, *n.*, the state or quality of being trim.

tri'nal, *adj.*, rel. to three.

trine, *adj.*, consisting of three; *n.*, a triad.

trinerv'ate, *adj.*, three-nerved.

trinerved', *adj.*, *i.q.* trinervate.

trin'gle, *n.*, a rod for curtain-rings.

Trinita'rian, *adj.*, rel. to the Holy Trinity and Trinitarian doctrine.

Trinita'rianism, *n.*, belief in the Holy and Undivided Trinity.

Trin'ity, *n.*, the union of Three Persons in One Godhead.

trin'ity, *n.*, a group of three.

trin'ket, *n.*, a little jewel or ornament of no great value.

trin'ketry, *n.*, trinkets collectively.

trinoc'tial, *adj.*, lasting three nights.

trino'mial, *adj.*, involving three terms.

tri'o, *n.*, a group of three; a musical composition for three voices or instruments; a special musical form.

tri'olet, *n.*, an eight-lined stanza of peculiar construction.

tri'onal, *n.*, a narcotic drug.

tri'or, *i.q.* trier (*leg.*).

trip, *n.*, a short, quick step; a slip; an error; a short excursion; *v.i.*, to step quickly; to slip; to err; to go for a short excursion.

tripar'tite, *adj.*, in three parts.

triparti'tion, *n.*, division into three parts.

tripe, *n.*, a cow's stomach.

trip'edal, *adj.*, on three feet.

tripen'nate, *adj.*, three times pinnate.

tripet'alous, *adj.*, having three petals.

trip'-hammer, *n.*, a machine hammer.

tri'phone, *n.*, a Pitman shorthand sign for three vowels.

triph'thong, *n.*, a union of three vowels.

triphthon'gal, *adj.*, of the nature of a triphthong.

triph'ylline, *adj.*, *s.q.* triphyllous.

triphyl'lous, *adj.*, with three leaves.

trip'le, *adj.*, threefold; three times over; *v.i.*, to increase threefold.

trip'led, *p.p.*, triple.

trip'let, *n.*, three taken together; in pl., three children at a birth.

trip'licate, *adj.*, threefold; *n.*, a third example of the same original.

trip'licate, *v.t.*, to increase threefold.

triplica'tion, *n.*, the act or result of triplicating.

triplic'ity, *n.*, the state or quality of being threefold.

trip'ling, *pr.p.*, triple.

tri'pod, *n.*, a three-legged stool or table; the sacred seat of the oracular Pythoness at Delphi.

tripo'dian, *n.*, an ancient musical instrument.

trip'ody, *n.*, a verse containing three feet.

trip'oli, *n.*, rotten stone.

tri'pos, *n.*, a list of persons gaining honours in the University examinations at Cambridge.

tripped, *p.p.*, trip.

trip'per, *n.*, one who trips; a tourist.

trip'ping, *pr.p.*, trip.

trip'pingly, *adv.*, in a tripping way.

trip'sis, *n.*, massage.

trip'tote, *n.*, a noun having only three cases.

trip'tych, *n.*, a picture or writing-tablet in three compartments, of which the two outer ones usually fold over the middle one.

tri'reme, *n.*, an ancient Greek war galley with three banks of oars.

trirhomboid'al, *adj.*, with three rhombic faces.

Trisag'ion, *n.*, an ancient hymn of the Eastern liturgies, not to be confused with the Sanctus.

trisect', *v.t.*, to cut equally into three parts.

trisect'ed, *p.p.*, trisect.

trisect'ing, *pr.p.*, trisect.

trisec'tion, *n.*, the act or result of trisecting.

trisep'alous, *adj.*, having three sepals.

trisper'mous, *adj.*, three-seeded.

triste, *adj.*, sad (*Fr.*).

trisul'cate, *adj.*, with three grooves.

trisyllab'ic, *adj.*, containing three syllables.

trisyl'lable, *n.*, a word of three syllables.

trite, *adj.*, worn; threadbare; commonplace.

trite'ly, *adv.*, in a trite way.

trite'ness, *n.*, the quality of being trite.

tri'theism, *n.*, the doctrine that there are three distinct Gods in the Trinity.

tri'theist, *adj.*, a believer in tritheism.

tritheist'ic, *adj.*, pert. to tritheism.

Tri'ton, *n.*, a marine demigod; a genus of molluscs; a newt.

tri'tone, *n.*, an interval of three full tones; augmented fourth (*mus.*).

trit'urable, *adj.*, able to be triturated.

trit'urate, *v.t.*, to crush; to reduce to powder.

trit'urated, *p.p.*, triturate.

trit'urating, *pr.p.*, triturate.

tritura'tion, *n.*, the act or result of triturating.

tri'umph, *n.*, a State ceremonial of rejoicing over a victory; victory; elation over a success; *v.i.*, to rejoice; to celebrate a victory.

trium'phal, *adj.*, of the nature of a triumph.

trium'phant, *adj.*, rejoicing over a conquest.

trium'phantly, *adv.*, in a triumphant way.

tri'umphed, *p.p.*, triumph.

tri'umpher, *n.*, one who triumphs.

tri'umphing, *pr.p.*, triumph.

trium'vir, *n.*, one of three colleagues in office (*triumviri*) in ancient Rome.

trium'viral, *adj.*, pert. to triumviri.

trium'virate, *n.*, the office of the triumviri; term of office.

tri'une, *adj.*, three in one.

triu'nity, *n.*, the unity of the Three Persons of the Blessed Trinity.

tri'valve, *adj.*, with three valves; *n.*, a three-valved shell.

trivalv'ular, *adj.*, having three valves.

triv'et, *n.*, an attachment to a grate for holding a kettle, etc.

triv'ial, *adj.*, trifling; ordinary; commonplace.

trivial'ity, *n.*, the state or quality of being trivial.

triv'ium, *n.*, the mediaeval curriculum comprising grammar, logic, and rhetoric. (This, with the *quadrivium*, i.e., geometry, astronomy, arithmetic and music, made up the complete system of the seven liberal arts.)

triweek'ly, *adj.*, occurring three times in the week.

tro'car, *n.*, a surgical draining instrument.

trocha'ic, *adj.*, pert. to a trochee.

trochan'ter, *n.*, a bony process on the upper thigh.

tro'chee, *n.*, a metrical foot consisting of a long syllable followed by a short one.

tro'chil, *n.*, *s.q.* trochilus.

troch'ilus, *n.*, the crocodile bird.

tro'chings, *n. pl.*, small antler-points.

troch'lea, *n.*, a pulley-like muscle.

tro'choid, *adj.*, pivotal.

trod, *p.t.*, tread.

trodd'en, *p.p.*, tread.

trog'lodyte, *n.*, a cave-dweller.

Tro'jan, *adj.*, pert. to Troy; *n.*, a native of Troy.

troll, *n.*, a fabulous giant; a powerful dwarf; a form of vocal music such as a catch; a fishing-reel; *v.t.*, to sing in the form of a troll; *v.i.*, to fish with a running line.

trolled, *p.p.*, troll.

trol'ley, *n.*, a special form of truck.

troll'ing, *pr.p.*, troll.

trol'lop, *n.*, a slut.

trom'bone, *n.*, a musical wind instrument of brass.

troop, *n.*, a host; a cavalry unit; a troupe; *v.i.*, to march in a multitude; to assemble in a large number; *v.t.*, to carry the colours (military) in ceremonious procession.

trooped, *p.p.*, troop.

troop'er, *n.*, a private soldier of cavalry; a troopship.

troop'ing, *pr.p.*, troop.

troop'ship, *n.*, a ship that conveys troops.

trope, *n.*, a figurative expression.

troph'ic, *adj.*, rel. to nutrition.

tro'phied, *adj.*, containing trophies.

tro'phy, *n.*, a memento of some achievement.

trop'ic, *adj.*, one of two circular areas N. and S. of the equator, where the sun's course appears to turn.

trop'ical, *adj.*, rel. to, bel. to, the tropics; figurative.

tro'pist, *n.*, one who makes use of tropes.

tropolog'ical, *adj.*, pert. to tropology.

tropol'ogy, *n.*, figurative expression.

trot, *n.*, a pace between walking and galloping or running; a short walk (*colloq.*); *v.i.*, to go at a trotting pace.

troth, *n.*, pledge; word of honour.

trot'ted, *p.p.*, trot.

trot'ter, *n.*, one who trots, esp. a horse; a pig's or sheep's foot.

trot'ting, *pr.p.*, trot.

trottoir', *n.*, the footpath (*Fr.*).

trou'badour, *n.*, an old French lyric poet.

troub'le, *n.*, distress; worry; painstaking; *v.t.*, to cause distress or wrong to; to entail labour upon; *v.i.*, to be painstaking.

troub'led, *p.p*, trouble

troub'ler, *n.*, one who troubles.

troub'lesome, *adj.*, annoying; worrying.

troub'ling, *pr.p.*, trouble.

troub'lous, *adj.*, disquieting; anxious.

trough, *n.*, a long, narrow tank for holding liquid; anything like a trough.

trounce, *v.t.*, to flog; to dress down with scolding or argument.

trounced, *p.p.*, trounce.

troun'cing, *pr.p.*, trounce.

troupe, *n.*, a theatrical or performing company.

trou'sers, *n. pl.*, a divided garment from the waist to the feet.

trousseau', *n.*, a bride's outfit of clothes.

trout, *n.*, a fresh-water fish.

trouvère, *n.*, one of the epic poets of mediaeval France.

tro'ver, *n.*, the act of finding lost property; a legal suit for the recovery of found property.

trow, *n.*, to think; believe.

trow'el, *n.*, an implement with which mortar is spread.

trow'el(l)ed, *adj.*, laid on with a trowel.

troy' weight, *n.*, a weight used in the jewellery and goldsmith's business; *adj.*, weighing 12 oz. to the lb.

tru'ancy, *n.*, playing the truant.

tru'ant, *n.*, one who shirks school or business; *adj.*, pert. to a truant; idle.

truce, *n.*, a suspension of hostilities.

truck, *n.*, a vehicle for goods; a railway goods-wagon; barter; *v.i.*, to barter goods.

truck'age, *n.*, cost of carriage by truck trucks collectively.

trucked, *p.p.*, truck.

truck'er, *n.*, one who trucks.

truck'ing, *pr.p.*, truck.

truck'le, *n.*, a small roller; *v.i.*, to give in in a servile way.

truck'le-bed, *n.*, a low bed on wheels that could be trundled under a taller bed when not in use.

truck'led, *p.p.*, truckle

truck'ler, *n.*, one who truckles.

truck'ling, *pr.p.*, truckle.

truck'man, *n.*, a man in charge of a truck.

tru'culence, *n.*, savage roughness; ferocity.

tru'culent, *adj.*, savage; ferocious.

trudge, *v.i.*, to tramp on foot.

trudged, *p.p.*, trudge.

trudg'ing, *pr.p.*, trudge.

true, *adj.*, veracious; correct; right.

tru'er, *adj.*, *comp.* of true.

tru'est, *adj.*, *super.* of true.

truf'fle, *n.*, a much appreciated fungus growing underground.

trug, *n.*, a wooden basket.

tru'ism, *n.*, a truth that no one can dispute.

trull, *n.*, a lewd woman.

tru'ly, *adv.*, in truth; sincerely.

trump, *n.*, a trumpet; a winning card; a suit superior to any other suit; *v.i.*, to take with a trump card; *v.i.*, to play out a trump.

trumped, *p.p.*, trump.

trump'ery, *n.*, cheap stuff; *adj.*, cheap; rubbishy.

trump'et, *n.*, a brass or silver musical instrument; *v.t.*, to proclaim aloud; to blazon abroad; *v.i.*, make trumpet-like sound (as elephant).

trump'eted, *p.p.*, trumpet.

trump'eter, *n.*, a performer on the trumpet; a species of pigeon.

trump'et - tongued, *adj.*, loud-voiced.

trump'ing, *pr.p.*, trump.

trun'cate, *adj.*, *i.q.* truncate; *v.t.*, to cut; lop.

trun'cated, *p.p.*, truncate; lopped.

trun'cating, *pr.p.*, truncate.

trunca'tion, *n.*, the act of truncating; state of being truncated.

trun'cheon, *n.*, a short staff; bâton; *v.t.*, to beat with a truncheon.

trun'dle, *v.t.*, to roll or push along on low wheels; *n.*, a truck.

trun'dle-bed, *n.*, *i.q.* truckle-bed.

trun'dled, *p.p.*, trundle.

trun'dling, *pr.p.*, trundle.

trunk, *n.*, a tree-stem; an animal's body apart from limbs and head; a proboscis; a box for traveling purposes.

trunk'-*call*, *n.*, a telephone message on a trunk line.

trunk'hose, *n.*, an old type of large breeches.

trunk'line, *n.*, a main railway, etc., line.

trun'nel, *n.*, a wooden nail. Also *treenail.*

trun'nion, *n.*, one of the projections from the sides of a cannon.

trun'nioned, *adj.*, provided with a trunnion.

truss, *n.*, a support; a surgical support in hernia cases; a bundle (as of hay); *v.t.*, to bind; tuck up.

trussed, *p.p.*, truss.

truss'el, *n.*, a tressel; bundle.

truss'ing, *pr.p.*, truss.

trust, *n.*, belief; confidence; faith; a combination for establishing a monopoly; the holding of a person's property in his behalf by another person.

trust'deed, *n.*, a document creating a trust.

trust'ed, *p.p.*, trust; *adj.*, confidential; to be relied on.

trustee', *n.*, one who takes the charge of another's property.

trustee'ship, *n.*, the office of a trustee.

trust'er, *n.*, one who trusts.

trust'ful, *adj.*, confiding; full of trust.

trust'fully, *adv.*, in a trustful way.

trust'ier, *adj.*, *comp.* of trusty.

trust'iest, *adj.*, *super.* of trusty.

trust'iness, *n.*, the quality of being trusty.

trust'ing, *pr.p.*, trust; *adj.*, confiding.

trust'ingly, *adv.*, in a trusting way.

trust'worthiness, *adj.*, the state or quality of being trustworthy.

trust'worthy, *adj.*, worthy of confidence.

trust'y, *adj.*, to be relied on; loyal.

***truth*,** *n.*, the quality of being true; that which is true; loyalty.

truth'ful, *adj.*, loyal to truth; speaking the truth.

truth'fully, *adv.*, in a truthful way.

***truth*'fulness,** *n.*, the quality of being truthful.

truth'less, *adj.*, false.

truths, *n. pl.*, accepted or revealed beliefs.

trutta'ceous, *adj.*, rel. to trout.

try, *v.t.*, to attempt; make trial of; judge; vex; refine; *n.*, an attempt.

try'ing, *pr.p.*, try; *adj.*, vexatious.

try'sail, *n.*, a sail on the fore and main masts.

tryst, *n.*, an appointed meeting.

tryst'ing, *adv.*, pert. to a rendezvous.

Tsar, *n.*, the title of the Russian Emperor. Also *Czar; Tzar.*

Tsarit'sa, *n.*, the Russian Empress. Also *Czaritsa; Tzarina.*

tset'se, *n.*, a fly that destroys horses and oxen in S. Africa.

tub, *n.*, an open vessel; a bath (*colloq.*); *v.t.*, to practise oarsmen; to give a bath to (*colloq.*).

tu'ba, *n.*, a trumpet (*Lat.*).

tu'bal, *adj.*, rel. to tubes and ducts.

tub'bing, *pr.p.*, tub.

tub'by, *adj.*, tub-shaped; short and stout.

tube, *n.*, a cylindrical pipe or passage.

tubed, *adj.*, having a tube.

tu'ber, *n.*, a plant with a thick stem underground.
tu'bercle, *n.*, a small tuber; a morbid growth on tissue.
tu'bercled, *adj.*, having a tubercle.
tuber'cular, *adj.*, *i.q.* tubercled.
tuber'culate, *adj.*, *i.q.* tubercled.
tuber'culin, *n.*, a liquid preparation from tubercle bacilli.
tuberculo'sis, *n.*, the disease of tubercle.
tuber'culous, *adj.*, pert. to tubercle.
tuberif'erous, *adj.*, producing tubers.
tu'berose, *n.*, a strong scented tuberous plant.
tuberos'ity, *n.*, the state or quality of being tuberous.
tu'berous, *adj.*, consisting of tubers.
tu'biform, *adj.*, like a tube.
tu'bing, *n.*, material of which tubes are made.
tu'bipore, *n.*, a kind of coral.
tu'bular, *adj.*, like a tube; composed of tubes.
tu'bule, *n.*, a small tube.
tu'buliform, *adj.*, like a tubule.
tu'bulous, *adj.*, containing tubules.
tuck, *n.*, a pleat; a fold; a roll of drum; food (*slang*); *v.t.*, to put a tuck in; to wrap closely.
tucked, *p.p.*, tuck.
tuck'er, *n.*, a frilling on a woman's dress.
tuck'et, *n.*, a roll of drum.
tuck'ing, *pr.p.*, tuck.
Tu'dor, *adj.*, rel. to the Tudor dynasty; *n.*, one of the Tudor family; the architectural style of the Tudor era.
Tues'day, *n.*, the third day of the week.
tu'fa, *n.*, a soft kind of stone; scoria.
tufa'ceous, *adj.*, like, consisting of, tufa.
tuff, *n.*, *i.q.* tufa.
tuft, *n.*, hair or other substances gathered into a bunch; *v.t.*, to make tufts of; to cover with tufts.
tuft'ed, *adj.*, covered with tufts.
tuft'-hunter, *n.*, one who runs after persons with titles.
tuft'-hunting, *adj.*, running after persons with titles.
tuft'ing, *pr.p.*, tuft.
tuft'y, *adj.*, wooded.
tug, *n.*, a pull; a vessel that tows other vessels; *v.t.*, to pull; draw; tow.
tug'boat, *n.*, a towboat.
tugged, *p.p.*, tug.
tug'ger, *n.*, one who, that which, tugs.
tug'ging, *pr.p.*, tug.
tui'tion, *n.*, teaching, instruction; a tutor's profession.
tui'tionary, *adj.*, pert. to tuition.
tu'lip, *n.*, a flowering bulb.
tu'lipist, *n.*, a grower of tulips.
tulipoma'nia, *n.*, a passion for tulip-growing.
tu'lip-tree, *n.*, a tree so named.
tulle, *n.*, a fine fabric of silk.
tum'ble, *n.*, a fall; *v.t.*, to throw down; to disorder; *v.i.*, to fall.
tum'bled, *p.p.*, tumble.
tum'ble-down, *adj.*, rickety; ruinous.
tum'bler, *n.*, one who tumbles; an acrobat who does tumbling-tricks; a drinking-glass; a variety of pigeon.
tum'blerful, *n.*, what a tumbler will contain.
tum'bling, *pr.p.*, tumble.
tum'brel, *n.*, a cart that tilts up; a military wagon.
tum'bril, *n.*, *i.q.* tumbrel.
tumefac'tion, *n.*, swelling.
tu'mefied, *p.p.*, tumefy.
tu'mefy, *v.i.*, to swell.
tu'mefying, *pr.p.*, tumefy.
tu'mid, *adj.*, in a swollen state; bombastic.
tumid'ity, *n.*, the state or quality of being tumid.
tu'mour, *n.*, a swelling.
tu'mular, *adj.*, like a tumulus.
tu'muli, *n.*, pl. of tumulus.
tu'mult, *n.*, a wild disturbance; a riot.
tumul'tuary, *adj.*, pert. to a tumult.
tumul'tuous, *adj.*, of the nature of a tumult; very disorderly.
tumul'tuously, *adv.*, in a tumultuous way.
tumul'tuousness, *n.*, the state or quality of being tumultuous.
tu'mulus, *n.*, a large artificial mound.
tun, *n.*, a large cask; a wine measure of 252 gallons.
tu'nable, *adj.*, able to be tuned; agreeable to hear.
tune, *n.*, a melodic series; true sound; a proper state; *v.t.*, to bring (instruments) to exact pitch.
tuned, *p.p.*, tune.
tune'ful, *adj.*, melodious.
tune'fully, *adv.*, in a tuneful way.
tune'less, *adj.*, not melodious.
tu'ner, *n.*, one who tunes organs, pianofortes, etc.
tung'state, *n.*, a tungstic acid salt.
tung'sten, *n.*, a white metal so named.
tung'stic, *adj.*, pert. to, composed of, tungsten.
Tun'gus, *n. pl.*, an Asiatic Turanian race.
tu'nic, *n.*, an ancient Roman inner garment; a loose garment; a soldier's coat; an outer covering or membrane.

tu'nicary, *adj.*, *i.q.* tunicate.

tu'nicate, *adj.*, covered with a membrane.

tu'nicated, *adj.*, *i.q.* tunicate.

tu'nicle, *n.*, the vestment of a subdeacon or epistoler, also a part of the episcopal vesture.

tu'ning, *pr.p.*, tune.

tu'ning-fork, *n.*, a metal two-pronged instrument, carefully tuned, and giving the pitch.

Tunis'ian, *adj.*, rel. to Tunis; *n.*, a native of Tunis.

tun'nage, *n.*, tax (by the tun) on wine imports.

tun'nel, *n.*, a bored passage underground; *v.t.*, to bore (a passage) through.

tun'nel(l)ed, *p.p.*, tunnel.

tun'nel(l)ing, *pr.p.*, tunnel.

tun'ny, *n.*, a seawater fish so named.

tup, *n.*, a ram.

tu'pelo, *n.*, a tree noted for the hardness of its wood.

Tura'nian, *adj.*, pert. to the races other than the Aryans and Semites.

tur'ban, *n.*, an Oriental head covering.

tur'baned, *adj.*, wearing a turban.

tur'bary, *n.*, right to cut turf; ground where it may be cut.

tur'bid, *adj.*, muddy.

turbid'ity, *n.*, the state or quality of being turbid.

tur'bidly, *adv.*, in a turbid way.

tur'bidness, *n.*, *i.q.* turbidity.

tur'binate, *adj.*, driven by a turbine.

tur'binate, *v.t.*, to supply with a turbine.

tur'binated, *p.p.*, turbinate.

tur'bine, *n.*, a wheel actuated by falling water.

tur'bit, *n.*, a breed of pigeons.

tur'bot, *n.*, a flat, edible fish.

tur'bulence, *n.*, disorderliness; riotous conduct.

tur'bulency, *n.*, *i.q.* turbulence.

tur'bulent, *adj.*, riotous; disorderly.

Turc'ism, Turk'ism, *n.*, a characteristic of the Turks; Turkish idiom.

Turco'man, *adj.*, a French Algerian infantry soldier.

tureen', *n.*, a kind of bowl for soup or sauce.

turf, *n.*, grass; a piece of earth with grass upon it; the business of horse-racing; *v.t.*, to lay down with turf.

turfed, *p.p.*, turf.

turf'iness, *n.*, the state or quality of being turfy.

turf'ing, *pr.p.*, turf.

turf'y, *adj.*, like turf; covered with turf.

tur'gent, *adj.*, swelling; inflated.

turges'cence, *n.*, the state of becoming turgent.

turges'cency, *n.* *i.q.* turgescence.

turges'cent, *adj.*, becoming turgent or inflated.

tur'gid, *adj.*, inflated; distended; bombastic.

turgid'ity, *n.*, the state or quality of being turgid.

Turk, *n.*, a native of Turkey; a Mohammedan; an unruly child.

tur'key, *n.*, a large bird so named.

Tur'key, *n.*, the country of the Turks.

tur'key-buzzard, *n.*, an Amer. vulture.

tur'key-cock, *n.*, a male turkey.

tur'key-trot, *n.*, a dance borrowed from the negroes.

Turk'ish, *adj.*, pert. to Turkey and the Turks.

Turk'ism, *n.*, Turkish idiom or characteristic.

Turk's'-cap, *n.* a fez.

tur'malin, *n.*, *i.q.* tourmaline.

tur'meric, *n.*, a plant that yields a yellow dye.

tur'moil, *n.*, disturbance; upset; confusion.

turn, *v.t.*, to make to go or point in a different direction, or completely round; to transform; to make a version of; to shape with a lathe; *v.i.*, to move round or in a different direction; *n.*, the act of turning a curve; a short period of action; a good or evil deed; a fright.

turn'coat, *n.*, one who changes his opinions and abandons his principles.

turned, *p.p.*, turn.

turn'er, *n.*, one who turns; a workman using a lathe.

turn'ery, *n.*, things made with a lathe; a turner's trade.

turn'ing, *pr.p.*, turn; *n.*, a bend in a road.

turn'ing-point, *n.*, a point where a turn is made; a crisis.

tur'nip, *n.*, an edible bulbous root.

turn'key, *n.*, a keeper of prison-cells; a warder.

turn'out, *n.*, equipment; show.

turn'over, *n.*, money receipts in a business; an apple roll, etc.

turn'pike, *n.*, a toll-bar across a road.

turn'plate, *n.*, a turntable.

turn'sole, *n.*, the name of some flowers that turn toward the sun (*e.g.*, the heliotrope).

turn'spit, *n.*, one who turns the roasting spit; a variety of dog trained for this purpose.

turn'stile, *n.*, a revolving barrier.

turn'stone, *n.*, a bird so named for its turning over stones in quest of food.

turn'table, *n.*, a revolving table used for reversing engines, etc., or turning them on to another line.

tur'pentine, *n.*, an exudation from pine and fir trees.

tur'peth, *n.*, an E. Indian drug.

tur'pitude, *n.*, baseness; infamy.

turquoise', *n.*, a blue precious stone.

tur'ret, *n.*, a little tower.

tur'reted, *adj.*, furnished with turrets.

tur'ret-ship, *n.*, a war-vessel provided with a revolving turret.

tur'tle, *n.*, *i.q.*, a turtle dove; a large kind of edible tortoise.

tur'tle-dove, *n.*, a very gentle breed of doves.

turves, *n. pl.*, sods; pl. of turf.

Tus'can, *adj.*, pert. to Tuscany or Etruria; *n.*, a native of Tuscany.

tush, *interj.*, expressing scorn or reproof, or commanding silence.

tusk, *n.*, a large tooth.

tusked, *adj.*, having tusks.

tusk'er, *n.*, a wild boar.

tusk'y, *adj.*, tusk-like.

tus'sle, *n.*, a fight; a struggle; *v.i.*, to struggle.

tus'sled, *p.p.*, tussle.

tus'sock, *n.*, a tuft or clump of grass; *i.q.* tussock-grass.

tus'sock-grass, *n.*, a special kind of grass used as fodder.

tus'socky, *adj.*, full of tussocks.

tut, *interj.*, commanding silence.

tu'telage, *n.*, the act of protecting; state of being under protection.

tu'telar, *adj.*, guarding; protecting.

tu'telary, *adj.*, *i.q.* tutelar.

tu'tenag, *n.*, a white alloy; spelter.

tu'tor, *n.*, an instructor; guardian; *v.t.*, to teach; to bring under discipline.

tu'torage, *n.*, a tutor's fee.

tu'tored, *p.p.*, tutor.

tu'toress, *n.*, fem. of tutor.

tuto'rial, *adj.*, pert. to tutors or tuition.

tu'toring, *pr.p.*, tutor; *n.*, the act or profession of a tutor.

tu'torship, *n.*, a tutor's appointment.

tut'san, *n.*, St. John's wort.

tut'ti, *n. pl.*, all (*mus.*)

tut'ty, *n.*, oxide of zinc ointment.

tu-whit', *n.*, the cry of an owl.

tu-whoo', *n.*, the cry of an owl.

tuyère', *n.*, a pipe conveying air into a furnace.

twad'dle, *n.*, silly talk; nonsense; *v.i.*, to talk twaddle.

twad'dled, *p.p.*, twaddle.

twad'dler, *n.*, one who twaddles.

twad'dling, *pr.p.*, twaddle.

twain, *n.* and *adj.*, two.

twaite, *n.*, a shad.

twang, *n.*, a peculiar quality of sound; a disagreeable intonation or pronunciation; *v.t.*, to sound with a peculiar tone.

twanged, *p.p.*, twang.

twang'ing, *pr.p.*, twang.

twan'gle, *v.t.*, *i.q.* twang.

twank, *v.t.* and *n.*, *i.q.* twang.

twan'kay, *n.*, a green tea.

twank'ing, *pr.p.*, twank.

'twas, phrase = it was.

twat'tle, *v.i.*, to tattle.

twat'tling, *pr.p.*, twattle.

tway'blade, *n.*, a two-bladed knife or sword.

tweak, *v.t.*, to pinch; *n.*, a pinch.

tweaked, *p.p.*, tweak.

tweak'ing, *pr.p.*, tweak.

tweed, *n.*, a woollen fabric.

twee'dle, *v.t.* and *i.*, *i.q.* twiddle.

twee'dled, *p.p.*, tweedle.

twee'dling, *pr.p.*, tweedle.

tweel, *n.*, *i.q.* twill.

twee'ny-maid, *n.*, an under house-servant.

tweer, *n.*, *i.q.* tuyère.

twee'zers, *n. pl.*, pincers.

twelfth, *adj.*, the ordinal of twelve; next after the eleventh; *n.*, a twelfth part.

twelfth'-night, *n.*, the Feast of the Epiphany, Jan. 6, being the twelfth day from Christmas.

twelve, *n.*, a cardinal number, next after eleven; *adj.*, containing one more than eleven.

twelve'-mo, *n.*, a duodecimo (*colloq.*).

twelve'month, *n.*, space of a year.

twelve'pence, *n.*, a shilling.

twelve'penny, *n.*, a shilling; *adj.*, costing a shilling.

twen'tieth, *adj.*, the ordinal of twenty; *n.*, the double of tenth; a twentieth part.

twen'ty, *adj.*, consisting of twice ten; *n.*, the cardinal number of twice ten.

twen'tyfold, *adj.*, twenty times as much.

twi'bill, twy'bill, *n.*, a double bladed battle axe.

twice, *adv.*, two times; doubly.

twice'-told, *adj.*, repeated; stale.

twid'dle, *n.*, a twist with the fingers; *v.t.*, to twist about in the fingers; *v.i.*, to twirl.

twid'dled, *p.p.*, twiddle.

twid'dling, *pr.p.*, twiddle.

twig, *n.*, a small branch; *v.t.* and *i.*, to understand; perceive (*colloq.*)
twig'gy, *adj.*, like, full of, twigs.
twi'light, *n.*, the time just before dawn and sunset; dim light; *adj.*, semi-obscure.
twill, *n.*, a marking as with diagonal lines in a cloth fabric; the fabric itself; *v.t.*, to weave with a twill.
twilled, *p.p.*, twill.
twill'ing, *pr.p.*, twill.
twin, *adj.*, in a pair; double; strongly alike; *n.*, one of two at a birth; a counterpart.
twine, *n.*, fine string; strong thread; *v.t.* and *i.*, to wind round.
twined, *p.p.*, twine.
twinge, *n.*, a short, sharp pain; *v.t.*, to cause such a pain; *v.i.*, to feel such a pain.
twinged, *p.p.*, twinge.
twinge'ing, *pr.p.*, twinge.
twi'ning, *pr.p.*, twine; *n.*, a turn in a road.
twin'kle, *n.*, an intermittent rapid movement; a tremulous gleam; a moment; *v.i.*, to open and close (the eyes) rapidly; to give forth a rapid intermittent light.
twin'kled, *p.p.*, twinkle.
twin'kling, *pr.p.*, twinkle.
twirl, *v.t.*, to cause to revolve rapidly; *v.i.*, to revolve rapidly; *n.*, a quick revolution.
twirled, *p.p.*, twirl.
twirl'ing, *pr.p.*, twirl.
twist, *n.*, the act of twisting; a turn; a convolution; twisted cord; coiled tobacco; *v.t.*, to wind together; to turn round; *v.i.*, to be twisted or turned round.
twist'ed, *p.p.*, twist.
twist'er, *n.*, one who, that which, twist.
twist'ing, *pr.p.*, twist.
twit, *v.t.*, to tease by recalling some act.
twitch, *n.*, a jerk; a short spasm; *v.t.*, to pull with a jerk; *v.i.*, to be affected by a short spasm.
twitched, *p.p.*, twitch.
twitch'er, *n.*, one who, that which, twitches.
twitch'ing, *pr.p.*, twitch.
twit'ted, *p.p.*, twit.
twit'ter, *n.*, a repeated small cry as of birds; *v.t.*, to express in twittering; *v.i.*, to keep up a succession of small sounds.
twit'tered, *p.p.*, twitter.
twit'tering, *pr.p.*, twitter.
twit'ting, *pr.p.*, twit.
'twixt, *prep.*, betwixt; between.
two, *n.*, the cardinal number next after one; *adj.*, consisting of one more than one.
two'-decker, *n.*, a ship with two decks.
two'-edged, *adj.*, double-edged.
two'fold, *adj.*, double.
two-handed, *adj.*, wielded by both hands.
two'-legged, *adj.*, having two legs.
two'-lobed, *adj.*, having two lobes.
two'pence, *n.*, the sum of two pence.
two'penny, *adj.*, costing twopence; not of any value.
two'some, *n.*, game or dance for two.
Tychon'ic, *adj.*, rel. to Tycho Brahe, the astronomer.
tycoon', *n.*, the old title of the Japanese Commander-in-chief.
tye, *n.*, a buddle used in washing ore.
ty'ing, *pr.p.*, tie.
ty'ler, *n.*, *i.q.* tiler.
tym'pan, *n.*, the parchment frame used by printers for laying sheets upon.
tym'panal, *adj.*, *i.q.* tympanic.
tym'pani, *n. pl.*, drums.
tympan'ic, *adj.*, rel. to the tympanum.
tympanit'ic, *adj.*, pert. to tympanitis.
tympani'tis, *n.*, inflammation of the tympanum.
tym'panum, *n.*, the drum of the ear; the surface of the space within a pediment; a drum-like wheel.
tym'pany, *n.*, conceit; self-glorification.
ty'pal, *adj.*, pert. to type.
type, *n.*, a pattern; model; emblem; prefigurement; structural form; letters for printing; *v.t.*, to prefigure; typify; copy with a typewriter.
type'writer, *n.*, a typewriting machine.
type'writing, *n.*, the use of a mechanical contrivance which makes letters by means of types.
type'written, *adj.*, written with a typewriter.
Typho'ean, *adj.*, pert. to Typhoeus.
ty'phoid, *adj.*, resembling typhus; *n.*, an enteric disease.
typhoon', *n.*, a tornado.
ty'phus, *n.*, a dangerous epidemic disease.
typ'ic, *adj.*, *i.q.* typical.
typ'ical, *adj.*, emblematic; prefigurative; ordinary.
typ'ically, *adv.*, in a typical way.
typifica'tion, *n.*, prefiguration.
typ'ified, *p.p.*, typify.
typ'ify, *v.t.*, to prefigure; foreshadow.
typ'ifying, *pr.p.*, typify.
ty'pist, *n.*, one who uses a typewriter.
ty'po-, *pr.fix*, rel. to type.

typog'rapher, *n.*, a printer.

typograph'ic, *adj.*, pert. to typography.

typograph'ical, *adj.*, *i.q.* typographic.

typog'raphy, *n.*, printing.

typ'olite, *n.*, a fossil or stone marked with an animal or plant figure.

typol'ogy, *n.*, the study or interpretation of the typical allusions in Holy Scripture.

tyran'nic, *adj.*, *i.q.* tyrannical.

tyran'nical, *adj.*, despotic; overbearing; cruel.

tyran'nically, *adv.*, in a tyrannical way.

tyran'nicide, *n.*, the murder or murderer of a tyrant.

tyr'annize, *v.i.*, to act despotically or with cruelty.

tyr'annized, *p.p.*, tyrannize.

tyr'annizing, *pr.p.*, tyrannize.

tyr'annous, *adj.*, *i.q.* tyrannical.

tyr'anny, *n.*, the rule of a tyrant; despotism.

ty'rant, *n.*, a despot; oppressor.

tyre, *n.*, *i.q.* tire.

Tyr'ian, *adj.*, rel. to Tyre and the Tyrians; purple; *n.*, a native of Tyre.

ty'ro, *n.*, a novice.

Tyrolese', *adj.*, pert. to the Tyrol and the Tyrolese; *n.*, a native of the Tyrol.

Tyrtae'an, *adj.*, rel. to Tyrtaeus, the martial poet of antiquity.

Tzar, *n.*, *i.q.* Tsar or Czar.

Tzari'na, *n.*, *i.q.* Tsarina or Czarina.

U

u'berous, *adj.*, fruitful.

ubi'ety, *n.*, whereness; the state of being locally.

u'biquist, *n.*, one who believes in the omnipresence of Our Lord's Body.

ubiquita'rian, *adj.*, pert. to the Ubiquists; *n.*, *i.q.* ubiquist.

ubiquita'rianism, *n.*, the teaching of the Ubiquists.

ubiq'uitary, *adj.*, *i.q.* ubiquitous.

ubiq'uitous, *adj.*, being everywhere.

ubiq'uity, *n.*, the state or quality of being ubiquitous.

u'dal, *adj.*, allodial.

ud'der, *n.*, the milk-secreting organ in mammals.

udom'eter, *n.*, a rain-gauge.

ug'lier, *adj.*, *comp.* of ugly.

ug'liest, *adj.*, *super.* of ugly.

ug'lily, *adv.*, in an ugly way.

ug'liness, *n.*, the state or quality of being ugly.

ug'ly, *adj.*, ill-favoured; unsightly; shocking to the moral sense.

uh'lan, **u'lan**, *n.*, a German lancer.

uit'lander, *n.*, an alien resident in a Boer country.

ukase', *n.*, an imperial decree in Russia.

ul'cer, *n.*, a malignant sore.

ul'cerate, *v.t.*, to produce an ulcer in; *v.i.*, to become ulcerated.

ul'cerated, *p.p.*, ulcerate.

ul'cerating, *pr.p.*, ulcerate.

ulcera'tion, *n.*, the process or result of forming an ulcer.

ul'cerous, *adj.*, of the nature of ulcer.

Ulema', *n.*, the collective Turkish hierarchy.

ulig'inous, *adj.*, moist.

ul'lage, *n.*, the difference between a full and an empty cask.

ulma'ceous, *adj.*, pert. to elms.

ul'mic, *adj.*, obtained from ulmin.

ul'min, **ul'mine**, *n.*, a substance derived from the elm and other trees; also from vegetable mould.

ul'na, *n.*, the large bone of the forearm (*Lat.*).

ul'ster, *n.*, a long heavy overcoat.

ulte'rior, *adj.*, further; remoter; secondary.

ulte'riorly, *adv.*, in an ulterior way.

ul'tima, *n.*, a word's final syllable.

ul'tima ra'tio, *n.*, the last resort; final argument.

ul'timate, *adj.*, last; furthest.

ul'timately, *adv.*, finally.

ultima'tum, *n.*, a final demand.

ul'timo, *n.*, the month before this one.

ul'tra, Lat. *prep.*, *adv.*, and *prefix*, beyond; *adj.*, excessive.

ul'traism, *n.*, going to extremes.

ul'traist, *n.*, an extremist.

ultramarine', *adj.*, beyond the seas; *n.*, a blue colour.

ultramon'tane, *adj.*, beyond the mountains (*i.e.*, the Alps); pert. to ultramontanism; *n.*, a supporter of ultramontanism.

ultramon'tanism, *n.*, the view concerning the Pope's authority held, or supposed to be held, South of the Alps.

ultramon'tanist, *adj.* and *n.*, *i.q.* ultramontane.

ultramun'dane, *adj.*, beyond the world or solar system.

ul'ulate, *v.i.*, to howl.

ulula'tion, *n.*, howling.

um'bel, *n.*, inflorescence in the shape of a fan.

um'bellar, *adj.*, like an umbel.

um'bellate, *adj.*, having umbels.

um'bellated, *adj.*, *i.q.* umbellate.

umbellif'erous, *adj.*, *i.q.* umbellate.

um'ber, *n.*, a brown colour; *adj.*, umber-coloured.

um'bered, *adj.*, stained umber.

umbil'ic, *adj.*, pert. to the umbilicus.

umbil'ical, *adj.*, *i.q.* umbilic.

umbil'icate, *adj.*, like a navel.

umbili'cus, *n.*, the navel.

um'bles, *n. pl.*, the viscera of a deer.

um'bo, *n.*, the boss of a shield; a projectile on the shell of a bivalve.

um'bonate, *adj.*, having a boss.

um'bonated, *adj.*, *i.q.* umbonate.

um'bra, *n.*, a shadow (*Lat.*).

umbrac'uliform, *adj.*, like an umbraculum.

umbra'culum, *n.*, an umbrella-like appendage.

um'brage, *n.*, offence; shelter afforded by foliage.

umbra'geous, *adj.*, shady.

umbrel'la, *n.*, a portable protection against rain and sun-heat.

umbrif'erous, *adj.*, shade-giving.
um'pirage, *n.*, the exercise of an umpire's authority.
um'pire, *n.*, an arbitrator; one who supervises the players of a game.
unabashed', *adj.*, unashamed.
unaba'ted, *adj.*, without ceasing; undiminished.
una'ble, *adj.*, not able.
unabridged', *adj.*, not abridged or shortened.
unaccent'ed, *adj.*, not accented.
unaccept'able, *adj.*, not acceptable; unpleasant.
unaccom'modating, *adj.*, inconsiderate.
unaccom'panied, *adj.*, alone; not accompanied.
unaccount'able, *adj.*, not to be explained or accounted for.
unaccount'ably, *adv.*, in an unaccountable way.
unaccus'tomed, *adj.*, strange; unused.
unacknowl'edged, *adj.*, not acknowledged.
unacquaint'ed, *adj.*, ignorant; not knowing.
unadorned', *adj.*, simple; without ornament.
unadul'terated, *adj.*, pure; not adulterated.
unadvi'sable, *adj.*, not to be recommended; unwise; unsafe.
unadvi'sedly, *adj.*, without considering
unaffect'ed, *adj.*, not affected; simple; natural.
unaffect'edly, *adv.*, in an unaffected way.
unaid'ed, *adj.*, without help.
unallied', *adj.*, not allied.
unalloyed', *adj.*, pure; unmixed; without alloy.
unal'terable, *adj.*, not able to be altered.
unal'terably, *adv.*, in an unalterable way.
unal'tered, *adj.*, unchanged.
unambi'tious, *adj.*, without ambition.
una'miable, *adj.*, disagreeable; lacking in kindness.
unanim'ity, *n.*, absolute agreement; being of one mind.
unan'imous, *adj.*, entirely agreed; without a dissentient.
unan'imously, *adv.* entirely in agreement; by a solid vote.
unan'swerable, *adj.*, incapable of being answered.
unan'swerably, *adv.*, in an unanswerable way.
unan'swered, *adj.*, not answered.
unappre'ciated, *adj.*, not appreciated.
unapprised', *adj.*, not informed.
unapproach'able, *adj.*, not to be approached; haughty and reserved.
unappro'priated, *adj.*, not appropriated.
unarmed', *adj.*, without armour; defenceless.
unascertained', *adj.*, not ascertained.
unasked', *adj.*, without being asked; voluntarily.
unaspi'ring, *adj.*, not ambitious.
unassail'able, *adj.*, safe against assault.
unassailed', *adj.*, not assailed.
unassist'ed, *adj.*, without help.
unassort'ed, *adj.*, not assorted; mixed up.
unassu'ming, *adj.*, modest; not giving oneself airs.
unattached', *adj.*, not attached; independent.
unattain'able, *adj.*, unreachable; not to be attained.
unattempt'ed, *adj.*, not attempted.
unattend'ed, *adj.*, alone; without attendants.
unattract'ive, *adj.*, not attractive; displeasing.
u'nau, *n.*, a variety of sloth.
unauthen'tic, *adj.*, not authentic; not genuine.
unau'thorized, *adj.*, not authorized; without permission.
unavail'able, *adj.*, not available.
unavail'ing, *adj.*, useless; done in vain.
unavoid'able, *adj.*, not able to be avoided.
unavoid'ably, *adv.*, in an unavoidable way
unaware', *adj.*, not aware; not cognisant.
unawares', *adv.*, off one's guard; without warning.
unbal'anced, *adj.*, not balanced; intemperate.
unbar', *v.t.*, to remove the bars from; to open.
unbear'able, *adj.*, intolerable.
unbear'ably, *adv.*, in an unbearable way.
unbecom'ing, *adj.*, not becoming; unseemly; not suiting.
unbefit'ting, *adj.*, unseemly; not proper.
unbegot'ten, *adj.*, not begotten.
unbelief', *n.*, refusal to believe; doubt.
unbeliev'er, *n.*, a sceptic; a doubter; a heathen.
unbeliev'ing, *adj.*, not believing.
unbeloved', *adj.*, loved by no one.
unbend', *v.t.*, to relax; *v.i.*, to be condescending; to become unbent.
unbend'ing, *adj.*, not bending; stiff; not condescending.
unbent', *adj.*, in a relaxed state.
unbi'assed, *adj.*, without bias; not prejudiced.
unbid'den, *adj.*, without invitation.
unbind', *v.t.*, to loosen what is bound.
unbitt', *v.t.*, to uncoil from the bitts.
unbleached', *adj.*, in the natural state; not bleached.

unblem'ished, *adj.*, spotless; without blemish.

unblest', *adj.*, not blest; unhallowed; miserable.

unblush'ing, *adj.*, unabashed; shameless.

unbolt', *v.t.*, to remove the bolts from; to open.

unborn', *adj.*, not yet born.

unbor'rowed, *adj.*, not borrowed; one's own.

unbos'om, *v.t.*, *reflex.*, to show one's feelings or secrets.

unbought', *adj.*, not bought.

unbound'ed, *adj.*, without limit; immense.

unbound'edly, *adv.*, in an unbounded degree.

unbri'dle, *v.t.*, to remove the bridle from.

unbri'dled, *p.p.*, unbridle; *adj.*, without restraint; excessive.

unbrok'en, *adj.*, not broken; continuous.

unbroth'erly, *adj.*, not like a brother; without brotherly feeling.

unbuck'le, *v.t.*, to loosen the buckles of.

unbur'den, *v.t.*, *reflex.*, to make confession.

unbur'ied, *adj.*, not buried.

unbut'ton, *v.t.*, to undo the buttons of.

un*called*', *adj.*, without being called.

uncan'did, *adj.*, not candid; disingenuous.

uncanon'ical, *adj.*, not in accordance with the canons; not recognized in the Canon of Scripture.

unceas'ing, *adj.*, without pause; never ending.

unceas'ingly, *adv.*, endlessly.

unceremo'nious, *adj.*, rude; ill-mannered.

uncer'tain, *adj.*, not certain; in doubt; doubtful.

uncer'tainly, *adv.*, in an uncertain way.

uncer'tainty, *n.*, the state or quality of being uncertain.

unchain', *v.t.*, to remove the chain from; to let loose.

unchal'lengeable, *adj.*, unable to be challenged.

unchal'lenged, *adj.*, not challenged.

unchange'able, *adj.*, unable to be changed; not changing.

unchange'ably, *adv.*, in an unchangeable way.

unchanged', *adj.*, not changed.

unchang'ing, *adj.*, not changing; remaining the same.

unchar'itable, *adj.*, not charitable; censorious.

unchar'itableness, *n.*, the state of being uncharitable.

unchar'itably, *adv.*, in an uncharitable way.

unchaste', *adj.*, not chaste; impure.

unchris'tian, *adj.*, not Christian.

unchurch', *v.t.*, to exclude from the Church.

un'cial, *adj.*, written in large Greek capitals; *n.*, an uncial letter.

un'ciform, *adj.*, like a hook.

un'cinate, *adj.*, having a hook at the end.

uncir'cumcised, *adj.*, not circumcised; Gentile.

unciv'il, *adj.*, rude; impolite.

unciv'ilized, *adj.*, rude; barbarous.

unciv'illy, *adv.*, in an uncivil way.

un'cle, *n.*, the brother of one's father or mother; the husband of one's aunt; a pawnbroker (*slang*).

unclean', *adj.*, not clean; ceremonially impure.

unclean'ly, *adj.*, not cleanly; filthy.

unclean'ness, *n.*, the state or quality of being unclean.

unclose', *v.t.* and *i.*, to open.

unclothed', *adj.*, naked.

unclouded', *adj.*, without a cloud; bright; clear.

uncoil', *v.t.* and *i.*, to release.

uncome'ly, *adj.*, wanting in grace or charm.

uncom'fortable, *adj.*, not comfortable; uneasy.

uncom'fortably, *adv.*, in an uncomfortable way.

uncom'mon, *adj.*, not common; rare.

uncom'monly, *adv.*, in an uncommon manner or degree.

uncomplain'ing, *adj.*, making no complaint; acquiescing; patient.

uncom'promising, *adj.*, unyielding; inflexible.

unconcern', *n.*, calm indifference.

unconcerned', *adj.*, calmly indifferent.

unconcern'edly, *adv.*, without any concern.

uncondi'tional, *adj.*, without conditions; absolute.

uncondi'tionally, *adv.*, absolutely; without conditions.

uncondi'tioned, *adj.*, without limitations; absolute.

unconge'nial, *adj.*, not congenial; not agreeable; not suited.

unconnect'ed, *adj.*, not connected; disjoined; separate.

uncon'querable, *adj.*, invincible.

uncon'scionable, *adj.*, unreasonable; not controlled by conscience.

uncon'scious, *adj.*, not conscious; insensible; unaware.

uncon'sciously, *adv.*, insensibly; not consciously.

uncon'sciousness, *n.*, the state of being unconscious.

unconstitu'tional, *adj.* not according to the constitution.

unconstitu'tionally, *adv.*, in an unconstitutional way.

uncontrol'lable, *adj.*, unable to be controlled; violent.

uncontrolled', *adj.*, not under control; excessive.

unconvert'ed, *adj.*, not converted.

uncord', *v.t.*, to untie.

uncord'ed, *adj.*, not tied; *p.p.*, uncord.

uncork', *v.t.*, to draw the cork from.

uncount'ed, *adj.*, not counted; innumerable.

uncourt'eous, *adj.*, uncivil; rude.

uncourt'ly, *adj.*, wanting in courtesy.

uncouth', *adj.*, ungainly; awkward.

uncouth'ness, *n.*, the quality of being uncouth.

uncov'enanted, *adv.*, not pledged; not under agreement or promise; not under the Divine covenant of grace.

uncov'er, *v.t.*, to remove the cover from.

uncrea'ted, *adj.*, not created.

unc'tion, *n.*, anointing; ointment; the Sacrament of anointing; fervour in speech; pretended fervour; cant.

unc'tuous, *adj.*, full of unction; fatty; canting.

uncul'tivated, *adj.*, rude; waste.

uncut', *adj.*, not cut; with the margins untrimmed.

unda'ted, *adj.*, not dated.

undaunt'ed, *adj.*, dauntless; without fear.

undaunt'edly, *adv.*, in an undaunted way.

undec'agon, *n.*, a figure having eleven angles and eleven sides.

undeceive', *v.t.*, to remove a misconception from.

undeci'ded, *adj.*, not decided; hesitating.

undefend'ed, *adj.*, not defended; where a person accused makes no defence.

undefiled', *adj.*, pure; unstained.

undefined', *adj.*, not defined; indefinite.

undeliv'ered, *adj.*, not delivered.

undeni'able, *adj.*, not to be denied; indisputable.

undeni'ably, *adv.*, indisputably.

undenomina'tional, *adj.*, not distinctive of any denomination.

un'der, *prep.*, beneath; lower than; subject to; in the time or reign of; *adv.*, in a lower state or position; *adj.*, inferior; lower.

un'der-agent, *n.*, sub-agent.

underbid', *v.t.*, to make a lower estimate than.

un'derbred, *adj.*, not thoroughbred; not well bred; vulgar.

un'derbrush, *n.*, undergrowth.

un'der-clerk, *n.*, an inferior clerk.

un'derclothing, *n.*, inner garments.

un'dercurrent, *n.*, a current beneath an upper current.

un'dercut, *n.*, the under part of a sirloin; *adj.*, carved so as to stand out in relief.

undercut', *v.t.*, to carve stone, etc., so that it stands out in relief.

un'derdone, *adj.*, not done enough; not properly cooked

underdose', *v.t.*, to administer an insufficient dose.

un'derdose, *n.*, an insufficient dose.

un'derdrain, *n.*, a drain under the surface.

underdrain', *v.t.*, to drain below the surface.

under-es'timate, *n.*, an estimate lower than it should be.

under-es'timate, *v.i.*, to form too low an opinion of.

under-es'timated, *p.p.*, under-estimate.

under-es'timating, *pr.p.*, under-estimate.

underfoot', *adv.*, beneath the feet; below.

undergo', *v.t.*, to go through; endure; submit to.

undergo'ing, *pr.p.*, undergo.

undergone', *p.p.*, undergo.

undergrad'uate, *n.*, an academic student not yet admitted to a degree, being still *in statu pupillari* (in the position of a pupil).

un'derground, *adj.*, subterraneous; *adv.*, below the ground.

un'dergrowth, *n.*, shrubs, etc., growing beneath higher plants.

un'derhand, *adj.*, done behind one's back; mean; delivered with the hand kept below the (cricket) ball and the elbow; *adv.*, secretly; clandestinely; in an underhand way.

un'derhanded, *adj.*, done clandestinely.

underhung', *adj.*, projecting further than the upper jaw.

underlay', *v.t.*, to lay under another thing; to put underlays under types; *p.t.*, underlie.

un'derlay, *n.*, paper, etc., laid underneath types.

un'derlease, *n.*, a sub-lease.

underlease', *v.t.*, to grant a sub-lease of.

underlet', *v.t.*, to sub-let.

un'derlet, *n.*, a sublet.

underlie', *v.t.*, to lie under; to support.

underline′, *v.t.*, to score a line under; to emphasize.

underlined′, *p.p.*, underline.

un′derling, *n.*, a subordinate.

underli′ning, *pr.p.*, underline.

underly′ing, *pr.p.*, underlie.

undermine′, *v.t.*, to lay a mine under; to excavate beneath; to weaken.

un′dermost, *adj.*, lowest.

underneath′, *prep.* and *adv.*, below; beneath.

underpin′, *v.t.*, to secure with props or piers.

underpin′ning, *pr.p.* underpin; *n.*, a structure in support from below.

underrate′, *v.t.*, to value too little.

underrun′, *v.t.*, to run beneath.

underscore′, *v.t.*, to underline.

under-sec′retary, *n.*, an assistant secretary.

un′dershot, *adj.*, driven by water that flows beneath.

un′dersized, *adj.*, below standard size; small; dwarfish.

un′dersoil, *n.*, subsoil.

understand′, *v.t.*, to perceive the meaning of; to suppose; to be informed; to take as meant though not expressed; *v.i.*, to have understanding.

understand′ing, *adj.*, intelligent; *n.*, intelligence; an agreement.

understood′, *p.p.*, understand.

un′derstrapper, *n.*, a subordinate.

un′derstudy, *n.*, one preparing or prepared to take another's rôle.

undertake′, *v.t.*, to take upon oneself; to assume; to contract for doing; *v.i.*, to promise; engage oneself.

underta′ken, *p.p.*, undertake.

un′dertaker, *n.*, one who undertakes; one who carries out funeral arrangements; a contractor.

underta′king, *pr.p.*, undertake; *n.*, an enterprise; contract.

undertook′, *p.t.*, undertake.

underval′ue, *v.t.*, to put too low a value on.

un′derwear, *n.*, inner garments.

underwent′, *p.t.*, undergo.

un′derwood, *n.*, *s.q.* underbrush.

underwork′, *v.t.*, to work for lower wages than; to scamp; *v.i.*, to do too little work.

underwrite′, *v.t.*, to subscribe; to execute an insurance policy on; to subscribe for company stock not taken by the public; *v.i.*, to be an underwriter.

un′derwriter, *n.*, one who executes and delivers insurance policies, esp. on shipping.

undeserved′, *adj.*, not merited.

undeserv′ing, *adj.*, not meriting; unworthy.

undesigned′, *adj.*, not designed; not intended.

undesign′ing, *adj.*, not intending; ingenuous.

undesir′able, *adj.*, not to be desired; unpleasant.

undetect′ed, *adj.*, not discovered.

unde′viating, *adj.*, keeping straight onwards; not turning aside.

undid′, *p.t.*, undo.

undigest′ed, *adj.*, not digested.

undig′nified, *adj.*, wanting in dignity.

undimin′ished, *adj.*, not diminished.

undimmed′, *adj.*, not dimmed.

undis′ciplined, *adj.*, uncontrolled; not under discipline.

undisguised′, *adj.*, open; not concealed.

undismayed′, *adj.*, unafraid.

undisturbed′, *adj.*, not disturbed; left in the original state.

undivi′ded, *adj.*, whole; not divided.

undo′, *v.t.*, to cancel; make undone; inflict irreparable injury on.

undo′er, *n.*, one who undoes.

undo′ing, *pr.p.*, undo; *n.*, ruin.

undone′, *p.p.*, undo; *adj.*, not done.

undoubt′ed, *adj.*, certain; beyond doubt.

undoubt′edly, *adv.*, certainly.

undress′, *v.t.* and *i.*, to remove the clothing; *adj.*, in mufti; *n.*, mufti.

undue′, *adj.*, not legally due; excessive.

un′dulant, *adj.*, undulating.

un′dulate, *v.t.*, to cause to wave or vibrate; *v.i.*, to move in waves.

un′dulated, *p.p.*, undulate.

un′dulating, *pr.p.*, undulate.

undula′tion, *n.*, a waving motion.

un′dulatory, *adj.*, vibrating.

undu′ly, *adv.*, improperly; excessively.

undu′tiful, *adj.*, without respect for parents.

undy′ing, *adj.*, not dying; never ending.

unearned′, *adj.*, not earned; obtained without labour.

unearth′, *v.t.*, to disclose; bring to light.

unearthed′, *p.p.*, unearth.

unearth′ing, *pr.p.*, unearth.

unearth′ly, *adj.*, unlike anything on earth.

uneas′ily, *adv.*, uncomfortably.

uneas'iness, *n.*, the state or quality of being uneasy.

uneas'y, *adj.*, uncomfortable; not at one's ease.

uned'ucated, *adj.*, ignorant; not educated

unembar'rassed, *adj.*, without embarrassment.

unemployed', *adj.*, without employment.

unencum'bered, *adj.*, without encumbrance.

unend'ing, *adj.*, unceasing.

unendur'able, *adj.*, intolerable.

unendur'ably, *adv.*, intolerably.

unengaged', *adj.*, disengaged; not engaged.

unenlight'ened, *adj.*, ignorant; barbarous; without enlightenment.

unen'viable, *adj.*, not to be envied.

unen'viably, *adv.*, in an unenviable way.

une'quable, *adj.*, not equable; of uncertain temper.

une'qual, *adj.*, not equal; not uniform; incapable.

un'equalled, *adj.*, not equalled; not matched.

une'qually, *adv.*, in an unequal way.

unequiv'ocal, *adj.*, not ambiguous; certain.

unequiv'ocally, *adv.*, in an unequivocal way.

uner'ring, *adj.*, certain; making no mistake.

uner'ringly, *adv.*, in an unerring way.

unessen'tial, *adj.*, not essential; immaterial.

une'ven, *adj.*, not even; rough; up and down.

une'venly, *adv.*, in an uneven way.

une'venness, *n.*, the state or quality of being uneven.

unevent'ful, *adj.*, quiet; with nothing happening.

unexam'pled, *adj.*, unequalled; unique.

unexcep'tionable, *adj.* to which or whom no one can take exception.

unexcep'tionably, *adv.*, in an unexceptionable way.

unexhaust'ed, *adj.*, not exhausted; not used up.

unexpect'ed, *adj.*, sudden; coming on one unawares.

unexpect'edly, *adv.*, in an unexpected way.

unexplained', *adj.*, not explained; mysterious.

unexplored', *adj.*, never travelled over; unknown.

unexpressed', *adj.*, not spoken.

unextin'guishable, *adj.*, that cannot be extinguished.

unextin'guished, *adj.*, burning; shining; not put out.

unfa'ded, *adj.*, still fresh and blooming.

unfa'ding, *adj.*, never fading.

unfail'ing, *adj.*, always to be relied on; never found wanting.

unfail'ingly, *adv.*, in an unfailing way.

unfair', *adj.*, unjust; partial.

unfair'ly, *adv.*, in an unfair way.

unfair'ness, *n.*, injustice; partiality.

unfaith'ful, *adj.*, disloyal; not keeping a promise or vow.

unfaith'fulness, *n.*, the state of being unfaithful.

unfamil'iar, *adj.*, strange; unknown.

unfamil'iarly, *adv.*, in an unfamiliar way.

unfash'ionable, *adj.*, not conforming to the fashion.

unfash'ionably, *adv.*, in an unfashionable way.

unfast'en, *v.t.*, to loose; untie.

unfast'ened, *p.p.*, unfasten.

unfast'ening, *pr.p.*, unfasten.

unfath'omable, *adj.*, that cannot be fathomed.

unfa'vourable, *adj.*, unpromising; adverse.

unfa'vourably, *adv.*, in an unfavourable way.

unfeel'ing, *adj.*, wanting in feeling; unsympathetic.

unfeel'ingly, *adv.*, in an unfeeling way.

unfeigned', *adj.*, sincere; genuine.

unfeign'edly, *adv.*, sincerely; genuinely.

unfelt', *adj.*, not felt; unperceived.

unfem'inine, *adj.*, unlike what a woman should be.

unfet'tered, *adj.*, free; loose.

unfil'ial, *adj.*, not filial; not dutiful to parents.

unfin'ished, *adj.*, incomplete.

unfit', *adj.*, not fit; incompetent; *v.t.*, to make unfit.

unfit'ly, *adv.*, in an unfit way.

unfit'ness, *n.*, the quality of being unfit.

unfit'ted, *adj.*, not suited; *p.p.*, unfit.

unfit'ting, *adj.*, unsuitable; *pr.p.*, unfit.

unfix', *v.t.*, to release what is fixed.

unfixed', *p.p.*, unfix.

unfix'ing, *pr.p.*, unfix.

unflag'ging, *adj.*, not flagging; keeping on without relaxing effort.

unflat'tering, *adj.*, uncomplimentary.

unfledged', *adj.*, raw; callow.

unflinch'ing, *adj.*, absolutely resolute.

unfold', *v.t.*, to open what is folded; to disclose; *v.i.*, to come unfolded.

unfold'ed, *p.p.*, unfold; *adj.*, not folded; flat.

unfold'ing, *pr.p.*, unfold.

unforeseen', *adj.*, sudden; coming on one unawares.

unforetold', *adj.*, not predicted.

unforgiv'en, *adj.*, not forgiven.

unforgiv'ing, *adj.*, implacable; persistently cruel.

unformed', *adj.*, not completely formed; undeveloped in character.

unfor'tunate, *adj.*, ill-fated; unlucky.

unfor'tunately, *adv.*, by ill-luck.

unfound'ed, *adj.*, not based on fact.

unfrequent'ed, *adj.*, solitary; rarely visited.

unfre'quently, *adv.*, seldom.

unfriend'ly, *adj.*, unsociable; bearing ill-will.

unfruit'ful, *adj.*, not productive.

unfruit'fulness, *n.*, the state of being unfruitful.

unfulfilled', *adj.*, never fulfilled.

unfurl', *v.t.*, to unroll (as a flag).

unfurled', *p.p.*, unfurl.

unfurl'ing, *pr.p.*, unfurl.

unfur'nished, *adj.*, without furniture.

ungain'ly, *adj.*, clumsy; awkward.

ungen'erous, *adj.*, lacking in generosity.

ungen'erously, *adv.*, in an ungenerous way.

unge'nial, *adj.*, cold; not kindly.

ungen'tle, *adj.*, rough.

ungen'tlemanly, *adj.*, unlike a gentleman.

ungod'liness, *n.*, the state of being ungodly.

ungod'ly, *adj.*, wicked; at enmity with God.

ungov'ernable, *adj.*, uncontrollable.

ungov'ernably, *adv.*, in an ungovernable way.

ungrace'ful, *adj.*, awkward; lacking in grace.

ungrace'fully, *adv.*, in an ungraceful way.

ungrace'fulness, *n.*, want of charm or elegance.

ungra'cious, *adj.*, lacking in courtesy or condescension.

ungra'ciously, *adv.*, in an ungracious manner.

ungrammat'ical, *adj.*, not according to the rules of grammar.

ungrate'ful, *adj.*, without gratitude; unpleasing.

ungrate'fully, *adv.*, in an ungrateful way.

unground'ed, *adj.*, wanting in support or proof.

ungrudg'ing, *adj.*, generous.

un'gual, *adj.*, pert. to a claw or nail.

unguard'ed, *adj.*, not protected; rash.

unguard'edly, *adv.*, in an unguarded way.

un'guent, *n.*, ointment.

un'guentary, *adj.*, pert. to unguent.

unguic'ulate, *adj.*, having claws; having a claw-like base (*bot.*).

unguic'ulated, *adj.*, *i.q.* unguiculate.

un'gulate, *adj.*, hoofed; hoof-like.

un'gulated, *adj.*, *i.q.* ungulate.

unhal'lowed, *adj.*, unblest; not consecrated.

unhand', *v.t.*, to let go of.

unhand'some, *adj.*, stingy; ungenerous; wanting good looks.

unhand'somely, *adv.*, in an unhandsome way.

unhan'dy, *adj.*, clumsy.

unhap'pily, *adv.*, sadly; unfortunately.

unhap'piness, *n.*, the state of being unhappy.

unhap'py, *adj.*, joyless; unfortunate.

unharmed', *adj.*, not hurt; not injured; safe and sound.

unhar'ness, *v.t.*, to remove harness from.

unhar'nessed, *p.p.*, unharness.

unhar'nessing, *pr.p.*, unharness.

unhealth'iness, *n.*, the state of being unhealthy.

unhealth'y, *adj.*, not in good health; unwholesome.

unheard', *adj.*, not heard; without a hearing.

unheed'ed, *adj.*, not noticed; not regarded.

unheed'ing, *adj.*, regardless; rash.

unhes'itating, *adj.*, prompt in decision.

unhes'itatingly, *adv.*, without hesitation.

unhinge', *v.t.*, to take off its hinges; to upset the balance of.

unhinged', *p.p.*, unhinge.

unhing'ing, *pr.p.*, unhinge.

unhitch', *v.t.*, to loose; unfasten.

unho'liness, *n.*, the state or quality of being unholy.

unho'ly, *adj.*, profane; not consecrated; irreligious.

unhon'oured, *adj.*, inglorious; without honour.

unhook', *v.t.*, to remove from a hook; to undo the hooks of.

unhooked', *p.p.*, unhook.

unhook'ing, *pr.p.*, unhook.

unhorse', *v.t.*, to unseat; throw from a horse.

unhorsed', *p.p.*, unhorse.

unhors'ing, *pr.p.*, unhorse.

unhurt', *adj.*, unharmed; without injury.

U'niate, u'niate, *adj.*, a term describing those Eastern Churches which have accepted the Roman supremacy, but retain their own liturgies, rites, ceremonies, practices, etc.; *n.*, a member of a Uniate communion.

uniax'ial, *adj.*, having but one axis.

u'nicorn, *n.*, a legendary beast with a single horn; a narwhal; a variety of beetles and gasteropods; three horses in harness, a pair and a leader.

unicorn'ous, *adj.*, having a single horn.

unide'al, *adj.*, the opposite to ideal; unimaginative; materialistic.

unifa'cial, *adj.*, having a single face.

unif'ic, *adj.*, unifying.

unifica'tion, *n.*, the act or result of unifying.

uniflo'rous, *adj.*, producing a single flower.

unifo'liate, *adj.*, having only one leaflet.

u'niform, *adj.*, always preserving a single form; never varying; in conformity with a standard; *n.*, dress of one and the same pattern; *v.t.*, to make uniform; to put into uniform.

uniform'ity, *n.*, the being of one pattern; standard, etc.; regularity.

u'niformly, *adv.*, regularly; in one and the same way or degree.

u'nify, *v.t.*, to make one; to bring into uniformity.

Unigen'itus, *n.*, the famous Bull of Pope Clement XI, issued against the Jansenists in 1713. (The word means *Only-begotten*. Bulls are named after their opening word or words.)

unig'enous, *adj.*, of the same genus.

unila'biate, *adj.*, with one lip.

unilat'eral, *adj.*, one-sided.

unilit'eral, *adj.*, containing a single letter.

unimpaired', *adj.*, uninjured; whole.

unimpeach'able, *adj.*, not to be impeached; without a flaw; blameless.

unimpor'tant, *adj.*, of no importance or significance.

unimproved', *adj.*, not improved; unamended.

uninflam'mable, *adj.*, that cannot be set on fire.

uninfluen'tial, *adj.*, not influential.

uninhab'itable, *adj.*, not fit to be lived in; desert.

uninstruct'ed, *adj.*, ignorant.

uninstruct'ive, *adj.* not informing.

unintel'ligible, *adj.* past understanding.

unintel'ligibly, *adv.* in an unintelligible way.

unintend'ed, *adj.*, not designed; not premeditated.

uninten'tional, *adj.*, *i.q.* unintended.

uninten'tionally, *adv.*, without intention.

unin'terested, *adj.*, taking no interest.

unin'teresting, *adj.*, not arresting; dull.

uninterrupt'ed, *adj.*, without interruption.

uninterrupt'edly, *adv.*, without a break or interruption.

uninvi'ted, *adj.*, unbidden; without invitation.

uninvi'ting, *adj.*, not attractive.

u'nion, *n.*, the act of uniting; state of being united; combination; junction; mixture; the workhouse; a low vat used in brewing.

U'nionism, *n.*, the principle of combination, esp. Trade Union; the principles of those who demand that Ireland remain united to Great Britain.

U'nionist, *n.*, an adherent of Unionism.

U'nion Jack, *n.*, the Jack or national flag, showing the national crosses of the countries of the United Kingdom.

unip'arous, *adj.*, having one stem.

u'niped, *adj.*, having a single foot.

uniper'sonal, *adj.*, consisting of a single person.

unique', *adj.*, being the only one; sole; unequalled.

unise'rial, *adj.*, single-ranked.

unise'riate, *adj.*, *i.q.* uniserial.

unisex'ual, *adj.*, of a single sex.

u'nison, *adj.*, vibrating in the same number; of identical pitch; sounding alone; *n.*, exact agreement; state of sounding alone, or of several voices or instruments sounding the same notes, if not at the same pitch; the interval of an octave.

unis'onance, *n.*, identity of musical pitch.

unis'onant, *adj.*, sounding in unison.

unis'onous, *adj.*, *i.q.* unisonant.

u'nit, *n.*, an individual person or thing; a particular group or body; a quantity or value taken as the standard to which other quantities or values must be referred; one of the first nine numbers.

Unita'rian, *adj.*, rel. to Unitarianism; *n.*, a member of the Unitarian body.

Unita'rianism, *n.*, the principles of the Unitarians, who deny the Deity of Christ.

u'nitary, *adj.*, rel. to units and unity; integral.

unite', *v.t.*, to join in one; to combine; to attach; *v.i.*, to combine; to join together.

uni'ted, *p.p.*, unite; *adj.*, harmonious; loving.

uni′tedly, *adv.*, in an united way.

uni′ter, *n.*, one who, that which, unites.

uni′ting, *pr.p.*, unite.

u′nity, *n.*, the state of being one; oneness; harmony; agreement; the number one.

u′nivalve, *adj.*, having a single valve; *n.*, a gasteropod; a mollusc with a single-valved shell.

u′nivalved, *adj.*, *i.q.* univalve.

univalv′ular, *adj.*, *i.q.* univalve.

univer′sal, *adj.*, bel. to, pert. to, all mankind; applicable to all; existing everywhere; *n.*, a logical proposition which predicates something of every individual denoted by the subject; philosophically, a general concept, predicable of many individual things.

Univer′salism, *n.*, the doctrine that all men will finally be saved.

Univer′salist, *n.*, one who accepts Universalism.

universal′ity, *n.*, the quality or state of being universal.

univer′salize, *v.t.*, to generalize.

univer′salized, *p.p.*, universalize.

univer′sally, *adv.*, in regard to all; with no exceptions.

u′niverse, *n.*, all created things; the visible world.

univer′sity, *n.*, a corporation or gild; now understood to be a corporation of teachers and scholars. (It happens that colleges are commonly associated with it, but the University exists apart as an institution in itself.)

univ′ocal, *adj.*, having only one meaning.

unjust′, *adj.*, not just; unfair; cruel.

unjust′ifiable, *adj.*, without justification; inexcusable.

unjust′ifiably, *adv.*, in an unjustifiable way.

unjust′ly, *adj.*, in an unjust way.

unkempt′, *adj.*, untidy; dishevelled.

unken′nel, *v.t.*, to bring or drive out of retreat.

unken′nel(l)ed, *p.p.*, unkennel.

unken′nel(l)ing, *pr.p.*, unkennel.

unkind′, *adj.*, harsh; cruel.

unkind′ly, *adj.*, wanting in kindliness; *adv.*, in an unkind way.

unkind′ness, *n.*, the state of being unkind.

unknit′, *v.t.*, to unravel.

unknow′able, *adj.*, not able to be known or recognized.

unknow′ingly, *adv.*, without knowing.

unknown′, *adj.*, not known; obscure.

unlace′, *v.t.*, to undo the laces of.

unlaced′, *p.p.*, unlace.

unla′cing, *pr.p.*, unlace.

unlade′, *v.t.*, to unload.

unlatch′, *v.t.*, to undo the latch of.

unlatched′, *p.p.*, unlatch.

unlatch′ing, *pr.p.*, unlatch.

unlaw′ful, *adj.*, not lawful; illegal.

unlaw′fully, *adj.*, illegally.

unlaw′fulness, *n.*, the state of being unlawful; illegality.

unlearn′, *v.t.*, to forget; banish from the mind.

unlearned′, *p.p.*, unlearn.

unlearn′ed, *adj.*, not educated; illiterate.

unleav′ened, *adj.*, not leavened; not containing leaven.

unless′, *conj.*, if not; except.

unlet′tered, *adj.*, illiterate.

unli′censed, *adj.*, not licensed.

unlike′, *adj.*, not like; different from.

unlike′ly, *adj.*, not probable.

unlike′ness, *n.*, the state of being not like.

unlim′ited, *adj.*, without limit.

unlink′, *v.t.*, to loosen.

unliq′uidated, *adj.*, not liquidated; not ascertained as regards amount.

unload′, *v.t.*, to remove a load from; to disburden; to take the charge from a firearm; *v.i.*, to discharge cargo.

unload′ed, *p.p.*, unload; *adj.* (of a firearm) not charged.

unload′ing, *pr.p.*, unload.

unlock′, *v.t.*, to unfasten the lock of; to disclose.

unlocked′, *p.p.*, unlock; *adj.*, not locked.

unlock′ing, *pr.p.*, unlock.

unloose′, *v.t.*, *i.q.* to loose.

unloved′, *adj.*, not loved.

unlove′liness, *n.*, the state or quality of being unlovely.

unlove′ly, *adj.*, not worthy to be loved.

unluck′ily, *adv.*, by ill-luck.

unluck′y, *adj.*, unfortunate; ill-starred.

unmade′, *adj.*, not yet made; taken to pieces.

unmaid′enly, *adj.*, unlike, or not befitting, a maiden.

unmake′, *v.t.*, to take to pieces.

unma′king, *pr.p.*, unmake.

unman′, *v.t.*, to take the courage out of; to conquer.

unman′ageable, *adj.*, uncontrollable.

unman′ly, *adj.*, not like a man; effeminate; cowardly.

unmanned′, *p.p.*, unman.

unman′nered, *adj.*, ill-bred.

unman'nerly, *adj.*, *i.q.* unmannered.

unmar'ried, *adj.*, not married.

unmask', *v.t.*, to remove the mask from; to reveal.

unmasked', *p.p.*, unmask; *adj.*, not wearing a mask.

unmask'ing, *pr.p.*, unmask.

unmatched', *adj.*, unequalled; without a rival.

unmean'ing, *adj.*, unintelligible; without any sense.

unmen'tionable, *adj.*, unfit to be mentioned.

unmer'ciful, *adj.*, cruel.

unmer'cifully, *adv.*, in an unmerciful way.

unmer'ited, *adj.*, undeserved.

unmind'ful, *adj.*, forgetful; disregarding.

unmin'gled, *adj.*, not mixed; unadulterated.

unmista'kable, *adj.*, that cannot be mistaken.

unmit'igated, *adj.*, in full force; without abatement.

unmixed', *adj.*, *i.q.* unmingled.

unmoor', *v.t.*, to loose from its mooring.

unmoth'erly, *adj.*, unlike a mother.

unmoved', *adj.*, not moved; firm, steady; calm.

unmur'muring, *adj.*, without complaining.

unmu'sical, *adj.*, lacking the musical sense or quality.

unmuz'zle, *v.t.*, to loose the muzzle of; to allow freedom of speech to.

unmuz'zled, *p.p.*, unmuzzle.

unnamed', *adj.*, not named; unmentioned.

unnat'ural, *adj.*, contrary to nature; monstrous.

unnat'urally, *adv.*, in an unnatural way.

unnec'essarily, *adv.*, needlessly.

unnec'essary, *adj.*, needless; not essential.

unneigh'bourly, *adj.*, not like a neighbour; churlish.

unnerve', *v.t.*, to upset the nerves of; to debilitate.

unnerved', *p.p.*, unnerve.

unnerv'ing, *pr.p.*, unnerve.

unno'ted, *adj.*, not noted; undistinguished; forgotten.

unno'ticed, *adj.*, not noticed; unperceived.

unnum'bered, *adj.*, not numbered; innumerable.

unobjec'tionable, *adj.*, to which no objection can be raised.

unobli'ging, *adj.*, churlish; selfish.

unobserv'able, *adj.*, unable to be observed.

unobserv'ant, *adj.*, not quick at taking notice of things; paying no regard.

unobserv'ing, *adj.*, *i.q.* unobservant.

unobtru'sive, *adj.*, not obtrusive; retiring.

unoc'cupied, *adj.*, without occupation; empty; at leisure.

unoffend'ing, *adj.*, harmless.

unoffi'cial, *adj.*, informal; not official.

unoffi'cious, *adj.*, not officious.

uno'pened, *adj.*, not opened; shut.

unor'ganized, *adj.*, not properly organized.

unostenta'tious, *adj.*, without ostentation; without pretentious display.

unostenta'tiously, *adv.*, in an unostentatious way.

unpack', *v.t.*, to remove the contents from a packed trunk, etc.

unpacked', *p.p.*, unpack.

unpack'ing, *pr.p.*, unpack.

unpaid', *adj.*, not paid; still owing; unsalaried.

unpal'atable, *adj.*, not pleasing to the palate; nauseous.

unpar'alleled, *adj.*, unequalled; without a parallel.

unpar'donable, *adj.*, unforgivable.

unpar'donably, *adv.*, in an unpardonable way.

unparliament'ary, *adj.*, not in accordance with the rules of Parliament; rude.

unpatriot'ic, *adj.*, lacking in patriotism.

unpaved', *adj.*, rough; not paved.

unperceiv'able, *adj.*, imperceptible; not able to be perceived.

unperceived', *adj.*, unobserved; unnoticed.

unphilosoph'ical, *adj.*, not philosophical.

unpin', *v.t.*, to take the pins out of.

unpinned', *p.p.*, unpin.

unpin'ning, *pr.p.*, unpin.

unpit'ied, *adj.*, pitied by no one.

unpit'ying, *adj.*, showing no pity.

unpleas'ant, *adj.*, disagreeable.

unpleas'antly, *adv.*, disagreeably.

unpleas'antness, *n.*, the quality of being unpleasant.

unpleas'ing, *adj.*, disagreeable; not pleasing.

unpoet'ical, *adj.*, prosaic; not poetical; unimaginative.

unpol'ished, *adj.*, in the rough state; dull; rude.

unpollu'ted, *adj.*, clear; pure.

unpop'ular, *adj.*, not approved by the people; disliked.

unpopular'ity, *n.*, the state of being unpopular.

unprac'tical, *adj.*, not practical; given to speculation rather than to action.

unprac'tised, *adj.*, unskilful.

unprec'edented, *adj.*, unexampled; without precedent.

unprej'udiced, *adj.*, free from bias or prepossessions.

unpremed'itated, *adj.*, not thought out beforehand; done or said on the impulse of the moment.

unprepared', *adj.*, unready; not prepared.

unprepossess'ing, *adj.* wanting in attractiveness.

unpretend'ing, *adj.*, simple; modest.

unprin'cipled, *adj.*, unscrupulous; wanting in principle.

unprint'ed, *adj.*, not printed.

unproduc'tive, *adj.*, barren; not fertile.

unprofes'sional, *adj.*, not professional; not in accordance with the rules of a profession.

unprof'itable, *adj.*, not profitable; not advantageous; useless.

unprof'itably, *adv.*, in an unprofitable way.

unprom'ising, *adj.*, unfavourable in appearance.

unpronounce'able, *adj.*, not able to be pronounced.

unpropi'tious, *adj.*, ill-omened; unfavourable.

unprotect'ed, *adj.*, without protection.

unprovi'ded, *adj.*, not provided.

unprovoked', *adj.*, unchallenged.

unpub'lished, *adj.*, not hitherto published.

unpun'ished, *adj.*, without punishment.

unqual'ified, *adj.*, absolute; without conditions.

unquench'able, *adj.*, inextinguishable.

unques'tionable, *adj.*, beyond question; indisputable.

unques'tionably, *adv.*, indisputably.

unques'tioned, *adj.*, not called in question.

unques'tioning, *adj.*, not calling in question.

unqui'et, *adj.*, disturbed; anxious; *n.*, a state of being unquiet.

unqui'etly, *adv.*, in an unquiet way.

unrav'el, *v.t.*, to disentangle.

unrav'el(l)ed, *p.p.*, unravel.

unrav'el(l)ing, *pr.p.*, unravel.

unread', *adj.*, not read; illiterate.

unread'able, *adj.*, illegible.

unread'y, *adj.*, unprepared; not ready; slow to act.

unre'al, *adj.*, without reality; non-existent; imaginary.

unreal'ity, *n.*, the quality of being unreal.

unre'alizable, *adj.*, that cannot be realized.

unre'alized, *adj.*, not realized.

unrea'sonable, *adj.*, perverse; irrational.

unrea'sonableness, *n.*, the quality of being unreasonable.

unrea'sonably, *adv.*, in an unreasonable way.

unredeemed', *adj.*, not redeemed; hopelessly bad.

unregen'eracy, *n.*, the state of being unregenerate.

unregen'erate, *adj.*, not regenerate; sinful.

unreg'istered, *adj.*, not registered.

unrelent'ing, *adj.*, ruthless; pitiless; unforgiving.

unreli'able, *adj.*, not to be relied upon.

unremem'bered, *adj.*, forgotten.

unremit'ting, *adj.*, never relaxing; continuous.

unremu'nerative, *adj.*, bringing no reward or profit.

unrepent'ing, *adj.*, not repenting.

unrepresent'ed, *adj.*, not represented.

unrequi'ted, *adj.*, unrewarded.

unreserve', *n.*, a want of reserve.

unreserved', *adj.*, not reserved; frank.

unreserv'edly, *adv.*, without reserve.

unresist'ing, *adj.*, not offering resistance; passive.

unrest', *n.*, disquietude.

unrest'ing, *adj.*, restless; without pause.

unrestrained', *adj.* violent; without restraint.

unrestraint', *n.*, want of control.

unrestrict'ed, *adj.*, without restriction.

unreward'ed, *adj.*, not recompensed.

unrig', *v.t.*, to remove the rigging from.

unright'eous, *adj.*, unjust; unholy.

unright'eously, *adv.*, in an unrighteous way.

unright'eousness, *n.*, wickedness; the state or quality of being unrighteous.

unripe', *adj.*, not yet ripe; immature; sour.

unri'val(l)ed, *adj.*, without a rival.

unrobe', *v.i.*, to divest oneself of clothing.

unroll', *v.t.*, to spread open that which is rolled up; *v.i.*, to unfold.

unrolled', *p.p.*, unroll.

unroll'ing, *pr.p.*, unroll.

unroman'tic, *adj.*, prosaic; without sentiment.

unroof', *v.t.*, to remove the roof from.

unroofed', *p.p.*, unroof.

unroof'ing, *pr.p.*, unroof.

unruf'fled, *adj.*, calm; without a ripple.

unru'liness, *n.*, the state of being unruly.

unru'ly, *adj.*, disorderly; turbulent.

unsad'dle, *v.t.*, to remove the saddle from.

unsad'dled, *p.p.*, unsaddle.

unsad'dling, *pr.p.*, unsaddle.

unsafe', *adj.*, insecure; dangerous.

unsafe'ly, *adv.*, in an unsafe way.

unsaid', *adj.*, not spoken; *p.p.*, unsay.

unsale'able, *adj.*, which no one would buy.

unsanc'tified, *adj.*, not sanctified; unholy.

un*satisfac'torily*, *adv.*, in an unsatisfactory way.

un*satisfac'tory*, *adj.*, not giving satisfaction.

unsat'isfying, *adj.*, not satisfying.

unsa'voury, *adj.*, not savoury; not pleasant to taste or smell.

unsay', *v.t.*, to recall what has been said.

unsay'ing, *pr.p.*, unsay.

unscathed', *adj.*, scatheless; unharmed.

unschol'arly, *adj.*, unlearned; not like a scholar.

un*schooled'*, *adj.*, not trained; not disciplined.

unscientif'ic, *adj.*, not scientific; inexpert.

unscrew', *v.t.*, to withdraw a screw from.

unscrewed', *p.p.*, unscrew.

unscrew'ing, *pr.p.*, unscrew.

unscrip'tural, *adj.*, contrary to Holy Scripture.

unscru'pulous, *adj.*, devoid of scruples.

unscru'pulously, *adv.*, in an unscrupulous way.

unscru'pulousness, *n.*, the state or quality of being unscrupulous.

unseal', *v.t.*, to break the seal of; to open.

unsealed', *p.p.*, unseal; *adj.*, not sealed up.

unseal'ing, *pr.p.*, unseal.

unsearch'able, *adj.*, past finding out.

unsea'sonable, *adj.*, untimely; inopportune; not in season.

unsea'sonably, *adv.*, in an unseasonable way.

unseat', *v.t.*, to displace from a seat; to throw from a saddle.

unseat'ed, *p.p.*, unseat.

unseat'ing, *pr.p.*, unseat.

unsea'worthy, *adj.*, unfit for going to sea; leaky.

unsec'onded, *adj.*, not supported.

unsecta'rian, *adj.*, not confined to the principles of a single sect.

unsee'ing, *adj.*, unobservant.

unseem'ly, *adj.*, indecorous.

unseen', *adj.*, not seen; invisible.

un*self'ish*, *adj.*, not selfish; considerate for others.

un*self'ishly*, *adv.*, in an unselfish way.

un*self'ishness*, *n.*, the state or quality of being unselfish.

unser'viceable, *adj.*, of no use.

unset'tle, *v.t.*, to disturb; upset.

unset'tled, *p.p.*, unsettle.

unset'tling, *pr.p.*, unsettle.

unsex', *v.t.*, to take away the sex characteristics of.

unshack'le, *v.t.*, to remove the shackles from.

unsha'ken, *adj.*, not shaken; immovable; firm.

unsheathe', *v.t.*, to withdraw from the sheath.

unsheathed', *p.p.*, unsheathe.

unsheath'ing, *pr.p.*, unsheathe.

unship', *v.t.*, to disembark.

unshipped', *p.p.*, unship.

unship'ping, *pr.p.*, unship.

unshod', *adj.*, without shoes.

unshrink'able, *adj.*, that cannot be shrunk.

unshrink'ing, *adj.*, not shrinking; fearless.

unshrink'ingly, *adv.*, in an unshrinking way.

unsight'liness, *n.*, the state or quality of being unsightly.

unsight'ly, *adj.*, unpleasant to the eye.

unskil'ful, *adj.*, clumsy; inexpert.

unskil'fulness, *n.*, the state or quality of being unskilful.

unskilled', *adj.*, not expert; requiring no skilled effort.

unsmoked', *adj.*, not smoked.

unso'ciable, *adj.*, not companionable, shunning society.

unso'cial, *adj.*, not social; not convivial.

unsoiled', *adj.*, unstained; fresh; clean.

unsold', *adj.*, not sold.

unsolic'ited, *adj.*, unasked for.

unsophis'ticated, *adj.*, unadulterated; simple.

unsort'ed, *adj.*, not sorted; mixed up.

unsought', *adj.*, not sought.

unsound', *adj.*, unhealthy; rotten.

unsound'ly, *adv.*, in an unsound way.

unsound'ness, *n.*, the state or quality of being unsound.

unspa'ring, *adj.*, not sparing; generous; lavish.

unspa'ringly, *adv.*, in an unsparing way.

unspeak'able, *adj.*, unutterable; shocking.

unspeak'ably, *adv.*, unutterably.

unspent', *adj.*, not spent; not wearied.

unspot'ted, *adj.*, without blemish.

unsta'ble, *adj.*, unsteady; fickle.

unstained', *adj.*, without a stain.

unstead'ily, *adv.*, in an unsteady way.

unstead'iness, *n.*, the state or quality of being unsteady.

unstead'y, *adj.*, not steady; inclined to fall.

unstint'ed, *adj.*, without stint; lavish.

unstop', *v.t.*, to remove the stopper from.

unstopped', *p.p.*, unstop.

unstring', *v.t.*, to loosen the strings of.

unstrung', *p.p.* unstring; *adj.*, in a state of nervous disorder.

unstud'ied, *adj.*, natural; unpremeditated.

un*substan'tial*, *adj.*, not substantial; etherial.

unsuccess'ful, *adj.*, not succeeding.

unsuccess'fully, *adv.*, without success.

unsuit'able, *adj.*, unfitting; improper.

unsuit'ably, *adv.*, in an unsuitable way.

unsuit'ed, *adj.*, unfitted.

unsul'lied, *adj.*, unstained; pure.

unsum'moned, *adj.*, not having been summoned.

unsung', *adj.*, not sung; not celebrated in song.

unsupport'ed, *adj.*, without support; baseless.

unsurpassed', *adj.*, not surpassed.

unsuscep'tible, *adj.*, not susceptible.

un*suspect'ed*, *adj.*, not suspected.

un*suspect'ing*, *adj.*, not mistrustful.

unsuspi'cious, *adj.*, *i.q.* unsuspecting.

unsuspi'ciously, *adv.*, in an unsuspicious way.

unsustained', *adj.*, not sustained.

unswathe', *v.t.*, to remove the bandages from.

unswathed', *p.p.*, unswathe.

unswa'thing, *pr.p.*, unswathe.

unswayed', *adj.*, unmoved.

unsweet'ened, *adj.*, without sweetening.

unswerv'ing, *adj.*, not bending to either side; keeping straight on; resolute.

un*sympathet'ic*, *adj.*, wanting in sympathy.

unsystemat'ic, *adj.*, not systematic; not methodical.

untaint'ed, *adj.*, without taint.

unta'mable, untame'able, *adj.*, not docile; impossible to tame.

untast'ed, *adj.*, not tasted.

untaught', *adj.*, not taught; unlearned.

unten'able, *adj.*, not tenable; unable to b · held.

un*thank'ful*, *adj.*, ungrateful.

un*thank'fully*, *adv.*, ungratefully.

un*thank'*fulness, *n.*, ingratitude.

un*think'*able, *adj.*, inconceivable.

un*think'*ing, *adj.*, inconsiderate; careless.

un*think'*ingly, *adv.*, in an unthinking way.

unthought'ful, *adj.*, inconsiderate.

unthrift'y, *adj.*, extravagant; not economizing.

unti'dy, *adj.*, disorderly; slovenly.

untie', *v.t.*, to unfasten; to loose.

untied', *p.p.*, untie.

until', *conj.*, *i.q.* till.

untime'ly, *adj.*, premature; inopportune.

unti'ring, *adj.*, indefatigable.

un'to, *prep.*, to.

un*told'*, *adj.*, not told; past all telling.

unto'ward, *adj.*, adverse; unpleasant.

untrained', *adj.*, not trained; amateur.

untram'mel(l)ed, *adj.*, free; unfettered.

untrav'el(l)ed, *adj.*, stay-at-home.

un*tried'*, *adj.*, strange; new.

untrod', *adj.*, *i.q.* untrodden.

untrod'den, *adj.*, never before trodden; unexplored.

untrue', *adj.*, false.

untru'ly, *adv.*, falsely.

untruth', *n.*, what is not true; a lie.

untu'tored, *adj.*, undisciplined.

untwine', *v.t.*, to disentangle.

untwined', *p.p.*, untwine.

untwi'ning, *pr.p.*, untwine.

untwist', *v.t.*, to restore to its original state what has become twisted.

untwist'ed, *p.p.*, untwist.

untwist'ing, *pr.p.*, untwist.

unty'ing, *pr.p.*, untie.

unused', *adj.*, not previously used; new; unaccustomed.

un*u'sual*, *adj.*, out of the ordinary.

un*u'sually*, *adv.*, in an unusual way or degree.

unut'terable, *adj.*, unspeakable.

unva'ried, *adj.*, without varying.

unvar'nished, *adj.*, not varnished; plain; not embellished.

unva'rying, *adj.*, unchanging.

unveil', *v.t.*, to remove the veil from; to reveal; disclose.

unveiled', *p.p.*, unveil; *adj.*, not wearing a veil.

unveil'ing, *pr.p.*, unveil.

unver'ified, *adj.*, not proved to be true.

unwa'rily, *adv.*, in an unwary way.

unwa'riness, *n.*, the state of being unwary.

unwar'like, *adj.*, not warlike.

unwar'rantable, *adj.*, without any justification.

unwar'rantably, *adv.*, in an unwarrantable way.

unwar'ranted, *adj.*, without warrant or justification.

unwa'ry, *adj.*, lacking caution.

unwa'vering, *adj.*, unhesitating.

unwea'ried, *adj.*, indefatigable; not tired.

unwear'iedly, *adv.*, indefatigably.

unwear'y, *adj.*, *i.q.* unwearied.

unweave', *v.t.*, to take to pieces what is woven.

unweav'ing, *pr.p.*, unweave.

unwel'come, *adj.*, not acceptable; not welcomed.

unwell', *adj.*, indisposed; sick.

unwept', *adj.*, not wept for.

unwhole'some, *adj.*, not wholesome; indigestible.

unwhole'someness, *n.*, the quality of being unwholesome.

unwield'iness, *n.*, the state of being unwieldly.

unwield'y, *adj.*, big and clumsy; awkward to handle.

unwill'ing, *adj.*, reluctant; not willing.

unwill'ingly, *adv.*, in an unwilling way; against one's will.

unwill'ingness, *n.*, the state of being unwilling.

unwind', *v.t.*, to loosen what is wound up.

unwind'ing, *pr.p.*, unwind.

unwise', *adj.*, not wise; indiscreet; foolish; imprudent.

unwise'ly, *adv.*, in an unwise way.

unwit'tingly, *adv.*, without one's knowledge.

unwom'anly, *adj.*, not as a woman should be or do.

unwont'ed, *adj.*, unaccustomed; unusual.

unwont'edness, *n.*, the quality of being unwonted.

unworld'ly, *adj.*, not given up to worldly pleasures.

unworn', *adj.*, never yet worn; new; not worn out.

unwor'thily, *adv.*, in an unworthy way.

unwor'thiness, *n.*, the quality of being unworthy.

unwor'thy, *adj.*, undeserving.

unwound', *p.p.*, unwind.

unwo'ven, *p.p.*, unweave.

unwrit'ten, *adj.*, not put down in writing.

unwrought', *adj.*, not wrought.

unyield'ing, *adj.*, inflexible.

unyoke', *v.t.*, to remove the yoke from.

unyoked', *p.p.*, unyoke.

unyo'king, *pr.p.*, unyoke.

up, *adv.*, high; upwards; from below to above.

u'pas, *n.*, a poisonous Javanese tree.

upbraid', *v.t.*, to reproach.

upbraid'ed, *p.p.*, upbraid.

upbraid'er, *n.*, one who upbraids.

upbraid'ing, *pr.p.*, upbraid; *n.*, reproach.

upcast', *adj.*, pointed upwards; *n.*, a ventilating shaft in a mine.

upheav'al, *adj.*, the act or result of upheaving.

upheave', *v.t.*, to heave up; lift up with a thrust from below.

upheaved', *p.p.*, upheave.

upheav'ing, *pr.p.*, upheave.

upheld', *p.p.*, uphold.

up'hill, *adj.*, going uphill; laborious; *adv.*, climbing upwards.

uphold', *v.t.*, to support; maintain.

uphold'er, *n.*, one who upholds.

uphold'ing, *pr.p.*, uphold.

uphol'ster, *v.t.*, to put coverings on furniture; to supply a house with furnishings.

uphol'sterer, *n.*, one who furnishes houses.

uphol'stery, *n.*, an upholsterer's business; house-furnishing.

up'land, *adj.*, rel. to the hills.

uplift', *v.t.*, to lift up; exalt; elevate.

uplift'ed, *p.p.*, uplift: *adj.*, being above oneself.

uplift'ing, *pr.p.*, uplift; *adj.*, inspiring; elevating.

upon', *prep.*, on; on the surface of; in regard to.

up'per, *adj.*, higher.

up'permost, *adj.*, the highest.

up'pers, *n. pl.*, the higher parts of boots.

upraise', *v.t.*, to raise up; lift up.

upraised', *p.p.*, upraise.

uprais'ing, *pr.p.*, upraise.

uprear', *v.t.* and *i.*, to rear up.

upreared', *p.p.*, uprear.

uprear'ing, *pr.p.*, uprear.

up'right, *adj.*, erect; vertical; honest; *n.*, a support; a piano with vertically placed strings.

up'rightly, *adv.*, in an upright way.

up'rightness, *n.*, the state or quality of being upright.

uprise', *v.i.*, to rise up; spring up.

upris'en, *p.p.*, uprise.

upri'sing, *pr.p.*, uprise.

up'roar, *n.*, a din; tumult.

uproar'ious, *adj.*, boisterous; noisy.

uproot', *v.t.*, to pull up by the roots; dislodge; eradicate.

uproot'ed, *p.p.*, uproot.

uproot'ing, *pr.p.*, uproot.

uprose', *p.t.*, uprise.

upset', *v.t.*, to overthrow; disturb; affect seriously.

up'set, *n.*, the act of upsetting; disturbance; state of being upset; *adj.*, fixed.

upset'ting, *pr.p.*, upset; *adj.*, disquieting.

up'shot, *adj.*, issue; result; purport.

up'side down, adverbial phrase = bottom upwards.

upspring', *v.i.*, to spring up.

upstairs', *adv.*, going up stairs; above stairs.

upstart', *v.i.*, to start up.

up'start, *n.*, one who has too suddenly emerged from obscurity.

up'-stroke, *n.*, an upward stroke with a pen or pencil.

up'town, *adj.*, bel. to the upper part of a city (*Amer.*).

up'-train, *n.*, a train going in the direction of the capital.

upturn', *v.t.*, to overthrow.

upturned', *p.p.*, upturn; *adj.*, turned upwards.

upturn'ing, *pr.p.*, upturn.

up'ward, *adj.*, tending towards a higher level.

up'wards, *adv.*, towards a higher level.

Ura'lian, *adj.*, pert. to the Ural Mountains.

ura'nium, *n.*, a metallic element.

uranog'raphy, *n.*, description of the heavens; the art of making celestial maps, etc.

uranol'ogy, *n.*, the science of the heavens.

uranos'copy, *n.*, the surveying of the heavens.

U'ranus, *n.*, a planet so named.

u'rate, *n.*, an uric acid salt.

ur'ban, *adj.*, pert. to the town as distinct from the country.

urbane', *adj.*, polite; courteous; cultivated.

urban'ity, *n.*, politeness.

ur'chin, *n.*, a small boy; a hedgehog.

Ur'du, *n.*, Hindustani

u'rea, *n.*, the chief constituent of urine.

ure'ter, *n.*, one of the urinary ducts.

ure'thra, *n.*, the duct by which urine is voided.

urge, *v.t.*, to push; impel; encourage; advise; demand.

urged, *p.p.*, urge.

ur'gency, *n.*, the state of being urgent.

ur'gent, *adj.*, insistent; imperative; immediately important.

ur'gently, *adv.*, in an urgent way.

ur'ging, *pr.p.*, urge.

u'ric, *adj.*, pert. to urea.

U'rim, *n. pl.*, one of the oracular ornaments (Urim and Thummim) worn by the Jewish High Priest.

u'rinal, *n.*, a convenience.

u'rinary, *adj.*, pert. to urine.

u'rinate, *v.i.*, to void urine.

u'rinative, *adj.*, promoting the flow of urine.

u'rine, *n.*, a kidney-excretion.

u'rinous, *adj.*, *i.q.* urinary.

urn, *n.*, a vessel of many sizes and shapes; a receptacle for the ashes of the dead.

uros'copy, *n.*, examination of urine for purposes of diagnosis.

Ur'sa Ma'jor, *n.*, the Great Bear.

Ur'sa Mi'nor, *n.*, the Little Bear.

ur'siform, *adj.*, like a bear.

ur'sine, *adj.*, pert. to bears.

Ur'suline, *adj.*, bel. to the Order of St. Ursula, founded for the double object of nursing and the instruction of girls.

u'rus, *n.*, *i.q.* aurochs.

us, *pron.*, *pers.*, the objective case of we.

u'sable, *adj.*, able to be used.

u'sage, *n.*, custom; treatment.

u'sance, *n.*, the stated period for paying bills of exchange.

use, *n.*, the act of using; custom; treatment; advantage.

use, *v.t.*, to employ; put to use; treat; accustom; *v.i.*, to be wont.

used, *p.p.*, use; *adj.*, accustomed.

use'ful, *adj.*, serviceable; advantageous.

use'fully, *adv.*, in a useful way.

use'fulness, *n.*, the state or quality of being useful.

use'less, *adj.*, of no use.

use'lessly, *adv.*, to no purpose.

use'lessness, *n.*, the state or quality of being useless.

u'ser, *n.*, one who uses; use; possession.

ush'er, *n.*, a doorkeeper; an undermaster in a school; an officer in a law court, etc.; *v.t.*, to introduce.

ush'ered, *p.p.*, usher.

ush'ering, *pr.p.*, usher.

u'sing, *pr.p.*, use.

us'quebaugh, *n.*, whisky.

ust'ion, *n.*, burning.

ustula'tion, *n.*, searing.

u'sual, *adj.*, customary; ordinary.

u'sually, *adv.*, customarily; commonly.

u'sufruct, *n.*, enjoyment; possession.

usufruct'uary, *adj.*, in temporary possession.

u'surer, *n.*, one who practises usury; an extortioner.

usu'rious, *adj.*, pert. to usury; practising usury.

usu'riously, *adv.*, in an usurious way.

usurp', *v.t.*, to take unlawful possession of.

usurpa'tion, *n.*, the act of usurping.

usurped', *p.p.*, usurp.

usurp'er, *n.*, one who usurps.

usurp'ing, *pr.p.*, usurp

u'sury, *n.*, lending money at interest; extortion.

uten'sil, *n.*, a domestic or culinary appliance.

u'terine, *adj.*, rel. to the womb; having a common mother but another father.

u'terus, *n.*, the womb (*Lat.*).

utilita'rian, *adj.*, rel. to utility; *n.*, one who professes utilitarianism.

utilita'rianism, *n.*, the doctrine of the greatest good for the greatest number, as taught by J. S. Mill.

util'ity, *n.*, advantage; usefulness.

utiliza'tion, *n.*, the act or result of utilizing.

u'tilize, *v.t.*, to put to use.

u'tilized, *p.p.*, utilize.

u'tilizing, *pr.p.*, utilize.

ut'most, *adj.*, furthest; to the largest extent.

Uto'pia, *n.*, the land of Nowhere; an ideal State.

Uto'pian, *adj.*, pert. to Utopia; visionary; ideal.

Uto'pianism, *n.*, idealism in politics and social affairs.

u'tricle, *n.*, a cell with a thin wall; fruit thin-skinned and with a single cell.

utric'ular, *adj.*, pert. to utricle.

ut'ter, *v.t.*, to publish; speak; pronounce; put in circulation; *adj.*, complete; absolute; without qualification.

ut'terable, *adj.*, able to be uttered.

ut'terance, *n.*, speech; manner of speaking.

ut'tered, *p.p.*, utter.

ut'terer, *n.*, one who utters.

ut'tering, *pr.p.*, utter.

ut'terly, *adv.*, entirely; absolutely.

ut'termost, *adj.*, extreme.

u'vea, *n.*, a layer of the iris.

u'veous, *adj.*, like a grape.

u'vula, *n.*, the fleshy appendage of the soft palate.

u'vular, *adj.*, rel. to the uvula.

uxo'rial, *adj.*, pert. to a wife.

uxo'rious, *adj.*, *i.q.* uxorial; doting on a wife.

uxo'riousness, *n.*, the state of being uxorious.

V

va'cancy, *n.*, emptiness; state of being vacant; an office without its incumbent; empty space.
va'cant, *adj.*, empty; unoccupied; unintellectual.
vacate', *v.t.*, to leave unoccupied; to resign (an office).
vaca'ted, *p.p.*, vacate.
vaca'ting, *pr.p.*, vacate.
vaca'tion, *n.*, the act of vacating; a time of holiday.
vac'cinate, *v.t.*, to inoculate with vaccine lymph.
vac'cinated, *p.p.*, vaccinate.
vac'cinating, *pr.p.*, vaccinate.
vaccina'tion, *n.*, the act of vaccinating.
vac'cinator, *n.*, one who performs vaccination.
vac'cine, *adj.*, rel. to cows; *n.*, vaccine lymph.
vac'illancy, *n.*, *i.q.* vacillation.
vac'illant, *adj.*, vacillating.
vac'illate, *v.i.*, to waver; fluctuate in mind.
vac'illated, *p.p.*, vacillate.
vac'illating, *pr.p.*, vacillate.
vacilla'tion, *n.*, the state of being unsteady in mind.
vacu'ity, *n.*, emptiness; the state of being vacuous.
vac'uous, *adj.*, empty; brainless; with an unintellectual look.
vac'uum, *n.*, a void space.
va'de-me'cum, *n.*, a pocket guide. (The name is derived from two Latin words = go with me.)
vag'abond, *adj.*, vagrant; good for nothing; *n.*, a vagrant; a ne'er-do-well.
vag'abondage, *n.*, the state of being a vagabond.
vag'abondism, *n.*, *i.q.* vagabondage.
vag'abondize, *v.i.*, to act as a vagrant.
vaga'ry, *n.*, an eccentric proceeding; a whim.
vagi'na, *n.*, a sheath (*Lat.*).
vagi'nal, *adj.*, pert. to the vagina.
vag'inate, *adj.*, having a sheath.
vag'inated, *adj.*, *i.q.* vaginate.
va'grancy, *n.*, the state of being a vagrant.
va'grant, *adj.*, wandering; homeless; *n.*, one who lives a wandering, unsettled life.
vague, *adj.*, obscure; uncertain; indefinite; hazy.
vague'ly, *adv.*, in a vague way.
vague'ness, *n.*, the state or quality of being vague.
vail, *n.*, a parting gift to a servant.
vain, *adj.*, useless; without result; ineffectual; conceited.
vain'er, *adj.*, *comp.* of vain.
vain'est, *adj.*, *super.* of vain.
vainglo'rious, *adj.*, boastful; ostentatious.
vainglo'riously, *adv.*, boastingly.
vainglo'ry, *n.*, boastfulness; self-glorification.
vain'ly, *adv.*, to no purpose.
vair, *n.*, fur (*her.*).
vair'y, *adj.*, furry: furred (*her.*).
vai'vode, *n.*, the title of a prince in Rumania and other countries. Also *waywode*.
vakeel', *n.*, an Indian attorney; delegate.
val'ance, *n.*, drapery hanging from a bed.
vale, *n.*, *i.q.* valley.
va'le, *v.i.*, imperative mood = farewell (*Lat.*).
valedic'tion, *n.*, a farewell.
valedic'tory, *adj.*, bidding farewell.
va'lence, *n.*, the combining powers of an atom.
Valenciennes', *n.*, a special kind of costly lace.
val'entine, *n.*, a sweetheart; a gift on St. Valentine's Day, Feb. 14.
vale'rian, *n.*, a medicinal plant.
val'et, *n.*, a male personal attendant or body-servant; *v.t.* to attend upon.
valetudina'rian, *adj.*, rel. to sickness and health; *n.*, a confirmed invalid.
valetudina'rianism, *n.*, excessive and habitual worrying about one's health.
valetu'dinary, *adj.*, *i.q.* valetudinarian.
Valhal'la, *n.*, the place of dead heroes, according to Scandinavian mythology.
val'iant, *adj.*, brave; stout-hearted.
val'iantly, *adv.*, heroically; stoutly.
val'id, *adj.*, strong; established; ratified; legally confirmed.
valid'ity, *n.*, the state or quality of being valid.
val'idly, *adv.*, in a valid way.
val'inch, *n.*, a sampling-tube.
valise', *n.*, a portmanteau.

Val'kyrie, *n.*, one of Odin's twelve maidens, whose mission it was to lead slain heroes to Valhalla.
val'ley, *n.*, a depressed tract between hills.
val'lum, *n.*, a rampart (*Lat.*).
valo'nia, *n.*, acorn-cup.
val'orous, *adj.*, brave; heroic.
val'orously, *adv.*, in a valorous way.
val'our, *n.*, bravery; heroism.
valse, *n.*, a waltz; *v.t.*, to dance the waltz.
val'uable, *adj.*, of worth; costly; precious.
valua'tion, *n.*, the act of appraising or estimating value; an estimate made.
val'uator, *n.*, one whose profession it is to appraise.
val'ue, *n.*, worth; price; *v.t.*, to appraise; esteem.
val'ued, *p.p.*, value.
val'ueless, *adj.*, worthless.
val'uer, *n.*, *i.q.* valuator.
val'uing, *pr.p.*, value.
val'vate, *adj.*, having a valve or valves.
valve, *n.*, a covering over an opening; a mechanical device for opening or closing a passage; a division in a shell.
valved, *adj.*, closed with a valve.
valv'let, *n.*, a little valve.
valv'ular, *adj.*, like a valve.
valv'ule, *n.*, a little valve.
vam'brace, *n.*, armour for the forearm.
vamose', *v.i.*, to abscond (*Amer.*).
vamp, *n.*, a boot's upper leather; a patch on an old garment, etc., intended to make it appear new; a made-up accompaniment; *v.t.*, to put a vamp on; to make up an accompaniment to a song.
vamped, *p.p.*, vamp.
vamp'er, *n.*, one who vamps.
vamp'ing, *pr.p.*, vamp
vam'pire, *n.*, a fearful ghost that sucks the blood.
vam'plate, *n.*, a plate to guard the hand in couching a lance. Also *vamplet*.
van, *n.*, the front of an army or fleet; a covered cart; a goods carriage on a train.
vana'dium, *n.*, a metallic element so named.
Van'dal, *n.*, one of the 5th cent. invading barbarians who ravaged Europe and destroyed libraries, works of art, etc.; anyone like a Vandal.
vandal'ic, *adj.*, pert. to the Vandals.
van'dalism, *n.*, a spirit opposed to art and literature; barbarism.
vandyke', *adj.*, rel. to the painter Vandyke and his style; *n.*, a picture by him; a particular kind of lace collar; *v.t.*, to cut an ornamental collar in points.
vane, *n.*, a weather-cock.
vang, *n.*, a steadying-rope (*naut.*).
van'*guard*, *n.*, the advance guard of an army.
vanil'la, *n.*, a flavouring made from a dried orchid-fruit.
van'ish, *v.i.*, to disappear.
van'ished, *p.p.*, vanish.
van'ishing, *pr.p.*, vanish.
van'ity, *n.*, emptiness; foolish conceit; a vain show.
van'quish, *v.t.*, to overcome; conquer.
van'quishable, *adj.*, able to be vanquished.
van'quished, *p.p.*, vanquish.
van'quishing, *pr.p.*, vanquish.
van'tage, *n.*, advantage; a lawn tennis term, meaning the first point scored after deuce.
van'tage-ground, *n.*, a position of advantage.
vap'id, *adj.*, tasteless; dull.
vapid'ity, *n.*, the quality of being vapid.
vap'idly, *adv.*, in a vapid way.
vaporif'ic, *adj.*, producing vapour.
va'porizable, *adj.*, able to be vaporized.
vaporiza'tion, *n.*, conversion into vapour.
va'porize, *v.t.* and *i.*, to turn to vapour.
va'porized, *p.p.*, vaporize.
va'porizing, *pr.p.*, vaporize.
va'porous, *adj.*, filled with, resembling, vapour.
va'pour, va'por, *n.*, the result of converting solids or liquids by means of heat; mist; *v.i.*, to become vapour; to hector.
va'po(u)r-bath, *n.*, a bath of steam.
va'po(u)red, *p.p.*, vapour.
va'po(u)rer, *n.*, one who vapours.
va'po(u)ring, *pr.p.*, vapour.
va'po(u)rish, *adj.*, like vapour.
va'po(u)rs, *n. pl.*, hysterical fancies; melancholia.
va'po(u)ry, *adj.*, filled with vapour.
variabil'ity, *n.*, the state or quality of being variable.
va'riable, *adj.*, changeable; fickle.
va'riableness, *n.*, *i.q.* variability.
va'riably, *adv.*, changeably.
va'riance, *n.*, difference; strife.
va'riant, *adj.*, different; *n.*, an alternative form.
varia'tion, *n.*, the act of varying; change; deviation.

var'ices, *n.*, pl. of varix.
var'icocele, *n.*, a swelling in the scrotum or spermatic cord.
var'icose, *adj.*, excessively swollen.
va'ried, *p.p.*, vary.
va'riegate, *v.t.*, to introduce a variety of colours in.
va'riegated, *p.p.*, variegate.
va'riegating, *pr.p.*, variegate.
variega'tion, *n.*, the act or effect of variegating.
vari'ety, *n.*, diversity; a blend of diverse things; a peculiar kind.
va'riform, *adj.*, of diverse forms.
va'riformed, *adj.*, *s.q.* variform.
vari'ola, *n.*, smallpox.
vari'olar, *adj.*, pert. to variola.
variola'tion, *n.*, marking with smallpox.
variol'ic, *n.*, marked with smallpox.
va'riolite, *n.*, a greenstone having a pustular appearance.
va'rioloid, *adj.*, like smallpox.
vari'olous, *adj.*, *s.q.* variolar.
vario'rum, *n.*, denoting that a book contains the notes of several or many authorities.
va'rious, *adj.*, different; several.
va'riously, *adv.*, differently; here and there.
va'rix, *n.*, distention of a vein.
var'let, *n.*, a footman; a scamp.
var'nish, *n.*, a liquid used to give a polished surface; *v.t.*, to apply varnish to; to gloss.
var'nished, *p.p.*, varnish.
var'nisher, *n.*, one who varnishes.
var'nishing, *pr.p.*, varnish.
va'ry, *v.t.*, to alter; diversify; *v.i.*, to change; deviate; disagree.
va'rying, *pr.p.*, vary.
vas'cular, *adj.*, containing vessels.
vascular'ity, *n.*, the state or quality of being vascular.
vasculif'erous, *adj.*, producing vessels.
vase, *n.*, a vessel, usually ornamental.
Vas'eline, *n.*, trade-mark for a petroleum jelly and other products.
vas'iform, *adj.*, like a duct.
vas'sal, *n.*, the tenant of a feudal lord; *adj.*, in subjection.
vas'salage, *n.*, the state of a vassal; servitude.
vast, *adj.*, wide; huge; *n.*, space; the sea.
vast'er, *adj.*, *comp.* of vast.
vast'est, *adj.*, *super.* of vast.
vast'ly, *adv.*, to a vast extent.
vast'ness, *n.*, spaciousness; extent.
vast'y, *adj.*, a poetical form of vast, as "the vasty deep."
vat, *n.*, a large vessel used by brewers and tanners.
Vat'ican, *n.*, the great palace of the Popes in Rome; the papal curia.
Vat'icanism, *n.*, the policy of the papal curia.
va'ticide, *n.*, the murder of a prophet; the murderer of a prophet.
vatic'inal, *adj.*, foreboding; soothsaying.
vatic'inate, *v.t.*, to predict.
vatic'inated, *p.p.*, vaticinate.
vatic'inating, *pr.p.*, vaticinate.
vaticina'tion, *n.*, soothsaying; prediction.
vaude'ville, *n.*, a short musical comedy; a topical song.
Vaudois', *n. pl.*, the Waldenses, or people of Vaud in Switzerland.
vault, *n.*, an arched roof; a vaulted cellar; a tomb; the vault of heaven (*i.e.*, the sky); a leap; *v.t.*, to construct an arched roof over; *v.i.*, to leap.
vault'ed, *p.p.*, vault; *adj.*, having an arched roof of masonry.
vault'er, *n.*, one who vaults.
vault'ing, *pr.p.*, vault.
vaunt, *n.*, a boast; *v.i.*, to boast.
vaunt'ed, *p.p.*, vaunt.
vaunt'er, *n.*, one who vaunts.
vaunt'ing, *pr.p.*, vaunt; *n.*, boasting.
vaunt'ingly, *adv.*, in a boastful way.
vav'asour, *n.*, a baron's vassal.
veal, *n.*, calf's flesh.
vec'tor, *n.*, a line conceived to have direction and length fixed but not its position; quantity determining position in space of one point in relation to another.
Ve'da, *n.*, one of the Vedas, the four sacred books of the Hindus.
vedette', *n.*, a sentinel on horseback. Also *vidette*.
veer, *v.i.*, to turn about; *v.t.*, to cause to turn about.
veered, *p.p.*, veer.
veer'ing, *pr.p.*, veer.
veg'etable, *adj.*, rel. to plants; *n.*, a plant growing in the ground; an edible plant for the table.
veg'etal, *adj.*, of the nature of a plant.
vegeta'rian, *adj.*, rel. to vegetable diet; *n.*, one who adopts a vegetable diet.
vegeta'rianism, *n.*, the principles of those who eschew flesh diet and live chiefly on fruit and vegetables.
veg'etate, *v.i.*, to grow; sprout; to live an unintellectual, uninteresting life.

veg'etated, *p.p.*, vegetate.
veg'etating, *pr.p.*, vegetate.
vegeta'tion, *n.*, the act of vegetating; plant-growth; collective plants.
veg'etative, *adj.*, growing like plants.
ve'hemence, *n.*, impetuosity; vigour; passion.
ve'hemency, *n.*, *i.q.* vehemence.
ve'hement, *adj.*, impetuous; ardent; passionate.
ve'hemently, *adv.*, in a vehement way.
ve'hicle, *n.*, a means of conveyance; a medium.
vehic'ular, *adj.*, pert. to vehicles.
vehm'gericht, *n.*, an old German secret council.
veh'mic, *adj.*, pert. to the Vehmgericht.
veil, *n.*, a covering for the head or face; anything like a veil; *v.t.*, to cover with a veil; to conceal.
veiled, *p.p.*, veil.
veil'ing, *pr.p.*, veil; *n.*, material of which veils are made.
vein, *n.*, a blood-vessel; a leaf-rib; a seam in a mine; mood; style; *v.t.*, to mark with veins.
veined, *p.p.*, vein.
vein'ing, *pr.p.*, vein.
vein'less, *adj.*, wanting veins.
vein'ous, *adj.*, filled with veins.
vein'y, *adj.*, veined.
veld, veldt, *n.*, wide, open country.
vel'licate, *v.t.*, to make to twitch convulsively; *v.i.*, to twitch.
vel'licated, *p.p.*, vellicate.
vellica'tion, *n.*, twitching.
vel'lum, *n.*, finer parchment.
veloc'ipede, *n.*, a vehicle driven by the feet.
veloc'ity, *n.*, speed; rate of speed.
ve'lum, *n.*, a membranous covering (*Lat.*).
vel'vet, *n.*, silk material with a close, soft nap.
vel'veted, *adj.*, covered with velvet.
velveteen', *n.*, a fabric like velvet.
vel'veting, *n.*, collective velvet goods; velvet fabric.
vel'vety, *adj.*, soft and smooth like velvet.
ve'nal, *adj.*, open for sale; mercenary.
venal'ity, *n.*, mercenariness.
venat'ic, *adj.*, rel. to hunting.
vena'tion, *n.*, the arrangement of veins.
vend, *v.t.*, to sell.
vend'ed, *p.p.*, vend.
vendee', *n.*, one to whom something is sold.
vend'er, *n.*, one who sells.
vendet'ta, *n.*, a system of vengeance; blood-feud.
vendibil'ity, *n.*, the state of being vendible.
vend'ible, *adj.*, saleable; marketable.
vend'ing, *pr.p.*, vend.
vendi'tion, *n.*, the act of vending.
vend'or, *n.*, *i.q.* vender.
vend'or, *n.*, in law, chiefly a seller of lands and tenements.
vendue', *n.*, an auction-sale.
veneer', *n.*, a thin layer of wood, ivory, etc., laid over an inferior surface; an outer coating; external polish concealing bad qualities; *v.t.*, to cover with veneer; to gloss over.
veneered', *p.p.*, veneer.
veneer'ing, *pr.p.*, veneer; *n.*, the process of adding veneer; material used for veneer.
ven'erable, *adj.*, worthy of veneration; to be honoured for old age; the honorific title of an Archdeacon; the earliest of the three degrees in canonization (Venerable; Blessed; Saint).
ven'erate, *v.t.*, to regard with great reverence.
ven'erated, *p.p.*, venerate.
ven'erating, *pr.p.*, venerate.
venera'tion, *n.*, reverence.
ven'erator, *n.*, one who venerates.
vene'real, *adj.*, rel. to sexual passion.
ven'ery, *n.*, hunting; the chase; sexual indulgence.
venesec'tion, *n.*, phlebotomy; blood-letting.
Vene'tian, *adj.*, rel. to Venice and the Venetians; *n.*, a native of Venice.
ven'geance, *n.*, revenge; retribution; requital.
venge'ful, *adj.*, vindictive.
venge'fully, *adv.*, in a vengeful way.
ve'nial, *adj.*, pardonable; excusable.
venial'ity, *n.*, the quality of being venial.
Ve'ni,Crea'tor, *n.*, the first two words of the great Latin hymn for Whitsuntide, *Veni, Creator Spiritus.* It appears in the English Ordinal as "Come, Holy Ghost, our souls inspire," etc.
veni're, *n.*, a writ bidding the sheriff or coroner call a jury. (The full phrase is, *venire facias*, cause to come.) (*Lat.*)
ven'ison, *n.*, deer's flesh.
ven'om, *n.*, poison; malice; spite.
ven'omed, *adj.*, *i.q.* venomous.
ven'omous, *adj.*, containing venom; poisonous; malicious.
ven'omously, *adv.*, in a venomous way.

ve'nous, *adj.*, full of veins; carried in the veins.

vent, *n.*, an opening for letting in or out; utterance; scent (of an animal); a sale-mark; *v.t.*, to utter; emit; *v.i.*, to take breath (said of a hunted animal); to sniff the air.

vent'age, *n.*, a small opening.

vent'ed, *p.p.*, vent.

ven'ter, *n.*, the belly; a belly-like protuberance (*Lat.*).

vent'-hole, *n.*, *i.q.* vent.

ven'tiduct, *n.*, an air-passage.

ven'til, *n.*, a shutter arrangement within the wind-chest of an organ, regulating the admission of air.

ven'tilate, *v.t.*, to cause the air to circulate in; to make publicly known.

ven'tilated, *p.p.*, ventilate.

ven'tilating, *pr.p.*, ventilate.

ventila'tion, *n.*, the act of ventilating; public discussion.

ven'tilator, *n.*, any appliance for freshening the air in a room or building; one who ventilates.

vent'ing, *pr.p.*, vent.

ven'tose, *adj.*, flatulent; windy.

vent'-peg, *n.*, a peg to stop up a vent.

ven'tral, *adj.*, rel. to the venter; situated on the anterior surface.

ven'tricle, *n.*, a small cavity in the body.

ven'tricose, *adj.*, with a large belly; inflated.

ventrilocu'tion, *n.*, *i.q.* ventriloquism.

ventrilo'quial, *adj.*, pert. to ventriloquism.

ventril'oquism, *n.*, the art of speaking so that the voice seems to come from some other source than oneself.

ventril'oquist, *n.*, one who practises ventriloquism.

ventril'oquize, *v.i.*, to practise ventriloquism.

ventril'oquized, *p.p.*, ventriloquize.

ventril'oquizing, *pr.p.*, ventriloquize.

ventril'oquy, *n.*, *i.q.* ventriloquism.

ven'ture, *n.*, a hazard; attempt; trial; *v.t.* and *i.*, to attempt; dare; risk.

ven'tured, *p.p.*, venture.

ven'turer, *n.*, an adventurer.

ven'turesome, *adj.*, daring; taking risks; risky.

ven'turin, *n.*, a yellow powder imitating gold.

ven'turing, *pr.p.*, venture.

ven'turous, *adj.*, *i.q.* venturesome.

ven'turously, *adv.*, in a venturous way.

ven'ue, *n.*, the place or district where a trial is appointed to be held.

ven'ulose, *adj.*, full of little veins.

Ve'nus, *n.*, the Roman goddess of love; one of the planets. [ful.

vera'cious, *adj.*, truthful.

vera'ciously, *adv.*, truthfully.

verac'ity, *n.*, truthfulness.

veran'dah, *n.*, an open, roofed portico or gallery of a house. Also *veranda*.

vera'tria, *n.*, *i.q.* veratrine.

ver'atrine, *n.*, a compound medicine derived from hellebore and other plants, and used in cases of rheumatism and neuralgia.

verb, *n.*, a part of speech which predicates something of the subject.

ver'bal *adj.*, rel. to a verb or to a word; spoken; oral; literal.

ver'balism, *n.*, something spoken; mere words.

ver'balist, *n.*, a merely verbal critic; one interested merely in words.

verbal'ity, *n.*, the state of being verbal.

ver'balize, *v.t.*, to convert into a verb; *v.i.*, to be wordy.

ver'balized, *p.p.*, verbalize.

ver'balizing, *pr.p.*, verbalize.

ver'bally, *n.*, by word of mouth; word for word.

verba'tim, *adv.*, word for word (a base *Lat.* word).

Verbe'na, *n.*, vervain.

ver'biage, *n.*, wordiness; using more words than the sense requires.

verbose', *adj.*, wordy; too fond of words.

verbose'ly, *adv.*, in a verbose style.

verbos'ity, *n.*, wordiness.

ver'dancy, *n.*, the state of being verdant; greenness.

ver'dant, *adj.*, green; fresh.

verd-antique', *n.*, a green building-stone, very decorative.

ver'dantly, *adv.*, in a verdant way.

ver'derer, *n.*, an official in the royal forests having judicial powers.

ver'dict, *n.*, the finding of a jury; judgment; decision.

ver'digris, *n.*, a deposit on sheet copper produced by the action of acetic acid; green rust.

ver'diter, *n.*, one of certain pigments obtained from copper nitrate.

ver'dure, *n.*, greenness; vegetation.

ver'dured, *adj.*, covered with verdure.

verge, *n.*, the edge, brink; an emblematic wand or staff (also *virge*); area; *v.i.*, to border on.

verged *p.p.*, verge.

ver'ger, *n.*, a wand-bearer; an official who bears a wand or staff before ecclesiastical and academic dignitaries. (More correctly spelt *virger*, being derived from *virgifer* or *virgarius*.)

Vergil'ian, *adj.*, pert. to Vergil, the great Roman poet. Also *Virgilian*.

ver'ging, *pr.p.*, verge.

verid'ical, *adj.*, speaking the truth.

ver'iest, *adj.*, *super.* of very.

ver'ifiable, *adj.*, capable of verification.

verifica'tion, *n.*, proving to be true; affidavit in proof.

ver'ified, *p.p.*, verify.

ver'ify, *v.t.*, to establish the truth of; bring to the test of truth or fact; bear out; add affidavit to pleadings.

ver'ifying, *pr.p.*, verify.

ver'ily, *adv.*, truly; really.

verisim'ilar, *adj.*, probable; likely.

verisimil'itude, *n.*, likeliness; nearness to truth; a thing resembling the truth.

ver'itable, *adj.*, genuine; actual.

ver'ity, *n.*, truth; a fact; an eternally true doctrine.

ver'juice, *n.*, the juice of sour fruit.

ver'meil, *n.*, silver gilt; a varnish that produces lustre.

vermeol'ogist, *n.*, one who studies worms.

vermeol'ogy, *n.*, the study of worms.

vermicel'li, *n.*, a finer kind of macaroni.

vermic'eous, *adj.*, pert. to, resembling, worms.

ver'micide, *adj.*, destructive of worms.

vermic'ular, *adj.*, pert. to worms; like worms.

vermic'ulate, *adj.*, *i.q.* vermicular; worm-eaten; ornamented with wavy lines.

vermic'ulate, *v.t.*, to ornament with wavy lines.

vermic'ulated, *p.p.*, vermiculate.

vermicula'tion, *n.*, worm-like motion.

ver'micule, *n.*, a little worm.

vermic'ulous, *adj.*, worm-eaten.

ver'miform, *adj.*, like a worm.

ver'mifuge, *n.*, a remedy against worms.

vermil'ion, *n.*, cinnabar; a bright-red pigment.

ver'min, *n.*, any noxious creature, whether beast or insect; such creatures collectively.

ver'minate, *v.i.*, to produce worms or parasites.

vermina'tion, *n.*, the act or state of verminating.

ver'minous, *adj.*, full of vermin.

vermiv'orous, *adj.*, eating worms.

ver'muth, *n.*, a liqueur flavoured with wormwood. Also *vermouth*.

vernac'ular, *adj.*, native; pert. to one's own country; local; *n.*, the language of a particular country.

ver'nal, *adj.*, pert. to spring.

verna'tion, *n.*, the disposition of leaves within the leaf-bud.

Ver'nicle, *n.*, the handkerchief of St. Veronica with which she is said to have wiped Our Lord's face as He went to His Passion, and on which a true likeness of the face was impressed.

ver'nicose, *adj.*, with the appearance of being varnished.

ver'nier, *n.*, a small, adjustable scale which ascertains fractional parts of the sub-divisions on a fixed scale.

Veronese', *adj.*, rel. to Verona; *n.*, a native of Verona.

veron'ica, *n.*, *i.q.* vernicle; *n.*, a plant so named.

verr'ucose, *adj.*, warty.

ver'sant, *n.*, a slope of land; *adj.*, conversant.

ver'satile, *adj.*, able to turn one's hand to anything; apt at many pursuits; turning on a pivot.

versatil'ity, *n.*, all-round aptitude.

verse, *n.*, a metrical line; poetry; a single stanza; one of the short sections into which a chapter of the Bible is divided; a short liturgical sentence; a part of an anthem that is reserved for single voices.

versed, *adj.*, familiar with; conversant with; steeped in; proficient.

ver'sicle, *n.*, a short verse; esp. the liturgical short sentences in which the people respond to the priest (as, *Versicle:* O Lord, open Thou our lips. *Response:* And our mouth shall show forth Thy praise).

ver'sicolour, ver'sicolor, *adj.*, variegated; of many colours.

ver'sicoloured, ver'sicolored, *adj.*, *i.q.* versicolour.

versifica'tion, *n.*, poetry-writing; the act of versifying.

ver'sified, *p.p.*, versify.

ver'sifier, *n.*, one who makes verses, esp. poor ones.

ver'sify, *v.t.*, to turn into metrical writing; *v.i.*, to compose poetry.

ver'sifying, *pr.p.*, versify.

ver'sion, *n.*, a turning; translation; special account.

verst, *n.*, a Russian measure of distance (1,166 yards).

ver'sus, *prep.*, against (*leg.*).

versute', *adj.*, cunning; tricky.

vert, *v.i.*, to change one's faith (*colloq.*); *n.*, the tincture green (*her.*); a convert to another faith (*colloq.*); all that grows green leaves in a forest, and the right to cut it (*leg.*).

ver'tebra, *n.*, one of the segments of the backbone.

ver'tebrae, *n.*, pl. of vertebra.

ver'tebral, *adj.*, pert. to the vertebrae.

Vertebra'ta, *n.*, the division of the animal kingdom distinguished by the possession of a spinal column.

ver'tebrate, *adj.*, possessing a spinal column; *n.*, one of the Vertebrata.

ver'tebrate, *v.t.*, to cause to be backboned; to invigorate.

ver'tebrated, *adj.*, *i.q.* vertebrate; *p.p.*, vertebrate.

ver'tex, *n.*, the turning point at the summit; the apex; crown of the head.

ver'tical, *adj.*, pert. to the vertex; pert. to the crown of the head; upright.

ver'tically, *adv.*, upright; perpendicularly.

ver'ticil, *n.*, a whorl.

vertic'illate, *adj.*, whorled.

vertig'inous, *adj.*, giddy.

ver'tigo, *n.*, giddiness.

ver'vain, *n.*, a weedy plant so named; *i.q.* verbena.

verve, *n.*, spirit enthusiasm, as shown in artistic or literary production.

ver'y, *adj.*, true; real; actual; *adv.*, really; in a high degree.

vesi'ca, *n.*, a bladder: cyst (*Lat.*).

Vesi'ca pis'cis, *n.*, a fish-bladder, a name given in art to the pointed oval glory within which a pictorial representation or emblem was painted or carved.

ves'ical, *adj.*, rel. to the bladder.

ves'icant, *adj.*, blistering; *n.*, a blister.

ves'icate, *v.t.*, to blister.

ves'icated, *p.p.*, vesicate.

ves'icating, *pr.p.*, vesicate.

vesica'tion, *n.*, blistering.

ves'icatory, *adj.*, producing a blister.

ves'icle, *n.*, a small cyst.

vesic'ular, *adj.*, rel. to, resembling, vesicles.

vesic'ulate, *adj.*, having vesicles.

vesic'ulous, *adj.*, *i.q.* vesiculate.

Ves'pa, *n.*, a wasp; hornet (*Lat.*).

ves'per, *adj.*, rel. to evening; *n.*, the evening star (Venus)

ves'peral, *n.*, a book containing the chants used at vespers.

ves'pers, *n. pl.*, the last but one of the Day Hours or divine offices.

ves'pertine, *adj.*, rel. to the evening; opening or flying in the evening, as flowers, birds, etc.

ves'piary, *n.*, a wasps' nest.

ves'sel, *n.*, a hollow receptacle to hold liquid; a ship; a duct or canal which conveys blood, etc.; a person viewed as in receipt of blessings poured into him

vest, *n.*, a robe; dress; a waistcoat; a close-fitting body undergarment; *v.t.*, to robe; bestow power or office on; confer ownership; *v.i.*, to assume a robe; (with the addition of *in*) to come to.

Ves'ta, *n.*, the Roman goddess of the hearth; a striking-match.

ves'tal, *adj.*, pert. to Vesta; chaste; *n.*, one of the Virgins who kept the sacred light in her temple burning.

vest'ed, *p.p.*, vest; *adj.*, fixed without contingency.

vestia'rian, *adj.*, pert. to vestments and dress.

ves'tiary, *n.*, *i.q.* vestiarian.

vestib'ular, *adj.*, rel. to a vestibule.

ves'tibule, *n.*, a porch; entrance-chamber; anatomically, a connecting chamber.

vestib'ulum, *n.*, *i.q.* vestibule (*Lat.*).

ves'tige, *n.*, a trace; footmark; an atrophied organ.

vest'ing, *pr.p.*, vest.

vest'ment, *n.*, a robe; dress; garment.

ves'try, *n.*, a room in a church where the clergy and others robe; the collective ratepayers of a parish; their assembly.

ves'tryman, *n.*, a member of vestry.

ves'ture, *n.*, clothing; raiment.

vest'ured, *adj.*, robed.

Vesu'vian, *adj.*, pert. to Mt. Vesuvius; volcanic; *n.*, a fusee.

vetch, *n.*, a bean-like plant, much used for forage.

vet'eran, *adj.*, of old standing; experienced; *n.*, an old soldier or sailor; one who has grown old in any service or employment.

veterina'rian, *adj.*, rel. to veterinary practice.

vet'erinary, *adj.*, rel. to the treatment of diseases in animals; *n.*, a veterinary surgeon.

ve'to, *v.t.*, to forbid; prohibit officially; throw out a measure; *n.*, the right of vetoing; the act of vetoing; a prohibition.

ve'toed, *p.p.*, veto.

ve'toer, *n.*, one who vetoes.

ve'toing, *pr.p.*, veto.

ve'toist, *n.*, *i.q.* vetoer.

vettu'ra, *n.*, a four-wheeled carriage (*Ital.*).

vetturi'no, *n.*, the driver of a vettura.

vex, *v.t.*, to annoy; harass; tease.

vexa'tion, *n.*, the act of vexing; disappointment.

vexa'tious, *adj.*, annoying; disappointing.

vexa'tiously, *adv.*, in a vexatious way.

vexed, *p.p.*, vex.

vex'er, *n.*, one who vexes.

vex'il, *n.*, *i.q.* vexillum.

vex'illar, *adj.*, rel. to a vexillum.

vex'illary, *n.*, a standard-bearer.

vexilla'tion, *n.*, a Roman army division grouped under one standard.

vexil'lum, *n.*, a Roman military standard; large upper petal of a papilionaceous flower; the pennon sometimes hung round a bishop's crozier; a processional cross, etc.

vex'ing, *pr.p.*, vex.; *adj.*, *i.q.* vexatious.

vi'a, *n.*, a road; way. In English use, the word occurs in the ablative (*viâ*), in the sense of "by the way of," "through" (*Lat.*).

viabil'ity, *n.*, the state of being viable.

vi'able, *adj.*, able to maintain life.

vi'aduct, *n.*, a road supported on arches and carried across a valley or a depression in the country.

vi'al, *n.*, a flask; bottle. Also *phial*.

viam'eter, *n.*, an appliance for measuring distance travelled.

vi'and, *n.*, food; meat.

viat'ic, *adj.*, rel. to a journey.

viat'icum, *n.*, the last Sacrament. (This use of the word is developed from the original *Lat.* meaning of provisions for a magistrate or ambassador setting out on a journey.)

via'tor, *n.*, a traveller (*Lat.*).

vi'brant, *adj.*, vibrating; resounding.

vi'brate, *v.i.*, to oscillate; quiver.

vi'brated, *p.p.*, vibrate.

vi'bratile, *adj.*, tending to vibrate.

vi'brating, *pr.p.*, vibrate.

vibra'tion, *n.*, the act of vibrating; resonance.

vi'brative, *adj.*, *i.q.* vibratory.

vi'bratory, *adj.*, making vibrations.

vibur'num, *n.*, the Guelder-rose and kindred plants.

vic'ar, *n.*, a deputy. Theoretically, the priest or curate of a parish is the rector, but many parishes were formerly appropriated by the religious houses, which corporately became the rector in each case, and put in a perpetual curate as the rector's deputy or Vicar. In France and Belgium the priest of the parish is the Curé (our curate) and his assistant is styled Vicaire. In England we have the strange inversion of Vicar and (assistant) Curate.

vic'arage, *n.*, the benefice or the residence of a vicar.

vica'rial, *adj.*, pert. to a vicar and a vicar's tithes.

vica'riate, *n.*, the office, and tenure of office, of a vicar.

vica'rious, *adj.*, in substitution; done by deputy.

vica'riously, *adv.*, by deputy.

vice, *n.*, a fault; evil habit; a clamp for firmly holding in its place anything that has to be worked upon. The word is also used as a prefix = in place of; deputy.

vi'ce, a *Lat.* ablative = in place of.

vice-ad'miral, *n.*, an admiral of the second rank; the next to a full admiral.

vice-*chair'*man, *n.*, a deputy chairman.

vice-cham'berlain, *n.*, a deputy chamberlain.

vice-chan'cellor, *n.*, a chancellor's deputy.

vice-con'sul, *n.*, a consul's deputy.

vicege'rency, *n.*, the office, and tenure of office, of a vicegerent.

vicege'rent, *n.*, one who is deputed to exercise authority in another's name.

vic'enary *adj.*, containing twenty.

vicen'nial, *adj.*, pert. to a period of twenty years.

vice-pres'ident, *n.*, one who ranks after a president.

vice-*prin'cipal*, *n.*, the second in command of an institution presided over by a principal.

vice-re'gal, *adj.*, pert. to a viceroy.

vice'roy, *n.*, the king's deputy in a subject or united country.

viceroy'alty, *n.*, the office or jurisdiction of a viceroy.

vi'ce ver'sa, adverbial phrase = exactly in the reverse way.

vic'inage, *n.*, neighbourhood.

vic'inal, *adj.*, neighbouring.

vicin'ity, *n.*, neighbourhood; proximity.

vic'ious, *adj.*, depraved; faulty.

vic'iously, *adv.*, in a vicious way.

vic'iousness, *n.*, the state of being vicious.

vicis'situde, *n.*, change

vic'tim, *n.*, a sacrifice; a person suffering

from cruelty, oppression, misfortune, etc.

vic'timize, *v.t.*, to make a victim of; to make to suffer; to cheat.

vic'timized, *p.p.*, victimize.

vic'timizing, *pr.p.*, victimize.

vic'tor, *n.*, a conqueror (*Lat.*).

Victo'ria, victo'ria, *n.*, victory (*Lat.*); an open, light carriage; a variety of water-lily.

Victo'rian, *adj.*, pert. to Victoria (the place name) or the era of Queen Victoria.

victorine', *n.*, a lady's small boa.

victo'rious, *adj.*, conquering.

victo'riously, *adv.*, in a victorious way.

vic'tory, *n.*, triumph; success in battle.

vict'ual, *v.t.*, to supply with food. *See* victuals.

vict'ualled, *p.p.*, victual.

vict'ualler, *n.*, a licensed inn-keeper, who is supposed to provide food as well as drink.

vict'ualling, *pr.p.*, victual; *n.*, a victualler's trade.

vict'uals, *n. pl.*, food; eatables.

vicu'ña, *n.*, a kind of llama, noted for its fleece.

vi'de, *v.t.*, imperative mood = see (*Lat.*).

videl'icet, *adv.*, namely (*Lat.*).

vidette', *n.*, *i.q.* vedette.

vie, *v.i.*, to engage in rivalry.

vied, *p.p.*, vie.

Viennese', *adj.*, pert. to Vienna and its inhabitants; *n.*, a native of Vienna.

view, *n.*, sight; scenery; the act of seeing; an opinion; a picture.

viewed, *p.p.*, view.

view'er, *n.*, one who views.

view'ing, *pr.p.*, view.

view'less, *adj.*, without a view.

vig'il, *n.*, a watching; the eve of a feast.

vig'ilance, *n.*, watchfulness; wariness.

vig'ilant, *adj.*, watchful; vigilant.

vig'ilantly, *adv.*, warily; with vigilance.

vignette', *n.*, a photograph or engraving not enclosed in a border; a picture of the head and bust; *v.t.*, to make a vignette of.

vig'orous, *adj.*, full of energy or health.

vig'orously, *adv.*, in a vigorous way.

vig'our, *n.*, strength; energy; robust health.

Vik'ing, *n.*, a pirate from the fjords or viks of Scandinavia. (Another explanation of the name connects it with *vig* = war.)

vile, *adj.*, worthless; depraved.

vile'ly, *adv.*, in a vile way.

vile'ness, *n.*, the quality of being vile.

vi'ler, *adj.*, *comp.* of vile.

vi'lest, *adj.*, *super.* of vile.

vilifica'tion, *n.*, the act or effect of vilifying.

vil'ified, *p.p.*, vilify.

vil'ifier, *n.*, one who vilifies.

vil'ify, *v.t.*, to slander; defame; take away the character of.

vil'ifying, *pr.p.*, vilify.

vil'la, *n.*, a country estate (*Lat.*); a suburban house, detached or semi-detached, with a certain amount of garden.

vil'lage, *n.*, a small settlement or community in the country.

vil'lager, *n.*, a dweller in a village.

vil'lain, *n.*, a worthless person; a scoundrel; formerly, a serf under feudal conditions.

vil'lainous, *adj.*, rascally; scoundrelly; vile.

vil'lainously, *adv.*, in a villainous way.

vil'lainy, *n.*, depravity; wickedness.

villat'ic, *adj.*, pert. to a villa.

vil'leinage, *n.*, the system of serfdom; condition of a serf.

vil'li, *n. pl.*, hairs; hairy growth on plants.

vil'lous, *adj.*, covered with villi.

vim, *n.*, force (a colloquialism).

vim'inal, *adj.*, pert. to vine shoots.

vimin'eous, *adj.*, *i.q.* viminal.

vina'ceous, *adj.*, pert. to vines and grapes; like grapes in colour.

vinaigrette', *n.*, a perforated box containing aromatic salts.

vincibil'ity, *n.*, the state of being vincible.

vin'cible, *adj.*, able to be conquered.

vin'culum, *n.*, a tie; bond (*Lat.*).

vin'dicable, *adj.*, able to be vindicated.

vin'dicate, *v.t.*, to defend; to prove the justice or truth of; to justify.

vin'dicated, *p.p.*, vindicate.

vin'dicating, *pr.p.*, vindicate.

vindica'tion, *n.*, the act or result of vindicating.

vin'dicative, *adj.*, vindicating.

vin'dicator, *n.*, one who vindicates.

vin'dicatory, *adj.*, justifying.

vindic'tive, *adj.*, revengeful.

vindic'tively, *adv.*, in a vindictive way.

vindic'tiveness, *n.*, the quality of being vindictive.

vine, *n.*, the plant which produces grapes. (The name is sometimes given to other varieties of climbing plants.)

vine'-clad, *adj.*, covered with vines.
vin'egar, *n.*, wine allowed to turn sour; also the acid product of malt liquors.
vi'nery, *n.*, a house in which grapes are cultivated.
vine'yard, *n.*, land on which vines are cultivated.
vi'nous, *adj.*, pert. to wine; addicted to wine.
vin'tage, *n.*, the time of gathering the grapes for wine; the crop; the wine of a particular year.
vin'tager, *n.*, one who gathers in the vintage.
vint'ner, *n.*, a wine-seller.
vi'ny, *adj.*, like a vine; full of vines.
vi'ol, *n.*, the family name of the violin, violoncello, etc.; specifically, the bass-viol.
vi'ola, *n.*, the tenor violin; a plant genus.
vi'olable, *adj.*, able to be violated.
viola'ceous, *adj.*, pert. to violets.
vi'olate, *v.t.*, to break; transgress; ravish.
vi'olated, *p.p.*, violate.
vi'olating, *pr.p.*, violate.
viola'tion, *n.*, the act of violating.
vi'olator, *n.*, one who violates.
vi'olence, *n.*, the state or quality of being violent; fury; brutality.
vi'olent, *adj.*, furious; vehement; impetuous.
vi'olently, *adv.*, in a violent way.
violes'cent, *adj.*, with a violent tinge.
vi'olet, *n.*, a plant of the Viola kind; the colour of the same.
violin', *n.*, a wooden musical instrument, having four strings and played with a bow.
violin'ist, *n.*, a player on a violin.
vi'olist, *n.*, a player on the viol.
violoncel'list, *n.*, a player on the violoncello.
violoncel'lo, *n.*, a four-stringed bass instrument, played with a bow and held between the knees.
violo'ne, *n.*, the double-bass (*mus.*).
vi'per, *n.*, a poisonous snake; a venomous person.
vi'perine, *adj.*, pert. to, resembling, a viper.
vi'perous, *adj.*, venomous.
vira'go, *n.*, a violent, noisy woman.
vires'cent, *adj.*, becoming green.
vir'gate, *n.*, an old land-measure; *adj.*, wand-like; straight.
vir'ger, *n.*, *i.q.* verger.
Virgil'ian, *adj.*, pert. to Vergil, the great Latin poet. Also *Vergilian.*
vir'gin, *n.*, one who is and has always remained chaste; a maiden; supremely, the Blessed Virgin Mary; *adj.*, chaste; maidenly; pure.
vir'ginal, *adj.*, pert. to, resembling, a virgin.
virgin'ity, *n.*, the state of being virgin; maidenhood.
vir'go, *n.*, a virgin (*Lat.*).
vir'gulate, *adj.*, like a small wand.
virid'ity, *n.*, greenness.
vir'ile, *adj.*, manly; masculine; vigorous.
viril'ity, *n.*, manliness; masculine character.
virtu', *n.*, the skill of an artist; a work of art; a curio. Also *vertu.*
vir'tual, *adj.*, essentially, though not actually, so and so.
vir'tually, *adv.*, essentially, though not actually; to all intents and purposes.
vir'tue, *n.*, goodness; merit; purity; essential spirit.
virtuo'so, *n.*, an expert in an art; specifically, a fine player on a musical instrument.
vir'tuous, *adj.*, good; pure.
vir'tuously, *adv.*, in a virtuous way.
vir'tuousness, *n.*, the state or quality of being virtuous.
vir'ulence, *n.*, the state or quality of being virulent.
vir'ulent, *adj.*, venomous; bitter; spiteful.
vir'ulently, *adv.*, in a virulent way.
vi'rus, *n.*, poison (*Lat.*); poisonous matter.
vis, *n.*, power (*Lat.*).
vi'sa, *v.t.*, *i.q.* visé.
vi'saed, *p.p.*, visa.
vis'age, *n.*, countenance.
vis-à-vis', *adv.*, face to face; *n.*, an opposite neighbour.
vis'cera, *n. pl.*, entrails; bowels.
vis'ceral, *adj.*, pert. to viscera.
vis'cid, *adj.*, sticky; glutinous.
viscid'ity, *n.*, the state or quality of being viscid.
viscos'ity, *n.*, the state or quality of being viscous.
vis'count, *n.*, a titled person ranking between an earl and a baron.
vis'countess, *n.*, fem. of viscount.
vis'cous, *adj.*, *i.q.* viscid.
visé', *n.*, the confirmation of a passport; *v.t.*, to endorse a passport after examination.
Vish'nu, *n.*, the second in rank of the three Hindu deities.
visibil'ity, *n.*, the state of being visible.
vis'ible, *adj.*, able to be seen; within sight; apparent.
vis'ibly, *adv.*, in a visible way.

Vis'igoth, *n.*, one of the Visigoths, a division of the Goths which settled in France and Spain.

Visigoth'ic, *adj.*, pert. to Visigoths.

vi'sion, *n.*, the act or power of seeing; a dream; an apparition; prophetic sight.

vi'sionariness, *n.*, the quality of being visionary.

vi'sionary, *adj.*, given to dreaming; imaginative; unreal; *n.*, one who indulges in fanciful schemes.

vis'it, *v.t.*, to go to see a person or to stay in a place; to punish; to inspect; *n.*, the act of calling on a person; a stay in a place; inspection.

vis'itable, *adj.*, able to be visited.

vis'itant, *n.*, *i.q.* visitor.

visita'tion, *n.*, the act of visiting; a visit of official inspection; punishment; chastisement.

visite', *n.*, a light, outdoor feminine costume, which was the mode in the early part of the 19th cent.

vis'ited, *p.p.*, visit.

vis'iting, *pr.p.*, visit.

vis'itor, *n.*, one who visits in any sense; specifically, a person authorized to visit a college or church, etc., for the purpose of official inspection.

visito'rial, *adj.*, pert. to an official visitor.

vis'or, viz'or, *n.*, the open-work in the front of a helmet.

vis'ored, viz'ored, *adj.*, furnished with a visor.

vis'ta, *n.*, a view.

vis'ual, *adj.*, pert. to vision or sight.

visual'ity, *n.*, the quality of being visual.

vis'ualize, *v.t.*, to form a mental picture of.

vi'tal, *adj.*, pert. to life; essential.

vi'talism, *n.*, the theory that life owes its origin to a vital, as distinct from a chemical or material, principle.

vi'talist, *n.*, a believer in vitalism.

vital'ity, *n.*, the state or quality of being vital; living power.

vitaliza'tion, *n.*, the act of vitalizing; state of being vitalized.

vi'talize, *v.t.*, to put life into.

vi'talized, *p.p.*, vitalize.

vi'talizer, *n.*, one who, that which, vitalizes.

vi'talizing, *pr.p.*, vitalize.

vi'tally, *adv.*, in a vital way or sense.

vi'tals, *n. pl.*, the vital parts of an animal organism (*i.e.*, on which life depends, as the heart, lungs, etc.).

vi'tiate, *v.t.*, to corrupt; debase.

vi'tiated, *p.p.*, vitiate.

vi'tiating, *pr.p.*, vitiate.

vitia'tion, *n.*, the act or effect of vitiating.

vit'iculture, *n.*, the cultivation of the vine.

vit'reous, *adj.*, pert. to glass; glassy.

vitres'cence, *n.*, the state of becoming vitreous.

vitres'cent, *adj.*, becoming vitreous.

vitres'cible, *adj.*, vitrifiable.

vitrifac'tion, *n.*, the act or effect of vitrifying.

vit'rifiable, *adj.*, able to be vitrified.

vitrifica'tion, *n.*, *i.q.* vitrifaction.

vit'rified, *p.p.*, vitrify; *adj.*, glazed.

vit'riform, *adj.*, of a glassy appearance.

vit'rify, *v.t.*, to turn into glass; to glaze; *v.i.*, to become glassy.

vit'rifying, *pr.p.*, vitrify.

vit'riol, *n.*, sulphuric acid.

vit'riolate, *v.t.*, to convert into a sulphate.

vit'riolated, *p.p.*, vitriolate.

vit'riolating, *pr.p.*, vitriolate.

vitriola'tion, *n.*, the act or effect of vitriolating.

vitriol'ic, *adj.*, pert. to vitriol; like vitriol.

vit'riolizable, *adj.*, able to be vitriolized.

vitrioliza'tion, *n.*, *i.q.* vitriolation.

vit'riolize, *v.t.* and *i.*, *i.q.* vitriolate.

vit'riolized, *p.p.*, vitriolize.

vit'riolizing, *pr.p.*, vitriolize.

vit'uline, *adj.*, pert. to a calf and veal; like veal or a calf.

vitu'perate, *v.t.*, to abuse; revile.

vitu'perated, *p.p.*, vituperate.

vitu'perating, *pr.p.*, vituperate.

vitupera'tion, *n.*, the act of vituperating; abuse; reviling.

vitu'perative, *adj.*, abusive; reviling.

vitu'perator, *n.*, one who vituperates.

viva'ce, *adv.*, in a lively manner; quickly (*mus.*).

viva'cious, *adj.*, lively; sprightly.

viva'ciously, *adv.*, in a vivacious way.

viva'ciousness, *n.*, *i.q.* vivacity.

vivac'ity, *n.*, liveliness; sprightliness.

viva'rium, *n.*, a place where live animals are kept.

viv'ary, *n.*, *i.q.* vivarium.

vi'va vo'ce, *adv.*, orally; *adj.*, oral.

vives, *n. pl.*, an ear disease, esp. in horses.

viv'id, *adj.*, with a look of life; exceedingly bright; realistic.

viv'idly, *adv.*, in a vivid way.

viv'idness, *n.*, the quality of being vivid.

vivifica'tion, *n.*, the act or result of vivifying.

viv'ified, *p.p.*, vivify.

viv'ify, *v.t.*, to put life into; animate.

viv'ifying, *pr.p.*, vivify.

vivip'arous, *adj.*, bringing forth living offspring.

vivisec'tion, *n.*, dissection of the living body.

viv'isector, *n.*, one who practises vivisection.

vix'en, *n.*, a female fox; a termagant woman.

vix'enish, *adj.*, like a vixen.

viz'ard, *n.*, a mask.

vizier', *n.*, a high Mohammedan state official.

vizier'ate, *n.*, the office of a vizier.

viz'or, *n.*, *i.q.* visor.

viz'ored, *adj.*, having a vizor.

vo'cable, *n.*, a word.

vocab'ulary, *n.*, a list of words in alphabetical order.

vocab'ulist, *n.*, the maker of a vocabulary.

vo'cal, *adj.*, pert. to the voice and utterance.

vocal'ic, *adj.*, pert. to, containing, vowels.

vo'calism, *n.*, *i.q.* vocalization.

vo'calist, *n.*, a singer.

vocal'ity, *n.*, the quality of being vocal; the quality of vowels.

vocaliza'tion, *n.*, the act of vocalizing.

vo'calize, *v.t.*, to make vocal; to form or utter with the mouth; to add vowel points to (in shorthand or in a language, such as Hebrew, which has only consonantal letters); *v.i.*, to give utterance.

vo'calized, *p.p.*, vocalize.

vo'calizing, *pr.p.*, vocalize.

vo'cally, *n.*, in a vocal way; orally; with the voice.

voca'tion, *n.*, a calling, esp. in the sense of a Divine call; a profession; career.

voc'ative, *adj.*, pert. to calling; *n.*, the vocative case, so named from its being used in direct addresses.

vocif'erate, *v.t.* and *i.*, to shout out; bawl.

vocif'erated, *p.p.*, vociferate.

vocif'erating, *pr.p.*, vociferate.

vocifera'tion, *n.*, the act of vociferating.

vocif'erous, *adj.*, loud; bawling.

vocif'erously, *adv.*, in a vociferous way.

vogue, *n.*, fashion; prevailing use.

voice, *n.*, sound produced by the mouth; the spoken word; a sound like a human voice; suffrage, or share in voting, etc.; a resonant vocal note; tone; a verb-form distinguishing between active and passive; *v.t.*, to give expression to; to adjust and regulate the tone of an organ pipe.

voiced, *p.p.*, voice.

voice'less, *adj.*, without a voice; silent.

voic'ing, *pr.p.*, voice; *n.*, the act of regulating the tone of an organ pipe.

void, *adj.*, empty; useless; invalid; without effect; *v.t.*, to make invalid; to excrete; *n.*, empty space.

void'able, *adj.*, able to be voided.

void'ance, *n.*, voiding; state of being void or vacant, esp. the vacancy of a benefice.

void'ed, *p.p.*, void.

void'er, *n.*, one who, that which, voids.

void'ing, *pr.p.*, void.

void'ness, *n.*, the state or quality of being void.

vo'lant, *adj.*, flying.

Volapuk', *n.*, an artificial universal language, the invention of Johann M. Schley (1879).

vol'atile, *adj.*, quickly evaporating; gay; fickle.

volatil'ity, *n.*, the quality or state of being volatile.

vol'atilizable, *adj.*, able to be volatilized.

volatiliza'tion, *n.*, the act or effect of volatilizing.

vol'atilize, *v.t.*, to make to evaporate; *v.i.*, to evaporate.

vol'atilized, *p.p.*, volatilize.

vol'atilizing, *pr.p.*, volatilize.

volcan'ic, *adj.*, pert. to volcanoes.

volcanic'ity, *n.*, the quality of being volcanic.

vol'canist, *n.*, one who investigates volcanic phenomena.

volcan'ity, *n.*, *i.q.* volcanicity.

vol'canize, *v.t.*, to expose to volcanic heat.

volca'no, *n.*, an opening in the earth's crust through which molten lava is ejected or, in the case of an extinct volcano, has at some time been ejected.

vole, *n.*, a field-mouse.

volée', *n.*, a rush of musical notes (*Fr.*).

volita'tion, *n.*, flight.

voli'tion, *n.*, an act of will; will-power.

vol'itive, *adj.*, pert. to the will.

volks'raad, *n.*, the Orange State's legislative assembly.

vol'ley, *n.*, a simultaneous discharge of missiles; the immediate return of a tennis-ball while it is in flight; *v.t.*, to discharge in a volley; to return a tennis-ball while in flight; *v.t.*, to be discharged or to sound together; to volley at tennis.

vol'leyed, *p.p.*, volley.

vol'leying, *pr.p.*, volley.

volt, *n.*, a quick movement to avoid a thrust in fencing; unit of electromotive force.

volta'ic, *adj.*, galvanic

Voltair'ism, *n.*, the scepticism of Voltaire.

vol'taism, *n.*, galvanism.

vol'taplast, *n.*, a battery used in the electrotype process.

vol'tatype, *n.*, electrotype.

voltigeur', *n.*, a vaulter; tumbler; an irregular sort of French rifleman.

volt'meter, *n.*, an apparatus for measuring the force of an electric current.

volubil'ity, *n.*, the quality of being voluble.

vol'uble, *adj.*, glib; talkative.

vol'ubly, *adv.*, in a voluble way.

vol'ume, *n.*, sheets or pages bound up together to make one book; a book; a coil; bulk; content; strength of sound.

vol'umed, *adj.*, convolute; bulky.

volumet'ric, *adj.*, pert. to the measurement of the volume of gases.

volu'minous, *adj.*, bulky; containing many volumes.

vol'untarily, *adv.*, of one's own free will.

vol'untary, *adj.*, done of one's own free will; *n.*, an organ solo.

vol'untaryism, *n.*, the principle of refusing Stateaid to religious or educational institutions.

volunteer', *n.*, one who offers his services gratuitously; *v.t.*, to offer; propose; *v.i.*, to offer oneself for doing anything; to undertake.

volunteered', *p.p.*, volunteer.

volunteer'ing, *pr.p.*, volunteer; *n.*, service as a volunteer.

volupt'uary, *adj.*, pert. to luxury; *n.*, one addicted to luxury and self-indulgence.

volupt'uous, *adj.*, pert. to sensual or sensuous pleasures.

volupt'uously, *adv.*, in a voluptuous way.

volupt'uousness, *n.*, the state of being voluptuous.

volute', *adj.*, spiral; *n.*, a classical architectural ornament curved like a scroll; a kind of gasteropod.

volu'ted, *adj.*, having a volute.

volu'tion, *n.*, *i.q.* convolution.

vom'it, *n.*, matter thrown up from the stomach; an emetic; *v.t.*, to throw up from the stomach; *v.i.*, to be sick.

vom'ited, *p.p.*, vomit.

vom'iting, *pr.p.*, vomit; *n.*, sickness.

vom'itive, *adj.*, causing vomiting; emetic.

vom'ito, *n.*, yellow fever (*Spanish*).

vom'itory, *adj.*, *i.q.* vomitive; *n.*, an emetic.

vomituri'tion, *n.*, retching.

vora'cious, *adj.*, greedy; with a huge appetite.

vora'ciously, *adv.*, in a voracious way.

vorac'ity, *n.*, greediness.

vor'tex, *n.*, a whirlpool; whirling motion.

vor'tical, *adj.*, pert. to a vortex.

vor'tically, *adv.*, in a vortical way.

vor'ticel, *n.*, a bell-animalcule.

vo'taress, *n.*, fem. of votary.

vo'tary, *n.*, one vowed to another person, a deity, a study, etc.; *adj.*, votive.

vote, *n.*, a written or spoken assent; *v.t.*, to grant; *v.i.*, to give a vote.

vo'ted, *p.p.*, vote.

vo'ter, *n.*, one who possesses or exercises the vote.

vo'ting, *pr.p.*, vote; *n.*, votes collectively.

vo'tive, *adj.*, given in performance of a vow.

vo'tively, *adv.*, in a votive way.

vouch, *v.t.* and *i.*, to confirm; support.

vouched, *p.p.*, vouch.

vouchee', *n.*, one who is called upon to defend a legal title.

vouch'er, *n.*, one who vouches; an attesting document, etc.; the calling in of a vouchee.

vouch'ing, *pr.p.*, vouch.

vouch'or, *n.*, *i.q.* voucher (in the legal sense).

vouchsafe', *v.t.*, to grant; condescend (to do or give).

vouchsafed', *p.p.*, vouchsafe.

vouchsafe'ment, *n.*, an act of condescension; the favour granted.

vouchsaf'ing, *pr.p.*, vouchsafe.

voussoir', *n.*, a wedge-shaped stone in an arch.

vow, *n.*, a solemn pledge; *v.t.*, to pledge; promise; *v.i.*, to declare.

vowed, *p.p.*, vow.

vow'el, *n.*, an open sound as distinguished from a consonant; the letter which names each vowel.

vow'elize, *v.t.*, *i.q.* vocalize in the sense of adding vowel points.

vow'el(l)ed, *adj.*, having vowels.

vow'er, *n.*, one who vows.

vow'ing, *pr.p.*, vow.

vox huma'na, *n.*, a reed-stop on the organ bearing some likeness to the human voice.

vox pop'uli, *Lat.* phrase = the popular voice.

voy'age, *n.*, a journey by water; *v.t.*, to traverse; *v.i.*, to go by water.

voy'aged, *p.p.*, voyage.

voy'ager, *n.*, one who voyages.

voyageur', *n.*, a fur-trader; a Canadian boatman (*Fr.*).

voy'aging, *pr.p.*, voyage.

vraisemblance', *n.*, appearance of truth; plausibility (*Fr.*).

Vulca'nian, *adj.*, pert. to Vulcan and metallurgy; also to Vulcanism.

Vulcan'ic, *adj.*, *i.q.* Vulcanian.

Vul'canist, *n.*, one who holds the Plutonic theory of rock formation.

vul'canite, *n.*, rubber vulcanized

vulcaniza'tion, *n.*, the act or effect of vulcanizing.

vul'canize, *v.t.*, to treat rubber with sulphur at a high temperature.

vul'canized, *p.p.*, vulcanize.

vul'canizing, *pr.p.*, vulcanize.

vul'gar, *adj.*, bel. to the people; vernacular; common; low; unrefined.

vulga'rian, *n.*, a rich person with unrefined manners.

vul'garism, *n.*, coarseness; vulgarity; mode of expression not in good literary taste.

vulgar'ity, *n.*, the state or quality of being vulgar; coarseness.

vul'garize, *v.t.*, to make vulgar; debase.

vul'garized, *p.p.*, vulgarize.

vul'garizing, *pr.p.*, vulgarize.

vul'garly, *adv.*, in a vulgar way; commonly.

Vul'gate, *n.*, the Lat. version of the Sacred Scriptures made by St. Jerome in the 4th cent.

vulnerabil'ity, *n.*, the state of being vulnerable.

vul'nerable, *adj.*, able to be wounded; not proof against attack.

vul'nerary, *adj.*, healing; *n.*, a remedy for wounds.

vul'pine, *adj.*, pert. to foxes; fox-like; crafty.

vul'ture, *n.*, a large bird of prey so named.

vul'turine, *adj.*, pert. to vultures.

vy'ing, *pr.p.*, vie.

W

wab'ble, *v.i.*, *i.q.* wobble.

wab'bled, *p.p.*, wabble.

wab'bling, *pr.p.*, wabble.

wack'e, *n.*, the German equivalent for trap-rock.

wad, *n.*, soft material used for stuffing; tow rammed into a gun to keep the powder in; *v.t.*, to use as a wad; to stuff with a wad.

wad'ded, *p.p.*, wad.

wad'ding, *pr.p.*, wad; *n.*, material for stuffing.

wad'dle, *v.i.*, to walk with a goose-like movement; *n.*, a walking from side to side.

wad'dled, *p.p.*, waddle.

wad'dler, *n.*, one who waddles.

wad'dling, *pr.p.*, waddle.

wade, *v.i.*, to walk through water; *v.t.*, to cross by wading.

wa'ded, *p.p.*, wade.

wa'der, *n.*, one who wades.

wa'ders, *n. pl.*, waterproof stockings used in fishing.

wa'ding, *pr.p.*, wade.

wa'dy, *n.*, a watercourse.

wa'fer, *n.*, a very thin piece of paste, used for various purposes; esp. the thin disc for the Eucharist; *v.t.*, to seal up with a wafer.

wa'fered, *p.p.*, wafer.

wa'fering, *pr.p.*, wafer.

waf'fle, *n.*, a cake made with batter.

waft, *v.t.*, to carry or send with a wind.

waft'age, *n.*, wafting; distance wafted.

waft'ed, *p.p.*, waft.

waft'er, *n.*, one who, that which, wafts.

waft'ing, *pr.p.*, waft.

wag, *n.*, the act of wagging; a funny fellow; *v.t.* and *i.*, to shake or nod backwards and forwards.

wage, *v.t.*, to carry on (a war or battle); to hazard; *n.*, pay of a servant.

waged, *p.p.*, wage.

wa'ger, *n.*, a bet; *v.t.* and *i.*, to bet.

wa'gered, *p.p.*, wager.

wa'gerer, *n.*, one who wagers.

wa'gering, *pr.p.*, wager.

wa'ges, *n. pl.*, wage. (This form is more commonly used than *wage*.)

wagged, *p.p.*, wag.

wag'gery, *n.*, drollery; playful joking.

wag'ging, *pr.p.*, wag.

wag'gish, *adj.*, droll; playful.

wag'gishly, *adv.*, in a waggish way.

wag'gle, *v.t.* and *i.*, to shake from side to side.

wag'gled, *p.p.*, waggle.

wag'gling, *pr.p.*, waggle.

wa'ging, *pr.p.*, wage.

wag'(g)on, *n.*, a large cart; a truck on a railway.

wag'(g)onage, *n.*, wagons collectively; charge for freight on wagons.

wag'(g)oner, *n.*, a wagon-driver.

wagonette', *n.*, a light carriage.

wag'tail, *n.*, a bird so named.

Waha'bi, *n.*, a member of the Arabian sect founded by Abd-el-Wahab.

waif, *n.*, a lost thing; a stray.

wail, *v.t.* and *i.*, to lament; *n.*, a cry in lament.

wailed, *p.p.*, wail.

wail'er, *n.*, one who wails.

wail'ing, *pr.p.*, wail; *n.*, loud lamentation.

wain, *n.*, a wagon.

wain'scot, *n.*, panelling of a wall; *v.t.*, to cover with panelling.

wain'scot(t)ed, *p.p.*, wainscot.

wain'scot(t)ing, *pr.p.*, wainscot; *n.*, panelling.

waist, *n.*, the part of the body immediately above the hips; the middle.

waist'band, *n.*, a belt.

waist'coat, *n.*, a vest.

wait, *v.i.*, to be in a state of expectancy; to stand still; to serve at a table; to attend on someone; *v.t.*, to await; *n.*, sing. of waits.

wait'ed, *p.p.*, wait.

wait'er, *n.*, one who waits in any sense, esp. who serves at table.

wait'ing, *pr.p.*, wait; *adj.*, serving at table; *n.*, a waiter's calling.

wait'ing-maid, *n.*, a female attendant.

wait'ress, *n.*, fem. of waiter.

waits, *n. pl.*, Christmas open-air singers and musicians.

waive, *v.t.*, to concede; resign one's claim to.

waived, *p.p.*, waive.

waiv'er, *n.*, voluntary renouncement of a right or claim (*leg.*).

waiv'ing, *pr.p.*, waive.

wake, *v.t.*, to rouse out of sleep; *v.i.*, to be awake; to arise from sleep; *n.*, the track of a vessel, etc.; a vigil for the dead.

waked, *p.p.*, wake.

wake'ful, *adj.*, sleepless; vigilant.

wake'fully, *adv.*, in a wakeful way.

wake'fulness, *n.*, the state of being wakeful.

wa'ken, *v.t.* and *i.*, *i.q.* wake.

wa'kened, *p.p.*, waken.

wa'kener, *n.*, one who wakens.

wa'kening, *pr.p.*, waken.

wa'ker, *adj.*, on the watch; vigilant.

wa'king, *pr.p.*, wake.

Walden'ses, *n.*, the name of the followers of Peter Waldo, a Piedmontese Protestant preacher who founded a sect *c.* 1170.

wale, *n.*, the scar or mark produced by a blow with a whip, etc.; *v.t.*, to scar.

waled, *p.p.*, wale.

Walhal'la, *n.*, *i.q.* Valhalla.

walk, *v.i.*, to move at a pace slower than trotting or running; to take walking exercise; to conduct oneself; *v.t.*, to make to walk; to travel over; *n.*, a movement slower than trotting or running; an act of walking; a place to walk in; a manner of life.

walked, *p.p.*, walk.

walk'er, *n.*, one who walks.

walk'ing, *pr.p.*, walk.

walk'ing-stick, *n.*, a stick used as a help in walking.

wall, *n.*, a defence round an enclosure; the side of a house or a room; *v.t.*, to furnish with a wall; to protect.

wal'laby, *n.*, a species of kangaroo.

Wal(l)a'chian, *adj.*, pert. to Wallachia; *n.*, a native of Wallachia.

walled, *p.p.*, wall; *adj.*, fortified.

wall'er, *n.*, a wall-builder.

wal'let, *n.*, a satchel; bag.

wall'-eye, *n.*, an eye with a white iris.

wall'-eyed, *adj.*, having a wall-eye.

wall'flower, *n.*, a fragrant flower so named.

wall'-fruit, *n.*, cultivated fruit grown against a wall.

wall'ing, *pr.p.*, wall.

Walloon', *adj.*, rel. to the Walloons (of Flanders) and to the Walloon language.

wal'lop, *v.i.*, to make a bubbling noise (said of anything boiling); *v.t.*, to thrash; *n.*, a thrashing.

wal'loped, *p.p.*, wallop.

wal'loping, *pr.p.*, wallop; *n.*, a beating.

wal'low, *v.i.*, to roll in mud; to revel in vice.

wal'lowed, *p.p.*, wallow.

wal'lower, *n.*, one who wallows.

wal'lowing, *pr.p.*, wallow.

wall'-paper, *n.*, paper hung on walls.

wal'nut, *n.*, a tree, its wood, and its fruit so named.

wal'rus, *n.*, a tusked marine mammal.

waltz, *n.*, a variety of dance; waltz music; *v.i.*, to dance a waltz.

waltzed, *p.p.*, waltz.

waltz'ing, *pr.p.*, waltz.

wam'ble, *v.i.*, to feel symptoms of nausea; to rumble internally; to roll.

wampee', *n.*, a Chinese fruit.

wam'pum, *n.*, the N. Amer. name for beads made of shells and used to decorate a belt or for barter.

wan, *adj.*, pale; sickly; *v.i.*, to become wan.

wand, *n.*, a rod.

wan'der, *v.i.*, to stray; ramble; become light-headed.

wan'dered, *p.p.*, wander.

wan'derer, *n.*, one who wanders.

wan'dering, *pr.p.*, wander.

wane, *v.i.*, to grow less; to decline; *n.*, a growing less, esp. to the diminution of the moon's brightness.

waned, *p.p.*, wane.

wanghee', *n.*, a bamboo cane.

wa'ning, *pr.p.*, wane; *adj.*, on the wane.

wan'ly, *adv.*, in a sickly way.

wan'ned, *p.p.*, wan.

wan'ness, *n.*, the state of being wan.

wan'ning, *pr.p.*, wan.

want, *n.*, lack; need; poverty; desire; *v.t.*, to be without; to desire; *v.i.*, to be lacking; to fail.

want'ed, *p.p.*, want.

want'ing, *pr.p.*, want.

wan'ton, *adj.*, lascivious; sportive; without restraint; *n.*, a lustful person; *v.i.*, to play the wanton.

wan'toned, *p.p.*, wanton.

wan'toning, *pr.p.*, wanton.

wan'tonly, *adv.*, in a wanton way.

wan'tonness, *n.*, the state of being wanton.

want'wit, *n.*, silliness; lack of sense.

wap'enshaw, *n.*, an old Scottish form of sports.

wap'entake, *n.*, an old county subdivision resembling the hundred.

wap'iti, *n.*, the elk of America.

war, *n.*, conflict between nations; any state of enmity; *v.i.*, to be engaged in conflict.

war'ble, *v.t.* and *i.*, to sing in a bird-like way; *n.*, singing with a trill; a bot.

war'bled, *p.p.*, warble.

war'bler, *n.*, one who warbles; a bird.

war'bling, *pr.p.*, warble; *n.*, song.

war'-cry, *n.*, words shouted in a fight to rally one's own side and strike terror into the enemy, as, "St. George for England," "St. Denis for France."

ward, *v.t.*, to guard; *v.i.*, to keep watch; *n.*, guard; a municipal division; prison; one under the care of a guardian; one of the divisions in a lock or key.

war'-dance, *n.*, the dance of warriors.

ward'ed, *p.p.*, ward.

ward'en, *n.*, a guardian; custodian; head of certain colleges, guilds, etc.; a churchwarden; a variety of pear.

ward'enry, *n.*, the office of a warden.

ward'er, *n.*, a keeper: guard.

ward'ing, *pr.p.*, ward.

ward'mote, *n.*, the meeting of the inhabitants in a ward.

ward'robe, *n.*, a place to keep robes in; personal clothing.

ward'room, *n.*, the mess-room of the lieutenants on a man-of-war.

ward'ship, *n.*, the position of a ward; guardianship.

ware, *adj.* and *v.*, *i.q.* aware; beware.

ware'house, *n.*, a store for wares; *v.t.*, to put into store.

ware'housed, *p.p.*, warehouse.

ware'houseman, *n.*, a storer of goods.

ware'housing, *pr.p.*, warehouse.

wares, *n. pl.*, goods; merchandise.

war'fare, *n.*, a state of war; conflict.

war'horse, *n.*, a charger.

wa'rily, *adv.*, in a wary way.

wa'riness, *n.*, the state of being wary.

war'like, *adj.*, brave; fierce.

war'lock, *n.*, a wizard.

warm, *n.*, moderately hot; excited; passionate; *v.t.*, to make warm; *v.i.*, to grow warm.

warmed, *p.p.*, warm.

warm'er, *adj.*, *comp.* of warm.

warm'est, *adj.*, *super.* of warm.

warm'-hearted, *adj.*, affectionate; kind.

warm'-heartedness, *n.*, the quality of being warm-hearted.

warm'ing, *pr.p.*, warm.

warm'ing-pan, *n.*, a pan to contain coals for warming a bed, etc.

warm'ly, *adv.*, with warmth.

warmth, *n.*, the quality of being warm; moderate heat; excitement; passion; rich colouring.

warn, *v.t.*, to admonish; caution; put on guard; summon officially.

warned, *p.p.*, warn.

warn'er, *n.*, one who warns.

warn'ing, *pr.p.*, warn; *n.*, a caution; admonition; notice of dismissal.

War'-Office, *n.*, the office of the War Minister.

warp, *n.*, lengthwise threads crossed by the woof; a twist; a rope for warping; *v.t.*, to twist awry; to haul a ship by means of a hawser round something fixed; to fertilize by means of flooding.

war'-paint, *n.*, N. Amer. face decoration of warriors.

war'-path, *n.*, an expedition of warriors.

warped, *p.p.*, warp.

warp'ing, *pr.p.*, warp.

war'rant, *n.*, a guarantee; security; authorization; commission; *v.t.*, to give authority for; to guarantee; assure.

war'rantable, *adj.*, able to be warranted.

war'ranted, *p.p.*, warrant.

warrantee', *n.*, one to whom a warranty is issued.

war'ranter, *n.*, one who warrants.

war'ranting, *pr.p.*, warrant.

war'rantor, *n.*, one who warrants.

war'ranty, *n.*, security; warrant.

warred, *p.p.*, war.

war'ren, *n.*, a preserve, esp. for rabbits; right to preserve wild animals (*leg.*).

war'rener, *n.*, the keeper of a warren.

war'ring, *pr.p.*, war.

war'rior, *n.*, a fighting man; soldier.

war'-song, *n.*, a song for warriors.

wart, *n.*, a morbid growth on the skin.

wart'wort, *n.*, one of several plants useful for the cure of warts.

wart'y, *adj.*, covered with, resembling, warts.

war'-whoop, *n.*, the yell of warriors fighting.

war'-worn, *adj.*, veteran.

wa'ry, *adj.*, discreet; cautious.

was, *p.t.*, be.

wase, *n.*, a porter's head-pad on which to rest a burden.

wash, *v.t.*, to cleanse with water; to bathe; to lay a thin surface over; to purify; *v.i.*, to perform the act of washing; *n.*, the act of washing; a shallow part of the sea, etc.; effect of displacement of water; a lotion; a thin layer or coating; indifferent drink (*colloq.*).

wash'-ball, *n.*, a form of toilet soap.

wash'-board, *n.*, a board used in washing clothes.

wash'-bowl, *n.*, a bowl to wash in.

washed, *p.p.*, wash.

wash'er, *n.*, one who washes; a device for making a screw, a joint, etc., secure.

wash'erwoman, *n.*, a woman who washes clothes.

wash'house, *n.*, a building where washing is done.

wash'ing, *pr.p.*, wash; *n.*, the act of washing; the employment of washing; clothes washed at a laundry.
wash'-leather, *n.*, chamois-leather.
wash'-stand, *n.*, a table on which washing utensils are placed.
wash'-tub, *n.*, a laundry tub.
wash'y, *adj.*, poor; thin (*colloq.*).
wasp, *n.*, a stinging winged insect.
wasp'ish, *adj.*, like a wasp; irritable and vexatious; thin about the waist.
wasp'ishly, *adv.*, in a waspish way.
was'sail, *n.*, Christmas merry-making and drinking; a drink of various ingredients; *v.i.*, to revel; feast; *v.t.*, to pledge in wine or ale.
was'sailer, *n.*, one who wassails.
wast, *p.t.*, be, *2nd pers. sing.*
waste, *n.*, loss; consumption; extravagance; country uncultivated; refuse; *adj.*, uncultivated; not in use; *v.t.*, to devastate; destroy; expend extravagantly; dissipate.
waste'book, *n.*, a day-book.
wast'ed, *p.p.*, waste.
waste'ful, *adj.*, extravagant; not thrifty.
waste'fully, *adv.*, in a wasteful way.
waste'-gate, *n.*, an escape for the surplus water of a dam, etc.
waste'ness, *n.*, the state of being waste.
waste'pipe, *n.*, a pipe to allow an overflow to escape.
wa'ster, *n.*, one who wastes.
wa'sting, *pr.p.*, waste.
wa'strel, *n.*, a spendthrift; a waif.
watch, *n.*, keeping a look-out; vigilance; one who keeps watch; a division of the night-time; a pocket time-keeper; *v.t.*, to observe closely; keep an eye on; protect; *v.i.*, to be awake; keep guard.
watch'-case, *n.*, the outer cover of a watch.
watch'-dog, *n.*, a dog that keeps guard.
watched, *p.p.*, watch.
watch'er, *n.*, one who watches.
watch'ful, *adj.*, wakeful; vigilant.
watch'fully, *adv.*, in a watchful way.
watch'fulness, *n.*, the state of being watchful.
watch'-glass, *n.*, the glass cover of a watch face.
watch'-*guard*, *n.*, a chain, etc., to secure a watch to one's person.
watch'-house, *n.*, a building in which watchmen secured persons they arrested.
watch'ing, *pr.p.*, watch.
watch'maker, *n.*, a maker of watches.
watch'man, *n.*, one who keeps watch; an older type of policeman.
watch'night, *n.*, the last night of the year, on which people often sit up to see the new year in.
watch'-tower, *n.*, a look-out place.
watch'*word*, *n.*, a password.
wa'ter, *n.*, a fluid containing two parts of hydrogen to one of oxygen; the sea; water-like fluid; a diamond's brilliancy; *v.t.*, to give to drink; irrigate; to supply with water; dilute; *v.i.*, to take in water; to discharge water.
wa'terage, *n.*, charge for carrying by water.
wa'ter-butt, *n.*, a butt to hold rain-water.
wa'ter-cart, *n.*, a cart used for watering streets.
wa'tercourse, *n.*, the course of a stream.
wa'tercress, *n.*, an aquatic, edible plant.
wa'tered, *p.p.*, water; *adj.*, wavy in appearance.
wa'terfall, *n.*, a fall of water from a height.
wa'terfowl, *n.*, a bird that lives on the water.
wa'teriness, *n.*, the quality or state of being watery.
wa'tering, *pr.p.*, water
wa'tering-place, *n.*, a seaside resort or a place where mineral baths can be obtained.
wa'tering-pot, *n.*, a pot used in gardening.
wa'terish, *adj.*, thin; watery.
wa'ter-lily, *n.*, a lily-like aquatic plant.
wa'ter-logged, *adj.*, filled or soaked with water.
wa'terman, *n.*, a boatman.
wa'ter-mark, *n.*, a peculiar mark in the texture of paper.
wa'termelon, *n.*, a melon containing a watery juice.
wa'ter-mill, *n.*, a mill driven by water.
wa'ter-plane, *n.*, the plane of a ship's water-line.
wa'ter-pot, *n.*, a pot to hold water.
wa'terproof, *adj.*, impervious to wet; *n.*, a coat, etc., of waterproof material
wa'ter-ram, *n.*, a hydraulic ram.
wa'ter-rat, *n.*, a rat that lives in the banks of rivers, etc.
wa'ter-rate, *n.*, the rate paid for the public supply of water.
wa'ter-rot, *v.t.*, to produce rottenness in by means of soaking.
wa'ter-rotted, *p.p.*, water-rot.

wa'ter-rotting, *pr.p.*, water-rot.

wa'tershed, *n.*, high ground from which water descends into a river; a division between two river basins.

wa'ter-soak, *v.t.*, to fill interstices of with water.

wa'terspout, *n.*, a cyclonic column of water; a spout to carry off water.

wa'ter-tight, *adj.*, able to keep out water.

wa'terway, *n.*, the fairway in a river; channel.

wa'terworks, *n. pl.*, pumping stations; in sing., an ornamental cascade, fountain, etc.

wa'terwort, *n.*, a marsh annual so named.

wa'tery, *adj.*, like water; rel. to water; thin; poor in taste.

Wat'teau, *adj.*, pert. to Watteau and the style of dress exhibited in his pictures (early 18th cent.).

wat'tle, *n.*, a flexible twig; hurdle; the growth beneath a turkey's or fowl's throat; acacia; *v.t.*, to fasten with wattles; *adj.*, made with wattle.

wat'tled, *p.p.*, wattle.

wat'tling, *pr.p.*, wattle; *n.*, wattle-work; the art of wattling.

waul, wawl, *n.*, a cat's cry.

wave, *n.*, an undulating movement of water; a like movement of light, sound, etc.; *v.t.*, to move this way and that; brandish; give a wavy appearance to; *v.i.*, to undulate.

waved, *p.p.*, wave.

wave'less, *adj.*, without waves; calm.

wave'let, *n.*, a little wave.

wave'-like, *adj.*, like a wave.

wave'-offering, *n.*, a Jewish offering by waving towards the points of the compass.

wa'ver, *v.i.*, to falter; hesitate between alternative choices; flicker; *n.*, one who waves.

wa'vered, *p.p.*, waver.

wa'verer, *n.*, one who wavers.

wa'vering, *pr.p.*, waver.

wave'son, *n.*, floating wreckage.

wa'viness, *n.*, the state or quality of being wavy.

wa'ving, *pr.p.*, wave.

wa'vy, *adj.*, like a wave; undulating.

wawl, *n.*, *i.q.* waul.

wax, *n.*, a thick clinging substance, such as bees-wax; a like substance formed in the ear; cerumen; a rage (*slang*); *v.i.*, to increase in growth, strength, etc.; become.

waxed, *p.p.*, wax.

wax'en, *adj.*, made of, resembling, wax.

wax'-end, *n.*, the end of a piece of thread stiffened with wax.

wax'iness, *n.*, the quality of being waxy.

wax'ing, *pr.p.*, wax.

wax'wing, *n.*, a bird so named from the resemblance of some of its feathers to sealing-wax.

wax'work, *n.*, anything made of wax.

wax'y, *adj.*, wax-like; made of wax; angry (*slang*).

way, *n.*, a road; direction; means; manner.

way'bill, *n.*, a list of places of call.

way'bread, *n.*, the plantain.

way'farer, *n.*, a traveller.

way'faring, *adj.*, travelling.

waylaid', *p.p.*, waylay.

waylay', *v.t.*, to attack on the road; to watch for.

waylay'er, *n.*, one who waylays.

waylay'ing, *pr.p.*, waylay.

way'-mark, *n.*, a mile stone; guide-post.

way'side, *n.*, the side of the road; *adj.*, beside the road.

way'ward, *adj.*, perverse; going one's own way.

way'wardly, *adv.*, in a wayward way.

way'wardness, *n.*, the state of being wayward.

way'wode, *n.*, a Wallachian or Roumanian lord.

way'worn, *adj.*, tired; weary.

wayz'goose, *n.*, a yearly outing or festivity, esp. of printers.

we, pers. pron., 1st person, pl.

weak, *adj.*, not strong; feeble; without influence; yielding; easily led astray.

weak'en, *v.t.*, to make weak; undermine; *v.i.*, to become weak; to yield.

weak'ened, *p.p.*, weaken.

weak'ener, *n.*, one who, that which, weakens.

weak'ening, *pr.p.*, weaken.

weak'er, *adj.*, *comp.* of weak.

weak'est, *adj.*, *super.* of weak.

weak'-eyed, *adj.*, having weak eyes.

weak'ling, *n.*, a poor, weak creature.

weak'ly, *adv.*, in a weak way; *adj.*, in frail health.

weak'ness, *n.*, the quality of being weak.

weal, *n.*, happiness; prosperity; *i.q.* wale; *v.t.*, *i.q.* wale.

weald, *n.*, a forest; *i.q.* wold.

weald'en, *adj.*, pert. to a weald; *n.*, the lower cretaceous strata, esp. of the weald.

wealth, *n.*, well-being; prosperity; riches.

wealth'ier, *adj.*, *comp.* of wealthy.

wealth'iest, *adj.*, *super.* of wealthy.
wealth'y, *adj.*, rich; affluent.
wean, *v.t.*, to cease suckling; to alienate.
weaned, *p.p.*, wean.
wean'ing, *pr.p.*, wean.
wean'ling, *n.*, an infant just weaned.
weap'on, *n.*, an instrument of destruction.
weap'oned, *adj.*, armed with a weapon.
wear, *v.t.*, to destroy by gradual friction, long use, etc.; to assume; to be clothed with; *v.i.*, to become worn; to stand wear; *n.*, the act of wearing; state of being worn.
wear'able, *adj.*, able to be worn.
wear'er, *n.*, one who wears.
wear'ied, *p.p.*, weary.
wear'ier, *adj.*, *comp.* of weary.
wear'iest, *adj.*, *super.* of weary.
wear'ily, *adv.*, in a weary way.
wear'iness, *n.*, the state of being weary.
wear'ing, *pr.p.*, wear; *adj.*, distressing.
wear'isome, *adj.*, tiring; tedious; boring.
wear'isomeness, *n.*, the quality of being wearisome.
wear'y, *adj.*, tired; fatigued; tiring; *v.t.*, to make weary; tire; *v.i.*, to grow tired.
wear'ying, *pr.p*, weary
wea'sand, *n.*, the windpipe.
wea'sel, *n.*, a small carnivore.
weath'er, *n.*, atmospheric state; *v.t.*, to waste by the action of the air; to overcome by enduring; *v.i.*, to be changed by exposure to the atmosphere; *adj.*, on the windward side.
weath'er-beaten, *adj.*, hardened by exposure to wind and rain; worn and ancient.
weath'er-board, *n.*, a horizontal board placed as the cover or protection of a wall, etc., to throw off the rain; *v.t.*, to protect with weather-boards.
weath'er-bound, *adj.*, unable to move by reason of the weather.
weath'ercock, *n.*, a vane.
weath'ered, *p.p.*, weather.
weath'er-gage, *n.*, a ship's position to windward of another ship.
weath'er-glass, *n.*, a scientific weather-indicator.
weath'ering, *pr.p.*, weather; *n.*, architecturally, a slight slant in a horizontal surface in order to throw off the water; decay, waste, etc., due to atmospheric action.
weath'erly, *adj.*, able to keep on its course without drifting to leeward.
weath'erwise, *adj.*, possessing, or affecting, a knowledge of weather-signs.
weave, *v.t.*, to intertwine; to work with a loom; *v.i.*, to do weaving.
weav'er, *n.*, one who weaves.
weav'ing, *pr.p.*, weave; *n.*, the weaver's art.
wea'zen, *adj.*, withered-looking.
web, *n.*, threads woven together; texture; anything web-like, as the membrane in web-footed creatures, etc.; *v.t.*, to form as a web.
webbed, *p.p.*, web.
web'bing, *pr.p.*, web; *n.*, strong, woven braid used in upholstering.
web'by, *adj.*, web-like; full of webs.
web'-foot, *n.*, a web-footed creature.
web'-footed, *adj.*, having a membrane between the divisions of the foot.
wed, *v.t.* and *i.*, to marry; *p.t.* and *p.*, wed.
wed'ded, *p.p.*, wed.
wed'ding, *pr.p.*, wed; *n.*, the marriage ceremony.
wedge, *n.*, a V-shaped piece of wood or metal, used for forcing into anything; anything wedge-shaped; *v.t.*, to drive a wedge into.
wedged, *p.p.*, wedge; *adj.*, *i.q.* wedge-shaped.
wedge'-shaped, *adj.*, like a wedge.
wedg'ing, *pr.p.*, wedge
Wedg'wood ware, *n.*, pottery made at Wedgwood's works, Etruria, Staffordshire. The founder of the firm was Josiah Wedgwood. Many of the beautiful designs used were by Flaxman.
wed'lock, *n.*, marriage.
Wednes'day, *n.*, the fourth day of the week, named after Woden or Odin.
wee, *adj.*, tiny.
weed, *n.*, a wild, useless plant; tobacco, a cigar (*colloq.*); a poor sort of animal; *v.t.*, to pull weeds up; *v.i.*, to do weeding.
weed'ed, *p.p.*, weed.
weed'er, *n.*, one who, that which, weeds.
weed'ery, *n.*, weeds growing in great numbers.
weed'ing, *pr.p.*, weed; *n.*, the act or employment of weeding.
weed'ing-hook, *n.*, a hooked implement used in weeding; bill-hook.
weed'less, *adj.*, free from weeds.
weeds, *n. pl.*, a mourning costume worn by a widow.
weed'y, *adj.*, full of weeds; weed-like, rank; overgrown and weakly (*colloq.*).
week, *n.*, a period of seven days; sennight.

week'-day, *n.*, one of the six days exclusive of Sunday.

week'ly, *adj.*, happening, being published etc., every week; once a week; lasting for a week.

weel, *n.*, a willow or rush fish-trap.

ween, *v.i.*, to think; have the opinion.

weened, *p.p.*, ween.

ween'ing, *pr.p.*, ween.

weep, *v.i.*, to shed tears; cry; *v.t.*, to lament for.

weep'er, *n.*, one who weeps; a mourning-band; in pl., the cuffs forming part of widows' weeds.

weep'ing, *pr.p.*, weep.

weep'ing wil'low, *n.*, a variety of willow distinguished by its pendulous branches.

weev'er, *n.*, a fish so named.

weev'il, *n.*, a beetle so named, destructive to grain, roots, etc.; any insect that gets into a grain store and destroys the grain.

wee'vil(l)ed, *adj.*, attacked by weevils.

weft, *n.*, the cross-threads of a web.

weige'lia, *n.*, a Chinese or Japanese honeysuckle.

weigh, *v.t.*, to balance for the purpose of ascertaining the weight; to balance in the mind; to ponder; to press down; to lift up (an anchor); *v.i.*, to be of a certain weight; to set sail; *n.*, the act of weighing.

weigh'able, *adj.*, able to be weighed.

weigh'age, *adj.*, market charge for weighing.

weigh'-bridge, *n.*, platform scales.

weighed, *p.p.*, weigh.

weigh'er, *n.*, one who weighs.

weigh'-house, *n.*, a building where freight, etc., can be weighed.

weigh'ing, *pr.p.*, weigh.

weight, *n.*, the measure of the force which attracts bodies to the earth's centre; the amount that a thing weighs; relative quantity or mass; a heavy object; a standard by which things are weighed, as a pound weight, etc.; influence; import; *v.t.*, to load; burden; adulterate.

weight'ed, *p.p.*, weight.

weight'ier, *adj.*, *comp.* of weighty.

weight'iest, *adj.*, *super.* of weighty.

weight'ily, *adv.*, in a weighty way.

weight'iness, *n.*, the quality of being weighty.

weight'ing, *pr.p.*, weight.

weight'less, *adj.*, without weight.

weight'y, *adj.*, ponderous; influential; important.

weir, *n.*, a dam across a river.

weird, *adj.*, strange; mysterious; uncanny.

welch'er, *n.*, *i.q.* welsher.

wel'come, *v.t.*, to greet on arriving; receive with hospitality; *n.*, a hospitable greeting; hospitality; *adj.*, gladly received or admitted; timely and agreeable; *interj.*, delighted to see you!

wel'comed, *p.p.*, welcome.

wel'comer, *n.*, one who welcomes.

wel'coming, *pr.p.*, welcome.

weld, *v.t.*, to join by hammering or by pressure; to combine pieces into a homogeneous whole; *n.*, the result of welding.

weld'ed, *p.p.*, weld.

weld'ing, *pr.p.*, weld.

wel'fare, *n.*, well-being; happiness; prosperity.

wel'kin, *n.*, the sky.

well, *n.*, a spring of water or oil; a shaft sunk into the ground down to the water or oil; anything like a well; *v.i.*, to gush forth; spring up; *adv.*, in a good state; in a good manner; satisfactorily; sufficiently; *adj.*, in good health; *n.*, that which is satisfactory; *interj.*, expressing surprise.

well'aday, *interj.*, expressing grief. Also *wellaway.*

well'-being, *n.*, *i.q.* welfare.

well'-bred, *adj.*, of good breeding; of good manners.

well'-doer, *n.*, a virtuous person; doer of good deeds.

well'-doing, *n.*, good conduct, good deeds.

well'-done, *adj.*, done well; rightly formed; sufficiently cooked.

well'-dressed, *adj.*, smartly attired.

welled, *p.p.*, well.

wel'ling, *pr.p.*, well.

Wellingto'nia, *n.*, a large Californian tree.

Wellingto'nian, *adj.*, pert. to Wellington, esp. to the Great Duke.

well'-known, *adj.*, celebrated; famous; familiar.

well'-met, *adj.*, welcome.

well'nigh, *adv.*, nearly; almost.

well'spring, *n.*, a fount; source.

well'-wisher, *n.*, a person with friendly intent.

Welsh, *adj.*, pert. to Wales and the people of Wales or their language; *n.*, the Welsh language; *v.t.*, to cheat on a race-course.

welsh'er, *n.*, one who welshes.

Welsh'man, *n.*, a native of Wales.

welt, *n.*, a piece of leather between the sole and the upper of a boot; *v.t.*, to put welts in.

welt'ed, *p.p.*, welt.
wel'ter, *v.i.*, to roll about in anything; wallow; *n.*, a state of weltering; turmoil; *adj.*, describing a race in which the contestants are of unusual weights.
wel'tered, *p.p.*, welter.
wel'tering, *pr.p.*, welter.
welt'ing, *pr.p.*, welt.
wen, *n.*, a fleshy tumour.
wench, *n.*, a girl; *v.i.*, to associate with loose women.
wend, *v.i.*, to go.
wend'ed, *p.p.*, wend.
wend'ing, *pr.p.*, wend.
wen'ny, *adj.*, like a wen; troubled with wens.
went, *p.t.*, go.
wept, *p.t.* and *p.p.*, weep.
were, *p.t.*, be; also the *subjunctive*.
were'wolf, *n.*, a human being changed into a wolf.
Werne'rian, *adj.*, pert. to Werner and his geological doctrines.
wert, *2nd sing.* of were.
Wes'leyan, *adj.*, pert. to John Wesley and Wesleyanism; *n.*, a follower of Wesley.
Wes'leyanism, *n.*, the principles of Wesley's followers; Methodism.
west, *n.*, one of the four points of the compass, opposite to the East; the quarter of the sky where the sun sets; the West country; a Western land; *adj.*, situated in the west, or to the west of some other place.
west'erly, *adj.*, from or towards the west.
west'ern, *adj.*, pert. to, toward, the West.
west'ing, *n.*, distance between east and west; distance covered going westward.
west'ward, *adj.*, towards the West.
wet, *adj.*, humid; damp; rainy; *n.*, moisture; rain; *v.t.*, to make wet; moisten.
weth'er, *n.*, a ram that has been castrated.
wet'ness, *n.*, the state of being wet; moisture; dampness.
wet'-nurse, *n.*, a nurse who suckles another person's child; *v.t.*, to suckle another person's child; *v.i.*, to act the wet-nurse.
wet'ted, *p.p.*, wet.
wet'ter, *adj.*, *comp.* of wet.
wet'test, *adj.*, *super.* of wet.
wet'ting, *pr.p.*, wet; *n.*, the result of exposure to wet.
wet'tish, *adj.*, inclined to be wet.
wey, *n.*, a varying measure of weight (from 2 cwt. to 3 cwt.).
whack, *v.t.*, to strike; *n.*, a blow; a big slice (*colloq.*).
whacked, *p.p.*, whack.
whack'er, *n.*, one who whacks; a big lie (*colloq.*).
whack'ing, *pr.p.*, whack; *n.*, a beating.
whale, *n.*, a huge cetaceous mammal.
whale'-boat, *n.*, a boat used in whale-fishing.
whale'bone, *n.*, a flexible material obtained from the upper jaw of a whale.
whale'man, *n.*, a whale-fisher; whaler.
wha'ler, *n.*, a boat used for whale-fishing; a whaleman.
wha'ling, *n.*, the occupation of catching whales.
whap, *v.t.*, *i.q.* whop.
wharf, *n.*, a landing-stage or quay; *v.t.*, to moor at a wharf; store on a wharf.
wharf'age, *n.*, toll on a wharf.
wharf'ing, *pr.p.*, wharf; *n.*, wharves collectively; a wharf-like erection.
wharf'inger, *n.*, a wharf-owner.
what, *interrog. adj.* and *pron.*, asking for specific information, as "What noise was that?"; *rel. pron.*, what being used for "that which"; *exclamation*, expressing surprise, doubt, etc.
whatev'er, *adj.* and *indef. rel. pron.*, anything which; no matter what.
what'-not, *n.*, a bracket or set of shelves for bric-a-brac.
whatsoev'er, *adj.*, *i.q.* whatever.
wheal, *n.*, a principle; a mine; esp. a tin-mine.
wheat, *n.*, the most important of the cereals and the grain it produces.
wheat'ear, *n.*, the stonechat.
wheat'en, *adj.*, made of wheat.
whee'dle, *v.t.*, to coax; cajole.
whee'dled, *p.p.*, wheedle.
whee'dling, *pr.p.*, wheedle; *n.*, coaxing.
wheel, *n.*, a circular, revolving disc, solid or with openings; *v.t.*, to turn round; to roll on wheels; to push a wheeled cart; *v.i.*, to swing round; gyrate; to ride a bicycle, etc.
wheel'barrow, *n.*, a kind of hand-cart mounted on a wheel or wheels.
wheel'-carriage, *n.*, a wheeled vehicle.
wheeled, *p.p.*, wheel; *adj.*, provided with wheels.
wheel'er, *n.*, one who wheels; *i.q.* wheel-horse.
wheel'-horse, *n.*, the horse in the shafts, or one of the pole-horses in a four-in-hand, etc.
wheel'-house, *n.*, the sheltered structure for the man at the wheel.

wheel'ing, *pr.p.*, wheel.
wheel'wright, *n.*, a maker of wheels and wheeled vehicles.
wheeze, *v.i.*, to breathe with a distressing sound; *n.*, the sound of wheezing.
wheezed, *p.p.*, wheeze.
wheezing', *pr.p.*, wheeze; *n.*, the act of wheezing.
wheez'y, *adj.*, suffering from wheezing.
whelk, *n.*, a pimple.
whelm, *v.t.*, to submerge; overwhelm.
whelmed, *p.p.*, whelm.
whelm'ing, *pr.p.*, whelm.
whelp, *n.*, the young of a dog, lion, wolf, etc.; a cubbish boy; *v.t.*, to give birth to; *v.i.*, to have cubs.
whelped, *p.p.*, whelp.
whelp'ing, *pr.p.*, whelp.
when *interrog.pron.*, at what time? *rel. pron.*, (at the time) in which.
whence, *interrog. pronominal adv.*, from which place? *rel. pronominal adv.*, from which (place); (the place) from which.
whencesoe'ver, *adv.*, from whatsoever place or source.
whenev'er, *adv.*, at whatever time.
whensoev'er, *adv.*, rather more emphatic than whenever = at any time whatever.
where, *interrog. adv.*, in which place, part, direction? *rel.pron. adv.*, (at the place, to the place, etc.) in which; *n.*, with *the* = locality.
where'about, *adv.*, in regard to which; *i.q.* whereabouts.
where'abouts, *adv.*, a vague equivalent of where; *n.*, locality.
whereas', *conj.*, the fact being considered that . . .; compared with the fact that . . .; seeing that.

whereat', *interrog. adv.*, at what? *rel. adv.*, at which.
whereby', *interrog. adv.*, by what? *rel. adv.*, by which.
where'fore, *interrog. adv.*, for what? why? *rel. adv.*, because of which.
where'in, *interrog. adv.*, in what? *rel. adv.*, in which.
whereinsoev'er, *rel. adv.*, in whatsoever particular or point.
whereof', *rel.pron.*, of which.
whereon', *rel. adv.*, on which.
wheresoev'er, *rel. adv.*, in whatever place.
whereto', *rel. adv.*, to which.
whereun'to, *rel. adv.*, *i.q.* whereto.
whereupon', *rel. adv.*, immediately after, or in consequence of, which.
wherev'er, *rel. adv.*, in whatever place.
wherewith', *rel. adv.*, with which.
wherewithal', *rel.adv.*, with which; *n.*, means.
wher'ry, *n.*, a light boat; a fishing-boat decked; a drink made from crab-apples.
whet, *v.t.*, to sharpen; to make keen.
wheth'er, *pron. interrog.*, which of two; *conj.*, which or in one of two courses or alternatives.
whet'slate, *n.*, a hard stone used for sharpening blades, etc.
whet'stone, *n.*, a stone on which knives, etc., are sharpened.
whet'ted, *p.p.*, whet.
whet'ter, *n.*, one who whets.
whet'ting, *pr.p.*, whet.
whew, *interj.*, expressing a feeling of heat, discomfort, etc.
whew'ellite, *n.*, a hydrous calcium oxalate.

whey, *n.*, the thin part of milk after the curd has been separated.
whey'ey, *adj.*, like, containing, whey.
whey'ish, *adj.*, like whey.
which, *pron. interrog.*, asking what person or thing; the *rel. pron.* stands as the neut. of who.
whichev'er, *rel. pron. indef.* any soever.
which**soev'er,** *i.q.* whichever, but slightly more emphatic.
whiff, *n.*, a slight puff; a small outrigger; *v.t.*, to draw or emit a whiff.
whiffed, *p.p.*, whiff.
whiff'ing, *pr.p.*, whiff.
whif'fle, *v.i.* and *t.*, to change capriciously.
whif'fled, *p.p.*, whiffle
whif'fler, *n.*, one who whiffles.
whif'fletree, *n.*, a crossbar swinging on a pivot, having the traces of a cart or plough attached to its ends. Also *swingletree*.
whif'fling, *pr.p.*, whiffle.
Whig, *n.*, a member of a political party opposed to the Tories. Its interests were largely bound up with certain powerful families.
Whig'garchy, *n.*, the rule of the Whigs.
Whig'gery, *n.*, the principles of Whigs.
Whig'gish, *adj.*, favourable, pert. to, Whiggery.
Whig'gism, *n.*, *i.q.* Whiggery.
while, *conj.*, during the time when; whereas; *n.*, a period of time; *v.t.*, to make time pass agreeably.
whiled, *p.p.*, while.
whil'ing, *pr.p.*, while.
whi'lom, *adv.*, in former time. The word is often used adjectivally.
whilst, *conj.*, *i.q.* while.

whim, *n.*, a caprice; freak; crotchet.

whim'brel, *n.*, a variety of curlew.

whim'per, *n.*, a low whine; *v.t.*, to utter with a whimper; *v.i.*, to make a low whine.

whim'pered, *p.p.*, whimper.

whim'pering, *pr.p.*, whimper; *n.*, *i.q.* whimper.

whim'sey, *n.*, *i.q.* whim.

whim'sical, *adj.*, full of whims; crotchety; fanciful.

whimsical'ity, *n.*, the state of being whimsical.

whim'sically, *adv.*, in a whimsical way.

whim'wham, *n.*, an absurd idea; a toy.

whin, *n.*, furze.

whin'chat, *n.*, a bird so named.

whine, *v.i.*, to cry in a self-pitying way; *n.*, a plaintive cry.

whined, *p.p.*, whine.

whi'ner, *n.*, one who whines.

whi'ning, *pr.p.*, whine.

whi'ningly, *adv.*, in a whining way.

whin'nied, *p.p.*, whinny.

whin'ny, *n.*, the sound a horse makes; *v.i.*, to make the sound; *adj.*, covered with whins.

whin'nying, *pr.p.*, whinny.

whin'stone, *n.*, a hard kind of rock.

whip, *n.*, an instrument for punishing or driving; a lash; a driver; a Parliamentary party summoner; the summons he sends out; *v.t.*, to punish, correct; drive; beat; to oversew.

whip'-cord, *n.*, cord with which whiplashes are made.

whip'-hand, *n.*, the superior position.

whipped, *p.p.*, whip.

whip'per, *n.*, one who whips.

whip'per-in, *n.*, a huntsman in charge of the hounds.

whip'per-snap'per, *n.*, a youngster; an insignificant little person.

whip'pet, *n.*, a breed of dogs.

whip'ping, *pr.p.*, whip; *n.*, punishment with a whip.

whip'ping-post, *n.*, a post to which a person is tied up when about to be whipped.

whip'pletree, *n.*, the cornel.

whip'poorwill, *n.*, a goat-sucker bird.

whip'powill, *n.*, *i.q.* whippoorwill.

whip'-staff, *n.*, a whip handle.

whip'-stick, *n.*, the handle of a whip.

whip'stitch, *v.t.*, to gather with overhand stitching; *n.*, an overhand stitch.

whip'-stock, *n.*, a receptacle for a whip.

whir, whirr, *n.*, a trilling noise; *v.i.*, to make the sound.

whirl, *v.t.* and *i.*, to turn; twist; hurry along; *n.*, a rapid twisting round.

whirl'about, *n.*, a whirligig.

whirled, *p.p.*, whirl.

whirl'igig, *n.*, a child's spinning toy.

whirl'ing, *pr.p.*, whirl.

whirl'pool, *n.*, a vortex in water.

whirl'wind, *n.*, a rotatory wind-storm.

whirred, *p.p.*, whir.

whir'ring, *pr.p.*, whir.

whisk, *v.t.*, to carry off, brush away, rapidly; *v.i.*, to move along rapidly; *n.*, a swift movement; a housemaid's brush; a kitchen implement for beating up.

whisked, *p.p.*, whisk.

whisk'er, *n.*, hair on the side of the face.

whisk'ered, *adj.*, having whiskers.

whis'key, whis'ky, *n.*, a spirituous liquor.

whisk'ing, *pr.p.*, whisk.

whis'per, *n.*, utterance in a subdued voice; *v.t.*, to say in a whisper or secretly; *v.i.*, to speak in a whisper.

whis'pered, *p.p.*, whisper.

whis'perer, *n.*, one who whispers.

whis'pering, *pr.p.*, whisper.

whist, *n.*, a game of cards; *interj.*, hush!

whis'tle, *n.*, a sound forced through the lips; a wind instrument for signalling, etc.; *v.t.* and *i.*, to force a sound through an aperture of the lips.

whis'tled, *p.p.*, whistle.

whis'tler, *n.*, one who whistles.

whis'tling, *pr.p.*, whistle; *n.*, the act of whistling.

whit, *n.*, a small portion.

white, *adj.*, colourless; like snow; pure; *n.*, a white man; the white part of an egg; *v.t.*, to make white.

white'bait, *n.*, a diminutive edible fish.

whi'ted, *p.p.*, white; *adj.*, whitewashed.

white'-feather, *n.*, a coward; fear.

White' Friars, *n.*, members of the Carmelite Order.

whi'ten, *v.t.*, to make white.

whi'tened, *p.p.*, whiten.

whi'tener, *n.*, one who whitens.

white'ness, *n.*, the state or quality of being white.

whi'tening, *pr.p.*, whiten; *n.*, a whitewash.

white'smith, *n.*, a tinsmith.

white'throat, *n.*, a bird so named.

white'wash, *n.*, a mixture used to whiten walls, ceilings, etc.; *v.t.*, to wash with the mixture; to clear a shady character.

white'washed, *p.p.*, whitewash.

white'washer, *n.*, one who whitewashes.

white'washing, *pr.p.*, whitewash; *n.*, the act of whitewashing.

white'weed, *n.*, oxeye daisy.

white'wood, *n.*, the wood of the tulip-tree.

whith'er, *adv.*, *interrog.*, towards what place? *adv. rel.*, (place) toward which

whithersoev'er, *adv. rel.*, towards whatsoever place.

whi'ting, *pr.p.*, white; *n.*, powdered chalk; a fish.

whi'tish, *adj.*, somewhat white.

whit'low, *n.*, a painful growth at the quick of the nail, or in a sheep's foot.

Whit'sun, *adj.*, rel. to Whitsuntide.

Whit'-Sunday, *n.*, the Church's Pentecostal Feast. White Sunday, because converts were baptized on that day in white garments.

Whit'suntide, *n.*, the week between Whit-Sunday and Trinity Sunday.

whit'tle, *v.t.*, to cut away bit by bit; to shorten.

whit'tled, *p.p.*, whittle.

whit'tling, *pr.p.*, whittle.

whi'ty-brown, *adj.*, white tinged with brown.

whiz, *n.*, a sound part hum, part hiss; *v.i.*, to make the sound; to fly with a whizzing sound.

whizzed, *p.p.*, whiz.

whiz'zing, *pr.p.*, whiz.

who, *interrog. pron.*, what or which person? *rel. pron.*, the person referred to.

whoa, *exclamation*, used by carters to their horses when they wish them to stop.

whoev'er, *rel. pron.*, any or every one who.

whole, *adj.*, entire; sound; in good health; *n.*, entirety; the entire collection.

whole'ness, *n.*, the state or quality of being whole.

whole'sale, *adj.*, sold in bulk; not retail; *n.*, sale in bulk, not retail.

whole'some, *adj.*, healthy; sound; salutary.

whole'someness, *n.*, the quality of being wholesome.

whol'ly, *adv.*, entirely; completely.

whom, *interrog.* and *rel. pron.*, *obj. case of* who.

whomsoev'er, *rel. pron.*, *obj. case of* whosoever.

whoop, *n.*, a yell; *v.i.*, to yell; shriek.

whooped, *p.p.*, whoop.

whoop'ing, *pr.p.*, whoop.

whoop'ing-cough, *n.*, a distressing cough, distinguished by a whooping sound.

whop, *v.t.*, to beat; *n.*, a fall; a blow.

whopped, *p.p.*, whop.

whop'per, *n.*, a big lie (*slang*); anything very big.

whop'ping, *pr.p.*, whop.

whore, *n.*, a prostitute; *v.i.*, to keep company with prostitutes.

whore'dom, *n.*, prostitution.

whore'monger, *n.*, one who has dealings with prostitutes.

whor'ish, *adj.*, like a prostitute.

whorl, *n.*, a ring of leaves or other growth round the stem of a plant; a turn of a spiral; the fly of a spinning wheel.

whorled, *adj.*, having whorls.

whort, *n.*, *i.q.* whortleberry.

whor'tleberry, *n.*, an edible fruit.

whose, *interrog. poss. pron.*, of whom? bel. to whom? *rel. poss. pron.* of whom; bel. to whom.

whosesoev'er, *rel. poss. pron.*, of whomsoever.

who'so, *indef. rel. pron.*, anyone who.

whosoev'er, *indef. rel. pron.*, somewhat more indefinite than whoso.

why, *interrog. adv.*, for what reason? with what purpose? *interj.*, expressing curiosity or surprise; *n.*, the reason; the wherefore.

wick, *n.*, the part of a candle or lamp that is lighted.

wick'ed, *adj.*, sinful; depraved; mischievous.

wick'edly, *adv.*, in a wicked way.

wick'edness, *n.*, the state or quality of being wicked.

wick'er, *n.*, osier; *adj.*, plaited with osier.

wick'ered, *adj.*, made of wicker-work.

wick'er-work, *n.*, plaited osier.

wick'et, *n.*, a little gate, sometimes forming part of a larger one; a cricket stump.

Wic'liffite, *n.*, a follower of Wiclif; *adj.*, pert. to Wiclif.

wide, *adj.*, broad; spacious; vast; away from a mark; *adv.*, to a distance; *n.*, in cricket, a ball bowled outside the limits of the ends of the crease.

wide'awake, *adj.*, on the alert; free from sleepiness; *n.*, a soft felt hat.

wide'ly, *adv.*, far; to a distance.

wi'den, *v.t.*, to make wider; *v.i.*, to become wider.

wi'dened, *p.p.*, widen.

wide'ness, *n.*, *i.q.* width.

wi'dening, *pr.p.*, widen; *n.*, the act of making or becoming wider or open.

wi'der, *adj.*, *comp.* of wide.

wide'spread, *adj.*, extending over a great distance.

wi'dest, *adj.*, *super.* of wide.

widge'on, *n.*, a variety of wild duck.

wid'ow, *n.*, a woman whose husband is dead, and who remains single; *v.t.*, to bereave of a husband or of a wife.

wid'owed, *p.p.*, widow; *adj.*, in the state of a widow or widower.

wid'ower, *n.*, a man whose wife is dead and who remains single.

wid'owhood, *n.*, the state or period of being a widow.

width, *n.*, breadth; stretch from side to side.

wield, *v.t.*, to brandish; move with the hands.

wield'ed, *p.p.*, wield.

wield'er, *n.*, one who wields.

wield'ing, *pr.p.*, wield.

wield'y, *adj.*, easy to handle.

wife, *n.*, a married woman.

wife'hood, *n.*, the state of being a wife.

wife'less, *adj.*, without a wife.

wife'like, *adj.*, as a wife should be.

wife'ly, *adj.*, *i.q.* wifelike.

wig, *n.*, a false head of hair; *v.t.*, to scold (*colloq.*).

wigged, *p.p.*, wig; *adj.*, wearing a wig.

wig'ging, *pr.p.*, wig; *n.*, a scolding (*colloq.*)

wight, *n.*, a being; person.

wig'wag, *adv.*, to and fro.

wig'wam, *n.*, a N. Amer. Indian's hut or tent.

wild, *adj.*, untamed; fierce; violent; blustering; dissipated; *n.*, the wilderness.

wild'cat, *adj.*, risky; too speculative.

wild'er, *adj.*, *comp.* of wild.

wil'der, *v.t.*, *i.q.* bewilder.

wil'dered, *p.p.*, wilder.

wil'dering, *pr.p.*, wilder; *adj.*, perplexing; bewildering.

wil'derness, *n.*, a desert.

wild'est, *adj.*, *super.* of wild.

wild'-fire, *n.*, an old destructive device, consisting of combustible material for setting fire to an enemy's ships; heat-lightning.

wild'ly, *adv.*, in a wild way.

wild'ness, *n.*, the quality of being wild.

wile, *n.*, a trick; cunning; *v.t.*, to deceive; entrap.

wil'ful, *adj.*, self-willed; obstinate.

wil'fully, *adv.*, in a wilful way.

wil'fulness, *n.*, the state of being wilful.

wi'lier, *adj.*, *comp.* of wily.

wi'liest, *adj.*, *super.* of wily.

wi'lily, *adv.*, in a wily way.

wi'liness, *n.*, cunning; craftiness.

will, *n.*, determination; mental power of choice; command; desire; testamentary disposition; *v.t.*, to resolve; determine; ordain; bequeath. The word is also used as an auxiliary to form the future tense.

willed, *p.p.*, will.

wil'ling, *pr.p.*, will; *adj.*, ready; complying.

wil'lingly, *adv.*, in a willing way; voluntarily; readily.

wil'lingness, *n.*, the state of being willing.

will-o'-the-wisp, *n.*, a curious, moving light that plays over marshes; *ignis fatuus*.

wil'low, *n.*, a tree so named; a cricket-bat (*colloq.*).

wil'lowed, *adj.*, planted with willows.

wil'lowy, *adj.*, like a willow.

wil'ly, *adj.*, *i.q.* wilful (*Scot.*).

wil'ly-nil'ly, *adv.*, whether one likes or not.

wil'some, *adj.*, obstinate; wilful.

wilt, *2nd per.* sing., will; *v.i.*, to droop; fade; *v.t.*, to cause to droop.

wilt'ed, *p.p.*, wilt.

wilt'ing, *pr.p.*, wilt.

wi'ly, *adj.*, crafty; cunning.

wim'ble, *v.t.*, to bore; *n.*, a boring-tool.

wim'ple, *n.*, a head-covering once commonly worn by women, and now retained by nuns; *v.t.*, to cover with a wimple; *v.i.*, to undulate.

wim'pled, *adj.*, wearing a wimple.

wim'pling, *adj.*, rippling.

win, *v.t.*, to gain; obtain; *v.i.*, to gain a victory or success; *n.*, achieved success.

wince, *v.i.*, to cower; shrink; *n.*, the act of wincing.

winced, *p.p.*, wince.

winc'er, *n.*, one who winces.

winch, *n.*, a windlass; crank; *v.t.*, to move by means of a winch.

winched, *p.p.*, winch.

winch'ing, *pr.p.*, winch.

winc'ing, *pr.p.*, wince.

wind, *n.*, movement of air; breath; air or gas in the stomach; *v.t.*, to take the breath from; to scent.

wind, *v.t.*, to twist; coil; *v.i.*, to revolve; to take a devious course.

wind'age, *n.*, difference between the diameter of a projectile and the bore of the gun; action of the wind on the flight of a projectile.

wind'-bound, *adj.*, held up by wind.

wind'ed, *adj.*, with the breath knocked out.

wind'er, *n.*, one who, that which, winds.

wind'fall, *n.*, fruit blown off a tree; a piece of good luck.

wind'gall, *n.*, a swelling on a horse's fetlock-joint.

wind'ier, *adj., comp.* of windy.
wind'iest, *adj., super.* of windy.
wind'iness, *n.,* the state of being windy.
wind'ing, *pr.p.,* wind; *adj.,* twisting; *n.,* a turning; twisting.
wind'ing-sheet, *n.,* the wrapping of a corpse; a cerecloth.
wind'lass, *n.,* a roller round which a rope or chain is wound.
win'dle, *n.,* a reel; spindle.
wind'mill, *n.,* a mill worked by the wind.
win'dow, *n.,* an opening in a building to let in light and air.
win'dow-glass, *n.,* glazing for a window.
win'dow-sash, *n.,* the frame of a window-pane.
win'dow-seat, *n.,* a seat in a window.
wind'pipe, *n., i.q.* trachea.
wind'row, *n.,* a row or pile shaped by the wind's action.
wind'ward, *adv.,* toward the wind; *n.,* the quarter from which the wind blows.
wind'y, *adj.,* pert. to, full of, wind; blowing; boisterous; empty.
wine, *n.,* the juice of the grape.
wine'-bibber, *n.,* one who is too much addicted to wine.
wine'-cellar, *n.,* an underground wine-store.
wine'-glass, *n.,* a glass from which wine is drunk.
wing, *n.,* a bird's pinion with which it flies; any wing-like thing, as the side of a building; an aisle; *v.t.,* to furnish with wings; to stop the flight of; *v.i.,* to fly.
winged, *p.p.,* wing.
wing'ed, *adj.,* having wings.
wing'ing, *pr.p.,* wing.
wing'less, *adj.,* lacking wings.
wing'y, *adj.,* having wings; swift.
wink, *n.,* a twitching movement with the eyelids; a suggestive look; *v.t.,* to twitch (the eye); *v.i.,* to twitch the eyelids; to give a hint; to pretend not to see; to connive.
winked, *p.p.,* wink.
wink'er, *n.,* one who winks.
wink'ing, *pr.p.,* wink.
win'kle, *n., i.q.* periwinkle; an edible sea-snail.
win'ner, *n.,* one who, that which, wins.
win'ning, *pr.p.,* win; *adj.,* engaging; attractive.
win'ning-post, *n.,* the end of a race.
win'now, *v.t.,* to separate (grain) from the husks; to fan; *v.i.,* to do winnowing.
win'nowed, *p.p.,* winnow.
win'nower, *n.,* one who, that which, winnows.
win'nowing, *pr.p.,* winnow; *n.,* the process of winnowing.
win'some, *adj.,* engaging; charming.
win'ter, *n.,* the coldest season of the year; *v.i.,* to spend the winter; *v.t.,* to protect or lay up for the winter; *adj.,* pert. to winter.
win'tered, *p.p.,* winter
win'ter-green, *n.,* the name of certain plants which are green through the winter.
win'tering, *pr.p.,* winter.
win'terly, *adj.,* like winter; cold.
win'try, *adj., i.q.* winterly.
wi'ny, *adj.,* like wine.
winze, *n.,* a ventilating shaft in a mine.
wipe, *v.t.,* to rub; cleanse or dry by rubbing; *n.,* the act of wiping; a hit; defeat in argument.
wiped, *p.p.,* wipe.
wi'per, *n.,* one who, that which, wipes.
wi'ping, *pr.p.,* wipe.
wire, *n.,* metal drawn out into a thread; a telegram (*colloq.*); *v.t.,* to fence with wire; snare with wire; telegraph (*colloq.*).
wire'draw, *v.i.,* to draw wire.
wire'drawer, *n.,* one who draws wire.
wire'drawing, *pr.p.,* wiredraw; *n.,* a wire-drawer's occupation.
wire'drawn, *p.p.,* wiredraw; *adj.,* subtle; excessively fine.
wire'-gauze, *n.,* gauze made of wire.
wire'less, *n.,* transmission of telegraphic messages without the use of wires; marconigraph; a message so sent; a marconigram.
wire'-puller, *n.,* an intriguer; one who uses secret influence.
wire'-pulling, *n.,* intriguing; using secret influence.
wire'worm, *n.,* a wire-like worm.
wir'iness, *n.,* the state or quality of being wiry.
wir'y, *adj.,* like wire; strong and flexible; able to stand strain; thin but strong.
wis'dom, *n.,* the quality of being wise; sagacity; experience; learning.
wise, *adj.,* sagacious; prudent; learned; experienced.
wise'acre, *n.,* one who lays an unfounded claim to wisdom.
wise'ly, *adv.,* in a wise way.
wi'ser, *adj., comp.* of wise.
wi'sest, *adj., super.* of wise.
wish, *n.,* a desire; something desired; *v.t.,* to desire; *v.i.,* to have a longing.
wished, *p.p.,* wish.
wish'er, *n.,* one who wishes.

***wish'*ful**, *adj.*, longing; desiring.

***wish'*fully**, *adv.*, longingly.

***wish'*ing**, *pr.p.*, wish.

wish'y-washy, *adj.*, poor, thin.

wisp, *n.*, a thin bunch.

wist, an obsolete word = knew.

Wista'ria, *n.*, a climbing plant with a beautiful lilac flower.

wist'ful, *adj.*, sad; longing.

wist'fully, *adv.*, in a wistful way.

wis'tonwish, *n.*, a prairie-dog. Also *wishtonwish*.

wit, *n.*, knowledge; good sense; talent; the power of saying a pointed or clever thing with a touch of the humorous; a person noted for his wit.

witch, *n.*, a woman supposed to possess supernatural powers through familiarity with evil spirits; a sorceress; a bewitchingly charming woman; *v.t.*, to fascinate.

witch'craft, *n.*, sorcery.

witch'-elm, *n.*, a tree so named.

witch'ery, *n.*, enchantment; power of fascinating.

witch'-hazel, *n.*, a tree so named, from which a medicinal extract is made.

witch'ing, *pr.p.*, witch; *adj.*, enchanting.

wit'enagemot, *n.*, the ancient Anglo-Saxon national council.

with, *prep.*, in the company of; by means of; as a *prefix* it indicates antagonism, removal, deprivation.

withal', *adv.*, likewise; also.

withdraw', *v.t.*, to take away; hold back; *v.i.*, to go away; recede.

withdraw'al, *n.*, the act of withdrawing.

withdraw'er, *n.*, one who withdraws.

withdraw'ing, *pr.p.*, withdraw.

withdraw'ing-room, *n.*, what is now called the drawing-room (*i.e.*, a room to which one withdraws from the banqueting-hall).

withdrawn', *p.p.*, withdraw.

withdrew', *p.t.*, withdraw.

withe, *n.*, a twig, usually of willow; twisted twigs.

withed, *adj.*, made of withes.

with'er, *v.t.*, to cause to fade; to dry up; *v.i.*, to fade away; decay.

with'ered, *p.p.*, wither

with'ering, *pr.p.*, wither; *adj.*, crushingly sarcastic.

with'ers, *n. pl.*, the part between a horse's shoulder-bones.

withheld', *p.p.*, withhold.

withhold', *v.t.* and *i.*, to keep back; refuse to give.

withhold'en, *p.p.*, withhold.

withhold'er, *n.*, one who withholds.

withhold'ing, *pr.p.*, withhold.

within', *adv.*, inside.

without', *adv.*, outside; *prep.*, not having; with the omission of.

withstand', *v.t.*, to oppose; resist.

withstand'ing, *pr.p.*, withstand.

withstood', *p.p.*, withstand.

with'y, *n.*, *i.q.* withe.

wit'less, *adj.*, lacking wits.

wit'ling, *n.*, an unintellectual person.

wit'ness, *n.*, one who testifies; testimony; evidence; *v.t.*, to see with one's own eyes; attest; *v.i.*, to act as a witness.

wit'nessed, *p.p.*, witness.

wit'nessing, *pr.p.*, witness.

wit'ted, *adj.*, possessed of understanding.

wit'ticism, *n.*, a witty saying.

wit'tier, *adj.*, *comp.* of witty.

wit'tiest, *adj.*, *super.* of witty.

wit'tily, *adv.*, in a witty way.

wit'tiness, *n.*, the quality of being witty.

wit'ting, *adj.*, with full knowledge.

wit'tingly, *adv.*, consciously.

wit'ty, *adj.*, full of wit; characterized by wit; smartly funny.

wit'wal, *n.*, a variety of woodpecker.

wive, *v.t.*, to find a wife for; *v.i.*, to marry.

wived, *p.p.*, wive.

wi'vern, *n.*, *i.q.* wyvern.

wi'ving, *pr.p.*, wive.

wiz'ard, *n.*, masc. of witch; a sorcerer; conjurer.

wiz'ardry, *n.*, the arts of a wizard; enchantment.

wiz'en, *v.t.*, to wither and shrivel up; *adj.*, shrivelled up and faded-looking.

wiz'ened, *p.p.*, wizen.

woad, *n.*, a plant so named and the blue dye it yielded. The Britons in Julius Caesar's time dyed themselves with woad.

Wo'den, *n.*, the Celtic god of war. Also *Odin*.

woe, *n.*, sorrow; grief; calamity.

woe'begone, *adj.*, full of misery.

woe'ful, wo'ful, *adj.*, full of woe; sad; pitiful.

woe'fully, wo'fully, *adv.*, in a woeful manner.

woke, *p.t.*, wake.

wold, *n.*, forest land; open country.

wolf, *n.*, a dog-like wild carnivore; *v.t.*, to eat ravenously.

wolf'-fish, *n.*, a fish so named.

wolf'ish, *adj.*, like a wolf; rapacious.
wolf'ram, *n.*, a variety of tungstate.
wolf's'-bane, *n.*, aconite.
wolverine', *n.*, a carnivore so named.
wom'an, *n.*, fem. of man.
wom'an-ha'ter, *n.*, a misogymist; one who hates (or pretends to hate) womankind.
wom'anhood, *n.*, the state of being a woman; female maturity.
wom'anish, *adj.*, like a woman; unmanly.
wom'ankind, *n.*, women collectively.
wom'anliness, *n.*, the qualities appropriate to a woman.
wom'anly, *adj.*, as a woman ought to be.
womb, *n.*, the uterus.
wom'bat, *n.*, a marsupial of Australia.
wom'en, *n.*, pl. of woman.
won, *p.t.* and *p.*, win.
won'der, *n.*, astonishment; surprise; a marvel; a prodigy; *v.i.*, to feel astonishment or surprise.
won'dered, *p.p.*, wonder.
won'derful, *adj.*, surprising; amazing.
won'derfully, *adv.*, in a wonderful way.
won'derfulness, *n.*, the quality of being wonderful.
won'dering, *pr.p.*, wonder.
won'deringly, *adv.*, in a wondering way.
won'derment, *n.*, astonishment; perplexity.
won'drous, *adj.*, marvellous.
won'drously, *adv.*, marvellously.
won't, a colloquialism for "will not."
wont, *n.*, usage; custom; *adj.* accustomed.
wont'ed, *adj.*, accustomed.
wont'edness, *n.*, the state of being wont.
woo, *v.t.*, to court; importune.

wood, *n.*, timber; a collection of trees; the hard part of a tree.
wood'-ashes, *n.*, ashes from burnt wood.
wood'bine, *n.* a creeping plant so named.
wood'chat, *n.* a small bird so named.
wood'-chuck, *n.*, a bird.
wood'cock, *n.*, a wild fowl.
wood'cut, *n.*, an engraving on wood.
wood'-cutter, *n.*, one who fells trees.
wood'ed, *adj.*, covered with timber.
wood'en, *adj.*, made of wood; stiff; stolid.
wood'house, *n.*, a building in which wood is stored.
wood'iness, *n.*, the quality of being woody.
wood'land, *n.*, country covered with woods.
wood'less, *adj.*, without wood.
wood'-louse, *n.*, an insect found in old timber.
wood'man, *n.*, a forester; a wood-cutter.
wood'-note, *n.*, the song of birds.
wood'-nymph, *n.*, a nymph that haunts a wood.
wood'pecker, *n.*, a bird which pecks trees with a tapping sound.
wood'-pigeon, *n.*, a wild pigeon.
wood'roof, *n.*, a herb so named.
woods'man, *n.*, *i.q.* woodman.
wood'ward, *n.*, a forester.
wood'work, *n.*, things constructed of wood.
wood'-worker, *n.*, a worker in wood.
wood'y, *adj.*, covered with timber; like wood.
wooed, *p.p.*, woo.
woo'er, *n.*, a suitor.
woof, *n.*, cross-threads; woven-work.
woo'ing, *pr.p.*, woo. *n.*, love-making; *adj.*, courting.

woo'ingly, *adv.*, in a wooing manner.
wool, *n.*, fleece.
wool'comber, *n.*, one who combs wool.
woold, *v.t.*, to wind round.
woold'er, *n.*, a pin or stick used in woolding.
woold'ing, *pr.p.*, woold.
wool'fell, *n* a fleece.
wool'-gathering, *adj.*, abstracted; not collected in thought.
wool'len, *adj.*, made of wool; *n.*, a woollen cloth; woollen materials.
wool'liness, *n.*, the quality of being woolly.
wool'ly, *adj.*, fleecy; soft; like wool.
wool'pack, *n.*, a bale of wool.
wool'sack, *n.*, a sack of wool; the Lord Chancellor's cushion; the emblem of the Lord Chancellor's office.
wootz, *n.*, a fine Indian steel.
word, *n.*, a spoken utterance; a message; command; tidings; discussion; *v.t.*, to express in words.
***word'*-book**, *n.*, a vocabulary; dictionary.
word'ed, *p.p.*, word; *adj.*, expressed in precise words.
word'ily, *adv.*, in a wordy way.
word'iness, *n.*, the state or quality of being wordy.
word'ing, *pr.p.*, word; *n.*, the exact words.
word'y, *adj.*, full of words; verbose.
wore, *p.t.*, wear.
work, *n.*, labour; toil; employment; duty; something worked; a book or other composition; in pl., mechanism; a manufactory; deeds as distinct from faith; *v.t.*, to effect; to cause to work; to sew, etc.; *v.i.*, to labour; to do work; to ferment.

work'able, *adj.* practicable; able to be worked.

work'aday, *adj.*, ordinary; everyday.

work'bag, *n.*, a bag in which work is carried.

work'-box, *n.*, a box containing sewing materials, etc.

work'-day, *n.*, one of the days in the week exclusive of Sunday.

worked, *p.p.*, work.

work'er, *n.*, one who works.

work'house, *n.*, a Poorhouse.

work'ing, *pr.p.*, work.

work'ing-day, *n.*, *i.q.* work-day.

work'ing-man, *n.*, *i.q.* workman.

work'man, *n.*, one engaged in manual labour.

work'manlike, *adj.*, skilful; done in finished style.

work'manly, *adj.*, *i.q.* workmanlike.

work'manship, *n.*, skill.

work'shop, *n.*, a place where manual work is carried on.

work'shy, *adj.*, not too fond of work; *n.*, a shirker.

work'woman, *n.*, fem. of workman.

world, *n.*, the universe; this earth; life on earth; society.

world'liness, *n.*, the quality of being worldly.

world'ling, *n.*, one who lives only for this world.

world'ly, *adj.*, pert. to the world; living only for this world.

world'ly-minded, *adj.*, having no thought for anything but this world.

world'-wide, *adj.*, extending over the whole world.

worm, *n.*, a creeping animal; the thread of a screw; a poor, mean creature; *v.t.*, to destroy gradually: *v.i.*, to creep in; to wriggle in.

worm'-eaten, *adj.*, destroyed by worms; old; decayed.

wormed, *p.p.*, worm.

worm'il, *n.*, a parasitic worm; a bot.

worm'ing, *pr.p.*, worm.

worm'like, *adj.*, like a worm.

worm'wood, *n.*, absinthe.

worm'y, *adj.*, like a worm; full of worms.

worn, *p.p.*, wear; *adj.*, weary looking.

worn'il, *n.*, *i.q.* wormil.

worn'-out, *adj.*, tired out; made useless by long wear.

wor'ried, *p.p.*, worry.

wor'rier, *n.*, one who worries.

wor'ry, *n.*, care; trouble; anxiety; *v.t.*, to harass; tear with the teeth; perplex; *v.i.*, to be over-anxious; to fret.

wor'rying, *pr.p.*, worry; *adj.*, harassing; vexing.

worse, *adj.*, *comp.* of bad or ill; *adv.*, *comp.* of badly or ill.

wor'ship, *n.*, adoration; divine service; honour; reverence; the title of mayors and other magistrates; *v.t.*, to adore; pay divine honour to; to reverence; *v.i.*, to engage in worship.

wor'shipful, *adj.*, worthy of reverence.

wor'shipfully, *adv.*, in a worshipful way.

wor'shipped, *p.p.*, worship.

wor'shipper, *n.*, one who worships.

wor'shipping, *pr.p.*, worship.

worst, *adj.*, *super.* of bad; *adv.*, *super.* of badly; *v.t.*, to defeat; get the better of.

worst'ed, *p.p.*, worst.

wors'ted, *n.*, twisted woollen thread; *adj.*, made of worsted.

worst'ing, *pr.p.*, worst.

wort, *n.*, a herb; infusion of malt.

worth, *n.*, *i.q.* worthiness; value; *adj.*, of such and such value; possessing so much wealth; deserving of.

wor'thier, *adj.*, *comp.* of worthy.

wor'thiest, *adj.*, *super.* of worthy.

wor'thily, *adv.*, in a worthy way.

wor'thiness, *n.*, the quality of being worthy; moral excellence.

worth'less, *adj.*, of no value; depraved.

worth'lessness, *n.*, the state or quality of being worthless.

wor'thy, *adj.*, deserving; morally excellent; *n.*, a person to be esteemed.

wot, *v.t.*, to know.

would, *p.t.*, will.

would'-be, *adj.*, desiring to be; making pretence; *n.*, one who pretends.

wound (a hurt), *n.*, a hurt that pierces the skin; mental injury; *v.t.*, to inflict a wound upon; to hurt the mind of.

wound, *p.t.* and *p.*, wind.

wound'ed, *p.p.*, wound.

wound'ing, *pr.p.*, wound.

wound'wort, *n.*, kidney-vetch.

woura'li, *n.*, curare.

wove, *p.t.*, weave.

wo'ven, *p.p.*, weave.

wrack, *n.*, drifted seaweed; destruction; a scudding cloud.

wraith, *n.*, a ghost; spirit.

wran'gle, *v.i.*, to squabble; *n.*, an angry dispute.

wran'gled, *p.p.*, wrangle.

wran'gler, *n.*, one who wrangles; one who is placed in the first class of the Mathematical Tripos at Cambridge.

wran'glership, *n.*, a place in the first class of the Mathematical Tripos.

wran'gling, *pr.p.*, wrangle.

wrap, *v.t.*, to fold something round another to cover it; *n.*, a covering; rug.

wrap'page, *n.*, a wrapper; wraps collectively.

wrapped, *p.p.*, wrap.

wrap'per, *n.*, a covering; a loose outer garment.

wrap'ping, *pr.p.*, wrap.

wrasse, *n.*, a fish so named.

wrath, *n.*, anger.

wrath'ful, *adj.*, angry.

wrath'fully, *adv.*, in a wrathful way.

wreak, *v.t.*, to carry out in revenge.

wreaked, *p.p.*, wreak.

wreak'ing, *pr.p.*, wreak.

wreath, *n.*, a garland; chaplet.

wreathe, *v.t.*, to encircle with a wreath; to entwine.

wreathed, *p.p.*, wreathe.

wreath'ing, *pr.p.*, wreathe.

wreath'y, *adj.*, like a wreath.

wreck, *v.t.*, to destroy utterly; drive to ruin; *n.*, destruction, esp. of a ship; a ship wrecked; ruin; anything ruined.

wreck'age, *adj.*, remains from a shipwreck.

wrecked, *p.p.*, wreck.

wreck'er, *n.*, one who causes wrecks; one who steals shipwrecked goods that come ashore.

wreck'ing, *pr.p.*, wreck.

wren, *n.*, a small bird.

wrench, *v.t.*, to pull by twisting; *n.*, a twisting pull; a tool for wrenching.

wrenched, *p.p.*, wrench.

wrench'ing, *pr.p.*, wrench.

wrest, *v.t.*, to seize away; to twist; to misinterpret intentionally; *n.*, a violent pull.

wrest'ed, *p.p.*, wrest.

wrest'er, *n.*, one who, that which, wrests.

wrest'ing, *pr.p.*, wrest.

wres'tle, *v.i.*, to struggle by grappling; *v.t.*, to contend earnestly; to join in a wrestling contest.

wres'tled, *p.p.*, wrestle.

wres'tler, *n.*, one who wrestles.

wrest'ling, *pr.p.*, wrestle; *n.*, the act of wrestling.

wretch, *n.*, one in misery; a worthless person.

wretch'ed, *adj.*, in great distress; poor; mean.

wretch'edly, *adv.*, in a wretched way.

wretch'edness, *n.*, the state of being wretched.

wrig'gle, *v.i.*, to twist about; *v.t.*, to give a wriggling motion to; *n.*, a twisting motion.

wrig'gled, *p.p.*, wriggle.

wrig'gler, *n.*, one who wriggles.

wrig'gling, *pr.p.* wriggle.

wright, *n.*, a workman; carpenter.

wring, *v.t.*, to squeeze with a twist; to excruciate; *n.*, a twisting squeeze.

wring'er, *n.*, one who, that which, wrings.

wring'ing, *pr.p.*, wring.

wrin'kle, *n.*, a corrugation; a crease; *v.t.*, to corrugate; make into folds; *v.i.*, to become wrinkled.

wrin'kled, *p.p.*, wrinkle.

wrin'kling, *pr.p.*, wrinkle.

wrin'kly, *adj.*, full of wrinkles.

wrist, *n.*, the part of the arm next to the hand.

wrist'band, *n.*, a cuff.

wrist'let, *n.*, anything worn round the wrist.

wrist'-shot, *n.*, a quarter-shot in golf.

writ, *p.p.*, write (*obs.*); *n.*, a legal document commanding or summoning.

write, *v.t.*, to set down words on paper with a pen or pencil; to indite; to compose; *v.i.*, to use the pen; to be an author or composer.

wri'ter, *n.*, one who, that which, writes; a clerk; an author.

wri'tership, *n.*, the status of a writer to the signet or legal practitioner (*Scots law*).

writhe, *v.i.*, to turn and twist as in pain; *v.t.*, to twist.

writhed, *p.p.*, writhe.

wri'thing, *pr.p.*, writhe.

wri'ting, *pr.p.*, write; *n.*, written work; script; composition; authorship; a written document.

wri'ting-book, *n.*, a book to write in.

wri'ting-desk, *n.*, a desk to write upon.

wri'ting-master, *n.*, a teacher of writing.

wri'ting-paper, *n.*, paper for letter-writing.

writ'ten, *p.p.*, write.

wrong, *adj.*, the opposite to right; wicked; false; mistaken; incorrect; *adv.*, erroneously; unjustly; *n.*, an injury; injustice; *v.t.*, to do unjustly to.

wrong'-doer, *n.*, one who does wrong.

wrong'-doing, *n.*, evil doing.

wronged, *p.p.*, wrong.

wrong'ful, *adj.*, injurious; unjust.

wrong'fully, *adv.*, in a wrongful way.

wrong'headed, *adj.*, perverse.

wrong'ing, *pr.p.*, wrong.

wrong'ly, *adv.*, in a wrong way.

wrote, *p.t.*, write.

wroth, *adj.*, angry.

wrought, *p.t.* and *p.*, work.

wrung, *p.t.* and *p.*, wring.

wry, *adj.*, twisted; expressive of disgust, nausea, etc.

wry'neck, *n.*, a bird so named; a neck that is twisted.

wyan'dotte, *n.*, a breed of poultry.

Wyke'hamist, *n.*, originally, founder's kin to William of Wykeham, the founder of the two Colleges at Winchester and Oxford. (The latter, being founded after Winchester, is commonly known as New College, though its proper dedication is to St. Mary, like that of the sister foundation.)

wy'vern, *n.*, a winged serpent, two-legged, and long-tailed (*her.*).

X

Xan'thian, *adj.*, pert. to Xanthus.

xan'thic, *adj.*, yellowish.

xan'thin, -thine, *n.*, yellow colouring matter.

Xanthip'pe, *n.*, the name of Socrates' wife, who was the type of all shrewish wives.

xan'thogen, *n.*, reputed to be the radical of xanthic acid.

Xan'thous, *adj.*, yellow.

xe'bec, *n.*, a small ship, three-masted, having lateen and square sails.

xe'nium, *n.*, the Greek term for a gift to a stranger or an envoy.

xenog'amy, *n.*, marrying with a foreigner; cross-fertilization.

xenogen'esis, *n.*, foreign origin.

xenoma'nia, *n.*, abnormal liking for things foreign.

xeroph'agy, *n.*, eating dried food.

xerophthal'my, *n.*, dryness of the eyeball.

xero'sis, *n.*, dryness.

xe'rotes, *n.*, a dry bodily habit.

Xiph'ias, *n.*, the sword-fish and others of the same genus.

xiph'oid, *adj.*, sword-like.

xy'lem, *n.*, wood tissue.

xy'lograph, *n.*, a wood engraving.

xylog'rapher, *n.*, a wood engraver.

xylograph'ic, *adj.*, pert. to xylography.

xylog'raphy, *n.*, wood engraving.

xyloi'dine, -din, *n.*, an explosive.

xy'lonite, *n.*, a sort of gun-cotton, imitating ivory; celluloid.

xyloph'agous, *adj.*, eating wood.

xy'lophone, *n.*, a musical instrument played with wooden hammers on wooden bars.

xyst, *n.*, *i.q.* xystus.

xys'ter, *n.*, a surgical scraping instrument.

xys'tus, *n.*, a covered portico; scraped lint.

Y

Ya'ca-wood, *n.*, a wood grown in Jamaica.

yacht, *n.*, a light vessel; *v.i.*, to sail or keep a yacht.

yacht'ed, *p.p.*, yacht.

yacht'er, *n.*, one who yachts.

yacht'ing, *pr.p.*, yacht; *n.*, the pastime of sailing a yacht.

ya'ger, *n.*, a German sharpshooter. Also *jäger*.

Yahoo', *n.*, one of a savage race described in *Gulliver's Travels*.

yak, *n.*, a variety of ox.

yam, *n.*, an edible tuber.

Yan'kee, *n.*, a colloquial name for an American; *adj.*, pert. to Yankees.

Yan'keeism, *n.*, Americanism.

yap, *n.*, to make the yelping noise of a dog; *n.*, a yelp.

yap'on, *n.*, a bush, from the leaves of which a kind of tea is made.

yap'ping, *pr.p.*, yap.

yard, *n.*, an enclosed space on a farm or near a house, etc.; a standard measure of length = 36 in.; the timber on which a sail is spread.

***yard*-arm,** *n.*, the end of a yard (*naut.*).

***yard*stick,** *n.*, a yard measure.

yarn, *n.*, spun thread; a strand; a story, usually an extravagant one as told by a sailor (*colloq.*); *v.i.*, to indulge in story-telling.

yar'row, *n.*, milfoil.

yash'mak, *n.*, a Moslem woman's veil.

yat'aghan, *n.*, a peculiar sword-dagger with a double curve.

yaup, *v.i.*, to yelp; *n.*, a yelp; a blue titmouse.

yaw, *v.i.*, to get out of the course; to zigzag.

yawed, *p.p.*, yaw.

yaw'ing, *pr.p.*, yaw.

yawl, *n.*, a small two-masted vessel.

yawn, *v.i.*, to gape; *n.*, a gape.

yawned, *p.p.*, yawn.

yawn'ing, *pr.p.*, yawn; *adj.*, open.

ycleped', yclept', *n.*, an old *past participle* = called; named.

ye, *2nd pers. pron.*, *pl.* of *thou* or *you*.

yea, *particle*, *i.q.* yes.

yean, *v.i.*, to give birth to a lamb.

yeaned, *p.p.*, yean.

yean'ing, *pr.p.*, yean.

yean'ling, *n.*, a newly born lamb.

year, *n.*, an annual period of time = 365¼ days.

***year*-book,** *n.*, a book brought up to date each year and relating to contemporary matters.

***year*'ling,** *n.*, a one-year old animal.

***year*'ly,** *adj.*, occurring every year; lasting for a year; *adv.*, occurring every year.

yearn, *v.i.*, to have a strong desire.

yearned, *p.p.*, yearn.

yearn'ing, *pr. p.*, yearn; *n.*, a longing.

yeast, *n.*, barm; froth; any substitute for yeast.

yeast'y, *adj.*, like yeast; foaming; frothing.

yelk, *n.*, *i.q.* yolk (*i.e.*, the yellow part of an egg).

yell, *n.*, a loud cry of pain, anger, etc.; *v.t.*, to utter in a yell; *v.i.*, to raise a loud cry.

yelled, *p.p.*, yell.

yell'ing, *pr.p.*, yell.

yel'low, *n.*, a colour as of saffron or gold; *adj.*, yellow-coloured; jaundiced.

yel'lower, *adj.*, *comp.* of yellow.

yel'lowest, *adj.*, *super.* of yellow.

yel'low fe'ver, *n.*, a deadly malarian disease.

yel'lowish, *adj.*, inclined to yellow.

Yel'low Per'il, *n.*, the danger from the development of the power of the yellow races.

yelp, *v.i.*, to make a sharp bark; *n.*, a sharp bark.

yelped, *p.p.*, yelp.

yelp'ing, *pr.p.*, yelp.

yen, *n.*, Japanese monetary unit.

yeo'man, *n.*, a farmer.

yeo'manry, *n.*, a military force raised among the farmer class.

yerk, *v.t.*, *i.q.* jerk; to give a quick push to; *v.i.*, to kick; *n.*, a quick push.

yerked, *p.p.*, yerk.

yerk'ing, *pr.p.*, yerk.

yes, a particle of affirmation.

yes'ter, *adj.*, pert. to the day before the present one.

yes'terday, *n.*, the day before the present one; *adv.*, on the day before this one.

yes'ternight, *n.* and *adv.*, last night.

yet, *adv.*, still; besides; moreover; up to this time; *conj.*, moreover; however.

yew, *n.*, the taxus; a dark-leaved evergreen tree.

yew'en, *adj.*, made of yew.

yew'tree, *n.*, *i.q.* yew.

Yid'dish, *n.*, a mixed language spoken by Jews in England.

yield, *v.t.*, to give up; surrender; produce; *v.i.*, to give in; to submit; *n.*, amount produced or returned.

yield'ed, *p.p.*, yield.

yield'er, *n.*, one who yields.

yield'ing, *pr.p.*, yield; *adj.*, compliant; submissive.

yield'ingly, *adv.*, compliantly.

yield'ingness, *n.*, a readiness to comply.

ylang'-ylang, *n.*, a Malayan perfume. Also *ihlang-ihlang*.

yo'del, *n.*, a song or cry of Swiss-Tyrolese dwellers in the mountains, natural and falsetto notes alternating; *v.t.* and *i.*, to sing yodel-fashion. Also *jodel*.

yo'del(l)ing, *pr.p.*, yodel; *n.*, the practice of yodelling.

yoke, *n.*, a contrivance for fastening draught oxen together by the necks; a wooden frame supported in the middle on a person's neck and having suspended from the ends pails, buckets, etc.; any kind of bond; *v t.*, to join with a yoke.

yoked, *p.p.*, yoke.

yoke'-fellow, *n.*, a close companion; fellow-slave.

yo'kel, *n.*, a rustic.

yo'king, *pr.p.*, yoke.

yolk, *n.*, *i.q.* yelk; the oil in a sheep's skin.

yon, *adj.*, that over there.

yon'der, *adj.*, that over there; *adv.*, over there.

yore, *adv.*, in long past time.

you, *pron.*, *2nd pers.*, thou, thee, ye.

young, *adj.*, youthful; early; immature; fresh; *n.*, young offspring.

youn'ger, *adj.*, *comp.* of young.

young'est, *adj.*, *super.* of young.

young'ish, *adj.*, rather young.

young'ling, *n.*, a young creature.

young'ster, *n.*, a child.

youn'ker, *n.*, a stripling.

your, *possess. adj.*, belonging to you.

yourself', *pers. pron.*, you individually or personally.

yourselves', pl. of yourself.

youth, *n.*, the early period of life; a young person; young persons collectively.

youth'ful, *adv.*, young; immature; young-looking.

youth'fulness, *n.*, the state of being youthful.

youths, *n.*, pl. of youth.

ytter'bium, *n.*, a rare metal.

yt'tria, *n.*, oxide of yttrium.

yt'trious, *adj.*, containing, pert. to, yttrium.

yt'trium, *n.*, a metallic base.

yuc'ca, *n.*, a S. Amer. plant so named.

yufts, *n.*, a variety of Russia leather.

yu'lan, *n.*, a kind of magnolia.

Yule, *n.*, Christmas.

Yule'log, *n.*, a log of wood burnt at Christmas.

Yule'-tide, *n.*, Christmas time.

yunx, *n.*, a wryneck.

yure, *n.*, a dug.

Yur'ga, *n.*, an Afghan pony.

y-wis', *adv.*, an obsolete phrase = certainly; truly.

Z

zac'cho, *n.*, a socle. Also *saccho.*

zaf'fre, *n.*, a cobalt oxide.

Zambo, *n.*, a negro; *i.q.* Sambo.

Zamindar', *n.*, *i.q.* Zemindar.

za'ny, *n.*, an idiot; a buffoon.

za'nyism, *n.*, buffoonery.

zare'ba, *n.*, a fortification hurriedly thrown up.

zar'nich, *n.*, an arsenic sulphide.

zax, *n.*, a hatchet used in slating.

za'yat, *n.*, a Burmese caravanserai.

Ze'a, *n.*, Indian maize and other grasses.

zeal, *n.*, enthusiasm; ardour.

zeal'ot, *n.*, an enthusiast; a fanatic.

zeal'otism, *n.*, the conduct of zealots; fanaticism.

zeal'otry, *n.*, *i.q.* zealotism.

zeal'ous, *adj.*, full of zeal; ardent.

zeal'ously, *adv.*, in a zealous way.

ze'bra, *n.*, a black and white striped African quadruped; a wood used in cabinet-making.

ze'bu, *n.*, an Indian ox with a hump.

zech'in, *n.*, *i.q.* sequin

zech'stein, *n.*, magnesium limestone.

zed, *n.*, the name of the letter Z.

zed'oary, *n.*, a digestive, aromatic root; also used in perfume.

zeit'geist, *n.*, the spirit of the age.

zemindar', *n.*, an Indian tenant of Government land.

zem'indary, *n.*, land held by a zemindar; area of a zemindar's jurisdiction.

zena'na, *n.*, women's quarters in an Indian house.

Zend, *n.*, the ancient language of Persia.

Zend-Aves'ta, *n.*, the writings deemed sacred by the followers of Zoroaster.

zen'dik, *n.*, an Eastern name for an unbeliever.

zen'ith, *n.*, the highest point in the heavens.

ze'olite, *n.*, a silicate so named from the fact that it froths when acted on by the blow-pipe.

zeolit'ic, *adj.*, pert. to zeolite.

zeph'yr, *n.*, a soft West wind.

Zeph'yrus, *n.*, the West wind (*Lat.*).

zeri'ba, *n.*, *i.q.* zareba.

ze'ro, *n.*, a cipher; nought; nothing.

zest, *n.*, keen relish; enjoyment.

zest'ful, *adj.*, relishing.

ze'ta, *n.*, the sixth letter of the Greek alphabet, corresponding to English Z.

zetet'ic, *adj.*, pert. to inquiry.

zeug'ma, *n.*, a figure of speech, in which two or more nouns are brought under the government of one verb or into relation with one adjective, the meaning of which fits only one of the nouns.

Zeus, *n.*, the king of gods in Greek mythology.

zeux'ite, *n.*, a ferriferous species of tourmalin.

zib'et, *n.*, the civet.

zie'ga, *n.*, curd produced in milk by acetic acid.

zif, *n.*, the second of the Jewish ecclesiastical, and eighth of the civil, months.

zigan'ka, *n.*, a Russian country dance; the music of the same.

zig'zag, *adj.*, twisting and turning; not keeping straight; *n.*, a path that twists and turns; *v.i.*, to move in twists and turns. [zag.

zig'zagged, *p.p.*, zig-

zig'zagging, *pr.p.*, zigzag.

zim'ent-water, *n.*, copper-impregnated water.

zinc, *n.*, a metal; spelter.

zincif'erous, *adj.*, producing zinc.

zinck'y, *adj.*, like, containing, zinc.

zin'co, *n.*, an impression from a zinc plate.

zin'code, *n.*, the positive pole in a galvanic battery.

zinc'ograph, *n.*, *i.q.* zinco.

zincog'rapher, *n.*, one who reproduces in zinco.

zincograph'ic, *adj.*, pert. to zincography.

zincog'raphy, *n.*, the art of reproducing from a zinc plate.

zinc'ous, *adj.*, of the nature of zinc.

zin'giber, *n.*, ginger and other related herbs.

Zi'on, *n.*, the hill on which Jerusalem stands. Also *Sion.*

Zi'onism, *n.*, a Jewish movement for the restoration of Palestine to the Jews.

zir'con, *n.*, a zirconium silicate.

zirco'nia, *n.*, oxide of zirconium.

zirco'nium, *n.*, a metallic element.

zith'er, *n.*, a musical stringed instrument

zith'ern, *n.*, *i.q.* zither.

zo'diac, *n.*, an area of the heavens embracing the twelve constellations through which the sun travels in the year.

zodi'acal, *adj.*, pert. to the zodiac.

zo'etrope, *n.*, a toy which by revolving, makes figures in pictures seem to move.

zo'fra, *n.*, a Moorish name for a carpet.

zo'har, *n.*, cabalistic notes on the Old Testament.

Zo'laism, *n.*, realistic writing in the manner of Emile Zola.

Zolaist'ic, *adj.*, pert. to Zolaism and Zola.

zoll'verein, *n.*, a customs union.

zo'nal, *adj.*, pert. to zones.

zone, *n.*, a belt; girdle; one of the great circular divisions of the earth's surface.

zoned, *adj.*, girdled.

zo'nular, *adj.*, pert. to a zonule.

zo'nule, *n.*, a small belt.

zo'ō, *prefix* = animal.

zoog'amy, *n.*, animal production.

zoog'eny, *n.*, the formation of animal organs.

zoog'ony, *n.*, *i.q.* zoogeny.

zoog'rapher, *n.*, one who studies zoography.

zoog'raphy, *n.*, the study of the distribution of fauna over the world.

zool'atry, *n.*, animal worship.

zo'olite, *n.*, a fossil animal.

zoolit'ic, *adj.*, pert. to zoolites.

zool'oger, *n.*, a student of zoology.

zoolog'ic, *adj.*, pert. to zoology.

zoolog'ical, *adj.*, *i.q.* zoologic.

zool'ogist, *n.*, *i.q.* zoologer.

zool'ogy, *n.*, the study of animals.

zoomor'phism, *n.*, representation of deity in animal form.

zoon'omy, *n.*, the study of natural laws in relation to animals.

zooph'agan, *adj.*, *i.q.* zoophagous.

zooph'agous, *adj.*, carnivorous.

zoophor'ic, *adj.*, pert. to zoophorus.

zooph'orus, *n.*, a frieze along which are shown figures of men or animals (*arch.*).

zo'ophyte, *n.*, a low-grade animal, hardly distinguishable from a plant.

zoophyt'ic, *adj.*, pert. to zoophytes.

zoophytol'ogy, *n.*, the study of zoophytes.

zo'osperm, *n.*, a spermatozoid.

zoot'omist, *n.*, a student of comparative anatomy.

zoot'omy, *n.*, comparative anatomy.

Zoroas'trian, *adj.*, pert. to Zoroaster and his teaching.

Zoroas'trianism, *n.*, the doctrines of Zoroaster (Sarathustra), the ancient Persian lawgiver and teacher.

zos'ter, *n.*, a girdle.

Zouave', *n.*, a French soldier of a regiment wearing an Arab uniform.

zounds, *n.*, an old exclamation of surprise, anger, etc.

zu'folo, *n.*, a small kind of flute.

Zu'lu, *n.*, a member of a warlike South African tribe.

zumolog'ical, *adj.*, *i.q.* zymological.

zumol'ogist, *n.*, *i.q.* zymologist.

zumol'ogy, *n.*, *i.q.* zymology.

zumom'eter, *n.*, *i.q.* zymometer.

zygodac'tyl, *adj.*, having toes in pairs.

zygodac'tylous, *adj.*, *i.q.* zygodactyl.

zygo'ma, *n.*, the bony arch of the cheek.

zygomat'ic, *adj.*, rel. to the zygoma.

zyme, *n.*, the germ of zymotic diseases.

zymolog'ic, *adj.*, pert. to zymology.

zymolog'ical, *adj.*, *i.q.* zymologic.

zymol'ogist, *n.*, a student of zymology.

zymol'ogy, *n.*, the study of the phenomena of fermentation.

zymom'eter, *n.*, an apparatus showing degrees of fermentation.

zymo'sis, *n.*, fermenting.

zymot'ic, *adj.*, pert. to zymosis; pert. to diseases in which virus acts upon the system as though it set up fermentation.

zy'murgy, *n.*, brewing.

zy'thum, *n.*, an Egyptian drink of malt and wheat.

zyxom'ma, *n.*, an Indian name for the dragon-fly.

Appendix

In addition to some further ordinary words not previously given in this Dictionary it has been thought desirable to include in this Appendix certain new words which came into use during recent years, and also some already familiar words to which new meanings have been attached. In the case of any old word found in the Appendix, the reader is referred for its fuller definition to the earlier pages of the Dictionary.

A

Abnormal'ity, *n.*, irregularity: monstrosity.

ae'rial, *n.*, antenna (in wireless telegraphy).

a'erobus, *n.*, an aerial omnibus.

a'ero-cam'era, *n.*, a type of camera suitable for use on an aeroplane.

a'erogram, *n.*, a wireless message.

a'erogun, *n.*, an anti-aircraft gun.

aflame', *adv.*, and *pred. adj.*, in flame, flaming.

ag'rimotor, *n.*, a motor or tractor for farm work.

ail'eron, *n.*, the movable hinder edge of the planes, or the wing-tip of the tail, of an aeroplane.

air'-base, *n.*, a place where aircraft is housed.

air'man, *n.*, an aviator.

air'-mechan'ic, *n.*, one who repairs aircraft.

air'-plane, *n.*, *i.q.*, aeroplane.

air'-pocket, *n.*, a space in the upper air where the atmosphere is more rarefied than the surrounding air.

air'-raid, *n.* an aircraft attack on a town or camp.

air'way, *n.*, recognized route for aircraft.

air'worthy, *adj.*, in a fit state to travel in the air (said of aircraft).

all'-round trav'erse, *n.*, a swivel machine gun.

Al'pinist, *n.*, a climber of Alps.

Alsa'tian, *adj.*, belonging to Alsatia; *n.*, a native of Alsatia; a dog of Alsatian breed.

al'ternator, *n.*, a dynamo which generates an alternating electric current.

am'busher, *n.*, one who lies in ambush.

Ano'pheles, *n.*, a malarial mosquito.

antenn'a, *n.*, a radiator set on a pole or suspended from aircraft.

antic'ipatively, *adv.*, with the purpose of forestalling.

antitet'anin, *n.*, a toxin used to prevent tetanus.

ar'tistry, *n.*, artistic skill, artistic expression.

ascend'ancy, *n.*, supremacy, superiority.

au'to-wheel, *n.*, a small motor attachable to the back wheel of a bicycle.

av'idly, *adv.*, greedily, with avidity.

av'ion, *n.*, a French word for aeroplane.

B

back-spacer, *n.*, typewriter key which, on pressure, reverses the movement of carriage.

backwarda'tion, *n.*, consideration by a seller of stock for power to delay delivery.

bacteriol'ogist, *n.*, one who studies bacteriology.

ballonet, *n.*, *i.q.*, balloonet.

balloonet', *n.*, a small balloon.

bar, *n.*, unit of atmospheric pressure.

barer, *adj.*, *comp.* of bare.

barest, *adj.*, *super.* of bare; *v.*, 2nd *pers. pr.t.* of bare, and of *p.t.* of bear.

bargee', *n.*, one who works on a barge.

bar'rage, *n.*, a defensive screen of gunfire, produced by the dropping of shells in front of advancing troops.

bask'er, *n.*, one who basks.

bean, *n.*, a slang term of greeting, usually with the epithet "old" prefixed.

bent'wood, *n.*, wood artificially bent; *adj.*; made of this material.

Berth'a, *n.*, a German long-range gun named after Bertha Krupp.

bi'oscope, *n.*, a toy or

appliance showing pictures in movement.

Black Mari'a, *n.*, British soldiers' slang for a big German shell, named after a prison-van, which is known in England by that slang name.

blank'et, *v.t.*, to confuse the gunfire of companion ships by coming into the line of fire.

blight'er, *n.*, slang for a scoundrel or other offensive person.

Blight'y, *n.*, soldiers' slang for home. (The word is of Urdu origin, corrupted.)

blimp, *n.*, a little scouting airship.

blinking, *adj.*, slang for infernal, confounded.

blister, *n.*, a protective hull below the water, defending a ship's inner hull.

blue'-eyed, *adj.*, having blue eyes.

Bohe'mianism, *n.*, the life and manners of Bohemians.

Bo'loism, *n.*, the principles of Bolo Pasha, a traitorous Frenchman.

Bol'shevik, *n.*, one belonging to the Russian revolutionary party, aiming at the universal extinction of the bourgeoisie and capitalism; *adj.*, relating to Bolsheviks.

Bol'shevism, *n.*, the principles of Bolsheviks.

Bol'shevist, *n.*, a member of the Russian Leninite party of extremists, *i.q.*, Bolshevik.

bot'ulism, *n.*, ptomaine poisoning, especially from eating sausages.

box-resp'irator, *n.*, a gas mask of which a box containing chemicals is a part.

brack'et, *n.*, space beyond and short of a target, *v.i.*, to shoot beyond and short of a target.

brain'y, *adj.*, possessing brains; intellectual.

bridge'-head, *n.*, fortification at the head of a bridge.

Brit'isher, *n.*, vulgarism for Briton.

budg'eting, *n.*, the act of drawing up a budget; *pres. part.* of *v.t.* to budget.

bulge, *n.*, *i.q.*, blister.

Bur'goyne, *n.*, a variety of trenching tool.

bus, *n.*, slang for an aeroplane.

buzz, *v.t.*, to transmit a telephone message in Morse.

C

Caesa'rean, *adj.*, relating to Caesar, imperial. The word is used particularly in the phrase, *Caesarean section,* the operation (by cutting) for the delivery of a child.

cal'orie, cal'ory, *n.*, a heat unit.

Cam'ion, *n.*, a French motor-lorry.

cam'ouflage, *n.*, disguise, deception, effected by painting, covering with boughs, etc., *v.t.*, to disguise.

canoe'ist, *n.*, one who paddles a canoe.

cap'tained, *v.t.*, *p.p.* of captain.

cas'ually, *adv.*, in a casual, offhand way.

cen'suses, *n.*, pl. of census.

chauf'fer, *n.*, a fire basket.

civv'ies, *n.*, *pl.*, mufti; civilian dress.

clear'-cole, *n.*, the first coat in house-painting, composed of size and white lead or whiting; *v.t.*, to coat with it.

clumped, *v.t.* and *i.*, *p.p.* of clump = to group in a cluster.

coal'-hole, *n.*, a coal-cellar.

coast'al, *adj.*, on or belonging to the coast.

col'onizer, *n.*, one who forms, or has a reputation for forming colonies.

com'pensator, *n.*, mechanical or electrical device for rectifying uneven running.

com'plimented, *v.t.*, *p.p.* and *p.t.* of compliment.

conch'y, *n.*, slang for Conscientious Objector to military service.

conge'nially, *adv.*, in a congenial way.

Contempt'ibles, *n.*, *pl.* "The Old Contemptibles" is the name adopted for the men of the British Expeditionary Force, whom the Kaiser sneeringly described as a "contemptible little army."

contin'uousness, *n.*, the state or quality of being continuous.

conversa'tionalist, *n.*, one who is clever at talking.

cot'ton-wool', *n.*, raw cotton, mostly used for wadding.

coulomb', *n.*, quantity of electricity which a current of one ampère conveys in a second.

creak'y, *adj.*, making a harsh noise of a peculiar kind, such as that made by new boots.

croquette', *n.*, a term in cooking for a savoury ball composed of rice, potatoes and meat.

cross'over, *n.*, an article of feminine attire, the ends of which overlap.

crump, *n.*, the noise of an exploding shell.

cubed, *v.t.*, *p.p.* of cube.

Cunard'er, *n.*, a vessel of the Cunard line.

cur'tain-fire, *n.*, *i.q.*, barrage.

curt'sied, *v.i.*, *p.p.* and *p.t.* of curtsy.

curt'sying, *v.i.*, *p.p.* of curtsy.

cush'y, *adj.*, slang for easy, pleasant, with an idea of softness suggested by the similar sound of "cushion." The word, however, is of Indian origin.

Cuth'bert, *n.*, one who held an easy post under Government, and so escaped military service.

cut'-out, *n.*, a form of electric switch.

Czech'o-Slovak', *n.*, one who belongs to the united nation of Czechs and Slovaks; *adj.*, pertaining to Czecho-Slovakia.

D

daz'zle, *n.*, the device of disguising a ship's line by painting.

debus', *v.i.*, to descend from a lorry, *v.t.*, to remove from a lorry.

declutch', *v.t.*, to release the clutch of.

decode', *v.t.*, to convert into ordinary words the agreed code signs.

decohe'rer, *n.*, an arrangement by which a coherer is again put into a state of high resistance.

decontrol', *v.t.*, to remove from under control; *n.*, the removal.

deduct'ible, *adj.*, able to be deducted.

defeat'ist, *n.*, one who advocates doctrines tending to the nation's loss of victory.

dekk'o, *interj.*, = "let's look"; *n.*, a look.

democ'ratize, *v.a.*, to change on democratic lines.

deportee', *n.*, a person deported, or banished.

depth'-charge, *n.*, an explosive in the form of a mine or bomb under water.

diamet'rically, *adv.*, directly opposite.

dib'ber, *n.*, an instrument used for dibbling, *i.e.*, for boring holes in the ground.

di'chord, *n.*, having two strings.

dichro'ic, *adj.*, presenting two colours.

dic'ta, *n.*, sayings (*pl.* of *dictum*).

dissim'ilarly, *adv.*, in a dissimilar way.

distrib'utively, *adv.*, separately.

divorcee', *n.*, a divorced person.

dog'ging, *v.t.*, *pr.p.* of dog.

dol'men, *n.*, a cromlech.

dope, *n.*, a varnish used in aeroplane construction; slang for a drug; *v.t.*, to drug.

Do'ra, *n.*, regulations enforced under the Defence Of The Realm Act, known as D.O.R.A.

doss'-house, *n.*, a cheap lodging-house.

dough'-boy, *n.*, an American private soldier.

dras'tically, *adv.*, in a drastic way.

drif'ter, *n.*, a fishing-boat used for catching enemy's mines.

dud, *n.*, a failure, such as a bomb that did not explode.

dug'-out, *n.*, a shelter in the trenches or elsewhere.

dural'umin, *n.*, an aluminium alloy, used in constructing aeroplanes.

E

elec'tron, *n.*, a silver and gold alloy; an atom of negative electricity; an atom's electric charge.

electrocu'tion, *n.*, capital punishment by means of electricity.

embus', *v.t.*, to put into a lorry; *v.i.*, to mount a lorry.

emplace'ment, *n.*, a platform on which guns are mounted.

Eng'lishwoman, *n.*, woman native of England.

enure', *v.t.* and *i.*, to accustom; to come into operation, become effective (also inure).

enured', *p.t.* and *p.* of enure.

Esperant'ist, *n.*, a student of Esperanto.

evercir'culator, *n.*, a hot water system, in which the water circulates; a manuscript magazine, written in shorthand.

ex cathed'ra, phrase, meaning "from the chair," *i.e.*, with authority.

eye'strain, *n.*, excessive use of the eyes.

F

fab'ulousness, *n.*, the character of being fabulous.

fag, *n.*, slang for a cheap and nasty cigarette.

fair'-haired, *adj.*, having fair hair.

feuds, *n.*, *pl.* of feud, state of hostility; land held in fee.

fi'lite, *n.*, an Italian smokeless powder.

find, *v.t.*, a euphemism for "to steal."

fire'-control, *n.*, the method of controlling from one place the firing of a group of guns.

flag'-wagger, *n.*, slang for a signaller.

flame'-projector, *n.*, a device for discharging liquid fire.

flash'-light, *n.*, a torch or lantern giving light in flashes.

flat'-bottomed, *adj.*, having a flat bottom.

flip, *n.*, a jaunt in an aeroplane (*slang*).

fo'ci, *pl.* of *focus*, points of convergence.

fond'er, *adj.*, compar. of fond.

food'-card, *n.*, a ration card used during the food shortage in the war.

food'stuff, *n.*, material for food.

fool'proof, *adj.*, safe from being bungled.

foot'-slogger, *n.*, slang for frozen meat.

forestalled', *p.t.* and *p.* of forestall.

fore'*word*, *n.*, a preface.

forgo'ing, *v.a.*, *pr.p.* of forgo.

fraz'zle, *v.t.* and *i.*, to fray; *n.*, a thing frayed; the state of being frayed.

free'*hand*, *adj.*, drawn without artificial aid.

French'woman, *n.*, a woman native of France.

fri'go, *n.*, slang for frozen meat.

Fritz, *n.*, slang for a German soldier, and a German submarine.

frow'ziness, *n.*, the state of being frowzy.

full'-sized, *adj.*, of full size.

func'tioned, *v.i.*, *p.t.* and *p.* of function.

funk'-hole, *n.*, any place or position of shelter from danger.

fuss'iness, *n.*, the character or state of being fussy.

fu'turism, *n.*, the doctrines of futurist art.

futuris'tic, *adj.*, rel. to futurism.

G

gadg'et, *n.*, slang for a tool.

gassed, *v.t.*, *p.p.* of gas, meaning poisoned with noxious gas.

gay'er, *adj.*, compar. of gay.

gipp'o, *n.*, slang for soup.

good'-sized, *adj.*, of a fair or moderate size.

guern'sey, *n.*, thick knitted woollen tunic.

gun'layer, *n.*, a gunner who sights and elevates a gun.

H

half'-sized, *adj.*, of half size.

***hand'*-made,** *adj.*, made with the hand

haugh'tier, *adj.*, compar. of haughty.

heart'en, *v.t.*, to cheer, encourage.

heart'ened, *v.t.*, *p.p.* of hearten.

heart'ening, *v.t.*, *pr.p.* of hearten; *adj.*, encouraging.

hef'ty, *adj.*, able to lift weights; strong.

helicop'ter, *n.*, a heavier-than-air machine, able to rise vertically under its own power.

here*to'*, *adv.*, to this point or matter.

here*un'der*, *adv.*, below.

hick'boo, *n.*, slang for an air-raid.

hike, *v.t.*, to hoist or jerk; *v.i.*, to bolt; to ramble.

hol'land, *n.*, a linen fabric so named.

honk, *n.*, the sound of a motor-car horn; *v.i.*, to make that sound.

hoot'er, *n.*, one who hoots; a steam-whistle.

huff, *v.t.* and *i.*, to bully, offend, take offence at, remove an opponents piece (in draughts) from the board; *n.*, a fit of petulance.

Hun, *n.*, the name given to Germans, the Kaiser and his troops reproducing the barbarous atrocities of Attila and the Huns.

hun'ger-strike, *n.*, a refusal to take food until demands have been granted; *v.i.*, to call a hunger-strike.

hurt'ling, *v.i.*, *pr.p.* of hurtle.

hush'-boat, *n.*, an armed ship made to look like an unarmed trading vessel.

hutment, *n.*, collected huts in a camp.

hyd'rovane, *n.*, a rudder working horizontally in depressing or raising a submarine.

I

I'do, *n.*, an artificial language so named.

incensed', *adj.*, *p.p.* (of incense), indignant, enraged.

incens'ing, *v.t.*, *pr.p.* of incense.

in'comer, *n.*, one who comes in, who enters.

***inconve'niently*,** *adv.*, in an inconvenient way.

inexact'itude, *n.*, inaccuracy.

inhumane', *adv.*, cruel.

ini'tial(l)ing, *v.t.*, *pr.p.* of initial; *n.*, the use of initial letters.

ink'er, *n.*, one who, that which, inks.

in'stancy, *n.*, urgency.

***instruct'ively*,** *adv.*, in an instructive manner.

***instruct'iveness*,** *n.*, the quality of being instructive.

in'sulin, *n.*, a remedy for the treatment of diabetes.

intelligent'zia, *n.*, the educated classes.

interned', *p.p.* of intern.

ital'ics, *n.* (*pl.* of italic) letters sloping, as in italic type.

J

jaboran'di, *n.*, dried leaflets of Pilocarpus, used as a diuretic and sudorific drug.

Jack John'son, *n.*, a large German shell of low velocity.

jazz, *n.*, a noisy nigger dance; *v.i.*, to dance to jazz music.

Jer'ry, *n.*, a German soldier.

jiu-jit'su, *n.*, the Japanese art of wrestling.

joy'-ride, *n.*, a jaunt in a motor-car.

joy'stick, *n.*, the lever for starting an aeroplane.

Ju'go-Slav, *adj.*, belonging to Jugo-Slavia; *n.*, one of the Southern Slavs.

K

kam'erad, *n.*, German for comrade.

kil'o, a prefix, signifying one thousand, as Kilolitre, a measure of 1,000 litres.

kul'tur, *n.*, the German ideal of civilization.

L

lance'-jack, *n.*, slang for a lance-corporal.

land'-girl, *n.*, a farm-girl.

***large'*-sized,** *adj.*, of a large size.

la'test, *adj.* and *adv.*, *super.* of late.

leapt, *v.t.*, *p.t.* and *p.* of leap.

Lew'is-gun, *n.*, a quick-firing mounted gun.

liais'on-officer, *n.*, an officer whose duty it is to keep different commands in touch with one another.

lineal'ity, *n.*, the quality or state of being lineal.

lin'gerer, *n.*, one who lingers.

li'no, *n.*, a popular abbreviation of linoleum.

list'eners-*in*, *n. pl.*, those who listen-in to wireless.

list'ening-*in*, *pr.p.* of listen-in; *n.*, the act of hearing by means of wireless.

li'ver, *n.*, a bird of fable, shown in the Liverpool City arms as explaining the name of Liverpool.

lo'ganberry, *n.*, a plant produced by crossing a raspberry and a blackberry.

Lusita'nia, *n.*, the famous liner which was torpedoed by the Germans during the first World War.

lyr'icist, *n.*, a writer of lyric poetry.

M

machine'-gun, *n.*, a light mounted gun, mechanically actuated.

magne'to, a form combined with certain words, as magneto-electricity, *i.e.*, electricity generated by electric conductors and magnets. Magneto is coming to be regarded as a noun, and signifies the magneto-electric apparatus on a motor engine, etc.

mar'mite, *n.*, a high explosive shell.

Marx'ian, *adj.*, relating to Marx and his doctrines (Marxianism); *n.*, a follower of Marx.

match'wood, *n.*, wood splintered small, and suitable for match-making.

mat'tered, *v.i.* *p.p.* of matter.

max'imalist, *n.* *i.q.* a Bolshevist.

May'-fly, *n.*, an ephemeral insect so named.

meat'less, *adj.*, without meat.

med'itatively, *adv.*, n a meditative way.

mediumis'tic, *adj.*, relating to spiritualistic mediums.

Men'shevist, *n.*, the opposite to a Bolshevist.

***mer'est*,** *adj.*, *super.* of mere.

Messrs., *n. pl.*, Sirs; gentlemen. (The singular is Monsieur.)

metic'ulous, *adj.*, over-scrupulous: fussy; finical.

miaul', *v.i.*, to make the cry of a cat ("miaow").

miauled', *p.t.* and *p.* of miaul.

mi'crophone, *n.*, a contrivance for intensifying a weak sound.

militaris'tic, *adj.*, relating to militarism and militarists.

mine'-crater, *n.*, a hole made by an exploding mine.

Minn'en-werfer, *n.*, an apparatus for throwing bombs.

Moroc'can, *adj.*, belonging or native to Morocco; *n.*, an inhabitant of Morocco.

Morse, *n.*, a system of telegraphy named after its inventor, G. F. B. Morse.

mov'ies, *n. pl.*, the pictures in a cinematic show.

muni'tioner, *n.*, a worker in a munition factory.

myst'ery-ship, *n.*, *i.q.*, hush-boat.

N

napoo', *interj.*, the British soldiers' version of *il n'y en a plus*, there is no more.

neurasthen'ic, *adj.*, suffering from nervous debility.

non-par'ty, *adj.*, not attached to any party.

non'-skid, *adj.*, free from a tendency to skid.

north-east'ward, *adv.*, in the direction of the North-East.

nose'-dive, *n.*, an aeroplane's downward plunge; *v.i.*, to plunge downward.

O

o'pen-eyed', *adv.*, having the eyes open.

out' ***building*****,** *n.*, a building detached from a house; an outhouse.

o'verlord, *n.*, a superior lord.

P

pacif'icism, *n.*, the principle of peace at any price.

pacif'icist, *n.*, a professor of pacificism.

pac'ifism, *n.*, an incorrect form for pacificism.

pac'ifist, *n.*, an incorrect form for pacificist.

par'ados, *n.*, a fortification against attack from the rear.

par'avane, *n.*, an appliance for catching submerged mines. It has flat vanes in front, and a rudder which keeps it at any required depth.

Pars'eval, *n.*, a smaller, non-rigid, airship.

part'-ow'ner, *n.*, one who shares ownership with another, or with others.

past'-mast'er, *n.*, one who has passed the chair of a master; one who has a thorough mastery of any given art or craft or subject.

Pel'manism, *n.*, a system of mental culture and memory training.

persist'ently, *adv.*, in a persistent way.

pese'ta, *n.*, a Spanish silver coin, the equivalent of a franc or mark.

piano'la, *n.*, a mechanical piano.

pian'o-or'gan, *n.*, a mechanical piano made on the lines of an organ.

pier'-head, *n.*, the end of a pier.

pil'ferage, *n.*, stealing.

pill'-box, *n.*, slang for a German block-house.

pip'squeak, *n.*, a high-explosive shell fired from a field gun.

plane, *n.*, *i.q.*, aeroplane.

plaquette', *n.*, a small plaque or tablet of metal, porcelain, etc.

plas'ticine, *n.*, a variety of modelling clay.

plumped, *v.t.* and *i.*, *p.p.* of plump.

pogrom', *n.*, a Russian organized massacre.

poilu', *n.*, a French Tommy.

pois'on-gas, *n.*, a poisonous gas introduced into warfare by the Germans.

pol'icy-hold'er, *n.*, the holder of a policy of insurance or assurance.

por'traitist, *n.*, one who makes portraits.

posi'tional, *adj.*, relating to position.

Post'master - *Gen'eral*, *n.*, the Minister in charge of the Postal Service department.

pourpar'ler, *n.*, an informal talk preceding negotiations.

pozz'y, *n.*, soldiers' jam or marmalade.

pre-war', *adj.*, belonging to the time before the War.

prince'let *n.*, a petty prince.

pro'cessed, *v.t.*, *p.p.* of process, to print from a block made by the process method.

profiteer', *n.*, one who makes excessive profit at the cost of the people; *v.i.*, to make such profit.

prospect'ed, *v.i.*, *p.p.* of prospect, to survey.

prospect'ing**,** *v.i.*, *pr.p.* of prospect.

Prus'sianism, *n.*, the spirit and character of Prussians.

Prus'sianize, *v.t.*, to alter by Prussian method.

Prus'sianized, *v.t.*, *p.p.* of Prussianize.

py'lon, *n.*, strictly, a gateway of the Egyptian type. Also a structure made in imitation of a pylon; a stake to mark the course in an aerodrome; a form of telegraph wire support.

pyorrhoe'a, *n.*, a disease affecting the gums and teeth.

Q

Q'-ship, *n.*, *i.q.*, hush-boat.

quaint'est, *adj.*, *super.* of quaint.

R

ra'dio, *adj.*, pertaining to wireless telegraphy.

radioactiv'ity, *n.*, the property of sending out rays that penetrate opaque bodies.

ra'diograph, *n.*, an actinograph; an instrument recording intensity and duration of sunshine; a negative produced by Röntgen rays, or a print from it; *v.t.*, to make such a print.

radiog'raphy, *n.*, the study of radiant light or heat.

radiother'apy, *n.*, medical treatment by means of rays.

ra'dium, *n.*, a radio-active metal like barium, found in pitch-blende.

raid'ed, *v.t.* and *i.*, *p.t.* and *p.* of raid.

raid'er, *n.*, one who makes raids or forays.

raid'ing, *v.t.* and *i.*, *pr.p.* of raid.

rail'head, *n.*, the starting-point of a railway system.

ram'la, *n.*, a fine fibre used instead of cotton. [rare.

rar'est, *adj.*, *super.* of

ra'tioned, *v.t.*, *p.t.* and *p.* of ration.

rat'-tat', *n.*, a quick succession of raps.
repa'triate, *v.t.*, to restore to one's country.
revalua'tion, *n.*, a further valuing.
reval'ue, *v.t.*, to assess a value afresh.
reval'ued, *v.t.*, *p.t.* and *p.* of revalue.
reval'uing, *v.t.*, *pr.p.*, of revalue.
revict'ualment, *n.*, the act of revictualling, *i.e.*, providing victuals anew.
rust'less, *adj.*, not liable to rust.

S

Sam-Brown', *n.*, an officer's belt and shoulder-strap.
scamped, *v.t.*, *p.t.* and *p.* of scamp.
scoot'er, *n.*, a two-wheeled vehicle, moved by one foot, or propelled by motor-power.
sev'ery, *n.*, one of the compartments or divisions of a vaulted roof.
shell'-crater, *n.*, a hole in the ground caused by a bursting shell.
shell'-hole, *n.*, a hole caused in an armour plate by a bursting shell.
shell'-shock, *n.*, nervous disorder resulting from the explosion of shells.
side'-car, *n.*, a small car attached to the side of a motor-cycle.
side'-light, *n.*, a light from the side; (metaphorically) light thrown on a subject incidentally.
side'-slip, *n.*, a skid; slip to one side.
sin'ewless, *adj.*, wanting sinews.
Sinn Fein', *n.*, the Gaelic name of a seditious party in Ireland; *adj.*, belonging to the Sinn Feiners.
siz'zle, *v.i.*, to make the noise of frying; *n.*, the noise of frying.
siz'zled, *v.i.*, *p.t.* and *p.* of sizzle.
siz'zling, *v.i.*, *p.p.*, of sizzle; *n.*, *i.q.*, sizzle.
skew'ing, *v.i.*, *p.p.* of skew (to swerve).
slow'er, *adj.*, *comp.* of slow.
slow'est, *adj.*, *super.* of slow.
smoke'-bomb, *n.*, a bomb discharging a cloud of smoke.
snoozed, *v.i.* *p.t.* of snooze.
snott'y, *n.*, slang for a midshipman.
soon'est, *adv.*, *super.* of soon.
sour'est, *adj.*, *super.* of sour.
Sov'iet, *n.*, a Russian committee of men in a regiment or a town, etc., who assume complete control of the troops or the local affairs.
spi'dery, *adj.*, spider-like.
spir'itism, *n.*, the belief that spirit alone is real: *i.q.*, spiritualism.
spoon'-fed, *adj.*, fed, like a child, on liquid food.
sta'bilize, *v.t.*, to make stable, unchanging.
stall, *v.t.*, to check an aeroplane's forward movement.
star'-shell, *n.*, a shell emitting high illuminants.
step'-ladder, *n.*, a ladder with flat rungs.
stone'less, *adj.*, not containing stones.
storiette', **storyette'**, *n.*, a short tale.
stradd'le, *v.t.* (*i.q.*, bracket) to get the range.
strafe, *v.t.*, to inflict severe punishment; to pay an enemy out. (A war word, from the German *Strafen*, to punish.)
strafed, *v.t.*, *p.t.* and *p.p.* of *strafe*.
strafing, *v.t.*, *pr.p.* of *strafe*.
straight'er, *adj.*, *comp.* of straight.
stran'gle-hold, *n.*, a choking grip.
sub'marine, *v.t.*, to sink a vessel by means of a torpedo from a submarine.
suggest'iveness, *n.*, the quality of being suggestive.
sul'tanate, *n.*, the office of Sultan; the term of office of Sultan.
sum'mer-time, *n.*, the period of summer; the arrangement for saving daylight.
swank, *v.i.*, to swagger; *n.*, swagger.
syn'dicalism, *n.*, the principle of participation in the control and profits of an industry by the workers, the principle to be enforced by means of sympathetic strikes.
syn'thetize, *v.t.*, to make a synthesis of, *i.e.*, to unite elements into a complex whole.

T

tail'-dive, *v.i.*, to fall tail downward (said of an aeroplane); *n.*, the drop tail downward.
tank, *n.*, a kind of armoured car.
taub'e, *n.*, a German monoplane.
tax'y, *v.i.*, to motor along the ground (said of an aeroplane).
ten'derfoot, *n.*, a novice (slang for one who has newly come into the Australian Bush; also for entrants into a Boy Scouts' company).
terrain', *n.*, territory, region.
ter'rorized, *v.t.*, *p.p.* and *t.* of terrorize.
tear'-shell, *n.*, a shell emitting a lachrymatory fluid.
thing, *n.*, a slang term of endearment, as "old thing."

thread'er, *n.*, one who, that which, threads.

tin'ful, *n.*, the total contents of a tin.

tom'bola, *n.*, a lottery, in which, to win a prize, the ticket-holder must draw a given set of numbers.

toot'sweet, *adv.*, British soldiers' rendering of *tout de suite*.

top, *n.*, the trench parapet.

to'talizator, *n.*, a method of ascertaining the total amount of bets made and of sharing them among the backers of a winner.

to'talizer, *n.*, *i.q.*, totalizator.

toured, *v.t.* and *i.*, *p.t.* and *p.* of tour.

trekked, *v.i.*, *p.t.* and *p.* of trek (a Dutch word).

trek'king, *v.i.*, *pr.p.* of trek.

tri'plane, *n.*, a three-planed aeroplane.

Tur'co, *prefix*, as Turcophil, a friend of Turkey and Turks.

twink, *v.i.* and *n.*, *i.q.*, twinkle.

type'script, *n.*, the character used in typewriting; a piece of typed work.

U

U'-boat, *n.*, a German submarine.

Ukrain'ian, *adj.*, relating to the Ukraine, a region of Russia, the capital being Kiev; *n.*, a native of the Ukraine.

um'laut, *n.*, modification of a German vowel sound, esp. *a*, *o*, *u*.

ump'teen, *num. adj.*, slang for an indefinite number.

uncount'able, *adj.*, incapable of being counted.

undenomina'tionalism, *n.*, the principle of not being denominational.

underpinned', *v.t. p.t.* and *p.* of underpin (to prop up with timber, masonry, etc.).

understaffed', *adj.*, supplied with an inadequate number of officers, employees, etc.

undeserv'edly, *adv.*, without being deserved.

undeterred', *adj.*, not frightened out of doing something.

un*discharged'*, *adj.* not discharged (used esp. of bankrupts who have not been certified).

unemploy'able, *adj.*, not fit for employment; not able to be employed.

unfamiliar'ity, *n.*, the state or quality of being unfamiliar.

unfla'vo(u)red, *adj.*, not flavoured.

un*in'fluenced*, *adj.*, not influenced.

unique'ly, *adv.*, in a unique way.

unsha'ven, *adj.*, not shaven; rough-chinned.

untaxed', *adj.*, not taxed or subject to taxation.

V

vertical'ity, *n.*, the quality or state of being vertical.

vil'lein, *n.*, a serf attached to a feudal estate.

visé(e)d', *v.t.*, *p.t.* and *p.* of visé (to certify officially by stamping with a visé = inspected).

vi'tagraph, *n.*, a form of cinematograph.

vi'tamine, *n.*, the name for certain food substances considered to be essential.

vol'plane, *n.*, a steep downward flight by an aeroplane; *n.*, to make such a flight.

vort'icist, *n.*, one who makes his pictures consist of vortices.

W

Waac, *n.*, one belonging to the Women's Army Auxiliary Corps.

wad'dy, *n.*, an Australian war-club so named.

wagg'er, *n.*, *i.q.*, flag-wagger.

wan'gle, *v.t.*, to achieve by cunning or any other skilful management.

wash'able, *adj.*, capable of being washed.

wash'-out, *n.*, a complete failure (*slang*).

wast'age, *n.*, loss through waste.

west, *adv.*, a metaphor for death, in the phrase "to go west."

wheat'meal, *n.*, meal made from wheat.

wheat'sheaf, *n.*, a sheaf of wheat.

whipp'et, *n.*, a quick-moving light tank.

whi'ter, *adj.*, *comp.* of white.

whole'-heart'ed, *adj.*, sincere, enthusiastic.

wind, *n.*, the phrase "to get the wind up" means to be nervous.

wire'less, *adj.*, without the use of wire; *n.*, the method of transmitting sound without the use of wires.

wooll'y-bear, *n.*, a large German shrapnel-shell.

work'less, *adj.* unemployed.

Wrens, *n.* members of the Women's Royal Naval Service.

X

x'-rays', *n. pl.*, Röntgen rays.

Z

zep'pelin, *n.*, a large type of German air-ship.

zoom, *v.i.*, to turn upward sharply or suddenly (said of an aeroplane).

Proper Names

A

Aar
Aar'on
Abbe'ville
Ab'botsford
Ab'diel
Ab'dul-Hamid'
Abed'nego
A'bel
Ab'elard
Abera'von
Ab'ercorn
Ab'ercrombie
Aberdare'
Aberdeen'
Aberdeen'shire
Aberdour'
Abergaven'ny
Ab'ernethy
Aberyst'with
Abie'zer
Ab'igail
Abim'elech
Ab'ingdon
Ab'inger
Ab'ney
Aboukir', Abukir'
A'braham
A'bram
Abruz'zo
Ab'salom
Abyssin'ia
Aca'dia
Acapul'co
Ac'cra, Ac'ra
Ac'crington
Achai'a
Ach'eron
Ach'ill, Ach'il
Achil'les
Achit'ophel
Ach'met
A'cis
Ack'ermann
Ack'worth
Ac'land
A'cre
Actæ'on
Ac'ton
A'da
Adair'
Ad'am
Ad'derbury
Ad'dingham
Ad'dington
Ad'dison
Ad'ela
Ad'elaide
Adeli'na
Adel'phi
A'delung
A'den
Adiron'dacks
Ad'ler
Adol'phus
Ado'nis
A'drian
Adria'na
Adriano'ple
Adriat'ic
Adul'lam
Æge'an
Æne'as
Æs'chylus
Æscula'pius
Æ'sop, E'sop
Afghanistan'
Af'rica
Africa'nus
Agamem'non
Ag'atha
Agincourt
Ag'lionby
Ag'nes
Ag'new
A'gra
A'gram
Agric'ola
Agrip'pa
Agrippi'na
A'hab
Ahasue'rus
A'haz
Ahazi'ah
Ahith'ophel
Ah'med
Ai'kin
Ains'worth
Air'drie
Aire'dale
Aix
Aix-la-Chapelle'
Aix-les-Bains'
Ajmir'
Ak'enside
Ak'ron
Alaba'ma
Alad'din
Al'aric
Alas'ka
Al'ban
Alba'ni
Alba'nia
Al'bans, St.
Al'bany
Al'bemarle
Al'bert
Alber'ta
Al'bigenses
Al'bion
Al'cester
Alces'tis
Alcibi'ades
Al'cides
Ald'borough
Ald'bourne
Aldeb'aran
Alde'burgh
Al'den
Al'derbury
Al'dermanbury
Al'derney
Al'dersgate
Al'dershot
Al'derson
Al'derston
Ald'gate
Al'dington
Al'dridge
Ald'wych
Alençon
Alep'po
Alessan'dria
Alexan'der
Alexan'dria
Alexandri'na
Alex'is
Alfie'ri
Alfon'so
Al'ford
Al'fred
Al'freton
Algeci'ras
Alge'ria
Al'gernon

Algiers'
Algo'a
Al'ice
Alic'ia
Al'ison
Allahabad'
Al'lan
All'church
All'cott
Al'leghany
Al'legheny (city)
Al'len
Al'lendale
Al'lerton
Al'lingham
Al'lington
Al'loa
Al'lonby
Al'mack's
Alm'ondbury
Aln'wick
Alon'zo
Alphe'us
Alphon'so
Alping'ton
Alps
Alsace'
Alsa'tia
Al'sop
Al'ston
Al'tenburg
Althæ'a
Al'thorp
Al'ton
Alto'na
Altoo'na
Al'trincham, Al'-
Al'va [tringham
Alve'ley
Al'verstoke
Al'verstone
Al'verthorpe
Amade'us
Am'adis
Amaryl'lis
Amazo'nia
Am'berg
Am'berley
Am'bleside
Am'brose
Ame'lia
Amer'ica
Am'ersham
Ames'bury
Am'herst
Amiens'
Am'lwch
Am'mon
A'mos
Ampt'hill
Am'sterdam
A'my
Anac'reon
A'nak
An'andale
Anani'as
Andalu'sia

An'daman
An'derson
An'derston
An'des
Andor'ra
An'dover
An'drew
An'drews, St.
Androm'ache
Androm'eda
Androni'cus
An'dros
Aner'ley
Angel'ica
Angel'ico
Angeli'na
An'gelo
An'glesey
Ango'la
Anguil'la
An'gus
Anjou
Ann *or* Anne
Annam'
An'nan
An'nandale
Annap'olis
Annes'ley
An'nibal
An'selm
An'son
An'sted
An'stey
An'struther
An'thony, -tony
Antig'onus
Anti'gua
Antilles
An'tioch
Antip'ater
Antip'atris
Antoinette'
Anto'nio
Anto'nius
An'tony
An'trim
Ant'werp
Aos'ta
Apach'e
Apel'les
Ap'ennines
Aphrodi'te
Apol'lo
Apollo'nius
Apol'lyon
Ap'pleby
Ap'pledore
Ap'plegate
Ap'pleton
Aps'ley
Aq'uila
Aqui'nas
Arabel'la
Ara'bia
Ar'agon
A'ram

Ar'arat
Ara'tus
Arbroath'
{ Ar'buthnot
{ Arbuth'not
Arca'dia
Archela'us
Arch'ibald
Archime'des
Arco'le
Arcot'
Arctu'rus
Ar'dagh
Ardee'
Ar'den
Ardennes'
Ard'glass
Ard'ing
Ard'leigh
Ardnamur'chan
Ardros'san
Ard'wick
Areop'agus
Arequi'pa
Arethu'sa
Ar'gentine
Ar'gos
Argyll'
Ariad'ne
A'riel
Arimathæ'a
Arios'to
Aristar'chus
Aristi'des
Aristoph'anes
Ar'istotle
Arizo'na
Ar'kansas
Ark'low
Ark'wright
Armaged'don
Armagh'
Arme'nia
Armin'ius
Arm'ley
Arm'strong
Arnaud'
Arne
Arn'heim
Ar'nold
Ar'not
Ar'ran
Ar'reton
Ar'rowsmith
Artaxerx'es
Ar'temis
Artemis'ia
Ar'thur
Arthu'rian
Ar'undel
As'aph
As'cham [tee
Ashan'ti, Ashan-

Ash'bourne
Ash'burnham
Ash'burton
Ash'by-de-la-Zouch
Ash'cott
Ash'er
Ash'ford
Ash'ley
Ash'over
Ash'ton
Ash'ton-*under*-Lyne
Ash'well
A'sia
As'kew
Asmode'us
Aspa'sia
As'quith
Assam'
Assi'si
Assump'tion
Assyr'ia
Ast'bury
Ast'ley
As'ton
Astrakhan'
Astu'rias

Asun'cion
Athana'sius
Ath'elstan
Athe'ne
Ath'ens
Ath'erstone
Ath'erton
Athlone'
Ath'ol
Athy'
At'kins
At'kinson
Atlan'ta
At'terbury
At'tercliffe
At'tica
At'tila
At'tleborough
At'wood
Au'brey
Au'burn
Auck'land
Au'denshaw
Aud'ley
Au'drey
Augs'burg
Augus'ta
Augus'tine

Augus'tine, St.
Augus'tus
Aumale'
Aure'lia
Aure'lius
Aus'tell, St.
Aus'terlitz
Aus'tin
Australa'sia
Austra'lia
Aus'tria
Autol'ycus
A'va
Ave'bury
Ave'ning
Aver'nus
Av'ignon
Av'ington
A'von
Ax'bridge
Ax'minster
Ayles'bury
Ayles'ford
Ayl'sham
Ayr
Ayr'shire
A'zof *or* A'zov
Azores'

B

Ba'al
Ba'alim
Bab'bage
Ba'bel
Bab-el-Man'deb
Bab'ington
Bab'ylon
Bac'chus
Bach
Ba'cup
Badajos'
Bad'cock
Ba'den
Ba'den-Pow'ell
Bad'ham
Bad'minton
Baed'eker
Baf'fin Bay
Bagdad', Bagh'dad
Bage'hot, Bag'ot
Bag'shaw
Bag'shot
Bag'ster
Baha'ma
Bail'don
Bai'ley
Bain'bridge
Baines
Bain'ton

Bai'reuth, Bay'reuth
Bake'well
Baku'
Ba'la
Ba'laam
Bal'beck
Bal'combe
Bal'dock
Bald'win
Bâle
Balfe
Bal'four
Bal'guy
Bal'ham
Ba'liol
Balkan'
Bal'lantyne
Ballarat'
Ballina'
Ballinasloe'
Ballymo'ney
Ballyshan'non
Balmor'al
Bal'tic
Bal'timore
Baluchistan'
Balzac'
Bam'berg

Bam'ford
Bamp'ton
Ban'bury
Ban'croft
Ban'don
Banff
Bangalore'
Bangkok'
Ban'gor
Ban'ham
Banks
Ban'nerman
Ban'nister
Ban'nockburn
Ban'quo
Ban'tam
Ban'try
Ban'well
Barab'bas
Barba'dos
Bar'bara
Barbaros'sa
Bar'bary
Bar'bauld
Barcelo'na
Bar'clay
Bar'dolph
Bar'ford
Bar'ham

Bar'low
Bar'mouth
Bar'nabas
Bar'naby
Bar'nard Castle
Barn'by
Barnes
Bar'net
Bar'ningham
Barns'bury
Barns'ley
Barn'staple
Barn'well
Baro'da
Bar'rett
Bar'rington
Bar'row-in-Fur'-[ness
Bar'ry
Barthol'omew
Bartimæ'us
Bart'lett
Bar'ton
Ba'ruch
Bas'church
Bas'ford
Ba'sel
Bas'il
Ba'singhall
Ba'singstoke
Bas'kerville
Bassa'nio
Basse'-Terre'
Bas'sett
Bas'singbourne
Bas'sora
Bast'wick
Basu'toland
Bata'via
Bat'combe
Bate'man
Bates
Bath
Batheast'on
Bathford'
Bath'gate
Bath'sheba
Bath'urst
Bathwick'
Bat'ley
Bat'tenberg
Bat'tersea
Bava'ria
Baw'try
Bax'ter
Bay'ard
Bayeux'
Bay'ley
Bayonne'
Bea'consfield
Beale
Bea'minster
Bea'mish
Be'atrice
Beat'tie

Beau'champ
Beau'fort [Hants
Beau'lieu (in
Beauma'ris
Beau'mont
Beb'ington
Bec'cles
Bechua'naland
{ Becke't
{ Beck'ett
Beck'ford
Beck'ingham
Beck'ington
Beck'ley
Beck'with
Be'dale
Bed'dington
Bed'does
Bede
Bed'ford
Bed'lington
Bed'minster
Bed'win
Bed'worth
Bee'cher
Bee'chey
Beel'zebub
Beer'sheba
Bees, St.
Bees'ton
Bee'thoven
Beh'men
Beh'ring
Beirut', Beyrout'
Belfast'
Bel'ford
Bel'gium
Belgrade'
Bel'grave
Be'lial
Belin'da
Belisa'rius
Belize'
Bel'la
Bel'lamy
Bel'larmine
Bel'lerby
Beller'ophon
Bel'lingham
Bel'more
Beloochistan'
Bel'per
Belshaz'zar
Bel'ton
Bel'voir
Belzo'ni
Bem'bridge
Bena'res
Ben'digo
Ben'edick
Ben'enden
Ben'gal
Bengue'lla

Ben Lo'mond
Ben Nev'is
Benin'
Ben'jamin
Ben'nett
Ben'nington
Ben'son
Ben'tham
Ben'tinck
Bent'ley
Bén'ton
Beranger'
Berar'
Ber'bera
Berbice'
Bere Al'ston
Bereni'ce
Bere Re'gis
Ber'esford
Beresi'na
Ber'gen
Berke'ley
Berkhamp'sted
Berks
Berk'shire
Ber'lin
Ber'mondsey
Bermu'das
Ber'nard
Berne
Bern'hardt
Ber'ridge
Ber'tha
Ber'tillon
Ber'tram
Ber'vie
Ber'wick
Bes'ant, Besant'
Bes'ley
Bess
Bes'sie
Beth'any
Beth'el
Bethes'da
Beth'lehem
Beth'nal Green
Beth'une
Bet'sey
Beu'lah
Bev'an
Bev'eridge
Bev'erley
Bewd'ley
Bex'hill
Bex'ley
Bey'rout
Be'za
Bhutan'
Biarritz'
Bices'ter
Bick'ersteth
Bick'ley
Bid'denden

Bid'dulph
Bid'dy
Bid'eford
Bid'stone
Bier'ley
Big'gleswade
Big'low
Bihar'
Bilba'o
Billeric'ay
Bil'linge
Bil'lingham
Bil'lingsgate
Bil'lingshurst
Bil'ston
Bin'field
Bing'ham
Bing'hamton
Bing'ley
Bin'ney
Bi'on
Birk'beck
Birk'enhead
Bir'kett
Bir'mah
Bir'mingham
Bir'rell
Bir'stall
Bis'cay
Bish'op's Cas'tle
Bish'opsgate
Bish'op's Stort'-ford
Bish'opthorpe
Bish'opton
Bis'ley
Bis'marck
Bit'ton
Black'burn
Black'friars
Black'heath
Black'ley
Black'lock
Black'more
Black'pool
Black'stone
Blackwall'
Black'wood
Blag'don
Blai'na
Blaine
Blair
Blairgow'rie
Blake
Blake'ney
Blan'chard
Blanche
Bland'ford
Blan'tyre
Blar'ney
Blay'don

Blen'heim
Blen'kinsopp
Bletch'ingley
Bloem'fontein
Blom'field
Bloom'field
Blooms'bury
Blount
Blu'cher
Blyth
Boadice'a
Boaner'ges
Bo'az
Boccac'cio
Bod'enham
Bod'min
Boe'thius
Bog'nor
Bogota'
Bogue
Bohe'mia
Boileau'
Bokha'ra
Bol'ingbroke
Bol'ivar
Boliv'ia
Bolo'gna
Bol'ton
Bo'ma
Bombay'
Bo'naparte
Bonar Law'
Bon'iface
Bonn
Bon'nycastle
Bon'sall
Bon'vilstone
Bootan'
Boo'tle
Bordeaux'
Bordes'ley
Bore'ham
Bor'gia
Bor'neo
Bornu'
Bor'oughbridge
Bor'oughgreen
Bor'stal
Bosanquet
Bos'castle
Bos'cawen
Bos'nia
Bos'phorus
Bossuet'
Bos'ton
Bos'well
Bos'worth
Botes'dale
Bo'tha
Both'well
Bot'ley
Bou'cher
Bough'ton
Boulanger'

Boulogne'
Bour'bon
Bour'chier
Bourn
Bourne'mouth
Bou'verie
Bo'vey Tra'cey
Bow
Bow'den
Bowes
Bow'ling
Bowness'
Box'ford
Boyd
Boyle
Brack'ley
Brad'bourne
Brad'field
Brad'ford
Brad'laugh
Brad'ley
Brad'ninch
Brad'shaw
Brad'well
Bra'dy
Braemar'
Brah'ma
Braid'wood
Brails'ford
Brain'tree
Braith'waite
Bram'field
Bram'ley
Bramp'ton
Bran'denburg
Bran'don
Bras'sey
Braun'ston
Brazil'
Breage
Brech'in
Breck'nock
Brec'on
Brem'en
Brem'ner
Brent'ford
Brent'wood
Bres'lau
Brest
Bre'ton
Brett
Bri'an
Bria'reus
Bridge'port
Bridg'et
Bridge'town
Bridg'north
Bridg'water
Brid'lington
Brid'port
Bri'erley
Brigg
Brig'ham
Brig'house
Bright'lingsea
Brigh'ton
Brig'stock

Brin'disi
Brind'ley
Bris'bane
Bris'lington
Bris'tol
Brit'ain
Britan'nia
Britan'nicus
Brit'tany
Brix'ton
Broad'stairs
Broad'water
Broad'way
Brob'dingnag
Brock'en
Brock'ley
Brock'ton
Bro'die
Brod'rick
Brom'ham
Brom'ley
Bromp'ton
Broms'grove
Brom'wich
Brom'*yard*
Bron'tё
Brook'land
Brook'lyn
Brook'man
Brose'ley
Broth'erton
Brough'ton
Brown'ing

Bruce
Bruges
Brunei'
Brunel'
Bruns'wick
Brus'sels
Bru'ton
Bru'tus
Bry'an
Bry'anston
Bry'ant
Bryce
Buccleuch'
Buceph'alus
Buch'an
Buchan'an
Bucharest'
Buck'ingham
Buck'land
Buck'nall
Bu'dapest
Bud'dha
Bud'worth
Bue'nos Ay'res
Buf'fon
Bulgar'ia
Bü'low
Buluway'o
Bul'well
Bul'wer
Bum'stead
Bun'bury

Bun'gay
Bun'ker Hill
Bun'tingford
Bun'yan
Bur'bage
Burdett'
Bu'ren
Bur'ford
Burgoyne'
Bur'gundy
Burke
Bur'lington
Bur'ma
Bur'net
Bur'ney
Burn'ham
Burn'ley
Burns
Burnt'island
Bur'rell
Burslem
Bur'ton
Bur'well
Bur'y
Bur'y St. Ed'-[munds
Bus'by
Bush'ey
Bute
But'ler
But'terley
Bux'ton
Byng
By'rom
By'ron
Byzan'tium

C

Cab'ot
Cabul'
Cad'bury
Cade
Cad'er Id'ris
Ca'diz
Cad'mus
Cadog'an
Caen
Cæ'sar
Cæsare'a
Caffra'ria
Ca'gliari
Caglios'tro
Ca'hir
Cai'aphas
Caine
Cairns
Cai'ro
Cais'tor
Caith'ness
Caius Col'lege
Calabar'

Cala'bria
Calais (*France*)
Calais (*Amer.*)
Cal'bourn
Calcut'ta
Cal'deron
Cal'dicott
Ca'leb
Caledo'nia
Cal'iban
Cal'icut
Califor'nia
Calig'ula
Cal'lan
Call'cott
Cal'lington
Calli'ope
Calne
Cal'thorpe
Cal'ton
Cal'vary

Cal'vert
Cal'vin
Cam
Cam'berwell
Cambo'dia
Cam'bourne
Cambrai'
Cam'bria
Cam'bridge
Cam'den
Cam'elford
Cam'elot
Cam'eron
Cameroons'
Camil'la
Camil'lus
Cam'oens
Camp'bell
Camp'belltown

Camp'den
Campea'chy
Campe'che
Cam'perdown
Ca'naan
Can'ada
Canber'ra
Candahar'
Can'dia
Can'dy
Cane'a
Can'ford
Cannes
Can'ning
Can'nington
Can'nock
Can'onbury
Canos'sa
Cano'va
Can'terbury
Can'ton
Canton'
Cantyre'
Canute'
Caper'naum
Cape Town
Cap'per
Ca'pri
Cap'ulet
Caracal'la
Cara'cas
Carac'tacus
Car'diff
Car'digan
Ca'rey
Carew'
Car'ibbee
Carin'thia
Car'isbrooke
Car'leon
Carlisle'
Car'low
Carls'bad
Carl'ton
Carlyle'
Carmar'then
Car'mel
Carnar'von
Carnat'ic
Carneg'ie
Carn'forth
Caroli'na
Car'oline
Carpa'thian
Carra'ra
Car'rick
Carrickfer'gus
Car'rington
Car'roll
Car'ron
Carruth'ers
Carshal'ton
Car'son

Car'thage
Carthage'na
Car'ton
Cart'wright
Cash'el
Cashmere'
Cas'pian Sea
Cas'quets
Cassan'dra
Cas'sel
Castile'
Castlebar
Cas'tleford
Castlerea'
Cas'tleton
Castries'
Cat'aline
Catalo'nia
Cat'ford
Cath'arine
Cathay'
Cath'erine
Ca'to
Ca'ton
Cat'tegat
Cat'terick
Catul'lus
Cau'casus
Caus'ton
Cav'an
Cav'endish
Cavour'
Caw'dor
Cawnpore'
Caw'thorne
Cax'ton
Cayenne'
Cay'ley
Cay'thorpe
Cec'il
Cecil'ia
Cel'ebes
Ce'lia
Cel'sus
Cen'ci
Cenis'
Cer'berus
Ce'res
Cervan'tes
Cetewa'yo
Cetin'je, Cet-[ti'nge
Ceylon'
Chad'wick
Chalde'a
Chal'font
Chal'lis
Chal'mers
Chalons'
Cham'berlain
Cham'bers
Chan'dos
Chan'ning
Chan'trey
Chap'lin
Chap'man
Chard

Char'field
Char'ing Cross
Charl'bury
Charlemagne'
Charles
Charles'ton
Charles'town
Charleville'
Char'lotte
Char'lottetown
Charl'ton
Char'minster
Char'mouth
Cha'ron
Char'terhouse
Charyb'dis
Chateaubriand'
Chat'ham
Chat'teris
Chat'terton
Chau'cer
Chautau'qua
Chea'dle
Cheapside'
Ched'dar
Cheet'ham
Chelms'ford
Chel'sea
Chel'tenham
Chep'stow
Cherbourg'
Cher'iton
Cher'rington
Cher'son
Chert'sey
Ches'ham
Chesh'ire
Ches'hunt
Ches'ter
Ches'terfield
Ches'terton
Chet'wynd
Chev'iot
Chey'ne
Chica'go
Chich'ester
Chilcomp'ton
Chil'ders
Chil'e, Chil'I
Chil'ham
Chill'cott
Chil'lingworth
Chimbora'zo
Ching'ford
Chip'penham
Chip'perfield
Chip'ping Norton
Chip'stead
Chis'holm
Chis'lehurst
Chis'wick
Chitral'
Chlo'e
Cholm'ondeley
Chopin'
Chorassan'

Chor'ley
Chor'leywood
Chorl'ton
Christ
Christ'church
Christia'na
Christia'nia
Chris'tie
Christi'na
Chris'topher
Chrys'ostom
Chubb
Church'ill
Chuz'zlewit
Cic'ero
Cimabu'e
Cincinna'ti
Cincinna'tus
Cinderel'la
Cin'derford
Circas'sia
Cir'ce
Ci'rencester
Clackman'nan
Clac'ton-on-Sea'
Clan'ricarde
Clap'ham
Clap'perton
Clap'ton
Cla'ra
Clare
Clare'mont
Clar'ence
Clar'endon
Claris'sa
Clark
Clark'son
Clat'worthy
Claude'
Clau'dio
Clau'dius
Clav'erhouse
Clavering
Clav'erton
Clay'ton
Clea'ton
Cleck'heaton
Clemenceau'
Clem'ent
Clementi'na
Clem'entson
Cleopa'tra
Clerk'enwell
Cler'mont
Cleve'don
Cleve'land
Cleves
Clif'ford
Clif'ton
Clin'ton
Cli'o
Clith'ero
Clive
Clogher
Clonmel'
Clo'vis
Cloyne
Clut'terbuck
Clyde
Coal'brookdale
Coat'bridge
Cobb
Cob'bett
Cob'den
Cob'lenz
Co'burg
Coch'in Chi'na
Coch'rane
Cock'burn
Cock'erham
Cock'ermouth
Cock'erton
Cod'rington
Cœur de Lion'
Cog'geshall
Co'gnac
Coh'en
Coke
Col'chester
Cold'stream
Cole'ford
Cole'man
Colen'so
Coleraine'
Cole'ridge
Coles'hill
Col'lard
Col'lett
Col'lier
Col'lingbrook
Col'lingham
Col'lingwood
Col'lins
Col'linson
Col'man
Colne
Cologne'
Colom'bia
Colom'bo
Colon'na
Colora'do
Colquhoun'
Col'ston
Col'ton
Colum'bia
Colum'bus
Col'ville
Col'vin
Co'mo
Comp'ton
Comte
Concor'dia
Conde'
Confu'cius
Con'gleton
Con'go
Con'greve
Con'naught
Connect'icut
Con'nell
Con'nor
Con'rad
Con'stable
Con'stance
Con'stantine
Constantino'ple
Con'way
Cooke
Cook'ham
Cooks'town
Coop'er
Coorg, Kurg
Co'os
Cope'land
Copenha'gen
Coper'nicus
Cop'ley
Cop'perfield
Cop'pleston
Copt'hall
Corday'
Corde'lia
Cordil'leras
Cor'dova
Core'a, Kore'a
Corel'li
Corfe
Corfu'
Cor'inth
Coriola'nus
Cork
Corna'ro
Corneille'
Corne'lia
Corne'lius
Corn'hill
Corn'wall
Cornwal'lis
Coroman'del
Correg'gio
Cor'sham
Cor'sica
Corun'na
Cos'ham
Cos'sington
Cos'ta Ri'ca
Cot'ham
Cots'wold
Cot'tenham
Cot'tesmore
Cott'rell
Cour'land
Courte'nay
Court'ney
Coutts
Cov'ent Gar'den
Cov'entry
Cov'erdale
Cov'erley
Cov'ington
Cow'bridge

Cow'den
Cow'en
Cowes
Cow'ley
Cow'per
Cox
Crabbe
Cra'cow
Craig
Craik
Crail
Cran'bourne
Cran'brook
Cran'field
Cran'ford
Cran'mer
Cras'sus
Cra'ven
Craw'ford
Creagh
Cré'cy
Cred'iton
Creech
Creigh'ton
Cremo'na
Cres'sida
Cres'sy
Crete
Crewe

Crew'kerne
Crich'ton
Crick
Crick'lade
Crime'a
Crip'plegate
Cris'pin
Croa'tia
Crock'ett
Crœ'sus
Croft
Crom'arty
Crom'bie
Cro'mer
Crom'well
Cron'stadt, Kron-
[stadt
Cros'by
Cross'land
Cross'ley
Cross'thwaite
Cros'ton
Crow'combe
Crow'land
Crow'ther
Croy'don
Cru'den
Cruik'shank
Cru'soe
Cu'ba
Cuck'field
Cud'worth

Cul'len
Cul'liford
Cullod'en
Cull'ompton
Cul'ross
Cum'berland
Cum'ming
Cum'nock
Cunard'
Cun'ningham
Cu'par
Cu'pid
Curie'
Cur'ran
Cur'rie
Cur'tis
Cur'tius
Cur'wen
Cur'zon
Cuth'bert
Cuvier'
Cux'ton
Cuz'co
Cyc'lades
Cym'beline
Cyn'thia
Cyp'rian
Cy'prus
Cyr'il
Cy'rus
Cythere'a
Czer'ny

D

Dac'ca
Dag'enham
Da'gon
Daho'my
Daim'ler
Dako'ta
Dalhou'sie
Dalkeith'
Dal'las
Dalma'tia
Dalrym'ple
Dal'ston
Dal'ton
Daly
Dal'ziel
Dam'aris
Damas'cus
Dam'ien
Damiet'ta
Dam'ocles
Da'mon
Dam'pier
Dan
Dan'bury
Dan'by
Dan'iel

Dan'te
Dan'ton
Dan'ube
Dan'vers
Dan'zig
Daph'ne
D'Arblay'
Dar'by
Dardanelles'
Dar'field
Da'rien
Dari'us
Darjee'ling
Dar'laston
Dar'lington
Darm'stadt
Dar'racq
Dart'ford
Dart'mouth
Dar'ton
Dar'wen
Dar'win
Dauphine'
Dau'phiny
Dav'enham
Dav'enport

Dav'entry
Da'vey
Da'vid
Da'vid's, St.
Da'vidson
Da'vies, Da'vis
Da'vison
Dav'itt
Da'vos
Da'vy
Daw'ley
Daw'lish
Daw'son
Day'ton
Dea'kin
Deans
Deb'enham
Deb'orah
Dec'ca
Dec'can
Deck'er
Ded'dington
Ded'ham
Dee
Defoe'
Delago'a
De la Rue'

Del'aware
Del'hi (India,
Del'hi (U.S.A.)
Deli'lah
Delisle'
Del'phi
Del'phos
Demera'ra
Deme'trius
Democ'ritus
Demos'thenes
Den'bigh
Den'ham
Den'is
Den'man
Den'mark
Den'sham
Den'ton
Den'ver
Dept'ford
De Quin'cey
Der'by
Dere'ham
Der'went
Des'borough
Descartes'
Desdemo'na
Des Moines
Det'mold
Detroit'
Det'tingen
Dev'ereux
De Vin'ne
Devi'zes
Dev'on
Dev'onport
Dew'ar
Dews'bury
Dia'na
Dib'din
Dick
Dick'ens
Dick'inson
Dick'see
Diderot'
Di'do
Didot'
Dids'bury
Dieppe
Dig'by
Dijon'
Dilke
Dil'lon
Di'nah
Din'gle
Ding'wall
Din'ton
Diocle'tian
Diodo'rus Sic'u-
Diog'enes (lus
Dionys'ius

Dip'lock
Dis'ley
Disrae'li
Diss
Di'ves
Dix'on
Dnie'per
Dnies'ter
Dodd
Dod'dington
Dodd'ridge
Dods'well
Dod'well
Dog'berry
Do'herty
Dolgel'ly
Dombey
Dom'inic
Domini'ca
Domit'ian
Donaghadee'
Don'ald
Don'aldson
Don'caster
Donegal'
Dongo'la
Don'nington
Don'oghue
Do'ra
Dor'cas
Dor'chester
Doré'
Dor'king
Dor'noch
Dor'othy
Dor'rington
Dor'rit
D'Orsay'
Dor'set
Dort
Douay'
Doug'las
Dove'dale
Do'ver
Dow'ling
Down'end
Down'ham
Downpat'rick
Down'shire
Down'ton
Doyle
Drake
Dray'ton
Dres'den
Dreyfus'
Drif'field
Drogh'eda
Droit'wich
Dro'more
Dron'field
Dront'heim

Drood
Drum'mond
Dru'ry
Drusil'la
Dry'den
Dub'lin
Duck'worth
Dud'dington
Dud'ley
Duf'ferin
Duf'field
Duk'infield
Duluth'
Dul'verton
Dul'wich
Dumas'
Dumbar'ton
Dumfries'
Dunbar'
Dunblane
Dun'can
Duncan'non
Dun'church
Dundalk'
Dundas'
Dundee'
Dundon'ald
Dune'din
Dunferm'line
Dungan'non
Dungar'van
Dungeness'
Dunkirk'
Dun'lop
Dunman'way
Dunmore'
Dun'mow
Dunn
Dunra'ven
Dun'stable
Dun'stan
Dun'ster
Dur'ban
Dü'rer
Dur'ham
Dur'rant
Durs'ley
Dur'ward
Dut'ton
Dvor'ak
Dwight
Dwi'na
Dym'oke
Dy'mond
Dy'sart
Dy'son

E

Ea'ling
Eames
Earl's Court
Earn'shaw
Ears'don
Eas'ington
Eas'ingwold
East'bourne
East' Ham
East In'dies
East'ington
Eas'ton
Ea'ton
Ebene'zer
E'bro
Ec'cles
Ec'clesfield
Ec'cleshall
Ecclesias'tes
Ecclesias'ticus
Ec'cleston
Ec'uador
Ed'dystone
Ed'gar
Edg'baston
Edge'combe
Edge'hill
Edge'worth
Edge'worthtown
Ed'inburgh
Ed'ison
E'dith
Ed'mondson
Ed'monton
Ed'mund
E'dom
Ed'ward
Ed'win
Eg'bert
Ege'ria
Eg'erton
Eg'ham
Eg'linton
Eg'remont
E'gypt
Eir'e
Elaine'
El'ba
Elbe
El'don
El Dora'do
El'eanor
Elea'zar
Elephan'ta
El'gar
El'gin
E'li
E'lia
Eli'as
El'ibank
Elie'zer
Eli'hu
Eli'jah
El'iot
Eli'sha
Eli'za
Eliz'abeth
El'land
El'len
El'lenborough
Elles'mere
El'liott
El'lis
El'lison
Elm'sley
El'phinstone
Elsinore'
El'tham
El'ton
E'ly
El'zevir
Eman'uel
Em'ary
Em'bleton
Em'den
Em'erson
Em'ery
Em'ily
Em'ma
Emman'uel
Ems'worth
En'dor
Endym'ion
En'field
Engadine'
Enghien'
Eng'land
E'nid
En'nis
Enniscor'thy
Enniskil'len
E'noch
En'sor
Eph'esus
E'phraim
Epicte'tus
Epicu'rus
Epping
Ep'som
Ep'worth
Eras'mus
Er'ato
Er'furt
Er'ic
E'rie
Er'in
E'rith
Er'nest
Er'skine
Erze'rum
E'sau
Escula'pius
Es'dras
Esh'er
Esk
Es'mond
Es'senden
Es'sex
Es'ther
Estremadu'ra
Eth'el
Eth'elbald
Eth'elbert
Eth'elred
Eth'elwald
Eth'elwulf
Ethio'pia
Et'na
Eto'lia
E'ton
Eu'clid
Eugene'
Eugénie'
Eu'nice
Euphra'tes
Eurip'ides
Eu'rope
Euryd'ice
Euse'bius
Eus'tace
Eus'ton
Eutro'pius
Eux'ine
E'va
Ev'an
Evan'geline
Ev'ans
Ev'ansville
Eve
Ev'elyn, *Eng.*
Ev'elyn, *Scotch*
Ev'erard
Ev'erest
Ev'erett
Ev'ersley

Ev'erton
Eve'sham
Ew'art
Ew'ell
Ew'ing
Ex'bourne
Ex'bury
Ex'eter
Ex'minster
Ex'mouth
Ex'ton
Ey'lau
Eyre
Eze'kiel
Ez'ra

F

Fa'bian
Fabric'ius
Fair'bairn
Fair'fax
Fair'field
Fair'ford
Fa'kenham
Fal'coner
Fal'kirk
Falk'land
Fallieres'
Fal'mouth
Fal'staff
Fan'ny
Far'aday
Fare'ham
Far'ingdon
Far'leigh
Farn'borough
Farn'don
Farn'ham
Farn'worth
Far'oe Is'lands
Far'quhar
Far'ragut
Far'rar
Far'ringdon
Fa'scist
Fasho'da
Faust
Faus'tus
Fav'ersham
Faw'cett
Fawkes (Guy)
Fayette'
Feath'erstone
Felic'ia
Fe'lix
Fel'lenberg
Felt'ham
Fel'ton
Fen'church
Fénelon'
Fen'ning
Fen'ton
Fen'wick
Fer'dinand
Fer'gus
Fer'guson
Ferman'agh
Fermoy'
Fernan'dez
Ferra'ra
Fer'riby
Fer'ro
Fer'ry
Fer'rybridge
Festin'iog
Fes'tus
Feth'ard
Fev'ersham
Fez
Fez'zan
Field'ing
Fie'sole
Figaro'
Fig'gins
Fi'ji
Fildes'
Fill'more
Fil'ton
Finch'ley
Find'lay
Fin'don
Fin'gal
Finisterre'
Fin'land
Fin'lay
Fins'bury
Fish'er
Fish'guard
Fitzclar'ence
Fitzger'ald
Fitzher'bert
Fitzmau'rice
Fitzos'born
Fitzpat'rick
Fitz'roy
Fitzwil'liam
Flamborough
Flan'ders
Flax'man
Flax'ton
Fleet'wood
Flem'ing
Fletch'er
Flint
Flix'ton
Flod'den
Flo'quet
Flo'ra
Flor'ence
Flor'ida
Flush'ing
Foles'hill
Fol'jambe
Folke'stone
Folk'ingham
Fol'let
Fontainebleau'
Fon'tenoy
Forbes
Ford
Ford'ham
Ford'ingbridge
For'dyce
For'far
Formo'sa
For'res
For'ster
Forsyth'
For'tescue
Forth
Fortrose'
Fortuna'tus
Fort Wayne
Fos'ter
Foth'ergill
Foth'eringay
Foulis
Fow'ler
Fox'hill
Fram'ingham
Fram'lingham
Framp'ton
France
Fran'ces
Fran'cis
Franco'nia

Frank
Frank'enstein
Frank'fort
Frank'lin
Fra'ser
Fred
Fred'erick
Fred'ericton
Free'ling
Free'man
Free'town

Fre'mantle
Frere
Freycinet'
Fri'bourg
Friend'ly Isles
Fries'land
Frod'sham
Froe'bel
Frog'more
Froissart'

Frome
Froude
Ful'ford
Ful'ham
Ful'larton
Ful'ler
Ful'ton
Fur'ness
Fur'nival
Fu'seli
Fust

G

Ga'briel
Gad
Gain'ford
Gains'borough
Ga'ius
Galashiels'
Galate'a
Ga'len
Galic'ia
Galigna'ni
Gal'ilee
Galile'o
Gallip'oli
Gal'loway
Gal'ton
Gal'way
Gama'liel
Gambet'ta
Gam'bia
Gan'ges
Garci'a
Gar'dener
Gar'diner
Gard'ner
Gar'field
Gar'grave
Garibal'di
Garonne'
Gar'rick
Gar'stang
Garth
Gas'cony
Gas'quet
Gates'head
Gaul
Gau'tama
Gay'ton
Ga'za
Geelong'
Geben'na
Gei'erstein

Gel'derland
Guel'derland
Gene'va
Genevieve'
Gennes'aret
Geno'a
Geof'frey
Geoghe'gan
George
George'town
Geor'gia
Georgia'na
Ger'ald
Ger'aldine
Ger'rard
Ger'man
Ger'many
Ger'trude
Ger'vase
Ges'ner
Gethsem'ane
Ghauts
Ghent
Gi'ant's Causeway
Gib'bon
Gibbs
Gib'eon
Gibral'tar
Gib'son
Gid'eon
Giffard
Gif'ford
Gig'gleswick
Gil'bert
Gil'by
Gil'ead
Giles
Gill
Gil'lies
Gil'ling
Gil'lingham

Gil'pin
Giot'to
Glad'stone
Glam'is
Glamor'gan
Glan'ville
Glas'gow
Glas'tonbury
Glencoe'
Glenelg'
Glent'ham
Glos'sop
Glouces'ter
Glouces'tershire
Glo'ver
Go'a
God'alming
God'dard
God'frey
Godi'va
God'manchester
Godol'phin
God'win
Goe'the
Gol'car
Golcon'da
Gold Coast
Gol'dic
Gol'gotha
Goli'ath
Gomor'rah
Gon'dar
Good Hope, Cape of
Good'enough
Good'rich
Good'year
Gor'bals
Gor'don
Goree'
Gorgonzo'la

Gör'litz
Gorst
Gortschakoff'
Gos'berton
Gos'chen
Gos'ford
Gos'port
Gosse
Gos'sett
Gos'well
Go'tha
Go'tham
Goth'ard, St.
Goth'land
Got'tenburg
Göt'tingen
Gough
Gould
Gounod'
Gow'er
Grac'chus
Grace'church
Graf'ton
Gra'ham
Gra'hamstown
Grain'ger
Gram'pian
Grana'da
Gran'by
Grand'ison
Grand Rap'ids
Grange'mouth
Grant'ham
Gran'ville

Gras'mere
Grat'tan
Graves
Graves'end
Gray's Inn
Gray'son
Great Brit'ain
Great'ham
Greaves
Greece
Green'land
Green'law
Green'ock
Green'wich
Green'wood
Greg'ory
Greig
Grena'da
Greno'ble
Gren'ville
Gres'ford
Gresh'am
Gret'na Green'
Grev'ille
Grey'stoke
Gries'bach
Grif'fin
Grif'fith
Grims'by
Grin'stead
Grin'ton
Gri'qualand
Grisel'da
Grisons'
Gro'ningen
Groom'bridge

Gros'venor
Grote
Gro'tius
Grun'dy
Guadalaja'ra
Guadalquiv'ir
Guadeloupe'
Guam
Guatema'la
Guel'derland
Guelph
Guerns'ey
Guia'na
Guild'ford
Guin'ea
Guin'evere
Guin'ness
{Guis'borough
{Gis'borough
Guise
Guizot'
Gul'liver
Gun'ning
Gun'ston
Gün'ther
Gun'ton
Gur'ney
Gusta'vus
Gu'tenberg
Guth'rie
Gut'tenberg
Guy
Guy'on
Guzerat'
Gwa'lior

H

Haar'lem
Habak'kuk
Häck'el
Hack'et, Hack'ett
Hack'ney
Had'den
Had'denham
Had'dington
Had'leigh
Ha'drian
Haeck'el
Ha'fiz
Ha'gar
Hagg'ai
Hague
Hah'nemann
Hail'sham

Hai'nau, -y'nau
Hai'ti, Hay'ti
Hak'luyt
Hal'dane
Hales
Hales'owen
Hal'ifax
Hal'lam
Hal'lett
Hal'ley
Hal'liford
Hal'liwell
Hal'sall
Hals'bury
Hal'stead
Hal'ton

Halt'whistle
Ham'bleton
Ham'brook
Ham'burg
Ham'erton
Ham'ilton
Ham'let
Ham'mersmith
Ham'mond
Hamp'den
Hamp'shire
Hamp'stead
Hamp'ton
Ham'stead
Han'cock
Han'del
Hand'ley
Hands'worth

Han'ley
Han'nah
Han'nan
Han'nibal
Han'over
Han'sard
Hants
Han'way
Han'well
Han'worth
Haps'burg
Har'borne
Har'court
Hard'castle
Hardicanute'
Har'ding
Hard'ing
Hard'wick
Har'dy
Hares'field
Hare'wood
Har'lech
Har'lem
Har'ley
Har'lington
Har'lowe
Har'man
Har'old
Har'penden
Har'riet
Har'rington
Har'ris
Har'risburg
Har'rison
Har'rogate
Har'row
Har'rowby
Har'ry
Hart'field
Hart'ford
Hart'ington
Hart'land
Hart'lebury
Hart'lepool
Hart'ley
Hartz
Har'vard
Har'vey
Har'well
Har'wich
Har'wood
Has'lingden
Has'tings
Hat'field
Hat'ton
Haugh'ton
Havan'a
Hav'ant
Hav'elock
Hav'erfordwest
Hav'erhill
Ha'vre
Hawai'i
Hawar'den
Hawes

Haw'ick
Hawkes'bury
Hawkes'worth
Haw'kins
Haw'ley
Haw'thorne
Hay'dn
Hay'don
Hayes
Hay'ley
Hay'man
Hay'ti
Hay'ward
Hay'wood
Haz'litt
Head'ingly
Head'ington
Hea'ly
Heath'cote
Heath'field
Hea'ton
Heav'itree
Heb'denbridge
He'be
He'ber
Heb'rides
He'bron
Hec'ate
Heck'ington
Hec'la
Hec'tor
Hec'uba
Hed'ingham
He'don
He'gel
Hei'delberg
Heigh'am
Hei'ne
Hel'en
Hel'ena
Hele'na, St.
Hel'ens, St.
Hel'iers, St.
Hel'igoland
Héloise'
Helps
Hel'ston
Hel'ton
Helve'tia
Hem'ans
Hem'el Hemp'-stead
Hem'merde
Hem'mings
Hems'well
Hems'worth
Hen'bury
Hen'derson
Hen'don
Hene'age
Hen'field
Hen'gist
Hen'ley
Henriet'ta
Hen'ry
Hen'singham

Hep'tonstall
Heracli'tus
Herat'
Her'bert
Hercula'neum
Her'cules
Her'eford
Her'komer
Her'mes
Herne
Her'od
Herod'otus
Her'rick
Herrn'hutt
Her'schell,-schel
Hert'ford
Hert'fordshire
Her'vey
Herzegovi'na
He'siod
Hes'se Cas'sel
Hes'se Darm'-stadt
Hes'ter
Hev'ersham
Hew'orth
Hex'ham
Heytes'bury
Hey'wood
Hezeki'ah
Hiawa'tha
Hiber'nia
Hicks
Hicks'-Beach
Hig'gins
High'bury
High'gate
High'lands
High'worth
Hil'ary
Hil'da
Hil'desheim
Hil'lier
Hil'lington
Hills'borough
Hil'perton
Hil'ton
Hima'laya
Him'malch
Hinck'ley
Hind'ley
Hin'du
Hindustan'
Hin'ton
Hippar'chus
Hippoc'rates
His'cock
Hispa'nia
Hitch'cock
Hitch'in
Hoad'ly
Ho'bart

Hobbes
Hob'house
Hobo'ken
Hodge
Hodg'es
Hod'son
Hoey
Ho'fer
Hoff'mann
Ho'garth
Hogg
Hohenlin'den
Hohenzol'lern
Hol'beach
Hol'beck
Hol'bein
Hol'born
Hol'brook
Hol'croft
Holds'worth
Hol'inshed
Hol'land
Hol'linwood
Hol'loway
Holl'ywood
Hol'man
Holmes
Hol'stein
Holt
Hol'yhead
Hol'yoake
Hol'yoke
Hol'y Land
Hol'ywell
Hom'burg
Ho'mer
Hom'erton
Hondu'ras
Hong Kong'
Hon'iton
Honolu'lu

Hook'er
Hoop'er
Hop'kins
Hor'ace
Hora'tio
Hora'tius
Hor'field
Horn'castle
Hor'ner
Horn'sey
Hor'sa
Horse'fall
Hor'sham
Hors'ley
Horten'sius
Hor'ton
Hor'wich
Hose'a
Hoth'am
Hot'spur
Hough
Hough'ton
Houns'low
Hous'ton
Hove
How'ard
How'den
Howe
How'ell
How'itt
Hox'ton
Hoy'land
Huas'car
Hub'bard
Hu'bert
Hud'dersfield
Hu'dibras
Hud'son

Huer'ta
Hugh
Hughes
Hu'gli
Hu'go
Hul'lah
Hulme
Hul'ton
Hum'ber
Hum'boldt
Hume
Hum'mel
Hum'phrey
Hum'phreys
Hun
Hun'fleet
Hun'gary
Hun'gerford
Hun'slet
Hun'stanton
Hunt'ingdon
Hunt'ingford
Hunt'ington
Hunt'ley
Hurd
Hu'ron
Hurst
Hu'sey
Hus'kisson
Huss
Hutch'ings
Hutch'inson
Hut'ton
Hux'ley
Huy'gens
Hyde
Hyderabad'
Hy'geia
Hy'men
Hypa'tia
Hythe

I

Ia'go
I'an
Ib'sen
Ice'land
Ich'abod
I'colmkill
I'da
I'daho
Id'desleigh
Igna'tius
Il'chester
Il'ford
Il'fracombe
Il'keston

Ilk'ley
Illinois'
Illyr'ia
Il'minster
Imman'uel
In'cledon
In'dia
India'na
Indianap'olis
In'dus
In'gelow
In'gersoll
Ing'ham
In'gleborough
In'gleton

In'glis
In'goldsby
In'gram
Ink'erman
In'man
Inns'bruck / Inns'pruck
Invera'ry
Invercar'gill
Inverness'
Io'na
Io'nian Isles
I'owa
Ips'wich

Iqui'que
Irawa'di
Ire'land
Ire'ne
Ire'ton
Irkutsk'
Iroquois'
Ir'vine
Ir'ving
Ir'win
I'saac
I'saacson

Is'abel
Isabel'la
Isai'ah
Iscar'iot
Ish'mael
Ish'maelites
I'sis
I'sla
Isle of Wight'
Isle'worth
Is'lington
Isoc'rates

Ispahan'
Is'rael
Is'sachar
Is'tria
It'aly
Itch'en
Itha'ca
Ithu'riel
I'vanhoe
Ives, St.
Iv'iza
I'vory Coast
Ixi'on

J

Ja'besh
Ja'bez
Jack'son
Ja'cob
Jae'ger
Ja'el
Jaf'fa
Ja'go, St.
Jamai'ca
James
Jame'son
James'town
Janei'ro, Rio de
Jan'et
Ja'nus
Japan'
Ja'pheth
Jaques
Jar'dine
Jar'row
Jar'vis
Ja'son
Jas'per
Jas'sy
Ja'va
Jay
Jebb
Jed'burgh
Jed'do
Jeff
Jef'ferson
Jef'feries
Jef'fries
Jef'frey
Jehoi'achin
Jehoi'akim
Jeho'vah
Je'hu
Jek'yll
Jel'licoe

Jemi'ma
Je'na
Jen'kins
Jen'kinson
Jen'ner
Jen'net
Jen'nings
Jen'ny
Jeremi'ah
Jer'emy
Jer'icho
Jerome
Jer'rold
Jer'ry
Jer'sey
Jeru'salem
Jer'vaulx
Jer'vis
Jes'se
Jes'sica
Jes'sie
Jes'sop
Je'sus
Jeune
Jew'ry
Jez'ebel
Jim
Jo'achim
Joan
Joan'na
Job
Joe
Jo'el
Johan'nesburg
John
John'son
John'stone
Johore'

Jonah
Jo'nas
Jon'athan
Jones
Jor'dan
Jor'tin
Jos'celyn
Jo'seph
Jo'sephine
Jose'phus
Josh'ua
Josi'ah
Josi'as
Jou'bert (Dutch)
Joubert'(French)
Jove
Joyce
Ju'an
Ju'ba
Ju'dah
Ju'das
Judd
Jude
Jude'a
Ju'dith
Ju'dy
Jugur'tha
Ju'lia
Ju'lian
Julia'na
Ju'liet
Ju'lius
Jung'frau
Ju'nius
Ju'no
Ju'piter
Ju'ra
Jus'tin
Justin'ian
Jus'tus
Jut'land
Ju'venal

K

Ka'bul
Kal'mucks
Kamchat'ka
Kampa'la
Kandahar'
Kan'sas
Kant
Karls'ruhe
Kars
Kars'lake
Kashmir'
Kate
Kath'arine
Kean
Kear'ley
Keat'ing
Keats
Ke'ble
Kedle'ston
Keel'ing
Keene
Keigh'ley
Keith
Keke'wich
Kel'loe
Kel'ly
Kel'sall
Kel'sey
Kel'son
Kelve'don
Kem'ble
Kemp
Kem'pis
Kemp'sey
Ken'dal
Ken'drick
Ken'elm
Ken'ilworth
Ken'nard
Ken'nedy
Ken'nerley
Ken'net
Ken'nington
Ken'rick
Ken'sal Green
Ken'sington
Ken'sit
Kent
Kent'ish Town
Kentuck'y
Ken'wyn
Ken'yon
Keogh
Kep'ler

Kerr
Ker'ry
Ker'shaw
Kes'teven
Kes'wick
Ketch
Ket'tering
Khartoum' Khar-[tum'
Khi'va
Khorassan'
Kid'derminster
Kid'welly
Ki'ef, Ki'eff
Ki'kuyu
Kilbir'nie
Kilbride'
Kil'burn
Kil'da
Kildare'
Kild'wick
Kilken'ny
Killal'a
Killaloe'
Killar'ney
Kil'lyleagh
Kilmain'ham
Kilmar'nock
Kilmore'
Kil'ner
Kil'rush
Kil'wyn
Kim'berley
Kimbolton
Kincar'dine
King'lake
Kings'bridge
Kings' Coun'ty
Kings'down
Kings'land
Kings'ley
King's Lynn
King's Norton'
Kings'ton
King'ston-on-Thames
Kings'town

Kingswin'ford
Kings'wood
King'ton
King' Will'iam's [Town
Kinross'
Kinsale'
Kin'son
Kintyre'
Kip'ling
Kirk'by
Kirkcal'dy
Kirkcud'bright
Kirk'dale
Kirk'ham
Kirkhea'ton
Kirk'lington
Kirkpat'rick
Kirkwall'
Kir'riemuir
Kir'wan
Kitch'ener
Klon'dike
Klop'stock
Knares'borough
Knel'ler
Knight'on
Knights'bridge
Knollys
Knot'tingley
Knowles
Knox
Knut
Knuts'ford
Koch
Kohat'
Kon'go
Kön'igsberg
Kore'a
Ko'riacs
Koss'uth
Kra'cow
Krapot'kin
Kron'stadt
Krug'er
Ku'belik
Kuch'ing
Kumas'si
Kurdistan'
Ku'rile
Kyrle

L

Labouchere'
Labrador'
Labuan'
Lac'cadive
Lace'by
Lacedæ'mon
La Chaise'
La'cy
Ladrones'
Lady'smith
Lafayette'
Lafontaine'
La'gos
Lahore'
Laing
La'kenham
Lamartine'
Lam'berhurst
Lam'bert
Lam'beth
Lam'bourne
Lamb'ton
Lammermoor'
Lammermuir'
Lam'peter
Lan'ark
Lan'cashire
Lan'caster
Lan'celot
Lan'chester
Land'port
Land'seer
Land's End
Lane' End
Lang
Lang'dale
Lang'ford
Lang'ham
Lang'horne
Lang'ley
Lang'port
Lan'gridge
Lang'ton
Languedoc'
Lans'downe
Laodice'a
Laplace'
Lap'land
La Pla'ta
Lapu'ta
Lar'bert
Laris'sa

Lark'field
Lark'ins
Las'celles
Las'sa
Lataki'a
La'tham
La'thom
Lat'imer
Lattakoo'
Lau'ban
Laud
Lau'der
Laugh'ton
Launces'ton
Lau'ra
Lau'rier
Lausanne'
Lavalette'
Lava'ter
La'venham
Lav'ington
Lavin'ia
Lavoisier'
Lawes
Law'rence
Law'rie
Law'son
Law'ton
Lay'cock
Lay'ard
Laz'arus
Leach
Lead'enhall
Le'ah
Leake
Leam'ington
Lea'nder
Lear
Leath'erhead
Leb'anon
Lebrun'
Leckhamp'ton
Leck'y
Leclerc'
Led'bury
Leeds
Leek
Lees
Lee'ward Is'lands
Lefe'vre
Legge
Leghorn'
Legrand'

Leib'nitz
Leices'ter
Leices'tershire
Leigh
Leigh'ton Buz'zard
Lein'ster
Leip'sic, Leip'zig
Leith
Lei'trim
Lel'and
Lem'nos
Len'nox, Len'ox
Len'ton
Le'o
Leom'inster (Eng.)
Leom'inster (U.S.A.)
Leon
Leon'ard
Leon'idas
Leono'ra
Le'opold
Lepan'to
Le Queux'
Ler'wick
Le Sage'
Les'lie
Les'seps
Les'sing
Le'the
Letit'ia
Levant'
Le'ven
Lev'eridge
Le'vi
Lew'enhoeck
Lew'es, Lew'is
Lew'isham
Lex'ington
Ley'burn
Ley'den
Ley'land
Ley'ton
Ley'tonstone
Lha'sa
Lib'anus
Libe'ria
Lib'ya
Lich'field
Lid'dell
Lid'don
Lidg'ett
Lie'big
Liége'
Lif'ford

Light'foot
Lil'lian
Lille
Lil'leshall
Lil'liput
Lil'ly
Li'ma
Lim'ber
Lim'burg
Lime'house
Limer'ick
Limps'field
Lincoln
Lin'colnshire
Lind'field
Lind'sey
Lin'ley
Linlith'gow
Linnæ'us
Lin'thwaite
Lin'ton
Lin'wood
Li'onel
Lip'ari
Lip'pe
Lip'ton
Lis'bon
Lis'burn
Lis'keard
Lisle
Lis'more
Lis'ter
Liszt
Lithua'nia
Lit'tlebury
Lit'tleham
Lit'tlejohn
Lit'tleport
Lit'tleton
Liv'erpool
Liv'ersedge
Liv'ingstone
Livo'nia
Liv'y
Llan'daff (And so with the eight following words)
Llando'very
Llanel'ly
Llanfyl'lin
Llangol'len
Llan'idloes
Llano'ver
Llanrwst'
Llewel'yn
Lloyd

Loan'go
Locha'ber
Lock'hart
Lock'wood
Lock'ver
Lo'di
Loffo'den
Lof'tus
Lo'gan
Loh'engrin
Loire
Lo'mas
Lo'max
Lom'bard
Lom'bardy
Lom'broso'
Lo'mond
Lon'don
Londonder'ry
Long'don
Long'fellow
Long'ford
Longi'nus
Long'ley
Long'man
Long'port
Long'ton
Lons'dale
Loo'choo
Lo'pez
Lore'burn
Loren'zo
Loret'to
Lorne
Lorraine'
Los An'geles
Lostwith'iel
Lothar'io
Loth'bury
Lo'thian
Lot'ty
Lou'don
Lough'borough
Loughrea'
Lough'ton
Lou'is
Loui'sa
Lou'isburg
Louise'
Louisia'na
Lou'isville
Lourdes
Louth
Louvre
Love'lace
Lov'ell
Low'ell

Lowes'toft
Lowndes
Lowth
Low'ther
Loyo'la
Lub'bock
Lü'beck
Lu'can
Lu'cas
Luc'ca
Lucerne'
Lu'cia
Lu'cian
Lu'cifer
Lu'cius
Luck'now
Lucre'tia
Lucre'tius
Lu'cy
Lud'denden
Lud'ford
Lud'gate
Lud'low
Lud'wick
Lud'wig
Luke
Lul'lington
Lum'ley
Lun'dy
Lu'nenbourg
Lup'ton
Lush
Lush'ington
Lusita'nia
Lu'ther
Lu'ton
Lut'terworth
Lux'emburg
Lux'or
Lyc'idas
Lycur'gus
Lydd
Lyd'gate
Lyd'ia
Lyd'ney
Ly'ell
Lyg'on
Lyl'y
Lyme
Lyme Re'gis
Lym'ington
Lyn'combe
Lynd'hurst
Lyne'ham
Lynn
Ly'ons
Lyt'tleton
Lyt'ton

M

Ma'bel
Macad'am
Macao'
Macar'thy
Macart'ney
Macas'sar
Macau'lay
Macbeth'
Mac'cabees
Mac'clesfield
Macdon'ald
Macduff'
Macedo'nia
Macgreg'or
Machiavel'li
Ma'chin
Mackay'
Macken'zie
Macknight'
Maclar'en
Maclean'
Macleod'
MacMah'on
Macmil'lan
Macnama'ra
Macpher'son
Macquar'ie
Macrea'dy
Macroom'
Madagas'car
Mad'an
Mad'dox
Madei'ra
Madeleine'
Made'ley
Mad'ison
Madras'
Madrid'
Mæce'nas
Maes'tricht
Mafeking'
Mag'dala
Mag'dalen
Mag'deburg
Magel'lan

Ma'gog
Mahan'
Mahom'et
Mahony
Mahrat'ta
Maida' Hill
Maid'enhead
Maid'stone
Maine
Main'waring
Mait'land
Major'ca
Maju'ba
Mal'abar
Malac'ca
Mal'achi
Mal'aga
Mal'aprop
Mala'ya
Mal'colm
Mal'den
Mal'dive
Mal'don
Mallin'son
Malmes'bury
Malone'
Malo'ny
Mal'pas
Mal'ta
Mal'thus
Mal'ton
Mal'vern
Malvi'na
Mana'gua
Manas'seh
Manas'ses
Man'chester
Man'dalay
Mandin'go
Mangotsfield'
Manil'la
Manitoba'
Man'ley
Man'nering
Mann'heim
Man'ning
Man'ningtree
Mans'field
Man'son
Man'ton
Man'tua

Marajo'
Marañon'
Mar'athon
Mar'burg
Marcel'lus
Marco'ni
Mar'den
Maren'go
Mares'field
Mar'garet
Mar'gate
Mar'gery
Mari'a
Mari'enburg
Mar'ion
Ma'rius
Marjori'banks
Mark
Mark'ham
Mark'land
Marl'borough
Mar'low
Mar'maduke
Mar'mion
Marmontel'
Mar'mora
Mar'ple
Marque'sas
Mars
Mars'den
Marseilles'
Mar'shall
Mar'shalsea
Mar'sham
Marsh'field
Mar'ston
Martaban'
Mar'tha
Mar'tin
Mar'tineau
Martinique'
Mar'tock
Mar'ton
Ma'ry
Ma'ryborough
Ma'ryland
Mar'ylebone

Ma'ryport
Mas'eru
Mash'am
Masho'naland
Massachu'setts
Masséna'
Mas'sey
Mas'singer
Mas'terman
Matabe'le
Math'er
Math'eson
Matil'da
Mat'lock
Matth'ew
Matthi'as
Maud
Maureta'nia
Mau'rice
Maurit'ius
Maw'gan
Maximil'lian
Max'well
Mayence'
May'field
May'hew
May'nard
May'nooth
May'o
Mazep'pa
Mazzi'ni
M'Car'thy
McCor'quodale
McCul'loch
McKay'
McKen'na
McKin'ley
McKin'non
Meagher
Meath
Mec'ca
Meck'lenburg
Mede'a
Med'ici
Medi'na
Mediterra'nean
Med'way
Mei'ningen
Melanch'thon
Mel'ba
Mel'bourne
Mel'combe
Mel'huish
Melic'ent
Melin'da
Melis'sa
Mel'moth
Melpom'ene
Mel'rose
Mel'tham
Mel'ton Mow'-bray

Mel'ville
Me'mel
Mem'phis
Men'ai
Men'delssohn
Menpes
Menton'
Mento'ne
Mentz
Men'zies
Mephistoph'eles
Merca'tor
Mer'edith
Merion'eth
Mer'lin
Mer'riman
Mer'ryweather
Mer'sey
Merthyr Tyd'fil
Mer'ton
Me'shech
Mes'mer
Mesopota'mia
Messi'na
Met'calfe
Methu'selah
Metz
Meux
Mex'borough
Mex'ico
Mey'er
Meyn'ell
Mi'cah
Micaw'ber
Mi'chael
Mich'ie
Mich'igan
Mick'lethwaite
Mi'das
Mid'delburg
Mid'dleham
Mid'dlesbrough
Mid'dlesex
Mid'dleton
Mid'dlewich
Mid'hurst
Mid'somer Norton'
Mil'an *or* Milan'
Mil'bourne
Mil'denhall
Mil'dred
Mile End
Miles
Mil'ford
Millais'
Mil'lard
Mills
Mil'ner
Miln'thorpe
Mil'ton
Mil'verton

Milwau'kee
Minchinhamp'-ton
Min'den
Mine'head
Miner'va
Minneap'olis
Minneso'ta
Minor'ca
Min'ories
Mi'nos
Min'to
Mirabeau'
Miran'da
Mir'field
Mir'iam
Mississipp'i
Missolong'hi
Missou'ri
Mitch'am
Mitch'ell
Mitch'elstown
Mit'ford
Mithrida'tes
Miz'pah
Mo'ab
Mobile'
Mo'cha
Mod'bury
Mod'der
Mode'na
Mof'fat
Mogador'
Moham'med
Mo'hawk
Moi'ra
Mold
Molda'via
Moles'worth
Molière'
Mol'ly
Mo'loch
Molt'ke
Mol'ton
Moluc'ca
Momba'sa
Mo'mus
Mon'aco
Mon'aghan
Monck
Moncrief'
Mond
Monde'go
Mongo'lia
Monk'house
Monk'land
Monk'ton
Mon'mouth
Monroe'
Monro'via
Mon'tagu
Montaigne'
Monta'na

Mont Blanc'
Montcalm'
Monte'go
Montene'gro
Monterey'
Montesquieu'
Montevide'o
Montgom'ery
Montpel'lier
Montreal'
Montrose'
Montserrat'
Moo'dy
Moore
Mora'via
Mor'ay
Mor'dan
Mor'decai
More
More'a
Moreau'
More'cambe
Mores'by
More'ton
Mor'gan
Mor'ison
Mor'land
Mor'ley
Morn'ington
Moroc'co
Mor'peth
Mor'ris
Mor'rison
Morse
Mor'timer
Mort'lake
Mor'ton
Mos'cow
Mose'ley
Moselle'
Mo'ses
Mos'heim
Moss'ley
Mo'sul
Mot'ley
Mot'tram
Moul'ton
Mountcas'tle
Mount'ford
Mow'bray
Mozambique'
Mozart'
Moz'ley
Mül'hausen
Mü'ller
Mullingar'
Mul'lins
Mum'ford
Munchau'sen
Mundel'la
Mu'nich
Munro'
Mun'ster
Murat'
Mur'cia
Mur'phy
Mur'ray
Muscat'
Mus'covy
Mus'grave
Mus'selburgh
Mus'well Hill
My'att
My'ers
My'ott
My'ra
Mysore'

N

Na'aman
Na'both
Nagpur'
Na'hum
Nails'worth
Nairn
Nai'robi
Na'mur
Nan'cy
Nanking'
Nan'ny
Nan'sen
Nantes
Nantuck'et
Nant'wich
Na'omi
Naph'tali
Na'pier
Na'ples
Napo'leon
Na'poli
Nar'beth
Narcis'sus
Nares
Nase'by
Na'smyth
Nash
Nash'ville
Nassau'
Natal'
Na'than
Nathan'iel
Nato'lia
Naum'burg
Nav'an
Navari'no
Navarre'
Nay'land
Nay'lor
Naz'areth
Neale
Neath
Nebras'ka
Nebuchadnez'zar
Neck'er
Need'ham
Nehemi'ah
Nel'son
Nemours'
Ne'nagh
Ne'ots, St.
Nepaul'
Nep'tune
Ne'ro
Nes'ton
Nes'tor
Neth'erlands
Neu'burg
Neuchâtel'
Neu'stadt
Neva'da
Nev'ille
Nev'in
Nev'is
New'ark
{ New'berry / New'bery }
New'borough
New'bridge
{ New'burgh / New'burg }
New'burn
New'bury
New'castle *or* Newcas'tle
Newcastle-on-Tyne
New'castle-*under*-Lyme'
{ New'comb / New'come }
New'digate
New'enden
New'ent

Newfound'land
New'gate
New Hamp'shire
Newha'ven
New'ington
New Jer'sey
New'land
New'man
New'market
New Mex'ico
Newnes
Newn'ham
New Or'leans
New'port
New'quay
New'ry
New South Wales
New'ton
New'town
Newtownards'
New York
New York City
New Zea'land
Ney
Nga'mi
Niag'ara
Nicara'gua
Nice
Nich'olas
Nich'ols
Nich'olson

Nick'leby
Nicobar'
Nicode'mus
Nicosi'a
Nie'buhr
Nie'per
Nie'ster
Ni'gel
Ni'ger
Nige'ria
Nile
Nil'sson
Nim'rod
Nine' Elms
Nin'eveh
Nin'field
Nin'ian, St.
Ni'obe
Nix'on
No'ah
Noakes
No'bel
No'el
Noot'ka Sound
No'ra
Nord'berg
Nor'dica
Nord'land
Nore
Nor'folk
Nor'ham
Nor'man
Nor'manby

Nor'mandy
Nor'manton
Nor'ris
Northal'lerton
North'am
Northamp'ton
North Caroli'na
North'cote
North Dako'ta
North'field
North'fleet
North'leach
Nor'throp
Northum'ber-land
North'wood
Nor'ton
Nor'way
Nor'wich
Nor'wood
Not'tingham
Not'ting Hill
No'va Sco'tia
No'va Zem'bla
Novgorod'
Nu'bia
Nu'gent
Nu'ma
Nun'eaton
Nune'ham
Nu'nemberg
Nu'remberg
Nut'tall
Nyas'saland
Ny'koping

O

Oak'ford
Oak'ham
Oak'hill
Oak'ingham
Oak'land
Oak'ley
Obadi'ah
O'ban
Oberam'mergau
O'berlin
O'beron
O'bi
O'Bri'en
Ocea'nia
Ock'brook
O'Con'nell
O'Con'nor
Octa'via
Octa'vius
Odell'
O'der

Odes'sa
Œd'ipus
O'gilby
O'gilvie
Ohi'o
Okehamp'ton
Okhotsk'
Oklaho'ma
Old'bury
Old'castle
Ol'denburg
Old'field
Old'ham
Old'land
Olds'worth
Ol'iphant
Olivet'
Oliv'ia
Ol'lendorff

Ol'lerton
Ol'mütz
Ol'ney
Ol'veston
Olym'pia
Olym'pus
Omagh
O'mah
O'mar
Omdurman'
Om'maney
On'ega
O'Neil'
On'gar
Ons'low
Onta'rio
O'penshaw
Ophe'lia
O'pie

Opor'to
O'ram
Oran'
Or'egon
O'Reil'ly
O'renburg
Or'ford
Or'igen
Orino'co
Oris'sa
Ork'ney
Orlan'do
Or'leans
Or'monde
Orms'by
Orms'kirk
Or'mus
Or'pen
Or'pheus
Or'pington
Or'ton
Os'borne
Os'car
Os'mington
Os'mond
Osnabrück
Os'naburg
Os'sett
Os'sian
Os'tend
Os'tiaks
Os'wald
Os'waldtwisle
Oswe'go
Os'westry
Otahei'te
Ot'ham
Othel'lo
Oth'man
O'tho
Ot'ley
Ot'tawa
Ot'tery St. Ma'ry
Ot'way
Oudh, Oude
Oui'da
Oul'ton
Oun'dle
Ou'ral
Ouse
Ou'tram
O'verbury
O'verend
O'verton
Overys'sel
Ov'id
Ovie'do
O'vingham
O'wen
Ows'ley
Ow'ston
Ox'enden
Oxford
Ox'ley

P

Pacif'ic
Pad'dington
Pad'dy
Pa'derborn
Paderew'ski
Pad'iham
Pad'stow
Pad'ua
Pagani'ni
Pag'et
Paine
Paign'ton
Pains'wick
Pais'ley
Pak'enham
Palermo'
Pal'estine
Pa'ley
Pal'grave
Pal'issy
Pal'las
Pal'liser
Pall Mall
Pal'mer
Palm'erston
Palmy'ra
Pamir'
Pam'pas
Pampelu'na
Pamphyl'ia
Panama'
Pan'cras, St.
Pando'ra
Pang'bourne
Pank'hurst
Pap'ua
Paracel'sus
Paraguay'
Paramar'ibo
Paramat'ta
Parana'
Par'fitt
Par'is
Par'ker
Park'gate
Park'hurst
Par'kinson
Par'ma
Parnas'sus
Par'nell
Pa'ros
Par'ry
Par'sons
Par'sonstown
Pas'cal
Pass'more
Pasteur'
Patago'nia
Pat'ernosterRow
Pat'erson
Pat'more
Pat'mos
Pat'na
Pa'ton
Pat'rick
Pat'ten
Pat'terson
Pat'ti
Pat'tingham
Pat'tison
Paul
Pauli'na
Pauline'
Paul'ton
Paunce'fote
Pausa'nias
Pavi'a
Pawtuck'et
Pax'ton
Payne
Pea'body
Pearce
Pear'son
Pear'y
Pease
Peck'ham
Peck'sniff
Pe'dro
Pee'bles

Peel
Peg'asus
Peg'gy
Pegu'
Pe'ipus
Pekin'
Peking'
Pela'gius
Pelew' Islands
Pel'ham
Pell
Pem'bertor
Pem'bridge
Pem'broke
Pem'bury
Penden'nis
Pen'dleton
Pene'lope
Penn
Pen'nant
Pen'nefather
Pen'nington
Pen'niston
Pennsylva'nia
Pen'rith
Pen'ryn
Pens'ford
Pent'land
Pen'tonville
Pen'wortham
Penzance'
Peo'ria
Pep'in
Pepys
Per'cival
Per'cy
Per'egrine
Per'gamos
Per'icles
Per'kins
Perks
Pernambu'co
Perranzab'uloe
Per'rin
Per'ry
Persep'olis
Per'sia
Perth
Peru'
Peru'gia
Peshaw'ar
Pestaloz'zi
Pesth
Pe'ter
Pe'terborough
Pe'terchurch
Pe'terhead
Pe'tersfield
Pe'tersham

Peth'erton
Pe'trarch
Pet'rograd
Pet'worth
Pev'ensey
Pev'eril
Pew'sey
Pha'raoh
Phe'be
Phelps
Pheni'cia, Phœni'cia
Phid'ias
Philadel'phia
Phile'mon
Phil'ip
Phil'ippine
Phil'ipstown
Philis'tia
Phil'lack
Phil'lips
Phil'lis
Phill'pott
Phin'ehas
Phin'eas
Phipps
Phryg'ia
Phyl'lis
Piccadil'ly
Pick'ering
Pick'ett
Pick'ford
Pick'wick
Pied'mont
Pierce
Pier'pont
Pietermar'itzburg
Pig'ott
Pi'late
Pil'kington
Pil'lau
Pil'ton
Pin'dar
Piner'o
Pin'kerton
Pin'ner
Pin'nock
Pir'ie
Pi'sa
Pit'man
Pit'tington
Pitts'burg
Pi'us
Pizar'ro
Plais'tow
Plantag'enet
Plas'sey
Pla'ta
Pla'to
Platt
Plau'tus
Play'fair
Plev'na

Plin'y
Plumb'land
Plump'tre
Plum'stead
Plun'ket
Plu'tarch
Plu'to
Plym'outh
Plymp'ton
Plym'stock
Plynlim'mon
Po
Pock'lington
Po'cock
Poe
Poincaré'
Poitiers'
Po'land
Pole'-Ca'rew
Polk
Pol'lard
Pol'lock
Pollokshaws'
Pol'ly
Po'lo
Polo'nius
Polyb'ius
Polyne'sia
Pomera'nia
Pomo'na
Pompadour'
Pompe'ii
Pom'pey
Pondicher'ry
Pon'doland
Pon'sanooth
Pon'sonby
Pon'tefract *or* Pom'fret
Pon'tesbury
Pon'typool
Poole
Poo'na
Pop'lar
Por'lock
Por'son
Portadown'
Port'au-Prince'
Port'bury
Port'chester
Por'teus
Port Glas'gow
Por'tia
Port'ishead
Port'land
Portmad'oc
Port'man

Por'tobel'lo
Por'to Ri'co
Port Said'
Port'sea
Ports'mouth
Por'tugal
Po'sen
Pos'tlethwaite
Pot'iphar
Poto'mac
Poto'si
Pots'dam
Pot'terne
Pot'tersham
Pou'lett
Poul'ton
Pow'ell
Pow'erscourt
Pow'ick
Pow'is, Powys
Pow'nall
Poyn'ter
Poyn'ton
Praed

Prague
Pratt
Preiss'nitz
Pren'dergast
Pres'burg
Pres'cott
Prest'bury
Presteign'
Pres'ton
Pres'tonpans
Prest'wich
Preto'ria
Pri'am
Prid'eaux
Priest'ley
Prin'gle
Pri'or
Pris'cian
Priscil'la
Pritch'ard
Procrus'tes
Proc'tor
Prome'theus
Pros'pero
Pros'ser
Proth'eroe
Prout

Provence'
Prus'sia
Psy'che
Ptol'emy
Pud'sey
Pu'gin
Pules'ton
Pull'man
Pu'lo Pinang'
Pulte'ney
Punjab'
Pur'beck
Pur'brook
Pur'cell
Pur'fleet
Pur'nell
Pu'sey
Put'ney
Put'son
Put'tenham
Puy de Dôme'
Pygma'lion
Pym
Pyr'enees
Pytch'ley
Pythag'oras

Q

Quarles
Quatre Bras'
Quebec'
Queen'borough
Queen'hithe
Queen's' Coun'ty

Queens'ferry
Queens'land
Queens'town
Quen'don
Quen'tin
Quet'ta
Queux

Qui'loa
Quin
Quin'cy
Quintil'ian
Quin'tin
Qui'to
Quix'ote

R

Rabelais'
Ra'chel
Racine'
Rad'cliffe
Rad'ford
Rad'ipole
Rad'nor
Rad'stock
Raf'fles

Rag'lan
Ragu'sa
Raikes
Rain'ford
Rain'ham
Rain'hill
Ra'leigh, -legh
Ralph
Ram'eses

Ram'illies
Rams'bottom
Rams'den
Ram'sey
Rams'gate
Ran'dall
Ran'dolph

Rangoon'
Ran'som
Raph'ael
Ra'pin
Ras'selas
Rat'cliffe
Rath'bone
Rath'down
Rathdow'ney
Rath'gar
Rathmines'
Rat'isbon
Ra'venglass
Raven'na
Ra'venscroft
Ra'vensworth
Raw'cliffe
Raw'don
Raw'lings
Raw'linson
Raw'son
Raw'tenstall
Ray'mond
Ray'ner
Reade
Read'ing
Reay
Rebec'ca
Red'bridge
Red'burn
Red'car
Red'fern
Red'gauntlet
Red'grave
Red'hill
Red'land
Red'mond
Red'ruth
Red Sea
Reeves
Reg'gio
Regi'na
Reg'inald
Reid
Rei'gate
Rem'brandt
Rem'ington
Re'mus
Renan'
Ren'del
Rend'ham
René'
Ren'frew
Ren'nell
Ren'nie
Ren'shaw
Ren'wick
Rep'ton
Ret'ford
Reu'ben
Reuss

Reu'ter
Reyk'javik
Reyn'olds
Rheims
Rhine
Rho'da
Rhode'sia
Rhode' I'sland
Rhodes
Rhon'dda
Rhone
Rhys
Rib'chester
Ricar'do
Rich'ard
Rich'ardson
Richelieu'
Rich'mond
Rich'ter
Rick'etts
Rick'mansworth
Ridd'ell
Ridge'mount
Ridge'way
Ridge'well
Rid'ley
Rien'zi
Riev'aulx
Ri'ga
Ril'lington
Ring'wood
Ri'o Janei'ro
Rip'ley
Rip'on
Rit'chie
Rit'son
Rivie'ra
Riv'ington
Riz'zio
Rob'ert
Rob'ertson
Rob'espierre
Rob'in Hood
Rob'inson
Rob Roy
Rob'son
Roch'dale
Rochefort'
Rochefoucauld'
Rochelle', La
Roch'ester
Rock Fer'ry
Rock'hampton
Rock'ingham
Rod'erick
Rodg'er
Rod'ney
Rog'er
Rog'ers
Ro'land
Rollin'

Rome
Ro'meo
Rom'ford
Rom'illy
Rom'ney
Rom'sey
Rom'ulus
Ron'aldshay
Ro'nan, St.
Roose'velt
Ro'per
Ro'sa
Ros'alind
Ros'amond
Roseau'
Ros'cius
Roscoe'
Roscom'mon
Rose'bery
Rosel'la
Roset'ta
Rosh'erville
Ross
Rosset'ti
Rossi'ni
Rosyth'
Roth'erfield
Roth'erham
Roth'erhithe
Rothe'say
Roths'child
Roth'well
Rot'terdam
Rouen'
Rouma'nia
Roume'lia
Rousseau'
Rowe'na
Row'land
Row'ley
Row'ton
Rox'burgh
Rox'bury
Rox'well
Roys'ton
Roy'ton
Rua'bon
Ru'bens
Ru'binstein
Ru'dall
Rudge
Rudg'wick
Ru'dolph
Rud'yard
Ru'fus
Rug'by
Ruge'ley
Rum'ford
Rum'sey
Run'ciman
Run'corn

Run'nymede
Ru'pert
Rush'ington
Rush'ton
Rus'kin

Rus'sell
Rus'sia
Ruth
Ruth'erford
Ruth'erglen
Ru'thin (or)

Ruth'ven
Rut'land
Ryde
Rye
Ry'mer
Rys'wick

S

Saar
Sabi'na
Sachev'erell
Sack'ville
Sad'dleworth
Saf'fron Wal'den
Sag'inaw
Saha'ra
St. John (or)
Sal'adin
Salaman'ca
Sal'amis
Sal'combe
Sa'lem
Saler'no
Sal'ford
Salis'bury
Salee'
Sal'lust
Sal'ly
Salm'on
Salo'me
Saloni'ca
Sal'taire
Salt'ash
Salt'er
Salt'ford
Salt' Lake Cit'y
Salvador'
Salz'burg
Samarkand'
Sama'ria
Samo'a
Sa'mos
Samp'son
Sam'son
Sam'uel
San Anto'nio
San'cho Pan'za
San'croft
Sandakan'
San'dall
San'deman
San'ders
San'derson
Sand'ford

Sand'gate
Sand'hurst
San'diford
San Domin'go
San'down
Sand'ringham
Sand'wich
Sandys
San Francis'co (or)
San José'
San'key
San Re'mo
San Sal'vador
San'ta Cruz
San'ta Fé
Santia'go
Sant'ley
Sapphi'ra
Sapph'o
Saragos'sa
Sa'rah
Saraje'vo
Sarato'ga
Sara'wak
Sardanapa'lus
Sardin'ia
Sark
Sa'rum
Saskatch'ewan
Saul
Saun'ders
Saun'derson
Sauterne'
Savan'nah
Savonaro'la
Savoy'
Saw'bridgeworth
Saw'ston
Saw'try
Saxe-Al'tenburg
Saxe-Co'burg Go'tha
Saxe-Mei'ningen
Saxe-Wei'mar

Sax'mundham
Sax'ony
Sayce
Scal'iger
Scandina'via
Scar'borough
Schaffhau'sen
Schil'ler
Schles'wig
Schoef'fer
Schrevel'ius
Schu'bert
Schus'ter
Schwartz
Schwarz'burg
Schwerin'
Scil'la
Scil'ly Isles
Sci'o
Scip'io
Sclavo'nia
Scot'land
Scott
Scran'ton
Scrym'geour
Scul'coates
Scu'tari
Scyth'ia
Sea'combe
Sea'ford
Sea'forth
Sea'ham
Searle
Sea'ton
Seat'tle
Sebas'tian
Sebas'topol
Sedan'
Sed'berg
Sedge'field
Sedge'moor
Sedg'ley
Sedg'wick
See'ley
Sego'via
Seine
Sel'borne
Sel'by
Sel'den

Seli'na
Sel'kirk
Selous'
Sel'wyn
Semir'amis
Senaar'
Sen'eca
Senegal'
Senegam'bia
Seoul'
Serampore'
Seringapatam
Serve'tus
Ser'via
Seth
Sev'enoaks
Sev'ern
Sev'ille
Sèvres
Seychelles
Sey'mour
Sha'drach
Shad'well
Shaftes'bury
Shak'spere
Shake'speare
Shanghai'
Shan'non
Shap'wick
Shar'land
Sha'ron
Shaw
She'ba
Sheep'shanks
Sheerness'
Shef'field
Shef'ford
Shel'burne
Shel'don
Shel'ley
Shel'ton
Shem
Shen'stone
Shep'pard
Shep'pey
Shep'ton Mal'let
Sher'borne
Sher'idan
Sher'lock
Sher'man
Sher'win
Sher'wood
Shet'land
Shil'lingstone
Ship'ton
Shiraz'
Shir'ley
Shoe'buryness
Shore'ditch
Shore'ham
Shot'ley
Shrews'bury
Shrop'shire
Shuttle'worth
Shy'lock

Siam'
Sibe'ria
Sib'ford
Sic'ily
Sid'bury
Sid'cot
Sid'dons
Sid'mouth
Sid'ney
Si'don
Sie'mens
Sien'a
Sier'ra Leo'ne
Sig'ismund
Sikhs
Sile'sia
Silk'stone
Silva'nus
Sil'verton
Silves'ter
Sil'via
Sim'eon
Sim'kin
Sim'la
Simms
Si'mon
Simp'kin
Sim'plon
Simp'son
Si'nai
Sin'clair
Sin'clairtown
Sind'bad
Sind, Sindh
Singapore'
Sin'gleton
Sing Sing
Si'on
Sioux
Si'rach
Sis'era
Sismon'di
Sis'yphus
Sith'ney
Sit'tingbourne
Ska'raborg
Skeat
Skel'ton
Skibbereen'
Skid'daw
Skin'ner
Skip'ton
Skye
Slade
Slap'ton
Slea'ford
Sles'wick
Sli'go
Sloane
Slo'per
Slough
Small'bridge
Smal'ley
Smar'den
Smea'ton
Smeth'wick
Smith
Smith'ers
Smith'field

Smolensk'
Smol'lett
Smyr'na
Smyth
Snaith
Snel'ling
Snen'ton
Snod'grass
Snow'don
Snow'hill
Soci'nus
Soc'rates
Sod'bury
Sod'om
Sofa'la
Sofi'a
So'ham
So'ho
So'lent
Soleure'
Solihull'
Sol'omon
So'lon
Sol'way Firth
Soma'liland
Som'ers
Som'erset
Som'ersham
Som'erstown
Som'erton
Som'erville
Sophi'a
Soph'ocles
Sophro'nia
So'phy
Soth'eby
Soudan'
South'am
Southamp'ton
South'borough
South'bourne
South Caroli'na
South'cott
South Dako'ta
Southend'
Sou'they
South'gate
South Mol'ton
South'port
South'sea
South Shields
South'wark
South'well
South'wick
South'wold
Sow'erby
Spain
Spal'ding
Spar'ta
Speen
Speen'hamland

Spen'cer
Spen'nithorne
Spen'ser
Spi'cer
Spils'by
Spino'za
Spi'on Kop
Spit'alfields
Spit'head
Spitzberg'en
Spoon'er
Spring'field
Spur'geon
Sta'cey
Staf'fa
Staf'ford
Staines
Stain'land
Stal'bridge
Sta'lybridge
Stamboul'
Stam'ford
Stand'ish
Stand'lake
Stan'field
Stan'ford
Stan'hope
Stan'ley
Stan'ningley
Stan'ton
Stan'well
Sta'plefield
Sta'pleford
Sta'pleton
Star'key
Staun'ton
Stave'ley
Steb'bing
Sted'man
Stel'la
Sten'nett
Ste'phen
Ste'phens
Ste'phens, St.
Ste'phenson
Step'ney
Sterne
Ste'vens
Ste'venson
Ste'venton
Stew'art
Stew'arton
Steyn
Stil'lington
Stil'ton
Stir'ling
Stock'bridge
Stock'holm
Stock'land
Stock'port
Stocks'field
Stock'ton
Stock'well
Stock'with
Stod'dart
Sto'gumber
Stoke
Stoke New'ington
Stokes'ley
Stone
Stone'bridge
Stone'ham
Stone'haven
Stone'henge
Stone'house
Stony'hurst
Stor'noway
Stort'ford
Stoth'ert
Stour
Stour'bridge
Stour'port
Stour'ton
Stow'ell
Stow'market
Strabane'
Stra'bo
Strachan
Stra'chey
Strad'brooke
Straf'ford
Stral'sund
Strang'ford
Stranraer'
Stran'ton
Stras'burg
Strat'ford
Strathco'na
Strat'ton
Strauss
Streat'ham
Stre'litz
Stret'ford
Stret'ton
Strick'land
String'er
Strom'boli
Stromness'
Strood
Stroud
Strutt
Stu'art
Stub'bing
Stubbs
Stud'ley
Stur'minster
Stutt'gart
Styr'ia
Styx
Sua'bia
Sua'kin
Su'cre
Sudan'
Sud'bury
Sude'ley
Sue
Sueto'nius
Su'ez
Suf'folk
Sul'livan
Sul'ly
Suma'tra
Sum'ner
Sun'derland
Surat'
Sur'biton
Surinam'
Sur'rey
Su'san
Susan'na
Sus'sex
Sut'cliffe
Suth'erland
Sut'ton Cold'field
Suva
Swaff'ham
Swain'son
Swam'merdam
Swan'age
Swan'bourne
Swan'sea
Swa'ziland
Swe'den
Swe'denborg
Swin'burne
Swin'don
Swine'fleet
Swin'ey
Swin'ford
Swin'stead
Swin'ton
Swith'in, St.
Swith'un, St.
Swit'zerland
Syd'enham
Syd'ney
Sykes
Syl'la
Syl'via
Sy'monds
Sy'mons
Sy'ra
Syr'acuse
Syr'ia

T

Taba'go
Tabas'co
Tab'itha
Ta'bor
Tac'itus
Tad'caster
Tad'more
Taft
Ta'gus
Tahi'ti
Tain
Tait
Talave'ra
Tal'bot
Talleyrand'
Ta'mar
Tamerlane'
Tam'worth
Tam'many
Tanganyi'ka
Tangier'
Tang'ye
Tanjore'
Tan'talus
Tap'lin
Ta'ranto
Tar'land
Tarle'ton
Tarn
Tar'porley
Tar'quin
Tar'rant
Tar'sus
Tar'tary
Tar'vin
Tasma'nia
Tas'so
Tate
Tat'tenhall
Tat'tersall
Tauch'nitz
Taun'ton
Tav'erner
Tav'istock
Ta'vy
Tay
Tay'ler
Tay'lor
Ted
Tees
Teheran'
Teign'mouth
Tel-el-Kebir'
Telem'achus
Tel'ford
Tell
Tem'pe
Tem'pleton
Ten'bury
Ten'by
Teneriffe'
Ten'nent
Tennessee'
Ten'niel
Ten'nyson
Ten'terden
Ter'ence
Terpsich'ore
Terr'a del Fue'go
Ter'ry
Tertul'lian
Tet'bury
Tewkes'bury
Tex'as
Tex'el
Thack'eray
Tha'les
Thame
Thames
Than'et
Thatch'am
Thebes
Thel'wall
Themis'tocles
The'obald
Theoc'ritus
Theodo'ra
The'odore
Theod'oret
Theodo'sia
Theodo'sius
Theoph'ilus
There'sa
Thermop'ylæ
Thes'saly
Thet'ford
Thibet', Tibet'
Thiers'
Thirsk
Thom'as
Thom'asine
Thomp'son
Thom'son
Thor
Thorn'aby
Thorn'bury
Thorne
Thor'ney
Thorn'hill
Thorn'ley
Thorn'ton
Thorpe
Thrap'stone
Thucyd'ides
Thur'low
Thur'so
Thwaites
Ti'ber
Tibe'rias
Tibe'rius
Tibet', Thibet'
Tibul'lus
Tice'hurst
Tich'borne
Tich'field
Tick'ell
Tid'denham
Tid'dington
Tides'well
Tien' Tsin
Ti'gris
Til'bury
Til'ley
Tillicoul'try
Til'lingham
Til'lotson
Timbuc'too
Timbuk'tu
Timo'leon
Ti'mon
Tim'othy
Tims'bury
Tin'dal
Tintag'el
Tippera'ry
Tippoo Sah'ib
Tip'ton
Tita'nia
Ti'tian
Ti'tus
Tiv'erton
Tiv'oli
Toba'go
Tobi'as
To'bit
Tobolsk'
To'by
Todd
Tod'morden

To'go
Tokay'
To'kyo
Tole'do
Tolle'mache
Tol'stoi
Tom
Tom'kins
Tom'linson
Tomp'kins
Ton'bridge
Ton'ga
Tongata'bu
Tonquin'
To'ny
Tooke
Toot'ing
Top'lady
Tops'ham
Top'sy
Torbay'
Tor'nea
Toron'to
Torquay'
Tor'rington
Torto'la
Tortu'ga
Tort'worth
Tot'nes
Tot'tenham
Tot'tington
Toulon'
Toulouse'
Tournay' / Tournai'
Tours
Towces'ter
Town'er
Town'ley
Towns'end

Tox'teth
Toyn'bee
Tra'cey
Trafal'gar
Tra'jan
Tralee'
Tran'mere
Transvaal'
Transylva'nia
Trapp
Travancore'
Treb'izond
Tred'egar
Trelaw'ny
Tren'chard
Trent
Trent'ham
Tren'ton
Trevel'yan
Treves
Trev'ithick
Tre'vor
Trichinop'oly
Triest', Trieste'
Tring
Trinidad'
Trip'oli
Tristan' da Cun'ha
Tris'tram
Tro'ilus
Trol'lope
Tromp
Tros'sachs
Trow'bridge
Troy
True'man
Trum'pington
Tru'ro
Truxil'lo
Tu'am
Tü'bingen

Tuck'er
Tud'denham
Tu'dor
Tuil'leries
Tullamore'
Tul'loch
Tul'ly
Tun'bridge Wells
Tu'nis
Tun'stall
Tup'per
Tu'rin
Turkestan'
Tur'key
Turn'bull
Tur'ner
Tur'pin
Tur'vey
Tur'ville
Tus'cany
Tussaud'
Tux'ford
Tweed
Tweed'mouth
Twer'ton
Twick'enham
Twi'ning
Twy'ford
Ty'burn
Tyldes'ley
Ty'ler
Tyn'dale / Tyn'dall
Tyne
Tyne'mouth
Tyr'ol
Tyrone'
Tyr'rel
Tyr'whitt
Ty'ssen
Tyt'ler

U

Ugan'da
Uist
Uji'ji
U'kraine
Ulles'thorpe
Ulls'water
Ulm
Ul'ster
Ul'verstone
Ulys'ses
U'na
Un'derwood

Undine'
Uni'ted States
Un'terwalden
Un'win
Up'ham
Up'hill
Upperkirk'gate
Up'pingham
Upsa'la

Up'ton-on-Sev'ern
Up'well
U'ral
Ur'ban
Ure
U'ri
Uri'ah
Urqu'hart
Ur'sula
Uruguay'
Ush'ant

Usk
Us'worth
U'tah
U'tica
U'trecht
Uttox'eter
Ux'bridge

V

Valais'
Valdiv'ia
Valence'
Valen'cia / Valen'tia
Val'entine
Valentin'ian
Vale'rius Maxi'mus
Valet'ta
Valladolid'
Valparai'so
Val'py
Van'brugh
Vance
Vancou'ver
Van'derbilt
Van Die'men's Land
Vandyke'
Vaughan
Vaux
Vauxhall'
Vav'asour
Ven'ables
Vendée'
Venezue'la
Ven'ice
Vent'nor
Ve'ra Cruz
Verd, Cape
Vermont'
Ver'non
Vero'na
Versailles'
Ver'ulam
Verviers'
Vespa'sian
Vesu'vius
Vick'ers
Vick'ery
Vic'tor
Vien'na
Vienne'
Villiers'
Vince
Vin'cent
Vines
Vi'ning
Vi'ola
Vir'gil
Virgin'ia
Virgin'ius
Vis'tula
Viv'ian / Viv'ien
Vizagapatam'
Vlad'imir
Vol'ga
Vol'ney
Volog'da
Voltaire'
Vosges
Voules
Vul'can

W

Wace
Wad'dington
Wade'bridge
Wad'ham
Wag'ner
Wag'staff
Wain'wright
Wake'field
Wake'ford
Wal'brook
Wal'cot
Wal'deck
Wal'degrave
Wal'denburg
Wales
Wal'ford
Walk'er
Walk'ingham
Wal'lace
Walla'chia
Wal'lasey
Wal'ler
Wal'lingford
Wal'lis
Walls'end
Wal'mer
Wal'mersley
Walmes'ley
Wal'pole
Wal'sall
Walsh
Wal'sham
Wal'singham
Wal'ter
Wal'tham
Wal'thamstow
Wal'ton
Wal'worth
Wands'worth
Wans'ford
Wan'tage
Wap'ping
War'beck
War'borough
War'burton
Ward
Ward'law
Ward'leworth
Ware
Ware'ham
War'grave
Wark'worth
War'lingham

War'minster
Warm'ley
War'ner
Warn'ford
War'ren
War'rington
War'saw
War'ton
War'wick
Wash'burne
Wash'ington
Wat
Wa'terbury
Wa'terford
Wa'terhouse
Waterloo'
Wa'terworth
Wat'ford
Wat'kins
Wat'son
Watt
Watteau'
Wat'ton
Watts
Wau'chope
Waugh
Wa'verley
Wear'mouth
Wea'verhead
Wea'vertree
Webb
Web'ber
We'ber
Web'ster
Wedg'wood
Wed'more
Wednes'bury
Wee'don
Weeks
Wei'-hai-wei
Wei'mar
Wel'bury
Welch
Wel'don
Wel'ford
Wel'ler
Welles'ley
Well'ingborough
Wel'lington
Wells
Welsh'pool
Wem
Wemyss
Wen'dover
Wen'lock
Went'worth
Wer'ner
Wert'heim
Wer'ther
Wes'ley
West'acott
West'bourne
West'bury
West'cott
West'field
West'gate
West In'dies
West'lake
West'land
West'ley
West'macott
West'meath
West'minster
West'morland
Wes'ton
Wes'ton-su'per-Mare
Westpha'lia
West'port
West Virgin'ia
Weth'erell
Wex'ford
Wey'man
Wey'mouth
Whal'ley
Whal'ton
Wharn'cliffe
Whar'ton
Whate'ly
Wheel'er
Whis'ton
Whit'aker
Whit'bread
Whit'by
Whit'church
White'chapel
White'hall
Whiteha'ven
White'head
White'house
Whit'field
Whit'horn
Whit'ley
Whit'man
Whit'minster
Whit'more
Whit'ney
Whit'taker
Whit'tier
Whit'tingham
Whit'tington
Whit'tlesea
Whit'wick
Wick
Wick'ham
Wick'low
Wic'liffe
Wid'combe
Wid'nes
Wiesba'den
Wig'an
Wight
Wight'man
Wig'ram
Wig'toft
Wigton' / Wig'town
Wil'berforce
Wil'cox
Wil'ford
Wil'frid
Wilhelmi'na
Wilkes
Wilkes'-Barre
Wil'kie
Wil'kins
Wil'kinson
Will
Wil'lenhall
Willes'den
Will'iam
Will'iams
Will'iamsburg
Will'iamson
Wil'lingdon
Wil'lingham
Wil'lington
Wil'lis
Will'oughby
Wills'bridge
Wil'ly
Wil'mington
Wil'mot
Wilms'low
Wil'na
Wil'son
Wil'ton
Wilt'shire
Wim'bledon
Wim'borne
Wincan'ton
Win'chelsea
Win'chester
Winch'more
Winck'worth
Win'dermere
Wind'ham
Wind'sor
Win'ford
Win'gate
Wing'field
Wing'ham
Win'grove
Win'ifred
Win'kle
Wink'ton
Win'laton
Winn'ipeg
Wins'low
Win'ster
Win'ston
Win'terbourne
Winter'ton
Win'wick

Wirks'worth
Wis'bech
Wiscon'sin
Wise'man
With'am
With'ers
Wit'ney
Wit'tenberg
Wi'tu
Wo'burn
Wode'house
Wo'king
Wo'kingham
Wol'ga
Wol'laston
Wolse'ley
Wol'sey
Wol'singham
Wol'stanton
Wolverhamp'ton
Wol'verton
Wol'viston
Womb'well

Wood'bridge
Wood'bury
Wood'church
Wood'fall
Wood'ford
Wood'side
Wood'stock
Wood'ward
Woolhamp'ton
Wool'ley
Wool'los
Wool'ston
Wool'wich
Woot'ton
Woot'ton Bas'sett
Worces'ter
Worces'tershire
Words'ley
Words'worth
Working'ton
Work'sop
Wor'lington
Wor'lingworth
Wor'num
Wors'borough

Wors'ley
Wor'then
Wor'thing
Wor'thington
Wot'ton-*un'der*-Edge
Wrag'by
Wray
Wren
Wren'bury
Wren'tham
Wrex'ham
Wring'ton
Wroth'am
Wur'temberg
Wurz'burg
Wy'att
Wych'erley
Wyc'lif
Wyc'ombe
Wye
Wymond'ham
Wynd'ham
Wynn
Wyo'ming

X

Xan'adu
Xan'thus
Xantip'pe
Xav'ier

Xe'nia
Xen'ocles
Xenoc'rates
Xen'ophon

Xe'res
Xerx'es
Xul'la
Xu'ry

Y

Yale
Yar'borough
Yard'ley
Yar'mouth
Yar'row
Yates
Yat'ton
Yax'ley
Yeats
Yel'lowstone
Yem'en

Yenise'i
Yeo'vil
Yer'burgh
Yokoha'ma
Yon'kers
Yor'ick
York
Yosem'ite
Yost

Yough'al
Youl'grave
Young
Young'husband
Youngs'town
Yox'all
Yox'ford
Yucatan'
Yu'kon
Y'verdon
Yvetot'

Z

Zach
Zacche'us
Zachari'ah
Zach'ary
Zad'kiel
Za'dok
Zambe'si
Zamen'hof
Zang'will
Zan'te

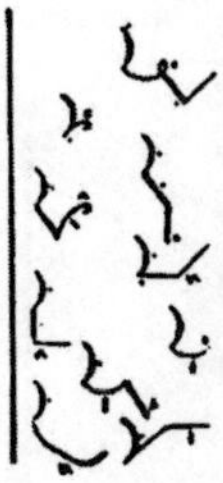

Zan'zibar
Zea'land
Zeb'edee
Zeb'ulon
Zechari'ah
Zedeki'ah
Ze'no
Zeno'bia
Zephani'ah
Zercho

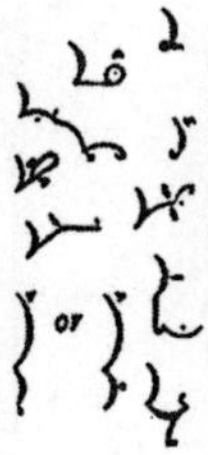

Zeus
Zeux'is
Zim'mermann
Zi'on
Zoroas'ter
Zu'luland
Zu'rich
Zut'phen
Zuyder' Zee
Zwing'li

Full List of Grammalogues

A

a *or* an
accord-ing
advantage
ah!
all
and
any
are
as
aught
awe
aye

B

balance
be
because
been
behalf
belief-ve-d
beyond
build-ing
but

C

call
called
can
cannot
care
cared
chair
chaired
cheer
cheered
child
circumstance
cold
come
could

D

dear
deliver-ed-y
deliverance
difference-t
difficult
do
doctor, Dr.
during

E

eh?
equal-ly
equalled

F

first
for
from

G

general-ly
generalization
gentleman
gentlemen
give-n
go
gold
great
guard

H

had
hand
has
have
he
him
himself
his
hour
how
however

I

importance-ant
impossible
improve-d-ment
in
influence
influenced
information
inscribe-d
inscription
instruction
instructive
is
it
itself

J

justification

L

language
large
largely
larger
liberty
Lord

M

me
member
mere
more
most
Mr.
much
myself

N

near
next
nor
northern
number-ed

O

O! oh!
of
on
opinion
opportunity
ought
our
ourselves
over
owe
owing
own

P

particular
people
pleasure
principal-ly
principle
put

Q

quite

R

rather
remark-ed
remember-ed

S

satisfaction
school
schooled
selfish-ness
sent
several
shall, shalt
short
should
significance
significant
signification
signify-ied
southern
speak
special-ly
spirit
subject-ed
subjection
subjective
sure
surprise
surprised

T

tell
thank-ed
that
the
their
them
themselves
there
therefore
thing
think
third
this
those
though
thus
thyself
till
to
to be
told
too
toward
towards
trade
tried
truth
two

U

under
usual-ly

V

- valuation
- very

W

- was
- we
- what
- when
- whether
- which
- who
- whose
- why
- wish
- wished
- with
- within
- without
- wonderful-ly
- word
- would
- writer

Y

- yard
- year
- you
- young
- your

Contractions

A

abandonment
acknowledge
administrator
administratrix
advertise-d-ment
altogether
amalgamate
amalgamation
anything
appointment
arbitrary
arbitrate
arbitration
arbitrator
architect-ure-al
assignment
attainment

B

bankruptcy

C

capable
certificate
character
characteristic
circumstantial
commercial-ly
contentment
contingency
cross-examination
cross-examine-d

D

danger
dangerous
defective
deficient-ly-cy
demonstrate
denomination-al
description
destruction
destructive
destructively
difficulty
discharge-d
distinguish-ed

E

efficient-ly-cy
electric
electrical
electricity
emergency
England
English
Englishman
enlarge
enlarger
enlightenment
entertainment
enthusiastic-iasm
especial-ly
esquire
establish-ed-ment
everything
exchange-d
executive
executor
executrix
exigency
expect-ed
expediency
expenditure
expensive
extinguish-ed

F

falsification
familiar-ity
familiarization
familiarize
February
financial-ly

G

govern-ed
Government

H

henceforward
howsoever

I

identical
identification
immediate
imperfect-ion-ly

imperturbable
incandescence
incandescent
inconsiderate
inconvenience-t-ly
incorporated
independent-ly-ce
indispensable-ly
individual-ly
influential-ly
inform-ed
informer
inspect-ed-ion
insurance
intelligence
intelligent-ly
intelligible-ly
interest
introduction
investigation
investment
ironmonger
irrecoverable-ly
irregular
irremovable-ly
irrespective
irrespectively
irresponsible-ility

J

January
jurisdiction

K

knowledge

L

legislative
legislature

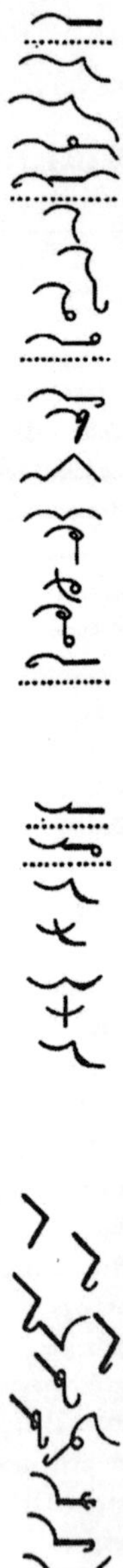

M

magnetic-ism
manufacture-d
manufacturer
manuscript
marconigram
mathematical-ly
mathematician
mathematics
maximum
mechanical-ly
messenger
metropolitan
minimum
ministry
misfortune
monstrous
mortgage-d

N

neglect-ed
negligence
never
nevertheless
nothing
notwithstanding
November

O

object-ed
objection
objectionable
objective
obstruction
obstructive
oneself
organization
organize-d
organizer

P

parliamentary
passenger
peculiar-ity
perform-ed
performance
performer
perpendicular
perspective
practicable
practice
practise-d
prejudice-d-ial-ly
preliminary
probable-ly-ility
production
productive
proficient-ly-cy
project-ed
proportion-ed
proportionate-ly
prospect
prospective
prospectus
public
publication
publish-ed
publisher

Q

questionable-ly

R

ratepayers
recoverable
reform-ed
reformer
regular
relinquish-ed
remarkable-ly

remonstrance
remonstrate
removable
represent-ed
representation
representative
republic
republican
respect-ed
responsible-ility
retrospect
retrospection
retrospective

S

satisfactory
sensible-ly-ility
something
stranger
stringency
subscribe-d
subscription
substantial-ly
sufficient-ly-cy
suspect-ed
sympathetic

T

telegram
telegraphic
thankful-ly
thenceforward
together

U

unanimity
unanimous-ly
uniform-ity-ly
universal-ly
universality
universe
university
unprincipled

W

whatever
whenever
whensoever
whereinsoever
wheresoever
whithersoever

Y

yesterday

Phrase Logograms

able to
according to
as has
as is
at all
at once
by all
did not
do not
from it
had been
had not
have been
if it
in order
in order to
in our
is as
is his
may not
out of
they are
till it
which have

Latin Prefixes

LATIN	MEANING	EXAMPLE
A-, ab-, abs- . .	from; away	avert; abduct; abstract
Ad- (taking by assimilation the forms, ac-, af-, ag-, al-, an-, ap-, ar-, as-, at-)	to; at	adhere; accede; affirm; aggregate; allude; annex; applaud; arrogant; assume; attribute.
Amb-, ambi- . .	on both sides	ambitious; ambidextrous.
Ante- . . .	before	antedate; antecedent.
Bi-, bis- . . .	twice; two ways; double	biennial; biscuit.
Circum- . . .	around; all round	circumspect.
Cis- . . .	on this side of	cisalpine.
Com-, col-, con-, cor-, co-	with; together; altogether (intensively)	combine; collect; connect; correspond; co-exist.
Contra-, contro-; Gallicized into counter-	against against	contradict; controvert. counterfeit.
De-	down; from; off	deduce.
Demi- . . .	half	demi-semiquaver, demi-god.
Dis-, di-, dif- . .	apart; asunder; not	disarm; divulge; differ.
Ex-,	out of; out; from	exacerbate.
e- before *d, l, m, n,*		educe; elucidate; emanate; enervate.
ef- before *f*		effect.
Equi- . . .	equally	equidistant.
Extra- . . .	beyond; without	extraordinary; extrajudicial.
In-	in; into; on; against	include.
Modified into		
il- before *l* .	(used with Verb)	illuminate.
im- before *m, p*	(used with Verb)	immure.
Gallicized into em-, en-		employ; enact.
In- before *h* and vowels	not	inhuman.
Modified into		
il- before *l* .	(used with Adj.)	illegal.
im- before *m* .	(used with Adj.)	immeasurable.
ir- before *r* .		irrational.
Inter-	between	intercede.
Gallicized into enter-	among	entertain.
Intro- . . .	within	introduce.
Juxta- . . .	near; nigh	juxtaposition

LATIN	MEANING	EXAMPLE
Mal- / Male- . . .	ill; badly	maladministration. / malefactor.
Manu- . . .	hand	manuscript.
Non- . . .	not	nonentity.
Ob- . . .	against; in front of	obstacle.
Modified into		
oc- before *c* .		occurrence.
of- before *f* .		offend.
op- before *p* .		opposition.
Omni- . . .	all	omniscient.
Per- . . .	through; thoroughly	perforate.
Post- . . .	after	post-mortem.
Pre- . . .	before	precede.
Preter- . . .	beyond; past	preternatural.
Pro- . . .	before; forth; torward	proceed
Gallicized into pur-		purpose.
Re-, red- . . .	back; again	rehearse; redeem.
Retro- . . .	backwards	retrospective.
Se-	apart	seclusion.
Semi- . . .	half	semicircle.
Sub- . . .	under	subject
Modified into		
suc- before *c* .		succour.
suf- before *f* .		suffice.
sug- before *g* .		suggest.
sup- before *p* .		support.
sur- before *r* .		surrender.
su(s)- before *s* .		su(s)-pect.
Super- . . .	above	superabundant.
Gallicized into sur- .		surfeit.
Trans-, tra- . .	across	transport; tramontane.
Gallicized into tres-		trespass.
Tri-	thrice	tricolour.
Ultra- . . .	beyond; advance	ultramarine.
Uni- . . .	one	university; uniform.

Greek Prefixes

GREEK	MEANING	EXAMPLE
A-	no; without	amorphous; apathy.
Modified into an- before vowels		anarchy; anonymous.
Amphi-	about; around; on both sides	amphitheatre; amphibious.
Ana-	up; through; according to	analogy, analysis.
Ant-, anti-	against; opposite to	antagonist; antiseptic; antipodes.
Apo-, aph-	away; apart; off	apostrophe; apostle; aphelion.
Arch-, archi-	chief; head; ruling	archbishop; architect.
Auto-	self	autograph, autobiography.
auth-, aut-, before a vowel	oneself	authentic; autopsy.
Cata-, cath-, cat-	down; through; according to	catastrophe; cathedral; cataract; categorical.
Deca-	ten	decagon; decametre.
Di-	two; double	dilemma; dimorphous; di(s)syllable.
Dia-	through; between	dialogue; diameter; diadem.
Dys-	bad; ill	dysentery; dyspeptic.
Ec-	out; forth	eclipse; ecstasy; eccentric.
Modified into ex- before a vowel		exodus.
En-	in; on	encomium; enthusiasm.
Modified into em- before *b*, *p*		emblem; emphasis.
el- before *l*		elliptical.
Endo-	within	endogenous; endogamous.
Epi-	upon; over	epistle; epitaph.
Modified into ep- before a vowel or *h*		epigram; epoch; ephemeral.
Eu-	well	eulogy; euphony.
Exo-	outside	exogenous; exotic.
Hemi-	half	hemisphere.
Hexa-	six	hexameter, hexagon.
Hetero-	other; different	heterodox; heterogeneous.
Hepta-	seven	heptagon.
Hier-	sacred	hierarchy.

GREEK	MEANING	EXAMPLE
Holo- . . .	whole; entire	holocaust.
Homo- . . .	same; similar; together	homonym; homogeneous.
Hyper- . . .	over; beyond; too	hyperborean; hypercritical.
Hypo- . . .	under; beneath	hypocrite; hypotenuse. hypothesis.
Modified into hyp- before *h* . .		hyphen.
Meta- . . .	beyond; after (denoting change)	metathesis; metaphor.
met- before vowel or *h* . . .		method; metonymy.
Mono- . . .	alone	monograph; monogram.
Modified into mon- before a vowel .		monarch; monk.
Ortho- . . .	right	orthoepy; orthography.
Oxy- . . .	sharp; acid	oxytone; oxygen.
Modified into ox- before a vowel .		oxalic.
Pan-, panto . .	all	Pan-Anglican; panoply; pantomime; panorama.
Para- . . .	beside	parasite; paraphrase.
Modified into par- before a vowel .		parable; paragraph; parallel.
Penta- . . .	five	pentameter.
Peri- . . .	round; around	perimeter; periphrasis; period.
Philo- . . .	love; loving	philology; philosopher.
Modified into phil- before a vowel .		philanthropy.
Poly- . . .	many	polyarchy; polygamy; polysyllable; polygon.
Pro- . . .	before	prophecy; programme; prologue.
Pros- . . .	towards	proselyte.
Pseudo- . . .	false	pseudo-metallic.
Modified into pseud- before a vowel .		pseudonym.
Syn- . . .	with	synthesis; synchronize.
Modified into		
syl- before *l* .		syllabus.
sym- before *b, m, p*		symbol; symmetry; sympathy.
sy- before *s, z* .		system; syzygy.
Tele- . . .	afar	telegram; telephone; telepathy; telescope.
Tri-	thrice; three	tripod; trigonometry; trihedral; trisyllable.

Commercial Terms and Phrases in Five Languages

Accept a Bill. *Fr.*, Accepter un billet, un effet; *Ger.*, einen Wechsel acceptieren; *Sp.*, Aceptar una letra de cambio; *Ital.*, Accettare una cambiale.

Acceptance for Honour. *Fr.*, Acceptation par honneur; *Ger.*, Ehrenannahme; *Sp.*, Aceptación por el honor de firma; *Ital.*, Accettazione per onor di firma.

Acceptance Supra Protest. *Fr.*, Acceptation par intervention; *Ger.*, Annahme (das Accept) per Intervention; *Sp.*, Aceptación por intervención; *Ital.*, Accettazione per intervento.

Accommodation Bill. (Sometimes called a " Kite"). *Fr.*, Billet de Complaisance; *Ger.*, Gefälligkeitswechsel; *Sp.*, Letra de acomodación; *Ital.*, Cambiale di Favore.

Account Days. *Fr.*, Jours de règlement, jours de paie, de liquidation; *Ger.*, Abrechnungstage, Zahltage, Liquidationstage, Skontrotage; *Sp.*, Dias de liquidación, de pago, de ajuste de cuentas; *Ital.*, Giorni di liquidazione.

Act of Bankruptcy. *Fr.*, Acte qui entraîne l'état de faillite; *Ger.*, Konkursgesetz; *Sp.*, Acto que constituye el estado de quiebra; *Ital.*, Atto che provoca o genera il fallimento.

" Act of God." *Fr.*, Acte de Dieu; *Ger.*, Fügungen Gottes; *Sp.*, Acto de Dios; *Ital.*, Caso fortuito.

Advice Note. *Fr.*, Note d'avis; *Ger.*, Benachrichtigungszettel; *Sp.*, Nota de aviso; *Ital.*, Biglietto d'avviso.

Agent. (*Lat.*, agens, agentis, present participle of ago, I do). *Fr.*, Représentant; *Ger.*, Agent; *Sp.*, Representante; *Ital.*, Agente, Rappresentante.

Agio. (Exchange, Discount). *Fr.*, *Ger.*, and *Sp.*, Agio; *Ital.*, Aggio.

Allotment. *Fr.*, Répartition; *Ger.*, Zuteilung; *Sp.*, Distribución; *Ital.*, Aggiudicazione, Assegnazione.

All Rights Reserved. *Fr.*, Tous droits reservés; *Ger.*, Alle Rechte vorbehalten; *Sp.*, Derechos de propiedad; *Ital.*, Riservati tutti i diritti.

Amalgamation. *Fr.*, Réunion, fusion; *Ger.*, Vereinigung, Amalgamierung; *Sp.*, Fusión, amalgamación; *Ital.*, Unione, fusione.

Ante-date. (*Lat.*, ante, before, and date). *Fr.*, Antidater; *Ger.*, vordatieren; *Sp.*, Anticipar la fecha; *Ital.*, Antidatare.

Articles of Association. *Fr.*, Statuts sociaux; *Ger.*, Gesellschaftsstatuten; *Sp.*, Artículos de asociación; *Ital.*, Statuto o Atto constitutivo della Società.

Assets. (*Lat.*, ad, to, and satis, enough). *Fr.*, Actif; *Ger.*, Activa; *Sp.*, Activo; *Ital.*, Attivo, Sostanze attive.

At Call. *Fr.*, À l'appel; *Ger.*, Auf Verlangen; *Sp.*, Á la demanda; *Ital.*, Alla domanda.

At Sight. *Fr.*, À vue; *Ger.*, a vista; *Sp.*, Á la vista; *Ital.*, A vista o a presentazione.

Audit. (*Lat.*, auditus, a hearing). *Fr.*, Audition; *Ger.*, Bücherrevision; *Sp.*, Ajuste de cuentas; *Ital.*, Verifica, Revisione di Conti.

Average. *Fr.*, Moyenne; *Ger.*, Durchschnitt; *Sp.*, Por medio; *Ital.*, Media, Ragguaglio.

Average Clause. *Fr.*, Clause de jet à la mer; *Ger.*, Havarieklausel; *Sp.*, Cláusula de avería; *Ital.*, Clausola di Avaria.

Backwardation. *Fr.*, Déport; *Ger.*, Deportgeschäft; *Sp.*, Interés que paga el bajista; *Ital.*, Deporto, Interesse pagato da chi giuoca al ribasso.

Balance Sheet. *Fr.*, Bilan; *Ger.*, Rechnungsabschluss; *Sp.*, Hoja del saldo; *Ital.*, Bilancio, Specchio Dell'Attivo e Passivo.

Bank Charter. *Fr.*, Privilège de la Banque; *Ger.*, Bankprivilegium; *Sp.*, Privilegio de Banco; *Ital.*, Privilegio della Banca.

Bankers' Clearing House. *Fr.* Comptoir général de virement, Chambre de liquidation; *Ger.*, Abrechnungsstelle; *Sp.*, Inspección de Liquidaciones; *Ital.*, Stanza di Compensazione dei Banchieri.

Bank Notes. *Fr.*, Billets de Banque; *Ger.*, Banknoten; *Sp.*, Billetes de Banco; *Ital.*, Biglietti di Banca, Banconote.

Bank Rate. *Fr.*, Taux; *Ger.*, Bankdiskont; *Sp.*, Tipo Bancario; *Ital.*, Tasso, Sconto della Banca.

Bankrupt. (From bank, a bench, and the *Lat.*, ruptus, broken). *Fr.*, Failli; *Ger.*, Bankrottierer; *Sp.*, Quebrado; *Ital.*, Fallito, Bancarottiere.

Barter. *Fr.*, Troquer; *Ger.*, Tauschhandel; *Sp.*, Baratar; *Ital.*, Barattare, Scambiare, Permutare merci.

Beerbohm's List. *Fr.*, Liste de Beerbohm; *Ger.*, Beerbohm's Liste; *Sp.*, Lista de Beerbohm; *Ital.*, Listino di Beerbohm.

Bill. *Fr.*, Note; *Ger.*, Nota, Schein; *Sp.*, Letra; *Ital.*, Cambiale, Cedola, Conto.

Bill Brokers. *Fr.*, Courtiers de change; *Ger.*, Wechselmakler; *Sp.*, Corredores de Letras; *Ital.*, Mediatori, Agenti di Cambio.

Bill of Exchange (B/E). *Fr.*, Lettre de Change; *Ger.*, Wechsel; *Sp.*, Letra de Cambio; *Ital.*, Lettera di Cambio, Cambiale.

Bill of Lading (B/L). *Fr.*, Connaissement; *Ger.*, Konnossement; *Sp.*, Conocimiento; *Ital.*, Polizza di carico.

Bill of Sale (B/S). *Fr.*, Contrat de vente; *Ger.*, Verkaufsbrief; *Sp.*, Escritura de venta; *Ital.*, Scrittura o Polizza di vendita, Ipoteca su merci.

Bonâ fide. *Fr.*, De bonne foi; *Ger.*, Bona fide; *Sp.*, De buena fé; *Ital.*, Bona Fide, In buona fede.

Book-keeping. *Fr.*, Comptabilité; *Ger.*, Buchführung; *Sp.*, Teneduría de Libros; *Ital.*, Contabilità, Ragioneria.

Broker. *Fr.*, Courtier; *Ger.*, Makler; *Sp.*, Corredor; *Ital.*, Mediatore, Sensale.

Bull. *Fr.*, Haussier; *Ger.*, Haussier; *Sp.*, Alcista; *Ital.*, Giuocatore di Borsa al rialzo.

Call (Stock Exchange). *Fr.*, Droit d'achat, prime; *Ger.*, Prämiengeschäft; *Sp.*, Derecho de Compra; *Ital.*, Diritti di compra.

Call (Companies). *Fr.*, Appel de fonds; *Ger.*, Einzahlungsaufforderung; *Sp.*, Citación; *Ital.*, Citazione, Richiesta di fondi.

Call Money. *Fr.*, Emprunt remboursable sur demande; *Ger.*, tägliches Geld; *Sp.*, Dinero en depósito para retirarlo sobre demanda; *Ital.*, Prestito rimborsabile a domanda.

Case of Need. *Fr.*, Au besoin; *Ger.*, Notadresse; *Sp.*, En caso necesario; *Ital.*, In caso di bisogno.

Charges Forward. *Fr.*, Port dû; *Ger.*, unter Nachnahme; *Sp.*, Gastos á pagar; *Ital.*, Spedizione contro Assegno, Spese di Assegno.

Chartered Accountant (C/A). *Fr.*, Expert-comptable; *Ger.*, behördlicher Bücherrevisor; *Sp.*, Perito mercantil; *Ital.*, Contabile approvato, patentato, Perito.

Charterer. *Fr.*, Fréteur, affréteur; *Ger.*, Befrachter; *Sp.*, Fletador; *Ital.*, Noleggiatore.

Charter Party (C/P). *Fr.*, Charte-partie (a document which can be divided into two parts); *Ger.*, Certepartie; *Sp.*, Póliza de fletamento; *Ital.*, Contratto di Noleggio.

Cheque (Chq.). *Fr.*, Chèque; *Ger.*, Check; *Sp.*, Cheque; *Ital.*, Cheque, Vaglia bancario, Assegno bancario.

Cheque Books. *Fr.*, Carnet de chèques; *Ger.*, Checkbuch; *Sp.*, Libros talonarios; *Ital.*, Libri degli Assegni, vaglia bancari.

A Cheque to Bearer. *Fr.*, Chèque non barré, au porteur; *Ger.*, Inhabercheck; *Sp.*, Cheque ó talon al portador; *Ital.*, Assegno, Cheque al portatore.

Clearing Banks. *Fr.*, Banques de virement; *Ger.*, Girobanken; *Sp.*, Bancos de liquidación; *Ital.*, Banche iscritte alla Stanza di Compensazione.

Commandite. Société en, or Partnership in (*Fr.*); *Ger.*, Kommanditgesellschaft; *Sp.*, Comandita; *Ital.*, Società in accomandita.

Commercial Crisis. *Fr.*, Crise commerciale; *Ger.*, Handelskrise; *Sp.*, Crisis comercial; *Ital.*, Crisi commerciale.

Committee. *Fr.*, Comité; *Ger.*, Komité, Ausschuss; *Sp.*, Comité; *Ital.*, Comitato.

Committee of Inspection. *Fr.*, Comité d'inspection; *Ger.*, Glaübigerausschuss; *Sp.*, Comité de Inspección; *Ital.*, Comitato d'Ispezione.

Company Promoter. *Fr.*, Promoteur d'une société; *Ger.*, Gründer einer Gesellschaft; *Sp.*, Fundador (promovedor) de una sociedad; *Ital.*, Promotore (fondatore) d'una società.

Consignment. *Fr.*, Consignation; *Ger.*, Konsignation; *Sp.*, Consignación; *Ital.*, Invio, Spedizione.

Consular Invoices. *Fr.*, Factures consulaires; *Ger.*, Konsulatsfakturen; *Sp.*, Facturas consulares; *Ital.*, Fatture vistate dal Console.

Contango. *Fr.*, Report; *Ger.*, Report; *Sp.*, Reporte; *Ital.*, Interesse o Premio per il Riporto.

Contingent Liability. *Fr.*, Responsabilité éventuelle; *Ger.*, Eventuelle Verantwortlichkeit; *Sp.*, Responsabilidad eventual; *Ital.*, Risponsabilità eventuale.

Corner. *Fr.*, Accaparement, Corner; *Ger.*, Corner, Kneife; *Sp.*, Acaparamiento, corner; *Ital.*, Accaparramento, Corner.

Cost and Freight (C. & F.). *Fr.*, Coût et frêt; *Ger.*, Kost und Fracht; *Sp.*, Costo y flete; *Ital.*, Spesa di Costo e nolo.

Cost, Freight, and Insurance (C.I.F. or C.F.I.). *Fr.*, Coût, frêt, et assurance (c.f.i. or c.i.f.); *Ger.*, Kost, Fracht und Assekuranz; *Sp.*, Costo, flete y seguro; *Ital.*, Costo nolo e assicurazione.

Costing. *Fr.*, Trouver le coût; *Ger.*, Den Kostpreis herausziehen; *Sp.*, Halar el costo; *Ital.*, Trovare il costo.

Crédit Mobilier, Société générale de. *Fr.*, Crédit Mobilier; *Ger.*, Mobiliarbank; *Sp.*, Crédito Mobiliario; *Ital.*, Società generale di Credito mobiliare.

Crossed Cheque. *Fr.*, Chèque barré; *Ger.*, gekreuzter Check; *Sp.*, Cheque Cruzado; *Ital.*, Cheque barrato.

Cum Dividend. *Fr.*, Dividende compris; *Ger.*, inklusive Dividende; *Sp.*, Dividendo incluso; *Ital.*, Col Dividendo.

Cumulative Preference Stocks and Shares. *Fr.*, Actions privilégiées cumulatives; *Ger.*, Aktien mit hinzugefügten Dividenden; *Sp.*, Valores cumulativos de prioridad; *Ital.*, Azioni e Titole cumulativi privilegiati.

Currency (from the *Lat.*, curro, I flow, or run). *Fr.*, Monnaie légale; *Ger.*, Währung; *Sp.*, Moneda Legal; *Ital.*, Circolazione monetaria, Valuta corrente, Numerario.

Currency Bonds. *Fr.*, Bons américains; *Ger.*, amerikanische Obligationen; *Sp.*, Bonos Americanos; *Ital.*, Obbligazioni Americane.

Currency of a Bill. *Fr.*, Temps à courir; *Ger.*, Laufzeit eines Wechsels; *Sp.*, Transcurso de una letra; *Ital.*, Decorrenza di una cambiale.

Day to Day Loans. *Fr.*, Emprunts de jour en jour; *Ger.*, Geld auf tägliche Kündigung; *Sp.*, Préstamo de día en día; *Ital.*, Prestiti di giorno in giorno.

Days of Grace. *Fr.*, Jours de grâce; *Ger.*, Fristtage; *Sp.*, Dias de gracia; *Ital.*, Giorni di favore.

Debenture. *Fr.*, Obligation; *Ger.*, Schuldschein, Obligation; *Sp.*, Obligación; *Ital.*, Obbligazione.

Del Credere Commission. *Fr.*, Ducroire; *Ger.*, Delcredereprovision; *Sp.*, Comision del Credere; *Ital.*, Provvigione Premio del Credere.

Demand Draft (D/D). *Fr.*, Traite à vue; *Ger.*, Sichtwechsel; *Sp.*, Libranza á presentación, Letra á la vista; *Ital.*, Tratta a vista o a presentazione.

Demurrage (from the *Fr.*, demeurer, to detain). *Fr.*, Surestarie; *Ger.*, Liegegeld; *Sp.*, Estadías; *Ital.*, Controstallie.

Discount (Bank Rate of). *Fr.*, Taux de l'escompte; *Ger.*, Bankdiskont; *Sp.*, Descuento bancario; *Ital.*, Tasso bancario di Sconto.

Dishonour. *Fr.*, Ne pas faire honneur à; *Ger.*, nicht honorieren; *Sp.*, Deshonrar; *Ital.*, Disonorare, Mancato pagamento, Rifiuto d'accettazione.

Dividend Warrant. *Fr.*, Coupon de dividende, coupon; *Ger.*, Dividendenschein; *Sp.*, Cédula, cupón; *Ital.*, Cupone di dividendo, cedola, cupone, tagliando.

Document Bills. *Fr.*, Billets documentés; *Ger.*, Wechsel mit Dokumenten; *Sp.*, Documentación; *Ital.*, Cambiali documentate.

Draft (Dft.)—

1. (*Fr.*, Mandat; *Ger.*, Anweisung; *Sp.*, Orden; *Ital.*, Tratta o Cambiale Tratta, Effetto). An order by which money is drawn from a bank, and also the money thus drawn.

2. (*Fr.*, Brouillon; *Ger.*, Entwurf; *Sp.*, Borrador; *Ital.*, Sfogliazzo, Copione). The first copy of a document.

3. (*Fr.*, Esquisse; *Ger.*, Skizze; *Sp.*, Diseño; *Ital.*, Schizzo, Bozzetto). Anything sketched roughly, or in outline.

4. (*Fr.*, Tirant; *Ger.*, Tiefgang; *Sp.*, Fondo; *Ital.*, Quanto pesca una nave.) The depth to which a ship sinks in the water.

5. (*Fr.*, Traite; *Ger.*, Tratte; *Sp.* Libranza; *Ital.* Tratta.) A bill of exchange (B/E).

6. (*Fr.*, Surusage; *Ger.*, Gutgewicht; *Sp.*, Merma; *Ital.*, Tara.) An allowance made by the wholesale merchant or manufacturer to a retailer for dust, waste by evaporation, and the turn of the scale.

Drawee. *Fr.* Tiré; *Ger.*, Acceptant, Trassat; *Sp.*, Aceptador, aceptante; *Ital.*, Trattario.

Drawer. *Fr.*, Tireur; *Ger.*, Aussteller, Trassant; *Sp.*, Girador, librador; *Ital.*, Traente.

Dutch Auction. *Fr.*, Adjudication au rabais; *Ger.*, holländische Versteigerung; *Sp.*, Almoneda; *Ital.*, Asta, Aggiudicazione al ribasso.

Endorse. *Fr.*, Endosser; *Ger.*, indossieren, girieren; *Sp.*, Endosar; *Ital.*, Girare, Eseguir la Girata.

Errors Excepted or Errors and Omissions Excepted (abbreviated thus, E.E., E. & O.E., or O.E.). *Fr.*, Sauf erreur; *Ger.*, Irrtum vorbehalten; *Sp.*, Salvo Error; *Ital.*, Salvo errore o Salvo Errore et Omissione.

Excise (now known as Inland Revenue). *Fr.*, Accise; *Ger.*, Accise, Verbrauchssteuer; *Sp.*, Sisa; *Ital.*, Dazio Consumo.

Ex-Dividend (abbreviated to Ex. Div. or to X.D.). *Fr.*, Coupon détaché; *Ger.*, ohne Dividende; *Sp.*, Cupón suelto; *Ital.*, Senza Dividendo, Cedola o Coupon staccato.

Ex Officio. *Fr.*, Officiellement; *Ger.*, Amtlich; *Sp.*, Oficialmente; *Ital.*, Ufficialmente.

Fiduciary Loan (*Lat.*, fiducia, trust). *Fr.*, Prêt fiduciare; *Ger.*, ungedeckte Anleihe; *Sp.*, Préstamo fiduciario; *Ital.*, Prestito fiduciario.

Fine Paper. *Fr.*, Papier de première valeur; *Ger.*, bestes Papier; *Sp.*, Papel de buena firma; *Ital.*, Carta con buone firme, di prim'ordine.

Firm. *Fr.*, Maison, raison sociale; *Ger.*, Firma; *Sp.*, Razón social, casa; *Ital.*, Ditta, Casa commerciale, Ragione Sociale.

First Class Paper. *Fr.*, Papier de première valeur; *Ger.*, feinstes Papier; *Sp.*, Papel de primera; *Ital.*, Carte con buone firme, di prim'ordine.

First of Exchange. *Fr.*, Première de change, première; *Ger.*, Primawechsel, Prima; *Sp.*, Primera de cambio, primera; *Ital.*, Prima di cambio, prima.

Fixed Capital. *Fr.*, Capital fixe, capital engagé; *Ger.*, festes Kapital; *Sp.*, Capital fijo; *Ital.*, Capitale fisso, Capitale impegnato o investito.

Floating Capital. *Fr.*, Capital circulant, fonds de roulement; *Ger.*, Betriebskapital; *Sp.*, Capital flotante; *Ital.*, Capitale circolante o in circolazione.

Floating Debt. *Fr.*, Dette non-consolidée, flottante; *Ger.*, Schwebende Schuld; *Sp.*, Deuda flotante; *Ital.*, Debito fluttuale, fluttuante.

Force Majeure. *Fr.*, Force majeure; *Ger.*, höhere Macht; *Sp.*, Fuerza mayor; *Ital.*, Forza maggiore.

Foreign Bills of Exchange. *Fr.*, Lettres de change sur l'étranger; *Ger.*, auswärtige Wechsel; *Sp.*, Letras de cambio sobre el extranjero; *Ital.*, Divisa estera di Cambio.

Founders' Shares. *Fr.*, Actions des fondateurs; *Ger.*, Gründeraktien; *Sp.*, Acciones de fundadores; *Ital.*, Azioni del Fondatori.

Fraudulent Preference. *Fr.*, Préférence frauduleuse; *Ger.*, Betrügerischer, betrüglicher Vorzug; *Sp.*, Preferencia fraudulenta: *Ital.*, Preferenza fraudolente.

Free Alongside Ship (abbreviated, F.A.S.). *Fr.*, Franco quai; *Ger.*, frei Längsseite; *Sp.*, Libre al costado; *Ital.*, Franco alla banda.

Free of all Average. *Fr.*, Franc-avarie; *Ger.*, frei von Havarie; *Sp.*, Franco de avería; *Ital.*, Franco da ogni avaria.

Free of Particular Average (abbreviated, F.P.A.). *Fr.*, Franc avarie partielle, or particulière; *Ger.*, frei von Beschädigung; *Sp.*, Libre de avería particular; *Ital.*, Franco d'avaria speciale.

Free on Board (abbreviated, F.O.B.). *Fr.*, Franco à bord; *Ger.*, frei an Bord (f.a.B.); *Sp.*, Franco á bordo (f.a.b.); *Ital.*, Franco a Bordo.

Free Overside. *Fr.*, Franco hors du navire; *Ger.*, frei ab Schiff; *Sp.*, Franco fuera del buque; *Ital.*, Franco fuori della nave.

Free Trade. *Fr.*, Libre commerce, Libre échange; *Ger.*, Freihandel; *Sp.*, Libre cambio; *Ital.*, Commercio libero, Libero scambio.

Freight Release. *Fr.*, Délivrance contre paiement du fret; *Ger.*, Freigabe; *Sp.*, Autorización de descarga; *Ital.*, Mandato di scarico, Consegna contro pagamento del nolo.

Futures. *Fr.*, Livraisons à terme; *Ger.*, Termingeschäfte; *Sp.*, Para llegar; *Ital.*, Consegne a termine.

Garnishee. *Fr.*, Tiers saisi; *Ger.*, Sequester; *Sp.*, Secuestro; *Ital.*, Sequestratario.

Garnishee Order. *Fr.*, Mandat de Saisie-arrêt; *Ger.*, Sequestrationsbefehl; *Sp.*, Orden de secuestro; *Ital.*, Mandato di Sequestro.

General Average (G.A.). *Fr.*, Avarie générale; *Ger.*, allgemeine Havarie; *Sp.*, Averia general; *Ital.*, Avaria generale.

Gilt Edged Securities. *Fr.*, Papier doré sur tranche; *Ger.*, Papiere erster Qualität; *Sp.*, Seguridades de gran valor; *Ital.*, Garanzie di prim' ordine.

Good Merchantable Quality and Condition (G.M.Q.). *Fr.*, Marchandises de bonne qualité vendable; *Ger.*, gute Qualität und Beschaffenheit; *Sp.*, Mercancías de buena calidad y acondicionadas; *Ital.*, Merci di qualità o condizioni vendibili facilmente.

Goodwill. *Fr.*, Clientèle; *Ger.*, Kundschaft; *Sp.*, Clientela; *Ital.*, Diritto di rilevare un negozio o commercio avviato e con clientela.

Guarantee. *Fr.*, Garantie, caution, aval; *Ger.*, Bürgschaft, Garantie, Kaution; *Sp.*, Garantía, caución; *Ital.*, Sicurta-Garanzia, Avalla.

Guarantor. *Fr.*, Garant; *Ger.*, Bürge, Garant; *Sp.*, Garante, fiador; *Ital.*, Garante, Mallevadore, Avallante.

Hire Purchase. *Fr.*, Par acompte; *Ger.*, Abzahlungsgeschäft; *Sp.*, Compra á plazos; *Ital.*, Compra a pagamento ateale.

Imports. *Fr.*, Importation; *Ger.*, Einfuhrwaren; *Sp.*, Importaciones; *Ital.*, Importazioni, Merci importate.

Inconvertible Paper Currency. *Fr.*, Papier-monnaie inconvertible; *Ger.*, nicht konvertierbares Papiergeld; *Sp.*, Papel moneda inconvertible; *Ital.*, Carta monetata inconvertibile.

Indent. *Fr.*, Commande; *Ger.*, Auftrag; *Sp.*, Orden por contrato; *Ital.*, Ordinazione, Contratto.

Indorse. *Fr.*, Endosser; *Ger.*, girieren, indossieren; *Sp.*, Endosar; *Ital.*, Girare, Eseguir la girata.

Injunction. *Fr.*, Arrêt de suspension; *Ger.*, Interlaut Verbot; *Sp.*, Injunción judicial; *Ital.*, Ingiunzione, Comando, Ordine.

Inland Bill. *Fr.*, Lettre de change sur l'intérieur; *Ger.*, inländischer Wechsel; *Sp.*, Letra de cambio sobre el interior; *Ital.*, Cambiale per l'interno.

Inscribed Stock. *Fr.*, Actions inscrites; *Ger.*, Inscriptionen; *Sp.*, Valores inscritos; *Ital.*, Capitale registrato.

Insurance, Marine. *Fr.*, Assurance maritime; *Ger.*, Seeversicherung; *Sp.*, Seguro Maritimo; *Ital.*, Assicurazione marittima.

Insurance or Assurance, Life. *Fr.*, Assurance sur la vie; *Ger.*, Lebensversicherung; *Sp.*, Seguro sobre la vida; *Ital.*, Assicurazione sulla vita.

Interim Dividend. *Fr.*, Dividendes par intérim (intérimaires); *Ger.*, Abschlagsdividende; *Sp.*, Dividendos provisorios; *Ital.*, Dividendo provvisorio.

In Transitu (abbreviated, in trans., *Lat.*). *Fr.*, En transit; *Ger.*, In transit; *Sp.*, En tránsito; *Ital.*, In transito.

Investment. *Fr.*, Placement; *Ger.*, (Kapital) anlage; *Sp.*, Invertir, empleo; *Ital.*, Investimento, Impiego di capitali.

Invoice (Inv.). *Fr.*, Facture; *Ger.*, Faktur, Rechnung; *Sp.*, Factura; *Ital.*, Fattura.

I.O.U. *Fr.*, Reconnaissance; *Ger.*, Schuldschein; *Sp.*, Vale; *Ital.*, Dichiarazione di debito, Pagherò.

Jobbers. *Fr.*, Agioteurs; *Ger.*, Effektenhändler; *Sp.*, Agiotistas; *Ital.*, Speculator sui Fondi pubblici, Giuocator alla Borsa.

Joint Account (J/A). *Fr.*, Compte à demi; *Ger.*, gemeinschaftliche Rechnung; *Sp.*, Cuenta á mitad; *Ital.*, Conto collettivo.

Joint Stock Banks. *Fr.*, Banque anonyme; *Ger.*, Aktienbank; *Sp.*, Banca Anónima; *Ital.*, Banche anonime.

Joint Stock Companies. *Fr.*, Sociétés par actions; *Ger.*, Aktiengesellschaften; *Sp.*, Sociedades por Acciones; *Ital.*, Compagnie anonime per Azioni, Società in nome collettivo.

Journal. *Fr.*, Journal; *Ger.*, Journal, Tagebuch; *Sp.*, Diario; *Ital.*, Giornale, Diario.

Kiteflying. *Fr.*, Émission de billets de complaisance; *Ger.*, Wechselreiterei; *Sp.*, Emisión de letras de acomodación; *Ital.*, Emissione di cambiali di favore.

Laches. *Fr.*, Négligence, retard; *Ger.*, Säumnis, Vernachlässigung; *Sp.*, Descuido, dilación; *Ital.*, Trascuranza, trascuratezza, indugio.

Lay Days. *Fr.*, Jours de planche; *Ger.*, Lade- or Liegetage; *Sp.*, Dias de plancha; *Ital.*, Stallie.

Legal Tender. *Fr.*, Monnaie légale; *Ger.*, gesetzliches Zahlmittel; *Sp.*, Moneda legal; *Ital.*, Moneta Legale.

Letter of Allotment. *Fr.*, Lettre de répartition; *Ger.*, Zuteilungsbrief; *Sp.*, Carta de repartición; *Ital.*, Lettera di assegnazione, di ripartizione.

Letter of Indemnity. *Fr.*, Garantie d'indemnité; *Ger.*, Schadloshaltungsbürgschaft; *Sp.*, Garantia de pérdida; *Ital.*, Garanzia d'Indemnita.

Letter of Regret. *Fr.*, Lettre de regret; *Ger.*, Ablehnung; *Sp.*, Carta de sentimiento ó condolencia; *Ital.*, Lettera di rincrescimento o condoglianza.

Letters of Administration. *Fr.*, Droit d'administrer la succession; *Ger.*, Verwaltungsrecht; *Sp.*, Derecho de administración; *Ital.*, Diritto di amministrazione.

Lex Mercatorum (or Lex Mercatoria, or the Law of Merchants). *Fr.*, Code commercial; *Ger.*, Handelsgesetz; *Sp.*, Código Mercantil; *Ital.*, Codice Commerciale.

Limited (Ltd.). *Fr.*, à responsabilité limitée, en commandite; *Ger.*, mit beschrankter Haftpflicht (m.b.H.); *Sp.*, Limitada, en Comandita; *Ital.*, In accomandita o a responsabilità limitata.

Liquidated Damages. *Fr.*, Dommages-interêts; *Ger.*, berechnete Entschädigung; *Sp.*, reclamaciones ajustadas; *Ital.*, Danni liquidati.

Loan. *Fr.*, Prct; *Ger.*, Anleihe; *Sp.*, Préstamo; *Ital.*, Prestito.

Long-dated Bill. *Fr.*, Papier à longue échéance, à long terme; *Ger.*, langlaufender Wechsel; *Sp.*, Letra á larga fecha; *Ital.*, Cambiale a lunga scadenza.

Making-up Price. *Fr.*, Cours de liquidation; *Ger.*, Liquidationskurs; *Sp.*, Curso de la liquidación; *Ital.*, Corso di Liquidazione.

Marine Insurance. *Fr.*, Assurance maritime; *Ger.*, Seeversicherung; *Sp.*, Seguro marítimo; *Ital.*, Assicurazione marittima.

Marked Cheques. *Fr.*, Chèques visés; *Ger.*, markierter Check; *Sp.*, Cheques visados; *Ital.*, Cheque bollati, vistati.

Market (*Ital.*, mercato; *Lat.*, mercatus, from merx, merchandise). *Fr.*, Marché; *Ger.*, Markt; *Sp.*, Mercado; *Ital.*, Mercato, Piazza.

Maturity. *Fr.*, Échéance; *Ger.*, Verfall (tag); *Sp.*, Vencimiento; *Ital.*, Maturità, Scadenza.

Memorandum of Association. *Fr.*, Bordereau d'association; *Ger.*, Gesellschaftsvertrag; *Sp.*, Memoria de Asociación; *Ital.*, Statuto o Atto constitutivo di Società.

Middlemen. *Fr.*, Intermédiaires; *Ger.*, Vermittler; *Sp.*, Intermediarios; *Ital.*, Agenti, Intermediari, Mediatori.

Mint Par of Exchange. *Fr.*, Cours de change au pair de monnaie; *Ger.*, Münzenparikurs; *Sp.*, Cambio al par de moneda; *Ital.*, Cambio al pari di moneta.

Money. *Fr.*, Argent, monnaie, pièces; *Ger.*, Geld, Valuta; *Sp.*, Dinero; *Ital.*, Denaro.

Mortgage (from the *Lat.*, mortuus, dead, and vas, a pledge; whence was derived the *Lat.*, mortuum vadium, a dead pledge, and the old *Fr.*, mortgage, literally a death-gage or pledge). *Fr.*, Hypothèque; *Ger.*, Hypothek; *Sp.*, Hipoteca; *Ital.*, Ipoteca.

Name Day. *Fr.*, Deuxième jour de liquidation; *Ger.*, Erfüllungstag; *Sp.*, Segundo día de liquidaciones; *Ital.*, Secondo giorno di liquidazione.

National Debt. *Fr.*, Dette publique; *Ger.*, Staatsschuld; *Sp.*, Deuda pública; *Ital.*, Debito Pubblico.

Negotiable Instruments, or Negotiable Paper. *Fr.*, Documents négociables or Papier négociable; *Ger.*, übertragbare Papiere; *Sp.*, Documentos negociables or Papel negociable; *Ital.*, Documenti, Effetti o carte girabili o negoziabili.

Nett, or Net. *Fr.*, Net (produit); *Ger.*, Nettobetrag; *Sp.*, Neto producto; *Ital.*, Netto, Esatto.

Noting a Bill. *Fr.*, Noter, protester; *Ger.*, notieren, protestieren;

Sp., Anotación, protesto; *Ital.*, appuntare una Cambiale nel Protocollo notarile (per il Protesto).

Not Negotiable. *Fr.*, Innégociable; *Ger.*, nicht übertragbar; *Sp.*, No negociable; *Ital.*, Non girabile, non negoziabile.

Novation. *Fr.*, Novation; *Ger.*, Neuerung; *Sp.*, Novación; *Ital.*, Novazione.

On Demand. *Fr.*, Sur demande, à présentation; *Ger.*, bei Sicht; *Sp.*, Á présentación, á vista; *Ital.*, A vista o a presentazione.

Options. *Fr.*, Réponse des primes; *Ger.*, Differenzgeschafte; *Sp.*, Privilegios; *Ital.*, Opzioni.

Overdraft. *Fr.*, Dépasser le crédit accordé; *Ger.*, Überschreitung des eingeräumten Kredits; *Sp.*, Girar en exceso del crédito concedido; *Ital.*, Eccedenza del credito accordato, oltrepassare il credito accordato.

Overtrading. *Fr.*, Commerce tropétendu, spéculations; *Ger.*, Überspekulation; *Sp.*, Especulaciones; *Ital.*, Traffico troppo esteso, Speculazione oltre il capitale disponibile.

Paid-up Capital. *Fr.*, Capital versé; *Ger.*, eingezahltes Kapital; *Sp.*, Capital pagado; *Ital.*, Capitale interamente versato.

Paper Credit. *Fr.*, Crédit sur effets, papier-monnaie; *Ger.*, Wechselkredit; *Sp.*, Efectos de créditos, papel moneda; *Ital.*, Effetti di Credito.

Pari Passu. *Fr.*, Au fur et à mesure, proportionnellement, marcher de pair; *Ger.*, Verhältnissmässig, gleichen Schritt halten; *Sp.*, En proporcion, ir de acuerdo; *Ital.*, Proporzionatamente, a proporzione, andare di pari.

Par of Exchange. *Fr.*, Pair; *Ger.*, Parikurs; *Sp.*, Par de cambio; *Ital.*, Pari di Cambio.

Particular Average (P.Av.). *Fr.*, Avarie particulière; *Ger.*, besondere or einfache Havarie; *Sp.*, Averia particular; *Ital.*, Avaria speciale o particolare.

Partnership. *Fr.*, Association; *Ger.*, Handelsgesellschaft; *Sp.*, Asociación; *Ital.*, Società, Associazione.

Par Value. *Fr.*, Pair; *Ger.*, Nennwert; *Sp.*, Par; *Ital.*, Pari.

Pawnbrokers. *Fr.*, Prêteur sur gage; *Ger.*, commissionnaire au mont-de-piété; *Ger.*, Pfandleiher; *Sp.*, Prestamista; *Ital.*, Pignoratario, Prestatore su Pegni, Monti di Pietà.

Payment for Honour Supra Protest. *Fr.*, Paiement par intervention, par honneur sous protêt; *Ger.*, Ehrenzahlung; *Sp.*, Pago por intervención, por el honor de firma; *Ital.*, Pagamento per intervento, per onore di firma.

Penalty Clause. *Fr.*, Clause de l'amande, la peine pécuniaire; *Ger.*, Geldstrafenklausel; *Sp.*, Cláusula de la multa, pena pecuniaria; *Ital.*, Clausola della multa, dell'amenda, della pena pecuniaria.

Perils of the Sea. *Fr.*, Dangers maritimes; *Ger.*, Seegefahr; *Sp.*, Riesgos de mar, Riesgos marítimos; *Ital.*, Pericoli marittimi.

Per Procuration. *Fr.*, Par procuration; *Ger.*, Per Prokura; *Sp.*, Por poder; *Ital.*, Per procura.

Personal Security. *Fr.*, Garantie mobilière; *Ger.*, persönliche Sicherheit; *Sp.*, Segurida personal; *Ital.*, Garanzia personale.

Petty Cash Book. *Fr.*, Frais généraux; *Ger.*, kleine Kasse; *Sp.*, Libro de gastos menores; *Ital.*, Libro dei piccoli pagamenti.

Plant. *Fr.*, Matériel, équipage, outillage, installation; *Ger.*, Betriebsanlage; *Sp.*, Planta, material; *Ital.*, Impianto, Materiale d'impianto.

Policy Proof of Interest. *Fr.*, Droit qui dépend de la police; *Ger.*, Beweis durch Police allein; *Sp.*, Derecho de posesión; *Ital.*, Diritto che deri a della Polizza.

Post-date. *Fr.*, Postdater; *Ger.*, nachdatieren; *Sp.*, Posdatar; *Ital.*, Posdatare.

Posting. *Fr.*, Porter au grand livre; *Ger.*, Übertragung; *Sp.*, Asiento; *Ital.*, Passare o portare al Libro Mastro, Trascrivere al Mastro.

Post Meridian (written P.M.). *Fr.*, Post méridien, de l'aprèsmidi; *Ger.*, nachmittags; *Sp.*, Después del mediodía; *Ital.*, Ore pomeridiane, Pomeriggio.

Post Obit Bond. *Fr.*, Contrat exécutoire après décès; *Ger.*, nach dem Tode zahlbare Verschreibung; *Sp.*, Escritura valable después de la muerte; *Ital.*, Obbligazione pagabile dopo la morte.

Poste Restante. *Fr.*, Poste restante; *Ger.*, postlagernd; *Sp.*, Lista de correo, Poste Restante; *Ital.*, Fermo in Posta.

Preference Stocks and Shares. *Fr.*, Actions privilégiées, actions de priorité; *Ger.*, Vorrechtsaktien; *Sp.*, Acciones privilegiados, acciones de prioridad; *Ital.*, Capitali e Azioni privilegiate.

Preferred Stock (sometimes called " B " Stock). *Fr.*, Actions privilégiées, actions de priorité; *Ger.*, Prioritätspapiere; *Sp.*, Valores privilegiados; *Ital.*, Capitali privilegiati, con diritto di priorità.

Prepay. *Fr.*, Payer d'avance; *Ger.*, vorausbezahlen; *Sp.*, Pagar por adelantado; *Ital.*, Pagare anticipatamente.

Principal may mean—

1. (*Fr.*, Chef, principal; *Ger.*, Prinzipal; *Sp.*, Jefe, principal; *Ital.*, Principale.) The head of or chief person in a firm.

2. (*Fr.*, Principal, capital; *Ger.*, Kapital; *Sp.*, Capital; *Ital.*, Capitale, Sorte.) Money on which interest is paid.

Private Banks. *Fr.*, Banque privée; *Ger.*, Privatbank; *Sp.*, Banco local; *Ital.*, Banche Private.

Private Companies. *Fr.*, Associations; *Ger.*, Privatgesellschaft; *Sp.*, Asociaciones; *Ital.*, Compagnie o Società private.

Private Limited Company. *Fr.*, Société anonyme particulière; *Ger.*, Privatgesellschaft mit beschränkter Haftung; *Sp.*, Compañía limitada particular; *Ital.*, Società anonima privata.

Profit. *Fr.*, Profit; *Ger.*, Gewinn, Nutzen; *Sp.*, Beneficios; *Ital.*, Profitto, Guadagno.

Profit and Loss Account. *Fr.*, Compte de profits et pertes; *Ger.*, Gewinn- und Verlustrechnung; *Sp.*, Cuenta de provechos y pérdidas; *Ital.*, Conto dei Profitti e Perdite.

Promissory Note (P/N). *Fr.*, Promesse, Billet à ordre; *Ger.*, Handschein; *Sp.*, Pagaré; *Ital.*, Pagherò, Vaglia cambiario.

Promotion Money. *Fr.*, Frais de fondation, frais (coût) d'établissement, de premier établissement; *Ger.*, Anlagekosten, Gründungskosten; *Sp.*, Gastos de primer establecimiento, de fundación, de constitución; *Ital.*, Spese d'impianto, di fondazione, di primo stabilimento.

Prompt. *Fr.*, Terme; *Ger.*, Ziel; *Sp.*, Tiempo de pago; *Ital.*, Termine, Respiro, Scadenza.

Pro Rata (*Lat.*). *Fr.*, Pro rata, proportionné; *Ger.*, pro rata, nach Verhältnis; *Sp.*, Pro rata; *Ital.*, Pro rata, Quota in proporzione.

Prospectus. *Fr.*, Prospectus; *Ger.*, Prospektus; *Sp.*, Prospecto; *Ital.*, Prospetto, Programma.

Protection. *Fr.*, Protection; *Ger.*, Schutzzoll; *Sp.*, Protección; *Ital.*, Protezionismo, Protezione.

Protest. *Fr.*, Protêt; *Ger.*, Protest; *Sp.*, Protesto; *Ital.*, Protesto.

Proximo (Prox.). *Fr.*, du mois prochain; *Ger.*, nächster Monat; *Sp.*, Próximo; *Ital.*, Prossimo mese.

Public Companies. *Fr.*, Sociétés en commandite; *Ger.*, Aktiengesellschaften; *Sp.*, Sociedades; *Ital.*, Società in accomandita.

Public Funds. *Fr.*, Fonds publics; *Ger.*, öffentliche Fonds; *Sp.*, Fondos publicos; *Ital.*, Fondi Pubblici, Cedole del Debito Pubblico.

Put. *Fr.*, Droit de vendre; *Ger.*, Verkaufsoption; *Sp.*, Derecho de vender; *Ital.*, Diritto di vendere.

Put and Call. *Fr.*, Double privilège; *Ger.*, Stellagegeschäft; *Sp.*, Derecho de comprar y vender; *Ital.*, Diritto di vendere e comprare, Doppio privilegio.

Put of More. *Fr.*, Droit de vendre le double; *Ger.*, Nochgeschäft; *Sp.*, Privilegio de doblar; *Ital.*, Diritto di vendere il doppio.

Pyx (The). *Fr.*, Boîte des monnaies à essayer; *Ger.*, Münzensammlung; *Sp.*, Caja de monedas para ensayar; *Ital.*, Scatola delle monete da saggiare.

Qualified Acceptance. *Fr.*, Acceptance specifiée; *Ger.*, bedingte Annahme; *Sp.*, Aceptación especificada; *Ital.*, Accettazione specificata o condizionata.

Quotation. *Fr.*, Citation, cote; *Ger.*, Kurs, Notierung; *Sp.*, Cotización, citación; *Ital.*, Quotazione, Listino o Distinta dei prezzi.

Rate of Exchange. *Fr.*, Cours; *Ger.*, Kurs; *Sp.*, Tipo de cambio; *Ital.*, Prezzo o Corso del Cambio.

Real Estate. *Fr.*, Biens immobiliers; *Ger.*, Grundeigentum; *Sp.*, Bienes inmuebles; *Ital.*, Beni, Sostanze immobili.

Registered Bonds. *Fr.*, Obligations nominatives; *Ger.*, eingetragene Obligationen; *Sp.*, Obligaciones certificadas; *Ital.*, Obbligazioni nominative.

Reserve Liability *Fr.*, Passif en réserve; *Ger.*, Reservepassiva; *Sp.*, Passivo en reserva; *Ital.*, passivo in riserva.

Restrictive Endorsement. *Fr.*, Endos restrictif; *Ger.*, beschränktes Indossament; *Sp.*, Endoso restringido; *Ital.*, Girata restrittiva.

Retire a Bill. *Fr.*, Retirer une traite; *Ger.*, einen Wechsel einlösen; *Sp.*, Retirar una letra; *Ital.*, Retirare une cambiale o tratta.

Ring. *Fr.*, Ligue coalition, bande noire; *Ger.*, Ring; *Sp.*, Liga, coalición; *Ital.*, Coalizione, Lega, Banda nera.

Rolling Stock. *Fr.*, Matériel roulant; *Ger.*, Betriebsmaterial; *Sp.*, Material de explotación; *Ital.*, Materiale roteante, circolante.

Royalty may mean—

1. (*Fr.*, Redevance; *Ger.*, Abgabe; *Sp.*, Privilegio; *Ital.*, Canone.) Dues paid by a person or company working a mine to the owners of the land for the privilege of working the ore, coal, etc.

2. (*Fr.*, Tantième; *Ger.*, Patentgebühr; *Sp.*, Patente; *Ital.*, Diritti di Brevetto.) Payments made to a patentee for the use of his patent.

3. (*Fr.*, Droits d'auteur; *Ger.*, Anteil des Verfassers; *Sp.*, Derechos de autor; *Ital.*, Diritti d'Autore.) Allowances made by a publisher to an author for the privilege of publishing and selling his book.

Run on a Bank. *Fr.*, Demandes générales de remboursement immédiat; *Ger.*, Bestürmen einer Bank; *Sp.*, Retiro de fondos en caso de pánico; *Ital.*, Ressa agli sportelli per immediato pagamento.

Salvage may mean—

1. (*Fr.*, Droit de sauvetage; *Ger.*, Bergelohn; *Sp.*, Salvamiento; *Ital.*, Diritti di salvataggio.) Money paid to those who assist in saving a ship or goods from the dangers of the sea.

2. (*Fr.*, Objets sauvés; *Ger.*, Geborgene Güter; *Sp.*, Objetos salvados; *Ital.*, Le merci salvate dal naufragio.) The goods so saved.

3. (*Fr.*, Objets sauvés; *Ger.*, vom Feuer gerettete Waren; *Sp.*, Objetos salvados; *Ital.*, Gli oggetti salvatti dall'incendio.) Property saved from a fire on land.

Sans Recours. (*Fr.*, without recourse.) *Ger.*, ohne Regress; *Sp.*, Sin recursos; *Ital.*, Senza ricorso.

Security. *Fr.*, Effet, titre, valeur; *Ger.*, Sicherheit; *Sp.*, Seguridad, título, valor; *Ital.*, Garanzia, Sicurtà, Effetto, Titolo.

Settlement is—

1. (*Fr.*, Règlement; *Ger.*, Ausgleichung; *Sp.*, Pago de Saldo; *Ital.*, Accomodamento, Accordo, Liquidazione.) The payment of an account or claim.

2. (*Fr.*, Douaire; *Ger.*, Versorgung; *Sp.*, Dotación; *Ital.*, Dote.) A deed made " upon consideration of marriage."

Settling Day. *Fr.*, Jour de règlement, jour de liquidation; *Ger.*, Stich- or Zalhtag; *Sp.*, Día de liquidación; *Ital.*, Giorno di liquidazione.

Shareholders. *Fr.*, Actionnaires; *Ger.*, Aktionäre; *Sp.*, Accionistas; *Ital.*, Azionisti.

Share Warrant. *Fr.*, Coupon (certificat), d'action; *Ger.*, Aktiencertificat, Aktienkupon; *Sp.*, Cupón (cédula) de acciones; *Ital.*, Cuponi (certificati) di azioni.

Ship's Husband. *Fr.*, Gérant à bord; *Ger.*, Korrespondenzreeder, Verfrachter; *Sp.*, Consignatario del vapor; *Ital.*, Gerente, Amministratore navale.

Short Bills. *Fr.*, Billets à courte échéance; *Ger.*, kurzsichtige Wechsel; *Sp.*, Letras á corta fecha; *Ital.*, Cambiali a breve scadenza.

Short Loans. *Fr.*, Prêts à courte date; *Ger.*, kurze Darlehen; *Sp.*, Préstamos á corta fecha; *Ital.*, Prestiti a breve scadenza o per breve periodo di tempo.

Sight Bills. *Fr.*, Billets à vue; *Ger.*, Sichtwechsel; *Sp.*, Letras á la vista; *Ital.*, Cambiali a vista.

Statute of Frauds. *Fr.*, Loi sur les fraudes; *Ger.*, Gesetz über Betrag; *Sp.*, Ley sobre los fraudes; *Ital.*, Legge sulle frodi.

Statute of Limitations. *Fr.*, Loi de prescription; *Ger.*, Verjährungsgesetz; *Sp.*, Estatuto de Limitaciones; *Ital.*, Legge di Prescrizione.

Statutory Declarations. *Fr.*, Déclarations sur parole au lieu de serment; *Ger.*, Erklärung auf Ehrenwort an Eides-statt; *Sp.*, Declaración sobre palabra en lugar de juramento; *Ital.*, Dichiarazione sulla parola invece del giuramento.

Sterling Bonds. *Fr.*, Obligations en sterling; *Ger.*, Sterlingobligationen; *Sp.*, Obligaciones en esterlina; *Ital.*, Obbligazioni pagabili in Sterline.

Stock is the term applied to—

1. (*Fr.*, Dette publique; *Ger.*, Staatspapiere; *Sp.*, Deuda pública; *Ital.*, Debito Pubblico). The national debt of any country.

2. (*Fr.*, Capital; *Ger.*, Kapital; *Sp.*, Capital; *Ital.*, Capitale, Valori). The capital raised in shares by a public company.

3. (*Fr.*, Marchandises en magasin; *Ger.*, Vorrat; *Sp.*, Existencias; *Ital.*, Merci in Magazzino). An accumulation of unsold goods.

Stock Exchange. *Fr.*, Bourse; *Ger.*, Fondsbörse; *Sp.*, Bolsa; *Ital.*, Borsa.

Stocktaking. *Fr.*, Inventaire; *Ger.*, Inventur, Lageraufnahme; *Sp.*, Inventario; *Ital.*, Inventario periodico.

Stop a Cheque. *Fr.*, Suspendre un chèque; *Ger.*, einen Check aufhalten; *Sp.*, Anular un cheque; *Ital.*, Sospendere un Cheque.

Stoppage in Transitu. *Fr.*, Arrêt, saisie; *Ger.*, Beschlagnahme unterwegs befindlicher Waren; *Sp.*, Suspensión de tránsito; *Ital.*, Arresto o sequestro della merce in transito in viaggio.

Straddle. *Fr.*, Double privilège; *Ger.*, Gegentransaktion, Eindeckung; *Sp.*, Doble privilegio; *Ital.*, Doppio privilegio.

Subpoena. *Fr.*, Citation; *Ger.*, Citation, Vorladung; *Sp.*, Citación; *Ital.*, Citare in giudizio, Citazione.

Subrogation. *Fr.*, Subrogation; *Ger.*, Einsetzung in eines anderen Stelle; Einschiebung eines dritten in die Stelle des eigentlichen Gläubigers; *Sp.*, Subrogación; *Ital.*, Surrogazione.

Sue. *Fr.*, Poursuivre; *Ger.*, Verklagen; *Sp.*, Procesar; *Ital.*, Citare, Processare, Contendere.

Surety is one who is bound by a legal document, called a bond, that—

1. (*Fr.*, Garant; *Ger.*, Gewährsmann; *Sp.*, Garantizador; *Ital.*, Garante), he will be answerable for the debt of another person if it is not paid when due; or

2. (*Fr.*, Répondant; *Ger.*, Bürge; *Sp.*, Fiador; *Ital.*, Mallevadore, Responsabile), he will be responsible for the performance of some duty undertaken by another.

Suspension of Payment. *Fr.*, Suspension de payements; *Ger.*, Zahlungseinstellung; *Sp.*, Suspensión de pagos; *Ital.*, Sospensione dei pagamenti.

Take up a Bill. *Fr.*, Faire honneur à un effet; *Ger.*, einen Wechsel einlösen; *Sp.*, Honrar une letra; *Ital.*, Onorare una cambiale o tratta.

Tale Quale. *Fr.*, Tel quel; *Ger.*, tale quale; *Sp.*, Tal cual; *Ital.*, Tale quale.

Telegraphic Transfers (or T.t's). *Fr.*, Transferts télégraphiques; *Ger.*, telegraphische Auszahlung; *Sp.*, Trasferencias por telégrafo; *Ital.*, Tassa per Vaglia telegrafici.

Tender may be either—

1. (*Fr.*, Soumission; *Ger.*, Angebot; *Sp.*, Apuesta; *Ital.*, Offerta, Esibizione scritta), a written offer to supply certain commodities upon specified terms.

2. (*Fr.*, Offre; *Ger.*, Angebot; *Sp.*, Oferta; *Ital.*, Offerta), an offer of money in payment of a debt.

Term of a Bill. *Fr.*, Terme d'un billet; *Ger.*, Ziel eines Wechsels; *Sp.*, Duración de una letra; *Ital.*, Scadenza o termine di una cambiale.

Ticket Day. *Fr.*, Deuxième jour de la liquidation; *Ger.*, zweiter Tag der Liquidation; *Sp.*, Segundo día de la liquidación; *Ital.*, Secondo giorno di liquidazione.

Token Money. *Fr.*, Jeton; *Ger.*, Scheidemünze; *Sp.*, Señal; *Ital.*, Gettoni, Monete di peso e titolo minori de egale.

Trade Discount. *Fr.*, Escompte commercial, escompte de revente; *Ger.*, Handelsskonto, Wiederverkaufsskonto; *Sp.*, Descuento comercial, descuento de reventa; *Ital.*, Sconto commerciale, sconto di rivendita.

Trade Mark. *Fr.*, Marque de commerce, marque de fabrique; *Ger.*, Schutzmarke; *Sp.*, Marca de fábrica; *Ital.*, Marca di fabbrica.

Trade Union. *Fr.*, Union ouvrière; *Ger.*, Handwerkerverband; *Sp.*, Unión obrera; *Ital.*, Corporazione, Maestranza, Camera del Lavoro, Consolato operaio.

Treasury Bills. *Fr.*, Billet du Trésor; *Ger.*, Schatzkammerschein; *Sp.*, Cédulas del Tesoro; *Ital.*, Boni del Tesoro.

Tret. *Fr.*, Réfaction; *Ger.*, Refaktie; *Sp.*, Rebaja; *Ital.*, Ribasso, Abbuono, Diffalco per tara o scarto.

Truck. *Fr.*, Payement en marchandises; *Ger.*, Tauschsystem; *Sp.*, Pago en mercancías; *Ital.*, Pagamento in generi o merci.

Trust. *Fr.*, Monopole; *Ger.*, Pfand, Ring; *Sp.*, Monopolio, unión de fabricantes; *Ital.*, Monopolio.

Turn. *Fr.*, Différence; *Ger.*, Unterschied; *Sp.*, Diferencia; *Ital.*, Differenza.

Ultra Vires. *Fr.*, En dehors de ses pouvoirs; *Ger.*, Ausserhalb der Ermächtigung; *Sp.*, En exceso de sus poderes; *Ital.*, fuori delle sue facoltà.

Uncalled Capital. *Fr.*, Fonds, capitaux pas appelés; *Ger.*, Unautgefordertes Kapital; *Sp.*, Fondos, capitales no llamados; *Ital.*, Versamenti, capitali non chiamati.

Underwriter. *Fr.*, Assureur maritime; *Ger.*, Assekurant, Versicherer; *Sp.*, Asegurador; *Ital.*, Assicuratore marittimo.

Undischarged Bankrupt. *Fr.*, Failli (banqueroutier) pas déchargé; *Ger.*, Entlassener Fallit, nicht freigesprochener Bankrottierer; *Sp.*, Fallido (quebrado) no descargado; *Ital.*, Fallito (bancarottiere) no scaricato.

Unfunded or Floating Debt. *Fr.*, Dette flottante; *Ger.*, schwebende Schuld; *Sp.*, Deuda flotante; *Ital.*, Debito oscillante o non consolidato.

Unlimited Company. *Fr.*, Compagnie (Société) à responsabilité illimitée; *Ger.*, Gesellschaft mit unbegrenzter Haftplicht, mit unbeschränkter Haftung; *Sp.*, Compañía (sociedad) de responsabilidad ilimitada; *Ital.*, Compagnia a responsabilità illimitata.

Value Received. *Fr.*, Valeur recue; *Ger.*, Wert erhalten; *Sp.*, Valor recibido; *Ital.*, Valuta ricevuta o riscossa.

Vendee. *Fr.*, Acheteur; *Ger.*, Käufer; *Sp.*, Comprador; *Ital.*, Compratore, Acquirente.

Vendor. *Fr.*, Vendeur; *Ger.*, Verkäufer; *Sp.*, Vendedor; *Ital.*, Venditore.

Visé. *Fr.*, Visa; *Ger.*, Visa; *Sp.*, Viso; *Ital.*, Vistato, Visto.

Voyage Policy. *Fr.*, Police de voyage; *Ger.*, Reisepolice; *Sp.*, Póliza de viaje; *Ital.*, Polizza di viaggio.

Warrant. *Fr.*, Warrant; *Ger.*, Warrant, Lagerschein; *Sp.*, Warrant, Orden; *Ital.*, Mandato di Procura.

Warranty. *Fr.*, Conditions d'assurance; *Ger.*, Bürgschaft, Garantie; *Sp.*, Condiciones de seguro; *Ital.*, Condizioni d'Assicurazione.

Wholesale. *Fr.*, Gros, commerce de gros; *Ger.*, en gros, im grossen; *Sp.*, al por mayor; *Ital.*, Vendita all'ingrosso.

Winding Up. *Fr.*, Liquidation; *Ger.*, Liquidation; *Sp.*, Liquidación; *Ital.*, Liquidazione.

Without Recourse. *Fr.*, Sans recours; *Ger.*, ohne Regress; *Sp.*, Sin recursos; *Ital.*, Senza ricorso.

Without Reserve. *Fr.*, Sans mise à prix; *Ger.*, ohne Vorbehalt, unbedingt; *Sp.*, Sin reserva; *Ital.*, Senza riserva.

Foreign Words, Phrases and Sayings

à bas (*Fr.*). Down, down with.
à bon marché (*Fr.*). Cheap; a good bargain.
ab ovo usque ad mala (*Lat.*). From the egg to the apples (as in Roman banquets); from first to last.
absence d'esprit (*Fr.*). Absence of mind.
absente reo (*Lat.*). The accused being absent.
ab urbe conditâ (*Lat.*). From the building of the city, i.e. Rome.
à compte (*Fr.*). On account; in part payment.
ad hominem (*Lat.*). To the man; to an individual's interests or passions; personal.
ad infinītum (*Lat.*). To infinity.
ad kalendas Graecas (*Lat.*). At the Greek calends; i.e. never, as the Greeks had no calends in their mode of reckoning.
à droite (*Fr.*). To the right.
adsum (*Lat.*). I am present; here!
aere perennius (*Lat.*). More lasting than brass; everlasting.
à gauche (*Fr.*). To the left.
à haute voix (*Fr.*). Aloud.
à la bonne heure (*Fr.*). Well timed; all right; very well; as you please.
à l'abri (*Fr.*). Under shelter.
à la Française (*Fr.*). After the French mode.
à la mode (*Fr.*). According to the custom or fashion.
al fresco (*It.*). In the open air; out-of-doors.
alter ego (*Lat.*). Another self.
amor patriae (*Lat.*). Love of country.
amour propre (*Fr.*). Self-love; vanity.
anno aetatis suae (*Lat.*). In the year of his or her age.
anno Domini (*Lat.*). In the year of our Lord.
anno urbis conditae (*Lat.*). In the year from the time the city (Rome) was built.
ante meridiem (*Lat.*). Before noon.
à outrance (*Fr.*). To the utmost; to extremities; without sparing.
à perte de vue. (*Fr.*). Till beyond one's view; out of sight.
à peu près (*Fr.*). Nearly.
à pied (*Fr.*). On foot.
à propos de bottes (*Fr.*). Apropos to boots; foreign to the subject.
à propos de rien (*Fr.*). Apropos to nothing; without a motive; for nothing at all.
aqua vitae (*Lat.*). Water of life; brandy.
argent comptant (*Fr.*). Ready money.
argumentum ad hominem (*Lat.*). An argument to the individual man; i.e. to his interests and prejudices.
argumentum ad ignorantiam (*Lat.*). An argument founded on the ignorance of the person addressed.
ariston metron (*Gr.*). The middle course is the best; the golden mean.

arrière pensée (*Fr.*). Hidden thought; mental reservation.
ars est celare artem (*Lat.*). It is art to conceal art.
ars longa, vita brevis (*Lat.*). Art is long, life is short.
artium magister (*Lat.*). Master of Arts.
à tout prix (*Fr.*). At any price.
au courant (*Fr.*). Fully acquainted with matters.
au fait (*Fr.*). Well acquainted with; expert.
au pis aller (*Fr.*). At the worst.
au revoir (*Fr.*). Adieu until we meet again.
autant d'hommes, autant d'avis (*Fr.*). So many men, so many minds.
aut Caesar aut nullus (*Lat.*). Either Caesar or nobody.
avant propos (*Fr.*). Preliminary matter; preface.
a vinculo matrimonii (*Lat.*). From the bond of matrimony.

bas bleu (*Fr.*). A blue-stocking; a literary woman.
beau monde (*Fr.*). The world of fashion.
beaux yeux (*Fr.*). Fine eyes; good looks.
ben trovato (*It.*). Well invented.
bis dat qui cito dat (*Lat.*). He gives twice who gives quickly.
bon jour (*Fr.*). Good day.
bonne bouche (*Fr.*). A delicate or tasty morsel.
bon soir (*Fr.*). Good evening.
bon vivant (*Fr.*). A good liver; a gourmand.
brevis esse laboro, obscurus fio (*Lat.*). I try to be brief, I become obscure.

caelum non animum mutant qui trans mare currunt (*Lat.*). They who cross the sea change their sky but not their nature.
caeteris (ceteris) paribus (*Lat.*). Other things being equal.
carpe diem (*Lat.*). Enjoy the present day; improve time.
casus belli (*Lat.*). That which causes or justifies war.
causa sine quâ non (*Lat.*). An indispensable cause or condition.
caveat emptor (*Lat.*). Let the buyer beware (or look after his own interests).
cedant arma togae (*Lat.*). Let arms yield to the gown; let military authority yield to the civil power.
cela va sans dire (*Fr.*). That goes without saying; needless to say.
ce n'est que le premier pas qui coûte (*Fr.*). It is only the first step that is difficult.
chacun à son goût (*Fr.*). Every one to his taste.
chateaux en Espagne (*Fr.*). " Castles in Spain "; castles in the air.
cogito, ergo sum (*Lat.*). I think, therefore I exist.
comme il faut (*Fr.*). As it should be.
compos mentis (*Lat.*). Sound of mind; quite sane.
conditio sine quâ non (*Lat.*). A necessary condition.
consule Planco (*Lat.*). When Plancus was consul; when I was a young man.
cordon bleu (*Fr.*). Blue ribbon; a cook of the highest class.
corps de ballet (*Fr.*). A body of ballet-dancers.
corrigenda (*Lat.*). Things to be corrected.
couleur de rose (*Fr.*). Rose colour; attractive aspect.
coup (*Fr.*). A stroke.

coup de grâce (*Fr.*). A finishing stroke.
coup d'état (*Fr.*). A sudden decisive blow in politics; a stroke of policy.
coup de main (*Fr.*). A sudden attack or surprise.
coup de maître (*Fr.*). A master stroke.
coup de théâtre (*Fr.*). A theatrical effect.
credat Judaeus Apella (*Lat.*). Let Apella, the superstitious Jew, believe it, (I won't); tell that to the Marines.
cucullus non facit monachum (*Lat.*). The cowl does not make the friar.
cui bono? (*Lat.*). For whose advantage is it?
cum grano salis (*Lat.*). With a grain of salt; with some allowance.
cum notis cariorum (*Lat.*). With the notes of various (critics).
currente calamo (*Lat.*). With a running or rapid pen.

damnant quod non intelligunt (*Lat.*). They condemn what they do not comprehend.
dare pondus fumo (*Lat.*). To give weight to smoke; to give importance to trifles.
de bonne grâce (*Fr.*). With good grace; willingly.
de die in diem (*Lat.*). From day to day.
de facto (*Lat.*). In point of fact; actual or actually.
de gustibus non est disputandum (*Lat.*). There is no disputing about tastes.
dei gratiâ (*Lat.*). By the grace of God.
de jure (*Lat.*). From the law; by right.
de mal en pis (*Fr.*). From bad to worse.
de minimis non curatur (*Lat.*). No notice is taken of trifles.
de mortuis nil nisi bonum (*Lat.*). Say nothing but good of the dead.
Deo adjuvante, non timendum (*Lat.*). God assisting, nothing is to be feared.
Deo gratias (*Lat.*). Thanks to God.
Deo volente (*Lat.*). God willing; by God's will.
de profundis (*Lat.*). Out of the depths.
desipere in loco (*Lat.*). To jest or be merry at the proper time.
de trop (*Fr.*). Too much; more than is wanted; out of place.
dies non (*Lat.*). A day on which judges do not sit.
Dieu est toujours pour les plus gros bataillons (*Fr.*). God is always on the side of the largest battalions; the largest army has the best chance of victory.
Dieu et mon droit (*Fr.*). God and my right.
diis aliter visum (*Lat.*). The gods thought otherwise.
docendo discimus (*Lat.*). We learn by teaching.
dolce far niente (*It.*). Sweet doing-nothing; sweet idleness.
dorer la pilule (*Fr.*). To gild the pill.
double entente (*Fr.*). A double meaning; a play upon words.
dramatis personae (*Lat.*). Characters of the drama or play.
dulce et decorum est pro patriâ mori (*Lat.*). It is sweet and glorious to die for one's country.
dum spiro spero (*Lat.*). While I breathe I hope.

ecce homo! (*Lat.*). Behold the man!
eheu! fugaces labuntur anni (*Lat.*). Alas! the fleeting years glide by.

en arrière (*Fr.*). In the rear; behind; back.
en attendant (*Fr.*). In the meantime.
èn effet (*Fr.*). In effect; substantially; really.
en famille (*Fr.*). With one's family; in a domestic state.
enfant gâté (*Fr.*). A spoiled child.
enfants perdus (*Fr.*). Lost children; (military), a forlorn hope.
enfant terrible (*Fr.*). A terrible child, or one that makes disconcerting remarks.
enfin (*Fr.*). In short; at last; finally.
en grande tenue (*Fr.*). In full dress.
en passant (*Fr.*). In passing; by the way.
en plein jour (*Fr.*). In broad day.
en route (*Fr.*). On the way.
entente cordiale (*Fr.*). Cordial understanding, especially between two states.
entêté (*Fr.*). Obstinate; headstrong.
entre nous (*Fr.*). Between ourselves.
eo nomine (*Lat.*). By that name.
e pluribus unum (*Lat.*). One out of many; one composed of many.
errare est humanum (*Lat.*). To err is human.
esprit de corps (*Fr.*). The animating spirit of a collective body.
et caetera, (et cetera) (*Lat.*). And the rest.
et hoc genus omne (*Lat.*). And everything of the sort.
et tu, Brute! (*Lat.*). And thou, also, Brutus.
exceptio probat regulam (*Lat.*). The exception proves (or tests) the rule.
ex delicto (*Lat.*). From the crime.
exegi monumentum aere perennius (*Lat.*). I have reared a monument more lasting than brass.
exempla sunt odiosa (*Lat.*). Examples are offensive.
exempli gratiâ (*Lat.*). By way of example.
exeunt omnes (*Lat.*). All go out or retire.
exitus acta probat (*Lat.*). The event justifies the deed.
ex necessitate rei (*Lat.*). From the necessity of the case.
ex officio (*Lat.*). In virtue of his office.
ex parte (*Lat.*). From one party or side.
ex pede Herculem (*Lat.*). From the foot we recognize a Hercules; we judge the whole from the specimen.
experientia docet stultos (*Lat.*). Experience instructs fools.
experimentum crucis (*Lat.*). The experiment of the cross; a crucial experiment.
experto crede (*Lat.*). Trust one who has tried or had experience.

faber suae fortunae (*Lat.*). The maker of his own fortune; a self-made man.
facile est inventis addere (*Lat.*). It is easy to add to things already invented.
façon de parler (*Fr.*). Manner of speaking.
faire mon devoir (*Fr.*). Do my duty.
fait accompli (*Fr.*). A thing already done.
fama nihil est celerius (*Lat.*). Nothing travels swifter than scandal.
fas est et ab hoste doceri (*Lat.*). It is right to be taught, even by an enemy.

faux pas (*Fr.*). A false step; a slip in behaviour.
festina lente (*Lat.*). Hasten slowly.
fiat experimentum in corpore vili (*Lat.*). Let trial or experiment be made on a worthless body.
fiat justitia, ruat caelum (*Lat.*). Let justice be done, though the heavens should fall.
fiat lux (*Lat.*). Let there be light.
fidei defensor (*Lat.*). Defender of the Faith.
finem respice (*Lat.*). Look to the end.
finis coronat opus (*Lat.*). The end crowns the work.
flagrante delicto (*Lat.*). In the commission of the crime.
fons et origo (*Lat.*). The source and origin.
fortes fortuna juvat (*Lat.*). Fortune helps the brave.
fortiter in re (*Lat.*). With firmness in acting.
froides mains, chaud amour (*Fr.*). Cold hands and a warm heart.
fruges consumere nati (*Lat.*). Born to consume fruits; born only to eat.
furor arma ministrat (*Lat.*). Rage provides arms.
fuyez les dangers de loisir (*Fr.*). Avoid the dangers of leisure.

garçon (*Fr.*). A boy; a waiter.
genius loci (*Lat.*). The genius or guardian spirit of a place.
gibier de potence (*Fr.*). A gallows-bird.
gli assenti hanno torto (*It.*) The absent are in the wrong.
gloria in excelsis (*Lat.*). Glory to God in the highest.
gradus ad Parnassum (*Lat.*). A step to Parnassus; aid in writing Greek or Latin poetry.
grande parure (*Fr.*). Full dress.
graviora quaedam sunt remedia periculis (*Lat.*). Some remedies are worse than the disease.
guerre à mort (*Fr.*). War to the death.
guerre à outrance (*Fr.*). War to the uttermost.
haec olim meminisse juvabit (*Lat.*). It will delight us to remember this some day.

hic et ubique (*Lat.*). Here and everywhere.
hic jacet (*Lat.*). Here lies.
hinc illæ lacrimæ (*Lat.*). Hence these tears.
hoc genus omne (*Lat.*). All of this sort or class.
hoi polloi (*Gr.*). The many; the vulgar; the rabble.
hominis est errare (*Lat.*). To err is human.
homo homini lupus (*Lat.*). Man is a wolf to man.
homo solus aut deus aut daemon (*Lat.*). A man alone is either a god or a devil.
homo sum; humani nihil a me alienum puto (*Lat.*). I am a man; I count nothing human indifferent to me.
honi soit qui mal y pense (*O. Fr.*). Evil to him who evil thinks.
horresco referens (*Lat.*). I shudder as I relate.
hors de combat (*Fr.*). Out of condition to fight.
hors de propos (*Fr.*). Not to the point or purpose.
humanum est errare (*Lat.*). To err is human.

ich dien (*Ger.*). I serve.
id est (*Lat.*). That is.
ignorantia legis neminem excusat (*Lat.*). Ignorance of the law excuses no one.
il ne faut jamais défier un fou (*Fr.*). Never defy a fool.
imperium in imperio (*Lat.*). A state within a state; a government within another.
in articulo mortis (*Lat.*). At the point of death; in the last struggle.
in capite (*Lat.*). In chief.
in esse (*Lat.*). In being; in actuality.
in extremis (*Lat.*). At the point of death.
in formâ pauperis (*Lat.*). As a poor man.
infra dignitatem (*Lat.*). Below one's dignity.
in loco parentis (*Lat.*). In the place of a parent.
in medias res (*Lat.*). Into the midst of things.
in medio tutissimus ibis (*Lat.*). You will walk safest in the middle.
in perpetuum (*Lat.*). For ever.
in puris naturalibus (*Lat.*). Quite naked.
inter alia (*Lat.*). Among other things.
inter arma silent leges (*Lat.*). Laws are silent in the midst of arms.
inter canem et lupum (*Lat.*). Between dog and wolf; at twilight.
in terrorem (*Lat.*). As a means of terrifying; by way of warning.
inter se (*Lat.*). Among themselves.
in transitu (*Lat.*). On the passage.
in vino veritas (*Lat.*). There is truth in wine; truth is told under the influence of intoxicants.
ipse dixit (*Lat.*). He himself said it; a dogmatic saying or assertion.
ipsissima verba (*Lat.*). The very words.
ira furor brevis est (*Lat.*). Anger is a short madness.
ita est (*Lat.*). It is so.

jacta est alea (*Lat.*). The die is cast.
je ne sais quoi (*Fr.*). I know not what.
jeu de mots (*Fr.*). A play on words; a pun.
jeu d'esprit (*Fr.*). A display of wit; a witticism.
jus gentium (*Lat.*). The law of nations.

laborare est orare (*Lat.*). To labour is to pray.
labor omnia vincit (*Lat.*). Labour conquers everything.
la critique est aisée, et l'art est difficile (*Fr.*). Criticism is easy, and art is difficult.
l'allegro (*It.*). The merry man.
lapsus calami (*Lat.*). A slip of the pen.
lapsus linguae (*Lat.*). A slip of the tongue.
lares et penates (*Lat.*). Household gods.
laudator temporis acti (*Lat.*). One who praises time past.
le beau monde (*Fr.*). The fashionable world.
le jeu n'en vaut pas la chandelle (*Fr.*). The game is not worth the candle; the object is not worth the trouble.
le roy (or la reyne) le veult (*Norm. Fr.*). The king (or the queen) wills it; the formula expressing the sovereign's assent to a Bill which has passed both Houses of Parliament.

les absents ont toujours tort (*Fr.*). The absent are always in the wrong.
lèse majesté (*Fr.*). High treason.
les murailles ont des oreilles (*Fr.*). Walls have ears.
lex scripta (*Lat.*). Written law; statute law.
lex non scripta (*Lat.*). Unwritten law; common law.
l'homme propose, et Dieu dispose (*Fr.*). Man proposes, and God disposes.
lite pendente (*Lat.*). During the trial.
litera scripta manet (*Lat.*). The written letter remains.

magna civitas, magna solitudo (*Lat.*). A great city is a great solitude.
magna est veritas, et prevalebit (*Lat.*). Truth is mighty, and will prevail.
magni nominis umbra (*Lat.*). The shadow of a great name.
magnum est vectigal parsimonia (*Lat.*). Economy is itself a great income.
malgré nous (*Fr.*). In spite of us.
malheur ne vient jamais seul (*Fr.*). Misfortunes never come single.
mardi gras (*Fr.*). Shrove Tuesday.
materiam superabit opus (*Lat.*). The workmanship will prove superior to the material.
mea culpa (*Lat.*). My fault; by my fault.
medio tutissimus ibis (*Lat.*). In a medium course you will be safest.
memento mori (*Lat.*). Remember death.
mens sana in corpore sano (*Lat.*). A sound mind in a sound body.
mirabile dictu (*Lat.*). Wonderful to relate.
mont de pieté (*Fr.*). A pawnshop.
monumentum aere perennius (*Lat.*). A monument more lasting than brass.
mors janua vitae (*Lat.*). Death is the gate of life.
multum in parvo (*Lat.*). Much in little.
mutatis mutandis (*Lat.*). With the necessary changes.

naturam expellas furca tamen usque recurret (*Lat.*). Though you drive out nature with a pitchfork, it will always return; nature will always assert itself.
necessitas non habet legem (*Lat.*). Necessity has no law.
nec scire fas est omnia (*Lat.*). It is not permitted to know all things.
nemine contradicente (*Lat.*). No one speaking in opposition; without opposition.
nemine dissentiente (*Lat.*). No one dissenting; without a dissenting voice.
nemo mortalium omnibus horis sapit (*Lat.*). No one is wise at all times.
nemo repente fuit turpissimus (*Lat.*). No one ever became a thorough villain in an instant.
ne plus ultra (*Lat.*). Nothing further; the utmost point; perfection.
ne quid detrimenti respublica capiat (*Lat.*). Lest the state receive any detriment.
nil desperandum (*Lat.*). There is no reason for despair.
n'importe (*Fr.*). It matters not.
nitor in adversum (*Lat.*). I strive against opposition.
noblesse oblige (*Fr.*). Rank imposes obligations; much is expected from one in good position.
nom de guerre (*Fr*). A war name; a pen name.

nom de plume (*Fr.*). An assumed name of a writer; incorrect for a *nom de guerre*.
non compos mentis (*Lat.*). Not in sound mind.
non omne licitum honestum (*Lat.*). Not every lawful thing is honourable.
non omnia possumus omnes (*Lat.*). We cannot, all of us, do everything.
non sequitur (*Lat.*). It does not follow.
nosce teipsum (*Lat.*). Know thyself.
noscitur e (*or* **a**) **sociis** (*Lat.*). He is known by his companions.
nota bene (*Lat.*). Mark well.
n'oubliez pas (*Fr.*). Don't forget.
nous avons changé tout cela (*Fr.*). We have changed all that.
nous verrons (*Fr.*). We shall see.
novus homo (*Lat.*). A new man; one who has raised himself from obscurity.
nudum pactum (*Lat.*). A mere agreement (i.e. one without benefit to the promiser).
nunquam minus solus, quam cum solus (*Lat.*). Never less alone than when alone.

obiter dictum (*Lat.*). A thing said by the way.
obscurum per obscurius (*Lat.*). Explaining an obscurity by something more obscure still.
odi profanum vulgus (*Lat.*). I loathe the profane rabble.
omne ignotum pro magnifico (*Lat.*). Whatever is unknown is held to be magnificent.
omne solum forti patria (*Lat.*). Every soil is a brave man's country.
omne tulit punctum qui miscuit utile dulci (*Lat.*). He gains complete approval who mixes the useful with the agreeable.
omnia mutantur, nos et mutamur in illis (*Lat.*). All things change, and we change with them.
omnia vincit amor (*Lat.*). Love conquers all things.
on connait l'ami au besoin (*Fr.*). A friend is known in time of need.
orator fit, poeta nascitur (*Lat.*). An orator may be made by training; a poet is born a poet.
O! si sic omnia (*Lat.*). Oh! if all things so; Oh! if he had always so spoken or acted.
otium cum dignitate (*Lat.*). Ease with dignity; dignified leisure.
ouvrage de longue haleine (*Fr.*). A work of long breath; a long or tedious business.

pace (*Lat.*). By leave of; not to give offence to.
pace tua (*Lat.*). With your consent.
palmam qui meruit ferat (*Lat.*). Let him who has won the palm wear it.
par excellence (*Fr.*). By way of eminence.
pari passu (*Lat.*). At an equal pace or rate of progress.
parva componere magnis (*Lat.*). To compare small things with great.
passim (*Lat.*). Everywhere; in all parts of the book, chapter, etc.
per angusta ad augusta (*Lat.*). Through trials to triumph.
per aspera ad astra (*Lat.*). Through rough ways to the stars; through suffering to renown.
petitio principii (*Lat.*). A begging of the question.
pied à terre (*Fr.*). A resting-place; a temporary lodging.

pis aller (*Fr.*). The worst or last shift.
poeta nascitur, non fit (*Lat.*). The poet is born, not made; nature, not study, must form the poet.
pour prendre congé (*Fr.*). To take leave.
pro bono publico (*Lat.*). For the good of the public.
pro rege, lege, et grege (*Lat.*). For the king, the law, and the people.
pro tempore (*Lat.*). For the time being.

qualis ab incepto (*Lat.*). The same as at the beginning.
quam diu se bene gesserit (*Lat.*). As long as he shall behave well; during good behaviour.
quantum meruit (*Lat.*). As much as he deserved.
quantum mutatus ab illo ! (*Lat.*). How changed from what he once was.
quid pro quo (*Lat.*). One thing for another; tit for tat; an equivalent.
qui m'aime, aime mon chien (*Fr.*). Love me, love my dog.
quis custodiet ipsos custodes (*Lat.*). Who shall keep the keepers themselves.
qui va là ? (*Fr.*). Who goes there ?
qui vive ? (*Fr.*). Who is there ?
quod erat demonstrandum (*Lat.*). Which was to be proved or demonstrated.
quod non opus est, asse carum est (*Lat.*). What is not wanted (or is of no use to a person) is dear at a copper.
quod scripsi scripsi (*Lat.*). What I have written, I have written.
quod vide (*Lat.*). Which see; refer to the word just mentioned.
quo fas et gloria ducunt (*Lat.*). Whither duty and glory lead.
quorum pars magna fui (*Lat.*). Of whom or which I was an important part.
quos Deus vult perdere, prius dementat (*Lat.*). Those whom God wishes to destroy, he first makes mad.
quot homines, tot sententiae (*Lat.*). Many men, many minds.

raison d'être (*Fr.*). The reason for a thing's existence.
reculer pour mieux sauter (*Fr.*). To draw back in order to make a better spring.
reductio ad absurdum (*Lat.*). The reducing of a position to a logical absurdity.
répondre en Normande (*Fr.*). To give an evasive answer.
requiescat in pace (*Lat.*). May he (or she) rest in peace.
res angusta domi (*Lat.*). Narrow circumstances at home, poverty.
res judicata (*Lat.*). A case or suit already settled.
respice finem (*Lat.*). Look to the end.
revenons à nos moutons (*Fr.*). Let us return to our sheep; let us return to our subject.
rien n'est beau que le vrai (*Fr.*). There is nothing beautiful except the truth.
rira bien, qui rira le dernier (*Fr.*). He laughs well who laughs last.
ruat coelum (*Lat.*). Let the heavens fall.

salus populi suprema est lex (*Lat.*). The welfare of the people is the supreme law.
salvo jure (*Lat.*). The right being safe.

sans façon (*Fr.*). Without ceremony or formality.
sans peur et sans reproche (*Fr.*). Without fear and without reproach.
sauve qui peut (*Fr.*). Let him save himself who can.
savoir faire (*Fr.*). The knowing how to act; tact.
semper idem (*Lat.*). Always the same.
se non è vero, è ben trovato (*It.*). If not true it is cleverly invented.
seriatim (*Lat.*). In a series; one by one.
sic itur ad astra (*Lat.*). Such is the way to the stars, or to immortality.
sic transit gloria mundi (*Lat.*). Thus passes away the glory of this world.
sic vos non vobis (*Lat.*). Thus you labour but not for yourselves.
silent leges inter arma (*Lat.*). Amidst arms, or in war, laws are silent, or disregarded.
si monumentum quàeris, circumspice (*Lat.*). If you seek his monument, look around you.
sine die (*Lat.*). Without a day being appointed.
sine qua non (*Lat.*). Without which, not.
si vis pacem, para bellum (*Lat.*). If you wish for peace, prepare for war.
solitudinem faciunt, pacem appellant (*Lat.*). They make a wilderness and call it peace.
sotto voce (*It.*). In an undertone.
souffler le chaud et le froid (*Fr.*). To blow hot and cold.
splendide mendax (*Lat.*). Nobly untruthful; untrue for a good object.
statu quo ante bellum (*Lat.*). In the state in which things were before the war.
suaviter in modo, fortiter in re (*Lat.*). Gentle in manner, resolute in execution or action.
sub judice (*Lat.*). Under consideration.
sub rosa (*Lat.*). Under the rose; privately.
summum jus, summa injuria (*Lat.*). The rigour of the law is the height of oppression.
suppressio veri, suggestio falsi (*Lat.*). A suppression of the truth is the suggestion of a falsehood.
sursum corda (*Lat.*). Lift up your hearts.

tant pis (*Fr.*). So much the worse.
tel maître, tel valet (*Fr.*). Like master, like man.
tempus edax rerum (*Lat.*). Time the devourer of all things.
tertium quid (*Lat.*). A third something; a nondescript.
tot homines, quot sententiae (*Lat.*). So many men so many minds.
tour de force (*Fr.*). A feat of strength or skill.
tout le monde est sage après coup (*Fr.*). Everybody is wise after the event.

uberrima fides (*Lat.*). The utmost good faith.
ultra vires (*Lat.*). Beyond powers or rights conferred by law.
un bien fait n'est jamais perdu (*Lat.*). A kindness is never lost.
un "tiens" vaut mieux que deux "tu l'auras" A bird in the hand is worth two in the bush.

vacuus cantat coram latrone viator (*Lat.*). The traveller with an empty purse sings in presence of the highwayman.
vade in pace (*Lat.*). Go in peace.

varium et mutabile semper faemina (*Lat.*). Woman is ever a changeful and capricious thing.
verbatim et literatim (*Lat.*). Word for word and letter for letter.
verbum sat sapienti (*Lat.*). A word is enough for a wise man.
vestigia nulla retrorsum (*Lat.*). No returning footsteps; no traces backward.
video meliora proboque, deteriora sequor (*Lat.*). I see and approve the better things, I follow the worse.
vi et armis (*Lat.*). By force and arms; by main force; by violence.
vires acquirit eundo (*Lat.*). As it goes it acquires strength.
vir sapit qui pauca loquitur (*Lat.*). He is a wise man who says but little.
vis medicatrix naturae (*Lat.*). The healing power of nature.
vita brevis, ars longa (*Lat.*). Life is short, art is long.
vivat regina! (*Lat.*). Long live the queen!
vivat rex! (*Lat.*). Long live the king!
vive la bagatelle! (*Fr.*). Success to trifles, or frivolity!
voir le dessous des cartes (*Fr.*). To see the under side of the cards; to be in the secret.
volenti non fit injuria (*Lat.*). No injustice is done to the consenting person.
vox et praeterea nihil (*Lat.*). A voice and nothing more; sound but no sense.
vox populi, vox Dei (*Lat.*). The voice of the people is the voice of God.